GLENN GOULD

A LIFE AND VARIATIONS

Also by Otto Friedrich

GLENN GOULD

A LIFE AND VARIATIONS

OTTO FRIEDRICH

KEY PORTER BOOKS

Canadian Cataloguing in Publication Data

Friedrich, Otto, 1929
Glenn Gould: a life and variations

ISBN 1-55263-153-2

Gould, Glenn, 1932-1982. 2. Pianists – Canada – Biography. I. Title.

ML417.G69F899 2000   786.2'092   C00-931024-X

The Publisher gratefully acknowledges the support of the Canada Council
for the Arts and the Ontario Arts Council for its publishing program.

We acknowledge the financial support of the Government of Canada
through the Book Publishing Industry Development Program (BPIDP)
for our publishing activities.

Key Porter Books Limited
70 The Esplanade
Toronto, Ontario
www.keyporter.com

00 01 02 03 04 6 5 4 3 2 1

Printed in Canada

To Priscilla

"The really important things in any biography are what someone thinks and feels and not what he has done. . . ."

—GLENN GOULD

"Perhaps the author of the second book on Glenn Gould will attempt a 'conventional' biography. He will fail. Gould has protected his private life from public scrutiny, firmly but courteously, as no other celebrity among artists in our time has done. Moreover, unless I am much in error, his private life is in fact austere and unremarkable. A book on his life and time would be brief and boring. . . ."

—*Glenn Gould, Music and Mind,* by Geoffrey Payzant

" . . . Payzant, in fact, provides ample evidence for this contention with his own first chapter, a quick-and-dirty sketch of Gould's early years—which is indeed rather boring and by no means as brief as it should be."

—Gould's review of Payzant's book

Preface

I had just taken a leisurely sip of coffee and unfolded the Paris *Herald-Tribune* at a café in the Milan airport when I saw the front-page headline announcing that Glenn Gould was dead. It was like a physical blow. I remember saying aloud—with a sense of not only loss but anger at that loss—"Oh, God *damn* it!"

Gould had been a hero of mine for more than twenty-five years, ever since my friend Martin Mayer, then a music critic for *Esquire,* had manifested his enthusiasm for this young newcomer by giving me a copy of *The Goldberg Variations.* Like most people discovering that incredible performance, I was overwhelmed. I played the record over and over. I went and bought a copy of the music and practiced it for months, knowing perfectly well that I would never be able to play it, or anything else, the way Gould did. There was nothing left but to imitate Mayer and give away copies. Over the years, I have handed out perhaps twenty copies of *The Goldberg Variations,* thinking each time that there was no better present I could give to anyone.

When Gould died, I thought that would be the end of that particular obsession. I could still play the favorite records late at night, the Bach partitas or the Beethoven Second Concerto or the Wagner transcriptions, but there would no longer be the haunting sense of that mysterious presence somewhere up in Canada, that unseen force from which new ideas and new creations periodically emanated. That was all over.

About two years later, I got a telephone call from my daughter Molly, a literary agent in New York, who coolly asked whether I

would be interested in writing a biography of Gould. Only then did
I learn that when Gould died, he left the execution of his will to a
Toronto lawyer named J. Stephen Posen, and that Posen was now
looking for a biographer. Yes, I was definitely interested.

Posen's first problem had been to find out exactly what Gould's
"estate" contained, apart from five pianos and a certain flow of
record royalties. The explorers who went through Gould's Toronto
apartment and his studio in a nearby hotel soon discovered that he
rarely threw anything away and rarely paid much attention to where
anything was. They came upon plastic garbage bags filled with unanswered mail, sheaves of manuscripts, heaps of unworn clothing.
Ruth Pincoe, a professional bibliographer, took charge of cataloguing and dating, insofar as it was possible, the accumulation of letters,
program notes, newspaper clippings, and all the rest of what eventually became "The Glenn Gould Collection" at the National
Library of Canada in Ottawa. Perhaps the most remarkable of these
papers was an assortment of lined note pads, scores of them. Gould
never kept a real diary, but on these undated note pads, he scribbled
whatever came to mind, ideas, letters, drafts of interviews, revisions
of articles, stock-market holdings, medical symptoms, his own temperature, and the temperature of various cities in Canada as reported
by his radio in the small hours of the morning.

Before opening Gould's papers to the public, Posen and the estate
decided to commission some writer to go through all this material,
to interview Gould's friends and relatives, and to write what might
be described as the "official" or "authorized" biography. Posen
assigned the task of finding this biographer to a Toronto agent,
Lucinda Vardey, and she started on her assignment by writing to a
lot of other literary agents to ask whether they had clients whom
they would like to recommend as Gould's biographer. One of these
inquiries almost inevitably ended on Molly's desk, and she
responded with an impassioned letter declaring that she had been
raised on the recordings of Glenn Gould. Ever since the appearance
of *The Goldberg Variations,* when she was four, she had been hearing
Bach partitas and Beethoven sonatas and whatever other new Gould
recordings her father kept bringing home.

Molly's letter had a certain effect. Though a number of other
names were recommended to the authorities in Toronto, Posen kept

remembering Molly's heartfelt enthusiasm and wondering whether I might be the answer to his search. It was apparently not an easy decision to make. One problem, according to Posen himself, was that I was not a Canadian, and therefore there might be criticisms about his surrendering one of Canada's great cultural heroes to an outsider. Another problem was that I was not a professional musician or musicologist, and there might be criticisms about putting a great artist into the hands of a mere journalist. I could not deny the charges. I am an American and I have spent much of my life working for such periodicals as *Time, The Saturday Evening Post,* and the New York *Daily News.* On the other hand, I was ready to argue rather strenuously that art is international, that Gould was an international figure, that I had known and loved music all my life, and that journalism consists mainly of getting at the truth and reporting it in an interesting way.

After summoning me to a very pleasant interrogation over lunch at the Windsor Arms Hotel in Toronto, Posen and his associates decided to take their chances on me. In the contract that Posen drafted and I signed, we agreed on certain ground rules for this biography of Gould. Among other things, we agreed that I would "endeavour to be sensitive to, to look carefully into and to give close attention in the Biography to the impact of the country of Canada and way of life of Canada on Glenn Gould's development, life and work." I had no doubts or hesitations in signing such a pledge, for I do know that being a Canadian was important to Gould, and I also like Canada very much.

The Glenn Gould Estate gave me exclusive access to Gould's papers in the National Library, and so I spent the fall of 1986 in Ottawa, reading and listening and taking what finally amounted to about one thousand pages of typewritten notes. The Glenn Gould Estate also promised to help open whatever doors needed to be opened to whatever friends and relatives I wanted to interview. And all of this was done, and after more than eighty tape-recorded interviews, I amassed nearly two thousand pages of transcripts.

Despite the estate's official involvement, however, Posen's contract promised me that this would be my book, and that all the judgments in it would be my judgments. "Subject to the foregoing," as the document declares, "it is understood that the final decision on the content of the Biography will be yours. . . ." The contract called for my manuscript to be sent to Posen for his inspection, it gave him the right to point out anything he considered inaccurate or defamatory, and it required that I "act reasonably in considering any such notice." That is the extent of our agreement.

So this is my book, representing my views and my judgments, and if anyone is displeased by anything I have written, I alone am responsible. I hope, of course, that no such reactions will occur.

This book, finally, has required a good deal of help from a good many people, and now it is time to thank them. Thanks first to Steve Posen for his trust and confidence in me. Thanks to Russell Herbert Gould and Vera Gould for their help and cooperation; and to Ray Roberts, Gould's friend and assistant, for the hours he spent in answering my questions.

The process of interviewing has been a long and interesting one. For assistance of all kinds, large and small, I owe a debt of gratitude to (in alphabetical order): John Barnes, John Beckwith, Leonard Bernstein, Boris Brott, Martin Canin, Sam Carter, Schuyler Chapin, Robert Craft, David Diamond, Timothy Findley, Winston Fitzgerald, Elizabeth Fox, Malcolm Frager, Robert Fulford, Monica Gaylord, Nicholas Goldschmidt, Gary Graffman, Jessie Greig, Morris Gross, George Roy Hill, Dr. Fred Hochberg, Paul Hume, Don Hunstein, Deborah Ishlon, Andrew Kazdin, Nicholas Kilburn, Jon Klibonoff, Susan Koscis, Franz Kraemer, Polly Kraft, Jaime Laredo, William Littler, James Lotz, John McGreevy, Karen McLaughlin, Peter Mak, Sir Neville Marriner, Lois Marshall, Martin Mayer, Bruno Monsaingeon, Paul Myers, Nancy Newman, Richard Nielsen, Harvey Olnick, David Oppenheim, Dr. Peter Ostwald, Margaret Pacsu, Tim Page, Dr. Emil Pascarelli, Geoffrey Payzant, Judith Pearlman, R.A.J. Phillips, Ruth Pincoe, Mario Prizek, Alan Rich, John Peter Lee Roberts, Joseph Roddy, Roger Rosenblatt, Roxolana Roslak, Lillian Ross, Edward Rothstein, Alexander Schneider, Harold Schonberg, Richard Sennett, Robert Silverman, Robert Skelton, Janet Somerville, Dr. Irvin Stein, Frederic Steinway, Dr. Joseph Stephens, Annalyn Swan, Vincent Tovell, Lorne Tulk, Kurt Vonnegut, and Ronald Wilford.

A special word of thanks to Dr. Helmut Kallmann, head of the music department at the National Library of Canada, and to his staff, notably Stephen Willis, curator of the Gould collection, and Gilles St. Laurent, who runs the machines in the tape vault.

Thanks to Nancy Canning, who produced the bibliography and discography at the end of this book.

Thanks to Dorothy Marcinek, who transcribed many of the interview tapes and retyped the manuscript.

Thanks to Lucinda Vardey for originally discovering me. And, of course, to Molly.

Otto Friedrich

Locust Valley, New York
December 1, 1988

Contents

GLENN GOULD

A LIFE AND VARIATIONS

I

The Legacy

The television cameras came to watch the memorial service for Glenn Gould, to observe everything and to record everything that they observed. They silently inspected the stained-glass windows that color St. Paul's Anglican Church in downtown Toronto. They silently surveyed the gathering of about three thousand friends and admirers, some of whom had known Gould well, some who had known him only in passing, and some who had known only his music, all crowded into that monumental church to pay homage. While the TV cameras watched, the microphones listened. They listened to Gould's admirers singing the "Old Hundredth," one of those stately hymns that he had loved ever since his childhood. "All people that on earth do dwell,/Sing to the Lord with cheerful voice:/Him serve with fear, his praise forth tell,/Come ye before him and rejoice."

The television cameras are always intruders, always asserting that all of life—even a memorial service for the dead—is mere raw material, fodder, film to be processed in the entertainment factory that serves us all. But the television cameras deserved their place as observers at the Gould service, for though the celebrated pianist had lived an unusually private and solitary life, though he had abandoned his extraordinary career as a concert performer, he had never abandoned what he once called "my love affair with the microphone." To him, the microphone and the camera brought a kind of artistic freedom that could be achieved in no other way. "I believe in 'the intrusion' of technology," he once wrote, "because, essentially, that intrusion imposes upon art a notion of morality which transcends the idea of art itself."

The television cameras know nothing of such things. They only watch and record. "Time present and time past/ Are both perhaps present in time future," as T. S. Eliot wrote at the start of *Burnt Norton*, "And time future contained in time past./ If all time is eternally present/ All time is unredeemable./ What might have been is an abstraction/ Remaining a perpetual possibility. . . ." Now, in October of 1982, now that Glenn Gould was dead, killed by a stroke just a few days after his fiftieth birthday, now the television cameras in the crowded Church of St. Paul watched Robert Aitken play a Bach flute sonata and the Orford Quartet play the cavatina from Beethoven's Opus 130. They watched Maureen Forrester, in tears, sing "Have Mercy, Lord," from the *St. Matthew Passion*, that beautiful lament in which Gould had accompanied her at one of her earliest concerts nearly thirty years earlier. They watched John Peter Lee Roberts, a Canadian Broadcasting Corporation executive who had been one of Gould's best friends, delivering his tribute. "When Glenn performed . . ." Roberts said, "he stood outside himself in an ecstasy which brought together music, mind and what I can only describe as a reaching toward God. The result was not so much an interpretation as a realization or re-creation of the music. . . . Glenn has gone now, but we must be grateful for his life and the rich legacy he has left us. . . ."

Then there sounded through the vaulted church a taped recording of the theme that symbolized that whole legacy, the stately saraband that Bach had used as the foundation of *The Goldberg Variations*. This had been Gould's choice for his spectacular debut on Columbia Records a quarter-century earlier, when he was a bold newcomer of twenty-three, and his reflective reinterpretation of that famous performance had just appeared on the market as the last of his fourscore recordings—and thus his testament.

And now, far more than when he was alive a decade ago, Gould has become the heroic icon to an increasingly widespread cult. This cult is based on the perfectly sound view that Gould was an extraordinary pianist, but it also extends considerably beyond that. It suggests that Gould's mastery of recording technology, his imaginative experiments in radio and television, and his extensive writings on all the communications media combine to make him a major contemporary thinker, an important theoretician of the postindustrial era. It also implies that in his much-publicized withdrawal from the competitive life, in his insistence on the value of solitude, Gould acquired a somehow superhuman persona, a spiritual power of the kind that would once have been attributed to martyred saints but now is more commonly ascribed to fallen movie stars—and that, accordingly, every relic of his private life deserves public enshrinement.

The rituals of ceremonial worship in our time are gigantically visual (even for classical pianists), and so when the New York Metropolitan Museum of Art invited Gould's admirers to come and hear him play a series of eight concerts in September of 1987, it invited them to watch him play on a screen about twenty feet high. The rituals are also intensely institutional. There is now a Glenn Gould Foundation and a Glenn Gould Prize, and the Canadian government extended the full weight of its beneficence in 1986 by sending a Glenn Gould exhibition to be seen by large crowds in Paris, Italy, and Eastern Europe. The institutional enthusiasm for organized discourse seems insatiable. The Canadian Society for Esthetics writes to invite one's participation in a "colloquium" on "the numerous facets of Gould's genius" at the University of Quebec in October of 1987. The Glenn Gould Society in the Netherlands, which publishes a glossy magazine about its hero, requests one's assistance in a Glenn Gould Symposium in Amsterdam in May of 1988. The National Library of Canada, in announcing a Gould exhibition to run throughout the summer of 1988, also announces a symposium on "Gould the Communicator."

In addition to all these official ceremonies, a number of admirers worship the icon in their oddly personal ways. The authorities guarding the relics receive frequent inquiries from supplicants who want to engage in various kinds of Gouldian research, Gould studies, Gould books, Gould catalogues. "There is a lady from Texas whose mother saw Gould in a dream," one of the pianist's friends writes from Toronto. "They were on a train, and he was telling the old Texas lady (who had never heard or seen Gould) that her daughter should work on a film project about his 'methods of creation. . . .'"

It may be useful to reassert the basic facts underlying the mythology. Gould was inexplicably gifted in childhood with a phenomenal natural talent for playing the piano. Blessed with understanding parents and a sympathetic teacher, he flowered, in his early twenties, into one of the world's very greatest pianists, one of the very greatest interpreters of both Bach and such modern masters as Schoenberg and Hindemith. Cursed, however, with a fear and even hatred of his natural environment, the concert hall, he managed to discover a way of escaping from the stage into the recording studio and continuing his career, behind clouds of self-created publicity, entirely in private. He made more than eighty records, which range across an enormous repertoire from Byrd and Gibbons through most of Bach, Mozart, and Beethoven and on into Wagner, Strauss, and Sibelius. These recordings, some of them glorious, all of them interesting, and now artfully preserved on compact disks, represent Gould's major contribution to art in our time.

There is something both exaggerated and poisonous, however, in our fascination with performing artists. As with our political leaders, we yearn both to idolize them and to possess them, and finally to degrade and destroy them. Gould's achievements would have been enough for most musicians to die rich and happy, but he was one of those restless souls who can see the falsities in the public admiration and who keep searching for new purposes in life. He worked hard at becoming a composer and even harder at creating compositions out of radio voices; he dreamed of writing both religious music and historical novels; he was beginning, in his last years, to create a new career as a conductor. And just as Gould rejected the richly rewarded role of virtuoso, the public that wanted to lionize him onstage eventually started to share his own idea that he was destined for greater things than performance, perhaps as a philosopher, perhaps as a saint.

But perhaps Gould finally saw through all such ambitions as well. There are many who thought he was crazy to give up a life that others keep struggling to achieve; there are some who believe that his undeniable eccentricity was simply his own way of dealing with life, and mastering it. The Canadian friend who wrote about the woman from Texas writes again to report that "a musician I know wrote a piece a while back called, 'Glenn Gould is alive and well in Orillia.' The basic premise is that he got bored, staged his own death, and is now sitting up in Orillia [the lakeside town where he spent his boyhood summers], watching all the fuss."

It is a pleasant thought, that Gould is alive and well in Orillia, but he is not. He is dead, dead, dead. And now it is time to start examining the legacy.

Bits and pieces of the Glenn Gould legacy survive in a large and silent room overlooking the lazy flow of the Ottawa River. On the fifth floor of the National Library of Canada, just a bit beyond the Supreme Court and the Justice Ministry and the splendidly Gothic revival Parliament—where a statue of a sword-wielding Sir Galahad commemorates the unsuccessful attempt by a young man named Henry Harper to rescue a girl named Bessie from the flooding river in 1901—there lie all of Gould's papers, boxes and boxes of letters ("Seventy-two meters of shelves," one librarian says proudly), radio scripts, canceled checks, Grammy nominations, newspaper clippings, medical prescriptions, and much more.

Some of the old passions still breathe. "You can't imagine the effect, the cheers, the happiness and the overwhelming joy . . . [you] produced upon me, my colleagues, and our students!" an admirer named Kitty Gvozdeva wrote from Leningrad. "We all welcome and greet you with the greatest love, admiration and affection we are capable of. . . ." Or from Budapest, in broken French: "Je suis Hongroise. J'aime beaucoup la musique. J'ai en entendu le votre concert en la radio. Je suis la votre appassioné ammiratrice. . . ." Or from somewhere in America, from an eighteen-year-old student: "Dear Glenn, You know, you make love to the piano keys, and it is the most beautiful thing I have ever seen." And from somewhere else in America: "Dear Mr. Gould: Please complete the following questionnaire and return to me at once, since my future depends entirely upon your answers: 1) Have you written any string quartets since your Opus 1? 2) Are you engaged? 3) Are you married? 4) If I come to Toronto, will you permit me to see you?"

He saved all these things. He saved a check stub for ten dollars, the first money he ever earned by playing the piano, when he won a Kiwanis prize back in the 1940's. He saved four battered leather wallets that the archivists have now labeled A through D, and a small earthenware mug that offers the familiar plea: "Please don't shoot the piano player. He's doing the best he can." And then there is a box containing several of those famous scarves and mufflers that he wore around his neck on the hottest days of summer. And a tan-covered book filled with blank pages and bearing the "humorous" title, *Essence of an Enigma.*

And half a dozen cardboard cartons full of Gould's own compositions, the surprisingly Brahmsian string quartet, the complex cadenzas to Beethoven's first piano concerto, even a mimeographed copy of a march entitled "Our Gifts," which states on the cover that it was composed by Glenn H. Gould in 1943, when he was a ten-year-old student at the Williamson Road Public School in Toronto. "We are the boys, we are the girls of all the Public Schools," he had written in a burst of wartime patriotism. "We have a Red Cross job to do, to furnish all the tools. . . ." And more than twenty cartons full of the music that he played, Bach, Beethoven, Mendelssohn, Hindemith, more Bach. There are several battered copies of the classic Ralph Kirkpatrick edition of *The Goldberg Variations,* one of them covered with Gould's private notations, like, at the bottom of *Variatio 3:* "N.B.—this is n.n. per se, but it needs a greater sense of cadence. . . ."

And here on these silent shelves in this silent room is a box containing a barometer and thirty-two black felt-tipped pens, the kind that Gould liked to use not only as a marker but as a baton, when he conducted his own recorded performances while listening to playbacks in the shrouded solitude of the studio control booth. And a box containing four pairs of sunglasses and another with three wristwatches, one stopped at quarter past one, one at quarter past five, and one at quarter past six. And a box containing nothing but "miscellaneous keys," dozens and dozens of them, on rings and chains and various bits of string, door keys, car keys, trunk keys, keys to God knows what forgotten cupboards or closets.

And cuff links, dozens of them too, squirreled away in three small containers, not chained sets of cuff links but the spiked kind that can be inserted hastily into the cuffs of white evening dress, pearl and mother-of-pearl, amethyst, gold, brass. He probably never wore a single one of them after that day in 1964 when, at the age of thirty-one, he walked off the concert stage forever. But he saved them. One unmatched cuff link has a rectangular plaque with a G clef inscribed on it; another bears the head of a goddess haloed by a ring of stars. ¡Each single cuff ¡link means that the other in the pair was lost somewhere in the scramble of the concert tour. And somewhere in the correspondence files, there is an unhappy letter from a young stage manager in Winnipeg, who wrote to remind Gould that he had loaned him a pair of his own cuff links, that "I was too excited by the whole thing to remember, and when I did you had gone." These cuff links had "only sentimental value to me," the manager wrote, but could Gould, wherever he now was, please send them back? "I do this so often that I can no longer remember which cuff links are mine . . ." Gould wrote back, barely acknowledging that the sentimental value was now a value forever lost. "The only thing I can suggest is that you go out and buy a pair like you had before and please send the bill to me. . . ."

And a jumble of books. The memoirs of Turgenev, Philippe Halsman's *Jump Book,* a deluxe edition of *Walden,* six plays of Strindberg, Waugh's *The Loved One,* a review copy of H. H. Stuckenschmidt's biography of Schoenberg, Goncharov's *Oblomov.* An inscribed copy of Lillian Ross's *Picture;* an inscribed copy of Yehudi Menuhin's *The Music of Man.* A paperback edition of Robert Nozick's *Anarchy, State and Utopia,* marked only by Gould's interest in a passage about animals. "Because people eat animals, they raise more than otherwise would exist without this practice," Nozick had written. "To exist for a while is better than never to exist at all." With one of his black felt pens, Gould heavily underlined that last sentence.

And then there are several copies of Geoffrey Payzant's intellectual study, *Glenn Gould, Music and Mind,* and there is Tim Page's *Glenn Gould Reader,* which contains the review that Gould, who had read and approved Payzant's book before publication, wrote of it after publication. "Professor Payzant makes clear that he . . . has not attempted a biographical study," Gould observed, with the academic owlishness that he loved to affect, "that Gould's private life is, in fact, 'austere and unremarkable,' and that 'a book on his life and times would be brief and boring.'" Chinese boxes contain nests of smaller and still smaller boxes. How many men ever get a chance even to see their own biographies, much less to write reviews criticizing them? (And just as Gould had approved Payzant's book, Payzant had approved Gould's review of it.)

But Gould's dedication to technology provides even stranger

forms of Chinese boxes. Here, on a library shelf containing more than 150 of Gould's videotapes, cassettes that range from Bernstein performances of Beethoven symphonies to the insomniac Gould's tapings of *The Mary Tyler Moore Show,* here is a TV series called *Glenn Gould Plays Bach,* which begins with the camera staring at the score of Bach's *Art of the Fugue.* Then it stares at a portrait of Gould in profile, superimposed on the Bach fugue. Then the image of Gould in profile suddenly comes to life and begins playing the Bach score. Then the camera pulls back to show a TV screen, to demonstrate that what we had been watching was only an image of Gould playing Bach on that screen, and now the camera pulls back still farther to show us Gould's performance on the screen being watched by Gould in an easy chair, ready to discuss all these complexities with Bruno Monsaingeon, the French TV producer who arranged the whole affair.

Such are the marvels that technology can produce at the flick of a switch, but they have no substance, no reality, no life. Flick the switch again, and the music of Bach immediately stops, the image quickly shrinks to a shining dot at the center of the TV screen, and we are left sitting in the comfortable silence of the National Library of Canada. Silence—in the stillness of this shrine, one must keep reminding oneself that Gould's greatness derived from the sounds that he created, the patterns of sound, the music.

Gould's piano, his battered black Steinway grand, now stands in a lonely place of honor on the library's ground floor, in a kind of niche at the foot of a circling stairway. It is a ceremonial stairway for state occasions, all walled and floored in what appears to be white marble, and the ordinary visitors who use the nearby elevators rarely catch a glimpse of either the stairway or of Gould's piano. Actually, this is only one of five pianos that could be designated as "Glenn Gould's piano." Another Steinway that he kept in his apartment was sold to the governor-general's residence to be played on such ceremonial occasions as Canada Day. Another Gould piano was loaned to the Vancouver Museum, and still others are regularly sent out to various exhibitions of Gould memorabilia.

But this warm instrument under the stairway of the National Library was the one Gould loved best, and it bears its official Steinway name, "CD 318," stamped in gold letters deep in its covering top. It was built in 1945, and once Gould discovered it, he made it his own. He used it for most of his recordings, shipping it to and fro between Toronto and New York, until there inevitably came the day when careless movers dropped it from a considerable height and then shoved it into place and pretended that nothing had happened. "The plate is fractured in four critical places," Gould reported bitterly to Steinway in December of 1971 after examining the ruins of his piano. "The lid is split at the bass end and there also is considerable damage to it toward the treble end as well. The sounding board is split at the treble end. Key slip pins are bent out of line. . . ." Technicians labored for months over the carcass of 318, but it could never be restored to Gould's satisfaction. His last recording of *The Goldberg Variations* was made on a Yamaha.

Still, CD 318 is, more than any other instrument, except perhaps the tinkly old Chickering that he used throughout his boyhood, Glenn Gould's piano. So when the executor divided up the estate and consigned CD 318 to the National Library, he stipulated that it should not be treated simply as an object of veneration but worked on and played by other pianists. And so, in the fall of 1986, we gathered in the auditorium of the National Library to hear a young pianist named Angela Hewitt give CD 318 its first public workout.

She was very engaging, attractive, buoyant, confident. She had won the 1986 International Bach Piano Competition in Toronto, and now she had come to the shrine to perform for us. Gould's father, Russell Herbert Gould, was there to listen, an aged but still erect figure in evening dress, and so were Miss Hewitt's own parents. She looked charming, in a black velvet tuxedo and an absurd red bow tie, and she played beautifully—one of the French Suites and a Weber sonata—with just the right combination of precision and ardor. We were all filled with admiration, and with a sense of the occasion, and we all knew that her last encore would have to be, as it of course was, the theme of *The Goldberg Variations*.

There was a wine-tasting reception afterward, and then they took Gould's piano away, and soon it was once again standing in isolation at the foot of the stairway, with a great steel clamp holding the keyboard shut and silent.

But there are always the tapes, boxes and boxes of tapes, shelf upon shelf of tapes—miles of tape. We are now in the audio archive, on the third floor of the National Library, an archive walled by rows of cinder blocks all painted in baby blue. Somebody tried to use paint to bring light to this vault, but there is no real light except what comes from three or four unshaded bulbs hanging in the darkness and silence. Here is a shelf entirely devoted to rows of seven-inch tapes, each bearing a label that tells and does not tell what the box contains: Haydn piano sonata, Elizabethan keyboard music, Anhalt fantasia, Prokofiev piano music, Beethoven variations in C minor, Hindemith piano sonata No. 1, Schumann piano quartet. . . .

There is another Glenn Gould here too, the Gould who built a whole new career for himself, after his retirement from the concert stage, as an explorer at the outer limits of radio and television, an explorer who first interviewed and then cut and spliced and wove until he had achieved another kind of music that he liked to call "contrapuntal radio." Here the labels on the boxed reels of tape tell their story of work completed: "Quiet in the Land," Freissan interview; "Quiet in the Land," Horsch interview; "Quiet in the Land," Mrs. Toews interview; "Quiet in the Land," Hiebert interview. . . . "Quiet in the Land," which Gould worked on for several years, was a documentary about the Mennonites, who, as he quoted one of them saying, were "in this world but not of it." This was the conclusion of the series that Gould called his "solitude trilogy," all symbolically set in the Canadian North. The idea of North—that was his title for the first in the series—was very important to Gould. So was the idea of solitude.

When we enter the cinder-block vaults of the National Library of Canada, we come there not just to survey the rows on rows of more than fifteen hundred tapes but to hear, in the midst of the all-enveloping silence, the sound of one of the great artists of our time. On the machines that Gould loved, one can play not only such familiar wonders as Bach's partitas but also such unfamiliar wonders as the Gould version of Beethoven's *Hammerklavier Sonata*. And then there are half-remembered tapes of half-remembered Canadian television shows—Gould playing Scriabin preludes in front of a swirling cloud of Scriabinesque colors, Gould dressed up in a white suit to recite bits of William Walton's *Façade*. And in and out of the music, one keeps intermittently hearing that odd, nervous, clipped, self-conscious voice—returned, for a moment, from the dead—saying, "This is Glenn Gould—"

II

The Prodigy

Not long after Glenn Gould's extraordinary New York debut in 1955, when it first became internationally known that this young Canadian pianist could play like an angel, and looked rather like an angel too, Florence Gould received a letter from an old friend named Pearl. "How my heart leaped with joy knowing how delighted his dear little mother would be . . ." she wrote. "Knowing as I do what a good Christian girl you are I couldn't help but recall the words no good thing will He withhold from them that walk uprightly."

Pearl had not seen her friend since one summer day in the 1920's, when Florence was still Florence Greig and had come to visit her at her father's house in Moncton, New Brunswick. Pearl's aunt had been sick, and the girls' chattering disturbed her. "My father who loved music and thought so much of you told us to go outside and sing," Pearl wrote, "so we went out and sat on the back fence and sang. You told me some day you were going to marry and have a little boy and his name would be Glenn. I said I suppose he will be musical. You quickly said I'll see to that, with a twinkle in your eye. I shall never forget that day. You were never satisfied with just anything, you wanted only the best. . . ."

Florence Greig, who worked for many years as a teacher of singing, was proud to claim a dim connection to Edvard Grieg. Her only child, Glenn, occasionally joked about his own reluctance to record the famous Piano Concerto in A minor by the Norwegian composer, whom he liked to describe as one of his mother's cousins. Both Florence Greig and Edvard Grieg were actually descended from a fierce

Scottish tribe known as the MacGregors, who claimed a royal descent from Griogair, son of Alpin, King of the Scots in the eighth century. The family motto is "'S Rìoghal mo dhream" (Royal is my race). The MacGregors once owned much of Argyll and Perthshire, but they were such a warlike clan that they were entirely proscribed in the seventeenth century, in the reign of King James VI (James I of England). The use of the family name was decreed punishable by death, and so the MacGregors became Gregs and Gregsons and Greigs.

Family legend claimed that the MacGregors rose up to fight for Bonnie Prince Charlie at Culloden in 1746, and that one of the survivors fled to Norway and eventually became the great-grandfather of Edvard Grieg. There are always scholars who devote their efforts to investigating such legends—in this case, J. Russell Greig, author of *Grieg and His Scottish Ancestry*, 1952—and the investigation unfortunately demonstrated that Alexander Greig, who was only six when the Scots fought at Culloden, probably emigrated to Norway simply to seek his fortune. He made it as an exporter of Norwegian lobster and stockfish.

Most family histories are equally prosaic. Peter Greig, one of thirteen children of a Scottish farmer, emigrated to Canada in the mid-nineteenth century. He and his wife, Emma, had ten children, one of whom was Charles Holman Greig, who married Mary Catherine Flett, whose father, a carpenter from the Orkneys, died in a fall from the roof of the Bank of Montreal. One of their children, Florence, duly met and married Russell Herbert Gould, whose father's business card said: "Thomas G. Gould, Fur Salon, Designers and Manufacturers of Quality Fur Garments." Bert Gould inherited and managed that prosperous fur business. His wife was forty-two when their only son was born. But even before he was born, according to her niece, Jessie Greig, "she did play music all the time she was carrying Glenn, with the hope that he was going to be a classical pianist."

Q: You think she had that in mind from the beginning?

A: I *know* she did.

And what can Bert Gould remember of his son's earliest days? Sitting with a cup of coffee in his sunny living room in Toronto, the old man smiles at the familiar question and offers a familiar answer. "When Glenn was just a few days old," he says, "he would reach up his arms like this. . . ." He raises his own aged arms toward the ceiling and wiggles his fingers to illustrate the idea of a week-old infant playing Bach. "Just a minute," he says, hurrying away to look for supporting evidence. "Here, this is something I did for that exhibition in France."

"As soon as he was old enough to be held on his grandmother's knee at the piano," the handsomely printed statement by Bert Gould declares, "he would never pound the key board as most children will with the whole hand, striking a number of keys at a time, instead he would always insist on pressing down a single key and holding it down until the resulting sound had completely died away. The fading vibration entirely fascinated him. . . ."

This is the stuff of legends, of course, a Christ child raising a hand to bless his worshipers, a boyish Napoleon brandishing a sword, a diminutive Mozart mesmerizing the courts of Europe by his agility at the harpsichord. But Glenn Gould really did have a talent that defied ordinary explanations. His father, who had played the violin in boyhood until he injured his hand, saw that easily. His mother soon realized that he had perfect pitch, and she began giving him piano lessons when he was three. He could read music before he could read words. She "used to play a game of note recognition with Glenn," according to Bert Gould's recollections. "He would go to a room at the far end of the house and his mother would strike a different chord on the piano in the living room. Invariably Glenn would call the correct answer."

The Goulds were obviously quite aware that their very left-handed child was unlike any others, and the child, though lucky in having such perceptive parents, was also quite aware of his own differentness, separateness, uniqueness. His father recalls that even as a baby, he wouldn't catch or play with a rubber ball. "And as he grew up," Bert Gould says, "if you threw a tennis ball—tried to get him to catch it—he'd turn his back and let it hit him, but he wouldn't catch it. Never would." Jessie Greig remembers when he came to her house for a visit at Easter time, when he was seven or eight, and he went outside to watch Jessie and her brothers playing marbles. "He watched for a long time, with his hands in his pockets," Miss Greig recalls, "and then he said, 'I'd like to play.' So we handed him some marbles, and he just put his hand down once to the cold earth, and he withdrew it *so* quickly—and he put his hands back in his pockets and said, 'I'm afraid I can't.' Even at that age, his hands must have been very, very sensitive, and he just said, 'I can't.' And he really wanted to. I can see him yet, kicking the earth with one toe, and wanting to join in and not being able to."

By then, the child seemed to have already decided on his future. "Oh, there was no doubt about that from the time he was three to five, anywhere in there," says Bert Gould. "In fact, at five years old, Glenn told me himself, 'I'm going to be a concert pianist.' He never changed his mind." But it was only a little later, when he was six, that the child was taken to his first concert, a recital by the legendary Josef Hofmann. "It was a staggering impression," Gould said later. "The only thing I can really remember is that, when I was being brought home in the car, I was in that wonderful state of half-awakeness in which you hear all sorts of incredible sounds going through your mind. They were all *orchestral* sounds, but *I* was playing them all, and suddenly I was Hofmann. I was enchanted."

There was something uncanny, unnatural, about Glenn Gould's gift. Most child prodigies work like galley slaves, many of them driven by their authoritarian parents or teachers, but Gould largely created himself. His indulgent mother was his only teacher until he was ten, by which time he had already mastered all of the first book of Bach's *Well-Tempered Clavier,* and then she turned him over to the almost equally indulgent Alberto Guerrero at the Toronto Conservatory. An émigré from Chile, Guerrero had conventionally definite views about how things should be played, but he easily recognized the uniqueness of the young Gould. "If Glenn feels he hasn't learned anything from me as a teacher, it's the greatest compliment anyone could give me," Guerrero's widow, Myrtle, once quoted him as saying. "The whole secret of teaching Glenn is to let him discover things for himself."

Gould not only taught himself, in the special music room that his father built so that the boy could play late at night, but he rarely worked very hard on anything that he wanted to learn. "I go days—not only days, but weeks—without touching the piano," he said to a slightly shocked interviewer in 1970. "I've never seen why it's necessary.... I play best after the two weeks or so that I've laid off." And he said it was that simple from the beginning. "I never bothered to practice very much—I now practice almost not at all—but even in those days I was far from being a slave of the instrument," he said in one of his long telephone talks with Jonathan Cott (*Conversations with Glenn Gould*). Gould professed to believe, in fact, that there was little to be taught or learned in the way of technique. "Given half an hour of your time and your spirit and a quiet room," he once said to a room full of educators, "I could teach any of you how to play the piano—everything there is to know about playing the piano can be taught in half an hour, I'm convinced of it."

Gould quickly added that he had never tried this experiment on any pupil, and there may have been a certain amount of hyperbole in his statement, perhaps a certain desire to *épater le pédagogue*. It seems more likely, however, that Gould's claim reflected a desire to generalize from his own experience, to deny the strangeness of his gift. After all, Bach himself had once said of his own skill as a keyboard virtuoso: "There is nothing to it. You have only to hit the right notes at the right time, and the instrument plays itself." But Bach also attributed his ability to hard work—"Whoever is equally industrious will succeed just as well"—whereas Gould seemed to feel very little need, at least on technical details, to work at all.

He could sight-read anything, and memorize at sight. John Roberts recalls Gould "flawlessly sight-reading" the Grieg concerto and then saying, "I just try not to look at the battlefield." Roberts also remembers an occasion when Gould challenged him to name any piece of music that Gould could not instantly play from memory. Roberts asked for specific sections of Strauss's *Burleske*, Prokofiev's Seventh Sonata, Beethoven's Opus 31, No. 3, "as well as other works, all of which he could do instantly."

These are all part of a fairly standard piano repertoire, of course, but Gould's head was full of orchestral and operatic works too. Roberts used to visit him at the summer home that Bert Gould had built on Lake Simcoe, about sixty miles north of Toronto, and there would be "sessions" at the piano that lasted until 3 A.M., sessions in which Gould seemed to transcribe the most complex orchestral scores as he went along. "I can remember him performing *Pelleas und Melisande* by Schoenberg with his eyes mostly closed . . ." Roberts recalled later. "Another example was the 'Four Last Songs' of Richard Strauss. He also had whole opera scores in the back of his head. Once he started Wagner's *Tristan und Isolde,* Glenn would be lost in another world, often oblivious to the presence of anyone else."

Judith Pearlman, the TV producer who made a television version of Gould's radio documentary, "The Idea of North," had a similar experience during her stay in Toronto. "After he had finished his recording session, I was in the control room, on the phone to New York, and he just sat down at the piano and started to play—all kinds of things. I knew he didn't like to have anybody listen to him, but after a while, I decided to come out of the control room. I *sneaked* out. I was terrified. Hearing him play live, which nobody ever heard—but he went right on playing. He said, 'Do you know this?' He was playing something from *Der Rosenkavalier.* And I said, 'Do you know *Die Frau ohne Schatten?'* And he just looked at me and then started playing the whole thing, from memory, and singing all the parts. I couldn't *move.* This is a big chunk of music, you know, and for him to have the whole thing in his head—"

Even that is not unique. Arthur Rubinstein once took the score of an unknown piano concerto aboard a plane to Spain and then performed it from memory, and without any rehearsal. Alicia de Larrocha has reported much the same thing. The pianist John Browning recalls that George Szell could sit down at a piano and play Beethoven string quartets from memory, or his own transcriptions of Strauss tone poems. "He could isolate on the piano, the viola part for a Schubert or Mozart quartet that he hadn't thought of in twenty years," Browning told David Dubal *(Reflections from the Keyboard).* These are no ordinary gifts, of course, but neither are they unimaginable. Gould's gift virtually was. He seems to have heard and perceived and taken in sound in a way that was quite different from the way these things are done by ordinary people. He himself became aware of this strange faculty when he was about thirteen, when he was working on a Mozart fugue in C minor (K. 394), and a surly household maid was determined to interrupt his work by turning on her vacuum cleaner.

"Well, the result was," as Gould recalled in an address to the graduating class at the Toronto Conservatory in 1964, "that in the louder passages, this luminously diatonic music ... became sur-rounded with a halo of vibrato, rather the effect that you might get if you sang in the bathtub with both ears full of water and shook your head from side to side all at once. And in the softer passages I couldn't hear any sound that I was making at all. I could feel, of course—I could sense the tactile relation with the keyboard ... and I could imagine what I was doing, but I couldn't actually hear it. But the strange thing was that all of it suddenly sounded better than it had without the vacuum cleaner, and those parts which I couldn't actually hear sounded best of all."

John Cage, during his period of absorption with aleatory music, or music of chance, was once reported to have listened with an expression of boredom to a recording of a familiar Brahms sym-phony—then to have smiled with pleasure when he heard the sym-phony suddenly interrupted by a doorbell. This was not because he welcomed the prospect of a visitor but because he welcomed the opportunity to hear for the first time the chance combination of a Brahms symphony and a ringing doorbell. Gould's perception of Mozart and the vacuum cleaner was not just an acceptance of an odd combination of sounds but an almost complete separation of his sense of music from his sense of hearing.

He liked to play two radios simultaneously, he once told Richard Kostelanetz, and "quite mysteriously, I discovered that I could better learn Schoenberg's difficult piano score, Opus 23, if I listened to them both at once, the FM to hear music and the AM to hear the news." Kostelanetz further recorded that Gould could read maga-zines while talking on the telephone and could "learn a Beethoven score while carrying on a conversation." Gould was not doing this to show off; he had simply discovered in himself a remarkable capac-ity to hear different things at once (notably the intertwining voices in Bach's fugues), and he found that this capacity somehow helped him to absorb music almost instantaneously. "If I am in a great hurry to acquire an imprint of some new score on my mind," he told the students at the Toronto Conservatory as an elaboration on his story of the vacuum cleaner, "I simulate the effect of the vacuum cleaner by placing some totally contrary noises as close to the instrument as I can. It doesn't matter what noise, really—TV westerns, Beatles records; anything loud will suffice—because what I managed to learn through the accidental coming together of Mozart and the vacuum cleaner was that the inner ear of the imagination is very much more powerful a stimulant than is any amount of outward observation."

Gould not only could hear and take in and memorize several things at once, but he heard with an incredible precision. Karen McLaughlin, who worked on the second recording of *The Goldberg Variations*, recalls that the sound engineers were amazed to find that Gould could differentiate between the playbacks from two different digital recording systems. "One was a Sony and one was a Mitsubishi, and the technical specifications were identical," she says, "and yet Glenn could unerringly tell them which was which. And that just amazed them. Nobody else could hear that kind of thing."

Despite a certain amount of theorizing and rationalizing, Gould seems to have been unable to understand the mysterious workings of his mysterious gift. "He was never terribly conscious of landing on right notes or worrying about that kind of thing," John Roberts remembers. "Once he began to think pianistically, it was destructive. I actually believe that at a certain moment, Glenn began to wonder, 'Well, how do I do this?' But he could never know how he did it. He just did it. And any kind of questioning, any conversation which veered toward how things are done really brought quite a reaction. He couldn't stand to talk about anything like that. That's why he disliked talking to other pianists. He had to try and protect himself from that."

Even for these disturbing aspects of his gift, though, Gould developed a theory, a metaphor, a source of authority. "Schoenberg once said," he observed, "that he would not willingly be asked by any of his composition students exactly why such-and-such a process served him well, because the question made him feel like that centipede who was asked in which order it moved its hundred legs, and afterwards he could move no legs at all—there's something impotent-making about that question. I'm rather afraid of it."

Perhaps the best analogy to Gould's strange gift lies in the ability to play chess blindfolded, even to play several such games simultaneously. This is not something that can be taught; it is simply there or not there. The prize example is Paul Morphy, of whom it has been said that having his mind must have been like having the boxing ability of Joe Louis when everyone else in the world was five feet high. Morphy took up chess at eight and could defeat anyone in his native New Orleans when he was ten. At nineteen, having won his law degree but being too young to practice, he went to New York to compete in the first American Chess Congress, which he won easily. Moving on to Europe, where he soon defeated the unofficial world champion, Adolf Anderssen, Morphy gave an exhibition in Paris by playing blindfolded against eight opponents at once, a world record at that time. The next day, he could still recite all the moves in all the games. He then planned to play blindfolded against twenty opponents, but friends dissuaded him on the ground that such an effort might cause a mental breakdown.

Thwarted in his ambition to overthrow his last rival, the British champion Howard Staunton, who evaded every challenge from the young American, Morphy sailed back to a hero's welcome in New York ("One smile, one glow of pride and pleasure, runs all over the land ..." wrote James Russell Lowell). But after a competitive career that had lasted only about a year and a half, Morphy gave up chess, with a Gouldian abandon, and never again played a major match. Indeed, he seems to have acquired an intense distaste for the game. Even his friends could see that something had gone wrong. Morphy returned to his mother's home in New Orleans, dabbled at the law, engaged in a protracted litigation against a brother-in-law who he thought had defrauded him. He claimed that enemies were trying to poison his food. For two decades, he emerged from his mother's house at noon every day, walked alone through the streets, swinging his cane, often talking to himself. At night, he went to the opera. One summer morning in 1884, when Morphy was forty-seven, his mother found him dead of a stroke in his bathtub.

One cannot help wondering what chess meant to Morphy. (Ernest Jones once wrote an elaborate psychoanalytic study, *The Problem of Paul Morphy*, suggesting that "the unconscious motive activating the players is not the mere love of pugnacity characteristic of all competitive games but the grimmer one of father-murder.") How would his life have been different if chess had been more systematically organized in those days, and if it had been possible for him to become the world champion? Conversely, what would his life have been like if he had never seen a chessboard, if he had lived in a society where the game of chess was completely unknown? Would that extraordinary brain have turned to some other form of strategic planning—to the manipulation of the stock market, for example—or would it have remained forever passive, dormant? And what of Glenn Gould, if, say, his mother had never owned a piano? Might that piercing mind have devoted itself to chess (Bert Gould did teach his son to play)? Or to investment banking (Gould later did invest his earnings very profitably)? Or to who knows what?

From another perspective, of course, Gould was destined to spend much of his early life as just another little boy growing up in just another neighborhood. The Goulds lived in an intensely WASP area known as The Beaches, and it was just a short walk from their modest house at 32 Southwood Drive down to the amiable streetcar line on Queen Street and then to the even more amiable boardwalk along the shore of Lake Ontario. Even now, if one looks westward toward downtown Toronto, a spit of land blocks the entire city from sight. One is completely cut off, in a very pleasant enclave.

Outside that enclave lay a world strange and ominous. "The most vivid of my childhood memories in connection with Toronto have to do with churches," Gould recalled in his script for a television show, "Glenn Gould's Toronto." "They have to do with Sunday evening services, with evening light filtered through stained-glass windows, and with ministers who concluded their benedictions with the phrase, 'Lord, give us the peace that the earth cannot give.' Monday mornings, you see, meant that one had to go back to school and encounter all sorts of terrifying situations out *there*. . . ."

Single children almost always encounter difficulties in their first collisions with other children, but Gould's collisions at the Williamson Road Public School, a three-story brick fortress about two blocks from his home, seem to have been particularly bruising. "I found going to school a most unhappy experience," he once told an interviewer, "and got along miserably with most of my teachers and all of my fellow students." The fellow students had similar memories. "He was somewhat isolated from the rest of us," Wayne Fulford, general manager of a bus equipment firm, told a reporter after Gould's death. "I mean, he wasn't somebody who pretended to be interested in hockey or baseball when he wasn't. . . . He didn't always mix in."

Gould was often bullied, sometimes came home crying. "I can remember him saying that the worst bully followed him nearly home and finally took a swing at Glenn," John Roberts recalls. "And Glenn just went for him. And hit him so hard that this kid wondered what had struck him. Then Glenn grabbed him by the lapels and shook him and said, 'If you ever come near me again, I will kill you.' And this kid was absolutely scared out of his mind, and the thing which also frightened Glenn was that he realized that it was true."

The Fulfords lived next door to the Goulds on Southwood Drive, and Wayne Fulford's older brother Robert, former editor of the Toronto magazine *Saturday Night,* has similar memories of the young pianist's loneliness. "I remember him as a child being much more puritanical than our district and our time in history would require," Fulford says. "He was a boy very much unlike other boys in that regard, as in a thousand others. Couldn't stand to hear boys blaspheme or use obscenities. And he would actually beg you not to. His mother had a kind of idea of what was a good child, and he bought it and internalized it. She was a bit of a dragon."

Q: But she wasn't harsh with him, was she?

A: Can't remember her being harsh with Glenn, but there's a way of nagging without being harsh that can be pretty controlling. I can remember her saying, "Glenn, you should do this, Glenn, you should do that." You don't need harshness if you're persistent. And she didn't like him to have opinions that were too confident.

Q: Too confident?

A: Too showing off. She was a real old-fashioned Canadian in that way. Don't come out of hiding too much, and never give an opinion that isn't well considered, and probably don't give it at all. I'd say she was a very narrow person in every way except musically, and maybe musically she was narrow too.

Elizabeth Fox, a CBC producer who became friends with Gould a few years later, has somewhat more amiable memories. "When you'd go to his home, it was just so warm and nice," she says. "I can remember eating well and being treated well, lots of lights on. I liked both his parents. I don't know what they were like with other people, but they were sure nice when I was there. But they constantly— they certainly deferred to him. I thought later of E. B. White's *Stuart Little,* about these people who have a mouse as a child. And he's dressed up as a human being, but he goes up and down the drains and all the rest. Well, when you were at the Goulds' house, you'd think, these people have produced something that is not of them. He's dressed *somewhat* like a human being, and he plays the piano, but it was—they were constantly in awe."

In this difficult period, Jessie Greig came into Gould's life as a kind of rescuer. He had always known her as a cousin living in nearby Uxbridge, but when he was thirteen and she was eighteen, the Goulds invited her to live with them while she attended teacher's college in Toronto. "We were very, very close, and our closeness came from my year there," she says. "He was sort of a capricious, very outgoing child, outgoing in the sense that he could join in any conversation, and did. He was interested in everything. And he had great confidence in everything. And his desire to learn everything was just boundless."

The Goulds clearly thought it would be a good idea for their rather lonely adolescent to acquire a big sister, and that is what Jessie soon became. She taught him, and took care of him, and fought with him, and loved him. "One night," she recalls with a laugh, "I had scrubbed the kitchen floor and waxed it and got the vegetables on. They were going out after dinner, so I said, 'I'll do the dishes,' and they said, 'Glenn will help you.' Well, after they'd left, he took and threw water on the freshly waxed floor, just to make me angry, and so I started to chase him. I grabbed a wax rag from under the sink, and I caught him on the stairs, and I waxed his face, you know, just like two kids would do. And he was very upset. He said he was going to die of germs.

"He said he was going to wring my neck—that was always his favorite expression—so I ran upstairs, and I got in the bathroom, and I locked the door. He went in my room, and he got my notebooks from school, and he kept ripping out a page and putting it under the bathroom every hour or so. I kept saying, 'Glenn, I'll fail.' And he'd say, 'That's all right. If I studied as much as you, I'd be through the university by now.' Then another page ripped, and under the door. Then we both heard the car come in, and we both flew to our respective rooms, and he slept all night in his clothes. And the next morning, his mother said, 'How did things go?' And Glenn said, 'Fine, just fine.'"

Apart from Jessie, Gould had few close friends. He easily persuaded himself, as he often told interviewers, that he liked animals
better than people. One of the first long newspaper stories about
him, in the Toronto *Star* of February 21, 1946, reported that the
thirteen-year-old pianist kept goldfish named Bach, Beethoven,
Chopin, and Haydn, as well as a budgerigar named Mozart. The
bird, according to the *Star,* "perched on the score [and] attempted
to accompany him." "He can't talk yet," Gould was quoted as saying, "but he knows his music." The Toronto *Telegram* took a similar approach a few years later and photographed Gould's shaggy
dog next to him at the piano. "The English setter, Nick, sat motionless as Glenn played variations of La Ricordanza by Carl Czerny,"
the *Telegram* reported, in that infinitely patronizing tone that newspapers use toward both musicians and children, "and seemed to
enjoy watching his master's fingers race over the keyboard."

Gould created his own journalistic account of these years by
founding a newspaper that he named "THE DAILY WOOF—The
Animals Paper, Etided [sic] by Glenn Gould." Only one neatly penciled issue survives. The two lead stories are headlined BACH DIES OF
FUNGUS and MOTZY BELIEVED TO HAVE LICE. The latter goes on to
report: "AAP Jan. 4 A matter still under examined [sic] is whether
or not Motzy, the budgy has lice. His recent scratchings have given
the impression that he had." At the bottom of the page, under the
headline SQUIRREL ATTRACTS ATTENTION, and the logo "Special to
the WOOF," the paper reported: "A black squirrel attracted much
attention here yesterday P.M. when he dragged a large chunk of
bread across the street spreading crumbs on the lawn. He is wanted
for questioning by local authorities in other recent thefts."

Most children quickly learn that their parents claim a God-given
right to kill any animals they choose. Gould never really learned
that, or never accepted it. Gould's father, the furrier, was a devoted
fisherman, as were many of the neighbors who lived near the
Goulds' summer cottage on Lake Simcoe, and Gould was just six
when one of these neighbors took him out on the lake for his first
actual fishing expedition. "I was the first to catch a fish," Gould
remembered years later, when he was a famous pianist being interviewed by the Toronto *Star.* "And when the little perch came up
and started wiggling about I suddenly saw this thing entirely from

the fish's point of view. And it was such a powerful experience, I sort of picked up my fish and said I was going to throw it back. At that moment—this has remained with me as a sort of block against people who exert influence over children—the father suddenly pushed me back into my seat, probably for the sensible reason that I was rocking the boat. Then he took the fish out of my reach, at which I went into a tantrum and started jumping up and down, stamping my feet and pulling my hair and stuff like that. And I kept at it until we got in to shore. . . ."

Gould's father, who did subsequently give up fishing at his son's urgings, remembers that there was once a skunk prowling for garbage outside the cottage, and the boy built a trap that would catch the animal without harming it. When the skunk was duly trapped, the father told the boy to go and deal with it, assuming that the confrontation would soon lead to the skunk being turned loose. "Within a few minutes, Glenn had him eating out of his hand," Bert Gould recalls. Skunks are handsome animals, but they can be fierce as well as smelly, and perhaps there was something about the wildness of the animal he had trapped that appealed to the boy. There remains in the archives of the National Library of Canada a fragment of a song that Gould wrote in honor of his new friend. "I am a skunk, a skunk am I," it goes, "skunking is all I know, I want no more, I am a skunk, a skunk I'll remain. . . ."

Near the end of his life, when he appeared in "Glenn Gould's Toronto," the pianist recalled that one of the unfinished works of his childhood was an opera that "was to deal with the ultimate catastrophe of nuclear destruction. In Act I the entire human population was to be wiped out and in Act II they were to be replaced by a superior breed of frogs." Gould claimed that he had actually composed "a few bars" of a chorus for frogs in the key of E major, "which I always felt to be a benign and sympathetic key," but he acknowledged that there would have been a "casting problem."

These few remnants of genocidal childhood fantasy finally served only as an introduction to an unusual scene in "Glenn Gould's Toronto," in which Gould, after recalling that he had once sung Mahler songs to some cattle grazing in a field, ventured out to the Toronto zoo in the silent emptiness of dawn and sang these same Mahler songs to a troop of captive elephants. The elephants listened in wonder for a few moments, then turned and flapped their giant ears and wandered away.

For the most part, Gould's summers on Lake Simcoe were idyllic. "Glenn was very proud of his first boat," according to Bert Gould, "which was a fifteen-foot cedar skiff which I had equipped with an electric motor and two twelve-volt storage batteries. This boat Glenn steered and controlled from a wheel at the bow. . . . Glenn was never happier than when on the water with his boat and his dog Nick in charge of the front deck. . . ." Bert also remembers one stormy day when he feared that his son might be lost, and so he set out in another boat to find him—and did find him, waving like a conductor at the waves that broke over the bow.

This amiable lakeside life led to an accident that was to become quite important in Gould's later years. His father built a rail from the house to the beach, to help Glenn haul his boat up out of the water. When the boy was about ten, his father recalls, something went wrong. "Glenn and a number of others got on the boat and started it down the rail," he says, "and somehow Glenn slipped and fell off the back of it and hit his spine on the rocks."

Q: How high a fall was that?

A: Well, it's not a great fall, I suppose a couple of feet, but a vertical drop to the rocks.

Q: Did he complain of pain then?

A: Oh, yes.

Q: Did you take him to a doctor then?

A: Oh, yes, we took him to doctors for a long time afterwards. . . . We had him to every specialist we could think of. Started with the medical men and then osteopaths and chiropractors—the works.

Q: How long did that go on?

A: I'd say two or three years anyway.

Such back injuries are mysterious and powerful—this may well have been the "obscure hurt" that haunted Henry James all his life— for they periodically seem to be cured, for months on end, and then the pain suddenly returns and seizes the victim, as though he were being grasped by a giant claw. Beyond that, the injury affects the neck, the arms, the wrists, the hands.

Gould's health was to remain something of an enigma throughout most of his life, to himself as well as to his doctors, his friends, and his public. Bert Gould still says emphatically that he "was never really sick a day in his life," but from the earliest concerts on, Gould often complained of debilitating ailments, and often canceled performances because of them. He seems to have suffered from some kind of circulatory problem that made his hands feel cold, and so he began using mittens, hot water, various pills. He felt susceptible to drafts, which led to sore throats and chills. He lived in dread of germs, viruses, infections. It is quite possible that these difficulties were largely imaginary, or a response to the stresses of playing in public—and Gould freely admitted to hypochondria—but just as a hypnotized man's arm can turn red and blistered when he is told that he is being burned by a cigarette, so a hypochondriac's imagined pains really do hurt. Gould consulted many doctors throughout his life; few brought him any real relief.

Like any other schoolboy, though, the vulnerable young pianist set off every day to learn spelling and fractions and all those other disciplines that the adult world considered necessary. After Gould had served his apprenticeship at the Williamson Road Public School, he moved on to a nearby public high school named Malvern Collegiate, but he went there only in the mornings, so that his afternoons could be reserved for the piano. The teaching at Malvern was rigorous. What was the Concordat of 1801? What was the Directory? What was the effect of the American Civil War on the development of the Canadian West? "In Kipling's address on Values in Life, what type of man does the author hold up for our admiration? Why is he admirable? What *advice* and what *comfort* does he offer to youth when depressed by a sense of his own worthlessness?" What is the difference between the Shakespearean sonnet and the Petrarchan sonnet? "Qu'est-ce que vous prenez comme petit déjeuner?" "Je prends d'habitude du céreal chaud, de la pain et du café. . . ." The teacher duly noted Gould's mistake in the gender of the word for bread. "Qu'avez-vous l'intention de faire l'année prochaine?" "J'ai l'intention étudier la musique."

Most of Gould's schoolbooks show a dutiful dedication to his work, extended notes on *Pride and Prejudice* and the history of Canada, but there was also a deplorable tendency toward romantic rhetoric. "Far down, through the concrete channel, a myriad of flustered flotsam floundered against a flurry of the windsquall," one paper for his English class began. "From far up, I saw a vacillating abstract of surrealistic shape whose every minute movement only multiplied my misconceptions of their unity. For I, a stranger to their city, saw a mass—controlled, directed, pushed—as one. I felt the incessant onward motion of the crowd, but I, aloof then, failed to see that each small, separate movement was a symbol of their individuality...." And so on. Gould's teachers did not encourage this sort of thing. "In this paragraph you are using words for their own sakes," one of them commented on one of his efforts. "The result is that your style is obscure and seems forced." Another judgment was even more blunt: "Vague answers will not suffice." And another still more so: "Just stuff and nonsense." The cruelest of these comments came from a teacher who quite accurately declared that much of Gould's paper on *Macbeth* was a "waste of words," and who then added: "You are absent too often and miss too much work. Your knowledge is not thorough, nor your application of it sufficiently exact. Your bad spelling also has contributed toward your failure as you see...."

As with the school bully whom he threatened to kill, Gould stood ready to combat his teachers. In one of those standard assignments on "my plans for the school year," he defiantly wrote: "I am at something of a disadvantage in writing on this subject, for my adventures in the halls of learning are curtailed at the close of the fourth period each morning. The remainder of my day is spent in music, with the exclusion of an hour or so in the evening which I rather grudgingly bequeath to Macbeth, the Treaty of Ghent and the subjunctive mood.... My plans for this season include a number of solo recitals and appearances with the Hamilton and Toronto Symphony Orchestras. Although very little of this is relevant to the title, I think it will be sufficient to show why I have not a moment to spend on extra-curricular activities at school. My plans for the school year, therefore, are nonexistent." To this bitter observation, the teacher wrote in the margin, "That cannot be." At the end, this same teacher wrote, "Clever," and graded the paper B-minus.

If the piano added something of a burden during Gould's school years, it was also an escape. "I think I was truly determined upon a career in music at the age of nine or ten," he told an interviewer, Bernard Asbell, in 1962. "I was determined to wrap myself up in music because I found it was a damned good way of avoiding my schoolmates, with whom I did not get along." He did not see himself specifically as a concert pianist, however. "I saw myself as a sort of musical Renaissance Man, capable of doing many things. I obviously wanted to be a composer. I still do. Performing in the arena had no attraction for me. This was, at least in part, defensive. Even from what little I then knew of the politics of the business, it was apparent that a career as a solo pianist involved a competition which I felt much too grand ever to consider facing."

Gould's mother was the most encouraging of teachers, and it was probably important that she was both a professional piano teacher and a singing coach. "His mother did a very important thing," John Roberts observes. "She made him sing, all the time. As he played notes, as a small child, he had to sing them. I think that had some-thing to do with his being able to hear in his mind as well as he could. And his mother used to listen to all his playing—he played rather than practiced—and if she thought something was not right, she would call out to him immediately. So as a small child, he never learned mistakes, because they were always perceived instantly. It wasn't until Glenn was ten that there was any need for him to go to another teacher. Glenn always said to me that he considered himself self-taught."

Raising a child endowed with such gifts is not easy. (What must Leopold Mozart have wondered in the darkness of some sleepless night?) The desire to protect and shelter and defend is repeatedly challenged by self-accusation, by the anxiety that one may not be doing enough to help the child become whatever it is destined to become. Mrs. Gould took her son to the Toronto Conservatory to be examined, like some medical wonder. "Dear Mr. Gould," said the letter to the seven-year-old boy from Fredk. C. Silvester, Exam-ination Registrar, "We have pleasure in informing you that the mark you received in your recent examination for Grade IV piano was the highest in the Province of Ontario. This entitles you to the Con-servatory's Silver Medal, which you will receive in the early part of October. . . ."

After a good deal of consultation, the Goulds decided to consign their prodigy to the care of Alberto Guerrero. It seems to have been a wise choice. By then already in his middle fifties, with a balding head and rimless spectacles, Guerrero had once founded and conducted the first symphony orchestra in Santiago, Chile. He gave premiere performances of Debussy and Ravel. In the 1920's, he migrated northward, and, according to an obituary notice in the Toronto *Star* in 1959, it was through his performances that "Toronto heard for the first time the major piano works of Hindemith, Schoenberg, Stravinsky, Milhaud, and others."

Guerrero also had some important idiosyncrasies that he taught to his pupils. "He sat lower in relation to the keyboard and played with flatter fingers than most players," according to another one of his students, John Beckwith, now a composer and professor at the University of Toronto. "His performances of light rapid passages had not only fluency and great speed but also exceptional clarity and separation of individual notes. . . . One practice-technique for finger separation consisted of playing the music for each hand separately, very slowly, but making the sound by tapping each finger with the non-playing hand. One learned from this how very precise and economical the muscle movements needed for fast playing really could be. It was indeed a 'pure finger-technique' in that virtually no hand-action was applied—the fingers did it all."

"Glenn was not taught in the usual way, 'Do this' or 'Do that,'" according to the recollections of Guerrero's widow, Myrtle. "Alberto exposed him to all kinds of music, and they would enjoy analyzing the music together. . . . The lessons were of great duration because Glenn insisted on getting every sound just right. He would linger over just one or two things until he had it. Alberto would say, 'Oh, it's all right, Glenn,' but Glenn would say, 'No, it's not!'" "My studies with Guerrero, in my later teens, were essentially exercises in argument," Gould recalled many years later. "They were attempts to crystallize my point of view versus his on some particular issue, whatever it was, and . . . I think that for me, anyway, it worked very well."

There still survive some amateur recordings of the two of them playing piano duets, the first movements of the great Mozart four-hand sonatas in C and F, the young Gould playing the upper part brightly and eagerly, like a yearling newly turned loose on a race-track, and Guerrero providing a watchful accompaniment, knowing full well how this animal could run. They played croquet together too, the Guerreros and Glenn and his mother, for the Guerreros had a cottage not far from the Goulds' place on Lake Simcoe. Like any boy who announces a hatred of competition, Gould also hated losing, and croquet, like chess, brings out the worst instincts. "Glenn was a furious competitor," Mrs. Guerrero recalled, "and if he didn't win, it was a tragedy."

The Goulds did not want their son to be a public prodigy, committed to the public rituals of a Rubinstein or a Menuhin, but they inevitably began wondering whether it was fair to a child of such enormous talent to keep that talent hidden. The Goulds were devoted churchgoers, so it seemed natural to them to offer up their son's talents on the altar of the church's social evenings. One elderly lady who heard Gould perform at a meeting of the Women's Missionary Society at the Emmanuel Presbyterian Church in Toronto recalled to an interviewer just a few years ago that the boy wore a white satin suit with short pants. A surviving letter from the Reverend W. J. Johnston of the Eglinton United Church thanks the Goulds for bringing their eleven-year-old son to "our church social last evening" and for making him "entertain us so wonderfully at the piano. He certainly is a lad of parts."

Gould's first formal public appearance, in 1945, came not at the piano but at the organ. He had been studying both instruments at the Toronto Conservatory, and he liked to claim in later years that his labors at the organ had taught him the significance of a bass line, and of a detached touch, and, of course, of the genius of Bach. The organ also provided Gould with his first (and last) job. He was hired to accompany the services at an Anglican church, but he had a habit of losing his place when the congregation sang. There was an embarrassing mistake, a rustle of disapproval, and then an abrupt dismissal. In his solo premiere, though, one newspaper review praised "Glenn Gould, a nipper who looks about 11, may be older, but announced his encore in a voice which has not yet changed. . . ." Edward Wodson of the *Telegram,* on the other hand, was astute enough to see that although Gould was "just a child, really, a loose-jointed, gracious, smiling boy . . . he played the organ last evening as many a full-grown concert organist couldn't if he tried. A genius he is . . . and in every detail his playing had the fearless authority and finesse of a master." Gould first attracted serious attention as a pianist when he entered a Kiwanis festival in February of 1946 and emerged as one of the thirty-two winners out of nine thousand contestants. "Serious attention" is perhaps too strong a term for a competition on which the Toronto *Star* reported only that "Gould was a poetic wizard with a Bach prelude, but too sinuously intense for the Fugue." The newspaper's critic, Augustus Bridle, devoted far more attention to "Miriam Smith, age 6, [who] dangled her bootees far above the pedals to play a Bach Gavotte," which Bridle said she had turned into "a fairyland fandango." A somewhat less idiotic review in the *Telegram* reported that the thirteen-year-old Gould had played a Bach prelude and fugue "with remarkable feeling and finesse, these characteristics in a degree rather beyond his years." The critic went on to conclude that "his performance at the piano as a whole, however, was too consciously mannered." Gould preserved the stub of the ten-dollar check that he won for this performance, but it may be possible to glimpse in these accounts of the Kiwanis festival one of the origins of his lifelong dislike of both competition and newspaper critics. "The Scribbler," he wrote years later in an unpublished fantasy entitled *The Gouldberg Variations,* "[was] a noxious little wart from, of all venalities, the daily press—that loathsome compendium of assaults, insults, vagaries, untruths, half-truths, libels, vulgarities, pomposities and even dichotomies.... There was not an ounce of goodness in this wretched chap, not from the greasy morass that stood proxy for his hair to his syphilitic little toe."

It was only a matter of time, and not too much time, before Guerrero wrote to Gould in 1946 to report the Toronto Symphony Orchestra's invitation to a major piano debut. "You have been chosen to play in the opening concert of the Secondary School Series ..." he wrote. "You would play the G Major Beethoven concerto. Sir Ernest [MacMillan] will conduct. There is a nominal fee of $75.... I have missed very much a game of croquet."

How casually it is said. You would play the G major Beethoven Concerto, a work that happens to be one of the masterpieces in the literature of the piano, and also a work to which thousands of amateurs have devoted many thousands of wasted hours. Gould was then thirteen, still writing school papers on Kipling and the history of Canada. Like every young pianist of that period he knew and played and loved Artur Schnabel's recording of the Beethoven Fourth with the Chicago Symphony Orchestra under Frederick Stock. "Almost every day," he later recalled, "some or all eight 78-rpm sides served as accompaniment for practice sessions in which I faithfully traced every inflective nuance of the Schnabelian rhetoric, surged dramatically ahead whenever he thought it wise . . . and glided to a graceful cadential halt every four minutes and twenty-five seconds or so while the automatic changer went to work on the turntable."

Gould claimed—his memory on these matters was not infallible—that Guerrero forced him to surrender his beloved Schnabel recording and to bow down to the teacher's authority, and that the teacher professed himself satisfied only when Gould played the concerto at the more brisk tempo recorded by Rudolf Serkin. "On the day of my debut it rained," Gould later wrote, "and that evening— it was early May, the first week of daylight saving, and the sun set at eight—the low-pressure area moved eastward, the ceiling lifted, and the skyline of Toronto took on that misty, orange-shaded cyclorama effect that Walt Kelly would soon celebrate in the color installments of 'Pogo' at Okefenokee. . . . This was a time for personal statement—a moment to grasp and to make one's own." Gould walked onto the stage and began playing the Beethoven concerto exactly as he pleased. He remembered long afterward that "I left in high spirits, my teacher was shattered, and the press, on the whole, was quite kind." There was only one small annoyance in the Toronto *Globe and Mail,* which reported that this great concerto had been "left in the hands of a child," and the reviewer wondered, "Who does the kid think he is, Schnabel?"

Even at this age, the child was already becoming a hero. Fourteen years later, a housewife in New Westminster, who had been fifteen years old on the occasion of Gould's concert, wrote him to tell him not only that she had been there but that she had recorded the event in her diary. "Glenn is fourteen but he looks much younger," she had written. "I think he must have been scared because at the beginning . . . after he had played a few chords, and was sitting while the orchestra was playing, he was sort of fidgety—kept pushing his hair back and mopping his brow with a large white handerchief. He was round-shouldered and seemed to bend over the piano as he played; his playing, however, more than made up for his idiosyncrasies. He was marvelous! The audience nearly brought the house down. Finally he played an encore—a Chopin Valse. His fingers moved like lightning. . . . I wonder whether, 10 or 15 years from now, we'll be hearing from him on the concert stages of the world?"

That performance in May of 1946 actually involved only the first movement of the concerto, and it was not until the following January that Gould played the entire work with the Toronto Symphony under the baton of an Australian guest conductor, Bernard Heinze. Pearl McCarthy then wrote in the *Globe and Mail* that "the boy played it exquisitely," but she also sounded a theme that was to become an obsession among reviewers throughout Gould's concert career. "Unfortunately," she wrote, "the young artist showed some incipient mannerisms and limited his self-control to the period when he himself was playing. As he approaches adult status, he will undoubtedly learn to suppress this disturbing fidgeting. . . ."

Gould, as usual, had an explanation, and in this case it involved his English setter, Nick (officially Sir Nickolson of Garelocheed), who was in the process of shedding hair. "As I was getting into my best dark suit prior to the concert," Gould later recalled, "my father cautioned me to keep my distance from Nick, but that, of course, was easier said than done. Nick was an affectionate and concerned animal and not one to see a friend off on an important mission without offering his good wishes." Gould's trousers, in short, were covered with long white dog hairs, but it was only during a pause in the slow movement of the concerto that be became aware of the dog's contribution. One of the strangest things about public performance is that one is capable of losing all sense of where one is, and just as it becomes possible to play a difficult piano concerto without even noticing the hundreds of watching faces, so it is also possible to start wondering, in the middle of that concerto, whether one should try to remove some dog hairs from one's trousers.*

Gould came to the absurd decision that the third movement would give him an opportunity, for there is a long orchestral tutti after each

---

*Gould retained a lifelong practice of thinking about different things at once. When an admiring friend once said that his playing showed "incredible powers of concentration" on the work being performed, Gould retorted, "That's not true at all. I just played with the Chicago Symphony, and during the last movement of the concerto, all I was thinking was, Is the driver that I hired going to be backstage when I'm finished so I can make a quick getaway?"

statement of the rondo theme. The one problem, which had never occurred to him, was that each statement of the theme was identical but then led to a different interlude, and that a pianist engaged in picking dog hairs from his trousers might lose track of which tutti the orchestra was playing. And so it happened. "Major tuttis went by and the [hair-removal] operation was ninety percent complete," Gould recalled. "Only one question remained in my mind: how complete was the concerto? Was this the tutti which, upon my entrance, I lead toward the dominant? Was it the one which I echo in the minor key? Or was it the one which points the way to the cadenza? The problem didn't occur to me until the last few bars of whichever tutti it was. I tried desperately to remember what besides picking setter hairs I'd been doing for the last five minutes or so and placed an inspired bet on tutti no. 3. The cadenza lead-in was, indeed, upcoming, but I had learned the first valuble lesson of my association with the T.S.O.—either pay attention or keep short-haired dogs."

Gould enjoyed his early success. "Performing before an audience gave me a glorious sense of power at fifteen," he told one interviewer. He probably had very little idea what an arduous process the climb to worldwide fame would become. The first solo recital was a student concert in April of 1947, which Gould later described only as "a brace of fugues and some Haydn, some Beethoven, some Mendelssohn, some Liszt (which I haven't played since in public)." GOULD DISPLAYS GROWING ARTISTRY, said the *Globe and Mail*. Looking back at his young self, Gould later declared that he was "not nervous at all. It was all part of a game, really. . . . In those days, one was blissfully unaware of the responsibility. I just wish I could feel that way again. Now you accomplish the same thing by sedatives."

Gould's memories of those days are not completely reliable. He did play Liszt's *Au Bord d'une Source* at his first official recital under the management of an energetic young Toronto impresario named Walter Homburger in the Eaton's department store auditorium in October of 1947. He also offered a rather un-Gouldian assortment of works by Scarlatti, Couperin, Beethoven, Mendelssohn, and Chopin. (Yes, the Impromptu in F-sharp major, Opus 36, and the Waltz in A flat, Opus 42. And Robert Fulford, who lived next door, says that his strongest memories of summer evenings on the veranda

were "the sound of him playing Chopin.") But while Gould's memories are selective, the Toronto music critics of the time are hardly
more reliable. Bridle of the *Star,* for example, wrote of that October
recital: "Spiderlike fingers, flexible rubberish wrists, pedals infallible, nose a foot above the keys, he was like an old man on a music
spree. . . . In a Beethoven sonata, Opus 37 [he meant Opus 31], he
outdid Rachmaninoff for intensively supple art. Vivid re-etching,
such as Ludwig never dreamed into a sonata, was the essence of this
youth-technique. . . ." And so on. But Bridle did add, after all that
gushing, "This boy is on the road to pianistic fame."

Radio provided another road, an important road, to that fame. For
those who have grown up with television, it is hard to understand
how important radio was in the 1940's. It was everything that TV
is today, plus whatever radio still is, plus a lot more. It was the one
national and even international system of communication, of both
messages and fantasy. It alone brought us the soothing voice of President Roosevelt at his fireside and the shrieking voice of Hitler on
his rostrum—both of whom derived a lot of their political power
from their mastery of radio—as well as the weekly chatter of Walter
Winchell's news broadcasts to "Mr. and Mrs. America and all the
ships and clippers at sea," and the weekly absurdities of Fred Allen
interviewing Senator Claghorn or the boxes and baskets tumbling
out of Fibber McGee's hall closet. TV destroyed all this phantas-
magoria by its relentless insistence on what TV people call "the
visuals," on showing us exactly what everything looks like, which
is usually less than we had imagined. Imagine a TV adaptation of
Orson Welles's *War of the Worlds* setting off a nationwide panic.

Radio also served to unite people. It created, among other things,
a standardized national accent and also a national schedule. Sunday
afternoon was the time for the New York Philharmonic—and thousands later remembered the news from Pearl Harbor as an interrup-
tion of Arthur Rubinstein's performance of the Brahms B flat
Concerto—just as Sunday night was the time for Winchell (who
sold Jergens lotion), Charlie McCarthy (who sold Chase and San-
born coffee), and Jack Benny (who sold Jell-O). Nowhere was this
more true than in the Canada of Gould's youth, a vast and relatively
empty land that was still rather nervously examining the connective
fibers of its own identity. "So I went back to my work in CBC and

stayed with the organization throughout the war," says the radio broadcaster who serves as hero of Hugh MacLennan's novel, *The Watch That Ends the Night*. "Strange years which now have become a blur. While the war thundered on, Canada unnoticed grew into a nation at last. This cautious country which had always done more than she had promised, had always endured in silence while others reaped the glory—now she became alive and to us within her excitingly so. . . . And sometimes, thinking with shame of the Thirties when nothing in Canada had seemed interesting unless it resembled something in England or the States, I even persuaded myself that here I had found the thing larger than myself to which I could belong. . . ."

Unlike anything south of the border, the CBC is, of course, a government-funded national network, and the people in charge of it were fully aware of their role in this national awakening. The organization had been founded in 1936, according to a magazine article recently tacked to the door of the CBC radio archives in Toronto, for the official purpose of "fostering national spirit and interpreting national citizenship." Over those great spaces, it was the CBC radio that provided the neurons to connect Montreal and Toronto with Winnipeg, Moose Jaw, Yellowknife. And against the constant buzz of broadcasting from the United States, the CBC needed and searched out and supported Canadian journalists, Canadian talkers and tellers, and, of course, Canadian musicians. Gould, unlike some of his admirers, was never a Canadian nationalist. "Our country," he wrote to a young American pianist in the 1950's, "having passed out of the stage when the foreign-born were considered indispensible, is now in an equally revolting nationalist stage in which all outside attractions ought to be dispensed with." Still, the young Gould, that nipper, that lad of parts, seemed made to order for the Canadian radio network's needs.

And it for him. "One Sunday morning in December 1950," he wrote in an essay titled "Music and Technology," "I wandered into a living-room-sized radio station, placed my services at the disposal of a single microphone belonging to the Canadian Broadcasting Corporation, and proceeded to broadcast 'live' two sonatas: one by Mozart, one by Hindemith. It was my first network broadcast, but it was not my first contact with the microphone; for several years

I'd been indulging in experiments at home with primitive tape recorders—strapping the mikes to the sounding board of my piano, the better to emasculate Scarlatti sonatas, for example.... But the CBC occasion ... was a memorable one: not simply because it enabled me to communicate without the immediate presence of a gallery of witnesses ... but rather because later the same day I was presented with a soft-cut 'acetate,' a disc which dimly reproduced the felicities of the broadcast in question and which, even today, a quarter-century after the fact, I still take down from the shelf on occasion in order to celebrate that moment in my life when I first caught a vague impression of the direction it would take ... when my love affair with the microphone began."

So he knew even then, at the age of eighteen, that technology could provide him with an alternative method of performing music, a method that could do away with all the staring faces, all the coughs and rustlings, all the anxieties. But he also knew perfectly well that he still had a great deal to learn. It is all too easy for an inexperienced youth to devote himself to the official classics, Bach and Beethoven, to become a specialist and even a partisan of what little he already knows. Gould was more ambitious. "My first experience of contemporary music was via Paul Hindemith and particularly *Matthias the Painter*," he later recalled. "I was 15 at the time, a complete reactionary. I hated all music after Wagner, and a good deal of Wagner, and suddenly I heard *Matthias the Painter,* in a recording with Hindemith conducting, and flipped completely. This suddenly was the recreation of a certain kind of Baroque temperament that appealed to me tremendously, and I, as a 15-year-old, came alive to contemporary music...." And so he became alive to Schoenberg and Webern and Prokofiev, even to Krenek, Casella, and Anhalt.

Hindemith's Third Sonata became one of Gould's basic works when he started giving local concerts. He played it at the University of Toronto early in 1950, along with Bach's *Italian Concerto* and Beethoven's *Eroica Variations,* and the young reviewer for *Varsity* declared that "one can only shout superlatives." He played the same Hindemith sonata at the University of Western Ontario a few months later, together with the Bach Toccata in E minor, a Mozart fantasia and a Chopin étude. The London *Free Press* praised his "singing tone."

By now, Gould had to decide on his future course. He had already decided that Malvern was of no future use to him, and that the only question was how to devote his life to music. "I was rather young to have taken a step like that," he later recalled. "I did so, I think, very much over the objections of my family, who thought it was an outrageous token of presumption for any kid of 19 to decide that he had had enough book learning." At the same time, though, Gould also decided that he had had enough conservatory learning, and his parents opposed that decision too. "I can still see tears in Glenn's eyes," Jessie Greig remembers. "He never really cried, but there'd be tears—he'd get so angry about it, because he felt he had outgrown Guerrero."

No matter what anyone else thought, Gould simply broke off his studies with Guerrero and retired to the cottage on Lake Simcoe. "I didn't approve of my teacher," he later wrote to a friend. And to another: "I was equipped with everything except the kind of solidarity of the ego which is, in the last analysis, the one important part of an artist's equipment." He now spent endless hours playing Bach on the old Chickering, endless hours going for walks with his dog (Nick had developed a growth on his back, and so he had been superseded by a collie named Banquo), and then still more hours playing Bach on the Chickering. He may have been undergoing a kind of crisis over the question of what to do with his life, but his father remembers that time with equanimity. "He was just practicing," says Bert Gould, "and preparing himself."

No longer under the tutelage of Guerrero, Gould looked toward Homburger for guidance, and Homburger decided that it was time for the nineteen-year-old virtuoso to explore a bit of the world beyond Toronto. He sent Gould, under the watchful care of his mother, to play the Beethoven Fourth in Vancouver, where he received what the Vancouver *Daily Province* described as "a rousing five curtain calls." And to Calgary, where the *Herald* bravely called his playing of the Bach Fifth Partita, the *Eroica Variations*, and the Hindemith sonata "one of the finest performances ever heard on the Calgary stage." The local press was hungry for more details. The *Albertan* asked Mrs. Gould "if she had any advice to hand on to mothers of other musical children," and Mrs. Gould promptly replied "that mothers must sacrifice and give of their time, often to the curtailment of social activity.... 'When Glenn practiced at noon I was always there and when he came home after school to practice again I was always home,' she commented." And now that he had reached the age of nineteen, was he "interested in girls"? the *Albertan* inquired. "No, he hasn't time for them yet, his mother says, adding with a smile, 'And I'm glad he hasn't right now.'"

Gould returned to Toronto to play the Beethoven Second Concerto. ("The Glenn Gould touch was a caress—" the *Telegram* gushed, "forceful as compulsion of tyranny, but lovely as faith, hope and charity in perfect unison....") And the Canadian premiere of Schoenberg's Suite for Piano, Opus 25. And Beethoven's Opus 101, and the Berg Sonata, and some short pieces by Orlando Gibbons for the Ladies' Morning Musical Club in Montreal. ("One of the great musical personalities of this generation," said the Montreal *Star*.) And Beethoven's Opus 109, at the Technical School Auditorium in Ottawa. ("Fascinating to watch the long, sensitive, animated hands of this slight, unassuming young man," said the Ottawa *Citizen* in one of the silliest of the many silly newspaper commentaries on the young Gould. "A Surrealist painter might feel tempted to paint these two hands, fantastically enlarged, as two huge living beings, with a small human body attached to them.")

That sonata had given Gould problems far beyond the Surrealist imaginings of the Ottawa critic, problems that only Gould could have created and only Gould could have solved. There is a difficult passage in the fifth variation of the last movement, an upward run in the right hand, which Gould described as "a positive horror." "You have to change from a pattern in sixths to a pattern in thirds, and you've got to do that in a split second," Gould later told Cott. "I had always heard this piece played by people who, when that moment arrived, looked like horses being led from burning barns— a look of horror would come upon them."

When Gould began a little practicing on Opus 109, just two or three weeks before his first public performance of it, he made the mistake of beginning with that difficult passage, "just to make sure there's no problem." As he tried it, "one thing after another began to go wrong," and within a few minutes he discovered that he had "developed a total block about this thing." That block paralyzed him until three days before the concert—"I couldn't get to that point without literally shying and stopping"—and so he decided to re-create the lesson of the maid with the vacuum cleaner and try what he called the Last Resort method. "That was to place beside the piano a couple of radios [and] turn them up full blast." This helped, but only partly. Keeping the radios on as loud as possible, Gould then concentrated all his attention on four unimportant accompanying notes in the left hand, and concentrated on playing them "as unmusically as possible." When he had mastered that, and finally turned off the radios, the block about the difficult right-hand run was gone.

And then Stratford. It had been founded as a Shakespeare festival, about seventy-five miles west of Toronto, but someone had inevitably had the idea of adding music, and so Stratford soon became the kind of festival where musicians could experiment, relax, enjoy themselves. Some veterans still recall the extraordinary 1954 production of Stravinsky's *A Soldier's Tale*, starring Marcel Marceau in his first North American appearance, and featuring Alexander Schneider as the wandering violinist. And that was how Schneider met Glenn Gould.

Sitting now by the picture window overlooking the shrill traffic on Manhattan's East Twentieth Street, he remembers the twenty-one-year-old pianist as "a very strange guy." Schneider was supposed to give a recital of Bach, Beethoven, and Brahms, and so he was introduced to the local prodigy. "And he came without any music," Schneider recalls. "He said, 'I play by heart.'" Schneider had never before encountered a pianist who knew the whole violin repertoire by heart. He himself prefers to play with the score in front of him, "so you can relax, you know, and make music." Gould was not like other musicians, as Schneider soon learned, and "he played *very* well."

So the word kept spreading. Another American musician, Harvey Olnick, who had come to teach at the University of Toronto, heard Gould play *The Goldberg Variations* at a small university recital. "I was bowled over, absolutely," he recalls. "I was absolutely thunderstruck. After the concert, he was just standing there, as you went out, and I said, 'I'd like to talk to you sometime. I don't understand this. Where did you come from? I know your teacher. He's a Romantic. Where did you learn to play Bach like this?'"

Olnick sent a pseudonymous review to the *Musical Courier,* the first report on Gould in an American periodical. "The public will soon be confronted with an artist in no way inferior to such artists as Landowska and Serkin," it said. That confrontation was soon scheduled when Walter Homburger booked his young client into the Phillips Collection in Washington and Manhattan's Town Hall early in 1955. Olnick went on beating the drums. "I called Winnie Leventritt in New York and I said, 'Winnie, go to this concert. This guy's a kook, but he's fantastic! Incredible!' And she had a party at her house, and so news got around."

With all the confidence of a youth of twenty-two, Gould ignored the traditional debut repertoire of a little Mozart, a little Chopin, and chose for his first American appearance in Washington only a few of his own favorites, a pavane by Orlando Gibbons and a Sweelinck fantasia, Bach's Fifth Partita, and five of the Three-Part Inventions, Beethoven's Opus 109 (difficult run and all), the thorny Berg Sonata, and the even more thorny Variations by Anton Webern. The most important witness to all this was Paul Hume, who wrote a remarkable review in the next day's Washington *Post.* "January 2 is early for predictions," Hume began, "but it is unlikely that the year 1955 will bring us a finer piano recital than that played yesterday afternoon in the Phillips Gallery. We shall be lucky if it brings us others of equal beauty and significance."

It is rare for a music critic to abandon all the usual cautions and hedgings and commit himself so boldly to a newcomer. The classic instance was Robert Schumann's marvelous salute to the appearance of Chopin's Opus 2 Variations on *Là Ci Darem la Mano:* "Hats off, gentlemen, a genius!" Gould was no Chopin, and Hume no Schumann, but there still is something moving in the critic's attempt to describe an extraordinary experience. "Gould is a pianist with rare gifts for the world," Hume concluded. "It must not long delay hearing and according him the honor and audience he deserves. We know of no pianist like him at any age."

"I had not listened for two minutes before I thought, I am listening to something more than extraordinary," Hume still recalls. Now retired, he is sitting in the boardroom of a Toronto bank, where the first Glenn Gould Prize of fifty thousand dollars has just been awarded to the Canadian composer R. Murray Schafer. "I thought,

I have never heard *this* kind of playing before," Hume says. "Gould made some of the *most* glorious music I have ever heard from any piano. The gift of prophecy is one that a critic must use with great care, but there was no question that he could have the greatest career in the world. I just sat there and thought, My God, how beautifully this piano is being played by this man."

The musical world is not very large, at its upper levels, and Hume's review very quickly became known in New York. The musical capital of the world was always ready to listen to a new challenger, to listen with skepticism and arrogance, but to listen. Like all young musicians, Gould had to pay his own expenses, had to pay $450 to rent Town Hall, and about $1,000 more for advertising, programs, and promotion. But New York was willing to pay attention. David Oppenheim, the director of Columbia Records' Masterworks division, was visiting Sasha Schneider's house on East Twentieth Street, and they listened to a recording by the great Romanian pianist Dinu Lipatti, who had died just five years earlier at the age of thirty-three. "I think I had maybe brought the Lipatti record to him," Oppenheim recalls. "And I said, 'Why can't we find another one like that?' And he said there was one, a person in Toronto named Glenn Gould, who was, alas, a little crazy but had a remarkable, hypnotic effect at the piano." Schneider remembers the discussion in much the same way. "So I said, 'Well, why don't you go and listen to—there is a boy coming from Canada. Go and take a contract with you right away, and sign him up, because if you liked Lipatti, you may like him.' So he went. . . ."

So he went. And others went too—not a great many, perhaps two hundred at most, but they were interested and important listeners. The young pianist Paul Badura-Skoda was there ("I marvel at his ability to give expression to three voices"). Eugene Istomin was there, with his colleague Gary Graffman. "It was a fantastic concert," Graffman still recalls. He is sitting now in his apartment near Carnegie Hall, which is filled with Chinese art, and he is sipping a mixture of tea and apple juice. "He had a hand in his pocket as he walked out. And as soon as he started to play, everybody—or at least *I*—sat on the edge of the chair, and I just listened to music and was absolutely floored. It was more than just hearing a very talented newcomer. It was a unique personality already."

And Winston Fitzgerald of the house of Steinway remembers the occasion just as vividly.

Q: What was the atmosphere at that debut?

A: Electric.

Gould's father, Bert, sat proudly in the audience on that memorable evening, but most of his Toronto friends were present only in the telegrams they showered upon him. ALL OUR VERY WARMEST WISHES FOR TREMENDOUS SUCCESS TONIGHT and KNOW YOUR CONCERT WILL BE WONDERFUL and ALL GOOD WISHES FOR A GREAT NY DEBUT AND BRILLIANT CAREER and ARISE AND SHINE FOR THY LIGHT HAS COME. And though it was not a big event by New York standards, the Toronto press covered it with characteristic enthusiasm. The *Star*'s Hugh Thomson described the young hero as "Toronto's 22-year-old pianist and composer, Glenn Gould, the youngest student to graduate from the Royal Conservatory." The *Telegram*'s George Kidd not only called him a "Toronto-born pianist" but felt compelled to appear blasé about the atmosphere of excitement. "For Canadians, it was no surprise that the 22-year-old pianist received such a response," he wrote. "His work has long been known from coast to coast. . . ."

Taking no chances before this important audience, Gould played the same pieces he had played so successfully in Washington. The *Telegram* correspondent noted that he wore a dark business suit instead of the customary white tie and tails. "His shyness was apparent as he stepped onto the large stage with its gleaming white walls and brown backdrop," Kidd wrote. "There was a hesitancy as he acknowledged the warm applause that swept up to him from the other side of the footlights. But once he began to play, the shyness departed. . . ."

The applause demanded an encore even at the intermission, and when the recital was all over, more than a hundred people crowded backstage to shake Gould's hand and congratulate the new star. The great rite of passage had been passed. Even the imperious New York *Times* was moderately impressed. "A debut recital of unusual promise," said the critic who signed himself "J.B." (John Briggs). "The challenging program Mr. Gould prepared was a test the young man met successfully, and in so doing left no doubt of his powers as a technician. The most rewarding aspect of Mr. Gould's playing, however, is that technique as such is in the background. The impression that is uppermost is not one of virtuosity but of expressiveness. One is able to hear the music." The *Herald-Tribune* was equally appreciative: "This young pianist is clearly a dedicated, sensitive poet of the keyboard; he has a wonderful control of finger articulation and tonal levels, while every fragile nuance . . . bespeaks the real artistic nature."

These were both rather short reviews, however, of the kind that get published every day. Both the *Times* and *Herald-Tribune* devoted more space and attention to a Carnegie Hall recital by a violinist named Julian Olevsky. Neither of them seemed to realize that a major event had just occurred. One man who did realize it, though, was David Oppenheim of Columbia Records, who decided that night that the great Lipatti was not without successors. A tall man, graying now, Oppenheim still remembers the very first notes of Gould's recital. "It started with something very slow—Sweelinck, I think it was," he says, "but it might have been someone else from that period—something that, in anyone else's hands, would have been just a crushing bore. And he did it in such a—he set such a religious atmosphere that it was just mesmerizing. And it didn't take more than five or six notes to establish that atmosphere, by some magic of precise rhythm and control of the inner voices. . . . And I was—thrilled. And looked around to see if there were any of my colleagues from other record companies there—didn't see them— and moved as quickly as I could to get to his manager the next day to propose a deal."

Nobody could remember a major recording contract ever having been offered after just one Town Hall recital. It was a contract that was to bring Gould worldwide fame, and to endure for more than twenty-seven years, until the day of his death.

III

The Goldberg Variations (I)

When Gould met with an executive of Columbia Records to decide what he should play for his first recording, he startled the executive by announcing that he would like to begin with Bach's *Goldberg Variations*. The executive, whom Gould did not identify in his subsequent account of this meeting, objected. Surely, he said, Gould would not want to stake his fledgling career on something so obscure, so difficult, so complex. ("It may be doubted," Sir Donald Francis Tovey had written, "whether any great classic is really so little known. . . .") The executive also felt obliged to observe that the redoubtable Wanda Landowska had already recorded *The Goldberg Variations* on her redoubtable harpsichord, and that most connoisseurs associated the work with her. "Don't you think the Two-Part Inventions would make a better debut choice?" he asked.

"I'd rather record *The Goldberg Variations*," Gould persisted, politely deaf to all objections.

"You really would, eh?" the executive said. "Well, why not? Let's take a chance."

It is, as Gould was to teach us, a magnificent, magical work. *Aria mit verschiedenen Veraenderungen*, Bach had modestly called it, an aria with different variations. As with many masterpieces, it is now encrusted by legends, which are not necessarily false. Legend reports that Bach journeyed from Leipzig to Dresden in 1741 and there visited one of his young pupils, Johann Gottlieb Goldberg, who was employed as a harpsichordist by Count Hermann Karl von Keyserling, the Russian ambassador to the court of Saxony. Count Keyserling suffered from neuralgia, which kept him awake at night.

Legend says that he asked Goldberg's teacher to write him something that would help him pass through these dark hours.

We do not know why this mundane request inspired Bach to write one of the masterpieces of Western music. Probably he himself did not know. He took as his theme a little saraband that he had already jotted down some fifteen years earlier in the *Notenbuch* that he provided for his twenty-year-old second wife, Anna Magdalena. Then, in contrast to most other variations by most other composers, he never again used his theme as the material to be varied. Instead, he relied only on the bass line, beginning with that stately progression downward from G to D, tonic to dominant, as the foundation for the thirty variations that were to become a kind of cathedral of sound, and of the Baroque imagination.

Perhaps the most extraordinary aspect of this cathedral is that every third variation, every third vault and groin in the construction, was a canon, a perfect replication of itself, at intervals that extended from a canon at the unison to a canon at the second and on to a canon at the octave, and then, as a kind of proof of Bach's unmatchable virtuosity, a canon at the ninth. But these are all technicalities. In between such casual demonstrations of virtuosity, Bach wrote a gorgeous collection of songs, dances, declamations, meditations, all based on that rudimentary progression downward from G to D. And yet it was emblematic of Bach's genius that the canons are among the most beautiful of all the variations. Count Keyserling was pleased. He sent Bach a golden goblet containing 100 louis d'or, apparently the biggest payment that Bach ever received for any single composition in his life. And according to legend, the count loved to listen to Bach's creation in the dark of a sleepless night. "Dear Goldberg," he would say, "please come and play me my variations."

It is difficult now to determine just how the young Gould acquired his passion for *The Goldberg Variations*. They really were very rarely played in those days, and they did have a reputation for being austere and academic, like some combination of Palestrina and Schoenberg. Guerrero occasionally performed them, so he may well have recommended them to his pupil, but Gould often roamed through volumes of Bach on his own, so he may have discovered them by himself, may have instinctively seen in that elaborate structure something that appealed to his sense of pattern and control.

He first performed them outside Toronto, two months after his New York debut, at an assembly of the Morning Musical Club at the Technical High School in Ottawa. The only record we have of this occasion is in the commentary of local critics like Lauretta Thistle of the Ottawa *Citizen*. "In the vast fairy cavern of The Goldberg Variations Mr. Gould is completely at home," she wrote, "and he makes an admirable host, communicating his own enjoyment in the treasures."

To make his first recording of *The Goldberg Variations*, Gould arrived that June of 1955 at the Columbia studio in an abandoned Presbyterian church at 207 East Thirtieth Street in New York, bringing with him a large supply of personal idiosyncrasies. He brought his own personal chair, which his father had built for him, which enabled him to sit just fourteen inches off the floor, so that he could keep his wrists at or below the level of the keyboard. ("I tried to find something fairly light in a folding chair," according to Bert Gould, "and then I had to saw about four inches off each leg, and I made a brass bracket to go around each leg and screw into it, and then welded the half of a turnbuckle to the brass bracket so that each leg could be adjusted individually.") He brought a bulky collection of sweaters and scarves in even the warmest weather, and he brought a large assortment of pills. When he played, he often gestured like a conductor with one hand while he attacked the keyboard with the other. And he sang, groaned, sighed. Gould had fairly good reasons for his odd behavior—it was easier to bring along his own low chair than to hunt for one in each new city, for example, and the scarves and pills all reflected a justifiable anxiety about his uncertain health—but many observers regarded all this as pure eccentricity, either a manic desire for self-indulgence or a manic yearning for publicity. Or perhaps those were both the same thing. In either case, Columbia was eager to publicize its boy wonder, to publicize him not only as a splendid pianist but as a bizarre personality.

"Columbia Masterworks' recording director and his engineering colleagues are sympathetic veterans who accept as perfectly natural all artists' studio rituals, foibles or fancies," said a Columbia press release about the recording of *The Goldberg Variations*. "But even these hardy souls were surprised by the arrival of young Canadian pianist Glenn Gould and his 'recording equipment.' . . . It was a balmy June day, but Gould arrived in coat, beret, muffler and gloves. 'Equipment' consisted of the customary music portfolio, also a batch of towels, two large bottles of spring water, five small bottles of pills (all different colors and prescriptions) and his own special piano chair. Towels, it developed, were needed in plenty because Glenn soaks his arms and hands up to the elbows in hot water for twenty minutes before sitting down at the keyboard.... Bottled spring water was a necessity because Glenn can't abide New York tap water. Pills were for any number of reasons—headaches, relieving tension, maintaining circulation. The air-conditioning engineer worked as hard as the man at the recording studio control panel. Glenn is very sensitive to the slightest changes in temperature, so there was constant adjustment of the vast studio air conditioning system...."

Columbia not only sent out this kind of publicity but invited musical journalists to come and see for themselves, and the journalists, sensing a good story, were glad to cooperate. "Debbie Ishlon at Columbia called me and said, 'There's something *happening* at the studio on Thirtieth Street,'" says Martin Mayer, who was then writing a monthly music column for *Esquire*. "She said, 'We're doing these recording sessions, *The Goldberg Variations,* and we've got this nut, and everybody's talking about how absolutely marvelous he is, you never heard anything like this.' So I went down there, to Thirtieth Street. Gould was listening to tapes when I came, and he didn't like some of what he heard. The producer would say, 'That's good,' and he would say, 'We'll see.'

"There was a little room off in a corner of this church—which was what this studio had been, you know—and there was a hot plate, and there was a kettle on the hot plate that was simmering, and there was a ewer on the table, a pitcher and a basin, and Gould came and put his hands in the basin and he poured in *scalding* water, and he said, 'This relaxes me.' Then he went out, and his hands were relaxed, and *red* they were. And the first thing I noticed was the way he played—like this—with his wrists below the level of the keyboard, which I'd never seen before. I watched and listened for about an hour and a half.

"Debbie had arranged for us to have lunch, and the first question I asked him was, 'Isn't it terribly hard to play the piano that way, not being able to put any of your upper body into getting a forceful action?' And he said, 'Oh, yes, you have to develop a lot of muscles behind your back, but that's the way my teacher taught me, and I can't change now.' And I said, 'I should think that would distort the way all the muscles in your arms and shoulders work.' And he said, 'My teacher's the biggest hunchback in Canada.'

"We went back to Gould's hotel in the Fifties, on Central Park— was that the St. Moritz? It might have been the St. Moritz. Anyway, he went to the bathroom and opened an attaché case, which opened up into a triple layer of medications. He reached in and took a bottle and took two pills. He said, 'These are my blood circulation pills. If I don't take them, I don't circulate.' I said, 'Well, by all means take them.' I really thought he was unique, a very, very great artist."

Gould was, of course, a willing participant in all this publicity. "My policy," as Joseph Roddy quoted him in a *New Yorker* profile, "has long been to cut the cloth to fit the corner newsstand." And so the press kept being invited to ogle his "eccentricities." "Gould puts on an astonishing and vivid show for those who attend record-ing sessions . . ." Herbert Kupferberg wrote in the *New York Her-ald-Tribune*. To the familiar tales of scarves and hats, he added that Gould "spurns the sandwiches sent in to the recording crew, sub-sisting instead on arrowroot biscuits washed down with his special spring water or skimmed milk." Jay Harrison went to cover the spectacle for *The Reporter* and noted that "a small Oriental rug had been placed beneath the pedals, for Mr. Gould finds himself unhappy when his feet rest on bare wood; and directly to his right, though the day was mild, an electric heater had been set up to keep him ultra-warm. . . . Gould finally began to play. He got through his opening phrase and then, without warning, flung his arms up. 'I can't,' he said plaintively. 'I can't. There is a draft. I feel it. A strong draft.' At this, a flock of workmen poured into the hall to track down the mysterious wind. . . ."

This kind of behavior naturally inspired the press to extravagant commentary. One Toronto columnist observed that Gould's melo-dramatic swaying over the keyboard resembled a combination "of the last act of *Macbeth* with an imitation of a proposal of marriage by a man who had just swallowed a fly." The press was also pleased to find that Gould could provide snappy answers to its questions.

When Ronald Collister of the Toronto *Telegram* asked him why he liked to take his shoes off during recording sessions, Gould replied, "I am naturally a foot-loose type." In repartee like that, Gould was starting to sound like another new keyboard phenomenon named Liberace.

But he did keep trying to explain himself. He knew that his hands were capable of a kind of magic that he could not fully understand, and so he naturally felt an extraordinary need to protect them. He tried to avoid shaking hands because some men like to apply crushing grips. He wore several pairs of gloves, he told Collister, because "My hands react badly to air-conditioning and dampness." "The melted paraffin wax he rubs on his hands 'makes me feel that I have new hands,'" Collister's story went on. "And the circulation pills he takes keeps his arms and hands supple. They are not studied eccentricities, he explains. 'I don't think about them. If I did, I would become so self-conscious I would have to give up this business.'"

As for Gould's use of pills, it is worth recalling that this was the era of Miltown, a time when the newly discovered tranquilizers and energizers seemed to provide everyone with a harmless method of dealing with the stresses of life. Gould joked about this in a letter to a young pianist in Washington, on which he inscribed the heading, GOULD'S CLINIC FOR PSYCHOPSEUMATIC [sic] THERAPY. "Due to my experience with internal medicine practice I am unusually alert to the problems of neurotic artists . . ." Dr. Gould wrote in his recommendation of various pills. "The yellow sleeping pills are called Nembutal. The white sedatives are called Luminal. I believe that both will have to be obtained through your doctor. Luminal is perfectly harmless and can be taken generally three times a day;—one after the noon meal and two at bedtime. I strongly advise however that you do not make a habit of Bevutal. It should definitely be reserved for the nights before special occasions and to break chronic sleeplessness. . . ."

The press kept wanting to know more. PIANIST USES 'STOP,' 'GO' PILLS, said a headline that December in Victoria, where Gould went to play the *Emperor Concerto*. "The tensions of traveling and playing concerts make a pianist's life an artificial existence, says Glenn Gould of Toronto . . ." the newspaper reported. "To keep up the pace, Mr. Gould has a bag-full of pills to stop perspiration before a concert, to increase circulation temporarily, stimulants 'to keep going' and sedatives fast and slow."

All this publicity, this kind of publicity, helped to make Gould, still in his early twenties, an international star. "Men we'd like you to meet," sighed a headline in *Glamour* in April of 1956, "A frail, loose-jointed Canadian with a bumper crop of light-brown hair, he bolsters legend with idiosyncracies: carts around pills, bottled spring water, a special chair; his views on diet (A friend: 'What did you eat that disagreed with you, Glenn? Food?')." *Vogue* the following month sounded even more feverish: "Glenn Gould ... has caused this year a glow of jubilant bonfires among American critics. . . . Tense, emaciated, with blueberry-blue eyes, Gould approaches his piano as he might an unbroken horse, bringing forth a tone both strong and lyrical. . . ."

The important thing, though, was that Gould's version of *The Goldberg Variations* was a great performance and a great recording, one of the greatest ever made. We who had not been present at Town Hall, the thousands of us, now had our first chance to discover Glenn Gould. Here we learned for the first time that Bach's variations (and, by implication, all of Bach) were not some cerebral construction to be respected from a respectful distance but rather a creation of passionate intensity and immense beauty. Here we learned too that Gould could play the piano like nobody else in the world. He had all the essential talents, a singing tone, a very precise articulation, a skillfully controlled dynamic range, but he also had two gifts that were rare if not unique. One was the ability to give this benign music an incredibly propulsive rhythmic drive. Being able to play with such precision even at high speed, he could make Bach's creation leap and plunge and fly; he filled it with a nervous energy that filled it with life. Gould's other extraordinary gift was the ability to make all three voices in three-part counterpoint remain completely independent even as he wove them inextricably together. The canons of *The Goldberg Variations* acquired an implicitly religious quality—as they must once have had in the mind of Bach—of being simultaneously one in three and three in one.

It took Gould just a week to make this extraordinary recording, and the last thing he taped was the opening theme itself. "I found that it took me twenty takes," he recalled later, "in order to locate a character for it which would be sufficiently neutral as not to prejudge the depth of involvement that comes later in the work. It was a question of utilizing the first twenty takes to erase all superfluous expression from my reading of it, and there is nothing more difficult to do. The natural instinct of the performer is to add, not to subtract." When the last notes of the "Aria da Capo" had finally died away, Gould shook hands with all the technicians and smiled and departed, with all his pills and his special chair in hand, and returned to Canada, to the summer cottage on Lake Simcoe.

The reviewers were reasonably appreciative, though none of them had the judgment or courage to commit themselves in the way Paul Hume had done when he wrote: "We know of no pianist like him at any age." Harold Schonberg of the New York *Times*, who was to become a kind of mossy boulder in Gould's path, began a record roundup in the Sunday edition by saluting Vlado Perlemuter's performance of the complete piano music of Ravel, and only after praising Robert and Gaby Casadesus's version of the Mozart four-hand sonatas did he get around to noting that there was "rather unusual playing" in a young Canadian's account of *The Goldberg Variations*. "Gould has skill and imagination, and the music appears to mean something to him," Schonberg acknowledged. "He also has a sharp, clear technique that enables him to toss off the contrapuntal intricacies of the writing with no apparent effort. Best of all, his work has intensity. . . . Obviously, a young man with a future."

The other reviews were rather similar, full of praise but mainly offering encouragement for the future rather than recognition of a great achievement. "This 23-year-old Canadian pianist has more promise than any young North American keyboard artist to appear since the war," said *Newsweek*. "His Bach is sensitive and superb, and with his musicianship and technique further revelations are to be expected. . . ." And Irving Kolodin in *The Saturday Review:* "Gould not only has all the finger discipline that can be taught, but also a kind of darting finesse that cannot. . . . He has made a mark for himself with this clean-lined, soberly expressive effort that will take considerable doing to excel."

And perhaps he never did. That extraordinary album of thirty variations, with that cover containing thirty snapshots of the shirt-sleeved young Gould playing, singing, explaining, listening, arguing—that record changed many people's lives, changed their ideas and feelings about Bach, about music, about themselves. It became a kind of talisman, something that had been mysteriously seen out at the edge of the universe and then brought back to us. It was a commercial phenomenon too, of course. The best-selling classical record in the year of its appearance, 1956, it never went out of print during the following quarter of a century, and the only man who would try to drive it out of print was Gould himself, when he rerecorded it shortly before his death. Even then, there are those of us who still prefer the original version, who prefer to the acutely self-conscious Gould of fifty the brashly confident Gould of twenty-two, the brilliant young virtuoso who felt, believed, knew that he could do anything.

In practical terms, though, what the huge success of *The Goldberg Variations* meant was that the young pianist who had delighted a few hundred people at his concerts in New York or Washington or Toronto now confronted the demands of the whole world. What did that success mean to you? Gould was asked by one interviewer. "Well, it meant a great deal to me," Gould confessed. "But it also launched me into the most difficult year I have ever faced."

IV

The Virtuoso on Tour

In the popular imagination, a concert pianist lives a rich and glamorous life. He strides onstage, under the spotlights, with the mysterious authority of a Lohengrin. Outfitted in the most elegant white tie and tails, he sits down at the piano, silences the expectant audience, and begins, with complete ease, to play. Almost by magic, from memory, the Chopin preludes flow forth, or the *Appassionata*. The audience explodes into applause, the men admiring, the women adoring. The pianist bows graciously and disappears into the night.

The reality is quite different. There is, of course, great music, and sometimes great emotion on both sides of the footlights, but there are also leaden pianos, coughing audiences, witless newspaper reviews, delayed flights, lonely hotel rooms, bad food, and constant anxiety. "We're just slave labor," John Browning once said to Elyse Mach *(Great Pianists Speak for Themselves)*. "We go to a hall and practice; then we rest, eat, and dress for the concert. We play the concert, go to an after-theater party, retire for a few hours' sleep, then catch a morning plane to the next stop. It becomes very routine.... On the other hand, no performing artist is ever in complete control over a situation, either. I think stage fright plays some part in the final product. Every performance has some of that. It begins to build in the morning and reaches a climax by mid-afternoon. That's when it's worst. I don't have bad nerves, but I often wake up with a tight knot in the stomach which gets tighter as the day progresses. . . ."

Many other pianists report similar difficulties. "It can get to you, year in and year out," Leon Fleisher told David Dubal. "It's terribly stressful to go from one imperfect situation to another, lousy piano, noisy audiences, drafts—you name it." And Philippe Entremont: "People think the life of a touring musician is glamorous. They don't realize the enormous amount of work involved, the incredible toll on the nerves. . . ." And Paul Badura-Skoda: "There are times when you feel that the public is just waiting for your slightest mistake. Concert halls are not always benevolent places." And Ruth Laredo: "I remember listening to Gina Bachauer on the radio . . . describing the life of a woman on the road, and what it's like after the concert, going back to your hotel room, and being alone so much of the time. It can be a very . . . difficult life." Fleisher recalled that when he was six or seven, his mother took him to hear Rachmaninoff and then rushed him backstage to shake the great man's hand. "Suddenly, in between encores, he came over to me," Fleisher said, "he peered down at me and asked, 'Are you a pianist?' And I looked up at this Empire State Building of a figure, and nodded my head. He then shook his head and said, 'Bad business.'"

Many artists nonetheless love to perform. The excitement overwhelms all difficulties. Arthur Rubinstein was perhaps the best example, and so when Gould undertook an interview with him, the two soon found themselves totally at odds. Rubinstein, like Madame Sosostris, had a bad cold, but he had nonetheless given his annual recital in Toronto, and when Gould came to meet him backstage, Rubinstein said, "You would have canceled the concert, wouldn't you?"

Gould equivocated. "I'm not sure, actually," he said. "I suppose that I. . . ."

"Of course you would have . . ." Rubinstein said. "I see it in your eyes."

Rubinstein then began interviewing his interviewer. "Was there never a moment when you felt that very special emanation from an audience?" he added.

"There really wasn't . . ." said Gould, who by then had not appeared in a concert hall for seven years.

"But you never felt that you had the soul of those people?" Rubinstein persisted.

"I didn't really want their souls, you know," Gould said. "Well, that's a silly thing to say. Of course, I wanted to have some influence, I suppose, to shape their lives in some way ... but I didn't want any power over them, and I certainly wasn't stimulated by their presence as such. ..."

"There we are absolute opposites, you know," Rubinstein said. "We are absolute opposites! ... If you would have followed the pianistic career for many years as I have—over sixty-five years, you know—you would have experienced this constant, constant, constant contact with the crowd that you have to, in a way, persuade, or dominate, or get hold of. ..."

Gould never wanted that. He never had the slightest intention of giving concerts for sixty-five years or of dominating crowds. He saw public performance only as a phase to be passed through, a phase that would bring him the money and celebrity to do other things. "For practical reasons, if nothing else, I suppose I will always remain to some extent a performer," he told an interviewer from the Toronto *Globe and Mail* in 1956, his first year on the concert tour. "One can too easily become enamored of the glamor, which I think is non-existent. My interests lie more in the literature of music, in composition, in conducting. ... "

Gould's next big expedition after the New York debut was to Detroit in March of 1956, his first American appearance with orchestra, and that involved a fairly typical series of mishaps. Originally, he was supposed to play the Beethoven Fourth Concerto with the Detroit Symphony Orchestra across the river in Windsor, Ontario, but when a French pianist named Eliane Richepin cabled that she was unable to make a scheduled appearance in Detroit, Gould was asked to fill in. He arrived at the Masonic Temple auditorium to try out the piano but found that it was being tuned for a recital by Arthur Rubinstein. "Mild-mannered and agreeable," according to a report in the Detroit *News*, "Gould agreed to go away until the tuner had finished, and to end his own practicing in time for the stage to be set for Rubinstein."

Gould's concert was a public triumph, but the reviewers' criticisms of his physical mannerisms at the keyboard came close to being personal attacks. "Seldom has a more exquisite performance been heard ... or a worse one witnessed," wrote J. Dorsey Callaghan in the Detroit *Free Press*. "Gould's storm-tossed mane of hair, his invertebrate posture at the keyboard and his habit of collapse at the end of each solo line were sheer show business. His interpretation and performance of the music . . . sheer genius." Harvey Taylor of the Detroit *Times* was even more patronizing. "The Beethoven fourth piano concerto . . . emerged with stunning beauty," he wrote. "He has obviously conquered the piano and now, to flower fully as a performing musician, he has only to conquer himself. In his current phase of development it is his tragedy that his behavior at the piano produced laughter in his audience. . . . Why do pianists feel that they can indulge in these fantastic emotional ecstasies?"

The Windsor *Daily Star* took a patriotic approach. "Canada triumphed last evening," its account began. The *Star* went on to describe Gould as "Canada's finest concert pianist and Canada's greatest contributor to the perfect interpretation and development of piano literature," and it reported that "our young Canadian artist captivated an audience which virtually filled the 5,000-seat auditorium. His ovation was tremendous. He took eight curtain calls. There were bravos, whistles, cheers." When Gould arrived in Windsor to play there three days later, however, the pressures upon him had apparently become nearly unbearable. In the dressing room before the concert, he suffered what the *Detroit News* called a seizure of "nervous tension" and announced that he could not play. "After extended discussion with symphony officials and insistence that he was too ill to play, Gould consented to 'try' and went to the piano," the newspaper reported. As for the actual performance of the Beethoven Fourth, the *News* said that "the extraordinary contortions and twitchings were missing," but it added that the "quiet and sedate" Gould gave "a performance that was almost colorless and marked by little of the brilliance for which Gould has been uproariously acclaimed. . . . He was far less of a pianist than he had been the preceding Thursday night."

Looking back on these difficult early years on the concert stage, Gould said that he had originally been quite unconscious of the physical mannerisms that many critics regarded as an attempt to attract publicity. (In surviving tapes of Gould's concerts, the most disturbing distraction is actually the ceaseless coughing from the audience.) "I had not regarded any of the things attendant upon my playing—my eccentricities, if you like—as being of any particular note at all," the pianist told Bernard Asbell. "No one made any fuss about them. Then suddenly a number of well-meaning . . . people in the arts . . . said, 'My dear young man, you must pull yourself together and stop this nonsense. . . .' The fact that I tend to sing a great deal while I'm playing, that I tend to conduct myself with one hand—all that sort of thing. . . . I had never given any thought to the importance, at least to some people, of visual image. When I suddenly was made aware of this in about 1956, I became extremely self-conscious about everything I did. The whole secret of what I had been doing was to concentrate exclusively on realizing a conception of the music, regardless of how it was physically achieved. This new self-consciousness was very difficult."

Musical commitments are generally made a year or more in advance, and Gould was now committed to endless touring. A solo recital in Toronto's Massey Hall. Bach's Fifth Partita, and the Beethoven Opus 109, and the Hindemith Third Sonata. "Mr. Gould employed a new gimmick," the *Telegram* reported. "During the entire work, his left leg was carelessly draped over his right knee."

The Beethoven Third Concerto in Pittsburgh. "He played brilliantly," said the *Press,* but "why must he crouch like a panther over the keys? Why should he pounce upon the notes like a leopard leaps upon its prey for the kill?" And the *Sun-Telegraph:* "He seems to forget that he is on a concert platform, that sort of exhibitionism having gone out more than 40 years ago. The discovery of new drugs and vitamins can cure such contortions, much as the witches exorcised them centuries ago." In Montreal, he played the Bach Concerto in D minor and the Strauss *Burleske.* "Canadians are unused to the possibility of a native excelling in the arts," said the *Star.* And a recital at Ohio Wesleyan. "There was hardly a listener who was not overwhelmed," said the Delaware *Gazette.*

That was a test run for his first reappearance at a recital in New York, where he played all of Bach's fifteen Three-Part Inventions, four pieces from *The Art of the Fugue,* and the third sonatas of both Hindemith and Krenek. "Astounding," said the *Herald-Tribune.* Then to Dallas for what the *Morning News* called an "interesting and provocative" performance of Beethoven's *Emperor Concerto.* Then a recital in Spokane, which included Beethoven's Opus 110, Mendelssohn's *Variations sérieuses,* and two Brahms intermezzi.

"Gould has marvelous talent and a masterful technique," said the *Daily Chronicle,* adding, as usual, that his "unusual mannerisms had most of the large audience buzzing by intermission time."

The journalistic obsession with Gould's "mannerisms" led to problems of a kind that no other pianist had to face. George Szell, the brilliant but irascible conductor of the Cleveland Orchestra, apparently took offense at Gould's hiring a carpenter to build blocks under his piano during a rehearsal of a concerto they were to play together. This incident took place during a break in the rehearsal, and Szell never said anything at the time, but a subsequent *Time* cover story on the conductor reported that Gould's fussiness had wasted so much of the orchestra's rehearsal time that Szell had angrily told him, "Perhaps if I were to slice one-sixteenth of an inch off your derrière, Mr. Gould, we could begin." Szell had never said any such thing, Gould told Jonathan Cott, so when Gould later met the man who had written the *Time* story, he asked him the source of this anecdote and learned that Szell had told it himself. The press not only prints authoritative lies but feeds on them. When Szell died in 1970, Gould was dismayed to see the same anecdote reappearing not only in the *Time* obituary, but also in slightly different form in *Newsweek,* and then in *Esquire.* There the quotation was substantially altered into what Gould recalled as "'I vill personally stick . . .'—I can't remember the exact words but it really doesn't matter—'stick one of zose legs up your rear end.'"* Gould finally wrote, and *Esquire* printed, his categorical denial of the scene. It included Gould's vow that if Szell had ever made such a remark, the Cleveland Orchestra "would have been obliged to find themselves a new guest in a hurry."

Fairly often, Gould rebelled at the whole system and canceled his concerts, sometimes because he felt bad, sometimes because he said he felt bad. "He became a notorious canceler," says Morris Gross, who was then Gould's attorney, "and I would get calls from all over the place. He would arrive in some major center in the United States and find himself unwilling—or he would say unable—to play. I

---

*These are Gould's versions, but such stories change in the retelling. As a matter of record, the *Esquire* version said: "Accounts vary as to whether [Szell said that Gould] should take the handle that adjusted the height and 'screw it up your ass' or whether he merely suggested that if the bench were too high Gould should simply 'squeeze down on your asshole.'"

would have to try to—provide a scenario which was acceptable to the impresario who was going to be losing a lot of money each time. And Glenn would promise to return, and sometimes he wouldn't even play the return concert. But sometimes, it was his offbeat appearance that would get him in trouble. I remember once he was doing a concert in Sarasota, Florida, and I got a phone call from him, and he said, 'I was sitting out on this park bench, and I guess they're trying to preserve their image of being a very warm area in the middle of winter. I was sitting there in my usual—doing nothing unusual—and they've run me in. The police.'"

Q: He was wearing all his coats and mittens, damaging the image of the city?

A: Exactly. I said, "What were you wearing?" That's exactly what happened.

And then came the news that the Soviet Union had invited Gould to play in Moscow and Leningrad in the spring of 1957. Russia in those days was still a land of fear and mystery. Scarcely four years had passed since the death of the terrible Stalin and the beginning of what Ilya Ehrenburg christened "the thaw." Westerners had barely heard of names like Gilels and Richter, and Russians had just experienced their first encounter with an American troupe that had come to perform *Porgy and Bess*. "When the cannons are silent, the muses are heard," as Truman Capote entitled his marvelous account of that Gershwin expedition. Gould, by now twenty-four, was the first classical musician from North America to be invited behind what was persistently called the Iron Curtain. He was delighted. Taking along his manager, Homburger, he flew to Moscow and established himself in the Canadian embassy. Officials there persuaded him that his Communist audiences would be offended if he clung to his habit of performing in a dark business suit, and so he reluctantly agreed to white tie and tails.

MOSCOW HAILS GOULD, cried the headline in the Toronto *Star*. At a time when the heavily censored Western press coverage of Moscow was minimal, the *Star* had shrewdly signed up Homburger as a special correspondent, and Homburger now reported on Gould's concert with breathless enthusiasm. "The famed Bolshoi Hall of the Tchaikowsky Conservatory of Music in Moscow was filled to capacity last night as Toronto's Glenn Gould became the first Canadian musician . . . to perform here," said the story under Homburger's by-line, which actually sounds rather like the work of a rewrite man on the *Star*'s cable desk. Gould had chosen several of his favorites, four selections from Bach's *Art of the Fugue,* the Sixth Partita in E minor, Beethoven's Opus 109, and the Berg Sonata. "By intermission, bravos could be heard all over the hall," Homburger reported. "As Gould took his second bow a huge basket of blue chrysanthemums was carried up the aisle toward the stage. . . . During intermission the director of the Moscow Philharmonic came to pay his compliments and said, 'Bach must be your great passion; we have never heard fugues like this.'

"At the end of the recital, bravos and applause again echoed through the hall," Homburger went on. "Soon the applause turned into a rhythmic clapping, the greatest compliment an artist can be paid in this country. And then the encores began: First a fantasia by Sweelinck, then two of the Goldberg Variations by Bach. Still the audience clamored for more and Gould added another set of three variations. . . . Even after the house lights had been put on the audience did not wish to leave and Gould had to take innumerable bows. By the time he came back to the dressing room many musicians were crowded into the dressing room to congratulate him. Still the audience persisted in their applause, so in the middle of receiving congratulations Gould was rushed out on the stage once more and as a final encore he played another five of the Goldberg Variations. . . ."

Even the most triumphant concerts remain fairly standard public rituals (performed in white tie and tails), but in this era of the thaw, the people who most passionately hungered to hear the young visitor from the West were the students at the Moscow Conservatory. Gould willingly agreed to go and play for them, on condition that he be allowed to choose whatever he pleased, with no program announced in advance. He then decided to play only modern music, meaning only music of the twentieth century.

"When I first announced what I was going to do, i.e. that I was going to play the sort of music that has not been officially recognized in the U.S.S.R. since the artistic crises in the mid thirties, there was a rather alarming and temporarily uncontrollable murmuring from the audience," Gould later reported in a letter to Yousuf Karsh, the photographer. "I am quite sure that many of the students were uncertain whether it was better for them to remain or walk out. As it turned out, I managed to keep things under control by frowning ferociously now and then and the only people who did walk out were a couple of elderly professors who probably felt that I was attempting to pervert the taste of the young. However, as I continued playing music of Schoenberg ... Webern and Krenek, there were repeated suggestions from the student body, mostly in the form of discreet whispers from the committee on the stage but occasionally the odd fortissimo suggestion from the audience, that they would prefer to spend their time with Bach and Beethoven. . . ."

Gould had a grand time in Russia. "It was a sensation equivalent to that of perhaps being the first musician to land on Mars or Venus ..." he wrote to Karsh. "It was a great day for me!" It was also a great day for the inhabitants of Mars. The pianist Bella Davidovich recalled that her husband was in the hospital and heard Gould's first Moscow concert on the radio, and he told her, "When you get to Leningrad, Glenn Gould will be there. Please stay one more day, you must not miss him, you cannot imagine the concert he gave." Mrs. Davidovich did stay on and did go to hear Gould, though she had great difficulty in getting a ticket. "After he played in Moscow," she recalled, "everybody was calling Leningrad, saying, 'Run to the concert—go to hear Gould.' The tickets were gone in a minute. We had never heard such playing."

Everywhere Gould appeared, he was greeted by cheering crowds. Women handed him bouquets of lily of the valley. In Leningrad, extra seats were installed onstage, an unusual concession to popular demand, and extra police had to be assigned to the crowds that milled around the lobby. For his last orchestral concert, when he played the Bach D minor Concerto and the Beethoven Second, the management had not only sold all 1,300 seats but also 1,100 standing-room tickets, which meant that the crowds jammed into every bit of floor space, and still more waited outside in vain hopes of getting in.

"It was a sight I shall not soon forget," Homburger cabled back to the Toronto *Star*. "Even those orchestra members who were not required during the concertos stood backstage to listen and gave Gould an ovation as he came offstage. The crowd once again was most demonstrative with immense bunches of flowers being tossed onstage and the hall resounding to the continuous roar of applause and bravos.

"Gould had originally decided not to play any encores after the concertos," Homburger went on. "However, the following message was delivered to him during intermission: 'Dear Sir, We implore you to play some Bach without the orchestra. Many of us had no opportunity of attending your concert on the 16th and had been waiting in the street for a long time and all in vain. [Signed] Your Russian admirers.' Of course, Gould did not want to disappoint anyone and so began another marathon of encores.

"At one point, Mr. Slovak, the conductor of the concert, said to me, 'I think I might as well go home. Gould can finish the concert. I don't think the public wants to hear the last orchestral piece.' I finally convinced the stage manager to move the piano to the side of the stage and Gould and I went back to the dressing room. It must have been all of five minutes when the stage manager returned and informed us that the audience was still applauding. So Gould took a final bow in his overcoat, cap and gloves."

Neither in Toronto nor in New York had Gould experienced anything quite like this, this outpouring of adulation and admiration, even love. "It was overwhelming and just a bit frightening," he later said. Canadians like to complain that their artists are not taken seriously until they achieve success in New York, but as Van Cliburn was to discover a year later, neither Canadians nor Americans stage the rituals of artistic triumph with the éclat of the Russians. Gould's family was well pleased too. "I am very proud of you and the work you are doing," his father said in an oddly formal cable to Moscow. "Every thinking Canadian has reason to thank you. Your music may have a very real part in establishing a better feeling between east and west. We do hope and pray that it will." The Canadian press took it all as a national event. "Mr. Gould represents Canada abroad with distinction," said the Toronto *Telegram*, "and in doing so he broadcasts the message that Canadians are interested in a world climate where music and its artistic allies can flourish uninterruptedly. Canada is proud of Glenn Gould. . . ."

The Russians were more warmly represented by Kitty Gvozdeva, a middle-aged teacher and translator in Leningrad. "I wish you, Glenn, darling, golden boy, all the love, and luck and happiness of this best of all possible worlds!" she wrote in one of the first of her many effusions. Gould was touched, and wrote back, and their affectionate correspondence lasted the rest of his life. Despite Kitty Gvozdeva's warmest pleadings for another visit, Gould never returned to the Soviet Union, but he always retained an affection for all those Russians who had showered him with lily of the valley, and they for him.

Gould was by now committed to the international concert track, and the track led next to Berlin, to a performance of the Beethoven Third Concerto with Herbert von Karajan and the Berlin Philharmonic. Gary Graffman recalls meeting Gould several times in Berlin because the two pianists were both practicing in the Steinway building.

Q: But he often said that he practically never practiced at all.

A: He was practicing a lot.

Q: He was practicing a lot?

A: He was practicing a lot.

Graffman also recalls that Gould "had a thing about adjusting to time changes and adjusting to food and adjusting to water," and when they went out to dinner together Gould wanted only a well-done steak. "I remember ordering escargots," Graffman says, "and when they came, I said to him, obviously not seriously, I said, 'I hope this doesn't disgust you.' And he said, 'Oh, that's perfectly all right. I just won't look while you're eating.' He was serious."

Gould's Berlin debut was a triumph. "A young man in a strange sort of a trance ..." wrote the doyen of German critics, H. H. Stuckenschmidt. "His technical ability borders on the fabulous; such a combination of fluency in both hands, of dynamic versatility, and of range in coloring represents a degree of mastery which in my experience has not appeared since the time of Busoni. A marvel, an experience, an incomparable delight...." Then southward-bound to Vienna, and Gould, having caught another cold, decided to take the train. "My cold is still lousy ..." he wrote to his father. "Sympathy but no flowers please.... Actually I spent a pretty miserable day with sinus pain—much like the time I came home from Texas and was deaf.... Aeroplanes can wreak havoc with a cold. Anyhow I stayed in Frankfurt (which is a very beautiful city from what little I saw of it)—then took the train last night to Wien."

Gould loved the Germanic landscape ("Beautiful forests and any number of quaint little towns dominated by Baroque churches," he wrote to his father), and it inevitably reminded him of a Germanic past to which he felt mysteriously attached. "I stayed up till 11:30 specially to sing *Die Meistersinger* as we went through Nürnberg," he wrote. Then came a painful dawn. "This morning at 6:30 the porter came around to give me back my passport when we had crossed into Austria and as I was opening the door of my compartment he suddenly pushed it shut again on my left thumbnail. Said thumbnail is now turning slightly blue and making it a bit difficult to write. . . ."

Gould found the legendary Vienna of Mozart and Haydn a little disappointing ("Too much rococo architecture for my rather severe tastes"), but his concert there was another triumph. "Encores upon encores," Homburger reported, "cheers upon cheers, house lights on, stage lights out, more applause, and a final bow in overcoat, hat, and gloves." From all this, Gould might have expected a triumphant welcome back to Toronto, something between a press conference and a ticker-tape parade, but he characteristically slipped home almost in secret. He didn't even give advance notice to his parents, with whom he still lived. "It was deliberate," he subsequently told an inquiring reporter from the Toronto *Telegram*. "I didn't want any fanfare. I was in New York, and it was hot, so I decided to come home. . . . I feel that I did the best playing of my career over there. Now that I'm home I just want to get away from everything for a while."

For a star pianist, though, there is no such thing as getting away from everything for a while. Gould returned to Toronto in June of 1957, and the *Telegram* reported that same week that he would hit the trail again in August, and the trail would take him that season to Montreal, Hollywood, Washington, Syracuse, Rochester, Pittsburgh, Cincinnati, St. Louis, New York, Oberlin, Miami, Philadelphia, New Orleans, Kingston, Buffalo, Winnipeg, Saskatoon, Seattle, Tacoma, Boston, Lexington, Ottawa. . . .

Gould's contract with Columbia called for him to make three records in two years, and his next choice was no less daring than his insistence on *The Goldberg Variations*. It was also a major miscalculation. He came to New York in February of 1956 and proceeded to record the last three sonatas of Beethoven, Opus 109 in E major, Opus 110 in A flat, and Opus 111 in C minor, all works of extreme subtlety and beauty and complexity. It was then considered rather bold for anyone to play any one of the three sonatas as the climax of a recital, and there were some critics who thought it presumptuous for any pianist to attempt a public performance of these masterpieces before having attained a considerable maturity.

Gould had played the Opus 109 often, the others rarely, and his conceptions of all three included some ideas that were extremely unorthodox. Much of his Opus 109 was splendid, but when he ventured into the beautiful variations in the final movement, he began violating what Beethoven had written, not just misinterpreting but violating. At the start of the fourth variation, specifically, Beethoven had carefully noted that it should be played "Un poco meno andante ciò è un poco più adagio come il tema," and he added, since he was then in a patriotic phase, a German equivalent, "Etwas langsamer als das Thema." Somewhat slower than the theme, which is andante. Since this beautiful piece comes between the vivace third variation and the stern counterpoint of the allegro fifth variation, it is obvious that Beethoven wanted to emphasize the contrast in the marvelous serenity of this variation. Ignoring the composer's written wishes, Gould played it at high speed, made it glib, superficial, flashy.

His hurried version of Opus 111 was still worse. This is one of Beethoven's very greatest works, one of those grand statements of heroic purpose, like the Fifth Symphony and the *Emperor Concerto*, and Gould only later acknowledged that he disliked this most popular aspect of Beethoven. ("The supreme historical example of a composer on an ego trip," he said, " a composer absolutely confident that whatever he did was justified simply because he did it.") Whenever Gould performed a piece that he disliked but didn't want to admit disliking, he tended, for mysterious reasons of his own, to speed up the tempo. (Some months later, when a critic in Cincinnati ventured to ask him why he had raced through the Opus 111, Gould first "put his hands in his pockets and said he felt it that way," then "explained further [that] the piece was weak in spots; it needed greater speed. . . .") Conversely, Gould said many years later, when discussing his rerecording of *The Goldberg Variations*, that the music he loved best was music that he wanted to hear played slowly. He attributed this feeling to his recollections of the old Presbyterian hymns of his boyhood.

Now he played the heroic first movement of Opus 111 at a frantic speed that deprived it of all its grandeur, made it sound like a stunt. Perhaps only Gould could play it that fast; only Gould would want to. He had said more than once that there was no reason to record a classic work unless one had a new interpretation to offer. "If there's any excuse at all for making a record, it's to do it differently," he declared in a recorded interview entitled "Glenn Gould: Concert Dropout," "to approach the work from a totally recreative point of view, that one is going to perform this particular work as it has never been heard before. And if one can't quite do that, I would say, abandon it, forget about it, move on to something else. . . ." These Gouldian theories were essentially misconceived, however. While an interpreter should have considerable latitude, there is really no reason for any pianist to ignore Beethoven's clearly stated wishes simply for the sake of expressing his own wishes, or simply for the sake of being different. There are limits, in other words, on the interpreter's freedom; the theme of *The Goldberg Variations* must not be played presto, not even by Glenn Gould. Heard today, more than thirty years after he made the recording, Gould's rushed and crashing performance of the Opus 111 remains a botch. It is a botch, one should add, that could only have been perpetrated by someone who was twenty-three years old, and a genius, but it is still a botch.

Partly because the Beethoven sonatas are so well known, in contrast to *The Goldberg Variations,* the critics were quick to pounce. "Unfortunately, his new Beethoven recording is more notable for eccentricity than for musical substance . . ." said one of the first newspaper reviews, in the Baltimore *Morning Sun.* "The whole impression, despite technical accomplishment, is one of childishness." *Time* accused Gould of merely "skimming the surface." "At every point one hears his mind operating attentively and independently," B. H. Haggin wrote in *The New Republic,* "and since the mind is not only powerful but willful and even eccentric, its operation is interesting but the result is largely unacceptable." And Harold Schonberg of the New York *Times* was as lordly as ever: "Not only are the performances immature; they are actually inexplicable.

The scramble through the finale of Op. 109 and the last variation of Op. 111 are something that the young Canadian pianist will look back on as an aberration in about ten years."

Gould was not someone who enjoyed admitting mistakes. In a letter to John Roberts, he sounded quite defiant: "I can only say that those alterations of dynamic or tempo indications with which I took license were the result, not of whims, but of rather careful scrutiny of the scores. . . . Since so many listeners and critics (trustworthy ones too) have taken exception to my conception of late Beethoven I cannot claim that it is the most convincing recording that I have made. However, I do feel that, if only as a personal manifesto, it is the most convinced." In a later letter to John Conly at *High Fidelity*, Gould said that his conception of late Beethoven "does come from an abiding personal conviction," and that he hoped to record more of it, even "if, as I expect, it will be similarly condemned." Gould never fulfilled that plan. Though he performed both the Opus 101 and the *Hammerklavier*, Opus 106, he never made a commercial recording of either one, nor indeed of any sonata after the *Appassionata*. And with the coming of stereo, Gould never rerecorded Beethoven's last three masterpieces; the original mono versions were quietly allowed to go out of print.

Nearly a year after this miscarriage, Gould made his New York orchestral debut in January of 1957 with Leonard Bernstein and the Philharmonic, and they reached the happy choice of Beethoven's Second Concerto. It was and perhaps still is the least known and least appreciated of Beethoven's five concerti, but Gould loved it, played it brilliantly, and made it virtually his own. His performance also illustrated some of the lesser known of his own qualities: charm, gaiety, effervescence. Even the dour Harold Schonberg was impressed, somewhat. "Mr. Gould strolled on stage," he wrote, with the customary atmospherics, "sat at the piano, crossed his legs during the opening tutti, gazed calmly upon audience and orchestra, and then untangled his legs and got to work. He presented a sharp, clear-cut reading that had decided personality." Leonard Bernstein was characteristically more effusive about Gould's performance. "He is the greatest thing that has happened to music in years . . ." he said.

Bernstein, like so many people, had first encountered Gould

through his recording of *The Goldberg Variations*. It had appeared when Bernstein's wife, Felicia, was pregnant with their first son; while she had to wait out the last month during a New York heat wave, that record "became 'our song.'" Bernstein's most vivid personal memory of the young Gould came slightly later, when they were preparing to record the Beethoven C minor Concerto, and Bernstein invited the pianist to dinner at his place in the Osborne apartment house, just across from Carnegie Hall. "He was all bundled up," Bernstein recalls, sipping on his Scotch and soda and taking another cigarette from his silver cigarette box, "and he had an astrakhan hat over some other kind of cap, doubly hatted, doubly mittened, and endlessly muffled and mufflered. And Felicia said, 'Aren't you going to take your hat off?' He said, 'No, no, that's all right, I'll keep it on.' A few minutes later, she asked me, in an aside, over drinks, whether this was a religious matter with him, and I said, 'As far as I know, it isn't!' So she brought it up again to him and said, 'Really, I think you ought to take your hat off, if you don't have any reason for having it on, because it's very warm.'

"And you know, he did. And when he had taken his hat off, Felicia said, 'But this is impossible!' I mean, he had—this was a mat of hair, soaking wet, and just unnourished, and no air. It was hair that hadn't breathed in God knows how long. And while I was fixing drinks or something, she lured him into the bathroom, sat him down at a stool, and cut his hair. And washed it, and combed it. And he came out looking like some kind of archangel, radiant, with this beautiful hair, which one had never seen the color of, quite blond, and shining, haloed-ish. It was really a very beautiful thing to see, what she did, his acceptance, equally beautiful, and the result, which was thrillingly beautiful."

When Gould and Bernstein appeared at the Columbia recording studio on Thirtieth Street, though, there were other dramas of a kind that everyone who worked with Gould was beginning to recognize. For their first collaboration, on the Beethoven Second, Gould arrived with the usual collection of scarves and pills and briefly took up his position at the piano. "With the opening tutti under way," Jay Harrison wrote in *The Reporter*, "Mr. Gould, having nothing to do during the first portion of the concerto, slid out from behind the piano and loped casually about the hall. He shook his head, waved his arms, beat time, and acted generally in a manner that any conductor less accustomed to the ways of genius might have found trying in the extreme. Bernstein, who was himself a prodigy once, took no notice. . . ." When they were finally ready for Gould to start taping, he couldn't be found. A Columbia salesman reported that he was in the men's room soaking his hands in scalding water.

"I love him, you know I love him," said Howard Scott, the recording director for Columbia, banging his head in exasperation. "But why does he have to soak his hands now. Why?"

"Don't rattle him," said the salesman. "He'll sell like crazy— thousands of albums, thousands. He's great and Columbia's got him."

The recording session, when it finally got under way, went well. Gould, for all his oddities, was a consummate professional. But also a perfectionist. Bernstein, very pleased with the performance, declared that "if we can't get great Beethoven out of what we've already done, we never will," but Gould dismayed everyone by saying, "I noticed some trills I'd like to redo."

"Trills," Scott muttered. "We just recorded fifteen of the best trills on records and he wants to redo them. Glenn, take it from me, we'll put together a record from out of all this that you'll be proud of, Lennie will love, and the critics will adore. I know."

He was right. Gould was proud of it, and Bernstein loved it. "I am as proud as you are . . ." he wrote to Gould, "and I hope the critics get the point & perceive for once in their lives what is really going on." The only taint was a bit of gossip, repeatedly told, most fully reported by Abram Chasins in *Speaking of Pianists*, and strenuously denied by Gould. The story was that in the exhilaration of their first public performance of the concerto, Bernstein had urged that they record it together "while it was hot," and that Gould declined, and that Bernstein bewilderedly asked why, and that Gould coolly said, "Because Bernstein isn't ready." B. H. Haggin maliciously repeated the tale, which Bernstein now says he never heard, and went on to comment on the recording: "The orchestra's tense, hard-driven, harsh-sounding playing make it evident that Bernstein still wasn't ready, but Gould makes Bernstein's unreadiness glaring with each piano phrase that he articulates and shapes so perfectly and with such repose and executes with such precision and such beauty of sound." Schonberg of the *Times* was for once more gracious: "The results are beautiful ... Mr. Gould can play with considerable dash, and he does when necessary; but the overall impression is one of well-balanced plasticity, of piano merging with orchestra and veering out again, of fine ensemble and musical finesse."

Only after that triumph, at the end of 1957, did Columbia release the third of Gould's great early recordings, the Fifth and Sixth of the Bach partitas, which he had actually taped somewhat earlier. As with the Beethoven sonatas, this combined a piece that Gould had performed a lot, the Fifth Partita in G major, with one that he had hardly played at all, the Sixth Partita in E minor. And as with *The Goldberg Variations* and the Beethoven Second Concerto, Gould was now taking hold of a relatively neglected part of the piano repertoire, demonstrating that both of these partitas were masterpieces, and making them unmistakably and forever his own. Thousands of people who had never before heard a Bach partita would hear them forever after as Gould alone had articulated and dramatized them.

The only one who disapproved of this superb recording was, strangely enough, Gould himself. He even made his dissatisfaction part of his subsequent indictment of the whole process of concert performances. "I had just returned from my first European tour ..." he told an interviewer, Elyse Mach, "and during that tour ... the Fifth Partita, which is a great favorite of mine, was an integral part of almost every program.... During those concert experiences I had to project that particular piece to a very large audience in most cases and, as a consequence, I had added hairpins—crescendi and diminuendi, and similar un-Bachian affectations—where they didn't need to be. I had exaggerated cadences in order to emphasize the separation of sentences or paragraphs, and so on. In other words, I was making an unnecessarily rhetorical statement about the music, simply as a consequence of having attempted to project it in very spacious acoustic environments.... So the result is that the record made in the summer of '57 is a very glib, facile effort, because a series of little party tricks which just don't need to be there had been added to the piece. Now the interesting thing is that, at the same time, I also recorded the Sixth Partita, which I had played very rarely in public ... and that's a good recording. No party tricks."

They are both far more than good recordings; they are both great recordings. The strange thing is that Gould, who couldn't see how he had gone terribly wrong on the late Beethoven sonatas, also could see only flaws and failures in his marvelous recording of the Fifth Partita. For once, the critics were more perceptive than he. "One is electrified . . . by the very first phrase of Bach's Partita No. 5 . . ." Haggin wrote in *The New Republic,* "by the power, the authority, the sustained tension that compel one's continued fascinated intellectual attention. . . . Both his intellectual power and his technical mastery are evident. . . . I can't recall another pianist achieving anything like this playing of counterpoint."

"Gould is back on the high road to enduring accomplishment . . ." Irving Kolodin wrote in *The Saturday Review.* "It is an enlivening experience to hear the music take shape under his hands, disciplined yet flexible, thoughtful but animated, properly restrained and still possessed of a dynamic rise and fall. . . . An interpreter who can conceive of a printed page with this much sophistication need only be true to his own best impulses. . . ."

Back on tour in August of 1957, Gould appeared to Canadians as a national hero. When he joined the Montreal String Quartet in playing the Brahms Quintet in F minor, Eric McLean of the *Star* reported not only that the performance was "electrifying" but that scalpers had been hawking tickets for as much as thirty dollars apiece, "something unheard of in the local history of chamber music."

South of the border, things were somewhat more difficult, for while the press fanned Gould's celebrity, it also seemed totally obsessed with what it kept calling his "mannerisms" or "eccentricities." Even Paul Hume, who had written that prescient review in the *Washington Post* three years earlier, now turned on Gould. After the usual complaints about the pianist's low chair and his little rug, after grumbling that Gould crossed his legs and massaged his wrists while the orchestra was playing, Hume went on to say that "for him these habits may now be necessities. But nothing like them has ever been needful to many pianists who have played this music more powerfully, more beautifully, and more poetically than Glenn Gould." On the other hand, celebrity begat celebrity. Gould's performance of *The Goldberg Variations* (and the Schoenberg Suite, Opus 25) attracted to Carnegie Hall an audience that included Arthur Rubinstein, Leonard Bernstein, Dimitri Mitropoulos, and Elisabeth Schwarzkopf, and it began winning more serious respect from Schonberg of the *Times*. "Always there was variety, a fine musical intelligence, an extraordinary ability to separate voices and a pair of hands that were unerring," Schonberg wrote. "For this kind of Bach playing one is content to put up with all the personal idiosyncrasies that Mr. Gould can conceive; though, in truth, it is difficult to see how he can conceive any more."

Most of the piano tour, though, involved provincial critics and provincial audiences in provincial cities. "The fabulous young Canadian pianist with the currently soaring reputation played his debut recital in the Miami area Friday night," the Miami *Herald* said of the man who had already dazzled New York, Washington, Berlin, and Moscow. Then came a recital in Philadelphia, and an orchestral concert in New Orleans, and then a performance of the Beethoven Third Concerto in Buffalo inspired the sage of the Buffalo *Evening News* to declare that Gould "has nothing like the technique of a young Horowitz [and] the Third Concerto in the hands of the incomparable Backhaus is undoubtedly closer to the wisdom involved in the Beethoven poetry."

Still, the New York press could be equally problematic. When Gould played the Schoenberg concerto and the Bach D minor with Dimitri Mitropoulos and the New York Philharmonic in March of 1958, Paul Henry Lang of the *Herald-Tribune* became positively indignant. "I found the performance nothing less than shocking," he wrote. "The same Glenn Gould who played the Schoenberg concerto with fine musicianship pounded and punched his way through this intimate chamber piece. His tone was harsh, at times downright brutal. . . . The whole thing was a caricature of a baroque concerto." Winthrop Sargeant of *The New Yorker*, by contrast, found the same performance "a masterpiece of coherence, control and fine musical taste." It was left to Hugh Thomson of the Toronto *Star* to report that Gould was "so carried away" in his performance of the Bach concerto that "he cut his thumb on the keys in the excitement of the finale. Then, when he began to play this Schoenberg concerto, blood kept spreading over the keys. This was probably all to the good, because if there ever was a work that needed some blood, it's Schoenberg's piano concerto."

Gould again appeared to be nearing a breaking point, both physically and psychologically, though he seems not to have realized what was happening. The first major symptom was an unusual sort of indifference to the quality of his own public performances. In Boston that same March, he came out after intermission and announced that he would play the Mozart Sonata in C major (K. 330) instead of Beethoven's Opus 110 because he hadn't practiced the Beethoven. "With innocent good humor," the Boston *Globe* reported, "he added that he hadn't practiced the Mozart either." And in Montreal, when he once again played *The Goldberg Variations,* Eric McLean shrewdly observed not only that "the finger work in the fast movements was not as clean as usual" but that Gould seemed to be getting bored. "It was as though excessive familiarity had caused Gould to lose interest in the primary melody of the movement," McLean wrote, "and had transferred all his attention to the tenor part. This is cavilling, of course. By general standards it was unusually brilliant and musical playing. It was only by the Gould standard that it fell short of perfection."

To Gould, of course, the Gould standard was the only standard, and he now felt a strong conflict between the drumming sense of duty and commitment and the desire to escape from that same drumming sense. In the summer of 1958, he had promised to return to Europe, to perform the Bach D minor at the Salzburg Festival with Mitropoulos and the Concertgebouw Orchestra, and then on to Brussels for Canada Day at the World's Fair, on to Berlin and Stockholm and Wiesbaden, Florence, Tel Aviv. . . . Looking back on that frantic period in his life, Gould daydreamed about the attractions of being some kind of a prisoner locked in a cell.

"I've never understood the preoccupation with freedom as it's reckoned in the Western world . . ." Gould wrote in a rather peculiar work, "Glenn Gould Interviews Glenn Gould about Glenn Gould." "To be incarcerated would be the perfect test of one's inner mobility and of the strength which would enable one to opt creatively out of the human situation." Gould found another way to opt creatively out of the human situation: he got sick, a severe attack of tracheitis that he blamed on the air conditioning in the Salzburg

Festspielhaus. Testifying on his own behalf, Gould described this illness as a reprieve. "My tracheitis was of such severity," he said, "that I was able to cancel a month of concerts, withdraw into the Alps, and lead the most idyllic and isolated existence."

Gould actually canceled only one recital in Salzburg, and two weeks later he got himself to Brussels to play the Bach D minor with Boyd Neel at the World's Fair. *Le Soir* aped the American newspaper coverage of Gould by complaining of his "orang-outang style," and the Toronto press aped its own coverage by reporting the Brussels attack as though it were significant news. Gould drove himself on. "I was terribly depressed," he later told Bernard Asbell. "I was going to be there [in Europe] for three months, terribly out of touch with all the life that I knew, and everything seemed ridiculous and I wished I were home. Before the first concert . . . in Berlin, I was walking to the rehearsal and suddenly said to myself, 'Well, who the hell said it was supposed to be fun anyway?' I must say this pulled me through several weeks. I settled on it as a motto."

Gould needed that motto during his actual concert with Karajan and the Berlin Philharmonic. Once again, the Bach D minor. It should perhaps be explained that this concerto begins with both piano and orchestra playing the sturdy main theme in unison, but that Bach himself later used the theme canonically, that is, restating it two beats after the original statement so that the theme accompanies itself. Now, on the stage of the Hochschule für Musik, after a speech by Mayor Willy Brandt, after the world premiere of an overture by Wolfgang Fortner, Gould and Karajan joined in what Gould later called "one of the most embarrassing beginnings this concerto has ever had."

What was embarrassing was that Gould misunderstood Karajan's cues. "I looked up at K," Gould later wrote in one of his many unfinished manuscripts, "saw, or thought I saw, his preparatory upbeat, and three-quarters of a second later, as his arms emphatically described the bottom of their trajectory, I made my entrance— alone—For K., up is down and vice versa—in the matter of prep. beats. The orch entered as I answered at the second beat—Happily canonic voice-leading met all academic requirements—I took ¾ of a second off to compensate and rejoined them in the middle of the bar. Apart from that, the afternoon was quite uneventful. We exchanged a final glance of mutual support, indicating to each other that a state of mutual preparedness was at hand. He then, as is his wont, closed his eyes for the duration. . . ."

And so, on to Stockholm. There is probably no way to capture all the turmoil and anxiety of this concert tour, or any concert tour, but among Gould's miscellaneous papers there is a memorandum, apparently written many years later,* which gives some sense of the young man on the run. It bears the title "A Season on the Road," and it is nothing but a series of notes, scraps. "Preambule," it begins, "summer of 58 Salzburg—Mitrop [Dimitri Mitropoulos]—Concertgebouw. . . . Premonitions of disaster. El Al Flt (J-Pl-R-Z) Berlin (the sweat in the night) Hochschule Karajan. . . . the continuing unwellness; contrast Berlin reaction to Spr 1957 (first exp. etc.). The chiropractor; Stockholm George-Walter (?) Jochum's lebensraum lecture from Nietzsche; 'the flu;' Bechstein-Steinway; the dinner party; Nordic hedonism; the letter 'flying under the flag;' 'Gt.' Dictator Chaplin . . . Wiesbaden, Sawallisch; cut finger, the drive down the Rhine; Koln, the paternoster; cancellation No. 1; the endless bath; chess . . . the flight to Hamburg—fever and pain; the chiropractor (Palmer method); 102 in the eve.; sweat in the morning; to Vierjahreszeiten—the Inner Harbor. Dr. Storgaharm: 'Remember Chopin.'"

Gould probably knew in Stockholm that he was getting seriously ill. "I have fallen victim to another flu à la Salzburg (current temperature 101 degrees)," he wrote to Homburger on October 2. "Sunday's concert may have to be canceled." But he pressed on to Wiesbaden and Cologne and then collapsed completely at the Hotel Vier Jahreszeiten in Hamburg. "I have chronic bronchitis in the right lung," he wrote to Homburger on October 18. "This we found out by X-rays yesterday. Since I don't know too much about this I am not sure that the practitioner who is seeing me is the best person for the job. . . . [He] is very much a Nature Boy type—milk and honey, cold cloths on the right side—all that sort of thing—I

---

*This probably was a set of notes for Gould's unwritten autobiography. Robert Silverman, editor of *The Piano Quarterly*, repeatedly pressed him to write his memoirs, and when they met in 1981, Silverman recalls, "He said, 'I'm going to write my biography in sections. I'm going to write about every year of my career when I was touring. . . . I'm going to work backwards and forwards, and I'm going to re-create a diary of my life.'"

am sure this kind of doctoring would suit you perfectly but it doesn't seem to be getting me any improvement. . . . I have a high fever every evening (last night up to 100.8). . . . If I see no hope of speedy recovery, I am going to cancel the works and head for Die Zauberberg." And then on October 24: "The doctor concluded his diagnosis yesterday and I have been put to bed for ten days on a no-protein diet. The idea seems to be to give the kidneys a rest as much as possible. X-rays showed there was nothing wrong with them whatever organically but that they had some way been affected by this virus. Quite frankly, I don't think I can stand ten days with nothing substantial to eat. . . ."

Gould's many friends and admirers were eager to offer advice. "We are all very sad about your illness," wrote a Berlin harpsi-chordist named Sylvia Kind, who recommended massages. "When the circulation is intensive, the poison goes out from the body," she wrote. "The masseur who saved my health (a half-Indian) . . . will come to your hotel. I rang him up and told him about you. . . ." Gould's grandmother wrote him about "that lame back" and said: "Next time, try my remedy, a *thin* coating of mustardine or muster-ole spread on a cloth and worn over the achy spot. It eases all my aches. . . ." From New York, the Columbia Records publicist Deb-bie Ishlon cabled: HAVE YOU TRIED YOGI EXERCISES?

The most concerned of these well-wishers was the impresario Wolfgang Kollitsch, who had organized Gould's concerts in Ger-many. "During the first days of the treatments he drove us crazy by phone begging us to come back to Berlin where he was sure there were better doctors," Gould wrote to Homburger. "Finally he called again on Monday night and announced, and I quote, 'I feel that in this hour of decision it is my duty to stand by your side.' No protests were any use and at 8:00 the next morning he arrived in Hamburg. He accompanied us to the hospital and when the doctor told him I really had been sick he was quite thunderstruck. (I found out afterwards that he had begged the doctor to change his mind while I was off having an X-ray or something.) Anyway when the doctor stood firm Kollitsch acquiesced entirely. . . . He stayed in Hamburg till evening and after dinner . . . I saw a new side of Kol-litsch—the hard-headed businessman in the guise of the Viennese gallant—He spoke of his loss of the amount he had spent to book the tour, of the commissions he had lost. . . ." On his sickbed, Gould agreed to a settlement in which Kollitsch kept all the money he already owed Gould, a matter of perhaps one thousand dollars, a settlement that Homburger described as "most generous—but definitely uncalled for."

Despite all these harassments, though, Gould loved playing the role of convalescent at the Vier Jahreszeiten in Hamburg. It is one of the great hotels of Europe, with marvelous chandeliers, and huge claw-footed bathtubs, and a superb view out over Hamburg's inner harbor. To live there in such splendor, with that wonderful sense of irresponsibility that comes with illness, could only have struck Gould as a blessing. "The best month of my life," he once described it to Cott, "—in many ways the most important precisely because it was the most solitary. . . . Knowing nobody in Hamburg turned out to be the greatest blessing in the world. I guess this was my Hans Castorp period; it was really marvelous. There is a sense of exaltation . . . it's the only word that really applies to that particular kind of aloneness." Nor was Gould fazed by the mysteriousness of his illness. A couple of years later, on hearing that Leonard Bernstein was suffering from "an exotic ailment," Gould wrote him a jocular (and prophetic) inquiry: "Do you have a title for it yet? If you are stuck in that department I have several titles for diseases which I am expecting to have in later life and have not yet had occasion to make use of. I always find that a good disease title will impress your average concert manager no end. . . ."

The only thing that could have made Gould's incarceration even better was a sense of the admiration of the outside world. And this too came to him in the new recording of his glittering performance of Beethoven's First Concerto, which included his own rather densely contrapuntal cadenzas. "I have been exulting for two days now in our Beethoven #1, which was sent me," he wrote to Vladimir Golschmann, who had provided the orchestral accompaniment. "I hope you have heard it and are as proud of it as I am. There is a real joie de vivre about it from beginning to end." And then there occurred a charming scene, when Gould was playing his new record of the Beethoven concerto in his hotel sickroom, and a chambermaid stopped to listen. "The maid," he wrote, "is standing entranced in the doorway with a mop in her hands, transfixed by the cadenza to movement #1 which is on the phonograph—it's just ended and she's just bowed and gone on to the next room."

After a month in the Hamburg hotel, Gould was ready to resume his tour in Italy, but he wanted to abandon the idea of going to Israel. Homburger was aghast. "Your suggestion of getting out of the Israeli tour, but continuing in Europe, is based on dreams rather than reality," he wrote. "It just can't be done. They would know about your playing and it would antagonize them to such a degree that it might even have reverberations over here."

It was in Italy, actually, that Gould encountered some novel difficulties. The Accademia Santa Cecilia in Rome didn't want him to play a Bach concerto and proposed instead that he perform Liszt, Chopin, or Mendelssohn. "While I should like to do everything possible to accommodate the Accademia," Gould rather stiffly responded, "I regret that it will not be possible for me to program any of the concerti which they suggested. My repertoire is built almost exclusively around preromantic music. . . ." They eventually compromised on the Beethoven Second.

But then, when Gould played a recital in Florence, he underwent for the first time the very unpleasant experience of being booed. "I had just concluded a performance of the Schoenberg suite, Op. 25," he later wrote, "which, although it was at the time thirty-five years old, had not yet been admitted to the vocabulary of the Florentines. I arose from the instrument to be greeted by a most disagreeable chant from the upper balcony, which was at once contradicted by feverish encouragements from the lower levels. Although I was new to this experience, I instinctively realized that no harm could come to me so long as I permitted the spectators to vent their fury upon each other. Therefore, I cunningly milked the applause for six curtain calls. . . ."

When Gould finally got to Israel, they loved him, as only the Israelis (or the Russians) could love a young Canadian who had come to play them *The Goldberg Variations*. Gould was heavily booked for other things too—the Beethoven Second Concerto three times in four days in Tel Aviv, then the Bach F minor and the Mozart C minor the following day, and then the Beethoven Second in Jerusalem the day after that, and so on, eleven concerts in eighteen days. Every performance was sold out, and the critics struggled to find their way into the transcendental. "Only words from the theological terminology would express this unique manifestation of the spirit from a higher sphere," wrote the reviewer for *Haaretz*. "This is indeed religious music; those are religious sounds.... Gould's playing comes nearest to the conception of prayer.... No praise, however high, could do it justice."

Israel was still a fledgling nation, still only ten years old, still surrounded and beleaguered, and that perilous condition colored the Israelis' perception of Gould, and his of them. "He made front-page news in the local papers," Homburger reported back to the Toronto *Star*, "when it was discovered that, unannounced and unescorted, he had visited a communal settlement within one mile of the Jordanian border. Glenn was exploring the countryside in his rented car. He picked up a hitch-hiker, who turned out to be an immigrant from India, returning to his communal settlement.... Gould was invited in and offered tea. When he requested milk, his host, without batting an eye, rolled up his sleeves, set off for the barn and called over his shoulder: 'Just a moment, I'll get it.'"

This frontier quality in Israel also affected Gould's customary idiosyncrasies. When he was supposed to play the Beethoven Second in Jerusalem on a cold December day, he found the hall impossible. "I don't think I'll play in Jerusalem tonight," he said. "I've just been with my manager to see the hall and it's too cold. There's no heating in it at all." He was told, of course, that the concert had been sold out, and that thousands of ticket-holders were coming to sit in the frosty hall to hear him. "Well, look, I'm susceptible to colds," Gould said. "I see no point in being heroic about it. If I get sick, I won't be able to go through with the rest of my concerts here."

They put eight heaters on the stage in the hope of providing a Gouldian environment, but nobody knew what the visitor would do. When he had not arrived at the scheduled time, a member of the orchestra walked to the front of the stage and announced to the shivering audience that Gould was "suffering from a cold." At that very moment, according to an Israeli reporter, "In loped Mr. Gould, wrapped in a long overcoat and a muffler. He slouched into his unique position at the piano and proceeded to turn in an unforgettable rendition of Beethoven's Second Piano Concerto."

That Beethoven concerto gave Gould difficulties that his Israeli audiences never imagined, or rather it was the "absolutely rotten" piano that the Israelis provided that gave him those difficulties. "I'd gone through a miserable rehearsal," Gould later told Jonathan Cott, "at which I really played like a pig because this piano had finally gotten to me. I was playing on *its* terms ... and I was really very concerned because I simply couldn't play a C-major scale properly."

Gould was then staying at a resort about fifteen miles outside Tel Aviv, and he decided to get into his Hertz car and seek a solution out in the wilderness. "I went out to a sand dune," he said, "and decided that the only thing that could possibly save this concert was to recreate the most admirable tactile circumstances I knew of." In other words, he decided to rehearse the Beethoven concerto by *imagining* himself playing it on his favorite piano, the turn-of-the-century Chickering that stood on short, stubby legs in his parents' cottage on Lake Simcoe.

"When you were sitting in the car in the desert," Cott asked, "were you performing the piece in the air, on the dashboard, or . . ."

"Neither, neither," Gould said. "The secret is that you must never move your fingers. If you do, you will automatically reflect the most recent tactile configurations that you've been exposed to."

So Gould sat in his rented car, looking out at the Mediterranean Sea, and imagined the living room in the cottage on Lake Simcoe, imagined each piece of furniture, imagined the old Chickering piano, imagined himself playing through the Beethoven concerto from beginning to end. "I ... got the entire thing in my head and tried desperately to live with that tactile image throughout the balance of the day," he said. "I got to the auditorium in the evening, played the concert, and it was without question the first time that I'd been in a really exalted mood throughout the entire stay there— I was *absolutely* free of commitment to that unwieldy beast. Now, the result, at least during the piano's first entrance, really scared me. There was a minimal amount of sound—it felt as though I were playing with the soft pedal down. . . . I was shocked, a little frightened, but I suddenly realized: Well, of course, it's doing that because I'm engaged with another tactile image, and eventually I made some adjustment, allowed for some give-and-take in relation to the instrument at hand. And what came out was really rather extraordinary— or at least I thought so."

Others thought so too, among them Max Brod, Franz Kafka's friend and literary executor, who came wandering backstage with a woman whom Gould took to be his secretary. Aping her German accent, Gould remembered her saying that they had heard several of his performances but that this concert "vas somehow, in some vay, somesing vas different, you vere not qvite one of us, you vere—your being vas *removed*." Gould bowed deeply and said thank you, "realizing of course that she had in fact put her finger on something that was too spooky to talk about." Kafka's friend's friend—and Gould was a great admirer of Kafka—rather spoiled this moment of insight by saying that Gould's performance of the Beethoven concerto was "unquestionably ze finest Mozart I haf ever heard."

When Gould returned to Toronto in December, the *Telegram* quoted him as saying that his touring had been "a little hectic," that he had lost twelve pounds, "but I still reach 160," and that he hadn't even had time to get his hair cut. "This is the remains of a production number a Berlin barber gave me, slightly overgrown," he said. He added that he planned to cut down the number of his performances in the coming year to perhaps no more than twenty-five in North America and ten in Europe, but now his schedule called him, and, on Christmas Day, he set out to play the Bach F minor and the Mozart C minor in Detroit. "Unfortunately Gould affects strange mannerisms to his own detriment," the Detroit *Free Press* said in that familiar litany. "The tittering audience is too busy wondering what he'll do next to appreciate his skilled playing. . . ."

In January of 1959, Pierre Berton of the Toronto *Star* caught Gould back at the family cottage on Lake Simcoe and persuaded him to talk about some of his childhood fears. "When he was a boy of eight, a schoolmate standing near him was physically ill," Berton wrote. "All eyes turned on the wretched child and from that instant on Gould was haunted by the spectre of himself being ill in public. That afternoon he returned to school with two soda mints in his pocket, a small tousled boy on guard against the moment when he might lose face. The soda mints were soon supplemented by aspirins and then by more pills. In school, Gould literally counted each second until lunch hour (10,800 seconds at 9 a.m., a comforting four-figure 9,900 at 9:15), and prayed that nothing might happen to humiliate him. Nothing ever did. He has never been ill in public. . . ."

But every time he walked onto the concert stage, before a hushed and expectant audience, Gould saw himself walking into a gladiatorial arena, where the audience sat ready to give the thumbs-down signal for his death. Even the piano that he had learned to master then seemed a wild beast. "It is very easy to let the piano become your enemy when you have lived with it and worked with it—especially when the majority of the pianos are ones you don't like," Gould said to Berton. "The piano symbolizes the terror of the performance and the only thing you can do is hypnotize yourself so the actual ordeal is less great."

Up until now, in his late twenties, Gould still lived at home with his parents. Or rather, he lived in a ragged series of hotel rooms in Chicago and San Francisco and London and Dallas, and then returned to seek haven in his parents' home in Toronto. Now he began thinking that it was time to live on his own, but even though he almost inevitably had become somewhat estranged from his father, he found the break difficult. "At one stage, he had a room in the Windsor Arms Hotel in Toronto," John Roberts recalls, "and he had another room in which he had a piano, at a certain point, when he was trying to find a way of living away from home. And then he took an apartment. And then he decided he didn't like it so he never moved in."

Then came what Gould himself called "a longing for grandeur," and so, "more or less on a whim," he rented a riverside estate called Doncherry, fifteen miles outside Toronto. Writing to a friend in Germany, he reported that Doncherry had twenty-six rooms, "if one counts the seven bathrooms, the breakfast room, the scullery." It also had a swimming pool and a tennis court, for a man who rarely swam or played tennis. And a view. "The view from down below looking up, and especially at night with flood lights, was like looking at Salzburg castle from your own strawberry patch," Gould wrote. "Oh, yes, there was one of those too." His manager, Homburger, apparently expressed misgivings about this château, which Gould took to mean that he "was terrified that I was giving up the piano." Homburger's secretary, Gould went on, "was convinced that I was having an affair with the upstairs maid (who hadn't yet been engaged, to do housework, that is) and my mother, I'm sure, was convinced that I was secretly married. . . ."

Gould invited Winston Fitzgerald of Steinway & Sons to come and admire his new palace. "He said, 'I'm going to take you for a ride,'" Fitzgerald recalls. "We drove out to this neocolonial house, and I thought he was going to introduce me to some friends of his. When we got to the door, he reached in his pocket and took out a key and opened the house, and it was empty. So he was showing me around the house and asking me how I liked it. We went upstairs and—there were two wings to the house, and he was telling me where he was going to have his studio, where his piano would be, and his new recording studio. It was all going to be in one wing of this house, and then we went to this other wing, and I said, 'What are you going to do here?' He said, 'Oh, this is going to be—my manager's going to live here.' And I said, 'You mean to tell me Walter Homburger's going to come out here and live?' He said, 'No, I mean my personal manager.' And I said, 'Who's that? I didn't know you had one.' And he looked me square in the face and said, 'You.' That was the way Glenn did things. Well, of course, I almost went through the floor. But I ultimately did not go to manage him, for many reasons, not the least of which was that he had a habit of calling me at two or three o'clock in the morning, and this happened several times a week for years. I did not tell him that I was afraid of being a prisoner of his whims. I said I had a lifelong obligation to Steinway's, and I just couldn't leave, and he accepted that."

Even in less baronial circumstances, the process of establishing a home is more complicated than somebody who has always lived with his parents might realize. John Roberts, who had helped Gould in his house-hunting, now watched him confront the problems of furnishing his château. "And of course, poor Glenn, whenever he went into a department store, he was instantly recognized, and people rushed and asked for his autograph, which he got very tired of. And so I began to organize things—we bought a stove, and a fridge, and I can't remember what, just reams and reams of things. And then he rang me up and said he'd changed his mind. And I said, 'Well, what did it?' And then there was great laughter, and he said to me, 'Well, it's when the brooms crossed the threshold that I realized that

domesticity had hit me, and I realized that this is not for me at all.'
So eventually he settled on this six-room penthouse on St. Clair
Avenue. But to get used to it, he didn't actually live there at first. He
would go and sleep there, but he also had the Windsor Arms situation, and he phased himself in. . . ."

Not too long after the move to St. Clair, Gould learned that another
tie to his youth had been cut. Banquo, the last of his pet dogs, was
hit by a car. "I was taking Banquo out for his walk at night," Bert
Gould recalls, "and he heard another dog yelping, as though he'd
been hit or something, and Banquo just left me on the sidewalk and
dashed across the street. He ran right in front of a car and was killed
on the spot. I went back home, got the wheelbarrow, and took him
back to the house, but he was gone. I called Glenn and told him, and
he was terribly upset. . . ."

Q: And he never wanted another dog?

A: Well, I won't say he didn't want another one, but he wasn't at
home for me to get him another one. I had an oil painting of Banquo
done especially to give to Glenn. It's down in the basement.

And at the end of 1959, Gould suddenly found himself unable to
give any more piano concerts. The implications of that discovery
must have been devastating, but what had actually happened was
almost ludicrous. After playing Beethoven's Fourth Concerto in
Oklahoma City that December, Gould went to New York for some
discussions at the house of Steinway, whose pianos he always used,
and there he had an ill-fated encounter with the chief Steinway technician, William Hupfer. Though Gould's subsequent lawsuit treated
Hupfer like some sort of a ruffian, he was scarcely that. Schuyler
Chapin, who had by now succeeded Oppenheim as head of Columbia Masterworks, described him as "a quiet, thoroughly professional
man" and "the only one allowed to tune and regulate Horowitz's
piano." Exactly what Hupfer did to Gould we do not know for sure
(a recent inquiry at Steinway prompted a suave young man in a pin-
striped suit to say regretfully that Hupfer "passed away about five
years ago"), but the affidavit that Gould filed in federal court
charged that Hupfer had engaged in "unduly strong handshakes and
other demonstrative physical acts." Ignoring widespread reports

that Gould was a man of "extreme and unusual sensitivity to physical contact," the complaint said, Hupfer approached him from behind and "recklessly or negligently let both forearms down with considerable force on the plaintiff's neck and left shoulder, driving the plaintiff's left elbow against the arm of the chair in which he was sitting."

Winston Fitzgerald, the Steinway official in charge of artists and repertory, and the man at whose desk the incident took place, dismisses Gould's whole account as fanciful. According to Fitzgerald, Gould and Hupfer had increasingly sharp professional disagreements, which they both repressed. "They had distinctly different ideas about the voicing of pianos," Fitzgerald says, "and Glenn wanted all sorts of things done to pianos that Mr. Hupfer would not do, did not consider good piano practice, and so this friction developed."

On the day of their encounter at Fitzgerald's desk, Fitzgerald recalls nothing "reckless or negligent." "Mr. Hupfer just laid his hand gently on Glenn's shoulder, and Glenn suddenly went into a state of gloom," Fitzgerald says. "And when Mr. Hupfer left, I said, 'Glenn, what's wrong?' And he said, 'He *hurt* me.' Well, I saw this, and I mean, he just put his—he *couldn't* have hurt him."

Q: But something happened. Gould *was* injured.

A: So he *said*.

Q: You think he didn't have injuries? He had to cancel a whole lot of concerts.

A: Well, I don't know. Certainly they didn't ensue from that incident. He may indeed have had some problems, but I can assure you that it was not from this incident with Mr. Hupfer. Hupfer was barely there two seconds. He just walked by and sort of lightly patted Glenn on the shoulder, and immediately there was this cloud of gloom hanging over him, and he said, "He *hurt* me."

Fitzgerald expressed some of his skepticism in a letter to Gould at the time, and Gould replied rather sharply that he "was a little surprised at the tone of your letter in so far as you seem to express some bafflement about the nature of my malaise." The only reason that several newspapers had been told that he had suffered from a "fall," he said, "was to avoid a fuller explanation which would perhaps cause some embarrassment to Steinway & Sons."

The only other surviving witness to the encounter, Frederick (Fritz) Steinway, corroborates Fitzgerald's account. "Fitzgerald said no, and I believe it," Steinway says.

Q: Then why did Gould claim to be so seriously injured?

A: Because he was a hypochondriac, as you well know.

Q: Why did he cancel a lot of concerts on account of this?

A: Artists are very apt to do that sort of thing for all kinds of reasons, some of which make sense and some of which do not.

When Gould eventually sued Steinway for $300,000 in damages, the press treated the whole affair as a light comedy. Gould really did feel, however, that he had suffered a serious injury to that fragile mechanism with which pianists perform their art. "The initial injury was to the left shoulder and when X-rayed the shoulder blade was shown to have been pushed down about one-half inch," Gould wrote to a friend a month after the incident. "That problem has basically been cleared up now but has caused a secondary reaction much more troubling. The nerve which controls the fourth and fifth fingers of my left hand has been compressed and inflamed or whatever, with the result that any movement involving a division of the left hand, as in a sudden leap to the left side of the keyboard, is, if not actually impossible, accomplished only by a considerable effort of will. . . . I have been having two treatments per day on different aspects of it—one medical and one chiropractic—and while no one seems to feel that it is likely to become permanent, I must say I am becoming rather dissatisfied with the relative lack of improvement."

Gould blamed his condition on "what may gallantly be called an 'accident' . . . entirely due to the idiocy of one of Chez Steinway's senior employees." He said this nemesis "may have forced me to become a full time composer," but he remained reluctant to announce any details in public. He simply canceled all concerts for the next three months ("I am back to cancelling concerts for a living," he wrote to Bob Barclay, the music publisher who had recently produced the score of his string quartet), and when he reappeared to perform the Beethoven Fourth in Baltimore, he said to the *Morning Sun* only that he had been "seeking relief from the effects of a strained shoulder." To a friend in Berlin, he attributed his recovery to cortisone. "It has really worked a miracle with the arm," he wrote. "I still am not able to give recitals because I don't feel that I can play for a whole evening without great fatigue, but I did play my first concerto appearance in three months last week. It was with the Baltimore Symphony and it was a great success despite the fact that my arm was quite sore and tired by the time I was finished. Nonetheless, to have got through it was something of an achievement and I am feeling much more optimistic about the full recovery of my arm."

Cortisone is an unreliable friend, however. "The arm is very, very much better," Gould wrote to Schuyler Chapin at Columbia in March. "The cortisone is having a truly miraculous effect, except that it makes me wretchedly nauseous but I have developed a system of taking it one day, being sick the second day, eating the third day, taking cortisone the fourth etc." And then it didn't work. "The temporary improvement during March, which enabled me to play some concerts, turned out to have been due to the taking of cortisone," Gould wrote to Robert Craft that May, "but it was a temporary improvement only and the trouble came back in full force."

Yet there remained a certain element of mystery as to what was really wrong with Gould, if anything. Dr. Joseph Stephens, a friend who both played the harpsichord and taught psychiatry at Johns Hopkins, speaks somewhat derisively of Gould's "imaginary illnesses."

Q: Were they really imaginary?

A: Oh, well, he became so obsessed by this shoulder thing that I had him seen at Hopkins by a very fancy neurologist, and he insisted that I sit with him while he was being examined, and the neurologist said to me, "Not a thing wrong with him."

Eugene Ormandy, the conductor of the Philadelphia Orchestra, warmly recommended in May an orthopedist named Irvin Stein, and so Gould went to Philadelphia to see him. "It was in relation to a difficulty with his neck and arm, which he had developed, according to him, subsequent to an extremely hearty push and slap on the top of his shoulder," Dr. Stein recalls from his retirement in Florida. "And it was associated with an immediate pain on the left side of his neck that went into his arm and affected his playing."

Q: Did you have any reason to doubt his story about how the injury was caused?

A: Well, I don't know. This is what he described to me.

Dr. Stein declared that the only solution was to encase Gould's whole arm and shoulder in a plaster cast, a cast that held the arm upward and outward. There is a photograph in the Ottawa Library that shows Gould in this portable prison, naked to the waist, the precious arm outstretched and immobilized, like the branch of an espaliered apple tree. He is somewhat unshaven in this photograph, and he looks terrified, like a trapped animal. To some extent he was.

Dr. Stein remembers those months with tranquility. "He tolerated very well having the shoulder in a plaster," he says, "so that we could bring his shoulder up toward his neck and reduce the stretch on the nerves in the brachial plexus, which is the thing that goes from the spine into the upper extremities. And he did very well after a few weeks of that, and then some gradual exercises. It apparently cleared up." In Gould's letters of that year, however, there is a good deal of agitation and anxiety. "I finally had to cancel the balance of the season and try to get this thing put in shape once and for all . . ." he wrote to a friend in early May. "What a season this has been!" And to another friend at the end of May: "I have just returned from Philadelphia and regret to say that . . . the treatment there was by no means wholly successful. . . . There has been, however, some improvement in the arm, I believe, and I am beginning to wear a metal cervical collar." And in early June: "When the arm was completely at rest in the cast, there was indeed a great deal of relief but, unfortunately, when it was taken out and once again required full support from the shoulder, the problem returned. . . . The problem is essentially one of endurance. Due to the stretching of the muscle complex of the shoulder, the arm fatigues terribly quickly."

By July, he felt well enough to go to New York for a recording session. "My arm, I think, was in the best shape it has been since last winter," he wrote Homburger. "I have been wearing the collar at all times when practising and having a great deal of physiotherapy, and I was quite sure that I could get through the recording with no difficulty. . . . The Monday session went very well indeed. I did Opus 31, No. 2 [Beethoven's Sonata No. 17 in D minor, the so-called *Tempest Sonata*] . . . and I think it will be a superb recording but by Tuesday with the exposure to air-conditioning (possibly), and without as much physiotherapy as I had been used to, the arm had tightened up again in exactly the same way and finally on

Wednesday we abandoned the recording of the Eroica variations [by Beethoven, Opus 35], cancelled Thursday's session and will take up again the end of August. This is, needless to say, very disappointing because I had certainly expected better results by this time. The symptoms are exactly the same as before—same knot, same aches, same fatigue. Next week Stratford begins and I am determined to try to get through it . . . but at this point I frankly don't see how."

He got through it by willpower, and because Stratford represented an odd kind of liberation. The authorities of the annual Shakespeare Festival had had the inspired idea in 1956 of making Gould a codirector of the new musical programs (along with the violinist Oscar Shumsky and the cellist Leonard Rose), and so he acquired the authority to organize unusual programs, all Mendelssohn, for example, or all Hindemith. But even before that, he enjoyed the idea of taking part in a festival. Instead of endlessly repeating his concert repertoire, endlessly playing Beethoven's Opus 109 and the Berg Sonata, he could try out all kinds of things. At this 1960 festival, for instance, he joined with Oscar Shumsky in playing Beethoven's Violin Sonata in C minor, and then with Shumsky and Leonard Rose in Beethoven's *Ghost Trio*. With the festival orchestra, he played not only Bach's D minor Concerto but also the Fifth Brandenburg Concerto, conducting both from the keyboard of a specially doctored piano that he called a "harpsipiano." GLENN GOULD AT STRATFORD 'BETTER THAN EVER,' said a headline in the Toronto *Star*. "It is perhaps conceivable that somewhere in the world one might hear greater performances of chamber music than those presented at the Festival Theatre here this afternoon," John Kraglund wrote in the Toronto *Globe and Mail*. "I have neither heard them nor heard of them, so I can only sympathize with the more than 1,000 persons who made fruitless efforts to secure tickets to a concert that had been sold to its capacity of nearly 2,300 seats several weeks ago."

And so Gould was back on the road. Mozart's C minor Concerto in Vancouver, and the same in New Haven, and the Strauss *Burleske* in Detroit, and the following night the Beethoven Second, and then the *Emperor* in Buffalo. "Having once experienced the threat and fear of not being able to play," he wrote to a friend, "has, understandably, made me perhaps for the first time really anxious to do so and I feel that some of the best performances I have given have been in these last few months." But there was still that inescapable sense of routine. "In South Bend, Indiana, if I remember correctly," says John Roberts, "he was climbing the stage to perform at a concert, and he said, 'Glenn Gould, what in God's name are you doing? Another platform, another place.'"

And there were the same old aggravations. Not only his shaky health ("I still have good days and bad days," he wrote to a friend in Berlin in September), not only the sometimes idiotic newspaper reviews ("I have never heard a concert with monotony carried to such extremes," said the Akron *Beacon Journal*), but sometimes moments of pure terror. One night, flying into Toronto, the plane coming in ahead of Gould's plane crash-landed, and Gould's flight had to be diverted to Ottawa. "Another time," according to Bert Gould, "they had the trays on their laps, and all the trays flew up and hit the ceiling, and stuff came down. It scared him, you know, and two or three times something like that gets you."

Then there were still the importunings of his admirers. A woman in Bethesda, Maryland, wrote to complain that she and a friend had driven all the way to Philadelphia to hear Gould play. "It wasn't until we were seated in the hall that we discovered a substitution had been made two days before," she wrote. "What induced our feeling of real shock, however, was the fact of having seen you just a few hours earlier at the Drake Hotel—you were checking out as we were checking in. . . . Please understand I have no wish to intrude. It's simply that the incident has left an uneasiness that refuses to subside. . . ." Gould felt obliged to explain to her that he had been visiting his Philadelphia doctor. "That, then, was the reason for my presence at the Drake Hotel on November 3 and the reason that you observed me checking out of the hotel that afternoon."

The following month, December of 1960, Gould finally filed his damage suit against Steinway in federal court in New York. He said that Hupfer's overly "demonstrative" salutation had cost him $3,600 in medical bills and $21,400 in lost earnings, and he asked $300,000 in compensation. Steinway hemmed and hawed for about nine months and then settled. "They wanted him in their stable," says Fitzgerald. "He was a star." "To all to whom these Presents shall come or may concern, greetings," the settlement proclaimed. "Know ye, that Glenn Gould, over the age of 21 years ... for and in consideration of the sum of nine thousand three hundred seventy-two and 35/100 ($9,372.35) lawful money of the United States of America, to him in hand paid by Steinway & Sons and William Hupfer, the receipt whereof is hereby acknowledged, have remised, released and forever discharged and by these Presents do for his heirs and executors and administrators remise, release and forever discharge the said Steinway & Sons and William Hupfer ... from all, and all manner of action and actions, cause and causes of actions, suits, debts, dues, sums of money, accounts, reckonings, bonds, bills, specialties, covenants, contracts, controversies, arguments, agreements, promises, variances, trespasses, damages, judgments, extents, executions, claims, and demands, whatsoever in law or in equity, which ..." And so on.

But the injury was not so completely healed. There was by now almost no part of Gould's soul and spirit—and perhaps this is just as true for all of us—that did not show signs of scar tissue. He was supposed to go to Philadelphia late in 1961 to play the *Emperor* with Ormandy and the Philadelphia Orchestra, but shortly after the Steinway settlement, he suddenly decided that he couldn't bear the idea of playing in Philadelphia. "Dear E," he wrote to Ormandy, "I imagine you have received some strange requests from time to time, but I daresay that few will be as startling as the one I am now going to make. I have been trying to summon courage to call you ... but I feel that what I have to ask you is so unusual that only by writing can I give it some kind of form. I have developed (if that's the word) over the past months what I can only describe to you as a great apprehension in regard to giving concerts in Philadelphia. Never before in my life have I experienced anything at all similar to it, for I have come to feel something approaching terror at the thought of playing in Philadelphia. I'm afraid that the association of Philadelphia in my imagination has become inextricably confused with my weeks there and with the fact that during those weeks I was immobilized, at least pianistically. . . ."

Gould was writing on the stationery of the Edgewater Hotel on Lake Mendota in Madison, Wisconsin, and he had great difficulty in saying what he wanted to say. "Dear E," he began again. "I hope when you read this that you will forgive me for having written instead of called. To be honest, I have tried to find the courage to telephone you for some days but I felt that it would be most difficult to give an intelligent presentation which I must describe to you. I have developed over the past few months what I can only describe as a very great apprehension about giving concerts in Phil. Never in—similar to it [sic] for I have come to feel something approaching terror.... What has happened is that in my imagination the assoc. of Phil has become hopelessly confused with the memories of the weeks I spent there in a cast last year.... The more I try to argue with myself against the illogic of this assoc. the worse it becomes. I had a dream for instance just a few nights ago in which I seemed to be walking just offstage in the Academy [the Philadelphia Academy of Music] and as I moved toward the stage I fell over a rope of some kind and the dream ended as I apparently broke my arm. Believe me, Eugene, I know how foolish this all is, and I would feel greatly embarrassed to detail such unreasoned fears to anyone but you. . . ."

But then he also had to write to the woman who had organized this concert, Emma Feldman, director of the Philadelphia All Star Forum Series, Inc. "Dear Emma," he began, on the stationery of the Greater Radisson Hotel in Minneapolis, "I imagine this letter will come as something of a shock to you and I can only assure you that it is no easy letter for me to write.... I have tried desperately but unsuccessfully to rid myself of a totally foolish and illogical phobia about giving concerts in Philadelphia.... As I am sure you will guess it is inextricably confused with the unpleasant memories of those very difficult weeks which I spent in a cast in Philadelphia last year, and in some mysterious way I have come to feel a great inhibition, even horror, of playing there. However idiotic this sounds to you I hope you will realize that in writing this I am in fact understating the case rather than exaggerating it. . . .

"As I said to Eugene there are only two courses open to me," he went on. "One, the sensible, maybe even restorative one, I suppose would be—" At that point, Gould reached the end of the second page of this letter. He then began the third page by writing, "Onl," and then stopped. He began again by writing on a new sheet of the stationery of the Greater Radisson Hotel, "Only two courses open to me," and then he stopped again. There were finally six different versions of this critical third page (and he saved all the drafts), and he finally said, "When one has dwelt upon this sort of phobia so intensely the very concentration on its circumstances is likely to produce an atmosphere of unusual tension and I should be most reluctant to give a concert on an important series like yours under such circumstances. . . . I am sure you know that I will make every possible effort to reimburse you for any loss on this engagement. . . ."

The Philadelphians did their best to help. Emma Feldman denied that she was "shocked" by Gould's cancellation of the concert and said only that she was "both sad and upset about your—shall we say attitude about Philadelphia. . . . You should have a very warm feeling about Philadelphia, since I believe we did get you practically cured here." Eugene Ormandy was more understanding, in a rather strange way. When Gould had canceled his performance of the *Emperor*, Ormandy had recruited Van Cliburn to replace him, and now he wrote to Gould: "Perhaps it will give you a chuckle when I tell you that every time I talked to Van, for some psychological reason, I called him Glenn. The third time it happened, he said he didn't mind at all because he loved Glenn and he considered it an honor and a pleasure to be called by that name. So in the subconscious, you are really still with us. . . ."

It was not true. In the subconscious, Gould was already seeking his freedom from "the terror of the performance." At the end of *Lohengrin*, when Elsa breaks her pledge and asks the mysterious knight who he is, she then can only watch helplessly as he renounces her and sails away.

V

The Abdication

From the very beginning of his concert career, Gould talked freely about abandoning it. "I went on record once saying to a reporter from the Toronto Telegram that I would retire at 23," he wrote to Karsh. "Unfortunately I said it when I was 22, and he reminded me of it when I was 24." Not long after his New York debut, Gould told an interviewer in Winnipeg: "I'm more convinced than ever that I'd rather be a composer. I don't particularly care to play before the public. I love playing for myself." And back in Toronto early in 1956: "I am not very fond of the concert business. I am not endeared to the footlights at all. And it is a devastating road if you can't endure traveling."

By 1959, when he was not yet twenty-seven, Gould was talking quite openly about a complete withdrawal. "He is making plans to retire," Jay Harrison wrote in the New York *Herald-Tribune.* "Or so he says, with something less than the ultimate in conviction. As he put it last week: 'I certainly don't intend to work beyond my thirty-fifth year—not if I can help it. I really would like the last half of my life to myself. Then I could do what I can only do part-time now—compose.'" And a month later, to Dennis Braithwaite of the Toronto *Star:* "I hope that I will be able to retire by the time I am 35. If I can't I shall be very disappointed in myself and go out selling insurance or something else. But I want to be in a position to give up playing the piano, at least publicly, altogether."

Though he joked about selling insurance "or something else," the prospect of abandoning a very lucrative career (his fee had climbed to $3,500 per concert, and he earned more than $100,000 per year) was a little frightening. How would he make a living? Would any-one buy the recordings of an unseen artist? Would a fickle public turn away and reject him just as he had rejected it? Retirement at such an age was virtually unprecedented. Franz Liszt had more or less abandoned the concert stage at thirty-six, but only to become court conductor and composer at Weimar. Still, the idea of retire-ment kept ripening in Gould's head. In April of 1962, when he was just a few months short of his thirtieth birthday, he made what seems to have been his first definite (though private) announcement in a letter to Humphrey Burton at the BBC in London: "I am not, at the moment, planning any tour in Europe for next season, or indeed at the moment for any season. This is due to the fact that, as of two months ago, I decided that when next season is over, I shall give no more public concerts. Mind you, this is a plan I have been announcing every year since I was 18, and there is a part of my public here that does not take these pronouncements too seriously, but this time I think I really mean it."

Gould made no official announcement. The plan just sort of solid-ified, like ice congealing in a river. Sometimes he spoke of it as lim-iting himself to a minimal number of concerts, sometimes as a total withdrawal but only for a short period of time, a year or two. He couldn't be sure. Early in 1963, he wrote to a fan who had asked him to play in Prince Edward Island: "I have remained quite firm up to now about my semiretirement plans. As a matter of fact, next year I am doing only a very few engagements in the major American cit-ies—just by way of reminding myself how to do a concert, and really intending to spend a year thinking and composing." To an interviewer in Portland, Oregon, he was still more specific. "His own plans call for retirement from the concert stage next year," she wrote, "save for a token 15 appearances, in order to devote more time to television and composing. 'After all, one must quit by 30,' he mused." And then, to a friend in New York: "I have, as you know, attempted to maintain a semiretired state so far as concert-giving is concerned, and ... I have accepted only a minimum num-ber of concerts next year ... and I really feel that I must stick to this resolve. In Canada, for instance, I do no public concerts now except Stratford. The reason for all of this is that I felt it was essen-tial, sooner or later, to find out what sort of a composer I could become and to also have as much time for writing as possible."

Part of Gould's dislike of the concert tour was his dislike of travel, or rather his dislike of travel under pressure. He dreaded airplanes (that whole generation of touring pianists was acutely aware that one of its most brilliant members, William Kapell, had been killed in a plane crash at thirty-one), and after 1962, he simply refused to fly. But travel also meant missed connections, unheated trains, flat tires, second-rate hotels, and second-rate food. "Usually, whenever musicians get together and talk about our traveling," says Jaime Laredo, a cheerful soul who recorded the Bach violin sonatas with Gould, "we always somehow manage to talk about this great restaurant in this city, or that wonderful hotel or that wonderful hall. But with Glenn, every city that you mentioned was some terrible experience. 'That's where I came down with the worst cold in my life,' or 'That's where the hotel bed was so soft that I couldn't sleep.' And it made me feel bad because I realized how much he had suffered, what an incredible ordeal it had been for him."

Gould's determination to abandon the concert stage appeared to many such observers at the time as a bizarre renunciation of everything to which young musicians should and did aspire. What was it, if not the chance to perform great music before applauding audiences, that drove Gould's contemporaries to spend long hours in arduous and disciplined practicing? And they were indeed a talented group—Gary Graffman, Leon Fleisher, Van Cliburn, Eugene Istomin, Julius Katchen, Jacob Lateiner, Seymour Lipkin, Lorin Hollander—all young and energetic and ambitious and eager to compete for the rewards of success. Yet the mere recitation of such names today suggests a whole generation devastated by the demands of the competition that Gould rejected. Graffman and Fleisher were both stricken by crippling hand injuries, and though they still perform the limited repertoire for left hand, both of these highly gifted artists now devote most of their time to teaching. ("Yes, I think perhaps we were driven more than the previous generation," says Graffman. "I wonder whether recordings had something to do with it. Audiences now expect a note-perfect performance.") Cliburn, who once received a ticker-tape parade down Broadway after his spectacular triumph in Moscow, has remained mysteriously absent from the stage for most of the last ten years. Katchen is dead. And the others? Their careers tend to corroborate Gould's judgment and to imply that his act of apparent abnegation was actually an act of affirmation, of prudence, of survival.

Apart from all questions of personal convenience, Gould had acquired a real loathing for the gladiatorial aspects of the concert hall. The audience's eager participation in all "those awful and degrading and humanly damaging uncertainties," Gould felt, made a piano recital one of "the last blood sports." "Some people feel," an interviewer argued in 1962, "that one of the joys of listening to music arises from the 'one-chance' risk of performance—that no one, neither player nor listener, knows quite how it will come out."

"To me this is heartless and ruthless and senseless," Gould said in a great rush of feeling. "It is exactly what prompts savages like Latin Americans to go to bullfights. When I hear it I want to retire. The spectator in the arena who regards musical performance as some kind of athletic event is happily removed from the risk, but he takes some kind of glee in what goes on there. This is entirely separate from what is really going on: an effort by the performer to form a powerful identification with the music. A performance is not a contest but a love affair. . . ."

And then there always came that dismal ritual of the newspaper critics publishing their commentaries on the love affair. In retrospect, these critics' obsession with Gould's platform behavior seems to fluctuate between the rude and the silly. "He was a joy to hear," Howard Taubman wrote in the New York *Times*, for example. "But his mannerisms at the piano were not a joy to see. If Mr. Gould cannot help himself, one can only sympathize. If, during rests, he must fling himself back like an exhausted gladiator, if he must cock his head to one side like an absorbed parrot, if he must fuss with his handkerchief and look as if he will miss the start of the cadenza, why then he must. He had better realize, however, that he is not only doing himself a disservice but also distracting attention from the music. On all sides, one could see listeners smirking and giggling at Mr. Gould's extra-musical behavior instead of paying heed to Mr. Gould's celestial song. . . ." But imagine if Mr. Taubman were expected to dress up in white tie and tails to write *his* celestial song, if he were permitted no mistakes and no rewritten sentences in the creation of his review, and if some other critic, assigned to the maintenance of Grub Street's highest standards, then published a commentary not only on Taubman's views and Taubman's prose but also on his haircut, his costume, and any gestures he might happen to make while at work.

Like most artists, Gould professed indifference to these tiresome observations on his performances; like most artists, he was fibbing. Beyond the pretense of indifference to public attacks on one's personal behavior, there are only three alternatives: to suffer in silence, to talk back, or to revel in the role that has been assigned. Gould intermittently tried all four courses, notably the last.

In London in 1959, for example, he appeared at a press conference tousled and unshaven, and wearing a knee-length jacket, heavy overcoat, and two pairs of gloves. "What makes you think I'm eccentric?" he inquired of the reporters who had assembled to record his eccentricities. One reporter pointed out to Gould that his right shoelace was untied, apparently hoping that Gould would live up to his reputation by trying to tie it with his gloved hands. "The pianist shrugged it off," according to the Associated Press report published back in Toronto, "put down his drink (a glass of pineapple juice), and kept his gloved hands—insured with Lloyd's for $100,000—in his pants pockets." The swaddled Gould did in fact have a fever from flu and subsequently had to cancel one of his London concerts, but if the London press wanted to patronize this visitor from the colonies, the Canadian press was prepared as always to defend him as a national treasure. "So they've been having a gay time in Britain, tagging our Glenn Gould with the label eccentric . . ." said an editorial in the Toronto *Star*. "Canadians should always remember why he's really unusual: Because he's a great pianist, a genius. . . . Mr. Gould admits being 'a hypochondriac, in a small way.' Maybe. Without any doubt, however, he is an artist and Canadian in a big way."

Perhaps the most controversial of the public criticisms involved one of the most unusual of Gould's concert imbroglios, his very public disagreement with Leonard Bernstein in 1962 about how to play the Brahms Concerto in D minor. Gould strongly disliked all the competitive and heroic aspects of the Romantic piano concerto, and he never performed any of those beloved war-horses by Chopin, Liszt, Schumann, Tchaikowsky, or his distant cousin Grieg. But he loved Brahms, and he knew that Brahms had originally conceived his first concerto as a kind of symphony for piano and orchestra, and he himself had been "gradually evolving" a new view of this music. "I have begun to find, I think, a way of playing the middle and late 19th century repertoire," he wrote to a friend, "in which the predominant characteristic will be the presence of organic unity and not the continual . . . coalition of inequalities which, it seems to me, underlies most interpretations of 19th century music. If this sounds fancy and a bit arbitrary, it is not really. All that I am doing is deliberately reducing the masculine and feminine contrast of theme-areas in favour of revealing the correspondence of structure material between thematic blocks. . . ."

The most dramatic aspect of Gould's interpretation of the Brahms D minor was his insistence that it be played very, very slowly. Brahms's only indication of the tempo he wanted was *maestoso*, which could mean almost anything, but Gould's interpretation of "majestic" was worthy of the marble statue of the Commendatore in *Don Giovanni*. "Glenn had called me a week or two earlier from Toronto," Bernstein recalls, lighting another cigarette, "and said, 'Oh, Lenny, get ready for this! Have I got news for you about Brahms! Wait till you hear the D minor Concerto. I've discovered it. I know how it has to go, finally.' And I said, 'I'll bet slow,' knowing about his Mozart sonatas. And he said, 'Forget everything you ever heard about the D minor. This will shock you.' And I said, 'Well, I'm ready for anything. You can't shock me. *You* can't shock me.' He said, 'Believe me, this will throw you.'

"So he came to the house, and we played on the two little pianos that I had back-to-back. And I was really amazed at how slow it was.* And he played the first movement, almost all of it, in six [beats per measure], so that the second movement, the adagio which is also in six-four time, sounded like a continuation of the first movement. That was one of his big points, you see, that the quarter-note remains consistent throughout and holds this whole huge thing together. And I said, 'Of course, you're exaggerating. You're not

---

* "Gould was wrong, and I can prove it," says the pianist Malcolm Frager. "Because if you've ever been to Vienna—the manuscript of the first movement has a metronome marking, which is not in any printed score, but it's in Brahms' handwriting. It's 56 to the dotted half, and it's quite fast—*Pom*—pom—pom—pom—pom so playing it twice that slow is *not* what Brahms had in mind. It's provable."

going to really do it this way. You're just showing me what you've found, with these mathematical relationships between one movement and another.' And he said, 'No, this is the way we'll play it.' And I said, 'All right.'"

Bernstein believed that the Philharmonic could not play the concerto at Gould's tempo without a special rehearsal, and at that rehearsal, he tried to give the players some extra encouragement. "I told the orchestra to be ready for this," Bernstein says, "and that we must take it very seriously because this guy is such a genius. And even if he's *wrong*, it's going to be gorgeous, and we must go along with him. He's adventurous, I'm adventurous, and let's do it."

Bernstein apparently felt that his audiences needed similar reassurances, and since he had begun a tradition of giving informal talks during his Thursday night concerts, which were treated partly as dress rehearsals, Bernstein decided to talk about "this extraordinary performance." He insists that he told Gould exactly what he was going to say, and that Gould agreed completely. By now, after all these years, Bernstein remembers Gould as the most enthusiastic of collaborators. *"Together,"* he says, "we wrote on the back of an envelope some notes for what I was going to say, and he was simply delighted. Because he was made of that kind of sportsman's stuff, he was taking a chance on everything."

The event really does not sound quite the way Bernstein remembers it. Listening to a tape of this bizarre occasion a quarter of a century later, one feels a sense of shock at the announcer suddenly declaring, "I think Mr. Bernstein will have something to say to the audience," and then Bernstein starting to propose, in that mellifluous voice, what he called "this small disclaimer." He praised Gould as "a thinking performer," and said that his version of the Brahms concerto had "moments . . . that emerge with astonishing freshness and conviction." But he also declared that this would be "a rather—shall we say—unorthodox performance . . . a performance distinctly different from any I've ever heard, or even dreamt of, for that matter." Two artists are entitled to a difference of opinion, of course. Yet Bernstein not only made a public spectacle of the difference but publicly wondered why he took part in a performance of which he disapproved. Partly because Gould was "so valid and serious an artist," he said, and partly because "there is in music what

Dimitri Mitropoulos used to call 'the sportive element,' that factor of curiosity, adventure, experiment, and I can assure you that it *has* been an adventure this week collaborating with Mr. Gould."

That was perhaps the worst of it, that Bernstein played to his audience and played it for laughs. There were chuckles when he started by saying, "Don't be frightened—Mr. Gould is here." There was laughter when he asked about this controversial conception of Brahms, "What am I doing conducting it?" There was loud and prolonged laughter when he said that he had only once before in his life "had to submit to a soloist's wholly new and incompatible concept, and that was the last time I accompanied Mr. Gould."

What could Gould—touchy, nervous, mercurial Glenn Gould—have thought about all these witticisms as he waited in the wings of Carnegie Hall and listened to the audience laugh? He later said, surprisingly enough, or perhaps not so surprisingly, that he didn't at all resent being the butt of Bernstein's humor. "Despite all the wild accusations that have been flying about, the speech was completely charming," he wrote to a friend. "Indeed, done with great generosity, and far from having precipitated a feud (as the newspapers suggest) we have never been better friends." Bernstein too took pains later to proclaim that he had not tried to degrade or embarrass Gould. After Gould's death, he kept saying that Gould had approved of his talk, that he had meant no harm. "It was a marvelous evening," he says. "And it was something very fresh. He really did find wonderful things in that concerto, and I *adored* him for it. But that *goddamned story* that I can never seem to get rid of. I tell you, that story drives me crazy. It makes me—uh—inarticulate to talk about it."

Everyone who was at the concert remembers it differently, each perhaps according to his own prejudices, but we have the surviving testimony of the tape recorder. On first hearing the incredibly slow opening to this concerto, one is almost inevitably overwhelmed by the lumbering and ungainly tempo. It seems almost absurd, and it certainly fails to achieve Gould's concept of a symphony. Yet as the movement proceeds, one begins to appreciate other aspects of Gould's performance. The slow tempo enables him to bring to this music a clarity that is rarely heard in more conventional versions, and he plays the lyrical passages with an unsentimental sweetness that is extremely beautiful. Finally even the heroic sections, which seem so awkward at first, acquire a stately majesty of their own.*

The audience's applause at the end was enthusiastic—an ovation—but the tradition-minded critics were predictably merciless. Irving Kolodin wrote in *The Saturday Review* that Gould's performance was "slow to the point of sluggishness," and Winthrop Sargeant of *The New Yorker* was even more harsh. "The pace, indeed, was such that all the work's stirring momentum was lost, and a kind of agony set in, similar to the feeling of impatience one experiences while riding in a delayed commuter train and counting off the interminable stops that separate one from one's goal." Paul Henry Lang wrote in the New York *Herald-Tribune* that he must "strenuously protest" because Bernstein had "violated elementary obligations of professional conduct" and because his disavowal of Gould was "an irresponsible act of high-handedness." But Lang's view of Gould was even more critical. "Mr. Gould is indeed a fine artist, unfortunately at present suffering from music hallucinations that make him unfit for public appearances. . . ."

Harold Schonberg, probably the most powerful critic in New York, was inspired to a ponderous attempt at humor. "Such goings-on at the New York Philharmonic concert yesterday afternoon!" his review in the *Times* began. "I tell you, Ossip, like you never saw. But maybe different from when we studied the Brahms D Minor Concerto at the Hohenzellern [sic] Academy." This Ossip, whom Schonberg kept addressing throughout the review in the tones of a Borscht Belt comic, was apparently meant to invoke Ossip Gabrilowitsch, a famous virtuoso who had often played the Brahms, but since Gabrilowitsch died in 1936, when Schonberg was twenty-one, it remained unclear what the fancied relationship between them was supposed to be, or what role Schonberg imagined himself to be playing, or what any of this *commedia dell'arte* had to do with Gould's

---

*The controversy over this performance never seems to die. Alan Rich, who never even heard the concert, wrote in *Keynote* in 1985 to take issue with Bernstein's public statement that the Gould version had required "well over an hour." With stopwatch in hand, Rich reported that Gould had taken only fifty-three minutes and fifty-one seconds, which was twenty-three seconds less than a recent recording by Krystian Zimmerman, for which Bernstein had felt no need to make a speech. Bernstein's angry defense against this clockwork is that Gould had played considerably faster at his second performance on Friday afternoon, the one that was taped and broadcast.

performance of the Brahms concerto. But Schonberg pressed relentlessly on. "So then the Gould boy comes on, and you know what, Ossip? . . . The Gould boy played the Brahms D Minor Concerto slower than the way we used to practice it. (And between you, me, and the corner lamppost, Ossip, maybe the reason he plays it so slow is maybe his technique is not so good.)"

"Isn't that awful?" Bernstein observes when the twenty-five-year-old review is quoted to him.

"Yes."

"How dare he? Really! That goes too far."

Schonberg's celebrated review was so malevolent—"that disgusting and supercilious review," as Schuyler Chapin refers to it—that one cannot help wondering about the origins of the critic's hostility. Schonberg himself says that the only time he ever met Gould was at a lunch organized by a Columbia publicist. "Debbie Ishlon thought that life in the Western Hemisphere would not be complete until Gould and I were brought together," the critic recalls. "We looked at each other, and I won't say it was hate at first sight, but we certainly operated on different frames of reference. Now, I'm primarily a nineteenth-century man, and you know what he thought of the nineteenth century. So there were some stabs at conversation, and his lip curled, especially when I—he was talking about concertos to record, and I mumbled something about the Hummel A minor, which I think is a masterpiece that leads straight to Chopin. He broke into laughter. And the lunch went downhill from there. And that was it."*

Q: And why Ossip?

A: What happened—I came back to the office, and I had plenty of time, instead of my normal forty minutes, and I wrote a normal review, and then I looked at it and said, "Oh, for God's sake," and I threw the thing out and went for the Ossip review. That was all.

Q: But why Ossip?

A: I don't know, I thought the name was funny.

For Leonard Bernstein to take a serious artistic disagreement and make a joking public disclaimer was bad enough, but for the senior

---

*In private, Gould liked to refer to Schonberg as Homer Sibelius, and he once wrote to Diana Menuhin: "It is my unshakable conviction that anything Homer Sibelius can know about on Monday, I can know about on Sunday."

music critic of the most important newspaper in the United States to review this performance with an elephantine version of Yiddish humor, and to say in the course of all this humor that one of the world's great keyboard technicians played the Brahms concerto so slowly because he didn't have the technical ability to play it properly—well, is it really so surprising that retirement from the concert stage came to seem more and more attractive? "He was *very*, very upset by that Harold Schonberg comment that suggested that maybe he couldn't play the Brahms, which was completely absurd," says Dr. Stephens, the Johns Hopkins psychiatrist. "It was so stupid, it really was a terrible thing to write, but he was very hurt by that, I mean more hurt than angered." This is not to suggest that Gould retired because he couldn't stand newspaper criticisms, only that the critics' inanities were yet another element among the many that made his life on the concert tour acutely unpleasant. "At live concerts I feel demeaned, like a vaudevillian," he said.

And the harassment went on and on. In Chicago later that month, the critic for the *American,* a Hearst paper that liked to print headlines in red ink, said of Gould's concert: "His appearance is careless and somehow disheveled. His clothes don't fit, his hair needs cutting and grooming, he appears to have his trouser pockets stuffed with grapefruits, and he walks like an impersonation of Henry Fonda impersonating the young Abe Lincoln. By being himself a parody, he is beyond parody. . . ." Donal Henahan of the *News* was a little better but not much: "Music's most successful hipster, Glenn Gould, finally slouched onto the Orchestra Hall stage after three cancellations. . . . Seating himself at the Ouija board on a sawed-off rickety relic of a chair that was held together with wires, the disheveled recitalist sang and stomped and conducted. . . ."

It was perhaps appropriate that Chicago was the site, two years later, of Gould's next-to-last public recital, on March 29, 1964, and that Henahan was one of those who reviewed the performance. It was Easter Sunday, and it snowed, and Henahan began by saying, "To point out at this late date that Glenn Gould plays extraordinary Bach is like saying that it sometimes snows on Easter Sunday, but in both cases the obvious still comes as a shock when it happens. For it is an elemental excitement that Gould's Bach exudes. . . . In the Bach of no other pianist today will you find the pulse of the

composer beating so powerfully. . . ." Gould played the Fourth Partita, and four fugues from *The Art of the Fugue* (and Beethoven's
Opus 110, and the Krenek Third Sonata). "For the record," Henahan concluded, "yes, the man did have the piano up on blocks; he
did sit on his wobbly chair; he did have a glass of water at the ready
(not used this time); he did sing intermittently; he did conduct with
whatever hand was not busy at the moment, and he did sit side-sad-
dle most of the time, knee almost to the floor. So all right if it makes
him happy."

There was only one last commitment, in Los Angeles, a fortnight
later, April 10, 1964. Gould played the same Bach he had played in
Chicago, but he substituted, as he often did, Hindemith's Third
Sonata for the Krenek and Beethoven's Opus 109 for Opus 110.
The *Herald-Examiner* found his Beethoven "the ultimate of poetry
and eloquence," but in the larger and more important *Times,* Dion
Winans wrote of the same piece that it was "a misfortune throughout . . . headlong . . . sentimental . . . hardly Beethoven to
remember."

None of them realized—possibly Gould did not realize it himself—that when he bowed and smiled and walked off the stage of
the Wilshire Ebell Theater in Los Angeles that April evening, he
was departing from the concert stage forever, at the age of thirty-
one. The waves of applause that bade him farewell would never be
heard again.

VI

The New Life

The first thing that Gould did after his retirement was to do nothing, or nothing professional. He spent a lot of time at the cottage on Lake Simcoe, still rather wintry in those lengthening days of early April. He had not yet figured out exactly how he wanted to spend the rest of his life. He wanted to write, to make radio and television shows, to lecture—to teach, in effect—but the details were vague. He had no master plan ready to be carried out. He wasn't even completely certain that he would never give another public concert.

"He did a lot of thinking," Jessie Greig recalls. "His mind was made up that there would be no more travel, that he would stay right here. He never said it in as many words, but it was quite evident in conversations that he had made up his mind that he was going to leave the stage and just be himself, you know. He felt that onstage he wasn't himself. He was someone else. I think that he was really deep in thought about it, but he knew where he was going. He was studying all the time. I went to the cottage once, and I can remember seeing the pile of books that he had to read. It was just an enormous amount."

Q: What were they? Can you remember some of the titles?

A: I really can't remember. I just remember the enormous pile of books. I think it covered everything.

When Gould felt a need for personal contact, he turned to the telephone. Unlike ordinary social intercourse, the telephone brought him immediately into contact with friends in New York or London or Berlin. The cost of long-distance calls was no obstacle— he willingly paid monthly bills of hundreds and hundreds of dollars—and so he developed a habit of spending long evening hours on the telephone, not just talking but reading aloud, singing, playing games.

And although Gould liked to wear old clothes and let his hair grow, his life in retirement was by no means ascetic. A listing of his possessions for an insurance company included not only two pianos and a Zao Wou-Ki painting that he valued at $4,500 but also "one four-seater Chesterfield . . . one small mahogany chest of drawers, two fruitwood tables, two lamp tables, one walnut and one mahogany, two lamp tables with marble base, one table lamp with gold leaf design," and so on. Also one Siemens diathermy unit and one ultrasonic therapy unit. He valued the whole array at $19,800, which, for a bachelor in 1962, was a not inconsiderable sum.

Gould emerged from his privacy that June to give a graduation address at the University of Toronto, and to receive an honorary degree as doctor of law. He did the same, in red robes, at the conservatory that November. "I am compelled to realize," he said to the graduates, perhaps referring to his own uncertainties, "that the separateness of our experience limits the usefulness of any practical advice that I could offer you. Indeed, if I could find one phrase that would sum up my wishes for you on this occasion, I think it would be devoted to convincing you of the futility of living too much by the advice of others." A reporter from the Toronto *Star* interviewed him after his address and quoted him as saying "that he's definitely giving up concert work 'after I finish the few obligations I still have left over. Nobody will believe me when I say it, but it's true.'"

His TV recital for the CBC that June may have been one of those "few obligations." He played once again some of his most familiar pieces, the Sweelinck fantasy, some of *The Goldberg Variations*, Beethoven's Opus 109, and the Berg Sonata. A reviewer in the *Globe and Mail* complained once again of his "mannerisms." It was clearly time for things to change. And yet because Gould had never officially announced his permanent retirement, only a reduction in commitments or a temporary "sabbatical," nobody took his absence too seriously. His manager, Walter Homburger, wrote to an official at Schirmer's in the fall of 1964 that Gould would perform the Schoenberg Concerto in Cincinnati the following January. Indeed, even a year later, Homburger was announcing that Gould would play the Schoenberg with the Baltimore Symphony in April of 1966. By this time, Gould was formally rejecting all such invitations. "I am afraid that I am not able to accept any engagements for next season," he wrote to Cincinnati. And to Newfoundland: "I am not able to accept any engagements for this coming season." And to Cleveland: "I am not by any means reneging on my promise to you that if I decide once again to give some concerts the Cleveland Symphony will certainly be among them, should you so desire, but my sabbatical is proving so productive in so many ways that I have not for the moment at least much intention of altering course."

The course was still not completely clear, though. Gould had already begun, for example, a sporadic and rather ill-conceived career as a lecturer (why should a man who does not want to play the piano in public want to read a lecture in public?). In February, a few months before his retirement, he had appeared at Hunter College in New York to talk about piano music, and particularly about Beethoven's Opus 109. It was not a very happy occasion. Gould began by leaning against his piano, announcing what he wanted to talk about in the first of two lectures and adding, "You may not see me next time." Raymond Ericson of the *Times* reported that Gould then "moved to the lectern and to the reading of his script. There he stayed, with occasional trips to the piano to illustrate a point, at which he might stay on the piano bench and continue reading. It was obvious that some listeners would have preferred to hear Mr. Gould make music and not talk. After he had played just a few measures early in the evening, he was greeted with prolonged applause. To this he merely shook his head, indicating that he was intent on giving his lecture.... Several persons walked out because they apparently had expected more music." Eric Salzman of the *Herald-Tribune* wrote even more sharply of the disparities between Gould and his listeners. "The large audience at Hunter College, which had obviously come to hear him play, were restless and bored ..." he reported. "Gould was talking about the whole subtle relationship of tonal and harmonic thinking to musical structure and expression in an age of rationality and revolution; it was brilliant, stimulating, informative and nearly totally lost on the audience.... One had the uneasy feeling that maybe five people in the audience were interested, alert and able to follow."

Gould tried this lecture again at the Gardner Museum in Boston two days later, and then began working on something quite different. When an admirer at the University of Cincinnati invited him to lecture there, he lectured on the works of Schoenberg. There are no surviving reports of bored listeners, and Gould must have been pleased when the University of Cincinnati published his lecture in book form in November of 1964, Gould's first, last, and only book. "Gould's view of Arnold Schoenberg is that he is much less revolutionist than inspired seer," said Arthur Darack, who had also written a foreword to the book, in the Cincinnati *Enquirer*, "a composer who pointed the way out of the dilemma of all artists who find themselves in a cul de sac imposed by the sterility of their times."

Gould liked writing, liked both the analytical and the hortatory aspects of the craft, and he liked the fact that a writer generally works alone, keeping his own pace, free to revise his creations again and again. Indeed, Gould periodically told interviewers that if he had not been a pianist, he would have been a writer, as though it were a simple matter of free choice. He had, in fact, been writing about his own performances from the beginning, and he would go on providing liner notes for his recordings until the end. The only Grammy he ever won during his entire life was for these liner notes. And in the rather specialized world of musical journals, Gould found the doors wide open to such periodicals as *High Fidelity* or *Musical America*. Robert Silverman, who paid him no money but published seventeen of Gould's articles in *The Piano Quarterly*, recalls the terms he offered: "I said to him at the beginning, 'You can write about anything you want. It doesn't have to be about music—anything you want to write, I'll publish. Carte blanche. No editing and there's no limit to the length.'

"The telephone calls were almost always in the same pattern," Silverman goes on. "He would call, and he would start off by saying, 'I've written the following, and I'd like to know if you like it.' And then he'd start, and he'd read the whole thing. He'd always tell me it was a draft, but I could not detect if there was anything different when I got the typed-up manuscript."

Q: And you had to accept it on the phone?

A: It didn't matter what he wrote—I was going to publish it. I took everything as a gift.

Yet the gap between Gould's piano-playing and his writing about that playing is a large one. It is the gap between an enormously gifted musician and an intelligent but rather inhibited literary amateur. Compare, for example, the enthusiastic brilliance of his performance of *The Goldberg Variations* with the affected pedantry of his commentary: "One hears so frequently of the bewilderment which the formal outline of this piece engenders among the uninitiated who become entangled in the luxuriant vegetation of the aria's family tree that it might be expedient to examine more closely the generative root in order to determine, with all delicacy, of course, its aptitude for parental responsibility."

That demonstrates not only Gould's weakness for pedantry but also those same faults that his schoolteachers had complained about, a prose style that attempted witty elegance but actually sounded mannered and artificial. Only occasionally does one catch glimpses of a slightly manic clown kept prisoner inside Gould's head. This alter ego made one of his first appearances in an article about the CBC written late in 1964 for *Musical America*. It appeared under the pseudonym of Herbert von Hochmeister (Gould's clowning was often ethnic, often Germanic), "the fine-arts critic of *The Great Slave Smelt*, perhaps the most respected journal north of latitude 70°." (Gould's clowning, somewhat mysteriously, often involved the Arctic.) "From beneath the High Victorian turrets of a folksy house in downtown Toronto, known affectionately—and nationally—as the Kremlin, a shrewd covey of white-collar conciliators devote themselves with dedicated anonymity to governing our cultural life. . . ." Perhaps inevitably, Gould's humor was not appreciated everywhere. He never forgave John Kraglund of the *Globe and Mail* for having once written that it was "as light and frothy as a tub of wet cement."

More interesting than this essay itself is Gould's subsequent analysis of his shift in identity. "I . . . was incapable of writing in a sustained humorous style until I developed an ability to portray myself pseudonymously . . ." he told Jonathan Cott about the creation of Herbert von Hochmeister of the Northwest Territories. "The reason for that metaphor was that Herbert could thereby survey the culture of North America from his exalted remove, and pontificate accordingly. The character was also vaguely based on Karajan. Von

Hochmeister was a retired conductor and was always spouting off about Germanic culture and things of that nature. At least that's how I got into the character. . . . Once I did that, I found it no problem at all to say what I wanted to say in a humorous style. Until then, there was a degree of inhibition that prevented me from doing so. But then the floodgates were open, and subsequently I developed a character for every season."

It all sounds very lighthearted, but these were rather uncertain times. "The last year has been quite awful for me," Gould confessed early in 1965 to Kitty Gvozdeva, who had the merit of living in faraway Leningrad. "I've written a great deal for one thing—many lectures and magazine articles of one kind or another, and my first book—a small one and on Schoenberg, so you won't approve! And it's given me the urge to publish more. The last year has also crystallized my feelings about travelling and concert giving. . . . I simply can't conceive of going back to that awful, transient life." And change seemed to bring a remarkable improvement in his somewhat fragile health. "Since I stopped giving concerts, I've scarcely had so much as a sniffle," he told one interviewer, Richard Kostelanetz. "Most of my earlier illnesses were psychosomatic—a sheer protest against my regimen."

At about this same time, Gould wrote to a friend in Berlin that he had just finished a ninety-minute radio documentary "about the recording industry and its effect upon the lives of modern man. It is a rather fascinating program, I think. [It was made] with interview material taken from conversations with a number of friends as well as a good deal of my own narration." A year later, Gould reorganized these views into an article featured in the fifteenth-anniversary issue of *High Fidelity* magazine. Entitled "The Prospects of Recording," it was one of the most interesting and important pieces he ever wrote.

Gould began this long essay, as he began many of his early writings, with a defense of his retirement from the stage. More specifically, he repeated an earlier prediction "that the public concert as we know it today would no longer exist a century hence, that its functions would have been entirely taken over by electronic media." This, he said, appeared to him "almost as self-evident truth," but it had been widely disputed, and so he wanted to elaborate on it. He recalled how brief the supposedly eternal tradition of the concert hall actually was, no more than about a hundred years, and he ridiculed almost every aspect of that tradition. Why, indeed, should it be necessary, with or without tuxedo, to trek through the snow at some fixed time to some cavernous hall to hear the same old repertoire played to an accompaniment of rustling and coughing? (Gould himself almost never went to concerts.) The only thing that kept the concert tradition alive, he argued, was the oligarchy of the music business, plus what Gould called "an endearing, if sometimes frustrating, human characteristic—a reluctance to accept the consequences of a new technology."

Recording in itself was hardly a very new technology. Thomas Alva Edison built and named his first phonograph in 1877, primarily as a dictating device, and so the machine preserved the voice of Gladstone and the piano-playing of Brahms. What was remarkable in the technology of recording was that it kept changing, radically, repeatedly devouring all its children. In 1888 came the shellac disk to replace Edison's waxed cylinder. Enter Caruso, Joachim, Grieg. In 1925 came the first electric records, which rotated at a standard 78 r.p.m. In 1948, Columbia introduced the LP, which turned at 33⅓ r.p.m., contained a whole Mozart symphony on one side instead of eight, and could not be broken. All 78 r.p.m. records had to be thrown away. At the same time, acetate and shellac began to be replaced in the 1940's by magnetic tape, which could be spliced to get rid of all mistakes.

In 1958 came another revolution, stereophonic sound from different speakers, which made all previous monaural recordings obsolete. In 1965, just as Gould was writing about the resistance to new technology, the tape cassette began to threaten the record itself. Now you could hear Beethoven not only in your own home but in your car, and, eventually, even while jogging through the park. In 1979, during Gould's last years, Decca introduced digital tapes, much clearer than anything before, and in 1983, after Gould's death, Sony and Philips brought forth the even clearer compact disk, yet another revolution, yet another devaluation of all previous recordings.

One of the most controversial aspects of this evolving technology was that splicing led to charges of trickery and even fraud. The classic case occurred when Elisabeth Schwarzkopf was hired to sing a high C that was secretly spliced into a Kirsten Flagstad recording of *Tristan*. But Gould was heartily in favor of what he called "creative cheating." In his article "Music and Technology," when Gould recalled how he had recorded a 1950 CBC performance of Mozart and Hindemith on a second-rate studio piano, he reveled in the accidental discovery "that if I gave [the acetate] a bass cut at a hundred cycles or thereabouts and a treble boost at approximately five thousand, the murky, unwieldy, bass-oriented studio piano could be magically transformed." Splicing and editing tapes, like altering pitch, enabled Gould to achieve combinations that he had hardly imagined while actually playing a piece. The goal of a recording, he believed, should be not historical authenticity but the highest possible quality.

Critics of such "creative cheating"—and there were and still are many—insist that there is a kind of mystical unity and power in an uninterrupted performance, particularly a live performance, that there is an arching melodic line that cannot be mechanically imitated. Gould had an answer to that too, which he entitled "The Grass Is Always Greener in the Outtakes: An Experiment in Listening." He began with a quotation from the enemy, specifically André Watts: "I can't help wishing that all recordings were live performances.... If this is totally unfeasible, then at least I'd like to know that there was no splicing within movements.... The whole intimidating idea of having all those guys around while you have to stop and ask for a retake ... can be pretty terrible, especially if you have to start again and again. It can get you very uptight." Gould's answer was to explore the basic question: Can anybody really tell the difference?

With a weightiness worthy of Herbert von Hochmeister, Gould created a test panel from among his friends and acquaintances: six professional musicians, six audio experts, six "laymen." Half were men, half women. To all of these, he presented a tape of eight performances ranging from Byrd and Bach to Scriabin and Schoenberg, from a Gould solo to a George Szell performance of part of Beethoven's Fifth. Each panelist was asked to play the half-hour tape three times and then tell how many splices could be detected (they ranged from zero to thirty-four per piece). "That took a prodigious number of hours and hours and hours," says Steve Posen, Gould's attorney, who was one of the panelists, "first to prepare the material and then to sit with people as they went through it—hours and hours to come up with this information. He was infinitely patient when he got onto something." Gould was happy to report that nobody came even close to counting the splices correctly, and in elaborate breakdowns of the results, he was also happy to report that the professional musicians fared worst, and the "laymen" best. The two highest scores went to a male physician and a female librarian.

While Gould was trying so hard to demonstrate that the studio recording was artistically superior to the live concert, the great piano event of 1965, the year after Gould's retirement, was the return of Vladimir Horowitz to Carnegie Hall after an absence of twelve years. Columbia released a two-record album of "an historic return," and that inspired a wave of new recorded concerts, in which the coughs and clinkers were all treated as part of the atmospherics. This was, of course, a recording trend diametrically opposed to Gould's beliefs. His shift from the concert hall to the recording studio was not just a matter of personal convenience but of artistic conviction (if, indeed, the two can be separated). In contrast to all those who took pride in the possibilities of re-creating a live recital, Gould objected to what he called "the non-taketwoness" of the concert stage. A recording, he insisted, should be completely different from a recital, not simply reproducing a live performance but perfecting it, exploiting all the technical possibilities that could not even be attempted in the concert hall.

Gould was not, of course, entirely alone in these beliefs. As early as the 1930's, the English impresario and recording executive Walter Legge had committed himself to the basic proposition: "I wanted better results than are normally possible in public performance: I was determined to put onto disc the best that artists could do under the best possible conditions." Legge was not a believer in splicing, which was then just beginning to become possible; "the best possible conditions" meant to him primarily a studio where the artists could record take after take in the search for perfection. Far more Gouldian was John Culshaw (1924–1980), who produced for Decca between 1958 and 1964 the first complete recording of Wagner's *Ring* (conducted by Sir Georg Solti). Culshaw passionately believed that the coming of stereo made it possible to record operas that would sound quite different from theatrical performances. "It can bring opera to life in the home in a way that was quite unimaginable twenty years ago," he wrote in *Ring Resounding*. "The effect is nothing like that of the opera house, for several reasons. The listener at home is not a member of a community, and whether he admits it or not his reactions in private are not the same as his reactions in public. . . . The sound of a good stereo recording . . . will tend to engulf the listener, and may draw him psychologically closer to the characters of the opera than when he is in the theater. The sense of being inside the drama is heightened by the absence of a visual element. . . . Instead of watching someone else's production, he is unconsciously creating his own."

Andrew Porter, reviewing Culshaw's version of *Das Rheingold*, captured the idea perfectly. "Listening to these records is not like going to the opera house without looking at the stage," he wrote in *The Gramophone*. "In some mysterious way they seem to catch you up in the work . . . more intimately than that." Opera conductors and singers do not greatly appreciate having their physical appearance be made secondary to the positioning of microphones, but Culshaw affected to scorn all such objections. "As a rule," he wrote, "artists today understand that the actual techniques of recording are best left to those who understand them."

Gould, of course, was one of those who understood them completely, and his mastery of recording technology gave him something that was psychologically very important to him: total control over his own musical performances. But to return to "The Prospects of Recording," Gould wanted to demonstrate not that miking and splicing could provide technical benefits to him but that recording had changed the whole nature of music. Purely in terms of the music played, the enormous broadening of the available repertoire— specifically the popularity of early music—occurred entirely after World War II and as a direct result of the LP record. Composers like Vivaldi and Telemann, not to mention Josquin or Machaut, rather suddenly became once again part of the culture.

No less significant was the change in the way music was performed, and thus heard and understood. Because the musicians no longer had to fill large spaces with sound, the whole process of making music began to put more emphasis on clarity of tone, and particularly clarity of polyphony. Chamber music flourished. Old instruments came back to life. Though Gould resisted that last tendency, insisting that Bach could be played on any instrument, that it was part of Bach's genius to ignore the special characteristics of various instruments, he nonetheless insisted on playing pianos that were dry and clear and light-toned. So the sound of a Horowitz playing a Rachmaninoff concerto by now sounds to the contemporary listener almost as deliciously old-fashioned as Stokowski's lush sonorities in Bach.

"One of the first musicians to grasp the significance of recording to the composing process," Gould said, "was Arnold Schoenberg, who ... remarked: 'In radio broadcasting, a small number of sonic entities suffice for the expression of all artistic thoughts; the gramophone and the various mechanical instruments are evolving such clear sonorities that one will be able to write much less heavily instrumented pieces for them.' Intentionally or not, the development of Schoenberg's own style demonstrates his understanding of the medium and its implications. . . ." This evolution became all the more clear when Schoenberg's works were performed by musicians who really understood and appreciated them, specifically not just Gould but also Robert Craft, with whom Gould had recorded the Schoenberg Piano Concerto back in 1961.

"For Craft, the stopwatch and the tape splice are tools of his trade," Gould said, "as well as objects of that inspiration for which an earlier generation of stick wielders found an outlet in the opera cape and temper tantrums." Gould compared Craft's recording of Schoenberg's *Pelleas und Melisande* with the "glowingly romantic" account of the same score by an older German conductor, Winfried Zillig. "Craft applies a sculptor's chisel to these vast orchestral complexes of the youthful Schoenberg," Gould wrote admiringly, "and gives them a determined series of plateaus on which to operate—a very baroque thing to do. He seems to feel that his audience—sitting at home, close up to the speaker—is prepared to allow him to dissect this music and to present it to them from a strongly biased conceptual viewpoint, which the private and concentrated circumstances of their listening make feasible. . . . We must be prepared to accept the fact that, for better or for worse, recording will forever alter our notions about what is appropriate to the performance of music."

One of the strangest aspects of technology is not only that it creates new processes but that it cancels—or makes possible the cancellation—of widely accepted older processes. The computer revolution supersedes the industrial revolution, making obsolete all that centralization and standardization that led to the assembly line; the computer can just as easily make a suit or an automobile to "customized" individual measurements as to uniform measurements, and so farewell to Blake's dark Satanic mills. Gould's theories of technology similarly implied a reversal of a musical tradition that dated all the way back to the Renaissance. It was then, according to Gould's historical vision, that Western music took a radically wrong turn, toward specialization. All the milestones that are usually treated in musical-history classes as cultural triumphs—the arrival of the professional composer like Haydn or Mozart, the professional orchestra like that of the Esterhazys, the professional piano virtuoso, the professional conductor whose musical performance consists of waving a baton—all these impressed Gould as steps downhill toward the large and competitive musical marketplace of today. Impresarios send vainglorious virtuosos out on tour, star conductors jet from one guest appearance to another, composers remain largely ignored, and the audience consists of thousands of automatons assembled in uncomfortable culture palaces.

What had been lost in the Renaissance—which also created, along with a lot of great art, the capitalist system that thereafter bought and sold art—was the tradition of artistic community. Just as the great Gothic cathedrals had been largely built by anonymous designers and volunteer labor, music in the precapitalist age was an art in which composers, performers, and listeners were all more or less the same. Whether it was a case of a market crowd listening to a street band or a king singing his own songs—is it conceivable to imagine any president of the United States performing in public, like King Frederick II of Prussia, a flute concerto of his own composition?—music had once been a shared and communal activity, not a spectacle provided by a hired specialist.

Gould's visions of this pre-eighteenth-century Utopia may have been quite unrealistic, but the interesting thing is that Gould believed it could all be re-created by the wonders of recording technology. Some of this was already happening. New composers like

Boulez and Stockhausen had long since introduced taped sounds into the concert hall, and now they were playing their own compositions on synthesizers. Gould was particularly impressed by a fad recording of 1968, *Switched-on Bach*, in which a gifted amateur musician named Walter Carlos bleeped and pinged his way through various Bach selections on a Moog synthesizer. Gould called it "the record of the year (no, let's go all the way—the decade!)." He went further and organized a CBC radio show in which he combined selections from *Switched-on Bach* and interviews with Carlos and a Canadian visionary, Jean Le Moyne. Carlos, in a high-pitched voice that heralded his coming transformation into Wendy Carlos, rattled on about the technical details of his synthesizer: "The keyboards don't generate sounds—they're nothing but voltage sources. . . . So that C might be three volts, and the C above that might be four volts and D is four volts plus one twelfth of four volts. . . ." Le Moyne went on to hymn the glories of technology. "Machines in themselves are good," he declared, and even "the much-maligned mills of the Victorian era . . . have clothed more men . . . than all the charity of all the kings and all the lords and all the saints of humanity." Indeed, Le Moyne seemed to believe that machines had replaced saints as mediators between God and man. "What the machine teaches us," he said, "is a kind of . . . commentary on that passage of Saint Paul to the Philippians when he said about Christ that he did not hold himself jealous of the rank that equaled him to God, but he went down and became man and became obedient. . . . And in that way, I think there is a kind of Christification going on in the machine world, in technology. . . ."

Gould himself was hardly less visionary. The culmination of this technological revolution in music, he believed, would be the liberation of the listener, or rather the transformation of the listener from a passive into an active participant. "Dial twiddling is in its limited way an interpretive act," he wrote in "The Prospects of Recording." "Forty years ago the listener had the option of flicking a switch marked 'on' and 'off' and, with an up-to-date machine, perhaps modulating the volume just a bit. Today, the variety of controls made available to him requires analytical judgment. And these controls are but primitive, regulatory devices compared to those participational possibilities which the listener will enjoy once current laboratory techniques have been appropriated by home playback devices."

The highest delight, in Gould's view, would come when this "new kind of listener" could reedit all the tapes in his vast collection. "Let us say, for example, that you enjoy Bruno Walter's performance of the exposition and recapitulation from the first movement of Beethoven's Fifth Symphony but incline toward Klemperer's handling of the development section, which employs a notably divergent tempo. . . . With the pitch-speed correlation held in abeyance, you could snip out these measures from the Klemperer edition and splice them into the Walter performance without having the splice procedure either an alteration of tempo or a fluctuation of pitch. . . ."

It is probably inevitable that any vision of paradise shows primarily what the visionary wishes for himself; he tacitly assumes that everyone else would like the same. Brünhilde promises to the warrior Siegmund a Valhalla where "dead heroes in a splendid body will embrace you kindly and welcome you solemnly." T. S. Eliot, on the other hand, predicts that the hippopotamus will eventually take his place among the saints, "performing on a harp of gold," washed as white as snow and "by all the martyred virgins kist." So Gould dreamed of a day when the music lover might return home from a hard day at the office and proceed forthwith to his Gouldian studio to spend his evening splicing tapes. "The listener," said Gould, "can ultimately become his own composer."

Gould was spinning out this fantasy during a BBC television interview with Humphrey Burton in 1966 when Burton interrupted with a fundamental objection. He said he had no desire whatever to hear a self-created pastiche of Walter and Klemperer, he wanted to hear Klemperer's Beethoven exactly as Klemperer chose to play it. But when it was possible to buy and edit ten different versions of a Beethoven sonata, Gould insisted, Burton *should* want to. To another interviewer, Richard Kostelanetz, Gould imagined all ten versions emerging from one of his own recording sessions. "I'd love to issue a kit of variant performances and let the listener assemble his own performance," he said. And so Gould went right on preaching and proselytizing for the technological paradise that lay just beyond the horizon.

Not long after the Burton encounter, Gould was conducting a radio interview with Leopold Stokowski, whom he revered partly because of his pioneering broadcasts and recordings of the 1930's, when he misguidedly referred to the fashionable theories of Marshall McLuhan. What did Stokowski think, Gould inquired, about Professor McLuhan's view that we were nearing a time when there would be no need for any professional performers, only the creators, the consumers, and the computers? This was seven years after *The Gutenberg Galaxy* and five years after *Understanding Media,* and various experts had exhausted themselves in debating the significance of "hot" and "cold" media in "the universal village." It is hard to believe that Stokowski wasn't fully aware of this, but he answered Gould's question by calmly saying, "Who is Professor McLuhan?"

When Gould informed him, Stokowski dismissed the theorist with a lordly declaration that "he has a right to his opinion." Later on, though, when he grandly acknowledged uncertainty on some point, he added another jab. "I don't know," he said, "but I doubt if Professor—what is his name? McLuhan?—knows either."

It is easy enough now to observe that Gould's prophecies about the end of the concert have not come true—any more than the appearance of the new listener in his secluded electronic studio—and the conservatories still turn out virtuosos ready to don their tuxedoes and fly to Omaha for yet another *Emperor Concerto.* Remember, though, that Gould's prophecies applied not to the present but to the coming century. And although a Brendel or Barenboim can still fill Carnegie Hall with the familiar fans listening to the familiar pieces—"We have been, let us say, to hear the latest Pole/," as Eliot wearily wrote, "Transmit the Preludes. . . ."—we also hear cries of alarm about the declining interest in such things. "Pianists . . . are thus even more susceptible than others to certain market considerations . . ." said one such threnody in the New York *Times* late in 1987. "Pressures from managers and presenters, especially outside of New York, dictate that standard fare is essential to attract what seems to be an ever-dwindling audience for piano recitals. . . ."

While the subsidized conservatories still feed the subsidized concert machine—and what could be more unreal than the process of young black singers being elaborately trained to sing German or Italian in an art form to which virtually no major new works have been added in nearly half a century?—much of Gould's philosophy is now taken for granted in the admittedly simpler recording of popular music. It goes without saying that the best and most successful pop singers write their own material, sing their own creations, and it took the Beatles very little time to evolve from pink-cheeked guitar strummers into the technicians who created the synthetic sounds of *Sergeant Pepper's Lonely Hearts Club Band* inside their electronic laboratory. Evan Eisenberg, who has explored what he calls the phonography of both classical and popular music, has even written in *The Recording Angel* that Gould "as a classical pianist . . . could not construct records as ambitiously as people like . . . Phil Spector and Frank Zappa could." On the basic point, though, Eisenberg suggests a very Gouldian conclusion: "History may conclude that Gould was the one sane musician of the century; and his colleagues who work the continents like traveling salesmen, unpacking their hearts from Altoona to Vancouver, may seem as pathetic to our grandchildren as the bowing and scraping geniuses of the eighteenth century seem to us."

Such judgments may seem to imply that Gould believed not only in art for art's sake but in the coronation of art's sake over everything else, that Gould believed art to represent the highest good, the godhead of its own religion. In fact, he believed quite the opposite. He might well have read with sympathy Plato's arguments on why Homer should be censored for the sake of public virtue in the Utopian Republic, or how the sensuous sound of flutes should be forbidden, except to shepherds, or how even subversive harmonies should be outlawed. "Which are the harmonies expressive of sorrow . . . ?" Socrates asks. "The harmonies which you mean are the mixed or tenor Lydian, and the full-toned or bass Lydian, and such like," says Glaucon. "These, then, I said, must be banished. . . ."

Gould might well have listened just as sympathetically to the outcries of Pozdnuishef, the tormented hero of Tolstoy's *The Kreutzer Sonata,* who was driven to frenzies of jealousy by hearing his wife perform Beethoven's violin sonata with another man. "That sonata is a terrible thing," he says. "And especially that movement. And music in general is a terrible thing. . . . They say music has the effect of elevating the soul—rubbish! falsehood! . . . Its effect is neither to elevate nor to degrade, but to excite. . . . It transports me into another state . . . under the influence of music it seems to me that I feel what I do not really feel, that I understand what I do not really understand, that I can do what I can't do. . . ."

Perhaps Gould might have sympathized even with the angry reflections of Lenin on Beethoven. "I don't know of anything greater than the Appassionata," as Tom Stoppard quotes Lenin in his recounting of the famous scene in *Travesties*. "Amazing, super-human music. It always makes me feel, perhaps naïvely, it makes me feel proud of the miracles that human beings can perform. But I can't listen to music often. It affects my nerves, makes me want to say nice stupid things and pat the heads of those people who while living in this vile hell can create such beauty. Nowadays . . . we've got to *hit* heads, hit them without mercy. . . ."

In all these quotations, music appears not as purely something of beauty—of a beauty that serves as an end in itself—but rather as something essentially false, something that falsifies the truth as it seduces the true believer. The church had good reasons for forbidding any counterpoint or other artistic complications in the musical settings of its liturgy. Gould's private cosmology remains uncertain, for he had long since left behind the devout Methodism of his parents, but he continued searching after some kind of spiritual truth. He read a great deal of theology, Kierkegaard and Tillich, late at night. He explored the outer edges of spiritualism, astrology, mind reading, prophecies. One aspect of his childhood Methodism that remained extremely strong was his yearning for virtue, to do good, to be good. He repeatedly referred to himself by the title of George Santayana's sole novel, *The Last Puritan*. His ethical system remained as undefined and unformulated as his cosmology, but it seems to have been based on a rigidly controlled code of behavior, a code that prescribed isolation from others. To thine own self be true.

All of Western society has been organized on a completely different basis, however, on the basis of relationships with other people, at best love and communion, but in everyday life competition and commerce. In one of his most forthright and striking statements, Gould once declared in an interview: "I happen to believe that competition rather than money is the root of all evil." He had undeniably known and thrived on competition since his childhood, from the days when he won the Kiwanis piano competition for ten dollars, when he won the highest marks ever scored in earning his diploma at the conservatory, when he concentrated fiercely on defeating his elders and betters on the croquet field, but as he looked back across that world from which he had done his best to retire, the competitive instinct struck him as destructive, sterile, evil. And since he was an artist, he expressed that moral judgment in terms of art, and vice versa. "To rephrase the fashionable cliche," he wrote in "Glenn Gould Interviews Glenn Gould about Glenn Gould," "I do try as best I can to make only moral judgments and not esthetic ones. . . ."

That dictum sent Gould spiraling off (he was interviewing himself, after all) into an increasingly bizarre series of declarations of belief. Starting with the statement that all houses should be painted battleship gray, because "it's my favorite color," he proclaimed that anyone who wanted to paint his house red should be prevented from doing so, not only for aesthetic reasons but because such a change "would . . . foreshadow an outbreak of manic activity," and ultimately, "a climate of competition and, as a corollary, of violence." Interrogator Gould protested that this represented "a type of censorship that contradicts the whole post-Renaissance tradition of Western thought." Gould easily retorted that "it's the post-Renaissance tradition that has brought the western world to the brink of destruction." Or as he put it in a much later interview with Tim Page, "I would like to see a world where nobody cared what anybody else was doing."

The ultimate goal of art, Gould believed, was "the gradual, lifelong construction of a state of wonder and serenity." More immediately, its purpose was "essentially therapeutic and remedial." As for all its competitive forms, its concerts, shows, exhibitions, prizes, applauding audiences, all of that, those were simply flowerings from the root of all evil. "I feel that art should be given a chance to phase itself out," Gould finally said to himself in his self-interview. "I think that we must accept the fact that art is not inevitably benign, that it is potentially destructive. We should analyze the areas where it tends to do least harm, use them as a guideline, and build into art a component that will enable it to preside over its own obsolescence. . . ."

Earlier in this interview, Gould had seemed to startle his interviewer by proclaiming that one of his ambitions in life was "to try my hand at being a prisoner ... on the understanding, of course, that I would be entirely innocent of all charges brought against me...." Now it only remained for the interviewer to suggest that Gould should return to the drafty Salzburg Festspielhaus and give another concert there, so that he could once again catch a virus that would bring him the martyrdom he so clearly sought. "There could be no more meaningful manner in which to scourge the flesh," said Interviewer Gould, "and certainly no more meaningful metaphoric mise en scene against which to offset your own hermetic life-style, through which to define your quest for martyrdom autobiographically, as I'm sure you will try to do, eventually."

"But ... I have no such quest in mind," Gould protested.

"Then and only then," said the interviewer, "will you achieve the martyr's end you so obviously desire...."

VII

The Classical Records

It was not at all certain that an unseen pianist could earn a living from nothing but recordings. Virtually nobody had ever done it before. But Gould was determined to make the attempt, and Columbia, though it regretted the loss of concert publicity, was ready to back him up. "We used to talk about it a lot, about his hatred of the stage," says Schuyler Chapin, the head of Columbia's classical music department. "Because he wanted reassurance that his retirement from the stage was not retirement from the piano. And his records had sold pretty well. There was no question about the fact that the company was anxious to keep him."

Q: But he did take a big drop in pay, didn't he, when he first retired?

A: Yes. But he had saved his money, made a good start.

Gould also enjoyed proving the skeptics wrong. Walter Homburger had strongly advised him not to leave the stage, says John Beckwith. "Homburger said, 'That's a very risky thing to do, the public forgets about you, and you can't pick it up again—be careful.' And the next five or six years, Glenn would phone him every year and say, 'Walter, I just got my check from Columbia. Guess.' And Walter would guess, and it was always ten thousand dollars higher than Walter guessed."

Since Columbia gave Gould a very free hand in choosing what he wanted to record, he happily chose large quantities of Schoenberg. In 1964 alone, the year of his retirement from the stage, he recorded the *Phantasy* for violin and piano (with Israel Baker), the Suite for Piano, Opus 25, and two groups of songs, Opus 2 and 3 (sung by

Ellen Faull, soprano; Helen Vanni, mezzo-soprano; Donald Gramm, bass-baritone). The following year, he added four sets of piano pieces, Opus 11, 19, 23, and 33, *The Book of the Hanging Gardens* (Helen Vanni), and the *Ode to Napoleon Bonaparte*, (with John Horton as speaker and the Juilliard Quartet). Under the benign reign of Goddard Lieberson, who was then president of Columbia Records, the company felt a now-forgotten obligation to record major contemporary composers even if their works did not bring large profits. Lieberson committed Columbia to Stravinsky's authoritative performances of everything he wrote, so he felt no qualms about encouraging Gould in his passion for Schoenberg.

Most of Gould's labors during the later 1960's, however, were devoted to the fundamentals of the classical repertoire. He had already recorded the Beethoven First Concerto with Golschmann, and the next three with Bernstein; his performance of the *Emperor* with Stokowski would complete that cycle in 1966. Having miscalculated in his distorted early reading of the last three Beethoven sonatas, he now turned back and began a fairly systematic recording of the more congenial early sonatas, the three of Opus 10 in 1964, the two of Opus 14 and the *Pathétique* in 1966. And the following year, he began the ambitious and somewhat ambiguous project of recording all the Mozart sonatas.

The bedrock of Gould's career, though, was his unique mastery of Bach. He played Bach unlike anyone else, and he probably understood Bach better than anyone else. After the spectacular recording of *The Goldberg Variations*, his hardly less spectacular performance of the fifth and sixth partitas implied that he would record them all, which he completed in 1963. His admirable readings of the concerti in D minor (with Bernstein in 1957) and F minor (with Golschmann in 1958) implied that he would record all the concerti too, which he finished in 1969. Not all of these implications were inevitably fulfilled. He had often performed excerpts from *The Art of the Fugue* in his concerts, and he began recording this work on the organ in 1969, but although his splendid album of the first nine fugues cried out to be completed, Gould inexplicably left the project unfinished.

The main implication, though, was that Gould was planning to become the first pianist ever to record the complete keyboard works of Bach, and that inevitably brought him face to face with what Robert Schumann had called "this work of works," *The Well-Tempered Clavier*. Gould seems to have been a little hesitant, possibly even a little overawed. He had learned all the twenty-four preludes and fugues of Book I under the aegis of his mother before he was ten years old, and Alberto Guerrero must have devoted many of their hours together to the wonders and mysteries of Book II. Yet Gould almost never played any of these marvelous pieces on the concert stage. And it is remarkable that although he loved to indulge himself in both pedantries and parodies in the liner notes to his recordings, he left the liner notes for Bach's masterpiece to someone else.

To write about *The Well-Tempered Clavier* is indeed difficult. "The fact that the work today has become common property may console us for the other fact that an analysis of it is almost as impossible as it is to depict a wood by enumerating the trees and describing their appearance," Albert Schweitzer wrote back in 1905 in his rather quirky biography of Bach. Unlike Gould, though, Schweitzer had no qualms about undertaking the impossible. "We can only repeat again and again—take them and play them and penetrate into this world for yourself," he wrote. "Aesthetic elucidation of any kind must necessarily be superficial here. What so fascinates us in the work is not the form or the build of the piece, but the world-view that is mirrored in it. It is not so much that we enjoy the *Well-Tempered Clavichord* [sic] as that we are edified by it. Joy, sorrow, tears, lamentation, laughter—to all these it gives voice, but in such a way that we are transported from the world of unrest to a world of peace, and see reality in a new way, as if we were sitting by a mountain lake and contemplating hills and woods and clouds in the tranquil and fathomless water." Perhaps this is just the transcendental style of the period—Thomas Mann wrote similarly about Wagner—but there seems to be something in Bach that inspires the Germanic soul to ululate. "I said to myself," Goethe wrote after hearing some of Bach's organ works, "it is as if the eternal harmony were conversing within itself, as it may have done in the bosom of God just before the Creation of the world. . . ."

Gould was not like that. He did write a preface for a new Peters edition of *The Well-Tempered Clavier*, but it was, as might be expected, restrained, respectful, even reticent. He wrote mainly about the fugues, often citing examples not from *The Well-Tempered*

Clavier but from *The Art of the Fugue*. And he was technical to the point of scholasticism: "The very first fugue of volume one, for example, tolerates only the most modest of modulations and in its stretto-ridden way resourcefully characterizes the fugue subject itself—a bland diatonic model of academic primness. Other fugues, like that in E Major from Book II, exhibit the same sort of modulatory disinclination and here so tenacious is Bach's loyalty to his six-note theme, and so diffident the modulatory program through which he reveals it to us, one has the impression that the intense and fervently anti-chromatic ghost of Heinrich Schütz rides again. . . ." Or consider this: "He sets forth his material in many different harmonic guises and spot-lights some structural phenomena latent within it at each of the major modulatory turning-points. Thus, when he dissolves into the mediant and establishes his theme for the first time in a major key (D flat) a canonic duet ensues between the theme itself, now ensconced in the soprano part and, one beat delayed and two octaves plus one note lowered, an imitation in the bass. For this episode the chromatic counter-theme temporarily vacates the scene and in its stead, subsidiary voices append their own quasi-canonic comments. . . ." And so on.

Gould's recordings of *The Well-Tempered Clavier*, begun shortly before his retirement, are similarly idiosyncratic. Some of the preludes and fugues are quite miraculous—those in both C-sharp major and C-sharp minor, for example, sound tense and energetic and full of feeling. Some others are interesting but distinctly peculiar. Gould believed, for example, that the lyricism of the famous C major Prelude was "just prosaically prefatory," and that he could enliven the piece by playing the flowing figure in the right hand partly staccato. He seems to have thought too that he could improve the Prelude in F-sharp major by playing it at half speed, and the Fugue in A flat by playing it at double speed. Bach allowed him much more latitude than other composers, of course, for he rarely specified how fast he wanted his music played, or how loud or soft, or even on what instrument. Then there were other pieces that Gould simply played rather dutifully, as though they had to be included just to make the work complete. Let it be remembered, though, that Gould being peculiar or even just dutiful generally meant piano-playing at a level that virtually nobody else could approach.

Some critics rebelled at the eccentricities in this new version of *The Well-Tempered Clavier*. "A resounding 'nuts!' to Gould," said an unsigned review of the first album in the Washington *Post*. "He has tampered with the tone of the piano, and with Bach's phrasing, producing a caricature in many cases, and rarely offering insights of value. The tone is unpleasant, the performances a constant irritation." B. H. Haggin of *The New Republic* sounded almost equally fretful. "Admirer though I am of Gould's playing," he wrote, "I find that the carefully thought-out peculiarities of touch and phrasing in some of the performances . . . make it impossible for me to go along with them as convincing and acceptable statements of the pieces."

Most critics were far more approving. "Few pianists match Gould in the discipline, sharp focus and scrupulous artistry he brings to Bach," said the Minneapolis *Tribune*. "Played in compelling style, with a rhythmic flexibility that maintains the tension in each complex work," said the Philadelphia *Inquirer*. "One can hardly wait for the rest of the series," said the Detroit *Free Press*. And in *The Saturday Review*, Irving Kolodin offered his magisterial endorsement: "This introduction is as stimulating to the attention as it is unconventional to the ear. One thing is certain: at his most forthright and unsentimental, Gould is nevertheless deeply involved with the music's meaning as he conceives it; passionately pursuing the ebb and flow of thought wherever it may lead. . . ."

In contrast to the concert hall, where only one star performer is out onstage alone under the spotlights, the recording studio is a somewhat more collaborative scene. The pressure is still there. "Gould is tense and anxious at recording sessions—sometimes desperately so, and much more than he was when he played concerts," according to Geoffrey Payzant. But the pianist shares the arena with engineers and technicians. The chief of these, throughout most of Gould's long recording career, was Andrew Kazdin, a heavyset and thickly bearded man who had the unusual credentials of both a music degree from the New England Conservatory and an engineering degree from the Massachusetts Institute of Technology. He was two years younger than Gould, but he also had a remarkable authority and a mastery of detail, and in the year of Gould's retirement from the stage, Columbia hired Kazdin, not yet thirty, to help produce records.

By some accounts, Kazdin could be a stern taskmaster. Helen Epstein's *Music Talks,* for example, contained a scene in which the highly gifted Ruth Laredo spent four and a half hours making forty takes and inserts for Rachmaninoff's thirty-minute *Variations on a Theme by Chopin.* "I'm not sure we're covered on the first bar of the seventh variation," Kazdin said at one point. "I'm certain," Mrs. Laredo answered wearily. "I'm not. Maybe we should hear it," Kazdin repeated. "Look—I'm sure I didn't play any wrong notes," Mrs. Laredo protested. "I'm not talking about wrong notes," Kazdin insisted, "I'm talking about notes that didn't speak. Can we do it again?"

It is hard to imagine Gould accepting that much direction, and Kazdin makes no attempt to imagine it. "Two different cases," he says. "As record producers you have to be in a kind of communion and fit yourself to the artist you're going to work with in the way that will allow that artist to function—you know, the freest, the most comfortably—in what the artist has to do, which is to record an interpretation that is faithful to the artist's conception."

At the same time, though, Kazdin feels that "it's always the responsibility of the producer to try to at least point out technical flaws, and hopefully get them fixed. There have been rare instances where an artist will refuse to fix it. I haven't been so afflicted, but I've seen it in recording sessions. . . . When it came to wrong notes, nobody needed to tell Gould, because the way we recorded was such that he had a chance to listen to everything right on the spot. . . . Occasionally, I do remember— He almost always played from memory, and occasionally he memorized something wrong. Sometimes it was very insignificant, a question of whether there was supposed to be a little *Pause* or not. When I saw that happen, I would always— I figured it was my responsibility at least to mention it once."

Q: You were following with the score then?

A: Oh, *yes.* Oh, *yes.* That question means that as soon as I finish this sentence, I'm going to have to tell you a whole lot of stuff. So if I saw that he was doing something that *may* have been an oversight, you just stated, you know, "Are you aware that my score"— you put it as tactfully as possible—"my score has a *Pause* in bar 42?" And then you could have two kinds of answers: "Yes, I know, but it doesn't make any sense to me, so I'm going—" Fine. Or, "It *does?*" And then that kind of answer yields part A and part B. "My gosh, so it does. Doesn't make sense, so I won't do it." Or, "Oh, my gosh, I never saw that. Sure, I'll start doing it." So you feel the responsibility of at least mentioning it. But from an interpretive point of view, it was your life's blood not to mention anything.

Q: You never would say, "I don't think that's right"?

A: No. That's the way to make that your last session. You could feel it through the soles of your feet—that you just didn't tell him how to play the piece. . . . That's suicide.

Fundamental, says Kazdin, is the score itself. Not only the pianist but also the producer must have studied it, analyzed it, annotated it. It carries notes not just on how a piece should be played but where technical mistakes have occurred, where engineering changes have been made, where future splices should come. "The score becomes the bible of that particular record," Kazdin says. "It becomes, like *the* one document."

After the recording sessions comes the elaborate process of editing, splicing, and mixing. Some musicians leave that part mostly or entirely to the producer. Gould did it all himself. "Gould was the only one who could choose his own takes," Kazdin says. "We supplied him with copies of everything that had taken place, but he was the only one who was able to—because only in his head could reside— You see, the splicing with Gould wasn't just to eliminate wrong notes or fix fluffs of any sort. It also very often was the way that the profile of the piece was established. I mean, the interpretation of the piece emerged sometimes only in the juxtaposition of various takes. This was only in his head. Nobody could second-guess that. So what would happen is, we'd supply him with copies of everything that took place in the recording session, which he would hopefully file away (or sometimes lose). Because the record wasn't always issued with any kind of close proximity to the recording sessions themselves—it could be a matter of years. And he preferred to let years pass. In other words, if the choice was, edit it now and then put it away and wait, or put it away now and then edit it when CBS says they want to release it, he preferred the latter. He felt it gave him perspective, you know. He was too close to it sometimes. Later, he could see more what he wanted to do with a piece, or what he had in fact done with the piece at the recording sessions. So when it came time, he would exhume those tapes, listen to them, put whatever hours into them—and this is rather rare among artists. Few of them go to the trouble he went to."

Gould himself once offered a striking example of how he edited his tapes, not to correct mistakes but to create a completely new version of what he had recorded. The piece in question was the monumental Fugue in A minor from Book I of *The Well-Tempered Clavier*. It was "a contrapuntal obstacle course . . ." Gould recalled in "The Prospects of Recording," "even more difficult to realize on the piano than are most of Bach's fugues, because it consists of four intense voices that determinedly occupy a register in the center octaves of the keyboard—the area of the instrument in which truly independent voice leading is most difficult to establish." Gould recorded eight different versions of this fugue at one session in 1965, then decided that takes 6 and 8 (both made without any breaks or splices) were the best, and about equally good. Then he decided to wait for several weeks before trying to decide between them. When he came to make that decision, he discovered a surprising new element. "It became apparent that both had a defect of which we had been quite unaware in the studio: both were monotonous."

Both versions of this fugue had been played at the same speed (which, let it be noted, was considerably too fast) but in very different styles. "Take 6," Gould wrote, "had treated it in a solemn, legato, rather pompous fashion, while in take 8 the fugue subject was shaped in a prevailingly staccato manner which led to a general impression of skittishness." Without saying who actually made the final decision—one can guess—Gould reported that "it was agreed that neither the Teutonic severity of take 6 nor the unwarranted jubilation of take 8 could be permitted to represent our best thoughts on this fugue," and that "someone noted" that both versions were the same speed, and so "it was decided" to combine them.

The final version begins with the Teutonic severity of take 6, but at the end of the exposition, "the more effervescent character of take 8 was a welcome relief in the episodic modulation with which the center portion of the fugue is concerned." Gould then cut back to the solemnities of take 6 for the recapitulation and conclusion. And he was very proud of all this, not only what had been done but the way it had been done. "What had been achieved," he wrote, "was a performance of this particular fugue far superior to anything that we could at the time have done in the studio. . . . By taking advantage of the post-taping afterthought . . . one can very often transcend the limitations that performance imposes upon the imagination."

This decision sounds as though it had been made rather easily in some conference, dominated by Gould, but much of Kazdin's work with his star performer was more complicated than that. "With him being a resident of Toronto and me being a resident of New York," Kazdin recalls, "we operated on the telephone. I would have my score, he would have his score, and he could read me what he wanted. Splice—"

Q: Like "splice at bar 42"?

A: Sometimes more than that. Something on the fourth 16th of bar 32, on the E flat, we change from take 3 to insert 4 in take 2. And I would duplicate in my score what he had painstakingly worked out in his score. Then I would do the work, and then I would play it to him. I worked out a way of playing him the tapes on the telephone. I made a direct connection on my end, which bypassed the weakest link, which is the microphone. The earphone actually isn't too bad. Certainly there were niceties about the sound that could not be detected this way, but who cared—he *knew* what the tapes sounded like, so we'd go on making improvements, and then he'd approve it, and that would be that.

For all his pride and willfulness and eccentricity, Gould was remarkably adept at chamber music, which requires exactly the opposite characteristics: restraint, diplomacy, modesty, a sense of communion. Gould delighted in accompanying singers in the rather difficult songs of Schoenberg, and he made beautiful recordings of chamber works as diverse as the three Bach sonatas for viola da gamba and harpsichord (with Leonard Rose) and the Brahms Quintet in F minor (with the Montreal String Quartet).

Jaime Laredo had never even met Gould when somebody at Columbia suggested in the mid-1970's that they join forces to record the six Bach violin sonatas. "I was very apprehensive when I went to Toronto," Laredo says of what had become Gould's newest recording operation, "because, you know, one heard all sorts of stories about Glenn Gould, and I had no idea what to expect. And from the very beginning, I was amazed at how well everything went—how nice he was, how amenable he was. It was not the kind of situation where, you know, 'This is my show and we play things my way.' Not at all. It was very much give-and-take. Not one argument or impasse or anything. It was all really enjoyable. The only thing I didn't find enjoyable was working in the middle of the night."

Q: It started at 4 P.M. or something?

A: Oh, how I wish it had started at 4 P.M.! In those days, you know, he used to make all his records in the auditorium at Eaton's department store, so we had to wait for the store to close, which was 9 o'clock. We never really started the first tape until around 11 P.M., and we worked until 4 or 5 in the morning. And I wasn't *used* to that. I had to switch gears every time I went to Toronto and sort of, you know, night is day and day is night.

"We had done a little bit of rehearsing over the phone," Laredo goes on, "and he would actually sing through an entire movement, because he wanted to talk about, you know, are you happy with this tempo, or how does this seem? Knowing Glenn's mind, how brilliant he was, I thought there would be a lot of analysis at the recording session, but we just started playing. And we played over and over again. The way of rehearsing was not taking things apart or analyzing, but we'd play a movement, and we'd play it again, and then we'd play it a third time or a fourth time. If either of us thought, Well, that really wasn't very good, then we didn't even bother listening to the tape. When we did a take that both of us thought, Hey, that was pretty good, then we'd go and we'd listen to that take. Then we'd come back out and do another one.

"I had always thought of Glenn as this intellectual, thinking musician, but until I actually heard him in the studio, I never really appreciated what a fabulous, great pianist he was. You know, when we were—two or three or four in the morning, and we were waiting for Andy to change tapes or whatever—and Glenn would start playing the piano and rambling on. I remember one night he started playing me some Liszt transcriptions, and I tell you, it was absolutely— I mean, I was just—I was sitting there with my mouth open. I'd never heard piano-playing like that. I mean, I'd never heard anybody with a technique like that. The control that he had of the piano, and the sounds were so beautiful. It was absolutely astounding. Absolutely astounding.

"Then we'd go back to Bach. There were some movements of certain sonatas that he felt very strongly about, and he said, 'Oh, it really just must be this way.' But many others he was very willing to, you know—'Oh, you really want to do it a little faster? Or a little slower? Fine.' Whatever. And there were a lot of things that we played quite differently. By differently, I mean that whereas my playing in certain movements tended to be a little bit warmer, a little more romantic, his tended to be a little bit more detached, a little bit more aloof. It was not that we were at odds in any way—it just, you know, the combination really worked. And there was not one unpleasant moment."

The music critics only gradually became aware of Gould's disappearance. In the New York *Times* of December 5, 1965, more than a year after Gould's retirement, under a headline that said, "The Vanishing Glenn Gould," Howard Klein reported, mistakenly, that "there have been no announcements . . . but the 33-year-old Canadian pianist has let it be known that he will appear in public now just often enough to keep in minimal touch with his public." Klein went on to praise the new recording that completed Book I of *The Well-Tempered Clavier,* but still with the familiar references to the famous eccentricities. "As usual he can be heard singing lustily away in the background," Klein wrote. "His engineers must have some time keeping his vocal counterpoint to the minimum they achieve. . . . But give him a really complex fugue, such as the C sharp minor, No. 4, and he is in his element, separating lines with his well-regulated control and putting them back together with master's concentration. And his virtuoso sprint with the B flat (No. 21) is all dash and pianistic bravura. . . ."

The new reviews of Gould's recordings generally demonstrated a somewhat changed attitude on the part of the music critics. Gradually, they began to show an increasing respect and restraint. There are several possible explanations for this. It may have been simply that the critics no longer could see Gould, weaving to and fro on his pygmy piano stool, and so they no longer felt the need to report on his physical behavior. Perhaps they sensed that he would never again appear among them, and that their caustic commentaries might have had something to do with his disappearance. Or perhaps it was simply that many record reviewers remain on a somewhat lower level than concert reviewers, and so they feel less need to assert their own personalities. All of these possibilities, of course, confirmed Gould's own view that the public piano recital was "the last blood sport," and that the mysteries of art could best be fulfilled in the privacy of the recording studio.

Klein returned to Gould's recordings the following year with a glowing account of his Schoenberg. "Gould achieves in his Schoenberg recordings what may be his best recordings to date . . ." he wrote. "Gould plays Schoenberg with love, not just affinity. . . . There is a profound technical, intellectual, and emotional identification with the music." The year after that, Klein somewhat more restrainedly praised Gould's Beethoven, in this case the *Pathétique* and the two sonatas of Opus 14. "Gould, as everyone knows, is an iconoclast," he wrote, "with an enormous talent for music as well as iconoclasm. The direction the talent takes is sometimes questionable. . . . But the talent is still there, as can be heard on this new disk. The Pathetique . . . is given a stormy, quasi-operatic performance that, despite departures from Beethoven's own markings, creates a spontaneous and dramatic effect. . . ."

The ambiguity in some of Gould's Beethoven recordings reflected his views on the composer himself. "I have very ambivalent feelings about Beethoven," he told one interviewer. Though he did not like all of Bach—he made several derogatory remarks about the improvisations in the Chromatic Fantasy and the fugues in the early toccatas, for example—he almost always spoke of the composer with admiration and affection. But there was something about the theatrical, self-important side of Beethoven that irritated him. He liked the bright and cheerful compositions of Beethoven's youth very much—and even the *Moonlight Sonata*—but as Beethoven grew more complex and more grandiose, Gould liked only the enigmatic and eccentric transitional works like the *Les Adieux Sonata* and the F minor Quartet, the Eighth Symphony rather than the Seventh or Ninth. Of the mighty *Hammerklavier Sonata,* by contrast, he wrote that "it is . . . the longest, most inconsiderate, and probably least rewarding piece that Beethoven wrote for the piano."

Gould nourished a special dislike for one of Beethoven's greatest and most popular masterpieces, the *Appassionata*. He criticized it, quite possibly because of its popularity, on rather obscure technical grounds: "The relation of first and second themes, both of them spawned by an arpeggiated triad figure, is somehow out of focus. . . . The development segment is similarly disorganized. . . ." As though aware that such objections would win little support, Gould then attacked the piece on personal and emotional grounds: "At this period of his life Beethoven was not only preoccupied with motivic frugality; he was also preoccupied with being Beethoven. And there is about the 'Appassionata' an egoistic pomposity, a defiant 'let's just see if I can't get away with using that once more' attitude, that on my own private Beethoven poll places this sonata somewhere between the *King Stephen* Overture and the *Wellington's Victory* Symphony."

This diatribe appeared, oddly enough, in Gould's liner notes to his own recording of the despised sonata. And as though to demonstrate what a bad piece it was—and to carry out his theory that there was no point in playing a familiar piece unless it could be played differently—Gould proceeded to play the *Appassionata* rather badly. He adopted a funereal tempo, so that the grand first movement sounded halting and hesitant, broken into fragments, and completely lacking the one thing that the *Appassionata* must have, namely passion.

Yet in the same year in which he recorded this burlesque of the standard Beethoven, 1967, Gould perversely brought forth from relative obscurity one of his oddest triumphs, the Liszt transcription of the Fifth Symphony. In theory, every criticism that Gould had made of the *Appassionata* applied just as well to the Fifth Symphony—was ever a work more imbued with "egoistic pomposity"?—and the clangor of that famous opening theme became all the more clangorous by being transferred from the orchestral strings to the piano. And all this from Liszt, a composer whom Gould never otherwise recorded and never mentioned without a sneer. Yet because Gould now took both Beethoven and Liszt at their own self-valuations, because he played this almost-laughable combination with the utmost seriousness, he brought it off with complete success. It is one of his most admirable recordings.

And because he recognized this success, and recognized the ele-ments of tacit parody in it, he shrewdly avoided in his liner notes the temptation to defend his work. Instead, he wrote a series of par-ody reviews attacking his own performance. "No keyboard version of this work has previously been available in our shops," Sir Hum-phrey Price-Davies is quoted from *The Phonograph*, "and I fancy that the current issue will find little favour in this country. The entire undertaking smacks of that incorrigible American pre-occupation with exuberant gesture. . . ." And in the *Münch'ner Musikologische Gesellschaft*, Prof. Dr. Karlheinz Heinkel begins by quoting from another Gouldian creation, Karlheinz Klopweisser: "Is it not notable that in his poetic-cycle 'Resonance-on-Rhine' *(Resonanz-am-Rhein)* Klopweisser's second stanza concludes the thought: 'With this oft-strident note let man now pause. . . .'"

This is Gouldian wit of a kind that only Gould could love, and yet the best joke is that Gould's silly ethnic parodies served to blur the real joke, which was simply that the celebrated classicist was presenting, completely deadpan, a brilliant performance of Liszt's transcription of that most venerable of romantic clichés, Beethov-en's Fifth Symphony.

After Beethoven, Gould's judgments on composers changed from unusual to bizarre. He denounced Chopin, Schumann, and Liszt, and more mildly dismissed Schubert. Indeed, of all the early Romantics, the only one he admired was Mendelssohn. He derided Verdi and all the Italian operatic masters. Among the early twentieth-century composers, he despised both Debussy and Ravel, and among con-temporaries, he disliked Stravinsky, Bartok, Poulenc. On the other hand, he praised and recorded Oscar Morawetz, Jacques Hétu, and István Anhalt, Canadians all. Of all composers of all times, he insisted his favorite was Orlando Gibbons.

The strangest of all these judgments was Gould's lifelong dislike and disapproval of Mozart. He enjoyed telling interviewers that Mozart was "a bad composer," and that he had "died too late rather than too early." His reasoning for that uncharacteristically heartless declaration was that Mozart's best works were those of his early twenties, that what Gould "hated" were the later masterpieces like the G minor symphony and *The Magic Flute,* and that if Mozart had lived to threescore years and ten, he "would have turned into a sort of cross between Weber and Spohr." When challenged on such denunciations, Gould would offer a series of unconvincing rationalizations to the effect that Mozart's music was "hedonistic" (one of Gould's pet pejoratives), or that Mozart had failed to conform to Gould's dictum that all piano music should be contrapuntal. Yet it is not too difficult to see in all these accusations an echo of a childish desire to shock the grownups, and perhaps a touch of envy toward music's most celebrated child prodigy.

"Were you always out of sympathy with Mozart, even in your student days?" asked Bruno Monsaingeon, a cherubic French violinist who had become interested in televised musical interviews and would become a major collaborator in Gould's later video work. Their "interviews," after some preliminary discussions, were generally written out in advance by Gould, questions as well as answers.

"As far back as I can remember . . ." Gould replied.

"But, as a student, you must have had to learn to play these works. . . . And you always disliked them?"

"What I felt at the time, I think, was dismay. I simply couldn't understand how my teachers, and other presumably sane adults of my acquaintance, could count these pieces among the great musical treasures of Western man."

In 1961, Gould recorded one of Mozart's greatest concerti, the 24th in C minor, K. 491, with the CBC Symphony Orchestra under Walter Susskind, "as sort of an experiment." Or, as he told another interviewer, Jonathan Cott, "because it's the only one that I sort of halfway like." It was a strong and stirring performance, and we can easily ignore Gould's compulsion to "improve" the score with various minor revisions, extra chords, trills, and arpeggiations. But after he had recorded this masterpiece, Gould also felt compelled to use it as the centerpiece of the TV show that he titled "How Mozart Became a Bad Composer."

This began with one of Gould's attempts to appear worldly and *au courant*. He flippantly described Mozart as someone "who could knock out a divertimento the way an accounts [sic] executive dispatches an inter-office memo. But in a way, that's his problem. Too many of his works sound like inter-office memos. . . . Like an executive holding forth upon the ramifications of a subject no one in the

front office is much concerned with anyway. 'Yeah, well, Harry, as I see it, J.B. has got this thing about replacing the water cooler. . . .'"
And so on.

From this nadir, Gould went on to make a number of interesting, if misguided, points. Starting with his view that Mozart's brilliant use of eighteenth-century conventions represented "an appalling collection of clichés," Gould went on to inquire how this had happened, how "those prodigious gifts which made Mozart as a young man the toast of Europe [had been] reduced in the end to skillful self-parody," how everything had finally succumbed to "that jaded, world-weary approach which beset Mozart in his later years." Gould's conclusion was that Mozart's "decline can be blamed on what should have been his greatest natural asset—a fantastic facility for improvisation." Public improvisation was a required skill among the musicians of Mozart's time (as among jazz musicians of our own time), but Gould naturally found this abhorrent. Improvisation, he wrote, is "pretty well limited to the sort of music-making that results from split-second reaction, and it must rely heavily on devices that have already secured a place in the mainstream of musical activity." In other words, clichés.

This view of Mozart led Gould on into an odd inquiry as to "whether the composer is, in fact, really necessary." We had already entered, after all, the age of aleatory art, in which John Cage wrote down whatever notes he received from the *I Ching*, and Jackson Pollock sprayed paint in all directions, and the devotees of "mixed media" danced under various combinations of flashing lights. The reigning theory was that the audience's reaction to a work of art was part of the art itself. Gould, who liked to imagine a future age when listeners would splice together different versions of some symphony to suit their own tastes, approved of any efforts "to draw the audience into the making of a work of art," but as an artist who privately enjoyed his own remarkable gifts as an improviser, Gould saw hidden dangers that others might never have noticed. "Not least among those dangers may be the hedonistic pursuit of improvisation as a way of life," he wrote. "And that's why I think we can learn from Mozart, why his reliance in his late works on a facility for improvisation provides a real object lesson for the Twentieth Century."

One of the listeners to this broadcast in 1968 was an Amherst professor who reported Gould's views to B. H. Haggin, the pedantic but respected music critic for *The New Republic* ("H. B. Haggle" was to become Gould's private name for him). Haggin, in turn, reported the Amherst professor's account back to Gould: " 'He'd play something marvelous from K. 491 and say "Nothing here. Arid. Mechanical clichés like inter-office memos." ' " Haggin sent Gould an article he had written about Mozart in the *Sewanee Review* and solemnly asked him "if you would be kind enough to mark on it any passages I refer to that you consider to be mechanical clichés like inter-office memos. . . . And while you are at it, would you add bar references to the passages in K. 491 that you so characterized in your television talk?"

Haggin had admired some of Gould's early recordings of Bach, but he believed strongly that a pianist had a duty to follow whatever instructions a composer had left for the performance of his music. Now, while he challenged Gould to document his personal attacks on Mozart, he also wanted to know why Gould so frequently ignored Mozart's instructions in his new recording of the first five Mozart sonatas. "I was of course surprised by your treatment of the opening statement of the first movement of K. 282," Haggin wrote with the most courtly pretense that he and Gould were talking the same language. "I looked at my *Urtext* edition, and found that the specified tempo was Adagio, and that the markings indicated that the statement was to be played legato. I would appreciate your telling me your reasons for making the tempo Andantino—not to say Allegretto—and playing the statement with a light non-legato touch, so that instead of the serious and even poignant *espressivo* that Mozart seems to have intended, the effect is *scherzando*. And concerning the passages after the opening statement, in K. 282's first movement, I have the same question as I asked about the Adagio of K. 280: what are your reasons for giving the left hand's mere accompaniment figuration without melodic significance emphasis equal to, and even greater than, that of the melody? These are serious questions, to which I hope you will give me serious answers."

Gould did answer seriously and even a bit defensively. He suggested that the broadcast had "suffered to a degree from that lack of distance and perspective which can help a program realize its own structural rhythm." But he added that "much (most?) of what I said

I meant, and I was careful I think to confine the less appreciative remarks to Mozart's concerto writing and to be (relatively) enthusiastic about the sonata output." As for his habit of playing Mozart accompaniments in a contrapuntal relationship to the melodies ("adding vitamins to the music," Gould once called this), he stood his ground: "The whole idea of a melodic attribute as distinguished from the component parts of a harmonic environment has always seemed to me anti-structural and even, dare I say it, undemocratic. . . . The more singable, likeable and memorable the tune one encounters the less likely it is that that particular melodic strain will require any special emphasis. . . ." But on the more important question of why Gould felt himself free to change or ignore what Mozart had actually written, the pianist offered no answer.

Nearly ten years later, Gould wrote somewhat differently about this "rather rocky relationship" with Haggin. There had been problems as early as 1965, when *High Fidelity* wanted to accompany Gould's article on "The Prospects of Recording" with some brief comments from other authorities. One of those authorities had been Haggin, who then charged that his comment had been taken out of context and distorted. Both Gould and the editors of *High Fidelity* apologized profusely. On the subject of Mozart, though, Gould now reported to a friend that Haggin "wrote essay-length letters, complete with manuscript enclosures, showing how things *should* be phrased, dynamically graded, etc. I seem to recall also that he expressed his deep concern about my fondness for inner-voice manipulation and my indifference, as he saw it, toward melodic invention. These later letters, of course, went unanswered. . . ."

It remains something of a mystery why Gould should have undertaken to record the complete sonatas of a composer he disliked, disapproved of, and, as a necessary consequence, didn't understand. He did like the early sonatas, the most inconsequential ones. "These are glorious pieces," he wrote, "lean, fastidious, and possessed of that infallible tonal homing instinct with which the young Mozart was so generously endowed." He even wrote to Haggin, after the first volume was issued, that "the sonata project in general has been a joyous task." And he did have a grand time with those early sonatas. He played them all briskly—a bit too briskly—but with enthusiasm and affection.

As Mozart matured and his sonatas became more complex, however, Gould seemed more and more determined, as with the later Beethoven sonatas, to deconstruct them. Some, like the A minor (K. 310) and the C major (K. 330), he played at blazing speed, which tended to reduce them to empty glitter. And the tone here was everything that Mozart should not be: cold, hard, distant, unfeeling. Gould's attitude seemed to be not just indifference or even dislike but actual contempt.* "The later sonatas I do *not* like," Gould later said to an interviewer, Tim Page. "I find them intolerable, loaded with quasitheatrical conceit, and I can certainly say that I went about recording a piece like the Sonata in B-flat major, K. 570, with no conviction whatsoever. The honest thing to do would have been to skip those works entirely, but the cycle had to be completed."

Some of these sonatas, Gould simply rewrote. The celebrated A major (K. 331), for example, begins with a theme and variations, *andante grazioso*. Gould played it about as slowly as is humanly possible ("so maddeningly slowly that I had to get everyone's hackles aroused," as he told one interviewer, Humphrey Burton), because he had adopted a theory that, regardless of what Mozart wrote, each variation should be faster than the preceding one. So when he came to the penultimate fifth variation, which Mozart, with his own sense of contrasts, marked *adagio,* Gould undertook what he called "a really perverse thing" and played it *allegro.*

"Well, the idea behind that performance," Gould said in his interview with Monsaingeon, "was that, since the first movement is a nocturne-cum-minuet rather than a slow movement, and since the package is rounded off by that curious bit of seragliolike exotica [he meant the famous concluding *Rondo alla turca*], one is dealing with an unusual structure, and virtually all of the sonata-allegro conventions can be set aside. . . . I admit that my realization of the first movement is somewhat idiosyncratic."

Monsaingeon: It certainly is. . . . Did you assume that the melody was so well known that it did not need to be heard again?

Gould: Something like that, yes. I wanted—if I can invoke the name of Webern once more—to subject it to a Webern-like scru-

---

*On a much smaller scale, Gould had similar problems with Scarlatti, whom he also didn't understand or like or play well.

tiny in which its basic elements would be isolated from each other and the continuity of the theme deliberately undermined. The idea was that each successive variation would contribute to the restoration of that continuity and, in the absorption of that task, would be less visible as an ornamental, decorative element.

And as for the extremely slow pace of the concluding rondo, Gould added, "it seemed important to establish a solid, maybe even stolid, tempo, partly because, to my knowledge, anyway, nobody had played it like that before. . . ."

In his conversations with Jonathan Cott, Gould was more accusatory, and even more paradoxical. "I had more fun with those things," he said of the Mozart sonatas, "than anything I've ever done, practically, mainly because I really don't like Mozart as a composer." Gould did not seem to realize that his dislike was perfectly evident in the recordings, and that this dislike would prevent a listener from enjoying the performance. What pleasure can there be, after all, in seeing or hearing someone express his dislike for a great artist?

There is yet another mystery here: Did Gould play Mozart so glibly and harshly because he disliked it, or did he dislike it because he mistakenly thought that what he heard in his inner ear was what Mozart had intended? Did he hear the Platonic ideal of a Mozart sonata only in the unfeeling tones that he himself brought to Mozart's heartfelt music? Gould avoided such questions. He preferred to veer off into a simplistic differentiation between early and late Mozart, and he reasserted his notion that Mozart's growth and maturity was one long decline. "I love the early sonatas—I love the early Mozart, period," he said to Cott. "I'm very fond of that period when he was either emulating Haydn or Carl Philipp Emanuel Bach but had not yet found himself. The moment he did find himself, as conventional wisdom would have it, at the age of eighteen or nineteen or twenty, I stop being so interested in him, because what he discovered was primarily a theatrical gift which he applied ever after not only to his operas but to his instrumental works as well, and given the rather giddy hedonism of eighteenth-century theater, that sort of thing doesn't interest me at all."

From there on, Gould simply became abusive. Declaring his preference for the sonatas of Haydn (of which, necessarily, he made a far better recording toward the end of his life), he said, "One never gets the feeling that any two are cut from the same cookie stamp. I do get that feeling in Mozart, I'm afraid. I get the feeling that once he hit his stride, they're *all* cut from the same cookie stamp." And of Mozart's development sections: "Mozart never really did learn to write a development section, because, of course, you don't have to write a development section unless you've got something to develop." And finally, of the whole recording project: "I had fun with it precisely because you can play the damn things in the most deliciously straightforward manner, never yielding at a cadence . . . just going straight through to the end. . . . Now, the horror and the outcry that resulted from my Mozart recordings—I think it was the critic Martin Mayer who said about Volume 2: 'Finally, this is madness!' or something to that effect—is to me terribly funny, because all the critics are really responding to is a denial of a certain set of expectations that have been built into their hearing processes."

To claim amusement at being criticized is a fairly standard defense, but the "fun" was rather joyless. "Laughter is supposed to keep a man young," as Ring Lardner wrote in *Symptoms of Being 35,* "but if its forced laughter it works the opp." And Mayer was by no means alone in his condemnation of Gould's Mozart recordings. "Entering the Mozart lists once more, Glenn Gould delivers Volume Two of the Piano Sonatas . . ." Donal Henahan wrote in the New York *Times* in July of 1969, "with performances of expectably brilliant pianism. Brilliant, and yet disconcerting. Gould seems to see these sonatas . . . as technical challenges, which they seldom are in normal performance. And since the Canadian can perhaps play more notes in less time than anyone alive, the results here can be distressing. . . . Even when one grows more or less used to runaway tempos and loses himself in admiration at Gould's fantastic ability to hold a pulse rock-firm while bringing out every detail of embroidery, the voice of Mozart is hard to hear. . . . Gould misses the aristocratic note that Mozart's sonatas strike. . . ."

Worse reviews were to come. We are still among the early sonatas, which Gould said he loved, and if his glittering performances do not really demonstrate love, they do demonstrate interest and respect, which is more than these boyish works usually receive. And sometimes Gould did reach a level far beyond that. His version of the Sonata in D major (K. 311), for example, is completely admirable, beautiful, and full of verve. Henahan at the *Times* remained quite respectful through the third Mozart album in 1972. "Gould is at his mercurial best in these four Mozart sonatas . . ." he wrote, "flinging himself into the pieces with evident (sometimes audible) glee. It is impossible not to be infected by his joy in playing this music, even if one's own idea of Mozart is less headlong and clipped in phrase."

In the following year, 1973, the *Times'* coverage of the Gould/ Mozart recordings fell into the hands of Peter G. Davis, who was considerably less sympathetic to Volume IV than Henahan had been to its predecessors. Davis was also reviewing Gould recordings of Beethoven and Hindemith, but he wrote that "the loudest anathemas will undoubtedly be reserved for the Mozart record, the fourth in an ongoing project. . . . One critic even went so far as to brand the previous disk in this series as 'the most loathsome record ever made.' The performances of Sonatas K. 331, K. 533, K. 545 and the D Minor Fantasy here will not make this sensitive soul any happier. They don't make me very happy either. It is very difficult to see what Gould is out to prove, unless the rumor that he actually hates this music is true. Tempos are painfully slow, the clipped, détaché articulation violates phrase structure (and many of Mozart's specific markings). . . . It all conjures up an image of a tremendously precocious but very nasty little boy trying to put one over on his piano teacher."

Nobody was more surprised by Gould's decision to record the complete Mozart sonatas than Andy Kazdin, his producer at Columbia. But Kazdin did not question the plan. "You know the joke—" Kazdin says. "'Where does your pet gorilla sleep?' 'Anywhere he wants.' It was, like, 'What's he going to record next?' 'Whatever he feels like.' Columbia was very enlightened that way. Basically, whatever he would do, they would accept. I mean, they knew they had something rather unique, and they would just sort of let him go."

Columbia indulged Gould even to the extent of moving the whole recording process from New York to Toronto. Ever since Gould had retired from the concert tours in 1964, he had chafed at the need to travel to taping sessions in New York about twenty times every year. He had not flown since 1962, and the train service all across the United States was becoming increasingly erratic, and the drive between Toronto and New York took at least ten boring hours each way. Then there was the nuisance and expense of shipping his piano to and fro, and of clearing it through customs each time.

Gould liked the acoustics in Toronto's Eaton Auditorium at least as well as those in any hall in New York, and so he began urging Columbia to let him make his recordings there. He was even willing to buy all his own equipment. "We came up with the plan that he would buy anything I told him to buy, which would be of a quality equivalent to what he could have used in New York," Kazdin says. "He would then charge back to CBS exactly the same hourly rates that our own engineering department charged the Masterworks department." Gould was boyishly proud of his new machinery. "It includes," he wrote to Ronald Wilford, who had become his manager after his retirement from the stage, "a Studer 8-track, 2 Ampex AG 440s, U87 microphones, matched sets of KLH speakers in my office and at Eaton auditorium, an extremely efficient cue-speaker system whereby the 'green room' is connected to the stage and insert takes are provided with the proper feeds from backstage. . . ." And so, from 1971 on, instead of Gould trekking to New York twice a month, Andy Kazdin made the trek to Toronto. "I was never crazy about flying either," says Kazdin.

As Gould acquired more and more control over his recordings, he seemed to work more and more slowly, more and more determined to achieve his own version of perfection, no matter what the cost. "I am by no means a fast worker in the studio," he wrote to Wilford in 1973. "A good session will consist of 2½ to 3 minutes per recording hour and, consequently, assuming the average record to include 50 minutes of recorded material, the best figure I can arrive at would be approximately 18 recording hours per album. . . ." (Gould's later radio work became comparably elaborate. William Littler of the *Star* noted that Gould had boasted of making 131 edits in a speech of 2 minutes and 43 seconds in his show on Richard Strauss, "about one edit per second. And you wonder why his documentaries take hundreds of hours to produce.")

And as Gould became more and more a media producer, he found more and more uses for a burly assistant named Ray Roberts. "It happened by a fluke," Roberts recalls over a pot of tea at the Windsor Arms Hotel in Toronto. "Glenn was recording in the old Eaton's Auditorium, and he had a whole lot of technical problems. An old friend of mine, Lorne Tulk, was doing the setups for him, and he asked me to just assist him on one particular occasion, and Glenn and I started talking, just in a casual way, and it became a regular occasion. This was in about 1970, when I was a salesman for Coca-Cola.

"Glenn had continual problems with his cars, and I started giving him advice on how to keep them running. I'm not a musician in any way, but I could make sure that things happened. We got equipment, we got transport, all of that, okay? I was a glorified gofer. But he also used me as a sounding board, to bounce ideas off. What do you think of X? Okay? He was very good to me, financially and in a lot of other ways. So that was fine."

Moving the recording sessions to Toronto brought an unusual dividend: Kazdin was now able to do the engineering work himself. As long as Gould recorded in New York, union regulations governed the editing process. "The physical act of splicing together tapes had to be done by a union engineer," Kazdin says. "There were some engineers who could read music, most often could not, and they had to work under the direction of the producer." Kazdin understandably felt that he could do all this work better himself. "When one does it oneself, there's a certain efficiency," he says. "It can be done faster than having to communicate to someone who, even if he's perfect, *some* part of the time there'll be a communications failure, and he won't understand, and you'll have to go back and do something again." But the union rules were the rules, and the rules forbade producers to work on tapes. "It was unheard of to even think about it," Kazdin says. "I couldn't even touch the tapes."

The union's jurisdiction did not extend to Toronto, however, and on anything recorded there, Kazdin became free to edit as he pleased, or as Gould pleased. "Then it occurred to me that there was absolutely no way they could tell whether I did it in Toronto or in my basement at home," he says, " and so in fact I did it there." And so it came to pass that the fourth volume of the Mozart sonatas included a credit for engineering by Kent Warden. "Warden I see as an anagram for Andrew," says Kazdin, "and Kent is a contraction of my middle name and my last name. I still am amused talking about this. My real masterpiece was the name for the editor, which was a complete anagram for all three of my names, which was Frank Dean Dennowitz."

Q: What is your middle name?

A: Fenton. So if you take Andrew Fenton Kazdin, you can unscramble that and come out with Frank Dean Dennowitz. Glenn, of course, knew all of this.

And how could Gould object to Kazdin's perhaps unintentional parody of Gould's schizophrenic love of alternate identities? How could the creator of Frank Dean Dennowitz receive anything but a wave of recognition from the creator of Herbert von Hochmeister (and, in future years, Teddy Slotz of New York, Sir Nigel Twitt-Thornwaite of London, and all the others)?

Kazdin, who is proud of his abilities, also gets satisfaction from the fact that he produced more than forty recordings by the head-strong Glenn Gould. "I've tried to figure out how it is that we made it work for fifteen years," he says, "and it must have been the fact that I was—to the extent that any human being can—just completely sublimating any form of ego. Just not intruding myself. Just knowing that my contribution to his record was going to be on the technical side, and that was fine. And if he was happy, then I was happy, and we were turning out very good records. I don't think two people can work together for that long without, you know, somewhere along the line, we must have bumped up against each other. I mean, there must have been some friction over maybe something foolish, you know, but it had nothing to do with the records. I mean, the facts speak for themselves."

Are we perhaps once again bumping up against something? Bumping up against memories of a Gould who was more than just eccentric? Kazdin is not surprised or thrown off balance by the suggestion. "Well, that's a good question because you're even asking it," he says. "You've already made an assumption in the asking of it. You want to know if his eccentricities went beyond— If you want to know how much your children have grown, you won't know as well as Uncle Fred, who sees them every three months. When you were thrown together with Glenn with such frequency, as I was in those years, as each new little thing came up, it was seemingly insignificant compared to what we had before. Nothing ever seemed to be terribly significant or important, and then, like the emperor's new clothes, some guy would walk in, and I'd be talking in a rather casual way, and I'd mention this or that, and he'd say, 'You mean he does that? And he does that? He sounds crazy!' And I'd say, 'No, no, no, no, no. He's just—' And then you'd start to think. You'd start to add up those things which snuck up on you, little by little, and you'd get into his way of working and thinking and being. So it's not a matter of whether I thought any of the things exceeded eccentricity, it's whether— Sometimes, I was unable to notice even the eccentricities, which got sort of caught up in the momentum of whatever the project was. The project would be his life, and you'd get caught up with him, and everything was supremely rationalized. He could rationalize anything, anything, better than anyone I've ever met in my life."

Q: That's also sometimes a mark of crazy people. Their most extreme crazinesses always make perfect sense to them. I'm not saying he was crazy, I'm just asking you about him.

A: You'll find people who are positive he was crazy, but I don't feel that I'm qualified, from a medical, psychological standpoint, to say when one crosses the line. I don't know. Eccentric was no question. Whatever that means. I mean that he had modes of behavior that seemed to defy logic but seemed to work for him, and he was happy, so you'd stand back and give him a little extra room. But while all that was going on, there was a supremely rational—I'm not talking about the artistic side, and I'm not talking about rationalizing—I'm saying there was a very rational person in there, who was very intelligent on many subjects besides music—could respond to logic, which many artists can't—and it was hard to believe that that person could be crossing the line. But he might have been. I didn't know then, and I don't know now. I'm sure there were many strange things that paraded under the banner of eccentricity. And, you know, you just let them go. I mean, in its own joky way, what I said to you how many minutes ago—"Where does your pet gorilla sleep?" "Anywhere he wants." He was a very valuable property to the record company, but he was—he was certainly unique in many ways.

About twenty years after Bach finished the complete and self-contained twenty-four preludes and fugues of *The Well-Tempered Clavier*, he mysteriously started all over again and wrote in the same sequence of major and minor semitones the even more complex and elaborate and beautiful preludes and fugues that constitute what we now know as Book II of the same *Well-Tempered Clavier*. "I have just this week finished Volume I of the W.T.C., thank goodness," Gould wrote to an admirer in August of 1965, "and now I have little choice but to proceed onward into Book II."

Once again, some of his performances were miraculous, some peculiar, some dutiful. But no critic's commentary could provide so interesting a view of what was going on in Gould's mind as did Gould's own analysis, on a subsequent television show with Bruno Monsaingeon, of one fugue he particularly loved. Gould character- istically began by playing a rather hackneyed early fugue and denouncing what he described as the standard view that "because Bach turned out to be, arguably, the greatest craftsman of all time, he started out that way and produced masterpieces in his playpen, and *he did not*." That declaration led Gould, the great believer in rigorous counterpoint, into a rather emotional testimonial: "What he had, right from the earliest days, was the ability to write music of *incredible* intensity and pathos. The kind of recitatives that you get in the toccatas, even the earliest ones, could virtually have gone into the *Matthew Passion*—I mean, they're *extraordinary* things. But he did *not* have the ability to integrate that intensity with a real fugal craft until he was, I think, close to forty."

Monsaingeon's main function was to serve as straight man in these prewritten conversations. "Well, is there an example of inte- gration that you could give us now?" he inquired.

"How about the—um—" Gould paused as though thinking about various alternatives, "the E major fugue from the second volume of *The Well-Tempered Clavier*?"

Despite Gould's theatrics, this is a splendid fugue, a brief and rather underestimated fugue, and Gould had thought deeply about it, and loved it passionately, and that all becomes clear in his presen- tation. These complementary elements are impossible to reproduce away from the television set, because Gould keeeps playing while he talks, and so his extremely technical analysis makes sense because he keeps illustrating what he is intently describing. And he keeps singing too, not in the strangulated tones of a concert virtuoso trying to suppress his instincts but in the full-throated enthusiasm of someone trying to express more contrapuntal voices than any piano can.

So imagine that you can see him playing and singing his way through the exposition of this stately and rather liturgical four-part fugue—he is wearing horn-rimmed glasses and one of his dark blue Viyella shirts, unbuttoned at the cuffs—and then listen to him start talking as he plays. "You know, it isn't exactly the world's most original thought," he says, "but what a choral piece this would have made! It's conceived vocally."

"Yes, yes," says the dutiful Monsaingeon.

"And maybe because he wasn't trying to cater to an instrument in any way," says Gould, still playing the exposition, "there's the sense that there isn't a wasted note, there isn't an artificial or superficial note. Everything is material to the material, everything absolutely grows out of the original subject, out of the original six notes which started it all [he plays that]. Even the first countertheme does [plays and sings that], because that countertheme is just the transposition of the subject [sings and plays it] to [sings and plays that] with a little bit of ornamentation."

Now things get more complicated. The first episode after the exposition is a stretto, that is, the theme is stated in one voice, and then, before that statement is finished, another voice echoes it, so that it moves in counterpoint to itself. This is, Gould says, "one of the first of those wonderfully compact, convoluted—in the best sense of the word—stretto overlaps. [He plays and sings it without comment for a while.] Only in this one, the countertheme gets its own stretto as well."

"The two ideas seem to develop in tandem," Monsaingeon offers.

"Exactly," Gould says. "And in tandem or otherwise, they move—well, one can't say they modulate together [continues playing], but they sort of bump into [laughs] the submediant key, C-sharp minor, thusly. And when he gets there, he does something rather cute. He takes the original subject and the original answer, starting on the original notes which they had started on, E and B respectively, and—transforms them, reharmonizes them, and finds a way of giving them a sort of tonal visa to pass through C-sharp minor. . . ."

It is possible that other pianists perform this brief fugue over an equally dense subtext of analysis, but it is hard to believe that many of them ever see so much in it as Gould saw, and amiably explained while he played. "Then they leave the orbit of C-sharp minor, if they were ever in fact in it," he observes, "and move, to the same extent that they were in C sharp, toward F-sharp minor. In which key, he does something very nice." Nice but very complex. Gould stops playing for a moment as he starts explaining. "He takes the theme, deprives it of the one expressive interval it had, the minor third [he plays that], and fills it in, as one would sing it in a scale [sings and plays], then makes the alto comment on that, also sort of filling in the pattern [plays and sings]. Except that in the alto, he starts to play around with the modes and goes up one way [plays a rising scale] and comes back down another. *Then* he adds a new countertheme in the bass [plays and sings], also based on the original idea, also expanding it to the interval of a fifth, and then puts *that* into a canon, in the tenor, just in case anybody'd missed the point. [He plays and sings that.] Then we leave F-sharp minor [still playing] by the same submediant C-sharp minor exit.

"Then you get another one of those glorious stretto occasions, as in the second sentence of the piece. And then, he does something very, very interesting—forgive me—after that stretto, for the first time, he introduces six diatonic notes in a row. Which doesn't seem like doing anything very special, but up till then, every motive that he's used has either been delineated by a fourth [he demonstrates] or by a fifth, as in the case of the countersubject [demonstrates]. He suddenly adds six notes successively [playing the fugue again now], then, in canon, seven [playing and singing], as though he were celebrating the ending that *seems* to be close by."

Monsaingeon has been allowing all this to run on far beyond the comprehension of anyone but a graduate student in harmonic analysis because he realizes that Gould is vividly demonstrating how his own mind works. This is where Gould lives, the interior citadel from which he observes a world unlike anything that anyone else sees or knows.

The "seeming" approach to the end of the fugue was, of course, only a seeming approach. There is still a coda to be explored and analyzed, and Gould continues full of enthusiasm. "So we have first the six-note thing, the seven-note extension, the eight-note extension," he says, "and—it's rudimentary material, but it makes for one of the most gloriously fulfilled codas he ever wrote, I think."

Monsaingeon is ready with his cue: "What about playing the whole fugue now?" Gould politely agrees that it is time to shift from analysis to performance. "One masterpiece coming up," he says. Then he begins to play.

VIII

The Composer

Gould had often declared that the main purpose in his retirement from the concert stage was to gain time to compose music of his own. "I saw myself as a sort of musical Renaissance Man, capable of doing many things," he told one interviewer. "I obviously wanted to be a composer. I still do." One can hear in such a declaration a certain hunger for a fame that would last. In no other art is there such a split between the immediate celebrity of the performer and the rewards that posterity grants to a great composer. Can we imagine a system in which a writer could become famous only by offering public readings of other men's works? Or a painter by staging slide shows? And what musicians do we remember from the past, some blazing piano virtuoso like Thalberg or Tausig (or Gould) or some relatively obscure creator like Franz Schubert? Yet it is Horowitz and not Elliott Carter who inspires people to stand in line all night outside Carnegie Hall.

To the young Gould, the idea of actually being a composer, of doing what Bach and Beethoven had done, was probably at least as important as the desire to compose something. "It's not that he wanted to become a composer—he wanted to become immortal," says Harvey Olnick. "Composition was a way of becoming more immortal." In "Glenn Gould's Toronto," the pianist very candidly recalled his youthful yearning to have his creations make an impression on the world. Before actually writing any music, he said, he would create elaborate title pages, which "were rather interesting because along with the name of the author in very large print there was also a totally fictitious publishing firm (always a different one) which was usually located in El Alamein or Murmansk or someplace I considered equally exotic."

Aside from a number of songs, which his mother had encouraged him to write ever since his childhood, Gould's boyhood compositions were mostly conservatory assignments. "The manuscript remnants of junior masterpieces occupy many drawers in my home," he later wrote. "They are tokens of that swift moving parade of enthusiasms which constitute the student life and they exhibit an attempt at every style from Palestrina (which was done to please my teachers) to Webern (which was done to annoy them). There were a great many quite professionally polished fughettas among them (I was good at fughettas, it was sort of like solving a jigsaw puzzle . . .)."

The first composition that actually got finished and performed was a suite of incidental music that the Malvern Dramatic Society asked Gould to write for a school production of Shakespeare's *Twelfth Night*. He was still only sixteen, but he had already performed Beethoven's Fourth Concerto, and he lived at such a level of publicity that the Toronto *Telegram* reported in February of 1949 that his music for *Twelfth Night* was "almost completed but not written down." This was not really incidental music in the traditional sense of accompaniment to a play but rather a piano suite that Gould played during intermission at the performance later that month. It contained four parts entitled "Regal Atmosphere," "Elizabethan Gaiety," "Whimsical Nonsense," and "Nocturne." Everybody was appropriately impressed.

As Gould's concert career became more and more complex, he often spoke of composing pieces that may have existed largely as sketches, or largely in his own imagination, a string trio that broke off after four pages, a clarinet sonata that no one ever seems to have heard. Early in 1950, he said he had written a piano sonata in the style of Schoenberg. The sonata was never finished, but there still survives a penciled manuscript entitled "5 Short Piano Pieces" and dated "1951–2." The piano pieces are each only about twenty bars long and resolutely written in the twelve-tone method, the resolute work of a resolute student.

At about this same time, Gould suddenly moved to a somewhat higher level by composing an atonal sonata for bassoon and piano.

Why the bassoon, that ungainly instrument that is so often used for comic or weird effects (e.g., the opening of Stravinsky's *Rite of Spring*)? One theory is that Gould's admiration for Alban Berg had led him to explore the possibilities inherent in Berg's Four Pieces for clarinet and piano; another is that his admiration for Hindemith led him to Hindemith's somewhat didactic but interesting series of sonatas for the flute, the horn, the oboe, the clarinet, and even the bassoon. Or perhaps it was simply that one of Gould's friends at the conservatory was a bassoonist.

Nicholas Kilburn is still a bassoonist. A taut, muscular man with a fierce white moustache, he makes his living with the Toronto Symphony Orchestra. He was once a pianist, but after he met and heard the young Gould—they were both then twelve—he decided to take up some other instrument. The bassoon seemed a good, remote choice, and so he eventually found himself giving a joint recital with the famous Glenn Gould. Now they were both nineteen. "The concert was very funny," Kilburn recalls, over a Greek salad in a restaurant across the street from the Toronto Symphony's rehearsal. "We walked out on the stage, and I looked at the audience, and I thought, What in heaven's name is going on? This room, the concert hall at the Royal Conservatory, was jammed to the rafters. But it wasn't jammed with my peers; it was jammed with all the intelligentsia, the musical intelligentsia of Toronto. Anybody who was anybody was there at that concert. I was staggered. . . .

"We did the Hindemith sonata, and the other one was Glenn's. How well it went, I don't recall. I do recall this—that the bow tie I was wearing was a clip-on. I'd never worn a bow tie in my life, and every time L took a breath, the clip-on bow tie would unclip, so I kept attempting to do the thing up. And finally, in a dudgeon, I just took it off and put it on the music stand. But it fell on the floor, and it looked to everyone as though I had just thrown it down.

"But the silliest thing of all was— You know, moisture collects in the crook of the bassoon, and the usual practice is that you remove the reed, and you blow into the crook to get the water past the S, or you take it off and you shake it. Well, I was so damn nervous that I took the crook with the reed in it, and I shook it. And the reed flew off, and flew back into the pipes of the organ at the back of the stage. Glenn was playing, and I hadn't another reed that

I could play. I had to retrieve that one. So I stood up, and Glenn looked up at me, wondering what in heaven's name I was doing. And as I went by him, I said, 'Vamp till ready.' That's a jazzer's term that says, 'Just keep going with that refrain until I get myself reorganized here, and we'll carry on.' Glenn didn't know what the hell I was talking about. I went back and picked up the reed, dusted it off, put it back on the bassoon, and we carried on with the performance. The poor chap didn't— Here was his great Toronto debut as a composer, and he's got some clown on the bassoon who's never played in public before."

Q: What did you finally think of the sonata? Is it a good piece?

A: Well, I've never played it again.

Q: Did you want to?

A: Not particularly. . . . I think Glenn was seeking something that he didn't quite achieve. Whatever it was. In fact, he was never happy with that bassoon sonata. Of course, he was very rarely happy with anything he wrote. After we'd finished performing the work, he insisted that it never be performed again. And any copies that I had, he wanted back. And the signature copy that I had, he destroyed.*

And then, almost out of nowhere, came a remarkable string quartet in F minor.† The most remarkable thing about it is that it is very beautiful. The disciple of Schoenbergian atonalism had suddenly regressed to an earlier Viennese tradition, that of Richard Strauss, Mahler, and particularly Bruckner, whose gorgeous Quintet in F major Gould had recently discovered.

Over a sustained pedal point on a low F, Gould made the second violin declaim a majestic four-note theme on which he constructed his entire quartet. (Perhaps unconsciously, Gould wrote a theme very similar to that of Beethoven's *Grosse Fuge* and also to the opening cello line in the A minor Quartet, Opus 132.) "This figure," Gould later wrote, "undergoes every adventure and enticement that

---

*Informed that a copy of the score and a recording still exist in the Gould archives, Kilburn said, "Well, that's his father's doing . . . part of this *history* that Bert was in the process of achieving."

†F minor was the key that expressed his own personality, according to one of the many such games that Gould liked to play. Asked by an interviewer to explain this statement, Gould said that F minor was "halfway between complex and stable, between upright and lascivious, between gray and highly tinted. . . . There is a certain obliqueness."

my technique would allow. All of the main sections of the work present themes which owe their derivation to this motive, however whimsically and fancifully its contours are altered in the progress of the work. . . . I was really attempting a giant romantic canvas to be composed of many minute pointillistic strokes."

Gould was almost too eager to be considered scandalous, scandalously melodious. He liked to compare his anachronistic quartet to the pictures of Hans van Meergeren, that unfortunate Dutch painter who achieved fame only in creating fraudulent pictures that he succeeded in selling as works by Vermeer. "How, in the midst of enthusiasm for the avant-garde movements of the day, could one find a work which would have been perfectly presentable at a turn-of-the-century academy . . . ?" Gould wrote in his liner notes to the Columbia recording of his quartet. "Well, the answer is really quite simple. Unlike many students, my enthusiasms were seldom balanced by antagonisms. My great admiration for the music of Schoenberg, for instance, was not enhanced by any counter-irritation for the Viennese romanticism of a generation before Schoenberg." Or, as he summed it up in an early draft of this essay, "I am constitutionally unfit to be a true rebel."

Gould claimed that his artful excursion into the 1890's soon became entirely spontaneous. "If this sort of theorizing suggests the same grim resolve with which every composer sets about an exercise in style," he wrote, "I must state that whatever may have been my academic motive initially, within a very few measures I was completely in the throes of this new experience. . . . I felt myself to be saying something original and my artistic conscience was clear. Whatever I had set out to prove pedagogically, it was soon evident that I was not shaping the Quartet—it was shaping me."

Well, perhaps, but the image of a creator in the throes of creation is not quite accurate. Donizetti wrote his marvelous *Don Pasquale* in eleven days, and when somebody mentioned that it had taken Rossini two weeks to finish *The Barber of Seville,* he said, "Rossini was always a slow worker." Gould spent two years laboring over his one-movement, half-hour-long quartet, and though he liked to consider himself a master craftsman, he had to keep telephoning friends to ask for guidance on the technical intricacies of bowing and double-stopping. Joseph Roddy remembers Gould even taking the manuscript to New York with him. "He was looking for some bowing advice," Roddy says, "and one night up in the Drake Hotel, I think it was, Sasha Schneider came up, and Debbie Ishlon of Columbia was there, and I was there, and there was the editing of the quartet to get the bowings right." Roddy tries mimicking their talk: "'I don't feel a down bow there— No, I don't— Are you sure?'"

"He used to call me sometimes at one o'clock in the morning because he had written three more bars to the quartet and he wanted to play the whole thing," Harvey Olnick recalls. "He wanted admiration the whole time, and indeed I thought it was miraculous. But as a piano piece, not as a quartet. Because he didn't really learn that you have to move registers around in order to make things interesting. And the composition was an act of will, of deciding beforehand that he wanted to do this."

So the work progressed. And there is probably no better way to describe it than to let Gould describe it, as he did in the long draft for his record-liner notes. "The development section in the classical symphonic structure is traditionally that place where the composer exerts all of his technical resources to elaborate and expand individually all the various themes and motives with which he has been working. It's obvious, I think, that this approach, this dissection of component parts, would be superfluous in my work since that is exactly what I have been doing from the beginning. Therefore, I allowed the development section to take an independent form—that of a fugue—indeed a very strict fugue. . . . The remainder of the development section of the Quartet is taken up with a series of chorales, three of them actually, whose function is to effect the return to the home key of F minor and hence the beginning of the recapitulation. . . ."

The supreme problem of any composer, of course, is to get his compositions performed. If Gould had written a piano sonata, he could have played it from Vancouver to Moscow, but since he had written a string quartet, he had to undertake the unfamiliar role of impresario for his own work. "Imagine then if you will the astonishment with which this work was met when I first played it on the piano for anyone that I could drag in to listen," he later wrote. "I well remember the first few piano read-throughs with some friends or other hapless callers in which the general tone of appreciation was something like, 'Ah, quit kidding.' 'Where did you dig this up?'"

That was in early 1955, when Gould was still just a Toronto prodigy, but 1955 was also the year in which Gould conquered Washington and New York, and so his quartet rather suddenly changed from the experiment of a provincial youth into the creation of an international celebrity. The following year, on May 26, it received its world premiere in Montreal by the Montreal Quartet (Hyman Bress, Mildred Goodman, Otto and Walter Joachim). Their performance prompted Marcel Valois of *La Presse* to high praise: "Serious, of high inspiration, pensive rather than lively, bathed in a discreet and slightly saddened coloring, the work . . . is of extraordinary interest."

When Gould became a codirector of the Stratford Festival, he brought along his quartet and put it in the middle of an unusual concert that also featured him playing the Berg Sonata and conducting from the keyboard Schoenberg's *Ode to Napoleon Bonaparte*. "Even though the [quartet] has a frankly acknowledged indebtedness to Bruckner and Richard Strauss, it was a moving and impressive work," Ross Parmenter wrote in the New York *Times*. Another listener, Walter Kaufmann, the conductor of the Winnipeg Orchestra, wrote his praises directly to Gould: "Three days ago I heard your String Quartet . . . a most remarkable work. . . . You have much to say, and although you may say it differently in the years to come, whatever you say in your Quartet is good, solid, and honest music."

Gould found a small New York publisher, Barger and Barclay, who brought out the quartet in 1956, and then he began the long process of sending out copies and spreading the word. He hopefully sent it, for example, to Lukas Foss, then at Tanglewood. "It is a work that I am proud of but not altogether happy with," he wrote. "It was my first attempt at writing for strings and my old organist's habit of seeing the cello line as a pedal-board induced me to keep it for long stretches on the C string, among many other faults." And to Vladimir Golschmann. "I read the score," the conductor wrote back, "and feel delighted to realize that a very great pianist can be more than a very great pianist." Gould was "so happy" that Golschmann had "found some interest in my String Quartet." The next time they met, he wrote, "I would love to play it for you, either via the transcription which was made of it by the Montreal String Quartet or my much more exciting and much more inaccurate piano reduction."

And to David Diamond, to whom Gould somewhat mysteriously said that he was now struggling with a sonata for clarinet and piano, "which I am desperately trying to prevent from becoming a quintet." Diamond was rather chillingly professional: "I would like to discuss with you the voice-leading, notation for strings, and in general what I find is a very restricted range coverage of the instruments," but he did add: "I want to know more of your music." They next met, Diamond recalls, after a Carnegie Hall performance of Diamond's Sixth Symphony by Charles Munch and the Boston Symphony, a performance in which "Mr. Munch lost his place, and it was sort of a mess." Diamond, Munch, Gould, and others gathered in Leonard Bernstein's apartment across the street. Diamond remembers talking with Gould about his efforts to escape from atonalism. "I said, 'Although your texture is quite simple, and you use it very, very well, did you consciously work through the entire quartet in serial technique?' He said, 'Yes, I did. I even have twelve-tone serial charts.' Overall, I found his quartet a little on the dry side, and yet quite expressive, and for some strange reason I felt there was a kind of Wagnerian *melos* in it, especially in the slow sections."

All this lobbying finally helped persuade Columbia to bring out a recording, early in 1960, by the Symphonia Quartet (Kurt Loebl, Elmer Seltzer, Tom Brennand, and Thomas Liberti, all members of the Cleveland Orchestra), which had given the work its American premiere in Cleveland the previous year. ("While addressing women's associations is not one of my favorite pastimes," Gould wrote to Louis Lane, the associate conductor of the Cleveland Orchestra, "I am more than happy to barter a lecture on Schoenberg for a performance of the quartet.") This recording, of course, brought Gould's composition an international audience. The *Christian Science Monitor* found the quartet "an intensely beautiful work," and *The Saturday Review* was equally impressed: "Gould's materials have a shape and character of their own, beautifully suited, incidentally, to the medium in which he is working. . . . The impulse to 'sing' is also strong in him, and it comes as a sample of refreshing aesthetic candor to find a composer who dares to write what he feels."

Not everyone was so enthusiastic, of course. Eric McLean of the

Montreal *Star* raised some serious objections: "It is touched with genius like everything Mr. Gould sets out to do.... But its faults are great ones too. The string writing is almost completely out of character, with the instruments crowded into a narrow tessitura. Whenever he ventures into such things as double-stopping, tremolos at the bridge, or even pizzicato, the effect is rather self-conscious.... I still believe that the best way to hear this work is to have the composer play it on the piano, singing whatever his fingers cannot encompass, and cursing the page-turner." Despite such criticisms, though, Gould's quartet lingers in the memory of anyone who hears it. Writing in *Commentary* at the time of Gould's death a quarter of a century later, Samuel Lipman judged his Opus 1 "an enormously talented reworking of early Schoenberg, deeply moving, for all its derivativeness, and never less than brilliantly accomplished as a composition."

Gould was pleased and proud with the success of his first major composition. "Despite its atmosphere of faded elegance and rather bittersweet fin-de-siecle idiom, [it] has received on the whole marvelous critical notices," he wrote to a friend in Berlin. "There have been a few 'fashionable' reviews which have pointed out that it is rather inappropriate to revive the spirit of Richard Strauss in the age of Karlheinz Stockhausen (or is it really his age?), but the 'progressive' voices have, fortunately, been in the minority and have helped stir up reasonably healthy controversy."

More important, Gould saw this first substantial creation as the first milestone on the road to a career as a composer. "This Quartet represents a part of my musical development which I cannot but regard with some sentiment," he wrote in his characteristically formal liner notes for the Columbia recording. "It is certainly not unusual to find an Op. 1 in which a young composer inadvertently presents a subjective synthesis of all that has most deeply affected his adolescence.... Sometimes these prodigal summations are the harbingers of the true creative life. Sometimes the brilliance with which they reflect the past manages to excel all that their composer will do thereafter. In any event ... it's Op. 2 that counts."

Although Gould did write other music, there was never to be any Opus 2. "I specialize in unfinished works," he confessed at one point. Except for his densely contrapuntal 1954 cadenzas to Bee-thoven's first piano concerto, which Gould himself described as "vastly inappropriate cadenzas ... in the general harmonic idiom of Max Reger," his only other published composition was a mildly amusing little neo-Baroque exercise entitled "So You Want to Write a Fugue?"

For just a trifle, this proved a remarkably popular work. Origi-nally written as a five-minute finale for a television show called "The Anatomy of Fugue," which Gould did for the CBC in 1963, it was recorded for Columbia the following year by an ensemble consisting of Elizabeth Benson-Guy, soprano; Anita Darian, mezzo-soprano; Charles Bressler, tenor; Donald Gramm, baritone, and the Juilliard Quartet, all conducted by Vladimir Golschmann. *HiFi/ Stereo Review* published a substantial article by Gould about this work in April of 1964 and bound into that issue a thin plastic copy of the recording. G. Schirmer published the score that same year, with a pink cover ornamented by two angels. And Columbia finally reissued the recording in 1980 as part of its *Glenn Gould Silver Jubi-lee Album*.

Gould's own description of this ponderous little fugue shows how seriously he took his own attempts at humor, particularly on the rather arcane (for television audiences) subject of counterpoint. "The basso begins by suggesting that a certain degree of courage is involved: 'You've got the nerve to write a fugue, so go ahead.' The tenor is concerned with the utility of the finished product: 'So go ahead and write a fugue that we can sing.' The contralto ... advo-cates an audaciously antiacademic method: 'Pay no mind to what we've told you, give no heed to what we've told you and the theory that you've read.' ... As a gesture of tribute ... the string quartet now renders a quodlibet of four of Bach's more celebrated themes (you'll note, among them, the second Brandenburg Concerto). Then, appropriately, the quartet turns to the contralto for a brief lecture on the perils of exhibitionism: 'But never be clever for the sake of being clever.' This, with its attendant warning—'For a canon in inversion is a dangerous diversion and a bit of augmenta-tion is a serious temptation'—creates an entirely new thematic sub-stance. Hereupon the string quartet renders a grandiose if minor-inflected quotation from *Die Meistersinger*—the archtypical example of musical cleverness—after which all concerned engage in joyous recapitulation. . . ."

This "joyous recapitulation" ends on a note of whistling-in-the-dark determination: "We're going to write a fugue. . . . We're going to write a good one now." That determination, of course, is exactly what was lacking in Gould's attempts to become a composer. "So go ahead," as the singers urged in the beginning, was an order that Gould could carry out only in terms of parody and pastiche. Near the end, he ventured warily into a mention of his own difficulties. "When you've finished writing it," the soprano promises, "I think you'll find great joy in it." The baritone can only answer: "Hope so. Well, nothing ventured, nothing gained, they say, but it really is rather hard to start."

Trio: Well?

Baritone: Let us try. Right now.

Trio: Now. We're going to write a fugue. . . .

And so on. Gould was a perfectionist, and perhaps he knew too much great music too well to accept the dispiriting contrast between his own efforts and those of the masters. He could obviously see the differences quite clearly, and he could not see much hope for narrowing them. For all his cleverness and skill, he knew that the innate gifts of a Beethoven or even a Scriabin—that compulsive creativity that Schoenberg once compared to an apple tree's need to flower and produce apples—was not in him. "I found that other men's music kept coming out," he admitted to William Littler of the Toronto *Star*. And so he fell back on the evasions of wit and humor. The sad question about the musical clowning in "So You Want to Write a Fugue?" is whether Gould knew how cruelly he was mocking his own failures.

As he got older, Gould kept returning to this kind of burlesque but for smaller and smaller audiences. Among his papers there remains an elaborately copied "Lieberson Madrigal," written for a testimonial dinner for Goddard Lieberson, who reigned as the king of Columbia Records for a quarter of a century. This starts with a four-part chorale of celebration: "Goddard, we wish you a happy anniversary, this is indeed a time for true rejoicing." But conflicting voices soon start bringing in office politics and inside jokes about "doting A & R . . . publicity that's seldom up to par, Creative Services that don't create, and sales force that gave poor John (and Frank) the gate. . . ." This inevitably leads into a fugue, to a text of "Lennie Bernstein wants to do Boulez, no Stockhausen . . ." over a sustained bass on a rival text: "No, no, Lennie, no you can't, why must you be so damn avant, damn avant, damn avant garde?"

In later years, Gould continued writing such things only for his friends. In one folder of his compositions, for example, there are ten pages of ink sketches leading up to "Monica—Her Madrigal" (presumably Monica Gaylord, a talented young black pianist from New York). The four-part lyrics are on Gould's standard level of comic verse: "Monica Anne, we've tried our best to guide you/ And though you've gone your own way, we've defied you./ Through every season, you've called it treason, yet we've still sought to reason with you./ We've clearly failed, for you have paled,/ You have now turned blue. . . ."

Gould's unfinished works were often ambitious (that may indeed be why they remained unfinished), from the boyhood chorus of postnuclear frogs to a cantata on Stalingrad that he took up in his thirties. "Future plans?" Gould was quoted as saying to an interviewer from the *CBC Times* in May of 1964, just after his retirement from the stage. "I'm recording like mad and working frantically on *A Letter from Stalingrad*, which I'm writing for soprano Lois Marshall. It's a very personal piece for me. The text is a letter from a German officer killed at Stalingrad, an extraordinarily moving thing, in which he instructs his wife in how she must conduct herself in the catastrophe of their world. He exhibits the remarkable schizophrenia of the German military character, coupling sentimental nostalgia with arrogant autocracy. My music is loose variations on a theme of Richard Strauss' *Metamorphosen*.* I've also written the first draft of a short, quasi-autobiographical opera. . . ."

But what ever happened to "A Letter from Stalingrad"? One can try asking Lois Marshall on the telephone.

A: I really don't know. It's something I know nothing about.

Q: You never sang it?

A: No indeed. I never saw it, nor ever heard of it. It may be a myth. . . .

*Oddly enough, Gould also talked of writing a TV opera on Franz Kafka's *Metamorphosis*.

The "quasi-autobiographical opera" is about a Straussian com-poser who wants, like the composer of Gould's quartet, to write old-fashioned music. This brings him a certain success. "Think of all the performances of your works,/" runs one fragment of the pro-spective libretto, "Your symphony given by Bernstein,/ Your piano sonata played by Cliburn. . . ." But now the composer insists on writing an antiquarian opera, including a fugue, and his daughter anticipates nothing but trouble from fashionable critics. These early drafts can be dated to the early 1960's, since they were scribbled on the stationary of TWA and Continental Airlines, but other folders contain very different drafts.

In one of these, the composer's identity becomes quite clear, since it is entitled "Dr. Strauss Writes an Opera" (presumably based on Strauss's *Capriccio,* for the stage is set in Garmisch in 1940). It begins—cliché of clichés—with the telephone ringing and the aged composer crossing the stage to take a call from his English pub-lisher: "Yes, yes, it is—uh—very good—yes, that is right, put him on, please—Herr Hawkes, *grüss Gott, wie geht's,* Herr Hawkes. . . ." In another version, the situation becomes more abstract, and Gould describes his cast of characters only as "the composer, the compos-er's daughter, her husband, a 12-tone composer. . . ." The plot remains roughly the same: "Comp. about 60 lives with daughter and her husband, who is reluctantly supporting him, and who is ambi-tious for . . . recognition of his talent. . . . He, however, lives a stormy interior life which is almost untouched by the daughter's plans for him. . . ." In one of Gould's fragmentary lyrics, the daugh-ter denounces the composer with considerable bitterness: "Old man, you're failing,/ Old man, you're dying,/ Old man, your world will simply fade away. . . ." If Gould ever wrote any music for this "quasi-autobiographical opera," there is no evidence of it.

Perhaps the most extraordinary of Gould's unfinished composi-tions—unstarted compositions—was one that he planned for the end of his life. "Glenn said that at fifty he would retire and write," Jessie Greig recalls her cousin echoing the predictions of his youth. "And one of the things that he told me he was going to do was, he was going to write—he was fascinated by the book of Revelation in the Bible, and he was going to write something akin to Handel's *Messiah.*"

. . . And I stood upon the sand of the sea, and saw a beast rise up out of the sea, having seven heads and ten horns, and upon his horns ten crowns, and upon his heads the name of blasphemy . . .

"We talked about it a couple of years, about the book of Revelation, about what it meant," says Miss Greig. "He had his own interpretations."

Q: What was his religion, exactly?

A: He believed in God, he believed in a hereafter. And you know that after his mother died [in 1975], I think that it was a more important part of his life, and he talked about it more often. He wanted to discuss certain things with me about the hereafter. His dreams were often about that.

Q: What dreams?

A: After his mother died, he dreamed about her a great deal, and he would tell me in great detail about this dream, about where she was living, and how she knew what we were doing, and so, you know, he really had a belief in the hereafter.

. . . And he showed me a pure river of water of life, clear as crystal, proceeding out of the throne of God and of the Lamb. . . . And on either side of the river, was there the tree of life, which bare twelve manner of fruits . . . and the leaves of the tree were for the healing of the nations. . . .

We can never know why so little of the music that Gould thought of writing, and talked of writing, ever got written. "Between the idea/ and the reality/," as Eliot wrote, "Between the motion/ And the act/ Falls the Shadow. . . ." Part of Gould's failure as a composer perhaps did come from the distractions of other activities, of radio and writing and all the disturbances of daily life. "I have the feeling that he was the kind of person who was constantly engaged in research," Diamond says, "constantly writing these lectures or these liner notes, and you know how time-consuming these things are. And that was a kind of avoidance of getting to composition. When you have that kind of musical intelligence, composing is not hard. What *is* hard is just getting to that paper and sitting down with the ink or the pencils and *composing*."

Part of Gould's failure undoubtedly came from the curse of per-

fectionism, part perhaps from a deeply felt lack of first-rate creative
talent—creative genius—part simply from a reluctance to explore
the limits of his own imperfections. "He *hated* it that everything
came out sounding like everybody else," says Leonard Bernstein,
who has known his own conflicts between performing and composing, between one's own work and the influence of masters. "He
said, 'I can't bear it.' I said, 'Well, a lot of Beethoven comes out
sounding like Haydn, a lot of Schubert comes out sounding like
Mozart—what're you going to do?' A lot of Mahler comes out
sounding like everybody who ever wrote music before Mahler. But
there's a personal voice there, in Schubert and in Beethoven and
Mahler. It's a deep inner sound that a composer makes, which comes
from the depths of him. Stravinsky stole from Tchaikowsky and
Beethoven and Bach and Rimsky-Korsakov and Ravel and—*but*
there's that *Igor* screaming through it all, an amazingly individual
voice. And Glenn said, 'Well, I guess that's what I don't have.' And
he couldn't stand it. He said, 'It's all either Schoenberg or Brahms,
what I write.' He showed me some sketch of something he had
worked on, as if to prove how *bad* he was as a composer. He said,
'Look at this—' I wish he had gone on, because I think he would
have arrived—he would have written some fascinating music. That
I'm sure of."

Lacking that personal voice—or feeling that he lacked it—Gould
got great satisfaction in his later years by adapting the ideas of others
and creating those marvelous transcriptions of Strauss and Wagner.
But as for original work, he finally decided on a completely different
course, rejecting all the overworked conventional forms of musical
composition and starting to experiment with something quite new,
a quite different kind of music.

"The Idea of North"

"What I have in mind, believe it or not," Gould wrote to a friend in San Francisco early in 1965, less than a year after his retirement, "is a trip to the Arctic. I have an enormous compulsion to look upon the Polar seas and I find that this is growing apace each year, so that I really must get it out of my system somehow."

Now that he was free to come and go as he pleased, he really did head north that June to fulfill his "enormous compulsion." To his admirer in Leningrad, Kitty Gvozdeva, he provided a few details: "I went to Hudson's Bay to a point just a few miles above the most northerly growth of forest in that area, which is for the moment the most northern point to which you can take a train in Canada. . . . This train, although it has one car with sleeping accommodations, is not really intended for tourists. Everyone seemed to think I was just slightly mad to be on it in the first place—and practically every member of its crew turned out to be fabulously gifted as a raconteur, in the way that people who have experienced great isolation tend to be. And so for approximately 1000 miles and for two nights and a day (each way), I was able to see an aspect of Canada with which very few people concern themselves. And I have come away from it with an enthusiasm for the North which may even get me through another winter of city living which, as you know, I loathe. . . ."

It was true, at least as of that time, that very few Canadians concerned themselves with the North. "We have administered these vast territories of the north in an almost continuing state of absence of mind," Prime Minister Louis St. Laurent said in 1953, when he first created the Department of Northern Affairs. Yet the North has long haunted the Canadian imagination, not just the Arctic territories themselves but the fundamental idea of North. The North is everything beyond the horizon, beyond the comfortable and the familiar, everything frozen and dark, treeless and windswept. It is a little like the American image of the western frontier, but unlike the compliant West, the hostile Arctic still presents an enormous wilderness. It has no San Diego, no Las Vegas, no Disneyland. "The North is always there," as André Siegfried once wrote. "It is the background of the picture without which Canada would not be Canada."

"It includes great, unrelieved stretches of snow and ice . . ." Barry Lopez wrote in *Arctic Dreams*. "But there are, too, surprising and riveting sights: Wilberforce Falls on the Hood River suddenly tumbles 160 feet into a wild canyon in the midst of the Canadian tundra, and its roar can be heard for miles. . . . The badlands of east-central Melville Island, an eroded country of desert oranges, of muted yellows and reds, reminds a traveler of canyons and arroyos in southern Utah. And there are places more exotic, like the Ruggles River, which flows out of Lake Hazen on Ellesmere Island in winter and runs 2,000 feet through the Stygian darkness, wreathed in frost smoke, before it disappears underneath its own ice. . . ."

In an obscure way, the history of the North makes Canada's national origins older and quite different from those of the United States. "The ferment that led explorers to the Canadian frontier did not begin in the fifteenth-century courts of Lisbon and Madrid, or in the counting houses of London and Bristol," as R.A.J. Phillips wrote in *Canada's North*. "It started much earlier, in Scandinavia." Five centuries before Columbus set sail, Eric the Red had led the Vikings to Greenland. They built settlements there, and on the coast of Newfoundland, which they called Markland. They erected stone houses and barns, brought in farm animals, cut down forests. Throughout the Middle Ages, the Viking settlements in northern Canada were known in Europe as a source of two treasured animals: falcons and polar bears. Canada, then, was not an obstacle discovered during the search for a new route to the Indies but rather, as Phillips put it, "the frontier of northern Europe."

Yet even after the gold rush in the Klondike at the end of the nineteenth century, even after the building of roads and airfields during World War II, the North remained largely untouched. When the Canadian government recovered from its "absence of mind" and began a decade of building and development, the entire population of this vast region still amounted to no more than 25,000. In all the Northwest Territories, there were exactly eight doctors. Education was provided by Anglican and Catholic missionaries, administration by the Royal Canadian Mounted Police. Even today, when icebreakers can force their way through the legendary Northwest Passage, now known as Lancaster Sound, and when trash and garbage can be found littering the bare tundra, there remains a mysterious attraction.

"The towns and telephones, the sound of generators, the grinding of sewage trucks, the ugliness of oil tanks: all this human defilement has not robbed the North of its strange power," Phillips wrote. "When men live in the North, their values change. . . . They live a lifetime alone, and die when they emerge. They become citizens of a different kind of country, a country where nature is overwhelmingly stronger than man. . . . Northern travellers seem to have found an extraordinary fulfillment in this unlikeliest of lands and seas. . . . In success or failure, almost all become missionaries for their cause. When they could return, they did. When they could not return, they relived their northern voyagings throughout their days, the way other men have spent their lives experiencing over and over the trauma of wartime."

Gould, with his Scottish origins, felt an almost mystical sense of that Canadian North and of its connections to the rest of the northern world. If you look at the globe from the North Pole rather than the Equator, Canada joins Russia, Scandinavia, Britain, and Germany on the peripheries of that frozen Mare Nostrum. This international idea of North was never fully articulated in Gould's writings, but it is hardly accidental that he not only loved Bach and Beethoven and Wagner but also recorded less universally admired Scandinavian composers like Grieg and Sibelius and even performed the music of the reclusive and eccentric Norwegian atonalist Fartein Valen. He thoroughly disapproved of the French, Debussy and Ravel, and he seems to have known very little of the great Italian opera composers.

Typically enough, Gould never actually went to the Arctic North.

Most of this frozen wilderness can be reached only by airplane, and nothing could now make Gould get into an airplane. The nearest to the Arctic that he ever ventured was that trip aboard the train known as the *Muskeg Express,* which ran and still runs from Winnipeg a thousand miles north to Churchill, on the southwestern shore of Hudson's Bay. The railroad ends there, and so does the highway system. From a southern perspective, Churchill is almost at the end of the world. But although the tree line ends here, this is barely the beginning of the Canadian North. There are about another 100 miles to the 60th parallel, the southern border of the Northwest Territories, another 200 miles beyond that to Repulse Bay, another 600 miles or so to Resolute Bay and Lancaster Sound and the Northwest Passage, and another 400 miles beyond that to the glaciers of Ellesmere Island. And only there lie the "polar seas" that Gould said he felt "an enormous compulsion to look upon." For an inhabitant of Toronto to describe one train trip to Churchill as a voyage to the North is a little like a Bostonian thinking (as any true Bostonian would think) of a visit to Washington as a journey south, or of a trip to Cleveland as the West.

Still, it was not the reality of the North that fascinated Gould, and he admitted as much, *en passant,* in the introduction to his extraordinary radio documentary, "The Idea of North": "I've been intrigued for quite a long time . . . by that incredible tapestry of tundra and taiga country, as they call it. . . . I've read about it, written about it occasionally, and even pulled up my parka once and gone there. But like all but a very few Canadians, I guess, I've had no direct confrontation with the northern third of our country. I've remained of necessity an outsider, and the north has remained for me a convenient place to dream about, spin tall tales about sometimes, and, in the end, avoid."

"He said, 'Let's go for an automobile ride, and I'll show you Toronto,'" Leonard Bernstein recalls. "So, well, what is there to see? It was cold, and it was getting dark, and I had sort of seen it the day before. So we went out, Glenn in his usual three coats and two hats, and I don't know how many pairs of gloves. We got into his car, which was a black sedan. He turned the heat up to maximum, and the radio volume up to maximum, and he got a station that was playing pop tunes, and Petula Clark was singing, and I said, 'Do you really want to hear this?' It was so hot in that car, I can't tell you, and the music was so loud, and there was nothing to see—it was growing dark—but we drove around for maybe half an hour, having a conversation by shouting over this radio full blast, and that was our tour of Toronto.

"One of the things we talked about was his new love affair with the Arctic. This man who was so afraid of cold, and so geared against it—and I mean literally, the gear he traveled with was immense—why would he seek it out, why would he seek out this enemy? Which was the enemy of his fingers, which were always getting cold at a recording session or a rehearsal, so that he had to have hot water, and many, many mittens. And he tried to answer it in—I don't know—without turning off the radio. It's very hard to tell you what was actually said, but what I came away with was a feeling of a kind of cosmic exploration. There was something spiritual about it. Elements of magic, having to do with the magnetic pole.

"I was terribly moved by it, because I'd have thought that the only explanation would be to seek out the thing that hurts you the most and confront it, in a sort of good old-fashioned Freudian way. The only way you can conquer your fear of elevators is to get into one and say, 'This is an elevator, I'm here, and everything's all right.' But it wasn't that. It was something much more magical and mystical."

"It was through me that Glenn encountered the concept of the radio documentary," says John Roberts of the CBC. "It was in sixty-one, I think—I produced a program called *Music by Royal Composers,* and it was just that, you know, all kinds of interesting people, in all varieties of monarchies of Britain, and it was an exploration of that area. Glenn was very fascinated. He asked me how it was put together, and I explained in immense detail, and he was very, very fascinated. He said, 'You know, I'd like to do that.' And then not long afterwards, he said to me, 'Look, I would like to try and put together a documentary on Schoenberg. Would you be interested?' And I said, 'Terribly interested.' And so, his first Schoenberg documentary was the result of that. And of course, having gone through all that, he was absolutely bitten by the bug, and he wanted to continue, and then other departments were interested in him and what he was doing, and so his scope widened. . . ."

Gould himself recalled his involvement with documentary radio beginning much earlier, in 1945 or 1946. Indeed, there was something about the medium itself, something about hearing a disembodied voice trying to make a connection, that had attracted and delighted the lonely schoolboy. Radio brought him the outside world, and yet it did so without violating his strong sense of privacy. "It's always seemed to me," he wrote, "that when that first person heard that second person's voice by virtue of a crystal set, or whatever it was heard on, that they had not only the most unique experience in music—of music in the sense of voice as sound, obviously, but that they had the one true approach to radio. They were able to get at something quite special . . . that original human contact, that incredible, spine-tingling sense of awareness of some other human voice and persona."

Gould remembered his first documentary on Schoenberg with some dismay, however. "I was always dissatisfied with the kind of documentaries that radio seemed to decree," he said. "You know, they very often came out sounding . . . —okay, I'll borrow Mr. McLuhan's term—linear. They came out sounding 'Over to you, now back to our host, and here for the wrap-up is'—in a word, predictable. I wrote the script, for instance, for a program on Schoenberg in sixty-two . . . [and] it seemed that one had to accept a linear mold in order to pursue any kind of career in radio at that time. So I was very dissatisfied with the available techniques, and in 1967, for the first time, I got a chance to try my hand at producing something on my own."

This was to become "The Idea of North." "What I would most like to do," Gould wrote to a friend in the summer of 1967, "is to examine the effects of solitude and isolation upon those who have lived in the Arctic or Sub-Arctic. In some subtle way, the latitudinal factor does seem to have a modifying influence upon character, although I have no editorial axe to grind in the matter. . . ." And to another friend: "My Arctic bluff has finally been called by Mother CBC, no less. They have suggested that I really do go ahead. . . ."

Gould's plan was to interrogate a number of people who had lived and worked in the North. "Something really does happen to people who go into the north," Gould later wrote, "—they become . . . in effect, philosophers." Then, with razors and glue, he would see what he could make of their taped recollections. One of his first choices was Bob Phillips, who had worked in the Department of Northern Affairs and was now assistant secretary of the cabinet, Privy Council Office. He was also a perceptive and sympathetic observer whose new book on the North had undoubtedly attracted Gould's attention.

"I remember so vividly the first contact," says Phillips, a graying, craggy-faced man who now devotes much of his time to renovating old houses. "It was a Sunday evening when we happened to have guests in, and the phone rang, and it was somebody from—he identified himself as from CBC in Toronto, called Gould, and he said he was doing a series of programs on the North, and asked my help. A couple of years had gone by since I'd been professionally associated with the North, so I offered to introduce him to other people, authorities on the North, but he was very insistent. He said, no, it doesn't matter if you're not up-to-date—it isn't about being up-to-date. It's more philosophical.

"So since we had guests waiting, I finally took the line of least resistance and agreed to meet him at the CBC studios in a day or two, and that was that. Or then—I remember the next stage even more vividly because I think it was the greatest *gaffe* in my life. I met this strange character up on the seventh floor of the Château Laurier, and we first went through a *strange* performance, in which there were more microphones than I'd ever seen laid out before, and finally he said, 'Well, may we talk?' And then he asked really quite penetrating, interesting questions about the North, which required very long answers. And while I was answering, I was astonished at his attitude. He was sort of shaking his head, and smiling, and shaking his head some more, affirmatively, and he seemed to be sort of happy, and then at times it was almost as though he were directing an orchestra, with his hands.

"And so it went, fairly intensely, for about an hour. I had no idea it was so long. And he said, 'Well, look, this is just absolutely marvelous, just what I wanted. Now why don't we take a break? You must be tired.' And so coffee was produced. And so, making conversation over the coffee, I asked him, I said, 'Excuse me, Mr. Gould, but are you related to the pianist?' And he then said that he *was* the pianist. Well, it seemed to me the most extraordinary thing. I had no idea. . . .'"

By some mysterious system of his own, Gould chose four other "participants" who had spent substantial amounts of time in the North. "We wanted," he said later, "an enthusiast, a cynic, a government budget-watcher, as well as someone who could represent that limitless expectation and limitless capacity for disillusionment which inevitably affects the questing spirit of those who go north seeking their future." For these roles, he picked, in addition to Bob Phillips, Marianne Schroeder, a nurse; Frank Vallee, a professor of sociology in Ottawa; James Lotz, a British anthropologist; and W. V. (Wally) Maclean, an aged surveyor whom Gould had met on the *Muskeg Express,* an autodidact who loved to quote Shakespeare and to hold forth on the symbolic meanings of the North.

It was Maclean, in a way, who had given Gould the idea for "The Idea of North." A railroad steward had introduced them at the breakfast table, and after some talk about the prospects of the North, Maclean startled Gould by asking, "Are you aware, Mr. Gould, that both Thoreau and Kafka practiced my profession? That both were surveyors?" Gould confessed that he was not. Maclean went on to argue that "there's a real connection between surveying and literature." Gould was fascinated. "For me, to encounter this suddenly in the middle of nowhere was amazing," he later told an interviewer. "And we started an eight-hour conversation—we didn't rise from that table after mid-morning tea, after lunch, or afternoon tea, until four o'clock, by which time I had a headache from the weight of ideas. . . . That was the genesis of his participating."

As usual, though, Gould made of his characters what he imagined in himself. "I think he split his own psyche up into different parts to make the show," Jim Lotz recalls. "The nurturer (the nurse), the objective critic (university professor), the pontificator (the civil servant), and the antiestablishment adventurer (is that me, or am I the idealist?). Then he had the old man in the cave as the commentator. You must see what Glenn did in Jungian terms, not Freudian ones. We were not matched off against each other, but rather set up to complement each other. Glenn played me like a piano, and in fact the program should have been called 'The Idea of Glenn Gould.'"

Still, Gould organized "The Idea of North" by getting each of these people to talk about the North, about their own experiences of loneliness and isolation. Thus Nurse Schroeder: "I didn't have to go to somebody in Coral [Harbor] and say I'm lonesome or I'm depressed. I just had to go and visit them, play a game of chess, whatever they wanted to do, and right away there was a sense of sharing this life. One could realize the value of another human being. You're excluding the rest of the world that will never understand, and you've made your own world with these people, and probably what you'll never know, and what nobody else will ever know, is whether you're kidding yourself or not. Have you really made your peace with these other people . . . because the only alternative to peace is a kind of crackup?"

And Lotz: "I was in many respects solitary, but in a strange way the North has made me more sort of gregarious, because the North does show you exactly how much you rely on your fellow man. What the sense of community means in the North is a matter of life and death. . . . It's so big, it's so vast, it's so immense, it cares so little, and this sort of diminishes you. And then you think, 'My God, I am here. I've got here, I live here. . . .'"

Such observations were reasonably interesting, reasonably perceptive, but they were still only raw material, reels of unedited tape, fodder. Once Gould had his interviews all recorded and transcribed in the south, he once again headed northward, on Route 17, a road that he loved, skirting the shores of Lake Superior. "No. 17 defines for much of its passage across Ontario the northernmost limit of agrarian settlement," he wrote some years later. "It is endowed with habitation, when at all, by fishing villages, mining camps, and timber towns that straddle the highway every fifty miles or so. Among these, names such as Michipicoten and Batchawana advertise the continuing segregation of the Canadian Indian; Rossport and Jackfish proclaim the no-nonsense mapmaking of the early white settlers; and Marathon and Terrace Bay . . . betray the postwar influx of American capital (Terrace is the Brasilia of Kimberly-Clark's Kleenex-Kotex operation in Ontario)."

While driving north, Gould heard on his car radio so many CBC renditions of Petula Clark singing "Who Am I?" that he decided to write an inquiry entitled "The Search for Petula Clark." But on this trip, the singer's question of "Who am I?" led Gould to a little coastal town named Wawa, where he enjoyed tramping along the lakefront piers built of giant timbers. "It's an extraordinary place . . ." he later said, "to sort out some thoughts and try to get some writing done."

"What did he do?" says Lorne Tulk, the skilled editor-engineer who worked with Gould on "The Idea of North." "He rented a motel room, and he sat in the motel room and wrote."

Q: What's up there, in Wawa?

A: Nothing.

Q: He just went up there for a visit?

A: No, he went to Wawa and wrote "North." He had all of his interviews transcribed, and he took all the transcripts with him, locked himself in a motel room in Wawa for two or three weeks, and came back with a program.

If the interviewing had been only a beginning, however, the writing was still only a beginning. In creating what he called "a documentary which thinks of itself as a drama," Gould had made a point of interviewing his five dramatis personae separately; they never met. He had originally planned these five separate interviews as five separate segments, perhaps even to be broadcast on five separate evenings. "And that remained true until something like six weeks prior to broadcast time," Gould later wrote, "which is pretty frightening when you come to think of it. *Five* weeks prior to broadcast time, I suddenly decided that that wasn't at all what I wanted to do—that, obviously, it had to be an integrated unit of some kind in which the texture, the tapestry of the words themselves would differentiate the characters and create dreamlike conjunctions within the documentary. These, of course, would have to be achieved through some rather prodigious editing, and I spent something like two to three weeks occupied with fine editing, still all the while being unsure as to the eventual form that the piece was going to take."

Since Gould had asked his chamber-music players roughly the same questions, he could organize his material into a half-dozen scenes, in which all the characters addressed themselves to the same general point. But when he had finished all this, he found that his hour-long show ran to nearly an hour and a half. "So I thought, 'Well, obviously, one scene has got to go.' We had a scene on the Eskimo—couldn't lose that; we had a scene on isolation and its effects—that had to stay, obviously; we had our closing soliloquy, we had our opening trio and other indispensables—and I couldn't part with any of them. . . . I thought to myself, 'Look, we really could hear some of these people speaking simultaneously—there is no particular reason why not.'"

After telling this story, in "Radio as Music," Gould admitted that "perhaps I exaggerate ever so slightly," but that was essentially how he invented what he later took to calling "contrapuntal radio." Almost nothing, of course, is ever "invented" just like that. Frank Capra, for one, was experimenting with simultaneous dialogue in films as far back as the early 1930's, and all such experimenters were quite aware that even the most banal statements somehow sound, when juxtaposed against other banal statements, less banal. Gould was nonetheless the first professional musician to edit the tapes of spoken words as though they were the notes in a contrapuntal composition.

"The Idea of North" begins with Nurse Schroeder saying, somewhat wistfully: "I was fascinated by the country as such. I flew north from Churchill to Coral Harbor . . . at the end of September. [Note how casually she names as her starting place the northernmost point that Gould ever reached.] Snow had begun to fall, and the country was partially covered by it. Some of the lakes were frozen around the edges, but towards the center of the lakes you could still see the clear, clear water. . . ."

After about a minute of this, Professor Vallee's rather gruff voice begins speaking (Gould, for some reason, never specifically identified any speakers, or any music being played, in any of his radio documentaries): "I don't go—let me say this again—I don't go for this northmanship bit at all. . . ." And so the duet continues:

Schroeder: We seemed to be going into nowhere, and the further north we went . . .

Vallee (simultaneously): I don't knock those people who do claim that they want to go farther and farther north, but . . .

These two people who have never met continue speaking simultaneously for a minute or so, and then, soon after Vallee says, "And the other fellow says, 'Well, I did one of thirty days,'" Bob Phillips's mellow voice starts saying, "And then for another eleven years, I served the North in various capacities. . . ."

This may all seem rather commonplace, but Gould edited these taped observations with a meticulous sense of both meaning and sound. Nurse Schroeder's voice begins almost pianissimo, then very gradually gets louder, and each new voice in this spoken fugato comes in on a specific tangent. Gould described this as "a kind of trio sonata texture." Speaking of Vallee's entrance in the midst of Nurse Schroeder's monologue, he said, "By this time we have become aware of a gentleman who has started to speak and who upon the word 'further' says 'farther'—'farther and farther north' is the context. At that moment, his voice takes precedence over hers in terms of dynamic emphasis. Shortly after, he uses the words 'thirty days,' and by this point we have become aware of a third voice which immediately after 'thirty days' says 'eleven years'—and another crossover point has been effected. The scene is built so that it has a kind of—I don't know if you have ever looked at the tone rows of Anton Webern as distinguished from those of Arnold Schoenberg, but it has a kind of Webern-like continuity-in-cross-over in that motives which are similar but not identical are used for the exchange of instrumental ideas. . . ."

It is a little difficult for an ordinary listener to accept Gould's assessment of "The Idea of North" as a musical composition. Granted that it is perfectly possible to treat the speaking voice as a musical instrument, granted that Gould edited his interview tapes just as skillfully and as imaginatively as he edited the tapes of his own performances on the piano, it nonetheless remains true that when Nurse Schroeder observes that "we seemed to be going into nowhere," these are neither abstract sounds being organized according to Gould's aesthetic plan nor are they Gould's words expressing Gould's ideas. Instead of composing a piece of verbal music, in other words, Gould was simply playing the role of editor, and succumbing, as editors often do, to the idea that what he had edited had become his own creation. A professional music critic like William Littler of the Toronto *Star* can be more understanding. "It rather depends on how deeply you want to argue what composition consists of," he says. "If it means the ordering of materials, with a sense of structure, to produce an overall statement—yes, compositional principles were involved in 'The Idea of North.' He's working with words, so he's composing with words. Obviously, if you take it much further and try to analyze it in terms of sonata form, you can't do it. But the general principles of composition are there." Besides, in an era when John Cage composes an *Imaginary Landscape* that includes twelve radios simultaneously playing at random, in an era when Steve Reich takes a taped confession of an accused murderer and then reproduces one or two phrases in a googol of repetitions, how is one to define music, except that it is whatever a gifted musician says it is?

Gould himself indisputably believed that his radio documentaries were musical compositions. "Taking . . . an interview like this one into the studio after the fact," he said not long afterward, "chopping it up and splicing here and there and pulling on this phrase and accentuating that one, throwing some reverb in there and adding a compressor here and a filter there . . . it's unrealistic to think of that as anything but a composition. . . . And . . . it is the way of the future. . . . I think our whole notion of what music really is has forever merged with all the sounds around us, you know, everything our environment makes available." And when he learned in 1972 that a young student named Robert Skelton was planning to write a detailed analysis of his string quartet, he promptly sent him tapes of "The Idea of North" and its sequel, "The Latecomers." "There are . . . certain connecting links," Gould wrote, "which should, I think, be noted: perhaps, most obviously, a concentration on aspects of counterpoint . . . and perhaps, less obviously, a tendency in each case to celebrate, if not precisely a fin de siecle situation, then at least a philosophy which deliberately sought an isolated vantage-point in relation to its time and milieu. . . . There is a true fraternal link, both in subject matter and technique, between the vocal polyphony of 'The Idea of North' . . . and the chromatically constructed counterpoint of the quartet."

When all the theorizing has been done, a radio show depends on one man (or woman) who knows what he (or she) wants, and one who can carry out those wishes. In this case, Lorne Tulk saw his job as the translation into sound of anything that Gould could imagine. "My only function is to play the console, the way you play a piano," says Tulk, a short, stocky man, curly-haired, full of energy. "The difference is that instead of black and white keys, I have turntables and tape recorders. . . . You just say, 'I want something that sounds like—'"

Q: Like what? Can I say that I want it to sound like New York City? Or I want it to sound like blue?

A: Sure. Any of those things.

And so they set to work, night after night. Though Jessie Greig vividly remembers the young Gould playing the piano long after everyone else in the family had gone to bed, Tulk thinks that he was the one who introduced Gould to the rich possibilities of the night. "You can get more done in that time," he says, matter-of-factly. "There's less interruptions. The place is quiet. I don't think Glenn had ever thought in terms of working all night, but once he started doing it, he discovered he loved it. The only thing he didn't like, he didn't like to see the sun come up. So he'd try to get finished and get home before the sunrise."

Q: Like a vampire.

A: It's the one thing that for some reason he found depressing, to see the sun come up. I don't know why.

Q: Perhaps it just meant that the night was gone, and now he had to stop everything and go to bed.

A: I don't know. He just used to say that he didn't want to see the sun rise.

As the deadline approaches, as the opening night draws near, all attention must be focused on getting the job done. The *Star*'s Littler paid a visit to the CBC's Studio K on a pre-Christmas night in 1967 and found a scene of controlled chaos. "By 3 A.M., everyone in Studio K was beginning to look a little like last week's cut flowers," he wrote. "[Producer] Janet Somerville, leaning against the control room wall, stared blankly ahead. Lorne Tulk, bending over his knobs and dials, wore an equally expressionless gaze. And the man in charge, shoes off and shirt hanging out of his trousers, held his face in his hands. The man in charge was Glenn Gould. He had been sitting in CBC Studio K's control room since 6 P.M., drinking coffee, taking tranquilizers, and editing tapes. . . ."

The show was supposed to be broadcast in a couple of days, but it was still far from finished. "You vant qvality, baby? It takes time," Gould offered in yet another of his ethnic impersonations. His listeners smiled weakly. Gould turned serious: "I started Thanksgiving Day, and except for my recording trips to New York, we've been working on this every night since then—last night until 2:30 A.M., the night before 3 A.M. I only regret we didn't start a week earlier to take the pressure off."

Gould then went back to work. Littler watched him and his crew labor over their four Ampex tape machines. "It was quite an operation to observe," he wrote. "Gould would sit up on the control panel, his script resting on a music stand, and cue Tulk with a vocabulary of gestures not unlike those of an orchestral conductor. They would talk together about crescendos and diminuendos, Gould would refer to a particular sequence as ternary or a particular voice as lyrical, and in general he seemed to be playing the role of composer-conductor. . . . Every now and then, when frustration threatened to erupt, he would break into an extravagant German-accented monologue or recall an anecdote associated with his research. His concentration was relentless. Each break would last only a minute or two, until the laughter died down. But he seemed to sense just when that break had to come. His coworkers never questioned him. They were there to help, to tell him what could be done, to activate his ideas. The ideas were almost invariably his."

Gould sustained these late-night sessions by his own enthusiasm, but there were limits. "Toward 5 A.M. . . . ," Littler reported, "Gould was still patient with his colleagues and they were still willing to go on as long as he wanted. But reactions were slowing and Gould's lack of sleep had already reduced his eyes to near-slits. 'It's beginning to catch up with me,' he smiled. 'I usually get by on seven or eight hours and can make out on four or five for a stretch. But I've stretched the stretch to the limit. Shall we call it a night?'"

Janet Somerville remembers those late-night editing sessions from a somewhat different perspective. "Lorne and Glenn loved each other, and so between them there was utter peace," she says. "It wasn't sick, it wasn't homosexual, it wasn't any of the things we put in a twentieth-century context. It was like a knight and a page, you know, on a great adventure. Lorne should have lived in the Middle Ages. I mean, he has that kind of loyal devotion, which was *the* human virtue of that relationship. And Lorne is just so rich in it. And Glenn found it all totally normal. I mean, he felt that of *course* people would feel that way about him."

A small white parrot suddenly flutters out of a corner of Miss Somerville's living room and swoops past her visitor. "Since it will go on doing that as long as you're here, I might as well put it away," she says, opening the door to the bird's cage and letting it take refuge. She remembers now that she had other work to do besides the

Gould show. She was the producer on a nightly program called *Ideas*, of which "The Idea of North" was just one installment, and she was particularly engrossed at that point in taping Martin Luther King's Toronto lectures on nonviolence. But even after working all day, she felt an obligation to spend her nights in the nocturnal world of Glenn Gould. "I was a tired, very hardworking producer who was concerned with five hours a week of other programming at the same time," she says, "but still fascinated by the aesthetic elegance and technical precision of what Glenn was doing. And I enjoyed those all-night sessions, just watching the two of them.

"They would turn out the studio lights and just go by the lights from the console, which was— They were both sort of lit from beneath, and they both have lovely faces, with, you know, strong bone structures. And I would sit there, very tired, having been working all day, and being about to work all the next day, watching the light on their bones and their skin, and watching their fascination. . . ."

Gould never played the piano for her, and now that he is dead, she can only watch him perform on television from time to time. "He looks beautiful," she says. "I mean, in a way, I sometimes feel a little embarrassed, as I sometimes did in watching him edit 'The Idea of North.' Because his physical reaction to beautiful sound, to making beautiful sound—or, in the case of editing, to *hearing* great sound—was so strong that I wanted to look away, sometimes. It was so autoerotic."

Q: Autoerotic?

A: Yes. I felt—you know, I felt sometimes that I was crossing that fine line of voyeurism. Because, I mean, *that's* where Glenn lived, you know, in that *total* response to what he had just created, and in its correspondence to what he had already previously heard in there, inside his head. And that was *so* much more important to him than personal relationships, or money, or, you know, the other things that we mortals get caught up in. That was—that was his *passion* in a very, very full sense.

The show did get done, and it got done just barely in time for Canada's celebration of its own centennial. It is sometimes a little difficult to remember how new the Canadian nation is. Not until well after the battle of Gettysburg, when Americans spent three days slaughtering each other in their struggle over the assertion of a national identity, was the Canadian federation born in 1867. And even then, the provinces of Manitoba and Saskatchewan did not yet exist, nor Alberta, nor British Columbia. So the centennial celebrations of 1967 were an important milestone in the Canadians' still evolving sense of their own identity. The Toronto *Telegram* printed a special magazine section that July 1, Canada Day, and asked various notables like Robertson Davies and Morley Callaghan to explain what it all meant. Gould's views were typically idiosyncratic: "Canada's a place to live comfortably, amicably, and with reasonable anonymity. And I think the latitudinal factor is important to me—the fact we're a northern people, cross-pollinated by influences from the south. But for the moment we're in danger of losing . . . something we Canadians could capitalize on: A synoptic view of the world we live in."

Gould said it all much better in "The Idea of North," which was finally broadcast at the very end of the anniversary year, on December 28. "I found myself listening at two levels simultaneously," Barbara Frum wrote in a clumsy but perceptive review in the Toronto *Star*, "—to the stream of ideas but just as compelling in this production, to the pattern of sounds Gould wove out of his speakers' voices. Using the hypnotic drone of moving train wheels as a bass, Gould wove the voices of the five persons he interviewed into a thick and moody line, fading the voices in and out, under and over each other. . . . There was no attempt to define a 'problem.' No urge to give climatic conditions, population statistics, recent history of the region. . . . Instead Gould used his interviews to create a sound composition about the loneliness, the idealism and the letdowns of those who go North." And the Ottawa *Citizen:* "A poetic and beautiful montage of the North emerged that. . . was more real and honest than the entire ten-foot shelf of standard clichés about Canada's northlands." And the Montreal *Star:* "The Gould broadcast . . . is likely to stand as the forerunner of a new radio art, a wonderfully imaginative striving for a new way to use the only half-explored possibilities of an established form."

Most of Gould's major radio documentaries were inevitably about music, and therein lay both their strengths and their weaknesses.

Strengths because music was Gould's passion, and he had a profound knowledge and experience of it. Weaknesses because music is very hard to capture in the alien language of words. And so Gould's documentaries often turned into music-appreciation seminars, in which various experts sat around and offered comments, until they were all overpowered by the background sounds of the music itself. "Casals: A Portrait for Radio" (1973) was appropriately reverent, and so was "Richard Strauss: The Bourgeois Hero" (1979).

Still, Gould was marvelously inventive. Dissatisfied with his first Schoenberg show in 1962, he eagerly accepted the invitation from John Roberts to celebrate Schoenberg's hundredth birthday in 1974. "It should not be a repeat of our 1962 program, or even a major revision of that very substantial effort," he wrote to Roberts, "though needless to say I would cull from that program such irreplaceable mementoes as Schoenberg's own voice, and almost certainly that of the late Frau Gertrude as well. Basically . . . I would prefer . . . to start from scratch. First of all . . . I would like to make it, overall, a more 'integral' structure—'symphonicizing' it, so to speak, somewhat along the lines of the Stokowski project. . . ."

The standard radio talk show consists of various guests being assembled in a studio and then encouraged to say whatever comes into their heads. Gould's concept of radio was totally different, totally controlled, with himself as the controller. Instead of assembling his experts to chatter at random, Gould interviewed them one by one, recorded them one by one, and then set to work splicing his tapes of these conversations. In contrast to the usual babble, Gould's carefully edited radio documentaries provided the totally implausible (but totally convincing) sound of a half-dozen very interesting people engaged in a very interesting discussion.

And then there was the music that Gould dubbed in, without ever explaining what he was doing. Thus in "Schoenberg: The First Hundred Years," Gould created the remarkable scene of Ernst Krenek recalling how he once went to visit Schoenberg to tell him about his recent discovery of some thirteenth-century motets, and how the atonality of this music provided a background to Schoenberg's own work. And while Krenek's *Mitteleuropäische* voice rolled on, telling how Schoenberg had proved completely uninterested in his visitor's discoveries, Gould dubbed in some of the strange medieval music that the great innovator had refused to hear.

Gould's reference to "the Stokowski project" recalled one of his most remarkable documentaries, "Stokowski: A Portrait for Radio" (1970). In contrast to Schoenberg, who could only be talked about, Stokowski was still there to be questioned. He was eighty-seven years old by now, but nonetheless flourishing, and full of octogenarian opinions. Gould had long admired him. He could remember that he had "hated every minute" of *Fantasia,* which had opened in Toronto when Gould was eight, but Stokowski took pride in unconventional programming, and the new technologies spread his unconventionalities far and wide. "My first encounters with masterpieces I'd read about and wondered about—Schoenberg's *Gurrelieder,* for example, or Mahler's eighth—were via his broadcasts and recordings," Gould later wrote in "Stokowski in Six Scenes," "and after such radio or phonograph exposures I invariably found myself in a state that I can only call exalted. . . . Stokowski was, for want of a better word, an ecstatic."

They had met, rather absurdly, at the Frankfurt railroad station in 1957. While waiting to board the Amsterdam–Vienna express, the twenty-five-year-old Gould recognized the white-haired conductor pacing to and fro. After trying in vain to think of some elegant means of introducing himself, he finally maneuvered his way into the great man's path, then dropped his ticket and stooped down to retrieve it. "I did manage (or at least I like to think I did) a look of genuine incredulity. 'Why, it's—it's—it's Maestro Stokowski, isn't it?'" Stokowski regarded his interrogator without great interest and said in a "benignly weary" voice, "It is, young man."

An ordinary admirer might have fled at that point, but Gould coolly introduced himself. He was pleasantly surprised to hear the maestro say, "I have read that you were recently in Leningrad." "It was incredible," Gould recalled. "He knew who I was; he knew what I'd been doing." Stokowski even proposed a rendezvous. "'Perhaps, then, later in the evening, I will visit with you. I would be interested to learn your impressions of Leningrad today, and perhaps you might have some interest in my impressions of Leningrad many years ago.' I assured him I would: I would have been interested in his impressions of Mickey Mouse if it had made a visit with him possible."

So they met again when the train was under way, and Stokowski politely inquired where and what Gould had most recently played.

Gould answered "rather proudly" that he had just performed Beethoven's Third Concerto with Herbert von Karajan in Berlin. "The
Beethoven third," Stokowski mused. "Is that not the lovely concerto in G major?" Gould was impressed. "It was a superb gam-
bit . . ." he said later. "Lovely or otherwise, the Beethoven third is
in the key of C minor, as Stokowski knew all too well; but in one
seemingly innocuous, skillfully indirect sentence, he had let me
know that he was not in awe of the 'Generalmusikdirektor of
Europe [Karajan],' that soloists, as a breed, were to be shunned on
principle, and that concertos, as a symphonic subspecies, were quite
beneath his notice."

Gould being Gould, he proposed, almost a decade later, after his
retirement from the stage, that they record the *Emperor Concerto*
together. "With pleasure," said Stokowski, who hadn't accompanied a soloist since working with Rachmaninoff in the 1930's. So it
was done, and a splendidly majestic recording it is. There also
remains of that 1966 recording session an odd footnote: During a
break, someone knocked at the door, and then a woman came in and
said to Gould, "Hi. I just wanted to say hello, because I'm a fan, and
since we were leaving, I thought I'd just stop by and tell you that."
Nobody seemed to know quite what to say, Gould recalled, and so
"the lady was finally reduced to adding, 'I'm Barbra Streisand.' And
I remember, to my eternal embarrassment, contributing the most
maladroit moment of that or any other conversation by saying, 'I
know.'" In this odd meeting of mutual fans—for Gould intensely
admired Miss Streisand's singing ("With the possible exception of
Elisabeth Schwarzkopf," he later wrote, "no vocalist has brought me
greater pleasure")—the pianist also became aware that Stokowski
"appeared vaguely annoyed about the whole thing—about the inter-
ruption of his discourse . . . about the appearance of this talkative
young woman whose name he either did not catch or did not know,
and that he drummed his fingers on the arm of his chair—more or
less in the rhythm of the timpani solo—to indicate his displeasure."

Three years later, John Roberts proposed a radio documentary on
Stokowski, and Gould asked the old man whether he would agree
to a lengthy interview, for what Gould had in mind now was a kind
of monologue in which Stokowski would talk about his view of life
while Gould dubbed in background music from Stokowski's recordings. Stokowski agreed, but there was a new difficulty. The New

York educational television station WNET was also planning a documentary on Stokowski, and after some negotiations with CBC, it was agreed that the television cameras would film Gould doing his radio interview. Even though only a bit of this film would be used, Gould and Stokowski were now both prisoners of forces beyond their control. There was a long wait, unsettling, exasperating, while the technicians set up their cameras in Stokowski's elegant Fifth Avenue apartment. Stokowski inquired of Gould what he planned to ask him. Gould artfully took out several pages of notes and read off a few questions. "'Of course,' I smiled, 'I really shouldn't tell you my questions in advance—I should try to surprise you.' (I could afford to smile—I still intended to surprise him.)"

The standard technique is to start with innocuous questions, and then to lead the way gradually into more difficult terrain, and if there is any question that may cause a disaster, save that until the end. Gould loved to overturn standard techniques, though, so now that the TV lights and cameras were all set up, and the irritable old man was impatient to do his turn, Gould started out with a completely incredible question. "Maestro, I have this recurring dream," he began, possibly recalling his triumphant visit to Russia. "In it, I appear to be on some other planet, perhaps in some other solar system, and, at first, it seems as though I am the only Earthman there. And I have a tremendous sense of exhilaration because I seem to believe, in the dream, that I have been given the opportunity—and the authority—to impart my value systems to whatever forms of life there might be on that planet; I have the feeling that I can create a whole planetary value system in my own image. . . ."

Stokowski, who had been staring nervously at the camera while waiting for one of the customary introductory cues ("How did you happen to take up conducting?"), turned in wonderment toward this bizarre interrogator. He began "moving his lips without uttering a word," Gould recalled, "and for some moments I thought that he was not going to answer at all." The extraordinary question that Gould was asking, in his windy and circuitous way, was, What would Stokowski do if he somehow landed on a distant planet where the inhabitants had no knowledge whatever of the arts. What—if anything—would he tell them?

The egomaniac in Stokowski paused for a moment and took a deep breath, and then the old man began an extraordinary peroration: "Think of our solar system, its colossal size," he said. "I have the impression that there are many solar systems, that ours is a very big one, but that there are others which are much larger. . . . I have also the impression that not only is there endless space and the endless mass of the solar systems that are in that space, but there is endless time and endless mental power, that there are great masses of mind, of which ours, in this little Earth that we live on, is only a small part. . . ."

"It was perfect," said Gould, the master manipulator, having gambled that he could surprise this old eagle into expressing the exaltation that nobody had ever before recorded, "it was poetry, it was exactly what I'd come for; if he could keep it up, I had a program."

Keep it up? Stokowski could hardly stop. "Art is like the deep roots of a great oak tree," he said, "and out of these roots grow many branches. . . . If I did have that possibility, I would do my best to give a clear impression to what other form of life there might be on that planet, of what I think is beautiful and orderly, what I think is creative and what I think is destructive. It would be possible, I hope, to let them see what is happening on this Earth—so much destruction, so little that is creative."

Stokowski stopped there, after nearly ten minutes, and eventually Gould took over, first with more questions and finally with razor and glue. He "could not bear to take my leave of Stokowski while he mused upon man's capacity for self-destruction," Gould said, and so he resorted once again to "creative cheating," re-editing the tape to make Stokowski end where he had begun: "Think of our solar system, its colossal size, its possibility." Then, as always, Gould edited himself out of the program, so that Stokowski, instead of answering a provocative question, appeared to be simply prophesying in the manner of some new Ezekiel. And then Gould added music, so that Stokowski's visionary outpourings soared over a background of Schoenberg's *Verklärte Nacht*, Holst's *The Planets*, and Scriabin's *Poem of Ecstasy*.

It was only some months after Gould had sent a tape of this really admirable documentary to Stokowski, and after it had been broadcast to considerable acclaim, that Gould learned that Stokowski, with the serene indifference of old age, had never listened to it.

Before, during, and after the making of the Stokowski program, Gould was deeply involved in extending "The Idea of North" into a number of sequels. The first of these dealt with another remote region, Newfoundland, the land of the Viking settlements, which had joined the Canadian federation only in 1949. Gould called his program "The Latecomers." Newfoundland was considerably more accessible than the Arctic, and more inhabited. Gould actually went there in August of 1968 "in search of characters for a documentary, the subject of which was by no means clear to me."

The subject was, of course, perfectly clear. Once again, Gould was seeking to portray solitude, isolation. Though Newfoundland was less frozen than northern Ontario, it had the additional barrier of the ocean, which Gould used as an underlying *basso continuo* throughout his program. "The reality is in its separateness," he later wrote. "The very fact—the inconvenience—of distance is its great natural blessing. Through that fact, the Newfoundlander has received a few more years of grace—a few more years in which to calculate the odds for individuality in an increasingly coercive cultural milieu."

Gould used thirteen characters this time, and once again none of them ever met. By now, he was seeing in this separateness of his characters all kinds of opportunities. One of the unnamed men he interviewed, for example, compared Newfoundland to Thoreau's Walden and observed that "people who are removed from the center of a society are always able to see it more clearly." One woman, on the other hand, disliked the isolation and felt that she had to escape every once in a while. "I kept saying, 'But why?' and naïve things of that kind," Gould later recalled. "She kept repeating herself, essentially, though with infinite variations . . . and finally turned on me with a fine fury, stopped short of insult, but indicated that my line of questioning was foolish." By splicing these two interviews together, with the interviewer once again removing himself, Gould managed to suggest that the woman who was annoyed at him was actually annoyed at the other man, and that this scene "would appear to be taking place between, I suppose, a man and wife, certainly a lady and gentleman who are engaged in rather intimate conversation. . . . The dialogue represented in that scene never took place as dialogue, and yet I have a strange feeling that had they met, it would have."

Technology gave Gould an even more remarkable opportunity for "creative cheating" in the episode of the fake wave. Gould used the waves on the coast of Newfoundland much as he had used the clacking railroad in "The Idea of North," and since the ocean offers a far greater variety of sounds, Gould taped hours of possibilities, pounding waves, lapping waves, sighing waves, grinding waves. Only when he got back to the editing room in Toronto did he find, as he later confessed, that "there was one scene for which I just couldn't find the right surf sound; I tried everything, every tape of sound we'd recorded in Newfoundland, and nothing quite matched the mood of the voices in that particular scene."

Gould grumbled to someone at the studio about his problem, and so he learned that the CBC had other tapes of other waves beating on other shores. Specifically, he learned that a TV crew had recently returned from making a show about Charles Darwin's voyage aboard the S.S. *Beagle* to the Galápagos Islands off the coast of Ecuador. He couldn't resist listening. "So," he said, "we ended up borrowing a tape from someone who had just returned from the Galápagos, and that worked perfectly."

But what does it actually mean for something to "work perfectly"? One wave in the background may seem a very small point of contention, and yet all the traditions of history, scholarship, and even journalism dictate that every statement must at least try to be true, that the thing should be what it pretends to be. No matter how awkward or implausible it may sound, this is what happened. *"Wie es eigentlich gewesen,"* as Leopold von Ranke said of his history of Rome, "how it really was." So if we are to hear waves beating on the shores of Newfoundland, they are supposed to be waves actually recorded on the shores of Newfoundland. Whether the taped sounds "quite matched the mood of the voices" is quite secondary, tertiary. Indeed, there is no comparison. To "match the mood" of a Newfoundlander's voice with the sound of a wave breaking on the Galápagos Islands is almost a contradiction in terms, an absurdity.

One of the wonders of technology, though, is that it denies the very idea of historical truth. Since everything on tape is a simulation, and since everything can be dubbed, redubbed, overdubbed, what actually happened is of almost no importance. Just as Elisabeth Schwarzkopf could be employed to sing a certain high note that Kirsten Flagstad could no longer reach, and nobody could tell the difference. When this operatic event leaked out as gossip, purists complained that a Flagstad performance should not include a high note secretly sung by Schwarzkopf, but what were the alternatives? No Flagstad performance? A Flagstad performance with mangled high notes? To Gould, such arguments were antiquarian. The goal was not historical accuracy but artistic perfection, and while there might well be very different visions of perfection, Gould was determined to follow his own.

So were the Mennonites, those remarkable descendants of the sixteenth-century Anabaptists, who believed passionately that every injunction of the New Testament must be carried out exactly as written. Gould made these onetime heretics the subject of "Quiet in the Land" (1973), his second sequel to "The Idea of North." It is the most complicated and in some ways the most interesting of these three radio shows because the separateness of the Mennonites is spiritual rather than physical, and chosen rather than compelled.

And Gould's mastery of his medium had by now become overwhelming. The beginning of "Quiet in the Land" is one of the most beautiful things he ever did, first the slow tolling of a church bell, pianissimo, as though from a great distance; then faint chirpings, which sound vaguely like sea gulls but gradually reveal themselves to be the voices of children at play; then, with the church bell still tolling, a sound that resembles surf but is actually the rush of highway traffic; and then the jubilation of a Mennonite congregation singing a hymn.

"Let us bow for prayer," the minister declares. "Lord God, the Holy Ghost, in this accepted hour, as on the day of Pentecost, descend in Thy power. . . ." And as the minister speaks those words, another voice is saying, "I think there is a conflict on the idea of Utopianism versus scattering into the world. . . ." And as the earnest voices continue their explorations of these churchly matters, the music in the background keeps veering between a solo cello playing a reflective Bach saraband and Janis Joplin singing, "Oh, Lord, won't you buy me a Mercedes-Benz?"

Gould was by now possessed by the idea of pushing "contrapuntal radio" to its absolute limits, and beyond. "There's going to be a scene in there which will drive you crazy . . ." he said to a CBC "interviewer" in one of those promotional shows for which he now wrote out both questions and answers. "It's a scene in which nine characters . . . talk about the church's relationship to pacifism at what appears to be a church meeting. It's all hooked up from the eight-track, of course. But it's going to make everything I've done up till the present seem like Gregorian chant by comparison."

It is a most impressive scene, about ten minutes long, and almost completely incomprehensible. At one point, for example, while one character says, "The Catholic Church takes a hard teaching like 'You shall not kill,'" a second character simultaneously says, "To me Christianity means unselfishness," and a third says, "When I am threatened as an individual, maybe then we had better reexamine how we have been doing things." Precisely because each of these speakers is saying something that requires concentration and reflection, the simultaneity of their words contradicts their purpose. Gould acknowledged that in such scenes "not every word is going to be audible," but he argued that "by no means every syllable in the final fugue from Verdi's *Falstaff* is either," and "I do believe that most of us are capable of a much more substantial information intake than we give ourselves credit for." The analogy to Verdi is a very debatable one. It does not matter greatly whether we know that the cast of *Falstaff* is singing "Tutto nel mondo è burla" (The whole world is but a joke), for the music is telling us much the same thing, and the music is what we have come to hear. The voices of two or three Christians speaking seriously at cross-purposes is itself almost a *burla*, indeed almost diabolical in its reduction of spiritual statements into spiritual babble.

And Gould's view of himself as the master of these revels did not go unchallenged. Jim Lotz found, on rehearing himself in "The Idea of North," that he could "become a little irritated at the absence of a coherent series of statements." One of Gould's Mennonite subjects, Roy Vogt, a professor of economics at the University of Manitoba in Winnipeg, complained even before the tapes were edited that Gould was manipulating people. "Several times in our conversation," he wrote to Gould, "I was led to believe that my ideas would be used not as the expression of an individual but as a foil for the ideas of others. You can't abstract an individual much more than that, even in a totalitarian society. The musical analogy of counterpoint which you used very often reinforces this impression. Each person becomes a note in a larger symphony, which in social terms is perhaps as good a way as any of describing the underlying assumptions of a totalitarian state. The dictator is a social composer."

Touché. Looking down at his arm and seeing that his accuser had drawn blood, Gould answered with a slashing counterattack. "Counterpoint is not a dry academic exercise . . ." he wrote to Vogt, "but rather a method of composition in which, if all goes well, each individual voice leads a life of its own. Naturally, even in the most complex contrapuntal textures, certain concessions must be demanded of each musical strand as an accommodation to the harmonic and rhythmic pace of the whole. . . . I do not, however, feel that my personal convictions encourage me to distort the interview-material which is made available to me. Quite frankly—and to put it in the most selfish terms—I would do less than justice to my role as a producer if I were to deliberately sacrifice the 'contrapuntal' integrity of one value-system in order to enhance another."

"Quiet in the Land" should have been the end of Gould's exploration of the northlands, but he received a letter from Peking in July of 1978, from John Fraser of the Toronto *Globe and Mail*, suggesting that he do a radio documentary on China. An unusual idea, which Gould inevitably found "fascinating." What made it somewhat absurd, however, was that Gould proposed to add this to his trilogy on solitude—the billion inhabitants of China as an example of solitude!—and the only thing even more absurd was that he contemplated making this documentary on China without leaving Canada. "The prospects for a visit by me to the Orient are nil," he wrote to Fraser. "As you know, I don't fly—haven't for sixteen years—and no assignment, no matter how enticing, will get me aloft again. Furthermore, with each passing year, I become more committed to a sedentary existence and less willing to contemplate any form of travel. . . . Even if a slow boat to China did exist, I would not be on it."

Still, Gould wanted to look into the possibilities. "The big question is: can we find an approach, however oblique, which justifies such a program?" he wrote. "What intrigues me is the possibility of relating a China-essay to the general theme of my so-called 'Solitude Trilogy.' . . . Suppose—and this is strictly off the top of my head—

we would do a program about 'The Last Puritans'—with apologies to George Santayana. Matter of fact, I like the title and I particularly like the relationship it could have to my 'Solitude Trilogy' (Quartet!)—i.e. the political dimension of isolation. What say you?"

Whatever Fraser may have said, nothing ever came of this bizarre project. The "Solitude Trilogy" remained a trilogy.

Since this is the age of television, somebody (possibly Gould himself) decided sometime in 1968 that "The Idea of North" should somehow be converted from "contrapuntal radio" into a television show. Gould was discussing this idea with a friend and producer at Columbia named Paul Myers, and Myers mentioned one of his friends, Judith Pearlman. She was just getting started in television, and she felt passionately about music in general and Gould's music in particular. So they all met and listened to a tape of "The Idea of North."

"That made me pretty nervous," Miss Pearlman recalls. "Because Gould was watching me like a hawk. And at the end, he said, 'Well, what do you think?' And I said, 'I think it's very hard to come to a decision after just hearing it once, and I'd like to listen to it again for the next two weeks.' So that's what I did. I took the tape home and made it my matins and evensong, lauds and complines, for two weeks. As I listened, the patterns of sound became clearer, along with the personalities of the five characters. Then I wrote a treatment, and Glenn read that and liked it."

"At the core of the film is a train journey north to Hudson Bay," the treatment begins. "It is, of course, a real train on a scheduled run—yet also a train of mind and mythology, carrying men still seeking the last frontier as trial or escape. . . ." Miss Pearlman barely realized that she had become a pawn in a complicated power struggle typical of television. The New York public broadcasting executives at WNET wanted to make a deal with the CBC for a series of ten coproduced shows, one of which would almost inevitably feature Glenn Gould, and the fact that Miss Pearlman had written a treatment that Gould had liked gave her a quasi-legal hold on "The Idea of North." It was a hold that was strong enough to survive several shifts and transfers among the executives who were supposed to decide things, and after nearly two years of negotiations and delays, she found herself in Ottawa, bargaining with the Canadian National Railways about what it would cost to rent a railroad car to carry a film crew from Winnipeg to Churchill.

Gould, who was busy making new recordings, elegantly removed himself from all these difficulties. While he sang the praises of technology, he liked to spend hours editing radio tapes with one technician in a studio but not in negotiating the price of a railroad car that would convert a fantasy of sound into a visual reality, or simulation of reality. "So I went over to talk to them, and they wanted five thousand dollars," Miss Pearlman recalls. "Well, my whole budget for such things was only eighteen thousand dollars, so we just kept on negotiating. They said we could have it for four thousand dollars, so I thought, We're making progress. And this went on for *days*. Finally, they said, 'Okay, you can have it for five hundred dollars.'

"So I went back to the CBC studio, and I could hear the producer shouting, the producer they had assigned to take charge of this project, and I knew he was drunk. He shouted that he would do all kinds of lascivious things to me. I was afraid of him, because of the way he talked, and because he was so big. He was about six feet four, and about two hundred fifty pounds. He had made his reputation producing sports events. So I got on the phone to New York, and I said, 'I don't think I can work with this guy.' And then I just held up the phone."

She demonstrates, holding her hand up over her head, holding up the telephone that carried the drunken bellowing of her assigned producer to the ears of supposedly protective coproducers in New York. "And the next Monday," she says, "I was told that he was off the show. Then they just left me on my own." This was not by any means the end of her social problems. She recalls that there was a certain amount of he-man drinking among the technicians, and that drinking repeatedly led to challenges to her authority. "Remember, I was a woman, one of the very few on an executive level at CBC," she says, "and I was from New York, and I was a Jew. I was everything you weren't supposed to be. It was not a good time to be in Canada, at least not for me."

But the work progressed. She hired an actor to play the homespun philosopher, Wally Maclean, and another to play the mute role of a

symbolic young man going north for the first time. There had been
no such character in the radio drama—he was just somebody
Maclean talked about—but TV always needs to *show* everything that
radio leaves to the imagination. And occasionally this has a miraculous effect. Miss Pearlman was determined to transfer Gould's
whole opening "trio sonata" onto film, so when Nurse Schroeder
started talking about the geese flying over Hudson Bay, Miss Pearlman showed us the geese in the air, and when Professor Vallee
started grumbling about the North, she showed us the grumbling in
a clubby Toronto bar. When Phillips then began talking about the
government's role in the North, the camera wandered into Ottawa's
Department of Northern Affairs and showed us row on row of filing
cabinets. And since Gould wanted his three characters talking simultaneously, Miss Pearlman very skillfully managed to get her three
images on the screen simultaneously. Gould's trio sonata thus
became a kind of sextet. When he saw it, he loved it. After looking
at seven hours of unedited rushes, he pronounced them "absolutely
remarkable."

Getting photographic material for such sequences was a lot more
complicated than taping five interviews for radio. While Gould had
made his one jaunt to Churchill in June, and later done his interviews at his convenience, Miss Pearlman had to take her actors and
her TV crew northward on her rented railway car in November. "It
was forty-five degrees below zero when we got there," she recalls.
"If you took off your glove, your hand began to feel burning. The
only hotel was a Quonset hut, but there was a telegram waiting for
me:

MAY WE RECOMMEND THE MONTEVIDEO EXCELSIOR—EIGHT PRESIDENTIAL
SUITES, 3 BANQUET ROOMS, 2 SALTWATER SWIMMING POOLS, SEASIDE
DINER . . . FOR YOUR MID-SEASON VACATION.

CORDIALLY,
G. GOULD, MANAGER

"Churchill was a town of about two thousand souls, and there was
just one main street," Miss Pearlman says. "Beyond that, on the
edge of town, there was a ring of shacks where the Indians lived,
and many of them had no windows. I mean, they were open to the

air, at forty-five below zero. I don't know how they survived. A lot of them were drunk all the time. I felt very bad. And another thing was that there were all these abandoned dogs up there. I remember one of them was a Great Dane, and Danes don't have the skin for that kind of weather. They were all scarred and starving and desperate. We were filming there for five days. I felt very bad."

Back in the semitropical metropolis of Toronto, Miss Pearlman found Gould "charming, nourishing, and supportive," but also very busy with his recordings. The language they had in common, while she worked on her film about solitude under his rather distant scrutiny, was not television but music. "It had to do with how lonely I was," she recalls. "I didn't know anyone in Toronto. He knew how I felt, not very happy." This was the occasion on which he played her *Die Frau ohne Schatten,* and the following week there occurred an even more remarkable scene.

Once again, Gould arranged for Miss Pearlman to use a piano in an empty CBC studio, looked in on her after his late-night recording session, and found her on the telephone to New York. Once again, he began to play, this time a Hindemith sonata. Once again, Miss Pearlman emerged from the control room. She happened to mention that she had heard that he had recently taped for the CBC something that nobody could imagine Gould playing, Chopin, the Sonata in B minor.

"Without saying anything, he started playing it," Miss Pearlman recalls. "Then all of a sudden, he got serious about it. It was like a switch being turned on. And he played the whole piece through from beginning to end. And it was the greatest performance I've ever heard in my life. I was more than stunned. At the end, he said, 'What do you think?' I said it was the best performance I'd ever heard. He said, 'Oh, it's not so good as the tape.' But I didn't agree. This was a live performance, and I told him that sometimes, even when he was recording, he should record a straight-through performance. Obviously, it made him acutely uncomfortable to play for a live audience. I remember going to his last performance of the Brahms concerto with Bernstein, and it was obvious that the person playing it was in great pain. But his playing for me now meant that he knew I was feeling awful. It was his gift to me, meaning, 'Hang in there.'"

The reviews in the summer of 1970 were generally favorable. The Toronto *Telegram*'s Kenneth Winters rightly judged that the television version was less daring than the radio original, but he added that it was "the first television production I have ever seen ... which is a complete, organic and lyrical composition in sounds as well as a composition in pictures." But because television must show what it describes, the cameras showed the snow and ice that the radio had ignored, and this demonstration of what the fabled North actually looks like raised chauvinist hackles. "'The Idea of North' emerges as a foreigner's idea of Canada," the Toronto *Star* complained. "Still and icy landscapes stretch before the camera. Defensively dressed in hooded parkas and boots, inhabitants of shanty towns bustle along bleak streets. And it looks cold. So cold that you wouldn't want to live there. . . ."

Such chamber-of-commerce carping overlooks the most important weakness in "The Idea of North"—and by implication in the whole "solitude trilogy"—which is that Gould never really told us what he thought about solitude. "I've always had some sort of intuition," he once said, "that for every hour that you spend in the company of other human beings you need X number of hours alone." And on another occasion, he declared that the basic theme of this whole trilogy was "that isolation is the indispensable component of human happiness." But how does solitude actually help or harm a man? How does it liberate him or cripple him? How does it enable him to see or prevent him from seeing? Is it a necessity or an accident? These would be difficult questions even if Gould were writing about them in the most straightforward way, but a radio drama spun out of other people's words was obviously the most ambiguous of approaches.

Janet Somerville astutely observed that Gould's passions concerned mainly the sounds that he heard inside his own head, and if this seems bizarre, it is only because we have all been trained in recent years to judge everyone in terms of his relations with other people. Anthony Storr, a lecturer in psychiatry at Oxford, argues that this is a major misconception, and he likes to cite Edward Gibbon's observation that "solitude is the school of genius." "It is widely believed that interpersonal relationships of an intimate kind are the chief, if not the only, source of human happiness," Storr wrote recently in *Solitude, A Return to the Self.* "Yet the lives of creative individuals often seem to run counter to this assumption. For example, many of the world's greatest thinkers have not reared families or formed close personal ties. This is true of Descartes, Newton, Locke, Pascal, Spinoza, Kant, Leibniz, Schopenhauer, Nietzsche, Kierkegaard and Wittgenstein." One could say much the same of Beethoven, Haydn, and Brahms, yet Gould never really tried to formulate or document any such theory, except as a personal preference of his own.

"I think for Gould the question of solitude must have been absolutely central," says Richard Sennett, the N.Y.U. sociology professor who has been working for several years on a book on the subject. "What solitude really does to people's sense of creativity—you can't really create difference without creating the sense of being alone. When you're in a community with other people, when what you express is what could be shared among all of them, that tends to be flat, tends to be ironed out. How does a person get the freedom to reflect, to be self-doubting without being self-indulgent? I suppose the writer who most resembles Gould is Wallace Stevens, with that notion of perfection in retreat. You also hear the silences of that kind of withdrawal in his poetry. Nothing escapes Stevens that isn't deeply, deeply considered. There's a kind of almost supernatural calm in his writing, and yet there's nothing studied about it. You just feel the lines flow one from the other, rather like what you sense in Gould's recording process. . . ."

"Yes, it's very much me, in terms of what it says," Gould told one interviewer about his enigmatic explorations of the North, "—no matter how long Wally Maclean may take to say it—it's about as close to an autobiographical statement as I am likely to make at this stage of my life." As spoken, as broadcast, the aged surveyor's final peroration on the meaning of going north sounds shrewd and sagacious. And perhaps to prevent us from listening too closely, Gould suddenly dubbed in the Arctic strains of Sibelius's Fifth Symphony. But when one reads the actual words that Maclean was declaiming through all that Sibelius—supposedly representing Gould's "autobiographical statement"—they come perilously close to gibberish: "A few years back, certainly in human memory, people thought that this—well, what we call our North—presented a real challenge. Well, what form did they take? Hah! What form? As if everything must somehow have a form. This is hard, this is hard on you. He must notice that you're struggling a bit, eh? But what you're really saying then is something like this: That there was a time when the challenge was understandable. What challenge then? Oh, well, here you have to take it easy. . . ." And so on.

In the way Gould presented "The Idea of North," he made it seem that these were his own ideas, his own creation. And yet he never signed the check. After Gould's brief opening statement, the listener never again hears him express any opinions whatever, never even hears him ask any questions. If anyone wants to take Wally Maclean's peroration as an expression of Gould's own views, all well and good, but Gould never committed himself to that. He remained offstage, the marionette-master, the magician. "Sure, he was a thinker, but very much a by-the-seat-of-the-pants thinker," says Littler of the *Star*. "He thought deeply, but he wasn't as worried by the contradictions in what he was saying as some people with more formal training in logical thought might be. There's an affinity between him and Marshall McLuhan, and I think he admired McLuhan's feeling that everything is provisional, that you make probes. . . ." "What Glenn really thought about solitude, only Glenn knows," Miss Pearlman adds. "He designed his solitude to suit himself, like a pearly shell. He made it a work of art. He distanced himself from other people's emotions—and then he was brilliant."

Yet there were other people who could see through Gould's pearly shell, and read his invisible writings on the walls. More than a decade after making "The Idea of North," when Gould played a tape of it to Margaret Pacsu, who was collaborating with him on his jubilee record album, she began crying. "I suddenly understood what he was trying to do with these voices," she recalls. "It was a quartet of these beautifully balanced—there was a rhythm and a melody to it. Plus the underlying— Now careful, because I'm a good Hungarian-American here, and I will burst into tears in a minute. The sadness of this man was that he was unable to reach out and make a—a—an intimate, warm contact with anyone. That's why I found that devastating. Plus to be sitting there in front of the man and have this happen. He was—surprised, and quite pleased, and quite comforting— Excuse me—" Remembering that moment when she burst into tears while Gould played her "The Idea of North," she bursts into tears all over again.

X

The TV Star

Music is one of the mysteries that television has never been able to solve. Television exists to show a series of pictures, and music is invisible. The cameras do quite well with opera, since the singers provide something to look at—though long close-ups of a figure like Luciano Pavarotti are a mixed blessing—but when they present a Leonard Bernstein conducting the Vienna Philharmonic, for example, they can only offer those endless shots of violinists sawing and flutists tootling and the white-haired maestro waving, gasping, pointing, sighing, leaping. And when they want to show a pianist, they can only show, from the left side and the right side, from above and below, from front and back and overhead, the pianist belaboring the keyboard. Gould was perfectly aware of this, of course, and when he let patterns of dots drift across the screen while the camera showed his hands playing *The Well-Tempered Clavier*, he told an interviewer, "I had done several TV concerts, and they were static, dull, I wondered if there wasn't a more imaginative way to present good music on TV. . . ."

Gould's first experiments were actually quite conservative. When the CBC first signed him up in 1961 to do four musical specials on its *Festival* series, he originally could think of nothing more imaginative than to create a special stage set for his piano and to talk about what he was going to play. Thus on his second program, when he performed the Shostakovitch Quintet and the Prokofiev Seventh Sonata, he not only gave an informal lecture on Soviet musical life but appeared on what one critic called "a set suggesting the opulence of the court of Peter the Great. . . ." And his commentaries tended to be, like his record-liner notes, somewhat pretentious and somewhat banal.

The CBC authorities were inclined to let Gould do pretty much what he wanted, but these early adventures in television were something less than a triumph. After his third program, entitled "Richard Strauss, A Personal View," the Toronto *Star*'s Roy Shields complained about "having Glenn Gould exercise his ego for an hour on prime time. . . . It is difficult to understand why Mr. Gould was allowed to write his own script. . . . His use of language . . . is quite unintelligible." When the fourth of these shows appeared in the spring of 1963 and included Gould's "So You Want to Write a Fugue?," Shields reluctantly conceded that "it was quite good, if you happened to be a fugue fan," but John Kraglund of the *Globe and Mail* couldn't resist borrowing part of Gould's libretto to accuse him of trying to "be clever for the sake of showing off."

Gould was inevitably making the discovery that TV critics could be even more exasperating than music critics. While most music critics made some pretense of knowing something about their subject, the TV critics felt it their assignment to make bright remarks about whatever appeared on their television screens, whether they knew anything about the subject or not. But the critics were not the only ones who felt that Gould's first TV shows were exercises in self-indulgence. "There's nothing wrong with him chatting," said Eric Till, who had just produced Gould's "Anatomy of Fugue," "but there are times, and last night was one, when even I couldn't understand what he was talking about. And I had it all explained to me." Kraglund of the *Globe* said Till then offered a parody, "in familiar Gould style," about "motivic experimentation, motivic compromise and so on." And was Gould difficult about making changes? Kraglund inquired. "No, he's most cooperative," the producer said. "But all we could do was suggest changes. And let's face it, if you had to say what he says in Gouldese, with all these favorite words of his, could any changes make it very different?"

Gould was undaunted. In November of that year—just six months before his retirement from the stage—he turned up in New York with a tape of his "Anatomy of Fugue," which he persuaded Yehudi Menuhin to come and watch in a closet-sized room at the CBC offices. Menuhin made a great show of being impressed by Gould's *savoir-faire.* "I find it rather difficult," he said, according to Lillian Ross of *The New Yorker,* "when they put you in front of the camera and say, '*Do* something.'"

Gould smiled. He, of course, had never been put in front of a camera and told to do something. He informed Menuhin that this show had taken two months of conferences, two days of shooting, and thirty thousand dollars. "I don't know if my film is for the mass public," Gould added. "Sometimes I think they don't know what the hell I've said, but they feel elevated."

Throughout this special showing for Menuhin, Gould periodically hopped up from his seat to ask the projectionist to get a sharper focus or to turn up the volume of sound. Miss Ross could not resist comparing images, the confident performer on the screen and the slightly nervous real-life master of ceremonies fidgeting as he watched his own taped performance. Menuhin beamed approval of every piece, following each with a murmur of "Lovely, lovely" or "It comes over beautifully."

"And you spoke throughout so *smoothly,*" Menuhin purred. "Was it impromptu?"

"I had it on the TelePrompTer," said Gould, all guilelessness. ("Glenn and Yehudi were always excessively polite to each other," one TV producer observed. "They respected each other greatly, but there was always that sort of top-dog syndrome, always walking around and looking at each other.") And Gould could not stop explaining. "I looked at it often enough to pick up all the cues, but I forced myself to invent phrases as I went along, to keep it sounding natural and not too formal."

"Yes, wonderful," Menuhin said. "Especially if the words are your own."

Gould, according to Miss Ross, "laughed shyly" at the praise for his script-writing. But he also had a plan, and his invitation to Menuhin had clearly been part of it.

"Next year, if you're going to have some time, we might do one together," he said offhandedly. "You ever done the Schoenberg *Fantasia?*"

Gould probably suspected that Menuhin had never played a lot of Schoenberg—and what better way to assert his own initiative?—but Menuhin was quite ready for him.

"Oh!" he said. "What a splendid idea! I must look at the music."

Menuhin tried to reinforce his position by inviting Gould to play the Schoenberg as part of one of Menuhin's concerts in England that summer, but Gould brushed the invitation aside. "I'm finished with concerts," he said. "I'm bored with them. It's animal. It's all a circus. It's immoral."

"Yes, I do know what you mean," Menuhin hastened to agree.

They ended with a pledge to meet in front of TV cameras in Toronto. "The Schoenberg, in July," said Gould. "It will be lovely," said Menuhin.

Two years passed before Gould got Menuhin before the cameras for a TV recital of Bach, Beethoven, and the Schoenberg *Phantasy*, a thorny and disagreeable piece that might be said to express all the tormented rage of Schoenberg's last years of obscurity in Hollywood. When Menuhin arrived in Toronto with only one day to rehearse this difficult work, Gould found to his dismay that the violinist still had not done any practicing, indeed "literally did not know [it] at all."

Gould, however, had already written a little script in which he would make Menuhin explain himself.

"You don't really like the Schoenberg, do you?" he asked, a rather remarkable question for two musicians to discuss just before they perform a piece of music.

"Well, Glenn," Menuhin answered (one can generally identify a Gould script by the fact that he thought it highly idiomatic for people to address each other as "Well, Glenn" and "Well, Yehudi," but there are traces of Menuhin's own style in the extreme courtliness of his answers), "I was very anxious to take up your invitation to play it because I admire you, and you know more about Schoenberg . . . than anyone else."

"What disturbs you most?" Gould persisted.

"There is this curious discrepancy between the gesture and the words," Menuhin replied, in a marvelously oblique effort to say that he found the piece senseless. "It's as if you had taken the words of *Hamlet* and then merely strung together a series of syllables that had no meaning as such. . . ."

After all of Gould's anxieties on the eve of taping, however, he found Menuhin's actual performance "one of the great experiences of my life. In some miraculous way, Yehudi had absorbed that extraordinary piece literally overnight and played it with absolutely reckless virtuosity. What was more important, though . . . was that he played it as though for that moment, at least, he loved it." Some critics agreed. Pat Pearce of the Montreal *Star,* for example, called this "an hour of TV grandeur . . . an hour of magnificence. . . . They gave TV a true moment of glory. For this could have been done only by TV." But Dennis Braithwaite of the *Globe and Mail* demonstrated once again that TV could provoke more brutal attacks than anything a music critic could imagine. "The program was really terrible," he wrote. "Worst of all, Glenn Gould was mostly what was wrong with it. . . . Certainly the producer, Eric Till, must be rapped for that nightmarish Victorian set . . . for photographing Gould from the back, thus making him look like something from the Cabinet of Dr. Caligari; for permitting him, while playing tender bits of Bach and Beethoven, to flop his mouth open and shut like a beached bass. . . . All this disarray wouldn't have mattered had their playing been beautiful and moving or if that famous talk had been arresting, or even made some kind of sense. But they fulfilled neither condition."

Many of Gould's thirty or so television shows were simply concerts, some with and some without commentary. The year after the Menuhin recital, for example, he joined the Toronto Symphony in playing the Bach G minor Concerto and the Strauss *Burleske.* In one sense, it was completely contradictory for Gould to be willing to play before the cameras what he refused to play before an audience. This was no longer a matter of not wanting to travel, for he traveled regularly to New York to make records, and a single recital at Carnegie Hall would have sold out within a few hours. Indeed, if he had simply announced that he would give one concert a year in Toronto's Massey Hall, the world would have thronged to fill Massey Hall. Nor was it a matter of his needing privacy or solitude. A pianist taping a concerto in the midst of a hundred orchestral musicians and a platoon of prowling TV technicians can hardly be said to be playing in private. And the camera eye, which brought his image to more people than could ever have watched him in a concert hall, brought that image in intense close-ups, publicizing and exaggerating all those celebrated gestures, the swaying, the singing, the self-conducting, that the critics so obsessively emphasized.

Gould, as usual, followed a logic of his own about these things. The fact that he was surrounded by studio listeners could be ignored because the listeners all had professional reasons to be there; they were not idle spectators who had paid just to watch. "If they were there to do a function, he didn't mind that," as Ray Roberts puts it. "He looked at them and said to himself, 'Oh, well, they're doing a job, the same as I'm doing a job.'" And though the audiences who watched him were now enormous, the TV camera provided a kind of mediation, at least a simulation of protection. If anything went disastrously wrong—though nothing ever did—it could be repaired. Gould could hardly help being amused, though, when the currents of the concert world brought to Toronto in 1970 a pianist just as eccentric as Gould himself, and just as famous for his eccentricity, the Italian virtuoso Arturo Benedetti Michelangeli.

"Much against the warnings of a number of more expert people," says John Barnes, the retired head of musical programs at CBC-TV, "I had engaged Michelangeli to do two things, a solo half-hour thing, a Beethoven sonata, and a concerto with the Toronto Symphony. He wanted to do the *Emperor*. I wasn't that keen on it, but he wanted to do the *Emperor*, so, you know—if he was going to do anything, it had to be on his terms, because he was a very difficult person.

"So he came. And one of the sidelights was that he had bought a new piano in Hamburg, insisted on flying it over and having it cleared through customs, but he'd never played it in public before, and he was dissatisfied with the tuning. So it sat in our main studio for two days whilst a tuner he'd brought in from Montreal hammered away at it, tried to get it corrected. But Michelangeli got more and more agitated. With some difficulty, he did the sonata. He only played it once for us, and we had to tape it live, and that was it.

"Then he announced that he wasn't going to play any more in the studio—that we had ruined his piano by the air conditioning, or something like that, and we were going to have to move to Massey Hall. By this time, I'd got kind of fed up with him. And coincidentally, we had been doing a series of programs with Glenn, and Glenn called, on a Tuesday morning, and wanted to speak to Mario Prizek, the producer. And I said 'Glenn, he's tied up to the teeth with Michelangeli, who's proving very difficult.'

"'Oh, yes,' says Glenn. 'I understand he can be tough. Good *luck!'*

"'Well, we'll need that on the show now,' I said. And Glenn said:

"'Well, John, if he doesn't show, I'll do it.' I said:

"'Glenn, I *heard* you. *Don't leave town!'*

"And he laughed. But it all came to a head on Thursday. There was an impasse. We couldn't book Massey Hall, it wasn't available, and we had the Toronto Symphony standing by for Friday morning. So I simply called in the impresario, a chap named Kudriatsev, from Montreal, who has now died. And the manager of Michelangeli. And I said, 'Look, I have to know, *now,* whether your artist is going to perform tomorrow, because otherwise the deal is off.' Kudriatsev was wringing his hands—'Vould you vait till tonight?' I said, 'No, I can't, I have to know now.' Well, they couldn't tell me—so I canceled the contract. Amazement on both their faces.

"'But vot vill you do?' I said:

"'I've got someone else to do it.'

"'But who? *Who?'* And I said:

"'Well, Mr. Gould is going to perform here.'

"There was a long pause by Kudriatsev, and then he *heaved* himself to his feet—he was a great, big, fat, big, big man— He bowed low, and he said, 'I con-*grat*-u-late you!' So I phoned Glenn, and I said, 'Glenn, you're on.'

"'What do you mean, "You're on?"' I said:

"'You said you'd do the *Emperor Concerto* for us.' He said:

"'You're kidding.' I said:

"'No, I'm not.'

"So Gould was as good as his word. He said, 'My God, just think that the Number One pianist is going to substitute for Number Two.' He canceled a radio show, and sat up most of the night, you know, preparing himself. [Gould had not performed the *Emperor* since recording it with Stokowski four years earlier.]

"The next morning, I went over to the studio with my unit manager, Lad Klimek, who was a Czech, and the orchestra was there, and the conductor, Karel Ancerl, and I said to Mario Prizek, 'You'd better get up and announce that it isn't Michelangeli that's playing this morning, it's going to be Glenn Gould.' So he got up and announced this, and Ancerl was standing there next to my unit manager, and he said something in Czech, and Lad said to me afterward, 'Maybe it's a good thing nobody understood what Ancerl said.' And I said, 'No, what was it?' And he said, 'Ancerl turned to me, and he said, "Michelangeli? *Gould?* Where do you people *get* such kooks?"'"

When the tape of Gould's overnight *Emperor Concerto* was finally broadcast several months later, it was—at safe remove—a triumph. "He was in superb form . . ." Littler wrote in the *Star.* "The camera, all the while, circled the piano, peered into the orchestra, and managed, without getting too fussy about it, to relate its vision to what was happening musically. Glenn Gould, as we all know by now, is television's pianist." Ken Winters of the *Telegram* agreed that Gould was "in stunning form," but he found the recorded sound a "matter for discouragement" and the whole program "discouragingly orthodox television." Talking with Gould afterward, Winters quoted him as saying that "it wasn't quite the kind of televised concert he'd like to do some day. I gathered that he had in mind something more enterprising and more inventive."

Artistic memories are fallible. Mario Prizek tells much the same story about Michelangeli's visit but presents himself rather than Barnes as the principal figure in the negotiations. Well, perhaps he is right. He and Gould worked closely on a number of productions. "The first concert was in 1962," says Prizek, starting to read from a list. He is a rather swarthy man with curling gray hair; he wears a chocolate-colored shirt, chocolate-colored slacks, and a gold necklace. ". . . and then 'Glenn Gould Plays Strauss.' That was with Lois Marshall and an orchestra conducted by Oscar Shumsky . . . And 'Conversations with Glenn Gould.' These were two one-hour shows for WNET in New York. . . ."

Prizek is a professional, and he understands what Gould saw in the possibilities of "creative cheating." There was a spectacular example—far more daring than the Galápagos wave in Newfoundland—during a show on Beethoven. "We were editing a Beethoven sonata," Prizek says, "and at one point the picture on both tapes we had was faulty—it was faulty video—and there was no way we could correct it with the existing materials. And I remembered that a few months before, Glenn had performed a Mozart sonata that had exactly the same beat, and in which he was working the same part of the keyboard. I called up that tape, and we looked at it, and my God, just for those three or four seconds that we needed to cover— It worked beautifully. And so we dropped in the Mozart shot for about three seconds in the middle of the Beethoven, and Glenn was delighted. Not in the fact of trickery but in making right something that wasn't right. When anyone would happen into the editing session while we were still working on other parts of the show, he'd want to show them the Mozart to see if they could notice it. And they couldn't."

Prizek is a gifted painter (he also knows eight languages), and not too long after the *Emperor Concerto*, he had an idea that he wanted to persuade Gould to undertake. "I knew of his interest in contemporary music," Prizek says, "and I wanted to deal, in an interesting, nonacademic way, with the various developments, decade by decade. I compiled a lot of data on the first two decades of this century, what was going on in music and literature and the arts, a sort of calendar of events, and changes in ideas about art. I showed this to Glenn, and he became more and more excited, so we concocted the first episode for John Barnes at CBC."

Barnes was very receptive. "I felt that we wanted to do something with Gould on a more sustained basis," he says. "As with any big artist, you don't just announce what you're going to do, you discuss what they'd like to do and see if you can come to a meeting of minds. So I phoned Glenn and suggested we have a talk, and this was one of the few occasions, by the way, on which *he* invited *me* to lunch. He stopped and picked me up in his car, and we went to lunch at the Westbury Hotel, and he said he was interested in doing some things that involved modern music."

Out of this idea came a series of four extraordinary hour-long shows called *Music in Our Time*. When the first of them, "The Age of Ecstasy (1900–1910)," appeared in 1974, it presented a Gould quite unlike anything ever seen before. For one thing, he was dressed in a neatly buttoned suit. No less unusual, he appeared in a sort of "Age of Ecstasy" living room, with *fin-de-siècle* paintings on the wall, ivory chessmen arrayed on a side table, and a fire burning in the marble fireplace. Most striking of all was that when Gould began playing Scriabin preludes, clouds of colored light began slowly swirling around behind his head, and not just swirling but constantly changing their shapes and their colors.

Gould had good reasons for this extravaganza. He explained to his audience that Scriabin thought musical keys implied equivalents in color, that he believed C major represented red, and D major yellow, and so on, and that he even tried unsuccessfully to invent a color keyboard. If he had succeeded, Gould said from his handsome armchair, the results "might have been something like this." The display of lights was organized by Prizek, who had commissioned Earl Reiback of the Electric Gallery in Toronto to create the chroma-keyed light sculptures. Gould was delighted. "Given the limitations of video-tape," he wrote to Paul Myers in London, "it was, I think, the most effective mating of music and camera we've managed to date and . . . some of the most effective television I've ever seen." Though this program contained other interesting examples of Gould's fascination with musical ecstasy—the Berg Sonata, four Schoenberg songs, and the Debussy Clarinet Rhapsody against a background of Monet water lilies—it was Gould's sensuous version of Scriabin that remains in the memory. "Not everyone will share his enthusiasm for the music of Scriabin," Kraglund wrote in the *Globe and Mail,* "but when he has finished introducing and performing that composer's preludes . . . there is a good chance the viewers will begin to develop an appreciation. That is one of the things about Gould—his ability to command attention in anything for which he has developed a passion."

And for what had Gould not developed a passion? On his second show, "The Flight from Order (1910–1920)," in which Gould's living room had evolved into Jugendstil and boasted a wind-up phonograph with a large trumpet to spread the new sounds, the pianist began with several of Prokofiev's magical *Visions fugitives,* then accompanied his friend Roxolana Roslak in Strauss's *Ophelialieder,* then conducted from the keyboard a dazzling version of *Pierrot Lunaire.* As soon as Patricia Rideout began singing each of Schoenberg's songs, the camera showed hallucinatory images illustrating the text. In "The Washerwoman," for example, the heroine knelt by a stream, scrubbing a piece of cloth, which she then held up and showed to be full of holes. Even when Gould hated a piece, that too was a passion. Thus, after announcing that the music of Stravinsky "sends me up the wall," he walked offstage and left the marvelous *Histoire du soldat* to be conducted by an associate, Boris Brott. He soon returned, though, to sail through his own spectacular transcription of Ravel's *La Valse* (a work of which more will be heard).

Most of the critics remained sympathetic, though some were getting restless. "How many viewers . . . had the slightest idea of what Glenn Gould was talking about . . . ?" Braithwaite complained in the *Star*. "Glenn Gould is a genius. Glenn Gould is a valuable Canadian national resource. But Glenn Gould is a hard man to follow through an analysis of even the familiar classics, let alone one of the twelve-tone labyrinths contrived by Arnold Schoenberg." The CBC didn't seem to mind such outbursts. "Glenn was someone whom we knew and trusted," John Barnes recalls. "He'd worked a great deal with radio. He'd produced things on radio. He'd grown up with us, and we with him, so we treated him very—with a good deal of respect, and let him be part of the team in a way that we probably wouldn't have done with someone else."

The third installment, "New Faces, Old Forms (1920–1930)," required all of the CBC's patience. "Visualize, if you will," Littler wrote in the *Star*, " a potted-palm scene with a vested Boris Brott conducting a chamber ensemble while a deadpan, ice-cream suited Glenn Gould and an eye-bulging Patricia Rideout brogue-accent their way through the Scottish Rhapsody from William Walton's *Façade*. If that isn't the unlikeliest opening for a CBC television music special I don't know what is. And the shenanigans don't end there. Messrs. Brott and Gould wind up in an argument about tempo, Gould and Rideout reappear as arthritic senior citizens, and all this happens within the first few minutes. . . ."

There were other shenanigans that never appeared on camera. During a rehersal, while Brott was preparing *Façade*, Gould went wandering around and finally sat down on the dais, just behind the conductor, with his fragile hands stretched out on the floor as props. "I was not aware of where Glenn was," Brott recalls, "and I stepped backwards, and I felt my heel just—well, my heel came down on—"

Q: On something squishy?

A: On something squishy. I didn't put my weight on it—thank God!—but Glenn was sitting on the floor, like this, with his hands behind him, and I had landed on one of them. And of course, all the stories that I had heard about various people flashed before my eyes—and the room went dead silent. All the cameramen and gaffers and everybody—the room went absolutely dead quiet. And he blanched. But then he sort of went like this and shook his hand and smiled and said, "It's all right. Don't worry."

And so, after some Bartok, some Schoenberg, some Hindemith and Copland, the program finished with Poulenc's bizarre "choreographic concerto" called *Aubade*. The uninjured Gould played several flashy cadenzas, Brott conducted eighteen instrumentalists, and a half dozen dancers spun and whirled through the roles of Acteon, Diana, and Diana's handmaidens. Poulenc, Gould warned his audience, wrote "some rather lovely things" but also "some of the most shameless claptrap of his time."

The furniture kept changing, so while the Gould of the 1920's sat in a white chair with a curving silver armrest, the Gould of the 1930's lounged in a tan Barcelona chair as he narrated "The Artist as Artisan" and offered Alfredo Casella's *Ricercare on the Name of Bach*, the Hindemith Trumpet Sonata, some Krenek songs, and the Webern Concerto for Nine Instruments. Any pianist might have had difficulties with this repertoire, but Gould's difficulties were of a unique sort. He told a friend that he had to go and practice the Webern, and when the friend expressed surprise at this, since Gould hardly ever practiced, and since he had often played this work during his concert years, Gould confessed. He confessed that he now had the complete score for all nine instruments in his head, "and I have to go and unlearn all the other parts." Yet another unique difficulty was how to translate Webern's abstract score into television. For that, Gould had himself accompanied not only by eight other instruments but by rapidly changing patterns of colored dots, squares, triangles, diamonds, simple shapes that kept expanding and contracting, multiplying and dividing, changing into each other. Gould's TV music had undergone a considerable evolution from the swirling clouds of color that had enveloped Scriabin.

This fourth installment, broadcast in 1977, was as imaginative as ever, but there was something a little perfunctory about it, as though Gould were losing interest, or simply not concentrating, as though his mind were on other things. "It all went along swimmingly for three or four productions, and then Gould had a sort of bad period," John Barnes recalls. "I guess it was maybe when his mother died. And he was ill himself. I don't know what it was, but he claimed to me that he just wasn't feeling well enough to do these things. So he canceled out a couple of times, over a couple of years. We got half of one of them done, but in the end, it just drifted away. It became fairly obvious after a while that he'd kind of lost interest in completing the whole thing."

Even when Gould was not working for the CBC, he had an office there, received mail there, left papers there to be typed, and he was generally treated like what Barnes called "a member of the team." It was because of this that a young director named John McGreevy felt entitled to call on Gould for help with an unusual problem. A newcomer from England, McGreevy had found himself a job in the CBC mailroom, then gotten a chance as a cameraman, then as a director.

"The CBC in the sixties was a place of extraordinary talent and creative vitality," McGreevy recalls, "and of course, coming with that, a lot of wild neurotics populated the corridors. And Glenn was the most exotic of all the neurotics who populated the corridors. I was aware of him long before he was aware of me, because his performances in the studio were always high theatre. And so I became fascinated by this phenomenon.

"Eventually we were aware of each other through the grapevine, but we never really talked until I had a musical problem with a show that I was working on, a one-hour drama called 'Mandelstam's Witness.' This was seventy-five, seventy-six. It was an adaptation of Nadezhda Mandelstam's memoirs, and I got the great Polish actress Ida Kaminska to present a portrait of Mandelstam in her Moscow apartment, describing her life, that fifty years of horror. But it needed something behind it, and the normal musical approaches just weren't going to work. I tried all kinds of things. And so I finally phoned Glenn, right out of the blue, and told him about it. And as it was Christmas Eve when I phoned him, I said, 'Glenn, you know, I would love you to come down and watch this sometime after the holidays.' And he said, 'Well, what are you doing this evening?'"

The idea that Gould had nothing better to do on a Christmas Eve is a little odd, but so is the idea that McGreevy would be similarly unoccupied, and so is the idea that the CBC studios would be wide open for business, but the two of them agreed to meet there. "He came down with stopwatches," McGreevy recalls, "with pencils and papers and so on. And we locked ourselves in a small booth at the CBC. And he was absolutely captivated by the show, and I think we ran it three times that evening. We got out of the booth at four o'clock in the morning—which was a great time for Glenn—and he said, 'I know what you must do. Imagine, in the apartment next door, which we never see, there is a young cellist, a student, and he is rehearsing over and over again a Shostakovitch cello concerto. And then at the very end, he starts to play the slow movement over the closing titles.' And of course it was perfect. When you see the show, you are persuaded that right next door to Mandelstam is a student working away on the cello, and you never need to see him. It was just the most sublime solution to a very, very difficult problem."

McGreevy then became one of the people whom Gould liked to call late at night. "Always at about one o'clock in the morning. 'I hope I'm not disturbing you, John, but I've just finished the first edit of whatever, and it only runs three hours, and I'd like you to hear it.' So one would hang up at four o'clock in the morning. But of course I had a tremendous appetite for all of his gifts and his outpouring of creativity. Being very new to the business myself, I found it grist for the mill for me to be able to listen to somebody in full flight, and in full command of his creative powers, and really pressing the boundaries of what is permissible, in terms of the amount of material you could lay on any individual at any one time. I was fascinated by that whole approach."

McGreevy was just beginning an ambitious project of his own, a series of portraits of the world's great cities, each one to be seen through the eyes of one idiosyncratic observer. Without telling Gould "what the hidden agenda was," McGreevy invited him to look at a show he had just finished. "And up came 'Peter Ustinov's

Leningrad,' with the great man sailing down one of the canals. And
Glenn leaped up and said, 'I know exactly why I'm here! You want
me to do 'Glenn Gould's Orillia.'* I said, 'Well, not quite Orillia,
but almost.' And from there we struck up the arrangement by which
he would do this inimitable portrait of Toronto—that was in sev-
enty-eight, I believe, or seventy-nine. And it was a glorious
experience."

Q: To what extent was that his own work, and to what extent did
you change it around, or redirect it?

A: It was very much a collaboration. His problem was that he
really didn't know Toronto today, so I had to—I mean, his Toronto
was the Toronto of the forties and fifties—the Toronto that he
remembered.

Q: Like so much else in his life, it was all inside his head.

A: Right.

The Toronto of the 1940's, the commercial capital of British
Canada, was by most accounts rather stodgy, rather provincial,
rather prudish, and rather pleased with itself. It didn't mind the fact
that other Canadians often called it "Hogtown," and it didn't mind
the fact that other Canadians jeered at the myriad blue laws—no
concerts on Sundays, no beer at baseball games—that characterized
"Toronto the Good." "In my youth," Gould himself recalled, "it
was said that for a really lively weekend, what you had to do was
drive to Buffalo."

World War II inevitably began changing Toronto, and the opening of the St. Lawrence Seaway in 1959 changed it still more, turning Hogtown into an international port. "I can still remember, when
the Seaway had been completed," Gould said, "how exciting it was
to prowl the Toronto waterfront and encounter ships that had
brought Volkswagens from Germany or TV sets from Japan and
had names like *Wolfgang Russ* or *Munishima Maru*." And as the
British influence faded, Toronto's powerful money suddenly
asserted itself in the form of exultant skyscrapers. Mies van der
Rohe's fifty-four-story Toronto-Dominion Bank became the highest office building in the entire Commonwealth; then I. M. Pei built
a slightly higher tower just across Bay Street for the Bank of Com-

*The town nearest to the Goulds' cottage on Lake Simcoe.

merce; and then Edward Durrell Stone a still higher one for the Bank of Montreal.

This economic boom attracted whole new populations. One quarter of all postwar immigrants to Canada came to Toronto, until the city's two million inhabitants included more Italians than there are in Florence, more West Indians than in Grenada. The Hungarian revolt of 1956 brought in swarms of refugees from Budapest, and the fall of South Vietnam filled Chinatown with Vietnamese. Despite all the changes and growth, however, Toronto was one of the few major cities in the world where the official passion for bulldozing and skyscraping was stoutly resisted by community opposition in raffish neighborhoods with names like Cabbagetown. The American urbanologist Jane Jacobs not only declared that Toronto was "the most hopeful and healthy city in North America," she went to live there herself. Even now, tourists from south of the border can only marvel at a metropolis where the streets are clean, the storekeepers courteous, the subways safe, and the parks in flower.

Gould could hardly remain unaware of the sudden growth of the cosmopolitan Toronto—he lived there virtually all of his life, and he loved the place—but it is quite possible to ignore such things. Or not ignore, but fail to take in, just as one can fail to notice in the mirror that one has passed from youth into middle age. So while McGreevy's cameras could follow Gould into a number of Toronto institutions that had remained largely unchanged—the zoo, for example, where Gould sang Mahler songs to the mistrustful elephants—the cameras remained somewhat baffled by the Toronto that existed inside Gould's head, the sound of the Sunday-night hymns, for example, that had offered him peace before the return to school on the following morning.

Since TV must show and keep showing, there were only two solutions. One was to illustrate Gould's visions with abstract or symbolic illustrations, as Gould himself had illustrated Scriabin with swirling colors and Webern with dancing dots. The other was to supplement Gould's intangible memories by steering the cameras into the Toronto of today. McGreevy naturally chose the second alternative, took Gould to the megalopolitan Eaton shopping center, and recorded his wonderment—"I don't believe it! It's absurd!" In this rather conventional travelogue of the tourist's Toronto, the

A left-handed child, unlike all others. Gould at eighteen months (*above, left*) and the prodigy with his guardian, Nick (*above, right*).

The only two teachers. Alberto Guerrero and his prize pupil (*above, left*) enjoyed croquet, while Gould's mother, Florence (*above, right*), did not allow mistakes.

"He really did wonderful things in the Brahms D-minor concerto, and I adored him for it," says Leonard Bernstein; seen here (*top*) rehearsing with Gould in the early 1960's, the conductor once made controversial public remarks about his performance of the piece with the pianist. (*Bottom*) Gould testing pianos at Columbia's Thirtieth Street studio in New York in 1957.

A genius for collaboration. Rehearsing chamber music with Yehudi Menuhin (*top*) and preparing for a radio interview with Leopold Stokowski.

The sound of a radio was, to Gould "the most unique experience in music." The pianist strikes an Arctic pose on the *Muskeg Express* while making his sound documentary, "The Idea of North" (*top*), which he spent months editing with engineer Lorne Tulk (*bottom, right*).

New Directions: A warmly gloved Gould discussing his string quartet with members of the Cleveland Orchestra (*top*) and working with producer Bruno Monsaingeon to translate his Bach into television.

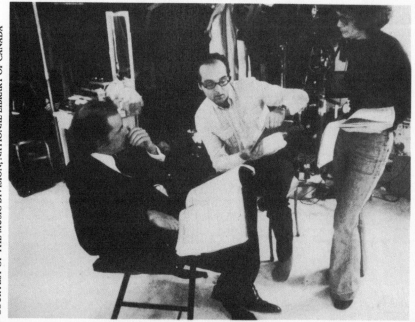

Breakthrough: Gould at his original recording session for the *Goldberg Variations* in 1955.

Final Days: Gould was near death when he re-recorded the *Goldberg Variations* in 1981.

cameras even recorded Gould's distaste for the sleazy naughtiness of the city's "strip"—"I always felt that 'Toronto the Good' was a very nice nickname"—and then relentlessly dollied on through the neon-lit vulgarities of Yonge Street. "Glenn Gould's Toronto," in other words, was in many ways not Glenn Gould's Toronto.

But Gould himself was fascinated by the challenge of trying to film his own sense of his own city. He knew that the elaborate technologies of television were far more complex (and more expensive) than anything he had mastered in radio, but he first tried to control the show by writing it. "I told him that these films run about 4,500 words, and so if he did an essay of about 7,000 words, then it gives us a little bit of room to edit," McGreevy recalls. "I went away and shot another couple of episodes of the series and came back to him three months later and he had written about 45,000 words. *And* he said, 'You can't touch a thing.' And I said, 'Well, Glenn, 45,000 words, that's a ten-hour film.' So we spent one very long night hacking our way through it, and he took it all in very great spirit because he knew it had to be done."

Even after all that cutting, there were scenes that Gould couldn't bear to kill, scenes that McGreevy knew he would somehow have to strangle in secrecy. "He had this awful Brando character, Teddy Slutz. And we did shoot a scene where Glenn is driving himself down Yonge Street and suddenly Teddy Slutz comes out of the crowd, hits the car, and they have a huge row with one another. And we double-shot it so that Glenn played all of his stuff [both roles], and quite frankly it was god-awful. So to save him from himself, we left it on the cutting-room floor. I said to him that we had technical problems. I wasn't going to tell him that it was god-awful."

Though Gould could freely indulge himself in such fantasies, the great problem in shooting a nonmusical TV documentary, outside the soundproofed sanctuary of the CBC studios, was that Gould once again had to confront the mindless crowd, the crowd that had once provided his concert audiences and now flowed through the streets. "I mean, one never physically touched Glenn," McGreevy says. "Real, genuine terror about that, and then you multiply that into a crowd, and being trapped in a crowd would be, I imagine, for Glenn, the ultimate horror. . . . The Eaton Center has thousands of people there all the time, and I think the claustrophobia of that was a problem. If I did things with him, it would draw a crowd, and he'd be very paranoid about everybody looking at him."

McGreevy was shrewdly protective. "I promised him," he recalls, "that I would do everything in such a way that there would be no attention drawn to us. We had to do some very clever and fast foot-work to get him in and out of these places without anybody realizing what we were up to. A lot of that stuff was shot with a concealed camera and Glenn on a radio mike, miles away. We hid behind pot-ted plants and so on, and so people didn't really know. All they saw was another nut talking to himself, and there are many of those."

Gould had other problems as well. McGreevy wanted to shoot the singing-to-the-elephants sequence in the dawn emptiness of the zoo, approximately when Gould went to bed, so they all agreed to meet at the zoo at 5 A.M. "At one o'clock in the morning, my phone rang, and it was Glenn," McGreevy says. "'John, I hope I'm not disturbing you, but I've got a problem, and you may want to start calling the crew because I *may* not be able to make it tomorrow morning. I don't wish to alarm you—' And by that time, of course, I'm sitting up. I said, 'What's the problem?'

"He said, 'Well, I have just contracted all of the symptoms—bar one—of what attacked me in Amsterdam (or was it Copenhagen?), in 1957, in October, when I was on tour, and I was doing the Strauss, I was doing the Schoenberg—I can't remember which opus I was doing—' And going on and on about this. I said, 'Glenn, what is it that you've contracted?' He said, 'Well, subclinical polio.'

"I said, 'I beg your pardon?' He said, 'Well, all the symptoms are there, except for one, and I don't know if it's going to come on, and it may be all right, but I thought I'd better alert you.' I'd never heard of subclinical polio. It sounded—well, he invented a lot of syn-dromes. I wasn't sure if he would actually show, but I arrived on location and set up the equipment, and then Glenn arrived, on time, a little shy, and said, 'I think I'm going to be all right.'"

Q: Could that have been pure stage fright?

A: Yes. Because he was with new people, and he was very, very shy, and he hadn't met my film crew before.

Gould was accustomed to controlling everything, to editing every take of every recording, every tape of his radio interviews, but this was all beyond his grasp. McGreevy was in charge, and McGreevy only let Gould see his editing after the process was all finished. "For Glenn, who had a tremendous desire for control over all the creative elements of his work," McGreevy says, "it was an incredible experience to come in and see the first cutting of this and see a thing that he had spent many hours working on with me, and see that the architecture had completely flown around.... Given that he was obsessed by process and structure and architecture within any given piece, this was for him quite fascinating. And so I spent months fending off all kinds of creative brilliance that he applied to me because of what I had done."

When it was all complete, it was, predictably, a big event for Toronto's civic authorities. "I went down to City Hall and persuaded the mayor to let me use the council chamber," McGreevy says. "Have you been in the modern City Hall? Oh, it's quite marvelous—it's *2001*. And to convert the rotunda into a movie theatre and invite several hundred people down to watch 'Glenn Gould's Toronto.'..." Gould heard about all this installation of huge screens, and he wanted, within his own rules, to know more. "He said, 'Do you think I could come?'" McGreevy recalls. "'I've never been in City Hall, and I'd just love to see myself thirty feet high.' And so he came and sat through it, an audience of one, and he had the time of his life. But there was no way he could be there with several hundred other people."

GOULD DOESN'T SHOW AT THE PARTY was the headline in the Toronto *Star*. "The big question at City Hall last night was: Would Glenn Gould show up? At least 300 people were on hand in the council chamber for a private screening of Glenn Gould's Toronto.... But of course Gould, who is the most reclusive of all performing artists, wasn't there. 'I was hoping this was going to be my chance to meet Glenn Gould but he was smarter than that and decided not to come,' Mayor John Sewell said in welcoming guests. And then Sewell added: 'But someone said it's still daylight out.'"

If such mockery seems unduly patronizing, as though Gould had some kind of moral obligation to stand in the mayor's receiving line and shake the outstretched hands of Toronto's cultural establishment, the newspaper reviews of "Glenn Gould's Toronto" went even further in a new series of personal attacks. The Toronto papers had always been quick to leap to Gould's defense against any outside criticisms, but now that he had made a TV show about their fair city, they found it almost treasonous. "Gould may well be one of the world's greatest interpreters of Bach, yet he has always struck me as a particularly pretentious recluse, cursed with intellectual snobbery," Bob Pennington wrote in the *Sun*. "Failing to show at last week's party in his honor at City Hall seemed just another example of the Garbo syndrome being used as an excuse for poor manners." The *Globe and Mail* was equally disapproving. "He ... ridicules Toronto's approach to its financial institutions," Don Downey wrote, "and sneers at the city's foundations.... There is little, in fact, that escaped Gould's acid tongue."

The *Star* chose to emphasize the fact that Gould was beginning to show his years, that the handsome young virtuoso had grown into a somewhat paunchy and pasty middle age. DRACULA LIVES AS TOUR GUIDE TO TORONTO, the *Star*'s headline proclaimed. "What a marvelous performance it is ..." wrote TV columnist Ron Base. "Gould announces that he does not arise until after dark. Nosferatu indeed lives! He skulks around Toronto and its shady suburban environs, his hatchet-sharp face shadowed by a floppy cap, his gaunt form swathed in formless overcoat and dark scarf, his wispy hands covered by gloves. Dracula is alive and well and showing us the view from the CN Tower. There is something infinitely cheeky about using a renegade, more concerned with revealing his eccentricities ... than the city in which he lives.... He merely sneers at it all."

Cheeky, yes, infinitely cheeky.

During the mid-1970's, when Gould was beginning to get tired of *Music in Our Time*, when he was deeply disturbed by the death of his mother, and when he began undergoing a number of mysterious medical difficulties, there suddenly came into his life the admiring figure of the French TV producer Bruno Monsaingeon.

Monsaingeon recalls that his own life had been completely overturned by the discovery of Gould's music. "I was in Moscow on a visit in 1965, just to learn the language," he says. "And records were extremely cheap there, so I was buying them by the kilo. I never had heard the name of Gould, but I had a little machine, and I played one of these new records, a live performance of the Bach Inventions that he did in Moscow in fifty-seven. And what happened then is almost indescribable. It was, for me, something of the intensity of a religious revelation. And you know, it completely altered my life. . . . There was something behind the dimensions of the pianist which was of much greater importance than just the genius of the pianist."

Q: What does that mean, exactly? What do you mean when you say it was like a religious experience?

A: My idea was that I heard a voice saying to me, "Come and follow me."

Q: Was that Gould's voice or just a voice?

A: A voice. I hadn't yet met Gould.

Q: But the voice referred to Gould?

A: Yes, yes, it meant that, exactly that.

In the next couple of years, while he still gave violin concerts, Monsaingeon got more and more involved in creating musical programs for French television, first organizing them, then directing them, then realizing that he could produce them on his own. "I was absolutely fascinated by the medium, you know," he says, "and when it appeared that I could have my own projects, the first thing I wanted to do was to try and approach that man of legend whom I'd never met, about whom I knew absolutely nothing, who was Glenn Gould. So I wrote him a long letter, about the way I conceived of television, or music on television, and so on, and could we possibly envision something together, in which you would be *the* subject. . . . I didn't expect an answer, really. It was just like a bottle thrown into the sea. And then six months later, I got a reply from him, an enormous letter, fifteen or twenty pages, saying, 'Well, I'm rather intrigued by your ideas. Why don't you come and see me?'"

If there was one thing that Gould recognized and responded to and appreciated, it was devotion. He needed it. He had received it from his parents, particularly his mother, and from Jessie Greig, and from Lorne Tulk, and from a few other colleagues and comrades, and now he recognized it again in Bruno Monsaingeon. And if Monsaingeon felt overtones of religious inspiration, Gould was not inclined to scorn the idea.

What Monsaingeon had to offer, though, was very practical. He now represented a German corporation named Classart, and Classart wanted to film a series of shows on Gould the hermit, Gould the exile, Gould the lord of the hidden empire. Gould happily agreed, and so Monsaingeon arrived in Toronto in 1974 with a ten-man French film crew. "Starting at two o'clock in the afternoon, we would work until six o'clock in the morning," Monsaingeon recalls. "Every day. And extremely—you know, never tired, simply because the intensity was there. And we also founded a trio at that point, which was—we discovered that my script assistant could read music, and so when there were technical problems, and the technicians were arranging things, we would sing *The Goldberg Variations.* The three of us together. We would give Glenn any part, you know, the soprano as well as the alto or bass, and he was relaxing in his armchair, singing whichever part we gave him to do, and so we sang the complete work. And then one day, Glenn said, 'I've found a title for our trio, for our debut in Town Hall. K for Karen, G for Glenn, and B for Bruno, our trio's going to be called The KGBs.'"

Monsaingeon called his series *Les Chemins de la Musique,* which, by its very insistence on direction, implies a certain disorder. Monsaingeon started like a documentary-maker, with shots of some moving men unloading a piano and carrying it into an empty studio. A narrating voice explains that Gould has not played in public for a number of years, and so we are following him into "La Retraite," as this first installment is called. Gould appears in his usual cap and scarf, takes them off, and starts playing Bach's Partita in E minor.

The documentary approach continues, on a fairly basic level. Why did Gould retire from the concert stage? "I found it an appalling experience, and essentially antimusical.... Giving up the concerts was simply a way of giving up an intensely unpleasant experience." These familiar questions and answers serve mainly as accompaniment. Monsaingeon's camera is there primarily to watch Gould play the piano, and so, as it watches, he plays Schoenberg's Suite, Opus 25, and a pavane by Orlando Gibbons, and a bit of his own transcription of Wagner's overture to *Die Meistersinger,* all with a great deal of auxiliary humming and moaning at the keyboard.

Filming with Gould was often less casual than it seemed. "When we had that first session," Monsaingeon recalls, "he hit the microphone at some point—very, very gently—and he collapsed into a chair and said, 'My God, a concussion.' And then he said, 'Well, look, in two hours there should be this effect; in four hours, that; in twelve hours— Now in thirteen hours, if this has not happened, then I'm all right.' And then I—you know, I was terrified. And he said, 'Well, I know, I know, once I let my imagination go, I'm lost.'"

If the first installment seemed diffuse and impressionistic, the second, entitled "L'Alchimiste," was designed to show the master technician pulling all the strands together. Better than any other film, in fact, it did show Gould at work as editor, cutter, mixer, technological creator. The basic subject was a fragment from one of Bach's English Suites, which Gould played in several different ways and then settled down to work on. The dialogue served as illustration:

Gould: Did you manage to get things sharpened up a bit? Is the center mike . . . attenuated now?

Technician: The center mike is a little bit above the other two, to enhance the middle frequencies. . . .

Gould: Are you cued to feed me about ten after the double bar? Okay, if the level isn't right, I'll stop you, but let's see what we can get. . . . Give me about two bars before the splice.

This devotion to the technology of recording reached a still higher point when Gould and his crew moved on from Bach to Scriabin. Camera on Lorne Tulk, moving microphones from place to place. *Gould* (his voice full of enthusiasm): "We're going to try something that may not work at all . . . because we've never done it before. It will involve a whole sequence of different mike perspectives. . . . One very close to the piano, almost like a jazz pickup, the kind of thing where you put the mike right inside the piano instead of in the lower strings, as Oscar Peterson* would do it. . . . Another at the discreet Deutsche Grammophon perspective, you know, a nice view from the balcony. And then, a more distant perspective still, one possibly that will pick up just resonance, just reverb from the back of the walls—and mix all these perspectives. . . . And the music that we're going to do all this for, with, to, is Scriabin. Because I don't think that any other composer has ever needed that

---

*The fact that Gould and one of the most popular jazz pianists both lived in Toronto inspired a number of editors to attempt to sponsor some kind of interview or encounter. Though both pianists were acutely aware of each other, nothing ever came of the idea. After Gould died, Peterson told an interviewer, "I was supposed to do a piano show with him . . . and I am sorry I did not."

help from technology as badly as Scriabin does. . . ." Scriabin, whose music generally sounds beautiful under almost any technological circumstances, sounded very beautiful indeed through Gould's network of microphones.

While Gould was the absolute master of sound, though, one senses that visual technology always remained slightly beyond his reach, a toy to be played with, puzzled over, explored. Monsaingeon's third installment began with a bass singing the opening of "So You Want to Write a Fugue?," and Gould watching on another screen, and then the tenor taking up the fugue theme on a different screen, and Gould watching that on yet another screen. Then Gould started to talk, over the multiplicity of singing voices, and described all of this as "the demolition of a fugue" and also as "a bit of *Waiting for Godot*." This show careened on through Webern and Berg, and then the fourth installment finally returned to the tonic key by showing nothing but Gould again playing Bach's Partita in E minor, Gould's own favorite (with which, remember, the series had begun). Not a word was spoken. Not a word needed to be spoken.

"As the last days approached," Monsaingeon recalls, "everybody was feeling very, very sad because they knew that they would probably never see him again. And unbeknownst to me and to Glenn, the crew had prepared a kind of farewell party. So when the last note or last word or last shot had been completed, a table was pushed forward, and there was plenty of drinks and nuts and all kinds of food and so on, and Glenn was horrified. He said, 'I'm sorry, I can't see all of this, and I have to say good-bye to everybody.' So it was a very abrupt kind of end, and then he wrote to everyone, very wonderful letters. But the feeling of sadness on the part of these people—it was extreme. It was extraordinary to have lived that period of time with that extraordinary man."

The Monsaingeon series had its modest success on European television, but both Gould and Monsaingeon felt that they had barely begun to explore what they and their cameras might create. After all the excursions into Beethoven, Wagner, and Berg, they decided to go back to bedrock and start planning a series on the idea of Gould playing Bach. Because of the nature of television—and because of the nature of Gould, who felt a lifelong yearning to teach, or perhaps to preach, to explain the nature and meaning of his art—Gould could not simply play Bach without writing everything down beforehand. "As is my habit," he wrote in another context in 1977, "the 'dialogue' was entirely scripted by me—I have, in fact, not spoken a spontaneous word via the airwaves for at least a decade. . . . In any case, all of the lines are mine."

Gould's insistence on total control could be disconcerting to his associates. "What about the text on Mozart and Mozart's piano sonatas?" Monsaingeon wrote to him in 1976 about the article that was eventually published under the title "Of Mozart and Related Matters: Glenn Gould in Conversation with Bruno Monsaingeon." "You had said that you would send it to me but it has not arrived. As you may imagine I am very anxious to know what my opinion is and how beautifully 'you' expressed 'my' thoughts." Looking back on these "interviews" now, Monsaingeon sees them as a kind of collaboration. "We spent three years drafting that before we actually started shooting," he says of the TV series, "so that, you know, we spent complete evenings at his studio at the Inn on the Park. And the show was to be very simple, playing and talk and play and talk. Nothing more complicated. What he did at the end was that he made the final draft, you know. And the final draft came from many versions that we had written together."

This final draft consisted mainly of cues. "Glenn, what is it about the fugue that gave it such a central role . . . ?" "Yes, I agree, but don't you think . . . ?" Once Gould picked up his cue, he was almost unstoppable. And sometimes Gould taught more than he realized. Monsaingeon happened to mention, in Gould's script, the beautiful *Chromatic Fantasy*, and Gould proceeded to denounce it in the most extreme terms.

Monsaingeon: You mean that you don't like it?

Gould: Oh, I quite cordially hate it.

Gould went on to call this masterpiece "a monstrosity," to declare that its harmony "wanders all over the lot" (shouldn't fantasies wander?), and even to ridicule its emotional intensity. "If Hitchcock had been working in the eighteenth century," Gould jeered, "Bach would have been working full-time on the Universal lot, writing backgrounds, for sure. I mean, can't you see Peter Lorre or Vincent Price sitting at the manual organ . . . as the clock strikes midnight?" Gould then proceeded to play this splendid piece ("My first and last performance of any part of the *Chromatic Fantasia*") in much the same way that he played the despised sonatas of Mozart, much too fast, with great contempt, and with virtually no sense of the beauties that he was racing through.

Gould's approach to *The Art of the Fugue*, on the other hand, was almost awestruck, and all the more courageous for that. He had often played parts of this monumental work during his concert years, but when he began to record it, in 1962, he took the somewhat evasive step of performing it on an organ, and then, after finishing the first nine of the fifteen fugues, he abandoned the whole project. Now, however, he determined to confront that majestic final fugue that had been interrupted in midmeasure by Bach's death.

"He had never played it before in public," Monsaingeon recalls, "and he said to me, the day before, on the telephone, 'It's the most difficult thing I've ever approached. It's—you've got to keep it going—how do you do that?' He was terribly intimidated. And he said to me, 'I've got several versions—one which would sound like a pavane and another one like a gigue, all very different in tempi and phrasing and articulation and so on. So I'd like to offer you a few, and you tell me which one you choose.'" So they went to the studio, and Gould played and played and played. "And I've never had the same sense of ecstatic abandon as on that particular day," Monsaingeon says. "When he reached the point where Bach introduces the theme of his own name, B-A-C-H, which is an extraordinarily moving passage, Glenn was just in another world, and he started to talk about what he was feeling, and he said, 'There's never been anything more beautiful in all of music.'" That performance too is on the tape, and that performance tells us a great deal about how Gould felt about Bach, about art, about life.

The end of any television series on Gould playing Bach naturally had to present Gould playing *The Goldberg Variations*. The middle-aged man, rather heavy now, and bespectacled, and getting bald, and even relying on makeup—

Q: Did he really use makeup?

A: Oh, always, always.

The middle-aged man had to confront the great triumph of his own youth, at least match it and perhaps somehow surpass it. But between the idea and the reality, nowadays, lies technology, and technology often means breakdown and failure. "I would like to comment in the strongest possible way upon the deplorable state of the physical plant and on the inadequate maintenance of the production hardware in Studio 7," Mario Prizek wrote to the CBC authorities after a taping of Gould's Bach series. There followed, then, a long chronicle of how contemporary technology generally works: On the first day of taping, one of the four cameras broke down, and when the director reorganized everything to work with three cameras, a second camera failed. "Three hours were wasted before the first take could be finished," Prizek said. "On the second day, we had barely started when the Studer began to malfunction. It 'gave up the ghost' before we could get our first 'take.' A maintenance crew was called. They had to disassemble the Studer completely before they could get it into operational condition. . . ." On the third day: "All our 'takes' after the supper-break were aborted by a loud hum and buzz on all tracks. . . ." And so on. "The nature of the delays caused by technical failures would be unacceptable even for an in-house production," Prizek declared, "but for a show which is done as a co-production (in this case with a West German production house) they were both shameful and shaming."

So when Gould began thinking about how to rerecord *The Goldberg Variations,* he began thinking about going back to New York, back to the obsolescent Columbia studio on East Thirtieth Street, back to that onetime church where he had first recorded those marvelous variations so many years ago.

XI

The Romantic Records

In the midst of his early recordings of Bach and Schoenberg and more Bach, Gould surprised many of his admirers by producing late in 1960 a collection of Brahms intermezzi. He might have impressed them by performing these beautifully windblown autumnal trifles in an austerely classical manner, but he indulged himself instead in the most lavish and luscious romanticism. And he was proud of it.

"I have received the test pressing of my latest recording—the first one made since the shoulder trouble—and I really think it is perhaps the best piano playing I have done . . ." he wrote to a friend in Berlin. "I think that you will be quite surprised not only with the repertoire but also with the style of playing which is, if I might say so, rather aristocratic. Come to think of it, I don't really think you will be surprised either. You know what an incurable romantic I am anyway."

To an interviewer, Bernard Asbell, Gould called this "the sexiest interpretation of Brahms intermezzi you have ever heard."

"How do you mean, 'sexiest'?" Asbell asked.

"I have captured, I think, an atmosphere of improvisation which I don't believe has ever been represented in Brahms recordings before," Gould said. "There is a quality as though—this isn't an original comment, but something one of my friends said—as though I were really playing for myself, but left the door open. I think a lot of people are going to hate it, but—"

"But you love it?"

"Yes, I love it. This is one of the things I am most proud of."

Gould's predictions of public rejection were obviously hyperbolic. Raymond Ericson of the New York *Times* found the new record a revelation "that the young Canadian pianist is at heart a highly romantic individual. . . . The Brahms performances are never less than absorbing, for here is an interesting mind at work. Most of them are convincing as interpretations and beautiful to hear." "The reviews of the Brahms, which are now beginning to arrive in force, are almost unanimously glorious . . ." Gould wrote happily to Homburger. "The only exception is the unpredictable Mr. Kolodin, who is violently opposed and says that my view of Brahms' last years is clearly that of a stodgy mooning old codger. . . . The Chicago Sun, which arrived this morning, said 'Gould has the kind of exceptional musicianship that can make him a specialist in any type of music he wishes to cultivate.'"

The Romantic era was, of course, the golden age of piano music, but in belatedly announcing his own romanticism, Gould felt a characteristically wayward impulse to denounce the great piano composers of the period. He repeatedly criticized Chopin, Schumann, and Liszt, and generally ignored Schubert. Just as waywardly, he made an exception of Mendelssohn and announced a recording of his organ sonatas. "I adore Mendelssohn," Gould declared, adding a pugnacious and wholly wrongheaded comparison. "He is a much greater composer than Schumann, for instance."

While Gould scolded the early nineteenth-century masters for their relative indifference to counterpoint, he offered exaggerated praise to the composers who flowered during the decaying years of the Romantic movement. "Actually, I am very much a romantic," he said in one typical outburst. "There are a great many composers of the 19th century whom I would play with the greatest pleasure had they provided any substantial literature for the piano. I think Tchaikowsky was a great composer, one it is now fashionable to dislike on all sorts of grounds such as sentimentality. But I think he was one of the really great symphonic composers, after Beethoven, and I love his music, but not his piano music."*

This particular interviewer, Dennis Braithwaite of the Toronto *Star*, told Gould that Sibelius had once been asked what melody he

---

*There is no evidence that Gould even considered playing Tchaikowsky's popular Concerto in B-flat minor, not to mention the two lesser ones or his voluminous solo pieces.

would take to a lifetime exile on a desert island. "One thing I would take with me," said Gould, "is Strauss' last opera, Capriccio, which I think is one of the most fantastically beautiful works ever written. I have been completely possessed by this work ever since I heard it in Berlin a couple of years ago. . . ." The interviewer casually informed Gould that Sibelius's choice had been the famous Handel "Largo," and then asked him, "What do you say to that?" Gould: "I'm speechless."

Gould was possessed not only by *Capriccio* but by all of Strauss. He once recalled that he had first heard *Ein Heldenleben* when he was seventeen, and he suggested that every adolescent musician probably heard this tone poem as "the work most likely to incorporate all of the doubts and stresses," and that every adolescent musician must grow out of that phase, and that he, Gould, never had. "I believe, quite simply, that Strauss was the greatest musical figure who has lived in this century," he wrote. But one of the elements in Strauss that most appealed to Gould was that he didn't really live in this century, that he turned his back on both the fads and the revolutions and wrote exactly as he pleased. This was the man about whom Gould tried unsuccessfully to write an opera, the man whose richly romantic orchestral scores Gould carried in his head and played on the piano in the small hours of the morning. But Strauss thought in terms of the Wagnerian orchestra, played the piano poorly, and took only a meager interest in it. He wrote little for the instrument, and what he did write was inconsequential.

Gould happened to be in the office of Schuyler Chapin, then the head of Columbia Masterworks, when Chapin got a telephone call from Eugene Ormandy about Strauss's musical setting to Alfred Lord Tennyson's *Enoch Arden*. "It seems difficult to imagine what could have attracted him to Tennyson's drawing-room epic," Gould later wrote of Strauss's extravaganza, but he suggested that "the melodrama setting was a vogue much admired in those days." *Enoch Arden*—has anyone read it since the darkest days of high school English?—tells in the most sonorous Victorian rhetoric the tale of an English sailor who is lost at sea in the far Pacific. He returns home many years later to find his wife happily married to someone else, then decides that she must never know of his survival, and so dies unrecognized and alone. For some reason, Strauss wrote a piano accompaniment—"most uncomfortably sentimental music," as Gould put it—and then took it on tour through Germany, playing the trills and tremolos while a friend declaimed Tennyson's dramatic verses.

"Ormandy wanted to record it," Chapin recalls. "He'd just had Claude Rains as a guest doing an orchestral version in Philadelphia, and they wanted to record it, and no *way* was I interested in that. But Glenn was in my office, and he heard the conversation, and he said, '*Enoch Arden*—it's really a lot of fun. I'd love to do it.' So this was the moment. Claude Rains had just finished it. Why not? I said, 'I can't pay you.' He said, 'I understand, just union scale.' So then I got hold of Rains, and he was a great admirer of Gould's, so all this was tickety-boo. Until we came to Mrs. Claude Rains."

"Mrs. Rains was quick to imagine slights to her husband and right away she picked up the idea that the atmosphere was not right," Chapin wrote in his memoirs, *Musical Chairs*. To keep the two collaborators separate, each was surrounded by a series of screens. "They could look over at one another but pursue their individual parts without distraction . . ." Chapin recalled. "They set to work with mutual suspicion. Gould would romp through the florid piano part while Rains rolled out the language with suppressed chokes and sobs that were so much a part of nineteenth-century declamation. Mrs. Rains was constantly furious and the conversations between the two artists were peppered with her comments. . . . But they did finish it and at the end stiffly acknowledged that they had both done some service to Tennyson and Strauss."

"I thought it was a very amusing thing to do," Chapin says now, "and we got it done at a cost of $1,500, which wasn't much even for those days. It sold about, I don't know, two thousand copies, something like that, but now it has become a collector's item. On Glenn's fiftieth birthday, we were talking on the phone about various things. We talked about *Enoch Arden,* and he said that his 'record spotter' in Toronto had told him it was now going for $150 a copy."

In confronting the world of romantic piano music, Gould confronted a scene completely dominated by two older masters, Arthur Rubinstein and Vladimir Horowitz. They were the most successful instrumentalists of their time, the most extravagantly admired, the most highly paid. They also had their passionate antagonisms. "Horowitz and I were close friends," Rubinstein wrote in his memoirs. "We called each other by our first names with the familiar 'thou,' and he would come some mornings to my place to consult me on his repertoire of effective encores; but I began to feel a subtle difference between us. His friendship for me was that of a king for his subject, which means he *befriended* me and, in a way, used me. In short, he did not consider me his equal. . . . Deep within myself, I felt I was the better musician."

Gould hated such competitive instincts, hated them in himself as well as in others. His friends almost invariably recall his generosity toward other pianists, his reluctance ever to criticize anyone. When he first met Rubinstein, he repeatedly addressed him as "Maestro," and when he later interviewed the famous virtuoso for *Look* in 1971, he offered effusive praises for Rubinstein's new recording of Brahms's F minor Quintet: "I'm drunk on it. I've now heard it five times in the last few weeks. . . . It's the greatest chamber-music performance with piano that I've heard in my life." But when Rubinstein finally wrote his autobiography in the late 1970's, the puritanical Gould could not resist creating a parody that struck directly at Rubinstein's greatest vulnerability, his vulgar boasting about his own celebrity, his popularity, and his romantic conquests. "I had scarcely begun the first supper show of my gala season at the Maude Harbor Festival," Gould began his "Memories of Maude Harbor," "when, as was my habit, I glanced toward the boxes. And there, seated on one marked 'Live Bait—Do Not Refrigerate,' was a vision of such loveliness that it instantly erased from my mind the memory of all four amorous adventures which had befallen me between lunch and five o'clock tea. . . ."

That is still fairly good-natured mockery, but toward Horowitz, Gould felt something more malevolent, something rather like envy, not only envy of Horowitz's transcendent gifts but envy of the admiration that they inspired. Gould probably felt a benign indifference to Rubinstein's cheery love of showmanship and applause, whereas he may have seen darker parallels in Horowitz's tortured retirement from the concert stage. What seems to have plagued him, though, was the widespread view that Horowitz possessed a matchless command of keyboard sonorities, that what he did could not be analyzed or understood, only marveled at.

"I told him once," says Robert Silverman, who published the Rubinstein parody and more than a dozen of Gould's other articles in his *Piano Quarterly*, "about listening to Horowitz play the Tchaikowsky concerto with Toscanini, with my family in the living room and my ear pressed up against the ten-dollar radio, and I'd gone out of my mind at the performance. I can't remember what he said then, but when I mentioned it another time, he *reacted*. He said, 'You *told* me that two years ago.' And then I heard that tone in his voice, and this is the way he sounded—if I can imitate him—'And I have a better technique than Horowitz.' And I laughed. He was so petulant, the way he said it. It was like a little boy saying, you know, 'Doesn't anybody realize that *I* have such a great technique?'"

Joseph Roddy, a graying but ebullient figure who wrote the first major profile of Gould in *The New Yorker* back in 1960, is walking along West Forty-third Street after a pleasant lunch of scampi and white wine when he suddenly remembers a similar scene. He can't recall exactly where it took place, somewhere in New York, when Gould was in town for one reason or another, and he sat down at a piano and whirled through a thunderously Horowitzian chain of double octaves. "And he said, 'I can do *that*,'" Roddy recalls. "'Anybody can do *that*.'" Silverman, sitting on the front porch of the large-beamed house that he built for himself in distant Vermont, laughs at the story. "Yes, right," he says. "As a matter of fact, he said it to me. He said, 'Horowitz's octaves stink.' Or—he'd never use a word like that—I have to be careful because I use my own language in there, but he said, 'Horowitz can't play octaves—he *fakes* them.' I remember him using the word fake."

"He told me," says Roddy, "that he had once done a great service for Horowitz. He had finished a little phrase for one of the Horowitz recording sessions." That seems hardly possible, but Roddy recalls that Gould had rented some space in the RCA Victor studio in New York, "just for some technical stuff that had to be done," and he went there late at night and found one of the engineers in despair. "He was splicing together some Horowitz tapes," Roddy says, "and he had reached the despondency point, because it couldn't be done, because each piece of tape had something wrong with it.

But Gould was as experienced as anyone could be with this whole splicing of tapes, so he sat in and got his brains around what the problem was, and then he said, 'Well, if you do this and this, and get that off there and this off here, then that's it, and you've got it, except that you'll be missing this bar, which I will get for you.' So there exists—" Roddy bursts out laughing, suggesting that somewhere in the legendary recordings of Vladimir Horowitz there is one measure of pure Gould. But *caveat emptor*: Funny stories tend to exfoliate in the retelling. Roddy acknowledges that the authorities at RCA don't "ever recall anything like this ever happening." Bob Silverman says Gould told him the same story about helping to edit a Horowitz tape but without any mention of adding a bit of his own playing. "I don't believe that part," says Silverman. "That part's not true."

Gould never felt any desire to challenge Rubinstein by recording, say, Chopin's Polonaise in A flat or a sheaf of the most beautiul mazurkas, but Horowitz represented a deeper challenge. Just a year after Gould had abandoned the concert stage in the spring of 1964, Horowitz emerged from more than a decade of retirement to appear once again at Carnegie Hall. The clamor surrounding that highly publicized return violated everything that Gould most deeply believed in. "I knew he was getting tired of playing only for a microphone in a studio," Wanda Horowitz was quoted as saying. "He talked of the difference when you play for people in a hall." And then there was all that newspaper publicity about the lines forming outside Carnegie Hall through the night, and Mrs. Horowitz providing the pilgrims with hot coffee, the whole circus atmosphere that Gould feared and loathed.

Gould's response—and it may not even have been a conscious response—was to issue his own recordings of two works that Horowitz virtually owned. One was Prokofiev's Seventh Sonata, one of the three "war sonatas" composed during the dark days of 1942 and given its American premiere by Horowitz. His spectacular recording had been sent to Prokofiev, who sent back a copy of the score inscribed with thanks "to the miraculous pianist from the composer." The second piece was Scriabin's no less miraculous Sonata No. 3 in F-sharp minor. Again, Horowitz seemed to be the unchallengeable champion. The liner notes told the familiar story of how his uncle Alexander, one of Scriabin's pupils at the Moscow Conservatory, had taken the eleven-year-old Vladimir to play for the master, and how Scriabin had told the prodigy's parents not to neglect his literary education. "Your son will always be a good pianist, but that is not enough," Scriabin had said, according to the Horowitz family scripture. "He must be a cultured man also."

Gould recorded the Prokofiev in 1967, the Scriabin in 1968, and both performances were issued in 1969. Since comparisons are said to be odious—"I happen to believe that competition . . . is the root of all evil," said Gould—let us not try to judge whether Gould's recordings are better than those of Horowitz. Both versions are marvelous. If Horowitz is more dramatic and more richly sonorous, the nervous energy and crystalline clarity of Gould's performances make them quite the equals of the older recordings. And though Gould made no mention of any competition, the challenge scarcely went unnoticed. "Choosing no small targets, Gould now has taken on the legend of Vladimir Horowitz by recording two works identified in the public mind with the Russian pianist . . ." Donal Henahan wrote in the New York *Times*. And Henahan was greatly impressed. About the popular finale to the Prokofiev, he wrote: "Who has ever heard this battered, bloodied movement played as a rather giddy, infectious dance? Gould makes it into one, without sacrificing an ounce of its power or motor excitement."

Gould had still further plans for Horowitz, much stranger plans. He wanted to create a parody of that famous Carnegie Hall recital, which Columbia had issued in a very successful two-record album solemnly entitled *An Historic Return*. Gould first suggested his parody in June of 1966 as one of his rather private northern jokes. He made no specific reference to Horowitz, only to the popular practice of recording virtuosos on tour, live, mistakes and all. "I would be presented in recital at White Horse, Yukon Territories; Yellow Knife, Northwest Territories, or some other such romantic spot," Gould wrote. He had originally thought of actually giving such a concert, but, as usual, he now wanted simply to tape it in a Toronto studio because this would be "an opportunity to spoof in a delicious way the whole absurd contradiction of the recorded public recital (Sviatoslav [Richter] at Sofia etc.). . . . It would, of course, be recorded to the best of our ability with perhaps just a few conspicuous clinkers left in to give it credence. . . . Then we would overdub the splutters, sneezes, and sighs of the noisiest damn audience since Neville Chamberlain was shouted down in the House."

Columbia was monumentally uninterested. But Gould would not give up. Writing about future projects in 1972 to Thomas Frost, a producer at Columbia, Gould openly referred to his idea as a burlesque of Columbia's own Horowitz record. "I'd still like to opt for a parody of the Horowitz 'Return' album—set in Moosonee, Ontario, perhaps and, even though several of your colleagues glanced nervously over their shoulders when mention was first made of this five years or so ago—I still like the idea and think it might solve our repertoire problems in a delightfully offbeat way." The repertoire problem was that Gould had intermittently taped a number of short pieces—three Scarlatti sonatas, two Scriabin *poèmes*— that didn't conveniently fit into any marketable package and therefore lay unreleased.

Columbia remained monumentally uninterested. Gould would not give up. Late in 1973, he wrote an eight-page letter to Frost to argue once again for this bizarre project. He enclosed a complete pseudo-Horowitz program, ranging from Scarlatti and Carl Philipp Emanuel Bach to Sibelius and a contemporary Canadian, Barbara Pentland. He even offered suggestions about the printed program notes, which he thought should largely ignore his recital. "I have always felt that one delightfully zany touch should be its almost total absorption with matters anthröpological, sociological, and geographical," he wrote. "Through contacts at the Department of Northern Affairs, I have managed to make friends with several people in each of the above-mentioned fields who could, I'm sure, be persuaded to contribute unimpeachably scholarly, but utterly irrelevant, essays on such subjects as, for example, 'the future of permafrost.'"

Despite the manic elements in Gould's obsession with such details, there was a completely serious idea at the core of this project, a new variation on his often-proclaimed idea of how music should be made and how it should not be made. "The joy of the record," he wrote, "would be to invest studio performances with an ambiance which would suggest every conceivable disadvantage of the live concert occasion—a predominantly tubercular audience, a recital hall seemingly in danger of imminent invasion by a pack of

timber wolves—indeed the collage possibilities are infinite...."
Gould knew, though, that the odds against him were long. He ended
with a plea: "Do please let me have some feedback. Eight years and
seven months is a long time to wait."

Columbia remained monumentally uninterested.

In July of 1975, Gould's mother, who had begun teaching him at the
keyboard forty years earlier, teaching him and singing to him and
making him sing to her, suffered a massive stroke. It hadn't yet happened when Bert Gould telephoned her to tell her that he would be
home from work within half an hour.

"When I drove into the yard," Gould recalls, "I went to the side
door, and she met me at the door and unlocked the door from the
inside. And I saw her start to fall. She didn't hit the floor, but she
would have if I hadn't caught her. And she never regained consciousness. I sat there in the hospital with her, most of the time, for
five days anyway. I guess you really know."

Q: Did she have more strokes, a sequence of strokes?

A: No, just the one, just the one.

Mrs. Gould was 83 then, and she had been failing for some years.
Indeed, the struggle to keep up two houses had already become too
much for her, and so Bert Gould, earlier in 1975, had sold the lakeside cottage where Glenn had spent his boyhood summers.

"She was *very* attached to it," Jessie Greig recalls, "but I know
that she knew that she couldn't do it any longer, keep up two places,
packing and going every weekend. I think it played a tremendous
part in her death, though. So did Glenn. We talked about it. I said,
'Well, why don't you buy the place?' And he said, 'I'm thinking
about it.' I said, 'You should keep it because, you know—' And he
said, 'Well, I'm thinking about it, but I don't think I—want—property—there—right—now.'"

To most of his friends, Gould said little or nothing about his
mother's death. Even Ray Roberts, who by now worked as his paid
factotum and spoke with him several times every day, can recall no
signs of the effects of that death. "He went through her funeral and
her death with dignity," Roberts told a CBC interviewer. "And one
of the things I learnt very early on was not to poke into the personal
feelings too— He didn't like that." But Jessie Greig saw more and

knew more: "He was really devastated by her death. . . . He missed her terribly, he really did. She was the one to whom he spoke most about his musical accomplishments, and she was the one he shared his reviews with. It was a very traumatic experience for him. And he became more introspective. . . ."

Four years later, Bert Gould decided to marry a family friend, Vera Dobson. He invited his son to act as best man. Gould was quite disturbed by this prospect. His papers contain several drafts of his attempts to answer, and even scraps of real or imagined family dialogue on the subject. Finally, he wrote out his answer in longhand: "Dear Father—I've had an opportunity to give some thought to the matter of your wedding and specifically to the invitation to serve as your best man. I'm sure that, under the circumstances, you would prefer to arrange a private service—one in which any such conventional ceremonial gesture would be inappropriate; in any case, while I appreciate your kindness in extending the invitation, I regret that I must decline. Needless to say, I wish you every happiness, and I would ask you to pass on my good wishes to Mrs. Dobson."

What John Barnes called "a sort of bad period" struck Gould rather suddenly during the summer of 1976. He was at work on the fourth installment of *Music of Our Time* when he suddenly discovered that he couldn't play the piano properly. "During 2nd TV taping (first week in June) lack of coordination was imm. apparent," he scribbled on the legal pads that were to become a year-long journal of diagnosis and desperation. "Opening theme of Casella was unbalanced—notes appeared to stick and scale-like passages were uneven and uncontrolled. . . . An unpleasant experience, and seemingly immune to solution by ad hoc pressures, finger (thumb indent) etc. During next 2 wks., which separated 2nd taping and commentary, problems increased. It was no longer poss. to play even Bach chorale securely—Parts were unbalanced, progression from note to note insecure. . . ."

It is impossible to determine exactly what was the matter with Gould, but his journal records all kinds of problems in his hands and arms, exhausting tensions, tingling in his fingertips, and loss of what had always been Gould's specialty: control. The journal also records apparently related problems, pains in the neck and back, serious eye trouble, an inner-ear disturbance known as labyrinthitis, and disturbances that Gould guardedly mentioned by saying, "It is quite poss., even likely, however, that it had a psychological base."

Gould confided in virtually no one about his difficulties. He did tell Jessie Greig that his legs kept going to sleep, that "he'd go to get up and there'd be absolutely no feeling in his legs." He told her that he thought the tingling "was a form of arthritis, or else poor circulation." She says that she repeatedly urged him to see a doctor. "And he said, 'They don't listen to me. I tell them about it, but they don't listen to me.'" He treated himself with a wax bath, and he got Ray Roberts to apply a thermal device to his stiff arm and shoulder almost every day. "It was a sort of microwave thing, and we'd put pads on," Roberts recalls, "and I used to assist him in doing that. I didn't think it was the healthiest thing in the world, but I have to tell you that I aided and abetted him because he asked me to." Although Gould consulted several doctors about lesser ailments, however, there is no evidence that he ever went to see one of them about this crippling disability. Only the journal tells, in endless and sometimes incomprehensible detail, about his nightly struggles to overcome whatever it was that afflicted him.

The journal discloses Gould's remarkable dependence on visual "images" of himself playing any given passage, as though the ability to see himself playing it were the only prerequisite for actually playing it. And now he seemed to be losing that magical ability. "Nothing prevented the gradual deterioration of image," he wrote in one typical passage, "and, finally, I returned to whole-body system, employing h-k-b rise, high wrist monitor, and constant adjustment re back." This is written mostly in a kind of private code (h-k-b, for example, means hand-knuckle-bridge). Indeed, the whole journal is mostly in code, for Gould was writing this entirely for himself. We can only guess at the possibilities. "Still point," for example, seems to be Gould's shorthand for a passage from Eliot's *Burnt Norton:* "At the still point of the turning world. Neither flesh nor fleshless;/ Neither from nor towards; at the still point, there the dance is,/ But neither arrest nor movement. . . ." "Process—The motto 'still point of the turning world' defines it . . ." Gould wrote. "It related to the revelation that fingers, ideally, should not be required to move—only, so to speak, to 'be there'—and that all other adjustments should be accommodated by body-adjustments."

This is a rather mystical view of the pianist's art, but Gould believed in it strongly. He liked to quote Arnold Schoenberg's story of the centipede "who was asked in which order it moved its hundred legs, and afterwards he could move no legs at all." Yet although Gould seemed to imagine the playing of the piano as a kind of vision, he devoted infinite attention to all the mechanical workings of both the piano and the pianist. And so his journal of this plague year is an exhaustive chronicle of physical details.

"During mid-summer, much effort was directed to the hand knuckles," he wrote in one early entry, "and, initially, it appeared that some progress was made when these were subject to indent pressure. This seemed to foster, on occasion, crescent-like sensation which was sometime solution. . . . In late summer . . . experiments which elevated wrist were tried. These were inaugurated to alleviate unnatural burden in indented fingers, thumbs and knuckles; the experiment resulted only in a complete loss of control. . . ."

That is the heartbreaking thing about this journal, the constant struggle toward a solution, the theorizing and rationalizing about each new experiment, the repeated glimpses of success, the repeated failures. All through that fall and winter, Gould worked on his problem, every night, and by the following April he was reporting a new experiment of relying only on his fingers. "There was initially no neck tension, no vision restriction, no limitation on hovering above keyboard. Beginning on the 2nd or 3rd day, however, there were wrist tightness problems, and, gradually, the separation into bumpy grouping and a general lack of fluidity." And then a breakthrough: "Suddenly, last night, I determined that *the* common denominator in *all* these problems (famous last words?) was the lack of *constancy* in shoulder elevation. For one brief moment, and only in r-h- [right hand] I *had* it; that gleaming lustrous sound was back and I realized, more than ever, that *that* was the sound of control. . . ."

For a time, the recovery seemed like a miracle. Thus, on April 26: "For most of the past 10 days, I was almost afraid to jinx what seemed like the perfect solution by setting down a desc. in these pages. It (the apparent solution) began the day after prev. entry. It involved tipping the head towards right shoulder and moving it as a unit in consequence. . . ." And then, on June 1: "I did try finger-thumb indent in coord with genl top-of-hand pressure—2 or 3 good days ensued. I did try holding wrist tightly from beneath so as to use *it* as a fulcrum-like constant. One day wonder. I did try relating body movt. to *stable* elbows so as to ensure height limitations and legislate front-back polarity.... We may, I think, conclude that nothing has worked."

June 16: "Let us hope there will be no more entries. I do believe the solution has been found. I will have to research these diaries to discover how many times I may have come close to it during the past year.... Without further procrastination, the solution is in the h-k-b response. It involves letting the h-k-b *rise* (exactly the opposite of the indent theories to which so many pages have been devoted) but *rise* as a result of finger indent motivation. The rise ... treats the hand (from h-k-b to wrist) as a platform from which fingers reach out and explore the keys below.... Obv., there is a need for further observation and testimony, but I think that the secret of May '67 [there are several mysterious references to some apparently similar breakdown and recovery in 1967] has been rediscovered—I hope and pray that it may not be lost ever again. I do believe it will be poss. to resume work almost imm."

June 23: "I am not sure that everything mentioned in the foregoing entry is beside the point, but it is, unfortunately, far from the last word. Last nite, in a session of close to 3 hrs., every conceivable variant was employed—none with success— For the last several days, right wrist had been unbearably sore after any 10 or 15 min. practice period. It was not partic noticeable *during* performance ... but imm. upon cessation of activity, the pain was intense."

That very same week, Gould's journal reported that "during taping re 'Music of Man,' no clear 'image' re this system was available; I resorted to wrist control (h-k-b relaxed and relieved)...." This casual reference to taping a TV show, in the midst of long descriptions of incapacity, seems to imply that Gould's difficulties were largely imaginary, but he apparently relied once again on a bit of "creative cheating," using a considerably earlier bit of tape for his performance of Scriabin's "Désir."

The Music of Man was the CBC's grandiose, eight-part TV series on the history of music from the earliest Neanderthal pipings to the latest Beatles strummings, all as conceived, organized, and narrated by Yehudi Menuhin. Since Gould and Menuhin were friends, or at least mutual admirers, and since this was a Canadian project, the history of music could not be considered complete without Gould holding forth on the subject. The original script by Curtis Davis says rather vaguely, "We join the YM/Gould conversation. (The talk will include Glenn Gould's reasons for choosing the media as his forum ...)." Gould, however, had to write his own script, which begins with his private notation that this is "a spontaneous, extemporaneous, off-the-cuff, top-of-our-heads conversation between Yehud (Ad lib) Menuhin and Glenn (Wing it) Gould— Commisioned by, and dedicated to Curtis *D*amned *A*udio *V*erité *I*s *S*inful." After the camera watches Gould and Menuhin both listening to a playback of a Bach gigue, the "spontaneous, extemporaneous, off-the-cuff" script calls for Gould to say, "Now, Yehudi, you've got to admit that you would not get to hear a sound like *that* in a concert."

Menuhin balked, though, at having Gould tell him what to say on his own television series. "Yes, I'm not sure I'd want to, actually, Glenn," he says in Gould's script, but what he actually said before the cameras was, "I would still recognize your playing. Whatever you've added electronically...." And so on. The memories of the witnesses differ as to whether this was a divergence of musical judgments, or literary judgments, or simply a conflict over turf: Who should write the words that both would agree to speak? There are always intermediaries who can work out compromises, and so when Menuhin said that "machinery" seemed to him "almost an intrusion" on the intimacy of the violinist's art, Gould was allowed to say, "It matters not to me whether I am 'successful' in creating a performance through one take, or whether I do it with 262 tape splices." Menuhin then observed that Gould's radical views on recording were actually becoming commonplace in pop music, almost cripplingly so. "Take the Beatles, who started out playing in public spontaneously; by the time they became accustomed to crutches, which enable them to record tracks separately and put them all together, to add notes and take them away, they could no longer play in public because the public expected something else." Gould: "In a sense, that is also what happened to me."

With both Gould and Menuhin jousting for control over their dialogue, the exchanges sometimes became quite highly charged.

Menuhin: That still doesn't invalidate the concert hall, the experience of which is essential, and remains the standard against which everything else is judged.

Gould: Nonsense, Yehudi. It was the standard until something else came along to replace it, which is exactly what the recording did; and the recording, surely, is now the standard against which the concert must be judged.

Menuhin: If no one is ever going to climb a mountain again, and we have to be satisfied with films about it, where are we?

Gould: We are without people who can climb mountains, which I think is a profoundly good thing. It will save any number of deaths per year.

Though Gould got through that show by playing an old tape of one of his favorite Scriabin pieces, he still had to return home to his piano in the penthouse on St. Clair Avenue, and to his treasury of preludes and fugues and toccatas and fugues and suites and variations and still more fugues, and to find that he could no longer control them as he once had. "Last night witnessed, among other things, a return to shoulder systems . . . back-rod, back-rod with collapsed chest, back-rod-head-immobile, with or without collapsed chest, r-shoulder elevation with head tipped to right, etc. In short, everything was tried and nothing worked. . . . It's back to the drawing board."

June 25: "2 days—2 systems—Day before yesterday, I concentrated on wrist control. . . . Wrist pain was largely alleviated. . . . Nevertheless, it, too, appeared a one-day wonder. . . . Nothing prevented the gradual (!) deterioration of image. . . ."

July 1: "It seemed as though everything had returned to normal. . . . New rep.—f—tocc. fugue [Gould means Bach's Toccata in F-sharp minor, which he was planning to record soon], for ex., was studied and everything made sense. I was about to call A.K. [Andrew Kazdin of Columbia] and set up July sessions. Yesterday evening, however, I sensed that all was not well; there was no spec. 'image' threat, just a genl feeling of unease. Being reluctant to admit any extra-psychic principle at work, I went to apt. at 11:30 p.m. The results were horrendous. G [major] Tocc. fugue, which had become a showpiece, was bumpy, inacc., uncertain, unrythmical and ditto everything else that was played. The weird thing was that, so far as I could see, no system-changes were employed. Further tests will follow. . . ."

July 6: "The results desc. in last para have not been repeated. . . .

I am not unmindful of the fact that past 2 wks have, by and large, and excl (very real) problem with wrist, been the most sustained period since problems began. . . ."

July 9: "Wrists were sore and stiff almost from outset. . . ."

July 11: "Last nite (40 min sess) began with arm-drag (shoulder-connect) system. Relaxation ensured—wrist flexibility relieved r-wrist tension *completely,* but usual penalties (overweighted staccato, etc.) followed. . . ."

July 12: "As usual! 2 hr. sess—provided unstable results. Rep. [repertoire] was varied—Bach as usual & Ruggles—Krenek—and, at no point, were results disastrous—merely unimpressive and, in Ruggles-Kreneck, inacc. . . . It *was* poss to switch, from moment to moment, to arm-drag systems; these, thru practice, ensured reasonable stability with Bach rep. but similar results were erratic and unfocussed in Krenek etc. . . ."

And here this long chronicle of suffering simply breaks off. Since Gould went on playing and recording to the end of his life, about five years later, we can only surmise that he somehow found a solution to his problem, or that, as sometimes happens, it simply went away. But exactly what was the problem? Dr. Emil Pascarelli suspects a collapsed spine, quite possibly a result of Gould's fall off that boat rail outside the Goulds' summer cottage on Lake Simcoe. Dr. Pascarelli is an easygoing man with a gray moustache, the medical director of the Kathryn and Gilbert Miller Health Care Institute for Performing Artists at St. Luke's/Roosevelt Hospital on West Fifty-ninth Street in Manhattan. He has read Gould's journal, but he has not been told the name of the patient.

Q: What is a collapsed spine?

A: Well, the vertebrae can erode and cause nerve compression. Maybe I should get a book.

Dr. Pascarelli rummages around in his cluttered office and then returns with a large book on the spine, richly illustrated with skeletal figures, skeletal nerves and tendons. He opens it up and pushes it forward. "The spine is made up of the vertebral body and the tail, and then in between are the disks, okay?" Dr. Pascarelli says. "Now, usually by collapsed spine is meant that a disk erodes, and it collapses. This is a spongy, cartilaginous substance, very rubbery, that acts as a shock absorber between the vertebral bodies. Now in front here is the medullary nervous system. It runs down there, so that if you have a bulge in here, it can compress the spinal column and cause nerve compression, which is—which can be very serious."

Q: He had some kind of spinal injury in his childhood. Could that—?

A: There might have been an exacerbation of the childhood injury, with nerve-root compression, that caused this problem. I don't know.

Q: Is it very painful?

A: It can be painful, but usually it's not. It's usually accompanied by a numbness and a tingling, a discomfort.

Gould's exact symptoms. There are operations to deal with such problems, but back injuries can remain as mysterious in their workings as in their origins. And there is no indication that Gould, although he went to many doctors about many afflictions, real and imaginary, ever consulted anyone about his spine. Yet the illustrations in Dr. Pascarelli's textbook are quite clear: Each cervical nerve affects a specific area of the wrist and hand. "This would be C-5, C-6, C-7," Dr. Pascarelli says as he points to each tentacle in the book. "In other words, these would be—C-7 would be up here in the neck, and these nerves innervate the arm and eventually get down to the muscles in the hand. . . ."

Dr. Pascarelli disapproves of anyone trying, as this nameless pianist did, to treat himself. "One gets the feeling," he says, "that this was a rather weird guy, who had his own notions about—I mean, he did not have too much of a working knowledge of his own body, of physiology and functional anatomy, and he was probably creating new problems. . . . He was trying to change the configuration of his hands, and these kinds of repositioning create more tensions on the tendons. . . . He was experimenting on himself in a pseudo-scientific way, and he didn't have any basic knowledge about what he was doing."

Q: Do you get any sense that any of this is imaginary?

A: I wouldn't say it was imaginary. I would say it's a man struggling with a problem. . . . He's very fearful, and he's attempting to solve it on his own. . . . There's a psychologic overlay here, a very heavy psychologic overlay. . . . Was he going through personal problems at this time? Divorce? Or a wife die, or lover die, or whatever? I mean, these are things you have to think about.

Dr. Fred Hochberg, an eminent neurologist who teaches at the

Harvard Medical School and heads a group of specialists in musicians' ailments at Massachusetts General Hospital, has similar suspicions. He and his colleagues studied Gould's journals (without knowing his name) for several months. After considering the possibility of epilepsy, Hochberg and his associates concluded only "that the individual was unusually preoccupied with medical function and difficulties and that there probably were some features of a paranoid nature." Beyond that, said Dr. Hochberg, no doctor was willing to go.

In sickness and in health, sometimes only after considerable delay, Gould kept on making record after record. He finished *The Well-Tempered Clavier* in 1971, the French and English suites during the early 1970's, and the complete sonatas of Mozart in 1974, but along with these standard classics, he also began producing a strange and hypnotically beautiful series of Romantic works. No Chopin or Schumann, of course. Instead, Gould came forth in 1973 with a gorgeous performance of the Sonata in E minor by his distant relative, Edvard Grieg, and on the back of that he provided a stunning version of Georges Bizet's *Variations chromatiques*. This almost unknown work, he announced, "is one of the very few masterpieces for solo piano to emerge from the third quarter of the 19th century; its almost total neglect is a phenomenon for which I can offer no reasonable explanation."

If Gould could find few masterpieces for solo piano in the third quarter of the nineteenth century (how could he have overlooked, for example, Brahms's Handel Variations?), he could relish the orchestral masterpieces of the period. And so he produced in 1973 his astonishing transcriptions of Wagner's *Meistersinger* prelude, the Rhine journey from *Götterdämmerung*, and the *Siegfried Idyll*. "It was a real labor of love," Gould said later. "I simply wanted to have something of Wagner's I could play."

To achieve that labor of love, Gould discovered that he had to rewrite a lot of Wagner's music, and so he coolly did so, subsequently explaining it all by a theory of his own. According to this theory such old-time transcribers as Franz Liszt had followed their originals too closely. "The Liszt transcriptions . . . tend to be relentlessly faithful . . ." he told Jonathan Cott, just as though he had never heard of such free-form Liszt creations as the *Reminiscences de Lucia di Lammermoor* or *Rigoletto: Paraphrase de Concert.* "If the orchestral texture is thick, Liszt will reproduce the thickness on the piano, and of course a thickness on the piano doesn't sound good, let's face it." And in a long drum roll, "Liszt usually falls back on a tremolando, which is so turn-of-the-century I can't stand it." Instead of such literal copying, Gould said, he "took a solemn oath" that he "would try to re-create the pieces as though somebody like Scriabin, who really knew something about the piano, as Wagner did not, had had a hand in it."

In his revisions of the *Siegfried Idyll*, Gould avoided most of Wagner's doublings of the bass and cello, on the ground that the piano would give this too percussive a sound, and he decided instead "to have the contrabass always enter on the offbeat." That, he said, was just "the prototype for several other little inventions along the way." Since Wagner's long-held chords would die away on the piano, for instance, "what I did was to invent whole other voices that aren't anywhere in the score, except that they are convincingly Wagnerian." At one point, he went even further. "What I did . . . was to invent a dialogue between two offstage horns, one in the tenor and one in the alto, that try to mimic each other, and they go on like this between themselves, and it's gorgeous. . . . Forgive me for saying so, but it's gorgeous!"

Ultimately, Gould's "creative cheating" reached a point where he was not only rewriting Wagner's music for the piano but writing music that the piano could not play. When he had performed the *Meistersinger* prelude for friends, he had always reached a point near the end when the multiplicity of voices becomes so great that "then you say, 'Okay, which themes are we leaving out tonight'?" The recording studio now made all forms of cheating possible, of course. "In order to accommodate the extraordinarily dense polyphony in the 'Meistersinger vorspiel,'" he wrote to a friend, "[I] wrote the last three minutes or thereabouts as though for a piano primo-piano secundo duet . . . and simply over-tracked the material when recording. Consequently, the transcription, strictly speaking, would not be reproducible—except, of course, by two pianists playing in concert—and is effectively realisable only via recording."

Such legerdemain raised a few eyebrows when Gould's Wagner

record appeared, as did his incredibly slow tempo in the *Siegfried Idyll*. ("I've always felt that the piece has an indigenous languor," Gould wrote, "which the 'ruhig bewegt', or whatever, in the score does not adequately delineate.") But the most remarkable thing about Gould's meltingly lyrical performance of Wagner was that it existed at all. Could anything be less likely from the hard-edged master of *The Goldberg Variations?* Could any other pianist even conceive of such a project?

Only an explorer of the Arctic would then have undertaken the task of recording three sonatinas by Sibelius, together with three lyric pieces called *Kyllikki*. And only Gould would have recorded them in a manner wholly divorced from concert performance. As he had done with Scriabin on television, he placed one microphone right inside the piano, another at a respectable distance, and still another in the equivalent of a balcony seat. In praising the results, Joseph McLellan of the Washington *Post* quoted Kazdin's explanation: "Kazdin calls it 'acoustic orchestration' and explains that the performance was recorded 'in a simultaneous variety of perspectives' and then edited to give each passage its ideal acoustic context, like a movie camera shifting from long shots to closeups. . . . It works particularly well with Gould's performance, which also examines the music 'in a simultaneous variety of perspectives.'"

This late Romantic and "post-Romantic" music was what preoccupied Gould during his last years. When he occasionally played the piano for a friend late at night, he was most likely to play one of his transcriptions of Strauss or Wagner. And when he considered further transcriptions, this was the kind of music that he worked on. Joe Roddy recalls him "playing recordings of Bruckner, or, for maybe the ten thousandth time in his life, the *Metamorphosen* of Strauss, which he decided at that point was the ultimate—was the piece that mattered to him more than any other. The trouble was that Strauss wrote it for twenty-three stringed instruments, and Glenn found that, try as he would, he couldn't really do that on the piano. He just couldn't make it work, and that's why he played it all the time, because it was his food."

Gould did finally record Strauss's youthful Sonata in B minor, Opus 5, along with five *Klavierstücken*, Opus 3, but this was his last recording, taped just a month before his death late in 1982. This and his performance of the Brahms ballades and rhapsodies appeared only after he was gone.

At dawn of May 20, 1980, after six or seven hours spent in editing tapes, Gould left his studio to drive home. "The body of a tiny, presumably new-born squirrel was on the roof of Lance (It had apparently dropped on it from above)," he wrote on a pad later that day, using his private name for one of his cars. "It was an immensely touching sight and, although I was momentarily startled and even frightened by it when I moved the car just before dawn, it was, I think, that sight and the reflections that stemmed from it which was finally resp. [responsible] for the launching of this journal."

The connection is elusive, for Gould kept this new journal for less than two months; it is mostly a chronicle of chores and vexations. It had been twenty-five years since that first recording of *The Goldberg Variations*, and Gould and Columbia had somehow agreed to clean out the cupboard by combining all the unissued miscellany into something to be called *The Glenn Gould Silver Jubilee Album*. So now he was editing those three Scarlatti sonatas that he had taped back in 1968, and a C.P.E. Bach sonata from that same period, and the two Scriabin *poèmes* he had done on TV in 1974, and his 1968 performance of the first movement of Liszt's transcription of Beethoven's Sixth Symphony, and even his 1966 accompaniment to Elisabeth Schwarzkopf's performance of Strauss's "Ophelialieder." This rather strange collection would also include a reissuing of "So You Want to Write a Fugue?"

The only thing it lacked was the repeatedly suppressed parody of Horowitz's "historic return." Seven years after the last rejection of this project, fifteen years after the historic return itself, Gould once again began doggedly pressing CBS for a chance to carry out his strange idea. Horowitz had by now returned to RCA Victor, which made the plan a little bit less implausible, but the general manager of CBS Records remained as monumentally uninterested as ever. Gould and CBS were now discussing the possibility of including some kind of interview or discussion in the jubilee album, but, as Gould noted in his 1980 journal, "Joe Dash has decreed that I must *not* spoof the Horowitz return on the talk disk. . . ."

Gould went to New York that June, partly to talk with CBS,

partly to look for a new piano, and somehow he kept the Horowitz parody alive. Now there was going to be a panel discussion, in which Gould would be the only sane participant, politely parrying the lunacies of his alter egos, Karlheinz Klopweisser, composer of the *Panzersymphonie* that had premiered at El Alamein in 1942; Theodore Slutz, the fine arts editor of New York's *Village Grass Is Greener;* and Sir Nigel Twitt-Thornwaite, conductor laureate of the BBC Light Orchestra (Orkneys) and author of *Beethoven's English Years: The Untold Story.* "It is very difficult," as Gould noted in his journal about his talks at CBS, "to maintain an acceptable level of sobriety at app. moments. I then embellished the idea with one further step—add a compère (real, live-type host) who can control and/ or act as a buffer for me vis a vis the panel. I decided to invite Margaret Pacsu; she's delighted with the idea and will bring along at least one of her own characters, Márta Hortávanyi, to sit in with the panel. . . ."

"I joined the CBC in seventy-two and was in television and moved over to radio and have been in radio ever since," says Miss Pacsu, an extremely attractive brunette who originally came from Princeton, New Jersey. "And one of those days, somewhere around 1976, I was working afternoons, and he came in, what was early for him, and he just bumbled into the music department. It was a hot summer day, and he was in his overcoat and his gloves, all shredded and whatever. He looked like a hobo, to use an Old World word, and we instantly—it was as if I'd known him all my life. Nobody introduced us, he didn't introduce himself, but we started doing these voices, almost instantaneously. He could do Russian, and he did everybody else, but the one he couldn't do was the Hungarian voice, which is my parents' accent, because the darn accent's on the first syllable, and he just couldn't quite get that.

"So I teased him about his ear and his accent, just banter, just jolly conversation, but I knew that he listened to our broadcasts. We had a contest on my program, and we played a brand-new recording— it was some very, very early Schoenberg—and we asked everybody to guess what it was. Well, we had one phone call, from one listener, and it was Glenn. But unfortunately, our free giveaway records were some of his, so we couldn't give them to him. But he loved to do that. I mean, he loved to sort of part the curtains and just emerge and step full-blown into somebody's life.

"Then when he started doing some of his comedy things for radio, he asked me to be his straight man, which I suppose should be a straight person now. Anyway, he was all of the voices, and he wrote all of the sketch and wrote my answers. And before we recorded this, he went into the bathroom and washed his hands, and they were *scarlet* red, and I just said, 'But Glenn, you know, this isn't a concert, this is taped radio. We can redo anything, any mistake.' And he said, 'Well, I suppose that is mildly neurotic, isn't it?' And I said nothing, one of the few times in my life when I said absolutely nothing. . . .

"He called me up—I guess it was the summer of eighty—it was the twenty-fifth of June, two days before my birthday—and he read me the script which he had written. I think he had written it in a matter of hours, or a couple of days, and there were barely any corrections between what he wrote, and what he read me on the phone, and what we finally did. So he must have been thinking about it for a long time.

"We did the record at night, at the Inn on the Park, and I remember he always ordered only *fresh* orange juice for his supper, or whatever meal that was to be at that time, which was about ten o'clock at night, and which he really enjoyed. You could just see that he was really enjoying that one meal, mixed with his—whatever they were, either uppers or slower-downers. I think he was slowing himself down most of the time.

"The pace was really horrendous, and he was very hard to work with, not from my point of view but the technical point of view, because he knew everything, he could hear everything that he wanted. You know, every edit, every single sentence. There weren't four or five versions, there were twenty-five and thirty-five and forty-five. But it was a very satisfactory experience. We were both silly. I mean, we did all kinds of funny things while we were doing this. We were doing animal noises, we did every accent we knew. He sang me a country-and-western song that he had written when he was fifteen. At the same time, he was practicing the next pieces he was going to record, the Haydn sonatas. And this is what happened to me. This whole thing represents three days in my life, from four in the afternoon until two in the morning, in which I did nothing else but that. It was totally focused. I don't remember anything else that happened."

Gould was similarly focused, and when he returned to his journal in mid-August, he was "amazed" to note that he had made no entries since early July. "The reason that I have not written relates ... directly to the chief product of the intervening wks ... the talk disc—if one can poss. refer to so magnif. (pardon my modesty) a creation by such a title.... Though we hit all manner of snags initially as well as some others subseq., it was apparent early on that we would survive and that the product would be superb.... Hilarious and serious by turns, it is, as M.P. [Margaret Pacsu] said at the office meeting (i.e. dub session yesterday) the perfect summing up of 25 yrs."

There are many clever moments in the talk-show section of *A Glenn Gould Fantasy,* but most of the record dealt with questions that Gould had lectured on many times before, his preference for recordings rather than live performances, his belief in the musical possibilities of radio documentaries, and so on. It obviously amused Gould vastly to put his own ideas mainly into the Teutonic accents of Karlheinz Klopweisser, and the attacks of his critics into the Blimpian tones of Sir Nigel Twitt-Thornwaite (the album even includes photographs of Gould schizophrenically playing all these roles, in long white locks as Klopweisser and in walrus moustache as Sir Nigel). Miss Pacsu joined in as not only the mistress of ceremonies but also the Hungarian critic Márta Hortaványi, author of *Fascistic Implications of the 6/4 Chord in Richard Strauss.*

Only when Miss Hortaványi finally asked Gould whether "it is not possible, like other artists who withdraw for a time from the public, that you make then a hysteric return," only then did Gould embark on his long-suppressed Horowitz parody, a piece of wildly surrealistic abandon unlike anything else he ever attempted. For this man who yearned for total control, it was an excursion into the nightmare of total loss of control. The hysteric return had to be set in the Arctic, of course, with Gould performing on the drilling platform of Geyser Petroleum's Exploratory Rig XB 67, while the Aklavic Philharmonic accompanied him via closed-circuit TV from the nuclear submarine *Inextinguishable,* two miles away.

The tape begins with Gould performing the last few bars of Weber's *Konzertstück,* of all things, and then an oleaginous CBC newcaster named Byron Rossiter offers one of those high-toned descriptions of how the audience has been "treated to a veritable feast for eye and ear; they watched as the midnight sun performed its annual mid-summer flirtation with the Beaufort Sea—dipping seductively toward the eager whitecaps on the horizon. . . ." A wave of applause then demonstrates that Gould has returned for an encore, and as he begins to play his spectacular transcription of Ravel's *La Valse,* the CBC commentator goes on describing the scene, telling us not only that Gould is playing on his knees because his famous folding chair was washed overboard but also that the directors of Geyser Petroleum are abandoning Oil Rig XB 67 "even as our soloist, totally absorbed in his performance, continues unaware of their departure." Rossiter then calls in an American correspondent, Cassie Mackerel, for an interview with the president of Geyser Petroleum, while, according to Gould's script, we hear "sounds of high-powered diesel engine with appropriate wave and wind effects; 'La Valse' is still heard, very distantly, in the background."

Miss Mackerel's interview discloses that Geyser has just discovered a major oil field, and all the corporate executives are rushing to call their stockbrokers before the news spreads, but the CBC announcer now takes us back to Gould spraying Ravel in all directions. "It does seem that Mr. Gould is aware that he no longer has an audience; he's increasing the tempo dramatically and—yes, yes, he's made a major cut in the work. . . . However, I've just been notified that, since Mr. Gould no longer has an audience on the rig, and since his recital therefore can no longer be classified as a public event under the provisions of the Public Events Statutes of the Broadcasting Act, our transmission must be terminated forthwith. So on behalf of our host, Geyser Petroleum. . . ." (*"Music up for final seconds to end of* 'La Valse,'" the script concludes, *"after which GG is heard walking off stage to the accompanying applause and barks of a solitary seal."*)

GG: Thank you, thank you, thank you very much.

Gouldian humor is occasionally quite funny, in an Arctic sort of way, and one can only wonder what Horowitz might have made of it. (Horowitz's manager, Peter Gelb, says that he cannot be interviewed.) Intensely aware of each other, these two great virtuosos apparently never met, but John Roberts recalls that Gould's death finally brought them together. "When Glenn died, one of the first

telegrams which came was from Horowitz," he says. "They also
sent flowers."

Q: But Gould never thought much of Horowitz.

A: Well, yes and no, yes and no. Horowitz pursued a repertoire
which Glenn was not very much interested in, but Glenn was full
of contradictions. . . .

XII

The Movies

One September day in 1971, without any explanation, a package arrived in Gould's mail. He opened it up and found that someone had sent him a copy of Kurt Vonnegut's *Slaughterhouse-Five*. And so he began reading: "All this happened, more or less. The war parts, anyway, are pretty much true. One guy I knew really *was* shot in Dresden for taking a teapot that wasn't his. Another guy I knew really *did* threaten to have his personal enemies killed by hired gunmen after the war...."

Only a day or two later did Gould receive an explanatory letter from George Roy Hill, the director, whose string of successful movies had recently included *Butch Cassidy and the Sundance Kid*. He was now editing his recently shot film of *Slaughterhouse-Five*, Hill wrote, and "I am starting to think about who is going to do the music for it." Since the major event in the novel was the Allied bombing of Dresden during the last days of World War II, Hill wanted the music to reflect the Baroque style of the ruined city. "I have been thinking of Bach and possibly improvisations on Bach themes throughout the film," he wrote. "Since my knowledge of Bach is closely associated with all your Bach recordings, I thought of you and hope to ask your advice ... and whether you would be interested in participating in some capacity in this project...."

By this time, Gould had read the novel—indeed, he read it three times—and he didn't much like it. *Slaughterhouse-Five* might have been—should have been—Vonnegut's best and most important novel, for the disaster at Dresden was central to both his own experiences and his view of the world. As a war prisoner, Vonnegut himself had survived the most concentrated destruction of the entire war because he had been confined in an underground slaughter-house. As a German-American, he was all too well qualified to see the ironies in the carnage. Perhaps because of that, Vonnegut avoided any real confrontation with his experience, first by not writing about it for many years, or rather by writing and then throwing away what he had written.

"I thought it would be easy for me to write about the destruction of Dresden," he finally declared at the start of *Slaughterhouse-Five*, "since all I would have to do would be to report what I had seen. . . . But not many words about Dresden came from my mind then. . . . I must have written five thousand pages by now, and thrown them all away. . . . There is nothing intelligent to say about a massacre." Vonnegut finally solved his problem only by framing his half-suppressed recollections within the familiar amiabilities of his science-fiction fantasies, of magical flights to the planet Tralfamadore. If Billy Pilgrim's space travels were fantasy, then so was the bombing of Dresden, or if the space travel was symbolic, then so too was Dresden. Either way, we all escape the realities of the firestorm that killed more than 135,000 people in a single night.

Gould seems to have had more general objections to Vonnegut's work, though he encountered some difficulties in formulating his criticisms. "Vonnegut, of course, is to the current crop of college frosh as J. D. Salinger was to the youth of my day—a dispenser of those too-easily accessible home truths that one somehow never does get at home," Gould wrote in a CBC commentary after the film was released. "And precisely because he quite ruthlessly exploits certain aspects of the generation gap . . . I suspect that much of his work will date quickly and reveal the supposed profundities of an opus like *Slaughterhouse-Five* as the inevitable clichés of an overgeneralized, underparticularized view of humanity."

But to create a musical score for the movie—how could Gould not be tempted? From the earliest beginnings in the age of silent films, celebrated musicians had been lured into collaboration with the camera. Prokofiev had provided the music for Sergei Eisenstein's *Alexander Nevsky* and *Ivan the Terrible*, and other film makers hired Shostakovich, Poulenc, Honegger. Aaron Copland wrote the score for *Of Mice and Men* and Darius Milhaud for *The Private*

Affairs of Bel-Ami. Even Stravinsky and Schoenberg underwent interviews in Hollywood. Part of the temptation was simply money, of course, but part was also the challenge of mastering a new medium, of exploring the possibilities of film, just as Monteverdi and the earliest opera composers had once explored the possibilities of the stage. Gould, who had spoken of his love affair with the microphone, who exulted in his exploits on radio and television, could hardly resist the invitation from George Roy Hill. "I'd be most intrigued to learn about the cinematic notions you intend to apply . . ." he wrote back. "Certainly a baroque ambience for the Dresden sequences sounds both appealing and appropriately ironic. . . ."

Gould later claimed that he imagined great possibilities for *Slaughterhouse-Five.* "I conceived of vast montages," he told William Littler of the Toronto *Star,* "while Hill, who doesn't like much music, thought in terms of set pieces. He kept telling me, 'Keep it simple, keep it simple!'" Hill, savoring a cup of coffee in a sunny office overlooking Rockefeller Plaza, offers no objection to Gould's account, but his own account is quite different. "What happened was—" he says, "I wanted to use Bach throughout, and I wanted to use Glenn Gould throughout. So what I did was, when I scored it, when I cut it, when I edited it, I put in Glenn Gould's records, so that when he—he had already scored it. He just didn't know it. But you can't take records and just use them, and so—I was really kind of afraid, because I didn't have his permission, so I wanted to be on his good side."

Hill diplomatically suggested that he would be happy to make a pilgrimage to Toronto, and Gould graciously agreed to receive him. "So I went up there, and he met me," Hill says. "He had taken a room in a motel that was near the airport, and we just sat there and talked, in this motel room, and I told him what I had done. I told him that I would be perfectly open to suggestions, as long as they were by Bach."

Q: Was he surprised that you'd gone so far ahead without him?

A: He didn't seem to be. In fact, he seemed to take it all in good part, and we sat there and talked for about five hours.

Q: About the movie?

A: About everything. He just started—he was a great raconteur, and he just kept going and going and going. I was fascinated, because I love his music. I think he was one of the giants of the age. So I was listening to this, seated at the foot of Gamaliel.

Despite his admiration and awe, Hill knew exactly what he wanted, and he skillfully maneuvered Gould into both approving what had already been chosen and agreeing to patch over a few gaps. The most difficult of these gaps, which was not really very difficult, was a marching scene in which a selection from Bach's Concerto in D major had to be grafted onto the Fourth Brandenburg Concerto.

"As you can imagine," Gould later told an interviewer, "there is no convenient way of getting from F sharp minor to G major in 18 seconds—not to mention going from 3/8 time to 2/2." Gould proposed that the first section simply fade into the second, but Hill vetoed that. He had permitted no dissolves in his hard-edged filming, and he wanted none on the sound track. He asked Gould to try again, so Gould tried bridging the gap by virtuosity. "I wrote a wildly imaginative canon with themes from the Brandenburg and the other concerto," he said. "George thought that was too sophisticated. We got together in a tiny studio at Film House in downtown Toronto. I felt like Ira Gershwin. I improvised a few versions and George said, 'That's it.'" But that wasn't it. The scene was cut from eighteen seconds to fourteen, and these are big changes in movie music. Gould attempted to make a recording of the agreed-on scene in the Eaton Auditorium in Toronto, and then the phone rang, and Hill reported that yet another four seconds had to be trimmed from the scene.

Gould finally came to New York for the final recording, in which he sat at the harpsichord and conducted a group of musicians from the New York Philharmonic. Gould was by now using the click-track, that movie-musical marvel that a conductor can slip over his ears to synchronize his music with what the film projector shows. "After 35 takes, they told me the click-track was wrong!" Gould marveled. "Now you can't rent the New York Philharmonic for nothing. That cost the studio about $1,000 in overtime pay." The studio, it is probably safe to say, hardly noticed. Bach's music, Gould's version of Bach's music, was a relatively minor part of *Slaughterhouse-Five*.

Hill still retained total control. "The music is all in and it's gorgeous—it exceeds everything I had hoped for," he wrote to Gould in March of 1972. Only then did he confess that he had overruled his hero's wishes on how the music was to be presented. Gould, who had consistently played Bach's harpsichord music on the piano, who had repeatedly declared that it didn't matter what instruments were used in such performances, now felt that the main themes of *Slaughterhouse-Five* should be played on a harpsichord. He recorded both piano and harpsichord versions, but after he was safely back in Toronto, Hill decided on the piano. "I can only say that I took these decisions knowing how strongly you felt, and was willing to make almost any compromise in the world dramatically in order to please you," Hill wrote to him. "However, I am not using the harpsichord in the first arrival of the star. I mixed it and loved it. Then I played the whole picture with it and . . . it failed to do one thing dramatically—the sound of the harpsichord is so different, particularly with the ornamentations, that it simply did not connect. . . ."

Having asserted his view, Hill was quite willing to let Gould take all the credit for the score, and Gould, having been pushed around a bit, was just as willing to take the credit. Indeed, the listings at the start of *Slaughterhouse-Five* ignore Bach and simply announce: "Music: Glenn Gould." According to Littler of the *Star*, the music for *Slaughterhouse-Five* represented "one of the briefest, aptest and most widely praised film scores of the season. As the New Yorker's Penelope Gilliatt writes, 'Bach's music is splendiferously used.'" Littler's own description of the Gould-Hill (Bach) creation was warmly admiring: "His entire score lasts less than a quarter hour and . . . consists entirely of bits of Bach. But what inspired bits! And how crucially placed! The first bit we encounter is the Largo from Bach's F minor Concerto, BWV 1056, which accompanies Billy's wandering, shell-shocked, through the snow-covered Ardennes forest during the war. Not only does this theme offer a marvelous sense of timelessness, its very shape and rhythm seem to pace the figure meandering through the snow. . . . [Music] in this film . . . simultaneously gives added meaning to the setting and an ironic counterpoint to the screen actions."

After such praises, what could Gould say, except that he really didn't like the movie because he really hadn't liked Vonnegut's novel? He liked Hill's direction, he liked all the technical aspects of the film, he felt that everyone had been remarkably faithful to Vonnegut's work, but he didn't think much of that work. "*Slaughterhouse-Five* . . . is a film about the banalities of Middle America which have impeded the moral and cultural evolution of that country," he concluded. "But it's a film produced for, and by, an elitist America, which, instead of turning sympathetically to its past in the hope of achieving some synthesis that might represent its true heritage, diminishes its present and jeopardizes its future by a total lack of faith in the incomparable virtue of charity. It's a film that was challenging and stimulating to work on, superbly crafted within the limits of its genre. . . . But it's not a work of art that one can love."

Vonnegut has become reasonably stoical about such things over the years. "Yes, I know what he said about my novel," he writes in answer to an inquiry. "I do not reply to critics unless they have misrepresented a book some way. His opinion does not offend me. It is yet another idiosyncratic little work of art by a passionate genius. The tone of it is that I have not built on the past, which is what most musicians do. One message of my book, however, is that much of what we have inherited, not music, though, will kill us if we don't stop treating it so respectfully."

Moviemakers periodically thought of Gould's Bach whenever they wanted a sound of coolness and detachment. Thus Warner Brothers used excerpts from *The Goldberg Variations* in the sound track for *The Terminal Man* (1974). Yet it was not until early in 1982, Gould's last year, that a producer actually asked him to provide some music for a film. This was Richard Nielsen, who had been a coproducer of "Glenn Gould's Toronto," and who now was engaged in filming Timothy Findley's *The Wars*. There are curious similarities between Findley's novel and *Slaughterhouse-Five*. Both are portraits of young men very unwillingly at war; both focus on images of fire; both treat war itself as brutal, meaningless, and absurd. *The Wars* was particularly Gouldian in that its hero's act of heroism was a doomed effort to save a troop of horses from German shelling.

Nielsen sent a rough cut of the film to Gould to see if he would like it. Gould liked it very much, Nielsen recalls, but he had one objection. "He said, 'There's a dead horse in one scene, and there is also a scene where a rabbit looks as if it's about to be killed.' He said, 'I know the horse is dead, but if it was killed for the film, I couldn't work on it. That is, if you actually killed that animal—' I said, 'Oh, no.' The horse had long been dead. I think he probably expired from natural causes. I think we got him from an abattoir, where they kill old horses for horsemeat. So we stuck him in a freezer until we needed him. And so Glenn said, 'Well, fine, then we'll do it.'"

Timothy Findley, a very amiable man who lives in an Ontario farmhouse with thirty-three cats, one of whom he claims to have taught to play soccer, remembers his anxiety at meeting Gould even though he had heard that Gould admired both his novel and his film script. "We were supposed to see it together and then talk about the music," Findley recalls. "And I felt: I can't live up to what he thinks of my work. So I was scared of him, and I was scared of the moment. I was sitting in the dimly lit screening room, looking around out of the corner of my eye, and I saw this person come through. And I could hear galoshes. You could hear the galoshes before anything."

Q: Slop-slop-slop?

A: And I thought, It's all true.

Q: This was in midsummer?

A: I can't remember what time of year it was, but he didn't need to dress that way—that was crazy. And so he came in, and my first impression was, He's sick—he's really ill. He looked ill, because the color of his skin was so alarming. And his hair looked dead. It really had that awful look of someone who's been ill in a very major way, so that their hair dies. And it looked like that—it looked like dead hair. . . .

"He was bigger than I thought he would be," Findley goes on, "and he sort of plunked himself down there on my left, and didn't say anything, and I thought, Oh, God! Now I'm going to have to do it all. I'm going to have to lean across and say, 'How do you do? I'm Timothy Findley.' And the joke in all this is that everybody said you never touch his hands, you never try to shake hands with him, but the first thing he did to me was to offer to shake hands. He offered me his hand in a very definite way, none of this tentative, 'don't-touch-me' stuff. Which was lovely, I thought."

It is no longer clear whether anyone really expected Gould to write a musical score for *The Wars*. He was by now less celebrated as a composer than as a kind of virtuoso of technology and pastiche. Gould's own idea was to create a score that would be, like the movie itself, a World War I period piece. That meant Brahms and people like that, and Victorian hymns, "Abide with Me." "I remember him pointing at the screen," Findley recalls, "and saying, 'All the music in the film will come out of that piano bench.' Meaning that everything would be accessible to the people in the film. Nothing would be imposed on them as characters. In other words, there would be no music coming from outside their lives. And I kind of liked that idea."

What Gould did then was to invite Nielsen and his director, Robin Phillips, to his studio for what Nielsen remembers as "really one of the most fascinating nights of my life." Gould had arranged recordings of his own performances to fit each important scene in the movie. "So Glenn did this absolute *tour-de-force* thing that night," Nielsen says, "of taking us through everything he had ever recorded, putting it up on his own electronic equipment, timing it before your eyes with the picture, playing it and modulating it. He literally took us through a whole range of suggestions, from things he had recorded. I remember we had some argument about the Strauss, the Richard Strauss thing in the opening [the third of the *Fünf Klavierstücken*, Opus 3], and he was so delighted with that because he said no one will ever know what this is. 'No one will believe this is Richard Strauss, because he wrote it when he was fourteen.'

"Anyway, we finally finished, and it was agreed that in certain passages, Glenn would compose certain things. Which he did. Sort of cello and bass sequences toward the end. And also the voices that we decided to use for the hymns, Glenn ended up directing those. But anyway, we staggered out of there at seven o'clock in the morning. Robin said, 'He's immensely impressive, but I need to think about him.' And he phoned me at about noon, and he said, 'I'm convinced we've made a mistake.' And I said, 'Well, I have just the opposite reaction.' I said, 'I'm still resonating.'"

Like Dmitri Tiomkin, who startled an Academy Awards audience by crediting his own Oscar to the help of such friends as Beethoven and Wagner, Gould decided to rely mainly on Brahms and Strauss.

Thus one of Brahms's late piano intermezzi (Opus 117, No. 1) became "Rowena's theme," and another one (Opus 118, No. 6) became the "Hospital ashes sequence." This was not plagiarism, for Gould (like Bach) made no secret of his borrowings, but one can hardly help wondering why, when he was finally given such an opportunity to compose whatever he wanted, he limited himself to making a series of arrangements. Even when he undertook to compose a fragment for a soldier to play on a harmonica in one of the nearby trenches, Gould fell back on one of the Brahms intermezzi as his starting point. "The first excerpt is a short set of variations on the theme of Brahms," he wrote to a friend, "the second an arrangment of 'Abide with Me' (both of which themes play a significant leitmotivic role in the score) and together, needless to say, they constitute my first professional exposure to the harmonica. In fact, my ignorance of the instrument was such that I had to ask what the lowest note of the average government-issue harmonica might be—middle C, it turns out, but it's not covered in your average text on orchestration."

Gould put a good deal of work into the performance of this music, not only his piano pieces but the hymns that had helped inspire Canadians to send their youth into the carnage. There is a particularly notable scene in which the hero's despairing mother sits drinking from a flask on the stone stairs of the church while the choir inside sings of patriotic dedication. This was the music, remember, in which Gould heard echoes of his own youth, of those Sunday-night prayers for "the peace that earth cannot give," before the Monday-morning return to school and the "terrifying situations out *there*." "Ever since I was a child," he said in one of his talks with Bruno Monsaingeon, "the music to which I've responded most deeply, the music which has moved me most, is not found in fugues or canons or whatever—it's found in chorales, hymns." Now, in March of 1982, just a few months before that same music sounded at Gould's memorial service, a reporter for the *Star* found the famous recluse out at the distant church of St. Martin-in-the-Fields, overseeing the Canadian Children's Opera Chorus and the choir of St. Simon the Apostle in recording the hymns he had chosen. "Gould specifically worked with three boys . . ." the reporter wrote, "on a piece of music he re-arranged for their voices." "It was a bizarre scene," Dick Nielsen adds, "because Glenn was conducting these boys but he was crouched down in a pew where you couldn't see him. All you could see was a hand reaching out—looked like a totally disembodied hand. Utterly mesmerizing to watch."

Performance, by now, was only the beginning of a Gould creation. After the music had been played and recorded, he started the infinitely detailed process of manipulating the tapes. Of that Strauss *Klavierstück* that he had used in the opening scene of the film, he wrote to the engineer: "Both segments of the Strauss should be dubbed again and/or run straight from the master during the mix. . . . If you do choose to go with the master for the mix, it will involve the all-important pitch alteration (Studer 500 to 504) which occurs at the end of bar 18, immediately before a cut to bar 47; otherwise expressed, it occurs 1 minute, 51 seconds into the opening segment. The other general comment about the Strauss is that, in the Soundmix Theatre, at least, it seemed decidedly bass-oriented. I recall that, during the dubbing session at my studio, I urged Kevin [Doyle, a sound engineer] to effect a steeper bass cut in order to compensate for the dynamic characteristics of the dubber itself. . . ." And so on. That one specimen of engineering instructions continues for seven single-spaced pages.

The Wars was a rather good movie, well acted by various members of Phillips's Stratford repertory company, and ultimately quite moving. Gould liked it a lot. "I think it's a remarkably fine picture," he wrote to a friend, "—very understated, rather slow-moving, interesting particularly for what it leaves unsaid and unshown." That is the kind of praise that implies commercial troubles, however, and those troubles duly arrived. *The Wars* did reasonably well in Toronto and other Canadian cities, but the reviews were mixed, as the phrase goes, and despite Nielsen's best efforts in Los Angeles, he could not find anyone to distribute the picture in the United States at all. In such circumstances, everyone tends to blame everyone else, including Gould. "Robin Phillips said at one point, 'I think the music's too good for the movie,' Nielsen recalls. "And I absolutely love what Glenn did, but I understand. Robin, I think, retains a view that a much more popular music score would have helped the film more."

Gould probably could never have provided that. ("How angry

Glenn was with Robin Phillips!" Jessie Greig recalls. "Glenn would just launch into this tirade on the phone about their working problems. And he would be so angry. . . .") But the most important thing about Gould's role in *The Wars* is that he never really wrote any score at all. Long ago, in his youth, he had talked often about his yearning to become a composer. As a famous virtuoso, he had renounced the concert stage in order to devote his time to composition. He had experimented with various kinds of nonmusical compositions in sound, but *The Wars* represented a kind of last chance, and it was a last chance declined. Sam Carter, Gould's final producer at CBS, later saw just a glimpse of the possibilities when he asked Gould, during a break in a recording session, to improvise on "Abide with Me." "And he did, for twenty minutes," Carter recalls. "And it was beautiful."

The Wars was only a movie, of course, and some authority or other has declared that the basic function of good movie music is to be ignored, not noticed, not heard. That is probably true for believers in the supremacy of visual images, though a rival theory would suggest that the function of a movie composer is to create and exploit one grand idea, the zither theme in *The Third Man,* for example, or the Lara theme in *Doctor Zhivago.* Gould was not really very much interested in such questions. It probably never occurred to him that Nielsen would be the last man to ask him to be what he had once said he wanted to be. Perhaps he had given up such ambitions. In any case, he had quite different plans for his future.

XIII

The Conductor

In one of the lined pads where Gould kept jotting down random thoughts, blood-pressure readings, first drafts of essays, stock-market statistics, letters, shopping lists, and anything else that crossed his restless mind, he now began writing lists of "dream pgms." The first one consisted of Wagner's *Siegfried Idyll,* Schoenberg's First Chamber Symphony, and Strauss's *Metamorphosen.* The second listed Schubert's Fifth Symphony, Strauss's Oboe Concerto, and Schoenberg's *Verklärte Nacht.* Not until the third program did Gould revert to Bach, the Third Brandenburg Concerto, and not until then did he include the first piano work, Bach's Concerto in D minor.

Gould's dream programs no longer featured the piano because he was dreaming of a whole new career for himself as a conductor. In this, he was hardly unique. Liszt had loved conducting; so had Mozart, Schumann, Rachmaninoff, not to mention Bernstein, Ashkenazy, Barenboim. Still, it seems a little strange for someone who had devoted so much of his life to the piano to switch entirely to conducting, to give up the actual performance of music for the sake of directing others in performance.

The main attraction seems to have been the enormously enlarged body of music that would be available to him. This was one of the indirect consequences of Gould's insistence on playing the piano only in the recording studio. It was true, as he had long argued, that the pressures of the concert stage constrained a pianist to perform the same few works over and over again, and thus imposed on him a narrow conservatism. An enthusiastic concert performer like Rubinstein could play some cherished favorite like the A-flat Polonaise again and again without ever tiring of it. For Gould, on the other hand, once he had performed a work, taped it, edited it, spliced it, and put it, as he liked to say, "in the can," that was generally the end. He not only never performed it again but never even looked at it for years on end. And so, once *The Well-Tempered Clavier*, once the partitas and toccatas and the English Suites and French Suites were done, all of Mozart and all of Schoenberg, the prospects seemed to be shrinking.

There were, to be sure, large areas still unfinished. Gould's traversal of the Beethoven sonatas never got much beyond the *Appassionata*, his complete Scriabin sonatas included only the Third and Fifth of the ten, and his beautiful account of the last six Haydn sonatas barely began his idea of recording all sixty. Beyond that, there were those many Romantic masterpieces that Gould professed to despise, the Schubert sonatas, the Chopin études, Schumann's *Carnaval* and *Etudes symphoniques*. Nonetheless, as Gould looked toward his future as a pianist, and as he began recording the oddities of Sibelius and early Strauss, he was apparently beginning to feel a bit hemmed in, restricted, even bored. "I've done it," he said of his entire piano career to Littler of the *Star* in 1981. "It was never something I wanted to spend my entire life doing. To devote the middle thirty years of your life to doing that [playing the piano] is a lot of time—especially the last 20 years, without concerts and other silly diversions. I have pretty well exhausted the music that interests me...."

Gould meant piano music, and he now concentrated much of his emotional energy on the orchestral literature of the late nineteenth century. He kept transcribing Strauss and Wagner on the piano, but why not go back to the original scores, and the sounds that the creators had originally imagined? "I know he was experimenting," says Ronald Wilford, his manager in these later years, "to see whether he wanted to be a conductor, and he was a very great Romantic, and he was having fun. He had done piano transcriptions, and I think what interested him now was doing these pieces in the original orchestration. So whether he was interested in being a conductor or whether he was interested in the original music, I know he was very interested in *his* experimenting to discover whether he could bring it off...."

In a sense, Gould had been conducting all his life. Anyone who ever saw him perform in public saw the extraordinary spectacle of a pianist waving one hand to demonstrate a rhythm while he played the opening statement of a Bach fugue with the other. And when he appeared with an orchestra, he was apt to conduct both himself and the orchestra, regardless of what the official conductor of record might be doing. When he actually mounted the podium, however, there were strange disturbances. He had looked forward "very eagerly," he wrote to a CBC executive in the spring of 1957, to conducting a concert at the Vancouver festival that fall, and on being asked to suggest some programs, he answered that "several ideas have occurred to me—among which would be a Bach or Mozart concerto (from the keyboard)—an all-Bach program—or a more general repertoire, possibly a Mozart or Schubert symphony plus an overture." When that concert was all over, though, his main recollection was of physical torment, "due to a rather involved muscular reaction." There was something about the arm and back muscles that he used in conducting that conflicted with the muscles he used in playing the piano.

"I became quite alarmed," he wrote to Vladimir Golschmann, a fellow conductor at the St. Louis Symphony, "about the danger of conducting at any time close to piano performances. . . . My retirement after a successful career of one concert which was at once my debut and my farewell appearance will, I am sure, be an irreparable loss in the music world. The one logical alternative is to retire from the piano world and devote myself to conducting, which I am seriously considering. . . ."

He was not seriously considering any such thing, of course, and yet the challenge kept luring him back to the podium. There still survives a 1957 TV tape of Gould conducting one movement of Mahler's Second Symphony, with Maureen Forrester as the soloist. Gould conducts without a baton, and he conducts left-handed, with deep, flowing gestures of his arms. One can imagine the back muscles protesting. Once again, Gould announced his retirement. "I had many plans for myself as a conductor," he told an interviewer, "but having done it twice this year, I've given them up. The concerts, in Toronto and Vancouver, were quite successful and I had a wonderful time. But after they were over, I couldn't go near a piano for two weeks. So I cancelled all my other conducting engagements. Don't ask me why; I don't even like to think about it." The reporter added a little elaboration: "A member of Mr. Gould's management organization later explained . . . that the gestures involved in conducting—the strong upbeats, downbeats and cue-throwing—had given Mr. Gould such cramps in his arms that he could scarcely move them, much less play a full recital."

Yet the lure kept reappearing. The Stratford Festival was where Gould liked to relax every summer in the 1950's and early 1960's, liked to concoct imaginative programs, engage in chamber music. Here, in one typical festival, he played parts of Strauss's *Capriccio* on the piano, joined Leonard Rose in a Brahms cello sonata, and even sang bits of *Elektra* while accompanying a soprano ("Seeing Glenn Gould through his current Richard Strauss phase," John Beckwith wrote sardonically in the *Star*, "is for the Canadian public somewhat like seeing a difficult child through mumps . . ."). And he again took up conducting, leading two Bach concerti from the keyboard and then the Cantata No. 54, "Thou shalt oppose sin."

And now in his last year, he began making notes on all the possibilities. "Scores to learn," one page in the legal pads begins, and then this remarkable list:

"Beethoven Egmont
"Fidelio
"Coriolanus
"Leonore #3
"Or King Stephen
"Symphony 2, 8
"Grosse Fuge
"Mendelssohn Hebrides . . .
"Ruy Blas
"Symphony 3, 4
"Brahms Symphony 3
"Vln Conc
"Tragic Overture
"Alto Rhapsody
"Song of Destiny?
"Strauss Metamorphosen . . ."

And so on. The list is two pages long, ending with Bach's B minor Mass and all the orchestral suites and Brandenburg Concerti, plus

Krenek's *Symphonic Elegy*, on the death of Anton Webern. Then Gould began writing down the amounts of time to be devoted to studying each of these composers, two hours for Beethoven, one hour and forty minutes for Mendelssohn, thirty minutes for Gluck and Handel. . . .

In all these plans to become a conductor, Gould resolutely ignored many of the most fundamental aspects of that role, those deriving from its intensely public nature. Not only does a conductor create music by extracting it from a hundred more or less willing colleagues but he must serve as the embodiment of his orchestra. He makes speeches, he raises funds, he exchanges ceremonial toasts with dowagers, he is, in every sense of the term, a public figure. Gould, on the other hand, planned to become a conductor in secret. With his own money, about five thousand dollars for an afternoon, he hired an orchestra so that he could rehearse, while his taping machines recorded every fragment. He did not even try this experiment in Toronto but drove thirty miles down the shore of Lake Ontario, in the spring of 1982, to the city of Hamilton.

"He said that he wanted to try," says Boris Brott, the conductor of the Hamilton Philharmonic Orchestra, who had once achieved the unwelcome distinction of having stepped on Gould's hand. "He wasn't sure whether he was going to be successful, or whether he could be successful, in communicating with large groups of people. I think he was a very shy individual, all in all, and yet so much of a showman, as it were. I hate to use the word showman, because it's not the right word. He was very anxious. . . ."

Q: Was there an element of secretiveness in it?

A: Oh, my God, yes! Was there ever! I mean, we literally had to close the hall, and we had security guards. . . .

Apart from having enough money to hire an orchestra—which is how Serge Koussevitzky (with a rich wife) became a conductor, and Sir Thomas Beecham too—how does one actually become a conductor? Is there not a craft and a technique to be learned, for a conductor as much as for a pianist? Brott, who won a post as assistant conductor of the Toronto Symphony at eighteen, is skeptical. "Conducting is such a hit-or-miss affair," he says. "There are so few conductors, if you go through history, who ever really studied conducting. You can learn in a conservatory the basis of conducting—

you know, sort of, what's piano, what's forte, what's four in a bar, what's three in a bar—but that's where it stops. I mean, interpretation, communication, physical communication, all of those things are never taught.

"Glenn had a very gesticulative, naturally gesticulative technique," Brott goes on. "Not a technique per se but an expression. I think, you know, one of the things that's most difficult for young conductors to learn, or for any conductors to learn, is to be uninhibited gesticulatively. That's part of—that's at least fifty percent of the battle. And he had that naturally. It was not a schooled conducting style. It was making music with your hands. At the same time, I didn't find his conducting all that natural or relaxed, to be honest. I felt there was a lot of tension. And one of the things I suppose we all have to learn as conductors is to relax while communicating tension."

Q: But he did get through to the orchestra, what he really wanted from them?

A: Oh, yes. . . . They loved working with him. They adored him. They found him fascinating. As did I.

Brott remembers that Gould wanted to rehearse a Schoenberg piece for piano and wind ensemble, and they talked about how it should go, and Gould was having some kind of difficulty in grasping the complex score. "Finally," Brott recalls, "he said, 'You know, this is ridiculous, but I can't seem to learn this. The only way I'm going to do this is if I play everything.' And so he just sat there at the piano and reduced everything, played his part and everybody else's part at the same time. And without having practiced. He had just decided—you know—it was mind-boggling. The thing that always amazed me about him, both as a pianist and as a musician generally, was that he had an ability to hear contrapuntally, so that all of the polyphonic lines, every line, was so clear in his mind—what was important, what wasn't important, and how it was to come out."

Whether such expensive experiments could ever have led to a career as a conductor remains open to question. Such a question naturally leads to Gould's manager, Ron Wilford of Columbia Artists Management Inc., a silver-haired man in a pin-striped gray suit, who is ready and able to parry any question about anything.

Q: It does seem very odd, when Gould was so reluctant to appear in public, that he should undertake a conducting career, which is a public sort of thing.

A: (Long pause) I don't know what your question is.

Q: How seriously did Gould plan to become a conductor, and what were the possibilities that he would have been successful as a conductor?

A: It depends on how you define the word conductor.

Q: Leading an orchestra.

A: As a music director?

Q: No, standing in front of the orchestra.

A: In a studio?

Q: Well, anywhere. In a studio or—

A: He did that.

Q: Do you think it would have been possible for him to have a career of just recording in a studio?

A: Recording? Yes.

Q: And live on the proceeds of the records?

A: What do you mean by "live on the proceeds of the records"?

Q: I mean, earn a satisfactory income from them.

A: (Long pause) Why not?

Q: Because it had never been done before that I know of.

A: What's never been done?

Q: Having a career as a conductor who doesn't appear in public.

A: (Long pause) The other part of Glenn Gould had never been done either. . . . Every career is unique to itself.

Gould's rehearsals with the Hamilton orchestra lasted no more than a few sessions, and then Gould began working with a free-lance group derived largely from the Toronto Symphony. The only orchestra recording he actually completed, shortly before his death, was a very slow and very beautiful (and still unreleased) perfor-mance of *The Siegfried Idyll.* When it was over, the microphones remained open, and Gould's voice can still be heard saying, spon-taneously and emotionally, "Gorgeous! Magnificent! Heart-breaking!"

Apart from making orchestral recordings of his own, Gould got interested in the idea of recording a piano concerto without ever seeing the conductor or the orchestra. Specifically, Beethoven and

Herbert von Karajan. This is not an unknown technology. Opera recordings sometimes include dubbed-in arias by singers who have conflicting commitments to perform in the Outer Antipodes. Still, Gould's interest in recording a concerto without ever seeing the orchestra illustrated either his interest in extending the boundaries of technology or his interest in making his life increasingly hermetic, or perhaps simply his interest in experimenting for the sake of experimenting.

The idea was born in 1976, when Karajan was conducting in New York, and Gould wrote out an elaborate scenario for their collaboration on the Bach D minor Concerto and the Beethoven Second, a collaboration that clearly established Gould as the director and Karajan as his deputy:

"Step 1. HvK and GG would first discuss, via phone if poss., all relevant interpretive aspects—temp, dyn. relationships etc.

"2. GG would then proceed to pre-record piano part, editing a two-track submaster which could be approp. leadered, either for tracking or a mix, for stop-tape cues (during tuttis), or . . . in relation to brief orch-solo exchanges (these, if they do not work, could of course be tracked subseq.).

"3. HvK would then record orch. part, using piano pre-tape (and audio feed ear-phone). The procedure would def. necc. stop-tape points so that piano track could be recued etc.

"4. Some segments would clearly benefit by being done the other way around—i.e. orch. material recorded first. . . .

"Thesis and Resolution: That HvK and GG could have a meeting of minds without a meeting.

"Antithesis and Retribution: The result could sound goddamn awful."

These alternative possibilities remained unresolved because of Gould's physical difficulties at the keyboard during the late 1970's. "The project, of course, was canceled due to the problems with my health at that time," he wrote. But when another possibility came up again two years later, when Karajan wanted to bring the Berlin Philharmonic to a taping session with Gould in Toronto, Gould raised objections about the pace of production. "In recent years," he wrote to the prospective producer in Munich, "I have made no recordings with orchestra—the last one, in fact, was in 1969—because of the necessity to adopt a product-per-hour ratio which I find simply unacceptable. I do realize, of course, that the economics of orchestral recording and taping make impractical the sort of leisurely schedule which I insist upon for solo material—a maximum of 10–12 recorded minutes per studio day. However, although in the past, I have worked at a much more accelerated pace in deference to the exigencies of orchestral recording, I am no longer willing to attempt that sort of feat. As I recall, during our ill-fated attempt to tape with the Berlin Philharmonic in the fall of 1976, two concertos—the Bach D minor and the Beethoven B flat major—were tentatively scheduled and two days set aside. This already seemed a breakneck pace to me but within the realm of the possible, nonetheless. In your recent letter, however, you proposed Beethoven No. 1 and 2 plus Bach's D minor and D major 'in a couple of days,' and I frankly cannot imagine committing music to tape at such a pace. . . . I am not willing to tape an average of more than 10 minutes of music per day."

So nothing ever came of the Karajan project, though the exact reasons remain somewhat mysterious. Gould's manager, Wilford, remains reticent.

Q: Do you know why all that came to nothing?

A: (Long pause) Yes. (Longer pause) But nothing which I can tell you.

If Karajan was too difficult, then maybe somebody else could be found. Gould had met Neville Marriner back in the 1950's, when Marriner was a violinist in Josef Krips's London Symphony Orchestra and Gould had performed a cycle of the Beethoven concerti. Despite all of Gould's fascination with novelties and experiments, there remained one part of his mind that always remembered familiar paths and old acquaintances. Marriner, the onetime violinist, had become very successful as the conductor of the London chamber orchestra of St. Martin-in-the-Fields, and Gould kept track of such things. Marriner was serving as guest conductor of the Cleveland Orchestra early in 1982 when Gould telephoned him.

"He said he had his fiftieth birthday coming up, and he was planning to give up playing the piano when he was fifty," Marriner recalls, on a telephone line from Los Angeles, where he is rehearsing Rossini's La Cenerentola. "But before he did that, he said, he'd like to make some records with me, and could we talk about it? So I flew up to Toronto one evening, got there about six o'clock, and we settled down to talk. He showed me some of his videos, played me a few records, and then we discussed the possibility of recording the Beethoven concertos. All five.

"It was very difficult," Marriner continues. "I mean, he said that he made one minute's music every hour, and I explained that we couldn't possibly keep an orchestra around for sixty hours, you know, just to make one record. And he agreed. And at about four o'clock in the morning, when I left, we had tentatively decided that he would record the solo parts and then send me the tapes, and I would then put the orchestra around them. And then shortly after that, of course, he died."

While Gould kept mulling over these possibilities, there remained in his mind an idea more radical than anything he had ever attempted. Now that the technology of recording on different tape tracks was perfectly familiar to him, now that he was thinking about recording concerti with different orchestras in different cities at different times, why couldn't he play the roles of both conductor and soloist himself? Not conducting from the keyboard, a part-time, hand-waving sort of effort, but conducting from the podium on one tape track and then performing at the piano on another? What better way could there be to control everything?

Gould had the Hamilton orchestra at his paid command, so all he needed was some young pianist to fill in for himself, some willing impersonator who could play the piano part while Gould conducted the orchestra, and who could then be erased, overdubbed, eliminated, when Gould decided to play the piano part himself. And what better work could be chosen for the experiment than the Beethoven Second Concerto, that bright and beautiful work that Gould had long ago unearthed and made his own? This was what Gould had chosen a quarter of a century ago for his brilliant New York orchestral debut with Bernstein and also for his first brilliant orchestral recording. All he needed now was a dummy, a ghost pianist, an alter ego.

Gould telephoned Martin Canin, a gifted musician whom he had once known on the young-pianists circuit in the 1950's and who now taught at Juilliard. Did Canin know anybody who had completely mastered the Beethoven Second and would like to come to Toronto to play it, knowing that his performance would eventually be erased? Yes, Canin had a pupil named Jon Klibonoff, who knew the work well and would perform the work well and would submit well to being erased.

Gould telephoned Klibonoff, who was then twenty-two, an eager beginner vastly impressed by a call from the master. "It was April Fool's Day, and I couldn't believe it," Klibonoff recalls. Gould wanted to talk. He did one of his Teddy Slutz routines. "In a little while, I'll be able to tell where you come from by your accent," Klibonoff recalls Gould saying. And then, after ten or fifteen minutes, Gould suddenly said, "I'll bet you come from about forty-five minutes west of the Lincoln Tunnel." "And I do," says Klibonoff. "Now that's fantastic, to have that kind of an ear."

So they talked on the telephone from Toronto to New York, talked and sang and rehearsed the whole concerto on the telephone. "Gould just started in and sang the entire orchestral tutti," Klibonoff recalls, "and then I came in, and we sang the whole movement on the telephone. If anybody had heard us, he'd have thought we were crazy."

For what he calls "a handsome honorarium," Klibonoff flew to Toronto. He went to the rehearsal hall in Hamilton, found it empty, climbed up onstage, tried out the piano for a while, and then sat down in the empty auditorium and began reading a book. In due time, a door opened, and the maestro appeared. "He was in a long coat and a hat," Klibonoff recalls, "and I figured, 'That must be him.'" Klibonoff stepped forward, and the coated figure said, "You must be Jon." Gould asked Klibonoff how he liked the piano onstage. Klibonoff, not knowing that the piano had once belonged to Gould, said he had found it rather dry. "I think it will do fine for this Beethoven, or for Bach," he said, "but I don't think you could get a very good Romantic tone from it."

"You couldn't get a good Romantic tone?" Gould echoed. He pushed away the standard-size piano stool and knelt down in front of the piano. "Then he started playing—*very* Romantic," Klibonoff recalls. "He asked me what it was, and I didn't know. I said, 'It doesn't sound like something written for the piano, it sounds like something for orchestra, probably Strauss.' And he said, 'Right. *Elektra.*'"

So they began rehearsing the Beethoven for the taping machines, take after take. Gould had many novel ideas about Beethoven's work. The pace, Klibonoff recalls, was "more stately" than that of the recording Gould had once made with Bernstein, more stately and more articulated, and Gould ignored Beethoven's markings whenever he chose. Klibonoff goes to his piano to demonstrate. "This is what Beethoven wrote," he says, playing the opening march theme and then the smoothly gentle response from the violins. "And this is the way Gould played it." He repeats the sequence, and the slur has disappeared from the violin response. It has become precise and almost staccato, like something from one of the Bach partitas.

The second movement, which Beethoven had marked *adagio*, Gould wanted extremely adagio. The orchestra had some difficulty with this tempo, Klibonoff recalls, difficulty in keeping the melodic line from breaking down. Gould also had some trouble in keeping control of the musicians with the gestures of his hands. In the technique of conducting, Klibonoff recalls, pausing to select the properly diplomatic phrase, Gould still "had a way to go." And Klibonoff himself had trouble with the extremely slow tempo that Gould demanded. Gould's solution, of course, was to go to the keyboard and play the piece himself. "And *he* didn't have any difficulty in giving it a line at that tempo," Klibonoff says. "He could do anything."

Orchestral musicians have labor unions, and labor unions have rules, and the rules would not allow Gould and Klibonoff to continue rehearsing Beethoven's Second on into the night. They had played only a few bars of the concluding rondo when Gould called a halt. He sent the orchestra home, and then he and Klibonoff went down into the basement to listen to the tapes. Were there any disagreements about the interpretation? "No, I knew from the beginning that there weren't going to be any disagreements," Klibonoff says with a wry smile. "I knew I was there 'at your service.'"

Gould seemed pleased. He said to Klibonoff that they should get together again and work on Beethoven's Third Concerto. Klibonoff would have been delighted, but this was in the spring of Gould's last year, and there were other things on his mind, and Klibonoff never heard from him again.

XIV

The Private Life

"Apart from all his work, wasn't there anybody Gould really cared about—passionately?"

"I was afraid you might ask me something like that," says John Roberts, the CBC executive. There is a pause. He offers a faint smile.

"Well, what's the answer?"

"That is the answer," says Roberts.

Gould was an extremely private man. While he fully understood all the techniques for manipulating the media, and while he exploited all those techniques in publicizing his work, he stoutly resisted all intrusions into his private life. Once, during his concert years, when an interviewer hopefully inquired whether Gould was engaged, or even had a steady girl friend, Gould gave a succinct answer: "I am not engaged." Gould's friends continue to guard that sense of privacy, and personal questions are almost invariably met by some variant of the statement that the pianist's private life is nobody's business. Not relevant to his art.

Still, we now live in the age of celebrity, when nothing is conceded to be nobody's business, when all the public heroes pay the price for their fifteen minutes of Warholian fame (and their riches) by permitting the cameras to photograph their mistresses, and even their illegitimate children, all happily at play. For someone to have neither wife nor children, nor acknowledged girl friends, invites dark suspicions that something perverse is being kept secret from the inquiring media. Perhaps inevitably, there has been a certain amount of speculation about Gould's real feelings.

"Glenn came out sort of swishy, and I said, 'Oh, one of those,'" Harvey Olnick says of Gould's first appearance at the University of Toronto. "I always thought he was gay," says Richard Sennett, the sociologist, who knew Gould during his concert years. "Because he seemed so completely indifferent to those vast numbers of fawning women, you know, in the green room." Many women, however, did not find Gould at all indifferent. "Glenn was an eighteenth-century man," says Judith Pearlman, the TV producer, "particularly in his extreme politesse and gallantry toward women. He got along much better with women than with men and was reluctant to be harsh to them in any way."

It is always possible that Gould felt latent homosexual inclinations—many people do, after all—and that he simply suppressed them. Some of the evidence in his private papers is a little ambiguous, and what is one to make of a man naming his two automobiles Lance and Longfellow? When *People* magazine inevitably came to write about Gould, late in his life, Joseph Roddy's story included a slightly enigmatic remark that his "monastic . . . solitude is occasionally broken by friends of both sexes, for varying lengths of time." Gould, who had rather naïvely hoped that this article would primarily publicize his new recording of *The Goldberg Variations*, was bitterly dismayed when Roddy first read the story to him over the telephone. "Damn right he hated that," says Ray Roberts. "It was a very clear inference that he was a homosexual. Glenn hit the *ceiling* at that."

Roddy insists that he intended no such thing. But he could sense Gould's dismay about the whole article when he read it to him on the phone. ("I felt sort of terrible about it," he recalls with a laugh. "I felt like a shit, is what I felt.") But on the question of Gould's sexuality, Roddy suddenly mimics Gould's practice of writing out questions for interviewers to ask him. "Why don't you say to me— here's your question—'Why did you *do* that?' And I'll tell you. What I felt, and I felt it with some conviction at that time, was that the homosexual community had swept up Glenn Gould, and I regarded that as wrong. I didn't think he was their property at all."

Q: What you wrote certainly could be construed as suggesting that he was a homosexual—but you didn't intend that?

A: No, I intended just the opposite.

Ray Roberts is even more emphatic. "Just for the record," he says vehemently, "Glenn was *not* a homosexual, absolutely not." Quite apart from the question of homosexuality, Gould undoubtedly found all inquiries about his most private concerns acutely distasteful. "I think Glenn had a tremendous fear of sex, colossal," says one Toronto executive who knew Gould quite well in his later years. "He feared his own sexuality, and he was not naïve or stupid or unsophisticated, so if he feared it, he feared something. There were some huge devils he was fighting. But don't misunderstand me, I think that Glenn would have *expired* before he would actually have done anything wrong." Gould often praised the straitlaced Calvinist morality that had been traditional in Ontario, often criticized Mozart and the whole Mediterranean culture for what he called "hedonism," often referred to himself as a reincarnation of George Santayana's "last Puritan." It seems rather unlikely that anyone who put such nervous emphasis on his own Puritanism might also have been leading a secret life of, shall we say, hedonism.

Still, there seems to have been something strange about Gould's sexuality, or lack of it, or about its direction, or lack of direction. A number of women who were very fond of him, admired him, sensed and felt puzzled by this strangeness, from the beginning and all through his life. Elizabeth Fox, a cheery blonde who now works as a producer of children's shows at the CBC, went out with Gould fairly often when he was twenty and twenty-one, and their dates consisted mainly of listening to music and talking about literature (Gould was in the process of discovering Thomas Mann). "The really personal impression that sticks in my mind is that I didn't know what he was, sexually," she recalls. "I always felt he didn't even shave. He had really smooth skin, and he *looked* sort of androgynous, though I didn't even know what the word was at the time." Repression takes many odd forms. Dr. Joseph Stephens, the Johns Hopkins psychiatrist, recalls that every time he visited Toronto, Gould regularly summoned a Dutch masseur. "And I would sit there with him while he was being massaged," Stephens says. "And I thought, What is this all about? Because my theory, which is absolute theory, is that everybody must be starved for human physical contact, and since he had no other physical contact that I knew of, he had physical contact with this masseur, and these sessions would go on and on." And Nicholas Kilburn, the bassoonist who knew Gould in those same years, recalls that they once were talking about sex, and Gould said, "My ecstasy is my music."

If women seemed threatening, they sometimes really were threatening. All celebrities attract a certain number of demented admirers, but there was something about Gould's remoteness that seemed particularly magnetic. "There was a woman from Boston who must have been around seventy years old," according to Bert Gould, "and she'd drive up to the cottage every summer in a station wagon loaded with her dogs and cats and everything else. She'd park her car over on the road about fifty yards from our door, and every time a boat came to our dock, she'd race down to see if Glenn was on it. It just got so sickening. I remember one day, she parked right in our driveway and started walking across the lawn. I was out sprinkling with the hose, and I just kept going in bigger circles until she walked back to her car. Oh, we'd get so sick of it."

"On a couple of occasions, we had a couple of crazies trying to get at him," says Ray Roberts. "He called me in the middle of the night one night. Some woman was pounding and scratching at his door. And then there was that crazy woman from Texas who kept writing him letters. She wrote him every day. She said she was going to come up and start shooting people on the corner of Bloor and Yonge unless he agreed to marry her."

Other women saw Gould's remoteness in a very different way. "I think Glenn was one of those people who take vows," says Margaret Pacsu, the CBC broadcaster who collaborated on Gould's jubilee record. "I mean, there *are* people who take vows. Buddhists do this, and there are Catholic priests who become devout and secluded people. I think Glenn made a kind of intellectual decision to concentrate entirely on his art." And Gould had once written: "Art on its loftiest mission is scarcely human at all."

Janet Somerville, the producer of "The Idea of North," saw the same dedication but she regards it as less ascetic. "When you watch him playing the piano on television," she says, "that sort of thing is pretty clearly woven into what he's doing. I mean, sexuality can be very *deeply* engaged in a lot of things other than sexual intercourse, and it certainly is engaged in making music. For Glenn and for lots of other people. For all of us, to some extent. I mean, this is not unusual, it's very human. But yes, Glenn had it to an unusual degree. . . ."

Gould did, in fact, have a long romance with the wife of a rather prominent musician, but she is reluctant to talk about any of the details. It began, in a way, when she and her husband were driving to dinner in Los Angeles, and the car radio suddenly began playing a new recording by an obscure young pianist performing *The Goldberg Variations*. The husband pulled up at the side of the road and sat listening, spellbound. The wife recalls that they were very late in arriving at the dinner party. She met Gould at a concert not long afterward, and an elaborate courtship began. She did not like the way he played Bach; he could hardly resist trying to reeducate her. He was always on tour in those days, and so the courtship took elaborate turns. Roddy's article in *People* offered one carefully disguised example. Gould liked to introduce himself on the telephone as one of his many alter egos, Herbert von Hochmeister, the sage of the Arctic, Sir Nigel Twitt-Thornwaite, the dean of British conductors, and so on. When he called his friend and identified himself as one of his comic creations, he often found his call taken by the woman's Chinese maid. It was apparently only when the irritating *People* story appeared that Gould learned that the simpering Chinese maid had actually been the cuckolded husband, who didn't greatly enjoy his own role and therefore inflicted this peculiar revenge on the great impersonator.

In the mid-1960's, shortly after Gould retired from the concert stage, his friend decided to move to Toronto with her two children. She rented a place near his apartment on St. Clair Avenue, and she lived there for four years. "She was a very, very lovely—a nice lady, and I liked her a lot," says Lorne Tulk, the engineer who worked on many of Gould's radio shows during this period. "In some respects, she was something like him. She was—how do I say the words?—'zingy'—would be the wrong word, because it has a bad connotation—"

Q: Lively?

A: Lively. Her mind was going all the time, and his mind was going all the time, so the two of them got on very well.

Gould wanted very much to marry her, she recalls, but she finally decided against it. She decided that he was too—what?—too unstable, too strange, too difficult. And so she returned, with the children, to her patient husband. Gould telephoned her every night for two years, she says, until she finally persuaded him to stop. They never saw each other again.

Despite Gould's self-promoted image as a "recluse," however, he naturally encountered other young women in the course of his work. Toronto is as full of attractive females as any other city, after all, and Glenn Gould's reputation in Toronto was very large indeed. "He was not what you would call a smart dresser," says one of these admirers, a professional singer, as she fingers the yellow beads around her neck, "or cared much about what he looked like, or anything like that, but I found him one of the most glamorous people I'd ever known. Glamorous in the sense that—it was the glamour of his intellect, the glamour of his talent, and even the glamour of his personality. He was a superstar, and he had a superstar personality."

Q: I don't quite know how to ask this, but I feel I have to ask it. Did you have a love affair with him?

A: Oh—uh—I don't think that's—I'm not about to tell you that.

Q: The reason that it's a problem is that one sometimes gets the sense of a man completely cut off from emotional relationships with other people. There have been rumors that he was a homosexual, or that he never had any sex at all.

A: I would prefer not to discuss his sexual life. . . . I have a very strong memory of Glenn, but whether or not he was a homosexual or a heterosexual or asexual or any kind of sexual, that is not the kind of thing that figures very prominently in my recollections. So I'm—you know—I mean, I think he was a very romantic figure. Yes, definitely.

And then there was always Cousin Jessie, who had once waxed his face for dirtying her kitchen floor, who loved him dearly all his life, and who demanded nothing of him. When asked why Gould never got married, the equally unmarried Jessie laughs and says, "Well, I think I would have pitied the woman he was married to. Because he was really married to his music." Jessie could never have married him; she was his cousin, and five years older, but Jessie had something else, her warmth and sympathy and affection.

"You know, I really believe that I was closer to him than any other living person," she says. "He wasn't demonstrative at all, but I remember. . . . I went to Cannington with him when his aunt on

his father's side died. He phoned and asked me if I'd go. . . . He was
very upset . . . and he reached over and ran his hand down my arm,
and he said, 'Jessie, I'll always be good to you.' And I knew he would
be. . . . The depth of the love he felt for me is really something,
because of the—you know—it was just something special. I've been
really fortunate. . . ."

Gould loved games, all kinds of games. He loved to invent new ones.
He loved to turn everything he encountered into some kind of a
game, which was a little strange for someone who professed to hate
all forms of competition. His father still recalls the three-year-old
child's fondness for his first piano book, by J. W. Ditson, "because
it's more or less a game the whole way through." Gould went on
playing musical games all his life. Ray Roberts recalls that he would
turn on the radio during the long drives to recording sessions in
New York, and he, Roberts, would have to name every piece being
played. Like most games, knowledge games are power games—I
know something that you don't know. All this was a little unfair to
Roberts, since he had no special background in music, but Roberts
did his best to learn different styles. "I was a musical nudnick for
starters," he says, "but after a while I got a feel for certain periods
of time. I got to be pretty good."

A more expert friend, the young New York pianist Monica Gaylord, turned the tables on Gould. She made a tape of twenty selections from her record collection and invited Gould to identify them.
She was a little surprised—Gould was probably even more surprised—to find that he knew only three of them. The man who
could play Strauss's *Elektra* from memory did not recognize such
familiar trifles as Chopin's Nocturne in E minor or Schubert's
Impromptu in G flat major.*

But Gould had other ways of playing this game with experts too.
"He knew he was a genius, and he loved to exhibit his genius," says
Dr. Stephens. "He played that game of 'Play such-and-such in the

---

*This was not the only time Gould revealed strange gaps in his seemingly encyclopedic
knowledge of music. Shortly before recording a Beethoven sonata, Opus 31, No. 1, he
acknowledged to a colleague that he had "never played it." After listening to a telecast of
Wagner's *Tannhäuser* from the Metropolitan Opera, he observed that he had "never even
known what it was about."

style of so-and-so,' and he was just incredible at improvising. I have never met anybody who could even vaguely begin to do anything like that. I would say, 'Play me a Beethoven sonata which was not written by Beethoven.' I would say, 'Play a fugue,' and he would just make up all this contrapuntal music, just like that. I said, 'Play me a Chopin nocturne,' and he just made up a Chopin nocturne that was absolutely gorgeous."

Then there was the color game, a supposedly scientific test devised by a Swiss German psychologist named Max Lüscher, in which participants pick their favorite colors and then elaborate psychological analysis ensues. "It is NOT a parlor game, and most emphatically it is not a weapon to be used in a general contest of 'one-upmanship,'" say the publishers of *The Lüscher Color Test*, who report that Dr. Lüscher has been employed as a "color consultant" by firms ranging from Parke-Davis to Volkswagen. Gould similarly used the test on prospective recording engineers, but also, of course, on his friends. Gould's favorite colors were those Arctic shades of gray and black, and he loathed the "aggressive" red. Monica Gaylord likes to wear bright red. Gould was baffled.

Some of Gould's games were quite esoteric. "He would say, 'I'll be Mozart, and you be Beethoven,' and then we would have a philosophical discussion," recalls Nicholas Goldschmidt, the conductor. Most of his games, however, were variations on Twenty Questions or I've Got a Secret. Again, power: I know something that you don't know; try to guess what it is. Gould didn't seem to care, though, whether he played the keeper of the secret or the one trying to discover it. Lorne Tulk recalls that during their midnight dinners while they worked on "The Idea of North," they repeatedly played a game that Gould called Identifications. "I tell you that I am thinking of someone," Tulk says, "and the only clue I give you is that it's either somebody you know or somebody you know of. It's not Twenty Questions because you can take as many questions as you want, but there is a hitch. The hitch is that you can't ask me a direct question. Your questions must be indirect."

Q: Like what? I mean, if I'm thinking of General de Gaulle, can you ask, "Is he an American?"

A: No, that would be a direct question. An indirect question would be: "If you were a dog, what kind of a dog would you be?"

Q: Well, if you were thinking of De Gaulle, what would the answer be?

A: I have a hard time thinking of De Gaulle in terms of a dog.

Q: A bloodhound?

A: I might say, you know, "An oversized French poodle." That's quite a clue, if you see what I'm saying.

Q: Complicated. Was it permissible to give up?

A: Well, that would be—the ultimate humiliation. I don't think Glenn ever gave up. I never knew him to give up.

Gould's games took many forms. He once decided to challenge Columbia Records' nearly incomprehensible royalty statements, and so he wrote a letter of seventeen single-spaced pages debating all the intricacies of payments due from Japan and Australia. He regarded the stock market as a wonderful game, and he played it very shrewdly. ("He used to eat frequently at the Royal York Hotel because the headwaiter there was a stock market buff," says Mario Prizek, "and they spent most of the meal time exchanging stock market tips.") During the troubled economic times in the two years before his death, according to Gould's stockbroker, the pianist was the only one of the broker's clients who made a profit on his trading. His estate, when he died, totaled about $750,000, and much of that came from playing the market.

If all of life is a game, of course, the great question is what the rules are. Gould believed in God, but despite his sternly Methodist upbringing, he believed in neither Christianity nor its churches. He believed in extrasensory perception. And in ghosts. He was profoundly superstitious. About the flight times of his friends' airplanes (which he refused to use) or the colors of their cars. "He was terrible about writing checks," says Ray Roberts, who took care of Gould's finances. "He would write a check, and he'd even give it to me sometimes, and then he'd say, 'No, no, it doesn't feel right. Give it back to me.' Sometimes, it would take him six or seven times writing a check before he decided that it was all right."

He adamantly refused to fly anywhere, and yet he drove his cars with wild abandon, repeatedly getting involved in speeding, wrong turns, even occasional collisions. "He learned to drive sitting on my knee," Bert Gould once recalled proudly. "Driving back and forth to the cottage. I'd be controlling the car but he'd be up on my knee, steering it." A little older, Gould absentmindedly steered his father's car into the lake. Older yet, he terrified friends by the heedless way he drove, and yet he refused to let anyone else drive. "I remember when he had that enormous Lincoln Continental which he ultimately smashed up," Harvey Olnick says, "which he liked because he said, 'It gives me more protection.' He went like a madman, and he would cross his legs, and talk and wave, and I would say, 'My God, Glenn, I'd rather take a bus, if you don't mind.'" Dr. Stephens recalls that the first time he ever met Gould, backstage after a concert in Baltimore, Gould proposed that they drive in Stephens's car to Stephens's house. "It was snowing," the psychiatrist says, "and I started to drive through the snow, and he said, 'You don't know anything about how to drive a car in the snow, and I think that *I* should drive.' So we stopped, and he began driving, quite recklessly, I thought. He skidded on the ice at an intersection, and I thought we were going to be killed."

The police record steadily grew. In the mid-1970's, for instance, it read: "25-07-73, speeding 72 mph in 55 mph zone; 25-10-73, speeding 40 mph in 30 mph zone; 29-11-73, speeding 40 mph in 30 mph zone; 05-04-74, prohibited turn; 09-01-75, speeding 44 mph in 30 mph zone; 31-01-75, disobeyed red traffic light. . . ." And so on. None of these were very serious offenses, but the multiplicity of charges is striking. And there were other accidents that never got onto his record. "He tended to bang cars up," Ray Roberts says, recalling an occasion when Gould bumped into somebody and "didn't want to stay around, so I had to get in touch with him and say, 'Get your car fixed, and we'll pay for it.'" Then Cousin Jessie remembers the time Gould hit a truck. "There was a snowstorm, and I'm not sure whether Glenn slipped sideways or the truck slipped sideways or they both slipped sideways," she says. "The truck took to the ditch, and there was nowhere for Glenn to go except into the river."

"He was operating on a different plane, on a different level," Roberts tries to explain, "He had so many things going on up here that he wasn't, you know, that he was sort of accident-prone, bashing things with his car. He drove fast, and sometimes he wouldn't pay attention, he'd have the radio on, and often he'd be conducting." Morris Gross, the attorney, remembers a time when he had to defend Gould for one such episode of "erratic driving." "He was a congenitally absentminded driver, putting it charitably," Gross says. "In this case, there was a police car that followed him for some time, and the policeman couldn't figure out what this crazy driver ahead of him—i.e., Gould—was doing. And when he asked Gould for an explanation, he said, 'Well, I had the radio on, and I was conducting Mahler.' And that was why his arms were waving crazily, both arms, and that's how he got into trouble. My recollection is that the judge hearing the case was very, very sympathetic and let Gould off."

Roberts repeatedly tried to persuade Gould that he would be far safer on an airliner than on the New York Thruway, but his arguments had little effect. Gould, who always wanted to be in control, thought that as long has he had one hand on the wheel of his speeding car, he really was in control. Perhaps to reinforce that idea, he installed a telephone near the wheel. "Yes, he thought he was in control," Harvey Olnick says. "And he loved to risk it. To be in control and yet to be on the edge of out of control. He played the piano that way too. He was always in control, but it seemed reckless at points, didn't it?"

Many of Gould's personal relationships had similar patterns of control and risk, games of discovery and revelation, played according to mysterious rules that Gould invented. As an international celebrity, he was constantly pursued by people who wanted something from him, at the very least his time, but also his ideas, his praise, his emotional energy, his affection. He often had to say no, which he found difficult, and so he found people to say no for him. But when some new acquaintance interested or attracted him, he could suddenly become overwhelmingly friendly. He generally tried to keep his friends separated from each other, but his enthusiasm was a quality that many of them later remarked on. Enthusiasm and encouragement and humor and charm. Gould would ask of a new friend all his time and attention; he would draw him into the Gouldian world of brilliant conversation, and complex games, and late-night music. He talked passionately about God, art, computers, politics (he regarded himself as a Socialist, though he played the stock market and never voted). And then, almost inevitably, there would come a break, and Gould would turn away, turn to other things and other people, and the abandoned friend would never be able to find out what he had done wrong, what mysterious rule he had mysteriously broken. One man who knew Gould well recalls, for example, that a celebrated musician was reported by some third party to have told a joke involving "some kind of cruelty to animals," and so Gould silently broke off all relations with the unsuspecting ex-friend because "this was no longer a person that he wanted to associate with."*

On rare occasions, Gould might try to explain, or explain his lack of explanations. In the National Library in Ottawa, there is a remarkable specimen of Gould telling some unidentified woman who had once thought herself important to him that she was not important after all. "I gather you tried to call me yesterday, so this letter—though difficult—is necessary," Gould begins. "You are as well aware as anyone by what intuition I am sometimes governed, upon what 'unreason' my decisions are sometimes based. And this intuition in the business of human relations is a force which I serve quite without question, and when it seems to demand isolation from one person or from everyone—that too is observed. However illogical and unpredictable and infuriating this may be to others, I have found in this obedience . . . a source of immense strength. And I can only ask you to be charitable and forgive me, and *believe* me when I tell you that you are in no way responsible for this . . . [and] that I hold you in as much affection as ever."

"He would burn—now, I don't want this taken out of context— but he would sort of burn people up," says Roberts. "I mean, he'd literally go at it night and day, night and day, night and day, until the person would be dropping from exhaustion, and he'd still be raring to go, you know? He once said to me that people ultimately disappoint you. One of the things I recognized very early on was that you didn't make demands on him. He liked my relationship because he could turn me on and off at will. I tried to make things as good for him as I could, but probably I would have been burned out sometime. You just couldn't keep up with his ongoingness. And what he

*Though Gould had no elaborate philosophy on the subject, he did write to a friend in 1973 that he had "become virtually a vegetarian in the past decade." This was simple enough for a man who described himself as "almost totally indifferent to the process of eating and quite frankly, can just barely manage to open cans." Mario Prizek reports that Gould had virtually no sense of taste.

wanted all the time was control. His whole life was tied up with control."

Control—the word keeps reappearing in almost everyone's recollections of Gould. He had always wanted to control all the circumstances of his life, and over the years it became a passion, an obsession. It was the need to be in control, really, that drove him from the concert stage to the recording studio. And in the recording studio, he had to control all the engineering, where the mikes were placed and how they were used, to make the recording companies come to his native city, to his own studio, where his own equipment would be the only equipment, with everything under his control.

It was the obsessive need for control that made him refuse virtually all interviews unless he could first know all the questions in advance and then eventually write all the questions himself. It was the need for control that made him conduct most of these interviews by means of the telephone and the tape recorder. Gould thought that he was a master of faked improvisation ("Well, Glenn, don't you think . . . ?"), but it is startling to hear some of the tapes that were occasionally made of genuine conversations, and to hear how much more genial and friendly he could become when the interviewing stopped. Similarly, his letters, even to strangers, are much warmer and sunnier than any of his published prose.

Still, the telephone not only preserved his sense of privacy but gave him great opportunities for variety in his social life. Toronto might be a little provincial but the telephone made it possible to have long and frequent conversations with friends in Montreal, New York, London. Gould's rules were, as usual, quite rigid. You did not call him; he called you. If you called him, you got an answering service (though he often eavesdropped on another phone). He might or might not call back, when he chose (always late at night), and for as long as he chose. Often for hours on end, Gould would read some new manuscript that he had just written, or some new version of some manuscript, or he would sing at great length some new musical discovery. Occasionally, at two or three in the morning, one of his listeners would drift off to sleep, and then wake to the sound of Gould sharply asking, "Hello? Hello? Are you there?"

And would it be possible to control people even after one's own death? Well, why not? Margaret Pacsu, in the midst of answering a question about Gould's fondness for Barbra Streisand, suddenly offers a theory: "How much of this was calculated, for *you* to be sitting here asking these questions and falling into this? I mean, you know, did he set this all up?"

Q: Are you talking about us?

A: I'm talking about you, the chosen biographer, who now has to sift through all this material. Did this man—look at that face on the jubilee album. Didn't he just set this all up so that you'd be sitting here asking—

Q: It *is* a rather malicious-looking face.

A: Well, but it's naughty too. Could you imagine that you'd be asking questions about Barbra Streisand? Or that he had carefully set this up so that historians and biographers in future years would be asking *these* very questions? You can go around in circles with that.

The weirdness and intensity of Gould's eccentricities suggest all too easily that these supposed eccentricities were actually symptoms of something more serious. One friend who knew him very well describes him quite bluntly as "a paranoid psychotic," using that term not as some loosely hyperbolic description but as an attempt at clinical diagnosis. Asked to provide specific evidence, this friend snaps back: "You know what a paranoid psychotic is, don't you? They're afraid that somebody is trying to poison their food. They're afraid to go out because somebody might try to kill them."

Q: And you're saying that Gould behaved that way?

A: Yes.

Corroborating evidence seems scarce. Geoffrey Payzant, in his book on the "music and mind" of Gould, which Gould read and okayed, carefully noted that the pianist had "never undergone psychoanalysis," carefully noted that he "has not discussed the psychological significance of his doodling with his friendly neighborhood psychoanalyst," carefully noted that Gould "cheerfully talks about his physical disorders, his hypochondria and his dependence upon tranquilizers and sedatives." And he carefully added: "Perhaps he will let us know about it in the same uninhibited way if ever he should have psychiatric treatment."

"Troubles with Glenn?" says David Oppenheim, the Columbia executive who first signed him up to record *The Goldberg Variations.* "Yeah, there were always troubles with Glenn, but you knew from the beginning that you were dealing with some special breed that had to be handled in a certain way. And this wasn't ever a person who was at peace, even troubled peace. . . . He made demands on the studio environment, on the piano, on the chair, on the temperature, on the— It was always trouble, in that sense. But it was not the kind of trouble that *people* make but just the kind of trouble that a different kind of creature gives us. We have troubles of that kind with our dogs and cats. They are what they are. And he was very much that way. . . . Glenn was queer, and I don't mean that in the sexual sense of the word but the traditional sense, just *queer*."

"What *is* the connection between insanity and imagination?" John McGreevy asks. "We have to be mad to imagine things that have never imagined before, and then to insist on the realization of those imaginings. So in that sense Glenn was one of the maddest hatters around, because he did dare to go out onto the furthest rim of what was previously accepted as tolerable behavior, and to live that life. Now the tension of persisting and insisting on that— I'm not talking about his art now, I'm talking about the life that he found for himself—must have induced in him extreme states of anxiety and panic and loneliness and terror from time to time. It must have been unbearable at times—I think he was exhausted by the effort of being Glenn Gould—but I never had a sense that he would have it any other way. Whether he ever went over the edge, I wouldn't say, but he was a fully creative person to the end."

"I certainly never thought of him as crazy," says Leonard Bernstein, but then there are qualifications. "I thought he was eccentric and compulsive, obsessive, contradictory, deliberately contradictory, just to mix people up. That had something to do with his identity. He had some kind of identity problem, and maybe the people he tried to mix up were, number one, himself. I don't like that sort of dime-store psychiatry based on hearsay, but I feel that he had a big problem about who he was, which may have affected every department of his life. Relationships, self-presentation on the stage, sexual life—is he going to be a kid or a grown-up man, is he always going to be this adventurous, surprising little fellow, or is he going to be a serious man? Is he ever going to live with anybody? Get married?

"But you see, I don't have enough evidence. I wouldn't *dare* use the word 'psychotic' about somebody that I had not seen for so long, and based only on tales of peculiarities and sudden shifts of intentions. You could make a convincing case for it. *You* could; I can't, I wouldn't. . . . Why don't you work on the— Take as a totem, as an example, the cold, this tremendous relationship he had with cold, and follow that through. That somebody who would be that fearful of the cold, and at such odds with it, at war with it all the time, should then have gone to seek it out and find magical—and *maybe* even *curative*—powers in the kind of coldness, the extremes of cold that you and I never even experienced— Okay. I loved him very much. And I'm sorry that our relationship stopped, when it did, but it was certainly not of my doing."

To the mystery of Gould's own personality, we must add the mystery of drugs, medications, particularly Valium, which Gould took in large quantities for most of his life. We now know that Valium can be addictive, which we didn't know when it first appeared as a popular psychological panacea in the 1960's, and we now know that there are a number of indeterminate side effects that we also didn't know about then, immeasurable disturbances, irrationalities—what do you call these things? Gould was always tense, intense, and Valium came to seem a necessity. One friend frankly called him "addicted," but these terms are ambiguous.

"He said he wasn't addicted, but he certainly was," says Jessie Greig.

Q: Addicted?

A: Well, I don't know. I thought he was. To me, anybody that takes it is addicted. . . . But he couldn't sleep. You know, his mind seemed to be always restless, probing, and he couldn't sleep without it, I guess. . . .

All these conflicts are at least partly a matter of interpretation. If a friend is discarded for some imagined slight, is that really paranoia or just the artistic personality? If someone insists on eating exactly the same food every day, washes his hands over and over, and follows the injunctions of astrology, numerology, and a theory of colors, is that compulsive neurosis or just whimsicality? At what level does the fear of flying pass from the rational to the irrational? At what level does hypochondria become itself a form of illness, particularly when it leads to self-diagnosis and self-medication? And to what extent do these various peculiarities have a synergistic effect, in which one or two eccentricities might be simply eccentric but the whole array of peculiarities implies a personality almost out of control, held together only by an iron sense of discipline?

If we accept Freud's hypothesis that sanity or normality can be defined as the ability to work and to love, we can look at the aging Gould and suspect that he had become psychologically impaired in both. Psychologically incapable of performing music in public and psychologically incapable of loving anyone as an equal. "If Glenn had managed, in his personal life, to just be a little bit less of a genius, a little bit more normal, I think he'd probably still be with us," says Malcolm Frager, the pianist. "I mean, if he'd settled down, gotten married and had children, and had something to think about besides himself, he probably would have— It could only have helped his playing, could have lent it greater warmth, greater humanity. And I think to have a happy family life is *much* more of a challenge than to have a career."

Many of Gould's friends and admirers feel that conventional psychological judgments simply do not apply to him. Timothy Findley, for example, still recalls his first meeting with the pianist at the screening of *The Wars* as a glimpse of one of "the god-people."

Q: What are god-people?

A: Well, the god-people are the truly, absolutely gifted, almost beyond human dimension or human comprehension. And they are— we might not all know who all of them are, but I think pretty nearly everybody would acknowledge the same ones, the Mozarts and the Shakespeares. There are probably, you know, ten of them in the whole history of the human race. But the substrata, just under them, and so far up that they're beyond all of us, are the people like Beethoven, and I would put Gould almost in that category. It's a quality of mind. When he talked about music, he was incapable of talking about it as a man. He was incapable of talking about it in any terms but his own. And you had to rise to that or you were lost. And as with all of those god-people—not unlike God himself, if you have that kind of belief—if they say things, your striving to understand them delivers what they're saying to you. Do you understand that?

Even in less exalted terms, though, Gould seems to have behaved just as most people would like to behave: He lived exactly as he pleased. He got up when he liked, ate what he liked, worked at what he wanted to work at, whenever he felt like it and however long he felt like it, answered to no bosses, saw or talked with whomever he wanted to talk with, achieved great performances of great music, hugely enjoyed himself, and earned a very good living for doing so. How could anyone ask for more?

Tim Page, the young New York music critic who first visited Gould late in his life, was shocked by the pianist's deteriorating physical appearance ("haggard, weathered, decayed"), but he saw the rich paradoxes in Gould's behavior. "I don't want to be like the people who say there was never anything strange about him," Page reflects. "There was a *lot* that was strange about him, I mean, a weird guy. There must have been a great deal of fear there—you know, fear in airplanes, in enclosed places, in concerts, and they all sort of boiled down to the same fear, which is, I think, a fear of death.

"He was certainly neurotic, and definitely drugged in his later years, but the weird thing is that he was so much *saner* than most people, in a lot of ways. I mean, he was so much more thoughtful and funny and friendly and kind, on his own terms, on his own carefully controlled terms, than most people. He was really jolly, and a really damned good companion."

XV

The Goldberg Variations (II)

Nobody knows exactly what inspired Gould to rerecord his first great triumph, *The Goldberg Variations*. Perhaps it was the spur of devising programs for Monsaingeon's video series. Perhaps it was simply the spur of technology in general, not only Monsaingeon's cameras but Columbia's new digital recording equipment. Perhaps, as he himself said, he had been rethinking the whole work, rethinking the relationship of the parts to the whole. Perhaps he was, like the novelist in Henry James's *The Middle Years*, "a passionate corrector, a fingerer of style." Given an opportunity to revise all his own works for the twenty-three-volume New York edition, James extensively fingered, retouched, and rewrote, adding to the fresh narratives of his youth the complexities of his older vision. In actual fact, Gould almost never recorded anything more than once—two sonatas by Mozart and Haydn were the only examples he cited when the question was raised—but *The Goldberg Variations* represented a kind of challenge. His most popular record, still selling well after a quarter of a century, the variations threatened to define and thus confine him. If he could not surpass the recording he had made at twenty-three, then he had learned and gained very little in all the years since then.

Gould had apparently not even played that famous recording for a long time. According to his own almost unbelievable account, he did not listen to it until three or four days before he went to New York in April of 1981 to redo it. "I just wanted to remind myself of what it was like," he said in a taped interview with Tim Page, "and, to be honest . . . it had, at that point, been so many years since

I'd heard it, that I really was curious about what I'd find." It had been, Gould said, "a rather spooky experience." He had felt "great pleasure in many respects." He had found the performance touched with "a real sense of humor," and he recognized in the actual playing "the fingerprints of the party responsible." There was one very important difference, however. "I could *not* recognize, or identify with, the *spirit* of the person who made that recording. It really seemed like some other person, some other spirit had been involved."

Gould now became very critical of this wonderful recording. Of his beautiful performance of the fifteenth variation, for example, he said contemptuously that it "sounds suspiciously like a Chopin nocturne, doesn't it?" When Page dutifully said, "It's not that bad," Gould retorted, "Would you believe a Bizet nocturne?" And when Page said, "I think, on its own terms, it's lovely," Gould insisted on attacking himself: "There's quite a bit of piano-playing going on there—and I mean that as the most derogatory comment possible." The reason that this "interview" comes to us in such precise detail, complete with underlinings for emphasis, is that Gould wrote it all himself, the questions as well as the answers. "It was about ninety percent Glenn, maybe ninety-five," says Page, "with some additions by me as we were working it out. But he did not want anything spontaneous."

Page had an odd relationship with Gould. He had been a young music critic on a short-lived New York paper called *The Soho Weekly News* when he got a call from a CBS publicist, Susan Koscis, who was trying to drum up some stories to help sell Gould's jubilee album. Everything was to be very tightly controlled. Anyone who would like to inverview Gould should write a letter saying what he would like to talk about, and then Gould would decide whom he wanted as an interlocutor, by telephone only. Page asked for an interview "entirely on your terms," and he felt honored to be chosen. "I was just, you know, a new kid in town," he says. He felt even more honored when his allotted hour on the telephone stretched out to about four hours. He was correspondingly horrified when his newspaper published his much-cut interview under a headline that identified Gould as "Recluse, Philosopher, TV Visionary and Crank." Page telephoned Toronto to apologize for his employers, Gould answered that he understood the wicked ways of the press, and so, without ever meeting, they became friends. Gould added Page to that diverse collection of people he lived with on the telephone, calling as often as once or twice a week, always at times of his own choosing, always late at night.

Page shared Gould's infatuation with the odd possibilities of technology. "He called my telephone-answering machine once," Page recalls, "and I had a—I was going through that phase with answering machines where you try to think of cute messages, and I got John McCormack's old recording of 'I hear you calling me,' and I thought it'd be a funny thing to put at the start of a tape. So when Glenn called me, he went—you know, you heard this sharp intake of breath and then 'Good heavens!' And he hung up, but I knew it was him. And then a day later, he called up, and there was John McCormack singing, 'I hear you calling me,' and then the beep, and then Glenn started singing, 'I had expected—' And *foolishly* I interrupted him, because I'd heard his voice, and I thought, My God, it's Glenn, and I'd better pick it up. And he said, 'Oh, you're there. I was just going to leave you a song I'd written.' And I said, 'Oh, well, please, I want to get this on tape.' And he said, 'No, no, no.' And he sang it to me, but I didn't tape it."

To launch the new *Goldberg Variations*, Gould wanted to make sure that all the critics understood what he was doing, so he wrote a self-interview that could be taped and sent out with the recording itself. To play the part of the questioner, he needed a docile collaborator, and so Miss Koscis once again called Page. "It was a typical CBS sleazy maneuver," Page recalls. "I don't mean Susan is sleazy, I mean the company is sleazy. They were willing to pay me seventy-five dollars to go up there and do the interview (they eventually paid a good deal more). They were not willing to pay expenses. They were not willing to pay for my hotel. Glenn called me and said, 'Let's talk about what we want to say. Do you have any questions you'd like to ask me?' I gave him a couple, and we talked about it briefly. He then sat down and wrote out the whole script. Then we both amended it. I finally agreed to go up there even though I had no money, *no* money, because the *Soho News* had folded, but then I thought, Somebody will want this interview with Glenn Gould. I nearly didn't go, but I had just finally qualified for an American Express card, so I put the whole thing on American Express."

Gould's draft of Page's interview is headed, just like his draft of the Menuhin interview, with the ironic notation that this is "a spontaneous, off-the-cuff, top-of-our-heads conversation between Tim (Wing It) Page and Glenn (Ad Lib) Gould." What Gould wanted Page to ask him to explain to the music critics was his new conception of *The Goldberg Variations*. He wanted to explain that the original version that they had loved all these years was simply a collection of unconnected piano pieces, and that he now had a theory that imposed a new relationship on all the variations.

This required, at the beginning, that the saraband theme be played extremely slowly, specifically taking three minutes rather than the one minute and forty-seven seconds of the early version. "I think that the great majority of the music that moves me very deeply is music that I want to hear played—or want to play myself, as the case may be—in a very ruminative, very deliberate way . . ." Gould said. "As I've grown older, I find . . . the great majority of my own early performances too fast for comfort. . . . With really complex contrapuntal textures, one does require a certain deliberation and I think that, to come full circle, it's the . . . lack of that deliberation that bothers me in the first version of the Goldberg."

Even more important, though, was Gould's new view that the tempo of each variation should be closely connected to the tempi of all the others. This was not exactly a new idea. Those few pianists who attempted *The Goldberg Variations* in earlier years had generally followed much the same prescription until Gould himself overturned all the traditions with the bold impetuosity of his 1955 recording. But now that he had made his own way back to the pre-Gould tradition, he saw it as a rare discovery. "I've come to feel, over the years, that a musical work, however long, ought to have basically one—I was going to say tempo but that's the wrong word—one pulse-rate, one constant rhythmic reference point," he said in this spontaneous, off-the-cuff, top-of-our-heads conversation with Page. "Now, obviously, there couldn't be anything more deadly dull than to exploit one beat that went on and on and on, indefinitely. . . . But you can take a basic pulse, and divide it or multiply it—not necessarily on a scale of 2-4-8-16-32, but often with far less obvious divisions—and make the result of those divisions or multiplications act as a *subsidiary* pulse for a particular movement. . . ."

Then he offered examples, starting with Variation 16, the "French Overture." "As you know," Gould's script said, "the French Overture is divided into two sections—the dotted rhythm sequence which gave it its name—which came from French opera tradition—and a little fughetta for the second half. The first section is written with four quarter notes to the bar (sings it) while the fughetta, on the other hand, is in 3/8 time—in other words, each bar in the fughetta contains one and a half quarter notes—a dotted quarter, as musicians like to call it (sings). . . ." And so on, until Page is made to say, "Well, Glenn, I don't think I can keep much more of this in my head at the moment." So they play three variations, and then Page, who already knows the recording perfectly well, now simulates a moment of recognition: "You know something, I felt it; I don't know if I would have actually been able to spot what you did just listening to it—but there *was* a link between those variations— I could feel it in my bones."

Though there are obviously elements of make-believe in all this, Page does not think he said anything that he does not really believe.

Q: He wrote that script for himself to tell you how much better the new version is than the old one, and you agreeing. Is that actually your view?

A: Yes.

Q: I must say that I like the old version much better.

A: Uh-huh, it's a controversial thing, I think. Ivo Pogorelich is with you, and I think a number of other people are too, but yeah, I have to say I really do like the second version better. It doesn't have the same buoyancy and devil-may-care quality, but it's so serene and so reflective.

Having decided that the CBC's recording facilities were technically inadequate, Gould returned to the old Columbia studio on East Thirtieth Street in Manhattan, which CBS, for economic imperatives of its own, was about to shut down. *The Goldberg Variations* was one of the last few recordings made there. But Gould had another reason for this trip to New York. After all his years with Steinway, he wanted to look for a new piano, and though he wanted to try more Steinways, and particularly German-made Steinways, he also wanted to try Bechsteins and other brands. His search eventually brought him to a new Yamaha in the window of the Ostrovsky

Piano Company, just behind Carnegie Hall. He tried playing that new Yamaha and some of the other instruments on display, a spectacle so unusual that the store sought to provide camouflage. "In order to insure his privacy," according to Robert Silverman, who had arranged the tryout, "Mrs. Ostrovsky had sheets hung over the front picture windows. I wonder what people walking along that busy street must have thought as Glenn played—with just some plate glass acting as a sound barrier."

Gould wasn't captivated by any of the pianos on display in the Ostrovsky window, but as he was about to leave, he spotted a much-used Yamaha standing in a back corridor, and he decided to try that. Nobody wanted him to use such an aged instrument, but he insisted. It was like a rediscovery of the battered Chickering in the lakeside cottage of his youth, like the moment in which the prince finds that the glass slipper fits Cinderella's foot. It was "just the instrument he'd been searching for," Silverman said. "He called to report that the long search was at last over." Gould bought the aged Yamaha on the spot and ordered it shipped to East Thirtieth Street for his recording of *The Goldberg Variations*. "We feel a great joy and fulfillment," Debbi Ostrovsky wrote to Gould, "in having nurtured an instrument which ultimately will find its home with you."

"So we went to Thirtieth Street with *tons* of equipment," says Sam Carter, a courtly, graying Southerner who acted as producer on Gould's last records. "We were just entering into the digital period, and so we had two modes of this Sony—we had the first one that they'd come up with, and then we had a 1610, which was a refinement on that, and then we were trying out the Mitsubishi system, and all these systems were still unproved, so every artist insisted that we must still have plenty of analog material, so we'd take along some multitrack tape to be very sure that we were really covered. And at the same time, Mr. Monsaingeon's video truck was sitting out in the street, and we were piping this signal to them."

The basic plan was that Gould would perform *The Goldberg Variations* for both Monsaingeon's cameras and Carter's recorders simultaneously. One variation at a time. Monsaingeon was not a film zealot who wanted his camera to keep nervously moving around to new perspectives; he liked to maintain one documentary point of view for several minutes at a time. And Gould liked that. If some aspect of his own performance before the cameras dissatisfied him, he played the whole variation over again. Only for the recording machines did he later insist on retake after retake. "Some of the variations he'd want to do again and again, until he got just what he wanted," Carter recalls. "A lot of people thought that he just stuck things together, and Glenn talked so much about technology, and he *loved* fooling around with tape, and he *loved* editing, and so some people got the impression that that must be the way he made his records, but that was far from the truth, you know. He had as many one-takers as anybody, and damn near any take he made would have stood on its own."

"The first thing that I became aware of really quickly," says Karen McLaughlin, who worked as Monsaingeon's assistant director, "was that Gould wasn't a kook, you know. He was a very straightforward, lovely guy, who I think had some really serious medical difficulties, which he didn't talk about. I think a lot of what people thought were his little eccentricities and crazinesses were, you know, genuine problems. I think he did have some kind of circulatory trouble because his hands were always cold, and they really *were*, you know. It wasn't a joke. Something in his central nervous system just didn't function as it normally would. He started out saying that he tried to eat moderately and be pretty careful about his diet, but by the—oh, the third day, I'd say, he was eating pizza with the rest of us. We were eating at two in the morning because we always worked at night."

The whole process of rerecording *The Goldberg Variations* was a kind of collective festivity. Even the most unschooled members of the crew felt a certain awe at Gould's performances but also a certain sense of communion. "One day as we were leaving the studio to have a bite to eat," Monsaingeon recalls, "one technician said to me, 'Do you know that piece that goes *Pam*-papa, pa-pa-pa-pa-pa-*pam*-pa-pa?' I said, 'Well, sure, it's Chopin's *Polonaise militaire*,' and he said, 'Do you think he might play that for us?' I said, 'Well, you know, I don't think that he's got any kind of love for Chopin, but why don't you ask him?' When we came back to the studio, that cameraman or cableman or whoever it was said to Glenn, 'Do you know this piece?' And he hummed it. And Glenn said, 'No.' The technician said, 'Well, too bad, I would have liked you to play it for us.' Glenn didn't say a thing, but when the shot was ready, and I said, 'Well, let's do the first take,' or the eighteenth take or whatever, Glenn, instead of playing the variation, made an improvisation on that Chopin theme. And played for about twenty minutes. It was absolutely unbelievable."

Q: In the manner of Bach?

A: No, no, no, it was very Brahmsian, Wagnerian, that kind of harmonic vocabulary. The Chopin theme was there, but he twisted it to all kinds of degrees and made it into a very chromatic piece. And when he finished, you know, he just roared in laughter, and everybody was—it was an incredible piece of display, of pianistic and musical display. And Glenn said to me, "Bruno, I hope you taped that." And, of course, I didn't, so it's gone forever.

Sam Carter recalls that *The Goldberg Variations* was recorded in six very separate sessions. Specifically, they were done from 4 P.M. to midnight on April 22, 23, 24, and May 12, 13, 14, 1981. "We would get a kind of basic thing from our sessions, but then he'd like to take the two-track tape home to Toronto with him and rethink the whole thing," Carter says. "And then we'd discuss it on the phone, and he'd try to put things together himself, and then he'd call me and say, 'Now try this, and see if you can do that, and see if there's any problem about the digital edit.' It wouldn't always work out exactly, because digital editing is a little bit different.

"Actually, I don't know how much you know about recording," Carter goes on, "but when we first started with the digital, it was a circus. Sony only had one digital editing machine making the rounds of Europe and the United States. They had another one in Tokyo. They'd give the machine to us for three days, say, and our engineers had only very brief sessions on how to use it. So we'd get the machine for a weekend, and each of the producers had maybe two or three records to try and edit during that time. So we'd sort of line up, and you'd come in at seven in the morning, or whatever time, you'd try to go through the night, even, as much as you could, because you'd only have a few hours to try desperately to do the records that you were responsible for. And then you'd get in and start, and the machine would break down, or it would not behave properly—it was a *circus*."

Gould seems to have observed a kind of double standard about the video and audio versions of *The Goldberg Variations*. Because he could be seen playing the music in the filmed version, he was slightly less demanding about the quality of the sound; because the recording depended entirely on sound, he wanted that perfect. "They were both meant to be the same," Monsaingeon recalls, "but what happened in fact was that there are a few notes in the record which are different from the film. But just a few notes. For example, one is the final note of the twenty-fifth, the slow variation in G minor. On the film, you can see him, with his right hand, doing this—well, actually, what he's doing, he's conducting a cello. Because he felt that last note was always slightly too loud, and he wanted to keep the cello down. So he redid that last note for the recording. He thought it was quite good enough for the film, because, you know, the picture compensates, but he felt that this particular note should be redone for the record."

The whole process of filming, taping, recording, lasted two months, with Gould traveling to and fro between Toronto and New York. Then he and Monsaingeon, who had collaborated on a detailed shooting script before any taping started, spent that June making the final edit of the video version. It was a kind of milestone, and they both knew it. "When we finally finished the editing," Monsaingeon says, "I remember being on the huge parking lot outside Glenn's studio, the two of us alone, early morning light, extraordinarily exhausted. And Glenn looked *very* tired. I remember looking into his eyes from very close, and seeing those wonderful eyes, very much inside the orbits, looking extremely intense and affectionate. And I felt that I didn't know where I was in the world. You know, I was escaping from some womb, some extraordinary hole in the earth, and landing again in the sunlight."

Now that *The Goldberg Variations* was finished, the beating of drums had to begin, and Gould, for all his reputation as a recluse, was quite an expert at beating drums. (Indeed, his reputation as a recluse was part of the publicity game.) So, for the edification of the prospective reviewers, he began writing that interview with himself, and then summoned Tim Page to Toronto in August of 1982 to play the part of the interviewer. "I was basically an actor," says Page, "an actor who brought something of himself, but an actor.

"So I went up there," Page goes on, "and we spent the first day watching films, watching *The Wars*, watching various tapes, watching him walk around the room, absolutely ecstatic, listening to Barbra Streisand and singing Carl Orff, I mean going around with just this *blissful* look on his face." Page subsequently wrote an account of this visit that provided a rather bleak portrait of the aging virtuoso. "He looked older than his forty-nine years," Page reported. "Gone was the slim, mercurial, oddly beautiful young man whose keyboard acrobatics had dazzled audiences in the late '50s and early '60s. In his place was a stooped, paunchy, rumpled, balding man. . . . Gould's tiny hotel studio was cell-like—the windows blocked, the curtains drawn. His desk was covered with bills, unanswered letters, and penciled first drafts. . . . The bathroom was littered with empty Valium bottles." Yet in the midst of all this, there were touches of something else. "'These are the happiest days of my life,' Gould said suddenly. . . ."

"And then the next night we went to the studio," Page continues, "and we started taping about one-thirty in the morning. We finished about three-thirty. It was a rock studio in downtown Toronto, and, you know, we went through it fairly quickly. I mean, I can tell that there are signs of fatigue in my voice, but it's still a pretty damn good interview, and ninety-five percent of the credit for that goes to Glenn. So what happened then was, I left the room for a minute to get a soda, and then I heard piano music. You know, all night, I'd been thinking, 'Gee, there *is* a piano in that corridor, and maybe he'll go over and play.' And then he sat down, and he started playing through his own transcription of Strauss's *Elektra*. Which is magnificent. And I'm just sitting there and thinking, My God, I'm hearing Glenn Gould play! Wake up! Because, you know, it's four in the morning. Then he played some of the overture of Strauss's *Capriccio*, and then he played Variation Nineteen of *The Goldberg Variations* . . . and then the night was over.

"And one of the things that struck me about all this," Page says, "was that you really had a sense that, for all his solitude, he desperately wanted to be liked. And wanted to be loved. And wanted people really to enjoy him. He was—when I finally said, 'Look, it's six o'clock in the morning, I've got to go to sleep,' it was, like, 'Okay, but I've got these wonderful things, which, you know, I could show you.' He was like a kid, a very sort of self-oriented kid, but he really wanted just to continue."

In contrast to the youthful enthusiasm of Tim Page, the publicity dragnet also brought to Toronto the worldly professionalism of Joe Roddy, on assignment for *People*. "I went up there with Alfred Eisenstadt," Roddy recalls, "and Gould liked the idea of dealing with Eisenstadt. He felt that they had sent the inventor of the camera to take his picture, so he felt very good about that. I think the pictures were for the most part failures, but the visit was excellent, and then I came back without Eisenstadt. We had dinner about ten o'clock that night. In comes the hotel cart with a splendid meal for me. A boiled egg for him. And I sit there like Falstaff, eating, and this conversation goes on, this fantastic discussion of the difference between the two recordings of *The Goldberg Variations*, and the justification for what he had done. He was pointing out what a shabby piece of music *The Goldberg Variations* were, in the early version. One or two of them were of a little interest, but for the most part it was a grab-bag bunch of subgrade Bach. I loved the subject, and so I let him go on and on, and I thought, How false of me. I thought, There isn't going to be one syllable of this in the story."

The surviving tape of that interview contains Gould's astonishing attack not only on his original performance of *The Goldberg Variations* but on the work itself. He accuses Roddy of mistakenly supposing "that I think it's a great work, and I don't. I think it's a very oversold work." He says there are some works that have haunted him for years—notably Strauss's *Metamorphosen*—but *The Goldberg Variations* is not one of them. "There are in the Goldbergs, I think, some of the very best moments in Bach, which is saying an awful lot, but I think there are also some of the silliest. Things such as the canon at the fifth really do move me in an extraordinary way, in as intense a way as anything in *The Art of the Fugue* does, and *The Art of the Fugue* is my favorite Bach work. However, there are also things such as Variations 28 and 29, which are as capricious and silly and dull and as balcony-pleasing as anything he wrote.... As a piece, as a concept, I don't really think it quite works." Since Roddy assumed that the readers of *People* magazine would not be interested in such things, the secret of Gould's real opinion of *The Goldberg Variations* went with him to the grave.

By the time this recording neared the market, Tim Page had become a critic at the New York *Times*, and so he was able to use that powerful position to publicize it even before it was officially released. Writing only about the 1955 version in June of 1982, he proclaimed it "a performance of intelligence, originality and fire. I continue to find fresh delights on every rehearing." The *Times* review of the new version was by Edward Rothstein, who took the opportunity to produce a retrospective survey of Gould's career. "The early performance is rambunctious, exuberant, relishing its power and freedom," he wrote. "This record is less viscerally intoxicating, but more affecting, more *serious,* more seductive in its depth. . . . The contemplative meditation of the Aria, the splendid varieties of attack in the 15th variation, the detached and crystalline character of the epic 25th, the almost frightening clarity in the virtuosic parts—all create a 'Goldberg' that gives both a sense of ecstasy and of quiet repose."

Susan Koscis, the CBS publicist, read the Rothstein story over the telephone to Gould. "I was always a little nervous when I had to read him an article," she recalls, "because if he didn't like it, I would feel terribly responsible, and I never wanted to displease him. Anyway, at the end of this reading, there was silence, and I thought, Oh-oh, he doesn't like it. But then, after a little while, he said that Ed had completely understood him, had grasped the importance of what was important to Glenn, and he said that no journalist had ever written an article with such understanding, and how wonderful it was to finally be understood." When the article itself reached Toronto a day or so later, Gould began reading it aloud over the telephone. He read every word to Jessie Greig, and they both exulted in it. A week later, he had the devastating stroke.

Most of the obituaries noted the ironies of *The Goldberg Variations* being Gould's first and last recordings. Eric McLean of the *Montreal Gazette* noted some deeper oddities. "The album had already been printed, so there could be no question of revamping the cover or the program notes to take his death into account," McLean wrote. "However, you will find in the packaging strange presentiments of what was about to happen. On the back of the album, there is the picture of Gould's piano, and what is obviously Gould's chair . . . but no Gould. Although the program notes make no mention of his death, they are enclosed in a black frame of the sort associated with obituaries. The performance? The 30 variations are played with the same intelligence and clarity that informed the original version. In fact the new interpretation approaches perfection more closely than the first. . . ."

Everything that Rothstein and others heard in this recording is even more explicitly present in Monsaingeon's video version. Gould looks terrible—fat, puffy, pasty, partly unshaven. His dark blue Viyella shirt, with the cuffs unbuttoned, looks simply sleazy. And all the celebrated "mannerisms" are on display; he sways and sings and sighs and makes gestures of conducting himself and more gestures that seem to signify his going into a trance. Yet as one watches, one gradually abandons all these prejudiced observations and becomes a participant in Gould's extraordinary performance. Not only is he playing beautifully, and passionately, but he looks serenely and profoundly happy in his transcendental ability to do what he is doing. Never before has he so clearly achieved his youthful goal of ecstasy. And yet there is also something else. More than a decade earlier, in one of his interviews with himself, Gould had sardonically questioned himself about attempting "to define your quest for martyrdom autobiographically, as I'm sure you will try to do eventually."

"For me," says John McGreevy, the TV director, "it speaks volumes about where he was headed. He's going to another place. This is his farewell. Absolutely. I can hardly bear to listen to it, even today, particularly the closing aria, knowing that he was saying farewell. The prolonged, drawn-out, agonizing poignancy of it. There's a man who was determined to impose, aesthetically and emotionally, his sensibility on his listeners. And he was saying, 'Good-bye.' And this was such an exquisite way of doing it."

Q: I like the first version much better. It had all that courage and enthusiasm.

A: Yes, and life. It's life, whereas the second version is death. He's going away, to another place.

Timothy Findley, the novelist who worked with Gould on *The Wars*, feels much the same way. "I couldn't stop crying when I watched him doing the last moments of *The Goldberg Variations*," he says.

Q: But he's terribly happy there—

A: Of course. He's gone into another dimension. Yes. He's found sainthood.

Q: Even though he's all alone.

A: Yes, of course. As all saints are. But how ghastly!

XVI

The End

Perhaps the most extraordinary thing about Glenn Gould's last year of life was the diversity of projects to which various people thought he had committed himself. It was like the six blind men and the elephant. Sam Carter of CBS Records, for example, thought Gould was so bewitched by digital records that he wanted to make new versions of Bach's Two- and Three-Part Inventions, and perhaps the *Italian Concerto*. Jessie Greig recalls him talking at length about writing a historical novel set in Scotland. Neville Marriner believes that he and Gould were going to record all the Beethoven concerti; Jaime Laredo hoped to record more violin sonatas. Bruno Monsaingeon, on the other hand, is one of several people who remember Gould saying, as he approached his fiftieth birthday, that he was going to stop playing the piano, and devote himself to writing, and conducting, and other things. "Just before he died," says Monsaingeon, "we had an appointment to start working on the script of the film that we wanted to do about the *Siegfried Idyll*, with Glenn conducting. And then we wanted to do a film on the B minor Mass of Bach." John McGreevy, the TV director, hoped to make a sequel to "The Idea of North." "We had wanted to do a film on the North," he says, "and, alas, we never got around to it. His radio documentary was fabulous, but I would have done something quite different. I really would have taken him right up to the Arctic, and—

Q: Would he have gone?

A: Yes, he would.

Q: But he'd have to go there by plane, and he wouldn't get into a plane.

A: I know, but we would find some way to get him up there—if it meant taking off by dogsled. He was very, very romantic about the North.

Q: How far north would you have gone?

A: Oh, I'd have taken him right to the roof of the world.

Gould had other plans for the future that were even stranger fantasies. After persuading Ray Roberts to buy a border collie for his children from the Humane Society, Gould began talking about an Arctic animal shelter. "The grand plan—tongue in cheek—was to go to Manitoulin Island, up north, and open the Glenn Gould Puppy Farm," Roberts recalls. "And guess who was going to be the manager? The idea was that we'd keep all the stray dogs from everywhere, and never put a dog out of its misery or anything like that." To Jessie Greig, Gould proposed yet another design for the future. "He said, 'When we get old and senile, I'll buy a house, and you can have the bottom floor, and I'll have the top floor,'" she remembers. "And I said, 'That won't do, because you make too much noise.' And he said, 'Well, then we'll change about.' And I said, 'Still, you'll play the piano all night.' So he was looking forward to being eighty, and at the time, now when I think about it, maybe he really wasn't, maybe that was a cover-up."

Miss Greig remembers that Gould looked much worse in that last summer of 1982. "When I saw him in June, I was absolutely downright floored," she says. "He had gone downhill so much, and just in a few months. His hair had thinned, he was stooped, and his whole face was drawn, you know. I couldn't believe how he'd aged. He'd been so boyish-looking, and he became like an old man. All during that summer, I kept saying to the family, 'I think Glenn's driven.' It's almost as if he was driven to finish those things that he was doing—the Bach and those other ones that he was getting ready to put out. Because he was—he just hardly had time to talk, he was so driven to complete them. And once he did say to me—he gave a big sigh and said, 'I'm *so* tired, Jessie.'"

The lined pads, on which Gould talked to himself, contain endless lists of medical symptoms, tests, medications. One typical specimen says:

"Palpitations

"Heat in arm

"Indigestive-style pains in chest

"Wake-up pulse rate—dream episodes. . . .

"High pulse diminishing with activity

"Freezing sensations—shivers—top of nose. . . .

"Ankle-foot phenomenon

"Recent month's lower abdomen problem—liquid consumption triggers pockets of 'ulcer-like' pains through to back—congestive sensation re bending over. . . ."

Part of this general sense of disintegration was purely the hypochondriac's imagination. At one point, for example, Gould wrote on his pad that he had just discovered some suspicious bluish spots on his stomach, and he wondered what that might portend. Before reporting this to his doctor, he wrote, he would go to the bathroom and check whether the spots might be merely a smear from the ballpoint pen with which he was writing this note. Then he wrote that he did go to the bathroom, and that the spots were indeed just some ink, and that he had washed them away.

Just as paranoiacs do have real enemies, though, hypochondriacs do have real illnesses. Gould did have dangerously high blood pressure, and he did have a whole array of other medical problems: a hyaline hernia, circulation trouble, tingling nerves in his arms and legs, an inner-ear problem called labyrinthitis which affected his sense of balance, eye trouble, hemorrhoids, intestinal gas pains, chronic sore throat, wheezing and shortness of breath, prostatitis, chest pains, and so on and so on. These were both painful and embarrassing. "Heat applied—pain excruciating when lying down in any pos.—and stiff . . . at rest of times," one entry on these pads reads. "3 hrs. sleep tonight . . . spasm effect on waking (r. side, in part., at the moment, is intense) is distressing in the extreme—medication—how many Fiorinal can one take (not that they seem to be doing any good) . . . ?"

He kept compulsively recording how many hours he slept, often three hours on a sofa and three hours in bed, with the radio going, and then he recorded his own pulse rate, sometimes every half hour, and then, when he intermittently woke up, the temperatures in Winnipeg or Calgary. Thus:

"3 A.M. Temp. —7

"HI Vancouver 7

"LO Timmins — 30

"Sleep 4½ (interr. hammering) & 2½ est. intermittent. . . ."

And he recorded even the embarrassments. "Interim wakeup almost invariably assoc. with bladder pressure. . . . On two occ. (succ. nights) in June, this resulted in urination while asleep— unprecedented since childhood."

Gould was by now going to no less than four Toronto doctors, but he was also telephoning Cousin Jessie with questions to ask her nephew, who was another doctor. "He'd say, 'Ask Dave this and ask Dave that,'" she says, "about this sensation he was having in his hands and feet and arms and legs." He also acquired weird ideas from various magazine articles. He thought, according to John Roberts, that it was "important to live as close as possible to the summit of a hill because one was less likely to develop cancer." And the doctors kept prescribing drugs. Aldomet for the high blood pressure, Nembutal for sleep, tetracycline and chloromycetin for his constant colds and infections. And Serpasil and Largostil and Stelazine and Resteclin and Librax and Clonidine and Fiorinal and Inderal and Inocid and Aristocort cream and Neocortef and Zyloprim and Butazolidin and Bactra and Septra and phenylbutazone and methyldopa and allopurinol and hydrochlorothiazide. And always, in addition to everything else, lots and lots of Valium.

What are we to make of all this? Mainly, perhaps, that Gould had very little idea of the side effects that might be caused by all these drugs, and that his various doctors may have remained almost equally innocent. In addition, of course, he led a naturally unhealthy life, late hours and bad food. "He did zero exercise," as Ray Roberts puts it, "and he ate scrambled eggs every damn day." For an outside view, we can solicit once again the judgments of Dr. Pascarelli in New York, who is moderately impressed as he reads through Gould's listings of his own symptoms. "'Chest, periodic tightness.' He might have developed angina, coronary insufficiency, so the chest pain might have been a harbinger of cardiac problems. 'Bladder activated wakeup.' He probably had prostatic problems, prostate blockage. 'Some finger pains equivalent to first uric acid findings.' He's alluding to the possibility that he's got some gouty arthritis. 'Stomach pains' could be anything from tension to a serious gastrointestinal problem. He goes and he has heart tests and cholesterol tests, tests for uric acid. 'Hyaline hernia.' That may have been the chest pains. There's a flat valve between the stomach and the esophagus, which allows acid contents of the stomach to regurgitate into the esophagus, and can give heartburn and pain. Particularly a problem at night, when you're lying flat, and the stomach contents can regurgitate into the esophagus. He's using Placido, which is a tranquilizer, to sleep, and he's waking up in the middle of the night, probably from his prostate."

Dr. Pascarelli continues flipping through pages and pages of self-diagnosis. "Okay, here we're talking about epicondylitis, an inflammation of the epicondyles, here in the elbow, which is sometimes called tennis elbow, so he apparently was given steroids, cortisone, muscle relaxant. And he still has urinary tract problems. And he's getting up in the middle of the night. He's on Aldomet. That's for blood pressure. And he refers to myalgia, which is muscle aches. And he says he also has twitches, spasms, and stiffness.

"And he has a bad cold, a virus, which may have caused him to get this arthralgia, pain in the joints. He's striving to keep his blood pressure under control. So then he gets notice of weight increase. . . . Now it seems that he's developed conjunctivitis, which he was treated for, and a middle-ear infection, and then he developed a tingling sensation in the left foot. . . . Black markings on his tongue, which is probably from the antibiotics. He's having trouble with his gastrointestinal tract, his hands and his legs. . . . I don't know what to tell you. I don't think you can really pull this together. I think that you have to just describe it as what it is. I get the feeling that this is a very frightened man, who, for a variety of reasons, is trying to seek a solution to perceived problems by doing a whole series of contrived experiments on himself."

Gould's fiftieth birthday fell on a Saturday, September 25, 1982. He heard vague reports that people were planning festivities in his honor, and he strongly opposed any such idea. "He phoned me a week before his birthday," Jessie Greig recalls. "He knew that his dad was planning a birthday party, and he didn't want *any* birthday party. He said that he knew that some of the people at CBS were planning a birthday party, and he said, 'I really don't want any birthday party. And if they invite you, don't go.' And I said, 'Well, okay.' He didn't even want you to send him a birthday card, you know. It really was funny. He never wanted you to mention his birthday."

Q: Was that a dislike of growing older?

A: I don't know. I don't know. I think he hated any celebration or anything that set him apart, you know. He really disliked celebrations.*

And he really was quite sick, with a bad cold or a flu. He was dosing himself with Vitamin C compounds, but they didn't help, and people did keep calling, from all over, to wish him happy birthday. Geoffrey Payzant recalls that Gould "thanked me for writing my book because it meant that he wouldn't have to spend a lot of time answering questions from the media on turning fifty." Edward Rothstein called and arranged to talk again at greater length later that week. "I looked forward, with eagerness, to a developing friendship," Rothstein says. John McGreevy called, and Rothstein's article had to be read to him. And Bob Silverman recalls that he and Gould discussed the Rothstein article "sentence by sentence, literally." Schuyler Chapin called, and said, as one always does, that he "couldn't believe Glenn was fifty." Gould sang parts of the new version of *The Goldberg Variations*, which Chapin had not yet heard. They talked for nearly an hour about the old days at Columbia, and Gould recalled having told somebody that "the really exciting days were when Schuyler Chapin was there."

"And then he said, 'Tell me about your children,'" Chapin recalls. "He was particularly interested in our youngest, Miles. And I'd forgotten a little incident when Miles was five. . . ." Chapin had been at home, sick, and Gould had come to visit, wearing "his raggedy overcoat and his gloves," and they had talked, and then Gould had spotted a collection of Strauss songs near the piano, and he wanted to play them. "Well, our piano stool was an ordinary Steinway piano stool," Chapin says. "No, no, no, of course that wouldn't do. We

---

*Another invitation that Gould scorned came from Jack Behrens, dean of the faculty of music at the University of Western Ontario, who had the marvelous idea of asking Gould to come on the day after his birthday and perform John Cage's *4′ 33″*, that celebrated oddity in which a pianist sits motionless before a piano throughout three silent movements of 33 seconds, 2 minutes 40 seconds, and 1 minute 20 seconds. The world's most famous nonperformer was not amused.

had to look around the apartment to find an adequate stool, and we did. It was the wastebasket in the library, so I emptied the wastebasket, put it down, and there he sat. He must have spent nearly an hour, playing and singing, with that awful voice, but absolutely on pitch. Then he said, 'I'm hungry,' so I scrambled some eggs. And suddenly I looked over, and Glenn had ceased talking and was sort of looking this way. Standing in the doorway was my little boy, Miles, absolutely mesmerized by this strange apparition in the kitchen. I introduced them, and Miles walked in, and kept looking at Glenn, and hopped into a chair, and had a glass of milk and a cookie while we were having scrambled eggs. And Glenn started to talk to him, while this kid started to talk right back to him, and they had a very interesting—you know, I mean, it's just an incident in one's life that is pleasurable and nice at the time, without one's thinking very much about it. But now Glenn went through the whole thing on the phone, chapter and verse—wastebasket, Strauss—"

Q: You mean ten years later?

A: More than ten years later. Twenty years later, I would say.

Gould's relations with his father were somewhat less tender, but Bert Gould thought he should do something to observe his son's fiftieth birthday. Gould played turtle, hard-shelled, withdrawn. "He phoned us that he was—he had a bad cold and wasn't feeling too good," Bert Gould recalls. Vera Gould nonetheless made him some cookies, and bought him a sweater, and then they both took the short drive over to the Inn on the Park to present their birthday presents. Gould remained wary. "He wasn't laid up or anything like that," Bert Gould recalls. "He came up to the car—outside—with us—and so on."

Gould had rather reluctantly made a will, two years earlier, leaving everything to the Salvation Army and the Toronto Humane Society, those guardians of the destitute and the helpless. Steve Posen pushed him into making the will ("He was angry at me for having suggested it to him from time to time"), but the attorney balked at Gould's peremptory instructions. "I said to him, 'Glenn, I'm sorry, but I need to be able to discuss with you what your assets and liabilities are, who are the people who could be dependent upon you, discuss with you what it is that you're doing.' He said something like, 'You have your instructions, sir.' He also said, 'When we are in our eighties, we will sit down together and make out the perfect will.' He said, 'This isn't for anything that we need. This isn't going to happen.'"

But Gould was superstitious, and the will haunted him. "I remember when Glenn told me on the phone that he had been asked to make up a will," Ron Wilford recalls. "He said, 'I've just come from signing my will, and it bothers me. I hope it isn't prophetic. It gives me a very bad feeling.'"

Two days after his birthday, on Monday, September 27, Gould woke up at about 2 P.M. and realized that there was something very wrong. That is the way strokes often come, not in some dramatic collapse but simply a sudden realization that something is very wrong. "He went to the bathroom," Roberts says, trying to reconstruct the critical moment, "and that's when he realized—he was sitting there—he was sleeping and woke up and realized that he'd had a stroke. He called me at my office."

Q: How did he realize it?

A: Well, he had a numbness down one side. So he called me at the office, and I tore right over to the Inn on the Park. And he actually got up and unlocked the door and let me in. We started calling doctors and everything else—trying to get—what to do—because he wanted the doctors to come over there. He didn't want to go down to the hospital. And the more calling around I did, trying to get hold of these various people, the more I became convinced that there was no way—we had to go down to the hospital. But the last thing he wanted was an ambulance pulling up, and that whole bit, so what I did was contact the management of the hotel, who very discreetly brought him up a chair, a wheelchair, and we took him down and put him into the Lincoln. *I* put him in the car. I don't know how in hell I ever did that, but I got him into the car and drove him down to the hospital.

Q: Was he conscious during all this?

A: Oh, yes.

Q: Was he talking?

A: Yes, oh, yes.

Q: But he knew it was serious?

A: Oh, yes. Well, he didn't think it was *that* serious, okay? He certainly didn't think it was life-threatening. Not at that point. So I got him down to the hospital, and got him admitted, and started making calls, you know, his father and that sort of thing. We took him upstairs, and they examined him, and put him in a room—not intensive care, I don't think—and he seemed quite normal. I mean, he was, you know, he slurred his speech—one side was—but he was fine.

Roberts stayed at the hospital, alone, until about midnight, then went home, then returned early the next morning to deal with things. He had called Jessie Greig the night before—she was in the midst of the laborious process of moving into a new apartment—and told her about the stroke. "Then they phoned me again at about six in the morning—I was so tired from moving—and said that Glenn had been asking for me all night long," Miss Greig recalls. "I went to the hospital, and they allowed me three minutes. I went over to his bed. I said, 'It's Jessie.' And he said, 'I know.' He said, 'I sent for you.' He had one hand behind his head, and I could see there was a swelling in his head, you know, and his eyes would close, but then they'd open again. And so I put my hand down, and he gripped it real tight, and he held my hand, and he said, 'I'm terribly ill.' And I said, 'I know you're terribly ill, but we Greigs are fighters, you know.' And he said, 'Yes, but it's too late now. It's just too late.'

"I only stayed—I was so tired I could hardly stand up—and they only allowed me three minutes. And I came out really upset. I think he knew from my face that I was upset. I didn't cry. I didn't do anything to show him I was upset. But we knew each other well enough for him to know I was upset."

Bert Gould came to the hospital with his wife, but she remained outside. Gould seemed to be asleep. "I sat there beside the bed and held his hand some," Bert Gould recalls, "but he wasn't conscious at all. Except in this way: I was talking to him, trying to make him hear or understand, and all of a sudden, one arm came up and started conducting." The old man, remembering, waves his own arm up in the air, to and fro. "Which he always did, you know, even driving the car or the boat or anything—he'd conduct. But you can't say that he was conscious. I presume that somehow he knew it was me. I don't know."

Gould did come awake again, after his father had gone, and he began struggling to resume his ordinary activities. "At one point there, he was still carrying on business things," Roberts recalls. "He wanted me to go and get in touch with his lawyers and get power of attorney so I could carry on those—we had to get all his income tax paid. There were going to be some fairly heavy fines if you didn't get it paid by the end of the company year. So he wanted to get this money issue cleared up, and he wanted to know what the stock market was doing, and, you know. But he was also dozing a lot, sleeping a tremendous amount. And he's having, you know, he's numb on one side. And he just deteriorated. Late Tuesday evening, we got him a TV set so he could watch, and he kept talking about wanting to tape some guy that was on some channel. Things started to get less and less coherent."

"At ten o'clock that Tuesday night," Jessie Greig says, "he had Ray phone me. Ray apparently was there the whole time. And Glenn wanted to play a guessing game. He wanted me to guess who else was at the hospital. There was a Catholic priest that he wasn't very fond of, and he was mixed up, because that priest wouldn't be at that hospital. He'd be at St. Mike's; he wouldn't be at Toronto General. Anyway, we played Twenty Questions through Ray. He sent Ray to the phone, and I was to guess who was there, and Ray went back and forth with the answers. And I came off the phone, and I was so happy. I said to my sister Betty, 'Glenn is going to be all right.' And Betty said, 'I hate to tell you, Jessie, but, you know, they quite often do that, and have a lucid time before they—' And then the next morning, they phoned and said that he had slipped into another deep coma."

Q: Did he have another stroke?
A: Yes.
Q: That second night?
A: Yes.

"It works this way," says Ray Roberts. "What happens is, when you have a stroke, one side of the brain swells up. And eventually what will happen, as it did in Glenn's case, it causes pressure on the other side, cuts the circulation on the other side, and the other side has a stroke. What happened was that that swelling was so extreme— He had a lot of headaches and things, you know, and his headaches were getting stronger, and by Tuesday night, he was getting to the point where you couldn't make any sense—"

Q: He was trying to talk?

A: Very much. He was crying out things like, "Ray, where are you?" But what he said didn't make any sense. He was very clear— you could understand him well enough—but, you know, like when somebody has a fever, they start making silly requests and things like that. That's what we were getting.

Q: And you stayed there that night?

A: I stayed up until about tennish.

Q: And on Wednesday what happened?

A: By Wednesday, he was into a—

Q: Coma?

A: He was basically completely incoherent, and everything else that's evident in a coma.

"It's funny how life—you know, it's funny in life what happens," says Jessie Greig. "A friend of mine who's a teacher here visited a friend at a cottage in Finland, and this girl there had nursed Glenn in the hospital. And she said, 'I never saw a man so at peace with himself.' She said the only thing he wasn't at peace with was that he wanted Jessie, and the nurses thought I must be a girl friend or something. But he said that when they talked to him, they had never seen a man so at peace with himself. So, you know, he must have come to accept it really quickly, in those two days."

Gould's stroke was kept secret from the press all during these first days. "We did ask the hospital authorities to keep it quiet, not announce it to the public," Bert Gould says. "We didn't want the press to get it because we knew there'd be no peace at all after that, so they held it up for several days until they came to us and said they felt they'd really have to announce it or they'd be in trouble. So they went and had it announced. I figured at the time that within an hour after the press had published it here we'd have telephone calls from Europe—friends there, and so on."

GOULD SUFFERS STROKE said the front page of the *Globe and Mail* on October 2. "Pianist Glenn Gould is in the intensive care ward of Toronto General Hospital after suffering 'a severe stroke' on Monday, his family revealed yesterday. A terse announcement issued by the hospital on the Gould family's behalf said it was 'still too early to determine if there will be any residual problems.'" And the phones began ringing, and kept ringing.

"I got a call to come in to Joe Dash's office [the general manager of CBS Records]," Susan Koscis recalls. "They said it was very important, some other people were there waiting for me, and I thought, That's it, they're going to tell me I'm fired. I was absolutely sure. I prepared myself. I walked in, sat down, and I saw all these somber faces, and I thought, Oh, for sure, I'm being fired. And then they told me that Glenn had had a stroke. And it didn't register, because I was so prepared to be fired. I said, 'What did you say?' And they said, 'Glenn had a stroke, and he's going to die, it is only a matter of time, so would you please prepare the press release, update the bio, get the photos ready?' You know, all that kind of thing. Oh, it was unbelievable."

When the hospital announced that it was "still too early to determine if there will be any residual problems," Gould was lying in a coma in the intensive care unit, kept alive by the hospital's life-support systems, and it was becoming increasingly clear that he was not going to recover, ever. Should the machinery go on indefinitely, pumping Gould's blood, breathing his air, when there was no hope that he could recover, or even regain consciousness? No, it was decided to end the torment, and at 11:30 A.M. on Monday, October 4, Gould was allowed to die.

It was Ray Roberts who reported that the life-support systems had been deliberately shut off, and he wanted that kept confidential. "Why do you need to include that anyway?" he asked.

Q: Because I want to tell the complete story, and that's part of it.

A: Yes, that's part of it.

Roberts did not then know that this part of the story had already been published in the Anglican magazine *Canadian Churchman*, in its obituary in November of 1982. "The massive stroke he suffered . . . left him almost totally paralyzed," it said. "He sank into a coma, was put on life-support systems, but within a few days his family made the agonizing decision to withdraw those systems."

Q: So what is the confidentiality here?
A: I guess there isn't any. Sure as hell I didn't tell them. Damn!

"I worked all weekend long, updating the bio and all this kind of thing," Susan Koscis recalls, "and I remember thinking, How strange I haven't heard from him. But I thought, Well, okay, he's working on a project, and he'll call me when he's finished. Then after working on the bio all weekend, I was at my desk typing it, and Joe Dash came in and said, 'Well, he's dead. Get the press release ready.' Just like that."

Many people heard about Gould's death not from newspapers or television but from calls from friends. Tim Page remembers that he turned on his answering machine and heard two messages, one from the New York *Times* announcing that he had just been formally hired, the second from a friend at CBS Records telling him of Gould's stroke. "So it was like these two pieces of news which were just bizarre," Page says. "I spent that weekend in just this state of frenzy and fury. Because I cared a lot for Glenn. I mean, it hit me very, very hard. I went out with Susan Koscis, and we just said, you know, 'What are we going to *do?*' This man who we barely ever saw—it was not like some kind of hero worship—it was real, genuine fondness, even love.

"I covered a couple of concerts that weekend, and then I came into the office just as the news came through that he had died. I'll never forget how eerie it felt to go to the *Times,* pick up the first copy of an edition with my writing in it as a regular critic, and to see that the front page has Glenn's obit."

So they took Gould's body out to the graveyard, Mount Pleasant Cemetery, and they buried him there, near his mother. Mount Pleasant is an enormous place, stretching east from Yonge Street to Bayview Avenue, not far from the Inn on the Park, not far from the apartment on St. Clair, not far from Bert and Vera Gould's house in Don Mills, not far from most of the places where Gould lived most of his life. The authorities at the cemetery take pride in the distinguished figures buried there, who range from William Lyon Mackenzie King, the onetime prime minister, to Zlitcho Demitro, identified as "world king of the gypsies," to Alexander Muir, who wrote "The Maple Leaf Forever." The rows and rows of less exalted graves reflect the cosmopolitanism of contemporary Toronto. Near Gould's grave are those of Veronica Molnar, Stephen Ching, Olga Vool, Heinz Rothermel, Stuart MacNaughton, John Haluza.

The Gould family plot contains one simple granite gravestone, with rosebuds carved along the edges. It says:

GOULD
Florence E.
July 26, 1975
Beloved wife of
Russell H. Gould

Their dearly loved son
Glenn H. Gould
Oct. 4, 1982

Seven or eight feet in front of that gravestone, and just a bit to the right, there is a granite plaque in the ground, about one foot by two. The plaque itself is dark gray granite. Mortised into it, in lighter gray, is the outline of a piano top. Inside that figure are the words:

Glenn Gould
1932–1982

Just below that date is a musical stave, in the treble clef, and upon it the opening notes of *The Goldberg Variations*.

Here lies Glenn Gould, his bones—*Requiescat in pace*—but he is not really here. Or rather, he is and is not. It is like and not like the National Library in Ottawa, which has collected and preserved his letters, his note pads, his scores, his books, his cuff links, his tapes, his piano. He is there and not there.

It is easy enough to say that he is in every house that has a record player and a recording of *The Goldberg Variations* or the partitas or the Beethoven Second Concerto or the Schoenberg Suite, and there are many of those. There was in Gould's recordings, in that detachment that could swerve into passion, in that coolness, that serenity, that ecstasy—there was a strange power unlike anything in the work of any other pianist. It was a power that made many people feel that their lives had somehow been changed, deepened, enriched. One woman, for example, told Bert Gould that she had recovered from a nervous breakdown by spending hours with Gould's Bach. A heart surgeon in London made it a practice to operate only after he and his patient had both listened to Gould recordings.

All during his last years, people kept writing to Gould to try to tell him what his music had meant to them. They always failed, and Gould, trying to answer them, also failed. "I most certainly agree with you about the therapeutic effects of music and musical performance," he wrote to one inquiring admirer two years before his death. "I have always believed that if this relationshp does not exist, it *should* exist. At the same time, vis-a-vis my own work, I prefer not to attempt to ascertain from precisely what sources any therapeutic value might be forthcoming. . . ." Therapeutic is perhaps too technical a term. Lillian Ross of *The New Yorker* expressed a more general feeling when she said, "I always feel grateful when listening to Gould play on records or over the radio these days."

In all those houses, on all those records and tapes, Gould is and is not there.

And then there are the *Voyagers*. In fall of 1977, while Gould was still alive, the United States government sent off into the unknown two spacecraft destined for Jupiter, Saturn, and beyond. In the hope that somebody somewhere might eventually intercept these spacecraft, they were loaded with a variety of messages that were supposed to report the existence of thinking beings on a planet known as earth. Official committees met to decide on what should be said. The messages included a golden plaque showing what a human male and female looked like, though there was considerable congressional opposition to such "smut." Official committees continued their studies. What resulted was a twelve-inch copper recording, together with a record-playing machine and pictorial instructions on how the machine could be made to play.

The record included a declaration of good cheer from President Jimmy Carter ("This is a present from a small, distant world . . ."), and another from U.N. Secretary General Kurt Waldheim, who was not then suspected of being a Nazi war criminal, but perhaps that is all too richly part of the earth's message. Then came a series of greetings in a series of languages, starting with Sumerian, the oldest one known, and ending with a child saying in English, "Hello from the children of planet earth." Then came something called "sounds of earth," which included whales breathing, volcanoes rumbling, dogs barking, trains whistling, trucks roaring, people laughing, kissing. And then, finally, the intergalactic language of music: pygmy girls in Zaire singing an initiation song, Louis Armstrong crooning "Melancholy Blues," a Japanese flute "depicting the cranes in their nest," the Queen of the Night aria from *The Magic Flute,* a woman's wedding song from Peru, and Glenn Gould playing the prelude and fugue in C major from the first book of Bach's *Well-Tempered Clavier.*

The two *Voyager* spacecraft, designed to last nearly a billion years, sailed past Jupiter and Saturn on schedule, passed Pluto and departed from the solar system late in 1987 and 1989. Remember now how Gould had once told Stokowski that he had "this recurring dream," that he had gone to "some other planet, perhaps in some other solar system," and that he had been "given the opportunity—and the authority—to impart my value systems to whatever forms of life there might be. . . ."

According to Michael R. Helton, of the Jet Propulsion Laboratory in California, who ran a computer analysis of where the two *Voyager* spacecraft were going, *Voyager I* would head toward the constellation Ophiuchus and *Voyager II* toward Capricornus. "In about 40,000 years," according to a report in *Science News,* "both craft should pass within 1 to 2 light years of a fourth-magnitude star (AC +79 3888)—not exactly grabbing distance. Voyager II should pass a similar distance to another star (AC −24 2833-183) 110,000 years later, and about 375,000 years after that, Voyager I will pass perhaps 1.5 light years from DM +21 652 in Taurus."

If some space patrol in Taurus ever gathers in one of these *Voyager* vehicles some 500,000 years from now, and if the authorities there ever crack open their catch, and if they manage to decipher the pictorial instructions and figure out how to play the copper record that contains the first prelude and fugue from Bach's *Well-Tempered Clavier,* God knows what they will make of Glenn Gould, who is and is not there, or of us.

A Note on Sources

It is not easy to determine how the traditional kind of scholarly documentation could be provided for this book. Most of it is based on great quantities of material that were privately obtained and not systematically organized. There are three basic areas to be considered.

I. The Gould papers at the National Library of Canada in Ottawa. About a year after Gould's death, in November 1983, the library acquired for an undisclosed sum the complete collection of Gould's writings, tapes, letters, and other papers, as well as many of his personal possessions (as described in Chapter I). Ruth Pincoe, the Toronto researcher assigned to sort out these papers, has written a striking description of the confusion she found in Gould's apartment: "Most of the papers, especially those dating back more than five years or so, were stored in one room, in boxes, in filing cabinets, and piled on shelves. Some were in file folders (quite probably arranged by someone else); many more were stuffed in large envelopes with vague titles indicating their contents. Some of the correspondence was separated out; much more of it bore every evidence of being completely accidental."

Ms. Pincoe apparently tried to follow whatever Gouldian organizational patterns she could discern, rather than trying to create one of her own. When I looked through all these papers in the fall of 1986, they were collected in rows of large cardboard boxes, all filled with folders. Some of these boxes were of relatively little interest (e.g., three filled with material on various Grammy nominations). The significant ones were: Outgoing correspondence, four boxes; incoming correspondence, six boxes; manuscript pads (restricted), three boxes; manuscript fragments (restricted), two boxes; scripts, sixteen boxes; drafts of articles and scripts, nineteen boxes; music manuscripts, five boxes. Perhaps of interest, though not to me, were seven boxes of financial papers and four boxes of canceled checks. Not "significant" but a great convenience were ten boxes of newspaper clippings, two boxes of magazine articles, and two boxes of photos.

When I studied all these papers, the boxes were simply standing on shelves, and I could look at anything I wanted to see. Though some other researchers have also been granted access to most or all of these papers, the collection was not opened to public use until the spring of 1988. As noted above, certain papers were and still are "restricted," which basically means that the library and the Glenn Gould Estate retain the right to control who sees them and what use may be made of them, if any. I do not really know why any such restrictions should exist. The restricted papers do confirm the reasonably obvious fact that Gould had many real medical problems, but if anyone comes here looking for anything scandalous, he will find precious few signs of it.

The letters, which I have generally identified as such in the course of this book, are numerous but only moderately interesting—much routine business correspondence, a surprising number of detailed answers to fan mail. There are occasionally letters of substance to faraway friends like John Roberts or Paul Myers, but nothing either confessional or revelatory. Ms. Pincoe has written that "it is strongly suspected he did his own weeding during his life," and Ray Roberts confirms that Gould destroyed a certain amount of correspondence that he did not want preserved.

The restricted pads and fragments are more complicated. They include many pages of preliminary drafts of various articles but also school papers and endless listings of Gould's blood pressure, hours of sleep, and repetitions of his own signature. Gould almost never dated any of these entries, and a disquisition on Schoenberg that begins in the midst of a list of stock market holdings may suddenly break off ten pages later in the midst of a list of medications, only to reappear just as suddenly in the midst of another pad containing shopping lists. Clearly, Ms. Pincoe's original ordering of all these documents could only be provisional, and one periodically hears talk that more comprehensive cataloguing is planned or under way, even that someone is transcribing all the scrawls on Gould's pads. One also hears that everything will be or is being computerized, which may or may not be an improvement. In any case, there seems no purpose in my trying to specify here which box contains which quotation. The general reader can reasonably trust my reliability, and any scholar who wants to undertake similar research will simply have to do the digging for himself.

II. The interviews. I conducted more than eighty interviews for this book, a number of them two or three hours in length. They were all done on tape (except twice when the tape recorder broke) and the tapes were then transcribed, but since all this material remains in my attic, there again seems little point in offering detailed documentation. It should be clear enough that when anyone starts talking at length, and in the present tense or in Q and A, this material comes from my interviews.

My heavy use of Q and A is a little unorthodox, but I like it partly because it conveys a sense of process, of a search for Gould actually taking place, and partly because the information being conveyed often derives from the questions as well as from the answers, or else from the interplay between the two. I think there is considerable value in reporting these things pretty much as they occur rather than simply mixing them into a smoothly homogenized account. And one does not have to look at many transcripts before one realizes that most people do not speak in complete sentences or with any great regard for the rules of syntax. In quoting what people said exactly as they said it, I have no intention of belittling or mocking any irregularities of speech, only of recording everything accurately.

I should add that in a very few instances, I have quoted from interviews conducted by other people and kindly loaned to me. Specifically, Tim Page conducted long interviews with Bert Gould and Jessie Greig, which the Glenn Gould Estate made available to me; Joe Roddy sent me the tape of the *People* interview in which Gould denounced *The Goldberg Variations;* and Vincent Tovell gave me a transcript of the excellent TV show "Glenn Gould: A Portrait" that he and Eric Till produced for the CBC.

III. Printed materials. There are four basic Gould books. First on any list, of course, is *The Glenn Gould Reader,* skillfully compiled and edited by Tim Page (1984). This substantial volume contains just about all of Gould's most significant writings, including notably "The Prospects of Recording," "Radio as Music," "Music and Technology," "Stokowski in Six Scenes," the self-interviews, the parody of Rubinstein, the essay on Toronto, the conversation with Bruno Monsaingeon on Mozart, the record-liner commentaries, and several major articles on Strauss and Schoenberg. This is the basic Gouldian canon.

(Monsaingeon has assembled and translated into French a somewhat larger but essentially similar collection of Gould's writings and interviews, published in Paris in three volumes: *Le Dernier Puritain* [1983], *Contrepoint à la Ligne* [1985], and *Non, Je Ne Suis Pas du Tout un Excentrique* [1986].)

The pioneering *Glenn Gould, Music and Mind*, by Geoffrey Payzant (1978), contains a certain amount of biographical material but is essentially an analysis of Gould's aesthetic philosophy, and Payzant is quite adept in pulling together the ideas in Gould's scattered writings. Since he was working on this during Gould's lifetime, he did not have any access to private or unpublished papers, but conversely he did have the advantage of getting Gould's views about his manuscript.

Glenn Gould Variations, By Himself and His Friends, edited by John McGreevy (1983), contains a number of valuable memoirs, notably Leonard Bernstein's "The Truth about a Legend," Robert Silverman's "Memories," and John Peter Lee Roberts's "Reminiscences." It also reprints several important earlier accounts, particularly Joseph Roddy's *New Yorker* profile, "Apollonian," Richard Kostelanetz's "Glenn Gould: Bach in the Electronic Age," and Robert Fulford's "Growing Up Gould."

Conversations with Glenn Gould, by Jonathan Cott (1984), reflects the kind of situation that Gould liked best: an intelligent and admiring interviewer, an open telephone line, an endless amount of time, and a verbatim tape transcript (subject to editorial retouching). Cott covers a great deal of territory, often, as in his account of the Wagner transcriptions or the George Szell episode, more thoroughly than anyone else.

More modest Q & A interviews with Gould appear in *Reflections from the Keyboard, The World of the Concert Pianist*, by David Dubal

(1984), and *Great Pianists Speak for Themselves,* by Elyse Mach (1980). Several recent books also contain interesting chapters on Gould, notably *The Recording Angel, Explorations in Phonography,* by Evan Eisenberg (1987); *The House of Music, Art in an Era of Institutions,* by Samuel Lipman (1984); and *The Solitary Outlaw,* by B. W. Powe (1987).

I should perhaps mention here one mysterious Gould book that I deliberately did not quote, a novel of sorts entitled *Der Untergeher* (1986), by Thomas Bernhard. The narrator is much involved with a fictitious character named Glenn Gould, "the most important piano virtuoso of the century," whom he supposedly met when they were both pupils of Vladimir Horowitz at a master class at the Salzburg Festival. Bernhard's Gould also has a Rockefeller Foundation grant, practices Chopin for hours on end, and in general bears no relation to reality. I wrote to Bernhard to ask him to explain why he had created this fantasy, but he never answered.

On the general and more or less recent music scene, I have read with interest *Musical Chairs, A Life in the Arts,* by Schuyler Chapin (1977); *Current Convictions, Views and Reviews,* by Robert Craft (1977), and *Present Perspectives, Critical Writings,* by Robert Craft (1984); *Music Talks, Conversations with Musicians,* by Helen Epstein (1987); *Out of Character, A Memoir,* by Maureen Forrester, with Marci McDonald (1986); *I Really Should Be Practicing, Reflections on the Pleasures and Perils of Playing the Piano in Public,* by Gary Graffman (1981); *Understanding Toscanini, How He Became an American Culture-God and Helped Create a New Audience for Old Music,* by Joseph Horowitz (1987); *Bernstein, A Biography,* by Joan Peyser (1987); and *My Many Years,* by Arthur Rubinstein (1980).

Some major interviews and commentaries on Gould have never been collected, of course. One good one that I have quoted often is "An Interview with Glenn Gould," by Bernard Asbell, an early and lengthy Q & A that appeared in *Horizon* in January of 1962. And since no record of Gouldian interviews should be confined to the printed page, I should mention that among TV and radio interrogations, the best was a series of four conducted for BBC-TV by Humphrey Burton in 1966. It is remarkable for the fact that Burton, unlike many interviewers, often challenged Gould and made him explain and defend his views.

Other notable press accounts of Gould's activities include "Making a Record with Leonard Bernstein," by Jay Harrison, in *The Reporter*, July 11, 1957; "Inner Voices of Glenn Gould," Harold Schonberg's controversial review of the Brahms D minor Concerto in the New York *Times*, April 7, 1962; "The Glenn Gould Contrapuntal Radio Show," by Robert Hurwitz, New York *Times*, January 5, 1975; "Glenn Gould," by Joseph Roddy, *People*, November 30, 1981; "Glenn Gould Revisits a Masterwork," by Edward Rothstein, New York *Times*, September 26, 1982; and "Pilgrim Pianist," by Sanford Schwartz, *The New Republic*, September 1, 1986.

All the main music critics wrote repeatedly about Gould's concerts and recordings, so the files in Ottawa bulge with their observations. Since New York is indisputably the musical capital of the continent, I have quoted mainly from the New York critics, particularly Harold Schonberg, Donal Henahan, Tim Page, and Edward Rothstein of the *Times*, Jay Harrison and Paul Henry Lang of the *Herald-Tribune*, Winthrop Sargeant of *The New Yorker*, B. H. Haggin of *The New Republic*, Irving Kolodin of *The Saturday Review*, and Martin Mayer of *Esquire*. In Canada, Gould naturally received even heavier press coverage. Perhaps the best of it came from William Littler of the Toronto *Star*, though there were also good stories by his predecessors, John Beckwith and Dennis Braithwaite, and Eric McLean of the Montreal *Star*.

On the general subject of Canada, I have done my best to rise from a characteristically American state of abysmal ignorance to one of merely woeful ignorance. Works of use in that rise have included *France and England in North America* by Francis Parkman; *O Canada, An American's Notes on Canadian Culture*, by Edmund Wilson; *The Scotch*, by John Kenneth Galbraith; *Canada's North*, by R.A.J. Phillips; and *Northern Realities*, by Jim Lotz, the latter two being both participants in Gould's "The Idea of North."

Gould's Concerts

Date	Place	Main works performed (titles abbreviated when repeated)
May 8	Toronto (Massey Hall)	Beethoven Concerto #4 (1st mvt.) (Ettore Mazzoleni conducting Toronto Conservatory Symphony Orchestra)
Oct. 28	Toronto	Beethoven Sonata Op. 2 #3 (last mvt.), Chopin Impromptu

1947

Jan. 14, 15	Toronto	Beethoven #4 (Bernard Heinze, Toronto Symphony)
April 10	Toronto	Haydn Sonata in E flat; Bach Preludes and Fugues in B-flat minor, C-sharp minor; Beethoven Sonata Op. 10 #3, Chopin Impromptu; Mendelssohn Andante and Rondo Capricioso
May 1	Toronto	Recital, program unknown
June 8	Toronto	Organ recital: Dupuis Concerto; Mozart Romanze; four Bach chorale preludes
Oct. 20	Toronto (Eaton Auditorium)	Five Scarlatti sonatas; Beethoven Tempest Sonata; Couperin Passacaille (arr. Guerrero); Chopin Waltz in A flat (Op. 42), Impromptu; Liszt Au Bord d'une source; Mendelssohn Rondo (official debut solo recital)
Nov. 16	Toronto	Same as Oct. 20 recital
Dec. 3	Hamilton	Beethoven Concerto #1 (Sir Ernest MacMillan, Toronto Symphony)

1948

| Nov. 4 | Toronto | Mozart Fantasia in C minor; Czerny Variations on a Theme of Rodé; Chopin Etude, Op. 10 #7 |
| Nov. 11 | Toronto | Dupuis Organ Concerto; MacDowell "To a Wild Rose" |

Date	Place	Main works performed (titles abbreviated when repeated)
1949		
March 6	Toronto	Two Scarlatti sonatas; Beethoven Sonata, Op. 81a; Mendelssohn *Variations sérieuses*
April 21	Toronto	Program unknown
May 3	Toronto	Two Scarlatti sonatas; two Chopin waltzes; Czerny
Oct. 9	Toronto	Beethoven Variations in F; Prokofiev Sonata #7
1950		
Jan. 19	Toronto	Hindemith Sonata #3
Feb. 12	Toronto	Bach *Italian Concerto*; Beethoven *Eroica Variations*
April 21	Toronto	*Italian Concerto*; Beethoven variations; Prokofiev
May 18	Toronto	Beethoven #4 (Ettore Mazzoleni, Conservatory Symphony)
Sept. 1	Toronto	Bach Toccata in E minor; Czerny Variations on "La Ricordanza"; Chopin Etude in C-sharp minor
Nov. 26	London, Ont.	Bach Toccata; Mozart Fantasia; *Eroica Variations*
1951		
Jan. 4	Toronto	Hindemith Sonata #3; Gould Bassoon Sonata (with Nicholas Kilburn); Gould Five Short Piano Pieces; Morawetz Fantasy in D minor; Krenek Sonata #3
Jan. 23	Toronto	Beethoven #1 (MacMillan, Toronto Symphony)
March 6	Toronto	Weber *Konzertstück* (MacMillan, Toronto Symphony)

Date	Place	Main works performed (titles abbreviated when repeated)
May 2	Hamilton	Beethoven #3 (Jan Wolanek, Hamilton Philharmonic)
May 27	St. Catherines, Ont.	Beethoven #3 (Wolanek, St. Catherines Civic Orchestra)
Oct. 28, 29	Vancouver	Beethoven #4 (William Steinberg, Vancouver Symphony)
Nov. 7	Calgary	Bach Partita #5; Beethoven Op. 81a; Variations in F
Dec. 12	Toronto	Beethoven #2 (MacMillan, Toronto Symphony)

1952

Feb. 10	Toronto	Sweelinck Fantasia; Partita #5; Brahms intermezzi; Berg Sonata
Aug. 30	Toronto	Beethoven three bagatelles, Op. 126; Prokofiev Sonata #7
Oct. 4	Toronto	Schoenberg six miscellaneous songs (with Elizabeth Benson Guy), Piano Pieces Op. 11, Piano Suite Op. 25, *Ode to Napoleon Bonaparte* (Victor Feldbrill, chamber group)
Nov. 6	Montreal	Partita #5; Beethoven Sonata Op. 101; Brahms intermezzi; Berg

1953

Feb. 16	Ottawa	Toccata, Partita; Beethoven Sonata Op. 109; Brahms; Berg
July 31	Stratford Festival	Beethoven Trio Op. 70 #1; Brahms Op. 101 (with Albert Pratz, violin, and Isaac Mamott, cello)
Aug. 4	Stratford Festival	Bach three Sinfonias, Partita #5; Op. 109; Berg Sonata
Oct. 3	Toronto	Webern Variations Op. 27; Berg; Schoenberg *Hanging Gardens* (with Roma Butler)

Date	Place	Main works performed (titles abbreviated when repeated)
Oct. 19	Peterborough	Gibbons Pavane; Partita #5; Beethoven Sonata Op. 110; Berg
Nov. 19	Toronto	Partita #5; Op. 110; Schoenberg Pieces Op. 11; Berg
Nov. 23	St. John, N.B.	Bach four Sinfonias, Partita #5; Op. 110; Berg

1954

Date	Place	Main works performed
Jan. 24	Montreal	Bach fifteen Sinfonias; Schoenberg Suite Op. 25; Hindemith Sonata #3
April 1	Brantford, Ont.	Bach fifteen Sinfonias; Op. 109; Brahms intermezzi; Berg
Oct. 16	Toronto	All-Bach concert (no details)
Oct. 25	Toronto	Bach fifteen Sinfonias; Beethoven *Eroica Variations;* Morawetz Fantasy
Nov. 4	Montreal	Morawetz; Bach three *WTC* preludes and fugues; *Eroica Variations*
Nov. 15	Winnipeg	Webern Variations; Partita #5; Berg; Op. 109
Dec. 14, 15	Montreal	Beethoven #1 (Désiré Defauw, Montreal Symphony)

1955

Date	Place	Main works performed
Jan. 2	Washington	Gibbons Pavane; Sweelinck Fantasia; Bach five Sinfonias, Partita #5; Webern Variations; Op. 109; Berg (U.S. debut)
Jan. 11	New York	Same as Washington
March 14	Ottawa	Bach *Goldberg Variations;* Hindemith #3; Krenek #3
March 29	Toronto	Bach D minor; Strauss *Burleske* (MacMillan, Toronto Symphony)
July 12	Stratford	Beethoven #2 (Boyd Neel, Hart House Orchestra)
July 29	Stratford	*Goldberg Variations*

Date	Place	Main works performed (titles abbreviated when repeated)
Aug. 8	Montreal	Beethoven #4 (Jean Marie Beaudet, Toronto Symphony)
Nov. 7	Montreal	*Goldberg Variations;* Beethoven Sonata Op. 111; Hindemith #3
Nov. 10	Ottawa	Beethoven #2 (Eugene Kash, Ottawa Philharmonic)
Nov. 15	Sherbrooke	Beethoven #4 (Sylvio Lacharité, Sherbrooke Symphony)
Dec. 4, 5	Victoria	Beethoven #5 (Hans Gruber, Victoria Symphony)
Dec. 11	Edmonton	Beethoven #4 (Lee Hepner, Edmonton Symphony)
Dec. 12	Winnipeg	Beethoven #1 (Walter Kaufmann, Winnipeg Symphony)

1956

Date	Place	Main works performed
March 15	Detroit	Beethoven #4 (Paul Paray, Detroit Symphony)
March 18	Windsor	Repetition of Detroit concert
March 21	Hamilton	Bach D minor (MacMillan, Toronto Symphony)
April 16	Toronto	Bach *Art of the Fugue* (#2, 4, 7) Partita #5; Op. 109; Hindemith #3
May 7	New York	Bach *Art of the Fugue* (excerpts)
July 9	Stratford	Krenek #3; Berg. Also conducted Schoenberg *Ode to Napoleon Bonaparte.* Gould String Quartet also performed
Oct. 10	Mount Lebanon, Pa.	Beethoven #3 (William Steinberg, Pittsburgh Symphony)
Oct. 15	Watertown, Conn.	Bach fifteen Sinfonias; Op. 109; Hindemith #3
Oct. 23, 24	Toronto	Beethoven #2 (Walter Susskind, Toronto Symphony)

Date	Place	Main works performed (titles abbreviated when repeated)
Oct. 30, 31	Montreal	Bach D minor; Strauss *Burleske* (Milton Katims, Montreal Symphony)
Nov. 2	Delaware, Ohio	Bach fifteen Sinfonias, *Art of the Fugue* (#1, 2, 4, 7); Op. 109
Nov. 16	New York (Metropolitan Museum)	Bach fifteen Sinfonias; Krenek #3; Hindemith #3
Nov. 19	Dallas	Beethoven #5 (Walter Hendl, Dallas Symphony)
Nov. 26	Niagara Falls, Ont.	Not known
Nov. 28	Hamilton	Bach *Italian Concerto*; Op. 110; Mendelssohn *Variations sérieuses*
Dec. 5	Spokane	Op. 110; Mendelssohn Variations; two Brahms intermezzi
Dec. 9	Vancouver	Beethoven #3 (Irwin Hoffman, Vancouver Symphony)
Dec. 11	Vancouver	Beethoven #5 (1st mvt.); Bach *Goldberg Variations* (excerpts) (Hoffman, etc.)
Dec. 13	Winnipeg	Bach D minor (Walter Kaufmann, Winnipeg Symphony)
Dec. 29, 30	St. Louis	Beethoven #4 (Vladimir Golschmann, St. Louis Symphony)

1957

Jan. 26, 27	New York	Beethoven #2 (Leonard Bernstein, N.Y. Philharmonic)
Feb. 4	Burlington, Vt.	Op. 109; Hindemith #3
Feb. 11	Quebec	Bach fifteen Sinfonias; Op. 109; Berg
Feb. 14	Brockville, Ont.	Partita #6; Op. 109; Hindemith #3
Feb. 28, March 1, 2	San Francisco	Bach F minor; *Burleske* (Enrique Jordá, San Francisco Symphony)

Date	Place	Main works performed (titles abbreviated when repeated)
March 8	Pasadena	Partita #6; Op. 109; Berg
March 17, 18	Victoria	Beethoven #4 (Hans Gruber, Victoria Symphony)
March 28, 30	Cleveland	Beethoven #2 (George Szell, Cleveland Orchestra)
May 7	Moscow	Partita #6; Op. 109; Berg
May 8	Moscow	Beethoven #4, Bach D minor (Moscow Philharmonic, conductor ??)
May 11	Moscow	Goldberg Variations; two Brahms intermezzi; Hindemith #3
May 12	Moscow	Berg; Schoenberg excerpts; Webern Variations; Krenek #3; Bach Art of the Fugue (excerpts)
May 14	Leningrad	Partita #6; Op. 109; Berg
May 16	Leningrad	Berg Sonata (rest unknown)
May 18	Leningrad	Bach D minor; Beethoven #2 (Vladislav Slovak, Leningrad Philharmonic)
May 19	Leningrad	Informal student concert; program unknown
May 24, 25, 26	Berlin	Beethoven #3 (Von Karajan, Berlin Philharmonic)
June 7	Vienna	Bach fifteen Sinfonias; Op. 109; Webern Variations
Aug. 20	Montreal	Brahms Quintet in F minor (with Montreal Quartet)
Aug. 27	Hollywood	Not known
Sept. 11	Toronto	Bach F minor; Beethoven #4 (Nicholas Goldschmidt, CBC Symphony)
Oct. 29, 30, 31	Washington	Beethoven #2 (Howard Mitchell, National Symphony)
Nov. 3	Syracuse, N.Y.	Partita #5; Mozart Fantasy in C minor and Sonata K. 330; two Brahms intermezzi; Hindemith #3

Date	Place	Main works performed (titles abbreviated when repeated)
Nov. 7	Rochester, N.Y.	Beethoven #2 (Gerard Samuel, Rochester Philharmonic)
Nov. 11	Toronto	*Goldberg Variations;* Haydn Sonata in E flat; K. 330
Nov. 16	Pittsburgh	*Goldberg Variations;* Haydn sonata; Schoenberg Piano Suite Op. 25
Nov. 20	Cincinnati	*Goldberg Variations;* Schoenberg Suite; Haydn sonata
Dec. 7	New York	Schoenberg Suite; K. 330; *Goldberg Variations*
Dec. 13	Miami	Partita #5; K. 330; two Brahms intermezzi; Berg

1958

Date	Place	Main works performed
Jan. 23	Philadelphia	Haydn sonata; K. 330; *Goldberg Variations*
Jan. 28	New Orleans	Beethoven #2 (Alfred Wallenstein, New Orleans Philharmonic)
Feb. 7	Buffalo	Beethoven #3 (Josef Krips, Buffalo Philharmonic)
Feb. 12	Kingston	*Goldberg Variations;* Beethoven Sonata Op. 10 #2; K. 330
Feb. 17	Winnipeg	Same as Kingston
Feb. 20	Saskatoon	Partita #5; Haydn sonata; Op. 110; Berg
Feb. 24, 25	Vancouver	Bach D minor; *Burleske* (Milton Katims, Seattle Symphony)
Feb. 26	Tacoma	Same as Vancouver
March 7	San Francisco	Bach F minor; Strauss *Burleske* (Enrique Jordá, San Francisco Symphony)
March 13, 14, 16	New York	Bach D minor; Schoenberg Concerto (Dimitri Mitropoulos, New York Philharmonic)

Date	Place	Main works performed (titles abbreviated when repeated)
March 21	Boston	*Goldberg Variations;* K. 330; Berg
March 23	Montreal	Same as Boston
March 28	Lexington, Ky.	*Goldberg Variations;* Op. 111
April 3	Ottawa	Bach fifteen Sinfonias, Partita #6; Beethoven Op. 111
May 4	Ann Arbor	Beethoven #4 (Eugene Ormandy, Philadelphia Orchestra)
May 27	Toronto	Bach Partitas #1 and 6
July 23	Vancouver	Haydn sonata; Op. 110; *Goldberg Variations*
July 27	Vancouver	Beethoven #2 (Irwin Hoffman, Vancouver Festival Orchestra)
July 30	Vancouver	Bach D minor, Brandenburg Concerto #5 (John Avison, CBC Chamber Orchestra)
Aug. 10	Salzburg	Bach D minor (Dimitri Mitropoulos, Concertgebouw Orchestra)
Aug. 25	Brussels	Bach D minor (Boyd Neel, Hart House Orchestra)
Sept. ?	Stockholm	Program not known
Sept. 21, 22	Berlin	Bach D minor (Von Karajan, Berlin Philharmonic)
Oct. 9	Wiesbaden	Beethoven #3 (Wolfgang Sawallisch, orchestra uncertain)
Nov. 15	Florence	Schoenberg Suite; K. 330; *Goldberg Variations*
Nov. 30	Tel Aviv	Beethoven #2 (Jean Martinon, Israel Philharmonic)
Dec. 4	Jerusalem	Same as Tel Aviv
Dec. ?	Tel Aviv	Three recitals; programs unknown
Dec. ?	Haifa	Three recitals; programs unknown

Date	Place	Main works performed (titles abbreviated when repeated)
Dec. 14, 16	Tel Aviv	Schoenberg Suite; K. 330; *Goldberg Variations*
Dec. 26, 27	Detroit	Bach F minor; Mozart C minor (Paul Paray, Detroit Symphony)

1959

Date	Place	Main works performed
Jan. 2	Minneapolis	Beethoven #4 (Antal Dorati, Minneapolis Symphony)
Jan. 5, 6	Houston	Beethoven #5 (André Kostelanetz, Houston Symphony)
Jan. 9	Pasadena	Schoenberg Suite; K. 330; *Goldberg Variations*
Jan. 14, 15, 16	San Francisco	Beethoven #3 (Enrique Jordá, San Francisco Symphony)
Jan. 24, 25	St. Louis	Beethoven #5 (Harry Farbman, St. Louis Symphony)
Jan. 31	Edmonton	Not known
Feb. 2	Calgary	Not known
Feb. 13	New York	Partita #6; Schoenberg Piano Pieces Op. 19; Op. 110; Berg
Feb. 18	Salt Lake City	Beethoven #3 (Maurice Abravenel, Utah Symphony)
Feb. 19	Ogden, Utah	Not known
Feb. 24	Buffalo	Op. 110; *Goldberg Variations*
March 1	Washington	Schoenberg Suite; K. 330; *Goldberg Variations*
March 3	Oberlin	Not known
March 8	Boston	Partita #6; Op. 110; two Brahms intermezzi; Hindemith #3
March 10	Quebec	Partita #6; Op. 110; Schoenberg Six Pieces; Hindemith #3
April 2, 3, 4	New York	Mozart C minor (Bernstein, New York Philharmonic)

Date	Place	*Main works performed* (titles abbreviated when repeated)
April 5	New York	Beethoven #3 (Bernstein, New York Philharmonic)
April 7, 8	Montreal	Beethoven #5 (Igor Markevich, Montreal Symphony)
April 14, 15	Toronto	Beethoven #3 (Walter Susskind, Toronto Symphony)
April 18	Birmingham, Ala.	Not known
April 20	Knoxville, Tenn.	Not known
April 22	Columbia, S.C.	Not known
May 16	Berlin	Schoenberg Suite; K. 330; *Goldberg Variations*
May 20	London	Beethoven #4 (Josef Krips, London Symphony)
May 22	London	Beethoven #1 (Krips, London Symphony)
May 30	London	Beethoven #2 (Krips, London Symphony)
June 1	London	Beethoven #3 (Krips, London Symphony)
Aug. 25	Salzburg	Schoenberg Suite; K. 330; *Goldberg Variations*
Aug. 31	Lucerne	Bach D minor (Von Karajan, Philharmonia Orchestra)
Oct. 8	Winnipeg	Brahms Concerto #1 in D minor (Victor Feldbrill, Winnipeg Symphony Orchestra)
Oct. 12	Ann Arbor	Sweelinck; Schoenberg Suite; K. 330; *Goldberg Variations*
Oct. 14	London, Ont.	Beethoven #2 (Martin Boundy, London Symphony)

Date	Place	Main works performed (titles abbreviated when repeated)
Oct. 25	Berkeley	Berg; Schoenberg Pieces; Hindemith #3; Krenek #3; Morawetz
Oct. 27	Denver	Bach D minor; *Burleske* (Saul Caston, Denver Symphony)
Nov. 1	San Francisco	Sweelinck; Schoenberg Suite; K. 330; *Goldberg Variations*
Nov. 5, 6	Atlanta	Beethoven #4 (Henry Sopkin, Atlanta Symphony)
Nov. 9	Rock Hill, S.C.	Partita #1; Berg; K. 330; Schoenberg Pieces; Op. 110
Nov. 20, 21	Cincinnati	Beethoven #4 (Max Rudolf, Cincinnati Symphony)
Nov. 23	Bloomington, Ind.	Partita #1; K. 330; Op. 110; Berg
Nov. 26	Cleveland	Schoenberg Concerto; Brandenburg #5 (Louis Lane, Cleveland Orchestra)
Dec. 10	Syracuse	Partita #1; Haydn sonata; Schoenberg Pieces; Op. 110; Berg
Dec. 17	Oklahoma City	Beethoven #4 (Guy Fraser Harrison, Oklahoma City Symphony)

1960

Date	Place	Main works performed
March 2	Baltimore	Beethoven #4 (Peter Herman Adler, Baltimore Symphony)
March 18	Toledo	Beethoven #4 (Joseph Hawthorne, Toledo Orchestra)
March 27, 28	Victoria	Beethoven #3 (Hans Gruber, Victoria Symphony)
April 5	Washington	Beethoven #1 (Howard Mitchell, National Symphony)
April 9	Rochester	Partita #1; *Eroica Variations*; Berg
April 19	Montreal	Beethoven #5 (Igor Markevich, Montreal Symphony)

Date	Place	Main works performed (titles abbreviated when repeated)
April 24	South Bend, Ind.	Brahms D minor (Edwyn H. Hames, South Bend Symphony)
July 24	Stratford	Bach D minor, Brandenburg #5 (Oscar Shumsky, National Festival Orchestra)
July 27	Vancouver	Beethoven #4; Mozart C minor (Louis Lane, Vancouver Festival Chamber Orchestra)
July 29	Vancouver	Beethoven *Tempest Sonata, Eroica Variations*; Berg
Aug. 2	Vancouver	Schoenberg songs, *Book of Hanging Gardens*, Suite, *Ode to Napoleon Bonaparte*
Aug. 7	Stratford	All Beethoven; details not known
Oct. 4	New Haven	Mozart C minor (Frank Brieff, New Haven Symphony)
Oct. 12	Detroit	*Burleske* (Paray, Detroit Symphony)
Oct. 13	Detroit	Beethoven #2; Brandenburg #5 (Paray, Detroit Symphony)
Nov. 6	Buffalo	Beethoven #5 (Krips, Buffalo Philharmonic)
Nov. 15	Cincinnati	*Tempest Sonata, Eroica Variations*; Brahms three intermezzi; Berg
Nov. 29	Akron	Same as Cincinnati
Dec. 1	Minneapolis	Not known
Dec. 6, 7	Toronto	Schoenberg Concerto; Mozart C minor (Susskind, Toronto Symphony)

1961

Date	Place	Main works performed
Jan. 31	Denver	Beethoven #3 (Saul Caston, Denver Symphony)
Feb. 5	St. Louis	Beethoven #2, #4 (Edouard van Remoortel, St. Louis Symphony)
Feb. 8	St. Louis	Beethoven #1, #5 (van Remoortel, St. Louis Symphony)

Date	Place	*Main works performed* (titles abbreviated when repeated)
Feb. 11	St. Louis	Beethoven #3, Triple Concerto (van Remoortel, St. Louis Symphony, and Harry Farbman, violin; Leslie Parnas, cello)
Feb. 20	Houston	Bach D minor (Sir Malcolm Sargent, Houston Symphony)
Feb. 23, 24	Tulsa	Beethoven #4 (Franco Autori, Tulsa Philharmonic)
March 4	Minneapolis	*Tempest Sonata, Eroica Variations;* Brahms intermezzi; Berg
March 12	Boston	Partita #3; Haydn sonata; *Tempest Sonata;* Berg
March 17, 18, 19	New York	Beethoven #4 (Bernstein, New York Philharmonic)
March 22	Miami	Partita #3; *Tempest Sonata, Eroica Variations;* Haydn sonata
March 25	Atlanta	Byrd three pieces; Partita #3; K. 330; Op. 109; Berg
April 9	Montreal	Krenek #3; Partita #3; Haydn sonata; Op. 110
April 25	Los Angeles	*Goldberg Variations;* Webern Variations; Op. 110; Berg
May 2	Cleveland	Partita #3; K. 330; Op. 109; Berg
July 16	Stratford	Brahms Cello Sonata #1, Violin Sonata #1, Trio #3 (Oscar Shumsky, violin, Leonard Rose, cello)
July 23	Stratford	Strauss songs, Violin Sonata, Op. 18, *Capriccio* (arr. Gould) (Ellen Faull, Victor Braun, Oscar Shumsky)
Aug. 4	Vancouver	Beethoven Sonata Op. 31 #3
Aug. 9	Vancouver	Bach Cantata #54 and unspecified concerto (Gould as pianist and conductor)

Date	Place	Main works performed (titles abbreviated when repeated)
Aug. 13	Stratford	Bach Concerto in D minor, Sonata #3 for gamba and harpsichord (Leonard Rose, cello, National Festival Orchestra)
Aug. 17	Vancouver	Brahms D minor (with Zubin Mehta, Vancouver Symphony)
Oct. 8	White Plains, N.Y.	Beethoven #5 (Simon Asen, Symphony of the Air)
Oct. 12, 14	Madison, Wis.	Not known
Oct. 22	Boston	Brandenburg #5; *Burkeske* (Paray, Detroit Symphony)
Oct. 26, 28	Cincinnati	Beethoven #5 (Max Rudolf, Cincinnati Symphony)
Nov. 3, 4	Madison, Wis.	Partita #3; K. 330; Op. 109; Berg
Nov. 17	Minneapolis	Beethoven #5 (Stanislaw Skrowa-czewski, Minneapolis Symphony)

1962

Date	Place	Main works performed
Jan. 2	Baltimore	Brandenburg #5; *Burleske* (Peter Herman Adler, Baltimore Symphony)
Feb. 6	Oakland	Beethoven #4 (Gerhard Samuel, Oakland Symphony)
Feb. 11	Berkeley	*Tempest Sonata*, Op. 110, *Eroica Variations*
Feb. 27	Winnipeg	Partita #3; *Tempest Sonata*; Prokofiev Sonata #7
March 5, 6	Portland, Ore.	Brahms D minor (Gregory Millar, Portland Symphony)
March 22, 24	Cleveland	Bach D minor; *Burleske* (Louis Lane, Cleveland Orchestra)
March 25	Cleveland	Bach D minor; Beethoven #3 (Louis Lane, Cleveland Orchestra)
April 6, 8	New York	Brahms D minor (Bernstein, New York Philharmonic)

Date	Place	Main works performed (titles abbreviated when repeated)
April 12	Toledo	Beethoven #3 (Joseph Hawthorne, Toledo Symphony)
April 14	Columbus, Ohio	Bach D minor; Beethoven #2 (Evan Whallon, Columbus Symphony)
April 22	Chicago	Byrd three pieces; Schoenberg Suite; Partita #3; Op. 109; Berg
April 26	Lexington, Ky.	Byrd three pieces; Partita #3; Haydn sonata; Op. 109; Berg
July 8	Stratford	Bach *Musical Offering, Art of the Fugue* (1-8) (Shumsky, Rose, members of National Festival Orchestra)
July 29	Stratford	Hindemith *Das Marienleben*, Sonata #3 (Lois Marshall)
Aug. 5	Stratford	Mendelssohn Trio in D minor, songs (Shumsky, Rose, Leopold Simoneau)
Aug. 10	Stratford	Not known
Oct. 9, 10	Baltimore	Brahms D minor (Adler, Baltimore Symphony)
Oct. 23	Atlanta	Beethoven #5 (Sopkin, Atlanta Symphony)
Nov. 8	Detroit	Beethoven #3 (Paray, Detroit Symphony)
Nov. 20	Cincinnati	*Art of the Fugue* (four fugues), Partita #4; Op. 109; Hindemith #3
Nov. 23	Kansas City	Byrd three pieces; Haydn sonata; Op. 109; Berg
Nov. 27	Louisville, Ky.	*Art of the Fugue* (four), Partita #4; Brahms three intermezzi; Hindemith #3

1963

Date	Place	Main works performed
Feb. 13, 14, 15	San Francisco	Bach D minor; Schoenberg (Jordá, San Francisco Symphony)
March 5	Denver	Brahms D minor (Caston, Denver Symphony)

Date	Place	*Main works performed* (titles abbreviated when repeated)
April 16	Rochester	*Art of the Fugue* (four), Partita #4; Op. 109; Hindemith #3
July 7	Stratford	Bach Violin Sonata #1, Concerto #6 (Shumsky, violin; Mario Bernardi, conductor; National Festival Orchestra)
July 28	Stratford	Glinka *Trio Pathétique*; Prokofiev Violin Sonata, Op. 94 (Shumsky; Sol Schoenbach, bassoon)
Oct. 26	Detroit	*Art of the Fugue* (four); Op. 109; Hindemith #3

1964

| March 29 | Chicago | *Art of the Fugue* (four); Partita #4; Krenek #3; Op. 110 |
| April 10 | Los Angeles | *Art of the Fugue* (four); Partita #4; Op. 110; Hindemith #3 |

Discography
by Nancy Canning

NOTE:

1. This catalogue is organized chronologically by recording date. Where possible, cuts from the same album have been grouped together to avoid redundancy in release information.
2. All recordings were released by CBS Masterworks on 33⅓ rpm discs unless otherwise specified.
3. With the exception of the non-CBS recordings, all release dates refer to first releases in North America. Only the first release of each piece is listed, with the exceptions of the non-CBS and CBS collections, e.g., *The Glenn Gould Legacy* series.

Abbreviations
  * Recorded in New York City, usually at CBS's 30th Street Studio
 ** Recorded in Toronto at Eaton Auditorium, unless otherwise specified
  § Unreleased: in CBS archives
   Produced by:
  1 Samuel H. Carter
  2 Thomas Frost
  3 Glenn Gould
  4 Andrew Kazdin
  5 John McClure
  6 Paul Myers
  7 Joseph Scianni
  8 Howard Scott
  9 Richard Killough

CBS Catalogue Numbers
  BS Bonus Special
  IM Digital
  ML Mono
  MS Stereo
  Mn Stereo, with multiple (n = number) discs
 MnX Stereo series
   S Soundtrack

RECORDING DATE	COMPOSER	WORKS	CATALOGUE NUMBER	RELEASE DATE	NOTES
1940s**	Mozart	Fantasy No. 1 in F minor (Four Hands), KV 594	TV 34793X	1983	With Alberto Guerrero, piano. Released by Vox as *The Young Glenn Gould: In Memoriam 1932–1982, Vol. 2*
	Mozart	Five Variations in G major (Four Hands), KV 501			
	Mozart	Sonata No. 4 in F major (Four Hands), KV 497			
	Mozart	Sonata No. 5 in C major (Four Hands), KV 521			
1951**	Berg	Sonata, Op. 1	RS3	1953	Released by Hallmark
	Prokofiev	"The Winter Fairy" from *Cinderella*			With Albert Pratz, violin
	Shostakovich	Three Fantastic Dances			With Albert Pratz, violin
	Taneyev	The Birth of the Harp	TV 34792X	1982	With Albert Pratz, violin. Released by Vox as *The Young Glenn Gould: In Memoriam 1932–1982, Vol. 1*
Oct. 1954	Bach	Partita No. 5 in G major, BWV 829	120	1954	Released by the CBC Transcription Service Program
	Morawetz	Fantasy in D minor			

Date	Composer	Work	Catalogue	Year	Notes
June 1955*	Bach	Goldberg Variations, BWV 988	ML 5060[8]	1956	
			S 31333[8]	1972	Var. 18 and 25 included on the sound track for *Slaughterhouse-Five*
			M4X 38616[8]	1984	*The Glenn Gould Legacy, Vol. 1*
1956	Gould	String Quartet, Op. 1	142	1956	Montreal String Quartet. Released by the CBC International Service Program
Feb./June 1956*	Beethoven	Sonata No. 30 in E major, Op. 109	ML 5130[8]	1956	
			M3 39036[8]	1985	*The Glenn Gould Legacy, Vol. 2*
Feb. 1956, July/Aug. 1957*	Bach	Partita No. 5 in G major, BWV 829	ML 5186[8]	1957	
	Bach	Partita No. 6 in E minor, BWV 830	M4X 38616[8]	1984	*The Glenn Gould Legacy, Vol. 1*
June 1956*	Beethoven	Sonata No. 32 in C minor, Op. 111	ML 5130[8]	1956	
			M3 39036[8]	1985	*The Glenn Gould Legacy, Vol. 2*

RECORDING DATE	COMPOSER	WORKS	CATALOGUE NUMBER	RELEASE DATE	NOTES
June 1956*	Beethoven	Sonata No. 31 in A-flat major, Op. 110	ML 5130ᵡ	1956	
			M3 39036ᵡ	1985	*The Glenn Gould Legacy, Vol. 2*
April 1957*	Beethoven	Concerto No. 2 in B-flat major, Op. 19	ML 5211ᵡ	1957	With Leonard Bernstein conducting the Columbia Symphony Orchestra
	Bach	Concerto No. 1 in D minor, BWV 1052			With Leonard Bernstein conducting the Columbia Symphony Orchestra
May 1957, Moscow	Bach	Three-Part Inventions, Nos. 2–15, BWV 788–801		§	Not released
May 1957, Moscow Conservatory	Bach	*Art of the Fugue*, BWV 1080	LDX 78799	1986	Nos. 1, 2, and 4. Gould comments between pieces, and speaks about composers of the New Viennese School of twelve-tone composers and Ernst Krenek. Released by Harmonium Mundi/France as *Concert du Moscou*. Produced by Nicholas Saba
	Bach	*Goldberg Variations*, BWV 988			Variations 3, 9, 10, 18, 24, and 30
	Berg	Sonata, Op. 1			

358

Date	Composer	Work	Catalog No.	Year	Notes
	Krenek	Sonata No. 3, Op. 92, No. 4			Excerpt
	Webern	Passacaglia for Orchestra			Excerpt
	Webern	Variations for Piano, Op. 27			
May 1957, Leningrad	Bach	Concerto No. 1 in D minor, BWV 1052	M4X 38616	1984	Live performance with Vladislav Slovak conducting the Leningrad Philharmonic Orchestra. *The Glenn Gould Legacy, Vol. 1*
May 1957, Leningrad	Beethoven	Concerto No. 2 in B-flat major, Op. 19	M3 39936	1985	Live performance with Vladislav Slovak conducting the Academic Symphony Orchestra. *The Glenn Gould Legacy, Vol. 2*
May 1957, Berlin	Beethoven	Concerto No. 3 in C minor, Op. 37	013.6323	1988	Live performance with Herbert von Karajan conducting the Berlin Philharmonic. Released by Nuova Era on CD only
July/Aug. 1957*	Bach	*The Well-Tempered Clavier,* Book II: Fugue No. 14 in F-sharp minor, BWV 883	ML 5186*	1957	
	Bach	*The Well-Tempered Clavier,* Book II: Fugue No. 9 in E major, BWV 878	M4X 38616*	1984	*The Glenn Gould Legacy, Vol. 1*

RECORDING DATE	COMPOSER	WORKS	CATALOGUE NUMBER	RELEASE DATE	NOTES
Aug. 1957	Brahms	Quintet in F minor, Op. 34	140	1957	With the Montreal String Quartet. Released by the CBC Transcription Service Program
Jan. 1958*	Haydn	Sonata No. 59 in E-flat major, XVI/49	ML 5274ᴿ	1958	
	Mozart	Sonata No. 10 in C major, KV 330			
	Mozart	Fantasia and Fugue in C major, KV 394	M3 39936ᴿ	1985	*The Glenn Gould Legacy, Vol. 2*
March 1958*	Schoenberg	Piano Concerto, Op. 42	013-6306	1986	Live performance with Dimitri Mitropoulos conducting the New York Philharmonic Orchestra. Released by Nuova Era on CD only
Apr./July 1958*	Beethoven	Concerto No. 1 in C major, Op. 15	ML 5298/MS 6017ᴿ	1958	With Vladimir Golschmann conducting the Columbia Symphony Orchestra. Cadenza by Gould
			M3 39936ᴿ	1985	*The Glenn Gould Legacy, Vol. 2*

Date	Composer	Work	Catalogue	Year	Notes
May 1958*	Bach	Concerto No. 5 in F minor, BWV 1056	ML 5298/MS 6017[R]	1958	With Vladimir Golschmann conducting the Columbia Symphony Orchestra
			S31333[R]	1972	Included on the sound track for *Slaughterhouse-Five*
June/July 1958*	Krenek	Sonata No. 3, Op. 92, No. 4	ML 5336[R]	1959	
			M3 42150[R]	1986	*The Glenn Gould Legacy, Vol. 4*
June/July 1958*	Schoenberg	Three Piano Pieces, Op. 11	ML 5336[R]	1959	
			M3 42150[R]	1986	*The Glenn Gould Legacy, Vol. 4*
July 1958*	Berg	Sonata, Op. 1	ML 5336[R]	1959	
			M3 42150[R]	1986	*The Glenn Gould Legacy, Vol. 4*
Aug. 1958, Salzburg	Bach	Concerto No. 1 in D minor, BWV 1052	013.6306	1986	Live performance with Dimitri Mitropoulos conducting the Concertgebouw Orchestra of Amsterdam. Released by Nuova Era on CD only
			D15119	1986	Released by Price Less on CD only

RECORDING DATE	COMPOSER	WORKS	CATALOGUE NUMBER	RELEASE DATE	NOTES
Sept. 1958, Stockholm	Mozart	Concerto No. 24 in C minor, KV 491	CD 323	1986	With Georg Ludwig Jochum conducting the Swedish Radio Symphony Orchestra at the Musical Academy in Stockholm. Released by BIS on CD only as *Glenn Gould in Stockholm 1958*
Oct. 1958, Stockholm	Beethoven	Concerto No. 2 in B-flat major, Op. 19			
Oct. 1958, Stockholm	Beethoven	Sonata No. 31 in A-flat major, Op. 110	CD 324	1986	Released by BIS on CD only as *Glenn Gould in Stockholm 1958*
	Berg	Sonata, Op. 1			
	Haydn	Sonata No. 59 in E-flat major, XVI/49			
May/Sept. 1959*	Bach	Partita No. 1 in B-flat major, BWV 825	ML 5472/MS 6141[6]	1960	
May 1959, July/ Sept./Nov. 1960*	Brahms	Intermezzi, Op. 76, Nos. 6 and 7, Op. 116, No. 4, Op. 117, Nos. 1–3, Op. 118, Nos. 1, 2, and 6, Op. 119, No. 1	ML 5637/MS 6237[7]	1961	
			M3 42107[7]	1986	*The Glenn Gould Legacy, Vol. 3*

Date/Location	Composer	Work	Catalogue	Year	Notes
May 1959*	Beethoven	Concerto No. 3 in C minor, Op. 37	ML 5418/MS 6096[8]	1960	With Leonard Bernstein conducting the Columbia Symphony Orchestra
June 1959*	Bach	Partita No. 2 in C minor, BWV 826	ML 5472/MS 6141[8]	1960	
	Bach	Italian Concerto (in F major), BWV 971			
Aug. 1959, Salzburg	Bach	*Goldberg Variations*, BWV 988	D15119	1986	Live performance. Released by Price Less on CD only
	Mozart	Sonata No. 10 in C major, KV 330			
Aug. 1959, Salzburg	Bach	*Goldberg Variations*, BWV 988	CMG1	1986	Live performance. Released by Frequenz on CD only as *Glenn Gould in Salzburg*
	Mozart	Sonata No. 10 in C major, KV 330			
	Schoenberg	Suite for Piano, Op. 25			
	Sweelinck	Fantasia in D minor for Organ (arr. for Piano)			
Aug. 1959, Salzburg	Bach	Brandenburg Concerto No. 5 in D major, BWV 1050		§	
March 1960, Cleveland, Severance Hall	Gould	String Quartet, Op. 1	ML 5578/MS 6178[8]	1960	Symphonia Quartet

RECORDING DATE	COMPOSER	WORKS	CATALOGUE NUMBER	RELEASE DATE	NOTES
July/Sept. 1960, Jan 1967, Aug. 1971*	Beethoven	Sonata No. 17 in D minor, *Tempest*, Op. 31, No. 2	M 32349ˣ	1973	—
July/Aug. 1960, Feb. 1967*	Beethoven	*Eroica Variations*, Op. 35	M 30080⁴	1970	
July 1960, May 1967*	Beethoven	Variations in F major, Op. 34			
Jan. 1961, Toronto, Massey Hall**	Mozart	Concerto No. 24 in C minor, KV 491	ML 5739/MS 6339²/ᴿ	1962	With Walter Susskind conducting the CBC Symphony Orchestra
	Schoenberg	Piano Concerto, Op. 42			With Robert Craft conducting the CBC Symphony Orchestra
March 1961*	Beethoven	Concerto No. 4 in G major, Op. 58	ML 5662/MS 6262⁸	1961	With Leonard Bernstein conducting the New York Philharmonic
Oct. 1961	Strauss	*Enoch Arden*, Op. 38	ML 5741/MS 6341⁷	1962	With Claude Rains, narrator
1962, Stratford, Ontario	Beethoven	Sonata No. 3 for Cello and Piano in A major, Op. 69	234	1986	With Leonard Rose, cello, at the 1962 Stratford Festival. Released by Melodram
	Beethoven	Trio in D major, *Ghost*, Op. 70, No. 1			With Leonard Rose, cello, and Oscar Shumsky, violin

Date	Composer	Work	Catalogue	Year	Notes
Jan./Feb. 1962	Bach	Art of the Fugue, Nos. 1-9, BWV 1080	ML 573[8]/MS 6338[7]	1962	Fugues I-IX played on organ. Recorded at All Saint's Church in Kingsway, Ontario
June/Sept. 1962*	Bach	The Well-Tempered Clavier, Book I: Nos. 1-8, BWV 846-853	ML 5808/MS 6408[6]	1963	
Sept. 1962*	Brahms	Concerto No. 1 in D minor, Op. 15	234	1986	With Leonard Bernstein conducting the New York Philharmonic. Released by Melodram
				1987	*Radiothon Special Edition Historic Recordings, Vol. 7.* A joint release between the New York Philharmonic and radio station WQXR
Oct. 1962*	Bach	Parita No. 3 in A minor, BWV 827	ML 5898/MS 6498[6]	1963	
Dec. 1962, March/ Apr. 1963*	Bach	Parita No. 4 in D major, BWV 828			
Apr. 1963*	Bach	Toccata in E minor, BWV 914			
Apr./June 1963, Aug. 1964*	Bach	The Well-Tempered Clavier, Book I: Nos. 9-16, BWV 854-861	ML 5938/MS 6538[6]	1964	
June 1963, Feb./ Aug. 1965*	Bach	The Well-Tempered Clavier, Book I: Nos. 17-24, BWV 862-869	ML 6176/MS 6776[6]	1965	

RECORDING DATE	COMPOSER	WORKS	CATALOGUE NUMBER	RELEASE DATE	NOTES
Dec. 1963, Jan. 1964*	Bach	Two- and Three-Part Inventions, BWV 772–801	ML 6022/MS 6622[6]	1964	
	Bach	Two- and Three-Part Inventions: No. 4 in D minor, BWV 775/790; No. 6 in E major, BWV 777/792; and No. 13 in A minor, BWV 784/799	M4X 38616[6]	1984	*The Glenn Gould Legacy, Vol. 1*
Dec. 1963*	Gould	"So You Want to Write a Fugue?"	M2X 35914[6]	1980	With Vladimir Golschmann conducting the Juilliard String Quartet, Elizabeth Guy-Benson (soprano), Anita Darian (mezzo-soprano), Charles Bressler (tenor), and Donald Gramm (baritone). *The Glenn Gould Silver Jubilee Album*
Jan. 1964*	Schoenberg	Suite for Piano, Op. 25	ML 6217/MS 6817[2]	1966	
			M3 42150[2]	1986	*The Glenn Gould Legacy, Vol. 4*
Jan. 1964, Jan. 1965*	Schoenberg	Six Songs, Op. 3	M 31312[2]	1972	With Donald Gramm, baritone, and Helen Vanni, soprano

Date/Location	Composer	Work	Catalog	Year	Notes
June 1964, Jan. 1965*	Schoenberg	Four Songs, Op. 2	ML 6216/MS 6816[2/4]	1966	With Ellen Faull, soprano
June 1964, Manhattan Center*	Beethoven	Sonata No. 6 in F major, Op. 10, No. 2	ML 6086/MS 6686[2]	1965	
June 1964, Sept. 1965*	Schoenberg	Six Little Piano Pieces, Op. 19	ML 6217/MS 6817[2]	1966	
July 1964*	Schoenberg	*Phantasy* for Violin and Piano, Op. 47	ML 6436/MS 7036[6]	1967	With Israel Baker, violin
Sept. 1964, Manhattan Center*	Beethoven	Sonata No. 5 in C minor, Op. 10, No. 1	ML 6086/MS 6686[2]	1965	
Nov. 1964, Manhattan Center*	Beethoven	Sonata No. 7 in D major, Op. 10, No. 3			
Jan./Nov. 1965*	Schoenberg	Two Songs, Op. 1	ML 6216/MS 6816[2/4]	1966	With Donald Gramm, bass-baritone
Feb. 1965*	Schoenberg	*Ode to Napoleon Bonaparte*, Op. 41	ML 6437/MS 7037[9]	1967	With the Juilliard String Quartet and John Horton, speaker
March/Aug. 1965, May 1966, Jan./Aug. 1970*	Mozart	Sonata No. 13 in B-flat major, KV 333	M 31073[4]	1972	*The Mozart Piano Sonatas, Vol. 3*
June 1965*	Schoenberg	*Das Buch der hängenden Garten*, Op. 15	ML 6216/MS 6816[4]	1966	With Helen Vanni, mezzo-soprano
June/Sept. 1965, May 1966*	Mozart	Sonata No. 12 in F major, KV 332	M 31073[4]	1972	*The Mozart Piano Sonatas, Vol. 3*

RECORDING DATE	COMPOSER	WORKS	CATALOGUE NUMBER	RELEASE DATE	NOTES
Sept./Nov. 1965*	Schoenberg	Five Piano Pieces, Op. 23	ML 6217/MS 6817[4]	1966	
			M3 42150[4]	1986	*The Glenn Gould Legacy, Vol. 4*
Nov. 1965*	Schoenberg	Piano Pieces, Op. 33[a] and b	ML 6217/MS 6817[4]	1966	
			M3 42150[4]	1986	*The Glenn Gould Legacy, Vol. 4*
Dec. 1965, Aug. 1970*	Mozart	Sonata No. 11 in A major, KV 331	M 32348[4]	1973	*The Mozart Piano Sonatas, Vol. 4*
Jan. 1966*	Strauss	Three Ophelia Songs, Op. 67	M2X 35914[6]	1980	With Elisabeth Schwarzkopf, soprano. *The Glenn Gould Silver Jubilee Album*
Jan. 1966*	Strauss	Four Songs, Op. 27, No. 4: "Morgen"		§	With Elisabeth Schwarzkopf, soprano
Jan. 1966*	Strauss	Eight Songs, Op. 49, No. 7: "Wer lieben will, muss leiden"		§	With Elisabeth Schwarzkopf, soprano
Jan. 1966*	Strauss	Four Songs, Op. 27, No. 3: "Heimliche Aufforderung"		§	With Elisabeth Schwarzkopf, soprano
Jan. 1966*	Strauss	Five Songs, Op. 48, No. 4: "Winterweihe"		§	With Elisabeth Schwarzkopf, soprano

Date	Composer	Work	Catalog No.	Year	Notes
Feb. 1966*	Beethoven	Sonata No. 9 in E major, Op. 14, No. 1	ML 6345/MS 6945[4]	1967	
Feb./May 1966*	Beethoven	Sonata No. 10 in G major, Op. 14, No. 2			
March 1966, Manhattan Center*	Beethoven	Concerto No. 5 in E-flat major, *Emperor*, Op. 73	ML 6288/MS 6888[4]	1966	With Leopold Stokowski conducting the American Symphony Orchestra
Apr. 1966, Oct. 1967*	Beethoven	Sonata No. 23 in F minor, *Appassionata*, Op. 57	MS 7413[4]	1970	
Apr. 1966*	Beethoven	Sonata No. 8 in C minor, *Pathétique*, Op. 13	ML 6345/MS 6945[4]	1967	
June 1966*	Morawetz	Fantasy in D minor	32110045/46[4]	1967	*Canadian Music in the 20th Century*
Aug. 1966, Jan./Feb. 1967*	Bach	*The Well-Tempered Clavier*, Book II: Nos. 1–8, BWV 870–877	MS 7099[4]	1968	
Oct. 1966, Feb. 1973*	Hindemith	Sonata No. 1 in A major	M 32350[4]	1973	
Nov. 1966*	Beethoven	Thirty-two Variations in C minor, WoO. 80	M 30080[4]	1970	
Nov. 1966*	Mozart	Fantasia in C minor, KV 475	M 33515[4]	1975	*The Mozart Piano Sonatas, Vol. 5*

RECORDING DATE	COMPOSER	WORKS	CATALOGUE NUMBER	RELEASE DATE	NOTES
Dec. 1966, Jan. 1967*	Hindemith	Sonata No. 3 in B-flat major	M 32350[4]	1973	
			M3 42150[4]	1986	*The Glenn Gould Legacy, Vol. 4*
March 1967*	Beethoven	Sonata No. 18 in E-flat major, Op. 31, No. 3	M 32349[4]	1973	
May 1967*	Bach	Concerto No. 3 in D major, BWV 1054	ML 6401/MS 7001[4]	1967	With Vladimir Golschmann conducting the Columbia Symphony Orchestra
			S 31333[4]	1972	Included on the sound track for *Slaughterhouse-Five*
May 1967*	Bach	Concerto No. 7 in G minor, BWV 1058	ML 6401/MS 7001[4]	1967	With Vladimir Golschmann conducting the Columbia Symphony Orchestra
May 1967*	Beethoven	Sonata No. 14 in C-sharp minor, *Moonlight*, Op. 27, No. 2	MS 7413[4]	1970	
May 1967*	Mozart	Sonata No. 5 in G major, KV 283	MS 7097[4]	1968	*The Mozart Piano Sonatas, Vol. 1*
May/Nov. 1967*	Mozart	Sonata No. 3 in B-flat major, KV 281			

Date	Composer	Work	Catalogue	Year	Album
May 1967*	Byrd	A Voluntary	M 30825[4]	1971	*A Consort of Musicke Bye William Byrde and Orlando Gibbons*
	Byrd	Sixth Pavan and Galliard			
June/July 1967*	Prokofiev	Sonata No. 7 in B-flat major, Op. 83	MS 7173[4]	1969	
			M3 42150[4]	1986	*The Glenn Gould Legacy, Vol. 4*
July 1967*	Byrd	First Pavan and Galliard	M 30825[4]	1971	*A Consort of Musicke Bye William Byrde and Orlando Gibbons*
July 1967*	Anhalt	Fantasia for Piano	32110045/46[4]	1967	*Canadian Music in the 20th Century*
July 1967*	Mozart	Sonata No. 15 in C major, KV 545	MS 7323/MGP 13[4]	1969	
			M 32348[4]	1973	*The Mozart Piano Sonatas, Vol. 4*
July 1967*	Pentland	*Shadows (Ombres)*		§	
July/Nov. 1967*	Mozart	Sonata No. 4 in E-flat major, KV 282	MS 7097[4]	1968	*The Mozart Piano Sonatas, Vol. 1*
Aug. 1967*	Hétu	*Variations pour piano*	32110045/46[4]	1967	*Canadian Music in the 20th Century*

371

RECORDING DATE	COMPOSER	WORKS	CATALOGUE NUMBER	RELEASE DATE	NOTES
Aug./Oct./Nov. 1967*	Mozart	Sonata No. 2 in F major, KV 280	MS 7097[4]	1968	The Mozart Piano Sonatas, Vol. 1
Nov. 1967*	Mozart	Sonata No. 1 in C major, KV 279	MS 7095[4]	1968	
Nov./Dec. 1967, Jan 1968*	Beethoven/Liszt	Symphony No. 5 in C minor, Op. 67	MS 7095[4]	1968	
Jan. 1968*	Schoenberg	Two Songs, Posth. / Two Songs, Op. 14	M 31312[4]	1972	With Helen Vanni, soprano
Jan. 1968*	Schumann	Quartet in E-flat major for piano and strings, Op. 47	MS 7325[9]	1969	With the Juilliard String Quartet
Jan. 1968, Sept. 1970*	Schoenberg	Three Songs, Op. 48	M 31312[4]	1972	With Helen Vanni, soprano
Jan. 1968*		Glenn Gould: Concert Dropout; Glenn Gould in Conversation with John McClure	BS 15[4]	1968	Bonus record included with MS 7095
			M4X 38616[4]	1984	The Glenn Gould Legacy, Vol. 1
Jan./Feb. 1968*	Scriabin	Sonata No. 3 in F-sharp minor, Op. 23	MS 7173[4]	1969	
			M3 42150[4]	1986	The Glenn Gould Legacy, Vol. 4

Date	Composer	Work	Catalog	Year	Album / Notes
Jan. 1968*	Scarlatti	Sonata in D major, L. 465		§	
Jan. 1968*	C.P.E. Bach	*Würtemburg* Sonatas: No. 1 in A minor, WQ 49	M2X 35914[4]	1980	*The Glenn Gould Silver Jubilee Album*
Jan. 1968, Feb. 1980*/**	Scarlatti	Sonata in D minor, L. 413			
	Scarlatti	Sonata in D major, L. 463			
	Scarlatti	Sonata in G major, L. 486			
Feb. 1968*	Beethoven	Sonata No. 24 in F-sharp major, Op. 78		§	
Feb. 1968*	Schoenberg	Eight Songs, Op. 6	M 31312[4]	1972	With Helen Vanni, soprano
Apr. 1968*	Schoenberg	Two Ballads, Op. 12, No. 1: "Jane Grey"			
July 1968*	Mozart	Sonata No. 9 in D major, KV 311	MS 7274[4]	1969	*The Mozart Piano Sonatas, Vol. 2*
July/Aug. 1968*	Beethoven/Liszt	Symphony No. 6 in F major, *Pastoral*, Op. 68: First Movement	M2X 35914[4]	1980	*The Glenn Gould Silver Jubilee Album*. Fifth movement recorded, but not released
Aug. 1968*	Gibbons	Lord of Salisbury Pavan and Galliard	M 30825[4]	1971	*A Consort Of Musicke Bye William Byrde and Orlando Gibbons*

RECORDING DATE	COMPOSER	WORKS	CATALOGUE NUMBER	RELEASE DATE	NOTES
Aug. 1968*	Gibbons	Allemand, or Italian Ground			
	Gibbons	Fantasy in C major			
Sept./Oct. 1968*	Mozart	Sonata No. 6 in D major, KV 284	MS 7274[4]	1969	*The Mozart Piano Sonatas, Vol. 2*
Sept. 1968*	Mozart	Sonata No. 7 in C major, KV 309			
1969	Gould	The Idea of North	PR8[3]	1971	Released by CBC Learning Systems
Jan./Feb. 1969*	Mozart	Sonata No. 8 in A minor, KV 310	M 31073[4]	1972	*The Mozart Piano Sonatas, Vol. 3*
Feb. 1969*	Bach	Concerto No. 2 in E major, BWV 1053	MS 7294[4]	1969	With Vladimir Golschmann conducting the Columbia Symphony Orchestra
	Bach	Concerto No. 4 in A major, BWV 1055			
Sept./Dec. 1969*	Bach	*The Well-Tempered Clavier,* Book II: Nos. 9–16, BWV 878–885	MS 7409[4]	1970	
Sept. 1969, Jan. 1971**	Bach	*The Well-Tempered Clavier,* Book II: Nos. 17–24, BWV 886–893	M 30537[4]	1971	

Date	Composer	Work	Catalog	Year	Collection
July 1970*	Scriabin	Sonata No. 5, Op. 53	M3 42150[4/8]	1986	*The Glenn Gould Legacy, Vol. 4*
Aug./Sept. 1970, Nov. 1974**	Mozart	Sonata No. 16 in B-flat major, KV 570	M 33515[4]	1975	*The Mozart Piano Sonatas, Vol. 5*
Aug. 1970*	Mozart	Sonata No. 10 in C major, KV 330	M 31073[4]	1972	*The Mozart Piano Sonatas, Vol. 3*
1971	Gould	The Latecomers	PR9[3]	1971	Released by CBC Learning Systems
Jan./Feb. 1971, Nov. 1973**	Bach	Overture in the French Style, BWV 831	M 32853[4]	1974	
Feb./May 1971, Feb. 1973**	Bach	French Suite No. 5 in G major, BWV 816			
March/May 1971**	Bach	French Suite No. 6 in E major, BWV 817	M 32853[4]	1974	
			M4X 38616[4]	1984	*The Glenn Gould Legacy, Vol. 1*
March/May 1971**	Grieg	Sonata in E minor, Op. 7	M 32040[4]	1973	
			M3 42107[4]	1986	*The Glenn Gould Legacy, Vol. 3*
Apr. 1971**	Bach	Variations in the Italian Style, BWV 989	[4]	§	

RECORDING DATE	COMPOSER	WORKS	CATALOGUE NUMBER	RELEASE DATE	NOTES
Apr. 1971**	Byrd	Hughe Ashton's Ground	M 30825[4]	1971	*A Consort of Musicke Bye William Byrde and Orlando Gibbons*
	Byrd	Sellinger's Round			
May 1971**	Bizet	*Variations chromatiques*, Op. 3	M 32040[4]	1973	
May 1971**	Schoenberg	Two Ballads, Op. 12, No. 2: "Der verlorene Haufen"	M 31312[4]	1972	With Cornelius Opthof, baritone
May 1971**	Bach	English Suite No. 2 in A minor, BWV 807	M2 34578[4]	1977	
			M4X 38616[4]	1984	*The Glenn Gould Legacy, Vol. 1*
Aug. 1971, May 1973**	Beethoven	Sonata No. 16 in G major, Op. 31, No. 1	M 32349[4]	1973	
March 1972, Feb. 1973**	Hindemith	Sonata No. 2 in G major	M 32350[4]	1973	
March/May 1972**	Handel	Suites for Harpsichord, Nos. 1-4	M 31512[4]	1972	Played on harpsichord

Date	Composer	Title	Record No.	Year	Collection
Apr./Nov. 1972, March 1973*/**	Mozart	Sonata in F major with Rondo, KV 533/494	M 32348[4]	1973	*The Mozart Piano Sonatas, Vol. 4*
Nov. 1972**	Mozart	Fantasia in D minor, KV 397			
Nov. 1972**	Bach	French Suite No. 2 in C minor, BWV 813	M 32347[4]	1973	
	Bach	French Suite No. 1 in D minor, BWV 812			
Dec. 1972, Feb. 1973**	Bach	French Suite No. 3 in B minor, BWV 814			
Dec. 1972**	Bizet	*Premier Nocturne* in D major	M 32040[4]	1973	
Dec. 1972**	Scriabin	Two Pieces, Op. 57, "Désir" and "Caresse dansée"	M2X 35914/M 36504[4]	1980	*The Glenn Gould Silver Jubilee Album*
			M3 42150[4]	1986	*The Glenn Gould Legacy, Vol. 4*
Feb./May/June 1973**	Wagner/Gould	*Siegfried Idyll*	M 32351[4]	1973	
Feb./May/June 1973**	Wagner/Gould	"Dawn" and "Siegfried's Rhine Journey" from *Götterdämmerung*	M 32351[4]	1973	
	Wagner/Gould	*Meistersinger* Prelude	M3 42107[4]	1986	*The Glenn Gould Legacy, Vol. 3*

RECORDING DATE	COMPOSER	WORKS	CATALOGUE NUMBER	RELEASE DATE	NOTES
Feb. 1973**	Bach	French Suite No. 4 in E-flat major, BWV 815	M 32347[4]	1973	
March/May 1973**	Bach	English Suite No. 1 in A major, BWV 806	M2 34578[4]	1977	
Nov. 1973, June/Sept. 1974**	Mozart	Sonata No. 14 in C minor, KV 457	M 33515[4]	1975	*The Mozart Piano Sonatas, Vol. 5*
Dec. 1973**	Bach	Sonata for Viola da Gamba and Keyboard: No. 3 in G minor, BWV 1029	M 32934[4]	1974	With Leonard Rose, cello
	Bach	Sonata for Viola da Gamba and Keyboard: No. 2 in D major, BWV 1028			
May 1974**	Bach	Sonata for Viola da Gamba and Keyboard: No. 1 in G major, BWV 1027			
May/June 1974**	Beethoven	Bagatelles, Op. 33 and 126	M 33265[4]	1975	
June 1974**	Bach	English Suite No. 3 in G minor, BWV 808	M2 34578[4]	1977	
Sept. 1974**	Mozart	Sonata No. 17 in D major, KV 576	M 33515[4]	1975	*The Mozart Piano Sonatas, Vol. 5*

Date	Composer	Work	Catalog	Year	Performers
Nov. 1974**	Beethoven	Sonata No. 1 in F minor, Op. 2, No. 1	M2 35911$^{3/4}$	1980	
Dec. 1974, May 1976**	Bach	English Suite No. 5 in E minor, BWV 810	M2 34578^4	1977	
	Bach	English Suite No. 4 in F major, BWV 809			
Jan. 1975**	Hindemith	Sonata for Trumpet in B-flat major and Piano	M2 33971/M 33973^4	1976	With Gilbert Johnson, trumpet
Feb. 1975**	Bach	Sonata for Violin and Harpsichord: No. 1 in B minor, BWV 1014	M2 34226^4	1976	With Jaime Laredo, violin
	Bach	Sonata for Violin and Harpsichord: No. 2 in A major, BWV 1015			
July 1975**	Hindemith	Sonata for Horn and Piano	M2 33971/M 33972^4	1976	With Mason Jones, horn
Sept. 1975**	Hindemith	Sonata for Bass Tuba and Piano			With Abe Torchinsky, tuba
Sept. 1975, Feb. 1976**	Hindemith	Sonata for Alto Horn in E-flat and Piano			With Mason Jones, horn
	Hindemith	Sonata for Trombone and Piano			With Henry Charles Smith, trombone
Oct. 1975, May 1976**	Bach	English Suite No. 6 in D minor, BWV 811	M2 34578^4	1977	

RECORDING DATE	COMPOSER	WORKS	CATALOGUE NUMBER	RELEASE DATE	NOTES
Nov. 1975**	Bach	Sonata for Violin and Harpsichord: No. 4 in C minor, BWV 1017	M2 34226[4]	1976	With Jaime Laredo, violin
	Bach	Sonata for Violin and Harpsichord: No. 3 in E major, BWV 1016			
Jan. 1976**	Bach	Sonata for Violin and Harpsichord: No. 5 in F minor, BWV 1018			
	Bach	Sonata for Violin and Harpsichord: No. 6 in G major, BWV 1019			
July 1976**	Beethoven	Sonata No. 2 in A major, Op. 2, No. 2	M2 35911[3/4]	1980	
Aug. 1976, Aug. 1979**	Beethoven	Sonata No. 3 in C major, Op. 2, No. 3			
Oct. 1976**	Bach	Toccata in D minor, BWV 913	M 35144[4]	1979	
Oct./Nov. 1976**	Bach	Toccata in F-sharp minor, BWV 910			
Oct./Nov. 1976**	Bach	Toccata in D major, BWV 912	M 35144[4]	1979	
			M4X 38616[4]	1984	*The Glenn Gould Legacy, Vol. 1*

Date	Composer	Work	Catalogue	Year	Notes
Nov. 1976, Jan./March 1977**	Hindemith	Das Marienleben, Op. 27	M2 34597[4]	1978	With Roxolana Roslak, soprano
Dec. 1976/March 1977**	Sibelius	Sonatine, Op. 67, Nos. 1–3	M 34555[4]	1977	
			M3 42107[4]	1986	The Glenn Gould Legacy, Vol. 3
March 1977**	Sibelius	Kyllikki: Three Lyric Pieces for Piano, Op. 41	M 34555[4]	1977	
1977	Bach	Fugue in A major on a Theme by Albinoni, BWV 950		§	
Apr./Aug. 1979**	Strauss	Five Piano Pieces, Op. 3	IM 38659[3/4]	1984	Nos. 1 and 3 recorded in April at the St. Lawrence Town Hall
May 1979**	Bach	Toccata in G major, BWV 916	M 35831[4]	1980	
June 1979**	Bach	Toccata in C minor, BWV 911			
June 1979**	Bach	Toccata in G minor, BWV 915			
June 1979**	Bach	Concerto in B-flat major after Marcello, BWV 974		§	
June/July 1979**	Beethoven	Sonata No. 15 in D major, Pastoral, Op. 28	M2 35911[3/4]	1980	

RECORDING DATE	COMPOSER	WORKS	CATALOGUE NUMBER	RELEASE DATE	NOTES
July 1979, Feb. 1980	Beethoven	Sonata No. 11 in B-flat major, Op. 22		§	Second and fourth movements only
Aug. 1979**	Bach	Fugue in B minor on a Theme by Albinoni, BWV 951		§	
Sept. 1979**	Beethoven	Sonata No. 12 in A-flat major, Op. 26	M 37831 ¾	1983	
Oct. 1979, Jan./ Feb. 1980**	Bach	Preludes and Fughettas, BWV 899, 902, and 902A	M 35891 ¾	1980	
	Bach	Preludes and Fugues, BWV 895 and 900			
	Bach	Six Little Preludes, BWV 933–938			
	Bach	Three Little Fugues, BWV 952, 953, and 961			
	Bach	Nine Little Preludes, BWV 924–928 and 930			
Oct. 1979**	Bach	Chromatic Fantasy and Fugue in D minor, BWV 903		§	
Apr. 1980	Bach	Fantasia in C minor, BWV 919		§	

Date	Composer	Work	Catalogue	Year	Notes
Apr. 1980	Bach	Fantasia in G minor, BWV 917			§
Apr. 1980	Bach	Prelude and Fugue on BACH, BWV 898			§
July/Aug. 1980**	Gould	A Glenn Gould Fantasy	M2X 35914[3]	1980	*The Glenn Gould Silver Jubilee Album*
Oct. 1980*	Haydn	Sonata No. 61 in D Major, XVI/51	I2M 36947/IM 37559[1/3]	1982	
Feb. 1981*	Haydn	Sonata No. 60 in C major, XVI/50			
Feb./March 1981	Haydn	Sonata No. 59 in E-flat major, XVI/49			
March 1981*	Haydn	Sonata No. 62 in E-flat major, XVI/52			
March/May 1981*	Haydn	Sonata No. 56 in D major, XVI/42			
	Haydn	Sonata No. 58 in C major, XVI/48			
Apr./May 1981*	Bach	*Goldberg Variations*, BWV 988	IM 37779[1/3]	1982	In co-production with Clasart Films
Aug. 1981**	Beethoven	Sonata No. 13 in E-flat major, Op. 27, No. 1	M 37831[3/4]	1983	
Aug. 1981	Bach	*Italian Concerto*, BWV 971			§

383

RECORDING DATE	COMPOSER	WORKS	CATALOGUE NUMBER	RELEASE DATE	NOTES
Feb. 1982, RCA Studio A*	Brahms	Ballades, Op. 10	IM 37800¹ᐟ³	1983	
Apr. 1982	Beethoven	Concerto No. 2 in B-flat major, Op. 19		§	With Gould conducting members of the Hamilton Philharmonic and Jon Klibanoff, piano
June/July 1982, RCA Studio A*	Brahms	Rhapsodies, Op. 79	IM 37800¹ᐟ³	1983	
			M3 42107¹ᐟ³	1986	No. 1 only. *The Glenn Gould Legacy, Vol. 3*
July 1982, Toronto	Wagner	*Siegfried Idyll*		§	With Gould conducting members of the Toronto Symphony Orchestra
Sept 1982, RCA Studio A*	Strauss	Sonata in B minor, Op. 5	IM 38659¹	1984	
			M3 42107¹	1986	*The Glenn Gould Legacy, Vol. 3*

CBC Radio and TV Shows

by Nancy Canning

NOTE:
1. All entries are live performances unless otherwise noted.
2. Virtually all broadcasts after 1957 include Gould introducing each work, and in many cases commenting extensively upon them.
3. All programs written or produced by Gould are so noted.

SOURCE	AIRDATE	SERIES NAME	COMPOSER	WORKS	NOTES
Radio	1950's		Bach	Fifteen Sinfonias, BWV 787–801	
			Bach	The Well-Tempered Clavier, Book II: Fugue No. 14 in F-sharp minor, BWV 883	
Radio	1950's		Beethoven	Concerto No. 2 in B-flat major, Op. 19	Roland Leduc conducting the CBC Little Symphony Orchestra
Radio	1950's		Scarlatti	Sonata in F minor, L. 475	
Radio	1950's		Webern	Variations for Piano, Op. 27	
Radio	3-6-51		Weber	*Konzertstück*	Sir Ernest MacMillan conducting the Toronto Symphony Orchestra in Massey Hall, Toronto. Gould plays a fragment of this recording in *The Glenn Gould Silver Jubilee Album*
Radio	10-29-51	Vancouver Symphony Orchestra	Beethoven	Concerto No. 4 in G major, Op. 58	William Steinberg conducting the Vancouver Symphony
Radio	9-28-52	Distinguished Artists	Beethoven	Six Bagatelles, Op. 126	
			Beethoven	Variations in F major, Op. 34	

Radio	10-5-52	Distinguished Artists	Beethoven	*Eroica Variations*, Op. 35	
			Beethoven	Sonata in G minor, Op. 49, No. 1	
Radio	10-12-52	Distinguished Artists	Beethoven	Sonata No. 28 in A major, Op. 101	
			Beethoven	Sonata No. 4 in E-flat major, Op. 7	Largo
Radio	10-14-52	CBC Concert Hall	Berg	Sonata, Op. 1	
			Schoenberg	Suite for Piano, Op. 25	
Radio	10-21-52	CBC Concert Hall	Sweelinck	Fantasia in D minor for Organ (arr. for Piano)	
Radio	1953	CBC Recital	Brahms	Sonata for Violin No. 2, Op. 100	With Morry Kernerman, violin
Radio	12-21-53	CBC Symphony Orchestra	Schoenberg	Piano Concerto, Op. 42	Canadian premiere of this work, Jean-Marie Beaudet conducting the CBC Symphony Orchestra
Radio	2-28-54		Bach	*The Well-Tempered Clavier*, Book II: Fugue No. 14 in F-sharp minor, BWV 883; Fugue No. 22 in B-flat minor, BWV 891; Fugue No. 7 in E-flat major, BWV 876	
			Bach	No. 11 in G minor, No. 14 in B-flat major, No. 4 in D minor, No. 7 in E minor, No. 8 in F major	

SOURCE	AIRDATE	SERIES NAME	COMPOSER	WORKS	NOTES
Radio	6-7-54	Distinguished Artists	Bach	Partita No. 5 in G major, BWV 829	
			Bach	No. 13 in A minor, BWV 799	
			Hindemith	*Ludus Tonalis*: Fugue No. 1 in C major	
			Hindemith	Sonata No. 3 in B-flat major	Incomplete
Radio	7-18-54	Summer Festival	Beethoven	Trio in B-flat major, WoO. 39	With Alexander Schneider, violin, and Zara Nelsova, cello
			Beethoven	Trio in D major, *Ghost*, Op. 70, No. 1	
TV	12-16-54	L'Heure du Concert	Beethoven	Concerto No. 1 in C major, Op. 15	First movement only, with Paul Scherman conducting an unidentified orchestra. Plays own cadenza. Only video of Gould in performance before a live audience
Radio	2-21-55	CBC Symphony Orchestra	Beethoven	Concerto No. 3 in C minor, Op. 37	Heinz Unger conducting CBC Symphony Orchestra
Radio	3-29-55	Toronto Symphony Orchestra	Bach	Concerto No. 1 in D minor, BWV 1052	Sir Ernest MacMillan conducting Toronto Symphony Orchestra
Radio	10-19-55	CBC Wednesday Night	Beethoven	Sonata No. 32 in C minor, Op. 111	

Radio	1-17-56	CBC Concert Hall	Bach	Partita No. 6 in E minor, BWV 830	
			Gibbons	Pavan and Galliard for the Lord of Salisbury	
Radio	4-25-56	Glenn Gould Interview			Gould interviewed by Eric McLean
Radio	10-23-56	Toronto Symphony Orchestra	Beethoven	Concerto No. 2 in B-flat major, Op. 19	Incomplete. Walter Susskind conducting Toronto Symphony
Radio	1957	Glenn Gould Interview			Interviewed by Ted Viets in Vienna during 1957 European tour
TV	2-20-57	Chrysler Festival	Bach	Partita No. 5 in G major, BWV 829	Allemand, Sarabande, and Courante movements
			Mahler	Symphony No. 2 in C minor, *Resurrection*	Gould conducting an unidentified orchestra with Maureen Forrester, soprano, in the fourth movement, "*Uhrlicht*"
Radio	5-26-57		Beethoven	Concerto No. 3 in C minor, Op. 37	Herbert von Karajan conducting the Berlin Philharmonic
Radio	9-11-57	International Geophysical Year Concert	Bach	Concerto No. 5 in F minor, BWV 1056	Nicholas Goldschmidt conducting the CBC Orchestra in Massey Hall, Toronto
TV	10-22-57	L'Heure du Concert	Bach	Concerto No. 1 in D minor, BWV 1052	Thomas Mayer conducting the Ottawa Symphony Orchestra in Montreal

SOURCE	AIRDATE	SERIES NAME	COMPOSER	WORKS	NOTES
Radio	7-15-58	Assignment			Interviewed by Hugh Thomson
TV	1959	On the Record	Bach	*Italian Concerto*, BWV 971	Excerpt. National Film Board production, filmed in CBS Studios, New York
TV	1959	Off the Record	Bach	Partita No. 2 in C minor, BWV 826	Excerpt
			Bach	*The Well-Tempered Clavier*, Book I: Fugue No. 6 in D minor, BWV 851	
Radio	1959		Mozart	Symphony No. 1 in E-flat major, KV 16	Gould conducting the CBC Vancouver Orchestra
			Schubert	Symphony No. 4	
Radio	8-59	Glenn Gould at Salzburg Festival, 1959	Bach	*Goldberg Variations*, BWV 988	
Radio	12-4-59	Project 60/At Home with Glenn Gould			Interviewed at his Lake Simcoe home by CBC producer Vincent Tovell, with brief musical examples transcribed for piano from a Bruckner Quintet, Sibelius's Fifth Symphony, and Gould's own Quartet
Radio	12-30-59	Glenn Gould Interview			American music critic Alan Rich interviews Gould in Berkeley, California

Medium	Date	Program	Composer	Work	Notes
Radio	1960's	Summertime/Vancouver International Festival	Schoenberg	Das Buch der hängenden Garten, Op. 15; Eight Songs: Op. 6 "Traumleben"; Four Songs: Op. 2 "Waldsonne"	With Kerstin Meyer, soprano
			Schoenberg	Ode to Napoleon Bonaparte, Op. 41	With Donald Brown, narrator, and the Vancouver String Quartet
			Schoenberg	Suite for Piano, Op. 25	
TV	7-26-60	Special/Stratford Festival	Beethoven	Violin Sonata in C minor, Op. 30, No. 2	In rehearsal of third movement with violinist Oscar Shumsky. Opens with Gould playing excerpts from Tchaikowsky's Romeo and Juliet
TV	10-11-60	Recital	Beethoven	Sonata No. 17 in D minor, Tempest, Op. 31, No. 2	
			Brahms	Intermezzo in E-flat major, Op. 117, No. 1	Excerpt
			Sweelinck	Fantasia in D minor in Organ (arr. for Piano)	
TV	2-6-61	Festival 61/The Subject Is Beethoven	Beethoven	Sonata for Cello and Piano No. 3 in A major, Op. 69	With Leonard Rose, cello
			Beethoven	Eroica Variations, Op. 35	
			Mendelssohn	Variations sérieuses	Excerpt
TV	1-14-61	Parade	Beethoven	Sonata in E-flat major, Op. 31, No. 3	Gould in comedy routine for children, filmed in Vancouver. Plays brief excerpt

SOURCE	AIRDATE	SERIES NAME	COMPOSER	WORKS	NOTES
Radio	1962	Stratford Music Festival 1962	Beethoven	Sonata for Cello and Piano No. 3 in A major, Op. 69	With Leonard Rose, cello
			Beethoven	Trio in D major, *Ghost*, Op. 70, No. 1	With Leonard Rose, cello, and Oscar Shumsky, violin
TV	1-14-62	Sunday Concert/ Music in the USSR			Includes discussion and excerpts from Balakirev, Glinka, and Tchaikowsky
			Prokofiev	Sonata No. 7 in B-flat major, Op. 83	
			Shostakovich	Piano Quintet, Op. 57	With the Symphonia Quartet
Radio	3-13-62	Ten Minutes with.../National School Telecast			Vincent Tovell interviews Gould on music and instruction
TV	4-8-62	Sunday Concert/ Glenn Gould on Bach	Bach	*Art of the Fugue:* No. 4, BWV 1080	Played on Gould's "harpsipiano" CD-318
			Bach	Brandenburg Concerto No. 5 in D Major, BWV 1050	Gould conducts from piano, with Oscar Shumsky, violin, and Julius Baker, flute
			Bach	St. Anne Fugue in E-flat major, BWV 552	On organ
			Bach	*Widerstehe doch der Sünde,* BWV 54	With Russell Oberlin, countertenor

Medium	Date	Program	Composer	Work	Notes
Radio	8-8-62	CBC Wednesday Night/Arnold Schoenberg: The Man Who Changed Music			Documentary on Schoenberg's life and works written and narrated by Gould. Includes interviews with Gertrude Schoenberg, Aaron Copland, Goddard Lieberson, Peter Ostwald, Istvan Anhalt, and Winthrop Sargeant. Some material used for 1974 *Music of Schoenberg* series
Radio	9-4-62		Brahms	Concerto No. 1 in D minor, Op. 15	Leonard Bernstein conducting the New York Philharmonic
TV	10-15-62	Festival/Richard Strauss: A Personal View	Strauss	Four Last Songs: No. 3, "Beim Schlafengehen"	With Lois Marshall, soprano. Interprets and talks about his affinity for Strauss's music
			Strauss	Four Songs Op. 27: No. 2, "Cäcilie"	With Lois Marshall
			Strauss	Le Bourgeois Gentilhomme Suite, Op. 60	With Oscar Shumsky playing violin and conducting an unidentified orchestra
			Strauss	Three Ophelia Songs, Op. 67	With Lois Marshall, soprano
			Strauss	Violin Sonata in E flat, major Op. 18	First movement, with Oscar Shumsky, violin
Radio	12-5-62	CBC Wednesday Night/Glenn Gould Recital	Bach	Partita No. 4 in D major, BWV 828	15th anniversary of this program series

SOURCE	AIRDATE	SERIES NAME	COMPOSER	WORKS	NOTES
TV	10-15-63	Festival/The Anatomy of Fugue	Bach	*The Well-Tempered Clavier*, Book II: Fugue No. 22 in B-flat minor, BWV 891; Fugue No. 7 in E-flat major, BWV 876	Introduces works and discusses the history and development of fugues and counterpoint. Program includes extensive discussion by Gould, using Elizabeth Benson-Guy and Patricia Rideout's performance of Lassus's "Who Followeth Me?" and Marenzio's "Spring Returns," madrigals, the fugue from Mozart's Adagio and Fugue in C minor performed by the Canadian String Quartet, Do Re Mi, and his own contrapuntal improvisation developed from the American and British national anthems as illustration
			Beethoven	Sonata No. 29 in B-flat major, *Hammerklavier*, Op. 106; Sonata No. 31 in A-flat major, Op. 110	
			Gould	"So You Want to Write a Fugue?"	Gould introduces his work and conducts the Canadian String Quartet and Concert Singers
			Hindemith	Sonata No. 3 in B-flat major	Last movement

TV	6-17-64	Festival/Concert for four Wednesdays	Bach	Goldberg Variations, BWV 988	Speaks about the Goldbergs and then performs Variation No. 30 and the Nine Canonic Variations
			Beethoven	Sonata No. 30 in E major, Op. 109	
			Sweelinck	Fantasia in D minor	
			Webern	Variations for Piano, Op. 27	
Radio	1-10-65	CBC Sunday Night/ Dialogues on the Prospects of Recording			Program written and narrated by Gould. Explores the roles of artists, editors, critics and engineers in the music of modern society. Includes interviews with Schuyler Chapin, John Hammond, Paul Myers, Marshall McLuhan, Diana Menuhin, Robert Offergeld, Leon Fleisher and Ludwig Diehn. Musical illustrations from Foss, Raaijmaker, Martin, Pousseur, and Stravinsky
Radio	1-27-65	Glenn Gould Interview			Interviewed by Patricia Moore of the CBC International Service Bureau on Schoenberg, Stravinsky, and recording. Broadcast in Moscow as five separate programs

SOURCE	AIRDATE	SERIES NAME	COMPOSER	WORKS	NOTES
TV	1966	Conversations with Glenn Gould: Bach			First of a four-part program co-produced by the BBC and PBS/Washington, D.C., of Gould in conversation with Humphrey Burton of the BBC. Opens with *Goldberg Variation* No. 4. They discuss the role of the performer and listener, and the advantages of recording over the concert experience.
TV	1966	Conversations with Glenn Gould: Beethoven			Focuses on tempi, using illustrations from the Third and *Emperor* Concerti, Op. 10, Nos. 1 and 2, and Op. 109
TV	1966	Conversations with Glenn Gould: Richard Strauss			Gould speaks of his love for Strauss's music. Plays excerpts from *Metamorphosen* and the Three Ophelia Songs
TV	1966	Conversations with Glenn Gould: Arnold Schoenberg			Discusses his view of Schoenberg's development, using excerpts from *Ode to Napoleon Bonaparte*, Op. 41, and Suite for Piano, Op. 25, and the Second Chamber Symphony, Op. 38

Medium	Date	Program	Composer	Works	Notes
TV	5-18-66	Festival/Duo: Yehudi Menuhin and Glenn Gould	Bach	Sonata for Violin and Harpsichord: No. 4 in C minor, BWV 1017	Gould and Menuhin discuss each piece before their performance
			Beethoven	Violin Sonata in G major, Op. 96, No. 10	
			Schoenberg	*Phantazy* for Violin and Piano, Op. 47	
TV	11-9-66	Intertel/The Culture Explosion			Gould is one of many interviewed by Alan Trebek on whether a cultural explosion has occurred
Radio	11-13-66	The Art of Glenn Gould/On Records and Recording			First of a weekly program series which ran from 11-13-66 to 4-30-67 which aired all of Gould's CBS recordings. The four programs listed below include Gould's comments. On this broadcast Gould explored the question of honesty in recording versus live performance
			Bach	*Art of the Fugue:* No. 3, BWV 1080; *Goldberg Variations*, BWV 988; Partita No. 5 in G major, BWV 829; *The Well-Tempered Clavier*, Book I: Prelude No. 8 in E-flat minor, BWV 853	Excerpts
					Aria
					Preambulum

SOURCE	AIRDATE	SERIES NAME	COMPOSER	WORKS	NOTES
			Beethoven	Concerto No. 5 in E-flat major, *Emperor*, Op. 73	With Leopold Stokowski conducting the American Symphony Orchestra
			Schoenberg	Five Piano Pieces, Op. 23, No. 2; Three Piano Pieces, Op. 11	Excerpts
			Strauss	*Enoch Arden*, Op. 38	Excerpt, with Claude Rains, narrator
Radio	11-23-66	Ideas/The Psychology of Improvisation			Discusses the nature of improvisation
Radio	11-29-66	CBC Tuesday Night/Glenn Gould in Recital	Bach	*The Well-Tempered Clavier*, Book II: Fugues No. 1 in C major, BWV 870; No. 2 in C minor, BWV 871; No. 6 in D minor, BWV 875; No. 7 in E-flat major, BWV 876	
			Hindemith	Sonata No. 1 in A major	
			Mozart	Fantasia in C minor, KV 475	

Medium	Date	Program	Composer	Work	Notes
Radio	1967	CBC Tuesday Night/ Glenn Gould in Recital	Beethoven	Sonata No. 29 in B-flat major, *Hammerklavier*, Op. 106	
			Mozart	Fantasia in C minor, KV 396	
Radio	3-12-67	The Art of Glenn Gould	Bach	*The Well-Tempered Clavier*, Book I: No. 1 in C major, BWV 846; No. 2 in C minor, BWV 847; No. 3 in C-sharp major, BWV 848; No. 4 in C-sharp minor, BWV 849	
			Gould	String Quartet, Op. 1	Discusses the structure of his quartet
TV	3-19-67	Music for a Sunday Afternoon	Beethoven	Sonata No. 17 in D minor, *Tempest*, Op. 31, No. 2; Thirty-two Variations in C minor	Excerpts
			Mozart	Sonata No. 13 in B-flat major, KV 333	
Radio	3-19-67	The Art of Glenn Gould	Bach	Two- and Three-Part Inventions, BWV 772–801	
			Gould	"So You Want to Write a Fugue?"	Discusses the theory and structure of his composition

SOURCE	AIRDATE	SERIES NAME	COMPOSER	WORKS	NOTES
TV	3-29-67	Festival/To Every Man His Own Bach			Discusses the obsolescence of the concert hall and the future of recording with Humphrey Burton of the BBC
			Bach	*Goldberg Variations*, BWV 988	Performs Variation No. 4 for the opening and Variation No. 30 for the closing of the program
			Beethoven	Concerto No. 5 in E-flat major, *Emperor*, Op. 73	Excerpt
			Beethoven	Sonata No. 5 in C minor, Op. 10, No. 1; Thirty-two Variations in C minor	
Radio	4-2-67	The Art of Glenn Gould	Gould	Conference at Port Chillkoot	Satirical documentary written by Gould on music critics' conference. Musical illustrations are from Schoenberg's Songs, Op. 2, and Book I of *The Well-Tempered Clavier*
Radio	5-7-67	Master Musician/Yehudi Menuhin			Gould introduces this series airing Menuhin's complete discography. Plays a recording of Menuhin at 14 performing Elgar's Violin Concerto
Radio	5-23-67	CBC Tuesday Night/Glenn Gould in Recital	Beethoven	Bagatelles, Op. 126: No. 1 in G major; No. 2 in G	

minor, No. 5 in C major; *Eroica Variations*, Op. 35; Sonata No. 18 in E-flat major, Op. 31, No. 3

Radio	9-19-67	CBC Tuesday Night/ Glenn Gould in Recital	Anhalt	Fantasia for Piano	
			Byrd	My Ladye Nevelle's Booke: Sixth Pavan and Galliard; A Voluntary; First Galliard	
			Mozart	Sonata No. 5 in G major, KV 283	
			Prokofiev	Sonata No. 7 in B-flat major, Op. 83	
TV	11-15-67	Centennial Performance	Bach	Concerto No. 7 in G minor, BWV 1058	Vladimir Golschmann conducting the Toronto Symphony Orchestra
			Strauss	*Burleske* for Piano and Orchestra in D minor	
Radio	11-23-67	CBC Centenary Concerts/Glenn Gould in Recital	Bach	*Art of the Fugue:* Nos. 9, 11, 13, BWV 1080; English Suite No. 1 in A major, BWV 806; Toccata in D minor, BWV 913	

SOURCE	AIRDATE	SERIES NAME	COMPOSER	WORKS	NOTES
Radio	12-11-67	The Best of Ideas		The Search for Petula Clark	Discusses the music and image of Petula Clark
Radio	12-28-67	Ideas	Gould	The Idea of North	The first documentary in the *Solitude Trilogy*, written and produced by Gould. Cast: Wally Maclean (narrator), R.A.J. Phillips, James Lotz, Frank Vallee, Marianne Schroeder
TV	1968	World of Music			Host for weekly series which ran from 2-4 to 3-17-68. On the last program, Gould introduces and comments extensively between acts of Mozart's *Abduction from the Seraglio*, KV 384
Radio	2-8-68	CBC Thursday Night/Glenn Gould in Recital	Beethoven	Sonata No. 24 in F-sharp major, Op. 78	Written and introduced by Gould
			C.P.E. Bach	*Würtemburg* Sonata No. 1 in A minor, WQ 49	
			Scarlatti	Sonata in D major, L. 463; Sonata in G major, L. 486	
			Scriabin	Sonata No. 3 in F-sharp minor, Op. 23	
Radio	5-20-68	Ideas		Anti Alea	Written and produced by Gould. Interviews Milton Babbitt, James Lyons, and Paul Myers on the subject of "chance" in music

Radio	6-11-68	CBC Tuesday Night/ Glenn Gould in Recital	Beethoven/ Liszt	Symphony No. 6 in F major, *Pastoral*, Op. 68	Outlines the background of Liszt's transcriptions of Beethoven's nine symphonies
Radio	6-11-68	CBC Tuesday Night/ The Stratford Festival			Discusses music festivals with Louis Applebaum
Radio	11-10-68	Sunday Supplement			A news magazine and public affairs program hosted and co-produced by Gould. Subjects include Walter Carlos's *Switched-on Bach*, the closing of the mines on Belle Isle, Newfoundland, and the movie *Charge of the Light Brigade*
Radio	12-3-68	CBC Tuesday Night	Mozart	Sonata No. 6 in D major, KV 284; No. 7 in C major, KV 309; No. 8 in A minor, KV 310	Discusses Mozart with James Kent
Radio	12-26-68	CBC Thursday Music	Gibbons	Fantasy in C major; Pavan and Galliard for the Earl of Salisbury; Italian Ground Bass	Discusses the music of Gibbons and Hindemith's *Gebrauchsmusik* with James Kent
			Haydn	Sonata No. 59 in E-flat major, XVI/49	
			Hindemith	Sonata No. 3 in B flat	

SOURCE	AIRDATE	SERIES NAME	COMPOSER	WORKS	NOTES
Radio	3-13-69	CBC Thursday Music/Glenn Gould in Recital	Bach	Overture in the French Style, BWV 831	Discusses the role of keys in diatonic music, Bach's affinity for B minor, and Berg's "tonal feelings" with James Kent
			Berg	Sonata, Op. 1	
			Brahms	Intermezzo in B minor, Op. 119, No. 1	
TV	5-8-69	Telescope/Variations on Glenn Gould	Beethoven/Liszt	Symphony No. 6 in F Major, *Pastoral*, Op. 68	Excerpt acts as backdrop
Radio	5-20-69	The Art of Glenn Gould/Take One	Bach	Concerto No. 1 in D minor, BWV 1052	Incomplete rehearsal with Vladimir Golschmann conducting Columbia Symphony Orchestra. Gould and co-host Ken Haslam discuss concert versus live performance
			Bach	Partita No. 5 in G major, BWV 829	
Radio	5-27-69	The Art of Glenn Gould/Take Two	Brahms	Intermezzo in A minor, Op. 76, No. 7	Gould and Hasdam perform a skit on concert-going public
			Prokofiev	Sonata No. 7 in B-flat major	
Radio	6-3-69	The Art of Glenn Gould/Take Three	Gould	The Search for Petula Clark	Rebroadcast
			Strauss	*Enoch Arden*, Op. 38	Claude Rains, narrator; Gould and Haslam discuss Strauss

Radio	6-10-69	The Art of Glenn Gould/Take Four	Schoenberg	Piano Concerto, Op. 42	Robert Craft conducting the CBC Symphony Orchestra. Gould and Haslam play tapes of Arnold and Gertrude Schoenberg
Radio	6-17-69	The Art of Glenn Gould/Take Five	Mozart	Concerto No. 24 in C minor, KV 491	Walter Susskind conducting the CBC Symphony Orchestra in Massey Hall, Toronto. Gould and Haslam discuss Mozart
			Mozart	Sonata No. 15, KV 545; No. 3 in B-flat major, KV 281; No. 5 in G major, KV 283	
Radio	6-24-69	The Art of Glenn Gould/Take Six	Bach	Concerto No. 7 in G minor, BWV 1058	Vladimir Golschmann conducting the Columbia Symphony Orchestra
			Bach	Sinfonia and Invention in B minor, BWV 786; E minor, BWV 778; G minor, BWV 782; G major, BWV 781	
			Bach	The Well-Tempered Clavier, Book I: Fugues No. 1 in C major, BWV 846; No. 2 in C minor, BWV 847; No. 3 in C-sharp major, BWV 848	

SOURCE	AIRDATE	SERIES NAME	COMPOSER	WORKS	NOTES
Radio	6-31-69	The Art of Glenn Gould/Take Seven	Anhalt	Fantasia for Piano	Gould and Lamont Tilden, co-hosts. Gould interviews Anhalt about his *Cento* (excerpt played)
			Brahms	Intermezzo in A major, Op. 118, No. 2	
			Scriabin	Sonata No. 3 in F-sharp minor, Op. 23	
Radio	7-8-69	The Art of Glenn Gould/Take Eight	Beethoven	Concerto No. 4 in G major, Op. 58	Gould discusses with co-host Bill Hawes his trouble with the opening of the 4th Concerto
Radio	7-15-69	The Art of Glenn Gould/Take Nine	Beethoven	Concerto No. 5 in E-flat major, *Emperor*, Op. 73	Leopold Stokowski conducting the American Symphony. Gould plays his interview with psychiatrist Joseph Stevens about the psychology of the virtuoso
Radio	7-22-69	The Art of Glenn Gould/Take Ten	Gould	Anti-Alea	Rebroadcast
			Krenek	Sonata No. 3	First and last movements. Gould discusses twelve-tone music
Radio	7-29-69	The Art of Glenn Gould/Take Eleven			Gould discusses with cohost Alan Maitland his desert island discography

			Composer	Work	Description
Radio	8-5-69	The Art of Glenn Gould/Take Twelve	Beethoven/ Liszt	Symphony No. 5 in C minor, Op. 67	Co-hosts Gould and Haslam play a skit on a musicologists' conference evaluating Gould's recording, featuring Gould as Sir Humphrey Pryce-Davies
Radio	8-12-69	The Art of Glenn Gould/Take Thirteen	Schoenberg	*Das Buch der hängenden Gärten*, Op. 15	Gould discusses with Haslam how a rift developed with the Juilliard Quartet over interpretation of the Schumann Quartet
			Schumann	Quartet in E-flat major	
Radio	8-19-69	The Art of Glenn Gould/Take Fourteen	Brahms	Intermezzo in E-flat major, Op. 117, No. 1; Intermezzo in B-flat minor, Op. 117. No. 2	Co-hosted by Gould and Bill Hawes. Gould interviews pianist David Bar-Illan about new approaches to concert programs
			Hétu	*Variations pour piano*	
			Mozart	Sonata No. 9 in D major, KV 311	
Radio	8-26-69	The Art of Glenn Gould/Take Fifteen	Beethoven	Concerto No. 3 in C minor, Op. 37	Co-hosted by Gould and Bill Hawes. Gould interviews Norman McLaren about the soundtracks for his films *Spheres, Pas de Deux, Mosaic,* and *Canon*
Radio	9-2-69	The Art of Glenn Gould/Take Sixteen	Bach	Partita No. 5 in G major, BWV 829; Partita No. 6 in E minor, BWV 830	Gould and cohost Ken Haslam discuss the relationship between harmonic and rhythmic elements in Bach, and Schoenberg's use of the dance form in his Suite
			Schoenberg	Suite for Piano, Op. 25	

SOURCE	AIRDATE	SERIES NAME	COMPOSER	WORKS	NOTES
Radio	9-9-69	The Art of Glenn Gould/Take Seventeen	Beethoven	Sonata No. 32 in C minor, Op. 111; No. 4 in C-sharp minor, *Moonlight*, Op. 27, No. 2; No. 8 in C minor, *Pathétique*, Op. 13	Host Ken Haslam with Gould as Theodore Slutz
Radio	9-16-69	The Art of Glenn Gould/Take Eighteen	Gould	The Idea of North	Gould rebroadcasts and talks about his documentary
Radio	9-23-69	The Art of Glenn Gould/Take Nineteen	Bach	*Art of the Fugue*, BWV 1080	Gould speaks with co-host Ken Haslam about the fugues of Bach, Mozart, Bartok, Verdi, Buxtehude, and Beethoven
			Gould	"So You Want to Write a Fugue?"	
Radio	9-30-69	The Art of Glenn Gould/Take Twenty	Gould	Conference at Port Chillkoot	Gould and Haslam discuss critics and criticism. Rebroadcast of 4-2-67 program
			Mozart	Sonata in D major, KV 284	Last movement
Radio	10-7-69	The Art of Glenn Gould/Take Twenty-one	Gould	On the Moog	Gould and Haslam talk about Walter Carlos's recordings. Rebroadcast of 11-10-68 program

Radio	11-12-69			The Latecomers	Broadcast in Ottawa, Vancouver, and Winnipeg only. Gould's contrapuntal documentary on Newfoundland, the second in his *Solitude Triology*
Radio	11-29-69	CBC Tuesday Night/ Glenn Gould in Recital	Gould		Includes Gould discussion with Haslam on Scriabin in relation to the Impressionists
			Brahms	Intermezzo in A major, Op. 118, No. 2	
			Mozart	Sonatas in B-flat major, KV 333; B-flat major, KV 570	
			Pentland	Shadows (Ombres)	
			Scriabin	Sonata, No. 5, Op. 53	
Radio	1970's	EBU Recital	Bach	Variations in the Italian Style, BWV 989	Co-production with the European Broadcast Union and CBC
			Beethoven	Variations in F major, Op. 34	
			Bizet	*Variations chromatiques*, Op. 3	
			Byrd	My Ladye Nevelle's Booke: Hugh Ashton's Ground; Sellinger's Round	
			Webern	Variations for Piano, Op. 27	

SOURCE	AIRDATE	SERIES NAME	COMPOSER	WORKS	NOTES
TV	2-18-70	Special/The Well-Tempered Listener			Conceived and developed by Gould. Talks with Curtis Davis about counterpoint and its demise with the development of the sonata form
			Bach	*The Well-Tempered Clavier*, Book II: Fugue No. 14 in F-sharp minor, BWV 883	Played on harpsichord
			Bach	*The Well-Tempered Clavier*, Book II: Fugue No. 22 in B-flat minor, BWV 891	First 25 bars played alternately on piano and harpsichord
			Bach	*The Well-Tempered Clavier*, Book II: Fugue No. 3 in C-sharp major, BWV 872	Excerpt, combination of harpsichord and piano performances
			Bach	*The Well-Tempered Clavier*, Book II: Fugue No. 9 in E major, BWV 878	Excerpt, combination of piano, harpsichord, and organ performances
Radio	7-23-70	CBC Thursday Night/Glenn Gould in Recital	Chopin	Sonata No. 3 in B minor, Op. 58	Gould in conversation with Haslam on the revival of interest in Romantic composers. Gould plays tape he has prepared on the music of the 1960's, which includes composers Terry Riley, Boulez, Barber, and Babbitt
			Mendelssohn	Songs Without Words, Op. 19, No. 1; Op. 19, No. 2; Op. 30, No. 3; Op. 85, No. 2; Op. 85, No. 5	

	Date	Program	Composer	Work	Notes
TV	8-5-70	Special		The Idea of North	Television version of original radio broadcast, directed by Judith Pearlman
TV	12-9-70	Special/Glenn Gould Plays Beethoven	Beethoven	Bagatelles, Op. 126: No. 3 in E-flat major	
			Beethoven	Concerto No. 5 in E-flat major, *Emperor*, Op. 73	Karel Ancerl conducting the Toronto Symphony
			Beethoven	Variations in F major, Op. 34	
Radio	2-2-71	CBC Tuesday Night/Encore		On Stokowski	Documentary written and produced by Gould in cooperation with the BBC, CBC, and NET/Boston
Radio	9-30-71	Musicscope	Bach	English Suite No. 2 in A minor, BWV 807; French Suites No. 5 in G major, BWV 816; No. 6 in E major, BWV 817	Gould interviews Hans Eichner of the University of Toronto on the influences of French culture on Germany in Bach's time
Radio	7-18-72	CBC Tuesday Night/Glenn Gould in Recital	Grieg	Sonata in E minor, Op. 7	Program on Norwegian composers, written and produced by Gould. Also aired by Norwegian radio NRK
			Valen	Sonata No. 2, Op. 38	
Radio	8-26-72	The Scene			Interviewed about his sound track for the film of Vonnegut's *Slaughterhouse-Five*

SOURCE	AIRDATE	SERIES NAME	COMPOSER	WORKS	NOTES
Radio	10-7-72	The Scene			Debate with Harry Brown on the value of competitive sports and games. Gould impersonates boxer Dominico Pastrono and others
Radio	2-27-73	CBC Tuesday Night/ Glenn Gould in Recital	Bach	French Suites No. 1 in D minor, BWV 812; No. 2 in C minor, BWV 813	
			Scriabin	Two Pieces Op. 57: "Désir" and "Caresse dansée"	
			Wagner/ Gould	*Siegfried Idyll*	Discusses his Wagner transcription with Ken Haslam, playing a few bars "straight," and then showing how he transcribed them
TV	1974	Chemins de la Musique/Glenn Gould: La Retraite	Bach	Partita No. 6 in E minor, BWV 830	First of four shows directed by Bruno Monsaingeon for ORTF
			Byrd	Sixth Galliard	
			Gibbons	Pavane for the Earl of Salisbury	
			Schoenberg	Suite for Piano, Op. 25.	
			Wagner/ Gould	*Meistersinger* Prelude	Excerpts

TV	1974	Chemins de la Musique/Glenn Gould: L'Alchimiste	Bach	English Suite No. 1 in A major, BWV 806	Recording session in Eaton Auditorium of Sarabande, and Bourées I and II with Engineer Lorne Tulk and Producer James Kent. Directed by Bruno Monsaingeon for French national television, ORTF
			Scriabin	Two Pieces Op. 57: "Désir" and "Caresse dansée"	
TV	1974	Chemins de la Musique/Glenn Gould: 1974	Berg	Sonata, Op. 1	Discusses "So You Want to Write a Fugue?"; shows kinescope, and The Idea of North. Directed by Bruno Monsaingeon for ORTF
			Schoenberg	Suite for Piano, Op. 25	Intermezzo
			Webern	Variations for Piano, Op. 27	
TV	1974	Chemins de la Musique/Glenn Gould: Partita No. 6	Bach	Partita No. 6 in E minor, BWV 830	Directed by Monsaingeon for ORTF
Radio	1-15-74	CBC Tuesday Night		Pablo Casals: A Radio Portrait	Written and produced by Gould. Uses the same contrapuntal radio techniques as in his Solitude Trilogy. Includes interviews with Casals' biographer Albert Kahn, several of his Marlboro Music Festival students, and Casals in rehearsal talking about Bach

SOURCE	AIRDATE	SERIES NAME	COMPOSER	WORKS	NOTES
TV	2-20-74	Musicamera/Music in Our Time: No. 1 The Age of Ecstasy, 1900–1910	Berg	Sonata, Op. 1	First of an unfinished series in which Gould discusses modern art and music, decade by decade. Directed by Mario Prizek
			Debussy	Rhapsodie for Clarinet, No. 1	With James Campbell, clarinet
			Schoenberg	Eight Songs, Op. 6: No. 1, "Traumleben"; No. 4, "Verlassen"; No. 7, "Lockung"; No. 8, "Der Wanderer"	With Helen Vanni, soprano
			Scriabin	Albumleaf, Op. 58; Prelude in E major, Op. 33, No. 1; Prelude in C major, Op. 33, No. 2; Prelude in E-flat major, Op. 49, No. 2; Prelude in F major, Op. 45, No. 3; Two Pieces: "Désir" and "Caresse dansée," Op. 57	
Radio	9-11-74	Music of Today/Schoenberg Series: No. 1			Series commemorating the 100th anniversary of Schoenberg's birth, written and hosted by Gould. Entire series uses recordings and includes no live performance. In this first program, Gould discusses the accessibility of Schoenberg's music

Medium	Date	Series	Composer	Work	Notes
			Schoenberg	Eight Songs Op. 6: No. 4, "Verlassen"	With Helen Vanni, soprano
Radio	9-18-74	Music of Today/Schoenberg Series: No. 2 A Schoenberg Liederabend	Schoenberg	Eight Songs Op. 6: No. 1, "Traumleben"; No. 7, "Lockung"; No. 8, "Der Wanderer"	With Helen Vanni, soprano. Gould discusses early vocal composition
			Schoenberg	Four Songs Op. 2: No. 4 "Waldsonne"	With Ellen Faull, soprano
			Schoenberg	Six Songs Op. 3: No. 4, "Hochzeitslied"	With Helen Vanni, soprano
			Schoenberg	Two Songs Op. 1: No. 1, "Dank"	With Donald Gramm, bass-baritone
Radio	9-25-74	Music of Today/Schoenberg Series: No. 3 Schoenberg the Inventor	Schoenberg	Six Little Piano Pieces, Op. 19	Gould discusses Schoenberg's middle period, his early experiments with vocal composition, and the "ten silent years."
			Schoenberg	Suite for Piano, Op. 25	
Radio	10-2-74	Music of Today/Schoenberg Series: No. 4 The Crusader	Schoenberg	*Ode to Napoleon Bonaparte*, Op. 41	Gould's recording, with the Juilliard Quartet and John Horton, reciter. Discusses Schoenberg's American period with Eric Leinsdorf.
Radio	10-9-74	Music of Today/Schoenberg Series: No. 5 The Symphonist Part 1	Schoenberg	*Pelleas und Melisande*, Op. 5	Excerpts. Gould discusses Strauss's and Mahler's influence on Schoenberg's symphonic style and their personal relationships

SOURCE	AIRDATE	SERIES NAME	COMPOSER	WORKS	NOTES
Radio	10-16-74	Music of Today/ Schoenberg Series: No. 6 The Symphonist Part 2	Schoenberg	Piano Concerto, Op. 42	Robert Craft conducting the CBC Symphony Orchestra. Gould discusses Schoenberg's American compositions and the 19th-century traditions
Radio	10-23-74	Music of Today/ Schoenberg Series: No. 7 Operatic Works	Schoenberg	*Moses und Aaron* and *Erwartung*, Op. 17	Excerpts. Show includes clips from 1962 interviews between Gould and Gertrude Schoenberg and others
Radio	10-23-74	Musicamera			Gould introduces the series that is to follow, excerpting clips from each program
Radio	10-30-74	Music of Today/ Schoenberg Series: No. 8 The Transcriptionist			Co-hosts Gould and Haslam discuss Schoenberg's transcriptions, including those of Bach and Brahms
Radio	11-6-74	Music of Today/ Schoenberg Series: No. 9			Includes clips from Gould's 1962 interview with John Cage, discussing his study with Schoenberg
Radio	11-13-74	Music of Today/ Schoenberg Series: No. 10	Schoenberg	*Phantasy* for Violin and Piano, Op. 47	With Israel Baker, violin.

Type	Date	Program/Title	Composer	Work	Notes
Radio	11-19-74			Schoenberg, the Firs[t] Hundred Years—A Documentary Fantasy for Radio	Written and produced by Gould, using his contrapuntal radio construction. Includes interviews with Krenek, Cage, and Leinsdorf. Music includes excerpts from eleven works by Schoenberg
Radio	1-27-75	CBC Tuesday Night/Music of Schoenberg	Schoenberg	Six Little Piano Pieces, Op. 19; Suite for Piano, Op. 25	
TV	2-5-75	Musicamera/Music in Our Time: No. 2 The Flight From Order, 1910–1920	Prokofiev	Visions fugitives, No. 2, Op. 22	
			Ravel/Gould	La Valse, Op. 45	Gould performs his own transcription
			Schoenberg	Pierrot Lunaire, Op. 21	"Introduction," "Columbine," "The Dandy," "Washerwoman," "Chopin Waltz," "Madonna," and "The Sick Moon." With Patricia Rideout, narrator, and instrumental ensemble
			Strauss	Three Ophelia Songs, Op. 67	With Roxolana Roslak, soprano
TV	8-29-75	Radio As Music			Documentary of Gould discussing the construction of his radio documentaries "The Idea of North" and "Quiet in the Land" with engineers Donald Logan and John Thomson

SOURCE	AIRDATE	SERIES NAME	COMPOSER	WORKS	NOTES
TV	11-26-75	Musicamera/Music in Our Time: No. 3 New Faces, Old Forms, 1920–30	Hindemith	*Das Marienleben*, Op. 27	With Roxolana Roslak, soprano
			Poulenc	*Aubade*	Boris Brott conducting an unidentified orchestra and the Robyn Lee and Jeremy Blanton dancers
			Schoenberg	Suite for Piano, Op. 25	Intermezzo
			Walton	*Façade Suite*	Boris Brott conducting unidentified excerpts. Gould performs in duet with Patricia Rideout, soprano, for the Rhapsody
TV	1976	Musicanada	Bach	Overture in the French Style, BWV 831	Recording session in Eaton Auditorium in Toronto with engineer Lorne Tulk
Radio	1976		Gould	Documentary: Ernst Krenek	Written, produced and performed by Gould. Rejected by the BBC, and never aired
Radio	4-25-77	Ideas	Gould	Quiet in the Land	Last part of the *Solitude Trilogy*, written and produced by Gould. Explores a Mennonite community

Radio	8-22-77	August Arts National			As host, Gould plays recordings of some favorite composers, Mendelssohn and Sibelius
Radio	8-23-77	August Arts National			As host, Gould plays recordings of some favorite composers, Gibbons, Schoenberg, Bruckner
Radio	8-24-77	August Arts National			As host, Gould plays recordings of music he doesn't particularly like, but played by performers he does: Krips conducting Mozart's *Haffner* and *Jupiter* symphonies, and Alexis Weissenberg playing Schumann's *Carnaval*
Radio	8-25-77	August Arts National			As host, Gould plays recordings of late Richard Strauss: *Deutsche Motet*, Oboe Concerto, *Capriccio*, and *Metamorphosen*
Radio	8-26-77	August Arts National			As host, Gould plays recordings of Streisand and Bach
TV	12-14-77	Musicamera/Music in Our Time: No. 4 The Artist As Artisan, 1930–40	Casella	*Due ricercari sul nome BACH*, No. 1	
			Hindemith	Sonata for Trumpet in B-flat major and Piano	First and third movements, with Raymond Crisera, trumpet
			Krenek	*Wanderlied im Herbst*, Op. 71	With Patricia Rideout, soprano

SOURCE	AIRDATE	SERIES NAME	COMPOSER	WORKS	NOTES
			Prokofiev	Sonata No. 7 in B-flat major, Op. 83	First movement
			Webern	Concerto for Nine Instruments	With Boris Brott conducting an unidentified ensemble
Radio	4-2-79	Mostly Music		Le Bourgeois Hero, Part I	Contrapuntal documentary written by Gould, on Richard Strauss. Includes interviews with composers Wolfgang Sawallisch, Stanley Silverman, and Wolfgang Fortner, producer John Culshaw, Strauss biographer Norman Del Mar
Radio	4-9-79	Mostly Music		Le Bourgeois Hero, Part II	
TV	9-27-79	Cities/Glenn Gould's Toronto			Written and narrated by Gould. Directed by John McGreevy
TV	12-12-79	The Music of Man/Sound or Unsound	Scriabin	Two Pieces Op. 57, No. 1: "Désir"	As part of Yehudi Menuhin's TV series, Gould discusses recording with Menuhin and illustrates mixing Scriabin's "Désir" CBC-MAET-OECA co-production
Radio	12-81	Booktime	Gould	The Three-Cornered World	Against a musical backdrop, Gould reads selections from the first chapter of Soseki's novel

TV	9-29-83	Glenn Gould Plays Bach/No. 1: Gould Plays Bach	Bach	*Art of the Fugue:* No. 1, BWV 1080	First of four Clasart co-productions, directed by Bruno Monsaingeon, who interviews Gould about Bach
			Bach	Chromatic Fantasy and Fugue in D minor, BWV 903; Partita No. 4 in D major, BWV 828; *Italian Concerto,* BWV 971; Overture in the French Style, BWV 831; Partita No. 6 in E minor, BWV 830; *The Well-Tempered Clavier,* Book II: Fugue No. 3 in C-sharp major, BWV 872	Excerpts in several cases
TV	10-6-83	Glenn Gould Plays Bach/No. 2: Bach and the Fugue	Bach	*Art of the Fugue:* Nos. 2, 4, 15, BWV 1080; Fugue from Fantasia and Fugue on the Name BACH, BWV 898; Sinfonia No. 1 in C major, BWV 787; *The Well-Tempered Clavier,* Book II: No. 19 in A major, BWV 888; Book II: No. 22 in B-flat minor, BWV 891; No. 9 in E major, BWV 878	Clasart co-production, directed by Bruno Monsaingeon. Excerpts in several cases
TV	10-17-83	Glenn Gould Plays Bach/No. 3: The Goldberg Variations	Bach	*Goldberg Variations,* BWV 988	Clasart coproduction, directed by Bruno Monsaingeon. Filmed in CBS Studios, New York, simultaneously with CBS recording of this work

421

Gould's Published Writings

by Nancy Canning

Note: This chronological bibliography contains published material only, and does not list the radio transcripts, and unpublished items included in Tim Page's anthology, *The Glenn Gould Reader*. Several articles which were either reworked under the same or different titles are noted as such.

Books

Arnold Schoenberg—A Perspective, University of Cincinnati Press, 1964

Periodicals, Program and Liner Notes

"A Consideration of Anton Webern," program notes for the New Musical Associates' second annual presentation at the Royal Conservatory, January 9, 1954

"The Goldberg Variations," liner notes on Gould's CBS recording ML 5060, March 1956

"Beethoven's Last Three Piano Sonatas," liner notes on Gould's CBS recording ML 5130, September 1956

"The Dodecacophonist's Dilemma," *Canadian Music Journal*, Autumn 1956

"Some Beethoven and Bach Concertos," liner notes on Gould's CBS recordings ML 5211, October 1957, and ML 5298, May 1958

"Piano Music of Berg, Schoenberg, and Krenek," liner notes on Gould's CBS recording ML 5336, July 1958

"String Quartet, Op. 1," program notes for a concert of chamber music at the Cleveland Institute of Music, March 25, 1960

   Also as "Gould's String Quartet, Op. 1," liner notes on CBS recording MS 6178, October 1960

"Bodky on Bach," book review of *The Interpretation of Bach's Keyboard Works* by Erwin Bodky in *Saturday Review*, November 26, 1960

"Let's Ban Applause!" *High Fidelity*, February 1962

"An Argument for Strauss," *High Fidelity*, March 1962

"Piano Concertos by Mozart and Schoenberg," liner notes on Gould's CBS recording MS 6339, May 1962

"Richard Strauss's *Enoch Arden*," liner notes on Gould's CBS recording MS 6341, May 1962

"The Schoenberg Heritage," program notes for 1962 Stratford Festival, July 13, 1962

"Hindemith—The Early Years," program notes for 1962 Stratford Festival, July 29, 1962

"Bach and Schoenberg Concertos," program notes for a San Francisco Symphony concert, February 13–15, 1963

"Not Defector," letter to the editor in Toronto *Daily Star*, May 27, 1963

"A Strauss and Schoenberg Concert," program notes for Strauss Festival Concert, July 7, 1963

"Russian Concert," program notes for 1963 Stratford Festival, July 28, 1963

"Bach: The Six Partitas; Glenn Gould Interviewed by David Johnson," liner notes on Gould's CBS recording M2S 693, September 1963

"So You Want to Write a Fugue?," *High Fidelity*, April 1964

"Strauss and the Electronic Future," *Saturday Review*, May 30, 1964
   Also as "An Argument for Music in the Electronic Age," *Varsity Graduate*/University of Toronto, December 1964

"Advice to a Graduation," *Bulletin of the Royal Conservatory of Music of Toronto*, December, 1964

"The CBC, Camera-Wise,"* *Musical America*, March 1965

"Dialogue on the Prospects of Recordings," *Varsity Graduate: Explorations*/University of Toronto, April 1965
   Also as "The Prospects of Recording," *High Fidelity*, April 1966

"Ives' Fourth," *High Fidelity*, July 1965

"Of Time and Time Beaters,"* *High Fidelity*, August 1965

"L'Esprit de jeunesse, et de corps, et d'art,"* *High Fidelity*, December 1965

"We, Who Are About to Be Disqualified, Salute You!" *High Fidelity*, December 1966

"The Piano Music of Arnold Schoenberg," liner notes on Gould's CBS recording M2S 736, April 1966

"Yehudi Menuhin: Musician of the Year," *High Fidelity*, December 1966

"The Search for Petula Clark," *High Fidelity*, November 1967
   Also as "Why Glenn Gould *Loves* Petula Clark," Toronto *Daily Star*, November 18, 1967

"Canadian Music in the Twentieth Century," liner notes on Gould's CBS recording 32110046, November 1967

*Published under the pseudonym Dr. Herbert von Hochmeister

"Arnold Schoenberg's Chamber Symphony No. 2," liner notes on *The Music of Arnold Schoenberg*, Volume 3, M2S 709, 1967

"Beethoven's 5th Symphony on the Piano: Four Imaginary Reviews," liner notes on Gould's CBS recording MS 7095, March 1968

"Recording of the Decade . . . Is Bach Played on, of All Things, a Moog Synthesizer?" *Saturday Night*, December 1968

"Piano Sonatas by Scriabin and Prokofiev," liner notes on Gould's CBS recording MS 7173, January 1969

"'Oh, For Heaven's Sake, Cynthia, There Must Be Something Else On,'" *High Fidelity*, April 1969

"The Well-Tempered Synthesizer," liner notes on Walter Carlos's CBS recording MS 7286, October 1969

"Should We Dig Up the Rare Romantics? . . . No, They're Only a Fad," New York *Times*, November 23, 1969

"Beethoven's *'Pathétique,' 'Moonlight,'* and *'Appassionata'* Sonatas," liner notes on Gould's CBS recording MS 7413, February 1970

"Beethoven: The Man and His Time," The Guelph Spring Festival program, May 1–16, 1970

> Also as "Admit It, Mr. Gould, You Do Have Doubts About Beethoven," Toronto *Globe and Mail Magazine*, June 6, 1970
>
> > "Gould Quizzed: (a Gouldish Encounter)," *American Guild of Organists and Royal Canadian College of Organists Magazine*, November 1971
> >
> > "Glenn Gould Interviews Himself About Beethoven," *Piano Quarterly*, Fall 1972

"His Country's 'Most Experienced Hermit' Chooses a Desert Island Discography," *High Fidelity*, June 1970

"Liszt's Lament? Beethoven's Bagatelle? Or Rosemary's Babies?" review of Rosemary Brown's Philips recording PHS-900256, *High Fidelity*, December 1970

"The Idea of North," liner notes on Gould's recording, CBC Learning Systems PR-8, 1971

"The Latecomers," liner notes on Gould's recording, CBC Learning Systems PR-9, 1971

"Rubinstein: Interview," *Look*, March 9, 1971

"Radio as Music: Glenn Gould in Conversation with John Jessop," *Canada Music Book*, Spring/Summer 1971

"William Byrd and Orlando Gibbons," liner notes on Gould's CBS recording M 30825, September 1971

"Gould's Second Choice Is a Heintzman," letter to the editor, Toronto *Telegram*, September 4, 1971

"Art of the Fugue," introduction to *The Well-Tempered Clavier, Book I*, 1972

"Wagner Transcriptions," liner notes on Gould's CBS recording M 32351, 1973

"Piano Music by Grieg & Bizet, with a Confidential Caution to Critics," liner notes on Gould's CBS recording M 32040, February 1973

"Hindemith: Will His Time Come? Again?" liner notes on Gould's CBS recording M 32350, September 1973

Also as "Hindemith: Kommt seine Zeit (wieder)?" *Hindemith-Jahrbuch,* 1973, trans. Peter Mueller

"Glenn Gould: Hindemith," *Stereo Guide,* Winter 1974

"Data Bank on the Upward Scuttling Mahler," book review of *Mahler, Volume 1,* by Henry-Louis de la Grange in Toronto *Globe and Mail,* November 10, 1973

Also in *Piano Quarterly,* Spring 1974

"Glenn Gould Interviews Glenn Gould about Glenn Gould," *High Fidelity,* March 1974

"Conference at Port Chillkoot," *Piano Quarterly,* Summer 1974

"Today, Simply Politics and Prejudices in Musical America Circa 1970 . . . but for Time Capsule Scholars It's Babbitt vs. Flat Foot Floogie," book review of *Dictionary of Contemporary Music,* edited by John Vinton, in Toronto *Globe and Mail,* July 20, 1974

Also as "The Future and 'Flat-Foot Floogie'" in *Piano Quarterly,* Fall 1974

"A Festschrift for 'Ernst Who'???" book review of *Horizons Circled: Reflections on My Music* by Ernst Krenek in *Piano Quarterly,* Winter 1974/75

Also as "Krenek, the Prolific, Is Probably Best Known to the Public at Large as—Ernst Who?" in Toronto *Globe and Mail,* July 19, 1975

"An Epistle to the Parisians: Music and Technology, Part 1," *Piano Quarterly,* Winter 1974/75

"Korngold and the Crisis of the Piano Sonata," liner notes on Anton Kubalek's recording, produced by Gould, GENESIS GS1055, 1974

"Glenn Gould Talks Back," letter to the editor in Toronto *Star,* February 9, 1975

"The Grass Is Always Greener on the Outtakes: An Experiment in Listening," *High Fidelity,* August 1975

"Streisand as Schwarzkopf," *High Fidelity,* May 1976

"Back to Bach (and Belly to Belly)," book review of *The Definitive Biography of P.D.Q. Bach (1807–1742)?* by Peter Schickele in Toronto *Globe and Mail,* May 29, 1976

Also as "Fact, Fancy, or Psychohistory: Notes from the PDQ Underground," in *Piano Quarterly,* Summer 1976

"Of Mozart & Related Matters: Glenn Gould in Conversation with Bruno Monsaingeon," *Piano Quarterly,* Fall 1976

Also as "Mozart: A Personal View . . . A Conversation with Bruno Monsaingeon," liner notes on Gould's CBS recording M 35899, July 1979

"Boulez," book review of *Boulez* by Joan Peyser in *New Republic*, December 25, 1976

"Critics," *The Canadian*, February 2, 1977

"Sibelius and the Post-Romantic Piano Style," *Piano Quarterly*, Fall 1977

"The Piano Music of Sibelius," liner notes on Gould's CBS recording M 34555, November 1977

"Portrait of a Cantankerous Composer," book review of *Schoenberg: His Life, World and Work* by H. H. Stuckenschmidt in Toronto *Globe and Mail*, March 18, 1978

"In Praise of Maestro Stokowski," New York *Times Magazine*, May 14, 1978

    Also as "Stokowski in Six Scenes, Part I," *Piano Quarterly*, Winter 1977–78, "Part II," Spring 1978, and "Part III," Summer 1978

    "Stokowski: A Recollection," *Toccata: The Magazine of the Leopold Stokowski Society*, Spring 1982

"Glenn Gould," book review of *Glenn Gould: Music and Mind* by Geoffrey Payzant in Toronto *Globe and Mail*, May 27, 1978

    Also as "A Biography of Glenn Gould," in *Piano Quarterly*, Fall 1978

"A Tale of Two *Marienlebens*," liner notes on Gould's CBS recording M 234597, July 1978

"A Hawk, a Dove, and a Rabbit Called Franz Joseph," *Piano Quarterly*, Fall 1978

"Memories of Maude Harbour, or Variations on a Theme of Rubinstein," *Piano Quarterly*, Summer 1980

"The Glenn Gould Silver Jubilee Album," liner notes on Gould's CBS recording M 35914, 1980

"What the Recording Process Means to Me," *High Fidelity*, January 1983

Index

About the Author

Otto Friedrich was born in 1929 in Boston. He graduated magna cum laude from Harvard University. He was a senior writer for *Time*, and was the author of many works of nonfiction, including *City of Nets, Before the Deluge, Going Crazy*, and *Decline and Fall*, which won the George Polk Award for best book on the press. He wrote extensively for magazines, including *Harper's, The Atlantic*, and *Esquire*, and was the former managing editor of the old *Saturday Evening Post*. Otto Friedrich died in 1995.

Für Marie-Claire, meinen Augapfel

Von Ken Follett sind bei BASTEI-LÜBBE erschienen:

10026 Die Nadel
10321 Dreifach
10531 Der Mann aus St. Petersburg
10481 Der Schlüssel zu Rebecca
10704 Auf den Schwingen des Adlers
11388 Die Löwen
11675 Der Modigliani-Skandal

Ken Follett

DIE SÄULEN
DER ERDE

Aus dem Englischen von
Gabriele Conrad, Till Lohmeyer
und Christel Rost

Illustriert von
Achim Kiel und Thomas Przygodda

BASTEI
LÜBBE

BASTEI-LÜBBE-TASCHENBUCH
Band 11 896

1. + 2. Auflage September 1992
3. + 4. Auflage November 1992
5. Auflage Februar 1993
6. Auflage März 1993
8. Auflage Juni 1993
9. Auflage Juli 1993
10. Auflage August 1993

Titel der Originalausgabe:
The Pillars of the Earth
© 1989 by Ken Follett
Originalverlag: McMillan London Limited
© 1990 für die deutschsprachige Ausgabe
by Gustav Lübbe Verlag GmbH, Bergisch Gladbach
Printed in Great Britain
Einbandgestaltung und Illustrationen:
Pencil Corporate Art, Braunschweig
Achim Kiel und Thomas Przygodda
Autoren-Foto: Wendy Carrig
Satz: Kremerdruck GmbH, Lindlar
Druck und Bindung: Cox & Wyman Ltd.
ISBN 3-404-11896-0

P R O L O G

1123

Die kleinen Jungen waren die ersten, die zum Richtplatz kamen.

Es war noch dunkel, als sie aus ihren Verschlägen schlüpften. Lautlos wie Katzen huschten sie in ihren Filzstiefeln über den jungfräulichen Schnee, der sich wie Linnen über die kleine Stadt gebreitet hatte,
und entweihten ihn mit ihren Schritten. Ihr Weg führte sie, vorbei
an windschiefen Holzhütten und über Sträßchen und Gassen, die von
gefrorenem Matsch bedeckt waren, zum stillen Marktplatz, auf dem
der Galgen bereits wartete.

Die Jungen verachteten alles, was den Älteren lieb und teuer war.
Für Schönheit und Rechtschaffenheit hatten sie nur Hohn und Spott
übrig. Sahen sie einen Krüppel, so brüllten sie vor Lachen, und lief
ihnen ein verletztes Tier über den Weg, so bewarfen sie es mit Steinen,
bis es tot war. Sie waren stolz auf ihre Narben. Besonders angesehen
aber waren Verstümmelungen: Ein Junge, dem ein Finger fehlte,
konnte es leicht bis zu ihrem Anführer bringen. Sie liebten nichts so
sehr wie die Gewalt und liefen meilenweit, um Blut zu sehen.

Und niemals fehlten sie, wenn der Henker kam.

Einer der Jungen pinkelte an das Gerüst, auf dem der Galgen
stand. Ein anderer kletterte die Treppen hinauf, griff sich mit beiden
Daumen an den Hals und ließ sich fallen wie einen nassen Sack, das
Gesicht abstrus verzerrt; die andern johlten vor Vergnügen und lockten damit zwei Hunde an, die kläffend über den Marktplatz rannten.
Einer der jüngeren Burschen biß unbekümmert in einen Apfel, da
kam ein älterer, versetzte ihm einen Schlag auf die Nase und nahm
ihm den Apfel weg. In seiner Wut ergriff der Kleine einen spitzen
Stein und brannte ihn einem der Köter aufs Fell; der jaulte auf und
machte sich davon.

Dann gab's nichts mehr zu tun. Die Horde ließ sich auf den trokkenen Steinplatten im Portal der großen Kirche nieder und wartete darauf, daß irgend etwas geschah.

Hinter den Fensterläden der ansehnlichen Holz- und Steinhäuser, die den Marktplatz säumten, flackerte Kerzenschein auf. Die Küchenmägde und Lehrbuben der wohlhabenden Händler und Handwerker machten Feuer, setzten Wasser auf und kochten Hafergrütze. Der schwarze Himmel färbte sich langsam grau. Gebeugten Hauptes erschienen die Frühaufsteher in den niedrigen Türen ihrer Häuser und gingen hinab zum Fluß, um Wasser zu holen. Obwohl sie in schwere Mäntel aus grober Wolle gehüllt waren, zitterten sie vor Kälte.

Eine Weile später betrat eine Gruppe junger Männer den Platz – Knechte, Arbeiter und Lehrburschen. Sie lärmten und taten sich groß, vertrieben mit Tritten und Schlägen die Kinder aus dem Portal, lehnten sich selbst gegen die gemeißelten Steinbögen, kratzten sich, spuckten aus und redeten mit aufgesetzter Kaltschnäuzigkeit über den Tod am Galgen.

»Wenn er Glück hat, bricht der Hals gleich beim Fall«, sagte einer, »das ist kurz und schmerzlos. Aber wenn er Pech hat und der Hals bricht nicht, dann hängt er am Strick, wird puterrot im Gesicht, und er schnappt nach Luft wie ein Fisch auf dem Trockenen. Bis er dann endlich erstickt.« – »Und das kann so lange dauern, wie ein Mann braucht, um eine Meile zurückzulegen!« fiel ein anderer ein, und ein Dritter meinte, es könne alles noch viel schlimmer kommen, er selbst hätte schon einmal gesehen, wie ein Gehenkter erst gestorben sei, als sein Hals schon eine Elle lang war!

Am anderen Ende des Marktplatzes kamen die alten Weiber zusammen, soweit als irgend möglich entfernt von den jungen Männern, denen jede Grobheit und jedes böse Wort gegenüber ihren Großmüttern zuzutrauen war. Die alten Frauen waren immer schon früh auf den Beinen. Längst brannte das Feuer im Herd und war die Stube gefegt.

Die Witwe Brewster, eine kräftige Person, die sie alle als ihre Wortführerin anerkannten, gesellte sich zu ihnen. Mühelos rollte sie ein Fäßchen Bier vor sich her wie ein Kind seinen Reifen. Kaum machte sie sich daran, es zu öffnen, da standen die Kunden auch schon mit Krügen und Eimern Schlange.

Der Büttel des Vogts öffnete das Haupttor und ließ die Bauern ein, die in den Häuschen vor der Stadtmauer lebten. Einige von ihnen wollten Eier, Milch und frische Butter verkaufen, andere kamen, um sich mit Bier und Brot zu versorgen, wieder andere aber blieben einfach auf dem Marktplatz stehen und warteten auf die Hinrichtung.

Von Zeit zu Zeit verrenkten die Leute die Hälse wie vorsichtige Spatzen und spähten zur Burg hinauf, die auf einer Anhöhe über dem Städtchen thronte. Gleichmäßig stieg der Rauch aus dem Küchentrakt, hie und da blakte Fackelschein hinter den schmalen Fensterschlitzen des Wohnturms auf. Dann – hinter der dicken grauen Wolke mochte gerade die Sonne aufgehen – öffneten sich die mächtigen Holztore, und eine kleine Prozession verließ die Burg. Voran ritt auf einem feinen schwarzen Roß der Vogt, gefolgt von einem Ochsenkarren mit dem gefesselten Delinquenten. Dem Karren folgten drei Reiter, ihre Gesichter waren auf die Entfernung nicht zu erkennen, doch verriet ihre Kleidung, daß es sich um einen Ritter, einen Priester und einen Mönch handelte. Die Nachhut bildeten zwei Bewaffnete.

Sie waren alle dabeigewesen, als tags zuvor im Kirchenschiff Gericht gehalten worden war. Der Priester hatte den Dieb auf frischer Tat ertappt: Der Mönch hatte bezeugt, daß der silberne Kelch dem Kloster gehörte; der Ritter war des Diebes Herr und hatte bestätigt, daß ihm der Bursche davongelaufen sei, und der Vogt hatte das Todesurteil gefällt.

Während die kleine Gruppe langsam den Burgberg heruntergeritten kam, strömten immer mehr Menschen auf dem Marktplatz zusammen und versammelten sich um den Galgen. Zu den letzten, die kamen, gehörten die führenden Bürger der Stadt: der Schlachter, der Bäcker, zwei Ledergerber, zwei Schmiede, der Messerschmied und der Bogner. Und alle brachten sie ihre Weiber mit.

Die Menge sah der Exekution mit gemischten Gefühlen entgegen. Normalerweise genossen es die Leute, dem Henker bei der Ausübung seiner Pflicht zuzusehen, denn die Delinquenten waren meistens Diebe, und Diebe wurden von ihnen, die ihre Habe im Schweiße ihres Angesichts erwarben, mit unversöhnlichem Haß verfolgt. Der Dieb allerdings, dem es an diesem Tage an den Kragen gehen sollte, war kein gewöhnlicher Dieb. Niemand wußte, wer er war und woher er kam. Er hatte keinen Menschen aus dieser Stadt bestohlen, sondern Mönche in einem zwanzig Meilen entfernten Kloster. Und was er gestohlen hatte, war ein mit Juwelen verzierter Silberkelch von so unermeßlichem Wert, daß er nie im Leben einen Käufer dafür gefunden hätte. Das war schon etwas anderes als der Diebstahl eines Schinkens, eines neuen Messers oder eines guten Gürtels, der für seinen rechtmäßigen Besitzer einen echten Verlust bedeutete. Nein, eines so unsinnigen Vergehens wegen konnten sie den Mann nicht hassen. Gewiß, als der Ochsenkarren mit dem Gefangenen auf dem Marktplatz eintraf, johlten und pfiffen einige, aber es waren im Grunde nur halbherzige Mißfallenskundgebungen. Die einzigen, die den Dieb mit sichtlicher Begeisterung verhöhnten, waren die Gassenjungen.

Von den Bewohnern der Stadt hatte kaum einer an der Gerichtsverhandlung teilgenommen. Gerichtstage waren keine Feiertage, und sie alle hatten ihre Arbeit. Sie sahen den Dieb jetzt zum ersten Male. Er war noch ziemlich jung, zwischen Zwanzig und Dreißig; von durchschnittlicher Größe und Gestalt zwar, ansonsten aber eine recht merkwürdige Erscheinung. Seine Haut war so weiß wie der Schnee auf den Dächern, die Augen – von leuchtendem Grün – standen vor, und sein Haar war von der Farbe einer geschabten Mohrrübe. Die jungen Mädchen fanden ihn häßlich, den alten Frauen tat er leid, und die Gassenjungen lachten und lachten, bis sie umfielen.

Den Vogt kannten die Leute alle. Die drei anderen Männer jedoch, die das Schicksal des Diebes besiegelt hatten, waren Fremde. Der Ritter, ein feister Mann mit strohblondem Haar, war offenbar eine nicht unbedeutende Person, kam er doch auf einem riesigen Schlachtroß daher, das gut und gerne ebensoviel kostete, wie ein Zimmermann in zehn Jahren verdiente. Der Mönch war um vieles älter, fünfzig oder fünfundfünfzig vielleicht, ein hochgewachsener, hagerer Mann, der vornübergebeugt im Sattel saß, als mache ihm die Last des Lebens schwer zu schaffen. Am auffallendsten war der Priester. Er war noch jung, mit scharfgeschnittener Nase und glattem schwarzem Haar. Er trug ein schwarzes Gewand und einen schwarzen Umhang und ritt auf einem dunklen Fuchshengst. Sein Blick war hellwach, so lauernd und bedrohlich wie der einer Katze, die ein Nest mit jungen Mäusen wittert.

Ein kleiner Junge zielte sorgfältig und spuckte dem Gefangenen ins Gesicht – kein schlechter Schuß, denn er traf genau zwischen die Augen. Der Delinquent stieß einen Fluch aus und wollte auf den Spucker losgehen, doch die Seile, mit denen er an beiden Seiten des Karrens festgebunden war, hinderten ihn daran. Der Zwischenfall war nicht weiter bemerkenswert – nur fiel den Leuten auf, daß der Gefangene normannisches Französisch gesprochen hatte, die Sprache der Herren. So war er wohl ein Sproß aus hohem Hause? Oder bloß ein Ausländer, der von weither kam? Niemand wußte es.

Der Ochsenkarren zockelte bis zum Galgen und hielt dort an. Mit der Schlinge in der Hand stieg der Büttel des Vogts auf die Ladefläche. Der Gefangene wehrte sich. Die Gassenjungen jubelten; sie wären enttäuscht gewesen, hätte der Mann alles widerstandslos über sich ergehen lassen. Der Gefangene, durch Fesseln an seinen Hand- und Fußgelenken in seiner Bewegungsfreiheit eingeschränkt, verstand es dennoch, durch heftige Kopfstöße nach links und rechts der Schlinge zu entgehen. Da trat der Büttel, ein hünenhafter Mann, ein paar Schritte zurück, holte aus und versetzte ihm einen kräftigen Hieb in die Magengrube. Der Fremde krümmte sich; schon war der Büttel zur Stelle, warf ihm die Schlinge über den Kopf und zog den Knoten fest. Dann sprang er vom Karren herab, zog das Seil stramm und befestigte das andere Ende an einem Haken am Grunde des Galgens.

Das war der Wendepunkt. Wenn der Gefangene jetzt noch zappelte, schnürte es ihm um so schneller die Luft ab.

Die Bewaffneten nahmen ihm die Fußfesseln ab und ließen ihn dann allein auf dem Karren stehen, die Hände auf dem Rücken gebunden. Die Menge war auf einmal totenstill.

An dieser Stelle kam es bei Hinrichtungen gelegentlich zu Zwischenfällen: Die Mutter des Verurteilten bekam einen Schreikrampf, oder sein Eheweib sprang in einem letzten verzweifelten Versuch, sein Leben zu retten, mit gezücktem Messer aufs Schafott. Manchmal flehte der Verurteilte Gott um Vergebung an, in anderen Fällen brach er in wüste Verwünschungen gegen seine Henker aus. Die Bewaffneten nahmen, auf alles gefaßt, zu beiden Seiten des Schafotts Aufstellung.

Da fing der Verurteilte auf einmal zu singen an.

Er hatte eine hohe, ganz reine Tenorstimme. Er sang auf französisch, doch selbst jene, denen diese Sprache fremd war, hörten der wehmütigen Weise an, daß sie von Trauer und Abschied sprach.

> Ein Lerchenvogel tat sich einst
> im Jägernetz verfangen.
> Und singt so süß und singt so rein,
> als ob der Stimme Zauberklang –
> ihn wieder könnt' befrein.

Sein Blick ruhte dabei unentwegt auf einer Person inmitten der Menge. Die Leute wichen zurück, so daß sie alsbald für jedermann zu erkennen war.

Es war ein Mädchen, kaum mehr als fünfzehn Jahre alt. Die Menschen auf dem Marktplatz fragten sich, warum sie ihnen nicht schon früher aufgefallen war. Sie hatte langes, dunkelbraunes Haar, das ihr in üppiger Fülle über die Schultern wallte und oberhalb der breiten Stirn einen Wirbel bildete, den man im Volksmund »Teufelsmütze«

hieß. Ihre Gesichtszüge waren ebenmäßig, die Lippen voll. Die alten Frauen schlossen aus der fülligen Mitte und den schweren Brüsten sofort, daß das Mädchen schwanger und der Verurteilte der Vater ihres ungeborenen Kindes war. Allen anderen jedoch fielen nur ihre Augen auf: Sie paßten nicht recht zu dem sonst durchaus hübschen Gesicht. Sie lagen tief in ihren Höhlen und waren von außergewöhnlichem, goldenem Glanz. Wer sie ansah, wandte alsbald den Blick wieder ab, denn diese Augen schienen jedermann tief ins Herz zu schauen und auch die geheimsten Geheimnisse zu entdecken. Das Mädchen war in Lumpen gehüllt, und Tränen liefen ihre weichen Wangen herab.

Der Ochsentreiber blickte den Büttel erwartungsvoll an. Der Büttel sah den Vogt an und harrte des vereinbarten Kopfnickens. Der unheimliche junge Priester stieß den Vogt voller Ungeduld verstohlen in die Seite, doch der Vogt schenkte ihm keine Beachtung. Er ließ den Dieb weitersingen, und so gelang es dem häßlichen Mann mit seiner schönen Stimme, sich den Tod noch wenige furchtbare Augenblicke lang vom Leibe zu halten.

> Es graut der Tag, der Jäger kommt,
> um ihm den Tod zu geben.
> Es stirbt der Vogel, stirbt der Mensch –
> mein Lied wird ewig leben.

Als das Lied zu Ende war, sah der Vogt den Büttel an und nickte. Der Büttel rief: »Hopp!« und hieb dem Ochsen mit einem Seil in die Flanke, während der Ochsentreiber seine Peitsche knallen ließ. Der Ochse zog an, der Mann taumelte, der Wagen glitt ihm unter den Füßen weg, und er fiel ins Bodenlose. Der Henkerstrick spannte sich, und dann brach das Genick des Diebes mit hörbarem Knacken.

Ein Schrei ertönte, und alle starrten die junge Frau an.

Nicht sie hatte geschrien, sondern das Weib des Messerschmieds, das neben ihr stand, sie aber war der Anlaß gewesen: Vor dem Galgen war sie auf die Knie gesunken und reckte die Arme vor, bereit zum Fluch. Die Leute wichen vor ihr zurück, wußte doch ein jeder, daß der Fluch eines Menschen, dem Unrecht geschah, besondere Kräfte besaß. Und daß es bei dieser Hinrichtung nicht mit rechten Dingen zuging – den Verdacht hegten sie ohnehin. Die Gassenjungen packte das Grauen.

Das Mädchen richtete den beschwörenden Blick ihrer hellgoldenen Augen nun auf die drei Fremden – den Ritter, den Mönch und den

Priester. Und dann verhängte sie ihren Fluch über sie – furchtbare Worte in hellem, klingendem Ton:

»Krankheit und Sorge, Hunger und Schmerz beschwöre ich auf Euch herab. Euer Haus soll vom Feuer verzehrt werden, und Eure Kinder sollen am Galgen enden. Euren Feinden soll es wohl ergehen, während Ihr in Gram und Trauer alt werdet und in Siechtum und Elend dahinfault ...« Noch während sie sprach, griff das Mädchen in einen Sack, der neben ihr auf dem Boden lag, und zog einen lebenden Hahn heraus.

Und mit einemmal hielt sie ein Messer in der Hand. Eine einzige rasche Bewegung – da hatte sie auch schon dem Tier den Kopf abgeschnitten, den blutenden Rumpf gepackt und nach dem schwarzhaarigen Priester geschleudert. Das kopflose Tier traf ihn zwar nicht, doch das Blut bespritzte nicht nur den Priester, sondern auch den Mönch und den Ritter, in deren Mitte er stand.

Voller Abscheu und Ekel wandten sich die drei Männer ab, doch das Blut traf sie alle, befleckte ihre Gewänder und zeichnete ihre Gesichter.

Das Mädchen machte kehrt und rannte um ihr Leben.

Die Menge öffnete ihr eine Gasse, die sich hinter ihr wieder schloß. Danach herrschte das reine Chaos, bis es dem Vogt gelang, die Aufmerksamkeit seiner Bewaffneten auf sich zu lenken. Wütend befahl er ihnen, das Mädchen einzufangen. Gehorsam kämpften sie sich durch die Menge, drängten rüde Frauen und Kinder beiseite, doch ehe sie sich's versahen, war das Mädchen verschwunden. Der Vogt hieß sie weitersuchen, aber er wußte genau, daß sie nicht gefunden würde.

Angewidert wandte er sich ab. Der Ritter, der Mönch und der Priester hatten die Flucht des Mädchens nicht weiter verfolgt. Statt dessen starrten sie allesamt auf den Galgen. Der Vogt folgte ihrem Blick. Der tote Dieb hing am Strick, sein blasses, junges Gesicht bereits blau verfärbt. Unter seiner sanft hin und her pendelnden Leiche drehte der kopflose Hahn im blutbefleckten Schnee zackige Kreise.

Buch 1 1135-36

In einem weiten Tal am Fuße eines Hanges, gleich neben einem Bach mit frischem, perlendem Wasser, errichtete Tom ein Haus.

Die Mauern waren bereits drei Fuß hoch und wuchsen schnell. Die Sonne schien, und die beiden Maurer, die Tom angeworben hatte, arbeiteten in gleichbleibendem Rhythmus. Ratsch – platsch – peng machten ihre Kellen, während der Träger unter dem Gewicht der schweren Steinblöcke schwitzte. Alfred, Toms Sohn, mischte den Mörtel und zählte Schaufel um Schaufel den Sand, den er gerade auf ein Brett häufelte. Auch ein Zimmermann war zugegen; er stand neben Tom an der Werkbank und bearbeitete sorgfältig einen Buchenholzblock mit einem Breitbeil.

Der vierzehnjährige Alfred war groß und schlank wie sein Vater. Tom überragte die meisten Männer um Haupteslänge, und Alfred, der noch im Wachsen war, hatte ihn schon fast erreicht. Die beiden sahen einander überhaupt sehr ähnlich, hatten beide hellbraunes Haar und grünliche Augen mit braunen Flecken. Ein hübsches Paar, die zwei, sagten die Leute, wenn sie ihnen begegneten. Sie unterschieden sich im wesentlichen dadurch, daß Tom einen lockigen, braunen Bart trug, während sich auf Alfreds Oberlippe erst ein feiner blonder Flaum zeigte. Tom erinnerte sich voller Zärtlichkeit daran, daß einst auch das Haupthaar seines Sohnes so blond gewesen war.

Alfred wurde nun langsam zum Mann, und Tom hätte es gern gesehen, wenn sein Sohn mit etwas mehr Fleiß und Bedacht bei der Sache gewesen wäre. Der Junge mußte noch eine Menge lernen, wenn er ein Steinmetz werden wollte wie sein Vater. Bisher hatten ihn die Regeln der Baukunst allenfalls verwirrt oder gelangweilt.

Das Haus, an dem sie gerade arbeiteten, würde nach seiner Fertigstellung das schönste und größte Herrenhaus im Umkreis von vielen

Meilen sein. Das Erdgeschoß war als geräumiger Speicher angelegt, in dem Vorräte und Gerätschaften gelagert werden konnten. Die gewölbte Decke diente als Brandschutz. Über dem Speicher sollte dann die eigentliche Wohnstube entstehen, die über ein außerhalb der Mauern zu errichtendes Treppenhaus erreichbar war. Da sie so hoch lag, war sie nur schwer anzugreifen und um so leichter zu verteidigen. An der Außenwand der Wohnstube sollte sich ein Schornstein erheben, durch den der Rauch vom Kamin abzog – eine wahrhaft umwälzende Neuerung. Bisher hatte Tom nur ein einziges Mal ein Haus mit Schornstein gesehen. Es war ihm jedoch so einleuchtend erschienen, daß er sich sofort zum Nachbau entschlossen hatte. Im zweiten Stock, also oberhalb der großen Wohnstube, sollte ein kleines Schlafzimmer entstehen; die jungen Damen von Adel waren sich zu gut, um gemeinsam mit Männern, Mägden und Jagdhunden in der großen Stube zu schlafen.

Die Küche sollte in einem eigenen Gebäude untergebracht werden, denn irgendwann ging jede Küche einmal in Flammen auf. Um Schlimmeres zu verhüten, legte man sie daher meist ein gutes Stück entfernt vom Wohnhaus an – und begnügte sich mit lauwarmen Mahlzeiten.

Tom war damit beschäftigt, den Eingang des Hauses zu errichten. Die Türpfosten sollten rund sein und wie Säulen aussehen; das betonte die Würde des jungvermählten Paares von adeligem Geblüt, das hier Wohnung nehmen wollte. Mit Blick auf das vorgeformte hölzerne Simsbrett, das ihm als Richtschnur diente, setzte Tom seinen Eisenmeißel an und klopfte vorsichtig mit dem großen Holzhammer darauf. Viele kleine Splitter und Bruchstücke rieselten herunter, und die behauene Fläche war ein wenig deutlicher gerundet als zuvor. Er hatte es wieder einmal geschafft. Die glatte Bruchfläche war gut genug für eine Kathedrale.

In Exeter hatte Tom einst am Bau der Kathedrale mitgewirkt. Anfangs war es für ihn ein Auftrag wie jeder andere gewesen, und er hatte mit Ärger und Verdrossenheit die Ermahnungen des Baumeisters hingenommen, der immer wieder etwas an seiner Arbeit auszusetzen hatte. Tom kannte seine Stärken und wußte, daß er ein überdurchschnittlich guter und gewissenhafter Steinmetz und Maurer war. Erst allmählich ging ihm auf, daß die Mauern einer Kathedrale eben nicht nur gut, sondern *tadellos* zu sein hatten, denn eine Kathedrale wurde zu Ehren Gottes errichtet und war zudem so groß, daß die geringste Abweichung zum vielleicht tödlichen Konstruktionsfehler werden konnte.

Toms Ärger verwandelte sich in Faszination. Die gnadenlose Detailbesessenheit im Verbund mit einem äußerst anspruchsvollen Bauvorhaben öffnete ihm die Augen für die Wunder seines Handwerks. Bei dem Baumeister in Exeter lernte er die Bedeutung der Proportionen kennen, die Symbolik verschiedener Zahlen, die nahezu magischen Formeln zur richtigen Berechnung der Dicke einer Mauer oder des Winkels einer Stufe in einer Wendeltreppe. All diese Dinge fesselten ihn, und es erstaunte ihn, als er erfuhr, daß viele Steinmetzen unfähig waren, sie zu begreifen.

Nach einiger Zeit wurde Tom zur rechten Hand des Baumeisters und war nun auch imstande, dessen Schwächen zu erkennen. Der Mann war ein hervorragender Handwerker, aber ein unfähiger Organisator. Zur rechten Zeit die richtige Menge Steine zu beschaffen, um mit den Maurern Schritt halten zu können, stellte für ihn ein schier unüberwindliches Problem dar. Wie brachte man die Schmiede dazu, in ausreichender Zahl das gerade benötigte Werkzeug herzustellen? Wie schaffte man genügend gebrannten Kalk und Sand für den Mörtel her? Wer fällte das Holz für die Zimmerleute, und wer beschaffte vom Domkapitel das Geld, um alles zu bezahlen?

Wäre Tom bis zum Tode des Dombaumeisters in Exeter geblieben, hätte er gut und gerne dessen Nachfolger werden können. Doch es kam anders. Dem Domkapitel ging – nicht zuletzt infolge der Mißwirtschaft des Baumeisters – das Geld aus, und die Handwerker waren gezwungen, sich anderswo nach Arbeit umzusehen.

Der Kastellan von Exeter bot Tom die Stelle des Baumeisters an. Seine Aufgabe hätte darin bestanden, die Befestigungen der Stadt zu renovieren und auszubauen – eine Lebensaufgabe, falls nichts dazwischenkam.

Doch Tom hatte das Angebot abgelehnt. Er wollte wieder eine Kathedrale bauen.

Agnes, seine Frau, hatte diesen Entschluß nie verstanden. Als Festungsbaumeister in Exeter hätte er mit seiner Familie in einem guten Steinhaus leben können. Sie hätten Diener gehabt und eigene Ställe und jeden Tag Fleisch auf dem Tisch. Nie hatte sie Tom verziehen, daß er diese einmalige Gelegenheit ausgeschlagen hatte. Der unwiderstehliche Drang, einen Dom erbauen zu wollen, war ihr unbegreiflich; sie verstand weder die organisatorische Vielfalt noch die intellektuelle Herausforderung, die in den Berechnungen lag. Weder die gewaltige Höhe der Mauern noch die atemberaubende Schönheit und Größe des fertigen Bauwerks vermochten sie zu begeistern. Tom dagegen, der einmal an diesem Wein genippt hatte, würde sich nie wieder mit etwas Geringerem zufriedengeben.

Das alles lag jetzt zehn Jahre zurück, und seitdem waren sie weit herumgekommen. Hier entwarf er ein neues Kapitelhaus für ein Kloster, dann arbeitete er ein oder zwei Jahre an einer Burg oder errichtete für einen reichen Kaufmann ein Stadthaus. Doch sobald er ein wenig Geld gespart hatte, nahm er seinen Abschied und zog mit Frau und Kind weiter – immer auf der Suche nach einer Kathedrale.

Er sah von der Werkbank auf und erblickte Agnes, die am Rand der Baustelle stand. In der Rechten trug sie einen Vesperkorb und in der Linken einen großen Krug Bier, den sie mit der Hüfte abstützte. Es war Mittag. Er sah sie liebevoll an. Niemand wäre so vermessen gewesen, Agnes hübsch zu nennen, doch verrieten die breite Stirn, die großen braunen Augen, die gerade Nase und die starke Kieferpartie enorme innere Kraft. Ihr dunkles, drahtiges Haar war in der Mitte gescheitelt und auf dem Hinterkopf zusammengebunden. Agnes war Toms Seelengefährtin.

Sie schenkte Tom und Alfred Bier ein. Einen Augenblick standen sie wortlos beisammen, die beiden großen Männer und die kräftige Frau, und tranken Bier aus hölzernen Bechern. Da kam aus einem Weizenfeld die siebenjährige Martha gesprungen, das vierte Mitglied der Familie. Sie war so hübsch wie eine Narzisse – freilich eine Narzisse, der ein Blütenblatt fehlt, denn zwei Milchzähne waren ihr ausgefallen und die neuen noch nicht nachgewachsen. Sie rannte auf Tom zu, küßte ihn auf den staubigen Bart und nippte an seinem Bier. Er zog ihren knochigen Körper an sich und drückte sie. »Trink du nur nicht zuviel«, sagte er, »sonst fällst du in den Graben!« Die Kleine torkelte im Kreis umher und spielte die Betrunkene.

Sie ließen sich auf dem Holzstoß nieder. Agnes reichte Tom ein großes Stück Weißbrot, eine dicke Scheibe gekochten Schinkenspeck und eine kleine Zwiebel. Tom ließ sich das Fleisch schmecken und begann die Zwiebel zu schälen. Agnes gab den Kindern zu essen und bediente sich dann auch selbst. Vielleicht war es wirklich verantwortungslos, um der unsicheren Hoffnung auf eine neue Kathedrale willen den langweiligen Posten in Exeter auszuschlagen, dachte Tom bei sich. Aber wie dem auch sei, Hunger hat meine Familie trotz dieser Leichtfertigkeit nie leiden müssen.

Er zog sein Eßmesser aus der Tasche seiner Lederschürze, schnitt sich eine Scheibe Zwiebel ab und verzehrte sie mit einem Stück Brot. Die Zwiebel brannte süß in seinem Mund.

Da sagte Agnes auf einmal: »Ich bin wieder schwanger.«

Tom hörte auf zu kauen und starrte sie an. Ein Freudenschauer durchfuhr ihn, und weil er nicht wußte, was er sagen sollte, grinste er sie nur dümmlich an. Agnes errötete schließlich und fügte hinzu: »*So* überraschend ist es ja nun auch wieder nicht!«

Tom umarmte sie. »Schön, schön«, sagte er, noch immer vor Freude strahlend. »Ein Kindchen, das mir den Bart zausen kann! Und ich dachte schon, das nächste Kind in der Familie würde Alfreds sein.«

»Freu dich nicht zu früh«, ermahnte ihn Agnes. »Einem ungeborenen Kind soll man noch keinen Namen geben. Das bringt Unglück.«

Tom nickte zustimmend. Agnes hatte eine Totgeburt und mehrere Fehlgeburten hinter sich, und ein kleines Mädchen, Matilda, war im Alter von zwei Jahren gestorben. »Wär' trotzdem schön, wenn es ein Junge wird«, sagte er, »jetzt, wo Alfred schon so groß ist. Wann ist es denn soweit?«

»Nach Weihnachten.«

Tom fing an zu rechnen. Der Rohbau des Hauses sollte vor dem ersten Frost stehen und zum Schutz gegen den Winter mit Stroh bedeckt werden. Die Steinmetzen sollten in den kalten Monaten die Steine für Fenster, Gewölbe, Türfassungen und den Kamin schneiden, die Zimmerleute Dielenbretter, Türen und Fensterläden zimmern, während er selbst das Gerüst für die Arbeiten in den oberen Stockwerken vorbereiten wollte. Die folgenden Arbeiten standen dann im nächsten Frühjahr an: die Fertigstellung der Gewölbe im Erdgeschoß, das Einziehen des Bodens im ersten Stock sowie die Errichtung des Daches. Bis Pfingsten nächsten Jahres würde der Bau die Familie ernähren. Dann war das Kleine ein halbes Jahr alt, und sie konnten mit ihm weiterziehen. »Schön«, sagte er zufrieden, »das ist schön«, und schob sich noch einen Zwiebelschnitz in den Mund.

»Ich werde langsam zu alt zum Kinderkriegen«, sagte Agnes. »Das muß jetzt das letzte sein.«

Tom dachte über ihre Worte nach. Er wußte nicht genau, wie alt sie war, jedenfalls nicht nach Jahren, doch daß Frauen ihres Alters Kinder bekamen, war durchaus keine Seltenheit. Je älter sie waren, das stimmte allerdings, desto schwerer fiel es ihnen und desto schwächer waren die Kinder. Gewiß hatte Agnes recht.

Aber wie will sie eine neue Schwangerschaft verhindern? Als ihm die Antwort einfiel, legte sich ein Schatten auf sein sonniges Gemüt.

»Vielleicht finde ich Arbeit in einer Stadt«, sagte er, um sie zu besänftigen, »an einer Kathedrale oder einem Bischofssitz. Dann können wir in einem großen Haus mit Holzdielen wohnen und uns ein Mädchen leisten, das dir zur Hand geht.«

Ihr Ausdruck verhärtete sich, und ihre Antwort klang skeptisch: »Vielleicht.« Sein Gerede über Kathedralen behagte ihr nicht.

Ihre Miene schien zu sagen: Wenn du niemals an einer Kathedrale gearbeitet hättest, dann lebten wir wahrscheinlich längst in einem Stadthaus, hätten genug gespartes Geld unter der Feuerstelle vergraben und brauchten uns um unsere Zukunft nicht zu sorgen.

Tom wandte den Blick von ihr und biß ein Stück Schinkenspeck ab. Sie hatten Anlaß zum Feiern, und dennoch herrschte Mißstimmung zwischen ihnen. Er kam sich gedemütigt vor. Wortlos kaute er an dem zähen Fleisch. Dann hörte er plötzlich Pferdegetrappel und hob lauschend den Kopf. Der Reiter kam von der Straße her, vermied jedoch das Dorf, indem er die Abkürzung durch den Wald nahm.

Einen Augenblick später erschien ein junger Mann auf einem Pony und sprang ab. Er sah aus wie ein Knappe, eine Art Ritterlehrling. »Euer Herr kommt«, sagte er.

Tom erhob sich. »Ihr meint Lord Percy?« Percy Hamleigh war einer der wichtigsten Männer der Grafschaft. Ihm gehörte das Tal – und nicht nur dieses –, und er war es auch, der den Hausbau in Auftrag gegeben hatte und bezahlte.

»Sein Sohn«, sagte der Knappe.

»Der junge William.« Percys Sohn William sollte das Haus nach seiner Hochzeit beziehen. Er war mit Lady Aliena, der Tochter des Grafen von Shiring, verlobt.

»Eben derselbe«, antwortete der Knappe. »Und er ist sehr erbost.«

Tom erschrak. Verhandlungen mit einem Bauherrn waren im günstigsten Fall schwierig. Ein wütender Bauherr war schlicht und einfach unerträglich. »Worüber ist er erbost?«

»Seine Braut hat ihn zurückgewiesen.«

»Die Tochter des Grafen?« erwiderte Tom überrascht und spürte auf einmal Angst. Hatte er sich nicht eben erst in Sicherheit über seine Zukunft gewiegt? »Ich dachte, die Ehe sei längst vereinbart.«

»Das dachten wir alle – nur Lady Aliena nicht, wie es scheint«, sagte der Knappe. »Sie hatte ihn kaum erblickt, da verkündete sie auch schon, daß nichts in der Welt sie dazu bewegen könne, ihn zu heiraten.«

Tom runzelte die Stirn. Die Sache gefiel ihm ganz und gar nicht. »Soweit ich mich entsinne, sieht der junge Herr doch gar nicht übel aus«, sagte er.

»Als ob es darauf ankäme, in ihrer Stellung«, bemerkte Agnes. »Wo kämen wir hin, wenn Grafentöchter sich ihre Ehemänner selbst aussuchen könnten? Fahrende Sänger und dunkeläugige Spitzbuben würden uns regieren!«

»Vielleicht ändert das Mädchen seine Meinung ja noch«, meinte Tom hoffnungsvoll.

»Ja, wenn ihre Mutter die Birkenrute sprechen läßt, dann schon«, ergänzte Agnes.

»Ihre Mutter lebt nicht mehr«, sagte der Knappe.

Agnes nickte. »Kein Wunder, daß ihr der Blick für die Realitäten des Lebens fehlt. Aber warum weist ihr der Vater nicht den Weg? Das verstehe ich nicht.«

»Es hat den Anschein, daß er ihr versprochen hat, sie niemals einem Mann zur Frau zu geben, den sie nicht mag.«

»Ein törichtes Versprechen!« schimpfte Tom. Wie konnte sich ein mächtiger Herr den Launen eines jungen Mädchens ausliefern? Militärische Allianzen, die gräflichen Finanzen, ja, sogar die Fertigstellung des Hauses konnten in der einen oder anderen Weise von dieser Eheschließung betroffen sein.

»Sie hat einen Bruder«, sagte der Knappe. »Insofern ist es nicht gar so wichtig, wen sie heiratet.«

»Trotzdem ...«

»Der Graf ist ein unbeugsamer Mann«, fuhr der Knappe fort. »Er steht zu seinem Wort – selbst wenn er es nur einem Kind gegeben hat.« Er zuckte mit den Schultern. »So heißt es jedenfalls.«

Tom betrachtete die niedrigen Grundmauern des künftigen Hauses. Ich habe noch nicht genug Geld gespart, um die Familie gut über den Winter zu bringen ... Der Gedanke ließ ihn frösteln.

»Vielleicht wird der junge Herr eine andere Braut finden, die bereit ist, hier mit ihm zu leben. Er hat die Wahl – die ganze Grafschaft steht ihm zur Verfügung.«

Mit der krächzenden Stimme des Heranwachsenden rief Alfred: »Jesus Christus! Ich glaube, da kommt er.«

Sie alle folgten seinem Blick. Vom Dorf her kam ein Pferd übers Feld herangaloppiert und zog eine Wolke aus Staub und aufgewirbelter Erde hinter sich her. Sowohl die Größe als auch die Geschwindigkeit des Pferdes hatten Alfred erschreckt: Es war geradezu riesig. Tom hatte solche Tiere schon gesehen, Alfred wahrscheinlich nicht. Es handelte sich um ein Schlachtroß, am Widerrist so hoch wie das Kinn eines Mannes und unverhältnismäßig breit gebaut. In England wurden solche Pferde nicht gezüchtet; sie stammten aus dem Ausland und waren sündhaft teuer.

Tom ließ die Reste seiner Mahlzeit in der Schürzentasche verschwinden und kniff die Augen zusammen, um im Gegenlicht besser sehen zu können. Das Pferd hatte die Ohren angelegt, und seine Nüstern bebten, doch aus dem hoch getragenen Kopf glaubte Tom schließen zu können, daß der Reiter es noch unter Kontrolle hatte. Der Eindruck bestätigte sich, als Roß und Reiter näher kamen: Der Reiter lehnte sich zurück und zerrte an den Zügeln, das Pferd schien tatsächlich etwas langsamer zu werden. Tom spürte jetzt, wie die trommelnden Hufe den Boden unter seinen Füßen erzittern ließen. Er sah sich nach Martha um, wollte sie auf den Arm nehmen, damit sie nicht in Gefahr geriet, doch Martha war verschwunden.

»Sie ist im Getreidefeld«, sagte Agnes, doch darauf war Tom schon selbst gekommen. Rasch lief er zum Rain des Feldes, das unmittelbar an die Baustelle anschloß, und spähte besorgt über den wogenden Weizen. Von Martha keine Spur. Jetzt sah er nur noch eine Möglichkeit, das drohende Unheil abzuwenden: Er mußte dem Pferd Einhalt gebieten, mußte zumindest versuchen, es in seinem wilden Lauf zu bremsen.

Er trat auf den Feldweg hinaus und ging mit ausgebreiteten Armen auf Pferd und Reiter zu. Das Tier bemerkte ihn, hob den Kopf, um besser sehen zu können, und wurde tatsächlich langsamer. Doch dann sah Tom zu seinem großen Entsetzen, wie der Reiter dem Pferd die Sporen gab.

»Verdammter Narr!« brüllte er ihm entgegen, obwohl der Reiter ihn gar nicht hören konnte.

In diesem Augenblick schlüpfte Martha aus dem Weizenfeld auf den Weg, nur ein paar Meter vor Tom.

Der war im ersten Moment wie gelähmt vor Schreck. Dann sprang er vor, schreiend und wild mit den Armen fuchtelnd, um das Tier abzulenken. Doch das Pferd war ein Schlachtroß; es war darauf dressiert, johlende Kriegerhorden zu attackieren, und ließ sich durch nichts beirren. Mitten auf dem schmalen Weg stand Martha wie angewurzelt und starrte auf das Untier, das auf sie zustürmte. Tom erkannte verzweifelt, daß er seine Tochter nicht mehr rechtzeitig erreichen konnte. Er wich nach links aus, geriet beinahe ins Weizenfeld, und da, im allerletzten Moment, machte auch das Pferd einen leichten Schwenk zur Seite. Der Steigbügel des Reiters streifte Marthas Goldhaar, dicht neben ihren nackten Füßen fuhr ein Huf auf den Boden und trat ein tiefes Loch hinein. Dann war das Pferd vorüber, und aufgewühlte Erde regnete auf die beiden herab. Tom riß seine Tochter an sich und drückte sie fest an sein wild klopfendes Herz.

Die Erleichterung drohte ihn zu überwältigen. Die Glieder wurden ihm schwach, und ihm war, als rönne Wasser durch seine Adern. Doch gleich darauf kam die Wut – Wut auf diesen rücksichtslosen Dummkopf auf seinem gewaltigen Schlachtroß. Er sah sich nach ihm um. Lord William lehnte sich im Sattel ein wenig zurück und streckte die Füße in den Steigbügeln vor. Das Pferd warf unruhig den Kopf hin und her und bockte, doch William blieb im Sattel. Er ließ das Pferd kantern, dann fiel es in einen leichten Trab. In einem weiten Kreis führte er es an die Baustelle heran.

Martha weinte. Tom überließ sie ihrer Mutter und wartete auf William. Der junge Herr war groß und gut gebaut. Er mochte um die zwanzig Jahre alt sein und hatte strohblonde Haare. Seine engstehenden Augen erweckten den Eindruck, als blinzele er unablässig in die Sonne. Gewandet war er in einen kurzen schwarzen Waffenrock, schwarze Kniehosen und Lederschuhe mit Kreuzbändern bis über die Waden. Selbstzufrieden und sichtlich unbeeindruckt von dem Zwischenfall saß er im Sattel. Der dumme Kerl weiß nicht einmal, was er angerichtet hat, dachte Tom voller Grimm. Ich könnte ihm den Hals umdrehen!

Vor dem Holzstoß brachte William sein Pferd zum Stehen und sah auf die Bauleute herab. »Wer hat hier das Sagen?« fragte er.

Wenn du mein kleines Mädchen verletzt hättest, wärst du jetzt schon ein toter Mann! wollte Tom sagen, doch er schluckte seinen Zorn herunter. Es fiel ihm schwer genug. Er trat vor und griff das Pferd am Zaum. »Ich bin der Baumeister«, sagte er gepreßt. »Ich heiße Tom.«

»Das Haus wird nicht mehr gebraucht«, sagte William. »Du kannst deine Leute entlassen.«

Genau das hatte Tom befürchtet. Aber er gab die Hoffnung noch nicht auf. Vielleicht ließ William sich in seinem Zorn zu voreiligen Entschlüssen hinreißen und konnte eines Besseren überzeugt werden. Es kostete ihn einige Überwindung, seine Stimme freundlich und vernünftig klingen zu lassen. »Aber die Arbeiten sind schon weit fortgeschritten«, sagte er. »Wollt Ihr das alles verfallen lassen? Über kurz oder lang werdet Ihr das Haus doch ohnehin brauchen.«

»Spar dir deine Ratschläge, Baumeister Tom. Ich weiß selbst, was ich zu tun habe. Ihr seid alle entlassen.« Er riß am Zügel, doch Tom hielt das Pferd noch immer am Zaum. »Laß mein Pferd los!« befahl William drohend.

Tom schluckte. Gleich würde William das Tier veranlassen, den Kopf hochzunehmen. Er fingerte das Brot aus seiner Schürzentasche und hielt es dem Pferd hin, das prompt den Kopf senkte und ein Stück abbiß. »Es gibt noch einiges zu bereden, Herr, bevor Ihr uns verlaßt«, sagte er leise.

»Wenn du nicht sofort mein Pferd losläßt, schlage ich dir den Kopf ab!« brauste William auf.

Tom sah ihm direkt in die Augen, bemüht, seine Furcht zu verbergen. Zwar war er größer als William, doch wenn der junge Herr sein Schwert zog, half ihm das gar nichts.

»Tu, was der Herr sagt, Mann«, stammelte Agnes angsterfüllt.

Es herrschte Totenstille. Reglos wie Statuen standen die Arbeiter da und verfolgten die Szene. Die Vernunft gebot Nachgeben. Tom wußte es. Doch Williams Pferd hätte um ein Haar sein Töchterchen totgetrampelt, und das konnte Tom ihm so schnell nicht vergessen. Er war noch immer aufs höchste erregt, und so antwortete er mit klopfendem Herzen: »Ihr müßt uns noch bezahlen.«

William zog erneut an den Zügeln, doch Tom ließ das Zaumzeug nicht los, und das Pferd war abgelenkt, weil es in Toms Schürzentasche nach weiterer Nahrung suchte. »Holt euch euern Lohn bei meinem Vater!« fauchte William wütend.

Tom hörte, wie der Zimmermann mit vor Angst zitternder Stimme sagte: »Das werden wir tun, mein Herr, habt vielen Dank.«

Armseliger Feigling, dachte Tom, aber er zitterte selbst. Dennoch rang er sich die Erwiderung ab: »Wenn Ihr uns entlassen wollt, müßt Ihr uns auszahlen, so ist es Brauch. Das Haus Eures Vaters liegt zwei Tagesmärsche von hier entfernt. Wer weiß, ob er überhaupt anwesend ist, wenn wir dort eintreffen.«

»Es sind schon Männer aus geringerem Anlaß gestorben«, gab William zurück, die Wangen gerötet vor Wut.

Aus dem Augenwinkel sah Tom, wie die Hand des Knappen an den Schwertknauf fuhr. Er wußte, daß jetzt der Punkt erreicht war, an dem er aufgeben und sich demütig zeigen sollte, doch der Zorn auf William saß wie ein hartnäckiges Geschwür in seiner Magengrube, und so brachte er es trotz seiner Furcht einfach nicht über sich, das Zaumzeug loszulassen.

»Zuerst bezahlt uns, dann könnt Ihr mich töten«, sagte er kühn.

»Ob man Euch deswegen hängt oder nicht, ist mir gleich. Früher oder später sterbt Ihr ohnehin, und dann werde ich im Himmel sein und Ihr in der Hölle.«

Plötzlich war Williams höhnisches Grinsen wie weggewischt, und er erbleichte. Tom war verblüfft: Was hatte den Burschen dermaßen erschreckt? Bestimmt nicht der Hinweis auf den Galgen – damit, daß ein Edelmann wegen der Ermordung eines Handwerkers gehängt wurde, war kaum zu rechnen. Konnte es sein, daß er sich vor der Hölle fürchtete?

Wortlos starrten sie sich in die Augen. Ebenso erstaunt wie erleichtert sah Tom, daß der von Hoffart und Zorn gezeichnete Ausdruck in Williams Gesicht nicht wiederkehrte, sondern endgültig dahinschmolz und durch panikartige Furcht ersetzt wurde. Schließlich zog William einen ledernen Geldbeutel aus dem Gürtel, warf ihn dem Knappen zu und sagte: »Gib ihnen ihr Geld!«

Und da forderte Tom sein Schicksal heraus. Als William die Zügel wieder anzog, worauf das Pferd seinen schweren Kopf hob und seitwärts tänzelte, da gab der Baumeister das Zaumzeug noch immer nicht frei, sondern bewegte sich mit dem Tier mit und sagte: »Einen vollen Wochenlohn. So ist es Brauch bei Entlassungen.« Er hörte, wie Agnes dicht hinter ihm angstvoll nach Luft schnappte, und wußte, daß sie ihn für verrückt hielt, weil er die Auseinandersetzung mutwillig fortsetzte. Dennoch ließ er nicht locker. »Das heißt also: sechs Pence für den Arbeiter, zwölf für den Zimmermann und jeden Maurer, dazu vierundzwanzig Pence für mich. Macht zusammen sechsundsechzig.« Niemand konnte Beträge so schnell zusammenrechnen wie er.

Der Knappe sah seinen Herrn und Meister fragend an, und William schnaubte: »Sei's drum!«

Tom ließ das Zaumzeug los und wich einen Schritt zurück.

William wendete sein Pferd und trat ihm heftig in die Flanken. Dann sprengten Roß und Reiter über den Feldweg davon.

Tom ließ sich auf den Holzstoß fallen. Was war bloß in ihn gefahren? Es war schierer Wahn, Lord William so frech die Stirn zu bieten! Er konnte von Glück sagen, daß er noch am Leben war.

Wie fernes Donnergrollen verklangen die Hufschläge. Williams Knappe schüttete den Inhalt der Geldbörse auf ein Brett. Erst jetzt, als er die Silberpennys im Sonnenschein glitzern sah, überkam Tom ein Gefühl des Triumphes: Der Wahn hatte sich auf jeden Fall ausgezahlt! Er hatte sich und seinen Leuten eine angemessene Bezahlung erstritten. »Selbst hohe Herren sind an die alten Bräuche gebunden«, sagte er halb zu sich selbst.

Agnes hatte ihn sehr wohl gehört: »Gebe Gott, daß du nie wieder für Lord William arbeiten mußt«, sagte sie mürrisch.

Tom lächelte sie an. Er konnte gut verstehen, daß sie sich nach all den ausgestandenen Ängsten nicht bester Laune erfreute. »Runzle du nur nicht zu oft die Stirn, sonst hast du für den Säugling nur klumpige Milch in deinen Brüsten«, sagte er.

»Wenn du im Winter keine Arbeit findest, kann ich keinen von uns ernähren«, gab sie zurück.

»Bis zum Winter ist es noch lange hin«, sagte Tom.

Den Sommer über blieben sie im Dorf. Später betrachteten sie diesen Entschluß als furchtbaren Fehler, doch vorerst sprach alles dafür, denn außer Martha konnten sie alle bei der Ernte jeden Tag einen Penny verdienen. Als der Herbst kam und sie weiterziehen mußten, besaßen sie ein fettes Schwein und ein schweres Säckchen voller Silberpennys.

Die erste Nacht verbrachten sie im Portal einer Dorfkirche. Am zweiten Abend fanden sie eine kleine Priorei und genossen die Gastfreundschaft der Mönche. Am dritten Tag wanderten sie durch den riesigen Chute Forest, ein dichtbewachsenes, urwaldartiges Gebiet, und die Straße, die hindurchführte, war kaum breiter als ein Ochsenkarren. Unter den Eichen zu beiden Seiten des Weges prunkte das üppige Grün des zur Neige gehenden Sommers.

Tom trug seine kleineren Werkzeuge in einem Ranzen bei sich, die Hämmer baumelten an seinem Gürtel. Unter dem linken Arm trug er seinen zum Bündel zusammengerollten Mantel, in der rechten Hand, gleichsam als Spazierstock, seine Eisenpike. Er war froh darüber, daß sie wieder auf Wanderschaft waren. Vielleicht wartete ja irgendwo schon eine Kathedrale auf ihn? Er konnte es zum Dombaumeister bringen und bräuchte bis zu seinem Lebensende nie wieder Arbeit zu suchen. Die Kirche, die er bauen wollte, war so groß und schön, daß er sich um sein Seelenheil keine Sorgen mehr machen mußte.

Agnes trug ihre wenigen Haushaltsgegenstände in einem Kochtopf auf dem Rücken. Alfred waren die Werkzeuge anvertraut, die ihnen beim Bau eines Unterschlupfs behilflich sein würden: ein Beil, eine Krummaxt, eine Säge, einen kleinen Hammer, einen Spaten und eine Ahle, mit der man Löcher in Holz und Leder bohren konnte. Martha war noch zu klein für schwerere Lasten; sie trug lediglich ihre Eßschüssel und ihr Messer am Gürtel und ihren Wintermantel auf dem Rücken. Zudem hatte sie sich um das Schwein zu kümmern, das sie bei Gelegenheit auf einem Markt verkaufen wollten.

Auf ihrem Weg durch die schier endlosen Wälder ließ Tom seine Frau nie aus den Augen. Sie war jetzt schon im fünften Monat und schleppte nicht nur auf ihrem Rücken, sondern auch in ihrem Bauch eine beträchtliche Last mit sich herum. Dennoch zeigte sie keinerlei Anzeichen von Müdigkeit. Auch Alfred ging es gut; er war ja auch in einem Alter, in dem die jungen Burschen oft nicht wissen, wohin mit ihren Kräften. Nur Martha ermüdete recht schnell. Ihre dünnen Beinchen waren wie geschaffen zum Rennen und Spielen, doch fehlte ihnen die Ausdauer für lange Wanderungen. Immer wieder fiel Martha hinter den anderen zurück, so daß sie stehenbleiben und auf das Kind mit dem Schwein warten mußten.

Wieder schweiften Toms Gedanken ab. Einmal mehr dachte er an den Dom, den er eines Tages bauen wollte. Wie immer errichtete er zunächst einen imaginären Bogengang. Das war ganz einfach: zwei senkrechte Säulen, die einen Halbkreis trugen. Eine zweite, identische Konstruktion kam hinzu. In seiner Phantasie schob er die beiden Bögen einfach zusammen und fügte noch eine ganze Reihe weiterer hinzu, so daß sie schließlich ein tunnelartiges Gewölbe bildeten. Das Gewölbe war die Grundidee des Baus, denn es besaß ein Dach, das den Regen fernhielt, und zwei Wände, die das Dach trugen. Eine Kirche war nichts anderes als ein verfeinertes Tunnelgewölbe.

Ein Gewölbe indes war dunkel. Die erste Verfeinerung bestand demnach im Einbau von Fenstern. Waren die Wände stark genug, so konnte man Löcher hineinschneiden. Sie sollten oben abgerundet, senkrechte Seiten haben und eine flache Fensterbank – kurzum die gleiche Form aufweisen wie der ursprüngliche Bogengang. Gleiche Formen bei Bögen und Fenstern waren eines der Geheimnisse, die die Schönheit eines Gebäudes bestimmten. Gleichmäßigkeit war ein anderes; Tom stellte sich auf jeder Seite des Gewölbes zwölf identische Fenster in regelmäßigen Abständen vor.

Auch die Simse oberhalb der Fenster malte er sich schon aus, konnte sich jedoch plötzlich nicht mehr richtig konzentrieren. Er hatte das Gefühl, daß ihn jemand beobachtete. Das ist doch albern, dachte er – und wenn schon … Natürlich werde ich beobachtet – von den Vögeln, den Füchsen und Wildkatzen, den Eichhörnchen, Ratten, Mäusen, Wieseln, Hermelinen und was sonst noch so kreucht und fleugt hier im Wald.

Zur Mittagszeit rasteten sie am Rande eines kleinen Bachs. Sie tranken das klare Wasser und aßen kalten Speck und Holzäpfel, die sie vom Waldboden klaubten.

Am Nachmittag war Martha sehr müde. Einmal fiel sie fast hundert Schritt zurück. Während sie auf das Mädchen warteten, dachte Tom daran, was für ein hübscher, kräftiger Blondschopf Alfred in jenem Alter gewesen war. Mit einer Mischung aus Zärtlichkeit und Verärgerung sah er seiner Tochter zu, die langsam aufschloß und dabei lauthals das Schwein ob seiner Trägheit beschimpfte. Plötzlich brach, nur wenige Schritte vor Martha, eine Gestalt aus dem Unterholz, und dann geschah alles so schnell, daß Tom glaubte, seinen Augen nicht trauen zu können: Der Mann, der dem Kind so unvermittelt in den Weg getreten war, schwang eine Keule hoch über seine Schultern. Ein Entsetzensschrei wollte sich Toms Kehle entringen, doch noch ehe er sich Bahn brechen konnte, schlug der Mann zu. Die Keule traf das Mädchen so wuchtig an der Schläfe, daß Tom den furchtbaren Aufschlag hörte. Martha stürzte zu Boden wie eine fallengelassene Puppe.

Tom rannte den Weg zurück; seine Füße trommelten auf dem harten Erdboden wie die Hufe von Lord Williams Schlachtroß. Er rannte, so schnell er nur konnte, und dabei war ihm, als sähe er die Geschehnisse, die sich vor seinen Augen abspielten, hoch oben auf einem Fresko an einer Kirchenwand: Er sah sie, aber er konnte nichts daran ändern. Der Wegelagerer, daran konnte kein Zweifel bestehen, war ein Outlaw, ein Vogelfreier. Es war ein kleiner, untersetzter Mann in einem braunen Rock. Seine Füße waren nackt. Für Bruchteile eines Augenblicks sah er Tom direkt an. Das Gesicht des Mannes war grauenvoll verstümmelt: Man hatte ihm die Lippen abgeschnitten – wahrscheinlich als Strafe für ein Delikt, das eine grobe Lüge einschloß. Die entstellte, von wulstigem Narbengewebe umgebene Mundpartie verwandelte das Gesicht in eine unablässig grinsende Fratze. Wäre da nicht die am Boden liegende Martha gewesen – allein der entsetzliche Anblick hätte Tom zurückschaudern lassen.

Der Wegelagerer wandte den Blick von Tom: Das Schwein war ihm wichtiger. Er trieb es mit einem Stock in das dichte Unterholz und war gleich darauf verschwunden.

Tom fiel neben Martha auf die Knie. Er legte ihr seine breite Hand auf die schmale Brust und spürte den Herzschlag; kräftig und regelmäßig wie er war, vertrieb er Toms schlimmste Befürchtungen. Marthas Augen waren jedoch geschlossen, und hellrotes Blut sickerte in ihr blondes Haar.

Schon kniete auch Agnes neben ihm. Sie berührte Marthas Brust, prüfte den Puls, legte ihr die Hand auf die Stirn. Dann sah sie Tom an; ihr Blick war hart und gefühllos. »Sie wird's überleben«, sagte sie. »Hol uns das Schwein jetzt zurück!«

Rasch schnallte Tom seinen Ranzen mit den Werkzeugen ab und ließ ihn auf den Boden fallen. Mit der Linken zog er den großen Eisenhammer aus dem Gürtel, in der Rechten trug er nach wie vor die Pike. Am niedergetrampelten Buschwerk erkannte er, wohin der Dieb geflohen war, und dann quiekte das Schwein vernehmlich.

Tom nahm die Verfolgung auf. Der Fluchtweg ließ sich kaum verfehlen, denn der Wegelagerer war ein gewichtiger Mann und hatte mit dem Schwein eine unverkennbare Spur aus niedergetretenen Blumen, Sträuchern und jungen Bäumen hinterlassen. Tom jagte ihm hinterher, getrieben von rasender Wut und dem inbrünstigen Wunsch, den Kerl zu erwischen und niederzumachen. Er brach durch einen niedrigen Jungbirkenwald, stürmte einen Abhang hinunter und stampfte durch einen kleinen Sumpf, an dessen jenseitigem Ende ein Pfad weiterführte. Hier gab es keine zertrampelten Pflanzen mehr; der Dieb mochte sich nach links oder rechts gewendet haben. Tom blieb stehen und lauschte. Irgendwo zu seiner Linken quiekte das Schwein, und hinter ihm rannte noch jemand durch den Wald, vermutlich Alfred. Tom wandte sich nach links.

Der Pfad führte durch eine Senke und nach einer scharfen Biegung einen Hügel empor. Das Schwein war jetzt ganz deutlich zu hören. Tom keuchte schwer, als er den Hang hinaufjagte; das jahrelange Einatmen von Steinstaub hatte seine Lungen geschwächt. Dann hatte er die Steigung bewältigt und konnte den Dieb sehen. Er war nur zwanzig oder dreißig Schritt vor ihm und rannte, als sei der Teufel hinter ihm her. Tom legte einen Zwischenspurt ein und verringerte den Abstand. Wenn er nicht lockerließ, mußte er den Dieb über kurz oder lang erwischen, denn ein Mann mit einem Schwein unterm Arm kann nicht so schnell laufen wie ein Mann ohne Schwein. Seine Brust schmerzte. Der Dieb war noch fünfzehn Schritt entfernt, noch zwölf ... Tom hob die Pike wie einen Speer. Nur noch ein kleines Stückchen näher, dann ... Noch elf Schritt, zehn ...

Da tauchte im Gebüsch am Wegrand plötzlich ein schmales Gesicht unter einem grünen Hut auf; Tom nahm es gerade noch am Rande seines Blickfelds wahr, bevor die Pike seiner wurfbereiten Hand entglitt. Es war zu spät, beiseite zu springen. Ein derber Ast wurde ihm in den Weg geworfen. Tom stolperte und stürzte zu Boden.

Die Pike war verloren, aber er hatte ja noch seinen Hammer. Er rollte sich ab und kam wieder auf die Beine. Erst jetzt merkte er, daß er es mit zwei Gegnern zu tun hatte – dem Mann mit dem grünen Hut und einem Glatzkopf mit verfilztem, weißem Bart. Sie gingen gleichzeitig auf ihn los.

Tom sprang beiseite und holte aus. Sein Hammer sauste auf den grünen Hut nieder, doch der Mann wich im letzten Moment aus, so daß ihn der schwere eiserne Hammerkopf nur an der Schulter traf. Mit einem Schmerzensschrei ging er zu Boden, wobei er sich den Arm hielt, als wäre er gebrochen. Um ein zweites Mal auszuholen, fehlte die Zeit, denn inzwischen war der Glatzkopf näher gerückt. Tom stieß ihm den Hammerkopf ins Gesicht und brach ihm den Backenknochen.

Die beiden Wegelagerer hielten sich ihre Wunden und machten sich davon; von ihnen war kein Widerstand mehr zu erwarten. Tom sah sich nach dem Schweinedieb um. Er rannte noch immer den Pfad entlang, hatte jetzt aber wieder einen größeren Vorsprung. Ohne Rücksicht auf die Schmerzen in seiner Brust nahm Tom die Verfolgung wieder auf. Doch schon nach wenigen Schritten hörte er hinter sich eine vertraute Stimme.

Alfred.

Tom blieb stehen und sah sich um.

Die beiden Halunken schlugen auf Alfred ein, der sich mit Händen und Füßen wehrte. Drei-, viermal erwischte er den Kerl mit dem grünen Hut am Kopf, dann trat er dem Glatzkopf gegen das Schienbein. Doch keiner der beiden ließ von ihm ab. Es gelang ihnen, sich so nahe an ihn heranzudrängen, daß er nicht mehr weit genug ausholen konnte und seine Schläge wirkungslos blieben. Tom zögerte, hin und her gerissen zwischen der Entscheidung, entweder den Schweinedieb zu verfolgen oder seinen Sohn zu retten. Schließlich gelang es dem Kahlköpfigen, Alfred ein Bein zu stellen. Der Junge stürzte zu Boden. Sofort waren die beiden Wegelagerer über ihm und prügelten wie besessen auf ihn ein.

Tom eilte ihm zu Hilfe. Er rammte den Kahlkopf mit dem ganzen Gewicht seines Körpers, so daß der Mann in hohem Bogen ins Gebüsch flog. Dann drehte er sich um und visierte einmal mehr mit dem Hammer den grünen Hut an. Der Angreifer hatte die Wucht des Hammers schon einmal geschmeckt und konnte sich ohnehin nur noch mit einem Arm verteidigen. Dennoch gelang es ihm, dem ersten Hieb auszuweichen und, noch ehe Tom ein zweites Mal ausholen konnte, im Unterholz zu verschwinden.

Tom drehte sich nach den beiden anderen Wegelagerern um: Der Kahlkopf machte sich über den Pfad davon; von dem Schweinedieb, der sich in entgegengesetzter Richtung aus dem Staub gemacht hatte, war nichts mehr zu sehen.

Ein bitterer, gotteslästerlicher Fluch entfuhr seinen Lippen: Das Schwein entsprach der Hälfte ihrer Ersparnisse, die sie in diesem Sommer zurückgelegt hatten. Schwer keuchend sank Tom zu Boden.

»Wir haben drei Männer in die Flucht geschlagen«, sagte Alfred aufgeregt.

Tom sah ihn an. »Aber sie haben unser Schwein.« Die Wut brannte in seinem Magen wie saurer Most. Sie hatten das Schwein im Frühjahr von ihren ersten Ersparnissen gekauft und es den ganzen Sommer über gemästet. Ein fettes Schwein brachte sechzig Pence auf dem Markt. Sein Fleisch konnte, zusammen mit ein paar Kohlköpfen und einem Sack Getreide, eine ganze Familie über den Winter bringen. Aus seiner Haut ließen sich ein Paar Lederschuhe und ein oder zwei Beutel fertigen. Der Verlust des Schweins war eine Katastrophe.

Neidvoll betrachtete Tom seinen Sohn: Alfred hatte sich von der Verfolgungsjagd und dem anschließenden Kampf schon wieder erholt und wartete nun ungeduldig auf seinen Vater. Einst konnte ich laufen wie der Wind, ohne mein Herz zu spüren, dachte Tom. Wie lange mag das her sein? Vor zwanzig Jahren war ich in seinem Alter ... vor zwanzig Jahren! Mir ist, als wäre es erst gestern gewesen.

Er rappelte sich auf. Auf dem Rückweg, der sie zunächst wieder den Pfad entlang führte, legte er den Arm um Alfreds breite Schultern. Der Junge war noch etwa eine Spanne kleiner als er, aber das würde sich bald ändern. Gut möglich, daß Alfred ihm eines Tages sogar über den Kopf wuchs. Ich hoffe, sein Verstand wächst ebenso schnell, dachte Tom und sagte: »Jeder Narr kann in eine Schlägerei geraten. Der kluge Mann weiß sich herauszuhalten.« Alfred sah ihn verwirrt an.

Sie verließen den Pfad, stapften durch den Morast und kletterten den angrenzenden Hang empor. Erst als sie das Dickicht aus jungen Birken erreichten, fiel Tom Martha wieder ein, und erneut stieg die Wut in ihm hoch: Der Wegelagerer hatte das unschuldige Kind, das nie eine Gefahr für ihn war, ohne jeden Grund niedergeschlagen und verletzt.

Tom beschleunigte seine Schritte, und wenige Augenblicke später stand er zusammen mit Alfred wieder auf der Straße. Martha lag noch unverändert an derselben Stelle auf dem Boden. Ihre Augen waren geschlossen, und das Blut in ihrem Haar trocknete bereits. Agnes kniete neben ihr – und neben Agnes kniete, zu Toms größter Überraschung, eine fremde Frau, die einen kleinen Jungen bei sich hatte. Kein Wunder, daß ich mich heute morgen immer wieder beobachtet fühlte, dachte er, in diesem Wald scheint es ja vor Menschen zu wimmeln! Er bückte sich und legte Martha die Hand auf die Brust. Ihr Atem ging gleichmäßig.

»Sie wird bald aufwachen«, sagte die Fremde mit einer Stimme, die keinen Widerspruch zuließ. »Und dann wird sie kotzen. Danach ist alles wieder gut.«

Tom betrachtete die Fremde neugierig. Sie war ziemlich jung, vielleicht ein Dutzend Jahre jünger als er. Ihr kurzes ledernes Überkleid enthüllte geschmeidige, gebräunte Glieder. Ihr Gesicht war hübsch, und ihr dunkelbraunes Haar bildete über der Stirn eine Teufelsmütze. Tom spürte einen Anflug von Begehren. Doch da hob die Fremde den Kopf und sah ihn an. Sie hatte tiefliegende Augen von seltsam honiggoldener Farbe, die ihrem Antlitz einen magischen Zug verliehen, und ihr Blick war von ungewöhnlicher Intensität. Tom war in diesem Augenblick überzeugt, daß die Frau seine Gedanken gelesen hatte.

Peinlich berührt, wandte er seinen Blick ab und sah Agnes an. »Wo ist das Schwein?« fragte sie vorwurfsvoll.

»Da waren noch zwei andere Outlaws«, erwiderte Tom, und Alfred fügte hinzu: »Wir haben die beiden niedergeschlagen, aber der mit dem Schwein ist uns entkommen.«

Agnes quittierte die Worte mit einem finsteren Blick, sagte aber kein Wort mehr.

»Wir sollten das Mädchen in den Schatten legen«, bemerkte die Fremde. »Allerdings müssen wir dabei vorsichtig sein.«

Sie erhob sich, und Tom erkannte, daß sie nicht besonders groß war, gut einen Fuß kleiner als er selbst. Er bückte sich und nahm Martha behutsam auf. Ihr kindlicher Körper kam ihm beinahe gewichtslos vor. Ein paar Schritt weiter bettete er das nach wie vor völlig kraftlose Mädchen auf eine grasbewachsene Stelle am Fuße einer alten Eiche.

Alfred sammelte die Werkzeuge ein, die seit dem Überfall auf der Straße lagen. Der fremde Knabe sah ihm mit weit aufgerissenen Augen und offenem Mund zu. Er mochte ungefähr drei Jahre jünger sein als Alfred und sah recht merkwürdig aus. Tom fiel auf, daß ihm der sinnliche Reiz seiner Mutter völlig fehlte. Er hatte sehr blasse Haut, hellrote Haare, leicht hervortretende grüne Augen und den stierendblöden Blick eines Dummerjans. Eines dieser Kinder, die, wenn sie nicht jung sterben, später als Dorftrottel enden, dachte Tom. Alfred fühlte sich unter diesem Blick sichtlich unwohl.

Unvermittelt riß der fremde Knabe ohne ein Wort der Erklärung Alfred die Säge aus der Hand und betrachtete sie, als habe er so etwas noch nie gesehen. Alfred, wütend über diese Ungehörigkeit, nahm ihm die Säge wieder ab, was der Junge ohne Gemütsbewegung zuließ. Die Mutter rief: »Jack! Benimm dich!« Sein Verhalten war ihr offensichtlich peinlich.

Tom sah sie an. Zwischen ihr und dem Kind bestand nicht die geringste Ähnlichkeit. »Seid Ihr die Mutter?« fragte er.

»Ja, die bin ich. Ich heiße Ellen.«

»Wo ist Euer Mann?«

»Er ist tot.«

Das war eine Überraschung. »Seid Ihr etwa alleine unterwegs?« fragte Tom ungläubig. Diese Wälder waren schon für einen Mann wie ihn gefährlich genug – eine Frau konnte kaum darauf hoffen, sie lebend wieder zu verlassen.

»Wir sind nicht unterwegs«, antwortete Ellen. »Wir leben hier im Wald.«

Tom war entsetzt. »Das heißt, Ihr seid ...« Er sprach nicht weiter, weil er die Frau nicht beleidigen wollte.

»Outlaws, jawohl«, sagte Ellen. »Oder meint Ihr etwa, alle Outlaws sehen so aus wie Faramond Openmouth, der Euch das Schwein gestohlen hat?«

»Ja«, sagte Tom, obwohl er eigentlich hätte sagen wollen, *ich hätte nie gedacht, daß es unter den Outlaws so schöne Frauen gibt.* Unfähig, seine Neugier zu zügeln, fragte er: »Was war Euer Vergehen?«

»Ich habe einen Priester verflucht«, sagte sie, ohne ihn dabei anzusehen.

Gar so schlimm war dieses Vergehen in Toms Augen nicht. Vielleicht war es ja ein sehr mächtiger Priester gewesen – oder ein überempfindlicher. Oder aber Ellen zog es vor, die Wahrheit für sich zu behalten.

Er sah Martha an. Kurz darauf öffnete das Mädchen die Augen. Sie war verwirrt und hatte wohl auch ein wenig Angst. Agnes kniete sich neben sie. »Es ist alles gut«, sagte sie. »Du bist in Sicherheit.«

Martha setzte sich auf und übergab sich. Agnes hielt sie im Arm, bis die Krämpfe vorüber waren. Tom dachte: Alle Achtung, Ellens Voraussage hat sich erfüllt. Und wenn sich auch der zweite Teil erfüllt, wird es Martha gleich wieder bessergehen. Er fühlte sich auf einmal ungeheuer erleichtert und war selbst überrascht von der Stärke dieser Empfindung. Ich hätte es nicht ertragen, wenn ich mein kleines Mädchen verloren hätte, dachte er und kämpfte mit den Tränen. Ellen bedachte ihn mit einem mitfühlenden Blick, und erneut war ihm, als schauten ihm ihre blaßgoldenen Augen direkt ins Herz.

Er brach einen Zweig von der Eiche, streifte die Blätter ab und reinigte damit Marthas Gesicht. Das Mädchen war noch immer sehr blaß.

»Sie braucht jetzt Ruhe«, sagte Ellen. »Laßt sie ausruhen – so lange, wie ein Mann braucht, um drei Meilen zurückzulegen.«

Tom prüfte den Sonnenstand. Der Tag war noch lang. Er beschloß zu warten und machte es sich bequem. Agnes wiegte Martha sanft in ihren Armen. Der Knabe Jack richtete seine Aufmerksamkeit jetzt auf die kleine Verwundete und starrte sie mit demselben Idiotenblick an wie zuvor Alfred. Tom hätte gern mehr über Ellen erfahren und fragte sich, ob sie sich vielleicht dazu bewegen ließ, ihre Geschichte zu erzählen. Er wollte unter keinen Umständen, daß sie jetzt fortging.

»Wie ist denn das alles soweit gekommen?« fragte er unbestimmt.

Wieder sah sie ihm in die Augen. Und dann fing sie an zu erzählen.

Ihr Vater war ein Ritter gewesen, ein großer, starker, gewalttätiger Mann, der sich Söhne wünschte, mit denen er reiten und ringen und jagen konnte, Gefährten, die des Abends mit ihm zechten. Doch die Erfüllung seiner Wünsche blieb ihm versagt, denn er bekam eine Tochter, Ellen, und dann starb seine Frau. Er heiratete wieder, doch seine zweite Frau war unfruchtbar. Es kam so weit, daß er Ellens Stiefmutter verabscheute, und schließlich jagte er sie gar aus dem Haus. Er mußte ein sehr grausamer Mensch gewesen sein, obgleich Ellen davon nichts merkte. Sie verehrte ihn und teilte seine Abneigung gegen die zweite Gemahlin, und so blieb sie auch bei ihrem Vater, als die Stiefmutter endlich ging. Sie wuchs nun in einem reinen Männerhaushalt auf. Ellen spielte nicht mit Kätzchen und kümmerte sich nicht um alte blinde Hunde, sondern sie ließ sich die Haare stutzen und trug einen Dolch. Als sie Marthas Alter erreicht hatte, spuckte sie aus wie ein Mann, vertilgte die Äpfel mitsamt dem Kerngehäuse, und war ihr ein Pferd nicht zu Willen, so trat sie es so heftig in den Bauch, daß es vor Schreck die Luft anhielt und ihr gestattete, den Sattelgürtel noch ein Loch fester zu zurren. Sie wußte, daß alle Männer, die nicht zum Gefolge ihres Vaters gehörten, Schwanzschlecker hießen und alle Frauen, die sich nicht mit ihnen abgeben wollten, Schweinehuren.

Die tiefere Bedeutung dieser Schimpfworte blieb ihr damals zwar noch schleierhaft, interessierte sie aber auch gar nicht.

Der gleichmäßige Klang ihrer Stimme in der milden Luft des Herbstnachmittags lullte Tom ein. Er schloß die Augen und sah Ellen als kleines, flachbrüstiges Gör mit dreckigem Gesicht bei ihrem Vater und seinen Spießgesellen am langen Tisch sitzen. Sie goß starkes Bier in sich hinein, rülpste und grölte wilde Kampfgesänge, in denen es um Plündern, Rauben und Schänden, um Pferde und Burgen und edle Jungfrauen ging ... bis sie zu guter Letzt umfiel und auf den harten Brettern ihren Rausch ausschlief.

Wäre sie nur immer so flachbrüstig geblieben, ihr Leben hätte einen weit glücklicheren Verlauf genommen! Doch mit den Jahren änderte sich das Verhalten der Männer in ihrer Gegenwart. Sie sahen sie mit anderen Augen an und brüllten nicht mehr vor Lachen, wenn Ellen zu ihnen sagte: »Haut ab, sonst schneid' ich euch die Eier ab und werf' sie den Schweinen zum Fraß vor!« Die Männer glotzten sie an, wenn sie des Abends ihr wollenes Überkleid auszog und sich in ihrem langen Leinenhemd zum Schlafen niederlegte. Und wenn sie draußen im Wald ihr Wasser abschlugen, wandten sie ihr im Gegensatz zu früher den Rücken zu.

Mit der Kirche hatte der Vater sonst wenig im Sinne, doch eines Tages überraschte Ellen ihn im Gespräch mit dem Dorfpfarrer – und die beiden sahen sie an, als unterhielten sie sich gerade über sie. Am nächsten Morgen sagte ihr Vater zu ihr: »Nun geh mit Henry und Everard und tu, was sie dir anschaffen.« Dann küßte er sie auf die Stirn. Ellen fragte sich, was in ihn gefahren sein mochte – wurde er auf seine alten Tage plötzlich sanft und milde? Sie sattelte ihren schnellen Grauschimmel – einen Zelter oder ein Pony zu reiten lehnte sie ab – und machte sich mit den beiden Bewaffneten auf den Weg.

Die Männer lieferten Ellen in einem Nonnenkloster ab und ritten wieder zurück. Sie tobte und schrie und fluchte gotteslästerlich. Mit ihrem Dolch verletzte sie die Äbtissin, dann rannte sie davon und lief nach Hause. Ihr Vater schickte sie wieder zurück – auf dem Rücken eines Esels, an Händen und Füßen gefesselt und an den Sattel gebunden. Im Kloster wurde sie in eine Büßerzelle gesteckt und darin festgehalten, bis die Wunde der Äbtissin geheilt war. Es war ein kaltes, feuchtes und dunkles Loch. Sie bekam Wasser, aber nichts zu essen. Kaum war sie aus dem Karzer entlassen, lief sie wieder davon, doch ihr Vater sandte sie umgehend zurück. Diesmal wurde sie ausgepeitscht, bevor man sie wieder in die dunkle Zelle steckte.

Es gelang ihnen schn...
Ellen legte den Habit der No...
lernte die Gebete auswendig, obg...
die Nonnen haßte, die Heiligen ver...
glaubte, was ihr über Gott erzählt wurde. ...
Schreiben, Musizieren und Rechnen, Zeichnen...
Vaterhaus hatte man Englisch und Französisch gesp...

Das Klosterleben erwies sich schließlich als gar nich...
war eine reine Frauengesellschaft mit eigenen Regeln und R...
anders zwar, aber in vielfacher Hinsicht ähnlich der vertrauten M.n-
nergesellschaft daheim. Alle Nonnen mußten ein gewisses Pensum an
körperlicher Arbeit leisten. Ellen wurde schon bald mit der Pferde-
pflege betraut und brachte es binnen kurzem zur Stallmeisterin.

Armut war nie ein Problem für sie. Gehorsam fiel ihr schon erheblich schwerer, aber sie lernte ihn mit der Zeit. Das dritte Gelübde,
die Keuschheit, nahm sie weniger ernst, und es kam hin und wieder
durchaus vor, daß sie – allein schon, um der Äbtissin zu trotzen –
die eine oder andere Novizin einweihte in die Freuden der ...

An dieser Stelle unterbrach Agnes Ellens Erzählung. Sie nahm
Martha bei der Hand und zog sie fort, um ihr irgendwo an einem
Wasserlauf das Gesicht zu waschen und ihr Kleid zu reinigen. Zu
ihrem Schutz nahm sie auch Alfred mit, obgleich sie versprach, in
Rufweite zu bleiben. Selbst Jack erhob sich und traf Anstalten, ihr zu
folgen, doch Agnes wollte ihn nicht dabei haben und sagte es ihm
deutlich. Jack schien sie zu verstehen, denn er setzte sich sofort wieder
hin. Tom war klar, daß es seiner Frau einerseits darum ging, ihren
Kindern den Fortgang dieser ebenso gottlosen wie unzüchtigen Geschichte vorzuenthalten – und daß sie ihn andererseits nicht mit Ellen
allein lassen wollte.

Eines Tages, fuhr Ellen fort, hatte der Zelter der Äbtissin gelahmt.
Es geschah einige Tagesreisen vom Kloster entfernt. Da sie sich unweit
der Abtei von Kingsbridge befand, lieh sich die Äbtissin vom dortigen
Prior ein anderes Pferd. Nach ihrer Rückkehr befahl sie Ellen, das
geborgte Pferd heimzuführen und dann den lahmen Zelter zurück-
zubringen.

Im Pferdestall des Klosters, in Sichtweite der verfallenden alten
Kathedrale von Kingsbridge, begegnete Ellen einem jungen Mann, der
aussah wie ein geprügelter kleiner Hund. Er hatte die tapsige Anmut
und witternde Wachsamkeit eines Welpen, wirkte jedoch schüchtern
und verschreckt, als ob man ihm all seine Verspieltheit mit Prügeln

ansprach, verstand er sie nicht. Sie
........em, doch er war kein Mönch. Schließlich sagte
..... Worte auf französisch, da strahlte er sie freudig an und
antwortete in derselben Sprache.

Ellen kehrte nie wieder in das Nonnenkloster zurück und lebte
seither im Wald. Anfangs hauste sie in einem primitiven Unterschlupf
aus Laub und Zweigen, später fand sie eine trockene Höhle. Ellen
hatte die männlichen Fertigkeiten, die sie im Hause ihres Vaters gelernt hatte, nicht vergessen: Sie wußte, wie man Rehe erlegte, konnte
Kaninchenfallen bauen und Schwäne mit Pfeil und Bogen zur Strecke
bringen. Sie konnte das gejagte Wild ausnehmen und das Fleisch
kochen, ja sie verstand sich sogar aufs Säubern und Gerben der Felle
und stellte daraus ihre Kleidung her. Außer von Wild ernährte sie
sich von den Früchten des Waldes, von Nüssen, Kräutern und Wildge-
müse. Alles, was sie sonst noch brauchte – Salz, Wollkleidung, ein
Beil oder ein neues Messer –, mußte sie stehlen.

Sie brachte Jack zur Welt; das war für sie die schlimmste Zeit ...

Und der Franzose? wollte Tom fragen. Was war mit dem? War er
Jacks Vater? Und wenn – wann war er gestorben? Und wie? Aber er
behielt die Fragen für sich. Er las es ihr am Gesicht ab, daß sie über
diesen Teil der Geschichte Stillschweigen bewahren wollte, und zu
den Leuten, die sich gegen ihren Willen zu etwas überreden ließen,
gehörte diese Frau bestimmt nicht.

Inzwischen war Ellens Vater gestorben, und seine Gefolgschaft
hatte sich in alle Himmelsrichtungen zerstreut. Sie hatte nun auf der
ganzen Welt keine Verwandten und Freunde mehr. Als sie die Stunde
ihrer Niederkunft kommen fühlte, machte sie vor dem Eingang ihrer
Höhle ein großes Feuer, das die ganze Nacht über brannte. Sie hatte
genug Wasser und Nahrung, Pfeil und Bogen sowie ein Messer zur
Abwehr der Wölfe und streunender Hunde lagen griffbereit. Sie besaß
sogar einen schweren roten Mantel, den sie einem Bischof gestohlen
hatte; in ihn wollte sie den Säugling wickeln. Womit sie nicht gerechnet hatte, waren die Schmerzen und Ängste der Geburt. Lange Zeit
glaubte sie, sterben zu müssen, doch als alles vorüber war, war sie
noch am Leben und das Neugeborene gesund und munter.

In den folgenden elf Jahren führten Ellen und Jack ein einfaches,
bescheidenes Leben. Der Wald bot ihnen alles, was sie brauchte,
solange sie sich darum kümmerten, rechtzeitig Wintervorräte anzulegen – Äpfel, Nüsse und gepökeltes oder geräuchertes Wildbret. Gäbe
es keine Könige und Edelleute, keine Bischöfe und Vögte, dachte Ellen

mitunter, dann könnte ein jeder so leben wie wir und damit glücklich und zufrieden sein.

Tom fragte sie, wie sie mit den anderen Outlaws im Walde auskam, mit Männern wie Faramond Openmouth zum Beispiel. Er stellte sich vor, wie sie des Nachts an ihre Lagerstelle schlichen, um ihr Gewalt anzutun, und obwohl er nie in seinem Leben eine Frau gegen ihren Willen besessen hatte – nicht einmal seine eigene –, spürte er jetzt die Lust in seinen Lenden.

Die anderen Outlaws, erklärte Ellen, fürchteten sich vor ihr. Er sah ihr in die leuchtenden, hellen Augen und wußte warum: Sie hielten Ellen für eine Hexe. Den gesetzestreuen Bürgern, die durch den Wald reisten und genau wußten, daß sie mit einem Vogelfreien tun und lassen konnten, was sie wollten, und nicht einmal dann, wenn sie ihn totschlugen, eine Strafe zu befürchten hatten, ging Ellen einfach aus dem Weg. Und warum hatte sie sich vor ihm, Tom, nicht versteckt? Sie habe das verwundete Kind gesehen, sagte sie, und ihre Hilfe anbieten wollen; schließlich habe sie selbst ein Kind.

Sie hatte ihren Sohn in allem unterwiesen, was man ihr im Vaterhaus über die Jagd und den Umgang mit Waffen beigebracht hatte. Und dann hatte sie ihn gelehrt, was sie bei den Nonnen gelernt hatte: Schreiben und Lesen, Musik und Zahlen, Französisch und Latein, Zeichnen und sogar die Geschichten aus der Bibel. An langen Winterabenden hatte sie ihm zudem das Vermächtnis seines französischen Vaters anvertraut, der mehr Legenden, Gedichte und Lieder kannte als jedermann sonst auf der Welt.

Tom glaubte ihr nicht, daß der Knabe Jack schreiben und lesen konnte. Er selbst konnte gerade seinen Namen und eine Handvoll anderer Wörter wie *Pence* und *Schritt* und *Scheffel* schreiben. Agnes, die Tochter eines Priesters, war da schon geschickter, doch auch ihr fiel es schwer genug; sie schrieb sehr langsam und bemüht, und die Zungenspitze sah ihr dabei aus dem Mundwinkel. Alfred konnte überhaupt nicht schreiben, ja er war kaum imstande, seinen eigenen Namen zu erkennen, und Martha konnte nicht einmal das. Unvorstellbar, daß dieses blöde wirkende Kind mehr vom Schreiben und Lesen verstehen sollte als Toms gesamte Familie!

Ellen forderte ihren Sohn auf, etwas zu schreiben. Jack glättete mit der Hand einen Fleck Erde und kratzte mit den Fingern Buchstaben hinein. Tom erkannte das erste Wort – *Alfred* –, mußte danach jedoch passen und kam sich dabei wie ein Narr vor. Ellen befreite ihn aus seiner peinlichen Lage, indem sie ihm den ganzen Satz vorlas:

»Alfred ist größer als Jack.« Dann zeichnete der Junge flink zwei Figuren in den Sand, eine große und eine kleine, und obwohl es sich um ziemlich einfache Gestalten handelte, konnte man gut erkennen, daß die eine breitschultrig war und ziemlich dämlich guckte, während die andere, kleinere, offensichtlich grinste. Tom, der selber über ein gewisses Zeichentalent verfügte, war von der Einfachheit und Kraft der in die Erde gekratzten Figuren beeindruckt.

Und doch wirkte das Kind auf ihn wie ein Idiot.

Ellen ahnte, was Tom dachte, und bekannte, daß ihr das kürzlich auch aufgefallen sei. Jack hatte nie in seinem Leben mit anderen Kindern gespielt, ja ihm fehlte – außer mit seiner Mutter – jeglicher Umgang mit anderen Menschen. Infolgedessen war er wie ein wildes Tier aufgewachsen und hatte trotz all seiner erlernten Kenntnisse nicht die geringste Ahnung, wie er sich in Gegenwart anderer Menschen benehmen sollte – und deshalb redete er kein Wort, stierte nur großäugig vor sich hin und schnappte sich Gegenstände, ohne zu fragen.

Zum erstenmal seit Beginn ihrer Geschichte wirkte Ellen bei diesen Worten verletzlich, und die Aura der durch nichts zu bezwingenden Unabhängigkeit fiel von ihr ab. Tom erkannte, daß sie im Grunde ebenso besorgt wie ratlos war. Um Jacks willen mußte sie sich wieder der menschlichen Gesellschaft anschließen – bloß wie? Einem Mann war es vielleicht möglich, einen Grundherrn dazu zu bewegen, ihm einen kleinen Hof zu verpachten – vor allem, wenn er ihm überzeugend vorlog, er sei gerade von einer langen Pilgerfahrt nach Jerusalem oder Santiago de Compostela zurückgekehrt. Gewiß gab es auch Bauernhöfe, die von Frauen bewirtschaftet wurden, doch handelte es sich dabei ausnahmslos um Witwen mit erwachsenen Söhnen. Kein Mensch, weder in der Stadt noch auf dem flachen Land, würde ihr Arbeit geben – ganz abgesehen davon, daß sie keine Unterkunft besaß und ungelernte Arbeitskräfte von ihrem Herrn nur selten ein Obdach gestellt bekamen. Sie war ein Mensch ohne Namen, ein Nichts.

Tom empfand Mitleid mit ihr. Sie hatte ihrem Kind alles gegeben, was sie konnte, aber das reichte nicht aus. Sie sah nirgendwo einen Ausweg. Sie war schön, gescheit und stark – und dennoch dazu verurteilt, bis zum Ende ihrer Tage gemeinsam mit ihrem seltsamen Sohn im tiefen Waldversteck zu hausen.

Agnes kam mit Martha und Alfred zurück. Tom musterte Martha nicht ohne Sorge, doch sie sah aus, als sei ihr noch nie etwas Schlimmeres widerfahren als eine gründliche Gesichtswäsche. Ellens Kummer hatte

Tom für eine Weile abgelenkt, doch nun holte ihn die eigene Misere wieder ein: Er hatte keine Arbeit, und sein Schwein war ihm gestohlen worden. Die Schatten wurden bereits merklich länger. Tom begann die geringe Habe zusammenzusuchen, die ihnen noch verblieben war.

»Wo zieht Ihr hin?« fragte Ellen.

»Nach Winchester«, antwortete Tom. In Winchester gab es eine Burg, einen bischöflichen Palast, verschiedene Klöster – und vor allem eine Kathedrale.

»Salisbury ist näher«, erwiderte Ellen. »Und als ich zum letztenmal dort war, wurde am Dom gerade gebaut. Sie waren dabei, ihn zu erweitern.«

Tom hörte es voller Freude: genau das, was er suchte! Gelang es ihm, einen Arbeitsplatz an einer Dombauhütte zu bekommen, konnte er seine Fähigkeiten unter Beweis stellen und es über kurz oder lang zum Baumeister bringen. »Wie kommen wir von hier aus nach Salisbury?« fragte er aufgeregt.

»Ihr müßt umkehren. Nach drei oder vier Meilen erreicht Ihr dann eine Weggabelung – erinnert Ihr Euch?«

»Ja, da war doch ein Teich mit übelriechendem Wasser ...«

»Ganz recht. Wenn Ihr Euch dort nach rechts wendet, gelangt Ihr nach Salisbury.«

Sie verabschiedeten sich. Agnes hatte Ellen von Anfang an nicht gemocht, aber sie überwand sich und sagte höflich: »Ich danke Euch, daß Ihr mir bei Marthas Pflege zur Hand gegangen seid.«

Ellen lächelte und sah ihnen sehnsuchtsvoll nach.

Nach einiger Zeit warf Tom einen Blick zurück. Ellen stand noch immer am selben Fleck, die Beine leicht gespreizt und eine Hand schattenspendend über den Augen, den merkwürdigen Knaben an ihrer Seite. Tom winkte ihr, und sie winkte zurück.

»Eine bemerkenswerte Frau«, sagte er zu Agnes.

Agnes erwiderte nichts darauf, doch Alfred sagte: »Der Junge war vielleicht komisch ...«

Sie gingen der tiefstehenden Herbstsonne entgegen. Was für eine Stadt mag Salisbury wohl sein? fragte sich Tom; er war noch nie dort gewesen. Natürlich war er aufgeregt. Zwar träumte er davon, eine von Grund auf neue Kathedrale zu errichten, doch wann gab es schon einmal eine solche Gelegenheit? Viel eher fand sich ein altes Gebäude, das restauriert, erweitert oder umgebaut wurde. Ihm war jetzt alles recht – Hauptsache, die Aussicht, später einmal eine Kirche nach eigenen Plänen bauen zu können, blieb ihm erhalten.

»Warum hat der Mann mich geschlagen?« fragte Martha.

»Weil er unser Schwein stehlen wollte«, gab Agnes zur Antwort.

»Soll er sich doch ein *eigenes* Schwein besorgen!« erwiderte das Mädchen empört. Es klang, als sei ihr gerade erst aufgegangen, daß der Wegelagerer ihnen ein Unrecht angetan hatte.

Wenn Ellen ein Handwerk erlernt hätte, brauchte sie sich keine Sorgen mehr zu machen, dachte Tom. Ein Steinmetz, ein Zimmermann, ein Weber oder ein Gerber konnte kaum in eine vergleichbare Lage geraten – er zog einfach in die nächste Stadt und suchte sich dort Arbeit. Gewiß, es gab auch ein paar Handwerkerinnen, aber das waren zumeist die Ehefrauen der Meister oder ihre Witwen. »Was sie braucht«, sagte Tom laut, »das ist ein Ehemann.«

»Meinen bekommt sie nicht«, bemerkte Agnes spröde.

Der Tag, an dem sie das Schwein verloren, war auch der letzte milde Herbsttag. Die Nacht verbrachten sie in einer Scheune. Als sie am nächsten Morgen wieder ins Freie traten, wölbte sich der Himmel über ihnen wie ein bleiernes Dach. Ein kalter Wind jagte Regenschauer über das Land. Sie packten ihre dicken, filzigen Winterumhänge aus, legten sie an und schnürten sie unter dem Kinn fest. Zum Schutz gegen die Nässe zogen sie sich die Kapuzen tief ins Gesicht, dann machten sie sich in gedrückter Stimmung auf den Weg – vier schwermütige Gespenster in einem Regensturm. Die Straße war matschig und mit Pfützen übersät; bei jedem Schritt spritzte Wasser unter ihren Holzschuhen auf.

Tom versuchte sich die Kathedrale von Salisbury vorzustellen. Im Prinzip war ein Dom oder eine Kathedrale das gleiche wie jede andere Kirche – der Unterschied bestand lediglich darin, daß eine Kathedrale auch Bischofssitz war. In der Praxis allerdings waren Kathedralen die größten, reichsten, erhabensten und vollkommensten Kirchen. Einfache Gewölbe mit Fenstern fand man unter ihnen kaum. In den meisten Fällen bestanden sie vielmehr aus drei Gewölben – einem großen, das die beiden kleineren zu seinen Seiten überragte wie das Haupt eines Menschen seine Schultern. Sie hießen Hauptschiff und Seitenschiffe. Das mittlere Gewölbe besaß keine Seitenwände, sondern ruhte auf Säulen, die durch Bögen miteinander verbunden waren und eine Arkade bildeten. Die Seitenschiffe dienten hauptsächlich zu Prozessionen – in Kathedralen oft sehr eindrucksvolle Ereignisse –, boten aber auch Raum für kleine Seitenkapellen, die bestimmten Heiligen geweiht waren und zusätzliche Spenden einbrachten. Kathedralen waren die kostspieligsten Gebäude der Welt – viel teurer noch als Bischofspaläste oder Burgen –, daher mußten sie entsprechend einträglich sein.

Salisbury lag näher, als Tom gedacht hatte. Gegen Mittag gelangten sie auf eine kleine Anhöhe, von der sich die Straße in einem langen, weiten Bogen abwärts zog. Jenseits der regengepeitschten Felder erhob sich die Hügelfestung Salisbury aus der Ebene wie ein Boot auf einem See. Der Regenschleier ließ keine Einzelheiten erkennen, doch Tom zählte vier oder fünf Türme, die hoch über die Stadtmauer emporragten. Der Anblick von soviel Mauerwerk ließ das Herz des Steinmetzen höher schlagen.

Ein eisiger Wind fegte über die Ebene, als sie ihren Weg fortsetzten, und ließ Gesichter und Hände frostkalt werden. Am Fuße des Hügels, zwischen vereinzelten Häusern, die aussahen, als seien sie aus der überquellenden Stadt herausgespült worden, trafen vier Straßen zusammen. Andere Reisende schlossen sich ihnen an. Gesenkten Hauptes und mit hochgezogenen Schultern trotteten die Menschen auf das Osttor zu, um hinter den hohen Mauern Schutz vor den Unbilden des Wetters zu suchen.

Auf dem steil ansteigenden Wegstück vor dem Tor holten sie einen mit Steinen beladenen Ochsenkarren ein. Tom sah darin ein gutes Zeichen. Der Fuhrmann ging gebeugt hinter dem Gefährt her und half mit der Schulter nach, doch auch so kamen die Ochsen nur sehr langsam voran. Tom erkannte, daß er hier einen Freund gewinnen konnte: Er gab Alfred einen Wink, und gemeinsam stemmten sie sich mit der Schulter gegen den Karren und halfen schieben.

Wenig später rumpelten die riesigen Holzräder über eine hölzerne Brücke, die einen tiefen und breiten, trockengefallenen Burggraben überspannte. Gewaltige Erdarbeiten waren nötig gewesen, um diesen Graben zu schaffen und mit dem Aushub die Stadtwälle aufzuschütten. Hunderte von Arbeitern mußten daran mitgewirkt haben. Das ist weit mehr Aufwand, dachte Tom, als es zum Ausheben der Fundamente für eine Kathedrale bedarf. Die Brücke knarrte und ächzte unter dem Gewicht des Karrens und der beiden mächtigen Zugtiere.

Vor dem Tor endete die Steigung, so daß der Ochsenkarren wieder aus eigener Kraft vorankam. Der Fuhrmann richtete sich auf, und Tom und Alfred taten es ihm nach. »Ich danke Euch herzlich«, sagte der Fuhrmann.

»Wofür sind die Steine eigentlich?« fragte Tom.

»Für die neue Kathedrale.«

»Neu? Ich dachte, die alte würde lediglich erweitert.«

Der Fuhrmann nickte. »Ja, so hieß es ursprünglich. Aber das ist schon zehn Jahre her. Inzwischen ist mehr neu als alt.«

Auch das war für Tom eine gute Nachricht. »Wer ist der Dombaumeister?« fragte er.

»John von Shaftesbury. Um die Planung kümmert sich allerdings auch Bischof Roger.«

Das war durchaus nichts Ungewöhnliches. Es kam nur selten vor, daß ein Bischof seinem Baumeister freie Hand ließ; viel öfter mußten die Baumeister die überschäumende Phantasie der Kleriker dämpfen und ihren hochfliegenden Plänen realistische Grenzen setzen. Die Handwerker warb allerdings wahrscheinlich John von Shaftesbury an.

Der Fuhrmann wies mit dem Kinn auf Toms Werkzeugranzen. »Steinmetz?« fragte er.

»Ja. Ich suche Arbeit.«

»Na, vielleicht habt Ihr Glück«, antwortete der Fuhrmann nüchtern. »Und wenn's an der Kathedrale nicht klappt, dann vielleicht an der Burg.«

»Wer ist der Burgherr?«

»Besagter Roger, er ist sowohl Bischof als auch Kastellan.«

Natürlich, dachte Tom. Von dem mächtigen Roger von Salisbury, der von jeher zum engsten Freundeskreis des Königs zählte, hatte er auch schon gehört.

Sie passierten das Tor und betraten die Stadt, die auf den ersten Blick ganz überfüllt wirkte, so eng drängten sich die Gebäude, die Menschen und die Tiere in ihren Mauern. Sie sah aus, als könne sie jederzeit aus den Nähten platzen und alles, was nicht niet- und nagelfest war, in den Burggraben stürzen. Dicht an dicht standen die Holzhäuser, als stritten sie sich um einen guten Standplatz wie Zuschauer bei einer Hinrichtung. Jedes verfügbare Fleckchen Erde war genutzt. Wo zwei Häuser ursprünglich durch ein schmales Gäßchen getrennt waren, hatte irgendwer einen halbhohen Unterschlupf gebaut, der – da die Tür fast die gesamte Vorderfront beanspruchte – nicht einmal Fenster besaß. Wo beim besten Willen keine menschliche Behausung mehr hineinpaßte, hatte man Verkaufsstände für Bier, Brot oder Äpfel aufgeschlagen, und war der Platz auch dafür zu eng, so fand sich ein Stall, ein Schweinekoben, ein Misthaufen oder ein Wasserfaß.

Und es war unbeschreiblich laut in der Stadt. Der Regen trug nur wenig dazu bei, den Lärm zu dämpfen, der aus den Werkstätten drang und sich mit den Rufen der Straßenhändler mischte, die lauthals ihre Ware anpriesen; die Menschen grüßten sich, verhandelten und stritten miteinander; dazwischen ertönte Gewieher, Gebell und wütendes Gefauche.

Marthas Stimme erhob sich über den Lärm: »Was stinkt denn hier so fürchterlich?«

Tom lächelte. Sie war seit Jahren in keiner Stadt mehr gewesen. »Das ist der Geruch der Menschen«, erklärte er.

Die Straße war nur wenig breiter als der Ochsenkarren, was den Fuhrmann jedoch nicht davon abhielt, seine Tiere stetig voranzutreiben, denn standen sie erst einmal still, so war zu befürchten, daß sie sich nicht mehr zum Weitergehen bewegen ließen. Unablässig hieb er mit der Peitsche auf sie ein, ohne auf Hindernisse zu achten, und die beiden Ochsen trotteten stumpfsinnig weiter durch die Menge und drängten alles beiseite, was ihnen in den Weg kam – einen Ritter auf einem Schlachtroß, einen Förster mit Pfeil und Bogen, einen feisten Mönch auf einem Pony, Bewaffnete und Bettler, Hausfrauen und Huren.

Eine kleine Schafherde trippelte vor ihnen her. Der alte Schäfer hatte alle Hände voll zu tun, die Tiere beisammen zu halten. Bestimmt ist heute Markttag, dachte Tom.

Als der Ochsenkarren vorbeirumpelte, sprang eines der Schafe durch die offenstehende Tür in eine Bierstube. Im Nu stürmte die ganze blökende Herde hinterher und richtete ein heilloses Durcheinander an. Bierkrüge fielen zu Boden, Tische kippten und Stühle stürzten um.

Die Straße war ein einziger Sturzbach aus Schlamm und Unrat. Tom hatte einen Blick für die Regenmenge, die auf die Dächer herabfiel, und er wußte, wie breit eine Dachrinne sein mußte, um mit einem starken Guß fertig zu werden. Er erkannte sofort, daß alles Wasser, das in diesem Teil der Stadt von den Dächern floß, durch eben die Straße ablief, auf der sie sich gerade befanden. Bei starkem Gewitterregen, dachte er bei sich, braucht man hier ein Boot, um auf die andere Seite zu gelangen.

Erst in der Nähe der Burg, die auf dem höchsten Punkt des Hügels thronte, wurde die Straße breiter. Hier gab es auch Steinhäuser, von denen nur wenige reparaturbedürftig waren. Sie gehörten den Handwerkern und Händlern, die ihre Werkstätten und Läden zu ebener Erde eingerichtet hatten und in den Wohnstuben darüber lebten. Am Warenangebot erkannte Tom sogleich, daß Salisbury eine wohlhabende Stadt sein mußte. Messer und Töpfe brauchte jeder – bestickte Schals, verzierte Gürtel und silberne Schnallen dagegen wurden nur von reichen Leuten gekauft.

Vor der Burg bog der Fuhrmann mit seinem Gespann rechts ab. Tom und seine Familie folgten ihm. Die Straße führte hier in einem Viertelkreis um die äußeren Begrenzungsmauern. Dann kamen sie durch ein weiteres Tor, und mit einemmal war von dem rastlosen Gewimmel in der Stadt kaum noch etwas zu spüren. Statt dessen herrschte ein anderes Gedränge: die hektische, aber geordnete Vielfalt einer großen Baustelle.

Sie befanden sich jetzt auf dem eingefriedeten Gelände der Kathedrale, welches das gesamte Nordwestviertel der kreisrund angelegten Stadt einnahm. Tom blieb einen Augenblick stehen, um das Bild in sich aufzunehmen. Alles, was er hier hören, sehen, schmecken konnte, erwärmte sein Herz wie ein sonniger Sommertag. Dem eintreffenden Ochsenkarren mit seiner Steinfracht kamen zwei leere Karren entgegen, die gerade die Baustelle verließen. In den Bauhütten an der Kirchenmauer waren die Steinmetzen an der Arbeit; mit Eisenmeißeln und großen Holzhämmern behauten sie gezielt die schweren Blöcke, so daß sie zu Plinthen, Säulen, Kapitellen, Schäften, Strebepfeilern, Bögen, Fenstern, Schwellen, Fialen und Brüstungen zusammengefügt werden konnten. In der Mitte des Platzes – in sicherem Abstand zu allen anderen Gebäuden – stand die Schmiede. Durch die offenstehende Tür sah man den Feuerschein, und der helle Klang des Hammers auf dem Amboß hallte weithin über das Gelände. Da sich die Werkzeuge der Steinmetzen rasch abnutzten, mußte der Schmied unentwegt neue schaffen. Unbeteiligten Zuschauern mochte die Baustelle als reinstes Chaos erscheinen, Tom hingegen durchschaute auf einen Blick den großen, komplizierten Mechanismus, den zu beherrschen seine größte Sehnsucht war.

Jeder Handgriff der Männer war ihm vertraut, und er sah auf Anhieb, wie weit die Arbeit bereits gediehen war. Gegenwärtig errichtete man die Ostfassade.

Dort war in fünfundzwanzig bis dreißig Fuß Höhe ein Gerüst angebracht. Während die Maurer im Kirchenportal auf das Ende des Regens warteten, stiegen unablässig Träger mit Steinen auf den Schultern die Leitern hinauf und hinunter. Weiter oben kletterten Dachdecker und Klempner übers Dachgebälk wie Spinnen in einem riesigen hölzernen Netz. Sie nagelten Bleiplatten auf die Verstrebungen und brachten Abflußrohre und Dachrinnen an.

Mit Bedauern stellte Tom fest, daß die Kathedrale nahezu fertig war. Mehr als zwei Jahre Arbeit konnte er sich hier nicht erhoffen – kaum genug, um zum leitenden Steinmetz aufzusteigen, geschweige denn zum Dombaumeister. Trotzdem wollte er um Arbeit nachsuchen, denn der Winter stand vor der Tür. Mit Hilfe des Schweins hätte er seine Familie auch ohne Arbeit über die kalte Jahreszeit gebracht – ohne das Schwein war es aussichtslos.

Sie folgten dem Ochsenkarren bis zu jener Stelle, an der die Steine abgeladen und gestapelt wurden. Dankbar senkten die Ochsen ihre Köpfe in den Wassertrog. Der Fuhrmann rief einem vorbeigehenden Maurer zu: »Wo ist der Baumeister?«

»In der Burg«, antwortete der Maurer.

Der Fuhrmann nickte und wandte sich an Tom. »Ihr findet ihn vermutlich im Bischofspalast.«

»Habt Dank.«

»Ganz meinerseits.«

Erneut drängten sie sich durch die verstopften, engen Gassen bis zum Eingang der Burg. Sie war durch einen weiteren trockenen Graben und einen zweiten, riesigen Erdwall gesichert. Die Familie überquerte die Zugbrücke. In einem Wachhäuschen saß ein untersetzter, mit einer Ledertunika bekleideter Mann auf einem Hocker und blickte hinaus in den Regen. Er war mit einem Schwert bewaffnet. Tom sprach ihn an.

»Guten Tag. Tom Builder werde ich genannt. Ich möchte gerne den Dombaumeister sprechen, John von Shaftesbury.«

»Beim Bischof«, antwortete der Wachhabende gleichgültig.

Sie betraten den Hof. Bei der Burg handelte es sich, wie bei den meisten anderen Burgen auch, um eine Ansammlung unterschiedlicher Gebäude hinter einem großen Erdwall. Der Burghof maß im Durchmesser etwa hundertfünfzig Schritt. Auf der dem Tor gegenüberliegenden Seite stand der wuchtige Wohnturm, die letzte Zuflucht bei einem Angriff. Er erhob sich hoch über die Befestigungsanlagen und gewährte einen weiten Ausblick auf die Umgebung. Linker Hand befand sich eine Reihe von Gebäuden, die überwiegend aus Holz gezimmert waren: ein langer Stall, ein Backhaus und verschiedene Vorratslager. In der Mitte des Burghofs stand ein Brunnen. Auf der rechten Seite nahm ein großes Steinhaus, bei dem es sich offensichtlich um den bischöflichen Palast handelte, fast die gesamte Nordhälfte der Anlage ein. Es war im gleichen Stil wie die Kathedrale gehalten: Die kleinen Türen und Fenster schlossen oben mit Rundbögen ab.

Das Haus hatte zwei Stockwerke und war noch ziemlich neu, ja an einer Ecke waren sogar noch Maurer am Werk, die allem Anschein nach einen Turm anbauten. Trotz des Regens war der Burghof recht bevölkert. Leute kamen und gingen, eilten von Haus zu Haus: Bewaffnete, Priester, Händler, Bauleute, Palastgesinde.

Der Palast besaß mehrere Eingänge, die, wie Tom auffiel, allesamt offenstanden. Er war sich nicht ganz sicher, wie er nun vorgehen sollte. Wenn der Bischof gerade mit dem Baumeister sprach, wollte er vielleicht nicht gestört werden. Andererseits war ein Bischof kein König, und Tom war ein freier Bürger und Steinmetz mit einem legitimen beruflichen Anliegen – kein kriecherischer Leibeigener, der irgendeine Klage vorzubringen hatte. Tom entschloß sich daher für den direkten Weg. Er hieß Agnes und Martha warten. Dann ging er mit Alfred über den matschigen Hof zum Palast und trat durch die erstbeste Tür ein.

Sie gerieten in eine kleine Kapelle mit einer gewölbten Decke und einem Fenster hinter dem Altar. An einem hohen Pult neben dem Eingang saß ein Priester, der mit flinker Hand ein Pergament beschrieb. Beim Eintritt der beiden sah er auf.

»Wo finde ich den Baumeister John?« fragte Tom ohne Umschweife.

»In der Sakristei«, antwortete der Priester und wies mit einer ruckartigen Kopfbewegung auf eine Seitentür.

Tom bat nicht eigens darum, vorgelassen zu werden. Bei einer formgemäßen Anmeldung lassen sie uns warten, und wir verlieren bloß Zeit, dachte er. Mit entschlossenen Schritten durchquerte er die Kapelle und betrat die Sakristei.

Es war ein kleiner Raum mit quadratischem Grundriß, der durch zahlreiche Kerzen erhellt wurde. Einen Großteil seiner Bodenfläche bedeckte ein flacher Sandhaufen, der mit einem Richtscheit sauber geglättet worden war. Die beiden Männer, die sich im Zimmer befanden, sahen Tom nur kurz an, ehe sie ihre Aufmerksamkeit wieder auf den Sand richteten. Der Bischof, ein alter Mann mit runzligem Gesicht und funkelnden schwarzen Augen, zeichnete mit einem angespitzten Holzstab etwas in den Sand. Der Baumeister – er trug eine Lederschürze – sah ihm dabei zu. Er gab sich geduldig, doch seine Miene verriet Skepsis.

Tom wartete unruhig. Alles hing davon ab, daß er jetzt einen guten Eindruck machte, sich höflich, aber nicht kriecherisch gab, sein Wissen erwies, aber sich nicht damit brüstete. Ein Handwerksmeister forderte von seinen Untergebenen ebensoviel Gehorsam wie Geschick, das war ihm klar. Er hatte ja selbst schließlich schon Arbeitskräfte angeworben.

Bischof Roger entwarf ein zweistöckiges Gebäude, das auf drei Seiten große Fenster zeigte. Er war ein guter Zeichner; seine Linien waren gerade, die rechten Winkel exakt. Er zeichnete einen Grundriß und eine Seitenansicht, aber Tom erkannte sofort, daß dieses Gebäude niemals errichtet werden würde.

Schließlich war der Bischof fertig. »So«, sagte er.

John wandte sich an Tom. »Was führt Euch her?«

Tom tat so, als habe er ihn um seine Meinung gebeten. »Ein Gewölbe mit so großen Fenstern ist ein Ding der Unmöglichkeit.«

Der Bischof sah ihn empört an. »Das ist kein Gewölbe, sondern eine Schreibstube.«

»Das spielt keine Rolle. Auch sie wird einstürzen.«

»Er hat recht«, bemerkte John.

»Aber die Schreiber brauchen doch Licht!«

John zuckte mit den Schultern und wandte sich wieder an Tom: »Wer seid Ihr?«

»Mein Name ist Tom. Ich bin Steinmetz.«

»Das dachte ich mir. Was führt Euch zu uns?«

»Ich suche Arbeit«, antwortete Tom und hielt den Atem an.

John schüttelte sofort den Kopf. »Ich habe keine Arbeit für Euch.«

Seine Worte trafen Tom wie Keulenschläge. Am liebsten hätte er auf dem Absatz kehrtgemacht. Doch er wahrte die Form und hörte sich die Begründung an.

»Wir arbeiten seit zehn Jahren hier«, fuhr John fort. »Die meisten Steinmetzen besitzen ein Haus in der Stadt. Mittlerweile nähert sich der Bau der Vollendung, und ich habe schon jetzt mehr Leute, als ich eigentlich brauche.«

Es war aussichtslos. Tom wußte es. Dennoch fragte er: »Und der Palast?«

»Für den gilt dasselbe«, erwiderte John. »Am Palast beschäftige ich die überzähligen Leute. Ohne den Palast und Bischof Rogers andere Burgen hätte ich längst schon Steinmetzen entlassen müssen.«

Tom nickte. Bemüht, sich seine Verzweiflung nicht anmerken zu lassen, fragte er: »Ist Euch vielleicht bekannt, wo es sonst Arbeit gibt?«

»Am Kloster von Shaftesbury wurde Anfang des Jahres gebaut, soviel ich weiß. Vielleicht sind sie noch nicht fertig. Das ist eine Tagesreise von hier.«

»Ich danke Euch.« Tom wandte sich zum Gehen.

»Tut mir leid!« rief ihm der Dombaumeister nach. »Ihr scheint ein guter Mann zu sein.«

Tom gab darauf keine Antwort mehr. Niedergeschlagen sah er ein, daß er sich zu große Hoffnungen gemacht hatte. Eine Absage war durchaus nichts Ungewöhnliches, doch seine Begeisterung für den Dombau hatte ihn blind gemacht ... Jetzt öffnete ihm die Wirklichkeit wieder die Augen, und er sah sich schon an einer langweiligen Stadtmauer oder dem häßlichen Wohnhaus eines Silberschmieds arbeiten.

Auf dem Weg zurück über den Burghof gab er sich einen Ruck. Er ließ es Agnes nie wissen, wenn er eine Enttäuschung erlebt hatte. Stets tat er, als wäre alles in bester Ordnung. Wenn es hier keine Arbeit für ihn gab – na gut, dann fand sich bestimmt in der nächsten oder übernächsten Stadt etwas. Sobald er sich auch nur das geringste Zeichen von Kummer anmerken ließ, das wußte er, würde Agnes ihn wieder drängen, sich endlich etwas Dauerhaftes zu suchen und mit dem unruhigen Wanderleben aufzuhören. Doch genau das wollte er nicht – es sei denn, er fände eine Stadt, in der eine Kathedrale gebaut wurde.

»Hier gibt es für mich nichts zu tun«, sagte er zu Agnes. »Laß uns weiterziehen.«

Agnes verbarg ihre Enttäuschung nicht. »Man sollte meinen, wo ein Dom und ein Palast gebaut werden, müßte es allemal Arbeit für einen Steinmetz geben«, sagte sie.

»Beide Gebäude sind schon fast fertig«, erklärte Tom. »Sie haben mehr Leute, als sie brauchen.«

Die Familie überquerte die Zugbrücke und tauchte wieder ein in das geschäftige Hin und Her auf den Straßen der Stadt. Durch das Osttor hatten sie Salisbury betreten, durch das Westtor wollten sie es verlassen, denn dort begann die Straße nach Shaftesbury. Tom wandte sich nach rechts und führte die Seinen durch jenen Teil der Stadt, den sie bisher noch nicht kannten.

Vor einem baufälligen Steinhaus blieb er stehen. Der Mörtel, den die Maurer benutzt hatten, war zu schwach gewesen; nun war er mürbe und bröckelte aus den Fugen. In die entstandenen Löcher war der Frost gedrungen und hatte einige Mauersteine bersten lassen. Wenn nichts geschah, würde der Schaden nach dem nächsten Winter noch größer sein. Tom beschloß, den Eigentümer des Hauses darauf aufmerksam zu machen.

Ein breiter Bogen überspannte den ebenerdigen Eingang. Die Holztür stand offen. Gleich dahinter saß ein Handwerker, in der Rechten einen Hammer, in der Linken eine Ahle. Er schnitzte ein kompliziertes Ornament in einen hölzernen Sattel, der vor ihm auf der Werkbank lag. Im Hintergrund erkannte Tom Holz- und Ledervorräte sowie einen Lehrjungen, der Hobelspäne zusammenkehrte.

»Guten Tag, Meister Sattler«, sagte Tom.

Der Sattler sah auf. Mit einem einzigen Blick schätzte er Tom richtig ein – nämlich als einen Mann, der sich selber einen Sattel machen konnte, sofern er einen brauchte –, und er begnügte sich mit einem kurzen Nicken.

»Ich bin Baumeister«, fuhr Tom fort. »Wie ich sehe, bedürft Ihr meiner Dienste.«

»Wie das?«

»Der Mörtel an Eurem Haus bröckelt, die Steine bersten. Kann sein, daß das Haus den kommenden Winter nicht übersteht.«

Der Sattler schüttelte den Kopf. »Es wimmelt in dieser Stadt nur so von Steinmetzen und Maurern. Warum sollte ich da einen Fremden anstellen?«

»Ich verstehe.« Tom wandte sich zum Gehen. »Gott mit Euch.«

»Hoffentlich«, antwortete der Sattler.

»Der Kerl hat kein Benehmen«, murmelte Agnes, als sie weitergingen.

Die Straße führte auf einen Marktplatz – eine wahre Schlammwüste –, auf dem die Bauern aus der Umgebung ihren geringfügigen Überschuß an Fleisch, Getreide, Milch oder Eiern gegen Dinge eintauschten, die sie brauchten, aber nicht selbst herstellen konnten, darunter Töpferware, Pflugscharen, Seile und Salz. Auf solchen Märkten ging es gemeinhin lebhaft und geräuschvoll zu. Da wurde gefeilscht, gestritten und gescherzt. Manche Standbesitzer lieferten sich heftige Scheingefechte mit ihren Nachbarn; es gab billiges Backwerk für die Kinder; hier spielte ein fahrender Musikant auf, dort bot eine Akrobatentruppe ihre Künste dar. Allenthalben sah man grell geschminkte Huren, und nur selten fehlte der kriegsversehrte Soldat mit seinen Geschichten über die Wüsten des Orients und rasende Sarazenenhorden. Wer ein gutes Geschäft gemacht hatte, gab nur allzuoft der Versuchung nach, den Handel entsprechend zu feiern, und legte seinen Gewinn in Starkbier an, so daß gegen Mittag die Stimmung meist schon recht hitzig war. Andere verloren ihr Geld beim Würfelspiel, was mitunter zu Schlägereien führte. Heute jedoch, an einem verregneten Vormittag und zu einer Jahreszeit, da die Ernte bereits eingefahren oder verkauft war, war die Stimmung eher gedämpft. Bis auf die Haut durchnäßte Bauern und vor Kälte schlotternde Händler tätigten ihre Geschäfte in wortkargem Zwiegespräch, und jeder sehnte sich nach seinem warmen Heim und Herd.

Tom und die Seinen bahnten sich ihren Weg durch die trübsinnige Menge, ohne den halbherzigen Schmeicheleien des Wurstverkäufers und des Messerschleifers Beachtung zu schenken. Sie hatten den Marktplatz schon fast hinter sich gelassen, da entdeckte Tom sein Schwein.

Im ersten Moment war er so überrascht, daß er seinen Augen nicht zu trauen wagte. Doch dann raunte Agnes ihm zu: »Tom! Schau!«, und ihm war klar, daß auch sie das Tier gesehen hatte.

Es bestand nicht der geringste Zweifel – er kannte das Schwein so gut wie seine eigenen Kinder. Ein Mann mit der rosigen Gesichtsfarbe und der üppigen Mitte eines Menschen, der ausreichend Fleisch zu essen hat und sich jedesmal noch einen Nachschlag genehmigt, hielt das Schwein mit fachmännischem Griff im Arm; es handelte sich zweifellos um einen Schlachter. Tom und Agnes standen da wie vom Schlag gerührt und starrten den Mann an, und da sie ihm den Weg versperrten, ließ es sich gar nicht vermeiden, daß auch er sie bemerkte.

»Nun ...«, sagte er. Es verwirrte ihn, daß er so angestarrt wurde. Außerdem hatte er es eilig und wollte vorbei.

Es war Martha, die das Schweigen brach. »Das ist doch unser Schwein!« schrie sie aufgeregt.

»So ist es«, bestätigte Tom und sah dem Schlachter geradewegs in die Augen.

Ein Ausdruck der Verschlagenheit huschte über die Miene des Mannes. Der weiß genau, daß das Schwein gestohlen ist, dachte Tom. Doch der Schlachter sagte: »Ich habe soeben fünfzig Pence dafür bezahlt, und deshalb gehört es jetzt mir.«

»Wem immer Ihr Euer Geld gegeben habt: Er hatte kein Recht, Euch das Schwein zu verkaufen. Gewiß habt Ihr es nur deshalb so billig bekommen. Von wem habt Ihr es?«

»Von einem Bauern.«

»Kennt Ihr ihn persönlich?«

»Nein. Hört zu, ich bin der Schlachter, der die Festung mit Fleisch versorgt. Ich kann nicht von jedem Bauern, dem ich ein Schwein oder eine Kuh abkaufe, verlangen, daß er ein Dutzend Zeugen beibringt, die hoch und heilig versichern, daß es auch wirklich seins ist!«

Der Mann wandte sich ab, als wollte er sich entfernen, doch da packte Tom ihn am Ärmel und hielt ihn fest. Der Schlachter war sichtlich erbost, sah jedoch schnell ein, daß er, kam es zu einem Handgemenge, das Schwein loslassen mußte. Gelang es aber dieser Familie erst einmal, sich des Tieres zu bemächtigen, so lag der Fall andersherum. Dann war es an *ihm,* seine Ansprüche auf das Schwein zu beweisen. Er zügelte also seinen Zorn und sagte: »Wenn Ihr Anzeige erstatten wollt, wendet Euch an den Vogt.«

Nach kurzem Überlegen verwarf Tom den Vorschlag. Ihm fehlten die Beweise. Statt dessen fragte er: »Wie sah der Mann aus, von dem Ihr mein Schwein gekauft habt?«

Wieder dieser verschlagene Blick. »Wie alle andern.«

»Hatte er seinen Mund verhüllt?«

»Wenn ich's mir recht überlege – ja, hatte er.«

»Er war ein Outlaw, der seine Verstümmelung verbarg«, sagte Tom voller Verbitterung. »Das ist Euch natürlich nicht aufgefallen, oder?«

»Heute regnet's doch Bindfäden!« protestierte der Schlachter. »Da laufen doch alle vermummt herum.«

»Wann habt Ihr den Handel geschlossen?«

»Gerade eben.«

»Und wo ist der Mann hingegangen?«

»In eine Schenke, vermute ich.«

»Um dort mein Geld zu versaufen!« sagte Tom angewidert. »Macht, daß Ihr fortkommt, ich laß Euch laufen. Vielleicht werdet Ihr eines Tages selbst mal beraubt. Dann wird's Euch hart ankommen, daß so viele Leute billige Ware kaufen, ohne zu fragen, woher sie stammt.«

Der Schlachter sah ihn wütend an und zögerte, als wolle er noch etwas entgegnen. Doch dann besann er sich eines Besseren und machte sich aus dem Staub.

»Warum läßt du ihn ziehen?« fragte Agnes.

»Weil er hier bekannt ist wie ein bunter Hund«, antwortete Tom. »Ich bin fremd hier. Wenn ich mich mit ihm schlage, gelte ich als der Angreifer. Außerdem – wie soll ich beweisen, daß das Schwein mir gehört? Steht ihm vielleicht mein Name auf dem Hintern geschrieben?«

»Aber unsere Ersparnisse ...«

»Kann immer noch sein, daß wir das Geld wiederbekommen. Schweig jetzt still und laß mich nachdenken.« Der Streit mit dem Schlachter hatte Tom aufgeregt, und der rauhe Ton, in dem er Agnes anfuhr, verschaffte ihm eine gewisse Erleichterung. »Irgendwo in dieser Stadt läuft ein Kerl ohne Lippen herum, der fünfzig Silberpennys im Beutel hat. Wir müssen ihn bloß finden und ihm das Geld abnehmen.«

»Genau«, sagte Agnes entschlossen.

»Geh du zurück zum Kirchhof – den Weg, auf dem wir gekommen sind. Ich gehe weiter und komme dann von der anderen Seite zur Kathedrale. Danach kehren wir dann durch die nächste Straße hierher zurück – und so weiter. Womöglich hockt er schon in einer Schenke. Wenn du ihn siehst, bleib in der Nähe und schick Martha nach mir. Alfred nehme ich mit. Sieh zu, daß der Kerl dich nicht erkennt.«

»Keine Sorge«, erwiderte Agnes mit finsterer Entschlossenheit. »Ich will das Geld zurück. Ich brauche es, um meine Kinder zu ernähren.«

Tom berührte ihren Arm und lächelte. »Du bist eine Löwin, Agnes!«

Sie sah ihm in die Augen, hob sich unvermittelt auf die Zehenspitzen und küßte ihn kurz, aber fest auf den Mund. Dann drehte sie sich um und ging mit Martha im Schlepptau über den Marktplatz. Tom blickte ihnen nach, bis sie außer Sichtweite waren; erst dann setzte er mit Alfred seinen Weg fort. Trotz des Mutes, den Agnes bewiesen hatte, machte er sich Sorgen um sie.

Der Dieb fühlte sich offenbar sicher. Kein Wunder: Zum Zeitpunkt seines Überfalls hatten sich Tom und seine Familie auf dem Weg nach Winchester befunden. So war er einfach in entgegengesetzter Richtung davongelaufen und hatte das Schwein in Salisbury verhökert. Tom hatte ja erst, nachdem er von Ellen auf den Umbau der Kathedrale von Salisbury hingewiesen worden war, seine Pläne geändert. Ohne es zu wissen, war er damit dem Wegelagerer auf den Fersen geblieben. Der Dieb dachte nicht im Traume daran, daß er Tom je wiederbegegnen würde, und genau darin lag ihr Vorteil: Sie konnten ihn überraschen.

Langsam zogen sie durch die matschigen Straßen. Tom spähte verstohlen in alle Häuser, deren Tür offenstand, bemühte sich aber sorgsam darum, nicht aufzufallen. Es war nicht auszuschließen, daß die Angelegenheit mit einer gewaltsamen Auseinandersetzung endete; da konnte es nur von Nachteil sein, wenn sich alle Welt an einen hochgewachsenen Steinmetz erinnerte, der die halbe Stadt durchsucht hatte. Die meisten Behausungen waren elende Hütten aus Holz, Lehm und Schilf mit einer Feuerstelle in der Mitte und ein paar einfachen, selbstgefertigten Möbeln auf dem strohbedeckten Fußboden. Ein Faß und ein paar Bänke bedeuteten eine Schenke; ein mit einem Vorhang verhängtes Bett in der Ecke verriet die Hure; lärmendes Volk, das sich um einen einzelnen Tisch drängte, die Würfelstube.

Eine Frau mit rotbemalten Lippen ließ ihn ihre Brüste sehen, doch Tom schüttelte nur den Kopf und ging rasch weiter. Insgeheim verlockte ihn zwar die Vorstellung, es am hellichten Tag mit einer ihm gänzlich unbekannten Frau zu treiben und sie dafür zu bezahlen, doch hatte er es noch nie in seinem Leben getan.

Ellen fiel ihm ein, die Vogelfreie. Auch sie hatte ihn gereizt. Sie war von verführerischer Schönheit, doch der durchdringende Blick ihrer tiefliegenden Augen hatte etwas Einschüchterndes. Das freizügige Angebot einer Hure irritierte Tom nur vorübergehend; der Zauber Ellens hingegen wirkte nach. Urplötzlich packte ihn der unsinnige Wunsch, in die Wälder zurückzulaufen, sie zu suchen und über sie herzufallen.

Sie erreichten die Kathedrale, ohne den Dieb gefunden zu haben. Tom beobachtete die Dachdecker, die das dreieckige Holzdach über dem Mittelschiff mit Bleiplatten versahen. Da die Pultdächer der Seitenschiffe noch nicht gedeckt waren, ließen sich noch die Halbbögen ausmachen, welche die Seitenschiffe mit der Mauer des Hauptschiffs verbanden und die obere Hälfte des Langhauses trugen. Er machte Alfred darauf aufmerksam: »Ohne diese Stützen würde das Gewicht der steinernen Gewölbe im Innern der Kirche die Mauer des Hauptschiffs nach außen drücken«, erklärte er. »Siehst du, daß sich die Halbbögen auf einer Linie mit den Strebepfeilern in der Mauer des Seitenschiffs befinden? Innen wird diese Linie durch die Säulen der Arkaden im Hauptschiff fortgesetzt. Und die Fenster im Seitenschiff liegen auf der gleichen Höhe wie die Bögen der Arkade. Stärke verbindet sich mit Stärke und Schwäche mit Schwäche.« Alfred hatte nichts begriffen und empfand die Erklärung offensichtlich als Zumutung. Tom seufzte.

Die Gegenwart holte ihn wieder ein, als er Agnes entdeckte, die ihnen entgegenkam. Zwar war ihr Gesicht durch die Kapuze verhüllt, doch erkannte er sie an ihrem selbstsicheren, zielstrebigen Gang. Sogar breitschultrige Arbeiter traten zur Seite, um ihr Platz zu machen. Wenn Agnes der Dieb über den Weg läuft und es kommt zum Kampf, dachte Tom, dann kann er sich auf einiges gefaßt machen.

»Habt ihr ihn gesehen?« fragte Agnes.

»Nein. Und ihr auch nicht, wie's scheint.« Man konnte nur hoffen, daß der Dieb die Stadt nicht schon verlassen hatte. Es war indes kaum anzunehmen, daß er sich aus dem Staub machte, ohne wenigstens ein paar von seinen Pennys auszugeben. Im Wald ließ sich mit Geld nichts anfangen.

Agnes dachte nicht anders darüber. »Er *muß* hier irgendwo sein. Suchen wir weiter!«

»Wir durchstreifen jetzt andere Straßen und treffen uns am Marktplatz wieder.«

Tom und Alfred machten kehrt und verließen den Kirchplatz durch das Tor. Der Regen durchweichte ihre Umhänge, und Tom fühlte sich vorübergehend verlockt, in einer Schenke vor dem Feuer Platz zu nehmen und sich einen Krug Bier und eine Rinderbrühe zu gönnen. Doch dann fiel ihm wieder ein, wie hart er für das Schwein hatte arbeiten müssen, und er sah den Mann ohne Lippen vor sich, der mit der Keule auf Marthas unschuldiges Köpfchen einschlug. Die Wut auf den Kerl brachte sein Blut in Wallung und wärmte ihn.

Eine systematische Suche ließ sich kaum bewerkstelligen, denn die Gassen der Stadt folgten keiner bestimmten Ordnung. Sie führten mal hierhin, mal dorthin – je nachdem, wo die Häuser und Hütten standen, und es gab zahlreiche scharfe Biegungen und Sackgassen. Die Straße, die vom Osttor zur Zugbrücke der Burg führte, war die einzige in der Stadt, die durchgehend gerade angelegt war.

Auf dem Herweg hatten sich Tom und Alfred an die äußeren Befestigungswälle der Burg gehalten. Jetzt liefen sie kreuz und quer durch die Vorstadt und machten immer erst kehrt, wenn sie die Stadtmauer erreichten. Es war eine armselige Gegend, mit den baufälligsten Hütten, den lautesten Schenken und den ältesten Huren. Unterhalb des Stadtkerns gelegen, wurde dieses Viertel vom Unrat aus den wohlhabenderen Bezirken geradezu überschwemmt; er staute sich am Fuß der Mauer. Auch den Menschen, die hier hausten, schien es ähnlich ergangen zu sein, sah man doch weit mehr Krüppel, Bettler, hungrige Kinder, geschlagene Frauen und hilflose Säufer als in anderen Teilen der Stadt.

Nur der Kerl ohne Lippen war nirgends zu finden.

Zweimal entdeckte Tom einen Mann mit vergleichbarem Körperbau und ähnlicher Gestalt, stellte aber jedesmal bei näherem Hinsehen fest, daß das Gesicht nicht verunstaltet war.

Die Suche endete am Marktplatz, wo Agnes schon ungeduldig auf sie wartete. Ihre Augen funkelten. »Ich habe ihn gefunden«, raunte sie.

In Toms Erregung mischte sich eine beklemmende Vorahnung. »Wo?«

»Vor einer Garküche am Osttor. Er ging gerade hinein.«

»Führ mich hin.«

Sie umrundeten die Burg bis zur Zugbrücke, erreichten über die Hauptstraße das Osttor und tauchten ein in das Gewirr der von der Stadtmauer überragten Sträßchen und Gäßchen. Gleich darauf hatte Tom die Garküche auch schon erspäht. Es war nicht einmal ein richtiges Haus, lediglich ein schräges Dach auf vier Pfosten, dessen Rückwand die Stadtmauer bildete. Im Hintergrund brannte ein gewaltiges Feuer, über dem ein großer Kessel bullerte und ein Hammel an einem Spieß gebraten wurde. Es war Mittagszeit und der Stand voller Menschen, überwiegend Männer. Der Geruch des gebratenen Fleisches stieg Tom in die Nase und ließ seinen Magen knurren.

Angestrengt spähte er in die Menge. Er fürchtete, der Dieb könne sich in der Zwischenzeit wieder aus dem Staub gemacht haben. Aber er entdeckte ihn sofort: Der Mann saß ein wenig abseits auf einem Hocker und löffelte Eintopf aus einer Schüssel. Er hielt sich den Schal vors Gesicht.

Tom wandte sich rasch ab, um nicht selbst erkannt zu werden. Er mußte sich jetzt überlegen, wie er vorgehen wollte.

Aufgebracht wie er war, hätte er den Halunken am liebsten ohne viel Federlesens niedergeschlagen und ihm seine Geldkatze abgenommen. Aber die Menge würde ihn nicht so ohne weiteres davonkommen lassen; er hätte Erklärungen abgeben müssen, nicht nur vor den Umstehenden, sondern auch vor dem Vogt. Ein solches Vorgehen war durchaus rechtmäßig, und da der Dieb vogelfrei war, würde niemand für seine Ehrlichkeit bürgen. Er dagegen, Tom, war Steinmetz und ganz offenkundig ein ehrenwerter Mann ... Doch bis das alles klargestellt und bewiesen war, konnten Wochen vergehen, zumal wenn der Vogt gerade durch die Grafschaft streifte. Und wenn es zu einem Tumult kam, war allemal noch mit einer Anklage wegen Landfriedensbruchs zu rechnen.

Nein – es war auf jeden Fall besser, unter vier Augen mit dem Dieb abzurechnen.

In der Stadt übernachten konnte der Wegelagerer nicht; er hatte hier keine Bleibe, und da er sich nicht als rechtschaffener Mann ausweisen konnte, würde er auch keine finden. Es blieb ihm also nichts anderes übrig, als am Abend rechtzeitig vor Toresschluß die Stadt zu verlassen.

Und es gab nur zwei Stadttore.

»Wahrscheinlich kehrt er auf dem gleichen Weg zurück, auf dem er gekommen ist«, sagte Tom zu Agnes. »Ich warte auf ihn vor dem

Osttor. Alfred soll das Westtor im Auge behalten. Du bleibst in der Stadt und beobachtest ihn. Martha bleibt bei dir, aber paß auf, daß er sie nicht sieht. Wenn du mir oder Alfred Nachricht geben willst, schick uns Martha.«

»Wird gemacht«, antwortete Agnes knapp.

»Was soll ich tun, wenn er an mir vorbeikommt?« fragte Alfred aufgeregt.

»Nichts«, erwiderte Tom bestimmt. »Merk dir, welchen Weg er einschlägt und warte, bis Martha mich geholt hat. Dann stellen wir ihn gemeinsam.« Alfreds enttäuschter Blick ließ ihn hinzufügen: »Du tust, was ich dir sage. Nach meinem Schwein will ich nicht auch noch meinen Sohn verlieren.«

Alfred nickte widerstrebend.

»Und jetzt verschwinden wir besser, bevor er sieht, wie wir hier zusammenglucken und Pläne schmieden. Auf, auf!«

Tom entfernte sich, ohne sich noch einmal umzuschauen. Agnes war auf jeden Fall zuverlässig! Auf schnellstem Wege marschierte er zum Osttor und verließ die Stadt über die wackelige Holzbrücke, über die sie am Morgen den Ochsenkarren geschoben hatten. Vor ihm erstreckte sich wie ein schnurgerader, langer Teppich, der über Täler und Hügel ausgerollt worden war, die Straße nach Winchester. Am Fuße des Stadtbergs zweigte linker Hand der sogenannte Portway ab, die Straße, auf der sie selbst (und vermutlich auch der Dieb) nach Salisbury gelangt waren. Er wand sich eine Anhöhe hinauf, hinter der er verschwand. Aller Wahrscheinlichkeit nach würde der Spitzbube wieder denselben Weg nehmen.

Bei der Weggabelung am Fuße des Hügels, die von einzelnen Häusern umstanden war, wandte sich Tom nach links und hielt nach einem geeigneten Versteck Ausschau. Nach ungefähr zweihundert Schritten machte er halt und sah zurück. Er war schon zu weit gegangen, denn von hier aus waren die Gesichter der Leute, die die Weggabelung passierten, nicht mehr zu erkennen. Die Straße war von tiefen, wasserführenden Gräben gesäumt, die allenfalls bei trockenem Wetter Tarnung geboten hätten. Die Böschungen auf der gegenüberliegenden Seite waren ziemlich hoch und gingen in Felder und Wiesen über. Auf dem Stoppelfeld südlich der Straße weideten ein paar Rinder. Eine Kuh lag, von der Böschung halb verdeckt, unmittelbar am Feldrand. Von dort aus mußte sich die Straße gut überblicken lassen. Mit einem Seufzer der Erleichterung lief Tom den Weg zurück, sprang über den Graben, kletterte die Böschung hoch und versetzte der Kuh einen

Tritt. Das Tier stand auf und trottete davon. Tom legte sich in die trockene, noch warme Kuhle, zog sich die Kapuze tief ins Gesicht und richtete sich auf eine längere Wartezeit ein. Er hätte jetzt gerne etwas zu sich genommen, hatte jedoch versäumt, sich in der Stadt noch Brot zu besorgen.

Er war unruhig und nicht ohne Furcht. Der Dieb war zwar kleiner als er, dabei aber, wie sein Überfall auf Martha bewiesen hatte, flink und heimtückisch. Weit mehr als körperliche Verletzungen fürchtete Tom jedoch, der Versuch, sein Geld wiederzubekommen, könnte mißlingen.

Er dachte an Agnes und Martha und hoffte, daß alles gutging. Agnes wußte sich zu helfen, soviel war klar. Und was konnte der Dieb schon tun, selbst wenn er sie entdeckte? Ein bißchen mehr aufpassen, das war alles.

Von seinem Lagerplatz aus waren die Türme der Kathedrale zu erkennen, und Tom bedauerte inzwischen, daß er sich nicht die Zeit genommen hatte, hineinzuschauen. Besonders neugierig war er auf die Pfeiler der Arkaden. Gewöhnlich handelte es sich um dicke Säulen, aus deren oberen Enden die Bögen hervorwuchsen: nach Norden und Süden die Verbindungsbögen zu den benachbarten Arkadensäulen sowie ein weiterer, entweder nach Osten oder nach Westen geführter Bogen, der die Verbindung zum Seitenschiff schuf. Tom gefiel diese Lösung nicht; ein Bogen, der einer runden Säule entsprang, bot nach seinem Gefühl keinen schönen Anblick. In *seiner* Kathedrale würden Bündelpfeiler stehen, und jede einzelne Rippe sollte am oberen Ende in einen Bogen übergehen – eine Lösung, die ebenso elegant wie logisch war.

Er malte sich die Ornamente der Bögen aus. Geometrische Formen waren am häufigsten, denn das Meißeln von Zickzacklinien und Rautenmustern erforderte nur wenig künstlerisches Geschick. Tom indessen schwebten Blattfriese vor; sie milderten die kantige Regelmäßigkeit der Steine und verliehen ihnen einen Hauch Natur.

Bis weit in den Nachmittag hinein beschäftigte er sich im Geiste mit seiner imaginären Kathedrale. Dann trippelte eine schmale, blonde Gestalt über die Brücke und passierte die Häuser an der Kreuzung. Martha! An der Abzweigung zögerte sie kurz, bevor sie sich für den richtigen Weg entschied. Tom beobachtete, wie sie die Stirn runzelte; sie war offensichtlich beunruhigt, weil sie ihn noch nicht gefunden hatte. Erst als sie gleichauf mit ihm war, rief er sie mit leiser Stimme an: »Martha!«

Sie stieß einen Freudenschrei aus, als sie seiner ansichtig wurde, und sprang über den Graben. »Das ist von Mama«, sagte sie und holte aus ihrem Umhang eine Pastete mit Rindfleisch und Zwiebeln.

»Beim Heiligen Kreuz!« rief Tom und biß herzhaft in das noch warme Backwerk. »Deine Mutter ist wahrlich eine gute Frau!« Es schmeckte himmlisch.

Martha setzte sich neben ihren Vater ins Gras. »Und nun hör, was der Mann, der unser Schwein stahl, getan hat«, sagte sie und zog, während sie überlegte, was die Mutter ihr zu berichten aufgetragen hatte, die Nase kraus. Sie war so entzückend, daß es Tom beinahe den Atem verschlug. »Er ist aus der Garküche rausgegangen und hat sich mit einer Frau mit angemaltem Gesicht getroffen und ist in ihr Haus gegangen. Wir haben draußen gewartet.«

Während der Halunke unser Geld verhurt hat, dachte Tom grimmig. »Erzähl weiter!«

»Er ist nicht lange im Haus von der Frau geblieben. Danach ist er in eine Schenke gegangen, und da sitzt er immer noch. Er trinkt nicht viel, aber er würfelt die ganze Zeit.«

»Hoffentlich gewinnt er«, sagte Tom finster. »Ist das alles?«

»Ja, das ist alles.«

»Hast du Hunger?«

»Ich hab' ein Brötchen gegessen.«

»Hast du Alfred schon Bescheid gesagt?«

»Nein, noch nicht. Ich wollte erst zu dir.«

»Sag ihm, er soll zusehen, daß er irgendwo ein trockenes Plätzchen findet.«

»... ein trockenes Plätzchen findet«, wiederholte Martha. »Soll ich ihm zuerst das sagen, oder soll ich ihm erst erzählen, was der Mann macht, der unser Schwein gestohlen hat?«

»Erzähl ihm erst vom Schweinedieb«, erwiderte Tom. Die Reihenfolge war natürlich vollkommen gleichgültig, aber Martha hatte nach einer klaren Antwort verlangt. Er lächelte ihr zu. »Bist ein kluges Köpfchen, mein Kind. Aber jetzt mach dich auf den Weg.«

»Mir gefällt das Spiel«, sagte sie und winkte ihm zum Abschied zu. Als sie zierlich über den Graben setzte, blitzten ihre nackten Beinchen auf.

Tom sah ihr nach. Die Liebe zu ihr und die Wut auf den Spitzbuben erfüllten sein Herz. Wie hart wir arbeiten mußten, um uns das Schwein leisten zu können! dachte er. Wenn wir unsere Kinder ernähren wollen, brauchen wir das Geld dringend.

Inzwischen war er sogar bereit, den Dieb zu töten, falls es keine andere Möglichkeit gab, das Geld wiederzubeschaffen. Allerdings würde vermutlich auch Faramond Openmouth aufs Ganze gehen. Er war ein Outlaw, stand also außerhalb von Recht und Gesetz. Outlaws schreckten vor keiner Gewalttat zurück. Es war durchaus möglich, daß Faramond Openmouth schon früher einmal einem seiner Opfer wiederbegegnet war. Eines stand jedenfalls fest: Der Mann war brandgefährlich.

Das Tageslicht begann überraschend früh zu schwinden, und Tom fürchtete, den Dieb bei Regen und Dunkelheit nicht mehr erkennen zu können. Je dunkler es wurde, desto weniger Menschen betraten oder verließen die Stadt. Die meisten Auswärtigen hatten sich längst auf den Heimweg in ihre Dörfer gemacht. In den höhergelegenen Häusern der Stadtmitte sowie in den elenden Hütten am Rand flakkerte Lampen- und Kerzenschein auf. Tom war nahe daran, die Hoffnung aufzugeben, und fragte sich, ob der Dieb nicht vielleicht doch eine Bleibe gefunden hatte. Vielleicht hatte er Spießgesellen in der Stadt, die sich nicht darum scherten, daß er ein Outlaw war. Vielleicht ...

Und da sah er auf einmal einen Mann, dessen Mund mit einem Schal verhüllt war.

Der Mann überquerte gerade die Holzbrücke, anscheinend in Gesellschaft zweier anderer Männer. Tom fielen jetzt die beiden Komplizen des Wegelagerers ein – der Glatzkopf und der Mann mit dem grünen Hut. Waren sie vielleicht gemeinsam in die Stadt gekommen? Tom hatte keinen der beiden in Salisbury gesehen, aber was besagte das schon? Vielleicht hatten sie sich vorübergehend getrennt und zum gemeinsamen Rückmarsch verabredet? Tom unterdrückte einen Fluch; mit drei Männern konnte er es kaum aufnehmen. Doch als die drei Wanderer näher kamen, trennten sie sich voneinander, und Tom erkannte zu seiner großen Erleichterung, daß sie doch nicht zusammengehörten.

Die ersten beiden waren Vater und Sohn – zwei Bauern, der Kleidung nach, mit dunklen, engstehenden Augen und Hakennasen. Sie bogen in den Portway ein, und der Mann mit dem Schal folgte ihnen in einiger Entfernung.

Tom beobachtete den Gang des Diebs. Der Mann wirkte nüchtern. Das war schade.

Auf der Brücke waren zwei weibliche Gestalten aufgetaucht – Agnes und Martha. Tom war entsetzt: Mit ihnen als Zuschauern bei der bevorstehenden Auseinandersetzung hatte er nicht gerechnet. Allerdings hatte er ihnen das Kommen auch nicht ausdrücklich untersagt.

Alle fünf näherten sich jetzt seinem Schlupfwinkel. Tom straffte sich. Weil er so groß war, ließen es seine Gegner meist nicht auf eine direkte Konfrontation mit ihm ankommen. Outlaws aber kämpften mit dem Mut der Verzweiflung; bei ihnen mußte man auf alles gefaßt sein.

Die beiden Bauern waren inzwischen auf gleicher Höhe. Sie unterhielten sich friedlich über Pferde. Tom zog seinen Schlaghammer aus dem Gürtel und wog ihn in der rechten Hand. Er haßte Diebe, die nicht arbeiteten, sondern rechtschaffenen Menschen das Brot stahlen. Er hatte keine Bedenken mehr, diesem Halunken den Schädel einzuschlagen.

Es war, als spürte der Dieb die drohende Gefahr, denn er ging plötzlich langsamer. Tom wartete ab, bis er nur noch vier oder fünf Schritte entfernt war – dann ließ er sich die Böschung hinunterrollen, setzte über den Bach und trat dem Mann in den Weg.

Der Dieb blieb stocksteif stehen und starrte ihn an. »Was soll das?« fragte er beunruhigt.

Er erkennt mich nicht, dachte Tom. »Du hast gestern mein Schwein gestohlen«, sagte er. »Und heute hast du es einem Schlachter verkauft.«

»Nein, ich …«

»Streite es nicht ab!« sagte Tom. »Gib mir das Geld, das du dafür erlöst hast, und ich tue dir nichts.«

Im ersten Moment glaubte er, der Dieb wolle seiner Aufforderung Folge leisten. Der Mann zögerte, und Toms Erregung ebbte ein wenig ab. Doch dann machte der Dieb auf dem Absatz kehrt und lief geradewegs in Agnes hinein.

Um sie über den Haufen zu rennen, war er nicht schnell genug – es gehörte ohnehin einiges dazu, eine Frau wie Agnes über den Haufen zu rennen –, und so taumelten die beiden wie in einem ungelenken Tanz von einer Wegseite zur anderen. Dann merkte der Dieb, daß die Frau ihm ganz bewußt den Weg versperrte, und stieß sie beiseite. Doch Agnes streckte das Bein aus und erwischte ihn zwischen den Knien. Beide stürzten sie zu Boden.

Tom schlug das Herz bis zum Hals, als er ihr zu Hilfe eilte. Der Dieb rappelte sich gerade auf, das Knie auf Agnes' Rücken. Tom packte ihn am Kragen, schleuderte ihn zur Seite und warf ihn, ehe er sein Gleichgewicht wiedergewann, in den Graben.

»Bist du wohlauf?« fragte Tom hastig.

»Ja«, antwortete Agnes.

Die beiden Bauern waren inzwischen stehengeblieben und hatten sich umgedreht. Mit weit aufgerissenen Augen beobachteten sie die Szene. Der Spitzbube hockte noch im Graben. »Er ist ein Outlaw!« rief Agnes ihnen zu, um zu verhindern, daß sie Partei für ihn ergriffen. »Er hat unser Schwein gestohlen!« Der Bauer und sein Sohn zeigten keine Regung. Sie blieben einfach stehen und warteten ab, was als nächstes geschah.

Noch einmal versuchte Tom es mit gutem Zureden: »Gib mir mein Geld, und ich laß dich laufen!«

Schnell wie eine Ratte kam der Mann aus dem Graben. Er hatte ein Messer gezückt und wollte Tom an die Gurgel. Agnes schrie auf. Tom duckte sich. Das Messer blitzte auf, und er spürte einen brennenden Schmerz am Unterkiefer. Wieder blitzte das Messer auf, doch diesmal sprang Tom rechtzeitig zurück und holte gleichzeitig mit dem Hammer aus. Da auch der Dieb zurücksprang, pfiffen Messer und Hammer durch die feuchte Abendluft, ohne zu treffen.

Einen Augenblick lang standen die beiden Männer einander schwer keuchend gegenüber und starrten sich an. Toms Wange schmerzte. Der Gegner war ihm durchaus gewachsen, zwar kleiner, aber mit einem Messer bewaffnet, das erheblich gefährlicher war als Toms Schlaghammer. Todesangst ergriff Tom und nahm ihm den Atem.

Aus dem Augenwinkel gewahrte Tom eine plötzliche Bewegung. Auch der Dieb bemerkte sie. Er sah sich nach Agnes um und duckte sich: Der Stein, den sie geworfen hatte, flog haarscharf an seinem Kopf vorbei.

Tom nutzte die Gelegenheit mit der Geschwindigkeit eines Mannes, der weiß, daß es um sein Leben geht. Er holte aus, ließ den Hammer auf den gebeugten Kopf des Diebes niedersausen und traf ihn im selben Augenblick, da er sich wieder aufrichten wollte. Es war ein hastig geführter Schlag, in dem längst nicht alle Kraft lag, die aufzubringen Tom imstande war. Der Mann taumelte, fiel aber nicht.

Tom schlug ein zweites Mal zu.

Er konnte sich Zeit nehmen. Er konnte weit ausholen und gut zielen und dachte an Martha, als er zuschlug. Diesmal traf der eiserne Hammerkopf den noch ganz benommenen Dieb mit voller Wucht an der Stirn, genau auf den Haaransatz. Er stürzte zu Boden wie ein nasser Sack.

Tom war so erregt, daß er keinerlei Erleichterung verspürte. Er kniete neben dem Wegelagerer nieder und durchsuchte ihn. »Wo ist seine Geldtasche?« rief er. »Wo, zum Teufel, hat er unser Geld?« Der schlaffe Körper ließ sich nur mühsam bewegen. Schließlich gelang es Tom, ihn auf den Rücken zu wälzen. Er öffnete den Umhang. Am Gürtel war ein großer, lederner Geldbeutel befestigt. Tom öffnete die Schnalle. Im Beutel befand sich ein weiches Wollsäckchen, das mit einer Zugschnur versehen war. Tom zog das Säckchen heraus. Es war sehr leicht. Er sah hinein. »Leer! Er muß noch eine andere Tasche haben!«

Er zog dem Mann den Umhang aus und tastete ihn sorgfältig ab. Es gab keine versteckten Taschen, keine harten Stellen. Er zog ihm die Stiefel aus. Nichts. Er zog sein Eßmesser aus dem Gürtel und schlitzte die Sohlen auf: wieder nichts. Ungeduldig fuhr er mit dem Messer in die Wolltunika des Diebes und schlitzte sie bis zum Saum auf. Aber der Mann trug auch keinen verborgenen Leibgurt, in dem er das Geld verwahrte.

Der Dieb lag jetzt mitten auf der Straße im Matsch, nackt bis auf die Strümpfe. Der Bauer und sein Sohn glotzten Tom an wie einen Verrückten. »Er hat nicht einen Penny bei sich!« schrie Tom Agnes zu. Er war außer sich vor Wut.

»Dann hat er alles verspielt«, erwiderte sie bitter.

»Ich hoffe, er muß dafür im tiefsten Höllenfeuer brennen«, sagte Tom.

Agnes kniete nieder und legte dem Dieb die Hand auf die Brust.

»Genau das tut er jetzt«, gab sie zur Antwort. »Du hast ihn umgebracht.«

Zu Weihnachten litten sie Hunger.

Der Winter kam in jenem Jahr früh, und er war so kalt und hart und unnachgiebig wie der eiserne Meißel des Steinmetzen. Als erster Reif Felder und Wiesen überzuckerte, hingen noch Äpfel an den Bäumen. Die Leute sagten, das geht vorüber, aber der Frost blieb. In manchen Dörfern, wo man das herbstliche Pflügen ein wenig zu lange hinausgezögert hatte, brachen die Pflugscharen bei dem Versuch, die steinharte Erde aufzulockern. Eilig schlachteten die Bauern ihre Schweine und pökelten sie ein, und die Grundherren schlachteten ihre Rinder, weil das Weidegras nicht ausreichte, die Herden vollzählig über den Winter zu bringen. Aber sogar das wenige Gras, das noch verfügbar war, welkte unter dem endlosen Frost dahin, so daß noch viele Rinder starben, die dem Schlachterbeil entgangen waren. Hungrige Wölfe drangen in der Dämmerung in die Dörfer ein und holten sich so manches magere Huhn und unvorsichtige Kind.

Überall im Land hatte man auf den Baustellen beim ersten Frosteinbruch die im Sommer errichteten Mauern hastig mit Stroh und Dung bedeckt und sie auf diese Weise gegen die ärgste Kälte geschützt, denn der Mörtel war noch nicht ganz trocken und durfte, sollte er nicht brüchig werden, keinen Frost bekommen. Erst im Frühjahr konnten die Mörtelarbeiten wieder aufgenommen werden. Einige Maurer und Steinmetzen waren lediglich für den Sommer angeworben worden. Sie kehrten in ihre Dörfer zurück, wo man sie als Handwerker schätzte, und fertigten den Winter über Pflüge, Sättel, Pferdegeschirre, Wagen, Schaufeln, Türen und was sonst noch der kundigen Hand eines Mannes bedurfte, der mit Hammer, Meißel und Säge umzugehen verstand. Die anderen Steinmetzen zogen sich in die Bauhütten zurück und behauten während der lichten Stunden des Tages Steine in bisweilen recht komplizierten Formen. Aber weil der Frost schon so früh eingesetzt hatte, kamen sie mit ihrer Arbeit zu schnell voran, und weil die Bauern hungerten, hatten die Bischöfe, Burgherren und Kastellane weniger Geld für Bauarbeiten zur Verfügung als erhofft. Also wurden im weiteren Verlauf des Winters einige Steinmetzen entlassen.

Tom wanderte mit seiner Familie von Salisbury nach Shaftesbury und von dort nach Sherborne, Wells, Bath, Bristol, Gloucester, Oxford, Wallingford und Windsor. Überall brannten die Feuer in den Dombauhütten, und an Kirchen- und Burgmauern hallte der Klang von Eisen auf Stein wider. Die Baumeister formten mit ihren kunstfertigen, in fingerlosen Handschuhen steckenden Händen kleine originalgetreue Modelle der Bögen und Gewölbe. Einige Meister waren ungeduldig, kurz angebunden oder unhöflich; andere bedachten Tom, die Kinder und die schwangere Frau mit bedauernden Blicken und wechselten ein paar freundliche Worte mit ihnen. Doch wenn man zur Sache kam, lautete die Antwort überall gleich: Nein, tut mir leid, Arbeit habe ich für Euch keine.

Wo immer es möglich war, machten sie sich die Gastfreundschaft der Klöster zunutze, in denen jeder Reisende ein Essen und einen Schlafplatz erhielt – wenn auch streng nur für eine einzige Nacht. Als die Brombeeren gereift waren, hatten sie sich wie die Vögel tagelang von nichts anderem ernährt. Im Wald konnte Agnes ein Feuer entzünden, den eisernen Kochtopf daraufsetzen und einen Brei kochen, doch oftmals blieb ihnen nichts anderes übrig, als sich beim Bäcker Brot oder beim Fischhändler eingelegte Heringe zu besorgen. Oder sie mußten in Schenken und Garküchen essen, was natürlich erheblich teurer war als sich selbst zu verpflegen. Unwiederbringlich schmolzen ihre Spargroschen dahin.

Martha war von Natur aus dünn, doch wurde sie jetzt noch magerer. Alfred wurde immer größer und wirkte inzwischen schlaksig. Agnes aß nur wenig, doch das Kind in ihrem Leib war gierig, und es entging Tom nicht, daß der Hunger sie quälte. Manchmal befahl er ihr, mehr zu essen, und dann beugte sie tatsächlich ihren eisernen Willen der vereinten Autorität von Ehemann und ungeborenem Kind. Doch rund und rosig wie in ihren früheren Schwangerschaften wurde sie diesmal nicht; vielmehr wirkte sie trotz ihres geschwollenen Leibes hager und hohlwangig wie ein Kind während einer Hungersnot.

Von Salisbury aus hatten sie ungefähr drei Viertel eines großen Kreises zurückgelegt, so daß sie gegen Ende des Jahres wieder die ausgedehnten Waldungen erreichten, die sich von Windsor bis fast vor die Tore von Southampton erstreckten. Ihr Ziel war Winchester. Tom hatte seine Werkzeuge verkauft, und der Erlös dafür war bereits bis auf wenige Pennys aufgezehrt. An seiner nächsten Arbeitsstelle würde er sich Werkzeuge borgen müssen – oder aber Geld, um sich neue zu kaufen. Er wußte nicht mehr ein noch aus; Winchester war seine letzte Hoffnung. In seiner Heimatstadt lebten noch Geschwister von ihm – aber er stammte aus dem Norden des Landes, und die Reise dauerte mehrere Wochen. Bis dahin wäre die Familie längst verhungert. Agnes war ein Einzelkind. Ihre Eltern waren tot. Feldarbeit gab es während des Winters keine. Vielleicht konnte Agnes in einem wohlhabenden Haus in Winchester eine Anstellung als Magd oder Küchenmädchen finden und auf diese Weise ein paar Pennys zusammenkratzen. Eins stand jedenfalls fest: Von Ort zu Ort ziehen konnte sie nicht mehr lange, denn ihre Stunde nahte.

Aber auch nach Winchester waren es noch drei Tagesreisen, und der Hunger quälte sie. Brombeeren gab es keine mehr, es gab in der Nähe auch kein Kloster und keine Haferflocken mehr im Kochtopf, den Agnes auf dem Rücken trug. Am Abend zuvor hatten sie ein Messer gegen einen Laib Roggenbrot, vier Teller Suppe ohne Fleisch und ein Nachtlager in einer Bauernhütte eingetauscht. Seither hatten sie keine menschliche Siedlung mehr zu Gesicht bekommen. Am Spätnachmittag erspähte Tom allerdings eine Rauchsäule, die sich über die Baumwipfel erhob, und sie fanden das einsame Haus eines königlichen Jagdaufsehers, der ihnen für Toms kleine Axt einen Sack Steck-rüben gab.

Nur etwa drei Meilen später sagte Agnes, sie sei zu müde zum Weitergehen. Tom war überrascht: In all den Jahren, die sie nun schon zusammenlebten, hatte er dergleichen noch nie von ihr gehört.

Sie setzte sich unter eine große Roßkastanie am Wegesrand. Mit Hilfe eines der letzten Werkzeuge, die ihnen verblieben waren – einer abgenutzten Holzschaufel, die niemand hatte kaufen wollen –, hob er eine flache Grube für das Lagerfeuer aus. Die Kinder sammelten Rei-sig, und Tom entzündete das Feuer. Dann nahm er den Kochtopf und machte sich auf die Suche nach einem Bach. Nach einer Weile kehrte er zurück; der Topf war mit eiskaltem Wasser gefüllt. Martha sammelte Kastanien auf, die vom Baum gefallen waren, und Agnes zeigte ihr, wie man sie schälen und das weiche Innere zu einem groben Mehl zermahlen konnte, mit dem sich die Steckrübensuppe ein wenig an-dicken ließ. Tom schickte Alfred nach mehr Feuerholz aus, während er selbst einen Stock zur Hand nahm und im Fallaub herumzustochern begann. Er hoffte, einen Igel oder ein Eichhörnchen im Winterschlaf aufzustöbern; es hätte die Suppe ein bißchen angereichert. Aber er hatte kein Glück.

Langsam senkte sich die Dunkelheit über die Wälder herab. Tom setzte sich neben Agnes ans Feuer.

»Haben wir noch Salz?« fragte er.

Sie schüttelte den Kopf. »Du ißt den Brei schon seit Wochen ohne Salz. Ist dir das noch nicht aufgefallen?«

»Nein.«

»Hunger ist der beste Koch.«

»Nun, davon haben wir mehr als genug.« Tom war auf einmal müde. Zu viele Enttäuschungen hatte er in den vergangenen Monaten erfahren. Er empfand sie als eine schwere Last. Er konnte einfach nicht länger den Tapferen spielen. Tiefe Niedergeschlagenheit lag in seiner Stimme, als er Agnes fragte: »Was ist nur schiefgegangen, Agnes?«

»Alles«, antwortete sie. »Du hattest schon im letzten Winter keine Arbeit. Im Frühjahr bekamst du dann welche, und dann ließ die Toch-ter des Grafen die Verlobung platzen, und Lord William verzichtete auf das neue Haus. Daß wir uns damals entschlossen, noch zu bleiben und bei der Ernte zu helfen, war ein Fehler.«

»Ja, das stimmt. Im Sommer hätte ich woanders viel eher eine Arbeit gefunden als im Herbst.«

»Und dann kam der frühe Wintereinbruch. Doch selbst den hätten wir noch überstanden, wenn uns das Schwein nicht gestohlen worden wäre.«

Tom nickte trübsinnig. »Mein einziger Trost ist der, daß der Dieb nun alle Qualen der Hölle über sich ergehen lassen muß.«

»Hoffentlich.«

»Zweifelst du etwa daran?«

»Die Priester wissen gar nicht soviel, wie sie immer vorgeben. Mein Vater war schließlich auch einer ...«

Tom konnte sich noch sehr gut an seinen Schwiegervater erinnern. Eine Mauer der Gemeindekirche war eingestürzt und konnte nicht mehr ausgebessert werden. Er, Tom, hatte den Auftrag erhalten, eine neue zu errichten. Zu heiraten war den Priestern untersagt, doch jener Priester hatte eine Haushälterin, und die Haushälterin hatte eine Tochter. Im Dorf war es ein offenes Geheimnis, daß der Priester der Vater des Kindes war. Agnes war keine Schönheit, schon damals nicht, doch sie schien vor Energie und Tatkraft schier zu bersten, und ihre Haut hatte den schimmernden Glanz der Jugend. Sie besuchte Tom auf der Baustelle und unterhielt sich mit ihm. Manchmal preßte der Wind ihr das Kleid hautnah an den Leib, so daß Tom die Formen ihres Körpers sehen konnte, als ob sie nackt gewesen wäre, sogar den Nabel. Eines Nachts kam sie zu ihm in seine kleine Hütte, legte ihm die Hand auf den Mund, um ihn am Reden zu hindern, und zog dann ihr Kleid aus, so daß er sie nackt im Mondlicht sehen konnte. Da nahm er ihren starken, jungen Körper in die Arme, und sie liebten sich.

»Wir waren beide noch völlig unerfahren«, sagte er laut.

Agnes wußte sofort, woran er dachte, doch ihr Lächeln hielt nicht lange vor. »Es ist so lange her«, sagte sie.

»Können wir jetzt essen?« fragte Martha.

Tom knurrte der Magen, als ihm der Geruch der Suppe in die Nase stieg. Er tauchte seinen Napf in die blubbernde Flüssigkeit und fischte ein paar Rübenscheibchen mit dünnem Brei heraus. Mit der stumpfen Seite seines Messers prüfte er die Rüben. Sie waren noch nicht ganz durch, aber er wollte die anderen nicht länger warten lassen. Alfred und Martha bekamen ihre Näpfe gefüllt, dann war Agnes an der Reihe.

Sie wirkte sehr erschöpft und hing ihren Gedanken nach, als Tom ihr den Napf reichte. Bevor sie die Suppe an die Lippen hob, blies sie hinein, um sie ein wenig zu kühlen.

Die Kinder waren rasch fertig und baten um einen Nachschlag.

Tom schützte seine Hände mit dem Mantelsaum, nahm den Topf vom Feuer und teilte den Rest der Suppe unter Alfred und Martha auf.

Als er zu Agnes zurückkehrte, fragte sie ihn: »Und du?«

»Ich esse morgen was«, gab er zur Antwort.

Sie war zu müde, um zu widersprechen.

Tom und Alfred schürten das Feuer und sammelten gemeinsam Holz für die Nacht. Dann wickelten sie sich in ihre Mäntel und legten sich ins Laub.

Tom fiel in einen unruhigen Schlaf. Als er Agnes stöhnen hörte, war er sofort hellwach.

»Was ist los?« flüsterte er.

Wieder stöhnte sie auf. Ihr Gesicht war bleich, die Augen hielt sie geschlossen. Nach einer Weile antwortete sie: »Das Kind kommt.«

Tom schlug das Herz bis zum Hals. Nicht hier, dachte er, nicht hier auf dem gefrorenen Boden mitten im Wald. »Es ist doch noch gar nicht fällig«, sagte er.

»Es kommt vor der Zeit.«

Tom gab sich alle Mühe, ruhig und besonnen zu klingen. »Ist das Wasser schon abgegangen?«

»Schon kurz hinter der Hütte des Jagdaufsehers.« Agnes keuchte, die Augen waren noch immer geschlossen.

Tom erinnerte sich, daß sie plötzlich im Gebüsch verschwunden war. Er hatte geglaubt, ein natürliches Bedürfnis habe sie überkommen. »Hast du Wehen?«

»Ja, die ganze Zeit schon.«

Es paßte zu ihr, daß sie kein Wort darüber verloren hatte. Inzwischen waren auch Alfred und Martha erwacht. »Was ist denn los?« fragte Alfred.

»Das Kind kommt«, sagte Tom.

Martha brach in Tränen aus.

Tom runzelte die Stirn. »Meinst du, du schaffst es noch zurück bis zur Försterhütte?« fragte er Agnes. Dort gab es wenigstens ein Dach, ein bißchen Stroh zum Daraufliegen – und jemanden, der ihnen helfen konnte.

Agnes schüttelte den Kopf.

»Dann wird es also nicht mehr lange dauern.« Sie befanden sich im einsamsten Teil des Waldes. Den ganzen Tag über hatten sie kein Dorf gesehen, und der Jagdaufseher hatte gemeint, sie würden auch am kommenden Tag keines zu Gesicht bekommen. Es bestand nicht die geringste Aussicht, eine Frau zu finden, die etwas von der Hebammenkunst verstand. Er selbst würde Agnes entbinden müssen, hier draußen in der Kälte, und nur die Kinder würden ihm beistehen. Und falls es Schwierigkeiten gab … Er hatte keinerlei Medizin – und keine Ahnung dazu.

Es ist alles meine Schuld, dachte er bei sich. Ich habe sie geschwängert, ich habe sie ins Elend gebracht. Sie hat sich auf mich verlassen, und nun muß sie das Kind mitten im Winter unter freiem Himmel auf die Welt bringen! Männer, die Kinder in die Welt setzten und sie später verhungern ließen, hatte Tom zeitlebens verachtet. Jetzt mußte er einsehen, daß er selbst um keinen Deut besser war. Er empfand tiefe Scham.

»Ich bin so müde«, sagte Agnes, »ich glaube, ich schaffe es nicht. Ich möchte Ruhe, nur Ruhe …« Ein dünner Schweißfilm ließ ihr Gesicht im Feuerschein erglänzen.

Ich muß mich zusammenreißen, dachte Tom. Ich muß ihr Mut zusprechen, damit sie bei Kräften bleibt. »Ich helfe dir«, sagte er. Es war im Grunde nichts Besonderes oder Geheimnisvolles, was ihnen jetzt bevorstand; er selbst hatte schon mehrmals miterlebt, wie Kinder auf die Welt kamen. Die Hebammenarbeit freilich war normalerweise Frauensache: Frauen wußten, wie der werdenden Mutter zumute war; sie konnten daher auch besser auf sie eingehen. Nichts sprach jedoch dagegen, daß im Notfall auch ein Mann den nötigen Beistand leistete.

»Mir ist kalt«, sagte Agnes.

»Komm näher ans Feuer«, antwortete er, zog seinen Umhang aus und breitete ihn gleich neben dem Feuer auf den Boden. Agnes versuchte aufzustehen. Tom nahm sie auf die Arme und bettete sie vorsichtig auf das neue Lager. Dann kniete er neben ihr nieder. Unter ihrem Winterumhang trug sie eine von oben bis unten durchgeknöpfte Wolltunika. Tom öffnete zwei Knöpfe und ließ seine Hände hineingleiten. Agnes hielt die Luft an.

»Tut es weh?« fragte er erschrocken.

»Nein«, erwiderte sie und lächelte kurz. »Deine Hände sind so kalt.«

Er tastete ihren Bauch ab. Die Schwellung war höher und spitzer als in der Nacht zuvor, als sie auf einem Haufen Stroh in der Bauernhütte geschlafen hatten. Tom verstärkte den Druck und konnte knapp unterhalb des Nabels das ungeborene Kind spüren. »Ich glaub', ich fühle das Hinterteil, aber nicht den Kopf.«

»Das kommt, weil es herauswill«, erwiderte Agnes. Tom wickelte sie wieder in ihren Umhang und deckte sie zu. Es war höchste Zeit, die notwendigen Vorbereitungen zu treffen. Er sah sich nach den Kindern um. Martha schniefte; Alfred schien sich zu fürchten. Er mußte den beiden etwas zu tun geben.

»Alfred, nimm den Kochtopf und geh zum Bach. Wasch ihn säuberlich aus und füll ihn mit frischem Wasser. Du, Martha, sammelst ein paar Schilfhalme und flichtst mir daraus zwei Schnüre, beide lang genug für eine Schlinge. Macht schnell! Wenn der Morgen graut, habt ihr ein neues Geschwisterchen.«

Die Kinder verschwanden. Tom zog sein Eßmesser und schärfte es an seinem Schleifstein. Als Agnes erneut aufstöhnte, legte er das Messer beiseite und hielt ihre Hand.

So hatte er auch bei der Geburt der anderen Kinder neben ihr gesessen: Alfred, Matilda – die im Alter von zwei Jahren gestorben war –, dann Martha und zuletzt der kleine Junge, der tot auf die Welt kam; Tom hatte insgeheim schon beschlossen gehabt, ihn Harold zu nennen. Doch bei jeder Geburt hatten Agnes kundige Frauen mit Rat und Tat zur Seite gestanden – bei Alfred noch ihre eigene Mutter, bei Matilda und Harold die Hebamme des Dorfes und bei Martha keine geringere als die Gutsherrin. Diesmal hing alles an ihm – und er durfte sich seine Besorgnis nicht anmerken lassen, sondern mußte ihr trotz der widrigen Umstände Mut und Zuversicht einflößen.

Ein Wehenkrampf ging vorüber, und Agnes entspannte sich.

»Erinnerst du dich noch an Marthas Geburt, als Lady Isabella Hebamme spielte?« fragte Tom.

Agnes lächelte. »Ja, ich weiß es noch genau. Du hast damals eine Kapelle für den Lord gebaut und sie gebeten, ihre Magd nach der Hebamme zu schicken ...«

»... worauf Lady Isabella antwortete: ›Nach dieser trunkenen alten Hexe? Der würde ich nicht einmal erlauben, einen Wurf Wolfshunde zu entbinden!‹ Und dann hat sie uns in ihre eigene Schlafkammer gebracht. Lord Robert konnte erst zu Bett gehen, als Martha geboren war.«

»Sie war eine gute Frau.«

»Ladys wie sie gibt es nicht viele.«

Alfred kam mit dem Wassertopf zurück. Tom stellte ihn in die Glut, nicht über die offene Flamme. Das Wasser sollte nicht kochen, sondern nur heiß werden. Agnes holte aus ihrem Umhang einen kleinen Leinenbeutel, in dem sie einige saubere Tücher bereithielt.

Martha kam mit einer Handvoll Schilfhalme zurück und begann sie zu flechten. »Wozu brauchst du die Schnüre?« fragte sie.

»Zu etwas sehr Wichtigem«, sagte Tom. »Du wirst es schon sehen. Achte darauf, daß sie gut und fest werden.«

Alfred wirkte unruhig; ihm war offensichtlich nicht wohl in seiner Haut. »Los, hol noch mehr Holz, Junge!« sagte Tom. »Wir wollen das Feuer größer machen.« Alfred verschwand, froh darüber, daß er etwas zu tun bekam.

Jetzt kam eine heftige Wehe. Die Anstrengung, die es Agnes kostete, das Kind aus ihrem Schoß zu pressen, zeichnete ihr Gesicht, und sie ächzte wie ein sturmgeschüttelter Baum. Tom sah, daß sie alles gab, was ihr an körperlichen Kräften noch verblieben war. Wie gern hätte er ihr geholfen, hätte die Wehen selbst auf sich genommen, es ihr leichter gemacht!

Endlich schienen die Schmerzen ein wenig nachzulassen, und Tom atmete tief durch. Agnes war in eine Art Halbschlaf gefallen.

Alfred brachte einen Armvoll Feuerholz.

Agnes war auf einmal wieder hellwach. »Mir ist so kalt«, klagte sie.

»Schüre das Feuer, Alfred«, sagte Tom. »Und du, Martha, legst dich neben deine Mutter und wärmst sie.« Die Kinder gehorchten mit furchtsamem Blick. Zitternd vor Kälte, nahm Agnes Martha in die Arme und zog sie an sich.

Die Sorge um Agnes machte Tom fast krank. Das Feuer loderte hoch auf, doch die Luft wurde immer kälter. Sie war jetzt schon so kalt, daß sie imstande war, das Neugeborene bei seinem ersten Atemzug zu töten. Daß Kinder im Freien auf die Welt kamen, war an sich nichts Ungewöhnliches und geschah vor allem während der Erntezeit, wenn die Frauen bis zur letzten Minute auf den Feldern draußen arbeiteten, gar nicht selten. Doch zur Erntezeit war die Erde trocken, das Gras weich und die Luft lau. Von einer Wintergeburt unter freiem Himmel hatte Tom noch nie gehört.

Agnes stützte sich auf ihre Ellbogen und spreizte die Beine.

»Was ist?« fragte Tom mit Furcht in der Stimme, doch Agnes brachte vor Anstrengung kein Wort heraus.

»Alfred, knie dich hinter deine Mutter auf den Boden, so daß sie sich anlehnen kann!«

Kaum hatte Alfred die ihm zugewiesene Stellung eingenommen, öffnete Tom Agnes' Umhang und knöpfte ihre Tunika auf. Er kniete zwischen ihren Beinen nieder und sah die Haare auf dem Kopf des Kindes. »Jetzt ist es bald vorüber, Liebling«, murmelte er beruhigend.

Agnes entspannte sich wieder, schloß die Augen und lehnte sich zurück. Im Wald war es ganz still, nur das Prasseln des Feuers war zu hören. Tom fiel plötzlich wieder ein, daß auch die verfemte Ellen ihr Kind im Freien geboren hatte, ohne jede Hilfe. Es mußte entsetzlich gewesen sein. Sie hatte von ihrer Angst erzählt, daß ein Wolf hätte kommen und ihr in ihrer Hilflosigkeit das Neugeborene wegschnappen können ... In diesem Winter, so hieß es, waren die Wölfe von besonderer Kühnheit. Allerdings war kaum damit zu rechnen, daß sie eine Gruppe von vier Menschen angriffen.

Die nächste Wehe kam, und auf Agnes' schmerzverzerrtem Gesicht bildeten sich neue Schweißperlen. Jetzt ist es soweit, dachte Tom. Wieder konnte er im flackernden Licht das feuchte schwarze Kopfhaar des Kindes erkennen. Er wollte beten, doch dazu war nun keine Zeit mehr. Agnes' Atem ging hastig, stoßweise. Immer weiter kam der Kopf zum Vorschein. Tom sah schon die faltige Nackenhaut.

»Der Kopf ist da«, sagte er. Agnes entspannte sich wieder etwas. Langsam drehte Tom das Kind um, so daß die geschlossenen Augen und der mit Blut und Schleim verschmierte Mund des Kindes zu sehen waren.

»O seht doch!« rief Martha. »Schaut euch das kleine Gesichtchen an!«

Agnes hörte es und lächelte, doch schon kündigte sich die nächste Wehe an. Die Schultern erschienen, erst die eine, dann die andere, und Tom beugte sich vor und hielt den kleinen Kopf mit der linken Hand. Der Rest des Körpers kam mit einem Schwung. Tom hielt die Rechte unter die Hüften des Kindes, als die winzigen Beinchen in die kalte Welt glitten.

»Gib mir jetzt die Bänder, die du geflochten hast«, sagte Tom zu Martha. »Gleich wirst du sehen, wozu man sie braucht.«

Sie reichte ihm die geflochtenen Halme. Tom band an zwei Stellen die Nabelschnur ab, nahm sein Messer zur Hand und durchtrennte sie zwischen den beiden Knoten.

Tom hob das Kind hoch und betrachtete es von allen Seiten. Es war voller Blut, so daß er schon das Schlimmste fürchtete, doch als er genauer hinsah, fanden sich keinerlei Verletzungen.

Das Kind war ein Junge.

»Das sieht ja furchtbar aus«, sagte Martha.

»Der ist gesund und munter«, sagte Tom, ganz schwach vor Erleichterung. »Ein Prachtkerl!«

Das Kind öffnete den Mund und fing an zu schreien.

Tom sah sich nach Agnes um. Sie lächelten einander zu. Er zog das winzige Wesen an seine Brust. »Martha, hol ein Schüsselchen

Wasser aus dem Topf.« Das Mädchen sprang auf, um seinen Wunsch zu erfüllen. »Agnes, wo sind die Tücher?« Agnes deutete auf den Leinenbeutel, der neben ihrer Schulter auf der Erde lag. Alfred nahm ihn auf und reichte ihn seinem Vater. Sein Gesicht war tränenüberströmt; es war das erstemal, daß er eine Geburt miterlebte.

Tom tauchte ein Tuch in die Schüssel und wusch dem Kleinen vorsichtig Blut und Schleim aus dem Gesicht. Agnes knöpfte das Oberteil ihrer Tunika auf, und Tom legte ihr den brüllenden Säugling in den Arm.

Dann setzte er sich erleichtert nieder. Sie hatten es geschafft! Das Schlimmste war überstanden und das Kind wohlauf. Er war stolz.

Agnes legte sich das Kind an den Busen. Das Schreien hörte auf, als der winzige Mund die Brustwarze fand und zu saugen begann.

»Woher weiß das Kindchen, daß es saugen muß?« fragte Martha erstaunt.

»Das ist ein unergründliches Rätsel«, sagte Tom, gab ihr die Schüssel und fügte hinzu: »Hol deiner Mutter frisches Wasser. Sie möchte sicher etwas zu trinken.«

»O ja«, stimmte Agnes dankbar zu, als hätte sie eben erst gemerkt, wie durstig sie war. Als Martha ihr das Wasser brachte, trank sie die Schüssel in einem Zug leer. »Oh, tut das gut«, sagte sie. »Vielen Dank!«

Sie betrachtete den Säugling an ihrer Brust. Dann sah sie Tom an. »Du bist ein guter Mann«, sagte sie mit leiser Stimme. »Ich liebe dich.«

Tom spürte, wie ihm die Tränen in die Augen stiegen. Er lächelte ihr zu. Doch dann fiel ihm auf, daß sie nach wie vor ziemlich stark blutete. Die verschrumpelte Nabelschnur, die noch immer aus ihrem Schoß hing, kringelte sich in einer kleinen Blutlache auf Toms Umhang.

Kurz darauf fragte Martha ihren Vater: »Wartest du noch auf etwas?«

»Ja«, erwiderte Tom. »Auf die Nachgeburt.«

»Was ist das?«

»Du wirst's schon sehen.«

Mutter und Kind ruhten eine Weile. Dann schlug Agnes unvermittelt die Augen auf. Ihre Muskeln verkrampften sich, und der Mutterkuchen erschien. Tom nahm ihn auf und betrachtete ihn. Er sah aus wie vom Hackbrett des Schlachters gefallen und war auf einer Seite eingerissen. Man hätte meinen können, daß ein Stück fehlte, doch war Tom sich dessen nicht sicher, schließlich hatte er nie zuvor eine

Nachgeburt so genau angesehen. Wahrscheinlich war das immer so – irgendwie mußte sie sich ja schließlich vom Körper losgerissen haben.

Er warf die Nachgeburt ins Feuer. Ein unangenehmer Geruch entströmte ihr, als die Flammen sie erfaßten. Sie einfach in den Wald zu werfen, war nicht ratsam; sie hätte Füchse oder gar Wölfe anlocken können.

Agnes blutete immer noch. Daß mit der Nachgeburt stets ein Blutschwall abging, war Tom noch geläufig, nur erinnerte er sich nicht an solche Mengen. Er wußte jetzt, daß die Krise noch nicht überstanden war. Vor Hunger und Erschöpfung schwindelte ihn, doch der Anfall war nur von kurzer Dauer. Er riß sich zusammen.

»Du blutest noch immer ein bißchen«, sagte er zu Agnes, wobei er sich bemühte, seine Sorge nicht durchklingen zu lassen.

»Das hört sicher bald auf«, sagte sie. »Deck mich zu.«

Tom knöpfte ihr das Oberteil der Tunika zu und wickelte ihr den Umhang um die Beine.

»Kann ich mich jetzt etwas ausruhen?« fragte Alfred.

Er kniete noch immer hinter Agnes und stützte sie. Er hat so lange in derselben Stellung verharrt, daß ihm alle Glieder abgestorben sein müssen, dachte Tom und sagte: »Ich löse dich ab.« Für Agnes, die ja den Säugling halten mußte, war es bequemer, halb aufgerichtet zu bleiben. Außerdem hielt der Körper des Stützenden ihren Rücken warm und schützte sie vor dem Wind. Tom und Alfred tauschten die Plätze. Alfred streckte ächzend seine jungen Beine. Tom legte die Arme um Agnes und das Kind. »Wie geht es dir?« fragte er.

»Ich bin entsetzlich müde.«

Der Säugling schrie. Agnes legte ihn aufrecht, so daß er ihre Brust finden konnte. Während das Kind zu nuckeln begann, schlief sie ein.

Tom war beunruhigt. Die Erschöpfung nach einer Geburt war normal, doch Agnes' ungewöhnliche Teilnahmslosigkeit machte ihm Sorgen. Sie war zu schwach.

Der Säugling schlief, und nach einer Weile schliefen auch die anderen beiden Kinder ein. Martha kuschelte sich an Agnes, Alfred streckte sich auf der anderen Seite der Feuerstelle aus. Tom hielt Agnes in den Armen und streichelte sie sanft, hin und wieder küßte er ihren Scheitel. Er spürte, wie sich ihr Körper zunehmend entspannte und immer tiefer in Schlaf sank. Wahrscheinlich ist es das Beste für sie, dachte er. Er berührte ihre Wange. Obwohl er alles getan hatte, um sie warmzuhalten, war die Haut kalt und klamm. Er suchte den Säugling unter ihrem Gewand und legte ihm die Hand auf die Brust. Das Kind war warm, sein Herz schlug fest und regelmäßig. Tom lächelte. Ein kräftiges Kind, dachte er. Stark genug zum Überleben.

Agnes regte sich. »Tom?«

»Ja?«

»Erinnerst du dich an die Nacht, als ich zu dir in deine Hütte kam? Damals, als du an der Kirche meines Vaters gearbeitet hast?«

»O ja, natürlich«, sagte er und tätschelte sie. »Wie könnte ich diese Nacht jemals vergessen?«

»Ich habe es nie bereut, daß ich deine Frau geworden bin. Nicht ein einziges Mal. Und jedesmal, wenn ich an diese Nacht zurückdenke, fühle ich mich froh und glücklich.«

Er lächelte. Es tat ihm gut. »Mir geht es genauso«, sagte er. »Ich bin froh, daß du damals zu mir gekommen bist.«

Sie schwieg, verloren in ihren Gedanken. Dann sagte sie: »Ich hoffe, du wirst eines Tages deine Kathedrale bauen.«

Tom war überrascht. »Ich dachte, du wärst dagegen.«

»War ich auch, aber das war nicht recht. Du verdienst etwas Schönes.«

Er verstand nicht, was sie damit meinte.

»Bau eine schöne Kathedrale für mich.«

Sie wußte nicht, was sie sagte. Tom war froh, als sie wieder einschlief. Diesmal wurde ihr Körper ganz schlaff, und ihr Kopf fiel zur Seite. Hätte Tom ihn nicht festgehalten, wäre der Säugling ihr von der Brust gefallen.

So lagen sie eine lange Zeit. Schließlich fing das Kind wieder an zu schreien, doch Agnes reagierte nicht darauf. Alfred wurde von dem Geschrei geweckt; er drehte sich nach seinem kleinen Bruder um.

Tom rüttelte Agnes vorsichtig. »Wach auf!« sagte er. »Der Kleine hat Hunger.«

»Vater!« rief Alfred mit erstickter Stimme. »Ihr Gesicht!«

Eine böse Vorahnung beschlich Tom. Sie hatte zu stark geblutet. »Agnes!« wiederholte er. »Wach auf!« Sie rührte sich nicht. Sie mußte das Bewußtsein verloren haben. Tom erhob sich und ließ ihren Oberkörper sanft zu Boden gleiten, bis sie flach auf dem Rücken lag. Ihr Gesicht war gespenstisch bleich.

Mit dem Schlimmsten rechnend, wickelte Tom den um ihre Hüften geschlungenen Umhang auf.

Überall war Blut.

Alfred hielt den Atem an und wandte sich ab.

»Lieber Herr Jesus, steh uns bei!« flüsterte Tom.

Das Geschrei des Säuglings hatte inzwischen auch Martha geweckt. Sie sah das Blut und fing an zu kreischen. Tom packte sie und schlug ihr ins Gesicht. Sie war sofort still. »Kein Geschrei!« befahl er ruhig und gab sie wieder frei.

Alfred fragte: »Stirbt Mutter?«

Tom legte Agnes die Hand auf die Haut unterhalb ihrer linken Brust. Er spürte nichts.

Das Herz hatte aufgehört zu schlagen.

Tom verstärkte den Druck seiner Hand. Agnes' Haut war warm, und er spürte die Schwere ihrer Brust. Aber sie atmete nicht mehr, und das Herz stand still.

Wie Nebel senkte sich eine dumpfe Kälte um Tom. Agnes war von ihm gegangen. Er starrte in ihr Gesicht. Wie war es möglich, daß sie nicht mehr bei ihnen war? Er wollte, daß sie sich bewegte, die Augen aufschlug, ein- und ausatmete. Er ließ seine Hand auf ihrer Brust liegen. Es hieß, daß stillstehende Herzen mitunter wieder zu schlagen begannen ... Aber sie hatte so viel Blut verloren.

Er sah Alfred an. »Mutter ist tot«, flüsterte er.

Alfred starrte ihn begriffsstutzig an, Martha fing an zu weinen. Auch der Säugling wimmerte. Ich muß mich um die Kinder kümmern, dachte Tom. Ich darf jetzt keine Schwäche zeigen.

Insgeheim jedoch empfand er ein fast unstillbares Bedürfnis danach zu weinen. Er wollte die Tote umarmen, bis der Körper kalt und steif war. Er wollte an das junge Mädchen Agnes denken, an die lachende Frau, an die Frau, die er leidenschaftlich geliebt hatte. Er wollte seine Wut aus sich herausschluchzen und die Fäuste recken gegen den unbarmherzigen Himmel. Aber er versagte es sich und wappnete sein Herz. Er durfte jetzt unter keinen Umständen den Kopf verlieren, sondern mußte Stärke zeigen – der Kinder wegen.

Keine Träne trat ihm in die Augen.

Was ist jetzt zu tun? fragte er sich.

Wir müssen ein Grab schaufeln.

Ich muß ein tiefes Loch graben und Agnes hineinlegen, damit sie von den Wölfen verschont bleibt und ihre Gebeine am Tag des Jüngsten Gerichtes wiederauferstehen können. Am Grab muß ich für ihre Seele beten. O Agnes, warum hast du mich verlassen?

Der Säugling schrie unentwegt. Seine Augen waren fest geschlossen, der Mund öffnete und schloß sich regelmäßig, als schöpfe er Kraft aus der Luft. Er brauchte unbedingt Nahrung. Agnes' Brüste waren voller warmer Milch. Warum nicht? dachte Tom und bettete das Kind so, daß es eine Brustwarze erreichen konnte. Es begann sofort zu saugen.

Martha sah mit großen Augen zu und lutschte dabei am Daumen.

»Halt das Kind fest, so daß es nicht herunterfällt!« trug Tom ihr auf.

Sie nickte und kniete neben der Toten und dem Kind nieder.

Tom holte den Spaten. Agnes hatte den Ruheplatz unter der großen Roßkastanie selbst ausgewählt. Wohlan – so sollte er auch zu ihrer letzten Ruhestätte werden. Er schluckte und überwand den schier unwiderstehlichen Drang, sich einfach auf den Boden zu setzen und zu weinen. Einige Schritte vom Stammgrund entfernt – weit genug, um das Wurzelwerk nicht zu verletzen – kratzte er ein Rechteck in die Erde. Dann fing er an zu graben.

Die Arbeit tat ihm gut. Indem er all seinen Willen und all seine Konzentration darauf verwandte, den Spaten ins frostharte Erdreich zu treiben, gelang es ihm, alle anderen Gedanken zu vergessen und neue innere Kraft zu schöpfen. Ab und zu ließ er sich von Alfred ablösen, dem die eintönige körperliche Arbeit ebenfalls einen gewissen Trost verschaffte. Sie gruben, so schnell sie konnten, und gerieten bald trotz der bitteren Kälte ins Schwitzen.

Irgendwann fragte Alfred: »Meinst du nicht, es ist groß genug?«

Tom nickte widerstrebend. Am liebsten hätte er weitergegraben, doch das Loch war inzwischen schon fast mannstief. »Ja, das genügt«, sagte er und kletterte hinaus.

Inzwischen dämmerte der Morgen herauf. Martha hatte den Säugling aufgenommen. Sie saß am Feuer und wiegte ihn auf den Armen. Tom kniete neben Agnes nieder und wickelte sie fest in ihren Umhang, achtete jedoch darauf, daß das Gesicht frei blieb. Dann hob er sie auf, legte sie neben das Grab, stieg wieder in die Grube und holte sie zu sich. Er bettete sie behutsam auf die Erde und kniete neben ihr in ihrem kalten Grab. Sanft küßte er sie noch einmal auf die Lippen, dann schloß er ihr die Lider.

Er kletterte wieder hinaus. »Kommt her, Kinder«, sagte er.

Alfred und Martha stellten sich neben ihn, und Tom legte seine Arme um sie. Martha hielt den Säugling im Arm. Sie starrten in das Grab. »Sagt jetzt: ›Gott segne unsere Mutter.‹!« befahl er.

Die Kinder sagten: »Gott segne unsere Mutter.«

Martha schluchzte, und Alfreds Augen waren tränenfeucht. Tom drückte sie an sich und schluckte seine eigenen Tränen.

Als die erste Schaufel Erde ins Grab fiel, schrie Martha auf. Alfred nahm seine Schwester in die Arme, Tom schaufelte weiter. Der Gedanke, Erde auf Agnes' Gesicht werfen zu müssen, war ihm unerträglich, und so bedeckte er zunächst ihre Füße, dann ihre Beine und ihren Rumpf, und er türmte die Erde so hoch, daß sie bald einen großen Hügel bildete, der sich mit jeder neu hinzukommenden Schaufel verbreiterte. Die Erde rieselte über den Hals, den Mund, den er geküßt hatte, und schließlich war das Gesicht auf Nimmerwiedersehen verschwunden.

Rasch füllte Tom das Grab auf.

Als er fertig war, verstreute er die restliche Erde, so daß sich das Grab nicht mehr von der Umgebung abhob. Den Outlaws hier im Wald war durchaus zuzutrauen, daß sie es in der Hoffnung, einen Ring an der Leiche zu finden, wieder aufscharrten.

Dann stand er neben dem Grab. »Lebwohl, meine Liebe«, flüsterte er. »Du warst eine gute Frau. Ich liebe dich.«

Mit Mühe riß er sich los.

Sein Umhang lag noch immer dort, wo er Agnes entbunden hatte. Die untere Hälfte war getränkt mit geronnenem, trocknendem Blut. Tom nahm sein Messer zur Hand, schnitt den Umhang in der Mitte durch und warf die blutgetränkte Hälfte ins Feuer.

Martha hielt nach wie vor den Säugling im Arm. »Gib ihn mir!« sagte Tom. Martha sah ihn an, die Augen voller Furcht. Tom wickelte den nackten Säugling in die unbefleckte Hälfte des Umhangs. Das Kind schrie. Zu Alfred und Martha, die ihn mit stumpfen Blicken anglotzten, sagte er: »Wir haben keine Milch, um ihn am Leben zu halten. Er muß hierbleiben, bei seiner Mutter.«

»Aber da stirbt er doch!« rief Martha.

»Ja«, sagte Tom mit gepreßter Stimme. »Er stirbt auf jeden Fall, wie immer wir uns verhalten.« Er wünschte, der Säugling hörte auf zu schreien.

Er sammelte seine Habseligkeiten zusammen, steckte sie in den Kochtopf und schnallte sich den Topf auf den Rücken, ganz so, wie Agnes es immer getan hatte.

»Laßt uns gehen«, sagte er.

Martha fing an zu schluchzen. Alfreds Gesicht war totenbleich. Im grauen Licht eines kalten Morgens brachen sie auf. Das Geschrei des Kindes wurde leiser und leiser, bis es schließlich nicht mehr zu hören war.

Es hätte nichts genützt, noch länger am Grab zu bleiben. Die Kinder hätten kein Auge mehr zugetan, und den Rest der Nacht am

Grab zu wachen, wäre sinnlos gewesen. Es war gut, daß sie wieder unterwegs waren; es lenkte sie ab.

Tom schlug einen schnellen Schritt an, doch seine Gedanken waren nun frei und ließen sich nicht mehr bändigen. Gehen, gehen ... sie konnten nichts anderes tun als gehen. Es gab keinerlei Vorbereitungen zu treffen, keine Arbeit, kein Ziel und nichts zu sehen als einen düsteren Wald und zittrige Schatten im Fackelschein. Immer wieder dachte er an Agnes, an dieses oder jenes gemeinsame Erlebnis, und bei manchen Erinnerungen, die sich einstellten, lächelte er und drehte sich nach ihr um, um ihr zu sagen, woran er gerade gedacht hatte ... Da traf ihn dann jedesmal die Erkenntnis, daß sie gestorben war, wie ein Schlag. Er war vollkommen durcheinander, als sei etwas gänzlich Unbegreifliches geschehen, obwohl es zu den natürlichsten Dingen der Welt gehörte, daß Frauen ihres Alters im Kindbett starben und Ehemänner seines Alters als Witwer zurückließen. Das Gefühl des Verlusts schwärte wie eine offene Wunde. Er hatte einmal gehört, daß Menschen, denen man an einem Fuß die Zehen abgeschnitten hatte, ständig hinfielen und das Gehen unter großen Mühen neu erlernen mußten. So ähnlich erging es ihm jetzt auch; es war, als hätte man ihm einen Teil seines Körpers amputiert, und er hatte sich mit der Endgültigkeit des Verlusts noch nicht abgefunden. Er versuchte, nicht mehr an Agnes zu denken, doch ließ sich die Erinnerung nicht abschütteln. Er sah sie vor sich, wie sie kurz vor ihrem Tod ausgesehen hatte ... Es war schier unglaublich, daß sie vor wenigen Stunden noch gelebt hatte und nun unwiederbringlich von ihm gegangen war. Er sah ihr vom Geburtsschmerz verzerrtes Gesicht und das stolze Lächeln, als es vorüber war und sie den neugeborenen Sohn in den Armen hielt. Er hörte ihre Worte danach: *Ich hoffe, du wirst eines Tages deine Kathedrale bauen.* Und: *Bau eine schöne Kathedrale für mich.* Es waren die Worte einer Frau gewesen, die wußte, daß sie im Sterben lag.

Je weiter sie gingen, desto öfter mußte Tom an den zurückgelassenen Säugling denken. In einen halben Mantel gehüllt, lag er auf dem frischen Grab. Wahrscheinlich lebte er noch, es sei denn, ein Fuchs hatte bereits seine Witterung aufgenommen. Auf jeden Fall würde er sterben, noch bevor es richtig Tag geworden war. Er würde noch ein wenig schreien und dann seine Augen schließen. Im Schlaf würde er erkalten und sein junges Leben aushauchen.

Es sei denn, ein Fuchs hätte ihn bereits gewittert ...

Es gab nichts, was Tom für den Säugling hätte tun können. Um zu überleben, brauchte das Kind Milch, und Milch gab es keine. Es gab kein Dorf, wo man eine Amme hätte finden können, es gab weder ein Schaf noch eine Ziege oder eine Kuh. Alles, was Tom seinem jüngsten Sohn hätte geben können, waren Rüben, und die hätten das Kind mit ebenso großer Sicherheit umgebracht wie der Fuchs.

Weiter und weiter gingen sie, und immer mehr peinigte Tom der Gedanke an das ausgesetzte Kind. Es geschah oft genug, gewiß: Vor allem unter Bauern mit kleinen Höfen und großen Familien war Kindesaussetzung gang und gäbe, und manchmal sah sogar der Priester darüber hinweg. Aber ich gehöre nicht zu diesen Leuten, dachte Tom. Es wäre meine Pflicht gewesen, das Kind bis zu seinem Tode in den Armen zu halten und es dann zu begraben. Nicht, daß es einen Sinn gehabt hätte – aber nur so und nicht anders hätte sich ein rechtschaffener Mann verhalten müssen.

Inzwischen war es Tag geworden.

Tom blieb unvermittelt stehen.

Auch die Kinder gingen nicht weiter. Sie starrten ihn an und warteten, zu allem bereit, auf alles gefaßt.

»Ich hätte das Kind nicht aussetzen dürfen«, sagte Tom.

»Aber wir können es nicht ernähren«, erwiderte Alfred. »Es muß ja doch sterben.«

»Trotzdem hätte ich es nicht aussetzen dürfen.«

»Laßt uns zurückgehen«, sagte Martha.

Tom zögerte noch. Es wäre ein Eingeständnis seiner Schuld. Aber es stimmte ja. Er hatte gesündigt.

Er drehte sich um. »Gut«, sagte er. »Gehen wir zurück.«

Alle Gefahren, die er zuvor als Hirngespinste hatte abtun wollen, waren auf einmal wieder greifbare, unmittelbare Drohungen. Gewiß hatte der Fuchs – oder sogar ein Wolf – den Säugling längst gewittert und ihn fortgeschleppt in sein Lager. Auch die Wildschweine waren gefährlich, obwohl sie keine Fleischfresser waren. Und die Eulen? Zwar waren Eulen kaum imstande, einen Säugling fortzutragen, aber sie konnten ihm gewiß die Augen aushacken …

Tom ging schneller. Er fühlte sich benommen vor Hunger und Erschöpfung. Martha mußte rennen, um mit ihm Schritt zu halten, aber sie beklagte sich nicht.

Er fürchtete sich vor dem, was ihn am Grab seiner Frau erwartete. Raubtiere waren gnadenlos – und sie merkten es sofort, wenn ein Lebewesen wehrlos war.

Er wußte nicht mehr, wie lange sie schon unterwegs waren, denn er hatte jedes Zeitgefühl verloren. Der Wald rechts und links des

Weges kam ihm völlig unbekannt vor, obwohl sie von dorther kamen. Schon hielt er angestrengt Ausschau nach dem Grab. Das Feuer mußte eigentlich noch brennen ... Sie hatten die Reiser so hoch geschichtet. Tom suchte nach der großen Roßkastanie, nach ihren unverwechselbaren Blättern im abgefallenen Laub. Der Weg machte eine Biegung, an die er sich nicht erinnern konnte, und Tom fragte sich in seiner Verwirrung bereits, ob sie nicht doch schon an Agnes' Grab vorübergegangen waren, ohne es zu erkennen. Dann plötzlich glaubte er weit vor sich einen schwachen orangefarbenen Schimmer zu sehen.

Ihm war, als setze sein Herz aus. Er ging schneller und kniff die Augen zusammen. Ja, es war ein Feuer. Er fing an zu laufen. Er hörte Martha hinter sich aufschreien, als fürchte sie, er wolle sie im Stich lassen. »Wir sind da!« rief er über die Schulter zurück. Die Kinder rannten hinter ihm her.

Keuchend erreichte er den Kastanienbaum. Das Feuer brannte munter vor sich hin. Da war der Stapel mit dem aufgeschichteten Holz, dort der dunkle Fleck, auf dem Agnes verblutet war. Und da war auch das Grab; es sah aus wie ein flaches, unbepflanztes Beet. Und auf dem Grab war – nichts.

Tom sah sich um. Er war vollkommen außer sich. Keine Spur von dem Säugling – nirgends. Seine Augen füllten sich mit Tränen der Verzweiflung. Selbst der halbe Umhang, in den er das Kind noch gewickelt hatte, war verschwunden ... und dabei war das Grab gänzlich unberührt. Es gab keine Tierfährten auf dem weichen Boden, kein Blut, keine Schleifspuren ...

Tom hatte plötzlich das Gefühl, nicht mehr richtig zu sehen. Auch sein Verstand schien ihn im Stich zu lassen. Er wußte jetzt, daß er den Säugling unter keinen Umständen hätte aussetzen dürfen. Erst wenn er die Gewißheit hätte, daß das Kind tot war, würde er Ruhe finden. Doch so, wie es aussah, ließ sich nicht ausschließen, daß das Kind noch lebte – irgendwo in der Nähe. Er beschloß, die Umgebung abzusuchen.

»Wo gehst du hin?« fragte Alfred.

»Wir müssen das Kind suchen«, sagte Tom, ohne sich noch einmal umzudrehen. Er schritt die kleine Lichtung ab, spähte ins Gebüsch. Noch immer fühlte er sich schwach und schwindelig. Er fand nichts, nicht den geringsten Hinweis auf die Richtung, in welcher der Wolf mit dem Neugeborenen verschwunden war. Es mußte ein Wolf gewesen sein, er war jetzt ganz sicher. Und das Lager der Bestie war vermutlich nicht allzuweit entfernt.

»Wir müssen den Kreis erweitern«, sagte er zu den Kindern.

Er ging voran, und sie folgten ihm. Von Mal zu Mal wurde der Kreis um das Feuer größer. Tom ließ sich weder vom Unterholz noch vom dichten Buschwerk aufhalten. Obwohl er spürte, daß sein Geist sich zunehmend verwirrte, gelang es ihm, das einzig entscheidende Gebot der Stunde im Gedächtnis zu behalten: Er mußte den Säugling finden. Trauer war ihm in diesen Augenblicken fremd; er empfand vielmehr eine wilde, wütende Entschlossenheit, genährt durch die furchtbare Erkenntnis der eigenen Schuld. Und so stolperte er durch den Wald, spähte verbissen in alle Richtungen und blieb alle paar Schritte stehen, um zu lauschen, ob irgendwo das unverkennbare Wimmern eines Neugeborenen zu hören war. Aber wann immer er und die Kinder innehielten und lauschten – sie hörten nichts als das Schweigen des Waldes.

Er wußte nicht mehr, wieviel Zeit seit Beginn ihrer Suche verstrichen war. Da sie im Kreis gingen, überquerten sie immer wieder den Weg, doch die Zeitspannen dazwischen wurden immer länger, und irgendwann verstärkte sich der Verdacht, daß sie ihn überhaupt nicht mehr erreichten. Tom fragte sich, wieso sie noch nicht an der Kate des Jagdaufsehers vorbeigekommen waren, und es keimte der Gedanke in ihm auf, daß sie vielleicht gar nicht mehr das Grab umkreisten, sondern sich längst verlaufen hatten und ziellos im Wald hin und her irrten. Im Grunde war es ihm gleichgültig – wichtig war lediglich, daß sie die Suche fortsetzten.

»Vater«, sagte Alfred.

Tom sah ihn ungnädig an; er wollte sich durch nichts und niemanden bei seiner Suche stören lassen. Alfred trug Martha, die anscheinend fest eingeschlafen war, auf dem Rücken. »Was gibt's?« fragte Tom.

»Können wir eine Pause machen?«

Tom zögerte. Er wollte keine Rast einlegen, aber Alfred sah aus, als sei er am Rande der Erschöpfung. »Gut«, antwortete er widerstrebend. »Aber nur eine ganz kurze.«

Sie befanden sich gerade an einem Hang, an dessen Fuß möglicherweise ein Bach floß. Tom hatte Durst. Er übernahm Martha und trug sie auf den Armen den Hang hinunter. Tatsächlich fand sich im Tal ein kleiner, klarer Bach mit eisumsäumten Ufern. Er legte Martha auf der Böschung ab, ohne daß sie aufwachte. Dann knieten Tom und Alfred nieder und schöpften mit den Händen das kalte Wasser.

Alfred legte sich neben Martha und schloß die Augen, während

Tom sich umsah. Sie standen auf einer kleinen Lichtung, die ein Teppich aus abgefallenen Blättern bedeckte. Der Wald rundum bestand aus niedrigen, stämmigen Eichen, deren kahle Kronen sich zu einem engen Geflecht verdichteten. Tom überquerte die Lichtung. Er wollte hinter den Bäumen nach dem Kind suchen, doch am Waldrand versagten ihm die Beine den Dienst, und er mußte sich setzen.

Es war inzwischen hellichter Tag, wenngleich die Sonnenstrahlen durch einen leichten Nebel gedämpft wurden. Seit Mitternacht schien es kaum wärmer geworden zu sein. Tom schlotterte vor Kälte, und ihm wurde klar, daß er die ganze Zeit ohne seinen Umhang umherlief. Er wußte nicht mehr, wo er ihm abhanden gekommen war. Entweder wurde auf einmal der Nebel dichter – oder mit seinen Augen war etwas nicht mehr in Ordnung, denn er konnte die Kinder auf der anderen Seite der Lichtung nicht mehr sehen. Er wollte aufstehen, doch seine Beine ließen ihn im Stich.

Kurz darauf brach die Sonne durchs Gewölk, und dann erschien der Engel.

Sie kam von Osten her über die Lichtung und trug einen langen Wintermantel aus gebleichter, nahezu weißer Wolle. Tom sah sie kommen, ohne Überraschung oder Neugier zu empfinden – er war längst jenseits von Verwunderung oder Furcht. Er sah ihr entgegen mit dem gleichen starren und leeren Blick, mit dem er zuvor die kräftigen Eichenstämme gemustert hatte. Ihr üppiges dunkles Haar umrahmte das ovale Gesicht, und der bodenlange Mantel verbarg ihre Füße, so daß man hätte meinen können, sie schwebe über das Laub.

Unmittelbar vor ihm blieb sie stehen. Ihre blaßgoldenen Augen schienen ihm in die Seele zu schauen und seinen Schmerz zu verstehen. Sie kam ihm seltsam bekannt vor – so als ob er ein Bild dieses Engels erst kürzlich irgendwo in einer Kirche gesehen hätte.

Dann öffnete sie den Mantel. Darunter war sie nackt. Es war der durchaus weltliche Körper einer Frau von Mitte Zwanzig, mit blasser Haut und rosigen Brustwarzen. Tom hatte bisher immer geglaubt, Engel in ihrer Reinheit seien frei von jeglicher Körperbehaarung. Dieser hier war offenbar eine Ausnahme.

Sie kniete vor ihm nieder, der er mit gekreuzten Beinen unter einer Eiche saß, beugte sich vor und küßte ihn auf den Mund. Die furchtbaren Erfahrungen der vergangenen Nacht hatten ihn so benommen gemacht, daß ihn selbst das nicht mehr überraschte. Sie schob seinen Oberkörper mit sanfter Gewalt zurück, bis er flach auf dem Rücken lag, und schmiegte ihren nackten Körper an ihn. Sogleich spürte er durch seine Tunika hindurch ihre Wärme, und dann hörte er auf zu zittern.

Sie nahm sein bärtiges Gesicht in die Hände und küßte ihn gierig, wie jemand, der nach einem langen, heißen Tag kühles Wasser gereicht bekommt. Dann glitten ihre Finger an seinen Armen entlang bis zu den Gelenken und führten seine Hände an ihre Brüste. Tom umfaßte sie wie in Trance. Sie waren weich und nachgiebig, doch wurden die Brustwarzen unter seinen Fingerspitzen groß und hart.

Auf einmal schoß ihm der Gedanke durch den Kopf, daß er gestorben sein mußte. Gewiß – das, was er gerade erlebte, entsprach nicht den herkömmlichen Vorstellungen vom Himmel, aber das war ihm gleichgültig. Auf sein Denk- und Wahrnehmungsvermögen war ohnehin schon seit Stunden kein Verlaß mehr. Nun schwanden auch die letzten Reste von Verstand und Vernunft. Tom überließ sich ganz und gar seinem Körper, und dieser spannte sich und preßte sich gegen den der Frau, zog Kraft aus ihrer Hitze und ihrer Nacktheit. Sie öffnete den Mund, ihre Zunge stieß vor und wurde bereitwillig von der seinen empfangen.

Plötzlich zog der Engel sich zurück und gab seinen Körper frei. Tom sah, wie sie den Rock seiner Tunika bis zur Gürtellinie hochschob und mit gespreizten Beinen über ihn kam. Als ihre Körper sich in qualvoller Wonne berührten, zögerte sie kurz, und ihre alles durchdringenden Augen suchten seinen Blick. Dann spürte er, wie er in sie eindrang. Es war ein Gefühl von so unendlicher Lust, daß er schier zu vergehen fürchtete. Sie bewegte ihre Hüften, lächelte und küßte sein Gesicht.

Nach einer Weile wurde ihr Atem heftiger, und Tom merkte, daß sie die Herrschaft über ihren Körper verlor. Er beobachtete sie voller Lust und Faszination. Im Rhythmus ihrer immer schneller werdenden Bewegungen stieß sie kurze, spitze Schreie aus. Ihre Ekstase berührte Tom im tiefsten Innern seiner verwundeten Seele, so daß er nicht wußte, ob er vor Verzweiflung weinen, vor Freude schreien oder hysterisch lachen sollte. Dann schüttelte die gemeinsame Lust sie wie Bäume im Sturm, wieder und wieder, bis endlich ihre Leidenschaft gesättigt war und der Engel auf seine Brust sank.

So lagen sie lange Zeit beieinander, und ihr heißer Körper wärmte ihn durch und durch. Er glitt in eine Art Dämmerzustand, mehr Tagträumerei denn Schlaf, und als er die Augen wieder öffnete, war er bei klarem Verstand.

Er betrachtete die junge schöne Frau über sich und wußte sofort, daß es sich nicht um einen Engel handelte, sondern um die verfemte Ellen, die ihnen damals, als der Wegelagerer ihr Schwein geraubt hatte, in diesem Teil der Wälder begegnet war. Sie spürte, daß er sich bewegte, öffnete die Augen und sah ihn an mit einem Blick, in dem sowohl Zuneigung als auch Furcht lag. Tom mußte plötzlich an seine Kinder denken. Er schob Ellen sanft von sich und setzte sich auf. Alfred und Martha lagen, in ihre Umhänge gewickelt, im Laub; die Sonne schien auf ihre schlafenden Gesichter. Und wie ein böser Traum waren ihm auf einmal die Ereignisse der vergangenen Nacht wieder gegenwärtig: Agnes war tot, das neugeborene Kind – sein Sohn! – war verschwunden ... Er barg sein Gesicht in den Händen.

Ellen stieß einen merkwürdigen Pfiff aus, der aus zwei Tönen bestand. Als Tom aufsah, entdeckte er eine Gestalt zwischen den Bäumen, die sich rasch als Ellens seltsamer Sohn entpuppte, der Knabe Jack mit der leichenblassen Haut, den karottenfarbenen Haaren und den hellen, grünen Augen. Tom stand auf und zog seine Kleidung zurecht. Auch Ellen erhob sich und knöpfte ihren Mantel zu.

Der Junge trug etwas in der Hand. Er ging auf Tom zu und zeigte es ihm. Es war der halbe Umhang, in den der Vater den Säugling eingewickelt hatte, bevor er ihn auf dem Grab der Mutter zurückließ.

Tom begriff nicht, was das zu bedeuten hatte. Er starrte erst den Jungen an und dann Ellen. Sie nahm ihn bei den Händen, erwiderte seinen Blick und sagte: »Dein Kind lebt.«

Tom wagte es nicht, ihren Worten Glauben zu schenken. Das wäre einfach zu schön, zuviel des Glücks für diese Welt. »Das kann nicht wahr sein«, sagte er.

»Doch, es ist wahr.«

Hoffnung keimte auf. »Wirklich?« fragte er. »Wirklich?«

Sie nickte. »Wirklich. Ich werde dich zu ihm führen.«

Tom erkannte, daß sie es ernst meinte. Eine Welle der Erleichterung und des Glücks erfaßte ihn. Er fiel auf die Knie, und dann, endlich, konnte er weinen.

»Jack hörte das Kind schreien«, erklärte Ellen. »Er war unterwegs zum Fluß. Nördlich von hier gibt es eine Stelle, wo ein guter Werfer Enten mit Steinen erlegen kann. Er wußte nicht, wie er sich verhalten sollte, deswegen rannte er nach Hause und holte mich. Doch auf dem Weg dorthin sahen wir einen Priester. Er ritt auf einem Zelter und hielt das Kind im Arm.«

»Ich muß ihn finden ...«, fuhr Tom dazwischen.

»Übereile nichts«, erwiderte Ellen. »Ich weiß, wo er sich befindet. Unweit des Grabes deiner Frau bog er von der Hauptstraße ab. Der Pfad führt zu einem kleinen Kloster mitten im Wald.«

»Das Kind braucht Milch.«

»Die Mönche haben Ziegen.«

»Dem Himmel sei Dank«, sagte Tom inbrünstig.

»Ich führe dich hin, sobald ihr etwas zu euch genommen habt«, fuhr Ellen fort. »Aber ...« Sie runzelte die Stirn. »Sag deinen Kindern noch nichts von dem Kloster.«

Tom warf einen Blick zurück. Am anderen Rand der Lichtung lagen Alfred und Martha noch immer in tiefem Schlaf. Jack war inzwischen bei ihnen und starrte sie mit jenem leeren Blick an, der für ihn so bezeichnend war. »Warum nicht?« fragte Tom.

»Ich bin mir nicht sicher ... Ich glaube einfach, es ist besser, damit noch ein wenig zu warten.«

»Aber dein Sohn wird es ihnen sagen.«

Sie schüttelte den Kopf. »Er hat den Priester zwar gesehen, aber ich glaube nicht, daß er daraus die entsprechenden Schlüsse zieht.«

»Na gut.« Tom wurde ernst. »Wenn wir gewußt hätten, daß du in der Nähe bist, hättest du vielleicht meine Agnes retten können.«

Erneut schüttelte Ellen den Kopf, und ihr dunkles Haar umtanzte das Gesicht. »Da gibt es keine Hilfe. Man muß die Frau möglichst warm halten, und das hast du ja getan. Wenn eine Frau innerlich blutet, hört es entweder von selbst auf und sie erholt sich, oder aber es hört nicht mehr auf und sie stirbt.« Tränen traten Tom in die Augen, und Ellen fügte hinzu: »Es tut mir so leid.«

Tom nickte trübsinnig.

»Aber die Lebenden müssen sich um die Lebenden kümmern«, fuhr sie fort. »Du brauchst ein warmes Mahl und einen neuen Mantel.« Sie stand auf.

Gemeinsam weckten sie die Kinder. Tom sagte ihnen, daß der Kleine wohlauf sei; Ellen und Jack hätten einen Priester gesehen, der ihn zu sich genommen hätte. Er und Ellen wollten den Mann später aufsuchen, doch zuvor seien sie bei Ellen zum Essen eingeladen. Alfred und Martha vernahmen die Neuigkeiten ohne große Gemütsbewegung; sie konnte jetzt nichts mehr schrecken. Tom war kaum weniger verwirrt als sie. Sein Leben veränderte sich so schnell, daß er die einzelnen Ereignisse kaum noch nachvollziehen konnte. Ihm war, als säße er auf dem Rücken eines ungestümen Pferdes: Die Dinge flogen

nur so an ihm vorbei und gaben ihm keine Möglichkeit, auf sie einzugehen. Er konnte nichts anderes tun, als sich festzuhalten und zu
versuchen, bei klarem Verstand zu bleiben. Agnes hatte mitten in der
kalten Winternacht ein Kind geboren, das allen Widrigkeiten zum
Trotz gesund und munter war. Alles schien in bester Ordnung zu sein,
doch dann war Agnes, seine treue Seelengefährtin, in seinen Armen
verblutet, und er hatte den Verstand verloren. Das Schicksal des Kindes schien besiegelt, und sie ließen es auf dem Grab zurück. Später
hatten sie es vergeblich gesucht. Plötzlich war Ellen vor ihm erschienen, und Tom hatte sie für einen Engel gehalten. Sie hatten sich
geliebt wie in einem Traum, und schließlich hatte sie ihm gesagt, daß
das Kind lebte und geborgen sei. Würde das Leben ihm je wieder Zeit
lassen, über die Flut der Ereignisse nachzudenken?

Sie machten sich auf den Weg. Tom hatte immer geglaubt, daß
Verfemte in Schmutz und Elend lebten, doch Ellen paßte ganz und
gar nicht in dieses Bild. Er fragte sich, wie ihre Wohnung aussehen
mochte. Sie führte ihre Gäste kreuz und quer durch den Wald. Es
gab weder Weg noch Steg, doch sie bewegte sich mit traumwandle-
rischer Sicherheit. Sie wußte trockenen Fußes Bäche zu überqueren,
duckte sich unter tiefhängenden Zweigen, umging einen gefrorenen
Sumpf, zwängte sich durch ein dichtes Gebüsch und überkletterte
flink den gewaltigen Stamm einer vom Sturm gefällten Eiche. Schließlich erreichten sie ein Brombeergestrüpp, in dem Ellen zu verschwinden schien. Tom folgte ihr und erkannte, daß sich durch das auf den
ersten Blick so undurchdringliche Dickicht ein schmaler Pfad wand.
Die Dornen schlossen sich über ihren Köpfen zu einem Gewölbe, in
dem nur mehr trübes Licht herrschte. Tom blieb stehen und wartete,
bis sich seine Augen an die Düsternis gewöhnt hatten. Jetzt erst merkte
er, daß er sich in einer Höhle befand.

Die Luft war warm. Vor ihnen glühte auf einem Herd aus flachen
Steinen ein Feuer. Der Rauch stieg senkrecht empor; es gab also irgendwo einen natürlichen Abzug. Die Höhlenwand war auf der einen
Seite mit einem Wolfsfell und auf der anderen mit einer Hirschdecke
bespannt, welche von hölzernen Pflöcken gehalten wurden. Von der
Decke herab hing eine geräucherte Wildbretkeule. Tom sah eine selbst-
gezimmerte Kiste voller Holzäpfel, Binsenlichter auf einem Vorsprung
in der Wand. Den Boden bedeckte trockenes Schilf. Am Rand des
Feuers stand wie in jedem anderen Haushalt auch ein Kochtopf, in
dem, nach dem Geruch zu urteilen, derselbe dicke Eintopf brodelte
wie anderswo – Gemüse mit Suppenknochen und Kräutern. Tom war

verblüfft: Dieses Heim hier war gemütlicher als die armseligen Hütten vieler Leibeigener.

Auf der anderen Seite des Feuers lagen zwei Matratzen aus Hirschfell, die vermutlich mit Schilf ausgestopft waren. An beiden Kopfenden lag, sorgfältig zusammengerollt, ein Wolfspelz. Das waren die Schlafplätze von Ellen und Jack. Im hinteren Teil der Höhle war eine beachtliche Sammlung von Waffen und Jagdgeräten zu erkennen: ein Bogen, mehrere Pfeile, Netze, Kaninchenfallen, einige gefährlich aussehende Dolche, eine mit großer Sorgfalt gefertigte hölzerne Lanze mit feuergehärteter, scharfer Spitze – und, mitten unter diesen einfachen Gebrauchsgegenständen, auch drei Bücher. Tom traute seinen Augen nicht: Noch nie hatte er in einem privaten Heim – geschweige denn in einer Höhle – Bücher gesehen. Bücher gehörten seiner Meinung nach in die Kirche.

Der Knabe Jack ergriff eine hölzerne Schüssel, tauchte sie in den Kochtopf und begann zu trinken. Alfred und Martha sahen ihm mit knurrendem Magen zu. Ellen bedachte Tom mit einem Blick, der um Nachsicht zu bitten schien. Dann sagte sie zu ihrem Sohn: »Wenn wir Besuch haben, Jack, bekommen die Gäste zuerst.«

Der Junge starrte sie an. Er begriff nicht, was sie damit meinte. »Warum?«

»Weil es zur Gastfreundschaft gehört. Gib den Kindern jetzt auch von der Suppe.«

Jack war noch nicht überzeugt, doch tat er, was seine Mutter ihm aufgetragen hatte. Ellen reichte Tom eine Schüssel mit Suppe. Er setzte sich auf den Boden und schlürfte sie in sich hinein. Sie schmeckte nach Fleisch und wärmte ihn innerlich. Ellen legte ihm ein Fell um die Schultern. Als er die Flüssigkeit ausgetrunken hatte, fischte Tom Fleisch und Gemüse mit den Fingern heraus. Wann habe ich zum letztenmal Fleisch gegessen? fragte er sich. Es muß Wochen her sein. Es schmeckte nach Ente – wahrscheinlich hatte Jack das Tier mit seiner Steinschleuder erlegt.

Sie aßen den ganzen Topf leer. Als sie satt waren, legten Alfred und Martha sich auf das Schilf. Bevor sie einschliefen, sagte Tom ihnen noch, daß er mit Ellen zusammen nun den Priester aufsuchen wolle und daß Jack bis zu ihrer Rückkehr dableiben und auf sie aufpassen würde. Die beiden erschöpften Kinder nickten zustimmend und schlossen die Augen.

Tom und Ellen verließen die Höhle. Tom trug den Pelz, den sie ihm über die Schultern gelegt hatte. Sie hatten das Brombeerdickicht kaum hinter sich, als Ellen auch schon stehenblieb, sich Tom zuwandte, seinen Kopf zu sich herabzog und ihn auf den Mund küßte.

»Ich liebe dich«, sagte sie voller Leidenschaft. »Ich liebe dich, seit ich dich zum erstenmal sah. Ich habe mir immer einen Mann gewünscht, der sowohl stark als auch zärtlich ist, und ich dachte schon, daß es so etwas gar nicht gibt. Doch dann sah ich dich. Ich wollte dich, aber ich sah, daß du deine Frau geliebt hast. Mein Gott, wie habe ich sie beneidet. Es tut mir leid, daß sie sterben mußte, wirklich, denn ich sehe die Trauer in deinen Augen und all die Tränen, die darauf warten, vergossen zu werden. Es bricht mir das Herz, dich so traurig zu sehen. Aber nun, da deine Frau von dir gegangen ist, will ich dich für mich haben.«

Tom wußte nicht, was er sagen sollte. War es möglich, daß eine so schöne, kluge und selbständige Frau sich gleichsam auf den ersten Blick in ihn verliebt hatte? Kaum zu glauben. Und noch schwerer fiel es ihm, seine eigenen Gefühle zu beschreiben. Er litt furchtbar unter dem Verlust seiner Frau. Es stimmte nur zu sehr, was Ellen gesagt hatte: Er spürte den Druck der unvergossenen Tränen hinter seinen Augen. Auf der anderen Seite verzehrte ihn die Sehnsucht nach Ellen mit ihrem heißen Körper, ihren goldenen Augen und ihrer schamlosen Lust. Doch Agnes war erst seit ein paar Stunden unter der Erde. Er schämte sich seiner eigenen Begehrlichkeit.

Er starrte Ellen an, und ihre Augen sahen einmal mehr in seine Seele hinein. »Du brauchst jetzt nichts zu sagen, aber du brauchst dich auch nicht zu schämen. Ich weiß, daß du sie geliebt hast. Sie hat dich auch geliebt, ich konnte es ihr ansehen. Du liebst sie noch immer, ja, gewiß. Du wirst nie aufhören, sie zu lieben.«

Sie hatte ihm eine Antwort erspart, aber er hätte auch nichts zu antworten vermocht. Diese außergewöhnliche Frau raubte ihm schlichtweg die Sprache. Alles schien besser zu werden – dank ihr. Schon die Tatsache, daß sie offenbar genau wußte, was ihn bedrückte, empfand er als Erleichterung. Ihm war, als gebe es nichts mehr, dessen er sich schämen mußte. Er seufzte.

»So ist es gut«, sagte sie und nahm ihn bei der Hand.

Nach einem Marsch von ungefähr einer Meile, der sie durch reinsten Urwald führte, erreichten sie die Straße. Unterwegs riskierte Tom immer wieder Seitenblicke auf Ellen. Er erinnerte sich an ihre erste Begegnung. Damals hatte er noch gemeint, die merkwürdigen Augen beeinträchtigten ihre Schönheit. Inzwischen war es ihm ein Rätsel, wie er je auf diesen Gedanken hatte kommen können. Ihre erstaunlichen Augen erschienen ihm nun als Ausdruck ihrer einzigartigen Persönlichkeit und sie selbst als die Schönheit in Vollendung. Rätselhaft blieb nur, warum sie bei ihm war.

Sie legten weitere drei oder vier Meilen zurück. Tom war zwar nach wie vor müde, doch die Suppe hatte ihm neue Kraft verliehen. Obwohl er Ellen vollständig vertraute, lag ihm daran, sein Kind mit eigenen Augen zu sehen.

Als das Kloster vor ihnen durch die Bäume schimmerte, sagte Ellen zu ihm: »Wir wollen uns den Mönchen nicht sofort zeigen.«

Tom begriff es nicht. »Warum?« fragte er.

»Du hast einen Säugling ausgesetzt. Das gilt als Mord. Ich schlage vor, wir sehen uns das Kloster erst einmal etwas näher an und schauen, um was für Leute es sich handelt.«

Tom rechnete angesichts der Umstände der Kindesaussetzung nicht mit Schwierigkeiten, aber eine gewisse Vorsicht konnte sicher nicht schaden. Er nickte zustimmend und folgte Ellen ins Unterholz. Kurz darauf lagen sie gut versteckt am Rande der Lichtung.

Es war ein sehr kleines Kloster. Tom hatte Erfahrungen im Klosterbau und nahm daher an, daß es sich um eine sogenannte Zelle handelte, die Zweig- oder Außenstelle einer größeren Abtei. Es verfügte lediglich über zwei Steinhäuser, die Kapelle und das Dormitorium. Alles andere – eine Küche, die Ställe und verschiedene andere landwirtschaftliche Gebäude – bestand aus Holz oder mit Lehm beworfenem Flechtwerk. Häuser und Umgebung wirkten sauber und gepflegt; man gewann den Eindruck, daß die Mönche ebensoviel Zeit bei der Arbeit wie beim Gebet verbrachten.

Es waren nicht viele Leute zu sehen. »Die meisten Mönche sind bei der Arbeit«, sagte Ellen. »Sie errichten dort hinten auf dem Hügel eine Scheune.« Sie spähte himmelwärts. »Zum Mittagessen werden sie zurückkommen.«

Tom sah sich die Lichtung genauer an. Zur Rechten, teilweise verdeckt durch eine kleine Herde angepflockter Ziegen, fielen ihm zwei Gestalten auf. »Sieh mal dort!« sagte er zu Ellen und wies mit dem Finger auf die beiden Menschen. »Der eine, der da sitzt, das ist ein Priester«, sagte er, »und er ...«

»... er hat etwas auf seinem Schoß.«

»Wir müssen näher heran.«

Im Schutz der Bäume schlichen sie um die Lichtung herum, bis sie sich schließlich ungefähr auf gleicher Höhe mit den Ziegen befanden. Tom klopfte das Herz bis zum Hals, als er den Priester auf seinem

Hocker genauer ins Auge faßte. Der Mann hielt ein Kind auf dem Schoß. Mein Sohn! dachte Tom und spürte einen Kloß im Hals. Es stimmte, es stimmte wirklich! Mein Sohn ist noch am Leben! Am liebsten wäre er dem Priester um den Hals gefallen.

Neben dem Priester kniete ein junger Mönch. Beim näheren Hinsehen erkannte Tom, daß der junge Mann ein Tuch in einen Eimer tauchte und dann dem Kind einen vermutlich mit Ziegenmilch getränkten Zipfel in den Mund steckte.

»Wohlan«, sagte Tom nicht ohne Beklemmung. »Ich werde mich jetzt zu erkennen geben, meine Schuld bekennen und meinen Sohn wieder zu mir nehmen.«

Ellen sah ihn kritisch an. »Augenblick, Tom! Denk erst einmal nach, was *dann* geschehen soll.«

Er wußte nicht genau, worauf sie hinauswollte. »Ich werde die Mönche um Milch bitten«, sagte er. »Daß ich ein armer Mann bin, sieht man mir an. Sie geben Almosen.«

»Und danach?«

»Nun, ich hoffe, sie geben mir genug Milch für drei Tage, so daß ich damit bis Winchester komme.«

»Und danach?« Sie ließ nicht locker. »Womit willst du das Kind dann ernähren?«

»Nun ja – ich werde mir eine Arbeit suchen ...«

»Seit unserer ersten Begegnung im vergangenen Herbst bist du ununterbrochen auf Suche nach Arbeit«, sagte Ellen. Sie schien sich ein wenig über ihn zu ärgern, und Tom wußte nicht, warum. »Du hast weder Geld noch Werkzeug«, fuhr sie fort. »Was wird mit dem Kind geschehen, wenn du auch in Winchester keine Arbeit findest?«

»Ich weiß es nicht.« Ihr harter Ton tat ihm weh. »Was soll ich denn tun? Vielleicht so leben wie du? Ich kann keine Enten mit Steinschleudern erlegen – ich bin Steinmetz.«

»Du könntest das Kind hierlassen.«

Tom war, als hätte ihn der Blitz getroffen. »Hierlassen? Wo ich es gerade erst wiedergefunden habe?«

»Hier ist dein Sohn gut aufgehoben. Er hat es warm und bekommt genug zu trinken. Du brauchst ihn auf der Arbeitssuche nicht mit dir herumzuschleppen – und wenn du was gefunden hast, kannst du zurückkommen und das Kind holen.«

Alles in Tom sträubte sich gegen diesen Vorschlag. »Ich weiß nicht«, sagte er. »Die Mönche müßten mich ja für einen Rabenvater halten ...«

»Sie wissen ohnehin, daß du es ausgesetzt hast«, erwiderte Ellen ungeduldig. »Ob du es nun heute eingestehst oder später.«

»Können Mönche überhaupt mit so kleinen Kindern umgehen?«

»So gut wie du allemal.«

»Ich habe da meine Zweifel.«

»Immerhin haben sie schon herausgefunden, wie man einen Säugling ohne Amme füttern kann.«

Sie hatte ihn schon fast überzeugt. So sehr Tom sich auch danach sehnte, das kleine Bündel in die Arme zu schließen – er konnte nicht leugnen, daß ein neugeborenes Kind bei den Mönchen besser aufgehoben war als bei ihm. Er hatte weder Nahrung noch Geld und nur wenig Hoffnung auf Arbeit. »Lassen wir ihn hier«, sagte er traurig. »Ich fürchte, es gibt keinen anderen Weg.« Noch einmal warf er einen Blick über die Lichtung, sah die kleine Gestalt auf dem Schoß des Priesters. Das Kind hatte dunkles Haar, wie Agnes. Tom hatte sich nun zwar entschieden, aber er konnte sich noch immer nicht losreißen.

Auf der gegenüberliegenden Seite der Lichtung tauchte eine größere Gruppe von Mönchen auf, fünfzehn bis zwanzig an der Zahl. Sie trugen Äxte und Sägen bei sich. Tom und Ellen mußten jetzt mit ihrer Entdeckung rechnen und zogen sich daher tiefer ins Unterholz zurück. Das Kind verschwand aus ihrem Blickfeld.

Sie entfernten sich, auf allen vieren kriechend. Als sie die Straße erreichten, richteten sie sich auf und rannten Hand in Hand los. Nach drei- oder vierhundert Schritten war Tom erschöpft, doch inzwischen bestand keine Gefahr mehr. Sie schlugen sich in die Büsche und fanden ein von der Straße aus nicht einsehbares Fleckchen, das zur Rast einlud.

Das Sonnenlicht sprenkelte den grasigen Hang, auf dem sie sich niederließen. Tom sah Ellen an. Sie lag auf dem Rücken; ihr Atem ging schnell. Die Wangen waren leicht gerötet, und ihre Lippen lächelten ihn an. Der Umhang klaffte am Hals auseinander und enthüllte den Ansatz ihrer Brüste. Er begehrte, sie nackt zu sehen, und seine Begierde war weit stärker als alle Schuldgefühle. Er beugte sich über sie, um sie zu küssen, und hielt dann inne, weil allein ihr Anblick schon von verführerischer Schönheit war. Und dann sprach er – sprach, ohne seine Worte zuvor gewogen zu haben, und war daher selbst überrascht von dem, was er sagte.

»Ellen«, sagte er. »Willst du meine Frau werden?«

KAPITEL II

Peter von Wareham war der geborene Unruhestifter.

Die Mutterabtei in Kingsbridge hatte ihn in die kleine Zelle im Wald versetzt. Warum der Prior von Kingsbridge heilfroh gewesen war, ihn loszuwerden, war leicht einzusehen: Der hochgewachsene, etwas schlaksig wirkende Endzwanziger war ebenso intelligent wie anmaßend und hatte an allem und jedem etwas auszusetzen. Schon kurz nach seiner Ankunft hatte er sich wie ein Besessener in die Feldarbeit gestürzt und seinen Mitbrüdern vorgehalten, sie seien faul. Dann hatte er zu seiner Überraschung feststellen müssen, daß die anderen durchaus mit ihm Schritt halten konnten und die jüngeren ihn sogar noch übertrafen. Er sah ein, daß der Vorwurf der Untätigkeit ein Schlag ins Wasser gewesen war, und suchte nach einem anderen Haar in der Suppe: Sein zweiter Anklagepunkt hieß Völlerei.

Er aß nur noch die Hälfte seiner Brotration und verzichtete auf jegliches Fleisch. Er trank tagsüber Wasser aus den Bächen, verdünnte sein Bier und rührte keinen Wein an. Er kanzelte einen jungen, gesunden Mönch ab, den es nach einer zweiten Portion Porridge verlangte. Einem anderen, der aus Jux und Tollerei das Weinglas eines Mitbruders leerte, machte Peter so heftige Vorwürfe, daß der junge Mann in Tränen ausbrach.

Äußerlich merkt man unseren Brüdern die Völlerei jedenfalls nicht an, dachte Prior Philip auf dem Weg zum Mittagessen. Die jungen sind schlank und kräftig, die älteren sonnengebräunt und drahtig. Nicht einer unter ihnen ist von jener bläßlichen, weichen Beleibtheit, die von zu üppiger Nahrung und körperlicher Untätigkeit herrührt. Eigentlich sollten alle Mönche schlank und rank sein, dachte Philip. Dicke Mitbrüder erzeugen unter den Armen des Landes nur Neid und Haß auf die Diener des Herrn.

Bezeichnend für Peter war, daß er seine Anklage ins Gewand einer Beichte kleidete. »Ich habe mich der Sünde der Völlerei schuldig gemacht«, hatte er am Vormittag bekannt. Sie saßen auf dem Hügel, wo sie die Scheune bauten, auf frisch gefällten Baumstämmen, aßen Roggenbrot und tranken Bier. »Ich habe die Regel des heiligen Benedikt mißachtet, der zufolge ein Mönch weder Fleisch essen noch Wein trinken darf.« Mit hocherhobenem Kopf ließ er seine stolzen, dunklen Augen in die Runde schweifen, bis sein Blick auf Philip zu ruhen kam. Mit den Worten »Und jedermann hier im Kreise hat sich derselben Sünde schuldig gemacht« beendete er sein Bekenntnis.

Es ist ein Jammer, daß Peter immer wieder aus der Rolle fällt, dachte Philip. Er hat sich dem Werke Gottes verschrieben, hat einen klugen Kopf und verfügt über feste Grundsätze … Die guten Eigenschaften gingen freilich einher mit einem geradezu zwanghaften Geltungsbedürfnis, das ihn immer wieder dazu verleitete, Unfrieden zu stiften. In dieser Hinsicht war Peter ein wahrer Tunichtgut, was Philip jedoch nicht daran hinderte, ihn genauso zu lieben wie alle anderen Mitbrüder auch, erkannte er doch hinter der anmaßenden und höhnischen Fassade eine bekümmerte Seele, die nicht glauben konnte, daß es Menschen gab, die sie mochten.

Philip hatte gesagt: »Nun, das gibt uns die Gelegenheit, uns ins Gedächtnis zu rufen, was der heilige Benedikt zu diesem Thema sagte. Erinnerst du dich an den genauen Wortlaut, Peter?«

»Er sagte: ›Jeder, der nicht krank ist, soll sich des Fleisches enthalten.‹ Und dann: ›Der Wein ist nicht das Getränk der Mönche.‹«

Philip nickte. Wie vermutet, kannte Peter die Regel doch nicht so gut wie er selbst. »Fast richtig, Peter«, erwiderte er. »Der Heilige meinte allerdings nicht das Fleisch schlechthin, sondern ›das Fleisch unserer vierfüßigen Tiere‹ und er nahm nicht nur die Kranken, sondern auch die Schwachen aus. Wen wird er wohl mit ›den Schwachen‹ gemeint haben? Wir hier in unserer kleinen Gemeinde sind der Ansicht, daß Männer, die von harter Feldarbeit ermattet sind, bisweilen durchaus ein wenig Rindfleisch essen sollten, um bei Kräften zu bleiben.«

Peter hatte ihm schweigend zugehört. Die gerunzelte Stirn und die buschigen, zusammengekniffenen schwarzen Augenbrauen, welche die große, gebogene Nase überbrückten, brachten seine Mißbilligung deutlich genug zum Ausdruck. Sein von mühsam unterdrücktem Widerspruchsgeist gezeichnetes Gesicht wirkte maskenhaft.

Philip hatte seine Ausführung fortgesetzt: »Was nun den Wein betrifft, so sagt uns der Heilige: ›Wir lesen, daß der Wein nicht das Getränk der Mönche ist.‹ Die Benutzung der Worte *Wir lesen* heißt ja nun, daß er die Verordnung eben nicht in vollem Umfang billigt. Schließlich sagte er an anderer Stelle, daß ein Schoppen Wein am Tag für jedermann genügen sollte, und warnt uns davor, uns zu betrinken. Den Aufruf zur vollständigen Enthaltsamkeit vermag ich diesen Worten nicht zu entnehmen. Was meinst du?«

»Aber er trägt uns auf, in allen Dingen Genügsamkeit zu wahren«, sagte Peter.

»Und du meinst, daß wir hier nicht genügsam leben?«

»Jawohl, das meine ich«, verkündete Peter mit volltönender Stimme.

»›Laßt jene, denen Gott die Gabe der Enthaltsamkeit verliehen hat, wissen, daß ihnen gebührender Lohn zuteil werden wird‹«, zitierte Philip. »Wenn du meinst, daß das Essen hier bei uns zu üppig ist, so hindert dich niemand daran, weniger zu dir zu nehmen. Aber vergiß nicht, was der Heilige noch sagt. Er zitiert den ersten Korintherbrief, in welchem der heilige Paulus sagt: ›Ein jeder hat von Gott eine Gabe erhalten, der eine diese und der andere jene.‹ Und dazu meint der Heilige: ›Aus diesem Grunde läßt sich die Menge an Speis und Trank, derer ein anderer Mensch bedarf, nicht über alle Zweifel erhaben festlegen.‹ Dies, Bruder Peter, solltest du beim Fasten und bei deinen Meditationen über die Sünde der Völlerei stets im Gedächtnis behalten.«

Danach waren sie wieder an die Arbeit gegangen. Peter hatte die Miene eines Märtyrers aufgesetzt. Philip war klar, daß sich der schwierige Mitbruder nicht so leicht zum Schweigen bringen ließ. Von den drei mönchischen Gelübden Armut, Keuschheit und Gehorsam kam letzteres Bruder Peter am schwersten an.

Gegen ungehorsame Mönche ließen sich natürlich gewisse Maßnahmen ergreifen: Man konnte sie bei Wasser und Brot in den Karzer stecken, man konnte sie auspeitschen lassen, und schließlich blieben immer noch der Verweis aus dem Kloster und die Exkommunikation. Philip war durchaus nicht zimperlich mit der Verhängung solcher Strafen – besonders in Fällen, in denen seine Autorität herausgefordert wurde –, weshalb ihm auch der Ruf eines strengen Disziplinators vorauseilte. In Wirklichkeit sprach er harte Strafen nur sehr ungern aus. Sie brachten Mißstimmung in die klösterliche Gemeinschaft und machten alle Betroffenen unglücklich. Im Falle Peters war mit Strafen überhaupt nichts auszurichten – sie würden allenfalls dazu führen, seinen Stolz und seine Unnachgiebigkeit ins Unermeßliche wachsen zu lassen. Philip sann darüber nach, wie er Peter gefügiger machen und ihn milder stimmen könnte. Eine leichte Aufgabe war das gewiß nicht. Indes, so dachte er, wenn alles im Leben leicht wäre, bedürften die Menschen nicht der Führung Gottes.

Sie erreichten die Lichtung, auf der das Kloster stand. Auf dem Weg über das offene Feld bemerkte Philip Bruder John, der ihnen vom Ziegenpferch her heftig zuwinkte. Johnny Eightpence – so sein richtiger Name – galt als nicht ganz richtig im Kopf. Warum ist er nur so aufgeregt? fragte sich Philip. Neben Johnny saß ein Mann im Priestergewand, den Philip schon einmal irgendwo gesehen zu haben glaubte. Der Abt beschleunigte seine Schritte.

Der Priester war ein kleiner, untersetzter Mann von ungefähr fünfundzwanzig Jahren mit kurzgeschnittenem schwarzem Haar und hellblauen, funkelnden Augen, die eine rasche Auffassungsgabe und einen klaren Verstand verrieten. Philip war, als schaue er in einen Spiegel: Verblüfft erkannte er in dem Priester Francis, seinen jüngeren Bruder.

Und Francis hielt in den Armen ein neugeborenes Kind.

Philip hätte nicht sagen können, was ihn mehr überraschte – Francis oder der Säugling. Inzwischen waren auch die anderen Mönche herangekommen. Francis erhob sich, gab Johnny das Kind und wurde von Philip umarmt.

»Was führt dich hierher?« fragte Philip freudestrahlend. »Und wie kommst du zu diesem Kind?«

»Über die Gründe meines Kommens laß uns später reden«, erwiderte Francis. »Und was das Kind betrifft – ich habe es gefunden. Im Wald, mutterseelenallein. Es lag neben einem lodernden Feuer ...« Er hielt inne.

»Und?« drängte Philip.

Francis zuckte mit den Schultern. »Mehr kann ich dir auch nicht sagen, denn das ist alles, was ich weiß. Ich wollte eigentlich schon gestern abend hier sein, schaffte es aber nicht ganz und verbrachte daher die Nacht in der Hütte eines Jagdaufsehers. Heute früh im Morgengrauen machte ich mich wieder auf den Weg. Auf einmal hörte ich gleich neben der Straße ein Kind schreien. Einen Augenblick später sah ich es dann auch. Ich hob es auf und brachte es hierher. Mehr kann ich beim besten Willen nicht dazu sagen.«

Philip betrachtete das winzige Bündel in Johnnys Armen voller Staunen. Vorsichtig streckte er die Hand aus und lüpfte einen Zipfel der Decke, in die das Kind gehüllt war. Er sah ein runzliges, rosafarbenes Gesichtchen mit geöffnetem, zahnlosem Mund und Haaren auf dem Kopf. Er wickelte das Bündel noch ein bißchen weiter auf. Kleine, zarte Schultern, zappelnde Ärmchen und geballte Fäustchen kamen zum Vorschein. Philip sah den Rest der Nabelschnur am Bauch des Kindes und empfand ein leichtes Ekelgefühl dabei. Ist das natürlich? fragte er sich. Es sah aus wie eine gut verheilende Wunde, die man am besten sich selbst überließ. Er zog die Decke noch ein Stückchen weiter zurück. »Ein Junge«, bemerkte er mit verlegenem Hüsteln und deckte das Kind wieder zu. Ein Novize kicherte.

Philip fühlte sich hilflos. Was, um alles in der Welt, soll ich damit? dachte er. Soll ich es stillen?

Der Säugling weinte, und sein Jammern rührte Philips Herz. »Es ist hungrig«, sagte er und dachte bei sich: Woher weiß ich das eigentlich?

Ein Mönch sagte: »Wir können es nicht nähren.«

Philip wollte gerade sagen: Warum nicht? Doch da fiel ihm die Antwort auch schon ein: Es gab weit und breit keine einzige Frau.

Wie sich jedoch herausstellte, hatte Johnny bereits eine Lösung gefunden. Er setzte sich auf den Melkschemel und nahm den Säugling auf den Schoß, in der Hand ein Tuch, dessen einen Zipfel er zusammengezwirbelt hatte. Den tauchte er nun in einen Milchkübel und wartete, bis er mit Flüssigkeit durchtränkt war. Dann steckte er dem Kind den Zipfel in den Mund, und der Kleine begann sofort zu saugen und zu schlucken.

Philip hätte jubeln können. »Das ist wirklich eine gute Idee, Johnny«, sagte er.

Johnny grinste. »Hab' ich früher schon mal gemacht«, sagte er stolz. »Bei einem Zicklein, dessen Mutter starb, bevor es entwöhnt war.«

Wie gebannt sahen die Mönche zu, wie Johnny ein zweites Mal die einfache Handlung vollzog. Als er mit dem Tuch die Lippen des Säuglings berührte, öffneten, wie Philip amüsiert feststellte, unwillkürlich auch einige Mönche den Mund. Das Kind auf diese Weise zu ernähren, war eine recht langwierige Angelegenheit – aber wahrscheinlich ging es auch unter normalen Umständen nicht wesentlich schneller.

Peter von Wareham, der zunächst der allgemeinen Verwunderung anheimgefallen war und dementsprechend seine Kritik an allem und jedem vorübergehend vergessen hatte, kam wieder zu sich und sagte: »Leichter wäre es wohl, die Mutter des Kindes ausfindig zu machen.«

»Das bezweifle ich«, meinte Francis. »Ich nehme an, die Mutter ist nicht verheiratet und ließ sich zu einer moralischen Verfehlung hinreißen. Ich nehme an, sie ist noch recht jung. Vielleicht ist es ihr gelungen, ihre Schwangerschaft geheimzuhalten. Als ihre Zeit gekommen war, schlich sie sich in den Wald und errichtete sich ein großes Feuer. Dann gebar sie ohne Hilfe das Kind, überließ es den Wölfen und kehrte zurück. Sie hat gewiß Vorsorge getroffen, daß man sie nicht finden kann.«

Der Säugling war eingeschlafen. Aus einer Eingebung heraus nahm Philip ihn Johnny ab, zog ihn an die Brust, stützte das Köpfchen mit der Hand und wiegte das kleine Bündel sanft hin und her. »Armes kleines Wesen«, sagte er, »armes, armes kleines Wesen.« Er war hingerissen von dem heftigen Verlangen, dem Kind Schutz und Pflege angedeihen zu lassen. Es entging ihm nicht, daß die Mönche ihn verdutzt anstarrten; derartige Zärtlichkeitsbekundungen waren sie von ihm nicht gewohnt. Selbstverständlich hatten sie ihn noch nie zuvor einen Menschen streicheln sehen, war doch jede Form der körperlichen Zuwendung im Kloster streng verboten. Sie hielten ihn schlichtweg solcher Anwandlungen für unfähig. Wohlan denn, dachte er bei sich, dann habe ich sie soeben eines Besseren belehrt.

Da ergriff Peter von Wareham wieder das Wort: »Wir müssen das Kind nach Winchester bringen und ihm eine Pflegemutter suchen.«

Wäre es nicht ausgerechnet Peter gewesen, der diese Worte gesprochen – Philips Widerspruch hätte möglicherweise auf sich warten lassen. Aber es war eben Peter – daher ging Philip sofort darauf ein, und von Stund an veränderte sich sein Leben. »Dieses Kind ist ein Geschenk Gottes.« Er blickte in die Runde. Mit weit geöffneten Augen sahen ihn die Mönche an und hingen an seinen Lippen. »Wir werden uns selbst um den Knaben kümmern«, fuhr Philip fort. »Wir werden ihn ernähren, ihn lehren und ihn in gottgefälliger Weise großziehen. Sobald er zum Mann gereift ist, wird er selbst die Gelübde ablegen. Auf diese Weise geben wir ihn dem Herrn zurück.«

Es herrschte verwundertes Schweigen.

Dann erhob jedoch Peter von Wareham seine zornige Stimme: »Das ist unmöglich!« rief er. »Mönche taugen nicht dazu, Kinder aufzuziehen!«

Philip fing einen Blick seines Bruders Francis auf, und die beiden lächelten sich in Erinnerung an gemeinsam Erlebtes an. Als Philip wieder sprach, war seine Stimme schwer vom Gewicht der Vergangenheit. »Unmöglich? Nein, Peter, im Gegenteil. Ich bin sicher, daß sie es können, und mein Bruder teilt meine Meinung. Wir haben da unsere eigenen Erfahrungen, nicht wahr, Francis?«

An jenem Tag, den Philip seither insgeheim den »letzten Tag« nannte, war sein Vater schwerverletzt nach Hause gekommen.

Philip hatte ihn zuerst gesehen. Sie lebten damals in einem kleinen Weiler im gebirgigen Norden von Wales, und sein Vater kam über den gewundenen Pfad an der Flanke des Berges ins Dorf geritten. Wie immer lief der Sechsjährige dem Vater entgegen. Doch anders als sonst hob der Vater seinen kleinen Jungen nicht aufs Pferd, um ihn das letzte Stück des Weges mitreiten zu lassen. Vielmehr saß er zusammengesunken im Sattel und hielt die Zügel in der rechten Hand, während der linke Arm schlaff herabbaumelte. Sein Gesicht war bleich, seine Kleider blutverschmiert. Philip empfand ebensoviel Neugier wie Furcht, denn er hatte seinen Vater noch nie schwach gesehen.

»Hol deine Mutter!« sagte Papa.

Nachdem sie ihn glücklich ins Haus gebracht hatten, schnitt Mutter ihm das Hemd vom Leibe. Philip war entsetzt: Mehr noch als das viele Blut schockierte ihn die Tatsache, daß seine sonst so auf Sparsamkeit bedachte Mutter vorsätzlich die guten Kleider zerstörte. »Macht euch bloß keine Sorgen meinetwegen«, hatte Papa gesagt, doch seine gemeinhin rauhe Stimme war nur mehr ein schwaches Gemurmel, dem obendrein niemand Beachtung schenkte – eine weitere erschreckende Erkenntnis für den kleinen Philip, denn Vaters Wort war stets Gesetz gewesen. »Laßt mich in Ruhe, und bringt die anderen alle ins Kloster«, fuhr Papa fort. »Die verdammten Engländer werden gleich hier sein.« Das Kloster, zu dem auch eine Kirche gehörte, lag hoch oben auf dem Berg. Philip begriff nicht, wieso sie dort hinaufsteigen sollten, obgleich es doch gar nicht Sonntag war. Mama erwiderte: »Wenn du noch mehr Blut verlierst, wirst du niemals mehr irgendwohin gehen können.« Tante Gwen indes sagte, sie wolle Alarm schlagen, und verließ das Haus.

Wenn Philip in späteren Jahren über die nun folgenden Ereignisse nachdachte, war ihm klar, daß er und sein vierjähriger Bruder Francis in der damaligen Aufregung schlicht vergessen worden waren. Niemand dachte daran, die beiden in Sicherheit zu bringen. Die Leute kümmerten sich um ihre eigenen Kinder und nahmen an, Philip und Francis seien bei ihren Eltern gut aufgehoben – doch Papa verblutete, und Mama versuchte, ihn zu retten, und so kam es, daß die Engländer sie alle vier erwischten.

Nichts in Philips kurzem Leben hatte ihn auf den Anblick der zwei Bewaffneten vorbereitet, die unvermittelt die Tür einschlugen und in sein nur aus einem großen Raum bestehendes Elternhaus eindrangen. Unter anderen Umständen hätte er vor den beiden gar keine Angst gehabt, denn es handelte sich um stämmige und etwas linkische Halbwüchsige, wie es sie überall gibt. Burschen ihres Schlages pflegten gemeinhin alte Frauen zu verspotten, Juden zu mißhandeln und sich um Mitternacht vor den Schenken in Raufhändel einzulassen. Doch die beiden, die an jenem Tag ins Haus stürmten, waren (wie Philip erst viele Jahre später einsah, als er endlich vernünftig darüber nachdenken konnte) vom Blutrausch wie besessen. Sie hatten gerade eine Schlacht hinter sich, die Schreie der Sterbenden klangen ihnen noch in den Ohren, Kameraden waren neben ihnen gefallen, und sie selbst hatten vor Angst buchstäblich den Verstand verloren. Immerhin, die Schlacht war siegreich beendet worden; sie hatten überlebt und hetzten nun die in die Flucht geschlagenen Feinde. Es gab nur eines, was ihre Gier befriedigen konnte, und das war Blut, immer mehr Blut, das waren noch mehr Todesschreie, noch mehr Wunden und noch mehr Sterbende ... und all das war ihren verzerrten Gesichtern anzusehen, als sie zur Tür hereinstürmten wie Füchse in einen Hühnerstall.

Es ging alles sehr schnell, obwohl Philip sich später an jeden einzelnen ihrer Schritte erinnern konnte, als hätte es sehr lange gedauert. Die beiden Männer trugen nur leichte Rüstung – ein kurzes Kettenhemd und mit Eisenbändern verstärkte Lederhelme. Sie hatten die Schwerter gezückt. Der eine war häßlich, hatte eine große, gebogene Nase, schielte und bleckte die Zähne, so daß sein Gesicht einer grinsenden Fratze glich. Der andere hatte einen üppigen, ganz mit Blut verklebten Bart; da er selbst jedoch allem Anschein nach unverletzt war, mußte das Blut von jemand anderem stammen. Ihre gnadenlosen, berechnenden Augen erfaßten sofort, worauf es ankam. Sie taten Philip und Francis als unbedeutend ab, nahmen von Mama kaum Notiz und gingen, noch ehe die Familie sich rühren konnte, auch schon auf Vater los.

Mama hatte sich gerade über den Verwundeten gebeugt und seinen linken Arm verbunden. Sie richtete sich auf und trat den Angreifern entgegen; in ihren Augen funkelte der Mut der Verzweiflung. Papa sprang auf, seine unversehrte rechte Hand fuhr an den Schwertknauf. Philip stieß einen Entsetzensschrei aus.

Der häßliche Mann hob sein Schwert, ließ es mit dem Knauf voran auf Mamas Kopf niedersausen und drängte sie beiseite, ohne zuzustechen. Wahrscheinlich wollte er, solange Papa noch lebte, nicht riskieren, daß seine Waffe in einem anderen Körper steckenblieb – so jedenfalls erklärte sich Philip Jahre später das Verhalten des Mannes. Der kleine Philip rannte damals bloß zu seiner Mutter, ohne zu begreifen, daß sie ihn nicht mehr schützen konnte. Mama taumelte. Der häßliche Mann kümmerte sich nicht mehr um sie und holte zum nächsten Hieb aus. Philip klammerte sich an Mamas Rocksaum und starrte wie gebannt auf seinen Vater.

Papa war es gelungen, sein Schwert aus der Scheide zu ziehen. Es klang wie ein Glockenschlag, als die Klingen aufeinanderschlugen und Vater den ersten Hieb parierte. Wie alle kleinen Jungen hielt Philip seinen Vater für unbezwingbar, doch jetzt war die Stunde der Wahrheit gekommen. Der Blutverlust hatte den Vater geschwächt, und schon bei der Abwehr des ersten Schlages fiel ihm das Schwert aus der Hand. Der Angreifer holte nur kurz aus und schlug sofort wieder zu. Der Hieb traf Papa genau dort, wo die kräftigen Halsmuskeln in den Schultergürtel übergingen. Als Philip sah, wie die scharfe Schneide in Vaters Fleisch fuhr, begann er zu schreien. Der häßliche Mann zog das Schwert zurück und stieß es Philips Vater tief in den Bauch.

Vor Entsetzen wie gelähmt, sah Philip zu seiner Mutter auf. Ihre Blicke trafen sich just in dem Augenblick, als der Bärtige Mama niederschlug. Sie stürzte neben Philip zu Boden; aus ihrer Kopfwunde floß Blut. Der Bärtige hatte sein Schwert inzwischen umgedreht, so daß die Spitze nach unten zeigte. Er packte es mit beiden Händen und hob es hoch in die Luft, fast wie ein Mann, der sich selbst entleiben will, und ließ es dann mit aller Kraft niederfahren. Unter dem grauenvollen Geräusch brechender Knochen durchbohrte die Klinge Mamas Brust – und dies mit solcher Gewalt, daß sie (wie Philip trotz seiner alles verzehrenden Angst bemerkte) am Rücken wieder hervortrat und Mutters Körper buchstäblich am Boden festnagelte.

Verzweifelt sah Philip sich wieder nach seinem Vater um. Er sah, wie Papa über dem Schwert des häßlichen Mannes zusammensackte und ein gewaltiger Blutschwall aus seinem Mund drang. Der Angreifer trat einen Schritt zurück und zerrte an seinem Schwert, doch Papa vollzog diese Bewegung unwillkürlich nach, so daß sich der Abstand zwischen ihnen nicht verringerte. Der häßliche Mann schrie wütend auf und drehte das noch immer in Papas Bauch steckende Schwert hin und her, bis er es schließlich frei bekam. Papa stürzte zu Boden, die Hände über dem offenen Unterleib verkrampft. Philip hatte immer geglaubt, die inneren Teile des Menschen seien mehr oder weniger

fest, weshalb ihn der Anblick der häßlichen Schläuche und unförmi-
gen Organe, die aus seinem Vater herausquollen, gleichermaßen verwunderte wie anekelte. Dann riß der Angreifer das Schwert beidhän-
dig in die Höhe und beendete sein grausames Werk auf die gleiche
Weise wie zuvor sein bärtiger Spießgeselle.

Die beiden Engländer sahen einander an, und Philip bemerkte,
sehr zu seiner Verblüffung, daß sich eine gewisse Erleichterung auf
ihren Mienen abzeichnete. Dann drehten sie sich nach den beiden
Kindern um. Der eine nickte, der andere zuckte mit den Schultern,
und Philip war mit einem Male klar, daß sie nun auch ihn und seinen
Bruder mit ihren scharfen Schwertern aufschlitzen wollten. Ihm ging
auf, wie grauenvoll weh das tun würde, und die Todesangst, die von
ihm Besitz ergriff, wollte ihm schier den Kopf zerspringen lassen.

Der Mann mit dem blutverkrusteten Bart bückte sich plötzlich,
packte Francis am Fußknöchel und riß ihn hoch. Der Kleine hing
mit dem Kopf nach unten in der Luft und schrie nach seiner Mama;
daß sie tot war, hatte er noch gar nicht begriffen. Der häßliche Mann
zog sein Schwert aus Papas Körper, zielte mit der Spitze auf Francis'
Herz und holte aus.

Der Todesstreich wurde nie ausgeführt. Eine befehlsgewohnte
Stimme ertönte, und die beiden Männer erstarrten mitten in der Bewegung. Das Geschrei verstummte, und Philip merkte, daß er selbst es
war, der geschrien hatte. In der Tür stand Abt Peter in seiner Kutte
aus grober Wolle, und der Zorn des Herrn funkelte in seinen Augen.
In seiner Hand hielt er ein hölzernes Kreuz wie ein Schwert.

Wenn Philip in späteren Jahren in seinen Alpträumen jenen Tag
nachvollzog, wenn er des Nachts schreiend und in Schweiß gebadet
aus dem Schlaf fuhr, dann gelang es ihm stets, sich wieder zu beruhigen, indem er sich jenes abschließende Bild ins Gedächtnis zurückrief:
Ein unbewaffneter Mann mit einem Kreuz beendete das Schreien,
machte die Wunden vergessen.

Abt Peter hob die Stimme. Philip konnte nicht verstehen, was er
sagte – der Abt sprach natürlich Englisch –, doch die Bedeutung seiner
Worte war klar, denn die beiden Männer schämten sich offensichtlich,
und der Bärtige setzte Francis behutsam wieder ab. Ohne in seiner
Rede innezuhalten und ohne das geringste Zögern betrat der Abt die
Wohnstube. Die beiden Bewaffneten traten einen Schritt zurück. Es
sah fast so aus, als hätten sie Angst vor ihm – sie, die sie Rüstung
und Schwert trugen, hatten Angst vor dem Abt in seiner wollenen
Kutte, fürchteten das hölzerne Kreuz! Er wandte ihnen verächtlich

den Rücken zu und ging in die Hocke, um mit Philip zu sprechen. Seine Stimme klang ganz ruhig.

»Wie heißt du?«

»Philip.«

»Ach ja, ich erinnere mich. Und wie heißt dein Bruder?«

»Francis.«

»Ja, richtig.« Sein Blick fiel auf den blutenden Körper der Mutter. »Das ist deine Mama, oder?«

»Ja«, antwortete Philip. Er deutete auf den übel zugerichteten Körper seines Vaters, und das Grauen sprang ihn an. »Das da drüben ist mein Papa.«

»Ich weiß«, sagte der Mönch, und seine Stimme klang beruhigend. »Du brauchst jetzt nicht mehr zu schreien. Aber beantworte mir meine Fragen. Begreifst du, daß deine Eltern tot sind?«

»Ich weiß nicht«, erwiderte Philip kläglich. Er wußte, was es bedeutete, wenn Tiere starben – aber konnte so etwas auch Mama und Papa zustoßen?

Abt Peter sagte: »Sterben ist wie Einschlafen.«

»Aber ihre Augen sind doch offen!« kreischte Philip.

»Pssst! Du hast recht. Am besten, wir schließen sie ihnen.«

»Ja«, sagte Philip. Das war eine beruhigende Lösung.

Abt Peter erhob sich, nahm Philip und Francis an der Hand und führte sie zur Leiche ihres Vaters. Dort kniete er nieder und nahm Philips rechte Hand in die seine. »Ich zeige dir, wie man es macht«, sagte er und führte die Hand des Jungen über das väterliche Gesicht. Philip zuckte zurück. Er traute sich nicht, seinen Vater zu berühren, er war so merkwürdig bleich, so schlaff, so entsetzlich verstümmelt. Angstvoll sah er zu Abt Peter auf – einem Mann, dem niemand zu widersprechen wagte. Aber der Abt war gar nicht böse auf ihn. »Komm«, sagte er freundlich und ergriff wieder Philips Hand, und diesmal sträubte sich Philip nicht. Der Mönch führte den Zeigefinger des Knaben an Vaters linkes Augenlid und drückte es über die Pupille, die schauerlich ins Leere starrte. Dann gab er Philips Hand frei und sagte zu ihm: »Nun schließe auch das andere Auge.«

Erneut streckte Philip, diesmal ungeleitet, die Hand aus und schloß Vaters rechtes Auge. Danach ging es ihm etwas besser.

Abt Peter fragte: »Sollen wir auch deiner Mama die Augen schließen?«

»Ja.«

Sie knieten neben der Mutter nieder. Mit den Ärmeln seiner Kutte wischte ihr der Abt das Blut aus dem Gesicht. »Und Francis?« fragte Philip.

»Ja, er kann uns vielleicht helfen«, sagte der Mönch.

»Tu, was ich bei Papa gemacht habe, Francis«, sagte Philip zu seinem Bruder. »Mach Mamas Augen zu, damit sie schlafen kann.«

»Schlafen Mama und Papa?« fragte Francis.

»Nein, aber es ist *wie* Schlafen«, gab Philip bestimmt zurück, »und deshalb sollen ihre Augen zu sein.«

»Na gut«, sagte Francis, streckte, ohne zu zögern, sein Patschhändchen aus und drückte der Mutter die Augen zu.

Der Abt nahm die beiden Knaben auf, in jeden Arm einen, und trug sie aus dem Haus, ohne die beiden Bewaffneten noch eines Blickes zu würdigen. Er trug sie den steilen Pfad zum Kloster empor und setzte sie unterwegs nicht ein einziges Mal ab. Sie waren in Sicherheit.

Er gab ihnen in der Klosterküche zu essen und trug ihnen, als sie satt waren, auf, dem Koch bei der Zubereitung des Abendessens zu helfen; er wollte nicht, daß sie mit ihren Gedanken allein waren. Am nächsten Tag ließ er sie noch einmal ihre toten Eltern sehen. Die Leichen waren gewaschen und gekleidet, die Wunden, soweit noch sichtbar, gesäubert. Die offenen Särge waren nebeneinander im Kirchenschiff aufgebahrt. Es waren nicht die einzigen. Eine Reihe von Verwandten und Bekannten aus dem Dorf hatte es ebenfalls nicht mehr geschafft, sich vor den marodierenden Soldaten der Invasionstruppen in Sicherheit zu bringen. Abt Peter begleitete die Buben zur Beerdigung und achtete darauf, daß sie sehen konnten, wie die beiden Särge nebeneinander in das gemeinsame Grab gelassen wurden. Als Philip zu weinen anfing, stimmte auch Francis ein. Irgend jemand machte »Psst!«, doch Abt Peter sagte: »Laßt die Kinder weinen.« Erst als kein Zweifel mehr daran bestehen konnte, daß die Kinder den Tod ihrer Eltern und die Endgültigkeit des Abschieds begriffen hatten, sprach er mit ihnen über ihre Zukunft.

Unter ihren Verwandten gab es nach dem Überfall keine einzige unversehrte Familie mehr. Alle hatten den Verlust der Mutter oder des Vaters zu beklagen, und niemand war bereit oder imstande, sich um die beiden Jungen zu kümmern. Damit standen nur noch zwei Möglichkeiten offen: Sie konnten entweder einem Bauern überlassen (oder gar verkauft) werden, der sie als Arbeitssklaven benutzen würde, bis sie alt und stark genug waren, um davonzulaufen. Oder aber sie kamen in die Obhut des Herrn.

Daß Kinder im Kloster aufgenommen wurden, geschah durchaus

nicht selten. Das Eintrittsalter lag gemeinhin bei elf Jahren und das Mindestalter – da die Mönche im Umgang mit Säuglingen und Kleinkindern nicht geübt waren – bei fünf. Einige der Zöglinge waren Waisen, andere Halbwaisen, und wieder andere stammten aus Familien, in denen es zu viele Söhne gab. Im Regelfall bekam das Kloster von den Eltern noch eine üppige Mitgift – einen Hof, eine Kirche oder sogar ein ganzes Dorf, doch konnte bei nachgewiesener Armut darauf verzichtet werden. Da Philips Vater seinen Kindern ein bescheidenes Gehöft in den Bergen hinterlassen hatte, waren Francis und Philip nicht einmal mittellos. Abt Peter machte den Vorschlag, das Gehöft und die beiden Jungen dem Kloster zu überlassen, und die überlebenden Verwandten erklärten sich damit einverstanden. Man setzte einen Vertrag auf, der durch die Unterschrift des Fürsten von Gwynedd, Gruffyd ap Cynan, bestätigt wurde, der durch König Henrys Invasionstruppen zwar eine zeitweilige Demütigung hatte hinnehmen müssen, seinen Thron aber nicht verloren hatte.

Trauer und Sorge waren für Abt Peter nichts Unbekanntes, doch auch er war auf das, was Philip in der Folgezeit durchmachen mußte, nicht vorbereitet. Ungefähr ein Jahr nach den schrecklichen Ereignissen, als die Kinder sich an das Klosterleben gewöhnt hatten und die Trauer um die Eltern nicht mehr gar so schwer auf ihnen zu lasten schien, wurde Philip urplötzlich von einer Art unversöhnlichen Zorns erfaßt. Die Lebensbedingungen in der Gemeinschaft auf dem Klosterberg rechtfertigten seine Wut nicht: Es gab genug zu essen und anzuziehen, während der Wintermonate brannte im Dormitorium ein warmes Feuer, und den Kindern wurde sogar ein wenig Liebe und Zuneigung entgegengebracht. Die strenge Disziplin und die ermüdenden Rituale sorgten zumindest für eine gewisse Ordnung und Regelmäßigkeit. Philip indessen benahm sich, als sei er schuldlos ins Gefängnis geworfen worden. Er weigerte sich, Befehle auszuführen, und untergrub bei jeder sich bietenden Gelegenheit die Autorität der Klosteroffizialen. Er stahl Lebensmittel, zerbrach mutwillig Eier, ließ Pferde von der Leine, verhöhnte die Kranken und bedachte alle, die älter waren als er, mit Beleidigungen. Das einzige Vergehen, dessen er sich nicht schuldig machte, war Gotteslästerung, daher verzieh ihm der Abt alles andere, und eines Tages war Philip diesem Zustand von ganz allein entwachsen. Als er sich am Weihnachtsfest die vergangenen zwölf Monate ins Gedächtnis zurückrief, wurde ihm plötzlich klar, daß er nicht eine einzige Nacht im Karzer verbracht hatte.

Seine Rückbesinnung auf einen gesitteten Lebenswandel ließ sich nicht auf ein bestimmtes Ereignis zurückführen, doch trug unter anderem wahrscheinlich der Umstand dazu bei, daß der Unterricht ihn mehr und mehr zu fesseln begann. Die mathematische Seite der Musiktheorie faszinierte ihn, und selbst in der Konjugation lateinischer Verben erkannte er eine gewisse Logik, an der er Gefallen fand. Er war beauftragt worden, dem Cellerar zur Hand zu gehen, also jenem Mönch, der für die Versorgung des Klosters von Sandalen bis zum Saatgut zuständig war, und auch diese Aufgabe erregte seine Neugier. Er entwickelte eine an Heldenverehrung grenzende Bewunderung für Bruder John, einen gutaussehenden, kräftigen jungen Mönch, der ihm geradezu als Inbegriff der Gelehrsamkeit, Frömmigkeit, Klugheit und Freundlichkeit erschien. Sei es aus Nachahmung, sei es aus persönlicher Neigung (oder aber aus dem einen und dem anderen Grunde) – er begann, in den sich Tag für Tag wiederholenden Andachten und Gebeten einen gewissen Trost zu finden.

Als die Jahre der Reife kamen, beherrschten die klösterlichen Rituale sein Denken, und die heiligen Harmonien erfüllten sein Ohr.

Sowohl Philip als auch Francis waren allen anderen Knaben ihres Alters weit voraus, jedenfalls soweit sie es selbst beurteilen konnten. Daß sie Ausnahmetalente waren, ahnten sie damals noch nicht; vielmehr schrieben sie ihre Fähigkeiten dem Leben und der Ausbildung im Kloster zu. Auch als sie selbst immer mehr Lehraufgaben in der kleinen Schule übernahmen und nicht mehr von dem pedantischen alten Novizenmeister, sondern vom Abt persönlich unterrichtet wurden, meinten sie, ihr Vorsprung vor ihren Altersgenossen sei lediglich darauf zurückzuführen, daß sie schon so früh mit dem Lernen begonnen hätten.

Wenn Philip an seine Jugend dachte, dann erschien ihm die Spanne zwischen dem Ende seiner Rebellion und der ersten Attacke der fleischlichen Lust als eine Art Goldenes Zeitalter – obgleich sie insgesamt höchstens ein Jahr umfaßt hatte. Danach begann die qualvolle Zeit der unkeuschen Gedanken und nächtlichen Entladungen, die Zeit entsetzlich peinlicher Beichten (sein Beichtvater war der Abt persönlich), endloser Bußen und Geißelungen. Die Lust blieb ihm ein ständiger Begleiter, verlor jedoch mit den Jahren an Bedeutung und suchte ihn schließlich nur noch in seltenen Augenblicken geistiger und körperlicher Untätigkeit heim, wie eine alte wetterfühlige Verwundung.

Francis hatte etwas später mit denselben Anfechtungen zu kämpfen. Obwohl sein Bruder sich ihm nie anvertraute, gewann Philip den Eindruck, daß Francis den bösen Gelüsten weniger Widerstand entgegenbrachte als er selbst und ihnen gelegentlich gar nicht so ungern auch erlag ... Doch darauf kam es inzwischen nicht mehr an. Wichtig war, daß sie beide ihren Frieden mit jenen Leidenschaften gemacht hatten, die mehr als alles andere das klösterliche Leben gefährdeten.

So wie Philip dem Cellerar, war Francis dem Prior zugeordnet, dem Stellvertreter des Abtes. Nach dem Tode des Kellermeisters übernahm Philip sein Amt, obwohl er erst einundzwanzig Jahre alt war. Als Francis einundzwanzig wurde, wollte der Abt eigens für ihn das neue Amt eines Subpriors einrichten. Der Vorschlag führte jedoch zu einer unerwarteten Krise. Francis bat darum, aus der Verantwortung entlassen zu werden. Er wollte sich zum Priester weihen lassen und dem Herrn fortan außerhalb der Klostermauern dienen.

Philip war ebenso verblüfft wie entsetzt über das Vorhaben seines Bruders. Nicht im Traum hätte er gedacht, einer von ihnen käme je auf die Idee, das Kloster zu verlassen, und nun war ihm, als habe er soeben erfahren, er sei zum Thronerben bestimmt worden. Nach einigem Hin und Her war es dann soweit: Francis zog hinaus in die weite Welt. Es dauerte nicht lange, und er fand eine Anstellung als Hofkaplan beim Grafen von Gloucester.

Philips Vorstellungen von seiner eigenen Zukunft waren bis zu diesem Moment – soweit er sich überhaupt darüber Gedanken gemacht hatte – immer recht einfach gewesen: Er wollte Mönch sein und bleiben und ein demütiges, gottesfürchtiges Leben führen; vielleicht konnte er später sogar einmal Abt werden und dem Vorbild Peters nacheifern. Nun jedoch fragte er sich unwillkürlich, ob Gott ihm nicht eine andere Bestimmung zugedacht hatte. Das Gleichnis von den Talenten fiel ihm ein: Gott erwartete von seinen Dienern nicht nur die Erhaltung, sondern auch die Mehrung seines Reichs. Nicht ohne Furcht vertraute er Abt Peter seine Gedanken an, mußte er doch damit rechnen, ob seines Stolzes zurechtgewiesen zu werden.

Die Antwort überraschte ihn. »Ich habe mich schon gefragt«, sagte der Abt, »wann du endlich darauf kommen wirst. *Selbstverständlich* bist du zu Höherem berufen! Unweit eines Klosters geboren, im Alter von sechs Jahren verwaist, von Mönchen aufgezogen, mit einundzwanzig zum Cellerar ernannt ... Nein, wer einen solchen Werdegang nimmt, den hat Gott nicht dazu ausersehen, sein ganzes Leben in einem kleinen Kloster auf einem öden Berggipfel zu verbringen! Der Acker hier ist viel zu klein für dich. Auch du mußt uns verlassen.«

Philip war wie vor den Kopf geschlagen. Doch die Frage, die ihm eingefallen war, mußte er unbedingt noch stellen. »Wenn dieses Kloster hier so unbedeutend ist ... Warum hat Gott dann Euch hierher bestellt?«

Abt Peter lächelte. »Vielleicht, damit ich mich um dich kümmere.«

Später in jenem Jahr reiste der Abt nach Canterbury, um dem Erzbischof seine Aufwartung zu machen. Nach seiner Rückkehr sagte er zu Philip: »Ich habe dich dem Prior von Kingsbridge überlassen.«

Philip erschrak. Kingsbridge war eines der größten und bedeutendsten Klöster des Landes. Es war eine Kathedralenpriorei; seine Kirche war eine Kathedrale, ein Bischofssitz. Abt des Klosters war nominell der Bischof, doch wurde es de facto von seinem Stellvertreter, dem Prior geleitet.

»Prior James ist ein alter Freund von mir«, fuhr Abt Peter fort. »In den letzten Jahren hat er, ich weiß nicht warum, viel von seinem früheren Mut und seiner Tatkraft eingebüßt. Kingsbridge, soviel steht fest, braucht frisches Blut. Besonderen Kummer macht James seit einiger Zeit eine kleine Außenstelle seines Klosters draußen im Wald. Er braucht dort einen absolut zuverlässigen Mann, der die Zelle wieder auf den Pfad der Tugend und Gottgefälligkeit zurückführen kann.«

»Und ich soll der Prior dieser Zelle werden?« fragte Philip erstaunt.

Der Abt nickte. »So ist es. Und wenn es stimmt, daß Gott mit dir noch eine Menge vorhat, so darfst du gewiß sein, daß er dir bei der Lösung der dortigen Schwierigkeiten seine Hilfe nicht versagen wird.«

»Und wenn es nicht so ist?«

»Dann kannst du jederzeit hierher zurückkehren und mein Cellerar sein. Aber wir irren uns bestimmt nicht, mein Sohn, du wirst schon sehen.«

Es gab einen tränenreichen Abschied. Siebzehn Jahre hatte Philip im Kloster gelebt. Die Mönche waren seine Familie und standen ihm inzwischen näher als seine Eltern, die man ihm weiland auf so furchtbare Weise genommen hatte. Es war gut möglich, daß er seine Mitbrüder nie wiedersehen würde, und diese Aussicht betrübte ihn zutiefst.

Kingsbridge wirkte zunächst einschüchternd und erdrückend auf ihn. Das von hohen Mauern umgebene Kloster war größer als manch ein Dorf, die Kathedrale eine gewaltige, düstere Höhle und das Haus des Priors ein kleiner Palast. Doch nachdem Philip sich erst einmal an die enormen Dimensionen gewöhnt hatte, fielen ihm bald auch schon jene Zeichen der Entmutigung auf, die Abt Peter an seinem alten Freund wahrgenommen hatte. Die Kirche war baufällig und hätte dringend renoviert werden müssen, die Gebete wurden heruntergeleiert, das Schweigegebot immer wieder gebrochen, und es gab viel zu viele Diener – mehr Diener gar als Mönche. Philips anfängliche Schüchternheit wandelte sich rasch in Zorn. Am liebsten hätte er Prior James am Schlafittchen gepackt, ihn kräftig durchgeschüttelt und angeschrien: ›Was fällt Euch ein? Wie könnt Ihr es wagen, Gott mit so hastig heruntergeplapperten Gebeten zu beleidigen? Was untersteht Ihr Euch, Novizen das Würfelspiel und Mönchen die Haltung von Schoßhunden zu erlauben? Woher nehmt Ihr die Kühnheit, von Dienerscharen umgeben in einem Palast zu leben, während Gottes Kirche zur Ruine verkommt?‹ Er sagte natürlich nichts von alledem. Er hatte eine kurze, förmliche Unterredung mit Prior James, einem hochgewachsenen, hageren und gebeugten Mann, der auf seinen gerundeten Schultern das ganze Leid der Welt zu tragen schien. Danach sprach er mit dem Subprior, Remigius. Zu Beginn des Gesprächs ließ Philip durchblicken, daß sich nach seiner Überzeugung im Kloster einiges ändern müsse. Er hatte fest mit der freudigen Zustimmung des zweiten Mannes gerechnet, doch Remigius sah ihn nur von oben herab an, als wolle er sagen: ›Für wen haltet Ihr Euch eigentlich, junger Mann?‹, und wechselte rasch das Thema.

Remigius erklärte ihm, die Zelle St.-John-in-the-Forest sei vor drei Jahren gegründet und mit Land und Gerätschaften ausgestattet worden. Obwohl sie inzwischen längst hätte autark sein sollen, müsse sie nach wie vor von der Mutterabtei unterstützt werden. Andere Unannehmlichkeiten kämen hinzu: Da hätte ein Diakonus in der Zelle übernachtet und sich über die schlampigen Gottesdienste beschwert; es lägen Klagen von Reisenden vor, die behaupteten, in jener Gegend von Mönchen ausgeraubt worden zu sein; und dann gäbe es auch noch Gerüchte über ›Unreinheit‹ … Remigius konnte oder wollte sich darüber nicht näher auslassen – ein Umstand, in dem Philip nur mehr ein weiteres Zeichen für die Gleichgültigkeit erkannte, mit der das Kloster Kingsbridge seine Geschäfte führte. Nach dem Gespräch mit Remigius zitterte er vor Wut. Ein Kloster diente der höheren Ehre Gottes. Wenn es diesem Anspruch nicht gerecht wurde, taugte es nichts. Die Priorei Kingsbridge war noch schlimmer. Der allenthalben zu erkennende Schlendrian war gotteslästerlich, und Philip konnte nichts dagegen tun. Im günstigsten Fall konnte er ein Filialkloster der Abtei reformieren.

Auf dem zweitägigen Ritt zu seiner neuen Wirkungsstätte im Wald grübelte er über die spärlichen Informationen nach, die er erhalten hatte, und überlegte sich in Demut, wie er sein neues Amt erfüllen könnte.

Ein Prior wurde gemeinhin von den Mönchen gewählt, doch bei kleineren Außenposten einer großen Abtei konnte der Prior des Mutterhauses nach eigenem Gutdünken entscheiden. Philip war daher nicht gebeten worden, sich zur Wahl zu stellen – was wiederum bedeutete, daß er nicht von vornherein auf die Kooperation der Mönche zählen konnte. Langsam und vorsichtig würde er sich in dem neuen Amt vorantasten müssen. Er mußte zuerst die Schwierigkeiten besser kennenlernen, mit denen sich das kleine Kloster im Wald plagte; erst später, wenn er über alles Bescheid wußte, konnte er sich daran machen, sie zu bewältigen. Er mußte den Respekt und das Vertrauen der Mönche erringen und sich vor allem der Mitarbeit jener versichern, die älter waren als er und ihm sein Amt vielleicht nicht gönnten. Sobald ich mich auskenne und meine Führerschaft unbestritten ist, dachte er, werde ich handeln – und zwar entschieden.

Doch dann kam alles ganz anders.

Die Dämmerung hatte bereits eingesetzt, als er am zweiten Tage die Lichtung erreichte. Er zügelte sein Pony und betrachtete seine neue Heimat. Es gab damals nur ein Steinhaus und die Kapelle (das ebenfalls steinerne Dormitorium ließ Philip erst ein Jahr später errichten). Die aus Holz gezimmerten Hütten und Scheunen wirkten baufällig und heruntergekommen. Philip gefiel das nicht: Was Mönche errichteten, sollte von Dauer sein – gleichgültig, ob es sich um Schweinekoben oder Kathedralen handelte. Er sah sich um und entdeckte weitere Belege für jene Nachlässigkeit, die ihn bereits in Kingsbridge entsetzt hatte: Es gab keine Zäune, aus einem Scheunentor quoll das Heu heraus, und gleich neben einem Fischteich dampfte ein Misthaufen. Er spürte, wie sich seine Gesichtsmuskeln vor unterdrückter Wut spannten, und er flüsterte sich zu: »Bleib ruhig, bleib bloß ruhig!«

Kein Mensch war zu sehen. Das hatte durchaus seine Ordnung, denn es war die Zeit der Vesper. Die meisten Mönche befanden sich demnach in der Kapelle. Philip versetzte seinem Pony einen leichten Peitschenhieb in die Flanke und ritt auf eine Hütte zu, die wie ein Stall aussah. Ein junger Bursche mit Stroh in den Haaren linste über die Tür und glotzte Philip mit leerem Blick an.

»Wie heißt du?« fragte Philip und fügte nach einem Moment der Verlegenheit hinzu: »Mein Sohn.«

»Man nennt mich Johnny Eightpence«, sagte der Bursche.

Philip saß ab und überließ dem Jungen die Zügel. »Wohlan, Johnny Eightpence, du kannst mein Pferd absatteln.«

»Jawohl, Vater.« Johnny schlang die Zügel um einen vorstehenden Balken und entfernte sich.

»He, wo willst du hin?« rief Philip ihm in scharfem Ton nach.

»Ich will den Brüdern sagen, daß ein Fremder gekommen ist.«

»Du wirst dich zunächst in Gehorsam üben, Johnny. Sattle jetzt mein Pferd ab. Ich werde die Brüder selbst über meine Ankunft unterrichten.«

»Jawohl, Vater.« Eingeschüchtert kehrte Johnny zurück und tat wie ihm geheißen.

Philip sah sich um. In der Mitte der Lichtung befand sich ein Gebäude, das wie eine lange Halle aussah. Nicht weit davon entfernt stand ein kleines rundes Gebäude mit einem Loch auf dem Dach, dem Rauch entwich; es handelte sich höchstwahrscheinlich um die Küche. Philip wollte wissen, was es zum Abendessen gab. In streng geführten Klöstern gab es nur eine Mahlzeit am Tag, das Mittagessen. Hier herrschten jedoch ganz offensichtlich weniger strenge Sitten, und so gab es vermutlich nach dem Abendgebet noch ein leichtes Mahl – Brot mit Käse oder gesalzenem Fisch, vielleicht auch eine Schüssel Gerstengrütze mit Kräutern. Als Philip sich jedoch der Küche näherte, stieg ihm unverwechselbarer Bratengeruch in die Nase und ließ ihm das Wasser im Munde zusammenlaufen. Er blieb stehen und runzelte die Stirn, dann betrat er das kleine Gebäude.

Zwei Mönche und ein Knabe saßen um den Herd, der mitten im Raum aufgestellt war. Philip sah, wie einer der beiden Mönche seinem Mitbruder einen Krug reichte, den dieser sofort an die Lippen setzte. Der Junge drehte einen Spieß über dem Feuer, und auf dem Spieß steckte ein kleines Schwein.

Als Philip ins Licht trat, blickten die drei überrascht auf. Ohne ein Wort zu sagen, nahm er dem Mönch den Krug aus der Hand und roch daran.

»Warum trinkt Ihr Wein?«

»Weil er das Herz stärkt, Fremder«, erwiderte der Mönch. »Na los, koste ihn. Tu einen langen Zug!«

Niemand, soviel stand fest, hatte sie vor dem Eintreffen des neuen Priors gewarnt. Und vor den Berichten, die ein zufällig des Weges kommender Mönch nach Kingsbridge bringen würde, fürchteten sie sich offenbar auch nicht. Philip verspürte den Drang, dem Mann den Weinkrug über den Schädel zu schlagen. Doch er beherrschte sich, holte tief Luft und sagte mit sanfter Stimme: »Die Kinder der Armen hungern, damit wir genügend Fleisch und Wein bekommen«, sagte er. »Dies geschieht indessen zur höheren Ehre Gottes – und nicht dazu, uns in bessere Stimmung zu versetzen. Für heute habt Ihr genug Wein getrunken.« Den Krug noch immer in der Hand, wandte er sich zum Gehen.

Auf dem Weg zur Tür hörte er, wie einer der Mönche hinter ihm herrief: »Für wen haltet Ihr Euch eigentlich?« Philip gab darauf keine Antwort. Sie würden es noch früh genug erfahren.

Er stellte den Krug vor der Küche auf dem Erdboden ab und begab sich als nächstes zur Kapelle. Wütend ballte er die Hände zu Fäusten und öffnete sie wieder; es war ein Versuch, seinen Zorn im Zaum zu halten. Du darfst nichts überstürzen, sagte er sich. Sei vorsichtig. Laß dir Zeit.

Im Portal der kleinen Kapelle hielt er einen Augenblick inne, um sich zu beruhigen. Dann schob er leise die schwere Eichentür auf und trat ein.

Vor ihm standen in unregelmäßigen Reihen ungefähr ein Dutzend Mönche und einige Novizen. Er sah sie nur von hinten. Vorne, am Altar, stand der Sakristan und las laut aus einem aufgeschlagenen Buch. Er leierte seinen Text schnell herunter, und die Antworten der Mönche kamen ebenso leiernd und gelangweilt. Auf einem schmutzigen Altartuch flackerten drei ungleich lange Kerzen.

Im Hintergrund standen zwei junge Mönche und unterhielten sich angeregt. Das Abendgebet interessierte sie kaum. Als Philip sie erreichte, machte einer von ihnen gerade einen Witz, worauf der andere laut auflachte und das Geplapper des Sakristans übertönte. Diese Szene brachte für Philip das Faß zum Überlaufen, und alle seine guten Vorsätze waren wie weggewischt. »RUHE!« brüllte er, so laut er konnte.

Das Gelächter brach ab. Der Sakristan verstummte. Grabesstille herrschte auf einmal in der Kapelle, und alle Mönche wandten sich zu Philip um.

Philip packte den Mann, der so dreist gelacht hatte, am Ohr. Der Mönch war ungefähr im gleichen Alter wie er selbst, aber merklich größer. Philip zog seinen Kopf herunter. »Auf die Knie!« schrie er. Einen Augenblick lang sah es aus, als wolle sich der junge Mann losreißen. Doch er wußte, daß er im Unrecht war, und das schlechte Gewissen lähmte, wie Philip erwartet hatte, seinen Widerstandsgeist. Philip verstärkte seinen Griff, und der Mönch fiel auf die Knie.

»Das gilt für euch alle«, befahl Philip. »Auf die Knie!«

Sie hatten allesamt Gehorsam gelobt, und die skandalöse Disziplinlosigkeit, die sich in jüngster Zeit im Kloster breitmachte, hatte die jahrelange Gewohnheit noch nicht zu erschüttern vermocht. Gut die Hälfte der Mönche und alle Novizen fielen auf die Knie.

»Ihr alle habt euer Gelübde gebrochen«, sagte Philip und ließ sie seine Verachtung spüren. »Ihr seid Gotteslästerer, alle miteinander.« Er sah sie alle der Reihe nach an. »Eure Buße beginnt sofort.«

Nun beugten auch diejenigen, die zuvor gezögert hatten, die Knie, bis schließlich nur noch der Sakristan stand. Er war ein feister Mann mit schläfrigen Augen und mochte etwa zwanzig Jahre älter sein als Philip, der nun auf ihn zuging.

»Gib mir das Buch!« befahl Philip.

Der Sakristan starrte ihn trotzig an und würdigte ihn keiner Antwort.

Philip war mit einem Schritt bei ihm und griff nach dem großen Band, doch der Sakristan ließ ihn nicht los. Philip zögerte. Zwei Tage lang hatte er sich selbst Vorsicht und Bedächtigkeit geschworen – und nun stand er hier, die Schuhe noch voller Straßenstaub, und setzte in einem Machtkampf mit einem ihm gänzlich unbekannten Mann alles aufs Spiel. »Das Buch her, und dann runter auf die Knie!« wiederholte er.

Ein höhnischer Zug lag in der Miene des Sakristans. »Wer seid Ihr?« fragte er.

Philip zögerte erneut. Daß er Mönch war, verrieten seine Kutte und sein Haarschnitt, und daß er eine höhere Stellung bekleidete, mußte sein Auftreten ihnen klargemacht haben. Unklar war nach wie vor, ob er einen höheren Rang innehatte als der Sakristan. Philip hätte jetzt nur zu sagen brauchen *Ich bin euer neuer Prior*, aber das wollte er nicht. Es erschien ihm plötzlich sehr wichtig, sich allein mittels moralischer Autorität durchzusetzen.

Der Sakristan spürte seine Unsicherheit und machte sie sich sofort zunutze. »Hättet Ihr vielleicht die Güte«, fragte er mit gespielter Höflichkeit, »uns mitzuteilen, wer da gekommen ist und wünscht, daß wir in seiner Gegenwart niederknien?«

Das reichte, um Philips letzte Bedenken zu vertreiben. Gott steht auf meiner Seite, dachte er, wovor also fürchte ich mich? Er holte tief Luft und sprach mit donnernder Stimme, die hoch oben im steinernen Gewölbe widerhallte: »Gott ist es, der euch befiehlt, in *seiner* Gegenwart niederzuknien!«

Der Sakristan schien eine Spur seiner Selbstsicherheit verloren zu haben. Philip nutzte die Gelegenheit und entriß ihm das Buch. Nun war dem Mann der Rest seiner Autorität genommen. Jetzt kniete auch er nieder.

Philip ließ sich seine Erleichterung nicht anmerken. Er ließ seinen Blick über die Anwesenden schweifen und verkündete: »Ich bin euer neuer Prior.«

Er las das Gebet und ließ die Mönche bis zum Ende knien. Es dauerte lange, denn Philip ließ sie alle Antworten so lange wiederholen, bis sie in absoluter Einstimmigkeit ertönten. Danach führte er sie schweigend zum Refektorium. Er ließ das gebratene Schwein zurück in die Küche bringen und bestellte statt dessen Brot und Leichtbier. Ein Mönch erhielt den Auftrag, während des Abendessens laut vorzulesen. Gleich nach Beendigung der Mahlzeit führte Philip die Mönche, ohne ein Wort zu verlieren, ins Dormitorium.

Er befahl, die Bettstatt des Priors, die in einem eigenen Gebäude untergebracht war, herbeizuschaffen, denn er wollte im gleichen Raum wie seine Mönche schlafen. Auf diese Weise ließ sich der Sünde der Unkeuschheit am einfachsten und wirksamsten vorbeugen.

In der ersten Nacht tat er kein Auge zu. Bis Mitternacht saß er neben einer brennenden Kerze und verharrte in stillem Gebet. Dann weckte er die Mönche zur Matutin, die er jedoch zum Zeichen, daß er nicht gnadenlos war, recht schnell abwickelte. Danach gingen die Mönche wieder zu Bett, doch Philip schlief auch jetzt noch nicht.

Im Morgengrauen, noch ehe die Mitbrüder wieder erwachten, ging er hinaus, sah sich in der Umgebung ein wenig um und machte sich Gedanken über den kommenden Tag. Mitten auf einem Feld, das erst in jüngster Zeit gerodet worden war, fiel ihm ein riesiger Stumpf auf, der anscheinend von einer uralten Eiche stammte. Da kam ihm plötzlich eine Idee.

Nach der Prim und dem Frühstück schickte er die Mönche mit Seilen und Äxten hinaus aufs Feld. Die Rodung des gewaltigen Baumstumpfs nahm den gesamten Vormittag in Anspruch. Eine Gruppe zog nach Kräften an den Seilen, eine andere rückte dem Wurzelwerk mit Äxten zu Leibe. Als die Arbeit schließlich vollbracht war und der Stumpf nachgab, ließ Philip Bier und Brot austeilen und genehmigte allen eine Scheibe von dem Braten, den er ihnen am Abend zuvor vorenthalten hatte.

Damit lösten sich zwar nicht sämtliche Schwierigkeiten in Luft auf, doch zumindest wußte jetzt ein jeder, woran er war. Von Anfang an weigerte sich Philip, das Mutterkloster um Versorgungsgüter anzugehen. Lediglich Saatgut für den Anbau von Getreide und Kerzen für

113

die Kapelle ließ er sich noch liefern. Wollten die Mönche fortan Fleisch auf dem Tisch haben, so mußten sie sich selber darum kümmern. Allein diese Erkenntnis wirkte Wunder: Die Brüder verwandelten sich in gewissenhafte Viehzüchter und kenntnisreiche Fallensteller, und hatten sie zuvor in den Gebetsstunden eine willkommene Ablenkung von der Arbeit gesehen, so waren sie nun dankbar, wenn Philip die Andachten ein wenig verkürzte, so daß ihnen mehr Zeit zur Feldarbeit blieb.

Zwei Jahre später war das Kloster von fremder Hilfe unabhängig, und nach zwei weiteren Jahren konnte es bereits Fleisch, Wildbret und einen hochbegehrten Ziegenkäse an das Mutterkloster in Kingsbridge liefern. Die Zelle im Wald prosperierte, die Gottesdienste waren feierlich und ernst, und die Brüder waren gesund und guter Dinge.

Philip hatte allen Anlaß, zufrieden zu sein, und er wäre es vielleicht auch gewesen – hätten sich die Verhältnisse im Mutterkloster nicht rapide verschlechtert.

Kingsbridge hätte einer der geistigen Mittelpunkte des Königreichs sein können, ein Ort voller Leben und Lebendigkeit. Wissenschaftler aus aller Herren Länder hätten die Bibliothek besuchen können und der Prior ein Ratgeber an Fürstenhöfen sein müssen. Die Reliquienschreine waren dazu angetan, Pilger aus dem ganzen Land anzulocken, und die Gastfreundschaft der Mönche hätte beim Adel in ebenso gutem Rufe stehen können wie ihre Mildtätigkeit bei den Armen ... Welch anderes Bild bot indessen die Wirklichkeit! Die Kirche verfiel zusehends, die Hälfte der Gebäude stand leer, und die Priorei stand bei verschiedenen Geldverleihern tief in der Kreide. Mindestens einmal im Jahr stattete Philip dem Mutterhaus einen Besuch ab, und jedesmal kehrte er wutentbrannt zurück: Es war nicht mit anzusehen, wie der von gläubigen Menschen zusammengetragene und von beherzten Mönchen gemehrte Wohlstand dort verschleudert wurde – wie das Erbe des rechtschaffenen Mannes im Gleichnis vom verlorenen Sohn.

Einer der Gründe für die Misere war in der Lage der Priorei zu suchen.

Kingsbridge war ein kleines Dorf am Ende einer Nebenstraße, die nicht weiterführte. Seit den Zeiten des ersten Königs Wilhelm – den die einen den ›Eroberer‹, die anderen aber, je nach ihrem persönlichen Standpunkt, den ›Bastard‹ nannten – waren die meisten Kathedralen in die größeren Städte verlegt worden. Das Kloster Kingsbridge gehörte zu den wenigen Orten, die von dieser Entwicklung nicht betroffen waren. Philip sah darin allerdings kein unüberwindliches Problem: Seiner Überzeugung nach war ein geschäftiges Kloster mit einer Kathedrale eine Stadt für sich.

Der Hauptgrund für die Häufung von Schwierigkeiten lag in der Untätigkeit des alten Priors James. Die Hand, die das Ruder führte, war kraftlos, das Schiff ein willenloser Spielball der Gezeiten.

Und zu Philips tiefer Betrübnis ließ sich keine Wendung zum Besseren absehen – im Gegenteil: Solange Prior James lebte, würde sich der Niedergang des Klosters unaufhaltsam fortsetzen.

Sie wickelten das Kind in sauberes Linnen und legten es in einen großen Brotkorb, der auch als Wiege dienen konnte. Den kleinen Bauch voller Ziegenmilch, schlief der Knabe ein. Philip übertrug Johnny Eightpence die Verantwortung für den neuen Mitbruder, denn wiewohl Johnny nicht ganz richtig im Kopf war, verstand er sich doch bestens auf den Umgang mit kleinen, schwachen Lebewesen.

Philip war überaus neugierig zu erfahren, was Francis zu ihm geführt hatte. Im Laufe des Mittagessens spielte er mehrfach darauf an, doch Francis ging darauf nicht ein, so daß Philip nichts anderes übrigblieb, als sich weiterhin zu gedulden.

Dem Essen folgte das Studium. Es gab keine Wandelgänge hier draußen im Wald, doch war es den Mönchen gestattet, sich im Portal der Kapelle niederzulassen und zu lesen oder aber auf der Lichtung spazierenzugehen. Auch durften sie ab und an das Küchengebäude betreten und sich nach altem Brauch am Feuer wärmen. Philip und Francis umrundeten die Lichtung Seite an Seite, wie einst im Kreuzgang ihres walisischen Heimatklosters. Endlich ergriff Francis das Wort.

»König Heinrich hat die Kirche immer wie einen untergeordneten Teil seines Reiches behandelt. Er erteilte Bischöfen Befehle, belegte die Kirche mit Steuern und Abgaben und hintertrieb die Autorität des Papstes.«

»Das ist mir bekannt«, erwiderte Philip. »Was willst du damit sagen?«

»König Heinrich ist tot.«

Philip verhielt den Schritt. Damit hatte er nicht gerechnet!

»Er starb in seiner Jagdhütte bei Lyons-la-Forêt in der Normandie«, fuhr Francis fort. »Er hatte gerade ein Gericht von Neunaugen zu sich genommen, die er so gerne mochte, obwohl sie ihm nie recht bekommen sind.«

»Und wie lange ist das her?«

»Heute ist der erste Tag des neuen Jahres – er starb vor genau einem Monat.«

Philip war aufrichtig erschrocken. Er hatte noch nie den Tod eines Königs miterlebt, denn Heinrichs Thronbesteigung lag in der Zeit vor seiner Geburt. Andererseits wußte er: Der Tod eines Königs bedeutete Unruhe, vielleicht sogar Krieg. »Und was geschieht jetzt?« fragte er bestürzt.

Sie setzten ihren Weg fort. »Das Schlimme ist«, sagte Francis, »daß der rechtmäßige Erbe des Königs vor vielen Jahren im Meer ertrank. Du erinnerst dich?«

»Ja, ich erinnere mich.« Philip war damals zwölf Jahre alt gewesen. Der Tod des Thronfolgers war das erste Ereignis von landesweiter Bedeutung, das sich seinem Gedächtnis eingeprägt und ihn auf die Welt außerhalb der Klostermauern aufmerksam gemacht hatte. Der Königssohn war vor Cherbourg beim Untergang des ›Weißen Schiffes‹ zu Tode gekommen. Abt Peter, der nach dem Ableben des Thronfolgers den Ausbruch von Krieg und Anarchie befürchtete, hatte dem jungen Philip von den Ereignissen berichtet. Letztlich war es König Heinrich jedoch gelungen, die Zügel in der Hand zu behalten, so daß das Leben von Francis und Philip in denselben geordneten Bahnen weiterlief wie zuvor.

»Der König hat natürlich noch zahlreiche andere Kinder«, fuhr Francis fort, »insgesamt mindestens zwanzig, darunter meinen eigenen Herrn, Graf Robert von Gloucester. Aber bei ihnen handelt es sich samt und sonders um illegitime Sprosse ... Außer dem verstorbenen Sohn hat König Heinrich trotz seiner gewaltigen Fruchtbarkeit nur noch ein einziges legitimes Kind hinterlassen, und zwar ein Mädchen namens Mathilde. Bastarde sind von der Thronfolge ausgeschlossen – doch eine Frau ist fast genauso schlimm.«

»Hat König Heinrich denn keinen Erben ernannt?« fragte Philip.

»Doch, doch, er bestimmte Mathilde zur Erbin. Sie hat einen Sohn, der ebenfalls Heinrich heißt. Daß sein Enkelsohn dereinst den Thron besteigen wird, war des verblichenen Königs sehnlichster Wunsch, doch gegenwärtig zählt er noch keine drei Jahre! Der König hat daher die Barone Mathilde Treue schwören lassen.«

Philip begriff nicht, worum es ging. »Wenn der König Mathilde als Erbin eingesetzt hat und die Barone ihr bereits den Treueid geschworen haben ... dann ist doch alles in Ordnung, oder?«

»So einfach ist das Leben bei Hofe noch nie gewesen«, antwortete

Francis. »Mathilde ist mit Gottfried von Anjou verheiratet, und das Anjou und die Normandie sind seit Generationen verfeindet. Unsere normannischen Herren hassen die Angeviner. Offen gestanden – die Einschätzung unseres alten Königs, die anglonormannischen Barone könnten einem aus dem Hause Anjou widerspruchslos England und die Normandie überlassen, war sehr blauäugig – Treueid hin oder her.«

Die ebenso kundige wie respektlose Rede seines Bruders über die bedeutendsten Persönlichkeiten des Landes brachte Philip ein wenig durcheinander. »Woher weißt du das nur alles?« fragte er.

»Die Barone trafen sich in Le Neubourg, um über ihr weiteres Vorgehen zu entscheiden. Es versteht sich von selbst, daß auch mein eigener Herr, Graf Robert, an dieser Besprechung teilnahm. Ich begleitete ihn und diente ihm als Sekretär für seine Korrespondenz.«

Philip warf einen Seitenblick auf seinen Bruder. Was für ein unterschiedliches Leben wir doch führen! dachte er. Dann kam ihm ein neuer Gedanke. »Graf Robert ist der älteste Sohn des verstorbenen Königs, nicht wahr?«

»Ja, und er ist von großem Ehrgeiz besessen. Aber er hält sich an die weitverbreitete Meinung, daß illegitime Sprosse des Königs sich ihr Reich erstreiten müssen. Erben können sie es nicht.«

»Wer kommt sonst noch in Frage?«

»König Heinrich hatte drei Neffen, die Söhne seiner Schwester. Der älteste ist Theobald von Blois, der zweite Stephan, der bei seinem Onkel in hoher Gunst stand und von ihm mit ausgedehnten Ländereien hier in England bedacht wurde, und dann ist da noch Henry, der Benjamin der Familie, der dir als Bischof von Winchester vertraut ist. Die Barone sprachen sich für den ältesten aus, also für Theobald, und zwar unter Berufung auf eine Tradition, die du wahrscheinlich vollauf billigst ...« Francis sah Philip an und grinste.

Philip lächelte zurück. »In der Tat«, sagte er und fügte hinzu: »So heißt unser neuer König also Theobald?«

Francis schüttelte den Kopf. »Das bildete er sich zunächst auch ein – nur haben wir jüngeren Söhne nun einmal die Art, uns in den Vordergrund zu drängen.« Die beiden Brüder erreichten den Rand der Lichtung und machten kehrt. »Während Theobald gnädigst die Huldigung der Barone entgegennahm, überquerte Stephan den Kanal, begab sich schnurstracks nach Winchester und besetzte mit Hilfe von Bischof Henry, dem Nesthäkchen der Familie, die dortige Burg. Vor allem aber bemächtigte er sich dort des königlichen Schatzes.«

Philip wollte Francis schon unterbrechen und sagen: ›So ist also

Stephan unser neuer Herrscher!«, doch diesmal hütete er seine Zunge: Schon bei Mathilde und Theobald hatte er sich zu voreiligen Schlüssen hinreißen lassen.

Francis fuhr fort: »Zur endgültigen Absicherung seines Sieges fehlte Stephan nur noch der Segen der Kirche, denn um wirklich König zu sein, muß er in Westminster vom Erzbischof gekrönt werden.«

»Nun, das dürfte ihm nicht schwergefallen sein«, sagte Philip, »immerhin ist sein Bruder Henry einer der führenden Priester im Lande – als Bischof von Winchester und Abt von Glastonbury ist er fast so mächtig wie der Erzbischof von Canterbury. Wobei noch hinzukommt, daß er ein wahrer Krösus ist. Und warum sollte Bischof Henry Stephan seine Unterstützung versagen? Er hat ihm schließlich schon bei der Besetzung Winchesters geholfen.«

Francis nickte. »Ich muß gestehen, daß Bischof Henry während der Nachfolgekrise geradezu hervorragend taktiert hat. Allerdings hat er Stephan gewiß nicht aus brüderlicher Liebe unterstützt.«

»Warum denn?«

»Eben erst habe ich dich darin erinnert, wie der verstorbene König mit der Kirche und ihren Repräsentanten umzuspringen pflegte. Bischof Henry möchte nun sicherstellen, daß der nächste König, wer immer es auch sein mag, die Kirche besser behandelt. Als Bedingung für seine Unterstützung nahm er seinem Bruder den feierlichen Schwur ab, daß die Rechte und Privilegien der Kirche unter einem König Stephan stets beachtet und gewahrt blieben.«

Philip war beeindruckt. Stephans Verhältnis zur Kirche war gleich zu Beginn seiner Herrschaft klar umrissen – und zwar nach Bedingungen, die die Kirche gestellt hatte. Das Wichtigste daran mochte jedoch der Präzedenzfall sein: Zwar war die Krönung der Könige schon vorher Aufgabe der Kirche gewesen, doch nie zuvor hatte sie Bedingungen stellen können. Eines nicht allzu fernen Tages mochte es sogar so weit kommen, daß kein König mehr ohne vorherige Absprache mit der Kirche die Macht ergreifen konnte. »Das kann für uns von großer Bedeutung sein«, sagte Philip.

»Es ist natürlich möglich, daß Stephan sich nicht an sein Versprechen hält«, erwiderte Francis. »Doch du hast auf jeden Fall recht: So wie sein Vorgänger Heinrich wird er mit der Kirche niemals umspringen können. Es besteht indessen eine andere Gefahr. Zwei Barone waren über Stephans Vorgehen aufs höchste entrüstet. Der eine von ihnen ist Bartholomäus, Graf von Shiring.«

»Ich kenne ihn. Er lebt nur eine Tagesreise entfernt von hier und gilt als ein gottesfürchtiger Mann.«

»Das mag schon sein. Ich weiß nur, daß er ein selbstgerechter, starrsinniger Baron ist, der trotz der versprochenen Generalamnestie nie von seinem Treueid auf Mathilde abrücken wird.«

»Und wer ist der andere Gegner von Stephan?«

»Graf Robert von Gloucester, mein Herr. Ich habe dir ja schon von seinem Ehrgeiz berichtet. Er quält sich ständig mit dem Gedanken, daß er – wäre er nur legitim geboren – längst die Krone trüge. Er möchte seine Halbschwester Mathilde auf dem Thron sehen, denn er glaubt, sie wäre von seinem Rat und Beistand abhängig. Damit wäre er dann de facto König, wenngleich nicht dem Namen nach.«

»Wird Graf Robert konkrete Schritte in dieser Richtung unternehmen?«

»Ich fürchte ja.« Francis senkte die Stimme, obwohl niemand in ihrer Nähe war. »Robert und Bartholomäus planen gemeinsam mit Mathilde und ihrem Gemahl einen Aufstand, der Stephan stürzen und Mathilde an seiner Statt auf den Thron setzen soll.«

Philip blieb stehen. »Das würde ja alle Errungenschaften des Bischofs von Winchester zunichte machen!« rief er und packte seinen Bruder am Arm. »Aber, Francis ...«

»Ich weiß, woran du denkst.« Alle Anmaßung war von Francis abgefallen; aus seinem Blick sprach nackte Angst. »Wenn Graf Robert erfährt, daß ich mit dir über seine Pläne gesprochen habe, läßt er mich sofort aufhängen. Er vertraut mir voll und ganz – doch ich bin in letzter Instanz der Kirche verpflichtet, ich kann nicht anders.«

»Was willst du tun?«

»Ich dachte daran, mich um eine Audienz beim neuen König zu bemühen und ihm alles zu erzählen. Die beiden rebellischen Grafen würden natürlich alles abstreiten, und ich würde als Verräter gehenkt. Der Aufstand indessen wäre verhindert – und ich käme sogleich in den Himmel.«

Philip schüttelte den Kopf. »Man hat uns gelehrt, daß es eitel ist, das Martyrium zu suchen.«

»Ich weiß. Und außerdem glaube ich, daß Gott hier auf Erden auch noch einige Aufgaben für mich bereithält. Ich habe eine Vertrauensstellung am Hofe eines einflußreichen Barons, und wenn ich bei ihm bleibe und meine Position durch harte Arbeit festige, so werde ich dort für die Rechte der Kirche und die Herrschaft des Gesetzes einiges tun können.«

»Gibt es irgendeine andere Möglichkeit ...?«

Francis sah Philip in die Augen. »Ja. Und darum bin ich hier.«

Ein Angstschauer lief Philip über den Rücken. Francis war gekommen, ihn um Unterstützung zu bitten, andernfalls hätte er ihn nie in dieses furchtbare Geheimnis eingeweiht.

»Ich kann den Aufstand nicht verraten«, fuhr Francis fort. »Du hingegen kannst es.«

»Jesus Christus und alle Heiligen, steht mir bei!« entfuhr es Philip.

»Wenn der Plan hier unten im Süden enthüllt wird, bleibt das Haus Gloucester von jedem Verdacht verschont. Niemand weiß, daß ich hier war, und daß wir Brüder sind, weiß auch kaum einer. Du findest sicher eine glaubwürdige Erklärung für deine Informationen. Vielleicht hast du gesehen, wie sich ein Haufen Bewaffneter zusammenrottet. Oder ein Mitglied des Haushalts von Graf Bartholomäus hat einem dir bekannten Priester während der Beichte das Geheimnis anvertraut.«

Philip zog die Kutte fester um sich. Ihn schauerte. War es urplötzlich kälter geworden? Francis zog ihn da in eine äußerst gefährliche Affäre hinein. Es ging um eine unmittelbare Einmischung in die Angelegenheiten des Hofes – und das war ein Spiel, dem oft genug schon die erfahrensten Köpfe zum Opfer gefallen waren. Wer sich als Außenseiter in diese Dinge einmischte, war ein Narr.

Andererseits: Es stand eine Menge auf dem Spiel. Philip konnte nicht einfach die Hände in den Schoß legen und mit ansehen, wie ein von der Kirche ausgewählter Monarch durch eine Rebellion gestürzt wurde – nicht jedenfalls, solange ihm Mittel und Wege offenstanden, es zu verhindern. Und so gefährlich die Aufdeckung des Komplotts für ihn auch sein mochte – für Francis wäre es reiner Selbstmord.

»Was haben die Rebellen vor?« fragte Philip.

»Graf Bartholomäus befindet sich gegenwärtig auf der Rückreise nach Shiring. Von dort aus wird er Botschaften an seine Anhänger im Süden Englands aussenden. Graf Robert wird ein oder zwei Tage später nach Gloucester zurückkehren und seine Anhänger im Westen des Landes mobilisieren. Zuletzt wird Brian Fitzcount, der Herr von Wallingford Castle, seine Tore schließen, so daß der gesamte Südwesten Englands kampflos in Rebellenhand fällt.«

»Dann ist es ja fast schon zu spät«, wandte Philip ein.

»Noch nicht ganz. Es bleibt uns ungefähr noch eine Woche. Allerdings darfst du nicht mehr lange zögern.«

Philip gestand sich resigniert ein, daß er seine Entscheidung bereits so gut wie getroffen hatte. »Ich weiß nicht, wem ich es sagen soll«, antwortete er. »Üblicherweise würde man derartige Dinge mit dem Grafen besprechen – aber in diesem Fall geht das natürlich nicht. Der Vogt steht wahrscheinlich auf seiner Seite. Kennst du jemanden, der garantiert auf unserer Seite steht?«

»Wie wär's mit dem Prior von Kingsbridge?«

»Mein Vorgesetzter ist alt und müde. Er würde wahrscheinlich in Untätigkeit verharren.«

»Dann müssen wir jemand anderen finden.«

»Da wäre zum Beispiel noch der Bischof ...« Philip hatte mit dem Bischof von Kingsbridge bislang noch kein einziges Wort gewechselt, war sich jedoch sicher, bei ihm vorgelassen zu werden und Gehör zu finden. Da sich die Kirche für König Stephan entschieden hatte, stand der Bischof gleichsam von Amts wegen auf seiner Seite. Außerdem war er mächtig genug, entsprechende Maßnahmen zu ergreifen.

»Wo lebt der Bischof?« fragte Francis.

»Anderthalb Tagereisen von hier.«

»Dann machst du dich am besten noch heute auf den Weg.«

»Gewiß«, erwiderte Philip schweren Herzens.

Bedauern spiegelte sich in Francis' Miene. »Ich wünschte, es hätte einen anderen getroffen«, sagte er.

»Ich auch«, gab Philip aus vollem Herzen zurück. »Ich auch.«

Philip rief die Mönche in der kleinen Kapelle zusammen und berichtete ihnen vom Tod des Königs. »Beten wir nun für eine friedliche Nachfolge und dafür, daß der neue König die Kirche mehr lieben möge als der verstorbene König Heinrich«, sagte er. Doch er verschwieg ihnen, daß der Schlüssel für eine friedliche Thronfolge auf seltsamem Weg in seine Hand geraten war. Statt dessen verkündete er: »Andere Botschaft, die ich erhielt, erfordert meine sofortige Abreise zu unserem Mutterhaus nach Kingsbridge.«

Der Subprior sollte während seiner Abwesenheit die Chorgebete lesen, dem Cellerar oblag die Verantwortung für die Landwirtschaft. Keiner von beiden war jedoch imstande, es mit Peter von Wareham aufzunehmen. Wenn ich zu lange fortbleibe, dachte Philip, stellt Peter das ganze Kloster auf den Kopf ... Gut möglich, daß es dann bei meiner Rückkehr gar kein Kloster mehr gibt. Er hatte bisher noch keine Antwort auf die Frage gefunden, wie sich Peter im Zaum halten ließ, ohne daß seine Selbstschätzung darunter litt. Jetzt mußte alles plötzlich ganz schnell gehen, und so blieb Philip nichts anderes übrig, als sich eine Notlösung einfallen zu lassen.

»Wir sprachen heute vormittag über die Völlerei«, sagte er nach einer Pause. »Bruder Peter verdient unser aller Dank, weil er uns daran erinnerte, daß Gott der Herr unsere Äcker gesegnet und uns Wohlstand geschenkt hat – und dies, wohlgemerkt, nicht, damit wir nun feist und bequem werden, sondern allein zu seinem höheren Ruhm. Zu unseren heiligen Pflichten gehört es, unsere Reichtümer mit den Armen zu teilen. Wir haben diese Pflicht bislang vernachlässigt, vor allem deshalb, weil es hier draußen im Wald niemanden gibt, mit dem wir teilen könnten. Bruder Peter hat uns jedoch darauf hingewiesen, daß es unsere Pflicht ist, hinauszugehen und die Armen zu suchen, denn nur so können wir ihnen helfen.«

Die Mönche waren überrascht, denn sie waren doch davon ausgegangen, das Thema Völlerei sei am Vormittag erschöpfend behandelt worden. Peter von Wareham wirkte unsicher. Es gefiel ihm, daß er auf einmal wieder im Mittelpunkt des Interesses stand, doch argwöhnte er, daß Philip noch eine weitere Überraschung im Ärmel hatte. Seine Ahnung trog ihn nicht.

»Ich habe beschlossen«, fuhr Philip fort, »daß wir fortan jede Woche einen Penny pro Mitbruder für die Armen zurücklegen. Sollten wir dadurch ein bißchen weniger zu essen haben, so werden wir diese Einschränkung freudig hinnehmen, wird sie uns doch dereinst im Himmel vergolten. Noch wichtiger jedoch ist, daß wir auf die sinnvolle Verwendung unserer Pennys achten. Gibt man einem armen Mann einen Penny, damit er für sich und seine Familie Brot kaufen kann, so mag es durchaus geschehen, daß er schnurstracks zur Schenke läuft, sich betrinkt und schließlich nach Hause zurückkehrt, um sein Weib zu schlagen. Die gute Frau wäre ohne unsere milde Gabe besser gefahren. Es ist also ratsam, dem Armen – oder besser gleich seinen Kindern – Brot zu geben. Das Verteilen von Almosen ist eine heilige Aufgabe, derer wir uns mit der gleichen Sorgfalt widmen müssen wie der Heilkunst und der Erziehung der Jugend. In vielen Klöstern gibt es daher einen eigens zu diesem Zweck bestallten Almosenier, und so werden auch wir es in Zukunft halten.«

Philip sah sich in der Runde um. Die Mönche hörten ihm mit gespannter Aufmerksamkeit zu. Peter blickte recht zufrieden drein; er sah inzwischen in Philips Ausführungen einen persönlichen Sieg. Mit dem, was nun folgte, hatte niemand gerechnet.

»Die Aufgabe des Almoseniers ist alles andere als einfach. Er wird sich in den umliegenden Dörfern und Städten umtun müssen, vor allem in Winchester. Dort wird er sich unter das niedrigste Volk, die gemeinsten, häßlichsten und übelsten Menschen zu begeben haben, denn sie sind die Armen in unserem Land. Er muß für sie beten, wenn sie Gott lästern, muß die Kranken unter ihnen besuchen und allen vergeben, die ihn betrügen und berauben. Er wird Kraft, Demut und unendliche Geduld brauchen, und die Geborgenheit unserer Gemeinschaft wird ihm fehlen, denn er wird öfter unterwegs als hier sein.«

Wieder sah Philip in die Runde. Jetzt war allen Mönchen unbehaglich zumute. Keiner von ihnen strebte nach diesem Amt. Er ließ seinen Blick auf Peter von Wareham ruhen. Peter wußte jetzt, was auf ihn zukam, und machte ein langes Gesicht.

»Peter war es, der uns auf unsere Unzulänglichkeiten hinwies«, fuhr Philip schließlich mit gemessenen Worten fort. »Ich habe daher beschlossen, ihn mit der ehrenvollen Aufgabe des Almoseniers zu betrauen.« Er lächelte. »Bruder Peter, dein Dienst beginnt mit dem heutigen Tag.«

Du wirst so oft unterwegs sein, daß du hier im Kloster kaum noch Unruhe stiften kannst, dachte Philip bei sich, und dein Zorn auf unser beschauliches Leben wird sich mäßigen, je öfter du dich in den stinkenden Gassen von Winchester unter den Abschaum des Menschengeschlechts mischen mußt.

Peter sah in seiner Ernennung zum Almosenier eindeutig eine Bestrafung, sonst nichts. Der haßerfüllte Blick, mit dem er Philip bedachte, ließ den Prior fast verzagen.

Philip riß den Blick von seinem Widersacher los und widmete sich wieder den anderen. »Nach dem Tode eines Königs folgt stets eine Zeit der Gefahr und Ungewißheit«, sagte er. »Betet in meiner Abwesenheit für mich.«

Am zweiten Tag seiner Reise, gegen Mittag, befand sich Prior Philip nur mehr wenige Meilen vom bischöflichen Palast entfernt. Je näher er kam, desto mulmiger ward ihm zumute. Der Bischof würde wissen wollen, woher die Nachricht von dem geplanten Aufstand stammte, und Philip hatte sich auch schon eine halbwegs plausible Geschichte ausgedacht. Nur – was sollte er tun, wenn der Bischof ihm diese Geschichte nicht abnahm? Was, wenn er ihm zwar glaubte, aber Beweise sehen wollte? Und wenn es auch kaum wahrscheinlich

123

war, so ließ es sich doch nicht ganz ausschließen, daß der Bischof in die Verschwörung eingeweiht war und sie sogar unterstützte (auf diese Möglichkeit war Philip erst gekommen, nachdem Francis sich verabschiedet hatte). Vielleicht war er ein alter Freund des Grafen von Shiring. Daß Bischöfe ihre eigenen Interessen über die der Kirche stellten, war durchaus nichts Ungewöhnliches.

Der Bischof konnte Philip auf der Folter zur Preisgabe seines Informanten zwingen. Er war dazu zwar nicht berechtigt – doch was hieß das schon? Zur Verschwörung gegen den König war er auch nicht berechtigt ... Vor Philips geistigem Auge stellten sich die Bilder von Folterinstrumenten ein, wie man sie gelegentlich auf den Bildern der Maler sehen konnte, die das Fegefeuer darstellten. Gemälde dieser Art waren der Wirklichkeit nachempfunden, wie sie in den Verliesen der Bischöfe und Barone herrschte. Philip glaubte nicht, daß ihm die Kraft zum Martyrium gegeben war.

In einiger Entfernung vor sich erblickte er eine Gruppe von Reisenden, die zu Fuß unterwegs waren. Sein erster Impuls war anzuhalten, um sie nicht überholen zu müssen, denn er war allein, und es gab genügend Wegelagerer, die ohne jeden Skrupel auch einen Mönch überfallen hätten. Dann jedoch erkannte Philip, daß sich eine Frau und zwei Kinder unter den Wanderern befanden, und von reisenden Familien ging gemeinhin keine Gefahr aus. Im Trab setzte er ihnen nach.

Bald konnte er Einzelheiten erkennen: Die Gruppe bestand aus einem hochgewachsenen Mann, einem fast ebenso großen Jungen, einer auffallend kleinen Frau und zwei Kindern. Es handelte sich ganz offensichtlich um arme Leute, denn sie waren in lumpenartige Gewänder gehüllt und trugen keinerlei Wertgegenstände mit sich. Der Mann war von kräftigem Körperbau, aber so ausgemergelt, als ob er an einer zehrenden Krankheit litte – oder aber ganz einfach an Hunger. Als Philip die Familie erreichte, sah ihn der Mann wachsam an und murmelte den Kindern etwas zu, so daß sie sich um ihn scharten. Philip hatte ihn anfangs auf fünfzig Jahre oder mehr geschätzt.

Erst jetzt erkannte er, daß er trotz seines sorgenzerfurchten Gesichts noch kaum die Vierzig erreicht hatte.

»Heda, Mönch!« sagte die Frau.

Philip sah sie kritisch an. Daß eine Frau noch vor ihrem Ehemann das Wort ergriff, war ungewöhnlich. Und *Mönch* war zwar nicht direkt unhöflich, doch hätte *Bruder* oder *Vater* mehr Respekt bewiesen. Die Frau war ungefähr zehn Jahre jünger als der Mann und hatte tiefliegende Augen von ungewöhnlich hellgoldener Farbe, die ihr eine besondere Anziehungskraft verliehen. Philip empfand die Frau als gefährlich.

»Guten Tag, Vater«, sagte der Mann, und es klang, als wolle er sich für das vorlaute Benehmen seiner Frau entschuldigen.

»Gott segne Euch!« sagte Philip und zügelte seine Stute. »Wer seid Ihr?«

»Baumeister Tom nennt man mich. Ich suche Arbeit.«

»Und findet keine, nicht wahr?«

»So ist es.«

Philip nickte. Es war immer dasselbe. Handwerker, die im Baugewerbe tätig waren, wanderten von Arbeitsstelle zu Arbeitsstelle. Und immer wieder kam es vor, daß sie keine Arbeit fanden – entweder, weil es nicht genügend Baustellen gab, oder aber, weil sie einfach Pech hatten. Auf ihren Wanderungen nahmen diese Leute oftmals die Gastfreundschaft der Klöster in Anspruch. Hatten sie zuvor gut verdient, so erhielt man von ihnen zum Abschied eine üppige Spende; waren sie indessen schon eine Weile unterwegs, erwiesen sie sich oftmals als völlig mittellos. Die einen wie die anderen mit der gleichen Herzlichkeit zu empfangen, gehörte bisweilen zu den schwierigeren Aufgaben der klösterlichen Mildtätigkeit.

Dieser Baumeister Tom gehörte mit Sicherheit zu den armen Schluckern seiner Zunft, wenngleich sein Weib wesentlich gesünder aussah als er. »Ich habe Speis und Trank in meiner Satteltasche«, sagte Philip. »Es ist Essenszeit, und die Nächstenliebe ist eine heilige Pflicht. Wenn Ihr und Eure Familie mein Brot mit mir teilen wollt, wird es mir im Himmel dereinst gelohnt – und außerdem habe ich dann jemanden, der mir beim Essen Gesellschaft leistet.«

»Ihr seid sehr freundlich«, erwiderte Tom und sah seine Begleiterin an. Sie zuckte andeutungsweise mit den Schultern und nickte knapp. Fast ohne Pause fuhr der Mann fort: »Wir nehmen Euer Angebot gerne an und danken Euch sehr dafür.«

»Dankt Gott dem Herrn, nicht mir«, antwortete Philip wie immer in solchen Fällen.

»Danken wir den Bauern, aus deren Zehnt die Speisen stammen«, sagte die Frau.

Sie hat Haare auf den Zähnen, dachte Philip bei sich, verkniff sich aber jede Bemerkung.

Auf einer kleinen Lichtung, auf der Philips Pony sich am winterschlaffen Gras gütlich tun konnte, machten sie Rast. Philip war insgeheim froh über die Verzögerung, sie bedeutete einen kleinen Aufschub der gefürchteten Unterredung mit dem Bischof. Der Baumeister erzählte, daß auch er unterwegs zum bischöflichen Palast sei. Er hoffte, der Bischof habe einige Ausbesserungen zu erledigen oder plane vielleicht sogar einen kleinen Anbau. Philip beobachtete die Familie während des Gesprächs genau, ohne sich jedoch seine Neugier anmerken zu lassen. Es war kaum vorstellbar, daß die Frau die Mutter des älteren der beiden Jungen war; dazu war sie viel zu jung. Der Bursche war wie ein Kalb – stark und täppisch, mit blödem Blick. Der andere Junge war wesentlich kleiner und schmächtiger, er hatte karottenrotes Haar, schneeweiße Haut und vorstehende hellgrüne Augen. Sein Blick war merkwürdig starr und wirkte irgendwie geistesabwesend: Er erinnerte Philip ein wenig an den armen Johnny Eightpence, mit dem Unterschied jedoch, daß der seltsame Knabe, wenn man ihm in die Augen sah, den Blick erwiderte und dabei den Eindruck erweckte, als sei er schon sehr erwachsen und habe viel erlebt. Auf seine Art war er eine genauso beunruhigende Erscheinung wie seine Mutter. Das dritte Kind war ein kleines Mädchen von ungefähr sechs Jahren. Sie fing immer wieder an zu weinen. Ihr Vater behielt sie stets im Auge und kümmerte sich liebevoll um sie. Hin und wieder tätschelte er sie, um sie zu trösten. Einmal berührte der Mann auch seine Frau, und es entging Philip nicht, daß die Blicke der beiden voller Sinnlichkeit waren, als sie sich begegneten.

Die Frau schickte die Kinder große Blätter suchen, die als Teller benutzt werden konnten. Philip öffnete seine Satteltaschen. Tom fragte ihn: »Wo liegt Euer Kloster, Vater?«

»Mitten im Wald, eine Tagesreise westlich von hier«, antwortete Philip. Die Frau blickte auf, und Tom hob die Brauen. »Kennt Ihr es?« fragte Philip.

»Wir kommen aus Richtung Salisbury und müssen daran vorbeigekommen sein«, sagte Tom.

»In der Tat, das müßt ihr. Allerdings liegt es noch ein gutes Stück von der Hauptstraße entfernt. Wer das Kloster nicht kennt, geht daran vorbei, denn von der Straße aus ist es nicht zu sehen.«

»Ach so«, erwiderte Tom, war mit seinen Gedanken jedoch anscheinend ganz woanders.

Philip hatte auf einmal eine Idee. »Sagt an«, begann er, »ist Euch unterwegs vielleicht eine Frau begegnet? Eine sehr junge Frau möglicherweise und – nun ja – gesegneten Leibes ...?«

»Nein«, erwiderte Tom wie beiläufig, doch Philip hatte das Gefühl,

126

daß den Baumeister das Thema brennend interessierte. »Wieso fragt Ihr?«

Philip lächelte. »Hört zu, ich werde es Euch erzählen. Gestern am frühen Morgen wurde im Wald ein Säugling gefunden und in mein Kloster gebracht. Es handelt sich um einen kleinen Jungen, der nach meinem Dafürhalten kaum einen Tag alt war. Er muß in der Nacht zuvor auf die Welt gekommen sein. Seine Mutter muß sich demnach zur gleichen Zeit wie Ihr in jenem Teil des Waldes aufgehalten haben.«

»Uns ist keine Frau dort begegnet«, wiederholte Tom. »Aber sagt uns – was habt Ihr mit dem Säugling gemacht?«

»Wir haben ihn mit Ziegenmilch gefüttert, die ihm außerordentlich gut zu bekommen scheint.«

Mann und Frau hingen an Philips Lippen. Das ist eine Geschichte, die an jedermanns Herz rührt, dachte er. Nach einer kurzen Pause fragte Tom: »Und jetzt sucht Ihr seine Mutter, wie?«

»O nein, ich fragte nur aus Neugier. Falls sie mir zufällig über den Weg liefe, würde ich der Frau das Kind natürlich zurückgeben. Doch so wie die Dinge liegen, will sie es gar nicht haben. Sie hat gewiß Sorge dafür getragen, daß niemand sie findet.«

»Was geschieht denn mit dem Jungen?«

»Wir werden ihn bei uns im Kloster aufziehen – als ein Kind Gottes. Auch mein Bruder und ich wuchsen in einem Kloster auf. Unsere Eltern wurden uns schon früh genommen. Danach wurde der Abt unser Vater, und die Mönche waren unsere Familie. Wir bekamen zu essen, brauchten nicht zu frieren und erhielten eine gute Ausbildung ...«

»... und wurdet beide Mönche«, warf die Frau ein. Es klang leicht ironisch, als wollte sie damit sagen, daß die klösterliche Barmherzigkeit letztlich von Eigennutz bestimmt war.

Philip war froh, ihr widersprechen zu können. »Nein«, sagte er, »mein Bruder verließ den Orden.«

Die Kinder kehrten zurück. Sie hatten keine großen Blätter gefunden – was im Winter auch gar nicht so leicht war. Es blieb ihnen nichts anderes übrig, als ohne Teller zu essen. Philip verteilte Brot und Käse, und die Familie fiel darüber her wie hungrige Raubtiere.

»Der Käse stammt aus meinem Kloster«, erläuterte er. »Viele mögen ihn frisch, so wie diesen hier, doch schmeckt er noch besser, wenn man ihn eine Weile reifen läßt.«

Seine Gäste beeindruckte das wenig. In kürzester Zeit hatten sie ihre Portionen verzehrt. Philip hatte noch drei Birnen dabei. Er holte sie aus den Satteltaschen und reichte sie Tom, der sie den Kindern weitergab.

Schließlich erhob sich Philip. »Ich werde dafür beten, daß Ihr Arbeit findet.«

»Wenn Ihr daran denkt, Vater«, sagte Tom, »dann erwähnt mich doch dem Bischof gegenüber. Ihr wißt, daß wir Not leiden, und habt gesehen, daß wir anständige Menschen sind.«

»Ich werde daran denken.«

Tom hielt das Pferd am Zügel, während Philip aufsaß. »Ihr seid ein guter Mensch, Vater«, sagte er, und Philip sah auf einmal Tränen in seinen Augen.

»Der Herr sei mit Euch.«

Tom gab das Pferd noch nicht frei. »Dieser Säugling ... ich meine, das Findelkind, von dem Ihr uns erzählt habt ...« Er sprach ganz leise, als wollte er die Kinder nicht mithören lassen. »... habt Ihr ihm schon einen Namen gegeben?«

»Ja, das haben wir. Er heißt Jonathan – das Geschenk Gottes.«

»Jonathan. Der Name gefällt mir.« Tom gab die Stute frei.

Philip betrachtete ihn neugierig. Dann trat er dem Pferd in die Flanken und trabte davon.

Der Bischof von Kingsbridge lebte nicht in Kingsbridge. Sein Palast stand am Südhang eines üppig begrünten Tals, das eine gute Tagesreise von der kalten Kathedrale und ihren jammervollen Mönchen entfernt lag. Dem Bischof war das ganz recht so, denn allzu viele Gottesdienste hätten ihn nur abgelenkt von anderen Pflichten, zu denen unter anderem das Eintreiben von Pachtgeldern, die Rechtsprechung und ein aktives Interesse an den Geschehnissen am königlichen Hof gehörten. Auch die Mönchen waren's zufrieden, denn je weiter der Bischof entfernt war, desto weniger kam er ihnen in die Quere.

Es hätte ohne weiteres Schnee fallen können, so kalt war es, als Philip am Nachmittag den Bischofspalast erreichte. Ein eisiger Wind fegte durch das Tal, und tiefhängende graue Wolken lagen wie Stirnrunzeln über dem herrschaftlichen Haus am Hang, das, obwohl es keine Burg war, nichtsdestoweniger über ausgezeichnete Befestigungen verfügte. Im Umkreis von ungefähr hundert Schritten war der Wald gerodet, und das Haus selbst war von einem starken, gut mannshohen Staketenzaun umgeben, den seinerseits ein mit Regenwasser gefüllter Graben umschloß. Der Wachhabende am Tor zeigte sich höflich und entgegenkommend, führte jedoch ein schweres Schwert.

Der Palast selbst war ein schönes Steinhaus in der Form des Buchstabens E. Das Erdgeschoß war ein fensterloses Gewölbe, dessen starke Mauern lediglich von mehreren schweren Türen durchbrochen wurden, von denen eine offenstand. Philip konnte im düsteren Licht zahlreiche Fässer und Säcke ausmachen. Die anderen Türen waren geschlossen und mit Ketten gesichert. Philip fragte sich, was sie verbargen: Wenn der Bischof Gefangene hatte, so schmachteten sie vermutlich dort im Verlies.

Der kurze Mittelstrich des E war eine Außentreppe, die zu den Wohnstuben im ersten Stock führte. Der lange, aufrechte Strich des E war vermutlich der Saal, der obere respektive untere mochten die Kapelle und das Schlafgemach enthalten. Die Fenster waren klein und mit Läden versehen; sie wirkten auf Philip wie funkelnde Äuglein, die mißtrauisch die Außenwelt betrachteten.

Zum Palast gehörten ferner eine Küche und ein steinernes Backhaus sowie ein aus Holz gezimmerter Stall und eine Scheune. Alle Baulichkeiten waren in gutem Zustand. Pech für Baumeister Tom, dachte Philip.

Im Stall standen mehrere gute Pferde, darunter zwei Schlachtrösser. Außerdem lungerten ein paar Bewaffnete herum und schlugen die Zeit tot. Vielleicht hatte der Bischof Besuch.

Philip überließ seine Stute dem Stalljungen und stieg die Treppe hinauf. Eine düstere Vorahnung hatte ihn beschlichen. Die Szenerie wurde in bedrückender Weise von Soldaten und Kriegsgerät beherrscht. Wo waren die Schlangen der Bittsteller, wo die Mütter, die ihre Neugeborenen segnen lassen wollten? Philip betrat eine ihm fremde Welt und trug ein gefährliches Geheimnis mit sich. Es kann lange dauern, bis ich diesen Ort wieder verlasse, dachte er voller Angst. Ich wünschte, Francis hätte mich mit seinem Anliegen verschont.

Das Ende der Treppe war erreicht. Welch unwürdige Gedanken, schalt er sich. Da bekomme ich die Gelegenheit, Gott und der Heiligen Kirche zu dienen, und ich mache mir Sorgen um meine persönliche Sicherheit! Wie viele Menschen gibt es, die tagtäglich ihr Leben riskieren – in der Schlacht, auf hoher See und bei halsbrecherischen Pilgerfahrten und Kreuzzügen. Auch ein Mönch muß gelegentlich die Angst am eigenen Leibe erfahren, und wenn ihm dabei die Knie schlottern ...

Er holte tief Luft und betrat das Haus.

Der Saal war düster und rauchig. Um die kalte Luft draußen zu halten, schloß Philip rasch die Tür hinter sich. Seine Augen gewöhnten sich nur langsam an die Dunkelheit. Am anderen Ende des Saals brannte ein großes Kaminfeuer; sein Schein und das spärliche Tageslicht, das durch die kleinen Fenster fiel, sorgten für die einzige Beleuchtung. Um den Kamin herum saßen mehrere Männer, einige in geistlicher Tracht, andere in den teuren, aber abgetragenen Gewändern des niederen Adels. Sie waren in ein ernstes Gespräch vertieft, ihre Stimmen klangen leise und geschäftsmäßig. Ihre Sessel standen in keiner besonderen Ordnung, doch waren aller Augen und Worte an einen Priester gerichtet, der in ihrer Mitte saß wie eine Spinne im Netz. Der Mann war auffallend dünn, und so wie er die Beine hielt und seine langen Arme über den Sessel breitete, hatte es den Anschein, als sei er jederzeit zum Sprung bereit. Sein glattes Haar war pechschwarz, sein Gesicht bleich, die Nase spitz. Seine schwarze Kleidung ließ ihn gleichermaßen elegant wie bedrohlich erscheinen.

Der Bischof aber war er nicht.

Ein Dienstbote erhob sich von einem Stuhl neben der Tür und sprach Philip an. »Guten Tag, Vater. Wen wünscht Ihr zu sprechen?« Im gleichen Augenblick hob ein großer Hund, der neben dem Feuer lag, sein Haupt und fing an zu knurren. Der Mann im schwarzen Gewand sah auf, erblickte den Besucher und gebot den anderen mit erhobener Hand Schweigen.

»Guten Tag«, erwiderte Philip höflich. »Ich wollte mit dem Bischof sprechen.«

»Der Bischof ist nicht hier«, sagte der Mann herablassend.

Philip war enttäuscht. Er hatte sich vor dem Gespräch und den damit verbundenen Gefahren gefürchtet, gewiß, doch jetzt hatte er das Gefühl, vergeblich gekommen zu sein. An wen sonst sollte er sich mit seinem schrecklichen Geheimnis wenden? »Wann erwartet Ihr ihn zurück?« fragte er den Priester.

»Wir wissen nicht, wann er zurückkommt. Was führt Euch zu ihm?«

Der Ton des Priesters war abweisend, und Philip fühlte sich getroffen. »Ich bin unterwegs im Namen des Herrn«, erwiderte er scharf. »Wer seid Ihr?«

Der Priester hob die Brauen; die Herausforderung schien ihn zu überraschen. Die anderen Männer im Saal schwiegen still, als erwarteten sie einen plötzlichen Ausbruch. Der Priester indessen antwortete nach einer kleinen Pause in halbwegs verbindlichem Ton: »Ich bin sein Erzdiakon. Mein Name ist Waleran Bigod.«

Für einen Priester gerade der richtige Name, dachte Philip.

»Mein Name ist Philip«, sagte er. »Ich bin der Prior des Klosters St.-John-in-the-Forest, einer Zelle der Priorei Kingsbridge.«

»Ich habe von Euch schon gehört«, sagte Waleran. »Ihr seid Philip von Gwynedd.«

Das war eine Überraschung. Philip wußte nicht zu sagen, wie ein leibhaftiger Erzdiakon dazu kam, den Namen eines um so viel niedriger gestellten Gottesdieners zu kennen. Immerhin war sein bescheidener Rang gut genug, um Walerans Verhalten zu ändern. Er gab sich auf einmal freundlich und zuvorkommend. »Setzt Euch zu uns ans Feuer«, sagte er. »Gegen einen guten Schluck Glühwein habt Ihr gewiß nichts einzuwenden, oder? Er wärmt das Blut.« Auf seinen Wink sprang eine zerlumpte Gestalt auf, die auf einer Bank an der Wand gesessen hatte.

Philip ging zur Feuerstelle. Waleran flüsterte den anwesenden Männern etwas zu, worauf diese aufstanden und sich verabschiedeten. Philip nahm Platz und wärmte sich die Hände, während Waleran seine Gäste zur Tür begleitete. Philip fragte sich, was das Thema ihres Gesprächs gewesen war und warum der Erzdiakon die Unterredung nicht mit einem Gebet beendet hatte.

Der Diener in den zerlumpten Kleidern reichte ihm einen hölzernen Becher. Philip nippte am heißen, würzigen Glühwein und bedachte seine nächsten Schritte. An wen sollte er sich wenden, wenn der Bischof nicht erreichbar war? Sollte er sich direkt an Graf Bartholomäus wenden und ihn einfach darum bitten, von seiner Rebellion Abstand zu nehmen? Nein, diese Idee war lächerlich: Der Graf würde ihn sofort ins Loch stecken und den Schlüssel fortwerfen. Eigentlich blieb nur noch der Vogt, der – zumindest in der Theorie – die Krone in der Grafschaft vertrat, wobei jedoch niemand voraussagen konnte, auf welche Seite er sich, solange die Thronfolge noch unklar war, schlagen würde. Wie dem auch sei, dachte Philip bei sich, letztlich werde ich das Risiko wohl eingehen müssen. Er sehnte sich bereits nach dem einfachen Leben im Kloster zurück, wo sein gefährlichster Feind Peter von Wareham war.

Walerans Gäste waren verschwunden, die Tür wurde geschlossen, und das Pferdegetrappel unten im Hof verstummte. Waleran kehrte zum Kamin zurück und schob sich einen großen Sessel zurecht. Philip war so sehr mit seinem Problem beschäftigt, daß ihm an einem Gespräch mit dem Erzdiakon wenig lag. Andererseits fühlte er sich zu einem höflichen Auftreten verpflichtet. »Ich hoffe, Ihr habt Eure Unterredung nicht meinetwegen abgebrochen«, sagte er.

Waleran machte eine wegwerfende Handbewegung. »Es war ohnehin an der Zeit«, sagte er. »Diese Angelegenheiten ziehen sich immer ungebührlich in die Länge. Wir sprachen über die Verlängerung der Pachten für Diözesanland. Dergleichen könnte in wenigen Augenblikken geregelt werden, wenn die Beteiligten nur ein wenig mehr Entschlußkraft an den Tag legen wollten.« Er wedelte mit seiner knochigen Hand, als wolle er alle Pachten und Pächter ein für allemal aus seinem Gedächtnis vertreiben. »Wie ich höre, habt Ihr in jener kleinen Zelle im Wald gute Arbeit geleistet.«

»Es überrascht mich, daß Ihr davon gehört habt«, antwortete Philip.

»Der Bischof ist *ex officio* Abt von Kingsbridge. Es ist also seine Pflicht, daran Interesse zu nehmen.«

Vielleicht hat er auch nur einen gut informierten Erzdiakon, dachte Philip bei sich. Doch er sagte: »Der Segen des Herrn lag auf unserer Arbeit.«

»In der Tat.«

Sie unterhielten sich in normannischem Französisch, jener Sprache also, derer sich Waleran auch im Gespräch mit seinen Gästen bedient hatte. Es war die Sprache der Herrschenden. Allerdings glaubte Philip aus einem kleinen Akzent in Walerans Redeweise heraushören zu können, daß seine Muttersprache Englisch war. Er war demnach kein normannischer Aristokrat, sondern ein Engländer, der den Weg nach oben durch eigene Anstrengung geschafft hatte – wie Philip auch.

Philips Vermutung bestätigte sich bereits im nächsten Satz, denn Waleran verfiel von sich aus ins Englische und sagte: »Ich wünschte, der Herr würde seinen Segen auch der Priorei Kingsbridge nicht versagen.«

Ich bin offensichtlich nicht der einzige, der sich über die Zustände in Kingsbridge Gedanken macht, dachte Philip. Waleran weiß anscheinend besser Bescheid als ich. »Wie geht es Prior James?« fragte er.

»Er ist krank«, erwiderte Waleran knapp.

Demnach ist er mit Gewißheit nicht imstande, etwas gegen die Rebellion des Grafen Bartholomäus zu unternehmen, dachte Philip bedrückt. Es bleibt mir nichts anderes übrig – ich muß nach Shiring reiten und mein Glück beim dortigen Vogt versuchen.

Waleran kannte gewiß alles, was Rang und Namen hatte in der Grafschaft. »Kennt Ihr den Vogt von Shiring?« fragte Philip. »Was ist das für ein Mann?«

Der Erzdiakon zuckte mit den Schultern. »Ein gottloser, anmaßender, gieriger und bestechlicher Kerl – wie alle Vögte. Warum fragt Ihr?«

»Wenn ich nicht mit dem Bischof sprechen kann, sollte ich mich vielleicht mit dem Vogt unterhalten.«

»Ich habe das Vertrauen des Bischofs«, sagte Waleran, und ein Lächeln spielte um seine Lippen. »Wenn *ich* Euch behilflich sein kann ...« Er machte eine einladende Handbewegung, wie ein Mann, der weiß, daß seine Großzügigkeit vielleicht gar nicht erwünscht ist.

Philip hatte sich ein wenig beruhigt, hatte es doch anfänglich so ausgesehen, als sei die Stunde der Wahrheit um ein oder zwei Tage aufgeschoben. Jetzt kehrte die innere Angst zurück. Konnte er Erzdiakon Waleran vertrauen? Walerans Gelassenheit war vermutlich gespielt: Er gab sich zurückhaltend, brannte jedoch insgeheim wahrscheinlich darauf zu erfahren, was Philip dem Bischof mitzuteilen hatte.

Es gab eigentlich keinen Grund, ihm zu mißtrauen; er wirkte wie ein Mann, der weiß, was er tut. Aber hatte er wirklich die Macht, den Aufstand zu unterbinden? Wenn nicht, so war er vielleicht imstande, den Bischof aufzutreiben. Waleran das Geheimnis anzuvertrauen, hatte einen entscheidenden Vorteil: Der Bischof hätte darauf bestehen können, daß Philip ihm seine Informationsquelle benannte. Der Erzdiakon hatte dazu nicht das Recht. Er würde sich also mit der Geschichte, die Philip ihm auftischte, zufriedengeben müssen – ob er sie nun glaubte oder nicht.

Wieder lächelte Waleran. »Wenn Ihr noch länger zögert, muß ich wohl annehmen, daß Ihr mir mißtraut!«

Philip hatte Verständnis für den Erzdiakon. Waleran war ihm nicht unähnlich: Er war jung, gut ausgebildet und intelligent und stammte aus einfachen Verhältnissen. Für Philips Geschmack gab er sich ein wenig zu weltlich, doch war dies eine läßliche Sünde für einen Priester, dessen Amtspflichten einen regen Umgang mit Damen und Herren aus höheren Ständen erforderlich machten. Die Abgeschiedenheit des mönchischen Lebens, die auch einen gewissen Schutz bot, war ihm verwehrt. Im Herzen ist Waleran ein gottesfürchtiger Mann, sagte sich Philip. Er wird gewiß im Sinne der Kirche handeln.

Noch zögerte er. Bisher kannten nur Francis und er selbst das Geheimnis. Sobald ein Dritter eingeweiht wurde, war alles möglich. Er holte tief Luft.

»Vor drei Tagen kam ein verletzter Mann in mein Kloster«, begann er schließlich und leistete schweigend Abbitte für seine Lüge. »Er trug

Waffen und ritt auf einem guten und schnellen Pferd. Ein oder zwei Meilen zuvor war er schwer gestürzt. Er muß recht schnell geritten sein, als es passierte, denn er hatte sich nicht nur den Arm, sondern auch einige Rippen gebrochen. Den Arm konnten wir wieder richten, was die Rippen betraf, waren wir jedoch hilflos. Zudem hustete er Blut, was auf innere Verletzungen hindeutete ...« Philip beobachtete während seiner Rede aufmerksam Walerans Miene, die bislang allenfalls höfliches Interesse verriet. »Er war zweifellos in Lebensgefahr, weshalb ich ihm riet, seine Sünden zu bekennen. Und daraufhin vertraute er mir ein Geheimnis an.«

Philip zögerte, denn er wußte nicht, inwieweit Waleran über die neuesten politischen Entwicklungen informiert war. »Ich nehme an, Ihr wißt, daß Stephan von Blois mit dem Segen der Kirche Ansprüche auf den englischen Thron erhebt.«

Waleran wußte sogar mehr als Philip. »Er wurde drei Tage vor Weihnachten in Westminster gekrönt«, ergänzte er.

»Ach ja?« Das hatte selbst Francis noch nicht gewußt.

»Was war das für ein Geheimnis?« fragte Waleran ungeduldig.

Philip nahm seinen Mut zusammen. »Kurz bevor er starb, sagte mir der Reiter, daß sein Herr, der Graf von Shiring, und Robert von Gloucester sich verschworen hätten, einen Aufstand gegen Stephan anzuzetteln.« Philip hielt den Atem an.

Walerans blasse Wangen erbleichten noch mehr. Er beugte sich im Sessel vor und fragte: »Glaubt Ihr, daß der Reiter die Wahrheit gesagt hat?«

»Sterbende pflegen ihrem Beichtvater gegenüber meistens die Wahrheit zu sagen.«

»Vielleicht hat er lediglich ein Gerücht wiedergegeben, das im gräflichen Haushalt herumschwirrte?«

Mit Skepsis von seiten Walerans hatte Philip nicht gerechnet. »Oh, nein«, improvisierte er hastig. »Graf Bartholomäus hatte ihn ausgesandt, um seine Truppen in Hampshire zu alarmieren.«

Walerans kluge Augen prüften Philips Gesicht. »Führte er eine schriftliche Botschaft mit sich?«

»Nein.«

»Kein Siegel oder sonstiges Zeichen der gräflichen Autorität?«

»Nein, nichts.« Philip geriet ins Schwitzen. »Ich nehme an, er war bekannt genug bei den Leuten, die er aufsuchen sollte. Wahrscheinlich war er der offizielle Vertreter des Grafen.«

»Wie hieß er?«

»Francis«, entfuhr es Philip unwillkürlich. Schon im nächsten Augenblick hätte er sich deshalb am liebsten die Zunge abgebissen.

»Sonst nichts?«

»Einen anderen Namen hat er mir nicht genannt.« Philip hatte das Gefühl, Waleran zwinge ihn mit seinen gezielten Fragen zur Preisgabe aller Einzelheiten.

»Und seine Waffen und seine Rüstung? Ließen sie keinen Schluß auf seine Herkunft zu?«

»Eine Rüstung trug er nicht«, erwiderte Philip verzweifelt. »Wir haben ihn mit seinen Waffen beerdigt – Mönche haben keine Verwendung für das Schwert. Man könnte sie natürlich wieder ausgraben – doch ich kann Euch versichern, daß sie keinerlei besondere Kennzeichen trugen. Sie würden Euch mit Sicherheit nicht weiterhelfen ...« Er mußte Waleran irgendwie ablenken. »Was ist, Eurer Ansicht nach, zu tun?«

Waleran runzelte die Stirn. »Das ist schwer zu sagen, zumal uns echte Beweise fehlen. Die Verschwörer können einfach alles abstreiten – und dann muß der Ankläger sich verteidigen.« Die Ergänzung ›... vor allem, wenn sich der Vorwurf als ungerechtfertigt erweist‹, stand unausgesprochen im Raum. »Habt Ihr schon mit jemand anderem darüber gesprochen?« fuhr Waleran fort.

Philip schüttelte den Kopf.

»Wo wollt Ihr denn von hier aus hin?«

»Nach Kingsbridge. Da ich meine Zelle Hals über Kopf verließ, brauchte ich eine glaubhafte Ausrede. Ich sagte also, ich wollte die Priorei besuchen – und das will ich jetzt auch tun, auf daß die Lüge nachträglich zur Wahrheit wird.«

»Sprecht dort zu niemandem über das, was Ihr mir eben erzählt habt.«

»Ihr habt mein Wort.« Philip wunderte sich, warum Waleran darauf so großen Wert legte. Vielleicht aus Eigeninteresse: Wenn er schon das Risiko auf sich nahm, die Verschwörung aufzudecken, dann wollte er auch die Lorbeeren einheimsen. Ehrgeizig war er zweifellos – und das kam Philips Absichten durchaus entgegen.

»Überlaßt diese Angelegenheit mir!« Waleran war auf einmal wieder sehr kurz angebunden. Der krasse Unterschied zu seinem gerade zuvor noch zur Schau getragenen Benehmen verriet Philip, daß Waleran seine Freundlichkeit an- und ablegen konnte wie seine Kleider. Der Erzdiakon fuhr fort: »Nun reitet nach Kingsbridge, aber vergeßt den Vogt.«

»Gewiß.« Philip spürte, daß er die erste Hürde genommen hatte. Ein Stein fiel ihm vom Herzen. Niemand ließ ihn ins Verlies werfen, niemand folterte ihn, um ein Geständnis zu erpressen, niemand warf ihm Verrat vor. Obendrein war er die Verantwortung los – hatte sie abgetreten an jemanden, der anscheinend ganz froh darüber war.

Er erhob sich und ging zum nächsten Fenster. Es war jetzt Nachmittag, würde aber noch eine ganze Weile hell bleiben. Es drängte ihn fortzukommen, nur fort, und das Geheimnis, das ihn belastete, hätte er am liebsten dagelassen ... »Wenn ich jetzt losreite, schaffe ich bis heute abend noch acht bis zehn Meilen«, sagte er.

Waleran hielt ihn nicht auf. »Das heißt, Ihr erreicht gegen Abend den Weiler Bassingbourn. Dort findet Ihr ein Bett für die Nacht. Wenn Ihr Euch im Morgengrauen wieder auf den Weg macht, könnt Ihr mittags in Kingsbridge sein.«

»Ja.« Philip wandte sich vom Fenster ab und sah den Erzdiakon an. Waleran starrte gedankenverloren ins Feuer; er hatte die Stirn gerunzelt. Nur allzugern hätte Philip gewußt, was im Kopf des Mannes vorging, doch Waleran schwieg sich darüber aus. »Ich werde sofort aufbrechen«, sagte er.

Waleran erwachte aus seiner Versonnenheit und war auf einen Schlag wieder freundlich und zuvorkommend. Er lächelte und stand auf. »Wohlan denn!« sagte er, begleitete Philip zur Tür und folgte ihm die Treppen hinab in den Hof.

Ein Stalljunge führte Philips Pferd vor und sattelte es. Waleran hätte sich nun ohne weiteres verabschieden und zum Kaminfeuer zurückkehren können, zog es jedoch vor zu warten. Wahrscheinlich will er ganz sicher sein, daß ich tatsächlich nach Kingsbridge und nicht doch nach Shiring reite, dachte Philip.

Er saß auf und gestand sich ein, daß er sich erheblich wohler fühlte als bei seiner Ankunft. Er wollte sich gerade verabschieden, als er Tom Builder erkannte, den Baumeister, der in diesem Augenblick mit seiner Familie im Schlepptau durchs Tor schritt. Philip wandte sich an Waleran: »Da kommt ein Mann, den ich unterwegs getroffen habe. Er ist Baumeister. Ein anständiger Kerl, wie's scheint, und er hat's nicht leicht in diesem Winter. Vielleicht habt Ihr ein paar Ausbesserungsarbeiten zu erledigen. Ihr werdet bestimmt mit ihm zufrieden sein.«

Waleran gab darauf keine Antwort. Er wirkte völlig fassungslos, all seine Gelassenheit war von ihm abgefallen. Mit offenem Mund starrte er die Familie an. Es war, als habe ihn der Schlag gerührt.

»Was ist Euch?« fragte Philip besorgt.

»Die Frau!« Walerans Stimme war kaum mehr als ein Flüstern. Philip sah sie an. »Sie ist recht hübsch«, sagte er; es war ihm bei ihrer ersten Begegnung gar nicht aufgefallen. »Indes hat man uns gelehrt, daß es für einen Priester ratsam ist, in Keuschheit zu leben. Wendet Euern Blick von ihr, Erzdiakon.«

Waleran hörte ihm gar nicht zu. »Ich dachte, sie sei längst tot«, stammelte er. Dann sah er zu Philip auf und gab sich einen Ruck. »Grüßt mir den Prior von Kingsbridge!« Er versetzte Philips Pferd einen heftigen Schlag aufs Hinterteil; das Tier machte einen Satz und trabte zum Tor hinaus. Als Philip es wieder unter Kontrolle hatte, war er bereits zu weit fort, um sich zu verabschieden.

Zur Mittagsstunde des folgenden Tages lag Kingsbridge vor ihm, genau wie Erzdiakon Waleran vorausgesagt hatte. Von einer bewaldeten Anhöhe bot sich ein weiter Blick über eine leblose, gefrorene Landschaft, deren Eintönigkeit nur durch vereinzelte kahle Baumskelette ein wenig aufgelockert wurde. Nirgendwo war ein Mensch zu sehen, es gab ja keine Feldarbeit, die mitten im Winter zu verrichten gewesen wäre. Ungefähr zwei Meilen weiter, ebenfalls auf einer Anhöhe, ragte die Kathedrale von Kingsbridge empor, ein gewaltiges, gedrungenes Bauwerk, das Philip an ein Denkmal auf einem Grabhügel erinnerte.

Die Straße führte durch eine Senke, und Kingsbridge verschwand vorübergehend aus seinem Blickfeld. Das Pony, ein ruhiges Tier, suchte sich vorsichtig seinen Weg zwischen den gefrorenen Wagenspuren. Philip mußte an Erzdiakon Waleran denken. Der Mann war so selbstsicher und gewandt in seinem Auftreten, daß Philip sich ihm gegenüber jung und naiv vorkam, obwohl der Altersunterschied zwischen ihnen nicht groß sein konnte. Mühelos und ohne seine Gäste zu verprellen, hatte er die Besprechung beendet, hatte aufmerksam angehört, was Philip ihm mitzuteilen wußte, hatte sogleich herausgefunden, daß der schwache Punkt im Mangel an handfesten Beweisen lag – und Philip schließlich fortgeschickt, ohne sich in irgendeiner Form auf eine bestimmte Handlungsweise festzulegen.

Philip verzog das Gesicht zu einem schmerzlichen Grinsen. Erst jetzt erkannte er, wie sehr er sich hatte nasführen lassen. Waleran hatte ihm nicht einmal versprochen, den Bischof über den Verschwörungsplan in Kenntnis zu setzen. Daß Waleran die Informationen nutzbringend einsetzen würde, stand andererseits so gut wie fest – dafür würde schon sein Ehrgeiz sorgen. Vielleicht, dachte Philip, ist er mir sogar dankbar und zeigt sich bei Gelegenheit erkenntlich.

Der Erzdiakon hatte ihn mächtig beeindruckt, das stand fest. Um so mehr verwunderte ihn die einzige Blöße, die Waleran sich gegeben hatte – seine Reaktion auf das Eheweib des Tom Builder. Die Frau war ihm, Philip, gleich bei der ersten Begegnung in einer gewissen, unbestimmten Weise gefährlich erschienen. Waleran war offenbar für ihre Reize empfänglich, was unter dem Strich natürlich auf dasselbe hinauslief. Aber da mußte noch etwas anderes sein, hatte der Erzdiakon doch gesagt: *Ich dachte, sie sei längst tot.* Es klang fast, als hätte er in weit zurückliegender Zeit mit ihr gesündigt. Nach der Art zu urteilen, wie er mich fortschickte, muß er ein schlechtes Gewissen haben, dachte Philip. Er wollte zweifellos vermeiden, daß ich noch mehr erfuhr ...

Insgesamt vermochte aber auch die Episode mit der Frau das Bild, das Philip sich von Waleran gemacht hatte, nicht sonderlich zu beeinträchtigen. Waleran war ein Priester, kein Mönch. Keuschheit war von jeher ein wesentlicher Bestandteil des klösterlichen Lebens gewesen, den Priestern jedoch niemals zwingend auferlegt worden. Bischöfe hatten Mätressen und Dorfpfarrer Haushälterinnen. So wie es unmöglich war, böse Gedanken zu untersagen, war auch der Zölibat ein Gesetz, das sich kaum durchsetzen ließ. Wenn der Herr lüsternen Priestern nicht vergeben konnte, dann kamen nur sehr wenige Gottesdiener in den Himmel.

Von der nächsten Anhöhe aus war Kingsbridge wieder zu sehen. Die gewaltige Kirche mit ihren vielen Rundbögen und kleinen, tiefliegenden Fenstern beherrschte die ganze Umgebung. In gleicher Weise dominierte das Kloster das Dorf. Die Westfassade der Kathedrale, die sich Philips Blicken bot, war mit gedrungenen Zwillingstürmen versehen, von denen einer vor vier Jahren vom Blitz getroffen und eingestürzt war. Er war noch immer nicht wiederaufgebaut worden und trug wesentlich zu dem erbärmlichen Erscheinungsbild der Kathedrale bei. Philip regte sich bei jedem Besuch von neuem darüber auf, für ihn war der Trümmerhaufen vor dem Portal eine ständige, beschämende Erinnerung an den Verfall der klösterlichen Moral in Kingsbridge.

Um die Kirche herum gruppierten sich, wie Verschwörer um einen Thron, die aus dem gleichen hellen Kalkstein errichteten Klostergebäude, und außerhalb der niedrigen Mauer, die das Klostergelände umgab, standen vereinzelte reetgedeckte Hütten aus Lehm und Holz. Hier wohnten die Bauern, die die Felder in der Umgebung bestellten, sowie die Diener der Mönche. Ein schmales, ungeduldiges Flüßchen plätscherte durch die Südwestecke des Dorfs und versorgte das Kloster mit Wasser. Eine alte Holzbrücke führte hinüber. Als Philip sie erreichte, spürte er einmal mehr, wie gallebitterer Zorn sich seiner bemächtigte. Die Priorei Kingsbridge war ein Schandmal der Kirche und des Klosterwesens, und er, Philip, konnte nichts dagegen tun. Seine Wut und die Erkenntnis seiner Machtlosigkeit stießen ihm bitter im Magen auf.

Die Priorei war Eigentümerin der Brücke und erhob einen Brückenzoll. Die Bohlen knackten und quietschten unter dem Gewicht von Philip und seinem Pferd. Das Geräusch lockte am jenseitigen Ufer einen alten Mönch aus seinem Verschlag. Er erkannte Philip, winkte ihm zu und entfernte den alten Weidenast, der als eine Art Schranke diente. Philip fiel auf, daß der alte Mann hinkte. »Was ist mit deinem Fuß, Bruder Paul?«

»Bloß eine Frostbeule. Das wird sich im nächsten Frühjahr schon geben.«

Er trug lediglich Sandalen an den Füßen. Paul war ein zäher Bursche. Trotzdem war es im Grunde unbarmherzig, einen Mann im fortgeschrittenen Alter bei dieser Kälte den ganzen Tag im Freien zubringen zu lassen. »Du solltest ein Feuer haben, an dem du dich wärmen kannst«, sagte Philip.

»Das wäre ein Segen!« seufzte Paul. »Aber Bruder Remigius meint, das Feuerholz wäre teurer als die gesamten Einkünfte aus dem Brückenzoll.«

»Wieviel verlangen wir denn?«

»Pro Mann einen Farthing. Und einen Penny fürs Pferd.«

»Wird die Brücke von vielen Menschen benutzt?«

»O ja, von sehr vielen.«

»Wieso können wir uns dann kein Feuerholz leisten?«

»Nun ja – die Mönche bezahlen natürlich keinen Brückenzoll, genausowenig wie die Diener der Priorei und die Dorfbewohner. Alle paar Tage kommt einmal ein fahrender Ritter vorbei oder ein Kesselflicker auf Wanderschaft. Ja, und dann natürlich an hohen Feiertagen, wenn Leute aus der ganzen Grafschaft zum Gottesdienst in die Kathedrale streben, da kommen 'ne Menge Farthings zusammen.«

»Da wär's doch wohl am besten, die Brücke nur an Feiertagen zu bemannen und dir von den Einkünften Feuerholz zu kaufen.«

»Bitte, Bruder«, erwiderte Paul ängstlich, »sag Remigius nichts davon! Wenn er glaubt, ich hätte mich beklagt, wird er sehr ungehalten sein.«

»Keine Sorge«, sagte Philip und trat seinem Pferd in die Flanken. Er wollte nicht, daß Paul sein Gesicht sah. Unfähigkeit und Dummheit regten ihn maßlos auf. Sein ganzes Leben hatte Paul dem Herrn und dem Kloster gedient, und nun, im Herbst seines Lebens, zwang man ihn dazu, wegen ein oder zwei Farthing am Tag bei klirrendem Frost im Brückenhäuschen auszuharren. Das war nicht nur grausam, sondern auch völlig überflüssig. Ein geduldiger alter Mann wie Paul konnte viel sinnvollere Aufgaben erfüllen – Hühner züchten zum Beispiel –, was auch von den Einkünften her für die Priorei viel günstiger wäre als der kümmerliche Brückenzoll. Doch der Prior war eben zu alt und zu träge, und für Remigius, den Subprior, galt offenbar das gleiche.

Es ist eine schwere Sünde, dachte Philip, so nachlässig mit den menschlichen und materiellen Werten umzugehen, die aus tiefer Frömmigkeit und Liebe dem Herrn überantwortet sind.

In unversöhnlicher Stimmung dirigierte er sein Pony an den einfachen Hütten vorbei zum Tor der Priorei. Der Klosterhof bildete ein Rechteck, in dessen Mitte sich die Kathedrale erhob. Alle Gebäude nördlich und westlich der Kirche dienten weltlichen und praktischen Zwecken, während die Baulichkeiten im Osten und Süden privat oder zu geistlichen Verrichtungen genutzt wurden.

Der Eingang zum Klosterhof befand sich aus diesem Grunde an der Nordwestecke des Rechtecks. Das Tor stand offen, und der junge Mönch im Wachhäuschen winkte Philip zu. Gleich hinter dem Tor, an der Westmauer, war der Stall, ein massiver Holzbau, der stabiler wirkte als so manch eine menschliche Unterkunft jenseits der Mauer. Auf Strohballen hockten zwei Stallburschen – keine Mönche, sondern weltliche Hilfskräfte der Priorei. Als Philip mit seinem Pferd eintrat, erhoben sie sich widerwillig, sichtlich wenig erfreut über die zusätzliche Arbeit, die ihnen der Besucher einbrockte.

Ein scharfer Geruch drang Philip in die Nase. Er erkannte sofort, daß der Stall schon drei oder vier Wochen nicht mehr ausgemistet worden war. In seiner ohnehin schon gereizten Laune fand er sich nicht bereit, den Burschen ihre Nachlässigkeit durchgehen zu lassen. »Bevor ihr mein Pony einstellt«, sagte er daher zu ihnen, »mistet den Stellplatz aus und streut frisches Stroh. Danach säubert auch den Rest des Stalls. Dauerfeuchtes Stroh führt zu Huffäule. Ihr seid nicht so überarbeitet, daß ihr nicht ab und zu den Stall ausmisten könntet!« Griesgrämig und verstockt sahen die beiden ihn an, so daß Philip drohend hinzufügte: »Tut, was ich euch sage, sonst sorge ich dafür, daß euch wegen Faulheit ein ganzer Tageslohn gestrichen wird.« Er wandte sich zum Gehen, doch dann fiel ihm noch etwas ein: »In meiner Satteltasche findet sich ein Käse. Bringt ihn in die Küche zu Bruder Milius.«

Er ging, ohne eine Antwort abzuwarten. Sechzig Hilfskräfte waren in der Priorei angestellt und bedienten fünfundvierzig Mönche – ein schandbares Mißverhältnis in Philips Augen. Unterbeschäftigtes Personal neigte dazu, aus lauter Trägheit die wenigen ihm verbliebenen Pflichten auch noch zu vernachlässigen; die beiden Stallburschen bewiesen es einmal mehr.

Philip ging an der Westmauer entlang, bis er das Gästehaus erreichte. Er fragte sich, ob außer ihm noch andere Besucher im Kloster weilten. Der große Innenraum des Hauses war jedoch kalt und unbelebt; auf der Schwelle staute sich vom Wind zusammengetriebenes Laub aus dem vergangenen Herbst. Er wandte sich nach links und überquerte den großen, mit spärlichem Gras bewachsenen Platz, der das Gästehaus – wo mitunter wenig frommes Gelichter oder gar Frauen übernachteten – von der Kirche trennte. Der Haupteingang befand sich auf der Westseite. Die Trümmer des eingestürzten Turms lagen immer noch dort, wo sie hingefallen waren, und bildeten einen großen, doppelmannshohen Haufen.

Wie die meisten Kirchen hatte auch die Kathedrale von Kingsbridge einen kreuzförmigen Grundriß. Der Westteil öffnete sich zu einem Schiff, das dem senkrechten Kreuzbalken entsprach. Der waagerechte Balken zweigte in Höhe des Altars ab und bestand aus dem nördlichen und dem südlichen Arm des Querschiffs. Der Chor jenseits der Querschiffe war im wesentlichen den Mönchen vorbehalten. Am äußersten Ende lag das Grabmal des heiligen Adolphus, das gelegentlich noch Ziel von Pilgerfahrten war.

Philip betrat das Mittelschiff. Zur Rechten und zur Linken lagen die düsteren Alleen der Rundbögen und mächtigen Säulen. Ihr Anblick war nicht dazu angetan, seine Stimmung zu heben, im Gegenteil. Der Zustand des Gebäudes hatte sich seit seinem letzten Besuch noch verschlechtert. Die Fenster in den niedrigen Seitenschiffen wirkten in den ungeheuer dicken Mauern wie schmale Tunnelröhren. Hoch oben im Dach fiel durch die größeren Fenster des Obergadens genug Licht auf die Deckengemälde, um zu zeigen, wie stark sie bereits verblaßt waren. Die Apostel- und Heiligengestalten waren nur mehr trübe Schatten, die sich stellenweise kaum noch vom Hintergrund abhoben. Trotz des kalten Winds, der durch die scheibenlosen Fensterhöhlen fegte, hing ein leicht modriger Geruch wie nach verrottenden Kleidern in der Luft. Vom anderen Ende her, wo gerade ein Hochamt gehalten wurde, drang der feierliche Sprechgesang der lateinischen Liturgie herüber. Philip durchmaß das Mittelschiff. Der Boden war nie gepflastert worden; in Ecken und Winkeln, die von den Holzschuhen der Bauern und den Sandalen der Mönche nur selten betreten wurden, wuchs Moos auf dem nackten Erdboden. Die gemeißelten Spiralen und Kannelierungen der massiven Säulen sowie die Zackenfriese, die die verbindenden Bögen schmückten, waren einstmals bemalt und vergoldet gewesen. Geblieben waren lediglich hier und da einige Reste papierdünnen Blattgolds, und ein unregelmäßiges Fleckenmuster deutete an, wo einst Farbe gewesen war. Der Mörtel zwischen den Steinen war bröckelig, fiel heraus und stapelte sich am Fuß der Mauern zu kleinen Häufchen. Philip spürte, wie der nun schon vertraute Zorn von neuem in ihm hochstieg. Die Besucher dieser Kirche sollten eigentlich Ehrfurcht empfinden vor der Majestät des Allmächtigen. Aber die Bauern waren einfache Leute, die die Dinge nach dem Augenschein beurteilten. Beim Anblick dieser Kirche hielten sie den Herrn wahrscheinlich für eine nachlässige, gleichgültige Gottheit, die nicht imstande war, ihre Sünden zu erkennen und die Verehrung, die sie ihm entgegenbrachten, zu würdigen. Und gerade sie, die Bauern, waren es doch, die mit ihrer Arbeit und ihrem Schweiß die Kirche trugen! Es war eine Schande, es ihnen mit diesem zerfallenen Mausoleum zu lohnen!

Philip kniete vor dem Altar nieder und verharrte dort eine Weile, denn Zorn, so berechtigt er sein mochte, vertrug sich nicht mit Andacht und Gebet. Erst als er sich ein wenig beruhigt hatte, erhob er sich wieder und ging weiter.

Der Ostflügel der Kirche war zweigeteilt. Gleich hinter der Mitte befand sich der Chor mit hölzernem Gestühl; dort saßen und standen während der Gottesdienste die Mönche. Dahinter lag der Schrein mit dem Grabmal des Heiligen. Philip ging um den Altar herum. Er wollte sich im Chor einen Platz suchen. Doch dann blieb er unwillkürlich stehen, denn ein Sarg versperrte ihm den Weg.

Er war vollkommen überrascht. Niemand hatte ihm gesagt, daß ein Mönch gestorben war – aber er hatte ja seit seiner Ankunft auch nur mit drei Personen gesprochen, mit dem alten Paul, der schon ein bißchen geistesabwesend war, und mit den beiden Stallburschen, die er nicht eben zu Vertraulichkeiten ermuntert hatte. Er trat näher an den Sarg heran, um zu sehen, wer der Tote war. Ihm stockte der Atem.

Es war Prior James.

Mit offenem Mund starrte Philip die Leiche an. Mit einemmal sah alles anders aus! – Ein neuer Prior würde Einzug halten, es gab neue Hoffnung ...

Die heimliche Freude war eine unbillige Reaktion auf den Tod eines verehrungswürdigen Bruders, und mochte er noch so gefehlt haben, Philip zwang sich zu einer Haltung, die dem traurigen Anlaß angemessen war. Aufmerksam studierte er den Ausdruck des Toten. In seinen letzten Jahren war James ein gebeugter, schmalgesichtiger Mann mit schlohweißem Haar gewesen. Von der für ihn so typischen Leidensmiene war jetzt nichts mehr zu sehen; aller Kummer und alle Verzweiflung waren aus seinem Antlitz gewichen. Er hatte Frieden gefunden. Philip kniete neben der Totenbahre nieder und fragte sich, worunter der alte Mann in seinen späten Jahren so gelitten hatte. Gab es da vielleicht eine Sünde, die er nie zu bekennen gewagt hatte? Hatte er um eine Frau getrauert oder einem Unschuldigen Unrecht zugefügt? Was immer es sein mochte – James würde erst am Tag des Jüngsten Gerichts darüber sprechen.

Die Gedanken über die Zukunft ließen sich trotz bester Absichten nicht vertreiben. Prior James, ein furchtsamer Mann ohne Entschlußkraft und Rückgrat, hatte das Kloster langsam verfallen lassen. Nun würde ein frischer Wind wehen. Ein neuer Mann würde kommen, die arbeitsscheuen Diener und Knechte in die Pflicht nehmen, den eingestürzten Kirchturm wieder aufbauen lassen und den gewaltigen natürlichen Reichtum der Priorei sinnvoll nutzen. Das Kloster würde wieder zu einer großen moralischen Macht werden. Philip war zu aufgeregt, um länger stillzuhalten. Er erhob sich und schritt mit ungewohnter Leichtigkeit zum Chor, wo er sich auf einer der hinteren Bänke einen freien Platz suchte.

Andrew von York, der Sakristan, leitete den Gottesdienst. Er war ein leicht erregbarer, rotgesichtiger Mann, der immer so aussah, als würde ihn im nächsten Augenblick der Schlag treffen. Er gehörte zu den Klosteroffizialen, die für die Verwaltung zuständig waren. In seinen Verantwortungsbereich fielen die Gestaltung der Gottesdienste, die heiligen Bücher und Reliquien, die liturgischen Gewänder und die Kirchendekoration, vor allem aber auch die Instandhaltung der Kirche. Er hatte einen Kantor unter sich, der für die Musik zuständig war, und einen Schatzmeister, dem die Aufsicht über die juwelenge-schmückten goldenen und silbernen Kerzenhalter und Kelche und die anderen geweihten Gefäße oblag. Über dem Sakristan standen ledig-lich noch der Prior und Subprior Remigius, mit dem Andrew seit langem eng befreundet war.

Andrew las die Psalmen mit kaum verhülltem Zorn, so wie es seine Art war. Philip war noch immer ganz durcheinander, weshalb ihm erst nach geraumer Zeit auffiel, daß der Gottesdienst nicht in der gebote-nen Form stattfand. Da gab es eine Gruppe jüngerer Mönche, die herumalberten und sich ungeniert unterhielten. Philip erkannte bald, daß sie sich über den alten Novizenmeister lustig machten, der auf seinem Sitz eingenickt war. Die meisten von ihnen waren erst vor kurzem aus seiner Obhut entlassen worden und erinnerten sich wahr-scheinlich noch gut an die harte Hand, mit der er sie geführt hatte. Sie schnippten Dreckkügelchen nach ihm. Jedesmal, wenn sein Ge-sicht getroffen wurde, zuckte er zusammen und bewegte sich unruhig hin und her, ohne jedoch aufzuwachen. Andrew schien von alledem nichts zu bemerken. Philip hielt nach dem Cirkator Ausschau, der für die Aufrechterhaltung der Disziplin zuständig war. Der Mönch saß auf der anderen Seite des Chors und war in die Unterhaltung mit einem Mitbruder vertieft. Er achtete weder auf den Gottesdienst noch auf das ungebührliche Benehmen der jungen Mönche.

Philip wartete noch einen Augenblick, obgleich seine Geduld schon am Ende war. Anführer der Rabauken war, wie es schien, ein gutaussehender Bursche von vielleicht einundzwanzig Jahren, der ein besonders unverschämtes Grinsen zur Schau trug. Philip sah, wie er mit seinem Eßmesser in eine brennende Kerze langte und dem Novi-zenmeister flüssigen Talg auf die Glatze spritzte. Mit einem Schrei fuhr der alte Mann aus dem Schlaf, als das heiße Fett auf seiner Kopfhaut landete. Die jungen Mönche platzten schier vor Lachen.

Philip erhob sich seufzend. Er packte den Rädelsführer von hinten am Ohr und zerrte ihn unsanft aus dem Chor ins südliche Querschiff. Andrew sah von seinem Gebetbuch auf und runzelte die Stirn, als er Philip erblickte. Die Unruhe zuvor war ihm völlig entgangen.

Außer Hörweite der anderen Mönche blieb Philip stehen und ließ das Ohr des jungen Mannes los. »Name?« fragte er.

»William Beauvis.«

»Welcher Teufel ist während des Hochamts in dich gefahren?«

»Die Messe ödet mich an«, gab William mürrisch zurück.

Für Mönche, die sich über ihr Schicksal beklagten, hatte Philip nicht das geringste Mitgefühl. »Ödet dich an?« wiederholte er mit erhobener Stimme. »Was hast du denn heute sonst noch getan?«

Trotzig erwiderte William: »Matutin und Laudes mitten in der Nacht, Prim vor dem Frühstück, dann Terz, Hauptmesse, Studium und nun das Hochamt ...«

»Hast du auch gegessen?«

»Ja, Frühstück.«

»Und jetzt willst du zu Mittag essen?«

»Ja.«

»Die meisten Menschen deines Alters arbeiten von Sonnenaufgang bis Sonnenuntergang im Schweiße ihres Angesichts auf den Feldern, um sich ihr Frühstück und ihr Mittagessen zu verdienen ... Und dabei fällt auch immer noch etwas für dich mit ab! Weißt du eigentlich, warum sie das tun?«

»Ja«, sagte William, trat unruhig von einem Fuß auf den anderen und blickte zu Boden.

»Also?«

»Sie tun es, weil sie wollen, daß die Mönche für sie beten.«

»Richtig. Brot, Fleisch und das aus Steinen erbaute Dormitorium, in dem im Winter ein warmes Feuer brennt, verdankst du der harten Arbeit der Bauern. Und du bist so müde und angeödet, daß du für sie nicht einmal während des Hochamts stillhalten kannst!«

»Es tut mir leid, Bruder.«

Philip betrachtete den jungen Mann aufmerksam. William war kein böswilliger Kerl. Die Hauptschuld lag bei seinen Oberen, deren lasches Regiment ein solches Betragen in der Kirche duldete. »Warum bist du Mönch geworden, wenn dich der Gottesdienst langweilt?« fragte Philip in milderem Ton.

»Ich bin meines Vaters fünfter Sohn.«

Philip nickte. »Dafür, daß die Priorei dich aufnahm, hat er ihr bestimmt ein gutes Stück Land übereignet, wie?«

»Ja, einen ganzen Hof.«

Es war immer die gleiche Geschichte: Ein Mann, der zu viele Söhne hatte, schenkte einen von ihnen dem Herrn. Und um sicherzustellen, daß dieser das Geschenk nicht zurückwies, gab er ihm noch ein Stück Land mit, das groß genug war, um dem Sprößling ein karges Auskommen in mönchischer Armut zu ermöglichen. Auf diese Weise wurden viele junge Leute Mönche, obwohl ihnen die innere Berufung dazu fehlte. Kein Wunder, daß sie es mit dem Gehorsam nicht so genau nahmen.

»Angenommen«, sagte Philip, »du würdest versetzt – auf einen kleinen Gutshof vielleicht, oder du kämest zu mir in meine kleine Zelle im Wald, wo es eine Menge Feldarbeit gibt und die Andachten vergleichsweise wenig Zeit in Anspruch nehmen – was meinst du, würde es dir da leichter fallen, in Frömmigkeit und Anstand an den Gottesdiensten teilzunehmen?«

Williams Miene hellte sich auf. »Ja, Bruder, ich glaube, es würde mir leichter fallen.«

»Das dachte ich mir. Ich werde sehen, was sich tun läßt. Mach dir aber keine allzu großen Hoffnungen. Vielleicht mußt du warten, bis wir einen neuen Prior haben, und bei ihm selbst um die Versetzung einkommen.«

»Ich danke Euch auf jeden Fall sehr.«

Der Gottesdienst war vorüber, und die Mönche verließen die Kirche in einer kleiner Prozession. Philip legte zum Zeichen, daß er die Unterredung für beendet hielt, den Zeigefinger auf die Lippen. Als die Mönche vorbeikamen, schlossen sich Philip und William an und folgten ihnen hinaus in den quadratischen Kreuzgang, der an die Südflanke des Kirchenschiffs anschloß und ringsum von Arkaden umgeben war. Dort löste sich die Prozession auf. Philip wollte sich Richtung Küche entfernen, sah sich jedoch urplötzlich dem Sakristan gegenüber. Breitbeinig, die Hände in die Hüften gestemmt, versperrte der Mann ihm den Weg. »Bruder Philip«, tönte er.

»Bruder Andrew ...«, antwortete Philip und dachte bei sich: Was ist denn in den gefahren?

»Was fällt dir ein, mein Hochamt zu stören?«

Philip wußte nicht, wie ihm geschah. »Dein Hochamt zu stören?« wiederholte er ungläubig. »Der junge Mann betrug sich höchst ungebührlich. Er ...«

»Ich bin durchaus imstande, mit ungebührlichem Betragen während meines Gottesdienstes selbst fertig zu werden«, unterbrach ihn Andrew mit erhobener Stimme. Die Mönche, die begonnen hatten, sich zu zerstreuen, hielten inne und blieben in der Nähe, um ja nichts zu versäumen.

Philip konnte die Aufregung nicht verstehen. Junge Mönche und Novizen mußten gelegentlich während der Gottesdienste zur Ordnung gerufen werden, das blieb nicht aus, und diese Aufgabe fiel nun einmal den älteren Brüdern zu. Es gab keine Regel, die besagte, daß nur der Sakristan das Recht dazu hatte. »Du hast doch gar nicht gesehen, was geschehen ist ...«, begann Philip.

»Vielleicht doch, Bruder Philip. Vielleicht hatte ich lediglich vor, die Angelegenheit später zu bereinigen ...«

Er hat bestimmt nichts bemerkt, dachte Philip und stellte die herausfordernde Frage: »Gut, dann sag es mir. Was hast du gesehen?«

»Bilde dir ja nicht ein, du könntest mich einem Verhör unterziehen!« brüllte Andrew, und sein Gesicht lief purpurrot an. »Du magst in deiner kleinen Zelle draußen im Wald Prior sein, meinetwegen. Aber ich bin hier seit zwölf Jahren Sakristan und werde die Gottesdienste in dieser Kathedrale nach meinem eigenen Gutdünken halten – und ohne die Einmischung von Fremden, die nicht halb so alt sind wie ich.«

Vielleicht habe ich mich wirklich nicht ganz korrekt verhalten, dachte Philip. Warum wäre Andrew sonst so wütend? Was jedoch viel wichtiger war: Ein Streit im Kreuzgang war für die anderen Mönche alles andere als erbaulich und durfte nicht fortgeführt werden. Zähneknirschend schluckte Philip seinen Stolz hinunter und beugte untertänig das Haupt. »Ich sehe meine Verfehlung ein, Bruder, und erbitte demütig deine Verzeihung.«

Andrew hatte sich auf ein längeres Wortgefecht eingerichtet, weshalb ihm der frühe Rückzug seines Kontrahenten überhaupt nicht gefiel. »Sieh zu, daß so etwas nicht noch einmal geschieht«, sagte er ungnädig.

Philip verzichtete auf eine Antwort. Es stand außer Frage, daß Andrew das letzte Wort haben mußte, so daß jede weitere Bemerkung nur wieder eine neue Replik herausfordern würde. Er blieb noch ein paar Augenblicke mit gesenktem Blick an Ort und Stelle stehen und biß sich auf die Zunge, während Andrews strafender Blick auf ihm ruhte. Endlich drehte sich der Sakristan auf dem Absatz um und schritt hocherhobenen Hauptes von dannen.

Die Mönche starrten Philip an. Die Erniedrigung, die er soeben erfahren hatte, ärgerte ihn, doch nahm er sie hin, denn ein stolzer Mönch war ein schlechter Mönch. Ohne ein weiteres Wort zu verlieren, verließ er den Kreuzgang.

Die Wohnquartiere der Mönche befanden sich auf der Südseite des Klostergeländes: das Dormitorium in der Südost-, das Refektorium in der Südwestecke. Philip wandte sich nach Westen, durchquerte das Refektorium und trat ins Freie, so daß sein Blick nun wieder auf das Gästehaus und die Stallungen fiel. Hier in der Südwestecke des Geländes lag der Küchenhof, der von drei Seiten eingefaßt war: von der Küche selbst, vom Refektorium, vom Backhaus und von der Brauerei.

Ein hoch mit Rüben beladener Karren stand im Hof und wartete darauf, entladen zu werden. Philip stieg die Treppen zur Küchentür empor und trat ein.

Drinnen herrschte eine fast erstickende Atmosphäre. Der Geruch nach bratendem Fisch hing schwer in der Luft; es klirrten und klapperten die Pfannen, und durch die Hitze gedämpfte Befehle und Anweisungen schwirrten durch den Raum. Drei Köche, ein jeder vor Eile rotgesichtig und verschwitzt, bereiteten mit Hilfe von sechs oder sieben Küchenjungen das Mahl. An beiden Enden der Küche befand sich eine große Feuerstelle; die Flammen loderten hell auf, und darüber brutzelten je zwanzig oder mehr Fische an Spießen, die von zwei Küchenjungen, denen der Schweiß in Strömen übers Gesicht lief, langsam gedreht wurden. Der Fischgeruch ließ Philip das Wasser im Munde zusammenlaufen. In großen Eisentöpfen, die über den Flammen hingen, kochten Karotten. An einem Hackbrett standen zwei junge Männer und schnitten armlange Weißbrote auf, die als Unterlagen für die Speisen benutzt wurden. Aufseher über das scheinbare Chaos war Bruder Milius, der Küchenmeister, ein Mann ungefähr in Philips Alter. Er thronte auf einem hohen Stuhl und betrachtete das aufgeregte Hin und Her mit seelenruhigem Lächeln, als wäre alles in bester Ordnung (was nach seiner persönlichen Erfahrung wahrscheinlich sogar stimmte). Er lächelte auch Philip an und sagte: »Vielen Dank für den Käse.«

»Ach ja!« Philip hatte sein Mitbringsel schon fast vergessen – so viel war seit seiner Ankunft geschehen. »Er ist ausschließlich aus Morgenmilch gemacht. Du wirst es am Geschmack merken, er ist ein bißchen anders.«

»Ich bin schon ganz versessen darauf. Aber sag an, Bruder, warum schaust du so verdrießlich drein? Ist etwas geschehen?«

»Nein, nichts. Ich hatte lediglich eine Auseinandersetzung mit Andrew.« Philip machte eine abfällige Handbewegung. »Kann ich mir einen heißen Stein vom Feuer nehmen?«

»Natürlich.«

Im Küchenfeuer pflegten immer einige Steine zu liegen, die man zum schnellen Erhitzen kleinerer Mengen Wasser oder Suppe herausnehmen konnte. »Bruder Paul, der Mann im Brückenhäuschen, hat eine Frostbeule, und Remigius gibt ihm kein Feuerholz«, erklärte Philip. Er ergriff eine langarmige Zange und zog einen der heißen Steine aus dem Feuer.

Milius öffnete einen Schrank und holte ein Stück altes Leder hervor, das früher einmal eine Schürze gewesen sein mochte. »Hier«, sagte er, »da hast du was zum Einwickeln.«

»Ich danke dir.« Philip legte den Stein in die Mitte des Lederstücks und hob es vorsichtig an den vier Zipfeln auf.

»Beeil dich«, sagte Milius. »Es gibt gleich Essen.«

Philip winkte ihm kurz zu. Über den Küchenhof erreichte er das Tor. Zu seiner Linken, gleich neben der Westmauer, stand die Mühle. Vor vielen Jahren hatte man oberhalb der Priorei einen Kanal gegraben, der den Mühlenteich mit Flußwasser versorgte. Das Wasser trieb das Mühlrad an und floß von dort aus unterirdisch zur Brauerei und zur Küche. Es speiste auch den Brunnen im Kreuzgang, wo sich die Mönche vor dem Essen die Hände wuschen, sowie die neben dem Dormitorium gelegene Latrine. Dahinter bog der Kanal gen Süden und mündete wieder in den Fluß. Die Anlage entsprang der weitsichtigen Planung eines ehemaligen Priors.

Vor dem Stall lag ein Haufen schmutziges Stroh. Die Burschen folgten also Philips Befehl und misteten aus. Philip durchschritt das Tor und begab sich zur Brücke; der Weg führte ihn durch das Dorf.

War es anmaßend von mir, den jungen William Beauvis zu tadeln? fragte er sich. Nein, ich habe mir nichts vorzuwerfen. Im Gegenteil, es wäre sündhaft gewesen, wenn ich eine derartige Störung des Gottesdienstes tatenlos hingenommen hätte.

Er erreichte die Brücke und steckte den Kopf in Pauls kleinen Unterschlupf. »Hier, wärme daran deine Füße!« sagte er und reichte ihm das Lederbündel mit dem heißen Stein. »Wenn er ein bißchen abgekühlt ist, nimm ihn heraus und stell deine Füße direkt auf den Stein. Die Wärme müßte eigentlich bis heute abend vorhalten.«

Bruder Paul schlüpfte aus den Sandalen und stellte seine Füße sofort auf das warme Bündel. »Ich spüre schon, wie der Schmerz nachläßt«, sagte er dankbar.

»Wenn du den Stein heute abend ins Küchenfeuer legst, ist er morgen früh wieder heiß«, bemerkte Philip.

»Und Bruder Milius ist damit einverstanden?« fragte Paul aufgeregt.

»Mein Wort darauf.«

»Du bist sehr gut zu mir, Bruder Philip.«

»Das ist doch selbstverständlich.« Philip verabschiedete sich, bevor Pauls Dankesbekundungen peinlich wurden. Es ging schließlich nur um einen heißen Stein.

Er kehrte zurück in die Priorei, wusch sich im steinernen Becken an der Südwand des Kreuzgangs die Hände und betrat das Refektorium. An einem Stehpult stand ein Mönch und las mit lauter Stimme vor. Das Essen sollte, so wollte es die Regel, abgesehen von der Tischlesung, schweigend eingenommen werden. Dennoch hörte man nicht nur die Eßgeräusche der ungefähr vierzig Mönche, sondern auch ständiges, regelwidriges Geflüster. Philip ließ sich an einem der langen Tische auf einem freien Platz nieder. Der Mönch neben ihm verspeiste sein Mahl mit sichtlichem Behagen. Er sah Philip an und murmelte: »Heute gibt es frischen Fisch!«

Philip nickte. Er wußte es bereits. Sein Magen knurrte.

»Wie ich höre, gibt es bei euch draußen im Wald täglich frischen Fisch«, sagte der Mönch nicht ohne neidvollen Unterton in der Stimme.

Philip schüttelte den Kopf. »Jeden zweiten Tag gibt es Geflügel«, flüsterte er.

Seine Antwort machte den Mitbruder nur noch neidischer. »Hier gibt's sechsmal in der Woche Pökelfisch.«

Ein Diener legte eine große Weißbrotscheibe vor Philip auf den Tisch und belegte sie mit einem gebratenen Fisch, der nach Bruder Milius' Kräuterwürze duftete. Philip holte sein Eßmesser hervor und wollte gerade zulangen, als sich am anderen Ende des Tisches ein Mönch erhob und mit dem Finger auf ihn zeigte. Es war der Cirkator oder Aufseher. Was gibt's jetzt schon wieder? dachte Philip.

Der Cirkator brach – wozu er berechtigt war – das Schweigegebot: »Bruder Philip!«

Alle Mönche hörten auf zu essen, und es herrschte absolute Stille im Refektorium.

Auch Philip, das Eßmesser noch auf den Fisch gerichtet, hielt inne und blickte erwartungsvoll auf.

»Wer zu spät kommt, bekommt nichts zu essen«, sagte der Cirkator. »So will es die Regel.«

Philip seufzte. An diesem Tag schien wirklich alles schiefzugehen. Er legte das Messer beiseite, gab dem Diener das Brot mitsamt dem Fisch zurück und beugte den Kopf, um der Tischlesung zu lauschen.

In der Ruhestunde nach dem Essen ging Philip ins Vorratslager unterhalb der Küche und unterhielt sich mit Cuthbert Whitehead, dem Cellerar. Das Lager war ein großes, dunkles Gewölbe mit winzigen Fenstern, das von kurzen, stämmigen Pfeilern getragen wurde. Die Luft war trocken und gesättigt vom Duft der hier lagernden Schätze: Hopfen und Honig, eingelagerte Äpfel und getrocknete Kräuter, Käse und Essig. Bruder Cuthbert war meistens hier unten zu finden, denn seine vielfältigen Pflichten ließen ihm nicht viel Zeit für Gottesdienste, was jedoch seinen Neigungen durchaus zupaß kam: Er war ein fähiger Bursche, der mit beiden Beinen im Leben stand und für spirituelle Dinge nicht allzuviel übrig hatte. Als Cellerar war er gleichsam das für die materiellen Dinge zuständige Pendant des Sakristans, denn in seinen Aufgabenbereich fielen alle praktischen Bedürfnisse der Mönche: Er mußte die auf den Klostergütern hergestellten Waren zum Markt bringen und jene Versorgungsgüter herbeischaffen, die von den Mönchen und ihren Bediensteten nicht selbst produziert wurden. Es war eine Aufgabe, die großes Organisationstalent und sorgfältige Berechnungen erforderte. Cuthbert war allerdings nicht ganz auf sich allein gestellt: Milius, der Küchenmeister, trug die Verantwortung für die täglichen Mahlzeiten, und es gab auch einen Kammerdiener, der sich um die Kleidung der Mönche kümmerte. Beide unterstanden sie Cuthberts Oberaufsicht. Daneben gab es noch drei weitere Klosteroffiziale, die ihm nominell unterstanden, jedoch über eine gewisse Unabhängigkeit verfügten: den Gästemeister, den Infirmarius, der sich in einem separaten Gebäude um die alten und kranken Mitbrüder kümmerte, und den Almosenpfleger. Obwohl er also über eine Reihe von Mitarbeitern verfügte, blieb Cuthberts Verantwortung gewaltig. Dabei behielt er mit dem Argument, Pergament- und Tintenverschwendung sei eine Schande, alle Zahlen und Informationen im Kopf. Philip argwöhnte, daß Bruder Cuthbert nie richtig Schreiben und Lesen gelernt hatte. Seinen Zunamen ›Whitehead‹ verdankte Cuthbert im übrigen dem Umstand, daß er von früher Jugend an weißhaarig gewesen war. Inzwischen war er über sechzig, und die einzigen Haare, die ihm verblieben waren, entsprossen in dichten Büscheln seinen Ohren und Nasenlöchern; es war, als wollten sie seine Glatze wettmachen. Philip, der in dem Kloster in Wales selber Cellerar gewesen war, hatte Verständnis für Cuthberts Sorgen und Launen, weshalb Cuthbert ihn auch sehr mochte. Da ihm nicht entgangen war, wie man Philip um seine Mahlzeit gebracht hatte, griff er nun in ein Faß und holte ein halbes Dutzend Birnen heraus. Sie waren ein wenig verschrumpelt, schmeckten jedoch recht gut. Philip verspeiste sie mit Behagen, während Cuthbert sich über die wirtschaftliche Lage des Klosters beklagte.

»Es ist mir gänzlich unverständlich, wie die Priorei zu so vielen Schulden kommen konnte«, bemerkte Philip, den Mund voll Fruchtfleisch.

»Sie sollte auch keine haben«, sagte Cuthbert. »Sie besitzt mehr Land und treibt mehr Abgaben ein als je zuvor.«

»Eben – warum aber sind wir dann trotzdem nicht reich?«

»Du kennst doch unser hiesiges System: Das Klostereigentum wird zum größten Teil unter die Offizialen aufgeteilt. Der Sakristan hat seine Ländereien, ich habe die meinen, der Novizenmeister, der Gästemeister, der Infirmarius und der Almosenpfleger sind etwas weniger üppig ausgestattet. Der Rest gehört dem Prior. Jeder von uns zieht das Einkommen aus seinem Eigentum zur Erfüllung seiner Verpflichtungen heran.«

»Na und?«

»Nun, all dieses Eigentum will gepflegt werden! Nehmen wir einmal an, wir verpachten eine bestimmte Fläche Landes für eine bestimmte bar zu zahlende Summe. Da wäre es nicht recht, es einfach dem höchsten Anbieter zuzuschlagen und das Geld dann einzusacken. Wir sollten uns vielmehr um einen besonders *guten* Pächter bemühen und ihm bei seiner Arbeit auf die Finger sehen. Er muß sich auch um die Felder kümmern – sonst kann es passieren, daß eine Weide versumpft, daß sich der Boden erschöpft und so weiter. Der Pächter kann dann auf einmal die Pachtsumme nicht mehr tragen, so daß er uns das Land wieder zurückgibt – nur eben in einem erheblich schlechteren Zustand als zuvor. Oder nimm ein anderes Beispiel – einen kleinen Gutshof, der von unserem Gesinde bearbeitet und von Mönchen geleitet wird: Wird der Hof immer nur dann besucht, wenn jemand die Erzeugnisse abholt, so sehen sich die Mönche um ihren Lohn betrogen und werden nachlässig, das Gesinde stiehlt die Feldfrüchte und der Ertrag des Guts sinkt von Jahr zu Jahr. Selbst der Kirche muß man stets auf die Finger sehen – und man sollte nicht immer nur das Eintreiben des Zehnten im Kopf haben. Ein guter Priester muß her, der sein Latein beherrscht und ein heiligmäßiges Leben führt. Ist dem nicht so, verfallen die Menschen in Gottlosigkeit, sie heiraten, gebären und sterben ohne den Segen der Kirche und versuchen uns bei der Berechnung des Zehnten zu betrügen.«

Philip verzehrte gerade die letzte Birne. »Die Klosteroffizialen sollten sich mit besonderer Sorgfalt um die Bestellung ihrer Güter kümmern«, sagte er.

Cuthbert zapfte einen Becher Wein vom Faß und reichte ihn Philip. »In der Tat, das sollten sie, aber sie haben ja so viele andere Dinge im Kopf! Und überhaupt: Was versteht ein Novizenmeister schon vom Ackerbau? Wie soll ein Infirmarius ein Gut verwalten? Natürlich, ein strenger Prior wird seine Untergebenen zum haushälterischen Umgang mit seinen Reichtümern veranlassen, jedenfalls bis zu einem gewissen Grade. Aber wir hatten eben dreizehn Jahre lang einen sehr schwachen Prior, und so fehlt es uns jetzt an Geld zur Renovierung der Kathedrale, sechsmal die Woche steht Pökelfisch auf dem Tisch, die Klosterschule hat immer weniger Novizen, und das Gästehaus steht verwaist!«

Philip versank in düsteres Schweigen und nippte an seinem Wein. Es fiel ihm schwer, angesichts dieser erschreckenden Vergeudung von Werten, die dem Herrn gehörten, einen kühlen Kopf zu bewahren. Am liebsten hätte er die Verantwortlichen allesamt am Kragen gepackt und sie kräftig durchgeschüttelt, bis sie wieder zur Besinnung kamen.

Aber in diesem Fall lag der Verantwortliche aufgebahrt hinter dem Altar, und allein aus dieser Tatsache ergab sich ein kleiner Hoffnungsschimmer. »Wir werden ja bald einen neuen Prior bekommen«, sagte Philip. »Neue Besen kehren gut.«

Cuthbert bedachte ihn mit einem skeptischen Blick. »Remigius? Ein neuer Besen?«

Philip war sich nicht ganz klar, worauf Cuthbert hinauswollte. »Remigius wird doch nicht Prior – oder?«

»Wir müssen damit rechnen.«

Philip war entsetzt. »Aber der ist doch um keinen Deut besser als Prior James. Was kann denn die Mitbrüder bewegen, ausgerechnet ihn zu wählen?«

»Nun ja, da ist vor allem einmal ein großes Mißtrauen gegenüber Fremden. Sie wählen bestimmt keinen, den sie nicht kennen, was wiederum heißt, daß die Wahl auf einen von uns fallen wird. Und Remigius ist Subprior, das heißt der ranghöchste Mönch in unserem Kreis.«

»Aber es gibt keinerlei Regel, die besagt, daß wir den ranghöchsten Mönch zum Prior wählen müssen«, protestierte Philip. »Es kommen ebensogut alle anderen Offiziale in Frage. Zum Beispiel du.«

Cuthbert nickte. »Man hat mich bereits gefragt. Ich habe abgelehnt.«

»Und warum?«

»Ich werde langsam alt, Philip. Schon meine jetzige Tätigkeit wächst mir im Grunde über den Kopf. Jede zusätzliche Verantwortung gäbe mir den Rest. Mir fehlt ganz einfach die Kraft dazu, ein heruntergewirtschaftetes Kloster zu leiten und wieder auf Trab zu bringen.

Nimm alles in allem, und du wirst finden, daß ich für diese Aufgabe auch nicht besser tauge als Remigius.«

Philip wollte es immer noch nicht wahrhaben. »Es gibt doch noch andere ... den Sakristan, den Cirkator, den Novizenmeister ...«

»Der Novizenmeister ist ein alter Mann und noch müder als ich. Der Gästemeister ist ein Vielfraß und ein Säufer. Und der Sakristan und der Cirkator haben sich bereits auf Remigius festgelegt. Warum? Ich weiß es nicht, aber ich habe so meine Vermutungen. Wahrscheinlich hat Remigius dem Sakristan die Stelle des Subpriors und dem Cirkator das Amt des Sakristans versprochen – jeweils zum Lohn für ihre Unterstützung.«

Philip ließ sich rücklings auf die Mehlsäcke fallen, die ihm als Sitzgelegenheit dienten. »Du willst damit also sagen, daß Remigius die Nachfolgefrage längst in seinem Sinne geregelt hat, oder?«

Cuthbert ließ sich mit seiner Antwort Zeit. Er erhob sich und ging zur anderen Seite des Lagerraumes, wo bereits ein hölzerner Wassertrog voller lebendiger Aale, ein Eimer mit klarem Wasser und ein etwa zu einem Drittel gefülltes Faß mit Salzlake bereitstanden. »Komm, hilf mir!« sagte er zu Philip und zog ein Messer heraus. Dann fischte er einen Aal aus dem Trog, hieb den Kopf des Tieres auf den Steinboden, schnitt ihm den Leib auf und nahm ihn aus. Schließlich schob er Philip den noch immer leicht zuckenden Fischkörper zu und sagte: »Wasch ihn im Eimer, und schmeiß ihn dann ins Faß. Der wird uns zur Fastenzeit schon den Appetit verderben!«

Philip wässerte und wusch den halbtoten Aal, so gut er konnte, und warf ihn dann in die Salzlake.

Cuthbert war schon beim nächsten Aal, als er wieder auf die Nachfolgefrage zu sprechen kam: »Es gibt noch einen weiteren Kandidaten: Er würde einen guten Prior abgeben und sich mit Sicherheit um grundlegende Reformen bemühen. Und vom Rang her kann er es zwar nicht mit dem Subprior aufnehmen, durchaus aber mit dem Sakristan und dem Cellerarius.«

Philip tauchte den Aal in den Eimer. »Wen meinst du?«

»Dich.«

»Mich?« Philip war so überrascht, daß er den Aal auf den Fußboden fallen ließ. Rein formal gehörte er zu den Offizialen der Priorei, doch wäre es ihm nie in den Sinn gekommen, sich auf eine Stufe mit dem Sakristan und den anderen Amtsträgern zu stellen – vor allem, weil sie alle viel älter waren als er.

»Ich bin zu jung ...«, stammelte er.

»Denk mal drüber nach«, erwiderte Cuthbert. »Du hast von Kindesbeinen an im Kloster gelebt. Schon mit einundzwanzig Jahren warst du Cellerarius. Seit vier oder fünf Jahren bist du Prior einer kleinen Außenstelle unseres Hauses – und du hast deine Zelle vortrefflich reformiert. Es ist für jedermann ersichtlich, daß der Herr seine Hand über dich hält.«

Es gelang Philip, den entwischten Aal wieder einzufangen und im Faß zu verstauen. »Der Herr hält seine Hand über uns alle«, sagte er ausweichend. Cuthberts Vorschlag kam wie ein Keulenschlag. Er, Philip, hatte sich immer einen energischen neuen Prior für Kingsbridge gewünscht – aber an sich selbst hatte er nie gedacht. Nach einer Weile fügte er nachdenklich hinzu: »Es ist wohl richtig, daß ich ein besserer Prior wäre als Remigius.«

Cuthbert war's offenbar zufrieden. »Wenn du einen Fehler hast, Philip, dann ist das deine Unschuld.«

Philip hielt sich nicht für unschuldig oder naiv. »Was soll das heißen?« fragte er.

»Du suchst bei anderen Leuten niemals nach niedrigen Beweggründen. Die meisten von uns tun das schon. So ist jedermann hier im Kloster fest davon überzeugt, daß du auf das Amt des Priors spekulierst und nur gekommen bist, weil du um Stimmen werben willst.«

Philip war ungehalten. »Wie kommen die denn *darauf*?«

»Versuch dich doch mal mit den Augen eines niedrigen, argwöhnischen Geistes zu sehen! Du tauchst hier auf, völlig unerwartet und nur wenige Tage nach dem Ableben von Prior James, so daß man unwillkürlich annehmen muß, ein Informant hier aus dem Kloster habe dich heimlich benachrichtigt.«

»Und wie, glaubt man, soll ich das alles eingefädelt haben?«

»Das weiß doch keiner! Sie halten dich ganz einfach für viel raffinierter als du bist.« Cuthbert schlitzte einen weiteren Aal der Länge nach auf und weidete ihn aus. »Denk doch mal nach, wie du dich hier aufführst seit deiner Ankunft: Kaum hast du das Klostergelände betreten, befiehlst du den Stallburschen auszumisten. Dann rufst du die Burschen zur Ordnung, die während des Hochamts Unfug treiben. Du sprichst mit dem jungen William Beauvis über dessen mögliche Versetzung, obwohl jedermann weiß, daß die Entscheidung in dieser Frage dem Prior vorbehalten ist. Du bringst Bruder Paul draußen an der Brücke einen heißen Stein und kritisierst damit indirekt Remigius. Und schließlich lieferst du auch noch in der Küche einen vorzüglichen Käse ab, von dem wir alle nach dem Essen kosten durften. Und obwohl uns natürlich niemand ausdrücklich *gesagt* hat, woher der Käse stammte, so ist das vorzügliche Aroma doch ein unverkennbares Markenzeichen der Käserei von St.-John-in-the-Forest ...«

Eine Verkettung von peinlichen Mißverständnissen, dachte Philip und erwiderte: »All diese Dinge hätte auch jeder andere von uns tun können.«

»*Eines* vielleicht, ja, das mag für uns Ältere, die wir ein Amt ausüben, zutreffen. Aber ich wüßte keinen, der all diese Dinge auf einmal getan hätte. Du kommst daher und ergreifst die Initiative! Das war ja schon ein erstes Probefegen mit dem neuen Besen. Kein Wunder, daß sich Remigius' Busenfreunde auf die Hinterbeine stellen! Was glaubst du, warum dich Sakristan Andrew im Kreuzgang so ausgescholten hat?«

»Ach so ... nun, das erklärt manches! Ich habe mich schon gefragt, was eigentlich in ihn gefahren ist.« Philip wusch gedankenverloren einen ausgenommenen Aal. »Und aus demselben Grund hat mir wohl der Cirkator das Essen verboten, wie?«

»Ganz recht. Er wollte dich vor den Augen aller Mitbrüder demütigen. Ich glaube allerdings, daß der Schuß nach hinten losgegangen ist, denn der Tadel war in beiden Fällen an den Haaren herbeigezogen. Außerdem hast du ihn nobel über dich ergehen lassen. Um ehrlich zu sein, du hast ihn mit wahrhaft heiligmäßiger Miene ertragen.«

»Es ging mir nicht um den äußeren Eindruck.«

»Das war bei den Heiligen genauso. Hörst du? Es läutet zur Non. Am besten läßt du mich jetzt mit meinen Aalen allein. Nach dem Gebet ist Studium, und im Kreuzgang darf disputiert werden. Viele Mitbrüder werden sich mit dir unterhalten wollen.«

»Nicht so schnell!« sagte Philip besorgt. »Daß einige Leute sich einbilden, ich wolle Prior werden, heißt noch lange nicht, daß ich mich auch tatsächlich zur Wahl stelle.« Die Aussicht auf eine harte Wahlauseinandersetzung war ihm alles andere als angenehm. Außerdem war er mit sich selbst noch nicht im reinen: Bin ich wirklich bereit, meine inzwischen so gut funktionierende Zelle im Wald gegen die gewaltigen Probleme hier in Kingsbridge einzutauschen? fragte er sich. Er bat Cuthbert um Verständnis. »Ich brauche Zeit zum Nachdenken.«

»Ich weiß.« Cuthbert richtete sich auf und sah Philip in die Augen. »Bedenke aber bei all deinen Überlegungen folgendes: Überzogener Stolz ist eine bekannte Sünde – doch läßt sich der Wille Gottes durch überzogene Bescheidenheit genauso leicht durchkreuzen.«

Philip nickte. »Ich werde mich deiner Worte erinnern. Vielen Dank.«

Er verabschiedete sich und schloß sich vor dem Lager den anderen Mönchen an, die ebenfalls unterwegs zur Kirche waren. Die aberwitzigsten Gedanken schossen ihm durch den Kopf. Jahrelang hatte er sich darüber geärgert, wie schlecht und würdelos die Priorei Kingsbridge geführt wurde, und nun bot sich ihm unvermittelt eine Chance, die Dinge selbst in die Hand zu nehmen und zum Besseren zu wenden. Würde er es wirklich schaffen? Er war plötzlich unsicher. Die Mißstände zu erkennen, war eine Sache – sie auch zu beheben eine ganz andere. Die Leute mußten überzeugt werden, die Liegenschaften erforderten eine kundige Verwaltung, Geld mußte aufgetrieben werden … Die Aufgabe verlangte einen klugen Kopf, und die Last der Verantwortung wog schwer.

In der Kirche fand er, wie immer, Frieden. Nach den unerfreulichen Vorfällen vom Vormittag betrugen sich die Mönche diesmal anständig und gesittet. Philip hörte die vertrauten Sätze des Chorgebets und murmelte die ihm seit so vielen Jahren vertrauten Antworten. Die Gedanken beruhigten sich, sein Kopf wurde wieder klar.

Möchtest du Prior von Kingsbridge werden? fragte er sich, und die Antwort kam unverzüglich: Ja! Allein, um dem Verfall dieses Gotteshauses Einhalt zu gebieten, seine Mauern instandzusetzen, es neu zu bemalen und es zu füllen mit dem Gesang von hundert Mönchen und den Stimmen von tausend Gläubigen, die das Vaterunser sprechen – allein deshalb ersehne ich dieses Amt! Und dann sind da die Klostergüter, die neu geordnet und mit neuem Leben erfüllt werden müssen, auf daß sie wachsen und gedeihen können. In einem Winkel des Kreuzgangs sah Philip schon eine kleine Schülergruppe beieinanderstehen, denen Lesen und Schreiben beigebracht wurde. Hell und warm sollte das Gästehaus sein, so daß Barone und Bischöfe dort logieren konnten, bevor sie der Priorei zum Abschied wertvolle Dotationen machten … Er wollte eine Bibliothek einrichten und sie mit vielen schönen Büchern füllen, in denen das Wissen der Welt gesammelt war. Jawohl, er wollte Prior von Kingsbridge werden, er wollte es von ganzem Herzen.

Gibt es noch andere Gründe, die mich bewegen? fragte er sich. Wenn ich mir vorstelle, der Prior zu sein, der all diese Verbesserungen zur höheren Ehre Gottes in die Wege leitet – erfüllt da nicht auch eitler Stolz mein Herz?

O ja.

In der kalten, ehrfurchtgebietenden Atmosphäre der Kathedrale war es ihm unmöglich, sich der Selbsttäuschung hinzugeben. Sein Ziel war es, den Ruhm Gottes zu mehren – aber der Ruhm Philips hatte auch seinen Reiz. Der Gedanke, Befehle erteilen zu können, die keinen Widerspruch duldeten, gefiel ihm. Er sah sich als Entscheidungsträger, Rechtswalter, Ratgeber und Anreger, der nach eigenem Wissen und Gewissen strafte und verzieh. Schon hörte er die Menschen sagen: ›Philip von Gwynedd hat dieses Kloster reformiert. Es war ein Schandfleck, als er es übernahm – und schaut euch an, was er daraus gemacht hat!‹

Ja, ich wäre ein guter Prior, dachte er. Gott schenkte mir die Geistesgaben, ohne die es nicht möglich ist, so große Werte zu verwalten. Er verlieh mir auch die Gabe, Menschen zu führen; ich habe das als Cellerarius in Gwynedd und als Prior in St.-John-in-the-Forest bewiesen. Die Mönche in den von mir geführten Häusern sind froh und glücklich; die alten haben keine Frostbeulen, und die jungen schlagen nicht aus Arbeitsmangel über die Stränge. Ich kümmere mich um meine Leute.

Andererseits – verglichen mit Kingsbridge waren die Ämter in Gwynedd und St.-John-in-the-Forest geradezu harmlos. In Gwynedd hatte niemals solche Schluderei geherrscht. In der Zelle draußen im Wald hatte anfangs einiges im argen gelegen, doch war sie klein genug gewesen, so daß man stets den Überblick behielt. Demgegenüber war die Reform der Priorei Kingsbridge eine Herkulesarbeit. Es konnte Wochen dauern, bis allein der Besitzstand genau festgestellt war: wo überall die Ländereien, die Wälder, Weiden und Getreidefelder lagen und was im einzelnen zu tun war, um aus den weit zerstreuten Liegenschaften eine prosperierende Einheit zu schaffen. Bis man das alles erfaßt hatte, konnten Jahre ins Land gehen! In seiner kleinen Zelle im Wald dagegen hatte Philip lediglich ein gutes Dutzend Mönche zu harter Feldarbeit und diszipliniertem Gebet anhalten müssen.

Gut, gestand er sich ein, meine Motive sind nicht nur uneigennützig, und es sind durchaus Zweifel angebracht, ob ich die nötigen Fähigkeiten besitze. Also ist es vielleicht doch besser, auf die Kandidatur zu verzichten? Die Sünde der Hoffart ließe sich auf diese Weise vermeiden. Doch wie sagte Cuthbert? *Der Wille Gottes läßt sich durch überzogene Bescheidenheit genauso leicht durchkreuzen.*

Was ist der Wille Gottes? fragte sich Philip schließlich. Möchte er, daß Remigius Prior wird? Von den Fähigkeiten her bin ich Remigius überlegen – und was die Motive angeht, nun, die dürften bei ihm kaum reiner sein als bei mir. Gibt es noch einen anderen Kandidaten? Gegenwärtig nicht. Solange uns der Herr keine dritte Möglichkeit offenbart, müssen wir davon ausgehen, daß die Wahl auf mich oder Remigius fällt. Wie die Amtsgeschäfte unter Remigius geführt werden, ist klar – er hat es ja während der langen Krankheit von Prior James bewiesen. Schluderei und Untätigkeit gehen weiter, nichts wird unternommen gegen den zunehmenden Verfall der Priorei. Und unter mir? Ich bin stolz, und meine Talente müssen sich erst noch beweisen. Aber ich werde auf jeden Fall *versuchen,* das Kloster zu reformieren. Und wenn Gott mir die Kraft gibt, werde ich dabei Erfolg haben.

So sei es denn, sagte er zu Gott, als das Gebet sich seinem Ende näherte. Ich werde mich zur Kandidatur bereiterklären, und ich werde mich mit allen Kräften dafür einsetzen, daß ich die Wahl gewinne. Und wenn Du, Herr, aus unergründlichem Ratschluß mich nicht willst – nun, dann liegt es an Dir, mich zurückzuhalten, auf welche Art auch immer.

Zweiundzwanzig Jahre lebte Philip nun schon im Kloster, doch da all seinen Vorgesetzten eine lange Lebensdauer beschieden war, hatte er noch nie eine Abtwahl miterlebt. Es war ein einzigartiges Erlebnis im mönchischen Leben, denn die Brüder waren bei der Stimmabgabe frei und niemandem Gehorsam schuldig. Einer galt auf einmal soviel wie der andere.

Vor langer, langer Zeit führten die Mönche, soweit man den Legenden trauen konnte, ein Leben in absoluter Gleichheit. Da beschloß eine Gruppe Gleichgesinnter aus freien Stücken, der Welt und ihren fleischlichen Genüssen den Rücken zu kehren und sich irgendwo in der Wildnis eine geweihte Zufluchtsstätte zu errichten. Sie führten dort ein entsagungsvolles, frommes Leben, rodeten den Wald oder legten einen Sumpf trocken, ackerten und pflügten und bauten sich in gemeinsamer Arbeit ihre Kirche. In jenen Tagen waren sie tatsächlich wie Brüder zueinander. Der Prior war, wie schon der Titel sagt, lediglich der *Primus inter pares,* und Gehorsam schworen sie nur der Ordensregel des heiligen Benedikt, nicht jedoch den Offizialen des Klosters. Von all diesen urdemokratischen Regeln existierte mittlerweile jedoch nur noch die freie Wahl des Abts und des Priors.

Manche Mönche wußten mit der ungewohnten Macht gar nicht richtig umzugehen; es war ihnen unbehaglich dabei. Sie wollten genauso Anweisungen haben oder schlugen vor, die Entscheidung einem Wahlgremium zu überlassen, das sich aus den älteren und erfahreneren Mitbrüdern zusammensetzte. Wieder andere mißbrauchten das Privileg und wurden anmaßend; sie verlangten Gegenleistungen für ihre Unterstützung. Die meisten waren allerdings vor allem daran interessiert, eine vernünftige Entscheidung zu treffen.

Philip unterhielt sich an jenem Nachmittag im Kreuzgang mit fast allen, entweder unter vier Augen oder in kleinen Gruppen. Offen bekannte er ihnen, daß er sich um das Amt bewerben wolle und daß er sich trotz seiner Jugend für einen besseren Kandidaten als Remigius halte. Er beantwortete ihnen ihre Fragen, die sich vor allem um die Lebensmittelversorgung der Priorei drehten, und beendete jede Unterredung mit der Bemerkung: »Wenn jeder einzelne von uns seine Entscheidung nach reiflicher Überlegung und innigem Gebet trifft, wird der Herr dem Gewählten seinen Segen gewiß nicht versagen.« Philip wußte, daß dieser Satz dem Anlaß angemessen war, und er glaubte an ihn.

»Wir werden gewinnen«, sagte Milius, der Küchenmeister, am nächsten Morgen zu ihm. Die Küchenjungen schürten gerade das Feuer, und die beiden Männer versorgten sich zum Frühstück mit dunklem, grobem Brot und Bier.

Philip biß ein kräftiges Stück ab und weichte es im Mund mit einem Schluck Bier auf. Milius war ein gescheiter, lebhafter junger Mann; er galt als Schützling Cuthberts und bewunderte Philip. Er hatte glatte, dunkle Haare und ein kleines Gesicht mit hübschen, ebenmäßigen Zügen. Wie Cuthbert diente auch er dem Herrn lieber durch praktische Arbeit und mied auf diese Weise die meisten Gottesdienste. Philip traute seinem Optimismus nicht. »Wie kommst du denn darauf?« fragte er ihn voller Skepsis.

»Cuthbert und alle, die auf seiner Seite stehen, unterstützen dich – der Ökonom, der Infirmarius, der Novizenmeister und ich. Wir wissen, daß du etwas von der Versorgung eines Klosters verstehst – und darin liegt derzeit eines unserer größten Probleme. Die meisten einfachen Mönche werden dir aus einem ganz ähnlichen Grund ihre Stimme geben: Sie trauen dir zu, die Klostergüter besser zu verwalten, und erwarten sich von daher angenehmere Lebensumstände und besseres Essen.«

Philip runzelte die Stirn. »Ich möchte niemandem falsche Vorstellungen machen. Zuallererst möchte ich die Kirche renovieren lassen und dafür sorgen, daß die Gottesdienstordnung eingehalten wird. Das Essen kommt erst danach.«

»Recht so, das wissen die anderen auch«, gab Milius ein wenig zu hastig zurück. »Daher werden zum Beispiel der Gästemeister und zwei oder drei andere auch für Remigius stimmen. Ihnen ist ein bequemes Leben unter einem schwachen Prior lieber. Die anderen, die ihn unterstützen, sind allesamt seine persönlichen Freunde, die sich von seiner Wahl besondere Privilegien erhoffen, der Sakristan zum Beispiel, der Cirkator, der Schatzmeister und so weiter. Der Kantor ist mit dem Sakristan befreundet, aber ich glaube, wir könnten ihn auf unsere Seite ziehen. Vor allem, wenn du versprichst, einen Bibliothekar zu ernennen.«

Philip nickte. Der Kantor war mit musikalischen Aufgaben ausgelastet und fühlte sich mit der zusätzlichen Arbeit eines Bibliothekars überfordert. »Das ist auf jeden Fall eine gute Idee«, sagte er. »Der Aufbau unserer Bibliothek erfordert einen eigenen Mann.«

Milius erhob sich von seinem Stuhl und fing damit an, ein Küchenmesser zu schleifen. Er hat zu viel überschüssige Kraft, dachte Philip, und muß sich mit körperlicher Arbeit ablenken.

»Insgesamt«, rechnete Milius vor, »sind vierundvierzig Mönche stimmberechtigt. Nach meiner Schätzung sind zur Zeit günstigstenfalls achtzehn auf unserer und zehn auf Remigius' Seite. Das bedeutet, daß sechzehn ihre Entscheidung noch nicht getroffen haben. Da wir zur Mehrheit dreiundzwanzig Stimmen brauchen, mußt du von denen, die noch schwanken, fünf gewinnen.«

»So, wie du es sagst, klingt es nicht allzu schwer«, meinte Philip. »Wieviel Zeit bleibt uns denn noch?«

»Das kann ich nicht genau sagen. Für die Festsetzung des Wahltermins sind die Mönche selbst zuständig. Wenn wir jedoch vorschnell handeln, kann es passieren, daß sich der Bischof weigert, unsere Wahl zu bestätigen. Umgekehrt kann er uns auch zu größerer Eile anhalten, falls wir die Wahl zu lange hinauszögern. Der Bischof hat zudem das Recht, einen eigenen Kandidaten zu ernennen. Im Augenblick weiß er noch nicht einmal, daß der alte Prior gestorben ist.«

»Dann kann es noch eine Weile dauern bis zur Wahl, nicht wahr?«

»Ja. Und was dich betrifft, so mußt du, sobald du dir deiner Mehrheit einigermaßen sicher bist, zurückkehren in deine Zelle im Wald und dort abwarten, bis alles vorüber ist.«

Philip war verwirrt. »Warum das?« fragte er.

»Allzugroße Vertrautheit erzeugt Verachtung!« Aufgeregt fuchtelte Milius mit dem geschärften Messer hin und her. »Vergib mir, wenn meine Worte respektlos klingen, aber du hast mich ja direkt danach gefragt. Momentan bist du mit einer Aura umgeben. Für uns Jüngere bist du eine entrückte, verehrungswürdige Person. In deiner kleinen Zelle hast du geradezu Wunder gewirkt, indem du das Unterste nach oben gekehrt und sie autark gemacht hast. Du bist ein strenger Disziplinator, sorgst aber gleichzeitig dafür, daß deine Mönche immer gut zu essen haben. Du bist ein geborener Führer – und dennoch imstande, dein Haupt zu beugen und demütig Tadel zu ertragen wie der jüngste Novize. Du bist mit den Heiligen Schriften vertraut – und machst den besten Käse in der Grafschaft ...«

»Und *du* übertreibst!«

»Nur ein bißchen.«

»Ich kann es einfach nicht glauben, daß die Leute so von mir denken. Es ist unnatürlich.«

»Da stimme ich dir zu«, meinte Milius und zuckte leicht mit der Schulter. »Und wenn sie dich erst einmal besser kennen, verfliegt der Zauber ja auch. Deshalb sage ich doch: Willst du deine Aura behalten, mußt du so bald wie möglich verschwinden. Bleibst du hier, so sehen alle, wie du dir in den Zähnen herumpolkst und dich am Hintern kratzt. Sie hören dich schnarchen und furzen, lernen deine Launen kennen und wissen, wie du reagierst, wenn du dich in deinem Stolz verletzt fühlst oder Kopfweh hast. Das bringt uns nicht weiter. Sollen sie doch Remigius von einem Fettnäpfchen ins andere stolpern sehen – während dein Bild rein und unbefleckt bleibt!«

»Mir gefällt das nicht«, sagte Philip, und seine Stimme klang besorgt. »Es kommt mir irgendwie unehrlich vor.«

»Ist es aber nicht!« widersprach Milius. »Es ist vielmehr ein anschauliches Beispiel dafür, wie sehr Gott dem Herrn und diesem Kloster gedient wäre, wenn du Prior würdest – und wie miserabel wir alle dran sind, wenn Remigius die Oberhand behält.«

Philip schüttelte den Kopf. »Ich bin nicht bereit, mich als Engel darstellen zu lassen. Aber gut, ich werde nicht hierbleiben; meine Pflichten daheim im Wald rufen mich ohnehin zurück. Nur werden wir den Mitbrüdern nichts vorgaukeln. Wir bitten sie darum, einen fehlbaren, unvollkommenen Mann zu wählen, der dringend ihrer Hilfe und ihrer Gebete bedarf.«

»Ja, so mußt du es ihnen sagen!« rief Milius begeistert aus. »Genau so! Das wird ihnen gefallen.«

Er ist unverbesserlich, dachte Philip und wechselte das Thema. »Diese Mitbrüder, die sich noch nicht entschieden haben – was sind das eigentlich für Leute?«

»Sie hängen am Althergebrachten«, erwiderte Milius, ohne zu zögern. »Für sie ist Remigius eben der Ältere, der Mann, von dem die geringsten Veränderungen zu erwarten sind. Sie können ihn besser einschätzen und haben sich schon an sein Regiment gewöhnt.«

Philip nickte zustimmend. »Ich spüre ihre mißtrauischen Blicke. Sie schauen mich an wie einen fremden Hund, von dem man nicht weiß, ob er bissig ist.«

Die Glocke läutete zum Kapitel. Milius trank sein Bier aus. »Sie planen eine Attacke gegen dich, Philip. Ich kann nicht genau sagen, in welcher Form, aber auf jeden Fall werden sie versuchen, dich als jungen und unerfahrenen Dickkopf darzustellen, auf den kein Verlaß ist. Halte dich möglichst zurück, sei vorsichtig, überleg dir genau, was du sagst – aber überlaß es bitte Cuthbert und mir, dich zu verteidigen.«

Philip verspürte eine gewisse Beklemmung. Er war es nicht gewohnt, jede Handlung abzuwägen und daraufhin zu überprüfen, wie andere vielleicht reagieren würden. Mit einem skeptischen Unterton in der Stimme erwiderte er: »Bisher habe ich mir immer nur darüber Gedanken gemacht, wie Gott mein Handeln beurteilt.«

»Ich weiß, ich weiß«, gab Milius ungeduldig zurück. »Aber es ist doch keine Sünde, wenn man einfacheren Gemütern ein wenig dazu verhilft, dich und dein Tun im rechten Licht zu sehen.«

Sie machten sich auf den Weg zum Kreuzgang. Philip war jetzt sehr besorgt. Eine Attacke? Was hatte das zu bedeuten? Werden sie irgendwelche Lügen über mich verbreiten? Und wie soll ich darauf reagieren? Wenn jemand Unwahrheiten über mich erzählt, werde ich wütend. Soll ich meine Wut unterdrücken, um nach außen hin den Schein des Besonnenen zu bewahren und um die Stimmen der Konservativen zu buhlen? Nein, denn wenn ich schweige, werden die Mitbrüder meinen, an den Lügen sei doch etwas dran.

Philip entschloß sich, er selbst zu bleiben – und sich vielleicht ein kleines bißchen ernster und würdiger zu geben als bisher.

Das Kapitel war ein kleines, rundes Gebäude, das an den Ostumlauf des Kreuzgangs anschloß. Die Sitzbänke im Inneren waren in konzentrischen Ringen angeordnet. Da kein Feuer brannte, war es empfindlich kalt. Das Licht kam durch Fenster, die so hoch saßen, daß ein Blick nach draußen nicht möglich war: Man hatte im Kapitelsaal also nur seine Mitbrüder vor Augen.

Philip machte aus der Not eine Tugend: Er sah sich um. Fast die gesamte Klosterbelegschaft war anwesend. Alle Altersstufen zwischen siebzehn und siebzig, große und kleine Gestalten, dunkle und helle.

Alle trugen sie Ledersandalen und die Kutte aus rauher, ungebleichter Wolle. Da war zum Beispiel der Gästemeister mit kugelrundem Bauch und roter Nase als Zeichen seiner Laster – Laster, die unter Umständen verzeihlich wären, dachte Philip, vorausgesetzt, er könnte wenigstens ab und zu mal ein paar Gäste vorweisen ... Da war der Garderobenmeister, der zu Weihnachten und Pfingsten Kuttenwechsel und Rasur befahl (ein Bad wurde ebenfalls angeraten, war aber nicht vorgeschrieben). An der Mauer gegenüber lehnte der älteste Mitbruder, ein schmächtiger, nachdenklicher Mann mit nach wie vor mehr grauen als weißen Haaren, der nur selten das Wort ergriff, dann aber immer etwas zu sagen hatte. Er wäre wahrscheinlich ein guter Kandidat für das Amt des Priors gewesen, galt jedoch als zu zurückhaltend. Da war ferner Bruder Simon mit dem verstohlenen Blick und den rastlosen Händen, der (wie Milius Philip zuflüsterte) so oft die Sünde der Unkeuschheit beichtete, daß man fast schon annehmen mußte, er habe mehr Gefallen an der Beichte als an der Sünde. Auch William Beauvis war da und benahm sich anständig. Bruder Paul erschien, er hinkte kaum noch. Cuthbert Whitehead wirkte ruhig und selbstbeherrscht. John Small, der winzige Schatzmeister, war da, und Pierre, der Cirkator, der Philip tags zuvor daran gehindert hatte, sein Essen einzunehmen. Philip sah sich um – und merkte auf einmal, daß alle ihn ansahen. Peinlich berührt senkte er den Blick.

Remigius betrat den Kapitelsaal in Begleitung Andrews, des Sakristans. Sie setzten sich zu John Small und Pierre. Immerhin, dachte Philip, sie geben wenigstens zu, daß sie alle unter einer Decke stecken.

Das Kapitel begann mit einer Lesung über Symeon Stylites, den Heiligen des Tages. Symeon war ein Eremit gewesen, der den Großteil seines Lebens auf einer hohen Säule verbracht hatte. Obgleich an seiner Fähigkeit zur Selbstentsagung kein Zweifel bestehen konnte, hatte Philip immer einen heimlichen Zweifel am tatsächlichen Wert seines Bekenntnisses gehegt. In Scharen waren die Menschen zu ihm geströmt – aber waren sie wirklich gekommen, weil sie sich von ihm geistige Erbauung erwarteten, oder trieb sie bloß die Neugier, einen Sonderling zu sehen?

Nach dem Gebet wurde ein Kapitel aus dem Buch des heiligen Benedikt vorgetragen. Diesem alltäglichen Brauch verdankten die Versammlung und der Versammlungssaal ihren Namen. Remigius stand auf und sammelte sich, bevor er zu lesen begann. Philip sah ihn im Profil – und zum erstenmal mit den Augen des Rivalen. Sein Auftreten und seine Redeweise ließen Remigius stets als einen Mann erscheinen, der genau weiß, was er will; im Widerspruch zu seinem wahren Charakter und seiner Amtsführung gelang es ihm somit, den Eindruck von Sachverstand und Kompetenz zu erwecken. Aber die genauere Betrachtung ließ bereits ahnen, was hinter dieser Fassade steckte: Seine ein wenig vorstehenden blauen Augen waren in ständiger, flatterhafter Bewegung; der schwache Mund zuckte oft nervös, bevor er zu sprechen begann, und die Hände öffneten und schlossen sich unwillkürlich, obwohl Remigius ansonsten einen ruhigen Stand hatte. Seine Autorität beruhte auf einem anmaßenden, oft launenhaften Wesen und einem herablassenden Umgang mit seinen Untergebenen.

Philip wunderte sich, daß Remigius sich dazu entschlossen hatte, das Kapitel selbst vorzutragen. Einen Augenblick später war ihm klar, warum. »Der erste Schritt zur Demut ist unbedingter Gehorsam«, las Remigius. Er hatte das fünfte Kapitel ausgewählt, das vom Gehorsam handelte, um allen Anwesenden seinen hohen Rang und ihre untergeordnete Stellung ins Gedächtnis zu rufen. Es war die Strategie der Einschüchterung – und ein raffinierter Taktiker war Remigius allemal. »Sie leben nicht, wie sie selbst leben wollen, noch gehorchen sie ihren eigenen Wünschen und Begehren; vielmehr folgen sie in den Klöstern dem Befehl und der Richtung, die andere für sie vorgeben, und ihr Streben ist darauf aus, von einem Abt geführt zu werden.« Remigius machte eine kleine Pause. »Ohne Zweifel halten sie, die sie so handeln, sich an das Wort des Herrn: *Ich bin nicht gekommen, nach meinem eigenen Willen zu handeln, sondern erfülle den Willen Dessen, Der mich gesandt hat.*«

Remigius gab die erwarteten Vorgaben für die entscheidende Schlacht: Er, soviel stand fest, wollte in der bevorstehenden Auseinandersetzung die althergebrachte Ordnung repräsentieren.

Dem Kapitel folgte die Fürbitte für die Verstorbenen. Alle Gebete, das verstand sich von selbst, galten an jenem Tag der Seele des verstorbenen Priors James. Der lebhafteste Teil der Kapitelversammlung war stets der Schluß: Man diskutierte über allgemeine Fragen des Klosters, bekannte seine Sünden und brachte Fehlverhalten zur Sprache.

Remigius begann die Aussprache mit den Worten: »Gestern während des Hochamts gab es eine Störung.«

Philip fühlte sich fast erleichtert. Endlich wußte er, welcher Art die angekündigte Attacke war. Er war sich nach wie vor nicht ganz sicher, ob er sich bei jenem Vorfall richtig verhalten hatte – doch er kannte seine Motive und war bereit, sich zu verteidigen.

»Ich selber war leider nicht anwesend«, fuhr Remigius fort. »Dringende Geschäfte hielten mich im Hause des Priors fest. Der Sakristan erstattete mir jedoch Bericht.«

Cuthbert Whitehead unterbrach ihn. »Mach dir deswegen keine Vorwürfe, Bruder Remigius«, sagte er in versöhnlichem Ton. »Zwar ist uns allen bekannt, daß klösterlichen Geschäften im Prinzip nie der Vorrang gegenüber dem Hochamt eingeräumt werden soll, doch wissen wir auch, daß dir durch den Tod unseres geliebten Priors viele Aufgaben zugefallen sind, die sonst gar nicht in deine Zuständigkeit fallen. Ich bin überzeugt, daß niemand hier im Saal meint, dir eine Buße auferlegen zu müssen.«

Du geriebener alter Fuchs! dachte Philip. Natürlich hatte Remigius nicht im Traum daran gedacht, einen Fehler zu bekennen – was Cuthbert freilich nicht davon abhielt, ihm großmütig Verzeihung zu gewähren. So entstand der Eindruck, als habe es sich tatsächlich um ein Schuldeingeständnis gehalten. Selbst wenn Philip nun eines Fehltritts überführt werden sollte, so stand er damit allemal noch auf derselben Stufe wie Remigius. Darüber hinaus hatte Cuthbert mit seiner Bemerkung Zweifel daran gesät, ob Remigius überhaupt imstande war, die Pflichten eines Priors zu bewältigen. Mit einigen wenigen, im freundlichsten Ton formulierten Worten hatte er schlicht Remigius' Autorität untergraben. Remigius schäumte, und Philip spürte, wie ihm die Vorfreude auf den Sieg fast die Luft benahm.

Sakristan Andrew sah Cuthbert vorwurfsvoll an. »Ich bin allerdings ebenfalls fest davon überzeugt, daß niemand der Anwesenden die Absicht hat, unseren verehrten Subprior zu kritisieren«, sagte er. »Der Vorfall während des Hochamts wurde von Bruder Philip verursacht, der aus seiner Zelle St.-John-in-the-Forest angereist ist und uns einen Besuch abstattet. Philip hat unseren jungen Mitbruder William Beauvis von seinem Platz im Chor fortgezerrt und ihm, noch während ich die Messe zelebrierte, im südlichen Querschiff schwere Vorhaltungen gemacht.«

Remigius hatte sich wieder gefaßt und eine sorgenvoll-tadelnde Miene aufgesetzt. »Wir dürften darin übereinstimmen, daß Philip mit seinem Eingreifen bis zum Ende des Gottesdienstes hätte warten sollen.«

Philip studierte die Gesichter der anderen Mönche, vermochte jedoch nicht zu sagen, ob sie dem Gesagten zustimmten oder nicht. Sie verfolgten den Schlagabtausch mit der Neugier von Zuschauern bei einem Turnier, bei dem es nicht um Recht und Unrecht geht, sondern einzig und allein darum, wer am Ende den Sieg davonträgt.

Philip wollte protestieren – *Wenn ich gewartet hätte, wäre das doch bis zum Ende des Gottesdienstes so weitergegangen!* –, doch dann erinnerte er sich an den Ratschlag des Milius und schwieg. Und tatsächlich ergriff nun Milius für ihn das Wort.

»Auch ich habe das Hochamt versäumt«, begann er, »wie leider schon des öfteren zuvor – findet das Hochamt doch immer kurz vor dem Essen statt. So kannst du, Bruder Andrew, mir vielleicht kurz sagen, worum es ging. Was veranlaßte eigentlich Bruder Philip zum Eingreifen?«

»Die jungen Mitbrüder verhielten sich in der Tat etwas unruhig«, antwortete der Sakristan finster. »Ich hätte ihnen später schon meine Meinung gesagt.«

»Ich verstehe durchaus, daß dir die Einzelheiten nicht ganz vertraut sind – du warst eben mit Leib und Seele bei deinem Gottesdienst. Doch haben wir ja glücklicherweise einen Cirkator, zu dessen ausdrücklichen Pflichten die Aufrechterhaltung der Disziplin zählt. Bruder Pierre – erzähl uns doch, was du beobachtet hast.«

Der Cirkator war aufgebracht. »Genau dasselbe, was der Sakristan eben schon berichtet hat.«

»Wie's scheint, müssen wir uns wegen der Einzelheiten an Bruder Philip persönlich wenden«, sagte Milius.

Gut gemacht, dachte Philip. Milius hat für jedermann erkennbar festgestellt, daß weder der Sakristan noch der Cirkator wußten, was die jungen Mönche während des Gottesdienstes eigentlich getrieben hatten. Doch trotz seiner Bewunderung für Milius' rhetorische Fähigkeiten hatte Philip Skrupel, das Spiel mitzuspielen. Die Wahl eines Priors war kein intellektueller Wettstreit, sondern vielmehr der Versuch, den Willen Gottes zu erforschen. Er zögerte. Milius warf ihm einen Blick zu, der soviel besagte wie *Jetzt ergreife die Gelegenheit beim Schopfe!* – aber Philip verfügte über eine gewisse Sturheit, die vor allem dann zum Tragen kam, wenn jemand versuchte, ihn in eine moralisch zweideutige Stellung zu manövrieren. Er sah Milius an und sagte: »Es verhielt sich so, wie meine Mitbrüder es eben geschildert haben.«

Milius war sichtlich entsetzt und starrte Philip ungläubig an, öffnete sogar den Mund, wußte jedoch nicht, was er sagen sollte. Philip machte sich schon Vorwürfe, daß er ihn so bloßgestellt hatte.

Remigius wollte gerade in seiner Anklage fortfahren, als sich eine weitere Stimme meldete. »Ich möchte bekennen.«

Alle sahen auf oder drehten sich um. Es war William Beauvis, der mit seinen Faxen während des Hochamts den Stein erst ins Rollen gebracht hatte. Er hatte sich erhoben und wirkte sehr zerknirscht. »Ich habe den Novizenmeister mit Dreckkügelchen beworfen und dabei gelacht«, gestand er mit leiser, aber klarer Stimme. »Bruder Philip hat mir die Augen geöffnet. Ich schäme mich. Ich flehe den Herrn um Vergebung an und bitte die Mitbrüder, mir eine Buße aufzuerlegen.« Er setzte sich wieder hin.

Ehe Remigius auf das Bekenntnis reagieren konnte, stand ein zweiter junger Mönch auf und sagte: »Auch ich möchte bekennen. Ich habe dasselbe getan wie William. Ich bitte um eine Buße.« Er setzte sich. Der plötzliche Ausbruch des schlechten Gewissens erwies sich geradezu als ansteckend: Ein dritter Mönch stand auf und bekannte, dann ein vierter, ein fünfter …

So kam die Wahrheit ans Licht – trotz der Vorbehalte Philips, der über den Verlauf der Dinge hochzufrieden sein konnte. Er sah, daß Milius mühevoll ein triumphierendes Grinsen unterdrückte. Die Bekenntnisse ließen keinen Zweifel mehr daran, daß unter den Augen von Cirkator und Sakristan ein mittlerer Aufruhr stattgefunden haben mußte.

Remigius war über die Wende, die die Dinge genommen hatten, natürlich alles andere als begeistert. Er verurteilte die Übeltäter zu einer Woche absoluten Schweigens, das heißt, sie durften weder selbst sprechen noch angesprochen werden. Die Strafe war härter, als es im ersten Augenblick klang. Philip selbst hatte sie in seiner Jugend über sich ergehen lassen müssen. Schon bei eintägigem Schweigegebot geriet man in bedrückende Vereinsamung; eine ganze Woche war etwas ganz Entsetzliches.

Im Grunde traf die jungen Mönche lediglich Remigius' Zorn darüber, daß man ihm ein Schnippchen geschlagen hatte. Nach dem Bekenntnis blieb ihm nichts anderes übrig, als die Schuldigen zu bestrafen – obwohl er damit vor allen Mönchen offen zugab, daß Philip von Anfang an recht gehabt hatte. Seine Attacke hatte sich als übler Fehlschlag erwiesen. Trotz eines leichten Anflugs von schlechtem Gewissen genoß Philip seinen Triumph.

Doch die Erniedrigung des Subpriors war damit noch nicht zu Ende.

Cuthbert ergriff das Wort. »Es gab da noch einen weiteren Vorfall, über den wir sprechen sollten. Er ereignete sich gleich nach dem Hochamt im Kreuzgang.« Philip fragte sich, was der alte Mönch nun schon wieder im Schilde führte. »Bruder Andrew machte Bruder Philip schwere Vorwürfe wegen ungebührlichen Benehmens.« Das wissen doch alle längst, dachte Philip, doch Cuthbert fuhr fort: »Ort und Zeit für die Erörterung solcher Vorwürfe ist, wie wir alle wissen, die Kapitelversammlung. So haben es unsere Vorfahren im Orden beschlossen, und sie hatten gute Gründe dafür. Erhitzte Gemüter pflegen sich über Nacht ein wenig abzukühlen, so daß man am nächsten Morgen *sine ira et studio* über die geführten Klagen sprechen kann. Zudem kann die Klostergemeinschaft in der Kapitelversammlung ihr vereintes Wissen einbringen und somit gemeinsam zu einer Lösung der strittigen Frage beitragen. Zu meinem tiefen Bedauern hat Andrew sich über diese kluge Regel höhnisch hinweggesetzt, indem er Philip im Kreuzgang mit unbeherrschter Rede angriff und jedermanns Ruhe und Frieden störte. Es wäre ungerecht gegen die jungen Brüder, die soeben für ihr Tun bestraft wurden, wenn Andrew ohne Buße davonkäme.«

Cuthberts Argumentation war ebenso brillant wie gnadenlos. Die Frage, ob Philip rechtmäßig gehandelt hatte, als er William während des Hochamts aus dem Chor holte, war bisher überhaupt noch nicht erörtert worden – vielmehr hatte jeder Versuch, sie zur Sprache zu bringen, sogleich zu einer kritischen Befragung des Anklägers geführt. Philip empfand dies als gerechten Lohn, denn Andrews Vorwürfe waren unaufrichtig gewesen. Cuthbert und Milius war es gelungen, Remigius und seine beiden Hauptverbündeten, Andrew und Pierre, unglaubwürdig zu machen.

Andrews gemeinhin rotes Gesicht war mittlerweile vor Wut purpurfarben, während Remigius fast ängstlich aussah. Philip war es zufrieden – sie verdienten es nicht anders –, doch sah er auch eine Gefahr: Die Erniedrigung der Gegenspieler konnte zu weit getrieben werden. »Es ziemt sich nicht für jüngere Brüder, über die Bestrafung ihrer Vorgesetzten zu diskutieren«, sagte er. »Überlaßt es dem Subprior, diese Angelegenheit für sich zu entscheiden.« Ein Blick in die Runde verriet ihm, daß die Mönche seine Großmut guthießen – unbeabsichtigt hatte er einen weiteren Teilerfolg errungen.

Alles schien gelaufen. Philip war überzeugt, die meisten der zuvor noch Unentschiedenen auf seine Seite gezogen zu haben. Doch da erhob noch einmal Remigius die Stimme und sagte: »Es gibt da noch eine weitere Angelegenheit, auf die ich zu sprechen kommen möchte.«

Philip sah den Subprior an; der Mann wirkte verzweifelt, Sakristan Andrew und Cirkator Pierre waren sichtlich überrascht. Was nun kam, war demnach nicht von langer Hand geplant.

»Den meisten unter euch dürfte bekannt sein, daß der Bischof das Recht hat, uns Kandidaten seiner Wahl vorzuschlagen«, sagte Remigius. »Er hat darüber hinaus das Recht, die Bestätigung unserer Wahl abzulehnen. Diese Teilung der Macht kann zu Auseinandersetzungen zwischen Bischof und Kloster führen – wie einige ältere Mitbrüder aus leidvoller Erfahrung wissen. Da der Bischof uns nicht dazu zwingen kann, seinen Kandidaten zu akzeptieren, wir aber gegen seinen Willen auch nicht auf dem unseren bestehen können, gibt es im Streitfall nur eine Verhandlungslösung, deren Ausgang zu einem Gutteil von der Entschlossenheit und Einigkeit der Brüder bestimmt wird – vor allem von ihrer *Einigkeit*.«

Philip war nicht ganz wohl bei den Worten des Subpriors. Remigius hatte sich beruhigt, zumindest nach außen hin, und kehrte wieder die alte hochmütige Erhabenheit hervor. Obwohl Philip noch nicht genau wußte, worauf Remigius hinauswollte, verflog das Vorgefühl des sicheren Triumphs.

»Ich erwähne diese Dinge heute, weil mir zwei wichtige Informationen zu Ohren gekommen sind, die ich euch nicht vorenthalten möchte. Zum einen ist es denkbar, daß hier in unserer Runde nicht nur ein einziger Kandidat nominiert wird.« (Das überrascht nun wirklich keinen mehr, dachte Philip.) »Zum anderen wird auch der Bischof einen Kandidaten benennen.«

Remigius machte eine bedeutungsschwangere Pause. Diese Nachricht war wirklich neu – und für beide Lager unangenehm. Irgend jemand fragte: »Weißt du, um *wen* es sich handelt?«

»Ja«, antwortete Remigius, doch Philip war in diesem Augenblick überzeugt, daß er log. »Die Wahl des Bischofs fiel auf Bruder Osbert von Newbury.«

Ein oder zwei Mönche schnappten hörbar nach Luft. Entsetzt waren alle. Osbert von Newbury war ihnen gut bekannt, war er doch eine Zeitlang Cirkator in Kingsbridge gewesen. Er war der illegitime Sohn des Bischofs. Er mißbrauchte die Kirche dazu, ihm ein müßiggängerisches Leben in materiellem Überfluß zu ermöglichen. Nie hatte er auch nur den ernsthaften Versuch unternommen, sich an seine Gelübde zu halten. Nach außen hin umgab er sich mit einer leicht durchschaubaren Scheinheiligkeit, und wenn er in Schwierigkeiten geriet, verließ er sich auf seinen Vater. Die Vorstellung, ihn zum Prior zu haben, war furchterregend – selbst für die Anhänger des Remigius. Allenfalls dem Gästemeister und einem oder zwei seiner unrettbar verderbten Spießgesellen war zuzutrauen, daß sie sich in der Hoffnung auf eine disziplinlose und schludrige Amtsführung für Osbert aussprachen.

Remigius streute Salz in die frische Wunde. »Wenn wir zwei Kandidaten aufstellen, Brüder«, fuhr er fort, »dann ist es möglich, daß der Bischof sagt, sie sind entzweit und können sich nicht auf einen guten Mann einigen … Man muß ihnen also die Entscheidung abnehmen. Wenn wir die Ernennung Osberts verhindern wollen, tun wir folglich gut daran, nur einen einzigen Kandidaten aufzustellen – und zwar einen, wie ich hinzufügen sollte, der auch ernstgenommen wird. Jugend und Unerfahrenheit wären hier zum Beispiel äußerst abträglich.«

Zustimmendes Gemurmel erhob sich. Eben noch hatte Philip wie der sichere Sieger ausgesehen – und nun diese Wendung! Alle Mönche, die er schon gewonnen glaubte, standen auf einmal wieder hinter Remigius und sahen ihn als den sicheren Kandidaten, den Mann, auf den man sich einigen mußte, um Osbert zu verhindern. Philip war nach wie vor überzeugt, daß Remigius gelogen hatte, aber darauf kam es jetzt gar nicht mehr an. Er hatte den Mönchen einen gehörigen Schrecken eingejagt und sich auf diese Weise ihrer Unterstützung versichert. Damit stand fest, daß der Niedergang der Priorei Kingsbridge auch in den kommenden Jahren unaufhaltsam fortschreiten würde.

Ehe noch jemand anders das Wort ergreifen konnte, sagte Remigius: »Laßt uns nun auseinandergehen und im Gebet und bei der Arbeit auf dem Weinberg des Herrn über das Gesagte nachdenken.« Er stand auf und verließ mit Andrew, Pierre und John Small im Gefolge den Kapitelsaal. Seine drei Mitstreiter wirkten ebenso verblüfft wie siegessicher.

Kaum waren die vier fort, erhob sich sogleich wieder aufgeregtes Stimmengewirr. »Soviel Raffinesse hätte ich Remigius nie zugetraut«, sagte Milius zu Philip.

»Er lügt«, erwiderte Philip bitter, »ich bin mir dessen ganz sicher.«

Cuthbert, der zu ihnen getreten war, hatte die Bemerkung mitbekommen. »Und wenn schon«, sagte er. »Die Drohung alleine genügt.«

»Eines Tages wird die Wahrheit schon ans Licht kommen«, meinte Philip.

»Nicht unbedingt«, antwortete Milius. »Nehmen wir an, der Bischof verzichtet auf die Nominierung Osberts. Da wird Remigius dann einfach behaupten, er habe aus Furcht vor einem Streit mit dem einmütigen Kloster einen Rückzieher gemacht.«

Philip blieb hart. »Ich gebe noch nicht auf«, sagte er.

»Was können wir noch tun?« fragte Milius.

»Wir müssen die Wahrheit herausfinden.«

»Und wie?«

Philip überlegte angestrengt. Die Ausweglosigkeit bereitete ihm physische Schmerzen. »Warum können wir ihn nicht einfach fragen?«

»Fragen? Wen?«

»Den Bischof. Wir können uns doch bei ihm selbst nach seinen Absichten erkundigen.«

»Wie stellst du dir das vor?«

»Wir können eine Botschaft an den bischöflichen Palast schicken, oder?« Philip sah Cuthbert an.

Cuthbert dachte nach. »Ja, das ist möglich. Ich sende ohnehin dauernd Botschafter aus. Da kann ich auch einen zum Bischof schikken.«

»Und den Bischof fragen lassen, was er vorhat?« fragte Milius skeptisch.

Philip runzelte die Stirn. Genau das war der kritische Punkt.

Cuthbert stimmte Milius zu. »Der Bischof wird uns keine Antwort geben«, meinte er.

Philip hatte eine Idee, und seine finstere Miene hellte sich auf. Aufgeregt hieb er mit der geballten rechten Faust in die linke Handfläche. »Nein«, sagte er, »der Bischof nicht. Aber sein Erzdiakon.«

In dieser Nacht träumte Philip von Jonathan, dem ausgesetzten Säugling. In seinem Traum lag das Kind im Portal der Kapelle von St.-John-in-the-Forest, während Philip im Inneren der Kirche die Prim las. Da erschien auf einmal ein Wolf am Waldesrand und schlich sich geschmeidig wie eine Schlange über das Feld, um das Kind zu holen. Philip unternahm nichts; er hatte Angst, den Gottesdienst zu stören und von Remigius und Andrew, die beide zugegen waren, gescholten zu werden. (In Wirklichkeit war keiner von beiden jemals in Philips Zelle gewesen.) Philip entschloß sich zu schreien, doch als er es versuchte, entrang sich, wie so oft in Träumen, kein Laut seiner Kehle. Er versuchte es wieder und wieder – und strengte sich dabei so an, daß er erwachte. Zitternd lag er auf dem Bett und hörte die Atemzüge der schlafenden Mönche um ihn herum. Erst langsam gelang es ihm, sich davon zu überzeugen, daß der Wolf nur eine Ausgeburt seines Traums war.

Seit seiner Ankunft in Kingsbridge hatte er kaum noch an den kleinen Jungen gedacht. Nun fragte er sich, was er mit dem Knaben machen sollte, falls er doch noch zum Prior gewählt würde. Die Voraussetzungen wären gänzlich andere. In einem kleinen Kloster im Wald fiel ein Säugling nicht sonderlich auf. Derselbe Säugling in Kingsbridge würde dagegen für erhebliche Aufregung sorgen. Und wenn schon, dachte Philip. Es ist keine Sünde, den Leuten Anlaß zum Klatschen zu geben. Wenn ich Prior bin, kann ich tun und lassen, was mir gefällt. Ich kann Johnny Eightpence nach Kingsbridge holen und ihn weiterhin für das Kind sorgen lassen ...

Philip empfand eine ungebührliche Freude bei diesem Gedanken und war fest entschlossen, ihn in die Tat umzusetzen. Erst dann fiel ihm ein, daß er aller Wahrscheinlichkeit nach gar nicht Prior werden würde.

Den Rest der Nacht über lag er wach, von fiebriger Ungeduld erfüllt. Es gab nichts, was er hätte tun können, um sein Anliegen voranzutreiben. Gespräche mit den Mitbrüdern würden nichts einbringen, denn deren Denken wurde beherrscht von der Furcht vor Osbert. Einige von ihnen hatten ihn nach der Versammlung sogar noch angesprochen und ihm gesagt, wie sehr sie seine Niederlage bedauerten – ganz so, als hätte die Wahl längst stattgefunden. Mit Mühe hatte er der Versuchung widerstanden, sie alle als treulose Feiglinge zu bezeichnen, und ihnen statt dessen lächelnd beschieden, daß sie sich vielleicht noch wundern würden. In Wirklichkeit war seine Zuversicht schwer erschüttert. Wer konnte schon sagen, wie Erzdiakon Waleran reagieren würde? Vielleicht war er gar nicht anwesend, wenn die Botschaft im Bischofspalast eintraf, und selbst wenn er anwesend war, konnte es durchaus sein, daß er aus bestimmten Gründen dagegen war, daß Philip von den Plänen des Bischofs erfuhr. Am wahrscheinlichsten war freilich, daß Waleran, seiner Natur entsprechend, eigene Pläne verfolgte.

Als der Morgen graute, stand Philip zusammen mit den Mitbrüdern auf und ging in die Kirche zur Prim, dem ersten Gebet des Tages. Danach wollte er gemeinsam mit den anderen das Frühstück einnehmen, wurde jedoch auf dem Weg zum Refektorium von Milius aufgehalten und mit einer verschwörerischen Geste in die Küche gebeten. Philip folgte ihm; seine Nerven waren zum Zerreißen gespannt. Der Botschafter war offenbar schon zurück. Doch selbst wenn er sofort Antwort bekommen und noch am gleichen Nachmittag den Rückweg angetreten hatte, war er ungewöhnlich schnell gewesen. Nach Philips Kenntnis stand im Klosterstall kein Pferd, dem ein so rasanter Ritt zuzutrauen war. Oder steckte etwas anderes dahinter?

Nicht der Botschafter stand in der Küche und wartete auf ihn. Es war der Erzdiakon persönlich, Waleran Bigod.

Philip starrte ihn voller Überraschung an. Die hagere, schwarzgekleidete Gestalt hockte auf einem Stuhl wie eine Krähe auf einem Baumstumpf. Die Spitze der schnabelartig gekrümmten Nase war rotgefroren. Waleran wärmte seine knochenbleichen Hände an einem Becher mit heißem Glühwein.

»Wie gut, daß Ihr gekommen seid!« platzte Philip heraus.

»Ich danke Euch für Eure Nachricht«, erwiderte Waleran kühl.

»Stimmt es wirklich«, fragte Philip ungeduldig, »daß der Bischof Osbert von Newbury als Kandidat für die Nachfolge von Prior James nominieren will?«

Waleran hob die Hand, um Philips Ungestüm zu bremsen. »Darauf komme ich noch«, sagte er. »Bruder Cuthbert war gerade dabei, mich über die gestrigen Ereignisse zu informieren.«

Philip verbarg seine Enttäuschung. Er hatte sich eine direkte Antwort erhofft. Vergeblich studierte er Walerans Miene. Der Erzdiakon verfolgte in der Tat seine eigenen Pläne – nur war ihm beim besten Willen nicht anzumerken, welche.

Cuthbert, den Philip zunächst gar nicht gesehen hatte, saß am Feuer und tauchte sein Brot ins Bier, um es für seine altgewordenen Zähne aufzuweichen, und fuhr mit seinem Bericht über die Kapitelversammlung fort. Philip trat unruhig von einem Fuß auf den anderen und versuchte, Walerans Miene zu enträtseln. Er probierte ein Stück Brot, fand es jedoch zu hart. Nur um seine Hände irgendwie zu beschäftigen, griff er schließlich zum Bierkrug und trank einen Schluck.

»Und so«, sagte Cuthbert schließlich, »sahen wir nur eine einzige Möglichkeit: Wir mußten versuchen, die wahren Absichten des Bischofs zu ergründen. Bruder Philip sah sich in der glücklichen Lage, Euch jüngst persönlich kennengelernt zu haben. Deshalb sandten wir die Botschaft an Euch.«

»Und nun sagt Ihr uns, was wir wissen wollen?« fragte Philip ungeduldig.

»Ja, ich werde es euch sagen.« Waleran stellte den Becher mit Glühwein ab, ohne einen Schluck getrunken zu haben. »Der Bischof möchte, daß sein Sohn Prior von Kingsbridge wird.«

Philip sah seine Hoffnungen schwinden. »So hat Remigius also die Wahrheit gesagt.«

»Allerdings«, fuhr Waleran fort, »ist der Bischof nicht bereit, es auf einen Streit mit den Mönchen ankommen zu lassen.«

Philip runzelte die Stirn. Auch dies entsprach mehr oder weniger dem, was Remigius gesagt hatte. Trotzdem war irgend etwas an der Sache faul. »Nur um uns das zu erzählen, habt Ihr den weiten Weg hierher sicher nicht auf Euch genommen.«

Waleran sah Philip an, und eine gewisse Anerkennung lag in seinem Blick. »Nein«, sagte er. »Der Bischof hat mich gebeten, die Stimmung hier im Kloster zu ergründen. Zudem hat er mir die Vollmacht erteilt, in seinem Namen einen Kandidaten zu nominieren. Ich führe das bischöfliche Siegel bei mir, so daß ich das Nominierungsschreiben hier an Ort und Stelle verbindlich ausfertigen kann.«

Es dauerte einen Augenblick, bis Philip die ganze Tragweite des Gesagten begriff. Waleran war bevollmächtigt, mit Brief und Siegel des Bischofs einen Kandidaten zu nominieren. Der Bischof hatte die gesamte Angelegenheit seinem Erzdiakon überlassen, der folglich mit allerhöchster Autorität schalten und walten konnte.

Philip holte tief Luft und sagte: »Seht Ihr ein, was Cuthbert gerade zu erklären versuchte: daß nämlich Osberts Kandidatur zu eben jenem Streit führen würde, den der Bischof zu vermeiden trachtet?«

»Ja, durchaus.«

»Dann werdet Ihr Osbert also nicht nominieren?«

»Nein.«

Philip war gespannt wie eine Bogensehne. Wenn ihnen Osbert erspart blieb, würden die Mönche aus lauter Dankbarkeit jeden anderen Kandidaten wählen, den Waleran ihnen präsentierte.

Die Entscheidung über den neuen Prior von Kingsbridge lag in Walerans Hand.

»Wen dann?« fragte Philip.

»Euch ... oder Remigius ...«

»Remigius' Fähigkeiten ...«

»Seine Fähigkeiten sind mir ebensogut bekannt wie die Euren«, unterbrach ihn Waleran mit erhobener weißer Hand. »Und ich weiß auch, wer von euch beiden der bessere Prior wäre. Aber darum alleine geht es nicht.«

Was soll das nun schon wieder? fragte sich Philip. *Darf* es überhaupt noch um etwas anderes gehen? Er blickte in die Runde. Milius war nicht minder verblüfft als er, doch der alte Cuthbert lächelte, als wisse er genau, worum es ging.

»Mir ist wie Euch daran gelegen, daß wichtige kirchliche Ämter nicht generell an ältere Würdenträger vergeben werden, deren Heiligmäßigkeit größer sein mag als ihre administrativen Fähigkeiten ... Es gilt vielmehr, kraftvolle und fähige Persönlichkeiten zu fördern, auch wenn sie an Jahren noch recht jung sein mögen.«

»Natürlich«, bestätigte Philip ungeduldig, ohne die tiefere Bedeutung von Walerans Rede zu begreifen.

»Wir vier, die wir hier versammelt sind, sollten zu diesem Behufe zusammenarbeiten«, fuhr Waleran fort.

»Ich weiß nicht, worauf Ihr hinauswollt«, sagte Milius.

»Ich schon«, bemerkte Cuthbert.

Waleran bedachte Cuthbert mit einem dünnen Lächeln und wandte sich wieder an Philip. »Laßt mich offen zu Euch sprechen«, sagte er. »Der Bischof selbst ist schon recht alt. Eines Tages wird er sterben, und dann wird sich die Frage nach einem Nachfolger stellen, genauso wie jetzt im Amt des Priors. Die Wahl des Bischofs vollziehen die Mönche von Kingsbridge, denn der Bischof von Kingsbridge ist gleichzeitig ihr Abt.«

Philip runzelte die Stirn. Was sollte das alles nur? Es ging um die Wahl des Priors, um sonst nichts.

Doch Waleran fuhr fort: »Natürlich sind die Mönche in ihrer Wahlentscheidung nicht vollkommen frei, denn auch der Erzbischof und der König haben ihre Vorstellungen von der Besetzung des Bischofsstuhls. In letzter Instanz müssen jedoch die Mönche mit ihrer Stimme die Ernennung legitimieren. Ihr drei werdet, wenn die Zeit gekommen ist, großen Einfluß auf die Entscheidung haben.«

Cuthbert nickte; seine Vermutungen schienen sich bestätigt zu haben. Jetzt dämmerte auch Philip, worauf der Erzdiakon hinauswollte.

Waleran kam zum Ende: »Ihr wollt, daß ich Euch zum Prior von Kingsbridge mache. Ich will, daß Ihr mich zum Bischof macht.«

Das also steckte dahinter!

Unfähig, ein Wort zu sagen, starrte Philip Waleran an. Es war alles ganz einfach. Der Erzdiakon schlug ihnen einen Kuhhandel vor. Das war zwar nicht unbedingt dasselbe wie die Sünde der Simonie, also der Kauf und Verkauf kirchlicher Ämter, hatte aber dennoch einen unangenehm geschäftlichen Beigeschmack. Er bemühte sich um eine nüchterne Betrachtung des Angebots. Seine Wahl zum Prior wäre damit gesichert. Mit klopfendem Herzen gestand sich Philip ein, daß ihm unter diesen Voraussetzungen nicht der Sinn danach stand, spitzfindige Bedenken zu formulieren.

Waleran, auch dies stand fest, würde zu einem späteren Zeitpunkt Bischof werden. Ob er ein guter Bischof sein würde? An Kompetenz mangelte es ihm gewiß nicht, und so, wie es schien, war er auch frei von ernsten Lastern. Er hatte eine eher weltliche, praktische Einstellung, was den Dienst am Herrn betraf, aber das konnte Philip auch von sich selbst sagen.

Sicher, da war eine gewisse Rücksichtslosigkeit im Auftreten des Erzdiakons, die Philip fremd war, doch beruhte sie allem Anschein nach auf der festen Entschlossenheit, die Interessen der Kirche zu wahren und zu fördern.

Wer sonst kam als Nachfolger des Bischofs in Frage? Wahrscheinlich Osbert. Daß kirchliche Ämter vom Vater auf den Sohn vererbt wurden, war trotz der offiziellen Forderung nach Einhaltung des Zölibats keineswegs unüblich. Osbert als Bischof wäre indessen eine noch größere Belastung für die Kirche als ein Prior Osbert, dachte Philip. Allein, um seine Wahl zu verhindern, wären wir möglicherweise sogar gezwungen, einen erheblich schwächeren Kandidaten als Waleran zu unterstützen.

Und sonst? Es war unmöglich vorauszusagen, wie sich die Lage nach dem Ableben des Bischofs darbieten würde. Auf jeden Fall konnten noch Jahre ins Land gehen, bis es soweit war.

»Wir können Euch nicht garantieren, daß Ihr gewählt werdet«, sagte Cuthbert zu Waleran.

»Das weiß ich wohl«, erwiderte der Erzdiakon. »Ich bitte Euch auch lediglich um die Nominierung – was, streng genommen, genau meinem Angebot an Euch entspricht.«

Cuthbert nickte. »Ich bin einverstanden«, sagte er feierlich.

»Ich auch«, pflichtete Milius ihm bei.

Der Erzdiakon und die beiden Mönche sahen Philip an, der sichtlich hin und her gerissen war. Das war alles andere als eine ordnungsgemäße Bischofswahl, er machte sich da nichts vor. Andererseits: Das erhoffte Amt lag greifbar nahe. Es war gewiß nicht recht, daß kirchliche Ämter gehandelt wurden wie Pferde auf dem Roßmarkt – doch wenn er jetzt nein sagte, stand zu erwarten, daß Remigius Prior und Osbert Bischof würde!

Indes, was galten in dieser Stunde schon vernünftige Argumente! Philip war von dem brennenden Wunsch erfüllt, Prior von Kingsbridge zu werden, und dieser Wunsch war eine unwiderstehliche Kraft, egal, was im einzelnen dafür oder dagegen sprach. Er erinnerte sich an sein Gebet vom Vortag: Ich habe Gott versprochen, um dieses Amt zu kämpfen. Nun hob er die Augen und schickte ein Stoßgebet zum Himmel: *Wenn Du es nicht geschehen lassen willst, dann lähme meinen*

Mund und meine Zunge, lasse meinen Atem stocken und mach, daß ich nicht mehr sprechen kann.

Dann sah er Waleran in die Augen und sagte: »Ich bin einverstanden.«

Das Bett des Priors war riesig – mindestens dreimal so breit wie das größte Bett, in dem Philip je zuvor geschlafen hatte. Der hölzerne Bettkasten war halb so hoch wie ein Mann, und darüber lag noch eine Federmatratze. Um zu verhindern, daß der Schläfer des Nachts Zug bekam, war es rundum mit Vorhängen umgeben, die von der geduldigen Hand einer frommen Frau mit biblischen Motiven bestickt worden waren.

Philip betrachtete das Bett nicht ohne Vorbehalte. Daß ihm als Prior ein eigenes Schlafzimmer zustand, empfand er bereits als genug der Ehre. Er hatte nie zuvor ein eigenes Schlafzimmer gehabt und folglich noch kein einziges Mal in seinem Leben alleine geschlafen. Das Bett war schlichtweg zu üppig ... Er überlegte, ob er sich eine Strohmatratze aus dem Dormitorium bringen und das Bett ins Infirmarium schaffen lassen sollte, wo es die Leiden eines siechen alten Mönchs lindern helfen mochte. Aber das Bett war ja nicht nur für ihn selbst da: Wenn hoher Besuch angesagt war – ein Bischof, ein Lord oder sogar ein König –, suchte sich der Prior irgendwo anders eine Lagerstatt und überließ sein Schlafzimmer dem Gast. Man konnte das Bett also nicht so ohne weiteres entfernen.

»Ihr werdet heute nacht gewiß gut schlafen«, sagte Waleran Bigod nicht ohne einen neidvollen Unterton.

»Ja, das sollte ich eigentlich«, antwortete Philip, doch es klang nicht sehr überzeugt.

Alles war ganz schnell gegangen. Noch in der Küche hatte Waleran einen Brief an die Priorei verfaßt, in dem er die Mönche aufforderte, sofort zur Wahl zu schreiten, und Philip für das Amt des Priors nominierte. Er hatte den Brief mit dem Namen des Bischofs gezeichnet und mit dem bischöflichen Siegel versehen.

Sie hatten sich dann gemeinsam zum Kapitelsaal begeben, wo Remigius sofort bei ihrem Eintritt erkannte, daß die Schlacht für ihn verloren war. Waleran trug den Brief vor. Als er Philip für das Amt des Priors vorschlug, applaudierten die Mönche. Remigius war klug genug, auf eine formelle Abstimmung zu verzichten, und gestand seine Niederlage ein.

Philip war Prior.

Er hatte sofort den Vorsitz über die Kapitelversammlung übernommen und sie wie in Trance zu Ende geführt. Dann war er über die Wiese zum Haus des Priors gegangen, das in der Südostecke des Klostergeländes stand, und hatte dort offiziell Wohnung genommen.

Erst beim Anblick des Bettes wurde ihm klar, daß sein Leben eine tiefgreifende, unumkehrbare Wandlung erfahren hatte. Er war jetzt etwas Besonderes, erhaben über die anderen Mönche. Er verfügte über Macht und Privilegien. Und er trug Verantwortung. Ihm allein oblag die Sorge über das Wohl und Wehe jener kleinen Gemeinschaft von fünfundvierzig Männern: Litten sie Hunger, so war es seine Schuld; verlotterten sie an Leib und Seele, traf ihn der gerechte Tadel; machten sie der Kirche des Herrn Schande, so würde der Herr ihn, Philip, zur Rechenschaft ziehen. Du hast dich nach dieser Last gedrängt, erinnerte er sich – nun mußt du sie auch tragen.

Seine erste Pflicht bestand darin, die Mönche zum Hochamt in die Kirche zu führen. Es war Dreikönigstag, der zwölfte Tag nach Weihnachten, ein Feiertag. Alle Dorfbewohner und zahlreiche Menschen aus der näheren und weiteren Umgebung würden den Gottesdienst besuchen. Eine gute Kathedrale mit einer ansehnlichen Mönchsgemeinschaft und einem Ruf für besonders feierliche Messen konnte tausend Menschen und mehr anziehen. Selbst die trostlose Kirche in Kingsbridge zog noch einen Großteil des lokalen Adels an, war doch der Gottesdienst gleichzeitig ein gesellschaftliches Ereignis, bei dem man Nachbarn, Freunde und Geschäftspartner traf.

Philip indessen hatte vor der Messe, nun da sie endlich allein waren, noch etwas mit Waleran zu besprechen. »Erinnert Ihr Euch an die Nachricht, die ich Euch kürzlich überbrachte?« begann er. »Ihr wißt, die Sache mit dem Grafen von Shiring ...«

Waleran nickte. »Und ob ich mich erinnere! Ja, diese Angelegenheit mag in der Tat von größerer Bedeutung sein als die Frage, wer Prior und wer Bischof wird. Graf Bartholomäus ist bereits in England eingetroffen. Man erwartet ihn morgen in Shiring.«

»Was habt Ihr vor?« fragte Philip besorgt.

»Ich möchte mich Sir Percy Hamleighs bedienen«, erwiderte Waleran. »Ich hoffe, daß er heute zur Messe kommen wird.«

»Ich habe von ihm gehört, kenne ihn jedoch nicht persönlich«, sagte Philip.

»Haltet Ausschau nach einem dicken Lord mit einem scheußlichen Weib und einem hübschen Sohn. Die Frau ist unübersehbar in ihrer Häßlichkeit.«

»Was veranlaßt Euch zu dem Glauben, daß sich die beiden auf König Stephans Seite schlagen könnten?«

»Sie hassen den Grafen leidenschaftlich.«

»Warum?«

»Ihr Sohn, William, war mit der Tochter des Grafen verlobt. Sie wandte sich jedoch von ihm ab, und die Hochzeit wurde abgesagt. Für die Hamleighs war dies eine schwere Demütigung. Sie leiden noch heute darunter und warten nur darauf, sich an Graf Bartholomäus rächen zu können.«

Philip nickte befriedigt. Er war froh, wenigstens dieses Problem vom Hals zu haben; es gab, weiß Gott, allein in Kingsbridge genügend andere. Sollte sich Waleran um die Welt außerhalb der Klostermauern kümmern.

Sie verließen das Haus des Priors und begaben sich zum Kreuzgang, wo die Mönche bereits warteten. Philip übernahm die Spitze, und die kleine Prozession setzte sich in Bewegung.

Philip genoß den Einzug in die Kirche mit den singenden Mönchen in seinem Gefolge ... ja, er gestand sich ein, daß seine Freude daran größer war, als er zuvor geahnt hatte. Er suchte nach einer Erklärung für dieses überschwengliche Glücksgefühl. Es muß daran liegen, sagte er sich, daß meine neue, hervorgehobene Stellung die Macht, Gutes zu tun, symbolisiert. Ich wünschte, Abt Peter von Gwynedd könnte mich jetzt sehen ... Wie stolz er wäre, der alte Mann!

Er führte die Mönche zu ihren Bänken im Chor. An bedeutenden Feiertagen wie diesem wurde die Messe oft vom Bischof persönlich gehalten. Heute hielt sie der Stellvertreter des Bischofs, Erzdiakon Waleran. Als Waleran begann, ließ Philip seinen Blick über die Gemeinde der Gläubigen schweifen und versuchte, die Familie Hamleigh ausfindig zu machen. Ungefähr hundertfünfzig Menschen standen im Schiff. Die Reichen unter ihnen waren an ihren schweren Wintermänteln und Lederschuhen zu erkennen, die Bauern trugen Filzstiefel oder Holzschuhe und grobe Jacken. Es war nicht schwer, die Hamleighs zu finden. Sie standen ziemlich weit vorn in der Nähe des Altars. Waleran hatte nicht übertrieben. Die Frau war von geradezu abstoßender Häßlichkeit. Obwohl sie eine Haube trug, war ihr Gesicht zum größten Teil frei. Philip konnte sehen, daß es mit großen Geschwüren übersät war, an denen sie fortwährend herumfingerte. Neben ihr stand ein gewichtiger Herr von ungefähr vierzig Jahren; das mußte Percy sein. Seine Kleider verrieten, daß er ein Mann von beträchtlichem Wohlstand und Einfluß war, aber nicht zur allerersten Garnitur der Grafen und Barone zählte. Der Sohn lehnte an einer der gewaltigen Säulen, die das Kirchenschiff trugen – ein gutgewachsener junger Mann mit hellblondem Haar, engstehenden Augen und hochmütigem Blick. Die Einheirat in eine Grafenfamilie hätte den Hamleighs eine Brücke über jene Kluft geschlagen, die die kleinen Landedelleute vom Hochadel des Königreichs trennte. Kein Wunder, daß sie sich über die geplatzte Hochzeit ärgerten.

Philip konzentrierte sich wieder auf den Gottesdienst. Für seinen Geschmack zelebrierte Waleran die Messe ein wenig zu hastig. Einmal mehr fragte sich Philip, ob er recht daran getan hatte, sich auf die Nominierung Walerans zum Nachfolger des Bischofs einzulassen. An seiner Strebsamkeit bestand kein Zweifel – nur schien der Erzdiakon die Bedeutung der Liturgie zu unterschätzen. Die Macht und der Reichtum der Kirche waren schließlich nur ein Mittel zum Zweck: Das eigentliche Ziel war die Rettung der Seelen. Ich sollte mir über Waleran nicht den Kopf zerbrechen, dachte Philip. Geschehen ist geschehen – und wahrscheinlich dämpft der Bischof Walerans Ehrgeiz schon allein dadurch, daß er noch zwanzig Jahre am Leben bleibt!

Die Gemeinde war unruhig. Eine aktive Beteiligung am Gottesdienst wurde nur von Priestern und Mönchen erwartet; die Gläubigen waren nur mit einigen wenigen bekannten Gebeten vertraut und stimmten ansonsten nur beim Amen ein. Manche verfolgten den Ablauf der Messe in ehrfürchtigem Schweigen, andere aber liefen von einem zum anderen, begrüßten einander und unterhielten sich. Es sind einfache Leute, dachte Philip bei sich. Man muß ihnen etwas *bieten,* wenn man ihre Aufmerksamkeit wachhalten will.

Der Gottesdienst näherte sich seinem Ende. Erzdiakon Waleran sprach zu den Versammelten: »Die meisten von euch werden wissen, daß unser geliebter Prior von Kingsbridge von uns gegangen ist. Sein Leichnam ist hier in der Kirche aufgebahrt und wird heute mittag nach dem Essen auf dem Klosterfriedhof zur letzten Ruhe gebettet. Der Bischof und die Mönche von Kingsbridge haben Bruder Philip von Gwynedd, der uns heute morgen in die Kirche führte, zu seinem Nachfolger gewählt.«

Waleran hielt inne, und Philip erhob sich, um die Prozession wieder hinauszugeleiten. Da ließ sich Waleran erneut vernehmen: »Ich habe eine weitere traurige Nachricht bekanntzugeben.«

Völlig überrascht setzte sich Philip wieder.

»Ich erhielt soeben eine Botschaft«, sagte Waleran.

Das stimmt nicht, dachte Philip. Wir waren den ganzen Morgen zusammen. Was hatte dieser durchtriebene Erzdiakon denn nun schon wieder vor?

»Die Botschaft wird uns alle in tiefe Trauer stürzen.« Wieder machte er eine Kunstpause.

Irgend jemand war gestorben – bloß wer? Waleran mußte es schon bei seiner Ankunft gewußt haben, doch hatte er kein Wort darüber verloren. Warum?

Philip fiel nur eine einzige Antwort ein – und wenn sich dieser Verdacht bewahrheitete, dann war Waleran weit ehrgeiziger und skrupelloser, als Philip es sich je hätte träumen lassen. Hatte er sie wirklich alle getäuscht und manipuliert? War er, Philip, nichts als ein Spielstein auf Walerans Brett gewesen?

Walerans abschließende Worte bestätigten die schlimmsten Befürchtungen. »Liebe Gemeinde«, sagte er feierlich, »der Bischof von Kingsbridge ist tot.«

»Das Luder wird auch dasein«, sagte Williams Mutter. »Ich bin mir ganz sicher.«

Mit einer Mischung aus Beklemmung und Sehnsucht musterte William die drohend vor ihnen aufragende Fassade der Kathedrale von Kingsbridge. Wenn Lady Aliena auch an der Dreikönigsmesse teilnimmt, dachte er, wird das für uns alle furchtbar peinlich. Dennoch beschleunigte der Gedanke, er könne sie vielleicht wiedersehen, seinen Herzschlag.

Im Trab näherten sie sich Kingsbridge: William und sein Vater auf Schlachtrössern, seine Mutter auf einem feinen Rennpferd. Drei Ritter und drei Bedienstete folgten ihnen. Sie bildeten einen eindrucksvollen, ja – zu Williams heimlichem Vergnügen – einen geradezu furchterregenden Trupp; die Bauern, die zu Fuß nach Kingsbridge unterwegs waren, stoben erschrocken auseinander, wenn hinter ihnen der Hufschlag der stattlichen Rösser erklang.

Williams Mutter schäumte vor Wut. »Sie alle wissen Bescheid«, fauchte sie mit zusammengebissenen Zähnen, »selbst diese elenden Leibeigenen. Sie machen sich über uns lustig. ›Wann ist eine Braut keine Braut?‹ fragen sie und antworten: ›Wenn der Bräutigam Will Hamleigh heißt.‹ Ich habe einen Kerl deswegen auspeitschen lassen, aber nicht einmal das half. Wenn dieses Luder mir in die Hände fällt, zieh’ ich ihr bei lebendigem Leib die Haut ab, hänge sie an einen Nagel und laß die Raben ihr bloßes Fleisch zerhacken!« Hoffentlich hört sie bald auf damit, dachte William. Die Familie war gedemütigt worden, und schuld daran war er – jedenfalls behauptete das seine Mutter. Er wollte nicht dauernd daran erinnert werden.

Die alte Holzbrücke über dem Fluß dröhnte unter den Huftritten. Auf dem Gräberfeld nördlich der Kirche taten sich bereits zwanzig oder dreißig Pferde am spärlichen Gras gütlich, doch keines darunter konnte es mit den Tieren der Hamleighs aufnehmen.

Sie ritten vor bis zum Stall und überließen die Pferde den Stallknechten der Priorei. Dann schritten sie in strenger Formation über die Grünfläche: zur Rechten und zur Linken der Mutter Vater und Sohn, dahinter die Ritter und als Nachhut die Bediensteten. Die Leute öffneten ihnen eine Gasse, doch William konnte sehen, wie sie sich gegenseitig anstießen, verstohlen mit dem Finger auf sie zeigten und miteinander tuschelten. Er war fest davon überzeugt, daß sie nur ein Thema hatten: die geplatzte Verlobung, die Hochzeit, aus der nichts geworden war. Er riskierte einen Seitenblick auf seine Mutter und erkannte an ihrem Gewitterblick, daß sie das gleiche dachte wie er.

Dann betraten sie die Kirche.

William haßte Kirchen. Selbst bei schönem Wetter war es darin düster und kalt, und aus dunklen Winkeln und den niedrigen Gewölben der Seitenschiffe waberte Modergeruch. Vor allem aber erinnerten ihn Kirchen immer an die Qualen der Hölle – und vor der Hölle fürchtete er sich.

Er ließ seinen Blick in die Runde schweifen. Anfangs fiel es ihm schwer, die Gesichter der Gläubigen zu erkennen, doch auch, nachdem sich seine Augen an die Dunkelheit gewöhnt hatten, konnte er Aliena nirgends entdecken. Sie hatten das Seitenschiff fast durchschritten. Nirgendwo eine Spur von ihr. William war gleichermaßen erleichtert wie enttäuscht. Doch dann erspähte er sie, und sein Herz setzte einen Schlag aus.

Aliena stand ziemlich weit vorn im südlichen Teil des Schiffs, eskortiert von einem Ritter, den William nicht kannte, und umgeben von Bewaffneten und Zofen. Obwohl sie ihm den Rücken zuwandte, war sie an ihrer dunklen, wallenden Lockenpracht leicht zu erkennen.

Er hatte Aliena kaum erblickt, als sie sich umdrehte. William sah die sanft geschwungene Linie ihrer Wange und die gerade, gebieterische Nase im Profil. Der Blick aus ihren dunklen, fast schwarzen Augen begegnete dem seinen. William hielt den Atem an. Die dunklen, ohnehin schon großen Augen weiteten sich noch, als Aliena ihn erkannte. William wollte desinteressiert an ihr vorbeischauen und so tun, als habe er sie nicht gesehen, aber er war nicht imstande, seine Augen von ihr abzuwenden. Er sehnte sich nach einem Lächeln von ihr, wenigstens einem angedeuteten, einer gerade noch wahrnehmbaren Krümmung ihrer vollen Lippen, das nichts weiter besagen mochte als höfliche Kenntnisnahme. Er neigte den Kopf – es war eher ein

Nicken als eine Verbeugung. Alienas Züge verhärteten sich, und sie drehte sich wieder um.

Wie von einem plötzlichen Schmerz getroffen, zuckte William zusammen. Er kam sich vor wie ein getretener Hund und hätte sich am liebsten in eine dunkle Ecke verkrochen. Vorsichtig sah er sich nach allen Seiten um. Ob jemand den Blickwechsel beobachtet hatte? Die Leute sahen von ihm zu Aliena und wieder zu ihm. Sie stießen einander in die Rippen und flüsterten. Um niemanden ansehen zu müssen, hielt William den Blick starr geradeaus gerichtet. Es kostete ihn Überwindung, den Kopf hochzuhalten. Wie konnte sie uns das nur antun? fragte er sich. Wir sind eine der stolzesten Familien in Südengland, und ihretwegen kommen wir uns jetzt klein und unbedeutend vor. Allein der Gedanke daran trieb ihm die Zornesröte ins Gesicht. Am liebsten hätte er sein Schwert gezogen und wäre damit auf jemanden losgegangen – egal, auf wen.

Der Vogt von Shiring begrüßte Williams Vater mit Handschlag. Die Leute wandten sich ab und suchten sich etwas anderes, worüber sie klatschen konnten. Williams Wut war ungebrochen. Aliena wurde von jungen Adligen begrüßt; einer nach dem anderen verneigte sich vor ihr. *Denen* lächelt sie bereitwillig zu, dachte William.

Die Messe begann. Warum nur mußte das alles so entsetzlich schiefgehen? fragte er sich. Graf Bartholomäus hatte einen Sohn, der einst sein Vermögen und seinen Titel erben würde. Seine Tochter taugte also für eine lohnende politische Verbindung. Aliena war sechzehn Jahre alt und noch Jungfrau. Da sie fürs Klosterleben nichts übrighatte, ging jedermann davon aus, daß ihr der Heiratsantrag eines gesunden, neunzehnjährigen Edelmanns gerade recht kommen mußte – schließlich hätte ihr Vater ihr aus politischen Erwägungen auch einen feisten, gichtigen Vierzigjährigen oder gar einen kahlköpfigen sechzigjährigen Baron aussuchen können.

Als der Ehevertrag besiegelt war, hatten William und seine Eltern kein Geheimnis mehr daraus gemacht, im Gegenteil: In allen Grafschaften nah und fern hatten sie die große Neuigkeit verbreitet. Das erste Treffen der Neuverlobten wurde allenthalben nur als reine Formalität betrachtet – nur nicht von Aliena, wie sich herausstellen sollte.

Sie kannten einander natürlich schon länger. William konnte sich noch gut an das kleine Mädchen Aliena mit dem schelmischen Gesicht und der Stupsnase erinnern. Die widerspenstigen Haare trug sie damals kurz geschnitten. Sie war ein streitlustiger, draufgängerischer

Dickkopf gewesen, und alle anderen Kinder tanzten nach ihrer Pfeife. Aliena bestimmte, welche Spiele gespielt wurden und wer in welche Mannschaft kam; sie schlichtete Streitigkeiten und zählte Punkte und Tore. Ihre dominierende Art hatte William einerseits fasziniert, andererseits aber auch abgestoßen. Wenn man einen Streit vom Zaun brach, konnte man Aliena aus dem Tritt bringen und sich selbst in Szene setzen – aber immer nur vorübergehend. Über kurz oder lang nahm sie unweigerlich das Heft wieder in die Hand – und er, William, saß da und fühlte sich besiegt, verschmäht, verärgert – und verzaubert, ganz ähnlich wie auch jetzt wieder.

Nach dem Tode ihrer Mutter begleitete Aliena ihren Vater auf vielen Reisen. William bekam sie daher nicht mehr so oft zu Gesicht wie früher – aber immer noch oft genug, daß ihm auffiel, zu welch atemberaubender Schönheit sie heranwuchs. Als man ihm eröffnet hatte, sie solle seine Braut werden, war er daher hocherfreut gewesen. Was Aliena davon hielt, kümmerte ihn nicht; schließlich, so hatte er geglaubt, bestimme nicht sie über die Auswahl ihres künftigen Gemahls. Trotzdem wollte er sie besuchen, bevor er sie zum Altar führte. In bester Absicht machte er sich auf den Weg.

Aliena war noch Jungfrau, er jedoch hatte schon seine Erfahrungen. Unter den Mädchen, die er umworben hatte, waren einige fast so hübsch wie Aliena gewesen, darunter allerdings keine von so hoher Geburt. Er hatte die Erfahrung gemacht, daß Mädchen sich vor allem von seinen feinen Kleidern und feurigen Rössern beeindrucken ließen; auch mochten sie es, wenn er ihnen süßen Wein spendierte und bunte Bänder kaufte, wie sie überhaupt seinen freigebigen Umgang mit Geld bewunderten. Gelang es ihm dann, sie in eine einsame Scheune zu locken, fügten sich die meisten, mehr oder minder bereitwillig, seinen Wünschen.

Im Grunde seines Herzens war William Mädchen gegenüber ein wenig schüchtern, und wenn ihn eine interessierte, ließ er es sie zunächst nicht wissen. Doch kaum war er mit Aliena allein, war es um seine Zurückhaltung geschehen. Sie trug ein hellblaues Seidenkleid, das in freiem Fall ihre Figur umschmeichelte, doch William konnte nur an den nackten Körper darunter denken, den er alsbald würde sehen können, so oft ihm der Sinn danach stand. Er hatte sie mit einem Buch in der Hand angetroffen. Sie las – eine höchst merkwürdige Beschäftigung für eine Frau, die keine Nonne war. Nur um sich von der Bewegung ihrer Brüste unter der blauen Seide abzulenken, hatte er sie nach dem Titel des Buches gefragt.

»Es heißt *Das Alexanderlied* und handelt von einem König namens Alexander der Große. Es beschreibt, wie er ganz wundersame Länder im Osten erobert hat, wo wertvolle Edelsteine an Rebstöcken wachsen und die Blumen sprechen können.«

Es war William unbegreiflich, wie man mit derartigem Blödsinn seine Zeit vertun konnte. Er verzichtete freilich auf einen Kommentar und erzählte ihr statt dessen von sich – von seinen Pferden und Hunden sowie seinen Erfolgen auf der Jagd, beim Ringen und auf Turnieren. Indessen zeigte sich Aliena weniger beeindruckt, als er gehofft hatte. Er berichtete von dem Haus, das sein Vater für sie beide bauen ließ, und erklärte ihr, gleichsam als Vorbereitung auf ihre neue Aufgabe als Gemahlin, wie er sich ihre künftige Haushaltsführung vorstellte. Doch je länger er auf sie einredete, desto stärker spürte er, daß sie ihm gar nicht mehr richtig zuhörte, ohne daß er wußte, warum. Er rückte so nah wie möglich an sie heran, denn er wollte sie packen, an ihr herumfummeln und herausfinden, ob diese Titten wirklich so groß waren, wie er sich das einbildete ... Aliena jedoch verschränkte die Arme, schlug die Beine übereinander und rückte von ihm ab. Sie wirkte so abweisend, daß er widerstrebend von ihr abließ und sich mit dem Gedanken tröstete, daß er in Kürze ohnehin mit ihr treiben konnte, was er wollte.

Nichts deutete zu diesem Zeitpunkt auf die große Szene hin, die Aliena, kaum daß William die Burg verlassen hatte, ihrem Vater vorspielen sollte. Sie sagte lediglich zu William: »Ich glaube, wir passen nicht zueinander«, und wirkte dabei ganz gefaßt. Er, William, hielt das für jungmädchenhafte Bescheidenheit und fand es ganz entzückend. Er fände, sie passe ganz ausgezeichnet zu ihm, hatte er ihr versichert ...

Kaum war er fort, da stürmte Aliena zu ihrem Vater und verkündete dem bestürzten Mann, daß sie um nichts in der Welt diesen William Hamleigh heiraten wolle. Niemand könne sie von diesem Entschluß abbringen, lieber gehe sie noch ins Kloster, und wenn sie sie in Ketten vor den Altar schleifen wollten, so käme doch das Ehegelübde nie über ihre Lippen ... Dieses Luder, dachte William, dieses verdammte Luder! Dennoch verfolgte er Aliena nicht mit der gleichen Gehässigkeit wie seine Mutter. Nein, er wollte ihr nicht bei lebendigem Leib die Haut abziehen. Er wollte auf ihrem heißen Körper liegen und ihren Mund küssen.

Am Ende des Dreikönigsgottesdienstes wurde der Tod des Bischofs offiziell bekanntgegeben. Hoffentlich lenkt das die Leute von dieser verfluchten Verlobungsgeschichte ab, dachte William. Die Mönche verließen in geschlossener Prozession die Kirche, die erfüllt war vom aufgeregten Stimmengewirr der Gläubigen, welche sich nun ebenfalls auf den Weg machten. Viele von ihnen waren dem alten Bischof nicht nur spirituell, sondern auch materiell verbunden – als Pächter oder als Beschäftigte auf seinen Gütern –, und alle waren brennend an der Frage interessiert, wer ihm wohl im Amte nachfolgen würde und mit welchen Änderungen man unter dem neuen Bischof rechnen mußte. Der Tod eines hohen Herrn barg stets Gefahren für die von ihm Beherrschten.

Als William seinen Eltern auf ihrem Weg durch das Kirchenschiff folgte, sah er zu seiner Überraschung den Erzdiakon auf sie zukommen. Mit geschmeidigen Bewegungen, wie ein schwarzer Hund auf einer Kuhweide, bahnte er sich seinen Weg durch die Menge, und die Leute wichen eilfertig zur Seite. Waleran würdigte die Bauern keines Blickes, wechselte aber ein paar Worte mit jedem einzelnen der ihm begegnenden Landadeligen. Als er die Hamleighs erreichte, begrüßte er Williams Vater, ignorierte den Sohn und wandte sich an die Mutter: »Eine Schande, diese Sache mit der Ehe, nicht wahr?«

William errötete. Glaubte dieser Narr vielleicht, seine Beileidsbekundungen seien ein Gebot der *Höflichkeit*?

Mutter war an einem Gespräch über dieses Thema genausowenig gelegen wie William. »Ich bin nicht nachtragend«, log sie.

Waleran ging nicht auf ihre Bemerkung ein. »Mir ist da etwas zu Ohren gekommen, was Euch vielleicht interessieren wird«, sagte er und senkte die Stimme, damit kein Unberufener ihn verstehen konnte. Selbst William mußte sich anstrengen, um mitzubekommen, worum es ging. »Wie es scheint, ist Graf Bartholomäus nicht bereit, von seinem Treueid auf den verstorbenen König Abstand zu nehmen.«

»Bartholomäus war schon immer halsstarrig und ein Heuchler obendrein«, sagte der alte Hamleigh.

Waleran rang sich ein schmerzliches Lächeln ab. Er wollte, daß sie ihm zuhörten. Auf ihre Kommentare konnte er verzichten.

»Bartholomäus und Graf Robert von Gloucester akzeptieren Stephan nicht als Thronfolger – und Stephan ist, wie Ihr wißt, die Wahl der Kirche und der Barone.«

Was soll das? fragte sich William. Wieso belämmert uns ein Erzdiakon mit einer der üblichen Streitereien unter den Baronen? Auch sein Vater wußte mit der Bemerkung nichts anzufangen, denn er erwiderte: »Na und? Was können die Grafen schon dagegen tun?«

»Hör jetzt endlich zu!« zischte Mutter ihn an. Sie teilte Walerans Abneigung gegen die Einwürfe ihres Mannes.

»Wie ich höre, planen die beiden einen Aufstand gegen Stephan. Sie wollen an seiner Statt Mathilde auf den Thron setzen.«

William glaubte im ersten Augenblick, sich verhört zu haben. War das möglich? Eine derart törichte Bemerkung aus dem Mund des Erzdiakons und das hier, mitten in der Kathedrale von Kingsbridge? Ob es nun stimmte oder nicht – dafür konnte man gehängt werden!

Auch Vater Hamleigh war bestürzt. Ganz anders dagegen seine Frau. Nachdenklich sagte sie: »Robert von Gloucester ist Mathildes Halbbruder ... Das gibt durchaus einen Sinn.«

»Jeder, der Graf Bartholomäus erledigt«, fuhr Waleran fort, »und damit die Rebellion im Keim erstickt, kann sich der ewigen Dankbarkeit König Stephans und der Heiligen Mutter Kirche gewiß sein.«

»Wirklich?« fragte Vater benommen. Mutter hingegen nickte verständnisinnig.

»Bartholomäus wird noch heute zurückerwartet.« Bei diesen Worten blickte Waleran auf und nickte irgend jemand anderem zu. Dann sah er wieder Williams Mutter an und sagte: »Ich dachte mir, daß vor allen anderen Euch diese Nachricht interessieren müßte.« Ohne ein weiteres Wort zu verlieren, wandte Waleran sich einem anderen Gesprächspartner zu.

William blickte ihm nach. War das alles, was er uns zu sagen hat? fragte er sich. Seine Eltern setzten ihren Weg fort, und er folgte ihnen durch das mächtige Bogenportal ins Freie. Keiner der drei sprach ein Wort. William hatte in den vergangenen fünf Wochen die verschiedensten Gerüchte über den möglichen Thronfolger gehört. Dann aber war Stephan drei Tage vor Weihnachten in der Abtei zu Westminster gekrönt worden, und die Debatte schien beendet. Wenn Waleran mit seinen Andeutungen recht hatte, war auf einmal alles wieder offen. Die Frage war nur, warum der Erzdiakon ausgerechnet die Hamleighs eingeweiht hatte.

Sie betraten den großen freien Platz vor der Kirche, den sie überqueren mußten, um zu den Ställen zu gelangen. Kaum hatten sie die Menge vor dem Portal hinter sich gelassen und waren wieder unter sich, rief der alte Hamleigh aus: »Welch eine glückliche Schicksalsfügung! Ausgerechnet der Mann, der unsere Familie aufs Schlimmste beleidigt hat, wird des Hochverrats überführt!«

William verstand nicht, was daran so erfreulich war. Mutter hingegen nickte zustimmend.

»Wir können ihn mit gezücktem Schwert festnehmen und ihn am nächsten Baum aufknüpfen«, fuhr Vater fort.

Ach so! Mit einem Schlag war William alles klar. Wenn Bartholomäus ein Verräter war, durfte man ihn töten. »Endlich können wir uns rächen!« platzte er heraus. »Und statt einer Bestrafung wartet eine königliche Belohnung auf uns ...«

»Ihr Narren! Ihr verdammten Narren!« unterbrach ihn seine Mutter wütend. »Ihr blinden, hirnlosen Idioten! Ihr wollt Bartholomäus also am nächstbesten Baum aufknüpfen, ja? Soll ich euch sagen, was dann als nächstes geschieht?«

Die beiden Männer schwiegen. Wenn Mutter in dieser Gemütsverfassung war, widersprach man ihr am besten nicht.

»Robert von Gloucester wird abstreiten, daß es jemals eine Verschwörung gegeben hat. Er wird König Stephan in die Arme schließen und ihm ewige Treue schwören – und das wär's auch schon, abgesehen davon, daß man euch zwei als Mörder hängen würde.«

William schauderte. Die Vorstellung, er könne eines Tages am Galgen enden, entsetzte ihn und verfolgte ihn bis in seine Träume. Daß Mutter recht hatte, war nicht von der Hand zu weisen: Der König mochte glauben – oder zumindest nach außen hin so tun –, daß niemand im Lande so verwegen sein könne, sich gegen ihn zu erheben. Zum Beweis seiner Glaubwürdigkeit würde er jederzeit zwei Menschenleben opfern.

»Du hast recht«, sagte Percy Hamleigh zu seiner Frau. »Dann fesseln wir Bartholomäus eben wie ein schlachtreifes Schwein, schleppen ihn lebendigen Leibes zum König nach Winchester, tragen dort unsere Anklage vor und kassieren die Belohnung gleich an Ort und Stelle.«

»Du kannst doch wirklich nicht bis drei zählen«, schnaubte Mutter verächtlich. William merkte, daß sie mindestens genauso aufgeregt war wie Vater, nur äußerte sich die Spannung bei ihr anders. »Warum läßt sich eigentlich Erzdiakon Waleran diese fette Beute entgehen?« fragte sie. »Wäre doch sehr vorteilhaft für ihn, wenn er dem König einen gefesselten Verräter präsentieren könnte, nicht wahr? Weißt du nicht, daß er mit Leib und Seele danach giert, Bischof von Kingsbridge zu werden? Warum hat er ausgerechnet *dir* das Privileg eingeräumt, Bartholomäus festzunehmen? Warum ist er nicht nach Hamleigh gekommen, sondern tut so, als träfe er uns rein zufällig hier in der Kirche? Warum hat er das Gespräch so schnell beendet und im Grunde alles offengelassen?«

Sie machte eine rhetorische Pause, als warte sie auf eine Antwort. Vater und Sohn wußten jedoch, daß sie in Wirklichkeit gar keine hören wollte. William erinnerte sich, daß Priester sich von Amts wegen nicht an blutigen Auseinandersetzungen beteiligen sollten, und fragte sich, ob Waleran vielleicht deshalb mit Bartholomäus' Festnahme nichts zu tun haben wollte. Es war eine abwegige Vermutung; er brauchte nicht lange, um das einzusehen. Derartige Skrupel waren Waleran gewiß unbekannt.

»Ich sag' euch warum«, fuhr Mutter fort. »Waleran ist sich seiner Sache nicht sicher. Er weiß nicht genau, ob Bartholomäus wirklich ein Verräter ist. Seine Quelle ist nicht zuverlässig. Ich habe keine Ahnung, wie er an die Information gekommen ist – vielleicht hat er zufällig zwei Trunkenbolde darüber schwadronieren hören, oder er hat eine zweideutige Botschaft abgefangen. Kann auch sein, daß er's von einem Kundschafter hat, dem er nicht über den Weg traut. Auf jeden Fall ist er nicht bereit, sich selbst die Hände schmutzig zu machen. Nie würde er Graf Bartholomäus offen des Verrats bezichtigen, stünde er dann doch, wenn sich die Vorwürfe gegen den Grafen als haltlos erweisen sollten, als Verleumder da. Waleran sucht ganz einfach jemanden, der für ihn die Dreckarbeit erledigt. Wenn alles vorbei ist und Bartholomäus zweifelsfrei des Hochverrats überführt, dann wird er sich schon melden und seinen Lohn einfordern. Ist der Graf allerdings unschuldig, so wird Waleran von dem Gespräch, das er heute mit uns geführt hat, nichts mehr wissen wollen.«

So, wie sie es darstellte, klang es ganz folgerichtig. Ohne Mutter, gestand sich William ein, wären Vater und ich Waleran auf den Leim gegangen. Wir hätten uns vor seinen Karren spannen lassen und das gesamte Risiko auf uns genommen. Doch auf Mutters politische Urteilskraft war Verlaß.

»Soll das nun heißen, daß wir die ganze Angelegenheit auf sich beruhen lassen?« fragte Percy Hamleigh.

»Nein, gewiß nicht.« Ihre Augen funkelten. »Wenn wir Glück haben, liegt darin trotz allem eine große Chance, den Leuten, die uns so erniedrigt haben, den Garaus zu machen.« Ein Roßknecht führte ihr Pferd vor; sie nahm die Zügel entgegen und entließ ihn mit einer Handbewegung, stieg aber noch nicht auf. Nachdenklich tätschelte sie den Hals des Tieres und flüsterte: »Wir brauchen handfeste Beweise für den Verrat, so daß Bartholomäus alles Leugnen nicht mehr hilft. Allerdings müssen wir uns die Beweise heimlich beschaffen. Kein Mensch darf davon erfahren. Sobald wir sie haben, können wir Bartholomäus festnehmen und ihn dem König überstellen. Ihm wird dann nichts anderes übrigbleiben, als zu gestehen und um Gnade zu winseln – und wir können Anspruch auf die uns zustehende Belohnung erheben.«

»Und jede Beteiligung Walerans an der Aufdeckung des Komplotts abstreiten«, fügte Vater hinzu.

Mutter schüttelte den Kopf. »Warum? Soll er doch seinen Teil bekommen. Er steht dann in unserer Schuld – und das kann nie schaden, nicht wahr?«

Percy Hamleigh sah seine Frau unsicher an. »Aber wie sollen wir das anstellen?« fragte er. »Wie kommen wir an die Beweise?«

Mutter runzelte die Stirn. »Wir müssen uns unter irgendeinem Vorwand auf seiner Burg einschleichen und uns dort umsehen. Leicht ist das nicht, soviel steht fest. Einen Freundschaftsbesuch nimmt uns kein Mensch ab. Jedermann weiß, daß wir Bartholomäus hassen.«

William hatte auf einmal eine Idee. »Ich kann doch hinreiten«, sagte er.

Überrascht sahen seine Eltern auf. »Nun, du erregst gewiß weniger Aufmerksamkeit als dein Vater. Nur – du bräuchtest einen bestimmten Anlaß ...«

Mit diesem Einwand hatte William gerechnet. »Ich kann sagen, daß ich Aliena besuchen will«, gab er zur Antwort, und allein der Gedanke daran brachte sein Blut in Wallung. »Ich könnte sie bitten, sich ihren Entschluß noch einmal zu überlegen. Sie hat mich damals völlig falsch eingeschätzt. Ich glaube immer noch, daß ich ihr ein guter Ehemann sein könnte. Vielleicht will sie bloß ein bißchen mehr umworben werden.« Er verzog das Gesicht, in der Hoffnung, ein zynisches Lächeln hervorzubringen. Die Eltern sollten nicht merken, daß er es bitterernst meinte.

»Eine geradezu perfekte Ausrede!« sagte Mutter und bedachte William mit einem anerkennenden Blick. »Herr im Himmel, vielleicht hat der Junge ja doch eine Spur von der Intelligenz seiner Mutter geerbt.«

Als William sich am Tag nach dem Dreikönigsfest auf den Weg nach Earlscastle machte, war er zum erstenmal seit vielen Monaten guten Mutes. Es war ein klarer, kalter Morgen; der Nordwind brannte in seinen Ohren, und unter den Hufen seines Schlachtrosses knirschte das gefrorene Gras. Über einer scharlachroten Tunika trug er einen mit Kaninchenfell gefütterten Mantel aus bestem flandrischem Tuch.

Walter, sein Bediensteter, begleitete ihn. William war zwölf Jahre alt gewesen, als Walter sein Waffenlehrer wurde. Reiten, Jagen, Fechten und Ringen hatte er von ihm gelernt. Inzwischen war Walter Pferdeknecht, Gefährte, Leibwächter in einem. Er war so groß wie William, jedoch viel breiter gebaut als er, ein wahrer Kleiderschrank. Neun oder zehn Jahre älter als sein Herr, war Walter immer noch jung genug, um jedem Saufgelage standzuhalten und sich als Schürzenjäger hervorzutun, andererseits aber auch schon so abgeklärt, daß er den jungen William, wenn's hart auf hart kam, aus der Schußlinie ziehen konnte. Walter war Williams bester Freund.

Obwohl ihm klar war, daß er erneut mit Zurückweisung und Erniedrigung rechnen mußte, ergriff William bei dem Gedanken an das bevorstehende Wiedersehen mit Aliena eine merkwürdige Erregung. Der eine kurze Blick in ihre dunklen Augen hatte seine Sehnsucht von neuem entfacht. Er konnte es kaum erwarten, mit ihr zu sprechen, ihr nahe zu sein, die wilde, wogende Lockenpracht zu sehen und den Bewegungen ihres Körpers unter dem Kleid nachzuspüren.

Die andere Seite der Medaille war, daß die unerwartete Gelegenheit zur Rache auch seinen Haß von neuem entzündet hatte. Es lag an ihm, die schlimme Demütigung seiner Familie ein für allemal vergessen zu machen, und die Aussicht darauf erfüllte ihn mit ungeheurer Spannung. Allerdings hätte er gerne eine etwas deutlichere Vorstellung davon gehabt, was er in Earlscastle eigentlich suchte. Er war sich ziemlich sicher, daß er herausfinden würde, ob an Walerans Geschichte etwas dran war, ließen sich doch Kriegsvorbereitungen auf einer Burg kaum verheimlichen. Da mußten Pferde zusammengetrieben und ausgerüstet, Waffen gereinigt und Vorräte angelegt werden. Freilich: Sich selbst von der Verschwörung zu überzeugen, war eine Sache – unwiderlegbare Beweise beizubringen eine ganz andere. William hatte noch nicht die geringste Vorstellung, wie ein echter Beweis auszusehen hatte. Er beschloß daher, einfach die Augen offenzuhalten und die Dinge auf sich zukommen zu lassen; irgend etwas würde sich schon finden. Ein besonders raffinierter Plan war das nicht, und William war sich dieser Schwäche voll bewußt. Heimliche Zweifel beschlichen ihn, und er fürchtete, die einmalige Gelegenheit zur Rache könne schließlich doch noch ungenutzt verstreichen.

Je näher er Earlscastle kam, desto beklommener ward ihm zumute. Was ist, wenn sie mich gar nicht erst in die Burg hineinlassen? fragte er sich in einem Anfall von Panik, und es kostete ihn ein paar Minuten, bis er sich wieder beruhigt hatte. Eine Burg war ein allgemein zugänglicher Ort. Sie ohne Begründung zu schließen, wäre einer öffentlichen Bekanntmachung der Verschwörung gleichgekommen.

Während in der Burg von Shiring der Grafschaftsvogt residierte, lebte Graf Bartholomäus ein paar Meilen außerhalb der Stadt. Das kleine Dorf, das rund um die Mauern seiner Burg entstanden war, nannte sich Earlscastle. Zum erstenmal sah William den Ort aus der Perspektive des Angreifers.

Ein breiter und tiefer Burggraben, wie eine Acht mit einem kleinen oberen und einem großen unteren Kreis geformt, umgab die Anlage. Das Erdreich, das beim Ausheben der Gräben angefallen war, hatte man innerhalb der beiden Ringe zu hohen Wällen aufgeschüttet. Den einzigen Zugang zur Burg bildeten am Grund der Acht eine Brücke über den Graben und eine daran anschließende Bresche im Wall. Der obere Ring, gewissermaßen das Allerheiligste, war nur über den unteren sowie über eine weitere Brücke zu erreichen.

Es herrschte reges Kommen und Gehen, als William und Walter über das freie Feld, das Burg und Dorf umgab, auf die Anlage zutrabten. Zwei Bewaffnete auf schnellen Pferden überquerten gerade die Brücke und galoppierten in verschiedenen Richtungen davon, und unmittelbar vor den beiden Neuankömmlingen betraten vier fremde Reiter die Burg.

William bemerkte, daß sich der letzte Abschnitt der Brücke in das gewaltige steinerne Torhaus hochziehen ließ. Die Wälle waren in regelmäßigen Abständen mit steinernen Wachtürmen versehen, so daß im Verteidigungsfall das gesamte Umfeld von Bogenschützen bestrichen werden konnte. Wer diese Burg erstürmen will, muß sich auf einen langen und blutigen Kampf gefaßt machen, dachte William bedrückt, und es ist keineswegs sicher, ob wir die dafür erforderlichen Truppen zusammenbekommen.

Im Augenblick dachte natürlich kein Mensch daran, die Zugbrücke hochzuziehen. Die Burg war offen, und die Wache im Torhaus ließ William und Walter anstandslos passieren. Im unteren Ring, der durch die Erdwälle von der Außenwelt abgeschnitten war, lagen wie üblich Ställe, Küchen, Werkstätten, ein Wohnturm für das Gesinde und eine Kapelle. Eine gewisse Spannung lag in der Luft. Die Pferdeknechte, Diener und Mägde wirkten ungewöhnlich aufgekratzt; sie unterhielten sich laut und waren zu allerlei Späßen aufgelegt. Der unbefangene Betrachter mochte darin nichts als eine normale Reaktion auf die Rückkehr des Burgherrn sehen; William freilich vermutete, daß mehr dahintersteckte.

Er ließ Walter bei den Pferden zurück und begab sich zur zweiten Brücke, die den unteren Ring der Anlage mit dem oberen verband. Diesmal hielt ihn der Torwächter an und fragte nach seinem Begehr. »Ich möchte mit Lady Aliena sprechen«, antwortete William.

Der Torwächter, der ihn nicht kannte, musterte ihn von oben bis unten und schätzte ihn, nicht zuletzt wegen seines feinen Mantels und der eleganten roten Tunika, als hoffnungsvollen Bewerber ein. Er grinste und sagte: »Wahrscheinlich findet Ihr die junge Dame im großen Saal.«

In der Mitte des oberen Kreises stand ein zweistöckiger Wohnturm mit quadratischem Grundriß, in dessen Erdgeschoß sich, wie üblich, ein Vorratslager befand. Eine hölzerne Außentreppe führte hinauf in den großen Saal und konnte bei Bedarf eingezogen werden. Im zweiten Stock lag das Schlafgemach des Grafen. Wenn die Hamleighs kommen, ihn zu holen, wird er sich zum Schluß dort verschanzen, dachte William.

Wer immer diese Burg erstürmen wollte, sah sich mit einer Fülle von ausgeklügelten Hindernissen konfrontiert. William, der sich darüber noch nie Gedanken gemacht hatte, erkannte jetzt die genauen Funktionen der verschiedenen Bollwerke: Selbst nach erfolgreicher Besetzung des unteren Rings war die Schlacht noch nicht gewonnen. Die zweite Brücke und das Torhaus mußten auch erst erobert werden, und selbst wenn es gelang, den trutzigen Wohnturm zu stürmen, kam es aller Wahrscheinlichkeit nach noch zu einem erbitterten Kampf um den Zugang zum zweiten Stock. Wenn es überhaupt eine Möglichkeit gab, diese Burg einzunehmen, dies wurde William jetzt klar, dann nur mit Hilfe einer List. Man mußte irgendeinen Vorwand finden, um sich einzuschleichen ...

Er stieg die Treppe hinauf und betrat den Saal. Der große Raum war voller Menschen, doch der Graf war nirgendwo zu sehen. Der Aufgang zum Schlafgemach befand sich ganz links an der gegenüberliegenden Wand. Auf den unteren Stufen und drum herum saßen fünfzehn bis zwanzig Ritter und Bewaffnete und unterhielten sich in gedämpftem Ton. Das war recht ungewöhnlich, denn Ritter und Bewaffnete waren nicht vom gleichen Stand: Die Ritter waren Grundbesitzer, die ihren Lebensunterhalt aus Pachteinnahmen bestritten, während Bewaffnete täglich für ihre Dienste entlohnt wurden. Nur wenn Kriegsgeruch in der Luft lag, entstand so etwas wie Kameradschaft zwischen den beiden Gruppen.

Einige Männer waren William persönlich bekannt, darunter Gilbert Catface, ein übellauniger alter Haudegen mit altmodischem Bakkenbart und üppigem Schnäuzer. Er hatte die Vierzig bereits überschritten, war aber immer noch stramm und kräftig. Ralph von Lyme, der für seine Garderobe mehr Geld ausgab als eine Braut, war ebenfalls zugegen; diesmal trug er einen blauen, mit roter Seide verbrämten Mantel. Neben einigen anderen, die William schon irgendwo einmal gesehen zu haben glaubte, hockte auch Jack fitz Guillaume auf den Stufen. Obwohl kaum älter als William, hatte er schon den Ritterschlag empfangen.

Die jungen Männer reagierten kaum, als William ihnen zum Gruß zunickte. Zwar war er allgemein bekannt, doch galt er seiner Jugend wegen noch nicht viel.

Er sah sich weiter im Saal um und entdeckte auf der gegenüberliegenden Seite Aliena. Das Mädchen sah heute ganz anders aus als am Tag zuvor: Hatte sie zum Festtagsgottesdienst in der Kathedrale ein Kleid aus Samt und Seide, spitz zulaufende Stiefel und allerlei Ringe und hübsche Bänder getragen, so war sie jetzt barfuß und trug die einfache Tunika einer Bauersfrau oder eines Kindes. Sie saß auf einer Bank, allem Anschein nach in ein Brettspiel vertieft. William sah, wie sie die Nase kraus zog und die Beine übereinanderschlug; dabei rutschte die Tunika hoch und entblößte ihre Knie. Gestern noch ganz die feine Dame aus gutem Hause, war sie heute nur mehr ein verletzliches Kind, und das machte sie für William noch begehrenswerter. Er empfand es auf einmal als eine Schande, daß dieses Kind ihm und seiner Familie so viel Kummer hatte bereiten können. Er sehnte sich mit aller Macht nach einer Gelegenheit, ihr zu zeigen, daß er doch stärker war als sie, und diese Sehnsucht war fast so süß wie die Lust.

Sie spielte mit einem Jungen, der ungefähr drei Jahre jünger war als sie. Er wirkte unruhig und ungeduldig; offensichtlich machte ihm das Spiel keinen Spaß. William erkannte die Familienähnlichkeit zwischen den beiden: Der Junge erinnerte ihn mit seiner Stupsnase und dem kurzgeschnittenen Haar an die kleine Aliena in seinem Alter. Das muß Richard sein, ihr Bruder, dachte er, der Erbe des Grafentitels.

William ging etwas näher heran. Richard sah kurz auf und blickte ihn an, nur um seine Aufmerksamkeit gleich wieder dem Spiel zuzuwenden. Aliena konzentrierte sich. Das bemalte Spielbrett war wie ein Kreuz geformt und in verschiedenfarbige Quadrate aufgeteilt. Die schwarzen und weißen Spielsteine schienen aus Elfenbein zu bestehen. Offenbar handelte es sich um ein Geschenk, das Alienas Vater seinen Kindern aus der Normandie mitgebracht hatte.

William hatte nur noch Augen für Aliena. Als sie sich ein wenig weiter über das Brett neigte, wölbte sich der Ausschnitt ihrer Tunika vor, und William konnte den Ansatz ihrer Brüste sehen. Ja, sie waren so groß, wie er sie sich vorgestellt hatte. Sein Mund wurde trocken.

Richard setzte einen Spielstein auf ein anderes Feld. Aliena sagte: »Nein, das darfst du nicht.«

Der Junge protestierte: »Warum nicht?«

»Weil das gegen die Regeln verstößt, du Dummkopf.«

»Ich finde diese Regeln blöd«, gab Richard trotzig zurück. Aliena brauste auf: »Du mußt dich aber dran halten!«

»Warum?«

»Das muß man eben. Deshalb.«

»Ich muß gar nichts«, erwiderte er und kippte das Brett um. Die Steine kullerten über den Boden.

Aliena holte blitzschnell aus und verpaßte ihm eine Ohrfeige.

Richard schrie empört auf – sein Stolz war ebenso getroffen wie seine Wange. »Du …« Er zögerte. »Du … Teufelshure!« schrie er dann, drehte sich auf dem Absatz um und lief davon, nur um nach ein paar Schritten heftig mit William zusammenzustoßen.

William packte den Jungen am Arm und hob ihn hoch. »Paß bloß auf, daß kein Priester in der Nähe ist, wenn du deine Schwester mit solchen Ausdrücken beschimpfst«, sagte er.

Richard zappelte hin und her. »Du tust mir weh!« jammerte er. »Laß mich gehen!«

Erst als der Junge seinen Widerstand aufgegeben und zu weinen begonnen hatte, setzte William ihn wieder ab. Heulend lief Richard davon.

Das Spiel war vergessen. Aliena starrte William an. Die gerunzelten Brauen verrieten ihre Verblüffung. »Wie kommst du denn hier her?« fragte sie. Die ruhige, besonnene Stimme paßte nicht zu ihrer Jugend.

William nahm auf der Bank Platz. Er war sehr zufrieden mit sich selbst: Dem Bengel hatte er es gezeigt. »Ich bin gekommen, weil ich dich sehen wollte.«

Ihre Miene verriet, daß sie jetzt auf der Hut war. »Warum?« fragte sie.

William setzte sich so, daß er die Treppe zum Gemach des Grafen gut überblicken konnte. In diesem Augenblick kam ein Mann mittleren Alters die Treppe herunter. Er trug die Kleidung eines höhergestellten Bediensteten: eine runde Mütze und eine kurze Tunika aus gutem Tuch. Auf seinen Wink hin erhoben sich ein Ritter und ein

Bewaffneter und folgten ihm die Treppe hinauf. William wandte sich wieder an Aliena.

»Ich möchte mit dir reden.«

»Worüber?«

»Über uns beide.« Er sah, wie hinter Alienas Rücken der Diener auf sie zukam. Sein Gang hatte etwas Geziertes an sich. In einer Hand trug er einen Zuckerhut von schmutzig-brauner Farbe, in der anderen eine seltsam urwüchsige Ingwerwurzel. Der Mann war demnach der Haushofmeister, der aus dem streng gehüteten Gewürzschrank im Gemach des Grafen den Tagesbedarf an wertvollen Ingredienzen abgeholt hatte, um sie dem Küchenmeister zu bringen: den Zucker vielleicht zum Süßen von Apfeltörtchen, den Ingwer zur Würze eines Neunaugengerichts.

Aliena drehte sich um und folgte Williams Blick. »Hallo, Matthew!« rief sie aus.

Der Haushofmeister lächelte, brach ein Stück Zucker ab und reichte es ihr. William hatte den Eindruck, daß Matthew ganz vernarrt in Aliena war. Irgend etwas in ihrem Verhalten mußte ihm verraten haben, daß das Mädchen sich nicht ganz wohl in seiner Haut fühlte, denn sein Lächeln verwandelte sich unvermittelt in ein besorgtes Stirnrunzeln. »Alles in Ordnung?« fragte er sie mit weicher Stimme.

»Ja, danke.«

Jetzt erst nahm Matthew von William Notiz. Er war sichtlich überrascht. »Der junge William Hamleigh, nicht wahr?«

Es war William peinlich, daß man ihn erkannt hatte, obwohl er wußte, daß es sich gar nicht vermeiden ließ. »Behalt deinen Zucker für die Kinder«, sagte er, obgleich ihm Matthew gar nichts angeboten hatte. »Ich mag das Zeug nicht.«

»Sehr wohl, der Herr.« Matthews Blick verriet, daß es nicht seine Art war, sich mit den Söhnen des Landadels anzulegen; er verdankte seine Stellung anderen Qualitäten. »Euer Vater hat wunderbar weiche Seidenstoffe von seiner Reise mitgebracht«, sagte er, an Aliena gewandt. »Ich werde sie Euch später zeigen.«

»Danke«, sagte Aliena.

Matthew ging.

»Weibischer Tölpel«, bemerkte William.

»Wieso bist du so unhöflich zu ihm?« fragte Aliena.

»Ich dulde es nicht, daß Domestiken mich ›der junge William Hamleigh‹ nennen.« Schon im nächsten Atemzug bereute er den Satz. So wirbt man nicht um eine junge Dame, schalt er sich. Der Anfang ist mißlungen. Du mußt charmant sein, zuvorkommend! Er lächelte und fügte hinzu: »Wenn du meine Frau wärst, würden meine Diener ›Lady‹ zu dir sagen.«

»Bist du gekommen, um noch einmal über die Heirat zu sprechen?« fragte sie ungläubig.

Er hatte das Gespräch mit einer harmlosen Plauderei einleiten wollen. Mit ihrer Direktheit und Offenheit brachte sie ihn ganz durcheinander; er spürte selbst, daß er die Kontrolle über das Gespräch verlor.

»Du kennst mich doch gar nicht!« rief er erregt aus. »Du hast mich von Anfang an falsch eingeschätzt! Ich weiß nicht, was dich im einzelnen damals so gegen mich aufgebracht hat, doch was immer es war: dein Urteil war voreilig.«

Aliena wandte sich ab; sie dachte über eine passende Antwort nach. Hinter ihr kamen der Ritter und der Bewaffnete die Treppe herunter und verließen den Saal. Ihre Mienen wirkten ernst und entschlossen. Einen Augenblick später erschien ein weiterer Mann auf der Treppe; er trug die Soutane eines Priesters und war vermutlich der Privatsekretär des Grafen. Auf seinen Wink hin standen zwei Ritter auf und stiegen die Treppe hinauf: Ralph von Lyme im leuchtend rot gesäumten Mantel und ein älterer Mann mit kahlem Kopf. Für William war jetzt klar, daß die im Saal wartenden Männer einzeln oder zu zweit zum Grafen gerufen wurden. Die Frage war nur, warum.

»Nach so langer Zeit«, sagte Aliena. Sie unterdrückte eine Gemütsbewegung. Es mochte Wut sein, doch konnte William sich des Eindrucks nicht erwehren, daß sie ihn am liebsten ausgelacht hätte. »Nach all dem Theater, den Haßtiraden, dem Skandal … Ausgerechnet jetzt, da sich die ganze Aufregung endlich ein wenig legt, da kommst *du* und sagst mir, ich hätte einen Fehler gemacht …«

So, wie sie es ausdrückt, klingt es nicht sehr überzeugend, dachte William. »Überhaupt nichts hat sich gelegt«, antwortete er erregt. »Die Leute reden nach wie vor darüber, meine Mutter schäumt noch immer vor Wut, und mein Vater wagt sich bis heute nicht erhobenen Hauptes in die Öffentlichkeit. Nichts hat sich geändert für uns, gar nichts.«

»Dann geht es dir wohl nur um die Familienehre, wie?«

William ignorierte den drohenden Unterton in ihrer Stimme. Ihm war auf einmal eingefallen, was der Graf mit all diesen Rittern und Bediensteten vorhatte: Er sandte Boten aus. »Familienehre?« wiederholte er geistesabwesend. »Ja.«

»Ich weiß, daß auch ich mehr auf Dinge wie Familienehre, nützliche Verbindungen und so weiter achten sollte«, sagte Aliena. »Aber man heiratet doch nicht nur deshalb.« Sie zögerte einen Moment, dann gab sie sich einen Ruck. »Vielleicht sollte ich dir von meiner Mutter erzählen. Sie haßte meinen Vater. Mein Vater ist kein schlechter Mann, wirklich nicht. Er ist sogar ein sehr bedeutender Mann, und ich liebe ihn sehr. Nur ist er eben auch furchtbar ernst und streng. Er hat Mutter einfach nie verstanden. Sie war eine frohe, glückliche Frau, die gerne lachte, wunderbare Geschichten erzählen konnte und die Musik liebte. Vater hat ihr das alles ausgetrieben.« Aliena hatte Tränen in den Augen, doch William nahm sie kaum wahr. Er dachte nur an die Botschaften, die Graf Bartholomäus zu versenden hatte. »Und daran ist sie schließlich auch gestorben«, fuhr Aliena fort. »Weil er sie einfach nicht so sein ließ, wie sie war. Ich weiß das ganz genau – und er auch, siehst du? Und deshalb hat er mir versprochen, daß er mich nie einem Mann zur Frau geben wird, den ich nicht mag. Verstehst du mich jetzt?«

Diese Botschaften sind Befehle, dachte William, Stellungsbefehle an seine Freunde und Mitstreiter. Er bereitet sie auf die bevorstehende Rebellion vor. Und die Boten sind lebendige *Beweise*.

Erst jetzt merkte er, daß Aliena ihn anstarrte. »... den du nicht magst«, stammelte er. »Magst du mich etwa nicht?«

Ihre Augen funkelten. »Du hast mir überhaupt nicht zugehört«, sagte sie wütend. »Du bist dermaßen von dir selbst eingenommen, daß du für die Gefühle anderer Menschen nicht das geringste Verständnis aufbringst. Wie war's denn das letztemal, als du hier warst? Pausenlos hast du geredet und geredet – und immer nur über dich. Du hast mir nicht eine einzige Frage gestellt!«

Ihre Stimme war immer lauter geworden. Als sie verstummte, merkte William, daß auch die Männer auf der anderen Seite des Saals ihre Gespräche eingestellt hatten und zuhörten. »Nicht so laut!« raunte er ihr zu.

Sie hörte nicht auf ihn. »Du willst also wissen, warum ich dich nicht mag. Gut, ich sag's dir. Ich mag dich nicht, weil du nicht die geringste Spur von Kultur und Bildung besitzt. Ich mag dich nicht, weil du kaum lesen kannst. Ich mag dich nicht, weil du nichts anderes im Kopf hast als deine *Hunde*, deine *Pferde* und *dich selbst*!«

Gilbert Catface und Jack fitz Guillaume lachten inzwischen vernehmlich. William spürte, wie ihm das Blut ins Gesicht schoß. Diese Kerle waren *nichts*, sie waren *Ritter*, und sie lachten *ihn* aus – ihn,

Lord Percy Hamleighs Sohn! Er erhob sich. »Gut«, sagte er in dem verzweifelten Versuch, Aliena zum Schweigen zu bringen. »Laß es jetzt gut sein!«

Aber Aliena schenkte ihm nichts. »Ich mag dich nicht, weil du selbstsüchtig, langweilig und entsetzlich dumm bist«, brüllte sie, und alle Ritter im Saal lachten aus vollem Halse. »Ich kann dich nicht ausstehen. Ich hasse dich. Ich verachte dich. Ich verabscheue dich! Und *deshalb* werde ich dich nicht heiraten – nie und nimmer!«

Die Ritter jubelten und applaudierten ihr. William krümmte sich innerlich. Ihr Gelächter ließ ihn sich klein, schwach und hilflos vorkommen, wie damals, als er ein kleiner Junge war und vor allem und jedem Angst hatte. Er wandte sich von Aliena ab. Krampfhaft darum bemüht, sich seine wahren Gefühle nicht anmerken zu lassen, durchquerte er den Saal. Das Gelächter um ihn herum nahm noch an Lautstärke zu. Endlich erreichte er die Tür. Er riß sie auf, stolperte hinaus und schmetterte sie hinter sich zu. Wut und Scham schnürten ihm fast den Atem ab, als er die Außentreppe hinunterstürmte. Das allmählich verklingende Hohngelächter verfolgte ihn noch über den ganzen schmutzigen Burghof bis hin zum Tor.

Ungefähr eine Meile hinter Earlscastle kreuzte der Weg nach Shiring eine Hauptstraße. Der Reisende, der sich hier nach Norden wandte, gelangte über Gloucester an die walisische Grenze. Südwärts führte die Straße nach Winchester und an die Küste, und diese Richtung schlugen William und Walter ein.

Williams Kummer hatte sich in stille Raserei verwandelt und ihm die Sprache verschlagen. Er sehnte sich danach, Aliena weh zu tun, und wollte all diese Ritter töten. Am liebsten hätte er sein Schwert in jede einzelne dieser lachenden Fratzen gebohrt, und wenn dies schon nicht möglich war, so wollte er sich zumindest an einem von ihnen rächen. William hatte einen Plan, der, falls er aufging, in doppelter Hinsicht nützlich war, denn er würde ihm nicht nur Genugtuung, sondern auch die gesuchten Beweise für die Verschwörung verschaffen. Die Aussicht darauf war Balsam für seine Wunden und erfüllte ihn mit wölfischer Vorfreude.

Zunächst jedoch mußten sie einen von ihnen erwischen. Die Straße führte sie alsbald an den Rand eines großen Waldes. William saß ab und ging zu Fuß weiter; sein Pferd führte er am Zügel. Walter, der die üble Laune seines Herrn respektierte, folgte ihm schweigend. Nach einer Weile verengte sich die Straße zu einem schmalen Weg.

William blieb stehen, drehte sich um und sagte zu seinem Gefährten: »Wer kann besser mit einem Messer umgehen, du oder ich?«

»Im Nahkampf bin ich besser«, sagte Walter vorsichtig. »Ihr, Herr, versteht Euch dafür besser aufs Werfen.« Wenn William wütend war, redeten ihn alle mit ›Herr‹ an.

»Ich nehme an, du weißt, wie man ein durchgehendes Pferd zu Fall bringt, wie?« fragte William.

»Ja. Man braucht dazu einen kräftigen, derben Pfahl.«

»Gut. Such dir jetzt einen geeigneten kleinen Baum und schneid ihn dir zurecht. Dann hast du, was du brauchst.«

Walter verschwand.

William führte die beiden Pferde tiefer in den Wald hinein und band sie ein gutes Stück von der Straße entfernt an einen Baum. Dann zog er verschiedene Riemen und Schnüre aus Sattel- und Zaumzeug – genug, um einen Mann an Händen und Füßen zu fesseln, und noch ein bißchen mehr. Sein Plan war simpel; aber William hatte nicht die Zeit, sich etwas Raffinierteres einfallen zu lassen. Es kam auf einen Versuch an – und dann mußte man das Beste hoffen.

Auf dem Weg zurück zur Straße fand er einen kräftigen, abgefallenen Eichenast. Der Prügel war trocken und hart und ließ sich schwingen wie eine Keule.

Walter wartete bereits mit seinem Pfahl. »Leg dich hinter der Buche dort auf die Lauer!« sagte William und deutete auf einen dicken Stamm unmittelbar am Wegesrand. »Und denk daran, daß du den Pfahl nicht zu früh vorstößt, sonst springt das Pferd bloß drüber. Zu lange darfst du aber auch nicht warten, weil es bei der Hinterhand meist nicht klappt. Am besten, du erwischst den Gaul zwischen den Vorderbeinen und rammst die Spitze auf der anderen Seite in den Boden, so daß der Pfahl nicht einfach beiseite fliegt.«

Walter nickte. »Ich hab' schon mal gesehen, wie's gemacht wird.«

William ging ungefähr dreißig Schritt zurück in die Richtung, aus der sie gekommen waren, und suchte sich ein ähnliches Versteck. Er hatte dafür zu sorgen, daß das Pferd durchging – nur wenn es galoppierte und nicht mehr zu bremsen war, würde Walter es zu Fall bringen können. Über kurz oder lang mußte einer der gräflichen Boten auftauchen. William hoffte inständig, daß es nicht zu lange dauern würde. Er brannte darauf, seinen Plan in die Tat umzusetzen.

Die Ritter, die mich ausgelacht haben, hatten ja keine Ahnung, daß ich als Kundschafter in der Burg war, dachte er und zog daraus einen gewissen Trost. Aber einer von ihnen wird es bald erfahren.

Sein Lachen wird ihm noch leid tun. Es wird ihm leid tun, daß er nicht vor mir auf die Knie gesunken ist und meine Stiefel geküßt hat. Heulen wird er und mich um Gnade anwinseln, aber ich werde nicht lockerlassen und ihn quälen bis aufs Blut ...

Als tröstend empfand William auch die Vorstellung, daß sein Plan, wenn alles nach Wunsch verlief, den Anfang vom Ende des Grafen Bartholomäus bedeuten konnte – und damit den späten Triumph und neue Machtfülle für die Hamleighs. Dann würden alle, die sich über die geplatzte Verlobung lustig gemacht hatten, vor Furcht beben – und so manch einer müßte sich auf weit Schlimmeres gefaßt machen.

Wenn Bartholomäus stürzt, dann stürzt auch Aliena, dachte William, und das ist das Schönste an der Sache. Wenn ihr Vater als Verräter am Galgen hängt, dann helfen ihr ihr aufgeblasener Stolz und ihre Überheblichkeit auch nicht mehr weiter. Wenn ihr der Sinn dann immer noch nach weicher Seide und Zuckerwerk steht – dann wird ihr nichts anderes übrigbleiben, als mich zu heiraten. Schon sah er Aliena, wie sie ihm demütig und reuevoll ein heißes Pastetchen aus der Küche servierte und alles tat, um ihn zufriedenzustellen; Aliena, wie sie mit weichen, leicht geöffneten Lippen nach einer kleinen Zärtlichkeit gierte, um einen Kuß bettelte ...

Pferdegetrappel auf dem winterharten Straßendreck riß ihn aus seinen Träumereien. Er zog sein Messer und wog es in der Hand, um sich Gewicht und Gewichtsverteilung wieder ins Gedächtnis zu rufen. Die Spitze war beidseitig geschliffen. Er richtete sich auf und preßte seinen Rücken gegen den Baum, hinter dem er Deckung gesucht hatte. Er packte das Messer zwischen Daumen und Zeigefinger an der Schneide, atmete nur noch ganz flach und wartete. Er war aufgeregt. Der Wurf konnte sein Ziel verfehlen. Vielleicht mißlang der Anschlag auf das Pferd, vielleicht gelang es dem Reiter, Walter mit einem glücklichen Stich zu töten, so daß William allein mit ihm fertig werden mußte ... Irgend etwas stimmte nicht mit den Hufschlägen. Auch Walter war es aufgefallen; mit kritisch gerunzelter Stirn spähte er aus seinem Versteck. Ach so! Es war nicht nur ein Pferd, was da auf sie zukam. Eine schnelle Entscheidung tat not. Nehmen wir es auch mit zwei Leuten auf? William schwankte. Klingt ein bißchen zu sehr nach ehrlichem Kampf, dachte er. Lassen wir sie laufen und warten auf einen einzelnen Boten. Das ist zwar eine Enttäuschung, aber mit Sicherheit das Klügste in dieser Situation. Mit einer unmißverständlichen Geste winkte er Walter ab. Sein Gefährte nickte verständnisvoll und verschwand wieder in seinem Versteck.

Kurz darauf erschienen zwei Reiter auf dem Weg. Rote Seide blitzte auf: William erkannte Ralph von Lyme und hinter ihm den kahlen Schädel seines Begleiters. Die beiden Männer trabten vorüber und verschwanden rasch wieder aus seinem Blickfeld.

Trotz der Ernüchterung, die sich seiner bemächtigte, war William froh über die Bestätigung der These, daß der Graf Boten aussandte. Die Frage war allerdings, ob Bartholomäus sie aus Vorsicht nur paarweise auf den Weg schickte. Wer immer die Gelegenheit dazu hatte, schloß sich auf seinen Reisen einer Gruppe an; es war ganz einfach sicherer. Andererseits gab es gewiß eine Menge Leute, die Bartholomäus unterrichten wollte, und es stand ihm nur eine beschränkte Anzahl an Boten zur Verfügung. Unter diesen Voraussetzungen wäre es fast Luxus gewesen, jeweils zwei an denselben Ort zu schicken. Hinzu kam, daß Ritter kampferprobte Burschen waren, die jedem herkömmlichen Wegelagerer einen harten Kampf liefern würden – einen Kampf zumal, bei dem für einen Wegelagerer nicht allzuviel herausspringen konnte, denn außer seinem Schwert und seinem Pferd führte ein Ritter kaum Wertgegenstände mit sich. Ein Schwert aber war schwer verkäuflich für jemanden, der sich vor peinlichen Fragen fürchten mußte, und Pferde wurden bei Überfällen oft verletzt. Alles in allem war ein Ritter im Wald weniger gefährdet als andere Personen.

William kratzte sich mit dem Messergriff am Kopf. Beides ist möglich, dachte er.

Er ließ sich nieder und wartete. Eine tiefe Stille lag über dem Wald. Eine schwache Wintersonne kam hervor und schickte zitternde Strahlen durch das Geäst, bevor sie wieder verschwand. Sein Magen erinnerte William daran, daß die Mittagessenszeit bereits vorüber war. Ein paar Meter vor ihm überquerte ein Reh den Weg und ahnte nicht, daß es von den Blicken eines hungrigen Menschen verfolgt wurde. Williams Ungeduld wuchs.

Wenn sie das nächste Mal wieder zu zweit kommen, müssen wir's trotzdem riskieren, dachte er bei sich. Das ist gewiß ein Wagnis, aber zum einen spricht das Überraschungsmoment für uns, und zum anderen ist Walter ein sagenhafter Kämpfer. Was sollen wir auch sonst machen? Es ist wahrscheinlich unsere letzte Chance. William war sich durchaus darüber im klaren, daß er sein Leben aufs Spiel setzte – doch was war das schon für ein Leben, in dem man ständig gedemütigt wurde und Spott und Hohn über sich ergehen lassen mußte? Da war ein Tod im Kampf schon ehrenvoller.

Am besten wäre es freilich, dachte er, wenn Aliena jetzt allein auf ihrem weißen Pony dahergesprengt käme. Im hohen Bogen fliegt sie vom Pferd und schrammt sich Arme und Beine auf. Sie landet in einem Brombeergestrüpp, und die Dornen dringen tief in ihre weiße Haut. Sie blutet aus vielen kleinen Wunden. Und dann bin ich plötzlich über ihr ... William weidete sich an ihrem Entsetzen und malte sich Alienas Verletzungen in allen Einzelheiten aus. Er sah, wie sich ihre Brust unter ihm hob und senkte, sah den namenlosen Schrecken, den ihr die Erkenntnis, daß sie ihm auf Gedeih und Verderb ausgeliefert war, ins Gesicht schrieb ... Dann hörte er wieder Hufschläge.

Diesmal war es nur ein Pferd.

Er richtete sich auf, zog sein Messer, preßte den Rücken wieder an die Rinde des Baums, lauschte ...

Es war ein gutes, schnelles Tier, kein Schlachtroß, aber ein solides Rennpferd, das sich im gleichmäßigen Trab näherte und nicht einmal besonders schwer atmete. William sah sich nach Walter um und nickte ihm zu: Jetzt war es soweit, da kam der Beweis! Er faßte das Messer an der Spitze und hob den rechten Arm.

Da wieherte in einiger Entfernung ein Pferd. Es war weithin hörbar im stillen Wald und übertönte mühelos das leichte Hufgeklapper. Das näher kommende Tier reagierte sofort, indem es die Gangart wechselte. Der Reiter rief »Brrr!«, und sein Pferd verfiel in einen langsamen Schritt. William fluchte verhalten. Der Reiter war jetzt auf der Hut. Zu spät erkannte William, daß er sein eigenes Roß noch weiter in den Wald hätte führen müssen.

Nun, da das Pferd im Schritt ging, ließ sich die Entfernung nicht mehr abschätzen. William widerstand der Versuchung, hinter seinem Baum hervorzulugen, und lauschte mit äußerster Anspannung. Plötzlich hörte er das Pferd in unmittelbarer Nähe schnauben, und dann sah er es, gerade noch einen Schritt von seinem Schlupfwinkel entfernt – und das Pferd sah ihn. Es scheute, und der überraschte Reiter stieß einen unartikulierten Grunzlaut aus.

William fluchte. Er erkannte die Gefahr sogleich: Das Pferd konnte sich umdrehen und in die falsche Richtung durchgehen. Mit einem Satz umrundete er den Baum und sprang, den Arm bereits zum Wurf erhoben, hinter dem Pferd auf den Weg. Jetzt erkannte er auch den Reiter, einen bärtigen Mann, der mit verkniffener Miene an den Zügeln zerrte. Es war der alte, zähe Kämpe Gilbert Catface. William schleuderte sein Messer.

Das Pferd schien zusammenzufahren wie ein erschrockener Mensch. Ehe Gilbert etwas dagegen unternehmen konnte, verfiel es in einen panikartigen Galopp und jagte in höchster Geschwindigkeit auf Walters Hinterhalt zu.

William rannte hinterher. Gilbert war so sehr damit beschäftigt, sich im Sattel zu halten, daß er gar nicht erst den Versuch unternahm, das Tier wieder unter Kontrolle zu bringen. Schon waren die beiden auf gleicher Höhe mit Walters Versteck. Jetzt, Walter, dachte William, jetzt ...

William bekam gar nicht genau mit, wie der Pfahl vorgestoßen wurde. Er sah nur, daß Walter ganze Arbeit geleistet hatte. Die Vorderläufe des Pferdes knickten ein, als wäre urplötzlich alle Kraft aus ihnen entwichen. Die Hinterläufe holten auf einmal die vorderen ein, so daß sie für kurze Zeit miteinander verknäuelt schienen. Zuletzt senkte sich der Pferdekopf nach unten, das Hinterteil stieg hoch, und das Tier stürzte schwer zu Boden.

Gilbert flog durch die Luft. William wollte ihn gleich gebührend in Empfang nehmen, doch versperrte ihm das am Boden liegende Pferd den Weg. Gilbert landete unverletzt, überschlug sich und war schon wieder auf den Knien. Einen Augenblick lang fürchtete William, der Ritter könnte davonlaufen und entkommen, doch da schoß auch schon Walter aus dem Unterholz hervor, sprang Gilbert von hinten an und warf ihn um.

Beide Männer kamen gleichzeitig wieder auf die Füße. William sah zu seinem Entsetzen, daß Gilbert, der alte Fuchs, auf einmal ein Messer in der Hand hielt. Entschlossen übersprang er das Pferd, holte mit dem Eichenprügel aus und erwischte Gilbert just in dem Moment, da dieser das Messer hob, seitlich am Kopf.

Gilbert taumelte, aber er fiel nicht um. Verdammt zäh, der Kerl, dachte William und holte zu einem neuen Schlag aus. Gilbert kam ihm jedoch zuvor und sprang ihn mit gezücktem Messer an. William trug Freierskleider, keinen Kampfanzug. Die scharfe Schneide fuhr in die feine Wolle seines Mantels und schlitzte sie auf. Seine Haut hatte er nur gerettet, weil er im entscheidenen Moment zurückgesprungen war.

Aber Gilbert ließ nicht locker. William war gezwungen, ständig auszuweichen, und kam gar nicht mehr dazu, seinen Knüppel zu schwingen. Ein ums andere Mal sprang Gilbert ihn an, und jedesmal mußte William einen Schritt zurückweichen. Er spürte, daß er in die Enge getrieben wurde, und wurde plötzlich von Todesangst befallen. Doch dann tauchte auf einmal Walter hinter Gilbert auf und riß ihm mit einem gewaltigen Tritt die Beine vom Boden.

William atmete auf und dankte Gott, daß er ihm Walter gerade noch rechtzeitig geschickt hatte.

Gilbert versuchte, sich aufzurappeln, doch Walter trat ihm ins Gesicht, und William zog ihm sicherheitshalber noch zweimal den Knüppel über den Schädel. Danach rührte sich der Ritter nicht mehr.

Sie drehten ihn auf den Bauch, und Walter setzte sich auf seinen Kopf. William fesselte Gilbert die Hände auf dem Rücken, zog ihm danach die langen schwarzen Reitstiefel aus und band ihm schließlich die nackten Knöchel mit einem starken Lederriemen zusammen. Dann erhob er sich und grinste Walter an. Walter lächelte. Es tat gut, den geschmeidigen alten Haudegen kampfunfähig am Boden liegen zu sehen.

Jetzt mußten sie ihn nur noch zum Reden bringen.

Gilbert kam schon wieder zu sich. Walter drehte ihn um. Als Gilbert William erkannte, verwandelte sich seine Verblüffung schnell in Furcht. William war hocherfreut. Er bereut sein Gelächter schon, dachte er. In Kürze wird er es verfluchen ...

Gilberts Pferd hatte sich wieder aufgerappelt. Es war ein paar Schritt gelaufen und dann stehengeblieben. Jetzt sah es sich um. Es atmete schwer und zuckte jedesmal zusammen, wenn ein Windstoß durch die Zweige fegte. Das Messer steckte nicht mehr in der Wunde. William fand es nach kurzer Suche und nahm es an sich, während Walter das Pferd einfing.

Sie mußten jederzeit mit einem weiteren Boten des Grafen rechnen und waren darauf gefaßt, ihr Opfer schleunigst ins Gebüsch zu ziehen und ihm den Mund zuzuhalten. William lauschte angestrengt, doch es war nichts zu hören.

Sie banden Gilbert auf den Rücken seines Pferdes und begaben sich zu der Lichtung, auf der William ihre eigenen Tiere angebunden hatte. Die Rösser rochen das Blut, das aus der Wunde des Neuankömmlings sickerte, und wurden so unruhig, daß William nichts anderes übrigblieb, als Gilberts Pferd in einiger Entfernung von den anderen festzubinden.

Dann sah er sich nach einem Baum um, der für die Ausführung seines Plans geeignet war. Seine Wahl fiel auf eine Ulme mit einem kräftigen Seitenast in acht oder neun Fuß Höhe. Er zeigte sie Walter und sagte: »Wir hängen Gibert jetzt an diesen Ast.«

Walter grinste in lustvoller Vorfreude. »Was habt Ihr mit ihm vor, Herr?« fragte er.

»Das wirst du gleich sehen.«

Gilberts wettergegerbtes Gesicht war totenbleich vor Furcht. William zog ein Seil unter seinen Achseln durch, band es auf dem Rücken zusammen und warf das freie Ende über den Ast.

»Heb ihn jetzt hoch!« sagte er zu Walter, und dieser tat, wie ihm geheißen. William warf das freie Ende des Seils noch mehrere Male über den Ast und zog es dann fest. Walter ließ los, und Gilbert baumelte am Seil, die Fußspitzen etwa schritthoch über dem Boden.

»Geh jetzt und sammle Brennholz!« befahl William seinem Begleiter.

Sie schichteten die Reiser unter Gilbert zu einem Stoß auf, und William entzündete sie mit Hilfe eines Feuersteins. Kurz darauf züngelten die ersten Flammen hoch, und die entstehende Hitze weckte Gilbert aus seinem Dämmerzustand.

Als er erkannte, was seine Peiniger mit ihm vorhatten, stöhnte er entsetzt auf. »Bitte!« flehte er. »Bitte laßt mich wieder runter. Es tut mir leid, daß ich Euch ausgelacht habe. Bitte habt Gnade mit mir!«

William sagte kein Wort. Gilberts Unterwürfigkeit tat ihm wohl, doch war sie nicht der Zweck der Übung.

Als die Hitze Gilberts nackte Zehen erreichte, winkelte er die Knie an. Sein Gesicht war schweißüberströmt. In der Luft hing ein leichter Geruch nach angesengtem Stoff, denn die Hitze erfaßte auch die Kleider.

Ich glaube, es ist an der Zeit, mit dem Verhör zu beginnen, dachte William und sagte: »Warum warst du heute auf der Burg?«

Gilbert starrte ihn mit weit aufgerissenen Augen an: »Um dem Grafen meine Aufwartung zu machen«, sagte er. »Was ist daran so schlimm?«

»Warum hast du dem Grafen deine Aufwartung gemacht?«

»Der Graf ist gerade aus der Normandie zurückgekehrt.«

»Du bist nicht ausdrücklich zu ihm gerufen worden?«

»Nein.«

Kann sein, daß er recht hat, dachte William. So ein Verhör ist gar nicht so einfach, wie ich es mir vorgestellt habe ...

»Was hat der Graf zu dir gesagt, als du zu ihm vorgelassen wurdest?«

»Er hat mich begrüßt und mir für meinen Willkommensgruß gedankt.«

»Was noch?«

»Er hat sich nach meiner Familie und nach meinem Heimatdorf erkundigt.«

»Sonst noch was?«

»Nein.«

»Was hat er dir von König Stephan und Kaiserin Mathilde erzählt?«

»Nichts! Ich versichere es Euch!«

Gilbert konnte die Knie nicht länger anziehen, und die Füße sackten zurück in die höher schlagenden Flammen. Er stieß einen gellenden Schmerzensschrei aus, und sein Körper zog sich krampfhaft zusammen. Die Füße entkamen dadurch für einen Augenblick dem Feuer, und Gilbert erkannte, daß er die Schmerzen, indem er seinen Körper in schwingende Bewegungen versetzte, ein wenig lindern konnte. Er schrie jedoch jedesmal auf, wenn er beim Zurückpendeln unweigerlich wieder in die Flammen geriet.

Ob er die Wahrheit sagt? fragte sich William einmal mehr. Wie läßt sich das herausfinden? Irgendwann ist er wahrscheinlich so weit, daß er alles zugibt, was ich ihm in den Mund lege. Ich darf ihm nicht zu deutlich sagen, was ich von ihm hören will … Er begann, sich Sorgen zu machen. Wer hätte gedacht, daß Foltern ein so schwieriges Geschäft ist? dachte er.

Ruhig, fast im Plauderton, stellte er die nächste Frage. »Wo willst du jetzt hin?«

Gilbert kreischte vor Schmerzen und Seelenqual. »Was spielt denn das für eine Rolle?«

»Wo willst du hin?«

»Nach Hause!«

Der Mann war fast am Ende. William wußte, wo Gilbert zu Hause war – in einem Dorf im Norden. Sie hatten ihn aber auf dem Weg nach Süden abgefangen.

»Wo willst du hin?« fragte William noch einmal.

»Was wollt Ihr von mir?«

»Die Wahrheit, das ist alles«, erwiderte William. »Ich merke es sofort, wenn du lügst.« Walter bekundete mit einem Brummen seine Zustimmung. Ich werde langsam besser, dachte William.

»Wo willst du hin?« fragte er zum viertenmal.

Gilbert verließen die Kräfte, er konnte kaum noch hin und her schwingen. Vor Schmerzen stöhnend, pendelte er über dem Feuer aus und riß noch einmal die Unterschenkel hoch, um die Füße vor den Flammen zu bewahren. Diese loderten inzwischen aber schon so hoch, daß sie auch seine Knie versengten. Ein nicht ganz unbekannter, leicht ekelerregender Geruch stieg William in die Nase. Er brauchte nicht lange, um ihn zu erkennen: Es war der Geruch nach brutzelndem

Fleisch, wie er ihm von den Mahlzeiten her vertraut war. Die Haut an Gilberts Beinen und Füßen wurde braun und platzte auf. Die Härchen auf den Schienbeinen verfärbten sich schwarz, erste Fetttröpfchen lösten sich und fielen zischend ins Feuer. Gilberts Qualen faszinierten William. Jeder Schrei seines Opfers ließ ihn innerlich erbeben. Er hatte die Macht des Schmerzes über einen Menschen und genoß sie in vollen Zügen. Ein ähnliches Gefühl überkam ihn, wenn er mit einem Mädchen allein war, an einem Ort, wo kein Mensch ihr Jammern hören konnte, und wenn er sie dann zu Boden warf und ihr die Röcke hochschob und wußte, daß niemand und nichts mehr ihn daran hindern konnte, sie zu besitzen.

Fast widerstrebend wiederholte er seine Frage noch einmal. »Wo willst du hin?«

»Nach Sherborne.«

»Warum?«

»Holt mich hier raus, um Jesu Christi willen, und ich erzähl' Euch alles.«

Der Sieg war in greifbarer Nähe. Es war zutiefst befriedigend. Doch ganz war das Ziel noch nicht erreicht. »Zieh seine Füße aus dem Feuer!« sagte William zu Walter.

Walter packte Gilbert an der Tunika und zog ihn zu sich, so daß die Beine nicht mehr über den Flammen hingen.

»Also?«

»Graf Bartholomäus hat fünfzig Ritter in Sherborne und Umgebung«, sagte Gilbert mit erstickter Stimme. »Ich soll sie sammeln und nach Earlscastle bringen.«

William lächelte. Es war höchst erfreulich, daß all seine Vermutungen sich bestätigten. »Und was beabsichtigt der Graf mit diesen Rittern zu tun?«

»Hat er nicht gesagt.«

»Walter, laß ihn noch ein bißchen schmoren.«

»Nein!« brüllte Gilbert. »Ich sag' Euch alles.«

Walter zögerte.

»Jetzt aber schnell«, drohte William.

»Sie wollen gegen König Stephan ins Feld ziehen. Für die Kaiserin Mathilde.«

Endlich war er heraus, der gesuchte Beweis. William kostete seinen Triumph aus. »Wenn ich dir die Frage in Gegenwart meines Vaters noch einmal stelle – wirst du dieselbe Antwort geben?«

»Ja. Ja doch!«

»Und wenn dir mein Vater die Frage in Gegenwart des Königs noch einmal stellt – wirst du dann immer noch die Wahrheit sagen?«

»Ja.«

»Schwör es beim heiligen Kreuz!«

»Ich schwöre beim heiligen Kreuz, daß ich die Wahrheit sagen werde.«

»Amen«, sagte William zufrieden und begann, das Feuer auszutreten.

Sie banden Gilbert auf den Sattel seines Pferdes und legten dem Tier einen Leitzügel an. Dann ritten sie im Schritt weiter. Der Ritter vermochte sich kaum aufrecht zu halten. William packte ihn nicht allzuhart an. Er wollte nicht, daß Gilbert starb, denn ein toter Gilbert war zu nichts mehr nütze. Beim nächsten Wasserlauf bespritzte er die angebrannten Füße und Beine des Ritters mit kaltem Wasser, und obwohl Gilbert vor Schmerzen aufschrie, tat ihm die Roßkur wahrscheinlich gut.

In Williams überschwengliches Triumphgefühl mischte sich ein Wermutstropfen. Noch nie in seinem Leben hatte er einen Menschen getötet. Nur allzugerne hätte er Gilbert jetzt umgebracht. Einen Menschen foltern und ihn dann nicht töten können – das war dasselbe, wie einem Mädchen die Kleider vom Leibe reißen und es dann doch nicht vergewaltigen zu können. Je mehr er darüber nachdachte, desto stärker verlangte ihn nach einer Frau.

Vielleicht zu Hause, dachte er ... Aber nein, da muß ich sofort den Eltern Bericht erstatten. Und dann wollen sie sicher gleich, daß Gilbert sein Geständnis vor einem Priester und womöglich noch anderen Zeugen wiederholt. Sobald das geschehen ist, wird sich alles nur noch um die Gefangennahme des Grafen drehen. Wir müssen ihn uns so bald wie möglich schnappen, am besten schon morgen, bevor er eine zu große Streitmacht um sich versammelt hat ...

William hatte sich noch immer keine List einfallen lassen, mit deren Hilfe man die Burg ohne lange Belagerung einnehmen konnte. Verdrossen gestand er sich ein, daß es noch lange hin sein mochte, bevor er die nächste hübsche Frau auch nur *erblickte* – doch genau in diesem Augenblick kam sie ihm schon entgegen.

Eine Gruppe von fünf Menschen kam auf William zu, darunter eine dunkelhaarige Frau von ungefähr fünfundzwanzig Jahren, nicht gerade ein junges Mädchen mehr, aber jung genug allemal. Je näher sie kam, desto neugieriger wurde William. Sie war in der Tat recht hübsch – mit ihrem dunkelbraunen Haar, das auf der Stirn einer Teufelsmütze entsprang, und den tiefliegenden, blaßgoldenen Augen. Ihre Figur war schlank und geschmeidig, die sonnengebräunte Haut seidig-weich.

»Bleib hier!« sagte William zu Walter. »Und sieh zu, daß die Leute den Ritter nicht sehen, solange ich mit ihnen rede.«

Bei den Reisenden, die inzwischen stehengeblieben waren und den auf sie zukommenden Reiter aufmerksam beobachteten, handelte es sich offenbar um eine Familie: ein hochgewachsener Mann, ein ausgewachsener, aber noch bartloser Jüngling und zwei halbwüchsige Bälger gehörten dazu. Den Mann habe ich doch irgendwo schon einmal gesehen, dachte William verblüfft.

»Kenne ich dich?« fragte er unverblümt.

»Ich kenne *Euch*«, erwiderte der Mann. »Und Euer Pferd ebenso. Ihr hättet nämlich um ein Haar meine Tochter umgebracht.«

Die Erinnerung kehrte zurück. Mein Roß hat das Kind nicht berührt, dachte William, aber es war verflucht knapp. »Du hast mein Haus gebaut«, sagte er. »Und als ich dich entließ, verlangtest du Geld und hast mir fast gedroht.«

Der Mann widersprach nicht und hielt seinem Blick stand.

»Jetzt bist du nicht mehr so keck, wie?« sagte William und rümpfte die Nase. Die ganze Familie schien Hunger zu leiden. Wie's scheint, ist heut der Tag der Abrechnung mit allen, die mich je beleidigt haben, dachte William und fragte: »Habt ihr Hunger?«

»Ja, wir haben Hunger«, bestätigte der Baumeister mit verhaltenem Zorn.

William besah sich die Frau. Mit leicht gespreizten Beinen und vorgeschobenem Kinn stand sie vor ihm und blickte ihm furchtlos in die Augen. Aliena hatte seine Lust entfacht, jetzt wollte er sie an dieser Frau stillen. Das ist eine ganz muntere, dachte er, die zappelt und kratzt, wenn's zur Sache geht – na, um so besser …

»Verheiratet seid ihr beiden nicht, wie, Baumeister? Ich kann mich noch an deine Frau erinnern. Das war eine häßliche Kuh.«

Schmerz verdüsterte des Baumeisters Gesicht. »Meine Frau ist tot.«

»Und die hier hast du noch nicht vor den Altar geschleppt, nicht wahr? Bettelarm, wie du bist, fehlt dir sogar das Geld, um den Priester zu bezahlen.« Im Hintergrund tänzelten die Pferde ungeduldig hin und her, und Walter hustete vernehmlich. »Soll ich dir Geld geben, damit du was zu essen kaufen kannst? Was meinst du?«

»Ich würde es dankbar entgegennehmen«, erwiderte der Baumeister, doch William merkte genau, daß dem Mann seine unterwürfige Haltung schwerfiel.

»Du bekommst es nicht geschenkt. Ich kauf' dir das Weib ab.«

Die Betroffene antwortete selbst: »Ich bin unverkäuflich, mein Junge«, sagte sie in spöttischem Ton.

Sie hatte einen wunden Punkt getroffen. William wurde zornig. Wart's ab, bis wir allein sind, dachte er. Dann werd' ich dir schon zeigen, ob ich ein Mann oder ein Junge bin. Er wandte sich an den Baumeister: »Ich gebe dir ein Pfund Silber für sie.«

»Sie ist unverkäuflich.«

William platzte der Kragen. Da bietet man einem Verhungernden ein Vermögen an und dann so eine Abfuhr! »Entweder du nimmst jetzt das Geld, du Idiot, oder ich hau' dir mein Schwert zwischen die Rippen und rammle das Weib gleich hier vor den Augen der Kinder.«

Der Baumeister bewegte seinen Arm unter dem Umhang. Wahrscheinlich hat er eine Waffe dabei, dachte William. Und überhaupt … Er ist zwar klapperdürr, aber ziemlich groß. Kampflos gibt er das Weib nicht her … In diesem Augenblick schob die Frau ihren Umhang hoch und legte ihre Hand an den Griff eines Dolches von beachtlicher Länge, der in ihrem Gürtel steckte. Auch der ältere der beiden Jungen war schon so groß, daß er Schwierigkeiten machen konnte.

»Herr, wir haben dafür jetzt keine Zeit!« Es war Walter, der sich mit leiser, aber tragender Stimme zu Wort meldete.

William nickte widerstrebend. Wir müssen Gilbert bei den Eltern abliefern, sagte er sich. Die Sache ist zu wichtig, als daß sie wegen eines Weibes Aufschub duldet. Es hilft nichts, ich muß noch eine Weile darben.

Da standen sie vor ihm, diese fünf zerlumpten Hungerleider, und waren allesamt dazu bereit, den Kampf gegen zwei wohlgenährte und mit Schwertern bewaffnete Reiter aufzunehmen. William konnte diese Leute einfach nicht verstehen. »Gut, wenn ihr wollt – dann verhungert eben«, sagte er, trat seinem Pferd in die Flanken und ritt weiter. Kurze Zeit später war die Familie außer Sicht.

Ungefähr eine Meile hinter dem Ort, an dem sie William Hamleigh begegnet waren, fragte Ellen: »Können wir wieder ein bißchen langsamer gehen?«

Tom merkte erst jetzt, daß er unwillkürlich einen recht strammen Schritt angeschlagen hatte, und er gestand sich ein, daß Angst dahintersteckte. Hatte es doch kurzzeitig so ausgesehen, als müßten er und Alfred sich mit zwei bewaffneten Reitern schlagen ... Dabei hatte er nicht einmal mehr eine Waffe. Er hatte unter dem Mantel nach seinem Maurerhammer getastet, nur um schmerzlich daran erinnert zu werden, daß er das gute Stück schon Wochen zuvor gegen einen Sack Haferflocken eingetauscht hatte. Warum William schließlich nachgegeben hatte, war ihm unklar. Auf jeden Fall wollte Tom den Abstand zu ihm so schnell wie möglich vergrößern – wer vermochte schon zu sagen, ob sich der Bösewicht nicht noch anders besann?

Tom hatte am Palast des Bischofs von Kingsbridge ebensowenig Arbeit gefunden wie überall sonst, wo er es versucht hatte. Schließlich hatte er von einem Steinbruch in der Nähe von Shiring gehört. In Steinbrüchen wurde – anders als auf Baustellen – die Zahl der Beschäftigten im Winter nicht verringert. Gewiß, von seinem Können und seiner Ausbildung her war Tom andere und besser bezahlte Arbeiten gewohnt als die Steinhauerei – aber das kümmerte ihn längst nicht mehr. Er wollte seine Familie ernähren, das war alles. Der Steinbruch bei Shiring gehörte Graf Bartholomäus, der, wie Tom erfahren hatte, auf einer Burg einige Meilen westlich der Stadt lebte.

Seine Lage war, seit Ellen ihn begleitete, noch verzweifelter als zuvor. Er wußte, daß sie sich aus Liebe – und ohne die möglichen Folgen zu bedenken – dazu entschlossen hatte, ihr Schicksal mit ihm zu teilen. Vor allem besaß sie keine klare Vorstellung davon, wie schwer es für Tom war, Arbeit zu finden, und hatte sich daher auch niemals ernsthaft mit dem Gedanken auseinandergesetzt, daß sie den Winter vielleicht nicht überleben würden. Tom seinerseits, der sie nicht mehr verlieren wollte, hatte es nicht über sich gebracht, ihr reinen Wein einzuschenken – eine Frau war imstande, wenn die Lage kritisch wurde, das Wohl ihres Kindes über alles zu stellen. Er fürchtete, Ellen könnte ihn wieder verlassen.

Eine Woche lang waren sie jetzt zusammen: sieben verzweifelte Tage und sieben wundervolle Nächte. Wenn Tom des Morgens erwachte, war er glücklich und sah die Zukunft in rosigem Licht. Mit fortschreitendem Tag kam dann der Hunger, die Kinder wurden müde, und Ellens Stimmung erreichte einen Tiefpunkt. An manchen Tagen – zum Beispiel als ihnen der Mönch mit dem Käse begegnete – bekamen sie etwas zu essen, an anderen mußten sie sich mit sonnengetrockneten Rindfleischstreifen aus Ellens Notvorrat zufriedengeben. Die waren zäh wie Hirschleder und schmeckten auch nicht viel anders, doch das war immer noch besser als gar nichts. Abends aber, wenn es dunkel wurde und sie sich niederlegten, elend und kalt, und sich aneinanderkuschelten, um sich gegenseitig zu wärmen, dann dauerte es nicht lange, und sie fingen an sich zu streicheln und zu küssen. Anfangs wollte Tom immer gleich zu ihr kommen. Ellen wies ihn jedoch sanft zurück: Sie wollte mehr Küsse und ein viel längeres Vorspiel. Tom ging auf ihre Wünsche ein – und war begeistert. Kühn erforschte er ihren Körper und liebkoste ihn an Stellen, an denen er Agnes nie berührt hatte. Er streichelte und küßte ihre Ohren, ihre Achselhöhlen und die Spalte zwischen ihren Hinterbacken. In manchen Nächten steckten sie die Köpfe unter der Decke zusammen und kicherten ausgelassen, dann wieder beschenkten sie einander mit reiner Zärtlichkeit. Einmal – sie nächtigten allein im Gästehaus eines Klosters, und die Kinder schliefen den Schlaf der Erschöpften – übernahm Ellen die Führung. So zeigte sie ihm, wie er sie mit seinen Fingern erregen konnte, und er folgte ihren Anweisungen bereitwillig, von ihrer Schamlosigkeit gleichermaßen verwirrt wie entflammt. War es dann vorbei, versanken sie in einen tiefen, erholsamen Schlaf; die Liebe hatte allen Kummer und Ärger des Tages hinweggespült.

Es war jetzt Mittag. William Hamleigh dürfte jetzt weit genug fort sein, dachte Tom und beschloß, eine Rast einzulegen.

Wieder hatten sie nur Trockenfleisch zu essen. Am Morgen erst war es ihnen gelungen, bei einem einsam gelegenen Bauernhof ein wenig Brot zu erbetteln. Die Bäuerin hatte ihnen darüber hinaus in einer großen Holzflasche ohne Stöpsel etwas Bier mitgegeben und ihnen erlaubt, die Flasche zu behalten. Ellen hatte die Hälfte des Inhalts für das Mittagessen aufbewahrt.

Tom ließ sich auf dem Rand eines uralten Baumstumpfs nieder, und Ellen setzte sich neben ihn. Sie nahm einen kräftigen Schluck Bier zu sich und reichte die Flasche an Tom weiter.

»Möchtest du auch etwas Fleisch?« fragte sie.

Er schüttelte den Kopf und trank. Es wäre ihm nicht schwergefallen, die Flasche auszutrinken, doch bezwang er sich und ließ noch etwas für die Kinder übrig. »Bewahr das Fleisch lieber auf«, sagte er zu Ellen. »Vielleicht bekommen wir heute abend auf der Burg was zu essen.«

Alfred setzte die Flasche an die Lippen und leerte sie in einem Zug.

Jack wirkte erschrocken und enttäuscht, und Martha brach in Tränen aus. Alfred grinste dämlich.

Ellen sah Tom an. Als er nicht reagierte, sagte sie: »Das solltest du ihm eigentlich nicht durchgehen lassen.«

Tom zuckte mit den Schultern. »Er ist größer als die anderen beiden. Er braucht auch mehr.«

»Er bekommt sowieso immer das meiste. Die Kleinen brauchen wenigstens *etwas*.«

»Die Kinder sollen ihre Streitigkeiten unter sich austragen. Es ist Zeitverschwendung, sich da einzumischen.«

Ellens Stimme wurde hart. »Soll das heißen, daß Alfred die beiden Jüngeren nach Belieben schikanieren kann, ohne daß du dagegen einschreitest?«

»Er schikaniert sie nicht. Kinder zanken sich andauernd.«

Ellen schüttelte den Kopf. Sie war offenbar ganz durcheinander. »Ich verstehe nicht«, sagte sie. »Du bist ein rundum netter und verständiger Mann – nur wenn es um Alfred geht, bist du blind!«

Jetzt übertreibt sie aber, dachte Tom. Um sie nicht noch weiter gegen ihn aufzubringen, sagte er: »Gib den Kleinen eben ein bißchen Fleisch.«

Ellen öffnete ihre Tasche. Sie war noch immer eingeschnappt. Sowohl für Martha als auch für Jack schnitt sie einen Streifen Trockenfleisch ab, aber die ausgestreckte Hand Alfreds ignorierte sie geflissentlich. Tom fand das nicht recht. Sie hätte ihm ruhig etwas geben können, dachte er. Alfred ist kein schlechter Kerl; Ellen versteht ihn bloß nicht. Er ist ein großer Junge, auf den ich stolz sein kann. Er hat einen großen Appetit und ein hitziges Gemüt – aber wenn das eine Sünde ist, dann fällt jeder zweite junge Mann seines Alters der Verdammnis anheim ...

Sie ruhten sich noch eine Weile aus und machten sich dann wieder auf den Weg. Jack und Martha gingen voran; sie kauten noch immer auf dem ledrigen Fleisch herum. Die beiden kamen trotz des Altersunterschiedes – Martha war sechs und Jack vielleicht elf oder zwölf – recht gut miteinander aus. Martha war von Jack ganz hingerissen – und Jack genoß die für ihn völlig neue Erfahrung, eine Spielgefährtin zu haben. Ein Jammer, daß Alfred Jack nicht mochte! Alfred war natürlich der Stärkere, aber der kleine Jack war ein heller Bursche.

Tom wollte sich nicht länger darüber den Kopf zerbrechen. Er hatte weiß Gott andere Sorgen, als sich mit den Kabbeleien der Kinder zu belasten. Insgeheim fragte er sich manchmal schon, ob er überhaupt je wieder Arbeit finden würde. Vielleicht müssen wir ewig so weiterwandern, tagein, tagaus, bis wir nacheinander tot umfallen: An einem frostigen Morgen liegt ein Kind vor mir, kalt und leblos. Das andere hat nicht mehr die Kraft, ein plötzliches Fieber zu überstehen.

Ellen geschändet und ermordet von einem zufällig des Weges kommenden Schuft wie William Hamleigh ... Und ich – ich werde dünner und dünner, bis ich eines Morgens zu schwach bin, um auf die Beine zu kommen, und einfach im Wald liegen bleibe und langsam das Bewußtsein verliere ...

Bevor es so weit käme, dies war ihm klar, hätte Ellen ihn längst verlassen. Sie würde rechtzeitig in ihre Höhle zurückkehren, wo immerhin noch ein Faß Äpfel und ein Sack Nüsse standen, die ausreichten, zwei – aber nicht fünf – Menschen über den Winter zu bringen. Es bricht mir das Herz, wenn sie geht, dachte Tom.

Wie es wohl dem kleinen Jungen im Kloster ergehen mochte? Die Mönche hatten ihn Jonathan genannt. Tom gefiel der Name, der nach Auskunft des Mönchs mit dem Käse ›Geschenk Gottes‹ bedeutete. Er sah den kleinen Kerl vor sich, wie er nach der Geburt ausgesehen hatte – rot, runzelig und kahl. Inzwischen hatte er sich bestimmt verändert; eine Woche war im Leben eines Neugeborenen eine lange Zeit. Er war gewiß schon gewachsen, konnte die Lider weiter öffnen als zuvor und fing an, von seiner Umgebung Notiz zu nehmen: Ein lautes Geräusch schreckte ihn auf, ein Gutenachtlied beruhigte ihn. Manchmal, vor dem Aufstoßen, kräuselten sich seine Mundwinkel, so daß die Mönche in ihrer Unwissenheit meinten, er lächle ...

Hoffentlich behandeln sie ihn gut, dachte Tom. Der Mönch mit dem Käse hatte den besten Eindruck auf ihn gemacht; wenn alle so waren wie er, dann handelte es sich durchwegs um nette und fähige Männer. Auf jeden Fall war Jonathan bei ihnen besser aufgehoben als bei seinem leiblichen Vater, der weder Geld noch Obdach hatte. Wenn ich jemals wieder eine große Baustelle unter mir habe, gelobte sich Tom, und zusätzlich zu freier Unterkunft und Verpflegung die Woche vier Shilling verdiene, dann werde ich dem Kloster Spenden zukommen lassen.

Sie erreichten den Waldrand, und kurz darauf erhob sich vor ihnen die Burg des Grafen Bartholomäus.

Tom faßte neuen Mut, aber er ließ sich nichts anmerken. Seine Lektion nach Monaten der Enttäuschung war die, daß allzu große Erwartungen zu Beginn die Zurückweisung am Ende nur noch schlimmer machten.

Der Weg zur Burg führte durch kahle Felder. Martha und Jack fanden ein kleines, verletztes Vögelchen, und die ganze Familie blieb stehen, um es sich anzusehen. Es war ein winziger Zaunkönig. Als Martha sich über ihn beugte, hüpfte er davon; anscheinend konnte er nicht mehr fliegen. Das Mädchen fing den Vogel ein und barg ihn in ihren Händen.

»Er zittert ja«, sagte sie. »Ich kann es fühlen. Er muß furchtbare Angst haben.«

Der Vogel machte keinerlei Anstalten mehr zu fliehen, sondern saß still in Marthas Hand und starrte mit hellen Augen die vielen Menschen an, die sich um ihn drängten. »Ich glaube, er hat sich den Flügel gebrochen«, sagte Jack.

»Laß mal sehen!« sagte Alfred zu seiner Schwester und nahm ihr den Vogel weg.

»Wenn wir uns um ihn kümmern, wird er vielleicht wieder gesund«, sagte Martha.

»Nein, wird er nicht«, gab Alfred zurück und drehte dem Tierchen mit seinen großen Händen den Hals um. Alles geschah ganz schnell.

»Herrgott noch mal!« sagte Ellen.

Zum zweitenmal an diesem Tag brach Martha in Tränen aus.

Alfred lachte und warf den toten Vogel auf den Boden.

Jack hob ihn auf. »Tot«, sagte er.

»Was ist eigentlich los mit dir, Alfred?« fragte Ellen.

»Gar nichts ist los mit ihm«, antwortete Tom anstelle seines Sohnes. »Der Vogel wäre sowieso nicht zu retten gewesen.«

Er ging weiter, und die anderen trotteten hinterher.

Daß Ellen schon wieder auf Alfred wütend war, ärgerte ihn. Was sollte dieses Theater um einen toten Zaunkönig? Tom erinnerte sich daran, wie er sich selbst mit vierzehn Jahren gefühlt hatte, als Halbwüchsiger im Körper eines Mannes: unbehaglich und unsicher. *Wenn es um Alfred geht, bist du blind,* hatte Ellen ihm vorgeworfen. Sie hatte ja keine Ahnung!

Die Holzbrücke, die über den Burggraben zum Torhaus führte, war schwach und baufällig. Der Graf hatte höchstwahrscheinlich nichts dagegen, denn Brücken verschafften auch möglichen Angreifern Einlaß. Je eher sie einstürzten, desto sicherer war die Burg. Die hohen Erdwälle waren in regelmäßigen Abständen mit steinernen Wachtürmen bestückt. Das Torhaus jenseits der Brücke sah aus wie zwei mit einem Bogen verbundene Türme. Viel Mauerwerk aus Stein, dachte Tom bei sich, keine von diesen Burgen, die nur aus Lehm und Holz bestehen ... Morgen habe ich vielleicht schon Arbeit. Allein der Gedanke daran, endlich wieder einmal gute Werkzeuge in der Hand zu haben, erfüllte ihn mit Begeisterung. Er sah sich die Vorderseite eines Steinblocks glätten und hörte den Meißel über die rauhe Fläche schaben; schon spürte er das trockene Gefühl, das der Steinstaub in seinen Nasenlöchern verbreitete ... Morgen abend habe ich vielleicht endlich mal wieder einen vollen Magen – und habe die Speisen nicht erbettelt, sondern verdient ...

Als sie näher kamen, erkannte Tom mit geschultem Blick, daß der Zustand der Zinnen auf dem Torhaus sehr zu wünschen übrigließ. Einige größere Steine waren herausgebrochen, so daß die Brüstungen stellenweise fast eingeebnet waren. Auch im Torbogen hatten sich Mauersteine gelockert.

Die beiden Wachposten am Tor waren ungewöhnlich aufmerksam. Einer von ihnen fragte Tom, was er auf der Burg wolle.

»Bin Steinmetz«, erwiderte er. »Hoffe auf eine Anstellung im Steinbruch des Grafen.«

»Da wendet Ihr Euch am besten an den Haushofmeister«, meinte der Wachposten hilfsbereit. »Er heißt Matthew. Wahrscheinlich findet Ihr ihn im großen Saal.«

»Danke«, sagte Tom. »Was ist das für ein Mann?«

Der Posten grinste seinen Kollegen an und antwortete: »Von ›Mann‹ kann man da eigentlich nicht sprechen ...« Die beiden lachten.

Ich werde schon herausfinden, was das zu bedeuten hat, dachte Tom und betrat mit Ellen und den Kindern im Gefolge den Innenhof. Die Wirtschaftsgebäude waren überwiegend aus Holz; einige von ihnen verfügten allerdings über steinerne Sockel. Bei dem einzigen echten Steingebäude handelte es sich allem Anschein nach um die Kapelle. Auf dem Weg über den Burghof stellte Tom fest, daß die Zinnen und Brüstungen aller Wachtürme reparaturbedürftig waren. Sie überquerten die Brücke, die zum oberen Ring führte, und meldeten sich beim Wachposten im Torhaus. Tom erklärte, daß er Haushofmeister Matthew sprechen wolle. Sie wurden eingelassen, begaben sich ohne Umschweife zum Wohnturm und stiegen die Holztreppe empor, die zum großen Saal führte.

Tom erkannte den Grafen und seinen Haushofmeister sofort an ihren Kleidern. Graf Bartholomäus trug eine lange Tunika mit bauschigen Ärmelaufschlägen und besticktem Saum. Matthews Tunika war kürzer. Sie entsprach im Schnitt Toms eigener, war aber aus weicherem Stoff geschneidert. Auf dem Kopf trug Matthew eine kleine runde Mütze. Die beiden Männer hielten sich unweit der Feuerstelle auf – der Graf saß, der Haushofmeister stand. Tom ging auf sie zu, blieb dann aber in respektvoller Entfernung stehen, um zu warten, bis man auf ihn aufmerksam wurde. Graf Bartholomäus war ein hochgewachsener Mann über Fünfzig. Er hatte schlohweiße Haare und ein hageres, blasses Gesicht. Seine hochmütige Miene verriet keine Spur von Großherzigkeit. Der Haushofmeister war jünger. So, wie er dastand, erinnerte er Tom an die Bemerkung des Torwächters: Er wirkte feminin. Tom wußte nicht, was er davon halten sollte.

Im Saal befanden sich noch verschiedene andere Personen, die jedoch allesamt von Tom keine Notiz nahmen. Das Gespräch zwischen dem Grafen und seinem Haushofmeister dauerte schier endlos und stürzte den wartenden Tom in ein Wechselbad aus Angst und Hoffnung. Als es endlich zu Ende war, verneigte sich der Haushofmeister und wandte sich zum Gehen. Tom faßte sich ein Herz, trat vor und sagte: »Seid Ihr Matthew?«

»Ja, der bin ich.«

»Ich heiße Tom Builder, bin Steinmetz und Baumeister. Ich bin ein tüchtiger Handwerker. Meine Kinder hungern. Wie ich hörte, besitzt Ihr einen Steinbruch …« Er hielt den Atem an.

»In der Tat, den besitzen wir«, antwortete Matthew. »Aber ich glaube nicht, daß wir gegenwärtig weitere Steinbrecher benötigen.« Er sah sich nach dem Grafen um, der kaum merklich den Kopf schüttelte. »Nein«, fuhr er dann fort. »Wir können Euch nicht anstellen.«

Es war die Schnelligkeit der Entscheidung, die Tom das Herz brach. Ablehnungen, die in ernstem Ton oder nach einiger Bedenkzeit ausgesprochen wurden, vielleicht auch mit einigen Worten des Bedauerns, waren leichter zu ertragen. Dieser Matthew war kein schlechter Kerl, das hatte Tom sofort erkannt. Aber er war sehr beschäftigt. In Tom und seiner Familie sah er ein neues Problem auf sich zukommen, daß er sich so schnell wie möglich vom Hals schaffen wollte.

»Ich könnte hier auf der Burg verschiedene Reparaturen durchführen«, sagte Tom in seiner Verzweiflung.

»Solche Dinge erledigt unser Stellmacher«, sagte Matthew.

Die Stellmacher waren auf den Burgen oft Mädchen für alles und verstanden vom Bauhandwerk meist herzlich wenig. »Ich bin Maurer und Steinmetz«, sagte Tom. »Meine Mauern sind stark.«

Es gefiel Matthew nicht, daß Tom ihm so hartnäckig widersprach. Er wollte grob werden, doch dann fiel sein Blick auf die Kinder, und seine Züge entspannten sich wieder. »Ich würde Euch ja gerne nehmen«, sagte er, »aber wir können Euch nicht gebrauchen.«

Tom nickte. Bei diesem Stand der Dinge war es ratsam, sich zu fügen, einen mitleidheischenden Blick aufzusetzen und um eine Mahlzeit sowie ein Obdach für die kommende Nacht zu bitten. Aber diesmal war Ellen bei ihm, und er fürchtete, sie könnte ihn verlassen, und deshalb entschloß er sich zu einem letzten Versuch. Laut genug, daß auch der Graf es hören konnte, sagte er: »Ich hoffe nur, daß Ihr Euch in naher Zukunft nicht schlagen müßt!«

Die Reaktion übertraf alle seine Erwartungen. Matthew fuhr erschrocken zusammen, und der Graf stand auf und sagte mit scharfer Stimme: »Was soll das? Warum sagt Ihr das?«

Da habe ich anscheinend einen wunden Punkt getroffen, dachte Tom und antwortete: »Weil sich Eure Verteidigungsanlagen in einem sehr schlechten baulichen Zustand befinden.«

»Inwiefern?« fragte der Graf. »Drückt Euch gefälligst etwas deutlicher aus, Mann!«

Der Graf war aufgebracht, hörte jetzt aber genau zu. Tom holte tief Luft. Eine zweite solche Chance bekomme ich bestimmt nicht, dachte er.

»Aus den Mauern des Torhauses bröckelt vielerorts der Mörtel heraus. Das sind prächtige Ansatzstellen für die Brechstange. Hat der Feind erst einmal ein, zwei Steine ausgehebelt, fällt die Mauer schnell. Außerdem ...« Um zu verhindern, daß ihm jemand ins Wort fiel, sprach Tom jetzt sehr schnell. »Außerdem sind die Zinnen und Brüstungen der Türme beschädigt. An manchen Stellen gibt es kaum noch welche. Im Falle eines Angriffs sind Eure Ritter und Bogenschützen also ohne Deckung ...«

»Ich weiß, wozu man Brüstungen braucht«, unterbrach ihn der Graf pikiert. »Sonst noch was?«

»Ja. Das Vorratslager hier im Wohnturm ist nur durch eine Holztür gesichert. Wenn ich das Gebäude angreifen wollte, würde ich dort eindringen und Feuer legen.«

»Und was würdet Ihr tun, wenn Ihr der Graf wäret und einen solchen Angriff verhindern wolltet?«

»Ich würde ausreichend Sand und Kalk und einen Haufen passender Steine beschaffen lassen und dafür sorgen, daß ein Maurer bereitsteht, der bei Gefahr im Verzug den Eingang sofort dichtmacht.«

Graf Bartholomäus starrte Tom an. Er hatte die blaßblauen Augen zusammengekniffen und runzelte die weiße Stirn. Tom wußte mit dieser Miene nichts anzufangen. Ist er böse auf mich, weil ich mich so kritisch über die Verteidigungsanlagen seiner Burg geäußert habe? fragte er sich. Man konnte nie wissen, wie die hohen Herren auf Kritik reagierten ... Im allgemeinen war es günstiger, sie ihre Fehler machen zu lassen. Aber Tom trieb der Mut der Verzweiflung.

Der Graf schien sich endlich zu einer Entscheidung durchgerungen zu haben. Er wandte sich an Matthew und sagte: »Stell den Mann ein!«

Tom unterdrückte mit Mühe einen Jubelschrei. Er konnte es kaum fassen. Überglücklich lächelte er Ellen zu, und sie lächelte zurück. Unbelastet von den Hemmungen der Erwachsenen, schrie Martha laut: »Hurra!«

Graf Bartholomäus hatte sich abgewandt und unterhielt sich mit einem Ritter. Mit dem freundlichsten Lächeln fragte Matthew Tom: »Habt Ihr heute schon zu Mittag gegessen?«

Tom schluckte. Vor lauter Glück kamen ihm beinahe die Tränen. »Nein«, sagte er.

»Dann kommt, ich zeige Euch die Küche.«

Der Haushofmeister führte sie über die Brücke zum unteren Ring. Die Küche war ein großes Holzhaus mit einem Sockel aus Stein. Matthew hieß sie vor der Tür warten. Ein süßlicher Geruch hing in der Luft und verriet, daß gerade Törtchen gebacken wurden. Toms Magen knurrte heftig, und das Wasser lief ihm im Munde zusammen. Kurz darauf kehrte Matthew zurück und reichte Tom einen großen Krug Bier. »Man wird Euch gleich Brot und kalten Speck bringen«, sagte er und ließ sie allein.

Tom trank einen Schluck Bier und gab den Krug an Ellen weiter, die zunächst Martha trinken ließ, bevor sie ihn selbst an den Mund setzte. Als sie fertig war, kam Jack an die Reihe, doch ehe er trinken konnte, griff Alfred zu, um ihm den Krug zu entreißen. Jack hatte offenbar damit gerechnet; er drehte sich rasch um, so daß Alfred den Krug verfehlte. Bloß nicht schon wieder eine Streiterei, dachte Tom, ausgerechnet jetzt, da sich alles zum Guten wendet! Schon wollte er dazwischenfahren und seinem Grundsatz, sich nicht in die Auseinandersetzungen der Kinder einzumischen, untreu werden, als Jack sich wieder umdrehte und mit lammfrommer Miene Alfred den Bierkrug entgegenstreckte.

Alfred setzte ihn an die Lippen und trank. Tom, der selbst nur einen kleinen Schluck getrunken hatte, war davon ausgegangen, der Krug käme wieder zu ihm zurück; Alfred indessen sah nicht so aus, als wolle er ihm noch etwas übriglassen. Und dann geschah auf einmal etwas Merkwürdiges. Als Alfred den Krug immer höher hob, um ihn bis auf den letzten Tropfen zu leeren, fiel ihm plötzlich etwas ins Gesicht.

Erschreckt schrie Alfred auf, ließ den Krug fallen und wischte sich mit einer raschen Handbewegung das weiche, flaumige Etwas aus dem

Gesicht. »Was ist das?« kreischte er. Das Ding war auf den Boden gefallen, und Alfred starrte es, vor Ekel zitternd, an. Er war käsebleich im Gesicht.

Alle starrten sie auf den Boden. Es war der tote Zaunkönig.

Tom warf Ellen einen schnellen Blick zu, dann sahen sie beide Jack an. Der hatte den Krug von Ellen entgegengenommen und sich rasch umgedreht, um Alfreds Attacke zu entgehen, um ihm kurz darauf mit überraschender Bereitwilligkeit den Krug zu überreichen ...

Und da stand er jetzt und blickte den entsetzten Alfred an. Auf seinem jungen und doch schon so alten Gesicht lag ein sanftes, zufriedenes Lächeln.

Jack wußte, daß er für seinen Streich würde büßen müssen. Alfred wird sich irgendwie rächen, dachte er, wird mir vielleicht, wenn von den anderen gerade niemand hinsieht, in den Magen boxen ... Das war einer von Alfreds Lieblingsschlägen, denn er war einerseits sehr schmerzhaft und hinterließ andererseits keine sichtbaren Spuren. Jack hatte schon mehrfach beobachtet, wie Alfred Martha auf diese Weise mißhandelte.

Trotzdem – die Sache hatte sich gelohnt. Alfreds entsetzte, angstverzerrte Miene, als der tote Vogel ihm ins Gesicht fiel – dafür ließ sich sogar ein Schlag in den Magen verschmerzen ...

Alfred haßte Jack, und daß man ihn hassen konnte, war für Jack eine vollkommen neue Erfahrung. Seine Mutter hatte ihn stets geliebt, und andere Menschen, die ihm Gefühle entgegenbrachten, hatte er nie gekannt. Einen verständlichen Grund für Alfreds Feindseligkeit gab es nicht, zumal er sich Martha gegenüber ganz ähnlich verhielt. Bei jeder sich bietenden Gelegenheit kniff oder zwickte er sie, zog sie an den Haaren oder stellte ihr ein Bein. Wenn Martha an etwas Gefallen fand, gab es für Alfred nichts Schöneres, als ihr die Freude daran zu vergällen. Ellen konnte sein Benehmen nicht ausstehen; sein Vater hingegen tat, als hielte er es für die normalste Sache der Welt, und das, obwohl er selbst ein netter und freundlicher Mann war, der Martha zweifellos sehr gern hatte. Jack konnte das nicht begreifen. Trotzdem – oder gerade deswegen – fand er es hochinteressant.

Alles war interessant. Nie zuvor hatte Jack eine so aufregende Zeit erlebt. Trotz Alfred, trotz seines ständig knurrenden Magens und obwohl er darunter litt, daß sich seine Mutter viel mehr um Tom kümmerte als um ihn, war Jack von der Flut der auf ihn einströmenden neuen Erfahrungen und Ereignisse wie gebannt.

Das vorläufig letzte Wunder war diese Burg. Jack hatte natürlich schon viel von Burgen gehört: An langen Winterabenden im Wald hatte seine Mutter ihm *Chansons* beigebracht, französische Verserzählungen über Ritter und Zauberer, von denen manche Tausende von Zeilen umfaßten. Burgen waren in diesen Erzählungen Stätten der Zuflucht und der Liebe. Und da er nie eine Burg mit eigenen Augen gesehen hatte, stellte er sich darunter so etwas wie eine vergrößerte Version der eigenen Wohnhöhle vor.

Wie anders sah jetzt die Wirklichkeit aus! So riesengroß, mit so vielen Gebäuden und vielen, vielen Menschen, die alle einer bestimmten Beschäftigung nachgingen ... Die einen beschlugen Pferde, die anderen holten am Brunnen Wasser, wieder andere fütterten Hühner oder backten Brot. Und immer wieder kamen Leute, die etwas trugen oder schleppten – Stroh für die Lager, Feuerholz, Mehlsäcke, Stoffballen, Schwerter, Sättel, Post. Tom erklärte ihm, daß der Burggraben und die Wälle keine natürlichen Bestandteile der Landschaft waren, sondern von Dutzenden von Männern in gemeinsamer Arbeit geschaffen worden waren. Jack zweifelte nicht am Wahrheitsgehalt seiner Worte, konnte sich aber nicht vorstellen, wie diese Arbeit im einzelnen vor sich gegangen war.

Am Spätnachmittag, als es für die Arbeit langsam zu dunkel wurde, strebten die fleißigen Menschen alle zum großen Saal des Wohnturms. Binsenlichter wurden entzündet und das Feuer neu entfacht. Selbst die Hunde flohen jetzt vor der Kälte und kamen herein. Männer und Frauen holten Bretter und Böcke, die auf einer Seite des Saals aufgestapelt waren, und errichteten damit einen großen, T-förmigen Tisch. Dann stellten sie Stühle an den Schmal- und Bänke an den Längsseiten auf. Jack hatte noch nie so viele Menschen zusammenarbeiten sehen und staunte darüber, mit welcher Begeisterung sie bei der Sache waren. Lachend hoben sie die schweren Bretter vom Stapel, riefen »Hau ruck!« und »Zu mir her!« und »Runter jetzt, vorsichtig!«. Jack beneidete sie um ihre Kameradschaft und fragte sich, ob er auch eines Tages daran würde teilhaben dürfen.

Nach einer Weile ließen sich alle Leute auf den Bänken nieder. Ein Diener verteilte große Holzschüsseln und Holzlöffel, wobei er mit lauter Stimme mitzählte. Dann ging er noch einmal von einem zum anderen und warf je eine dicke Scheibe altbackenes Brot in die Schüsseln. Ein anderer Diener verteilte hölzerne Becher und schenkte aus großen Krügen Bier ein. Jack, Martha und Alfred, die gemeinsam am Grund eines großen ›T‹ saßen, bekamen alle eigene Becher, so daß es keinen Anlaß zum Streit gab. Jack griff zu und wollte trinken, doch seine Mutter bat ihn, noch einen Augenblick zu warten.

Nachdem alle Anwesenden mit Bier versorgt waren, wurde es auf einmal still. Graf Bartholomäus schritt die Treppen, die zu seinem Schlafgemach führten, herab. Ihm folgten Haushofmeister Matthew, drei oder vier andere gutgekleidete Herren, ein Junge – und das schönste menschliche Wesen, das Jack in seinem Leben je gesehen hatte.

Es war ein Mädchen oder eine Frau, er wußte es nicht genau zu sagen. Sie war ganz in Weiß gekleidet, und ihre Tunika hatte erstaunlich weite Ärmel, welche, als sie die Treppe hinabschwebte, hinter ihr über den Boden schleiften. Ihre dunklen Haare umspielten in üppig wallender Lockenpracht das Gesicht. Jack wußte sofort, wer diese Feengestalt war: Es war die schöne Prinzessin aus den *Chansons*. Kein Wunder, daß alle Ritter weinten, wenn sie starb!

Als die Prinzessin den Saal betrat, erkannte Jack, daß sie noch recht jung war, bloß ein paar Jahre älter als er, doch sie hielt den Kopf hoch erhoben und schritt wie eine Königin zur Schmalseite des Tisches. Dort nahm sie an der Seite des Grafen Platz.

»Wer ist das?« flüsterte Jack.

»Das muß die Tochter des Grafen sein«, antwortete Martha.

»Wie heißt sie?«

Martha zuckte mit den Schultern, doch ein kleines Mädchen mit ungewaschenem Gesicht, das neben Jack saß, hatte die Frage gehört und sagte: »Sie heißt Aliena. Sie ist wunderschön.«

Der Graf hob seinen Becher aufs Wohl seiner Tochter. Dann sah er langsam von einem zum anderen und trank. Auf dieses Zeichen hatten alle gewartet. Sie hoben die Becher und tranken.

Das Abendessen wurde in gewaltigen, dampfenden Kesseln hereingetragen. Zuerst wurde dem Grafen serviert, dann seiner Tochter, dem Knaben und den Männern, die bei ihnen am Kopf des Tisches saßen. Alle anderen bedienten sich selber. Es gab einen würzigen Eintopf mit gesalzenem Fisch. Jack füllte seine Schüssel und aß mit großem Appetit. Schnell war er bei der Brotscheibe angelangt, die inzwischen mit öliger Suppe getränkt war. Beim Kauen starrte er Aliena an. Alles, was sie tat, faszinierte ihn – von der gezierten Art, wie sie kleine Fischbrocken aufs Messer spießte und zwischen den blendend weißen Zähnen hindurch in den Mund schob, bis hin zu ihrer befehlsgewohnten Stimme, mit der sie die Diener herumkommandierte. Alle schienen sie sie zu mögen: Sie kamen sofort, wenn Aliena sie rief, lächelten, wenn sie zu ihnen sprach, und führten ihre Aufträge mit größter Eile und Gewissenhaftigkeit aus. Die jungen Männer, die am Tisch saßen, bewunderten Aliena ebenfalls, und Jack merkte, wie sie sich aufspielten, wenn sie glaubten, die Tochter des Grafen blicke in ihre Richtung. Sie schenkte ihnen allerdings kaum Beachtung, sondern widmete ihre Aufmerksamkeit vorrangig den älteren Herren aus der Begleitung ihres Vaters. Sie achtete darauf, daß sie immer genug Brot und Wein hatten, stellte ihnen Fragen und lauschte aufmerksam ihren Antworten. Wie das wohl wäre, dachte Jack, wenn sich eine so schöne Prinzessin einmal mit mir unterhalten und mich dabei mit ihren großen, dunklen Augen anschauen würde ...

Nach dem Abendessen kam die Musik. Zwei Männer und eine Frau spielten mit Schafglocken, einer Trommel und Flöten, die aus Tierknochen gefertigt waren, verschiedene Melodien. Der Graf hielt die Augen geschlossen und schien sich ganz in der Musik zu verlieren. Jack hingegen mochte die sehnsuchtsvollen, melancholischen Klänge nicht; ihm waren die frohen Lieder, die er von seiner Mutter kannte, lieber. Den anderen Menschen im Saal erging es anscheinend ähnlich. Sie rückten unruhig auf den Bänken hin und her, und als die Musik endlich vorbei war, herrschte allgemeine Erleichterung.

Jack hatte gehofft, Aliena noch aus der Nähe anschauen zu können, wurde jedoch enttäuscht. Die Tochter des Grafen verließ den Saal, gleich nachdem die Musik verklungen war, und stieg wieder die Treppe hinauf. Wahrscheinlich hat sie dort oben ihr eigenes Schlafzimmer, dachte Jack.

Die Kinder und ein paar Erwachsene verbrachten den Abend beim Schach- und Damespiel, während geschäftigere Naturen die freie Zeit vor dem Schlafengehen zur Herstellung von Gürteln, Mützen, Socken, Handschuhen, Schüsseln, Pfeifen, Würfeln, Schaufeln und Pferdepeitschen nutzten. Jack spielte einige Partien Schach, die er samt und sonders gewann, verlor dann aber gegen ein fremdes Kind beim Damespiel und geriet darüber so in Wut, daß ihm seine Mutter das Weiterspielen verbot. Da trieb er sich dann ziellos im Saal herum und horchte, was die Leute einander zu sagen hatten. Einige führten vernünftige Gespräche über Ackerbau und Tiere, Bischöfe und Könige, andere neckten einander, prahlten oder erzählten lustige Geschichten. Jack fand das eine wie das andere ungemein spannend.

Die Binsenlichter brannten schließlich herunter, der Graf zog sich zurück, und wenig später wickelten sich auch die letzten der sechzig oder siebzig Personen im Saal in ihre Mäntel und Umhänge und legten sich auf dem strohbedeckten Boden zur Ruhe.

Tom und Jacks Mutter legten sich, wie immer, gemeinsam nieder, und Ellen umarmte Tom so, wie sie früher einmal den kleinen Jack umarmt hatte. Neidisch sah der Junge ihnen zu. Er hörte, wie sie miteinander sprachen und wie seine Mutter auf einmal verhalten kicherte. Nach einer Weile fingen ihre Körper unter den Kleidern an, sich rhythmisch auf und ab zu bewegen. Als er sie zum erstenmal dabei beobachtet hatte, war Jack furchtbar besorgt gewesen, denn was immer es war, es sah so aus, als müsse es ihnen sehr weh tun. Aber dann war ihm aufgefallen, daß sie sich dabei küßten, und Mutter stöhnte zwar gelegentlich, aber gewiß nicht vor Schmerz, dessen war er sich ganz sicher. Er wußte nicht warum, aber er scheute sich, sie darüber auszufragen. Jetzt sah er auf einmal im matten Licht des heruntergebrannten Feuers ein anderes Paar, das sich genauso verhielt, und schloß daraus, daß es sich um eine ganz normale Sache handeln mußte. *Noch* so ein Rätsel, dachte er und war kurz darauf fest eingeschlafen.

Die Kinder erwachten schon früh am Morgen, doch durfte das Frühstück erst aufgetragen werden, wenn die Messe gelesen war, und die Messe konnte erst gelesen werden, wenn der Graf aufgestanden war. So blieb ihnen nichts anderes übrig als zu warten. Ein Diener, der ebenfalls schon in aller Frühe auf den Beinen war, trug ihnen auf, das Feuerholz für den beginnenden Tag heraufzuholen. Die Erwachsenen regten sich, als kalte Morgenluft durch die offenstehende Tür drang. Kaum hatten die Kinder genug Holz herbeigeschafft, da begegnete ihnen Aliena.

Sie kam die Treppe herab wie am Abend zuvor, sah aber ganz anders aus. Sie trug eine kurze Tunika und Filzstiefel. Die wilden Locken waren zurückgebunden und ließen den weißen Hals, die kleinen Ohren und die elegant geschwungenen Wangen frei. Die großen dunklen Augen, die am vergangenen Abend noch so ernst und erwachsen gewirkt hatten, funkelten lustig. Hinter Aliena kam der Junge die Treppe herunter, der beim Abendessen neben ihr gesessen hatte. Er war vielleicht ein oder zwei Jahre älter als Jack, aber längst nicht so groß wie Alfred. Neugierig sah er die drei ihm unbekannten Kinder an, doch war es Aliena, die als erste das Wort ergriff. »Wer seid ihr?« fragte sie.

»Mein Vater ist Steinmetz und wird die Burg ausbessern«, gab Alfred ihr zur Antwort. »Ich bin Alfred. Meine Schwester heißt Martha. Der da heißt Jack.«

Jack merkte, daß Aliena nach Lavendel duftete, und verging fast vor Ehrfurcht. Wie war es möglich, daß jemand nach Blumen roch?

»Wie alt bist du?« fragte Aliena Alfred.

»Vierzehn.« Auch Alfred war von großer Scheu ergriffen, Jack konnte es ihm ansehen. Es kostete Toms Sohn einige Überwindung, bevor er zurückfragte: »Und wie alt bist du?«

»Fünfzehn. Habt ihr Hunger?«

»Ja.«

»Dann kommt mal mit.«

Aliena voran, verließen sie den Saal und stiegen die Außentreppe hinunter. Alfred sagte: »Aber es gibt doch erst Frühstück, wenn die Messe gelesen ist.«

»Wann es hier was gibt, bestimme ich«, erwiderte Aliena mit einer herrischen Kopfbewegung.

Sie führte die Kinder über die Zugbrücke in den unteren Ring und ließ sie vor der Küche warten. »Ist sie nicht hübsch?« flüsterte Martha Jack zu, und der nickte verträumt. Kurz darauf kehrte Aliena mit einem Weißbrot und einem Krug Bier zu ihnen zurück. Sie brach einige große Brocken ab und verteilte sie, dann ließ sie den Bierkrug kreisen.

Nach einer Weile fragte Martha schüchtern: »Wo ist denn deine Mutter?«

»Meine Mutter ist tot«, erwiderte Aliena kurz angebunden.

»Bist du nicht traurig darüber?«

»Ich war traurig. Aber es ist schon lange her.« Sie verwies auf den Jungen neben ihr. »Richard kann sich gar nicht mehr an ihren Tod erinnern.«

Richard muß ihr Bruder sein, dachte Jack.

»Meine Mutter ist auch tot«, sagte Martha, und Tränen stiegen ihr in die Augen.

»Seit wann?« fragte Aliena.

»Sie starb vorige Woche.«

Marthas Tränen scheinen sie kaum zu rühren, dachte Jack, es sei denn, sie gibt sich so streng, um ihren eigenen Kummer zu verbergen.

»Was ist das dann für eine Frau bei euch?« fragte Aliena brüsk.

»Das ist meine Mutter«, sagte Jack, ganz begeistert darüber, daß es etwas gab, was er ihr sagen konnte.

»So? Und wo ist *dein* Vater?«

»Ich habe keinen Vater.« Wie aufregend es war, daß die Prinzessin mit ihm sprach!

»Ist er auch tot?«

»Nein«, sagte Jack. »Ich habe niemals einen Vater gehabt.«

Einen Augenblick herrschte Schweigen. Dann prusteten Aliena, Richard und Alfred plötzlich vor Lachen. Jack wußte nicht, wie ihm geschah, und starrte sie mit offenen Augen an. Aber ihr Gelächter wurde immer lauter, so daß er sich schließlich gedemütigt fühlte. Was ist daran so komisch, daß ich nie einen Vater gehabt habe? fragte er sich. Selbst Martha hatte ihre Tränen vergessen und lächelte auf einmal.

»Und woher kommst du dann, wenn du nie einen Vater hattest?« fragte Alfred höhnisch.

»Aus meiner Mutter. Alles was jung ist, kommt aus den Müttern.« Jack war völlig verstört. »Was haben denn Väter damit zu tun?«

Jetzt brüllten die anderen schier vor Lachen. Richard hüpfte vor lauter Vergnügen auf und ab und zeigte mit dem Finger auf Jack. Alfred sagte zu Aliena: »Der hat keine Ahnung. Wir haben ihn im Wald aufgelesen.«

Jacks Wangen brannten vor Scham. Es war so schön gewesen, mit Aliena sprechen zu können – und nun hielt sie ihn für den größten Narren, einen Dummerjan aus dem Wald. Das Schlimmste aber war, daß er einfach nicht verstand, was für einen Fehler er gemacht hatte. Er hätte losheulen können, wollte es auch, aber ein Stück Brot steckte ihm im Hals, und er bekam es nicht herunter. Er sah Alienas belustigte Miene und konnte es nicht mehr ertragen. Wütend warf er sein Brot auf den Boden, drehte sich um und lief davon.

Irgendwohin – nur fort! Er erreichte den Wall, der die Burganlage umgab, und kletterte mühsam die steile Böschung hinauf. Oben angelangt, setzte er sich auf die kalte Erde, ließ seinen Blick über die Umgebung schweifen und bemitleidete sich selbst. Er war furchtbar wütend auf Alfred und Richard, sogar Martha und Aliena waren ihm auf einmal verhaßt. Prinzessinnen sind herzlos, dachte er.

Die Glocke läutete zur Frühmesse. Gottesdienste waren auch so eine rätselhafte, merkwürdige Angelegenheit. Die Priester sprachen und sangen in einer Sprache, die weder Englisch noch Französisch war, und schienen sich dabei an Statuen und Bilder zu wenden oder gar an gänzlich unsichtbare Wesen. Seine Mutter vermied Gottesdienste, wann immer es ihr möglich war. Als Jack sah, wie unter ihm die Bewohner der Burg zur Kapelle strömten, huschte er über die Wallkrone und hockte sich auf die Außenböschung, wo man ihn nicht mehr sehen konnte.

Die Burg war von ebenen, kahlen Feldern umgeben, die am Horizont von Wäldern begrenzt wurden. Zwei frühe Besucher kamen über das flache Vorfeld auf die Burg zu. Der Himmel war mit tiefhängenden grauen Wolken bedeckt. Vielleicht gibt es bald Schnee, dachte Jack.

Zwei weitere Neuankömmlinge, Reiter diesmal, rückten in sein Blickfeld. Sie waren so schnell, daß sie die ersten beiden noch vor dem Eingang überholten. Sie saßen ab und überquerten die Holzbrücke vor dem Torhaus zu Fuß. Da außer den Wachposten alle Burgbewohner bei der Frühmesse waren, mußten sich die Besucher gedulden, bis sie ihre Anliegen vorbringen konnten.

Jack sprang erschrocken auf, als hinter ihm plötzlich eine Stimme ertönte. »Hier hast du dich also versteckt!« Es war seine Mutter. Er drehte sich nach ihr um. Ellen erkannte sofort, daß ihren Sohn etwas bedrückte. »Was hast du denn?« fragte sie.

Er hätte sich am liebsten von ihr trösten lassen, überwand sich jedoch und fragte statt dessen: »Habe ich einen Vater?«

»Ja«, antwortete Ellen. »Jeder Mensch hat einen Vater.« Sie kniete neben ihm nieder.

Er wandte sich von ihr ab. Es ist ihre Schuld, daß sie mich so gedemütigt haben, dachte er. Warum hat sie mir nie etwas von meinem Vater erzählt? »Was ist mit ihm geschehen?«

»Er ist gestorben.«

»Wann? Als ich klein war?«

»Du warst noch nicht geboren.«

»Wie kann er dann mein Vater sein?«

»Kinder entstehen aus einem Samen. Der Same kommt aus dem Glied des Mannes und wird in die Spalte der Frau gepflanzt. Dann wächst er im Bauch der Frau zum Kind heran. Wenn das Kind fertig ist, kommt es heraus.«

Jack brauchte eine Weile, um die Neuigkeit zu begreifen. Hatte das vielleicht mit den nächtlichen Bewegungen unter den Mänteln zu tun? Nach einer Pause fragte er sie: »Pflanzt Tom auch einen Samen in dich?«

»Kann sein.«

»Dann wirst du wieder ein Kind bekommen.«

Sie nickte. »Ein Brüderchen für dich – was hältst du davon?«

»Mir egal«, sagte Jack. »Tom hat dich mir sowieso schon weggenommen. Bruder hin, Bruder her, darauf kommt es auch nicht mehr an.«

Sie nahm ihn in die Arme und drückte ihn an sich. »Niemand wird mich dir wegnehmen, niemals!«

Jetzt ging es ihm wieder ein bißchen besser.

Ellen setzte sich neben ihren Sohn. Nach einer Weile sagte sie: »Es ist kalt hier draußen. Laß uns zurückgehen. Wir können uns vor dem Frühstück noch ein wenig am Feuer wärmen.«

Jack nickte. Sie standen auf und rannten die Wallböschung hinunter. Von den vier Besuchern war nirgendwo etwas zu sehen. Vielleicht waren sie in die Kapelle gegangen.

Auf der Brücke zum oberen Ring fragte Jack seine Mutter: »Wie hat mein Vater denn geheißen?«

»Jack, wie du«, antwortete sie. »Die Leute nannten ihn Jack Shareburg.«

Das gefiel ihm. Er hatte den gleichen Namen wie sein Vater. »So kann ich mich Jack Jackson nennen, wenn ich einmal einem anderen Jack begegne, oder?«

»Ja, das kannst du. Die Leute nennen einen allerdings nicht immer so, wie man es sich wünscht. Aber versuchen kannst du es auf jeden Fall.«

Jack nickte. Es tat ihm gut. Von nun an konnte er sich selbst als Jack Jackson fühlen und brauchte sich nicht mehr so zu schämen. Wenigstens weiß ich jetzt, was es mit den Vätern auf sich hat, dachte er. Und ich weiß, wem ich meinen Namen verdanke – Jack Shareburg ...

Sie erreichten das Torhaus der inneren Burg. Nirgendwo war ein Wachposten zu sehen. Ellen blieb stehen. »Ich habe das dumpfe Gefühl, daß hier etwas nicht stimmt«, sagte sie und kniff die Brauen zusammen. Ihre Worte klangen ruhig und besonnen, aber Jack spürte die Angst in ihrer Stimme und fürchtete Schlimmes.

Seine Mutter betrat die Wache im Erdgeschoß des Torhauses. Gleich darauf hörte Jack, wie sie vor Schreck den Atem anhielt und sah, wie ihre rechte Hand zum Mund fuhr. Er folgte ihr in den kleinen Raum. Sie starrte auf den Boden.

Der Wachposten lag flach auf dem Rücken, die ausgestreckten Arme waren schlaff. Seine Kehle war durchgeschnitten, und auf dem Erdboden neben seinem Hals hatte sich eine frische Blutlache gebildet.

Der Mann war zweifellos tot.

Gegen Mitternacht waren William Hamleigh und sein Vater in Begleitung von fast hundert Rittern und berittenen Bewaffneten (sowie Mutter Hamleigh in der Nachhut) aufgebrochen. Mit Donnergetöse rumpelte die Streitmacht, die ihre Gesichter der Kälte wegen verhüllt hatte und ihren Weg mit Fackeln beleuchtete, durch die Dörfer, zum namenlosen Entsetzen der Bewohner. Es war noch pechschwarze Nacht, als sie die Kreuzung erreichten. Sie saßen ab und führten fortan ihre Pferde am Zügel, zum einen, damit die Tiere sich erholen konnten, zum anderen, weil sie auf diese Weise wesentlich leiser vorankamen. Als der Tag heraufdämmerte, verbargen sie sich in den Wäldern vor der offenen Feldflur, in deren Mitte die Burg des Grafen Bartholomäus lag.

William hatte bei seinem Besuch versäumt, die genaue Zahl der auf der Burg versammelten kampffähigen Männer festzustellen. Trotz seiner Beteuerung, daß viele von ihnen Kuriere waren, die noch am gleichen Tag ausgeschickt wurden, und daß eine verläßliche Zählung daher ohnehin nicht möglich gewesen wäre, hatte ihm diese Unterlassung eine gnadenlose Abfuhr seitens seiner Mutter eingetragen. Immerhin hatte er sich auf eine Schätzung eingelassen; etwa vierzig Mann. Wenn sich diese Zahl in den wenigen seither verflossenen Stunden nicht allzusehr verändert hatte, konnten die Hamleighs mit einer Überlegenheit von mehr als zwei zu eins rechnen.

Für eine Belagerung der Burg reichte ihre Streitmacht natürlich bei weitem nicht aus. Sie hatten sich deshalb einen Plan ausgedacht, der eine erheblich schnellere Eroberung der Burg vorsah. Das Hauptproblem bestand darin, daß jede heranrückende Truppe von den Wachposten auf den Türmen frühzeitig erspäht werden konnte, was zwangsläufig die sofortige Schließung der Burg zur Folge haben würde. Genau dies galt es also zu verhindern: Wenn die Streitmacht ihre Schlupfwinkel in den Wäldern verließ und über das freie Vorfeld zum Sturm auf die Burg antrat, durfte niemand mehr die Zugbrücken hochziehen und die Tore schließen.

Es war natürlich Mutter Hamleigh gewesen, die des Rätsels Lösung gefunden hatte.

»Wir brauchen eine Ablenkung«, hatte sie gesagt und sich dabei einen dicken Pickel an ihrem Kinn aufgekratzt. »Sie müssen regelrecht in Panik verfallen, so daß sie die Truppe erst bemerken, wenn es bereits zu spät ist. Wie wär's mit einem Feuer?«

»Wenn da plötzlich ein Fremder kommt und Feuer legt, sind sie doch alle gewarnt«, hielt Vater Hamleigh dagegen.

»Er darf sich halt nicht erwischen lassen«, meinte William.

»Das versteht sich von selbst«, fuhr Mutter ungeduldig dazwischen und sagte, an ihren Sohn gewandt: »Du mußt es während der Frühmesse tun.«

»Ich?« hatte William gefragt.

Er war justament zum Befehlshaber der Vorhut ernannt worden.

Langsam, sehr langsam kroch die Morgendämmerung über den Horizont. William fieberte vor Unruhe. Sie hatten ihren Plan im Laufe der Nacht noch ein wenig ausgefeilt. Dennoch gab es noch eine Menge Unwägbarkeiten: Vielleicht kommen wir aus unvorhersehbaren Gründen gar nicht in die Burg hinein, dachte er. Oder man schöpft Verdacht und beobachtet uns, so daß wir den Anschlag nicht ausführen können. Oder man setzt uns sogar gefangen ... Und selbst, wenn alles nach Plan verläuft, wird es zum Kampf kommen – zu meiner ersten richtigen Schlacht! Es wird Verwundete und Tote geben, und wenn ich Pech habe, erwischt es mich auch ...

Die Angst zog ihm die Eingeweide zusammen. Aliena ist dort, und wenn wir in die Flucht geschlagen werden, wird sie es miterleben. Umgekehrt wird sie auch unseren Triumph mit ansehen müssen ... Er sah sich schon mit blutverschmiertem Schwert in ihr Schlafgemach stürmen. Da wird auch sie bereuen, daß sie mich ausgelacht hat ...

In der Burg bimmelte die Glocke zur Frühmesse. William nickte, und zwei Männer aus der Truppe verließen die Deckung und schritten über das freie Feld auf die Burg zu. Es waren Raymond und Rannulf, zwei starke Kerle mit harten Zügen und harten Muskeln, beide um einige Jahre älter als William. Sie waren von ihm persönlich für diese Aufgabe ausgewählt worden, denn sein Vater, der die Attacke der Hauptstreitmacht führen würde, hatte ihm freie Hand gelassen.

William sah Raymond und Rannulf nach, die in schnellem Schritt das gefrorene Feld überquerten. Bevor sie die Burg erreichten, wechselte er einen Blick mit Walter und trat seinem Pferd in die Flanken. Im Trab setzten sie den anderen nach. Die Wachposten auf den Türmen sahen nun im ersten Morgenlicht zwei getrennte Paare auf die Burg zukommen, das eine zu Fuß, das andere zu Pferde. Nichts konnte harmloser erscheinen ...

Williams Schätzung stimmte: Er und Walter überholten Raymond und Rannulf ungefähr hundert Schritt vor dem Eingang zur Burg. An der Brücke saßen sie ab. Das Herz schlug ihm bis zum Hals. Wenn er jetzt versagte, war der gesamte Angriffsplan zum Scheitern verurteilt.

Das Tor war mit zwei Wachposten besetzt. William war besessen von der alptraumhaften Vorstellung, sie könnten in einen Hinterhalt geraten sein ... Schon sah er ein Dutzend Bewaffnete aus ihren Verstecken stürmen und spürte, wie sie ihn in Stücke hackten ... Die Posten waren wachsam, ahnten jedoch nichts Böses. Sie trugen keine Rüstung. William und Walter hatten Kettenhemden unter ihre Umhänge gezogen.

Williams Eingeweide schienen sich in Wasser aufgelöst zu haben. Er konnte nicht mehr schlucken. Einer der Wachposten erkannte ihn und grüßte ihn kumpelhaft: »Hallo, Lord William! Wieder auf Freiersfüßen, he?«

»Oh, mein Gott!« sagte William mit schwacher Stimme und hieb dem Posten seinen Dolch in den Leib. Die Klinge drang unterhalb des Brustkorbs in den Körper ein und fuhr aufwärts bis in die Herzgegend.

Der Mann rang nach Luft, sackte zusammen und öffnete den Mund wie zum Schrei. Ein falsches Geräusch konnte alles verderben. William wußte nicht, was er tun sollte. In seiner Panik riß er den Dolch aus der Wunde und rammte ihn dem Mann tief in den geöffneten Rachen. Ein Blutstrom schoß hervor, aber der gefürchtete Schrei blieb aus. Die Augen des Mannes schlossen sich. William zog den Dolch wieder hervor, und der Posten stürzte zu Boden.

Williams Pferd war, durch die plötzlichen Bewegungen erschreckt, ein paar Schritte zur Seite gewichen. William ergriff es am Zaumzeug und sah sich nach Walter um. Der hatte ›seinem‹ Mann fachkundig die Gurgel durchgeschnitten; der Posten war gestorben, ohne auch nur einen Mucks von sich zu geben. So muß ich's auch machen, dachte William, das nächste Mal, wenn ich jemanden zum Schweigen bringen will ... Dann überkam ihn ein Triumphgefühl: Ich habe es geschafft! Endlich habe ich eigenhändig einen Menschen getötet!

Auf einmal war alle Angst verflogen.

Er überließ Walter die Zügel seines Pferdes und rannte die Wendeltreppe zum Turm des Torhauses hinauf. Ganz oben befand sich die Winde, mit deren Hilfe die Zugbrücke hochgezogen werden konnte. Zwei Schwerthiebe genügten, um die Trosse zu kappen. Er warf das lose Ende zum Fenster hinaus; es fiel auf die Wallböschung und glitt nahezu lautlos in den Burggraben. Die Zugbrücke konnte Vaters Streitmacht jetzt nicht mehr den Weg versperren.

Als Raymond und Rannulf gerade das Torhaus erreichten, kam William wieder die Treppe herunter. Ihre erste Aufgabe bestand darin, die riesigen, eisenbeschlagenen Eichenholztore, welche den Torbogen zwischen Brücke und vorderem Burghof verschlossen, zu demolieren. Sie zogen jeder einen Holzhammer und einen Meißel hervor und begannen, den Mörtel zu entfernen, der die gewaltigen eisernen Türangeln hielt.

Die dumpfen Hammerschläge klangen in Williams Ohren furchtbar laut. Er schleifte rasch die beiden Toten in den Wachraum. Da die Burgbewohner noch immer bei der Frühmesse waren, bestand durchaus die Chance, daß die Leichen erst gefunden wurden, wenn alles bereits zu spät war.

Er nahm die Zügel wieder an sich. Gemeinsam durchschritt er mit Walter den Torbogen und erreichte den Burghof. Gemessenen Schritts gingen sie auf den Stall zu. Es kostete William eine Menge Überwindung, sich den Anschein eines ganz normalen, ruhigen Besuchers zu geben. Verstohlen schielte er hinauf zu den Posten in den Wachtürmen. Hatte einer von ihnen vielleicht die Zugbrückentrosse in den Graben rutschen sehen? Kamen ihnen die Hammerschläge nicht merkwürdig vor? Einige Posten beobachteten William und Walter in der Tat, schienen sich aber nicht sonderlich über sie aufzuregen. Die Hammerschläge waren selbst für William kaum noch vernehmbar; dort oben in luftiger Höhe konnte man sie vermutlich gar nicht hören. William war erleichtert. Der Plan schien aufzugehen.

Sie hatten den Stall erreicht, traten ein und hängten die Zügel ihrer Pferde locker über eine Stange, so daß sich die Tiere selbst befreien konnten. Dann zog William seinen Feuerstein aus der Tasche und schlug Funken, die das Stroh in Brand setzten. Da es mit Erde vermischt und ziemlich feucht war, begann es mancherorts nur zu glimmen; sie legten daher noch an verschiedenen Stellen Feuer. Die Pferde witterten den Rauch und wurden unruhig. William und Walter warteten noch, bis sie sicher waren, daß das Feuer sich von alleine weiterentwickeln würde. Bisher verlief alles genau nach Plan.

Sie traten wieder ins Freie. Raymond und Rannulf waren im Schutze des Torbogens noch immer damit beschäftigt, die Türangeln freizuhämmern. William und Walter gingen jetzt auf die Küche zu; es sollte so aussehen, als hätten sie Hunger und wollten sich etwas zu essen holen. Von ihnen abgesehen, war der Burghof menschenleer: Alle Einwohner waren bei der Messe. Ein beiläufiger Blick hinauf zu den Turmzinnen verriet William, daß die Wachen sich nicht mehr um ihn und seinen Begleiter kümmerten, sondern wieder, wie es ihre Aufgabe war, das Vorfeld der Burg beobachteten. William hielt die Ruhe trotz allem für trügerisch und rechnete jederzeit mit einer Attacke. Wenn sich uns hier mitten im Hof einer entgegenstellt, dachte er, dann müssen wir ihn gleichsam vor aller Augen töten. In dem Fall wäre das Spiel so gut wie verloren ...

Sie umrundeten die Küche und gingen auf die zweite Brücke zu. Als sie an der Kapelle vorbeikamen, konnten sie die gedämpften Klänge des Gottesdienstes hören. Dort drinnen sitzt jetzt Graf Bartholomäus, dachte William erregt, und er hat nicht die geringste Ahnung, daß drei Meilen von hier eine feindliche Streitmacht lauert. Er weiß nicht, daß sich vier Angreifer bereits in seine Burg eingeschlichen und den Stall in Brand gesetzt haben ... Auch Aliena ist in der Kapelle. Sie kniet vor dem Altar und betet. Bald wird sie vor *mir* knien ... Das Blut pochte in seinen Schläfen, daß ihn schwindelte.

Sie betraten die zweite Brücke. Der Weg über die erste war der Streitmacht der Hamleighs nach dem Kappen der Trosse kaum noch zu verwehren, doch konnte der Graf sich immer noch in den zweiten Ring der Burganlage flüchten. Gelang es jedoch – und diesen Plan verfolgte William –, die zweite Brücke hochzuziehen, so wäre Bartholomäus der Fluchtweg versperrt. Er wäre dann mehr oder weniger schutzlos den Eroberern ausgeliefert.

Ein Posten verließ die Wachstube im Torhaus und trat ihnen entgegen. »Ihr seid früh dran«, sagte er.

»Der Graf hat uns so früh bestellt«, sagte William und ging auf den Posten zu, doch der Wachhabende wich sofort einen Schritt zurück. Sehr viel weiter zurück darf er nicht, dachte William, sonst erreicht er das Ende des Torbogens und kann von oben gesehen werden.

»Der Graf befindet sich zur Zeit in der Kapelle«, sagte der Wachposten.

»Dann müssen wir auf ihn warten.« Der Mann mußte schnell und geräuschlos beseitigt werden – nur wußte William nicht, wie er nahe genug an ihn herankommen sollte. Er warf Walter einen fragenden Seitenblick zu, doch sein Gefährte stand mit unerschütterlicher Miene neben ihm und schien nicht die geringste Eile zu haben.

»Im Wohnturm brennt ein Feuer«, sagte der Mann. »Da könnt Ihr Euch aufwärmen.«

William zögerte. Der Wachposten wurde mißtrauisch und fragte leicht gereizt: »Worauf wartet Ihr noch?«

William suchte verzweifelt nach einer Antwort. Endlich fiel ihm eine Gegenfrage ein: »Können wir hier irgendwo etwas zu essen bekommen?«

»Ja, aber erst nach dem Gottesdienst. Das Frühstück wird im großen Saal aufgetragen.«

William bemerkte erst jetzt, daß Walter kaum merklich zur Seite gerückt war. Nur noch ein kleines Stückchen ... William machte ein paar Schritte in die entgegengesetzte Richtung, ging an dem Posten vorbei und sagte: »Die Gastfreundschaft eures Grafen ist nicht gerade sehr beeindruckend ...« Der Mann drehte sich nach ihm um. »Wir haben einen weiten Weg hinter uns ...«, fuhr William fort.

Da schlug Walter zu.

Blitzartig sprang er den Wachposten von hinten an und umklammerte mit beiden Armen dessen Schultern. Dann riß er mit der Linken das Kinn des Mannes hoch und schnitt ihm mit dem Messer in seiner Rechten die Kehle durch. Ehe William sich versah, war alles vorbei.

William seufzte erleichtert auf. Gemeinsam haben wir vor dem Frühstück drei Männer getötet, dachte er und genoß das in ihm aufwallende Gefühl grenzenloser Macht. Nach dem heutigen Tag lacht mich niemand mehr aus!

Walter schleifte die Leiche in die Wachstube. Das Torhaus hatte denselben Grundplan wie das vorherige. Eine Wendeltreppe führte hinauf zu dem kleinen Raum, in dem sich die Brückenwinde befinden mußte.

Gefolgt von Walter, stürmte William die Stufen empor. Er kannte den Mechanismus der Zugbrücke nicht und hatte bei seinem Besuch am Tag zuvor auch nicht daran gedacht, ihn auszukundschaften. Es wäre ohnehin schwer genug gewesen, einen plausiblen Grund für die Inspektion des Turms zu finden. William rechnete mit einer Radwinde. Als die beiden oben ankamen, fanden sie aber lediglich eine Seiltrommel ohne Winde vor. Die Brücke ließ sich also nur mit Muskelkraft hochziehen. William und Walter warfen sich ins Seil, doch die Brücke quietschte nicht einmal. Diese Aufgabe hätte zehn starke Männer erfordert.

William brauchte eine Weile, bis er begriff, warum nur die erste Zugbrücke mit einer Radwinde versehen war: Sie wurde Abend für Abend hochgezogen, die zweite dagegen nur in Notfällen. Aber was half es, sich darüber den Kopf zu zerbrechen? Sie mußten sich eben etwas anderes einfallen lassen. Ließ sich die Brücke nicht hochziehen, so konnten sie doch auf keinen Fall das Tor verschließen und auf diese Weise die Flucht des Grafen verzögern. William rannte die Wendeltreppe wieder hinunter, und Walter blieb ihm auf den Fersen. Unten angekommen, traf es ihn wie ein Schlag. Nicht alle Burgbewohner waren bei der Frühmesse: Vor seinen Augen verließen gerade eine Frau und ein Kind die Wachstube. William erkannte sie sofort. Es war das Weib des Baumeisters, das er tags zuvor für ein Pfund Silber hatte kaufen wollen. Sie starrte ihn aus durchdringenden, honigfarbenen Augen an. Er wußte, daß er vor ihr nicht den harmlosen Besucher zu spielen brauchte; nie und nimmer würde sie ihm das abnehmen. Entscheidend war, daß sie keinen Alarm schlug – und dafür gab es nur eine Garantie: Sie mußte ebenso schnell und geräuschlos getötet werden wie die Torwächter.

Aber diesen Augen entging nichts. Sie erkannte an seiner Miene, was er vorhatte, packte das Kind bei der Hand, drehte sich um und rannte auf den Wohnturm zu.

Die beiden Angreifer nahmen sofort die Verfolgung auf, wurden jedoch durch ihre Kettenhemden und ihre schweren Waffen behindert. Hinzu kam, daß sich die Frau und das Kind als ungewöhnlich flink erwiesen. Schon hatten sie die Außentreppe des Wohnturms erreicht. Die Frau stürmte hinauf und begann zu schreien. Keuchend blieben William und Walter am Fuß der Treppe stehen und sahen sich um. Das Spiel war aus. Die Wächter auf den Türmen waren durch die Schreie alarmiert worden. Erst zwei, dann drei, dann vier von ihnen verließen ihre Posten und stürmten herunter in den Hof. Die Frau verschwand, das Kind noch immer an der Hand, im Innern des Wohnturms. Auf sie kam es jetzt nicht mehr an. Nun, da die Wachposten alarmiert waren, ergab ihr Tod keinen Sinn mehr.

William und Walter zogen ihre Schwerter. Seite an Seite standen sie im Hof – bereit, um ihr Leben zu kämpfen.

Der Priester hielt gerade die Hostie über den Altar, als Tom merkte, daß mit den Pferden etwas nicht stimmte. Sie wieherten und stampften ungewöhnlich heftig mit den Hufen. Kurz darauf unterbrach jemand den leisen lateinischen Singsang des Priesters mit den Worten: »Es riecht nach Rauch!«

Jetzt nahmen auch Tom und die anderen Gottesdienstbesucher den Brandgeruch wahr. Tom, der die meisten anderen um Haupteslänge überragte, stellte sich auf die Zehenspitzen und sah zum Fenster der Kapelle hinaus. Der Stall brannte lichterloh.

»Feuer!« sagte er, doch als er noch etwas hinzufügen wollte, ging seine Stimme im Chor zahlloser aufgeregter Rufe unter.

Die Messe war mit einem Schlag vergessen. Alles strömte zum Ausgang. Tom hielt Martha zurück, weil er fürchtete, sie könnte sich in dem Gedränge verletzen, und befahl auch Alfred dazubleiben. Wo stecken nur Ellen und Jack? fragte er sich.

Einen Augenblick später war die Kapelle bis auf sie drei und einen verärgerten Priester leer.

Tom führte die Kinder hinaus. Einige Leute befreiten gerade die Pferde, um ihnen den Flammentod zu ersparen, andere waren zum Brunnen gelaufen und schöpften Löschwasser. Ellen war nirgendwo zu sehen. Von Panik ergriffen, jagten die freigelassenen Pferde über den Burghof, das Trommeln der Hufe auf dem Boden verursachte einen Höllenlärm. Tom runzelte die Stirn und hörte genau hin: Der Lärm war zu laut; es klang eher nach hundert Pferden als nach zwanzig oder dreißig. Eine furchtbare Vorahnung beschlich ihn. »Ihr zwei wartet hier«, sagte er zu den Kindern. »Alfred, du paßt auf Martha auf.« Er selbst rannte den steilen Wall hinauf und kam, nach Luft ringend, oben an.

Seine schlimmsten Befürchtungen wurden bestätigt, und kalte Todesangst ergriff sein Herz. Über die braunen Felder vor der Burg stürmte eine Streitmacht von vielleicht achtzig oder hundert hochgerüsteten Reitern heran. Der Anblick allein war furchterregend: Die Kettenhemden und die gezückten Schwerter schimmerten in der Morgensonne. Die Pferde liefen im gestreckten Galopp, aus ihren Nüstern wölkte heißer Atem. Die Reiter duckten sich, zu allem entschlossen, in ihren Sätteln. Man hörte keinerlei Anfeuerungsrufe oder Geschrei, allein das ohrenbetäubende Donnern der Hufe erfüllte die Luft.

Tom drehte sich um und blickte in den Burghof. Warum hörte nur er die anstürmende Armee? Weil die dicken Mauern der Burg den Hufschlag dämpften und im Burghof selbst die Hölle los war. Warum hatten die Wachhabenden nichts gesehen? Weil sie alle ihre Posten verlassen hatten, um bei den Löscharbeiten zu helfen. Hinter der Attacke steckte ein raffinierter Plan. Es war jetzt an Tom, Alarm zu schlagen.

Und wo war Ellen?

So sehr er sich auch bemühte, er konnte sie nirgends sehen. Große Teile des Burghofs waren jetzt von dickem weißem Rauch verhüllt. Graf Bartholomäus stand unweit des Brunnens und bemühte sich, eine Eimerkette zu organisieren. Tom rannte die Böschung hinunter, lief auf den Grafen zu und packte ihn rauh an der Schulter. »Das ist ein Angriff!« brüllte er ihm ins Ohr.

»Was?«

»Wir werden angegriffen!«

Der Graf war in Gedanken noch immer bei dem brennenden Stall. »Angegriffen? Von wem?«

»So hört mir doch zu!« schrie Tom. »Hundert Reiter stürmen auf die Burg zu!«

Jetzt endlich horchte der Graf auf. Das blasse Aristokratengesicht verriet auf einmal Furcht. »Habt Ihr sie gesehen?«

»Ja.«

»Wer ... ach, egal! Hundert Reiter, sagt Ihr?«

»Ja, doch!«

Der Graf wandte sich von Tom ab und befahl seine Kommandanten herbei. »Peter! Ralph! Das ist ein Überfall, das Feuer ist nur ein Ablenkungsmanöver. Wir werden angegriffen.« Die beiden Männer erwiesen sich als ebenso begriffsstutzig wie ihr Befehlshaber. Dann hörten sie genauer hin und bekamen es mit der Angst zu tun. Der Graf schrie: »Sagt den Männern, sie sollen ihre Schwerter ergreifen! Und beeilt euch, um Gottes willen!« Er wandte sich wieder an Tom. »Kommt mit mir, Baumeister. Ihr seid stark. Wir können die Tore schließen.« Schon rannte er los, und Tom folgte ihm. Bei geschlossenen Toren und hochgeklappter Zugbrücke war man durchaus imstande, hundert Gegnern Paroli zu bieten.

Als sie das Torhaus erreichten, war die gegnerische Streitmacht durch den Bogen bereits zu erkennen. Sie war jetzt keine ganze Meile mehr von der Burg entfernt. Weil sich die schnellen Pferde mittlerweile abgesetzt hatten, zog sich die vordem geschlossene Truppe inzwischen etwas in die Länge.

»Die Tore – seht!« brüllte der Graf.

Die beiden großen, eisenbeschlagenen Tore lagen flach auf dem Boden. Tom erkannte sofort, daß die Angeln aus der Mauer gemeißelt worden waren. Die Feinde hatten eine Vorhut eingeschleust, die ganze Arbeit geleistet hatte. Toms Magen verkrampfte sich vor Angst.

Er blickte zurück. Noch immer keine Spur von Ellen. Was war los mit ihr? Jetzt war alles möglich. Er mußte zu ihr und sie beschützen.

»Die Zugbrücke!« rief der Graf.

Der beste Schutz für Ellen bestand darin, daß man die Angreifer gar nicht erst in die Burg hereinließ. Der Graf rannte bereits die Wendeltreppe empor. Tom gab sich einen Ruck und folgte ihm. Wenn es gelang, die Zugbrücke hochzuziehen, konnte das Torhaus von wenigen Männern verteidigt werden. Doch als er den Raum mit der Winde erreichte, stockte ihm fast das Herz: Die Trosse war gekappt, die Brücke ließ sich nicht mehr hochziehen.

Graf Bartholomäus stieß einen bitteren Fluch aus. »Wer immer diesen Überfall geplant hat ... Der Bursche ist schlau wie Luzifer.«

Tom machte eine andere Überlegung zu schaffen: Wer immer die Tore demoliert, die Brückentrosse gekappt und den Stall in Brand gesetzt hatte, befand sich längst innerhalb der Burg. Angstvoll sah er sich um. Wo mochten sich die Eindringlinge verborgen halten?

Der Graf äugte durch eine Schießscharte. »O Gott, sie sind gleich hier!« stöhnte er und rannte die Treppe hinunter.

Tom folgte ihm auf dem Fuße. Im Torbogen waren mehrere Ritter versammelt, die sich hastig ihre Schwerter umschnallten und die Helme aufsetzten. Graf Bartholomäus erteilte Befehle. »Ralph und John, treibt ein paar Pferde auf die Brücke, auf daß sie dem Feind den Weg versperren. Richard, Peter und Robin – holt Verstärkung und haltet hier die Stellung! Ihr, Baumeister, sammelt das Gesinde und die Kinder und schickt sie über die Brücke in den oberen Burghof!«

Tom war's zufrieden: Endlich hatte er einen Vorwand, um nach Ellen zu suchen. Als erstes rannte er zur Kapelle. Alfred und Martha warteten noch immer dort, wo er sie zurückgelassen hatte. Sie hatten Angst. »Zum Wohnturm, schnell!« rief er ihnen zu. »Und heißt alle Frauen und Kinder, die ihr seht, euch folgen – auf Befehl des Grafen!«

Die Kinder stürmten davon. Auch er wollte ihnen so bald wie möglich folgen. Vorerst blieben ihm aber noch ein paar Augenblicke zur Durchführung des gräflichen Befehls. Er rannte zum Stall, wo die Leute noch immer eimerweise Wasser in die Flammen gossen. »Kümmert euch nicht mehr um das Feuer!« schrie er. »Die Burg wird angegriffen! Bringt eure Kinder in den Wohnturm!«

Überall war Rauch. Die Augen tränten ihm, und er konnte nicht mehr richtig sehen. Nahebei standen ein paar Leute und schauten tatenlos zu, wie die Flammen den Stall verzehrten. Tom wiederholte seine Botschaft und sagte auch den Stallknechten Bescheid, die die freigelassenen Pferde wiedereinzufangen versuchten. Ellen war nirgends zu sehen.

Der Rauch stieg ihm in die Lungen. Tom mußte husten. Schwer atmend rannte er zur Brücke, die in den oberen Burghof führte. Dort blieb er stehen, holte tief Luft und blickte sich um. Von allen Seiten strömten jetzt die Menschen zusammen und liefen auf die Brücke zu. Er war sich inzwischen fast sicher, daß Ellen und Jack bereits im Wohnturm Zuflucht gesucht hatten, aber allein die Vorstellung, er könne sie übersehen haben, war kaum erträglich. Am unteren Torhaus standen die Ritter des Grafen dicht an dicht. Ein erbitterter Kampf

Mann gegen Mann war entbrannt. Auf einmal tauchte Graf Bartholo-
mäus mit tränenden Augen und blutverschmiertem Schwert neben
Tom aus dem Rauch auf und rief ihm zu: »Bringt Euch in Sicherheit!«
In diesem Augenblick gelang den Angreifern am unteren Torhaus der
Durchbruch. Die Verteidiger wichen zurück. Tom rannte über die
Brücke.

Am zweiten Torhaus standen fünfzehn oder zwanzig Männer bereit, um den oberen Burghof zu verteidigen. Sie bildeten für Tom und
den Grafen eine Gasse. Als sich die Reihen hinter ihm wieder schlossen, hörte Tom Hufgetrappel auf den Holzbohlen der Brücke. Die Lage
der Verteidiger war aussichtslos. Hundert blutrünstige Bewaffnete
stürmten auf sie ein ... und damit auch auf Ellen und die Kinder.

Sie liefen die Treppe zum Wohnturm hinauf. Auf halber Höhe
drehte Tom sich um. Die Verteidiger wurden von den Angreifern praktisch überrannt. Mit großen Schritten nahm er die letzten Stufen und
rannte vor zum großen Saal – nur, um dort feststellen zu müssen,
daß man ihnen auch hier zuvorgekommen war.

Die Vorhut der Feinde hatte den Wohnturm besetzt und alle Menschen, die hier Zuflucht gesucht hatten, als Geiseln genommen. Überall lagen tote und verwundete Ritter, überall war Blut. Und gleich am
Eingang des Saals standen vier finster dreinblickende Männer in Kettenhemden. Entsetzt erkannte Tom ihren Anführer – William Hamleigh.

Tom war vor Schreck wie gelähmt. In Williams Augen funkelte die
Mordlust. Schon fürchtete Tom, William wolle sich auf ihn stürzen
und ihn umbringen, doch da wurde er von zwei Spießgesellen Williams am Arm gepackt, in die Halle gezogen und aus dem Weg gezerrt.

Die Hamleighs steckten also hinter dem Überfall auf die Burg des
Grafen Bartholomäus. Aber warum?

Das gräfliche Gesinde, die Frauen und Kinder drängten sich an
der gegenüberliegenden Wand des Saals zusammen. Mit grenzenloser
Erleichterung stellte Tom fest, daß sich auch Alfred, Martha, Ellen
und Jack unter den Gefangenen befanden. Die Angst stand ihnen ins
Gesicht geschrieben, doch waren sie allem Anschein nach unverletzt.

Am Saaleingang kam es zu einem Tumult: Graf Bartholomäus und
zwei seiner Ritter stürmten herein, wurden jedoch schon an der Tür
von William Hamleighs Leuten abgefangen. Einer der Leibwächter
wurde sofort niedergestochen. Der zweite verteidigte seinen Herrn mit
erhobenem Schwert. Als kurz darauf noch weitere Ritter des Grafen
eintrafen und in den erbitterten Nahkampf eingriffen, sah es vorüber-

gehend so aus, als gerieten William und seine Leute in die Defensive. Dann aber mußten sich die Ritter des Grafen plötzlich nach zwei Seiten verteidigen: Die Feinde hatten den Burghof erobert, und die ersten erstürmten den Wohnturm.

Auf einmal rief eine machtvolle Stimme: »Halt!«

Die Kampfhandlungen wurden eingestellt, die Ritter beider Lager nahmen eine Verteidigungsstellung ein.

»Bartholomäus von Shiring!« rief die Stimme. »Ergebt Ihr Euch?«

Tom sah, wie der Graf sich umdrehte und zur Tür blickte. Die Ritter traten zur Seite. »Hamleigh«, murmelte der Graf ungläubig. Dann antwortete er klar und deutlich: »Werdet Ihr meine Familie und meine Dienerschaft unbehelligt lassen?«

»Ja.«

»Schwört es.«

»Ja, wenn Ihr Euch ergebt. Ich schwöre es beim heiligen Kreuz.«

»Ich ergebe mich«, sagte Graf Bartholomäus.

Vor dem Saal ertönte Jubelgeschrei.

Tom wandte sich ab. Martha rannte quer durch den Saal auf ihn zu. Er nahm sie auf den Arm. Kurz darauf war auch Ellen bei ihm und fiel ihm in die Arme.

»Wir sind in Sicherheit«, sagte Ellen mit Tränen in den Augen. »Wir alle ...«

»In Sicherheit ...«, wiederholte Tom bitter. »Und wieder bettelarm.«

Unvermittelt verstummte William. Er war der Sohn von Lord Percy Hamleigh. Es ziemte sich für ihn nicht, in hemmungsloses Jubelgeschrei zu verfallen und sich auf diese Weise mit jedem einfachen Bewaffneten gemein zu machen. Er riß sich zusammen und setzte eine herrische Miene auf, die vor Selbstzufriedenheit nur so strotzte.

Sie hatten gesiegt. Er hatte seinen Plan ausgeführt – nicht ohne Rückschläge, aber erfolgreich. Vor allem aber war der Sieg der von ihm und seinen drei Mitstreitern geleisteten Vorarbeit zu verdanken. William wußte nicht mehr, wie viele Männer er getötet oder verstümmelt hatte – er hatte zu zählen aufgehört. Bei allem war er selbst unverletzt geblieben. Allerdings ... woher kam das viele Blut in seinem Gesicht? Kaum hatte er es mit dem Ärmel fortgewischt, war schon wieder neues da. Vorsichtig tastete er sein Gesicht und seinen Kopf ab. An einer Stelle fehlten die Haare, und die Kopfhaut brannte wie Feuer, als er sie berührte. Um keinen Verdacht zu erregen, hatte er auf das Tragen eines Helms verzichtet. Nun, da er wußte, daß er verwundet war, spürte er auch die Schmerzen. Er ertrug sie mit Fassung – schließlich war eine Wunde so etwas wie eine Tapferkeitsauszeichnung.

In diesem Moment traten sein Vater und Graf Bartholomäus einander gegenüber. Bartholomäus streckte Percy in einer Geste der Unterwerfung mit dem Knauf voraus sein Schwert entgegen. Percy nahm es an sich, und seine Leute brachen erneut in Begeisterung aus.

Als der Lärm sich gelegt hatte, hörte William Bartholomäus fragen: »Warum habt Ihr uns das angetan?«

Und Vater Hamleigh antwortete: »Ihr habt Euch gegen den König verschworen.«

Bartholomäus erkannte, daß sein Plan verraten war, und er konnte sein Entsetzen darüber nicht verbergen. Ob er sich vor all diesen Leuten hier zu der Verschwörung bekennen wird, fragte sich William und hielt den Atem an. Doch Graf Bartholomäus bewahrte Haltung. »Ich verteidige meine Ehre vor dem König, nicht hier«, sagte er.

Vater Hamleigh nickte. »Wie Ihr wünscht. Befehlt Euren Leuten, die Waffen niederzulegen und die Burg zu verlassen.«

Graf Bartholomäus tat, wie ihm geheißen, und einer nach dem anderen traten die Männer vor und warfen vor Percy Hamleigh ihre Schwerter auf den Boden. William genoß die Szene. Zu sehen, wie sich die Feinde vor seinem Vater erniedrigten, war eine Augenweide.

Percy Hamleigh rief einen seiner Ritter zu sich. »Fang die Pferde ein und binde sie irgendwo fest. Und nehmt den Toten und Verwundeten die Waffen ab.« Waffen und Pferde der Besiegten gehörten den Siegern: Die Männer des Grafen mußten zu Fuß und ohne Waffen das Weite suchen. Mit den eroberten Pferden sollte das reiche Beutegut aus den Vorratsspeichern der Burg nach Hamleigh transportiert werden. Vater winkte einem weiteren Ritter und sagte zu ihm: »Schick das Küchenpersonal an die Arbeit. Wir wollen schmausen. Der Rest der Dienerschaft kann verschwinden.« Nach der Schlacht hatten die Männer Hunger: Wohlan denn, sie sollten ihr Gelage haben! Die erlesensten Weine des Grafen und die besten Speisen aus Küche und Keller standen zur Verfügung.

Die Ritter, die Percy Hamleigh und Graf Bartholomäus umstanden, bildeten eine Gasse: Williams Mutter trat ein.

Sie wirkte sehr klein unter so vielen kräftigen Kämpfern, doch als sie den Schal abnahm, fuhren alle, die sie zum erstenmal sahen, erschrocken zurück. Ihr entstelltes Gesicht entsetzte jedermann.

Lady Hamleigh sah ihren Mann an und sagte in zufriedenem Ton: »Ein großer Triumph!«

Weil ich so gute Vorarbeit geleistet habe, nicht wahr, Mutter? wollte William sagen, doch sein Vater kam ihm zuvor.

»William hat dafür gesorgt, daß wir anstandslos reinkamen.«

»So, hat er?« erwiderte sie und drehte sich nach ihrem Sohn um. Inständig hoffte William auf das verdiente Lob.

»Jawohl«, bestätigte Vater Hamleigh. »Der Junge war hervorragend.«

Mutter nickte. »Nun, vielleicht hast du recht.«

William wurde warm ums Herz. Er grinste tölpelhaft.

Mutter wandte sich an Graf Bartholomäus. »Der Graf verneige sich vor mir!« sagte sie.

»Nein«, erwiderte der Graf.

»Holt mir die Tochter!« befahl Mutter Hamleigh.

William sah sich um. Vorübergehend hatte er Aliena ganz vergessen. Er entdeckte sie sofort. Sie stand neben Matthew, dem weibischen Haushofmeister. William ging zu ihr, packte sie am Arm und brachte sie zu seiner Mutter. Matthew folgte ihnen.

»Schneidet ihr die Ohren ab!« sagte Mutter.

Aliena schrie auf.

William spürte eine merkwürdige Regung in seinen Lenden.

Das Gesicht des Grafen wurde aschfahl. »Ihr habt versprochen, uns nichts anzutun«, sagte er trotzig. »Ihr habt es geschworen.«

Auf wen wird die Wahl fallen? dachte William. *Wer wird ihr die Ohren abschneiden dürfen? Vielleicht erlaubt Mutter es mir ...* Seine Erregung wuchs.

»Kniet nieder!« sagte Mutter zu Bartholomäus.

Zögernd folgte der Graf ihrem Befehl und beugte sein Haupt.

William verspürte eine gewisse Enttäuschung.

»Schaut ihn euch an!« rief Mutter mit erhobener Stimme in den Raum. »Und merkt euch, wie es einem Mann ergeht, der die Hamleighs beleidigt!« Herrisch blickte sie um sich. Williams Herz erfüllte Stolz. Die Familienehre war wiederhergestellt.

Mutter wandte sich ab. Nun war wieder Percy Hamleigh an der Reihe. »Bring ihn in sein Schlafgemach!« sagte er zu William. »Und paß gut auf ihn auf!«

Der Graf erhob sich.

»Nimm das Mädchen gleich mit!« fügte Vater Hamleigh hinzu.

William packte Aliena hart am Arm. Es war schön, sie so zu berühren. Rauf mit ihr ins Schlafgemach, dachte er. Wer weiß, ob sich nicht eine Gelegenheit ergibt. Wenn ich mit ihr allein bin, kann ich mit ihr machen, was ich will ... Ich kann ihr die Kleider vom Leib reißen, so daß sie nackt vor mir steht ... Ich kann ...

»Erlaubt, daß mein Haushofmeister uns begleitet«, bat der Graf. »Matthew soll sich um meine Tochter kümmern.«

Vater Hamleigh sah Matthew an und sagte: »Meinetwegen. Der Kerl sieht harmlos aus.«

William betrachtete Alienas Gesicht. Es war noch immer leichenblaß. In ihrer Angst gefiel sie ihm besser als je zuvor. Sie war so scheu, so verletzlich ... Er wollte ihren üppigen Körper mit dem seinen zerquetschen, ihr die Schenkel auseinanderzwingen und dabei das Entsetzen in ihrem Gesicht sehen. Überwältigt von seinen Gefühlen beugte er sich zu ihr und wisperte ihr ins Ohr: »Ich will dich immer noch heiraten.«

Sie entzog sich ihm. »Heiraten?« wiederholte sie voller Verachtung und so laut, daß jeder es hören konnte. »Bevor ich dich heirate, sterbe ich lieber, du widerlicher, aufgeblasener Kröterich!«

Die Ritter grinsten, einer hämischer als der andere, und ein paar Dienstboten fingen an zu kichern. William stieg die Schamröte in den Kopf.

Mutter Hamleigh trat einen Schritt vor und schlug Aliena ins Gesicht. Graf Bartholomäus, der seiner Tochter zu Hilfe kommen wollte, wurde von den ihn bewachenden Rittern zurückgehalten. »Halt dein Maul!« fuhr Williams Mutter das Mädchen an. »Du bist jetzt nicht mehr die feine Dame! Du bist die Tochter eines Verräters. Wart's nur ab – in Kürze gehst du am Bettelstab und hast nichts mehr zu beißen! Für meinen Sohn bist du nicht mehr gut genug. Und jetzt verschwinde, und untersteh dich, noch einmal den Mund aufzumachen!«

William gab ihren Arm frei, und Aliena folgte ihrem Vater. Als er sie gehen sah, gestand William sich ein, daß die süße Rache auf einmal gallebitter schmeckte.

Sie geht wie eine Heldin, genau wie die Prinzessin in einem Versepos, dachte Jack. Ergriffen sah er ihr nach, wie sie mit hocherhobenem Kopf die Treppe emporstieg. Im Saal herrschte Schweigen, bis sie nicht mehr zu sehen war. Es war, als sei unvermittelt eine Lampe ausgegangen. Wie benommen starrte Jack auf die Stelle, an der Aliena eben noch gestanden hatte.

Ein Ritter kam auf sie zu und fragte: »Wer von euch ist der Koch?«

Der Koch selbst hatte zuviel Angst, sich freiwillig zu melden, aber jemand anders deutete auf ihn.

»Du bereitest jetzt das Frühstück«, befahl ihm der Ritter. »Geh in die Küche und nimm deine Helfer mit!« Der Koch suchte ein halbes Dutzend Leute aus. Dann brüllte der Ritter: »Ihr anderen verlaßt auf der Stelle die Burg! Und wenn euch euer Leben lieb ist, dann rührt ihr nichts an, was euch nicht gehört! Unsere Schwerter triefen von Blut – da kommt es auf ein bißchen mehr oder weniger nicht an! Verschwindet!«

Einer nach dem anderen trotteten sie zur Tür hinaus. Ellen nahm ihren Sohn, Tom seine Tochter bei der Hand. Alfred hielt sich dicht bei ihnen. Alle trugen sie ihre Winterumhänge. Außer ihren Eßmessern besaßen sie jetzt nur noch das, was sie am Leib trugen. Mit den anderen Entlassenen gingen sie die Treppe hinunter, überquerten die Brücke zum unteren Burghof, stolperten über die nutzlos am Boden liegenden Tore und verließen, ohne noch einmal innezuhalten, das umwallte Gelände. Auf dem freien Feld hinter dem Burggraben zerriß die Spannung wie eine Bogensehne und löste ihre Zungen. Aufgeregt unterhielten sie sich über den Überfall und die grauenvollen Erlebnisse der letzten Stunden. Teilnahmslos hörte Jack zu, wie jeder seine Tapferkeit rühmte. Er selbst war nicht tapfer gewesen – er war bloß davongelaufen.

Und stimmte das überhaupt? Er, Jack, hatte den Eindruck, die einzig wahrhaft Tapfere sei Aliena gewesen. Wie war es denn, als sie in den Wohnturm kamen und feststellen mußten, daß die erhoffte Zuflucht zur Falle geworden war? Da hatte Aliena sofort das Heft in die Hand genommen und dafür gesorgt, daß Dienerschaft und Kinder ruhig blieben und sich von den Kämpfenden fernhielten. Sie hatte die Ritter der Hamleighs angeschrien, wenn diese ruppig mit den Gefangenen umgingen oder ihre Schwerter gegen Frauen und unbewaffnete Männer erhoben. Sie hatte gehandelt, als sei sie selber unverletzlich.

Zärtlich fuhr ihm seine Mutter über den Schopf. »Woran denkst du?« wollte sie wissen.

»Ich frage mich, was mit der Prinzessin geschehen wird.«

Ellen wußte sofort, wer gemeint war. »Mit Lady Aliena«, sagte sie.

»Sie ist wie eine Prinzessin im Gedicht. Sie lebt in einer Burg. Nur die Ritter sind nicht so heldenhaft wie in der Dichtung.«

»Da hast du allerdings recht«, stimmte seine Mutter ihm zu. Ihre Stimme klang hart.

»Was wird mit ihr geschehen?«

Ellen schüttelte den Kopf. »Ich weiß es nicht, Jack.«

»Ihre Mutter ist tot.«

»Dann kommen schwere Zeiten auf sie zu.«

»Das hab' ich mir schon gedacht.« Jack machte eine Pause. »Sie hat mich ausgelacht, weil ich nicht wußte, wie das mit den Vätern ist. Aber ich hab' sie trotzdem gemocht.«

Seine Mutter legte den Arm um ihn. »Es tut mir leid, daß ich es dir nicht rechtzeitig erklärt habe«, sagte sie.

Zum Zeichen, daß er ihre Entschuldigung akzeptierte, berührte er ihre Hand. Wortlos setzten sie ihren Weg fort. Die Schar der Vertriebenen wurde langsam kleiner; immer wieder bog der eine oder andere oder auch eine ganze Familie vom Weg ab und strebte querfeldein auf das einsame Haus eines Verwandten oder Bekannten zu, um ein Frühstück zu erbitten und darüber nachzudenken, was als nächstes geschehen sollte. An der Kreuzung zerfielen sie in drei Gruppen: Die einen wandten sich nach Süden, die anderen nach Norden, und der Rest ging geradeaus weiter, Richtung Shiring. Ellen löste sich von Jack und faßte Tom am Arm. Tom blieb stehen. »Wo sollen wir hin?« fragte sie.

Die Frage schien ihn zu überraschen; es war, als setzte er voraus, daß alle ihm folgten, ohne Fragen zu stellen. Jack kannte diese überraschte Miene schon; sie zeigte sich recht oft, wenn Mutter Tom ansprach. Vielleicht hat ihm seine erste Frau solche Fragen nie gestellt, dachte der Junge.

»Wir gehen nach Kingsbridge«, sagte Tom, »zum Kloster.«

»Kingsbridge?« wiederholte Ellen erschrocken.

Jack konnte sich ihre Aufregung nicht erklären, und Tom ging nicht darauf ein. »Sie haben dort, wie mir gestern zu Ohren kam, einen neuen Prior«, erklärte er. »Ein neuer Mann in diesem Amt hat oft große Pläne. Kann sein, daß er die Kirche renovieren oder umbauen will.«

»Ist der alte Prior gestorben?«

»Ja.«

Die Antwort schien Ellen ein wenig zu beruhigen. Mutter muß den alten Prior gekannt haben, dachte Jack. Und gemocht hat sie ihn bestimmt nicht ...

Jetzt war auch Tom der besorgte Unterton in ihrer Stimme aufgefallen. »Stimmt etwas nicht mit Kingsbridge?« fragte er.

»Ich war schon mal dort«, antwortete sie. »Es ist weiter als eine Tagesreise von hier.«

Jack wußte, daß der weite Weg ihr nichts ausmachte. Tom indessen nahm sie beim Wort. »Ein bißchen weiter, ja. Bis morgen mittag können wir es aber schaffen.«

»Einverstanden.«

Tom ging weiter.

Kurze Zeit später bekam Jack auf einmal Bauchschmerzen. Eine Weile lang überlegte er, woran es liegen mochte. Auf der Burg hatte ihm niemand etwas getan, und auch Alfred hatte ihn schon seit zwei Tagen nicht mehr in den Magen geboxt. Er brauchte nicht lange, bis ihm die Antwort einfiel.

Er hatte wieder Hunger.

KAPITEL IV

Die Kathedrale von Kingsbridge bot alles andere als einen erfreulichen
Anblick. Der niedrige, gedrungene Bau mit dicken Mauern und winzigen Fenstern stammte aus einer Zeit lange vor Toms Geburt; aus
Tagen, da den Baumeistern die Bedeutung der Proportionen noch
nicht klar gewesen war. Toms Generation wußte, daß eine gerade,
echte Wand stärker war als eine dicke Mauer und daß man die Wände
durchaus mit großen Fenstern versehen konnte, solange diese nur
über perfekte Rundbogen verfügten. Aus der Entfernung betrachtet,
wirkte die Kathedrale zudem leicht windschief. Beim Näherkommen
erkannte Tom, warum: Einer der beiden Zwillingstürme auf der Westseite war eingestürzt. Die Entdeckung erfüllte ihn mit heimlicher
Freude: Dem neuen Prior war sicher an einem raschen Wiederaufbau
gelegen. Hoffnung beflügelte seine Schritte. Die Ereignisse auf Earlscastle hatten ihm arg zugesetzt: Kaum hatte er die langersehnte Anstellung gefunden, da wurde sein neuer Arbeitgeber überfallen und gefangengesetzt. Noch eine solche Enttäuschung überlebe ich nicht, dachte
Tom bei sich.

Sein Blick fiel auf Ellen. Sie wird mich verlassen, dachte er voller
Angst. Sobald sie glaubt, daß ich keine Arbeit mehr finde und folglich
mitsamt meinen Angehörigen verhungern muß, wird sie gehen ...
Ellen lächelte ihn an, doch als sie sich abwandte und wieder die
wuchtige, düstere Kathedrale vor Augen hatte, verfinsterte sich ihre
Miene wieder. Es war Tom nicht entgangen, daß sie sich in Gegenwart
von Priestern und Mönchen nicht wohl in ihrer Haut fühlte, und er
fragte sich, ob Ellen vielleicht ein schlechtes Gewissen hatte, weil sie
ohne den Segen der Kirche mit ihm zusammenlebte.

Auf dem Klostergelände herrschte geschäftiges Kommen und Gehen. Tom wußte aus eigener Erfahrung, daß es solche und solche

Klöster gab, verschlafene und aktive, doch das Bild, das sich ihnen in Kingsbridge bot, übertraf alles, was er bisher erlebt hatte. Es sah so aus, als sei drei Monate vor der Zeit ein gründlicher Frühjahrsputz im Gange. Vor den Ställen, die gerade von einigen Novizen ausgemistet wurden, standen zwei Mönche und striegelten die Pferde, während ein dritter Zaumzeug reinigte. Das Gästehaus neben den Ställen wurde gefegt und geschrubbt, und vor der Tür stand ein Wagen mit frischem Stroh.

Kein Mensch arbeitete indessen an dem eingestürzten Turm. Fachmännisch begutachtete Tom den Trümmerhaufen, der von ihm übriggeblieben war. Der Einsturz mußte schon einige Jahre zurückliegen, denn Frost und Regen hatten die scharfen Kanten der Steine abgeschliffen, der bröckelige Mörtel war fortgeschwemmt und der gesamte Steinhaufen schon ein oder zwei Zoll tief in dem weichen Boden eingesunken. Merkwürdig, daß man so lange nichts daran getan hat, dachte Tom, Kathedralen gelten doch gemeinhin als etwas Besonderes. Der verstorbene Prior muß faul, unfähig oder beides gewesen sein ... Wahrscheinlich werden die Mönche jetzt an den Wiederaufbau denken – das heißt, ich komme gerade zur rechten Zeit. Nach soviel Pech ist eine Glückssträhne ja auch überfällig ...

»Niemand erkennt mich«, sagte Ellen.

»Wann warst du denn zum letztenmal hier?« fragte Tom.

»Vor dreizehn Jahren.«

»Kein Wunder, daß sie sich nicht mehr an dich erinnern können.«

Sie schritten gerade an der Westfassade entlang. Tom öffnete eine der großen Holztüren und warf einen Blick ins düstere Innere. Sogleich erkannte er die dicken Säulen und die alte Holzdecke. Doch auch hier tat sich einiges: Da waren Mönche, die mit langstieligen Pinseln die Wände weißelten, während andere den aus gestampftem Lehm bestehenden Boden fegten. Der neue Prior war offensichtlich bestrebt, das Kloster rundum aufzumöbeln. Auch das gab Anlaß zur Hoffnung. Tom schloß die Tür wieder.

Im Küchenhof auf der anderen Seite der Kirche standen mehrere Novizen vor einem großen Trog voll schmutzigem Wasser und kratzten mit scharfrandigen Steinen Ruß- und Fettreste von Kochtöpfen und anderem Küchengeschirr. Ihre Fingerknöchel waren wundgescheuert und vom eiskalten Wasser gerötet. Als sie Ellen erblickten, kicherten sie und trauten sich nicht, sie offen anzusehen.

Tom fragte einen errötenden Novizen, wo der Cellerar zu finden sei. Strenggenommen hätte er sich nach dem Sakristan erkundigen müssen, in dessen Verantwortungsbereich alle baulichen Maßnahmen auf dem Klostergelände fielen, doch Kellermeister waren generell leichter ansprechbar. Das letzte Wort lag ohnehin beim Prior. Der Novize verwies ihn auf den Lagerraum eines in der Nähe stehenden Hauses. Gefolgt von Ellen und den Kindern betrat Tom das Gebäude durch die offenstehende Tür. Drinnen blieben sie zunächst einmal stehen und starrten ins dämmrige Licht.

Tom fiel sofort auf, daß das Haus, in dem sie sich jetzt befanden, neuer war als die Kirche. Auch war es solider gebaut. Die Luft war trocken, und es roch nicht nach Fäulnis, sondern nach den eingelagerten Speisen und Gewürzen, die seinen Magen sogleich schmerzhaft aufbegehren ließen: Er hatte schon wieder zwei Tage lang nichts gegessen. Nachdem sich seine Augen an die Düsternis gewöhnt hatten, erkannte Tom, daß der Boden des Lagerraums sorgfältig gepflastert war und daß die kurzen, stämmigen Säulen ein Tonnengewölbe trugen. Kurz darauf erspähte er einen hochgewachsenen Mann mit Stirnglatze und weißem Haarkranz, der aus einem großen Faß Salz in einen Topf löffelte.

»Seid Ihr der Cellerar?« fragte Tom, doch der Mann gebot ihm mit erhobener Hand Schweigen. Er zählte die Salzportionen und wollte nicht unterbrochen werden. Wortlos warteten sie ab, bis er fertig war.

»... achtundfünfzig, neunundfünfzig, sechzig!« sagte er schließlich und legte den Löffel beiseite.

»Mein Name ist Tom. Ich bin Baumeister. Ich würde gerne den Nordwestturm Eurer Kathedrale wieder aufbauen.«

»Ich heiße Cuthbert Whitehead und bin der Cellerar. Wenn's nach mir ginge, könntet Ihr gleich anfangen. Wir werden jedoch zuvor Prior Philip fragen müssen. Euch ist doch bekannt, daß wir einen neuen Prior haben, nicht wahr?«

»Ja.« Dieser Cuthbert gehört zu den angenehmen Vertretern seiner Zunft, dachte Philip. Ein weltlicher, umgänglicher Mensch, einem kleinen Schwatz gewiß nicht abgeneigt.

»Dem neuen Mann scheint sehr daran gelegen zu sein, das äußere Erscheinungsbild des Klosters zu verbessern.«

Cuthbert nickte. »Das schon, nur möchte er dafür kein Geld ausgeben. Habt Ihr bemerkt, daß alle Arbeiten hier auf dem Gelände von Mönchen ausgeführt werden? Er möchte keine Handwerker anwerben. Die Priorei hat ohnehin zu viele Diener, meint er.«

Das war eine schlechte Nachricht. »Was halten denn die Mönche davon?« fragte Tom, wohl wissend, daß er damit einen wunden Punkt berührte.

Cuthbert lachte, und sein runzeliges Gesicht zeigte noch ein paar Fältchen mehr. »Ihr seid mir ein taktvoller Mann, Baumeister Tom! Ich weiß, was Ihr denkt: So viele arbeitende Mönche habt Ihr noch nie gesehen, nicht wahr? Nun denn, der neue Prior zwingt niemanden zur Arbeit. Allerdings weiß er die Regel des heiligen Benedikt auf seine Weise auszulegen: Wer körperliche Arbeit leistet, so sagt er, darf rotes Fleisch essen und Wein trinken. Wer hingegen nur betet und studiert, muß sich mit gesalzenem Fisch und Dünnbier zufriedengeben. Wenn Ihr ihn fragt, wird er Euch eine ausgefeilte theologische Begründung geben. Entscheidend ist jedoch, daß sich viele Freiwillige für die harte Fron gemeldet haben, vor allem jüngere Mönche.« Cuthbert schien nichts dagegen zu haben; er wirkte lediglich etwas verdutzt.

»Aber Mönche können keine Steinmauern errichten«, erwiderte Tom, »da können sie essen, was sie wollen.« Er hatte noch nicht ausgesprochen, als er in der Ferne ein Kind schreien hörte. Das Geräusch rührte an sein Herz. Ein Kind? Hier im Kloster? Er brauchte eine Weile, bis er merkte, wie ungewöhnlich das war.

»Fragen wir den Prior«, sagte Cuthbert, aber Tom hörte ihm kaum zu. Die Stimme schien einem sehr kleinen Kind zu gehören, einem Säugling vielleicht, und sie kam näher. Tom sah Ellen an; auch sie hatte es gehört und war sichtlich überrascht. Auf einmal verdüsterte ein Schatten den Eingang. Tom spürte einen Kloß im Hals. Ein Mönch mit einem Säugling auf dem Arm betrat das Lager. Tom erkannte das kleine Gesicht. Es war sein Sohn.

Tom schluckte. Das Gesichtchen war krebsrot, die Fäustchen waren geballt, der Mund stand offen und zeigte den zahnlosen Gaumen. Das Kind schrie, aber es war kein kränkliches oder schmerzvolles Schreien, sondern die kräftige, lustvolle Forderung nach Nahrung. Der kleine Kerl war rundum gesund. Tom wurden die Knie schwach, so froh und erleichtert war er.

Der Mönch, der den Säugling trug, war ungefähr zwanzig Jahre alt, hatte einen wirren Haarschopf und strahlte dümmlich über das ganze Gesicht. Die Anwesenheit einer Frau schien ihn – im Gegensatz zu den meisten anderen Mönchen – nicht befangen zu machen. Er lächelte in die Runde und sagte zu Cuthbert: »Jonathan braucht mehr Milch.«

Am liebsten hätte Tom das Kind in die Arme geschlossen. Er gab sich alle Mühe, seine Gefühle zu verbergen, und sah verstohlen die Kinder an. Sie wußten nur, daß ein reisender Priester den ausgesetzten

Säugling gefunden hatte. Daß sein Retter ihn in einem kleinen Kloster im Wald abgeliefert hatte, war ihnen unbekannt. Ihre Mienen verrieten nur mäßige Neugier; anscheinend kam keines von ihnen auf die Idee, das Kind auf dem Arm des Mönchs könnte dasselbe sein wie das, welches sie im Wald zurückgelassen hatten.

Cuthbert ergriff einen Schöpflöffel und füllte aus einem bereitstehenden Eimer Milch in einen kleinen Krug. Ellen wandte sich an den jungen Mönch und fragte ihn: »Darf ich das Kindchen mal halten?« Sie streckte die Arme aus, und der Mönch reichte ihr den Säugling. Tom beneidete sie. Wie gerne hätte er das kleine warme Bündel an sein Herz gedrückt! Ellen wiegte den Säugling in den Armen, so daß er vorübergehend verstummte.

Cuthbert sah auf. »Wohlan, Johnny Eightpence, ein braves Kindermädchen ist er! Aber ihm fehlt die Wärme und Weichheit des Weibes.«

Ellen lächelte den jungen Mann an. »Warum nennt man Euch Johnny Eightpence?«

Cuthbert antwortete an seiner Statt. »Weil er nur acht Pence auf den Shilling bringt«, sagte er und tippte sich mit dem Finger an die Schläfe. »Aber auf die Bedürfnisse eines so kleinen dummen Wesens scheint er sich besser zu verstehen als wir, die wir mit allen Geistesgaben gesegnet sind.« Er machte eine kurze Pause und fügte dann unbestimmt hinzu: »Das ist wohl alles Teil einer höheren göttlichen Fügung ...«

Ellen stand inzwischen neben Tom und hielt ihm das Kind mit ausgestreckten Armen entgegen. Sie hatte seine Gedanken gelesen. In tiefer Dankbarkeit sah er sie an und nahm das kleine Menschlein in seine großen Hände. Durch die Decke, in die der Säugling gewickelt war, spürte er das Herz des Kindes schlagen. Die Decke war aus teurem Tuch, und eine Frage schoß ihm durch den Kopf: Woher die Mönche wohl so weiche Wolle haben? Er drückte das Kind an seine Brust und wiegte es hin und her. Seine Methode war jedoch offenbar nicht so gut wie die Ellens, denn der Kleine begann wieder zu schreien. Tom hatte nichts dagegen. Das kräftige Gebrüll war Musik in seinen Ohren, bedeutete es doch nichts anderes, als daß das Kind, das er im Wald ausgesetzt hatte, gesund und munter war. Schweren Herzens gestand er sich ein, daß die Entscheidung, den Kleinen in der Obhut der Mönche zu lassen, die einzig richtige gewesen war.

»Wo schläft er denn?« fragte Ellen Johnny.

Diesmal beantwortete Johnny die Frage selbst: »Sein Kinderbettchen steht bei uns im Dormitorium.«

»Dann weckt er Euch doch jede Nacht auf.«

»Um Mitternacht müssen wir ohnehin aufstehen, zur Frühmesse«, erklärte Johnny.

»Natürlich! Ich vergaß, daß die Nächte der Mönche so ruhelos sind wie die der Mütter!«

Cuthbert gab Johnny den Milchkrug. Der junge Mönch nahm ihn entgegen – und holte sich mit der freien Hand und geübtem Griff den Säugling zurück. Tom war darauf nicht gefaßt; er wollte seinen Sohn noch nicht wieder fortgeben, doch was konnte er tun? In den Augen der Mönche hatte er nicht die geringsten Ansprüche auf das Kind. Einen Augenblick später war Johnny mitsamt seinem Schützling verschwunden – sehr zum Leidwesen Toms, der nur mit Mühe der Versuchung widerstand, hinterherzulaufen und zu rufen: *So wartet doch, halt! Es ist mein Sohn! Gebt ihn mir zurück!* Ellen packte ihn am Arm und drückte ihn; es war wie ein stummer Zuspruch.

Wieder ein Hoffnungsschimmer, dachte Tom. Wenn ich hier Arbeit bekomme, kann ich Jonathan jeden Tag sehen. Es war fast *zu* schön – ein Traum, an dessen Erfüllung er kaum zu denken wagte.

Dem lebenserfahrenen Cuthbert war nicht entgangen, wie sich die Augen von Martha und Jack beim Anblick des mit fetter, cremiger Milch gefüllten Krugs geweitet hatten. »Mögen Eure Kinder vielleicht ein wenig Milch?« fragte er.

»O ja doch, gewiß, ich bitte Euch, Vater«, erwiderte Tom. Er hätte selber gerne etwas davon gehabt.

Cuthbert füllte zwei Holzschüsselchen mit Milch und reichte sie Martha und Jack. Gierig stürzten die beiden das Getränk herunter. Um ihre Münder bildeten sich große weiße Ringe. »Noch ein bißchen?« fragte Cuthbert.

»Ja, bitte«, antworteten sie einstimmig. Tom sah Ellen an und wußte, daß sie wie er tiefe Dankbarkeit darüber empfand, daß die Kinder endlich wieder etwas in den Magen bekamen.

Ein zweites Mal schöpfte Cuthbert Milch in die Schüsselchen. Beiläufig fragte er: »Sagt, Freunde, wo kommt Ihr denn her?«

»Von Earlscastle bei Shiring«, erwiderte Tom. »Gestern morgen sind wir dort aufgebrochen.«

»Habt Ihr seitdem schon etwas gegessen?«

»Nein«, antwortete Tom ohne Umschweife. Obwohl er wußte, daß Cuthbert es gut mit ihnen meinte, fiel ihm das Eingeständnis, daß er die Kinder nicht hatte ernähren können, schwer.

»Dann nehmt Euch fürs erste ein paar Äpfel«, sagte Cuthbert und deutete auf das Faß neben der Tür. »Damit Ihr bis zum Abendessen durchhaltet.«

Während Martha und Jack ihre zweite Portion Milch tranken, begaben sich Alfred, Ellen und Tom zum Apfelfaß. Alfred langte kräftig zu und wollte einen ganzen Armvoll davontragen, doch Tom schlug ihm die Äpfel aus der Hand und raunte ihm zu: »Nicht mehr als zwei oder drei, hast du mich verstanden?« Alfred nahm drei.

Tom ließ sich die Äpfel schmecken, und sein Magen beruhigte sich ein wenig. Trotzdem konnte er nicht umhin, sich insgeheim zu fragen, wie lange es noch hin war bis zum Abendessen. Als ihm einfiel, daß Mönche, um Kerzenlicht zu sparen, gemeinhin vor Einbruch der Dunkelheit zu speisen pflegten, war er glücklich.

Cuthbert sah Ellen kritisch an. »Kenne ich Euch?« fragte er nach einer Weile.

Ihr war unbehaglich zumute. »Nicht, daß ich wüßte«, sagte sie.

»Ihr kommt mir irgendwie bekannt vor.«

»Ich habe meine Kindheit hier in der Gegend verbracht.«

»Ach so, das wird's wohl sein«, sagte Cuthbert. »Deswegen habe ich das Gefühl, Ihr seid älter als Ihr sein solltet.«

»Ihr müßt ein sehr gutes Gedächtnis haben.«

Er runzelte die Stirn. »Es könnte besser sein. Da war doch noch etwas anderes ... Ich bin mir ganz sicher ... Aber sei's drum. Warum habt Ihr Earlscastle verlassen?«

»Die Burg wurde gestern früh im Morgengrauen angegriffen und erobert«, berichtete Tom. »Graf Bartholomäus wird des Hochverrats bezichtigt.«

»Die Heiligen stehen uns bei!« rief Cuthbert bestürzt aus und sah auf einmal aus wie eine alte Jungfer, die sich vor einem Stier fürchtet. »Des Hochverrats!«

Von draußen näherten sich Schritte. Tom drehte sich um und sah einen weiteren Mönch eintreten. »Das ist unser neuer Prior«, sagte Cuthbert.

Tom erkannte den Mann sofort. Es war Philip, der Mönch, der ihnen unterwegs begegnet war und ihnen den köstlichen Käse gegeben hatte. Auf einmal war ihm alles klar: Der neue Prior von Kingsbridge war zuvor Prior des kleinen Waldklosters gewesen und hatte Jonathan bei seiner Übersiedlung mitgenommen!

Welch glückliche Fügung des Schicksals! Philip war ein freundlicher Mann. Er hat mich von Anfang an gemocht und mir vertraut, dachte Tom bei sich. Er wird mir gewiß eine Arbeit geben ...

Auch Philip erkannte ihn auf Anhieb. »Seid gegrüßt, Baumeister«, sagte er. »Da war's wohl nichts mit Arbeit am bischöflichen Palast, wie?«

»Nein, Vater. Der Erzdiakon wollte mir keine Arbeit geben. Der Bischof selbst war gar nicht da.«

»Da habt Ihr wohl recht«, erwiderte Philip. »Der Bischof war bereits im Himmel. Wir wußten das damals freilich noch nicht.«

»Der Bischof ist tot?«

»Jawohl.«

»Das ist doch ein alter Hut!« fuhr Cuthbert ungeduldig dazwischen. »Tom und seine Familie kommen gerade aus Earlscastle. Die Burg wurde erobert – und Graf Bartholomäus gefangengenommen!«

Philip blieb unbewegt. »Schon …«, murmelte er vor sich hin.

»Schon?« wiederholte Cuthbert. »Wieso sagst du ›schon‹?« Der Cellerar schien den jungen Prior zu mögen, war aber auf der Hut – wie ein Vater, dessen Sohn aus dem Krieg heimkehrt und nicht nur ein scharfes Schwert im Gürtel trägt, sondern einen merkwürdigen Ausdruck im Gesicht. »Hast du gewußt, was da im Busch war?«

Philip war ein wenig durcheinander. »Nein, nein, nicht genau«, wiegelte er ab. »Mir kam nur gerüchteweise zu Ohren, daß Bartholomäus mit Stephans Krönung nicht einverstanden war.« Er hatte sich wieder gefangen. »Wie dem auch sei, wir können nur dankbar sein. Stephan hat versprochen, die Rechte der Kirche zu achten. Mathilde dagegen hätte uns vermutlich genauso unterdrückt wie einst ihr verstorbener Vater. Ihr bringt gute Botschaft, Baumeister, in der Tat.« Der Prior freute sich, als habe er selbst den Überfall ausgeführt.

Tom wollte sich nicht in ein Gespräch über Graf Bartholomäus verwickeln lassen. »Der Graf hatte mich am Tag vorher mit dem Ausbau der Verteidigungsanlagen beauftragt«, sagte er. »Aber ich bekam nicht einmal einen Tageslohn.«

»Wie bedauerlich«, sagte Philip. »Übrigens – von wem wurde die Burg eigentlich angegriffen?«

»Von Lord Percy Hamleigh.«

»Aha!« Philip nickte, und einmal mehr hatte Tom den Eindruck, daß er dem Prior mit seinem Bericht lediglich bestätigte, was dieser ohnehin erwartete. Er wollte jetzt endlich auf seine eigenen Sorgen zu sprechen kommen.

»Ihr seid dabei, die Kathedrale zu renovieren …«

»Ja, ich tue, was ich kann«, erwiderte Philip.

»Gewiß wollt Ihr auch den Turm wiederaufbauen.«

»Den Turm wiederaufbauen, das Dach ausbessern, den Boden pfla-
stern … ja, das habe ich vor.« Erst jetzt schien ihm der Grund für
Toms Anwesenheit aufzugehen. Rasch fügte er hinzu: »Und Ihr be-
werbt Euch um die Stelle des Baumeisters, habe ich recht? Entschuldigt meine Unaufmerksamkeit. Ich würde Euch wirklich sehr gerne
anstellen. Das Problem ist nur: Ich kann Euch nicht bezahlen. Die
Klosterkasse ist leer, absolut leer.«

Für Tom kam die Antwort wie ein Schlag ins Gesicht. Alles hatte
darauf hingedeutet, daß hier in Kingsbridge endlich Arbeit auf ihn
wartete. Er wollte seinen Ohren nicht trauen und starrte den Prior
an. Das Kloster sollte kein Geld haben? Das war doch unfaßbar! Gewiß, der Cellerar hatte gesagt, daß all die zusätzlichen Arbeiten ausschließlich von Mönchen erledigt würden … Doch selbst, wenn es
stimmte, was der Prior sagte: Ein Kloster konnte sich allemal beim
Juden Geld borgen. Das ist das Ende, dachte Tom. Er hatte das Gefühl,
von allen Kräften, die ihn bislang durch den Winter gebracht hatten,
verlassen zu werden. Er fühlte sich schwach und hilflos. Ich kann
nicht mehr, dachte er, es ist aus und vorbei.

Philip erkannte seine Not. »Ich kann Euch ein Abendbrot anbieten
und einen Schlafplatz, auch Frühstück könnt Ihr haben.«

Bitterer Zorn übermannte Tom. »Ich nehme Euer Angebot an«,
sagte er. »Aber lieber tät’ ich’s mir verdienen!«

Philip hob die Brauen, als er merkte, welche Gefühle Tom bewe-
ten. Dennoch antwortete er mit sanfter Stimme: »Wendet Euch an
Gott – das nennt man beten, nicht betteln.« Mit diesen Worten verließ
er den Raum.

Auch den anderen war Toms Erregung aufgefallen; sie wirkten alle
ein wenig verschreckt. Es ärgerte ihn, daß sie ihn alle anstarrten. Nur
wenige Schritte hinter Philip trat er hinaus ins Freie, blieb im Hof
vor der Tür stehen, sah die große alte Kirche vor sich aufragen und
rang um Fassung.

Ellen und die Kinder folgten ihm wenige Augenblicke später nach.
Ellen legte ihm tröstend den Arm um die Taille – eine Geste, die die
Novizen sogleich wieder dazu veranlaßte, einander anzustoßen und
zu tuscheln. Tom achtete nicht darauf. »Ich werde beten«, sagte er
mit grimmiger Entschlossenheit. »Ich werde beten, daß ein Blitz vom
Himmel fährt und die Kirche hier in Schutt und Asche legt.«

Seit zwei Tagen wußte Jack, was es bedeutete, die Zukunft fürchten
zu müssen.

Nie zuvor in seinem bisherigen kurzen Leben hatte er weiter als einen Tag vorausdenken müssen – und wäre er je in die Verlegenheit geraten, so hätte er gewußt, was ihn erwartete. Im Wald war ein Tag wie der andere, und die Jahreszeiten gingen unmerklich ineinander über. Hier draußen war alles anders: Da wußte man heute nicht, wo man morgen sein, was man tun und ob man etwas zu essen bekommen würde.

Das Schlimmste daran war das dauernde Hungergefühl. Um die Schmerzen zu lindern, hatte Jack heimlich Gras und Blätter gegessen – mit dem Ergebnis, daß die Schmerzen nicht ausblieben, sondern sich lediglich etwas veränderten. Und übel wurde einem obendrein. Martha weinte oft vor Hunger. Sie und er gingen immer gemeinsam. Martha sah zu ihm auf – er hatte so etwas noch nie erlebt. Daß er nicht imstande war, ihr zu helfen, quälte ihn noch mehr als sein eigener Hunger.

Wären sie daheim, in der Umgebung der Höhle, geblieben, da hätte er schon Abhilfe geschaffen: Er hätte Enten jagen, Nüsse sammeln und Eier stehlen können; er kannte die Stellen und wußte, wie es ging. In Städten und Dörfern und auf den unbekannten Straßen und Wegen dazwischen war er dagegen völlig hilflos. Das einzige, was er wußte, war, daß Tom unbedingt Arbeit finden mußte.

Sie verbrachten den Nachmittag im Gästehaus des Klosters. Es war ein schmuckloses Gebäude mit einem einzigen Raum. In der Mitte befand sich eine Feuerstelle, und der Boden bestand aus gestampfter Erde. In nichts unterschied sich das Gästehaus von einem einfachen Bauernhof, doch Jack, der sein Leben lang in einer Höhle gewohnt hatte, fand es wunderbar. Er wollte wissen, wie man ein solches Haus errichtete, und Tom gab ihm bereitwillig Auskunft. Zunächst, so erklärte er ihm, müsse man zwei junge Bäume fällen, sie entasten, in einem rechten Winkel aneinanderlehnen und dasselbe vier Schritt weiter wiederholen. Die beiden auf diese Weise entstandenen Dreiecke gelte es, durch einen Firstbalken miteinander zu verbinden. Parallel dazu würden leichte Äste oder Holzleisten an den jeweils gegenüberstehenden Stämmen befestigt, so daß schließlich ein beidseitig bis auf den Erdboden reichendes, schräges Dach entstünde. Das Dach müsse dann mit rechtwinkligen Rahmen aus geflochtenem Dachdeckerstroh bedeckt und mit Lehm wasserdicht gemacht werden. Die Giebelwände bestünden aus in den Boden gerammten Pfählen; die Ritzen und Spalten dazwischen würden mit Lehm verschmiert. Die Tür komme in eine der beiden Giebelwände. Fenster gäbe es keine.

Jacks Mutter streute frisches Stroh auf dem Boden aus, und Jack entzündete ein Feuer mit Hilfe des Feuersteins, den er stets bei sich führte. Als die anderen außer Hörweite waren, fragte er seine Mutter, warum der Prior Tom nicht anstellen wolle, obwohl es doch genug zu tun gebe. »Solange die Kirche noch benutzbar ist, will er wohl Geld sparen«, antwortete Ellen. »Wäre die ganze Kirche eingestürzt, so bliebe ihnen gar nichts anderes übrig, als sie wiederaufzubauen – aber mit dem eingefallenen Turm können sie leben …«

In der Abenddämmerung kam ein Küchenjunge und brachte den Gästen einen Kessel voll Eintopf und einen Laib Brot, der so lang war wie ein ausgewachsener Mann groß – und das alles für sie allein! Der Eintopf bestand aus Gemüse, Kräutern und Suppenknochen mit viel Fleisch, und obenauf schillerten die Fettaugen. Das Brot war sogenanntes Pferdebrot; es setzte sich zusammen aus den verschiedensten Getreidesorten wie Roggen, Gerste und Hafer, enthielt aber auch getrocknete Erbsen und Bohnen. »Das ist das billigste Brot, das es gibt«, sagte Alfred. Jack, der vor ein paar Tagen zum erstenmal in seinem Leben Brot gegessen hatte, fand es großartig. Er aß und aß, bis ihm der Bauch weh tat. Alfred aß, bis nichts mehr übrig war.

Danach saßen sie am Feuer und versuchten, das ungewohnte Festmahl zu verdauen. »Warum ist der Kirchturm eigentlich eingestürzt?« fragte Jack.

»Wahrscheinlich hat der Blitz eingeschlagen«, antwortete Alfred. »Oder es war ein Feuer.«

»Aber der Turm besteht doch nur aus Steinen«, sagte Jack. »Die brennen doch gar nicht.«

»Das *Dach* ist nicht aus Stein, du Dummkopf«, sagte Alfred voller Verachtung. »Das Dach besteht aus Holz.«

Jack dachte einen Augenblick nach. »Wenn das Dach brennt – stürzt dann immer gleich das ganze Gebäude ein?«

Alfred zuckte mit den Schultern. »Manchmal jedenfalls.«

Eine Weile lang sprach keiner von beiden ein Wort. Tom und Ellen, die auf der anderen Seite der Feuerstelle saßen, unterhielten sich in gedämpftem Ton.

Plötzlich sagte Jack unvermittelt: »Ist das nicht komisch mit dem Kind?«

»Was ist komisch?« fragte Alfred nach einer Pause.

»Na ja, euer Kind ist damals im Wald verlorengegangen, viele Meilen von hier. Und nun ist da plötzlich ein kleines Kind hier im Kloster.«

Weder Alfred noch Martha schien dieser Zufall besonders bemerkenswert, so daß auch Jack nicht weiter darüber nachdachte.

Die Mönche begaben sich sofort nach dem Abendessen zur Ruhe. Gästen niederen Standes wurden keine Kerzen zur Verfügung gestellt. Tom und seine Familie blieben daher noch eine Weile beim langsam ersterbenden Feuer sitzen und legten sich dann ins Stroh.

Jack konnte lange nicht einschlafen. Er dachte nach. Wenn heute nacht die Kathedrale niederbrennt, sind alle unsere Sorgen mit einem Schlag beseitigt, sagte er sich. Der Prior wird Tom mit dem Neubau der Kirche beauftragen. Wir könnten alle hier in diesem schönen Haus wohnen bleiben, und jeden Tag gäbe es Eintopf mit Fleisch und Pferdebrot ... Wenn ich Tom wäre, würde ich die Kirche selbst anzünden. Ich würde warten, bis alle eingeschlafen sind, und dann heimlich in die Kirche schleichen und mit meinem Feuerstein einen Brand entfachen ... Bevor irgend jemand etwas merken und Alarm schlagen würde, wäre ich längst wieder hier und könnte mich schlafend stellen ... Und wenn sie dann alle anfangen würden, eimerweise Wasser in die Flammen zu schütten, wie gestern, als der Stall von Graf Bartholomäus brannte, dann würde ich natürlich mitmachen, und alle würden denken, ich wolle das Feuer löschen, genau wie sie ...

Alfred und Martha schliefen bereits tief – Jack merkte es an ihren Atemzügen. Tom und Ellen taten unter Toms Umhang das, was sie normalerweise um diese Zeit taten (Alfred nannte es ›ficken‹), dann schliefen auch sie ein. Tom hatte offenbar doch nicht vor, heimlich aufzustehen und die Kathedrale anzuzünden.

Was *hat* er eigentlich vor? fragte sich Jack. Will er weiter von Ort zu Ort wandern, bis wir alle verhungert sind?

Als die langsamen, regelmäßigen Atemzüge ihm verrieten, daß alle vier in tiefstem Schlummer lagen, kam Jack auf die Idee, *er selbst* könnte die Kathedrale anzünden.

Der Gedanke allein war so furchterregend, daß sein Herz plötzlich wie wild zu schlagen begann.

Ich müßte ganz leise aufstehen, sagte er sich. Die Fenster des Gästehauses sind wegen der Kälte alle fest geschlossen, und die Tür ist aus Sicherheitsgründen verriegelt, aber ich glaube, ich kriege sie schon irgendwie auf und komme raus, ohne jemanden zu wecken. Die Kirchentüren sind vielleicht auch verschlossen, aber auch da wird sich ein Weg finden, vor allem für jemanden, der so klein ist wie ich ... Und wenn ich erst einmal drin bin, finde ich auch den Weg hinauf zum Dach ...

Jack hatte in den zwei Wochen, die er inzwischen mit Tom unterwegs war, eine Menge gelernt. Tom hatte fast immer vom Bauen und von Gebäuden gesprochen – meistens in der Absicht, Alfred etwas beizubringen. Während Alfred jedoch nicht das geringste Interesse zeigte, hatte Jack genau zugehört. Unter anderem hatte er erfahren, daß alle größeren Kirchen über in die Mauern eingelassene Treppen verfügten. Sie dienten dazu, die oberen Bereiche für Renovierungsarbeiten leichter zugänglich zu machen. Jack wollte sich eine solche Treppe suchen und über sie das Dach erreichen.

Er setzte sich auf. Es war jetzt finstere Nacht. Er lauschte den Atemzügen der anderen und erkannte Tom an dem leichten Rasseln in seiner Brust, das – wie Ellen ihm erklärt hatte – von dem vielen Steinstaub herrührte, den Tom im Laufe seines Lebens eingeatmet hatte. Alfred schnarchte laut, drehte sich dann auf die Seite und war wieder still.

Sobald ich das Feuer gelegt habe, dachte Jack, muß ich auf schnellstem Wege ins Gästehaus zurück. Was wohl die Mönche mit mir tun werden, wenn sie mich erwischen? In Shiring hatte Jack einmal erlebt, wie ein Junge seines Alters ausgepeitscht wurde, weil er in einem Gewürzladen einen Zuckerhut gestohlen hatte. Der Junge hatte gebrüllt wie am Spieß, als die geschmeidige Rute ihm das Hinterteil blutig schlug. Die Prügelei war Jack viel grausamer vorgekommen als das gegenseitige Totschlagen in der Schlacht von Earlscastle, und das Bild des blutenden Knaben verfolgte ihn noch immer. Die Vorstellung, ihm könne dasselbe widerfahren, erfüllte ihn mit Entsetzen.

Wenn ich das wirklich tue, wird keine Seele je davon erfahren.

Er legte sich wieder hin, wickelte sich in seinen Umhang und schloß die Augen.

Ob die Kirchentür wirklich verschlossen ist? Wenn ja, dann klettere ich durchs Fenster. Wenn ich auf der Nordseite der Kirche bleibe, entdeckt mich niemand ... Das Dormitorium ist auf der Südseite und wird auch noch durch den Kreuzgang verdeckt. Auf dieser Seite befindet sich nur noch der Friedhof.

Ich stehe auf und sehe mich mal um. Ich will nur wissen, ob es überhaupt möglich ist ...

Er zögerte noch einen Augenblick. Dann stand er auf.

Das frische Stroh knisterte unter seinen Füßen. Einmal mehr lauschte er auf die Atemgeräusche der vier Schlafenden. Es war jetzt sehr still; nicht einmal mehr die Mäuse raschelten im Stroh. Er wagte sich einen Schritt vor, hielt inne, lauschte. Die anderen schliefen und schliefen. Jack verlor die Geduld und war mit drei schnellen Schritten an der Tür. Wieder spitzte er die Ohren: Die Mäuse scharrten und raschelten wieder; offenbar waren sie zu dem Schluß gekommen, daß sie nichts zu befürchten hatten. Die Menschen schliefen.

Mit den Fingerspitzen tastete er die Tür ab, bis er den Eichenholzbalken fand, mit dem sie verriegelt war. Der Balken ruhte in zwei Trägern und erwies sich als unerwartet schwer. Jack konnte ihn gerade ein paar Zoll weit anheben und mußte ihn dann wieder fallen lassen. Scheppernd plumpste er in die Träger zurück. Es klang furchtbar laut. Jack erstarrte und lauschte angespannt. Toms rasselnder Atem geriet aus dem Takt. Was soll ich sagen, wenn sie mich erwischen? dachte er, der Verzweiflung nahe. Ich sage, ich wollte rausgehen … aber warum? Ich werde sagen, ich mußte mal. Erleichtert atmete er auf. Die Ausrede war glaubwürdig. Er hörte, wie Tom sich umdrehte, und wartete auf seine tiefe, rauhe Stimme, aber sie blieb aus. Die Atemzüge wurden wieder gleichmäßig.

Gespenstischer Silberglanz umspielte die Tür. Das muß der Mond sein, dachte Jack. Er holte tief Luft, packte zu und hob den Balken hoch. Diesmal war er auf das Gewicht vorbereitet. Noch einen Zoll, und er war frei. Jack preßte den Balken an seine Brust, ging dann vorsichtig in die Knie und legte ihn auf den Boden. Er wartete, bis der Schmerz in seinen Armen ein wenig nachgelassen hatte und horchte. Außer den gleichmäßigen Schlafgeräuschen der anderen war nichts zu hören.

Behutsam öffnete Jack die Tür einen Spaltbreit. Die eisernen Angeln quietschten leise, und ein kalter Luftzug drang herein. Jack schauderte, wickelte den Umhang fester um seinen Körper, zog die Tür ein Stückchen weiter auf und schlüpfte hinaus.

Die Wolkendecke brach auf, und der Mond rollte in den unruhigen Himmel. Ein eiskalter Wind fegte über das Klostergelände. Einen Augenblick lang war Jack versucht, in die stickige Wärme des Hauses zurückzukehren. Schwarzsilbrig im Mondlicht ragte die gewaltige Kirche vor ihm auf. Mit ihren dicken Mauern und den winzigen Fenstern wirkte sie auf ihn eher wie eine Burg. Sie ist richtig häßlich, dachte Jack.

Alles war still. Allenfalls außerhalb der Umfriedung, im Dorf, mochten noch ein paar Leute am Feuer sitzen und Bier trinken oder sich im Schein eines Binsenlichts mit Näharbeiten beschäftigen. Noch immer zögerte Jack und starrte die Kirche an, und die Kirche starrte vorwurfsvoll zurück, als wisse sie genau, was er im Schilde führte.

Mit einem Achselzucken befreite er sich von der unheimlichen Vision. Dann trat er den Weg über den weiten Vorplatz an.

Die Tür auf der Westseite des Gebäudes war verschlossen. Jack begab sich zur Nordflanke und sah zu den Fenstern auf. Auf den anderen Seiten waren einige Fenster mit großen, durchscheinenden Leintüchern bespannt, um die Kälte fernzuhalten, diese hier jedoch schienen frei zu sein. Er hätte ohne weiteres hindurchgepaßt, konnte sie aber nicht erreichen, weil sie zu hoch waren. Jack tastete das Mauerwerk ab und fand hier und da Spalten, aus denen sich der Mörtel gelöst hatte, aber keiner war groß genug, um seinen Zehen Halt zu bieten. Er brauchte eine Leiter oder etwas Ähnliches.

Er überlegte, ob sich aus Trümmern des eingestürzten Turms eine behelfsmäßige Treppe bauen ließ, doch die Steine, die ganz geblieben waren, erwiesen sich als zu schwer, und die geborstenen waren zu uneben. Er wurde das Gefühl nicht los, daß er am vergangenen Tag irgendwo etwas Geeignetes gesehen hatte, konnte sich aber, so sehr er sich auch bemühte, nicht genau erinnern. Dann fiel sein Blick auf den Stall jenseits des im Mondschein liegenden Gräberfelds, und er wußte Bescheid: ein Holzblock mit zwei oder drei Stufen, der es kleinwüchsigen Menschen ermöglichte, große Pferde zu besteigen. Ein Mönch hatte darauf gestanden und eine Mähne gestriegelt. Ein solcher Tritt war kein lohnendes Diebesgut; es bestand also durchaus die Möglichkeit, daß er über Nacht nicht weggeschlossen wurde.

Auf leisen Sohlen schlich Jack sich an die Stallungen heran. Aber die Pferde hörten ihn und wurden unruhig. Ein Tier schnaubte, ein anderes hustete. Jack blieb besorgt stehen. Ob die Pferdeknechte im Stall übernachteten? Er rührte sich nicht vom Fleck und horchte, doch keine menschliche Bewegung war zu vernehmen, und auch die Pferde beruhigten sich wieder.

Aber wo war der Tritt? Er konnte ihn nirgends sehen. Vielleicht stand er an der Stallwand, die im tiefschwarzen Mondschatten lag. Jack erreichte sie und ging sie ab. Wieder wurden die Pferde aufmerksam; sie spürten seine Nähe und waren unruhiger als zuvor. Eines von ihnen wieherte gar auf. Jack erstarrte. Eine Männerstimme rief: »Ruhig! So gebt doch Ruhe!« Im gleichen Augenblick, noch immer reglos wie eine Salzsäule, entdeckte Jack, was er suchte: Der Trittblock stand direkt vor seiner Nase – ein Schritt weiter, und er wäre darüber gestolpert. Er wartete, bis im Stall wieder Ruhe herrschte; dann bückte er sich und lud sich das Gestell auf die Schultern. Langsam tappte er zurück zur Kirche. Im Stall rührte sich nichts mehr.

Es war zum Verzweifeln: Selbst von der obersten Stufe des Trittblocks ließ sich das Fenster nicht erreichen! Er konnte nicht einmal hineinschauen. Er war zwar noch immer unschlüssig, ob er seinen Plan tatsächlich ausführen sollte, wollte aber auf keinen Fall vor den äußeren Umständen kapitulieren. Wäre ich doch so groß wie Alfred, dachte er.

Er wollte nichts unversucht lassen. Er sprang herunter, nahm einen kurzen Anlauf, schnellte sich mit dem Sprungbein von der obersten Stufe ab und erreichte ohne Mühe den Fenstersims. Mit einem Klimmzug zog er sich hoch. Doch als er durch die Öffnung kriechen wollte, erlebte er eine böse Überraschung: Ein Eisengitter verwehrte ihm den Einlaß. Wahrscheinlich war es schwarz gefärbt und deshalb bei den herrschenden Lichtverhältnissen von unten nicht zu erkennen. Jack kniete auf dem Sims und ertastete die Umrisse des Gitters. Es gab kein Durchkommen.

Enttäuscht sprang Jack wieder herunter, nahm den Trittblock und brachte ihn dorthin zurück, wo er ihn gefunden hatte. Die Pferde verhielten sich diesmal ruhig.

Linker Hand des Haupteingangs türmte sich der Trümmerhaufen. Vorsichtig kletterte Jack auf die am Rand liegenden Brocken und spähte ins Kircheninnere. Vielleicht bot sich hier ja ein Weg. Als der Mond hinter einer Wolke verschwand, hielt der Junge, vor Kälte zitternd, inne. Er fürchtete, mit seinem Gewicht die Steine ins Rutschen zu bringen. Es wäre lebensgefährlich – und selbst wenn er unverletzt bliebe, würde das Kollern und Rumpeln doch jedermann aus dem Schlaf reißen. Als der Mond wieder zum Vorschein kam, spähte Jack zum Gipfel des Trümmerhaufens hinauf und beschloß, den Versuch zu wagen. Das Herz schlug ihm bis zum Hals. Die meisten Steine rührten sich nicht, einige jedoch wackelten unter seinem Gewicht bedenklich hin und her. Am Tag hätte ihm eine solche Klettertour sogar Spaß gemacht, aber da wäre im Notfall gleich Hilfe zur Stelle gewesen, und außerdem hätte er ein reines Gewissen gehabt … Jetzt war er viel zu ängstlich und aufgeregt, und mit seiner Trittfestigkeit war es nicht weit her. Als er auf der glitschigen Oberfläche eines großen Steins ausrutschte und um ein Haar gestürzt wäre, blieb er stehen.

Er war jetzt so hoch, daß er auf das Dach des nördlichen Seitenschiffs herabschauen konnte. Vielleicht hatte es irgendwo ein Loch, oder vielleicht gab es einen Spalt zwischen dem Gipfel des Trümmerhaufens und dem Dach … Doch nichts von alledem: Das Dach ging nahtlos in die Turmruine über, nirgends zeigte sich eine Lücke, durch die man in die Kirche hätte einsteigen können. Jack war gleichermaßen enttäuscht wie erleichtert.

Ständig um sich blickend, um ja trittfeste Steine zu finden, kletterte er rückwärts wieder herunter. Je näher er dem festen Boden kam, desto besser fühlte er sich. Zum Schluß sprang er – und landete wohlbehalten im Gras.

Er kehrte zur Nordfassade zurück und setzte die Umrundung der Kirche fort. Er hatte in den vergangenen zwei Wochen mehrere Kirchen gesehen, die alle mehr oder weniger über den gleichen Grundriß verfügten. Das Schiff bildete jeweils den größten Teil und war immer nach Westen ausgerichtet. Nach Norden und Süden ragten zwei ›Arme‹ hervor, die Tom ›Querschiff‹ nannte. Das Ostende hieß ›Apsis‹ und war kürzer als das Langhaus. Das Besondere an Kingsbridge war lediglich, daß die Kathedrale zwei Türme besaß, auf jeder Seite des Eingangs einen.

Im nördlichen Querhaus befand sich eine Tür. Jack versuchte, sie zu öffnen, fand sie jedoch verschlossen. Er ging weiter, die Ostseite entlang: Dort gab es überhaupt keine Tür. Er blieb stehen und spähte über den grasbewachsenen Hof. Im südöstlichen Winkel des Klostergeländes standen noch zwei Gebäude, das Hospital und das Haus des Priors. Nichts rührte sich dort, auch sah man kein Licht. Auf der Südseite der Apsis setzte Jack seinen Streifzug fort, bis er das südliche Querhaus erreichte. An dessen äußerem Ende schloß, wie die Hand am Arm, jenes Gebäude an, das die Erwachsenen ›Kapitelhaus‹ nannten.

Jack schlug die schmale Gasse ein, die zwischen Querhaus und Kapitelhaus zum Kreuzgang führte, und erreichte alsbald eine quadratische Rasenfläche, die rundum von einem Bogengang umschlossen war. Gespenstisch schimmerte der blasse Stein der Bogen im Mondlicht, während undurchdringliche Schwärze den im Schatten liegenden Gang verhüllte. Jack wartete, bis sich seine Augen an die Düsternis gewöhnt hatten.

Die Gasse hatte ihn zum Ostrand des Kreuzgangs geführt. Linker Hand konnte er die Tür des Kapitelhauses erkennen. Dahinter, am Südende des Ostgangs, befand sich eine weitere Tür, von der Jack annahm, daß sie zum Dormitorium führte. Rechter Hand führte eine dritte Tür ins südliche Querhaus, aber auch sie war verschlossen, ebenso eine vierte, an der Jack im Nordgang sein Glück versuchte.

Schließlich kam er in der Südwestecke des Kreuzgangs an eine fünfte Tür. Sie führte zum Refektorium. Jack fragte sich, wieviel Lebensmittel wohl herbeigeschafft werden mußten, um so viele Mönche tagein, tagaus zu ernähren. Neben der Tür befand sich ein kleiner Brunnen mit einem Becken: Die Mönche wuschen sich vor dem Essen die Hände.

In der Mitte des Südgangs war seitwärts ein Bogen eingelassen. Jack betrat einen schmalen Korridor, der das Refektorium auf der rechten vom Dormitorium auf der linken Seite trennte. Er stellte sich die schlafenden Mönche vor, die gleich hinter der Mauer auf dem Boden lagen. Der Korridor endete unmittelbar vor der morastigen Uferböschung des von dort aus noch ungefähr hundert Schritt entfernten Flusses. Jack schaute auf das Wasser hinab, und mußte, ohne zu wissen warum, an die Geschichte von dem Ritter denken, dem man den Kopf abgeschlagen hatte und der dennoch weiterlebte. Und er hatte auf einmal die Vision, der Ritter ohne Kopf entsteige dem Fluß und komme über die Böschung auf ihn zu. In Wirklichkeit rührte sich nichts, doch die Angst war da und ließ sich nicht vertreiben. Rasch drehte er sich um und lief zum Kreuzgang zurück. Dort fühlte er sich sicherer.

Er zögerte, als er das vom Mondlicht übergossene Viereck wieder vor sich sah. Es muß doch irgendeine Möglichkeit geben, sich in ein so großes Gebäude einzuschleichen, dachte er, wußte aber nicht, an welcher Stelle er noch suchen sollte. In gewisser Hinsicht war er ganz froh darüber. Er hatte mit dem Gedanken gespielt, eine furchtbar gefährliche Tat zu begehen. Um so besser, wenn sich jetzt herausstellte, daß diese Tat undurchführbar war ... Andererseits: Die Vorstellung, bei Tagesanbruch das Kloster verlassen und weiterwandern zu müssen, war ihm ein Graus. Diese endlose Marschiererei, der Hunger, Toms Wut und Enttäuschung, Marthas Tränen ... Ein kleiner Funke aus dem Feuerstein, den er in einem Beutel an seinem Gürtel trug, konnte dies alles verhindern!

Eine Bewegung am Rande seines Blickfelds schreckte ihn auf. Sein Herz schlug schneller. Jack drehte den Kopf und erblickte eine geisterhafte Gestalt mit einer Kerze in der Hand, die geräuschlos über den Ostgang auf die Kirche zu glitt. Nur mit Mühe gelang es ihm, einen Schrei zu unterdrücken. Eine zweite Gestalt folgte der ersten nach. Jack trat zurück in den Schatten des Torbogens und biß sich, um nicht vor Angst zu weinen, in die geballte Faust. Ein unheimlicher, klagender Laut erfüllte auf einmal den Kreuzgang. Das nackte Entsetzen hatte Jack gepackt – doch dann dämmerte ihm langsam, was sich da vor seinen Augen abspielte: Es war die Prozession der Mönche vom Dormitorium zur Kirche. Die Zeit der Mitternachtsmesse war gekommen, und die Brüder sangen ein frommes Lied. Obwohl er nun wußte, worum es ging, dauerte es noch eine ganze Weile, bis er sich von seinem Schrecken erholt hatte. Er begann am ganzen Leib zu zittern und konnte nichts dagegen tun.

Der Mönch, der die Prozession anführte, sperrte mit einem riesengroßen, eisernen Schlüssel die Kirchentür auf. Einer nach dem anderen verschwanden die Brüder in der Kathedrale. Kein einziger von ihnen drehte sich um und sah in Jacks Richtung. Die meisten erweckten den Eindruck, als schliefen sie noch halb, und niemand dachte daran, die Tür wieder zu verschließen.

Als Jack wieder zu sich fand, merkte er sofort, daß ihm jetzt der Weg in die Kirche offenstand.

Aber seine Beine versagten ihm den Dienst.

Ich brauche doch nur einmal hineinzuschauen, sagte er sich, sonst nichts. Ich schaue hinein und sehe nach, ob es irgendwo einen Aufgang zum Dach gibt. Niemand zwingt mich, dort Feuer zu legen ... Ich schaue es mir nur an ...

Er holte tief Luft, verließ seinen Schlupfwinkel unter dem Torbogen und schlich quer über den Kreuzgang. Vor der offenstehenden Tür zögerte er und steckte zunächst einmal nur die Nase hinein. Der Altar und der Chor, wo die Mönche vor ihren Bänken standen, waren mit Kerzen erleuchtet, Inseln des Lichts in einem großen schwarzen Raum. Die Mauern und die Seitenschiffe lagen in tiefer Düsternis. Ein Mönch stand am Altar und verrichtete dort irgendwelche Handlungen, die Jack nicht begriff. Die Mitbrüder stimmten hin und wieder einen unverständlichen Sprechgesang an. Wie ist das möglich, dachte Jack, daß sie sich wegen so etwas mitten in der Nacht aus den warmen Betten scheuchen lassen?

Er schlüpfte durch die Tür.

Jetzt war er drinnen, und die Dunkelheit verbarg ihn. Nur: dort, wo er jetzt stand – gleich neben der Tür an der Mauer –, durfte er nicht stehenbleiben. Die Brüder hätten ihn beim Verlassen der Kirche gesehen. Er schlich weiter. Die flackernden Kerzen warfen unruhige Schatten. Hätte der Mönch am Altar den Kopf gehoben, so wäre Jack ihm vielleicht aufgefallen. Doch der Mann war allem Anschein nach von seiner Tätigkeit vollauf in Anspruch genommen. Die mächtigen Säulen boten Jack Deckung. Schnell huschte er von einer zur anderen, wobei er jedoch darauf achtete, unterschiedlich lange Pausen einzulegen. Seine Bewegungen sollten unregelmäßig und unberechenbar bleiben, den irrlichternden Schatten entsprechend. Je näher er der Vierung kam, desto heller wurde das Licht. Schon fürchtete er, der Mönch am Altar würde plötzlich aufblicken, ihn sehen, auf ihn zustürzen und ihn am Schlafittchen packen ...

Er erreichte die andere Seite und verschwand erleichtert in den tiefen Schatten, die das Mittelschiff verdunkelten. Er blieb kurz stehen und atmete auf. Dann zog er sich in den Schutz des Seitenschiffs zurück und schlich sich heimlich und immer wieder nach allen Seiten sichernd zum Westende vor. Im hintersten und dunkelsten Teil der Kirche setzte er sich auf die Fußplatte einer Säule, um dort auf das Ende der Messe zu warten.

Er zog den Umhang über das Kinn hoch und hauchte den Atem gegen seine Brust, um sich ein wenig zu wärmen. Wie sehr sich doch mein Leben in den letzten beiden Wochen verändert hat, dachte er. Es kommt mir vor, als seien seit dem Tag, an dem Mutter und ich unser beschauliches Leben im Wald aufgegeben haben, schon Jahre vergangen ... Der Junge wußte, daß es kein Zurück in die gewohnte Geborgenheit gab. Er hatte Hunger, Kälte, Gefahr und Verzweiflung kennengelernt und wußte, daß ihm die Angst davor von nun an ständiger Begleiter sein würde.

Er riskierte einen Blick hinter der Säule hervor. Über dem Altar, wo das Kerzenlicht am hellsten war, ließ sich gerade noch die hohe Holzdecke erkennen. Neue Kirchen, das wußte Jack, verfügten über steinerne Gewölbe. Aber die Kathedrale von Kingsbridge war uralt. Die Holzdecke würde brennen wie Zunder ...

Ich tu's sowieso nicht, dachte er.

Freilich ... Tom wäre heilfroh, wenn die Kirche abbrennen würde. Jack war sich nicht ganz sicher, ob er Tom überhaupt mochte – stark, hart und befehlsgewohnt, wie der nun einmal war, so ganz anders als Mutter, die eher die leiseren Töne bevorzugte. Brachte Jack Tom also nicht unbedingt Zuneigung entgegen, so doch auf jeden Fall Bewunderung, ja sogar eine gewisse Ehrfurcht. Die einzigen Männer, mit denen Jack es bislang in seinem Leben zu tun bekommen hatte, waren Outlaws gewesen – gefährliche, rohe Kerle, bei denen nur Gewalt und Verschlagenheit zählten und für die es nichts Schöneres gab, als andere Leute hinterrücks zu erstechen. Ein Mensch wie Tom – stolz und furchtlos, obwohl er keine Waffen trug – war Jack bisher noch nicht begegnet. Nie würde er vergessen, wie Tom William Hamleigh entgegengetreten war, als der ihm Mutter abkaufen wollte. *Lord William hatte sich gefürchtet* – das hatte Jack nachhaltig beeindruckt. Seiner Mutter hatte er damals gesagt, nicht im Traum habe er geglaubt, daß man so tapfer sein könne wie Tom, und Ellen hatte darauf geantwortet: »Deshalb mußten wir auch den Wald verlassen. Du brauchst einen Mann, zu dem du aufsehen kannst.«

Jack rätselte noch heute über den Sinn dieser Bemerkung. Eines stand jedenfalls fest: Er wollte Tom imponieren – irgendwie. Die Brandstiftung in der Kathedrale war dazu allerdings wenig geeignet, denn davon durfte – zumindest auf absehbare Zeit – niemand etwas erfahren. Später, in vielen Jahren, dachte Jack, wird dann vielleicht einmal der Tag kommen, an dem ich zu Tom gehe und sage: »Erinnerst du dich an jene Nacht, in der die Kathedrale von Kingsbridge abbrannte und der Prior dir den Auftrag gab, eine neue zu errichten? Und wie unser Elend dadurch ein Ende fand und wir fortan immer genug zu Essen und ein Dach über dem Kopf hatten? Weißt du eigentlich, wie der Brand damals entstanden ist …?« Da würde der Augen machen!

Aber ich trau' mich ja ohnehin nicht.

Der Gesang erstarb, und Füße scharrten über den Boden. Die Messe war vorüber. Die Mönche verließen ihre Bänke und strebten dem Ausgang zu. Jack rutschte um die Säule herum, so daß er nicht gesehen werden konnte.

Die Mönche löschten die Kerzen im Chor, ließen aber eine einzelne auf dem Altar brennen. Die Tür fiel krachend ins Schloß. Jack verharrte noch eine Weile an seinem Platz; vielleicht befand sich ja noch ein Nachzügler in der Kirche. Doch es blieb alles still. Endlich wagte er sich hinter seiner Säule hervor.

Es war ein merkwürdiges Gefühl, so ganz allein in diesem gewaltigen kalten und leeren Gebäude. Ich komme mir vor wie ein Mäuschen, dachte er. Ich verberge mich in dunklen Winkeln und komme erst hervor, wenn die großen Menschen fortgegangen sind. Er hatte mittlerweile den Altar erreicht und nahm die dicke, hell leuchtende Kerze an sich. Jetzt fühlte er sich ein wenig sicherer.

Mit dem Licht setzte er seine Erkundung der Kirche fort. An der Ecke der Vierung, also dort, wo Hauptschiff und südliches Querhaus aneinandergrenzten, entdeckte er eine Tür in der Wand, die nur mit einer einfachen Klinke verschlossen war. Er drückte die Klinke herunter, und die Tür öffnete sich.

Seine Kerze erhellte eine Wendeltreppe, die so schmal war, daß ein dicker Mann sie nie hätte besteigen können. Auch war die Decke so niedrig, daß ein Mann von der Größe Toms nur tief geduckt hinaufgekommen wäre. Jack stieg die Treppe empor.

Die Treppe führte zu einer schmalen Galerie, die zum Schiff hin durch aneinandergereihte kleine Bögen abgeschlossen wurde. Die schräge Decke verband die Oberseite der Bögen mit dem Fußboden auf der gegenüberliegenden Seite.

Der Fußboden selbst war nicht flach, sondern beidseitig abwärts gewölbt. Jack brauchte eine Weile, bis er sich orientiert hatte. Er befand sich direkt über dem südlichen Seitenschiff. Das Tunnelgewölbe des Seitenschiffs bildete den Boden unter Jacks Füßen, das auch von außen sichtbare Schrägdach die Decke über seinem Kopf. Da das Seitenschiff erheblich niedriger war als das Hauptschiff, war der Dachstuhl noch ein gutes Stück entfernt.

Jack wandte sich nach Westen und erkundete die Galerie. Nun, da die Mönche fort waren und die Gefahr der Entdeckung gebannt, fand er seinen Ausflug richtig spannend. Ihm war, als wäre er auf einen Baum geklettert und hätte hoch oben im Geäst eine von unten nicht einsehbare Verbindung zwischen allen Wipfeln des Waldes entdeckt – einen Pfad durch eine Welt in luftiger Höhe, die dem normalen Sterblichen verborgen bleibt.

Am Ende der Galerie stand er wieder vor einer kleinen Tür. Er ging hindurch und gelangte ins Innere des erhalten gebliebenen Südwestturms. Der Raum, in dem er sich nun befand, war gewiß nicht für die Öffentlichkeit bestimmt. Er war unverputzt und wirkte unfertig. Anstelle eines geschlossenen Fußbodens gab es hier nur Balken, zwischen denen große Lücken klafften. Allerdings war auf der Innenseite der Mauer eine schmale Holztreppe ohne Geländer angebracht. Sie führte aufwärts.

Ungefähr auf halbem Weg zur Turmspitze bemerkte Jack eine schmale, gewölbte Öffnung gleich neben der Treppe in der Mauer. Er zwängte seinen Oberkörper hindurch und hielt die Kerze hoch. Er war im Dachstuhl; unter ihm befand sich die Holzdecke und über ihm das Bleidach.

Im ersten Augenblick konnte er sich aus dem Gewirr der Balken und Streben kein rechtes Bild machen. Dann jedoch erkannte er rasch die Konstruktion: Riesige Eichenbalken, von denen jeder gut einen Fuß breit und zwei Fuß hoch war, überspannten das Hauptschiff in Querrichtung von Nord nach Süd. Jeder Balken bildete mit je zwei mächtigen Streben, die oben einander berührten, ein Dreieck. Soweit das Licht der Kerze reichte, sah Jack daher eine gleichmäßige Folge

271

von Dreiecken vor sich. An der Unterseite der Querbalken war die bemalte Holzdecke des Mittelschiffs befestigt.

Am Rand des Dachstuhls, im Winkel zwischen Querbalken und Streben, befand sich eine Laufplanke, die Jack erreichte, nachdem er sich vollends durch die Maueröffnung gezwängt hatte. Klein, wie er war, konnte er gerade noch aufrecht stehen. Schon nach ein paar Schritten war ihm klar, daß ein Feuer hier reichlich Nahrung finden würde: Rundherum gab es trockenes Holz in Hülle und Fülle. Er hob die Nase, prüfte den merkwürdigen Geruch, der in der Luft hing, und kam zu dem Schluß, daß es sich um Pech handeln mußte. Das Dachgebälk war geteert. Es würde brennen wie Zunder.

Ein unerwartetes Rascheln auf dem Boden schreckte ihn auf. Er mußte an den kopflosen Ritter im Fluß und die gespenstische Prozession im Kreuzgang denken. Dann sagte er sich, wahrscheinlich sind es Mäuse, und beruhigte sich. Erst, als er genauer hinsah, merkte er, daß das Geräusch von Vögeln stammte, die unter den Balken nisteten.

Der Dachstuhl entsprach in seinem Grundriß dem gemauerten Bau, den er bedeckte. In Höhe der Vierung zweigten dementsprechend die Dächer der Querhäuser ab. An der Ecke blieb Jack stehen. Wenn ihn sein Ortssinn nicht trog, mußte er sich jetzt direkt oberhalb der kleinen Wendeltreppe befinden, über die er die Galerie erreicht hatte. Wäre es ihm mit dem Feuer ernst gewesen, so war er nun an der richtigen Stelle, denn die Flammen konnten sich von hier aus in alle vier Himmelsrichtungen ausbreiten – sowohl über das Hauptschiff und die Apsis sowie in beide Querhäuser hinein.

Die Tragbalken des Dachs bestanden aus Eichenkernholz, und es war trotz ihres Teeranstrichs keineswegs sicher, daß sie sich mit einer einfachen Kerzenflamme entzünden ließen. Aber unter den Balken lag allerhand Unrat herum – Hobelspäne und Reste von alten Säcken und Tauen, auch ein altes, verlassenes Nest. Das ideale Material ... Er brauchte es nur zu einem kleinen Haufen zusammenzutragen.

Seine Kerze war schon ziemlich weit heruntergebrannt.

Es schien alles so einfach ... Den Unrat zusammentragen – die Flamme dranhalten – abhauen. Wie ein Geist über den Klosterhof gehuscht, auf leisen Sohlen ins Gästehaus geschlüpft, die Tür verriegeln, ins Stroh fallen und abwarten, bis Alarm geschlagen wurde ...

Aber wenn jemand mich sieht ...

Wenn mich *jetzt* jemand erwischt, dachte Jack, kann ich mich immer noch herausreden. Ich wollte mir nur einmal die Kathedrale bei Nacht ansehen. Mehr als eine Tracht Prügel hätte ich nicht zu befürchten. Aber wenn sie mich dabei ertappen, wie ich gerade die Kirche in Brand stecke, dann ist es mit Prügeln nicht getan. Jack dachte an den Zuckerdieb mit dem blutenden Hintern. Er erinnerte sich auch an verschiedene grausame Strafen, denen die Outlaws im Wald unterworfen gewesen waren: Faramond Openmouth hatte man die Lippen abgeschnitten und Jack Flathat eine Hand abgehackt. Alan Catface war in den Stock gelegt und mit Steinen beworfen worden, so daß er danach nie wieder richtig sprechen konnte. Schlimmer noch waren Berichte über Menschen, die die ihnen zugedachten Strafen nicht überlebt hatten: Einen Mörder hatte man gefesselt in ein Faß gesteckt, dessen Innenseite rundum mit Eisendornen versehen war, und dann hatte man das Faß einen Abhang herunterrollen lassen ... Ein Pferdedieb war bei lebendigem Leib verbrannt, eine diebische Hure gepfählt worden ... Was werden sie mit einem Jungen anstellen, der eine Kathedrale in Schutt und Asche gelegt hat?

Nachdenklich begann er, den leicht entzündbaren Unrat auf der Laufplanke zusammenzutragen, direkt unter einer der mächtigen Streben.

Als der Haufen ungefähr fußhoch war, setzte Jack sich hin und starrte ihn an.

Seine Kerze flackerte. In wenigen Augenblicken würde sie ausgehen, und die Chance war vertan.

Kurz entschlossen hielt er die Kerzenflamme an einen Fetzen altes Sackleinen, der sogleich Feuer fing. Die Flamme griff auf ein paar alte Hobelspäne über, erfaßte ein ausgetrocknetes Vogelnest und flackerte lustig auf.

Ich kann es immer noch austreten, dachte Jack.

Das Anfeuermaterial verbrannte ein wenig zu schnell: Es stand zu erwarten, daß es aufgezehrt war, bevor das Dachgebälk Feuer fing. Eilig sammelte Jack noch Nachschub und warf es in den Brandherd. Die Flammen stiegen höher. Ich kann es immer noch austreten, dachte Jack noch einmal. Das Pech, mit dem der Balken verschmiert war, begann zu qualmen. Der Unrat war schon fast verbrannt. Ich könnte es einfach wieder ausgehen lassen, dachte Jack, doch dann bemerkte er, daß die Laufplanke Feuer gefangen hatte. Mit meinem Umhang kann ich die Flammen wahrscheinlich noch ersticken ... Doch statt dessen warf er noch ein paar Hände voll Späne hinein und sah tatenlos zu, wie die Flammen höher und höher stiegen.

Rauch erfüllte die Luft, und es wurde merklich wärmer, ja heiß in dem kleinen Winkel zwischen den Dachsparren, obwohl die eiskalte

Nacht nur zollweit entfernt war. Einige kleinere Holzleisten, auf die die bleiernen Dachplatten genagelt waren, hatten inzwischen Feuer gefangen, und dann, endlich, flackerte auch an einem schweren Tragbalken ein erstes kleines Flämmchen auf.

Die Kathedrale brannte.

Es war geschehen und ließ sich nicht mehr zurücknehmen.

Jack fürchtete sich. Er hatte es plötzlich sehr eilig, wollte hinaus, zurück ins Gästehaus, seinen Umhang um sich ziehen, sich ins Stroh verkriechen, die Augen ganz fest zumachen und den gleichmäßigen Atemzügen der anderen lauschen ...

Er eilte über die Laufplanke zurück zu der kleinen Öffnung in der Mauer und drehte sich um. Das Feuer breitete sich überraschend schnell aus, teils wohl wegen der gepechten Balken, aber auch über die Laufplanke. Die kleineren Verstrebungen brannten schon alle lichterloh.

Jack kletterte in den Turm, lief die Treppe hinunter, eilte über die Galerie zur Wendeltreppe. Unten angekommen, rannte er auf schnellstem Wege zur Tür, durch die er hereingekommen war.

Sie war verschlossen.

Er schimpfte sich einen Dummkopf. Die Mönche hatten die Tür beim Betreten der Kathedrale auf- und beim Verlassen natürlich wieder zugesperrt.

Wie Galle stieg die Angst in ihm auf. Er hatte die Kirche angezündet und saß nun in ihr fest.

Es gelang ihm, die panische Furcht, die ihn ergriff, niederzukämpfen und seine Lage ruhig zu überdenken. Er hatte von außen an sämtlichen Türen gerüttelt und dabei festgestellt, daß alle verschlossen waren. Es war jedoch denkbar, daß die eine oder andere nicht durch ein Schloß, sondern durch einen von innen zu öffnenden Riegel versperrt war.

Er rannte durch die Vierung ins nördliche Querhaus und überprüfte das Nordportal. Es war verschlossen. Er rannte zum Haupteingang auf der Westseite – alle drei der Öffentlichkeit zugänglichen Tore waren verschlossen. Zuletzt probierte er es an der kleinen Tür, die das südliche Seitenschiff mit dem Kreuzgang verband. Auch sie war verschlossen.

Am liebsten hätte er einfach losgeheult. Er spähte zur Decke hinauf. Stimmte es, daß unweit des Übergangs zum südlichen Querhaus aus einer Ritze Rauch hervorquoll? Oder spielte ihm seine Phantasie einen Streich?

Was soll ich tun? dachte er.

Vielleicht kommen die Mönche, sobald sie das Feuer bemerkt haben, in solcher Hast herbeigestürmt, um zu löschen, was noch zu löschen ist, daß sie gar nicht merken, wie ein kleiner Junge zur Tür hinausschlüpft? Oder aber sie entdecken mich sofort, packen mich und überschütten mich mit Vorwürfen ... Aber vielleicht schlafen sie ja auch so tief, daß sie erst aufwachen, wenn die Kathedrale eingestürzt ist und mich unter einem riesigen Trümmerhaufen begraben hat ...

Die Augen wurden ihm feucht, und Jack wünschte, den Unrathaufen im Dachstuhl nie angezündet zu haben.

Verzweifelt blickte er um sich. Ob man mich hören wird, wenn ich mich an ein Fenster stelle und laut schreie?

Ein Rumpeln, gefolgt von einem Krachen, schreckte ihn auf. Als er nach oben blickte, sah er, daß ein großer Balken auf die Holzdecke gefallen war und diese durchbohrt hatte. Das Loch bildete einen roten Fleck vor einem schwarzen Hintergrund. Kurz darauf krachte es erneut, und ein riesiger Balken durchbrach die Decke, drehte sich im Fallen um sich selbst und stürzte mit solcher Wucht zu Boden, daß die gewaltigen Säulen des Kirchenschiffs erzitterten. Ein Regen aus Funken und glühender Asche folgte nach. Jack lauschte; er wartete auf Rufe oder Hilfeschreie, auf das schrille Rasseln einer Glocke, doch nichts geschah. Niemand hatte etwas gehört – und wenn schon der Lärm des herabstürzenden Balken die Mönche nicht aufweckte, so würde sein Schreien erst recht vergeblich sein.

Ich sterbe, ich muß sterben ... Er war wie von Sinnen. Ich verbrenne oder werde von den Trümmern zermalmt ... Es sei denn, ich finde doch noch einen Weg hinaus!

Der eingestürzte Turm ... Jack hatte zwar den Steinhaufen von außen überprüft und keinen Eingang gefunden, aber da er sich aus Angst vor einem Geröllsturz nicht allzuweit vorgewagt hatte, war es immerhin möglich, daß sich von innen noch etwas finden ließ – und vielleicht gelang es ihm, sich mit dem Mut der Verzweiflung doch noch irgendwo hindurchzuquetschen, wo er zuvor nicht einmal einen Spalt gesehen hatte.

Er rannte hinüber auf die Westseite. Der Feuerschein aus dem Loch in der Decke sowie die Flammen, die an dem am Boden liegenden Balken leckten, überstrahlten das Mondlicht, und die Arkade des Mittelschiffs war nun mit Gold statt mit Silber übergossen. Der Trümmerhaufen, der vom Nordwestturm übriggeblieben war, sah aus wie eine solide Mauer. Da führte kein Weg hindurch. »Mama!« brüllte

Jack aus vollem Hals, obwohl er genau wußte, daß Ellen ihn nicht hören konnte.

Einmal mehr kämpfte er die Panik nieder. Da war doch noch etwas gewesen im Zusammenhang mit dem eingestürzten Turm ... er konnte sich bloß nicht genau erinnern. In den anderen Turm war er über die Galerie des südlichen Seitenschiffs gelangt. Dementsprechend mußte der eingefallene Turm ursprünglich über die nördliche Galerie erreichbar gewesen sein. Auf jeden Fall lohnte es sich, einmal nachzusehen, ob sich dort nicht ein von unten unsichtbares Schlupfloch verbarg.

Um nicht von fallendem Gebälk erschlagen zu werden, rannte Jack im Schutz des Seitenschiffs zurück zur Vierung. Irgendwo hier auf der Nordseite mußte doch auch eine kleine Tür sein, die zu einer Wendeltreppe führte. Er sah sich um. Vor der Ecke, an der das nördliche Querhaus abzweigte, war keine Tür. Und dahinter auch keine. Wie konnte ein Mensch so viel Unglück auf einmal haben? Es war nicht zu fassen: Nirgends fand sich ein Aufstieg zur Galerie, obwohl nach allem menschlichen Ermessen irgendwo einer sein *mußte*.

Er zermarterte sich den Kopf. Es gab einen Zugang zum Nordwestturm, man mußte ihn bloß finden. Ich muß zurück in den Dachstuhl, dachte er. Dort oben muß auf jeden Fall ein Übergang sein, eine kleine Öffnung, wie auf der anderen Seite.

Angstvoll starrte er zur Decke hinauf. Dort oben herrschte jetzt ein Inferno. Aber Jack sah keinen anderen Ausweg mehr.

Wegen der herabstürzenden Balken war schon die Überquerung des Mittelschiffs lebensgefährlich. Noch einmal warf er einen Blick nach oben. Im Augenblick sah es nicht so aus, als stünde der nächste Trümmersturz unmittelbar bevor. Jack holte tief Luft, überquerte die Gefahrenzone, so schnell er konnte, und kam unbeschadet auf der anderen Seite an.

Schon hatte er die kleine Tür erreicht. Er riß sie auf und stürmte die Wendeltreppe empor. In der Galerie war die Wärme, die vom brennenden Dachstuhl ausstrahlte, bereits fühlbar. Über die Treppe im Südwestturm gelangte er zu der kleinen bogenförmigen Öffnung. Mit eingezogenem Kopf kroch er hindurch. Hitze und Rauch erfüllten den Dachstuhl. Die höheren Dachsparren standen alle in Flammen, und auch einige der großen Balken hatten Feuer gefangen. Ein beißender Geruch nach brennendem Pech hing in der Luft. Jack mußte husten. Er zögerte nur einen Augenblick, dann betrat er einen der Querbalken, die das Mittelschiff überspannten, und ging los. Binnen kürzester Zeit war er schweißüberströmt, und seine Augen tränten so sehr, daß er kaum noch etwas sehen konnte. Als ihn ein unerwartet heftiger Hustenanfall überfiel, geriet er ins Stolpern. Sein rechter Fuß rutschte ab, stieß auf den Boden – und brach, ohne auf starken Widerstand zu stoßen, durch die morsche Holzdecke. Namenloses Entsetzen ergriff den Jungen. Schon sah er sich zappelnd und zeternd in die Tiefe stürzen, Kapriolen schlagend wie zuvor der brennende Balken, dessen Fall er beobachtet hatte. Er schrie auf, taumelte mit ausgestreckten Armen vorwärts … Doch das Holz hielt.

Er war vor Schreck wie gelähmt. Die Hände und das linke Knie trugen sein Gewicht, der rechte Fuß steckte noch im Loch. Erst die schier unerträgliche Hitze ließ Jack wieder zu sich kommen. Vorsichtig befreite er seinen Fuß und kroch auf allen vieren weiter.

Er hatte die andere Seite fast erreicht, als mehrere schwere Balken zusammenbrachen und hinabstürzten. Das ganze Gebäude schien zu schwanken, und der Balken unter Jack zitterte wie eine Bogensehne. Der Junge hielt inne und klammerte sich fest. Das Beben legte sich. Jack kletterte weiter und erreichte kurz darauf die Laufplanke auf der Nordseite.

Wenn ihn seine Vermutung trog und es keinen Durchgang zum ehemaligen Nordwestturm gab, mußte er auf dem gleichen Weg zurück, auf dem er gekommen war.

Er richtete sich auf. Kalte Nachtluft wehte ihn an. Irgendwo mußte ein Spalt sein. Aber war er groß genug?

Drei Schritte weiter in westlicher Richtung blieb Jack stehen. Noch einen Schritt, und er wäre ins Nichts gestürzt.

Vor ihm gähnte ein großes Loch und gab den Blick auf die vom Mondlicht beschienene Turmruine frei. Jack atmete tief durch. Das Inferno lag hinter ihm.

Aber er befand sich sehr hoch oben. Auf Dachhöhe. Tief unten – zum Springen viel zu weit – war der Gipfel des Trümmerhaufens zu erkennen. Dem Feuer bin ich vorerst entkommen, dachte er – doch wie komme ich da runter, ohne mir den Hals zu brechen? Hinter dem Jungen wogte ein Flammenmeer, und aus der Maueröffnung, in der er stand, wölkte dichter Rauch.

Auch der eingefallene Turm war vormals mit einer Holztreppe versehen gewesen, die jedoch beim Einsturz zum größten Teil mit heruntergerissen worden war. Und jene Stellen, wo die Stufen in die Mauer eingelassen und mit Mörtel befestigt waren, maßen nicht mehr als ein oder zwei Zoll. Jack fragte sich, ob er es schaffen würde; gefährlich war es auf jeden Fall. Ein beißender Geruch stieg ihm in die Nase: Sein Umhang wurde langsam heiß und würde bald Feuer fangen. Er hatte keine andere Wahl.

Er setzte sich hin und tastete mit dem Fuß nach dem ersten Stumpf. Dann drehte er sich um, hielt sich mit beiden Händen fest und belastete die ungewöhnliche Stufe. Sie hielt. Auch die nächste war stabil. Die dritte kam ihm dagegen ziemlich locker vor. Mit beiden Händen klammerte er sich an die vorige und verstärkte langsam den Druck. Er mußte damit rechnen, im nächsten Augenblick ohne Fußhalt an der Mauer zu baumeln. Aber es ging noch einmal gut, und mit jedem Schritt kam er der Spitze des Trümmerhaufens näher.

Weiter unten wurden die abgebrochenen Reste der Stufen immer kleiner, als ob die Wucht des Einsturzes hier noch stärker gewesen wäre. Jack erreichte einen Stumpf, der, wie er durch den Filzstiefel hindurch fühlte, gerade so breit war wie sein großer Zeh. Als er sein Gewicht darauf verlagerte, rutschte sein Fuß ab. Der andere Fuß befand sich noch auf einer breiteren Stufe, die der plötzlichen Belastung durch Jacks volles Gewicht nicht gewachsen war und brach. Vergeblich versuchte der Junge, mit den Händen irgendwo Halt zu finden – die Stümpfe waren alle viel zu klein. Er fiel in die Tiefe.

Er landete hart auf Händen und Knien, genau auf dem Gipfel des Trümmerhaufens. Entsetzt, wie er war, glaubte er, dies wäre nun das Ende und er sei tot. Erst nach einer Weile dämmerte ihm, daß er unwahrscheinliches Glück gehabt hatte. Seine Hände schmerzten, und er hatte sich übel die Knie aufgeschlagen – doch ansonsten hatte er den Sturz unbeschadet überstanden.

Er rappelte sich auf und kletterte vom Trümmerhaufen hinunter; die letzten Blöcke übersprang er. Er war noch einmal davongekommen.

Ich bin in Sicherheit, dachte er, und die Knie wurden ihm schwach. Am liebsten hätte er blindlings drauflos geheult. Ich habe es geschafft! Stolz mischte sich in das Gefühl der grenzenlosen Erleichterung. Was für ein Abenteuer!

Doch das Abenteuer war noch nicht vorüber. Hier draußen hing nur ein schwacher Brandgeruch in der Luft, und das ohrenbetäubende Brausen der Flammen im Dachstuhl klang wie das ferne Rauschen des Windes. Daß die Kirche in Flammen stand, bewies lediglich der rötliche Feuerschein hinter den Fenstern. Dennoch war es nur noch eine Frage der Zeit, bis die ersten Klosterbewohner aus dem Schlaf schreckten. Die von den stürzenden Balken ausgelösten Erschütterungen mußten über kurz oder lang jemanden aus dem Schlaf schrecken. Jeden Augenblick konnte ein verschlafener Mönch, der nicht wußte, ob sich tatsächlich ein Erdbeben ereignet oder ob er es nur geträumt hatte, aus dem Dormitorium gestolpert kommen ... Jack hatte die Kathedrale angezündet – ein verabscheuungswürdiges Verbrechen in den Augen eines Mönchs. Er mußte so schnell wie möglich verschwinden.

Er lief über den Rasen zum Gästehaus. Alles war still und ruhig. Keuchend blieb er vor der Tür stehen. Wenn ich so schnaufe, wachen sie alle gleich auf, dachte er. Er versuchte, sich wieder zu beruhigen, doch dadurch wurde die Keucherei nur noch schlimmer. Ihm blieb nichts anderes übrig, als abzuwarten.

Eine Glocke begann zu läuten und schallte durch die stille Nacht. Es war ein drängendes, unnachgiebiges Geläute, ein Hilferuf, der keinen Fehlschluß mehr zuließ. Jack erstarrte. Wenn ich jetzt reingehe, wissen sie sofort Bescheid. Aber wenn ich nicht reingehe ...

Die Tür des Gästehauses öffnete sich, und heraus trat Martha. Entsetzt starrte Jack sie an.

»Wo warst du denn?« fragte sie mit sanfter Stimme. »Du riechst nach Rauch.«

Jack suchte eine glaubhafte Ausrede. »Ich bin gerade erst rausgekommen«, sagte er in seiner Verzweiflung. »Ich habe die Glocke läuten hören.«

»Lügner«, erwiderte Martha. »Du bist schon ewig lang fort, das weiß ich genau. Ich war nämlich wach.«

Jack sah ein, daß er ihr nichts vormachen konnte. »War sonst noch jemand wach?« fragte er angstvoll.

»Nein, nur ich.«

»Sag keinem, daß ich fort war, Martha. Bitte!«

Sie spürte die Furcht in seinen Worten und sagte in beruhigendem Ton: »Ja, Jack, ich schweige. Hab keine Angst!«

»Danke!«

In diesem Augenblick erschien Tom neben ihnen. Er kratzte sich am Kopf. »Was geht hier vor?« fragte er verschlafen und hob die Nase. »Hier riecht's irgendwie brenzlig.«

Jack deutete auf die Kathedrale; sein Arm zitterte. »Ich glaube ...«, begann er und mußte schlucken. Es klappt, dachte er insgeheim. Tom denkt sicher, daß ich gerade erst aufgestanden bin, kurz vor Martha. Als er weitersprach, klang seine Stimme zuversichtlicher. »Die Kirche, schau! Ich glaube, sie brennt.«

Philip hatte sich noch nicht ans Alleinschlafen gewöhnt. Er vermißte die stickige Dormitoriumsluft, das Geraschel und Geschnarche der schlafenden Mitbrüder, auch die Unruhe, die entstand, wenn ein älterer Mönch aufstand und zur Latrine schlurfte (meistens gefolgt von anderen Brüdern im fortgeschrittenen Alter – eine regelmäßig wiederkehrende Prozession, über die sich die jüngeren Brüder immer sehr amüsierten). Am Abend störte ihn das Alleinsein noch nicht; da war er immer todmüde. Nachts jedoch, wenn ihn die Frühmesse geweckt hatte, fiel es ihm seit einiger Zeit schwer, wieder einzuschlafen. Anstatt wieder ins große weiche Bett zurückzukehren (es war ihm ein wenig peinlich, wie schnell er sich *daran* gewöhnt hatte), blieb er oft wach. Er machte sich ein Feuer, vertiefte sich bei Kerzenschein in seine Lektüre, kniete zum Beten nieder oder saß ganz einfach da und dachte nach.

Es gab eine Menge, worüber er nachdenken mußte. Die finanzielle Lage der Priorei war noch viel schlimmer, als er befürchtet hatte. Das Hauptproblem war, daß das Kloster in seiner Gesamtheit zu niedrige Einkünfte erwirtschaftete. Es fehlte überall an Bargeld. Zwar verfügte man über große Ländereien, doch waren die meisten Höfe langfristig zu niedrigem Zins verpachtet, und manche von ihnen lieferten den Pachtzins in Naturalien ab – so und so viele Sack Mehl, so und so viele Faß Äpfel, so und so viele Fuhren Rüben. Die nicht verpachteten Höfe wurden von Mönchen geführt, die jedoch nicht imstande zu sein schienen, gut verkäufliche Überschüsse zu erwirtschaften. Die zweite Einnahmequelle der Priorei waren die ihr gehörenden Kirchen, die zur Ablieferung des Zehnten verpflichtet waren. Unglücklicherweise unterstanden sie dem Sakristan. Wieviel genau er einnahm und was er mit dem Geld machte, ließ sich nicht so ohne weiteres feststellen. Aus dem miserablen baulichen Zustand der Kathedrale konnte man nur schließen, daß die Einkünfte nicht sehr hoch waren – oder aber der Sakristan ging mit dem Geld schlecht um, was um so verblüffender war, als er über die Jahre eine eindrucksvolle Kollektion juwelengeschmückter Gefäße und anderer Kirchengeräte zusammengetragen hatte.

Philip wußte, daß er sich die Zeit nehmen mußte, den weit verstreuten Klosterbesitz persönlich in Augenschein zu nehmen; erst dann würde er genauer Bescheid wissen. Fest stand nur soviel: Um die täglich anfallenden Kosten bestreiten zu können, hatte der alte Prior über Jahre hinaus bei Geldverleihern in Winchester und London große Summen geborgt. Dementsprechend hoch war die Verschuldung. Die Erkenntnis hatte Philip mit tiefer Niedergeschlagenheit erfüllt.

Er dachte viel darüber nach, suchte Trost im Gebet, und nach einer Weile begann sich eine Lösung abzuzeichnen. Er entwickelte einen Dreistufenplan. Zunächst wollte er die Finanzverwaltung des Klosters an sich ziehen. Bisher war es so, daß jeder Klosteroffiziale für bestimmte Bereiche zuständig war und mit den Einkünften aus seinem Bereich auch die fälligen Ausgaben bestritt. Der Cellerar, der Sakristan, der Gästemeister, der Novizenmeister und der Krankenmeister – alle hatten sie ihre ›eigenen‹ Bauernhöfe und Kirchen. Natürlich würde keiner von ihnen je zugeben, daß er zuviel Geld hätte. Wer Überschüsse erwirtschaftete, gab das Ersparte aus Furcht, man könne es ihm fortnehmen, schnell wieder aus. Philip beschloß, das neue Amt eines Kämmerers einzuführen, dessen Aufgabe es sein sollte, sämtliche Einkünfte des Klosters zu verwalten und den Offizialen nur das Geld auszubezahlen, das sie tatsächlich brauchten.

Der Kämmerer mußte natürlich einer von Philips Vertrauten sein. Zuerst dachte er, Cuthbert Whitehead, den Kellermeister, mit dem Amt zu betrauen, doch dann fiel ihm Cuthberts Abneigung gegen schriftliche Aufzeichnungen ein. Das war schlecht. Über alle Einkünfte und Ausgaben sollte forthin genau Buch geführt werden. So fiel Philips Wahl auf Bruder Milius, den jungen Küchenmeister. Eines stand fest: Gleichgültig, wer das neue Amt nun erhielt – allein seine Einführung würde den Offizialen des Klosters übel aufstoßen. Philip fürchtete ihren Widerstand jedoch wenig: Er war jetzt Prior und hatte das Sagen – und die Mehrzahl der Mönche wußte oder ahnte zumindest, wie es um das Kloster bestellt war. Sie würden seine Reformen gutheißen.

Sobald Philip die Finanzen des Klosters unter Kontrolle hatte, wollte er den zweiten Teil seines Dreistufenplans in die Tat umsetzen.

Die Pacht für alle entfernt gelegenen Klostergüter sollte fürderhin in Bargeld bezahlt werden. Damit entfielen zunächst einmal die umständlichen Warentransporte. Es gab zum Beispiel ein Gut in Yorkshire, dessen ›Pacht‹ sich auf zwölf Lämmer im Jahr belief. Treu und brav lieferte der Pächter also Jahr für Jahr zwölf Lämmer nach Kingsbridge, obwohl die Transportkosten den Wert der Tiere überstiegen und die Hälfte von ihnen unterwegs krepierte. In Zukunft sollte das Kloster ausschließlich von Höfen aus der näheren Umgebung versorgt werden.

Des weiteren beabsichtigte Philip, das herkömmliche Bewirtschaftungssystem der Klostergüter zu ändern. Jeder Hof produzierte zur

Zeit noch von allem etwas – ein wenig Getreide, ein wenig Fleisch, ein wenig Milch und so weiter. Seit Jahren schon hielt Philip diese Methode für unwirtschaftlich. Der Ertrag der Höfe reichte immer gerade für den Eigenbedarf – oder, anders ausgedrückt: Jeder Hof schaffte es, immer gerade soviel zu verbrauchen, wie er erwirtschaftete. Philip wollte erreichen, daß die Höfe sich auf bestimmte Erzeugnisse spezialisierten. So sollte sich der Getreideanbau auf eine Reihe von Dörfern in Somerset konzentrieren, wo die Priorei auch einige Mühlen besaß. In den üppig begrünten Hügeln von Wiltshire sollte die Fleisch- und Milchwirtschaft erblühen, und in der Zelle St.-John-in-the-Forest auch weiterhin die Ziegenzucht und die Herstellung von Ziegenkäse betrieben werden.

Hauptpunkt der landwirtschaftlichen Reformen war jedoch die Umwandlung aller kleineren und mittleren Höfe mit armen, unergiebigen Böden in Schafzuchten.

Philip hatte seine Jugend in einem Kloster verbracht, zu dem eine Schafzucht gehörte (in jenem Teil von Wales lebten alle Bauern von der Schafzucht). Langsam, aber stetig war der Wollpreis gestiegen, Jahr für Jahr, seit Philip sich erinnern konnte, und bis in die Gegenwart hinein. Mit Schafen ließ sich die dauernde Geldknappheit des Klosters in absehbarer Zeit beheben.

Die dritte Stufe des Plans sah den Abriß der Kathedrale und die Errichtung einer neuen vor.

Die alte Kirche war ebenso häßlich wie unpraktisch, und der Umstand, daß der Nordwestturm eingestürzt war, deutete darauf hin, daß das ganze Gebäude morsch und baufällig war. Moderne Kirchen waren höher, länger und – vor allem – heller. Sie boten Platz für alles, was Pilger, die von weither kamen, sehen wollten – für bedeutende Grabmäler und Heiligenreliquien. Die Kathedralen der neuen Zeit waren mit zusätzlichen kleineren Altären ausgestattet und besaßen Seitenkapellen, die bestimmten Heiligen geweiht waren. Eine unter Berücksichtigung neuester Erkenntnisse errichtete Kathedrale würde den immer vielfältigeren Anforderungen moderner Gottesdienste gerecht werden und weit mehr Gläubige und Pilger nach Kingsbridge führen, als dies bisher der Fall war. Langfristig würde sie auf diese Weise sogar die Baukosten wieder einspielen. Zuerst, dachte Philip, saniere ich die Klosterfinanzen – und dann erbaue ich als Symbol für die Wiedergeburt des Klosters eine neue Kathedrale.

Sie soll die Krönung meines Lebenswerks sein.

Zehn Jahre werde ich brauchen, bevor ich genug Geld habe, um mit dem Bau beginnen zu können, dachte er und erschrak. Da bin ich dann ja schon fast vierzig! Die Vorstellung war nicht sehr erbauend. Er tröstete sich mit dem Gedanken, daß er vielleicht schon in einem Jahr soweit sein würde, ein paar unerläßliche Renovierungsarbeiten an der alten Kirche durchführen zu lassen. Zum übernächsten Pfingstfest würde sie dann immerhin schon ganz manierlich aussehen.

Sein Plan war fertig. Philip war wieder froh und zuversichtlich. Er war bereits dabei, sich in Detailfragen zu vertiefen, als er in der Ferne ein dumpfes Krachen hörte; es klang, als habe jemand eine große Tür zugeworfen. War jemand wach und machte sich im Dormitorium oder im Kreuzgang zu schaffen? Wenn es was Ernstes ist, werde ich's früh genug herausfinden, dachte er bei sich, und seine Gedanken schweiften ab und befaßten sich wieder mit Pacht- und Zehntzahlungen. Eine weitere wichtige Geld- und Wohlstandsquelle der Klöster waren Schenkungen von seiten der Eltern junger Zöglinge – nur: wer Novizen aus den entsprechenden Familien bekommen wollte, brauchte eine attraktive Klosterschule …

Erneut wurde er in seinen Überlegungen gestört. Das Krachen war lauter als beim erstenmal und ließ sogar die Wände seines Hauses leicht erbeben. Das war bestimmt *keine* Tür, dachte er. Was geht denn da drüben vor? Er ging zum Fenster und öffnete den Laden. Der kühle Nachtwind blies herein und ließ ihn schaudern. Vom Fenster aus konnte er die Kirche, das Kapitelhaus, den Kreuzgang, das Dormitorium und die Küchengebäude dahinter überblicken. Alles schien in tiefstem Frieden zu liegen. Die Luft war so kalt, daß ihm beim Atmen die Zähne weh taten. Aber da war noch etwas in der Luft. Er hob den Kopf und prüfte den Geruch. Es war Rauch.

Aufgeregt kniff er die Brauen zusammen. Nirgendwo war ein Feuer zu erkennen.

Er zog den Oberkörper zurück. Vielleicht ist es der Rauch von meiner eigenen Feuerstelle, dachte er, aber dem war nicht so.

Er wußte nicht, woran er war. In höchster Beunruhigung schlüpfte er in seine Stiefel, ergriff seinen Umhang und verließ im Laufschritt das Haus.

Philip rannte über den grasbewachsenen Vorplatz zum Kreuzgang. Unterwegs wurde der Rauchgeruch stärker. Es konnte jetzt kein Zweifel mehr daran bestehen, daß irgendwo auf dem Klostergelände ein Brand ausgebrochen war. Die Küche! war sein erster Gedanke – fast alle Feuersbrünste gingen von einer Küche aus. Er lief durch die schmale Gasse zwischen südlichem Querhaus und Kapitelhaus und dann quer über den Klosterhof. Am Tag wäre er durchs Refektorium in den Küchenhof gegangen, doch war die Tür nachts verschlossen. Durch den Boden im Südgang kam er zur Rückseite der Küche. Nichts deutete auf ein Feuer hin, weder in der Brauerei noch im Backhaus, und es roch auch nicht mehr so stark nach Rauch. Er rannte noch ein Stück weiter und späte über den Rasen zum Gästehaus und zu den Ställen hinüber. Nichts rührte sich, alles war still.

Konnte das Feuer im Dormitorium ausgebrochen sein? Es war das einzige Klostergebäude mit eigener Feuerstelle, das er noch nicht überprüft hatte. Allein der Gedanke an einen Brand im Dormitorium war haarsträubend. Ihn überkam die schauerliche Vision von lauter Mönchen, die vom Rauch betäubt auf ihren Lagern ruhten, während das Gebäude lichterloh brannte ... Kurz bevor er die Tür des Dormitoriums erreichte, wurde diese von innen geöffnet, und Cuthbert Whitehead trat ihm entgegen. Er trug ein Binsenlicht in der Hand.

»Riechst du's?« fragte Cuthbert ohne Umschweife.

»Ja – was ist mit den Brüdern?«

»Hier brennt's nicht.«

Philip war erleichtert. Wenigstens war seine Herde wohlauf. »Wo dann?«

»Vielleicht in der Küche ...«, sagte Cuthbert.

»Nein, da habe ich schon nachgesehen.« Nun, da er wußte, daß keine Menschenleben in Gefahr waren, sorgte sich Philip um seinen Besitzstand. Er hatte sich die ganze Zeit mit der Finanzlage des Klosters befaßt und wußte, daß er sich keine Gebäudereparaturen leisten konnte. Sein Blick fiel auf die Kathedrale. War da ein leichter roter Schimmer hinter den Fensterlöchern?

»Geh zum Sakristan und hol den Kirchenschlüssel, Cuthbert«, sagte er.

Cuthbert eilte schon voraus. »Ich hab' den Schlüssel bei mir«, rief er.

»Guter Mann!«

Über den Kreuzgang liefen sie zum südlichen Eingang des Querschiffs. Hastig steckte Cuthbert den Schlüssel ins Schloß und drehte ihn um. Kaum hatten sie die Tür geöffnet, da wallten ihnen Rauchschwaden entgegen.

Philip stockte das Herz. Seine Kirche brannte! Wie konnte das geschehen?

Er trat ein. Seinen Augen bot sich ein verwirrendes Bild: Gleich vor ihnen, im südlichen Querhaus und um den Altar herum lagen riesige brennende Balken auf dem Boden. Wo kamen sie her? Und woher kam der donnernde Lärm, der doch von einem viel größeren Feuer herzurühren schien?

Cuthbert rief: »Da oben! Sieh doch!«

Philip hob den Kopf und fand mit einem Schlag all seine Fragen beantwortet. Die bemalte Holzdecke brannte lichterloh, von unten sah es aus wie das Fegefeuer. Der größte Teil war bereits verbrannt und gab den Blick auf die lodernden Balken und Streben des Dachstuhls frei, um die herum Flammen und Rauch einen wahren Teufelstanz aufführten. Philip war vor Schreck wie gelähmt. Erst, als ihn seine Halsmuskeln zu schmerzen begannen, kam er wieder zu sich.

Er rannte weiter, hielt in der Vierung kurz inne, lief weiter, blieb auch vor dem Altar kurz stehen, sah sich in der ganzen Kirche um. Das gesamte Dach stand in Flammen, vom Portal im Westen bis zur Apsis im Osten sowie über den beiden Querhäusern. *Wie kriegen wir das Wasser rauf?* fragte er sich in einem Anflug von Panik … mit einer Eimerkette über Wendeltreppe und Galerie? Unmöglich. Selbst mit hundert Mann bekommen wir nicht die Wassermengen hinauf, die wir bräuchten, um dieses donnernde Inferno zu löschen. Das Dach ist nicht mehr zu retten; er sah es ein. Und bis wir das Geld für ein neues Dach haben, ist die Kirche Schnee und Regen schutzlos preisgegeben …

Direkt über seinem Kopf ertönte ein Bersten und Krachen. Als er nach oben blickte, sah er, wie sich ein schwerer Balken langsam nach unten senkte und ihm auf den Kopf zu fallen drohte. So schnell ihn seine Beine trugen, rannte er zurück ins südliche Querhaus, wo Cuthbert schreckensbleich auf ihn wartete.

Ein ganzer Abschnitt des Dachstuhls brach ein – drei Dreiecke aus Balken und Streben samt den daran festgenagelten Bleiplatten. Ohne an ihre eigene Gefährdung zu denken, starrten Philip und Cuthbert wie gebannt auf die Szenerie. Das Dach stürzte auf einen der großen Rundbogen der Vierung, und das Mauerwerk barst mit einem explosionsartigen Knall, der widerhallte wie Donnerrollen. Alles ging merkwürdig langsam vor sich: Die Balken senkten sich langsam, der Bogen brach langsam, und die zerborstenen Steine taumelten langsam zu Boden. Weitere Dachbalken lösten sich, und dann stürzte mit tiefem Grollen ein Teil der Nordmauer der Apsis ein und rutschte seitwärts ins nördliche Querschiff.

Philip war wie vom Schlag gerührt. Der Anblick eines in sich zusammenstürzenden Gebäudes von solcher Größe war von schrecklicher, bewegender Kraft. Es war wie ein Berg, der ins Rutschen geriet, oder ein Fluß, der auf einmal austrocknete. Nie, in seinen schlimmsten Träumen nicht, hatte Philip ein solches Ereignis vorausgesehen, ja, er zweifelte noch immer daran, ob das, was sich vor seinen Augen abspielte, Wirklichkeit war. Er wußte nicht mehr ein noch aus.

Cuthbert zog ihn am Ärmel. »Komm raus, schnell!« schrie er. Philip konnte sich nicht von dem Anblick lösen. Er mußte an die Rechnung denken, die er gerade erst aufgestellt hatte: Die finanzielle Sanierung des Klosters sollte zehn Jahre dauern – zehn Jahre voller Einschränkungen und harter Arbeit ... Und jetzt kamen plötzlich neue Aufgaben auf ihn zu: ein neues Dach, eine neue Nordmauer ... und vielleicht noch mehr, ein Ende war gar nicht abzusehen. Das ist Teufelswerk, dachte er. Wie sonst ist es möglich, daß der Dachstuhl ausgerechnet in einer frostkalten Januarnacht Feuer fängt?

»Wir kommen hier noch um!« schrie Cuthbert, und die Angst in seiner Stimme rührte Philips Herz. Er wandte sich ab. Gemeinsam verließen sie die Kirche und rannten in den Kreuzgang.

Auch die Mitbrüder waren inzwischen alarmiert. Einer nach dem anderen tappten sie aus dem Dormitorium und hielten an der Tür unwillkürlich inne, um zur brennenden Kirche aufzusehen. Um zu verhindern, daß es zu einem Gedränge kam, hatte Küchenmeister Milius neben der Tür Aufstellung genommen und scheuchte die Brüder weiter. Seinen Anweisungen folgend, entfernten sie sich über die Südseite des Kreuzgangs. Dort stand auf halbem Wege Tom Builder und wies sie an, sich durch den Torbogen in Sicherheit zu bringen. Philip hörte ihn sagen: »Geht zum Gästehaus und haltet Euch unter allen Umständen von der Kirche fern!«

Er übertreibt, dachte Philip. Hier im Kreuzgang besteht doch gewiß keine Gefahr – oder? Andererseits – es schadete nicht und war vielleicht eine ganz vernünftige Vorsichtsmaßnahme. Eigentlich, gestand er sich ein, hätte ich selber darauf kommen müssen ...

Toms Vorsicht brachte ihn auf einen anderen schlimmen Gedanken: Was war noch alles von dem verheerenden Feuer bedroht? Wenn schon der Kreuzgang nicht absolut sicher war – wie verhielt es sich dann mit dem Kapitelhaus? In einem kleinen, fensterlosen Seitenzimmer mit dicken Steinmauern bewahrten sie die eisenbeschlagene Eichenholzkiste auf, in der sich nicht nur das geringe Barvermögen des Klosters und die juwelengeschmückten Gefäße des Sakristans befanden, sondern auch wertvolle Urkunden wie königliche Privilegien und Besitztitel.

Philip erblickte Schatzmeister Alan, einen jungen Mönch, der für den Sakristan arbeitete und mit der Beaufsichtigung der Kirchengeräte betraut war. Er rief ihn zu sich. »Der Klosterschatz muß in Sicherheit gebracht werden. Er kann nicht länger im Kapitelhaus bleiben. Wo ist der Sakristan?«

»Er ist fort, Vater.«

»Dann suche ihn, laß dir die Schlüssel geben und bring den Schatz ins Gästehaus. Und nun lauf!«

Während Alan sich im Laufschritt entfernte, wandte Philip sich an Cuthbert und sagte: »Du behältst ihn am besten im Auge!« Cuthbert nickte und folgte Alan.

Philip sah wieder in die Höhe. In den wenigen Augenblicken, in denen seine Aufmerksamkeit abgelenkt gewesen war, hatte das Feuer sich noch verstärkt. Wild schlugen die Flammen empor, und der Feuerschein ließ alle Fenster erstrahlen. Der Sakristan hätte sich eigentlich um den Schatz kümmern müssen, dachte er. Statt dessen hatte er nichts Eiligeres zu tun, als seine Haut zu retten ... Haben wir sonst noch etwas vergessen? Angesichts der Schnelligkeit, mit der sich die Dinge entwickelten, fiel es ihm schwer, folgerichtig zu denken. Die Brüder bringen sich in Sicherheit, der Schatz wird geholt ...

Ich habe den Heiligen vergessen!

Hinter dem Bischofsthron in der Apsis befand sich das steinerne Grabmal des heiligen Adolphus, eines frühen englischen Märtyrers. Das Skelett des Heiligen ruhte in einem Holzsarg innerhalb des Grabmals. In regelmäßigen Abständen wurde die schwere Steinplatte des Grabmals gehoben und der Sarg öffentlich zur Schau gestellt. Obwohl aus früheren Zeiten überliefert war, daß Kranke, die sein Grabmal berührt hatten, auf wundersame Weise geheilt wurden, war Adolphus in den vergangenen Jahren ein wenig in Vergessenheit geraten. Die sterblichen Überreste eines Heiligen konnten eine große Attraktion für eine Kirche sein. Sie lockten nicht nur viele Pilger an, sondern stärkten auch den Glauben allgemein. Da sie sehr viel Geld einbrachten, kam es sogar vor – welch eine Schande! –, daß Mönche Heiligenreliquien aus anderen Kirchen stahlen. Philip hatte vor, das Interesse an Adolphus wiederzubeleben. Er mußte das Skelett retten.

Da er die Steinplatte allein nicht heben und den Sarg allein nicht tragen konnte, brauchte er Hilfe. Im Grunde hätte der Sakristan auch an den Heiligen denken können, aber er war nirgends zu sehen. Der nächste Mönch, der das Dormitorium verließ, war Remigius, der eingebildete Subprior. Nun mußte eben er mit anpacken. Philip rief ihn zu sich und sagte: »Komm, hilf mir, das Skelett des Heiligen zu bergen!«

Angstvoll blickte Remigius mit seinen blaßgrünen Augen auf die brennende Kathedrale, doch nach kurzem Zögern überwand er sich und folgte Philip ins Innere.

Das Feuer hatte sich, obwohl Philip die Kirche erst vor kurzer Zeit verlassen hatte, enorm ausgeweitet. Ein stechender Geruch, wie von Pechfackeln, stieg Philip in die Nase. Trotz der Flammen fegte ein kühler Zug durch das Gebäude: Während der Rauch durch die klaffenden Löcher im Dach entwich, sog das Feuer kalte Luft durch die Fenster. Der aufsteigende Wind fachte die Flammen zusätzlich an. Glühende Asche regnete herab, und verschiedene schwere Balken im Dachstuhl erweckten den Eindruck, als könnten sie jeden Augenblick herunterstürzen. Bisher hatte Philip sich nur um seine Mitbrüder und um den Klosterschatz gesorgt – jetzt fürchtete er zum erstenmal um sein eigenes Leben. Er zögerte, unschlüssig, ob er sich noch weiter in das Inferno vorwagen sollte.

Je länger ich warte, desto größer wird das Risiko, dachte er. Und wenn ich noch lange grübele, verliere ich vollends die Nerven ... Er hob seine Kutte an, rief Remigius zu: »Folge mir!« und rannte ins Querhaus. Überall am Boden brannten kleine Feuerchen, die er sorgsam umging. Er wußte, daß er jeden Augenblick damit rechnen mußte, von herabstürzendem Gebälk erschlagen zu werden. Das Herz klopfte ihm bis zum Hals; am liebsten hätte er der inneren Spannung, die ihn beherrschte, mit einem lauten Schrei Erleichterung verschafft. Doch dann war er auch schon auf der anderen Seite und im Schutz des Seitenschiffs angelangt.

Er blieb stehen. Die Seitenschiffe besaßen steinerne Gewölbe, weshalb das Feuer dort keine Nahrung fand. Remigius war an seiner Seite. Philip hatte Rauch eingeatmet; er hustete und keuchte.

»Hier kommen wir nicht mehr lebendig raus«, sagte Remigius.

»Der Herr wird uns beschützen«, erwiderte Philip – und dachte im gleichen Augenblick: Wieso fürchte ich mich dann?

Doch für theologische Fragen war jetzt keine Zeit.

Im Schutz des Seitenschiffs erreichte er die Apsis. Das mit kunstvollem Schnitzwerk versehene Chorgestühl stand in Flammen, und Philip spürte die davon ausgehende Hitze. Er empfand den Verlust wie einen körperlichen Schmerz, verdrängte ihn jedoch und konzentrierte sich auf seine Aufgabe.

Der Sarkophag stand auf einem niedrigen Sockel. Philip und Remigius mußten die Steinplatte abheben, den Sarg herausholen und ihn ins Seitenschiff schaffen, während sich das Dach über ihnen in seine Bestandteile auflöste. Philip sah Remigius an. Die etwas hervorstehenden grünen Augen des Subpriors waren vor Angst geweitet. Um Remigius nicht noch zusätzlich zu verschrecken, verbarg Philip seine eigene Furcht. »Pack du an diesem Ende an, ich greif' mir das andere!« sagte er und wartete nicht erst auf Zustimmung. Remigius folgte seinen Anweisungen.

Die schwere Steinplatte rührte sich nicht vom Fleck.

Philip sah ein, daß er mehr Helfer hätte mitnehmen müssen.

Er hatte einfach nicht gründlich nachgedacht. Zurücklaufen und Hilfe holen konnte er jetzt nicht mehr, denn es stand zu befürchten, daß das Querhaus in Kürze nicht mehr passierbar war. Aber wir können doch die Gebeine des Heiligen nicht hierlassen, dachte er. Über kurz oder lang wird ein Balken auf das Grabmal stürzen und die Steinplatte zerschmettern, danach fängt der Holzsarg Feuer, und der Wind wird die Asche in alle Himmelsrichtungen zerstreuen ... ein furchtbares Sakrileg und ein entsetzlicher Verlust für die Kathedrale.

Plötzlich kam ihm eine Idee. Er ging um das Grabmal herum und winkte Remigius zu sich. Er kniete nieder und stemmte beide Hände unter das überstehende Ende der Steinplatte. Remigius tat es ihm nach, und mit vereinten Kräften gelang es den Männern, die Platte anzuheben. Schließlich konnten sie sich zunächst auf die Knie und dann auf die Füße erheben. Die Grabplatte stand senkrecht. Ein letzter Stoß, und sie überschlug sich, polterte auf der anderen Seite auf den Boden und brach in zwei Teile.

Philip warf einen Blick in den nun offenen Sarkophag. Der äußere Zustand des Sargs ließ nichts zu wünschen übrig. Das Holz wirkte fest, die eisernen Haltegriffe waren nur oberflächlich etwas angelaufen. Philip beugte sich hinein und packte zu, Remigius tat das gleiche auf der gegenüberliegenden Seite. Es gelang ihnen, den Sarg ein paar Zoll weit anzuheben, doch war er wesentlich schwerer, als Philip erwartet hatte. Remigius ließ los, und der Sarg fiel zurück.

»Ich kann das nicht«, sagte er. »Ich bin älter als Ihr.« Philip verkniff sich eine ärgerliche Bemerkung. Wahrscheinlich war der Sarg mit Blei ausgeschlagen. »Komm rüber!« rief er Remigius zu. »Wir versuchen, ihn aufzustellen!«

Gemeinsam fiel ihnen das Anheben des einen Endes verhältnismäßig leicht. Als der Sarg aufrecht stand, hielten sie kurz inne und verschnauften. Philip merkte erst jetzt, daß das Fußende nach oben zeigte – der Heilige stand also auf dem Kopf. Stumm leistete der Prior Abbitte. Eine nicht endenwollende Flut brennender oder glühender Holzstückchen regnete auf sie herab, und Remigius schlug jedesmal, wenn ein paar Funken seine Kutte trafen, wie besessen darauf ein. Bei jeder sich bietenden Gelegenheit warf er zudem angstvolle Blicke hinauf zum brennenden Dach. Philip entging nicht, daß den Mann rasch der Mut verließ.

Sie neigten den Sarg über den Rand des Sarkophags, so daß er wie eine Wippe auf die andere Seite kippte und dort auf dem Boden aufschlug. Die heiligen Knochen werden herumgewirbelt wie Würfel im Becher, dachte Philip und gestand sich ein, daß er noch nie etwas so Unheiliges getan hatte – aber es gab keine andere Lösung.

Sie schleiften den Sarg fort, wobei die eisenverstärkten Kanten kleine Furchen durch die festgestampfte Erde zogen. Sie hatten den relativen Schutz des Seitenschiffs noch nicht erreicht, als mit ohrenbetäubendem Krachen eine wirre Masse aus brennendem Holz und heißem Blei genau auf das offenstehende Grab des Heiligen fiel. Der Aufschlag ließ den Boden erzittern, und der Sarkophag zersprang in tausend Stücke. Ein großer Balken verfehlte Philip und Remigius nur um Haaresbreite und schlug ihnen den Sarg aus der Hand. Für den Subprior war das Maß voll.

»Das ist Teufelswerk!« schrie er wie von Sinnen und stürmte davon.

Es hätte nicht viel gefehlt, und Philip wäre blindlings hinterhergerannt. Wenn der Teufel in dieser Nacht wirklich mit im Spiel war, ließ sich nicht absehen, was noch alles geschehen konnte. Philip hatte noch nie einen bösen Geist gesehen, kannte jedoch zahllose Augenzeugenberichte. Er rief sich zur Ordnung: Wir Mönche sind dazu da, dem Satan entgegenzutreten, und nicht, um vor ihm davonzulaufen! Fast sehnsüchtig sah er sich nach dem Seitenschiff um. Dann holte er tief Luft, packte die beiden Griffe auf der Stirnseite und wuchtete den Sarg hoch.

Er schaffte es, ihn unter dem herabgestürzten Balken hervorzuziehen. Der Sarg wies einige Dellen und Absplitterungen auf, war aber überraschenderweise nicht zerbrochen. Glühende Asche regnete auf Philip herab. Er sah hinauf zum Dach. Tanzte da eine zweibeinige Gestalt in den Flammen – oder war es nur eine wirbelnde Rauchfahne? Als er den Kopf wieder senkte, sah er, daß der Saum seiner Kutte Feuer gefangen hatte. Er kniete nieder und schlug die brennenden Stellen auf den Boden. Die Flammen gingen sofort aus. Plötzlich ertönte ein merkwürdiges Geräusch, bei dem es sich um das Ächzen gemarterten Holzes oder das spöttische Lachen eines Dämons handelte. »Heiliger Adolphus, steh mir bei!« rief er aus und packte wieder an.

Bis zur nächsten Tür, die im südlichen Querhaus lag, war es noch weit. Philip wußte nicht, ob er es schaffen würde, bevor das, was vom Dach noch übriggeblieben war, in die Kirche stürzte. Vielleicht spekulierte der Teufel genau darauf. Unwillkürlich mußte er wieder nach oben schauen. Die zweibeinige, rauchumwaberte Gestalt verschwand blitzartig hinter einem geschwärzten Balken. Er weiß, daß ich's nicht schaffe, dachte Philip. Er spähte ins Seitenschiff, einmal mehr versucht, den Heiligen im Stich zu lassen und um sein Leben zu laufen, erblickte mit einemmal Bruder Milius, Cuthbert Whitehead und Tom Builder, drei höchst wirkliche Gestalten, die ihm zu Hilfe eilten. Sein Herz schlug plötzlich höher vor Freude und Erleichterung, und da war er sich gar nicht mehr so sicher, daß oben im Dachstuhl ein böser Geist herumturnte.

»Gott sei Dank!« rief er und fügte überflüssigerweise noch hinzu: »Kommt, helft mir!«

Tom prüfte das Dach mit kritischem Blick. Geister schien er dort nicht zu sehen, aber er sagte: »Beeilen wir uns!«

Sie hoben den Sarg hoch und luden ihn sich auf die Schultern, ein jeder an einer anderen Ecke. Selbst für vier Männer war das Gewicht noch gewaltig. »Vorwärts!« rief Philip, und sie strebten, gebeugt unter ihrer Last, dem Ausgang zu.

Kurz vor dem südlichen Querschiff rief Tom lauthals: »Wartet!« Der Boden war übersät mit Trümmern und kleineren Brandherden, und immer mehr brennendes Holz fiel von oben herab. Philip versuchte, irgendwo einen Pfad ausfindig zu machen. Sie waren noch nicht weitergegangen, als auf der Westseite der Kirche plötzlich lautes Gepolter anhub. Philip sah auf; ihn graute vor dem Geräusch. Das Gepolter schwoll zu Donnergetöse an.

»Er ist schwach«, sagte Tom Builder. »Genau wie der andere.«

Philip verstand nicht, worauf der Baumeister hinauswollte.

»Wen meint Ihr damit?« fragte er.

»Den Südwestturm.«

»O nein! Nein!«

Das Getöse wurde lauter und lauter. Voller Entsetzen beobachtete Philip, daß die gesamte Westmauer der Kirche, wie von Gottes Hand geschoben, ein Stück vorwärts rückte. Auf einer Länge von gut fünfzehn Schritt krachte der Dachstuhl ein, stürzte ins Hauptschiff und löste ein regelrechtes Erdbeben aus. Und dann knickte der Südwestturm um, und seine Trümmer ergossen sich wie ein Erdrutsch über die benachbarten Teile der Kirche.

Philip stand vor Schrecken wie gelähmt. Seine Kirche löste sich vor seinen Augen in ihre Bestandteile auf! Selbst wenn es mir gelingt, das erforderliche Geld aufzutreiben, wird die Wiederherstellung der Kirche Jahre in Anspruch nehmen, dachte er. Was soll ich nun tun? Wie soll das Kloster diese Katastrophe überleben?

Der Sarg bewegte sich auf Philips Schultern und riß den Prior aus seiner Erstarrung. Die anderen drei drängten weiter, und Philip ging einfach mit. Tom suchte und fand einen Weg durch das Chaos. Ein brennendes Scheit Holz fiel auf den Sarg und rutschte herunter, ohne einen der Träger zu treffen. Kurz darauf hatten sie die gegenüberliegende Seite erreicht. Durch die offenstehende Tür traten sie in die kalte Nachtluft hinaus.

Die Zerstörung der Kirche hatte Philip so mitgenommen, daß er nicht einmal mehr Erleichterung über die eigene Rettung empfand. Sie eilten durch den Kreuzgang und verließen ihn durch den Torbogen auf der Südseite. In sicherer Entfernung von den Gebäuden blieb Tom stehen und sagte: »Das genügt.« Vorsichtig setzten sie den Sarg auf dem gefrorenen Boden ab.

Philip brauchte eine Weile, bis er wieder zu Atem kam, und er nutzte die Pause, um sich auf die vor ihm liegenden Aufgaben zu konzentrieren: Den Verblüfften zu spielen – dafür war jetzt nicht die Zeit. Er war der Prior, er hatte das Sagen. Was war als nächstes zu tun? Vorrang hatte die körperliche Unversehrtheit der Mitbrüder. Philip holte noch einmal tief Luft, straffte die Schultern und sah die drei Männer an.

»Cuthbert«, begann er, »du bleibst hier und bewachst den Sarg des Heiligen. Die anderen folgen mir.«

Er führte sie hinter den Küchengebäuden entlang und zwischen der Brauerei und der Mühle hindurch auf die große Freifläche vor dem Gästehaus. Die Mönche, viele Dorfbewohner und die Familienangehörigen des Baumeisters standen in kleinen Gruppen beieinander, starrten mit weit aufgerissenen Augen die brennende Kirche an und unterhielten sich in gedämpftem Ton. Auch Philip drehte sich noch einmal um, bevor er zu ihnen sprach. Die Kathedrale bot inzwischen einen jämmerlichen Anblick. Der Westflügel war ein einziger Trümmerhaufen, und aus den Resten des Dachstuhls loderten riesige Flammen empor.

»Sind alle da?« rief er. »Wenn ihr jemanden zu vermissen glaubt, nennt seinen Namen!«

»Cuthbert Whitehead!« rief jemand.

»Er bewacht die Gebeine des Heiligen. Sonst jemand?«

Es fehlte niemand mehr.

»Zähl die Mönche durch«, sagte Philip zu Milius. »Wir wollen Gewißheit haben. Mit uns beiden müssen es fünfundvierzig sein.« Wohl wissend, daß er sich auf Milius verlassen konnte, ließ er es dabei bewenden und wandte sich an Tom. »Eure Familie ist vollzählig?«

Tom nickte und deutete auf die Seinen. Sie standen neben der Mauer des Gästehauses, die Frau, der große Sohn und die beiden Kleinen. Der Junge sah Philip angstvoll an. Für die Kinder muß es ein furchtbares Erlebnis sein, dachte Philip.

Der Sakristan saß auf der eisenbeschlagenen Kiste, die den Kloster-schatz enthielt. Philip, der gar nicht mehr daran gedacht hatte, war froh, daß der Schatz in Sicherheit war.

»Bruder Andrew«, sagte er zu dem Mann, »der Sarg mit den Gebei-nen des heiligen Adolphus befindet sich hinter dem Refektorium. Nimm dir ein paar kräftige Mitbrüder und bringe ihn ...« Er überlegte. Der sicherste Ort war wahrscheinlich das Wohnhaus des Priors. »... und bringe ihn in mein Haus!«

»In Euer Haus?« gab Andrew empört zurück. »Die sterblichen Überreste des Heiligen gehören in *meine* Obhut!«

»Es wäre auch an *dir* gewesen, sie aus der brennenden Kirche zu retten!« fuhr Philip ihn an. »Und nun tu, was ich dir aufgetragen habe. Kein Wort mehr!«

Widerstrebend erhob sich der Sakristan. Es war ihm anzusehen, daß er vor Wut kochte.

»Beeil dich, Mann!« rief Philip ihm zu. »Oder du verlierst auf der Stelle dein Amt!« Er wandte Andrew den Rücken zu und fragte Milius: »Wie viele?«

»Vierundvierzig – plus Cuthbert. Dazu elf Novizen und fünf Gäste. Niemand fehlt.«

»Der Herr hat Erbarmen mit uns.« Es kam Philip fast wie ein Wunder vor, daß es keine Toten, ja nicht einmal einen Verwundeten zu beklagen gab. Er spürte jetzt seine körperliche Erschöpfung, war jedoch innerlich viel zu aufgewühlt, um sich hinzusetzen und auszu-ruhen. »Gibt es sonst noch irgendwelche Wertgegenstände, die wir in Sicherheit bringen müssen?« fragte er. »Wir haben den Schatz, wir haben die Reliquien ...«

Alan, der junge Schatzmeister, meldete sich zu Wort. »Was ist mit den Büchern?«

Philip stöhnte auf. Natürlich, die Bücher! Sie befanden sich in einem verschlossenen Schrank im Kreuzgang, gleich neben der Tür zum Kapitelhaus, so daß die Mönche sie während der Studierzeiten rasch zur Hand hatten. Die Bücher einzeln aus dem Schrank zu holen, war jetzt kaum noch möglich – es würde gefährlich lange dauern. Aber vielleicht konnten ein paar starke junge Männer den Bücherschrank insgesamt in Sicherheit bringen. Philip sah sich um. Der Sakristan hatte ein halbes Dutzend Mönche ausgewählt und war mit ihnen bereits unterwegs. Philip suchte sich nun seinerseits drei junge Mönche und drei ältere Novizen aus und hieß sie, ihm zu folgen.

Er konnte nicht mehr rennen, er war einfach zu müde. Wieder wählte er den Weg vorbei an Mühle und Brauerei und an der Rückseite von Küche und Refektorium entlang. Cuthbert Whitehead und der Sakristan kümmerten sich gemeinsam um den Abtransport des Sarges. Philip führte seine Leute durch die schmale Gasse, die Refektorium und Dormitorium voneinander trennte und von Süden her unter einem Torbogen in den Kreuzgang mündete.

Die Hitze war jetzt deutlich spürbar. Die Tür des großen Bücherschranks war mit Schnitzwerk versehen: Es zeigte Moses mit den Gesetzestafeln. Philip befahl den jungen Männern, den Schrank nach vorne zu kippen und ihn auf die Schultern zu nehmen. Sie trugen ihn durch den Kreuzgang zum Südtor. Während die Mönche weitergingen, blieb Philip stehen und drehte sich um. Der Anblick der ruinierten Kirche erfüllte sein Herz mit tiefer Trauer. Die Rauchentwicklung war zurückgegangen, dafür gab es mehr Flammen. Weite Strecken des Daches waren verschwunden. Er sah, wie es sich nun auch über der Vierung senkte, und ahnte, daß diese Partie als nächste herabstürzen würde. Dann gab es einen donnernden Krach, der lauter war als alles andere, was er während des Brandes gehört hatte: Das Dach des südlichen Querhauses stürzte ein. Philip war, als stünde sein eigener Körper in Flammen, so sehr litt er unter den Schmerzen der Kathedrale. Einen Augenblick später hatte er plötzlich den Eindruck, als beulte sich die Wand des Querhauses über dem Kreuzgang aus. Gott helfe uns, sie stürzt ein! schoß es ihm durch den Kopf. Schon begann das Mauerwerk zu bröckeln ... Sie fällt genau auf mich, dachte er und wollte fliehen, doch er hatte noch keine drei Schritte getan, da traf ihn etwas am Hinterkopf, und er verlor das Bewußtsein.

Die Feuersbrunst, die die Kathedrale von Kingsbridge zerstörte, war für Tom ein Fanal der Hoffnung.

Er spähte über den weiten Vorplatz in die riesigen Flammen, die aus der Kirchenruine schlugen, und hatte dabei nur einen Gedanken: Das bedeutet Arbeit!

Der Gedanke hatte sich sofort, nachdem er mit verschlafenen Augen vor die Tür des Gästehauses getreten war und den ersten schwachen Rotschimmer hinter den Kirchenfenstern erblickt hatte, in seinem Bewußtsein eingenistet. Tom war die ganze Zeit über von einer schamlosen, glücklichen Zuversicht besessen gewesen, während er an der Evakuierung der Mönche beteiligt gewesen war, in der brennenden Kirche Vater Philip gesucht oder geholfen hatte, den Sarg des Heiligen in Sicherheit zu bringen.

Als er endlich die Zeit zum Nachdenken fand, schämte er sich plötzlich seiner klammheimlichen Freude über den Brand.

Andererseits – es war ja niemand verletzt worden, und der Klosterschatz war in Sicherheit; außerdem war die Kirche ohnehin uralt und baufällig. Warum also sollte er sich nicht freuen?

Die jungen Mönche mit dem schweren Bücherschrank auf den Schultern kamen über den Vorplatz. Ich muß nur noch dafür Sorge tragen, dachte Tom, daß auch wirklich ich den Auftrag zum Wiederaufbau der Kathedrale bekomme. Und der beste Zeitpunkt, Prior Philip darauf anzusprechen, ist jetzt ...

Philip befand sich allerdings nicht unter den Schrankträgern, die gerade das Gästehaus erreichten und ihre schwere Last abluden. »Wo ist Euer Prior?« fragte Tom.

Der Älteste unter den Mönchen drehte sich überrascht um.

»Ich weiß es nicht«, sagte er. »Ich dachte, er wäre hinter uns.«

Vielleicht ist er zurückgeblieben, um das Feuer besser beobachten zu können, dachte Tom. Hoffentlich ist ihm nichts passiert ...

Ohne weitere Umstände rannte Tom los. Nicht nur, weil Philip ein guter Mensch zu sein schien, war ihm an seinem Wohlergehen gelegen. Der Prior hielt ja auch seine schützende Hand über Jonathan. Es war unmöglich vorauszusagen, was ohne ihn mit dem Kind geschehen würde.

Er fand Philip in dem schmalen Gang zwischen Refektorium und Dormitorium. Zu seiner Erleichterung saß der Prior aufrecht da; er wirkte benommen, war aber äußerlich unverletzt. Tom half ihm auf die Beine.

»Mir ist was auf den Kopf gefallen«, sagte Philip stockend.

Tom blickte an ihm vorbei auf die brennende Ruine. Das südliche Querhaus war eingestürzt und auf den Kreuzgang gefallen.

»Ihr könnt von Glück reden, daß Ihr noch am Leben seid«, sagte er. »Der Herr muß noch einiges mit Euch vorhaben.«

Philip schüttelte den Kopf, um wieder zu sich zu kommen.

»Ich war kurze Zeit bewußtlos«, sagte er, »aber jetzt geht es mir wieder besser. Wo sind die Bücher?«

»Beim Gästehaus.«

»Dann laßt uns dorthin zurückkehren.«

Auf dem Rückweg hielt Tom Philips Arm. Der Prior war nicht ernsthaft verletzt, aber ziemlich durcheinander.

Als sie wieder beim Gästehaus ankamen, hatte das Feuer in der Kathedrale seinen Höhepunkt bereits überschritten. Tom wunderte sich, daß er die Gesichter der anderen so gut erkennen konnte, obwohl die Flammen längst nicht mehr so hell aufloderten wie zuvor. Erst dann fiel ihm auf, daß es allmählich tagte, und er erschrak.

Philip nahm sogleich wieder die Zügel in die Hand. Küchenmeister Milius trug er auf, für alle Brei zu kochen, und Cuthbert Whitehead erhielt die Erlaubnis, ein Faß mit starkem Wein zu öffnen, damit sie sich unterdessen ein wenig wärmen konnten. Philip befahl, im Gästehaus ein Feuer anzuzünden, und die älteren Mönche, die die Kälte kaum noch ertrugen, gingen hinein. Zu allem fing es jetzt auch noch an zu gießen. Windgepeitschte, eiskalte Regenböen fegten übers Klostergelände, und die Flammen an der Kirchenruine wurden kleiner und erstarben rasch.

Bald waren alle Mönche beschäftigt. Prior Philip verließ das Gästehaus und ging gemessenen Schritts zur Kirche. Tom folgte ihm. Das ist meine Chance, dachte er. Wenn ich jetzt keinen Fehler mache, kann ich auf Jahre hinaus hier arbeiten …

Philip war stehengeblieben und starrte auf den Trümmerhaufen, der einst die Westfassade gewesen war. Traurig schüttelte er den Kopf. Er sieht aus, als stünde er vor den Trümmern seines eigenen Lebens, dachte Tom, der schweigend neben dem Prior stand. Nach einer Weile ging Philip weiter, wanderte an der Nordseite der Kirche entlang und über das Gräberfeld. Tom begleitete ihn und schätzte mit fachmännischem Blick den Schaden ab.

Die Nordmauer des Langhauses stand noch, doch das nördliche Querschiff und die Nordwand der Apsis waren zum größten Teil eingestürzt. Der Ostflügel der Kirche war erhalten geblieben. Die beiden Männer umrundeten ihn und besahen sich die Südseite. Weite Teile der Südmauer waren eingefallen, und das südliche Querhaus hatte den Kreuzgang verschüttet. Das Kapitelhaus stand noch.

Vor dem Torbogen am Ostrand des Kreuzgangs versperrte ihnen ein Trümmerhaufen den Weg. Es sah schlimm aus, doch erkannte Tom sofort, daß der Kreuzgang selbst unter dem Schutt einigermaßen verschont geblieben war. Er kletterte über das geborstene Mauerwerk, bis er an einen Punkt gelangte, von dem aus er in die Kirche hineinsehen konnte. Gleich hinter dem Altar führte eine halb verdeckte Treppe hinab in die Krypta. Die Krypta lag direkt unter dem Chor. Tom spähte hinein und untersuchte den Steinboden oberhalb der Krypta auf Bruchstellen. Zum Glück fand er keine – wahrscheinlich war die Krypta unversehrt geblieben. Tom behielt die Entdeckung vorerst für sich; Philip sollte die erfreuliche Nachricht erst im entscheidenden Augenblick erfahren.

Der Prior war inzwischen weitergegangen. Tom sputete sich, ihn einzuholen. Auf der Rückseite des Dormitoriums schloß er zu ihm auf. Keines der Klostergebäude hatte, von einigen Kleinigkeiten abgesehen, Schaden genommen – weder das Dormitorium noch das Refektorium, weder die Küche noch das Backhaus oder die Brauerei. Philip hätte aus dieser Feststellung einen gewissen Trost ziehen können, aber seine Miene hellte sich nicht auf.

Sie beendeten ihren Rundgang, wo sie ihn begonnen hatten – vor der eingestürzten Westfassade. Unterwegs hatte keiner von beiden auch nur ein Wort verloren. Mit einem schweren Seufzer brach Philip jetzt das Schweigen. »Das war ein Werk des Teufels«, sagte er.

Jetzt ist meine Stunde gekommen, dachte Tom, holte tief Luft und sagte: »Es kann auch ein Werk Gottes gewesen sein.«

Philip sah ihn überrascht an. »Wie das?«

Tom wägte seine Worte genau. »Niemand ist verletzt worden. Die Bücher, der Klosterschatz und die Gebeine des Heiligen sind allesamt gerettet. Zerstört wurde nur die Kirche. Vielleicht wollte Gott eine neue.«

Philip lächelte skeptisch. »Und wahrscheinlich ist es auch Gottes Wille, daß Ihr diese Kirche erbaut ...« So sehr von Sinnen, daß ihm der Eigennutz in Toms Argumenten entgangen wäre, war er nun auch wieder nicht.

Tom ließ sich nicht beirren. »Das mag wohl so sein«, erwiderte er. »Schließlich war es auch nicht der Teufel, der Euch am Vorabend des Brandes einen Baumeister geschickt hat.«

Philip wandte sich ab. »Ja, gewiß wird es eines Tages eine neue

Kathedrale geben«, sagte er. »Ich kann Euch bloß nicht sagen, wann. Und was soll ich in der Zwischenzeit tun? Wie soll das Leben hier im Kloster weitergehen? Wir sind nur hier, um Gott zu dienen und Gelehrsamkeit zu üben.«

Der Prior war zutiefst verzweifelt. Für Tom war der Zeitpunkt gekommen, ihm einen Hoffnungsschimmer zu zeigen. »In zwei Wochen haben mein Sohn und ich den Kreuzgang so weit freigelegt, daß er wieder benutzbar ist«, sagte er in einem Ton, der zuversichtlicher klang, als es berechtigt gewesen wäre.

Überrascht blickte Philip auf. »Meint Ihr wirklich?« fragte er, doch sein Ausdruck hellte sich nur vorübergehend auf. »Aber wo sollen wir denn unsere Gottesdienste abhalten?« setzte er niedergeschlagen hinzu.

»In der Krypta. Die wäre doch dafür geeignet, nicht wahr?«

»Ja, das wäre sie in der Tat ...«

»Ich bin sicher, daß die Krypta kaum Schaden genommen hat«, sagte Tom.

Philip starrte ihn an, als wäre er der Engel der Barmherzigkeit.

»Zuerst räumen wir den Weg zwischen dem Kreuzgang und den Treppen zur Krypta frei«, fuhr Tom fort. »Das geht verhältnismäßig schnell. Es mag in Euren Ohren merkwürdig klingen, aber es ist ein wahres Glück, daß diese Seite der Kirche nahezu vollständig zerstört ist. So besteht nämlich keine Gefahr mehr durch einstürzendes Mauerwerk. Die stehengebliebenen Mauern muß ich mir genau ansehen. Es kann sein, daß wir die eine oder andere mit Streben abstützen müssen. Man sollte sie zudem jeden Tag auf neue Risse untersuchen, doch selbst dann ist es nicht ratsam, die Kirche bei Sturm zu betreten.« All diese Dinge waren sehr wichtig, aber Tom sah, daß Philip sie nicht aufnahm. Philip wollte von Tom nur Gutes hören, etwas Aufmunterndes, Hilfreiches. Die einzige Möglichkeit, den ersehnten Auftrag zu bekommen, bestand darin, Philips Wünsche zu erfüllen. Tom änderte seinen Tonfall. »Stellt mir ein paar von den jüngeren Mönchen zur Verfügung, und ich richte die Kirche so her, daß Ihr in zwei Wochen wieder ein halbwegs geregeltes Leben führen könnt.«

Philip sah ihn mit großen Augen an. »Zwei Wochen?« fragte er ungläubig.

»Gewährt mir und meiner Familie Unterkunft und Verpflegung. Meinen Lohn könnt Ihr mir zahlen, wenn Ihr das Geld dazu habt.«

»Ihr meint, Ihr könnt mir innerhalb von zwei Wochen meine Priorei wiedergeben?« fragte Philip noch einmal.

Tom war sich seiner Sache keineswegs so sicher – aber selbst wenn es drei Wochen dauerte, würde niemand ihm einen Strick daraus drehen. »Innerhalb von zwei Wochen, jawohl«, bestätigte er mit fester Stimme. »Danach können wir damit anfangen, die restlichen Mauern einzureißen – das ist, wohlgemerkt, eine Sache für Fachleute, wenn kein Unglück geschehen soll. Wir können die wiederverwendbaren Steine aussortieren und die unbrauchbaren fortschaffen lassen. Und während all dies geschieht, beginnen wir mit dem Plan für die neue Kathedrale.«

Tom hielt den Atem an. Er hatte sein Bestes getan. Nun wird er mir Arbeit geben *müssen,* dachte er.

Der Prior nickte und lächelte erstmals wieder. »Ich glaube, Gott hat Euch mir gesandt«, sagte er. »Kommt, wir frühstücken erst einmal. Danach können wir mit der Arbeit beginnen.«

Tom atmete hörbar aus; es war ein abgrundtiefer Seufzer der Erleichterung. »Ich danke Euch«, sagte er. Auch seine Stimme zitterte ein wenig, er konnte nichts dagegen tun. Doch plötzlich war ihm alles egal. Er schluchzte auf und schämte sich dessen nicht. »Ich vermag Euch gar nicht zu sagen, was Eure Worte für mich bedeuten«, fügte er hinzu.

Nach dem Frühstück hielt Philip in Cuthberts Lagerraum unter der Küche eine improvisierte Kapitelversammlung ab. Die Mönche waren nervös und aufgeregt. Sie hatten sich für ein sicheres, gleichförmiges, überschaubares und mithin ein wenig langweiliges Leben entschieden oder zumindest damit abgefunden. Die meisten von ihnen hatten keine Ahnung, wie es weitergehen sollte. Ihre Bestürzung berührte Philip tief. Mehr denn je kam er sich vor wie ein Schäfer, dem die Sorge um eine törichte, hilflose Herde anvertraut worden ist ... obgleich er natürlich wußte, daß er es nicht mit tumben Schafen, sondern mit seinen geliebten Brüdern zu tun hatte. Nach reiflicher Überlegung war er zu dem Schluß gekommen, der beste Trost liege in klaren Worten: Er mußte ihnen sagen, wie es weitergehen sollte, und ihre Aufgeschrecktheit durch harte Arbeit in sinnvolle Bahnen lenken. Darüber hinaus mußte so bald wie möglich wieder der gewohnte Alltag einziehen.

Philip änderte das Ritual der Kapitelversammlung trotz der ungewöhnlichen äußeren Umstände nicht. Er befahl die Verlesung des Martyrologiums des Tages, an das sich die Gebete für die verstorbenen Mitbrüder anschlossen: Aus dem Gebet zogen die Klöster ihre Existenzberechtigung. Als Philip merkte, daß einige Mönche ihre innere Unruhe noch immer nicht überwunden hatten, wählte er aus Kapitel 20 der Regel des heiligen Benedikt den Abschnitt mit der Überschrift *Von der Ehrfurcht beim Gebet.* Danach folgte der Nekrolog. Das vertraute Ritual beruhigte die Brüder. Philip beobachtete, wie mit der Zeit der verschreckte Ausdruck aus ihren Gesichtern wich – sie erkannten, daß ihre Welt nicht unterzugehen drohte.

Zum Schluß erhob sich Philip und sprach zu ihnen. »Die Katastrophe, die uns in der vergangenen Nacht heimgesucht hat, war glücklicherweise nur dinglicher Natur«, begann er und versuchte, soviel Wärme und Zuversicht in seine Stimme zu legen wie möglich. »Unser Leben aber ist ein geistiges, unsere Arbeit ist Gebet, Ritus und Meditation.« Er sah von einem zum anderen, versuchte, keinen auszulassen, und wartete, bis er sich der geschärften Aufmerksamkeit aller sicher sein konnte. Dann sagte er: »Es wird nur wenige Tage dauern, dann werden wir diese unsere gewohnte Arbeit wiederaufnehmen. Das verspreche ich euch.«

Er machte eine Pause, um seine Worte nachwirken zu lassen. Die allgemeine Erleichterung war fast mit Händen zu greifen. »Der Herr in seiner Weisheit«, fuhr Philip schließlich fort, »hat uns gestern einen Baumeister geschickt, der mir versichert hat, daß der Kreuzgang in einer Woche wieder benutzbar ist – vorausgesetzt, wir vertrauen uns seiner sachkundigen Leitung an.«

Ein unterdrücktes Gemurmel verriet, daß diese Nachricht die Brüder angenehm überraschte.

»In unserer Kirche wird, wie ich fürchte, nie wieder eine Messe stattfinden können. Wir werden eine neue Kathedrale bauen müssen, ein Unterfangen, das, wie ihr wißt, viele Jahre in Anspruch nehmen wird. Aber Tom Builder glaubt, daß die Krypta heilgeblieben ist. Die Krypta ist geweiht, wir können dort also Gottesdienste abhalten. Tom meint, er kann uns innerhalb von einer Woche nach der Freilegung des Kreuzgangs sicheren Zugang zu ihr verschaffen. Ihr seht, wir können unseren normalen Ritus rechtzeitig zum Sonntag Septuagesima wiederaufnehmen.«

Erneut war die Erleichterung hörbar, und Philip spürte, daß sein Versuch, die Mitbrüder zu besänftigen und sie mit neuem Mut zu erfüllen, Erfolg zeitigte. Zu Beginn der Kapitelversammlung noch ängstlich und verwirrt, waren sie jetzt ruhig und hoffnungsfroh. »Brüder, die sich harter körperlicher Arbeit nicht gewachsen fühlen, sind entschuldigt«, fügte er noch hinzu, »wer aber seine gesamte Arbeitskraft Tom Builder zur Verfügung stellt, darf rotes Fleisch essen und Wein trinken.«

Er setzte sich. Remigius war der erste, der nach ihm das Wort ergriff. »Wieviel Geld werden wir diesem Baumeister zahlen müssen?« fragte er argwöhnisch.

Man konnte sich darauf verlassen, daß Remigius immer ein Haar in der Suppe fand. »Nichts, vorerst«, erwiderte Philip. »Tom weiß, wie arm wir sind. Solange wir ihm keinen Lohn zahlen können, arbeitet er für freie Unterkunft und Verpflegung.«

Philip wußte, daß seine Aussage doppeldeutig war. Sie konnte besagen, daß Tom erst dann Anspruch auf Lohn erheben durfte, wenn die Priorei wieder zahlungsfähig war. In Wirklichkeit war es natürlich so, daß sich das Kloster vom ersten Tag an bei ihm verschuldete. Ehe Philip jedoch die Vereinbarung näher erläutern konnte, sprach bereits wieder Remigius.

»Und wo wird der Baumeister mit seiner Familie wohnen?«

»Ich habe ihm das Gästehaus überlassen.«

»Sie könnten auch bei einer Familie im Dorf Unterschlupf finden.«

»Der Baumeister hat uns ein großzügiges Angebot gemacht«, erwiderte Philip ungeduldig. »Wir können von Glück reden, daß wir ihn bei uns haben. Solange wir ihm ein anständiges Haus zur Verfügung stellen können, das ohnehin meistens leersteht, braucht er nicht bei anderen Leuten im Ziegen- oder Schweinestall zu nächtigen.«

»Zu dieser Familie gehören zwei Frauen …«, begann Remigius.

»Eine Frau und ein kleines Mädchen«, verbesserte ihn Philip.

»*Eine* Frau dann eben. Daß Frauen auf dem Klostergelände leben, ist unerwünscht.«

Die Mönche murrten; Remigius' Nörgelei mißfiel ihnen. »Daß Frauen im Gästehaus übernachten, ist absolut selbstverständlich«, sagte Philip.

»Aber nicht *diese* Frau!« entfuhr es Remigius im Zorn, doch hatte es den Anschein, als bereue er seinen Ausbruch sofort wieder.

Philip runzelte die Stirn. »Ist dir die Frau näher bekannt, Bruder?« fragte er.

»Sie lebte früher in dieser Gegend hier«, antwortete Remigius zögernd.

Was ist nur los mit dieser Frau? fragte sich Philip. Schon zum zweitenmal erlebte er eine ungewöhnliche Reaktion auf ihre Anwesenheit. Er konnte sich noch gut an die heillose Verwirrung erinnern, die Waleran Bigod bei ihrem Anblick überkommen hatte.

»Stimmt etwas nicht mit ihr, Bruder?« fragte er Remigius, doch ehe der Angesprochene antworten konnte, meldete sich Bruder Paul, der Alte vom Brückenhäuschen, zu Wort.

»Ich entsinne mich«, sagte er mit traumverlorener Stimme, »daß in den Wäldern der Umgebung einst ein Mädchen hauste, ganz im Freien. Das muß jetzt ungefähr fünfzehn Jahre her sein. Die Frau des Baumeisters erinnert mich an dieses Mädchen.«

»Die Leute sagen, es war eine Hexe«, sagte Remigius. »Wir können in unserem Kloster keine Hexe dulden!«

»Da bin ich mir nicht so sicher«, wandte Bruder Paul ein. Er sprach noch immer mit langsamer, meditativer Stimme. »Jede Frau, die in der Wildnis lebt, wird früher oder später als Hexe bezeichnet. Nur schafft die bloße Behauptung noch keine Wahrheiten. Ob diese Frau nun eine Gefahr ist für uns – ich vermag es nicht zu sagen und überlasse das Urteil darüber vertrauensvoll unserem Prior.«

»Die Übernahme eines klösterlichen Amts führt nicht unbedingt gleich zu höherer Weisheit«, fauchte Remigius.

»Nein, in der Tat nicht«, erwiderte Paul gedehnt und sah Remigius direkt in die Augen. »Gelegentlich kommt die Weisheit nie.«

Die Mönche lachten über diese Schlagfertigkeit. Daß die Antwort ausgerechnet von dem alten Paul kam, dem man so etwas nie zugetraut hätte, machte die Sache nur noch komischer. Philip sah sich gezwungen, den Ungehaltenen zu spielen. Er klatschte in die Hände und gebot Schweigen. »Genug!« sagte er. »Mit solchen Dingen spaßt man nicht. Ich werde die Frau befragen. Brechen wir nun auf und widmen wir uns wieder unseren Pflichten. Wer von der Arbeit entschuldigt werden möchte, begebe sich in die Krankenstube zu Gebet und Meditation. Die anderen kommen mit mir.«

Er verließ den Lagerraum und ging mit den Mönchen im Gefolge zum Kreuzgang. Nur einige wenige Mitbrüder – darunter Remigius und Sakristan Andrew – setzten sich ab und gingen zur Krankenstube. Die beiden kommen mir weder krank noch gebrechlich vor, dachte Philip, war aber andererseits ganz froh, daß die notorischen Unruhestifter sich entfernten.

Unter Toms Leitung hatten ein paar Klosterbedienstete bereits mit den Aufräumungsarbeiten begonnen. Der Baumeister selbst stand auf dem Schutthaufen im Kreuzgang und schrieb mit einem großen Stück Kreide den Buchstaben ›T‹ auf verschiedene Trümmersteine.

Zum erstenmal in seinem Leben stellte Philip sich die Frage, wie sich so schwere Steinbrocken überhaupt aus dem Weg schaffen und abtransportieren ließen. Viele von ihnen waren so groß, daß niemand sie auch nur anzuheben vermocht hätte. Er brauchte nicht lange auf eine Antwort zu warten: Ein Stein wurde auf zwei nebeneinander liegende Balken gerollt und von zwei Männern fortgetragen. Gewiß hatte Tom Builder ihnen gezeigt, wie man es anstellte.

Die Arbeit ging zügig voran, da die meisten der sechzig Klosterbediensteten mit anpackten. Ein ununterbrochener Strom von Menschen trug Steine fort und kam mit leeren Händen zurück, um neue zu holen. Der Anblick gab Philip Mut, und er sandte ein stummes Stoßgebet zum Himmel, in dem er dem Herrn für Tom Builder dankte.

Tom erblickte den Prior und kletterte vom Schutthaufen. Bevor er sich an Philip wandte, sagte er zu einem der Bediensteten (es war der Schneider, der die Mönchskutten nähte): »Sagt den Brüdern, daß sie Euch beim Forttragen der Steine helfen sollen. Aber gebt acht, daß sie nur die von mir markierten Brocken nehmen – sonst kann es passieren, daß der Haufen ins Rutschen kommt und jemanden erschlägt.« An Philip gewandt, fuhr er fort: »Ich habe genügend markiert – damit sind sie eine Zeitlang beschäftigt.«

»Wohin werden die Steine gebracht?« fragte Philip.

»Kommt mit, ich zeig's Euch. Ich wollte ohnehin schauen, ob sie sie richtig stapeln.«

Die beiden gingen los. Die Steine wurden an der Ostseite des Klostergeländes aufgeschichtet. »Eine Reihe von Bediensteten kann ich leider nicht freistellen«, sagte Philip. »Sie sind unabkömmlich. Die Stallknechte müssen sich um die Pferde kümmern, die Köche ums Essen, wir brauchen auch jemanden, der Feuerholz sammelt, die Hühner müssen gefüttert werden und so weiter. Überarbeiten tut sich dabei keiner. Die Hälfte könnt Ihr haben. Dazu kommen noch etwa dreißig Mönche.«

Tom nickte. »Das wird genügen.«

Die Männer stapelten die noch warmen Steine an der Ostmauer des Klostergeländes, nur wenige Schritt vom Hospital und dem Haus des Priors entfernt. »Wir müssen die alten Steine für den Neubau aufbewahren«, sagte Tom. »Für die Wände lassen sie sich nicht mehr gebrauchen, dazu sind sie zu verwittert. Aber für die Fundamente taugen sie allemal. Und die zerbrochenen Steine lassen sich auch noch verwenden. Mit Mörtel vermischt schütten wir sie als Füllung in den Hohlraum zwischen äußerer und innerer Mauerwand.«

»Ich verstehe«, sagte der Prior und sah zu, wie der Baumeister die Leute anwies, die Steine so zu schichten, daß der entstehende Haufen nicht wieder einstürzen konnte. Ohne Toms Rat und Erfahrung läuft hier gar nichts, dachte Philip, das steht schon jetzt fest.

Als Tom mit der Arbeit der Männer zufrieden war, nahm Philip ihn beim Arm und führte ihn zum Gräberfeld im Norden der Kirche. Der Regen hatte aufgehört, doch waren die Grabsteine noch feucht. Mönche wurden auf der Ostseite des Friedhofs, Dorfbewohner auf der Westseite bestattet. Philip und Tom blieben vor der Ruine des nördlichen Querhauses stehen, welche die beiden Abteilungen des Gräberfelds voneinander trennte. Ein schwacher Sonnenstrahl durchbrach die Wolken. Im hellen Licht des Tages wirkte das geschwärzte Gebälk des Dachstuhls nicht mehr ganz so unheimlich. Philip schämte sich jetzt fast, daß er noch während der Nacht geglaubt hatte, einen Teufel zu sehen.

»Einige meiner Mitbrüder haben gewisse Vorbehalte dagegen, daß eine Frau auf dem Gelände des Klosters leben wird.« Toms erschrokkener Blick verriet mehr als bloße Beunruhigung. Er hat Angst, dachte Philip, er ist fast außer sich ... Er muß die Frau wirklich sehr lieben. Hastig sprach er weiter. »Ich hingegen möchte es Euch nicht zumuten, irgendwo im Dorf mit einer anderen Familie die Hütte zu teilen. Um Ärger zu vermeiden, wäre es allerdings ratsam, wenn Euer Weib sich vorsichtig verhalten würde. Sagt ihr, sie möge sich von den Mönchen möglichst fernhalten, vor allem von den jüngeren. Wenn sie auf dem Klostergelände herumläuft, soll sie ihr Antlitz verhüllen. Vor allem aber darf sie nichts tun, was dazu angetan wäre, sie in den Verdacht der Hexerei zu bringen.«

»Es wird so sein, wie Ihr es wünscht«, sagte Tom mit fester Stimme, die nicht so recht zu seinem Aussehen passen wollte. Philip wußte, daß das Weib des Baumeisters eine gescheite Frau war, die durchaus ihre eigene Meinung hatte. Besonders begeistert wird sie über diese Verhaltensvorschriften nicht sein, dachte er. Andererseits – gestern ging diese Familie noch am Bettelstab. Da steht wohl zu erwarten, daß sie die Einschränkungen als kleinen Preis für Obdach und Sicherheit akzeptieren wird.

Sie setzten ihren Weg fort. In der Nacht hatte Philip in der Zerstörung der Kirche noch eine übernatürliche Tragödie gesehen, eine furchtbare Niederlage für die Kräfte des Fortschritts und die Verteidiger des wahren Glaubens, einen schweren Schlag gegen sein persönliches Lebenswerk. Inzwischen sah er darin nur mehr ein Problem, das zu lösen ihm aufgegeben war – ein gewaltiges Problem, gewiß, dessen Ausmaße einen erblassen lassen konnten, aber eben doch kein übermenschliches mehr. Den Wandel verdankte er im wesentlichen Tom. Philip empfand große Dankbarkeit gegenüber dem Baumeister.

Sie erreichten die Westseite der Ruine. Vor dem Stall wurde gerade ein schnelles Pferd gesattelt. Wer tritt denn heute eine Reise an, dachte der Prior, ausgerechnet heute? Er ließ Tom zum Kreuzgang zurückkehren und ging selbst zum Stall, um sich die Sache näher anzusehen.

Er fand schnell heraus, wer sich das Pferd hatte satteln lassen. Es war Alan, der junge Mitbruder und Helfer des Sakristans, der die Truhe mit dem Klosterschatz aus dem Kapitelhaus geborgen hatte.

»Und wohin führt dich dein Weg, mein Sohn?« fragte Philip.

»Zum Palast des Bischofs«, gab Alan zur Antwort. »Bruder Andrew schickt mich, Kerzen, Weihwasser und die Hostie zu holen, alldieweil wir bei dem Brand alles verloren haben und sobald wie möglich wieder einen geregelten Gottesdienst abhalten wollen.«

Das klang durchaus vernünftig. All diese Dinge waren in einer verschlossenen Kiste im Chor aufbewahrt gewesen und mit Sicherheit verbrannt. Es freute Philip, daß der Sakristan so schnell an die Erneuerung der Utensilien dachte. »Sehr gut«, sagte er zu Alan. »Aber warte noch ein Weilchen. Nimm bitte noch einen Brief an Bischof Waleran mit.« Dank seiner raffinierten, wenngleich nicht gerade sehr reputierlichen Winkelzüge war der durchtriebene Waleran inzwischen designierter Bischof. Philip konnte ihm die zugesagte Unterstützung nicht mehr entziehen und war daher verpflichtet, ihn ab sofort als Bischof zu behandeln. »Ich muß ihm von dem Brand berichten.«

»Ja, Vater«, erwiderte Alan. »Nur – ich habe schon einen Brief an den Bischof. Von Remigius.«

»Ach so!« Philip war überrascht. Das ist ja recht kühn von Remigius, dachte er und sagte: »Wohlan denn! Reite mit Umsicht – und der Herr sei mit dir!«

»Danke, Vater.«

Philip ging zur Kirche zurück. Remigius hatte es ja *sehr* eilig – und der Sakristan nicht minder! Warum nur? Philip fühlte sich nicht wohl in seiner Haut. Ob Remigius wirklich nur über den Brand der Kathedrale berichtet hat? Oder steht in dem Brief noch etwas anderes?

Auf halbem Wege blieb Philip stehen und drehte sich um. Als Prior stand ihm durchaus das Recht zu, Alan den Brief wegzunehmen und ihn zu lesen. Aber es war bereits zu spät: Alan trabte gerade zum Tor hinaus. Philip starrte ihm nach. In diesem Augenblick sah er das Weib des Baumeisters aus dem Gästehaus kommen. Sie trug einen Korb, der vermutlich die Asche von der Feuerstelle enthielt, und ging auf den Misthaufen neben dem Stall zu. Philip beobachtete sie. Sie hatte einen gefälligen Gang – wie der Schritt eines guten Pferdes.

Wieder mußte er an den Brief denken, den Remigius an Waleran geschrieben hatte.

Es war zwar nur ein Gefühl, beunruhigte ihn aber trotzdem: Er konnte sich des Verdachts nicht erwehren, daß der Brand der Kathedrale darin nur eine nebensächliche Rolle spielte.

Ohne dafür eine klare Begründung zu haben, war er sich sicher, daß der Hauptanlaß für das Schreiben das Weib des Baumeisters war.

Jack erwachte beim ersten Hahnenschrei. Er öffnete die Augen und sah, daß Tom gerade aufstand. Still blieb er liegen und hörte, wie Tom draußen vor der Tür auf die Erde pißte. Nur zu gern hätte er das verwaiste warme Plätzchen an der Seite seiner Mutter eingenommen und sich dicht an sie gekuschelt, aber er fürchtete Alfreds gnadenlosen Spott und blieb deshalb, wo er war. Tom kam wieder herein und rüttelte Alfred wach.

Vater und Sohn tranken Bier, das vom Vorabend übriggeblieben war, und aßen trockenes Pferdebrot. Dann gingen sie zur Arbeit. Da sie nicht alles Brot gegessen hatten, hoffte Jack noch etwas zu finden, mußte jedoch zu seiner Enttäuschung feststellen, daß Alfred auch dieses Mal alles mitgenommen hatte.

Alfred arbeitete den ganzen Tag über mit Tom auf der Baustelle. Jack ging manchmal mit seiner Mutter in den Wald. Während er mit seiner Schleuder auf Entenjagd ging, stellte Ellen Fallen auf. Alles, was sie fingen, verkauften sie an die Dorfbewohner oder an Cuthbert, den Kellermeister. Die kleinen Einkünfte waren ihre einzige Bargeldquelle, denn Tom verdiente keinen Penny. Sie kauften sich dafür Stoff, Leder oder Talg, woraus Mutter an den Tagen, an denen sie nicht in den Wald gingen, Schuhe, Unterhemden, Kerzen oder auch mal eine Mütze fertigte. Jack und Martha spielten unterdessen mit den Kindern aus dem Dorf. Am Sonntag, nach der Messe, saßen Tom und Ellen gern vor dem Feuer beisammen und unterhielten sich. Manchmal fingen sie auch an, miteinander zu schmusen, und Tom ließ seine Hand in Mutters Umhang verschwinden. Dann wurden die Kinder hinausgeschickt, und die Tür wurde von innen verriegelt. Das waren die schlimmsten Momente in der ganzen Woche, denn Alfred regte sich darüber immer furchtbar auf und ließ seine Wut an den beiden Jüngeren aus.

Heute indessen war ein normaler Werktag; Alfred war also vom Morgengrauen bis zur Abenddämmerung beschäftigt. Jack erhob sich und ging vor die Tür, wenig später folgte ihm Martha. Es war kalt, aber trocken. Die Ruine der Kathedrale war geradezu überlaufen, so viele Arbeiter waren dort am Werk. Sie trugen Steine, schaufelten Schutt beiseite, stützten unzuverlässige Mauern ab und rissen solche, die nicht mehr zu retten waren, nieder.

Zwischen Dorfbewohnern und Mönchen herrschte die stillschweigende Übereinkunft, daß die Kirche vom Teufel angezündet worden war, und über längere Zeiträume hinweg vergaß Jack tatsächlich, daß er selbst es getan hatte. Wenn dann die Erinnerung wiederkehrte, schreckte er immer erst auf – und war kurz darauf außerordentlich zufrieden mit sich selbst. Er hatte ein furchtbares Risiko auf sich genommen, aber es hatte sich gelohnt. Er, Jack, hatte die Familie vor dem Hungertod gerettet.

Die Mönche frühstückten vor Beginn der Arbeit, während die einfachen Arbeiter warten mußten, bis die Mönche im Kapitel waren. Die Wartezeit kam Jack und Martha immer schier unendlich vor. Jack wachte jeden Morgen mit leerem Magen auf, und die kalte Morgenluft regte seinen Appetit noch zusätzlich an.

»Gehen wir in den Küchenhof«, sagte Jack. »Vielleicht geben uns die Küchenjungen was zu knabbern.« Martha stimmte bereitwillig zu. Sie war sowieso ganz hingerissen von Jack und wäre auch auf alle anderen Vorschläge eingegangen.

Im Küchenhof entdeckten die beiden, daß Bruder Bernard, der für das Backhaus verantwortlich war, an diesem Tag Brot backte. Da all seine Gehilfen auf der Baustelle beschäftigt waren, mußte er das Feuerholz eigenhändig herbeischaffen. Bernard war ein junger, aber schon recht beleibter Mann. Er keuchte schwer unter der Last der schweren Äste und Scheite. »Wir helfen dir, Bruder«, sagte Jack. »Wir holen dir das Holz.«

Bernard kippte den breiten, flachen Tragekorb neben dem Ofen aus und reichte ihn Jack. »Ihr seid gute Kinder«, schnaufte er. »Gott segne euch.«

Die Kinder liefen zum Brennholzstapel hinter der Küche. Dort füllten sie den Korb und schleppten die schwere Last gemeinsam zurück zum Backhaus.

Der Ofen war bereits heiß, und Bernard schüttete das neue Holz gleich ins Feuer. Jack taten die Arme weh, aber sein Magen war noch übler dran. Rasch rannte er los, um den nächsten Korbvoll zu holen.

Als sie zum zweitenmal zurückkehrten, war Bernard gerade dabei, kleine Teiglaibe auf ein Blech zu legen. »Holt mir noch einen Korb, und ihr bekommt heiße Brötchen«, sagte er. Jack lief das Wasser im Munde zusammen.

Die Kinder beluden den Korb diesmal besonders hoch und stolperten gerade zurück, als ihnen im Hof Alfred über den Weg lief. Er trug einen Eimer bei sich und wollte anscheinend gerade Wasser aus dem Mühlteich holen. Seit dem Tag, da Ellens Sohn ihm einen toten Vogel ins Bier getan hatte, verfolgte Alfred Jack mit unversöhnlichem Haß. Wenn sie einander begegneten, drehte sich Jack meist wie beiläufig um und sah zu, daß er fortkam. Auch jetzt spielte er mit dem Gedanken, einfach den Korb fallen zu lassen und das Weite zu suchen, gestand sich dann aber ein, daß ihm ein solches Verhalten als Feigheit ausgelegt würde. Außerdem stieg ihm vom Backhaus her der Duft des frischgebackenen Brotes in die Nase. Mit klopfendem Herzen hielt er den Korb fest und versuchte, etwas schneller voranzukommen.

Alfred lachte die beiden Kinder aus, die sich zu zweit mit einer Last abplagten, welche er selbst ohne Schwierigkeiten allein hätte tragen können. Sie machten einen weiten Bogen um ihn, doch Alfred ging auf sie zu und schubste Jack um. Der Junge fiel auf sein Hinterteil und fühlte einen stechenden Schmerz im Lendenwirbel. Der Korb kippte um, und die gesammelten Holzscheite purzelten heraus. Weniger aus Schmerz denn aus Wut füllten sich Jacks Augen mit Tränen. Kein Mensch hat Alfred provoziert, dachte er. Es ist eine himmelschreiende Ungerechtigkeit, daß er ungestraft mit mir so umgehen kann. Er rappelte sich auf und sammelte das Holz wieder ein. Um Marthas willen unterdrückte er seine Erregung. Gemeinsam packten sie an und brachten den Korb ins Backhaus.

Die versprochene Belohnung wartete schon auf sie. Das Blech mit den frischgebackenen Brötchen kühlte auf einem steinernen Sims aus. Als die Kinder eintraten, nahm Bernard ein Brötchen fort, stopfte es sich in den Mund und sagte: »Sie sind gut. Bedient euch. Aber vorsichtig – sie sind noch heiß!«

Jack und Martha griffen zu. Weil er Angst hatte, sich den Mund zu verbrennen, kostete Jack zunächst nur behutsam. Das Backwerk schmeckte aber so köstlich, daß er seine Vorsicht schnell vergaß. Im Nu war das Brötchen verschlungen, und Jack stierte die verbleibenden neun mit sehnsüchtigen Augen an.

Bruder Bernard grinste. »Ich weiß, was du willst«, sagte er. »Nimm sie dir ruhig alle.«

Jack hob den Saum seines Umhangs und wickelte die Brötchen darin ein. »Wir bringen sie Mutter mit«, sagte er zu Martha.

»Braver Bub«, sagte Bernard. »Dann macht euch mal auf die Socken.«

Jack war begeistert. So ein Festessen, dachte er. Mutter wird sehr zufrieden mit mir sein. Gerne hätte er unterwegs noch ein Brötchen verzehrt, aber er bezwang sich. So viele auf einmal! Allein die Menge war schon eine Überraschung.

Auf der Freifläche vor dem Gästehaus begegnete ihnen Alfred ein zweites Mal.

Er hatte offenbar den Eimer gefüllt, ihn zur Baustelle gebracht und war nun unterwegs, um noch mehr Wasser zu holen. Jack beschloß, den Unbekümmerten zu spielen, und hoffte, Alfred würde ihn nicht beachten. Aber der geraffte Umhang, in dem er die Brötchen trug, war zu auffällig. Alfred steuerte direkt auf ihn zu.

Jack hätte ihm freiwillig ein Brötchen gegeben. Aber er wußte, daß Alfred jede Gelegenheit nutzen würde, ihm *alle* abzunehmen. Darum rannte er los.

Alfred nahm die Verfolgung auf, holte ihn nach kurzer Zeit ein und ließ ihn über das ausgestreckte Bein stolpern. Kopfüber stürzte Jack zu Boden, und die noch warmen Brötchen kullerten über das Gras. Alfred hob eines auf, wischte es ab und steckte es sich in den Mund. Seine Augen weiteten sich vor Überraschung. »Frisches Brot!« murmelte er und bückte sich nach den anderen.

Jack war wieder auf den Füßen und wollte ebenfalls ein Brötchen aufheben, aber Alfred schlug ihn mit der flachen Hand so heftig ins Gesicht, daß er gleich wieder hinfiel. Dann sammelte er die restlichen Brötchen ein und trollte sich – mit vollen Backen kauend. Jack brach in Tränen aus.

Martha sah ihn mitleidvoll an, aber Mitleid war jetzt das letzte, was Jack wollte. Er fühlte sich zutiefst erniedrigt. Er ging fort, und als Martha Anstalten traf, ihm zu folgen, drehte er sich um und sagte zu ihr: »Verschwinde!« Martha zuckte zusammen und blieb stehen. Kurz darauf war er allein.

Er ging auf die Ruine zu und wischte sich mit dem Ärmel die Tränen aus dem Gesicht. In seinem Herzen keimten Mordgedanken. Ich habe die Kathedrale zerstört, dachte er. Ich bin auch fähig, Alfred umzubringen.

Das Gelände um die Kirchenruine wurde gefegt und geputzt. Jack erinnerte sich, daß der Besuch eines kirchlichen Würdenträgers angesagt war; der Mann kam, um den entstandenen Schaden zu besichtigen.

Alfreds körperliche Überlegenheit war das Hauptproblem – es war zum Verrücktwerden. Bloß weil er so groß und stark war, konnte er sich das alles herausnehmen. Ziellos strich Jack umher. Er kochte vor Wut und bedauerte es aufrichtig, daß Alfred damals, als all diese Steine herunterfielen, nicht in der Kirche gewesen war.

Dann entdeckte er den Bösewicht. Alfred befand sich im nördlichen Querhaus und schaufelte Steinschutt auf einen Karren. Sein Gesicht war grau vor Staub. Nicht weit von dem Karren entfernt ragte ein Balken aus dem Schutt, der den Sturz vom Dach fast unbeschadet überstanden hatte. Er war lediglich etwas angesengt und rußgeschwärzt. Mit dem Finger fuhr Jack über die Oberfläche. Ein weißer Strich entstand. Plötzlich hatte er eine Idee: »Alfred ist ein Schwein«, schrieb er in den Ruß.

Einige Arbeiter wurden auf ihn aufmerksam. Es überraschte sie, daß der kleine Junge schreiben konnte. Ein junger Mann fragte ihn: »Was heißt das?«

»Fragt Alfred«, erwiderte Jack.

Alfred stierte auf das Geschriebene und runzelte ärgerlich die Stirn. Seinen Namen konnte er entziffern – aber das war auch schon alles. Er wußte, daß es sich um eine Beleidigung handeln mußte, konnte aber nicht genau sagen um welche, und das allein war schon demütigend genug und wurmte ihn furchtbar. Jacks Zorn legte sich dagegen ein wenig. Alfred sah einfach zu dämlich aus! Größer mag er ja sein, dachte der Junge, aber gescheiter bin ich.

Noch immer wußte niemand, was die Worte im Ruß bedeuteten. Da kam zufällig ein Novize vorbei, las sie und lächelte. »Wer ist Alfred?« fragte er.

»Der da«, sagte Jack und wies mit dem Daumen auf seinen Widersacher. Alfred wurde immer wütender. Da er aber nicht wußte, wie er sich verhalten sollte, stützte er sich linkisch auf seine Schaufel und blickte dumm aus der Wäsche.

Der Novize lachte. »Ein Schwein, wie? Wonach gräbt er denn? Nach Eicheln?«

»Wahrscheinlich«, sagte Jack, froh darüber, einen Verbündeten gefunden zu haben.

Alfred ließ die Schaufel fallen und versuchte, Jack zu packen. Aber der Junge war auf der Hut. Wie der Blitz fegte er davon. Offenbar um Ausgewogenheit bemüht, stellte der Novize ihm ein Bein, doch Jack sprang leichtfüßig darüber hinweg. So schnell er konnte, rannte er über das Gelände der ehemaligen Apsis, umkurvte Schutthaufen und sprang über am Boden liegende Dachsparren. Hinter sich hörte er die schweren Schritte und den grunzenden Atem Alfreds, der ihm dicht auf den Fersen war. Seine Angst lieh seinen Füßen Flügel.

Einen Augenblick später fiel ihm siedendheiß ein, daß er den falschen Weg eingeschlagen hatte. Auf dieser Seite der Ruine gab es kein Entkommen. Er verlor den Mut. Das wird diesmal verdammt wehtun, dachte er.

Die obere Hälfte des Ostflügels war eingestürzt, und der Schutt türmte sich vor dem stehengebliebenen Mauerrest. Da ihm kein anderer Ausweg offenstand, kletterte Jack hurtig den Trümmerhaufen empor.

Oben angekommen spähte er über die Mauer. Vor ihm gähnte ein ungefähr fünfzehn Fuß tiefer Abgrund – bei weitem zu tief, um ohne Risiko hinunterzuspringen. Er schwankte. Alfred hatte ihn fast erreicht, schon langte er nach Jacks Knöchel. Der Junge verlor das Gleichgewicht. Einen Augenblick lang stand er mit einem Fuß in der Luft auf der Mauerkrone und ruderte wie wild mit den Armen, während Alfred seinen Knöchel umklammerte. Dann spürte Jack, daß er sich nicht mehr halten konnte. Alfred riß noch einmal heftig an seinem Knöchel und ließ dann los. Jack stürzte ab und war während des Falls nicht einmal mehr imstande, die Füße nach unten zu bringen. Er hörte sich schreien und landete auf der linken Körperseite. Der Aufprall war furchtbar. Ein böser Zufall wollte es zudem, daß sein Gesicht auf einem Stein aufschlug.

Ihm wurde schwarz vor Augen.

Als er wieder zu sich kam und die Lider öffnete, stand Alfred direkt über ihm – er mußte irgendwo einen Abstieg gefunden haben. Neben Alfred befand sich ein älterer Mönch. Jack kannte ihn; es war Remigius, der Subprior. Remigius blickte ihn an und sagte: »Steh auf, Bursche!«

Jack wußte nicht, ob er es schaffen würde. Er konnte seinen linken Arm nicht bewegen, und seine linke Gesichtshälfte fühlte sich taub an. Er setzte sich auf. Er hatte mit dem Schlimmsten gerechnet und wunderte sich daher, daß er sich überhaupt rühren konnte. Mit dem rechten Arm stemmte er sich hoch. Unter großen Schmerzen, und indem er soviel Gewicht wie möglich auf sein rechtes Bein verlagerte, gelang es ihm, sich zu erheben. In seinem Gesicht wich die Taubheit dem Schmerz.

Remigius ergriff ihn am linken Arm. Es tat entsetzlich weh, und Jack schrie auf. Remigius ging darauf nicht ein. Er packte Alfred am Ohr. Wahrscheinlich werden wir jetzt ganz schlimm bestraft, dachte Jack, doch die Schmerzen waren so stark, daß ihm alles andere gleichgültig war.

»Nun, Kerl«, sagte Remigius zu Alfred, »sag mir mal, warum du versuchst, deinen Bruder umzubringen.«

»Das ist nicht mein Bruder!« erwiderte Alfred.

Remigius' Ausdruck veränderte sich. »Nicht dein Bruder?« fragte er. »Habt ihr etwa nicht dieselben Eltern?«

»*Sie* ist nicht meine Mutter!« rief Alfred aus. »Meine Mutter ist tot.«

Ein listiges Lächeln huschte über das Gesicht des Subpriors.

»Wann ist deine Mutter denn gestorben?«

»An Weihnachten.«

»*Letzte* Weihnachten?«

»Ja.«

Trotz seiner Schmerzen bemerkte Jack die auffallende Neugier des Subpriors. Wieso interessiert ihn das nur so? fragte er sich. Mit vor Aufregung zitternder Stimme setzte Remigius seine Befragung fort.

»So hat dein Vater die Mutter dieses Knaben hier erst kürzlich kennengelernt, wie?«

»Ja.«

»Und sind die beiden, seitdem sie ... zusammen sind, schon bei einem Priester gewesen, um sich nach Recht und Sitte trauen zu lassen?«

»Ich ... äh ... ich weiß nicht«, stotterte Alfred. Er versteht die Worte gar nicht, die der Mönch benutzt, dachte Jack. Er verstand sie allerdings selber nicht.

»Je nun!« sagte Remigius ungeduldig. »Ich meine: Gab es eine Hochzeitsfeier?«

»Nein.«

»Ich verstehe.« Der Subprior schien mit dieser Antwort rundum zufrieden, obgleich Jack eher mit dem Gegenteil gerechnet hätte. Einen Augenblick lang dachte der Mönch nach und sagte kein Wort. Dann schien er sich der beiden Knaben wieder zu erinnern. »Also, ihr zwei«, sagte er. »Wenn ihr weiterhin hier in der Priorei leben und das Brot der Mönche essen wollt, dann streitet euch nicht mehr so häßlich – selbst, wenn ihr keine Brüder seid. Wir Diener Gottes dürfen kein Blutvergießen sehen – das ist einer der Gründe dafür, daß wir ein zurückgezogenes, weltabgeschirmtes Leben führen.« Mit dieser kleinen Mahnrede gab Remigius die beiden frei und ging seiner Wege. Und endlich konnte Jack zu seiner Mutter laufen.

Es dauerte drei, nicht zwei Wochen, bis Tom und seine Helfer die Krypta so weit hergerichtet hatten, daß sie sich als behelfsmäßige Kirche benutzen ließ. Waleran, der designierte Bischof, hatte sein Kommen angekündigt und wollte die erste Messe lesen. Der Kreuzgang war von allem Schutt befreit, und Tom hatte die beschädigten Partien ausgebessert. Kreuzgänge waren vom Baulichen her recht einfach, nichts weiter als überdachte Gassen; die Arbeit war ihm leichtgefallen. Davon abgesehen bildete die Kathedrale über weite Strecken nach wie vor den Anblick eines Trümmerfelds. An manchen der noch stehenden Mauern bestand Einsturzgefahr. Zwischen dem Kreuzgang und den Treppen zur Krypta hatte Tom jedoch durch das ehemalige nördliche Querschiff einen gut begehbaren Gang freischaufeln lassen.

Tom sah sich um. Mit ihren annähernd fünfzig Quadratfuß Grundfläche bot die Krypta ausreichend Platz für die klösterlichen Gottesdienste. Der ziemlich düstere Raum war ein niedriges Gewölbe mit dicken, schweren Säulen, das dank seiner stabilen Konstruktion das Feuer ohne Schaden überstanden hatte. Als Altar diente ein auf Schragen gestellter Zeichentisch, und die Bänke hatte man aus dem Refektorium herbeigeschafft. Der Sakristan mußte nur noch die bestickten Altartücher auflegen und die juwelengeschmückten Kandelaber verteilen, dann würde ein vorzüglicher Eindruck entstehen.

Mit der Wiederaufnahme der Gottesdienste verlor Tom einen Großteil seiner Mitarbeiter. Die meisten Mönche würden von nun an wieder ihre gewohnten Riten pflegen und zu ihren angestammten Arbeiten in Landwirtschaft und Klosterverwaltung zurückkehren. Ungefähr die Hälfte der weltlichen Klosterbediensteten verblieb ihm. Prior Philip verfocht ihnen gegenüber eine harte Linie: Da er ohnehin glaubte, es seien ihrer zuviele, hatte er alle, die sich über die Versetzung aus Stall oder Küche beklagten, vor die Wahl gestellt, entweder zu gehorchen oder zu gehen. Ein paar waren gegangen, die meisten hatten sich jedoch gefügt.

Die Priorei schuldete Tom inzwischen bereits drei Wochenlöhne. Da einem Baumeister vier Pence pro Tag zustanden, belief sich die Summe mittlerweile auf zweiundsiebzig Pence und erhöhte sich von Tag zu Tag. Tom hatte vor, den Prior nach einem halben Jahr um Bezahlung zu bitten. Die Schuld würde mithin zweieinhalb Pfund

Silber betragen – und diese Summe mußte Philip erst einmal aufbringen, bevor er Tom entlassen konnte. So verliehen seine Rückstände dem Baumeister ein Gefühl der Sicherheit.

Es bestand sogar die entfernte Möglichkeit, daß er sich nie wieder im Leben eine andere Stelle würde suchen müssen. Tom wagte kaum, daran zu denken. Immerhin handelte es sich um eine Bischofskirche, eine Kathedrale. Wenn man sich zuständigenorts für die Errichtung eines repräsentativen Neubaus aussprach und die erforderlichen Gelder aufbrachte, dann konnte Kingsbridge durchaus zur größten Baustelle des Königreichs werden und auf Jahrzehnte hinaus Dutzenden von Steinmetzen Arbeit und Brot geben.

Aber das war weit mehr, als man erhoffen konnte. In Gesprächen mit Mönchen und Dorfbewohnern hatte Tom erfahren, daß die Kathedrale von Kingsbrigde nie sehr bedeutend gewesen war. Verborgen in ländlicher Einsamkeit und über mehrere Generationen von Bischöfen beherrscht, die es an jedem Ehrgeiz fehlen ließen, war der langsame Niedergang gar nicht mehr zu verkennen. Die Priorei war ebenso arm wie unscheinbar. Es gab Klöster, die durch üppige Gastfreundschaft, glänzende Schulen, umfangreiche Bibliotheken oder hervorragende philosophische Leistungen ihrer Prioren und Äbte die Aufmerksamkeit von Königen und Erzbischöfen auf sich zu ziehen wußten. Nichts dergleichen traf auf Kingsbridge zu. Aller Wahrscheinlichkeit nach würde Prior Philip sich mit einer kleinen, einfach gebauten und bescheiden ausgestatteten Kirche zufriedengeben müssen, deren Errichtung allenfalls zehn Jahre in Anspruch nehmen würde.

Doch selbst damit wäre Tom hochzufrieden gewesen. Er hatte, noch ehe die von Feuer geschwärzten Ruinen erkaltet waren, seine Chance erkannt: Hier würde er eine Kathedrale errichten – oder nirgends.

Prior Philip war längst davon überzeugt, daß Tom Builder vom lieben Gott persönlich nach Kingsbridge entsandt worden war. Tom wußte, daß er mit der gelungenen Organisation der Aufräumungsarbeiten und seiner wertvollen Hilfe bei der Normalisierung des klösterlichen Lebens Philips Vertrauen gewonnen hatte. Nun kam es darauf an, den richtigen Augenblick für ein erstes Gespräch über die Planung des Neubaus abzupassen. Wenn ich keinen Fehler mache, dachte er, wird der Prior mich mit der Erstellung der Pläne beauftragen. Gerade die Tatsache, daß die neue Kirche vermutlich eher bescheiden ausfallen würde, sprach für Tom – bei einem größeren Bauwerk war eher damit zu rechnen, daß man sich an einen erfahrenen Dombaumeister wandte. Tom war voller Hoffnung.

Die Glocke rief zur Kapitelversammlung und bedeutete den Arbeitern, daß sie sich zum Frühstück begeben durften. Tom verließ die Krypta und ging zum Refektorium. Unterwegs begegnete ihm Ellen.

Wutentbrannt trat sie ihm in den Weg, als wollte sie ihn keinen Schritt weitergehen lassen. In ihren Augen lag ein Blick, der nichts Gutes verhieß. Martha und Jack begleiteten sie. Ellens Sohn war übel zugerichtet: Ein Auge war geschlossen, die linke Gesichtshälfte stark geschwollen und durch Aufschürfungen entstellt. Aus seiner schiefen Haltung ließ sich schließen, daß er das rechte Bein nicht belasten konnte. Tom tat der kleine Kerl furchtbar leid. »Was ist denn mit dir passiert?« fragte er.

»Das war Alfred«, sagte Ellen.

Tom stöhnte innerlich auf. Einen Moment lang schämte er sich seines Sohnes, der soviel größer und stärker war als Jack. Aber Jack war auch kein Engel – vielleicht hatte er Alfred provoziert. Der Baumeister sah sich um und erblickte seinen Sohn unter den Arbeitern, die zum Refektorium strömten. »Alfred!« brüllte er. »Komm her!«

Alfred drehte sich um und kam langsam näher. Das schlechte Gewissen war ihm anzusehen.

»Warst du das?« fragte Tom und deutete auf Jack.

»Er ist von einer Mauer gefallen«, sagte Alfred verdrossen.

»Hast du ihn geschubst?«

»Ich war hinter ihm her.«

»Wer hat angefangen?«

»Jack hat mich beschimpft.«

Jacks geschwollene Lippen bewegten sich. »Ich hab' ihn ein Schwein geheißen, weil er unser Brot weggenommen hat.«

»Brot?« fragte Tom. »Wie kommt ihr denn vor dem Frühstück zu Brot?«

»Bruder Bernard, der Bäcker, hat es uns gegeben. Wir haben Brennholz für ihn geschleppt.«

»Ihr hättet das Brot mit Alfred teilen sollen«, meinte Tom.

»Hätt' ich ja auch.«

»Und warum bist du dann weggelaufen?« fragte Alfred.

»Ich wollte es Mutter zeigen!« rief Jack entrüstet. »Und da ist Alfred gekommen und hat es mir weggefressen.«

Aus vierzehnjähriger Erfahrung im Umgang mit Kindern wußte Tom, daß es aussichtslos war, im nachhinein herausfinden zu wollen, wer bei einem Streit der Schuldige war. »Ab mit euch zum Frühstück«, sagte er. »Und wenn ihr euch heute noch einmal kabbelt, dann siehst du, Alfred, heute abend genauso aus wie Jack, dafür trage ich Sorge. Und jetzt haut ab, alle drei!«

Die Kinder verdrückten sich.

Tom und Ellen gingen langsam hinter ihnen her. Kaum waren sie außer Hörweite, da fragte Jacks Mutter: »Ist das alles, was du dazu zu sagen hast?«

Tom sah sie an. Ellen war noch immer aufgebracht – doch was sollte er tun? Er hob die Schultern. »Das ist doch dasselbe wie immer. Unschuldslämmer sind sie beide nicht.«

»Tom! Wie kannst du so etwas sagen?«

»Der eine ist so schlimm wie der andere.«

»Alfred hat ihnen ihr Brot weggenommen, und Jack hat ihn ein Schwein geheißen. So etwas darf doch nicht mit Blutvergießen enden.«

Tom schüttelte den Kopf. »Jungen prügeln sich immer. Man könnte sein ganzes Leben damit vertun, ihre Streitereien schlichten zu wollen. Sie sollen das unter sich ausmachen.«

»Nein, Tom, das genügt mir nicht«, erwiderte Ellen mit einem drohenden Unterton in der Stimme. »Sieh dir Jacks Gesicht an und dann Alfreds. Das war keine harmlose Rauferei unter Kindern mehr, sondern der bösartige Überfall eines ausgewachsenen Mannsbilds auf einen kleinen Jungen.«

Tom konnte diese Argumentation nur schwer ertragen. Ein Waisenknabe war Alfred gewiß nicht, doch das galt ja für Jack genauso. Ich kann nicht zulassen, daß Jack zum verwöhnten Hätschelkind der Familie wird, dachte er. »Alfred ist kein ausgewachsenes Mannsbild. Er ist gerade mal vierzehn Jahre alt. Aber immerhin *arbeitet* er und leistet damit – im Gegensatz zu Jack – einen Beitrag zu unserem Lebensunterhalt. Jack spielt den ganzen Tag – wie ein Kind. Nach meinem Dafürhalten sollte er Alfred einen gewissen Respekt entgegenbringen, was er aber, wie du mir wohl bestätigen kannst, nicht tut.«

»Das ist mir vollkommen gleichgültig!« fauchte Ellen. »Du kannst mir erzählen, was du willst – ich sehe nur eines: Mein Sohn ist verletzt und hätte sich ohne weiteres auch den Hals brechen können. *Das lasse ich nicht zu!*« Sie brach in Tränen aus. Mit ruhigerer Stimme, aber immer noch wütend, fügte sie hinzu: »Jack ist mein Kind. Ich ertrage es nicht, ihn in solch einem Zustand zu sehen.«

Tom hatte Verständnis für sie und hätte sie gerne getröstet, fürchtete sich andererseits aber davor, zu nachgiebig zu erscheinen. Er hatte das Gefühl, die Auseinandersetzung mit Ellen könnte ein Wendepunkt sein. Jack war, da er immer nur mit seiner Mutter zusammengelebt hatte, ein sehr behütetes, ja ein überbehütetes Kind. Tom sah nicht ein, daß er eines besonderen Schutzes gegen die Widrigkeiten des täglichen Lebens bedurfte. Ließ man ihm das durchgehen, so schaffte man einen Präzedenzfall, der auf Jahre hinaus zu ständig neuem Ärger Anlaß geben würde. Im Innern seines Herzens wußte der Baumeister, daß Alfred diesmal zu weit gegangen war, und er war auch entschlossen, ihm ins Gewissen zu reden. Aber er hielt nichts davon, dies jetzt anzusprechen. »Prügel gehören zum Leben«, sagte er zu Ellen. »Jack muß lernen, sie entweder zu ertragen oder zu vermeiden. Ich kann nicht die ganze Zeit hinter ihm her sein und ihn beschützen.«

»Vor diesem Raufbold von Sohn könntest du ihn schon schützen!«

Tom zuckte zusammen. Er haßte es, wenn sie Alfred einen Raufbold nannte. »Ja, das könnte ich«, gab er verärgert zurück. »Aber ich werde es nicht tun. Jack muß lernen, sich selber zu schützen.«

»Ach, fahr doch zur Hölle!« fuhr Ellen ihn an, machte kehrt und ließ ihn stehen.

Tom betrat das Refektorium. Die Holzhütte, in der die Klosterbediensteten normalerweise ihre Mahlzeiten einnahmen, war beim Einsturz des Südwestturms beschädigt worden. Die Arbeiter warteten daher mit dem Essen, bis die Mönche fertig waren, und kamen dann ins Refektorium. Tom suchte sich einen Platz abseits. Ihm war jetzt nicht nach Gesellschaft zumute. Ein Küchenhelfer brachte ihm einen Krug Bier und stellte einen Korb mit ein paar Brotscheiben vor ihn hin. Tom tunkte ein Stück Brot ins Bier und begann zu essen.

Alfred ist ein großer Bursche mit zuviel überschüssiger Kraft, dachte er und seufzte in seinen Bierkrug. Die Vaterliebe wärmte sein Herz. Natürlich hat er etwas von einem Raufbold an sich, daran gibt es nichts zu rütteln. Aber mit der Zeit wird sich das schon legen. Ich werde meine Kinder nicht dazu zwingen, besondere Rücksichten auf diesen dahergelaufenen Jack zu nehmen, dachte Tom. Sie haben schon viel zuviel ertragen müssen. Sie haben ihre Mutter verloren, mußten monatelang von einem Ort zum anderen ziehen und wären ums Haar verhungert. Soweit es in meinen Kräften steht, werde ich ihnen weitere Belastungen ersparen. Nach allem, was geschehen ist, haben sie durchaus einen Anspruch auf etwas Nachsicht und Milde. Jack soll Alfred eben aus dem Weg gehen, das wird ihn schon nicht umbringen ...

Auseinandersetzungen mit Ellen erfüllten Tom regelmäßig mit Schwermut. Sie hatten sich schon des öfteren gestritten, und meistens war es dabei um die Kinder gegangen. Der jüngste Streit war der bislang schlimmste. Es war ihm schier unmöglich, die harten feindlichen Züge, die im Zorn ihr Antlitz beherrschten, mit der leidenschaftlichen Liebe in Einklang zu bringen, welche sie kurz zuvor noch miteinander verbunden hatte. In ihrer Wut kam sie ihm vor wie eine Fremde, die sich in böser Absicht in sein beschauliches Leben einmischte.

Mit seiner ersten Frau war es anders gewesen. Gewiß, es hatte Meinungsverschiedenheiten gegeben, aber nicht so hitzige, erbitterte Krächke. Im nachhinein kam es ihm vor, als hätten er und Agnes in allen wichtigen Dingen übereingestimmt und in den wenigen Ausnahmefällen mehr Rücksicht aufeinander genommen. So soll es auch sein im Zusammenleben von Mann und Frau, dachte er. Ellen wird lernen müssen, daß man in einer Familie nicht immer den eigenen Willen durchsetzen kann.

Es war nicht so, daß er Ellen fortwünschte, nicht einmal, wenn sie vor Wut tobte. Aber er konnte es nicht verhindern, daß sich immer häufiger sentimentale Erinnerungen an Agnes einstellten. Sie war fast sein gesamtes Erwachsenenleben an seiner Seite gewesen, und ihr Tod bedeutete für ihn einen schmerzhaften Verlust, den er noch lange nicht überwunden hatte.

Tagsüber, wenn die Arbeiter wußten, was sie zu tun hatten, und Tom sich mit Muße einer Tätigkeit zuwenden konnte, die sein fachmännisches Geschick erforderte – zum Beispiel der Ausbesserung einer Mauer im Kreuzgang oder der Restauration eines Pfeilers in der Krypta –, führte er bisweilen imaginäre Gespräche mit Agnes. Meistens erzählte er ihr dabei von Jonathan, ihrem jüngsten gemeinsamen Sohn. Tom sah den Kleinen jetzt fast täglich. Er wurde in der Küche gefüttert, im Kreuzgang herumgetragen und des Abends im Dormitorium zu Bett gebracht. Jonathan machte den Eindruck eines rundum gesunden und glücklichen Kindes. Kein Mensch im Kloster, von Ellen einmal abgesehen, wäre auf den Gedanken gekommen, daß Tom am Schicksal des Kleinen besonderen Anteil nahm. Auch über Alfred und Prior Philip, ja sogar über Ellen unterhielt sich Tom mit Agnes, genauso wie er sich – außer über Ellen – mit der Lebenden darüber unterhalten hätte. Er berichtete ihr von seinen Zukunftsplänen, von seiner Hoffnung, endlich eine dauerhafte Anstellung gefunden zu haben, und von seinem Traum, eine eigene Kathedrale entwerfen und bauen zu können. Agnes' Antworten hörte er in seinem Kopf. Sie klangen mal zufrieden und ermutigend, mal begeistert, mal skeptisch, mal ablehnend – je nachdem. Manchmal gab er ihr recht, manchmal widersprach er ihr. Hätte er jemandem von seinen Gesprächen mit Agnes erzählt, so wäre ihm der Vorwurf, er kommuniziere mit einem Geist, nicht erspart geblieben ... Ein Schwarm von Priestern hätte sich über ihn hergemacht und ihn mit Weihwasser und Exorzismus traktiert. Tom hingegen wußte genau, daß ihm nichts Übernatürliches widerfuhr. Er kannte Agnes eben so gut, daß er sich ihre Worte und Gefühle in praktisch jeder beliebigen Situation vorstellen konnte.

Agnes besuchte ihn ohne Vorankündigung und zu den merkwürdigsten Zeiten. Einmal schälte er mit seinem Eßmesser gerade eine Birne für Martha, da sah er plötzlich Agnes vor sich, sah, wie sie sich über ihn lustig machte, weil es ihm nicht gelang, die Schale in einem einzigen, ungebrochenen Streifen zu entfernen. Auch beim Schreiben mußte er immer an sie denken, denn sie hatte ihm alles beigebracht, was sie selbst bei ihrem Vater, dem Priester, gelernt hatte – wie man beispielsweise eine Feder spitzte oder *cementarius* buchstabierte, das lateinische Wort für ›Baumeister‹. Wenn er sich am Sonntag das Gesicht wusch und sich den Bart einseifte, fiel ihm ein, wie Agnes ihm, als sie jung verheiratet waren, erklärt hatte, daß das Gesicht bei regelmäßiger Bartwäsche von Läusen und Geschwüren verschont blieb. Kein Tag verging ohne die eine oder andere lebhafte Erinnerung an Agnes, oft aus den nichtigsten Anlässen.

Tom wußte sehr wohl, was er an Ellen hatte, und es bestand nie die Gefahr, daß er ihre Gegenwart als selbstverständlich betrachtete. Ellen war einzigartig. Sie hatte etwas Ungewöhnliches, Unfaßbares an sich – und gerade dies machte ihren besonderen Reiz aus. Er war ihr dankbar, daß sie ihn an jenem Morgen nach Agnes' Tod in seiner tiefen Trauer getröstet hatte. Manchmal allerdings wünschte er insgeheim, er wäre ihr erst ein paar Tage und nicht schon wenige Stunden, nachdem er seine Frau unter die Erde gebracht hatte, begegnet; er hätte dann ein wenig Zeit gehabt, in stiller Einsamkeit um Agnes zu trauern. Eine vorgeschriebene Trauerzeit hätte er gewiß nicht eingehalten – das war etwas für Mönche und höhere Herrschaften, nichts für den einfachen Mann. Aber er hätte, bevor er sich an das neue Leben mit Ellen gewöhnte, in Ruhe von Agnes Abschied nehmen und sich mit ihrem Fortsein abfinden können. In den ersten Tagen nach Agnes' Tod waren ihm solche Gedanken nicht gekommen. Da hatte die ständige Angst vor dem Hungertod in Verbindung mit dem erregenden neuen Liebestaumel eine Art übersteigerter Endzeitstimmung in ihm hervorgerufen. Doch seitdem er wieder Arbeit und Brot hatte, spürte er Gewissensbisse. Und manchmal war ihm, als trauere er nicht bloß Agnes nach, sondern auch seiner eigenen Jugend. Es gab kein Zurück mehr. Nie wieder würde er so jung und unerfahren, so aggressiv, lebenshungrig und stark sein wie damals, als er sich in Agnes verliebt hatte.

Er schluckte den letzten Bissen Brot herunter, verließ vor den anderen das Refektorium und begab sich zum Kreuzgang. Er war zufrieden mit der Arbeit, die er dort geleistet hatte: Kaum vorstellbar, dachte er, daß der quadratische Platz noch vor drei Wochen unter einem riesigen Schutthaufen begraben lag. Nur noch einige zersprungene Pflastersteine, für die er keinen Ersatz gefunden hatte, zeugten von der Katastrophe.

Allerdings war der Kreuzgang noch immer arg verstaubt. Ich werde ihn noch einmal ausfegen und mit Wasser ausspülen lassen, dachte er. Langsam wanderte er durch die Ruine. Im nördlichen Querhaus entdeckte er einen geschwärzten Balken. Ein paar Wörter waren in den Ruß geschrieben. Es gelang ihm, sie zu entziffern: ›Alfred ist ein Schwein.‹ Das war es also gewesen, was Alfred so in Rage gebracht hatte. Eine ganze Menge Holz vom Dachgebälk war nicht zu Asche verbrannt. Überall lagen noch solche geschwärzten Balken herum. Ich werde ein paar Leute beauftragen, das Holz einzusammeln und in den Brennholzschuppen zu bringen. ›Seht zu, daß die Baustelle ordentlich aussieht‹, hätte Agnes angesichts des bevorstehenden hohen Besuchs gesagt. ›Sie sollen merken, daß sich die Einstellung Tom Builders gelohnt hat.‹ – Du hast recht, meine Gute, dachte Tom. Als er sich wieder an die Arbeit machte, spielte ein Lächeln um seine Lippen.

Waleran Bigod und seine Begleitung waren noch ungefähr eine Meile entfernt, als sie gesichtet wurden. Es waren ihrer drei, die im strengen Galopp über die kahlen Felder auf das Kloster zuritten: Voran Waleran selbst auf einem schwarzen Roß, mit schwarzem, flatterndem Umhang. Philip und die höheren Klosteroffizialen warteten vor dem Stall, um die Gäste willkommen zu heißen.

Philip wußte nicht genau, wie er Waleran behandeln sollte. Es war unbestreitbar, daß der Erzdiakon ihn hinters Licht geführt hatte. Er hatte ihm den Tod des Bischofs einfach verschwiegen. Als später die Wahrheit herauskam, schien dies Waleran nicht im geringsten peinlich zu sein. Philip hatte schon damals nicht gewußt, wie er sich ihm gegenüber verhalten sollte. Inzwischen ging er davon aus, daß mit Klagen und Beschwerden kaum etwas zu erreichen war. Außerdem wurde die ganze Affäre inzwischen von der Brandkatastrophe überschattet. Philip nahm sich jedoch vor, gegenüber Waleran in Hinkunft höchste Vorsicht walten zu lassen.

Obwohl er eine Wegstrecke von mehreren Meilen hinter sich hatte, war Walerans Hengst nervös und leicht erregbar. Philip behagte das nicht: Es ziemte sich nicht für einen Kleriker, den feurigen Reiter zu spielen. Die meisten Diener Gottes ritten ruhigere Gäule.

Mit einer schwungvollen Drehung saß Waleran ab und übergab die Zügel einem Stallknecht. Philip entbot ihm einen förmlichen Gruß. Waleran drehte sich um und betrachtete die Kirchenruine. Sein Ausdruck verfinsterte sich. »Ein teures Feuer, Philip, in der Tat«, sagte er. Zu Philips gelinder Überraschung wirkte er aufrichtig bekümmert.

Bevor der Prior antworten konnte, meldete sich Remigius zu Wort. »Das Werk des Teufels, verehrter Herr Bischof«, sagte er.

»So, meint Ihr?« erwiderte Waleran. »Nach meiner Erfahrung hat der Teufel in solchen Fällen meistens Helfer – zum Beispiel Mönche, die in der Kirche Feuer entzünden, um sich bei der Morgenandacht ein wenig zu wärmen. Oder gedankenlos brennende Kerzen im Glockenturm stehenlassen.«

Philip gefiel, wie Waleran Remigius abfertigte. Dennoch konnte er die kaum verhohlenen Anschuldigungen Walerans nicht unwidersprochen lassen. »Ich habe eine Untersuchung der möglichen Ursachen des Brandes durchgeführt«, sagte er. »In jener Nacht wurden in der Kirche keine Feuer entzündet«, sagte er. »Ich weiß es genau, denn ich war selbst zugegen. Und oben auf dem Dach war schon monatelang kein Mensch mehr gewesen.«

»Womit erklärt Ihr Euch dann das Feuer?« fragte Waleran mißtrauisch. »War es Blitzschlag?«

Philip schüttelte den Kopf. »Wir hatten kein Gewitter. Das Feuer scheint in der Nähe der Vierung ausgebrochen zu sein. Wie üblich hatten wir auf dem Altar eine brennende Kerze stehenlassen. Ich halte es für möglich, daß das Altartuch Feuer fing und mit der aufsteigenden Luft Funken die Holzdecke erreichten. Sie war sehr alt und bestand aus äußerst trockenem Holz.« Philip hob die Schultern. »Ich weiß, daß diese Erklärung alles andere als befriedigend ist, aber wir haben zur Zeit keine bessere.«

Waleran nickte. »Sehen wir uns den Schaden etwas näher an.«

Sie gingen los. Bei den Männern in Walerans Begleitung handelte es sich um einen Bewaffneten und einen jungen Priester. Der Bewaffnete blieb beim Stall zurück, um sich um die Pferde zu kümmern.

Der Priester begleitete Waleran und wurde Philip als Dechant Baldwin vorgestellt. Sie überquerten die große Freifläche vor der Kathedrale. Plötzlich legte Remigius Waleran die Hand auf den Arm, veranlaßte ihn dadurch stehenzubleiben und sagte: »Das Gästehaus ist unbeschädigt, wie Ihr seht.«

Nun blieben auch die anderen alle stehen und drehten sich um. Gereizt fragte sich Philip, was Remigius nun schon wieder im Schilde führte. Die Frau des Baumeisters kam gerade vom Küchenhof her und verschwand vor aller Augen im Gästehaus. Philip riskierte einen Seitenblick auf Waleran und merkte, daß der hohe Gast sichtlich erschrocken war. Er mußte wieder an die unvergeßliche Szene am Bischofshof denken. Als Waleran damals der Frau ansichtig geworden war, hatte ihn schier das Entsetzen gepackt. Was war los mit dieser Frau?

Waleran nickte Remigius kaum merklich zu und wandte sich an Philip. »Wer wohnt zur Zeit im Gästehaus?« fragte er.

Philip war überzeugt, daß Waleran die Frau wiedererkannt hatte, ließ sich jedoch nichts anmerken und sagte: »Ein Baumeister mit seiner Familie.«

Waleran nickte, und sie setzten ihren Weg fort. Philip wußte jetzt, warum Remigius Waleran auf das Gästehaus aufmerksam gemacht hatte: Er wollte unbedingt, daß Waleran die Frau sah. Philip nahm sich vor, sie bei nächstbester Gelegenheit einem eingehenden Verhör zu unterziehen.

Sie betraten die Ruine. Unter Toms Leitung waren sieben oder acht Mann, ungefähr zur Hälfte Mönche und Klosterbedienstete, dabei, einen schweren, halb verbrannten Dachbalken hochzuheben. Es herrschte große Geschäftigkeit. Insgesamt wirkte die Abbruchstelle überraschend gut aufgeräumt. Philip hatte das Gefühl, daß die rege Betriebsamkeit vor Ort ihm zugute kam, obwohl doch eigentlich Tom dafür verantwortlich war.

Der Baumeister kam auf die Besucher zu und begrüßte sie. Er überragte sie alle um Haupteslänge. »Tom Builder, unser Baumeister«, sagte Philip zu Waleran. »Er hat dafür gesorgt, daß Kreuzgang und Krypta bereits wieder benutzbar sind. Wir sind ihm dafür sehr dankbar.«

»Ich erinnere mich an Euch«, sagte Waleran zu Tom. »Ihr machtet mir kurz nach Weihnachten Eure Aufwartung. Ich konnte Euch allerdings keine Arbeit anbieten.«

»Ja, das stimmt«, erwiderte Tom mit seiner tiefen, staubigen

Stimme. »Vielleicht war es Gottes Wille, mich in dieser schweren Zeit Prior Philip an die Seite zu stellen.«

»Ein theologischer Baumeister, hört, hört«, sagte Waleran spöttisch.

Ein leichter Anflug von Röte zeigte sich auf Toms staubverschmiertem Gesicht.

»Was habt Ihr als nächstes vor?« fragte Waleran.

»Aus Sicherheitsgründen müssen wir die noch stehenden Mauern niederreißen, sonst fallen sie eines Tages noch jemandem auf den Kopf«, antwortete Tom in gebührender Demut. »Danach sollten wir den Platz so weit aufräumen, daß wir mit dem Bau der neuen Kirche beginnen können. Außerdem wäre es ratsam, so schnell wie möglich große Bäume zu finden, die für den neuen Dachstuhl geeignet sind, je länger das Holz ablagert, desto besser wird das Dach ...«

»Wir können keine Bäume fällen, bevor wir das Geld haben, sie zu bezahlen«, fuhr Philip hastig dazwischen.

»Darüber unterhalten wir uns später«, sagte Waleran geheimnisvoll.

Die Bemerkung fesselte Philips Aufmerksamkeit. Er hoffte darauf, daß Waleran einen Plan zur Finanzierung der neuen Kirche hatte. War die Priorei auf ihre eigenen Mittel angewiesen, so konnte erst in vielen Jahren mit dem Bau begonnen werden. Seit drei Wochen schon schlug sich Philip erfolglos mit diesem Problem herum.

Er führte die kleine Gruppe über den freigeräumten Pfad zum Kreuzgang. Waleran genügte ein Blick, um festzustellen, daß dieser Bereich bereits wiederhergestellt war. Vom Kreuzgang aus begaben sie sich zum Haus des Priors.

Kaum waren sie eingetreten, entledigte sich Waleran seines Mantels, nahm Platz und wärmte seine bleichen Hände über dem Feuer. Bruder Milius, der Küchenmeister, servierte heißen Glühwein in kleinen Holzschalen. Waleran nippte ein Schlückchen und sagte zu Philip: »Habt Ihr Euch schon mal mit dem Gedanken befaßt, daß dieser Tom Builder das Feuer vielleicht selbst gelegt hat? Er brauchte dringend Arbeit ...«

»Ja, das habe ich«, erwiderte Philip. »Aber ich halte es für ziemlich abwegig. Die Kirche war während der Nacht stets verschlossen. Wie hätte er hineinkommen sollen?«

»Vielleicht tagsüber. Er könnte sich versteckt haben.«

»Aber dann wäre er später nicht mehr herausgekommen.« Philip schüttelte den Kopf. »Wie dem auch sei, nach meinem Dafürhalten ist der Mann zu einer solchen Tat schlichtweg nicht fähig. Er ist ein kluger Kopf – weitaus gescheiter übrigens, als man bei der ersten Begegnung vermuten möchte –, doch fehlt ihm jede Art von Gerissenheit. Ich habe ihn danach gefragt, wie seiner Meinung nach der Brand entstanden sein könnte, und ihm dabei direkt in die Augen gesehen. Wäre er schuldig – seine Miene hätte es mir verraten.«

Waleran lenkte zu Philips Überraschung sofort ein. »Ich glaube, Ihr habt recht«, sagte er. »Ich kann mir den Mann schlecht als Brandstifter vorstellen. Es paßt einfach nicht zu ihm.«

»Wahrscheinlich werden wir die genaue Brandursache nie erfahren«, meinte Philip. »Was uns jetzt vorrangig bewegt, ist die Frage der Finanzierung des Neubaus. Ich weiß nicht ...«

»Gut, gut!« Waleran unterbrach ihn mit erhobener Hand und wandte sich an die anderen Personen in der Runde: »Ich muß mich mit Prior Philip unter vier Augen unterhalten. Die übrigen mögen uns jetzt verlassen.«

Philip war neugierig. Was veranlaßt Waleran zu dieser Geheimniskrämerei? dachte er.

»Ein Wort noch, bevor wir gehen, ehrwürdiger Bischof«, sagte Remigius. »Meine Mitbrüder haben mich gebeten, Euch noch etwas mitzuteilen.«

Was hat der denn jetzt schon wieder vor? dachte Philip.

Waleran hob irritiert die Brauen. »Wie kommen die Brüder darauf, *Euch* mit dieser Mitteilung zu betrauen? Warum wenden sie sich nicht an ihren Prior?«

»Weil Prior Philip ihrer Sorge kein Gehör schenkt.«

Philip wurde ärgerlich. Er wußte noch immer nicht, worauf Remigius hinauswollte. Kein Mitbruder hatte sich bei ihm beklagt. Der Subprior hatte offenbar nichts anderes im Sinn, als ihn, den Prior, vor dem designierten Bischof bloßzustellen. Waleran bedachte ihn mit einem fragenden Blick. Philip hob die Schultern und versuchte, sich seine Erregung nicht anmerken zu lassen.

»Wohlan denn, Bruder Remigius, laßt hören!« sagte Waleran. »Ich bin begierig, es zu erfahren – vorausgesetzt, es handelt sich tatsächlich um eine Angelegenheit von so weitreichender Bedeutung, daß sie die Aufmerksamkeit des Bischofs erfordert.«

»Auf dem Gelände der Priorei lebt gegenwärtig eine Frau«, sagte Remigius.

»Nicht schon wieder!« stöhnte Philip. »Er meint die Frau des Baumeisters. Sie wohnt bekanntlich im Gästehaus.«

»Diese Frau ist eine Hexe«, sagte Remigius.

Was bewegt ihn nur, immer wieder auf diesem leidigen Thema herumzureiten? dachte Philip. Er hat es doch schon einmal versucht und damit Schiffbruch erlitten. Wir sind uns in diesem Punkt uneinig, gewiß – aber ich bin Prior und habe hier das Sagen. Waleran wird mich unterstützen müssen – es sei denn, er will jedesmal mit hineingezogen werden, wenn Remigius mit einer meiner Entscheidungen nicht einverstanden ist. »Die Frau ist *keine* Hexe«, sagte er, und seine Stimme verriet, daß er der Sache überdrüssig war.

»Hast du die Frau schon verhört?« bohrte Remigius nach.

Philip erinnerte sich jetzt daran, daß er zugesagt hatte, die Frau des Baumeisters zu befragen. Doch es war nie dazu gekommen. Er hatte sich statt dessen an ihren Ehemann gewandt und ihn gebeten, seiner Frau Vorsicht und Zurückhaltung anzuraten. Daß er auf das direkte Gespräch mit ihr verzichtet hatte, erwies sich jetzt als Vorteil für Remigius. Trotzdem war nicht zu erwarten, daß Waleran sich wegen dieser Kleinigkeit auf die Seite des Subpriors schlug. »Nein, ich habe sie nicht verhört«, gab Philip zu, »doch gibt es nicht das geringste Anzeichen für Hexerei. Die ganze Familie ist von Grund auf anständig und gottesfürchtig.«

»Die Frau ist eine Hexe – und eine Hure obendrein«, erwiderte Remigius. Die Empörung trieb ihm das Blut ins Gesicht.

»Was sagst du da?« fuhr Philip auf. »Mit wem hurt sie?«

»Mit dem Baumeister!«

»Das ist ihr Ehemann, du Narr!«

»Nein, das ist er nicht!« gab Remigius triumphierend zurück. »Die beiden sind nicht verheiratet und kennen sich überhaupt erst seit einem Monat!«

Philip blieb die Spucke weg. Damit hatte er nicht gerechnet. Remigius hatte ihn kalt erwischt. Wenn es stimmte, was er sagte, war die Frau strenggenommen tatsächlich eine Hure. Allerdings handelte es sich um eine Erscheinungsform der Hurerei, über die man gemeinhin hinwegsah. Viele Paare hatten keine Eile, ihre Verbindung vom Priester absegnen zu lassen, und dachten oft erst daran, wenn schon das erste Kind unterwegs war. In ärmlichen, abgelegenen Teilen des Landes lebten die Menschen nicht selten sogar jahrzehntelang als Mann und Frau zusammen und zogen Kinder groß. Da kam es dann schon mal vor, daß ein verdutzter Priester bei einer Kindstaufe gebeten wurde, auch dem Verhältnis der Großeltern seinen Segen zu erteilen. Aber die Nachsicht eines Dorfpriesters unter lauter armen Bauern in den

Randgebieten der christlichen Welt war eine Sache – ob ähnliche Zustände auch bei einem wichtigen Angestellten der Priorei und auf deren Gelände geduldet werden konnten, eine ganz andere.

»Wie kommst du darauf, daß die beiden nicht verheiratet sind?« fragte Philip argwöhnisch, obgleich er sich denken konnte, daß Remigius, ehe er im Beisein Walerans derlei Anklagen vorbrachte, den Sachverhalt genau geprüft hatte.

»Ich kam zufällig vorbei, als die beiden Knaben sich stritten. Da haben sie mir gesagt, daß sie gar keine Brüder sind. So kam das alles raus.«

Philip war von Tom tief enttäuscht. Hurerei oder Unzucht war eine weitverbreitete Sünde, die jedoch gerade von Mönchen, die aller fleischlichen Lust entsagt hatten, aufs äußerste verabscheut wurde. Wie konnte Tom sich nur darauf einlassen? Er hätte wissen müssen, dachte Philip, daß ich ein solches Verhalten nicht billigen kann. Sein Zorn auf den Baumeister war noch größer als seine Erregung über Remigius. Dessen Vorgehensweise empfand er indessen als heimtückisch. »Warum hast du mir nicht Bescheid gesagt?« fragte er ihn. »Ich bin dein Vorgesetzter.«

»Ich habe es erst heute vormittag erfahren.«

Philip lehnte sich geschlagen zurück. Remigius hatte ihm eins ausgewischt, und er, Philip, stand jetzt da wie ein Narr. Das war die Rache für die Niederlage bei der Priorwahl, dachte er und wandte seine Aufmerksamkeit Waleran zu. An ihn hatte sich die Klage gerichtet – sollte er jetzt das Urteil sprechen.

Waleran zögerte nicht. »Der Fall ist klar«, sagte er. »Die Frau muß ihre Sünde bekennen und öffentlich Buße tun. Sie muß die Priorei verlassen und ein Jahr lang getrennt von dem Baumeister in Keuschheit leben. Danach dürfen sie heiraten.«

Ein Jahr Trennung war ein hartes Urteil. Aber Philip fand es gerecht; die beiden hatten die Ehre des Klosters beschmutzt. Er fragte sich allerdings, wie die Frau das Urteil aufnehmen würde. »Was geschieht, wenn die Frau sich dem Spruch nicht beugt?« fragte er.

Waleran hob die Schultern. »Dann wird sie in der Hölle braten.«

»Ich fürchte, der Baumeister wird sie begleiten, wenn sie Kingsbridge verläßt.«

»Es gibt andere Baumeister.«

»Gewiß.« Philip wollte Tom nicht verlieren. Waleran hingegen war anzusehen, daß er nichts dagegen hätte, wenn Tom und seine Mätresse Kingsbridge den Rücken kehrten und auf Nimmerwiedersehen verschwänden. Einmal mehr fragte er sich, was für ein Geheimnis diese Frau umgab.

»Und nun verlaßt bitte diesen Raum, damit ich mich ungestört mit Eurem Prior unterhalten kann«, sagte Waleran.

»Augenblick noch!« fuhr Philip dazwischen. Es war *sein* Haus, und die Männer waren *seine* Mönche. Wenn hier jemand Kommen und Gehen heißt, dann bin das ich, dachte er, nicht Waleran. »Ich werde mit dem Baumeister über diese Sache reden«, sagte er. »Außerdem wünsche ich, daß nichts von dem, was hier gesprochen wurde, an die Außenwelt dringt, hört ihr? Wer gegen diese Anordnung verstößt, kann sich auf eine empfindliche Strafe gefaßt machen. Hast du das verstanden, Remigius?«

»Ja«, sagte Remigius.

Philip ließ ihn nicht aus den Augen. Er sagte kein Wort, doch sein Schweigen war beredt genug.

»Jawohl, *Vater*«, sagte Remigius endlich.

»Gut. Und jetzt geht.«

Sie gingen – Remigius, Andrew, Milius, Cuthbert und Dechant Baldwin. Waleran schenkte sich noch ein wenig Wein nach und streckte die Beine aus, so daß sie näher ans wärmende Feuer kamen. »Frauen stiften immer Unfrieden«, sagte er. »Ist eine rossige Stute im Stall, so schnappen die Hengste nach den Pferdeknechten, schlagen aus und sind kaum noch zu bändigen. Selbst die Wallache drehen durch. Zwar ist ihnen die körperliche Lust versagt, doch riechen können sie die heißen Fotzen allemal.«

Philip war peinlich berührt; er sah keinen Anlaß für so deftige Worte. »Wie steht's mit dem Neubau der Kirche?« fragte er.

»Ja, richtig. Ihr habt vermutlich gehört, daß diese Angelegenheit, wegen der Ihr kürzlich bei mir vorspracht, einen für uns günstigen Ausgang genommen hat? Ich spreche von der Verschwörung des Grafen Bartholomäus gegen den König.«

»Ja, ich weiß Bescheid.« Philip hatte das Gefühl, der Besuch im bischöflichen Palast läge schon eine Ewigkeit zurück. Er konnte sich noch gut daran erinnern, wie er, vor Angst zitternd, vorgebracht hatte, was er von dem Komplott gegen den von der Kirche gewählten Monarchen wußte. »Ich hörte, daß Percy Hamleigh die Burg gestürmt und den Grafen gefangengenommen hat.«

»So ist es. Bartholomäus sitzt in Winchester im Verlies und harrt seines Schicksals.« Waleran war mit dem Lauf der Dinge sichtlich zufrieden.

»Und Graf Robert von Gloucester? Er war der stärkere der beiden Verschwörer ...«

»... und kommt daher auch glimpflicher davon. Im Grunde so gut wie straffrei. Er hat König Stephan die Treue geschworen, worauf man über seine Beteiligung an der Verschwörung einfach hinwegsah ...«

»Aber was hat das mit unserer Kathedrale zu tun?«

Waleran erhob sich, ging zum Fenster und betrachtete die Ruine. Aufrichtige Trauer lag in seinem Blick, und Philip gestand sich ein, daß Waleran sich trotz seines weltlichen Gehabes ein frommes Herz bewahrt hatte. »Unser Beitrag zur Aufdeckung der Verschwörung bringt König Stephan in unsere Schuld. In nicht allzuferner Zeit werden wir beide, Ihr und ich, eine Audienz bei ihm haben.«

»Beim König?!« rief Philip, ein wenig beunruhigt über diese Perspektive.

»Er wird uns fragen, was wir uns zur Belohnung wünschen.«

Philip verstand jetzt, worauf Waleran hinauswollte, und war sofort aufs höchste erregt. »Und wir werden sagen, daß ...«

Waleran drehte sich um und sah Philip an. Seine Augen waren wie schwarze Juwelen und funkelten vor Ehrgeiz. »Wir werden ihm sagen, daß wir uns eine neue Kathedrale für Kingsbridge wünschen.«

Tom wußte, daß Ellen an die Decke gehen würde.

Sie regte sich schon genug auf über das, was mit Jack geschehen war – allein deswegen hätte er sie beruhigen müssen. Die Kunde von der ihr auferlegten ›Buße‹ mußte sie nun zusätzlich erzürnen. Am liebsten hätte Tom die Hiobsbotschaft noch ein oder zwei Tage für sich behalten. Aber das war unmöglich: Prior Philip hatte angeordnet, Ellen müsse bis zum Abend das Klostergelände verlassen haben. Er mußte es ihr also sofort sagen, und da Philip ihm zur Mittagsstunde Bescheid gegeben hatte, sagte er es ihr beim Mittagessen.

Wie üblich betraten sie das Refektorium gemeinsam mit den anderen Klosterbediensteten, nachdem die Mönche gespeist und den Saal verlassen hatten. Die Tische waren dicht besetzt. Das ist vielleicht ganz gut so, dachte Tom, in Gegenwart so vieler Leute hält sie sich vielleicht ein bißchen zurück ...

Er sollte schon bald erfahren, daß er sich in diesem Punkt gewaltig verrechnet hatte.

Er wollte es ihr schonend beibringen, in kleineren Portionen gewissermaßen, und so sagte er zunächst nur: »Sie wissen jetzt, daß wir nicht verheiratet sind.«

»Wer hat ihnen das gesagt?« fragte sie wütend. »Ein Hetzer?«

»Alfred. Aber du darfst ihm keinen Vorwurf machen – Remigius, dieser geriebene Bruder, hat es ihm aus der Nase gezogen. Wir haben den Kindern ja auch nie ausdrücklich verboten, darüber zu reden.«

»Ich mache dem Jungen keinen Vorwurf«, erwiderte sie etwas ruhiger. »Was sagen die Leute noch?«

Er beugte sich über den Tisch und flüsterte ihr zu: »Sie bezichtigen dich der Unzucht.«

»Der Unzucht?« wiederholte sie mit lauter Stimme. »Und was ist mit dir? Zur Unzucht gehören zwei! Wissen das diese Mönche etwa nicht?«

Die Arbeiter, die in der Nähe saßen, fingen an zu lachen.

»Pssst!« zischte Tom. »Sie sagen, wir sollen heiraten.«

Ihr Blick wurde hart. »Wenn das alles wäre, würdest du mich nicht so trübsinnig anschauen. Was sagen sie noch? Raus mit der Sprache!«

»Sie wollen, daß du deine Sünde bekennst.«

»Verdammte Heuchler«, entgegnete Ellen angewidert. »Des Nachts bebocken sie einander, und am Tag reißen sie's Maul auf und zeihen *uns* der Sünde!«

Das Gelächter wurde lauter. Die Arbeiter stellten ihre Gespräche ein und lauschten.

»Sprich etwas leiser, Ellen, bitte!« flehte Tom sie an.

»Wahrscheinlich verlangen sie von mir auch, daß ich Buße tue, wie? Die Demütigung gehört immer dazu. Na, was soll ich denn tun? Nun sag's schon. Einer *Hexe* kannst du ohnehin nichts vormachen ...«

»Nicht auch noch *das*!« zischte Tom sie an. »Du machst ja alles noch viel schlimmer!«

»Dann red jetzt endlich!«

»Wir müssen ein Jahr getrennt leben, und du mußt die ganze Zeit über keusch bleiben ...«

»Darauf pisse ich!« brüllte Ellen.

Nun blickte auch der letzte auf.

»Ich pisse auf dich, Tom Builder!« schrie sie. Dann wurde ihr bewußt, daß sie Publikum hatte. »Ich pisse auf euch alle«, fügte sie hinzu. Die meisten Anwesenden grinsten. Einer so hübschen Person mit vor Eifer geröteten Wangen und großen goldenen Augen konnte man kaum böse sein. Ellen stand auf. »Ich pisse auf die Priorei Kingsbridge!« Schon war sie auf den Tisch gesprungen und schritt zum Jubel der Arbeiter auf der Platte entlang. Hurtig brachte man Suppenschüsseln und Bierkrüge in Sicherheit und lehnte sich zurück. »Ich pisse auf den Prior!« sagte Ellen. »Und auf den Subprior, den Sakristan, den Kantor und den Kämmerer samt all ihrer Urkunden, Privilegien und Kisten voller Silbergeld!« Sie hatte das Ende des Tisches erreicht. Gleich daneben stand ein zweiter, kleinerer Tisch, an dem, wenn die Mönche speisten, ein Vorleser zu sitzen pflegte. Auf diesem Tisch lag ein aufgeschlagenes Buch.

Tom erkannte plötzlich, was sie vorhatte. »Ellen!« rief er. »Das nicht, bitte!«

Doch Ellen war nicht mehr zu halten. Sie sprang auf das kleine Tischchen, raffte ihren Rock, ging in die Hocke und urinierte auf das aufgeschlagene Buch. Dabei kreischte sie so laut sie konnte: »Ich pisse auf die Regel des heiligen Benedikt!«

Die Männer brüllten vor Lachen und hämmerten mit den Fäusten auf die Tische. Sie johlten, pfiffen und jubelten. Tom wußte nicht, ob sie Ellens Verachtung der Ordensregel teilten oder ob sie sich bloß darüber freuten, daß eine so schöne Frau sich vor ihnen entblößte. In ihrer Schamlosigkeit und Vulgarität lag durchaus ein gewisser sinnlicher Reiz.

Unter donnerndem Applaus sprang sie vom Tisch und rannte zur Tür hinaus.

Alle Anwesenden fingen zur gleichen Zeit an zu reden. Eine solche Szene hatte keiner von ihnen je erlebt. Tom war entsetzt und zutiefst beschämt. Er wußte, daß dieser Auftritt schlimme Folgen haben würde – und doch war da auch eine Stimme in ihm, die sagte: Was für eine Frau!

Einen Augenblick später stand auch Jack auf und folgte seiner Mutter hinaus. Sein verschwollenes Gesicht zeigte den Anflug eines Lächelns.

Tom sah Alfred und Martha an. Alfred war völlig verwirrt, Martha kicherte. »Kommt mit, ihr zwei« sagte Tom. Gemeinsam verließen sie das Refektorium.

Sie fanden Ellen im Gästehaus. Jacks Mutter saß auf dem Sessel und wartete auf Tom. Sie trug ihren warmen Mantel, hielt ihren großen Lederranzen in der Hand und machte einen ruhigen und gefaßten Eindruck. Tom wurde kalt ums Herz, als er den Ranzen sah, doch versuchte er, sich nichts anmerken zu lassen. »Das wird uns höllisch teuer zu stehen kommen«, sagte er.

»Ich glaube nicht an die Hölle«, sagte Ellen.

»Ich hoffe, sie erlauben dir noch, zu bekennen und Buße zu tun.«

»Ich werde nichts bekennen.«

Jetzt war es um seine Selbstbeherrschung geschehen. »Ellen, verlaß mich nicht!«

Sie sah ihn mit traurigen Augen an. »Hör zu, Tom. Bevor ich dich kennenlernte, hatte ich genug zu essen und ein Dach über dem Kopf. Ich war sicher und geborgen und konnte mich und meinen Sohn versorgen. Ich war auf niemanden angewiesen. Seitdem wir beide zusammen sind, habe ich stärker als je zuvor erfahren, was es heißt, dem Hungertod nahe zu sein. Inzwischen hast du zwar Arbeit gefunden, aber noch längst keine Sicherheit. Die Priorei kann dich nicht bezahlen, und es kann gut sein, daß du im nächsten Winter wieder auf der Straße stehst.«

»Philip wird schon irgendwo Geld auftreiben«, sagte Tom. »Davon bin ich fest überzeugt.«

»Deine Überzeugung kann trügen.«

»Du glaubst nicht an mich«, erwiderte Tom verbittert. Und ehe er es verhindern konnte, entfuhr ihm die Bemerkung: »Du bist genau wie Agnes. Du glaubst nicht an meine Kathedrale.«

»Ach, Tom«, antwortete Ellen betrübt. »Ginge es nur um mich, so bliebe ich ja hier. Aber sieh dir doch meinen Sohn an.«

Tom kam ihrer Aufforderung nach. Die Prellungen und Schürfwunden hatten sich verfärbt, so daß fast das gesamte Gesicht des Knaben purpurviolett war. Das linke Ohr war auf das Doppelte seiner ursprünglichen Größe angeschwollen. Die Nasenlöcher waren mit eingetrocknetem Blut verkrustet, und ein Schneidezahn war abgebrochen.

»Ich hatte Angst, er würde aufwachsen wie ein Tier, wenn wir weiterhin im Wald blieben«, fuhr Ellen fort. »Ich wollte, daß er den Umgang mit anderen Menschen lernt – aber nicht um diesen Preis. Deshalb kehren wir in den Wald zurück.«

»Sprich nicht davon, Ellen, ich bitte dich«, sagte Tom voller Verzweiflung. »Laß uns erst noch darüber reden. Triff keine übereilten Entscheidungen!«

»Das ist keine übereilte Entscheidung, Tom, gewiß nicht«, antwortete sie kummervoll. »Ich bin so traurig, daß ich nicht einmal mehr wütend sein kann. Ich wollte deine Frau sein, glaub mir. Aber nicht um jeden Preis.«

Wenn Alfred Jack nicht verfolgt hätte, wäre uns das ganze Theater erspart geblieben, dachte Tom. Aber das war doch nur Kinderkram – oder etwa nicht? Oder war doch etwas dran an Ellens Behauptung, daß ihn seine Vaterliebe blind machte? Zum erstenmal zweifelte er an der Richtigkeit seines Verhaltens. Vielleicht hätte ich strenger sein müssen mit Alfred, dachte er. Daß Buben in dem Alter sich prügelten, war zwar normal – nur waren Martha und Jack dem größeren und stärkeren Alfred körperlich weit unterlegen. Vielleicht war Alfred doch ein Raufbold ...

Aber was half die Einsicht? Sie kam zu spät. »Bleib wenigstens im Dorf!« bat er Ellen verzweifelt. »Wart ein Weilchen und sieh zu, wie sich die Dinge entwickeln.«

»Ich glaube nicht, daß die Mönche mir das jetzt noch gestatten werden.«

Er wußte, daß sie recht hatte. Das Dorf gehörte der Priorei, und alle Häusler waren zur Abgabe einer Pacht verpflichtet, welche sie meistens in Gestalt von Arbeitstagen ableisteten. Die Mönche konnten jedem Bewohner des Dorfes, der ihnen mißfiel, die Unterbringung verweigern. Nach allem, was geschehen war, hätte man ihnen die Zurückweisung Ellens nicht einmal übelnehmen können. Sie hatte ihren Entschluß gefaßt und auf alle denkbaren Möglichkeiten, wieder davon Abstand zu nehmen, buchstäblich – gepißt.

»Gut«, sagte Tom schließlich. »Ich begleite dich. Das Kloster schuldet mir bereits zweiundsiebzig Pennys. Wandern wir eben weiter – wir haben bisher überlebt und werden ...«

»Und deine Kinder?« fragte Ellen sanft.

Tom mußte an Martha denken, die vor Hunger geweint hatte. Er wußte, daß er ihr das nicht noch einmal zumuten konnte. Und da war ja auch noch der kleine Jonathan, der in der Obhut der Mönche lebte. Ich will ihn nicht noch einmal verlassen, dachte Tom, ich habe es einmal getan und mir das nie verziehen.

Dennoch konnte er den Gedanken, Ellen zu verlieren, nicht ertragen.

»Du kannst dich nicht zerreißen«, sagte sie. »Ich ziehe mit dir nie wieder von Ort zu Ort. Das ist keine Lösung – es wäre in jeder Hinsicht schlimmer als die Lage, in der wir uns gegenwärtig befinden. Ich kehre wieder in den Wald zurück, und zwar ohne dich.«

Er starrte sie an. Er wollte glauben, daß es ihr nicht ernst damit war, aber ein Blick in ihr Gesicht überzeugte ihn vom Gegenteil. Ihm fielen keine Argumente mehr ein. Er öffnete den Mund, um etwas zu sagen, doch kam kein einziges Wort über seine Lippen. Er fühlte sich hilflos.

Ellen atmete vernehmbar aus und ein; ihr Busen hob und senkte sich. Auch sie war innerlich aufgewühlt. Er wollte sie berühren, spürte jedoch, daß sie jetzt nicht berührt werden wollte. Vielleicht werde ich sie nie wieder in meine Arme schließen, dachte er. Es war kaum faßbar. Nacht für Nacht hatte er ihr beigelegen in den vergangenen Wochen, und er hatte sie mit einer Vertrautheit berührt, die er sonst nur seinem eigenen Körper entgegenbrachte. Und nun war sie ihm plötzlich versagt wie eine Fremde.

»Schau nicht so traurig«, sagte sie. Ihre Augen waren voller Tränen.

»Ich kann's nicht ändern«, sagte er. »Ich *bin* traurig.«

»Es tut mir leid, daß ich dich so unglücklich gemacht habe.«

»Es braucht dir nicht leid zu tun. Eher sollte dir leid tun, daß du mich so glücklich gemacht hast – das ist es nämlich, Weib, was jetzt so schmerzt. Daß du mich so glücklich gemacht hast.«

Ein Seufzer entrang sich ihrer Kehle. Dann stand sie auf und ging – ohne ein weiteres Wort.

Jack und Martha folgten ihr. Alfred zögerte und wußte nicht, wo er hinsehen sollte. Dann ging auch er.

Tom starrte auf den verlassenen Sessel. Nein, dachte er, es kann nicht wahr sein. Sie verläßt mich nicht.

Er setzte sich auf den Sessel. Er war noch warm von ihrem Körper, den er so sehr liebte. Mit Gewalt mußte er die Tränen unterdrücken. Daß sie von ihrer Entscheidung nicht mehr abrücken würde, war ihm klar: Ellen war eine Frau, die niemals schwankte. Wenn sie einen Entschluß gefaßt hatte, so setzte sie ihn auch in die Tat um.

Aber diesen würde sie eines Tages vielleicht bereuen.

Es war ein Hoffnungsschimmer. Er wußte, daß sie ihm mit Leib und Seele zugetan war, daran hatte sich nichts geändert. Erst in der vergangenen Nacht hatte sie ihn leidenschaftlich geliebt, mit der Gier einer Verdurstenden; hatte sich, als er seine Lust schon befriedigt hatte, über ihn gewälzt und weitergemacht, ihn wild geküßt und in seinen Bart gestöhnt, wenn sie kam ... Und sie war gekommen, ein ums andere Mal, bis sie endlich erschöpft war. Aber es war ja nicht nur das, was sie verband. Sie genossen jede gemeinsame Stunde. Sie redeten ununterbrochen miteinander – viel mehr, als Tom je mit Agnes geredet hatte, selbst als Jungverliebte. Ich werde ihr genauso fehlen wie sie mir, dachte er. Wenn ihr Zorn verflogen ist und sie sich wieder an das tägliche Einerlei gewöhnt hat, wird sie sich sehnen nach jemandem, mit dem sie sich unterhalten kann. Sie wird nach einem kräftigen Körper gieren und nach einem bärtigen Gesicht, das sie küssen kann. Und dann wird sie an mich denken.

Aber Ellen ist auch stolz. Ihr Stolz kann sie daran hindern, zu mir zurückzukehren – selbst wenn sie es im Grunde ihres Herzens will.

Er sprang auf. Ich muß mit ihr darüber sprechen, dachte er. Rasch verließ er das Haus. Ellen stand am Tor und verabschiedete sich von Martha. Tom rannte am Stall vorbei und erwischte sie gerade noch rechtzeitig.

Sie schenkte ihm ein trauriges Lächeln. »Leb wohl, Tom.«

Er ergriff ihre Hände. »Wirst du eines Tages zurückkehren? Nur auf Besuch? Wenn ich weiß, daß es kein Abschied für immer ist und daß du irgendwann wiederkommst, und sei es auch nur für eine kurze Frist ... Wenn ich das weiß, dann komme ich drüber hinweg.«

Sie zögerte.

»Bitte!«

»Gut«, sagte sie.

»Schwör es!«

»Ich halte nichts von Schwüren.«

»Aber ich.«

»Gut. Ich schwöre es.«

»Ich danke dir.« Zärtlich zog er sie an sich. Ellen ließ es geschehen. Er nahm sie in die Arme, und die Tränen strömten über sein Gesicht. Schließlich entzog sie sich ihm. Widerstrebend gab er sie frei, und Ellen wandte sich dem Tor zu.

Vom Stall her ertönte plötzlich ein Geräusch. Es war das Schnauben und Stampfen eines feurigen, ungehorsamen Rosses. Es handelte sich um Walerans Hengst, den der Bischof gerade besteigen wollte. Walerans und Ellens Blicke kreuzten sich, und er erstarrte.

Und in diesem Augenblick fing sie an zu singen.

Tom kannte das Lied nicht, obgleich er es schon des öfteren von ihr gehört hatte. Es hatte eine furchtbar traurige Melodie und einen französischen Text, doch Tom verstand genug, um zu wissen, worum es ging.

Ein Lerchenvogel tat sich einst
im Jägernetz verfangen.
Und singt so süß und singt so rein,
als ob der Stimme Zauberklang –
ihn wieder könnt' befreien.

Tom sah unwillkürlich den Bischof an. Waleran war bleich wie der Tod, sein Mund stand offen, die Augen waren vor Schreck geweitet. Tom war baß erstaunt: Wie war es möglich, daß ein einfaches Lied einem solchen Mann derart angst und bange machen konnte?

Es graut der Tag, der Jäger kommt,
um ihm den Tod zu geben.
Es stirbt der Vogel, stirbt der Mensch –
mein Lied wird ewig leben.

»Lebt wohl, Waleran Bigod!« rief Ellen. »Zwar verlasse ich Kingsbridge, doch nicht Euch. Ich werde bei Euch sein, in Euern Träumen!«

In meinen auch, dachte Tom. Einen Moment lang standen alle da wie vom Donner gerührt.

Ellen machte kehrt. Sie hielt Jack an der Hand. Niemand sprach ein Wort, als die beiden durchs Tor schritten und in der Abenddämmerung verschwanden.

Buch II | 1136-37

Nach Ellens Fortgang war es an Sonntagen im Gästehaus sehr still. Alfred spielte auf der Wiese am anderen Ufer des Flusses mit den Dorfburschen Fußball. Martha, die Jack arg vermißte, spielte Rollenspiele, wobei sie Gemüse sammelte, Brei kochte und eine Puppe anund auszog. Tom arbeitete an seinem Entwurf für die Kathedrale.

Ein- oder zweimal hatte er Philip darauf angesprochen, ob er ihm nicht seine Vorstellungen von der neuen Kirche etwas genauer auseinandersetzen könne, doch der Prior hatte alle diesbezüglichen Anspielungen bewußt oder unbewußt überhört. Philip war ein vielbeschäftigter Mann. Tom hingegen dachte – vor allem an Sonntagen – an kaum etwas anderes als an seinen Plan.

Am liebsten saß er gleich hinter der geöffneten Tür des Gästehauses und betrachtete die Ruine der Kathedrale. Gelegentlich skizzierte er etwas auf einer Schieferplatte; die Hauptarbeit geschah jedoch in seinem Kopf. Tom war es – im Gegensatz zu vielen anderen Menschen – immer leichtgefallen, sich feststehende Objekte und eine komplizierte Raumaufteilung bildlich vorzustellen.

Er hatte sich Philips Vertrauen und Dankbarkeit durch die fachmännische Organisation der Aufräumarbeiten erworben, galt jedoch beim Prior nach wie vor als einfacher Maurer und Steinmetz, der rastlos von einer Baustelle zur anderen zog. Es lag jetzt an ihm selbst, Philip davon zu überzeugen, daß er auch ein fähiger Architekt und Kathedralenbaumeister war.

An einem Sonntag, annähernd zwei Monate, nachdem Ellen ihn verlassen hatte, war Tom so weit, daß er glaubte, mit dem Grundriß beginnen zu können.

Er flocht sich eine ungefähr drei mal zwei Fuß große Matte aus Schilf und biegsamen Zweigen und umgab sie mit einem sauberen, am Rand hochstehenden Holzrahmen, so daß sie aussah wie ein Tablett. Dann verbrannte er etwas Kreide, mischte sich mit dem erhaltenen Kalk einen starken Mörtel zurecht und füllte damit das »Tablett«. Als der Mörtel zu binden begann, ritzte er mit einer Nadel Striche hinein. Für gerade Linien benutzte er sein eisernes, fußlanges Lineal, für rechte Winkel sein Winkeleisen und für Kurven seine Zirkel.

Er wollte drei Zeichnungen anfertigen: einen Schnitt, um die Bauweise zu erklären; einen Aufriß, um die schönen Proportionen aufzuzeigen; und einen Grundriß zur Erläuterung der Raumaufteilung. Mit dem Schnitt fing er an.

Er stellte sich die Kathedrale als länglichen Brotlaib vor und schnitt in Gedanken am Westende die Kruste ab. Der Blick ins Innere wurde frei, und Tom begann zu zeichnen.

Es war ganz einfach. Er zeichnete einen oben abgeflachten Bogengang: Das war, vom Ende aus gesehen, das Schiff. Wie die alte Kirche würde es eine flache Holzdecke haben. Tom hätte natürlich liebend gern ein steinernes Gewölbe errichtet, doch wußte er, daß Philip dazu die Mittel fehlten.

Über das Schiff zeichnete er ein dreieckiges Dach. Die Breite des Dachs bestimmte die Breite des Gebäudes, war ihrerseits aber abhängig von dem zur Verfügung stehenden Holz. Balken von mehr als fünfunddreißig Fuß Länge waren schwer zu bekommen und unerhört teuer. (Gutes Holz war so wertvoll, daß es in der Regel lange, bevor es die erforderliche Länge erreichte, von seinem Eigentümer geschlagen wurde.) Tom ging davon aus, daß das Schiff seiner Kathedrale wahrscheinlich an die zweiunddreißig Fuß breit sein würde.

Das Kirchenschiff auf der Skizze war hoch, unmöglich hoch. Aber eine Kathedrale war nun einmal ein aufregendes Gebäude, ehrfurchtgebietend in ihrer Größe, und in ihrer Höhe und Erhabenheit zog sie die Blicke der Betrachter himmelwärts. Ein Grund dafür, daß Kathedralen Besucher von weither anzogen, lag darin, daß sie die größten Bauwerke ihrer Zeit waren. Wer keine Domkirche kannte, hatte gute Aussichten, eines Tages sein Leben zu beenden, ohne je ein Gebäude gesehen zu haben, das die eigene Hütte merklich überragte.

Pech war nur, daß das Gebäude, das Tom gezeichnet hatte, zum Einsturz verdammt war: Das schwere Dach aus Holz und Blei war zu gewichtig für die Mauern, die sich zuerst nach außen wölben und dann zusammenbrechen würden. Sie bedurften einer Stütze.

Tom zeichnete daher zwei Bogengänge mit gewölbtem Dach, die gerade halb so hoch waren wie das von ihnen flankierte Kirchenschiff.

Es waren die Seitenschiffe. Weil sie auch erheblich schmaler waren als das Hauptschiff, kam auch die Deckenkonstruktion billiger: Man konnte sie mit steinernem Gewölbe versehen. Für beide Seitenschiffe war ein einfaches Pultdach vorgesehen.

Die Seitenschiffe sorgten für eine gewisse Stütze des Hauptschiffs, mit dem sie durch ihre Gewölbe verbunden waren. Allerdings waren sie nicht hoch genug. Es mußten daher in regelmäßigen Abständen oberhalb der Gewölbe und unterhalb der Dächer zusätzliche Streben eingefügt werden. Tom zeichnete einen Steinbogen, der den oberen Rand der Seitenschiffmauer mit der Wand des Hauptschiffs verband. Als weitere Klammer diente ein massiver, vorspringender Strebepfeiler an der Außenseite der Mauer, gleich unterhalb des Steinbogens, dem Tom, um ihm mehr Gewicht zu verleihen und weil es besser aussah, noch eine Fiale, ein Türmchen, aufsetzte.

Eine Kirche, die durch ihre Höhe beeindrucken sollte, war ohne Seitenschiffe und stützendes Strebewerk undenkbar. Nur – diesen Sachverhalt auch einem Mönch verständlich zu machen, konnte mit Schwierigkeiten verbunden sein. Zur Verdeutlichung hatte Tom die Zeichnung angefertigt.

Er zeichnete auch die Fundamente, die unterhalb der Wände tief in den Erdboden hineinreichten. Leute, die von seinem Handwerk nichts verstanden, wunderten sich immer darüber, *wie* tief.

Es war eine einfache Skizze, mit der ein Baumeister nicht viel hätte anfangen können. Um Prior Philip einen ersten Eindruck zu verschaffen, war sie gerade richtig. Tom wollte Philip so weit bringen, daß er seine Vorschläge begriff und imstande war, sich die fertige Kirche vorzustellen und sich dafür zu begeistern. Leicht war dies gewiß nicht, denn es gehörte eine gewaltige Vorstellungskraft dazu, von ein paar in Mörtel geritzten Strichen auf eine große, fertige Kathedrale zu schließen. Der Prior würde sämtliche Hilfe benötigen, die Tom ihm geben konnte.

Die Wände, die Tom gezeichnet hatte, wirkten von vorne fest und solide, obwohl sie es in Wirklichkeit nicht waren. Tom zeichnete nun die Seitenansicht der Mittelschiffswand, vom Inneren der Kirche aus gesehen. Sie war auf drei Ebenen unterbrochen: Die untere Hälfte ließ sich kaum als Wand bezeichnen, bestand sie doch nur aus einer Reihe von Pfeilern, deren obere Enden durch halbkreisförmige Bogen miteinander verbunden waren. Dieser Teil wurde Arkade genannt und gab den Blick frei auf die Rundbogenfenster der Seitenschiffe. Fenster- und Arkadenbogen mußten genau aufeinander abgestimmt werden, so daß das einfallende Licht ungebrochen das Mittelschiff erreichen konnte. Die Pfeiler der Arkade standen auf gleicher Höhe wie die äußeren Strebepfeiler.

Jeder Bogen der Arkade wurde von drei nebeneinanderliegenden kleineren Bogen gekrönt, dem sogenannten Triforium. Da sich hinter ihnen das Pultdach des Seitenschiffs befand, konnte durch diese Bogen kein Licht einfallen. Oberhalb des Triforiums schloß sich der mit Fenstern durchbrochene Ober- oder Lichtgaden an.

Die Baumeister und Steinmetzen früherer Tage, also auch die Erbauer der alten Kathedrale von Kingsbridge, hatten Stabilität durch dicke, schwere Mauern zu erreichen gesucht und aus diesem Grund nur sehr kleine, überaus armselige Fenster eingebaut, die kaum Licht hereinließen. Inzwischen wußte man jedoch, daß gerade und sorgfältig gemauerte Wände auch bei größeren Fenstern genügend Stabilität boten.

Nach Toms Plan betrug das Größenverhältnis der drei Elemente der Mittelschiffswand – Arkade, Triforium und Obergaden – genau 3:1:2. Die Arkade war also halb so hoch wie die Wand, und der Obergaden beanspruchte ein Drittel der Resthöhe. Die richtigen Proportionen waren das Entscheidende beim Kirchenbau: Sie vermittelten unterschwellig das Gefühl eines rundum harmonischen, in sich stimmigen Gebäudes.

Toms Zeichnung war fertig. Er prüfte sie mit kritischem Blick und fand sie tadellos. Aber was würde Philip davon halten? Er, Tom, konnte die Bogen sehen, von vorne bis hinten in langer Reihe aufmarschiert, mit der Nachmittagssonne auf Schnitzwerk und Gesimsen … Aber würde Philip dasselbe sehen wie er?

Er begann mit der dritten Zeichnung, dem Grundriß. Nach seiner Vorstellung sollten die Arkaden je zwölf Bogen umfassen. Die Kirche wurde dadurch in zwölf Abschnitte oder Joche aufgeteilt. Davon entfielen sechs Joche auf das Hauptschiff und vier auf den Chor. Die in Höhe des siebten und achten Jochs liegende Vierung öffnete sich nach beiden Seiten zum Querschiff hin. Oberhalb der Vierung erhob sich der Turm.

Alle Kathedralen, ja nahezu alle Kirchen überhaupt, hatten einen kreuzförmigen Grundriß. Das Kreuz war das bedeutendste Symbol der Christenheit, doch gab es auch praktische Gründe für diese Konstruktion: Die Querhäuser boten willkommenen Raum für zusätzliche Kapellen und Versammlungsräume wie die Sakristei.

Nach Beendigung des Grundrisses wandte Tom sich wieder der

Hauptskizze zu, die – von Westen her gesehen – das Innere der Kirche zeigte, und begann, den Turm einzuzeichnen.

Der Kirchturm sollte entweder anderthalbmal oder doppelt so hoch sein wie das Schiff. Die niedrigere Version führte zu einem eindrucksvollen regelmäßigen Profil, bei dem Seitenschiffe, Hauptschiff und Turm im Verhältnis 1:2:3 abgestuft waren. Aufregender war die höhere Version: Bei gleichbleibendem Verhältnis zwischen Hauptschiff und Seitenschiffen überragte der Turm das Hauptschiff um das Doppelte seiner Länge, so daß die Proportionen insgesamt dem Verhältnis 1:2:4 entsprachen. Tom hatte sich für die zweite Version entschieden: Dies war die einzige Kathedrale, die er je bauen würde – und da wollte er nach den Sternen greifen ... Er hoffte inständig, Philip möge es nicht anders ergehen.

Erklärte sich der Prior mit dem vorliegenden ersten Entwurf einverstanden, so mußte Tom sich erneut ans Werk machen und genauere, maßstabsgetreue Pläne anfertigen. Hinzu kämen Hunderte von Einzelzeichnungen – von Plinthen, Säulen, Kapitellen, Kragsteinen und Türeinfassungen, von Fialen, Treppen, Wasserspeiern und zahllosen anderen Einzelheiten; er würde jahrelang damit beschäftigt sein. Was er jetzt vor sich hatte, war indes das Wesentliche – und es konnte sich sehen lassen: Es war einfach, billig, elegant und genau proportioniert.

Er mußte seinen Entwurf jemandem zeigen – und zwar bald.

Ursprünglich hatte er warten wollen, bis der Mörtel hart war und sich eine passende Gelegenheit zum Gespräch mit Prior Philip bot. Jetzt änderte er seine Meinung: Philip sollte den Entwurf sofort anschauen.

Ob er mich für anmaßend hält? fragte er sich. Der Prior hat mich nicht gebeten, einen Entwurf zu zeichnen. Vielleicht denkt er an einen anderen Baumeister, einen, der schon einmal für ein Kloster gearbeitet und sich dort bewährt hat? Vielleicht verlacht er mich und meinen Ehrgeiz ... Andererseits: Wenn ich ihm nichts zeige, meint er vielleicht, ich sei den anstehenden Aufgaben gar nicht gewachsen, und holt sich einen anderen Baumeister, ohne mich überhaupt in Erwägung zu ziehen ... Tom war nicht bereit, dieses Risiko einzugehen. Eher nahm er es hin, als anmaßend zu gelten.

Es war Nachmittag, aber noch hell. Die Mönche versammelten sich um diese Zeit im Kreuzgang, während Philip sich meistens in seinem Haus aufhielt und in der Bibel las. Tom beschloß, an seine Tür zu klopfen.

Vorsichtig ergriff er sein Zeichenbrett und verließ das Haus.

Er mußte an der Ruine vorbei, und auf einmal kam ihm die ungeheure Aufgabe, die er sich aufladen wollte, schier unlösbar vor: diese vielen Steine, all das Holz und die Handwerker, all diese *Jahre* ... Was kommt da nur alles auf mich zu, dachte er. Ich muß für den stetigen Nachschub an hochwertigen Baumaterialien sorgen, muß Handwerker einstellen und entlassen und unermüdlich mit Senkblei und Wasserwaage deren Arbeit kontrollieren. Ich muß Lehrbretter für die Gesimse herstellen und Hebevorrichtungen konstruieren ...

Tom zweifelte an seiner Kraft und an seinen Fähigkeiten. Dann aber packte ihn wieder die Begeisterung: Wie großartig wäre es, aus dem Nichts heraus etwas Neues zu schaffen ... hier, an diesem Ort, wo sich zur Zeit nur ein einziger großer Trümmerhaufen befindet, eine neue Kathedrale entstehen zu sehen und dann, wenn sie fertig ist, sagen zu können: Das ist mein Werk!

Aber da rumorte noch ein anderer Gedanke in seinem Hinterkopf, ohne daß er ihn richtig fassen konnte. Er schob ihn von sich, wollte sich nicht zu ihm bekennen. Agnes war ohne priesterlichen Beistand gestorben und lag in ungeweihtem Boden. Am liebsten wäre er in Begleitung eines Priesters an den traurigen Ort zurückgekehrt, hätte ihn ein paar Gebete sprechen lassen und vielleicht einen kleinen Grabstein errichtet. Aber Tom hatte Angst, daß, wenn er andere auf die Grabstätte im Wald aufmerksam machte, auch die Geschichte mit dem ausgesetzten Säugling ans Tageslicht kommen würde. Kindesaussetzung galt nach wie vor als Mord. Von Woche zu Woche war seine Sorge um die Seele seiner verstorbenen Frau gewachsen: Wo war sie – an einem guten oder an einem schlechten Ort? Aus Furcht, nach genaueren Einzelheiten befragt zu werden, wagte er nicht, sich an einen Priester zu wenden, und tröstete sich mit dem Gedanken, daß Gott ihm gewiß wohlgesonnen sein werde, wenn er ihm eine Kathedrale errichtete. Ob ich den Herrn darum bitten darf, die mir gewährte Gunst Agnes zukommen zu lassen? fragte er sich. Er wollte seine Arbeit an der Kathedrale Agnes widmen – dann, so fühlte er, würde er sich um ihr Seelenheil keine Sorgen mehr machen müssen und selber Ruhe finden.

Er stand vor dem Haus des Priors, einem kleinen, ebenerdigen Steinhaus. Obwohl es recht kühl war, stand die Tür offen. Tom zögerte einen Moment. Bewahre deine Ruhe und kehre deinen Sachverstand und deine Erfahrung heraus, sagte er sich. Zeige ihm, daß du ein Baumeister bist, der mit allen neuen Erkenntnissen seiner Zunft vertraut ist. Gib dich als ein Mann, dem du selbst gern dein Vertrauen schenken würdest ...

Er trat ein. Das Haus hatte nur einen einzigen Raum. Auf der einen Seite stand ein großes Bett mit üppig dekorierten Vorhängen, auf der anderen ein kleiner Altar mit einem Kruzifix und einem Kerzenhalter. Prior Philip, die Stirn sorgenvoll gerunzelt, stand am Fenster und las in einem Pergament. Er blickte auf, lächelte Tom zu und fragte ihn: »Was gibt's?«

»Zeichnungen, Vater«, erwiderte Tom und bemühte sich, seine Stimme klar und ruhig klingen zu lassen. »Meine ersten Entwürfe für die neue Kathedrale. Darf ich sie Euch zeigen?«

Philip schien gleichermaßen überrascht wie neugierig. »Aber selbstredend!« sagte er.

In der Zimmerecke stand ein großes Stehpult. Tom rückte es ins Licht und legte seinen Rahmen auf die Schräge. Philip betrachtete die Zeichnungen, und Tom studierte Philips Miene. Er erkannte sogleich, daß der Prior noch nie eine Aufrißzeichnung, einen Grundriß und einen Gebäudequerschnitt gesehen hatte. Sein Gesicht verriet Ratlosigkeit.

Tom wollte ihm helfen. Er zeigte auf den Aufriß und erklärte: »Hier seht Ihr ein Joch des Mittelschiffs. Stellt Euch vor, Ihr steht mittendrin und betrachtet die Wand. Hier seht Ihr die Pfeiler der Arkade. Sie sind durch Bogen miteinander verbunden. Durch die Bogenöffnungen könnt Ihr die Fenster des Seitenschiffs erkennen. Oberhalb der Arkade seht Ihr das Triforium und darüber wiederum den Obergaden mit seinen Fenstern.«

Philips Miene hellte sich auf. Er begann zu verstehen und erwies sich als gelehriger Schüler. Als er sich jedoch dem Grundriß zuwandte, bemerkte Tom, daß auch der ihm ein Buch mit sieben Siegeln war.

»Einen solchen Plan brauchen wir draußen auf der Baustelle, wenn wir den genauen Standort der Wände und Säulen, der Türen und Strebepfeiler festlegen wollen. Er wird uns sagen, wo wir unsere Pflöcke einschlagen und unsere Schnüre spannen müssen.«

Wieder dämmerte die Erkenntnis in Philips Gesicht. Es ist gar nicht so schlecht, daß er die Zeichnungen von alleine nicht versteht, dachte Tom, da kann ich meine Zuversicht und meinen Sachverstand besser zur Geltung bringen ... Schließlich wandte sich Philip dem Querschnitt zu, und Tom fuhr mit seiner Erklärung fort. »Hier, in der Mitte, seht Ihr das Schiff. Es hat eine Holzdecke. Dahinter befindet sich der Turm. Das Hauptschiff wird – hier und hier – von den Seitenschiffen flankiert. Die Strebepfeiler sind außen an den Seitenschiffen angebracht.«

»Das sieht ja großartig aus«, sagte Philip. Der Querschnitt beeindruckte den Prior besonders. Es war, als habe jemand die Westfassade der Kirche wie eine Schranktür geöffnet, um den Blick auf das Innere freizugeben.

Philips Blick wanderte zum Grundriß zurück. »Das Mittelschiff besteht demnach nur aus sechs Jochen?«

»Jawohl. Der Chor hat deren vier.«

»Ist das nicht ziemlich klein?«

»Könnt Ihr Euch denn einen größeren Bau leisten?«

»Ich kann mir überhaupt keinen leisten«, erwiderte Philip. »Ich nehme an, Ihr habt keine Ahnung, wieviel dieser hier kostet.«

»Ich weiß ganz genau, was er kostet«, sagte Tom und bemerkte die Überraschung, die sich auf Philips Gesicht abzeichnete: Der Prior wußte nicht, daß Tom überhaupt mit Zahlen umgehen konnte. Viele Stunden hatte der Baumeister damit zugebracht, die Kosten des Kathedralenbaus zu errechnen – bis auf den letzten Penny. Jetzt gab er Philip einen Annäherungswert: »Ich schätze, daß Ihr mit dreitausend Pfund hinkommt.«

Ein hohles Lachen war die Antwort. »Ich habe in den vergangenen Wochen das Jahreseinkommen der Priorei berechnet«, sagte der Prior und schwenkte das Pergament, in dessen Lektüre er bei Toms Eintreffen vertieft gewesen war. »Hört, was dabei herausgekommen ist: Dreihundert Pfund. Von denen jeder Penny ausgegeben wird.«

Für Tom kam die Enthüllung nicht überraschend. Daß die Priorei in der Vergangenheit schlecht geführt worden war, sah man an allen Ecken und Enden. Der Baumeister war zuversichtlich, daß es Philip gelingen würde, die Finanzen wieder in Ordnung zu bringen. »Ihr werdet das Geld schon irgendwie zusammenbekommen, Vater«, sagte er und fügte fromm hinzu: »Mit Gottes Hilfe.«

Philip wandte seine Aufmerksamkeit wieder den Zeichnungen zu. Er wirkte noch nicht überzeugt. »Wieviel Zeit würde dieser Bau in Anspruch nehmen?« fragte er.

»Das hängt davon ab, wie viele Leute Ihr beschäftigt«, antwortete Tom. »Mit dreißig Steinmetzen und Maurern sowie einer ausreichenden Zahl an Tagelöhnern, Lehrburschen, Zimmerern und Schmieden, die ihnen zur Hand gehen, mag es fünfzehn Jahre dauern. Gebt ein Jahr für die Fundamente, je vier Jahre für Chor und Querschiff sowie sechs Jahre für das Langhaus.«

Die Rechnung verfehlte ihren Eindruck nicht. »Ich wünschte mir, unsere Klosteroffizialen wären mit Eurer Vorausschau und Eurer Zahlenkunst begabt«, sagte er und betrachtete sehnsuchtsvoll die Entwürfe. »Das hieße, ich müßte zweihundert Pfund im Jahr auftreiben. Wenn man's so nimmt, klingt es gar nicht mehr so schlimm ...« Er versank in Gedanken. Tom war aufgeregt: Philip sah in den vor ihm liegenden Zeichnungen nicht mehr nur abstrakte Entwürfe, sondern Vorlagen für ein durchführbares Projekt. »Gesetzt den Fall, ich könnte mehr Geld beschaffen – würde das die Arbeit beschleunigen?«

»Bis zu einem gewissen Grade, ja.« Tom war vorsichtig; er wollte nicht, daß Philip sich in übertriebene Begeisterung hineinsteigerte, der später zwangsläufig die Enttäuschung folgen mußte. »Ihr könntet zum Beispiel sechzig Steinmetzen und Maurer anstellen und überall gleichzeitig mit dem Bau beginnen. Dann dauert es vielleicht nur acht oder zehn Jahre. Mehr als sechzig Steinmetzen und Maurer auf einer Baustelle dieser Größenordnung würde ich nicht empfehlen: Sie stehen sich nur selbst im Weg.«

Philip nickte; er sah das offensichtlich ein. »Aber selbst mit dreißig Steinmetzen könnte der Ostflügel innerhalb von fünf Jahren fertig sein.«

»So ist es. Ihr könntet darin Gottesdienste abhalten und einen neuen Schrein für die Gebeine des heiligen Adolphus aufstellen.«

»O ja!« Nun hatte der Prior richtig Feuer gefangen. »Ich hatte schon gedacht, es würde Jahrzehnte dauern, bis in Kingsbridge wieder eine Kirche steht.« Er musterte Tom mit skeptischem Blick. »Habt Ihr schon einmal eine Kathedrale gebaut?«

»Nein, aber eine Reihe kleinerer Kirchen. Außerdem habe ich mehrere Jahre am Bau der Kathedrale von Exeter mitgewirkt. Zum Schluß war ich der Stellvertreter des Dombaumeisters.«

»Hier in Kingsbridge wollt Ihr selber Dombaumeister sein, wie?«

Tom zögerte. Alles andere als Offenheit war bei Philip fehl am Platze; der Mann hatte keine Geduld für lange Umschweife. »Ja, Vater«, sagte er so ruhig wie möglich. »Ich möchte, daß Ihr mich zum Dombaumeister bestimmt.«

»Warum?«

Mit dieser Frage hatte Tom nicht gerechnet. Es gab so viele Antworten ... *Weil ich schon erlebt habe, wie man es nicht machen soll, und glaube, daß ich es besser kann,* dachte er. *Weil es für einen Handwerksmeister, abgesehen vielleicht von der Liebe zu einer schönen Frau, nichts Befriedigenderes gibt als die tätige Ausübung seines Berufs. Weil eine Aufgabe wie diese das Leben eines Mannes mit Sinn und Bedeutung erfüllt.* Welche Antwort wollte der Prior hören? Wahrscheinlich eine fromme ... Unbekümmert entschied Tom sich für die einfache Wahrheit: »Weil sie so schön sein wird.«

Philip bedachte ihn mit einem merkwürdigen Blick, den Tom nicht zu deuten imstande war. *»Weil sie so schön sein wird«*, wiederholte er. Tom bereute seine Antwort schon; er hielt sie für töricht und wollte noch etwas hinzufügen. Doch dann merkte er, daß Philip ihm gar nicht gram war – im Gegenteil: Der Prior war bewegt. Toms Worte waren ihm zu Herzen gegangen. Schließlich nickte er, als stimme er nach längerer Überlegung Toms Bemerkung zu, und sagte: »Ja – und was könnte besser sein, als für Gott etwas Schönes zu tun?«

Tom schwieg. Philip hatte nicht gesagt: *Ja, Tom, Ihr sollt mein Dombaumeister sein!* Er wartete.

Philip schien sich zu einem Entschluß durchgerungen zu haben. »Ich werde in drei Tagen gemeinsam mit Bischof Waleran nach Winchester reisen und den König aufsuchen«, sagte er. »Ich kenne die Pläne des Bischofs noch nicht in allen Einzelheiten, doch bin ich sicher, daß wir König Stephan bitten werden, den Neubau einer Kathedrale zu Kingsbridge finanziell zu unterstützen.«

»Hoffen wir, daß er sich Euren Wünschen gewogen zeigt«, sagte Tom.

»Er ist uns noch einen Gefallen schuldig«, erwiderte Philip und lächelte dabei geheimnisvoll. »Er müßte eigentlich helfen.«

»Und wenn er es tut ...?«

»Ich glaube, Tom Builder, daß der Herr eine bestimmte Absicht verfolgte, als er mir Euch schickte«, sagte Philip. »Ihr könnt die Kirche bauen – vorausgesetzt, der König gibt uns das Geld.«

Nun war es an Tom, bewegt zu sein. Er wußte kaum, was er sagen sollte. Ihm war soeben sein Lebenswunsch erfüllt worden – allerdings nur unter einer bestimmten Bedingung. Alles hing jetzt vom Geld des Königs ab. Er nickte und akzeptierte damit sowohl das Versprechen als auch das Risiko. »Ich danke Euch, Vater«, sagte er.

Die Glocke läutete zum Vesper. Tom nahm seinen Rahmen auf.

»Braucht Ihr die Entwürfe?« fragte Philip. Die Idee ist nicht schlecht, dachte Tom. Wenn ich sie hierlasse, sind sie Philip eine ständige Mahnung. »Nein«, sagte er, »ich habe alles im Kopf.«

»Gut, ich hätte sie gerne hier.«

Tom nickte und ging zur Tür.

Dann fiel ihm etwas ein. Wenn ich jetzt nicht frage wegen Agnes, werde ich es wahrscheinlich nie tun, dachte er. Er drehte sich noch einmal um. »Vater?«

»Ja?«

»Mein erstes Weib ... sie hieß Agnes ... starb ohne einen Priester und liegt in ungeweihter Erde. Sie hatte nicht gesündigt – es waren ... die Umstände. Ich frage mich ... Es kommt doch immer wieder vor, daß jemand eine Kapelle baut oder ein Kloster gründet, weil er hofft, im Leben nach dem Tode Gnade vor den Augen des Herrn zu finden. Glaubt Ihr, daß ich mit meinem Entwurf zu Agnes' Seelenheil beitragen kann?«

Philip runzelte die Stirn. »An Abraham erging die Aufforderung, seinen einzigen Sohn zu opfern. Gott fordert heute keine Blutopfer mehr, denn das höchste Opfer wurde bereits gegeben. Die Lehre aus der Geschichte Abrahams ist die, daß Gott von uns das Beste verlangt, zu dem wir fähig sind, das, was uns mehr als alles andere am Herzen liegt. Ist dieser Entwurf das Beste, was Ihr Gott anbieten könnt?«

»Von meinen Kindern abgesehen, ja.«

»Dann geht in Frieden, Tom Builder. Gott wird Euer Angebot annehmen.«

Philip hatte keine Ahnung, warum Waleran Bigod ihn ausgerechnet in den Ruinen des Schlosses von Graf Bartholomäus treffen wollte.

Es war ihm nichts anderes übriggeblieben, als nach Shiring zu reiten, dort zu übernachten und sich am Morgen auf den Weg nach Earlscastle zu machen. Vor ihm ragten die Zinnen der Burg aus dem Morgennebel. Wahrscheinlich leiten ihn rein praktische Erwägungen, dachte Philip: Waleran reiste von einem Ort zum anderen. Kein Ort auf der Route lag näher an Kingsbridge als Earlscastle; zudem war die Burg ein nicht zu verfehlendes Ziel.

Nur allzugern hätte Philip genauer gewußt, was Waleran im Schilde führte. Seit dessen Besuch in Kingsbridge hatte er den designierten Bischof nicht mehr gesehen. Waleran wußte nicht, wieviel Geld Philip zum Bau der Kirche benötigte, und Philip wußte nicht, was Waleran vom König zu fordern gedachte. Waleran war, was seine Pläne betraf, ein furchtbarer Geheimniskrämer. Philip war innerlich aufs höchste angespannt.

Der Prior war froh, daß Tom Builder ihn genau über Kosten und Dauer des Kathedralenbaus aufgeklärt hatte. Der Mann legte Ansichten von bemerkenswerter Tiefe an den Tag und war immer wieder für Überraschungen gut. Er konnte kaum lesen und schreiben, war aber imstande, eine Kathedrale zu entwerfen, den Bedarf an Arbeitskräften, die voraussichtliche Bauzeit *und* die Kosten zu errechnen ... Der Baumeister war ein ruhiger Mann, aber eine ehrfurchtgebietende Erscheinung: Er war sehr groß, hatte ein bärtiges, wettergegerbtes Gesicht, scharfe Augen und eine hohe Stirn. Manchmal beschlich den Prior in Toms Gegenwart eine gewisse Beklommenheit, die er mit einem besonders herzlichen Ton zu überspielen versuchte. Tom indessen war sehr ernst und ahnte nichts von den Gefühlen, die Philip in seiner Anwesenheit überkamen. In dem Gespräch über seine verstorbene Frau, das Philip sehr berührt hatte, war eine bis dahin unerkannte Frömmigkeit zum Ausdruck gekommen. Tom war einer von jenen Menschen, die ihren Glauben im Innersten ihres Herzens verschlossen, und das waren allemal nicht die Schlechtesten.

Je näher Earlscastle kam, desto unbehaglicher war Philip zumute. Aus der blühenden, geschäftigen Burg, die einst das umgebende Land beschützt und vielen Menschen Arbeit und Brot gegeben hatte, war eine triste Ruine geworden, und die Hütten und Häuser im Schatten der Mauern waren verlassen wie leere Nester in den kahlen Zweigen. Und er, Philip, war dafür verantwortlich. Er hatte die Verschwörung verraten, die hier ausgebrütet wurde, und damit in Gestalt Percy Hamleighs und seiner Mannen den Zorn Gottes auf die Burg und ihre Bewohner herabbeschworen.

Ihm fiel auf, daß Mauern und Torhaus bei den Kämpfen kaum beschädigt worden waren. Aller Wahrscheinlichkeit nach waren die Angreifer eingedrungen, ehe man die Tore hatte schließen können. Philip führte sein Pferd am Zügel über die hölzerne Brücke und betrat den unteren Burghof. Hier waren die Spuren der Schlacht schon deutlicher: Unversehrt stand nur die steinerne Kapelle. Von den Wirtschaftsgebäuden waren nur noch verkohlte Reste übriggeblieben. Am Fuße der Mauer wirbelte der Wind Ascheflocken auf.

Vom Bischof war nirgendwo etwas zu sehen. Zu Pferd überquerte Philip das Gelände und gelangte zur Brücke, die zum oberen Burghof führte. Von dort aus war es nicht mehr weit zum trutzigen Wohnturm. Eine recht wackelig aussehende Holztreppe führte zum Eingang im ersten Stock. Streng und abweisend wirkte der Bau mit seinen schmalen Fenstern, die nicht viel mehr waren als Schießscharten ... und doch hatte er Graf Bartholomäus nicht beschützen können.

Immerhin – die Fenster versprachen einen weiten Blick über das

Land. Philip beschloß, von oben nach dem Bischof Ausschau zu halten. Er band sein Pferd ans Treppengeländer und stieg hinauf.

Die Tür öffnete sich, kaum daß er sie berührt hatte. Er trat ein. Der große Saal war dunkel und staubig, die Binsen auf dem Boden knochentrocken. Die Feuerstelle war kalt. Eine Wendeltreppe führte weiter hinauf. Philip trat ans Fenster. Der Staub stieg ihm in die Nase, und er mußte niesen. Da der Ausblick alles andere als überwältigend war, entschied er sich, ins nächste Stockwerk zu steigen.

Oben angekommen, sah Philip sich zwei geschlossenen Türen gegenüber. Er vermutete, daß die kleinere zur Latrine und die größere ins gräfliche Schlafgemach führte. Er öffnete die größere.

Das Zimmer war nicht leer.

Philip erstarrte vor Schreck. Mitten im Raum stand, das Gesicht ihm zugewandt, eine junge Frau von außergewöhnlicher Schönheit. Einen Augenblick lang glaubte der Prior an eine Vision, und sein Herz schlug ihm bis zum Halse. Üppige dunkle Locken umwallten ein bezauberndes Gesicht. Aus großen, dunklen Augen sah die Frau ihn an. Sie ist genauso überrascht wie ich, dachte Philip und löste sich aus seiner Starre. Er wollte einen Schritt auf sie zugehen, doch da wurde er unvermittelt von hinten gepackt und spürte die kalte Klinge eines langen Messers an seinem Hals. Eine männliche Stimme sagte: »Und wer, zum Teufel, seid Ihr?«

Das Mädchen kam auf ihn zu. »Nennt Euren Namen, sonst wird Matthew Euch töten«, sagte sie mit königlicher Würde.

Ihr Verhalten verriet die adlige Herkunft. Doch selbst Adligen war es untersagt, Mönche zu bedrohen. So antwortete Philip ruhig: »Sag Matthew, er möge den Prior von Kingsbridge sofort loslassen, widrigenfalls hat er mit schlimmen Folgen zu rechnen.«

Der Mann gab ihn frei. Ein Blick über die Schulter zeigte Philip, daß es sich bei diesem Matthew um einen schmächtigen Burschen handelte, ungefähr so alt wie er selbst. Er kam offenbar gerade aus der Latrine.

Das Mädchen mochte an die siebzehn Lenze zählen. Trotz ihres anmaßenden Benehmens war sie recht ärmlich gekleidet. Während er sie noch musterte, öffnete sich plötzlich der Deckel einer Truhe, die hinter dem Mädchen an der Wand stand, und ein halbwüchsiger, etwas belämmert dreinschauender Junge kroch heraus. In der Hand hielt er ein Schwert. Philip vermochte nicht zu sagen, ob er dort auf der Lauer gelegen oder sich bloß versteckt hatte.

»Und wer bist du?« fragte er.

»Ich bin die Tochter des Grafen von Shiring. Mein Name ist Aliena.«

Die Tochter! dachte Philip. Ich hatte keine Ahnung, daß sie noch immer auf der Burg lebt ... Er betrachtete den Jungen. Der war vielleicht fünfzehn Jahre alt und sah – bis auf die Stupsnase und die kurzen Haare – dem Mädchen sehr ähnlich. Fragend hob Philip die Brauen.

»Ich bin Richard, der Erbe der Grafschaft«, sagte der Junge im krächzenden Ton des Heranwachsenden.

Und auch der Mann, der hinter Philip stand, stellte sich vor. »Mein Name ist Matthew. Ich bin der Haushofmeister der Burg.«

Philip war jetzt klar, daß die drei sich seit der Gefangennahme des Grafen auf der Burg verborgen hielten. Der Haushofmeister kümmerte sich um die Kinder. Er mußte irgendwo Geld oder Vorräte versteckt haben.

»Ich weiß, wer dein Vater ist«, sagte Philip, an Aliena gewandt. »Doch wo ist deine Mutter?«

»Sie starb vor vielen Jahren.«

Der Prior spürte einen Stich im Herzen. Die Kinder waren praktisch Vollwaisen – und er war mitschuldig an ihrem Schicksal. »Habt ihr denn keine Verwandten, die sich um euch kümmern können?«

»Ich kümmere mich um die Burg, bis mein Vater wiederkommt«, erwiderte das Mädchen.

Die leben ja in einer Traumwelt, dachte Philip. Sie tun so, als seien sie noch immer Mitglieder einer reichen und mächtigen Familie. In Wirklichkeit ist Aliena, deren Vater in Ungnade gefallen ist und im Verlies sitzt, ein Mädchen wie jedes andere – und der Junge Erbe von gar nichts. Nie wieder wird Graf Bartholomäus Earlscastle betreten – es sei denn, der König beschließt, ihn hier zu hängen ...

Das Mädchen tat ihm leid, doch er empfand auch eine gewisse Hochachtung für die Willensstärke, mit der sie die Illusion aufrechterhielt und noch zwei andere Menschen in ihrem Bann hielt. Sie hat das Format einer Königin, dachte er.

Von draußen ertönte Hufgetrappel auf Holz: Mehrere Pferde überquerten die Brücke. »Was führt Euch hierher?« fragte Aliena.

»Eine Verabredung«, sagte Philip. Er drehte sich um und wollte zur Tür, doch Matthew versperrte ihm den Weg. Einen Moment lang standen sie sich Auge in Auge gegenüber. Wollen sie mich am Fortgehen hindern? fragte sich Philip, doch da trat der Haushofmeister auch schon zur Seite und ließ ihn passieren. Er verließ das Gemach, raffte seine Kutte und eilte die Wendeltreppe hinunter. Als er unten ankam, hörte er Schritte hinter sich. Matthew holte ihn ein.

»Erzählt niemandem, daß Ihr uns hier getroffen habt!« sagte er.

Philip erkannte, daß Matthew die Wirklichkeit durchaus begriff. »Wie lange wollt Ihr hierbleiben?« fragte Philip.

»So lange wie möglich«, antwortete der Haushofmeister.

»Und wenn Ihr die Burg verlassen *müßt*? Wohin wendet Ihr Euch dann?«

»Ich weiß es nicht.«

Philip nickte. »Ich wahre Euer Geheimnis«, versprach er.

»Danke, Vater.«

Philip durchquerte den staubigen Saal und trat ins Freie. Unten zügelten gerade Bischof Waleran und zwei andere Männer ihre Rösser neben Philips eigenem Pferd. Waleran trug einen schweren Mantel, der mit schwarzem Pelz besetzt war, und auf dem Kopf eine schwarze Pelzmütze. Er sah auf, und Philip blickte in seine blassen Augen. »Ehrwürdiger Herr Bischof«, sagte Philip respektvoll und schritt die Stufen hinunter. Das Bild des jungfräulichen Mädchens im gräflichen Schlafgemach stand noch immer lebhaft vor seinen Augen und ließ sich nicht so schnell abschütteln, wie es ihm liebgewesen wäre.

Waleran saß ab. Seine Begleiter waren dieselben wie beim letztenmal: Dechant Baldwin und der Bewaffnete. Philip nickte den beiden zu; dann kniete er vor Waleran nieder und küßte ihm die Hand.

Waleran akzeptierte die Ehrbezeigung, ohne sie besonders auszukosten: Rasch entzog er Philip seine Hand. Waleran liebte die reine Macht – die äußeren Insignien interessierten ihn nicht.

»Allein, Philip?« fragte er.

»Gewiß. Die Priorei ist arm. Eine Begleitung für mich wäre eine überflüssige Ausgabe. Als Prior von St.-John-in-the-Forest hatte ich nie eine Eskorte – und hab's dennoch überlebt.«

Waleran zuckte mit den Achseln. »Kommt mit«, sagte er. »Ich möchte Euch etwas zeigen.« Quer über den Hof schritt er auf den nächsten Turm zu, betrat ihn durch die niedrige Tür und stieg sogleich die Treppen empor. Philip folgte ihm. In dichten Trauben hingen Fledermäuse an der niedrigen Decke, und Philip zog den Kopf ein, um ihnen auszuweichen.

Dann standen sie hoch oben vor den Zinnen des Turms, und ihre Blicke schweiften über das sie umgebende Land.

»Es handelt sich um eine der kleineren Grafschaften im Königreich«, sagte Waleran.

»Ihr sagt es.« Philip schauderte. Es herrschte ein kalter, feuchter Wind, und sein Mantel war nicht so warm wie Walerans. Er fragte sich, warum ihn der Bischof hierhergeführt hatte.

»Die Ländereien sind zum Teil recht gut, doch gibt es auch viel Wald und steinige Höhen.«

»Ja.« Bei klarem Wetter hätte man viele Morgen Ackerland und Wald überblicken können. Die beiden Betrachter konnten jedoch im Süden, obwohl sich der Morgennebel inzwischen gelichtet hatte, kaum den Waldrand erkennen und sahen nur die flachen Felder in unmittelbarer Nähe der Burg.

»Zur Grafschaft gehört auch ein riesiger Steinbruch, aus dem hervorragende Kalksteinblöcke gefördert werden«, fuhr Waleran fort. »Die Wälder bergen prächtiges Holz in großer Menge, und die Höfe erwirtschaften einen beachtlichen Reichtum. Gehörte diese Grafschaft uns, Philip, so könnten wir unsere Kathedrale bauen.«

»Wenn Schweine Flügel hätten, könnten sie fliegen«, sagte Philip.

»Oh, du Kleingläubiger!«

Philip starrte Waleran an. »Ist das etwa Euer Ernst?«

»In der Tat.«

Philip war nach wie vor sehr skeptisch, doch keimte trotz allem eine gewisse Hoffnung in ihm auf. Ja, wenn das möglich wäre! Aber er sagte: »Der König braucht militärische Unterstützung. Er wird die Grafschaft jemandem zusprechen, der imstande ist, Ritter in die Schlacht zu führen.«

»Der König verdankt seine Krone der Kirche und Euch und mir seinen Sieg über Bartholomäus. Ritter sind nicht alles, was er braucht.«

Waleran meinte es tatsächlich ernst. War das überhaupt denkbar? War es möglich, daß der König die Grafschaft Shiring der Kirche übereignete, um auf diese Weise den Wiederaufbau der Kathedrale von Kingsbridge zu finanzieren? Es war schier unglaublich, trotz der Argumente, die Waleran angeführt hatte. Aber Philip konnte einfach nicht anders: Der Gedanke, wie großartig es wäre, wenn alle Steine, alles Holz *und* genügend Geld für die Handwerker zur Verfügung stünden, ließ ihn nicht mehr los. Was hatte Tom Builder gesagt? Mit sechzig Steinmetzen und Maurern kann der Bau in acht bis zehn Jahren vollendet sein. Allein die Vorstellung war atemberaubend.

»Was ist mit dem ehemaligen Grafen?« fragte er.

»Bartholomäus hat seinen Verrat bekannt. Die Verschwörung gab er von vornherein zu, nur hat er eine Zeitlang noch versucht, den

König als Usurpator darzustellen, um zu beweisen, daß seine Tat nicht als Hochverrat zu bezeichnen sei ... Die Folterknechte des Königs haben ihm aber schließlich auch diese Flausen ausgetrieben.«

Philip schauderte erneut. Er wollte nicht darüber nachdenken, wie man es angestellt hatte, einen so harten Mann wie Bartholomäus zum Einlenken zu zwingen.

Er schob den Gedanken von sich. »Die Grafschaft Shiring«, murmelte er vor sich hin ... Es war eine ungemein ehrgeizige Forderung. Eine eigenartige, ganz und gar unvernünftige Hochstimmung überkam ihn.

Waleran richtete die Augen himmelwärts. »Machen wir uns auf den Weg«, sagte er. »Übermorgen erwartet uns der König.«

Aus seinem Versteck hinter den Zinnen des nächsten Turms beobachtete William Hamleigh die beiden Gottesmänner. Er kannte den einen wie den anderen: Der große Schlanke, der mit seiner spitzen Nase und seinem schwarzen Mantel wie ein Amselmännchen aussah, war der neue Bischof von Kingsbridge. Der kleine Energische mit dem kahlrasierten Schädel und den hellblauen Augen war Prior Philip. Was treiben die zwei nur hier? fragte er sich.

Er hatte den Mönch kommen sehen. Philip hatte sich umgeschaut, als erwartete er jemanden, und war dann in den Wohnturm gegangen. Ob er den drei dort lebenden Menschen begegnet war, vermochte William nicht zu sagen, war doch der Prior schon nach kurzer Zeit wieder herausgekommen. Vielleicht hatten sie sich vor ihm versteckt. Philip jedenfalls hatte dann den Bischof begrüßt und war mit ihm auf den Turm geklettert, und da standen sie nun in luftiger Höh', und aus den ausladenden Gebärden, mit denen der Bischof über Feld und Flur deutete, hätte man schließen können, es gehöre alles ihm. Der Bischof, daran konnte kein Zweifel bestehen, war voller Überschwang, während bei Philip Zurückhaltung und Skepsis dominierten. Bestimmt schmieden die beiden ein Komplott, dachte William bei sich.

Doch er war nicht gekommen, um Waleran und Philip heimlich zu beobachten. Seine Neugier galt vielmehr Aliena.

Immer häufiger trieb es ihn hierher. Sie zehrte an seinem Gemüt. Tag und Nacht suchten ihn die wildesten Visionen heim: Aliena nackt und gefesselt in einem Kornfeld; Aliena wie ein furchtsamer junger Hund in einem Winkel seines Schlafgemachs kauernd; Aliena einsam und verloren im Wald, und es wird Nacht ... Es wurde so schlimm, daß er sie unbedingt sehen mußte, in Fleisch und Blut. Im Morgengrauen ritt er dann nach Earlscastle. Während Walter, sein Knecht, im Wald zurückblieb und sich um die Pferde kümmerte, schlich William sich in die Burg ein. Er hatte ein Versteck gefunden, von dem aus sich ein guter Überblick über den Wohnturm und den oberen Burghof bot.

Manchmal dauerte es sehr lange, bis er Aliena zu Gesicht bekam, und seine Geduld wurde arg auf die Probe gestellt, doch war ihm der Gedanke, wieder fortgehen zu müssen, ohne sie wenigstens ganz kurz gesehen zu haben, so unerträglich, daß er immer ausharrte. Wenn sie dann endlich erschien, wurden ihm der Hals trocken und die Handflächen feucht, und sein Herzschlag beschleunigte sich. Eines Nachmittags im Sommer – er lag schon seit dem frühen Morgen auf der Lauer – war sie zum Brunnen gegangen, hatte einen Eimer Wasser heraufgezogen und ihre Kleider abgelegt, um sich zu waschen. Allein die Erinnerung an diese Szene genügte, um William erneut in Erregung zu versetzen. Als Aliena die Arme hob, um sich die Haare einzuseifen, bewegten sich aufreizend ihre großen, stolzen Brüste, und es war eine Lust, mit anzusehen, wie die Brustwarzen kleiner wurden, als kaltes Wasser über sie spritzte. Das dunkel gelockte Dreieck zwischen ihren Beinen war überraschend groß, und als Aliena sich mit seifiger Hand dort wusch und rieb, hatte William nicht mehr an sich halten können und in seine Kleider ejakuliert.

Etwas so Hübsches wie damals war seitdem nicht mehr geschehen, und im Winter wusch sie sich gewiß nicht. Kleinere Freuden gab es hingegen durchaus. War Aliena allein, so pflegte sie oft zu singen oder gar Selbstgespräche zu führen. William hatte sie beim Flechten ihrer Haare beobachtet, hatte sie tanzen und wie ein kleines Kind die Tauben von den Wallanlagen scheuchen sehen. Und während er sie aus seinem Schlupfwinkel heraus bei all diesen kleinen, intimen Tätigkeiten mit seinen Blicken verfolgte, wuchs in ihm das keineswegs unangenehme Gefühl, daß sie ihm in gewisser Hinsicht ausgeliefert war.

Solange der Mönch und der Bischof sich auf dem Gelände der Burg aufhielten, würde sie sich natürlich nicht blicken lassen. Glücklicherweise verweilten die beiden nur kurze Zeit auf dem Turm, bestiegen dann ihre Pferde und ritten mit ihren Dienern davon. Waren sie wirklich nur wegen der schönen Aussicht nach Earlscastle gekommen? Wenn ja, dann hatte ihnen aber das Wetter einen Strich durch die Rechnung gemacht ...

Vor Ankunft der Besucher war der Haushofmeister im Haus gewesen und hatte Feuerholz geholt. Er war der Koch der kleinen Gruppe im Wohnturm. William wußte, daß Matthew bald wieder erscheinen würde, diesmal, um Wasser zu holen. Wahrscheinlich, dachte er, essen sie vornehmlich Brei, denn einen Backofen gibt es im Wohnturm nicht. Später am Tag pflegte der Haushofmeister die Burg zu verlassen und nahm dabei bisweilen den Jungen mit. Sobald die beiden gegangen waren, war es bis zu Alienas Erscheinen nur noch eine Frage der Zeit.

Als ihn die Warterei zu langweilen begann, beschwor William die Vision von dem sich waschenden Mädchen herauf. Die Erinnerung war fast so gut wie die Wirklichkeit. Nur – heute war er nicht ganz bei der Sache. Über der Burg und ihren drei Bewohnern hatte noch bis zum frühen Morgen eine merkwürdig verwunschene Stimmung gelegen, deren Zauber nun durch den Besuch dieser von Grund auf unzauberhaften Gestalten mit ihren schmutzüberkrusteten Gäulen ein für allemal gebrochen war. William war, als habe ihn ein häßlicher Lärm mitten aus einem wunderschönen Traum geschreckt: Wie sehr er sich auch bemühte – er konnte nicht mehr einschlafen.

Eine Zeitlang grübelte er darüber nach, was die Besucher vorgehabt haben mochten, fand aber, obwohl er sich sicher war, daß sie irgend etwas ausheckten, keine plausible Antwort. Es gab nur einen Menschen, der sich wahrscheinlich einen Reim darauf machen konnte, und das war seine Mutter. William beschloß, Aliena an diesem Tag allein zu lassen. Er wollte nach Hause reiten und Bericht erstatten.

Am zweiten Tag trafen sie gegen Abend in Winchester ein. Sie betraten die Stadt von Süden her durch das Königstor und gingen ohne Umwege zur Kathedrale. Dort angekommen, trennten sie sich: Waleran begab sich zur Residenz des Bischofs. Der Palast lag auf eigenem Grund am Rande der großen Freifläche, die die Kathedrale umgab. Philip wollte dem Prior seine Reverenz erweisen und um ein Nachtlager im Dormitorium nachsuchen.

Nach drei Tagen auf der Straße kam Philip die klösterliche Ruhe und Beschaulichkeit so erfrischend vor wie eine kühle Quelle an einem heißen Sommertag. Der Prior von Winchester war ein umgänglicher, rundlicher Mann mit rosiger Haut und weißem Haar. Zum Abendessen lud er Philip in sein Haus. Während des Mahls unterhielten sie sich über ihre Bischöfe. Der Prior von Winchester hatte große Ehrfurcht vor Bischof Henry und war ihm voll ergeben. Wahrscheinlich bringt es nicht viel, mit einem Bischof zu streiten, der so reich und mächtig wie Henry ist, dachte Philip. Trotzdem wollte er sich von *seinem* Bischof nicht in dieser Weise beherrschen und drangsalieren lassen.

Er schlief tief und fest. Kurz vor Mitternacht stand er auf und ging zum Frühgottesdienst.

Als er – zum erstenmal in seinem Leben – die Kathedrale von Winchester betrat, überkam ihn eine gewisse Beklemmung.

Der Prior hatte ihm gesagt, es handele sich um die größte Kirche der Welt, und der Augenschein hatte es bestätigt. Die Kathedrale war eine Achtelmeile lang – Philip kannte Dörfer, die man darin hätte unterbringen können! – und verfügte über zwei große Türme, einen über der Vierung und einen zweiten an der Westseite. Der Vierungsturm war dreißig Jahre zuvor eingestürzt und hatte das Grabmal von König William Rufus verschüttet, der freilich ein gottloser Mann gewesen war und von vornherein nicht in einer Kirche hätte bestattet werden dürfen. Inzwischen war der Turm wiederaufgebaut worden.

Während des Gottesdienstes stand Philip direkt unter dem neuen Turm. Er sang und empfand dabei die Würde und die gewaltige Kraft, die von dem mächtigen Bauwerk ausging. Die von Tom Builder entworfene Kathedrale würde sich im Vergleich zu Winchester geradezu bescheiden ausnehmen – vorausgesetzt, sie wurde je gebaut! Philip kam zu Bewußtsein, daß ihn seine Reise mit den allerhöchsten Kreisen des Landes in Verbindung brachte, und er war plötzlich ganz aufgeregt. Schließlich war er nur ein einfacher Junge aus den walisischen Bergen, der dank eines glücklichen Geschicks Mönch geworden war. Und heute würde er vor dem König stehen. Was gab ihm das Recht dazu?

Mit den anderen Mönchen kehrte er ins Dormitorium zurück. Aber er fand keinen Schlaf mehr. Er fürchtete, bei der Audienz etwas Falsches zu sagen oder zu tun und damit König Stephan oder Bischof Henry gegen Kingsbridge einzunehmen. In Frankreich geborene Herrschaften mokierten sich gerne über die Art, wie Engländer mit ihrer Sprache umgingen – was würden sie von einem walisischen Akzent halten? Frömmigkeit, Gehorsam und hingebungsvolle Arbeit für Gott, das waren die Kriterien, nach denen man Philip in der monastischen Welt bisher beurteilt hatte. Hier, in der Hauptstadt eines der größten Königreiche auf Erden, galten solche Eigenschaften gar nichts. Philip hatte das Gefühl, den Boden unter den Füßen zu verlieren, hielt sich mit einemmal für einen Hochstapler, einen Niemand, der vorgab, ein Jemand zu sein, und er war überzeugt, daß man ihn rasch entlarven und mit Schimpf und Schande davonjagen würde.

Als der Morgen graute, erhob er sich, nahm an der Prim teil und frühstückte im Refektorium. Das Kloster war wohlhabend: Die Mönche aßen Weißbrot und tranken Starkbier. Nach dem Frühstück begaben sich die Brüder in die Kapitelversammlung, während Philip den bischöflichen Palast aufsuchte. Der ansehnliche, mit weiten Fenstern versehene Steinbau lag in einem mehrere Morgen großen Garten, der von einer Mauer umschlossen war.

Waleran rechnete zuversichtlich mit Bischof Henrys Unterstützung bei seiner unerhörten Intrige. Mit Henrys Hilfe konnten alle Wünsche in Erfüllung gehen, denn schließlich war er nicht irgendwer, sondern Henry von Blois, der jüngere Bruder des Königs. Er war nicht nur der Kleriker mit den besten Verbindungen zum Hof, sondern in seiner Eigenschaft als Abt des wohlhabenden Klosters von Glastonbury auch der reichste Vertreter seines Standes in ganz England. Schon jetzt galt er als der nächste Erzbischof von Canterbury. Einen mächtigeren Verbündeten konnte Kingsbridge gar nicht bekommen.

Vielleicht geht ja doch alles gut, dachte Philip, vielleicht ermöglicht uns der König den Bau einer neuen Kathedrale ... Allein der Gedanke daran erfüllte ihn mit solcher Hoffnung, daß ihm das Herz schier zerspringen wollte.

Ein Diener beschied ihn, daß Bischof Henry voraussichtlich erst am späteren Vormittag Besuch empfangen könne. Philip war innerlich viel zu erregt, um zum Kloster zurückzukehren. Voller Unruhe beschloß er, sich die Stadt anzusehen – die größte Stadt, in der er je gewesen war.

Der Bischofspalast lag im äußersten Südosten von Winchester. Philip schritt zunächst an der östlichen Stadtmauer entlang. Nachdem er das Gelände eines weiteren Klosters, der St. Mary's Abbey, überquert hatte, gelangte er in ein Viertel, das ganz im Zeichen der Leder- und Wollverarbeitung stand und von zahlreichen Wasserläufen durchzogen war. Bei genauerem Hinsehen erkannte er, daß es sich nicht um natürliche Bäche, sondern um von Menschenhand geschaffene Kanäle handelte. Gespeist vom Itchen-Fluß, versorgten sie das Stadtviertel mit den großen Wassermengen, die zum Waschen der Felle und Gerben der Häute erforderlich waren. Normalerweise entwickelten sich solche Gewerbe in unmittelbarer Ufernähe. Philip staunte über die Kühnheit der Leute, die hier den Fluß zu den Werkstätten gebracht hatten – statt umgekehrt.

Trotz der vielen Handwerksbetriebe war Winchester ruhiger und weniger überfüllt als alle anderen Städte, die Philip bislang kennengelernt hatte. Orte wie Salisbury oder Hereford schienen in ihren Mauern eingezwängt wie ein dicker Mann in eine enge Tunika: Die Häuser standen dicht an dicht, die Hintergärten waren zu klein, der Marktplatz vermochte die Volksmenge nicht zu fassen. Mensch und Tier mußten um jeden Fußbreit Boden kämpfen, und dauernd hatte man das Gefühl, die gereizte Stimmung könne sich jederzeit in offenen Auseinandersetzungen entladen. Winchester indessen war so groß, daß niemand unter Platzmangel zu leiden schien. Ein Grund für das Gefühl der Weitläufigkeit lag, wie Philip nach einer Weile erkannte, darin, daß die Straßen wie ein Gitternetz angelegt waren. Sie waren größtenteils schnurgerade und bildeten mit den Querstraßen rechte Winkel. Philip hatte so etwas noch nie gesehen: Die ganze Stadt mußte nach einem Plan errichtet worden sein.

Kirchen gab es zu Dutzenden, in allen Formen und Größen, aus Holz oder aus Stein. Jede Kirche war für einen kleinen Stadtbezirk zuständig. Eine Gemeinde, die sich so viele Priester leisten konnte, mußte sehr reich sein.

Leichte Übelkeit beschlich Philip in der Straße der Fleischhauer. Noch nie hatte er soviel rohes Fleisch auf einem Fleck gesehen. Blut floß aus den Läden auf die Straße, und zwischen den Füßen der Käufer und Passanten huschten fette Ratten hin und her.

Die Straße der Fleischhauer mündete im Süden in die High Street, gleich gegenüber dem alten Königspalast. Philip wußte bereits, daß die Könige seit der Errichtung des neuen Wohnturms auf der Burg den alten Palast mieden, doch schlug die königliche Münze im Untergeschoß des von dicken Mauern und eisenbewehrten Toren geschützten Gebäudes nach wie vor Silberpennys. Eine Weile blieb Philip vor dem schmiedeeisernen Gatter stehen und sah den Funken zu, die aufsprühten, wenn der Hammer auf den Prägestock niederfuhr. Es war der bildhafteste Ausdruck des Reichtums dieser Stadt. Philip war überwältigt.

Es standen noch ein paar andere Leute vor dem Tor und sahen den Münzern bei der Arbeit zu. Wahrscheinlich handelte es sich um eine bekannte Attraktion der Stadt, die kein Besucher sich entgehen ließ.

Neben Philip stand eine junge Frau und lächelte ihm zu. Er erwiderte das Lächeln, und sie sagte: »Was du willst – für einen Penny.«

Was meinte sie damit? Philip lächelte wieder, unbestimmt. Da öffnete sie ihren Mantel, und er sah zu seinem Entsetzen, daß sie darunter splitternackt war. »Alles, was du willst – für einen Silberpenny!«

Begierde keimte in ihm auf wie das Gespenst einer lange verdrängten Erinnerung. Sie war eine Hure. Er spürte, wie er bis unter die Haarspitzen errötete. Rasch wandte er sich ab und eilte davon. »Sei kein Frosch!« rief sie ihm nach. Ihr spöttisches Gelächter verfolgte ihn noch ein gutes Stück.

Erregt und verärgert verschwand er in einer Seitengasse, die ihn nach kurzer Zeit auf den Marktplatz führte. Hinter den Ständen erhoben sich die Türme der Kathedrale. Er achtete nicht auf die Lockrufe der Händler, sondern drängelte sich rastlos durch die Menge. Bald darauf erreichte er wieder den Kirchplatz.

Die geordnete Ruhe des Kirchen- und Klosterbezirks war wie eine kühle Brise. Im Friedhof blieb Philip stehen und versuchte sich zu sammeln. Scham und Empörung beherrschten ihn. Wie konnte dieses Weib es wagen, einen Mann in Mönchskutte zu versuchen? Sie hatte ihn offensichtlich als auswärtigen Besucher erkannt. War es möglich, daß reisende Mönche fernab vom heimatlichen Kloster zu ihren Kunden zählten? Natürlich, gestand er sich ein, Mönche begehen genau die gleichen Sünden wie andere Sterbliche … Ihn hatte lediglich die Schamlosigkeit des Weibes erschreckt. Das Bild ihrer Nacktheit blieb bei ihm, so wie der heiße Kern einer Kerzenflamme hinter den geschlossenen Lidern des Betrachters weiterglüht.

Er seufzte. Was für Eindrücke! Die von Menschenhand geschaffenen Bäche, die Ratten in den Fleischerläden, die großen Stapel frischgeprägter Silberpennys, die Frau in ihrer Nacktheit … Philip wußte, daß die Bilder zurückkehren und ihn in seinen Meditationen heimsuchen würden.

Er betrat die Kathedrale. Er fühlte sich zu schmutzig, um einfach niederzuknien und zu beten, doch empfand er allein schon den langsamen Gang durchs Kirchenschiff als eine Art Läuterung. Durchs Südtor verließ er die Kathedrale. Übers Klostergelände erreichte er den bischöflichen Palast.

Im Erdgeschoß befand sich eine Kapelle. Philip stieg die Treppe hinauf und trat in den Saal. Hinter der Tür standen ein paar Diener und junge Geistliche herum, einige hockten auch auf einer Bank vor der Wand. Waleran und Bischof Henry saßen auf der gegenüberliegenden Seite des Saals an einem Tisch. Ein Diener trat Philip in den Weg. »Die Bischöfe sind beim Frühstück«, sagte er, als wollte er damit zum Ausdruck bringen, daß Philip sie nicht sprechen könne.

»Ich möchte mich zu ihnen setzen«, erwiderte Philip.

»Ihr wartet besser noch ein Weilchen.«

Der hält mich für einen einfachen Mönch, dachte Philip und sagte: »Ich bin der Prior von Kingsbridge.«

Der Diener zuckte mit den Schultern und ließ ihn durch.

Bischof Henry saß an der Schmalseite des Tisches, Waleran zu seiner Rechten. Henry war ein untersetzter, breitschultriger Mann mit streitlustiger Miene. Er mochte etwa so alt wie Waleran sein, also vielleicht ein oder zwei Jahre älter als Philip. Die Dreißig hatte er mit Sicherheit noch nicht erreicht. Sein rosiger Teint und die wohlgepolsterten Gliedmaßen wiesen ihn als einen Mann mit herzhaftem Appetit aus und bildeten einen merklichen Gegensatz zu dem leichenblassen Waleran und dem hageren Philip. Seine Augen waren wach und klug, das Gesicht verriet Entschlossenheit. Als jüngster von vier Brüdern hatte er vermutlich zeitlebens kämpfen müssen, um zu seinem Recht zu kommen. Überrascht stellte Philip fest, daß Henrys Kopf geschoren war – ein Zeichen dafür, daß der Bischof einst die Profeß abgelegt hatte und sich noch immer als Mönch betrachtete. Allerdings trug er kein härenes Gewand, sondern eine prunkvolle Tunika aus purpurfarbener Seide. Waleran trug unter seiner gewohnten schwarzen Tunika ein makelloses weißes Leinenhemd. Philip erkannte, daß die beiden sich bereits für die Audienz beim König zurechtgemacht hatten. Waleran und Henry aßen kaltes Rindfleisch und tranken Rotwein dazu. Philip, der nach dem langen Gang durch die Stadt großen Hunger verspürte, lief das Wasser im Munde zusammen.

Waleran blickte auf. Als er Philips ansichtig wurde, huschte ein unwilliger Zug über sein Gesicht.

»Guten Morgen«, sagte Philip.

»Das ist mein Prior«, sagte Waleran zu Henry.

Philip gefiel diese Bezeichnung wenig. »Philip von Gwynedd, ehrwürdiger Herr Bischof«, fügte er hinzu. »Prior von Kingsbridge.«

Er rechnete damit, daß der Bischof ihm seine beringte Hand zum Kusse reichen würde, doch Henry sagte nur »Na, prächtig!« und stopfte sich einen weiteren Brocken Rindfleisch in den Mund. Philip stand da und wußte nicht, wie er sich verhalten sollte. Will mich denn keiner bitten, Platz zu nehmen? dachte er.

»Wir kommen gleich, Philip«, sagte Waleran.

Das kam einem Hinauswurf gleich, Philip merkte es sofort. Gedemütigt wandte er sich ab und kehrte zu den Männern zurück, die vor der Tür herumlungerten. Der Diener, der ihn zuvor hatte abweisen wollen, grinste hämisch, als wollte er sagen: *Ich hatte dich ja gewarnt.* Philip hielt sich von den anderen fern. Er schämte sich auf einmal seiner fleckigen braunen Kutte, die er nun schon seit einem halben Jahr Tag und Nacht auf dem Leibe trug. Viele Benediktinermönche pflegten ihre Ordenskleidung schwarz zu färben, doch in Kingsbridge verzichtete man aus Ersparnisgründen schon seit Jahren darauf. Philip hatte immer geglaubt, daß feine Kleider nur der Eitelkeit Vorschub leisteten und sich für einen Diener Gottes nicht ziemten, wie hoch sein Rang auch sein mochte. Jetzt wurde ihm auf einmal klar, daß sie auch noch einen anderen Zweck erfüllten. In Samt und Seide gekleidet, hätte ich wahrscheinlich keine solche Abfuhr bekommen, dachte er, doch … Demut ist mönchische Pflicht. Also war es gut für mein Seelenheil …

Die beiden Bischöfe standen vom Tisch auf und schritten zur Tür. Ein Diener brachte eine fein bestickte scharlachrote Robe mit Seidenbesatz. Henry legte sie an und sagte: »Viel zu sagen werdet Ihr heute nicht haben, Philip.«

Und Waleran setzte hinzu: »Überlaßt das Reden uns.«

»Überlaßt das Reden mir«, sagte Bischof Henry mit leichter Betonung des *mir*. »Wenn der König Euch etwas fragt, gebt ihm einfache Antworten und schmückt die Dinge nicht zu sehr aus. Der König begreift Euren Wunsch nach einer neuen Kirche auch ohne viel Heulen und Zähneklappern.«

Das hätte er sich sparen können, dachte Philip, der Henrys Benehmen unangenehm herablassend fand. Er ließ sich seinen Unmut jedoch nicht anmerken, sondern beschränkte sich auf ein zustimmendes Nicken.

»Gehen wir jetzt«, sagte Henry. »Mein Bruder ist Frühaufsteher, und so wie ich ihn kenne, beschließt er sein Tagwerk rasch, um sich zur Jagd in den New Forest zu verfügen.«

Sie verließen den Palast. Ein Bewaffneter, der ein Schwert am Gürtel und in der Hand einen Stab trug, schritt Henry voran. Die High Street ging es entlang, dann bergauf Richtung Westtor. Die Menschen traten bereitwillig zur Seite für die beiden Bischöfe, nicht aber für Philip, der deshalb ein Stück zurückfiel. Hier und da bat jemand um einen Segen, worauf Henry, ohne seine Schritte zu verlangsamen oder gar stehenzubleiben, das Kreuzzeichen in die Luft hieb. Kurz vor dem Torhaus bogen sie von der Straße ab und betraten die Holzbrücke, die über den Burggraben führte. Obwohl man ihm versichert hatte, daß er nicht viel zu sagen habe, verspürte Philip ein flaues Gefühl im Magen: Gleich werde ich vor dem König stehen, dachte er.

Die Burg lag im äußersten Südwesten der Stadt; die Mauern auf der West- und der Südseite waren daher gleichzeitig Teile der Stadtmauer. Allerdings waren die Mauern, die die Rückseite der Burg von der Stadt trennten, ebenso hoch und stark wie die äußeren Verteidigungsanlagen. Es war, als müßte der König vor seinen Bürgern ebenso geschützt werden wie vor der Außenwelt.

Sie durchschritten einen in die Mauer eingelassenen niedrigen Torbogen, der sie direkt auf den wuchtigen Wohnturm zuführte. Das eindrucksvolle Bauwerk mit quadratischem Grundriß beherrschte den gesamten oberen Teil der Burganlage. Philip zählte die schießschartenartigen Fenster und schloß daraus, daß es über drei Stockwerke verfügen mußte. Im Erdgeschoß war, wie üblich, ein Vorratslager untergebracht; über eine Außentreppe gelangte man zum Haupteingang im ersten Stock. Am Fuß der Treppe standen zwei Posten, die sich vor Henry verneigten.

Der Fußboden im großen Saal war mit Binsenmatten bedeckt. Es gab eine Feuerstelle, Holzbänke und ein paar in die Steinmauer eingelassene Sitze. In einer Ecke standen zwei Bewaffnete und bewachten den ebenfalls in die Wand eingelassenen Treppenaufgang zu den oberen Stockwerken. Einer der beiden Männer sah Henry an, nickte und stieg die Treppe hinauf – vermutlich, um dem König die Ankunft seines Bruders zu melden.

Philip war übel vor Angst und Unruhe. In den nächsten Minuten konnte sich seine Zukunft entscheiden. Er wünschte nur, seinen beiden Begleitern besser trauen zu können, und machte sich Vorwürfe, weil er am Morgen in der Stadt herumgelaufen war, statt für den Erfolg seiner Mission zu beten. Er schämte sich seiner schmutzigen Kutte.

Zwanzig oder dreißig Personen befanden sich außer ihnen im Saal, fast ausschließlich Männer. Es war ein bunt zusammengewürfelter Haufen aus Rittern, Priestern und wohlhabenden Bürgern. Plötzlich schreckte er überrascht auf: Am Feuer stand Percy Hamleigh und unterhielt sich mit einer Frau und einem jungen Mann. Was führte den hierher? Die häßliche Frau war sein Weib, der junge Kerl sein verrohter Sohn. Sie hatten gemeinsam mit Waleran den Sturz des Grafen Bartholomäus herbeigeführt; so konnte es kaum Zufall sein, daß sie ebenfalls zum König gekommen waren.

An Waleran gewandt, fragte Philip: »Seht Ihr ...?« Er hätte gerne gewußt, ob der Bischof mit den Hamleighs gerechnet hatte.

»Ja, ich sehe sie!« zischte Waleran. Er war sichtlich ungehalten.

Philip empfand die Anwesenheit der Hamleighs als bedrohlich, obwohl er nicht hätte sagen können warum. Er beobachtete sie genauer. Vater und Sohn waren einander sehr ähnlich: wohlgenährt, mit strohgelbem Haar und sturem Blick. Die Frau sah aus wie einer jener Dämonen, welche auf Höllendarstellungen die armen Sünder quälen. Ununterbrochen fingerte sie mit skelettdürren Händen an den entstellenden Geschwüren in ihrem Gesicht herum. Das gelbe Kleid, das sie trug, machte sie nur noch häßlicher. Unruhig trat sie von einem Fuß auf den anderen; rastlos wanderten ihre Blicke im Saal umher und kreuzten sich schließlich auch mit Philips, der sich daraufhin rasch abwandte.

Henry begrüßte seine Bekannten und segnete alle anderen. Als plötzlich der Posten wieder erschien, wurde deutlich, daß der Bischof die ganze Zeit über die Treppe im Auge behalten haben mußte, denn er sah ihn sofort und brach, als der Mann nickte, das Gespräch, das er gerade führte, mitten im Satz ab.

Hinter Henry stieg Waleran die Treppe empor. Die Nachhut bildete Philip, dem das Herz bis zum Hals schlug.

Der Saal im zweiten Stock war von gleicher Größe und Gestalt wie der im ersten, doch herrschte eine vollkommen andere Atmosphäre. Die Wände waren mit Gobelins behangen, und auf den gewienerten Bodenbrettern lagen Schaffellteppiche. Das Feuer loderte hoch und sorgte zusammen mit Dutzenden von Kerzen für helles Licht. Neben der Tür stand ein Eichenholztisch mit Federn, Tinte und einem Stapel Briefbögen aus Pergament. Ein Schreiber hielt sich bereit, das königliche Diktat aufzunehmen. Der König saß in einem großen, mit Fellen bedeckten Holzsessel neben der Feuerstelle.

Das erste, was Philip auffiel, war, daß der König keine Krone trug. Zur purpurnen Tunika trug er hohe Ledergamaschen, als wolle er in Kürze ausreiten. Zu seinen Füßen lagen wie Höflinge, die sich besonderer Gunst erfreuen, zwei große Jagdhunde. Stephan ähnelte Bischof Henry, seinem Bruder. Er hatte die gleichen intelligenten Augen, insgesamt jedoch etwas feinere Züge und dichtes, hellbraunes Haar. Er saß zurückgelehnt in seinem großen Sessel (den Philip für einen Thron hielt), hatte die Ellbogen auf die Lehne gestützt und streckte die Beine weit von sich. Trotz seiner legeren Haltung lag eine gewisse Spannung in der Luft. Locker und gelöst wirkte nur der König.

Ein hochgewachsener Mann in teurer Kleidung verließ den Saal, den Philip und die beiden Bischöfe gerade betraten. Er nickte Henry zu wie einem alten Bekannten; Waleran wurde von ihm ignoriert. Wahrscheinlich ein mächtiger Baron, dachte Philip.

Bischof Henry trat vor den König, verneigte sich und sagte: »Guten Morgen, Stephan.«

»Ich hab' noch immer nicht diesen Schuft Ranulf zu sehen bekommen«, sagte der König. »Wenn er nicht bald auftaucht, laß ich ihm die Finger abschneiden.«

»Du kannst jetzt täglich mit ihm rechnen, das versprech' ich dir. Aber vielleicht solltest du ihm die Finger auf jeden Fall abschneiden lassen.«

Philip wußte nicht, wer Ranulf war und warum der König ihn sehen wollte, hatte jedoch den Eindruck, daß Stephan bei aller Entrüstung nicht ernsthaft daran dachte, den Mann zu verstümmeln.

Ehe er weiter darüber nachdenken konnte, trat Waleran vor und verneigte sich. »Waleran Bigod, der neue Bischof von Kingsbridge«, sagte Henry. »Du erinnerst dich?«

»Ja, ja«, erwiderte Stephan, »aber wer ist das?« Er sah Philip an.

»Das ist mein Prior«, sagte Waleran.

Da Waleran keinen Namen nannte, ergänzte Philip ihn selbst: »Philip von Gwynedd, Prior von Kingsbridge.« Seine Stimme kam ihm ungebührlich laut vor. Er verneigte sich.

»Tretet vor, Vater Prior!« sagte der König. »Ihr scheint Euch zu fürchten. Was bedrückt Euch so?«

Philip fiel keine passende Antwort ein. Ihn bedrückte so vieles … In seiner Verzweiflung sagte er: »Mich bedrückt, daß ich keine saubere Kutte besitze.«

Stephan lachte, doch klang es nicht unfreundlich. »Nun, das soll Euch nicht weiter betrüben«, sagte er und fügte mit einem Seitenblick auf seinen fein herausgeputzten Bruder hinzu: »Mir ist's lieber, wenn ein Mönch wie ein Mönch aussieht – und nicht wie ein König.«

Philip fühlte sich ein wenig besser.

»Ich hörte von dem Brand. Wie kommt Ihr denn jetzt zu Rande?«

»Am Vorabend des Brandes sandte Gott uns einen Baumeister. Er hat den Kreuzgang sehr schnell wieder instandgesetzt. Der Gottesdienst findet in der Krypta statt. Gegenwärtig räumen wir mit Unterstützung des Mannes den Bauplatz frei. Er hat auch schon Pläne für eine neue Kirche gezeichnet.«

Bei diesen Worten hob Waleran die Brauen. Von den neuen Plänen wußte er nichts. Wäre er gefragt worden, hätte Philip ihm davon berichtet – aber Waleran hatte nicht gefragt.

»Dann geht es ja lobenswert schnell voran«, sagte der König. »Wann wollt Ihr denn mit dem Neubau beginnen?«

»Sobald ich das Geld dafür habe …«

»Deshalb habe ich Prior Philip und Bischof Waleran mitgebracht«, fuhr Henry dazwischen. »Für ein Vorhaben dieser Größenordnung hat weder das Kloster noch die Diözese genügend finanzielle Mittel.«

»Die Krone auch nicht, mein lieber Bruder«, sagte Stephan.

Philip war enttäuscht: Das war alles andere als ein vielversprechender Anfang.

»Ich weiß«, erwiderte Bischof Henry. »Und deshalb habe ich darüber nachgedacht, ob du ihnen nicht auch ohne zusätzliche Kosten für dich selbst den Neubau der Kathedrale ermöglichen kannst.«

Stephan sah seinen Bruder skeptisch an. »Nun – wie steht's? Waren deine Bemühungen um einen so kunstfertigen, um nicht zu sagen zauberhaften Plan von Erfolg gekrönt?«

»Ja. Gib der Diözese die Ländereien des Grafen von Shiring. Mit den Einnahmen kann sie ihr Bauvorhaben finanzieren. Das ist mein Vorschlag.«

Philip hielt den Atem an.

Der König wirkte auf einmal sehr nachdenklich.

Waleran öffnete den Mund, um etwas zu sagen, doch Henry gebot ihm mit einer Handbewegung Schweigen.

»Die Idee ist gut«, sagte der König. »Ich hätte nichts dagegen … nur – ich habe die Grafschaft gerade vorhin Percy Hamleigh so gut wie versprochen.«

Philip stöhnte hörbar auf. Er hatte schon fest mit der Zustimmung des Königs gerechnet; die Enttäuschung traf ihn wie ein Messerstich.

Henry und Waleran waren wie vor den Kopf geschlagen. Diese Antwort hatten sie beide nicht erwartet.

Als erster fand Henry seine Sprache wieder. »So gut wie?« fragte er.

Der König hob die Schultern. »Ich kann mich vielleicht noch irgendwie herauswinden. Peinlich wird es auf jeden Fall. Andererseits – schließlich war Percy es, der den Verräter Bartholomäus seiner gerechten Strafe zugeführt hat.«

»Nicht ohne Hilfe, mein Herr und König!«

»Ich weiß, daß Ihr daran Anteil hattet …«

»*Ich* war derjenige, der Percy Hamleigh von dem Komplott gegen Euch in Kenntnis setzte!«

»Ja, richtig. Übrigens – woher wußtet *Ihr* denn davon?«

Philip trat unruhig von einem Fuß auf den anderen. Das kann gefährlich werden, dachte er. Niemand durfte erfahren, daß der erste

Hinweis von seinem Bruder Francis stammte, denn Francis arbeitete nach wie vor für Robert von Gloucester, dem der König die Teilnahme an der Verschwörung verziehen hatte.

»Von jemandem, der auf dem Sterbebett ein Bekenntnis ablegte«, antwortete Waleran.

Philip fiel ein Stein vom Herzen. Waleran wiederholte lediglich seine eigene Notlüge – mit dem Unterschied freilich, daß er so tat, als sei das ›Bekenntnis‹ vor ihm selbst abgelegt worden und nicht vor Philip.

»Wie dem auch sei«, fuhr der König fort, »es war Percy, nicht Ihr, der unter Einsatz von Leib und Leben die Burg des Grafen angriff und den Verräter festnahm.«

»Du könntest Percy auch irgendwie anders belohnen«, warf Henry ein.

»Percy wünscht sich ausdrücklich Shiring«, erwiderte Stephan. »Er kennt die Grafschaft und wird sie sicherlich gut führen. Ich könnte ihm natürlich auch Cambridgeshire geben – doch wer vermag schon zu sagen, ob ihm die Sumpfbewohner dort folgen werden?«

»Dein erster Dank sollte Gott gelten, nicht den Menschen. Schließlich verdankst du deine Krone Ihm.«

»Aber Percy hat Bartholomäus festgenommen.«

Das war eine Respektlosigkeit. Henry rümpfte empört die Nase. »Gott ist der Lenker aller Dinge ...«

Stephan hob die Hand. »Versuch nicht, mich unter Druck zu setzen«, sagte er.

»Gewiß nicht«, erwiderte Henry kleinlaut.

Es war eine sehr anschauliche Demonstration königlicher Macht. Vorübergehend hatte es so ausgesehen, als stritten sich zwei Männer gleichen Ranges – doch dann hatte Stephan ein einziger Satz genügt, um Henry in seine Schranken zu verweisen.

Philip war tief enttäuscht. Anfangs hatte er ihr Ansinnen für völlig aussichtslos gehalten. Im Verlauf des Gesprächs war dann jedoch Hoffnung aufgekeimt, und er hatte schon angefangen sich auszumalen, wie sich der neue Reichtum bestmöglich würde nutzen lassen ... Nun wurde er unsanft aus seinen Träumen gerissen.

»Mein Herr und König«, sagte Waleran. »Ich danke Euch für Eure Bereitschaft, noch einmal über die Zukunft der Grafschaft Shiring nachzudenken, und harre andächtig Eurer Entscheidung.«

Schön gesagt, dachte Philip. Waleran zieht sich elegant aus der Affäre, indem er den Nachgiebigen spielt und dabei so tut, als sei das letzte Wort noch nicht gesprochen ... Der König hat sich nicht in diesem Sinne ausgedrückt; alles, was *er* gesagt hat, kann nur als Ablehnung gedeutet werden ... Und doch ist der nochmalige Hinweis darauf, daß seine Entscheidung so oder so ausfallen kann, keinesfalls beleidigend. Ich muß mir das merken: Wenn die Gefahr besteht, abschlägig beschieden zu werden, versuche man die Entscheidung zu verschieben ...

Stephan zögerte einen Moment; es war, als hege er den Verdacht, man wolle ihm das Wort im Munde umdrehen. Doch dann schien er alle Zweifel von sich zu weisen. »Ich danke Euch allen für Euren Besuch«, sagte er.

Philip und Waleran wandten sich zum Gehen, Henry indes rührte sich nicht vom Fleck und stellte die Frage: »Wann können wir mit deiner Entscheidung rechnen?«

Wieder sah es so aus, als fühlte Stephan sich in die Enge getrieben. »Übermorgen«, sagte er.

Henry verneigte sich. Zu dritt verließen sie den Saal.

Die Ungewißheit war fast so schlimm wie eine Ablehnung. Philip fand die Warterei schier unerträglich. Den Nachmittag verbrachte er in der großartigen Bibliothek der Priorei Winchester, doch konnten ihn deren Schätze kaum ablenken; immer wieder fragte er sich, was wohl im Kopf des Königs vorgehen mochte. Konnte Stephan die Zusage, die er Percy Hamleigh gegeben hatte, wieder zurücknehmen? Wie wichtig war Percy überhaupt für ihn? Die Hamleighs gehörten dem Landadel an und spekulierten auf die Grafschaft. Angst davor, Percy vor den Kopf zu stoßen, brauchte der König doch gewiß nicht zu haben – oder?

Andererseits: Wie ernst war es ihm mit seinem Hilfsangebot für Kingsbridge? Könige waren dafür bekannt, daß sie gemeinhin erst im Alter fromm wurden ...

Stephan war noch jung.

Vor ihm lag der *Trost der Philosophie* des Boethius. Philip betrachtete das Buch, ohne darin zu lesen. Unablässig kreisten seine Gedanken um die möglichen Beweggründe des Königs. Da kam auf Zehenspitzen ein Novize zu ihm geschlichen und sprach ihn schüchtern an: »Im Außenhof steht jemand, der mit Euch sprechen möchte, Vater.«

»Wer?« fragte Philip. Da der Besucher draußen warten mußte, konnte es sich nicht um einen Mönch handeln.

»Eine Frau.«

Die Hure! dachte Philip entsetzt. Das Weib, das mich vor der Münze angesprochen hat ... Ein Blick ins Gesicht des Novizen verriet ihm, daß er sich getäuscht hatte. »Wie sieht sie aus?« fragte er.

Der junge Mann verzog angewidert das Gesicht.

Philip nickte. Er wußte Bescheid. »Regan Hamleigh.« Was führte sie nun schon wieder im Schilde? »Ich komme sofort.«

Langsam umrundete er den Kreuzgang und versuchte sich zu sammeln. Mit dieser Frau konnte man es nur aufnehmen, wenn man im Vollbesitz seiner geistigen Kräfte war.

In einen schweren Mantel gehüllt, stand sie vor dem Empfangszimmer des Kellermeisters und verbarg ihr Gesicht unter einer Kapuze. Sie bedachte Philip mit einem Blick von so unverhüllter Tücke, daß er am liebsten auf dem Absatz kehrtgemacht hätte. Nur weil er sich schämte, zum zweitenmal an diesem Tag vor einer Frau davonzulaufen, blieb er stehen und fragte: »Was wollt Ihr von mir?«

»Närrischer Mönch!« geiferte sie. »Wie könnt Ihr nur so dumm sein?«

Philip fühlte, wie ihm das Blut ins Gesicht schoß. »Ich bin der Prior von Kingsbridge«, antwortete er, »und Ihr redet mich gefälligst mit ›Vater‹ an.« Zu seinem Ärger klang seine Stimme eher mürrisch als gebieterisch.

»Bitte sehr, *Vater* ... Doch nun sagt mir, was in Euch gefahren ist, daß Ihr Euch von diesen beiden gierigen Bischöfen so *benutzen* laßt!«

Philip holte tief Luft. »Drückt Euch verständlich aus!«

»Bei solchen Einfaltspinseln, wie Ihr einer seid, ist das gar nicht so leicht. Aber ich werd's versuchen. Die niedergebrannte Kirche ist für Waleran nur ein willkommener Vorwand, sich die Ländereien der Grafschaft Shiring unter den Nagel zu reißen. Ist das verständlich genug? Habt Ihr jetzt begriffen, worum es geht?«

Ihr verächtlicher Ton ärgerte Philip nach wie vor. Aber er konnte der Versuchung, sich zu verteidigen, nicht länger widerstehen. »Da gibt's nichts zu verheimlichen«, sagte er. »Die Einkünfte aus den Ländereien sollen zur Finanzierung der neuen Kathedrale herangezogen werden.«

»Wie kommt Ihr denn darauf?«

»Nun, darum dreht sich doch alles!« protestierte Philip, während insgeheim schon die ersten Zweifel aufkeimten.

»Wem werden denn die neuen Ländereien gehören«, fragte Regan. »Der Priorei oder der Diözese?« Der beißende Spott in ihrer Stimme hatte sich in Gerissenheit verwandelt.

Philip starrte sie einen Moment lang ungläubig an. Dann wandte er sich ab: Ihr Gesicht war einfach zu abstoßend. Bei all seinen Überlegungen war er stets davon ausgegangen, daß die neuen Ländereien der Priorei gehören und von ihm persönlich verwaltet werden sollten. Jetzt erinnerte er sich, daß Bischof Henry während der Audienz beim König ausdrücklich darum gebeten hatte, die Länder der *Diözese* (und damit in Walerans Obhut) zu geben. Er, Philip, hatte dies als simplen Versprecher aufgefaßt, der freilich, wie er sich eingestehen mußte, weder sofort noch später korrigiert worden war.

Er musterte Regan Hamleigh voller Mißtrauen. Kaum denkbar, daß sie im voraus wußte, was Henry dem König sagen wollte. Möglicherweise hatte sie recht. Andererseits ließ sich nicht ausschließen, daß sie nur darauf aus war, Unfrieden zu stiften. Wenn es zu einem Zerwürfnis zwischen Philip und Waleran kam, waren die Hamleighs allemal die lachenden Dritten. »Waleran ist Bischof«, sagte er. »Er braucht eine Kathedrale.«

»Er braucht eine ganze Menge«, entgegnete sie. Nun, da sie vernünftig zu argumentieren begann, wirkte Regan auf einmal menschlicher. Trotzdem ertrug Philip ihren Anblick nur für kurze Zeit. »Für viele Bischöfe«, fuhr sie fort, »wäre eine schöne Kathedrale in der Tat das Allerwichtigste. Waleran setzt hingegen andere Prioritäten. Aber wie dem auch sei: Solange er an der Quelle sitzt, kann er Euch und Euren Baumeistern jederzeit den Geldhahn zudrehen ... ganz nach seinem Belieben.«

Da hatte sie recht, dachte Philip. Wenn Waleran die Pachtgelder einnimmt, behält er natürlich einiges davon für sich. Und wieviel das sein wird, entscheidet einzig und allein er selbst. Niemand könnte ihn daran hindern, Geld für Dinge abzuzweigen, die mit der Kathedrale nicht das Geringste zu tun haben. Und ich müßte mir Monat für Monat den Kopf darüber zerbrechen, wie ich meine Bauleute bezahlen soll ... Nein, am besten wäre es natürlich, wenn die Ländereien in den Besitz der Priorei übergingen ...

Klar war freilich, daß Waleran sich auf einen solchen Vorschlag nie und nimmer einlassen würde und daß Bischof Henry seinen Amtsbruder deckte. In diesem Fall blieb Philip nur noch der direkte Appell an den König, der sich allerdings dazu bewogen fühlen könnte, den Streit der Kirchenvertreter durch die Übertragung der Grafschaft Shiring an Percy Hamleigh ein für allemal zu schlichten.

Und das war genau das, was Regan wollte.

Philip schüttelte den Kopf. »Wenn Waleran mich wirklich täuschen will – warum hat er mich dann mitgenommen? Er hätte doch seine Bitte auch allein vortragen können.«

Sie nickte. »Hätte er, ja. Aber vielleicht hätte der König Zweifel an seiner Aufrichtigkeit gehabt und der Behauptung, er wolle die Grafschaft nur haben, um mit ihrer Hilfe eine Kathedrale zu bauen, keinen Glauben geschenkt. Alle Verdächte, die Stephan gehegt haben mag, habt Ihr zerstreut, indem Ihr Waleran begleitet und seinen Anspruch unterstützt habt.« Sie verfiel wieder in den verächtlichen Ton. »Und Ihr seht so jämmerlich aus in Eurer verdreckten Kutte! Der König bemitleidet Euch geradezu! Nein, es war wirklich ein geschickter Schachzug von Waleran, Euch mitzunehmen.«

Philip beschlich das entsetzliche Gefühl, Regan Hamleigh könne in allem, was sie sagte, recht haben, doch war er nicht bereit, es einzugestehen. »Ihr wollt ja nur, daß Euer Gemahl Graf von Shiring wird«, sagte er.

»Ich könnte Euch den Beweis für die Richtigkeit meiner Worte liefern«, sagte die Frau. »Vorausgesetzt, Ihr seid bereit, einen halbtägigen Ritt auf Euch zu nehmen ...«

In Regan Hamleighs Machenschaften hineingezogen zu werden, war das letzte, was Philip wollte. Aber er mußte herausfinden, ob an ihren Behauptungen etwas dran war, und so stimmte er widerstrebend zu. »Gut, ich komme mit.«

»Morgen?«

»Ja.«

»So haltet Euch im ersten Tageslicht bereit.«

William Hamleigh war es, der Sohn von Percy und Regan, der am nächsten Morgen, als die Mönche die Prim zu singen begannen, im Außenhof des Klosters auf Philip wartete. Die beiden verließen Winchester durch das westliche Stadttor und bogen unmittelbar dahinter in die gen Norden führende Straße nach Athelynge ein. Auch der Palast von Bischof Waleran lag, wie Philip wußte, in dieser Richtung und war ungefähr eine halbe Tagesreise entfernt. Dorthin bringt er mich also, dachte Philip. Aber warum? Er war zutiefst mißtrauisch und nahm sich vor, auf der Hut zu sein. Den Hamleighs war durchaus zuzutrauen, daß sie ihn vor ihren Karren spannen wollten – die Frage war nur, wie. Vielleicht waren die Hamleighs hinter einem bestimmten Dokument her, das sich in Walerans Besitz befand, und wollten es sehen oder sogar stehlen. Es konnte sich um einen Vertrag oder ein königliches Privileg handeln. Vielleicht wollte der junge Lord William der bischöflichen Kanzlei vorflunkern, er und Philip seien geschickt worden, das Dokument abzuholen ... und vielleicht schenkte man ihm sogar Glauben, weil der Prior von Kingsbridge ihn begleitete. Mit dieser oder einer ähnlichen List war bei William Hamleigh immer zu rechnen – und deshalb wollte Philip auf der Hut sein.

Es war ein trüber, grauer Morgen. Ein feiner, durchdringender Nieselregen fiel. William schlug auf den ersten paar Meilen ein forsches Tempo an. Um den Pferden Gelegenheit zum Verschnaufen zu geben, verlangsamte er schließlich den Schritt. Nach einer Weile sagte er zu Philip: »So wollt Ihr mir also die Grafschaft wegnehmen, Mönch, he?«

Der feindselige Ton verwirrte und empörte Philip; er hatte William keinerlei Anlaß dazu gegeben. Entsprechend scharf fiel seine Antwort aus: »Euch? Ihr bekommt sie doch ohnehin nicht, mein Junge! Ich, Euer Vater oder Bischof Waleran bekommen sie. Niemand hat den König ersucht, sie *Euch* zu geben.«

»Ich werde sie dereinst erben.«

»Warten wir's ab.« Es war sinnlos, sich mit William zu streiten. »Ich will Euch doch nichts Böses«, fuhr er in versöhnlichem Ton fort. »Ich will eine neue Kathedrale errichten, das ist alles.«

»Dann nehmt Euch eine andere Grafschaft«, erwiderte William. »Warum hacken die Leute bloß immer auf uns herum?«

Philip bemerkte die Verbitterung in der Stimme des jungen Mannes. »Tun sie das?« fragte er.

»Das Schicksal des Grafen Bartholomäus sollte ihnen eigentlich eine Lehre sein. Er hat unsere Familie beleidigt – Ihr seht ja jetzt, was er davon gehabt hat.«

»Die Kränkung ging ursprünglich doch wohl von seiner Tochter aus, oder?«

»Das Luder ist genauso stolz und eingebildet wie sein Vater. Aber auch sie wird dafür noch büßen. Wir zwingen jeden, der uns beleidigt, in die Knie, Ihr werdet schon sehen.«

Das sind die giftigen Worte eines mißgünstigen alten Weibes, dachte Philip, nicht die normalen Gefühle eines jungen Mannes um die Zwanzig. Die Unterhaltung gefiel ihm ganz und gar nicht. Die meisten Menschen verbargen ihren nackten Haß unter manierlichen Kleidern. William in seiner Einfalt war dazu nicht imstande. »Die Rache überläßt man am besten dem Jüngsten Gericht«, sagte er.

»Warum wartet Ihr mit dem Bau Eurer Kathedrale nicht auch bis zum Jüngsten Gericht?«

»Weil es dann zu spät ist, die Seelen der Sünder vor den Qualen der Hölle zu bewahren.«

»Fangt mir bloß damit nicht an!« rief William mit schriller Stimme. »Spart Euch das für Eure Predigten auf.«

Der Prior verbiß sich die scharfe Entgegnung, die ihm bereits auf der Zunge lag. Irgend etwas stimmte nicht mit diesem Burschen. Philip hatte den Eindruck, der Junge könne jeden Augenblick vom Jähzorn gepackt und in seiner Wut zum Äußersten getrieben werden – mit möglicherweise tödlichen Folgen. Dennoch fürchtete er sich nicht vor ihm. Er hatte überhaupt keine Angst vor Gewalttätern – vielleicht, weil er als Kind die furchtbarsten Gewalttaten erlebt und *über*lebt hatte. Doch was war schon damit gewonnen, wenn er William jetzt tadelte und zusätzlich erboste? Gar nichts. Er antwortete im freundlichsten Ton: »Himmel und Hölle sind mein Gewerbe – Tugend und Sünde, Vergebung und Strafe, Gut und Böse ... Ich fürchte, ich kann darüber nicht schweigen.«

»Dann unterhaltet Euch meinetwegen mit Euch selbst«, erwiderte William und gab seinem Pferd die Sporen.

Als sein Vorsprung ungefähr vierzig oder fünfzig Schritt betrug, zügelte er sein Tier wieder, und Philip fragte sich schon, ob William sein Verhalten bedauere und wieder an seine Seite kommen wolle. Aber dem war nicht so. Den Rest der Strecke legten sie getrennt zurück.

Philip war voller Unruhe und obendrein ziemlich niedergeschlagen. Er war nicht mehr Herr seines eigenen Schicksals. In Winchester hatte er das Feld Waleran Bigod überlassen, und nun ließ er sich von William Hamleigh irgendwohin führen, ohne zu wissen, warum. Alle versuchen sie, sich meiner zu bedienen, dachte er. Warum lasse ich das alles willenlos mit mir geschehen? Es wäre weiß Gott an der Zeit, selbst die Initiative zu ergreifen ...

Aber was sollte er tun? Umkehren und nach Winchester zurückkreiten? Das brachte jetzt auch nichts mehr.

So setzte er seinen Weg fort und starrte trübsinnig auf das auf und ab wippende Hinterteil von Williams Pferd.

Kurz vor Mittag erreichten sie das Tal, in dem der Bischofspalast lag. Philip wußte noch genau, wie er zu Beginn des Jahres zitternd vor Furcht hier eingetroffen war, belastet von der Bürde eines tödlichen Geheimnisses ... Was hatte sich seither nicht alles verändert!

Zu Philips Erstaunen ritt William am Sitz des Bischofs vorbei. Die Straße führte nun bergan und verengte sich zu einem schmalen Feldweg. Kurz vor dem Gipfel der Anhöhe kamen sie zu einer Art Baustelle. Ein Erdwall, der aussah, als wäre er erst vor kurzer Zeit aufgeschüttet worden, versperrte ihnen den Weg. Ein böser Verdacht keimte in Philip auf.

Sie bogen vom Weg ab und ritten am Fuße des Walls entlang, bis sie an eine Lücke kamen. Sie ritten hindurch und gelangten zu einem trockenen Burggraben, der an dieser Stelle noch gefüllt war, um den Zugang zum Innenraum zu ermöglichen.

»Habt Ihr mich deshalb hierhergebracht?« fragte Philip.

William beschränkte sich auf ein Nicken.

Philip fand seinen Verdacht bestätigt. Waleran baute eine Burg. Es war niederschmetternd.

Er trat seinem Pferd in die Flanken und überquerte den Graben. William folgte ihm. Graben und Wall umschlossen ringförmig den Gipfel der Anhöhe. Am inneren Grabenrand war eine zwei bis drei Fuß hohe Steinmauer errichtet. Sie war noch nicht fertig, doch ließ sich aus ihrer Dicke schließen, daß sie eines Tages sehr hoch sein würde.

Waleran ließ eine Burg erbauen, doch die Baustelle war verwaist. Weder Baumeister noch Werkzeuge, weder Steinhaufen noch Bauholz waren zu sehen. Nach schnellem, fleißigem Beginn waren die Arbeiten plötzlich eingestellt worden. Allem Anschein nach war Waleran das Geld ausgegangen.

»Daß Waleran der Bauherr ist, steht außer Zweifel – oder?« fragte Philip.

»Glaubt Ihr etwa, Waleran Bigod würde *jemand anderem* gestatten, in unmittelbarer Nähe seines Palasts eine Burg zu errichten?«

Philip fühlte sich erniedrigt und verletzt. Jetzt war alles kristallklar: Bischof Waleran strebte nach dem Besitz der Grafschaft Shiring samt Holzvorräten und Steinbruch, weil er eine Burg bauen wollte. Es ging ihm nicht um die Kathedrale. Er, Philip, diente lediglich als Mittel zum Zweck, der Brand der Kathedrale in Kingsbridge als willkommene Ausrede. Dahinter steckte die Absicht, die Gottesfurcht des Königs so anzuheizen, daß er Waleran die Grafschaft übertrug.

Nun sah sich Philip mit denselben Augen, mit denen Waleran und Henry ihn sehen mußten: Naiv, willfährig und jedermann freundlich zunickend, ließ er sich zur Schlachtbank führen. Ihr Urteil war ja so zutreffend! Er hatte ihnen vertraut und ihnen alle Entscheidungen überlassen, hatte sogar ihre Kränkungen mit tapferem Lächeln hingenommen, weil er glaubte, sie wollten ihn unterstützen … In Wirklichkeit hatten sie ihn von Anfang an hintergangen.

Walerans Skrupellosigkeit war erschütternd. Philip konnte sich noch gut an die traurige Miene des Bischofs beim Anblick der abgebrannten Kathedrale erinnern. Eine tiefverwurzelte Frömmigkeit hatte er damals an ihm wahrgenommen. Waleran glaubte offenbar, daß im Dienst der Kirche fromme Zwecke unfromme Mittel heiligten. Philip hatte sich diese Meinung nie zu eigen gemacht. Nie würde ich ihm das antun, was er mir anzutun versucht, dachte er bei sich.

Sich selbst hatte Philip nie für leichtgläubig gehalten. Jetzt fragte er sich: Wo lag mein Fehler? Er kam zu dem Schluß, daß er sich hatte blenden lassen – von Bischof Henry und seinen seidenen Gewändern, von der großen Stadt Winchester und ihrer großartigen Kathedrale, von den Silberhaufen in der Münze, den Fleischbergen in der Straße der Fleischhauer und von der bangen Erwartung einer Audienz beim König. Er hatte vergessen, daß Gott der Herr auch durch seidene Gewänder hindurch das sündhafte Herz erkannte; daß der einzige Reichtum, den anzustreben sich lohnte, himmlischer Reichtum war und daß in der Kirche selbst der König niederknien mußte. Geblendet von der Macht, der Weltläufigkeit und der Eleganz der anderen hatte er den Blick für seine wahren Ideale verloren, seine kritischen Fähigkeiten außer Kraft gesetzt und voll und ganz seinen Oberen vertraut – und war dafür belogen und betrogen worden.

Regenböen fegten über die verwaiste Baustelle. Nach einem letzten Blick wendete Philip sein Pferd und ritt tief betrübt davon. William folgte ihm. »Nun, Mönch, was sagt Ihr dazu?« johlte er hinter ihm her. Philip gab ihm keine Antwort.

Er selbst war es ja gewesen, der Waleran zum Bischofsamt verholfen hatte. *Ihr wollt, daß ich Euch zum Prior von Kingsbridge mache. Ich will, daß Ihr mich zum Bischof macht.* So hatten seine Worte gelautet. Gewiß, Waleran hatte ihnen damals verschwiegen, daß der alte Bischof bereits tot war; insofern war das Versprechen unter falschen Voraussetzungen gegeben worden. Aber so, wie es damals ausgesehen hatte, war die Zusage eben Voraussetzung für seine eigene Wahl zum Prior gewesen ... Alles Ausflüchte, erkannte Philip jetzt. Ich hätte die Wahl des Priors *und* des Bischofs in Gottes Händen lassen sollen. Die Strafe waren nun unabsehbare Auseinandersetzungen mit Bischof Waleran.

Der Gedanke an die Kränkungen, Abfuhren, Manipulationen und Täuschungen, die ihm widerfahren waren, brachte sein Blut in Wallung. Gehorsam ist eine mönchische Tugend, die einem freilich außerhalb der Klostermauern nicht zum Vorteil gereicht, dachte er verbittert. In einer von Machtstreben und Habgier beherrschten Welt mußte man argwöhnisch, anspruchsvoll und beharrlich sein, wenn man bestehen wollte.

»Diese verlogenen Bischöfe haben Euch zum Narren gehalten, he?« sagte William.

Philip zügelte sein Pferd. Vor Wut zitternd deutete er mit dem Finger auf William und brüllte: »Halt deinen Mund, Bursche! Du sprichst von den heiligen Priestern Gottes. Noch *ein* Wort, und du wirst brennen, das verspreche ich dir!«

William erbleichte vor Angst.

Philip gab seinem Pferd die Sporen. Williams Häme erinnerte ihn an die eigentlichen Motive der Hamleighs: Sie hatten ihn hierhergebracht, um einen Keil zwischen ihn und Waleran zu treiben. Ihr Ziel war es, sie so zu entzweien, daß die umstrittene Grafschaft Percy Hamleigh zufiel wie eine reife Frucht. Doch Philip war nicht gewillt, sich vor ihren Karren spannen zu lassen – weder vor ihren noch vor einen anderen! Die Zeiten, da er mit sich machen ließ, was andere wollten, waren ein für allemal vorbei. Von nun an würde er selbst die Zügel in der Hand behalten.

So weit, so gut – nur: Was konnte er tun? Wenn er, Philip, sich auf einen Streit mit Waleran einließ, bekam Percy die begehrten Ländereien. Verhielt er sich still, bekam sie Waleran.

Was waren die Motive des Königs? Er wollte einen Beitrag zur Errichtung einer neuen Kathedrale leisten: eine wahrhaft königliche Tat, von der seine Seele nach dem Tod nur würde profitieren können. Andererseits mußte er Percy Hamleigh für seine Treue belohnen. So seltsam es erscheinen mochte – eine besondere Notwendigkeit, den beiden im Grunde viel mächtigeren Bischöfen zu Gefallen zu sein, bestand für ihn nicht. Vielleicht, dachte Philip, lassen sich meine Ansprüche und die der Hamleighs in einer für den König annehmbaren Form befriedigen ...

Und da kam ihm auf einmal eine Idee. Sie gefiel ihm. Das letzte, womit seine Widersacher rechneten, war eine mögliche Allianz zwischen ihm und den Hamleighs. Und gerade deshalb war sie erfolgversprechend. Die Bischöfe, die auf einen solchen Fall nicht vorbereitet waren, würden gleichsam auf dem falschen Fuß erwischt werden ...

Wer zuletzt lacht, lacht am besten, dachte Philip.

Voraussetzung war allerdings eine entsprechende Vereinbarung mit den Hamleighs, und ob die zu erreichen war, stand in den Sternen. Percy begehrte das reiche Ackerland von Shiring, den Grafentitel, die

Macht und das Ansehen eines starken Ritterheeres unter seinem Befehl. Das reiche Ackerland begehrte auch er, Philip, darüber hinaus lag ihm an der Nutzung des Steinbruchs und der Wälder. Titel und Ritterheer reizten ihn dagegen nicht.

Vor seinem geistigen Auge begann sich ein Kompromiß abzuzeichnen. Es war noch nicht alles verloren.

Wie wonnig wäre ein später Triumph – nach all dem, was geschehen war!

Mit wachsender Begeisterung bedachte Philip nun sein Verhalten gegenüber den Hamleighs. Den demütigen Bittsteller würde er nicht spielen, soviel stand fest. Er wollte ihnen vielmehr einen Vorschlag machen, den abzulehnen sie sich einfach nicht leisten konnten.

Als sie wieder in Winchester ankamen, war Philips Pferd unwillig und er selbst bis auf die Haut durchnäßt, aber er hatte auch einen Plan.

Unter dem Bogen des Westtors sagte er zu William: »Bringt mich zu Eurer Mutter!«

William war überrascht. »Ich dachte, Ihr wolltet sogleich zu Bischof Waleran ...«

Diese Reaktion hat ihm sicher Regan vorausgesagt, dachte Philip. »Verschont mich mit Eueren Gedanken, Bursche!« fuhr er seinen Begleiter an. »Bringt mich zu Eurer Mutter, das genügt vollauf!« Er war mehr als bereit für die Auseinandersetzung mit Lady Regan. Lange genug hatte er sich zurückgehalten.

William wandte sich nach Süden und führte Philip zu einem Gebäude in der Gold Street, die zwischen der Burg und der Kathedrale lag. Es war ein großes Holzhaus mit hüfthohem Steinsockel. Sie betraten eine breite Diele, von der mehrere Wohnungen abzweigten. Wahrscheinlich logierten die Hamleighs hier zur Untermiete – zahlreiche Bürger der Stadt Winchester vermieteten Zimmer an Besucher des königlichen Hofs. Als Graf würde Percy über ein eigenes Stadthaus verfügen.

William führte Philip in einen zur Straße hin ausgerichteten Raum mit einem großen Bett und einem Kamin. Regan saß vor dem Feuer, Percy stand neben ihr. Philips unerwartetes Erscheinen überraschte Williams Mutter, doch faßte sie sich schnell und sagte: »Nun, Mönch, hatte ich recht?«

»Törichtes Weib!« herrschte er sie an. »Ärger als Ihr es getan habt, kann der Mensch kaum irren.«

Regan verschlug es die Stimme, so hatte sein scharfer Ton sie erschreckt.

Ich kuriere sie mit ihrer eigenen Medizin, dachte er befriedigt und fuhr im gleichen Ton fort: »Ihr bildet Euch ein, Ihr könntet mich und Waleran entzweien. Habt Ihr wirklich geglaubt, ich würde Euch nicht auf die Schliche kommen? Ihr seid ein geriebenes Weib, gewiß, aber *denken* können auch noch andere Menschen auf Gottes Erde!«

Ihre Miene verriet, was in ihr vorging: Sie wußte, daß ihr Plan gescheitert war, und suchte fieberhaft nach einem Ausweg. Er hakte nach, ehe sie sich wieder sammeln konnte.

»Ihr habt versagt, Regan. Jetzt stehen Euch noch zwei Wege offen: Entweder Ihr bleibt hier sitzen und erwartet ergeben des Königs Beschluß – vielleicht habt Ihr ja Glück, und er ist Euch morgen vormittag gewogen ...« Er hielt inne.

»Und der andere Weg?« fragte sie widerstrebend.

»Ein Geschäft. Zwischen Euch und mir. Wir teilen die Grafschaft untereinander auf und sorgen dafür, daß Waleran leer ausgeht. Wir gehen gemeinsam zum König, sagen ihm, daß wir einen Kompromiß geschlossen haben, und lassen ihn absegnen, bevor die Bischöfe etwas dagegen unternehmen können.« Philip ließ sich auf einer Bank nieder und gab sich zwanglos. »Im Grunde ist das Eure einzige Chance. Ihr habt gar keine andere Wahl.« Er blickte in die Flammen, um seine innere Anspannung zu verbergen. Eigentlich müßten sie darauf eingehen, dachte er. Es ist die Wahl zwischen dem Spatz in der Hand und der Taube auf dem Dach ... Aber sie sind furchtbar habsüchtig – vielleicht gehen sie doch aufs Ganze ...

Percy Hamleigh ergriff als erster das Wort. »Die Grafschaft aufteilen?« fragte er. »Wie?«

Immerhin, wenigstens sind sie neugierig, dachte Philip erleichtert. »Hört Euch an, was ich Euch vorzuschlagen habe«, erwiderte er. »Ihr werdet sehen, daß mein Angebot äußerst großzügig ist. Ihr wäret verrückt, wolltet Ihr es zurückweisen.« Er wandte sich wieder an Regan. »Ich biete Euch die bessere Hälfte.«

Erwartungsvoll blickten sie ihn an, aber Philip gab ihnen keine weiteren Erläuterungen. »Was soll das heißen – ›die bessere Hälfte‹?« fragte Regan schließlich ungeduldig.

»Was ist wertvoller – urbares Land oder Wald?«

»Mit Gewißheit urbares Land.«

»Gut. Ihr sollt das Ackerland haben. Ich nehme den Wald.«

Regan kniff die Augen zusammen. »Das heißt, Ihr wollt das Holz für Eure Kathedrale.«

»Ganz recht.«

»Was ist mit Wiesen und Weiden?«

»Was wollt Ihr haben – die Vieh- oder die Schafweiden?«

»Die Viehweiden.«

»Einverstanden. Dann nehme ich die Schafzuchten in den Hügeln. Wollt Ihr die Einkünfte von den Märkten oder den Steinbruch?«

Percy sagte: »Die Märk ...«, doch Regan unterbrach ihn. »Angenommen, wir wollen den Steinbruch?«

Sie weiß, worauf ich hinaus will, dachte Philip, der den Steinbruch für den Dombau benötigte. Ihm war klar, daß Regan hinter den Markteinkünften her war – das war leichter verdientes Geld –, und so antwortete er zuversichtlich: »Wollt Ihr aber nicht – oder?«

Sie schüttelte den Kopf. »Nein. Wir nehmen die Märkte.«

Percy zog ein langes Gesicht. »Ich brauche einen Wald für die Jagd«, sagte er. »Ein Graf muß über eigene Jagdgründe verfügen.«

»Jagen könnt Ihr dort«, erwiderte Philip rasch. »Ich will bloß das Holz.«

»Einverstanden«, sagte Regan – ein wenig zu schnell für Philip, dem sogleich Bedenken kamen. Habe ich unwissentlich auf ein wichtiges Recht verzichtet? fragte er sich. Oder ist sie bloß ungeduldig und will nicht lange über solche Nebensächlichkeiten streiten? Er hatte den Gedanken noch nicht zu Ende geführt, da fuhr Regan Hamleigh fort: »Angenommen, wir finden unter den Urkunden des Grafen Bartholomäus noch Hinweise auf weitere Ländereien, auf die dann sowohl Ihr als auch wir Anspruch erheben?«

Aus der Tatsache, daß sie sich auf solche Einzelheiten einließ, schloß Philip auf ihre Bereitschaft, seinen Vorschlag anzunehmen. Er versuchte, sich seine Erregung nicht anmerken zu lassen, und antwortete kühl: »Dann müssen wir uns auf einen Schiedsrichter einigen. Wie wär's mit Bischof Henry?«

»Einem Priester?« In Regans Stimme schwang ein Anflug der altgewohnten Verachtung mit. »Nein. Ich zweifle an seiner Objektivität. Wie wär's mit dem Vogt von Shiring?«

Der ist auch nicht objektiver als der Bischof, dachte Philip. Aber da ihm niemand einfiel, mit dem beide Seiten gleichermaßen zufrieden gewesen wären, stimmte er zu: »Einverstanden – unter einer Bedingung: daß wir gegen *sein* Urteil beim König Berufung einlegen können.« Diese Rückversicherung müßte genügen, dachte er.

»Einverstanden«, sagte Regan und fügte mit einem Seitenblick auf ihren Ehemann hinzu: »Wenn es meinem Gemahl so gefällt.«

»Ja, ja«, sagte Percy Hamleigh.

Philip wußte, daß der Erfolg nahe war. Er holte tief Luft und sagte: »In der Hauptsache sind wir uns also einig. Wir können demnach ...«

»Augenblick!« unterbrach ihn Regan. »Wir sind uns noch nicht einig.«

»Aber ich habe Euch alles gegeben, was Ihr wolltet.«

»Es ist immer noch möglich, daß uns der König die *gesamte* Grafschaft überträgt.«

»Oder überhaupt nichts.«

Regan zögerte. »Vorausgesetzt, wir werden handelseinig – wie gedenkt Ihr Euch dann zu verhalten?«

Philip hatte mit dem Einwand gerechnet. Er wandte sich an Percy. »Könnt Ihr heute abend noch beim König vorsprechen?«

Percy war sichtlich aufgeregt, aber er sagte: »Wenn ich einen guten Grund dafür habe, ja.«

»Geht zu ihm und teilt ihm mit, daß wir uns geeinigt haben. Er soll unseren Kompromiß morgen vormittag als seine eigene Entscheidung bekanntgeben. Versichert ihm, daß wir beide, Ihr und ich, uns mit dieser Entscheidung einverstanden erklären werden.«

»Und was soll ich sagen, wenn er mich fragt, ob die Bischöfe auch einverstanden sind?«

»Dann sagt, wir hätten noch nicht die Zeit gefunden, mit ihnen darüber zu sprechen. Ruft ihm ins Gedächtnis zurück, daß nicht der Bischof, sondern der Prior für den Bau der Kathedrale zuständig ist. Und laßt durchblicken, daß den Bischöfen, wenn ich zustimme, gar nichts anderes übrigbleibt, als ebenfalls zuzustimmen ...«

»Aber wenn die Bischöfe nach der Verkündung der Entscheidung Beschwerde führen?«

»Wie könnten sie!« rief Philip aus. »Sie geben doch vor, einzig und allein deshalb nach der Grafschaft zu trachten, weil sie mit den Einkünften die neue Kathedrale finanzieren wollen. Soll Waleran sich vielleicht beschweren, daß er nun keine Gelder mehr zweckentfremden kann?«

Regan kicherte. Philips Verschlagenheit gefiel ihr. »Der Plan ist gut«, sagte sie.

»Es gibt allerdings eine wichtige Bedingung«, sagte Philip und sah ihr in die Augen. »Der König muß ausdrücklich verkünden, daß mein Anteil der *Priorei* übertragen wird. Wenn er das nicht von sich aus tut, werde ich ihn darum bitten. Überträgt er meinen Anteil der Diözese, dem Sakristan, dem Erzbischof oder sonstwem, ist unsere gesamte Übereinkunft null und nichtig. Ist das klar?«

»Ich verstehe«, sagte Regan gereizt. Philip sah in ihrer Verstimmung ein Zeichen dafür, daß sie mit dem Gedanken gespielt hatte, dem König eine leicht abgewandelte Version der Übereinkunft zu präsentieren, und war froh, daß er für eine Klarstellung gesorgt hatte.

Er erhob sich, wollte aber nicht gehen, ohne den Pakt zuvor auf irgendeine Weise besiegelt zu haben. »Wir sind uns also einig«, sagte er, und es klang mehr wie eine Feststellung denn wie eine Frage. »Wir haben einen bindenden Vertrag geschlossen.« Er sah von einem zum anderen.

Regan nickte fast unmerklich, und Percy bestätigte: »Ja, wir haben einen Vertrag geschlossen.«

Philips Herzschlag beschleunigte sich. »Gut«, sagte er gepreßt. »Ich sehe Euch morgen vormittag auf der Burg.« Mit ausdruckslosem Gesicht verließ er das Zimmer. Draußen auf der dunklen Straße ließ er jedoch seinen Gefühlen freien Lauf und gestattete sich ein breites, triumphierendes Grinsen.

Nach dem Abendessen verfiel Philip in einen unruhigen, bangen Schlaf. Gegen Mitternacht erhob er sich für die Matutin, danach lag er wach auf seiner Strohmatratze und grübelte darüber nach, welchen Lauf die Dinge am kommenden Vormittag nehmen könnten.

Eigentlich, so dachte er, müßte König Stephan den Vorschlag gutheißen, bot dieser ihm doch einen Ausweg aus seinem Dilemma, indem er ihm einen neuen Grafen *und* eine neue Kathedrale verschaffte. Freilich war er sich längst nicht so sicher, wie er Regan gegenüber zum Ausdruck gebracht hatte, daß Waleran die Entscheidung tatenlos hinnehmen würde. Dem Bischof war durchaus zuzutrauen, daß ihm noch Argumente gegen die Übereinkunft einfielen. So mochte er, wenn er nur schnell genug dachte, einwenden, daß sich eine so eindrucksvolle, prestigeträchtige und reich geschmückte Kathedrale, wie er sie sich vorstellte, unter den Bedingungen des Abkommens zwischen den Hamleighs und der Priorei nicht finanzieren ließ. Möglicherweise kamen dem König dann noch einmal Bedenken.

Kurz vor Beginn der Morgendämmerung wurde Philip von einem weiteren Gedanken heimgesucht, der seine Pläne zu gefährden drohte: Regan konnte ihm einen Streich spielen und sich auf einen Kuhhandel mit Waleran einlassen. Angenommen, sie schlug dem Bischof den gleichen Kompromiß vor? Waleran bekäme dann die Steine und das Holz, die er für den Bau seiner Burg benötigte … Der Gedanke ließ Philip nicht mehr zur Ruhe kommen. Rastlos wälzte er sich auf seinem

Lager hin und her. Ich hätte selbst zum König gehen müssen, dachte er, obwohl ihm klar war, daß Stephan ihn wahrscheinlich gar nicht vorgelassen hätte und Waleran, hätte er von dem Besuch erfahren, nur mißtrauisch geworden wäre ... Nein, sichere Vorkehrungen gegen Verrat und Betrug gab es in diesem Falle nicht. Er konnte nur noch beten.

Und das tat er denn auch, bis der Morgen heraufdämmerte.

Er frühstückte mit den Mönchen. Das Weißbrot, so fand er, füllte den Magen weniger gut als das gewohnte Pferdebrot. Trotzdem brachte er kaum etwas herunter. Obgleich er wußte, daß der König zu so früher Stunde noch keinen Besuch empfing, begab er sich schon wenig später zur Burg und nahm auf einem in die Mauer geschlagenen Steinsitz im unteren Saal Platz.

Mit der Zeit füllte sich der Raum mit Höflingen und Bittstellern. Einige Leute waren sehr auffällig gekleidet – sie trugen gelbe, blaue und rosafarbene Tuniken und Mäntel mit üppiger Pelzverbrämung. Das berühmte *Doomsday Book* wurde, wie Philip jetzt wieder einfiel, irgendwo in der Burg aufbewahrt – wahrscheinlich in jenem ein Stockwerk höher gelegenen Saal, in dem der König ihn und die beiden Bischöfe empfangen hatte. Er hatte es zwar nicht gesehen, aber das wollte angesichts seiner inneren Anspannung während der Audienz nicht viel heißen. Der königliche Schatz befand sich ebenfalls hier, vermutlich ganz oben in einem verschlossenen Fach gleich neben dem Schlafgemach des Monarchen. Wieder empfand Philip die Umgebung als beklemmend, doch war er entschlossen, sich diesmal nicht mehr einschüchtern zu lassen. All diese Leute in ihren eleganten Kleidern, die Ritter und Lords, die Kaufleute und Bischöfe waren auch nur Menschen. Die meisten von ihnen waren gerade mal mit Mühe imstande, ihren eigenen Namen zu schreiben. Außerdem verfolgten sie hier bei Hofe samt und sonders nur eigennützige Ziele, während er, Philip, im Namen Gottes gekommen war. Seine Mission – und seine schmutzige Kutte! – erhoben ihn über alle anderen Bittsteller.

Dieser Gedanke machte ihm Mut.

Ein Priester erschien auf der Treppe zum oberen Saal und sorgte für gespannte Unruhe unter den Wartenden, die alle hofften, daß nun die Audienzzeit begann. Der Priester wechselte ein paar gemurmelte Worte mit einem der Bewaffneten, die unten an der Treppe Wache standen, und entschwand wieder in der Richtung, aus der er gekommen war. Der Bewaffnete rief einen Ritter auf. Der Mann gab sein Schwert ab und stieg die Treppe hinauf.

Ein eigenartiges Leben führen sie, diese Geistlichen am königlichen Hof, dachte Philip. Der König kam ohne sie natürlich nicht aus. Sie waren nicht nur da, um die Messe zu lesen, sondern es oblag ihnen auch der gesamte bei der Regierungsarbeit anfallende Schriftverkehr. Wer sonst hätte ihn erledigen können? Die paar Laien, die des Lesens und Schreibens kundig waren, beherrschten es nur unzureichend und waren dementsprechend langsam. Besonders heiligmäßig war das Leben der Hofkleriker gewiß nicht. Francis, Philips leiblicher Bruder, hatte sich dafür entschieden und arbeitete für Robert von Gloucester. Ich muß ihn mal nach seinen näheren Lebensumständen befragen, dachte Philip – falls ich ihn je wiedersehe.

Kurz nachdem der erste Bittsteller die Treppe hinaufgegangen war, trafen die Hamleighs ein.

Philip widerstand dem Impuls, sofort auf sie zuzugehen und sie zu begrüßen: *Noch* brauchte nicht alle Welt zu wissen, daß sie unter einer Decke steckten. Er betrachtete sie aufmerksam und versuchte, aus ihren Mienen auf ihre Gedanken und Gefühle zu schließen. William schien voller Hoffnung zu sein, Percy dagegen eher ängstlich, und Regan war angespannt wie eine Bogensehne. Philip wartete noch einen Augenblick, dann erhob er sich möglichst unauffällig und ging auf die Hamleighs zu. Er begrüßte sie höflich und sagte zu Percy: »Habt Ihr mit ihm gesprochen?«

»Ja.«

»Und?«

»Er hat gesagt, er wolle in der Nacht darüber nachdenken.«

»Wieso denn *das*?« fragte Philip gleichermaßen enttäuscht wie aufgebracht. »Was gibt's da noch lange nachzudenken?«

Percy zuckte mit den Schultern. »Fragt ihn doch selber.«

»Na – und was habt Ihr für einen *Eindruck* von ihm?« hakte Philip nach. Er war wütend. »Schien er Euch angetan von dem Vorschlag – oder was?«

»Ich glaube, er fand die Idee ganz gut, weil sie ihn aus einer Zwickmühle befreit. Andererseits war er mißtrauisch – die Lösung kam ihm irgendwie zu einfach vor.«

Das klingt glaubhaft, dachte Philip; dennoch ärgerte es ihn, daß König Stephan die Gelegenheit nicht beim Schopfe gepackt hatte. Nach einer kurzen Pause sagte er: »Lassen wir es fürs erste dabei bewenden. Die Bischöfe könnten Verdacht schöpfen. Es wäre nicht gut, wenn sie vor dem Spruch des Königs von unserer Zusammenarbeit erführen.«

Er nickte den Hamleighs höflich zu und kehrte zu seinem steinernen Sitz zurück. Dort versuchte er, sich die Wartezeit zu verkürzen, indem er überlegte, was im Falle einer für ihn günstigen Entscheidung als nächstes zu tun wäre. Wann würde man mit dem Bau der neuen Kathedrale beginnen können? Es hing davon ab, wie schnell sich aus den neuen Gütern bares Geld abzweigen ließ. Die Schafherden würden nach dem Verkauf der Wolle im Sommer einiges abwerfen. Einige der Höfe im Bergland waren gewiß verpachtet, und die Pacht war meistens nach der Ernte fällig. Wenn alles gutging, war im Herbst genug Geld vorhanden, um einen Forstmeister mit dem Beginn des Holzeinschlags und einen Steinbruchmeister mit der Förderung der Steine zu beauftragen. Zur gleichen Zeit konnten schon unter Tom Builders Leitung die Fundamente ausgeschachtet werden.

Ein schöner Traum ...

In beunruhigend rascher Folge gingen nun die Höflinge die Treppe hinauf und hinunter: König Stephan arbeitete heute recht schnell.

Philip fürchtete bereits, er könne noch vor Eintreffen der Bischöfe sein Tagewerk beenden und sich zur Jagd verfügen, als die beiden endlich kamen. Waleran wirkte sehr angespannt, Henry indessen nur gelangweilt. Für den Bischof von Winchester war die Angelegenheit zweitrangig. Gewiß, er war seinem Amtsbruder Unterstützung schuldig, doch konnte es ihm letztlich gleichgültig sein, welchen Ausgang die Affäre nahm. Für Waleran war der Spruch des Königs dagegen von entscheidender Bedeutung, stand und fiel damit doch sein Plan, eine Burg zu errichten – eine Burg, die nichts anderes war als ein weiterer Schritt des Bischofs auf dem steilen Weg zur Macht.

Philip wußte nicht genau, wie er sich verhalten sollte. Die beiden hatten versucht, ihn zu übervorteilen. Am liebsten hätte er sie zur Rede gestellt und ihnen ins Gesicht gesagt, daß er ihnen auf die Schliche gekommen war – nur wären sie in diesem Fall gewarnt gewesen. Er wollte sie jedoch ahnungslos in die Audienz gehen lassen, damit der königliche Kompromiß sie unvorbereitet traf und ihnen keine Zeit mehr für Gegenargumente ließ. Er ließ sich daher seine wahren Gefühle nicht anmerken, sondern lächelte den Bischöfen freundlich zu. Freilich erwiesen sich seine Bedenken als gegenstandslos: Die beiden Herren zogen es vor, ihn vollständig zu ignorieren.

Es dauerte nun nicht mehr lange, bis sie von der Wache aufgerufen wurden. Henry und Waleran schritten voran, Philip folgte ihnen, und die Hamleighs bildeten die Nachhut. Dem Prior von Kingsbridge schlug das Herz bis zum Hals.

König Stephan stand vor dem Kamin. Er wirkte diesmal kühler und geschäftsmäßiger als bei der ersten Audienz. Philip sah darin einen Vorteil: Sollten die Bischöfe versuchen, ihm mit Wortklaubereien zu kommen, so würde er sie kurz und bündig abfertigen. Bischof Henry ging auf seinen Bruder zu und blieb neben ihm vor dem Kamin stehen, die anderen nahmen in der Saalmitte Aufstellung. Philip verspürte auf einmal einen stechenden Schmerz in den Händen und erkannte, daß er vor lauter Aufregung seine Fingernägel in die Handflächen gebohrt hatte. Nur unter Aufbietung aller Willenskräfte gelang es ihm, die Fingermuskeln zu entspannen.

Der König flüsterte seinem Bruder etwas zu, das die anderen nicht verstehen konnten. Henry runzelte die Stirn und antwortete ebenso leise. Ohne daß einer von ihnen die Stimme hob, ging das Gespräch noch eine Weile hin und her. Dann gebot Stephan mit erhobener Hand seinem Bruder Schweigen und blickte Philip an.

Zu Scherzen war der König diesmal nicht aufgelegt. Er hüstelte und begann: »Mein treuer Untertan Percy Hamleigh wird mit dem heutigen Tag Graf von Shiring.«

Aus dem Augenwinkel sah Philip, daß Waleran drauf und dran war, nach vorne zu stürzen und dem König seinen Protest entgegenzuschreien, jedoch von Bischof Henry mit einer raschen, unmißverständlichen Geste zurückgehalten wurde.

Der König fuhr fort: »Aus dem Besitz seines Vorgängers erhält Graf Percy die Burg sowie alles urbare Land einschließlich der Güter, die an Ritter verpachtet sind, und die Viehweiden in der Ebene.«

Philip konnte seine Erregung kaum mehr verbergen. Der König hatte den Vorschlag offenbar akzeptiert! Er riskierte einen Seitenblick auf Waleran. Das Gesicht des Bischofs war von Wut und Verzweiflung gezeichnet.

Percy trat vor und kniete vor dem König nieder, die Hände zusammengelegt wie im Gebet. Der König legte seine Hände über Percys und sprach: »Ihr, Percy, Graf von Shiring, seid hiermit rechtmäßiger Besitzer der erwähnten Ländereien samt aller Einkünfte und möget Eure Freude daran haben.«

Und Percy antwortete: »Ich schwöre bei allem, was heilig ist, Euer getreuer Lehensmann zu sein und Euch gegen jedermann zu verteidigen.«

Der König gab Percys Hände frei, und der frischgebackene Graf erhob sich.

Stephan wandte sich an die übrigen Anwesenden. »Alle anderen

Ländereien aus dem Besitz des ehemaligen Grafen übereigne ich ...«
Er machte eine Pause. Sein Blick wanderte von Philip zu Waleran und
wieder zurück. »... übereigne ich der *Priorei* von Kingsbridge zum
Zwecke des Baus einer neuen Kathedrale.«

Philip unterdrückte mit Mühe einen Freudenschrei. Er hatte gewonnen! Er strahlte den König an – das ließ sich nicht vermeiden –
und drehte sich dann nach Waleran um. Der Bischof war erschüttert
bis ins Mark. Er versuchte gar nicht mehr, den Gleichmütigen hervor-
zukehren: Sein Mund stand offen, die Augen hatte er aufgerissen. Aus
dem Blick, mit dem er den König bedachte, sprach schiere Ungläubig-
keit. Dann sah er Philip an. Waleran wußte, daß er einen entscheidenden Fehler gemacht hatte, von dem Philip jetzt profitierte. Aber er
konnte sich nicht vorstellen, *wie* es geschehen war.

»Die Priorei Kingsbridge«, fuhr der König fort, »erhält darüber
hinaus das Recht, dem gräflichen Steinbruch in unbegrenzter Menge
Steine für den Kathedralenbau zu entnehmen. Desgleichen ist sie ermächtigt, in den gräflichen Wäldern Holz zu schlagen.«

Empörung wallte in Philip auf. Das widersprach der Vereinbarung!
Der Steinbruch und die Waldungen sollten in den Besitz der *Priorei*
übergehen – für Percy war lediglich das Jagdrecht vorgesehen! Also
hatte Regan die Vertragsbedingungen doch noch zu ihren Gunsten
verändert ... Philip blieben nur wenige Augenblicke Zeit: Sollte er
trotzdem zustimmen – oder sollte er die Übereinkunft in Bausch und
Bogen ablehnen? Der König sagte: »Zum Schiedsrichter im Falle von
Unstimmigkeiten bestimme ich den Vogt von Shiring, doch steht beiden Parteien in letzter Instanz das Recht zu, bei mir Berufung einzulegen ...« Regans Benehmen ist unverschämt, dachte Philip – aber so
wesentlich sind die Veränderungen nun auch wieder nicht. Die Vereinbarung nützt mir allemal ... Da sagte der König: »Wie ich vernommen
habe, sind sich beide Seiten bereits einig.« Jetzt blieb keine Zeit mehr.
Percy sagte: »Jawohl, mein Herr und König.«

Waleran öffnete den Mund zu einer Entgegnung, schließlich hatte
er dem Kompromiß nicht zugestimmt. Aber Philip kam ihm zuvor.
»Jawohl, mein Herr und König«, sagte auch er.

Sowohl Bischof Henry als auch Bischof Waleran fuhren herum und
starrten Philip an. Ihre Bestürzung war unverkennbar: Jetzt ging ihnen
auf, daß sich dieser jungenhafte Prior, der noch nicht einmal wußte,
daß man bei Hofe sauberen Habit anlegte, hinter ihrem Rücken mit
dem König geeinigt hatte. Henry entspannte sich schnell; seine Miene
verriet die Belustigung eines Mannes, der einem flinken Kind beim

Damespiel unterliegt. Walerans Ausdruck wurde dagegen böse. Philip glaubte, seine Gedanken lesen zu können. Der Bischof wußte jetzt, was sein Kardinalfehler gewesen war: Er hatte seinen Gegner unterschätzt und daraufhin eine demütigende Niederlage erlitten. Philip fühlte sich in diesem Augenblick für alles entschädigt, was er selber durchgemacht hatte: die Heimtücke, die Erniedrigung, die ständigen kleinen Seitenhiebe. Er hob das Kinn und riskierte die Sünde der Hoffart. Sein Blick war eine Botschaft an Waleran: *Wer Philip von Gwynedd übers Ohr hauen will, muß früher aufstehen*...

Der König sagte: »Teilt Bartholomäus, dem ehemaligen Grafen, meine Entscheidung mit.«

Philip vermutete, daß Bartholomäus irgendwo auf der Burg in einem Verlies saß. Die Kinder fielen ihm ein, die zusammen mit dem Diener in der Ruine hausten ... Er mußte an ihr zukünftiges Schicksal denken. Einmal mehr verspürte er Gewissensbisse.

Der König entließ die Anwesenden mit Ausnahme von Bischof Henry. Wie auf Wolken schritt Philip zum Ausgang. Gleichzeitig mit Waleran erreichte er die Treppe. Er blieb stehen, um dem Bischof den Vortritt zu lassen. Walerans Gesicht war eine haßverzerrte Maske, und als er den Mund öffnete, war es, als wolle er Gift und Galle spucken. »Ich schwöre Euch hoch und heilig, daß Ihr Eure Kirche niemals bauen werdet«, zischte er Philip an. Den Prior traf der Klang dieser Worte bis ins Mark.

Seine Hochstimmung war wie fortgeblasen.

Waleran zog seine schwarze Kutte fest um seine Schultern und stürmte die Treppe hinunter.

Philip wußte, daß er sich einen Feind fürs Leben gemacht hatte.

Als die Burg Earlscastle in Sicht kam, konnte William Hamleigh seine Erregung kaum noch zügeln.

Es war am folgenden Nachmittag, also am Tag nach der Entscheidung des Königs. Obwohl er und Walter seitdem fast ununterbrochen im Sattel saßen, fühlte William sich nicht müde. Ihm war, als schwelle ihm das Herz in seiner Brust und schnüre ihm den Atem ab. In Kürze würde er Aliena wiedersehen.

Er hatte sie einst heiraten wollen, weil sie die Tochter eines Grafen war, und sie hatte ihn dreimal zurückgewiesen. Die Erinnerung an ihre Hochnäsigkeit ließ ihn zusammenfahren. Wie ein absoluter Niemand, ein Bauer, war er sich vorgekommen; sie hatte so getan, als seien die Hamleighs eine Familie von niedrigstem Stand. Doch inzwischen hatten sich die Voraussetzungen von Grund auf geändert. Nun war es *ihre* Familie, die nichts mehr galt. Er war der Sohn eines Grafen – und sie ein Nichts. Aliena hatte keinen Titel mehr, keinen Rang, kein Land, kein Vermögen. Er, William, würde nun die Burg in Besitz nehmen und Aliena davonjagen – und dann hätte sie nicht einmal mehr ein Dach über dem Kopf. Es war fast zu schön, um wahr zu sein.

Sie hatten die Burg fast erreicht. William zügelte sein Pferd. Er wollte Aliena ohne Vorwarnung überraschen: Wie ein Blitz aus heiterem Himmel wollte er über sie kommen und ihr einen furchtbaren, vernichtenden Schlag versetzen.

Graf Percy und Gräfin Regan waren zu ihrem Stammsitz nach Hamleigh zurückgekehrt, um die ordnungsgemäße Überführung des Familienschatzes, der besten Pferde und des Gesindes in die Wege zu leiten. William sollte ein paar Dorfbewohner zu Aufräum- und Reinigungsarbeiten auf der Burg anwerben. Earlscastle mußte geheizt, gesäubert, kurz: bewohnbar gemacht werden.

Tiefhängende, bleigraue Wolken quollen über den Himmel – so niedrig, daß sie fast die Zinnen der Burg berührten. Für die kommende Nacht kündigte sich Regen an. Um so besser, dachte William. Ich werfe sie in ein Unwetter hinaus ...

Sie saßen ab und führten die Pferde am Zügel über die hölzerne Zugbrücke. Ich bin der Eroberer dieser Burg, dachte William voller Stolz. Im unteren Burghof sproß bereits frisches Grün. Sie banden ihre Pferde an und ließen sie grasen; William gab seinem Schlachtroß noch eine zusätzliche Handvoll Korn. Da kein Stall mehr vorhanden war, verstauten sie ihre Sättel in der Kapelle. Die Pferde schnaubten und stampften, doch verloren sich die Geräusche im böigen Wind. Zu Fuß überschritten William und Walter die zweite Brücke.

Nirgendwo war ein Lebenszeichen zu erblicken. Hat Aliena etwa die Burg verlassen? dachte William beklommen. Das wäre eine bittere Enttäuschung ... Schon fürchtete er, eine trostlose, hungrige Nacht in einer kalten, verdreckten Burg stünde ihnen bevor. Sie stiegen die Außentreppe zum großen Saal empor. »Still!« raunte er Walter zu, als sie vor der Tür standen. »Ich will, daß ihnen der Schreck in alle Glieder fährt.«

Er schob die Tür auf. Der große Saal war dunkel und leer, und es roch, als sei er schon monatelang nicht mehr benutzt worden. Vorsichtig schlich William auf die Treppe zu. Trockene Binsen knirschten unter seinen Füßen. Walter hielt sich dicht hinter ihm.

Sie schlichen die Treppe hinauf. Nichts war zu hören: Die dicken Mauern des Wohnturms verschluckten alle Geräusche. Auf halbem Wege blieb William stehen, drehte sich um, legte warnend den Finger auf die Lippen und wies auf den Lichtschimmer, der durch den Spalt am unteren Türrand drang: Es war also doch jemand anwesend.

Sie stiegen die letzten Stufen empor und verharrten vor der Tür. Drinnen erklang ein mädchenhaftes Gekicher. William lächelte glücklich. Er tastete nach dem Griff, drehte ihn vorsichtig herum und öffnete die Tür mit einem vehementen Tritt. Das Kichern verwandelte sich in einen Angstschrei.

Ein hübsches Bild bot sich ihren Augen: Aliena und Richard, ihr jüngerer Bruder, saßen an einem Tischchen unweit des Kamins bei einem Brettspiel. Hinter Aliena stand Haushofmeister Matthew und blickte ihr über die Schultern. Alienas Gesicht schimmerte rosa im Schein des Feuers, und hier und da setzten die Flammen ihrer üppigen Lockenpracht kastanienbraune Glanzlichter auf. Sie trug eine helle Leinentunika, und ihre roten Lippen formten vor Überraschung ein großes, rundes ›o‹. William sagte kein Wort. Er sah sie nur an und weidete sich an ihrer Furcht. Aliena brauchte nicht lange, um sich wieder zu fangen. »Was willst du hier?« fragte sie.

William hatte den Auftritt in seiner Phantasie schon mehrfach geprobt. Langsam betrat er den Raum, schritt zum Kamin und wärmte seine Hände über dem Feuer. Dann sagte er: »Ich wohne hier. Was willst *du* hier?«

Aliena sah von ihm zu Walter. Sie war verwirrt und fürchtete sich; dennoch hatte ihre Stimme einen herausfordernden Klang.

»Diese Burg gehört dem Grafen von Shiring. Sag, was du willst – und dann verschwinde!«

Triumphierend grinste William über sein ganzes Gesicht: »Der Graf von Shiring ist mein Vater«, sagte er. Der Haushofmeister gab ein brummendes Geräusch von sich, als habe er diese Antwort befürchtet. Aliena wirkte aufs äußerste bestürzt. »Mein Vater wurde gestern morgen in Winchester vom König zum Grafen von Shiring ernannt«, fuhr William fort. »Die Burg gehört uns, und bis zur Ankunft meines Vaters bin ich der Burgherr.« Er wandte sich an Matthew und schnippte mit den Fingern. »Ich habe Hunger. Bring mir Brot, Fleisch und Wein!«

Der Haushofmeister zögerte und warf Aliena einen besorgten Blick zu. Er wollte sie nicht allein lassen, sah aber ein, daß er keine Wahl hatte. Er ging zur Tür. Aliena traf Anstalten, ihm zu folgen, doch William rief ihr im Befehlston zu: »Du bleibst hier!«

Walter stand zwischen ihr und der Tür. Es gab kein Entkommen.

»Du hast kein Recht, mir Befehle zu erteilen!« sagte Aliena, und der altgewohnte, gebieterische Ton schwang in ihrer Stimme mit.

»Bleibt hier, Herrin«, sagte Matthew, sichtlich eingeschüchtert. »Regt sie nicht auf. Ich bin gleich zurück.«

Aliena warf ihm einen unwirschen Blick zu, blieb aber, wo sie war. Matthew verschwand.

William setzte sich an den Tisch, während Aliena neben ihrem Bruder am Spieltisch Platz nahm. Er musterte die beiden aufmerksam. Sie sahen einander ähnlich, doch alle Kraft schien dem Mädchen vorbehalten. Richard war in letzter Zeit stark aufgeschossen. Sein Gesicht war noch bartlos; seine Haltung verriet die ganze Unsicherheit des Heranwachsenden. William genoß das Gefühl, die Geschwister in seiner Gewalt zu haben. »Wie alt bist du, Richard?« fragte er.

»Vierzehn«, antwortete der Junge mürrisch.

»Schon mal wen getötet?«

»Nein«, gab Richard zurück, um mit bemühter Verwegenheit hinzuzufügen: »Noch nicht.«

Auch du wirst zu Kreuze kriechen, du aufgeblasener kleiner Furz, dachte William und wandte sich an Aliena: »Und wie alt bist du?«

Im ersten Moment sah es so aus, als weigere sie sich, mit ihm zu reden. Doch dann schien sie ihre Meinung zu ändern – vielleicht, weil sie an Matthews Warnung denken mußte – *Regt sie nicht auf…*

»Siebzehn«, sagte sie.

»Ei fein, die ganze Familie kann zählen!« sagte William. »Bist du noch Jungfrau, Aliena?«

»Natürlich!« fauchte sie.

Unvermittelt streckte William den Arm aus und faßte an ihren Busen. Die Brust füllte seine große Hand. Er packte zu. Das Fleisch war fest, aber nachgiebig. Aliena zuckte zurück. Seine Hand rutschte ab.

Viel zu spät fuhr Richard dazwischen und schlug Williams Arm zur Seite. Er hätte ihm keinen größeren Gefallen tun können. Wie der Blitz schoß er vom Stuhl hoch und schlug Richard die Faust ins Gesicht. Erwartungsgemäß erwies sich der Junge als Weichling: Er schrie auf und barg sein Gesicht in den Händen.

»Rühr ihn nicht an!« schrie Aliena.

Überrascht starrte William sie an. Sie schien sich mehr um ihren Bruder als um sich selbst zu sorgen. Das mußte man sich merken.

Matthew kehrte zurück. Er trug einen großen Holzteller mit einem Laib Brot, einem Schinken und einem Krug Wein. Als er Richard sah, wurde er blaß. Er stellte den Teller auf den Tisch, ging zu ihm hin und nahm ihm sanft die Hände vom Gesicht. Es war gerötet und unter dem linken Auge angeschwollen. »Ich sagte doch, Ihr solltet sie nicht aufregen«, murmelte er, schien aber erleichtert, daß die Verletzung nicht schlimmer war. William war enttäuscht: Er hatte gehofft, Matthew würde wütend aufbrausen. Der Kerl drohte zum Spielverderber zu werden.

Der Anblick der Speisen ließ William das Wasser im Munde zusammenlaufen. Er zog seinen Stuhl näher an den Tisch heran, kramte sein Eßmesser hervor und schnitt sich eine dicke Scheibe Schinken ab. Walter setzte sich ihm gegenüber. Mit vollen Backen Brot und Schinken kauend, forderte William Aliena auf: »Bring uns Becher und schenk uns ein.« Matthew, der bereits auf dem Sprung war, rief er zurück: »Nicht du – sie!« Aliena zögerte. Matthew sah sie an und nickte angstvoll. Da stand sie auf, ging zum Tisch und nahm den Krug auf.

Als sie sich über den Tisch lehnte, langte William mit raschem Griff unter den Saum ihrer Tunika und ließ seine Finger die schlanken Beine hinaufgleiten. Die Fingerspitzen ertasteten den weichen Flaum auf den Waden, spürten die Muskeln und Sehnen hinter dem Knie und die weiche Haut auf der Innenseite der Oberschenkel. Dann jedoch schnellte Aliena zurück, drehte sich blitzschnell um die eigene Achse und ließ den schweren Weinkrug auf seinen Schädel niederfahren.

Mit der linken Hand gelang es William, den Schlag zu parieren. Mit der Rechten schlug er ihr ins Gesicht, und zwar so hart er konnte. Ein angenehmes Brennen auf seiner Handfläche verriet ihm, daß er voll getroffen hatte. Aliena schrie auf. Am Rande seines Blickfelds sah William, daß Richard aufsprang. Das war genau das, worauf er gehofft hatte. Er gab Aliena einen heftigen Stoß, so daß sie mit einem dumpfen Aufprall zu Boden stürzte.

Wie ein Hirsch, der den Jäger annimmt, ging Richard auf ihn los. Nachdem William der ersten wütenden Attacke ausgewichen war, versetzte er Richard einen Hieb in die Magengrube, dem er, als der Junge sich vornüberkrümmte, einen ganzen Hagel von Schlägen auf Augen und Nase folgen ließ. Es war zwar nicht so schön, wie auf Aliena einzuschlagen, machte aber trotzdem Spaß. Nach wenigen Augenblicken war Richards Gesicht blutüberströmt.

Plötzlich stieß Walter einen Warnschrei aus und sprang auf. Er starrte über Williams Schulter. William wirbelte herum und sah Matthew mit gezücktem Messer auf sich zukommen. Der Angriff traf ihn unvorbereitet – Kühnheit hatte er dem weibischen Haushofmeister nicht zugetraut. Da Walter nicht mehr rechtzeitig um den Tisch herumkam, konnte William zur Abwehr nur noch die Hände heben. Der furchtbare Gedanke durchzuckte ihn, er könne in der Stunde seines höchsten Triumphs getötet werden. Ein stärkerer Angreifer hätte Williams Arme einfach beiseite geschlagen. Matthew hingegen war von schlanker Gestalt. Das angenehme Leben am Grafenhof hatte seinen Körper kaum gestählt, und so gelang es William, das Messer kurz vor seinem Hals abzufangen. Aber die Gefahr war noch nicht vorüber. Matthew hob zum zweitenmal den Arm. Doch ehe er zustechen konnte – und während William einen Schritt zurücktrat und sein Schwert zog –, hatte Walter ihn erreicht und rammte ihm seinen langen, spitzen Dolch in den Rücken.

Blankes Entsetzen zeichnete Matthews Blick. William sah, wie die Dolchspitze aus seiner Brust hervortrat und die Tunika zerriß. Matthew fiel das Messer aus der Hand und polterte auf die Dielenbretter. Er rang nach Luft – vergeblich, wie es schien; er brachte lediglich ein gurgelndes Geräusch hervor. Dann ging er in die Knie, aus seinem Mund floß Blut, die Augen schlossen sich. Während er zu Boden stürzte, riß Walter den Dolch aus seinem Rücken. Ein Blutstrahl schoß aus der Wunde, ebbte jedoch rasch wieder ab.

Alle starrten sie die Leiche an – Walter, William, Aliena und Richard. Nachdem er um Haaresbreite dem Tode entgangen war, fühlte sich William, als könne er Berge versetzen. Er packte den Kragen von Alienas Tunika. Der Stoff war weich und fein und sehr, sehr teuer, doch genügte ein scharfer Ruck, und die Tunika riß der Länge lang entzwei, und William hielt einen fußbreiten Streifen in der Hand. Aliena schrie und versuchte vergeblich, ihren Körper mit dem verbliebenen Teil der Tunika zu bedecken.

William schluckte. Ihre plötzliche Verwundbarkeit erregte ihn aufs höchste. Es war noch viel aufregender als damals, als er sie am Brunnen beobachtet hatte, wußte sie doch diesmal, daß er sie sah. Sie schämte sich vor ihm, und ihre Züchtigkeit erhitzte ihn noch zusätzlich. Mit einem Arm bedeckte sie ihre Brüste, mit der anderen Hand ihre Scham. William ließ den Stoffstreifen fallen, packte Aliena bei den Haaren, drehte sie um und riß ihr den Rest der Tunika vom Rücken.

Sie hatte hübsche weiße Schultern, eine schmale Taille und überraschend volle Hüften. Er zog sie an sich, drückte sich an sie und rieb seinen Unterleib an ihrem Hintern. Er beugte sich vor und biß in die weiche Haut ihres Nackens, bis sie wieder aufschrie und er Blut schmeckte. Richard bewegte sich.

»Halt den Jungen fest!«

Walter nahm Richard in den Schwitzkasten.

William preßte Aliena mit einem Arm an sich und ließ die freie Hand über ihren Bauch ins Dreieck zwischen den Schenkeln gleiten. Das buschige Haar war gekräuselt wie auf ihrem Kopf. Brutal drangen seine Finger in sie ein. Aliena fing an zu weinen. William hatte das Gefühl, noch nie im Leben so erregt gewesen zu sein.

Er trat einen Schritt zurück und riß Aliena nach hinten, so daß sie über sein ausgestrecktes Bein stolperte. Der Fall benahm ihr den Atem. Sie röchelte.

William hatte den Lauf der Ereignisse nicht vorausgeplant. Er hätte nicht einmal mehr sagen können, wie es soweit gekommen war. Er wußte nur eines: Nichts in der Welt konnte ihn jetzt noch zurückhalten.

Er hob seine Tunika und entblößte sich vor ihr. Alienas entsetzter Blick bestärkte ihn in der Vermutung, daß sie noch nie einen Steifen gesehen hatte. Eine echte Jungfrau also, dachte er. Um so besser.

»Bring mir den Jungen her!« sagte er zu Walter. »Ich will, daß er zuschaut.« Der Gedanke, es vor Richards Augen zu tun, kam William besonders reizvoll vor – er wußte selbst nicht, warum.

Walter schubste Richard vorwärts und zwang ihn auf die Knie. William kniete auf dem Boden und versuchte, Aliena die Schenkel auseinanderzuzwängen. Das Mädchen wehrte sich. Er warf sich auf sie, um sie mit seinem Gewicht zur Botmäßigkeit zu zwingen, aber es gelang ihm nicht, in sie einzudringen. William wurde wütend. Er stützte sich auf einen Ellbogen und schlug ihr die Faust ins Gesicht. Aliena schrie auf, und zorniges Rot überflammte ihre Wangen, aber ihr Widerstand war ungebrochen.

Walter, der sie hätte festhalten können, mußte sich um den Jungen kümmern.

Plötzlich hatte William eine Idee. »Schneid dem Burschen ein Ohr ab, Walter«, sagte er.

Aliena verhielt sich auf einmal still. »Nein!« sagte sie mit rauher Stimme. »Laßt ihn in Frieden. Tut ihm nicht mehr weh.«

»Also dann – Beine auseinander!« forderte William.

Sie starrte ihn mit weit aufgerissenen Augen an. Die furchtbare Wahl, vor die er sie stellte, steigerte ihr Entsetzen ins Unerträgliche.

William genoß ihre Pein. Walter erwies sich als idealer Mitspieler. Er zog sein Messer, hielt es an Richards rechtes Ohr und schnitt dem Jungen nach kurzem Zögern mit einer fast zärtlich wirkenden Bewegung das Ohrläppchen ab.

Richard kreischte auf. Aus der kleinen Wunde sprudelte Blut. Das kleine Stück Fleisch fiel auf Alienas Brust, die sich unter den schweren Atemzügen hob und senkte.

»Aufhören!« schrie sie. »Ich tu's!«

William spuckte in die Hand, rieb ihr die Flüssigkeit zwischen die Beine und bohrte seine Finger in sie hinein. Aliena schrie auf vor Schmerz, was seine Lust nur noch vergrößerte. Er warf sich über sie. Aliena verkrampfte sich, leistete aber keinen Widerstand mehr. Sie schloß die Augen. Obwohl ihr Körper nach dem vorausgegangenen Kampf schweißüberströmt war, zitterte sie. William brachte sich in die richtige Stellung, hielt inne, um Alienas Grauen und seine Vorfreude auszukosten, und sah sich nach den anderen um. Richard starrte voller Abscheu auf die Szene, Walter glotzte geil.

»Du bist der nächste, Walter!« rief William.

Aliena stöhnte vor Verzweiflung.

Dann drang er hastig und heftig in sie ein. Er spürte den Widerstand ihres Jungfernhäutchens und stieß brutal nach. Es tat ihm weh – aber ihr noch mehr. Aliena schrie. William verstärkte seine Anstrengungen – bis er spürte, daß in ihr etwas zerriß. Alienas Gesicht wurde totenblaß, ihr Kopf fiel zur Seite, das Mädchen verlor das Bewußtsein. Da, endlich, vergoß William seinen Samen in ihr, und er lachte und lachte dabei, trunken vor Lust und Siegesfreude, bis er sich vollkommen leergepumpt fühlte.

Der Sturm tobte fast die ganze Nacht hindurch und flaute erst kurz vor dem Morgengrauen ab. Die plötzliche Stille weckte Tom Builder auf. Im Dunkeln auf seinem Lager liegend, lauschte er Alfreds schweren und Marthas ruhigeren Atemzügen. Vielleicht haben wir einen klaren Morgen, dachte er – den ersten sichtbaren Sonnenaufgang nach zwei oder drei wolkenverhangenen Wochen. Darauf hatte er gewartet.

Er erhob sich und öffnete die Tür. Es war noch dunkel; sie hatten also noch viel Zeit. Mit dem Fuß stieß er seinen Sohn an: »Aufwachen, Alfred! Die Sonne geht bald auf.«

Alfred grunzte verschlafen und setzte sich auf. Martha drehte sich um, ohne zu erwachen. Tom ging zum Tisch. Er nahm den Deckel von einem Steinguttopf, holte einen halben Laib Brot hervor und schnitt davon zwei dicke Scheiben ab – eine für sich und eine für Alfred. Gemeinsam setzten sie sich auf die Bank und frühstückten.

Im Krug war Bier. Tom nahm einen tiefen Zug und reichte den Krug an Alfred weiter. Agnes hätte dafür gesorgt, daß sie aus Bechern tranken, und Ellen nicht minder – aber es war keine Frau mehr im Haus. Nachdem Alfred den Krug wieder abgesetzt hatte, verließen sie ihr Quartier.

Der schwarze Himmel wurde langsam grau, als sie die große Freifläche vor der Kathedrale überquerten. Eigentlich hatte Tom den Prior wecken wollen, doch als die beiden zur Ruine kamen, war Philip, von denselben Gedanken geleitet wie Tom, bereits an Ort und Stelle. In einen schweren Mantel gehüllt, kniete er auf dem feuchten Boden und betete.

Ihre Aufgabe bestand darin, eine Gerade festzulegen, die genau in Ost-West-Richtung verlief und die Achse der neuen Kathedrale bilden sollte.

Die notwendigen Vorbereitungen hatte Tom schon vor einiger Zeit getroffen: Am Ostende des Baues hatte er eine Eisenstange in den Boden gerammt, die an ihrer Spitze eine kleine, nadelöhrartige Öse trug. Der Stab war fast so hoch, wie Tom groß war; die ›Öse‹ befand sich demnach in Höhe seiner Augen. Um zu verhindern, daß die Stange versehentlich verrückt wurde, hatte er sie mit einer Mischung aus Mörtel und Trümmerschutt im Boden verankert. An diesem Morgen sollte nun eine zweite Stange aufgestellt werden, und zwar genau in westlicher Richtung, am gegenüberliegenden Ende der künftigen Kathedrale.

»Misch uns ein bißchen Mörtel, Alfred«, sagte Tom zu seinem Sohn.

Alfred ging, um Sand und Kalk zu holen. Tom holte die zweite Stange sowie einen kleinen Holzhammer aus seinem Werkzeugschuppen unweit des Kreuzgangs, brachte sie zum Westrand der Baustelle und wartete auf den Sonnenaufgang. Während Alfred auf einem Brett Sand, Kalk und Wasser zu Mörtel vermischte, beendete Prior Philip seine Gebete und gesellte sich zu Tom.

Der Himmel wurde heller. Die Spannung der drei Männer wuchs. Ihre Blicke waren auf die Ostmauer des Klostergeländes gerichtet. Endlich schob sich die rote Sonnenscheibe über die Mauerkrone.

Tom stellte sich so, daß er den Rand der Sonnenscheibe durch die Öse der Stange am Ostende sehen konnte. Dann bestimmte er, während Philip mit lauter Stimme ein lateinisches Gebet begann, den

Standort der zweiten: An jenem Punkt, an dem sie ihm den Blick auf die Sonne versperrte, senkte er sie langsam auf den Boden und drückte das zugespitzte Ende in die feuchte Erde. Er zog den Holzhammer aus dem Gürtel und klopfte den Stab in den Boden, bis sich die Öse genau in Augenhöhe befand. Wenn er gut gearbeitet und seine Hand nicht gezittert hatte, mußten die Sonnenstrahlen jetzt durch *beide* Ösen fallen.

Tom kniff ein Auge zu und spähte mit dem anderen durch die kleine Öffnung an der Spitze der zweiten Stange zur Öse der ersten hinüber. Das Sonnenlicht blendete ihn. Die beiden Stangen lagen genau auf der Ost-West-Achse, die für die Ausrichtung der neuen Kathedrale maßgebend war.

Tom erklärte dem Prior das Prinzip und trat dann zur Seite, um Philip die Gelegenheit zu geben, sich selbst zu überzeugen.

»Perfekt«, sagte Philip.

»So ist es«, bestätigte Tom und nickte.

»Wißt Ihr, was wir heute für einen Tag haben?« fragte Philip.

»Freitag.«

»Es ist darüber hinaus der Tag, an dem wir uns an das Martyrium des heiligen Adolphus erinnern. Gott schickte uns diesen Sonnenaufgang, damit wir die Lage der neuen Kirche am Tag unseres Heiligen bestimmen konnten. Ist das nicht ein gutes Zeichen?«

Tom lächelte. Nach seiner Erfahrung kam es im Bauhandwerk mehr auf gute Arbeit an als auf gute Vorzeichen – doch das hinderte ihn nicht daran, sich für Philip zu freuen. »Ja, in der Tat«, sagte er. »Es ist ein sehr gutes Zeichen.«

Aliena war fest entschlossen, nicht mehr daran zu denken. Die ganze Nacht hindurch hockte sie mit dem Rücken zur Wand auf dem kalten Steinfußboden der Kapelle und starrte in die Finsternis. Anfangs kreisten ihre Gedanken unablässig um die teuflischen Schrecken, die sie durchlitten hatte, doch ganz allmählich ließ der Schmerz ein wenig nach, und es gelang ihr, ihre Sinne den Geräuschen des Sturms zuzuwenden – dem Regen, der auf das Kapellendach trommelte, und dem Wind, der um die Wälle der verlassenen Burg heulte.

Zunächst war sie nackt gewesen. Als sie endlich von ihr abgelassen hatten, waren sie an den Tisch zurückgegangen und hatten sich über die Speisen und Getränke hergemacht, ohne noch einen Gedanken an Aliena und den blutenden Richard zu verschwenden, der neben ihr auf dem Boden lag. Die Geschwister hatten die Gelegenheit beim Schopf ergriffen und waren aus dem Zimmer geflüchtet. Zu diesem Zeitpunkt war der Sturm bereits losgebrochen, so daß sie in strömendem Regen über die Brücke gehastet waren und in der Kapelle Zuflucht gesucht hatten. Richard allerdings war umgehend in den Wohnturm zurückgekehrt. Dort mußte er in dem Raum, in dem sich die Männer aufhielten, seinen und Alienas Umhang vom Kleiderhaken neben der Tür gerissen und sich, noch ehe William und sein Reitknecht aufspringen konnten, wieder aus dem Staub gemacht haben.

Noch immer schwieg er beharrlich. Er hatte Aliena ihren Umhang gegeben und sich in seinen eigenen gehüllt. Nun hockte er, mit deutlichem Abstand zu seiner Schwester, ebenfalls auf dem Boden, den Rücken gegen dieselbe Wand gelehnt. Sie sehnte sich danach, von einem liebevollen Menschen in die Arme genommen und getröstet zu werden, aber Richard tat, als hätte sie etwas unsagbar Schändliches verbrochen. Und das Schlimmste daran war, daß sie selbst genauso empfand. Sie hätte sich nicht schuldiger fühlen können, wenn sie eine Todsünde begangen hätte. Sie verstand sehr gut, warum er sie nicht trösten, sie nicht einmal berühren wollte.

Die Kälte war eine Erleichterung. Sie half ihr, sich abzukapseln, sich in ihr Schneckenhaus zu verkriechen; außerdem schien sie den Schmerz zu betäuben. An Schlaf war gar nicht erst zu denken, doch irgendwann im Laufe der Nacht fielen die Geschwister in einen trance-ähnlichen Zustand und saßen lange Zeit vollkommen bewegungslos.

Das plötzliche Ende des Sturms brach den Bann. Jetzt erkannte Aliena, daß die bisher undurchdringliche Dunkelheit gewichen war, daß sich die Fenster der Kapelle als kleine, graue Flecken ausnahmen. Richard erhob sich und trat zur Tür. Sie beobachtete ihn, verärgert über die Störung. Am liebsten wäre sie an dieser Wand sitzen geblieben, bis sie erfroren oder verhungert wäre. Sie konnte sich nichts Schöneres vorstellen, als friedlich in ewige Besinnungslosigkeit hinüberzudämmern. Dann öffnete Richard die Tür, und das schwache Licht der Morgendämmerung fiel auf sein Gesicht.

Der Schock riß Aliena aus ihrer Trance. Richard war kaum wiederzuerkennen. Sein unförmig angeschwollenes Gesicht war blutverkrustet und mit blauen Flecken übersät. Sein Anblick rührte sie fast zu Tränen. Richard war von jeher ein Schaumschläger gewesen. Als kleiner Junge war er auf einem nur in seiner Phantasie existierenden Pferd um den Burghof gefegt und hatte imaginäre Feinde mit einer imaginären Lanze erstochen. Vaters Ritter hatten ihn noch dazu ermuntert, indem sie so taten, als fürchteten sie sich vor seinem hölzernen Schwert, wo ihn doch in Wirklichkeit schon jedes fauchende Kätzchen in die Flucht schlug. In dieser Nacht aber hatte Richard all seinen Mut zusammengenommen – und war dafür entsetzlich zugerichtet worden. Von nun an würde Aliena sich um ihn kümmern müssen.

Sie erhob sich langsam. Ihr ganzer Körper fühlte sich wund an, doch die Schmerzen waren nicht mehr so schlimm wie am Abend. Sie überlegte, wie es wohl im Wohnturm aussehen mochte. Vermutlich hatten William und sein Reitknecht im Laufe der Nacht den Krug mit Wein geleert und waren dann eingeschlafen. Bei Tagesanbruch würden sie erwachen.

Bis dahin mußte sie mit Richard verschwunden sein.

Sie ging zum Altar der Kapelle hinüber, einem schlichten, hölzernen Kasten, weiß gestrichen und ohne jegliche Verzierung. Sie stemmte sich dagegen und stieß ihn mit einem Ruck um.

»Was machst du da?« fragte Richard mit angsterfüllter Stimme.

»Dies war Vaters Geheimversteck«, erwiderte sie. »Er hat es mir verraten, bevor er gegangen ist.« An der Stelle, wo der Altar gestanden hatte, lag ein Bündel aus Tuch auf dem Boden. Aliena knüpfte es auf. Zum Vorschein kamen ein großes Schwert samt Scheide und Gürtel und ein tückisch aussehender, einen Fuß langer Dolch.

Richard trat hinzu, um die Stücke in Augenschein zu nehmen. Er war nicht eben ein Meister im Umgang mit dem Schwert. Er war zwar ein ganzes Jahr lang darin unterrichtet worden, stellte sich aber immer recht unbeholfen an. Doch Aliena konnte die Waffe auf gar keinen Fall handhaben, und so reichte sie sie an ihn weiter. Er schlang sich den Gürtel um die Mitte.

Aliena betrachtete den Dolch. Sie hatte noch nie eine Waffe getragen. Zeitlebens war sie behütet und beschützt worden. Die Einsicht, daß sie die tödliche Klinge zu ihrem eigenen Schutz brauchte, ließ sie noch deutlicher fühlen, wie vollkommen verlassen sie war. Ob sie je davon Gebrauch machen könnte? Ich habe eine hölzerne Lanze in ein Wildschwein gerammt, dachte sie; warum sollte ich hiermit nicht einen Menschen erstechen können – so einen wie William Hamleigh? Der Gedanke machte sie schaudern.

Die lederne Scheide für den Dolch war mit einer Schlaufe versehen, die man am Gürtel befestigte. Aliena konnte sie mühelos über ihr schmales linkes Handgelenk streifen. Die Klinge steckte sie in ihren Ärmel. Sie war so lang, daß sie über ihren Ellenbogen hinausragte. Selbst wenn sie es nicht fertigbrachte, einen Menschen zu erstechen, so mochte die Waffe doch dazu dienen, Angreifern einen Schrecken einzujagen.

Richard sagte: »Wir müssen fort, und zwar schleunigst.«

Aliena nickte, sie hielt aber auf dem Weg zur Tür inne. Inzwischen war es heller geworden, und sie machte auf dem Boden der Kapelle zwei schemenhafte Gegenstände aus, die ihr bislang entgangen waren. Bei näherer Betrachtung stellten sie sich als Sättel heraus, einer von mittlerer Größe, der andere von wahrhaft riesigen Ausmaßen. Sie konnte sich lebhaft vorstellen, wie William und sein Reitknecht am Abend zuvor noch voller Erregung über ihren Triumph in Winchester und ermüdet von ihrem Ritt hier angekommen waren, den Pferden die Sättel abgenommen und sie achtlos in die Kapelle geworfen hatten, bevor sie in den Wohnturm geeilt waren. Daß jemand wagen würde, sie zu bestehlen, wäre ihnen nie in den Sinn gekommen. Aber Verzweiflung macht mutig.

Aliena trat an die Tür und sah sich draußen um. Das Licht war schwach und farblos, aber hell genug. Der Wind war abgeflaut und der Himmel wolkenlos. In der Nacht hatte der Sturm etliche Holzschindeln vom Dach geweht. Nichts rührte sich um die Kapelle, nur die beiden Pferde weideten im nassen Gras. Sie sahen kurz zu Aliena auf, senkten aber gleich wieder die Köpfe. Eins der Pferde war ein riesiges Schlachtroß, daher also der übergroße Sattel. Das andere war ein gescheckter Hengst, nicht besonders edel, aber kompakt und solide. Aliena ließ ihren Blick von den Pferden zu den Sätteln und zurück schweifen.

»Worauf warten wir noch?« fragte Richard ängstlich.

Aliena hatte ihren Entschluß gefaßt. »Wir nehmen ihre Pferde«, sagte sie mit Entschiedenheit.

Richard sah verängstigt drein. »Die bringen uns um.«

»Sie werden uns nicht erwischen. Sie können uns nur einholen und töten, wenn wir ihnen die Pferde hierlassen.«

»Und wenn sie uns erwischen, bevor wir uns aus dem Staub machen können?«

»Wir müssen uns eben sputen.« Sie war bei weitem nicht so zuversichtlich, wie sie sich gab, aber sie mußte Richard Mut machen. »Den Renner satteln wir zuerst – er sieht ein bißchen freundlicher aus. Hol seinen Sattel.«

Sie huschte davon. Beide Pferde waren mit langen Seilen an Pfosten heruntergebrannter Gebäude gebunden. Aliena löste das Seil des Schecken und zog ihn sachte zu sich heran. Gewiß gehörte er Williams Reitknecht. Ein kleineres und sanfteres Tier wäre ihr lieber gewesen, doch Aliena traute sich durchaus zu, mit diesem Pferd fertig zu werden. Richard mußte eben zusehen, wie er mit dem Schlachtroß zurechtkam.

Der Schecke beäugte Aliena mißtrauisch und legte die Ohren an. Sie war extrem ungeduldig, zwang sich aber, besänftigend auf das Tier einzureden und weiter sachte an dem Seil zu ziehen, bis es sich schließlich beruhigte. Sie hielt seinen Kopf und streichelte seine Nüstern, dann streifte Richard ihm die Zügel über und schob ihm das Mundstück ins Maul. Aliena fiel ein Stein vom Herzen. Richard hob den kleineren der beiden Sättel auf den Pferderücken und zurrte ihn schnell und geübt fest. Den Umgang mit Pferden waren die Geschwister von Kindesbeinen an gewohnt.

An beiden Seiten des Sattels waren Taschen befestigt. Aliena hoffte nur, daß sie etwas Nützliches enthielten – einen Feuerstein vielleicht, ein wenig Nahrung oder etwas Pferdefutter –, aber zum Nachsehen blieb keine Zeit. Voller Unruhe überprüfte sie das Gelände bis zur Brücke, die zum Wohnturm hinaufführte. Niemand war in Sicht.

Das Schlachtroß hatte beobachtet, wie der Schecke gesattelt wurde, und wußte, was ihm bevorstand, legte jedoch keinen großen Eifer an den Tag, sich mit wildfremden Menschen einzulassen. Es schnaubte und widersetzte sich dem Zug am Seil. »Sch-sch«, machte Aliena. Sie hielt das Seil gestrafft, zog stetig an, und widerwillig näherte sich das Pferd. Es war ein sehr starkes Tier, das sie, sollte es ernsthaft Widerstand leisten, in die größten Schwierigkeiten bringen konnte. Aliena überlegte, ob nicht der Hengst sie beide tragen könnte. Doch dann bliebe William das Schlachtroß, um ihnen nachzusetzen.

Sobald sie das Roß nahe genug herangezogen hatte, schlang Aliena das Seil mehrfach um den Pfosten, so daß es nicht mehr weglaufen konnte. Aber als Richard versuchte, ihm Zügel anzulegen, warf es den Kopf zurück und wich ihm aus.

»Versuch es zuerst mit dem Sattel«, sagte Aliena. Beruhigend redete sie auf das Tier ein und tätschelte seinen mächtigen Hals, während Richard den Riesensattel hochhievte und festzurrte. Ein gewisser Ausdruck der Resignation bemächtigte sich des Rosses. »Ganz brav jetzt«, befahl Aliena mit fester Stimme, aber es ließ sich nicht hinters Licht führen und witterte die Angst, die insgeheim mitschwang. Richard näherte sich mit dem Zaumzeug, und das Pferd schnaubte und versuchte, sich davonzumachen. »Ich hab' was für dich«, sagte Aliena und griff in die leere Tasche ihres Umhangs. Das Roß ließ sich täuschen, beugte den Hals, drückte seinen Kopf in ihre leere Handfläche und suchte nach Futter. Aliena spürte seine rauhe Zunge auf ihrer Haut. Behende legte Richard ihm das Zaumzeug an, solange es noch mit gebeugtem Kopf und offenem Maul dastand.

Aliena warf erneut einen ängstlichen Blick auf den Turm. Nichts rührte sich.

»Steig auf«, sagte sie zu Richard.

Mit großer Mühe gelang es ihm, einen Fuß in den hohen Steigbügel zu setzen und sich auf das riesenhafte Tier zu schwingen.

Das Pferd wieherte laut.

Alienas Herz raste. War das Geräusch bis in den Wohnturm zu hören? Bestimmt erkannte ein Mann wie William sein Roß schon am Wiehern, vor allem, wenn es sich um ein solch wertvolles Tier wie dieses handelte. Hoffentlich war er nicht aufgewacht.

Sie rannte zu ihrem Pferd hinüber und fummelte mit kalten Fingern am Knoten des Sattels herum. Der bloße Gedanke, William könne wach geworden sein, verwandelte sie in ein Nervenbündel. Er würde die Augen aufmachen, sich aufsetzen und umsehen. Er würde sich erinnern, wo er war, und würde sich fragen, warum sein Pferd gewiehert hatte. Dann würde er sofort herunterkommen. Aliena fühlte sich noch nicht imstande, ihm entgegenzutreten. Unvermittelt überfiel sie wieder die unerträgliche, entsetzliche Schande, die er ihr angetan hatte, mit all ihren grauenvollen Einzelheiten.

Richard sagte drängend: »Nun mach schon, Allie!« Sein Pferd war mittlerweile nervös und ungeduldig geworden, und er hatte alle Hände voll zu tun, es zu beruhigen. Ein paar Meilen in gestrecktem Galopp würden es ermüden und fügsamer machen. Es wieherte noch einmal und tänzelte seitwärts.

Endlich hatte Aliena den Knoten gelöst. Sie war versucht, das Seil einfach liegenzulassen, doch dann hätte sie den Schecken nicht wieder anbinden können; also rollte sie das Seil hastig und unordentlich auf und befestigte es am Sattelriemen. Eigentlich hätte sie die Steigbügel richten müssen. Sie waren auf die Größe von Williams Reitknecht eingestellt, der sie um einiges überragte, und hingen deshalb viel zu tief für sie. Aber wenn sie sich bloß vorstellte, wie William die Treppe herunterrannte, den Saal durchquerte und ins Freie trat ...

»Lange kann ich dieses Pferd nicht mehr halten«, ließ Richard sich, vor Anstrengung keuchend, vernehmen.

Aliena war nicht weniger nervös als das Schlachtroß. Sie schwang sich auf den Hengst. Kaum war sie aufgesessen, tat ihr inwendig alles weh, und sie konnte sich nur mit größter Mühe im Sattel halten. Richard lenkte sein Tier zum Tor, und Alienas Pferd folgte ihm ohne jegliches Zutun von ihrer Seite. Die Steigbügel waren, wie erwartet, außer Reichweite, und sie mußte sich mit den Knien Halt verschaffen. Während sie sich langsam in Bewegung setzten, hörten sie plötzlich Rufe von irgendwo hinter sich. »Oh, nein!« stöhnte sie laut. Sie sah, wie Richard sein Pferd mit den Hacken antrieb. Das massige Tier fiel in leichten Trab. Der Schecke tat es ihm nach, und Aliena nahm dankbar wahr, daß es in allem dem Schlachtroß folgte, denn sie selbst war nicht in der Verfassung, das Tier zu beherrschen. Richard versetzte seinem Roß einen weiteren Tritt, und es beschleunigte seinen Schritt, als sie den Torbogen des Wachhauses passierten. Aliena hörte wiederum einen Ruf, und er klang, als hätten die Verfolger aufgeschlossen. Sie warf einen Blick über die Schulter und sah William mit seinem Reitknecht durch den Burghof hinter ihnen herrennen.

Richards unruhiges Pferd senkte, sobald es die offenen Felder vor sich sah, den Kopf und schlug einen Galopp an. Sie donnerten über die hölzerne Zugbrücke. Aliena spürte einen Druck an ihrem Oberschenkel und sah aus den Augenwinkeln eine Männerhand nach ihren Sattelgurten greifen, doch im Nu war sie wieder verschwunden. Sie waren entkommen! Eine Welle der Erleichterung überflutete sie, doch dann stellte sich der Schmerz wieder ein. Während ihr Pferd querfeldein galoppierte, fühlte sie sich innerlich wie gepfählt – so wie tags zuvor, als der Dreckskerl William in sie eingedrungen war; außerdem spürte sie etwas Warmes ihren Oberschenkel herabrinnen. Sie ließ die Zügel schießen und kämpfte mit geschlossenen Augen gegen den Schmerz. Doch das Entsetzen der vergangenen Nacht ließ sie nicht los und malte sich hinter ihren geschlossenen Augenlidern ab. Und als sie über das Feld setzten, skandierte sie im Takt mit den Hufschlägen: »Ich will nicht dran denken – will nicht dran denken – an nichts – an nichts – an nichts.«

Das Pferd schwenkte nach rechts, und Aliena spürte, daß es leicht bergauf ging. Sie öffnete die Augen und sah, daß Richard von dem schlammigen Pfad abgebogen war und den längeren Weg in die Wälder eingeschlagen hatte. Vermutlich wollte er ganz sichergehen, daß das Schlachtroß auch wirklich müde und folgsam war, bevor sie eine langsamere Gangart anschlugen. Beide Tiere würden sich nach einem harten Ritt einfacher handhaben lassen. Es dauerte nicht lange, und Alienas Pferd zeigte Ermüdungserscheinungen. Sie setzte sich im Sattel auf. Der Schecke kanterte, wechselte in einen leichten Trab und verfiel schließlich in Trott. Richards Pferd verfügte über mehr Ausdauer und gewann schnell an Vorsprung.

Aliena drehte sich um und blickte über die Felder. Die Burg lag nun eine Meile hinter ihnen, und sie war nicht ganz sicher, ob sie wirklich zwei Gestalten wahrnahm, die auf der Zugbrücke standen und ihnen nachsahen. Vielleicht war es nur Einbildung. Denen steht ein langer Fußmarsch bevor, ehe sie Ersatzpferde auftreiben können, dachte Aliena. Vorerst fühlte sie sich in Sicherheit.

Ihre Hände und Füße prickelten und wurden langsam warm. Die Hitze des Pferdeleibes stieg wie Feuer auf und hüllte sie in einen wärmenden Kokon. Richard zügelte endlich sein Roß, machte kehrt und gesellte sich zu ihr. Sein Pferd ging nun langsam und schnaubte heftig, als sie in den Schatten der ersten Bäume bogen. Die Geschwister kannten diesen Wald in- und auswendig, denn sie hatten den größten Teil ihres Lebens hier verbracht.

»Wo wollen wir hin?« fragte Richard.

Aliena runzelte die Stirn. Ja, wohin wollten sie eigentlich? Und was sollten sie tun? Sie hatten nichts zu essen und zu trinken, sie hatten nicht einmal Geld. Und sie, Aliena, hatte nichts außer dem Umhang, den sie trug – kein Unterkleid, kein Hemd, weder einen Hut noch Schuhe. Sie wollte für ihren Bruder sorgen – aber wie?

Plötzlich erkannte sie, daß sie in den vergangenen Monaten in einer Scheinwelt gelebt hatte. Irgendwo im Hinterkopf hatte sie gewußt, daß es mit dem gewohnten Leben ein für allemal vorbei war, aber sie hatte sich geweigert, der Realität ins Auge zu sehen. William Hamleigh hatte sie wachgerüttelt. Sie hatte nicht den geringsten Zweifel daran, daß seine Geschichte der Wahrheit entsprach: König Stephan hatte Percy Hamleigh zum Grafen von Shiring ernannt. Aber vielleicht war das nicht alles. Vielleicht hatte der König Vorsorge für sie und Richard getroffen. Wenn nicht, dann hätte er sie treffen müssen, und sie würden ein Bittgesuch an ihn stellen. Wie dem auch immer sei, sie mußten nach Winchester. Dort konnten sie zumindest herausfinden, was ihrem Vater zugestoßen war.

Plötzlich dachte sie: Oh, Vater, wann nahm das Unglück seinen Lauf?

Seit dem Tod ihrer Mutter hatte er sich ganz besonders um sie gekümmert. Sie wußte, daß er ihr mehr Aufmerksamkeit schenkte als andere Väter ihren Töchtern. Es quälte ihn, daß er nicht wieder geheiratet hatte, damit sie eine neue Mutter bekam; aber er hatte ihr erklärt, die Erinnerung an seine verstorbene Frau mache ihn glücklicher, als eine neue Ehe das könne. Und Aliena hatte nie den Wunsch nach einer Ersatzmutter verspürt. Ihr Vater hatte sich um sie gekümmert, sie hatte sich um Richard gekümmert, und keiner von ihnen hatte darunter gelitten.

Diese Zeiten waren unwiederbringlich vorbei.

»Wo wollen wir hin?« fragte Richard noch einmal.

»Nach Winchester«, antwortete sie. »Wir werden den König aufsuchen.«

Richard war sofort Feuer und Flamme. »Ja! Und wenn wir erst berichten, was William und sein Reitknecht vorige Nacht getan haben, dann wird der König gewiß –«

Heftige, unbändige Wut flammte in Aliena auf.

»Halt den Mund!« schrie sie. Die Pferde scheuten. Unbeherrscht riß sie an den Zügeln. »Kein einziges Wort darüber!« Sie kochte vor Zorn und brachte die Worte kaum über die Lippen. »Wir werden niemandem davon erzählen – niemandem! Niemals! Nie und nimmer!«

Die Satteltaschen des Reitknechts enthielten ein großes Stück Hartkäse, ein paar Schluck Wein in einer Lederflasche, einen Feuerstein und etwas trockenes Holz sowie ein oder zwei Pfund Mischgetreide, von dem Aliena annahm, es sei für die Pferde bestimmt. Gegen Mittag verzehrten die Geschwister den Käse und tranken den Wein, während die Pferde das spärliche Gras fraßen, an immergrünem Gesträuch knabberten und aus einem klaren Bach tranken. Alienas Blutfluß hatte aufgehört, und ihr Unterleib fühlte sich wie betäubt an.

Unterwegs waren sie anderen Reisenden begegnet, aber Aliena hatte Richard eingeschärft, mit niemandem zu reden. In den Augen eines flüchtigen Beobachters mochten sie wie ein imposantes Paar wirken, besonders Richard mit seinem Schwert auf dem riesigen Pferd; ein kurzer Wortwechsel hätte sie jedoch alsbald als zwei schutzlose Kinder bloßgestellt und sie unter Umständen in Gefahr gebracht. Deswegen machten sie einen großen Bogen um andere Menschen.

Sobald es dunkler wurde, sahen sie sich nach einem geeigneten Rastplatz für die Nacht um. Etwa hundert Meter neben der Straße fanden sie eine Lichtung am Ufer eines Baches.

Aliena verfütterte ein wenig Korn an die Pferde, während Richard Feuer machte. Ohne Kochgeschirr konnte sie noch nicht einmal Getreideschleim für sich kochen. Falls es ihnen nicht gelang, ein paar Eßkastanien zum Rösten zu finden, würden sie die Körner roh kauen müssen.

Während Aliena noch darüber nachdachte und Richard außer Sichtweite Feuerholz zusammenklaubte, wurde sie von einer tiefen, aus unmittelbarer Nähe kommenden Stimme aufgeschreckt. »Na, wen haben wir denn da, meine Kleine?«

Sie schrie auf. Das Pferd machte erschrocken einen Satz nach hinten. Aliena drehte sich um und erblickte einen schmutzigen, bärtigen Mann, von Kopf bis Fuß in braunes Leder gekleidet. »Haltet Euch von mir fern!« kreischte sie.

»Nur keine Angst«, sagte er.

Aus dem Augenwinkel nahm sie wahr, daß Richard mit Holz beladen hinter dem Fremden auf die Lichtung trat. Er blieb still stehen und beobachtete sie beide. Zieh dein Schwert! dachte Aliena, aber er wirkte zu ängstlich und unsicher, um irgend etwas zu unternehmen. Sie trat einen Schritt zurück und brachte das Pferd zwischen sich und den Fremden. »Wir haben kein Geld«, sagte sie. »Wir haben überhaupt nichts.«

»Ich bin der Jagdpfleger hier«, sagte er.

Aliena brach vor Erleichterung fast in die Knie. Ein Jagdpfleger stand in den Diensten des Königs und wurde dafür bezahlt, den Jagd- und Forstgesetzen Geltung zu verschaffen. »Warum hast du das nicht gleich gesagt, du dummer Kerl?« sagte sie, verärgert über ihre eigene Angst. »Ich hielt dich schon für einen Wegelagerer!«

Er schien überrascht und sogar beleidigt, als habe sie etwas Unhöf- liches gesagt, erwiderte jedoch lediglich: »Ihr seid dann wohl eine Dame von Stand.«

»Ich bin die Tochter des Grafen von Shiring.«

»Und der Knabe wird sein Sohn sein«, sagte der Jagdpfleger, ob- wohl er Richard gar nicht gesehen haben konnte.

Richard kam näher und ließ das Holz fallen. »Stimmt«, sagte er. »Wie heißt du?«

»Brian. Habt Ihr vor, die Nacht hier zu verbringen?«

»Ja.«

»Ganz allein?«

»Ja.« Aliena war klar, daß er sich fragen mußte, warum sie ohne Begleitung unterwegs waren, wollte sich aber nicht dazu äußern.

»Und Ihr sagt, Ihr habt kein Geld.«

Aliena blickte ihn stirnrunzelnd an. »Du zweifelst an meinen Worten?«

»O nein. Mir ist klar, daß Ihr von Adel seid. Das erkenne ich an Eurem Gebaren.« Schwang eine Andeutung von Ironie in seiner Stimme mit? »Falls Ihr allein und mittellos seid, würdet Ihr es viel- leicht vorziehen, die Nacht in meinem Haus zu verbringen. Es ist nicht weit von hier.«

Aliena hatte nicht die Absicht, sich diesem rauhen Gesellen anzu- vertrauen. Sie wollte das Angebot schon ablehnen, als er wieder das Wort ergriff.

»Meine Frau wird Euch mit Freuden bewirten. Außerdem habe ich ein warmes Nebengebäude, wo Ihr schlafen könnt, falls Ihr lieber allein seid.«

Die Erwähnung der Frau gab den Ausschlag. Die Gastfreundschaft einer achtbaren Familie sollten sie unbedenklich annehmen können. Doch Aliena zögerte immer noch. Dann stellte sie sich ein Kaminfeuer vor, eine Schale heiße Suppe, einen Becher Wein und ein Lager aus Stroh mit einem Dach über dem Kopf. »Wir wären dir sehr dankbar«, sagte sie. »Geben können wir dir nichts – ich habe die Wahrheit gesagt, wir haben kein Geld –, aber eines Tages kommen wir zurück und zeigen uns erkenntlich.«

»Das genügt«, sagte der Forstaufseher. Er ging zum Feuer und trat es aus.

Aliena und Richard schwangen sich auf ihre gesattelten Pferde. Der Jagdpfleger trat hinzu und sagte: »Gebt mir die Zügel.« Aliena war nicht sicher, was er vorhatte, gab ihm aber die Zügel, und Richard tat es ihr nach. Der Mann machte sich auf den Weg durch den Wald und führte die beiden Pferde. Aliena hätte lieber die Zügel selbst in der Hand behalten, aber sie ließ ihn gewähren.

Der Weg war weiter, als er gesagt hatte. Es war bereits dunkel und sie hatten drei oder vier Meilen zurückgelegt, bevor sie einen Feldrain erreichten, an dessen Rand ein kleines strohgedecktes Holzhaus stand. Durch die Fensterläden drangen Licht und Kochdünste, und Aliena stieg dankbar vom Pferd.

Die Frau des Jagdpflegers hatte die Pferde gehört und trat an die Tür. Der Mann sagte zu ihr: »Ein junger Lord und eine Lady, allein im Wald. Gib ihnen etwas zu trinken.« Er wandte sich an Aliena. »Geht schon hinein. Ich kümmere mich um die Pferde.«

Aliena behagte sein gebieterischer Tonfall nicht – sie war es gewohnt, selbst die Befehle zu geben –, aber sie hatte nicht das geringste Verlangen danach, ihr Pferd abzusatteln. Sie trat ein, und Richard folgte ihr. Das Haus war voller Rauch und dumpfer Gerüche, aber warm. In einer Ecke war eine Kuh angebunden. Aliena war froh, daß der Mann das Nebengebäude erwähnt hatte: Sie hatte noch nie mit Vieh in einem Raum geschlafen. Auf dem Feuer blubberte ein Topf. Sie setzten sich auf eine Bank, und die Frau reichte beiden eine Schale Suppe, die nach Wild schmeckte. Als die Frau Richards Gesicht im Licht sah, erschrak sie. »Was ist Euch zugestoßen?« fragte sie.

Richard setzte zu einer Antwort an, aber Aliena kam ihm zuvor.

»Uns sind etliche Mißgeschicke widerfahren«, sagte sie. »Wir sind auf dem Weg zum König.«

»Ich verstehe«, sagte die Frau. Sie war klein, hatte einen bräunlichen Teint und machte den Eindruck, als sei sie ständig auf der Hut. Sie stellte keine weiteren Fragen.

Aliena aß ihre Suppe auf und wollte mehr. Sie hielt der Frau die Schale hin, doch die sah weg. Aliena war verwirrt. Wußte die Frau nicht, was sie wollte? Oder hatte sie nicht mehr? Aliena wollte eben den Mund aufmachen, um sie anzufahren, als der Jagdpfleger eintrat.

»Ich zeige Euch die Scheune, in der Ihr schlafen könnt«, sagte er. Er nahm eine Laterne von einem Haken neben der Tür. »Kommt mit.«

Aliena und Richard erhoben sich. Aliena sagte zu der Frau: »Eine dringende Bitte habe ich noch. Kannst du mir ein altes Gewand geben? Ich habe nichts an unter diesem Umhang.«

Die Frau wirkte aus irgendeinem Grund ungehalten. »Ich schau' mal nach, was ich finden kann«, murmelte sie.

Aliena ging zur Tür. Der Jagdpfleger sah sie merkwürdig an, starrte auf ihren Umhang, als ob er, wenn er nur fest genug stierte, durch das Tuch hindurchsehen könnte. »Zeig uns den Weg!« fuhr sie ihn an. Er drehte sich um und verließ das Haus.

Er führte sie um das Haus herum und quer durch einen Gemüsegarten. Das unstete Licht der Laterne ließ eine Holzhütte erkennen, eher einen Schuppen denn eine Scheune. Er öffnete die Tür, und sie schlug gegen eine Regentonne, in der das Wasser aus der Dachrinne aufgefangen wurde. »Seht es Euch an«, sagte er. »Schaut, ob es Euch behagt.«

Richard ging zuerst hinein. »Bring die Laterne, Allie«, sagte er. Aliena drehte sich um und wollte dem Jagdpfleger die Laterne abnehmen. Im gleichen Augenblick gab er ihr einen kräftigen Stoß. Sie stürzte durch die offene Tür, prallte mit ihrem Bruder zusammen, und beide landeten kopfüber auf dem Boden. Die Tür schlug zu, und es wurde dunkel. Von draußen kam ein merkwürdiges Geräusch herein, als ob ein schwerer Gegenstand vor die Tür geschoben wurde.

Aliena rang um Fassung.

»Was war das, Allie?« rief Richard.

Sie setzte sich auf. War der Mann wirklich Jagdaufseher oder doch ein Wegelagerer? Ein Gesetzloser konnte er nicht sein – dazu wirkte sein Haus zu gediegen. Aber wenn er tatsächlich Jagdpfleger war – warum hatte er sie dann eingesperrt? Hatten sie gegen das Gesetz verstoßen? Hatte er erraten, daß die Pferde nicht ihnen gehörten? Oder hegte er unehrliche Absichten?

»Allie, warum hat er das getan?« fragte Richard.

»Ich weiß es nicht«, sagte sie matt. Sie hatte nicht mehr die Kraft, sich aufzuregen oder wütend zu werden. Sie stand auf und rüttelte an der Tür. Sie gab keinen Spaltbreit nach. Vermutlich hatte der Jagdpfleger die Regentonne von außen dagegengeschoben. In der Dunkelheit tastete Aliena die Wände ab. Sogar die untere Dachschräge konnte sie erfühlen. Der Schuppen bestand aus fugenlos zusammengesetzten Brettern und war mit großer Sorgfalt gebaut worden. Dies war das Verlies des Jagdaufsehers, in dem er Rechtsbrecher einsperrte, bevor sie dem Vogt vorgeführt wurden. »Hier kommen wir nicht raus«, sagte Aliena.

Sie setzte sich wieder. Der Boden war trocken und mit Stroh bedeckt.

»Wir sitzen hier fest, bis er uns freiläßt«, sagte sie entmutigt. Richard setzte sich neben sie. Nach einer Weile legten sie sich Rücken an Rücken nieder. Aliena glaubte, sie wäre viel zu zerschlagen, verängstigt und angespannt, um Schlaf zu finden. Doch außerdem war sie noch vollkommen erschöpft, und so versank sie schon nach wenigen Augenblicken in einen heilsamen Schlummer.

Sie erwachte erst, als die Tür geöffnet wurde und das Tageslicht auf ihr Gesicht fiel. Erschrocken setzte sie sich auf; sie wußte nicht, wo sie sich befand, noch, warum sie auf dem harten Boden schlief. Doch dann fiel ihr alles wieder ein, und sie bekam es mit der Angst zu tun: Was hatte der Jagdaufseher mit ihnen vor? Aber nicht er trat ein, sondern seine kleine, braunhäutige Frau; und obwohl ihre Miene ebenso verschlossen und unzugänglich war wie am Abend zuvor, so brachte sie ihnen doch einen Kanten Brot und zwei Becher.

Richard setzte sich ebenfalls auf. Argwöhnisch beobachteten sie die Frau. Sie sagte nichts, reichte beiden einen Becher, brach das Brot und gab es Aliena und Richard. Plötzlich merkte Aliena, wie unglaublich hungrig sie war. Sie tunkte ihr Brot in das Bier und begann zu essen.

Die Frau blieb an der Tür und beobachtete die Geschwister, wie sie Brot und Bier verzehrten. Dann reichte sie Aliena ein Stück zusammengefaltetes, verschlissenes und vergilbtes Linnen: Es war ein altes Kleid.

Die Frau sagte: »Zieht das an und macht Euch aus dem Staub.«

Aliena verwirrte die Gleichzeitigkeit von Güte und harten Worten, aber sie zögerte nicht, die Gabe anzunehmen. Sie drehte sich um, ließ ihren Umhang fallen, zog flink das Gewand über den Kopf und legte den Umhang wieder an.

Sie fühlte sich gleich besser.

Die Frau reichte ihr ein Paar abgetragene und viel zu große Holzschuhe.

Aliena sagte: »Darin kann ich nicht reiten.«

Die Frau lachte rauh: »Ihr werdet nicht reiten.«

»Wieso nicht?«

»Er hat Euch die Pferde genommen.«

Aliena war zutiefst getroffen. Wie ungerecht: Ihre Pechsträhne wollte einfach nicht abreißen: »Wo hat er sie hingebracht?«

»So was erzählt er mir nicht, aber er wird wohl auf dem Weg nach Shiring sein. Dort wird er die Tiere verkaufen und sich erkundigen, wer Ihr seid und ob aus Euch noch mehr herauszuschlagen ist als der Preis Eures Pferdefleisches.«

»Und warum läßt du uns dann gehen?«

Die Frau musterte Aliena von oben bis unten. »Weil es mir nicht gefiel, wie er Euch ansah, als Ihr ihm sagtet, daß Ihr nackt unter dem Umhang seid. Wahrscheinlich versteht Ihr das erst, wenn Ihr eine verheiratete Frau seid.«

Aliena verstand es durchaus, doch sie verlor kein Wort darüber.

Richard sagte: »Wird er dich denn nicht umbringen, wenn er herausfindet, daß du uns freigelassen hast?«

Sie lächelte zynisch. »Er jagt mir nicht annähernd soviel Angst ein wie anderen. Aber jetzt fort mit Euch.«

Sie verließen den Schuppen. Aliena begriff, daß diese Frau hatte lernen müssen, mit einem brutalen und herzlosen Mann auszukommen. Dennoch hatte sie sich ein Mindestmaß an Anstand und Mitgefühl bewahrt. »Ich danke dir für das Kleid«, sagte sie unbeholfen.

Der Frau lag nichts an ihrem Dank. Sie wies auf einen Pfad und sagte: »Nach Winchester geht's hier lang.«

Die Geschwister schritten von dannen, ohne noch einmal zurückzublicken.

Aliena hatte noch nie Holzschuhe getragen – Menschen ihres Standes trugen nur Lederstiefel oder Sandalen – und fand sie klobig und unbequem. Auf dem kalten Boden waren sie allerdings besser als nichts.

Erst außer Sichtweite des Hauses fragte Richard: »Allie, warum geschehen uns nur so schreckliche Dinge?«

Die Frage machte Aliena ganz niedergeschlagen. Kein Mensch war gut zu ihnen. Kein Mensch scherte sich darum, wenn sie wie Vieh geprügelt und ausgeraubt wurden. Niemand nahm sie in Schutz. Wir sind zu vertrauensselig gewesen, dachte sie. Drei Monate lang hatten sie auf der Burg gelebt, ohne je die Türen zu verschließen. Aliena nahm sich vor, von nun an niemandem mehr über den Weg zu trauen. Nie wieder würde sie jemandem erlauben, die Zügel ihres Pferdes zu ergreifen, und wenn sie noch so grob und unhöflich werden mußte. Nie wieder würde sie jemandem den Rücken zukehren – wie dem Jagdpfleger, der sie in den Schuppen gestoßen hatte. Nie wieder wollte sie die Gastfreundschaft eines Fremden annehmen, nie ihre Türe nachts unverschlossen lassen, sich nie wieder durch Freundlichkeit hinters Licht führen lassen.

»Laß uns schneller gehen«, sagte sie zu Richard. »Vielleicht können wir Winchester noch vor Anbruch der Dunkelheit erreichen.«

Sie folgten dem Pfad bis zu der Lichtung, auf der sie dem Forstaufseher begegnet waren, und fanden die Stelle, wo sie Feuer gemacht hatten. Von hier aus war die Straße nach Winchester leicht zu finden; sie waren mehrmals dort gewesen und kannten den Weg. Sobald sie den Weg erreicht hatten, kamen sie schneller voran. Der nach dem Sturm vor zwei Tagen einsetzende Frost hatte den lehmigen Boden bretthart gefroren.

Richards Gesicht nahm allmählich wieder normale Züge an. Tags zuvor hatte er sich an einem Bach im Wald mit kaltem Wasser gewaschen, so daß die Blutkrusten weitgehend verschwunden waren. Auf der Wunde an seinem rechten Ohrläppchen hatte sich häßlicher Schorf gebildet. Seine Lippen waren noch immer geschwollen, aber sein Gesicht war nicht mehr so aufgedunsen. Er hatte noch jede Menge blauer Flecken, deren schillernde Farben ihm einen ziemlich furchterregenden Ausdruck verliehen, aber das konnte nichts schaden.

Aliena vermißte die Wärme des Pferdeleibes. Zwar war ihr bei dem anstrengenden Marsch warm geworden, doch Hände und Füße schmerzten vor Kälte. Den ganzen Vormittag über herrschte eisiger Frost, der sich erst gegen Mittag ein wenig milderte. Inzwischen war sie hungrig geworden. Ihr fiel ein, daß sie erst gestern noch geglaubt hatte, es sei ihr völlig gleichgültig, ob sie je wieder ein warmes Dach über dem Kopf oder satt zu essen haben würde. Aber an gestern wollte sie nicht mehr denken.

Jedesmal, wenn sie das Trappeln von Pferdehufen vernahmen oder Leute auch nur von Ferne sahen, stahlen sie sich in den Wald und versteckten sich, bis die Reisenden an ihnen vorbeigezogen waren. Kamen sie an ein Dorf, so hasteten sie eilig hindurch und sprachen mit niemandem ein Wort. Richard hätte gern etwas zu essen erbettelt, doch Aliena erlaubte es nicht.

Gegen Mitte des Nachmittags hatten sie sich ihrem Ziel bis auf wenige Meilen genähert, ohne daß sie von irgend jemand belästigt worden wären. Allmählich gelangte Aliena zu der Überzeugung, daß es wohl doch nicht so schwierig war, jeden Verdruß zu vermeiden – da trat plötzlich ein Mann aus dem Gebüsch und stellte sich ihnen in den Weg.

Es war zu spät, sich zu verstecken, und weit und breit war keine

Menschenseele zu entdecken, die ihnen hätte zu Hilfe kommen können.

»Nicht stehenbleiben«, sagte Aliena zu Richard, aber der Mann blockierte den Weg. Sie mußten anhalten. Aliena sah sich nach einem Fluchtweg um, doch ein Stück hinter ihnen war ein zweiter Mann aus dem Wald getreten und vereitelte jedes Entkommen.

»Wen haben wir denn da?« sagte der Mann vor ihnen mit lauter Stimme. Er war ein fetter Kerl mit rotem Gesicht und einem verdreckten, verfilzten Bart. Er schob einen mächtigen Bauch vor sich her und trug eine schwere Keule bei sich. Das war ganz bestimmt ein Wegelagerer! Es war ihm anzusehen, daß er vor keiner Gewalttat zurückschreckte, und Aliena wurde angst und bange.

»Laß uns in Ruhe«, bat sie flehend. »Wir haben selbst nichts.«

»Da bin ich nicht so sicher«, sagte der Mann. Er tat einen Schritt auf Richard zu. »Das sieht mir ganz nach einem feinen Schwert aus und ist bestimmt ein paar Schilling wert.«

»Es gehört aber mir«, trotzte Richard, doch seine Stimme klang wie die eines verschreckten Kindes.

Es hat keinen Sinn, dachte Aliena. Wir sind einfach machtlos. Ich bin noch nicht einmal erwachsen, und Richard ist noch ein Kind, und jeder kann mit uns umspringen, wie's ihm gerade paßt.

Der Fettwanst hob mit überraschender Behendigkeit seine Keule und holte zum Schlag aus, doch Richard duckte sich flink. Der Hieb, der seinem Kopf galt, traf ihn nur an der Schulter. Aber der Dicke war stark, und Richard ging zu Boden.

Urplötzlich war es mit Alienas Selbstbeherrschung vorbei. Sie war ungerecht behandelt, gemeinstens mißbraucht und obendrein noch ausgeraubt worden, ihr war kalt, und sie hatte Hunger. Ihr kleiner Bruder war vor kaum zwei Tagen schon einmal halbtot geschlagen worden, und nun gab ihr der Anblick des Fettwanstes, der mit der Keule auf ihn losging, den Rest. Sie war wie von Sinnen. Im Nu hatte sie den Dolch aus dem Ärmel gezogen, war auf den Banditen losgegangen und stieß mit dem Messer nach seinem Bauch. »Laß ihn in Ruhe, du Schurke!« schrie sie.

Damit hatte er nicht gerechnet, und sie traf ihn wie ein Blitz aus heiterem Himmel: Vor einem jungen Mädchen, das noch dazu unbewaffnet schien, hatte er sich offenkundig sicher gefühlt. Sein Umhang war bei dem Angriff auf Richard aufgegangen, und er hielt noch immer die Keule in beiden Händen. Die Dolchspitze durchschnitt das wollene Gewand und das leinene Unterhemd und machte erst halt, als sie gegen die gespannte Haut seines Wanstes stieß. Ekel schüttelte Aliena, und sie durchlebte einen Moment blanken Entsetzens bei dem Gedanken, diese Haut zu durchbohren und einem lebendigen Menschen ins Fleisch zu stoßen; aber ihre Furcht gewann die Oberhand, und sie rammte ihm das Messer in die Weichteile. Gleich darauf überfiel sie die Angst, er könne am Leben bleiben und Rache nehmen, deshalb stieß sie den langen Dolch immer tiefer in seine Eingeweide, so tief, bis nur noch das Heft herausragte.

Aus dem furchterregenden, grausamen Mann war mit einemmal ein ängstliches, waidwundes Tier geworden. Er schrie vor Schmerzen, ließ die Keule fallen und starrte auf das Messer hinab, das in ihm steckte. Im selben Moment begriff Aliena: Ihm war vollkommen klar, daß seine Verletzung tödlich war. Entsetzt fuhr sie zurück, als der Wegelagerer taumelte. Dann fiel ihr wieder ein, daß in ihrem Rücken ein zweiter Strauchdieb lauerte. Von Panik ergriffen, er werde sich für den Tod seines Komplizen rächen, griff sie wieder nach dem Messer und zog daran. Der Verwundete hatte sich halb von ihr abgewandt, so daß sie die Waffe seitwärts herausziehen mußte. Dabei spürte sie, wie sie die weichen Eingeweide durchschnitt. Blut spritzte auf ihre Hand. Der Mann schrie wie am Spieß und stürzte zu Boden. Aliena wirbelte herum, das blutige Messer in der Hand, und sah sich dem anderen Mann gegenüber. Im gleichen Augenblick rappelte Richard sich auf und zog sein Schwert.

Der zweite Wegelagerer sah von einem zum anderen, dann auf seinen sterbenden Freund. Dann machte er auf dem Absatz kehrt und rannte in den Wald.

Aliena sah ihm ungläubig nach. Es war kaum zu fassen: Sie hatten ihn tatsächlich in die Flucht geschlagen!

Sie wandte den Blick dem zweiten Mann zu. Er lag flach auf dem Rücken, und aus der großen Stichwunde quollen seine Gedärme. Seine Augen waren weit aufgerissen, und sein Gesicht war von Angst und Pein verzerrt.

Aliena vermochte weder Erleichterung noch Stolz darüber zu empfinden, daß sie sich und ihren Bruder erfolgreich gegen die beiden Schurken verteidigt hatte: Der Anblick des Sterbenden war zu grausig.

Richard kannte solche Vorbehalte nicht. »Du hast ihn erdolcht, Allie!« rief er, zwischen Aufregung und Erleichterung schwankend. »Du hast es ihnen gezeigt!«

Aliena sah ihn an. Es war an der Zeit, daß er seine Lektion lernte. »Töte den hier«, sagte sie.

Richard starrte sie an. »Wie bitte?«

»Töte ihn«, wiederholte sie. »Gib ihm den Gnadenstoß. Mach ihn kalt!«

»Wieso denn ich?«

Sie gab ihrer Stimme bewußt einen harten Klang. »Weil du dich wie ein kleiner Junge aufführst. Aber ich brauche einen Mann. Und weil du mit deinem Schwert nie etwas anderes als imaginäre Kriege ausgefochten hast. Irgendwann mußt du es lernen. Was ist los mit dir? Wovor hast du Angst? Er stirbt sowieso. Er kann dir nichts mehr tun. Los, zieh dein Schwert! Du brauchst die Übung. Töte ihn!«

Richard hielt sein Schwert mit beiden Händen fest und sah unsicher drein. »Wie denn?«

Der Mann brüllte auf.

Aliena schrie Richard an: »Woher soll ich das wissen?! Schlag ihm den Kopf ab, oder stich ihm ins Herz! Egal, wie! Hauptsache, du bringst ihn zum Schweigen!«

Richard hob ratlos sein Schwert und ließ es wieder sinken.

Aliena sagte: »Wenn du es nicht tust, dann lasse ich dich im Stich, das schwöre ich dir bei allem, was mir heilig ist. Eines Nachts werde ich aufstehen und mich davonmachen, und wenn du am nächsten Morgen aufwachst, bin ich nicht mehr bei dir. Dann stehst du mutterseelenallein da. Bring ihn jetzt um, auf der Stelle!«

Wieder hob Richard sein Schwert. Und dann geschah das Unglaubliche: Der Sterbende hörte auf zu schreien und versuchte, sich aufzurappeln. Er rollte sich zur Seite und stützte sich mit dem Ellbogen ab. Richard stieß einen Laut aus, der halb Angstschrei und halb Schlachtruf war, und hieb das Schwert mit aller Macht in den entblößten Hals des Mannes.

Die Waffe war schwer und die Klinge scharf und trennte mehr als die Hälfte des feisten Halses vom Rumpf. Wie eine Fontäne schoß das Blut heraus, und der Kopf fiel grotesk verrenkt zur Seite. Der Körper sackte zu Boden.

Aliena und Richard starrten auf den Toten hinab. In der Winterluft bildeten sich Schwaden über dem warmen Blut. Beide Geschwister waren überwältigt von ihrer Tat. Plötzlich wollte Aliena nur noch weg. Sie fing an zu rennen, und Richard lief ihr nach.

Sie rannte, bis ihr die Puste ausging. Erst da fiel ihr auf, daß sie schluchzte. Langsam ging sie weiter. Diesmal kümmerte es sie nicht mehr, daß Richard sie weinen sah. Es schien ihn ohnehin nicht zu berühren.

Langsam beruhigte sie sich wieder. Ihre Füße taten weh. Sie blieb stehen, zog die Holzschuhe aus, nahm sie in die Hand und ging barfuß weiter. Nach Winchester war es nicht mehr weit.

Nach einer Weile sagte Richard: »Wir sind ganz schön dumm.«

»Wieso?«

»Der Mann da. Wir haben ihn einfach liegengelassen. Wir hätten seine Stiefel nehmen sollen.«

Aliena blieb stehen und starrte ihn entgeistert an.

Er drehte sich nach ihr um und lachte verhalten. »Dagegen ist doch nichts einzuwenden, oder?« meinte er.

Als sie bei Anbruch der Dunkelheit durch das westliche Stadttor von Winchester die High Street betraten, schöpfte Aliena neuen Mut. Draußen im Wald hätten sie ermordet werden können, ohne daß irgendwer davon erfuhr. Natürlich wimmelte es in der Stadt ebenfalls von Dieben und Gaunern, aber wenigstens konnten die ihre Verbrechen nicht dreist am hellichten Tag verüben. In der Stadt gab es Gesetze, und Gesetzesbrecher wurden verbrannt, verstümmelt oder aufgeknüpft.

Sie erinnerte sich, wie sie erst vor ungefähr einem Jahr mit ihrem Vater durch dieselbe Straße gekommen war. Sie waren natürlich zu Pferde gewesen; ihr Vater auf einem übernervösen Kastanienbraunen, sie auf einem wunderschönen grauen Zelter, und die Leute hatten ihnen auf ihrem Ritt durch die breiten Straßen Platz gemacht. Sie besaßen ein Haus im Süden der Stadt und wurden dort bei ihrer Ankunft von acht oder zehn Bediensteten begrüßt. Das Haus war frisch geputzt gewesen, frisches Stroh lag auf allen Böden, und in sämtlichen Kaminen brannte ein Feuer. Aliena hatte jeden Tag die schönsten Kleider getragen: feinstes Leinen, Seide und weiche Wolle in den prächtigsten Farbschattierungen, Stiefel und Gürtel aus Kalbsleder und mit Edelsteinen besetzte Broschen und Armreifen. Sie hatte dafür Sorge zu tragen, daß alle, die dem Grafen ihre Aufwartung machten, angemessen bewirtet wurden: Fleisch und Wein für die Reichen, Brot und Bier für die Ärmeren, ein Lächeln und ein Plätzchen vor dem Kamin für jedermann. Ihr Vater nahm es mit den Pflichten eines Gastgebers peinlich genau, entsprach aber selbst nicht annähernd seinen eigenen Vorstellungen – die meisten fanden ihn kühl und zurückhaltend, wenn nicht gar herablassend. Das machte Aliena wett.

Ihr Vater genoß allseits Respekt und wurde von den höchsten Würdenträgern aufgesucht: dem Bischof, dem Abt, dem Vogt und den Baronen, die bei Hofe verkehrten. Aliena fragte sich, wie viele von ihnen sie jetzt wohl wiedererkennen würden, wie sie barfuß durch den Schlamm und Schmutz der High Street watete, doch der Gedanke daran vermochte ihre Zuversicht nicht zu dämpfen. Das wichtigste war, daß sie ihr Leben wieder in den Griff bekam.

Sie gingen an ihrem Haus vorüber. Es war unbewohnt und verschlossen: Die Hamleighs hatten es wohl noch nicht in Besitz genommen. Aliena fühlte sich einen Augenblick lang versucht, dort einzudringen. Das ist mein Haus! dachte sie. Aber das stimmte natürlich nicht, und die Vorstellung, die Nacht dort zu verbringen, erinnerte sie an die vergangenen Monate auf der Burg, die sie blind gegenüber der Wirklichkeit verbracht hatte. Entschlossen ging sie weiter.

Ein weiterer Vorteil war die Tatsache, daß es in der Stadt ein Kloster gab. Die Mönche stellten jedem Bittsteller einen Schlafplatz zur Verfügung. Heute nacht würden Richard und sie ein Dach über dem Kopf haben, unter dem sie sicher und trocken schlafen konnten.

Sie fand die Kathedrale und betrat den Klosterhof. Zwei Mönche standen hinter einer aufgebockten Tischplatte und verteilten Bier und grobes Brot aus Bohnen und Weizen an mehr als hundert Menschen. Aliena staunte. Es war ihr nicht in den Sinn gekommen, daß eine solche Menge auf die Gastfreundschaft der Mönche angewiesen sein könnte. Richard und sie schlossen sich der Schlange an. Verblüfft stellte sie fest, daß alle Rempeleien und Rangeleien – wie sie gewöhnlich auftraten, wenn eine freie Mahlzeit ausgeteilt wurde – unterblieben. Das gesittete Verhalten der vielen Menschen war offenbar allein auf den Mönch zurückzuführen, der ruhig und bestimmt seine Anweisungen erteilte.

Sie bekamen ihr Abendessen und nahmen es mit in die Herberge hinüber, ein großer, scheunenartiger Holzbau ohne jegliches Mobiliar, der nur schwach von Binsenlichtern erleuchtet wurde und stark nach den Ausdünstungen eng zusammengepferchter Menschen roch. Zum Essen setzten sie sich auf den Boden, der gut und gerne eine frische Auslage mit Stroh vertragen hätte. Aliena überlegte, ob sie sich den Mönchen gegenüber zu erkennen geben sollte. Der Abt würde sich vielleicht an sie erinnern. In einem Kloster dieser Größe gab es bestimmt ein besseres Gästequartier für Besucher höherer Stände. Dennoch verspürte sie eine gewisse Abneigung gegen dieses Vorhaben, sei es, daß sie Angst davor hatte, sich der Lächerlichkeit preiszugeben, sei es, daß sie davor zurückschreckte, sich erneut Fremden anzuvertrauen; und wiewohl sie von einem Abt nichts zu befürchten hatte, zog sie es doch vor, anonym und unbemerkt zu bleiben.

Die anderen Gäste waren in der Mehrzahl Pilger, darunter wenige Handwerker, erkennbar an ihren mitgeführten Werkzeugen, sowie mehrere Hausierer – Männer, die über die Dörfer zogen und Dinge verkauften, die die Bauern selbst nicht herstellen konnten: Nadeln und Messer, Kochtöpfe und Gewürze. Einige von ihnen waren mit Kind und Kegel unterwegs. Die Kinder waren laut und aufgeregt, rannten hin und her, stritten sich und fielen auf die Nase. Ab und zu gab es einen Zusammenstoß mit einem Erwachsenen, eine Maulschelle und lautes Wehgeschrei. Ein paar Kinder waren noch nicht ganz stubenrein, und Aliena beobachtete, wie sie einfach ins Stroh auf den Boden pinkelten. In einem Haus, in dem das Vieh im selben Raum wie seine Besitzer schlief, fiel das wahrscheinlich nicht weiter ins Gewicht, aber in einem überbelegten Schlafsaal wie diesem war es ziemlich ekelerregend. Immerhin mußten sie später alle auf diesem Stroh schlafen.

Ein seltsames Gefühl beschlich Aliena, als sähen ihr alle Leute an, daß sie ihre Unschuld verloren hatte. Das war natürlich lächerlich, aber sie konnte sich nicht davon freimachen. Wiederholt überprüfte sie, ob sie wieder blutete. Sie blutete nicht. Doch jedesmal, wenn sie sich umdrehte, fiel ihr erneut irgendein Fremder ins Auge, der sie unverwandt und durchdringend anstarrte. Sobald sich ihre Blicke kreuzten, blickte ihr Gegenüber weg, doch wenig später ertappte sie schon wieder einen anderen bei seiner unangenehmen Musterung. Sie redete sich ein, sie sei albern, niemand starre sie an, und diese Leute sähen sich nur neugierig in dem vollen Raum um. Es gab ohnehin nichts Auffälliges an ihr zu entdecken: Sie war ebenso schmutzig, schlecht angezogen und müde wie alle anderen auch. Trotzdem wollte das merkwürdige Gefühl nicht weichen, so daß sie mit der Zeit wider ihren Willen immer wütender wurde. Besonders ein Mann fiel ihr auf, ein Pilger mittleren Alters in Begleitung einer vielköpfigen Familie. Schließlich riß ihr der Geduldsfaden, und sie fuhr ihn an: »Was glotzt du so? Hör sofort auf, mich anzustarren!« Er schien verlegen und wandte seine Augen ab, ohne etwas zu erwidern.

Richard sagte ruhig: »Warum hast du das getan, Allie?«

Sie hieß ihn den Mund zu halten, und er verstummte.

Bald nach dem Abendessen machten die Mönche die Runde und sammelten die Binsenlichter ein. Ihnen lag daran, daß die Gäste früh schlafen gingen: Das hielt sie des Nachts von den Bierstuben und Bordellen fern und erleichterte es am nächsten Morgen, die Besucher so früh wie möglich loszuwerden. Einige alleinstehende Männer verließen den Raum, sobald die Lichter verschwunden waren, und begaben sich zweifellos auf die Suche nach fleischlichen Genüssen, doch die meisten rollten sich auf ihren Umhängen auf dem Boden zusammen.

Aliena hatte seit Jahren nicht mehr in einem solchen Gemach geschlafen. Als Kind hatte sie die Leute unten im Saal beneidet, die Seite an Seite in einem verräucherten und nach Essensdünsten riechenden Raum mit den Wachhunden vor dem langsam erlöschenden Feuer lagen. Dieses Bild hatte ihr ein gewisses Zusammengehörigkeitsgefühl vermittelt, das in den weitläufigen Räumen ihrer adligen Familie nicht zu finden war. Damals war sie manchmal aus ihrem eigenen Bett geschlüpft und die Treppe heruntergeschlichen, um sich neben einer ihrer Lieblingsmägde, Madge Laundry oder Old Joan, schlafen zu legen.

Die Gerüche ihrer Kindheit in der Nase, schlief Aliena ein. Sie träumte von ihrer Mutter. Gewöhnlich fiel es ihr schwer, sich an ihre Mutter zu erinnern, aber diesmal sah sie Mamas Gesicht überraschend klar vor sich: die feinen Züge, das scheue Lächeln, die leichte Knochenstruktur, den ängstlichen Blick. Sie sah ihre Mutter gehen, sah, wie sie sich leicht zur Seite neigte und den anderen Arm, wie um das Gleichgewicht nicht zu verlieren, leicht abgewinkelt hielt, als suche sie Halt an der Mauer. Sie hörte ihre Mutter lachen mit dieser unerwartet vollen und sehr tiefen Altstimme, jederzeit bereit, in Gesang oder Gelächter auszubrechen, und doch immer zu ängstlich dazu. In diesem Traum verstand Aliena zum erstenmal, was ihr im Wachen nie klar geworden war: Ihr Vater hatte ihre Mutter dermaßen eingeschüchtert, ihre Lebensfreude so vollkommen unterdrückt, daß sie, wie eine Blume, der man das Wasser verweigert, verwelken und verdorren mußte. Aliena war, als habe sie das alles seit jeher gewußt, so vertraut kam es ihr vor. Neu und erschreckend allerdings war, daß sie selbst schwanger war. Ihre Mutter schien sich darüber zu freuen. Sie hielten sich in einem Schlafgemach auf. Alienas Bauch war derart angeschwollen, daß sie nicht anders als in der uralten Pose aller werdenden Mütter sitzen konnte, die Beine leicht geöffnet, die Hände still über dem gewölbten Bauch gefaltet. Plötzlich stürzte William Hamleigh ins Zimmer, einen langen Dolch in der Hand, und Aliena wußte sofort, daß er ihr den Bauch aufschlitzen würde – genauso, wie sie es mit dem feisten Räuber im Wald gemacht hatte. Ihre Entsetzensschreie waren so laut, daß sie aufrecht sitzend davon erwachte. Erst dann wurde ihr klar, daß William weit fort war, daß sie nicht wirklich geschrien, sondern all das sich nur in ihrem Kopf abgespielt hatte.

Danach lag sie wach und fragte sich, ob sie vielleicht tatsächlich schwanger war.

Dieser Gedanke war ihr nie zuvor gekommen, und sie erschrak zu Tode darüber. Allein die Vorstellung, von William Hamleigh ein Kind zu bekommen! Abscheulich! Aber vielleicht war es gar nicht von ihm, sondern von seinem Reitknecht? Das ließ sich womöglich nie genau feststellen. Aber wie sollte sie dieses Kind überhaupt lieben können? Jedesmal, wenn ich es ansehe, dachte sie, wird es mich an jene grauenvolle Nacht erinnern. Sie schwor sich, das Kind heimlich zur Welt zu bringen, es gleich nach der Geburt auszusetzen und erfrieren zu lassen – wie eine Bäuerin, die schon zu viele Kinder hatte. Erst als sie sich zu diesem Entschluß durchgerungen hatte, wurde sie wieder vom Schlaf übermannt.

Kaum war der Tag angebrochen, da kamen auch schon die Mönche mit dem Frühstück. Von den anderen Gästen waren die meisten wach, denn sie waren früh schlafen gegangen. Aliena hingegen, die den Schlaf der Erschöpfung schlief, wurde erst durch ihren Lärm geweckt.

Das Frühstück bestand aus warmer, gesalzener Hafergrütze, die von Aliena und Richard heißhungrig verschlungen wurde. Am liebsten hätten sie noch etwas Brot dazu gegessen. Aliena überlegte sich derweilen, was sie König Stephan sagen wollte. Höchstwahrscheinlich war ihm einfach entfallen, daß der Graf von Shiring zwei Kinder hatte. Sobald sie vor ihm erschienen und ihn daran erinnerten, würde er ohne weiteres Zögern für sie sorgen. Gesetzt den Fall jedoch, er mußte überredet werden, legte sich Aliena die passenden Worte zurecht. Sie beschloß, nicht auf der Unschuld ihres Vaters zu beharren, denn das ließe den Schluß zu, daß der König ein falsches Urteil gesprochen hätte, und das würde er als Beleidigung betrachten. Außerdem würde sie nicht dagegen protestieren, daß Percy Hamleigh zum Grafen ernannt worden war. Männer mit Macht und Einfluß konnten nichts weniger vertragen, als wenn bereits gefällte Entscheidungen im nachhinein in Frage gestellt wurden. »Entschieden ist entschieden«, pflegte ihr Vater zu sagen, »ob nun zum Guten oder zum Schlechten.« Nein, sie wollte den König schlicht darauf hinweisen, daß sie und ihr Bruder unschuldig waren, und ihn bitten, ihnen ein Rittergut zu überlassen, damit sie ein bescheidenes Auskommen hatten und Richard sich auf seine Laufbahn als Ritter des Königs vorbereiten konnte. Ein kleines Gut ermöglichte ihr außerdem, sich um ihren Vater zu kümmern, sobald es dem König gefiel, ihn freizulassen. Vater war keine Gefahr mehr. Weder besaß er einen Titel, noch Gefolgsleute oder Vermögen. Sie mußte dem König ins Gedächtnis rufen, daß ihr Vater dem alten König Heinrich, Stephans Onkel, stets treue Dienste geleistet hatte. Sie wollte sich nicht aufdrängen, aber sie wollte ihr Anliegen mit der gebotenen Demut eindringlich, klar und einfach vorbringen.

Nach dem Frühstück fragte sie einen der Mönche, wo sie sich das Gesicht waschen könne. Er schien überrascht: Diese Frage wurde ihm offensichtlich höchst selten gestellt. Doch da Mönche gemeinhin sehr reinlich waren, zeigte er ihr bereitwillig eine offene Wasserleitung, aus der klares, kaltes Wasser auf das Gelände der Priorei geleitet wurde. Allerdings ermahnte er sie, sich nicht, wie er sich ausdrückte, ›unzüchtig‹ zu waschen, damit keiner der Brüder sie zufällig sehen und seine Seele besudeln konnte. Mönche, dachte Aliena, tun viel Gutes, aber ihre Einstellung ist doch oftmals sehr lebensfremd.

Nachdem sie sich den Straßenstaub von den Gesichtern gewaschen hatten, verließen sie das Kloster und gingen die High Street hinauf zum Schloß, das sich neben dem Westtor der Stadt befand. Aliena hoffte, sich durch ihr frühes Erscheinen bei demjenigen, der für die Vorlassung von Bittstellern zuständig war, einschmeicheln zu können, so daß sie nicht in der Menge der später vorsprechenden, hochwichtigen Persönlichkeiten in Vergessenheit geriet. Doch dann war es innerhalb der Schloßmauern sehr viel ruhiger, als sie angenommen hatte. War König Stephan etwa schon so lange hier, daß ihn kaum jemand mehr aufsuchte? Sie hatte keine Ahnung, wann er eingetroffen war. Der König, glaubte sie, sei normalerweise die ganze Fastenzeit hindurch in Winchester, doch in der Zeit, in der sie mit Richard und Matthew allein und ohne Priester auf der Burg gelebt hatte, war ihr jegliches Zeitgefühl abhanden gekommen, so daß sie nun nicht hätte sagen können, wann die Fastenzeit tatsächlich begonnen hatte.

Am Fuß der Treppe, die zum Wohnturm hinaufführte, stand ein bulliger, graubärtiger Wachposten. Aliena machte Anstalten, an ihm vorbeizugehen, wie sie es an der Seite ihres Vaters gewohnt gewesen, doch der Posten versperrte ihr mit gesenkter Lanze den Weg. Sie schaute ihn gebieterisch an und sagte: »Ja?«

»Und wer bist du, daß du meinst, hier einfach durchspazieren zu können, mein Kind?« sagte der Wachposten.

Sinkenden Mutes erkannte Aliena, daß sie es mit jener Sorte

Mensch zu tun hatte, die ihre Genugtuung allein daraus zieht, daß sie andere Menschen von ihren Zielen abhalten kann.

»Wir wollen dem König ein Bittgesuch unterbreiten«, sagte sie kühl. »Laß uns also durch.«

»Du?« erwiderte der Posten verächtlich. »Mit Holzschuhen an den Füßen? Selbst meine Frau würde sich damit schämen. Mach, daß du wegkommst.«

»Geh mir aus dem Weg, Wachmann«, sagte Aliena. »Jeder Bürger hat das Recht, ein Gesuch an den König zu richten.«

»Doch die ärmeren Ausgaben werden, wenn sie töricht genug sind, davon Gebrauch machen zu wollen, im allgemeinen —«

»Wir gehören aber nicht zu den ärmeren Ausgaben!« fauchte Aliena. »Ich bin die Tochter des Grafen von Shiring, und mein Bruder ist sein Sohn. Laß uns also durch, sonst wirst du den Rest deiner Tage in einem Verlies dahinvegetieren!«

Der Posten blickte nicht mehr ganz so überheblich drein, sagte aber reichlich glatt: »Du kannst kein Gesuch an den König richten, weil er gar nicht hier ist. Er ist in Westminster. Und wenn du bist, wer du vorgibst zu sein, dann hättest du das selber wissen müssen.«

Aliena war wie vor den Kopf geschlagen. »Aber wieso ist er denn in Westminster? Er sollte doch über Ostern hier sein!«

Dem Wachposten dämmerte allmählich, daß sie kein Gossenkind war. »Zu Ostern hält er in Westminster hof. Sieht so aus, als wolle er sich nicht in allem nach dem alten König richten. Warum sollte er auch?«

Damit hatte er natürlich recht, aber es war Aliena nie in den Sinn gekommen, daß ein neuer König eine andere Zeiteinteilung haben könnte. Und da sie zu jung war, um sich an den Regierungsantritt von König Heinrich zu erinnern, wurde sie immer ratloser. Sie hatte einen ausgeklügelten Schlachtplan gehabt – und nun hatte er sich als verfehlt herausgestellt! Am liebsten hätte sie die Flinte ins Korn geworfen.

Sie schüttelte den Kopf, um die unheilvolle Mutlosigkeit zu verscheuchen. Dies war keine Niederlage, nur ein Rückschlag. Das Bittgesuch an den König war nur eine Möglichkeit, die sie für sich und ihren Bruder in Anspruch nehmen konnte. Nach Winchester war sie schließlich noch aus einem weiteren Grund gekommen: Sie wollte herausfinden, was mit ihrem Vater geschehen war; er konnte ihr bestimmt sagen, was sie tun sollte.

»Wer ist denn dann hier?« wandte sie sich wieder an den Wachposten. »Es muß doch irgendwelche Bedienstete des Königs hier geben. Ich will ja nur meinen Vater sehen.«

»Im Schloß oben gibt es einen Schreiber und einen Haushofmeister«, erwiderte der Posten. »Sagtest du, der Graf von Shiring sei dein Vater?«

»Ja.« Sie hielt den Atem an. »Weißt du etwas über ihn?«

»Ich weiß, wo er ist.«

»Wo denn?«

»Im Gefangenenhaus der Burg.«

So nahe! »Wie komme ich dort hin?«

Der Posten deutete mit dem Daumen über die Schulter. »Den Hügel runter, an der Kapelle vorbei, gegenüber vom Haupttor.« Daß er sie am Betreten des Wohnturms gehindert hatte, genügte ihm offenbar, denn nun gab er bereitwillig Auskunft. »Am besten wendet ihr euch an den Gefangenenaufseher. Er heißt Odo, und er hat tiefe Taschen.«

Letzteres verstand Aliena nicht, doch sie war zu aufgeregt, um es sich erklären zu lassen. Bis zu diesem Augenblick hatte sie ihren Vater an einem unbestimmten, weit entfernten Ort im Verlies geglaubt, und jetzt hieß es plötzlich, er sei hier in dieser Burg! Sie vergaß das Bittgesuch an den König: Sie wollte nur noch zu ihrem Vater. Allein der Gedanke, daß er in der Nähe war und ihr helfen konnte, machte ihr die Gefahren und die Ungewißheit der vorangegangenen Monate doppelt deutlich. Sie wollte sich in seine Arme stürzen und ihn sagen hören: »Jetzt ist alles wieder in Ordnung, jetzt wird alles wieder gut.«

Der Wohnturm stand etwas erhöht in einer Ecke der Burg. Aliena drehte sich um und betrachtete die ganze Anlage, eine bunt zusammengewürfelte Ansammlung von Gebäuden aus Stein und Holz, umgeben von hohen Mauern. Den Hügel hinunter, hatte der Wachposten gesagt: an der Kapelle vorbei – sie entdeckte ein gepflegtes kleines Steinhaus, das wie eine Kapelle aussah – und gegenüber vom Haupttor. Der Hauptzugang bestand aus einem Tor in der Außenmauer der Befestigung, so daß der König sie direkt und unter Umgehung der Stadt betreten konnte. Gegenüber dem Eingang, in unmittelbarer Nähe der rückwärtigen Mauer, die die Burg von der Stadt trennte, stand ein kleines Steinhaus, vermutlich das Gefängnis.

Aliena und Richard eilten den Hügel hinunter. Ob es Vater gutgeht? überlegte Aliena. Bekommt man im Gefängnis auch ordentlich zu essen? Die Gefangenen ihres Vaters in Earlscastle waren stets mit Suppe und Brot versorgt worden, aber sie hatte gehört, daß Gefangene anderswo manchmal schlecht behandelt wurden. Sie konnte nur hoffen, daß Vater wohlauf war.

Sie überquerten den Burghof mit bangem Herzen. Die Anlage war weitläufig und geradezu übersät mit Gebäuden: Küchen, Ställe, Soldatenquartiere, zwei Kapellen. Nun, da sie wußte, daß der König gar nicht da war, konnte Aliena unschwer die Anzeichen dafür erkennen, die sie auf ihrem Zickzackkurs zum Gefängnis eher beiläufig wahrnahm: Wildernde Hausschweine und Schafe hatten sich von den vor dem Tor gelegenen Siedlungen auf den Burghof verirrt und wühlten in den Abfallhaufen, Bewaffnete lungerten träge herum und fanden ihre einzige Beschäftigung darin, vorübergehenden Frauen zweideutige Bemerkungen nachzurufen, und im Portal einer der Kapellen wurden sogar Glücksspiele gespielt. Aliena störte die allgemeine Nachlässigkeit. Sie zog daraus den Schluß, daß sich niemand so recht um ihren Vater kümmerte, und fing an, das Schlimmste zu befürchten.

Das Gefängnis war ein baufälliges Haus aus Stein, das dereinst einem königlichen Beamten, einem Richter oder Amtmann etwa, gehört haben mochte. Das obere Stockwerk, vormals der Gemeinschaftsraum, jetzt nahezu dachlos, war beinahe völlig ruiniert, lediglich das Erdgeschoß war noch intakt. Das besaß zwar keine Fenster, dafür aber eine große Holztür mit Eisenbeschlägen, die nur angelehnt war. Während Aliena noch unschlüssig verharrte, ging eine hübsche Frau mittleren Alters in einem Umhang aus gutem Tuch an ihr vorbei, öffnete die Tür ganz und ging hinein.

Aliena und Richard folgten ihr.

Im Innern war es düster. Es roch nach abgestandenem Schmutz und Moder. Das Gewölbe, einst ein einziger Lagerraum, war offenbar mit hastig zusammengeschusterten Bruchsteinwänden unterteilt worden. Aus der Tiefe des Gebäudes ließ sich monotones Stöhnen vernehmen – es klang wie der Singsang eines Mönchs, der mutterseelenallein die Litanei eines Gottesdienstes abspult. Gleich hinter der Tür befand sich ein kleiner Raum, der nichts beherbergte außer einem Tisch und einem Stuhl. In der Mitte des Raumes brannte ein Feuer auf dem nackten Boden. Ein großer, einfältig wirkender Mann, der ein Schwert am Gürtel trug, fegte den Raum, als hätte er es nicht nötig. Er sah auf, begrüßte die Frau mit einem »Guten Morgen, Meg« und ließ sich einen Penny von ihr geben. Die Frau verschwand in der Dunkelheit. Dann nahm er Aliena und Richard wahr. »Was wollt ihr hier?«

»Ich will meinen Vater besuchen«, sagte Aliena. »Den Grafen von Shiring.«

»Er heißt jetzt schlicht und einfach Bartholomäus«, erwiderte der Gefangenenwärter.

»Deine Spitzfindigkeiten kannst du dir an den Hut stecken, Wärter. Wo ist er?«

»Wieviel Geld hast du denn?«

»Ich habe gar keins, deshalb solltest du dir erst gar keine Hoffnung auf ein Schmiergeld machen.«

»Wenn du kein Geld hast, kannst du deinen Vater nicht besuchen.« Stur machte er sich wieder ans Fegen.

Aliena hätte am liebsten losgebrüllt: Nur so wenige Meter, die sie von ihrem Vater trennten, und dieser Kerl ließ sie nicht zu ihm! Der Kerl war nicht nur groß und bullig, sondern auch bewaffnet – sie hatte also nicht die geringste Aussicht, ihn niederzuringen. Geld jedoch hatte sie auch nicht. Schon als sie gesehen hatte, daß die Meg genannte Frau einen Penny zahlte, waren ihr Befürchtungen gekommen – immerhin, hatte sie gedacht, kann es sich dabei auch um die Bezahlung für irgendeine besondere Vergünstigung handeln. Nun war klar, daß sie sich getäuscht hatte: Das war der Eintrittspreis.

»Ich werde mir einen Penny beschaffen«, sagte sie, »und ihn dir so schnell wie möglich bringen. Willst du uns nicht gleich zu meinem Vater lassen, nur für einen Augenblick?«

»Erst den Penny«, gab der Aufseher zurück, wandte sich ab und machte sich wieder ans Fegen.

Aliena kämpfte mit den Tränen. Sie war drauf und dran – in der Hoffnung, Vater könne sie hören –, eine Botschaft hinauszuschreien, doch dann machte sie sich klar, daß solch ein verworrenes Gerufe ihn nur ängstigen und entmutigen konnte, ohne daß er wirklich Wichtiges erfuhr. In ohnmächtiger Wut wandte sie sich zum Gehen.

Auf der Schwelle drehte sie sich noch einmal um. »Wie geht es ihm? Wenigstens das kannst du mir doch sagen – bitte! Geht es ihm gut?«

»Nein«, sagte der Gefangenenwärter. »Er liegt im Sterben. Und jetzt raus mit euch.«

Aliena schossen die Tränen in die Augen, und sie stolperte durch die Tür, ging blindlings weiter und stürzte beinahe über ein Schaf oder ein Schwein. Sie begann zu schluchzen. Richard nahm sie beim Arm, und sie ließ sich von ihm führen. Sie verließen die Burg durch das Haupttor, durchquerten die Siedlungen mit ihren ärmlichen Hütten und winzigen Feldern und machten schließlich auf einer Wiese halt, wo sie sich auf einem Baumstumpf niederließen.

»Dein Geheule läßt sich kaum noch ertragen, Aliena«, jammerte Richard.

Aliena riß sich zusammen. Immerhin hatte sie ihren Vater ausfindig gemacht – war das etwa nichts? Und sie hatte erfahren, daß er krank war – aber der Gefängnisaufseher war ein grausamer Kerl und hatte wahrscheinlich gewaltig übertrieben. Nun brauche ich nur noch einen Penny aufzutreiben, dachte sie, dann kann ich selber mit Vater sprechen, selber sehen, wie gut oder schlecht es ihm geht, und ich kann ihn fragen, was ich tun soll – seinetwegen und Richards wegen.

»Wie können wir einen Penny auftreiben, Richard?« fragte sie.

»Ich weiß nicht.«

»Wir haben nichts zu verkaufen. Niemand würde uns etwas leihen. Du bist nicht abgebrüht genug zum Stehlen ...«

»Wir könnten betteln«, schlug er vor.

Eine gute Idee! Soeben kam ein offensichtlich wohlhabender Bauer auf einem kräftigen kleinen Rappen den Hügel herunter. Aliena sprang auf und lief zur Straße. Kaum war der Bauer nahe genug, fragte sie ihn: »Gebt Ihr mir bitte einen Penny, mein Herr?«

»Scher dich zum Teufel«, knurrte der Mann und spornte sein Pferd zu schnellerer Gangart an.

Niedergeschlagen kehrte sie zu dem Baumstumpf zurück. »Bettler fragen immer nach Essen oder Kleidung«, sagte sie. »Ich habe noch nie gehört, daß man ihnen Geld gibt.«

»Aber wie kommt man denn an Geld?« wollte Richard wissen. Diese Frage hatte er sich offenkundig noch nie gestellt.

»Der König nimmt Steuern ein, die Grundherren kriegen Pacht, die Priester den Zehnten. Ladenbesitzer leben vom Verkauf, und Handwerker bekommen Lohn. Bauern brauchen kein Geld, weil sie ihre Felder haben«, zählte Aliena auf.

»Lehrlinge werden bezahlt.«

»Tagelöhner auch. Wir könnten arbeiten gehen.«

»Für wen?«

»In Winchester gibt es jede Menge kleiner Manufakturen, die Leder und Stoffe herstellen«, sagte Aliena mit frischem Mut. »In einer Stadt kann man leicht Arbeit finden.« Sie erhob sich behende. »Komm, versuchen wir's gleich!«

Richard zögerte noch. »Ich kann aber nicht wie jeder x-beliebige einfache Mann arbeiten«, sagte er. »Ich bin schließlich der Sohn eines Grafen.«

»Diese Zeiten sind vorbei«, gab Aliena unumwunden zurück. »Hast du nicht gehört, was der Aufseher gesagt hat? Du mußt einsehen, daß du nichts Besseres bist – jetzt nicht mehr.«

Er verzog mißmutig das Gesicht und schwieg.

»Also, ich gehe jetzt«, sagte sie. »Du kannst ja hierbleiben, wenn du willst.« Entschlossen ging sie auf das Westtor zu. Sie kannte Richards Launen und wußte, daß er niemals lange schmollte.

Und tatsächlich holte er sie ein, noch bevor sie die Stadt erreicht hatte. »Sei mir bitte nicht böse, Allie«, bat er. »Ich werde schon arbeiten. Eigentlich bin ich ganz schön stark – ich werd' bestimmt ein guter Arbeiter.«

Sie lächelte ihn an. »Das glaube ich auch.« Das stimmte zwar nicht, aber sie sah keinen Sinn darin, ihn zu entmutigen.

Sie traten auf die High Street hinaus. Aliena erinnerte sich, daß Winchester eine planvolle, rechteckige Anlage besaß. Nach Süden zu, nunmehr zur Rechten der Geschwister, war die Stadt in drei Teile gegliedert: Unweit des Westtors befand sich die Burg, im Anschluß daran kamen die Häuser der wohlhabenden Bürger und gen Südosten schließlich die Kathedrale und der Bischofspalast. Nördlich der High Street, zur Linken der Geschwister, fand sich zunächst das Judenviertel, woran sich ein Geschäftsviertel und im Nordosten die Manufakturen anschlossen.

Aliena ging zielstrebig die High Street hinunter, bog kurz vor dem Osttor nach links in eine Straße, durch die ein schmaler Bach lief. Auf der einen Seite war die Straße gesäumt von ganz gewöhnlichen Häusern aus Stein oder Holz; die andere Straßenseite beherbergte ein Gewirr seltsamer Hütten, von denen die meisten aus nicht mehr als einem von Pfosten getragenen Dach bestanden und wirkten, als drohten sie jeden Augenblick zusammenzufallen. Jede dieser Hütten war durch eine kleine Brücke oder durch quer übers Wasser gelegte Planken mit dem Bach verbunden oder aber direkt darüber errichtet. Überall gingen Männer und Frauen ihrer Arbeit nach, die enorme Mengen von Wasser erforderten. Sie wuschen Wolle, gerbten Leder, walkten und färbten Tuch, brauten Bier. Die Nasen der Geschwister erschnupperten unzählige Gerüche: beißende und gärende, schwefelige und rauchige, harzige und faulige. Die dort arbeitenden Menschen wirkten allesamt geradezu *ungeheuer* fleißig. Auch Bauern hatten natürlich immer sehr viel zu tun und faulenzten nie, aber sie pflegten ihre Aufgaben bedächtig anzugehen und fanden oft Zeit für einen Schwatz mit Vorübergehenden oder zur Beobachtung von Dingen, die ihre Neugier weckten. Die Menschen in den Manufakturen dagegen sahen kein einziges Mal von ihrer Arbeit auf. Sie schien ihre gesamte Konzentration und Energie in Anspruch zu nehmen. Sie bewegten sich ausnahmslos rasch und zielstrebig, ob sie nun Säcke trugen, große Wassereimer ausleerten oder Leder und Tuche bearbeiteten. Der Anblick, den sie in ihren windschiefen, düsteren Hütten boten, wo sie ihrer rätselhaften Beschäftigung nachgingen, erinnerte Aliena unwillkürlich an die wild in Kesseln rührenden Dämonen, die sie auf Bildern von der Hölle gesehen hatte. Dann machte sie halt an einer Hütte, wo sie erkennen konnte, was vor sich ging: Hier wurde Tuch gewalkt. Eine kräftige Frau schöpfte Wasser aus dem Becher, das sie in einen riesigen, mit Blei ausgeschlagenen Trog goß, hielt dabei ab und zu inne und gab aus einem Sack ein Scheffel Fullererde hinzu. Auf dem Boden des Bottichs lag, von Wasser durchtränkt, ein mehrere Ellen langes Tuch. Zwei Männer schlugen mit hölzernen Keulen heftig darauf ein. Diese Prozedur ließ das Tuch einlaufen und festigte es, wodurch es wetterbeständig wurde; außerdem entzog die Fullererde der Wolle das Fett. Am anderen Ende des Grundstücks stapelten sich Ballen unbehandelten, frisch und locker gewebten Tuchs neben Säcken voller Fullererde.

Aliena überquerte den Bach und näherte sich den am Trog arbeitenden Leuten. Sie blickten kurz auf, unterbrachen ihre Arbeit jedoch nicht. Der Boden um sie herum war naß, und Aliena sah, daß alle barfuß waren. Dann wurde ihr klar, daß niemand innehalten und sie nach ihrem Anliegen fragen würde, daher fragte sie mit erhobener Stimme: »Ist euer Meister hier?«

Die Frau gab ihr Antwort, indem sie mit dem Kopf auf den rückwärtigen Teil des Geländes wies.

Aliena bedeutete Richard, ihr zu folgen, und ging durch ein Tor auf einen Hof, auf dem Tuchbahnen auf hölzernen Gestellen getrocknet wurden. Sie entdeckte das Gesicht eines Mannes, der, über ein Gestell gebeugt, das Tuch zurechtrückte. »Ich suche den Meister«, sagte sie.

Er richtete sich auf und sah sie an, ein häßlicher Mann mit nur einem Auge und einem leichten Buckel, als hätte er sich jahrelang über Trockengestelle gebeugt und könnte sich nicht mehr gerade aufrichten. »Was gibt's?« fragte er.

»Bist du der Walkmeister?«

»Ich führ' die Arbeit jetzt seit fast vierzig Jahren aus, im Knaben- wie im Mannesalter«, sagte er. »Ich hoffe, ich bin ein anerkannter Meister meines Faches. Was willst du?«

Aliena wurde klar, daß sie an einen regelrechten Schlauberger geraten war. Sie schlug einen demütigen Tonfall an und fragte: »Mein Bruder und ich suchen Arbeit. Wirst du uns einstellen?«

Er antwortete nicht sofort, sondern musterte sie erst einmal von oben bis unten. »Herr im Himmel, was soll ich mit euch anfangen?«

»Wir tun jede Arbeit«, sagte Aliena beherzt. »Wir brauchen Geld.«

»Mit euch kann ich nichts anfangen«, sagte der Mann verächtlich und wandte sich wieder seiner Arbeit zu.

Aliena ließ sich nicht damit abspeisen. »Warum nicht?« sagte sie zornig. »Wir sind keine Bettler, wir wollen unser Geld *verdienen*.«

Er drehte sich zu ihr um.

»Bitte!« flehte sie, obwohl sie sich selber dafür haßte.

Er bedachte sie mit einem ungeduldigen Blick und mit einer Miene, als wäre er sich nicht schlüssig, ob die Kreatur vor ihm einen Fußtritt wert sei oder nicht; aber sie erkannte darin auch die Versuchung, aufzutrumpfen und ihr ihre eigene Dummheit vor Augen zu führen. »Na schön«, seufzte er. »Ich werde es euch erklären. Kommt mit.«

Er führte sie an den Trog. Die Männer und die Frau zogen gerade das Tuch aus dem Wasser und waren bemüht, es gleichzeitig aufzurollen. Der Meister wandte sich an die Frau: »Lizzie, komm her und zeig uns mal deine Hände.«

Gehorsam trat die Frau zu ihnen und streckte ihre Hände aus. Sie waren rauh und rot und dort, wo die Haut aufgesprungen war, mit offenen Stellen übersät.

»Fühl mal, wie das ist«, sagte der Meister zu Aliena.

Aliena berührte die Hände der Frau. Sie waren kalt wie Eis und sehr rauh, aber am auffälligsten war ihre ungewöhnliche Härte. Sie betrachtete ihre eigenen Hände, die ihr nun, da sie die der Frau hielt, plötzlich weich und weiß und sehr klein schienen.

»Sie hat ihre Hände im Wasser gehabt, seit sie ganz klein war«, erklärte der Meister, »deswegen macht es ihr nichts aus. Bei dir ist das anders. Du würdest diese Arbeit nicht einmal einen Vormittag lang aushalten.«

Aliena wollte ihm widersprechen. Sie würde sich schon daran gewöhnen, meinte sie, war aber nicht sicher, ob es stimmte. Bevor sie den Mund aufmachen konnte, mischte Richard sich ein. »Und ich?« sagte er. »Ich bin größer als die beiden Männer – ich könnte die Arbeit schon schaffen.«

Es stimmte tatsächlich, daß Richard größer und breiter war als die Männer, die die Keule schwangen. Wenn er mit einem Schlachtroß fertig wird, dachte Aliena, dann kann er auch Tuch walken.

Die beiden Männer hatten das nasse Tuch vollständig aufgerollt, und einer von ihnen schulterte nun die Rolle, um sie auf den Hof zum Trocknen zu bringen. Der Meister bot ihm Einhalt. »Laß den jungen Herrn mal spüren, was so ein Ballen wiegt, Harry.«

Der Angesprochene wuchtete den Tuchballen von seiner Schulter und legte ihn Richard auf. Der sackte unter dem Gewicht zusammen, richtete sich mühsam wieder auf, ging aber gleich wieder in die Knie, so daß das Ende des Ballens auf dem Boden ruhte. »Das kann ich nicht tragen«, keuchte er.

Die Männer lachten. Der Meister warf einen triumphierenden Blick in die Runde, und Harry nahm den Ballen wieder auf, legte ihn geübt über die Schulter und trug ihn weg.

»Das ist eine ganz andere Art von Stärke«, sagte der Meister. »Die kriegt man nur, wenn man arbeiten muß.«

Das machte Aliena wütend. Sie zu verspotten, wo sie sich doch nur auf ehrliche Weise einen Penny verdienen wollten! Ihr wurde klar, daß dieser Meister sie mit geradezu diebischer Freude aufzog und so lange weiter sticheln würde, wie sie ihn ließ. Einstellen würde er weder sie noch Richard. »Vielen Dank für deine Zuvorkommenheit«, sagte sie mit deutlichem Sarkasmus, machte kehrt und ging davon.

»Es war nur so schwer, weil es so naß war!« verteidigte sich Richard. »Damit hatte ich nicht gerechnet.«

Aliena erkannte, daß sie gute Miene zum bösen Spiel machen mußte, damit Richard nicht den Mut verlor. »Es gibt schließlich noch andere Arbeitsmöglichkeiten«, sagte sie, während sie die matschige Straße entlanggingen.

»Was können wir denn sonst noch tun?«

Aliena schwieg. Mittlerweile waren sie an der nördlichen Stadtmauer angelangt, so daß sie nun nach links gen Westen abbiegen mußten. Dies war offenbar die ärmlichste Gegend von Winchester. Die Häuser, unmittelbar an die Stadtmauer gelehnt, waren größtenteils nur windschiefe Schuppen und die Gassen mit Unrat übersät. Nach einer ganzen Weile sagte Aliena: »Erinnerst du dich noch an die Mädchen auf der Burg? Wenn sie zu Hause keinen Platz mehr hatten und auch noch keinen Ehemann, kamen sie zu uns, und Vater hat sie alle aufgenommen. Sie haben dann bei der Küchenarbeit geholfen, bei der Wäsche oder in den Ställen, und an Heiligentagen bekamen sie von Vater einen Penny.«

»Glaubst du etwa, daß wir auf der Burg von Winchester leben könnten?« fragte Richard zweifelnd.

»Nein. Die nehmen niemanden auf, solange der König abwesend ist – sie haben ohnehin mehr Leute, als sie brauchen. Aber in der Stadt gibt es viele Reiche. Ein paar von denen werden sicher noch Dienstmägde gebrauchen können.«

»Das ist aber keine Männerarbeit.«

Aliena lag es auf der Zunge, ihn zu fragen: Warum läßt du dir nicht selber etwas einfallen, statt immer nur an meinen Vorschlägen herumzumäkeln? Sie verkniff es sich jedoch und sagte statt dessen: »Es genügt, wenn einer von uns so lange arbeitet, bis er einen Penny bekommt; dann können wir Vater besuchen und ihn fragen, was wir weiter tun sollen.«

»Na gut.« Richard hatte nichts dagegen, daß nur einer von ihnen arbeitete, besonders dann nicht, wenn das Los auf Aliena fiel.

Sie wandten sich erneut nach links und betraten das sogenannte Judenviertel der Stadt. Aliena blieb vor einem großen Haus stehen. »Die haben hier bestimmt Bedienstete«, sagte sie.

Richard war entsetzt. »Du willst doch nicht etwa für Juden arbeiten, oder?«

»Warum nicht? Die Häresie anderer Leute schnappt man schließlich nicht so leicht auf wie ihre Flöhe.«

Richard zuckte die Achseln und folgte ihr in das Innere des Hauses.

Das Gebäude war aus Stein und wie fast alle Stadthäuser schmal, aber sehr tief. Die Diele, in der die Geschwister standen, erstreckte sich über die volle Breite des Hauses. Im Kamin brannte ein Feuer, und es gab ein paar Bänke zum Sitzen. Der Duft, der aus der Küche drang, ließ Aliena das Wasser im Mund zusammenlaufen, obwohl er mit fremdartigen Gewürzen durchsetzt war. Ein junges Mädchen kam aus dem rückwärtigen Teil des Hauses und begrüßte sie. Sie hatte dunkle Haut und braune Augen und sprach sie respektvoll an. »Ihr wünscht den Goldschmied zu sprechen?«

Das war also der Beruf des Hausherrn. »Ja, bitte«, erwiderte Aliena. Das Mädchen verschwand, und Aliena sah sich ein wenig um. Ein Goldschmied brauchte natürlich ein solides Steinhaus, um sein Gold sicher unterzubringen. Die Tür zwischen der Eingangshalle und dem rückwärtigen Teil des Hauses war aus schweren Eichenbrettern gezimmert und mit Eisen beschlagen. Die Fenster waren schmal und so klein, daß nicht einmal ein Kind hätte hindurchklettern können. Wie nervenaufreibend, dachte Aliena, wenn das gesamte Vermögen in Gold und Silber angelegt ist, das in kürzester Zeit gestohlen werden kann! Doch gleich darauf fiel ihr ein, daß auch ihr Vater, obwohl sein Reichtum nur aus ganz normalem Grundbesitz und einem Titel bestand, trotzdem von einem Tag auf den anderen alles verloren hatte.

Der Goldschmied trat ein. Er war klein und dunkelhäutig und musterte sie mit zusammengekniffenen Augen, als hätte er ein kleines Schmuckstück zu begutachten und zu taxieren. Sein Urteil war rasch gefällt und er fragte: »Ihr wünscht etwas zu verkaufen?«

»Ihr habt uns richtig eingeschätzt, Goldschmied«, sagte Aliena. »Ihr habt erraten, daß wir Edelleute sind, die sich in einer Notlage befinden. Leider haben wir nichts zu verkaufen.«

Der Mann sah sie beunruhigt an. »Wenn Ihr Geld leihen wollt, dann fürchte ich –«

»Nein, wir wollen uns auch kein Geld borgen«, fiel Aliena ihm ins Wort, »denn wir haben auch nichts zu verpfänden.«

Er wirkte erleichtert. »Womit kann ich Euch helfen?«

»Würdet Ihr mich als Dienstmagd einstellen?«

Der Mann war entsetzt. »Eine Christin? Gewiß nicht!«

Allein schon der Gedanke ließ ihn zurückschrecken.

»Warum nicht?« fragte Aliena kläglich enttäuscht.

»Das geht einfach nicht.«

Wollte er sie beleidigen? Die Vorstellung, *ihre* Religion könne jemandem zuwider sein, war erniedrigend. Aber hatte sie nicht eben erst so neunmalklug behauptet, die Häresie anderer Leute schnappe man nicht so leicht auf wie ihre Flöhe?

»Die ganze Stadt würde Sturm dagegen laufen.«

Aliena war überzeugt, daß ihm die öffentliche Meinung lediglich als Ausflucht diente – trotzdem hatte er höchstwahrscheinlich recht. »Dann machen wir uns wohl besser auf die Suche nach einem reichen Christen«, sagte sie.

»Ihr könnt es ja versuchen«, stimmte der Goldschmied halbherzig zu. »Aber eins will ich Euch ganz offen sagen: Ein weiser Mann würde Euch nicht als Dienstmagd einstellen. Ihr seid daran gewöhnt, Befehle zu geben, und fändet Euch nur sehr schwer drein, sie entgegenzunehmen.«

Aliena öffnete schon den Mund, um zu protestieren, doch er hob die Hand und gebot ihr Schweigen. »Oh, ich weiß, daß Ihr guten Willens seid. Aber Ihr seid zeitlebens von anderen bedient worden, und selbst jetzt noch habt Ihr in Eurem tiefsten Inneren das Gefühl, alles müsse Euch in den Schoß fallen. Menschen von hohem Stand geben keine guten Dienstboten ab. Sie sind ungehorsam, ungehalten, unbedacht und überempfindlich, und sie glauben, hart zu arbeiten, wenn sie in Wirklichkeit weniger tun als alle anderen; das führt zu Reibereien in der Dienerschaft.« Er zuckte mit den Schultern. »Meiner Erfahrung nach wenigstens.«

Aliena vergaß, daß sie sein Widerwille gegen ihre Religion beleidigt hatte. Immerhin war er der erste Mensch, der ihnen freundlich begegnete, seit sie die Burg verlassen hatten.

»Aber was können wir denn dann tun?« fragte sie.

»Ich kann Euch nur sagen, was ein Jude tun würde. Er würde sich nach etwas umsehen, das verkäuflich ist. Als ich in diese Stadt kam, fing ich damit an, Schmuck von Leuten aufzukaufen, die Geld brauchten. Dann habe ich das Silber eingeschmolzen und es an die Münzpräger verkauft.«

»Aber wo habt Ihr das Geld zum Kauf des Schmucks hergenommen?«

»Das habe ich von meinem Onkel geliehen – und ihm übrigens mit Zinsen zurückgezahlt.«

»Aber uns würde niemand Geld leihen!«

Er sah sie nachdenklich an. »Was hätte ich ohne den Onkel gemacht? Ich glaube, ich wäre in den Wald gegangen und hätte Nüsse gesammelt. Die hätte ich dann in der Stadt an die Hausfrauen verkauft, die in ihren Hinterhöfen vor lauter Unrat und Dreck keinen Platz für Bäume und überdies zu wenig Zeit haben, selbst in den Wald zu gehen.«

»Dafür ist jetzt nicht die richtige Jahreszeit«, gab Aliena zurück. »Im Augenblick wächst gar nichts.«

Der Goldschmied lächelte. »Die Ungeduld der Jugend«, meinte er. »Ihr müßt ein Weilchen warten.«

»Na schön.« Aliena schien es sinnlos, das Schicksal ihres Vaters zu erwähnen. Der Goldschmied hatte sich redliche Mühe gegeben, ihnen zu helfen. »Seid bedankt für Euren guten Rat.«

»Lebt wohl.« Er wandte sich zum Gehen und schloß die massive Tür mit den Eisenbeschlägen hinter sich.

Aliena und Richard traten wieder auf die Straße hinaus. Der Goldschmied hatte sich zwar sehr liebenswürdig verhalten – nichtsdestotrotz hatten sie den halben Tag damit vertan, Abfuhren einzustecken, und Aliena fühlte Hoffnungslosigkeit in sich aufsteigen. Ziellos wanderten sie durch das Judenviertel, bis sie wieder auf die High Street stießen. Aliena merkte plötzlich, wie hungrig sie war – es war bereits

Mittag. Und wenn ihr schon der Magen knurrte, so mußte Richard halb verhungert sein! Sie schlenderten die High Street entlang, voller Neid auf die wohlgenährten Ratten, die sich an den Abfällen gütlich taten.

Am alten Königspalast angekommen, hielten sie wie alle Fremden inne, um den Münzern hinter ihren Gitterstäben zuzusehen, wie sie Geld prägten. Aliena starrte wie gebannt auf die Stapel von Silberpennies – wenn sie doch nur einen einzigen davon haben könnte!

Nach einer Weile fiel ihr ein Mädchen in ihrer Nähe auf, das ungefähr so alt war wie sie selbst und das Richard anlächelte. Sie sah freundlich aus, und als sie zum zweitenmal lächelte, sprach Aliena sie an. »Lebst du hier?«

»Ja«, erwiderte das Mädchen. Sie war offenbar ausschließlich an Richard interessiert.

»Unser Vater ist im Gefängnis«, platzte Aliena heraus, »und wir suchen nach einer Möglichkeit, uns Geld zu verdienen, damit wir den Gefängnisaufseher bestechen können. Weißt du etwas für uns?«

Das Mädchen wandte endlich den Blick von Richard und fragte Aliena: »Ihr wollt wissen, wie ihr euch Geld verdienen könnt?«

»Richtig, und wir sind bereit, fleißig dafür zu arbeiten. Wir machen alles. Glaubst du, du weißt etwas für uns?«

Das Mädchen musterte Aliena eingehend von Kopf bis Fuß. »Ja, ich weiß schon«, sagte sie schließlich. »Ich kenne jemanden, der euch vielleicht helfen kann.«

Aliena war geradezu überwältigt: Zum erstenmal an diesem Tag war ihre Frage bejaht worden! »Wann können wir zu ihm gehen?« fragte sie eifrig.

»Ihr.«

»Wie bitte?«

»Es ist eine Frau. Und wenn ihr mit mir geht, kannst du wahrscheinlich gleich mit ihr reden.«

Aliena und Richard sahen sich entzückt an. Aliena konnte ihr plötzliches Glück kaum fassen.

Das Mädchen wandte sich zum Gehen, und sie folgten ihr. Sie führte sie zu einem großen Holzhaus, das an der Südseite der High Street stand. Es bestand im wesentlichen aus einem Erdgeschoß, besaß aber noch einen kleinen Ausbau im ersten Stockwerk. Das Mädchen erklomm eine Außentreppe und bedeutete ihnen, ihr zu folgen.

Das Obergeschoß bestand aus einer einzigen Schlafkammer. Aliena sah sich mit großen Augen um: Sie war weit aufwendiger ausgestattet, als alle Räume der väterlichen Burg selbst zu Mutters Lebzeiten es je gewesen waren. An den Wänden hingen Gobelins, der Boden war mit Fellen ausgelegt und das Bett mit bestickten Vorhängen umgeben. Auf einem thronähnlichen Stuhl saß eine Frau mittleren Alters in einem wunderschönen Kleid. Sie muß einmal sehr schön gewesen sein, dachte Aliena, auch wenn ihr jetzt die Haare ausfallen und ihr Gesicht schon Runzeln hat.

»Das ist Mistreß Kate«, stellte das Mädchen vor.

»Kate, dieses Mädchen besitzt keinen Penny, und ihr Vater sitzt im Gefängnis.«

Kate lächelte. Aliena lächelte zurück, mußte sich aber dazu zwingen: Irgend etwas an Kate wollte ihr nicht so recht behagen. »Nimm den Jungen mit in die Küche«, sagte Kate, »und gib ihm einen Becher Bier, während wir uns unterhalten.«

Das Mädchen führte Richard hinaus. Aliena war froh, daß er Bier bekam – vielleicht bekam er sogar etwas zu essen?

»Wie heißt du?« fragte Kate.

»Aliena.«

»Ein ungewöhnlicher Name. Aber er gefällt mir.« Sie stand auf und trat näher – für Alienas Geschmack etwas zu nah. Sie legte Aliena die Hand unters Kinn. »Du hast ein *sehr* hübsches Gesicht.« Ihr Atem roch nach Wein. »Leg deinen Umhang ab.«

Aliena verwirrte diese Untersuchung, aber sie fügte sich: Bis jetzt wirkte alles recht harmlos, und sie wollte auf keinen Fall die erste vielversprechende Aussicht auf Arbeit nach den morgendlichen Fehlschlägen durch etwaige Unbotmäßigkeit aufs Spiel setzen. Sie ließ ihren Umhang von den Schultern gleiten, legte ihn auf eine Bank und stand nun in dem alten Leinenkleid da, das ihr die Frau des Jagdpflegers gegeben hatte.

Kate ging einmal ganz um sie herum und schien aus irgendeinem Grund beeindruckt. »Mein liebes Kind, dir wird es nie an Geld mangeln und auch sonst an nichts. Wenn du für mich arbeitest, werden wir beide reich.«

Aliena runzelte die Stirn. Das klang ihr allzu verrückt. Sie wollte nichts weiter, als bei der Wäsche, beim Kochen oder Nähen helfen: Wie sollte sie da irgendwen reich machen? »Was für eine Arbeit meint Ihr?« sagte sie.

Kate, die hinter ihr stand, ließ die Hände an Alienas Seiten heruntergleiten, befühlte ihre Hüften und stand so dicht hinter ihr, daß Aliena ihre Brüste spürte, die sich gegen ihren Rücken preßten. »Du hast eine wunderbare Figur«, sagte Kate. »Und deine Haut ist genauso wunderbar. Du bist von adliger Geburt, nicht wahr?«

»Mein Vater war der Graf von Shiring.«

»Bartholomäus! Soso. Ich kann mich gut an ihn erinnern – nicht etwa, daß er einer meiner Kunden gewesen wäre. Ein tugendhafter Mann, dein Vater. Nun, jetzt verstehe ich auch, warum du in Not bist.«

Kate hatte also Kunden. »Was verkauft Ihr?« fragte Aliena.

Kate gab keine Antwort darauf. Sie trat wieder vor Aliena hin und sah ihr ins Gesicht. »Bist du noch Jungfrau, Kleine?«

Aliena wurde rot vor Scham.

»Du brauchst dich nicht zu genieren«, sagte Kate. »Du bist also keine mehr. Nun ja, das macht nichts. Jungfrauen werden hoch gehandelt, aber natürlich hält das nicht vor.« Sie umschlang Alienas Hüften mit den Händen, beugte sich vor und küßte sie auf die Stirn. »Du bist sehr üppig, auch wenn du es selber nicht weißt. Bei allen Heiligen, du bist einfach unwiderstehlich!« Sie ließ eine Hand von Alienas Hüften zu ihrem Busen hinaufgleiten, nahm behutsam eine Brust in ihre Hand, wog und drückte sie sachte, neigte sich schließlich vor und küßte Aliena auf den Mund.

Schlagartig fiel es Aliena wie Schuppen von den Augen: warum das Mädchen vor der Münze nur Richard zugelächelt hatte, woher Kate ihr Geld bezog, worin ihre eigene Arbeit für Kate bestehen sollte, ja, was für eine Frau diese Kate war. Sie kam sich töricht vor. Daß sie darauf nicht früher gekommen war! Einen Moment lang ließ sie Kate gewähren – ihr Kuß war so ganz anders als das, was William Hamleigh ihr angetan hatte, so gar nicht abscheuerregend. Aber es war nicht recht, und *damit* wollte sie auf gar keinen Fall ihr Geld verdienen. Sie entzog sich Kates Umarmung. »Ihr wollt mich zur Hure machen«, stellte sie fest.

»Zu einem Freudenmädchen, meine Liebe«, erwiderte Kate. »Spät aufstehen, jeden Tag wunderschöne Kleider tragen, Männer glücklich machen, reich werden. Du könntest es weit bringen. Du hast so ein gewisses Etwas ... Du könntest jeden Preis verlangen, jeden! Glaub mir, ich kenne mich aus.«

Aliena erschauderte. Auf der Burg hatte es stets ein oder zwei Huren gegeben – eine reine Notwendigkeit an einem Ort, wo sich so viele Männer ohne ihre Frauen aufhielten –, und sie hatten stets als die Niedrigsten der Niedrigsten gegolten, als die geringsten unter den Weibern, und standen im Rang sogar noch unter den Kehrern. Aber es war nicht der bescheidene Status, der Aliena vor Ekel erbeben ließ – es war die Vorstellung, daß jederzeit gemeine Kerle wie William Hamleigh hereinspazieren konnten und sie ihnen für einen Penny zu Willen sein mußte. Der Gedanke brachte die Erinnerung zurück, wie sein massiger Leib sich bedrohlich über sie schob – sie, die mit gespreizten Beinen auf dem Boden lag, zitternd vor Schreck und Abscheu, darauf wartend, daß er in sie eindrang ... Die grauenvollen Ereignisse drängten sich ihr unwillkürlich wieder auf und beraubten sie jeglichen Gleichmuts und Selbstvertrauens. Das Gefühl, ihr stieße, bliebe sie auch nur einen Moment länger in diesem Haus, das gleiche noch einmal zu, wurde übermächtig: Von Panik erfaßt, wollte sie nur noch hinaus ins Freie. Wo war die Tür? Rückwärts und vorsichtig ging sie darauf zu, fürchtend, sie könnte diese Kate erzürnen, fürchtend, irgend jemanden gegen sich aufzubringen.

»Es tut mir leid«, murmelte sie. »Bitte vergebt mir, aber das kann ich nicht, wirklich ...«

»Laß es dir noch mal durch den Kopf gehen!« sagte Kate heiter. »Solltest du deine Meinung ändern, kannst du jederzeit wiederkommen. Ich bin bestimmt noch hier.«

»Danke«, flüsterte Aliena. Endlich fand sie die Tür und stürzte hinaus. Noch vollkommen durcheinander rannte sie die Treppe hinunter auf die Straße und zum Haupteingang dieses Hauses. Die Tür war nur angelehnt, doch Aliena hatte zuviel Angst, um hineinzugehen.

»Richard!« rief sie, »Richard, komm raus!« – keine Antwort. Das Innere war schwach erleuchtet und sie konnte außer wenigen schemenhaften weiblichen Figuren nichts erkennen.

»Richard, wo bist du?« schrie sie mit sich überschlagender Stimme.

Sie bemerkte, daß sie von Passanten angestarrt wurde, und ihre Angst wuchs. Und endlich tauchte Richard auf, einen Becher Bier in der einen, ein Hühnerbein in der anderen Hand. »Was gibt's denn?« fragte er undeutlich mit vollem Mund. Sein Ton machte klar, daß ihn die Störung ärgerte.

Sie packte ihn am Arm. »Komm da raus«, sagte sie. »Das ist ein Hurenhaus!«

Die Umstehenden lachten laut auf, und mehrere zotige Bemerkungen flogen hin und her.

»Vielleicht geben sie dir auch ein Stück Fleisch«, meinte Richard.

»Die wollen mich hier zur Hure machen!« tobte sie.

»Gemach, gemach«, sagte Richard. Er leerte seinen Becher, stellte ihn auf den Fußboden gleich hinter der Tür und stopfte sich die Überreste des Hühnerbeins unter sein Hemd.

»Mach schon«, drängte Aliena, obgleich die Notwendigkeit, sich mit ihrem kleinen Bruder auseinanderzusetzen, wieder einmal beruhigend auf sie wirkte. Es schien ihn nicht weiter aufzuregen, daß seine Schwester zur Hure gemacht werden sollte – ihm schien nur leid zu tun, daß er ein Haus verlassen mußte, in dem man so freigebig mit Hühnchen und Bier umging.

Die Umstehenden erkannten, daß der Spaß ein Ende hatte, und gingen weiter, nur eine Frau blieb stehen – die gutgekleidete Frau, der sie im Gefängnis begegnet waren. Sie hatte dem Aufseher einen Penny gegeben, und er hatte sie Meg genannt. Sie bedachte Aliena mit einem Blick, in dem sich Neugier und Mitgefühl mischten, doch Aliena hatte mittlerweile eine Abneigung gegen Blicke jeglicher Art entwickelt und sah verärgert weg. Die Frau sprach sie an. »Du sitzt in der Patsche, ja?« fragte sie.

Der freundliche Unterton in Megs Stimme veranlaßte Aliena, sich umzudrehen. »Ja«, sagte sie nach einer Pause. »Wir sitzen in der Klemme.«

»Ich habe euch im Gefängnis gesehen. Mein Mann sitzt dort – ich besuche ihn jeden Tag. Warum wart ihr dort?«

»Unser Vater ist im Gefängnis.«

»Aber ihr seid nicht hineingegangen.«

»Wir haben kein Geld, um den Aufseher zu bezahlen.«

Megs Blick glitt über Aliena hinweg zur Tür des Freudenhauses. »Und deswegen bist du hier – um Geld aufzutreiben?«

»Ja, aber ich hatte nicht die geringste Ahnung, um was es sich handelt, bevor ...«

»Du armes Ding«, sagte Meg. »Meine Annie wäre jetzt in deinem Alter, wenn sie noch lebte ... Warum kommt ihr morgen früh nicht mit mir zusammen zum Gefängnis? Dann versuchen wir mit vereinten Kräften, Odo an seine Christenpflicht zu erinnern und Mitleid mit zwei mittellosen Kindern zu haben.«

»Oh, das wäre wunderbar«, antwortete Aliena gerührt. Viel Erfolg versprach dieser Vorschlag nicht, aber allein die Tatsache, daß ihnen jemand helfen wollte, ließ ihr das Wasser in die Augen schießen.

Meg sah sie immer noch prüfend an. »Habt ihr heute schon etwas gegessen?«

»Nein. Richard hat in dem ... da drin etwas bekommen.«

»Dann kommt ihr besser zu mir nach Hause, dort gibt's Brot und Fleisch.« Sie bemerkte Alienas zweifelnden Gesichtsausdruck und fügte hinzu: »Ohne daß ihr dafür etwas tun müßt.«

Aliena glaubte ihr. »Danke«, sagte sie. »Du bist sehr gütig. Das haben wir bislang noch kaum erlebt. Ich weiß gar nicht, wie ich dir danken soll.«

»Nicht nötig«, sagte sie. »Kommt mit.«

Megs Mann handelte mit Wolle. Er pflegte nicht nur in seinem Haus im Süden der Stadt, sondern auch an seinem Stand auf dem Wochenmarkt sowie auf dem alljährlich stattfindenden Großmarkt auf dem St.-Giles-Hügel die Schafvliese aufzukaufen, die ihm die Bauern aus der Umgebung brachten. Dann stopfte er sie in große Wollsäcke, von denen jeder die Vliese von zweihundertvierzig Schafen faßte, und lagerte sie in einer Scheune hinter seinem Haus. Wenn die flämischen Weber einmal im Jahr ihre Agenten auf der Suche nach der weichen, doch soliden englischen Wolle aussandten, verkaufte Megs Mann seine gesamte Ware und verschiffte sie über Dover und Boulogne nach Brügge und Gent, wo sie zu hochwertigen Tuchen verarbeitet und schließlich zu Preisen in alle Welt verkauft wurden, die für die Bauern mit ihren Schafen unerschwinglich waren.

Das alles erzählte Meg den Geschwistern im Laufe des Abendessens, und dabei lächelte sie die beiden so herzlich an, daß sie am Ende meinten, diese Frau könne, unter welchen Umständen auch immer, niemals einen Mitmenschen unfreundlich behandeln.

Ihr Mann war beschuldigt worden, falsch zu wiegen, ein Verbrechen, das in Winchester als gravierend galt, da der Reichtum der Stadt auf der Ehrlichkeit ihrer Händler beruhte. Aliena allerdings schloß aus der Art und Weise, wie Meg davon sprach, daß der Mann nicht unschuldig sein konnte. Seine Abwesenheit hatte jedoch kaum Auswirkungen auf die Geschäfte gehabt. Meg hatte ganz einfach seinen Platz eingenommen. Im Winter gab es sowieso nicht viel zu tun: Sie war nach Flandern gereist und hatte allen Agenten versichert, das Unternehmen liefe reibungslos weiter; außerdem hatte sie die Scheune reparieren und dabei gleich ein wenig vergrößern lassen. Sobald die Schafschur einsetzte, würde sie genau wie er Vliese kaufen. Sie konnte die Qualität beurteilen und die Preise festsetzen. Dem befleckten Ruf ihres Gatten zum Trotz war sie bereits in die Kaufmannsgilde der Stadt aufgenommen worden, denn die Tradition der Kaufleute besagte, daß man sich in Notzeiten unter die Arme zu greifen hatte, zumal Megs Gatte noch nicht seiner Schuld überführt war.

Richard und Aliena aßen und tranken dazu sogar Wein, wärmten sich an Megs Feuer und unterhielten sich mit ihr bis zum Anbruch der Dunkelheit; erst dann kehrten sie zum Schlafen ins Kloster zurück. Aliena wurde in dieser Nacht wieder von Alpträumen heimgesucht. Diesmal träumte sie von ihrem Vater. In ihrem Traum saß er, groß, bleich und gebieterisch wie eh und je, auf einem Thron im Gefängnis, und als sie ihn besuchte, mußte sie sich tiefer vor ihm verneigen als vor dem König. Er machte ihr Vorwürfe und behauptete, sie habe ihn seinem Schicksal überlassen und sei in ein Freudenhaus gezogen. Empört über diese Ungerechtigkeit erwiderte sie zornig, *er* habe schließlich *sie* im Stich gelassen. Beinahe hätte sie noch hinzugefügt, er hätte sie sogar William Hamleigh auf Gedeih und Verderb ausgeliefert, aber die Abneigung, ihrem Vater zu berichten, was William ihr angetan hatte, siegte. Erst dann sah sie, daß William ebenfalls anwesend war, auf einem Bett saß und Kirschen aus einer Schüssel mampfte. Er spuckte mit einem Kirschkern nach ihr, der schmerzhaft auf ihre Wange traf. Ihr Vater lächelte nur, worauf William begann, mit den weichen Kirschen nach ihr zu werfen. Sie trafen ihr Gesicht und ihr Kleid, und sie begann zu weinen, denn das Kleid war zwar alt, aber ihr einziges und jetzt über und über mit blutrotem Kirschsaft besudelt. Das machte sie so unbeschreiblich traurig, daß sie erwachte und erleichtert feststellte, daß sie ja nur geträumt hatte, wenngleich die Wirklichkeit – die Tatsache, daß sie heimat- und mittellos war – weitaus schlimmer war als ein Traum, in dem sie mit weichen Kirschen beworfen wurde.

Da stahl sich auch schon das Morgengrauen durch die Ritzen der Herberge. Um sie herum erwachten die anderen Schlafgäste und erhoben sich. Bald darauf kamen die Mönche herein, öffneten Türen und Fensterläden und riefen zum Frühstück.

Aliena und Richard schlangen es hastig hinunter und begaben sich zu Megs Haus, wo sie bereits erwartet wurden. Meg hatte einen würzigen Rindfleischeintopf gekocht, den ihr Mann nur noch aufwärmen mußte, und Aliena forderte Richard auf, den schweren Topf für Meg zu tragen, wobei sie wünschte, sie hätte selbst etwas für ihren Vater. Das war ihr bisher nicht in den Sinn gekommen, aber selbst dann hätte sie nichts für ihn kaufen können. Der Gedanke, daß sie nichts für ihn tun konnten, war kaum erträglich.

Sie gingen die High Street hinauf, betraten die Burg durch die Hinterpforte, passierten den Wohnturm und kamen zum Gefängnis. Aliena fiel wieder ein, was Odo ihr gestern, als sie sich nach ihrem Vater erkundigte, gesagt hatte: »Er liegt im Sterben.« Sie hatte angenommen, daß er aus purer Grausamkeit übertrieb, aber nun war sie doch besorgt und fragte Meg: »Mit meinem Vater ist doch alles in Ordnung, oder?«

»Das weiß ich nicht, meine Liebe«, sagte Meg. »Ich habe ihn noch nie zu Gesicht bekommen.«

»Der Aufseher sagte, er läge im Sterben.«

»Dieser Mann ist hundsgemein. Wahrscheinlich hat er das nur gesagt, um euch zu quälen. Aber gleich werdet ihr euch ja selbst ein Bild machen können.«

Megs tröstliche Worte konnten Aliena nicht beruhigen, so daß sie sich auf das Schlimmste gefaßt machte, als sie in die übelriechende Düsternis des Gefängnisses trat.

Odo wärmte gerade seine Hände über dem Feuer in der Mitte der Eingangshalle. Er nickte Meg zu und sah dann Aliena an. »Hast du das Geld?« fragte er.

»Ich zahle für sie«, sagte Meg. »Hier hast du deine zwei Pennies, einen für mich und einen für sie.«

Ein verschlagener Blick huschte über Odos dümmliche Visage, und er sagte: »Das macht zwei Pennies für die beiden – für jeden einen.«

»Sei nicht so stur«, sagte Meg. »Wenn du nicht beide einläßt, schwärze ich dich bei der Kaufmannsgilde an, und du wirst deinen Posten verlieren.«

»Schon gut, schon gut, du brauchst mir nicht zu drohen«, grunzte er und wies auf einen Torbogen in der Mauer zu seiner Rechten. »Bartholomäus ist da drin.«

»Ihr braucht ein Licht«, sagte Meg. Sie zog zwei Kerzen aus der Tasche ihres Umhangs, entzündete sie am Feuer und reichte Aliena eine davon. Sie wirkte beunruhigt. »Hoffentlich geht alles gut«, sagte sie und gab Aliena einen Kuß. Dann verschwand sie rasch unter dem zweiten Torbogen.

»Vielen Dank für den Penny«, rief Aliena ihr nach, doch Meg war bereits in der Dunkelheit verschwunden.

Aliena lugte ängstlich in die Dunkelheit, die Odo ihnen gewiesen hatte. Mit hocherhobener Kerze schritt sie durch den Torbogen und fand sich in einem winzigen, quadratischen Flur wieder. Im Kerzenlicht machte sie drei schwere, von außen durch je einen Querbalken verriegelte Türen aus. Odo rief: »Genau vor euch.«

Aliena sagte: »Heb den Riegel hoch, Richard.«

Richard hob das schwere Querholz aus der Halterung und lehnte sich gegen die Wand. Aliena stieß die Tür auf und schickte rasch ein Stoßgebet gen Himmel. In der Zelle war es stockdunkel. Zögernd blieb Aliena mit ihrer Kerze in der Tür stehen und starrte auf die unruhigen Schatten. Die ganze Zelle stank wie ein Abort. »Wer da?« kam es aus dem Dunkel. »Vater?« fragte Aliena. Dann sah sie eine dunkle Gestalt auf dem strohbedeckten Boden sitzen.

»Aliena?« Es klang ungläubig. »Bist du es, Aliena?« Die Stimme ihres Vaters, nur älter.

Sie trat näher und hielt die Kerze hoch. Er sah zu ihr auf, der Kerzenschein fiel auf sein Gesicht – und Aliena stockte der Atem vor Entsetzen. Er war kaum wiederzuerkennen.

Er war schon immer dünn gewesen, aber jetzt sah er aus wie ein Skelett .

Er starrte vor Dreck, und seine Kleider waren zu Lumpen zerfallen. »Aliena!« sagte er. »Du bist es wirklich!« Sein Gesicht verzog sich zu einem Lächeln, das auf Aliena wirkte, als grinse sie ein Totenschädel an.

Sie brach in Tränen aus. Der Schock traf sie völlig unvorbereitet: seine ungeheuerliche Veränderung übertraf noch ihre schlimmsten Befürchtungen. Sie erkannte sofort, daß er im Sterben lag; der bösartige Odo hatte die Wahrheit gesagt. Aber er war noch am Leben, litt noch immer Qualen und freute sich doch so schmerzlich, sie zu sehen. Sie hatte sich vorgenommen, ruhig und gefaßt zu bleiben, aber nun verlor sie jede Beherrschung, sackte vor ihm in die Knie und weinte, als wollten die Schluchzer, die tief aus ihrem Inneren drangen, sie schier zerreißen.

Er beugte sich vor und legte die Arme um sie und tätschelte ihr den Rücken, wie man ein Kind tröstet, das sich über ein angeschrammtes Knie oder ein kaputtes Spielzeug grämt. »Wein doch nicht«, sagte er sanft. »Nicht jetzt, wo du deinen Vater so glücklich gemacht hast.«

Aliena spürte, wie ihr die Kerze aus der Hand genommen wurde. Vater sagte: »Und dieser große junge Mann ist mein Richard?«

»Ja, Vater«, erwiderte Richard steif.

Aliena umarmte ihren Vater; seine Magerkeit fühlte sich an wie Stöcke in einem Sack. Er siechte dahin, war nur noch Haut und Knochen. Sie wollte sprechen, ihm etwas Liebes oder Tröstliches sagen, doch vor lauter Schluchzen brachte sie kein Wort heraus.

»Richard«, hörte sie ihn sagen, »wie groß du geworden bist! Hast du schon einen Bart?«

»Er sprießt schon ein bißchen, Vater, ist aber noch sehr spärlich.«

Aliena merkte, daß auch Richard den Tränen nahe war und darum kämpfte, nicht die Fassung zu verlieren. Wenn er es nicht schafft, dachte Aliena, wird er sich schämen, denn Vater wird ihm prompt befehlen, er solle sich zusammenreißen und wie ein Mann benehmen, und das macht alles nur noch schlimmer. Vor lauter Sorge um Richard hörte sie auf zu weinen und gewann mühsam ihre Fassung zurück. Sie drückte Vaters grausam dürren Körper noch einmal an sich, löste sich dann aus der Umarmung, wischte sich die Tränen aus den Augen und schneuzte sich in ihren Ärmel.

»Geht es euch beiden gut?« fragte Vater. Er sprach langsamer als früher und seine Stimme war zittriger geworden. »Wie seid ihr zurechtgekommen? Wo lebt ihr jetzt? Sie haben mir nicht das geringste über euch berichtet – das war die ärgste Tortur, die sie sich ausdenken konnten. Aber ihr scheint wohlauf zu sein – gesund und munter! Das ist wunderbar!«

Das Wort Tortur ließ Aliena zusammenzucken, und sie fragte sich, ob er tatsächlich gefoltert worden war, hakte jedoch nicht nach: Sie hatte Angst vor seiner Antwort. Statt dessen nahm sie Zuflucht zu einer Lüge: »Uns geht es gut, Vater.« Die nackte Wahrheit hätte ihm den Rest gegeben, das wußte sie genau. Sie hätte nicht nur das Glück zerstört, das er in diesem Moment empfand, sondern außerdem noch dazu geführt, daß er seine letzten Tage auf Erden voller quälender Selbstvorwürfe durchlitt. »Wir sind auf der Burg geblieben, und Matthew hat sich um uns gekümmert.«

»Aber da könnt ihr nicht mehr wohnen«, gab er zurück. »Der König hat diesen fetten Tölpel Percy Hamleigh zum Grafen ernannt – also bekommt er auch die Burg.«

Er wußte also Bescheid. »Es ist alles in Ordnung«, beruhigte sie ihn. »Wir haben die Burg verlassen.«

Er berührte ihr Kleid, das alte Leinending, das ihr die Frau des Jagdpflegers geschenkt hatte. »Was ist das?« fragte er streng. »Hast du etwa deine Kleider verkauft?«

Ihm entgeht immer noch nichts, dachte Aliena. Er läßt sich nicht so einfach hinters Licht führen. Sie entschied sich, ihm einen Teil der Wahrheit zu sagen. »Wir mußten die Burg überstürzt verlassen und haben keine Kleidung mitgenommen.«

»Wo ist Matthew? Warum ist er nicht bei euch?«

Diese Frage hatte sie befürchtet. Sie zögerte mit der Antwort, nur kurz zwar, aber es war ihm nicht entgangen.

»Na los! Ihr braucht mir nichts zu verheimlichen!« sagte er mit einem Anflug der gewohnten Autorität. »Wo ist Matthew?«

»Die Hamleighs haben ihn umgebracht«, erwiderte sie. »Aber uns haben sie kein Haar gekrümmt.« Sie hielt den Atem an. Ob er ihr das glaubte?

»Armer Matthew«, sagte er traurig. »Eine Kämpfernatur war er nie. Ich hoffe nur, daß er direkt in den Himmel gekommen ist.«

Er hatte ihr die Geschichte abgenommen! Erleichtert schlug Aliena ungefährlichere Themen an. »Wir sind nach Winchester gekommen, um den König zu ersuchen, gewisse Vorkehrungen für uns zu treffen, aber er ...«

»Zwecklos«, unterbrach er sie, bevor sie erklären konnte, warum der König nicht zu sprechen war. »Er wird keinen Finger für euch rühren.«

Sein harscher Ton wirkte verletzend auf Aliena. Hatte sie sich nicht alle Mühe gegeben, das Beste aus ihrer aussichtslosen Situation zu machen? Hatte sie dafür gar kein Lob verdient? Nur eine abfällige Bemerkung, die deutlich besagte: *Das war reine Zeitverschwendung.* Nun ja, mit Kritik war Vater stets schnell bei der Hand. Eigentlich sollte ich daran gewöhnt sein, dachte sie und fragte fügsam: »Was sollen wir jetzt tun, Vater?«

Er rutschte auf dem Stroh ein wenig hin und her, und dabei ertönte ein vernehmliches Klirren. Alienas Entsetzen nahm kein Ende: Sie hatten ihn tatsächlich in Ketten gelegt! »Mir blieb nur eine Möglichkeit, wenigstens etwas Geld zu verstecken. Nichts wirklich Sicheres, aber die einzige Gelegenheit, die sich bot. In der Geldkatze unter meinem Hemd hatte ich fünfzig Byzantiner, und die übergab ich einem Priester.«

»Fünfzig Byzantiner!« japste Aliena verblüfft. Das waren Goldstücke, die nicht in England geschlagen wurden, sondern aus Byzanz kamen. Sie hatte noch nie erlebt, daß jemand mehr als einen davon besaß. Ein Byzantiner war vierundzwanzig Silberpennies wert, dann waren fünfzig – nein, soweit reichten ihre Rechenkünste nicht aus.

»Welchem Priester?« wollte Richard vernünftigerweise wissen.

»Vater Ralph von der St.-Michaelis-Kirche am Nordtor.«

»Ist er ein guter Mensch?« fragte Aliena.

»Das kann ich nur hoffen, aber sicher bin ich nicht. An dem Tag, da die Hamleighs mich nach Winchester brachten, war ich zufällig ein paar Augenblicke allein mit ihm, bevor sie mich einsperrten. Ich wußte, daß das die letzte Gelegenheit für mich war. Also gab ich ihm meine Geldkatze und flehte ihn an, sie sicher für euch aufzubewahren. Fünfzig Byzantiner, das sind immerhin fünf Pfund Silber.«

Fünf ganze Pfund! Diese Neuigkeit mußte Aliena erst einmal verdauen, doch dann begriff sie sofort, daß dieses Geld ihr Leben von Grund auf verändern würde: Das war das Ende ihrer Armut! Von nun an mußten sie nicht mehr von der Hand in den Mund leben, sie konnten sich Brot kaufen und sogar die höllisch unbequemen Holzschuhe durch richtige Stiefel ersetzen. Ja, sie konnten sich, sollten sie wieder reisen müssen, zwei billige Ponys leisten. Gewiß, das Geld würde nicht ewig reichen, doch zunächst einmal enthob es sie des beängstigenden Gefühls, unentwegt am Rande des Abgrunds entlangzubalancieren. In Zukunft mußte sie nicht mehr all ihre Gedanken der Frage widmen, wie sie den nächsten Tag überstehen sollten. Statt dessen könnte sie sich den wesentlichen Dingen zuwenden – wie Vater aus diesem schrecklichen Gefängnis befreit werden konnte. »Was sollen wir anfangen, wenn wir das Geld haben?« fragte sie. »Wir müssen dich freibekommen.«

»Ich komme hier nicht mehr raus«, beschied er sie grob. »Daran ist überhaupt nicht zu denken. Sie hätten mich doch längst aufgeknüpft, wenn ich nicht im Sterben läge.«

Aliena rang um Luft. Wie konnte Vater nur derart reden?

»Was entsetzt dich daran?« fragte er sie. »Der König muß mich auf jeden Fall aus dem Weg schaffen, und auf diese Weise hat er mich nicht selbst auf dem Gewissen.«

»Vater«, schlug Richard vor, »ich glaube, ich kann dich hier herausholen. Die Wachleute sind nicht besonders aufmerksam, wenn der König nicht da ist, und mit ein paar Mann müßte ich es schaffen.«

Aliena brauchte nicht lange nachzudenken, um zu wissen, daß dieser Befreiungsplan scheitern mußte: Dazu besaß Richard weder die nötige Erfahrung noch die erforderlichen Fähigkeiten. Und davon ganz abgesehen, war er einfach zu jung – kein erwachsener Mann würde sich seinem Befehl unterordnen.

Sie befürchtete schon, Vater könne den Bruder durch eine seiner höhnischen Bemerkungen verletzen, aber er sagte nur: »Schlag dir das aus dem Kopf. Solltest du dennoch hier einbrechen, werde ich mich weigern, dir zu folgen.«

Es hatte keinen Sinn, sich noch mit ihm zu streiten, wenn er einmal eine Entscheidung getroffen hatte. Dennoch wollte Aliena schier das Herz brechen bei dem Gedanken, daß Vater seine letzten Tage in dieser stinkenden Zelle verbringen mußte. Aber konnte sie nicht doch einiges tun, um ihm das Leben zu erleichtern? »Gut«, sagte sie, »wenn du bleiben willst, machen wir hier sauber und besorgen frische Binsen. Und wir bringen dir jeden Tag warmes Essen. Wir können Kerzen mitbringen und vielleicht sogar eine Bibel für dich ausleihen. Du kannst ein Feuer machen ...«

»Nichts da!« fiel er ihr ins Wort. »Ihr werdet nichts dergleichen tun. Ich erlaube es euch nicht, daß ihr eure Zeit damit verschwendet, hier herumzulungern und zu warten, bis ich tot bin.«

Aliena kamen erneut die Tränen. »Aber wir können dich doch nicht einfach deinem Schicksal überlassen!«

Wie stets, wenn jemand ihm törichterweise zu widersprechen wagte, überhörte er den Einwand einfach. »Eure liebe Mutter hatte eine Schwester, eure Tante Edith. Sie lebt mit ihrem Mann, einem Ritter, in dem Dorf Huntleigh an der Straße nach Gloucester. Dort geht hin.«

Dann konnten sie Vater regelmäßig besuchen, fiel Aliena ein. Vielleicht gestattete er wenigstens seiner Schwägerin und ihrem Mann, ihm ein paar Erleichterungen zu verschaffen. Sie versuchte, sich Tante Edith und Onkel Simon ins Gedächtnis zu rufen, die sie seit Mamas Tod nicht mehr gesehen hatte. Sie entsann sich undeutlich einer schmalen, nervösen Frau, die ihrer Mutter glich, und eines großen, lebhaften Mannes, der bei Tisch kräftig zugelangt hatte. »Werden sie sich um uns kümmern?« fragte sie zweifelnd.

»Natürlich. Sie sind doch eure Verwandten.«

Aliena fragte sich, ob das ein hinreichender Grund war, daß eine in bescheidenen Verhältnissen lebende Ritterfamilie zwei hungrige Heranwachsende bei sich aufnahm; aber Vater hatte es behauptet, und sie vertraute ihm.

»Was sollen wir dort tun?« fragte sie.

»Richard wird Schildknappe seines Onkels und die Fertigkeiten des Rittertums erlernen. Und du wirst bis zu deiner Verheiratung Tante Ediths Kammerzofe sein.«

Im Laufe des Gesprächs überkam Aliena das Gefühl, sie hätte nun schon meilenweit eine schwere Last mit sich herumgetragen und spüre erst jetzt, da sie ihr von den Schultern genommen wurde, wie sehr ihr Rücken schmerzte. Jetzt hatte Vater wieder das Sagen und ihr wurde klar, daß die Verantwortung der letzten Tage viel zu groß für sie gewesen war. Wie beruhigend, daß er trotz Krankheit und Gefangensetzung alles zuverlässig im Griff hatte! Vor allem aber erleichterte sie, daß sie nun ihrer Hauptsorge ledig war – denn es schien höchst überflüssig, sich ausgerechnet um ihn zu sorgen, der so bereitwillig das Kommando übernahm.

Jetzt wurde er sogar noch herrischer. »Bevor ihr geht, werdet ihr mir beide einen Eid schwören.«

Aliena war entsetzt: Davor hatte er sie stets gewarnt. *Einen Eid schwören heißt, seine Seele aufs Spiel zu setzen,* pflegte er zu sagen. *Schwöre nur, wenn du absolut sicher bist, eher sterben zu wollen als den Schwur zu brechen.* Und genau eines solchen Schwurs wegen war er hier: Alle anderen Barone hatten ihr Wort gebrochen und König Stephan den Treueid geleistet, nur Vater hatte sich geweigert. Er wäre lieber gestorben, als seinen Schwur zu brechen – und genau das war jetzt der Fall.

»Gib mir dein Schwert«, sagte er zu Richard.

Richard zog sein Schwert und reichte es ihm.

Vater nahm es an sich, drehte es um und deutete mit dem Heft nach vorn. »Knie dich hin.«

Richard kniete vor seinem Vater nieder.

»Leg deine Hand auf das Heft.« Er hielt inne, um Kraft zu schöpfen. Dann ertönte seine Stimme so laut wie Glockenschläge: »Schwöre bei Gott, dem Allmächtigen, bei Jesus Christus und allen Heiligen, daß du nicht eher ruhen wirst, als bis du Graf von Shiring und Herr über alle Ländereien bist, über die ich einst gebot.«

Aliena vernahm es überrascht und betroffen. Sie hatte etwas Gewöhnlicheres von Vater erwartet, wie das Versprechen, stets die Wahrheit zu sagen und Gott zu fürchten; aber nein, er gab Richard einen genau umrissenen Auftrag, den zu erfüllen womöglich sein ganzes Leben lang dauerte!

Richard holte tief Luft und sprach mit leicht zitternder Stimme: »Ich schwöre bei Gott dem Allmächtigen, bei Jesus Christus und allen Heiligen, daß ich nicht eher ruhen werde, als bis ich Graf von Shiring und Herr über alle Ländereien bin, über die du einst gebotest.«

Vater stieß einen Seufzer aus, als wäre ihm ein Stein vom Herzen gefallen. Gleich darauf verblüffte er Aliena noch einmal. Er drehte sich um und hielt ihr das Heft des Schwertes entgegen. »Schwöre bei Gott dem Allmächtigen, bei Jesus Christus und allen Heiligen, daß du für deinen Bruder Richard Sorge tragen wirst, bis er sein Gelübde erfüllt hat.«

Aliena fühlte sich wie verurteilt. Das also war ihr bestimmt: Richard sollte Vater rächen, und sie hatte sich um Richard zu kümmern. Auf diese Weise konnte auch sie Vergeltung üben, denn wenn Richard Graf wurde, verlor William Hamleigh sein Erbe. Es kam ihr in den Sinn, daß niemand *sie* gefragt hatte, wie sie sich ihr Leben vorstellte, aber dieser dumme Einwand verflüchtigte sich ebenso schnell wie er gekommen war. Dies war ihre Bestimmung, und sie schien ihr nur rechtens. Aliena lehnte sich nicht dagegen auf, aber sie machte sich klar, wie schicksalsträchtig dieser Moment war: Ein Zurück gab es nicht mehr, und ihr Lebensweg wurde unwiderruflich vorherbestimmt. Sie legte ihre Hand auf das Heft und leistete den verlangten Eid. Die Klarheit und Stärke ihrer Stimme überraschte sie selbst. »Ich schwöre bei Gott dem Allmächtigen, bei Jesus Christus und allen Heiligen, daß ich für meinen Bruder Richard Sorge tragen werde, bis er sein Gelübde erfüllt hat.« Sie bekreuzigte sich. Es war vollbracht. Ich habe einen Eid geschworen, dachte sie, und lieber will ich sterben als mein Wort zu brechen. Der Gedanke erfüllte sie mit einer Art zorniger Befriedigung.

»Gut«, sagte Vater, und seine Stimme klang wieder ebenso schwach wie zuvor. »Von nun an braucht ihr nie wieder hierherzukommen.«

Aliena glaubte ihren Ohren nicht zu trauen. »Onkel Simon kann uns ab und zu herbringen, und wir kümmern uns darum, daß du es immer warm und genug zu essen hast ...«

»Nein«, sagte er entschieden. »Ihr habt jetzt eine Aufgabe zu erfüllen. Ihr werdet weder eure Zeit noch eure Kraft auf Besuche im Kerker verschwenden.«

Sie hörte ihm an, daß er keinen Widerspruch dulden würde, konnte aber nicht anders, als gegen seine harte Entscheidung zu protestieren.

»Dann laß uns wenigstens einmal noch herkommen, damit wir dir ein paar Erleichterungen verschaffen können!«

»Ich will keine Erleichterungen.«

»Bitte ...«

»Kommt nicht in Frage.«

Sie gab auf. Er pflegte gegen sich selbst mindestens ebenso hart zu sein wie gegen andere. »Wie du willst«, brachte sie schluchzend heraus.

»Ihr geht am besten wieder«, sagte er.

»Jetzt schon?«

»Ja. Hier herrscht nichts als Verzweiflung, Fäulnis und Tod. Nun, da ich weiß, daß es euch gut geht und ihr mir versprochen habt zurückzugewinnen, was uns zusteht, bin ich mit meinem Los zufrieden. Wenn ich jedoch zusehen müßte, wie ihr eure Zeit mit Besuchen hier vertut, wäre mein Glück schnell wieder dahin. Geht jetzt also.«

»Nein, Papa!« entgegnete Aliena wider besseres Wissen.

»Hör zu«, sagte er, und seine Stimme nahm endlich einen weicheren Klang an. »Ich habe ein ehrenhaftes Leben geführt und werde bald sterben. Ich habe meine Sünden bekannt und bin bereit für die Ewigkeit. Betet für meine Seele. Und geht.«

Aliena neigte sich vor und küßte ihn auf die Stirn. Ihre Tränen benetzten sein Gesicht. »Lebe wohl, liebster Vater«, flüsterte sie und erhob sich.

Richard beugte sich hinunter und küßte ihn. »Lebe wohl, Vater«, sagte er unsicher.

»Gott segne euch und helfe euch, euer Gelübde zu erfüllen«, sagte Vater.

Richard ließ ihm die Kerze da. Aliena drehte sich auf der Schwelle noch einmal um und warf in dem unsteten Licht einen letzten Blick auf ihn. Auf seinem eingefallenen Gesicht lag der wohlbekannte Ausdruck ruhiger Entschlossenheit. Sie betrachtete ihn, bis ihr Blick von Tränen verschleiert wurde. Dann drehte sie sich um, durchquerte den Vorraum und stolperte ins Freie.

Richard mußte sie führen, denn Aliena war wie betäubt vor Kummer. Es wollte ihr vorkommen, als wäre Vater schon tot, aber am schlimmsten empfand sie, daß er noch immer zu leiden hatte. Sie hörte, wie Richard sich nach dem Weg erkundigte, achtete aber nicht weiter darauf und fand sich schließlich vor einer kleinen Kirche wieder, an die eine windschiefe Hütte gebaut war. Erst da sah sich Aliena um und stellte fest, daß sie sich in einem Armenviertel mit winzigen, baufälligen Häusern befanden. Die Gassen waren mit Unrat übersät, in dem wilde Köter nach Ratten jagten und die Kinder im Schmutz spielten. »Das muß Sankt Michael sein«, sagte Richard.

Das Hüttchen neben der Kirche war offenbar das Haus des Priesters. Es hatte nur ein Fenster mit einem Fensterladen davor. Da die Tür offen stand, gingen sie hinein.

In der Mitte des einzigen Raums brannte ein Feuer. Die Einrichtung bestand aus einem groß gezimmerten Tisch, wenigen Schemeln und einem Bierfaß in einer Ecke. Der Boden war mit Binsen ausgelegt. Vor dem Feuer saß ein Mann auf einem Stuhl und trank aus einem großen Becher. Er war klein und mager und mochte um die Fünfzig sein; er hatte eine rote Nase und lichtes graues Haar. Er trug normale Alltagskleidung, ein schmuddeliges Unterhemd mit einer braunen Tunika und Holzschuhe.

»Vater Ralph?« fragte Richard unsicher.

»Und wenn ich der wäre?«

Aliena seufzte. Warum nur machten die Leute dauernd Schwierigkeiten, als gäbe es davon nicht schon mehr als genug auf der Welt? Im Augenblick jedoch fehlte ihr die Kraft, sich mit den Launen anderer auseinanderzusetzen, und sie überließ es Richard zu fragen: »Heißt das ja?«

Die Frage beantwortete sich von selbst. Von draußen rief eine Stimme: »Ralph? Bist du zu Hause?« Gleich darauf kam eine Frau mittleren Alters herein und gab dem Priester einen Kanten Brot und eine große Schale, aus der Fleischgeruch stieg. Zum erstenmal lief Aliena dabei nicht das Wasser im Mund zusammen: Sie fühlte sich viel zu betäubt, um hungrig zu sein. Die Frau gehörte wohl zu Ralphs Gemeinde, denn ihre Kleidung war von der gleichen Armseligkeit wie seine eigene. Wortlos nahm er ihr das Essen ab und ließ es sich schmecken. Die Frau bedachte die Geschwister mit einem gleichgültigen Blick und ging wieder hinaus.

»Nun, Vater Ralph«, sagte Richard, »ich bin der Sohn von Bartholomäus, dem ehemaligen Grafen von Shiring.«

Der Mann hielt inne und sah von seinem Essen auf. Aus seinem Gesicht sprach Feindseligkeit – und noch etwas, das Aliena nicht deuten konnte. Empfand er Furcht? Schuldgefühle? Er wandte sich wieder seiner Schüssel zu, murmelte aber: »Was wollt ihr von mir?«

Aliena wurde mulmig zumute.

»Du weißt genau, was ich will«, gab Richard zurück. »Mein Geld, die fünfzig Byzantiner.«

»Ich weiß nicht, wovon du redest«, sagte Ralph.

Aliena starrte ihn ungläubig an. Das darf doch nicht wahr sein! dachte sie. Vater hat bei diesem Priester Geld für uns hinterlegt – das hat er uns selbst erzählt! Und in solchen Sachen irrt er sich nie.

Richard war alle Farbe aus dem Gesicht gewichen. »Wie meinst du das?«

»Genauso, wie ich's sage: Ich weiß nicht, wovon du redest. Und jetzt raus mit euch.« Er löffelte wieder seinen Eintopf.

Der Kerl log natürlich; aber was war dagegen zu machen? Richard ließ nicht locker: »Mein Vater hat Geld bei dir hinterlegt – fünfzig Byzantiner. Und er hat dich angewiesen, es mir zu geben. Wo hast du es gelassen?«

»Dein Vater hat mir gar nichts gegeben.«

»Er hat aber gesagt, daß ...«

»Dann hat er gelogen.«

Das hatte Vater ganz bestimmt nicht! Aliena ergriff zum erstenmal das Wort. »Wir wissen, daß du lügst.«

Ralph zuckte die Achseln. »Ihr könnt euch ja beim Vogt beschweren.«

»Das könnte aber unangenehm für dich werden. In dieser Stadt hackt man Dieben die Hände ab.«

Ein Anflug von Angst machte sich auf seinem Gesicht breit, verflüchtigte sich aber sofort wieder, und er gab herausfordernd zurück: »Dann steht mein Wort gegen das eines eingekerkerten Verräters – falls euer Vater überhaupt lange genug lebt, um seine Aussage machen zu können.«

Er hat recht, dachte Aliena. Es gibt keinen einzigen Zeugen dafür, denn das Geld war Vaters Geheimnis – er wollte vermeiden, daß es dem König in die Hände fällt oder diesem Percy Hamleigh oder irgendwelchen anderen Aasgeiern, die sich um den Besitz eines in Ungnade Gefallenen scharen. Hier herrschen die gleichen Gesetze wie im Wald, erkannte sie voll Bitterkeit. Die Kinder eines eingekerkerten Adeligen darf man offenbar ungestraft ausplündern. Wieso habe ich eigentlich vor diesen Unmenschen Angst? fragte sie sich zornig. Wieso haben die keine Angst vor mir?

Richard sah sie an und flüsterte ihr zu: »Er hat recht, oder?«

»Ja«, erwiderte sie Gift und Galle spuckend. »Es hat gar keinen Zweck, daß wir uns beim Vogt beschweren.«

Ihr fiel wieder ein, wie sie ein einziges Mal jemandem Angst eingeflößt hatte: damals im Wald, als sie den fetten Banditen erstach und sein Komplize wie von Hunden gehetzt davonrannte. Dieser Priester ist keinen Deut besser als die Verfemten! dachte sie. Und er ist alt und schwach. Wahrscheinlich hat er nicht damit gerechnet, daß wir jemals bei ihm auftauchen. Vielleicht läßt er sich doch noch einschüchtern?

»Was sollen wir jetzt tun?« fragte Richard.

Aliena folgte einer plötzlichen Eingebung. »Sein Haus niederbrennen«, sagte sie wütend. Im Nu stand sie vor dem Feuer und trat mit ihren Holzschuhen nach den brennenden Scheiten, so daß sie nach allen Seiten flogen. Die Binsen um den Feuerplatz gingen sofort in Flammen auf.

»He!« brüllte Ralph. Er wollte aufstehen, doch dabei entglitt ihm das Brot, und der Eintopf ergoß sich über seinen Schoß, und bevor er noch richtig stand, hatte sich auch schon Aliena auf ihn gestürzt.

Sie versetzte ihm einen Stoß, so daß er das Gleichgewicht verlor und zu Boden fiel. Aliena, die blindwütig und ohne nachzudenken gehandelt hatte, beflügelte der Erfolg ihres Angriffs noch. Sofort warf sie sich über ihn, landete mit den Knien auf seiner Brust und schnürte ihm den Atem ab. Ihre Wut stieg ins Unermeßliche, und sie schrie ihm direkt ins Gesicht: »Du verlogener, diebischer, gottloser Heide, dich laß ich bei lebendigem Leib verbrennen!«

Er wandte die Augen ab – und verzog vor Entsetzen das Gesicht. Aliena, die seinem Blick folgte, sah, daß Richard sein Schwert gezogen und angriffsbereit erhoben hatte. Das schmutzige Gesicht des Priesters war ganz blaß geworden, und er flüsterte: »Du bist des Teufels!«

»Und du bestiehlst arme Kinder!« Aus dem Augenwinkel bemerkte sie einen langen Scheit, dessen eines Ende lichterloh brannte. Sie ergriff ihn beim anderen Ende und hielt dem Priester die brennende Seite vors Gesicht. »Jetzt brenn' ich dir die Augen aus, eins nach dem anderen. Erst das linke ...«

»Nein, bitte nicht«, wisperte er. »Tu mir nicht weh.«

Aliena konnte kaum fassen, wie schnell er klein beigab. Dann fiel ihr auf, daß die Binsen um sie herum alle Feuer gefangen hatten. »Wo ist das Geld?« fragte sie ihn plötzlich wieder in ihrem normalen Tonfall.

Dem Priester saß noch immer der Schreck in allen Gliedern. »In der Kirche.«

»Wo in der Kirche?«

»Unter dem Stein hinter dem Altar.«

Aliena sah Richard an. »Du bewachst ihn, während ich gehe und nachschaue«, befahl sie ihm. »Wenn er sich rührt, bringst du ihn um.«

»Allie«, sagte Richard, »bis du zurückkommst, wird das Haus abgebrannt sein.«

Aliena sah sich kurz um, ging zu dem Bierfaß und hob den Deckel. Es war noch halb voll. Sie packte es am Rand und kippte es um. Das Bier ergoß sich über den Boden, tränkte die Binsen und erstickte die Flammen.

Aliena verließ die Hütte. Sie wußte, daß sie ihre Drohung, dem Priester die Augen auszubrennen, wahr gemacht hätte; doch statt sich dessen zu schämen, empfand sie ein geradezu überwältigendes Machtgefühl. Sie hatte beschlossen, sich nicht mehr unterkriegen zu lassen, und sie hatte diesen Entschluß gleich in die Tat umgesetzt. Die Kirche besaß nur einen Eingang, der durch ein kleines Schloß gesichert war. Aliena hätte durchaus zurückgehen und den Schlüssel holen können, aber sie zog ihren Dolch aus dem Ärmel, schob die Klinge in die Türritze und brach das Schloß auf. Die Tür flog auf, und sie trat ein.

Die Kirche war wahrhaft erbärmlich. Außer dem Altar gab es praktisch nichts darin, und ihr einziger Schmuck bestand aus wenigen unbeholfenen Malereien auf den gekalkten Holzwänden. Es gab nur eine einzige Kerze, die in einer Ecke stand und mit ihrer flackernden Flamme ein geschnitztes Bildnis beleuchtete, das vermutlich den heiligen Michael darstellte. Die Einsicht, daß fünf Pfund Silber für einen so armen Mann wie Vater Ralph eine beinahe unüberwindliche Versuchung sein mußten, schmälerte Alienas Triumph vorübergehend ein wenig, doch in ihrer Lage verbot sich jegliches Mitgefühl von selbst.

Die Kirche stand auf nackter, festgestampfter Erde, doch hinter dem Altar lag eine Steinplatte. Kein besonders gutes Versteck, fand Aliena, aber wer kam schon auf die Idee, eine so offensichtlich arme Kirche auszurauben?

Sie kniete sich auf einem Bein nieder und versuchte, die Platte zu verrücken, doch sie war sehr schwer und rührte sich nicht vom Fleck. Aliena bekam es mit der Angst zu tun. Richard kann diesen Ralph schließlich nicht ewig in Schach halten, überlegte sie, und wenn der Kerl entkommt und Hilfe holt – dann muß *ich* beweisen, daß das Geld uns gehört! Und das dürfte sich womöglich noch als meine geringste Sorge herausstellen, denn immerhin habe ich schon einen Überfall auf einen Priester und einen Einbruch in seine Kirche auf dem Kerbholz. Die Erkenntnis, daß nunmehr sie selbst gegen das Gesetz verstieß, ließ sie frösteln. Der Anflug von Angst verlieh ihr zusätzliche Kraft. Mit einem gewaltigen Ruck gelang es ihr, die Platte ein kleines Stück zu verschieben. Die Aushöhlung war ungefähr einen Fuß tief, und nach einem weiteren Ruck an der Platte konnte Aliena ihre Hand hineinschieben und die Geldkatze herausholen.

»Na also!« sagte sie laut. »Da ist sie ja!« Sie empfand es als große Genugtuung, daß sie den unehrlichen Priester überwältigt und das Geld ihres Vaters zurückerobert hatte. Doch als sie sich erhob, merkte sie, daß ihr Sieg nicht unumschränkt war: Die Geldkatze fühlte sich verdächtig leicht an. Aliena schnürte sie auf und schüttelte den Inhalt heraus: Es waren nur zehn Münzen. Zehn Byzantiner entsprachen einem Pfund Silber.

Was war aus den anderen vierzig geworden? Vater Ralph hatte sie ausgegeben! Alienas Zorn flammte wieder auf. Das Geld ihres Vaters war alles, was sie auf dieser Welt besaß, und der diebische Priester hatte sie um vier Fünftel betrogen!

Den Gürtel der Geldkatze hin und her schwingend, verließ sie die Kirche. Auf der Straße zuckte ein Passant bei ihrem Anblick erschrocken zurück, als käme ihm ihre Miene nicht ganz geheuer vor. Aliena nahm keine Notiz von ihm und betrat das Haus des Priesters, wo Richard breitbeinig über Vater Ralph stand und ihm die Schwertspitze an die Kehle hielt. Aliena ging sofort wieder auf den Priester los. »Das ist nur ein kläglicher Rest!« schrie sie ihn an. »Was hast du mit unserem Geld gemacht?«

»Es ist weg«, flüsterte der Priester.

Sie kniete sich neben ihn auf den Boden und hielt ihm ihr Messer vors Gesicht. »Was heißt weg?«

»Ich habe es ausgegeben«, gestand er mit einer Stimme, die heiser vor Furcht war.

Aliena hatte das Gefühl, diesen Kerl erstechen, erschlagen und dann auch noch in einem Fluß ersäufen zu können – aber was hätte es schon geholfen! Davon bekam sie ihr Geld nicht wieder. Ihr Blick fiel auf das umgestürzte Faß: Ein Trinker hatte einen großen Bedarf an Bier. Sie hätte platzen können vor Wut und Enttäuschung. »Wenn sich dein Ohr für einen Penny verkaufen ließe, ich würde es dir abschneiden!« fauchte sie, worauf er sie ansah, als rechne er damit, daß sie es auch für nichts und wieder nichts täte.

»Allie«, wandte Richard furchtsam ein, »das Geld ist weg. Wir sollten den Rest nehmen und schnellstens verschwinden.«

Widerwillig gestand sich Aliena ein, daß er recht hatte. Ihre Wut verpuffte allmählich und hinterließ einen bitteren Nachgeschmack. Es brachte ihr nichts ein, wenn sie den Priester noch mehr einschüchterte: und je länger sie blieben, um so eher mochte jemand hereinkommen und sie ernsthaft in Schwierigkeiten bringen. Sie stand auf. »Na gut.« Sie verstaute die Goldmünzen in der Geldkatze, die sie sich unter ihren Umhang schnallte. Dann deutete sie mit dem Finger auf den Priester und drohte: »Kann sein, daß ich eines Tages wiederkomme und dich wirklich umbringe.«

Sie machte auf dem Absatz kehrt, verließ das Haus und marschierte die enge Gasse entlang. Richard setzte ihr nach. »Das hast du wunderbar gemacht, Allie!« stieß er aufgeregt hervor, als er sie eingeholt hatte. »Der Kerl war halb tot vor Angst – und du hast das Geld gekriegt!«

Sie nickte. »Ja, das habe ich«, erwiderte sie verbissen. Sie stand immer noch unter Spannung, fühlte sich aber, nachdem ihre Wut verraucht war, wie leergepumpt.

»Was sollen wir kaufen?« fragte Richard.

»Ein bißchen was zu essen für die Reise.«

»Keine Pferde?«

»Die kriegen wir nicht für ein Pfund.«

»Aber wir können dir wenigstens ein paar Stiefel kaufen.«

Sie dachte darüber nach. Ihre Holzschuhe waren die reinste Tortur und der Boden zu kalt, um barfuß zu gehen. Aber Stiefel waren teuer, und sie wollte das Geld nicht zu rasch ausgeben. »Nein«, entschied sie. »Ich werde es noch ein paar Tage länger ohne Stiefel aushalten. Wir behalten das Geld lieber.«

Er schien enttäuscht, focht ihre Autorität jedoch nicht an.

»Was sollen wir zu essen kaufen?«

»Grobes Brot, Hartkäse und Wein.«

»Wie wär's mit ein paar Pasteten?«

»Die sind zu teuer.«

»Oh!« Er schwieg einen Moment lang und sagte schließlich: »Du bist aber närrisch, Allie!«

Aliena seufzte. »Ich weiß.« Warum eigentlich? dachte sie. Ich hätte doch allen Grund, stolz auf mich zu sein. Ich habe uns von der Burg hierhergeführt, ich habe meinen Bruder verteidigt, ich habe meinen Vater gefunden, ich habe das Geld erobert. Ja, und ich habe einem Fettwanst mein Messer in den Bauch gerammt und meinen Bruder gezwungen, ihn zu töten; und einem Priester habe ich ein brennendes Holzscheit vors Gesicht gehalten, drauf und dran, ihm die Augen damit auszubrennen.

»Hat es mit Vater zu tun?« fragte Richard mitfühlend.

»Nein, nicht mit Vater«, erwiderte Aliena. »Nur mit mir selber.«

Aliena bereute, daß sie die Stiefel nicht gekauft hatte. Auf ihrem Marsch nach Gloucester trug sie die Botten, bis ihr die Füße bluteten, ging dann barfuß weiter, bis sie die Kälte nicht länger ertragen konnte, und schlüpfte schließlich doch wieder in die Holzschuhe. Sie fand heraus, daß es leichter ging, wenn sie gar nicht auf ihre Füße achtete; jedesmal, wenn sie die wunden Stellen und das Blut sah, empfand sie ihre Schmerzen stärker.

In der hügeligen Gegend, durch die sie kamen, gab es hauptsächlich ärmliche kleine Höfe, auf denen die Bauern nicht mehr als einen Morgen Hafer oder Roggen anbauten und nur wenige magere Tiere hielten. Als Aliena meinte, sie könnten nun nicht mehr allzu weit von Huntleigh entfernt sein, verweilte sie am Rande eines Dorfes und sprach einen Bauern an, der in einem eingezäunten Gehege neben einem niedrigen, aus Akaziengeflecht und Lehm gebauten Bauernhaus ein Schaf schor. Der Kopf des Tieres war in einer blockähnlichen Vorrichtung aus Holz gefangen, und die Wolle wurde mit einem langschneidigen Messer geschnitten. Zwei weitere Schafe harrten unruhig ihrer Schur, und ein viertes, bereits geschorenes Schaf tat sich auf der Weide gütlich und wirkte in der Kälte überaus nackt.

»Ein bißchen früh für die Schafschur«, bemerkte Aliena.

Der Bauer, ein junger Mann mit rotem Haar und Sommersprossen, blickte auf und grinste sie gutmütig an. Seine aufgekrempelten Ärmel entblößten behaarte Arme.

»Schon, aber ich brauche das Geld. Statt selber Hunger zu leiden, lasse ich lieber die Schafe frieren.«

»Wieviel bekommst du für die Wolle?«

»Einen Penny für ein Vlies. Aber dafür muß ich bis nach Gloucester gehen. Das kostet mich einen ganzen Arbeitstag auf dem Feld, ausgerechnet im Frühjahr, wenn es soviel zu tun gibt.« Das kam brummig heraus, schien aber nichts an seiner guten Laune zu ändern.

»Wie heißt dieses Dorf?« fragte Aliena ihn.

»Die Fremden nennen es Huntleigh«, sagte er. Bauern benutzten niemals den Namen ihres Dorfes – für sie war es einfach das Dorf. Namen bedeuten nur Reisenden etwas. »Wer bist du?« fragte er mit unverhohlener Neugier. »Was führt dich hierher?«

»Ich bin die Nichte Simons von Huntleigh«, erwiderte Aliena.

»Ach so. Nun, du findest ihn in dem großen Haus. Ein Stück die Straße zurück, dann den Pfad entlang, der zur Rechten durch die Felder führt.«

»Danke.«

Das Dorf lag behaglich inmitten seiner gepflegten Felder wie ein Schwein in seiner Suhle. Ungefähr zwanzig kleinere Behausungen drängten sich um das Herrenhaus, das nicht viel größer war als das eines wohlhabenden Bauern. Tante Edith und Onkel Simon konnten nicht sonderlich betucht sein.

Vor dem Gutshaus standen mehrere Männer bei einem Pferdegespann. Einer von ihnen schien der Lehnsherr zu sein, denn er trug eine scharlachrote Jacke. Aliena betrachtete ihn genauer. Es war zwölf oder dreizehn Jahre her, seit sie ihren Onkel Simon zum letztenmal gesehen hatte, aber sie glaubte, ihn zu erkennen. Sie hatte ihn als großen Mann in Erinnerung und er kam ihr jetzt kleiner vor, aber das lag sicher daran, daß sie selbst gewachsen war. Sein Haar begann sich zu lichten, und das Doppelkinn hatte er damals noch nicht gehabt. Dann hörte sie ihn sagen: »Dieses Tier hat einen sehr hohen Widerrist«, und erkannte ihn an der rauhen, leicht krächzenden Stimme zuverlässig wieder.

Allmählich wurde ihr wohler zumute. Von nun an werden wir verköstigt und gekleidet, versorgt und beschützt, dachte sie; mit grobem Brot und hartem Käse ist es jetzt ebenso vorbei wie mit den Nächten auf Stroh und langen Märschen mit der Hand am Messer. Hier wartete ein weiches Bett auf sie und ein neues Kleid, und zum Essen gab es gebratenes Fleisch.

Onkel Simon sah auf und in ihre Richtung. Zunächst wußte er nicht, wen er vor sich hatte. »Schaut euch das an«, sagte er zu seinen Männern. »Ein hübsches Mädchen und ein junger Soldat kommen zu Besuch!« Doch dann wurde sein Blick unstet; offenbar dämmerte ihm, daß er es nicht mit wildfremden Menschen zu tun hatte. »Ich kenne euch doch, oder?« sagte er.

»Ja, Onkel Simon, allerdings«, sagte Aliena.

Er zuckte zusammen, als sei ihm ein Geist erschienen.

»Bei allen Heiligen? Die Stimme einer Toten!«

Aliena verstand gar nichts, doch er lieferte ihr die Erklärung nach. Er trat auf sie zu und musterte sie so durchdringend, wie er ein Pferdegebiß begutachten mochte, und sagte schließlich: »Deine Mutter hatte die gleiche honigsüße Stimme. Und Herrgott noch mal, du bist genauso schön wie sie!« Er streckte die Hand aus, um ihr Gesicht zu berühren, aber sie trat eiligst einen Schritt zurück.

»Aber du bist auch genauso halsstarrig wie dein verdammter Vater, das sehe ich gleich. Er war es wohl, der euch hergeschickt hat, oder?«

Alles in Aliena sträubte sich. Es war ihr zuwider, daß er Papa als ihren »verdammten Vater« bezeichnete. Doch Widerspruch von ihrer Seite hätte ihn nur darin bestärkt, sie als halsstarrig zu bezeichnen; also biß sie sich auf die Zunge und antwortete bescheiden: »Ja. Er sagte, Tante Edith werde sich unserer annehmen.«

»Nun, da hat er sich geirrt«, sagte Onkel Simon. »Tante Edith ist tot. Und außerdem habe ich, seit euer Vater in Ungnade gefallen ist, die Hälfte meines Landes an Percy Hamleigh, diesen fetten Schurken, verloren. Hier sind harte Zeiten angebrochen. Ihr könnt also gleich wieder kehrtmachen und nach Winchester zurückgehen. Ich nehme euch jedenfalls nicht auf.«

Aliena war erschüttert. Wie hart er wirkte! »Aber wir sind doch mit dir verwandt!« sagte sie.

Er besaß Anstand genug, einen Anflug von Scham zu zeigen, doch seine Antwort fiel barsch aus. »Mit mir nicht. Du bist bloß die Nichte meiner ersten Frau, und die ist tot. Selbst als sie noch am Leben war, hat sie ihre Schwester nie besucht, nur wegen dieses aufgeblasenen Esels, den deine Mutter geheiratet hat.«

»Wir werden arbeiten«, bat Aliena. »Wir sind beide bereit ...«

»Spar dir deine Worte«, sagte er. »Ich nehme euch nicht auf.«

Aliena war fassungslos: Er klang so endgültig! Es hatte offensichtlich keinen Sinn, sich mit ihm zu streiten oder ihn anzuflehen. Doch mittlerweile hatte sie so viele Enttäuschungen und Rückschläge dieser Art einstecken müssen, daß sie eher Bitterkeit als Niedergeschlagenheit empfand. Noch vor einer Woche wäre sie in einer ähnlichen Situation in Tränen ausgebrochen. Jetzt war ihr eher danach, ihm ins Gesicht zu spucken. »Das vergesse ich dir nicht«, sagte sie. »Das bekommst du zu spüren, wenn Richard erst Graf ist und wir die Burg wiederhaben!«

Er lachte. »Ob ich das noch erlebe?«

Es hatte keinen Sinn, weiter herumzustehen und sich von diesem Menschen demütigen zu lassen. »Komm, wir gehen«, sagte sie zu Richard. »Wir kommen auch allein zurecht.«

Onkel Simon hatte sich bereits abgewandt und widmete sich wieder seinem Pferd mit dem hohen Widerrist. Den Männern in seiner Begleitung war ihre Verlegenheit anzusehen.

Kaum waren die Geschwister außer Hörweite, fragte Richard kläglich: »Was machen wir denn nun, Allie?«

»Wir werden diesen herzlosen Leuten beweisen, daß wir besser sind als sie«, erwiderte sie grimmig. Was sie fühlte war nicht Mut, sondern Haß, blanker Haß auf Onkel Simon, auf Vater Ralph, auf den Gefängnisaufseher Odo, auf die Banditen, auf den Jagdpfleger – und ganz besonders auf William Hamleigh.

»Nur gut, daß wir wenigstens Geld haben«, meinte Richard.

Das stimmte. Aber das Geld würde nicht ewig reichen.

»Wir können es nicht einfach so ausgeben«, sagte sie, während sie dem Pfad folgten, der zur Hauptstraße zurückführte. »Wenn wir es nur für Essen und solche Sachen ausgeben, dann sind wir, sobald es aufgebraucht ist, genauso arm dran wie zuvor. Wir müssen etwas damit anstellen.«

»Das sehe ich nicht ein«, sagte Richard. »Ich finde, wir sollten ein Pony kaufen.«

Sie starrte ihn an. War das ein Scherz? Doch sie konnte kein

Lächeln auf seinem Gesicht erkennen. Er verstand ganz einfach nicht, worum es ging. »Wir haben keine gesellschaftliche Stellung, keinen Titel, kein Land«, erklärte sie geduldig. »Der König wird uns nicht helfen. Als Hilfskräfte können wir uns nicht verdingen – das haben wir in Winchester schon versucht, und niemand wollte uns haben. Wir müssen aber nicht nur das tägliche Brot verdienen, sondern außerdem noch genug, um dich als Ritter auszustaffieren.«

»Ach so«, sagte er. »Jetzt verstehe ich.«

Sie sah ihm an, daß er es nicht wirklich begriff.

»Wir müssen uns in irgendeinem Beruf etablieren, damit wir genug zu essen haben und ausreichend Geld, um dir ein gutes Pferd zu kaufen.«

»Willst du damit sagen, daß ich bei einem Zimmermann in die Lehre gehen soll?«

Aliena schüttelte den Kopf. »Du mußt Ritter werden, nicht Zimmermann. Sind wir schon mal jemandem begegnet, der finanziell unabhängig war und keine Ausbildung hatte?«

»Ja«, erwiderte Richard unerwartet. »Meg aus Winchester.«

Er hatte recht. Meg war Wollhändlerin, obwohl sie nie in die Lehre gegangen war. »Aber Meg hat einen Marktstand.« Sie kamen an dem rothaarigen Bauern vorbei, der ihnen den Weg gewiesen hatte. Seine vier geschorenen Schafe befanden sich wieder auf der Weide, während er die Vliese mit geflochtenen Schilfrohrbändern zu einem Bündel schnürte. Er sah von seiner Arbeit auf und winkte ihnen zu. Leute wie er trugen ihre Wolle in die Stadt und verkauften sie an die Händler. Aber als Wollhändler braucht man ein Geschäft …

Oder vielleicht doch nicht?

Sie drehte sich abrupt um.

»Wo willst du hin?« fragte Richard.

Sie war zu aufgeregt, um zu antworten. Sie lehnte sich über den Zaun und fragte den Bauern: »Wieviel, hast du gesagt, kannst du für deine Wolle kriegen?«

»Einen Penny fürs Vlies«, erwiderte er.

»Aber der Hin- und Rückweg nach Gloucester kostet dich einen ganzen Tag Arbeit.«

»Genau da liegt der Hund begraben.«

»Und wenn ich dir deine Wolle abkaufe? Dann kannst du dir die Reise sparen.«

»Allie!« warf Richard ein. »Wir brauchen keine Wolle!«

»Halt den Mund, Richard.« Sie hatte jetzt keine Lust, ihm ihren

Plan zu erklären – sie brannte vor Ungeduld, ihn an dem Bauern auszuprobieren.

Der Bauer sagte: »Das wäre sehr nett von dir.« Aber er schaute zweifelnd drein, als traue er dem Braten nicht so recht.

»Einen Penny pro Vlies kann ich dir natürlich nicht geben.«

»Aha! Hab' ich mir doch gedacht, daß an der Sache etwas faul ist.«

»Ich könnte dir zwei Pennies für deine vier Vliese zahlen.«

»Aber jedes Vlies ist doch einen Penny wert!« wandte er ein.

»In Gloucester schon. Aber dies ist natürlich Huntleigh.«

Er schüttelte den Kopf. »Vier Pennies und ein Tag Arbeitsausfall sind mir lieber als zwei Pennies und ein gewonnener Tag.«

»Und wenn ich dir drei Pennies für deine vier Vliese biete?«

»Dann verlier' ich einen Penny.«

»Und gewinnst einen Arbeitstag.«

Er sah verwirrt aus. »Von so was hab' ich noch nie gehört.«

»Es ist genauso, als wenn ich Fuhrmann wäre und du mir einen Penny dafür gibst, die Wolle zu Markt zu tragen.«

Seine Begriffsstutzigkeit machte sie ärgerlich. »Die Frage ist, ob dir ein zusätzlicher Arbeitstag auf dem Feld einen Penny wert ist oder nicht?«

»Das hängt davon ab, was ich mit dem Tag anstelle«, erwiderte er nachdenklich.

Richard sagte: »Allie, was sollen wir denn mit vier Vliesen anfangen?«

»Sie an Meg verkaufen«, erwiderte sie ungeduldig. »Für je einen Penny. Auf diese Weise haben wir einen Penny verdient.«

»Aber dafür müssen wir auch den ganzen Weg nach Winchester zurücklaufen!«

»Nicht doch, du Dummkopf. Wir kaufen fünfzig Bauern ihre Wolle ab und nehmen alle Vliese mit nach Winchester. Verstehst du? Auf diese Weise können wir fünfzig Pennies Gewinn machen! Davon können wir uns ernähren *und* auf ein gutes Pferd für dich sparen!«

Sie wandte sich wieder dem Bauern zu. Sein fröhliches Grinsen war verschwunden und er kratzte sich seinen rotblonden Kopf. Es tat Aliena leid, ihn in solche Verwirrung gestürzt zu haben, aber ihr war daran gelegen, daß er ihr Angebot annahm. Tat er es, so hätte sie die Gewißheit, den ihrem Vater geleisteten Schwur halten zu können. Doch Bauern waren dickköpfig. Am liebsten hätte sie ihn am Kragen gefaßt und geschüttelt. Statt dessen griff sie in ihren Umhang und kramte in ihrer Geldbörse. Sie hatten die goldenen Byzantiner im

Haus des Goldschmieds in Winchester in Silberpennies umgetauscht; nun nahm sie drei heraus und hielt sie dem Bauern unter die Nase. »Da«, sagte sie. »Haben wir ein Geschäft gemacht oder nicht?«

Der Anblick des Silbers machte dem Bauern Beine. »Einverstanden«, sagte er und strich es ein.

Aliena lächelte. Es sah ganz so aus, als wären sie endlich auf dem richtigen Weg.

In der darauffolgenden Nacht benutzte sie ein gebündeltes Vlies als Kopfkissen. Der Schafsgeruch erinnerte sie an Megs Haus.

Beim Erwachen am nächsten Morgen entdeckte sie, daß sie nicht schwanger war.

Ein Silberstreif am Horizont!

Vier Wochen nach Ostern kamen Aliena und Richard mit einem handgezimmerten, von einem alten Klepper gezogenen Karren und einem riesigen Sack mit zweihundertvierzig Vliesen in Winchester an.

Und bemerkten zum erstenmal, daß es so etwas wie Zölle gab.

Bisher hatten sie die Stadt immer betreten, ohne irgendwelche Aufmerksamkeit auf sich zu ziehen, aber jetzt begriffen sie, warum die Stadttore schmal und Tag und Nacht mit Zöllnern besetzt waren. Für jede Wagenladung, die nach Winchester hineinfuhr, wurde eine Abgabe von einem Penny erhoben. Glücklicherweise hatten sie noch ein paar Pennies übrig und konnten den Zoll bezahlen; andernfalls hätten sie umkehren müssen.

Die meisten Vliese hatten sie zwischen einem halben und dreiviertel Penny gekostet. Für das alte Pferd hatten sie sechs Schillinge gezahlt und den holprigen Karren als Dreingabe bekommen. Den Rest des Geldes hatten sie fast gänzlich für Essen ausgegeben. Aber heute abend würden sie ein Pfund Silber *und* ein Pferd mit Karren besitzen.

Danach wollte Aliena wieder hinausfahren, einen weiteren Sack Vliese zusammenkaufen und das so lange wiederholen, bis alle Schafe geschoren waren. Bis zum Ende des Sommers wollte sie genug Geld für ein gutes Pferd und einen neuen Karren beisammen haben.

Aufgeregt lenkte sie ihren alten Klepper durch die Straßen auf Megs Haus zu. Heute noch würde sie beweisen, daß sie auf sich und ihren Bruder allein und ohne irgendwelche Unterstützung aufpassen konnte! Sie fühlte sich erwachsen und unabhängig. Sie hatte ihr Leben selbst in die Hand genommen. Sie hatte nichts vom König bekommen, brauchte keine Verwandten und kam sehr gut ohne Mann zurecht.

Sie freute sich darauf, Meg wiederzusehen. Meg war ihr Vorbild gewesen und eine der wenigen, die Aliena geholfen hatten, ohne den Versuch zu unternehmen, sie auszurauben, zu vergewaltigen oder auszunutzen. Aliena wollte sie über das Gewerbe im allgemeinen und den Wollhandel im besonderen ausfragen.

Weil Markttag war, dauerte es lange, bis sie ihren Karren durch die geschäftige Stadt bis in Megs Straße gelenkt hatten. Endlich kamen sie vor ihrem Haus an. Aliena betrat die Eingangshalle. Dort stand eine Frau, der sie noch nie zuvor begegnet war. »Oh!« stutzte Aliena.

»Was gibt's?« fragte die Frau.

»Ich bin eine Freundin von Meg.«

»Die wohnt nicht mehr hier«, gab die Frau barsch zurück.

»Ach, du meine Güte.« Aliena sah nicht ein, daß sie so kurz und bündig abgefertigt werden sollte. »Wo ist sie hingezogen?«

»Sie ist mit ihrem Mann fortgegangen, der die Stadt schmählich verlassen mußte«, erwiderte die Frau.

Aliena war enttäuscht und ihr wurde bang ums Herz: Sie hatte mit Megs Hilfe beim Verkauf der Wolle gerechnet.

»Das sind ja schreckliche Neuigkeiten!«

»Er war ein Betrüger, und an deiner Stelle würde ich mich nicht damit brüsten, mit ihr befreundet zu sein. Und jetzt raus hier.«

Aliena war empört, daß jemand schlecht über Meg sprach. »Mir ist ganz egal, was ihr Mann getan haben mag«, sagte sie. »Meg war eine feine Frau und den Tagedieben und Huren, die diese stinkende Stadt bewohnen, weit überlegen.« Sprach's und verließ das Haus, bevor die Frau sich eine Antwort zurechtlegen konnte.

Ihr verbaler Sieg war jedoch nur ein geringer Trost.

»Schlechte Nachrichten«, sagte sie zu Richard. »Meg hat Winchester verlassen.«

»Ist der jetzige Bewohner auch Wollhändler?« erkundigte er sich.

»Ich habe nicht gefragt. Ich war viel zu sehr damit beschäftigt, der Frau meine Meinung zu sagen.« Jetzt kam sie sich dumm vor.

»Was machen wir jetzt, Allie?«

»Wir müssen die Vliese verkaufen«, erwiderte sie besorgt. »Am besten, wir gehen auf den Markt.«

Sie drehten sich um und kehrten zur High Street zurück, von wo aus sie sich langsam einen Weg durch die Menschenmassen zum Marktplatz bahnten, der zwischen der High Street und der Kathedrale lag. Aliena führte das Pferd; Richard ging hinter dem Karren her und half schieben, wenn der Klepper es allein nicht schaffte, was nicht selten vorkam. Der Marktplatz wimmelte nur so von Menschen, die sich durch die engen Gassen zwischen den Ständen drängten und dabei von Karren wie dem Alienas unablässig aufgehalten wurden. Sie hielt an und erklomm ihren Wollsack, um von dort Ausschau nach Wollhändlern zu halten. Sie konnte nur einen einzigen entdecken. Sie kletterte wieder herunter und lenkte das Pferd zu dieser Bude.

Das Geschäft des Mannes lief gut. Er hatte ein großes, mit einem Seil markiertes Areal und dahinter einen Schuppen aus Hurden, leichten Holzrahmen und mit einem Geflecht aus Zweigen und Binsen. Dabei handelte es sich offensichtlich um eine Behelfskonstruktion, die an jedem Markttag neu errichtet wurde. Der Händler selbst war ein dunkelhäutiger Mann, dessen linker Arm in Höhe des Ellbogens in einem Stumpf endete, an dem ein Holzkamm befestigt war. Wurde ihm ein Vlies zum Kauf angeboten, so griff er die Wolle mit dem Arm, strählte ein Stück mit seinem Kamm heraus und betastete es mit der Rechten, bevor er seinen Preis nannte. Danach, wenn er den vereinbarten Preis auszahlte, nahm er sowohl den Kamm als auch seine unversehrte Rechte zu Hilfe. Bei größeren Einkäufen benutzte er eine Waage zum Abwiegen der Pennies.

Aliena drängte sich durch die Menge auf den Stand zu. Ein Bauer bot dem Händler drei ziemlich dünne, mit einem Ledergürtel zusammengebundene Vliese an. »Ein bißchen spärlich«, sagte der Händler. »Drei Viertelpennies pro Stück.« Er zählte zwei Pennies ab, nahm ein kleines Beil und zerteilte den dritten Penny mit einem gekonnten Hieb in vier Viertel. Er gab dem Bauern die beiden Pennies und eines der Viertel. »Dreimal drei Viertelpennies macht zwei Pennies und einen Viertelpenny.« Der Bauer nahm den Gürtel von den Vliesen und händigte sie ihm aus.

Als nächstes schleppten zwei junge Männer einen ganzen Sack voll Wolle herbei. Der Händler begutachtete die Ware sorgfältig. »Ein voller Sack, aber minderwertige Qualität«, sagte er. »Ich gebe euch ein Pfund.«

Aliena fragte sich, woher er genau wissen konnte, daß der Sack voll war. Wahrscheinlich war es reine Übungssache. Sie beobachtete ihn beim Auswiegen von einem Pfund Silberpennies.

Ein paar Mönche näherten sich mit einem riesigen Karren, auf dem sich die Wollsäcke stapelten. Aliena beschloß, ihr Geschäft vor den Mönchen zu tätigen. Sie gab Richard ein Zeichen, worauf er ihren Sack Wolle vom Karren hievte und ihn zum Stand brachte.

Der Händler prüfte die Wolle. »Gemischte Qualität«, sagte er. »Ein halbes Pfund.«

»Was?« sagte Aliena ungläubig.

»Einhundertzwanzig Pennies«, sagte er.

Aliena war entsetzt. »Aber ihr habt doch gerade ein Pfund für den Sack bezahlt!«

»Ist nur wegen der Qualität.«

»Ihr habt ein Pfund für schlechte Qualität bezahlt!«

»Ein halbes Pfund«, wiederholte er starrsinnig.

Die Mönche waren mittlerweile herangekommen und standen herum, aber Aliena rührte sich nicht vom Fleck: Ihr Lebensunterhalt stand auf dem Spiel, und ihre Furcht vor Armut überstieg die vor dem Händler bei weitem. »Sagt mir, warum«, beharrte sie. »An meiner Wolle ist doch nichts auszusetzen, oder?«

»Nein.«

»Dann gebt mir das gleiche wie den beiden Männern.«

»Nein.«

»Warum nicht?« Ihre Stimme überschlug sich fast.

»Weil niemand einem Mädchen den gleichen Preis zahlen würde wie einem Mann.«

Sie hätte ihn am liebsten erwürgt. Er bot ihr weniger als sie bezahlt hatte! Es war unfaßbar. Wenn sie seinen Preis akzeptierte, wäre ihre ganze Arbeit umsonst gewesen. Noch schlimmer war jedoch, daß ihr ausgeklügelter Plan, sich und ihrem Bruder ein Auskommen zu verschaffen, gescheitert und die kurze Zeitspanne der Unabhängigkeit und Selbständigkeit bereits vorüber war. Und warum? Weil er einem Mädchen nicht soviel wie einem Mann bezahlen wollte!

Der Anführer der Mönche sah sie an. Sie haßte es, angestarrt zu werden. »Schau mich nicht so an!« sagte sie grob. »Wickel lieber deine Geschäfte mit diesem gottlosen Krämer ab.«

»In Ordnung«, erwiderte der Mönch gutmütig. Er gab seinen Gefährten ein Zeichen, und sie schleiften einen Sack heran.

Richard sagte: »Nimm die zehn Shilling, Allie. Sonst bleiben wir noch auf diesem Sack Wolle sitzen!«

Aliena starrte den Händler wütend an, während er die Vliese der Mönche begutachtete. »Gemischte Qualität«, sagte er. Sie fragte sich, ob er wohl jemals eine Ware als gut bezeichnete. »Ein Pfund, zwölf Pennies pro Sack.«

Warum nur mußte Meg weggehen? dachte Aliena bitter. Wenn sie noch hier wäre, gäbe es diese Probleme nicht.

»Wieviel Stück habt ihr?« fragte der Händler.

Ein junger Mann, der sich durch seinen Habit als Novize auswies, sagte: »Zehn«, aber der Anführer korrigierte ihn und sagte: »Nein, elf.« Der Novize machte Miene, ihm zu widersprechen, sagte aber nichts.

»Das macht elfeinhalb Pfund Silber und zwölf Pennies.«

Der Händler begann, das Geld auszuwiegen.

»Ich laß mich von dem nicht ins Bockshorn jagen«, sagte Aliena zu Richard gewandt. »Wir versuchen es mit der Wolle anderswo – in Shiring oder vielleicht in Gloucester.«

»So weit! Und was, wenn wir sie dort auch nicht loswerden?«

Er hatte recht – woanders konnten sie unter Umständen auf die gleichen Schwierigkeiten stoßen. Sie hatten weder eine gesellschaftliche Stellung noch Unterstützung oder Protektion – das war der springende Punkt. Der Händler würde es nicht wagen, die Mönche zu beleidigen; und selbst die armen Bauern könnten ihm wahrscheinlich Unannehmlichkeiten bereiten, wenn er sie ungerecht behandelte. Ein Mann jedoch, der versuchte, zwei schutzlose Kinder zu betrügen, ging keinerlei Risiko ein.

Die Mönche trugen ihre Säcke in den Schuppen des Händlers. Jedesmal, wenn ein Sack verstaut war, händigte er dem Anführer der Mönche ein abgewogenes Pfund Silber und zwölf Pennies aus. Als alle Säcke untergebracht waren, blieb auf dem Tisch immer noch ein Säckchen Silber übrig.

»Das waren nur zehn Säcke«, sagte der Händler.

»Ich habe gleich gesagt, daß es nur zehn waren«, meinte der Novize.

»Hier ist der elfte«, sagte der Anführer der Mönche und legte eine Hand auf Alienas Wollsack.

Sie starrte ihn verblüfft an.

Der Händler war mindestens ebenso überrascht. »Ich hab' ihr ein halbes Pfund dafür geboten«, sagte er.

»Ich habe ihr die Ware abgekauft«, sagte der Mönch. »Und sie an dich weiterverkauft.« Er nickte den anderen Mönchen zu, und sie schafften Alienas Sack in den Schuppen.

Der Händler schien alles andere als erfreut, händigte jedoch anstandslos das letzte Pfund sowie zwölf Pennies aus. Der Mönch reichte das Geld an Aliena weiter.

Sie war wie vom Donner gerührt. Alles war schiefgegangen, und nun kam dieser Fremde daher und rettete sie – nachdem sie ihn so unfreundlich behandelt hatte!

Richard sagte: »Vielen Dank für Eure Hilfe, Vater.«

»Danke dem Herrgott«, erwiderte der Mönch.

Aliena hatte es die Sprache verschlagen. Sie war außer sich vor Freude. Sie drückte das Geld an ihre Brust. Wie konnte sie ihm je danken? Sie betrachtete ihren Retter. Er war ein kleiner, schmaler Mann mit starker Ausstrahlung. Er bewegte sich behende und sah sehr wach aus, wie ein Vogel mit mattem Gefieder und hellen Augen. Seine waren übrigens blau. Seinen schwarzen Haarkranz durchzogen bereits graue Strähnen, doch das Gesicht wirkte jung. Aliena kam er irgendwie bekannt vor. Wo war sie ihm nur schon einmal begegnet?

Der Mönch stellte gerade die gleiche Überlegung an.

»Ihr erinnert Euch nicht an mich, aber ich kenne Euch«, sagte er. »Ihr seid die Kinder von Bartholomäus, dem ehemaligen Grafen von Shiring. Ich weiß, daß Euch Schlimmes widerfahren ist, und bin froh, daß ich Gelegenheit hatte, Euch zu helfen. Ich werde Euch Eure Wolle jederzeit abkaufen.«

Aliena hätte ihn am liebsten umarmt und geküßt. Nicht nur, daß er sie soeben gerettet hatte – er war sogar bereit, ihre Zukunft sicherzustellen: Endlich fand sie ihre Sprache wieder. »Ich weiß nicht, wie ich Euch danken soll«, sagte sie. »Wir haben weiß Gott einen Beschützer gebraucht.«

»Nun, dann habt ihr jetzt gleich zwei«, erwiderte er, »Gott und mich.«

Aliena war tief gerührt. »Ihr habt mir das Leben gerettet, und ich weiß noch nicht einmal, wer Ihr seid«, sagte sie.

»Ich heiße Philip«, antwortete er. »Ich bin der Prior von Kingsbridge.«

Es war ein schöner Tag, als Tom Builder mit den Steinklopfern zum Steinbruch ging.

Es war kurz vor Ostern, fünfzehn Monate nach dem Brand der alten Kathedrale. Fünfzehn Monate hatte Prior Philip gebraucht, um das Geld für die Einstellung von Handwerkern aufzutreiben.

In Salisbury, wo der Bau des Bischofpalastes dem Ende zuging, hatte Tom einen Forst- und einen Steinbruchmeister auftreiben können. Ersterer war mit seinen Männern inzwischen schon seit zwei Wochen damit beschäftigt, in den flußnahen Wäldern oberhalb von Kingsbridge hohe Kiefern und ausgewachsene Eichen aufzuspüren. Der Transport von Baumaterial über die kurvenreichen, unbefestigten Straßen kam teuer zu stehen; es war erheblich billiger, das Holz flußabwärts zur Baustelle zu flößen. Je nach Verwendungszweck wurde das Bauholz fürs Gerüst einfach gestutzt oder für die Schablonen der Steinmetzen und Steinhauer sorgfältig modelliert. Die höchsten Bäume wurden als zukünftige Dachbalken beiseite gelegt. In Kingsbridge traf nun kontinuierlich gutes Holz ein, und Tom hatte nichts weiter zu tun, als die Forstarbeiter jeden Samstagabend zu bezahlen.

Die Steinbrecher waren in den vorangegangenen Tagen angekommen. Ihr Meister, Otto Blackface, hatte seine beiden Söhne, beides Steinklopfer, mitgebracht, dazu vier Enkel, allesamt Lehrlinge, und zwei Gehilfen, von denen einer sein Neffe und der andere sein Schwager war. Vetternwirtschaft dieser Art war nichts Ungewöhnliches, und Tom hatte nichts dagegen einzuwenden: Familienverbände arbeiteten in der Regel recht gut zusammen.

Auf der Baustelle selbst waren außer Tom und dem Zimmermann der Priorei bisher noch keine Handwerker beschäftigt. Zunächst galt es, einen Vorrat an Baumaterialien anzulegen. Bald jedoch mußten

die Leute angeworben werden, die das Rückgrat der Baukolonne bildeten: die Steinmetzen. Das waren die Männer, die Stein auf Stein fügten
und die Mauern hochzogen. Mit ihnen begann das großartige Abenteuer erst richtig. Tom ging mit federnden Schritten: Seit nunmehr
zehn Jahren hatte er auf diese Chance gehofft und hingearbeitet.

Er hatte beschlossen, als ersten Steinmetzen seinen eigenen Sohn,
Alfred, einzustellen, der jetzt – ungefähr – sechzehn Jahre alt war und
inzwischen die notwendigen Grundkenntnisse beherrschte: Er konnte
Steine glatt schneiden und eine Mauer errichten. Mit dem offiziellen
Baubeginn sollte Alfred auf vollen Lohn gesetzt werden.

Toms zweiter Sohn, Jonathan, war fünfzehn Monate alt und wuchs
schnell. Er war ein kräftiges Kind und wurde von allen Bewohnern
des Klosters nach Strich und Faden verwöhnt. Zunächst war Tom ein
wenig beunruhigt gewesen, daß man das Kind in die Obhut des
schwachsinnigen Johnny Eightpence gegeben hatte. Indes stellte sich
bald heraus, daß Johnny es in puncto Fürsorglichkeit mit jeder Mutter
aufnehmen konnte und überdies mehr Zeit als die meisten Mütter für
seinen Zögling hatte. Die Mönche hatten Tom bisher noch nicht der
Vaterschaft verdächtigt, und es sah so aus, als würden sie nie dahinter-
kommen.

Die siebenjährige Martha hatte eine Lücke in den Schneidezähnen
und vermißte Jack. Um sie machte sich Tom die meisten Sorgen, denn
sie brauchte eine Mutter.

An Frauen, die nur zu gerne Toms Frau geworden wären und sich
fortan um eine kleine Tochter gekümmert hätten, mangelte es nicht.
Er wußte, daß er keineswegs unattraktiv war, und außerdem schien
sein Lebensunterhalt nun, da Prior Philip den Startschuß für die Bauarbeiten gegeben hatte, ein für allemal gesichert. Tom war aus dem
Gästehaus ausgezogen und hatte sich im Dorf ein schönes Haus mit
zwei Zimmern und einem Kamin gebaut. Als leitender Dombaumeister
konnte er beizeiten mit einem Gehalt und weiteren Einkünften rechnen, die so manch einen kleinen Landadeligen vor Neid erblassen
lassen würden. Nur – er konnte sich nicht vorstellen, eine andere
Frau als Ellen zu heiraten. Er glich einem Mann, dem, da er sich an
den edelsten Wein gewöhnt hat, der herkömmliche Tafelwein wie Essig
schmeckt. Im Dorf wohnte eine Witwe, eine rundliche, hübsche Frau
mit nettem Lächeln, üppigem Busen und zwei wohlerzogenen Kindern. Sie hatte ein paar Pasteten für ihn gebacken und ihn auf der
Weihnachtsfeier sehnsuchtsvoll geküßt. Auf der Stelle hätte sie ihm
ihr Jawort gegeben. Tom aber wußte, daß er mit ihr nicht glücklich

werden, sondern sich unentwegt nach den Reizen der unberechenbaren, bezaubernden und leidenschaftlichen Ellen sehnen würde.

Ellen hatte versprochen, eines Tages auf Besuch zu kommen. Tom war felsenfest davon überzeugt, daß sie ihr Versprechen halten würde, und klammerte sich hartnäckig daran, obwohl es jetzt schon über ein Jahr her war, seit sie ihn verlassen hatte. Wenn sie kam, wollte er um ihre Hand anhalten.

Sie wird mich nicht zurückweisen, dachte er. Ich bin nicht länger mittellos, sondern kann uns alle ohne Schwierigkeiten ernähren. Tom hatte zudem das Gefühl, daß man Alfred und Jack mit einigem Geschick von ihren dauernden Streitereien abhalten konnte. Wenn man Jack zum Arbeiten bringt, dachte er, dann wird Alfred ihn nicht mehr so ablehnen. Ich werde Jack anbieten, bei mir als Lehrling anzufangen. Der Bursche hat schließlich schon Interesse am Bauhandwerk bekundet, ist blitzgescheit und in etwa einem Jahr auch groß und stark genug für die schwere Arbeit. Alfred kann ihm dann keine Faulheit mehr vorwerfen.

Das zweite Problem lag darin, daß Jack lesen konnte und Alfred nicht. Ich werde Ellen bitten, Alfred an den Sonntagen Lesen und Schreiben beizubringen, dachte Tom. Dann wird Alfred sich Jack ebenbürtig fühlen. Die Jungen werden auf einer Stufe stehen, beide eine gute Ausbildung haben, beide arbeiten und über kurz oder lang auch gleich groß sein.

Tom wußte, daß Ellen das Zusammenleben mit ihm trotz all ihrer Prüfungen genossen hatte. Sie mochte seinen Körper und schätzte seinen Verstand. Sie würde gerne zu ihm zurückkehren.

Ob sich die Sache mit Prior Philip ins reine bringen ließ, stand auf einem anderen Blatt. Ellen hatte Philips Religion zutiefst beleidigt und den Prior in kaum überbietbarer Weise gekränkt. Ob es für dieses Problem überhaupt eine Lösung gab? Tom wußte es nicht.

Vorerst jedoch wurden seine geistigen Kräfte voll und ganz von der Planung der Kathedrale in Anspruch genommen. Otto und seine Steinklopfer wollten sich am Steinbruch eine vorläufige Behausung bauen. Sobald sie sich dort eingerichtet hatten, würden sie mit dem Bau echter Häuser beginnen, und die Verheirateten unter ihnen konnten ihre Familie nachkommen lassen.

Von allen Bauhandwerkern erforderte die Arbeit im Steinbruch das geringste Geschick und die meiste Muskelkraft. Dem Steinbruchmeister oblag die Kopfarbeit. Er entschied, in welcher Reihenfolge der Abbau zu erfolgen hatte; er besorgte Leitern und Hebevorrichtungen;

wurde an einer Wand gearbeitet, entwarf er das Gerüst. Auch war er für den steten Werkzeugnachschub aus der Schmiede verantwortlich. Die Förderung der Steine selbst war verhältnismäßig einfach. Der Steinbrecher hieb zunächst mit einer eisernen Spitzhacke eine Kerbe in die Felsen und vertiefte sie dann mit Hammer und Meißel. Sobald sie groß genug war, trieb er einen hölzernen Keil in die Vertiefung. Wenn er das Gestein richtig eingeschätzt hatte, spaltete es sich genau an der vorgesehenen Stelle.

Arbeiter schafften die Steine entweder auf Tragen aus dem Steinbruch oder hoben sie mittels eines Seils, das über ein riesiges Drehrad lief, hinaus. In der Bauhütte wurden die Blöcke von den Steinklopfern mit Äxten annähernd in die vom Baumeister angegebenen Formen gehauen. Die Feinarbeit erfolgte natürlich erst an Ort und Stelle in Kingsbridge.

Die größte Schwierigkeit war der Transport. Der Steinbruch war eine Tagesreise von der Baustelle entfernt. Ein Fuhrmann verlangte voraussichtlich vier Pence pro Ladung – und konnte dabei nicht mehr als acht oder neun große Steine befördern, ohne daß Karren oder Pferd Schaden nahmen. Sobald sich die Steinbrecher eingerichtet hatten, wollte Tom das Gebiet nach Wasserläufen erkunden, die eine Verkürzung der Reise ermöglichten.

Sie hatten Kingsbridge im Morgengrauen verlassen. Auf ihrem Weg durch den Wald erinnerten Tom die Bäume, die sich über die Straße wölbten, an die Pfeiler der Kathedrale, die er bauen wollte. Überall sproß das frische Laub. Tom hatte gelernt, die Kapitelle mit Spiralen oder einem Zickzackmuster zu schmücken. Jetzt kam ihm der Gedanke, daß sich auch eine Blattornamentik anbot; sie würde sogar besonders ins Auge fallen.

Sie kamen gut voran und befanden sich gegen Mitte des Nachmittags bereits in der Nähe des Steinbruchs.

Zu seiner Überraschung vernahm Tom schon aus der Ferne den Klang von Metall auf Stein. Es hörte sich an, als würde dort eifrig gearbeitet. Rechtlich gehörte der Steinbruch Percy Hamleigh, dem Grafen von Shiring, doch der König hatte der Priorei in Kingsbridge das Privileg erteilt, dort Steine für ihre Kathedrale zu fördern. Vielleicht wollte Graf Percy gleichzeitig für seine eigenen Zwecke abbauen, was ihm der König vermutlich nicht ausdrücklich untersagt hatte. Lästig wäre es allemal.

Otto, ein Mann mit dunklem Teint und rauhen Sitten, runzelte unwillig die Stirn, sagte aber nichts. Die anderen Männer brummelten ungehalten vor sich hin. Tom schenkte ihnen keine Beachtung, sondern schritt ungeduldig schneller aus, um der Sache auf den Grund zu gehen.

Die Straße führte in einem weiten Bogen durch ein Waldstück und endete am Fuße eines Hügels. Der Hügel enthielt die begehrten Steine, und ein gewaltiges Stück war bereits von früheren Steinbrechern aus seiner Flanke genommen worden. Tom hatte den Eindruck, die Natur des Steinbruchs müsse die Arbeit erleichtern: Es war sicherlich einfacher, Steine aus der Höhe herabzulassen, als sie aus einem Loch heraufzuholen.

Im Steinbruch wurde gearbeitet, daran gab es nun keinen Zweifel mehr. Am Fuße des Hügels befand sich eine Hütte, ein massives Gerüst rankte sich etwa zwanzig Fuß den felsigen Hang empor, und unten lag ein Haufen Steine zum Abtransport bereit. Tom zählte mindestens zehn Steinbrecher. Zwei finster dreinblickende Bewaffnete lungerten vor der Bauhütte herum und bewarfen ein Faß mit Steinen.

»Das behagt mir überhaupt nicht«, meinte Otto.

Tom ging es ebenso; er ließ sich aber nichts anmerken. Selbstbewußt, als gehöre ihm der Steinbruch persönlich, ging er auf die beiden Posten zu. Die rappelten sich erschrocken auf und blickten wie alle Wachen, die nach endlosen ereignislosen Tagen plötzlich überrascht werden, recht betreten und schuldbewußt drein. Tom warf einen prüfenden Blick auf ihre Bewaffnung: Sie trugen Schwert, Dolch und schwere Lederwämse, aber keine Rüstung. Tom selbst trug einen Steinmetzhammer am Gürtel. Auf einen Kampf konnte er sich nicht einlassen. Er ging geradewegs und ohne ein Wort zu sagen auf die Männer zu, machte im letzten Augenblick einen Bogen um sie herum und setzte seinen Weg in Richtung Bauhütte fort. Die Wachen sahen einander ratlos an: Wenn Tom kleiner gewesen wäre oder keinen Hammer gehabt hätte, wären sie ihm vielleicht in den Weg getreten, aber dafür war es jetzt zu spät.

Tom betrat das großzügig angelegte Holzhaus mit einem offenen Herd. An den Wänden hingen saubere Werkzeuge, und in einer Ecke lag ein großer Stein, auf dem sie gewetzt werden konnten.

Zwei Steinklopfer standen vor einer großen Werkbank, Bossierstuhl genannt, und bearbeiteten Steine mit ihren Äxten. »Seid gegrüßt, Brüder!« Tom benutzte die unter Handwerkern übliche Anrede. »Wer ist hier der Meister?«

»Ich bin der Steinbruchmeister«, erwiderte einer von ihnen. »Mein Name ist Harold von Shiring.«

»Ich bin der Baumeister der Kathedrale in Kingsbridge. Ich heiße Tom.«

»Seid gegrüßt, Tom Builder. Was führt Euch zu uns?«

Tom musterte Harold einen Augenblick, bevor er antwortete. Er war ein bleicher, staubiger Mann mit kleinen, staubgrünen Augen, die sich beim Sprechen verengten, als ob er ständig gegen Steinstaub anblinzelte. Er lehnte lässig auf dem Bossierstuhl, war aber nicht so entspannt, wie er sich gab. Er weiß ganz genau, warum ich hier bin, dachte Tom. »Ich habe meinen Steinbruchmeister mitgebracht. Er möchte mit der Arbeit beginnen.«

Die beiden Wachposten waren Tom in die Hütte gefolgt; hinter ihnen traten jetzt Otto und seine Männer ein. Auch ein paar von Harolds Männern drängten sich herein; sie waren neugierig und wollten sich nichts entgehen lassen. Harold sagte: »Der Steinbruch gehört dem Grafen. Wenn Ihr Steine entnehmen wollt, dann müßt ihr mit ihm sprechen.«

»Nein, das werde ich nicht«, erwiderte Tom. »Als der König Graf Percy den Steinbruch überließ, gewährte er dem Kloster zu Kingsbridge die Schürfrechte. Wir brauchen keine weitere Erlaubnis.«

»Aber wir können doch nicht alle gleichzeitig hier arbeiten, oder?«

»Vielleicht doch«, sagte Tom. »Ich habe nicht die Absicht, Eure Männer um ihre Arbeit zu bringen. Der ganze Hügel besteht aus Stein; das reicht für zwei oder mehr Kathedralen. Es sollte uns gelingen, den Steinbruch so aufzuteilen, daß jeder von uns hier Steine schneiden kann.«

»Dem kann ich leider nicht zustimmen«, meinte Harold. »Ich stehe in den Diensten des Grafen.«

»Nun, und ich stehe in den Diensten des Priors von Kingsbridge, und meine Männer werden morgen früh mit der Arbeit beginnen, ob es Euch nun paßt oder nicht.«

Einer der beiden Bewaffneten meldete sich zu Wort: »Ihr werdet weder morgen noch sonstwann hier arbeiten.«

Bis zu diesem Augenblick hatte Tom sich daran geklammert, daß Percy, obwohl er den Geist des königlichen Edikts verletzt hatte, durch entschlossenes Auftreten dazu veranlaßt werden könnte, sich an die Vereinbarungen zu halten und der Priorei den Abbau der benötigten Steine zu erlauben. Die beiden Bewaffneten waren aber offenbar dazu angehalten worden, die Steinbrecher des Klosters abzuweisen. Entmutigt sah Tom ein, daß er ohne Kampf keinen einzigen Stein bekommen würde.

Der Wachposten, der das Wort ergriffen hatte, war ein kleiner, stämmiger Bursche von ungefähr fünfundzwanzig Jahren, dem die Rauflust aus den Augen sprach. Er wirkte dumm, aber stur – der schwierigste Menschenschlag für eine vernünftige Unterhaltung. Tom sah ihn herausfordernd an und sagte: »Wer seid Ihr?«

»Ich bin der Aufseher im Auftrag des Grafen von Shiring. Er hat mir befohlen, diesen Steinbruch zu bewachen, und genau das werde ich auch tun.«

»Und wie gedenkt Ihr das zu tun?«

»Mit diesem Schwert.« Er legte die Hand an seinen Gürtel.

»Und was glaubt Ihr, wird der König mit Euch anstellen, wenn Ihr ihm wegen Landfriedensbruchs vorgeführt werdet?«

»Das Risiko gehe ich ein.«

»Ihr seid nur zu zweit«, erwiderte Tom mit ruhiger Stimme. »Wir sind sieben Männer und vier Lehrjungen und haben eine königliche Erlaubnis, hier zu arbeiten. Niemand wird uns hängen, wenn wir Euch töten.«

Die beiden Bewaffneten wirkten betroffen, doch bevor Tom seinen Vorteil ausnutzen konnte, mischte Otto sich ein. »Augenblick«, sagte er, an Tom gewandt. »Ich habe meine Leute hierhergebracht, um Steine zu klopfen – nicht, um zu kämpfen.«

Tom verließ der Mut. Wenn die Steinbrecher nicht zum Kampf bereit waren, war alle Hoffnung umsonst.

»Seid doch nicht so furchtsam!« sagte er. »Oder wollt Ihr Euch von zwei Rabauken um die Arbeit bringen lassen?«

Otto blickte mürrisch drein. »Auf einen Kampf mit Bewaffneten laß ich mich nicht ein«, erwiderte er. »Ich habe seit zwanzig Jahren ununterbrochen Geld verdient und bin auf diese Arbeit nicht angewiesen. Und außerdem – was weiß ich denn, wer hier recht hat? Was mich betrifft, steht Euer Wort gegen seins.«

Tom sah Ottos Arbeiter an, einen nach dem anderen. Die beiden Steinklopfer wirkten genauso eigensinnig. Es stand außer Frage, daß sie sich an das hielten, was Otto ihnen vorgab, denn schließlich war er nicht nur ihr Vater, sondern auch ihr Meister. Tom hatte sogar Verständnis für Ottos Standpunkt und gestand sich ein, daß er an seiner Stelle wahrscheinlich nicht anders gehandelt hätte. Nur wenn's ums nackte Leben ging, konnte man einen Kampf gegen Bewaffnete riskieren.

Ein Trost war Ottos Vernünftigkeit für Tom nicht; vielmehr verstärkte sie sein Gefühl der Ohnmacht noch. Er unternahm einen letzten Versuch. »Es wird keinen Kampf geben«, sagte er. »Die Herren wissen genau, daß der König sie hängen lassen wird, wenn sie uns auch nur ein Haar krümmen. Laßt uns Feuer machen und uns zur Ruhe begeben. Morgen früh beginnen wir dann mit der Arbeit.«

Er erkannte sofort, daß er die Nacht nicht hätte erwähnen dürfen. Einer von Ottos Söhnen warf ein: »Wie sollen wir mit diesen Mordbuben in der Nähe Schlaf finden?«

Die anderen stimmten ihm zu.

»Wir werden Wachen aufstellen«, sagte Tom, der Verzweiflung nah.

Otto schüttelte entschieden den Kopf. »Wir kehren noch heute zurück, und zwar sofort.«

Tom sah von einem zum anderen und mußte sich eingestehen, daß er den kürzeren gezogen hatte. Mit welch hochgespannten Erwartungen war er am Morgen aufgebrochen! Es war unfaßbar, daß diese kleinmütigen Halunken seine Pläne zunichte machen konnten! Er konnte sich eine bissige Schlußbemerkung nicht verkneifen. »Ihr handelt gegen den Willen des Königs«, sagte er zu Harold, »und das kann Euch teuer zu stehen kommen. Richtet das dem Grafen von Shiring aus. Und sagt ihm, wer ich bin. Er soll sich hüten, Tom Builder von Kingsbridge in die Hände zu geraten. Er muß damit rechnen, daß ich ihm seinen fetten Hals so lange zudrücke, bis er verreckt.«

Johnny Eightpence fertigte für den kleinen Jonathan eine Mönchskutte in Miniaturausgabe an, einschließlich weiter Ärmel und Kapuze. Der kleine Knirps sah darin so entzückend aus, daß ihm alle Herzen zuflogen – nur, praktisch war seine Bekleidung nicht: Die Kapuze rutschte ihm ständig über die Augen und nahm ihm die Sicht, und beim Krabbeln geriet die Robe mit seinen Knien in Konflikt.

Am Nachmittag, nachdem Jonathan (und die Mönche) aus dem Mittagsschläfchen erwacht waren, stieß Prior Philip im ehemaligen Hauptschiff der Kirche, das den Novizen als Spielplatz diente, auf Johnny Eightpence und seinen Zögling. Die Novizen durften hier um diese Zeit ihre überschüssigen Kräfte austoben. Johnny sah ihnen gerne beim Fangenspielen zu, während Jonathan das Gewirr aus Pflöcken und Kordeln untersuchte, das Tom Builders Grundriß für den Ostflügel der neuen Kathedrale darstellte.

Philip blieb ein paar Minuten lang stillvergnügt stehen und sah den hin- und herrennenden Jungen zu. Er mochte Johnny, der seinen mangelnden Verstand durch ein ungewöhnlich gutes Herz wettmachte, sehr gern.

Jonathan hatte sich aufgerichtet und hielt sich an einem Pflock fest, umklammerte das daran befestigte Seil und machte zwei täppische, bedächtige Schritte.

»Bald kann er laufen«, sagte Philip zu Johnny.

»Er gibt sich redlich Mühe, Vater, aber meistens landet er auf dem Hintern.«

Philip ging in die Hocke und streckte seine Hände nach Jonathan aus. »Komm zu mir«, sagte er. »Na, komm!«

Jonathan grinste und entblößte seine ersten Zähnchen. Dann deutete er mit dem Finger auf Philip, ließ unvermittelt das Seil los und überwand die kurze Strecke in einem plötzlichen Anfall von Kühnheit mit drei raschen, entschlossenen Schritten.

Philip fing ihn in seinen Armen auf und rief: »Bravo!« Er drückte den Kleinen an sich und war auf dessen Leistung so stolz, als wäre es seine eigene gewesen.

Auch Johnny war ganz aus dem Häuschen. »Er läuft! Er läuft!« jubelte er.

Jonathan strampelte und wollte wieder auf den Boden. Philip stellte ihn auf seine Beine, um zu sehen, ob es noch einmal klappte. Aber Jonathan befand, er habe für heute genug geleistet. Er ließ sich sogleich auf die Knie fallen und krabbelte zu Johnny hinüber.

Philip konnte sich noch gut daran erinnern, wie empört einige Mönche gewesen waren, als er Johnny und den Kleinen nach Kingsbridge geholt hatte. Mit Johnny war jedoch leicht auszukommen, solange man nicht vergaß, daß er im Grunde genommen ein Kind im Körper eines Mannes war, und Jonathan hatte allein mit seinem Charme jeden Widerstand gebrochen.

Jonathan war allerdings nicht der einzige Stein des Anstoßes während des ersten Jahres geblieben. Die Mönche, die für Philip gestimmt hatten, weil sie sich von ihm eine spürbare Verbesserung der Versorgung erwarteten, fühlten sich an der Nase herumgeführt, als er, um die laufenden Ausgaben der Priorei einzuschränken, einschneidende Sparmaßnahmen ankündigte. Philip empfand dies als Kränkung: Seiner Meinung nach hatte er nie einen Zweifel daran gelassen, daß die neue Kathedrale Vorrang hatte. Die Klosteroffizialen hatten sich darüber hinaus gegen seinen Plan, ihnen ihre finanzielle Unabhängigkeit zu nehmen, gesträubt, obwohl sie ganz genau wußten, daß die Priorei ohne Reformen dem sicheren Ruin entgegenging. Als Philip schließlich Geld für die Vergrößerung der klösterlichen Schafherden ausgab, wäre es um ein Haar zu einer Meuterei gekommen. Doch Mönche waren im Grunde folgsame, gefügige Menschen, und Bischof Waleran, der sich vielleicht auf die Seite der Rebellen geschlagen hätte, war fast das ganze Jahr über unterwegs auf Romreise. Den Mönchen blieb schließlich nichts anderes übrig, als sich aufs Murren und Klagen zu beschränken.

Philip hatte manch einen Entschluß in Einsamkeit getroffen und bisweilen darunter gelitten, aber er war sicher, daß die Ergebnisse ihn entschädigen würden. Seine Maßnahmen trugen erfreulicherweise inzwischen bereits erste Früchte. Die Wollpreise waren wieder gestiegen, und Philip hatte rechtzeitig mit der Schur beginnen lassen: Nur deshalb konnte er es sich auch leisten, Forstarbeiter und Steinbrecher anzustellen. Je schneller sich die finanzielle Lage besserte, desto rascher festigte sich auch seine Stellung als Prior.

Er tätschelte Johnny Eightpence liebevoll den Kopf und setzte die Inspektion der Baustelle fort. Tom und Alfred hatten mit der Unterstützung von Priorbediensteten und einigen jüngeren Mönchen bereits mit dem Ausheben der Fundamente begonnen. Die Grube war jedoch erst fünf bis sechs Fuß tief. Tom hatte Philip erklärt, daß die Fundamente an manchen Stellen bis zu fünfundzwanzig Fuß tief im Boden verankert werden müßten. Dazu waren eine beträchtliche Zahl von Arbeitern und eine Hebevorrichtung erforderlich.

Die neue Kirche würde größer als die alte, für eine Kathedrale aber immer noch recht klein sein. Eine Stimme in Philip wünschte sich die längste, höchste, prächtigste und schönste Kathedrale im gesamten Königreich. Der Prior unterdrückte diesen Wunsch und rief sich zur Ordnung. Sei dankbar dafür, daß du überhaupt wieder eine Kirche bekommst, schalt er sich – ganz egal, wie sie ausfällt!

Er betrat Toms Arbeitsschuppen und betrachtete die Holzarbeiten auf der Werkbank. Der Baumeister hatte fast den gesamten Winter hier verbracht und mit einer eisernen Meßlatte und einer Garnitur scharfer Meißel sogenannte Schablonen angefertigt – hölzerne Modelle, an die sich die Steinmetzen beim Zurechtschneiden der Steine halten mußten. Voller Bewunderung hatte Philip gesehen, wie dieser große Mann das Holz mit seinen Riesenhänden präzise und gewissenhaft zu tadellosen Bogen, Kanten und genauen Winkeln zurechtgeschnitzt hatte. Er griff sich eine der Schablonen und sah sie sich näher an. Sie war wie ein Segment aus einer Margaritenblüte geformt – ein Viertelkreis mit mehreren runden Ausbuchtungen, die an Blütenblätter erinnerten. Wozu brauchte er einen solchen Stein? fragte sich Philip. Es fiel ihm schwer, sich diese Dinge auszumalen. Toms große

Vorstellungskraft war für ihn immer wieder Anlaß zur Bewunderung. Er warf einen Blick auf Toms holzgerahmte, in Mörtel geritzte Zeichnungen und fand heraus, daß er eine Schablone für die Pfeiler der Arkade in der Hand hielt. Sie würden wie gebündelte Schäfte aussehen. Philip war bisher davon ausgegangen, daß sich solche Pfeiler tatsächlich aus gebündelten Schäften zusammensetzten. Erst jetzt begriff er, daß es sich um eine optische Täuschung handelte: Die Pfeiler waren in Wirklichkeit massive Steinsäulen mit schaftähnlichen Dekorationen.

Fünf Jahre, und der Ostflügel ist fertig, hatte Tom gesagt. Fünf Jahre – und er, Philip, konnte wieder in einer Kathedrale die Messe lesen. Er mußte nur das Geld dafür auftreiben. Da seine Reformen eine gewisse Anlaufzeit brauchten, war es im laufenden Jahr noch recht schwierig, die Mittel für einen bescheidenen Anfang zu finden. Aber Philip war zuversichtlich. Nach dem Verkauf der Frühjahrswolle im nächsten Jahr werden wir uns mehr Handwerker leisten können, dachte er; dann können die Bauarbeiten richtig beginnen.

Die Glocke läutete zur Abendandacht. Philip verließ den kleinen Schuppen und ging zur Krypta. Er traute seinen Augen kaum, als er zur Klosterpforte hinüberblickte: Tom Builder und die Steinbrecher kehrten zurück! Was war geschehen? Tom hatte doch gesagt, er wolle eine Woche fortbleiben, und das Steinbrechergespann sollte sich doch an Ort und Stelle einquartieren! Philip eilte ihnen entgegen.

Beim Näherkommen bemerkte er, daß die Männer völlig erschöpft waren. Die Enttäuschung stand ihnen ins Gesicht geschrieben.

»Was gibt's?« erkundigte er sich. »Wieso seid Ihr schon zurück?«

»Schlechte Nachrichten«, erwiderte Tom Builder.

Während des Gottesdienstes kochte Philip vor Wut. Graf Percys Verhalten war eine Unverschämtheit. Die Rechtslage in diesem Fall war völlig klar; die Anweisungen des Königs waren unzweideutig. Der Graf war bei der Verkündung persönlich zugegen gewesen, und das Schürfrecht für den Steinbruch war der Priorei in einer Urkunde verbrieft worden. Unruhig klopfte Philips rechter Fuß auf den Steinfußboden der Krypta. Man bestiehlt uns, dachte er. Percy hätte ebensogut Geld aus einem Kirchenschatz stehlen können. Für sein Verhalten gibt es nicht die geringste Entschuldigung! Schamlos verweigerte er sowohl Gott als auch dem König den Gehorsam.

Das Schlimmste war, daß Philip die neue Kathedrale ohne die kostenlosen Steine aus dem Steinbruch nicht bauen konnte. Die Finanzierung war eine Gratwanderung. Falls die Steine zum gängigen Marktpreis gekauft und über noch weitere Strecken hertransportiert werden mußten, würde sich der Beginn der Bauarbeiten um etwa ein Jahr verzögern. Sechs oder sieben Jahre würde es dauern, bis die Gottesdienste wieder in einer Kathedrale abgehalten werden konnten. Allein der Gedanke daran war unerträglich. Gleich nach dem Abendgottesdienst berief er eine Notsitzung der Kapitelversammlung ein und teilte den Mönchen mit, was geschehen war.

Philip hatte inzwischen seinen eigenen Stil in der Kapitelversammlung durchgesetzt. Remigius, sein Stellvertreter, verübelte ihm immer noch, daß er bei der Wahl unterlegen war, und machte, wenn es um geschäftliche Dinge ging, keinen Hehl aus seiner Abneigung. Remigius war ein konservativer, phantasieloser Pedant, dessen Vorstellung von der Führung eines Klosters sich in keinem einzigen Punkt mit Philips Ansichten deckte. Die Brüder, die bei der Wahl für Remigius gestimmt hatten, gaben ihm auch im Kapitel zumeist Schützenhilfe: Andrew, der am Schlagfuß leidende Sakristan; Pierre, der engstirnige Cirkator, und John Small, der faule Ökonom. Philips engste Mitarbeiter waren diejenigen, die sich für seine Wahl eingesetzt hatten: Cuthbert Whitehead, der alte Kellermeister, und der junge Milius, den Philip mit dem neugeschaffenen Amt des Schatzmeisters betraut hatte und dem folglich die Verantwortung für die Finanzen der Priorei oblag. Die Streitereien mit Remigius überließ Philip stets ihm. Meistens sprach er alle wichtigen Punkte vor der Kapitelversammlung mit Milius durch. War das nicht der Fall, so konnte er sich darauf verlassen, daß Milius eine ähnliche Meinung wie er selbst vertrat. Philip sah sich auf diese Weise in der Lage, als unparteiischer Schiedsrichter am Ende der Sitzung ein Resümee zu ziehen. So setzte sich Remigius zwar so gut wie nie durch, doch konnte Philip das eine oder andere seiner Argumente aufnehmen und somit den Eindruck eines auf Konsens beruhenden Führungsstils bewahren.

Die Mönche ärgerten sich über Graf Percys Verhalten. So wie sie vormals gejubelt hatten, als König Stephan der Priorei freies Bauholz in unbegrenzten Mengen und kostenlose Steine zugesichert hatte, so tobten sie jetzt vor Wut, weil Percy sich der königlichen Order widersetzte.

Als die Unmutsäußerungen verstummt waren, meldete sich Remigius zu Wort: »Ich kann mich daran erinnern, dies schon vor einem Jahr vorgebracht zu haben«, hub er an. »Das Abkommen, demzufolge der Graf den Steinbruch besitzt und wir die Abbaurechte haben, war mir schon immer ein Dorn im Auge. Wir hätten von vornherein versuchen müssen, den Steinbruch in unseren Besitz zu bekommen.«

Die Bemerkung enthielt ein Körnchen Wahrheit und erwies sich daher für Philip als harter Brocken. Er hatte sich ja mit Lady Regan auf die vollständige Übernahme des Steinbruchs geeinigt – nur um von ihr in letzter Minute darum betrogen zu werden! Er war versucht zu erwidern, daß er unter den obwaltenden Umständen den besten Handel abgeschlossen hatte und daß Remigius seine Verhandlungskünste im gefährlichen Labyrinth des königlichen Hofes erst einmal unter Beweis stellen müsse, biß sich aber auf die Zunge – schließlich war er der Prior und trug die Verantwortung, auch und gerade dann, wenn etwas schiefging.

Milius kam ihm zu Hilfe. »Es ist ja schön und gut, im nachhinein zu bedauern, daß uns der König den Steinbruch nicht exklusiv übereignet hat. Wichtiger scheint mir freilich die Frage, wie wir uns nun verhalten sollen.«

»Das liegt ja wohl auf der Hand«, erwiderte Remigius sogleich. »Da wir die Männer des Grafen nicht selbst vertreiben können, müssen wir den König darum ersuchen. Wir müssen ein Abordnung entsenden, die ihn darum bittet, die Erfüllung des Vertrages zu erzwingen.«

Zustimmendes Gemurmel erhob sich. Andrew, der Sakristan, meldete sich zu Wort: »Wir sollten die klügsten und redegewandtesten Brüder entsenden.«

Philip begriff, daß Remigius und Andrew sich bereits als Anführer der Delegation betrachteten.

Remigius sagte: »Wenn der König erfährt, was vorgefallen ist, wird Percy Hamleigh wahrscheinlich nicht mehr lange Graf von Shiring sein.«

Philip war sich dessen nicht so sicher.

»Wo hält sich der König denn gegenwärtig auf?« fragte Andrew nachdenklich. »Weiß das jemand?«

Philip war vor kurzem in Winchester gewesen und hatte dort von den Reiseplänen des Königs erfahren. »Er ist in die Normandie aufgebrochen«, sagte er.

»Dann wird es ja ganz schön lange dauern, bis man ihn einholt«, warf Milius ein.

»Das Streben nach Gerechtigkeit erfordert stets Geduld«, verkündete Remigius salbungsvoll.

»Aber jeder Tag, den wir mit dem Streben nach Gerechtigkeit zubringen, geht uns beim Bau der neuen Kathedrale verloren«, antwortete Milius. Sein Tonfall ließ erkennen, daß ihn die Bereitwilligkeit, mit der Remigius den Aufschub in Kauf nahm, verärgerte. Philip konnte es ihm nachfühlen. Milius fuhr fort: »Und damit ist es ja noch nicht einmal getan. Wenn wir den König gefunden haben, müssen wir ihn erst einmal dazu bringen, daß er uns Gehör schenkt. Das kann Wochen dauern. Danach gibt er Percy vielleicht noch die Gelegenheit einer Rechtfertigung – das dauert und dauert ...«

»Wie sollte Percy das wohl zuwege bringen?« fragte Remigius gereizt.

»Ich weiß es nicht«, erwiderte Milius, »aber ich bin ganz sicher, daß er sich was einfallen lassen wird.«

»Aber schließlich wird der König nicht umhinkönnen, sein Wort zu halten.«

Eine neue Stimme ließ sich vernehmen: »Da wäre ich nicht so sicher.« Alle sahen sich nach dem Sprecher um. Es war Bruder Timothy, der älteste Mönch in der Priorei. Er war ein kleiner, bescheidener Mann, der nur selten das Wort ergriff; tat er es jedoch, so war sein Kommentar stets hörenswert. Manchmal dachte Philip, eigentlich hätte Timothy Prior werden sollen. Meistens ließ er die Kapitelversammlung teilnahmslos an sich vorüberziehen und verfiel in eine Art Dämmerzustand. Jetzt aber hatte er sich vorgebeugt, und seine Augen leuchteten vor Überzeugung. »Der König ist eine Kreatur des Augenblicks«, sagte er. »Er ist ununterbrochen bedroht, und zwar sowohl durch Rebellen innerhalb des eigenen Reiches als auch von den benachbarten Monarchen. Er braucht Verbündete. Graf Percy ist ein einflußreicher Mann mit vielen Rittern. Wenn der König zu dem Zeitpunkt, da wir unsere Eingabe vorbringen, gerade Percys Unterstützung benötigt, dann werden wir uns, ganz unabhängig von der Rechtmäßigkeit unseres Anliegens, eine Abfuhr holen. Der König ist auch nur ein Mensch. Es gibt nur einen wahren Richter, und das ist Gott.« Er lehnte sich zurück und ließ die Lider sinken, als interessierte es ihn nicht im geringsten, wie die Brüder seine Rede aufnahmen. Philip unterdrückte ein Lächeln: Präziser hätte er seine eigenen Befürchtungen nicht formulieren können.

Widerstrebend sah Remigius die Aussicht auf eine lange, aufregende Reise nach Frankreich und einen Aufenthalt am königlichen Hof entschwinden. Aber er hatte den Argumenten Timothys nichts entgegenzusetzen. »Was sollen wir dann tun?« fragte er.

Philip wußte es selber nicht. Der Vogt konnte ihnen in diesem Fall nicht helfen: Percy war zu mächtig, um sich von einem einfachen

Vogt in die Schranken weisen zu lassen. Und auf den Bischof war ebenfalls kein Verlaß. Es war zum Haareausraufen! Fest stand nur eines: Philip war nicht bereit, die Hände in den Schoß zu legen und sich mit der Niederlage abzufinden. Ich werde diesen Steinbruch bekommen – und wenn ich ihn selbst befreien muß ...

Das war überhaupt die Idee. »Augenblick«, sagte er.

Es ginge nur, wenn alle Brüder, deren Gesundheitszustand es erlaubte, mitmachten, und mußte sorgfältig geplant werden wie eine militärische Operation, allerdings ohne Waffen ... Sie brauchten Wegzehrung für zwei Tage ...

»Ich weiß nicht, ob etwas dabei herauskommen wird«, sagte er. »Aber es ist zumindest den Versuch wert. Hört zu.«

Er setzte ihnen seinen Plan auseinander.

Wenig später machten sie sich auf den Weg: dreißig Mönche, zehn Novizen, Otto Blackface mit seinen Steinbrechern, Tom Builder und Alfred, zwei Pferde und ein Karren. Als es dunkel wurde, zündeten sie zur besseren Orientierung ihre Laternen an. Um Mitternacht machten sie Rast und verzehrten ihre von der Küche eilig hergerichtete Verpflegung: gebratenes Huhn, Weißbrot und Rotwein. Philip hatte schon immer die Meinung vertreten, daß harte Arbeit mit gutem Essen belohnt werden sollte. Auf dem Weitermarsch stimmten sie die Messe an, die sie um diese Zeit abzuhalten pflegten.

Als die Nacht am schwärzesten schien, gab Tom Builder, der die Kolonne anführte, das Zeichen zum Anhalten und sagte zu Philip: »Noch eine Meile bis zum Steinbruch.«

»Gut«, sagte Philip und wandte sich an die Mönche. »Zieht eure Holzschuhe und Sandalen aus und die Filzstiefel an.« Er selbst war der erste, der aus seinen Sandalen schlüpfte und ein Paar weiche Filzstiefel von der Art, wie die Bauern sie im Winter tragen, überstreifte.

Er nahm zwei Novizen beiseite. »Edward und Philemon, ihr bleibt mit den Pferden und dem Karren hier. Verhaltet euch ruhig und wartet, bis es richtig hell geworden ist. Dann kommt uns nach. Habt ihr verstanden?«

»Ja, Vater«, erwiderten sie wie aus einem Munde.

»Und nun zu den anderen«, sagte Philip. »Folgt jetzt Tom Builder, und zwar mucksmäuschenstill, wenn ich bitten darf.«

Sie setzten ihren Weg fort.

Von Westen wehte eine leichte Brise, und das Rascheln des Laubes übertönte sowohl den Atem von fünfzig Männern als auch die Schlurf-geräusche von fünfzig Paar Filzstiefeln. Philip spürte eine gewisse Beklemmung. Jetzt, da es ernst wurde, erschien ihm sein Plan auf einmal halb verrückt. Stumm betete er für den Erfolg ihrer Mission.

Die Straße beschrieb eine Linkskurve, und im flackernden Licht der Laterne zeichneten sich die undeutlichen Umrisse eines Holz-schuppens, ein Haufen halbfertiger Steinblöcke, ein paar Leitern und Gerüste und im Hintergrund ein dunkler Hügelrücken mit häßlich weißen Steinbrechernarben ab.

Mann für Mann schlichen sie an der Hütte vorüber. Philip hielt den Atem an. Wenn sie Hunde haben, beginnt gleich ein Höllenspekta-kel, und alles war umsonst, dachte er. Aber es blieb still.

Unterhalb des Gerüstes gebot er seinen Leuten Einhalt. Er war stolz darauf, daß sie sich so ruhig verhalten hatten – das Schweigen fiel ihnen sonst schon in der Kirche schwer. Vielleicht lähmte die Angst ihre Zungen.

Tom Builder und Otto Blackface wiesen den Steinbrechern schwei-gend ihre Plätze zu. Sie wurden in zwei Gruppen geteilt: Die einen versammelten sich am Fuße des Steilhanges, die anderen erklommen das Gerüst. Als sie ihre Stellungen eingenommen hatten, bedeutete Philip den Mönchen, sich sitzend oder stehend um die Arbeiter zu gruppieren. Er selbst postierte sich auf halbem Wege zwischen Hütte und Hang.

Die zeitliche Planung war perfekt: Kurz nach Philips letzten Anord-nungen dämmerte der Tag herauf. Philip nahm eine Kerze aus seinem Umhang, entzündete sie an seiner Laterne und hob sie in die Höhe. Das war das abgesprochene Signal. Alle vierzig Mönche und Novizen holten nun ihrerseits eine Kerze hervor und entzündeten sie. Die Wirkung war spektakulär. Über einem Steinbruch, der von schweigen-den, gespenstischen Gestalten besetzt war, brach der Tag herein, und jede hielt ein kleines, flackerndes Licht in den Händen ...

Philip sah sich nach der Hütte um. Bisher war von dort noch kein Lebenszeichen gekommen. Sie würden noch eine Weile warten müs-sen, was Mönchen jedoch nicht allzu schwerfiel: Stundenlanges Still-stehen gehörte zu ihrem täglichen Leben. Die Arbeiter indessen wur-den bald ungeduldig; sie traten rastlos von einem Fuß auf den anderen und flüsterten miteinander, doch das spielte nun auch keine Rolle mehr.

Endlich erwachten die Bewohner der Hütte. Philip hörte jemanden husten und spucken und kurz darauf ein schleifendes Geräusch. Es klang, als würde hinter der Tür ein Querbalken angehoben. Mit erhobener Hand gab er das Zeichen für absolute Stille.

Die Hüttentür öffnete sich. Philip stand noch immer mit erhobener Hand da. Ein Mann trat heraus und rieb sich die Augen; nach Toms Beschreibung war es Harold von Shiring, der Steinbruchmeister. Harold bemerkte zunächst nichts Ungewöhnliches. Er lehnte sich gegen den Türpfosten und hustete tief und blubbernd wie ein Mann, der zuviel Steinstaub auf den Lungen hat. Philip ließ die Hand sinken. Weiter hinten gab der Kantor den Ton an, und die Mönche fingen an zu singen. Der Steinbruch füllte sich mit unheimlichen Klängen.

Die Wirkung auf Harold war überwältigend. Er riß den Kopf hoch und glotzte den Geisterchor, der wie von Zauberhand in seinem Steinbruch erschienen war, mit weit aufgerissenen Augen und hängendem Unterkiefer an. Ein Angstschrei entwich seinem offenen Mund, dann stolperte er durch die Tür zurück in die Hütte.

Philip gestattete sich ein zufriedenes Lächeln. So weit, so gut. Die Furcht vor dem Übernatürlichen würde allerdings nicht lang vorhalten. Wieder erhob er seine Hand. Die Steinbrecher begannen mit der Arbeit und untermalten den Chorgesang mit dem Klang von Eisen auf Stein.

Zwei oder drei Gesichter lugten ängstlich aus der Tür. Die Männer kamen schnell dahinter, daß sie es mit leibhaftigen Mönchen und Arbeitern und nicht mit Erscheinungen oder Geistern zu tun hatten, und traten vor die Hütte, um sich die Sache genauer anzusehen. Auch die beiden Bewaffneten traten auf den Plan. Sie schnallten sich ihre Schwerter um und starrten auf die seltsame Szenerie. Für Philip war der entscheidende Augenblick gekommen: Wie würden sich die beiden Posten verhalten?

Der Anblick der kräftigen, bärtigen und ungepflegten Männer mit ihren an Kettengürteln hängenden Schwertern und Dolchen und schweren Lederwämsen beschwor eine leidvolle Erinnerung herauf: Unwillkürlich mußte Philip an die beiden Soldaten denken, die sein Elternhaus überfallen und Vater und Mutter umgebracht hatten. Plötzlich und unerwartet überkam ihn eine tiefe Trauer um die Eltern, an die er sich kaum erinnern konnte. Und während er voller Abscheu auf Graf Percys Aufseher schaute, verwandelten sie sich plötzlich in einen häßlichen Mann mit einer Hakennase und einen anderen mit blutverschmiertem Bart. Wut und Verachtung erfüllten ihn und eine wilde Entschlossenheit, daß solchen blindwütigen, gottlosen Rohlingen das Handwerk gelegt werden mußte.

Eine Zeitlang verhielten sie sich still. Inzwischen waren sämtliche Steinbrecher des Grafen vor die Hütte getreten. Es waren insgesamt zwölf Arbeiter; hinzu kamen die beiden Bewaffneten.

Die Sonne schickte ihre Strahlen über den Horizont.

Die Steinbrecher aus Kingsbridge hatten bereits die ersten Steine gelockert. Wenn die Wachen sie an der Arbeit hindern wollten, mußten sie zunächst die Mönche vertreiben, die die Arbeiter schützend umringten. Philip hatte darauf gesetzt, daß sie es nicht wagen würden, sich an betenden Mönchen zu vergreifen.

Bisher war seine Rechnung aufgegangen: Sie zögerten.

Die beiden zurückgelassenen Novizen erschienen mit Pferden und Karren. Sie sahen furchtsam in die Runde. Philip bedeutete ihnen mit einem Handzeichen, wo sie den Karren abstellen sollten. Dann drehte er sich um, verständigte sich wortlos mit Tom Builder und nickte.

Zwischenzeitlich waren mehrere Steine geschnitten worden, und Tom wies einige der jüngeren Mönche an, sie aufzuheben und zum Karren zu tragen. Die Männer des Grafen sahen neugierig zu. Da die Steine für eine Person zu schwer waren, mußten sie mit Seilen vom Gerüst herabgelassen und auf Tragen zum Karren geschleppt werden. Die Posten lösten sich aus der Menge vor der Hütte und gingen auf den Karren zu. Philemon, einer der Novizen, kletterte hinauf und setzte sich mit trotziger Miene auf einen Stein. Tapferer Junge! dachte Philip und befürchtete das Schlimmste.

Die Männer näherten sich dem Karren, vor dem die vier Mönche, die die beiden Steine geschleppt hatten, eine Art Barriere bildeten. Philip wurde nervös. Die Männer blieben vor den Mönchen stehen und legten die Hand auf den Schwertknauf. Der Gesang brach ab.

Sie werden es nicht wagen, schutzlose Mönche mit dem Schwert zu bedrohen, dachte Philip, erkannte aber gleich, daß er sich von Wunschdenken leiten ließ. Die Männer waren hartgesottene Haudegen, die so manch eine blutrünstige Schlacht überstanden hatten. Es wäre ein leichtes für sie, Menschen, von denen sie noch nicht einmal Vergeltungsmaßnahmen zu befürchten hatten, mit ihren Schwertern zu durchbohren. Gewiß, sie mußten die Strafe Gottes bedenken, die ihnen sicher war, wenn sie seine Diener ermordeten. Sogar Verbrecher ihres Schlags mußten sich darüber im klaren sein, daß sie eines Tages vor dem Jüngsten Gericht stehen würden. Ob sie sich vor der Hölle fürchteten? Vielleicht – aber sie fürchteten auch Graf Percy. Philip vermutete, daß sie sich vor allem darüber Gedanken machten, ob Percy ihnen die nächtliche Besetzung des Steinbruchs durchgehen ließe oder nicht. Da standen sie, die rechte Hand am Schwertgriff, und wägten im Geiste die Strafe, die ihnen von Graf Percy drohte, gegen den Zorn Gottes ab.

Die beiden Männer sahen sich an. Der eine schüttelte den Kopf. Der andere zuckte die Achseln. Gemeinsam verließen sie den Steinbruch.

Der Kantor gab einen neuen Ton an, und die Mönche brachen in einen Triumphgesang aus. Die Steinbrecher stießen einen Siegesschrei aus, und Philip seufzte vor Erleichterung auf. Einen Augenblick lang war die Lage äußerst kritisch gewesen. Jetzt strahlte er vor Freude.

Er blies seine Kerze aus und begab sich zum Karren. Er umarmte jeden einzelnen der vier Mönche, die den Bewaffneten von Angesicht zu Angesicht gegenübergestanden hatten, sowie die beiden Novizen, die mit dem Karren nachgekommen waren. »Ich bin stolz auf euch«, sagte er herzlich. »Und Gott auch, glaube ich.«

Die Mönche und Steinbrecher schüttelten einander die Hände und beglückwünschten sich. Otto Blackface ging auf Philip zu und sagte: »Gut gemacht, Vater Philip. Ihr seid ein tapferer Mann, wenn ich mir erlauben darf, das zu sagen.«

»Gott hat uns beschützt«, sagte Philip. Sein Blick fiel auf die Steinbrecher des Grafen, die wie begossene Pudel in der Nähe der Hüttentür herumstanden. Er wollte sie sich nicht zu Feinden machen, zumal die Gefahr bestand, daß Percy sich ihrer bediente, um neuerlich Unruhe zu stiften. Philip beschloß, mit ihnen zu reden.

Er nahm Otto beim Arm und führte ihn zur Hütte hinüber. »Der Wille Gottes hat sich hier und heute durchgesetzt«, sagte er zu Harold. »Ich hoffe, Ihr seid uns nicht böse.«

»Wir sind arbeitslos«, erwiderte Harold. »Das ist böse genug.«

Einer plötzlichen Eingebung folgend, sagte Philip: »Wenn Ihr wollt, könnt Ihr schon heute wieder Arbeit haben. Ich werde Euch alle einstellen, Ihr braucht noch nicht einmal aus Eurer Hütte auszuziehen.«

Harold war im ersten Moment wie vor den Kopf geschlagen, gewann jedoch seine Fassung schnell wieder und fragte: »Zu welchem Lohn?«

»Wie üblich«, erwiderte Philip, ohne zu zögern. »Zwei Pence pro Tag für die Handwerker, einen Penny pro Tag für die Hilfskräfte, vier Pence für Euch selbst, und Ihr bezahlt Eure Lehrlinge.«

Harold sah sich nach seinen Mitarbeitern um, und Philip zog Otto beiseite, damit die Männer sich ungestört besprechen konnten. Im

Grunde konnte sich Philip zwölf zusätzliche Männer nicht leisten. Wenn Harold und seine Männer das Angebot annahmen, konnte die Einstellung der Steinmetzen nicht weiter hinausgeschoben werden. Hinzu kam, daß in diesem Fall die Steine schneller geschnitten als gebraucht wurden. Man schuf sich somit zwar einen Vorrat, hatte aber auch größere Ausgaben. Ein kluger Schachzug war es allemal, Percys Steinbrecher auf die Lohnliste der Priorei zu setzen, denn wenn der Graf doch noch einen weiteren Versuch unternehmen sollte, den Steinbruch auszubeuten, mußte er erst einmal neue Arbeitskräfte anwerben. Dies aber könnte sich, sobald die Kunde von den Ereignissen die Runde gemacht hatte, als recht schwieriges Unterfangen erweisen.

Harold und seine Männer waren sich offenbar nicht einig. Nach ein paar Minuten kam er auf Philip zu. »Wer hat hier das Sagen, wenn wir für Euch arbeiten?« fragte er. »Ich oder Euer eigener Steinbruchmeister?«

»Otto hat die Oberaufsicht«, erwiderte Philip, ohne zu zögern. Harold konnte er diese Aufgabe nicht anvertrauen, denn es war nicht auszuschließen, daß er sich wieder auf Percys Seite schlagen würde. Und zwei Verantwortliche waren undenkbar – das führte unweigerlich zu Streitereien. »Ihr könnt nach wie vor Eure eigenen Männer befehligen«, fügte Philip hinzu, »aber Otto steht über Euch.«

Harold kehrte enttäuscht zu seinen Mitarbeitern zurück. Die Diskussion begann von neuem. Tom Builder gesellte sich zu Philip und Otto. »Euer Plan ist aufgegangen, Vater«, sagte er mit breitem Grinsen. »Der Steinbruch ist wieder unser, ohne daß ein einziger Tropfen Blut vergossen wurde. Ihr seid großartig!«

Philip neigte dazu, ihm beizupflichten, und sah ein, daß er sich der Sünde des Hochmuts schuldig machte. Sich selbst und Tom zur Mahnung sagte er: »Gott ist es, der das vollbracht hat.«

Otto sagte: »Vater Philip hat Harold angeboten, ihn und seine Männer einzustellen. Sie sollen hier mit uns arbeiten.«

»Tatsächlich?« Tom wirkte ungehalten. Der Baumeister, nicht der Prior stellte die Handwerker ein, so wollte es der Brauch. »Ich hätte nicht gedacht, daß Ihr Euch das leisten könnt.«

»Kann ich auch nicht«, gab Philip zu. »Aber ich will nicht, daß diese Männer untätig herumlungern und sich von Percy zu einem Gegenschlag mißbrauchen lassen.«

Tom nickte nachdenklich. »Und es kann auch nicht schaden, wenn wir schon einen Vorrat an Steinen haben, falls Percy sich doch noch durchsetzen sollte.«

Es schien, als hätte Harold sich mit seinen Arbeitern geeinigt. Er kam wieder auf Philip zu und sagte: »Seid Ihr bereit, mir die Löhne auszuzahlen, so daß ich sie nach eigenem Gutdünken verteilen kann?«

Der Vorschlag gefiel Philip nicht, lief er doch darauf hinaus, daß der Meister seine Mitarbeiter übervorteilen konnte. »Fragt den Baumeister«, sagte er.

»Das ist durchaus üblich«, sagte Tom. »Wenn Eure Männer es so wollen, bin ich einverstanden.«

»Dann nehmen wir das Angebot an«, sagte Harold.

Harold und Tom schüttelten einander die Hand. »So ist's recht«, sagte Philip. »Jeder kommt auf seine Kosten.«

»Mit einer Ausnahme«, warf Harold ein.

»Wer denn?« fragte Philip.

»Regan, Graf Percys Frau«, sagte Harold unheilvoll. »Wenn sie erfährt, was heute hier geschehen ist, dann gibt es ein Blutbad.«

An jenem Tag ging man nicht auf die Jagd, und so spielten die jungen Männer auf Earlscastle »Katzensteinigen« – eine der Lieblingsbeschäftigungen William Hamleighs.

An Katzen gab es auf der Burg keinen Mangel, und auf eine mehr oder weniger kam es nicht an. Die Burschen schlossen die Türen und Klappläden im großen Saal des Wohnturms und rückten die Möbel gegen eine der Wände, so daß die Katze sich nirgends verstecken konnte. Dann trugen sie in der Saalmitte einen Haufen Steine zusammen. Die Katze, ein betagter Mäusefänger mit graumeliertem Fell, spürte die Blutrunst in der Luft und hockte sich, in der Hoffnung, doch noch entwischen zu können, in die Nähe der Tür.

Jeder Teilnehmer warf pro Steinwurf einen Penny in einen Topf. Wer der Katze schließlich den Rest gab, bekam den Topf.

Während sie die Reihenfolge auslosten, wurde die Katze zusehends unruhiger und tigerte vor der Tür auf und ab.

Walter warf als erster und hatte damit eine günstige Ausgangsposition. Die Katze war zwar auf der Hut, kannte das Spiel aber nicht und konnte vielleicht überrumpelt werden. Walter nahm, mit dem Rücken zum Opfer, einen Stein auf und verbarg ihn in seiner Hand; dann drehte er sich langsam um die eigene Achse, holte blitzschnell aus und warf.

Daneben. Der Stein polterte gegen die Tür, die Katze machte einen Satz und suchte das Weite. Die Männer johlten.

Als zweiter hatte man es nicht mehr so leicht. Die Katze war jetzt gewarnt, zudem war sie noch ausgeruht und leichtfüßig. Ein junger Knappe war an der Reihe. Er beobachtete, wie die Katze auf der Suche nach einer Fluchtmöglichkeit durch den Raum rannte, wartete, bis sie langsamer wurde, und zielte. Ein guter Wurf, aber das Tier sah den Stein kommen und rettete sich mit einem Sprung zur Seite. Die Männer stöhnten auf.

Die Katze raste in panischer Angst im Raum herum und sprang auf die an der Wand gestapelten Böcke und Planken und von dort wieder auf den Boden. Ein älterer Ritter war als nächster an der Reihe. Er täuschte einen Wurf an, um die Fluchtrichtung herauszubekommen. Als sie wieder loslief, zielte er auf eine Stelle zwischen der unmittelbaren und der vorausgeschätzten Position. Seine Kriegslist brachte ihm zwar den Beifall der anderen ein, aber die Katze sah auch diesmal den Stein kommen und mied ihn, indem sie mitten im Lauf stehenblieb.

Verzweifelt versuchte das Tier, hinter einer Kirchentruhe in der Ecke Zuflucht zu finden. Der nächste Schütze sah dann eine Chance darin und nutzte sie: Mit einem schnellen Wurf traf er das noch in der Ecke kauernde Tier am Hinterteil. Allgemeines Gejohle war die Antwort. Die Katze gab ihren Versuch, sich hinter die Truhe zu zwängen, auf und lief – langsamer jetzt und humpelnd – wieder im Raum hin und her.

Nun war William an der Reihe. Indem er sie zunächst anbrüllte und dann einen Wurf vortäuschte, machte er ihr wieder Beine und kam seinem Ziel, sie schneller zu ermüden, erheblich näher. Jeder andere, der die gleiche Verzögerungstaktik angewandt hätte, wäre ausgebuht worden, aber William war schließlich der Sohn des Grafen, und so faßte man sich in Geduld. Die Katze wurde langsamer; sie litt offenbar unter Schmerzen und drückte sich an die Wand neben der Tür. William holte aus und zielte. Ehe jedoch der Stein seine linke Hand verlassen hatte, ging unversehens die Tür auf, und im Rahmen erschien ein schwarzgekleideter Priester. William vollendete den Wurf, doch die Katze schnellte davon wie ein Pfeil und miaute triumphierend. Der Priester stieß einen schrillen Schreckensschrei aus und raffte den Rock seiner Soutane. Die jungen Kerle brachen in schallendes Gelächter aus, als die Katze zwischen den Beinen des Priesters landete und durch die offenstehende Tür davonschoß. Der Priester verharrte in der ängstlichen Pose eines alten Weibes, das sich vor einer Maus fürchtet, und die jungen Männer schütteten sich aus vor Lachen.

William erkannte den Priester. Es war Bischof Waleran.

Das stachelte ihn nun erst recht zum Lachen an. Die Tatsache, daß der weibische Priester, der sich von einer Katze so hatte erschrecken lassen, auch noch ein Rivale der Familie war, verlieh der Szene zusätzlichen Reiz.

Der Bischof hatte sich schnell wieder gefangen. Er errötete, drohte William mit dem Finger und verkündete mit schneidender Stimme: »Dafür werdet Ihr in den tiefsten Tiefen der Hölle ewige Qualen erdulden!«

Williams Gelächter verwandelte sich blitzartig in panische Angst. Von kleinauf hatte ihm seine Mutter mit ihrer drastischen Schilderung der Hölle Alpträume bereitet. Furchtbar, was die Teufel alles mit den armen Seelen anstellten! Sie rösteten sie in den Flammen des Höllenfeuers, stachen ihnen die Augen aus und säbelten den Männern mit scharfen Messern das Gemächt ab ... Seit jenen Tagen war William die bloße Erwähnung der Hölle aufs tiefste verhaßt. »Halt's Maul!« brüllte er den Bischof an, und auf einmal herrschte Grabesstille im ganzen Saal. William zog sein Messer und ging auf Waleran zu. »Mit Euren Predigten habt Ihr hier nichts verloren, alter Giftmischer!« Waleran wirkte keineswegs ängstlich, sondern allenfalls verwundert: Mit Interesse vermerkte er, wo Williams schwacher Punkt lag. William geriet dadurch nur noch mehr in Rage. »Euch werd' ich's zeigen, so wahr Gott mein –«

Drauf und dran, tatsächlich mit dem Messer auf den Bischof loszugehen, wurde er durch eine Stimme von der Treppe daran gehindert. »William! Schluß damit!«

Es war sein Vater.

William hielt inne, und nach kurzem Zögern steckte er sein Messer wieder in die Scheide.

Waleran betrat den Saal. Ein zweiter Priester folgte ihm und schloß die Tür hinter sich; es war Dechant Baldwin.

»Ich bin überrascht, Euch hier zu sehen, Bischof«, sagte Graf Percy.

»Etwa, weil Ihr den Prior von Kingsbridge bei unserem letzten Zusammentreffen dazu angestiftet habt, mich hinters Licht zu führen? Tja, daß Ihr überrascht seid, wundert mich nicht. Gemeinhin ist Nachsicht nicht meine Stärke.« Er streifte William mit einem eiskalten Blick. »Aber ich bin nicht nachtragend, wenn es meinen eigenen Interessen zuwiderliefe.«

Vater Hamleigh nickte nachdenklich. »Am besten gehen wir nach oben. Du auch, William.«

Bischof Waleran und Dechant Baldwin erklommen die Stufen zum Wohntrakt des Grafen, und William folgte ihnen. Noch immer bedauerte er, daß die Katze entkommen war. Andererseits war er sich auch darüber im klaren, daß er selbst nur um Haaresbreite davongekommen war: Hätte er Hand an den Bischof gelegt, so wäre er höchstwahrscheinlich dafür gehängt worden. Aber das Empfindliche, Gekünstelte an Waleran war ihm nach wie vor zuwider.

Sie betraten Vaters Zimmer, den gleichen Raum, in dem er Aliena vergewaltigt hatte. Jedesmal, wenn er hier war, hatte er die Szene unmittelbar vor Augen: ihren üppigen weißen Körper, die Angst in ihrem Gesicht, ihre Schreie, die verzerrte Miene ihres kleinen Bruders, der zum Zuschauen gezwungen war, und schließlich – sein Meisterstück! –, wie er sie Walter zu dessen eigenem Vergnügen überlassen hatte. Nur allzugern hätte er sie als Gefangene dabehalten, zur ständigen Verfügbarkeit.

Seit jenem Tag war er wie besessen von ihr. Er hatte sogar versucht, sie ausfindig zu machen. Ein Jagdpfleger, der dabei erwischt worden war, wie er Williams Schlachtroß in Shiring verkaufen wollte, hatte auf der Folter bekannt, es von einem Mädchen gestohlen zu haben, dessen Beschreibung auf Aliena paßte. Vom Gefängnisaufseher in Winchester hatte William erfahren, daß Aliena ihren Vater vor dessen Tod noch besucht hatte. Und seine Freundin Mistreß Kate, die Besitzerin eines von ihm gerne aufgesuchten Freudenhauses, hatte ihm erzählt, daß sie Aliena eine Stelle in ihrem Etablissement angeboten hatte. Letztlich hatte sich ihre Spur trotz aller Nachforschungen verflüchtigt. »Zerbrich dir nicht den Kopf darüber, Willy, mein Junge«, hatte Kate in ihrer ungerührten Art gesagt. »Du willst große Titten und langes Haar? Haben wir alles. Warum nimmst du heute abend nicht Betty und Millie zusammen, vier schwere Brüste, ganz für dich allein!« Aber Betty und Millie waren weder unschuldig, noch war ihre Haut schneeweiß, und ihnen stand auch nicht die Todesangst im Gesicht. Er hatte das Angebot angenommen, aber er hatte so gut wie nichts davon gehabt. Es war tatsächlich so, daß er seit jenem Abend mit Aliena hier im Zimmer des Grafen bei keiner einzigen Frau mehr Befriedigung gefunden hatte.

Er zwang die Gedanken an sie aus seinem Kopf. Bischof Waleran sprach mit seiner Mutter: »Ich nehme an, Ihr wißt, daß der Prior von Kingsbridge Euren Steinbruch an sich gebracht hat?«

Sie wußten nichts davon. William war überrascht, und seine Mutter schäumte vor Wut. »Was?« fragte sie ungläubig. »Wie das?«

»Angeblich gelang es Euren Wachposten zunächst, die Steinbrecher zu verscheuchen. Doch als sie am nächsten Morgen erwachten, wimmelte es im Steinbruch von psalmodierenden Mönchen, und sie hatten Angst davor, sich an Männern Gottes zu vergreifen. Daraufhin stellte Prior Philip Eure Steinbrecher ein, und jetzt arbeiten sie dort friedlich Seite an Seite mit den Seinen. Mich wundert nur, daß Eure Wachposten nicht zurückgekommen sind, um Bericht zu erstatten.«

»Wo sind sie, diese Feiglinge?« kreischte Mutter mit hochrotem Kopf. »Denen werde ich Beine machen – ich sorge dafür, daß sie sich selbst die Eier aufschneiden ...«

»Jetzt wird mir klar, warum sie nicht zurückgekommen sind«, bemerkte Waleran.

»Die Wachposten sind nicht der Rede wert«, sagte Vater. »Das sind nur Soldaten. Die Verantwortung liegt bei diesem mit allen Wassern gewaschenen Prior. Nicht im Traum hätte ich ihm das zugetraut! Er hat uns aufs Kreuz gelegt, das ist alles.«

»Genau«, erwiderte Waleran. »Hinter einer Fassade unschuldiger Frömmigkeit verbirgt er die Durchtriebenheit einer Hausratte.«

Waleran sieht ja selbst wie eine spitzschnäuzige schwarze Ratte mit glattem Fell aus, dachte William. Was kümmert es ihn, wem der Steinbruch gehört? Waleran ist genauso gerissen wie Prior Philip, und genau wie Philip führt auch er etwas im Schilde!

»Er soll uns nicht ungeschoren davonkommen«, sagte Mutter. »Wir Hamleighs dürfen uns nicht in aller Öffentlichkeit erniedrigen lassen! Diesem Prior muß eine Lektion erteilt werden!«

Vater hatte seine Zweifel. »Es geht doch bloß um einen Steinbruch«, sagte er. »Und der König hat ...«

»Hier geht es nicht nur um den Steinbruch, sondern um die Familienehre!« fuhr Mutter ihm ins Wort. »Was der König gesagt hat, ist Nebensache.«

William pflichtete seiner Mutter bei. Philip von Kingsbridge hatte den Hamleighs die Stirn geboten und mußte vernichtet werden. Wer nicht gefürchtet wurde, war ein Nichts. Doch was machten sie alle für ein Geschrei darum! Die Sache war doch ganz simpel zu lösen! »Warum gehen wir nicht einfach mit ein paar Männern hin und setzen die Steinbrecher des Priors vor die Tür?«

Vater schüttelte den Kopf. »Sich den Wünschen des Königs passiv zu widersetzen, indem man – wie wir in diesem Falle – den Steinbruch selbst ausbeutet, ist eine Sache. Bewaffnete zu entsenden und Arbeiter an die Luft zu setzen, die dort mit ausdrücklicher Erlaubnis des Königs tätig sind, eine ganz andere. Das kann mich meinen Titel und meine Grafschaft kosten.«

Widerstrebend mußte William ihm beipflichten. Vaters Vorsicht war in den meisten Fällen begründet.

»Ich habe einen Vorschlag«, sagte Bischof Waleran. »Ich bin der Meinung, diese Kathedrale sollte woanders errichtet werden. Nicht in Kingsbridge.«

William stutzte. Er begriff die Bedeutung dieser Bemerkung ebenso wenig wie sein Vater. Mutters Augen indessen weiteten sich; sie hörte einen Augenblick lang auf, sich im Gesicht zu kratzen, und sagte nachdenklich: »Eine höchst interessante Idee.«

»Früher standen die meisten Kathedralen in Dörfern wie Kingsbridge«, fuhr Waleran fort. »Unter dem ersten König William wurden vor sechzig bis siebzig Jahren viele in die Städte verlegt. Kingsbridge ist nichts weiter als ein kleines Dorf am Ende der Welt. Außer einem verwahrlosten Kloster, das viel zu arm ist, um eine Kathedrale zu unterhalten – geschweige denn zu bauen –, gibt's dort rein gar nichts.«

Mutter fragte: »Und wo würde es Euch belieben, sie zu erbauen?«

»In Shiring«, erwiderte Waleran. »Die Stadt ist groß genug – hat wohl an die tausend oder mehr Einwohner, und es gibt dort einen Markt und jedes Jahr eine Wollmesse. Außerdem liegt Shiring an der Hauptstraße. Und wenn wir uns beide dafür stark machen, wenn der Bischof und der Graf an einem Strang ziehen – dann könnten wir uns durchsetzen.«

»Aber wenn die Kathedrale in Shiring steht«, wandte Vater ein, »dann können sich die Mönche in Kingsbridge nicht darum kümmern.«

»Eben, eben!« rief Mutter ungeduldig. »Ohne die Kathedrale ist Kingsbridge keinen Pfifferling wert, die Priorei läuft unter ferner liefen und Prior Philip verschwindet wieder in Bedeutungslosigkeit – was ihm nur recht geschieht.«

»Und wer kümmert sich dann um die Kathedrale?« fragte Vater Hamleigh hartnäckig.

»Ein neues Domkapitel«, antwortete Waleran. »Von mir ernannt.«

Allmählich begann William Walerans Vorstellungen zu verstehen. Eine Verlegung der Kathedrale nach Shiring gäbe Waleran die Möglichkeit, die Kontrolle darüber an sich zu reißen.

»Und wie steht es mit dem Geld?« wollte Vater wissen. »Wer, wenn nicht die Priorei von Kingsbridge, wird die neue Kathedrale finanzieren?«

»Bei näherer Betrachtung wird sich erweisen, daß der Großteil der klösterlichen Besitztümer der Kathedrale zugeeignet ist«, sagte Waleran. »Wenn die Kathedrale umzieht, dann gehen sie mit. Als König Stephan die alte Grafschaft Shiring aufteilte, sprach er dem Kloster zu Kingsbridge, wie wir alle nur allzugut wissen, die Gutshöfe in den Hügeln zu. Das war sein Beitrag zur Finanzierung der neuen Kathedrale. Wenn nun jemand anders den Dom baut, so wird der König von der Priorei erwarten, daß sie dem neuen Bauherrn diese Ländereien überläßt. Die Mönche würden sich natürlich dagegen sträuben, doch bin ich überzeugt, daß eine genaue Prüfung der Verträge für klare Verhältnisse sorgen wird.«

Die weitreichenden Konsequenzen der Pläne Walerans zeichneten sich ab: Er will sich nicht die Kathedrale, sondern auch einen Großteil des Klostervermögens unter den Nagel reißen, dachte William.

Sein Vater sagte: »Soweit es Euch betrifft, Bischof, ein großartiger Plan – nur: Was habe *ich* davon?«

Mutter antwortete an Walerans Statt: »Begreifst du das denn nicht?« fragte sie gereizt. »Dir gehört Shiring. Stell dir mal vor, wie die Stadt mit dieser Kathedrale aufblühen wird! Hunderte von Handwerkern und Arbeitern werden über Jahre hinaus auf der Baustelle tätig sein. Alle müssen sie irgendwo wohnen und dir Miete zahlen. Lebensmittel und Kleidung müssen sie auf deinem Markt kaufen – ganz zu schweigen von den Domherren selbst und den Gläubigen, die zu Ostern und Pfingsten nach Shiring statt nach Kingsbridge strömen werden. Und vergiß nicht die Pilger, die die Reliquienschreine sehen wollen ... Sie alle haben Geld und geben es aus.« Ihre Augen blitzten vor Gier. William hatte seine Mutter lange nicht mehr so begeistert erlebt. »Wenn wir die Sache richtig anpacken, wird Shiring zu einer der bedeutendsten Städte im ganzen Königreich!«

Und sie wird mir gehören, dachte William. Nach Vaters Tod werde ich Graf.

»In Ordnung«, sagte Vater. »Euer Plan bringt Philip den Ruin, verschafft Euch, Bischof, mehr Macht und mir mehr Reichtum. Was ist zu tun?«

»Die Entscheidung über die Verlegung der Kathedrale liegt beim Erzbischof von Canterbury – zumindest theoretisch.«

Mutter sah ihn durchdringend an. »Wieso ›theoretisch‹?«

»Weil wir derzeit keinen Erzbischof haben. William von Corbeil ist Weihnachten gestorben, und der König hat noch keinen Nachfolger ernannt. Wir wissen jedoch, wer aller Wahrscheinlichkeit nach den

Posten bekommt: Unser Freund Henry von Winchester hat schon lange ein Auge darauf geworfen. Er wurde vom Papst bereits mit der Interimsverwaltung betraut. Zudem ist er ein Bruder des Königs.«

»Kann man auf seine Freundschaft zählen?« wollte Vater wissen. »Als Ihr Euch um diese Grafschaft bemüht habt, war er nicht sehr hilfsbereit.«

Waleran zuckte die Achseln. »Er wird mir helfen, so gut er kann. Wir müssen unser Anliegen eben überzeugend vortragen.«

»Wenn er auf den Stuhl des Erzbischofs spekuliert, wird ihm kaum daran gelegen sein, sich einflußreiche Persönlichkeiten zum Feinde zu machen«, sagte Williams Mutter.

»Stimmt. Aber Philip fällt nicht ins Gewicht. Bei der Wahl des Erzbischofs wird er kaum mitreden dürfen.«

»Und weshalb kann Henry uns dann nicht gleich geben, was wir wollen?« fragte William.

»Weil er nicht Erzbischof ist, noch nicht! Und weil er genau weiß, daß ihm während der Übergangszeit peinlich genau auf die Finger gesehen wird. Er muß alles daransetzen, als weiser und gerechter Richter zu gelten, und darf nicht als ein Mann erscheinen, der seinen Günstlingen Gefallen erweist. Dafür gibt es *nach* der Wahl ausreichend Gelegenheit.«

»Das heißt also«, meinte Mutter nachdenklich, »daß er sich unser Anliegen günstigstenfalls wohlwollend anhören wird. Und wie lautet unser Anliegen?«

»Daß wir eine Kathedrale bauen können und Philip nicht.«

»Und wie können wir ihn davon überzeugen?«

»Seid Ihr in letzter Zeit in Kingsbridge gewesen?«

»Nein.«

»Ich war Ostern dort.« Waleran lächelte. »Sie haben noch nicht mit dem Bau begonnen. Außer dem vorgesehenen Bauplatz mit ein paar in die Erde gehauenen Pflöcken und Seilen haben sie nichts vorzuweisen. Sie haben angefangen, die Fundamente zu graben, sind aber erst ein paar Zoll weit gekommen. Ein Steinmetz mit seinem Lehrling arbeitet dort und der Zimmermann der Abtei, gelegentlich geht ihnen der eine oder andere Mönch als Hilfsarbeiter zur Hand. Ein desolater Anblick, vor allem bei Regen. Am liebsten wäre mir, Bischof Henry würde sich selbst ein Bild machen.«

Mutter nickte weise. William sah ein, daß der Plan gut war, doch die Aussicht auf eine Zusammenarbeit mit dem abscheulichen Waleran Bigod war ihm von Grund auf verhaßt.

»Wir werden Henry im voraus darüber aufklären, wie klein und unbedeutend Kingsbridge und wie arm das Kloster dort ist«, fuhr Waleran fort. »Dann kann er sich mit eigenen Augen davon überzeugen, daß sie auf der Baustelle über ein Jahr gebraucht haben, um ein paar kleine Löcher zu graben. Zu guter Letzt laden wir ihn nach Shiring ein und legen ihm dar, wie schnell hier, wo der Bischof, der Graf und die Bevölkerung alle an einem Strick ziehen, eine Kathedrale hochgezogen werden kann.«

»Wird er denn kommen?« fragte Mutter besorgt.

»Wir müssen ihn fragen, mehr können wir nicht tun«, erwiderte Waleran. »Ich werde ihn einladen, uns am Pfingstsonntag in seiner Funktion als Erzbischof zu besuchen. Dadurch geben wir zu erkennen, daß wir ihn bereits als Erzbischof betrachten – und das wird ihm schmeicheln.«

Vater Hamleigh sagte: »Hauptsache, Prior Philip erfährt nichts davon.«

»Das läßt sich kaum machen«, gab Waleran zurück. »Der Bischof kann nicht unangemeldet in Kingsbridge erscheinen – das würde einen äußerst merkwürdigen Eindruck machen.«

»Aber Philip wird, sobald er von seinem Kommen erfährt, alles daransetzen, den Bau voranzutreiben.«

»Womit? Er hat kein Geld, vor allem jetzt nicht, nachdem er Eure Steinbrecher angestellt hat. Steinbrecher können keine Mauern bauen.« Waleran schüttelte langsam den Kopf und lächelte zufrieden. »Ihm sind die Hände gebunden. Ihm bleibt nur noch die Hoffnung, daß Pfingsten die Sonne scheint.«

Philips erste Reaktion auf die Nachricht, der Bischof von Winchester wolle Kingsbridge einen Besuch abstatten, war Freude. Es bedeutete natürlich, daß der Gottesdienst im Freien, und zwar an der Stelle, wo die Kathedrale gestanden hatte, gehalten werden mußte, aber dagegen war nichts einzuwenden. Für den Fall, daß es Pfingsten regnete, konnte der Zimmermann der Priorei über und unmittelbar um den Altar herum ein provisorisches Dach bereitstellen, so daß der Bischof nicht naß wurde. Der Besuch erschien Philip wie eine Vertrauensbekundung. Der Bischof will uns damit zu verstehen geben, daß er Kingsbridge nach wie vor als Domplatz und in dem Verlust des Gebäudes nichts weiter als einen vorübergehenden Zustand sieht, dachte er.

Doch als sich die erste Begeisterung gelegt hatte, kamen Philip ernste Zweifel. Gab es vielleicht noch andere Gründe für die Visite des Bischofs? Gemeinhin suchten Bischöfe Klöster auf, um für sich und ihr Gefolge die ihnen zustehende freie Unterkunft und Verpflegung in Anspruch zu nehmen. Kingsbridge war freilich berühmt oder, genauer gesagt, berüchtigt für seine karge Kost und seine spartanisch einfachen Unterkünfte. Philips Reformen hatten bisher nur bewirkt, das Niveau von fürchterlich auf gerade noch erträglich zu heben. Außerdem war Henry der reichste Kirchenfürst im gesamten Königreich und suchte schon aus diesem Grund Kingsbridge gewiß nicht auf, um sich an Speis und Trank gütlich zu tun. Andererseits war Henry ein Mann, der, so wie Philip ihn einschätze, für alles, was er tat, einen guten Grund hatte.

Je mehr Philip darüber nachdachte, um so mehr verstärkte sich sein Verdacht, daß Bischof Waleran seine Hände im Spiel haben mußte. Er hatte damit gerechnet, daß Waleran innerhalb von ein, zwei Tagen nach Erhalt des Briefes kommen würde, um mit ihm den Gottesdienst und protokollarische Fragen des hohen Besuchs zu besprechen. Bischof Henry sollte Kingsbridge in guter Erinnerung bleiben, soviel stand fest. Doch je mehr Tage ins Land strichen, ohne daß Waleran sich blicken ließ, um so stärker wurden Philips Bedenken.

Zehn Tage vor Pfingsten erhielt Philip einen Brief des Priors von Canterbury, der ihn über das ganze Ausmaß des gegen ihn gerichteten Komplotts aufklärte. Nicht in seinen düstersten Ahnungen hätte Philip mit einem solchen Schurkenstreich gerechnet! Die Kathedrale von Canterbury unterstand ebenso wie die von Kingsbridge Benediktinermönchen, und die Brüder standen einander, wann immer möglich, bei. Der Prior von Canterbury, der naturgemäß eng mit dem amtierenden Erzbischof zusammenarbeitete, hatte in Erfahrung gebracht, daß Waleran Henry nur deshalb nach Kingsbridge geladen hatte, weil er ihn für die Verlegung von Diözese und Kathedrale nach Shiring gewinnen wollte.

Philip war fassungslos. Sein Herzschlag beschleunigte sich, und die Hand, die den Brief hielt, zitterte. Mit diesem teuflischen Schachzug traf Waleran ihn völlig unvorbereitet.

Am meisten ärgerte er sich darüber, daß er das Unheil nicht hatte kommen sehen, war ihm doch Walerans Hinterhältigkeit sattsam bekannt. Es war gerade ein Jahr her, daß der Bischof versuchte hatte, ihn in der Auseinandersetzung um den Steinbruch und die Ländereien zu übervorteilen. Wie hatte Waleran getobt, als Philip ihm auf die Schliche gekommen war! Unvergeßlich war ihm sein wutverzerrtes

Gesicht ... *Ich schwöre bei allem, was mir heilig ist, daß Ihr Eure Kirche nie bauen werdet!* hatte Waleran gedroht ... Doch die Zeit hatte der Drohung ihre Schärfe genommen, und Philip war unvorsichtig geworden. Der Brief in seiner Hand war die brutale Erinnerung daran, daß Waleran ein gutes Gedächtnis hatte.

»Bischof Waleran sagt, daß du kein Geld hast und der Bau innerhalb von fünfzehn Monaten keinerlei Fortschritte gemacht hat«, schrieb der Prior von Canterbury. »Er fordert Bischof Henry auf, sich mit eigenen Augen davon zu überzeugen, daß die Priorei in Kingsbridge zum Bau einer Kathedrale gar nicht fähig ist. Und da noch kaum etwas geschehen sei, meint er, wäre es am besten, so bald wie möglich die Verlegung zu beschließen.« Waleran war viel zu gerissen, um sich bei einer plumpen Lüge erwischen zu lassen. Er hatte lediglich schamlos übertrieben. In Wirklichkeit hatte Philip schon eine Menge erreicht. Er hatte die Ruine abgetragen, die Baupläne verabschiedet und mit den Fundamenten begonnen. Die ersten Bäume waren gefällt und die ersten Steine gebrochen. Freilich – an Ort und Stelle war noch nicht viel geschehen; es gab nur wenig, was sich dem Besucher vorführen ließ. Kein Wunder bei den gewaltigen Hindernissen, die zu überwinden gewesen waren – von der Reform der Klosterfinanzen bis hin zum Sieg über Graf Percy im Kampf um den Steinbruch. Walerans Intrige war durch und durch ungerecht!

Mit dem Brief aus Canterbury in der Hand trat Philip ans Fenster und ließ den Blick über die Baustelle schweifen. Die Frühjahrsregenfälle hatten sie in einen einzigen Morast verwandelt. Zwei junge Mönche mit aufgesetzten Kapuzen schleppten vom Flußufer Bauholz herauf. Tom Builder hatte einen Flaschenzug konstruiert, mit dem sich die Erde aus den Gruben für die Fundamente hinaufbefördern ließ, und betätigte gerade das Drehrad, während sein Sohn Alfred in der Baugrube stand und Fässer mit Schlamm füllte. Man gewann den Eindruck, die beiden könnten im gleichen Tempo unentwegt weiterarbeiten, ohne je von der Stelle zu kommen. Jeder Betrachter der Szene, der nicht gerade ein Fachmann war, mußte zu dem Schluß kommen, daß sich hier vor dem Jüngsten Gericht keine Kathedrale erheben würde.

Philip kehrte an sein Schreibpult zurück. Was tun? Einen Augenblick war er versucht, die Hände einfach in den Schoß zu legen. Soll Bischof Henry ruhig kommen und sich ein eigenes Urteil bilden, dachte er. Und wenn die Kathedrale dann in Shiring gebaut werden soll – nun, dann wird sie eben in Shiring gebaut. Mag Waleran seinen

Willen haben und die Kathedrale für seine eigenen Zwecke nutzen, möge sie der Stadt Shiring und der bösen Dynastie derer von Hamleigh Wohlstand bringen. Gottes Wille geschehe.

Nein, so geht es nicht! Philip wußte, daß dieser Weg in die Sackgasse führte. Gottvertrauen bedeutete nicht, in Untätigkeit zu verharren; es äußerte sich vielmehr in der Überzeugung, daß ehrliches und energisches Bemühen letztlich doch zum Erfolg führt. Es ist meine heilige Pflicht, sagte sich Philip, alles zu tun, um zu verhindern, daß die Kathedrale von zynischen und gottlosen Menschen aus Selbstsucht mißbraucht wird. Bischof Henry muß sehen, daß die Bauarbeiten zügig vorangehen und daß die Priorei Kingsbridge über genügend Energie und Entschlossenheit verfügt, um das Vorhaben auch zu Ende zu führen.

Stimmte das überhaupt? Tatsache war, daß der Bau der Kathedrale Philip unsägliche Schwierigkeiten bereitete und auch weiterhin bereiten würde. Schon die Blockade des Steinbruchs hätte ihn fast in die Knie gezwungen. Philip war nach wie vor felsenfest davon überzeugt, daß er mit Gottes Wille Erfolg haben würde, doch seine Gewißheit allein würde bei weitem nicht ausreichen, um Bischof Henry zu überzeugen.

Er beschloß, ohne Rücksicht auf Verluste, der Baustelle ein imposanteres Gepräge zu geben. Ich werde in den verbleibenden zehn Tagen alle Mönche zur Arbeit abkommandieren. Vielleicht gelingt es ihnen, die Baugrube so weit auszuheben, daß Tom und Alfred schon die Fundamente legen können. Wenn sie es – an einer Stelle wenigstens – fertigbekommen, kann Tom mit dem Bau der Mauer beginnen. Das ist zwar nicht viel, aber immerhin besser als gar nichts.

Philip hätte hundert Arbeitskräfte benötigt, hatte aber noch nicht einmal genug Geld für zehn.

Bischof Henry, soviel stand fest, würde an einem Sonntag eintreffen, wenn keine Menschenseele bei der Arbeit war. Es sei denn, Philip appellierte an die Gemeinde, sich als Hilfskräfte zur Verfügung zu stellen ... Er malte sich aus, wie er den Gläubigen den neuen Pfingstgottesdienst erklären würde: Statt Gesang und Gebet werden wir Löcher graben und Steine schleppen. Nun, da würden sie vielleicht schauen ... Sie würden ...

Ja, wie würden sich die Menschen wohl verhalten?

Wahrscheinlich werden sie vorbehaltlos mitmachen.

Philip zog die Stirn kraus. Entweder ich bin verrückt, dachte er, oder es klappt tatsächlich ...

Er versank ins Grübeln. Am Ende der Messe werde ich verkünden, daß die Buße für die Vergebung aller Sünden diesmal in einem halben Arbeitstag auf der Dombaustelle besteht. Und zum Abendessen gibt es Brot und Bier.

Die Leute würden mitmachen, es gab keinen Zweifel.

Ich muß mit jemandem darüber reden, dachte er. Milius? Nein, der denkt ohnehin so wie ich. Ich brauche jemanden, der nicht von vornherein meine Ansichten teilt.

Philips Wahl fiel auf Cuthbert Whitehead, den Kellermeister. Er warf seinen Umhang über, zog die Kapuze zum Schutz gegen den Regen tief ins Gesicht und ging hinaus. Er eilte quer über die Baustelle, winkte Tom flüchtig zu und strebte dem Küchentrakt zu, dem inzwischen ein Hühnerhof, ein Kuhstall und eine Molkerei angeschlossen worden waren: Philip mochte das knapp bemessene Bargeld nicht für Waren des täglichen Gebrauchs ausgeben, die ohne Schwierigkeiten von den Mönchen selbst erzeugt werden konnten.

Er betrat den Lagerraum des Kellermeisters im Gewölbe unterhalb der Küche und schnupperte den trockenen aromatischen Duft von Kräutern und Gewürzen. Cuthbert zählte gerade Knoblauchzwiebeln, die auf lange Schnüre aufgezogen waren, und murmelte leise Zahlen vor sich hin. Er sah erschreckend alt aus und war nur noch Haut und Knochen.

»Siebenunddreißig«, sagte Cuthbert laut. »Wie wär's mit einem Becher Wein?«

»Nein, danke.« Philip wußte inzwischen aus Erfahrung, daß er tagsüber keinen Wein trinken durfte. Er machte ihn träge und reizbar. Der heilige Benedikt hatte genau gewußt, warum er die Mönche zur Mäßigung mahnte. »Ich bin nicht hier wegen deiner Vorräte, sondern ich brauche deinen Rat. Komm, setz dich!«

Cuthbert schob sich vorbei an Kisten und Fässern und stolperte über einen Sack, bevor er sich auf einem dreibeinigen Schemel niederließ. Das Lager war längst nicht mehr so gut aufgeräumt wie ehedem.

»Hast du Schwierigkeiten mit deinen Augen, Cuthbert?«

»Sie sind nicht mehr so gut wie früher, aber immer noch gut genug«, gab Cuthbert kurzangebunden zurück.

Um seine Sehkraft war es vermutlich schon seit Jahren schlecht bestellt – vielleicht mit ein Grund dafür, daß er nie richtig lesen gelernt hatte. Cuthbert war in diesem Punkt aber offenbar empfindlich, so daß Philip nicht weiter darauf einging, sondern sich lediglich vornahm, beizeiten einen Nachfolger für den Kellermeister heranzuziehen. »Der Prior von Canterbury hat mir einen sehr beunruhigenden Brief geschrieben«, sagte er und weihte Cuthbert in Walerans Komplott ein. Zum Schluß meinte er: »Ich sehe nur eine Möglichkeit, die Baustelle in einen Bienenstock zu verwandeln, in dem es brummt und summt vor Geschäftigkeit: Wir müssen die Gemeinde zur Mitarbeit anhalten. Spricht etwas dagegen?«

Cuthbert zögerte nicht eine Sekunde lang. »Gar nichts. Die Idee ist hervorragend!«

»Aber ein bißchen ungewöhnlich, wie?« meinte Philip.

»Es wäre nicht das erstemal.«

»Wirklich?« Philip war freudig überrascht. »Wo hat es denn so was schon gegeben?«

»Ich habe das schon von verschiedenen Stellen gehört.«

Philip war aufgeregt. »Und – klappt es?«

»Manchmal. Wahrscheinlich hängt es vom Wetter ab.«

»Und wie stellt man es am besten an? Genügt es, wenn es der Priester am Ende des Gottesdienstes ankündigt?«

»Ein bißchen mehr Vorbereitung ist schon erforderlich. Der Bischof oder der Prior entsendet zuvor Boten in die Gemeinden. Sie verkünden, daß die Vergebung der Sünden gegen Arbeit auf der Baustelle gewährt wird.«

»Eine großartige Idee«, sagte Philip begeistert. »Vielleicht kommen sogar mehr Menschen als sonst!«

»Oder weniger«, warf Cuthbert ein. »Es gibt Leute, die dem Priester lieber Geld zahlen oder einem Heiligen eine Kerze weihen, als den ganzen Tag im Schlamm herumzuwaten und sich mit schweren Steinen abzurackern.«

»Daran habe ich überhaupt nicht gedacht«, sagte Philip, den auf einmal der Mut verließ. »Vielleicht ist die Idee doch nicht so gut.«

»Hast du sonst noch andere Vorschläge?«

»Nein.«

»Dann mußt du es riskieren und das beste hoffen, nicht wahr?«

»Ja«, sagte Philip. »Hoffen wir das Beste.«

In der Nacht zu Pfingstsonntag fand Philip keinen Schlaf. Die ganze Woche über hatte die Sonne geschienen – ideale Voraussetzungen für seinen Plan. Doch mit beginnender Dunkelheit am Sonnabend setzte der Regen ein. Der Prior lag schlaflos da und hörte die Regentropfen aufs Dach trommeln und den Wind in den Bäumen rauschen. Er hatte das Gefühl, genug gebetet zu haben – Gott war jetzt gewiß darüber im Bilde, was auf dem Spiel stand.

Am Sonntag zuvor hatte jeder Mönch des Klosters ein oder zwei Dorfkirchen in der näheren und weiteren Umgebung aufgesucht, um den Gemeinden mitzuteilen, daß sie ihre Sünden durch sonntägliche Arbeit auf der Dombaustelle abbüßen konnten. Am Pfingstsonntag ginge es um die Sünden des vorangegangenen Jahres, danach rechne sich ein Arbeitstag gegen die Sünden einer Woche mit Ausnahme von Mord und Gotteslästerung. Philip selbst hatte sich nach Shiring begeben und in jeder der vier Kirchen das Wort ergriffen. Zwei Mönche hatte er nach Winchester geschickt. Ihr Auftrag lautete, in der Stadt so viele der schier unzähligen kleinen Kirchen aufzusuchen, wie ihnen möglich war. Winchester war zwei Tagesreisen entfernt, doch das Pfingstfest erstreckte sich über sechs Tage, und für einen großen Jahrmarkt oder einen außergewöhnlichen Gottesdienst nahm man durchaus die Strapazen einer solchen Reise in Kauf. Alles in allem hatten ein paar tausend Menschen von der Botschaft Kunde erhalten. Wie viele darauf reagieren würden, stand freilich in den Sternen.

Die übrige Zeit hatten die Mönche selbst auf der Baustelle gearbeitet. Das gute Wetter und die langen Tage des Frühsommers hatten das Ihrige getan, so daß fast alles, was Philip sich vorgenommen hatte, bewältigt worden war. Die Fundamente für die Ostwand des Altarraums waren gelegt. Die Löcher für die Fundamente der Nordwand waren großenteils ausgehoben, so daß die ersten Steine gelegt werden konnten. Tom hatte so viele Flaschenzüge gebaut, daß Dutzende von Hilfskräften bei den noch ausstehenden Ausschachtungsarbeiten eingesetzt werden konnten. Am Flußufer stapelten sich die von den Forstarbeitern herangeflößten Stämme sowie eine Fülle von Steinen, die zur Baustelle hinaufgeschleppt werden mußten. Arbeit gab es für Hunderte von Menschen.

Aber würde *überhaupt jemand* kommen?

Um Mitternacht stand Philip auf und stapfte durch den Regen in die Krypta zum Frühgebet. Als er nach der Frühmesse zurückkehrte, hatte der Regen aufgehört. Er ging nicht wieder zu Bett, sondern blieb auf und las. Die Stunden zwischen Mitternacht und Morgengrauen waren die einzige ihm verbliebene Zeit zum Studium und zur Meditation, denn den Tag über beanspruchte das Kloster seine gesamte Kraft.

In dieser Nacht fiel es ihm schwer, sich zu konzentrieren. Wieder und wieder kreisten seine Gedanken um den bevorstehenden Tag. Mit einem Schlag konnte er um die Früchte seiner einjährigen Arbeit gebracht werden. Ihm fiel ein – vielleicht aus einem Anflug von Fatalismus heraus –, daß es nicht rechtens war, sich Erfolg um des Erfolges willen zu wünschen. Ist es mein Stolz, der hier auf dem Spiel steht? fragte er sich. Stolz war von allen Sünden diejenige, für die er am anfälligsten war. Er dachte an die Menschen, die von ihm abhingen, die Mönche, die Dienstleute, die Steinbrecher, Tom und Alfred, die Einwohner des Dorfes und die Gläubigen in der gesamten Grafschaft. Von Bischof Waleran war nicht zu erwarten, daß er sich im gleichen Maße um sie kümmerte wie Philip. So wie Waleran den Dienst am Herrn verstand, konnte er über die Menschen nach eigenem Gutdünken verfügen. Für Philip bestand der Dienst am Herrn in der Fürsorge um den Nächsten. Dafür gab es die Erlösung. Nein, es konnte nicht Gottes Wille sein, daß Waleran aus diesem Wettstreit als Sieger hervorging. Mag sein, daß ein kleines bißchen Stolz auf dem Spiel steht, gestand Philip sich ein. Aber es geht auch um Menschenseelen.

Endlich brach der Tag an, und wieder ging er zur Krypta hinüber, diesmal zur Prim. Die Mönche waren unruhig und aufgeregt: Sie wußten genau, daß die Ereignisse des Tages von entscheidender Bedeutung für ihre Zukunft sein würden. Der Sakristan haspelte rasch die Messe herunter, und Philip kam nicht umhin, ihm diesmal seine Hast nachzusehen.

Als sie die Krypta verließen, erstrahlte der Himmel in hellem Blau. Sie begaben sich zum Frühstück ins Refektorium. Gott hatte ihnen wenigstens das Wetter geschickt, um das sie gebetet hatten. Ein guter Anfang.

Tom Builder wußte, daß es heute um seine Zukunft ging.

Philip hatte ihm den Brief des Priors von Canterbury gezeigt. Es stand für Tom außer Frage, daß Waleran im Falle der Verlegung der Kathedrale einen anderen Baumeister einstellen würde. Nie, so dachte er, wird Waleran einen von Philip gebilligten Bauplan verwenden, nie das Risiko eingehen, einen Mann anzuwerben, der möglicherweise noch zu Philip hielt. Für Tom hieß es Kingsbridge oder das Nichts. Entweder er baute diese Kathedrale oder keine. Eine solche Gelegenheit bot sich nur einmal im Leben, und heute stand sie auf dem Spiel.

Er war, was bisweilen vorkam, zur morgendlichen Kapitelversammlung geladen worden. Meist ging es um Probleme, die mit dem Bau zusammenhingen, wie Fragen zum Plan, zu den Kosten und zur Dauer bestimmter Bauabschnitte. Diesmal war es anders: Er war damit beauftragt worden, die Freiwilligen – so sie denn kamen – sinnvoll einzusetzen. Er wollte, daß es bei Bischof Henrys Ankunft auf der Baustelle summte und brummte wie in einem Bienenkorb ...

Geduldig wartete er die lateinischen Lesungen und Gebete ab, von denen er kein Wort verstand. Schließlich ging Philip jedoch zur englischen Sprache über und forderte Tom auf, in groben Zügen darzulegen, wie er sich den Einsatz der Hilfskräfte vorstellte.

»Ich werde an der Ostmauer der Kathedrale arbeiten, während Alfred die Steine für das Fundament legt«, begann Tom. »In beiden Fällen beabsichtigen wir, Bischof Henry vor Augen zu führen, wie weit die Bauarbeiten schon gediehen sind.«

»Wie viele Männer braucht Ihr zur Unterstützung?« wollte Philip wissen.

»Alfred braucht zwei Hilfskräfte, die ihm die Steine bringen. Er wird Baumaterial aus der Ruine der alten Kirche benutzen. Außerdem braucht er jemanden, der Mörtel für ihn anrührt – wie ich im übrigen auch. Ich brauche außerdem noch zwei Hilfskräfte. Alfred kann für das Fundament unregelmäßige Steine benutzen, solange sie nur oben und unten flach sind. Meine Steine müssen dagegen sorgfältig behauen werden, weil sie über der Erde liegen und deutlich sichtbar sind. Ich habe daher zwei Steinschneider aus dem Steinbruch kommen lassen.«

Philip ergriff das Wort. »Das ist zwar alles sehr wichtig, um vor Bischof Henry einen guten Eindruck zu machen«, sagte er, »aber die meisten Freiwilligen werden doch wohl die Fundamente ausheben.«

»Richtig. Die Fundamente für den Chor sind markiert, aber zum großen Teil erst ein paar Zoll tief. Die Mönche müssen die Hebevorrichtungen bedienen – ich habe einigen von euch beigebracht, wie man damit umgeht –, und die Freiwilligen können die Fässer füllen.«

»Und was passiert, wenn wir mehr Freiwillige als Arbeit haben?« fragte Remigius.

»Im Grunde können wir unbegrenzt viele beschäftigen«, erwiderte Tom. »Wenn wir nicht genug Hebemaschinen haben, kann der Aushub in Eimern und Körben weggetragen werden. Der Zimmermann muß sich bereithalten, um notfalls noch ein paar Leitern zu fertigen – das Holz dafür haben wir.«

Remigius ließ nicht locker: »Aber die Zahl der Leute, die in die Baugrube passen, ist doch sicherlich begrenzt.«

Tom hatte das Gefühl, daß Remigius nur um des Widersprechens willen widersprach, und gab gereizt zurück: »Ein paar hundert passen schon hinein. Die Grube ist groß.«

»Und außerdem gibt es noch andere Arbeiten als graben«, fügte Philip hinzu.

»In der Tat«, pflichtete Tom ihm bei. »Große Mengen von Holz und Steinen liegen am Fluß bereit und müssen heraufgeschleppt werden. Ihr müßt darauf achten, daß die Materialien an den richtigen Stellen gestapelt werden. Die Steine gehören neben die Baugruben, aber wohlgemerkt *außerhalb* der Kirche, sonst sind sie uns im Wege. Der Zimmermann wird Euch sagen, wo das Holz zu stapeln ist.«

»Ob alle Freiwilligen ungelernte Hilfskräfte sein werden – was meint Ihr?« fragte Philip.

»Nicht unbedingt. Es mag auch der eine oder andere Handwerker dabei sein – ich hoffe es jedenfalls. Wir müssen sie dann entsprechend einsetzen. Zimmerleute könnten Werkstätten für die Winterarbeit bauen. Alle Steinmetze können Steine schneiden und Fundamente legen. Falls ein Schmied dabei ist, lassen wir ihn in der Dorfschmiede Werkzeuge schmieden.«

Schatzmeister Milius meldete sich zu Wort: »Dann ist ja soweit alles klar. Ich möchte jetzt gerne anfangen. Ein paar Dorfbewohner sind bereits eingetroffen und warten darauf, eingewiesen zu werden.«

Tom hatte noch etwas auf dem Herzen. Es war eine wichtige, aber auch heikle Sache, und er suchte nach den richtigen Worten. Mönche konnten mitunter sehr anmaßend sein und die Freiwilligen mit ihrem Verhalten vor den Kopf stoßen. Tom wollte den Tag jedoch friedlich und harmonisch gestalten. »Ich habe in der Vergangenheit bereits mit Freiwilligen gearbeitet«, sagte er. »Es ist sehr wichtig, daß man sie nicht … wie niederes Gesinde behandelt. Wir mögen zwar der Meinung sein, daß der Himmel ihnen ihre Mühe lohnt und sie daher noch härter arbeiten sollten, als wenn ihnen ihr Lohn im Diesseits ausgezahlt würde. Nur – die Freiwilligen müssen diese Meinung nicht unbedingt teilen. Sie haben das Gefühl, unentgeltlich zu arbeiten und uns dadurch einen großen Gefallen zu erweisen. Zeigen wir uns undankbar, so werden sie langsamer arbeiten und Fehler machen. Schlagen wir daher leise Töne an, das ist das Beste.«

Tom bemerkte, daß der Prior ein Lächeln unterdrückte, als wüßte er genau, welche Vorbehalte sich hinter Toms honigsüßen Worten verbargen. »Ihr habt recht«, sagte Philip. »Wenn wir die Leute gut behandeln, werden sie froh und munter an die Arbeit gehen. Ihre gute Arbeitsmoral wird zweifellos auch Bischof Henry beeindrucken.« Er sah seine Mitbrüder der Reihe nach an. »Keine weiteren Fragen? Gut, dann laßt uns beginnen.«

Aliena hatte unter der schützenden Hand von Prior Philip ein sorgenfreies und erfolgreiches Jahr verbracht.

Im Frühjahr und Sommer war sie mit Richard unterwegs gewesen und hatte den Bauern Felle abgekauft. Wann immer ein handelsüblicher Wollsack gefüllt war, verkauften sie ihn an Philip weiter. Am Ende der Saison besaßen sie fünf Pfund Silber.

Zu Weihnachten erfuhr Aliena, daß ihr Vater wenige Tage nach ihrem Besuch gestorben war. Es kostete sie eine Menge Schmiergeld, um sein Grab ausfindig zu machen, das sich auf einem Armenfriedhof in Winchester befand. Sie weinte herzerweichend – nicht nur um Vater, sondern um ihr gemeinsames, sicheres und sorgenfreies Leben, das unwiederbringlich dahin war. In gewisser Weise hatte sie schon vor seinem Tode von ihm Abschied genommen, war ihr doch, als sie das Gefängnis verließ, klar, daß sie ihn nie wiedersehen würde. Andererseits war Vater noch immer bei ihr, denn der Eid, den er sie hatte schwören lassen, band sie. Aliena hatte sich damit abgefunden, den Rest ihres Lebens auf seine Erfüllung zu verwenden.

Richard und Aliena überwinterten in einem kleinen Häuschen an der Klostermauer. Sie hatten sich beim Stellmacher in Kingsbridge Räder gekauft und einen Karren gezimmert. Im Frühjahr erstanden sie einen jungen Ochsen als Zugtier. Inzwischen war die Zeit der Schafschur angebrochen, und sie hatten bereits mehr Geld eingenommen, als das Gespann gekostet hatte. Aliena dachte schon daran, im kommenden Jahr einen Gehilfen einzustellen. Für Richard wollte sie eine Anstellung als Page bei einem Landadeligen suchen, damit er seine Ausbildung zum Ritter beginnen konnte.

Alle ihre Pläne hingen jedoch von Prior Philip ab.

Ein achtzehnjähriges alleinstehendes Mädchen wie Aliena galt bei jedem Wegelagerer und vielen Kaufleuten als leichte Beute. Sowohl in Shiring als auch in Gloucester hatte sie probehalber versucht, einen Sack Wolle an einen Händler zu verkaufen, und beide Male hatte man ihr nur den halben Preis gegeben. Es gab in jeder Stadt immer nur einen einzigen Händler, der natürlich ganz genau wußte, daß sie ihm auf Gedeih und Verderb ausgeliefert war. Irgendwann einmal wollte Aliena ein eigenes Lager besitzen und direkt mit den flämischen Aufkäufern verhandeln, doch bis dahin würde noch viel Wasser die Themse hinunterfließen. Vorerst hing ihr Wohl und Wehe allein von Philip ab.

Und Philips Lage war auf einmal kritisch geworden.

Vor Rechtlosen und Dieben war sie beständig auf der Hut. Daß aber ihr Auskommen unvermittelt von einer ganz anderen Seite bedroht wurde, traf sie völlig unvorbereitet.

Richard hatte anfänglich keine Lust, am Pfingstsonntag auf der Dombaustelle zu arbeiten. Dankbarkeit war nicht gerade seine Stärke. Aliena hatte ihn schließlich mit sanfter Gewalt vom Gegenteil überzeugt, und so gingen sie kurz nach Sonnenaufgang die paar Schritte zur Klostereinfriedung hinüber. Zu Alienas Überraschung war fast das gesamte Dorf erschienen: etwa dreißig bis vierzig Männer, manche sogar mit Frau und Kind. Aber dann fiel ihr ein, daß Prior Philip ihr Lehnsherr war; seinem Ruf nicht Folge zu leisten, war unklug. Im Laufe des letzten Jahres hatte Aliena eine Vielzahl überraschender, neuer Einsichten in das Leben der einfachen Leute gewonnen.

Tom Builder wies die Dorfbewohner in ihre Arbeit ein. Richard ging sogleich auf Toms Sohn Alfred zu. Die beiden waren beinahe gleichaltrig – Richard fünfzehn, Alfred ungefähr ein Jahr älter –, und sie spielten jeden Sonntag mit den anderen Jungen aus dem Dorf Fußball. Die kleine Martha war ebenfalls da, doch Ellen, die Frau mit dem merkwürdig aussehenden, rothaarigen Jungen war verschwunden, und niemand wußte wohin. Aliena erinnerte sich noch gut daran, wie Tom mit seiner Familie nach Earlscastle gekommen war. Damals waren sie bitter arm gewesen. Prior Philip hatte ihn gerettet – ebenso wie sie selbst.

Aliena und Richard erhielten je eine Schaufel und die Aufgabe, Löcher für die Fundamente zu graben. Der Boden war feucht, doch schien die Sonne, so daß die Oberfläche rasch austrocknen würde. Aliena machte sich mit Feuereifer an die Arbeit. Selbst mit fünfzig Leuten dauerte es sehr lange, bis die Schächte sichtbar tiefer wurden. Richard mußte oft verschnaufen und stützte sich auf die Schaufel. »Wenn du ein Ritter werden willst, dann schaufel gefälligst!« schimpfte Aliena, ohne damit etwas zu bewirken.

Die langen Fußmärsche und die Arbeit mit den schweren Wollsäcken hatten ihren Körper gestählt. Sie war schlanker und kräftiger als im vergangenen Jahr. Dennoch bekam sie vom Schaufeln allmählich Rückenschmerzen und war daher froh und dankbar, als Prior Philip das Glockenzeichen für eine Pause gab. Ein paar Mönche brachten aus der Küche warmes Brot und schenkten Dünnbier aus. Die Sonne schien inzwischen stärker, und einige Männer zogen die Hemden aus.

Die Pause war noch nicht vorüber, als eine Gruppe Fremder durchs Tor kam. Aliena blickte ihnen hoffnungsvoll entgegen. Vielleicht waren diese wenigen ja die Vorboten einer noch viel größeren Menge. Prior Philip hieß sie willkommen.

»Woher seid ihr?« fragte er die Männer, die dankbar das ihnen angebotene Bier hinunterstürzten.

»Aus Horsted«, erwiderte einer von ihnen und wischte sich mit dem Ärmel über den Mund. Das klang vielversprechend: Horsted war ein Dorf mit zwei- bis dreihundert Einwohnern, ein paar Meilen westlich von Kingsbridge. Wenn sie Glück hatten, kamen vielleicht hundert Freiwillige.

»Und wie viele von euch kommen insgesamt?« fragte Philip.

Der Mann schien über die Frage erstaunt. »Nur wir vier«, erwiderte er.

Im Verlauf der nächsten Stunde trafen weitere vereinzelte Freiwillige ein, bis ihre Zahl, nachdem der Vormittag halb verstrichen war, auf siebzig bis achtzig angestiegen war. Dann brach der Strom völlig ab.

Das reichte nicht!

Philip stand am Ostende und sah Tom bei der Arbeit zu. Die Sockel zweier Strebepfeiler waren bis zur Höhe der dritten Steinreihe bereits fertig. Tom arbeitete an der Mauer, die beide Pfeiler miteinander verbinden sollte. Wahrscheinlich bleibt es bei den Anfängen, dachte Philip mutlos.

Jedesmal, wenn die Arbeiter ihm einen Quader brachten, nahm Tom sein eisernes, L-förmiges Instrument zur Hand und prüfte, ob die Seitenkanten des Steins gerade waren. Dann warf er mit der Schaufel eine Schicht Mörtel auf die Mauer, riefelte sie mit der Spitze seiner Kelle, setzte den Quader auf und strich den überschüssigen Mörtel ab. Beim Zusammenfügen der Steine richtete er sich nach einer straff zwischen die beiden Sockel gespannten Schnur.

Philip fiel auf, daß die Ober- und Unterseiten der Steine, die beim Bau in Mörtel gebettet wurden, fast genauso glatt waren wie die sichtbaren Außenflächen. Er fragte Tom nach dem Grund.

»Nie darf ein Stein den unterhalb oder oberhalb liegenden Stein berühren«, antwortete Tom. »Daher brauchen wir den Mörtel.«

»Warum dürfen sie sich nicht berühren?«

»Das führt zu Rissen.« Tom richtete sich auf. »Wenn man auf ein schiefergedecktes Dach tritt, bricht man mit dem Fuß ein. Legt man jedoch eine Planke darüber, so kann man es ohne Schaden betreten. Die Planke verteilt das Gewicht. Der Mörtel erfüllt die gleiche Aufgabe.«

Darüber hatte Philip noch nie nachgedacht. Die Baukunst war eine hochinteressante Tätigkeit, besonders bei einem Mann wie Tom, der imstande war, sehr anschaulich zu erklären, was er tat.

Auf der Rückseite waren die Steine am unebensten. Warum wohl? fragte sich Philip. Sie sind doch im Innern der Kirche sichtbar – oder? Erst nach einer Weile fiel ihm ein, daß Tom ja eine Doppelmauer mit einem Zwischenraum in der Mitte baute. Die Rückseiten der Quader waren im fertigen Bau demnach unsichtbar.

Tom hatte gerade wieder einen Stein auf den Mörtel gelegt. Er griff nach seiner Setzwaage, einem Dreieck aus Eisen, an deren Spitze ein Lederriemchen befestigt war. Ein Bleigewicht sorgte dafür, daß das Riemchen immer gerade hing. Tom setzte das Instrument auf den Stein und prüfte den Fall des Pendels. Je nachdem, wie weit das Gewicht rechts oder links von der Mittelmarkierung abwich, beklopfte er den Stein mit seinem Hammer. Saß der Quader gerade, schob Tom die Setzwaage seitwärts über den Spalt zum angrenzenden Stein und kontrollierte die Höhe. Zum Schluß überprüfte er die Seiten, um zu sehen, ob der Stein nach innen oder nach außen überhing. Bevor er einen neuen Quader zur Hand nahm, zupfte Tom an der straffgespannten Schnur und ließ sie zurückschnappen; er überzeugte sich damit, daß die Vorderseite der Steine eine gerade Linie bildete. Zum erstenmal ging Philip auf, wie sehr es beim Bau von Steinmauern auf äußerste Präzision ankam.

Er hob den Blick und sah sich auf der Baustelle um. Groß wie sie war, fielen die achtzig Männer und Frauen sowie die paar Kinder kaum ins Gewicht. Und obwohl die Sonne strahlte und alle Beteiligten mit großem Eifer an der Arbeit waren, konnte er sich des Gefühls nicht erwehren, daß alle Anstrengungen im Grunde sinnlos waren. Er hatte sich mindestens hundert Leute erhofft, sah aber inzwischen ein, daß selbst die nicht ausgereicht hätten.

Wieder kam ein kleiner Trupp durchs Tor. Philip bezwang sich und begrüßte sie mit einem Lächeln. Die Leute brauchten nicht zu wissen, daß ihre Mühe umsonst sein würde. Immerhin würden ihnen ihre Sünden vergeben. Als er auf die Neuankömmlinge zuging, fiel ihm auf, daß die Gruppe größer war, als er zunächst vermutet hatte. Er zählte zwölf Männer, denen noch zwei Nachzügler folgten. Vielleicht bringen wir es bis Mittag, wenn der Bischof kommt, doch noch auf hundert Leute, dachte er und sprach: »Gott segne euch.« Er hatte gerade begonnen, ihnen zu erklären, wo sie zu graben hatten, als er durch einen lauten Ruf unterbrochen wurde.

»Philip!«

Unwillig runzelte er die Stirn. Das war die Stimme von Bruder Milius, auch er hätte Philip in der Öffentlichkeit eigentlich mit ›Vater‹ anreden müssen. Philip sah sich um. Milius balancierte – nicht eben in würdevoller Haltung – auf der Klostermauer herum. Mit ruhiger, aber tragender Stimme rief Philip ihm zu: »Bruder Milius, kommt von der Mauer herunter!«

Milius blieb, wo er war, und rief zurück: »Komm her und schau dir das an!«

Kein gutes Beispiel für klösterliche Disziplin, dachte Philip, noch dazu vor all den Fremden hier. Was ist nur in Milius gefahren? Er benimmt sich doch sonst stets tadellos ... »Kommt sofort her und erstattet Bericht, Milius«, erwiderte er in einem Tonfall, wie er ihn gemeinhin nur unruhigen Novizen gegenüber an den Tag legte.

»Das mußt du mit eigenen Augen sehen!« brüllte Milius.

Ich hoffe nur, er hat eine gute Entschuldigung für sein Verhalten, dachte Philip verärgert. Andererseits wollte er seinem engsten Mitarbeiter eine öffentliche Zurechtweisung ersparen. Mit gezwungenem Lächeln, innerlich jedoch vor Ärger schon fast kochend, lief er zur Mauer. Mit einem Satz war er oben. »Was soll dieses Benehmen?« fauchte er Milius an.

»Sieh doch!« sagte Milius und deutete in die Ferne.

Philip blickte über die Dächer des Dorfes und jenseits des Flusses auf die Straße, die sich im Westen über die Hügel zog. Dann glaubte er, seinen Augen nicht trauen zu können: Die Straße, die sich durch die begrünten Felder schlängelte, war voller Menschen, eine einzige, wogende Masse, die sich auf Kingsbridge zu bewegte! »Ist das eine Armee?« Doch dann begriff er, daß die Menschen zu ihm kamen, daß es *seine* Freiwilligen waren, und sein Herz schlug höher vor Begeisterung.

»Schau nur!« rief er. »Das müssen fünfhundert sein – tausend – nein, mehr!«

»Stimmt«, sagte Milius überglücklich. »Nun kommen sie doch noch!«

»Wir sind gerettet!« Philip war so aufgeregt, daß sein Zorn auf Milius augenblicklich verflog. Die Straße war bis hin zur Brücke schwarz von Menschen. Die Leute, die er soeben begrüßt hatte, waren nur die Vorhut gewesen. Die ersten strömten bereits durchs Tor, und auf der Baustelle wimmelte es von Menschen, die darauf warteten, daß man sie anstellte. »Halleluja!« brüllte Philip verwegen.

Mit Euphorie allein war es nicht getan – die Leute mußten sinnvoll eingesetzt werden. Der Prior sprang von der Mauer. »Los!« rief er Milius zu. »Trommle alle Mitbrüder zusammen – wir brauchen sie jetzt als Aufseher, nicht mehr als Arbeiter! Sag dem Küchenmeister, er soll soviel Brot wie möglich backen und ein paar Extrafässer Bier bereitstellen! Wir brauchen mehr Eimer und Schaufeln! All diese Menschen müssen beschäftigt sein, wenn Bischof Henry eintrifft!«

In der nun folgenden Stunde hatte Philip alle Hände voll zu tun. Um Platz zu schaffen, schickte er sogleich an die hundert Freiwillige hinunter zum Fluß, Holz und Steine zu holen. Sobald Milius sein Trüppchen aufsichtführender Mönche beisammen hatte, schickte der Prior Freiwillige in die Baugruben. Es dauerte nicht lange, und Schaufeln, Fässer und Eimer wurden knapp. Philip befahl, sämtliche Kochtöpfe aus der Küche herbeizuschaffen, von ein paar Freiwilligen ließ er einfache Holzkästen zusammenzimmern und Tragen aus Korbgeflecht herstellen. Da auch die Leitern und Hebemaschinen nicht ausreichten, wurde die Wand der größten Grube an einer Seite abgeschrägt, so daß man mühelos hinein- und herausgehen konnte. Philip merkte jetzt, daß er sich noch nicht überlegt hatte, was mit den gewaltigen Mengen Erde geschehen sollte, die bei den Ausschachtungsarbeiten anfielen. Kurzentschlossen entschied er, den Aushub auf dem steinigen Grund am Flußufer aufzuschütten. Vielleicht ließ sich die Fläche später einmal als Garten nutzen. Er gab gerade die nötigen Anweisungen, als Küchenmeister Bernard in heller Aufregung auf ihn zustürzte. Er habe mit höchstens zweihundert Leuten gerechnet, rief er, aber inzwischen seien es schon tausend oder mehr! »Mach Feuer im Küchenhof und koch die Suppe in einem Eisenzuber!« ordnete Philip an. »Verdünn das Bier mit Wasser und scheu dich nicht, sämtliche Vorräte aufzubrauchen. Hol dir ein paar Dorfbewohner und sag ihnen, sie sollen zu Hause Essen kochen. Laß dir was einfallen!«

Der Küchenmeister war kaum fort, als Philip plötzlich jemand auf die Schulter tippte und ihn auf französisch ansprach: »Prior Philip, darf ich um Eure Aufmerksamkeit bitten?« Es war Waleran Bigods Mitarbeiter und Vertrauter, Dechant Baldwin.

Philip drehte sich um. Vor ihm, hoch zu Roß, standen die erwarteten Besucher und sahen sich erstaunt auf dem Bauplatz um. Da war zunächst Bischof Henry, ein stämmiger, untersetzter Mann mit kämpferischer Miene, dessen Tonsur einen auffälligen Kontrast zu seiner bestickten scharlachroten Robe bildete. An seiner Seite Bischof Waleran, wie gewöhnlich schwarz gewandet. Sein Gesicht war die übliche starre Maske aus verächtlicher Herablassung; dennoch gelang es ihm nicht, seine Bestürzung völlig zu verhehlen. Hinzu kamen der fette Percy Hamleigh, sein strammer Sohn William und seine häßliche Frau Regan: Percy und William hatten keine Ahnung, was hier gespielt wurde. Regan aber begriff Philips Schachzug und kochte vor Wut.

Henry gewährte Philip die Gunst eines unverwandt neugierigen Blickes, den der Prior offen erwiderte, obgleich ihn das unverhüllte Interesse des Bischofs überraschte. Auch eine Spur belustigter Anerkennung war dabei. Philip ging auf ihn zu und küßte die beringte Hand, die Henry ihm entgegenstreckte.

Behende und gewandt sprang Henry vom Pferd, und seine Begleiter taten es ihm nach. Philip befahl zwei Mönchen, die Pferde in den Stall zu führen. Henry und Philip waren ungefähr gleichaltrig, doch wirkte der Bischof infolge seiner rötlichen Gesichtsfarbe und seines üppigen Leibesumfangs wesentlich älter. »Wohlan, Vater Philip«, sagte er. »Ich bin gekommen, um mir ein eigenes Bild von den Berichten zu machen, denen zufolge Ihr nicht fähig sein sollt, hier in Kingsbridge eine Kathedrale zu bauen.« Er machte eine Pause, ließ seinen Blick über die vielen hundert emsigen Arbeiter schweifen und schaute Philip wieder an. »Mir scheint, man hat mich falsch informiert!«

Philips Herz setzte einen Schlag aus. Deutlicher konnte Henry es kaum sagen. Ich habe gewonnen, dachte er.

Philip drehte sich um und sah Bischof Waleran an. Dessen Gesichtszüge waren erstarrt vor unterdrückter Wut. Waleran wußte genau, daß er wieder einmal den kürzeren gezogen hatte. Philip kniete nieder, senkte den Kopf, um seinen Triumph zu verbergen, und küßte Walerans Hand.

Tom Builder genoß seine Arbeit. Es war lange her, seit er zum letztenmal eine Mauer gebaut und den tiefen inneren Frieden verspürt hatte, mit dem ihn das Aufeinanderfügen von Quadern in absolut geraden Reihen und das langsame Wachsen eines Bauwerks erfüllte.

Und als erst die Freiwilligen zu Hunderten herbeiströmten und er sah, daß Philips Plan aufging, da wuchs seine Freude an der Arbeit ins Unermeßliche. Diese Steine waren Teil *seiner* Kathedrale; diese Mauer, erst ein paar Fuß hoch, würde dereinst bis in den Himmel reichen. Tom spürte: Dies war der Höhepunkt, die Erfüllung seines Lebens.

Die Ankunft Bischof Henrys hatte er sofort bemerkt. Wie ein Stein, der in einen Teich fällt, hatte die Nachricht ihre Kreise gezogen: Die

Arbeiter hielten einen Augenblick lang in ihrer Arbeit inne und warfen einen Blick auf die prächtig gekleideten Gestalten, die sich geziert einen Weg durch den Schlamm suchten. Dem Bischof mußte es beim Anblick der tausend Freiwilligen, die in bester Laune und mit Feuereifer den Bau ihrer neuen Kathedrale vorantrieben, schier die Sprache verschlagen haben. Jetzt lag es an Tom, einen ähnlich guten Eindruck zu machen. In Gegenwart gut gekleideter Herrschaften hatte er sich noch nie wohlgefühlt – jetzt mußte er sachkundig, ruhig und selbstsicher vor ihnen auftreten und sich als ein Mann darstellen, dem man dankbar und mit ruhigem Gewissen ein so gewaltiges und kostspieliges Bauvorhaben anvertraut.

Er hielt die Augen offen und legte seine Kelle nieder, als er die Besucher näher kommen sah. Prior Philip stellte ihm Bischof Henry vor, und Tom kniete nieder und küßte ihm die Hand. »Tom ist unser Baumeister«, sagte er. »Er wurde uns von Gott an dem Tag gesandt, als die alte Kirche niederbrannte.«

Tom fiel auch vor Bischof Waleran auf die Knie und musterte die Begleiter. Übertriebene Unterwürfigkeit ziemt sich eigentlich nicht für einen Baumeister, dachte er bei sich. Er erkannte Percy Hamleigh, für den er einst ein halbes Haus gebaut hatte. »Lord Percy«, sagte er mit einer kleinen Verbeugung. Er sah Percys abstoßend häßliche Frau. »Lady Regan.« Sein Blick glitt weiter zum Sohn. Ihm fiel wieder ein, wie William mit seinem Schlachtroß damals beinahe die Kleine zermalmt hätte. Auch der Versuch des jungen Mannes, Ellen zu kaufen, war ihm wieder gegenwärtig. Dieser junge Bursche war ein durch und durch verworfener Kerl! Aber Tom machte gute Miene zum bösen Spiel. »Und der junge Lord William. Seid gegrüßt.«

Bischof Henry musterte Tom von oben bis unten. »Habt Ihr Eure Pläne gezeichnet, Tom Builder?«

»Ja, ehrwürdiger Vater. Wünscht Ihr, sie zu sehen?«

»Gewiß doch.«

»Wenn Ihr bitte hier herüber kommen möchtet.«

Henry nickte. Tom holte aus seiner Hütte den Grundriß, einen in Gips gezeichneten Plan, der von einem ungefähr vier Fuß langen Holzrahmen eingefaßt war. Er lehnte ihn gegen die Hüttenwand und trat ein paar Schritte zurück.

Es war ein heikler Augenblick. Die meisten Menschen konnten mit einem Grundriß nichts anfangen. Bischöfe und Adelige haßten es jedoch, ihre Unkenntnis einzugestehen, weshalb man ihnen das Vorhaben so erklären mußte, daß ihre Unwissenheit dem Rest der

Menschheit verborgen blieb. Andererseits gab es natürlich auch Bischöfe, die Baupläne lesen konnten und sich beleidigt fühlten, wenn ein einfacher Baumeister sich die Freiheit nahm, sie zu belehren.

Tom deutete nervös auf den Plan und sagte: »Dies hier ist die Mauer, an der ich gerade arbeite.«

»Ja, natürlich, die Ostwand«, sagte Henry. Damit hatte sich die Frage von selbst beantwortet: Der Mann kannte sich aus. »Warum hat das Querhaus keine Seitenschiffe?« fragte er.

»Aus Kostengründen«, erwiderte Tom ohne zu zögern. »Aber wenn wir in fünf Jahren mit ihrem Bau beginnen, und falls das Kloster auch weiterhin so gedeiht wie im ersten Jahr nach Prior Philips Amtsübernahme, dann ist es gut möglich, daß wir uns Seitenschiffe für das Querhaus leisten können.« Er hatte zwei Fliegen mit einer Klappe geschlagen – Philip gelobt und die Frage beantwortet – und kam sich sehr klug vor.

Henry nickte zustimmend. »Es ist nur vernünftig, bescheiden zu planen und Spielraum für Erweiterungen zu lassen. Zeigt mir die Vorderansicht.«

Tom holte die Vorderansicht hervor. Da er mittlerweile wußte, daß Henry das, was er vor sich sah, auch begriff, verzichtete er auf Erläuterungen. Henry bestätigte ihn, indem er sagte: »Die Proportionen sind gefällig.«

»Danke«, gab Tom zurück. Der Bischof schien mit allem zufrieden. »Es wird eine bescheidene Kathedrale sein«, fügte Tom noch hinzu, »aber sie wird lichter und schöner als die alte werden.«

»Und wie lange wird der Bau dauern?«

»Fünfzehn Jahre, wenn nichts dazwischenkommt.«

»Es kommt *immer* etwas dazwischen. Trotzdem. Könnt Ihr uns zeigen, wie sie *aussehen* wird – ich meine, für jemanden, der davorsteht?«

Tom verstand, was er wollte. »Ihr wollt eine Zeichnung sehen.«

»Ja.«

»Gewiß doch.« Tom kehrte mit dem bischöflichen Besuch im Gefolge zur Mauer zurück, kniete sich vor das Brett und strich den Mörtel glatt. Dann zeichnete er mit der Spitze seiner Kelle eine Ansicht des Westflügels in den Mörtel. Zeichnen konnte er, es war eine seiner Stärken. Der Bischof, sein Gefolge sowie alle Mönche und Freiwilligen, die in der Nähe standen, sahen fasziniert zu. In den Augen derjenigen, die nicht zeichnen konnten, grenzte diese Fähigkeit an ein Wunder. Tom brauchte nicht lange. Nach ein paar Minuten war die

Skizze der Westfassade mit ihren gewölbten Torbogen, großen Fenstern und Flankentürmen fertig. Ein einfacher Trick, der jedoch nie seine Wirkung verfehlte.

»Bemerkenswert«, sagte Bischof Henry. »Möge Gottes Segen Euer Geschick begleiten.«

Tom lächelte. Das war soviel wie eine hochamtliche Bestätigung seiner Ernennung zum Dombaumeister.

»Wollt Ihr, ehrwürdiger Bischof, eine Erfrischung zu Euch nehmen, bevor Ihr die Messe lest?« fragte Prior Philip.

»Ja, gern.«

Tom fiel ein Stein vom Herzen. Seine Prüfung war vorüber – und er hatte sie bestanden.

»So kommt ins Haus des Priors, gleich hier drüben, wenn ich bitten darf«, sagte Philip, und die bischöfliche Entourage setzte sich in Bewegung. Philip kniff Tom in den Arm und raunte ihm zu: »Wir haben's geschafft!« In seiner Stimme lag verhaltener Triumph.

Tom atmete leicht auf, als die Würdenträger sich entfernten. Er empfand Stolz und Zufriedenheit. Ja, dachte er, wir haben es geschafft. Bischof Henry hatte sich beeindruckt gezeigt – und mehr als das: Er war schlichtweg überwältigt, trotz seiner nach außen hin zur Schau getragenen Zurückhaltung. Waleran hatte ihn offenbar auf ein ganz anderes Bild vorbereitet – eine triste, halbverlassene Baustelle, auf der sich nichts tat. Um so größer mußte nun seine Überraschung sein. Der heimtückische Plan Walerans hatte sich gegen seinen Erfinder gekehrt und seinen Gegnern einen großartigen Sieg beschert.

Er sonnte sich noch im Glanz seines Erfolgs, als hinter ihm plötzlich eine vertraute Stimme erklang: »Hallo, Tom Builder!«

Er drehte sich um und erblickte Ellen.

Nun war es an ihm, überwältigt zu sein! Die dramatische Krise um den Dombau hatte ihn so sehr beschäftigt, daß er den ganzen Tag über nicht an sie gedacht hatte. Ellen sah genauso aus wie damals, als sie ihn verlassen hatte: schlank und rank, mit dunklem Haar, das sich bewegte wie Wellen auf einem Strand, die Haut bronzebraun, die tiefliegenden Augen von schimmerndem Gold ... Mit ihren vollen Lippen, bei deren Anblick er immer sofort ans Küssen denken mußte, lächelte sie ihn an.

Am liebsten hätte er sie sofort in die Arme genommen, aber er beherrschte sich. Mühsam brachte er ein »Hallo, Ellen!« hervor.

Ein junger Mann an ihrer Seite sagte: »Hallo, Tom.«

Tom sah ihn neugierig an.

»Du kennst doch Jack!« sagte Ellen.

»Jack!« rief Tom überrascht. Wie der Bursche sich verändert hatte! Er war jetzt ein wenig größer als seine Mutter und von jenem hageren Körperbau, über den Großmütter gemeinhin zu sagen pflegen: »Der Junge ist zu schnell in die Höhe geschossen.« Er hatte nach wie vor feuerrote Haare, einen hellen Teint und grüne Augen, aber seine Gesichtszüge waren insgesamt viel gefälliger als früher. Eines Tages mochte ein richtig hübscher Kerl aus ihm werden.

Tom sah wieder zu Ellen hinüber. Einen Moment lang genoß er es einfach, sie anzustarren. Am liebsten hätte er gesagt: Ich habe dich vermißt, ich kann dir gar nicht sagen, wie sehr ich dich vermißt habe, und beinahe tat er es auch, aber dann verließ ihn der Mut, und er sagte statt dessen: »Und wo bist du all die Zeit gewesen?«

»Wir haben im Wald gelebt, wie immer«, erwiderte sie.

»Und wieso seid ihr gerade heute zurückgekommen?«

»Wir hörten von dem Aufruf an die Freiwilligen; wir waren neugierig und wollten wissen, wie es dir geht. Außerdem habe ich mein Versprechen, eines Tages zurückzukommen, nicht vergessen.«

»Ich bin so froh, daß du es eingelöst hast«, sagte Tom. »Ich habe mich nach dir gesehnt.«

Sie schien auf der Hut. »Ach ja?«

Dies war der Augenblick, auf den er ein Jahr lang gewartet und hingearbeitet hatte, doch nun, da es drauf ankam, hatte er Angst. Bis zu diesem Zeitpunkt hatte er sich in der Hoffnung wiegen können, daß Ellen zu ihm zurückkehren würde, doch wenn sie ihm jetzt eine Abfuhr erteilte, hatte er sie für immer und ewig verloren. Er hatte Angst davor, den Anfang zu machen. Das Schweigen zog sich in die Länge. Tom holte tief Luft. »Hör zu«, begann er. »Ich möchte, daß du zu mir zurückkommst. Also. Sag jetzt bitte nichts, bevor du mich angehört hast – bitte!«

»Gut«, erwiderte sie zurückhaltend.

»Philip ist ein sehr guter Prior. Dank seiner Leitung wird das Kloster reicher und reicher. Meine Arbeit hier ist sicher. Wir werden nie mehr auf der Straße stehen, nie, das verspreche ich.«

»Es war nicht, weil ...«

»Ich weiß, aber ich will dir reinen Wein einschenken.«

»Gut.«

»Ich habe im Dorf ein Haus gebaut, mit zwei Räumen und einem Kamin, und ich kann es noch ausbauen. Wir brauchen nicht in der Priorei zu leben.«

»Aber Philip gehört das Dorf.«

»Philip steht im Augenblick in meiner Schuld.« Tom deutete mit einer weit ausholenden Armbewegung auf die Szenerie um sie herum. »Er weiß, daß er dies alles nicht ohne meine Hilfe auf die Beine hätte stellen können. Wenn ich ihn darum bitte, dir zu vergeben und das Jahr im Exil als Sühne anzuerkennen, so wird er damit einverstanden sein. Gerade heute wird er mir dieses Ansinnen nicht ausschlagen können.«

»Und was wird mit den Jungen?« fragte sie »Soll ich ruhig mitansehen, wie Alfred bei jedem Anfall von schlechter Laune Jack blutig schlägt?«

»Ich denke, ich habe auch dafür eine Lösung gefunden, glaub mir«, erwiderte Tom. »Alfred ist inzwischen Steinmetz. Wenn ich Jack als Lehrling einstelle, hat Alfred keinen Grund mehr, sich über seine Untätigkeit aufzuregen. Und du kannst Alfred Schreiben und Lesen beibringen, damit die Jungen einander ebenbürtig sind – beide arbeiten, und beide sind des Lesens und Schreibens kundig.«

»Du hast viel darüber nachgedacht, nicht wahr?« sagte sie.

»Ja.«

Er wartete auf ihre Reaktion. Er hatte kein großes Vertrauen in seine Überzeugungskraft. Er konnte ihr lediglich sagen, was er meinte. Ja, wenn man alle seine Pläne zeichnerisch darstellen könnte! Aber ich habe doch alles gesagt, dachte er, was kann sie dagegen noch einwenden? Sie mußte einfach zustimmen!

Doch Ellen zögerte noch immer. »Ich bin mir nicht sicher«, sagte sie.

Da war es um seine Selbstbeherrschung geschehen. »Oh, Ellen, sag das bitte nicht.« Schon fürchtete er, vor all diesen Leuten in Tränen auszubrechen. Nur stockend konnte er weitersprechen. »Ich liebe dich so sehr, bitte geh nicht wieder fort. Nur die Hoffnung auf deine Rückkehr hat mir den Mut zum Durchhalten gegeben. Ich kann einfach nicht ohne dich leben. Bitte, Ellen, verschließ mir nicht die Türen zum Paradies! Siehst du denn nicht, daß ich dich aus tiefstem Herzen liebe?«

Ihr Verhalten veränderte sich sofort. »Warum hast du das nicht gleich gesagt?« flüsterte sie und kam zu ihm. Tom nahm sie in die Arme. »Ich liebe dich auch, du Dummkopf«, sagte sie.

Ihm wurde ganz schwach vor Freude. Sie liebt mich wirklich! dachte er. Er drückte sie fest an sich und sah ihr ins Gesicht. »Willst du mich heiraten, Ellen?«

Sie hatte Tränen in den Augen – und lächelte. »Ja, Tom, ich heirate dich«, sagte sie und hob ihm ihr Gesicht entgegen.

Er drückte sie an sich und küßte sie auf den Mund. Ein Jahr lang hatte er von diesem Augenblick geträumt. Er schloß die Augen und genoß das Gefühl ihrer vollen Lippen auf seinem Mund. Ihr Mund war leicht geöffnet, und ihre Lippen waren feucht. Der Kuß war so wunderbar, daß er einen Augenblick lang alles um sich herum vergaß. Dann sagte jemand in der Nähe: »Verschluck sie nicht, Mann!«

Er befreite sich aus ihrer Umarmung und sagte: »Wir befinden uns in einer Kirche!«

»Na und?« erwiderte Ellen fröhlich und küßte ihn gleich noch einmal.

Prior Philip hat uns wieder einmal alle überlistet, dachte William verbittert. Er saß im Haus des Priors, trank Philips verwässerten Wein und naschte kandierte Früchte aus der Klosterküche. Er hatte eine Weile gebraucht, um Philips triumphalen Erfolg in seiner ganzen Tragweite zu verstehen. An Bischof Walerans ursprünglicher Einschätzung der Lage war nichts auszusetzen: Es stimmte ja, daß Philip knapp bei Kasse war und die Kathedrale in Kingsbridge nur unter den größten Schwierigkeiten würde errichten können. Dennoch hatte dieser listige Mönch verbissen weitergemacht, einen Baumeister angeheuert, mit dem Bau begonnen und mir nichts, dir nichts, nur um Bischof Henry aus dem Konzept zu bringen, ein Heer von Arbeitern zusammengezogen. Und das hatte seinen Eindruck auf Henry natürlich nicht verfehlt – allein schon deshalb, weil Bischof Waleran die Lage zuvor in den düstersten Farben geschildert hatte.

Dieser verfluchte Mönch wußte ganz genau, daß er den Sieg davongetragen hatte. Es fiel ihm sichtlich schwer, sein siegesgewisses Grinsen zu verbergen. Im Augenblick war er in ein Gespräch mit Bischof Henry vertieft und unterhielt sich angeregt über verschiedene Schafrassen und den Wollpreis. Henry hörte aufmerksam, ja beinahe respektvoll zu, während Williams Eltern, die weit bedeutender als dieser einfache Prior waren, rücksichtslos übergangen wurden.

Der Kerl wird diesen Tag noch bereuen, dachte William. Niemand darf die Hamleighs ungestraft zum Narren halten! Wir haben unseren heutigen Rang nicht dadurch erreicht, daß wir uns von hergelaufenen Mönchen übers Ohr hauen ließen. Bartholomäus von Shiring hat die Hamleighs beleidigt und ist dafür als Verräter im Gefängnis gestorben. Philip wird es nicht besser ergehen.

Auch Tom Builder schwor William Hamleigh insgeheim Rache. Nie hatte er vergessen, wie Tom ihm in Durstead Paroli geboten, sein Pferd festgehalten und ihn gezwungen hatte, die Arbeiter auszubezahlen. Heute, so dachte William voller Ingrimm, hat er mich respektlos mit »junger Lord William« angesprochen. Offensichtlich steckt er mit Philip unter einer Decke und baut jetzt Kathedralen anstelle von herrschaftlichen Häusern. Er wird noch zu spüren bekommen, daß er sich besser auf Gedeih und Verderb den Hamleighs ausgeliefert hätte, statt sich mit ihren Feinden zu verbünden!

So verzehrte sich William in stiller Wut, bis Bischof Henry sich erhob und verkündete, er sei nun bereit für den Gottesdienst. Auf einen Wink des Priors sprang ein Novize auf und verließ eilends den Raum. Wenig später erklang das Glockenzeichen.

Alle machten sich auf den Weg, Bischof Henry an der Spitze, Bischof Waleran als zweiter, dann Prior Philip und zuletzt die Laien. Die Mönche warteten draußen und fügten sich hinter Philip in die Prozession ein. Die Hamleighs bildeten notgedrungen die Nachhut.

Die Freiwilligen saßen auf Mauern und Dächern und füllten die gesamte Westhälfte des Klosterhofes. Henry bestieg eine mitten auf der Baustelle errichtete Plattform. Die Mönche nahmen hinter ihm Aufstellung, im zukünftigen Chor der Kathedrale. Die Hamleighs sowie die bischöfliche Entourage begaben sich ins künftige Mittelschiff.

Als sie dort Platz nahmen, entdeckte William Aliena.

Die junge Frau hatte sich sehr verändert. Sie trug grobe, billige Kleidung und Holzschuhe, und die Lockenpracht, die ihr Gesicht einrahmte, war schweißnaß. Aber sie war es, das stand außer Frage, und ihre Schönheit verschlug ihm den Atem. Er konnte den Blick nicht von ihr wenden, nicht einmal, als der Gottesdienst seinen Lauf nahm und das Klostergelände von einem aus tausend Kehlen kommenden Vaterunser widerhallte.

Sie schien zu spüren, daß sie beobachtet wurde, wirkte unruhig, trat von einem Bein aufs andere und sah sich schließlich suchend um. Endlich kreuzten sich ihre Blicke. Entsetzen zeichnete ihre Miene; obwohl bestimmt zehn Schritte oder mehr zwischen ihnen lagen und Dutzende von Menschen sie trennten, fuhr sie zusammen und schreckte zurück. In ihrer Angst war sie für William nur noch begehrenswerter, und er spürte seinen Körper reagieren wie schon seit einem Jahr nicht mehr. Doch in sein Begehren mischte sich Ablehnung; er haßte es, daß sie ihn wieder in ihren Bann zog. Aliena errötete und senkte den Blick; es war, als schäme sie sich. Sie wechselte ein paar

Worte mit einem Jungen, der neben ihr stand – natürlich, ihr Bruder, dachte William, dessen erotisches Gedächtnis sich auch an dieses Gesicht erinnerte –, machte kehrt und tauchte in der Menge unter.

William fühlte sich betrogen. Er war versucht, ihr zu folgen, aber das war unmöglich, nicht mitten im Gottesdienst und nicht unter den Augen seiner Eltern, zweier Bischöfe, vierzig Mönche und tausend Gläubiger. Enttäuscht wandte er sich wieder dem Altar zu. Die Chance, ihren Aufenthaltsort herauszufinden, war vertan.

Sie war verschwunden, aber er konnte sie nicht vergessen. Sein Glied war steif, und er fragte sich, ob das in der Kirche eine Sünde war. Seinen Vater schien irgend etwas zu beunruhigen. »Schau!« hörte William ihn zu Mutter sagen. »Schau dir diese Frau an!«

William glaubte zuerst, er meine Aliena, aber von ihr war weit und breit nichts mehr zu sehen. Als er dem starren Blick des alten Hamleighs folgte, erblickte er eine Frau von ungefähr dreißig Jahren. Sie hatte nicht die gleiche, sinnliche Ausstrahlung wie Aliena, zeichnete sich jedoch durch eine gewisse Ungebändigtheit und Beweglichkeit aus, die sein Interesse weckten. Sie stand neben Tom, was William zu der Annahme führte, es müsse sich wohl um die Frau des Baumeisters handeln – die gleiche also, die er ihm vor etwa einem Jahr abzukaufen versucht hatte. Aber woher kannte Vater sie?

»Ist sie das?« fragte Vater.

In diesem Augenblick – als hätte sie seine Worte gehört – drehte die Frau sich um und schaute die Hamleighs mit ihren durchdringend blaßgoldenen Augen an. »Um Gottes willen, sie ist es tatsächlich«, zischte Mutter.

Der starre Blick der Frau ging an Vater nicht spurlos vorüber: Sein gerötetes Gesicht wurde fahl, seine Hände zitterten. »Der Herr stehe uns bei«, sagte er. »Ich dachte, sie wäre längst tot!«

Und William dachte: Was, zum Teufel, hat das nun wieder zu bedeuten?

Genau das hatte Jack immer befürchtet.

Das ganze Jahr über hatte er gespürt, daß seine Mutter Tom Builder vermißte. Sie war nicht mehr so ausgeglichen wie früher; oft starrte sie verträumt in die Ferne, und nachts keuchte und stöhnte sie manchmal, als ob sie davon träumte oder sich einbildete, mit Tom zu schlafen. Die ganze Zeit über war Jack sich darüber im klaren gewesen, daß Ellen zu Tom zurückkehren würde. Und nun hatte sie eingewilligt, bei ihm zu bleiben.

Die bloße Vorstellung war ihm verhaßt.

Sie waren stets glücklich zusammen gewesen: Er liebte seine Mutter und seine Mutter liebte ihn, und niemand mischte sich ein.

Das Leben im Wald war ein bißchen fade, das war schon richtig. Jack gestand sich ein, daß er die vielen Menschen und das Leben in den Städten, die er in der kurzen Zeit mit Toms Familie kennengelernt hatte, gelegentlich vermißte. Auch Martha fehlte ihm. Tagträumereien von der »Prinzessin« – so nannte er Aliena für sich, obwohl er ihren richtigen Namen kannte – hatten ihm die Langeweile des Waldlebens versüßt. Es hatte durchaus etwas für sich, mit Tom zusammenzuarbeiten und das Baumeisterhandwerk zu erlernen – nur: Mit seiner Freiheit war es dann vorbei. Sie werden mir Vorschriften machen, dachte er, und ich muß arbeiten, ob ich nun will oder nicht. Und ich muß Mutter mit allen anderen teilen.

Er saß auf einem Mäuerchen neben dem Klostertor, überlegte und überlegte und kam zu keinem festen Schluß, und plötzlich entdeckte er zu seinem grenzenlosen Erstaunen die Prinzessin.

Er blinzelte. Sie drängte sich durch die Menschenmenge und strebte dem Tor zu. In jenen Tagen hatte sich unter ihren kostbaren Kleidern ein sinnlich-runder Mädchenkörper verborgen. Inzwischen war sie schlanker und wirkte viel erwachsener. Das durchgeschwitzte Leinenkleid klebte ihr am Körper, deutlich zeichneten sich ihre vollen Brüste, die Rippen, der flache Bauch, die schmalen Hüften und die langen Beine ab. Ihr Gesicht war schmutzverschmiert, der Lockenkranz unordentlich. Irgend etwas mußte die Prinzessin aus der Fassung gebracht haben; sie wirkte verängstigt und verstört. Jack war vollständig in ihren Bann geschlagen und verspürte auf einmal eine merkwürdige Regung in der Lendengegend, die ihm bisher völlig unbekannt gewesen war.

Er folgte der Prinzessin. Es war keine bewußte Entscheidung. Eben hatte er noch auf der Mauer gesessen und sie mit offenem Mund angestarrt – und nun rannte er auch schon hinter ihr her. Draußen auf der Straße holte er sie ein. Sie roch wie jemand, der harte körperliche Arbeit verrichtet hat. Er erinnerte sich daran, daß sie damals immer nach Blumen geduftet hatte. »Stimmt etwas nicht?« fragte er.

»Nein, es ist alles in Ordnung«, erwiderte Aliena kurzangebunden und beschleunigte ihre Schritte.

Jack ließ sich nicht abschütteln. »Ihr erinnert Euch nicht an mich. Als wir uns das letzte Mal gesehen haben, habt Ihr mir erklärt, wie Kinder gezeugt werden.«

»Ach, halt den Mund und verschwinde!« rief sie.

Er blieb stehen und ließ sie, tief enttäuscht, allein weitergehen. Ich habe alles falsch gemacht, dachte er. Sie hat mich wie ein lästiges Kind behandelt. Dabei bin ich schon dreizehn! Aber aus der luftigen Höhe ihrer achtzehn oder mehr Jahre genügt ihr das anscheinend nicht.

Er sah, wie sie auf ein Haus zuging, einen Schlüssel, den sie am Lederband um den Hals trug, hervorzog und die Tür aufschloß.

Sie lebte hier!

Das änderte natürlich alles.

Das Leben in Kingsbridge erschien ihm mit einem Schlag in einem anderen Licht. Ich werde die Prinzessin jeden Tag sehen können! Dafür lohnt es sich, das Waldleben aufzugeben!

Er blieb, wo er war, und ließ die Tür nicht aus den Augen, doch Aliena kam nicht wieder heraus. Schon merkwürdig, auf der Straße herumzustehen und sich Hoffnungen auf jemanden zu machen, der einen kaum kannte ... Jack wollte sich nicht vom Fleck rühren. Eine ganz neuartige Empfindung regte sich in ihm. Alles andere war plötzlich unwichtig. Nur auf die Prinzessin kam es ihm an. Er war wie verzaubert. Er war wie verzückt. Er war wie besessen.

Er war verliebt.

Buch III 1140-42

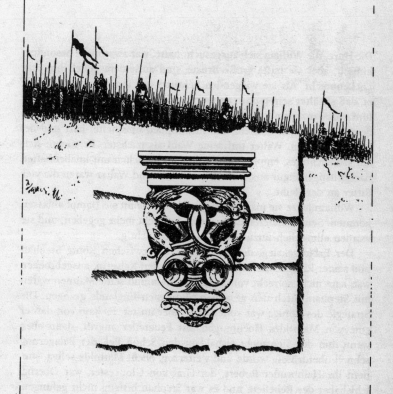

Die Hure, die William sich ausgesucht hatte, war zwar nicht besonders hübsch, aber sie hatte große Brüste, und außerdem gefiel ihm ihre Lockenpracht. Als sie wiegenden Schrittes auf ihn zukam, bemerkte er, daß sie älter sein mußte als ursprünglich angenommen – zwischen fünfundzwanzig und dreißig – und daß ihre Augen im Gegensatz zu dem unschuldigen Lächeln, das ihre Lippen umspielte, hart und berechnend waren. Walter traf seine Wahl als nächster. Er suchte sich ein schmächtiges, empfindlich wirkendes Mädchen mit knabenhafter, flachbrüstiger Figur aus. Erst nach William und Walter waren die vier Ritter an der Reihe.

William hatte sie ins Bordell geschleppt, damit sie Dampf ablassen konnten: Seit Monaten hatte es keine Schlacht mehr gegeben, und sie wurden allmählich unzufrieden und streitsüchtig.

Der Erbfolgekrieg, der vor einem Jahr zwischen König Stephan und seiner Rivalin Mathilde, der sogenannten Kaiserin, ausgebrochen war, kam nicht so recht vom Fleck. William und seine Mannen waren mit Stephan durch den gesamten Südwesten Englands gezogen. Die Strategie des Königs war voller Elan, aber unstet. Es kam vor, daß er eine von Mathildes Hochburgen mit Feuereifer angriff, dann aber, wenn ihm der Sieg nicht alsbald in den Schoß fiel, der Belagerung schnell überdrüssig wurde und weiterzog. Nicht Mathilde selbst, sondern ihr Halbbruder Robert, der Graf von Gloucester, war Oberbefehlshaber der Rebellen, und es war Stephan bislang nicht gelungen, eine Konfrontation mit ihm zu erzwingen: alles in allem ein halbherziger Krieg mit vielen Manövern und nur wenigen echten Schlachten; daher die Unruhe unter Williams Männern.

Das Bordell war in kleine, mit Strohmatratzen ausgelegte Nischen unterteilt. Williams Hure stellte den Wandschirm so auf, daß sie ungestört waren, ließ ihr Hemd fallen und entblößte ihre Brüste. Sie waren, wie er bereits vermutet hatte, riesig, doch nun stellte er leicht enttäuscht fest, daß ihre großen Brustwarzen und die sichtbaren Äderchen Indiz dafür waren, daß sie Kinder gestillt hatte. Trotzdem zog er sie an sich, nahm ihre Brüste in die Hände, knetete sie und kniff ihre Brustwarzen. »Sachte«, mahnte sie, schlang die Arme um ihn, zog seine Hüften zu sich heran und rieb sich an ihm. Wenig später zwängte sie eine Hand zwischen ihre Leiber und tastete nach seinen Lenden.

Er fluchte verhalten: Sein Körper reagierte nicht.

»Macht doch nichts«, murmelte sie. Ihr herablassender Ton ärgerte ihn, aber er protestierte nicht, als sie sich aus der Umarmung löste, sich vor ihn kniete, sein Hemd lüpfte und mit dem Mund an die Arbeit ging.

Zunächst fand er Gefallen daran und dachte schon, nun sei alles in Ordnung, verlor aber nach der anfänglichen Erregung rasch wieder das Interesse. Er beobachtete ihr Gesicht, weil ihn das bisweilen erregte, aber im Augenblick konnte er an nichts anderes denken als an die klägliche Figur, die er abgab. Wut stieg in ihm auf – und ließ ihn noch mehr zusammenschrumpfen.

Sie hielt inne und sagte: »Ihr müßt Euch entspannen.« Als sie wieder ans Werk ging, lutschte sie so fest, daß sie ihm weh tat. Er wich zurück und schrie leise auf, als sie seine empfindliche Haut mit ihren Zähnen streifte. Er versetzte ihr mit dem Handrücken einen Schlag ins Gesicht. Sie schnappte nach Luft und fiel zur Seite.

»Ungeschicktes Luder!« fauchte er. Sie lag auf der Matratze zu seinen Füßen und blickte ängstlich zu ihm auf. Mehr aus Ungehaltenheit als aus böser Absicht versetzte er ihr einen schlechtgezielten Tritt, der sie in der Magengrube traf, weit härter als ursprünglich beabsichtigt, und sie krümmte sich vor Schmerz.

Er kniete sich hin, rollte sie auf den Rücken und setzte sich rittlings auf sie. In ihrem Blick mischten sich Furcht und Schmerz. Er hob ihr das Kleid bis zur Mitte hinauf. Die Haare zwischen ihren Beinen waren dicht und kraus, ganz nach seinem Geschmack. Er spielte mit sich selbst, während er sich an ihrem Körper satt sah; er war noch nicht steif genug. Allmählich wich die Angst aus ihren Augen. Ihm fiel ein, daß sie es absichtlich darauf abgesehen haben mochte, ihn abzukühlen und seine Begierde zu zügeln, damit sie ihm nicht zu Willen sein mußte. Der Gedanke machte ihn so rasend, daß er ihr die geballte Faust ins Gesicht stieß.

Sie schrie gellend auf und versuchte, sich unter ihm hervorzuwinden. Er drückte sie mit seinem vollen Gewicht nieder, doch sie wehrte sich weiter und schrie dabei ununterbrochen. Jetzt war er voll erigiert. Er versuchte, ihre Oberschenkel gewaltsam auseinanderzudrücken, doch es gelang ihm nicht.

Der Wandschirm flog beiseite, und Walter in Stiefeln und Unterhemd, sein Glied wie einen Fahnenmast vor sich hertragend, kam herein, unmittelbar gefolgt von zwei Rittern: Ugly Gervase und Hugh Axe.

»Haltet sie fest, Jungs«, befahl William.

Die drei Ritter knieten sich um die Hure und drückten sie zu Boden.

William machte sich bereit, in sie einzudringen, hielt dann aber inne und kostete die Vorfreude aus.

»Was war los, Herr?« wollte Walter wissen.

»Hat ihre Meinung geändert, als sie mein Riesending sah«, erwiderte William grinsend.

Die Männer brachen in johlendes Gelächter aus, und William drang in die Frau ein. Es machte ihm Spaß, wenn er dabei Zuschauer hatte.

Walter sagte: »Ihr habt mich unterbrochen, als ich meinen gerade reinstecken wollte.«

William sah deutlich, daß Walter noch nicht befriedigt worden war. »Steck ihn ihr in den Mund«, sagte er. »Das gefällt ihr bestimmt.«

»Ich versuch's mal.« Walter wechselte die Stellung und zog den Kopf der Frau an den Haaren hoch. Mittlerweile war sie verängstigt genug, um auf alles einzugehen, und machte anstandslos mit. Gervase und Hugh brauchten sie nicht länger festzuhalten, blieben aber stehen und schauten begeistert zu: Wahrscheinlich hatten sie noch nie eine Frau gesehen, der es von zwei Männern gleichzeitig besorgt wurde. Das gleiche galt auch für William, und er fand es seltsam aufregend. Walter schien genauso zu empfinden, denn binnen kurzer Zeit fing er an zu keuchen und sich ruckartig zu bewegen, und dann kam er auch schon. William, der ihn nicht aus den Augen gelassen hatte, tat es ihm gleich darauf nach.

Als sie sich erhoben, war William noch immer in Hochstimmung. »Warum nehmt ihr sie nicht auch noch?« fragte er Gervase und Hugh. Die Vorstellung, das gleiche Schauspiel gleich noch einmal zu genießen, behagte ihm.

Doch die beiden waren nicht allzu erpicht darauf. »Auf mich wartet mein kleiner Liebling«, sagte Hugh, und Gervase fügte hinzu: »Auf mich auch.«

Die Hure stand auf und richtete ihre Kleidung. Ihr Gesicht verriet nicht die geringste Gefühlsregung. William sagte zu ihr: »Das war nicht schlecht, was?«

Sie starrte ihn einen Moment lang an, dann schürzte sie die Lippen und spuckte aus. William spürte eine warme, klebrige Flüssigkeit im Gesicht: Sie hatte Walters Samen im Mund behalten. Das Zeug nahm ihm die Sicht, und er hob wütend die Hand, um sie zu schlagen, aber sie duckte sich und glitt zwischen den Wandschirmen davon. Walter und die anderen Ritter brachen in schallendes Gelächter aus. William fand das überhaupt nicht komisch, aber er konnte schlecht mit Walters Samen im Gesicht hinter dem Mädchen herjagen; ja, wenn er sein Gesicht nicht verlieren wollte, mußte er gute Miene zum bösen Spiel machen, und so stimmte er in das Gelächter ein.

»Ich hoffe nur, Herr, daß Ihr jetzt kein Kind von Walter kriegt!« meinte Ugly Gervase, und alle brüllten vor Lachen; selbst William fand den Gedanken belustigend. Gemeinsam verließen sie den Alkoven, wobei sie sich gegenseitig stützten und sich das Wasser aus den Augen wischten.

Die anderen Mädchen starrten sie ängstlich an: Sie hatten Williams Hure schreien gehört und befürchteten Ärger. Andere Kunden äugten neugierig aus ihren Verschlägen. »Das war das erstemal, daß ich das Zeug aus einem Mädchen hab' schießen sehen!« sagte Walter, und wieder bogen sie sich vor Lachen.

Einer von Williams Knappen stand mit besorgter Miene an der Tür. Er war fast noch ein Kind und hatte wahrscheinlich noch nie ein Bordell von innen gesehen. Unsicher, ob es ihm ziemte, in die Heiterkeit einzustimmen, lächelte er halbherzig. »Was hast du hier zu suchen, du Arschgeige?« fuhr William ihn an.

»Für Euch ist eine Nachricht gekommen, Herr«, sagte der Knappe.

»Na, dann steh nicht so dumm herum, sag mir lieber, wie sie lautet!«

»Es tut mir sehr leid, Herr«, sagte der Junge. Er wirkte dermaßen verängstigt, daß William schon glaubte, er wolle gleich kehrtmachen und aus dem Haus laufen.

»Was tut dir leid, du Scheißkerl?« brüllte William. »Wie lautet die Nachricht?«

»Euer Vater ist tot, Herr«, platzte der Junge heraus und fing an zu weinen.

William stierte ihn an, wie vom Donner gerührt. Tot? dachte er. Tot? »Aber er ist doch kerngesund!« röhrte er einfältig. Es stimmte zwar, daß Vater nicht mehr in die Schlacht ziehen konnte, aber das nahm bei einem Mann von bald fünfzig Jahren kaum wunder. Der Knappe weinte noch immer. William rief sich ins Gedächtnis, wie sein Vater bei ihrem letzten Zusammentreffen ausgesehen hatte: massig, rotgesichtig und kraftvoll, leicht aufbrausend wie stets und geradezu strotzend vor Lebensfreude; und das war nicht einmal ... Erschüttert stellte er fest, daß es fast ein Jahr her war, seit er seinen Vater zum letztenmal gesehen hatte. »Was ist geschehen?« fragte er den Knappen. »Was ist ihm zugestoßen?«

»Er hat plötzlich einen Anfall bekommen«, schluchzte der Knappe.

Ein Anfall! Langsam ging ihm auf, daß Vater wirklich tot war. Dieser große, starke, polternde, jähzornige Mann hilflos und kalt auf einer Steinplatte –

»Ich muß nach Hause«, sagte William unvermittelt.

»Ihr müßt zunächst den König um Beurlaubung ersuchen«, riet Walter behutsam.

»Ja, richtig«, stimmte William geistesabwesend zu. »Ich muß um Erlaubnis bitten.« In seinem Kopf ging es drunter und drüber.

»Soll ich die Wirtin entlohnen?« fragte Walter.

»Ja.« William gab Walter seinen Geldbeutel. Irgendwer legte ihm seinen Umhang über die Schulter. Walter sprach im Flüsterton mit der Bordellbesitzerin und bezahlte sie. Hugh Axe hielt William die Tür auf.

Schweigend gingen sie durch die Straßen des kleinen Städtchens. William fühlte sich merkwürdig entrückt, als ginge ihn das Geschehen gar nichts an. Er konnte es immer noch nicht fassen, daß Vater nicht mehr sein sollte. Doch da sie sich dem Hauptquartier näherten, versuchte er, sich zusammenzureißen.

König Stephan hielt, in Ermangelung einer Burg oder eines Zunfthauses, in der Kirche hof, einem einfachen Steingebäude mit inwendig knallig rot, blau und karottenfarben gestrichenen Wänden. Inmitten der Kirche war auf dem Boden ein Feuer entzündet worden, neben dem der stattliche König mit seinem hellbraunen Haar in der für ihn üblichen lässigen Haltung auf einem hölzernen Thron saß, die Beine weit von sich gestreckt. Er trug Soldatenkleidung, hohe Stiefel und einen ledernen Waffenrock, doch statt des Helmes eine Krone. William und Walter drängten sich durch die Bittsteller um das Kirchenportal, nickten den Wachposten zu, die die Menge zurückhielten, und begaben sich in den inneren Zirkel. Stephan unterhielt sich gerade mit einem adligen Neuankömmling, unterbrach das Gespräch aber, als er William sah. »William, mein Freund! Ihr habt es also erfahren.«

William verneigte sich. »Ja, mein Herr und König.«

Stephan erhob sich. »Ich trauere mit Euch«, sagte er. Er legte seine Arme um William und hielt ihn einen Augenblick lang umschlungen, bevor er ihn wieder freigab.

Durch seine Anteilnahme fühlte sich William erstmals zu Tränen gerührt. »Ich muß Euch um Heimaturlaub bitten«, sagte er.

»Er sei Euch bereitwillig, wenn auch nicht freudigen Herzens gewährt«, erwiderte der König. »Wir werden Euren starken rechten Arm vermissen.«

»Ich danke Euch, Herr.«

»Außerdem gewähre ich Euch die Verwaltung der Grafschaft Shiring und aller damit verbundenen Einkünfte, bis die Frage der Nachfolge geklärt ist. Geht nach Hause, begrabt Euren Vater und kommt so schnell wie möglich wieder zu Uns zurück.«

William verneigte sich noch einmal und zog sich zurück. Der König vertiefte sich wieder in sein Gespräch mit dem Grafen, während sich die Höflinge um William scharten und ihn ihrer Anteilnahme versicherten. Erst da ging ihm die Bedeutung dessen, was der König gesagt hatte, auf. Er hatte ihm die Verwaltung der Grafschaft anvertraut, *bis die Frage der Nachfolge geklärt ist.* Welche Frage? William war das einzige Kind seines Vaters. Wie konnte es da eine Frage geben? Er betrachtete die Gesichter um sich herum, und sein Blick fiel auf einen jungen Priester, der als stets gut informiert galt. Er zog den Mann zu sich heran und fragte leise: »Was, zum Teufel, hat er mit dieser ›Frage um die Nachfolge‹ gemeint, Joseph?«

»Es gibt noch einen zweiten Anwärter auf die Grafschaft«, erwiderte Joseph.

»Einen zweiten Anwärter?« wiederholte William erstaunt. Er hatte weder Halbbrüder noch illegitime Brüder noch irgendwelche Vettern. »Wer ist es?«

Joseph deutete auf einen Mann, der ihnen den Rücken zukehrte und zu den Neuangekommenen gehörte. Er trug die Kleidung eines Knappen.

»Aber der ist ja nicht einmal Ritter!« sagte William laut. »Mein Vater war Graf von Shiring!«

Der Knappe hatte es gehört und drehte sich um. »Mein Vater war ebenfalls Graf von Shiring.«

Zunächst erkannte William ihn nicht. Er hatte einen breitschultrigen, etwa achtzehn Jahre zählenden jungen Mann vor sich, der für einen Knappen bestens gekleidet war und ein gutes Schwert besaß. Seine Haltung verriet Selbstvertrauen, ja sogar Arroganz. Vor allem aber bedachte er sein Gegenüber mit einem solchen Ausdruck blanken Hasses, daß William erschrocken zurücktrat. Das Gesicht kam ihm irgendwie bekannt vor. Trotzdem wußte William noch immer nicht, wen er vor sich hatte – bis er die rote Narbe am rechten Ohr des Knappen entdeckte, wo ihm das Ohrläppchen abgeschnitten worden war. Blitzartig überfiel ihn die Erinnerung an ein winziges Stück weißen Fleisches, das auf die schweratmende Brust einer von panischer Angst ergriffenen Jungfrau fiel, an die Schmerzensschreie eines Jungen: Dies war Richard, der Sohn des Verräters Bartholomäus, Alienas Bruder! Der Knabe, der gezwungen worden war zuzuschauen, wie zwei Männer seine Schwester vergewaltigten, war zu einem stattlichen Mann herangewachsen, dem der Rachedurst aus den blauen Augen loderte. William fühlte sich unvermittelt von Furcht gepackt.

»Ihr erinnert Euch, nicht wahr?« sagte Richard in leicht gedehntem Tonfall, der seine kalte Wut nicht vollkommen verdecken konnte.

William nickte. »Ich erinnere mich.«

»Ich auch, William Hamleigh«, sagte Richard. »Ich auch.«

William saß auf dem großen Stuhl am Kopfende des Tisches, dem ehemaligen Stammplatz seines Vaters. Er hatte seit jeher gewußt, daß er ihn eines Tages einnehmen würde, und sich dabei vorgestellt, wie ungeheuer mächtig er sich dann fühlen würde. Nun, da es Wirklichkeit geworden, empfand er eher eine gewisse Angst, mit seinem Vater verglichen, für unzureichend befunden und von niemandem respektiert zu werden.

Williams Mutter saß zu seiner Rechten. Zu Lebzeiten seines Vaters hatte er oft beobachtet, wie sie mit Vaters Ängsten und Schwächen Katz und Maus spielte und stets ihren eigenen Willen durchsetzte. Das sollte ihm nicht passieren, hatte er sich gelobt.

Zu seiner Linken saß Arthur, ein sanftmütiger, grauhaariger Mann, einst der Gutsverwalter des Grafen Bartholomäus, den Williams Vater, nachdem er Graf von Shiring geworden, wegen seiner profunden Kenntnis sämtlicher Ländereien übernommen hatte. Williams Zweifel an der Weisheit dieser Entscheidung hatten sich nie gelegt: Anderer Leute Diener blieben nicht selten den Methoden ihrer vormaligen Brotgeber treu.

»König Stephan kann Richard unmöglich zum Grafen ernennen«, sagte Mutter gerade wütend. »Er ist nichts weiter als ein Knappe!«

»Ich begreife nicht, wie er selbst das zuwege gebracht hat«, sagte William gereizt. »Ich dachte immer, sie seien an den Bettelstab geraten. Aber er trug feine Kleidung und ein gutes Schwert. Wo hat er das Geld her?«

»Er hat sich als Wollhändler etabliert«, erwiderte Mutter. »Er hat mehr Geld, als er braucht. Oder vielmehr seine Schwester – soviel ich höre, führt sie die Geschäfte.«

Aliena! Sie also steckte dahinter. William hatte sie nie ganz vergessen können, doch seit der Krieg ausgebrochen war, hatte sie nicht mehr all seine Gedanken beherrscht – bis er Richard begegnet war. Nun spukte sie ihm wieder ständig im Kopf herum, so frisch und schön, verletzlich und begehrenswert wie eh und je. Er haßte sie – schon allein der Macht wegen, die sie über ihn besaß.

»Dann ist Aliena jetzt also reich?« fragte er betont gleichgültig.

»Richtig. Aber du hast ein ganzes Jahr für den König gekämpft. Er kann dir dein Erbe nicht verwehren.«

»Richard hat sich angeblich ebenfalls tapfer geschlagen«, sagte William. »Ich habe mich erkundigt. Und obendrein ist seine Tapferkeit dem König zu Ohren gekommen.«

Mutters bislang ärgerlich verächtliche Miene wurde nachdenklich. »Dann hat er also tatsächlich gewisse Aussichten.«

»Das ist zu befürchten.«

»Nun gut. Dagegen müssen wir etwas tun.«

»Aber was?« fragte William unwillkürlich. Da hatte er sich nun vorgenommen, seiner Mutter keinesfalls das Kommando zu überlassen, und nun verfiel er schon wieder in alte Gewohnheiten!

»Du mußt dem König ein größeres Kontingent an Rittern, neuen Waffen, besseren Pferden sowie Knappen und Kriegern mitbringen, wenn du zurückkehrst.«

William hätte ihr liebend gern widersprochen, aber er wußte, daß sie recht hatte. Der König würde das Lehen letztendlich demjenigen geben, der versprach, ihm am wirkungsvollsten zur Seite zu stehen – unabhängig vom Für und Wider der rechtlichen Lage.

»Aber das ist noch nicht alles«, fuhr Mutter fort. »Du mußt wie ein Graf auftreten und auch so handeln. Dann wird der König deine Ernennung früher oder später als *fait accompli* ansehen.«

Trotz aller Vorbehalte siegte Williams Neugier. »Wie tritt man denn auf und handelt wie ein Graf?«

»Tu deine Meinung kund, zu allem und jedem: Wie der König den Krieg künftig führen sollte, was die beste Taktik für die jeweils bevorstehende Schlacht wäre, wie es um die politische Lage im Norden bestellt ist, und – das ist besonders wichtig! – äußere dich vor allem über die anderen Grafen, über ihr Können und ihre Loyalität. Mit denen sprich von Mann zu Mann, am besten über andere. Erzähl dem Grafen von Huntingdon, daß der Herzog von Warenne ein großartiger Kämpfer ist; und dem Bischof von Ely erzählst du, daß du dem Vogt von Lincoln nicht über den Weg traust. Dann wird man dem König berichten: ›William von Shiring steht auf der Seite des Herzogs von Warenne‹ oder ›William von Shiring und sein Gefolge sind gegen den Vogt von Lincoln‹. Wenn du auf diese Weise erst einmal einen bedeutenden Eindruck erweckt hast, wird der König dir auch bereitwillig mehr Macht verleihen.«

William hielt wenig von solchen Feinheiten. »Ich meine, die Stärke meiner Armee wird mehr ins Gewicht fallen«, sagte er. Er wandte sich an den Gutsverwalter: »Wieviel Geld haben wir, Arthur?«

»Nichts, Herr«, erwiderte Arthur.

»Was, zum Teufel, erlaubt Ihr Euch?« sagte William grob. »Es muß etwas dasein. Wieviel ist es?«

Arthur wirkte leicht überheblich, als habe er von Williams Seite nichts zu befürchten. »Herr, es ist absolut kein Geld vorhanden.«

William hätte ihn am liebsten erwürgt. »Dies ist die Grafschaft Shiring!« sagte er laut und vernehmlich, so daß selbst die Ritter und das Burggesinde am anderen Ende des Tisches aufschauten. »Da muß es doch Geld geben!«

»Natürlich, Herr, wir nehmen ständig Geld ein«, antwortete Arthur milde. »Aber wir geben es auch wieder aus, besonders in Kriegszeiten.«

William musterte das blasse, glattrasierte Gesicht. Arthur war viel zu selbstgefällig. Ob er wohl ehrlich war? Schwer zu sagen. William wünschte, er hätte Augen, die einem Mann ins Herz sehen konnten.

Seine Mutter wußte genau, was er dachte. »Arthur spricht die Wahrheit«, sagte sie und scherte sich keinen Deut darum, daß er mit ihnen am gleichen Tisch saß. »Er ist alt, faul und einfallslos, aber er ist ehrlich.«

William fühlte sich zutiefst getroffen. Kaum hatte er auf diesem Stuhl Platz genommen, da schrumpfte seine Macht auch schon wie durch Zauberhand. Es war wie verhext! Es schien kein Weg daran vorbeizuführen, daß er, gleichgültig, wie alt er auch wurde, immer ein Knabe unter Männern blieb. »Wie ist das nur gekommen?« fragte er schwach.

»Dein Vater war den größten Teil des Jahres vor seinem Tod krank«, erwiderte Williams Mutter. »Ich sah zwar, daß er die Zügel schleifen ließ, konnte ihn aber nicht dazu bewegen, etwas zu unternehmen.«

Seine allmächtige Mutter – und konnte sich nicht durchsetzen? Das war ja etwas ganz Neues! Nie zuvor hatte William erlebt, daß nicht alle nach ihrer Pfeife tanzten. Er wandte sich an Arthur: »Wir haben mit die besten Äcker im ganzen Königreich. Wie kann es angehen, daß wir ohne einen Penny dastehen?«

»Mehrere Höfe haben Schwierigkeiten, und viele Pächter sind mit ihren Abgaben ins Hintertreffen geraten.«

»Aber weshalb denn?«

»Ein Grund, der mir immer wieder zu Ohren kommt, ist der, daß die jungen Männer nicht auf dem Land arbeiten wollen, sondern in die Städte ziehen.«

»Dann müssen wir sie eben daran hindern!«

Arthur zuckte die Achseln. »Sobald ein Leibeigener ein Jahr lang in der Stadt gelebt hat, ist er ein freier Mann. Das ist Gesetz.«

»Und was ist mit den Pächtern, die nicht bezahlt haben? Was habt Ihr mit denen gemacht?«

»Was kann man da machen?« erwiderte Arthur. »Wenn wir ihnen ihren Lebensunterhalt wegnehmen, dann können sie nie bezahlen. Wir müssen uns in Geduld fassen und auf eine gute Ernte hoffen, damit sie den Rückstand aufholen können.«

Arthur nimmt seine eigene Unfähigkeit, mit all diesen Schwierigkeiten zu Rande zu kommen, viel zu leicht, dachte William wütend, aber noch beherrschte er sich. »Na gut, selbst wenn alle jungen Männer in die Städte gehen, wie steht es dann mit den Einkünften aus unserem Hausbesitz in Shiring? Wenigstens der sollte uns doch etwas eingebracht haben.«

»Seltsamerweise nicht«, antwortete Arthur. »In Shiring stehen viele Häuser leer. Die jungen Männer gehen wohl woanders hin.«

»Oder man hat Euch belogen«, sagte William. »Wahrscheinlich werdet Ihr mir gleich noch mitteilen, daß auch die Einkünfte aus dem Markt in Shiring und aus der Wollmesse zurückgegangen sind?«

»Ja –«

»Und weshalb erhöht Ihr dann die Mieten und Steuern nicht?«

»Das haben wir ja, Herr, und zwar auf Befehl Eures verstorbenen Vaters; trotzdem sind die Einkünfte zurückgegangen.«

»Wie hat Bartholomäus es bloß geschafft, bei einem solch uneinträglichen Lehen nicht den Grund unter den Füßen zu verlieren?«

Auch auf diese Frage war Arthur nicht um eine Antwort verlegen. »Er besaß außerdem noch den Steinbruch, der früher eine schöne Stange Geld einbrachte.«

»Und nun ist er in den Händen dieses verfluchten Mönchs.« William war am Ende seines Lateins. Ausgerechnet jetzt, wo er darauf angewiesen war, Pracht und Prunk an den Tag zu legen, mußte er erfahren, daß er keine Mittel dazu besaß! Diese Lage konnte sich zu einer regelrechten Gefahr auswachsen. Der König hatte ihn nur mit der vorläufigen Verwaltung der Grafschaft betraut. Das war eine Art Bewährungsprobe. Kehrte er mit einer kleineren Streitmacht an den Hof zurück, so erweckte er unweigerlich den Eindruck, er sei undankbar, wenn nicht gar treulos.

Außerdem mußte an Arthurs Schilderung der Lage etwas faul sein. William war ganz sicher, daß er betrogen wurde – wahrscheinlich lachten sie sich hinter seinem Rücken ins Fäustchen. Der Gedanke machte ihn wütend. Mit ihm nicht! Denen würde er es zeigen. Er würde nicht klein beigeben, selbst wenn es erst zum Blutvergießen kommen mußte.

»Ihr habt für alles eine Entschuldigung«, sagte er zu Arthur. »Tatsache ist, daß Ihr während der Krankheit meines Vaters, als Ihr eigentlich besonders wachsam hättet sein müssen, Euren Pflichten nicht nachgekommen seid.«

»Aber, Herr –«

William erhob seine Stimme. »Wenn Ihr nicht den Mund haltet, werde ich Euch auspeitschen lassen.«

Arthur erblaßte und schwieg.

William fuhr fort: »Morgen beginnen wir mit einer Rundreise durch die Grafschaft. Wir werden jedes einzelne meiner Dörfer besuchen und den Bauern die Leviten lesen. Mag sein, daß Ihr nicht wißt, wie man mit diesem jammernden, verlogenen Volk umgeht. Ich schon. Wir werden schnell herausfinden, wie verarmt meine Grafschaft in Wirklichkeit ist. Und falls Ihr mich belogen habt, dann gnade Euch Gott – Ihr werdet als erster hängen, das schwöre ich!«

Außer Arthur nahm er noch seinen Reitknecht Walter und die vier Ritter mit, die im vergangenen Jahr an seiner Seite gekämpft hatten: Ugly Gervase, Hugh Axe, Gilbert de Rennes und Miles Dice – samt und sonders bullige, gewalttätige Männer, leicht aufbrausend und stets kampfbereit. Sie nahmen ihre besten Pferde mit und waren, um die Bauernschaft in Angst und Schrecken zu versetzen, bis an die Zähne bewaffnet. Ein Mann, der nicht imstande ist, anderen Angst einzuflößen, war in Williams Augen eine Memme.

Es war ein heißer Spätsommertag und der Weizen stand in fetten Garben auf den Feldern. Der sichtbare Überfluß tat das seine, um Williams Wut über die eigene Geldknappheit noch zu schüren. Irgend jemand beraubte ihn, obwohl es eigentlich niemand wagen durfte, ihm die Stirn zu bieten. Seine Familie hatte die Grafschaft dem in Ungnade gefallenen Bartholomäus abgewonnen, und trotzdem stand er ohne einen Penny da, während Bartholomäus' Sohn aus dem Vollen schöpfte! Die Vorstellung, daß er bestohlen wurde und nichtsahnend zur Zielscheibe des Spottes geworden war, nagte an William, und je weiter er ritt, um so wütender wurde er.

Er hatte beschlossen, mit Northbrook anzufangen, einem kleinen, von der Burg ziemlich abgelegenen Dörfchen. Die Einwohnerschaft setzte sich aus Leibeigenen und Freisassen zusammen. Die Leibeigenen waren Williams Eigentum und durften ohne seine Einwilligung nichts unternehmen. Sie schuldeten ihm zu bestimmten Jahreszeiten eine festgelegte Zahl von Arbeitstagen und einen Teil ihrer Ernte. Die Freisassen zahlten ihm lediglich Pachtzins, und zwar in bar oder in Naturalien. Fünf von ihnen waren damit in Verzug geraten. William glaubte zu wissen, daß sie sich nur deshalb soviel Freiheiten herausnahmen, weil sie wußten, daß die Burg weit weg war. Dieses Dorf war bestimmt ein guter Ausgangspunkt für seine umfassende Aufräumaktion.

Es war ein langer Ritt, und die Sonne stand hoch am Himmel, als sie sich dem Flecken näherten, der aus zwanzig oder dreißig Häusern und drei riesigen, schon abgeernteten Feldern bestand.

Unweit der Häuser, am Rande eines der Felder, wuchs eine Gruppe von drei hohen Eichen. Als William mit seinen Mannen näher kam, sah er, daß der Großteil der Dorfbewohner im Schatten der Eichen zu sitzen und sein Vesper zu verzehren schien. Er gab seinem Pferd die Sporen, legte die letzten paar hundert Schritt in leichtem Galopp zurück und kam dann mit seinen Mannen in einer Staubwolke zum Stehen.

Während sich die Dörfler aufrappelten, ihr Brot hinunterwürgten und sich den Staub aus den Augen wischten, wurde William, dessen mißtrauischem Auge nichts entging, Zeuge einer merkwürdigen kleinen Begebenheit. Ein Mann mittleren Alters mit schwarzem Bart redete leise, aber eindringlich auf ein dralles, rotwangiges Mädchen mit einem drallen rotbäckigen Säugling ein. Ein junger Bursche, der sich dazugesellte, wurde von dem älteren Mann hastig davongescheucht. Dann ging das Mädchen, augenscheinlich widerstrebend, auf das Dorf zu und wurde von der Staubwolke verschluckt. Williams Neugier war geweckt: Irgend etwas war faul an der Sache. Welchen Reim sich Mutter wohl darauf gemacht hätte?

Er beschloß, die Angelegenheit für den Augenblick auf sich beruhen zu lassen. Mit lauter Stimme wandte er sich an Arthur, so daß alle ihn hören konnten: »Fünf meiner Pächter sind mit ihren Abgaben im Rückstand, stimmt's?«

»Ja, Herr.«

»Wer ist der säumigste Zahler?«

»Athelstan hat seit zwei Jahren nicht bezahlt, aber er hatte großes Pech mit seinen Schweinen.«

William fiel Arthur ins Wort und sprach über seinen Kopf hinweg: »Wer von euch ist Athelstan?«

Ein großer, gebeugter Mann um die Fünfundvierzig trat nach vorn. Er hatte lichtes Haar und wässerige Augen.

»Warum zahlst du mir keine Pacht?« fragte William.

»Herr, mein Hof ist klein und ich habe keine Hilfe, jetzt, wo meine Jungs in die Stadt arbeiten gegangen sind, und dann kam noch das Schweinefieber −«

»Moment mal«, unterbrach William. »Wohin sind deine Söhne gegangen?«

»Nach Kingsbridge, Herr, um dort auf der Dombaustelle zu arbeiten. Sie wollen heiraten, wie alle jungen Männer, und mein Land ist nicht groß genug für drei Familien.«

William merkte sich die Auskunft, daß die jungen Männer in Kingsbridge Arbeit gefunden hatten, für später vor. »Dein Gut ist auf jeden Fall groß genug, um eine Familie zu ernähren, und trotzdem hast du deine Pacht nicht bezahlt.«

Athelstan fing wieder mit seinen Schweinen an. William stierte ihn feindselig an und hörte gar nicht zu. Ich weiß, warum du nicht gezahlt hast, dachte er. Du wußtest, daß dein Herr zu krank war, um selbst nach dem Rechten zu sehen. Das hast du ausgenutzt und ihn betrogen − du und die vier anderen Missetäter. Wehe wir zeigen einmal eine Schwäche − sofort beraubt ihr uns!

Einen Moment lang badete er in Selbstmitleid, überzeugt, daß sich die fünf insgeheim ins Fäustchen gelacht hatten. Nun, sie sollten gleich ihre Lektion erteilt bekommen. »Gilbert und Hugh, ergreift diesen Bauern und haltet ihn fest«, befahl er in ruhigem Ton.

Athelstan redete immer noch. Die beiden Ritter saßen ab und näherten sich ihm. Seine Geschichte vom Schweinefieber verebbte, und die Ritter packten ihn an den Armen. Er wurde bleich vor Furcht.

William wandte sich mit der gleichen ruhigen Stimme wieder an Walter: »Hast du deine Kettenpanzerhandschuhe dabei?«

»Ja, Herr.«

»Zieh sie an. Erteile Athelstan eine Lektion. Aber laß ihn am Leben, damit er die Kunde davon verbreiten kann.«

»Jawohl, Herr.« Walter entnahm seiner Satteltasche ein paar lederne Handschuhstulpen mit feinem Kettenpanzer auf den Knöcheln und den Rückseiten der Finger. Bedächtig zog er sie an. Die versammelten Dorfbewohner beobachteten ihn mit Grauen, und Athelstan stöhnte auf.

Walter stieg vom Pferd, ging auf Athelstan zu und versetzte ihm mit einer gepanzerten Faust einen Schlag in den Magen. Der Aufprall klang ekelhaft laut.

Athelstan klappte zusammen, viel zu benommen, um aufschreien zu können. Gilbert und Hugh zogen ihn wieder auf die Beine, und Walter schlug ihm ins Gesicht. Blut sprudelte ihm aus Mund und Nase. Eine der Zuschauerinnen, wahrscheinlich seine Frau, kreischte auf und warf sich schreiend auf Walter: »Halt! Laßt ihn los! Bringt ihn nicht um!«

Walter schubste sie beiseite. Zwei andere Frauen ergriffen sie und hielten sie zurück. Sie ließ nicht locker und wehrte sich noch immer. Die anderen Bauern sahen feindselig schweigend mit an, wie Walter Athelstan systematisch bis zur Bewußtlosigkeit zusammenschlug.

»Laßt ihn los«, sagte William schließlich.

Gilbert und Hugh gaben Athelstan frei. Er sackte zu Boden und rührte sich nicht. Die beiden Weiber ließen seine Frau los, die zu ihm hinüberrannte und sich schluchzend neben ihm auf den Boden kniete. Walter streifte die Handschuhe ab und wischte das Blut und die Fleischfetzen aus den Panzerketten.

William hatte bereits das Interesse an Athelstan verloren. Er ließ seinen Blick über das Dorf schweifen und bemerkte am Ufer des Baches einen offensichtlich neuen, zweistöckigen Bau. Er deutete mit dem Finger darauf und fragte Arthur: »Was ist das?«

»Ich habe es noch nie zuvor gesehen, Herr«, erwiderte Arthur beunruhigt.

William glaubte ihm nicht. »Das ist doch eine Wassermühle, oder?«

Arthur zuckte mit den Achseln, aber seine Gleichgültigkeit überzeugte William nicht. »Ich wüßte nicht, was sonst dort unten am Wasserlauf stehen sollte.«

Wie konnte er nur so anmaßend sein, nachdem er gerade mit eigenen Augen gesehen hatte, wie ein Bauer auf Williams Befehl halbtot geschlagen worden war? Am Rande der Verzweiflung fragte William: »Dürfen meine Leibeigenen ohne meine Erlaubnis Mühlen bauen?«

»Nein, Herr.«

»Und wißt Ihr auch, *warum* es verboten ist?«

»Damit sie ihr Getreide in die Mühlen ihres Herrn bringen und ihn dafür bezahlen, daß es dort gemahlen wird.«

»Und der Herr profitiert davon.«

»Jawohl, Herr.« Arthur sprach mit der gleichen Herablassung, mit der man einem Kind die simpelsten Dinge erklärt: »Aber wenn sie für den Bau einer Mühle eine Buße zahlen, nimmt der Herr ebensoviel ein.«

William fand seinen Ton zum Verrücktwerden. »Nein, er nimmt *nicht* ebensoviel ein. Das Bußgeld ist stets geringer als das, was die Bauern andernfalls zu zahlen hätten. Und deswegen bauen sie so gerne Mühlen. Und deswegen hätte mein Vater das nie zugelassen.« Ohne Arthur Gelegenheit zu einer Erwiderung zu lassen, versetzte er seinem Pferd einen Tritt und ritt zur Mühle hinüber. Seine Ritter folgten, und der kunterbunte Haufen der Dorfbewohner schloß sich ihnen an.

William stieg ab. Das Gebäude ließ nicht den geringsten Zweifel an dem Zweck, dem es diente. Unter dem Druck des schnell fließenden Wassers drehte sich ein großes Schaufelrad, das wiederum eine Achse in Bewegung setzte, die durch die Seitenwand der Mühle ins Innere führte. Eine solide Holzkonstruktion, die die Planung auf Dauer verriet. Wer auch immer die Mühle errichtet, hatte damit gerechnet, sie jahrelang ungestört betreiben zu können.

Der Müller stand draußen vor der offenen Tür und trug einen Ausdruck gekränkter Unschuld zur Schau. In dem Raum hinter ihm stapelten sich fein säuberlich die Getreidesäcke. William stieg vom Pferd. Der Müller verneigte sich höflich, aber lag da nicht eine Spur von Verachtung in seinem Blick? Wieder einmal wurde William von dem schmerzlichen Gefühl übermannt, daß diese Leute ihn für eine Null hielten, und sein eigenes Unvermögen, ihnen seinen Willen aufzuzwingen, machte ihn hilflos, so daß er den Müller zornig anbrüllte: »Was hast du dir dabei gedacht? Daß du damit ungeschoren davonkommst? Du hältst mich wohl für dumm?« Dann schlug er dem Mann ins Gesicht.

Der Müller stieß einen übertriebenen Schmerzensschrei aus und fiel unnötigerweise zu Boden.

William stieg über ihn hinweg und betrat die Mühle. Die Achse des Wasserrades war durch eine Reihe hölzerner Verzahnungen mit der Achse des Mühlsteins im oberen Stockwerk verbunden. Das gemahlene Getreide fiel durch eine Schütte auf die Tenne zu ebener Erde. Das Obergeschoß, welches das Gewicht des Mühlsteins zu tragen hatte, ruhte auf vier kräftigen, zweifellos ohne Williams Erlaubnis in seinem Wald geschlagenen Stämmen. Schlug man die weg, so brachte man das gesamte Gebäude zum Einstürzen.

William trat vor die Tür. Hugh Axe führte die Waffe, der er seinen Namen verdankte, an den Sattel geschnürt mit sich. »Gib mir deine Streitaxt«, sagte William. Er begab sich wieder in die Mühle und begann, die hölzernen Stützpfosten des Obergeschosses mit der Axt zu bearbeiten. Wenn ich hier fertig bin, dachte er mit grausamer Genugtuung, wird keiner mehr über mich lachen!

Walter kam herein und sah ihm zu. William hieb eine tiefe Kerbe in einen der Pfosten und hatte sich halb durch einen zweiten gearbeitet, als die Plattform, die darauf ruhte und das ungeheure Gewicht des Mühlsteins trug, zu beben begann. »Hol mir ein Seil«, sagte William, und Walter ging nach draußen.

So weit wie er es nur wagen konnte, hackte William in die beiden Pfosten, bis das Gebäude über ihm zusammenzubrechen drohte. Als Walter mit dem Seil kam, schlang William es um einen der Stämme, ging mit dem anderen Ende nach draußen und band es seinem Schlachtroß um den Hals.

Die Bauern verfolgten das Treiben in feindseligem Schweigen.

Kaum war das Seil vertäut, fragte William nach dem Müller.

Der trat, immer noch bemüht, den Eindruck eines unschuldigen Opfers zu erwecken, näher.

»Gervase, fessle ihn und bring ihn nach drinnen«, befahl William.

Der Müller machte prompt einen Fluchtversuch, doch Gilbert stellte ihm ein Bein und setzte sich auf ihn, während Gervase ihn mit Lederriemen an Händen und Füßen fesselte. Als die beiden Ritter ihn hochhoben, wehrte er sich und flehte um Gnade.

Einer der Dorfbewohner trat vor und sagte zu William: »Das könnt

Ihr nicht tun. Das ist Mord! Selbst ein Graf darf niemanden umbringen.«

William drohte ihm mit vor Wut bebendem Finger. »Wenn du dein Maul noch ein einziges Mal aufreißt, dann steck ich dich auch noch mit in die Mühle!«

Der Mann hielt seinem Blick noch einen Moment lang trotzig stand, besann sich dann jedoch und wandte sich ab.

Dann kamen die Ritter wieder aus der Mühle, und William führte das Pferd vorwärts, bis das Seil straff gespannt war, versetzte dem Tier einen Schlag auf das Hinterteil, und es legte sich ins Zeug.

Drinnen begann der Müller gellend zu schreien. Die Laute, die er ausstieß, ließen das Blut gefrieren: Der Mann wußte genau, daß er innerhalb weniger Minuten zermalmt wurde, und litt Todesqualen.

Das Pferd warf den Kopf hin und her und versuchte, das Seil um seinen Hals zu lockern. William brüllte das Tier an und versuchte, es mit Tritten zum Ziehen zu bewegen. »Legt euch ins Seil, Männer!« rief er seinen Rittern zu. Die vier ergriffen das straff gespannte Seil und halfen dem Pferd ziehen. Unter den Dorfbewohnern wurden Stimmen des Protests laut, doch niemand wagte einzugreifen. Arthur hielt sich abseits; er sah elend aus.

Die Schreie des Müllers wurden immer schriller. William stellte sich vor, von welch blindem Entsetzen der Mann in Erwartung seines schrecklichen Endes erfaßt sein mußte. Das ist die Rache der Hamleighs, dachte er, und keiner von diesen Bauern hier wird sie jemals wieder vergessen!

Die Stämme knarrten hörbar, bevor sie mit lautem Knall brachen. Das Pferd machte einen Satz nach vorn, und Williams Ritter ließen das Seil fahren. Eine Ecke des Daches sackte ein, und sämtliche Frauen brachen in Wehklagen aus. Die Holzwände der Mühle schienen zu erzittern; die Schreie des Müllers schraubten sich noch höher; unter gewaltigem Getöse stürzte das Obergeschoß ein, die Schreie verstummten, und der Boden bebte, als der Mühlstein donnernd auf der Dreschtenne landete. Die Wände barsten, das Dach brach ein, und im Handumdrehen war von der Mühle nichts geblieben als ein Haufen Feuerholz, der eine Leiche unter sich begrub.

Endlich fühlte William sich wieder einigermaßen wohl.

Er sah, wie einige Dörfler auf die Trümmer zustürzten und anfingen, fieberhaft darin herumzuwühlen. Falls sie hofften, den Müller lebend zu finden, so stand ihnen eine Enttäuschung bevor. Seine Leiche mußte einen gräßlichen Anblick bieten. Um so besser!

540

Als William sich umsah, bemerkte er das rotwangige Mädchen, das sich, um keine Aufmerksamkeit zu erregen, mit ihrem rotwangigen Kind im Hintergrund hielt. Ihm fiel wieder ein, daß der Mann mit dem schwarzen Bart – wahrscheinlich ihr Vater – eifrig darauf bedacht gewesen war, sie ihm aus den Augen zu schaffen. William beschloß, dieses Rätsel noch zu lösen, bevor er das Dorf wieder verließ. Er sah das Mädchen direkt an und winkte es zu sich herüber. In der Hoffnung, nicht sie sei gemeint, sondern jemand anders, drehte sie sich um. »Du«, sagte William. »Komm her.«

Der Mann mit dem schwarzen Bart sah sie und knurrte ungehalten.

»Wer ist dein Mann, Mädchen?« fragte William.

Der Vater antwortete: »Sie hat keinen –«

Aber es war zu spät, denn das Mädchen hatte bereits erwidert: »Edmund.«

»Du *bist* also verheiratet. Und wer ist dein Vater?«

»Ich«, sagte der bärtige Mann. »Theobald.«

William wandte sich an Arthur. »Ist Theobald ein freier Mann?«

»Er ist Leibeigener, Herr.«

»Und wenn die Tochter eines Leibeigenen heiratet, ist es da nicht das Recht des Herrn und Besitzers, sich in ihrer Hochzeitsnacht als erster an ihr gütlich zu tun?«

Arthur war entsetzt. »Aber Herr! Dieser barbarische Brauch ist in diesem Teil der Welt seit Menschengedenken nicht mehr ausgeübt worden!«

»Stimmt«, sagte William. »Der Vater zahlt statt dessen eine Buße. Wieviel hat Theobald bezahlt?«

»Er hat noch nicht bezahlt, Herr, aber –«

»Noch nicht bezahlt! Dabei hat sie schon ein feistes, rotbackiges Kind!«

Theobald ergriff das Wort: »Wir hatten nie das Geld, Herr, und sie war schwanger von Edmund und wollte unbedingt getraut werden; aber jetzt, da die Ernte eingebracht ist, können wir zahlen.«

William lächelte das Mädchen an. »Laß mich mal dein Kindchen sehen.«

Sie starrte ihn nur angstvoll an.

»Komm schon, gib's mir.«

So sehr sie ihn auch fürchtete, sie konnte sich nicht dazu durchringen, ihm ihr Kind auszuhändigen. William trat auf sie zu und nahm ihr das Kind behutsam ab. Ihre Augen weiteten sich vor Furcht, aber sie widersetzte sich nicht. Das Kind fing sofort an zu schreien. William hielt es einen Moment lang fest, dann packte er es mit einer Hand bei den Knöcheln und warf es, so hoch er konnte, blitzschnell in die Luft.

Das Mädchen schrie wie am Spieß und verfolgte das Kind mit den Augen.

Der Vater stürzte mit ausgestreckten Armen hinzu, um es wieder aufzufangen.

Noch während das Mädchen nach oben starrte, griff William nach ihrem Kleid und riß es auf. Ihr Leib war rosig und rund.

Der Vater hatte den Säugling sicher aufgefangen, und das Mädchen wandte sich zur Flucht, doch William fing sie ab und warf sie zu Boden.

Der Vater reichte das Kind an eine Frau weiter und drehte sich zu William um. »Da ich in der Hochzeitsnacht nicht zu meinem Recht gekommen bin«, verkündete William, »und da auch keine Strafe gezahlt worden ist, nehme ich mir jetzt, was mir zusteht.«

Der Vater stürzte sich auf ihn.

William zog sein Schwert.

Der Vater blieb wie angewurzelt stehen.

William musterte die junge Frau, die vor ihm auf dem Boden lag und versuchte, ihre Blöße mit den Händen zu bedecken. Ihre Furcht erregte ihn. »Und wenn ich mit ihr fertig bin, können meine Ritter sie haben«, erklärte er mit einem selbstzufriedenen Lächeln.

In nur drei Jahren hatte sich Kingsbridge so sehr verändert, daß es kaum wiederzuerkennen war.

Seit jenem Pfingstsonntag, da Philip mit seinem Heer von freiwilligen Helfern Bischof Waleran Bigod einen Strich durch die Rechnung gemacht hatte, war William nicht mehr hier gewesen. Damals hatte es nicht mehr als vierzig oder fünfzig Häuser gegeben, von denen sich die meisten dicht um das Klostertor drängten und nur einzelne den schlammigen Pfad säumten, der den Hügel hinunter zur Brücke führte. Nun, da William sich durch die wogenden Felder dem Dorf näherte, zählte er mindestens dreimal so viele. Die Häuser wirkten wie braune Fransen an der grauen Klostermauer und beanspruchten das gesamte Areal zwischen Priorei und Fluß. Auch auf dem Prioreigelände waren neue Steingebäude entstanden, und die Mauern der Kirche schienen rasch in die Höhe zu wachsen. Am Flußufer gab es zwei neue Anlegeplätze. Aus Kingsbridge war eine richtige Stadt geworden.

Das äußere Erscheinungsbild dieser Ortschaft nährte einen Verdacht in ihm, der seit seiner Rückkehr aus dem Krieg immer stärker geworden war. Auf seiner Rundreise durch die Grafschaft, auf der er rückständige Pachten eingetrieben und unbotmäßige Leibeigene terrorisiert hatte, war immer wieder der Name Kingsbridge gefallen. Junge Männer ohne Landbesitz fanden dort Arbeit; wohlhabende Familien schickten ihre Söhne in der Priorei zur Schule; Kleinbauern verkauften den Bauarbeitern Eier und Käse; und alle Welt begab sich, wenn möglich, an jedem Heiligentag nach Kingsbridge, obwohl die Kathedrale noch gar nicht stand. Heute war ein solcher Heiligentag – Michaeli – der dieses Jahr auf einen Sonntag fiel. Das Reisewetter war gut an diesem milden Frühherbstmorgen, so daß mit einer großen Menschenmenge zu rechnen war. William wollte herausfinden, was sie nach Kingsbridge zog.

Er ritt in Begleitung seiner fünf Gefolgsleute, die auf den Dörfern erstklassige Arbeit geleistet hatten. Die Nachricht von Williams Inspektion hatte sich wie ein Lauffeuer verbreitet, und nach wenigen Tagen wußten die Leute, was sie von ihm zu erwarten hatten. Sobald er im Anzug war, schickten sie alle Kinder und jungen Frauen in die Wälder. William machte es Spaß, den Leuten Angst einzujagen: das wies sie gebührend in ihre Schranken. Und mittlerweile wußten sie nur zu gut, was es hieß, daß er das Sagen hatte!

Als sie sich der Stadt näherten, spornte William sein Pferd zum Trab an, und sein Gefolge setzte ihm nach. Mit Volltempo irgendwo einzureiten, machte immer großen Eindruck auf die Leute, die sich oft nur mit einem Satz zur Seite vor den gewaltigen Schlachtrössern retten konnten oder nach allen Seiten in die Felder flüchteten.

Mit ohrenbetäubendem Hufgetrappel ging es über die Holzbrücke, vorbei am Mauthaus, das sie samt Zöllner links liegenließen, doch versperrte ihnen ein mit Kalkfässern beladener, von zwei riesigen, langsam dahintrottenden Ochsen gezogener Karren den Weg, so daß sie ihre Pferde heftig am Zügel nehmen mußten.

Im Schritt ging es nun hinter dem Ochsenkarren her, und William hatte Muße, sich umzusehen. Neue, eiligst gebaute Häuser füllten die Lücken zwischen den alten Gebäuden. Er entdeckte eine Garküche, ein Wirtshaus, eine Schmiede und einen Schuster. Der sichtliche Wohlstand ließ William vor Neid erblassen.

Allerdings war kaum jemand auf der Straße zu sehen. Vielleicht waren sie alle oben in der Priorei.

Gefolgt von seinen Rittern, ritt er hinter dem Ochsenkarren durch das Klostertor – ganz und gar kein Einzug, wie William ihn liebte! Einen Moment lang befürchtete er schon heftig, die Leute hätten ihn dabei beobachtet und lachten ihn nun aus, aber glücklicherweise sah niemand zu ihnen her.

Im Gegensatz zur menschenleeren Stadt außerhalb der Mauern ging es auf dem Klostergelände zu wie in einem Bienenstock.

William zügelte sein Pferd und sah sich prüfend um. Die vielen Menschen und das rege Treiben verwirrten ihn zunächst, doch dann erkannte er, daß sich das Bild aus drei Teilen zusammensetzte.

In unmittelbarer Nähe am Westende des Klostergeländes fand ein Markt statt. Die Stände waren in ordentlichen Reihen aufgebaut, die von Norden nach Süden verliefen und zwischen denen sich mehrere hundert Leute tummelten, die Nahrung und Getränke, Hüte und Schuhe, Messer, Gürtel, Entenküken, Welpen, Töpfe, Ohrringe, Wolle, Garn, Seil und Dutzende anderer Gebrauchs- und Luxusgüter einkauften. Der Markt lief offensichtlich bestens, und die Penny-, Halb- und Viertelpennystücke, die ihre Besitzer wechselten, mußten ein erklecklichen Sümmchen ergeben.

Kein Wunder, dachte William erbittert, daß der Markt in Shiring auf dem absteigenden Ast ist, wenn die Konkurrenz in Kingsbridge dermaßen floriert! Die Gebühren der Standbesitzer, die Zölle für die Lieferanten und die Verkaufssteuern, die eigentlich dem Grafen von Shiring zufließen sollten, füllten statt dessen die Schatztruhen der Priorei von Kingsbridge.

Aber ein Markt bedurfte der Genehmigung des Königs, und William war sicher, daß Prior Philip keine hatte. Wahrscheinlich plante er, sich – wie der Müller in Northbrook – erst dann darum zu bemühen, wenn man ihm auf die Schliche gekommen war. Leider war es in Philips Fall für William nicht so einfach, ihm eine Lektion zu erteilen.

Hinter dem Markt gab es eine Ruhezone. Im Anschluß an den Kreuzgang, wo sich einst die Vierung der alten Kirche befunden hatte, war ein Altar mit einem Baldachin darüber errichtet worden. Vor dem Altar stand ein weißhaariger Mönch und las aus einem Buch, dahinter die Mönche, säuberlich in Reihen aufgestellt, und sangen Kirchenlieder, deren Klänge jedoch das Treiben auf dem Marktplatz schluckte. Die versammelte Gemeinde war sehr klein. Wahrscheinlich die Non der Mönche, dachte William. Zum Michaelisgottesdienst würde jede Arbeit ruhen und selbstverständlich auch das Treiben auf dem Markt eingestellt.

Am anderen Ende des Klosterhofs wurde der Ostteil der Kathedrale gebaut. Dort gibt Prior Philip das, was er am Markttag abgesahnt hat, wieder aus, dachte William ungehalten. Die Wände waren dreißig oder vierzig Fuß hoch gediehen und ließen bereits die Umrisse der Fenster und Arkadenbogen erkennen. Überall wimmelte es von Arbeitern. William fand, sie sähen ein wenig merkwürdig aus, und kam schließlich darauf, daß es an ihrer bunten Kleidung lag. Es handelte sich natürlich nicht um die regulären, bezahlten Arbeiter, die heute einen freien Tag hatten; diese Leute waren freiwillige Helfer.

Er hatte nicht damit gerechnet, daß sie *so* zahlreich wären – Hunderte von Männern und Frauen, die Steine schleppten, Holz spalteten, Fässer rollten und schwere Karrenladungen Sand vom Fluß heraufholten. Und sie alle arbeiteten unentgeltlich, nur für die Vergebung ihrer Sünden!

Dieser gerissene Prior hat das hervorragend eingefädelt, stellte William neidisch fest. Denn die Menschen, die zur Arbeit am Dom kamen, gaben außerdem noch Geld auf dem Markt aus, und die Besucher des Marktes ließen sich ihrem Seelenheil zuliebe gewiß nicht wegen ein paar Stunden Arbeit lumpen. So wusch eine Hand die andere.

Er setzte sein Pferd in Bewegung und ritt über den Kirchacker zur Baustelle, um sich dort genauer umzusehen.

Die acht massiven Säulen des Bogengangs standen sich in Zweierpaaren über die Gesamtlänge der Baustelle hinweg gegenüber. Aus der Entfernung hatte William gemeint, er könne bereits die Rundbogen sehen, die einen Pfeiler mit dem nächsten verbanden, aber bei näherer Betrachtung mußte er feststellen, daß sie noch gar nicht gebaut worden waren – das, was er dafür gehalten hatte, waren hölzerne, wie Rundbogen geformte Hilfsgerüste, auf denen die Steine ruhten, solange gebaut wurde und der Mörtel noch naß war. Das Hilfsgerüst stand nicht auf dem Boden, sondern lag auf den hervorspringenden Simsen der Kapitelle am oberen Ende der Säulen auf.

Parallel zum Bogengang wurden die Außenwände der Seitenschiffe mit regelmäßigen Aussparungen für die Fenster hochgezogen. Strebepfeiler ragten auf halbem Wege zwischen je zwei Fensteröffnungen aus der Wand. William betrachtete die offenen Enden der unvollendeten Wände: Sie bestanden nicht aus behauenen Steinen, sondern waren Doppelwände mit einem Hohlraum dazwischen, der anscheinend mit Bruchsteinen und Mörtel ausgefüllt wurde.

Das Gerüst bestand aus starken, mit Seilen zusammengebundenen Pfosten, die Laufbrücken aus biegsamen jungen Bäumchen und geflochtenem Schilf trugen.

Das alles muß eine schöne Stange Geld gekostet haben, stellte William insgeheim fest.

Seine Mannen im Gefolge, ritt er außen um den Altarraum herum. Dort schmiegten sich Holzhütten mit Pultdächern – die Werkstätten und Logen der Handwerker – an die Wände. Die meisten davon waren verschlossen, denn am heutigen Tag arbeiteten weder die Mauer an ihren Wänden noch die Zimmerleute an ihren Hilfsgerüsten. Die aufsichtführenden Handwerker jedoch – die Meister unter den Steinmetzen und Zimmerleuten – befehligten die freiwilligen Arbeitskräfte und zeigten ihnen, wo die vom Flußufer heraufgetragenen Steine und Stämme, der Sand und der Kalk zu lagern waren.

William lenkte sein Pferd um den Ostteil der Kirche gen Süden, wo ihm der Weg durch das Klostergebäude versperrt wurde. Er drehte um und konnte sich gar nicht genug über die Gerissenheit von Prior Philip wundern, der seine Meister an einem Sonntag zur Arbeit anhielt und seine Hilfskräfte umsonst bekam.

Das Gesehene hatte William nachdenklich gemacht, und nun schien ihm mehr als klar zu sein, daß niemand anders als Prior Philip die Schuld am Niedergang der Grafschaft Shiring trug. Die Bauernhöfe verloren ihre jungen Männer an die Baustelle, und Shiring, das Juwel der Grafschaft, wurde vom Aufschwung der neuen Stadt Kingsbridge in den Schatten gestellt. Die Einwohner zahlten ihre Mieten nicht an William, sondern an Philip, und die Käufer und Verkäufer auf dem Markt füllten nicht die Truhen der Grafschaft, sondern die der Priorei. Und überdies standen Philip das Holz, die Schafe und der Steinbruch zur Verfügung, die dereinst den Reichtum des Grafen gemehrt hatten.

William ritt mit seinen Männern quer über das Gelände zum Marktplatz zurück, den er sich genauer ansehen wollte. Er trieb sein Pferd in die Menge, kam jedoch nur schrittweise voran. Hier stoben die Leute nicht ängstlich zur Seite. Wurden sie von seinem Pferd geschubst, so blickten sie nicht furchtsam, sondern höchstens ungehalten oder gar verärgert zu ihm auf; und niemand überschlug sich, ihm Platz zu machen, sondern alle nahmen sich Zeit dafür und ließen ihn ihre Geringschätzung merken. Hier hatte niemand vor ihm Angst. Das beunruhigte ihn zutiefst: Furchtlose Menschen waren unberechenbar.

Er ritt eine Reihe von Ständen ab, dann die nächste wieder herauf, stets seine Ritter hinter sich. Das Schneckentempo der Menschenmenge machte ihn übellaunig. Zu Fuß wäre er schneller vorangekommen, aber bei diesem dreisten Volk von Kingsbridge konnte man nie wissen: Womöglich schreckte es nicht einmal davor zurück, ihn anzurempeln.

Er war die Seitenreihe halb heruntergeritten, als er Aliena erblickte.

Abrupt zügelte er sein Pferd und starrte sie wie gebannt an.

Das war nicht mehr das magere, überanstrengte und verängstigte Mädchen mit Holzschuhen an den Füßen, dem er hier am Pfingstsonntag vor drei Jahren begegnet war. Ihr Gesicht, damals angespannt und abgezehrt, war voller geworden, und sie wirkte glücklich und gesund. Ihre dunklen Augen blitzten vor guter Laune, und bei jeder Kopfbewegung fielen ihr die dichten Locken ins Gesicht.

Sie war so schön, daß William vor Begierde ganz schwindelig wurde.

Sie trug ein scharlachrotes, reich besticktes Gewand, und an ihren ausdrucksvollen Händen funkelten mehrere Ringe. Ihr zur Seite stand eine ältere Frau, wahrscheinlich eine Dienstmagd. Geld wie Heu, hatte Mutter gesagt; kein Wunder, daß es Richard mit seinen vorzüglichen Waffen zum Knappen gebracht und sich dem Heer König Stephans angeschlossen hatte. Der Teufel sollte sie holen! Wie hatte es dieses bettelarme, einflußlose Mädchen nur so weit bringen können?

Sie verweilte an einem Marktstand mit beinernen Nadeln, Seidengarn, hölzernen Fingerhüten und anderen Nähutensilien und unterhielt sich angeregt mit dem Verkäufer, einem stämmigen, dunkelhaarigen Juden. Ihre Haltung war respekteinflößend, sie hatte sich das sichere Auftreten, das sie als Tochter eines Grafen auszeichnete, erneut angeeignet.

Sie sah viel älter aus. Natürlich, sie war älter geworden. Er selbst war inzwischen vierundzwanzig, sie mußte also einundzwanzig sein. Aber sie wirkte älter. Keine Spur von Kindlichkeit mehr. Sie war eine erwachsene Frau.

Sie sah auf, und ihre Blicke kreuzten sich.

Das letzte Mal, als sie seiner ansichtig wurde, war sie vor Scham errötet und davongelaufen. Diesmal behauptete sie ihre Stellung und starrte zurück.

Er versuchte es mit einem wissenden Lächeln.

Ein Ausdruck tödlicher Verachtung machte sich auf ihrem Gesicht breit.

William spürte, wie er knallrot anlief. Sie war so hochmütig wie eh und je, verachtete ihn mit der gleichen Intensität wie vor fünf Jahren. Er hatte sie erniedrigt und entehrt, und trotzdem flößte er ihr keine Furcht mehr ein. Am liebsten hätte er ihr ins Gesicht gesagt, daß er jederzeit wieder ebenso mit ihr umspringen könne; über die Köpfe der Menschenmenge hinweg wollte er es ihr nicht zurufen. Unter ihrem unbeugsamen Blick kam er sich klein und unbedeutend vor. Vergebens bemühte er sich um ein höhnisches Lächeln; er brachte nur eine dümmliche Grimasse zustande, und das Wissen darum ließ ihn sich wie ein Tölpel fühlen. Peinlich berührt wendete er sein Pferd und trieb es an, doch die Menschenmenge hinderte ihn, so daß er sich im Schneckentempo entfernte und Alienas vernichtenden Blick noch lange im Nacken spürte.

Als er den Marktplatz endlich hinter sich gelassen hatte, sah er sich Prior Philip gegenüber.

Der kleine Waliser hatte die Arme in die Hüften gestemmt und das Kinn kampflustig vorgeschoben. William fiel auf, daß er nicht mehr so mager wie ehedem und daß sein spärliches Haar frühzeitig ergraut war. Auch sah er nicht mehr aus, als wäre er zu jung für seine Stellung. In seinen blauen Augen blitzte helle Wut. »Lord William!« rief er herausfordernd.

William riß sich in Gedanken von Aliena los und erinnerte sich daran, daß er ein Hühnchen mit Philip zu rupfen hatte. »Ich bin froh, Euch zu begegnen, Prior.«

»Ich ebenfalls«, gab Philip ärgerlich zurück, obwohl der Anflug eines unsicheren Stirnrunzelns über sein Gesicht huschte.

»Ihr haltet hier einen Markt ab!« beschuldigte William ihn.

»Na und?«

»Ich glaube nicht, daß König Stephan Kingsbridge je die Erlaubnis dazu gegeben hat. Noch einer seiner Vorgänger, soweit ich weiß.«

»Was erlaubt Ihr Euch?« sagte Philip.

»Ich oder sonstwer –«

»Ihr!« rief Philip und schnitt ihm das Wort ab. »Was fällt Euch eigentlich ein, hier aufzukreuzen und von einer Genehmigung zu faseln – Ihr, der Ihr in den vergangenen vier Wochen über das Land gefegt seid und Euch der Brandstiftung, des Diebstahls, der Vergewaltigung und mindestens eines Mordes schuldig gemacht habt?!«

»Das hat überhaupt nichts mit –«

»Wie könnt Ihr es wagen, in ein Kloster zu kommen und von einer Genehmigung zu faseln!« brüllte Philip. Er trat einen Schritt vor und drohte William mit dem Finger, worauf Williams Pferd nervös zur Seite tänzelte. Philips Stimme war von enormer Tragweite, so daß es William nicht gelang, ihn zu unterbrechen. Inzwischen hatte sich eine

Ansammlung von Mönchen, freiwilligen Helfern und Marktbesuchern eingefunden, um der Auseinandersetzung beizuwohnen. Philip war nicht zu halten: »Nach allem, was Ihr verbrochen habt, gibt es für Euch nur noch eines zu sagen: ›Vater, ich habe gesündigt!‹ Auf den Knien solltet Ihr liegen in diesem Kloster! Um Vergebung solltet Ihr beten, wenn Ihr dem ewigen Feuer der Hölle entrinnen wollt!«

William wurde leichenblaß. Das Wort »Hölle« flößte ihm jedesmal panische Angst ein. Verzweifelt versuchte er, Philips Redefluß zu unterbrechen, indem er rief: »Und was ist mit Eurem Markt? Und was ist mit Eurem Markt?«

Philip hörte ihn kaum. Er schäumte vor Zorn. »Bittet um Verzeihung für Eure Schandtaten!« rief er. »Auf die Knie mit Euch! Auf die Knie, wenn Ihr nicht in der Hölle brennen wollt!«

Die Angst hatte William schon beinahe überzeugt, er werde unweigerlich im Höllenfeuer enden, wenn er nicht sofort vor Philip auf die Knie fiel und betete. Er wußte, daß er längst hätte beichten sollen, denn er hatte nicht nur auf seinem Ritt durch die Grafschaft gesündigt, sondern obendrein auch noch im Krieg viele Menschen erschlagen. Wenn er nun starb, bevor er seine Sünden bekannt hatte? Bei dem Gedanken an die ewigen Flammen der Hölle und an die Teufel mit ihren scharfen Messern wurde ihm ganz schwach zumute.

Philip kam direkt auf ihn zu, wies mit dem Finger auf ihn und schrie: »Auf die Knie mit Euch!«

William lenkte sein Pferd rückwärts. Sein verzweifelter Blick irrte nach allen Seiten, doch die Menge schnürte ihn ein. Seine Ritter hinter ihm sahen höchst verdutzt drein, unschlüssig, wie auf die geistlichen Drohungen eines unbewaffneten Mönches zu reagieren war. William wurde es zuviel – er hatte jetzt genug Erniedrigungen eingesteckt! Erst Aliena, und nun dies! Heftig zerrte er an den Zügeln, und sein riesiges Schlachtroß bäumte sich gefährlich auf. Vor seinen mächtigen Hufen teilte sich die Menge. Sobald es mit den Vorderhufen wieder den Boden berührte, versetzte William seinem Pferd einen großen Tritt in die Flanken, daß es einen Satz nach vorn machte. Zuschauer stoben auseinander. William trat noch einmal zu, und das Tier fiel in leichten Trab. Brennend rot vor Scham ergriff er die Flucht durch das Klostertor, gefolgt von seinen Rittern, wie eine Meute zähnefletschender Hunde, die ein altes Weib mit dem Besen verjagt.

Zitternd vor Angst bekannte William seine Sünden auf dem kalten Steinfußboden der kleinen Kapelle im Bischofspalast. Schweigend und vor Ekel wie erstarrt hörte sich Bischof Waleran die Liste der Morde, Überfälle und Vergewaltigungen an, die William sich hatte zuschulden kommen lassen. Sogar während seiner Beichte empfand William nichts als Verachtung für den hochnäsigen Bischof mit den reinweißen, über der Brust gefalteten Händen und den durchscheinend hellen, leicht geblähten Nasenlöchern, die zu sagen schienen, ein schlechter Geruch läge in der staubigen Luft. Es bereitete William unendliche Qualen, Waleran um die Vergebung seiner Sünden bitten zu müssen, aber sie wogen zu schwer, als daß ein gewöhnlicher Priester ihm Absolution hätte erteilen können. So lag er also, von Furcht geplagt, auf den Knien, während Waleran ihm auftrug, in der Kapelle von Earlscastle ein ewiges Licht aufzustellen, und ihm erst danach mitteilte, seine Sünden seien vergeben.

Langsam wie Nebel wich die Angst von ihm.

Sie verließen die Kapelle und begaben sich in die rauchgeschwängerte große Halle, wo sie vor dem Kamin Platz nahmen. Der Herbst ging allmählich in den Winter über, und es war kalt in dem großen Steinhaus. Eine Küchenhilfe servierte ihnen warmes, mit Honig und Ingwer zubereitetes Gewürzbrot. William fing an, sich wieder wohlzufühlen.

Dann fiel ihm Richard ein, Bartholomäus' Sohn, der sich ebenfalls um die Grafschaft bewarb, während er, William, zu arm war, um ein großes Heer auf die Beine zu stellen, mit dem er dem König imponieren konnte. Zwar hatte er im Laufe des letzten Monats eine Menge Geld eingetrieben, aber immer noch nicht genug. Er seufzte und sagte: »Dieser verfluchte Mönch saugt der Grafschaft Shiring das Blut aus.«

Waleran griff mit blassen, klauenähnlichen Fingern nach einem Stück Brot. »Ich habe mich schon gefragt, wie lange Ihr wohl brauchen werdet, um zu diesem Schluß zu kommen.«

Natürlich – Waleran hatte sich schon längst seine eigene Meinung gebildet. Wenn er doch nur nicht so überheblich wäre! Gerne unterhielt William sich mit ihm nicht. Aber er wollte von ihm Gewißheit über eine rechtliche Frage haben. »Der König hat doch Kingsbridge nie die Marktrechte erteilt, oder?«

»Soweit ich weiß, gewiß nicht.«

»Dann verstößt Philip gegen das Gesetz.«

Waleran zuckte die knochigen, in schwarzes Tuch gehüllten Schultern. »Wenn Ihr so wollt, ja.«

Waleran schien die Sache nicht sonderlich zu bewegen, aber William ließ nicht locker. »Man sollte ihm Einhalt gebieten.«

Waleran verzog angewidert die Lippen. »Ihr werdet mit ihm kaum wie mit einem Leibeigenen umspringen können, der seine Tochter ohne Eure Erlaubnis verheiratet hat.«

William lief rot an: Waleran spielte auf eine seiner Sünden an, die er ihm eben erst gebeichtet hatte. »Wie kann man ihm sonst beikommen?«

Waleran dachte nach. »Das Marktrecht ist ein Vorrecht des Königs. Wären die Zeiten friedlicher, würde er sich vermutlich selbst darum kümmern.«

William lachte höhnisch auf. Trotz all seiner Klugheit kannte Waleran den König nicht halb so gut wie er selbst.

»Nicht einmal in Friedenszeiten könnte ich einen Dank von ihm erwarten, wenn ich mich über einen nicht genehmigten Markt beschwere.«

»Nun, dann ist eben sein hiesiger Stellvertreter, also der Vogt von Shiring, dafür zuständig.«

»Was kann der denn ausrichten?«

»Er könnte vor dem Grafschaftsgericht eine Verfügung gegen die Priorei erwirken.«

William schüttelte den Kopf. »Damit ist mir überhaupt nicht gedient. Das liefe lediglich darauf hinaus, daß das Gericht eine Geldstrafe verhängt, die die Priorei zahlt – und der Markt ginge trotzdem weiter. Das käme ja beinahe einer Genehmigung gleich.«

»Schade nur, daß es keinen vernünftigen Grund gibt, Kingsbridge seinen Markt zu verwehren.«

»Selbstverständlich gibt es einen!« schnappte William ungehalten zurück. »Er nimmt schließlich dem Markt in Shiring die Kunden weg.«

»Aber Shiring ist eine Tagesreise von Kingsbridge entfernt.«

»Die Leute nehmen auch einen langen Anweg in Kauf.«

Waleran zuckte wieder die Schultern und William wurde klar, daß er das jedesmal dann tat, wenn er abweichender Meinung war. »Es heißt«, sagte Waleran, »daß der Mensch einen Dritteltag auf den Anmarsch, einen Dritteltag auf den Markt selbst und das letzte Drittel auf den Heimweg verwendet. Daraus folgt, daß ein Markt ein Einzugsgebiet von sieben Meilen hat, was einem Fußmarsch von einem Dritteltag entspricht. Sobald zwei Märkte mehr als vierzehn Meilen voneinander entfernt liegen, überschneiden sich ihre Einzugsgebiete also nicht. Zwischen Shiring und Kingsbridge liegen zwanzig Meilen. Dem Marktregal zufolge hätte Kingsbridge durchaus Anspruch auf einen eigenen Markt, und der König müßte also die Erlaubnis dazu erteilen.«

»Der König tut, was ihm paßt«, polterte William, war aber doch unsicher geworden. Von diesem Marktrecht hörte er heute zum erstenmal. Es schien ihm nur allzu geeignet, Prior Philips Stellung noch zu festigen.

»Egal«, meinte Waleran, »wir haben es ohnehin nicht mit dem König, sondern mit dem Vogt zu tun.« Er runzelte die Stirn. »Der Vogt könnte der Priorei befehlen, keinen Markt mehr ohne Genehmigung abzuhalten.«

»Reine Zeitverschwendung«, schnaubte William verächtlich. »Wer hält sich schon an eine Anordnung, der nicht mit einer Drohung Nachdruck verliehen wird?«

»Philip möglicherweise.«

Das konnte William nicht glauben. »Wieso sollte er?«

Ein hämisches Lächeln umspielte Walerans blutleere Lippen. »Ich bin nicht sicher, daß ich es Euch erklären kann«, sagte er. »Aber Philip glaubt, daß das Gesetz König sein sollte.«

»Blödsinn«, sagte William ungeduldig. »Der König ist König.«

»Ich sagte doch, daß Ihr es nicht verstehen würdet.«

Walerans Besserwisserei machte William rasend. Er erhob sich und trat ans Fenster. Auf dem nahe gelegenen Hügel konnte er die Erdarbeiten ausmachen, die Waleran vor vier Jahren für den Bau seiner Burg in Auftrag gegeben hatte. Waleran hatte gehofft, ihn aus dem Einkommen aus der Grafschaft Shiring bestreiten zu können, doch Philip hatte ihm einen Strich durch die Rechnung gemacht; mittlerweile waren die Wälle mit Gras überwachsen und der trockene Graben mit Brombeersträuchern überwuchert. William entsann sich, daß Waleran gehofft hatte, für seinen Bau den Steinbruch des Grafen von Shiring in Anspruch nehmen zu können. Jetzt verfügte Philip über den Steinbruch. William sprach den nächsten Gedanken aus: »Wenn ich meinen Steinbruch noch hätte, könnte ich ihn als Sicherheit beleihen und ohne weiteres Geld zur Aufstellung eines Heeres bekommen.«

»Warum holt Ihr ihn Euch dann nicht zurück?« fragte Waleran.

William schüttelte den Kopf. »Das habe ich bereits versucht.«

»Und Philip hat Euch ein Schnippchen geschlagen. Aber jetzt sind dort keine Mönche mehr. Ihr könntet ein paar Männer ausschicken und die Steinklopfer vor die Tür setzen lassen.«

»Und wie soll ich Philip davon abhalten, daß er sich auf die gleiche Weise wie letztes Mal wieder dort einnistet?«

»Indem Ihr einen hohen Zaun um den Steinbruch zieht und ihn ständig bewachen laßt.«

Das ist die Lösung! dachte William eifrig. Damit wäre ich auf einen Schlag alle meine Sorgen los! Aber was mochte Waleran zu diesem Vorschlag bewogen haben? Mutter hatte ihn vor der Skrupellosigkeit des Bischofs gewarnt. »Es gibt nur eines, was du über Waleran Bigod wissen mußt«, hatte Mutter gesagt. »Er tut nichts, aber auch gar nichts, was er nicht vorher aufs gründlichste erwogen hätte. Bei ihm gibt es nichts Überhastetes oder Sorgloses, keinen Zufall, nichts Überflüssiges. Vor allem aber kennt er keine Großzügigkeit.« Doch Waleran haßte Philip, und er hatte geschworen, ihn am Bau der Kathedrale zu hindern. Wenn das kein ausreichender Beweggrund war!

William musterte Waleran nachdenklich. Er kam nicht mehr so recht voran. Er war schon in jungen Jahren Bischof geworden, aber Kingsbridge war eine unbedeutende und verarmte Diözese, und Waleran hatte sie gewiß nur als Trittbrett für Höheres betrachtet. Statt dessen war es der Prior, der es zu Reichtum und Ansehen brachte. Waleran stand ebenso im Schatten Philips wie er selbst. Sie hatten beide allen Grund, seinen Untergang herbeizuwünschen.

Wieder einmal kam William zu dem Entschluß, seine Abneigung gegen Waleran zugunsten seiner eigenen langfristigen Pläne hintanzustellen.

»In Ordnung«, sagte er. »Es könnte klappen. Aber was ist, wenn Philip sich beim König beschwert?«

»Dann sagt Ihr, es sei die Vergeltung für den ungenehmigten Markt«, antwortete Waleran.

William nickte. »Mir ist jede Ausrede recht«, sagte er, »solange ich nur mit einer genügend großen Armee wieder in den Krieg ziehen kann.«

Walerans Augen glitzerten boshaft. »Wenn mich mein Gefühl nicht trügt, so kann Philip seine Kathedrale nicht bauen, wenn er die Steine zum gängigen Marktpreis einkaufen muß. Und sobald die Bauarbeiten erst einmal eingestellt werden, geht es mit Kingsbridge bergab. Damit wäret Ihr alle Eure Sorgen auf einen Schlag los, William.«

William stand nicht der Sinn nach Dankbarkeitsbezeugungen. »Ihr haßt Philip aus tiefster Seele, nicht wahr?«

»Er steht mir im Wege«, sagte Waleran beiläufig, aber William hatte einen Moment lang Einblick genommen in die unverhohlene Grausamkeit, die sich hinter der kühlen, berechnenden Fassade des Bischofs verbarg.

William wandte sich wieder praktischen Erwägungen zu. »Alles in allem dürften es dreißig Steinbrecher sein, einige mit Frau und Kindern«, sagte er.

»Ja, und?«

»Es könnte ein Blutvergießen geben.«

Waleran hob die schwarzen Augenbrauen. »Tatsächlich?« meinte er. »Nun, dann werde ich Euch eben Absolution erteilen müssen.«

In der Nacht brachen sie auf, denn sie wollten ihr Ziel im Morgengrauen erreichen. Die brennenden Fackeln, die sie mitführten, ließen ihre Pferde scheuen. Außer Walter und den vier Rittern nahm William noch sechs Bewaffnete mit. Die Nachhut bildete ein Dutzend Bauern, die den Graben ausheben und den Zaun errichten sollten.

William war ein entschiedener Verfechter generalstabsmäßiger Planung – und daher samt seinen Mannen auch so nützlich für König Stephan –, doch diesmal hatte er ausnahmsweise keinen Schlachtplan. Sein Vorhaben war derart banal, daß er jegliche Vorbereitung, die auch nur entfernt an eine echte Schlacht denken ließ, als unter seiner Würde empfand. Ein paar Steinklopfer mit ihren Angehörigen hatten ihm nicht viel entgegenzusetzen; und ihr Anführer – hieß er Otto? Ja, richtig, Otto Blackface – hatte sich damals, als Tom Builder erstmals mit seinen Männern zum Steinbruch kam, ohnehin geweigert zu kämpfen.

Ein empfindlich kühler Dezembermorgen brach an, und der Nebel hing in Fetzen von den Bäumen wie armer Leute Wäsche. William mochte diese Jahreszeit nicht: Morgens war es kalt, abends früh dunkel und in der Burg stets feucht; zu oft bekam man gepökeltes Fleisch und gesalzenen Fisch vorgesetzt. Mutter war schlechter Laune, das Gesinde mürrisch und seine Ritter wurden streitsüchtig. Dieses kleine Gefecht würde ihnen guttun. Ihm selbst übrigens auch: Er hatte bereits alles in die Wege geleitet, um von den Juden in London zweihundert Pfund auf den Steinbruch zu leihen. Noch bevor dieser Tag zur Neige ginge, hatte er für die Zukunft ausgesorgt.

Sie waren noch etwa eine Meile vom Steinbruch entfernt, als William anhielt und zwei Männer bestimmte, die er zu Fuß vorausschickte. »Ihr müßt damit rechnen, auf einen Wachposten oder auf Hunde zu stoßen«, schärfte er ihnen ein. »Haltet Pfeil und Bogen schußbereit.«

Kurz darauf beschrieb die Straße einen Bogen nach links und endete abrupt vor dem steilen Abhang eines verstümmelten Hügels. Dies war der Steinbruch. Nichts regte sich. Am Straßenrand hielten Williams Männer einen verängstigten Jungen fest – wahrscheinlich ein Lehrling, der Wache geschoben hatte –, zu dessen Füßen ein Hund mit einem Pfeil im Genick verblutete.

Das Überfallkommando schloß zur Vorhut auf, ohne noch besonders auf Lautlosigkeit zu achten. William zügelte sein Pferd und sah sich um. Ein Großteil des Hügels war seit seinem letzten Besuch verschwunden. Hügelauf reihte sich Gerüst an Gerüst bis in die entlegensten Ecken und hinab in eine tiefe, am Fuß des Hügels ausgehobene Grube. Unweit der Straße stapelten sich Steinquader unterschiedlicher Größe und Form, daneben standen, beladen und abfahrbereit, zwei robuste Holzkarren mit riesigen Rädern.

Weit und breit war alles mit grauem Staub überzogen, selbst Büsche und Bäume. Ein großes Stück Wald war gerodet worden – *Mein Wald!* dachte William erbittert –, und es gab zehn oder zwölf Holzhäuser, manche mit Gemüsegärtchen und eins sogar mit einem Schweinekoben. Es war ein richtiges kleines Dorf.

Der Wachposten hatte wahrscheinlich geschlafen – und sein Hund ebenfalls. William wandte sich ihm zu. »Wie viele Männer gibt es hier, Bursche?«

Der Junge sah ihm furchtsam, doch beherzt ins Gesicht. »Ihr seid Lord William, nicht wahr?«

»Beantworte meine Frage, Junge, sonst nehme ich dieses Schwert und mach' dich einen Kopf kürzer!«

Er erbleichte vor Angst, erwiderte aber tapfer mit etwas zittriger Stimme: »Wollt Ihr etwa versuchen, Prior Philip diesen Steinbruch zu stehlen?«

Was ist nur los mit mir? dachte William. Ich kann ja nicht mal mehr einem halben Kind Angst einjagen, das noch feucht hinter den Ohren ist! Wieso glauben die Leute eigentlich, sie könnten mir trotzen? »Dieser Steinbruch gehört mir!« fauchte er. »Prior Philip kannst du vergessen – der kann dir jetzt auch nicht helfen. Wie viele Männer?«

Statt zu antworten, warf der Junge den Kopf in den Nacken und schrie lauthals: »Hilfe! Nehmt euch in acht! Angriff! Angriff!«

William packte sein Schwert. Er zögerte und sah zu den Häusern hinüber: Aus einer der Türen lugte ein ängstliches Gesicht. Er entschied, den Lehrling in Ruhe zu lassen, riß einem seiner Männer die brennende Fackel aus der Hand und trieb sein Pferd an.

Mit hocherhobener Fackel ritt er auf die Häuser zu und hörte, wie seine Männer ihm folgten. Die Tür der ihm an nächsten gelegenen Hütte ging auf und ein triefäugiger Mann im Unterhemd schaute heraus. William schleuderte die brennende Fackel über seinen Kopf. Sie landete auf dem Fußboden im Stroh, das sofort Feuer fing. William stieß ein Triumphgeheul aus und jagte an der Hütte vorbei.

Er ritt sämtliche Häuser der kleinen Siedlung ab, während hinter ihm seine Männer losstürmten und unter Kriegsgeheul ihre Fackeln auf die reetgedeckten Dächer schleuderten. Sämtliche Türen gingen auf und zu Tode erschrockene Männer, Frauen und Kinder strömten heraus, die gellend schrien und den hämmernden Hufen zu entgehen versuchten. Alles lief in panischer Angst durcheinander, während überall die Flammen hochschlugen. William zügelte sein Pferd und betrachtete das Tohuwabohu aus sicherer Entfernung. Die Haustiere hatten sich losgerissen, ein wildgewordenes Schwein raste blindlings hin und her, und inmitten des Durcheinanders stand wie angewurzelt eine Kuh, die ihren tumben Kopf verwirrt von einer Seite zur anderen schwenkte. Selbst die jungen Männer. die sich gemeinhin nicht so schnell ins Bockshorn jagen ließen, wirkten eingeschüchtert und verängstigt. Wahrhaftig, das Morgengrauen war die beste Tageszeit für derartige Aktionen: Menschen, die noch halbnackt waren, mangelte es entschieden an Angriffslust!

Ein dunkelhäutiger Mann mit schwarzem Haarschopf und Stiefeln an den Füßen stapfte aus einer der Hütten und fing sofort an, Befehle zu erteilen. Das mußte Otto Blackface sein. William konnte nicht hören, was er sagte. Seinen Gesten entnahm er, daß Otto den Frauen auftrug, sich mit den Kindern im Wald zu verstecken, aber was befahl er den Männern? Wenig später fand er es heraus: Zwei junge Männer rannten zu einer abseits gelegenen Hütte, entriegelten die Tür und tauchten kurz darauf mit schweren Steinklopfhämmern bewaffnet auf. Otto schickte noch weitere Männer zu der Hütte, bei der es sich offensichtlich um einen Geräteschuppen handelte. Sie wollten sich also wehren.

Vor drei Jahren hatte Otto sich geweigert, für Philip zur Waffe zu greifen – woher kam dieser Gesinnungswandel?

Worauf er auch immer zurückzuführen sein mochte, er besiegelte nur sein Ende. William verzog die Lippen zu einem grimmigen Lächeln und packte sein Schwert.

Inzwischen hatten sich sechs oder acht Männer mit Vorschlaghämmern und langstieligen Äxten bewaffnet. William gab seinem Pferd die Sporen und preschte auf die Gruppe vor dem Tor zum Geräteschuppen los. Die Männer sprangen beiseite, doch William holte mit dem Schwert aus und brachte einem von ihnen eine tiefe Wunde am Oberarm bei. Der Mann ließ sein Beil fallen.

William galoppierte weiter, bis er sein Pferd wenden konnte. Sein Atem ging stoßweise, und er fühlte sich blendend: In der Hitze einer Schlacht kannte er keine Furcht, nur noch Erregung. Ein paar seiner Männer hatten das Geschehen beobachtet und sahen ihn fragend an. Er bedeutete ihnen, sich ihm anzuschließen, und ritt eine weitere Attacke gegen die Steinbrecher. Sechs Rittern auszuweichen war schwieriger als einem. William stieß zwei Männer nieder, und ein paar andere wurden von seinen Gefolgsleuten mit dem Schwert erledigt; allerdings ging alles viel zu schnell, als daß er sie hätte zählen oder sich vergewissern können, ob sie lediglich verwundet oder tot waren.

Als er sich wieder umwandte, war Otto dabei, seine Männer um sich zu scharen. Sobald die Ritter wieder zum Angriff übergingen, verliefen sich die Steinklopfer zwischen den brennenden Häusern. Eine kluge Taktik, wie William voller Bedauern feststellte. Die Ritter machten sich an die Verfolgung, doch nun konnten die Arbeiter leichter ausweichen, und überdies scheuten die Pferde vor den lichterloh brennenden Häusern. William hatte es auf einen grauhaarigen, mit einem Hammer bewaffneten Mann abgesehen und verfehlte ihn mehrmals nur knapp, bevor er ihm entkam, indem er durch ein Haus lief, dessen Dach in Flammen stand.

William wurde klar, daß Otto sein Hauptgegner war: Er erteilte den Steinklopfern nicht nur kluge Anweisungen, er flößte ihnen auch Mut ein. War er erst einmal aus dem Weg geschafft, würden sich die anderen ergeben. William zügelte sein Pferd und hielt nach dem dunkelhäutigen Mann Ausschau. Die meisten Frauen und Kinder waren verschwunden; nur zwei Fünfjährige standen mitten auf dem Schlachtfeld, hielten sich an den Händen und weinten. Williams Ritter stürmten zwischen den Häusern hindurch und machten Jagd auf die Arbeiter. Bestürzt stellte William fest, daß einer seiner Bewaffneten von einem Hammer niedergestreckt worden war und nun stöhnend und blutend auf dem Boden lag. Mit Verlusten auf der eigenen Seite hatte er ganz und gar nicht gerechnet! Eine Frau rannte kopflos und ununterbrochen rufend von einem brennenden Haus ins andere. William verstand kein Wort, doch er begriff, daß sie nach jemandem suchte. Endlich hatte sie die beiden Fünfjährigen entdeckt, schnappte sie sich und trug sie davon, einen unter jedem Arm. Auf ihrer Flucht stieß sie beinahe mit Gilbert de Rennes zusammen, einem von Williams Rittern. Gilbert hob schon das Schwert, um sie niederzustrekken, als plötzlich Otto hinter einer Hütte hervorsprang und mit seinem Beil ausholte. Die Klinge durchschnitt glatt Gilberts Oberschenkel und blieb im Holz des Sattels stecken. Das Bein fiel zu Boden und Gilbert stürzte schreiend vom Pferd.

Er würde nie wieder kämpfen.

Gilbert war ein Ritter von unschätzbarem Wert. Wütend trieb William sein Pferd an. Die Frau mit den Kindern verschwand blitzschnell. Otto mühte sich mit seinem Beil ab, das noch immer in Gilberts Sattel steckte. Er sah auf und erkannte, daß William direkt auf ihn zuritt. Wäre er in diesem Augenblick davongerannt, hätte er vielleicht entkommen können, doch er rührte sich nicht vom Fleck und zerrte weiter an seinem Beil. William hatte ihn schon beinahe erreicht, als sich das Beil doch noch löste. Er hob sein Schwert, doch Otto wich und wankte nicht, sondern holte mit der Axt aus. Im letzten Moment begriff William, daß die Geste seinem Pferd galt und daß der Steinklopfer das Tier schwer treffen konnte, noch bevor er selbst nahe genug herangekommen war, um den Mann niederzustrecken. Verzweifelt zerrte William an den Zügeln, sein Roß kam rutschend zum Stehen, bäumte sich auf und wandte den Kopf. Ottos Hieb traf das Tier am Nacken. Das Beil drang tief in die starken Muskeln, und sofort sprudelte das Blut wie eine Fontäne aus der Wunde. Das Pferd sackte zu Boden. William konnte gerade noch abspringen, bevor der mächtige Leib auf dem Boden aufschlug.

Er war außer sich vor Wut. Dieses Schlachtroß hatte ihn ein Vermögen gekostet und ein ganzes Jahr lang durch den Krieg getragen; es nun durch das Beil eines Steinklopfers zu verlieren machte ihn rasend. Ein mächtiger Satz über den Kadaver – und schon hieb er wild auf Otto ein.

Der gab sich so schnell nicht geschlagen. Er hielt sein Beil mit beiden Händen fest und parierte Williams Schwerthiebe mit dem eichernen Stiel. William schlug immer wilder um sich, und es gelang ihm, Otto zurückzutreiben. Der Mann war bärenstark, trotz seines Alters, und zuckte mit keiner Wimper. Nun packte auch William sein Schwert mit beiden Händen und hieb noch fester drauflos. Wieder parierte Otto mit dem Axtstiel, aber diesmal blieb Williams Klinge im Holz stecken. Das Blatt wendete sich: Jetzt trieb Otto William vor sich her. William riß heftig an seinem Schwert und bekam es schließlich auch frei, aber Otto war ihm gefährlich nahe gerückt.

Urplötzlich fürchtete William um sein Leben.

Otto hob das Beil. William wich zurück. Er blieb mit der Ferse hängen, stolperte, fiel rücklings über den Pferdekadaver und landete in einer Lache warmen Bluts, hatte jedoch glücklicherweise sein Schwert nicht verloren. Otto stand mit hocherhobenem Beil über ihm. Der Schlag sauste nieder, und William rollte sich mit letzter Verzweiflung zur Seite. Er spürte den Sog, mit dem die Waffe unmittelbar neben seinem Gesicht die Luft zerschnitt; dann war er mit einem Satz wieder auf den Beinen und stieß mit dem Schwert nach dem Steinklopfer.

Jeder Soldat wäre längst zur Seite gesprungen, statt seine Waffe aus dem Boden zu ziehen, denn am größten war die Verwundbarkeit nach einer fehlgeschlagenen Attacke. Aber Otto war kein Soldat, bloß ein tapferer Dummkopf, und so stand er, eine Hand am Stiel seines Beils, mit dem anderen Arm um sein Gleichgewicht rudernd, da – eine leichte Beute für William. Hastig stieß er zu, beinahe blind, doch er traf sein Ziel. Die Schwertspitze traf Ottos Brust. William stieß noch einmal nach, und die Klinge glitt zwischen die Rippen des Mannes. Ottos Griff um das Beil lockerte sich, und sein Gesicht nahm einen Ausdruck an, den William nur allzu gut kannte: Der Blick verriet Überraschung, der Mund öffnete sich wie zum Schrei, gab jedoch keinen Ton von sich, und die Haut färbte sich plötzlich grau – der Anblick eines tödlich verwundeten Mannes. Um ganz sicherzugehen, stieß William die Klinge noch tiefer hinein, bevor er sie wieder herauszog. Ottos Augen rollten in ihren Höhlen nach oben, auf der Vorderseite seines Hemdes erschien ein roter, schnell größer werdender Fleck, und er stürzte zu Boden.

William drehte sich sofort um und ließ seinen Blick über den Schauplatz schweifen. Er sah zwei Steinklopfer davonrennen; wahrscheinlich hatten sie mit angesehen, wie ihr Anführer getötet wurde. Im Davonlaufen riefen sie den anderen etwas zu. Aus dem Kampf war ein Rückzug geworden. Die Ritter setzten den Flüchtenden nach. William stand schweratmend und unbeweglich da. Diese verdammten Steinbrecher hatten sich zur Wehr gesetzt! Er sah auf Gilbert hinab, der mit geschlossenen Augen bewegungslos in einer Blutlache lag. William legte ihm die Hand auf die Brust: kein Herzschlag. Gilbert war tot.

William streifte durch das Gelände zwischen den noch immer brennenden Häusern und zählte die Leichen. Drei Steinklopfer waren tot, dazu eine Frau mit Kind, die beide aussahen, als wären sie von Pferden zu Tode getrampelt worden. Drei von Williams Kriegern waren verwundet, vier Pferde verletzt oder tot.

Nach dieser Bestandsaufnahme trat er neben den toten Leib seines Schlachtrosses. Dieses Pferd war ihm lieber gewesen als die meisten Menschen. Gewöhnlich fühlte er sich nach einer Schlacht aufgekratzt, doch jetzt war er niedergeschlagen. Das reinste Schlachthaus! Was als simple Operation zur Vertreibung von ein paar hilflosen Arbeitern begonnen, hatte sich in eine hitzige Schlacht mit hohen Verlusten verwandelt.

Die Ritter jagten die Steinklopfer bis an den Waldrand, kamen mit ihren Pferden nicht weiter und kehrten zurück. Walter ritt auf William zu und sah, daß Gilbert tot dalag. Er bekreuzigte sich und sagte: »Gilbert hat mehr Männer getötet als ich.«

»Seinesgleichen gibt's nicht viele, und ich kann es mir nicht leisten, auch nur einen davon wegen eines Scharmützels mit einem verfluchten Mönch zu verlieren«, sagte William grimmig. »Von den Pferden ganz zu schweigen.«

»Die reinste Schweinerei«, meinte Walter. »Diese paar Leute haben uns eine heftigere Schlacht geliefert als die Rebellen Roberts von Gloucester.«

William schüttelte angewidert den Kopf. »Ich verstehe das nicht«, sagte er und ließ seinen Blick über die Toten schweifen. »Wofür, zum Teufel, glaubten die eigentlich, kämpfen zu müssen?«

Kurz nach Tagesanbruch, da sich die meisten Brüder in der Krypta zur Prim versammelten, hielten sich nur noch zwei Menschen im Dormitorium auf: Johnny Eightpence, der den Boden kehrte, an einem Ende des langgestreckten Raumes, am anderen Ende Jonathan, der Schule spielte.

Prior Philip verweilte einen Moment lang in der Türöffnung und sah dem Jungen zu. Jonathan war mittlerweile knapp fünf Jahre alt, ein aufgeweckter, selbstbewußter Knabe, dessen kindlicher Ernst ihm alle Herzen zufliegen ließ. Johnny kleidete ihn nach wie vor in Miniatur-Mönchskutten. Heute spielte Jonathan Novizenmeister und unterrichtete eine nur in seiner Einbildung bestehende Schülerschar. »Das ist falsch, Godfrey!« sagte er streng zu der leeren Bank. »Wenn du deine Berven nicht lernst, gehst du heute ohne Abendessen aus!« Er meinte *Verben*. Philip lächelte gerührt. Einen eigenen Sohn hätte er nicht mehr lieben können. Einzig Jonathan machte ihm in seinem Leben nichts als Freude, reine, unverdorbene Freude.

Das Kind konnte im ganzen Kloster frei herumlaufen wie ein junger Hund und wurde von allen Mönchen verhätschelt und verwöhnt. Die meisten betrachteten ihn als eine Art Schoßkind, als amüsantes Spielzeug, doch Philip und Johnny bedeutete er mehr als das. Johnny liebte den Jungen wie eine Mutter, und Philip fühlte sich wie sein Vater, obwohl er es zu verbergen suchte. Philip selbst war von frühester Kindheit an von einem gütigen Abt aufgezogen worden, und nichts schien ihm natürlicher, als Jonathan gegenüber die gleiche Rolle einzunehmen. Statt ihn, wie die anderen Mönche, zu kitzeln oder mit ihm Nachlaufen zu spielen, erzählte er ihm biblische Geschichten, unterhielt ihn mit Abzählreimen und hatte stets ein wachsames Auge auf ihn.

Er betrat den Raum, lächelte Johnny an und setzte sich zu den eingebildeten Schuljungen auf die Bank.

»Guten Morgen, Vater«, sagte Jonathan mit ernster Miene. Johnny hatte ihm beigebracht, stets betont höflich zu sein.

Philip sagte: »Was hieltest du davon, zur Schule zu gehen?«

»Latein kann ich schon«, brüstete Jonathan sich.

»Wirklich?«

»Ja. Hör zu: Omnius pluvius buvius nomine patri amen.«

Philip verbiß sich das Lachen. »Das *klingt* zwar wie Latein, aber so *ganz* stimmt es noch nicht. Bruder Osmund, unser Novizenmeister, wird es dir richtig beibringen.«

Jonathan wirkte ein wenig niedergeschlagen angesichts der Erkenntnis, daß er doch noch kein Latein konnte. Er sagte: »Ich kann aber ganz, ganz schnell laufen, schau!«

So schnell er konnte, rannte er von einem Ende des Raumes zum anderen.

»Wunderbar!« rief Philip. »Das ist wirklich sehr schnell.«

»Ja – und ich kann sogar noch schneller rennen –«

»Nicht jetzt«, sagte Philip. »Hör mir mal zu. Ich gehe für eine Weile weg.«

»Bist du morgen wieder da?«

»Nein, so bald nicht.«

»Nächste Woche?«

»Auch dann noch nicht.«

Jonathan sah ratlos drein. Eine Zeitspanne von mehr als einer Woche ging über seinen Verstand. Dann ergründete er ein anderes Rätsel: »Warum denn?«

»Ich muß den König sprechen.«

»Oh.« Auch damit konnte Jonathan nicht viel anfangen.

»Und ich hätte gerne, daß du in meiner Abwesenheit zur Schule gehst. Würde dir das Spaß machen?«

»Ja!«

»Du bist jetzt fast fünf. Nächste Woche hast du Geburtstag. Am ersten Tag des Jahres bist du zu uns gekommen.«

»Woher bin ich denn gekommen?«

»Von Gott. Alles kommt von Gott.«

Jonathan gab sich mit der Antwort nicht zufrieden. »Aber wo war ich denn *davor*?« hakte er nach.

»Ich weiß nicht.«

Jonathan runzelte die Stirn; auf seinem sorgenfreien, blutjungen

Gesichtchen sah das sehr komisch aus. »Aber irgendwo *muß* ich doch gewesen sein!«

Eines Tages, dachte Philip, wird irgendwer Jonathan erklären müssen, wo die kleinen Kinder herkommen. Bei dem Gedanken daran verzog er das Gesicht zu einer Grimasse. Nun, soweit war es, Gott sei Dank, noch nicht! Er wechselte das Thema. »Ich möchte, daß du während meiner Abwesenheit bis hundert zählen lernst.«

»Ich kann schon zählen«, sagte Jonathan. »Eins zwei drei vier fünf sechs sieben acht neun zehn elf zwölf grölf tölf mölf –«

»Nicht schlecht«, meinte Philip, »aber Bruder Osmund wird dir noch viel mehr beibringen. Du mußt bloß während des Unterrichts stillsitzen und ihm aufs Wort gehorchen, verstanden?«

»Ich werde bestimmt der Beste der ganzen Schule!« behauptete Jonathan.

»Warten wir's ab.« Philip betrachtete den Jungen noch eine Weile lang. Die Entwicklung des Kindes faszinierte ihn – die Art und Weise, wie er sich Wissen aneignete, welch unterschiedliche Phasen er durchlief. Gegenwärtig verwunderte Philip vor allem der Nachdruck, mit dem der Kleine ständig behauptete, schon Latein sprechen und zählen und schnell laufen zu können: Ob das wohl eine notwendige Vorstufe für echtes Lernen war? Irgendeinen Zweck mußte es in Gottes Plan wohl erfüllen. Eines Tages würde Jonathan ein erwachsener Mann sein. Philips Gedankengänge machten ihn so ungeduldig, daß er beinahe wünschte, Jonathan möge rascher heranwachsen.

Doch bis dahin würde noch ebensoviel Zeit vergehen wie beim Bau der Kathedrale.

»Dann gib mir einen Kuß zum Abschied«, sagte Philip.

Jonathan hob ihm das Gesichtchen entgegen, und Philip drückte ihm einen Kuß auf die weiche Wange. »Auf Wiedersehen, Vater«, sagte Jonathan.

»Auf Wiedersehen, mein Sohn«, antwortete Philip.

Er drückte Johnny Eightpence liebevoll den Arm und ging hinaus.

Die Mönche kamen aus der Krypta und begaben sich ins Refektorium. Philip schlug die entgegengesetzte Richtung ein; er wollte in der Krypta für den Erfolg seiner Mission beten.

Es hatte ihm schier das Herz gebrochen, als er erfuhr, was im Steinbruch vorgefallen war. Fünf Tote, darunter ein kleines Mädchen! Er hatte sich in sein Haus verkrochen und bitterlich geweint. Fünf seiner Schafe von William Hamleigh und dessen brutaler Meute niedergestreckt! Philip hatte sie alle gekannt: Harry von Shiring, den ehemaligen Steinbruchmeister von Lord Percy; den dunkelhäutigen Otto Blackface, der von Anfang an das Kommando über den Steinbruch geführt hatte; Ottos stattlichen Sohn Mark und dessen Frau Alwen, die abends auf den Schafsglocken zu spielen pflegte, und die kleine Norma, Ottos siebenjährige Enkelin, sein ein und alles. Gutherzige, gottesfürchtige und fleißige Menschen, die ein Recht darauf hatten, von ihrem Herrn Frieden und Gerechtigkeit zu erwarten. William hatte sie hingemetzelt wie ein Fuchs, der Hühner reißt. Das hätte selbst die Engel im Himmel zum Weinen gebracht.

Philip hatte um sie getrauert und sich dann nach Shiring begeben, um Gerechtigkeit zu fordern. Der Vogt hatte sich glattweg geweigert, auch nur einen Finger zu rühren. »Lord William verfügt über eine kleine Armee – wie soll ich ihn da wohl verhaften?« hatte Eustace gesagt. »Der König braucht Ritter für seinen Kampf gegen Mathilde – was würde er wohl sagen, würfe ich einen seiner besten Mannen in den Kerker? Wenn ich Mordanklage gegen William erhebe, werde ich entweder auf der Stelle von seinen Rittern getötet oder später von König Stephan als Verräter aufgeknüpft.«

Philip ging auf, daß die Gerechtigkeit in einem Erbfolgekrieg zu den ersten Todesopfern zählt.

Dann teilte der Vogt ihm mit, daß William offiziell Beschwerde gegen den Markt in Kingsbridge geführt hatte.

Es war natürlich absurd, daß William ungestraft morden konnte und gleichzeitig wegen einer reinen Formalität Anklage gegen Philip erhob; dennoch fühlte sich Philip hilflos. Es stimmte, daß er für den Markt keine Genehmigung hatte und genaugenommen im Unrecht war. Das Unrecht mußte beseitigt werden. Er war der Prior von Kingsbridge, er hatte nichts als seine moralische Autorität in die Waagschale zu werfen. William konnte auf ein ganzes Heer von Rittern zurückgreifen, Bischof Waleran seine Verbindungen an höchster Stelle spielen lassen, der Vogt sich auf seine königliche Vollmacht berufen – er, Philip, konnte nur Recht von Unrecht scheiden, und wenn er sich dieses Standpunkts begab, stand er wahrhaftig verlassen da. Also hatte er angeordnet, den Markt einzustellen.

Diese Entscheidung versetzte ihn in eine verzweifelte Lage.

Die Finanzen der Priorei hatten sich einerseits dank strengerer Kontrolle, andererseits dank stetig steigender Einkünfte aus dem Markt und der Schafzucht erheblich verbessert; aber Philip verwandte jeden Penny auf den Bau der Kathedrale und hatte sich bei den Juden in Winchester mit einer hohen Summe verschuldet, die noch zurückgezahlt werden mußte. Und nun verlor er auf einen Schlag nicht nur den Nachschub an kostenlosen Steinen, sondern auch die Einkünfte aus dem Markt – und möglicherweise sogar die freiwilligen Hilfskräfte, von denen viele hauptsächlich wegen des Marktes gekommen waren und künftig wohl ausblieben.

Er würde die Hälfte der Bauleute entlassen müssen und konnte die Hoffnung, den Dombau noch zu seinen Lebzeiten zu vollenden, in den Wind schreiben. Dazu war er nicht bereit.

Er fragte sich, ob ihn die Schuld an dieser Krise traf. War er allzu zuversichtlich, allzu ehrgeizig gewesen? Eustace, der Vogt, hatte sich jedenfalls so ausgedrückt. »Ihr zieht Euch viel zu große Stiefel an, Philip«, hatte er verärgert gesagt. »Ihr steht einem unbedeutendem Kloster vor und seid bloß ein unbedeutender Abt, aber Ihr bildet Euch ein, dem Bischof, dem Grafen und dem Vogt Vorschriften machen zu können. Ihr macht Eure Rechnung ohne den Wirt. Wir sind zu mächtig für Euch. Ihr macht uns nichts als Scherereien.« Eustace, ein häßlicher Mann mit schiefstehenden Zähnen und einem Schielauge, wirkte in seinem schmuddeligen gelben Gewand selber reichlich unbedeutend; dennoch fühlte sich Philip von seinen Worten tief getroffen. Ihm war schmerzhaft klar, daß keiner der Steinbrecher gestorben wäre, hätte nicht er sich William Hamleigh zum Feind gemacht. Aber blieb ihm denn eine andere Wahl? Wenn er die Flinte ins Korn warf, würden noch mehr Menschen zu Schaden kommen – wie der Müller, den William umgebracht hatte, wie die Tochter des Leibeigenen, die William und seine Ritter geschändet hatten. Er *mußte* weiterkämpfen.

Und das hieß, daß er den König aufsuchen mußte.

Gerne tat er es gewiß nicht. Schon einmal, vor vier Jahren in Winchester, hatte er sich an den König gewandt, und obwohl seiner Bitte damals stattgegeben wurde, hatte er sich doch am königlichen Hofe schrecklich unwohl gefühlt. Der König war von ebenso listigen wie skrupellosen Leuten umgeben, die um seine Aufmerksamkeit buhlten und sich um seine Gunst stritten; solche Menschen konnte Philip nicht ausstehen: Sie gierten nach Reichtümern und Stellungen, die ihnen nicht zukamen. Die höfischen Ränke durchschaute er ohnehin nicht: In seiner Welt hatte man sich das, was man wollte, gefälligst zu verdienen und mußte keinem Gönner Honig ums Maul schmieren. Nun allerdings blieb ihm nichts anderes übrig, als sich in diese Welt zu begeben und nach denselben Regeln mitzuspielen: Nur der König konnte ihm die Markterlaubnis erteilen. Nur der König konnte die Kathedrale noch retten.

Er beendete sein Gebet und verließ die Krypta. Die aufgehende Sonne tauchte die grauen Steinmauern der aufstrebenden Kathedrale in rosa Licht. Die Bauleute, die von Sonnenaufgang bis Sonnenuntergang werkten, sperrten ihre Bauhütten auf, schärften ihre Werkzeuge und mischten den ersten Schub Mörtel. Der Verlust des Steinbruchs hatte noch keine Auswirkungen auf den Bau gehabt; sie hatten von Anfang an mehr Quader als nötig gefördert und verfügten über einen Vorrat, der viele Monate lang reichen würde.

Es wurde Zeit zum Aufbruch. Die nötigen Vorkehrungen waren getroffen. Der König hielt sich in Lincoln auf. Philip nahm einen Reisebegleiter mit: Alienas Bruder Richard. Nachdem er ein Jahr lang als Knappe gekämpft hatte, war er vom König zum Ritter geschlagen worden. Er war heimgekehrt, um sich eine neue Ausrüstung zu beschaffen, und machte sich nun auf den Weg zurück zur königlichen Armee.

Aliena war im Wollgeschäft erstaunlich erfolgreich geworden. Sie verkaufte ihre Vliese längst nicht mehr an Philip, sondern verhandelte direkt mit den flämischen Händlern. Dieses Jahr hatte sie sogar die gesamte Wolle der Priorei aufkaufen wollen. Sie hätte weniger gezahlt als die Flamen, aber dafür hätte Philip sein Geld eher bekommen. Er hatte abgelehnt. Trotzdem war es als Anzeichen für ihren Erfolg zu werten, daß sie ihm überhaupt ein solches Angebot machen konnte.

Vor dem Stall warteten Aliena und ihr Bruder bereits auf Philip. Richard saß auf einem kastanienbraunen Schlachtroß, das Aliena zwanzig Pfund gekostet haben mußte. Er hatte sich zu einem stattlichen, breitschultrigen jungen Mann entwickelt, dessen regelmäßige Züge lediglich eine rote Narbe am rechten Ohr beeinträchtigte. Er war aufs prächtigste in Rot und Grün gekleidet und mit einem neuen Schwert, sowie mit Lanze, Streitaxt und Dolch ausgerüstet. Sein Gepäck wurde von einem zweiten Pferd getragen, das er am langen Zügel mit sich führte. Begleitet wurde er von zwei Bewaffneten auf schnellen Pferden und einem Knappen, der ein gedrungenes, kräftiges Pferd ritt.

Aliena war in Tränen aufgelöst, doch Philip hätte nicht zu sagen gewußt, ob es am Abschiedsschmerz lag, am Stolz auf Richards prächtige Erscheinung oder an der Angst, ihn nie wiederzusehen. Vielleicht an allem zusammen. Viele Dorfbewohner hatten sich zur Verabschiedung eingefunden, darunter fast alle jungen Männer und Knaben. Richard war ihr Held, das stand ganz außer Frage. Auch die Mönche waren vollzählig erschienen, um ihrem Prior eine gute Reise zu wünschen.

Die Stallburschen führten die beiden Pferde heran, einen für Philip bereits gesattelten Zelter und ein Lastpferd für sein bescheidenes Gepäck, das hauptsächlich aus Reiseproviant bestand. Die Handwerker legten ihre Werkzeuge nieder und kamen, angeführt vom bärtigen Tom und seinem rothaarigen Stiefsohn Jack, herüber.

Philip verabschiedete sich mit einer eher förmlichen Umarmung von Remigius, seinem Subprior, und um einiges herzlicher von Milius und Cuthbert, bevor er aufsaß. Grimmig stellte er fest, daß er nun vier Wochen lang tagtäglich in diesem harten Sattel sitzen mußte. Dann erteilte er allen Anwesenden seinen Segen. Die Mönche, Bauleute und Dorfbewohner winkten und riefen ihm und Richard ihr Adieu zu, als die beiden Seite an Seite durch das Klostertor ritten.

Dann ging's die enge Dorfstraße hinunter, wo sie den Leuten zuwinkten, die aus ihren Häusern schauten. Unter lautem Hufgetrappel überquerten sie die Holzbrücke und schlugen den Weg durch die Felder ein. Kurz darauf warf Philip einen Blick zurück und sah, wie die aufgehende Sonne durch die Fensteröffnung im halbfertigen Ostflügel der neuen Kathedrale schien. Wenn seine Mission mißlang, würde sie womöglich nie vollendet. Doch nach allem, was er durchgemacht hatte, mochte er sich nicht mit der Vorstellung befassen, er könnte letztendlich doch den kürzeren ziehen. Er drehte sich wieder um und richtete sein Augenmerk auf den vor ihm liegenden Weg.

Die Stadt Lincoln liegt auf einer Anhöhe. Philip und Richard näherten sich ihr von Süden auf der uralten und sehr belebten Ermine Street. Schon von weitem konnten sie den Hügel mit den Türmen der Kathedrale und den Burgzinnen sehen. Aber sie waren noch immer drei, vier Meilen entfernt, als sie, zu Philips Erstaunen, auch schon an einem Stadttor anlangten. Die Vororte müssen wahrlich riesig sein, dachte er; die Bevölkerung muß in die Tausende gehen.

Weihnachten war die Stadt in die Hände Ranulfs von Chester gefallen, der der mächtigste Mann in Englands Norden und ein Verwandter der Kaiserin Mathilde war. König Stephan hatte die Stadt zwar wieder an sich gebracht, aber Ranulfs Truppen hielten nach wie vor die Burg besetzt. Lincoln war, wie Philip und Richard unterwegs erfahren hatten, in der merkwürdigen Lage, zwei miteinander verfeindete Heerlager innerhalb seiner Stadtmauern zu beherbergen.

Philip hatte sich im Laufe der vergangenen vier Wochen nicht für Richard erwärmen können. Alienas Bruder war ein zorniger junger Mann, der die Hamleighs glühend haßte und nur auf Rache sann;

und er tat so, als dächte Philip nicht anders. Tatsächlich aber bestand ein großer Unterschied zwischen ihnen. Wenn Philip die Hamleighs haßte, so wegen der Greueltaten, die sie ihren Untertanen zufügten – die Welt konnte sehr viel besser ohne diese Familie auskommen. Richard hingegen würde niemals Ruhe finden, wenn es ihm nicht gelang, die Hamleighs aus dem Feld zu schlagen – sein Haß diente reinem Selbstzweck.

Richard war, wenn es um körperlichen Einsatz ging, tapfer und stets kampfbereit, doch auf anderen Gebieten zeigte er deutliche Schwächen. So verwirrte er seine Krieger, indem er sie einmal wie Ebenbürtige behandelte, dann aber wieder wie Bedienstete herumkommandierte. In den Gasthäusern versuchte er, auf Fremde Eindruck zu machen, indem er ihnen Bier spendierte. Er gab stets vor, den Weg genau zu kennen, auch wenn es gar nicht stimmte, so daß sie nicht selten einen weiten Umweg machten, nur weil er seinen Irrtum nicht eingestehen mochte. Lange bevor sie Lincoln erreichten, war Philip zu der Erkenntnis gekommen, daß Richard seiner Schwester Aliena nicht das Wasser reichen konnte.

Sie kamen an einem großen See vorbei, auf dem es von Schiffen nur so wimmelte, und überquerten am Fuße des Hügels einen Fluß, der die südliche Begrenzung des Stadtkerns bildete. Lincoln lebte offensichtlich von der Schiffahrt. Gleich bei der Brücke gab es einen Fischmarkt. Sie ließen die ausgedehnten Vororte hinter sich, passierten ein weiteres bewachtes Tor und betraten die belebte Stadt. Unmittelbar vor ihnen führte eine schmale Straße, die schwarz vor Menschen war, den Hang hinauf. Die dichtgedrängt stehenden Häuser zu beiden Seiten waren teilweise oder zur Gänze aus Stein gebaut, ein Zeichen beachtlichen Reichtums. Die Anhöhe war dermaßen steil, daß das Hauptstockwerk der meisten Häuser an einem Ende etliche Fuß über den Boden und am anderen Ende unter die Erde gebaut war. Das bergabwärts gelegene Geschoß diente unweigerlich als Laden oder Werkstatt. Die einzigen unbebauten Flächen fanden sich auf den neben den Kirchen gelegenen Friedhöfen, und auf jedem einzelnen wurde ein Markt abgehalten, für Getreide, Geflügel, Wolle, Leder und anderes mehr.

Philip bahnte sich mit Richard und dessen kleinem Gefolge mühsam den Weg durch das Gewimmel von Städtern, Bewaffneten, Tieren und Gespannen. Zu seinem Erstaunen bemerkte Philip, daß die ganze Stadt gepflastert war. Welch ein Reichtum muß hier herrschen, dachte er, wenn man sogar die Straße mit Steinen auslegen kann wie einen

Palast oder eine Kathedrale! Der Weg war zwar durch den vielen Unrat und Tierdung immer noch rutschig, aber weit besser als die Schlammströme, in die sich die Straßen anderer Städte winters aufzulösen pflegten.

Sie hatten den Bergrücken erreicht, passierten ein weiteres Tor und fanden sich im Herzen der Stadt. Schlagartig herrschte eine ganz andere Atmosphäre: Es war viel ruhiger, doch lag Spannung in der Luft. Unmittelbar zu ihrer Linken befand sich der Eingang zur Burg. Die große, eisenbeschlagene Tür im Durchgang war fest verschlossen. Schemenhafte Gestalten bewegten sich hinter den Schießscharten im Torhaus, und Wachposten in Panzerzeug, deren Eisenhüte das fahle Sonnenlicht widerspiegelten, patrouillierten auf der zinnenbesetzten Mauer. Philip beobachtete, wie sie auf und ab gingen: Sie führten keine Gespräche miteinander, es gab keine Witze und kein Gelächter, kein Hinauslehnen über die Brüstung, um den vorübergehenden Mädchen nachzupfeifen – diese Posten standen Wache, hielten mit Adleraugen, ja Besorgnis Ausschau und hatten für nichts anderes Zeit.

Zu Philips Rechter, knapp eine Viertelmeile vom Burgtor entfernt, war die Westfassade der Kathedrale zu sehen. Philip erkannte auf den ersten Blick, daß die Kirche dem König als militärisches Hauptquartier diente, trotz ihrer Nähe zur Burg. Die schmale Gasse, die zwischen den Häusern der Domherren zur Kathedrale führte, wurde durch eine Reihe von Wachposten versperrt. Hinter ihnen gingen Ritter und Bewaffnete durch die drei Portale in der Kathedrale ein und aus. Der Friedhof war ein einziges Heerlager aus Zelten und Kochfeuern und weidenden Pferden. Klostergebäude suchte man hier vergebens: Der Dom zu Lincoln wurde nicht von Mönchen, sondern von Domherren genannten Priestern geleitet, die in gewöhnlichen Stadthäusern unweit der Kirche wohnten.

Der Bereich zwischen Kathedrale und Burg war, von Philip und seinen Begleitern abgesehen, menschenleer, und der Prior merkte plötzlich, daß sie sowohl von den Wachposten des Königs als auch von jenen auf der gegenüberliegenden Burg nicht aus dem Auge gelassen wurden. Er befand sich im Niemandsland zwischen zwei Heeren und damit am gefährlichsten Ort in ganz Lincoln. Dann fiel ihm auf, daß Richard mit seinen Mannen schon vorausgeritten war. Eilends folgte er ihnen.

Die königlichen Wachen ließen sie anstandslos passieren: Richard war hier gut bekannt. Philip bewunderte die Westfront der Kathedrale. Der enorm hohe Portalbogen, flankiert von zwei halb so hohen Seitenbogen, wirkte geradezu ehrfurchtgebietend. Wie das Tor zum Himmelreich, dachte Philip, was es in gewisser Weise ja auch ist. Philip beschloß auf der Stelle, daß die Westfassade des Doms von Kingsbridge auch solche Bogen bekommen sollte.

Philip und Richard überließen dem Knappen ihre Pferde und begaben sich durch das Feldlager in die Kathedrale. Hier drinnen war es sogar noch voller als draußen. Die Seitenschiffe dienten als Ställe: Hunderte von Pferden waren an den Pfeilern des Bogengangs angebunden. Im Mittelschiff drängten sich die Bewaffneten, und auch hier gab es Kochfeuer und Bettstellen. Es wurde Englisch und Französisch durcheinander gesprochen, hin und wieder war sogar Flämisch zu hören, die gutturale Sprache der Wollhändler aus Flandern. Im großen und ganzen befanden sich die Ritter in und die Bewaffneten außerhalb der Kathedrale. Philip sah mit Bedauern, daß einige Männer um Geld spielten. Noch mehr befremdete ihn der Anblick einiger Frauen, die für diese Jahreszeit äußerst dürftig gekleidet waren und den Männern schöne Augen zu machen schienen – beinahe, als wären sie sündige Frauen, dachte er, oder sogar, Gott behüte, Huren.

Um ihren Anblick zu meiden, hob er die Augen zur Decke. Sie war aus Holz und mit leuchtenden Farben wunderschön bemalt, bildete allerdings, bei all den Leuten, die im Mittelschiff ihr Essen kochten, eine schreckliche Feuergefahr. Er folgte Richard durch die Menge. Der junge Mann fühlte sich hier offensichtlich wohl, wirkte selbstsicher und zuversichtlich, rief Grafen und Baronen Grußworte zu und hieb dem einen oder anderen Ritter kräftig auf den Rücken.

Die Vierung sowie der Ostflügel der Kathedrale waren durch Seile abgeteilt. Der Ostteil schien den Priestern vorbehalten – das will ich wenigstens hoffen! dachte Philip –, und die Vierung diente dem König als Quartier.

Die Absperrung war durch eine weitere Reihe Wachposten gesichert, dahinter drängten sich die Höflinge und schließlich saß, in einem Zirkel von Grafen, König Stephan auf einem hölzernen Thron in der Mitte.

Der König war in den fünf Jahren, seit Philip ihn in Winchester gesehen hatte, sehr gealtert. Sein attraktives Gesicht war von Sorgenfalten gezeichnet, sein lohfarbenes Haar wies Spuren von Grau auf, und das Kirchenjahr hatte ihn schmaler werden lassen. Er befand sich offensichtlich mitten in einer freundschaftlichen Auseinandersetzung mit seinen Grafen. Richard stellte sich an den Rand des inneren Zirkels und machte eine tiefe Verbeugung. Der König schaute auf, erkannte ihn und sagte mit dröhnender Stimme: »Richard von Kingsbridge: Wie gut, Euch wieder hier zu sehen!«

»Habt Dank, mein Herr und König«, sagte Richard.

Philip trat neben ihn und verbeugte sich ebenfalls.

Stephan sagte: »Habt Ihr Euch etwa einen Mönch als Knappen mitgebracht?«, und die Höflinge lachten prompt.

»Dies ist der Prior von Kingsbridge, Herr«, sagte Richard.

Stephan blickte genauer hin, und Philip sah ihm an, daß er sich erinnerte. »Natürlich, ich kenne doch Prior … Philip«, sagte er, wenn auch sein Tonfall nicht so herzlich klang wie bei Richards Begrüßung. »Seid Ihr gekommen, um für mich zu kämpfen?« Die Höflinge lachten wieder.

Es freute Philip, daß sich der König an seinen Namen erinnerte. »Ich bin gekommen, weil das Werk Gottes – der Wiederaufbau der Kathedrale von Kingsbridge – dringend der Hilfe meines Herrn und Königs bedarf.«

»Darüber müßt Ihr mir ausführlich berichten«, fiel Stephan hastig ein. »Kommt morgen wieder, dann habe ich mehr Zeit.« Er wandte sich erneut an seine Grafen und nahm die Unterhaltung in gedämpftem Tonfall wieder auf.

Richard verbeugte sich und zog sich zurück, und Philip tat es ihm nach.

König Stephan war weder am nächsten Tag, noch am Tag darauf noch am übernächsten Tag zu sprechen. Die erste Nacht verbrachte Philip in einem Gasthaus, doch dort bedrückte ihn der ständige Bratengeruch und das schrille Gelächter der Frauenzimmer. Leider gab es kein Kloster in der Stadt. Normalerweise hätte er beim Bischof Aufnahme gefunden, aber der König hatte sich im Bischofspalast einquartiert, und die Häuser in der Nähe der Kathedrale, die die Mitglieder der königlichen Entourage beherbergten, platzten bereits aus allen Nähten. Am zweiten Abend begab Philip sich weit außerhalb der Stadt, noch über den Vorort Wigford hinaus, in ein Kloster, dem ein Heim für Aussätzige angeschlossen war. Dort hatte er grobes Brot und Dünnbier zum Abendessen, als Nachtlager eine harte Matratze auf dem Fußboden, absolute Ruhe von Sonnenuntergang bis Mitternacht, Gebetsstunden in aller Herrgottsfrühe, zum Frühstück wässerigen, ungesalzenen Haferbrei – und war damit vollkommen glücklich.

Jeden Morgen nahm er die wertvolle Urkunde, die der Priorei das Recht zum Abbau des Steinbruchs verlieh, mit zur Kathedrale. Tag und Tag verging, ohne daß der König Notiz von ihm nahm. An den Gesprächen der anderen Bittsteller, in denen es nur darum ging, wer gerade des Königs Gunst genoß und wer in Ungnade gefallen war, beteiligte er sich nicht.

Er wußte, warum man ihn warten ließ. Mutter Kirche befand sich im Widerstreit mit dem König. Stephan hatte die großzügigen Versprechen, die ihm zu Beginn seiner Herrschaft entlockt worden waren, alle nicht gehalten. Seinen Bruder, den mit allen Wassern gewaschenen Bischof Henry von Winchester, hatte er sich zum Feind gemacht, indem er die Kandidatur eines anderen für das Amt des Erzbischofs von Canterbury unterstützte; damit hatte er auch Waleran Bigods Hoffnungen auf eine rasche Karriere in Henrys Kielwasser ein Ende gesetzt. Doch in den Augen der Kirche bestand Stephans größte Sünde in der fast gleichzeitigen Verhaftung Bischof Rogers von Salisbury und seiner beiden Neffen, den Bischöfen von Lincoln und Ely, wegen ungenehmigten Burgenbaus. Ein einstimmiger Chor der Entrüstung erhob sich landauf, landab in Kathedralen und Klöstern über diese Freveltat. Stephan war gekränkt. Er vertrat die Meinung, daß Bischöfe in ihrer Eigenschaft als Diener Gottes keine Burgen brauchten; wenn sie doch welche bauten, so durften sie nicht erwarten, weiterhin wie Diener Gottes behandelt zu werden. Das war ehrlich, aber naiv.

Der Riß war zwar wieder gekittet worden, aber König Stephans Bereitschaft, sich die Bittgesuche heiliger Männer anzuhören, war beträchtlich gesunken, daher mußte sich Philip in Geduld fassen. Er nutzte die Gelegenheit zur Meditation. Als Prior blieb ihm dazu leider nur wenig Zeit. Jetzt gab es auf einmal stundenlang nichts für ihn zu tun, so daß er sich in seine Gedanken versenken konnte.

Die Höflinge machten schließlich einen großen Bogen um Philip, was ihn auffällig machte und es dem König zunehmend erschwerte, ihn zu übersehen. Am Morgen seines siebten Tages in Lincoln war er gerade tief in Gedanken über das hehre Geheimnis der Dreifaltigkeit, als er plötzlich bemerkte, daß direkt vor ihm jemand stand, ihn ansah und mit ihm sprach – der König höchstselbst.

»Schlaft Ihr etwa mit offenen Augen, Mann?« fragte Stephan, zwischen Belustigung und Unmut schwankend.

»Ich bitte um Entschuldigung, Herr, aber ich habe nachgedacht«, sagte Philip und verneigte sich reichlich verspätet.

»Macht nichts. Ich will mir Eure Kutte borgen.«

»Was?« Philip war viel zu überrascht, um gute Manieren an den Tag zu legen.

»Ich will die Burg genauer in Augenschein nehmen. Wenn ich wie ein Mönch aussehe, schießen sie wenigstens nicht mit Pfeilen nach mir. Macht schon – geht in eine der Kapellen und zieht Euer Gewand aus.«

Philip trug nur ein Unterhemd unter seiner Kutte. »Aber Herr, was soll ich dann anziehen?«

»Ich vergaß, wie keusch Ihr Mönche seid.« Stephan schnipste mit den Fingern nach einem jungen Ritter. »Robert – leiht mir Euren Waffenrock, schnell.«

Der Ritter, der sich gerade mit einem Mädchen unterhielt, zog sich geschwind aus, reichte dem König mit einer Verbeugung seinen Rock und wandte sich mit einer obszönen Geste wieder dem Mädchen zu. Seine Freunde lachten und grölten.

Philip schlüpfte in die winzige Kapelle von Sankt Dunstan, bat den Heiligen mit einem hastig gemurmelten Gebet um Vergebung, zog seine Kutte aus und legte den kurzen, scharlachroten Waffenrock des Ritters an. Es war seltsam. Seit seinem sechsten Lebensjahr war er in Mönchsgewändern gegangen – nun hätte er sich nicht merkwürdiger fühlen können, hätte er sich als Frau verkleidet. Er verließ die Kapelle und reichte seine Kutte Stephan, der sie sich rasch über den Kopf zog.

Dann sagte der König zu seiner Überraschung: »Wenn Ihr wollt, könnt Ihr mit mir kommen und mir über die Kathedrale in Kingsbridge berichten.«

Philip war verblüfft. Im ersten Moment wollte er ablehnen. Durchaus denkbar, daß einer der Wachposten auf den Burgzinnen nun, da ihn seine Mönchstracht nicht mehr schützte, auf ihn zielte. Doch andererseits bot sich die Möglichkeit, mit dem König ungestört allein zu sein und ihm in aller Ruhe die Angelegenheit mit dem Steinbruch und dem Markt auseinanderzusetzen: Eine solche Gelegenheit käme wahrscheinlich nie wieder.

Stephan hob seinen purpurnen, an Kragen und Saum mit weißem Fell besetzten Umhang auf. »Legt ihn um«, sagte er zu Philip. »Damit lenkt Ihr die Aufmerksamkeit von mir ab und auf Euch.«

Sämtliche Höflinge waren verstummt und verfolgten neugierig den Gang der Dinge.

Philip begriff, daß der König ihm damit unmißverständlich zu verstehen gab, daß er in einem Heerlager nichts zu suchen hatte und nicht mit Privilegien auf Kosten derer rechnen durfte, die Kopf und Kragen für den König riskierten. Das war nichts Unbilliges verlangt.

Doch Philip wußte auch: Wenn er den Standpunkt des Königs einfach hinnahm, so konnte er ebensogut gleich den Heimweg antreten und jegliche Hoffnung auf die neuerliche Nutzung des Steinbruchs und die Wiedereröffnung des Marktes begraben. Ihm blieb nichts anderes übrig, als die Herausforderung anzunehmen. Er holte tief Luft und sagte: »Vielleicht ist es Gottes Wille, daß ich für den König sterbe.« Er griff nach dem purpurroten Umhang und legte ihn an.

Überraschtes Gemurmel erhob sich aus der Menge, und selbst König Stephan wirkte verdutzt. Sie hatten erwartet, Philip würde einen Rückzieher machen. Philip biß sich auf die Zunge und wünschte, er hätte sich aus der Affäre gezogen. Jetzt war es zu spät.

Stephan machte kehrt und ging auf das Nordportal zu. Philip folgte ihm. Einige Höflinge machten Anstalten, ihnen ebenfalls zu folgen, aber Stephan winkte ab und sagte: »In Begleitung des gesamten königlichen Hofes würde selbst ein Mönch Aufmerksamkeit erregen.« Er stülpte die Kapuze an Philips Kutte über den Kopf, und sie traten auf den Friedhof hinaus.

Philips kostbarer Umhang zog neugierige Blicke auf sich, als die beiden sich einen Weg durch das Heerlager bahnten: Die Männer hielten ihn für einen Baron und wunderten sich, warum sie ihn nicht kannten. Die Aufmerksamkeit, die ihm plötzlich entgegenschlug, während Stephan keines Blicks gewürdigt wurde, machte Philip schuldbewußt, als wäre er ein Hochstapler.

Sie gingen nicht direkt auf das Haupttor der Burg zu, sondern durch ein Gewirr von schmalen Gassen, bis sie unweit der Kirche St.-Paul-in-the-Bail gegenüber der Nordostecke der Burg herauskamen. Die Burgmauern waren auf soliden Erdwällen errichtet und von einem trockenen Graben umgeben. Zwischen dem Grabenrand und den nächstliegenden Gebäuden erstreckte sich etwa hundert Schritt weit unbebautes Gelände. Stephan trat auf die grasbewachsene Fläche hinaus und wandte sich gen Westen, wobei er die Nordmauer einer eingehenden Prüfung unterzog und sich dicht an die Rückwände der Häuser am Rande des offenen Geländes hielt. Stephan ließ Philip zu seiner Linken, also zwischen sich und der Burg gehen. Das unbebaute Gelände diente natürlich dazu, den Bogenschützen freies Schußfeld zu gewähren.

Philip hatte zwar keine Angst vor dem Tod, doch Schmerzen fürchtete er, so daß sein Hauptgedanke der Frage galt, wie weh ihm ein Pfeil wohl tun würde.

»Habt Ihr Angst, Philip?« fragte Stephan.

»Schreckliche Angst«, erwiderte Philip offen und fügte, durch die Flucht leichtsinnig geworden, hinzu: »Und Ihr?«

Der König lachte über die kecke Frage. »Ein wenig«, gab er zu.

Philip fiel wieder ein, daß er bei dieser Gelegenheit mit dem König über die Kathedrale sprechen wollte, aber er konnte keinen klaren Gedanken fassen, solange er in Lebensgefahr schwebte. Sein Blick glitt immer wieder zur Burg hinüber und suchte die Wallanlage nach einem schußbereiten Bogenschützen ab.

Die Burg nahm die gesamte Südostecke der Innenstadt ein und bildete im Westen sogar einen Teil der Stadtmauer, so daß man, wollte man sie umrunden, die Stadt verlassen mußte. Stephan führte Philip durch das Westtor in einen Vorort namens Newland. Hier ähnelten die aus Flechtwerk und Lehm gebauten Behausungen eher Bauernkaten und hatten große, sonst nur in Dörfern übliche Gärten. Über die offenen Felder wehte ein bitterlich kalter Wind. Stephan bog nach Süden ab, immer noch am Rand der Burg entlang. Er zeigte auf eine kleine Pforte in der Burgmauer. »Als ich die Stadt eroberte, muß Ranulf von Chester hierdurch geflohen sein«, sagte er.

Philips Angst hatte sich etwas gelegt. Außer ihnen benutzten noch andere den Pfad, und außerdem waren die Wallanlagen auf dieser Seite weniger stark bewacht, weil die Besetzer der Burg keinen Angriff vom offenen Lande, sondern aus der Stadt befürchteten. Philip holte tief Luft und platzte dann heraus: »Falls ich sterbe, werdet Ihr dann Kingsbridge einen Markt geben und William Hamleigh dazu bewegen, dem Kloster den Steinbruch zu überlassen?«

Stephan antwortete nicht gleich. Sie gingen nun bergab gen Südosten und schauten zum Wohnturm auf, der von ihrem Standpunkt aus ganz und gar uneinnehmbar wirkte. An der Ecke bogen sie durch ein weiteres Tor und betraten die Unterstadt, wo sie die Südseite der Burg abschritten. Philip fühlte sich erneut in Gefahr. Ein Burginsasse, der die beiden Männer auf ihrem Rundgang um die Mauer beobachtete, konnte ohne Schwierigkeiten den Schluß ziehen, daß sie einen Erkundungsgang machten, und sie als leichte Beute betrachten, vor allem ihn in dem purpurnen Königsmantel. Um sich von seiner Furcht abzulenken, musterte er den Wohnturm. Die Wand wies mehrere kleine Löcher auf, Abflüsse für die Latrinen. Der herausgespülte Dreck landete einfach auf Mauern und Wall, wo er liegenblieb, bis er verrottete. Kein Wunder, daß es hier so stank. Philip hielt den Atem an, und sie eilten weiter.

Am südöstlichen Ende gab es einen zweiten, kleineren Turm. Philip und Stephan hatten die Burg nun zu drei Vierteln umrundet. Philip fragte sich, ob Stephan seine Frage inzwischen vergessen hatte. Er wagte nicht, sie zu wiederholen. Der König könnte ihn für aufdringlich halten und sich womöglich gekränkt fühlen.

An der Hauptstraße, die mitten durch die Stadt führte, bogen sie erneut um die Ecke. Noch bevor Philip einen Seufzer der Erleichterung ausstoßen konnte, hatten sie ein weiteres Tor passiert und befanden sich wenige Augenblicke später wieder im Niemandsland zwischen Kathedrale und Burg.

Blankes Entsetzen erfaßte Philip, als der König ausgerechnet hier stehenblieb und sich dabei in eine Stellung manövrierte, die es ihm ermöglichte, dem Prior über die Schulter zu spähen und die Burg einer genauen Musterung zu unterziehen – die aber Philips auffälligen, in Purpur und Hermelin gewandeten Rücken praktisch zur Zielscheibe eines jeden Postens und Bogenschützen machte, von denen es im Torhaus nur so wimmelte. Jeden Moment konnte ihn ein Pfeil oder eine Lanze von hinten durchbohren! Vor Schreck erstarrte er zur Bildsäule, und trotz des eiskalten Windes brach ihm der Schweiß aus allen Poren.

»Ich gab Euch diesen Steinbruch schon vor Jahren, nicht wahr?« sagte König Stephan.

»Nicht ganz«, erwiderte Philip mit zusammengebissenen Zähnen. »Ihr habt uns das Recht verliehen, Steine für die Kathedrale zu brechen; den Steinbruch selbst gabt Ihr Percy Hamleigh. Percys Sohn William hat meine Steinbrecher überfallen, fünf Menschen umgebracht, darunter eine Frau und ein Kind, und nun verweigert er uns den Zugang.«

»So was sollte er lieber unterlassen«, sagte der König nachdenklich, »vor allem, wenn er von mir zum Grafen von Shiring ernannt werden will.« Philip wollte schon Hoffnung schöpfen, da fügte der König hinzu: »Verflucht noch mal, ich sehe beim besten Willen keine Möglichkeit, wie man in diese Burg eindringen könnte.«

»Ich bitte Euch, befehlt William, den Steinbruch wieder zu öffnen«, sagte Philip. »Er mißachtet Euch und bestiehlt unseren Herrgott.«

Stephan schien ihn nicht gehört zu haben. »Ich glaube, sie haben nicht sehr viele Männer da drin«, sagte er im selben sinnenden Tonfall. »Vermutlich sind sie fast alle auf den Wallanlagen, um einen starken Eindruck zu machen. Wie war das mit dem Markt?«

Philip kam zu dem Schluß, daß es wohl zu seiner Prüfung gehören mußte, ihn hier festzuhalten, den Rücken einer Schar von Bogenschützen ausgesetzt. Er wischte sich mit der Pelzmanschette des königlichen Umhangs die Stirn. »Mein Herr und König, jeden Sonntag kommen Menschen aus der ganzen Grafschaft nach Kingsbridge zum Gottesdienst und zur unentgeltlichen Arbeit am Dombau. Anfangs verkauften nur wenige einfallsreiche Männer und Frauen Fleischpasteten, Wein, Hüte und Messer an die freiwilligen Hilfskräfte, doch mit der Zeit wurde daraus ein richtiger Markt. Und nun bitte ich Euch, diesen Markt offiziell zu genehmigen.«

»Werdet Ihr für die Urkunde bezahlen?«

Philip wußte, daß eine Bezahlung durchaus üblich war, einer religiösen Körperschaft aber auch erlassen werden konnte. »Ja, Herr, ich werde zahlen – falls Ihr nicht wünscht, uns die Genehmigung zum höheren Ruhm des Herrn kostenlos zu gewähren.«

Zum erstenmal sah Stephan Philip direkt in die Augen. »Ihr seid ein tapferer Mann, wie Ihr vor mir steht, mit dem Rücken zum Feind, und dennoch mit mir handelt.«

Philip erwiderte seinen Blick offen. »Wenn es Gottes Wille ist, daß mein Leben zu Ende geht, dann kann nichts mich retten«, sagte er und klang dabei mutiger, als er sich fühlte. »Aber wenn Gott will, daß ich weiterlebe und den Dom in Kingsbridge baue, dann können zehntausend Bogenschützen nichts gegen mich ausrichten.«

»Gut gesagt!« bemerkte Stephan, schlug Philip auf die Schulter und wandte sich der Kathedrale zu. Philip ging mit vor Erleichterung weichen Knien neben ihm her und fühlte sich bei jedem Schritt, den er zwischen sich und die Burg legte, ein wenig besser. Anscheinend hatte er die Prüfung bestanden. Aber er mußte den König zu einer unzweideutigen Verpflichtung bewegen. Nur noch wenige Momente, und er würde wieder von Höflingen umringt sein. Als sie die Reihe der Wachposten passierten, nahm Philip all einen Mut zusammen und sagte: »Mein Herr und König, wenn Ihr einen Brief an den Vogt von Shiring schreiben würdet –«

Er wurde unterbrochen. Einer der Grafen eilte ihnen aufgeregt entgegen und sagte: »Robert von Gloucester ist auf dem Weg hierher, mein Herr und König.«

»Was? Wie weit von hier?«

»Nicht weit. Höchstens einen Tagesmarsch –«

»Wieso bin ich nicht gewarnt worden? Ich habe überall Posten aufstellen lassen.«

»Sie haben den Fosse Way genommen und dann die Straße verlassen, um sich querfeldein zu schlagen.«

»Mit wem hat er sich verbündet?«

»Mit sämtlichen Grafen und Rittern, die in den vergangenen zwei Jahren ihre Ländereien verloren haben. Und Ranulf von Chester ist ebenfalls –«

»Natürlich. Dieser gemeine Verräter.«

»Er hat alle seine Ritter aus Chester bei sich, dazu noch eine wilde Horde von raubgierigen Walisern.«

»Wieviel Mann insgesamt?«

»Um die tausend.«

»Verflucht – das sind hundert mehr als wir!«

Mittlerweile hatten sich mehrere Barone um sie geschart, und einer von ihnen ergriff das Wort. »Herr, wenn er übers flache Land kommt, muß er durch die Furt ziehen –«

»Gute Idee, Edward!« sagte Stephan. »Bezieht mit Euren Mannen Posten am Fluß und seht zu, daß Ihr die Furt halten könnt. Ihr werdet dazu Bogenschützen brauchen.«

»Wie weit sind sie schon vorgerückt, weiß das jemand?« fragte Edward.

Der Graf, der zuerst gesprochen hatte, sagte: »Der Späher meinte, sie seien schon sehr nah. Womöglich sind sie noch vor Euch bei der Furt.«

»Ich mache mich sofort auf den Weg«, sagte Edward.

»Bravo!« sagte König Stephan. Er schlug die zur Faust geballte Rechte in die linke Handfläche. »Endlich werde ich Robert von Gloucester auf dem Schlachtfeld begegnen. Ich wünschte nur, ich hätte mehr Männer. Aber dennoch – hundert Leute mehr fallen nicht so sehr ins Gewicht.«

Philip hörte sich das alles grimmig schweigend an. Eben war er noch drauf und dran gewesen, Stephans Einwilligung zu bekommen! Nun stand dem König der Kopf nach anderen Dingen. Doch Philip mochte sich nicht einfach geschlagen geben. Noch immer trug er den Purpurmantel des Königs. Er ließ ihn von den Schultern gleiten und hielt ihn dem König mit den Worten hin: »Wir schlüpfen besser wieder in unsere gewohnten Rollen, mein Herr und König.«

Stephan nickte zerstreut. Ein Höfling trat hinter ihn und half ihm beim Ausziehen der Mönchskutte. Philip reichte ihm die königliche Robe und sagte: »Herr, Ihr scheint meiner Bitte wohlgesonnen.«

Stephan wirkte ungehalten über die Mahnung. Er rückte seine Robe schulterzuckend zurecht und wollte gerade den Mund aufmachen, als sich eine neue Stimme vernehmen ließ.

»Mein Herr und König!«

Philip erkannte die Stimme, und sein Mut sank. Er drehte sich um und erblickte William Hamleigh.

»William, mein Junge!« rief der König in dem dröhnend-herzhaften Tonfall, den er seinen Kriegern gegenüber anzuschlagen pflegte. »Ihr kommt genau zur rechten Zeit.«

William verneigte sich und sagte: »Herr, ich habe fünfzig Ritter und zweihundert Männer aus meiner Grafschaft mitgebracht.«

Philips Hoffnungen zerfielen zu Staub.

Stephan war ganz offensichtlich hocherfreut. »Was für ein guter Mann Ihr seid!« sagte er herzlich. »Damit sind wir dem Feind überlegen!« Er legte William einen Arm um die Schulter und ging mit ihm in die Kathedrale.

Philip blieb wie angewurzelt stehen und sah ihnen nach. Um Haaresbreite hätte ich meine Mission erfüllt, dachte er voller Bitterkeit, doch dann kam William und hat mit seiner Armee den Sieg über die Gerechtigkeit davongetragen. Er sah, daß der Höfling noch immer seine Kutte hielt, nahm sie ihm ab und zog sie über. Der Höfling folgte dem König in den Dom. In Philips Enttäuschung mischte sich Bitterkeit, zumal ihm der Anblick der drei riesigen Bogenportale wieder seine Hoffnung in Erinnerung brachte, ebensolche Bogen in Kingsbridge bauen zu können. Doch König Stephan hatte sich auf William Hamleighs Seite geschlagen. Er hatte die Wahl gehabt: die Rechtmäßigkeit von Philips Anliegen gegen den Vorteil von Williams Armee. Der König hatte seine Prüfung nicht bestanden.

Nun blieb Philip nur noch eine Hoffnung: daß König Stephan die bevorstehende Schlacht verlor.

Der Himmel klarte ein wenig auf, als der Bischof in der Kathedrale die Messe zelebrierte. Die Pferde waren bereits gesattelt, die Ritter trugen Panzerhemden, die Bewaffneten waren verköstigt und mit einem Trunk starken Weins gelabt worden, der ihnen Mut einflößen sollte.

In den Seitenschiffen stampften und schnaubten die Schlachtrösser, während William Hamleigh noch inmitten der Ritter und Grafen im Mittelschiff kniete und der Bischof ihnen im voraus Absolution für all die Menschenleben erteilte, die sie im Laufe dieses Tages auf ihr Gewissen laden sollten.

William war vor Angst und Aufregung wie benommen. Trug der König heute den Sieg davon, so würde sein Name auf ewig mit dieser

Schlacht verbunden sein, denn dann würde es heißen, daß er mit seiner Verstärkung das Zünglein an der Waage gewesen sei. Sollte der König aber verlieren ... nichts war unmöglich. William zitterte auf dem kalten Steinfußboden.

Der König, in ein frisches, weißes Gewand gekleidet, stand vorne und hielt eine Kerze in der Hand. Als die Hostie emporgehalten wurde, brach die Kerze und erlosch. William wurde von Grauen erfaßt: Das war ein schlechtes Omen! Ein Priester kam mit einer neuen Kerze und entfernte die zerbrochene, und Stephan lächelte unbekümmert, doch das Gefühl einer übernatürlichen Bedrohung wollte nicht weichen, und als William sich verstohlen umsah, hätte er schwören können, daß es allen anderen ebenso erging.

Nach dem Gottesdienst legte der König mit Hilfe eines Dieners sein Panzerzeug an, eine knielange Brünne aus Leder mit aufgenähten Eisenringen. Sie war vorn und hinten bis in Hüfthöhe geschlitzt, damit sie ihn beim Reiten nicht behinderte. Der Diener schnürte sie am Hals fest zu. Dann setzte er dem König eine enganliegende Kappe mit langer Kettenkapuze auf, die sein helles Haar bedeckte und seinen Nacken schützte. Über die Kappe stülpte er einen eisernen Helm mit Nasenschutz. Die Lederstiefel waren mit Ketten und spitzen Sporen versehen.

Währenddessen scharten sich die Grafen um den König. William befolgte den Rat seiner Mutter und tat, als wäre er bereits einer von ihnen, drängte sich vor und gesellte sich zu der Gruppe um den König. Nachdem er eine Weile lang zugehört hatte, begriff er, daß Stephan zum Rückzug überredet werden und Lincoln den Rebellen überlassen sollte.

»Ihr gebietet über mehr Land als Mathilde – Ihr könnt ein größeres Heer ausheben«, sagte ein älterer Mann, in dem William Lord Hugh erkannte. »Zieht gen Süden, holt Verstärkung und kommt dann zahlenmäßig überlegen zurück.«

Nach dem bösen Vorzeichen mit der zerbrochenen Kerze war William selbst eher nach Rückzug zumute, aber der König bewies wenig Geduld für solches Gerede. »Wir sind stark genug, sie heute zu besiegen«, sagte er munter. »Wo habt Ihr Euren Kampfgeist gelassen?« Er schlang sich einen Gurt um, an dessen einer Seite sein Schwert, an der anderen ein Dolch hing; die dazugehörigen Scheiden waren aus Holz und Leder gefertigt.

»Die beiden Heere gleichen sich zu sehr in Umfang und Stärke«, meinte ein großer Mann mit kurzem, graumeliertem Haar und gestutztem Bart, der Graf von Surrey. »Es ist zu riskant.«

William wußte, daß dieses Argument bei Stephan nicht zog: Der König war viel zu ritterlich. »Gleichen sich zu sehr?« wiederholte er verächtlich. »Mir ist ein fairer Kampf lieber.« Er streifte lederne, an der Oberseite gepanzerte Fingerhandschuhe über. Der Diener reichte ihm einen hölzernen, mit Leder bespannten Schild. Der König schlang sich den Tragegurt um den Nacken und hielt den Schild in der Linken.

»Zum gegenwärtigen Zeitpunkt setzen wir durch einen Rückzug kaum etwas aufs Spiel«, beharrte Hugh. »Wir haben ja noch nicht einmal die Burg erobert.«

»Damit würde ich die Möglichkeit verschenken, mich endlich mit Robert von Gloucester auf dem Schlachtfeld zu messen«, sagte Stephan. »Zwei Jahre lang ist er mir stets nur ausgewichen. Und nun, da sich die Gelegenheit bietet, mit diesem Verräter ein für allemal abzurechnen, werde ich nicht den Schwanz einziehen, nur weil sich unsere Heere zu sehr gleichen.«

Ein Reitknecht führte sein gesatteltes Pferd vor. Stephan war schon im Begriff aufzusitzen, als am Westportal Unruhe entstand und ein kotbespritzter, blutender Ritter durch das Hauptschiff herbeieilte. William schwante nichts Gutes. Als der Mann sich vor dem König verneigte, erkannte William in ihm einen von Edwards Männern, die zur Verteidigung der Furt entsandt worden waren. »Wir kamen zu spät, Herr«, stieß der Mann heiser und keuchend hervor. »Der Feind hat den Fluß bereits überschritten.«

Noch ein böses Omen! William wurde kalt. Jetzt lagen nur mehr offene Felder zwischen dem Feind und der Stadt Lincoln.

Selbst Stephan wirkte einen Moment lang bestürzt, riß sich aber augenblicklich zusammen. »Macht nichts!« sagte er. »Um so eher geht es in die Schlacht!« Er schwang sich auf sein Schlachtroß.

An seinem Sattel hing eine Streitaxt. Der Diener reichte ihm eine hölzerne Lanze mit blitzender Eisenspitze und vervollständigte damit die Bewaffnung des Königs. Stephan schnalzte mit der Zunge, und das Roß setzte sich gehorsam in Bewegung.

Während er die ganze Länge des Mittelschiffs hinter sich legte, saßen auch die Grafen, Barone und Ritter auf und schlossen zu ihm auf, so daß sie den Dom wie in einer Prozession verließen. Draußen kamen noch die Fußsoldaten dazu. Dies war der Augenblick, in dem so mancher von Furcht ergriffen wurde und sich nach einer Fluchtmöglichkeit umsah. Doch das würdevolle Dahinschreiten, die beinahe feierlich anmutende Atmosphäre und die gaffende Stadtbevölkerung erschwerten den Hasenfüßen das Entkommen.

Die Zahl der königlichen Streitmacht erhöhte sich noch um hundert oder mehr Städter – dickwanstige Bäcker, kurzsichtige Weber und rotnasige Bierbrauer –, die sich, nur notdürftig bewaffnet, auf ihren Gäulen und Kleppern dem Heer anschlossen. Ihre Kampfbereitschaft bewies, wie unbeliebt sich Ranulf in Lincoln gemacht hatte.

Da das Heer nicht an der Burg vorbeiziehen konnte, weil ihm von dort die Bogenschützen drohten, verließ es die Stadt durch das Nordtor, den sogenannten Newport Arch, und wandte sich dann erst gen Westen. Dort sollte die Schlacht ausgetragen werden.

William musterte das Gelände mit wachen Augen. Hier gab es, im Gegensatz zum Süden der Stadt, wo der Hügel steil zum Fluß hin abfiel, eine langgestreckte Kuppe, die sachte in die Ebene überging. William erkannte sofort, daß Stephan die günstigste Stelle zur Verteidigung der Stadt gewählt hatte: Aus welcher Richtung der Feind auch kommen mochte, er hatte stets den Hang unterhalb des königlichen Heeres zu überwinden.

Stephan hatte die Stadt etwa eine Viertelmeile hinter sich gelassen, als ihm zwei Kundschafter eilig den Hang herauf entgegenritten kamen. Sie kannten den König und hielten direkt auf ihn zu. William drängte sich näher heran, um ihren Bericht ebenfalls zu hören.

»Der Feind nähert sich in Windeseile, Herr«, sagte einer der Späher.

William ließ seinen Blick über die Ebene schweifen. In der Ferne wälzte sich stetig eine schwarze Masse heran: der Feind. Furcht beschlich ihn. Er versuchte, sie abzuschütteln – vergeblich. Sobald die Schlacht begann, würde sie von allein weichen.

König Stephan fragte: »Wie sieht ihre Schlachtordnung aus?«

»Ranulf und die Ritter aus Chester bilden die Mitte, Herr«, begann der Kundschafter. »Sie sind zu Fuß.«

William fragte sich, woher der Späher das wissen konnte. Er mußte sich geradewegs ins feindliche Lager begeben und den Marschbefehlen gelauscht haben. Dazu gehörte schon einiges an Mut!

»Ranulf in der Mitte?« fragte Stephan verwundert. »Dann wäre ja nicht er, sondern Robert der Anführer!«

»Robert von Gloucester bildet mit einer Horde Männer, die sich ›Die Entrechteten‹ nennen, den linken Flügel«, fuhr der Späher fort. William wußte, warum sie sich diesen Namen gegeben hatten: Ein jeder von ihnen hatte seit Beginn des Krieges sein Land verloren.

»Dann hat Robert das Kommando an Ranulf abgegeben«, sagte Stephan nachdenklich. »Schade. Ich kenne Robert gut – bin praktisch mit ihm zusammen aufgewachsen – und hätte seine Absichten durchschauen können. Aber Ranulf ist mir fremd. Einerlei. Wer ist auf der Rechten?«

»Die Waliser, Herr.«

»Bogenschützen, nehme ich an.« Die Männer aus Südwales waren berühmt für ihre Geschicklichkeit im Umgang mit Pfeil und Bogen.

»Nicht die«, sagte der Kundschafter. »Ein wilder Haufen mit bemalten Gesichtern, die wüste Lieder schmettern und Hämmer und Keulen schwingen. Beritten sind sie so gut wie gar nicht.«

»Sie müssen aus dem Norden von Wales sein«, vermutete Stephan. »Ranulf hat ihnen vermutlich die Plünderung der Stadt versprochen. Gott stehe Lincoln bei, sollte es dazu kommen! Aber es wird ihnen nicht gelingen! Wie heißt Ihr, Kundschafter?«

»Roger, Lackland genannt«, erwiderte der Mann.

»Lackland? Für Eure Mühe sollt Ihr zehn Morgen Land bekommen.«

Der Mann war überglücklich. »Ich danke Euch, Herr!«

»Nun also.« Stephan wandte sich um und faßte seine Grafen ins Auge, um den Schlachtplan bekanntzugeben. William war gespannt, welche Rolle ihm zufallen würde. »Wo ist mein Lord Alan von der Bretagne?«

Alan näherte sich auf seinem Pferd. Er war der Anführer einer Schar bretonischer Söldner – entwurzelte Haudegen, die für Geld kämpften und niemandem zur Treue verpflichtet waren.

Stephan sagte zu Alan: »Ihr sollt mit Euren tapferen Bretonen im vorderen Glied zu meiner Linken sein.«

William empfand die Klugheit dieser Entscheidung nach: Bretonische Söldner gegen walisische Abenteuer, Unzuverlässigkeit gegen Undiszipliniertheit.

»William von Ypres!« rief Stephan.

»Mein Herr und König.« Ein dunkelhäutiger Mann auf einem schwarzen Schlachtroß erhob seine Lanze. Dieser William war Anführer einer weiteren, aus Flamen bestehenden Söldnertruppe, welcher der Ruf vorauseilte, um eine Spur zuverlässiger als die Bretonen zu sein.

Stephan sagte: »Ihr haltet Euch ebenfalls zu meiner Linken, aber hinter Alans Mannen.«

Die beiden Söldnerführer machten kehrt und ritten zum Heer zurück, um ihre Männer einzuteilen. William fragte sich, wo er wohl aufgestellt würde. Ihm stand absolut nicht der Sinn danach, im vorderen Glied zu kämpfen. Er hatte sich bereits genügend hervorgetan, indem er eine solch große Truppe einbrachte. Eine sichere, ereignislose Stellung im hinteren Glied käme ihm heute zupaß.

»Meine Grafen von Worcester, Surrey, Northampton, York und Hertford mit ihren Rittern«, befahl der König, »bilden meine rechte Flanke.«

William erkannte erneut, wie sinnvoll Stephans Anordnung war: Die mehrheitlich berittenen Grafen und Ritter sahen sich Robert von Gloucester und seinen verbündeten ›entrechteten‹ Adligen gegenüber, die großenteils ebenfalls beritten sein würden. Dennoch fühlte er sich enttäuscht, daß er nicht zusammen mit den Grafen aufgestellt worden war. Der König hatte ihn doch nicht vergessen, oder?

»Ich werde zu Fuß gemeinsam mit der Infanterie die Mitte halten«, verkündete Stephan.

Zum erstenmal war William nicht mit seiner Entscheidung einverstanden. Seiner Meinung nach war es stets besser, so lange wie möglich im Sattel zu bleiben. Aber Ranulf, der Anführer der feindlichen Streitmacht, war angeblich zu Fuß, und Stephans überspannter Sinn für Gerechtigkeit zwang ihn dazu, seinem Feind ebenbürtig gegenüberzutreten.

»An meiner Seite in der Mitte will ich William von Shiring mit seinen Mannen haben«, sagte der König.

William wußte nicht, ob er sich freuen oder entsetzt sein sollte. Auserwählt zu sein, an der Seite des Königs zu kämpfen, war eine große Ehre – Mutter wäre sicherlich hocherfreut –, setzte ihn aber auch höchster Gefährdung aus. Schlimmer war jedoch, daß er zu Fuß kämpfen mußte. Und um das Maß vollzumachen, würde der König ihn beobachten und seine Leistung aus unmittelbarer Nähe begutachten können. Er mußte einen furchtlosen Eindruck erwecken und auf den Feind zugehen, während seine bevorzugte Taktik sonst darin bestand, einen großen Bogen um jede brenzlige Situation zu machen und nur zu kämpfen, wenn es absolut nicht mehr zu umgehen war.

»Die treuen Bürger von Lincoln werden die Nachhut bilden«, verkündete Stephan. Diese Entscheidung zeugte sowohl von Rücksichtnahme als auch militärischem Geschick. Die Stadtbewohner waren nirgendwo von großem Nutzen, doch wenn sie im hinteren Glied blieben, konnten sie kaum einen Schaden anrichten und würden auch keine hohen Verluste zu beklagen haben.

William hißte das Banner des Grafen von Shiring – auch dies eine Idee seiner Mutter. Streng genommen hatte er kein Recht darauf, denn er war nicht der Graf; aber seine Leute waren es gewohnt, dem Banner von Shiring zu folgen – so oder ähnlich wollte er jedenfalls argumentieren, sprach man ihn darauf an. Und wenn sie die Schlacht gewonnen, war er am Ende dieses Tages vielleicht tatsächlich Graf von Shiring …

Seine Männer scharten sich um ihn. Walter war wie stets an seiner Seite, zuverlässig wie ein Fels in der Brandung. Das gleiche galt für Ugly Gervase, Hugh Axe und Miles Dice. Der im Steinbruch ums Leben gekommene Gilbert war durch Guillaume de St. Clair ersetzt worden, einen jungen Mann mit frischem Gesicht und einer Neigung zur Grausamkeit.

William sah sich um – und geriet in hellen Zorn beim Anblick Richards von Kingsbridge, der schimmerndes neues Panzerzeug trug und auf einem herrlichen Schlachtroß saß. Er gehörte zur Truppe des Grafen von Surrey. Zwar hatte er dem König keine Armee zugeführt wie William, wirkte jedoch ungemein imposant – unverbraucht, kraftvoll und tapfer –, und sollten ihm heute irgendwelche Heldentaten gelingen, konnte er durchaus die Gunst des Königs gewinnen. Schlachten waren unberechenbar, und Könige nicht minder.

Vielleicht würde Richard aber auch fallen. Das wäre ein *echter* Glücksfall! Nach Richards Tod gelüstete William mehr, als ihn je nach einer Frau gelüstet hatte.

Er hielt Ausschau gen Westen. Der Feind war näher gerückt.

Philip stand auf dem Dach der Kathedrale, und unter ihm lag, ausgebreitet wie auf einer Landkarte, die Stadt Lincoln. Der Dom war unmittelbar von der Altstadt mit ihren geraden Straßen und ihren ordentlichen Gärten umgeben, die Burg nahm den ganzen Südwesten ein. In den neueren Stadtteilen auf der nach Süden hin steil abfallenden Hangseite zwischen Altstadt und Fluß, ansonsten von reger Betriebsamkeit erfüllt, herrschte heute ängstliche Stille, die sich wie ein Leichentuch über die Stadt gesenkt hatte. Die Leute standen auf ihren Hausdächern, um von dort aus die Schlacht zu verfolgen. Der Fluß kam von Osten, schlängelte sich am Fuße des Hügels entlang und weitete sich dann zu einem Brayfield Pool genannten, großen natürlichen Hafen, der von Kaianlagen gesäumt war und in dem es von Schiffen und Booten nur so wimmelte. Ein Kanal, der sogenannte Fosdyke, verlief von Brayfield Pool aus in westlicher Richtung – bis hin zum Trent, hatte Philip sich sagen lassen. Aus seiner luftigen Höhe sah Philip staunend, wie schnurgerade sich der Kanal über viele

Meilen hinzog. Es hieß, er sei schon vor urdenklichen Zeiten gebaut worden.

Der Kanal bildete den Rand des Schlachtfeldes. Philip beobachtete, wie König Stephans Heer die Stadt in einem bunt zusammengewürfelten Haufen verließ und sich auf dem Hügelkamm allmählich zu drei ordentlichen Kolonnen formierte. An den roten und gelben Waffenröcken und den farbigen Bannern erkannte Philip, daß Stephan die Grafen zu seiner Rechten aufgestellt hatte. Hier herrschte auch die meiste Aktivität: Man ritt auf und ab, erteilte Befehle und schmiedete Pläne. Die Gruppe zur Linken des Königs, auf dem zum Kanal hin abfallenden Hang, war in gedämpftes Grau und Braun gekleidet, verfügte über weniger Pferde, wirkte weit weniger geschäftig und sparte sich ihre Kräfte offenbar für die Schlacht auf: Das waren gewiß die Söldner.

Jenseits von Stephans Heer, dort, wo die Umrisse des Kanals verschwammen und kaum mehr von den Hecken zu unterscheiden waren, tummelte sich das Heer der Rebellen gleich einem Bienenschwarm auf den Feldern. Zunächst hatte es ausgesehen, als käme es nicht recht vom Fleck, aber als Philip nach einer Weile wieder hinschaute, war es schon ein gutes Stück näher gerückt.

Philip blieb nichts anderes übrig, als untätig zuzuschauen – eine Situation, die er haßte. Er versuchte, den Ausgang der Schlacht geduldig und gefaßt abzuwarten: Wenn Gott eine neue Kathedrale in Kingsbridge wünscht, dachte er, so wird er selbst Sorge dafür tragen, daß König Stephan heute Robert von Gloucester unterliegt und ich die siegreiche Kaiserin Mathilde bitten kann, mir den Steinbruch zurückzugeben und den Markt zu genehmigen. Sollte aber Stephan siegen, so muß ich wohl den Willen Gottes hinnehmen und meine ehrgeizigen Pläne aufgeben. Aus Kingsbridge wird dann allerdings ein unbedeutendes, verschlafenes Nest ...

Doch so sehr sich Philip auch bemühte – damit konnte er sich nicht abfinden. Er wünschte sich sehnlichst, daß *Robert* siegte.

Ein bitterkalter Wind blies um die Türme der Kathedrale und drohte, die weniger robusten Zuschauer aus ihrer Höhe auf den Friedhof darunter zu fegen. Philip fröstelte und wickelte sich fester in seinen Umhang.

Die beiden Heere waren noch fast eine Meile voneinander entfernt.

Das Heer der Rebellen kam ungefähr eine Meile vor der Front des Königs zum Stehen. Es war eine Qual, den Gegner in voller Stärke sehen, aber keinerlei Einzelheiten ausmachen zu können. William hätte gerne gewußt, wie gut die Rebellen bewaffnet, ob sie guten Mutes und kampfbereit oder müde und widerwillig waren, ja sogar, wie groß sie waren. Sie schoben sich wieder langsam vorwärts, da die hinteren Reihen, beseelt von der gleichen Beklommenheit wie William, nach vorne drängten, um den Gegner in Augenschein zu nehmen.

Die Grafen und ihre Ritter in Stephans Heer reihten sich mit ihren Pferden auf und hielten die Lanzen angriffsbereit. William ließ seine Pferde hinter der Nachhut zurück. Er befahl den Knappen, sie nicht in die Stadt zu führen, sondern bereitzuhalten für den Fall, daß sie gebraucht wurden – für die Flucht bereitzuhalten, meinte er, sprach es jedoch nicht aus. Nach einer verlorenen Schlacht war es besser davonzulaufen, statt zu sterben.

Eine Weile lang geschah gar nichts, und es schien beinahe, als wolle der Kampf nie beginnen. Der Wind flaute ab und die Pferde beruhigten sich – ihre Reiter jedoch nicht. König Stephan nahm seinen Helm ab und kratzte sich am Kopf. Auch William wurde unruhig.

Dann kam aus unerfindlichen Gründen plötzlich wieder Spannung auf. Ein Schlachtruf ertönte, sämtliche Pferde scheuten. Gejohle erklang und wurde sogleich vom Donnern der Pferdehufe wieder verschluckt. Die Schlacht hatte begonnen. William witterte den süßsauren Geruch der Angst.

Er sah sich um und versuchte, Klarheit über die Lage zu gewinnen, aber überall herrschte Chaos, und da er zu Fuß war, konnte er nur seine unmittelbare Umgebung überblicken. Die Grafen hatten wohl das Startzeichen zur Schlacht gegeben, indem sie gegen den Feind vorgerückt waren. Vermutlich hatten die entrechteten Adligen aus Graf Roberts Heer entsprechend darauf reagiert und waren geschlossen zum Sturmangriff übergegangen. Fast zur gleichen Zeit erhob sich ein Geheul von links, und als William sich umdrehte, sah er, wie die Berittenen unter den bretonischen Söldnern ihren Pferden die Sporen gaben. Daraufhin erhob sich aus der entsprechenden Abteilung des feindlichen Heeres, wahrscheinlich also dem welschen Mob, ein unglaubliches Geheul, das einem fast das Blut in den Adern stocken ließ.

Richard hatte William ganz aus den Augen verloren.

Dutzende von Pfeilen stiegen gleich einer Vogelschar hinter den Linien des Feindes auf und prasselten nun überall herunter. William hielt sich seinen Schild über den Kopf. Er haßte Pfeile – sie töteten aufs Geratewohl.

König Stephan stieß einen Schlachtruf aus und stürmte vor. William zog sein Schwert, rannte ihm nach und rief seine Männer zu

sich. Aber die Berittenen zu seinen Seiten hatten sich bei ihrem Sturmangriff aufgefächert und gerieten zwischen ihn und den Feind.

Zur Rechten war das ohrenbetäubende Klirren von Eisen auf Eisen
zu hören, und die Luft war von dem metallischen Geruch erfüllt, den
er gut kannte. Die Grafen und die Entrechteten waren aufeinander
gestoßen. William sah nur noch Männer und Pferde, die aufeinanderprallten, herumwirbelten, angriffen und fielen. Das Wiehern der Tiere
war nicht mehr von den Schlachtrufen der Männer zu unterscheiden,
und von irgendwoher hörte William trotz des Getöses schon die entsetzten, markerschütternden Schreie der ersten Verwundeten. Hoffentlich hatte es Richard erwischt!

William wandte sich nach links und sah mit Entsetzen, daß die
Bretonen von den Keulen und Äxten der wilden Waliser zurückge-
trieben wurden, die wie Berserker wüteten, schrien und tobten und
sich vor lauter Kampfeifer gegenseitig über den Haufen rannten. Sie
brannten offenbar schon darauf, die reiche Stadt zu plündern. Die
Bretonen, die nichts als ihren nächsten Wochensold zu erwarten
hatten, kämpften defensiv und gaben Boden preis. William wandte
sich angewidert ab.

Es ärgerte ihn, daß er selbst noch nicht zum Zuge gekommen war,
umgeben von seinen Rittern, vor sich sowohl die berittenen Grafen
als auch die Bretonen. Er drängte sich bis zum König vor. Ringsum
tobte die Schlacht: gestürzte Pferde, wilde Zweikämpfe, der ohrenbetäubende Lärm aufeinanderschlagender Schwerter und der ekelerre-
gende Blutgeruch, nur William und König Stephan befanden sich in
einem toten Winkel.

Philip hatte zwar eine hervorragende Übersicht, konnte sich jedoch
keinen Reim auf die Geschehnisse machen. Da drunten herrschte ein
einziges Chaos: aufblitzende Klingen, vorpreschende Pferde, aufflat-
ternde und sinkende Banner und der Schlachtenlärm, den der Wind
gedämpft herübertrug. Es war zum Verrücktwerden! Männer fielen
und starben, andere rappelten sich wieder auf und fochten weiter,
doch Philip konnte beim besten Willen nicht erkennen, wer Sieger
und wer Verlierer war.

In seiner Nähe stand ein Dompriester, ganz in Pelz gehüllt, der
ihn ansah und fragte: »Wie läuft es?«

Philip schüttelte den Kopf und erwiderte: »Ich weiß es nicht.«

Er hatte den Satz noch nicht zu Ende gesprochen, da sah er links
vom Schachtfeld Männer den Hügel hinab auf den Kanal zu fliehen.

Philip meinte, in ihnen die Söldner des Königs zu erkennen, die von den Walisern in ihrer Kriegsbemalung verfolgt wurden. Ihr Siegesgeschrei drang vernehmlich herüber, und Philips Hoffnung stieg: Die Rebellen hatten die Oberhand!

Dann sprang der Funke auf die andere Seite über. Zur Rechten, wo die Berittenen kämpften, schien das Heer des Königs zurückzuweichen. Zunächst war es nur eine kaum wahrnehmbare Bewegung, die aber zunehmend deutlicher wurde; im Handumdrehen war aus dem geordneten Rückzug eine kopflose Flucht geworden, und die Ritter des Königs nahmen zuhauf Reißaus.

Philip fühlte sich selig: Das mußte der Wille Gottes sein!

Das Blatt wendete sich erschreckend schnell. Eben noch hatten die beiden Heere gleichermaßen erbittert gekämpft, und schon im nächsten Augenblick fielen die Männer des Königs zurück. William war zutiefst entmutigt. Zu seiner Linken flüchteten die bretonischen Söldner den Hügel hinunter und wurden von den Walisern in den Kanal gejagt; zu seiner Rechten suchten die Grafen ihr Heil im Rückzug nach Lincoln. Nur die Mitte hielt dem Ansturm noch stand: König Stephan, inmitten des Getümmels, hieb mit einem riesigen Schwert um sich, und die Männer aus Shiring kämpften wie die Berserker rings um ihn herum. Aber die Lage war brenzlig: Setzten die Seitenflügel ihren Rückzug fort, so wurde der König eingekesselt. William wünschte, der König möge zurückweichen, doch dessen Mut überwog seine Klugheit, so daß er unverdrossen weiterkämpfte.

Plötzlich verlagerte sich das Geschehen zur linken Seite hin. William blickte sich um und sah, daß die flämischen Söldner aus dem Hinterhalt über die Waliser herfielen, die notgedrungen von der Verfolgung der Bretonen abließen und sich ihrer eigenen Verteidigung widmeten. Einige Zeit ging alles drunter und drüber. Dann griff Ranulf von Chester aus der Mitte der feindlichen Front die Flamen an, die sich plötzlich von zwei Seiten attackiert sahen.

Stephan, des Getümmels gewahr geworden, trieb nun seine eigenen Mannen zum Nachrücken an, und William begann, an der Weisheit von Ranulfs Entscheidung zu zweifeln. Sollte es den Männern des Königs gelingen, zu Ranulf und seiner Truppe aufzuschließen, so würde diesmal Ranulf von zwei Seiten in die Zange genommen.

Dann stürzte, direkt zu Williams Füßen, einer seiner eigenen Ritter zu Boden, und im nächsten Moment befand er sich inmitten des Kampfgeschehens.

Ein grobschlächtiger Mann aus dem Norden ging mit blutverschmierten Schwert auf ihn los, doch William parierte den Stoß mit Leichtigkeit: Sein Angreifer war bereits abgekämpft, er hingegen ganz frisch. William stieß nach dem Gesicht des Mannes, verfehlte sein Ziel und parierte einen weiteren Schlag. Er hob sein Schwert in die Höhe und gab seine Deckung absichtlich preis; sobald der Mann, wie erwartet, wieder zum Angriff überging, wich William zur Seite und ließ sein Schwert mit aller Macht auf die Schulter des Mannes niedersausen. Der Hieb durchschlug seines Gegners Panzerhemd und brach ihm das Schlüsselbein; er stürzte zu Boden.

Zu seiner Rechten entstand plötzlich Gedränge, so daß sich einer seiner beiden Gegner abwenden und gegen einen rotgesichtigen, mit einem Hackebeil bewaffneten Mann zur Wehr setzen mußte, der aussah wie ein irrsinnig gewordener Schlachter. Damit blieb William nur noch ein Gegner. Bösartig grinsend ging er auf ihn los. Der Mann, von Panik ergriffen, schlug blind nach Williams Kopf. William duckte sich und trieb seine Schwertspitze genau unterhalb des kurzen Kettenhemdes in den Oberschenkel des Mannes. Das Bein knickte ein, und der Mann stürzte zu Boden.

Und wieder stand William ohne Gegner da. Schweratmend blieb er stehen. Einen Moment lang hatte er schon gedacht, das königliche Heer sei zersprengt worden, aber es hatte sich wieder gesammelt, und derzeit schien weder die eine noch die andere Seite an Boden zu gewinnen. Er wandte sich nach rechts, um zu sehen, wer den Angriff geführt, der einen seiner Gegner abgelenkt hatte, und stellte verblüfft fest, daß es die Bürger von Lincoln waren, die sich einen erbitterten Kampf mit dem Feind lieferten. Vermutlich glaubten sie, Heim und Herd verteidigen zu müssen. Aber wer hatte sie, nachdem die Grafen das Weite gesucht, so eilig aufgeboten? Die Antwort ließ nicht lange auf sich warten: Zu seinem großen Mißfallen sah er, wie Richard von Kingsbridge auf seinem Schlachtroß die Bürger anfeuerte. Williams Zuversicht welkte dahin. Wenn der König sah, wie tapfer sich Richard schlug, war all seine Mühe womöglich umsonst gewesen! Williams Blick suchte Stephan. Im selben Augenblick, da er ihn entdeckte, fiel Richard dem König auf, und Stephan winkte ihm ermunternd zu. William äußerte seinen Unmut in einem grollenden Fluch.

Der Angriff der Stadtbewohner verschaffte dem König eine Atempause, wenngleich nur eine kurze. Dann hatten auch schon Ranulfs Mannen die Flamen auf dem linken Flügel in die Flucht geschlagen, und Ranulf konnte sich der Mitte zuwenden. Gleichzeitig sammelten sich die sogenannten Entrechteten zum Angriff auf Richard und die Bürger von Lincoln, und der Kampf entbrannte erst richtig.

William sah sich plötzlich einem wahren Hünen mit einer Streitaxt gegenüber. Verzweifelt wich er dem Angriff aus, urplötzlich um sein Leben fürchtend. Jeder Hieb trieb ihn ein Stück zurück, und dann erkannte er entsetzt, daß nicht nur er, sondern die gesamte königliche Armee gleichermaßen zurückwich. Von links kamen die Waliser wieder den Hügel herauf und fingen erstaunlicherweise an, mit Steinen zu werfen. Das mochte lächerlich anmuten, verfehlte aber seine Wirkung nicht, denn nun mußte William sich nicht nur gegen den Riesen und dessen Streitaxt zur Wehr setzen, sondern auch noch die Wurfgeschosse im Auge behalten. Auf einmal schien es nur so von Feinden zu wimmeln, und William ahnte verzweifelt, daß sie den Männern des Königs zahlenmäßig überlegen waren. Die Angst drohte ihn zu überwältigen, als ihm klar wurde, daß die Schlacht schon so gut wie verloren war und er selbst in Todesgefahr schwebte. Warum floh der König nicht, bevor es zu spät war? Warum kämpfte er immer noch? Das war ja der helle Wahnsinn – er würde fallen – sie würden alle sterben!

Williams Gegner hob die Axt zum Schlag, und Williams Kämpfernatur gewann für einen Augenblick wieder die Oberhand: Statt wie bisher zurückzuweichen, tat er einen Satz nach vorn und stieß nach dem Gesicht des Hünen. Seine Schwertspitze bohrte sich genau unter dem Kinn in den Hals des Mannes. William stieß kraftvoll nach. Die Augen des Mannes schlossen sich. William überkam eine Welle dankbarer Erleichterung. Er zog sein Schwert heraus und wich der Streitaxt aus, die aus den Händen des Toten fiel.

Er warf einen verstohlenen Blick zum König hinüber, der nur ein paar Schritte entfernt kämpfte. Stephan führte soeben einen kraftvollen, auf den Helm seines Gegners zielenden Schlag aus, und seine Klinge brach in zwei Teile, als wäre sie aus morschem Holz. Das war's! dachte William erleichtert. Die Schlacht ist vorüber. Jetzt wird der König fliehen, sich in Sicherheit bringen und sich ein andermal wieder zum Kampf stellen ... Zu früh gehofft: William hatte sich noch nicht ganz umgedreht und zur Flucht gewandt, da bot einer der Stadtbewohner dem König eine langstielige Holzfälleraxt an. Stephan griff danach und kämpfte weiter. Das war doch unglaublich!

William war schon drauf und dran, das Weite zu suchen, als er zu seiner Rechten Richard erblickte, der zu Fuß war und wie besessen kämpfte; er preschte vorwärts, hieb wild mit dem Schwert um sich und erledigte einen Feind nach dem anderen. Solange sein Rivale noch kämpfte, konnte William unmöglich fliehen. Erneut wurde er angegriffen, diesmal von einem kleingewachsenen Mann in leichter Rüstung, der sich rasch und behende bewegte, wobei sein Schwert in der Sonne nur so blitzte. Als ihre Waffen aufeinanderschlugen, erkannte William, daß er es mit einem hervorragenden Kämpfer zu tun hatte. Wieder fühlte er sich in die Defensive gedrängt und fürchtete um sein Leben; dazu zehrte das Wissen um die bereits verlorene Schlacht an seinem Mut. Er parierte die flinken, gezielten Hiebe und Schläge und wünschte nichts sehnlicher, als die Panzerung seines Gegners mit einem einzigen, gewaltigen Hieb zerschmettern zu können. Dann witterte er eine Chance und holte aus. Der andere duckte sich, stieß nach ihm, und William spürte seinen linken Arm taub werden. Er war verwundet! Ihm wurde schlecht vor Angst. Immer weiter wich er vor den Attacken seines Gegenübers zurück und fühlte sich dabei merkwürdig unsicher auf den Beinen, als ob ihm der Boden unter den Füßen wegglitte. Sein Schild hing ihm lose um den Hals – mit seinem nutzlos gewordenen linken Arm konnte er ihn nicht mehr halten. Der kleine Mann fühlte sich dem Sieg nahe und griff mit doppelter Kraft an. William, erfüllt von schierer Todesangst, sah sich bereits auf dem Schlachtfeld fallen.

Da war plötzlich Walter an seiner Seite.

William trat zurück. Walter schwang sein Schwert mit beiden Händen. Der kleine Mann war viel zu überrascht, um sich zu wehren, und stürzte wie ein gefälltes Bäumchen. William, ganz schwindelig vor Erleichterung, legte Walter eine Hand auf die Schulter.

»Wir haben verloren!« schrie Walter ihm zu. »Nichts wie weg von hier!«

William riß sich zusammen. Der König gab noch immer nicht auf, obwohl die Schlacht längst verloren war. Wenn er doch nur die Waffen strecken und die Flucht ergreifen wollte! Je länger er weiterfocht, um so größer war die Wahrscheinlichkeit, daß er gefangengenommen oder getötet wurde, und das konnte nur eins bedeuten: daß Mathilde Königin wurde.

William und Walter zogen sich verstohlen zurück. Warum war der König nur so leichtsinnig? Mußte er unbedingt seinen Mut beweisen? Seine Ritterlichkeit würde ihn noch das Leben kosten! Erneut war William versucht, den König einfach im Stich zu lassen. Aber da war immer noch Richard von Kingsbridge, der die rechte Flanke des Königs hielt wie ein Fels in der Brandung und die Gegner mit seinem

Schwert nur so niedermähte. »Noch nicht!« sagte William zu Walter. »Behalte den König im Auge!«

Sie zogen sich Schritt für Schritt zurück. Die Gefechte verloren allmählich an Intensität: Die Schlacht war entschieden, niemand wollte sich noch unnötig in Gefahr bringen. William und Walter kreuzten ihre Klingen mit zwei Rittern, die sich allerdings damit zufriedengaben, sie zurückzutreiben.

William trat zwei Schritte zurück und äugte zum König hinüber. Im selben Moment kam ein großer Steinbrocken übers Feld geflogen und traf Stephans Helm. Der König stolperte und ging in die Knie. Williams Gegenüber hielt inne und wandte den Kopf, um zu sehen, was Williams Aufmerksamkeit in Anspruch nahm. Die Streitaxt entfiel den Händen des Königs. Ein feindlicher Ritter lief auf ihn zu und riß ihm den Helm vom Kopf. »Der König«, schrie er triumphierend. »Ich habe den König.«

William, Walter und das gesamte königliche Heer machten kehrt und ergriffen das Hasenpanier.

Philip war außer sich vor Freude. Der Rückzug begann in der Mitte der königlichen Armee und breitete sich wie ein Lauffeuer nach beiden Seiten aus. Binnen kürzester Frist war das gesamte königliche Heer auf der Flucht: Das war der Lohn für Stephans Ungerechtigkeit!

Die Angreifer nahmen die Verfolgung auf. In der Nachhut der königlichen Armee hielten Knappen vierzig oder fünfzig reiterlose Pferde; so mancher unter den Flüchtenden sprang in einen Sattel und suchte das Weite – nicht Richtung Lincoln, sondern übers freie Feld.

Philip fragte sich, was wohl aus dem König geworden sein mochte.

Die Bürger von Lincoln räumten hastig ihre Hausdächer. Kinder wurden gerufen, Tiere zusammengetrieben. Ganze Familien verschwanden im Innern ihrer Häuser, schlossen die Fensterläden, verrammelten die Türen. Auf den Booten am Seeufer brach wirre Betriebsamkeit aus: Nicht wenige Städter versuchten, auf dem Wasserweg zu fliehen. Vor dem Dom stauten sich die Menschen, die dort Zuflucht suchten.

Viele rannten los, um die riesigen, eisenbeschlagenen Stadttore zu schließen. Aus der Burg strömten plötzlich Ranulf von Chesters Mannen, die offenkundig einem vorher vereinbarten Plan folgten. Sie sammelten sich zu Gruppen, von denen jeweils eine auf ein bestimmtes Stadttor zumarschierte. Rücksichtslos drängten sie sich zwischen die Stadtbewohner, streckten jeden, der ihnen in die Quere kam, nieder und rissen die eben erst geschlossenen Stadttore wieder auf, um den Eroberern freien Zugang zu verschaffen.

Philip beschloß, das Dach der Kathedrale zu verlassen. Die Menschen um ihn herum, die meisten davon Domherren, kamen auf den gleichen Gedanken. Sie duckten sich unter dem niedrigen Türrahmen, der ins Innere des Turmes führte. Dort begegneten sie dem Bischof und den Archidiakonen, die die Turmspitze erklommen hatten. Bischof Alexander machte einen überängstlichen Eindruck auf Philip. Schade: An einem solchen Tage sollte ein Bischof eigentlich anderen Mut zusprechen.

Vorsichtig stiegen sie die lange, enggewundene Wendeltreppe hinab und kamen am Westende des Hauptschiffes heraus. Hundert oder noch mehr Bürger befanden sich bereits in der Kirche, und die Menge strömte unaufhaltsam weiter durch die drei großen Portale herein.

Als Philip einen Blick hinaus warf, sah er zwei Ritter, die blutverschmiert und dreckverkrustet in gestrecktem Galopp über den Domvorhof preschten; sie kamen offensichtlich direkt vom Schlachtfeld. Schnurstracks ritten sie in die Kirche. Sobald sie den Bischof erblickten, rief einer von ihnen: »Der König ist in Gefangenschaft geraten!«

Philips Herz tat einen Sprung. König Stephan war nicht nur geschlagen, sondern obendrein auch noch in die Hände des Feindes gefallen! Das konnte nichts anderes bedeuten, als daß die Front seiner Anhänger im gesamten Königreich zusammenbrechen mußte! In seinem Kopf überschlugen sich die möglichen Auswirkungen nur so, aber noch ehe er einen klaren Gedanken fassen konnte, hörte er Bischof Alexander rufen: »Schließt die Türen!«

Philip traute seinen Ohren nicht. »Nein!« schrie er zurück. »Das könnt Ihr nicht tun!«

Der Bischof stierte ihn an, das Gesicht schneeweiß vor Angst und Schrecken. Er wußte nicht einmal, wen er vor sich hatte. Zwar hatte ihm Philip eine Höflichkeitsbesuch abgestattet, doch seitdem hatten sie kein einziges Wort miteinander gewechselt. Allmählich und mit sichtlicher Mühe erinnerte sich Alexander. »Das ist nicht Eure Kathedrale, Prior Philip, sondern meine! Schließt die Tore!« Mehrere Priester machten sich daran, seinem Befehl Folge zu leisten.

Entsetzen erfaßte Philip angesichts solcher Zurschaustellung nackter Selbstsucht – durch einen Mann der Kirche! »Ihr könnt die Leute doch nicht abweisen!« rief er erzürnt. »Da draußen gehen sie elendig zugrunde!«

»Wenn wir die Türen nicht verschließen, gehen wir alle zugrunde!« quäkte Alexander außer sich.

Philip packte den Bischof an den Falten seiner Robe. »Vergeßt nicht, wer Ihr seid!« schnappte er. »Es steht Euch nicht zu, Angst zu haben – und schon gar nicht vor dem Tod. Reißt Euch gefälligst zusammen!«

»Schafft mir den Kerl vom Leibe!« kreischte Alexander.

Mehrere Domherren eilten ihm zu Hilfe und zerrten Philip fort.

Philip rief ihnen zu: »Seht Ihr denn nicht, was er tut?«

»Warum geht Ihr nicht selber hinaus und beschützt sie, wenn Ihr so tapfer seid?« erwiderte einer der Domherren.

Philip riß sich los. »Genau das habe ich vor«, antwortete er.

Er drehte sich um. Das große Hauptportal wurde gerade geschlossen. Drei Priester mühten sich mit dem Tor ab, während draußen immer mehr Menschen versuchten, sich durch den schmaler werdenden Spalt zu zwängen. Philip konnte sich gerade noch durchquetschen, bevor es endgültig zufiel.

Binnen kurzem entstand im Portal ein kleiner Menschenauflauf. Männer und Frauen hämmerten mit den Fäusten gegen die Tür und forderten schreiend Einlaß, doch drinnen rührte sich nichts.

Plötzlich wurde Philip von Furcht ergriffen. Die panische Angst auf den Gesichtern der ausgesperrten Menschen steckte ihn an, und er spürte, wie er zu zittern begann. Schon einmal war er – im Alter von sechs Jahren – mit einer siegreichen Armee in Berührung gekommen, und das Entsetzen, das ihn damals überwältigt hatte, steckte ihm noch immer in den Knochen. Die Erinnerung an den Augenblick, da die Bewaffneten in sein Elternhaus eingedrungen waren, überfiel ihn so plötzlich und mit solcher Deutlichkeit, als sei es erst gestern geschehen. Wie angewurzelt stand er da und bemühte sich, das Zittern seiner Glieder zu unterdrücken, während um ihn herum die Menschenmenge tobte. Es war schon lange her, daß ihn dieser Alptraum zum letztenmal heimgesucht hatte. Wieder sah er die blutrünstigen Gesichter der Männer vor sich, das Schwert, mit dem sie seine Mutter aufgespießt hatten, seinen Vater, dem die Eingeweide grausig aus dem Bauch quollen; wieder fühlte er dieses nichts verstehende, alles überwältigende, an Wahnsinn grenzende Entsetzen. Und dann sah er den Mönch, der mit einem Kreuz in der Hand durch die Tür kam – und das Geschrei verstummte. Der Mönch zeigte seinem Bruder und ihm, wie sie die Augen von Vater und Mutter zu schließen hatten, damit sie den ewigen Schlaf tun konnten … Wie erwacht aus einem langen

Traum, machte sich Philip klar, daß er kein verängstigtes Kind mehr war, sondern ein erwachsener Mann, ein Mönch. Und ebenso wie Abt Peter ihn und seinen Bruder an jenem schrecklichen Tag vor siebenundzwanzig Jahren gerettet hatte, so wollte der erwachsene, im Glauben gefestigte Philip mit Gottes Hilfe heute jenen zur Seite eilen, die um ihr Leben fürchten mußten.

Er zwang sich, den ersten Schritt zu tun; der zweite war schon weniger schwierig und der dritte beinahe ein Kinderspiel.

Als er auf die Straße stieß, die zum Westtor der Stadt führte, wurde er fast von einer Gruppe fliehender Stadtbewohner über den Haufen gerannt: davonjagende Männer und Knaben, ihre kostbarsten Besitztümer in Bündel gepackt; um Atem ringende Alte, schreiende Mädchen, Frauen mit kreischenden Kindern in den Armen. Der Ansturm warf ihn etliche Schritte zurück, bevor es ihm gelang, sich gegen den Strom zu stemmen. Die Flüchtenden hielten auf den Dom zu. Der sei geschlossen, wollte er ihnen zurufen; sie sollten in ihren eigenen Häusern bleiben, die Türen verbarrikadieren und sich still verhalten; aber alles schrie wild durcheinander, keiner hörte ihm zu.

Er hatte erst wenige Schritte zurückgelegt, als plötzlich vier Reiter die Straße entlanggaloppierten. Sie hatten also diese Massenflucht verursacht! Die Leute drückten sich flach gegen die Häuserwände, andere konnten nicht rechtzeitig entkommen und viele wurden von den hämmernden Hufen der Pferde niedergetrampelt. Philip packte blankes Entsetzen, aber hier konnte er nichts ausrichten. Er verdrückte sich in eine Seitengasse, um nicht selbst umgemäht zu werden. Wenig später war der Spuk vorbei, und die Straße lag wie verlassen da.

Die Opfer blieben auf der Straße liegen. Als Philip aus der Seitengasse kam, nahm er eine Bewegung wahr: Ein Mann mittleren Alters in einem scharlachroten Umhang versuchte, trotz eines verletzten Beins, kriechend vorwärts zu kommen. Philip, der den Mann tragen wollte, überquerte die Straße; doch bevor er sein Ziel erreichte, erschienen zwei Männer mit Eisenhüten und Holzschilden auf der Bildfläche. »Der ist noch am Leben, Jake«, sagte einer der beiden.

Philip erschauderte. Ihm schien, die beiden glichen in Auftreten, Stimmen, Kleidung, ja sogar in ihrem Aussehen jenen beiden, die seine Eltern gemordet hatten.

Der Mann namens Jake erwiderte: »Der ist bestimmt ein Lösegeld wert – schau dir bloß den roten Umhang an!« Er drehte sich um, steckte die Finger in den Mund und pfiff. Ein dritter Mann kam herbeigerannt. »Nimm den Rotrock hier mit zur Burg und binde ihn fest.«

Der dritte Mann schlang die Arme um die Brust des verwundeten Bürgers und zerrte ihn davon. Der Verletzte schrie vor Schmerzen, da sein Bein über die Steine schleifte. »Halt!« rief Philip. Die drei hielten kurz inne, sahen ihn an und brachen in Gelächter aus; dann machten sie weiter wie gehabt.

Philip rief ihnen noch einmal nach, aber sie kümmerten sich gar nicht um ihn. Hilflos mußte er zusehen, wie der Verletzte fortgeschleift wurde. Ein weiterer, in einen langen Pelzmantel gehüllter Bewaffneter trat mit sechs Silbertellern unter dem Arm aus einem der Häuser. Jake musterte die Beute. »Das sind reiche Häuser hier«, sagte er zu seinem Kameraden. »Wir sollten uns Einlaß verschaffen und sehen, was sich finden läßt.« Sie gingen auf die verschlossene Tür eines Steinhauses zu und bearbeiteten sie mit ihren Streitäxten.

Philip kam sich nutzlos vor, war jedoch nicht gewillt, die Flinte ins Korn zu werfen. Gott hatte ihn gewiß nicht hierher gestellt, damit er die Besitztümer der Reichen verteidigte, daher kehrte er Jake und seinen Kumpanen den Rücken zu und eilte auf das Westtor zu. Weitere Bewaffnete kamen die Straße entlanggerannt. Unter ihnen befanden sich viele kleine, dunkelhäutige Männer mit bemalten Gesichtern, in Schaffelle gekleidet und mit Keulen bewaffnet. Das sind die Waliser, stellte Philip fest, voller Scham darüber, daß er dem gleichen Land wie diese Wilden entstammte. Er drückte sich gegen eine Hauswand und versuchte, so unauffällig wie möglich zu wirken.

Zwei Männer kamen aus einem Steinhaus und schleiften einen Mann mit weißem Bart und einem Seidenkäppchen auf dem Haupt an den Beinen hinter sich her. Einer von ihnen hielt dem Mann sein Messer an die Gurgel und fragte: »Wo hast du dein Geld versteckt, Jude?«

»Ich habe kein Geld«, erwiderte der Mann kläglich.

Das nimmt ihm niemand ab, dachte Philip. Die Juden von Lincoln waren bekannt für ihren Reichtum; dazu wohnte der Mann in einem Haus aus Stein.

Ein dritter Bewaffneter trat aus dem Haus und schleifte eine Frau an den Haaren hinter sich her. Sie war in mittleren Jahren und wahrscheinlich mit dem Juden verheiratet. Der erste Kerle brüllte: »Sag uns, wo du dein Geld versteckt hast, sonst stoß ich ihr mein Schwert in die Fotze!« Er hob den Rock der Frau, entblößte ihre angegrauten Schamhaare und zielte mit seinen langen Dolch auf ihren Schoß.

Philip wollte sich schon einmischen, doch da gab der Alte nach. »Tut ihr nichts, das Geld ist da«, stieß er hervor. »Im Garten vergraben, gleich neben dem Brennholz, laßt sie in Ruhe, bitte!«

Die Kerle rannten zu dritt in das Haus. Die Frau half ihrem Mann auf die Beine. Eine weitere Reitergruppe donnerte die schmale Straße hinunter, und Philip warf sich zur Seite. Als er sich wieder aufrappelte, waren die beiden Juden spurlos verschwunden.

Ein junger Mann in Panzerzeug rannte, von drei oder vier Walisern verfolgt, um sein Leben. Er war gleichauf mit Philip, als sie ihn einholten. Der ihm nächste Verfolger schwang sein Schwert und streifte die Wade des Fliehenden. Die Wunde konnte nicht tief sein, aber ernst genug, um den jungen Mann zum Stolpern und zu Fall zu bringen. Ein weiterer Verfolger schloß auf und hob seine Streitaxt.

Mit vor Angst schlotternden Knien trat Philip vor und rief: »Halt!« Der Mann holte aus.

Philip stürzte sich auf ihn.

Der Mann setzte zum Schlag an, doch Philip gab ihm einen Schubs. Die Klinge der Streitaxt traf die Gehsteine, keinen Fuß vom Kopf des Opfers entfernt. Der Angreifer fing sich wieder und glotzte Philip baff an. Philip stierte schweigend zurück, versuchte, sein Zittern zu beherrschen, und wünschte sich sehnlichst, daß ihm ein paar Brocken Walisisch einfielen. Keiner von beiden hatte einen Finger gerührt, als auch schon die zwei anderen Verfolger aufschlossen, deren einer mit Philip zusammenstieß, so daß er der Länge lang hinschlug. Das rettete ihm wahrscheinlich das Leben, wie er gleich darauf feststellte: Als er sich aufrappelte, hatten die drei ihn bereits vergessen. Statt dessen metzelten sie den armen, hilflos auf dem Boden liegenden jungen Mann mit geradezu unvorstellbarer Brutalität nieder. Als Philip wieder auf die Beine kam, war es bereits zu spät. Die Hämmer und Äxte trafen nur noch eine Leiche. Philip hob den Blick zum Himmel und schrie in ohnmächtigem Zorn: »Warum hast du mich hierhergeschickt, wenn ich doch niemandem helfen kann?«

Wie zur Antwort hörte er einen Schrei aus einem nahe gelegenen Haus, einem ebenerdigen Gebäude aus Stein und Holz, nicht ganz so wohlhabend wie die anderen in der Umgebung. Die Tür stand offen. Philip stürmte ins Haus. Die beiden Räume waren durch einen Bogengang verbunden, der Boden mit Stroh ausgelegt. Eine Frau mit zwei kleinen Kindern kauerte, halb verrückt vor Angst, in einer Ecke. In der Mitte standen drei Bewaffnete einem kleinen, kahlköpfigen Mann gegenüber. Eine junge Frau, nicht älter als achtzehn, lag auf dem

Boden. Ihr Kleid war zerrissen, und einer der drei Bewaffneten kniete auf ihrer Brust und zwang ihre Oberschenkel auseinander. Der Kahle wollte die Kerle zweifellos daran hindern, seiner Tochter Gewalt anzutun. Als Philip hereinkam, ging er gerade auf einen von ihnen los. Der Soldat schüttelte ihn ab, der Vater taumelte zurück. Der Soldat stieß ihm sein Schwert in den Unterleib. Die Frau in der Ecke schrie wie am Spieß.

»Halt!« gebot Philip lauthals.

Sie sahen ihn an, als wäre er nicht ganz bei Trost. Donnernd fuhr er sie an: »Tut, was ihr vorhabt, und die Hölle gibt euch nie wieder preis!«

Der Mann, der den Vater gemordet hatte, hob sein Schwert gegen Philip.

»Moment mal«, sagte der Mann auf dem Boden, der immer noch die Beine des Mädchens festhielt. »Wer seid Ihr, Mönch?«

»Ich bin Philip von Gwynedd, Prior von Kingsbridge, und befehle Euch im Namen des Herrn, dieses Mädchen in Ruhe zu lassen, wenn Euch Eure unsterblichen Seelen etwas wert sind.«

»Ein Prior – das habe ich mir fast gedacht«, sagte der Kerl auf dem Boden. »Der ist sein Lösegeld wert.«

Der erste Mann steckte sein Schwert in die Scheide und sagte: »Geht rüber zu der Frau in die Ecke, wo Ihr hingehört.«

Philip sagte: »Vergreift Euch nicht an einem Mönch!« Er gab sich alle erdenkliche Mühe, seiner Stimme einen drohenden Klang zu geben, aber selbst er konnte den Unterton der Verzweiflung heraushören.

»Nimm ihn mit zur Burg, John«, sagte der Kerl auf dem Boden, der immer noch auf dem Mädchen saß. Er schien der Anführer zu sein.

»Fahr zur Hölle«, gab John zurück. »Erst will ich die hier vögeln.« Er packte Philip am Arm und schleuderte ihn, noch ehe er sich zur Wehr setzen konnte, in die Ecke. Philip strauchelte und fiel neben der Mutter zu Boden.

Der Mann namens John hob sein Hemd und fiel über das Mädchen her.

Die Mutter wandte den Kopf und fing an zu schluchzen.

»Das kann ich nicht mit ansehen!« sagte Philip. Er erhob sich, packte den Vergewaltiger beim Schopf und zog ihn von dem Mädchen fort. Der brüllte vor Schmerz.

Der dritte Kerl hob seine Keule. Zu spät sah Philip den Schlag kommen. Die Keule landete auf seinem Schädel. Einen Augenblick lang verspürte er einen unsäglichen Schmerz, dann wurde alles schwarz um ihn. Noch bevor er auf dem Boden aufschlug, hatte er das Bewußtsein verloren.

Die Gefangenen wurden auf die Burg gebracht und in Käfige gesperrt, stabile, wie Miniaturhäuser wirkende Holzkonstruktionen, sechs Fuß lang, drei Fuß breit und gerade so hoch, daß man darin stehen konnte. Die Seitenwände bestanden aus senkrechten Holzlatten in kurzen Abständen, so daß der Aufseher in den Käfig hineinschauen konnte. Unter normalen Umständen kamen, wenn es sich um Diebe, Mörder oder Häretiker handelte, nicht mehr als ein, zwei Personen in einen Käfig. Heute sperrten die Rebellen jedoch acht bis zehn in jeden Verschlag, und dennoch kamen immer mehr Gefangene dazu. Die Überzähligen wurden schließlich mit Seilen aneinander gefesselt und in einer Ecke des Burghofs zusammengetrieben. Sie hätten leicht entkommen können, machten aber keine Anstalten dazu – wahrscheinlich waren sie hier sicherer aufgehoben als draußen in der Stadt.

Philip hockte mit wahnsinnigen Kopfschmerzen in der Ecke eines Käfigs und kam sich wie ein Dummkopf und Versager vor. Letzten Endes hatte er sich als ebenso nutzlos erwiesen wie der hasenherzige Bischof Alexander. Kein einziges Menschenleben hatte er gerettet, keinen einzigen Schlag verhindert. Ohne ihn wären die Bürger von Lincoln keinen Deut schlechter gefahren. Im Gegensatz zu Abt Peter war es ihm nicht gelungen, der Gewalt Einhalt zu gebieten. Ich bin eben nicht aus dem gleichen Holz wie Vater Peter geschnitzt, dachte er.

Doch damit nicht genug: In seinem vergeblichen Bemühen, den Einwohnern der Stadt zu helfen, hatte er womöglich jede Chance vertan, von Mathilde, war sie erst Königin, irgendwelche Konzessionen zugestanden zu bekommen. Er war Gefangener ihrer Armee. Daraus würde man schließen, daß er zu König Stephans Streitkräften gehört hatte. Das Kloster in Kingsbridge würde ein Lösegeld für seine Freilassung bezahlen müssen. Und höchstwahrscheinlich würde die ganze Sache Mathilde zu Ohren kommen, so daß sie von vornherein gegen ihn eingenommen war. Philip fühlte sich elend, enttäuscht und zutiefst reumütig.

Im Laufe des Tages wurden noch mehr Gefangene gebracht. Der Strom riß zwar bei Anbruch der Nacht ab, doch die Plünderung der Stadt ging unvermindert weiter. Das Geschrei und Geheul und der zerstörerische Lärm waren bis in die Burg hinein zu hören. Erst gegen Mitternacht wurde es ruhiger; vermutlich, weil die Soldaten sich nunmehr an ihrem erbeuteten Wein so berauscht, an ihren Vergewaltigungen und Brutalitäten so übersättigt hatten, daß sie zu keinen weiteren Untaten mehr fähig waren. Einige taumelten und stolperten in den Burghof, wo sie sich lallend ihrer Heldentaten rühmten und heftig miteinander stritten, bis sie endlich umfielen, ins Gras kotzten und besinnungslos einschliefen.

Auch Philip schlief, obwohl er nicht genügend Platz hatte, um sich auszustrecken, und sich in seiner Ecke mit dem Rücken gegen das hölzerne Käfiggitter lehnen mußte. Im Morgengrauen erwachte er, schlotternd vor Kälte, aber der Schmerz in seinem Kopf war Gott sei Dank ein wenig abgeklungen. Er stand auf, vertrat sich die Beine, so gut er konnte, und schlug sich mit den Armen gegen den Körper, damit ihm wärmer wurde. Sämtliche Gebäude der Burganlage barsten schier vor Menschen. Nicht nur die Ställe waren voll schlafender Männer, die ihre Pferde draußen angebunden hatten, auch aus den offenen Türen des Backhauses und der Küche ragten die Beine der Schläfer. Die wenigen nüchtern gebliebenen Soldaten hatten Zelte aufgeschlagen. Und überall wimmelte es von Pferden. Im Südosten des Burggeländes stand der Wohnturm – eine Burg in der Burg – auf einer hohen Motte; seine mächtigen Mauern bargen ein halbes Dutzend oder mehr Holzhäuser. Dort schliefen wahrscheinlich die Grafen und Ritter ihren Siegesrausch aus.

Philips Gedanken wandten sich den Folgen der gestrigen Schlacht zu. Ob damit der Krieg zu Ende war? Vermutlich. Vielleicht würde Stephans Frau, Königin Matilda, noch weiterkämpfen: Sie war Gräfin von Boulogne, hatte zu Beginn des Krieges mit ihren französischen Rittern Dover erobert und herrschte, stellvertretend für ihren Mann, über einen Großteil von Kent. Allerdings dürfte es ihr schwerfallen, die Unterstützung der Barone zu gewinnen, solange Stephan gefangensaß. In Kent mochte sie sich noch eine Zeitlang behaupten, doch daß sie noch weitere Gebiete hinzugewann, war unwahrscheinlich.

Doch damit allein war die Kaiserin Mathilde noch lange nicht aller Sorgen ledig. Zunächst mußte sie ihren militärischen Erfolg konsolidieren, die Zustimmung der Kirche erlangen und sich in Westminster krönen lassen. Doch das erforderte nur ein wenig Entschlußkraft und eine Portion Klugheit und sollte ihr eigentlich nicht schwerfallen.

Damit stünden dann auch die Zeichen für Kingsbridge gut – vorausgesetzt Philip gelang es, aus der Gefangenschaft entlassen zu werden, ohne als Anhänger Stephans zu gelten.

Die Sonne war noch nicht aufgegangen, doch je heller es wurde, desto mehr erwärmte sich die Luft. Allmählich erwachten auch Philips

Mitgefangene und ächzten vor Schmerzen: Die meisten hatten leichte Verletzungen davongetragen und fühlten sich nach der kalten Nacht in diesem zugigen Holzkäfig eher schlechter als besser. Einige von ihnen waren reiche Bürger, andere während der Schlacht in Gefangenschaft geratene Ritter. Sobald so gut wie alle wach waren, fragte Philip: »Hat jemand gesehen, was aus Richard von Kingsbridge geworden ist?« Um Alienas willen hoffte er, daß Richard mit dem Leben davongekommen war.

Ein Mann mit einem blutbefleckten Verband um den Kopf sagte: »Er hat wie ein Löwe gekämpft – als die Lage brenzlig wurde, hat er die Städter mobilisiert.«

»Ist er gefallen oder lebt er noch?«

Der Mann schüttelte seinen verletzten Kopf. »Ich habe ihn am Ende aus den Augen verloren.«

»Und was ist mit William Hamleigh?« Wenn der doch gefallen wäre!

»Er kämpfte fast die ganze Zeit an der Seite des Königs. Aber am Schluß ist er entkommen – ich habe gesehen, wie er, der Meute weit voraus, im gestreckten Galopp über die Felder setzte.«

»Aha.« Philips schwache Hoffnung zerschlug sich. So einfach wurde er seine Sorgen nicht los.

Die Unterhaltung verebbte, und es wurde wieder still im Käfig. Draußen kam Bewegung auf: Die verkaterten Soldaten kontrollierten ihre Beute, vergewisserten sich, daß ihre Gefangenen noch sicher hinter Schloß und Riegel waren, und holten sich ihr Frühstück aus der Küche. Philip fragte sich, ob die Gefangenen ebenfalls verköstigt wurden. Wahrscheinlich, dachte er, denn sonst verhungern sie und sind als Geiseln keinen Pfifferling mehr wert ... Aber wer sollte die Verantwortung für die Verpflegung so vieler Menschen tragen? Und wie lange mußte er selbst wohl hier bleiben? Seine Häscher mußten zunächst eine Lösegeldforderung nach Kingsbridge schicken. Darauf würden die Brüder einen aus ihren Reihen damit beauftragen, die Verhandlungen vor Ort zu führen. Wen wohl? Am besten wäre Milius, doch wahrscheinlicher war, daß Remigius, der als Subprior in Philips Abwesenheit die Verantwortung trug, einen seiner Busenfreunde schickte oder sogar sich selbst auf den Weg machte. Remigius würde sich Zeit lassen: Rasche Entscheidungen zu treffen, war nicht seine Sache, nicht einmal dann, wenn es ihm persönlich zum Vorteil gereichte. Das alles konnte Monate dauern! Philips Stimmung sank auf den Nullpunkt.

Anderen Gefangenen erging es besser. Bald nach Sonnenaufgang erschienen die ersten Frauen, Kinder und Anverwandten, um über das Lösegeld für ihre teuren Angehörigen zu verhandeln – anfangs noch schüchtern und verängstigt, mit der Zeit jedoch immer energischer. Eine Weile lang verhandelten sie mit den Soldaten, beteuerten, kein Geld zu haben und boten dafür billigen Schmuck und andere Wertgegenstände an; schließlich einigte man sich, die Angehörigen verließen die Burg und kamen wenig später mit dem ausgemachten Lösegeld, meistens in bar, zurück. Die Beute türmte sich immer höher und die Käfige leerten sich zusehends.

Gegen Mittag war die Hälfte der Gefangenen verschwunden. Philip nahm an, daß es sich um Ortsansässige gehandelt hatte. Wer blieb, mußte von weither kommen; die meisten waren wohl während der Schlacht in Gefangenschaft geratene Ritter. Philips Vermutung bestätigte sich, als der Burgvogt von einem zum anderen ging und jeden nach seinem Namen fragte: lauter Ritter aus dem Süden. Dann entdeckte Philip, daß in einem der Käfige nur ein einziger Gefangener saß, dazu im Zwingblock – als wolle man doppelt sichergehen, daß er auf gar keinen Fall entfliehen konnte. Philip starrte den abgesonderten Mitgefangene eine ganze Weile lang an, bevor ihm dämmerte, wen er vor sich hatte.

»Seht nur!« sagte er zu den drei Männern in seinem Käfig. »Der einzelne Mann da drüben. Täusche ich mich, oder ist er es wirklich?«

»Herrje, der König!« sagte einer, und die anderen nickten zustimmend.

Philip musterte den dreckverkrusteten Mann mit dem hellen Haar, der mit Händen und Füßen in dem unbequemen Schraubstock steckte: Er sah nicht anders aus als andere Menschen. Gestern noch war er König von England gewesen; gestern hatte er Kingsbridge das Marktrecht verweigert – heute konnte er ohne Erlaubnis nicht einmal aufstehen. Er hat es nicht besser verdient, dachte Philip; dennoch empfand er Mitleid mit ihm.

Am frühen Nachmittag bekamen die Gefangenen etwas zu essen: nur die lauwarmen Reste von der Mittagstafel der Soldaten, über die sie jedoch hungrig wie die Wölfe herfielen. Philip hielt sich zurück und überließ den anderen den Löwenanteil, denn Hunger war in seinen Augen eine unrühmliche Schwäche, die man von Zeit zu Zeit überwinden sollte, so daß er jedes aufgezwungene Fasten als eine Gelegenheit zur Selbstkasteiung betrachtete.

Während sie noch ihre Schüssel auskratzten, entstand um den Wohnturm hektische Betriebsamkeit, und eine Gruppe von Grafen trat heraus. Philip beobachtete, wie sie die steinerne Treppe hinabstiegen und mit einer gewissen Ehrerbietung behandelt wurden. Das mußten Ranulf von Chester und Robert von Gloucester sein, aber Philip kannte sie nicht. Sie näherten sich Stephans Käfig.

»Guten Tag, Vetter Robert«, sagte Stephan mit starker Betonung auf dem Wort Vetter.

Der größere der beiden erwiderte: »Es war nicht meine Absicht, Euch die Nacht im Stock verbringen zu lassen. Ich befahl, Euch zu verlegen, aber man hat mir nicht gehorcht. Immerhin scheint Ihr es überlebt zu haben.«

Ein Mann in Priesterkleidung löste sich aus der Gruppe und ging auf Philips Käfig zu. Philip beachtete ihn zunächst nicht, da Stephan fragte, was mit ihm geschehen sollte, und er wollte sich die Antwort nicht entgegen lassen. Aber der Priester fragte: »Wer von Euch ist Philip von Kingsbridge?«

»Ich«, antwortete Philip.

Der Priester wandte sich an einen der Bewaffneten, die Philip auf die Burg gebracht hatten. »Laßt diesen Mann frei.«

Philip verstand überhaupt nichts mehr. Diesen Priester hatte er noch nie gesehen. Zweifellos hatte man seinen Namen der zuvor durch den Burgvogt aufgestellten Liste entnommen. Aber wozu? Gewiß, diesen Käfig verließ er nur allzu gerne, doch so recht freuen konnte er sich nicht darüber – wer wußte schon, was ihm noch alles bevorstand!

Der Bewaffnete protestierte: »Aber er ist mein Gefangener!«

»Das war einmal«, erwiderte der Priester. »Laßt ihn frei.«

»Und warum soll ich ihn ohne Lösegeld laufen lassen?« fragte der Mann kriegerisch.

Der Priester bot ihm nicht weniger entschieden Paroli: »Erstens, weil er weder für den König gekämpft hat noch ein Bürger dieser Stadt ist und Ihr Euch durch seine Gefangennahme eines Verbrechens schuldig gemacht habt. Zweitens, weil er ein Mönch ist, und einem Mann Gottes Gewalt anzutun, ist Frevel. Drittens hat Königin Mathildes Sekretär seine Entlassung angeordnet, und wenn Ihr Euch noch lange sträubt, landet Ihr im Handumdrehen selbst in diesem Käfig, *also sputet Euch!*«

»Schon gut«, brummte der Mann.

Philip war bestürzt. Da hatte er gehofft, Mathilde werde nie von seiner Gefangennahme erfahren – doch nun, da ihr Sekretär ihn zu sich bestellte, zerstoben seine Hoffnungen zu nichts. Als er aus dem Käfig trat, war ihm zumute, als ginge die Welt unter.

»Kommt mit«, sagte der Priester.

Philip folgte ihm. »Soll ich freigelassen werden?« fragte er.

Ich denke schon.« Den Priester schien seine Frage zu überraschen. »Wißt Ihr denn nicht, zu wem ich Euch bringe?«

»Ich habe nicht die geringste Ahnung.«

Der Priester lächelte. »Dann will ich ihm die Überraschung nicht verderben.«

Sie überquerten den Burghof und erklommen die lange Treppe, die über den Erdwall zum Tor des Wohnturms führte. Philip zermarte sich das Gehirn, aber er kam beim besten Willen nicht darauf, welches Interesse Mathildes Sekretär an ihm haben sollte. Der Priester geleitete Philip in eins der Häuser.

Drinnen stand mit dem Rücken zur Tür ein weiterer Priester vor dem Feuer. Er war gebaut wie Philip, klein und schmächtig, und hatte das gleiche schwarze Haar, das allerdings nicht geschoren war und auch keinerlei graue Spuren aufwies. Dieser Rücken war ihm doch vertraut! Philip konnte sein Glück kaum fassen, und ein breites Lächeln erhellte sein Gesicht.

Der Priester drehte sich um. Er hatte die gleichen strahlend blauen Augen wie Philip, und auch er strahlte über das ganze Gesicht. »Philip!« sagte er mit ausgebreiteten Armen.

»Gelobt sei der Herr!« sagte Philip erstaunt. »Francis!«

Die beiden Brüder fielen sich um den Hals, und Philip schossen vor Freude die Tränen in die Augen.

Der königliche Audienzsaal in der Burg von Winchester hatte sich sehr verändert. Verschwunden waren nicht nur die Hunde, sondern auch König Stephans einfacher Holzthron, die Bänke und die Tierfelle an den Wänden. Ihren Platz nahmen nun bestickte Wandbehänge, buntfarbige Teppiche, Schalen mit kandierten Früchten und bemalte Stühle ein. Der ganze Raum duftete nach Blumen.

Philip hatte sich am königlichen Hof noch nie wohlgefühlt, aber ein *weiblicher* Königshof versetzte ihn erst recht in Angst und Schrekken. Kaiserin Mathilde war seine letzte Hoffnung: Von ihr hing es ab, ob er den Steinbruch wiederbekam und den Markt wieder abhalten durfte, doch dieser hochmütigen, eigensinnigen Frau traute er nicht zu, Gerechtigkeit walten zu lassen.

Die Kaiserin saß auf einem fein geschnitzten, vergoldeten Thron und trug ein glockenblumenblaues Gewand. Sie war groß und schlank, hatte dunkle, stolze Augen und glattes, glänzend schwarzes Haar. Über dem Kleid trug sie einen knielangen Seidenmantel, der in der Taille eng anlag und sich dann zu einem glockig fallenden Rock erweiterte, eine Mode, die sie in England eingeführt hatte und die inzwischen eifrig kopiert wurde. Mit ihrem ersten Mann war sie elf, mit ihrem zweiten vierzehn Jahre lang verheiratet gewesen, aber sie sah immer noch nicht wie vierzig aus. Man schwärmte allerorten von ihrer Schönheit. Auf Philip wirkte sie eher hölzern und unfreundlich, aber er war, da im großen und ganzen immun dagegen, kein Kenner weiblicher Schönheit.

Philip, Francis, William Hamleigh und Bischof Waleran verneigten sich vor ihr und warteten. Die Kaiserin ignorierte sie und setzte ihre Unterhaltung mit einer ihrer Hofdamen fort. Es schien um Belanglosigkeiten zu gehen, denn beide lachten geziert; trotzdem machte Mathilde keine Anstalten, ihre Besucher zu begrüßen.

Francis arbeitete eng mit ihr zusammen und sah sie beinahe täglich, aber sie standen nicht gerade auf freundschaftlichem Fuß. Ihr Bruder Robert, in dessen Diensten Francis zuvor gewesen war, hatte ihn Mathilde überlassen, da sie bei ihrer Ankunft in England einen erstklassigen Sekretär benötigte, doch das war nicht sein einziger Beweggrund. Francis fungierte als Verbindungsmann zwischen Bruder und Schwester und behielt die impulsive Mathilde im Auge. Es wäre nicht das erste Mal in der Geschichte, daß Geschwister in der Ränkeschmiede des königlichen Hofes Verrat aneinander begingen, daher bestand Francis' Hauptaufgabe darin, Mathilde jedwede Geheimaktion zu erschweren.

Die Kaiserin wußte darüber Bescheid und akzeptierte seine Funktion, doch das machte die Beziehung zu Francis keineswegs leichter.

Zwei Monate waren seit der Schlacht in Lincoln vergangen, und für Mathilde war alles nach Plan verlaufen. Bischof Henry hatte sie in Winchester nicht nur willkommen geheißen (und damit *seinen* Bruder Stephan verraten), sondern auch einen großen Rat aus Bischöfen und Äbten einberufen, der sie zur Königin erkor; derzeit verhandelte sie mit der Bürgerschaft von London über ihre Krönung in Westminster. König David von Schottland, zufällig ihr Onkel, hatte sich bereits auf den Weg gemacht, um ihr einen offiziellen Besuch von Herrscher zu Herrscher abzustatten.

Bischof Henry wurde von Bischof Waleran von Kingsbridge unterstützt, dem es – Francis zufolge – gelungen war, William Hamleigh zu überreden, das Lager zu wechseln und sich auf Mathildes Seite zu schlagen. Nun war William erschienen, um seine Belohnung zu kassieren.

Die vier Männer standen herum und warteten: William mit seinem Hintermann, Bischof Waleran, und Prior Philip mit seinem Fürsprecher Francis. Philip sah Mathilde heute zum erstenmal. Ihre äußere Erscheinung flößte ihm kein Vertrauen ein: Sie wirkte trotz ihrer königlichen Erscheinung unberechenbar.

Als Mathilde ihr Schwätzchen beendet hatte, wandte sich sich ihnen mit einer triumphierenden Miene zu, die Bände sprach: Seht her, wie unbedeutend Ihr seid; sogar meine Hofdame hat Vorrang vor Euch! Sie musterte Philip so lange und gründlich, daß er ganz verlegen wurde, dann fragte sie: »Nun, Francis, hier haben wir wohl Euren Zwilling?«

Francis erwiderte: »Mein Bruder Philip, Lady, der Prior von Kingsbridge.«

Philip verneigte sich noch einmal und sagte: »Der ein bißchen zu alt und grau für einen Zwillingsbruder ist, Lady.« Solch läppische Bemerkungen auf Kosten der eigenen Person galten bei Hofe als beliebt, doch die Dame musterte ihn nur kühl und gab keine Antwort.

Philip beschloß, keine weitere Mühe mehr an höfische Floskeln zu verschwenden.

Sie wandte sich William zu. »Und Sir William Hamleigh, der in der Schlacht zu Lincoln so wacker gegen meine Truppen gekämpft und sich nunmehr eines Besseren besonnen hat.«

William verneigte sich und hielt schlauerweise den Mund.

Mathilde richtete das Wort wieder an Philip. »Ihr habt mich gebeten, Euch die Genehmigung für Euren Markt zu erteilen.«

»Ja, Herrin.«

Francis fügte hinzu: »Der Erlös aus dem Markt wird ausschließlich für den Bau der Kathedrale aufgewendet.«

»An welchem Wochentag wollt Ihr Euren Markt abhalten?« fragte sie.

»Am Sonntag.«

Sie zog die gezupften Augenbrauen in die Höhe. »Ihr Männer Gottes seid gemeinhin gegen Sonntagsmärkte. Werden die Leute dadurch nicht von der Kirche ferngehalten?«

»Nicht in unserem Fall«, antwortete Philip. »Die Menschen kommen, um auf der Baustelle zu arbeiten und dem Gottesdienst beizuwohnen; bei dieser Gelegenheit machen sie ihre Einkäufe oder bieten ihre Waren feil.«

»Das heißt also, der Markt findet bereits statt?« warf sie mit schneidender Stimme ein.

Philip begriff, daß er ins Fettnäpfchen getreten war. Er hätte sich dafür ohrfeigen können!

Francis kam ihm zu Hilfe. »Nein, Lady, derzeit findet der Markt nicht statt«, sagte er. »Ursprünglich hat er sich von selbst entwickelt, aber Prior Philip ließ ihn wieder schließen, bis die Genehmigung dazu erteilt ist.«

Das entsprach der Wahrheit, war aber nicht die ganze Wahrheit. Mathilde schien sich jedoch damit zufriedenzugeben. Philip betete stumm um Vergebung für Francis.

Mathilde fragte: »Gibt es sonst keinen Markt in der Gegend?«

William ergriff das Wort. »Doch, es gibt einen in Shiring. Und der Markt in Kingsbridge hat uns das Geschäft weggenommen.«

»Aber von Shiring nach Kingsbridge sind es zwanzig Meilen!« hielt Philip dagegen.

Francis vermittelte. »My Lady, den Regalien zufolge müssen zwei Märkte mindestens vierzehn Meilen Abstand voneinander haben. Nach diesem Kriterium sind Kingsbridge und Shiring keine Konkurrenten.«

Mathilde nickte: Anscheinend akzeptierte sie Francis' Urteil in diesem Punkt. So weit, so gut, dachte Philip.

»Ihr habt außerdem darum ersucht«, fuhr sie fort, »Steine aus dem Steinbruch des Grafen von Shiring entnehmen zu dürfen.«

»Dieses Recht stand uns seit Jahren zu. Erst kürzlich hat William unsere Steinbrecher vertrieben, dabei fünf Männer getötet –«

»Wer gab Euch das Recht, Steine zu fördern?« unterbrach sie ihn.

»König Stephan –«

»Der Usurpator!«

Francis warf eilig ein: »My Lady, Prior Philip akzeptiert natürlich, daß sämtliche Edikte des Kronprätendenten Stephan, soweit nicht von Euch bestätigt, ungültig sind.«

Philip akzeptierte nichts dergleichen, sah aber ein, daß er besser daran tat, sich nicht dazu zu äußern.

»Den Steinbruch habe ich als Vergeltungsmaßnahme für den illegalen Markt geschlossen!« platzte William heraus.

Einfach unglaublich, dachte Philip, wie ein klarer Fall von Unrecht vor Gericht verzerrt werden kann!

»Dieses ganze Hin und Her konnte nur entstehen, weil Stephans ursprüngliche Regelung Unsinn war«, stellte Mathilde fest.

Jetzt meldete sich Bischof Waleran zum erstenmal zu Worte: »Da kann ich Ihnen nur aus vollstem Herzen zustimmen, Herrin«, sagte er kriecherisch.

»Wer dem einen den Steinbruch zubilligt, dem anderen aber das Recht verleiht, dort Steine zu fördern, beschwört von vornherein Streitigkeiten herauf«, sagte sie. »Der Steinbruch darf nur einem von beiden gehören.«

Das stimmt, dachte Philip. Und wenn sie im Geiste von Stephans ursprünglicher Entscheidung handelt, wird er Kingsbridge zugesprochen!

»Meine Entscheidung lautet: Der Steinbruch soll meinem edlen Verbündeten Sir William gehören.«

Philips Hoffnung war dahin: Ohne freien Zugang zum Steinbruch wäre der Bau der Kathedrale niemals so gut vorangekommen – nun war es damit aus und vorbei! In Zukunft würde er alle Hände voll zu tun haben, Geld für den Kauf von Steinen zu beschaffen. Und alles nur wegen dieser launischen Frau! Insgeheim schäumte er vor Wut.

»Habt Dank, Herrin«, sagte William.

»Kingsbridge soll jedoch die gleichen Marktrechte wie Shiring erhalten«, verfügte Mathilde.

Philip atmete auf. Der Markt deckte zwar die Kosten der Steine nicht ganz, trug aber einen guten Teil dazu bei. Dies hieß, daß er wie zu Beginn Geld zusammenkratzen mußte, aber zumindest konnten die Bauarbeiten fortgesetzt werden. Mathilde war mit ihrer Entscheidung beiden Parteien ein Stück entgegengekommen. Vielleicht war sie doch kein solcher Hohlkopf ...

»Die gleichen Marktrechte wie Shiring, Lady?« hakte Francis nach.

»Genauso habe ich mich ausgedrückt.«

Warum hatte Francis den Satz wiederholt? Philip wußte, daß es üblich war, bei der Erteilung neuer Genehmigungen auf die Rechte anderer Städte zu verweisen: Das war nur recht und billig und sparte überdies viel Schreibarbeit. Er würde sich vergewissern müssen, wie die Rechte in Shiring im einzelnen aussahen. Einschränkungen waren ebenso möglich wie zusätzlich Privilegien.

Mathilde sagte: »Ihr habt also beide etwas bekommen, William den Steinbruch und Prior Philip den Markt. Dafür werdet Ihr mir je hundert Pfund bezahlen. Das ist alles.« Damit wandte sie sich ab.

Philip war wie vom Donner gerührt. Hundert Pfund! Die Priorei besaß im Augenblick nicht einmal hundert Pennies. Woher sollte er wohl soviel Geld nehmen? Der Markt brauchte Jahre, bis er das abwarf! Dies war ein vernichtender Schlag, der das Bauprogramm auf lange Sicht hinaus verzögerte … Mit offenem Mund starrte Philip Mathilde an, die sich aber schon wieder in die Unterhaltung mit ihrer Hofdame vertieft hatte. Francis stieß ihn leicht an. Philip öffnete den Mund, doch Francis hielt sich den Finger vor die Lippen. »Aber –«, fing Philip an, doch Francis schüttelte heftig den Kopf.

Mutlos ließ Philip die Schultern hängen, wandte sich ab und kehrte der Königin den Rücken.

Francis zeigte sich nach seinem Rundgang durch das Kloster zu Kingsbridge höchst beeindruckt. »Als ich vor zehn Jahren hier war«, meinte er respektlos, »war dies die reinste Bruchbude. Du hast sie wieder zum Leben erweckt.«

Besonderen Gefallen fand er an der Schreibstube, die Tom während Philips Aufenthalt in Lincoln fertiggestellt hatte. Der kleine Anbau am Kapitelhaus besaß hohe Fenster, einen Kamin mit Abzug, eine Reihe Schreibpulte und einen großen Bücherschrank aus Eichenholz. Vier Klosterbrüder waren bereits an der Arbeit und schrieben, vor den hohen Pulten stehend, mit Federkielen auf Pergamentbögen. Drei von ihnen waren mit Abschriften beschäftigt: einer mit den Psalmen Davids, der zweite mit dem Matthäusevangelium und der dritte mit der Ordensregel des heiligen Benedikt. Der vierte, Bruder Timothy, schrieb die Geschichte Englands nieder, die allerdings mit der Erschaffung der Welt einsetzte, so daß Philip befürchtete, der alte Knabe brächte sie nie zu Ende. Philip hatte nur wenige Steine von der Kathedrale abzweigen wollen, und so war die Schreibstube recht klein geraten, aber sie war warm, trocken und hell und erfüllte ihren Zweck. »Es ist eine Schande, wie wenig Bücher das Kloster hat«, erklärte Philip, »doch da sie unerschwinglich für uns sind, ist dies der einzige Weg, unsere Sammlung zu vergrößern.«

Das Erdgeschoß barg eine Werkstatt, in der ein alter Mönch zwei Novizen beibrachte, wie Schafshäute zur Herstellung von Pergament gespannt, Tinte gemischt und lose Blätter zu Büchern gebunden wurden. »Du wirst bald sogar Bücher verkaufen können«, meinte Francis.

»O ja – die Schreibstube wird sich über kurz oder lang doppelt und dreifach bezahlt machen.«

Sie verließen das Gebäude und spazierten durch den Kreuzgang. Dies war die Zeit, die dem Selbststudium gewidmet war, und die meisten Mönche lasen. Andere meditierten auch, was, wie Francis skeptisch bemerkte, einem Nickerchen verdächtig ähnlich sah. In der Nordwestecke leierten zwanzig Schuljungen ihre lateinischen Verben herunter. Philip blieb stehen und deutete auf einen von ihnen. »Siehst du den Kleinen dort am Ende der Bank?«

»Der auf seine Schiefertafel schreibt und dabei die Zunge herausstreckt?«

»Das ist der Knabe, den du im Wald gefunden hast.«

»Wie groß er geworden ist!«

»Fünfeinhalb Jahre und frühreif dazu.«

Francis schüttelte verwundert den Kopf. »Wie doch die Zeit vergeht! Wie macht er sich?«

»Die Mönche verhätscheln ihn nach Strich und Faden, aber er wird es überleben, genau wie wir beide auch.«

»Wer sind die anderen Schüler?«

»Teils Novizen, teils Söhne von Kaufleuten und hiesigen Adligen. Sie sollen bei uns Schreiben und Rechnen lernen.«

Vom Kreuzgang gingen sie zur Dombaustelle hinüber. Vom Ostteil der neuen Kathedrale stand nun schon mehr als die Hälfte. Die lange Doppelreihe mächtiger Säulen mit den bereits vollendeten Bogen ragte vierzig Fuß in die Höhe. Über der Arkade zeichnete sich andeutungsweise schon das künftige Triforium ab, und zu ihren beiden Seiten waren die niedrigeren Mauern der Seitenschiffe hochgezogen worden, aus denen die Strebepfeiler herausragten. Während des Rundgangs bemerkte Philip, daß die Steinmetzen an den Halbbogen bauten, welche die Strebepfeiler mit dem Triforium verbinden und das Gewicht des Daches tragen sollten.

Francis staunte nur so. »Was du alles auf die Beine gestellt hast, Philip!« sagte er. »Die Schreibstube, die Schule, die neue Kirche, ja sogar die neuen Häuser in der Stadt – ohne dich wäre das alles nicht entstanden.«

Philip war gerührt: Solch ein Lob hatte er noch nie zu hören bekommen. Wäre er gefragt worden, so hätte er gesagt, der Segen Gottes ruhe auf seiner Arbeit. Aber im Grunde seines Herzens wußte er, daß Francis recht hatte: Diese aufstrebende, geschäftige Stadt war sein Werk. Die Anerkennung tat ihm doppelt gut, weil sie aus dem Munde seines weltgewandten, zynischen jüngeren Bruders kam.

Tom Builder erblickte sie und kam herüber. »Ihr habt unglaubliche Fortschritte gemacht«, sagte Philip zu ihm. »Ja, aber seht Euch das an.« Tom deutete in die Nordostecke des Klostergeländes, wo die Quader aus dem Steinbruch gelagert wurden. Normalerweise befanden sich dort Hunderte, säuberlich in Reihen aufeinandergestapelte Blöcke; jetzt lagen kaum mehr als fünfundzwanzig herum.

»Wir sind zwar großartig vorangekommen, aber dabei haben wir leider auch unseren Vorrat an Steinen aufgebraucht.«

Philips Hochgefühl verflüchtigte sich. Mathildes harter Richtspruch setzte alles, was er erreicht hatte, wieder aufs Spiel!

Sie wandten sich der Nordseite der Baustelle zu, wo die besten Steinmetzen an ihren Werkbänken arbeiteten und die Blöcke mit Hammer und Meißel in die richtige Form brachten. Philip stellte sich hinter einen von ihnen und begutachtete sein Werk. Der Mann arbeitete an einem Kapitell, dem großen, vorspringenden Stein am oberen Ende jeder Säule. Mit Hilfe eines leichten Hammers und kleinen Meißels schnitt er ein Blattmuster aus dem Kapitell heraus. Die Blätter waren stark unterhöhlt und äußerst fein. Philip stellte überrascht fest, daß der junge Handwerker Jack war, Toms Stiefsohn. »Ich dachte, Jack ist noch in der Lehre«, sagte er.

»Ist er auch.« Tom ging weiter und sagte erst, als sie außer Hörweite waren: »Der Junge ist unglaublich. Es gibt Männer hier, die schon Steine geschnitten haben, bevor er auf die Welt kam, und trotzdem kann ihm keiner das Wasser reichen.« Er lachte verlegen. »Dabei ist er noch nicht einmal mein eigener Sohn!«

Toms Sohn Alfred war selbst Steinmetzmeister mit eigenen Lehrlingen und Gesellen, aber Philip wußte, daß Alfred mit seiner Gruppe nicht bei den schwierigen Arbeiten eingesetzt wurde. Unwillkürlich fragte er sich, was Tom im Grunde seines Herzens dabei fühlen mochte.

Tom war mit seinen Gedanken bereits bei den finanziellen Problemen. »Aber der Markt wird doch bestimmt eine schöne Stange Geld abwerfen«, sagte er.

»Schon, aber nicht genug. Zu Beginn allenfalls fünfzig Pfund im Jahr.«

Tom nickte beklommen. »Ungefähr soviel, wie wir für die Bezahlung der Steine brauchen.«

»Wenn ich Mathilde nicht hundert Pfund für die Marktrechte zahlen müßte, kämen wir gut zurecht.«

»Was ist mit der Wolle?«

Die Vliese, die sich in Philips Scheune stapelten, würden binnen wenigen Wochen auf der Wollmesse zu Shiring verkauft und sollten etwa hundert Pfund einbringen. »Damit werde ich Mathilde bezahlen, aber dann bleibt mir immer noch nichts für die nächsten zwölf Monatslöhne der Handwerker übrig.«

»Könnt Ihr Euch nichts leihen?«

»Das habe ich schon versucht. Die Juden geben mir nichts mehr.

Ich habe mich erkundigt, als ich in Winchester war. Wenn sie nicht sicher sind, daß man das Geld zurückzahlen kann, leihen sie einem nichts.«

»Und Aliena?«

Philip stutzte. Auf den Gedanken, von ihr zu leihen, war er noch nie gekommen. Sie hatte sogar noch mehr Vliese in ihren Scheunen. Nach der Wollmesse würden sie gut und gerne ihre zweihundert Pfund wert sein. »Aber sie braucht das Geld für ihren Lebensunterhalt. Und Christen dürfen keine Zinsen verlangen. Wenn sie ihr Geld an mich verleiht, bleibt ihr selbst nichts mehr für ihren Handel. Obwohl ...« Noch während er sprach, kam ihm eine neue Idee. Hatte Aliena ihm nicht angeboten, seine gesamte Wollproduktion dieses Jahres aufzukaufen? Vielleicht fiel ihnen gemeinsam eine Lösung ein ... »Ich denke, ein Besuch bei ihr könnte nicht schaden«, sagte er. »Ist sie zu Hause?«

»Ich glaube schon – heute morgen habe ich sie jedenfalls noch gesehen.«

»Komm, Francis – du wirst gleich die Bekanntschaft einer bemerkenswerten jungen Frau machen.« Sie ließen Tom stehen und eilten der Stadt zu. Aliena besaß zwei nebeneinanderliegende Häuser an der Westmauer des Klosters. Eines bewohnte sie selbst, das andere diente ihr als Lager. Sie war sehr wohlhabend. Es mußte doch eine Möglichkeit geben, mit ihrer Hilfe Mathildes Wucherpreis für die Marktrechte aufzubringen!

Aliena stand in ihrem Lager und beaufsichtigte das Entladen eines turmhoch mit Wollsäcken bepackten Ochsenkarrens. Sie trug einen Mantel aus Brokat, wie die Kaiserin Mathilde ihn getragen hatte, und ihr Haar steckte unter einer weißen Leinenhaube. Sie wirkte gebieterisch wie immer, und die beiden Männer, die den Karren entluden, gehorchten ihr aufs Wort. Jedermann zollte ihr Respekt, aber enge Freunde hatte sie merkwürdigerweise keine. Sie begrüßte Philip herzlich. »Als wir Kunde von der Schlacht zu Lincoln erhielten, haben wir schon befürchtet, Ihr wäret ums Leben gekommen!« sagte sie. Aus ihren Augen sprach echte Anteilnahme, und Philip war gerührt bei dem Gedanken, daß es Menschen gab, die sich um ihn sorgten. Er stellte sie Francis vor.

»Habt Ihr in Winchester Gerechtigkeit gefunden?« wollte Aliena wissen.

»Nur zum Teil«, erwiderte Philip. »Kaiserin Mathilde hat uns die Genehmigung für den Markt erteilt, aber den Steinbruch vorenthalten.

Das eine wiegt das andere mehr oder weniger auf. Allerdings verlangt sie hundert Pfund für die Gewährung der Marktrechte.«

»Das ist ja schrecklich!« sagte Aliena entsetzt. »Ihr habt ihr doch gesagt, daß der Erlös aus dem Markt für den Bau der Kathedrale verwendet wird, oder?«

»Selbstverständlich.«

»Aber wo wollt Ihr denn hundert Pfund hernehmen?«

»Ich dachte, Ihr könntet mir vielleicht helfen.«

»Ich?« meinte Aliena verblüfft.

»In ein paar Wochen, wenn Ihr Eure Wolle erst an die Flamen verkauft habt, verfügt Ihr über zweihundert oder mehr Pfund.«

Aliena sah bekümmert drein. »Die ich Euch nur allzugerne geben würde, aber ich brauche sie, um nächstes Jahr wieder Wolle kaufen zu können.«

»Erinnert Ihr Euch noch, daß Ihr meine Wolle kaufen wolltet?«

»Ja, aber dazu ist es jetzt zu spät. Ich wollte sie zu Beginn der Saison haben. Außerdem könnt Ihr sie jetzt bald selbst verkaufen.«

»Ich habe mir überlegt«, sagte Philip, »ob ich Euch vielleicht die Wolle aus dem *nächsten* Jahr verkaufen kann?«

Sie runzelte die Stirn. »Aber die habt Ihr ja noch nicht!«

»Kann ich sie Euch nicht im voraus verkaufen?«

»Ich wüßte nicht, wie.«

»Ganz einfach. Ihr gebt mir das Geld jetzt. Ich gebe Euch die Wolle nächstes Jahr.«

Aliena wußte ganz offensichtlich nicht, was sie von diesem Vorschlag halten sollte; auf solche Weise wurden normalerweise keine Geschäfte getätigt. Für Philip war dieses Gebaren nicht minder fremd: Die Idee dazu war ihm eben erst gekommen.

Aliena sprach langsam und bedächtig. »Ich müßte Euch einen geringfügig niedrigeren Preis bieten als den, den Ihr durch Warten selbst erzielen könnt. Außerdem ist es gut möglich, daß der Wollpreis bis zum nächsten Sommer noch steigt – seit ich im Geschäft bin, war das bisher jedes Jahr der Fall.«

»Also erleide ich einen kleinen Verlust, und Ihr erzielt einen kleinen Gewinn«, sagte Philip. »Aber zumindest kann ich ein Jahr lang weiterbauen.«

»Aber was werdet Ihr nächstes Jahr tun?«

»Das weiß ich noch nicht. Vielleicht verkaufe ich Euch dann wieder die Wolle des nächsten Jahres.«

Aliena nickte. »Das klingt vernünftig.«

Philip nahm ihre Hände in seine und schaute ihr in die Augen. »Wenn Ihr das tut, Aliena, dann rettet Ihr damit die Kathedrale«, sagte er eindringlich.

Aliena wirkte sehr ernst. »Einst wart Ihr es, der mich gerettet hat, nicht wahr?«

»Ja, das stimmt.«

»Dann sind wir jetzt quitt.«

»Gott segne Euch!« Im Überschwang seiner Dankbarkeit nahm Philip sie in die Arme und drückte sie an sich – bis ihm plötzlich einfiel, daß sie ja eine Frau war. Hastig rückte er wieder von ihr ab. »Ich weiß gar nicht, wie ich Euch danken soll«, sagte er. »Ich war mit meinem Latein völlig am Ende.«

Aliena lachte. »Ich glaube nicht, daß ich soviel Dankbarkeit verdiene. Wahrscheinlich fahre ich bei diesem Geschäft sehr gut.«

»Das will ich doch hoffen.«

»Laßt uns den Handel doch mit einem Becher Wein besiegeln«, schlug Aliena vor. »Ich bezahle nur eben noch den Fuhrmann.«

Der Ochsenkarren war leer und die Ladung Säcke fein säuberlich aufgestapelt. Philip und Francis gingen nach draußen, während Aliena mit dem Fuhrmann abrechnete. Die Sonne ging gerade unter, und die Bauleute traten den Heimweg an. Philip fühlte sich wieder obenauf: Trotz aller Rückschläge hatte er eine Lösung für seine Probleme gefunden! »Gott sei gedankt, daß es Aliena gibt!« entfuhr es ihm.

»Warum hast du mir nicht gesagt, wie schön sie ist?« wollte Francis wissen.

»Schön? Mag schon sein.«

Francis lachte. »Philip, du bist blind! Sie gehört zu den schönsten Frauen, die mir je begegnet sind. Bei ihrem Anblick könnte man glatt in Versuchung geraten, die Priesterwürde an den Nagel zu hängen.«

Philip sah ihn scharf an. »So solltest du nicht daherreden.«

»Entschuldige.«

Aliena verriegelte das Lager, und sie begaben sich in das große, mit einem Hauptraum und separatem Schlafzimmer ausgestattete Haus. In der Ecke stand ein Faß Bier, von der Decke hing ein ganzer Schinken, und der Tisch war mit einem weißen Leinentuch gedeckt. Eine Magd schenkte den Wein für die Gäste aus einer Karaffe in silberne Becher. Aliena lebte in guten Verhältnissen. Wenn sie so schön ist, sinnierte Philip, warum hat sie dann keinen Mann? An Bewerbern herrschte wahrlich kein Mangel: Sämtliche heiratsfähigen jungen Männer im Umkreis hatten ihr den Hof gemacht, doch sie hatte alle abgewiesen. Philip war ihr so dankbar, daß er sie ebenfalls glücklich sehen wollte.

Alienas Gedanken kreisten noch um ihre Abmachung. »Das Geld werde ich erst nach der Wollmesse in Shiring haben«, sagte sie, sobald sie auf ihren Handel angestoßen hatten.

Philip wandte sich an Francis. »Wird Mathilde so lange warten?«

»Wie lange?«

»Die Messe findet Donnerstag in drei Wochen statt.«

Francis nickte. »Ich werde es ihr ausrichten. Sie wird sich gedulden.«

Aliena löste ihre Haube, schüttelte ihre dunkle Lockenpracht und seufzte matt. »Die Tage sind viel zu kurz«, sagte sie. »Die Zeit reicht hinten und vorne nicht. Ich würde gerne mehr Wolle kaufen, aber ich muß erst genügend Fuhrleute finden, die sie mir nach Shiring transportieren.«

Philip sagte: »Und nächstes Jahr werdet Ihr sogar noch mehr haben.«

»Ich wünschte nur, wir könnten die Flamen nach Kingsbridge locken. Das wäre viel einfacher, als sämtliche Vliese nach Shiring zu schaffen.«

»Und warum tut Ihr das nicht?« warf Francis ein.

Die beiden sahen ihn verblüfft an. »Wie denn?« fragte Philip.

»Indem Ihr Eure eigene Wollmesse abhaltet.«

Philip dämmerte, worauf Francis hinauswollte. »Geht das denn?«

»Mathilde hat Euch die gleichen Rechte wie Shiring verliehen. Ich habe die Urkunde eigenhändig ausgefertigt. Wenn Shiring eine Wollmesse abhalten kann, dann könnt Ihr das auch.«

»Oh, das wäre wunderbar!« sagte Aliena. »Dann bräuchten wir nicht die ganze Ladung Säcke nach Shiring zu karren. Wir könnten unsere Geschäfte hier abschließen und die Wolle direkt nach Flandern verschiffen.«

»Das ist noch das Geringste«, wandte Philip aufgeregt ein. »Eine Wollmesse wirft in einer einzigen Woche mehr ab als ein Sonntagsmarkt im ganzen Jahr. Dieses Jahr wird es natürlich noch nicht klappen – niemand würde davon erfahren. Aber wir können schon auf der diesjährigen Wollmesse in Shiring für unsere eigene im nächsten Jahr werben und sicherstellen, daß wirklich alle Aufkäufer Bescheid wissen ...«

»Das wird erhebliche Auswirkungen auf Shiring haben«, sagte Aliena. »Wir beide zusammen haben die größte Menge an Vliesen in der ganzen Grafschaft zu verkaufen. Ohne uns ist die Wollmesse in Shiring nur noch halb soviel wert.«

»William Hamleigh wird also Verluste machen«, meinte Francis. »Der wird wütend wie ein Stier.«

Francis hat den Nagel auf den Kopf getroffen, dachte Philip und schüttelte sich unwillkürlich vor Widerwillen. William glich tatsächlich einem wütenden Stier.

»Na und?« meinte Aliena. »Wenn Mathilde uns die Erlaubnis gegeben hat, dann steht einer Wollmesse nichts im Wege. Und William kann uns nichts anhaben, oder?«

»Das will ich doch hoffen«, sagte Philip inbrünstig. »Das will ich doch stark hoffen.«

KAPITEL X

Am Gedenktag des heiligen Augustinus war Punkt zwölf Uhr Feier-
abend, und die Bauleute begrüßten das mittägliche Glockenzeichen
mit einem Seufzer der Erleichterung. Gewöhnlich arbeiteten sie an
sechs Wochentagen von Sonnenaufgang bis Sonnenuntergang, so daß
sie die Erholungspausen, die ihnen die Heiligentage boten, gut brauchen konnten. Allein Jack war so vertieft in seine Arbeit, daß er das
Läuten nicht hörte.

Die Herausforderung, harten Stein in weiche, runde Formen zu
verwandeln, hatte ihn völlig in Bann geschlagen. Der Stein hatte seinen eigenen Willen und setzte sich zur Wehr, wenn Jack ihm gewaltsam zu Leibe rückte: Entweder rutschte der Meißel ab oder der Ein-
schnitt wurde zu tief und das Muster mißlang. Aber wenn er mit dem
Klumpen Stein vor ihm erst einmal vertraut war, konnte er ihn auch
verwandeln. Je schwieriger die Aufgabe, um so größer Jacks Begeisterung.

Er bekam allmählich das Gefühl, die Ornamente, die Tom von ihm
verlangte, seien zu einfach. Er war der Zickzack- und Rautenmuster,
der Hundszahnfriese, Spiralen und einfachen Rundstäbe überdrüssig,
und selbst dieses Laubfries kam ihm ziemlich steif und eintönig vor.
Am liebsten hätte er natürlich aussehendes, geschmeidiges und unregelmäßiges Blattwerk aus dem Stein geschnitten und die unterschied-
lichen Formen echter Blätter von Eichen, Eschen und Birken imitiert,
doch Tom ließ ihn nicht. Viel lieber noch hätte er Szenen aus der
Bibel dargestellt: Adam und Eva, David und Goliath, das Jüngste
Gericht – vollständig mit Dämonen und Teufeln und nackten Menschen –, aber er wagte gar nicht erst darum zu bitten.

Schließlich kam Tom und gebot ihm Einhalt. »Heute ist Feiertag,
Junge«, sagte er. »Außerdem bist du noch mein Lehrling, und ich

618

brauche dich beim Aufräumen. Sämtliche Werkzeuge müssen vor dem Essen weggeschlossen werden.«

Jack legte seinen Hammer und die Meißel beiseite und deponierte den Stein, an dem er gearbeitet hatte, sorgfältig in Toms Bauhütte; dann folgte er Tom auf seinem Rundgang über die Baustelle. Die anderen Lehrlinge räumten schon auf und fegten Steinsplitter, Sand, Klümpchen getrockneten Mörtels und Holzspäne beiseite, die überall herumlagen. Tom sammelte seine Zirkel und sein Richtscheit ein, Jack seine Maßstöcke und seine Senkschnüre, und sie brachten alles in die Bauhütte.

In der Bauhütte bewahrte Tom seine Ruten auf, lange Eisenstäbe, die im Querschnitt quadratisch waren, dazu kerzengerade und von exakt gleicher Länge; sie steckten in einem verschließbaren Holzgestell und wurden zum Ausmessen verwendet.

Während sie weiter herumstreiften und Mörtelbretter und Schaufeln einsammelten, mußte Jack immerzu an die Ruten denken. »Wie lang ist so eine Rute?« fragte er.

Die Steinmetzen, die seine Frage hörten, brachen in Gelächter aus. Es war nicht das erste Mal, daß sie Jacks Fragen komisch fanden. Edward Short, ein wahrer Winzling von Steinmetz mit ledriger Haut und schiefer Nase, meinte: »Eine Rute ist ein Rute«, und das Gelächter begann von neuem.

Es machte ihnen Spaß, die Lehrlinge aufzuziehen, vor allem, wenn sie damit beweisen konnten, wie himmelhoch sie ihnen überlegen waren. Jack haßte es, um seiner Unwissenheit willen ausgelacht zu werden, fand sich jedoch damit ab, weil seine Neugier größer war. »Das verstehe ich nicht«, gab er geduldig zurück.

»Ein Zoll ist ein Zoll, ein Fuß ist ein Fuß und eine Rute ist eine Rute«, sagte Edward.

Die Rute war also eine Maßeinheit. »Und wieviel Fuß hat so eine Rute?«

»Aha! Das kommt ganz drauf an. In Lincoln sind es achtzehn, in Ostanglien sechzehn.«

Tom unterbrach den Wortwechsel und gab Jack eine Antwort, mit der er etwas anfangen konnte. »Auf dieser Baustelle kommen auf eine Rute fünfzehn Fuß.«

Eine Steinmetzin mittleren Alters fügte hinzu: »In Paris benutzen sie die Rute überhaupt nicht, nur den Maßstock.«

Tom sagte zu Jack: »Der Gesamtplan der Kirche basiert auf Ruten. Hol mir eine und ich zeig's dir. Es wird langsam Zeit, daß du dich mit diesen Dingen vertraut machst.« Er händigte Jack den Schlüssel aus.

Jack nahm eine Rute aus dem Gestell. Sie war ziemlich schwer. Tom gab gerne Erklärungen, und Jack hörte ihm gerne zu. Die Organisation der Dombaustelle war für ihn ein geheimnisvolles Muster, ähnlich dem eines Brokatmantels, und je mehr er davon verstand, desto mehr wollte er erfahren.

Tom stand im Seitenschiff am offenen Ende des halbfertigen Altarraums, der in der Mitte der künftigen Vierung lag. Er griff nach der Rute und legte sie quer durch das Seitenschiff auf den Boden. »Von der Außenwand bis zur Mitte des Bogenpfeilers ist es eine Rute.« Er stellte die Rute auf und legte sie in entgegengesetzter Richtung aus. »Von hier bis zum Mittelpunkt des Langhauses ist es eine Rute.« Er wiederholte den Vorgang, und das Ende der Stange markierte die Mitte des gegenüberliegenden Pfeilers. »Das Mittelschiff ist zwei Ruten breit.« Er legte die Rute wieder an und stieß an die Mauer des jenseitigen Seitenschiffes. »Insgesamt ist die Kirche vier Ruten breit.«

»Ja«, sagte Jack. »Und jeder Pfeiler hat eine Rute Abstand vom nächsten.«

Tom sah leicht verärgert drein. »Von wem hast du das denn?«

»Von niemandem. Aber die einzelnen Abschnitte des Seitenschiffs sind quadratisch; wenn sie also eine Rute breit sind, dann müssen sie auch eine Rute lang sein. Und die Abstände zwischen den Pfeilern des Mittelschiffs decken sich mit der Länge der Seitenschiffe, wie man sieht.«

»Wie man sieht«, wiederholte Tom. »Du hättest Philosoph werden sollen.« In seiner Stimme schwangen Stolz und Ärger mit. Es freute ihn, daß Jack so schnell von Begriff war, aber daß die Geheimnisse der Baukunst von einem bloßen Knaben durchschaut werden konnten, bereitete ihm Verdruß.

Jack jedoch nahm die ungeheure Logik des Gesamtplans viel zu sehr gefangen, als daß er sich über Toms Gefühle Gedanken gemacht hätte. »Der Altarraum muß demnach vier Ruten lang sein«, sagte er. »Und die Kirche insgesamt wird, wenn sie erst fertig ist, zwölf Ruten lang.« Schon kam ihm ein neuer Gedanke. »Und wie hoch soll sie werden?«

»Sechs Ruten. Die Arkaden drei, daß Triforium eine, der Lichtgaden zwei Ruten hoch.«

»Aber warum muß alles erst in Ruten berechnet werden? Wieso baut man nicht einfach Stein auf Stein drauflos, wie bei einem Haus?«

»Zunächst einmal, weil es so billiger ist. Alle Bogen der Arkade sind identisch, so daß wir die Vorlagen immer wieder verwenden können. Je weniger Steine wir verwenden, die sich in Form und Größe unterscheiden, desto weniger Schablonen muß ich herstellen, und so weiter. Zweitens vereinfacht es unsere Arbeit grundsätzlich, vom ursprünglichen Bauplan, der ausschließlich auf Quadraten aus Ruten basiert, bis hin zum Weißeln der Wände, denn wir können besser abschätzen, wieviel Kalktünche wir benötigen. Und je einfacher eine Sache ist, um so weniger Fehler werden gemacht. Das Teuerste an einem Bau sind die Fehler. Und drittens sieht eine Kirche, die in ihren Ausmaßen auf Ruten basiert, gut aus. Das Geheimnis wahrer Schönheit sind die richtigen Proportionen.«

Jack nickte wie verzaubert.

Die Mühe und das Wissen, die erforderlich waren, um einen so ehrgeizigen und anspruchsvollen Bau wie den einer Kathedrale zu leiten, bildeten einen Quell endlosen Staunens für ihn. Der Gedanke, daß Regelmäßigkeit und Wiederholung nicht nur die Arbeit vereinfachten, sondern überdies für ein harmonisches Gesamtbild sorgten, war geradezu verführerisch einleuchtend. Aber ob das Geheimnis wahrer Schönheit tatsächlich nur in den Proportionen zu suchen war? Seinem Geschmack nach lag es eher in den ungezähmten, überbordenden, ausufernden Dingen wie in Alienas Haar.

Jack schlang sein Essen hastig hinunter und verließ das Dorf Richtung Norden. Es war ein warmer Frühsommertag, und er ging barfuß. Seit er mit seiner Mutter in Kingsbridge lebte und dort arbeitete, gönnte er sich bisweilen das Vergnügen, in den Wald zurückzukehren. Anfangs hatte er diese Ausflüge dazu benutzt, um überschüssige Kraft auszutoben, war gerannt und herumgesprungen, hatte Bäume erklettert und mit seiner Schleuder Jagd auf Enten gemacht. Damals hatte er sich erst an den neuen, größeren und stärkeren Körper, den er nun hatte, gewöhnen müssen, doch das war längst vorbei. Wenn er jetzt in den Wald ging, dachte er nach: über die Schönheit, die in den richtigen Proportionen schlummern sollte, über die Frage, warum Gebäude nicht einstürzten, sondern stehen blieben, und wie es sich wohl anfühlen mochte, Alienas Brüste zu streicheln.

Seit Jahren schon betete er sie heimlich an. Das Bild, das sich ihm unauslöschlich eingeprägt hatte, rührte von ihrer ersten Begegnung her: Damals war sie in Earlscastle die Treppe zum Saal heruntergekommen, und er hatte sie für eine Märchenprinzessin gehalten. Und so entrückt wie damals war sie für ihn geblieben. Sie sprach mit Prior Philip, mit Tom Builder, mit dem Juden Malachi und mit allen anderen wohlhabenden und einflußreichen Leuten in Kingsbridge; er, Jack, hatte nie einen Grund gefunden, das Wort an sie zu richten. Er sah sie immer nur von weitem: Wenn sie in der Kirche war und betete, wenn sie auf ihrem Zelter über die Brücke ritt oder vor ihrem Haus in der Sonne saß; im Winter trug sie kostbare Pelze und im Sommer feinstes Leinen, und ihr schönes Gesicht war stets umrahmt von ihrer wilden Lockenpracht. Jeden Abend vor dem Einschlafen überlegte er, wie schön es sein mußte, wenn er ihr die Kleider abstreifen, sie nackt vor sich sehen und behutsam ihren weichen Mund küssen könnte.

Die Aussichtslosigkeit seiner Träumereien hatte ihn in letzter Zeit unzufrieden und niedergeschlagen gemacht. Es genügte ihm nicht mehr, Aliena aus der Ferne zu sehen, Brocken aus ihren Gesprächen mit anderen Leuten aufzuschnappen und sich vorzustellen, wie er sie lieben würde. Er wollte zur Tat schreiten.

Es gab etliche Mädchen seines Alters, bei denen er wohl zum Zuge gekommen wäre. Unter den Lehrlingen wurde ständig darüber geklatscht, welche der jungen Frauen von Kingsbridge entgegenkommend war und wie weit sie einen jungen Mann jeweils gehen ließ. Die meisten Mädchen waren fest entschlossen, bis zu ihrer Verheiratung, wie es die Kirche lehrte, Jungfrau zu bleiben, doch auch sie ließen einen dies oder jenes tun, Hauptsache, ihre Jungfernschaft blieb unangetastet. Jack hielten sie samt und sonders für komisch – und hatten damit, wie er meinte, nicht ganz unrecht –, aber ein oder zwei von ihnen fanden seine Fremdartigkeit anziehend. Eines Sonntags hatte er nach dem Kirchgang eine Unterhaltung mit Edith, der Schwester eines seiner Lehrlingskollegen begonnen; aber als er davon sprach, wie sehr er das Meißeln liebte, hatte sie angefangen zu kichern. Am darauffolgenden Sonntag war er mit Ann, der blonden Tochter des Schneidermeisters, in den Feldern spazierengegangen. Er hatte nicht viel gesagt, sondern sie geküßt und schließlich vorgeschlagen, sich in einem grünen Gerstenfeld auszustrecken. Er hatte sie noch einmal geküßt und ihre Brüste berührt, und sie hatte ihn bereitwillig wieder geküßt; aber nach einer Weile hatte sie sich ihm entzogen und gefragt: »Wer ist sie?« Jack, der gerade an Aliena gedacht hatte, war wie vom Donner gerührt. Er hatte versucht, die Angelegenheit herunterzuspielen und sie wieder zu küssen, doch sie hatte das Gesicht abgewandt und gesagt: »Wer sie auch immer sein mag, sie hat das große Los gezogen!« Sie waren gemeinsam nach Kingsbridge zurückgegangen, und Ann hatte beim Abschied gesagt: »Vergeude deine Zeit nicht damit, sie dir aus dem Kopf zu schlagen. Es wird dir nicht gelingen. Du willst sie und keine andere; bemüh dich also lieber, sie zu erobern.« Dann hatte sie ihn liebevoll angelächelt und hinzugefügt: »Du hast ein hübsches Gesicht. Wahrscheinlich ist es gar nicht so schwer, wie du glaubst.«

Ihre Herzensgüte verursachte ihm um so mehr Pein, als sie unter den Lehrlingen als besonders freizügig galt und er aller Welt erzählt hatte, er wolle sich an sie heranmachen. Jetzt kam ihm dieses Geschwätz dermaßen kindisch vor, daß er vor Scham am liebsten im Boden versunken wäre. Aber hätte er Ann den Namen der Frau genannt, die ihn Tag und Nacht verfolgte, hätte sie ihn gewiß nicht ermutigt. Eine unwahrscheinlichere Verbindung als zwischen Jack und Aliena ließ sich kaum vorstellen. Aliena war zweiundzwanzig, er siebzehn; sie war die Tochter eines Grafen, er ein Bastard; sie war eine reiche Wollhändlerin, er ein mittelloser Lehrling. Noch schwerer jedoch wog die Tatsache, daß sie geradezu berühmt war für die Zahl der Bewerber, die sich bei ihr einen Korb geholt hatten. In der ganzen Grafschaft gab es keinen vorzeigbaren jungen Herrn und keinen Erstgeborenen aus reichem Hause, der nicht schon nach Kingsbridge gekommen wäre, um ihr den Hof zu machen; und jeder hatte sich enttäuscht wieder auf den Heimweg gemacht. Wie sollte sich da ausgerechnet Jack, der außer einem »hübschen Gesicht« nichts aufzuweisen hatte, Hoffnungen machen?

Allerdings hatten Aliena und er eines gemeinsam: ihre Vorliebe für den Wald. Darin unterschieden sie sich von den meisten anderen Menschen, die die Sicherheit der Felder und Dörfer vorzogen und einen großen Bogen um den Wald machten. Aber Aliena machte häufig Spaziergänge in den Wäldern unweit von Kingsbridge, und sie hatte einen Lieblingsplatz, der abgeschieden lag und wo sie bisweilen Rast machte. Jack hatte sie ein- oder zweimal dort gesehen, war aber von ihr nicht bemerkt worden: Er bewegte sich so behutsam und lautlos, wie er es in der Kindheit gelernt hatte, als er sich seine Nahrung aus dem Wald hatte holen müssen.

Jetzt steuerte er auf die Lichtung zu, hatte aber nicht die geringste Ahnung, was er tun sollte, wenn er tatsächlich auf Aliena stieß. Was er tun *wollte,* wußte er genau: sich neben sie legen und ihren Körper streicheln. Vielleicht sollte er ein Gespräch mit ihr beginnen – aber worüber? Mit Mädchen seines Alters hatte er da keine Schwierigkeiten. Zu Edith hatte er neckend gesagt: »Dein Bruder erzählt die schlimmsten Sachen über dich, aber ich glaube ihm *kein einziges Wort*«, worauf sie prompt hatte wissen wollen, was ihr Bruder herumtratschte. Und Ann hatte er ganz direkt gefragt, ob sie ihn auf einem Spaziergang durch die Felder begleiten wolle. Aber wenn es darum ging, sich eine entsprechende Anrede für Aliena zurechtzulegen, war sein Kopf wie leergefegt. In seinen Augen gehörte sie, ihres ernsten und respekteinflößenden Gebarens wegen, schon zur älteren Generation. Dabei erinnerte er sich noch genau, wie verspielt sie mit siebzehn gewesen war. Seitdem hatte sie viel durchgemacht; trotzdem mußte sich irgendwo hinter der Maske der Ernsthaftigkeit noch das kleine, verspielte Mädchen verstecken. Das machte sie für Jack nur noch anziehender.

Er näherte sich der Lichtung. Um die Mittagszeit, wenn es am heißestens war, herrschte Stille im Wald, und Jack bewegte sich geräuschlos durch das Unterholz. Er wollte sich finden, bevor sie ihn entdeckte. Er war sich immer noch nicht sicher, ob er den Mut aufbringen würde, sie anzusprechen. Am meisten fürchtete er sich jedoch davor, einen schlechten Eindruck auf sie zu machen. Ein einzigesmal hatte er mit ihr geredet, und zwar an jenem Pfingstsonntag, als er nach Kingsbridge zurückgekehrt war; damals hatte er das Falsche gesagt, mit dem Ergebnis, daß sie seit vier Jahren kaum ein Wort gewechselt hatten. Dieses Mißgeschick sollte ihm nicht noch einmal passieren!

Wenige Augenblicke später äugte er hinter einer Buche hervor und erblickte sie.

Sie hatte sich ein außergewöhnlich schönes Plätzchen ausgesucht. Ein kleiner Wasserfall ergoß sich plätschernd in einen tiefen, von bemoosten Steinen umgebenen Teich, dessen Ufer in der Sonne lag. Aliena saß im Halbschatten unter einer Buche und las.

Jack war verblüfft. Eine Frau, die ein Buch las? Im Freien? Nur Mönche lasen Bücher, und auch die selten etwas anderes als Gebete. Alienas Buch war dazu noch ungewöhnlich, viel kleiner als die Bände in der Klosterbibliothek; es sah aus, als wäre es speziell für eine Frau gemacht worden oder für jemanden, der es mit sich herumtragen wollte. Jacks Überraschung war so groß, daß er seine Schüchternheit vergaß. Rasch trat er auf die Lichtung und fragte: »Was lest Ihr da?«

Sie fuhr zusammen und blickte erschrocken zu ihm auf. Herrje, er hatte ihr Angst eingejagt! Er fühlte sich unbeholfen und fürchtete schon, auch diesmal wieder ins Fettnäpfchen getreten zu sein, denn mit der Rechten griff sie blitzschnell in ihren linken Ärmel. Richtig, sie pflegte dort früher ein Messer zu tragen, und vielleicht tat sie das immer noch. Doch dann hatte sie ihn erkannt, und ihre Angst verflog ebenso schnell, wie sie gekommen war. Sie wirkte erleichtert, bedauerlicherweise aber auch ein wenig ungehalten. Er kam sich vor wie ein Störenfried und wäre am liebsten sofort wieder im Wald verschwunden. Doch das hätte es nur noch schwieriger gemacht, sie ein andermal anzusprechen, daher wich er nicht von der Stelle, nahm angesichts ihrer unfreundlichen Miene all seinen Mut zusammen und sagte: »Es tut mir leid, daß ich Euch erschreckt habe.«

»Ihr habt mich nicht *erschreckt*«, erwiderte sie rasch.

Er wußte, daß sie log, doch es lohnte nicht, mit ihr darüber zu streiten. Statt dessen wiederholte er seine ursprüngliche Frage: »Was lest Ihr da?«

Ihr Gesichtsausdruck veränderte sich, und sie betrachtete nachdenklich das gebundene Bändchen auf ihren Knien. »Mein Vater hat dieses Buch auf seiner letzten Reise in die Normandie erstanden und für mich mitgebracht. Ein paar Tage später wurde er ins Gefängnis gesteckt.«

Jack rückte ein wenig näher und warf einen Blick auf die aufgeschlagene Seite. »Das ist ja Französisch!« sagte er.

»Woher wißt Ihr das?« fragte sie erstaunt. »Könnt Ihr denn lesen?«

»Ja – aber ich dachte, es gäbe nur lateinische Bücher.«

»Das stimmt auch. Dies hier ist eine Ausnahme. Es ist ein Gedicht und heißt ›Das Alexanderlied‹.«

Ich habe es wahrgemacht, dachte Jack – ich rede mit ihr! Wie wunderbar! Aber was nun? Wie bringe ich sie zum Weiterreden? Verlegen fragte er: »Hm … äh, wovon handelt es denn?«

»Es ist die Geschichte von einem König, der Alexander der Große heißt und wunderbare Länder im Osten erobert, wo Edelsteine auf Weinstöcken wachsen und Blumen sprechen können.«

Jack war so beeindruckt, daß er seine Unsicherheit vergaß. »Wie sprechen die Blumen denn? Haben sie einen Mund?«

»Das wird nicht erklärt.«

»Glaubt Ihr, die Geschichte ist wahr?«

Sie sah ihn aufmerksam an, und er blickte in ihre wunderschönen Augen. »Ich weiß es nicht«, gab sie zurück. »Ich frage mich oft, ob die Geschichten wahr sind. Den meisten Leuten ist es egal, Hauptsache, die Geschichten gefallen ihnen.«

»Den Priestern ist es nicht egal. Die glauben, alle heiligen Geschichten sind wahr.«

»Die *sind* natürlich auch wahr!«

Jack hegte an den heiligen Geschichten die gleichen Zweifel wie an allen anderen auch; doch seine Mutter, die ihn diese Skepsis gelehrt, hatte ihn außerdem gelehrt, taktvoll zu schweigen, und so widersprach er nicht. Er gab sich alle Mühe, nicht auf Alienas Busen zu schauen, der sich genau am Rande seines Blickfelds befand: Wenn er den Blick senkte, hätte sie sofort gewußt, wo er hinsah. Er überlegte, was er ihr sonst noch sagen konnte. »Ich kenne viele Geschichten«, meinte er schließlich. »Ich kenne das ›Rolandslied‹, das ›Wilhelmslied‹ –«

»Wie meint Ihr das: Ihr *kennt* sie?«

»Ich kann sie rezitieren.«

»Wie ein Spielmann?«

»Was ist ein Spielmann?«

»Ein Mann, der herumreist und Geschichten erzählt.«

Das war neu für Jack. »Davon höre ich heute zum erstenmal.«

»In Frankreich gibt es viele. Als Kind bin ich mit meinem Vater oft hinübergefahren. Die Spielleute haben mir immer besonders gut gefallen.«

»Aber was tun sie? Auf der Straße stehen und reden?«

»Das kommt drauf an. An Festtagen kommen sie in die Halle des Herrn. Sie treten auf Märkten und Messen auf. Sie unterhalten die Pilger vor den Kirchen. Der hohe Adel hält sich mitunter seine eigenen Spielleute.«

Jack ging auf, daß er nicht nur mit ihr sprach, sondern eine richtige Unterhaltung mit ihr führte, die er mit keinem anderen Mädchen in Kingsbridge hätte führen können. Aliena und er waren außer seiner Mutter bestimmt die einzigen Menschen in der ganzen Stadt, die die französischen Heldenlieder kannten. Sie hatten etwas gemeinsam und konnten sich darüber unterhalten! Diese Erkenntnis war so überwältigend, daß Jack den Faden verlor und sich wie ein verwirrter Tölpel vorkam.

Glücklicherweise sprach Aliena schon weiter: »Normalerweise spielt der Spielmann die Geige zu seiner Geschichte. Erzählt er von einer Schlacht, so spielt er sehr schnell und hoch, sind zwei Menschen verliebt, spielt er langsam und betörend und an den lustigen Stellen kurze abgehackte Töne.«

Jack gefiel die Vorstellung, die Höhepunkte einer Geschichte mit Musik zu untermalen. »Ich wünschte nur, ich könnte Geige spielen.«

»Könnt Ihr wirklich Geschichten rezitieren?« fragte sie.

Er konnte sein Glück kaum fassen: Aliena war wirklich an ihm interessiert und fragte ihn sogar aus! Und ihr Gesicht war noch lieblicher, wenn die Neugier sie plagte. »Meine Mutter hat es mir beigebracht«, sagte er. »Wir haben im Wald gelebt, nur wir zwei. Sie hat mir die Geschichten immer wieder erzählt.«

»Aber wie könnt Ihr sie Euch merken? Es gibt Geschichten, für die man *Tage* braucht!«

»Ich weiß auch nicht. Es ist so ähnlich, wie man sich in einem Wald zurechtfindet. Man hat nicht den gesamten Wald im Kopf, aber wo man auch sein mag, man weiß von dort immer weiter.« Er sah wieder in ihr Buch – und machte eine Entdeckung. Er setzte sich neben sie ins Gras und schaute genauer hin. »Die Reime sind anders«, sagte er.

Sie wußte nicht genau, was er meinte. »Inwiefern?«

»Sie sind besser. Im ›Rolandslied‹ wird das Wort *König* mit *Richter* gereimt. In Eurem Buch reimt sich *Schwert* auf *Pferd*, auf *Herd*, auf *kehrt*, aber nicht auf *Herr*. Diese Reime sind ganz anders. Viel, viel besser. Mir gefallen sie.«

»Würdet Ihr …«, begann Aliena zaghaft. »Würdet Ihr mir ein Stück aus dem ›Rolandslied‹ vortragen?«

Jack setzte sich zurecht, so daß er sie dabei ansehen konnte. Die Intensität ihres Blickes und der Anflug von Eifer in ihren bezaubernden Augen machten ihm zu schaffen. Er schluckte heftig und begann:

Schöpfer aller Dinge,
Kaiser aller Könige
Wol, du oberster Richter
lehre mich selbst deine Worte.
Sende mir zu Munde
deine heilige Urkunde,
daß ich die Lüge vermeide,
die Wahrheit schreibe,
von einem theuerlichen Mann,
wie er das Reich Gottes gewann:
das ist Karl der Kaiser …

Jack machte eine Pause, und Aliena rief aus: »Ihr könnt es tatsächlich! Kaum zu fassen! Genau wie ein Spielmann!«

»Aber Ihr seht jetzt, was ich mit den Reimen meine, oder?«

»Ja, schon, aber mir kommt es auf die Geschichten an«, erwiderte sie. Ihre Augen blitzten vor Vergnügen. »Erzählt weiter.«

Jack hatte das Gefühl, vor Glück ohnmächtig werden zu müssen. »Wenn Ihr wollt«, gab er schwach zurück. Dann sah er ihr in die Augen und begann mit der zweiten Strophe.

Das erste Spiel der Sonnwendfeier bestand aus dem Verzehr des Wievielbrots. Wie den meisten dieser Spiele haftete auch ihm ein gewisser Aberglaube an, der Philip Kopfzerbrechen bereitete. Wenn er jedoch sämtliche Riten, die an die alten Religionen erinnerten, verbannen wollte, bliebe den Menschen nur noch die Hälfte ihrer Traditionen; außerdem würden sie sich ohnehin über sein Verbot hinwegsetzen. Also drückte er in den meisten Fällen beide Augen zu und schritt nur bei ein oder zwei Exzessen ein.

Die Mönche hatten auf dem Rasen im Westen des Klosterhofs Tische aufgestellt, und das Küchengesinde trug schon die dampfenden Kessel auf. Da der Prior gleichzeitig Gutsherr war, oblag es ihm, an hohen Feiertagen für das Festessen seiner Pächter zu sorgen. Philips Devise lautete: Großzügigkeit beim Essen und Geiz beim Trinken; also gab es Dünnbier und keinen Wein. Trotzdem gelang es an jedem Feiertag fünf oder sechs Unbelehrbaren, sich bis zur Besinnungslosigkeit zu besaufen.

Die angesehensten Bürger von Kingsbridge saßen an Philips Tisch: Tom Builder mit seiner Familie, die älteren Handwerksmeister einschließlich Toms ältestem Sohn Alfred und die Kaufleute, zu denen auch Aliena gehörte, nicht aber der Jude Malachi, der sich erst nach dem Gottesdienst zur Festgemeinde gesellen würde.

Philip bat um Ruhe, sprach das Tischgebet und reichte Tom das Wievielbrot. Im Laufe der Jahre hatte Philip Tom mehr und mehr zu schätzen gelernt: Es gab nicht viele, die offen und ehrlich ihre Meinung sagten und auch zu ihrem Wort standen. Toms Reaktion auf Überraschungen, Krisen und Unglücke bestand darin, daß er die Folgen ruhig abwog, den Schaden einschätzte und Vorkehrungen für die besten Gegenmaßnahmen traf. Philip betrachtete ihn liebevoll. Tom war nicht mehr derselbe Mann, der vor fünf Jahren um Arbeit bettelnd ins Kloster gekommen war. Damals war er erschöpft, abgezehrt und so mager gewesen, daß sich seine Knochen jeden Augenblick durch seine wettergegerbte Haut zu bohren drohten. In der Zwischenzeit war er fülliger geworden, vor allem, nachdem seine Frau zurückgekommen war. Nicht, daß er dick gewesen wäre, aber seine Knochen waren längst nicht mehr zu sehen, ebensowenig wie der einst verzweifelte Blick. Er trug teure Kleidung, einen Rock aus Lincoln-Tuch, weiche Lederschuhe und einen Gürtel mit Silberschnalle.

Philip mußte dem Wievielbrot die erste Frage stellen: »Wie viele Jahre wird es noch dauern, bis die Kathedrale fertig ist?« wollte er wissen.

Tom biß ein Stück von dem Brot ab. Kleine, harte Körner waren hineingebacken, und als Tom sie in seine Handfläche spuckte, zählten alle am Tisch laut mit. Es war schon vorgekommen, daß jemand bei diesem Spiel den ganzen Mund so voller Körner hatte, daß keiner der Anwesenden weit genug zählen konnte; doch bei all den heute versammelten Händlern und Handwerkern bestand diese Gefahr gewiß nicht. Sie zählten bis dreißig. Philip täuschte Bestürzung vor, und Tom meinte: »So lange werde ich also leben!« Allgemeines Gelächter erhob sich.

Tom reichte das Brot an Ellen weiter. Philip war vor dieser Frau auf der Hut. Sie besaß, ähnlich wie die Kaiserin Mathilde, Macht über Menschen – eine Macht, mit der Philip es nicht aufnehmen konnte. An jenem Tag, als Ellen der Priorei verwiesen worden war, hatte sie etwas Unsägliches verbrochen, etwas so Scheußliches, daß Philip noch immer kaum daran denken mochte. Er hatte geglaubt, sie sei auf Nimmerwiedersehen gegangen, doch zu seinem Entsetzen war sie wieder aufgetaucht, und Tom hatte ihn flehentlich gebeten, ihr zu vergeben. Tom hatte dabei klugerweise ins Feld geführt, daß Philip kein Recht hatte, ihr die Absolution zu verweigern, wenn Gott ihr ihre Sünde vergeben konnte. Philip hegte den Verdacht, daß Ellen nicht sonderlich reumütig war. Aber Tom hatte ihn am nämlichen Tag gefragt, da die freiwilligen Hilfskräfte eingetroffen waren und die Kathedrale gerettet hatten, und ehe Philip sich's versah, hatte er ihm, wider besseres Wissen, seinen Wunsch gewährt. Die beiden waren in der Gemeindekirche vermählt worden, einem kleinen Holzbau im Dorf, der älter war als die Priorei. Ellen hatte sich seit damals nichts zuschulden kommen lassen und Philip keinerlei Anlaß gegeben, seine Entscheidung zu bereuen. Dennoch fühlte er sich in ihrer Gegenwart nicht wohl in seiner Haut.

Tom fragte sie: »Von wie vielen Männern wirst du geliebt?«

Sie biß ein winziges Bröckchen Brot ab, was allgemeine Heiterkeit hervorrief. Alle Fragen in diesem Spiel neigten zur Zweideutigkeit, und Philip wußte, daß es nur seiner Anwesenheit zu verdanken war, wenn sie nicht ins Obszöne abglitten.

Ellen zählte drei Körner, und Tom mimte Entrüstung. »Ich will euch sagen, wer meine drei Liebsten sind«, erklärte Ellen, und Philip hoffte, ihre Antwort fiele nicht anstößig aus. »Der erste ist Tom. Der zweite ist Jack. Und der dritte ist Alfred.«

Man spendete ihrer Geistesgegenwart Beifall, und das Brot wurde weitergereicht. Als nächste war Toms Tochter Martha an der Reihe. Sie war zwölf Jahre alt und schüchtern. Das Brot sagte ihr drei Ehemänner voraus, was höchst unwahrscheinlich schien.

Martha reichte das Brot an Jack weiter, und Philip erkannte an ihrem verehrungsvollen Blick, daß sie ihren Stiefbruder wie einen Helden anhimmelte.

Jack war Philip ein Rätsel. Als Kind war er mit seinem karottenroten Haar, der bleichen Haut und den hervorstehenden grünen Augen geradezu häßlich gewesen, doch nun, da er zum jungen Mann herangewachsen, hatten sich seine Züge sozusagen harmonisch gefunden und waren so ansprechend, daß Fremde sich nach ihm umdrehten und ihn anstarrten. Ansonsten besaß er das gleiche Ungestüm wie seine Mutter, hielt wenig von Disziplin, und Gehorsam war für ihn ein Fremdwort. Zum Steinmetzgehilfen hatte er sich nicht geeignet: Statt für regelmäßigen Nachschub an Mörtel und Steinen zu sorgen, hatte er versucht, einen ganzen Tagesvorrat anzuhäufen und war dann fortgegangen, um etwas anderes zu tun. Er war ständig verschwunden. Eines Tages hatte er entschieden, keiner der vorhandenen Quader eigne sich für eine bestimmte Steinmetzarbeit, die er vorhatte, war daraufhin, ohne irgendwem Bescheid zu sagen, bis zum Steinbruch gelaufen, hatte sich den richtigen Stein ausgesucht und war damit zwei Tage später auf einem geliehenen Pony zurückgekehrt. Doch seine Eigenmächtigkeiten wurden ihm immer wieder nachgesehen, einmal seiner außerordentlichen Begabung zum Steinmetz wegen, zum anderen wegen seiner liebenswerten Natur – eine Eigenschaft, die er nach Philips Meinung ganz gewiß nicht von seiner Mutter geerbt hatte. Philip machte sich mitunter Gedanken darüber, was Jack wohl mit seinem Leben anfangen wollte. Wenn er sich Mutter Kirche anvertraute, könnte er es leicht zum Bischof bringen.

Martha fragte Jack: »Wie viele Jahre dauert es noch, bis du heiratest?«

Jack biß nur ein kleines Stück ab: Er schien darauf bedacht zu sein, möglichst bald zu heiraten. Philip fragte sich, ob er ein bestimmtes Mädchen im Sinn hatte. Jacks sichtliche Empörung zeigte, daß er den ganzen Mund voll Kerne hatte, und als sie gezählt wurden, malte sich pure Ablehnung auf seinem Gesicht. Die Endsumme lautete einunddreißig. »Aber dann bin ich ja schon achtundvierzig!« protestierte er. Das löste bei allen Anwesenden Heiterkeit aus, mit Ausnahme von Philip: Er hatte nachgerechnet, das Ergebnis für richtig gefunden und wunderte sich nun, wie flink Jack zu dem Ergebnis gekommen war. Selbst Milius, der Kämmerer, konnte nicht so schnell rechnen!

Jack saß neben Aliena. Philip fiel ein, daß er die beiden in diesem Sommer häufig zusammen gesehen hatte. Vielleicht deshalb, weil sie beide so gescheit waren. In Kingsbridge gab es kaum Leute, die Aliena das Wasser reichen konnten; und Jack war, im Gegensatz zu den anderen Lehrlingen, trotz all seiner Widerborstigkeit, seinen Jahren weit voraus. Dennoch gab ihre Freundschaft Philip Rätsel auf, denn in ihrem jugendlichen Alter machten fünf Jahre eine Menge aus.

Jack reichte Aliena das Brot und stellte ihr die gleiche Frage: »Wie viele Jahre, bis Ihr heiratet?«

Alles stöhnte und murrte: Dieselbe Frage noch einmal zu stellen, war zu simpel, das Spiel sollte schließlich für Witz und Spott sorgen. Doch Aliena, berüchtigt für die Zahl ihrer abgewiesenen Bewerber, brachte alle wieder zum Lachen, indem sie einen Riesenbatzen Brot abbiß und damit zu erkennen gab, daß sie gar nicht daran dachte, zu heiraten. Aber ihre Rechnung ging nicht auf: Sie spuckte einen einzigen Samenkern aus.

Wenn sie wirklich nächstes Jahr heiratet, dachte Philip, dann ist der Bräutigam bislang noch nicht in Sicht. Nicht, daß er an die Voraussagen des Brotes geglaubt hätte! Viel wahrscheinlicher war, daß Aliena als alte Jungfer starb, wenngleich sie, den Gerüchten zufolge, keine Jungfrau mehr war, da William Hamleigh sie, wie es hieß, verführt oder vergewaltigt hatte.

Aliena gab das Brot an ihren Bruder Richard weiter, aber Philip hörte ihre Frage nicht, denn er dachte noch immer über sie nach. Sowohl er als auch Aliena waren dieses Jahr völlig überraschend auf einem Teil ihrer Wolle sitzengeblieben. Der unverkaufte Rest war kaum der Rede wert – weniger als ein Zehntel von seiner und sogar noch weniger von Alienas Ware –, dennoch machte es ihm zu schaffen. Er hatte sich daraufhin Sorgen gemacht, Aliena könne ihre Abrechnung fürs nächste Jahr rückgängig machen, doch sie hatte zu ihrem Wort gestanden und ihm einhundertsieben Pfund ausbezahlt.

Philips Ankündigung, daß Kingsbridge im darauffolgenden Jahr eine eigene Wollmesse abhalten würde, hatte auf der Messe zu Shiring hohe Wellen geschlagen. Da die von William Hamleigh erhobenen Pachtgebühren und Standgelder eher Wucherpreisen glichen und Philip gedachte, seine Gebühren weit niedriger anzusetzen, war seine Ankündigung allgemein freudig aufgenommen worden. Graf William hatte bisher noch nicht zu erkennen gegeben, wie er darauf zu reagieren gedachte.

Im großen und ganzen hatte Philip das Gefühl, daß die Zukunft für die Priorei weit rosiger aussah als noch vor sechs Monaten. Er war nicht nur mit den durch die Schließung des Steinbruchs entstandenen Schwierigkeiten fertig geworden, sondern hatte darüber hinaus auch noch Williams Versuch abgewehrt, seinen Markt schließen zu lassen. Mittlerweile herrschte auf den Sonntagsmärkten wieder reges Treiben, und die Einnahmen hielten sich mit den hohen Ausgaben für die Steine aus Marlborough die Waage. Selbst in der Krisenzeit war auf dem Dombauplatz ununterbrochen weitergearbeitet worden. Philips einzige Sorge galt nun Mathilde, die, obwohl sie zweifelsohne das Heft in der Hand hatte, noch immer nicht gekrönt worden war. Ohne diese rechtmäßige Investitur beruhte ihre Herrschaft, wenngleich von den Bischöfen anerkannt, lediglich auf militärischer Stärke. Stephans Gemahlin hielt weiterhin Kent, und die Bürgerschaft von London hatte noch nicht Stellung bezogen. Ein unglücklicher Zufall, eine einzige Entscheidung konnte – ähnlich wie die Schlacht zu Lincoln, die Stephan zu Fall gebracht hatte – zum Sturz Mathildes und zu neuerlich chaotischen Zuständen führen.

Philip ermahnte sich, nicht allzu schwarz zu sehen. Er ließ seinen Blick über die um den Tisch Versammelten schweifen. Das Spiel war vorbei, der Festschmaus hatte begonnen. Dies waren ehrliche, gutherzige Männer und Frauen, die fleißig arbeiteten und zur Kirche gingen. Gott würde sich ihrer annehmen.

Es gab Gemüsesuppe, gebackenen, mit Pfeffer und Ingwer gewürzten Fisch, Ente und zum Nachtisch einen Pudding, der mit roten und grünen Streifen dekoriert war. Nach dem Essen trug man die Sitzbänke in die unvollendete Kirche, wo das Schauspiel stattfinden sollte.

Die Zimmerleute hatten zwei Wandschirme angefertigt, die von den Außenwänden bis zum ersten Pfeiler jedes Bogengangs reichten und so die jeweils erste Nische am Ostende der beiden Seitenschiffe vom Rest der Kirche trennten. Die mitwirkenden Mönche warteten bereits hinter den Schirmen auf ihren Auftritt im Mittelschiff. Ein junger Novize mit engelsgleichen Gesichtszügen, der die Rolle des heiligen Adolphus spielte, lag, in ein Leichentuch gehüllt, auf einem Tisch an der Rückwand des Mittelschiffs, stellte sich tot und verbiß sich nur mühsam das Lachen.

Ähnlich wie beim Wievielbrot sah Philip auch dem Stück mit gemischten Gefühlen entgegen. Wie leicht konnte es ins Respektlose und Vulgäre abrutschen! Aber Schauspiele waren ungeheuer beliebt; hätte er seine Einwilligung nicht gegeben, wäre sicher ein anderes Stück außerhalb der Kirche aufgeführt worden, bei dem es, in Ermangelung seiner Aufsicht, gewiß derb und zügellos zugegangen wäre. Im übrigen machte das Spiel den Mönchen beinahe noch mehr Spaß als ihren Zuschauern. Sich zu verkleiden, in eine andere Rolle zu schlüpfen, außer Rand und Band zu geraten, ja sogar gotteslästerisch zu handeln, schien ihnen eine gewisse Erleichterung zu verschaffen – vermutlich einen notwendigen Ausgleich zu ihrem ansonsten so strengen Lebenswandel.

Vor der Aufführung fand ein Gottesdienst statt, den der Sakristan kurz und bündig hielt. Danach gab Philip einen ebenso kurzen Bericht über das makellose Leben und die Wundertaten des heiligen Adolphus ab. Dann nahm er im Zuschauerraum Platz und machte es sich in Erwartung der Aufführung bequem.

Hinter dem linken Wandschirm trat eine Riesengestalt hervor, die auf den ersten Blick in formlose, bunt zusammengewürfelte Kleider gehüllt schien; bei näherer Betrachtung stellte sich heraus, daß der Darsteller in mehrere Bahnen schreiend bunter Stoffe gewickelt war, die mit Nadeln zusammengehalten wurden. Sein Gesicht war grell bemalt, und er schleppte einen prall gefüllten Geldsack mit sich herum. Das war der reiche Barbar. Sein Auftritt löste beifälliges Gemurmel aus, das sich, sobald die Zuschauer den Darsteller erkannten, in wogendes Gelächter wandelte: Es war Bruder Bernard, der allseits bekannte und ebenso beliebte wie beleibte Küchenmeister.

Er stolzierte ein paarmal beifallheischend auf und ab und stürzte sich auf die kleinen Kinder in der ersten Reihe, die vor Angst aufkreischten; dann schlich er sich, beständig auf der Lauer, an den Altar, hinter dem er seinen Geldsack deponierte. Schließlich wandte er sich ans Publikum und sagte laut und deutlich und mit dreister Miene: »Diese dämlichen Christen werden sich nicht an mein Silber herantrauen, denn sie glauben, es steht unter dem Schutz des heiligen Adolphus. Ha!« Damit zog er sich hinter den Wandschirm zurück.

Auf der anderen Seite tauchte eine mit hölzernen Schwertern und Beilen ausstaffierte Räuberbande auf, deren Gesichter mit Kreide und Ruß beschmiert waren. Zunächst marschierten sie mit grimmigen Mienen im Mittelschiff herum, bis einer von ihnen den Geldsack hinter dem Altar entdeckte. Ein Streit entspann sich: Sollten sie ihn stehlen oder nicht? Der gute Bandit vertrat die Meinung, der Diebstahl würde ihnen zum Verhängnis; der schlechte Bandit meinte, ein toter Heiliger könne ihnen nichts anhaben. Am Ende nahmen sie das Geld und zogen sich in eine Ecke zurück, wo sie es zählten.

Der Barbar erschien wieder, suchte überall nach seinem Geld und wurde, als er es nirgends finden konnte, fuchsteufelswild. Er trat an den Sarkophag des heiligen Adolphus und verfluchte ihn, da er seinen Schatz nicht gehütet hatte.

Da erhob sich der Heilige aus seinem Grab.

Der Barbar schlotterte vor Entsetzen. Der Heilige würdigte ihn jedoch keines Blickes, ging auf die Banditen zu und streckte sie einen nach dem anderen nieder, indem er mit bloßem Finger auf sie deutete. Die Getroffenen mimten Todesqualen, wälzten sich auf dem Boden, verrenkten sich aufs groteskeste und zogen gräßliche Fratzen.

Der Heilige verschonte nur einen, den guten Banditen, der das Geld wieder hinter dem Altar deponierte. Daraufhin wandte sich der Heilige an das Publikum und verkündete: »Ihr alle, die Ihr Zweifel hegt an der Macht des heiligen Adolphus, hütet Euch!«

Die Zuschauer kreischten und klatschten, während die Darsteller eine Weile lang im Mittelschiff herumstanden und verlegen grinsten. Der Sinn und Zweck des Spiels lag natürlich in der Moral der Geschichte, aber Philip wußte genau, daß die Zuschauer an den grotesken Szenen, dem Wutanfall des Barbaren und den Todeszuckungen der Banditen den meisten Spaß gehabt hatten.

Philip erhob sich, sobald der Applaus verstummt war, dankte den Darstellern und verkündete, daß in Kürze die Wettrennen auf der Weide am Flußufer stattfänden.

An diesem Tag mußte der fünfjährige Jonathan die Entdeckung machen, daß er trotz allem doch nicht der schnellste Läufer in Kingsbridge war. Er nahm, angetan mit seiner eigens für ihn angefertigten Mönchskutte, am Kinderrennen teil und löste allgemein Heiterkeit aus, als er sie lupfte und das Rennen vor aller Welt mit blankem Popo lief. Aber er trat gegen ältere Kinder an und erreichte das Ziel als einer der Letzten. Als er sich seiner Niederlage bewußt wurde, wirkte er dermaßen erschrocken und zerknirscht, daß Tom schier vor Mitleid zerfloß und ihn tröstend auf den Arm nahm.

Zwischen Tom und der Klosterwaise hatte sich mit der Zeit eine ganz besondere Beziehung entwickelt, aber im Dorf war noch niemand auf die Idee gekommen, dahinter ein Geheimnis zu vermuten. Tom verbrachte seine Tage auf dem Klostergelände, wo Jonathan nach Herzenslust herumtollte, und so war es nicht weiter verwunderlich, daß sie sich häufig begegneten; außerdem war Tom in jenem Alter, da die eigenen Kinder zu alt zum Verhätscheln, aber noch nicht alt genug für Enkelkinder waren, so daß es ganz natürlich schien, wenn er sich anderer Leute Kindern zuwandte. Soweit Tom wußte, war es bisher niemanden auch nur im Traum eingefallen, in ihm Jonathans Vater zu vermuten. Wenn überhaupt, dann wurde Philip mit dem Jungen in Verbindung gebracht – eine nicht allzu weit hergeholte Spekulation, auch wenn Philip, wäre sie ihm zu Ohren gekommen, bestimmt vor Entsetzen die Hände über dem Kopf zusammengeschlagen hätte.

Jonathan hatte Aaron, Malachis ältesten Sohn, entdeckt; sogleich war die Enttäuschung vergessen, und er entwand sich Toms Armen, um mit seinem Freund zu spielen.

Während die Lehrlinge ihre Wettrennen abhielten, kam Philip auf Tom zu und setzte sich neben ihn ins Gras. Es war ein heißer, sonniger Tag, und auf Philips geschorenem Kopf standen Schweißperlen. Toms Bewunderung für Philip hatte von Jahr zu Jahr zugenommen. Als er jetzt seinen Blick umherschweifen ließ, die jungen Männer bei ihren Wettkämpfen und die alten Leute im Schatten dösen sah, während die Kinder im Fluß planschten, mußte er unwillkürlich daran denken, daß es Philip war, der diese Gemeinschaft zusammenhielt: Er regierte das Dorf, sprach Recht, entschied, wo neue Häuser gebaut wurden, schlichtete Streitigkeiten; er beschäftigte die meisten der männlichen und sogar viele weibliche Dorfbewohner, entweder als Arbeiter auf der Baustelle oder als Bedienstete in der Priorei; und er stand dem Kloster vor, dem A und O des Ganzen. Er wehrte machtlüsterne Adlige ab, verhandelte mit dem Monarchen und hielt den Bischof in Schach. All diese wohlgenährten, im Sonnenschein miteinander wetteifernden Menschen verdankten mehr oder weniger ihren Wohlstand Philip.

Tom war sich der schier unglaublichen Nachsicht, die Philip in Ellens Fall an den Tag gelegt hatte, deutlich bewußt. Für einen Mönch war es beileibe kein Kinderspiel, ein solches Vergehen zu verzeihen. Dabei bedeutete es ihm so viel: Seine Freude am Bau der Kathedrale war durch seine Einsamkeit sehr überschattet worden. Erst seit Ellens Rückkehr fühlte er sich wieder wie ein ganzer Mensch. Und obwohl sie nach wie vor zum Verrücktwerden eigensinnig, streitsüchtig und unnachgiebig war, fiel es doch kaum ins Gewicht: In ihrem Innern brannte die Flamme der Leidenschaft, und mit diesem Licht hatte sie sein Leben erhellt.

Tom und Philip sahen einem Wettrennen zu, bei dem die Jungen auf den Händen laufen mußten. Jack gewann. »Dieser Junge ist wirklich ganz außergewöhnlich«, sagte Philip.

»Nicht jeder kann so schnell auf den Händen laufen«, meinte Tom.

Philip lachte. »Das stimmt – aber an seine akrobatischen Fähigkeiten habe ich dabei gar nicht einmal so sehr gedacht.«

»Ich weiß.« Jacks Klugheit war Tom seit langem sowohl ein Grund zur Freude als auch ein Dorn im Auge. Der Junge bewies lebhaften Wissensdurst an allem, was mit dem Bauen zusammenhing – eine Neugierde, die Alfred stets hatte vermissen lassen –, und Tom fand Vergnügen daran, Jack in die Geheimnisse seines Berufes einzuweihen. Aber Jack besaß keinerlei Taktgefühl und legte sich selbst mit jenen an, die ihm altersmäßig voraus waren. Man tat meistens besser daran, das eigene Licht unter den Scheffel zu stellen, doch das hatte Jack noch nicht einmal nach all den Jahren der Verfolgung durch Alfred gelernt.

»Der Junge braucht eine Ausbildung«, fuhr Philip fort.

Tom runzelte die Stirn. Jack war doch in der Ausbildung. Er war Lehrling. »Wie meint Ihr das?«

»Er sollte sich eine gute Handschrift zulegen, Latein lernen und die alten Philosophen studieren.«

Jetzt war Tom erst recht verwirrt. »Und zu welchem Zweck? Wo er doch Steinmetz wird?«

Philip sah Tom in die Augen. »Seid Ihr da so sicher?« fragte er. »Schließlich ist Jack immer für eine Überraschung gut.«

Daran hatte Tom noch nicht gedacht. Natürlich gab es junge Menschen, die genau das Gegenteil von dem taten, was von ihnen erwartet wurde: Grafensöhne weigerten sich zu kämpfen, Königskinder traten ins Kloster ein, Bastarde von Bauern wurden Bischöfe. Philip hatte recht, von Jack war Ähnliches zu erwarten. »Ja, was glaubt Ihr denn, welchen Weg er einschlagen wird?« fragte Tom schließlich.

»Das hängt davon ab, was er lernt«, erwiderte Philip. »Aber ich will ihn für die Kirche.«

Tom war überrascht. Als Mann der Kirche konnte er sich Jack nun gar nicht vorstellen. Außerdem machte ihn Philips Bemerkung betroffen: Es freute ihn, daß Jack Steinmetzmeister wurde; jede andere Entwicklung konnte ihm nur Enttäuschung bereiten.

Philip, der gar nicht bemerkte, was in Tom vorging, fuhr fort: »Gott braucht gerade die besten und gescheitesten jungen Männer. Seht Euch nur die Lehrlinge dort an, die darum wetteifern, wer am höchsten springt! Aus denen werden einmal gute Zimmerleute, Steinmetzen oder Steinschneider. Aber das Zeug zum Bischof? Das hat nur einer – Jack.«

Das stimmt, dachte Tom. Wenn Jack wirklich die Möglichkeit hat, mit Philips starker Rückendeckung eine Laufbahn in der Kirche einzuschlagen, dann sollte er sie wohl beim Schopfe packen; damit ist allemal mehr Reichtum und Macht verbunden als mit dem Beruf eines Steinmetzen. »Was genau habt Ihr mit ihm vor?« fragte er widerstrebend.

»Ich möchte, daß Jack als Novize ins Kloster kommt.«

»Mönch soll er werden?« Ein Mönchsdasein konnte er sich für Jack noch viel weniger vorstellen als das eines Priesters. Der Junge rebellierte ja sogar gegen die Disziplin auf der Baustelle – wie sollte er sich da wohl in die Klosterregeln fügen?

»Den Großteil seiner Zeit würde er beim Studium zubringen«, sagte Philip. »Er würde alles lernen, was unser Novizenmeister ihm beibringen kann, und darüber hinaus würde ich ihn noch selbst unterrichten.«

Wenn ein junger Mann ins Kloster eintrat, hatten seine Eltern der Sitte gemäß eine großzügige Spende zu machen. Tom fragte sich, was ihn dieser Vorschlag wohl kosten würde.

Philip erriet seine Gedanken. »Ich erwarte kein Geschenk an die Priorei von Euch«, sagte er. »Es genügt, daß Ihr Gott einen Sohn gebt.«

Natürlich wußte Philip nicht, daß er, Tom, der Priorei bereits einen Sohn geschenkt hatte: den kleinen Jonathan, der am Flußufer im seichten Wasser planschte und seine Kutte einmal mehr bis unter die Arme hochgezogen hatte. Aber Tom wußte, daß er seine persönlichen Gefühle in dieser Angelegenheit zurückstellen mußte. Philips Angebot war großzügig, offenbar war ihm sehr an Jack gelegen. Und für Jack bot es ungeheure Möglichkeiten. Andere Väter hätten ihren rechten Arm dafür gegeben, ihren Sohn so gut versorgt zu wissen. Tom verspürte allerdings einen Moment lang Unmut darüber, daß nicht sein leiblicher Sohn Alfred, sondern sein Stiefsohn Jack solch wunderbare Aussichten hatte. Aber auch solche Gefühle waren verwerflich, und er unterdrückte sie sogleich. Er sollte sich lieber freuen, Jack Mut zusprechen und hoffen, daß der Bursche sich bald mit den Klosterregeln abfinden würde.

»Es sollte aber bald geschehen«, fügte Philip hinzu.

»Bevor er sich in irgendein Mädchen verliebt.«

Tom nickte. Auf der Wiese steuerte das Wettrennen der Frauen seinem Höhepunkt zu, und er verfolgte es mit den Augen, noch immer in Gedanken versunken. Schließlich bemerkte er, daß Ellen in Führung lag. Aliena war ihr hart auf den Fersen, doch Ellen konnte ihren Vorsprung bis zur Ziellinie behaupten. Triumphierend riß sie die Arme hoch.

Aliena war verblüfft, daß Ellen sie geschlagen hatte. Zwar war sie als Mutter eines siebzehnjährigen Sohnes sehr jung, mußte aber dennoch mindestens zehn Jahre älter sein als Aliena. Schnaufend und schwitzend standen die beiden Frauen an der Ziellinie und lächelten sich an. Aliena fielen Ellens schlanke, sehnige braune Beine und ihre kompakte Figur auf. Die Jahre im Wald hatten sie gestählt.

Jack kam auf seine Mutter zu und beglückwünschte sie zu ihrem Sieg. Aliena konnte unschwer erkennen, daß sie einander sehr zugetan waren. Ähnlichkeit herrschte zwischen den beiden allerdings nicht: Ellen war eine sonnengebräunte Brünette mit tiefliegenden, goldbraunen Augen, Jack ein Rotschopf mit grünen Augen. Er wird wohl seinem Vater gleichen, dachte Aliena. Allerdings war über Jacks Vater, Ellens ersten Mann, nie ein Wort verloren worden. Vielleicht schämten sie sich seiner.

Mutter und Sohn so beieinander stehen zu sehen, brachte Aliena auf den Gedanken, daß Jack Ellen an ihren verlorenen ersten Mann erinnern mußte. Vielleicht hing sie deswegen so an ihm; vielleicht war ihr einzig der Sohn als Erinnerung an den geliebten Mann geblieben. Ähnlichkeit in der äußeren Erscheinung konnte sich in einem solchen Fall manchmal als ungeheuer starker Faktor erweisen. Ihr eigener Bruder Richard erinnerte sie bisweilen nur durch eine Geste oder einen Blick an ihren Vater, und dann flog ihm ihr Herz nur so zu; trotzdem wünschte sie sich bisweilen, er käme auch charakterlich mehr auf seinen Vater heraus.

Eigentlich hatte sie kein Recht, mit Richard unzufrieden zu sein. Er zog in den Krieg und schlug sich tapfer, und mehr konnte man von ihm nicht verlangen. Doch in letzter Zeit war sie häufig unzufrieden, trotz ihres Reichtums und ihrer Sicherheit, trotz ihres Hauses und ihrer Diener, trotz bester Kleidung, schönem Schmuck und einer angesehenen Stellung in der Stadt. Wäre sie gefragt worden, so hätte sie ohne zu zögern behauptet, glücklich zu sein. Aber unter der Oberfläche machte sich eine gewisse Unruhe breit. Sie verlor nie die Freude an ihrer Arbeit, aber stellte sich manchen Morgen die Frage, ob es wirklich darauf ankam, welches Gewand sie trug und ob sie überhaupt Schmuck anlegte. Es krähte ja doch kein Hahn danach, warum sollte sie sich also die Mühe machen? Trotz alledem war sie sich ihres Körpers bewußter geworden. Sie spürte genau, wie ihre Brüste sich beim Gehen bewegten. Wenn sie zum Baden an den Frauenstrand am Flußufer ging, schämte sie sich ihrer Behaarung. Beim Reiten spürte sie die Körperteile, die mit dem Sattel in Berührung kamen. Es war wirklich merkwürdig, fast, als würde sie ständig von einem Schnüffler verfolgt, der durch ihre Kleidung hindurch einen Blick auf ihren nackten Körper erhaschen wollte; der Schnüffler war sie selbst, und sie verletzte ihre eigene Intimsphäre.

Außer Atem ließ sie sich ins Gras fallen. Der Schweiß rann ihr zwischen den Brüsten und Schenkeln hinunter. Ungeduldig wandte sie ihre Gedanken einer wichtigeren Angelegenheit zu: Sie hatte dieses Jahr nicht ihren gesamten Wollbestand verkaufen können. Nicht, daß der Fehler bei ihr gelegen hätte: Die meisten Händler waren auf einem Teil ihrer Vliese sitzengeblieben, Prior Philip nicht ausgenommen. Er schien sich keine Sorgen zu machen, aber Aliena war beunruhigt. Was sollte sie mit der restlichen Wolle anfangen? Sie konnte sie natürlich bis zum nächsten Jahr lagern. Aber wenn sie dann wieder nicht alles verkaufte? Sie hatte keine Ahnung, wie lange sich Rohwolle unbeschadet hielt. Ihrem Gefühl nach würde sie austrocknen und spröde, was die Weiterverarbeitung nur erschweren konnte.

Wenn es weiterhin bergab ging, konnte sie Richard nicht länger unterstützen. Ritter zu sein, war ein kostspieliges Unterfangen. Das für zwanzig Pfund erstandene Schlachtroß hatte nach der Schlacht zu Lincoln die Nerven verloren und taugte fast nichts mehr; er würde bald ein neues haben wollen. Aliena konnte sich das zwar leisten, aber es riß dennoch ein tiefes Loch in ihren Beutel. Richard schämte sich, finanziell von ihr abhängig zu sein – eine ungewöhnliche Situation für einen Ritter –, und hatte gehofft, ausreichend Beute zu machen, um sich selbst über Wasser halten zu können, doch derzeit befand er sich auf der Seite der Verlierer. Wenn er die Grafschaft wirklich wiedergewinnen sollte, mußte Aliena weiterhin geschäftliche Erfolge aufweisen.

In ihren schlimmsten Alpträumen hatte sie all ihr Geld verloren und sah sie beide wieder als mittellose Beute ehrloser Priester, wollüstiger Adliger und blutrünstiger Banditen; am Ende landeten sie in dem stinkenden Verlies, dem letzten Aufenthaltsort ihres Vaters, wo sie, an die Wand gekettet, verreckten.

Dem Alptraum stand ein glücklicher Traum gegenüber, in dem sie und Richard gemeinsam auf der Burg, ihrer ehemaligen Heimat, lebten. Richard regierte ebenso weise wie einst ihr Vater, und Aliena half ihm dabei, hieß wichtige Besucher willkommen, erfüllte die Pflichten der Gastfreundschaft und saß bei den Mahlzeiten auf der Empore zu seiner Linken. Doch seit einiger Zeit hinterließ sogar dieser Traum einen faden Geschmack.

Sie schüttelte den Kopf, um ihre düsteren Gedanken zu vertreiben, und dachte wieder an die Wolle. Die simpelste Lösung bestand darin, die Hände einfach in den Schoß zu legen, die überschüssige Wolle bis zum folgenden Jahr aufzubewahren und sich für den Fall, daß sie ihre Ware auch dann nicht verkaufen konnte, mit dem Verlust abzufinden. Sie würde ihn schon verkraften. Dabei lief sie allerdings Gefahr, im darauffolgenden Jahr auf die gleichen Schwierigkeiten zu stoßen und somit am Beginn einer rückläufigen Geschäftsentwicklung zu stehen. Sie mußte sich nach einer anderen Lösung umsehen. Sie hatte bereits versucht, die Wolle an den ortsansässigen Weber zu verkaufen, aber sein Bedarf war gedeckt.

Der Anblick der Frauen von Kingsbridge, die sich von ihrem Wettlauf erholten, brachte sie auf den Gedanken, daß die meisten von ihnen wußten, wie man aus Rohwolle Tuch herstellt. Die Arbeit war langwierig, aber einfach: Die Bauersfrauen taten sie schon seit Adams und Evas Zeiten. Die Vliese mußten zunächst gewaschen werden, dann gekämmt, um die verfilzten Stellen zu entfernen, und schließlich versponnen. Daraufhin wurde das Garn zu losem Tuch verwebt, welches gewalkt werden mußte, damit es einlief und dichter wurde und zur Herstellung von Kleidung weiterverwendet werden konnte. Die Frauen der Stadt würden diese Arbeit wahrscheinlich für einen Penny am Tag verrichten. Aber wie lange brauchten sie wohl? Und wieviel brachte das fertige Tuch ein?

Sie würde ihren Plan erst einmal an einer kleinen Menge Wolle ausprobieren müssen. Sollte ihre Rechnung aufgehen, dann konnte sie mehrere Leute beauftragen, an den langen Winterabenden für sie zu arbeiten.

Sie setzte sich auf, voller Begeisterung über ihren neuen Plan. Ellen lag unmittelbar neben ihr. Jack saß auf der anderen Seite neben seiner Mutter. Ihre Blicke kreuzten sich; er lächelte leicht und schaute dann weg, als ob es ihn verlegen machte, wenn sie sah, wie er sie anschaute. Er war schon ein merkwürdiger Junge; an neuen Ideen herrschte bei ihm nie Mangel. Aliena konnte sich noch an den kleinen, seltsam aussehenden Knaben erinnern, der nicht wußte, wo die kleinen Kinder herkamen. In der ersten Zeit seines Aufenthalts in Kingsbridge war er ihr kaum aufgefallen. Inzwischen schien er sich dermaßen verändert zu haben, daß man fast meinen konnte, eine andere Person vor sich zu haben; es war beinahe, als wäre er aus dem Nichts aufgetaucht, einer Blume gleich, die eines Morgens erscheint, wo am Vortrag nichts als blanke Erde war. Vor allem sah er nicht mehr so komisch aus. Die Mädchen finden ihn wahrscheinlich sogar furchtbar nett, dachte sie und betrachtete ihn heiter. Sein Lächeln war auf jeden Fall sehr anziehend. Sie selbst schenkte seinem Äußeren kaum Beachtung, aber seine unglaubliche Phantasie nahm sie doch ein wenig gefangen. Mittlerweile hatte sie herausgefunden, daß er nicht nur mehrere Erzählungen in Versform auswendig wußte – und einige davon waren mehrere tausend Zeilen lang! –, sondern auch aus dem Stegreif dichten konnte, so daß sie nie wußte, ob er sich wirklich an den Text erinnerte oder dazuerfand. Und seine Geschichten waren nicht das einzig Überraschende an ihm: Auch seine Neugier war unbezähmbar, und er machte sich Gedanken über Dinge, die andere Leute als selbstverständlich hinnahmen. Eines Tages hatte er gefragt, woher all das Wasser im Fluß käme. »Stunde um Stunde, Tag und Nacht, jahrein, jahraus fließen abertausend Faß Wasser an Kingsbridge vorüber. Das geht nun schon so seit der Zeit vor unserer Geburt, vor der Geburt unserer Eltern, ja sogar vor der Geburt *ihrer* Eltern. Wo kommt es her? Gibt es irgendwo einen riesigen See, der den Fluß speist? Dann muß er so groß wie ganz England sein! Und was passiert, wenn er eines Tages austrocknet?« Er redete dauernd von solchen Dingen, wenn auch nicht immer so weit hergeholten, und Aliena merkte allmählich, wie sehr sie kluge Gespräche entbehrte. In Kingsbridge konnten die meisten Leute nur über Landwirtschaft und Ehebruch reden, und Aliena interessierte sich weder für das eine noch für das andere. Prior Philip war natürlich eine Ausnahme, gestattete sich aber nur selten das Vergnügen, ein Schwätzchen zu halten: Er hatte unentwegt alle Hände voll zu tun, mußte sich um den Dombau, die Mönche oder die städtischen Angelegenheiten kümmern. Aliena nahm an, daß Tom Builder ebenfalls einen klugen Kopf besaß, aber er war eher ein Denker denn ein Schwätzer. Jack war der erste Mensch, mit dem sie Freundschaft geschlossen hatte. Trotz seiner Jugend war er eine wunderbare Offenbarung Es war sogar vorgekommen, daß sie sich auf ihren Reisen darauf freute, nach Kingsbridge zurückzukehren und mit Jack reden zu können.

Sie fragte sich, woher seine Einfälle wohl kommen mochten. Bei diesem Gedanken nahm sie Ellen zum erstenmal wirklich wahr. Wer ein Kind allein im Wald aufzog, mußte erst recht merkwürdig sein! Aliena hatte sich mit Ellen unterhalten und war dabei auf eine Seelenverwandte gestoßen, eine unabhängige und eigenständige Frau, die mit der Art und Weise, wie das Leben mit ihr umgesprungen war, ein wenig haderte. Einer plötzlichen Eingebung folgend fragte Aliena sie jetzt: »Ellen, wo habt *Ihr* denn die Geschichten gelernt?«

»Von Jacks Vater«, erwiderte Ellen, ohne nachzudenken, doch gleich darauf verdüsterte sich ihr Gesicht, und Aliena wußte, daß sie besser daran tat, keine weiteren Fragen mehr zu stellen.

Ihr kam ein neuer Einfall. »Könnt Ihr weben?«

»Natürlich«, meinte Ellen. »Das kann doch jeder, oder?«

»Was hieltet Ihr davon, gegen Bezahlung zu weben?«

»Das kommt drauf an. Was habt Ihr im Sinn?«

Aliena erklärte es ihr. Ellen hatte natürlich genug Geld, aber das verdiente Tom, und Aliena vermutete, daß Ellen ein eigenes Einkommen nicht verschmähen würde.

Ihre Vermutung erwies sich als richtig. »Einverstanden, ich werde es versuchen.«

In diesem Augenblick kam Ellens Stiefsohn des Weges. Alfred war, ähnlich wie sein Vater, ein wahrer Hüne von einem Mann. Sein Gesicht war bis auf die eng beieinanderliegenden Augen von einem buschigen Bart bedeckt, was ihn listig erscheinen ließ. Er konnte lesen, schreiben und rechnen, war aber ansonsten ziemlich dumm. Dennoch hatte er es zu Wohlstand gebracht und verfügte über seine eigene Mannschaft von Steinmetzen, Lehrlingen und Gehilfen. Aliena hatte die Beobachtung gemacht, daß große Männer es, unabhängig von ihrer Klugheit, oft zu Macht und Einfluß brachten. Und außerdem zahlte sich Alfreds Position noch in anderer Hinsicht aus: Da sein Vater Dombaumeister von Kingsbridge war, liefen seine Männer nie Gefahr, ohne Arbeit dazustehen.

Er setzte sich neben sie ins Gras. Seine riesigen Füße steckten in schweren, mit grauem Steinstaub bedeckten Lederstiefeln. Sie redete kaum je mit ihm. Eigentlich sollten sie, die einzigen jungen Leute unter den bessergestellten Bürgern von Kingsbridge, die dazu alle in den der Klostermauer nächstgelegenen Häusern wohnten, etliches gemein haben, aber Alfred war einfach fade und langweilig. Nach einem Moment des Schweigens ergriff er das Wort. »Eigentlich sollten wir eine Kirche aus Stein haben«, sagte er völlig zusammenhanglos.

Er erwartete ganz offensichtlich von den Anwesenden, sich selbst ihren Reim auf diese Bemerkung zu machen. Aliena dachte einen Augenblick lang nach und sagte dann: »Meint Ihr damit die Pfarrkirche?«

»Was sonst?« gab er zurück, als wäre es die selbstverständlichste Sache der Welt.

Da die von den Mönchen in Anspruch genommene Krypta der Kathedrale sehr klein und stickig und die Bevölkerung von Kingsbridge gewachsen war, wurde die Pfarrkirche in jüngster Zeit immer häufiger benutzt. Und das, obwohl der alte Holzbau lediglich ein strohgedecktes Dach und einen festgestampften Lehmboden hatte.

»Da habt Ihr recht«, sagte Aliena. »Wir sollten wirklich eine Kirche aus Stein haben.«

Alfred sah sie erwartungsvoll an. Sie fragte sich, was er wohl hören wollte.

Ellen hatte offenbar mehr Übung darin, ihm alles aus der Nase zu ziehen. »Was hast du im Sinn, Alfred?« fragte sie ihn.

»Wie entsteht überhaupt eine Kirche?« wollte er wissen. »Will sagen, was müssen wir tun, wenn wir eine Kirche aus Stein haben wollen?«

Ellen zuckte die Achseln. »Keine Ahnung.«

Aliena runzelte die Stirn. »Ihr könntet eine Kirchengilde ins Leben rufen«, schlug sie vor. Kirchengilden waren Vereinigungen, deren Mitglieder ab und zu Bankette veranstalteten und untereinander Geld sammelten, das gemeinhin auf den Kauf von Kerzen für die Pfarrkirche oder zur Unterstützung von Witwen und Waisen in der Umgebung verwendet wurde. In kleinen Dörfern gab es nie eine Kirchengilde, aber Kingsbridge war schließlich kein Dorf mehr.

»Inwiefern wäre das der Kirche förderlich?« fragte Alfred.

»Die Gildenmitglieder würden das Geld für die neue Pfarrkirche aufbringen«, sagte Aliena.

»Dann sollten wir eine Kirchengilde ins Leben rufen«, meinte Alfred.

Aliena fragte sich, ob sie ihn falsch eingeschätzt hätte. Er war ihr nie sonderlich fromm vorgekommen, doch nun bemühte er sich offenbar ernsthaft darum, Geld für den Bau einer neuen Kirche aufzutreiben. Vielleicht gründeten stille Wasser tatsächlich tief? Doch dann fiel ihr ein, daß Alfred der einzige Baumeister in Kingsbridge war, der für den Bau der neuen Kirche in Frage kam. So sehr es ihm auch an Klugheit gebrach – gerissen war er allemal.

Trotzdem gefiel ihr sein Einfall. Kingsbridge entwickelte sich allmählich zu einer richtigen Stadt, und in jeder Stadt gab es mehr als eine Kirche. Solange es keine Alternative zur Kathedrale gab, wurde die Stadt quasi vom Kloster regiert. Im Augenblick war Philip ihr unbestrittener Herr und Meister. Und obwohl er ein mildtätiger Tyrann war, konnte sie sich doch eine Zeit vorstellen, da den Händlern der Stadt eine eigene Kirche durchaus zupaß käme.

Alfred sagte: »Vielleicht könntet Ihr den anderen die Sache erklären?«

Aliena hatte sich mittlerweile von ihrem Wettlauf erholt. Zwar tauschte sie die Gesellschaft von Ellen und Jack nur ungern gegen die von Alfred ein, aber seine Idee gefiel ihr; eine Ablehnung wäre außerdem mehr als grob erschienen. »Aber gerne«, sagte sie, erhob sich und ging mit ihm fort.

Die Sonne ging unter. Die Mönche hatten das Johannisfeuer entfacht und teilten das traditionelle, mit Ingwer gewürzte Bier aus. Jack war mit seiner Mutter allein und wollte die Gelegenheit nutzen, um ihr eine Frage zu stellen, aber er fand nicht die rechten Worte. Dann stimmte jemand ein Lied an, und da er wußte, daß sie jeden Augenblick einstimmen würde, platzte er übergangslos mit seiner Frage heraus: »War mein Vater ein Spielmann?«

Sie sah ihn an, überrascht, aber nicht verärgert. »Wer hat dir denn dieses Wort beigebracht?« wollte sie wissen. »Du hast doch noch nie einen gesehen.«

»Aliena. Sie ist mit ihrem Vater früher immer nach Frankreich gereist.«

Ellen ließ ihren Blick über die düstere Weide zum Lagerfeuer schweifen. »Ja, er war Spielmann. Er hat mir all die Geschichten beigebracht, genauso wie ich sie an dich weitergegeben habe. Und du erzählst sie jetzt Aliena?«

»Ja.« Jack fühlte sich beklommen.

»Du liebst sie sehr, oder?«

»Ist das so offenkundig?«

Sie lächelte liebevoll. »Ich glaube nicht, daß es außer mir jemandem aufgefallen ist. Sie ist erheblich älter als du.«

»Fünf Jahre.«

»Du wirst sie schon erobern. Du gleichst deinem Vater. Er konnte jede Frau haben, auf die er es abgesehen hatte.«

So verlegen es Jack machte, über Aliena zu reden, so überglücklich war er, Näheres über seinen Vater in Erfahrung zu bringen, und konnte es gar nicht abwarten, noch mehr zu hören, doch zu seinem großen Leidwesen kam in eben diesem Moment Tom daher und setzte sich zu ihnen. Er ergriff sogleich das Wort. »Ich habe mich mit Prior Philip über Jack unterhalten«, sagte er. Sein Tonfall klang unbeschwert, dennoch spürte Jack eine unterschwellige Spannung. Ihm schwante nichts Gutes. »Philip meint, der Junge braucht eine Ausbildung.«

Ellens Erwiderung fiel, wie nicht anders erwartet, ungehalten aus. »Er hat bereits eine Ausbildung genossen«, sagte sie. »Er kann Englisch und Französisch, lesen und schreiben. Er kann rechnen und außerdem noch ganze Gedichtbände auswendig –«

»Sachte, sachte, versteh mich nicht absichtlich falsch«, unterbrach Tom entschieden. »Philip hat nicht behauptet, Jack sei ein Dummkopf. Ganz im Gegenteil. Er meint, daß Jack intelligent genug ist, um noch *besser* ausgebildet zu werden.«

Jack machte sich gar nichts aus dieser Lobrede. Er teilte die Abneigung seiner Mutter gegen Geistliche. Irgend etwas war bestimmt faul an der Sache.

»Besser?« gab Ellen verächtlich zurück. »Was soll er denn nach Meinung dieses Mönches sonst noch lernen? Ich weiß schon. Theologie, Latein, Rhetorik, Metaphysik. Kuhscheiße.«

»Du solltest diesen Vorschlag nicht so schnell von der Hand weisen«, sagte Tom begütigend. »Wenn Jack Philips Angebot annimmt und zur Schule geht, dort eine gut lesbare Sekretärsschnellschrift lernt, Latein, Theologie und die anderen, von dir als Kuhscheiße bezeichneten Fächer studiert, dann könnte er bei einem Grafen oder Bischof eine Stellung als Schreiber bekommen und es schließlich zu Wohlstand und Einfluß bringen. Nicht alle Grafen sind Grafensöhne, wie es so schön heißt.«

Ellens Augen verengten sich gefährlich. »Wenn er Philips Angebot annimmt, hast du gesagt. Wie lautet denn Philips Angebot im Klartext?«

»Daß Jack Novize wird –«

»Nur über meine Leiche!« rief Ellen und sprang auf. »Die verdammte Kirche wird meinen Sohn nicht kriegen. Diese hinterhältigen, verlogenen Priester haben mir seinen Vater genommen, aber ihn werden sie mir nicht nehmen, und wenn ich Philip ein Messer in den Bauch rammen muß, das schwöre ich bei allen Göttern!«

Es war dies nicht der erste Wutanfall, den Tom an Ellen beobachtete, und er schien nicht sonderlich beeindruckt. Er sagte ruhig: »Was, zum Teufel, ist nur los mit dir, Weib? Diesem Jungen ist eine großartige Chance geboten worden.«

Auf Jack hatten die Worte *Diese hinterhältigen, verlogenen Priester haben mir seinen Vater genommen* den größten Eindruck gemacht. Was meinte sie damit? Er hätte am liebsten gefragt, kam aber nicht zu Wort.

»Jack wird kein Mönch, niemals!« schrie sie.

»Wenn er kein Mönch werden will, dann wird ihn auch niemand dazu zwingen.«

Ellen schaute mißmutig drein. »Dieser mit allen Wassern gewaschene Prior schafft es irgendwie immer, seinen eigenen Kopf durchzusetzen«, sagte sie.

Tom wandte sich an Jack. »Es ist langsam Zeit, daß du dich auch mal äußerst, Junge. Was willst *du* denn mit deinem Leben anfangen?«

Jack hatte noch nie über diese Frage nachgedacht, doch seine Antwort kam sofort und ohne Zögern, als hätte er seinen Entschluß schon seit langem gefaßt: »Ich will Baumeister werden wie du«, sagte er. »Ich will die schönste Kathedrale bauen, die die Welt je gesehen hat.«

Der rote Rand der Sonnenscheibe verschwand hinter dem Horizont, und die Nacht brach an. Es wurde Zeit für das letzte Ritual der Johannisfeier, für die schwimmenden Wünsche. Jack hatte schon einen Kerzenstumpf und ein Stück Holz bereit. Er sah Ellen und Tom an, die ihn beide ein wenig ratlos betrachteten. Die Bestimmtheit, mit der er über seine Zukunft gesprochen, hatte sie überrascht. Kein Wunder – ihn selbst auch.

Als er merkte, daß sie dem nichts mehr hinzuzufügen hatten, sprang er auf und lief quer über die Wiese auf das Feuer zu. Er entzündete einen trockenen Zweig, brachte das Ende der Kerze ein wenig zum Schmelzen und befestigte sie auf dem Holzstück; dann entzündete er den Docht. Die meisten Dorfbewohner waren ebenfalls damit beschäftigt. Wer sich keine Kerze leisten konnte, fertigte aus trockenem Gras und Binsen eine Art Boot und zwirbelte die Halme in der Mitte zu einem Docht zusammen.

Jack sah, daß Aliena nicht weit von ihm stand. Ihr Gesicht leuchtete im roten Schein des Johannisfeuers, und sie sah aus, als wäre sie tief in Gedanken versunken. »Was werdet Ihr Euch wünschen, Aliena?« platzte er heraus.

»Frieden«, sagte sie, und ihre Antwort kam ohne zu zögern. Dann wandte sie sich ein wenig erschrocken ab.

Jack fragte sich, ob es verrückt war, sie zu lieben. Sie mochte ihn, ja sie waren gute Freunde geworden; aber die Vorstellung, nackt nebeneinander zu liegen und heiße Küsse auszutauschen, war ihr ebenso fremd wie ihm nahe.

Sobald alle ihre Vorbereitungen getroffen hatten, knieten sie sich am Flußufer nieder oder wateten in das seichte Wasser hinein. Jeder hielt sein flackerndes Licht hoch und wünschte sich etwas. Jack schloß fest die Augen und stellte sich vor, wie Aliena, die Brüste von der Decke entblößt, im Bett lag, ihre Arme ausbreitete und sagte: »Komm und liebe mich, mein Gatte.« Dann ließen alle ihre Lichter vorsichtig ins Wasser gleiten. Wenn das Treibholz versank oder die Flamme erlosch, so bedeutete das, der Wunsch würde nie in Erfüllung gehen. Kaum hatte Jack sein kleines Boot zu Wasser gelassen, schwamm es auch schon fort, der hölzerne Unterbau verschwand aus seinem Blickfeld und nur die Flamme war noch sichtbar. Eine Weile lang beobachtete er sie gespannt, bis er sie unter den Hunderten tanzender Lichter, die auf dem Wasser hin und her schaukelten, nicht mehr ausmachen konnte; die flackernden Wünsche drifteten flußabwärts, bis sie in der Flußbiegung verschwunden und keiner mehr gesehen ward.

Den ganzen Sommer lang erzählte Jack Aliena Geschichten. Zunächst trafen sie sich gelegentlich, dann regelmäßig jeden Sonntag auf der Lichtung bei dem kleinen Wasserfall. Er erzählte ihr von Karl dem Großen und seinen Rittern, von Willehalm und von den Sarazenen. Dabei ging er völlig in seinen Geschichten auf. Aliena liebte es, zu beobachten, wie sich die Miene in seinem jungen Gesicht mit den wechselnden Geschicken des Liedes wandelte: Ungerechtigkeit wurde mit Empörung, Verrat mit Abscheu quittiert, die Tapferkeit eines Ritters brachte ihn schier aus dem Häuschen und ein Heldentod rührte ihn zu Tränen. Seine Gefühle waren so ansteckend, daß auch sie davon ergriffen wurde. Manche der Lieder waren zu lang, um sie an einem einzigen Nachmittag vorzutragen, und wenn er eine Geschichte unterbrach, so stets im spannendsten Moment, worauf Aliena sich die ganze Woche lang Gedanken darüber machte, wie sie wohl weiterginge.

Sie verriet nie auch nur ein Sterbenswörtchen von ihren Zusammenkünften. Über die Beweggründe dafür war sie sich nicht im klaren. Vielleicht, weil ihre Begeisterung für Jacks Geschichten bei niemandem auf Verständnis gestoßen wäre. Auf jeden Fall ließ sie die Leute, aus welchem Grund auch immer, stets in dem Glauben, sie begäbe sich auf ihren üblichen sonntäglichen Streifzug, und Jack hielt es, ohne daß sie sich miteinander abgesprochen hätten, ebenso; schließlich kam es so weit, daß sie niemandem mehr von ihren Treffen erzählen konnten, ohne den Eindruck zu erwecken, sie fühlten sich dessen schuldig. Ihre sonntäglichen Begegnungen wurden, ohne daß es je so geplant gewesen wäre, zu Geheimtreffen.

Eines Sonntags las Aliena ihm zur Abwechslung das Alexanderlied vor. Im Gegensatz zu Jacks Geschichten, in denen sich alles um höfische Intrigen, internationale Politik und gefallene Krieger drehte, ging es bei dieser um Liebeshändel und Magie. Jack zeigte sich von diesen neuen Elementen so beeindruckt, daß er am folgenden Sonntag zu einem neuen, selbst erfundenen Lied ansetzte.

Es war ein heißer Spätsommertag gegen Ende August. Aliena trug Sandalen und ein leichtes Leinenkleid. Im Wald war es, mit Ausnahme des plätschernden Wasserfalls und dem Auf und Ab von Jacks Stimme, mucksmäuschenstill. Die Geschichte begann wie die meisten anderen auch mit der Beschreibung eines tapferen Ritters – bärenstark, kampferprobt und im Besitz eines Zauberschwerts –, dem eine schwierige Aufgabe gestellt wird: in ein fernöstliches Land zu reisen und von dort einen Rebstock mitzubringen, an dem Rubine wuchsen. Doch dann war es auch schon vorbei mit der Ähnlichkeit: Der Ritter kam ums Leben, und in den Mittelpunkt rückte sein Knappe, ein tapferer, aber mittelloser junger Mann von siebzehn Jahren, der sich Hals über Kopf in die Tochter des Königs, eine wunderschöne Prinzessin, verliebt hatte. Trotz seiner Jugend und Unerfahrenheit und obwohl er nichts besaß als ein geschecktes Pony und seinen Bogen, schwor der Knappe, die seinem Herrn gestellte Aufgabe auszuführen.

Statt sich seiner Feinde, wie die gewöhnlichen Helden solcher Geschichten, mit einem einzigen, kraftvollen Hieb des Zauberschwerts zu entledigen, ließ dieser Knappe sich auf die aussichtslosesten Kämpfe ein, die er nur durch schieres Glück oder seinen Einfallsreichtum gewann und dabei dem sicheren Tod stets nur um Haaresbreite entging. Anders als die furchtlosen Ritter Karls des Großen hatte er nicht selten sogar Angst vor seinen Feinden, ließ sich aber durch nichts von seiner Mission abbringen. Und dennoch schien sie ebenso aussichtslos wie seine Liebe.

Aliena war von der Beherztheit des Knappen viel mehr angetan als von der Allmacht seines Herrn: Begab er sich auf feindlichen Boden, so biß sie sich vor Angst um ihn auf die Knöchel, verfehlte ihn der Schwertstreich eines Giganten wieder einmal nur um Haaresbreite, so japste sie aufgeregt, legte er sich einsam und allein schlafen und träumte von seiner unerreichbaren Prinzessin, so seufzte sie tief. Die Liebe, die er für die Dame empfand, schien ganz und gar untrennbar mit seiner Unbezwingbarkeit verwoben.

Am Ende brachte er zum denkbar größten Erstaunen des gesamten Hofes tatsächlich den Rebstock, an dem Rubine wuchsen, heim. »Dem Knappen jedoch galten die Barone und Grafen nicht soviel«, fuhr Jack fort und schnippte verächtlich mit den Fingern. »Ihm ging es allein um eine einzige Person. In derselben Nacht schlich er sich heimlich in ihre Gemächer, indem er die Wachen mittels einer klugen List, die er auf seiner Reise gen Osten gelernt hatte, übertölpelte. Endlich stand er vor ihrem Bett und betrachtete liebevoll ihr schlafendes Antlitz.« Dabei sah Jack Aliena in die Augen. »Sie erwachte sofort, aber sie fürchtete sich nicht. Der Knappe griff behutsam nach ihrer Hand.« Jack spielte die Geschichte mit, während er sprach, griff nach Alienas Rechter und hielt sie mit beiden Händen. Sie, im Bann seines Blickes und der machtvollen Liebe des jungen Knappen, bemerkte es kaum. »Ich liebe Euch so sehr«, sagte er zu ihr und küßte sie auf die Lippen. Jack beugte sich vor und küßte Aliena. Seine Lippen berührten sie so leicht, daß sie kaum etwas spürte. Und es war so rasch geschehen, daß die Geschichte auch schon weiterging. »Die Prinzessin fiel in einen tiefen Schlaf«, fuhr er fort. Habe ich mir das nur eingebildet? dachte Aliena. Hat Jack mich wirklich geküßt? Sie konnte es kaum glauben, spürte aber immer noch die Berührung seiner Lippen auf den ihren. »Am nächsten Tag hielt der Knappe zur Belohnung für den rubintragenden Rebstock beim König um die Hand der Prinzessin an.« Aliena kam zu dem Schluß, daß Jack sie geküßt hatte, ohne sich etwas dabei zu denken. Es gehörte wohl zu seiner Geschichte, dachte sie. Wahrscheinlich hat er es selber gar nicht gemerkt. Am besten denke ich nicht mehr daran. »Der König lehnte dieses Ansinnen ab, und dem Knappen wollte schier das Herz brechen. Die Höflinge wollten sich ausschütten vor Lachen. Noch denselbigen Tag ritt er auf seinem gescheckten Pony fort und verließ das Land; doch er schwor, eines Tages zurückzukehren und die schöne Prinzessin noch am gleichen Tag zu ehelichen.« Jack hielt inne und ließ Alienas Hand los.

»Wie ging es weiter?« wollte sie wissen.

»Ich weiß noch nicht«, erwiderte Jack. »Darüber habe ich mir noch keine Gedanken gemacht.«

Jeder, der in Kingsbridge auf sich hielt, trat der Kirchengilde bei. Den meisten war der Gedanke neu, doch die Vorstellung, daß aus dem Dorf Kingsbridge nun eine Stadt geworden war, fand allgemein Gefallen, und ihre angesehensten Bürger fühlten sich durch das Ansinnen, für eine Kirche aus Stein zu sorgen, in ihrer Eitelkeit bestärkt.

Aliena und Alfred warben um Mitglieder und trafen die Vorkehrungen für das erste, für Mitte September anberaumte Innungsessen. Durch Abwesenheit glänzten vor allem Prior Philip, der sich zwar mit dem Vorhaben nicht anfreunden konnte, jedoch nicht antagonistisch genug gestimmt war, um dagegen einzuschreiten; Tom Builder, der aus Rücksicht auf Philips Gefühle absagte; und Malachi, den seine Religionszugehörigkeit von vornherein ausschloß.

Ellen hatte mittlerweile aus Alienas unverkaufter Wolle einen Ballen Stoff gewebt. Er war rauh und ungefärbt, doch gut genug für Mönchskutten, und Cuthbert Whitehead, der Cellerar der Priorei, hatte ihn erworben. Trotz des sehr günstigen Preises erzielte Aliena das Doppelte des ursprünglichen Einkaufspreises der Wolle, und selbst, nachdem sie Ellen mit einem Penny pro Tag entlohnt hatte, blieb ihr noch ein Gewinn von einem halben Pfund. Cuthbert war darauf bedacht, noch mehr Stoff zum gleichen Preis kaufen zu können, so daß Aliena auch Philips unverkaufte Wolle erwarb und ein Dutzend Leute, meist Frauen, sich ans Weben machten. Ellen war bereit, einen weiteren Ballen herzustellen, weigerte sich jedoch entschieden, ihn zu walken; die Arbeit sei zu hart, sagte sie, und die meisten anderen pflichteten ihr bei.

Aliena hatte Verständnis dafür. Walken war Schwerarbeit. Sie konnte sich noch gut erinnern, wie sie und Richard in Winchester zu einem Walkmeister gegangen waren und ihn um Arbeit gebeten hatten. Zwei Männer hatten dort den Stoff in einem Trog mit Holzkeulen gewalkt, während eine Frau beständig Wasser nachgoß. Die Frau hatte Aliena ihre rissigen, roten Hände gezeigt, und Richard war, als man ihm den Ballen nassen Stoffs auf die Schultern gehievt hatte, in die Knie gesunken. Es gab viele Leute, die eine kleine Menge Tuch für ihren Eigenbedarf walkten, gewiß; um aber eine solche Arbeit den ganzen Tag lang auszuführen, mußte man schon aus besonderem Holz geschnitzt sein. Aliena beauftragte ihre Weber also mit der Herstellung lose gewebten Tuches und nahm sich vor, entweder selbst Walker einzustellen oder das Tuch an einen Walkmeister in Winchester zu verkaufen.

Das Gildenessen fand in der Holzkirche statt. Aliena kümmerte sich um die Zubereitung und verteilte sie auf die Gildenmitglieder, die zum Großteil mindestens einen Dienstboten hatten. Alfred und seine Leute errichteten einen langen Tisch aus Böcken und Brettern, besorgten Starkbier und ein Faß Wein.

Man nahm an beiden Seiten des Tisches Platz, und da es innerhalb der Gilde keine Rangunterschiede geben sollte, blieben die Plätze am Kopf- und Fußende frei. Aliena trug ein tiefrotes Seidengewand, an das sie eine rubinbesetzte Goldbrosche gesteckt hatte, und eine dunkelgraue Pelisse mit modisch weiten Ärmeln. Der Gemeindepriester sprach das Tischgebet; er war über das Zustandekommen der Gilde natürlich hocherfreut, würde eine neue Kirche doch nicht nur seinem Ansehen, sondern auch seinem Einkommen zugute kommen.

Alfred trug vor, wie die Pläne für den Geld- und Zeitaufwand zum Bau der neuen Kirche aussahen. Er tat, als wären sie auf seinem Mist gewachsen, doch Aliena war klar, daß den Großteil der Arbeit Tom geleistet hatte. Die Bauarbeiten sollten zwei Jahre dauern und neunzig Pfund kosten, und Alfred schlug vor, daß jedes der vierzig Gildenmitglieder jede Woche sechs Pence entrichten sollte. Das war mehr, als manche erwartet hatten, wie Aliena ihren Mienen entnahm. Der Beitrag wurde zwar von allen beschlossen, aber Aliena rechnete bereits mit ein oder zwei Absagen.

Sie selbst konnte das Geld leicht aufbringen, und wie sie sich so umschaute, fiel ihr auf, daß sie unter allen Anwesenden wahrscheinlich die Wohlhabendste war. Sie gehörte zu der kleinen Minderheit anwesender Frauen: Außer ihr gab es nur noch eine Braumeisterin, die für ihr gutes, starkes Bier berühmt war, eine Schneidermeisterin, die zwei Schneiderinnen und etliche Lehrlinge unter sich hatte, und die Witwe eines Schuhmachers, die das Geschäft ihres verstorbenen Mannes weiterführte. Aliena war die jüngste unter ihnen und sogar jünger als alle anwesenden Männer mit Ausnahme von Alfred, dem sie ein oder zwei Jahre voraus hatte.

Aliena vermißte Jack. Bisher hatte sie die Fortsetzung der Geschichte von dem jungen Knappen noch nicht gehört. Heute war ein Feiertag, und nichts wäre ihr lieber gewesen, als sich mit ihm auf der Lichtung im Wald zu treffen. Vielleicht konnte sie später noch hingehen.

Die Unterhaltung am Tisch drehte sich um den Krieg. Königin Matilda, Stephans Gemahlin, hatte sich wider Erwarten energisch zur Wehr gesetzt, erst kürzlich Winchester erobert und Robert von Gloucester gefangengesetzt. Robert war der Bruder der Kaiserin Mathilde und Oberkommandierender ihrer militärischen Streitkräfte. Einige Leute hielten Mathilde sogar für eine Galionsfigur und Robert für den eigentlichen Anführer der Rebellen. Wie dem auch immer war, die Gefangennahme Roberts kam für die Kaiserin ebenso ungelegen wie die Gefangensetzung Stephans für die Loyalisten, und die Meinungen darüber, welche Wendung der Krieg nehmen würde, gingen weit auseinander.

Die anläßlich dieses Festschmauses aufgetischten Getränke waren stärker als die, die Prior Philip ihnen gemeinhin vorsetzte, und je länger das Mahl sich ausdehnte, um so rauhbeiniger ging es zu. Selbst der Gemeindepriester wurde seiner mäßigenden Rolle nicht mehr gerecht – was wohl daran lag, daß er den Getränken nicht minder zusprach als alle anderen auch. Alfred, der neben Aliena saß, schien zwar in Gedanken versunken, aber auch sein Gesicht war gerötet. Aliena, die sich nichts aus starken Getränken machte, nahm während des Essens lediglich einen Becher Apfelmost zu sich.

Kurz vor Ende des Mahls brachte einer der Anwesenden einen Trinkspruch auf Alfred und Aliena aus. Alfred strahlte vor Freude. Danach wurden die ersten Lieder angestimmt, und Aliena überlegte, wie bald sie sich wohl davonschleichen konnte.

»Wir beide haben gute Arbeit geleistet«, sagte Alfred zu ihr.

Aliena lächelte. »Wir wollen lieber abwarten, wie viele nächstes Jahr um diese Zeit noch sechs Pence die Woche zahlen.«

Doch Alfred war im Augenblick nicht nach Befürchtungen und Einschränkungen.

»Wir haben gute Arbeit geleistet«, wiederholte er. »Wir sind ein großartiges Gespann.« Er hob sein Glas und trank ihr zu. »Glaubt Ihr nicht auch, daß wir ein gutes Gespann sind?«

»Sicher«, sagte sie, um ihm die Laune nicht zu verderben.

»Mir hat es Spaß gemacht«, fuhr er fort. »Das mit Euch – mit der Gilde, meine ich.«

»Mir hat es ebenfalls Spaß gemacht«, sagte sie höflich.

»Wirklich? Das macht mich sehr glücklich.«

Sie sah ihn abschätzend an. Warum beharrte er auf diesem Punkt? Seine Redeweise war klar und deutlich, und er machte nicht den Eindruck, als wäre er stockbetrunken. »Es war nett«, ergänzte sie abschwächend.

Er legte eine Hand auf ihre Schulter. Sie haßte nichts mehr, als angefaßt zu werden, konnte sich aber so weit beherrschen, daß sie nicht zusammenzuckte: Männer waren im Handumdrehen beleidigt.

»Sagt einmal«, sprach er und flüsterte dabei vertraulich, »wie muß Euer zukünftiger Ehemann beschaffen sein?«

Er wird mir doch um des Himmels willen keinen Heiratsantrag machen wollen, dachte Aliena mißmutig und tischte ihm ihre immer gleiche Antwort auf: »Ich brauche keinen Ehemann – mein Bruder macht mir genug Ärger.«

»Aber Ihr braucht Liebe«, meinte er.

Sie stöhnte innerlich.

Als sie antworten wollte, hob er eine Hand, um ihr Einhalt zu gebieten – eine männliche Angewohnheit, die sie zum Verrücktwerden fand. »Ihr wollt mir doch nicht weismachen, daß Ihr ohne Liebe auskommen könnt«, sagte er. »Jeder Mensch braucht Liebe.«

Sie blickte ihn geradeheraus an. Sie wußte, daß sie eine Ausnahme war: Die meisten Frauen konnten es gar nicht abwarten, bis sie unter die Haube kamen, und waren sie, wie in ihrem Fall, mit Zweiundzwanzig noch immer ohne Mann, konnten sie es nicht nur gar nicht erwarten, sondern waren geradezu versessen darauf. Was stimmt bloß nicht mit mir? dachte sie. Alfred ist jung, gesund und wohlhabend: Halb Kingsbridge macht ihm schöne Augen. Einen Augenblick lang geriet sie in Versuchung, ja zu sagen. Aber dann erregte allein der Gedanke an ein Leben mit Alfred – jeden Tag mit ihm zu Abend zu essen, mit ihm zur Kirche zu gehen, seine Kinder zur Welt zu bringen – äußersten Widerwillen in ihr. O nein, lieber einsam und allein bleiben! Sie schüttelte den Kopf. »Schlagt Euch das aus dem Kopf, Alfred«, sagte sie fest. »Ich brauche keinen Ehemann, weder für die Liebe noch für sonst etwas.«

Er ließ sich nicht so leicht entmutigen. »Ich liebe Euch, Aliena«, sagte er. »Es hat mich wahrhaft glücklich gemacht, mit Euch zusammenzuarbeiten. Ich brauche Euch. Wollt Ihr meine Frau werden?«

Er war also mit der Sprache herausgerückt. Bedauerlich, denn nun war sie gezwungen, ihn formell abzulehnen. Die Erfahrung hatte sie gelehrt, daß es keinen Zweck hatte, Verehrer mit Samthandschuhen anzufassen: Sie hielten eine freundliche Ablehnung für ein Zeichen von Entschlußlosigkeit und rückten ihr erst recht zuleibe. »Nein, das will ich nicht«, erwiderte sie. »Ich liebe Euch nicht, und es hat mir keine Freude gemacht, mit Euch zusammenzuarbeiten; ich würde Euch auch dann nicht heiraten, wenn Ihr der einzige Mann auf Erden wäret.«

Er war zutiefst gekränkt. Er mußte sich gute Chancen ausgerechnet haben. Dabei war sich Aliena ganz sicher, daß sie nichts getan hatte, das er als Ermunterung hätte auffassen können. Gewiß, sie hatte ihn als gleichberechtigten Partner behandelt, ihm zugehört, wenn er etwas zu sagen hatte, direkt und offen mit ihm geredet, ihre Verpflichtungen erfüllt und von ihm das gleiche erwartet. Aber es gab Männer, die das für einen Freibrief hielten. »Wie könnt Ihr so etwas sagen?« stammelte er.

Sie seufzte. Er war verletzt, und er tat ihr leid; aber im Handumdrehen würde er ungehalten werden und sich aufführen, als hätte sie ungerechtfertigte Vorwürfe gegen ihn erhoben; schließlich würde er sich einreden, grundlos von ihr beleidigt worden zu sein, und ausfallend werden. Nicht, daß sämtliche zurückgewiesenen Verehrer sich so benahmen; aber auf einen bestimmten Typus Mann traf dies zu, und Alfred gehörte einwandfrei zu diesem Typus. Sie mußte die Versammlung schnellstens verlassen.

Sie erhob sich. »Ich ehre Euren Antrag, und ich danke Euch dafür«, sagte sie. »Bitte nehmt auch meine Absage hin und fragt mich nie wieder.«

»Ihr rennt wohl davon, um meinen rotznasigen kleinen Stiefbruder zu sehen«, sagte er bösartig. »Ich kann mir vorstellen, daß er es Euch gut besorgt.«

Aliena wurde rot vor Scham. Man hatte also bemerkt, daß sie mit Jack befreundet war. Und Alfred sah es ähnlich, ihre Beziehung durch den Schmutz zu ziehen. Nun ja, sie rannte tatsächlich davon, um sich mit Jack zu treffen, und sie würde sich durch Alfred nicht davon abhalten lassen. Sie beugte sich vor, bis ihr Gesicht direkt vor seinem war und er verblüfft zurückfuhr. Ruhig und überlegt sagte sie: »Fahrt – zur – Hölle.« Dann wandte sie sich ab und ging hinaus.

Einmal im Monat saß Prior Philip in der Krypta zu Gericht. In früheren Zeiten hatte es lediglich einen Gerichtstag im Jahr gegeben, und selbst dann hatten die anliegenden Geschäfte so gut wie nie den ganzen Tag in Anspruch genommen. Aber die Verdreifachung der Bevölkerung hatte eine Verzehnfachung der Gesetzesverstöße mit sich gebracht.

Darüber hinaus hatte sich die Natur der Verbrechen verändert. Ehedem war es hauptsächlich um Land, Felderverträge oder Vieh gegangen. So versuchte ein gieriger Bauer etwa, die Grenzen eines Feldes heimlich zu verrücken, um sein Land auf Kosten seines Nachbarn zu vergrößern; ein Arbeiter stahl von der Witwe, für die er arbeitete, einen Sack Getreide; eine arme Frau mit zu vielen Kindern melkte eine Kuh, die ihr nicht gehörte. Heutzutage dreht es sich meistens um Geld, dachte Philip, während er an diesem ersten Dezembertag zu Gericht saß. Lehrlinge bestahlen ihre Meister, ein Ehemann brachte die Mutter seiner Frau um ihre Ersparnisse, Händler gaben in falscher Münze heraus, und reiche Frauen enthielten ihrem beschränkten Gesinde, das kaum bis drei zählen konnte, einen Teil des Lohnes vor. Solche Verstöße hatte es noch vor fünf Jahren, als kaum jemand in Kingsbridge über Bargeld verfügte, nicht gegeben.

Philip belegte fast alle Verbrechen mit einer Geldstrafe. Er hätte ebensogut die Prügelstrafe oder den Schraubstock verhängen oder jemanden in der Zelle unter dem Schlafsaal der Mönche einkerkern lassen können, aber solche Urteile fällte er eigentlich nur bei Gewaltverbrechen. Er hatte das Recht, Diebe hängen zu lassen, und die Priorei verfügte über einen soliden, aus Holz gefertigten Galgen; von diesem Recht hatte er allerdings – bislang – noch nie Gebrauch gemacht, und er hegte die stille Hoffnung, es auch nie zu müssen. Schwerere Verbrechen – wie Mord, Wilddieberei im königlichen Forst und Straßenraub – unterstanden der königlichen Gerichtsbarkeit in Shiring, vertreten durch Vogt Eustace, und der brachte schon mehr als genug Menschen an den Galgen.

An diesem Tag mußte Philip sich mit sieben Fällen unerlaubten Getreidemahlens befassen. Er stellte sie an den Schluß, um sie in einem Schwung abzuhandeln. Da Kingsbridge mittlerweile zwei Mühlen benötigte, hatte die Priorei erst kürzlich eine neue Wassermühle errichten lassen, die nun Seite an Seite mit der alten ihre Arbeit verrichtete. Aber die neue Mühle mußte sich erst bezahlt machen, und das hieß, daß jedermann sein Getreide zur Priorei bringen mußte, um es dort mahlen zu lassen. Genaugenommen war das schon immer so gewesen und wurde auf jedem Gut landauf, landab so gehandhabt: Den Bauern war es verboten, ihr Getreide zu Hause zu mahlen, und sie mußten ihren Herrn dafür bezahlen. In den vergangenen Jahren hatte Philip der steigenden Bevölkerungszahl und der häufigen Schäden an der alten Mühle wegen manches Mal beide Augen zugedrückt, doch nun war es an der Zeit, dem unerlaubten Mahlen ein Ende zu bereiten.

Die Namen der Schuldigen standen auf einer Schiefertafel, und er las sie einen nach dem anderen, beginnend mit dem Reichsten, vor. »Richard Longacre, Bruder Franziskus berichtet, daß Ihr einen von zwei Männern betriebenen großen Mahlstein hattet.« Franziskus war der Müller der Priorei.

Ein wohlhabend wirkender Freisasse trat vor. »Ja, mein Herr Prior, aber ich habe ihn zerstört.«

»Zahlt sechzig Pence Strafe. Enid Brewster, Ihr hattet eine Handmühle in Eurer Brauerei. Eric Enidson wurde beobachtet, wie er sie benutzte, und er ist ebenfalls angeklagt.«

»Ja, Herr«, sagte Enid, eine rotgesichtige Frau mit mächtigen Schultern.

»Und wo befindet sich die Handmühle jetzt?«

»Ich habe sie in den Fluß geworfen, Herr.«

Philip glaubte ihr kein Wort, aber was war schon dagegen zu tun? »Mit vierundzwanzig Pence Strafe belegt, dazu zwölf Pence für Euren Sohn. Walter Tanner?«

So hakte Philip allmählich die gesamte Liste ab und belegte die Täter, je nach der Schwere ihres Vergehens, mit Geldstrafen, bis er beim letzten und ärmsten ankam. »Witwe Goda?«

Eine alte, verkniffen aussehende Frau mit verblichenen schwarzen Gewändern trat vor.

»Bruder Franziskus hat Euch dabei ertappt, wie Ihr mit einem Stein Getreide gemahlen habt.«

»Ich hatte keinen Penny für die Mühle, Herr«, sagte sie vorwurfsvoll.

»Aber einen Penny für das Getreide hattet Ihr wohl«, meinte Philip. »Ihr sollt Eure Strafe erhalten wie jeder andere auch.«

»Wollt Ihr mich etwa verhungern lassen?« gab sie herausfordernd zurück.

Philip seufzte. Er wünschte sich, Bruder Franziskus hätte in diesem Fall einfach weggeguckt. »Wann ist das letzte Mal jemand in Kingsbridge verhungert?« fragte er. Er sah sich unter den versammelten Bürgern der Stadt um. »Erinnert sich einer der Anwesenden, wann zum letztenmal jemand in dieser Stadt vor Hunger umgekommen ist?« Er hielt einen Moment lang inne, als warte er auf Antwort, dann sagte er: »Ich glaube, das muß vor meiner Zeit gewesen sein.«

Goda warf ein: »Dick Shorthouse ist aber letzten Winter gestorben.«

Philip konnte sich an den Mann erinnern, einen Bettler, der in Schweinekoben und sonstigen Ställen zu schlafen pflegte. »Dick fiel um Mitternacht betrunken auf die Straße und erfror, da es zu schneien begann«, sagte er. »Aber verhungert ist er nicht, und wäre er nüchtern genug gewesen, um zur Priorei zu gehen, dann hätte er auch nicht zu frieren brauchen. Versucht nicht, mich zu hintergehen, wenn Ihr hungrig seid – kommt und macht von unserer Mildtätigkeit Gebrauch. Und wenn Ihr zu stolz dazu seid und statt dessen lieber gegen das Gesetz verstoßt, dann müßt Ihr eben bestraft werden, wie jeder andere auch. Habt Ihr verstanden?«

»Ja, Herr«, erwiderte die Alte mürrisch.

»Einen Viertelpenny Strafe für Euch«, sagte Philip. »Die Gerichtsverhandlung ist beendet.«

Damit erhob er sich, ging hinaus und stieg die Stufen der Krypta hinauf.

Es waren noch etwa vier Wochen bis Weihnachten, und die Arbeit an der Kathedrale war, wie immer um diese Jahreszeit, ins Stocken geraten. Die offenen, unvollendeten Mauern waren zum Schutz gegen Frost mit Stroh und Dung – dem Mist aus den Ställen der Priorei – abgedeckt worden. Bei Frost kann man nicht bauen, hieß es unter den Maurern. Philip hatte wissen wollen, warum sie die Mauern nicht jeden Morgen ab und abends wieder zudeckten, denn tagsüber gefror es so gut wie nie. Tom hatte behauptet, im Winter gebaute Mauern stürzten wieder ein. Philip zweifelte zwar nicht daran, führte es allerdings nicht auf den Frost zurück, sondern auf den Mörtel, der etliche Monate brauchte, um richtig fest zu werden, bevor die Mauern im neuen Jahr höher gezogen wurden. So ließ sich auch der Aberglaube der Maurer erklären, es brächte Unglück, mehr als zwanzig Fuß hoch im Jahr zu bauen: Ging man darüber hinaus, so lief man Gefahr, daß sich die unteren Reihen durch das Gewicht, das auf ihnen lastete, verschoben, weil der Mörtel sich noch nicht richtig gesetzt hatte.

Philip stellte überrascht fest, daß die Maurer sich samt und sonders im Freien, und zwar im zukünftigen Altarraum der neuen Kirche, versammelt hatten. Neugierig ging er hinüber.

Sie hatten einen aus Holz gefertigten Rundbogen auf zwei Pfosten gesetzt. Philip wußte, daß der Holzbogen Teil der von ihnen sogenannten Schablone war und dazu diente, den steinernen Bogen während der Bauarbeiten abzustützen. Im Augenblick allerdings fügten sie die Steine ohne Mörtel zusammen, um festzustellen, ob sie fugenlos paßten. Die Steinmetzen sahen kritisch zu, während die Lehrlinge und Arbeiter Stück für Stück auf die Schablone hievten.

Philip lenkte Toms Blick auf sich und fragte: »Wo gehört das hin?«

»Das ist ein Bogen fürs Triforium.«

Philip ließ seinen Blick nachdenklich in die Höhe schweifen. Die Arkade war im vergangenen Jahr fertiggestellt worden, und das darüberliegende Triforium sollte im nächsten Jahr in Angriff genommen werden. Dann blieb nur noch der Lichtgaden im Hauptschiff, bevor der Dachstuhl errichtet wurde. Da die Mauern den Winter über abgedeckt blieben, schnitten die Steinmetzen mittlerweile die nötigen Quader für das kommende Jahr. Wenn es mit diesem Bogen seine Richtigkeit hatte, konnten alle anderen nach dem gleichen Muster gearbeitet werden.

Die Lehrlinge, unter denen sich auch Toms Stiefsohn Jack befand, fügten den Bogen aus keilförmigen Steinen von beiden Seiten gleichzeitig zusammen. Obwohl er letztlich seinen Platz hoch oben in der Kirche finden würde, war er doch an den Stirnseiten mit komplizierten Friesen geschmückt, und jeder einzelne Stein wies ein Hundszahn-Ornament, darunter ein Scheibenfries und zum Abschluß am unteren Ende einen einfachen Rundstab auf. Zusammengefügt ergaben die gemeißelten Muster drei fortlaufende Bögen aus den drei verschiedenen Ornamenten, so daß beim Betrachter der Eindruck entstand, der Rundbogen bestehe aus mehreren halbrunden, übereinanderliegenden Steinreifen, während er sich in Wirklichkeit aus nebeneinanderliegenden Keilen zusammensetzte. Um diese optische Täuschung zu erzielen, mußten sowohl die Steine als auch die Ornamente exakt passen.

Philip sah zu, wie Jack den Schlußstein in der Mitte einfügte. Jetzt war der Bogen vollständig. Vier Steinmetzen griffen nach ihren Vorschlaghämmern und schlugen die Keile weg, die die hölzerne Schablone trugen. Es war ein atemberaubender Moment, als sie zu Boden fiel – und der Bogen hielt, auch ohne Mörtel! Tom Builder gab einen zufriedenen Grunzer von sich.

Philip spürte, daß ihn jemand am Ärmel zog. Er drehte sich um und erblickte einen jungen Mönch. »Ihr habt Besuch, Vater. Er wartet in Eurem Haus auf Euch.«

»Danke, mein Sohn.« Philip kehrte den Bauleuten den Rücken. Die Tatsache, daß die Mönche den Besucher ins Haus des Prior geführt hatten, ließ darauf schließen, daß es sich um eine wichtige Persönlichkeit handelte. Rasch überquerte er den Hof und betrat sein Haus.

Der Besucher war sein Bruder Francis, der einen sorgenvollen Eindruck machte. Philip umarmte ihn herzlich. »Hat man dir etwas zu essen angeboten?« wollte er wissen. »Du siehst erschöpft aus.«

»Man hat mich bereits mit Brot und Fleisch versorgt, danke. Ich habe den ganzen Herbst damit zugebracht, zwischen Bristol und Rochester hin- und herzureiten. König Stephan wurde in Bristol, Earl Robert in Rochester gefangengehalten.«

»Wurde, sagst du?«

Francis nickte.»Ich habe die Verhandlungen für den Austausch geführt: Stephan gegen Robert. Allerheiligen ist es dann geschehen. König Stephan ist mittlerweile wieder in Winchester.«

Philip war überrascht. »Da hat die Kaiserin Mathilde aber einen schlechten Tausch gemacht – einen König gegen einen Grafen!«

Francis schüttelte den Kopf. »Ohne Robert kommt sie nicht weiter. Sie ist unbeliebt und genießt außerdem kein Vertrauen. Und allmählich hat sie jeglichen Rückhalt verloren. Sie mußte Robert zurückhaben. Es war ein kluger Schachzug der Königin Matilda, keinen anderen als König Stephan im Austausch zu akzeptieren. Sie hatte es von vornherein auf ihn abgesehen und sich schließlich auch durchgesetzt.«

Philip trat ans Fenster und blickte hinaus. Es hatte angefangen zu regnen; ein kalter, schräg über die Baustelle peitschender Regen, der die hohen Mauern der Kathedrale in Dunkelheit tauchte und von den niedrigen, strohgedeckten Dächern der Bauhütten troff. »Und was hat das zu bedeuten?« fragte er schließlich.

»Das heißt, daß Mathilde einmal mehr nichts weiter als Anwärterin auf den Thron ist. Schließlich ist Stephan tatsächlich gekrönt worden, während Mathilde es nie so weit gebracht hat.«

»Aber sie war es, die mir die Genehmigung für den Markt gab.«

»Ja. Das könnte unangenehm werden.«

»Ist meine Genehmigung denn ungültig?«

»Nein. Sie ist durch eine legitime, von der Kirche bestätigte Herrscherin gewährt worden. Dabei macht es keinen Unterschied, ob sie gekrönt war oder nicht. Aber es könnte passieren, daß Stephan die Lizenz widerruft.«

»Mit den Einnahmen aus dem Markt bezahle ich die Steine«, sagte Philip besorgt. »Ohne ihn kann ich nicht weiterbauen. Das sind sehr schlechte Nachrichten!«

»Es tut mir leid für dich.«

»Und meine hundert Pfund?«

Francis zuckte die Achseln. »Stephan wird dir wahrscheinlich ans Herz legen, sie dir von Mathilde zurückzuholen.«

Philip wurde ganz elend. »Das ganze Geld«, murmelte er. »Es ist Gottes Geld, und ich habe es verloren.«

»Das ist nicht gesagt«, beschwichtigte Francis ihn. »Vielleicht nimmt Stephan die Genehmigung gar nicht zurück. Er hat nie ein sonderliches Interesse am Marktrecht bekundet, so oder so.«

»Graf William könnte Druck auf ihn ausüben.«

»William hat aber das Lager gewechselt, erinnerst du dich? Er hat sich auf Mathildes Seite geschlagen. Bei Stephan hat er bestimmt keinen Stein mehr im Brett.«

»Ich hoffe, du hast recht«, sagte Philip inbrünstig. »Bei Gott, ich hoffe wirklich, daß du recht hast.«

Als es zu kalt wurde, um auf der Lichtung zu sitzen, machte Aliena es sich zur Angewohnheit, abends bei Tom Builder hereinzuschauen. Alfred war gewöhnlich in der Schenke, und so bestand die Familie aus Tom, Ellen, Jack und Martha. Und da Tom mittlerweile gut verdiente, saßen sie gemütlich vor einem hell brennenden Feuer und verfügten über einen ausreichenden Vorrat an Kerzen. Ellen und Aliena beschäftigten sich mit Webarbeiten, Tom zeichnete gewöhnlich Pläne und Diagramme, die er mit einem scharfkantigen Stein auf ein poliertes Stück Schiefer ritzte. Jack erweckte zwar den Anschein, entweder einen Gürtel herzustellen, Messer zu schleifen oder einen Korb zu flechten, aber in Wirklichkeit verbrachte er die meiste Zeit damit, heimlich auf Alienas vom Kerzenlicht beschienenes Gesicht zu starren, die Bewegung ihrer Lippen beim Sprechen zu beobachten oder ihren weißen Hals zu betrachten, wenn sie an ihrem Bier nippte. Sie lachten viel in diesem Winter. Jack liebte nichts mehr, als Aliena zum Lachen zu bringen. Gewöhnlich war sie derart zurückhaltend und beherrscht, daß es eine wahre Freude war, wenn sie aus sich herausging – beinahe als erhaschte er einen Blick auf die nackte Aliena. Er ließ sich immer wieder etwas Neues einfallen, womit er sie belustigen konnte. Er imitierte die Handwerker auf der Baustelle, den Akzent eines Pariser Steinmetzen etwa oder die x-beinige Gangart eines Schmieds. Einmal gab er gar eine komische Version des mönchischen Lebens zum besten und stattete jeden einzelnen mit einem glaubwürdigen Laster aus – Remigius mit Hochmut, Bernard, den Küchenmeister, mit Völlerei, den Gästemeister mit Trunkenheit und Pierre, den Cirkator, mit Lüsternheit. Martha kugelte sich oft vor Lachen, und selbst der in sich gekehrte Tom konnte sich ein Grinsen nicht verkneifen.

Es war an einem dieser Abende, als Aliena plötzlich sagte: »Ich bin mir nicht sicher, ob ich all diesen Stoff überhaupt verkaufen kann.«

Ihre Bemerkung rief Bestürzung hervor, und Ellen meinte: »Warum weben wir dann überhaupt weiter?«

»Weil ich die Hoffnung noch nicht aufgegeben habe«, erwiderte Aliena. »Es gibt da eine Schwierigkeit, für die ich eine Lösung finden muß.«

Tom sah von seiner Schiefertafel auf. »Ich dachte, die Priorei kauft bereitwillig alles auf.«

»Das ist es auch nicht. Aber ich kann niemanden auftreiben, der den Stoff walken will, und die Priorei ist an lose gewebter Wolle nicht interessiert – und sonst auch niemand.«

»Walken ist die reinste Plackerei«, sagte Ellen. »Es wundert mich nicht, daß das niemand machen will.«

»Könnt Ihr denn dafür keine Männer einstellen?« schlug Tom vor.

»Nicht im wohlhabenden Kingsbridge. Die Männer hier haben Arbeit genug. In den großen Städten gibt es zwar richtige Walker, aber die meisten arbeiten für irgendwelche Weber und dürfen nicht für die Konkurrenten ihrer Brotherren walken. Außerdem wäre es viel zu teuer, den Stoff erst nach Winchester und dann wieder zurückzutransportieren.«

»Ein echtes Problem«, pflichtete Tom ihr bei und wandte sich wieder seiner Zeichnung zu.

Jack hatte eine Idee. »Schade, daß wir für die Arbeit keinen Ochsen nehmen können.«

Die anderen lachten. Tom sagte: »Das ist ja fast, als wolltest du einem Ochsen beibringen, Kirchen zu bauen.«

»Oder eine Mühle«, beharrte Jack. »Normalerweise gibt es gerade für die schwersten Arbeiten einfache Lösungen.«

»Aber sie will den Stoff walken, nicht mahlen«, wandte Tom ein.

Jack hörte nicht zu. »Schließlich benutzen wir Hebemechanismen und Winden, um die Steine auf die hohen Gerüste zu hieven.«

»Oh, das wäre einfach wundervoll, wenn dieser Stoff durch irgendeine geschickte Vorrichtung gewalkt werden könnte«, meinte Aliena.

Jack mußte daran denken, wieviel Freude er ihr bereiten würde, wenn er ihr diese Schwierigkeiten aus dem Weg räumen konnte. Er nahm sich vor, eine Lösung zu finden.

»Ich habe von einer Wassermühle gehört, die den Blasebalg in einem Hüttenwerk antreibt«, sagte Tom nachdenklich, »aber gesehen habe ich sie nicht.«

»Tatsächlich!« entfuhr es Jack. »Das ist der Beweis!«

Tom sagte: »Ein Mühlrad dreht sich im Kreis, und ein Mühlstein dreht sich ebenfalls im Kreis, und deswegen kann eins das andere antreiben; aber der Walkknüppel geht rauf und runter. Du kannst ein rundes Mühlrad nicht dazu bringen, einen Knüppel, der rauf- und runtergeht, anzutreiben.«

»Aber ein Blasebalg geht rauf und runter.«

»Stimmt, stimmt; aber ich habe das Hüttenwerk nie mit eigenen Augen gesehen, man hat mir lediglich davon erzählt.«

Jack versuchte, sich den Mechanismus einer Mühle vorzustellen: Das Mühlrad wurde durch die Kraft des Wassers angetrieben. Die Radachse war mit einem weiteren Rad in der Mühle verbunden. Dieses Rad, das aufrecht stand, hatte Zähne, die in die Zähne eines weiteren, flach liegenden Rades griffen. Das flache Rad trieb den Mühlstein an. »Ein aufrechtes Rad kann ein flachliegendes Rad antreiben«, murmelte Jack vor sich hin.

Martha lachte. »Jack, nun mach einen Punkt! Wenn Mühlen Stoff walken könnten, wäre bestimmt schon irgendein kluger Kopf darauf gekommen.«

Jack beachtete sie nicht. »Die Walkknüppel könnten an der Achse des Mühlrads befestigt werden«, sagte er. »Der Stoff könnte an der Stelle, wo die Knüppel aufprallen, flach hingelegt werden.«

Tom sagte: »Aber die Knüppel würden einmal zuschlagen und dann steckenbleiben; und das Rad ebenfalls. Wie oft muß ich es denn noch wiederholen – Räder drehen sich im Kreis, aber Knüppel müssen rauf- und runtergehen.«

»Es gibt aber keine«, sagte Tom mit Entschiedenheit; sein Tonfall ließ keine Widerrede zu.

»Ich gehe jede Wette ein, daß es doch eine gibt«, murmelte Jack aufsässig; Tom tat, als hätte er nichts gehört.

Am folgenden Sonntag verschwand Jack.

Morgens ging er wie gewöhnlich zur Kirche und aß daheim zu Mittag, aber zum Abendessen erschien er nicht. Aliena stand in der Küche ihres Hauses und bereitete gerade eine sämige Suppe mit Schinken, Kohl und Pfeffer zu, als Ellen auf der Suche nach Jack bei ihr hereinschaute.

»Ich habe ihn seit der Messe heute früh nicht mehr gesehen«, sagte Aliena.

»Er ist gleich nach dem Mittagessen verschwunden«, sagte Ellen. »Ich nahm an, er wäre bei Euch.«

Aliena geriet ein wenig in Verlegenheit darüber, daß Ellen ohne Umschweife zu diesem Schluß gekommen war. »Macht Ihr Euch Sorgen?«

Ellen zuckte die Achseln. »Als Mutter macht man sich immer Sorgen.«

»Hat er sich mit Alfred gestritten?« fragte Aliena besorgt.

»Das habe ich auch vermutet. Aber Alfred sagt nein.« Ellen seufzte. »Ich glaube nicht, daß ihm etwas zugestoßen ist. Schließlich ist es nicht das erste Mal, daß er verschwunden ist, und wahrscheinlich auch nicht das letzte Mal. Ich habe ihm einfach nie beigebracht, sich an geregelte Zeiten zu halten.«

Später am Abend, kurz vor dem Zubettgehen, schaute Aliena bei Tom herein, um sich nach Jack zu erkundigen: keine Spur von ihm. Besorgt ging sie schlafen. Richard hatte sich nach Winchester begeben, und sie war allein im Haus. Der Gedanke, Jack könnte in den Fluß gefallen und ertrunken oder ein anderes Unglück könne ihm zugestoßen sein, ließ sie nicht mehr los. Wie schrecklich das für Ellen sein mußte! Jack war schließlich ihr einziger Sohn. Bei der Vorstellung von Ellens Trauer um ihren Sohn schossen Aliena die Tränen in die Augen. Wie dumm, dachte sie, aus Mitgefühl für andere zu weinen, dazu über einen Unfall, der noch nicht einmal passiert ist! Sie rief sich zur Ordnung und versuchte, sich mit etwas anderem zu beschäftigen – mit dem ungelösten Problem des überschüssigen Stoffs. Normalerweise konnte sie sich mit geschäftlichen Sorgen die halbe Nacht um die Ohren schlagen, aber diesmal kehrten ihre Gedanken immer wieder zu Jack zurück. Und wenn er sich nun ein Bein gebrochen hatte und hilflos im Wald lag?

Endlich fiel sie in einen unruhigen Schlaf. Sie erwachte im ersten Morgengrauen und fühlte sich wie zerschlagen. Sie zog ihren schweren Umhang über ihr Nachthemd, stieg in ihre pelzgefütterten Stiefel und verließ das Haus, um nach Jack zu suchen.

Im Garten hinter der Schenke war er nicht – dort war schon manch einer eingeschlafen und nur durch die aus dem stinkenden Misthaufen aufsteigende Wärme vor dem Erfrieren gerettet worden. Sie lief zur Brücke hinunter und kämmte ängstlich das Flußufer ab bis zu einer Biegung, in der sich der angeschwemmte Unrat zu sammeln pflegte. Eine Entenfamilie stöberte in Holzspänen, abgetragen Schuhen, rostigen, weggeworfenen Messern und verwesenden Fleischknochen am Ufer herum. Von Jack keine Spur. Gott sei Dank!

Aliena stieg hügelan zum Klostergelände, wo die Dombauleute eben ihr Tagewerk begannen. Tom war in seinem Schuppen. »Ist Jack wieder da?«

Tom schüttelte den Kopf. »Noch nicht.«

Sie wandte sich schon zum Gehen, als der Zimmermannsmeister mit besorgter Miene hereintrat. »Sämtliche Hämmer sind verschwunden«, sagte er zu Tom.

»Wie merkwürdig«, erwiderte Tom. »Ich habe auch schon einen gesucht und konnte keinen einzigen finden.«

Alfred steckte seinen Kopf zur Tür herein und fragte: »Wo sind denn die Trummhölzer der Steinmetzen abgeblieben?«

Tom kratzte sich den Kopf. »Sieht fast so aus, als gäbe es auf der ganzen Baustelle keinen einzigen Hammer mehr«, sagte er verdutzt. Und fügte mit veränderter Stimme hinzu: »Dieser Jack steckt dahinter, darauf gehe ich jede Wette ein.«

Natürlich, dachte Aliena. Hämmer. Walken. Die Mühle!

Ohne ein Wort zu verlieren, verließ sie Toms Arbeitsschuppen und eilte an der Küche vorbei über das Klostergelände zur Südwestecke, wo ein vom Fluß abgezweigter Kanal zwei Mühlen antrieb, eine alte und eine brandneue. Ihre Vermutung bestätigte sich: Das Rad der alten Mühle war in Gang. Aliena ging hinein. Was sie drinnen erblickte, erschreckte und verwirrte sie zunächst einmal beträchtlich: Eine ganze Reihe Hämmer, befestigt an einer quer verlaufenden Stange, schien ganz aus eigenem Antrieb die Köpfe zu heben – wie Pferde, die alle gleichzeitig von der Futterkrippe aufsehen. Dann nickten sie mit den Köpfen, wiederum alle gleichzeitig, und schlugen an, mit einem ohrenbetäubenden Lärm, der Aliena schier die Besinnung raubte. Entsetzt schrie sie auf. Wie zur Antwort hoben die Hämmer erneut die Köpfe und schlugen an. Sie droschen auf eine Bahn ihres lose gewebten Stoffs ein, die, eben mit Wasser bedeckt, in einem flachen Holztrog jener Art lag, wie ihn die Mörtelmischer beim Dombau benutzten. Ihr wurde klar, daß die Hämmer den Stoff walkten, und das beruhigte sie, wenngleich das Ganze immer noch erschreckend lebendig wirkte. Aber wie kam das eigentlich zustande? Die Stange mit den Hämmern verlief parallel zur Achse des Mühlrades, an der wiederum eine Holzbohle befestigt war, die sich mit der Achse drehte. Bei jeder Drehung traf die Holzbohle auf die Hammerstiele und drückte sie nach unten, so daß die Köpfe aufsahen. Dann gab die sich weiterdrehende Bohle die Stiele wieder frei, so daß die Hammerköpfe herabsausten und auf den Stoff im Trog einschlugen. Genau das hatte Jack an jenem Abend gemeint – eine Mühle, die Tuch walken konnte.

Aliena hörte ihn sagen: »Die Hammerköpfe müßten noch beschwert werden, damit sie fester aufschlagen.« Als sie sich umdrehte, stand er müde, aber triumphierend vor ihr. »Ich glaube, ich habe das Problem gelöst«, sagte er und grinste scheu.

»Ich bin ja so froh, daß dir nichts zugestoßen ist – wir haben uns schon Sorgen um dich gemacht!« sagte sie. Ohne groß nachzudenken, umarmte und küßte sie ihn; es war nur ein flüchtiger Kuß, aber sobald sich ihre Lippen wieder trennten, umfaßte er ihre Taille mit den Armen und hielt sie behutsam, aber fest an sich gedrückt. Sie sah ihm in die Augen. Sie konnte an nichts anderes mehr denken als daran, wie froh es sie machte, daß er unversehrt und am Leben war. Liebevoll drückte sie ihn. Plötzlich war sie sich ihrer eigenen Haut bewußt: Sie spürte ihr rauhes Leinenhemd und das weiche Fell in ihren Stiefeln, und ihr Busen prickelte bei der Berührung seiner Brust.

»Du hast dich um mich gesorgt?« fragte er verwundert.

»Natürlich! Ich habe kaum ein Auge zugemacht!«

Sie lächelte glücklich, während er fürchterlich feierlich dreinblickte und sie schließlich mit seiner Laune ansteckte, so daß auch sie sich merkwürdig bewegt fühlte. Sie konnte ihr Herz schlagen hören, und ihr Atem beschleunigte sich. Hinter ihr dröhnten die Hämmer im Chor und brachten die Mühle mit jedem vereinten Schlag zum Zittern; die Erschütterungen gingen ihr durch Mark und Bein.

»Kein Grund zur Beunruhigung«, sagte er. »Mit mir ist alles in Ordnung.«

»Ich bin ja so froh«, wiederholte sie flüsternd.

Sie sah, wie er die Augen schloß und ihr sein Gesicht zuneigte; dann fühlte sie seinen Mund auf ihren Lippen. Er küßte sie behutsam. Er hatte volle Lippen und einen weichen Bart. Sie schloß die Augen, um sich ganz auf das Gefühl zu konzentrieren. Sein Mund bewegte sich auf ihrem, und es schien nur normal, ihm ihre Lippen zu öffnen. Ihr Mund war mit einemmal überempfindsam geworden, nahm die leichteste Berührung wahr, die kleinste Bewegung. Seine Zungenspitze liebkoste die Innenseite ihrer Oberlippe. Sie wurde von einem solchen Glücksgefühl erfaßt, daß sie am liebsten geweint hätte. Sie schmiegte sich an ihn, ihre weichen Brüste gegen seinen harten Brustkorb, fühlte, wie sich seine Hüftknochen in ihren Bauch drückten. Das war nicht mehr bloße Erleichterung darüber, ihn in Sicherheit zu wissen, nicht mehr bloße Freude, daß sie ihn gefunden hatte. Ein ganz neues Gefühl bemächtigte sich ihrer. Seine körperliche Gegenwart erfüllte sie mit einer solchen Ekstase, daß ihr schwindelte. Sie hielt ihn umschlugen, wollte ihn stärker, deutlicher fühlen, ihm noch näher sein. Sie liebkoste seinen Rücken mit ihren Händen. Sie wünschte sich, seine Haut fühlen zu können, aber seine Kleidung war im Weg. Ehe sie sich's versah, hatte sie ihren Mund geöffnet und war mit ihrer Zunge zwischen seinen Lippen. Er stieß einen kehligen tierähnlichen Laut aus, einen gedämpften Seufzer des Entzückens.

Die Tür der Mühle wurde aufgestoßen, und Aliena riß sich von Jack los. Es überkam sie wie ein Schock; ihr war, als habe sie tief geschlafen und sei durch ein paar Ohrfeigen aufgeweckt worden. Ihr Verhalten erfüllte sie mit Entsetzen – sie hatten sich aufgeführt wie eine Hure und ein Besoffener, die sich im Wirtshaus abknutschten und aneinander rieben! Sie trat einen Schritt zurück und drehte sich um. Am liebsten wäre sie vor Scham im Erdboden versunken: Bei dem Eindringling handelte es sich auch noch um Alfred! Schlimmer hätte es kaum kommen können. Erst vor drei Monaten hatte Alfred um ihre Hand angehalten, und sie hatte ihm hochmütig eine Abfuhr erteilt. Und heute hatte er mitbekommen, daß sie sich wie eine läufige Hündin benahm. Das reinste Paradox. Sie wurde rot vor Scham. Alfred starrte sie an, und in seinem Ausdruck, der sie lebhaft an William Hamleigh erinnerte, mischten sich Lüsternheit und hämische Verachtung. Sie war wütend auf sich selbst, weil sie Alfred einen Grund geliefert hatte, auf sie herabzusehen, und auf Jack, weil er seinen Teil dazu beigetragen hatte.

Sie kehrte Alfred den Rücken zu und sah Jack an, der unter ihrem Blick zusammenschrak. Sie wußte, daß ihr die Wut ins Gesicht geschrieben stand, aber das war nun nicht mehr zu ändern. Der Ausdruck benommener Glückseligkeit in Jacks Gesicht verwandelte sich, spiegelte Verwirrung und Gekränktsein wider. Unter normalen Umständen hätte sie das zum Einlenken gebracht, aber sie war zu aufgebracht. Sie haßte ihn für das, was er ihr aufgezwungen hatte. Blitzschnell ohrfeigte sie ihn. Er rührte sich nicht vom Fleck, doch sein Blick sprach Bände. Seine Wange rötete sich. Unfähig, den Ausdruck seiner Augen noch länger zu ertragen, wandte sie sich ab.

Hier konnte sie nicht bleiben. Verfolgt vom unaufhörlichen Aufschlagen der Hämmer, das ihr in den Ohren dröhnte, rannte sie zur Tür. Alfred trat rasch beiseite, mit beinahe ängstlicher Miene. Sie schoß an ihm vorbei und trat durch die Tür. Tom Builder war mit einer kleinen Gruppe Bauarbeiter soeben vor dem Gebäude angekommen. Alle Welt hatte sich auf den Weg zur Mühle gemacht, um herauszufinden, was dort vor sich ging. Aliena hastete wortlos an ihnen vorüber. Sie zog die Blicke von zwei Neugierigen auf sich und schämte sich schier in Grund und Boden; aber das Gehämmer, das aus der Mühle drang, war viel interessanter. Der eiskalt berechnende Teil von Alienas Verstand erinnerte sie daran, daß Jack das Problem des Tuchwalkens gelöst hatte; aber wenn sie daran dachte, daß er sich ihretwegen die ganze Nacht um die Ohren geschlagen hatte, fühlte sie sich noch elender. Sie rannte am Stall vorbei, durch das Klostertor und die Straße entlang; ihre Stiefel rutschten, und sie glitt immer wieder im Schlamm aus, bis sie endlich zu Hause ankam.

Richard war da. Er saß am Küchentisch und machte sich über einen Laib Brot und eine Schale Bier her. »König Stephan ist auf dem Vormarsch«, sagte er. »Der Krieg ist wieder ausgebrochen. Ich brauche ein neues Pferd.«

In den nächsten drei Monaten wechselte Aliena kaum zwei zusammenhängende Sätze mit Jack.

Er litt Liebeskummer. Sie hatte ihn geküßt, als ob sie ihn liebte, daran gab es nichts zu deuten. Als sie die Mühle verließ, war er ganz sicher gewesen, daß sie sich bald wieder so küssen würden. Er lief in einer erotischen Trance herum und dachte nur noch: Aliena liebt mich! Aliena liebt mich! Sie hatte seinen Rücken gestreichelt, ihre Zunge in seinen Mund geschoben und sich mit ihren Brüsten an seinen Körper geschmiegt. Als sie ihm aus dem Weg ging, dachte er zunächst, es geschähe aus Scham. Nach einem solchen Kuß konnte sie doch nicht so tun, als liebe sie ihn nicht! Er wartete: Sie würde ihre Scheu bald ablegen. Der Zimmermann der Priorei half ihm beim Bau eines stärkeren und beständigeren Mechanismus für die alte Mühle, und Aliena ließ ihren Stoff dort walken.

Sie bedankte sich aufrichtig bei ihm, aber ihre Stimme war kühl, und sie sah ihm nicht in die Augen.

Als dieser Zustand länger als ein paar Tage dauerte und sich schließlich wochenlang so hinzog, mußte er sich eingestehen, daß etwas nicht stimmte. Die Ernüchterung überkam ihn wie eine Woge, und er hatte das Gefühl, in Bedauern zu ertrinken. Er stand vor einem Rätsel. In seinem Elend wünschte er sich, älter zu sein oder mehr Erfahrung mit Frauen zu haben; dann hätte er wenigstens gewußt, ob ihre Haltung normal oder launisch war, ob es sich um etwas Vorübergehendes oder um einen Dauerzustand handelte, ob er es einfach ignorieren oder sie zur Rede stellen sollte. Aus Unsicherheit und aus panischer Angst, etwas Falsches zu sagen und damit alles noch schlimmer zu machen, tat er nichts. Ihr abweisendes Verhalten begann an ihm zu nagen, bis er sich nur noch wertlos, dumm und ohnmächtig vorkam. Wie hatte er nur auf die Idee verfallen können, die begehrenswerteste und unerreichbarste Frau der ganzen Grafschaft fände ausgerechnet an ihm, einem Knaben, Gefallen? Eine Zeitlang mochte er sie ja mit seinen Geschichten und Witzen amüsiert haben, aber sobald er sie wie ein Mann geküßt hatte, war sie davongelaufen. Geradezu närrisch, welche Hoffnungen er gehegt hatte!

Ein, zwei Wochen lang machte er sich Vorhaltungen wegen seiner Dummheit, dann gewann der Zorn die Oberhand. Bei der Arbeit war er gereizt und nur mit Vorsicht zu genießen. Seiner Stiefschwester Martha gegenüber benahm er sich so scheußlich, daß sie ebenso gekränkt reagierte wie er selbst auf Aliena. Die Sonntagnachmittage verbrachte er bei Hahnenkämpfen und verwettete seinen Lohn. Seine ganze Leidenschaft widmete er seiner Arbeit. Derzeit meißelte er Konsolen, die aus der Mauer hervorragenden Kragstücke, die den Anschein erweckten, Bogen oder Säulen abzustützen, die nicht bis auf den Boden reichten. Diese Konsolen wurden häufig mit Blattmustern dekoriert, stellten mitunter aber auch einen Menschen dar, der den Bogen mit seinen Händen zu stützen oder auf dem Rücken zu tragen schien. Jack veränderte das gewohnte Bild nur geringfügig, doch am Ende hatte er eine beunruhigend verrenkte menschliche Gestalt mit schmerzverzerrten Zügen geschaffen, ersichtlich dazu verdammt, das unmenschlich schwere Gewicht des Steins bis in alle Ewigkeit zu tragen.

Jack wußte, daß seine Arbeit hervorragend war: Niemand sonst konnte ein Gesicht meißeln, dem man den Schmerz ansah. Tom schüttelte den Kopf darüber, unfähig zu entscheiden, ob er die Ausdrucksstärke bewundern oder den Bruch mit der Tradition mißbilligen sollte. Philip war restlos begeistert. Jack scherte sich nicht um ihre Meinung; in seinen Augen war jeder, der die Figur nicht mochte, mit Blindheit geschlagen.

Eines Montags in der Fastenzeit, in der alle gereizt waren, weil sie schon seit drei Wochen kein Fleisch mehr gegessen hatten, kam Alfred mit geradezu triumphierender Miene zur Arbeit. Tags zuvor war er in Shiring gewesen. Jack wußte nicht, was er dort getan hatte, doch entging ihm nicht, wie höchst erfreut sich Alfred gab.

Während der Vormittagspause, in der Enid Brewster mitten im Altarraum Bier zapfte und an die Bauleute verkaufte, hielt Alfred einen Penny hoch und rief: »He, Jack Tomson, hol mir ein Bier!«

Jetzt fängt er von meinem Vater an, dachte Jack und machte keine Anstalten, Alfreds Aufforderung Folge zu leisten.

Einer der Zimmerleute, ein älterer Mann namens Peter, sagte: »Du tätest besser dran, ihm zu gehorchen, Lehrbube.« Lehrlinge waren den Meistern zu Gehorsam verpflichtet.

»Ich bin nicht Toms Sohn«, erwiderte Jack. »Tom ist mein Stief-vater, das weiß Alfred ganz genau.«

»Tu trotzdem, was er sagt«, gab Peter bedächtig zurück.

Widerwillig nahm er Alfreds Geld und stellte sich an. »Mein Vater hieß Jack Shareburg«, sagte er mit lauter Stimme. »Wenn du mich von Jack Blacksmith unterscheiden willst, kannst du mich Jack Jackson nennen.«

Alfred sagte: »Jack Bastard trifft wohl eher zu.«

Jack richtete das Wort an die Allgemeinheit: »Habt ihr euch je Gedanken darüber gemacht, warum Alfred nie seine Stiefel zu-schnürt?« Alle starrten auf Alfreds Füße. Und wirklich, seine schwe-ren, schlammverkrusteten Stiefel, die am Schaft mit einer Kordel zuge-bunden werden konnten, standen offen. »Damit er schneller an seine Zehen herankommt, wenn er mal weiter als bis zehn zählen muß.« Die Handwerker grinsten, und die Lehrlinge glucksten vor Vergnügen. Jack gab Enid den Penny und bekam das Bier. Er trug es zu Alfred hinüber und reichte ihm den Krug mit einer kleinen, spöttischen Verbeugung. Alfred war verärgert, aber nur ein wenig; er hatte offen-sichtlich noch einen Trumpf im Ärmel. Jack trollte sich, um sein Bier im Kreis der Lehrlinge zu trinken, und hoffte, Alfred würde ihn in Ruhe lassen.

Doch es kam anders. Wenig später gesellte sich Alfred zu ihm und sagte: »Ich an deiner Stelle wäre nicht so erpicht darauf, Jack Share-burg zum Vater zu haben. Weißt du denn nicht, was er war?«

»Er war Spielmann«, erwiderte Jack. Er gab seiner Stimme einen zuversichtlichen Klang, obwohl er sich schon vor Alfreds Antwort fürchtete. »Du weißt bestimmt nicht, was ein Spielmann ist.«

»Er war ein Dieb«, sagte Alfred.

»Ach, halt's Maul, du Trottel.« Jack wandte sich ab und nippte an seinem Bier, brachte es aber kaum hinunter.

Alfred hatte das nicht einfach dahingesagt.

»Weißt du denn nicht, wie er gestorben ist?« Alfred ließ nicht locker.

Das ist es, dachte Jack; das hat er gestern in Shiring herausgefun-den; und deswegen grinst er so dämlich. Widerwillig drehte er sich um und sah Alfred an. »Nein, ich habe keine Ahnung, wie mein Vater gestorben ist, Alfred. Aber ich bin sicher, daß du es mir bestimmt gleich sagen wirst.«

»Aufgeknüpft haben sie ihn, wie es sich für einen lausigen Dieb gehört.«

Unwillkürlich stieß Jack einen Schreckensschrei aus. Instinktiv wußte er, daß Alfred die Wahrheit sprach – er war sich seiner Sache viel zu sicher, als daß er die Geschichte erfunden haben konnte. Und mit einemmal war Jack auch klar, daß dies die Erklärung für die Verschwiegenheit seiner Mutter war. Schon seit Jahren vermutete er insgeheim etwas Derartiges, obwohl er stets so getan hatte, als wäre alles in Ordnung, als wäre er kein Bastard, sondern hätte einen richtigen Vater mit einem ehrlichen Namen. Doch in Wirklichkeit war die Furcht, der Name seines Vaters sei mit Schande befleckt und er habe allen Grund, sich seiner zu schämen, nie von ihm gewichen. Ausgerechnet jetzt, da er sich durch Alienas Zurückweisung ohnehin schon niedrig und klein fühlte, kam die Wahrheit über seinen Vater zutage! Sie traf ihn mit voller Wucht.

Alfred stand grinsend da, sichtlich zufrieden mit sich und der Welt und hocherfreut über die Wirkung, die er mit seiner Enthüllung erzielt hatte. Sein Anblick machte Jack fuchsteufelswild. Schlimm genug für ihn, daß sein Vater gehängt worden war – daß Alfred sich auch noch darüber freute, schlug dem Faß den Boden aus! Ohne nachzudenken, schüttete Jack ihm sein Bier in die grinsende Visage.

Die anderen Lehrlinge, die die beiden Stiefbrüder beobachtet und an deren Wortwechsel Gefallen gefunden hatten, wichen eiligst zurück. Alfred wischte sich das Bier aus den Augen, brüllte auf vor Wut und schlug mit seiner riesigen Faust zu, ungemein behende für einen derart bulligen Mann. Die Faust landete mit solcher Wucht auf Jacks Wange, daß er nicht einmal Schmerz empfand – sie wurde sofort taub. Und da hieb ihm Alfred auch schon die andere Faust in die Magengrube. Der Schmerz war so heftig, daß Jack meinte, nie wieder atmen zu können. Er sackte in sich zusammen und stürzte zu Boden. Sofort versetzte Alfred ihm mit seinem schweren Stiefel einen Tritt gegen den Kopf, so daß er einen Augenblick nur noch Sterne sah.

Blind rollte er sich zur Seite und kam mühselig wieder auf die Beine. Doch Alfred gab sich noch nicht zufrieden. Kaum richtete Jack sich auf, wurde er erneut gepackt. Verzweifelt und voller Angst wand er sich: Alfred kannte kein Erbarmen – er würde ihn zu Brei schlagen, wenn er sich nicht befreien konnte. Aber im Moment war Alfreds Griff zu stark. Erst als er mit seiner massigen Faust zum Schlag ausholte, gelang es Jack, sich loszureißen.

Er stürzte davon und Alfred setzte ihm nach. Jack drückte sich an einem Kalkfaß vorbei und stieß es, um Alfred den Weg zu versperren, absichtlich um, so daß sich der Kalk auf den Boden ergoß. Alfred machte zwar einen Satz über das Faß, prallte dann aber gegen die Wasserbutte, die ebenfalls umstürzte und den verschütteten Kalk zum Schäumen und Zischen brachte. Einige Handwerker protestierten lauthals gegen eine derartige Vergeudung teuren Materials, doch Alfred stellte sich taub, und Jack hatte nichts anderes im Sinn, als seinem Gegner zu entkommen. Zusammengekrümmt vor Schmerzen und noch halb blind von Alfreds Tritt, rannte er um sein Leben.

Alfred, ihm hart auf den Fersen, stellte ihm von hinten ein Bein, so daß Jack Hals über Kopf hinschlug. Jetzt bin ich erledigt, dachte er und rollte sich zur Seite, Alfred macht mich kalt. Er hangelte nach einer Leiter, die an das hohe Baugerüst gelehnt war, doch Alfred warf ihn nieder. Jack fühlte sich wie eine Maus in der Falle, aber die Leiter rettete ihn: Während Alfred sich dahinterklemmte, sprang Jack vor und nahm mit einem Satz mehrere Sprossen auf einmal. Dann raste er in Windeseile die Leiter hoch, die gleich darauf auch schon unter Alfreds schweren Schritten erbebte.

Sonst pflegte er Alfred, da er viel schneller war, stets mit Leichtigkeit zu entkommen, doch jetzt war er noch zu benommen und atemlos. Keuchend erreichte er das Ende der Leiter und schwang sich auf das Gerüst. Er stolperte und krachte gegen die Mauer, die erst diesen Morgen hochgezogen worden war. Der Mörtel, noch feucht, hielt keine Belastung aus. Die Mauer schwankte, mehrere Steinquader lösten sich und fielen hinunter. Jack, der glaubte, sie rissen ihn mit in den Abgrund, stand schwankend da und sah zu, wie die großen Steine durch die Luft taumelten und achtzig Fuß tiefer auf den Pultdächern der Bauhütten aufschlugen. Er richtete sich auf; hoffentlich war niemand in den Bauhütten gewesen! Im gleichen Moment hatte Alfred die Leiter überwunden und kam auf dem schwankenden Gerüst auf ihn zu, keuchend und hochrot im Gesicht. Seine Augen funkelten vor Haß, und Jack hegte nicht den geringsten Zweifel daran, daß er in diesem Zustand zu allem fähig war. Wenn er mich in die Finger kriegt, dachte Jack, schmeißt er mich glatt vom Gerüst! Alfred kam immer näher, Jack wich immer weiter zurück. Er trat in etwas Weiches: ein Häufchen Mörtel. Der kam ihm gerade recht! Blitzschnell bückte er sich, nahm eine Handvoll auf und zielte haarscharf auf Alfreds Augen.

Alfred, der nichts mehr sah, blieb stehen und schüttelte den Kopf, um sich von dem Mörtel zu befreien. Endlich die Gelegenheit zur Flucht! Jack raste auf das andere Ende des Gerüsts zu: Dort wollte er hinabsteigen, dem Kloster entfliehen und sich für den Rest des Tages im Wald verbergen. Zu seinem namenlosen Entsetzen stand jedoch keine Leiter dort. Nicht einmal am Gerüst konnte er hinabklettern, denn es reichte nicht bis zum Boden – es wurde von Querbalken getragen, die aus eigens dafür vorgesehenen Aussparungen in der Wand herausragten. Er saß in der Falle.

Er drehte sich um: Alfred war den Mörtel los und kam schon wieder auf ihn zu.

Es gab nur noch einen einzigen Fluchtweg. Am Ende der Mauer, dort wo der Altarraum an das Querschiff gebaut werden sollte, war jede Steinschicht eine halbe Quaderlänge kürzer als die darunterliegende, so daß sich eine senkrechte, sehr schmale Treppe gebildet hatte, die von tollkühnen Arbeitern bisweilen als Aufstieg benutzt wurde. Jack hielt vor Angst den Atem an, als er auf die Mauer hinaustrat, und setzte dann rasch, aber vorsichtig einen Fuß vor den anderen, wobei er sich davor hütete, nach unten zu schauen – ein Ausrutscher, und er würde in die Tiefe stürzen. Er erreichte das Ende, hielt einen Moment inne und blickte hinab. Ihm schwindelte. Doch ein Blick zurück sagte ihm, daß Alfred immer noch hinter ihm her war. Er begann mit dem Abstieg.

Es war ihm ein Rätsel, wieso Alfred, der sich noch nie durch besonderen Mut ausgezeichnet hatte, plötzlich so viel Kühnheit an den Tag legte. Es war, als hätte der Haß ihn jeglichen Gespürs für die Gefahr beraubt, ja, auf ihrem schwindelerregenden Abstieg schloß er sogar allmählich auf. Als Jack begriff, daß Alfred ihn so gut wie eingeholt hatte, trennten ihn immer noch zwölf Fuß vom Boden. Verzweifelt sprang er auf das strohgedeckte Dach der Zimmermannshütte, tat von dort einen Satz auf den Boden, landete aber so unglücklich, daß er sich den Knöchel verstauchte und stürzte.

Schnell rappelte er sich wieder auf. Die Zeit, die er durch seinen Sturz verloren, hatte Alfred gut genutzt, war inzwischen ebenfalls unten angekommen und zur Hütte gelaufen. Nun wartete er lauernd ab, welche Richtung Jack, der mit dem Rücken zur Wand stand, einschlagen würde. Einen schrecklichen Moment lang konnte Jack sich nicht entscheiden; dann folgte er einer Eingebung, tat einen Schritt zur Seite und zog sich rückwärts in die Hütte zurück.

Niemand war zu sehen, denn die Handwerker hatten sich alle um Enids Faß versammelt. Auf den Werkbänken lagen die Hämmer, Sägen und Meißel der Zimmerleute sowie die Holzstücke, an denen sie gearbeitet hatten. In der Mitte der Bauhütte lag ein Teil einer neuen Schablone auf dem Boden, die später zum Bau eines Bogens dienen sollte; ganz hinten an der Rückwand, wo die Hütte an die Kirche stieß, loderte ein Feuer, in dem die Zimmerleute ihre Sägespäne und unbrauchbare Holzstücke verbrannten.

Hier gab es kein Entkommen mehr.

Jack drehte sich um und sah sich Alfred gegenüber. Er saß in der Falle. Einen kurzen Augenblick lang war er vor Schrecken wie gelähmt, doch dann überkam ihn die kalte Wut. Egal, ob ich krepiere, dachte er, Hauptsache Alfred muß vorher noch bluten! Er wartete nicht, bis Alfred zum Schlag ausholte, senkte sofort den Kopf und stürmte los. Vor lauter Wut machte er nicht einmal von seinen Fäusten Gebrauch – er stürzte sich einfach mit voller Wucht auf ihn.

Damit hatte Alfred nun überhaupt nicht gerechnet.

Jack prallte mit der Stirn gegen Alfreds Mund, und wiewohl der eine halbe Handbreit größer und erheblich schwerer war, warf ihn die Gewalt der Attacke zurück. Jack erlangte sein Gleichgewicht wieder und sah befriedigt, daß Alfreds Lippen bluteten.

Alfred war immer noch zu überrascht, um zu reagieren. Da fiel Jacks Blick auf einen großen hölzernen Vorschlaghammer, der an einer der Werkbänke lehnte. Kaum hatte sich Alfred von seinem Schreck erholt und wollte wieder auf Jack losgehen, hob dieser den Hammer und holte ungestüm damit aus. Alfred wich aus, der Schlag ging daneben, doch plötzlich hatte Jack die Oberhand. Ermutigt und in freudiger Erwartung des Klanges von massivem Holz auf Alfreds knirschenden Knochen setzte er nach. Und wieder ging sein Schlag daneben – traf allerdings den Pfosten, auf dem das Dach der Bauhütte ruhte.

Die Bauhütte war beileibe nicht das, was man eine solide Konstruktion nennen konnte. Sie war schließlich keine Wohnung, sondern sollte den Zimmerleuten nur ermöglichen, auch bei Regen weiterzuarbeiten. Jacks Schlag brachte prompt den Pfosten ins Wanken. Die Wände – nichts als aus Weiden geflochtene Rahmen – gaben ebenfalls nach, das strohgedeckte Dach hing bereits durch, und Alfred blickte besorgt in die Höhe. Jack hob den Hammer, und Alfred trat eiligst den Rückzug durch die Tür an. Jack holte erneut aus. Alfred sprang zur Seite, stolperte über einen niedrigen Holzstoß und plumpste auf den Hosenboden. Jack hob schon den Hammer, um ihm den entscheidenden Schlag zu versetzen – da wurde er mit aller Kraft an den Armen gepackt. Er wandte den Kopf und erblickte Prior Philip, dessen Miene nichts Gutes verhieß. Er entwand den Hammer Jacks Händen.

Hinter dem Prior stürzte das Dach der Bauhütte ein. Sowohl Jack als auch Philip drehten sich um. Das trockene Stroh fing sofort Feuer und stand gleich darauf auch schon lichterloh in Flammen.

Tom tauchte auf und wies auf drei Arbeiter, die ihm am nächsten standen. »Ihr drei holt die Wasserbutte, die neben der Schmiede steht.« Den nächsten dreien befahl er: »Peter, Rolf, Daniel, holt Eimer. Und die Lehrlinge schaufeln Erde auf die Flammen – und zwar alle! Dalli, dalli!«

Jack und Alfred waren vergessen, denn alles widmete sich der Löschung des Feuers. Jack trat beiseite, sah zu und fühlte sich benommen und hilflos. Alfred stand ein wenig abseits.

War ich wirklich drauf und dran, Alfred mit einem Hammer den Schädel einzuschlagen? dachte Jack ungläubig. Es kam ihm gänzlich unwirklich vor. Er befand sich noch immer im Zustand lähmenden Entsetzens, als die Flammen unter den vereinten Kräften von Wasser und Erde erstickten.

Prior Philip betrachtete das Durcheinander, vor Anstrengung noch keuchend. »Seht Euch das bloß an«, sagte er zu Tom. Er war wütend. »Eine zerstörte Bauhütte. Die Arbeit der Zimmerleute ruiniert. Ein Faß Kalk vergeudet und ein ganzes Stück frischen Mauerwerks zusammengebrochen.«

Jack begriff, daß Tom in der Klemme saß: Ihm oblag es, für Ruhe und Ordnung auf der Baustelle zu sorgen, und Philip schrieb ihm die Schuld für den Schaden zu. Und außerdem handelte es sich bei den Übeltätern auch noch um Toms Söhne.

Tom legte eine Hand auf Philips Arm und sagte besänftigend: »Die Zunft wird sich der Sache annehmen.«

Aber Philip ließ sich nicht so leicht besänftigen. »Ich werde mich der Sache annehmen«, stieß er hervor. »Ich bin der Prior, und Ihr arbeitet schließlich alle für mich.«

»Dann erlaubt den Steinmetzen wenigstens, sich zu beratschlagen, bevor Ihr irgendwelche Entscheidungen trefft«, erwiderte Tom ruhig und besonnen. »Es ist gut möglich, daß wir uns auf einen Vorschlag einigen, der Eure Zustimmung findet. Und wenn nicht, dann habt Ihr immer noch freie Hand und könnt nach eigenem Gutdünken verfahren.«

Philip widerstrebte es offensichtlich, sich die Initiative aus der Hand nehmen zu lassen, aber Tom hatte die Tradition auf seiner Seite: Steinmetzen richteten sich selbst. Nach kurzer Bedenkpause meinte Philip: »Na gut. Aber ganz unabhängig von Eurer Entscheidung werde ich nicht dulden, daß Eure beiden Söhne weiter gemeinsam an diesem Dom bauen. Einer von ihnen muß gehen.« Immer noch kochend vor Wut wandte er sich zum Gehen.

Tom warf Jack und Alfred einen finsteren Blick zu, drehte sich um und schritt auf die größte Bauhütte der Steinmetzen zu.

Jack, der Tom folgte, ging allmählich auf, daß er ganz schön in der Tinte saß. Interne Disziplinarmaßnahmen der Steinmetzen betrafen gewöhnlich Vergehen wie Trunkenheit bei der Arbeit und Diebstahl von Baumaterial, und die Strafe bestand gemeinhin aus einer Geldbuße. Handgreifliche Auseinandersetzungen unter Lehrlingen pflegten damit zu enden, daß die beiden Streithähne einen Tag lang in den Stock gelegt wurden – doch Alfred war kein Lehrling, und derartige Rangeleien verursachten höchst selten solch große Schäden. Die Zunft konnte ein Mitglied, das für weniger als den vereinbarten Mindestlohn arbeitete, ausschließen und eines, das mit der Frau eines anderen Steinmetzen Ehebruch beging, bestrafen; ein solcher Fall war Jack allerdings noch nie zu Ohren gekommen. Über unbotmäßige Lehrlinge konnte gar die Prügelstrafe verhängt werden, doch wiewohl damit gedroht wurde, hatte Jack sie noch nie angewendet gesehen.

Die Meistersteinmetzen drängten sich in der Bauhütte, saßen auf den Werkbänken oder lehnten sich an die Rückwand. Sobald alle versammelt waren, ergriff Tom das Wort. »Unser Bauherr ist erbost, und das mit vollem Recht. Dieser Vorfall hat erheblichen Schaden angerichtet. Schlimmer noch, er hat uns Steinmetzen in Verruf gebracht. Wir dürfen mit den Schuldigen keine Milde walten lassen. Nur so können wir unseren guten Ruf als stolze und disziplinierte Handwerker, als Meister unserer selbst und unseres Faches, wiedergewinnen.«

»Gut gesagt!« rief Jack Blacksmith, und allgemein zustimmendes Gemurmel erhob sich.

»Ich habe nur das Ende des Streits mitbekommen«, fuhr Tom fort. »Hat einer von Euch gesehen, wie er begann?«

»Alfred hat sich auf den Burschen gestürzt«, sagte Peter Carpenter, der Mann, der Jack empfohlen hatte, Alfred zu gehorchen und ihm sein Bier zu holen.

Ein junger Steinmetz namens Dan, der für Alfred arbeitete, sagte: »Jack hat vorher Alfred sein Bier ins Gesicht geschüttet.«

»Nachdem er provoziert wurde«, warf Peter ein. »Alfred hat Jacks leiblichen Vater beleidigt.«

Tom sah Alfred an. »Stimmt das?«

»Ich habe nur gesagt, daß sein Vater ein Dieb war«, erwiderte Alfred. »Und das stimmt. Dafür ist er in Shiring gehängt worden. Das hat Vogt Eustace mir gestern erzählt.«

Jack Blacksmith meinte: »Wo kommen wir denn hin, wenn ein Handwerksmeister den Mund halten muß, nur weil einem Lehrling nicht paßt, was er sagt?«

Er erntete beifälliges Gemurmel. Jack erkannte mit Bangen, daß er so oder so nicht mit einem blauen Auge davonkommen würde. Vielleicht bin ich dazu verdammt, ein Verbrecher wie mein Vater zu werden, dachte er; vielleicht lande ich auch noch am Galgen.

Peter Carpenter, der sich zu Jacks Verteidiger aufschwang, ergriff erneut das Wort. »Und ich behaupte trotzdem, daß es ein Unterschied ist, ob der Meister den Lehrling absichtlich in Rage bringt oder nicht.«

»Auf jeden Fall muß der Lehrling bestraft werden«, beharrte Jack Blacksmith.

»Das bestreite ich ja gar nicht«, gab Peter zurück. »Allerdings sollte der Meister ebenfalls bestraft werden. Handwerksmeister sind verpflichtet, ihre mit den Jahren erworbene Weisheit dafür einzusetzen, daß Frieden und Einigkeit auf der Baustelle herrschen. Ein Meister, der selber einen Streit vom Zaun bricht, wird diesem Anspruch nicht gerecht.«

Zunächst hatte es den Anschein, als träfe Peter auf Zustimmung, dann meldete sich Dan, der auf Alfreds Seite stand, wieder zu Wort: »Es ist mir zu gefährlich, Nachsehen mit einem Lehrling zu haben, bloß weil der Meister ihn mal hart angefaßt hat. Alle Lehrlinge glauben, ihre Meister wären zu hart. Wenn Ihr so argumentiert, traut sich am Ende kein Meister mehr, seinem Lehrling die Meinung zu sagen, weil er Angst haben muß, daß der ihn wegen Unhöflichkeit schlägt.«

Jack erkannte voller Abscheu, wie beifällig diese Ansprache aufgenommen wurde – ein Beweis dafür, daß die Meister der Zunft nichts anderes im Sinn hatten, als ihre Autorität mit allen Mitteln zu hüten und zu stärken, ganz egal, wie es um Recht und Unrecht in seinem Fall bestellt war. Er fragte sich, welche Strafe sie ihm auferlegen würden. Eine Geldbuße konnte er nicht bezahlen. Hoffentlich legten sie ihn nicht in den Stock – was sollte Aliena von ihm denken? Noch schlimmer wäre, wenn sie ihn auspeitschten. Wahrscheinlich war, daß er auf jeden, der das versuchte, mit dem Messer losginge.

»Wir dürfen nicht vergessen«, sagte Tom, »daß unser Brotherr in dieser Sache eindeutig Stellung bezogen hat. Er sagte mir, er werde Jack und Alfred nicht länger gemeinsam auf dieser Baustelle dulden. Einer von ihnen muß also gehen.«

»Könnte man ihm das ausreden?« wollte Peter wissen.

Tom blickte nachdenklich drein, aber nach kurzer Bedenkpause meinte er: »Nein.«

Jack war entsetzt. Er hatte Prior Philips Ultimatum nicht ernstgenommen. Doch Tom tat es.

Dan meinte: »Wenn einer von beiden gehen muß, dann gibt es wohl keine Zweifel daran, wer das ist.« Dan arbeitete als Steinmetz für Alfred und unterstand nicht direkt der Priorei; wenn Alfred ging, würde er sicher ebenfalls gehen müssen.

Tom dachte wiederum nach und sagte schließlich: »Nein, natürlich nicht.« Er sah Jack an. »Jack muß gehen.«

Jack verstand allmählich, daß er die Folgen des Streits gefährlich unterschätzt hatte. Dennoch konnte er kaum glauben, daß sie ihn wirklich ausstoßen würden. Was sollte aus ihm werden, wenn er nicht mehr am Dom zu Kingsbridge bauen konnte? Seit Aliena sich in ihrem Schneckenhaus verkrochen hatte, war die Kathedrale sein ein und alles. Wie konnte er da fortgehen?

»Vielleicht läßt die Priorei sich ja auf einen Kompromiß ein. Wir könnten Jack einen Monat lang suspendieren«, schlug Peter Carpenter vor.

O ja, bitte! dachte Jack.

»Das reicht nicht«, gab Tom zurück. »Wir müssen schon den Eindruck erwecken, rigoros durchzugreifen. Prior Philip wird sich nicht mit weniger zufriedengeben.«

»Dann muß es wohl so sein«, meinte Peter seufzend. »Diese Kathedrale verliert den begabtesten jungen Steinmetzen, den die meisten von uns je gesehen haben, und warum? Weil Alfred sein dummes Maul nicht halten kann.« Mehrere Steinmetzen bekundeten Zustimmung, und Peter fuhr ermutigt fort: »Ich habe großen Respekt vor Euch, Tom Builder, mehr als vor jedem anderen Baumeister, für den ich je gearbeitet habe. Aber es muß einmal gesagt werden, daß Ihr einfach blind seid, wenn es um die Sturheit Eures Sohnes Alfred geht.«

»Keine persönlichen Angriffe, bitte«, sagte Tom. »Wir wollen doch bei den Tatsachen bleiben.«

»Schon gut«, gab Peter nach. »Ich meine, Alfred muß ebenfalls bestraft werden.«

»Ganz meine Meinung«, erwiderte Tom zur allgemeinen Überraschung. Die Bemerkung über seine Blindheit hat ihn getroffen, dachte Jack.

»Wieso das denn?« fragte Alfred verstimmt. »Bloß weil ich einen Lehrling verdroschen habe?«

»Er ist nicht dein Lehrling, sondern meiner«, sagte Tom. »Und du hast ihn nicht nur verdroschen. Du hast ihn über die ganze Baustelle gejagt. Hättest du ihn laufenlassen, wäre der Kalk nicht verschüttet worden, das Mauerwerk stünde noch und die Bauhütte der Zimmerleute wäre nicht niedergebrannt; und du hättest dein Hühnchen mit ihm rupfen können, sobald er wieder aufgetaucht wäre. Für das, was du getan hast, gibt es absolut keine Rechtfertigung.«

Die Steinmetzen pflichteten ihm bei.

Dan, der sich anscheinend zum Sprecher für Alfreds Steinmetze aufgeschwungen hatte, sagte: »Ich hoffe nur, daß Ihr nicht vorhabt, Alfred aus der Bauhütte auszuschließen. Ich zumindest würde mich dagegen energisch zur Wehr setzen.«

»Nein«, antwortete Tom. »Schlimm genug, daß wir einen begabten Lehrling einbüßen. Ich will nicht auch noch einen gestandenen Steinmetzen verlieren, der einer zuverlässigen Bautruppe vorsteht. Alfred muß bleiben – aber ich meine, er sollte eine Geldstrafe bekommen.«

Alfreds Männer wirkten erleichtert.

»Eine deftige Geldstrafe«, meinte Peter.

»Einen Wochenlohn«, schlug Dan vor.

»Einen Monatslohn«, gab Tom zurück. »Ich bezweifle, daß Prior Philip sich mit weniger zufriedengibt.«

»Aye«, bekundeten mehrere Männer.

»Sind wir uns also darüber einig, Brüder?« fragte Tom, indem er die hergebrachte Redewendung benutzte.

»Aye«, erscholl es von allen Seiten.

»Dann will ich dem Prior unsere Entscheidung mitteilen. Und Ihr begebt Euch besser wieder an die Arbeit.«

Jack sah mißmutig zu, wie die Steinmetzen einer nach dem anderen die Bauhütte verließen. Alfred warf ihm einen selbstgefällig triumphierenden Blick zu. Tom wartete, bis sie allein waren, und sagte dann zu Jack: »Ich habe für dich getan, was ich konnte – ich hoffe nur, deine Mutter begreift das.«

»Du hast nie auch nur einen kleinen Finger für mich gerührt!« brach es aus Jack heraus. »Du konntest mich nicht ernähren oder kleiden, noch mir ein Dach über dem Kopf verschaffen! Bevor du kamst, waren wir glücklich, danach sind wir verhungert!«

»Aber schließlich – «

»Du beschützt mich nicht einmal vor diesem hohlköpfigen Grobian, den du deinen Sohn nennst!«

»Ich habe versucht – «

»Und wenn ich die alte Kathedrale nicht niedergebrannt hätte, stündest du sogar ohne Arbeit da!«

»Was sagst du da?«

»Jawohl, ich habe die alte Kathedrale niedergebrannt.«

Tom erbleichte. »Das war ein Blitzschlag –«

»Geblitzt hat es überhaupt nicht. Es war eine klare Nacht. Und außerdem hat niemand in der Kirche Feuer gemacht. Ich habe das Dach in Brand gesteckt.«

»Aber warum denn?«

»Damit du Arbeit kriegst. Sonst wäre meine Mutter noch im Wald gestorben.«

»Das wäre sie nicht – «

»Aber deine erste Frau, die ist doch im Wald gestorben, oder nicht?«

Tom wurde leichenblaß. Plötzlich schien er um Jahre gealtert, und Jack begriff, daß er Tom zutiefst getroffen hatte. Das Wortgefecht hatte er zwar gewonnen, aber wahrscheinlich einen Freund verloren. Er fühlte sich schal und bedrückt.

»Mach, daß du rauskommst«, flüsterte Tom.

Jack ging.

Den Tränen nahe, entfernte er sich von den hochragenden Mauern der Kathedrale. Sein Leben war binnen weniger Momente zerstört worden. Unfaßbar, daß er dieser Kirche für immer den Rücken kehren sollte! An der Klosterpforte drehte er sich noch einmal um und sah zurück, dachte daran, was er alles vorgehabt hatte: ein großes Portal allein zu meißeln, Tom zu überreden, den Lichtgaden mit steinernen Engeln auszustatten und ihm seinen neuartigen Entwurf für Blendarkaden im Querschiff zu zeigen, über den er noch nie gesprochen hatte. Nun jedoch würde er nichts davon je in die Tat umsetzen können. Es war so ungerecht! Tränen schossen ihm in die Augen. Auf dem Heimweg nahm er seine Umgebung nur verschwommen wahr. Seine Mutter saß mit Martha am Küchentisch und brachte ihr mit einem scharfkantigen Stein und einer Schiefertafel das Schreiben bei. Seine Ankunft überraschte sie beide. Martha sagte: »Es kann doch unmöglich schon Mittag sein.«

Ellen sah Jack an, daß etwas nicht stimmte, und fragte besorgt:

»Was ist passiert?«

»Ich habe mich mit Alfred gestritten und bin von der Baustelle verbannt worden«, erwiderte er finster.

»Und Alfred nicht?« rief Martha aus.

Jack schüttelte den Kopf.

»Das ist gemein!« rief Martha aus.

»Und worüber habt ihr euch diesmal gestritten?« fragte Mutter müde.

Jack sagte: »Ist mein Vater in Shiring gehängt worden, weil er gestohlen hat?«

Martha schnappte nach Luft.

Mutter blickte traurig drein. »Ein Dieb war er nicht«, sagte sie. »Aber es stimmt, er wurde in Shiring gehängt.«

Jack hatte die rätselhaften Bemerkungen über seinen Vater satt und fragte erbost: »Warum sagst du mir nie die Wahrheit, wenn es um ihn geht?«

»Weil es mich unsäglich traurig macht!« brach es aus Ellen heraus, und zu Jacks Entsetzen begann sie zu weinen.

Er hatte sie noch nie weinen sehen. Normalerweise war sie die Stärke in Person. Er stand selbst kurz vor dem Zusammenbruch! Er schluckte den Kloß in seinem Hals und fragte beharrlich weiter: »Wenn er kein Dieb war, warum wurde er dann gehängt?«

»Ich weiß es nicht!« schrie Mutter. »Ich habe es nie gewußt. Und er selbst auch nicht. Sie haben behauptet, er hätte einen mit Edelsteinen verzierten Kelch gestohlen.«

»Wo?«

»Hier – in der Priorei zu Kingsbridge.«

»Kingsbridge! Hat Prior Philip ihn bezichtigt?«

»Nein, nein, das war lange vor Philips Zeit.« Sie sah Jack unter Tränen an. »Frag mich nicht, wer ihn beschuldigt hat und warum. Verfang dich nicht in einer solchen Falle. Sonst vertust du noch den Rest deines Lebens damit, ein Unrecht wiedergutzumachen, das schon geschah, bevor du geboren bist. Ich habe dich nicht aufgezogen, damit du Rache übst. Mach das bitte nicht zu deinem Lebensinhalt.«

Jack schwor sich, trotz ihrer Mahnung beizeiten mehr darüber in Erfahrung zu bringen; aber im Augenblick lag ihm nichts mehr am Herzen, als daß sie zu weinen aufhörte. Er setzte sich zu ihr auf die Bank und legte einen Arm um sie. »Nun, es sieht so aus, als würde die Kathedrale nun doch nicht mein Lebensinhalt.«

»Was wirst du jetzt tun?« wollte Martha wissen.

»Ich weiß nicht. In Kingsbridge kann ich schlecht bleiben, oder?«

Martha war bestürzt. »Aber warum denn?«

»Alfred hat versucht, mich umzubringen, und Tom hat mich aus der Bauhütte verbannt. Mit den beiden will ich nicht zusammenleben.

Und außerdem bin ich ein erwachsener Mann und sollte meine Mutter eigentlich verlassen.«

»Aber was wirst du tun?«

Jack zuckte die Achseln. »Außer dem Bauen habe ich nichts gelernt.«

»Du könntest an einer anderen Kirche arbeiten.«

»Mag schon sein, daß ich einen anderen Dom ebenso zu lieben lerne wie diesen«, sagte er verzagt. Und fügte in Gedanken hinzu: Aber nie werde ich eine andere Frau ebenso lieben, wie ich Aliena liebe.

Mutter sagte: »Wie konnte Tom dir nur so etwas antun?«

Jack seufzte. »Ich glaube nicht, daß es seine Absicht war. Prior Philip hat gesagt, daß er mich und Alfred nicht zusammen auf der Baustelle dulden wird.«

»Dieser verdammte Mönch steckt also dahinter!« sagte Mutter wütend. »Ich schwöre –«

»Er war über den Schaden, den wir angerichtet haben, sehr aufgebracht.«

»Ich möchte nur wissen, ob man ihn zur Vernunft bringen könnte.«

»Wie meinst du das?«

»Gott soll doch angeblich barmherzig sein – vielleicht trifft das auch auf Mönche zu.«

»Meinst du etwa, daß ich ihn anflehen sollte?« fragte Jack, den die Wendung in der Denkweise seiner Mutter überraschte.

»Ich dachte eher daran, selbst mit ihm zu reden«, erwiderte sie.

»Du?« Das sah ihr ganz und gar nicht ähnlich. Jack konnte es kaum fassen. Mutter mußte schon arg mitgenommen sein, um sich Philips Gnade auszuliefern.

»Was hältst du davon?« fragte sie ihn.

Jack erinnerte sich, daß Philip, soweit Tom es beurteilen konnte, nicht bereit gewesen war, Gnade vor Recht ergehen zu lassen. Doch Tom hatte ohnehin nur ein Ziel im Auge gehabt: daß die Zunft nicht lange fackelte, sondern schnell reinen Tisch machte. Und nachdem Tom Philip einmal versprochen hatte, sie würde kurzen Prozeß machen, konnte er im nachhinein schlecht um Nachsicht bitten. Mutters Fall lag anders, und Jack wurde etwas leichter ums Herz. Vielleicht würde er doch nicht gehen müssen. Vielleicht konnte er doch noch in Kingsbridge bleiben, in der Nähe der Kathedrale – und Alienas. Er hatte die Hoffnung aufgegeben, daß sie seine Liebe je erwidern würde; dennoch konnte er sich nicht mit dem Gedanken befreunden, sie auf Nimmerwiedersehen zu verlassen.

»Na schön«, meinte er. »Dann laß uns gehen und Prior Philip um Gnade bitten. Schließlich haben wir außer unserem Stolz nichts zu verlieren.«

Mutter hüllte sich in ihren Umhang, und die beiden verließen gemeinsam das Haus; Martha blieb bekümmert allein am Tisch zurück.

Es kam nicht oft vor, daß Jack Seite an Seite mit seiner Mutter ging; erst jetzt fiel ihm auf, wie klein sie war. Er kam sich wie ein Riese neben ihr vor. Plötzlich flog sein Herz ihr zu. Stets war sie bereit, wie eine Wildkatze für ihn zu kämpfen. Er legte seinen Arm um sie und drückte sie an sich. Sie lächelte ihn an, als wüßte sie, was in ihm vorging.

Sie betraten das Klostergelände und begaben sich zum Haus des Priors. Mutter klopfte und trat ein. Tom und Philip saßen beisammen, und Jack entnahm ihren Gesichtern, daß Tom sein Geständnis über den Kirchenbrand *nicht* hinterbracht hatte. Was für eine Erleichterung! Nun würde er wahrscheinlich nie mehr den Mut dazu finden. Jacks Geheimnis war bei ihm sicher aufgehoben.

Tom sah besorgt, ja fast ein wenig ängstlich drein, als er Mutter erblickte. Jack hatte noch seine Worte im Ohr: *Ich habe für dich getan, was ich konnte – ich hoffe nur, deine Mutter begreift das.* Tom hatte den letzten Streit zwischen Jack und Alfred bestimmt nie vergessen, denn Mutter hatte ihn daraufhin verlassen. Tom hatte Angst vor einer Wiederholung.

Jack fiel auf, daß der Zorn aus Philips Gesicht gewichen war. Ob die Entscheidung der Zunft ihn besänftigt hatte? Hatte er womöglich Gewissensbisse wegen der Härte seines Urteils?

Mutter eröffnete das Gespräch. »Ich bin gekommen, Euch um Nachsicht zu bitten, Prior Philip.«

Toms Gesicht spiegelte Erleichterung wider.

»Ich höre«, sagte Philip.

Mutter sagte: »Ihr tragt Euch mit der Absicht, meinen Sohn fortzujagen und ihn von allem zu trennen, was ihm lieb und teuer ist – seiner Heimat, seiner Familie und seiner Arbeit.«

Und der Frau, die er anbetet, dachte Jack bei sich.

»Wirklich?« erwiderte Philip. »Ich dachte, er sei lediglich entlassen worden.«

»Er hat außer der Baukunst nichts gelernt, und in Kingsbridge gibt es keine andere Arbeit für ihn. Außerdem hat er sich dieser riesigen Kirche mit Leib und Seele verschrieben. Es wird ihn stets dorthin ziehen, wo jemand eine Kathedrale baut. Er würde sogar bis nach Jerusalem ziehen, wenn er dort nur Steine findet, aus denen er Engel und Teufel herausmeißeln kann.«

Woher weiß sie das nur alles? fragte sich Jack. Er hatte selbst kaum je darüber nachgedacht – aber Mutter hatte vollkommen recht. »Ich werde ihn vielleicht nie wiedersehen«, fügte sie hinzu, und ihre Stimme bebte ein wenig. Staunend machte er sich klar, wie groß ihre Liebe zu ihm sein mußte: Um ihrer selbst willen hätte sie sich niemals so hingebungsvoll eingesetzt!

Philip sah sie mitfühlend an, doch es war Tom, der ihr antwortete. »Wir können einfach nicht zulassen, daß Jack und Alfred auf derselben Baustelle arbeiten«, sagte er störrisch. »Sonst kriegen sie sich nur wieder in die Haare, das weißt du ganz genau.«

»Dann kann Alfred ja gehen«, sagte Mutter.

Toms Miene betrübte sich. »Alfred ist *mein* Sohn.«

»Aber er ist zwanzig Jahre alt und ein hundsgemeiner Kerl!« Mutters Stimme klang zwar fest, aber ihr Gesicht war tränennaß. »Die Kathedrale liegt ihm keinen Deut mehr am Herzen als mir – er wäre vollauf zufrieden, wenn er in Winchester oder Shiring Häuser für Metzger und Bäcker bauen könnte.«

»Die Hütte kann aber nicht Alfred ausschließen und Jack behalten«, sagte Tom. »Überdies ist die Entscheidung bereits gefallen.«

»Aber die Entscheidung ist falsch!«

Philip mischte sich ein. »Vielleicht gibt es noch eine andere Möglichkeit.«

Sie blickten ihn gespannt an.

»In diesem Fall könnte Jack nicht nur in Kingsbridge bleiben, sondern sich auch der Kathedrale widmen, ohne daß Alfred ihm schaden könnte.«

Was das wohl sein mag? dachte Jack. Es klingt zu schön, um wahr zu sein!

»Ich brauche jemanden, der mir bei der Arbeit zur Hand geht«, fuhr Philip fort. »Ich vertue zuviel Zeit mit den baulichen Einzelheiten, über die entschieden werden muß. Ich brauche eine Art Assistenten, der den Bauaufseher für mich spielt, die meisten Entscheidungen selbst trifft und nur bei wichtigen Dingen meinen Rat einholt. Darüber hinaus müßte er sich um die Finanzen und die Rohmaterialien kümmern, Lieferanten und Fuhrleute auszahlen und natürlich auch die Löhne. Jack kann nicht nur lesen und schreiben, sondern ist obendrein der schnellste Rechner, der mir je untergekommen ist – «

»Und er ist mit allen Aspekten der Baukunst bestens vertraut«, warf Tom ein. »Dafür habe ich gesorgt.«

Jack wurde von Schwindel erfaßt: Nun durfte er doch bleiben! Sogar als Bauaufseher! Als solcher konnte er zwar keinen Stein mehr behauen, doch er hätte die Leitung des gesamten Kirchenbaus unter sich, in Philips Namen! Ein wahrhaft staunenswerter Vorschlag! Damit würde er mit Tom auf eine Stufe gestellt. Aber er wußte, daß er das Zeug dazu hatte. Und Tom wußte das ebenfalls.

Einen Haken hatte die Sache allerdings. Jack meldete sich zu Wort. »Ich kann nicht länger mit Alfred unter einem Dach leben.«

»Es ist ohnehin höchste Zeit, daß Alfred sich ein eigenes Heim schafft«, meinte Ellen. »Vielleicht bringt ihn das endlich dazu, daß er sich ernsthafter um eine Frau bemüht.«

»Dir fallen immer wieder neue Gründe ein, weshalb wir Alfred loswerden sollten«, sagte Tom ärgerlich. »Ich werde doch nicht meinen eigenen Sohn aus dem Haus werfen!«

»Ihr mißversteht mich beide«, sagte Philip. »Ihr habt meinen Vorschlag nicht ganz begriffen. Jack würde nicht bei Euch wohnen.«

Er hielt inne. Jack erriet, was kommen würde, und das war der letzte und schwerste Schlag dieses Tages.

Philip sagte: »Jack müßte natürlich hier in der Priorei leben.« Stirnrunzelnd sah er sie an, als überstiege es sein Fassungsvermögen, daß sie ihn immer noch nicht verstanden hatten.

Jack hatte ihn sehr gut verstanden. Er wußte noch genau, was seine Mutter beim Johannisfest im vergangenen Jahr gesagt hatte: *Dieser mit allen Wassern gewaschene Prior schafft es irgendwie immer, schließlich doch noch seinen Kopf durchzusetzen.* Sie hatte recht behalten. Philip wiederholte sein Angebot von damals, wenn auch unter anderen Vorzeichen. Jack stand vor einer schwierigen Wahl. Er konnte Kingsbridge verlassen und allem, was ihm lieb und teuer war, den Rücken kehren. Oder er konnte bleiben und seine Freiheit verlieren.

»Ich kann natürlich keinen Laien als Bauaufseher haben«, fügte Philip hinzu, und es klang, als wäre es die größte Selbstverständlichkeit der Welt. »Jack wird ins Kloster eintreten müssen.«

In der Nacht vor der ersten Wollmesse zu Kingsbridge blieb Prior Philip wie gewöhnlich nach den Vigilien auf, doch statt sich zum Lesen und Meditieren in sein Haus zurückzuziehen, begab er sich auf einen Rundgang durch das Kloster. Es war eine warme, sternenklare Sommernacht, und der Mond schien hell genug, so daß er keine Laterne brauchte.

Mit Ausnahme der geweihten, unmittelbar zum Kloster gehörigen Gebäude und des Kreuzgangs stand der Rest des Geländes für die Messe offen. Zur Reinhaltung war in jeder der vier Ecken eine tiefe Latrine ausgehoben worden, die man zudem, aus Rücksicht auf die in dieser Hinsicht empfindlichen Mönche, mit einem Sichtschutz umgeben hatte. Außerdem waren buchstäblich Hunderte von Marktständen errichtet worden. Die bescheidensten bestanden lediglich aus ungehobelten, auf Böcken ruhenden Ladentischen, doch die meisten waren mit etwas mehr Mühe gestaltet worden, besaßen ein Schild mit dem Namen des Standbesitzers, ein Bild mit dem Warenangebot, einen separaten Tisch zum Abwiegen und einen verschließbaren Schrank oder kleinen Schuppen für die Waren. Etliche Buden waren sogar mit Zelten versehen, sei es, um sich vor Regen zu schützen, sei es, um Geschäfte unter vier Augen abzuwickeln zu können. Die reichsten Stände allerdings entsprachen eher kleinen Häusern, ausgestattet mit großen Lagern sowie mehreren Ladentischen und Sitzecken, wo die Händler ihre wichtigsten Kunden standesgemäß empfangen und bewirten konnten. Zu Philips Überraschung war der erste, im Dienst eines Händlers stehende Zimmermann schon eine geschlagene Woche vor der Messe bei ihm aufgekreuzt und hatte sich nach dem genauen Standort des Verkaufsstands erkundigt; danach hatte er vier Tage zum Aufbau gebraucht, zwei weitere waren mit der Füllung des Lagers vergangen.

Ursprünglich hatte Philip die Anordnung der Stände so geplant, daß sie, ähnlich wie beim Wochenmarkt, zwei breite Gänge am Westende des Klostergeländes bildeten; er merkte allerdings schnell, daß der Platz nicht ausreichen würde. Nun reihten sich die Buden auch noch entlang der Kirchennordwand und in östlichem Bogen bis zu Philips Haus, ja sogar in der unfertigen Kirche waren zwischen den Pfeilern der Seitenschiffe noch welche aufgestellt. Ihre Besitzer waren nicht alle Wollhändler; auf einer solchen Messe wurde, von grobem Brot bis hin zu Rubinen, einfach alles feilgeboten.

Philip ging durch die vom Mondlicht beschienenen Reihen. Längst war alles fertig, denn heute durften keine Stände mehr errichtet werden. Die meisten waren auch schon mit Ware bestückt, und die Priorei hatte bis jetzt mehr als zehn Pfund an Zöllen und Gebühren eingenommen. Am Messetag selbst durften nur noch frisch zubereitete Nahrungsmittel – Brot, heiße Pasteten und Backäpfel – in die Stadt gebracht werden; selbst die Bierfässer waren am Vortag angeliefert worden.

Halbgeschlossene Augen verfolgten Philip auf seinem Rundgang, schlaftrunkene Grunzer grüßten ihn. Keiner der Standbesitzer ließ seine wertvollen Waren unbewacht, und so schliefen die meisten in ihren Buden, während die reicheren Händler ihre Dienstboten zum Wachdienst abkommandiert hatten.

Philip wußte nicht genau, wieviel die Messe ihm einbringen würde, aber an ihrem Erfolg konnte es kaum einen Zweifel geben, und er machte sich schon Hoffnungen auf erheblich mehr als die geschätzten fünfundzwanzig Pfund. In den vergangenen Monaten hatte er manches Mal bezweifelt, daß die Messe überhaupt stattfinden konnte. Der Krieg schleppte sich dahin, ohne daß Stephan oder Mathilde eindeutig die Oberhand gewannen, doch wenigstens war das Marktrecht nicht widerrufen worden. William Hamleigh hatte etliche Versuche zur Verhinderung der Messe unternommen und dem Vogt befohlen, sie zu unterbinden; der hatte sich an die rivalisierenden Monarchen gewandt, aber von keinem eine Antwort erhalten. William hatte seinen Pächtern untersagt, in Kingsbridge Wolle feilzubieten, doch da die meisten, statt ihre Vliese selbst zu vermarkten, ohnehin an Großhändler verkauften, hatte dieses Verbot vor allem dazu geführt, daß Aliena noch mehr Geschäfte tätigen konnte. Zu guter Letzt hatte er angekündigt, die Zölle und Pachtgebühren für die Messe in Shiring auf den gleichen Stand wie die von Philip erhobenen Abgaben zu senken; aber dieser Schritt kam zu spät, um noch ins Gewicht zu fallen, hatten doch die einflußreichen Käufer und Verkäufer längst ihre Dispositionen getroffen.

Nun, da sich der Himmel am östlichen Horizont merklich aufhellte und den Anbruch des großen Tages ankündigte, konnte William nichts mehr ausrichten: Die Händler mit ihren Waren warteten schon auf die ersten Kunden. Philip hoffte, William werde am Ende einsehen, daß die Wollmesse in Kingsbridge der Messe zu Shiring weit weniger Schaden zufügte, als er fürchtete. Der Wollhandel nahm unweigerlich von Jahr zu Jahr zu, so daß genug für zwei Märkte vorhanden war.

Er hatte seinen Rundgang fast beendet und blieb am südwestlichen Ende des Klostergeländes, wo sich die Mühlen und der Fischteich befanden, eine Zeitlang stehen und betrachtete das Wasser, das an den beiden stillstehenden Mühlen vorbeirauschte. Die eine diente nunmehr ausschließlich dem Walken von Tuchen und trug eine schöne Stange Geld ein. Das hatten sie Jack zu verdanken. Der Junge war unglaublich erfinderisch und würde sich mit der Zeit als enormer Gewinn für die Priorei erweisen. Er schien sich gut in sein Novizendasein eingelebt zu haben, obwohl er die Gebetszeiten noch immer als Störung beim Dombau empfand statt umgekehrt. Aber das würde er schon noch lernen; das klösterliche Leben übte einen läuternden Einfluß aus. Philip glaubte, daß Gott etwas Besonderes mit Jack vorhatte, und insgeheim hegte er die Hoffnung, Jack werde einmal seine Stelle als Prior von Kingsbridge einnehmen.

Jack erhob sich im ersten Morgengrauen und stahl sich aus dem Dormitorium, um vor der Prim noch einen allerletzten Kontrollgang über die Baustelle zu machen. Die Morgenluft war frisch und kühl wie klares Quellwasser. Ein warmer, sonniger Tag dämmerte herauf, gut für die Geschäfte und gut für die Priorei.

Er schritt die Mauern der Kathedrale ab und vergewisserte sich, daß sämtliche Werkzeuge und halbfertigen Arbeiten sicher in den Bauhütten verstaut worden waren. Tom hatte die vorrätigen Stein- und Holzstapel mit leichten Holzzäunen umgeben, um die Baumaterialien vor mutwilligen Beschädigungen durch gedankenlose oder betrunkene Besucher zu schützen. Und da ihnen nicht daran lag, daß irgendwelche tollkühnen Draufgänger auf die Mauern kletterten, waren alle Leitern in Sicherheit gebracht, die Wendeltreppen in den dicken Mauern mit provisorischen Türen verschlossen und die abgestuften Kanten der halbfertigen Mauern mit Holzblöcken versperrt worden. Mehrere Handwerksmeister sollten im Laufe des Tages Kontrollgänge machen und darauf achten, daß nichts beschädigt wurde.

Jack brachte es immer wieder fertig, die eine oder andere Gebetsstunde zu versäumen: Auf der Baustelle fand sich immer etwas zu tun. Zwar teilte er nicht den Haß seiner Mutter auf die christliche Religion, stand ihr aber mehr oder minder gleichgültig gegenüber. Begeistern konnte sie ihn nicht, aber er war bereit, sie hinzunehmen, solange es seinen Absichten diente. Er achtete darauf, daß er täglich wenigstens einem Gottesdienst beiwohnte – gewöhnlich jenem, bei dem Prior Philip oder der Novizenmeister zugegen waren, die beiden ranghöchsten Mönche, denen sein Fernbleiben am ehesten aufgefallen wäre. An sämtlichen Gebetsstunden teilzunehmen, hätte er nicht ertragen. Mönche führten das merkwürdigste und verdrehteste Leben, das sich vorstellen ließ: Die Hälfte ihrer Tage verbrachten sie mit selbstauferlegten Quälereien und Unannehmlichkeiten, die sie leicht hätten vermeiden können, die andere Hälfte damit, zu jeder Stunde, bei Tag und Nacht sinnlosen Hokuspokus in einer ansonsten leeren Kirche vor sich hin zu murmeln. Um alles Schöne und Angenehme machten sie einen großen Bogen – um Mädchen, Sport, Feste und Familienleben. Jack hatte allerdings beobachtet, daß die glücklichsten unter den Mönchen eine Aufgabe gefunden hatten, die sie zutiefst befriedigte: das Illustrieren von Manuskripten, Geschichtsschreibung, Kochen, das Studium der Philosophie oder – wie in Philips Fall – die Aufgabe, das verschlafene Dorf Kingsbridge in eine geschäftige Domstadt zu verwandeln.

Wenn Jack auch keine besondere Zuneigung für Philip empfand, so arbeitete er doch gern mit ihm zusammen. Männern, die ihr Leben der Kirche geweiht hatten, stand er mit der gleichen Zurückhaltung und Ablehnung gegenüber wie seine Mutter. Philips Frömmigkeit machte ihn verlegen, seine ehrliche Unschuld war ihm zuwider, und er mißtraute seiner Neigung zu glauben, Gott werde schon richten, was er, Philip, nicht selbst bewältigen konnte. Dennoch arbeitete Jack gern für ihn. Seine Anordnungen waren klar und durchdacht. Jack ließ er Raum für eigene Entscheidungen, und nie schob er die Schuld für eigene Fehler seinen Untergebenen in die Schuhe.

Jack war erst seit drei Monaten Novize und würde erst nach weiteren neun Monaten aufgefordert, Profeß abzulegen. Die drei Gelübde waren Armut, Keuschheit und Gehorsam. Was die Armut betraf, so trog der Schein: Mönche besaßen zwar keine persönliche Habe und auch kein Geld, lebten aber eher wie Herren denn wie Knechte – sie bekamen gut zu essen, warme Kleidung und stattliche Bauten aus Stein, in denen sie leben durften. Auch die Keuschheit macht mir nichts aus, dachte Jack bitter. Es hatte ihm eine gewisse kalte Genugtuung bereitet, Aliena höchstselbst mitzuteilen, daß er ins Kloster ging. Sie hatte erschrocken und schuldbewußt dreingesehen. Wenn er sich jetzt aus Mangel an weiblicher Gesellschaft ruhelos und gereizt fühlte, brauchte er nur daran zu denken, wie Aliena mit ihm umgesprungen war – ihre heimlichen Zusammenkünfte im Wald, die gemeinsamen Winterabende, die beiden Küsse; dann der plötzliche Umschwung, ihre Kälte und Härte; jedesmal, wenn er daran dachte, wollte er am liebsten nie wieder mit einer Frau zu tun haben. Nur mit dem dritten Gelübde – Gehorsam – würde er seine Schwierigkeiten haben. Philips Anordnungen, die von einem intelligenten und präzisen Menschen kamen, fügte er sich nur zu gerne; aber dem einfältigen Subprior Remigius, dem trunkenen Gästemeister oder dem aufgeblasenen Sakristan zu gehorchen, fand er äußerst schwer.

Nichtsdestotrotz trug er sich mit dem Gedanken, Profeß abzulegen. Schließlich brauchte er die Gelübde nicht zu halten. Ihm ging es ausschließlich um den Bau der Kathedrale. Die mit Nachschub, Konstruktion und Bauleitung verbundenen Probleme waren schier endlos und fesselnd. Einmal hatte er Tom helfen müssen, eine Methode zu finden, anhand derer sich die Anzahl der auf der Baustelle eintreffenden Steine mit der im Steinbruch verladenen vergleichen ließ – eine knifflige Sache, denn die Anfahrt dauerte zwischen zwei und drei Tagen, was die tägliche Zählung unmöglich machte. Ein andermal hatten sich die Steinmetzen über die Güte der von den Zimmerleuten gefertigten Schablonen beschwert. Die größte Herausforderung für Jack stellten jedoch die technischen Probleme dar, etwa die Frage, wie man die Steinfrachten in Tonnenschwere, die hoch oben auf der Mauer benötigt wurden, hinaufbeförderte, wenn dazu nur sehr einfache mechanische Hilfsmittel und ein ebenso einfaches Baugerüst zur Verfügung standen. All diese Fragen pflegte Tom Builder mit Jack wie mit einem Gleichgestellten zu besprechen. Tom schien Jack die wütende Behauptung, er habe nie auch nur den kleinen Finger für ihn gerührt, verziehen zu haben, und er tat, als hätte er Jacks Enthüllung, daß er die alte Kirche in Brand gesteckt hatte, vergessen. Die beiden arbeiteten froh und zufrieden Seite an Seite, und die Tage vergingen wie im Flug. Jack nutzte gar die langweiligen Gebetsstunden, um sich in Gedanken mit irgendwelchen verzwickten Konstruktions- oder Planungsfragen herumzuschlagen. Sein Wissensschatz vergrößerte sich ständig. Statt jahrelang nur Steine zu meißeln, lernte er nun, wie man eine Kathedrale baut. Eine bessere Lehre konnte man sich für jemanden, der einmal Baumeister werden wollte, gar nicht vorstellen. Und dafür war Jack bereit, sich durch zahllose mitternächtliche Vigilien zu gähnen.

Die Sonne lugte über die Ostwand des Klosterhofs. Auf der Baustelle war alles Ordnung. Die Budenbesitzer, die die Nacht neben ihren Waren verbracht hatten, begannen allmählich, ihr Bettzeug zusammenzufalten und ihre Artikel auszustellen. Die ersten Kunden würden nicht lange auf sich warten lassen. Eine Bäckerin ging mit einem Tablett frischer Brotlaibe auf dem Kopf an Jack vorbei. Der Geruch des ofenwarmen Brots ließ ihm das Wasser im Mund zusammenlaufen. Er machte kehrt und begab sich zum Refektorium, wo in Kürze das Frühstück aufgetragen wurde.

Bei den ersten Marktbesuchern handelte es sich um die Familienangehörigen der Budenbesitzer und um Leute aus der Stadt, die zwar neugierig auf die erste Wollmesse zu Kingsbridge, aber nicht sonderlich am Erwerb irgendwelcher Waren interessiert waren. Die Sparsamen unter ihnen hatten sich zu Hause den Bauch mit grobem Brot und Porridge vollgeschlagen, so daß sie die stark gewürzten und auffallend bunten Speisen an den Ständen nicht in Versuchung führten. Die Kinder machten große Augen und gingen wie benommen durch das verwirrende Angebot begehrenswerter Dinge. Eine früh aus den Federn gekommene, zuversichtliche Hure stolzierte mit rot angemalten Lippen und in roten Stiefeln herum und lächelte den Männern mittleren Alters hoffnungsvoll zu; aber zu solch früher Stunde stieß sie noch nicht auf Gegenliebe.

Aliena beobachtete dies alles von ihrer Bude aus, die eine der größten war. In den vergangenen Wochen hatte sie sämtliche Vliese der Priorei auf Lager genommen – die Wolle, für die sie letzten Sommer einhundertundsiebzig Pfund bezahlt hatte. Auch den Bauern hatte sie, wie üblich, ihre Vliese abgekauft, mehr als sonst sogar, denn William Hamleigh hatte seinen Pächtern verboten, ihre Ware selbst in Kingsbridge zu verkaufen, so daß sie sich alle an die Händler gewandt hatten. Aliena, die in Kingsbridge, wo die Messe stattfand, ansässig war, hatte von allen Händlern die meisten Geschäfte getätigt. Es war so gut gelaufen, daß ihr das Bargeld ausgegangen war und sie sich vierzig Pfund von Malachi hatte borgen müssen. In ihrem Lager, dem hinteren Teil der Messebude, stapelten sich einhundertundsechzig Sack Rohwolle, die Vliese von vierzigtausend Schafen; das hatte sie mehr als zweihundert Pfund gekostet, aber sie würde dreihundert dafür bekommen, genug Geld, um den Lohn eines gelernten Steinmetzen mehr als ein Jahrhundert lang zu bezahlen. Wann immer sie an diese Zahlen dachte, geriet sie in Staunen darüber, welche Größe ihr Geschäft erlangt hatte.

Mit den Aufkäufern rechnete Aliena erst kurz vor Mittag – nur fünf oder sechs, die sich alle kannten und von denen sie selbst die meisten aus dem Vorjahr kannte. Das Verhandlungsritual verlief immer gleich: Nach der Begrüßung kredenzte Aliena einen Becher Wein, sie setzten sich und plauderten eine Weile über dies und das, dann erst zeigte sie dem Aufkäufer ihre Wolle. Er bat sie, ein, zwei Säcke zu öffnen – niemals einen, der zuoberst lag! –, griff tief hinein und zog eine Handvoll Wolle heraus. Nun prüfte er die Länge, indem er an den Strähnen zupfte, beurteilte, wie weich sie war, indem er sie zwischen Daumen und Zeigefinger rieb, und machte zum Schluß noch eine Geruchsprobe. Dann ging das Feilschen los: Er bot an, den gesamten Lagerbestand zu einem geradezu lächerlich niedrigen Preis aufzukaufen – Aliena lehnte ab und nannte den Preis, den sie sich vorstellte. Darauf schüttelte er den Kopf, und sie setzten sich zu einem weiteren Becher Wein.

Bei jedem Aufkäufer wiederholte sich das Ritual. Wer sich bis zur Mittagszeit einfand, bekam ein Essen. Danach bot dann einer an, eine große Menge Wolle zu kaufen – zu wenig mehr, als Aliena selbst dafür gezahlt hatte. Sie hielt dagegen, indem sie mit ihrer Forderung ein wenig herunterging. Es wurde früher Nachmittag, bis der erste Kaufabschluß unter Dach und Fach war, der nur einen geringen Gewinn einbrachte, doch die anderen Händler begannen daraufhin, Aliena zu bedrängen, während sie ablehnte, noch mehr Wolle zu einem so niedrigen Preis zu verkaufen. Im Laufe des Nachmittags sollte er dann langsam anziehen, denn stieg er zu rasch, gingen die Geschäfte schleppend, da die Käufer in Gedanken schon überschlugen, wie schnell sie ihre Kontingente woanders auffüllen konnten. Verlangte Aliena einen geringeren Preis, als die Käufer zu zahlen bereit waren, erkannte sie es an der Hast, in der auf ihr Angebot eingegangen wurde. Also tätigte sie ihre Geschäfte wohlüberlegt eins nach dem anderen, bis sich die Knechte daranmachen konnten, die riesigen Wollsäcke auf die großrädrigen Ochsenkarren zu laden, dieweil Aliena Silberpennies und Gulden in Pfundsäcken wog.

Heute würde sie zweifellos mehr Geld denn je einnehmen: Sie hatte doppelt soviel wie im Vorjahr zu verkaufen, und die Wollpreise waren gestiegen. Sie hatte die Absicht, Philips Produktion wieder ein Jahr im voraus aufzukaufen, und spielte insgeheim mit dem Gedanken, sich ein Haus aus Stein bauen zu lassen – mit weiträumigen Kellerlagern für die Wolle, einer eleganten und komfortablen Halle und einem hübschen Schlafzimmer ganz für sich allein im Obergeschoß. Ihre Zukunft schien gesichert, und sie war überzeugt, daß sie Richard unterstützen konnte, so lange er ihre Hilfe brauchte. Alles lief hervorragend.

Um so rätselhafter, daß sie sich so entsetzlich elend fühlte.

Fast auf den Tag genau vier Jahre waren vergangen, seit Ellen nach Kingsbridge zurückgekehrt war, und für Tom waren es die besten vier Jahre seines Lebens gewesen.

Der Schmerz über Agnes' Tod war mit der Zeit dumpfer geworden, und Tom hatte nicht mehr das vertrackte Gefühl, hin und wieder ohne ersichtlichen Grund in Tränen ausbrechen zu müssen. In Gedanken hielt er noch immer Zwiesprache mit ihr, erzählte ihr von den Kindern, von Prior Philip und der Kathedrale, wenn auch seltener als früher. Und die bittersüßen Erinnerungen an seine erste Frau konnten die Liebe, die er für Ellen empfand, nicht überschatten; er lebte durchaus in der Gegenwart. Und Ellen zu sehen, zu berühren, mit ihr zu reden und zu schlafen war ein immerwährender Quell der Freude für ihn.

Wie tief ihn Jack damals, am Tag seiner schlimmen Auseinandersetzung mit Alfred, getroffen hatte, als er behauptete, er, Tom, habe sich nie richtig um ihn gekümmert! Sogar die folgende schreckliche Enthüllung, Jack hätte die alte Kathedrale in Brand gesteckt, war von diesem Vorwurf in den Schatten gestellt worden. Wochenlang hatte er sich damit herumgequält, bis er endlich entschied, Jack müsse unrecht haben: Er, Tom, hatte stets sein Bestes gegeben, und mehr konnte man wahrhaftig von niemandem verlangen. Danach hatte es ein Ende mit dem Kopfzerbrechen.

Der Dombau nahm ihn wieder gänzlich gefangen. Diese Aufgabe erwies sich mehr und mehr als die dankbarste Arbeit seines Lebens. Er allein trug die volle Verantwortung für Planung und Ausführung. Niemand redete ihm drein, und ging etwas schief, brauchte er den Fehler nur bei sich selbst zu suchen. Der Anblick der hochaufragenden, mächtigen Mauern mit ihren regelmäßig wiederkehrenden Bogen, den anmutigen Friesen und den schöpferischen Figuren ließ ihn zutiefst befriedigt denken: All das habe ich geschaffen, und siehe, es ist wohlgetan.

Sein alter Alptraum, eines Tages wieder mit hungernden Kindern, ohne Arbeit und ohne einen roten Heller auf der Straße zu stehen, schien nun, da unter dem Stroh in seiner Küche eine mächtige, mit Silberpennies gefüllte Truhe vergraben war, unwirklicher denn je. Dachte er an jene eisigkalte Nacht, da Agnes Jonathan geboren und den Tod gefunden hatte, so liefen ihm noch heute Schauer des Grauens über den Rücken; dennoch hatte er das sichere Gefühl, daß ihm derart Entsetzliches nie mehr widerfahren würde.

Mitunter kam ihm die Frage in den Sinn, warum Ellen und er eigentlich keine gemeinsamen Kinder hatten. Sie waren beide fruchtbar – die Vergangenheit bewies es –, und Ellen hatte reichlich Gelegenheit gehabt, schwanger zu werden – selbst jetzt noch, nach vier Jahren, liebten sie sich beinahe jede Nacht. Dennoch bereitete ihm ihre Kinderlosigkeit keinen Kummer: Der kleine Jonathan war sein ein und alles.

An einem Jahrmarkt, das wußte er aus Erfahrung, hatte man den meisten Spaß mit kleinen Kindern. Daher machte er sich, als der Vormittag zur Hälfte herum war und das Getümmel einsetzte, allmählich auf die Suche nach Jonathan, der als Miniaturmönch schon fast selbst zu den Attraktionen zählte. Jonathan hatte vor nicht allzu langer Zeit den Wunsch geäußert, sich den Kopf scheren zu lassen, und Philip, dem Knaben nicht weniger zugetan als Tom, hatte seinem Wunsch entsprochen mit dem Resultat, daß der Junge mehr denn je einem Zwergmönch glich. Etliche echte Zwergwüchsige hatten sich unter die Menschenmenge gemischt, zeigten ihre Kunststücke vor und bettelten. Jonathan war fasziniert von ihnen, und Tom mußte ihn eiligst von einem Zwerg wegdrängen, der eine große Zuschauerzahl anzog, indem er seinen normal großen Penis zur Schau stellte.

Jonglierkünstler, Akrobaten und Musikanten gaben ihr Können zum besten und ließen den Hut herumgehen; Wahrsager, Quacksalber und Huren drängten den Besuchern ihre Dienste auf; Kräfte wurden gemessen, Ringkämpfe ausgefochten und Glücksspiele veranstaltet. Die Leute trugen ihre farbenfrohsten Kleider, und wer es sich leisten konnte, hatte sich mit Duftstoffen überschüttet und das Haar geölt. Jedermann schien das Geld locker in der Tasche zu sitzen, und die Luft war erfüllt vom Klimpern der Silbermünzen.

Die Bärenhatz sollte beginnen. Jonathan hatte noch nie einen Bären gesehen und kam aus dem Staunen nicht heraus. Der graubraune Pelz des Tieres war an mehreren Stellen vernarbt und ließ darauf schließen, daß es zumindest einen Wettkampf überlebt hatte. Eine schwere Kette war um seine Mitte geschlungen und am anderen Ende an einem tief in den Boden gerammten Pfahl befestigt; der Bär selber stapfte an der straff gespannten Kette im Kreis herum und äugte bösartig in die wartende Menge. Tom vermeinte, ein verschlagenes Aufleuchten in seinen Augen ausgemacht zu haben; wäre er Glücksspieler gewesen, er hätte wohl auf den Bär gesetzt.

Von der Seite her scholl wütendes Gebell – die Hunde hatten die Witterung ihres Gegners aufgenommen. Hin und wieder verharrte der Bär in seinem Kreislauf, wandte den Blick der Kiste zu und brummte vernehmlich, danach schien sich das Gekläff jedesmal schier zu überschlagen.

Der Besitzer des Tieres, der Bärenführer, nahm noch immer Wetten entgegen. Jonathan wurde langsam ungeduldig, und Tom wollte sich schon zum Gehen wenden, als der Bärenführer endlich die Kiste öffnete. Der Bär stellte sich am äußersten Ende der Kette auf die Hinterbeine und fletschte die Zähne. Der Mann brüllte etwas Unverständliches und riß die Kiste auf.

Heraus quollen fünf Windhunde. Sie waren leicht und behende, und in ihren offenstehenden Mäulern blitzten spitze, scharfe Zähne. Ohne Umschweife gingen sie den Bären an, der mit seinen mächtigen Pranken nach ihnen schlug. Er landete einen Treffer, der Hund flog in vollem Bogen fort, und der Rest der Meute machte einen Rückzieher.

Die Menge schob sich näher an das Spektakel heran. Tom vergewisserte sich, daß Jonathan in Sicherheit war: Er stand ganz vorne, aber außer Reichweite des Bären. Der zog sich klugerweise bis an den Pfosten zurück, so daß die Kette am Boden lag und nicht bei jeder Bewegung an ihm zerrte. Die Hunde waren aber auch nicht auf den Kopf gefallen. Nach dieser ersten wirren Attacke formierten sie sich neu und verteilten sich im Kreis. Der Bär warf sich aufgeregt herum und versuchte, gleichzeitig in alle Richtungen zu spähen.

Einer der Hunde griff ihn mit wütendem Gekläff an. Der Bär stellte sich und holte aus, worauf sich der Hund rasch zurückzog und die anderen vier von allen Seiten auf den Bären losgingen. Der Bär drehte sich um sich selber, teilte mit seinen Pranken aus. Drei Hunde verbissen sich im Fleisch seiner Hinterbacken, was die Menge mit lebhaften Zurufen quittierte. Der Bär brüllte vor Schmerzen, stellte sich auf die Hinterbeine und schüttelte seine Quälgeister ab, die sich hastig in Sicherheit brachten.

Gleich darauf versuchte es die Meute erneut mit dieser Taktik. Tom meinte schon, der Bär werde auch diesmal wieder darauf hereinfallen, doch nachdem sich der erste Hund zurückgezogen hatte und die anderen nachsetzten, drehte sich der Bär flink um die eigene Achse und hieb dem erstbesten Kläffer seine Pranke in die Seite. Die Menge spendete ihm nicht weniger Beifall als vorher den Hunden. Die scharfen Krallen der Bärentatzen hinterließen auf der seidenweichen Haut des Hundes tiefe, blutige Striemen. Der Hund jaulte zum Herzerweichen, zog sich zurück und leckte seine Wunden. Die Zuschauer johlten und buhten.

Nun umkreisten die verbliebenen vier den Bären, wagten auch den einen oder anderen Ausfall, machten aber jedesmal kurz vor der Gefahrenzone kehrt. Irgendein Zuschauer fing an, langsam und rhythmisch in die Hände zu klatschen. Da griff einer der Hunde frontal an: Blitzschnell sprang er in den Kreis, duckte sich unter der erhobenen Pranke hindurch und ging dem Bären direkt an die Gurgel. Die

Menge tobte, als der Hund seine spitzen, weißen Zähne tief in den fleischigen Hals des Bären schlug, während nun auch die drei anderen Hunde zum Angriff übergingen. Der Bär richtete sich auf, prankte wild nach dem Hund an seiner Kehle, warf sich schließlich zu Boden und rollte sich heftig herum. Einen Moment lang nahm Tom nichts wahr außer einem einzigen Wirbel aus Tierfellen. Dann sprangen drei Hunde zur Seite, der Bär kam auf allen vieren zu stehen, und zurück blieb der vierte Hund, zu Tode gequetscht.

Die Spannung unter den Zuschauern wuchs: Der Bär hatte schon zwei Hunde aus dem Feld geschlagen, blutete aber selber aus mehreren Wunden an Rücken, Hals und Hinterbeinen und sah nun verängstigt aus. Die Meute hatte aufgehört zu kläffen und umkreiste den Bären schweigend. Auch sie wirkte ängstlich, hatte aber Blut geleckt, und ihre Mordlust war erwacht.

Ihr neuerlicher Angriff spielte sich auf die gleiche Weise wie zuvor ab: Einer flitzte in den Kreis und suchte sogleich wieder das Weite. Der Bär schlug nur halbherzig nach ihm und wandte sich dem zweiten Hund zu. Der jedoch zog sich ebenfalls sofort wieder zurück; und der dritte im Bunde tat es ihm gleich. Die Hunde wetzten, einer nach dem anderen, in den Kreis hinein und wieder heraus, so daß der Bär ständig auf Trab gehalten wurde. Bei jedem Vorstoß rückten sie ihm ein wenig näher auf den Leib, und seine Prankenhiebe verfehlten sie immer knapper. Die Zuschauer glaubten schon zu wissen, was kam, und ihre Erregung nahm noch zu. Jonathan stand noch immer in der vordersten Reihe, wenige Schritte von Tom entfernt; er wirkte gefesselt und ängstlich zugleich. Tom, der den Blick wieder dem Kampf zuwandte, bekam gerade noch mit, wie der Bär einen der Hunde mit der Tatze streifte, während ein zweiter zwischen seinen Hinterbeinen hindurchschlüpfte und sich in seinem weichen Bauch verbiß. Der Bär gab eine Art schrillen Schrei von sich. Sein Angreifer löste sich und nahm Reißaus. Sofort warf sich ein anderer auf ihn. Der Bär schlug nach ihm, verfehlte ihn jedoch, und der nämliche Hund wie zuvor ging ihm wieder an den Bauch. Diesmal brachte er seinem Opfer eine riesige, blutig klaffende Wunde sei, bevor er sich zurückzog. Der Bär bäumte sich auf und ließ sich dann auf alle viere fallen. Einen Augenblick lang meinte Tom, der Kampf sei nun zu Ende, aber so schnell gab der Bär nicht auf. Sobald der nächste Hund zum Angriff ansetzte, parierte er mit einem Scheinschlag, wandte den Kopf, sah den zweiten Hund auf sich zukommen, drehte sich überraschend schnell um und versetzte ihm einen machtvollen Hieb, der ihn durch die Luft segeln ließ. Die Menge tobte vor Begeisterung, als der Hund wie ein Klumpen Fleisch auf dem Boden landete. Tom beobachtete ihn einen Augenblick lang. Er war noch am Leben, schien sich aber nicht bewegen zu können. Vielleicht hatte der Hieb ihm das Rückgrat gebrochen. Der Bär beachtete ihn nicht weiter, denn er war nun außer Reichweite und konnte ihm nicht mehr gefährlich werden.

Zwei Hunde waren noch übrig. Beide sprangen mehrmals in Reichweite des Bären, zogen sich aber schnellstens wieder zurück, bis Meister Petz nur noch rein mechanisch reagierte; dann begannen sie, ihn schneller und immer schneller zu umkreisen. Der Bär tappte hierhin und dorthin, versuchte verzweifelt beide Gegner gleichzeitig im Auge zu behalten. Er war erschöpft, blutete stark und konnte sich kaum noch auf den Beinen halten. Die Hunde zogen ihre Kreise immer enger. Die Erde unter den mächtigen Bärentatzen hatte sich in blutigen Schlamm verwandelt. Wie immer es ausgehen mochte – das Ende des Kampfes war abzusehen. Schließlich griffen beide Hunde gleichzeitig an. Einer sprang dem Bären an den Hals, der andere attackierte seinen Bauch. Mit einem letzten verzweifelten Schlag hieb der Bär nach dem Hund an seinem Hals. Eine grausige Blutfontäne schoß hervor, und die Menge johlte begeistert auf. Tom meinte zunächst, der Hund hätte den Bären getötet, dann sah er, daß es umgekehrt war: Das Blut troff aus dem Hund, der nun mit aufgeschlitztem Hals zu Boden fiel. Kurz darauf versiegte der Blutstrom; der Hund war tot. Zwischenzeitlich hatte der letzte Hund aber dem Bären den Bauch aufgerissen, so daß die Gedärme herausquollen. Das Tier setzte sich nur noch mühselig zur Wehr. Der Hund konnte seinem Schlag mit Leichtigkeit ausweichen, griff erneut an und verbiß sich in seinen Gedärmen. Der Bär schwankte und schien kurz vor dem Ende. Die Menge tobte vor Begeisterung, und aus den aufgebissenen Gedärmen des Bären drang abscheulicher Gestank. Noch einmal sammelte er all seine Kraft und schlug nach dem Hund. Der Hieb hinterließ einen langen, blutenden Riß, der quer über den Rücken des Hundes verlief; aber die Wunde war nicht tief, und dem Jäger war klar, daß es mit dem Bären zu Ende ging. Sogleich griff er wieder an und verbiß sich in seinen Gedärmen, bis das mächtige Tier die Augen schloß und tot zu Boden sackte.

Der Bärenführer erschien und packte den siegreichen Hund am Halsband. Der Schlachter von Kingsbridge trat mit seinem Gehilfen heran, und sie begannen, den Bären zu zerlegen. Vermutlich haben sie sich mit dem Besitzer im voraus auf einen Preis geeinigt, dachte Tom. Die Zuschauer, die auf den Sieger gewettet hatten, forderten ihren Gewinn. Und alle wollten den siegreichen Hund streicheln. Tom sah sich nach Jonathan um. Jonathan war nirgends zu sehen.

Das Kind hatte während der Bärenhatz keine zehn Schritt von Tom entfernt gestanden. Wie war es ihm gelungen, sich einfach aus dem Staub zu machen? Es muß passiert sein, als das Spektakel seinem Höhepunkt zustrebte, dachte Tom und machte sich Vorwürfe. Suchend sah er sich in der Menge um. Zwar überragte er alle anderen um Haupteslänge, und Jonathan in seiner Mönchskutte und mit seinem geschorenen Kopf war leicht zu erkennen – dennoch war er nirgendwo zu entdecken.

Der Junge war auf dem Klostergelände verhältnismäßig sicher, konnte aber auf Dinge stoßen, von denen Prior Philip ihn lieber ferngehalten hätte: Huren beispielsweise, die es ihren Kunden im Stehen an der Klostermauer besorgten. Eher zufällig streifte Toms suchender Blick das Baugerüst – und blieb entsetzt an einer winzigen Gestalt in einer Mönchskutte hängen, die dort oben herumbalancierte.

Von Panik erfaßt, hätte er am liebsten hinaufgerufen: Bleib stehen, sonst fällst du! Aber jedes Wort wäre im Lärm des Marktes untergegangen. Hastig schob er sich durch die Menge zur Kathedrale. Jonathan, versunken in die Scheinwelt seines Spiels, hüpfte auf dem Gerüst herum, ungeachtet der Gefahr, jeden Moment ausrutschen, fallen und achtzig Fuß tief dem sicheren Tod entgegenstürzen zu können – Tom schluckte sein Entsetzen, das gallebitter in ihm aufstieg, hinunter.

Das Gerüst stand nicht auf dem Boden, sondern ruhte auf schweren Hölzern, die hoch oben in die Mauer eingelassen waren. Die Streben ragten etwa sechs Fuß weit hervor. Quer darüber lagen stabile, mit Tauen an den Streben befestigte Pfosten, auf denen wiederum die aus biegsamen Schößlingen und gewobenen Binsen gefertigten Gestelle ruhten. Normalerweise gelangte man über die in die dicken Mauern eingelassenen Wendeltreppen auf das Gerüst, die heute allerdings verbarrikadiert worden waren. Wie also war Jonathan nach oben gelangt? Leitern gab es keine – dafür hatte Tom Sorge getragen, und Jack hatte alles noch einmal überprüft. Der Junge mußte das abgestufte Ende der Mauer hochgestiegen sein. Die Enden waren zwar, um den Aufstieg zu erschweren, mit Holzblöcken abgedichtet worden, aber Jonathan konnte ohne weiteres daran hinaufgeklettert sein. Der Kleine war außerordentlich selbstbewußt – was aber nichts daran änderte, daß er mindestens einmal am Tag auf die Nase fiel.

Am Fuß der Mauer blieb Tom stehen und blickte besorgt in die Höhe. Achtzig Fuß über ihm spielte Jonathan vergnügt vor sich hin.

Die Angst legte sich wie eine kalte Hand um sein Herz, und er brüllte aus Leibeskräften: »Jonathan!«

Die Leute in der Nähe schraken zusammen und folgten Toms Blick. Kaum hatten sie das Kind auf dem Gerüst erkannt, machten sie auch ihre Freunde darauf aufmerksam, so daß es schnell zu einem kleinen Auflauf kam.

Jonathan hatte nichts gehört. Tom legte die Hände wie einen Schalltrichter vor den Mund und rief wieder: »Jonathan! Jonathan!«

Diesmal war es durchgedrungen. Das Kind sah hinab, erblickte Tom und winkte ihm zu.

»Komm da runter!« schrie Tom.

Jonathan schien bereit zu gehorchen, doch da fiel sein Blick auf die Wand und die steilen Stufen vor ihm, und er verlor den Mut. »Ich kann nicht!« rief er mit seinem hohen Stimmchen, das bis hinunter zu hören war.

Tom sah ein, daß er selbst hinaufklettern und den Jungen holen mußte. »Bleib, wo du bist, bis ich bei dir bin!« rief er hinauf. Er schob die Holzblöcke von den unteren Stufen und bestieg die Mauer.

Sie war anfangs gute vier Fuß breit, wurde aber mit zunehmender Höhe immer schmaler. Tom nahm eine Stufe nach der anderen. Am liebsten wäre er nach oben gestürmt, zwang sich aber, besonnen vorzugehen. Er warf einen Blick in die Höhe und sah, daß Jonathan am Rand des Gerüsts saß und seine kurzen Beinchen über den Abgrund baumeln ließ.

Ganz oben war die Mauer nur noch zwei Fuß breit und bot, wenn man wie Tom starke Nerven hatte, immer noch genügend Platz zum Gehen. Er schritt auf der Mauer entlang, sprang auf das Gerüst und schloß Jonathan in die Arme. Eine Welle der Erleichterung überflutete ihn. »Du dummer Junge«, sagte er, aber seine Stimme klang liebevoll, und Jonathan schmiegte sich an ihn.

Als er wieder hinabschaute, bemerkte er, daß sich hundert oder mehr Menschen die Hälse nach ihnen verrenkten. Wahrscheinlich hielten sie seinen Balanceakt, wie zuvor die Bärenhatz, für eine der Attraktionen des Jahrmarktes. »Also gut«, meinte Tom an Jonathan gerichtet, »dann laß uns mit dem Abstieg beginnen.« Er ließ den Jungen auf die Mauer nieder und sagte: »Ich bleibe dicht hinter dir, du brauchst dir also keine Sorgen zu machen.«

Doch Jonathan ließ sich nicht so leicht überzeugen. »Ich habe Angst«, sagte er. Er reckte Tom die Ärmchen entgegen und brach in Tränen aus, als dieser ihn nicht sofort hochhob.

»Na schön, dann trage ich dich eben«, sagte Tom. Glücklich war er darüber nicht, aber Jonathan wirkte zu mitgenommen, als daß er in dieser Höhe auf sich allein gestellt bleiben konnte. Tom stieg auf die Mauer, kniete sich neben Jonathan, nahm ihn auf den Arm und richtete sich wieder auf.

Jonathan klammerte sich an ihn.

Tom trat einen Schritt nach vorn. Das Kind im Arm versperrte ihm die Sicht auf die Steine unter seinen Füßen, doch damit mußte er sich wohl oder übel abfinden. Vorsichtig und mit wild klopfendem Herzen setzte er einen Fuß vor den anderen. Um sich selbst hatte er keine Bedenken, aber das Kind in seinem Arm ließ ihn in Angstschweiß ausbrechen. Endlich hatte er die erste Stufe erreicht. Zunächst war die Mauer dort zwar nicht breiter, doch die Stufen ließen sie weniger steil erscheinen. Erleichtert begann er mit dem Abstieg und fühlte sich mit jedem Schritt, den er tat, ruhiger. In Höhe des Triforiums, wo die Wand sich auf drei Fuß verbreiterte, hielt er einen Moment lang inne, um Atem zu schöpfen.

Müßig ließ er den Blick über das Klostergelände, Kingsbridge und die jenseitigen Felder schweifen – und was er dort erblickte, machte ihn stutzig. Eine riesige Staubwolke, etwa eine halbe Meile entfernt, hing über der Straße, die auf die Stadt zu führte. Erst nach einer Weile erkannte er, daß es sich um eine große Truppe Berittener handelte, die sich zügig näherte. Angestrengt spähte er in die Ferne und versuchte, sich einen Reim darauf zu machen. Zunächst meinte er, das müsse ein einzelner wohlhabender Kaufmann mit großem Gefolge sein, vielleicht gar eine Gruppe von Kaufleuten, doch dann wurde ihm klar, daß es viel zu viele waren, die überdies ganz und gar nicht wie Handelsleute wirkten. Angestrengt dachte er darüber nach, was ihn zu dem Schluß bewogen hatte, es könne sich auf keinen Fall um friedliche Kaufleute handeln – bis er in dem näher rückenden Haufen Schlachtrösser und Helme ausmachte und erkannte, daß die Männer bis an die Zähne bewaffnet waren.

Mit einemmal war ihm angst und bange zumute.

»Herr im Himmel, wer kann das sein«, sagte er laut.

»Du sollst nicht ›Herr im Himmel‹ sagen!« meinte Jonathan.

Wer immer das sein mochte – sie verhießen nichts Gutes.

Tom eilte die Stufen hinab. Die Menge spendete Beifall, als er auf den Boden sprang, aber er schenkte ihr keine Beachtung. Wo waren Ellen und die Kinder? Suchend sah er sich um, konnte sie aber nirgends entdecken.

Jonathan machte Anstalten, sich aus seinen Armen zu winden, doch Tom hielt ihn fest umschlungen. Da er seinen Jüngsten schon einmal bei sich hatte, bot es sich geradezu an, ihn zuallererst in Sicherheit zu bringen. Dann konnte er sich immer noch auf die Suche nach den anderen machen. Er zwängte sich durch die Menschenmenge auf die Tür zu, die zum Kreuzgang führte. Sie war von innen verriegelt, damit wenigstens ein Teil des Klosters vom lärmenden Treiben der Messe verschont blieb. Tom bollerte gegen die Tür und rief: »Macht auf! Macht auf!«

Nichts rührte sich.

Tom wußte nicht einmal, ob sich überhaupt jemand im Kreuzgang aufhielt. Doch für Mutmaßungen blieb keine Zeit. Er trat ein paar Schritte zurück, setzte Jonathan ab, hob seinen gestiefelten rechten Fuß und versetzte der Tür einen kräftigen Tritt. Rings um das Schloß barst das Holz. Er trat ein zweites Mal zu, noch fester, und die Tür flog auf. Genau dahinter stand ein älterer Mönch, der ihm verblüfft entgegensah. Tom hob Jonathan vom Boden und stellte ihn im Kreuzgang auf die Füße. »Behaltet ihn hier«, sagte er zu dem Alten. »Es sieht nach Ärger aus.«

Der Mönch nickte ergeben und nahm Jonathan bei der Hand.

Tom schloß die Tür.

Jetzt mußte er nur noch seine Familie finden – in einer Menge von tausend oder noch mehr Menschen!

Das erschien ihm schier aussichtslos, und seine Sorge wuchs. Weit und breit kein bekanntes Gesicht! Er stieg auf ein leeres Bierfaß, um einen besseren Überblick zu bekommen. Es war Mittagszeit, der Jahrmarkt hatte also seinen Höhepunkt erreicht. Wie ein träger Strom wälzte sich die Menschenmasse durch die Marktreihen, und vor den Buden, die Essen und Trinken feilboten, herrschte ein unbeschreiblicher Andrang. Tom durchkämmte die Menge mit den Augen, konnte aber keinen seiner Angehörigen ausmachen. Es war zum Verzweifeln! Er ließ seinen Blick über die Hausdächer schweifen: Die Reiter hielten mittlerweile im gestreckten Galopp auf die Brücke zu, ausnahmslos Bewaffnete, jeder mit einer brennenden Fackel in der Hand. Tom packte das Grauen: Das konnte nur zu einer Katastrophe führen!

Da fiel sein Blick auf Jack, der unmittelbar neben ihm stand und leicht belustigt zu ihm aufschaute. »Was stehst du denn auf einem Bierfaß herum?« wollte er wissen.

»Wir kriegen Ärger!« sagte Tom mit Nachdruck. »Wo ist deine Mutter?«

»Bei Aliena, an ihrem Stand. Was denn für Ärger?«

»Sieht schlimm aus. Wo sind Alfred und Martha?«

»Martha ist bei Mutter. Alfred schaut bei den Hahnenkämpfen zu. Was ist denn los?«

»Sieh selbst.« Tom reichte Jack die Hand und zog ihn auf das Faß, wo er mühsam balancierend vor Tom zu stehen kam. Die Reiter preschten bereits über die Brücke ins Dorf hinein.

»Um Himmels willen, wer ist das denn?« fragte Jack.

Tom heftete seinen Blick auf den Anführer, einen Hünen auf einem Schlachtroß. Er erkannte das gelbe Haar und die kräftige Statur. »Das ist William Hamleigh«, sagte er.

Die Männer ritten eben an den ersten Häusern vorbei, hielten ihre Fackeln an die Dächer und setzten das Stroh in Brand. »Die brennen ja die ganze Stadt nieder!« entfuhr es Jack.

»Das wird noch schlimmer, als ich dachte«, meinte Tom.

»Nichts wie runter hier!«

Sie sprangen gleichzeitig vom Faß herunter.

»Ich hole Mutter und Martha«, sagte Jack.

»Bring sie in den Kreuzgang«, drängte Tom. »Das ist der einzig sichere Ort. Wenn die Mönche sich widersetzen, dann sag ihnen, sie können dich mal.«

»Und wenn sie die Tür verriegeln?«

»Ich habe gerade erst das Schloß aufgebrochen. Mach schnell. Ich kümmere mich um Alfred. Beeil dich!«

Jack eilte davon. Tom arbeitete sich zum Hahnenkampfplatz durch und machte dabei ausgiebig von seinen Ellenbogen Gebrauch. Mehrere Männer verwünschten ihn lauthals, aber er hörte gar nicht hin, zumal sie seine Statur und seine finster entschlossene Miene rasch zum Verstummen brachte. Es dauerte nicht lange, da zog auch schon der Rauch von den Häusern bis über das Klostergelände. Tom roch ihn und sah, wie ein oder zwei Leute in seiner Nähe ebenfalls befremdet schnupperten. Nur noch wenige Augenblicke, und alles würde in Panik ausbrechen.

Die Hahnenkämpfe wurden gleich bei der Klosterpforte ausgetragen und waren umlagert von einer riesigen, lärmenden Menge. Tom drängte sich durch und hielt nach Alfred Ausschau. Die Menschenmenge hatte sich um ein flaches, etwa zwei Fuß messendes Loch gesammelt, in dem sich zwei Hähne mit Schnäbeln und bespornten Klauen gegenseitig zerfleischten. Blut spritzte und Federn flogen. Alfred stand in der ersten Reihe, völlig gefesselt von dem Kampf, und feuerte einen der beiden Unglücksraben – es war nicht ersichtlich, welchen – mit gellender Stimme an. Tom zwängte sich zu ihm durch und packte ihn am Arm. »Komm mit!« rief er.

»Ich hab' aber sechs Pennies auf den schwarzen gesetzt!« schrie Alfred zurück.

»Wir müssen schnellstens hier raus!« herrschte Tom ihn an. Im gleichen Augenblick trieb eine Rauchfahne über den Kampfplatz. »Riechst du denn das Feuer nicht?«

Ein, zwei andere Zuschauer hatten das Wort *Feuer* aufgeschnappt und sahen Tom neugierig an. Erneut wehte eine Rauchfahne herüber, und nun rochen es alle, auch Alfred. »Was ist das?« fragte er.

»Die Stadt brennt!« gab Tom zurück.

Plötzlich wollte niemand mehr bleiben. Schiebend und drängelnd zerstreuten sich die Männer in alle Himmelsrichtungen. Auf dem Kampfplatz machte der schwarze Hahn dem braunen den Garaus, doch das kümmerte niemanden mehr. Alfred schlug die falsche Richtung ein, und Tom packte ihn erneut. »Zum Kreuzgang!« befahl er. »Das ist der einzig sichere Ort.«

Der Rauch trieb nun in großen Schwaden herüber, und die Leute bekamen es mit der Angst zu tun. Alles lief kopflos durcheinander. Tom warf einen Blick über die wogenden Köpfe und sah, daß die Menge durch die Klosterpforte hinausdrängte; das war unklug, denn der Durchgang war schmal, und dort draußen waren sie auch nicht sicherer als auf dem Klostergelände. Trotzdem schlossen sich immer mehr dem Exodus an, so daß Tom mit Alfred schließlich gegen einen Menschenstrom ankämpfen mußte, der sich ihnen entgegenwälzte. Doch urplötzlich schlug die Stimmung um und alles drängte wieder zurück. Tom sah sich nach einem Grund für diesen überraschenden Sinneswandel um – und entdeckte den ersten Reiter, der auf den Klosterhof zupreschte. In diesem Moment wurde die Menge zur entfesselten Meute.

Die Krieger verbreiteten Angst und Schrecken. Ihre riesigen Pferde, nicht weniger furchtsam als die Menge, bäumten sich auf, wichen zurück, stürmten erneut los und stampften alles nieder, was ihnen zwischen die Hufe geriet. Ihre bewaffneten und behelmten Reiter schlugen mit Keulen und Fackeln um sich, mähten Männer, Frauen und Kinder um, setzten Marktstände, Kleidung und Haare in Brand. Es gab niemanden, der nicht wie am Spieß schrie. Noch mehr Berittene drängten nach, noch mehr Leiber fielen den malmenden Hufen zum Opfer. Tom brüllte Alfred ins Ohr: »Schlag dich zum Kreuzgang durch – ich will mich vergewissern, daß die anderen in Sicherheit sind. Lauf schon!« Er gab ihm einen Stoß, und Alfred machte sich davon.

Tom wollte sich zu Alienas Bude durchschlagen. Doch er hatte noch kaum zwei Schritte getan, als er über einen am Boden liegenden Körper stolperte und hinschlug. Fluchend rappelte er sich wieder auf; aber bevor er noch richtig zum Stehen kam, sah er, wie sich ein Schlachtroß mit angelegten Ohren und geblähten Nüstern vor ihm aufbäumte. Er sah das Weiße in den vor panischer Angst verdrehten Augen des Tieres, und über dem Pferdekopf sah er das vor Haß und Triumph zur Fratze verzerrte Gesicht von William Hamleigh. Es schoß ihm durch den Kopf, wie schön es wäre, Ellen noch einmal in seinen Armen zu halten, da traf ihn auch schon ein riesiger Huf mitten auf die Stirn. Ein furchtbarer, grauenvoller Schmerz drohte seinen Schädel zu sprengen, und alles wurde schwarz um ihn.

Als Aliena zum erstenmal den Brandgeruch wahrnahm, dachte sie noch, er käme von dem Essen, das sie servieren wollte.

Drei flämische Aufkäufer saßen vor ihrem Lagerhaus um einen Tisch, rundliche Männer mit schwarzen Bärten, deren Englisch einen starken germanischen Akzent hatte und deren Kleidung aus feinstem Tuch gefertigt war. Bisher lief alles nach Plan. Sie stand im Begriff, die ersten Verkäufe zu tätigen, hatte aber beschlossen, vorher das Mittagessen aufzutragen, um die Händler ein wenig auf die Folter zu spannen. Trotzdem würde sie einen Seufzer der Erleichterung tun, wenn dieses riesige Vermögen an Wolle endlich den Besitzer wechselte.

Sie setzte ihnen die Platte mit den in Honig gebratenen Schweinekoteletts vor: Das Fleisch, schön kroß und mit angebräuntem Fettrand, fand sogar vor ihrem kritischen Auge Gnade. Sie schenkte Wein nach. Einer der Flamen sog prüfend die Luft ein, worauf sich auch die anderen besorgt umsahen. Aliena bekam es plötzlich mit der Angst zu tun: Ein Brand war der Alptraum jedes Wollhändlers. Sie sah zu Ellen und Martha hinüber, die ihr beim Auftragen des Essens halfen. »Riecht ihr den Rauch auch?« wollte sie wissen.

Bevor sie noch antworten konnten, tauchte Jack auf. Aliena, die sich noch immer nicht an seine Mönchskutte und die Tonsur gewöhnt hatte, nahm die Angst in seiner Miene wahr. Am liebsten hätte sie ihn in den Arm genommen und ihm die Sorgenfalten von der Stirn geküßt. Aber dann fiel ihr wieder ein, wie sie sich damals vor sechs

Monaten in der alten Mühle hatte gehenlassen, und sie kehrte ihm rasch den Rücken. Die bloße Erinnerung daran trieb ihr noch immer die Schamröte ins Gesicht.

»Es gibt Ärger!« rief er gehetzt. »Wir müssen alle im Kreuzgang Schutz suchen!«

Sie sah ihn an. »Was ist passiert – brennt es irgendwo?«

»Graf William ist mit seinen Mannen eingefallen«, erwiderte er.

Aliena packte nacktes Entsetzen. William! Schon wieder William!

»Sie haben die Stadt in Brand gesteckt. Tom und Alfred sind schon auf dem Weg zum Kreuzgang. Kommt mit, bitte!« Die Worte sprudelten nur so aus Jack heraus.

Ellen fackelte nicht lange und ließ die Salatschlüssel, die sie gerade zu Tisch trug, den verdutzten Flamen vor die Füße fallen. »Herrje!« sagte sie und packte Martha beim Arm. »Nichts wie weg hier!«

Alienas Blick glitt sorgenvoll zu ihrem Lager. Dort stapelte sich Rohwolle im Wert von mehreren hundert Pfund, die sie vor dem Feuer bewahren mußte – nur wie? Jack sah sie erwartungsvoll an. Die Käufer verließen eilends die Tafel, und Aliena sagte zu Jack: »Geh nur. Ich muß bei meinem Stand bleiben.«

Ellen drängte: »Jack – komm schon!«

»Einen Augenblick noch«, sagte der und wandte sich Aliena zu.

Aliena entging nicht, daß Ellen zögerte, hin und her gerissen zwischen dem Drang, Martha in Sicherheit zu bringen, und dem Wunsch, auf Jack zu warten. »Jack! Jack!« mahnte sie.

Er drehte sich zu ihr um. »Mutter! Geh schon mit Martha voraus!«

»Na gut!« gab sie zurück. »Aber beeil dich. *Bitte!*« Und fort waren die beiden.

»Die ganze Stadt brennt«, erklärte Jack. »Der Kreuzgang ist die einzige Rettung – er ist aus Stein gebaut. Bitte komm mit, sofort!«

Vom Kloster her drangen die ersten Entsetzensschreie, und plötzlich war alles grau von Rauch. Wie gehetzt sah sich Aliena um und versuchte verzweifelt, sich ein Bild von der Lage zu machen. Inwendig schlotterte sie vor Angst. Und die Lagerbude barg die Früchte ihrer sechsjährigen, unermüdlichen Arbeit ...

»Aliena!« mahnte Jack. »Komm mit zum Kreuzgang – dort sind wir sicher!«

»Ich kann nicht!« schrie sie auf. »Meine Wolle!«

»Zum Teufel mit deiner Wolle!«

»Aber sie ist alles, was ich habe!«

»Wenn du tot bist, nützt sie dir auch nichts mehr!«

»Du hast leicht reden – ich habe jahrelang darum gekämpft, eine solche Position –«

»Aliena! *Bitte!*«

Plötzlich schrieen die Leute draußen in Todesangst auf. Die Reiter waren in das Klostergelände eingedrungen, preschten rücksichtslos durch die Menge, ritten alles nieder und steckten jede erreichbare Bude in Brand. Die Marktbesucher, von Panik ergriffen, unternahmen verzweifelte Versuche, den wild trommelnden Pferdehufen und flakkernden Fackeln zu entkommen, und trampelten sich dabei gegenseitig über den Haufen. Der leichte Zaun vor Alienas Stand brach unter dem Druck der Fliehenden zusammen. Ehe sie sich's versahen, wimmelte es auf dem Platz vor dem Lager vor Menschen; der Tisch samt den vollen Tellern und Weinbechern stürzte um, Jack und Aliena wurden zurückgedrängt. Zwei Reiter preschten auf den Stand zu, einer hieb wie wild mit der Keule um sich, der andere schwang drohend eine brennende Fackel. Jack schob sich vor Aliena, um sie mit seinem Körper zu schützen. Der erste Reiter zielte mit der Keule auf Alienas Kopf, doch Jack warf seinen Arm darüber und die Keule traf sein Handgelenk. Aliena spürte den Schlag noch, aber seine Wucht hatte Jack abgefangen. Sie sah auf und direkt in das Gesicht des zweiten Reiters.

William Hamleigh!

Aliena schrie auf.

Mit der lodernden Fackel in der Hand beobachtete er einen Moment lang ihr Gesicht und kostete seinen Triumph aus. Dann spornte er sein Pferd an und trieb es auf ihr Lager zu.

»Nein!« kreischte Aliena.

Verzweifelt versuchte sie sich aus dem Gedränge zu befreien und schlug wie wild um sich, wobei auch Jack nicht verschont blieb. Als sie sich endlich losgerissen hatte, stürzte sie zum Lager. William lehnte sich gerade aus dem Sattel und hielt die Flamme an die aufeinandergestapelten Wollsäcke. »Nein!« schrie sie wieder. Sie warf sich auf ihn, versuchte, ihn aus dem Sattel zu zerren, doch er stieß sie mühelos weg und sie fiel zu Boden. Noch einmal hielt er die Fackel an die Wollsäcke, und sie entflammten brausend. Das Roß, von den Flammen in Todesangst versetzt, bäumte sich auf und gab ein langgezogenes, schrilles Wiehern von sich. Plötzlich war Jack zur Stelle und zog Aliena von ihm fort. William riß sein Pferd herum und machte sich schleunigst aus dem Staub. Aliena rappelte sich auf. Sie griff nach einem leeren Sack und versuchte, die Flammen damit zu ersticken.

»Aliena, das ist Wahnsinn!« rief Jack. Die Hitze war schier unerträglich, dennoch griff sie nach einem Sack Wolle, der noch kein Feuer gefangen hatte, und versuchte, ihn davonzuschleifen – doch da dröhnten ihr die Ohren vom Tosen der Feuersbrunst, die Hitze griff auf ihr Gesicht über, und sie erkannte mit Entsetzen, daß ihr Haar in Flammen stand. Schon hatte sich Jack über sie geworfen, ihr beide Arme um den Kopf gelegt und sie dicht an sich gezogen. Gemeinsam fielen sie zur Erde. Er hielt sie noch eine Weile lang fest, dann löste er seinen Griff: Ihr Haar brannte nicht mehr, es roch nur noch versengt. Sie sah die Verbrennungen in Jacks Gesicht, seine Augenbrauen waren verschwunden. Da packte er sie auch schon am Knöchel und zerrte sie durch die Tür ins Freie, zog sie trotz ihres Widerstands so lange weiter, bis sie außer Gefahr waren.

Ihre Bude war inzwischen menschenleer. Jack ließ sie los. Sie versuchte sich aufzurappeln, aber er packte sie und hielt sie fest. Noch immer widersetzte sie sich, den Blick wie besessen auf die Flammen geheftet, die die Jahre härtester Arbeit mir nichts, dir nichts auffraßen – Jahren der Arbeit, Jahren der Sorgen, ihrem gesamten Besitz, all ihrer Sicherheit den Garaus machten. Alienas Kraft erlosch, ihr Widerstand versiegte. Sie lag nur noch da und schrie und schrie und schrie.

Philip war im Erdgeschoß unterhalb der Klosterküche und zählte mit Cuthbert Whitehead Geld, als er den Lärm hörte. Stirnrunzelnd sahen sie sich an und erhoben sich schließlich, um der Sache auf den Grund zu gehen.

Sie waren kaum durch die Tür getreten, als sie sich auch schon inmitten eines Aufruhrs befanden.

Philip sah mit fassungslosem Entsetzen, wie die Leute kopflos hin und her liefen, sich schoben und stießen, hinschlugen und über Gestürzte hinwegstiegen. Männer und Frauen brüllten, Kinder heulten, die Luft war voller Rauch. Alle Welt schien bestrebt, dem Klostergelände zu entfliehen. Außer dem Haupttor gab es nur noch einen Ausgang, und zwar den schmalen Spalt zwischen den Küchengebäuden und der Mühle. Dort war zwar keine Mauer, aber ein tiefer Graben, der das Wasser aus dem Mühlteich für die Brauerei heranführte. Philip wollte die Leute vor der Gefahr warnen, aber vergeblich: Niemand hörte hin.

Der Grund des Tumults war offensichtlich ein Feuer, und zwar ein sehr großes. Die Luft bestand nur noch aus Qualm und Rauch. Philip bekam es mit der Angst zu tun. Bei so vielen Menschen auf so engem Raum konnte es leicht zu zahlreichen Toten kommen. Was war zu tun?

Zunächst einmal mußte er sich ein genaues Bild der Lage machen. Er hetzte die Stufen zur Küchentür hinauf, um sich einen besseren Überblick zu verschaffen. Was er sah, erfüllte ihn mit schierem Grauen.

Ganz Kingsbridge stand in Flammen!

Ein verzweifelter Schreckensschrei entfuhr ihm.

Wie war es nur dazu gekommen?!

Dann fiel sein Blick auf die Reiter, die mit brennenden Fackeln durch die Menge preschten, und er begriff, daß es sich nicht um einen Unfall handelte. Sein erster Gedanke war, daß eine Schlacht zwischen den beiden Kriegsparteien entbrannt sein mußte, in die Kingsbridge aus unerfindlichen Gründen verwickelt worden war. Dann fiel ihm auf, daß die Bewaffneten es auf die Bürger von Kingsbridge abgesehen hatten. Das war keine Schlacht, das war ein Massaker!

Ein blonder, massiger Mann geriet in sein Blickfeld, der sein riesiges Schlachtroß rücksichtslos durch die Menschenmenge trieb. William Hamleigh.

Diese unschuldigen Menschen wurden mutwillig gemetzelt, diese umfassende Zerstörung der Stadt war Absicht – aus Habgier und Stolz! Der Gedanke trieb Philip schier zum Wahnsinn. Aus Leibeskräften brüllte er diesem Unmenschen zu: »Ich habe Euch erkannt, William Hamleigh!«

William hatte seinen Namen über die Schreie der Menge hinweg gehört. Er zügelte sein Pferd und sah in Philips Richtung.

»Dafür werdet Ihr zur Hölle fahren!« schrie Philip laut und deutlich.

Nackte Mordlust spiegelte sich in Williams Zügen. An diesem Tag zeitigte nicht einmal die Androhung dessen, was er sonst am meisten fürchtete, Wirkung. Er war wie besessen. Er schwenkte seine Fackel wie eine Fahne. »Dies *ist* die Hölle, Mönch!« brüllte er zurück, riß sein Pferd herum und ritt davon.

Mit einemmal waren sie alle verschwunden, die Reiter wie die panische Menge. Jack entließ Aliena aus seiner Umklammerung und stand auf. Seine rechte Hand fühlte sich taub an – richtig, er hatte den Schlag, der Alienas Kopf gegolten hatte, damit abgefangen. Er war froh über den Schmerz; hoffentlich würde er eine Weile lang vorhalten und ihn an den Vorfall erinnern.

Das Lagerhaus glich einem Inferno, und ringsum brannten kleine Feuer. Der Boden war mit Leibern übersät – ein paar rührten sich, andere bluteten, wieder andere lagen schlaff und unbeweglich da. Die Grabesstille wurde nur vom Knistern der Flammen unterbrochen. Der Mob war irgendwie entkommen und hatte die Toten und Verwundeten zurückgelassen. Jack fühlte sich benommen. Er hatte noch nie ein Schlachtfeld gesehen, aber so ähnlich, dachte er, muß es aussehen.

Aliena brach in Tränen aus. Jack legte ihr tröstend eine Hand auf die Schulter. Sie schob sie weg. Er hatte ihr das Leben gerettet, aber das war ihr völlig gleichgültig: Ihr ging es einzig und allein um ihre verdammte Wolle, die nun unwiderruflich in Flammen aufgegangen war. Einen Moment lang betrachtete er sie traurig. Ihr Haar war fast vollständig versengt, und sie sah überhaupt nicht mehr schön aus; aber er liebte sie. Es quälte ihn, daß sie so verzweifelt war und er ihr nicht helfen konnte.

Nun würde sie bestimmt nicht wieder versuchen, ins Lagerhaus zu gelangen. Er machte sich Sorgen um den Rest seiner Familie und ließ Aliena zurück, um nach ihnen zu suchen.

Sein Gesicht schmerzte. Er berührte seine Wange mit der Hand und zuckte zusammen. Auch er mußte sich verbrannt haben. Er betrachtete die auf dem Boden liegenden Leiber. Er hätte gerne etwas für die Verwundeten getan, aber wo sollte er beginnen? Er sah sich nach bekannten Gesichtern um und hoffte, keine zu finden. Mutter und Martha hatten sich in den Kreuzgang gerettet – sie müssen der Meute entkommen sein, dachte er. Ob Tom Alfred noch rechtzeitig gefunden hat? Er wandte sich dem Kloster zu. Da sah er Tom.

Sein Stiefvater lag in voller Länge auf dem schlammigen Grund. Von Leben keine Spur. Sein Gesicht war kenntlich, ja, wenn man einmal von der Partie der Augenbrauen absah, sogar friedlich zu nennen; aber seine Stirn war offen und der Schädel völlig zerschmettert. Jack konnte es kaum fassen. Tom war tot – unmöglich! Aber dann – dieser Körper da konnte unmöglich Leben in sich haben. Er sah weg und dann wieder hin. Es war Tom, und er war tot.

Jack kniete sich neben der Leiche nieder. Es drängte ihn, etwas zu tun, etwas zu sagen, und zum erstenmal verstand er, warum die Menschen für ihre Toten beteten. »Mutter wird dich schrecklich vermissen«, sagte er. Die bösen Worte fielen ihm wieder ein, die er Tom an den Kopf geworfen hatte, damals, als Alfred ihn schier umgebracht hatte. »Das war ja gar nicht wahr«, sagte er, und die Tränen liefen ihm nur so übers Gesicht. »Du hast mich nicht vernachlässigt. Du hast dich um mich gekümmert und mich ernährt, und du hast meine Mutter glücklich gemacht, wirklich und wahrhaft glücklich.« Aber das ist noch nicht alles, dachte er. Was Tom mir gegeben hat, sind nicht bloß Kleinigkeiten wie ein Dach über dem Kopf und das tägliche Brot. Tom hat mir etwas Einzigartiges gegeben; etwas, das kein anderer, nicht einmal mein eigener Vater, mir geben konnte, etwas, das eher einer Passion gleichkommt, einer Aufgabe, einer Kunst, einem Sinn fürs ganze Leben. »Du hast mir die Kathedrale gegeben«, flüsterte Jack dem Toten zu. »Dafür danke ich dir.«

Buch IV / 1142-45

Philips wütende Prophezeiung beraubte William jeglichen Triumphgefühls, und statt Zufriedenheit über die vollbrachte Tat zu empfinden, stand er nun Todesängste aus, daß er tatsächlich in die Hölle käme.

Mit seiner frechen Antwort: »Dies *ist* die Hölle, Mönch!« hatte er sich zwar gegen den Prior behauptet, aber das war nur der Hitze des Gefechts zuzuschreiben. Nun, da alles vorbei war, er seine Männer aus dem Flammenmeer der brennenden Stadt geführt, Pferde und Herzschlag sich beruhigt hatten, fand er die Zeit, über seinen Anschlag nachzudenken, zu erwägen, wie viele Menschen er wohl auf dem Gewissen hatte – verwundet, verbrannt, erschlagen –, und da fiel ihm Philips zorniges Gesicht wieder ein, der Finger, mit dem der Prior geradewegs in die tiefsten Tiefen der Erde zu weisen schien und dabei die schicksalsschweren Worte sprach: »Dafür werdet Ihr zur Hölle fahren!«

Gegen Abend war seine Stimmung auf dem Nullpunkt angelangt. Seine Krieger wollten mit ihm über den Überfall reden, die Höhepunkte im nachhinein noch einmal durchleben und in Erinnerungen an die Metzelei schwelgen, aber seine Stimmung steckte sie alsbald an, und sie versanken in düsteres Schweigen. Die Nacht verbrachten sie im Gutshaus eines der größeren Pächter Williams, und beim Abendessen betranken sich die Männer grimmig entschlossen bis zur Besinnungslosigkeit. Der Pächter, der die Bedürfnisse von Kriegern nach einer Schlacht genau zu kennen schien, hatte vorsorglich ein paar Huren aus Shiring kommen lassen, doch ihr Geschäft ging nur schleppend. William lag die ganze Nacht wach vor lauter Angst, er könne im Schlaf sterben und direkt zur Hölle fahren.

Am nächsten Morgen kehrte er nicht nach Earlscastle zurück, sondern begab sich statt dessen zu Bischof Waleran. Der war zwar bei seiner Ankunft nicht da, aber Dechant Baldwin teilte mit, er werde im Laufe des Nachmittags erwartet. William wartete in der Kapelle auf ihn, glotzte unentwegt auf das Kreuz über dem Altar und zitterte am ganzen Leibe, trotz der sommerlichen Hitze. Als Waleran erschien, hätte er ihm am liebsten die Füße geküßt.

Der Bischof kam, angetan mit schwarzen Gewändern, in die Kapelle gestürmt und sagte kalt: »Was habt Ihr hier zu suchen?«

William rappelte sich auf, krampfhaft bemüht, seine jämmerliche Angst hinter einer selbstbeherrschten Miene zu verbergen. »Ich habe gestern die Stadt Kingsbridge niedergebrannt.«

»Ich weiß«, fiel ihm Waleran ins Wort. »Den ganzen Tag schon bekomme ich nichts anderes zu hören. Was ist in Euch gefahren? Habt Ihr den Verstand verloren?«

Diese Reaktion kam für William völlig unerwartet. Er hatte den Überfall mit Waleran nicht im voraus besprochen, weil er sich dessen Billigung sicher geglaubt hatte – Waleran haßte alles, was mit Kingsbridge zusammenhing, besonders aber Prior Philip. William hatte erwartet, Waleran werde sich erfreut, wenn nicht sogar schadenfroh zeigen. Er sagte: »Ich habe Euren größten Feind ruiniert. Und nun muß ich meine Sünden bekennen.«

»Das wundert mich nicht«, gab Waleran zurück. »Es heißt, daß mehr als hundert Menschen in dem Feuer umgekommen sind.« Er schauderte. »Schrecklich, so zu sterben.«

»Ich bin zur Beichte bereit«, sagte William.

Waleran schüttelte den Kopf. »Ich weiß nicht, ob ich Euch Absolution erteilen kann.«

Ein Angstschrei bildete sich auf Williams Lippen. »Wieso nicht?«

»Ihr wißt, daß Bischof Henry von Winchester und ich uns wieder auf die Seite von König Stephan geschlagen haben. Ich glaube kaum, daß es der König gutheißen wird, wenn ich einem Verbündeten Mathildes die Absolution erteile.«

»Verflucht noch mal, Waleran, Ihr wart es doch, der mich bewogen hat, das Lager zu wechseln!«

Waleran zuckte die Achseln. »Dann wechselt Ihr es eben noch einmal.«

William begriff, daß dies von vornherein Walerans Ziel gewesen war: Ich soll mich also wieder mit Stephan verbünden, dachte er. Waleran sichtliches Entsetzen darüber, daß ich Kingsbridge in Schutt und Asche gelegt, war nur die Finte, mit der er sich eine gute Verhandlungsposition gesichert hat. Diese Erkenntnis löste eine Welle der

Erleichterung in ihm aus, hieß dies doch, daß Waleran nicht grundsätzlich dagegen war, ihm die Absolution zu erteilen! Aber wollte er wirklich wieder das Lager wechseln? Er schwieg und versuchte, in Ruhe darüber nachzudenken.

»Stephan hat den ganzen Sommer über einen Sieg nach dem anderen davongetragen«, fuhr Waleran fort. »Mathilde fleht ihren Ehemann an, ihr aus der Normandie zu Hilfe zu eilen, aber er weigert sich. Das Blatt hat sich zu unseren Gunsten gewendet.«

Schreckliche Aussichten taten sich plötzlich vor William auf: Die Kirche verwehrte ihm die Vergebung seiner Schandtaten; der Vogt klagte ihn des Mordes an; ein siegreicher König Stephan stellte sich hinter den Vogt und die Kirche; er selbst wurde verurteilt und gehängt ...

»Folgt meinem Beispiel und hört auf Bischof Henry – der weiß, aus welcher Richtung der Wind weht«, drängte Waleran. »Wenn alles klappt, wird Winchester zur Erzdiözese und Henry Erzbischof von Winchester – gleichrangig mit dem Erzbischof von Canterbury. Und wenn Henry stirbt, wer weiß? Gut möglich, daß ich dann Erzbischof werde. Und danach ... nun ja, es gibt bereits englische Kardinäle – eines Tages wird es vielleicht sogar einen englischen Papst geben ...«

Der unverhüllte Ehrgeiz, der sich plötzlich auf den ansonsten so steinernen Zügen Walerans malte, schlug William trotz seiner eigenen Befürchtungen in Bann. Waleran als Papst? Nichts war unmöglich. Aber was zählte, waren die unmittelbaren Folgen seiner Ambitionen, und es war nicht schwer zu erkennen, daß er selbst das Unterpfand in Walerans Ränkespiel darstellte. Waleran hatte durch seine Fähigkeit, ihn und seine Ritter aus Shiring jederzeit der einen oder anderen Seite in diesem Krieg zuzuführen, bei Bischof Henry an Ansehen gewonnen. Das ist also der Preis, den ich dafür zahlen muß, daß die Kirche zu meinen Taten beide Augen zudrückt, dachte William. »Soll das vielleicht heißen ...« Seine Stimme klang heiser. Er räusperte sich und nahm einen zweiten Anlauf. »Soll das vielleicht heißen, daß Ihr mir die Beichte abnehmt, wenn ich wieder zu Stephan überlaufe und ihm Treue schwöre?«

Das Glitzern in Walerans Augen erlosch, und sein Gesicht verwandelte sich wieder in eine steinerne Maske. »Genau das wollte ich damit sagen«, erwiderte er.

William blieb eigentlich keine Wahl, aber schließlich – welchen Grund hatte er, sich zu weigern? Als es so aussah, als trüge Mathilde den Sieg davon, war er auf ihre Seite übergewechselt, und nun, da

Stephan anscheinend die Oberhand hatte, war er nur allzugern bereit, sich wieder auf dessen Seite zu schlagen. Und überdies hätte er zu allem Ja und Amen gesagt, nur, um diese entsetzliche Furcht loszuwerden, er müsse in der Hölle braten. »Einverstanden«, erklärte er ohne Zaudern. »Wenn ich nur schnell beichten kann.«

»Na gut«, meinte Waleran. »Lasset uns beten.«

Schon während sie das Gebet hastig herunterleierten, spürte William, wie die Last seiner Schuld wich. Allmählich begann er gar, sich über seinen Erfolg zu freuen, und als er schließlich aus der Kapelle trat, war ihm die gehobene Stimmung so deutlich anzusehen, daß seine Männer lauthals ihre Freude kundtaten. William teilte ihnen mit, daß sie nach dem Willen Gottes, verkündet durch Bischof Waleran, künftig wieder für König Stephan kämpfen würden, und das genügte ihnen als Ausrede für eine Feier. Waleran ließ Wein kommen.

Während sie auf das Essen warteten, sagte William: »Stephan sollte mich jetzt in meiner Eigenschaft als Graf bestätigen.«

»Sollte schon«, bekräftigte Waleran. »Ob er es allerdings tut, ist eine andere Frage.«

»Aber ich bin doch zu ihm übergelaufen!«

»Richard von Kingsbridge ist ihm nie abtrünnig geworden.«

William gestattete sich ein selbstzufriedenes Grinsen. »Ich glaube, ich habe dafür gesorgt, daß Richard uns nicht mehr in die Quere kommen kann.«

»Ach ja? Wie das?«

»Richard hat nie Land besessen. Sein ritterliches Gefolge hat er sich nur auf Kosten seiner Schwester leisten können.«

»Eine unorthodoxe Methode, gewiß, allerdings auch eine erfolgreiche.«

»Aber seine Schwester hat kein Geld mehr. Ich habe gestern ihr Lagerhaus in Brand gesteckt. Jetzt steht sie ohne einen Heller dar und Richard ebenfalls.«

Waleran nickte anerkennend. »Dann ist es ja nur noch eine Frage der Zeit, bis er auf Nimmerwiedersehen verschwindet. Und dann, denke ich, wird Euch auch die Grafschaft zufallen.«

Das Essen wurde aufgetragen. Williams Krieger saßen am unteren Ende der Tafel und machten den Waschfrauen der Bischofsresidenz schöne Augen. William, der bei Waleran und den Erzdiakonen am oberen Ende saß, beneidete seine Männer ein wenig: Nun, da er seine Furcht losgeworden war, empfand er die Erzdiakone als langweilige Tischgenossen.

Dechant Baldwin reichte William ein Erbsengericht und sagte: »Lord William, wie wollt Ihr andere daran hindern, es Prior Philip gleichzutun und ihre eigene Wollmesse abzuhalten?«

Williams verblüffte die Frage. »Wer würde das schon wagen!«

»Ein Mönch sicherlich nicht mehr, aber vielleicht ein Graf.«

»Dazu bräuchte er eine Genehmigung.«

»Die könnte er bekommen, wenn er für König Stephan kämpft.«

»Nicht in dieser Grafschaft.«

»Baldwin hat recht«, mischte Bischof Waleran sich ein. »An der Grenze Eurer Grafschaft gibt es jede Menge Städte, die ihre eigene Wollmesse abhalten könnten: Wilton, Devizes, Wells, Marlborough, Wallingford ...«

»Wenn ich Kingsbridge niederbrennen konnte, kann ich auch jede andere Stadt niederbrennen«, sagte William verstimmt. Er nahm einen tiefen Schluck Wein. Es ärgerte ihn, seinen Sieg herabgemindert zu sehen.

Waleran griff nach einem Brötchen und brach es, aß jedoch nicht davon. »Mit Kingsbridge hattet Ihr leichte Beute«, führte er aus. »Es hat keine Stadtmauer, keine Burg, ja nicht einmal eine große Kirche, in der die Menschen Zuflucht suchen können. Überdies wird es von einem Mönch regiert, der weder über Ritter noch über Bewaffnete verfügt. Kingsbridge liegt, im Gegensatz zu den meisten anderen Städten, völlig schutzlos da.«

Dechant Baldwin fügte hinzu: »Und wenn der Krieg erst einmal vorbei ist, dann könnt Ihr auch eine Stadt wie Kingsbridge nicht mehr einfach niederbrennen und ungeschoren davonkommen – egal, wer dann auf dem Thron sitzt. Das ist dann Landfriedensbruch. Kein Herrscher kann dergleichen in Friedenszeiten dulden.«

William sah ein, daß sie recht hatten, und das ärgerte ihn. »Dann war die ganze Mühe womöglich umsonst«, sagte er und legte sein Messer nieder. Sein Magen verkrampfte sich vor Zorn, und er brachte keinen Bissen mehr hinunter.

»Wenn Aliena aber ruiniert sein sollte«, sagte Waleran, »dann ist dadurch natürlich so etwas wie eine Lücke entstanden.«

William verstand kein Wort. »Wie meint Ihr das?«

»Der Großteil der Wolle in dieser Grafschaft ist dieses Jahr an sie verkauft worden. Was aber wird nächstes Jahr?«

»Ich weiß nicht.«

Waleran fuhr nachdenklich fort: »Bis auf Prior Philip sind sämtliche Wollproduzenten im weiten Umkreis entweder Pächter des Grafen oder des Bischofs. Ihr seid, wenn schon nicht dem Namen nach, so doch zumindest faktisch der Graf, und ich bin der Bischof. Wenn wir unsere Pächter nun zwingen, ihre Vliese an uns zu verkaufen, dann haben wir zwei Drittel der gesamten Wollproduktion der Grafschaft, die wir selbstverständlich auf der Wollmesse zu Shiring verkaufen. Der Rest des Wollhandels ist dann so geringfügig, daß er auf keinen Fall eine weitere Wollmesse rechtfertigt, selbst wenn irgend jemand eine Genehmigung dafür erhalten sollte.«

Die Idee war brillant, das sah William sofort. »Und wir verdienen genausoviel Geld wie vordem Aliena«, fügte er noch hinzu.

»In der Tat.« Waleran nahm einen winzigen Bissen Fleisch vom Teller und kaute nachdenklich darauf herum. »Da habt Ihr also Kingsbridge niedergebrannt, Euren Erzfeind in den Ruin gejagt und Euch außerdem noch eine neue Einnahmequelle verschafft. Nicht schlecht für einen einzigen Tag.«

William genehmigte sich einen großen Schluck Wein und spürte, wie er seinen Magen erwärmte. Er ließ seinen Blick über das untere Ende des Tisches schweifen, und seine Augen leuchteten auf beim Anblick eines kräftigen, dunkelhaarigen Mädchens, das gerade zwei seiner Männer kokett anlächelte. Die wollte er sich heute abend herausgreifen. Er wußte jetzt schon, was geschehen würde: Hatte er sie erst einmal in eine Ecke gedrängt, sie zu Boden geworfen und ihren Rock angehoben, dann käme die Erinnerung an Alienas Gesicht, an den Ausdruck von Entsetzen und Verzweiflung, als sie ihre Wolle in Flammen aufgehen sah; und dann würde er es bestimmt schaffen. Die Aussicht darauf ließ ihn lächeln, und er nahm sich noch ein Stück von der Rehkeule.

Prior Philip hatten die Ereignisse zutiefst erschüttert. Williams unerwarteter Angriff, die Brutalität seines Überfalls, der schreckliche Anblick einer von Panik ergriffenen Menge, die gnadenlos hingemetzelt wurde, seine eigene Ohnmacht im Angesicht des Elends – das alles war zuviel zu ertragen, und er fühlte sich wie am Boden zerstört.

Am schlimmsten jedoch traf ihn Tom Builders Tod. Tom war auf dem Höhepunkt seines Könnens gewesen, ein wahrer Meister in allen Aspekten seines Handwerks, und hätte die Aufsicht über den Bau der Kathedrale bis zu ihrer Fertigstellung führen sollen. Darüber hinaus war er außerhalb des Klosters Philips engster Freund. Sie hatten sich mindestens einmal täglich beraten und gemeinsam um die Lösung der unendlich vielschichtigen Probleme, die ein solch umfangreiches Unternehmen mit sich brachte, gerungen. Tom vereinigte in sich sowohl Weisheit als auch Bescheidenheit, eine Verbindung, die die Arbeit mit ihm zu einer wahren Freude machte. Unfaßbar, daß er von ihnen gegangen sein sollte!

Philip fühlte sich mit seiner Weisheit am Ende; bitter empfand er, daß er keine wahre Macht besaß, und ohne Macht war er nicht einmal imstande, einen Kuhstall zu leiten, geschweige denn eine Stadt von der Größe Kingsbridges. Er hatte stets geglaubt, letzten Endes werde sich alles zum Guten kehren, solange er nur nach bestem Wissen und Gewissen handelte und sein Gottvertrauen nicht verlor. Die Brandschatzung der Stadt schien ihm nun das Gegenteil zu beweisen. Das nahm ihm allen Mut. Er saß den lieben langen Tag in seinem Haus herum, den Blick auf seinen Hausaltar geheftet, auf dem die Kerze allmählich herunterbrannte, legte die Hände in den Schoß und überließ sich seinen zerfahrenen, niederschmetternden Gedanken.

Es war der junge Jack, der überall nach dem Rechten sah. Auf seine Veranlassung wurden die Toten in die Krypta getragen, die Verwundeten in den Schlafsaal der Mönche gebracht und die Menschen, die am jenseitigen Flußufer auf der Wiese kampierten, notdürftig verköstigt. Glücklicherweise war es warm, so daß alle die Nacht im Freien verbringen konnten. Am Tag nach dem Massaker teilte Jack die immer noch benommenen Stadtbewohner in Gruppen ein und beschäftigte sie mit der Beseitigung von Schutt und Asche vom Klostergelände, während Cuthbert Whitehead und Milius Bursar bei den umliegenden Bauernhöfen Nahrungsmittel bestellten. Schon am zweiten Tag konnten die Toten in einhundertunddreiundneunzig frisch ausgehobenen Gräbern an der Nordmauer des Klosterhofs beigesetzt werden.

Jack ging mit seinen Vorschlägen zu Philip, und der gab sie einfach als Anordnungen weiter. Jack wies darauf hin, daß der Großteil der Überlebenden nur geringfügige materielle Verluste erlitten hatte: in den meisten Fällen lediglich eine Hütte und ein paar Möbel. Das Getreide stand noch auf dem Halm, das Vieh noch auf den Weiden, und die Ersparnisse der Leute befanden sich noch immer dort, wo sie vergraben worden waren – in der Regel unter der Feuerstelle ihres Hauses, wo sie den Brand, der die Stadt verwüstet, unbeschadet überstanden hatten. Die Kaufleute, deren Lager in Flammen aufgegangen waren, hatte es am schlimmsten getroffen; etliche standen, wie Aliena, vor dem blanken Nichts, andere hatten einen Teil ihres Reichtums in Form vergrabenen Silbers gerettet und konnten einen neuen Anfang machen. Jack schlug vor, die Stadt unverzüglich wieder aufzubauen.

Auf Jacks Vorschlag hin erteilte Philip die auf eine Woche befristete Ausnahmeerlaubnis, in den klösterlichen Wäldern beliebig viel Holz zum Wiederaufbau der Häuser zu schlagen. Daraufhin war Kingsbridge sieben Tage lang wie leergefegt, dieweil jede Familie die Bäume für ihr neues Haus auswählte und fällte. In diesen Tagen bat Jack Philip darum, einen Plan für die neue Stadt zu entwerfen. Diese Idee endlich erwies sich als zündend und riß Philip aus seiner lähmenden Lethargie.

Vier Tage lang arbeitete er unermüdlich an seinem Plan. Rings um die Klostermauern sollten die großen Häuser der reichsten Handwerker und Kaufleute stehen. Er besann sich auf das Gittermuster der Straßen in Winchester und entwarf das neue Kingsbridge nach den gleichen praktischen Erwägungen. Gradlinige Straßen, breit genug für zwei einander entgegenkommende Karren, sollten, von schmaleren Nebenstraßen gekreuzt, zum Fluß hinunterführen. Die Breite eines Baugrundstücks setzte er mit vierundzwanzig Fuß an – das bot genügend Raum für großzügige Fassaden. Jedes Grundstück sollte einhundertfünfundzwanzig Fuß tief sein und somit über ausreichend Platz für einen ordentlichen Hinterhof samt Abtritt, Gemüsegarten und Kuh- oder Schweinestall verfügen. Die alte Brücke war abgebrannt, die neue sollte an einem verkehrsgünstigen Platz am unteren Ende der Hauptstraße entstehen. Letztere sollte, dem Beispiel von Lincoln folgend, künftig gleich hinter der Brücke schnurgerade den Berg hinauf, an der Kathedrale vorbei und am anderen Ende der Stadt wieder hinausführen. Eine zweite breite Straße sollte vom Klostertor zu einem neuen Kai am Flußufer verlaufen, der stromabwärts unterhalb der Flußbiegung zu errichten war. Auf diese Weise konnten ganze Schiffsladungen unter Umgehung der Hauptgeschäftsstraße auf direktem Wege zum Kloster befördert werden. Unweit des neuen Kais sollte ein ganz neuer Stadtteil für die kleineren Häuser der Armen entstehen, die auf diese Weise ein ganzes Stück flußabwärts vom Kloster angesiedelt wurden und somit das Trinkwasser für die Mönche nicht mehr verunreinigen konnten.

Die Planung des Wiederaufbaus der Stadt vermochte Philip zwar aus seiner ohnmächtigen Versunkenheit zu reißen, doch sobald er einmal von seinen Entwürfen aufsah, überfielen ihn erneut Trauer und Zorn. War William Hamleigh in der Tat der Teufel in Menschengestalt? Er hatte mehr Unheil um sich verbreitet, als menschenmöglich schien. Philip las das gleiche Wechselspiel von Hoffnung und Kummer in den Gesichtern der Stadtbewohner, die schwerbeladen mit Bauholz aus dem Wald zurückkehrten. Jack hatte mit Hilfe der Mönche den Grundriß der neuen Stadt mit Pfählen und Seilen auf dem Boden markiert, und während die Leute ihre Wahl unter den verschiedenen Grundstücken trafen, konnte man den einen oder anderen düster sagen hören: »Wozu das alles? Wenn's nächstes Jahr nur doch wieder abbrennt?« Hätte es wenigstens die Aussicht auf Gerechtigkeit, auch nur den kleinsten Hoffnungsschimmer gegeben, daß die Übeltäter bestraft würden – die Menschen wären vielleicht nicht ganz so untröstlich gewesen. Philip hatte zwar viele Briefe geschrieben – an Stephan und an Mathilde, an Bischof Henry und an den Erzbischof von Canterbury, ja sogar an den Papst –, aber er wußte genau, daß in Kriegszeiten kaum Aussicht bestand, einen so mächtigen und einflußreichen Mann wie William zur Verantwortung zu ziehen.

Die größeren Grundstücke in Philips Plan waren trotz höherer Mieten sehr gefragt, so daß er seinen Entwurf änderte und noch mehr einzeichnete. Fast niemand wollte in dem ärmeren Viertel bauen, dennoch entschied Philip, es bei seinem ursprünglichen Plan zu belassen, um Raum für künftige Entwicklungen zu haben. Innerhalb von zehn Tagen nach dem Feuer wurden auf den meisten Grundstücken bereits Holzhäuser errichtet, und es dauerte keine weitere Woche, bis fast alle fertiggestellt waren. Sobald die Leute ihre Häuser bezogen hatten, wurde die Arbeit an der Kathedrale wiederaufgenommen. Die Bauleute erhielten ihre Löhne und wollten Geld ausgeben; folglich öffneten auch die Läden wieder ihre Pforten, die Kleinbauern brachten ihre Eier und Zwiebeln in die Stadt, dann nahmen auch die Küchenmädchen und Wäscherinnen ihre Arbeit bei den Kaufleuten und Handwerkern wieder auf, und mit der Zeit verlief das Leben in Kingsbridge wieder in den gewohnten Bahnen.

Aber es hatte so viele Tote gegeben, daß Kingsbridge einer Geisterstadt glich. Keine einzige Familie hatte nicht zumindest einen Angehörigen verloren, sei es ein Kind, die Mutter, den Ehemann oder eine Schwester. Die Menschen trugen zwar keine Trauerbinden, aber die Falten in ihren Gesichtern sprachen eine deutliche Sprache. Mit am schlimmsten hatte es den sechsjährigen Jonathan getroffen, der wie ein Häufchen Unglück über den Klosterhof schlich, bis Philip begriff, daß er Tom vermißte, der offenbar mehr Zeit mit dem Jungen zugebracht hatte als allgemein angenommen. Daraufhin reservierte Philip täglich eine Stunde allein für Jonathan, erzählte ihm Geschichten, brachte ihm Abzählreime bei und lauschte seinem unablässigen Geplapper.

Philip schrieb auch an die Äbte der größten Benediktinerabteien in England und Frankreich und fragte nach einem Baumeister, der Toms Stelle einnehmen könnte. Normalerweise hätte sich ein Prior in Philips Lage an seinen Bischof gewandt, denn Bischöfe reisten viel herum und hörten schon einmal von guten Baumeistern; aber Bischof Waleran würde für ihn natürlich keinen Finger rühren. Die Tatsache, daß die beiden Männer unwiderruflich miteinander zerstritten waren, erschwerte Philips Arbeit mehr, als nötig gewesen wäre.

Er hatte noch keine Antwort auf seine Briefe erhalten, da wandten sich die Handwerker auf ihrer Suche nach einem Baumeister instinktiv Alfred zu. Alfred war immerhin Toms Sohn, er war Steinmetzmeister und hatte seit einiger Zeit eine eigene, quasi eigenständige Bautruppe befehligt. Sein Verstand konnte sich zwar mit dem seines Vaters nicht messen und ließ leider viel zu wünschen übrig, aber er war des Lesens und Schreibens kundig, und mit der Zeit füllte er die Lücke aus, die durch Toms Tod entstanden war.

Eine Zeitlang hatte es den Anschein, als häuften sich die Fragen und Schwierigkeiten mehr denn zu Toms Zeiten, und Alfred rückte immer dann mit seinem Problem heraus, wenn von Jack weit und breit nichts zu sehen war. Das war zwar verständlich, denn jeder in Kingsbridge wußte, daß die beiden Stiefbrüder miteinander verfeindet waren, führte jedoch dazu, daß sich Philip wieder einmal mit unendlich vielen Einzelheiten belästigt fühlte.

Doch im Laufe der Wochen gewann Alfred immer mehr Selbstvertrauen und wandte sich schließlich eines Tages mit der Frage an Philip: »Hättet Ihr nicht lieber ein Gewölbe für die Kathedrale?«

Toms Bauplan sah eine Holzdecke für das Langhaus und steinerne Gewölbe für die schmaleren Seitenschiffe vor. »Ja, schon«, erwiderte Philip. »Aber wir haben uns für die Holzdecke entschieden, um Geld zu sparen.«

Alfred nickte. »Dabei gibt es nur ein Problem – eine Holzdecke kann abbrennen. Ein Gewölbe aus Stein ist feuerfest.«

Philip musterte ihn einen Moment lang und fragte sich, ob er Alfred wohl unterschätzt habe. Es überraschte ihn, daß er eine Änderung am Bauplan seines Vaters vorschlug; so etwas sah eher Jack ähnlich. Aber die Vorstellung einer feuerfesten Kirche gefiel ihm um so mehr, als die Stadt gerade gänzlich in Flammen aufgegangen war.

Alfred dachte ähnlich und sagte: »Das einzige Gebäude in der Stadt, das den Brand unbeschadet überstanden hat, ist die neue Pfarrkirche.«

Und die neue, von Alfred erbaute Pfarrkirche hat ein Steingewölbe, dachte Philip. Aber einen Haken hatte die Sache. »Sind die Mauern denn stark genug, um das zusätzliche Gewicht zu verkraften?«

»Wir müßten lediglich die Strebepfeiler verstärken, die dann etwas mehr hervorragen, das ist alles.«

Er hat sich das genau überlegt, stellte Philip fest. »Und die Kosten?«

»Auf lange Sicht kostet das natürlich mehr, und es wird drei oder vier Jahre länger dauern, bis die Kirche fertig ist. Aber auf die Höhe Eurer jährlichen Ausgaben hat das keinen Einfluß.«

Philip fand zunehmend Gefallen an Alfreds Vorschlag. »Heißt das, wir müssen ein Jahr länger warten, bevor wir den Gottesdienst wieder im Chorraum abhalten können?«

»Nein. Ob Stein oder Holz, das macht keinen Unterschied; wir können mit der Decke sowieso nicht vor nächstem Frühjahr beginnen, weil sich der Lichtgaden im Mittelschiff erst festigen muß, bevor wir ihn belasten können. Die Holzdecke ist schneller gebaut und spart dabei einige Monate; aber der Chorraum wird so oder so Ende nächsten Jahres überdacht sein.«

Philip überlegte. Es galt, die Vorteile eines feuerfesten Daches gegen den Nachteil abzuwägen, den eine vier Jahre längere Bauzeit mit sich brächte, ganz zu schweigen von den zusätzlichen Kosten. Letztere lagen jedoch in weiter Ferne, während die zusätzliche Sicherheit sofort ihre Wirkung haben würde. »Ich werde es mit den Brüdern in der Kapitelversammlung beraten«, sagte er. »Mir jedenfalls gefällt Euer Vorschlag.«

Alfred bedankte sich und ging hinaus. Philip starrte noch eine Weile lang auf die Tür und fragte sich, ob es nach all dem noch nötig war, sich nach einem neuen Baumeister umzusehen.

Am Erntedankfest zeigte sich Kingsbridge von seiner besten Seite. Des Vormittags wurde in jedem Haus ein Laib Brot gebacken – das Getreide war geerntet, und es gab billiges Mehl in Hülle und Fülle. Wer selbst keinen Ofen hatte, benutzte den des Nachbarn oder ließ das Brot in den großen Backhäusern des Klosters oder bei den Stadtbäckern, Peggy Baxter und Jack-atte-Noven, backen. Gegen Mittag roch es überall nach frischem Brot, und den Leuten lief das Wasser im Mund zusammen. Die Brotlaibe wurden auf Tischen ausgestellt, die auf der Wiese am gegenüberliegenden Flußufer aufgebaut worden waren, und von allen bewundert. Kein Brot glich dem anderen. Viele waren mit

Früchten oder Gewürzen gefüllt: Es gab Pflaumen- und Rosinenbrot, Ingwer- und Zuckerbrot, Zwiebel- und Knoblauchbrot und viele Sorten mehr. Einige Laibe waren petersiliengrün, eigelbgelb, sandelholzrot und sonnenblumenviolett. Hinzu kamen noch die unterschiedlichsten Formen: Dreiecke, Kegel, Kugeln, Sterne, Ovale, Pyramiden, Stangen, Brötchen, ja sogar Achten. Wieder andere waren in ihrem Ehrgeiz noch weiter gegangen und hatten wie Kaninchen, Bären, Affen und Drachen geformte Brote gebacken. Es gab Häuser und Burgen aus Brot. Aber der von Ellen gebackene Brotlaib schoß auf einstimmigen Beschluß den Vogel ab: die Darstellung der fertigen Kathedrale nach den Plänen ihres verstorbenen Mannes.

Ellens Kummer war unermeßlich gewesen. Nacht um Nacht hatte sie kläglich vor sich hin gewimmert, ohne daß irgend jemand sie hätte trösten können. Selbst jetzt noch, zwei Monate später, wirkte sie abgehärmt und verweint; aber Martha und Ellen schienen sich gegenseitig eine Stütze zu sein, und die Herstellung der Kathedrale aus Brot hatte ihnen einen gewissen Trost verschafft.

Aliena blieb lange vor Ellens Backwerk stehen und hatte nur einen Wunsch: eine Tätigkeit zu finden, die ihr selbst Trost spenden konnte. Sie hatte an nichts mehr Freude. Als man mit dem Kosten begann, ging sie lustlos von Tisch zu Tisch, ohne einen Bissen zu probieren. Nicht einmal das neue Haus hatte sie bauen wollen, bis Prior Philip ihr befohlen hatte, sich zusammenzureißen. Alfred hatte ihr das Holz gebracht und ein paar Männer für die Arbeit zur Verfügung gestellt. Sie aß immer noch tagtäglich im Kloster, wenn sie überhaupt daran dachte. Sie fühlte sich matt und kraftlos. Wenn sie schon einmal etwas für sich selbst tun wollte – aus dem restlichen Holz einen Küchenschemel bauen oder die Ritzen in den Wänden ihres Hauses mit Lehm aus dem Fluß füllen oder eine Schlinge für den Vogelfang basteln, so daß sie etwas zu essen hatte –, dann mußte sie jedesmal daran denken, wie unermüdlich sie gearbeitet hatte, um sich als Wollhändlerin zu etablieren, und wie unglaublich schnell alles in Schutt und Asche gelegt worden war, und dann verlor sie jedesmal wieder den Mut. So lebte sie also in den Tag hinein, stand spät auf, ging, wenn sie hungrig war, zum Essen ins Kloster, verbrachte den Tag damit, dem vorbeifließenden Fluß nachzuschauen, und schlief schließlich bei Anbruch der Dunkelheit auf dem strohbedeckten Fußboden ihres Hauses ein.

Bei aller Gleichgültigkeit war ihr dennoch klar, daß dieses Erntedankfest gar nichts besagte. Zwar war die Stadt wieder aufgebaut und die Menschen gingen wie zuvor ihren Geschäften nach, doch Williams

Massaker warf einen düsteren Schatten auf alles, und Aliena spürte sehr wohl die tiefsitzende Angst unter dem oberflächlichen Wohlergehen. Den meisten gelang das Verstellspiel besser als ihr, aber in Wirklichkeit fühlten sie sich genauso: daß es nicht so bleiben konnte und daß alles, was sie aufbauten, wieder vernichtet würde.

Während sie noch ausdruckslos auf die Unmenge an Broten starrte, traf ihr Bruder Richard ein. Er führte sein Pferd aus der menschenleeren Stadt hinaus und über die Brücke. Er hatte Kingsbridge schon einige Zeit vor dem Massaker verlassen und für König Stephan gekämpft, nun traute er kaum seinen Augen. »Was zum Teufel ist denn hier passiert?« sagte er zu seiner Schwester. »Ich kann unser Haus nicht mehr finden – die ganze Stadt hat sich verändert!«

»William Hamleigh ist während des Wollmarktes mit seinen Kriegern hier eingefallen und hat die Stadt niedergebrannt«, sagte Aliena.

Richard wurde vor Schreck weiß wie die Wand, und die Narbe an seinem rechten Ohr trat deutlich hervor. »William!« stieß er hervor. »Dieser Teufel!«

»Wir haben wieder ein neues Haus«, fuhr Aliena ausdruckslos fort. »Alfreds Leute haben es für mich gebaut. Aber es ist viel kleiner und liegt unten am neuen Kai.«

»Und du? Was ist mit dir?« fragte er und starrte sie an. »Du bist so gut wie kahl, und Augenbrauen hast du auch keine mehr.«

»Mein Haar hat Feuer gefangen.«

»Er hat doch nicht ...«

Aliena schüttelte den Kopf. »Diesmal nicht.«

Eins der Mädchen reichte Richard ein Stück Salzbrot zum Probieren. Er nahm es entgegen, ohne jedoch einen Bissen anzurühren. Er wirkte vollkommen überwältigt.

»Trotzdem, ich bin froh, daß du gesund und munter bist«, sagte Aliena.

Er nickte. »Stephan marschiert auf Oxford zu, wo Mathilde sich verschanzt hat. Vielleicht ist der Krieg bald vorüber. Aber ich brauche ein neues Schwert – ich bin gekommen, um Geld zu holen.« Er biß nun doch von seinem Brot ab und bekam auch wieder ein wenig Farbe. »Herrje, wie gut das schmeckt. Später kannst du mir ein Stück Fleisch braten.«

Plötzlich hatte sie Angst vor ihm. Sie wußte, daß er hart mit ihr ins Gericht gehen würde, und sie fühlte sich zu schwach, ihm Paroli zu bieten. »Ich habe kein Fleisch«, sagte sie.

»Na, dann geh halt zum Metzger und hol welches!«

»Sei mir bitte nicht böse, Richard«, sagte sie und fing an zu zittern.

»Ich bin dir nicht böse«, erwiderte er unwirsch. »Was ist denn nur los mit dir?«

»Meine gesamte Wolle ist bei dem Brand vernichtet worden«, sagte sie und starrte ihn ängstlich an, als rechne sie mit einem Wutausbruch.

Er runzelte die Stirn, blickte sie an, schluckte hart und warf die Kruste seines Brotes fort. »Die ganze Wolle?«

»Die ganze Wolle.«

»Aber ein bißchen Geld wirst du doch noch haben.«

»Keinen roten Heller.«

»Wieso? Du hattest doch immer eine große Truhe mit Silberpennies unter dem Fußboden vergraben –«

»Aber nicht im Mai. Ich habe es für Wolle ausgegeben – bis zum letzten Penny. Und außerdem habe ich mir vierzig Pfund von Malachi geliehen, die ich nicht zurückzahlen kann. Und ein Schwert kann ich dir ganz bestimmt nicht kaufen, ja, nicht einmal für ein Stück Fleisch zum Abendessen reicht es. Wir sind vollkommen mittellos.«

»Und wie soll ich dann weitermachen?« rief er wütend aus. Sein Pferd legte die Ohren an und scheute.

»Das weiß ich auch nicht!« gab Aliena weinerlich zurück. »Und schrei nicht so, du erschreckst nur das Pferd.« Sie brach in Tränen aus.

»William Hamleigh ist an allem schuld«, stieß Richard hervor. »Eines Tages werde ich ihn abstechen wie ein fettes Schwein, das schwöre ich bei allem, was mir heilig ist!«

Alfred kam auf sie zu. Sein buschiger Bart war voller Brotkrümel, und in der Hand hielt er einen Kanten Pflaumenbrot. »Probiert dies hier«, sagte er zu Richard.

»Ich habe keinen Hunger«, erwiderte Richard kurz angebunden.

Alfred sah Aliena an und fragte: »Was ist denn los?«

Richard antwortete an Alienas Statt: »Sie hat mir soeben mitgeteilt, daß wir keinen roten Heller mehr besitzen.«

Alfred nickte. »Alle haben etwas verloren, aber Aliena hat alles verloren.«

»Ihr begreift natürlich, was das für mich bedeutet«, sagte Richard. Er richtete die Worte an Alfred, sah dabei aber seine Schwester vorwurfsvoll an. »Ich bin am Ende. Wenn ich die Waffen nicht ersetzen, meine Männer nicht bezahlen und keine Pferde kaufen kann, dann kann ich auch nicht für König Stephan kämpfen. Meine Laufbahn als Ritter ist damit am Ende – und ich werde es nie zum Grafen von Shiring bringen.«

Alfred sagte: »Vielleicht heiratet Aliena ja einen reichen Mann.«

Richard lachte höhnisch auf. »Sie hat ihnen samt und sonders einen Korb gegeben.«

»Vielleicht wiederholt einer von ihnen sein Angebot.«

»Ja.« Richards Gesicht verzog sich zu einem grausamen Grinsen. »Wir können ja all ihren zurückgewiesenen Verehrern einen Brief schicken und ihnen mitteilen, daß sie ihr gesamtes Geld verloren hat und nun bereit wäre, sich die Sache noch einmal zu überlegen –«

»Genug«, sagte Alfred und legte seine Hand auf Richards Arm. Richard verstummte. Alfred wandte sich an Aliena. »Erinnert Ihr Euch noch daran, was ich Euch vor einem Jahr während des ersten Gilden-essens gesagt habe?«

Aliena verließ vollends der Mut. Es war unglaublich, daß Alfred wieder damit anfangen wollte. Sie hatte einfach nicht die Kraft, sich mit ihm auseinanderzusetzen. »Ich erinnere mich«, erwiderte sie. »Und ich hoffe, daß Ihr Euch an meine Antwort erinnern könnt.«

»Ich liebe Euch nach wie vor«, sagte Alfred.

Richard sah vollkommen verblüfft drein.

Alfred fuhr fort: »Ich möchte Euch immer noch heiraten. Aliena, wollt Ihr meine Frau werden?«

»Nein!« sagte Aliena. Gerne hätte sie mehr gesagt und die unange-nehme Sache ein für allemal entschieden, aber sie fühlte sich zu matt und zerschlagen. Ihr Blick flog von Alfred zu Richard und wieder zu Alfred zurück; sie hatte genug. Sie ließ die beiden wortlos stehen, ging schnellen Schritts über die Wiese und über die Brücke in die Stadt. Sie war der ganzen Sache überdrüssig und böse auf Alfred, daß er sein Angebot in Richards Gegenwart wiederholt hatte. Es wäre ihr lieber gewesen, wenn ihr Bruder nichts davon gewußt hätte. Drei Monate waren seit dem Brand vergangen – warum hatte Alfred sich bis jetzt damit Zeit gelassen? Es schien gerade so, als hätte er auf Richard gewartet.

Sie wanderte durch die menschenleeren neuen Straßen. Sämtliche Einwohner befanden sich am anderen Flußufer und kosteten die Brote. Alienas Haus lag in dem neuen Armenviertel unten am Kai. Die Mieten waren niedrig dort, aber sie wußte trotzdem nicht, woher sie das Geld dafür nehmen sollte.

Richard holte sie zu Pferde ein, stieg aus dem Sattel und ging neben ihr her. »Die ganze Stadt riecht nach neuem Holz«, sagte er im Plauderton. «Und alles ist so sauber!«

Aliena hatte sich bereits an das neue Stadtbild gewöhnt, aber jetzt sah sie zum erstenmal richtig hin. Es stimmte, alles war unglaublich sauber. Das Feuer hatte mit dem feuchten, modrigen Holz der älteren Gebäude, den reetgedeckten, vom jahrelangen Kochen schmierigen Dächern, den stinkenden, uralten Ställen und den übelriechenden Misthaufen kurzen Prozeß gemacht. Überall roch es neu: neues Holz, neue Reetdächer, neue Binsen auf den Fußböden, ja sogar frische Tünche auf den Wänden der wohlhabenderen Häuser. Es schien, als sei der Boden durch den Brand mit Nährstoffen angereichert worden, und aus allen Ecken sprossen die Wildblumen. Es war auffällig, wie wenig Leute seit dem Brand krank geworden waren, und man nahm allgemein an, daß dies eine Bestätigung der von vielen Philosophen vertretenen These war, nach der Krankheiten sich mittels übelriechender Dämpfe verbreiteten.

Aliena, tief in Gedanken versunken, merkte, daß Richard sie angesprochen hatte. »Was hast du gesagt?«

»Daß ich keine Ahnung hatte, daß Alfred letztes Jahr um deine Hand angehalten hat.«

»Damals hattest du andere Sorgen. Das muß ungefähr zur gleichen Zeit gewesen sein, als Robert von Gloucester gefangengesetzt wurde.«

»Es war nett von Alfred, dir ein Haus zu bauen.«

»Ja, das stimmt. Und hier ist es.« Sie betrachtete ihn, während er das Haus musterte. Er wirkte niedergeschlagen, und sie hatte Mitleid mit ihm – schließlich entstammte er einem Grafengeschlecht, und selbst das weiträumige Stadthaus, das sie vor dem Brand bewohnt hatten, war, verglichen mit der Burg, ein Abstieg für ihn gewesen. Und nun mußte er sich mit einem Haus begnügen, das eher dem eines Tagelöhners entsprach.

Sie ergriff die Zügel seines Pferdes. »Komm. Hinter dem Haus ist Platz für das Pferd.« Sie führte das große Tier durch den einzigen Raum im Haus und auf den rückwärtigen Hof, band es an einen Zaunpfosten und machte sich daran, den schweren hölzernen Sattel zu entfernen. Überall sprossen Gräser und Unkraut, die sich aus dem Nichts in der verbrannten Erde angesiedelt hatten. Die meisten Einwohner hatten inzwischen Latrinen gegraben, Gemüsegärten angelegt und Hühner- und Schweineställe gebaut, nur Alienas Hinterhof lag noch da wie am ersten Tag.

Richard verweilte einen Augenblick lang im Haus, aber es gab nicht viel zu sehen, und er folgte Aliena auf den Hof hinaus. »Das Haus ist ein bißchen kahl – keine Möbel, weder Töpfe noch Schüsseln ...«

»Ich habe kein Geld«, sagte Aliena teilnahmslos.

»Und im Garten hast du auch noch keinen Handstreich getan«, bemerkte er und blickte sich naserümpfend um.

»Mir fehlt einfach die Kraft dazu«, gab sie unwirsch zurück, reichte ihm den schweren Sattel und ging ins Haus.

Sie setzte sich mit dem Rücken zur Wand auf den Boden. Es war kühl hier drinnen. Sie hörte, wie Richard sich draußen im Hof mit dem Pferd zu schaffen machte. Sie hatte noch nicht lange so dagesessen, als eine Ratte die Schnauze aus dem Stroh steckte. Ratten und Mäuse mußten zu Tausenden in dem Feuer umgekommen sein, doch so langsam machten sie sich wieder bemerkbar. Aliena schaute sich suchend um, aber sie hatte nichts zur Hand, womit sie das Tier hätte töten können, das außerdem ebenso schnell, wie es gekommen war, wieder verschwand.

Was soll ich nur tun? dachte sie. Ich kann nicht bis zum Ende meiner Tage so weiterleben. Aber allein schon der Gedanke, ein neues Unternehmen aufzubauen, raubte ihr den Rest ihrer Kraft. Sie hatte ihren Bruder und sich bereits einmal aus bitterer Armut befreit; ihre Kraftreserven waren dabei zur Gänze erschöpft worden, und noch einmal würde sie es nicht zustande bringen. Sie mußte einen passiven Lebensstil finden und jemand anderem die Zügel überlassen, so daß sie frei von Entscheidungen und ohne Unternehmungsgeist leben konnte. Sie mußte an Madame Kate in Winchester denken, die sie auf die Lippen geküßt und ihre Brüste gedrückt hatte: »Mein liebes Kind, dir wird es nie an Geld oder sonst irgend etwas mangeln. Wenn du für mich arbeitest, werden wir beide reich.« Nein, dachte sie, bloß das nicht; nie und nimmer.

Richard kam mit den Satteltaschen herein. »Wenn du nicht für dich selbst sorgen kannst, dann such dir besser jemanden, der sich um dich kümmert«, sagte er.

»Ich habe ja dich.«

»Ich kann mich nicht um dich kümmern!« protestierte er.

»Wieso nicht?« gab sie unwirsch zurück. »Schließlich habe ich mich ganze sechs Jahre lang um dich gekümmert!«

»Ich habe schließlich im Krieg gekämpft – und du hast bloß Wolle verscheuert.«

Und einen Banditen erdolcht, dachte sie; und einen schurkischen Priester zu Boden gerissen, und dich ernährt und gekleidet und dich beschützt, als du vor lauter Angst auf deinen Knöcheln herumgekaut hast. Aber der leichte Anflug von Wut verpuffte ebenso rasch, wie er gekommen war, und sie erwiderte lediglich: »Ich hab' ja nur Spaß gemacht.«

Er grunzte, unsicher, ob er den Beleidigten spielen sollte oder nicht; dann schüttelte er unwillig den Kopf und meinte: »Wie dem auch sei, du solltest Alfred nicht so voreilig den Laufpaß geben.«

»Um Himmels willen, halt endlich den Mund«, sagte sie.

»Was hast du an ihm auszusetzen?«

»Ich habe überhaupt nichts an ihm auszusetzen. Verstehst du denn nicht? Es liegt an *mir*.«

Er ließ den Sattel sinken und zeigte mit dem Finger auf sie. »Stimmt genau. Und ich kann dir auch sagen, weshalb: Du bist vollkommen selbstsüchtig. Du denkst bei allem zuerst an dich selbst.«

Das war so himmelschreiend ungerecht, daß sie unfähig war, wütend zu werden. Statt dessen schossen ihr die Tränen in die Augen. »Wie kannst du nur so etwas behaupten?« widersprach sie schluchzend.

»Weil alles wunderbar wäre, wenn du Alfred nur heiraten wolltest. Aber was tust du? Du weigerst dich!«

»Und wenn ich Alfred zehnmal heirate – dir ist damit noch lange nicht geholfen.«

»Ei freilich.«

»Wie das denn?«

»Alfred hat mir gesagt, er will mich in meinem Kampf unterstützen, wenn ich sein Schwager werde. Ein wenig einschränken müßte ich mich schon – er kann sich nicht so viele Krieger leisten –, aber er hat mir ausreichend Mittel für ein Schlachtroß, neue Waffen und meinen eigenen Knappen zugesichert.«

»Wann?« fragte Aliena erstaunt. »Wann hat er das gesagt?«

»Gerade eben. Auf der Wiese.«

Aliena empfand diese Demütigung wie einen Schlag. Wenigstens besaß Richard soviel Anstand, einen Anflug von Scham zu zeigen – aber wie hatten die beiden um sie gefeilscht! Wie Pferdehändler! Sie erhob sich und verließ das Haus, ohne noch ein weiteres Wort zu verlieren.

Sie ging zur Priorei hinauf, sprang über den Graben bei der alten Mühle und betrat den Klosterhof. Die Mühle stand still, denn heute war Feiertag. Sonst hätte sie diesen Weg auch nicht gewählt, denn das Stampfen der Hämmer, die den Stoff walkten, bereitete ihr jedesmal Kopfschmerzen.

Der Klosterhof erwies sich, wie erwartet, als menschenleer. Auf der Baustelle herrschte Stille. Dies war die Stunde, in der die Mönche entweder ruhten oder lasen, und alle anderen befanden sich drüben auf der Wiese. Langsam wanderte Aliena über den Friedhof. Die gepflegten Gräber mit ihren ordentlichen Holzkreuzen und den frischen Blumen sprachen Bände: Die Stadt hatte das Massaker immer noch nicht verwunden. Sie verweilte neben Toms steinernem Grabmal, das von einem schlichten, von Jack gemeißelten Engel aus Marmor geschmückt wurde. Vor sieben Jahren, dachte sie, hat mein Vater eine völlig vernünftige Heirat für mich arrangiert. William Hamleigh war weder alt noch häßlich noch arm. Jedes andere Mädchen in meiner Lage hätte ihn mit einem Seufzer der Erleichterung akzeptiert. Aber ich habe ihm eine Abfuhr erteilt, und das war der Anfang allen Übels: Unsere Burg wurde angegriffen, mein Vater ins Gefängnis geworfen, mein Bruder und ich der Armut preisgegeben – selbst der verheerende Brand in Kingsbridge und Toms Tod sind im Grunde nur auf meine Halsstarrigkeit zurückzuführen ...

Daß Tom sterben mußte, schien, aus welchem Grund auch immer, schlimmer als alles andere – sei es, weil er allgemein so beliebt gewesen war, oder sei es, weil Jack mit ihm seinen zweiten Vater verloren hatte.

Und nun sträube ich mich schon wieder gegen eine ganz und gar vernünftige Heirat, dachte sie. Woher nehme ich nur das Recht, so wählerisch zu sein? Schließlich habe ich durch mein anspruchsvolles Wesen genug Unheil angerichtet. Ich sollte Alfred mein Jawort geben und ihm dankbar sein, daß ich nicht für Mistreß Kate arbeiten muß.

Sie wandte sich von der Grabstätte ab und ging zur Baustelle hinüber. Dort stellte sie sich in die künftige Vierung und betrachtete den Altarraum. Er war bis auf das Dach fertig, und die Bauleute hatten ihre Vorkehrungen für den nächsten Abschnitt getroffen, die Errichtung des Querschiffs: Rechts und links von ihr war der Grundriß mit Pfosten und Seilen markiert, und man hatte bereits mit dem Ausheben der Fundamente begonnen. Die steil vor ihr aufragenden Mauern warfen lange Schatten in der Spätnachmittagssonne. Das Wetter war mild, aber in der Kathedrale herrschte Kühle. Lange betrachtete Aliena versonnen die aneinandergereihten Rundbogen, die großen zuunterst, die kleinen darüber und die mittelgroßen obenauf. In der gleichmäßigen Wiederholung von Bogen und Pfeiler, Bogen und Pfeiler lag etwas unwiderstehlich Beruhigendes. Direkt vor ihr, in der Ostwand, befand sich ein wunderschönes Rundfenster, durch dessen Maßwerk die aufgehende Sonne die Morgengebete bescheinen würde.

Wenn Alfred tatsächlich gewillt war, dachte Aliena, Richard zu unterstützen, dann besteht doch noch eine Möglichkeit, den meinem Vater geleisteten Schwur zu erfüllen und für Richard zu sorgen, bis er die Grafschaft zurückerobert hat ... Im Grunde ihres Herzens war ihr klar, daß sie Alfred einfach heiraten mußte; sie wollte es nur nicht wahrhaben.

Sie ging durch das südliche Seitenschiff, ließ ihre Hand an der Wand entlanggleiten, spürte die rauhe Oberfläche der Steine und ließ ihre Fingernägel über die flachen, von den gezahnten Meißeln der Steinmetzen hinterlassenen Vertiefungen gleiten. In den Seitenschiffen war die Wand oberhalb der Fenster mit einer Blendarkade dekoriert. Sie erfüllte zwar keinen praktischen Zweck, trug aber viel zur Harmonie des Gesamtwerks bei. In Toms Kathedrale hatte selbst das kleinste Detail seinen Stellenwert und erweckte den Eindruck unabänderlicher Notwendigkeit. War ihr Leben genauso? Waren die Einzelheiten etwa Teil eines allumfassenden, vorherbestimmten Plans? Und glich sie dann nicht einem Baumeister, der eigensinnig auf einem Wasserfall im Altarraum bestand?

In der Südostecke der Kirche gab es eine niedrige Türöffnung, dahinter eine schmale Wendeltreppe. Aliena folgte einer plötzlichen Regung, trat durch die Öffnung und stieg hinauf. Sie war noch nicht allzu weit gekommen – die Tür war zwar nicht mehr zu sehen, aber auch noch kein Ende der Treppe in Sicht –, da beschlich sie ein merkwürdiges Gefühl, als winde sich die Treppe endlos bis in den Himmel hinein. Dann erblickte sie Tageslicht, das durch einen schmalen Schlitz in der Turmmauer fiel und die Stufen erhellte. Schließlich trat sie auf die breite Empore über dem Seitenschiff hinaus, die nach außen fensterlos war, nach innen aber den Blick auf die ungedeckte Kirche freigab. Sie machte es sich auf der Brüstung an einem Innenbogen bequem und lehnte sich gegen den Pfeiler. Der kalte Stein an ihrer Wange tat gut. Ob Jack ihn wohl bearbeitet hatte? Und dann plötzlich, aus dem Nichts, der Gedanke, daß sie sich von hier oben zu Tode stürzen könnte. Aber es war nicht wirklich hoch genug; womöglich brach sie sich nur die Knochen und mußte dann unter Schmerzen dort unten liegen, bis die Mönche kamen und sie fanden.

Sie beschloß, zum Lichtgaden hinaufzusteigen, und kehrte zur Wendeltreppe zurück. Diesmal hatte sie nicht so weit zu klettern, fand es aber doch beängstigend, und als sie oben ankam, schlug ihr das Herz bis zum Halse. Sie betrat den Umlauf, ein schmaler Tunnel in der Wand, und tastete sich Schritt für Schritt voran, bis sie die

Sohlbank eines der Zwillingsfenster erreichte, wo sie am Mittelpfeiler, der es unterteilte, Halt fand. Von hier fiel ihr Blick fünfundsiebzig Fuß ins Bodenlose, und unwillkürlich begann sie zu zittern.

Von der Wendeltreppe her erklangen Schritte. Alienas Atem ging plötzlich stoßweise, als wäre sie gerannt. Es war doch weit und breit niemand in Sicht gewesen! War ihr jemand gefolgt und versuchte nun, sich an sie heranzuschleichen? Jetzt kamen die Schritte aus dem dunklen Umlauf im Lichtgaden. Aliena ließ den Pfeiler los und stand unsicher schwankend am Rande des Abgrunds. Dann tauchte ein Gesicht ins Licht über der Sohlbank: Jack. Ihr Herz schlug so laut, daß es ihr in den Ohren dröhnte.

»Was machst du denn hier?« fragte er langsam.

»Ich ... ich wollte nur mal sehen, was deine Kathedrale für Fortschritte macht.«

Er wies auf das Kapitell über ihr. »Das habe ich gemacht.«

Sie sah hinauf. Der Stein stellte einen Mann dar, der das ganze Gewicht des Bogens auf seinem Rücken zu tragen schien, den Körper wie unter Schmerzen verkrümmt. Aliena betrachtete ihn lange. So etwas hatte sie noch nie zuvor gesehen. Ohne nachzudenken, sagte sie: »Genauso fühle ich mich auch.«

Als sie sich ihm zuwandte, stand er neben ihr und ergriff sie behutsam, aber fest am Arm. »Ich weiß«, sagte er.

Sie sah in die Tiefe. Die Vorstellung, aus dieser Höhe abzustürzen, machte sie krank vor Angst. Jack zog sie am Arm, und sie ließ sich von ihm zur Treppe zurückführen.

Unten angekommen, fühlte sich Aliena ganz schwach in den Knien. Jack drehte sich zu ihr um und sagte im Plauderton: »Ich habe im Kreuzgang gelesen, und wie ich aufblickte, sah ich dich im Lichtgaden stehen.«

Sie musterte sein jungenhaftes Gesicht, in dem sich Sorge und Zärtlichkeit spiegelten, und ihr fiel wieder ein, weshalb sie einfach losgegangen war und hier Zuflucht gesucht hatte. Sie sehnte sich danach, ihn zu küssen, und entdeckte die gleiche Sehnsucht in seinen Augen. Jede Faser ihres Körpers forderte sie auf, sich in seine Arme zu stürzen, aber sie wußte nun, was sie zu tun hatte. Wie gern hätte sie ihm erklärt: *Meine Liebe zu dir ist wie ein Sturm, wie eine Löwin, wie ohnmächtige Wut* – doch statt dessen sagte sie: »Ich glaube, ich werde Alfred heiraten.«

Wie vor den Kopf geschlagen, starrte er ihr ins Gesicht. Dann malte sich Trauer in seinen Zügen, eine uralte, weise Traurigkeit, die ihn reifer erschienen ließ, als seinen Jahren angemessen war. Sie dachte schon, er würde zu weinen anfangen, aber er tat es nicht. Statt dessen blitzte Zorn in seinen Augen auf. Er öffnete den Mund, um etwas zu sagen, besann sich, zögerte und sprach es endlich doch aus.

Mit einer Stimme so kalt wie der Nordwind sagte er: »Du hättest besser daran getan, aus dem Lichtgaden zu springen.«

Er ließ sie stehen und ging ins Kloster zurück.

Ich habe ihn auf ewig verloren, dachte Aliena, und ihr war, als müsse ihr das Herz brechen.

Jack hatte sich am Erntedankfest aus dem Kloster geschlichen. Das allein galt an sich nicht als schwerwiegendes Vergehen, aber die Tatsache, daß es nicht zum erstenmal vorgekommen und er überdies noch im Gespräch mit einer unverheirateten Frau gesehen worden war, ließ die Angelegenheit in einem strengeren Licht erscheinen. Seine Übertretung kam am darauffolgenden Tag im Kapitel zur Sprache, und man beschloß, ihn unter Hausarrest zu stellen; er durfte sich also nur in den Klostergebäuden, im Kreuzgang und in der Krypta aufhalten und nur in Begleitung eines Mönchs von einem Gebäude zum anderen gehen. Er nahm es kaum zur Kenntnis. Alienas Ankündigung hatte ihn dermaßen mitgenommen, daß alles andere dagegen verblaßte.

Daß er an der Kathedrale arbeitete, kam natürlich überhaupt nicht in Frage, aber seitdem Alfred dort das Kommando übernommen hatte, machte es ihm sowieso kaum noch Freude. Nun verbrachte er die freien Nachmittage mit Lesen. In Latein hatte er enorme Fortschritte gemacht und konnte, auch wenn es noch langsam ging, mittlerweile alles lesen, was ihm unter die Hände kam; und da die Lektüre zu nichts anderem dienen sollte, als seine Lateinkenntnisse zu verbessern, durfte er unter den Folianten seine eigene Wahl treffen. Und so klein die Bibliothek auch war, so verfügte sie doch über etliche philosophische und mathematische Werke, auf die Jack sich nun mit Feuereifer stürzte.

Viel von dem, was er las, war enttäuschend: seitenweise Genealogien, eintönige Berichte über die Wundertaten längst verstorbener Heiliger und endlose theologische Spekulationen. Das erste Werk, das ihn wirklich interessierte, war die Geschichte der Welt, von ihrer Erschaffung bis zur Gründung des Klosters in Kingsbridge, und nach Beendigung der Lektüre hatte er das Gefühl, nunmehr über alles, was sich jemals ereignet hatte, gründlich Bescheid zu wissen. Doch nach einer Weile ging ihm auf, daß das Buch dem selbstgestellten Anspruch, von *sämtlichen* Ereignissen zu berichten, nicht standhielt, denn schließlich trug sich überall – nicht nur in Kingsbridge und England, sondern auch in der Normandie, im Anjou, in Paris und in Rom, in Äthiopien und in Jerusalem – ständig irgend etwas zu; der Verfasser mußte also etliche Begebnisse ausgelassen haben. Trotzdem vermittelte das Werk Jack ein bis dahin unbekanntes Gefühl: daß die Vergangenheit einer Geschichte glich, in der eine Handlung die nächste bedingte, und daß die Welt kein grenzenloses Mysterium mehr, sondern ein endliches Etwas war, das sich begreifen ließ.

Die Rätsel waren noch faszinierender. Ein Philosoph stellte die Frage, warum ein schwacher Mann einen schweren Stein mit einer Brechstange bewegen kann. Darüber hatte Jack sich bisher noch nie Gedanken gemacht, aber nun ließ es ihn nicht mehr los. Einmal hatte er mehrere Wochen im Steinbruch verbracht und konnte sich noch gut erinnern, daß ein Stein, der nicht mit einer ein Fuß langen Brechstange bewegt werden konnte, gewöhnlich auf eine zwei Fuß lange Brechstange ansprach. Wie kam es, daß ein und derselbe Mann den Stein nicht mit dem kurzen, dafür aber mit dem langen Hebel bewegen konnte? Eine Frage führte zur nächsten. Die Dombauleute benutzten eine riesige Winde, um große Quader und Holz aufs Dach hinaufzuhieven. Die Last des Seils war für die bloßen Hände eines Mannes viel zu schwer, doch das Rad, mit dem das Seil eingeholt wurde, konnte er allein und ohne Hilfe drehen, und die Last wurde nach oben befördert. Wie war so etwas möglich?

Solche und ähnliche Spekulationen lenkten ihn eine Zeitlang ab, aber immer wieder kehrten seine Gedanken zu Aliena zurück. Oft genug stand er im Kreuzgang, vor sich auf dem Lesepult einen schweren Folianten, und ließ jenen Morgen in der alten Mühle, als er sie geküßt hatte, vor seinem geistigen Auge erneut ablaufen. Jede Einzelheit war ihm noch in Erinnerung, von der ersten sanften Berührung der Lippen bis zu der erregenden Empfindung, ihre Zunge in seinem Mund zu spüren. Er hatte sich eng an sie geschmiegt und konnte ihre Brüste und Hüften spüren. Die Erinnerung war so überwältigend, daß er beinahe glaubte, sie sei Wirklichkeit.

Was nur hatte sie so verändert? Er war nach wie vor der Überzeugung, daß der Kuß echt und Alienas darauffolgende Gefühlskälte falsch gewesen war. Er glaubte, sie zu kennen. Sie war liebevoll, sinnlich, romantisch, einfallsreich und warmherzig. Obendrein war sie noch gedankenlos und herrisch, und sie hatte gelernt, mit aller Härte zu kämpfen; aber sie war weder kalt noch grausam, und herzlos schon gar nicht. Einen Mann, den sie nicht liebte, allein wegen des Geldes zu heiraten, das paßte einfach nicht zu ihr. Es würde sie nicht nur unglücklich machen, sondern zur Verzweiflung treiben, das wußte er genau; und sie wußte es im Grunde ihres Herzens auch und würde diesen Schritt bis ans Ende ihres Lebens bereuen.

Eines Tages meinte einer der Klosterdiener, der gerade die Schreibstube ausfegte und sich zu einer kurzen Verschnaufpause auf seinen Besen lehnte: »Dann gibt es in eurer Familie ja bald ein großes Fest.«

Jack war in das Studium einer Weltkarte auf einem großen Pergament vertieft. Er hob den Blick. Der Sprecher war ein verwitterter alter Mann, längst zu schwach für schwere Arbeiten. Wahrscheinlich verwechselt er mich mit einem anderen, dachte Jack und fragte: »Wie das, Joseph?«

»Weißt du's denn nicht? Dein Bruder heiratet.«

»Ich habe keinen Bruder«, sagte Jack mechanisch, doch sein Herz zog sich zusammen.

»Also dann Stiefbruder.«

»Nein, davon hatte ich keine Ahnung.« Er mußte die Frage stellen! Er knirschte mit den Zähnen. »Wen heiratet er denn?«

»Diese Aliena da.«

Demnach war sie also entschlossen, ihre Absicht in die Tat umzusetzen. Insgeheim hatte Jack gehofft, sie werde ihren Entschluß noch ändern.

Er wandte sich ab, damit Joseph die Verzweiflung in seinem Gesicht nicht sah. »So, so«, murmelte er, krampfhaft bemüht, Gleichgültigkeit vorzutäuschen.

»Ja – wo sie doch immer so stolz und hochnäsig war, bis sie bei dem Brand alles verlor.«

»Wann – weißt du wann?«

»Morgen. Sie heiraten in der neuen Pfarrkirche, die Alfred gebaut hat.«

Morgen schon!

Aliena wollte Alfred schon morgen heiraten! Bis jetzt hatte Jack nie ernsthaft geglaubt, daß es tatsächlich soweit käme: Nun traf ihn die Wirklichkeit mit der Wucht eines Holzhammers. Aliena heiratete morgen. Mit seinem Leben war es ab morgen vorbei.

Er betrachtete die vor ihm auf dem Lesepult liegende Karte. Was kümmerte es ihn noch, ob Jerusalem oder Wallingford der Mittelpunkt der Welt war? Und würde es ihn wirklich glücklicher machen, wenn er wüßte, wie Hebel funktionieren? Er hatte Aliena gesagt, sie täte besser daran, aus dem Lichtgaden zu springen, als Alfred zu heiraten. Ich hätte hinzufügen sollen, dachte er, daß ich genausogutgleich mitspringen kann ...

Er verabscheute das Kloster. Das Mönchsdasein war eine ganz und gar idiotische Lebensweise. Und welchen Sinn hatte das Leben noch, wenn Aliena einen anderen heiratete und er selbst nicht einmal mehr am Dombau mitwirken durfte?

Daß er ganz genau wußte, wie sterbensunglücklich Aliena an Alfreds Seite würde, machte die Sache nur noch schlimmer. Und das lag nicht allein an seinem Haß auf Alfred. Es gab Mädchen, die eine Heirat mit Alfred mehr oder weniger zufriedengestellt hätte: Edith zum Beispiel, die nur gekichert hatte, als er, Jack, von seiner Leidenschaft fürs Meißeln sprach. Edith würde keine großen Ansprüche an Alfred stellen und ihm – solange sein Handwerk nur florierte und er die Kinder liebte – nur allzugern Honig um den Bart schmieren und ihm aufs Wort gehorchen. Aliena jedoch wird über kurz oder lang das Leben mit Alfred hassen, jeden einzelnen Moment, dachte Jack. Alfreds Grobschlächtigkeit muß sie verabscheuen, seine herrischen Manieren verachten, seine Gemeinheit wird sie anekeln und seine Begriffsstutzigkeit zum Wahnsinn treiben. Eine Ehe mit Alfred wäre die reinste Hölle für sie ...

Warum begriff sie das nicht? Jack stand vor einem Rätsel. Was ging nur in ihrem Kopf vor? Etwas Schlimmeres als die Ehe mit einem Mann, den sie nicht einmal liebte, konnte es doch gar nicht geben. Vor sieben Jahren hatte sie mit ihrer Weigerung, William Hamleigh zu heiraten, großes Aufsehen erregt, und nun nahm sie den Antrag eines Mannes an, der um keinen Deut besser zu ihr paßte. Was dachte sie sich dabei?

Jack mußte es einfach erfahren.

Kloster hin, Kloster her – er mußte mit ihr reden.

Er rollte die Karte zusammen, legte sie in den Schrank zurück und ging zur Tür. Joseph stand immer noch auf seinen Besenstiel gelehnt. »Geht Ihr etwa?« sagte er zu Jack. »Ich dachte, Ihr müßt hierbleiben, bis der Cirkator Euch holen kommt.«

»Der Cirkator kann mir den Buckel runterrutschen«, erwiderte Jack und verließ den Raum.

Sobald er den Ostflügel des Kreuzgangs betrat, geriet er in Prior Philips Blickfeld, der gerade von der Baustelle kam. Jack machte blitzschnell kehrt, doch Philip rief ihm nach: »Jack! Was treibst du da? Du stehst doch unter Hausarrest!«

Aber Jack stand jetzt nicht der Sinn nach klösterlicher Disziplin. Er schenkte dem Prior keine Beachtung, entfernte sich in entgegengesetzter Richtung und strebte dem Durchgang zu, der vom Südflügel zu den am neuen Kai gelegenen Häusern führte. Aber das Glück ließ ihn im Stich, den im gleichen Augenblick kam ihm Bruder Pierre, der Cirkator, gefolgt von seinen beiden Stellvertretern, entgegen. Kaum waren sie Jacks ansichtig geworden, blieben sie wie angewurzelt stehen.

Philip rief: »Halte diesen Novizen auf, Bruder Cirkator!«

Pierre streckte einen Arm aus, um Jack den Weg zu versperren, doch der stieß ihn beiseite. Pierre, rot vor Zorn, packte Jack am Arm, aber der entwand sich dem Zugriff und versetzte ihm einen Nasenstüber. Pierre schrie auf, allerdings mehr aus Wut als vor Schmerz. Dann warfen sich seine beiden Stellvertreter auf Jack.

Jack schlug wie ein Wilder um sich und hatte sich beinahe freigekämpft, als Pierre, von dem Schlag auf die Nase erholt, sich ebenfalls in das Getümmel stürzte; zu dritt brachten sie Jack zu Fall und warfen sich auf ihn. Jack wand sich wie ein Aal, fuchsteufelswild, weil ihn dieser Klosterquatsch nun auch noch daran zu hindern drohte, mit Aliena zu sprechen – und das war ihm wichtiger als alles andere. »Laßt mich los, ihr Idioten!« rief er ein ums andere Mal, doch die beiden Stellvertreter setzten sich einfach auf ihn, während Pierre sich aufrichtete und sich die blutige Nase am Ärmel seiner Kutte abwischte. Neben ihm tauchte Philip auf.

Jack erkannte trotz seiner unbändigen Wut, daß Philip ebenfalls außer sich war; er hatte ihn noch nie so gesehen. »Ein solches Verhalten dulde ich nicht, bei niemandem!« sagte er mit schneidender Stimme. »Du bist ein Novize, und du wirst mir gehorchen.« Er wandte sich an Pierre. »Steckt ihn in den Kerker!«

»Nein!« brüllte Jack. »Das könnt Ihr nicht!«

»Das kann ich sehr wohl«, gab Philip grimmig zurück.

Der Kerker war ein kleiner, fensterloser Raum unterhalb des Dormitoriums und neben den Latrinen. Normalerweise diente er als Aufenthaltsort für Gesetzesbrecher, die auf ihre Verhandlung vor dem Klostergericht oder auf den Weitertransport ins Gefängnis des Vogts von Shiring warteten; gelegentlich jedoch beherbergte er Mönche, die sich gravierender disziplinarischer Vergehen – etwa unkeuscher Handlungen mit Prioreibediensteten – schuldig gemacht hatten.

Jack hatte keine Angst vor der Einzelhaft; was ihn jedoch mit panischem Entsetzen erfüllte, war die Aussichtslosigkeit seiner Situation: Nun konnte er nicht mehr entfliehen und mit Aliena sprechen. »Ihr versteht überhaupt nichts!« brüllte er Philip an. »Ich muß mit Aliena reden!«

Etwas Schlimmeres hätte er kaum sagen können. Philip wurde jetzt erst recht wütend. »Genau dafür bist du ursprünglich bestraft worden«, gab er wutentbrannt zurück.

»Aber ich muß mit ihr reden!«

»Du *mußt* bloß eines: Dich in Gottesfurcht und in Gehorsam gegenüber deinen Oberen üben.«

»Ihr seid ein Esel, aber nicht mein Oberer! In meinen Augen seid Ihr eine Null. Laßt mich gefälligst gehen, verflucht noch mal!«

»Fort mit ihm«, gebot Philip finster.

Inzwischen war es zu einem rechten Auflauf gekommen, und mehrere Mönche ergriffen Jack an Armen und Beinen. Er wand sich wie ein Fisch an der Angel, vermochte aber gegen die Übermacht nichts auszurichten. Nicht zu fassen, daß dies ausgerechnet ihm zustieß! Widerborstig, wie er war, schleppten sie ihn durch den Gang bis vor die Tür der Zelle. Irgend jemand öffnete sie, und Bruder Pierre befahl schadenfroh: »Werft ihn hinein!« Sie schwangen ihn zurück, dann flog er auch schon im hohen Bogen durch die Luft. Er prallte hart auf dem Steinfußboden auf, rappelte sich jedoch ohne Rücksicht auf seine Blessuren sofort wieder hoch und warf sich gegen die Tür – die just in diesem Moment zugeschlagen wurde. Gleich darauf hörte er, wie der schwere Eisenriegel niederpolterte und der Schlüssel im Schloß umgedreht wurde.

Aus Leibeskräften hämmerte Jack gegen die Tür. »Laßt mich raus!« schrie er, und seine Stimme überschlug sich fast. »Ich muß sie von dieser Heirat abbringen! Laßt mich raus!« Kein Ton drang zu ihm herein. Er schrie und schrie und schrie, doch mit der Zeit verwandelte sich die Forderung in Flehen, sein Geschrei in Gejammer, bis seine Stimme zu heiserem Geflüster herabsank und er vor ohnmächtiger Wut nur noch weinen konnte.

Endlich hatte er sich ausgeweint, und seine Tränen versiegten.

Er sah sich um. Die Zelle war keineswegs stockfinster, denn unter der Tür drang ein schmaler Streifen Licht herein, so daß Jack die Umgebung schemenhaft ausmachen konnte. Mit den Händen tastete er sich ringsum die Wände entlang. Die Meißelspuren unter seinen Fingerspitzen sagten ihm, daß der Kerker schon vor langer Zeit gebaut worden war. Er maß ungefähr sechs Fuß im Quadrat. In einer der Decken fand sich eine Säule und ein Stück Gewölbedecke – zweifellos hatte die Zelle ursprünglich zu einem größeren Raum gehört und war später durch eine Mauer abgeteilt worden. Eine der Wände wies eine schmale Öffnung auf, beinahe wie eine Schießscharte, doch sie war fest verriegelt und wäre selbst ohne den Fensterladen auch für den Schlankesten zu eng gewesen, um sich hindurchzuzwängen. Der Steinboden fühlte sich feucht an, und Jack nahm erst jetzt das unablässige Rauschen war, aus dem er schloß, daß die Wasserrinne, die vom Mühlteich durch das Klostergelände zu den Latrinen führte, unterhalb der Zelle verlaufen mußte. Das bot auch die Erklärung dafür, daß der Boden nicht nur aus gestampfter Erde bestand, sondern gemauert war.

Er fühlte sich völlig ausgelaugt. Er setzte sich auf den Boden, den Rücken gegen die Wand gelehnt, und starrte auf den schmalen Lichtstreifen unterhalb der Tür, der ihn schmerzlich daran erinnerte, wo er jetzt eigentlich sein wollte. Wie war er nur in diese Klemme geraten? Vom Kloster hatte er nie viel gehalten und nie vorgehabt, sein Leben Gott zu weihen – an den er nicht einmal wirklich glaubte. Novize war er nur geworden, um ein drängendes Problem zu lösen, um in Kingsbridge, in der Nähe all dessen, was er liebte, bleiben zu können. Er hatte sich dem Wahn hingegeben, jederzeit gehen zu können. Und nun, da er diesen Ort verlassen wollte, gelang es ihm nicht: Er war gefangen. *Sobald ich hier rauskomme, drehe ich Prior Philip den Hals um*, dachte er, *und wenn ich dafür hängen muß!*

Das brachte ihn auf einen anderen Gedanken: *Wann* wollten sie ihn eigentlich freilassen? Er hörte die Glocke, die zum Abendessen rief. *Die kommende Nacht über werden sie mich bestimmt hierbehalten*, dachte er. *Wahrscheinlich beraten sie sich gerade über mich. Die unangenehmsten Mönche werden wohl die Forderung stellen, mich eine geschlagene Woche hier schmoren zu lassen – ha, ich sehe es genau vor mir, wie Pierre und Remigius nach schärfster Disziplin rufen! Aber es gibt auch andere, die mich besser leiden können, die halten vielleicht eine Nacht im Kerker für Strafe genug ...*

Was Philip wohl sagen würde? Er mochte Jack, war jetzt aber zweifellos sehr böse auf ihn, besonders nach der in der Wut hervorgestoßenen Bemerkung: *Ihr seid ein Esel, aber nicht mein Oberer! In meinen Augen seid Ihr eine Null!* Philip mochte durchaus versucht sein, jene, die mit harten Strafen stets schnell bei der Hand waren, gewähren zu lassen. Jacks einzige Hoffnung bestand darin, daß sie seinen sofortigen Hinauswurf aus dem Kloster fordern würden, die härteste Strafe, die sie sich denken konnten. In diesem Fall gelang es ihm vielleicht doch noch, vor der Hochzeit mit Aliena zu sprechen. Doch Philip wäre dagegen, kein Zweifel. Das käme in seinen Augen dem Eingeständnis einer Niederlage gleich.

Das Licht unterhalb der Tür wurde zunehmend schwächer. Draußen wurde es dunkel. Jack fragte sich, wo man als Gefangener wohl seine Notdurft verrichten sollte. Einen Topf gab es in der Zelle nicht. Es sah den Mönchen ganz und gar nicht ähnlich, gerade diesen Punkt zu übersehen: Von Reinlichkeit hielten sie viel, auch und gerade bei Sündern. Er inspizierte erneut den Fußboden, tastete ihn Stein um Stein ab und stieß schließlich auf ein Loch unweit einer Ecke. Das Wasser rauschte hier lauter, und er vermutete, daß der unterirdische Kanal direkt darunter verlief. Das mußte also seine Latrine sein.

Nicht lange nach dieser Entdeckung öffnete sich plötzlich die schmale Klappe. Jack sprang auf. Eine Schüssel und ein Kanten Brot wurden auf dem Fensterbrett abgestellt, doch das Gesicht des Mannes war nicht zu erkennen. »Wer bist du?« fragte Jack.

»Es ist mir verboten, mit dir zu reden«, leierte der Mann seine Anweisung herunter. Jack erkannte die Stimme trotzdem: Sie gehörte einem betagten Mönch namens Luke.

»Luke, haben sie gesagt, wie lange ich hier bleiben muß?« rief Jack.

Luke wiederholte die Formel: »Es ist mir verboten, mit dir zu reden.«

»Bitte, Luke, sag's mir, wenn du Bescheid weißt!« flehte Jack den alten Mann an, und es war ihm vollkommen gleichgültig, ob er dabei wie ein Jammerlappen klang oder nicht.

Luke erwiderte flüsternd: »Pierre forderte eine Woche, aber Philip hat zwei Tage daraus gemacht.« Die Klappe fiel wieder zu.

»Zwei Tage!« sagte Jack verzweifelt. »Aber bis dahin ist sie doch längst verheiratet!«

Er erhielt keine Antwort.

Jack stand still da und starrte ins Nichts. Das Licht, das durch den Spalt in die Zelle gedrungen war, hatte ihn so geblendet, daß er eine ganze Weile lang nichts mehr sah, bis er sich wieder an die Dunkelheit gewöhnt hatte; dann füllten sich seine Augen wiederum mit Tränen, und alles verschwamm.

Er streckte sich auf dem Boden aus. Er konnte nichts mehr unternehmen. Bis Montag saß er hinter Schloß und Riegel, und Montag war Aliena bereits Alfreds Frau und wachte in Alfreds Bett mit Alfreds Samen in sich auf ... Ihm wurde schlecht bei dem Gedanken.

Bald war es stockfinster. Er tastete sich zum Fensterbrett und trank aus der Schale. Sie enthielt klares Wasser. Er nahm ein Stückchen Brot und kaute darauf herum, hatte aber keinen Hunger und brachte es kaum hinunter, daher leerte er die Schale und legte sich wieder hin.

Er fand keinen Schlaf, sondern verfiel in eine Art Dämmerzustand, in dem er, ähnlich wie in einem Traum oder einer Vision, noch einmal die Sonntagnachmittage durchlebte, an denen er Aliena die Geschichte von dem Knappen erzählt hatte, der sich aus Liebe zu seiner Prinzessin auf die Suche nach dem edelsteintragenden Rebstock macht.

Die Mitternachtsglocke riß ihn aus seinem Dämmerschlaf. Er hatte sich mittlerweile so an den klösterlichen Tagesablauf gewöhnt, daß er um Mitternacht stets hellwach war; nachmittags mußte er allerdings, besonders dann, wenn er zu Mittag Fleisch gegessen hatte, oft ein Nickerchen machen. Die Mönche verließen jetzt ihre Betten und machten sich auf die Prozession vom Dormitorium zur Kirche. Sie mußten sich unmittelbar über Jack sammeln, aber er vernahm keinen einzigen Laut: Sein Kerker war schalldicht. Es schien kaum Zeit vergangen zu sein, bevor die Glocke erneut bimmelte und die Mönche zur Matutin rief. Die Zeit verging schnell, viel zu schnell; noch heute würde Aliena heiraten.

In den frühen Morgenstunden fiel er trotz seines Kummers in Schlaf.

Mit einem Ruck fuhr er hoch. Da war jemand in der Zelle!

Entsetzen erfaßte ihn.

Es war stockfinster, nur das Rauschen des Wassers kam ihm lauter vor. »Wer ist da?« fragte er mit zitternder Stimme.

»Ich bin's – du brauchst keine Angst zu haben.«

»Mutter!« Vor Erleichterung schwanden ihm beinahe die Sinne. »Woher weißt du denn, das ich hier bin?«

»Der alte Joseph ist zu mir gekommen und hat mir erzählt, was passiert ist«, sagte sie, ohne die Stimme zu senken.

»Nicht so laut; sonst hören dich noch die Mönche!«

»Bestimmt nicht. Hier drin kannst du singen und schreien, und niemand hört dich. Das weiß ich genau – ich habe es schließlich ausprobiert.«

Jack schossen so viele Fragen durch den Kopf, daß er gar nicht wußte, womit er beginnen sollte. »Wie bist du hier hereingekommen? Ist die Tür offen?« Mit ausgestreckten Armen tastete er sich zu ihr. »Oh – du bist ja naß!«

»Genau unter diesem Kerker verläuft der Kanal, und im Boden hier ist ein Stein locker.«

»Woher hast du das gewußt?«

»Dein Vater hat zehn Monate in dieser Zelle verbracht«, sagte sie, und die Bitterkeit, die sich in Jahren aufgestaut hatte, klang deutlich durch.

»Mein Vater? *In dieser Zelle?* Zehn Monate?«

»Damals hat er mir alle seine Geschichten und Lieder beigebracht.«

»Aber warum hat man ihn hier eingesperrt?«

»Wir haben es nie herausgefunden«, erwiderte sie voller Groll. »Man hat ihn in der Normandie entführt oder gefangengenommen – genau wußte er es selbst nicht – und hierhergebracht. Er konnte weder Englisch noch Latein und hatte nicht die geringste Ahnung, wo er sich befand. Etwa ein Jahr lang hat er in den Ställen gearbeitet, und dort haben wir uns kennengelernt.« Ihre Stimme wurde weich bei der Erinnerung daran. »Ich habe mich Hals über Kopf in ihn verliebt. Er war so sanftmütig und sah dermaßen verschreckt und unglücklich aus; und trotzdem sang er wie ein Vogel. Monatelang hatte kein Mensch mit ihm gesprochen. Wie er sich gefreut hat, als ich ihn auf französisch anredete! Ich glaube, er hat sich bloß deswegen in mich verliebt.« Ihre Stimme klang wieder grimmig. »Kurz darauf steckten sie ihn in diesen Kerker, und damals habe ich herausgefunden, wie man hier hereinkommt.«

Jack kam der Gedanke, daß er genau hier auf diesem Steinfußboden gezeugt worden sein mußte. Das machte ihn verlegen, und er war froh, daß sie sich in der Dunkelheit nicht gegenseitig sahen. »Aber mein Vater muß doch etwas angestellt haben, sonst hätten sie ihn doch nicht eingesperrt.«

»Er hat sich den Kopf zermartert, aber ihm fiel nichts ein. Schließlich erfanden sie ein Verbrechen. Jemand gab ihm einen mit Edelsteinen verzierten Becher und sagte ihm, er könne gehen. Er war noch keine zwei Meilen weit gekommen, da wurde er verhaftet und des Diebstahls angeklagt. Und dafür haben sie ihn gehängt.« Sie weinte jetzt.

»Wer hat das getan?«

»Der Vogt von Shiring, der Prior von Kingsbridge ... darauf kommt es jetzt auch nicht mehr an.«

»Und die Familie meines Vaters? Er muß doch Eltern gehabt haben, Brüder, Schwestern ...?«

»Ja, drüben in Frankreich hatte er eine große Familie.«

»Und warum ist er nicht entflohen und zu ihnen zurückgekehrt?«

»Er hat es einmal versucht, aber sie erwischten ihn und brachten ihn zurück. Dann haben sie ihn hier eingelocht. Er hätte es natürlich, nachdem ich den Fluchtweg entdeckt hatte, noch einmal versuchen können. Aber er wußte nicht, wie er hätte nach Hause finden sollen. Er sprach kein Wort Englisch und war arm wie eine Kirchenmaus – keine guten Voraussetzungen. Er hätte es trotzdem versuchen sollen, das wissen wir jetzt: aber damals sind wir nie auf den Gedanken gekommen, sie könnten ihn hängen.«

Jack nahm sie tröstend in die Arme. Sie war naß bis auf die Knochen und zitterte vor Kälte. Sie mußte hier heraus und ins Trockene. Dann fiel es ihm wie Schuppen von den Augen: Wenn sie diesen Kerker verlassen konnte, dann konnte er es auch! Solange seine Mutter von seinem Vater erzählte, hatte er Aliena beinahe vergessen gehabt; aber nun ging sein Wunsch doch noch in Erfüllung – er konnte mit Aliena sprechen, bevor sie sich auf diese Heirat einließ!

»Zeig mir, wie ich hier rauskomme«, sagte er unvermittelt.

Sie schniefte und schluckte ihre Tränen hinunter. »Gib mir deine Hand, ich zeige dir den Weg.«

Sie gingen quer durch die Zelle, und er spürte, wie sie durch das Loch glitt. »Laß dich in den Kanal hinunter«, sagte sie. »Dann hol tief Luft und steck den Kopf unter Wasser. Du mußt gegen den Strom kriechen. Laß dich ja nicht von ihm fortreißen, sonst landest du bei den Mönchen in der Latrine. Kurz vor Ende wird dir fast die Luft ausgehen, aber wenn du nicht in Panik gerätst und stetig weiterkriechst, schaffst du es.« Sie ließ sich noch weiter hinab, und der Kontakt brach ab.

Er fand das Loch und zwängte sich langsam hindurch.

Beinahe sofort hing er mit den Füßen im Wasser, und als er den Grund der Rinne ertastete, steckten seine Schultern noch immer in der Zelle. Bevor er sich endgültig hinabließ, suchte er den lockeren Stein und schob ihn wieder an seinen Platz: Die Mönche werden vielleicht Augen machen, wenn sie ihren Kerker verlassen vorfinden! dachte er übermütig.

Das Wasser war kalt. Er holte tief Luft, ließ sich auf alle viere nieder und kroch, so schnell es ging, gegen die Strömung an. Dabei stellte er sich die Gebäude vor, die über ihm lagen: den Gang, das Refektorium, die Küche und schließlich das Backhaus. Kein weiter Weg, dennoch schien er kein Ende zu nehmen. Bei dem Versuch, sich aufzurichten, stieß er mit dem Kopf gegen die Decke des Wasserschachts. Schon wollte ihn Panik erfassen, da fielen ihm die Worte seiner Mutter wieder ein: Er war beinahe am Ziel. Kurz darauf sah er vor sich einen Lichtschimmer. Während sie sich in der Zelle unterhalten hatten, mußte es hell geworden sein. Er kroch weiter, bis das Licht genau über ihm war, richtete sich auf und sog gierig die frische Luft ein. Sobald er zu Atem gekommen war, kletterte er aus dem Graben.

Seine Mutter hatte sich schon umgezogen. Sie trug ein sauberes, trockenes Kleid und wrang das nasse aus. Für ihn hatte sie ebenfalls trockene Kleidung bereitgelegt. Fein säuberlich zusammengefaltet lagen die Kleider, die er seit einem halben Jahr nicht mehr getragen hatte, am Ufer: ein Leinenhemd, ein grünes Wams aus Wolle, graue Kniehosen und Lederstiefel. Mutter wandte sich ab, und Jack entledigte sich in Windeseile der schweren Mönchskutte, zog die Sandalen aus und schlüpfte in seine eigenen Kleidungsstücke.

Die Kutte warf er in den Graben. Damit war es ein für allemal vorbei.

»Was hast du jetzt vor?« fragte Mutter.

»Ich muß zu Aliena.«

»Jetzt sofort? Es ist noch sehr früh.«

»Ich habe keine Zeit zu verlieren.«

Sie nickte. »Sei behutsam mit ihr. Sie hat schon genug mitgemacht.«

Jack hielt inne, um sie zu küssen, doch dann überlegte er es sich anders und umarmte sie ungestüm. »Du hast mich aus dem Gefängnis befreit«, sagte er lachend. »Du bist schon eine einzigartige Mutter!«

Sie lächelte, aber ihre Augen schimmerten feucht.

Er drückte sie noch einmal zum Abschied und machte sich auf den Weg.

Obwohl es inzwischen hell geworden war, ließ sich weit und breit keine Menschenseele blicken: Sonntags wurde nicht gearbeitet, und die Bewohner der Stadt nutzten die Gelegenheit, einmal bis nach Sonnenaufgang zu schlafen. Jack hatte keine Ahnung, ob es ihm schaden konnte, wenn er gesehen wurde. Hatte Prior Philip das Recht, einen entlaufenen Novizen einzufangen und zur Rückkehr zu zwingen? Und wenn er das Recht hatte, würde er es anwenden? Jack hatte keine Ahnung. Nichtsdestoweniger verkörperte Philip das Gesetz in Kingsbridge, und Jack hatte ihm Trotz geboten; es war also mit Ärger zu rechnen.

Im Augenblick jedoch, fand Jack, hatte er Besseres zu tun, als sich mit solchen Aussichten zu befassen.

Dann stand er auch schon vor Alienas Haus. Ob Richard wohl da war? Hoffentlich nicht. Und selbst wenn, daran war jetzt nichts mehr zu ändern. Er ging zur Tür und klopfte sachte an.

Er spitzte die Ohren und lauschte. Drinnen rührte sich nichts. Er klopfte erneut, diesmal lauter, und hörte erleichtert Stroh rascheln: Jemand rührte sich. »Aliena!« flüsterte er vernehmlich.

Er hörte sie auf die Tür zukommen und mit ängstlicher Stimme fragen: »Ja?«

»Mach auf!«

»Wer ist da?«

»Ich bin's, Jack.«

»Jack!«

Nichts geschah. Jack wartete.

Aliena schloß vor Verzweiflung die Augen und sackte gegen die Tür. Ihre Wange berührte das rauhe Holz. Nicht Jack, dachte sie; nicht heute, nicht jetzt.

Da war seine Stimme wieder, ein gedämpftes, eindringliches Wispern. »Aliena, bitte, mach auf, schnell! Wenn sie mich erwischen, stecken sie mich wieder ins Loch!«

Sie hatte gehört, daß er hinter Schloß und Riegel saß – die Spatzen pfiffen es von allen Dächern. Er mußte also geflohen sein. Und war schnurstracks zu ihr gekommen! Ihr Herz begann zu rasen. Sie konnte ihn unmöglich wegschicken.

Sie hob den Riegel und öffnete ihm.

Sein rotes Haar war klatschnaß, als hätte er gerade ein Bad genommen. Er trug keine Mönchskutte, sondern normale Alltagskleidung. Er lächelte sie an auf eine Weise, als wäre ihr Anblick das Schönste, das ihm je im Leben begegnen konnte. Dann runzelte er die Stirn und sagte: »Du hast ja geweint!«

»Was willst du hier?« fragte sie.

»Ich muß dich unbedingt sprechen.«

»Ich heirate heute.«

»Ich weiß. Darf ich hereinkommen?«

Sie wußte, daß es ein Fehler war, ihn einzulassen; doch dann erinnerte sie sich, daß ihr nur wenige Stunden blieben, bis sie Alfreds Frau wurde – dies war gewiß die letzte Gelegenheit, mit Jack unter vier Augen reden zu können. Fehler oder nicht, dachte sie, das ist mir egal, und machte die Tür ganz auf. Jack trat ein, sie schloß die Tür und schob den Riegel vor.

Da standen sie nun und sahen sich an. Aliena machte es ganz verlegen, denn wie er sie anstarrte – das war der verzweifelte sehnsuchtsvolle Blick eines Mannes, der kurz vor dem Verdursten einen Wasserfall entdeckt. »Sieh mich nicht so an«, sagte sie und wandte sich ab.

»Du darfst ihn nicht heiraten«, sagte Jack.

»Ich muß aber.«

»Er wird dich kreuzunglücklich machen.«

»Ich bin schon kreuzunglücklich.«

»Bitte, schau mich an!«

Sie wandte sich ihm zu und hob die Augen.

»Bitte sag mir, warum du das tust«, bat er.

»Warum sollte ich?«

»Weil du mich damals in der alten Mühle leidenschaftlich geküßt hast.«

Sie senkte die Augen und spürte, wie ihr die Schamröte ins Gesicht stieg. An jenem Tag hatte sie sich gehenlassen und seitdem nicht aufgehört, sich dessen zu schämen. Jetzt benutzte er es gegen sie. Sie sagte nichts. Sie war wehrlos.

»Und danach bist du zu Eis erstarrt«, fuhr er fort.

Sie hielt weiter die Augen gesenkt.

»Wir waren so gute Freunde«, fuhr er unerbittlich fort. »Den ganzen Sommer lang, auf deiner Lichtung, beim Wasserfall ... meine Geschichten ... wir waren so glücklich. Einmal habe ich dich dort geküßt, weißt du noch?«

Natürlich hatte sie es nicht vergessen, obwohl sie sich selbst eingeredet hatte, es sei nie geschehen. Die Erinnerung ging ihr zu Herzen, und sie sah ihn mit Tränen in den Augen an.

»Und dann habe ich die Mühle umgebaut«, fuhr er fort. »Ich war so froh, daß ich dir hatte helfen können! Und du warst ganz hingerissen davon. Und dann haben wir uns wieder geküßt, aber das war kein scheuer Kuß wie beim erstenmal. Diesmal war es ... leidenschaftlich.«

O Gott, ja, so war es! dachte sie und errötete erneut, und ihr Atem beschleunigte sich. Wenn er doch nur aufhören wollte! Aber er ließ nicht locker. »Wir haben uns fest umarmt und uns lange geküßt. Du hast deinen Mund geöffnet –«

»Hör auf damit!« schrie sie.

»Warum?« gab er unerbittlich zurück. »Was war daran falsch? Warum hast du dich abgewandt?«

»Weil ich Angst habe!« sagte sie, ohne nachzudenken, und brach in Tränen aus. Sie vergrub ihr Gesicht in den Händen und schluchzte. Gleich darauf spürte sie seine Hände auf ihren bebenden Schultern. Sie schüttelte sie nicht ab, und nach einer Weile schloß er sie in seine Arme. Sie ließ die Hände sinken, barg ihr Gesicht an seinem grünen Wams und weinte sich aus.

Sie schlang ihre Arme um seine Mitte.

Er legte seine Wange an ihr Haar – ihr kurzes, unschönes Haar, das nach dem Feuer noch immer nicht nachgewachsen war – und streichelte ihren Rücken, als wäre sie ein Kind. Am liebsten hätte sie sich nie mehr wieder vom Fleck gerührt. Aber er schob sie von sich, sah sie an und fragte: »Warum hast du solche Angst?«

Sie wußte warum, konnte es ihm aber nicht sagen. Sie schüttelte den Kopf und trat einen Schritt zurück; doch Jack hielt sie an den Handgelenken fest und ließ sie nicht los.

»Hör zu, Aliena«, sagte er. »Du sollst wissen, wie schrecklich das für mich war. Erst dachte ich, du liebst mich, dann dachte ich, du haßt mich, und jetzt willst du auch noch meinen Stiefbruder heiraten. Ich verstehe überhaupt nichts mehr. Ich habe keine Ahnung von solchen Dingen, ich war noch nie in meinem Leben verliebt. Aber es tut entsetzlich weh. Es ist so schlimm, daß ich einfach keine Worte dafür finde. Meinst du nicht, daß du wenigstens versuchen solltest, mir das alles zu erklären?«

Schuldgefühle drohten sie zu überwältigen. Wie hatte sie ihn nur so tief verletzen können, wo sie ihn doch über alles liebte? Es war beschämend, wie sie ihn behandelt hatte, ihn, der immer nur darauf bedacht gewesen, ihr zu helfen – und sie hatte alles zerstört! Sie schuldete ihm wirklich eine Erklärung. Sie nahm all ihre Kraft zusammen. »Jack, vor vielen Jahren ist mir etwas zugestoßen, etwas ganz Schreckliches, das ich jahrelang von mir geschoben habe. Ich wollte nie mehr daran denken, aber als du mich so geküßt hast, wurde ich plötzlich daran erinnert und konnte es einfach nicht länger ertragen.«

»Aber was denn? Was ist passiert?«

»Nachdem mein Vater eingekerkert wurde, lebten wir weiterhin auf der Burg, Richard und ich und unser Diener Matthew; und eines Abends kam William Hamleigh und hat uns hinausgeworfen.«

Er kniff die Augen zusammen. »Und?«

»Der arme Matthew kam dabei ums Leben.«

Er wußte, daß sie ihm nicht die ganze Wahrheit sagte. »Warum?«

»Wie meinst du das?«

»Warum haben sie euren Diener umgebracht?«

»Weil er versucht hat, sie davon abzuhalten.« Tränen liefen ihr über das Gesicht, und ihre Kehle fühlte sich an wie zugeschnürt, als müsse sie an jedem Wort ersticken. Hilflos schüttelte sie den Kopf und wollte sich schon abwenden, aber Jack ließ es nicht zu.

Seine Stimme klang sanft wie ein Kuß: »Wollte sie woran hindern?«

Plötzlich wußte sie, daß sie ihm alles erzählen konnte, und die Worte überstürzten sich geradezu. »Sie haben mich dazu gezwungen«, sagte sie. »Der Reitknecht hat mich festgehalten, und William hat sich auf mich geworfen, aber ich gab nicht nach, und dann haben sie Richards Ohrläppchen abgeschnitten und gedroht, sie würden ihn noch mehr verstümmeln.« Diesmal schluchzte sie vor Erleichterung, dankbar, sich endlich alles von der Seele reden zu können. Sie sah Jack in die Augen und fuhr fort: »Also habe ich meine Beine geöffnet, und William hat es mir angetan, während der Reitknecht Richard zwang, dabei zuzusehen.«

»Wie schrecklich für dich«, flüsterte Jack. »Ich habe zwar die Gerüchte gehört, aber ich hätte nie gedacht ... Liebste Aliena, wie konnten sie dir das antun?«

Sie mußte ihm nun alles sagen. »Und dann, als William mit mir fertig war, kam der Reitknecht an die Reihe.«

Jack schloß die Augen. Sein Gesicht war fahl und angespannt.

Aliena sagte: »Verstehst du, als wir beide uns dann geküßt haben, da wollte ich, daß du es mit mir tust, aber dann mußte ich an William und seinen Reitknecht denken, und da kam ich mir ganz schrecklich vor und hatte solche Angst, daß ich einfach davongelaufen bin. Deshalb war ich auch so gemein zu dir und habe dir das Leben so schwer gemacht. Es tut mir so leid.«

»Ich verzeihe dir«, flüsterte er. Er zog sie an sich, und sie wehrte sich nicht, als er sie in die Arme schloß. Sie konnte sich nichts Tröstlicheres vorstellen.

Sie fühlte, wie ihn schauderte. »Ekelst du dich vor mir?« fragte sie ängstlich.

Er sah sie an. »Ich bete dich an«, erwiderte er. Er neigte den Kopf und küßte sie auf den Mund.

Sie erstarrte. Das hatte sie nicht gewollt. Er rückte ein wenig von ihr ab und küßte sie wieder. Wie sanft sich seine Lippen auf ihrem Mund anfühlten! Sie war ihm so dankbar, daß sie die Lippen ein wenig schürzte, nur kurz, wie als Echo auf seinen Kuß. Ermutigt berührte er ihre Lippen wieder mit seinem Mund. Sie spürte seinen warmen Atem auf ihrem Gesicht, dann öffnete er seinen Mund ein wenig. Sofort wich sie zurück.

Er wirkte gekränkt. »Ist es denn so schlimm?«

Nein, sie empfand lange nicht mehr soviel Furcht wie früher. Sie hatte ihm die schreckliche Wahrheit erzählt, und er war keineswegs entsetzt zurückgewichen. An seiner Sanftheit und Liebenswürdigkeit hatte sich nichts geändert. Sie neigte den Kopf zur Seite, und er küßte sie noch einmal. Kein Grund zur Beunruhigung – an seiner Liebkosung war nichts Bedrohliches, nichts Gewalttätiges und Unbeherrschtes, weder rohe Kraft noch Haß noch Dominanz. Ganz im Gegenteil: Dieser Kuß war die reine, geteilte Freude.

Seine Lippen öffneten sich, und sie spürte seine Zungenspitze. Unwillkürlich verkrampfte sie sich. Er spielte mit ihren Lippen, und sie entspannte sich wieder. Er sog sachte an ihrer Unterlippe, und ihr wurde ein wenig schwindelig.

Er sagte: »Würdest du noch einmal das gleiche wie damals tun?«

»Was habe ich denn getan?«

»Ich zeig's dir. Öffne den Mund, ganz wenig nur.«

Sie tat, was er sagte, und spürte, wie seine Zunge ihre Lippen berührte, zwischen den leicht geöffneten Zähnen verschwand, in ihrem Mund nach ihrer Zunge forschte und sie fand. Sie entzog sich ihm.

»Genau«, sagte er. »Das hast du damals getan.«

»Wirklich?« fragte sie erschrocken.

»Ja.« Er lächelte, doch dann wurde sein Blick todernst. »Wenn du das nur noch einmal tun würdest – es würde den ganzen Kummer der letzten neun Monate aufwiegen.«

Sie neigte ihm ihr Gesicht entgegen und schloß die Augen. Dann fühlte sie seinen Mund auf ihrem. Sie öffnete die Lippen, zögerte kurz und ließ ihre Zunge unsicher in seinen Mund gleiten. Und mit einemmal kam die Erinnerung an damals, in der alten Mühle, und mit ihr die nämlichen ekstatischen Empfindungen. Sie bestand nur noch aus dem Bedürfnis, ihn festzuhalten, seine Haut und sein Haar zu berühren, seine Muskeln und Knochen zu ertasten, in ihn zu dringen und ihn in sich zu spüren. Ihre Zungen berührten sich, Scham und Ekel waren wie ausgelöscht – wie herrlich es war, etwas so Intimes mit ihm zu teilen!

Sie atmeten nun beide keuchend. Jack hielt ihren Kopf in seinen Händen. Sie streichelte seine Arme, seinen Rücken und schließlich seine Hüften, spürte, wie angespannt seine Muskeln waren. Atemlos löste sie sich von ihm; das Herz schlug ihr bis zum Halse.

Sie sah ihn an. Sie war erhitzt und atmete schwer, und sein Gesicht glühte vor Verlangen. Erneut beugte er sich vor, doch statt sie auf den Mund zu küssen, hob er ihr Kinn und liebkoste die zarte Haut ihres Halses mit seinen Lippen. Sie hörte sich vor Entzücken stöhnen. Er ließ seinen Kopf tiefer sinken und streifte die Wölbung ihrer Brüste mit dem Mund. Ihre Brustspitzen unter dem groben Nachthemd aus Leinen richteten sich auf und fühlten sich beinahe unerträglich empfindlich an. Seine Lippen umschlossen eine Brust, und sein Atem strich heiß über ihre Haut.

»Sachte«, flüsterte sie ängstlich. Er küßte ihre Brustwarze durch den Leinenstoff, und obwohl er so behutsam wie irgend möglich war, so durchfuhr sie doch eine so intensive Lustempfindung, als ob er sie gebissen hätte, und sie schnappte nach Luft.

Und dann ging er vor ihr auf die Knie.

Er drückte sein Gesicht in ihren Schoß. Bis zu diesem Augenblick hatte sich ihr gesamtes Wahrnehmungsempfinden auf ihre Brüste konzentriert, aber nun merkte sie plötzlich, daß ihre Lenden bebten. Er tastete nach dem Saum ihres Nachthemds und hob es bis zu ihrer Mitte hoch. Sie beobachtete ihn beklommen: Sie hatte sich stets geschämt, da unten so behaart zu sein. Aber es schien ihn nicht zu stören; er neigte sich vor und küßte sie behutsam, genau dort, als sei es die schönste Sache der Welt.

Sie sackte vor ihm in die Knie, keuchend, als wäre sie meilenweit gelaufen. Sie begehrte ihn. Ihre Kehle war trocken vor Verlangen. Sie legte ihre Hände auf seine Knie und ließ eine Hand unter sein Wams gleiten. Es war das erste Mal, daß sie das Glied eines Mannes berührte. Es fühlte sich heiß und trocken und hart an. Jack schloß die Augen und stöhnte aus tiefster Seele, während sie ihn mit den Fingerspitzen erkundete. Sie schob sein Wams hoch, beugte sich vor und küßte ihn, so wie er sie dort unten geküßt hatte, sanft und zärtlich. Sein Glied war an der Spitze zum Bersten geschwollen und ein wenig feucht.

Urplötzlich überkam sie das dringende Bedürfnis, ihm ihre Brüste zu zeigen, und sie richtete sich auf. Er sah ihr überrascht zu. Ohne ihn aus den Augen zu lassen, zog sie sich schnell das Nachthemd über den Kopf und ließ es einfach fallen. Nun war sie vollkommen nackt. Das machte sie überaus befangen, aber auf eine angenehme, köstlich schamlose Art. Jack betrachtete ihre Brüste wie verzaubert. »Wie schön sie sind«, sagte er.

»Findest du wirklich?« wollte sie wissen. »Ich dachte immer, sie seien zu groß.«

»Zu groß!« gab er zurück, und es klang, als hielte er alleine schon die Andeutung für ungeheuerlich. Er reckte sich und berührte ihre linke Brust mit seiner Rechten. Behutsam streichelte er ihre Haut mit den Fingerspitzen. Sie senkte den Kopf und beobachtete ihn dabei. Nach einer Weile ergriff sie seine Hände und drückte sie gegen ihre Brüste. »Stärker«, sagte sie heiser. »Ich will dich noch deutlicher spüren.«

Ihre Worte entfachten seine Leidenschaft. Er knetete ihre Brüste, nahm die Spitzen zwischen seine Finger und kniff sie leicht, so daß es gerade nur ein wenig schmerzte. Das ließ sie völlig außer Rand und Band geraten, und sie war nur noch von einem einzigen Gedanken beherrscht: seinen Körper ebenso zu ertasten wie er den ihren. »Zieh dich aus«, sagte sie. »Ich möchte dich ansehen.«

Wams und Unterhemd, Stiefel und Kniehose flogen beiseite, und er kniete sich wieder vor ihr hin. Sein rotes Haar trocknete allmählich zu wirren Kringeln. Er war schmal gebaut, seine Haut sehr hell, die Schultern und Hüften knochig. Er wirkte drahtig und agil, jung und frisch. Sein Glied ragte wie ein Baumstamm aus dem kastanienbraunen Schamhaar. Plötzlich hatte sie den Wunsch, seine Brust zu küssen. Sie neigte sich vor, streifte seine flachen, männlichen Brustwarzen mit den Lippen, und sie richteten sich auf, genau wie ihre. Sanft saugte sie daran, beseelt von dem Verlangen, ihm das gleiche Vergnügen zu bereiten wie er ihr. Er streichelte ihr Haar.

Sie wollte ihn in sich spüren, jetzt gleich.

Doch er schien nicht genau zu wissen, wie es weitergehen sollte. »Jack«, fragte sie, »hast du noch nie mit einer Frau geschlafen?«

»Nein«, erwiderte er und sah ein wenig töricht drein.

»Das macht mich so froh«, sagte sie inbrünstig. »So froh!«

Sie griff nach seiner Hand und führte sie zwischen ihre Beine. Sie war dort angeschwollen und überempfindlich, und bei seiner Berührung durchfuhr es sie wie ein Schock. »Fühl mich«, sagte sie. Er ließ seine Finger forschend herumwandern. »Fühl innendrin«, sagte sie. Zögernd führte er einen Finger ein. Sie war feucht vor Begierde. »Da«, sagte sie mit einem befriedigten Seufzer. »Da gehört es hin.« Sie schob seine Hand beiseite und streckte sich auf dem Stroh aus.

Er legte sich über sie, stützte sich auf einen Ellbogen und küßte sie auf den Mund. Sie fühlte, wie er ein wenig in sie eindrang und dann innehielt: »Was ist?« fragte sie.

»Es fühlt sich so eng an«, gab er zurück. »Ich habe Angst, dir weh zu tun.«

»Mach's ein bißchen stärker«, sagte sie. »Ich will dich so sehr, daß mir der Schmerz nichts ausmacht.«

Sie spürte, wie er sich in sie hineinstieß. Es tat weh, mehr als erwartet, aber nicht lange, und danach durchströmte sie ein Gefühl wunderbaren Erfülltseins. Sie sah ihm ins Gesicht. Er zog sich ein wenig zurück und schob sich wieder in sie hinein – und sie stemmte sich ihm entgegen. Sie lächelte. »Ich hätte nie gedacht, daß das so schön sein könnte«, sagte sie verwundert. Er schloß vor lauter Glück die Augen.

Nun begann er, sich rhythmisch zu bewegen. Die stete Reibung rief irgendwo in ihrer Lendengegend einen wunderbar angenehmen Puls ins Leben. Jedesmal, wenn ihre Körper aneinanderprallten, hörte sie sich vor Erregung leise aufstöhnen. Er neigte sich ihr entgegen, so daß er ihre Brustwarzen mit seinem Brustkorb berührte und sein heißer Atem sie streifte. Sie grub ihre Finger in seinen sehnigen Rükken. Ihr gleichmäßiges Stöhnen verwandelte sich in kurze Schreie. Plötzlich verspürte sie den Drang, ihn zu küssen. Sie schob ihre Hände in seine Locken und zog seinen Kopf zu sich herab, küßte ihn auf die Lippen, stieß mit der Zunge vor und bewegte sie in seinem Mund wie er sich in ihr, schneller und schneller. Das war ein so herrliches Gefühl, daß sie meinte, vor Erregung den Verstand zu verlieren. Lustvolle Schauder durchbebten sie, und dann krampfte sich alles in ihr zusammen, als wäre sie vom Pferd gefallen und auf dem Boden aufgeschlagen. Unwillkürlich schrie sie laut auf. Sie öffnete die Augen, sah ihn an und rief seinen Namen; eine zweite Welle riß sie hinfort, dann eine dritte; und dann spürte sie, wie sein Körper sich ebenfalls verkrampfte. Auch er schrie auf und sie spürte, wie sich ein heißer Strom in sie ergoß; das erregte sie so sehr, daß sie wieder und wieder von Krämpfen der Lust gepackt wurde, die ganz allmählich verebbten, bis sie schließlich ermattet und ruhig dalag.

Aliena konnte sich vor Erschöpfung nicht rühren, und ihr war auch nicht nach Reden zumute, aber sie fühlte Jacks Gewicht über sich, seine Hüftknochen drückten sich gegen sie, sein flacher Brustkorb lag auf ihren weichen Brüsten, sein Mund an ihrem Ohr, seine Finger hatten sich in ihr Haar verwickelt. Irgendwo im Hinterkopf formten sich undeutliche Gedanken: So also sollte es zwischen Mann und Frau sein; deshalb also macht alle Welt soviel Aufhebens darum; deshalb ist die Liebe zwischen Eheleuten so groß ...

Jacks Atem ging nun gleichmäßig und leicht, sein Körper entspannte sich, bis er völlig erschlaffte. Er war eingeschlafen.

Aliena drehte den Kopf zur Seite und küßte sein Gesicht. Er war ihr nicht zu schwer. Am liebsten wäre sie für immer und ewig so mit ihm liegengeblieben.

Bei diesem Gedanken kam die Erinnerung zurück.

Heute war ihr Hochzeitstag!

Herr im Himmel, dachte sie, was habe ich getan?

Sie brach in Tränen aus, und einen Moment später wachte Jack auf. Mit fast unerträglicher Zärtlichkeit küßte er ihr die Tränen fort.

»O Jack, ich möchte dich so gern heiraten«, sagte sie.

»Selbstverständlich heiraten wir«, gab er im Brustton tiefster Überzeugung zurück.

Er hatte sie mißverstanden, und das machte alles nur noch schlimmer. »Aber das geht nicht«, sagte sie und mußte noch mehr weinen.

»Aber jetzt, wo wir –«

»Ich weiß –«

»Jetzt mußt du mich heiraten!«

»Es geht nicht«, sagte sie. »Ich habe mein ganzes Vermögen verloren, und du hast auch nichts.«

Er stützte sich auf die Ellenbogen. »Ich habe immer noch meine Hände«, erwiderte er heftig. »Ich bin der beste Steinmetz weit und breit.«

»Aber du bist entlassen worden –«

»Das ist doch egal. Ich kann auf jedem Bauplatz der Welt Arbeit bekommen.«

Verzagt schüttelte sie den Kopf. »Das reicht nicht. Ich muß auch an Richard denken.«

»Wieso denn?« sagte er ungehalten. »Was hat das mit Richard zu tun? Der kommt doch gut alleine zurecht.«

Plötzlich wirkte Jack wie ein kleiner Junge, und Aliena fiel wieder der Altersunterschied zwischen ihnen ein: Er warf fünf Jahre jünger als sie und noch immer überzeugt, einen Anspruch auf ungetrübtes Glück zu haben. »Kurz vor seinem Tod«, erklärte sie, »habe ich meinem Vater geschworen, für Richard zu sorgen, bis er Graf von Shiring ist.«

»Aber das wird er womöglich nie!«

»Ein Eid ist ein Eid.«

Jack sah sie ratlos an und rollte sich zur Seite. Sein weicher Penis glitt aus ihr heraus, und Aliena empfand es wie einen schmerzlichen Verlust. Ich werde ihn nie wieder in mir spüren, dachte sie kummervoll.

»Das kann nicht dein Ernst sein«, sagte er. »Ein Eid, das ist doch nichts als hohles Gerede! Im Vergleich *hierzu* ist ein Eid gar nichts! Das hier ist wirklich, du und ich, das ist wirklich.« Er betrachtete ihre Brüste und faßte zwischen ihre Beine, um die krausen Haare zu streicheln. Die Berührung ging ihr durch Mark und Bein. Er sah, wie sie zusammenzuckte, und hielt inne.

Einen kurzen Moment lang fühlte sie sich versucht nachzugeben. *Ja, schön, laß uns zusammen davonlaufen, jetzt gleich.* Und hätte er sie weiter gestreichelt, hätte sie es vielleicht getan; aber die Vernunft gebot ihr zu sagen: »Ich werde Alfred heiraten.«

»Du bist nicht ganz bei Trost!«

»Das ist mein einziger Ausweg.«

Er starrte sie an. »Ich kann es einfach nicht glauben«, sagte er.

»Es geht nicht anders.«

»Ich kann dich doch nicht so einfach hergeben. Ich kann nicht. Ich kann einfach nicht.« Seine Stimme versagte.

Sie begann, an seine Vernunft zu appellieren – ebensosehr wie an ihre eigene. »Was nützt es schon, wenn ich das Versprechen, das ich meinem Vater gegeben habe, breche, um dir dann die Ehe zu versprechen? Sobald ich das erste breche, ist auch das zweite keinen Pfifferling mehr wert.«

»Das ist mir egal. Ich will kein Versprechen von dir. Ich will bloß, daß wir immer zusammenbleiben und uns lieben können, so oft wir wollen.«

Das ist die Vorstellung eines Achtzehnjährigen von der Ehe, dachte sie, aber sie sprach es nicht aus. Hätte sie frei entscheiden können – sie hätte sein Angebot nur allzugern angenommen. »Ich kann nicht einfach tun, was mir gefällt«, sagte sie traurig. »Das ist nun mal meine Bestimmung.«

»Was du tust, ist falsch«, gab er zurück. »Nicht nur falsch, es ist *schlecht*. Auf solche Weise dein ganzes Glück aufzugeben, das ist, als wenn du Edelsteine ins Meer wirfst. Das ist schlimmer als jede Sünde.«

Plötzlich durchzuckte sie der Gedanke, daß ihre Mutter ihm zugestimmt hätte. Sie hatte keine Ahnung, woher sie das so genau wußte, und sogleich schob sie den Gedanken beiseite. »Ich könnte niemals glücklich werden – nicht einmal mit dir –, wenn ich mit dem Wissen leben müßte, das Versprechen, das ich meinem Vater gab, gebrochen zu haben.«

»Dir liegt mehr an deinem Vater und deinem Bruder als an mir«, sagte er und klang zum erstenmal gereizt.

»Nein …«

»Was dann?«

Er war lediglich streitlustig, dennoch nahm sie seine Frage ernst. »Es bedeutet wohl, daß ich den Eid, den ich meinem Vater schwor, für wichtiger halte als meine Liebe zu dir.«

»Wirklich?« fragte er ungläubig. »Ist das dein Ernst?«

»Ja, das ist mein Ernst«, antwortete sie schweren Herzens, und die Worte klangen ihr wie eine Totenglocke.

»Dazu gibt es ja wohl nichts mehr zu sagen.«

»Nur … daß es mir leid tut.«

Er stand auf, wandte ihr den Rücken zu und griff nach seinem Unterhemd. Seine Beine waren überall übersät mit lockigen, rotblonden Härchen. Rasch schlüpfte er in Hemd und Wams, zog die Socken an und stieg in die Stiefel. Aliena ging es viel zu schnell.

»Du wirst schrecklich unglücklich sein«, sagte er.

Er legte es darauf an, ihr weh zu tun, doch der Versuch mißlang, denn sie hörte das Mitgefühl in seiner Stimme.

»Ja, das werde ich«, erwiderte sie. »Würdest du wenigstens … wenigstens so weit gehen zu sagen, daß du mich für diese Entscheidung achtest?«

»Nein«, gab er ohne Zögern zurück. »Das kann ich nicht. Ich verachte dich dafür.«

Sie saß da, nackt, wie sie war, sah ihn an und begann zu weinen.

»Am besten gehe ich jetzt«, sagte er, und seine Stimme drohte zu versagen.

»Ja, geh«, schluchzte sie.

Er ging zur Tür.

»Jack!«

Er drehte sich um.

Sie sagte: »Wünsch mir wenigstens alles Gute, ja, Jack?«

Er hob den Riegel. »Na gut –« Er hielt inne, brachte aber kein Wort heraus. Er sah zu Boden, dann wieder auf sie. Diesmal brachte er es heraus, wenn auch nur im Flüsterton: »Alles Gute.«

Damit ging er.

Toms ehemaliges Haus gehörte nun Ellen, aber da es gleichzeitig auch Alfreds Zuhause war, wimmelte es dort an diesem Morgen vor Menschen, die unter Anleitung von Alfreds dreizehnjähriger Schwester Martha den Hochzeitsschmaus vorbereiteten. Jacks Mutter sah betrübt zu. Alfred, ein Handtuch unter dem Arm, stand im Begriff, zum Fluß hinunterzugehen – die Frauen badeten einmal im Monat, die Männer nur Ostern und Michaeli, allenfalls noch am Morgen ihrer Hochzeit, wie es der Brauch wollte. Als Jack das Haus betrat, verstummte jede Unterhaltung.

»Was willst du denn hier?« fragte Alfred.

»Daß du diese Hochzeit abbläst«, gab Jack zurück.

»Verpiß dich«, sagte Alfred.

Jack begriff, daß er die Sache falsch angepackt hatte. Ihm war schließlich nicht an einer Auseinandersetzung gelegen. Sein Vorschlag mußte Alfred – vorausgesetzt, es gelang ihm, den Stiefbruder zur Einsicht zu bringen – ebenso recht kommen wie ihm selbst. »Alfred, sie liebt dich nicht«, sagte er so behutsam wie irgend möglich.

»Du hast doch keinen blassen Schimmer, Bürschchen.«

»Doch«, beharrte Jack. »Sie liebt dich nicht. Sie heiratet dich nur um Richards willen. Er ist der einzige, den diese Hochzeit glücklich machen wird.«

»Scher dich in dein Kloster zurück«, meinte Alfred verächtlich. »Wo hast du überhaupt deine Kutte gelassen?«

Jack holte tief Luft. Nun blieb ihm nichts anderes mehr übrig, als die Wahrheit zu sagen. »Alfred, sie liebt *mich*.«

Jack hatte mit einem Wutausbruch gerechnet, doch Alfred begnügte sich mit einem verschlagenen Grinsen. Jack kam sich vor wie der Ochs am Berge. Was sollte das denn? Allmählich dämmerte es ihm. »Du wußtest es die ganze Zeit!« sagte er ungläubig. »Du weißt, daß sie mich liebt, aber das ist dir vollkommen egal! Du willst sie auf jeden Fall, ob sie dich liebt oder nicht. Du willst sie ganz einfach besitzen.«

Alfreds verstecktes Grinsen wurde breiter und noch eine Spur hämischer, und Jack erkannte, daß er den Nagel auf den Kopf getroffen hatte; aber damit war es nicht getan: Alfreds Gesicht verriet noch mehr. Ein unerhörter Verdacht beschlich Jack. »Warum willst du sie überhaupt haben?« wollte er wissen. »Etwa, weil ... Ist es möglich, daß du sie nur heiraten willst, um sie mir wegzunehmen?« Seine Stimme hob sich im Zorn. »Daß du sie aus *Gehässigkeit* heiratest?« Die unverhohlene Genugtuung in Alfreds stupider Visage sprach Bände, und Jack wußte, daß er auch diesmal richtig lag. Das war ja verheerend! Die Vorstellung, daß Alfreds Beweggrund nicht einmal einer nur allzu verständlichen Begierde entsprang, sondern simpelster, reinster Bosheit – das überstieg sein Fassungsvermögen. »Du verfluchter Kerl – sieh bloß zu, daß du sie anständig behandelst!« brüllte er.

Alfred lachte.

Die bodenlose Gemeinheit, die darin zutage trat, traf Jack wie ein Faustschlag. Der Kerl hatte gar nicht die Absicht, Aliena gut zu behandeln! Dies sollte seine letzte Rache an Jack werden: Aliena zu heiraten und ihr das Leben zu vergällen. »Du Dreckstück«, sagte Jack grimmig. »Du Misthaufen. Du Scheißkerl. Du häßliches, dummes, gemeines, *abscheuliches* Ekel, du!«

Diese unverhohlenen Schmähungen endlich verstand selbst der begriffsstutzige Alfred. Er ließ sein Handtuch fallen und ging mit geballter Faust auf Jack los. Jack, längst darauf gefaßt, trat einen Schritt vor, um als erster zuzuschlagen. Doch plötzlich stand Jacks Mutter zwischen ihnen. So klein sie auch war – es bedurfte nur weniger Worte von ihr, und die Rauferei, die auszubrechen drohte, hatte auch schon ein Ende.

»Alfred! Geh baden.«

Alfred beruhigte sich schnell. Ihm war nur allzu klar, daß er es gar nicht mehr nötig hatte, Jack zu verprügeln: Er hatte so oder so den Sieg davongetragen und setzte eine selbstgefällige Miene auf, damit niemand einen Zweifel daran hegen konnte. Dann verließ er das Haus.

»Was hast du jetzt vor, Jack?« wollte seine Mutter wissen.

Jack, der noch immer vor Wut bebte, mußte mehrmals tief Luft holen, bevor er wieder sprechen konnte. Die Hochzeit war nicht mehr zu verhindern, das wußte er jetzt. Aber sollte er deswegen ohnmächtig dabei zusehen? »Ich muß fort aus Kingsbridge.«

Er bemerkte, daß ihr Gesicht sich kummervoll verzog, aber sie nickte. »Genau das habe ich befürchtet. Aber ich glaube, du hast recht.«

Die Klosterglocke läutete. Jack sagte: »Jetzt wird es nicht mehr lange dauern, bis sie meine Flucht entdecken.«

Ellen senkte die Stimme. »Dann geh geschwind und versteck dich unten am Fluß, in Sichtweite der Brücke. Ich bringe dir ein paar Sachen.«

»In Ordnung.« Er wandte sich zum Gehen.

Martha stand zwischen ihm und der Tür, und die Tränen liefen ihr übers Gesicht. Er umarmte sie, und sie drückte ihn fest an sich. Ihr kindlicher Körper war flach und knochig wie der eines Jungen. »Komm zurück, irgendwann«, sagte sie heftig.

Er gab ihr schnell einen Kuß und ging hinaus.

Draußen waren mittlerweile viele Leute unterwegs, holten Wasser und genossen die milde Herbstluft dieses Morgens. Die meisten wußten, daß Jack Novize geworden war – die Stadt war immer noch so klein, daß sich Neuigkeiten in Windeseile verbreiteten –, und wenn ihn auch niemand darauf ansprach, so zog er doch in seiner Alltagskleidung manch neugierigen Blick auf sich. Er eilte den Hügel hinunter, über die Brücke und am Ufer entlang, bis er ein Röhricht erreichte. Er suchte sich ein Plätzchen im Schilf, das ihm Sicht auf die Brücke bot, hockte sich nieder und wartete.

Er hatte nicht die geringste Ahnung, wohin er sich wenden sollte. Am besten ging er vielleicht immer geradeaus, bis er auf eine Stadt traf, in der ein Dom gebaut wurde. Es war ihm vollkommen ernst gewesen, als er zu Aliena gesagt hatte, er sei gut genug, um überall Arbeit zu finden. Er war überzeugt, daß ihn jeder Dombaumeister mit Handkuß nähme – selbst, wenn er niemanden brauchte –, führte er ihm nur vor, wie kunstfertig und geschickt er mit dem Meißel umging. Doch das alles schien nun sinnlos geworden. Niemals konnte er eine andere Frau als Aliena lieben, und mit der Kathedrale zu Kingsbridge ging es ihm ähnlich. *Hier* und nirgendwo sonst wollte er bauen.

Vielleicht gehe ich auch nur in den Wald, lege mich dort irgendwo unter die Bäume und warte auf den Tod ...

Die Vorstellung gefiel ihm, je mehr er darüber nachdachte. Das Wetter war mild, das Laub leuchtete grün und golden – ein friedliches Ende. Er bedauerte nur, nicht mehr über seinen Vater in Erfahrung gebracht zu haben, bevor er starb.

Er war gerade dabei, sich auszumalen, wie er auf einem Lager aus Herbstlaub sachte in den Tod hinüberglitt, da erblickte er seine Mutter auf der Brücke. Sie führte ein Pferd am Zügel.

Er sprang auf und lief ihr entgegen. Das Pferd war ihr eigenes, eine kastanienbraune Stute, die niemand außer Ellen ritt. »Du kannst mein Pferd haben«, sagte sie.

Er griff nach ihrer Hand und drückte sie dankbar.

In ihre Augen traten Tränen. »Ich hatte dir so wenig zu bieten«, sagte sie. »Erst ließ ich dich im Wald aufwachsen wie einen Wilden, dann zog ich mit Tom durchs Land und du wärest beinahe verhungert, und zu alledem mußtest du dich auch noch mit Alfred abfinden.«

»Du hast deine Sache sehr gut gemacht, Mutter«, gab er zurück. »Heute morgen habe ich mit Aliena geschlafen. Jetzt kann ich zufrieden sterben.«

»Du dummer Junge«, sagte sie. »Du bist genau wie ich. Wenn du deine Liebste nicht haben kannst, dann bleibst du lieber allein.«

»Geht es dir denn genauso?« wollte Jack wissen.

Sie nickte. »Nach dem Tod deines Vaters bin ich lieber allein geblieben, als mich mit dem Zweitbesten zufriedenzugeben. Nie wollte ich einen anderen Mann haben – bis ich Tom traf. Und das war elf Jahre später.« Sie entzog ihm ihre Hand. »Ich erzähle dir das nicht ohne Grund: Eines Tages wirst du eine andere lieben, selbst wenn es elf Jahre dauern sollte; das verspreche ich dir.«

Er schüttelte den Kopf. »Das scheint mir ganz unmöglich.«

»Ich weiß.« Sie warf einen beunruhigten Blick über die Schulter auf die Stadt. »Du mußt gehen.«

Jack wandte sich dem Pferd zu. Die Satteltaschen waren prall gefüllt. »Was ist da drin?« fragte er.

»Wegzehrung, ein bißchen Geld und ein voller Weinschlauch in dieser hier«, erwiderte sie. »In der anderen sind Toms Werkzeuge.«

Jack war gerührt. Mutter hatte nach Toms Tod darauf bestanden, seine Werkzeuge zu behalten, als Erinnerung. Daß sie sich nun davon trennte und an ihn weitergab! Er umarmte sie. »Danke«, sagte er schlicht.

»Wo willst du hin?«

Sein Vater fiel ihm ein. »Wo erzählen die Spielleute ihre Geschichten?« fragte er.

»Auf der Pilgerstraße nach Santiago de Compostela.«

»Glaubst du, daß sie sich an Jack Shareburg erinnern können?«

»Vielleicht. Sag ihnen, daß du ihm wie aus dem Gesicht geschnitten bist.«

»Wo liegt Santiago?«

»In Spanien.«

»Dann gehe ich nach Spanien.«

»Das ist ein weiter Weg, Jack.«

»Ich habe Zeit – mehr als genug.«

Sie schlang die Arme um ihn und drückte ihn an sich. Er fragte sich, wie oft sie das in den vergangenen achtzehn Jahren wohl getan, wie oft sie ihn über ein aufgeschlagenes Knie, ein verlorengegangenes Spielzeug oder irgendeine andere kindliche Enttäuschung hinweggetröstet haben mochte – und nun über diesen Schmerz, der nur allzu erwachsen war. Vor seinem inneren Auge zog alles vorbei, was sie je für ihn getan hatte – von seiner Kindheit im Wald bis zu seiner Flucht aus dem Kerker, stets bereit, wie eine Wildkatze für ihren Sohn zu kämpfen. Es tat unendlich weh, von ihr zu gehen.

Sie ließ ihn los, und er schwang sich aufs Pferd.

Einen Blick noch zurück, auf Kingsbridge! Bei meinem ersten Besuch, dachte er, war es ein kleines, verschlafenes Nest mit einer alten, baufälligen Kathedrale. Dann habe ich den alten Dom in Brand gesteckt, doch das weiß außer mir keine Menschenseele ... Und heute ist das Nest eine geschäftige, selbstgefällige kleine Stadt! Nun ja, es gibt schließlich noch andere Städte ... Der Abschied fiel ihm unendlich schwer, aber nun lockte das Unbekannte, das Abenteuer; darüber mußte der Schmerz, alles, was er je geliebt, zurückzulassen, verblassen.

Mutter sagte: »Komm bitte wieder, Jack, irgendwann.«

»Ich komme bestimmt wieder.«

»Versprochen?«

»Versprochen.«

»Wenn dir das Geld ausgeht, bevor du Arbeit findest, dann verkauf das Pferd, nicht das Werkzeug«, sagte sie.

»Ich liebe dich, Mutter«, sagte er.

Ihre Augen schwammen in Tränen. »Paß auf dich auf, mein Sohn.«

Er gab dem Pferd einen Tritt, und es setzte sich in Bewegung. Er drehte sich um und winkte. Sie winkte zurück. Dann spornte er das Pferd zum Trab an und ritt, ohne einen einzigen Blick zurück, von dannen.

Richard kam rechtzeitig zur Hochzeit heim.

König Stephan hatte ihm großzügig zwei Tage Urlaub gewährt, erklärte er. Die königliche Armee lag vor Oxford und belagerte die Burg, worin Mathilde in der Falle saß, und so gab es für die Ritter nicht viel zu tun. »Ich konnte doch unmöglich die Hochzeit meiner Schwester versäumen«, sagte er, und Aliena dachte verbittert: Du willst doch nur mit eigenen Augen sehen, daß sie auch wirklich stattfindet, damit du gewiß sein kannst, daß Alfred sein Wort hält.

Dennoch war sie froh, daß er sie zur Kirche und zum Altar führen würde. Sie hatte ja sonst niemanden.

Sie legte ein neues Leinenhemd an, darüber ein modisches weißes Gewand. Mit ihrem Stummelhaar ließ sich kein Staat machen, doch sie flocht die längsten Strähnen zu Zöpfen und umwickelte sie nach der neuesten Mode mit weißen Seidenbändern. Von der Nachbarin lieh sie sich einen Spiegel. Sie war blaß, und ihre Augen zeugten von einer schlaflosen Nacht. Nun ja, daran war jetzt nichts mehr zu ändern. Richard beobachtete sie. Er sah ein wenig einfältig drein, als wäre er sich seiner Schuld bewußt, und zappelte unruhig hin und her. Sorgte er sich, sie könnte die ganze Sache im letzten Moment abblasen?

Es gab Augenblicke, da war sie ernsthaft versucht, genau das zu tun. Sie malte sich aus, wie sie mit Jack Hand in Hand Kingsbridge den Rücken kehrte und irgendwo anders ein neues Leben begann, ein einfaches, ehrlich verdientes Leben ohne die Last alter Schwüre und toter Eltern. Was für ein törichter Traum! Ließ sie ihren Bruder im Stich, wurde sie nirgendwo glücklich, das war ihr klar.

Dann kam ihr in den Sinn, sie könnte zum Fluß hinuntergehen und sich hineinstürzen; sie sah sich schon stromabwärts treiben, eine aufgedunsene Wasserleiche im Hochzeitskleid, und sie begriff, daß die Heirat mit Alfred immer noch besser war, bot sie doch für so manche Schwierigkeit die beste Lösung.

Jack hätte dafür natürlich nur Hohn und Spott übrig.

Die Kirchenglocke begann zu läuten.

Aliena erhob sich.

So hatte sie sich ihre Hochzeit nie vorgestellt. Als kleines Mädchen hatte sie sich ausgemalt, wie sie einst am Arm ihres Vaters vom Wohnturm über die Zugbrücke zur Kapelle im tiefergelegenen Burghof schritte, wie sich Ritter und Krieger, Gesinde und Pächter in der Einfriedung drängten, ihr zujubelten und Glück wünschten. Der junge Mann, der in der Kapelle auf sie wartete, war in diesem Tagtraum verschwommen gewesen, aber sie wußte, daß er sie anbetete und sie zum Lachen brachte und daß sie ihn wundervoll fand. Aber nichts in ihrem Leben war so gekommen, wie sie sich's erhofft hatte. Richard hielt die Tür ihres kleinen Häuschens für sie auf, und sie trat ins Freie.

Zu ihrer Überraschung standen ihre Nachbarn vor den Türen ihrer Häuser, um sich von ihr zu verabschieden. Sie riefen ihr »Gott segne Euch!« und »Alles Gute!« zu, und Aliena empfand große Dankbarkeit. Auf ihrem Weg durch die Straße wurde sie mit Getreidekörnern überschüttet, dem Symbol für Fruchtbarkeit. Sie würde Kinder haben, und ihre Kinder würden sie lieben.

Die Pfarrkirche lag am anderen Ende der Stadt, im Viertel der Reichen, wo sie von heute abend an leben würde. Sie kam am Kloster vorbei. Die Mönche hielten gerade ihren Gottesdienst in der Krypta ab, aber Prior Philip hatte zugesagt, auf dem Hochzeitsfest zu erscheinen und das glückliche Paar zu segnen. Aliena hoffte, daß er es auch schaffte. Seit jenem Tag vor sechs Jahren, als er ihr in Winchester ihren ersten Wollsack abgekauft, war er aus ihrem Leben nicht mehr fortzudenken.

Vor der neuen Kirche, die Alfred mit Toms Hilfe gebaut, hatte sich eine kleine Menschenmenge versammelt. Die Eheschließung sollte auf englisch in der überdachten Vorhalle abgehalten werden, anschließend folgte eine lateinische Messe im Kirchenraum. Alfreds Bauleute waren gekommen und fast alle Frauen, die ehedem für Aliena gewebt hatten. Die Braut wurde mit Hochrufen empfangen.

Alfred stand schon bereit, begleitet von seiner Schwester Martha und Dan, einem seiner Steinmetzen. Er trug ein neues, scharlachrotes Wams und saubere Stiefel. Sein Haar war lang und schimmerte dunkel wie das von Ellen. Aliena fiel auf, daß Ellen fehlte, und sie war enttäuscht. Doch bevor sie Martha nach ihrer Stiefmutter fragen konnte, kam der Priester auch schon heraus, und der Gottesdienst begann.

Aliena wurde nachdenklich: Vor sechs Jahren hatte sie ihrem Vater einen Eid geschworen, der ihr Leben in völlig neue Bahnen gelenkt hatte; und nun begann ein neuer Lebensabschnitt für sie, und wiederum band sie sich durch ein Gelübde an einen Mann. Für sich selbst tat sie kaum je etwas. Heute morgen mit Jack hatte sie allerdings eine unerhörte Ausnahme gemacht. Das kam ihr noch immer ganz und gar verwunschen vor, wie ein Traum oder eine von Jacks abenteuerlichen Geschichten, die mit dem wirklichen Leben rein gar nichts zu tun hatten. Niemand sollte je davon erfahren! Dieses allerliebste Geheimnis wollte sie für sich behalten und höchstens ab und zu – wie ein Geizhals, der im Dunkel der Nacht seine versteckten Schätze zählt – aus ihrer Erinnerung hervorkramen.

Sie waren beim Ehegelübde angelangt, und auf des Priesters Wink hin sprach Aliena: »Alfred, Sohn von Tom Builder, ich nehme dich zu meinem Gemahl und gelobe, dir treu zu sein, heute und immerdar.« Danach wäre sie am liebsten in Tränen ausgebrochen.

Während Alfred dieses feierliche Gelübde wiederholte, wurde es unruhig unter den Anwesenden, und mehrere Köpfe drehten sich um. Aliena und Marthas Blicke kreuzten sich, und Martha wisperte: »Ellen ist da.«

Der Priester runzelte unwillig die Stirn und fuhr fort: »Hiermit erkläre ich euch, Alfred und Aliena, vor Gottes Angesicht zu Mann und Frau, und möge der Segen –«

Er sollte den Satz nie beenden. Hinter Aliena ertönte es laut und deutlich: »Ich verfluche diese Ehe!«

Ellen! Die Gemeinde stöhnte entsetzt auf.

Der Priester versuchte es noch einmal: »Und möge der Segen –« Er hielt inne, erblaßte und bekreuzigte sich.

Aliena drehte sich um: Die Anwesenden waren zurückgewichen, und Ellen stand direkt hinter ihr. In der einen Hand hielt sie einen lebendigen Hahn, in der anderen ein langes Messer. Blut tropfte vom Messer, und Blut schoß aus dem Hals des verwundeten Tieres. »Kummer und Sorge beschwöre ich auf diese Ehe herab!« rief sie, und ihre Worte ließen Aliena das Blut in den Adern gefrieren. »Unfruchtbar soll sie sein«, fuhr sie fort. »Bitterkeit und Haß, Trauer und Reue sollen niemals von ihr weichen. Geschlagen sein soll sie mit Impotenz.« Beim letzten Wort warf sie den Hahn hoch in die Luft. Die Leute schrien auf und duckten sich, nur Aliena stand still, wie vom Donner gerührt. Der Hahn segelte durch die Luft, verspritzte sein Blut und landete auf Alfred, der entsetzt zurücksprang. Das grausige Tier plumpste zu Boden, wo es sein Blut verströmte.

Als alle wieder aufblickten, war Ellen verschwunden.

Martha hatte Toms und Ellens altes Federbett, das nun Alfred und Aliena gehören sollte, mit frischen Leintüchern und einer neuen Wolldecke bezogen. Ellen war nach ihrem Auftritt in der Kirche spurlos verschwunden. Das Hochzeitsmahl war in gedrückter Stimmung verlaufen. Die Gäste, in Ermangelung anderer Unterhaltung, aßen und tranken mit grimmiger Entschlossenheit und brachen bei Sonnenuntergang auf, ohne die sonst üblichen groben Anzüglichkeiten über die Hochzeitsnacht von sich zu geben. Martha lag nun in ihrem eigenen Bett im Vorderzimmer, und Richard war in Alienas kleines Haus zurückgekehrt, das nun ihm gehörte.

Alfred sprach von dem Haus aus Stein, das er im nächsten Sommer für sie bauen wollte. Beim Festschmaus hatte er vor Richard damit geprahlt. »Es wird ein Schlafzimmer haben, eine Halle und ein Erdgeschoß«, hatte er gesagt. »Und wenn John Silversmiths Frau es erst sieht, wird sie auch ein solches Haus haben wollen. Dann wird es nicht lange dauern, und alle wohlhabenden Leute in der Stadt wollen auch ein Haus aus Stein haben.«

»Hast du denn schon einen Bauplan?« hatte Richard gefragt, und Aliena hatte die Skepsis aus seiner Stimme herausgehört, die allen anderen anscheinend entgangen war.

»Ich habe ein paar alte Tintenzeichnungen, die mein Vater auf Pergament gemacht hat. Eine davon mit dem Entwurf für das Haus, das wir vor Jahren für Aliena und William Hamleigh bauten. Danach werde ich mich bei meinem Entwurf richten.«

Aliena wandte sich angeekelt ab. Wie konnte man nur so taktlos sein? Und das an ihrem Hochzeitstag! Alfred hatte sich den ganzen Nachmittag über als rechtes Großmaul erwiesen, immer wieder Wein nachgeschenkt, Witze gerissen und seinen Arbeitskollegen verstohlen zugezwinkert. Er schien glücklich zu sein.

Nun saß er auf dem Bettrand und zog seine Stiefel aus. Aliena löste die Bänder in ihrem Haar. Sie war sich nicht schlüssig, was sie von Ellens Fluch halten sollte. Er hatte sie erschüttert, und sie hatte nicht die geringste Ahnung, was Ellen sich dabei gedacht haben mochte, doch das Grauen, das die meisten Leute erfaßt hatte, konnte sie nicht nachempfinden.

Von Alfred ließ sich das nicht behaupten. Als der geschlachtete Hahn auf ihm landete, war er in unverständliches Gebrabbel ausgebrochen. Richard hatte ihn handgreiflich zur Vernunft bringen müssen, indem er ihn am Wams packte und beutelte. Alfred war jedoch recht schnell wieder zu sich gekommen, und das einzige Anzeichen für seine Furcht war die Unermüdlichkeit, mit der er anschließend schulterklopfend und bierselig gute Laune verbreitet hatte.

Aliena fühlte sich merkwürdig gefaßt. Sie freute sich zwar nicht gerade auf das, was folgen würde, aber zumindest geschah es aus freiem Willen; selbst wenn es sie anekeln sollte, bliebe ihr doch jegliche Erniedrigung erspart. Schließlich hatte sie es nur mit einem einzigen Mann zu tun, und niemand anders würde dabei zusehen.

Sie zog ihr Kleid aus.

Alfred sagte: »Herr im Himmel, wenn das kein langes Messer ist!«

Sie löste den Riemen, der das Messer an ihrem linken Unterarm festhielt, und legte sich im Hemd aufs Bett.

Alfred hatte sich endlich seiner Stiefel entledigt. Er zog seine Kniehose aus, stand auf und warf ihr einen lüsternen Blick zu. »Zieh dein Unterzeug aus«, sagte er. »Ich habe ein Recht darauf, die Titten meiner Frau zu sehen.«

Aliena zögerte. Innerlich sträubte sie sich dagegen, sich nackt auszuziehen, aber es schien unklug, ihm seine allererste Bitte abzuschlagen. Gehorsam setzte sie sich auf und zog das Hemd über den Kopf. Heute morgen hatte sie das gleiche für Jack getan, und wie anders hatte sie sich dabei gefühlt! Entschlossen schob sie jeden Gedanken daran beiseite.

»Was für prachtvolle Möpse«, sagte Alfred. Er stellte sich neben das Bett und grapschte nach ihrer rechten Brust. Seine großen Hände waren rauh und rissig, die Fingernägel schmutzig. Er quetschte Alienas Brust, und sie zuckte zusammen. Er lachte und ließ von ihr ab.

Er zog sein Wams aus und hängte es an einen Haken. Dann kam er zum Bett zurück und zog die Decke weg.

Aliena schluckte. Sie fühlte sich hilf- und schutzlos, nackt seinem Blick ausgeliefert. »Herrgott, das ist ja eine ganz Haarige«, sagte er und faßte ihr zwischen die Beine. Unwillkürlich versteifte sie sich, zwang sich aber gleich wieder, die Beine zu öffnen. »So ist's brav«, sagte er und stieß einen Finger in sie hinein. Das tat weh, denn sie war trocken. Sie wußte nicht, wie sie sich das erklären sollte: Heute morgen, mit Jack, war sie feucht und schlüpfrig gewesen. Alfred grunzte und zwängte seinen Finger tiefer hinein.

Sie fühlte sich den Tränen nahe. Daß sie nicht viel Gefallen daran finden würde, war ihr von vornherein klar gewesen – mit soviel Grobheit allerdings hatte sie nicht gerechnet. Er hatte sie ja noch nicht einmal geküßt! Er liebt mich nicht, dachte sie; er mag mich noch nicht einmal. Für ihn bin ich nichts weiter als ein prachtvolles junges Pferd, das er zu reiten gedenkt. Ein Pferd hätte es sogar besser bei ihm – das würde er streicheln und auf den Hals klopfen, bis es sich an ihn gewöhnt, und beruhigend auf das Tier einreden, damit es sich beruhigt. Sie schluckte ihre Tränen hinunter. Es war meine eigene Entscheidung, dachte sie; niemand hat mich gezwungen, ihn zu heiraten; ich finde mich besser damit ab.

»Trocken wie Sägemehl«, brummte Alfred.

»Es tut mir leid«, flüsterte sie.

Er zog seine Hand zurück, spuckte zweimal hinein und rieb die Spucke zwischen ihre Beine. Das kam ihr vor wie der Gipfel der Verachtung. Sie biß sich auf die Zunge und sah weg.

Er drückte ihre Schenkel auseinander. Sie schloß die Augen, öffnete sie wieder und zwang sich, ihn anzusehen. Gewöhn dich dran, dachte sie, das wirst du bis an dein Lebensende tun müssen. Er schwang sich auf das Bett und kniete sich zwischen ihre Beine. Runzelte er die Stirn? Mit einer Hand griff er zwischen ihre Schenkel und spreizte sie, mit der anderen fuhr er unter sein Hemd. Sie sah, wie sich die Hand unter dem Linnen bewegte. Ja, er runzelte die Stirn. »Herr im Himmel«, murmelte er. »Du liegst da wie ein Brett, daß einem die Lust vergeht; da könnte man sich ja ebensogut an eine Leiche heranmachen.«

Wie ungerecht, ihr die Schuld zuzuschieben! »Ich weiß ja überhaupt nicht, was ich zu tun habe!« protestierte sie mit tränenerstickter Stimme.

»Andere Mädchen genießen es«, sagte er.

Genießen! dachte sie. Das glaube ich nicht! Doch dann erinnerte sie sich, wie sie diesen Morgen erst vor Entzücken gestöhnt und geschrien hatte. Doch zwischen dem, was sie noch am Morgen getan hatte, und dem, was jetzt vorging, schien ein himmelweiter Unterschied zu bestehen.

Das war einfach dumm! Sie setzte sich auf. »Laß mich das machen«, sagte sie und griff unter Alfreds Hemd. Sein Glied fühlte sich schlaff und leblos an. Sie war nicht sicher, was sie machen sollte. Sie drückte sanft zu und streichelte es mit den Fingerspitzen. Sie suchte in seinem Gesicht nach einer Antwort, doch darin war nur Wut zu lesen. Sie machte weiter, aber nichts änderte sich.

»Fester«, sagte er.

Sie drückte stärker zu. Sein Glied blieb schlaff, aber er wiegte seine Hüften, als fände er Gefallen daran. Ermutigt griff sie noch fester zu. Plötzlich schrie er auf und entzog sich ihr. Sie hatte des Guten zuviel getan. »Blöde Kuh!« zischte er und schlug ihr mit dem Handrücken ins Gesicht, so daß sie zur Seite fiel.

Sie lag auf dem Bett und wimmerte vor Angst und Schmerz.

»Du bist nichts wert, du bist verflucht!« stieß er wütend hervor.

»Ich habe mir alle Mühe gegeben!«

»Du bist ein vertrocknetes Luder«, wütete er, zerrte sie an den Armen hoch und stieß sie vom Bett. Sie landete im Stroh, das den Boden bedeckte. »Genau das hat diese Hexe Ellen gewollt«, schimpfte er. »Die hat mich noch nie ausstehen können!«

Aliena kniete sich auf den Boden und starrte ihn an. Er schien sie nicht noch einmal schlagen zu wollen. Seine Wut war verschwunden. »Du kannst da bleiben«, sagte er. »Zur Frau taugst du nicht, also hast du in meinem Bett auch nichts zu suchen. Du kannst wie ein Hund auf dem Boden schlafen.« Er hielt inne. »Hör schon auf, mich so anzustarren!« fuhr er sie an, doch seine Furcht war deutlich herauszuhören. Er sah sich suchend nach der Kerze um, fand sie und löschte die Flamme mit einem Schlag, der die Kerze zu Boden poltern ließ.

Aliena rührte sich nicht in der Dunkelheit. Sie hörte, wie Alfred sich auf dem Federbett bewegte, die Kissen zurechtrückte, sich hinlegte und die Decke hochzog. Ängstlich bemühte sie sich, leise zu atmen. Eine ganze Zeitlang warf er sich ruhelos hin und her, aber er stand nicht wieder auf und richtete auch kein Wort mehr an sie. Als sie sicher sein konnte, daß er eingeschlafen war, kroch sie quer durch den Raum, immer darauf bedacht, das Stroh nicht zum Rascheln zu bringen, und nahm Zuflucht in einer Zimmerecke. Dort rollte sie sich zusammen und lag lange hellwach. Schließlich begann sie zu weinen. Sie versuchte, dem Tränenstrom Einhalt zu gebieten, aus Angst, er könne davon aufwachen, aber es gelang ihr nicht, und so schluchzte sie leise vor sich hin. Wenn sie ihn aufgeweckt hatte, so ließ er es sich zumindest nicht anmerken. Auf dem Stroh in der Ecke weinte sie in sich hinein und endlich auch in Schlaf.

Den ganzen Winter über fühlte sich Aliena krank.

Die Nächte verbrachte sie, in ihren Mantel gehüllt, auf dem Boden vor Alfreds Bett. Ihr Schlaf war sehr unruhig, und tagsüber schien sie von hoffnungsloser Mattigkeit ergriffen. Oftmals war ihr so übel, daß sie kaum etwas aß – und dennoch schien sie zuzunehmen: Ihre Brüste waren größer, ihre Hüften breiter, die Taille runder geworden.

Eigentlich wäre es ihre Aufgabe gewesen, Alfred das Haus zu führen. Die meiste Arbeit tat jedoch Martha. Die drei bildeten eine recht trübsinnige Familie: Martha hatte ihren Bruder noch nie gemocht, und Alienas Abneigung hatte sich mittlerweile in leidenschaftliche Abscheu verwandelt. Unter diesen Voraussetzungen war es nicht weiter erstaunlich, daß Alfred soviel Zeit wie möglich außer Haus verbrachte: die Tage bei seiner Arbeit und die Abende in der Schenke. Martha und Aliena erledigten die Einkäufe und bereiteten die Mahlzeiten zu. Die Abende verbrachten sie mit Näh- und Schneiderarbeiten. Sehnsüchtig dachte Aliena an den Frühling und an warme Sonntagnachmittage auf ihrer Waldlichtung ... Da konnte sie dann friedlich im Gras liegen und von Jack träumen ...

Bis dahin blieb Richard ihr einziger Trost. Er besaß nun einen lebhaften, schnellen Rappen, ein neues Schwert und einen berittenen Schildknappen und zog wieder für König Stephan in den Kampf, wenngleich mit geringerem Gefolge. Der Krieg ging auch im neuen Jahr weiter. Mathilde war aus der Burg in Oxford entkommen und Stephan erneut durch die Lappen gegangen, und ihr Bruder, Robert von Gloucester, hatte Wareham zurückerobert. Das ewige Hin und Her nahm kein Ende. Unbedeutenden Siegen beider Seiten folgten Niederlagen und Verluste. Doch Aliena hielt sich treulich an ihren Schwur und fand wenigstens darin eine gewisse Befriedigung.

In der ersten Woche des neuen Jahres hatte Martha ihre erste Blutung. Um die Krämpfe zu mildern, bereitete Aliena ihr einen heißen Trank aus Kräutern und Honig. Sie beantwortete Marthas Fragen über das Kreuz, das zu tragen den Frauen auferlegt war, und machte sich auf die Suche nach dem Kästchen mit den Tüchern, die sie für ihre eigene Regel bereithielt. Als es sich im ganzen Haus nicht finden ließ, fiel ihr ein, daß sie es nach ihrer Heirat nicht mit ins neue Heim genommen hatte.

Das war schon drei Monate her.

Sie hatte also drei Monate lang keine Blutung gehabt.

Keine Blutung seit ihrem Hochzeitstag.

Keine Blutung, seit sie und Jack sich geliebt hatten.

Sie ließ Martha, die am Herdfeuer saß, ihre Zehen röstete und am Kräutertrunk nippte, wo sie war, und machte sich auf den Weg zu ihrem alten Haus am anderen Ende der Stadt. Richard war nicht da, aber sie besaß einen Schlüssel. Sie fand das Kästchen auf Anhieb, doch statt sofort wieder den Rückweg anzutreten, ließ sie sich vor der kalten Feuerstelle nieder, hüllte sich in ihren Mantel und ließ ihren Gedanken freien Lauf.

Michaeli hatte sie Alfred geheiratet, jetzt war Weihnachten vorbei. Dazwischen lag genau ein Vierteljahr. Dreimal war Neumond gewesen, dreimal hätte das Monatsblut fließen müssen, doch die ganze Zeit über hatte das Kästchen mit den Tüchern auf dem hohen Küchenbord neben dem kleinen Wetzstein gestanden, mit dem Richard die Küchenmesser schliff. Nun hielt sie es auf ihrem Schoß. Sie ließ den Zeigefinger über das rauhe Holz gleiten; er färbte sich schmutziggrau. Das Kästchen war mit Staub bedeckt.

Das Schlimmste daran war, daß sie und Alfred sich *nicht ein einziges Mal* geliebt hatten.

Nach jener schrecklichen Nacht hatte er es noch dreimal versucht: einmal gleich in der Nacht darauf, das zweite Mal in der nächsten Woche, und schließlich noch einmal einen Monat später, als er noch betrunkener als gewöhnlich aus der Schenke heimgekommen war. Jedesmal war er vollkommen unfähig gewesen. Anfangs hatte Aliena ihn aus einem gewissen Pflichtgefühl heraus sogar ermutigt, doch mit jedem neuerlichen Versagen war er noch wütender geworden, und sie hatte es mit der Angst zu tun bekommen. Es war sicherer, ihm aus dem Weg zu gehen, sich unauffällig zu kleiden und sich nie in seiner Gegenwart auszuziehen, so daß er erst gar nicht auf dumme Gedanken kam ... Hätte ich mir nicht vielleicht doch etwas mehr Mühe geben

sollen? fragte sie sich jetzt, obwohl sie genau wußte, daß es hoffnungslos gewesen wäre. Woran immer es liegen mochte – vielleicht an Ellens
Fluch, vielleicht schlicht und einfach an Alfreds Impotenz, vielleicht
aber auch an ihrer Erinnerung an Jack – Aliena fühlte sich ganz sicher,
daß Alfred sie fürderhin nicht mehr anrühren würde.

Das Kind, das sie unter dem Herzen trug, war nicht von ihm, und
es gab keine Möglichkeit, ihm das vorzuenthalten.

Unglücklich starrte Aliena auf die kalte Asche der Feuerstelle und
fragte sich, warum ausgerechnet sie immer so viel Pech haben mußte.
Sie hatte sich doch redlich Mühe gegeben, aus der schlechten Ehe
das Beste zu machen – doch da saß sie nun und war schwanger von
einem anderen Mann, nach einem einzigen Liebesakt!

Aber Selbstmitleid half nun auch nicht weiter. Sie mußte eine
Entscheidung treffen.

Sie legte eine Hand auf ihren Bauch. Kein Wunder, daß sie zugenommen, daß ihr ständig übel war, daß sie sich so matt fühlte! Da
drin entstand ein kleiner Mensch. Aliena lächelte. Wie schön es sein
würde, ein Kind zu haben!

Sie schüttelte den Kopf. Schön? Ach was, dachte sie, Alfred wird
wie ein gereizter Stier reagieren. Er ist imstande, mich aus dem Haus
zu werfen, ja ich traue ihm sogar zu, daß er mich, das Kind oder gar
uns beide tötet ... Eine entsetzliche Vision suchte sie heim: Alfred
könnte versuchen, das Kind schon vor der Geburt zu verletzen, indem
er meinen Bauch mit Fußtritten traktiert ... Sie wischte sich die Stirn:
der kalte Schweiß war ihr ausgebrochen.

Ich werde es ihm nicht sagen, dachte sie.

Ließ sich die Schwangerschaft geheimhalten? Vielleicht. Sie hatte
sich ohnehin schon angewöhnt, formlose, sackartige Gewänder zu
tragen. Und vielleicht wurde sie gar nicht so übermäßig dick – bei
manchen Frauen war das so. Zudem war Alfred nicht gerade der Auf-
merksamste. Vor den erfahrenen Frauen in der Stadt ließ sich eine
Schwangerschaft kaum verbergen, aber man konnte sich wohl einigermaßen darauf verlassen, daß sie ihr Wissen für sich behielten oder
doch wenigstens nicht mit dem Mannsvolk darüber redeten. Ja, dachte
Aliena, es kann klappen. Alfred wird erst von dem Kind erfahren,
wenn es geboren ist.

Und dann? Nun, zumindest hatte das kleine Würmchen erst einmal
wohlbehalten das Licht der Welt erblickt und wäre nicht schon im
Mutterleib totgetreten worden. Was blieb, war Alfreds Gewißheit, daß
das Kind nicht von ihm war. Ganz sicher wird er das arme Ding

hassen, dachte sie, gleichsam als ständige Erinnerung an seine fehlende Manneskraft. Er wird mir und meinem Kind das Leben zur Hölle machen.

Aliena mochte noch nicht so weit vorausdenken. Zunächst kam es darauf an, die nächsten sechs Monate unbeschadet über die Bühne zu bringen. Und bis zur Geburt blieb ihr noch genug Zeit, sich für die Zeit danach etwas auszudenken.

Ob es wohl ein Junge oder ein Mädchen wird? fragte sie sich. Sie stand auf, in der Hand das Kästchen mit den sauberen Tüchern für Marthas erste Monatsblutung. Arme Martha, dachte sie müde, das alles steht dir auch noch bevor.

Den ganzen Winter lang grübelte Philip über seinen Sorgen.

Ellens heidnischer Fluch unter dem Dach der Kirche, herausgeschrien während der Trauung, hatte ihn mit Entsetzen erfüllt. Er war nun überzeugt davon, daß sie eine Hexe war, und bedauerte es zutiefst, daß er damals, als sie die Ordensregel des heiligen Benedikt auf so abscheuliche Weise besudelt hatte, so dumm gewesen war, ihr zu vergeben. Er hätte wissen müssen, daß eine Frau, die zu solchen Handlungen imstande war, niemals echte Reue empfand. Es gab allerdings auch einen erfreulichen Aspekt an der Geschichte: Ellen hatte Kingsbridge wieder einmal verlassen und ward seitdem nicht mehr gesehen. Philip hoffte inständig, sie würde sich nie wieder blicken lassen.

Aliena war in ihrer Ehe mit Alfred sichtlich unglücklich, doch Philip glaubte nicht, daß der Anlaß dafür in Ellens Fluch zu sehen war. Zwar wußte Philip so gut wie nichts über die Probleme des ehelichen Zusammenlebens, doch konnte ihm nicht verborgen bleiben, daß eine so gescheite und lebhafte Person wie Aliena mit einem schwerfälligen, engstirnigen Tölpel wie Alfred einfach nicht glücklich werden *konnte* – ob sie nun Mann und Frau waren oder nicht.

Es wäre natürlich besser gewesen, wenn Aliena Jack geheiratet hätte, das sah Philip inzwischen längst ein. Er machte sich Vorwürfe, daß er sich von seinen eigenen Plänen für den Jungen hatte blenden lassen. Jack war einfach nicht für das Klosterleben geschaffen, und es war ein Fehler gewesen, ihn dazu zu nötigen. Nun mußte Kingsbridge ohne ihn, seine Ideen und seine Tatkraft auskommen.

Seit der Katastrophe am Tag des Wollmarktes war im Grunde alles schiefgegangen. Die Schulden des Klosters waren höher denn je. Philip hatte aus Geldmangel die Hälfte der Bauleute entlassen müssen, und dementsprechend war die Einwohnerzahl der Stadt gesunken. Dies wiederum hatte zur Folge, daß der Sonntagsmarkt kleiner wurde und die Einkünfte aus den Standmieten zurückgingen. Kingsbridge geriet allmählich ins Abseits.

Das Kernproblem war die fehlende Zuversicht der Bevölkerung. Zwar hatten die Leute ihre Häuser wiederaufgebaut und ihre kleinen Geschäfte wieder eröffnet, doch fehlte ihnen alles Vertrauen in die Zukunft. Was immer sie planen, was immer sie bauen mochten – es konnte an einem einzigen Tag wieder dahin sein, wenn es William Hamleigh so gefiel. Die unterschwellige Unsicherheit beherrschte das Denken aller und lähmte jeglichen Unternehmergeist.

Philip erkannte, daß es so nicht weitergehen konnte. Er mußte aktiv werden, mußte unbedingt dem schier unaufhaltsamen Abstieg Einhalt gebieten. Ein dramatisches Zeichen war erforderlich, das der Welt im allgemeinen und den Bewohnern der Stadt im besonderen deutlich machte, daß Kingsbridge nicht aufgab, sondern sich wehrte. Er verbrachte viele Stunden in Meditation und Gebet, um herauszufinden, wie dieses Zeichen aussehen könnte.

Im Grunde brauchte es nur ein Wunder. Wenn die Gebeine des heiligen Adolphus auch nur eine einzige Prinzessin von der Pest heilen, nur ein einziges Mal brackiges Brunnenwasser in frisches Süßwasser verwandeln würden, kämen die Menschen sogleich in Scharen nach Kingsbridge gepilgert. Aber der Heilige hatte schon seit Jahren keine Wunder mehr gewirkt. Mitunter fragte sich Philip, ob seine ruhige, praktische Art, das Kloster zu leiten, dem Heiligen womöglich nicht behagte, ereigneten sich doch Wunder allem Anschein nach häufiger an Orten, wo die Atmosphäre geprägt war von glühendem religiösem Eifer (um nicht zu sagen von schrankenloser Hysterie), wo ein vernunftbestimmtes Regiment jedoch wenig galt. Philip indes war durch eine Schule gegangen, die ihn gelehrt hatte, mit beiden Beinen auf der Erde zu bleiben. Vater Peter, sein erster Abt, pflegte zu sagen: »Betet um Wunder, aber vergeßt nicht, Kohl zu pflanzen.«

Das Symbol für die Lebenskraft von Kingsbridge war die Kathedrale. Konnte sie nicht durch ein Wunder vollendet werden? Eine ganze Nacht lang betete Philip um solch ein Wunder, doch am Morgen war der Chor immer noch dachlos dem Wetter preisgegeben, und dort, wo die Querschiffwände anschließen sollten, ragten die zackigen, offenen Mauerenden in die Luft.

Einen neuen Baumeister hatte der Prior noch nicht eingestellt. Mit Entsetzen hatte er vernommen, welch hohe Löhne sie forderten. Erst

allmählich wurde ihm klar, wie billig Tom gewesen war. Immerhin –
bisher kam Alfred mit den verbliebenen Arbeitskräften ganz gut zu
Rande. Seit seiner Heirat war Toms Sohn recht mürrisch und verschlossen – wie ein Mann, der sich vieler Rivalen entledigt, um König
zu werden, und dann erst herausfindet, daß ihm das Königtum eine
mühselige Last ist. Alfred war jedoch klar in seinen Befehlen und
Anweisungen und schien zu wissen, was er wollte. Die anderen Männer hatten Respekt vor ihm.

Die Lücke, die Tom hinterlassen hatte, schloß er freilich nicht.
Tom Builder fehlte Philip nicht nur als Baumeister, sondern auch als
Mensch. Tom hatte sich immer wieder mit der Frage beschäftigt,
warum große Kirchen nach einem ganz bestimmten Grundprinzip
errichtet werden mußten, und sich gemeinsam mit Philip in Spekulationen darüber ergangen, warum manche Bauten stehenblieben, während andere in sich zusammenfielen. Besonders fromm war der Baumeister nicht gewesen, doch gelegentlich hatte er Philip theologische
Fragen gestellt, die bewiesen, daß er dem Glauben dieselbe kritische
Intelligenz entgegenbrachte wie seinem eigenen Handwerk. Philip
hatte in ihm einen Gesprächspartner gesehen, der ihm geistig ebenbürtig war. Derlei Menschen gab es viel zu wenige in seinem Leben;
Jack hatte dazugehört, auch Aliena, aber letztere war fast versunken
in ihrer jammervollen Ehe. Cuthbert Whitehead wurde allmählich alt,
und Milius, der Kämmerer, war fast ständig unterwegs. Er reiste von
Schafzucht zu Schafzucht, zählte Morgen, Mutterschafe und Wollsäcke.

Ein lebendiges, geschäftiges Kloster in einer prosperierenden Domstadt würde in Hinkunft zweifellos Scholaren und andere kluge Köpfe
anziehen. Philip freute sich schon auf diese Zeit. Aber wenn es ihm
nicht gelang, Kingsbridge die alte Tatkraft und Zuversicht zurückzugeben, würde sie niemals kommen.

»Wir haben einen milden Winter«, sagte Alfred eines Morgens kurz
nach Weihnachten. »Wir können früher als sonst wieder mit der Arbeit
beginnen.«

Philip überlegte. Das Deckengewölbe sollte im kommenden Sommer errichtet werden. Sobald es fertig war, konnte das Chorhaus benutzt werden, und Kingsbridge wäre keine Domstadt mehr ohne Dom.
Das Chorhaus war der wichtigste Teil einer Kirche: Er barg in seinem
hinteren, Presbyterium genannten Ende den Hochaltar und die heiligen Reliquien, während vorne, im Chor, wo die Mönche saßen, die
meisten Gottesdienste stattfanden. Der Rest der Kirche wurde nur an

Sonn- und Feiertagen benutzt. War das Chorhaus erst einmal geweiht, so hatte sich die Baustelle in eine Kirche verwandelt – wenn auch vorerst nur in eine unvollendete.

Ein Jammer, daß es noch fast ein Jahr dauern sollte, bis es soweit war. Alfred hatte zugesagt, bis zum Herbst mit dem Gewölbe fertig zu sein. Meist konnte bis in den November hinein gearbeitet werden. Wurde nun, wie Alfred in Aussicht stellte, früher mit dem Bau begonnen, so mußte der Bau eigentlich auch früher fertig werden. Alle Welt wäre höchst erstaunt, wenn die Kirche bereits im Sommer geöffnet werden könnte. Nach solch einem Zeichen habe ich gesucht, dachte Philip – es wird die ganze Grafschaft in Erstaunen versetzen und allenthalben die Botschaft verkünden, daß Kingsbridge sich nicht lange hat in die Knie zwingen lassen.

»Könnt Ihr bis Pfingsten fertig sein?« fragte Philip.

Alfred sog zwischen zusammengepreßten Zähnen die Luft ein. Sein Blick verriet seine Zweifel. »Das Gewölbe ist der schwierigste Teil und erfordert größtes handwerkliches Geschick«, sagte er. »Da darf man nichts überstürzen und keine Lehrbuben dransetzen.«

Sein Vater hätte mit Ja oder Nein geantwortet, dachte Philip gereizt und erwiderte: »Angenommen, ich könnte Euch noch einige Mönche zur Verfügung stellen. Was würde das bringen?«

»Nicht viel. Wir bräuchten mehr Steinmetzen.«

»Einen oder zwei kann ich Euch vielleicht noch verschaffen«, antwortete Philip. Der milde Winter verhieß eine frühe Schafschur; er konnte also darauf hoffen, die Wolle ein wenig früher als sonst auf den Markt zu bringen.

»Ich weiß nicht …« Alfreds Skepsis war noch nicht verschwunden.

»Angenommen, ich setze den Steinmetzen eine Prämie aus?« fragte Philip. »Einen Wochenlohn zusätzlich, falls das Gewölbe bis Pfingsten fertig ist.«

»Prämie? Davon habe ich noch nie etwas gehört«, murmelte Alfred und zog ein Gesicht, als habe man ihm einen unsittlichen Antrag gestellt.

»Nun, alles geschieht irgendwann zum erstenmal«, gab Philip pikiert zurück. Alfreds übertriebene Vorsicht begann ihn aufzuregen. »Was meint Ihr?«

Alfred blieb stur. »Ich kann Eure Frage weder mit Ja noch mit Nein beantworten«, sagte er. »Ich werde mit meinen Männern darüber reden.«

»Heute noch?« fragte Philip ungeduldig.

»Heute noch.«

Und damit mußte Philip sich zufriedengeben.

William Hamleigh und seine Ritter erreichten Walerans Palast gleich hinter einem hoch mit Wollsäcken beladenen Ochsenkarren. Die Schafschur hatte bereits begonnen. Beide, William und Waleran, kauften den Bauern ihre Ware zu Vorjahrspreisen ab und spekulierten auf einen großen Zugewinn beim Wiederverkauf. Und keinem von beiden war es schwergefallen, die Pächter zum Verkauf zu bewegen. Anfangs hatten ein paar Bauern sich der Aufforderung widersetzt. Sie wurden davongejagt und ihre Höfe niedergebrannt. Danach begehrte niemand mehr auf.

William blickte die Anhöhe hinter dem Palast hinauf. Sieben Jahre lang befanden sich dort oben schon die kümmerlichen Wallanlagen der geplanten Burg, die nie fertiggestellt worden war – eine ständige Erinnerung an den Streich, den Prior Philip dem Bischof gespielt hatte. Wahrscheinlich würde Waleran, sobald der Wollhandel Gewinn abwarf, die Bauarbeiten wieder aufnehmen. In den Tagen des alten Königs Heinrich hatten Bischöfe außer einem einfachen Zaun aus locker aneinandergefügten Pfählen hinter einem schmalen Graben keine besonderen Verteidigungsanlagen für ihre Paläste gebraucht. Doch nachdem der Bürgerkrieg nun schon fünf Jahre währte, bauten sich selbst Männer, die weder Graf noch Bischof waren, gewaltige Burgen.

Waleran glückt offenbar alles, dachte William nicht ohne Neid, als er vor dem Stall vom Pferd stieg. Waleran hatte dem wetterwendischen Bischof Henry von Winchester stets die Treue gehalten und war somit zu einem seiner engsten Vertrauen geworden. Ein unablässiger Strom von zusätzlichen Besitztiteln und Privilegien hatte Waleran zu einem reichen Mann gemacht. Er war sogar schon zweimal nach Rom gereist.

William hatte nicht soviel Glück gehabt – daher seine Erbitterung. Obwohl er jeden Seitenwechsel Walerans mitvollzogen und beide kriegführenden Parteien mit stattlichen Armeen versorgt hatte, wartete er immer noch auf die Bestätigung seines Grafentitels. Als sich eine Zeitlang auf den Schlachtfeldern nichts tat, hatte er über seine Lage nachgedacht und war darob so wütend geworden, daß er beschloß, umgehend zu Waleran zu reiten und den Bischof zu stellen.

Mit Walter und den anderen Rittern im Gefolge stapfte er die Treppe zum Empfangssaal hinauf. Der Haushofmeister, der gerade Waschdienst hatte, trug Waffen – ein weiteres Zeichen der Zeit. Bischof Waleran saß wie immer auf einem großen Stuhl in der Mitte des

Saales, die knochigen Arme und Beine in merkwürdigem Winkel abgespreizt, als habe man ihn dort fallengelassen und nicht wieder richtig zusammengesetzt. Neben ihm stand Baldwin, inzwischen Erzdiakon, und wartete offenbar auf Anweisungen. Waleran selbst starrte, offenbar tief in Gedanken versunken, ins Feuer, doch als William näher trat, fuhr er ruckartig hoch und sah ihn an.

Während er Waleran begrüßte und Platz nahm, fühlte William jenen Widerwillen in sich aufsteigen, der ihn jedesmal ergriff, wenn er es mit diesem Mann zu tun hatte. Walerans weiche, schmale Hände, sein dünnes, schwarzes Haar, die leichenblasse Haut und die bleichen, bösartigen Augen jagten ihm eine Gänsehaut über den Rücken. Waleran vereinigte in sich alle Eigenschaften, die William zutiefst verhaßt waren: Gerissenheit, körperliche Schwäche, Hochmut und Klugheit.

Waleran, das wußte William, erging es in *seiner* Gegenwart nicht viel anders. Nie gelang es dem Bischof völlig, das Unbehagen zu verbergen, das ihn überfiel, wenn William den Saal betrat. Er setzte sich kerzengerade auf und verschränkte die Arme, seine Lippen kräuselten sich ein wenig, und er runzelte leicht die Stirn – man hätte meinen können, er leide an Magendrücken.

Eine Weile lang sprachen sie über den Krieg. Es war eine steife, schwerfällige Unterhaltung. William war daher heilfroh, als ein Bote eintrat und sie unterbrach. Der Mann überreichte Waleran eine mit Wachs versiegelte Pergamentrolle. Der Bischof schickte ihn in die Küche, wo er sich zu essen geben lassen sollte. Den Brief öffnete er nicht.

William ergriff die Gelegenheit beim Schopf und wechselte das Thema. »Ich bin eigentlich nicht gekommen, um mich mit Euch über die letzten Neuigkeiten von den Schlachtfeldern zu unterhalten«, sagte er. »Ich kam vielmehr, um Euch zu sagen, daß meine Geduld zu Ende ist.«

Waleran hob die Brauen, sagte aber nichts. Auf Themen, die ihm nicht behagten, reagierte er stets mit Schweigen.

William redete sich in Fahrt. »Seit dem Tode meines Vaters sind nun schon fast drei Jahre vergangen, doch König Stephan hat mich noch immer nicht als Graf von Shiring bestätigt. Ich finde das empörend.«

»Ich stimme Euch aus vollem Herzen zu«, erwiderte Waleran müde. Er spielte mit seinem Brief, untersuchte das Siegel, zupfte an der Verschnürung.

»Das freut mich«, sagte William, »denn Ihr werdet dieserhalb etwas unternehmen müssen.«

»Mein teurer William, ich kann Euch nicht zum Grafen machen.«

Mit dieser Antwort hatte William von vornherein gerechnet. Er war entschlossen, sich nicht damit abspeisen zu lassen. »Der Bruder des Königs hört auf Euch«, sagte er.

»Und was soll ich ihm sagen? Daß William Hamleigh dem König gute Dienste geleistet hat? Wenn es stimmt, so weiß es der König bereits – und wenn es nicht stimmt, weiß er es auch.«

William war Walerans Logik nicht gewachsen, folglich ging er auf die Argumente gar nicht erst ein. »Ihr seid es mir schuldig, Waleran Bigod.«

Waleran gab sich ungeduldig und wies mit der Pergamentrolle auf ihn. »Ich schulde Euch gar nichts. Selbst wenn Ihr hin und wieder meine Wünsche erfüllt habt, so behieltet Ihr doch stets Eure eigenen Ziele im Auge. Dankbarkeit schulden wir einander gewiß nicht.«

»Ich bin nicht mehr bereit, noch länger zu warten, soviel laßt Euch gesagt sein.«

»Was habt Ihr denn vor?« fragte Waleran mit leiser Verachtung in der Stimme.

»Zunächst werde ich Bischof Henry einmal persönlich aufsuchen.«

»Und?«

»Ich werde ihm sagen, daß Ihr Euch meinen Wünschen verschließt und daß ich infolgedessen ins Lager der Kaiserin Mathilde überwechseln werde.« William stellte mit Befriedigung fest, daß Walerans Miene sich veränderte: Er wurde noch ein wenig blasser und konnte seine Überraschung nicht verhehlen.

»Noch ein Seitenwechsel?« fragte er skeptisch.

»Nur einmal mehr als Ihr«, gab William derb zurück.

Walerans hochmütige Gleichgültigkeit war erschüttert, wenngleich nicht allzu sehr. Ihm und seiner Karriere war es sehr zugute gekommen, daß er William und seine Ritter immer derjenigen Seite zur Verfügung stellen konnte, die Bischof Henry gerade favorisierte. Wenn William sich nun selbständig machen wollte, so war dies zweifellos ein herber, wenn auch kein tödlicher Schlag. William ließ den Bischof nicht aus den Augen. Ihm war, als könne er dessen Gedanken lesen: Einerseits wollte er Williams Loyalität nicht verlieren, andererseits überlegte er, wieviel sie ihm wert war.

Um Zeit zu gewinnen, erbrach Waleran das Siegel und entrollte das Pergament. Er las, und ein Anflug von Zornesröte flammte über seine fischweißen Wangen. »Verdammt sei dieser Mann!« zischte er.

»Worum geht es denn?« fragte William.

Waleran hielt ihm das Schreiben hin. William ergriff es und stierte begriffsstutzig auf das Pergament. »An ... den ... geheiligten ... hochgnädigen Bischof ...«

Waleran, dem die Geduld für Williams unbeholfenen Leseversuch fehlte, nahm den Brief hastig wieder an sich. »Das Schreiben stammt von Prior Philip«, sagte er. »Er teilt mir mit, daß das Chorhaus der neuen Kathedrale bis Pfingsten fertiggestellt sei, und hat doch tatsächlich die Frechheit, mich darum zu bitten, die Messe zu lesen.«

William war verblüfft. »Wie hat er denn das schon wieder geschafft? Ich dachte, er hätte die Hälfte seiner Bauleute entlassen.«

Waleran schüttelte den Kopf. »Der Mann fällt doch immer wieder auf seine Füße, gleichgültig, was auch geschieht.« Er sah William nachdenklich an. »Euch haßt er natürlich. Er hält Euch für den Teufel in Menschengestalt.«

William fragte sich, welche Bosheit Waleran nun schon wieder aussheckte. »Na und?« sagte er.

»Wäre es nicht ein schöner Dämpfer für Prior Philip, wenn Ihr ausgerechnet zu Pfingsten als Graf bestätigt würdet?«

»Für mich allein wollt Ihr nichts unternehmen ... Aber wenn Ihr Philip damit kränken könnt, tut Ihr es doch ...« Es klang beleidigt, doch insgeheim fühlte William neue Hoffnung aufkeimen.

»Ich kann überhaupt nichts für Euch tun«, widersprach Waleran. »Aber ich werde mit Bischof Henry darüber reden.« Erwartungsvoll sah er zu William auf.

William zögerte. Nach einer Pause murmelte er widerstrebend: »Ich danke Euch.«

Der Frühling war kalt und trübe in diesem Jahr, und am Pfingstsonntag regnete es. Aliena war in der Nacht mit Rückenschmerzen aufgewacht, die sie auch, nachdem es längst Tag geworden war, nicht in Ruhe ließen. Sie kamen und gingen, wieder und wieder. Aliena saß in der Küche und flocht vor dem Kirchgang Marthas Haar, während Alfred ein üppiges Frühstück aus Weichkäse, Weißbrot und Starkbier zu sich nahm. Ein besonders unangenehmer Stich im Rücken ließ Aliena innehalten. Sie zuckte zusammen und richtete sich vorübergehend auf. Martha bemerkte es und fragte: »Was hast du?«

»Rückenschmerzen«, gab Aliena kurzangebunden zurück. Sie wollte nicht darüber reden. Die Schmerzen kamen sicher davon, daß sie in dem zugigen Hinterzimmer auf dem Fußboden schlief – und das wußte niemand, nicht einmal Martha.

Martha erhob sich und nahm einen heißen Stein vom Feuer, während Aliena sich wieder auf ihren Platz setzte. Sie wickelte den Stein in ein altes, versengtes Leder und drückte ihn Aliena in den Rücken. Der Schmerz ließ sofort nach. Nun war es an Martha, Alienas Haar zu flechten; die wilde, dunkle Lockenpracht war inzwischen nachgewachsen.

Seit Ellens Fortgang waren Martha und Aliena sich sehr nahegekommen. Arme Martha: Erst hatte sie ihre Mutter verloren, dann ihre Stiefmutter. Aliena hielt sich für einen schlechten Mutterersatz, war sie doch gerade zehn Jahre älter als Martha. Besser gefiel ihr die Rolle der großen Schwester. Am meisten vermißte Martha merkwürdigerweise Jack, ihren Stiefbruder.

Aber den vermißten sie ja eigentlich alle.

Wo mag er jetzt wohl sein? fragte sich Aliena. Es war nicht auszuschließen, daß er sich ganz in der Nähe befand, auf einer Dombaustelle in Salisbury oder Gloucester vielleicht. Wahrscheinlicher war indes, daß er in die Normandie gegangen war, doch konnte er sich auch sonstwo herumtreiben – in Paris, Rom, Jerusalem oder Ägypten. Aliena fielen die Erzählungen von Pilgern ein, die in fremden Ländern gewesen waren. Schon glaubte sie Jack zu sehen, wie er im gleißenden Sonnenlicht der Wüste Steine für eine Sarazenenfestung meißelte, und sie fragte sich: Ob er jetzt wohl an mich denkt?

Hufgetrappel unterbrach ihre Tagträumerei. Kurz darauf erschien, sein Pferd am Zügel haltend, ihr Bruder Richard in der Tür. Roß und Reiter waren durchnäßt und von oben bis unten mit Schlamm bespritzt. Aliena brachte ihm warmes Wasser von der Feuerstelle, so daß er sich wenigstens Gesicht und Hände waschen konnte, und stellte, während Martha das Pferd in den Hinterhof führte, Brot und kaltes Rindfleisch auf den Tisch. Dann füllte sie ihrem Bruder einen Becher mit Bier.

»Was tut sich im Krieg?« fragte Alfred. »Gibt's was Neues?«

Richard trocknete sich das Gesicht ab und ließ sich zum Frühstück nieder. »Wir haben eine Niederlage erlitten«, sagte er. »Bei Wilton.«

»Wurde Stephan gefangengenommen?«

»Nein, er ist entkommen, genau wie Mathilde kürzlich aus Oxford. Jetzt sitzt Stephan in Winchester und Mathilde in Bristol. Sie lecken ihre Wunden und versuchen, ihre gegenwärtigen Herrschaftsgebiete zu konsolidieren.«

Immer dasselbe, dachte Aliena. Die eine oder die andere Seite erringt einen bedeutungslosen Sieg oder erleidet eine bedeutungslose

Niederlage. Und nichts deutet darauf hin, daß dieser Krieg einmal ein Ende findet.

Richard sah sie an. »Du wirst dick«, stellte er fest.

Sie nickte, gab aber keine Antwort. Inzwischen war sie im achten Monat schwanger, und niemand wußte davon. Ein Glück, daß es noch immer so kalt war – so fiel es nicht auf, daß sie mehrere locker fallende Wintergewänder übereinander trug, die ihre Figur verbargen. In ein paar Wochen würde das Kind auf die Welt kommen – und die Stunde der Wahrheit schlagen. Aliena wußte noch immer nicht, wie sie sich nach der Geburt verhalten sollte.

Die Glocke läutete und rief die Bevölkerung der Stadt zur Pfingstmesse. Alfred schlüpfte in seine Stiefel und sah Aliena auffordernd an.

»Ich glaube, ich bleibe lieber hier«, sagte sie. »Mir geht's einfach zu schlecht.«

Gleichgültig zuckte er mit den Schultern und wandte sich ihrem Bruder zu. »Es wäre schön, wenn du mitkämst, Richard. Kaum einer wird heute fehlen. Es ist der erste Gottesdienst in der neuen Kirche.«

Richard war überrascht. »Ihr habt die Decke schon eingezogen? Ich dachte, Ihr würdet noch das ganze Jahr dazu brauchen.«

»Wir haben uns beeilt. Prior Philip versprach den Männern einen zusätzlichen Wochenlohn, falls sie bis heute fertig würden. Erstaunlich, wie schnell sie arbeiten konnten! Es war allerdings sehr knapp; das Gerüst haben wir erst heute morgen abgenommen.«

»Ja, das muß ich sehen«, sagte Richard. Er stopfte sich den letzten Bissen in den Mund und stand auf.

»Soll ich lieber bei dir bleiben?« fragte Martha Aliena.

»Nein, danke. Ich komme schon zurecht. Geh du nur. Ich werde mich ein bißchen hinlegen.«

Die drei schlüpften in ihre Mäntel und verließen das Haus. Aliena nahm den heißen Stein in seiner Lederhülle mit ins Hinterzimmer. Dort legte sie sich auf Alfreds Bett und schob sich den Stein unter den Rücken. Sie war seit ihrer Heirat furchtbar träge geworden. Früher hatte sie nicht nur einen Haushalt, sondern auch den erfolgreichsten Wollhandel der ganzen Grafschaft geführt – mittlerweile wuchs ihr schon Alfreds Haushalt über den Kopf, obwohl sie sonst gar nichts mehr zu tun hatte.

Eine Zeitlang lag sie still da, tat sich selber leid und wäre am liebsten eingeschlafen. Da spürte sie plötzlich, wie eine warme Flüssigkeit über die Innenseite ihrer Schenkel rann. Sie erschrak. Im ersten Moment fürchtete sie, unfreiwillig Wasser zu lassen, doch da verwandelte sich das Rinnsal in eine Sturzflut, und sie wußte Bescheid. Wie der Blitz fuhr sie hoch und setzte sich kerzengerade auf. Ihre Fruchtblase war geplatzt – das Kind kam!

Jähe Furcht überfiel sie. Ich brauche Hilfe! So laut sie konnte rief sie nach ihrer Nachbarin: »Mildred! Mildred, komm!« Aber nichts rührte sich – die Leute waren ja alle in der Kirche.

Der Fruchtwasserschwall war nun beinahe versiegt. Alfreds Bett troff vor Nässe. Er wird toben, dachte sie voller Angst – und nicht nur deshalb. Er wird außer sich sein, weil er sofort weiß, daß das Kind nicht von ihm ist ... O mein Gott, was soll ich nur tun?

Die Schmerzen im Rücken kehrten wieder. Aliena erkannte jetzt, daß es sich um jene Geburtsschmerzen handeln mußte, die gemeinhin als Wehen bezeichnet wurden. Sie vergaß Alfred. Sie war im Begriff zu gebären und hatte entsetzliche Angst, es alleine durchstehen zu müssen. Sie brauchte Beistand. Ich muß zur Kirche gehen und jemanden holen, dachte sie.

Sie schwang die Beine auf den Boden. Die nächste Wehe kam und schüttelte sie durch. Mit schmerzverzerrtem Gesicht blieb sie sitzen, bis es vorüber war. Dann stand sie auf und verließ das Haus.

Sie torkelte die schmutzige Straße entlang, und die aberwitzigsten Gedanken schossen ihr durch den Kopf. An der Klosterpforte wurde sie von der nächsten Wehe heimgesucht. Sie mußte sich an die Mauer lehnen und die Zähne zusammenbeißen. Als der Schmerz nachließ, betrat sie den Kirchhof.

Fast die gesamte Bevölkerung der Stadt drängte sich unter dem hohen Gewölbe des Chorhauses und den niedrigen Gewölben der Seitenschiffe. Am gegenüberliegenden Ende befand sich der Altar. Die neue Kirche bot einen seltsamen Anblick: Später sollte der gewölbten Steindecke noch ein dreieckiges Holzdach aufgesetzt werden – augenblicklich wirkte es ungeschützt wie ein Glatzkopf ohne Hut. Die Menschen wandten Aliena den Rücken zu.

Sie hatte die Kathedrale noch nicht erreicht, da erhob sich Waleran Bigod, der Bischof, und setzte zu einer Rede an. Daß neben ihm William Hamleigh stand, kam Aliena wie ein Alptraum vor. Trotz ihrer Pein verstand sie jedes Wort.

»... verkünde ich Euch mit Stolz und großer Freude, daß Stephan, unser gnädiger Herr, Lord William zum Grafen von Shiring ernannt hat.«

Aliena vergaß vor Entsetzen Schmerz und Angst. Sechs Jahre lang, seit jenem schrecklichen Tag, da sie ihren Vater im Verlies zu Winchester besucht hatte, war ihr ganzes Leben und Streben von dem Ziel beherrscht gewesen, wieder in den Besitz des familiären Erbes zu gelangen. Sie und ihr Bruder hatten Raub und Vergewaltigung, Feuersbrunst und Bürgerkrieg überstanden, und mehrere Male schien der Lohn für all ihre Mühen in greifbare Nähe gerückt. Jetzt war auf einmal alles verloren.

Ein ärgerliches Raunen erhob sich unter den Gläubigen. Da war kaum einer, der unter William nicht gelitten hatte, und alle lebten sie noch in Furcht vor ihm. Daß der König, der sie eigentlich beschützen sollte, ausgerechnet diesem Mann nun eine besondere Ehre zukommen ließ, mißfiel ihnen sehr. Aliena hielt nach Richard Ausschau; sie wollte wissen, wie er diesen letzten, entscheidenden Schlag gegen die Familie aufnahm. Aber sie konnte ihn nirgends entdecken.

Prior Philip erhob sich, das Gesicht wie vom Donner gerührt, und stimmte den Choral an. Halbherzig sang die Gemeinde mit. Von einer neuerlichen Wehe gepackt, lehnte Aliena sich an einen Pfeiler. Da sie ganz hinten stand, nahm niemand von ihr Notiz. Die schlimme Neuigkeit hatte sie seltsamerweise beruhigt. Ich bekomme ein Kind, dachte sie, so etwas geschieht doch jeden Tag. Ich muß jetzt nur noch Martha oder Richard finden. Sie werden schon dafür sorgen, daß alles gutgeht.

Aliena wartete, bis der Schmerz abgeklungen war, und drängte sich dann durch die Menge, um Martha zu finden. Sie entdeckte eine Gruppe von Frauen im nördlichen Seitenschiff und hielt, von neugierigen Blicken verfolgt, auf sie zu. Da wurde die Aufmerksamkeit der Menschen in der Kirche auf einmal von einem seltsamen Geräusch abgelenkt, das wie entferntes Donnergrollen klang. Zunächst übertönte es kaum den Gesang, doch dann wurde es lauter und lauter, und der Choral erstarb.

Aliena trat zu den Frauen, die sich ängstlich umsahen, weil sie nicht wußten, woher der Lärm kam. Sie berührte eine Schulter und fragte: »Habt Ihr meine Schwägerin Martha gesehen?«

Die Frau drehte sich um. Es war Hilda, das Weib des Gerbers. »Ich glaube, Martha steht drüben, auf der anderen Seite«, sagte sie und sah sogleich wieder weg. Das Grollen war inzwischen ohrenbetäubend.

Aliena folgte ihrem Blick. Alles starrte jetzt nach oben und auf die Mauern. In den Seitenschiffen reckten die Menschen die Hälse und lugten unter den Rundbogen hervor. Irgend jemand kreischte auf. Aliena sah, wie sich am anderen Ende der Kirche zwischen zwei Fenstern des Obergadens ein Riß bildete. Im nächsten Augenblick stürzten mehrere riesige Mauerstücke aus großer Höhe in die Tiefe und fielen auf die Menge in der Kirchenmitte. Schreie und Rufe ertönten, und mit einemmal herrschte ein unbeschreibliches Durcheinander. Wer konnte, wandte sich zur Flucht.

Der Boden unter Alienas Füßen bebte. Noch während sie versuchte, ins Freie zu gelangen, sah sie, daß die hohen Mauern am oberen Rand auseinanderklafften und das Deckengewölbe zerriß. Hilda, die Frau des Gerbers, stürzte vor ihren Füßen zu Boden. Aliena stolperte über den hingestreckten Körper und fiel selbst. Ehe sie sich wieder aufrichten konnte, ging ein Hagel von kleinen Steinen auf sie nieder. Schon zeigte auch das Dach des Seitenschiffs die ersten Risse und stürzte unmittelbar darauf ein. Irgend etwas traf Aliena am Kopf. Ihr wurde schwarz vor Augen.

Voller Stolz und Dankbarkeit hatte Philip den Gottesdienst begonnen. In einem Wettlauf mit der Zeit waren die Deckengewölbe gerade noch termingerecht fertig geworden. Von den vier Jochen waren allerdings erst drei überdacht, da der Bau des vierten erst beendet werden konnte, wenn das Querschiff errichtet und die unregelmäßigen Chorraumwände an dessen Mauern angeschlossen werden konnten. Alles, was bis zum Morgen noch an die Bauarbeiten erinnert hatte, war rücksichtslos fortgeräumt worden: die Werkzeuge, die Steinhaufen und Bauholzstapel, das Flechtwerk und die Pfosten der Gerüste, die Bruchsteine und der Schutt. Der Chor war aufgewischt, die Mauern von den Mönchen weiß getüncht, und über den Mörtel hatte man nach altem Brauch gerade rote Linien gezogen, wodurch das Fugenwerk gleichmäßiger wirkte, als es tatsächlich war. Während Altar und Bischofsthron aus der Krypta heraufgeschafft wurden, hatte man die Gebeine des Heiligen vorerst unten im Sarkophag gelassen – ihre Umbettung war einer feierlichen Zeremonie vorbehalten, der sogenannten ›Translation‹, die den Höhepunkt des Pfingstgottesdienstes bilden sollte. Zu Beginn der Messe – der Bischof saß auf seinem Thron, die Mönche standen in neuen Kutten hinter dem Altar, die Gläubigen drängten sich im Haupt- und in den Seitenschiffen – war Philip von tiefer Befriedigung erfüllt gewesen und hatte Gott für die erfolgreiche Beendigung des ersten, so wichtigen Bauabschnitts der neuen Kathedrale gedankt.

Dann war seine Hochstimmung allerdings rasch verflogen, weil Waleran gänzlich unerwartet die Erhebung Williams in den Grafenstand verkündet hatte. Es war nur allzu deutlich, was der Bischof mit dem Zeitpunkt der Ankündigung bezweckte: Er wollte ihm, Philip, den Tag seines Triumphs verderben und der Bevölkerung von Kingsbridge in Erinnerung rufen, daß sie noch immer der Gnade und Ungnade ihres grausamen Lehnsherrn ausgeliefert war. Philip grübelte noch nach einer angemessenen Replik, als unvermittelt das Grollen einsetzte.

Es war wie in einem jener Alpträume, von denen Philip bisweilen heimgesucht wurde: Da ging er hoch oben auf dem Baugerüst entlang und fühlte sich vollkommen sicher, bis er auf einmal bemerkte, daß sich in einem Seil, das die Gerüstbalken zusammenhielt, ein Knoten gelockert hatte. Es war nichts Ernstes – doch wenn er sich dann bückte, um den Knoten wieder festzuzurren, kippte das Brett unter seinen Füßen – nicht weit, aber doch so stark, daß er stolperte, das Gleichgewicht verlor und plötzlich mit rasender, Übelkeit erregender Geschwindigkeit in den weiten Kirchenraum hinabstürzte – im sicheren Bewußtsein seines unmittelbar bevorstehenden Todes.

Das Grollen war Philip zunächst ein Rätsel. Im ersten Moment glaubte er, ein Gewitter sei aufgezogen, doch das Donnern wurde immer lauter, und die Menschen in der Kirche hörten auf zu singen. Noch immer hielt Philip es für ein Phänomen, das sich rasch erklären würde und allenfalls dazu angetan war, den Gottesdienst zu stören. Dann sah er auf.

Im dritten Joch, wo das Baugerüst erst am Morgen entfernt worden war, erschienen hoch oben im Lichtgaden mehrere Risse im Mauerwerk. Urplötzlich waren sie da und vermehrten sich blitzartig wie züngelnde Schlangen, bis sie sich von einem Fenster zum anderen zogen. Philip empfand eine gewisse Enttäuschung: Er war so froh über die Vollendung des Chorhauses gewesen – und nun standen schon die ersten Reparaturen an. Er malte sich schon aus, was die Leute sagen würden, die von der Leistung der Baumeister bisher so beeindruckt gewesen waren: *Eile mit Weile* ... Doch da begannen auf einmal die Mauern der Kirche zu zittern, und mit heillosem Entsetzen erkannte Philip, daß von einer bloßen Unterbrechung des Gottesdienstes keine Rede sein konnte: Es bahnte sich eine Katastrophe an.

Nun zeigten sich auch an den verschiedensten Stellen des Deckengewölbes Risse. Ein gewaltiger Stein löste sich aus dem Mauerwerk und taumelte langsam herab. Die Menschen fingen an zu schreien und versuchten, aus der Fallinie zu kommen. Noch ehe Philip feststellen konnte, ob jemand verletzt war, lösten sich weitere Steine und stürzten in die Menge. Die Gemeinde geriet in Panik. Jeder versuchte, den herabfallenden Steinen auszuweichen, stieß rücksichtslos die anderen beiseite und trampelte über die zu Boden Gestürzten. Ist das vielleicht eine neue Teufelei des unberechenbaren William Hamleigh? dachte Philip, doch dann sah er den frischgebackenen Grafen in vorderster Reihe der Gläubigen. Wild schlug er um sich, um dem Verhängnis zu entkommen – nein, so etwas hätte William Hamleigh sich niemals angetan …

Die meisten Menschen hatten sich inzwischen umgedreht und versuchten, durch die noch offene Westflanke der Kathedrale zu entkommen. Doch ausgerechnet der Westteil brach in sich zusammen, das dritte Joch. Im zweiten Joch, wo Philip stand, schien das Gewölbe zu halten, und hinter ihm, im ersten Joch, wo die Mönche Aufstellung genommen hatten, wurden die Mauern von der soliden Ostfassade zusammengehalten.

Der kleine Jonathan und Johnny Eightpence kauerten im hintersten Winkel des nördlichen Seitenschiffs, wo sie nach Philips Dafürhalten noch am sichersten waren. Was konnte der Prior noch tun? Er mußte versuchen, so viele Schafe aus seiner Herde wie möglich in Sicherheit zu bringen. »Kommt hierher!« schrie er. Doch ob sie ihn hörten oder nicht – niemand achtete auf ihn.

Im dritten Joch kippte der obere Teil der Mauern nach außen um und stürzte ins Freie. Dann brach das gesamte Deckengewölbe auseinander, große und kleine Steine schossen durch die Luft und kamen wie ein tödlicher Hagelsturm über die verzweifelte Gemeinde. Pfeilschnell sprang Philip vor und packte einen Mann am Ärmel. »Zurück!« brüllte er und stieß ihn auf die Ostmauer zu. Der verblüffte Mann sah die Mönche an der Mauer kauern und hastete auf sie zu. Philip schnappte sich zwei Frauen und beförderte sie auf dieselbe Weise aus der Gefahrenzone. Die Umstehenden durchschauten seine Absicht und schlossen sich ohne weitere Aufforderung den beiden Frauen an. Weitere Menschen folgten, und alsbald strebten die meisten Gläubigen, die vorne gestanden hatten, ebenfalls auf die Ostmauer zu. Philip riskierte einen Blick in die Höhe, nur um zu seinem namenlosen Schrecken erkennen zu müssen, daß auch das zweite Joch nicht mehr zu retten war: Auch dort schlängelten sich Risse kreuz und quer durch den Lichtgaden und sprengten das Gewölbe über seinem Kopf. Rastlos trieb er immer mehr Menschen in die Sicherheit des Ostflügels, trieb sie wie ein Schäfer seine Herde in den Pferch. Ein Schauer aus Mörtelbrocken ging über seinem geschorenen Haupt nieder, dann prasselten auch schon die ersten Steine herunter. Die Menschen jagten auseinander. Manche suchten in den Seitenschiffen Zuflucht, andere – unter ihnen Bischof Waleran – drängten sich an die Ostwand, wieder andere versuchten noch immer, kletternd und kriechend über geborstene Steine und am Boden liegende Leiber die offene Westseite zu erreichen. Ein Stein streifte Philip an der Schulter; er war nicht schwer getroffen, aber es tat weh. Er legte die Hände über den Kopf und blickte erregt um sich: Allein stand er jetzt im zweiten Joch, alle anderen drängten sich am Rand der Gefahrenzone zusammen. Er konnte nichts mehr tun. So rannte er zur Ostseite hinüber und brachte sich selbst in Sicherheit.

Als er sich umdrehte und nach oben sah, stürzte gerade der Lichtgaden im zweiten Joch ein, und das Deckengewölbe fiel in den Altarraum – eine exakte Wiederholung dessen, was im dritten Joch geschehen war. Diesmal allerdings gab es weniger Opfer zu beklagen, weil die meisten Menschen hatten fliehen können und weil, anders als im dritten Joch, die Decken der Seitenschiffe zu halten schienen. Im Ostflügel drückten sich die Leute so eng wie irgend möglich an die Mauer. Aller Augen waren an die Decke gerichtet; alle fürchteten, auch hier, im ersten Joch, könne das Gewölbe nachgeben und auf sie herabstürzen. Das Getöse des fallenden Mauerwerks schien langsam leiser zu werden, doch war die Luft erfüllt von Staubwolken und nachrutschenden kleineren Steinen und Mörtelresten, so daß vorübergehend niemand etwas sehen konnte. Philip hielt den Atem an. Schließlich legte sich der Staub, die Luft war wieder klar, und das Gewölbe über ihnen erkennbar: Es war genau am Rand des ersten Jochs abgebrochen, der Rest schien jedoch zu halten.

Es herrschte absolute Stille. Wie gelähmt vor Entsetzen starrte Philip auf die Ruine seiner neuen Kirche. Außer dem ersten Joch war nichts stehengeblieben. Im zweiten Joch standen die Mauern noch bis zur Höhe der Galerie, während vom dritten und vierten nur noch die Seitenschiffe übrig waren, doch waren auch sie stark in Mitleidenschaft gezogen. Der Boden der Kirche war ein einziger Stein- und Schutthaufen und übersät mit den reglosen oder zuckenden Leibern der Toten und Verwundeten. Sieben Jahre fleißiger Arbeit, die Hunderte von Pfunden verschlungen hatte, waren mit einem Schlag dahin; Dutzende, wenn nicht Hunderte von Menschen in wenigen verhängnisvollen Augenblicken erschlagen. Philip tat das Herz weh ob all der vergeblichen Mühe, und er empfand tiefes Mitleid mit den Toten und Verletzten, mit den vielen Frauen und Kindern, die jetzt Witwen und Waisen waren. Seine Augen füllten sich mit bitteren Tränen.

Eine harte Stimme drang an sein Ohr. »Das habt Ihr nun von Eurer verdammten Überheblichkeit, Philip!«

Er drehte sich um und erkannte Bischof Waleran. Staub überzog die schwarzen Gewänder seines Widersachers, und in seinem Blick lag der Schimmer des Triumphs. Philip fühlte sich, als habe man ihm ein Messer zwischen die Rippen gestoßen. Es war grauenvoll genug, eine solche Tragödie miterleben zu müssen – dafür aber auch noch schuldig gesprochen zu werden, das war schlichtweg unerträglich. *Ich habe doch nur das Beste gewollt,* versuchte er zu sagen, aber die Worte blieben ihm im Halse stecken. Er brachte keinen Ton heraus.

Sein Blick fiel auf Johnny Eightpence, der in diesem Augenblick zusammen mit seinem Schützling seinen Schlupfwinkel im Seiten-schiff verließ. Die beiden erinnerten ihn wieder an seine Verantwor-tung. Die quälende Frage nach dem Schuldigen konnte später geklärt werden – fürs erste galt es, die Verletzten zu versorgen und die Ver-schütteten zu bergen. Ihm, dem Prior, oblag es, die Rettungsarbeiten in die Wege zu leiten. Wutentbrannt funkelte er Waleran an und brüllte: »Geht mir aus dem Weg!« Der Bischof trat verblüfft zur Seite. Mit einem Satz erreichte Philip den Altar und sprang hinauf.

»Hört mir zu!« rief er, so laut er konnte. »Wir müssen uns um die Verwundeten kümmern, die Verschütteten befreien und schließlich die Toten bestatten und für ihr Seelenheil beten. Ich werde jetzt drei Verantwortliche ernennen ...« Er ließ seinen Blick in die Runde schweifen, um zu sehen, wer von den Überlebenden die Katastrophe unbeschadet überstanden hatte. Er erkannte Alfred und sagte: »Alfred Builder ist für die Beseitigung der herabgestürzten Steine und die Bergung der Verschütteten zuständig. Ich fordere alle Steinmetzen, Maurer und Zimmerleute auf, ihm zur Hand zu gehen.« Zu Philips Erleichterung war auch sein alter Freund und Vertrauter Milius unver-letzt. »Milius, der Kämmerer, sorgt dafür, daß die Toten und Verwun-deten aus der Kirche geschafft werden. Er wird dabei kräftige junge Helfer brauchen. Randolph, der Infirmarius, wird sich der Verwunde-ten annehmen, sobald sie im Freien sind. Dabei können ihm die Älte-ren, vor allem die älteren Frauen, Hilfe leisten. Das mag genügen. Fangen wir an!«

Der Prior sprang vom Altar herunter. Befehle und Fragen hallten durcheinander und steigerten sich zum Tumult.

Alfred wirkte bis ins Mark erschüttert und entsetzt. Wenn irgend jemand Schuld an diesem Unheil trug, dann er, der Baumeister. Doch dies war nicht der Zeitpunkt für Vorwürfe. »Teilt Eure Leute in Gruppen ein und laßt sie an verschiedenen Stellen gleichzeitig mit der Arbeit beginnen«, sagte Philip.

Alfred starrte ihn mit leeren Augen an, dann kam er wieder zu sich. »Richtig, ja. Wir fangen an der Westseite an und schaffen den Schutt nach draußen.«

»Gut so.« Philip ließ ihn stehen und arbeitete sich zu Milius vor. Der Kämmerer erteilte bereits die ersten Befehle: »Tragt die Verwundeten alle vorsichtig aus der Kirche und legt sie dort aufs Gras. Die Toten bringt auf die Nordseite.«

Philip merkte, daß er sich, wie gewohnt, auf Milius verlassen konnte, und wandte sich ab. Randolph, der Infirmarius, kletterte über den Schutt. Philip eilte ihm nach. Draußen, auf der Westseite der Kirche, hatten sich die Menschen versammelt, denen es gelungen war, noch rechtzeitig vor dem Einsturz ins Freie zu entkommen. »Nimm dir diese Leute«, sagte Philip zu Randolph. »Schick sie ins Infirmarium nach Verbandszeug und deinen Instrumenten. Laß einige in der Küche heißes Wasser holen. Bitte den Cellerar um starken Wein für jene, die etwas Belebendes brauchen. Und sorge dafür, daß die Toten und Verwundeten sorgfältig und mit den entsprechenden Abständen aufgereiht werden, damit deine Helfer nicht über ihre Leiber stolpern.«

Die Rettungsarbeiten nahmen ihren Lauf. Viele der Überlebenden, die gleich ihm an der unversehrt gebliebenen Ostmauer Zuflucht gesucht hatten, waren ihm gefolgt und hatten bereits mit dem Abtransport der Toten begonnen. Ein, zwei Verwundete, die nur betäubt oder bewußtlos gewesen waren, kamen ohne Hilfe wieder auf die Beine. Philip fiel eine alte Frau ins Auge, die auf dem Boden saß und einen vollkommen verwirrten Eindruck machte. Es war Maud Silver, die Witwe eines Silberschmieds. Er half ihr auf und geleitete sie über das Trümmerfeld hinaus. »Was ist geschehen?« fragte sie, ohne ihn anzusehen. »Ich weiß gar nicht, was geschehen ist ...«

»Ich auch nicht, Maud«, sagte Philip.

Das habt Ihr nun von Eurer verdammten Überheblichkeit, Philip ... Die Worte von Bischof Waleran wollten ihm nicht mehr aus dem Kopf. Die Beschuldigung hatte ihn tief getroffen, zumal er ihr eine gewisse Berechtigung nicht absprechen konnte. Er war schon immer ein Antreiber gewesen, dem nichts gut genug war und nichts schnell genug ging. Er hatte Alfred dazu angetrieben, das Gewölbe schneller als geplant fertigzustellen, ebenso wie er andere dazu angetrieben hatte, einen Wollmarkt zu errichten und dem Grafen von Shiring den Steinbruch wegzunehmen. In jedem dieser Fälle hatte es am Schluß eine

Tragödie gegeben: die Niedermetzelung der Steinbrucharbeiter, die Brandschatzung der Stadt Kingsbridge – und nun dies! Und schuld daran war sein übertriebener Ehrgeiz, er sah es jetzt ganz deutlich. Ein Mönch tat besser daran, ein Leben der Entsagung zu führen und alles, was ihm an Rückschlägen und sonstigen Mißhelligkeiten widerfuhr, in stiller Demut als gottgegebene Lektionen in Geduld hinzunehmen.

Philip barg stöhnende Verwundete und widerstandslose Tote und half, sie aus den Ruinen seiner Kathedrale nach draußen zu tragen. Für sich faßte er bei dieser traurigen Arbeit den Entschluß, fürderhin jeglichen Ehrgeiz und alles Drängen dem Allmächtigen zu überlassen – er, Philip, wollte künftig passiv hinnehmen, was immer geschah. Wenn Gott eine Kathedrale wollte, so würde Er auch für einen Steinbruch sorgen. Sollte die Stadt niedergebrannt werden, so wollte er, Philip, es als Zeichen dafür nehmen, daß Gott keinen Wollmarkt wünschte. Und die eingestürzte Kirche wollte er nicht mehr aufbauen.

Kaum hatte Philip sich zu dieser Entscheidung durchgerungen, da erblickte er William Hamleigh.

Der neue Graf von Shiring saß nicht weit vom nördlichen Seitenschiff auf dem Boden des dritten Jochs. Sein Gesicht war aschfahl, und er zitterte vor Schmerzen, denn sein Fuß war unter einem großen Stein eingeklemmt. Philip half, den schweren Klotz beiseite zu wuchten, und dabei schoß ihm die Frage durch den Kopf, was den Herrn wohl dazu bewogen haben mochte, so viele gute Menschen sterben zu lassen – einem Aas wie diesem William aber das Leben zu schenken.

William jammerte erbärmlich über die Schmerzen in seinem Fuß, war ansonsten aber unversehrt. Sie halfen ihm wieder auf die Beine. Er stützte sich schwer auf einen etwa gleichgroßen, grobschlächtigen Mann und humpelte davon.

Und da schrie auf einmal ein kleines Kind.

Alle hörten es. Da nirgendwo ein Kind zu sehen war, schauten sich alle erstaunt um. Da – wieder! Die Stimme schien unter einem gewaltigen Stein- und Trümmerhaufen im Seitenschiff hervorzudringen. »Hier herüber!« rief Philip und befahl Alfred mit einem Wink an seine Seite. »Da drunter muß es sein – ein kleines Kind, es lebt...«

Wie gebannt lauschten alle dem Schreien. Es mußte sich in der Tat um ein sehr kleines Kind handeln, ein Säugling noch, bestimmt noch keinen Monat alt. »Ihr habt recht«, sagte Alfred. »Schieben wir erst einmal die größten Steine weg.« Der Schutt türmte sich so hoch, daß er den Bogen zum dritten Joch völlig blockierte. Philip half bei der Räumung nach Kräften mit. Er hatte keine Ahnung, welche Frau in der Stadt jüngst geboren hatte. Gewiß, es war durchaus möglich, daß ihm ein solches alltägliches Ereignis entgangen war. Zwar war die Einwohnerzahl der Stadt im vergangenen Jahr spürbar zurückgegangen, doch war sie immer noch so groß, daß er sich nicht jede Geburt merken konnte.

Urplötzlich hörte das Weinen auf. Die Männer hielten sofort inne und lauschten angestrengt, doch es kaum kein Laut mehr. Mit finsterer Entschlossenheit setzten sie ihre gefährliche Arbeit fort. Jeder Stein, den sie entfernten, konnte andere ins Rutschen bringen. Im Wissen um dieses Risiko hatte der Prior die Leitung der Aufräumarbeiten Alfred übertragen, der es nun aber zu Philips Leidwesen ganz an der gebotenen Vorsicht fehlen ließ: Er schien jeden tun zu lassen, was ihm gerade paßte. Ohne Plan und Ziel wurden die Steine vom Haufen gegriffen und fortgetragen. Als schließlich eine wahre Steinlawine ins Rollen zu kommen drohte, schritt Philip ein.

»Halt!«

Alfred, soviel war klar, stand noch viel zu sehr unter dem Eindruck der Katastrophe. Er war noch nicht wieder in der Lage, andere Leute vernünftig anzuleiten. Philip mußte selber in die Bresche springen. »Es kann sein, daß unter diesem Haufen noch Überlebende liegen«, sagte er. »Falls dem so ist, so muß sie irgend etwas vor den herabfallenden Steinen bewahrt haben. Wenn wir nicht aufpassen, gehen sie ihres Schutzes verlustig und werden durch unsere unbedachten Befreiungsversuche getötet. Geht also mit äußerster Behutsamkeit ans Werk!« Er deutete auf eine Gruppe von Steinmetzen, die müßig beieinanderstanden. »Ihr drei da, klettert vorsichtig auf den Haufen und hebt die obersten Steine herunter. Tragt sie aber nicht selber fort, sondern reicht sie Stück um Stück an andere Helfer weiter. Wir bringen sie dann von hier unten aus fort.«

Die Rettungsarbeiten wurden nach Philips Vorstellungen fortgeführt. Auf einmal ging alles schneller – und die Gefahr einer Rutschung schien gebannt.

Da das Kind nicht mehr schrie, ließ sich die Stelle, die freigelegt werden mußte, nicht mehr genau ausmachen. Sie trugen den Trümmerhaufen daher auf der ganzen Breite des Bogens ab. Da auch das Dach des Seitenschiffs teilweise eingefallen war, galt es nicht nur Steine und Mörtel beiseite zu räumen, sondern auch geborstene Balken und Dachplatten.

Philip schuftete unermüdlich: Er wünschte nichts sehnlicher, als daß das Kleine am Leben blieb. Er wußte, daß der Einsturz der Kirche Dutzende von Menschenleben gefordert hatte – dennoch schien ihm dieser unbekannte Säugling Vorrang vor allem anderen zu haben. Wenn dieses Kind gerettet wird, so empfand er, besteht noch eine gewisse Hoffnung auf die Zukunft. Und während er Stein um Stein abhob, hustend und beinahe blind vor Staub, sandte er in Gedanken inbrünstige Gebete gen Himmel, in denen er um das Leben des Kindes flehte.

Nach einiger Zeit war der Schuttberg so weit abgetragen, daß man die Außenmauern des Seitenschiffs und sogar den Teil eines tiefliegenden Fensters erkennen konnte. Tatsächlich hatte sich unter den Trümmern eine Art Hohlraum gebildet. Ob jemand darin überlebt hatte? Schon kroch ein Maurer vorsichtig in das freigelegte Loch ... und schon hörte man seinen Ruf: »Jesusmaria!«

Diesmal störte sich Philip nicht an der Blasphemie. »Was ist los?« fragte er. »Ist das Kind wohlauf?«

»Kann ich nicht genau sagen«, antwortete der Maurer und forderte seine Mithelfer im nächsten Atemzug auf, so schnell wie möglich weitere Steine abzutragen. Philip blieb nicht anderes übrig, als, beflügelt vom Fieber der Neugier, wieder zuzupacken.

Die Arbeit ging jetzt rascher voran. Sie hatten schon fast den Boden der Kathedrale erreicht, als ein riesiger Stein die Kräfte dreier gestandener Männer forderte. Er war noch nicht ganz fortgewuchtet, als Philip das Kind erblickte.

Es war nackt, und es war gerade erst geboren. Die weiße Haut war verschmiert mit Blut und Trümmerstaub, doch das karottenrote Haar war unverkennbar. Aus seinem kleinen runden Bäuchlein hing eine runzelige Nabelschnur, und ein näherer Blick verriet, daß es sich um einen Jungen handelte. Er lag am Busen einer Frau und saugte an einer ihrer Brüste. Das Kind lebte! Philips Herz schlug vor Freude höher. Er sah die Frau an – auch sie war am Leben. Sie blickte ihm in die Augen und verzog die Lippen zu einem schwachen Lächeln, aus dem das reinste Glück sprach.

Es war Aliena.

Aliena kehrte gar nicht erst in Alfreds Haus zurück.

Er erzählte überall herum, daß das Kind nicht von ihm war, und verwies zum Beweis auf den karottenroten Schopf. Es war die Haarfarbe Jacks. Abgesehen davon, daß er die beiden nicht in seinem Haus duldete, tat Alfred weder dem Kind noch Aliena etwas an.

Aliena zog wieder zu ihrem Bruder in das Haus im Armenviertel. Sie war erleichtert, daß Alfreds Rache so milde ausfiel, und froh darüber, daß sie nicht mehr vor seinem Bett auf dem Fußboden schlafen mußte wie ein Hund. Vor allem aber war sie stolz auf ihren kleinen Sohn und ganz hingerissen von ihm. Seine roten Haare, die blauen Augen und seine wunderbar weiße Haut erinnerten sie lebhaft an Jack.

Aus welchem Grunde nun die Kirche eingestürzt war, wußte niemand genau, wenngleich es natürlich die verschiedensten Vermutungen gab. Die einen behaupteten, Alfred sei ein schlechter Baumeister, die anderen gaben Philip die Schuld, weil er auf die Fertigstellung des Gewölbes bis zum Pfingstfest gedrängt hatte. Einige Maurer sagten aus, das Gerüst sei entfernt worden, ehe der Mörtel noch richtig getrocknet war, und ein alter Steinmetz behauptete, es habe ursprünglich gar nicht die Absicht bestanden, ein steinernes Gewölbe einzuziehen; die Mauern seien also von vornherein zum Tragen eines derartigen Gewichts gar nicht geeignet gewesen.

Neunundsiebzig Menschen waren bei dem Unglück umgekommen, jene mitgerechnet, die erst später ihren Verletzungen erlagen. Einig war man sich darüber, daß die Zahl der Opfer noch weit höher gewesen wäre, wenn Prior Philip nicht rechtzeitig so viele Leute in den Ostflügel geschickt hätte. Auf dem Klosterfriedhof war seit dem Feuer auf dem Wollmarkt kein Platz mehr frei, weshalb die meisten Toten neben der Gemeindekirche bestattet worden waren. Und viele Leute munkelten, auf der Kathedrale laste ein Fluch.

Alfred zog mit all seinen Maurern nach Shiring, wo er fortan Steinhäuser für die wohlhabenden Städter baute. Auch die anderen Handwerker kehrten Kingsbridge den Rücken. Kein einziger wurde wirklich entlassen, und Philip zahlte auch die Löhne weiter, doch nach der Beseitigung des Bauschutts gab es nicht mehr viel zu tun. Nach ein paar Wochen waren alle Arbeiter fort. Es kamen auch keine freiwilligen Helfer mehr an den Sonntagen, der Markt beschränkte sich auf ein paar lustlos zusammengezimmerte Stände, und schließlich packte auch Malachi Familie und Habseligkeiten auf einen großen, von vier Ochsen gezogenen Karren und verließ die Stadt, um sich eine fettere Weide zu suchen.

Richard verpachtete sein Schlachtroß an einen Bauern und lebte mit Aliena von den Einnahmen. Ohne Alfreds Unterstützung konnte er nicht mehr die Existenz eines Ritters führen, was freilich, nachdem William Graf geworden war, ohnehin keinen Sinn mehr ergab. Aliena fühlte sich zwar nach wie vor an den ihrem Vater geleisteten Schwur gebunden, sah jedoch unter den obwaltenden Umständen keine Gelegenheit mehr, ihn einzulösen. Richard verfiel zusehends in Trägheit und Lustlosigkeit. Er stand erst spät auf und verbrachte den größten Teil des Tages damit, faul in der Sonne zu sitzen. Abends ging er regelmäßig in die Schenke.

Im großen Haus des Steinmetzen lebte Martha nun allein mit einer ältlichen Dienerin. Die meiste Zeit allerdings war sie bei Aliena und kümmerte sich mit Begeisterung um deren Söhnchen – nicht zuletzt deshalb, weil es ihrem angebeteten Jack wie aus dem Gesicht geschnitten war. Sie drängte Aliena, das Kind Jack zu nennen, doch die junge Mutter wollte sich noch nicht festlegen und zögerte die Entscheidung aus Gründen, über die sie sich selbst nicht im klaren war, immer weiter hinaus.

Den ganzen Sommer über war Aliena erfüllt von mütterlichem Stolz und Eifer. Dann, als die Ernte eingebracht war, die Luft kühler und die Abende länger wurden, schwand ihre Zufriedenheit allmählich dahin.

Oft machte sie sich Gedanken über ihre Zukunft, und jedesmal kam ihr dabei Jack in den Sinn. Er war fort, sie hatte keine Ahnung, wo er sich aufhielt, und sie rechnete kaum noch mit seiner Rückkehr. Dennoch war er ihr ständiger Begleiter, voller Tatkraft und Leben, so deutlich und nah, als sei er erst tags zuvor von ihr gegangen. Sie erwog, in eine andere Stadt zu ziehen, wo sie sich als Witwe ausgeben könnte; sie dachte darüber nach, ob Richard sich nicht auf die eine oder andere Weise dazu bewegen ließe, seinen Lebensunterhalt zu verdienen; sie überlegte, ob sie nicht mit der Weberei beginnen oder als Wäscherin arbeiten könne, ja sie erwog sogar, sich bei einer der wenigen Familien in der Stadt, die sich so etwas noch leisten konnten, als Hausmagd zu verdingen. Doch alle Pläne, die sie schmiedete, quittierte ein stets präsenter Jack in ihrem Kopf mit höhnischem Gelächter. »Ohne mich geht alles schief«, behauptete er dreist. Das Schäferstündchen mit ihm am Morgen ihres Hochzeitstages war die ärgste Sünde, die sie in ihrem Leben je begangen hatte, davon war Aliena inzwischen überzeugt, und alles Unheil danach war ihre Strafe dafür. Dennoch gab es immer wieder Augenblicke, in denen sie das Gefühl hatte, eben jene Schandtat sei das einzig Gute in ihrem Leben gewesen – sie brauchte sich ja nur ihr Söhnchen anzusehen, und die Reue war wie fortgeblasen. Ihre Rastlosigkeit ließ sich indessen nicht mehr vertreiben. Ein Kind war nicht alles; sie fühlte sich unvollständig, unausgefüllt. Das Haus war ihr mit einemmal zu eng, Kingsbridge erschien ihr wie ausgestorben, ihr Leben langweilig und ereignislos. Es dauerte nicht lange, da bekam auch das Kind ihre Ungeduld zu spüren, und Martha mußte sich ein ums andere Mal bissige Bemerkungen gefallen lassen.

Als der Sommer vorüber war, brachte der Bauer Richards Schlachtroß zurück – es wurde nicht mehr gebraucht. Von einem Tag auf den anderen waren die Geschwister ohne Einkünfte. An einem Herbstmorgen machte sich Richard auf den Weg nach Shiring, um seine Rüstung zu verkaufen. Um Geld zu sparen, begnügte sich Aliena zum Abendbrot mit ein paar Äpfeln. Da ging auf einmal die Tür auf, und Jacks Mutter stand vor ihr.

»Ellen!« rief Aliena aus. Sie war mehr als erschrocken – sie war bestürzt. Ellen hatte eine kirchliche Heirat mit einem Fluch belegt und mußte daher noch immer mit einer Bestrafung durch Prior Philip rechnen.

»Ich möchte gerne meinen Enkel sehen«, sagte Ellen gelassen.

»Aber woher weißt du ...?«

»So etwas spricht sich herum, selbst draußen im Wald.« Ellen trat an die Wiege, die in der Ecke stand, und betrachtete das schlafende Kind. Ihre harten Züge entspannten sich. »Hübsch, hübsch ... nein, da besteht kein Zweifel, wer der Vater ist. Macht er sich gut?«

»Er war nicht einmal krank bisher«, sagte Aliena stolz. »Er ist zwar nicht groß, aber ungemein zäh.« Und rasch fügte sie noch hinzu: »Wie seine Großmutter.« Ellen war magerer geworden, ihre Haut dunkler. Sie trug eine kurze Ledertunika, die ihre braunen Waden freigab, und sie war barfuß. Sie wirkte jung und gesund – das Leben in den Wäldern schien ihr zu bekommen. Aliena rechnete nach und kam zu dem Ergebnis, daß Ellen jetzt fünfunddreißig Jahre alt sein mußte. »Du siehst gut aus«, sagte sie.

»Ihr fehlt mir«, erwiderte Ellen. »Ihr alle, du und Martha, ja sogar dein Bruder Richard. Jack fehlt mir sehr – und am meisten fehlt mir Tom.« Sie war auf einmal sehr traurig.

Aliena machte sich noch immer Sorgen um Ellens Sicherheit. »Hat dich irgendwer unterwegs gesehen? Die Mönche wollen dich vielleicht immer noch bestrafen.«

Ellen grinste. »In ganz Kingsbridge gibt es keinen einzigen Mönch, der es wagen würde, Hand an mich zu legen«, sagte sie. »Ich war aber trotzdem vorsichtig – kein Mensch hat mich gesehen.« Sie schwieg, ließ Aliena jedoch nicht aus den Augen. Der Blick ihrer honigfarbenen Augen war so streng, daß Aliena sich immer unbehaglicher fühlte.

Nach einer Weile sagte Ellen: »Du vergeudest dein Leben.«

»Wie meinst du das?« fragte Aliena, obwohl die Worte eine ganz bestimmte Saite in ihr zum Klingen gebracht hatten.

»Du solltest hier raus und Jack suchen.«

Es klang wie eine süße Verheißung, aber Aliena antwortete: »Das kann ich nicht.«

»Warum nicht?«

»Zunächst einmal deshalb, weil ich keine Ahnung habe, wo er sich befindet.«

»Ich weiß es.«

Alienas Herz schlug auf einmal schneller. Sie war davon ausgegangen, daß niemand über Jacks Verbleib Bescheid wußte, ja es war ihr, als sei er vollkommen vom Erdboden verschwunden. Ellens Enthüllung änderte alles. Jack konnte nicht weit sein – und sie, Aliena, konnte ihm seinen Sohn zeigen.

»Zumindest weiß ich, wo er hinwollte«, ergänzte Ellen.

»Wohin?« drängte Aliena.

»Nach Santiago de Compostela.«

»O du mein Gott!« Aliena hätte heulen können, so enttäuscht war sie. Santiago lag in Spanien und war die Grabstätte des heiligen Jakobus. Eine Reise dorthin dauerte mehrere Monate.

»Er hoffte, auf der Reise mit Spielleuten ins Gespräch zu kommen und etwas über seinen Vater zu erfahren.«

Aliena nickte betrübt. Das klang durchaus plausibel, denn daß er kaum etwas über seinen Vater wußte, hatte Jack schon immer bedauert. Mit seiner Rückkehr war nun wohl nicht mehr zu rechnen; höchstwahrscheinlich würde er unterwegs an einer Dombaustelle vorbeikommen, eine Stelle annehmen und sich dort niederlassen. Durch die Suche nach seinem Vater erfuhr er womöglich nie etwas von seinem eigenen Sohn.

»Ich würde ihm gerne nachreisen«, sagte Aliena. »Aber es ist so schrecklich weit!«

»Na und? Tausende haben die Strapazen einer Pilgerfahrt nach Santiago schon auf sich genommen. Warum solltest du das nicht auch können?«

»Ich habe meinem Vater geschworen, mich so lange um Richard zu kümmern, bis er Graf geworden ist«, gab Aliena zurück. »Ich kann ihn nicht allein lassen.«

Ellen betrachtete sie kritisch. »Und wie glaubst du ihm derzeit zu seiner Grafenwürde verhelfen zu können?« fragte sie. »Du besitzt keinen roten Heller, und außerdem heißt der neue Graf inzwischen William. Richard hat sämtliche Aussichten auf den Titel verloren – falls er jemals welche hatte. Du kannst ihm hier in Kingsbridge auch nicht mehr nützen als in Santiago. Du hast dein ganzes Leben diesem elenden Schwur untergeordnet, doch jetzt muß Schluß sein damit. Es ist aus und vorbei. Ich glaube nicht, daß dir dein Vater daraus irgendeinen Vorwurf machen könnte. Wenn du mich fragst, so könntest du Richard keinen größeren Gefallen tun, als ihn eine Zeitlang alleine zu lassen und ihm so die Gelegenheit zu geben, ein bißchen selbständiger zu werden.«

Sie hat recht, dachte Aliena, zur Zeit kann ich Richard ohnehin nicht helfen – weder in Kingsbridge noch anderswo. Ellen hatte ihr die Augen geöffnet: Sie hatte ihre Freiheit wiedererlangt – die Freiheit, Jack zu suchen. Allein der Gedanke daran stimmte sie froh. »Aber ich habe kein Geld für eine solche Pilgerfahrt«, wandte sie ein.

»Was ist denn aus eurem großen Schlachtroß geworden?«

»Das haben wir noch …«

»Dann verkauf es.«

»Das kann ich nicht. Es gehört doch Richard …«

»Verflixt und zugenäht, Aliena – wer hat es denn gekauft?« ereiferte sich Ellen. »Hat etwa Richard in jahrelanger harter Arbeit einen Wollhandel aufgebaut? Hat Richard mit habgierigen Bauern und sturen flämischen Kaufleuten verhandelt? Hat Richard die Wolle von überallher hier zusammengetragen, gelagert und schließlich auf einem eigens dafür gefertigten Marktstand verkauft? Mach mir ja nicht weis, das Pferd gehöre ihm …«

»Er wird sich furchtbar ärgern …«

»Um so besser. Hoffentlich ärgert er sich so sehr, daß er zum erstenmal in seinem Leben richtig arbeitet!«

Aliena öffnete den Mund, um weitere Einwände vorzubringen, schloß ihn aber wieder, ehe sie auch nur ein Wort gesagt hatte. Ellen hatte recht. Richard hatte sich in allem und jedem immer nur auf sie verlassen. Solange er um sein Erbe stritt, war sie verpflichtet gewesen, ihn zu unterstützen. Doch mittlerweile kämpfte er um gar nichts mehr; er hatte daher das Recht auf weitere Ansprüche an sie verwirkt.

Wie wäre es schön, Jack zu finden … Sie sah sein Gesicht vor sich, sein Lächeln. Wir werden uns küssen … Allein der Gedanke daran trieb ihr die Wollust in die Lenden und machte sie ganz verlegen.

»So eine Reise ist natürlich nicht ungefährlich«, sagte Ellen.

Aliena lächelte. »Das macht mir nicht die geringsten Sorgen. Ich bin das Reisen gewöhnt seit meinem siebzehnten Lebensjahr. Ich kann weiß Gott auf mich aufpassen.«

»Trotzdem. Auf dem Pilgerweg nach Santiago de Compostela treiben sich Hunderte von Leuten herum. Du solltest dich einer größeren Pilgergruppe anschließen, dann mußt du nicht allein reisen.«

Aliena seufzte. »Wenn der Kleine nicht wäre – ich wäre imstande, mich sofort auf den Weg zu machen.«

»Gerade um deines Söhnchens willen mußt du es tun«, hielt Ellen dagegen. »Es braucht einen Vater.«

Von dieser Seite hatte Aliena die Sache noch gar nicht betrachtet, ja, sie hatte ausschließlich eigennützige Motive in der möglichen Reise gesehen. Nun sah sie ein, daß auch das Kind Jack brauchte, nicht weniger als sie. Die tägliche Pflege des Kleinen hatte sie so in Anspruch genommen, daß sie über seine Zukunft noch nicht nachgedacht hatte. Auf einmal kam es ihr furchtbar ungerecht vor, daß ihr Sohn aufwachsen sollte, ohne seinen Vater zu kennen – dieses überschäumende, einzigartige, bewundernswerte Genie.

Sie spürte, daß Ellen sie schon fast überredet hatte. Plötzlich wurde ihr angst und bange zumute.

Ein weiterer Einwand fiel ihr ein: »Aber ich kann mein Söhnchen doch nicht mitnehmen!«

Ellen zuckte die Achseln. »Ihm wird der Unterschied zwischen Spanien und England nicht sonderlich auffallen ... Doch davon abgesehen: Niemand zwingt dich, den Kleinen mitzunehmen.«

»Wie könnte ich ihn hierlassen?«

»Laß ihn bei mir. Ich füttere ihn mit Ziegenmilch und wildem Honig.«

Aliena schüttelte den Kopf. »Die lange Trennung würde mir das Herz brechen. Ich liebe ihn viel zu sehr.«

»Wenn du ihn liebst«, sagte Ellen, »dann mach dich auf den Weg und suche seinen Vater.«

In Wareham fand Aliena ein Schiff, das sie mitnahm. Mit ihrem Vater hatte sie als junges Mädchen schon einmal den Ärmelkanal überquert; damals waren sie auf einem normannischen Kriegsschiff gefahren, einem jener langen, schmalen Boote, deren Seiten an Bug und Heck in einer hochgezogenen, aufwärts gekrümmten Spitze ausliefen. Sie besaßen ein quadratisches Ledersegel und zu beiden Seiten jeweils eine lange Reihe von Rudern. Das Schiff, das Aliena jetzt in die Normandie bringen sollte, war ähnlich gebaut, dabei aber um einiges breiter und vor allem tiefer, um möglichst viel Fracht aufnehmen zu können.

Es war aus Bordeaux gekommen, und Aliena hatte zugeschaut, wie barfüßige Seeleute große Weinfässer löschten, die für die Keller der Reichen bestimmt waren.

Aliena war klar, daß sie ihr Söhnchen zurücklassen mußte, doch es wollte ihr schier das Herz zerreißen. Jedesmal, wenn sie den Kleinen im Arm hielt, gingen ihr erneut alle Gründe durch den Sinn, die dafür sprachen, doch das änderte nichts: Sie wollte sich nicht von ihm trennen.

Ellen hatte sie nach Wareham begleitet, wo sich Aliena zwei Mönchen aus der Abtei von Glastonbury angeschlossen hatte; die frommen Brüder wollten ihre Güter in der Normandie aufsuchen. Es gab noch drei weitere Passagiere: einen jungen Knappen, der vier Jahre bei Verwandten in England verbracht hatte und nun zu seinen Eltern nach Toulouse zurückkehrte, sowie zwei junge Maurer, denen jemand erzählt hatte, daß auf der anderen Seite des Kanals die Löhne höher und die Mädchen hübscher seien. Am Morgen der Abreise hatten sie sich alle in einer Schenke versammelt und warteten, bis die Besatzung das Schiff mit schweren Barren kornischen Zinns beladen hatte. Die Maurer schütteten mehrere Krüge Bier in sich hinein, schienen davon jedoch nicht betrunken zu werden. Aliena liebkoste das Kind und weinte leise vor sich hin.

Endlich war das Schiff bereit zum Ablegen. Die stämmige schwarze Stute, die Aliena in Shiring erworben hatte, hatte noch nie das Meer gesehen und weigerte sich, die Laufplanke zu betreten. Der Knappe und die beiden Maurer boten jedoch begeistert ihre Hilfe an, und mit vereinten Kräften schafften sie das Tier schließlich an Bord.

Blind vor Tränen legte Aliena ihr Söhnchen in Ellens Arme. Ellen nahm den Kleinen entgegen, sagte jedoch: »Es geht nicht. Ich hätte es gar nicht erst vorschlagen sollen dürfen.«

»Aber was ist mit Jack?« schluchzte Aliena. »Ohne Jack kann ich nicht leben, ich kann's einfach nicht. Ich muß ihn unbedingt finden.«

»Selbstverständlich«, sagte Ellen. »Ich meine nicht, daß du auf die Reise verzichten sollst. Aber du kannst dein Kind nicht hierlassen. Nimm es mit.«

Nun kamen Aliena vor lauter Dankbarkeit erst recht die Tränen. »Glaubst du wirklich, daß es ihm nicht schadet?«

»Er hat doch auch den Weg hierher überstanden und sich dabei ausgesprochen wohlgefühlt. Die weitere Reise wird für ihn lediglich eine Fortsetzung des Gewohnten sein. Außerdem mag er die Ziegenmilch nicht besonders.«

Der Kapitän rief: »Beeilung, meine Damen, die Flut kommt!«

Aliena nahm ihren Sohn in die Arme und gab Ellen einen Kuß. »Ich danke dir. Jetzt bin ich wieder froh.«

»Viel Glück!« wünschte Ellen.

Aliena wandte sich ab und ging schnellen Schritts die Laufplanke hoch. Das Schiff legte sofort ab, und Aliena winkte, bis Ellen nur noch als kleines Pünktchen am Kai wahrzunehmen war. Sie hatten die Bucht noch nicht verlassen, als der Regen einsetzte. Da es auf Deck keinen Schutz gegen die Nässe gab, setzte sich Aliena in den Frachtraum zu den Pferden und der Ladung, obwohl sie auch dort nicht gänzlich vor dem Wetter geschützt war, denn das Deck, auf dem die Ruderer saßen, war nicht ganz abgeschlossen. Immerhin konnte sie das Kind unter ihrem Umhang warm und trocken halten. Das Schlingern des Schiffes schien ihm zu bekommen, es schlief bald ein. Als die Nacht hereinbrach und das Boot vor Anker ging, sprach Aliena die Gebete der Mönche mit. Den Rest der Nacht verbrachte sie in einem unruhigen Dämmerzustand, das Kind in ihren Armen.

Am nächsten Tag legten sie in Barfleur an, und Aliena fand in Cherbourg, der nächstgelegenen Stadt, eine Unterkunft. Einen ganzen Tag lang lief sie durch die Straßen und fragte Gastwirte und Baumeister nach einem durchreisenden jungen englischen Steinmetzen mit flammend rotem Haar. Niemand konnte sich an ihn erinnern – allerdings waren die meisten Normannen rothaarig, so daß Jack unter ihnen kaum aufgefallen wäre. Möglicherweise war er auch in einem anderen Hafen von Bord gegangen.

Aliena hatte im Grunde gar nicht damit gerechnet, schon so bald auf eine Spur von Jack zu stoßen; dennoch war sie ein wenig entmutigt. Schon am nächsten Morgen brach sie wieder auf und ritt gen Süden. Sie schloß sich einem Messerhändler mit seiner Familie an – einer stets fröhlichen dicken Frau und vier Kindern. Sie schlugen ein sehr gemächliches Tempo an, so daß Aliena ihr Pferd, das noch einen weiten Weg vor sich hatte, schonen konnte. Obwohl die Familie einen gewissen Schutz bot, trug Aliena ihr scharfes Messer mit der langen Klinge, festgebunden unter ihrem linken Ärmel, bei sich. Sie sah nicht wohlhabend aus. Ihre Kleidung war warm, aber nicht modisch, und ihr Pferd wirkte eher derb als feurig. Sie achtete darauf, stets ein paar

Münzen griffbereit in einer Börse zu tragen, so daß niemand die schwere Geldkatze zu sehen bekam, die sie sich unter ihrer Tunika um die Taille gebunden hatte. Ihr Kind stillte sie stets allein, damit keine fremden Männer ihre Brüste zu sehen bekamen.

Am Abend war ihr großes Glück beschieden und munterte sie beträchtlich auf. Sie hatten in einem Dörfchen namens Lessay halt-gemacht, und dort traf Aliena einen Mönch, der sich noch lebhaft eines jungen Engländers erinnerte – jawohl eines Steinmetzen, der das Rippengewölbe in der Klosterkirche, eine geradezu revolutionäre architektonische Neuerung, bewundert hatte. Aliena frohlockte. Der Mönch erinnerte sich sogar daran, daß Jack erzählt hatte, er sei in Honfleur an Land gegangen – eine Erklärung dafür, weshalb Aliena in Cherbourg keine Spur von ihm gefunden hatte. Obwohl die Bege-benheit nun schon ein Jahr zurücklag, berichtete der Mönch geläufig von Jack, offenkundig beeindruckt von seinem Charme. Aliena war überglücklich – hatte sie nun doch die Bestätigung dafür, daß sie auf dem richtigen Weg war.

Schließlich verabschiedete sie sich von dem Mönch und begab sich zur Nachtruhe ins Gästehaus der Abtei. Schon halb im Schlaf drückte sie ihr Söhnchen fest an sich und flüsterte in seine kleine rote Ohrmu-schel: »Jetzt finden wir deinen Vater bestimmt!«

In Tours wurde der Kleine krank.

Die Stadt war wohlhabend, schmutzig und dicht bevölkert. In Schwärmen huschten die Ratten um die riesigen Kornspeicher am Loireufer. Die Stadt war mit Pilgern überfüllt, denn Tours galt seit alters her als Ausgangspunkt für die Pilgerreise nach Santiago de Com-postela. Zudem stand das Fest des heiligen Martin, des ersten Bischofs der Stadt, unmittelbar bevor. Viele Leute strömten in die Abteikirche zu seinem Grabmal. Martins Berühmtheit rührte daher, daß er einst seinen Mantel zerteilt und die eine Hälfte einem nackten Bettelmann gegeben hatte. Alle Schenken und Herbergen in der Stadt waren be-legt, so daß Aliena froh sein mußte, in einer baufälligen, von zwei Schwestern älteren Jahrgangs geleiteten Kaschemme am Fluß Unter-schlupf zu finden. Die beiden alten Damen waren zu gebrechlich, um auch nur für die nötigste Sauberkeit sorgen zu können.

Aliena hielt sich nicht lange in der Unterkunft auf, sondern lief schon bald mit dem Säugling auf dem Arm in der Stadt umher und erkundigte sich nach Jack. Dabei wurde ihr rasch klar, daß sich die Wirtsleute in einer Stadt mit so vielen Besuchern und Durchreisenden schwerlich an einen bestimmten Gast aus dem Vorjahr erinnern konnten. Dennoch blieb sie an jeder Baustelle stehen und fragte nach einem rothaarigen jungen Steinmetzen aus England. Niemand hatte ihn eingestellt, niemand ihn gesehen.

Seit Lessay war sie nun ohne ein Zeichen von ihm. Wenn Jack wirklich nach Santiago de Compostela wollte, so hätte er nahezu zwangsläufig durch Tours kommen müssen. Vielleicht hat er seine Pläne noch geändert, dachte sie beklommen.

Wie alle anderen Reisenden suchte auch Aliena die Kirche des heiligen Martin auf. Das Bauwerk wurde gerade umfassend renoviert. Aliena fragte sich zum Baumeister durch und wurde an einen kleinen, übellaunigen Mann mit schütterem Haar verwiesen. Sie fragte ihn, ob er vor ungefähr einem Jahr einen Engländer beschäftigt habe.

»Ich beschäftige *niemals* Engländer«, sagte er, ohne sie aussprechen zu lassen. »Englische Maurer und Steinmetzen taugen nichts.«

»Der, den *ich* meine, taugt sehr viel«, erwiderte Aliena. »Außerdem spricht er so gut Französisch, daß Ihr vielleicht gar nicht gemerkt habt, daß er Engländer ist. Er hat rote Haare ...«

»Nie gesehen«, unterbrach sie der Baumeister rüde und wandte sich ab.

Niedergeschlagen kehrte Aliena in ihr Quartier zurück. Ohne jeden Anlaß hatte der Mann ihr eine regelrechte Abfuhr erteilt. Solche Erlebnisse stimmten einen nicht gerade zuversichtlich.

In der Nacht litt sie unter einer Magenverstimmung und tat kein Auge zu. Am nächsten Morgen fühlte sie sich so schlecht, daß sie sich nicht aus dem Haus wagte. Sie verbrachte den ganzen Tag im Bett. Durchs Fenster drang der Gestank vom Fluß, und über die Stiege krochen die üblen Gerüche aus der Taverne, ein widerwärtiger Dunst nach übergeschwapptem Wein und ranzigem Fett. Tags darauf war das Kind krank.

Sein Gewimmer weckte sie auf, ein armseliges, schwaches Klagen, das ganz und gar nichts zu tun hatte mit dem kräftigen, fordernden Gebrüll, das sie von ihm gewohnt war. Der Kleine hatte die gleiche Magenverstimmung wie sie, aber anders als seine Mutter fieberte er auch noch. Seine sonst so hellwachen Äuglein waren geschlossen, die Händchen zu Fäusten geballt. Die Haut war fleckig gerötet.

Aliena wußte nicht, wie sie sich verhalten sollte – er war ja noch nie krank gewesen.

Sie gab ihm die Brust. Der Kleine saugte begierig, jammerte und saugte wieder. Die Milch schien einfach durch ihn hindurchzurinnen.

In der Taverne arbeitete ein nettes junges Zimmermädchen. Aliena bat sie, zum Kloster zu laufen und geweihtes Wasser zu holen. Anfangs hatte sie auch erwogen, einen Arzt holen zu lassen, den Gedanken aber schnell wieder verworfen. Ärzte hatten die Angewohnheit, alle Leute zur Ader zu lassen, und sie konnte sich einfach nicht vorstellen, daß eine solche Kur dem Säugling zuträglich wäre.

Das Zimmermädchen kehrte in Begleitung ihrer Mutter zurück. Die Frau verbrannte ein Büschel getrockneter Kräuter in einer Eisenschüssel. Es entwickelte sich ein beißender Rauch, der die üblen Gerüche im Zimmer aufzusaugen schien. »Das Kind wird viel Durst haben«, sagte sie. »Gebt ihm die Brust, so oft es danach begehrt. Und trinkt auch selbst viel, so daß Ihr immer genug Milch habt. Mehr könnt Ihr nicht tun.«

»Wird er wieder gesund werden?« fragte Aliena beunruhigt.

Die Frau sah sie voller Mitgefühl an. »Das kann ich Euch leider nicht versprechen, meine Liebe. Bei so Kleinen läßt es sich nicht vorhersagen. Normalerweise überleben sie solche Sachen – aber manchmal eben auch nicht. Ist es Euer erstes?«

»Ja.«

»Dann denkt dran: es muß ja nicht das einzige bleiben.«

Aber es ist doch Jacks Sohn, dachte Aliena, und ich habe doch schon Jack verloren. Sie behielt ihre Gedanken jedoch für sich, dankte der Frau und bezahlte die Kräuter.

Als sie wieder allein waren, verdünnte sie das geweihte Wasser mit gewöhnlichem, tränkte ein Tuch darin und kühlte damit dem Kind den Kopf.

Im weiteren Verlauf des Tages schien sich der Zustand des Säuglings zu verschlechtern. Aliena stillte ihn, wenn er weinte, sang ihm etwas vor, wenn er wach lag, und kühlte ihn mit heiligem Wasser, wenn er schlief. Er suchte immer wieder ihre Brust, hatte jedoch wenig Ausdauer beim Saugen. Aliena war froh, daß sie soviel Milch hatte. Sie war selbst noch nicht gesund und ernährte sich nur mit trockenem Brot und verdünntem Wein. Das enge Zimmer mit den fliegendreckverschmutzten Wänden, der schief in den Angeln hängenden Tür, dem armselig kleinen Fenster und den groben Dielenbrettern wurde ihr mit jeder weiteren Stunde, die sie dort verbrachte, mehr verhaßt. Genau vier Möbelstücke befanden sich in dem Raum: ein wackeliges Bett, ein dreibeiniger Hocker, ein Kleiderständer und ein auf dem Boden stehender Leuchter mit drei Armen, aber nur einer Kerze.

Als es dunkel wurde, kam das Zimmermädchen herein und zündete die Kerze an. Das Kind lag auf dem Bett, strampelte mit Armen und Beinen und wimmerte jämmerlich. »Armes kleines Ding«, sagte sie. »Kannst einfach nicht verstehen, warum es dir so schlechtgeht.«

Aliena, die auf dem Hocker gesessen hatte, stand auf und legte sich ins Bett. Die Kerze ließ sie brennen, weil sie ihr Kind jederzeit sehen wollte. Die Nacht verbrachte sie in einem unruhigen Halbschlaf. Gegen Morgen atmete der Kleine flacher und zappelte nicht mehr. Auch das klägliche Wimmern hörte auf.

Aliena weinte lautlos. Sie hatte Jacks Spur verloren, und ihr Kind lag im Sterben – hier, in einem Haus voller Fremder und einer Stadt fern der Heimat. Es wird keinen anderen Jack mehr geben, dachte sie, und ich werde auch nie wieder ein Kind bekommen. Vielleicht sterbe ich auch – es wäre wahrscheinlich das Beste.

Als der Tag heraufdämmerte, blies sie die Kerze aus und sank in den Schlaf der Erschöpfung.

Ein lauter Lärm im Erdgeschoß ließ sie hochfahren. Die Sonne war aufgegangen, und an der Flußlände vor dem Fenster herrschte ein unruhiges, geschäftiges Hin und Her. Das Kind rührte sich nicht, seine Miene war friedlich und entspannt. Kalte Furcht ergriff Alienas Herz. Sie berührte seine Brust: Der Kleine war weder warm noch kalt. Die Angst benahm ihr den Atem. Da schlug der Knabe mit einem tiefen Seufzer, der den ganzen kleinen Körper durchschüttelte, die Augen auf, und Aliena wäre vor Erleichterung fast in Ohnmacht gefallen.

Sie nahm ihn auf und drückte ihn an sich. Der Säugling fing herzhaft an zu schreien. Er war wieder gesund, das Fieber war verflogen, die Schmerzen auch. Sie legte ihn an die Brust. Er saugte gierig und hörte diesmal erst auf, als nichts mehr kam. Und nachdem Aliena ihn umgebettet hatte, leerte er auch noch die andere Brust. Danach sank er in einen tiefen, zufriedenen Schlaf.

Auch Alienas Krankheit war vorüber, obgleich sie sich wie ausgewrungen fühlte. Sie schlief durch bis gegen Mittag, stillte das Kind erneut und ging dann hinunter in die Gaststube, wo sie eine Mahlzeit aus Ziegenkäse, frischem Brot und ein wenig Speck zu sich nahm.

War der Kleine am geweihten Wasser des heiligen Martin genesen? Aliena hielt das immerhin für möglich, und so begab sie sich am Nachmittag noch einmal zu seinem Grabmal, um sich zu bedanken.

In der großen Abteikirche fiel ihr beim Anblick der Bauarbeiten wieder Jack ein, der nun doch vielleicht eines Tages sein Kind zu sehen bekommen würde. Ob er aus einem bestimmten Grunde von der herkömmlichen Strecke nach Santiago abgewichen war? Vielleicht war er in Paris und schnitt dort Steine für eine neue Kathedrale. Ihr Blick fiel auf einen neuen Kragstein, der von den Arbeitern gerade angebracht wurde. Er war mit einer gemeißelten Männergestalt verziert, die das Gewicht des Pfeilers auf seinem Rücken zu tragen schien. Ohne den geringsten Schatten eines Zweifels erkannte Aliena, daß diese schmerzgebeugte Figur von Jack gemeißelt worden war. Er war also doch hiergewesen!

Mit aufgeregt pochendem Herzen ging sie auf die Arbeiter zu. »Dieser Kragstein ...«, sagte sie atemlos, »der stammt von einem Engländer, nicht wahr?«

Ein alter Arbeiter mit gebrochener Nase gab ihr Antwort: »Da habt Ihr recht – Jack Fitzjack hieß der Mann. Ich habe so etwas Feines noch nie in meinem Leben gesehen.«

»Wann war er denn hier?« fragte Aliena und hielt den Atem an. Der Alte kratzte sich seinen Grauschädel unter der speckigen Mütze.

»Na, das muß jetzt so ungefähr ein Jahr her sein. Aber der blieb nicht lange. Der Baumeister mochte ihn nicht.« Er senkte die Stimme. »Um die Wahrheit zu sagen: Der Jack, der war zu gut. Hat den Meister ja richtig vorgeführt. Deshalb mußte er gehen.« Er legte den Zeigefinger an die Nase, um Aliena zu verstehen zu geben, daß dieser Hinweis vertraulich gemeint war.

»Hat er Euch gesagt, wohin er von hier aus ziehen wollte?« fragte sie aufgeregt.

Der Alte betrachtete das Kind. »Wenn man nach der Haarfarbe geht, dann ist das seins.«

»Ja, Ihr habt recht.«

»Wird Jack Euch gerne wiedersehen wollen, was meint Ihr?«

Er denkt, daß Jack mich vielleicht absichtlich sitzengelassen hat, dachte Aliena. Sie lachte. »O ja!« sagte sie. »Er wird mich *sehr* gerne wiedersehen wollen!«

Der Mann zuckte mit den Schultern. »Sei's drum! Er sagte, er wolle nach Compostela.«

»Ich danke Euch!« jubelte Aliena und küßte den alten Mann zu dessen Verblüffung und Freude auf die Wange.

Die verschiedenen Wege der Jakobspilger durch Frankreich liefen in Ostabat zusammen, einem Ort in den Ausläufern der Pyrenäen. Dort schwoll die Gruppe von ungefähr zwanzig Pilgern, denen Aliena sich angeschlossen hatte, auf mehr als siebzig an. Sie bildeten einen fußkranken, aber fröhlichen Verein: ein paar wohlhabende Städter, einige Leute auf der Flucht vor dem Arm des Gesetzes, ein paar Trunkenbolde und viele Mönche und Priester. Die Gottesmänner waren natürlich aus Frömmigkeit unterwegs, die meisten anderen hingegen schienen fest entschlossen, das größtmögliche Vergnügen aus ihrer Pilgerfahrt zu ziehen. Alle möglichen Sprachen wurden durcheinander gesprochen, darunter sogar Flämisch und die südfranzösische Langue d'Oc – dennoch fiel es niemandem schwer, sich verständlich zu machen, und auf dem Weg durch die Pyrenäen sangen sie gemeinsam Lieder, spielten Spiele, erzählten sich Geschichten, ja, es gab sogar die eine oder andere Liebelei.

Aliena war nicht ganz so glücklich, denn hinter Tours war ihr niemand mehr begegnet, der sich an Jack erinnerte. Allerdings traf sie auch bei weitem nicht so viele Spielleute, wie sie angenommen hatte. Ein flämischer Pilger, der die gleiche Wallfahrt schon einmal gemacht hatte, sagte ihr, sie würden auf der spanischen Seite der Pyrenäen noch genügend Spielleute zu Gesicht bekommen.

Er behielt recht. In Pamplona erfuhr Aliena von einem Spielmann, er sei von einem rothaarigen jungen Engländer angesprochen worden; der Mann habe sich nach seinem Vater erkundigt.

Auf der beschwerlichen Pilgerstraße durch den Norden Spaniens erinnerten sich die meisten Spielleute, die Aliena befragte, an Jack. Ihre Aufregung wuchs, als ihr auffiel, daß alle behaupteten, Jack auf dem Weg *nach* Santiago de Compostela getroffen zu haben – nicht einer sagte, er sei auf der Rückreise gewesen.

Das konnte nur bedeuten, daß er noch immer dort war!

Je stärker sie die Strapazen der Reise spürte, desto größer wurde ihre Zuversicht. In den letzten Tagen vor der Ankunft ließ sie sich kaum noch bezähmen. Es war um die Wintermitte, doch das Wetter war angenehm mild und sonnig. Das Kind war nun ein halbes Jahr alt, gesund und munter. Aliena war felsenfest davon überzeugt, sie werde Jack in Santiago finden.

Sie erreichten ihr Ziel genau am Weihnachtstag und gingen ohne Umschweife zur Kathedrale, um an der Christmette teilzunehmen. In der Kirche drängten sich die Gläubigen. Aliena ging unablässig auf und ab und starrte in jedes Gesicht – doch Jack war nirgends zu finden. Sie mahnte sich selbst zur Geduld; schließlich war Jack nicht sonderlich fromm und ging eigentlich nur dann in die Kirche, wenn er dort arbeitete.

Bis sie eine Unterkunft gefunden hatte, war es dunkel geworden.

Aliena legte sich zu Bett, doch die Vorstellung, daß Jack womöglich nur ein paar Schritte von ihr entfernt wohnte, daß sie ihn vielleicht schon am nächsten Tag sehen, ihn küssen und ihm seinen Sohn zeigen konnte, ließ sie vor Aufregung keinen Schlaf finden.

Schon im ersten Morgengrauen war sie wieder auf. Das Kind, das ihre Ungeduld spürte, saugte unregelmäßig und biß ihr sogar mit seinem kleinen Gaumen in die Brust. Hastig wusch sie den Kleinen, nahm ihn auf den Arm und machte sich auf den Weg.

In der ständigen Erwartung, Jack um die nächste Ecke biegen zu sehen, streifte sie durch die Straßen und Gassen. Wie er bei ihrem Anblick staunen würde! Und wie froh er wäre! Doch da sie ihn nirgends entdecken konnte, begann sie schließlich, in den Herbergen nach ihm zu fragen, und sprach auf den Baustellen die Leute an. Sie kannte die kastilischen Worte für *Steinmetz* und *Rotschopf*, und da die Bewohner Santiagos ohnehin Fremde gewöhnt waren, bereitete ihr die Verständigung kaum Schwierigkeiten. Doch nirgends fand sich ein Hinweis auf den Gesuchten.

Sie fing an, sich Sorgen zu machen: Jack war nicht so leicht zu übersehen, und nach allem, was sie bisher hatte in Erfahrung bringen können, mußte er sich schon seit einigen Monaten hier aufhalten. Sie sah sich sogar nach seinen unverkennbaren Steinmetzarbeiten um – doch vergeblich.

Gegen Mittag sprach sie mit einer nachlässig gekleideten Frau mittleren Alters, einer Tavernenwirtin, die Französisch konnte und sich tatsächlich an Jack erinnerte.

»Ein hübscher Bursche – Eurer, ja? Nun ja, es konnte auch keines der hiesigen Mädchen bei ihm landen. Er war um Mittsommer herum hier, aber er ist nicht lange geblieben, tut mir leid. Er hat auch nicht gesagt, wohin er gehen wollte. Ich hab' ihn gemocht. Wenn Ihr ihn findet, gebt ihm einen dicken Kuß von mir.«

Aliena kehrte in ihre Unterkunft zurück und legte sich aufs Bett. Sie starrte an die Decke, erschöpft, enttäuscht und krank vor Heimweh. Das Kind greinte, doch zum erstenmal achtete sie nicht darauf. Es war so ungerecht: Da war sie den ganzen weiten Weg bis Santiago de Compostela auf seiner Spur gewesen – und nun hatte er sich wer weiß wohin gewandt!

Immerhin: Über die Pyrenäen war er nicht wieder gezogen, und westlich von Santiago konnte er sich auch kaum aufhalten, denn da gab es nur noch einen schmalen Küstenstreifen und das Meer, das bis ans Ende der Welt reichte. Jack mußte sich also nach Süden gewandt haben. Sie würde sich also auf ihrer schwarzen Stute und mit dem Kind im Arm erneut auf den Weg machen müssen, diesmal ins tiefste Spanien hinein.

Wie weit fort von Zuhause werde ich wohl sein, wenn diese Pilgerfahrt ihr Ende findet? fragte sie sich.

Jack verbrachte den Weihnachtstag bei seinem Freund Raschid Al-Harun in Toledo. Raschid war ein getaufter Sarazene, der aus dem Osten Gewürze importierte – vor allem Pfeffer – und ein Vermögen damit verdiente. Sie hatten sich zur Mittagsmesse in der großen Kathedrale getroffen und schlenderten nun in der warmen Wintersonne durch die engen Gassen und über den von vielfältigen Düften und Gerüchen durchzogenen Basar zum Viertel der Reichen.

Raschids Haus war aus blendend weißem Stein erbaut und umschloß einen Innenhof mit einem Brunnen. Die schattigen Arkaden des Innenhofs erinnerten Jack an den Kreuzgang im Kloster zu Kingsbridge. Dort allerdings sorgten sie für Schutz vor Regen und Wind – hier dienten sie dazu, die Sonnenhitze abzuhalten.

Raschid und seine Gäste saßen auf Kissen am Boden und speisten von einem niedrigen Tisch. Die Männer wurden von seiner Frau und seinen Töchtern bedient sowie von mehreren Dienerinnen, deren Stellung in diesem Haushalt durchaus Zweifel aufkommen ließ. Zwar war Raschid Christ und durfte nur eine Ehefrau haben, doch hegte Jack den Verdacht, er setze sich stillschweigend darüber hinweg, daß die Kirche Konkubinen mißbilligte.

Die Frauen stellten die größte Attraktion in Raschids gastfreundlichem Hause dar. Sie waren alle schön, ohne jede Ausnahme. Raschids Gattin war eine üppige, anmutige Frau mit glatter dunkelbrauner Haut, glänzendem schwarzem Haar und feucht schimmernden braunen Augen. Seine drei Töchter waren schlankere Ausgaben der Mutter. Die älteste war einem weiteren Mittagsgast anverlobt, dem Sohn eines Seidenhändlers in der Stadt. »Meine Raya ist eine vollkommene Tochter«, bemerkte Raschid, als sie mit einer Schüssel voller Duftwasser um den Tisch ging, damit die Gäste ihre Hände hineintauchen konnten. »Sie ist aufmerksam, gehorsam und schön. Josef kann sich glücklich schätzen.« Der Verlobte neigte zustimmend den Kopf.

Die Zweitälteste war stolz, ja hochmütig. Sie nahm es offenbar übel, daß ihre Schwester so mit Lob überhäuft wurde. Von oben sah sie auf Jack herab und goß ihm aus einer Kupferkanne ein Getränk in den Becher.

»Was ist das?« fragte er.

»Pfefferminzlikör«, sagte sie verächtlich. Sie wartete ihm höchst ungern auf – schließlich war sie die Tochter eines angesehenen Mannes und er nur ein mittelloser Vagabund.

Jack mochte Ayscha, die jüngste Tochter, am liebsten. Er hatte sie in den vergangenen drei Monaten, die er hier verbracht, recht gut kennengelernt. Sie war fünfzehn oder sechzehn Jahre alt, klein, lebhaft und stets gutgelaunt. Obwohl sie drei oder vier Jahre jünger war als er, kam sie ihm nicht wie eine Jugendliche vor. Sie besaß einen wachen, wißbegierigen Kopf und löcherte ihn oft endlos mit Fragen über England und das Leben dort. Nicht selten machte sie sich über die gute Gesellschaft von Toledo lustig – über aufgeblasene Araber, über Juden, die am Essen herummäkelten, und über den schlechten Geschmack der neureichen Christen –, so daß Jack sich manches Mal ausschütten wollte vor Lachen. Von allen drei Schwestern wirkte sie, obwohl die jüngste, am wenigsten zurückhaltend. Die Art, wie sie Jack ansah, als sie sich über ihn beugte und ihm gewürzte Steingarnelen servierte, verriet unmißverständlich, daß sie zu zügelloser Ausgelassenheit neigte. Ihre Blicke kreuzten sich, und sie sagte in gekonnter Imitation ihrer hochnäsigen Schwester: »Pfefferminzlikör!« Jack mußte lachen. In Ayschas Gesellschaft gelang es ihm oft für mehrere Stunden, nicht an Aliena zu denken.

War er indes nicht bei Raschid zu Gast, beherrschte Aliena seine Gedanken, als hätte er sie erst tags zuvor verlassen. Weit über ein Jahr hatte er sie nun nicht mehr gesehen, und doch war die Erinnerung an sie schmerzhaft lebendig. Mühelos wußte er sich jederzeit jede Variante ihrer ausdrucksvollen Mimik auszumalen: die lachende oder nachdenkliche, mißtrauische oder ängstliche, erfreute oder erstaunte und, am deutlichsten von allen, die leidenschaftliche Aliena. Er hatte nichts vergessen, keine Einzelheit ihres Körpers – die Rundung ihrer Brust, die weiche Haut ihrer Schenkel, den Geschmack ihres Kusses, den Duft ihrer Erregung. Wie schmerzlich sehnte er sich nach ihr!

Manchmal stellte er sich, um sein fruchtloses Verlangen nach ihr zu mildern, vor, was sie in besagtem Augenblick gerade tat. Dann sah er sie im Geiste des Abends Alfred die Stiefel ausziehen und sich mit ihm zu Tische setzen, sah, wie die beiden sich küßten und liebten, und wie Aliena einem kleinen Sohn die Brust gab, der genauso aussah wie Alfred. Derlei Bilder quälten und verfolgten ihn – seine Sehnsucht nach Aliena stillten sie nicht.

Am heutigen Weihnachtstag würde Aliena einen Schwan braten und für die Festtafel wieder mit seinen Federn bekleiden; dazu würden sie Molke trinken, die mit Bier, Eiern, Milch und Muskat vermischt war. Einen größeren Unterschied zu den Speisen, die Jack vor sich stehen hatte, konnte es kaum geben. Das Wasser lief ihm im Munde zusammen angesichts der Gerichts aus fremdartig gewürztem Lammfleisch oder Reis mit Nüssen oder den Salaten, die mit Zitronensaft und Olivenöl angerichtet waren. Es hatte einige Zeit gedauert, bis Jack sich an die spanische Küche gewöhnt hatte. Die großen Lendenstücke vom Rind, die Schweinsfüße und Hirschkeulen, ohne die in England kein Festtag denkbar war, wurden hier ebensowenig gereicht wie in dicke Scheiben geschnittenes Brot. Hier unten im Süden Spaniens gab es weder üppige Viehweiden, die große Rinderherden ernährten, noch den fetten Boden, auf dem der Weizen gedieh. Die vergleichsweise kleinen Fleischportionen wurden daher mit unzähligen Kräutern und Gewürzen angerichtet, und statt des in England allgegenwärtigen Brots wurde eine unüberschaubare Vielfalt an Gemüsen und Früchten gereicht.

Die Tage verbrachte Jack in Gesellschaft einer kleinen Gruppe englischer Geistlicher. Sie gehörten einer internationalen Gemeinschaft von Scholaren an, die auch Juden, Muslims und getaufte Araber einschloß. Die Engländer waren damit beschäftigt, die Werke der alten Mathematiker vom Arabischen ins Lateinische zu übersetzen, auf daß sie auch von Christen gelesen werden könnten. In fiebriger Erregung entdeckten sie Stück für Stück die Schätze arabischer Gelehrsamkeit, und Jack war von ihnen ohne viel Aufhebens als Studiosus aufgenommen worden. Sie nahmen jedermann in ihren Zirkel auf – Hauptsache, er verstand, was sie taten, und er teilte ihre Begeisterung. Sie kamen ihm vor wie Bauern, die jahrelang mühselig einem kargen Boden Früchte abgerungen hatten und sich urplötzlich in fruchtbarem Schwemmland wiederfinden.

Jack hatte die Baukunst aufgegeben und widmete sich dem Studium der Mathematik. Bislang war es ihm erspart geblieben, für Lohn zu arbeiten, denn die Geistlichen versorgten ihn mit Kost und Logis und hätten ihm wohl auch eine neue Kutte und Sandalen gegeben, wenn er der Kleidung bedurft hätte.

Raschid gehörte zu ihren Förderern. Da seine Handelsgeschäfte die ganze bekannte Welt umspannten und er daher mehrere Sprache sprach, begriff er sich als Weltbürger. Zu Hause sprach er Kastilisch, die Sprache der getauften Spanier, statt des üblichen Mozarabisch.

Die ganze Familie sprach außerdem Französisch, die Sprache der Normannen, die wichtige Handelspartner waren. Und wiewohl Raschid ein Mann der Geschäfte und des Handels war, besaß er doch einen hervorragenden Geist und eine unersättliche Wißbegier. Nichts liebte er mehr, als mit den Scholaren über ihre Theorien zu disputieren. Jack hatte er auf Anhieb gemocht, und so kam es, daß Jack mehrmals in der Woche bei ihm zu Gast war.

Raschid leitete das Tischgespräch ein, indem er Jack fragte: »Nun, was haben uns die Philosophen diese Woche beigebracht?«

»Ich habe sie mit dem Studium des Euklid verbracht.« *Die Elemente* des Euklid gehörte zu den ersten übersetzten Büchern.

»Euklid? Komischer Name für einen Araber«, bemerkte Raschids Bruder Ismail.

»Er war Grieche«, erklärte Jack. »Er lebte lange vor Christi Geburt. Bei den Römern gingen seine Werke verloren, doch die Ägypter hielten sie in Ehren – daher ist er uns in arabischer Sprache überliefert.«

»Und jetzt werden sie von Engländern ins Lateinische übersetzt«, kommentierte Raschid. »Höchst amüsant.«

»Aber was habt Ihr *gelernt*?« fragte Josef, Rayas Verlobter.

Jack zögerte – es war schwer zu erklären. Dann versuchte er es auf praktische und anschauliche Weise. »Mein Stiefvater, der Baumeister war, hat mich verschiedene Verfahren der Geometrie gelehrt – wie man eine Gerade genau kalibriert, wie man einen rechten Winkel zieht und wie man ein Quadrat in ein anderes zeichnet, so daß das kleinere genau der halben Fläche des größeren entspricht.«

»Wozu dienen denn derartige Fertigkeiten?« unterbrach ihn Josef ein wenig verächtlich. Er betrachtete Jack als Emporkömmling und war überdies eifersüchtig, weil Raschid Jacks Gesprächsbeiträgen so viel Aufmerksamkeit widmete.

»Diese Fertigkeiten sind sehr wichtig bei der Planung von Gebäuden«, erwiderte Jack freundlich und tat, als wäre ihm der mißgünstige Unterton nicht aufgefallen. »Nehmen wir diesen Innenhof. Die Fläche der überdachten Arkaden entspricht genau der unüberbauten Fläche im Inneren. Auf diese Art sind fast alle Innenhöfe gebaut, auch die Kreuzgänge in den Klöstern. Das liegt daran, daß dieses Flächenverhältnis dem Auge am gefälligsten ist. Wäre die freie Fläche in der Mitte größer, so sähe sie aus wie ein Marktplatz, wäre sie kleiner, so wirkte sie wie ein Loch im Dach. Um genau das richtige Gleichmaß zu finden, muß der Baumeister die freie Fläche so zeichnen können, daß sie exakt der Hälfte der Gesamtfläche entspricht.«

»Das habe ich noch nicht gewußt!« stieß Raschid triumphierend hervor – nichts erfreute ihn mehr, als etwas zu lernen, was er noch nicht kannte.

»Euklid gibt uns eine Erklärung dafür, warum diese Vorgehensweise stimmig ist«, fuhr Jack fort. »So sind zum Beispiel die beiden Teile der halbierten Geraden deshalb gleich lang, weil sie zu zwei kongruenten Dreiecken gehören, deren Schenkel jeweils die gleiche Länge haben.«

»Kongruent?« fragte Raschid.

»Das bedeutet deckungsgleich.«

»Aha – jetzt verstehe ich.«

Aber niemand sonst, darauf hätte Jack schwören mögen.

»Ihr konntet doch aber all diese geometrischen Sachen auch schon durchführen, bevor Ihr Euklid gelesen hattet«, wandte Josef ein. »Ich sehe also nicht ganz, welchen Gewinn Ihr davon habt.«

»Ein Mann hat immer einen Gewinn davon, wenn er eine Sache von Grund auf versteht!« protestierte Raschid.

»Außerdem bin ich nun, da ich die Prinzipien der Geometrie verstehe, vielleicht imstande, eine Lösung für andere, neuere Probleme zu finden, die meinen Stiefvater stets verwirrten.« Jack fühlte sich einigermaßen enttäuscht von diesem Gespräch – Euklid war über ihn gekommen wie der blendende Blitz der Erkenntnis, doch gelang es ihm offenbar nicht, den Anwesenden die atemberaubende Bedeutung seiner Entdeckungen verständlich zu machen. Er versuchte es auf anderem Weg: »Am interessantesten ist die Methode, die Euklid anwendet. Er stellt fünf Axiome auf – das sind Grundsätze, die keines Beweises bedürfen – und leitet davon alles andere logisch ab.«

»Nennt mir ein Beispiel für ein Axiom«, bat Raschid.

»Eine Gerade kann bis ins Unendliche verlängert werden.«

»Das ist unmöglich«, bemerkte Ayscha, die soeben mit einer Schüssel Feigen die Runde machte.

Die männlichen Gäste waren etwas pikiert darüber, daß sich ein Mädchen in ihre Diskussion mischte, doch Raschid lachte nachsichtig: Ayscha war seine Lieblingstochter. »Und warum ist das unmöglich?« fragte er.

»Irgendwann muß sie einmal ein Ende haben«, gab sie zurück.

»Aber in deiner Vorstellung kann sie unendlich weitergehen«, sagte Jack.

»In meiner Vorstellung können Flüsse bergauf fließen und Hunde Latein sprechen«, erwiderte sie schlagfertig.

Das hörte ihre Mutter, die soeben das Zimmer betrat. »Ayscha!« mahnte sie streng. »Hinaus mit dir!«

Die Männer lachten. Ayscha zog eine Grimasse und verließ den Raum. »Wer die einmal heiratet«, bemerkte Josefs Vater, »wird alle Hände voll zu tun haben!« Wiederum lachten alle. Auch Jack lachte mit – bis ihm aufging, daß alle ihn ansahen, als hätte der Witz ihm gegolten.

Nach dem Essen führte Raschid seine Sammlung mechanischen Spielzeugs vor. Er besaß einen Behälter, in dem man Wasser mit Wein mischen und beides wieder getrennt ablassen konnte; ein wunderbares, mit Wasser betriebenes Uhrwerk, das die Tagesstunden mit ungeheurer Genauigkeit anzeigte; einen Krug, der sich von selbst füllte, doch niemals überlief; sowie eine hölzerne Frauenstatuette, deren Augen aus einer Art Kristall waren, das in den warmen Tagesstunden Feuchtigkeit absorbierte und sie in der Abendkühle wieder von sich gab; es sah dann so aus, als weine sie. Jack war von diesen Dingen ebenso bezaubert wie Raschid, doch am meisten beschäftigte ihn die weinende Frau. Die Mechanismen der anderen Spielzeuge waren leicht verständlich, sobald man sie einmal erklärt bekommen hatte – aber niemand konnte genau sagen, wie die Holzfigur funktionierte.

Den Nachmittag verbrachten sie unter den Arkaden des Innenhofs mit müßigem Geplauder, mit Spielen oder Dösen. Jack verspürte den Wunsch, zu einer großen Familie wie dieser zu gehören – mit Schwestern und Onkeln und Schwägern –, ein Heim zu besitzen, in dem sie alle zusammenkommen konnten, und eine angesehene Stellung in einer kleinen Stadt. Dabei fiel ihm plötzlich wieder das Gespräch ein, das er mit seiner Mutter in jener Nacht, in der sie ihn aus der Arrestzelle des Klosters befreit, geführt hatte. Er hatte sie nach den Verwandten seines Vaters gefragt, und sie hatte geantwortet: *Ja, drüben in Frankreich hatte er eine große Familie.* Irgendwo habe ich also eine Familie wie diese, erkannte Jack. Die Brüder und Schwestern meines Vaters sind meine Onkeln und Tanten. Vielleicht habe ich sogar Vettern und Basen, die in meinem Alter sind. Ob ich sie jemals finden werde?

Er fühlte sich wie ein Blatt im Winde. Er konnte sich überall durchschlagen – aber er gehörte nirgendwo hin. Er war ein Steinmetz gewesen und ein Baumeister, dann ein Mönch und schließlich Mathematiker, aber wer und was war er wirklich? Ob er Spielmann werden sollte wie sein Vater oder ein Verfemter wie seine Mutter? Er war jetzt neunzehn Jahre alt, ein Heimat- und Wurzelloser ohne Familie und ohne ein Ziel im Leben.

Er spielte eine Partie Schach mit Josef, die er gewann. Dann trat Raschid zu ihnen und sagte: »Laß mich bei Jack sitzen, Josef – ich will noch etwas mehr über Euklid erfahren.«

Fügsam überließ Josef seinem zukünftigen Schwiegervater den Platz und entfernte sich: was *er* über Euklid wissen wollte, hatte er bereits vernommen. Raschid setzte sich und fragte Jack: »Ihr amüsiert Euch gut, ja?«

»Eure Gastfreundschaft ist unübertrefflich«, gab Jack geschmeidig zurück. Er hatte höfische Manieren in Toledo gelernt.

»Danke, aber ich meinte – mit Euklid.«

»Gewiß. Ich glaube, es ist mir nicht gelungen zu erklären, wie wichtig dieses Buch ist. Seht Ihr –«

»Ich denke, ich verstehe«, unterbrach ihn Raschid. »Ebenso wie Ihr erwerbe auch ich gerne Wissen um des Wissens willen.«

»Ja.«

»Dennoch muß sich ein Mann seinen Lebensunterhalt verdienen.«

Jack sah keinen Sinn in dieser Bemerkung, daher wartete er darauf, daß Raschid weitersprach. Der lehnte sich jedoch mit halb geschlossenen Augen zurück, offenkundig damit zufrieden, das kameradschaftliche Schweigen zu genießen. Jack fragte sich willkürlich, ob Raschid ihm vorwarf, keinen Handel zu betreiben, und bemerkte schließlich: »Eines Tages werde ich mich wohl wieder der Baukunst zuwenden.«

»Fein.«

Jack lächelte. »Als ich Kingsbridge verließ – auf dem Pferd meiner Mutter und mit den Werkzeugen meines Stiefvaters in einem Säckchen über der Schulter –, da dachte ich noch, es gäbe nur eine Art, eine Kirche zu bauen: dicke Wände mit Rundbögen und kleinen Fenstern, das Ganze gekrönt von einer Holzdecke oder einem steinernen Tonnengewölbe. Und die Kathedralen, die ich auf dem Weg von Kingsbridge nach Southampton sah, lehrten mich nichts anderes. Die Normandie hat mein ganzes Leben verändert.«

»Das kann ich mir vorstellen«, murmelte Raschid schläfrig. Da er kein großes Interesse zeigte, besann sich Jack jener Tage in Schweigsamkeit. Nur Stunden, nachdem er in Honfleur an Land gegangen war, hatte er die Abteikirche von Jumièges besichtigt. Das war die höchste Kirche, die er je gesehen hatte, und trotzdem besaß sie die üblichen Rundbogen und die hölzerne Decke. Eine Ausnahme war das Kapitelhaus, in dem Abt Urso eine geradezu revolutionäre Steindecke errichtet hatte: Statt eines glatten, fortlaufenden Tonnengewölbes oder eines gerippten Kreuzgewölbes bestand diese Decke aus Rippenbogen, die aus den Säulen entsprangen und im Scheitelpunkt des Daches zusammenliefen. Die Rippenbogen waren dick und stark, die dreieckigen Deckenteile zwischen ihnen dünn und leicht. Der Mönch, der Jack durch den Bau führte, erklärte ihm, das diese Bauweise leichter sei als die herkömmliche – die Rippenbogen wurden zuerst errichtet, danach waren die Zwischenräume leichter aufzufüllen. Auch wogen derartige Kreuzgewölbe weniger. Der Mönch erhoffte sich von Jack einen Bericht über bautechnische Neuerungen in England, wurde aber von ihm enttäuscht. Denn Jacks offenkundige Freude an dem Kreuzgewölbe schmeichelte dem Mönch, so daß er Jack erzählte, im nahe gelegenen Lessay gebe es eine Kirche, die ganz und gar mit Rippenbogen ausgestattet sei.

Tags darauf war Jack nach Lessay weitergezogen und hatte den ganzen Nachmittag in der dortigen Kirche verbracht. Das Deckengewölbe erschien ihm wie ein Wunder, und er hatte es ausgiebig studiert. Vor allem begeisterte ihn die Art, wie die Rippenbogen aus dem Scheitelpunkt des Dachgewölbes auf die Säulenkapitelle herabliefen und somit die Tatsache, daß das Gewicht des Daches von den stärksten Baugliedern getragen wurde, besonders betonten. Die Rippenbogen hoben die Logik der Konstruktion hervor.

Danach war Jack weiter gen Süden gezogen, in die Grafschaft Anjou. An der Abteikirche von Tours, die gerade ausgebessert wurde, fand er eine Stellung. Es fiel ihm nicht schwer, den Baumeister zu überreden – die Werkzeuge, die er bei sich führte, wiesen ihn als Steinmetz aus. Schon nach dem ersten Arbeitstag war dem Baumeister klar, daß er einen guten Griff getan hatte. Jacks Prahlerei vor Aliena, er könne überall auf der Welt Arbeit finden, war kein leeres Gerede gewesen.

Unter den geerbten Gerätschaften befand sich auch Toms Zollstock, ein Werkzeug, das gemeinhin nur Baumeister besaßen. Kaum sahen die Kollegen das kostbare Stück, da fragten sie auch schon, wie Jack in so jungen Jahren daran gekommen sei. Jack wollte es ihnen wahrheitsgemäß erklären, entschied sich jedoch im letzten Moment anders; schließlich hatte er als Mönch den Dombau zu Kingsbridge de facto geleitet, und Baupläne zeichnen konnte er ebenso gut wie Tom. Er verriet also nicht, daß er in Wirklichkeit gar kein Meister war – mit der Folge, daß der Baumeister, der ihn angeheuert hatte, fortan einen möglichen Rivalen in ihm sah.

Eines Tages schlug Jack dem für den Bau verantwortlichen Mönch eine kleine Änderung vor und verdeutlichte sie mittels einer Skizze.

Von Stund an hatte er keine Ruhe mehr – der Baumeister war nun endgültig davon überzeugt, Jack wolle ihn um seine Stellung bringen. An allem, was Jack tat, fand er etwas auszusetzen, und schließlich durfte Jack nur noch Quadersteine zuschneiden – eine höchst eintönige Aufgabe, die ihn bald weitertrieb.

Diesmal zog er nach Osten, nach Cluny. Die dortige Benediktinerabtei war das Mutterhaus eines klösterlichen Imperiums, das in der gesamten christlichen Welt vertreten war. Der Kluniazenserorden hatte die mittlerweile berühmte Wallfahrt zum Grab des heiligen Jakob in Santiago de Compostela angeregt und gefördert. Entlang der Pilgerstraßen nach Santiago gab es überall Kirchen, die dem heiligen Jakob geweiht waren, und kluniazensische Klöster, die sich der Wallfahrer annahmen. Und da Jacks Vater Spielmann an der Pilgerstraße gewesen war, lag der Schluß nahe, er könne ebenfalls in Cluny gewesen sein.

Diese Vermutung erwies sich indes als Trugschluß. In Cluny gab es überhaupt keine Spielleute, und Jack konnte nichts über seinen Vater in Erfahrung bringen.

Umsonst war die Reise dennoch nicht. Hatte Jack bisher nur halbkreisförmige Bogen gesehen und waren alle Gewölbe, die er kannte, entweder tunnelförmig – wie eine lange Reihe hintereinandergesetzter Rundbogen – oder, wenn sich zwei Tunnel trafen und ein Kreuzrippengewölbe entstand, gerippt gewesen, so sah es in Cluny anders aus.

Dort liefen die Bogen spitz aus.

Alle großen Bogengänge waren mit Spitzbogen versehen; die Kreuzgewölbe der Seitenchöre hatten Spitzbogen, und was das Verblüffendste war: Über dem Mittelschiff erhob sich eine Steindecke, die sich nur als spitzes Tonnengewölbe beschreiben ließ. Jack hatte von Jugend auf gelernt, ein Kreis sei »stark«, weil er *perfekt* war, und ein Rundbogen sei stark, weil er Teil eines Kreises war. Hätte er je darüber nachgedacht, so hätte er Spitzbogen für »schwach« gehalten. Tatsächlich aber waren die Spitzbogen, wie Jack von den Mönchen erfuhr, erheblich tragfähiger als die alten Rundbogen. Die Kirche in Cluny lieferte den Beweis, denn trotz des großen Gewichtes seiner spitz zulaufenden Steindecke war der Bau auch noch sehr hoch.

Lange hielt sich Jack in Cluny nicht auf. Er folgte nun der Pilgerstraße gen Süden und Westen, wich aber nach Lust und Laune von ihr ab. Es war Frühsommer, und an allen Pilgerwegen, in jeder größeren Stadt und bei den Kluniazenser-Klöstern fanden sich Spielleute und Troubadoure. Vor Kirchen und Kapellen unterhielten sich die Pilgerscharen mit Rezitationen und Liedern, und manche begleiteten ihren Vortrag auf der Viola. Es war genauso, wie Aliena es ihm erzählt hatte. Jack sprach jeden einzelnen an und fragte, ob er einen gewissen Jack Shereburg gekannt hätte. Keiner sagte ja.

Die Kirchen, die er auf seinem Weg durch den Südwesten Frankreichs und den Norden Spaniens zu sehen bekam, versetzten ihn ein ums andere Mal in Erstaunen. Sie waren ohne Ausnahme viel höher als englische Kathedralen. Manche der tonnenförmigen Deckengewölbe waren mit Querbändern versehen, die von Pfeiler zu Pfeiler reichten. Diese Einteilung machte es möglich, eine Kirche abschnittweise zu bauen, also Joch um Joch. Und sie veränderte das Aussehen einer Kirche. Die Hervorhebung der einzelnen Bauabschnitte zeigte, daß der ganze Bau aus einer Reihe vollkommen gleicher Einheiten bestand – wie ein in Scheiben geschnittenes Brot. Der gewaltige Innenraum erhielt dadurch eine logisch gegliederte Einteilung.

Jack traf im Hochsommer in Santiago ein. Die Hitze war gewaltig – nie hätte er geglaubt, daß es irgendwo auf der Welt derartig heiß werden konnte! Auch die Kathedrale von Santiago war atemberaubend, und das Tonnengewölbe des noch im Bau befindlichen Langhauses war ebenfalls mit Querbändern versehen.

Von hier aus zog Jack gen Süden.

Die Königreiche Spaniens hatten lange Zeit unter maurischer Herrschaft gestanden, und in den Gebieten südlich von Toledo waren die Muselmanen noch immer tonangebend. Jack war schlichtweg begeistert von der maurischen Bauweise, ihren hohen, kühlen Innenräumen, den Bogengängen und den im Sonnenlicht blendend weißen Mauern. Am meisten jedoch fesselte ihn die Entdeckung, daß die Sarazenen sowohl Rippen- als auch Spitzbogen verwendeten. Ob sich die Franzosen hier ihre Anregungen geholt hatten?

An einer Kirche wie dem Dom zu Kingsbridge werde ich nie wieder arbeiten können, dachte Jack. Er saß in der warmen spanischen Nachmittagssonne und achtete kaum auf das Gelächter der Frauen, das aus dem Inneren des großen, kühlen Hauses an sein Ohr drang. Noch immer wollte er die schönste Kathedrale der Welt bauen – und die würde gewiß nichts mehr mit den in England üblichen soliden, ja festungsähnlichen Gemäuern zu tun haben. Er wollte neue Ideen und Methoden anwenden, Rippengewölbe und Spitzbogen. Dabei dachte er nicht daran, das bisher Gesehene einfach zu kopieren. In keiner der Kirchen, die er studiert hatte, hatte man die neuen Möglichkeiten optimal genutzt. Vor seinem geistigen Auge formte sich das Bild eines Doms. Die Einzelheiten waren noch verschwommen, der Gesamteindruck jedoch klar: ein raumgreifender, luftiger Bau, durch dessen hohe Fenster das Sonnenlicht strömte und dessen Gewölbe so hoch war, daß es bis an den Himmel zu reichen schien.

»Josef und Raya werden ein Haus brauchen«, sagte Raschid unvermittelt. »Wenn Ihr es baut, werden gewiß weitere Aufträge folgen.«

Jack erschrak. An den Bau einfacher Wohnhäuser hatte er bisher niemals gedacht. »Meint Ihr denn, sie sind damit einverstanden, daß ich ihr Haus baue?« fragte er.

»Das könnte durchaus sein.«

Erneut machte sich Schweigen breit, und Jack dachte schon an eine Zukunft als Baumeister für die reichen Kaufleute von Toledo.

Dann schien Raschid endgültig aufzuwachen. Er setzte sich auf und öffnete die Augen. »Ich mag Euch, Jack«, sagte er. »Ihr seid ein ehrenwerter Mann, und ein Gespräch mit Euch ist immer ein Gewinn, was weit mehr ist, als sich über die meisten Leute in meiner Bekanntschaft sagen läßt. Ich hoffe, wir werden auf alle Zeiten gute Freunde werden.«

»Das hoffe ich auch«, erwiderte Jack ein wenig überrascht über die unerwartete Lobpreisung.

»Ich bin Christ, daher schließe ich meine Frauen nicht weg, wie es manche meiner muselmanischen Brüder tun. Aber ich bin auch Araber, und das heißt, daß ich ihnen nicht so viele ... vergebt mir: Zügellosigkeiten gestatte, wie sie anderen Frauen erlaubt sein mögen. In meinem Hause können sie meine männlichen Gäste kennenlernen und mit ihnen sprechen. Ich habe auch nichts dagegen, wenn sich hie und da eine Freundschaft entwickelt. Doch sobald sich die Freundschaft vertieft, wie es zwischen jungen Menschen ganz natürlich ist, erwarte ich von dem jungen Mann, daß er sich an die Gepflogenheiten hält. Alles andere müßte ich als Beleidigung auffassen.«

»Selbstverständlich«, sagte Jack.

»Ich wußte, daß Ihr mich richtig verstehen würdet.« Raschid erhob sich und legte eine Hand auf Jacks Schulter – eine Geste der Zuneigung. »Leider bin ich nicht mit einem Sohn gesegnet. Hätte ich einen, so wäre er Euch sicher ähnlich.«

»Aber dunkler, will ich hoffen«, gab Jack schlagfertig zurück.

Einen Moment lang sah Raschid ihn verständnislos an, dann brach er in brüllendes Gelächter aus, das die anderen Gäste im Innenhof aufschrecken ließ. »Richtig!« japste er erheitert. »Dunkler!« Dann verschwand er, noch immer prustend vor Lachen, im Innern des Hauses.

Die älteren Gäste begannen sich zu verabschieden. Jack saß allein in der kühler werdenden Nachmittagsluft und überdachte, was Raschid ihm gleichsam durch die Blume zu verstehen gegeben hatte. Kein Zweifel, es war ein Angebot gewesen: Wenn er, Jack, Ayscha heiratete, so war Raschid gewillt, ihn als Baumeister für die Reichen in Toledo ins Geschäft zu bringen. Auch die Warnung war unmißverständlich: Wenn er Ayscha nicht heiraten wollte, so sollte er sich künftig von ihr fernhalten. Die Manieren der Spanier mochten geschliffener sein als die der Engländer – doch wenn es nötig war, wußten sie ihre Meinung durchaus deutlich zu machen.

Als Jack nun genauer über das Ganze nachdachte, fand er es beinahe unglaublich. Bin das wirklich ich, dachte er, Jack Jackson, Bastard eines Gehenkten, aufgewachsen im Walde, Steinmetzlehrling und entflohener Mönch? Hat man tatsächlich *mir* angeboten, die schöne Tochter eines reichen arabischen Kaufmanns zu heiraten, und will mir obendrein noch meinen Lebensunterhalt als Baumeister in dieser Stadt der Düfte sichern? Es klingt zu schön, um wahr zu sein! Und dabei mag ich das Mädchen sogar!

Langsam ging die Sonne unter. Der Innenhof lag bereits im Schatten. Unter der Arkade saßen nur noch zwei Personen – er selbst und Josef. Gerade, als Jack sich zu fragen begann, ob dahinter vielleicht ein Plan steckte, tauchten – wie als Beweis für seine Vermutung – Raya und Ayscha auf. Trotz ihrer strengen Ansichten über zärtliche Beziehungen zwischen jungen Mädchen und jungen Männern wußte ihre Mutter mit Sicherheit genau, was vor sich ging – und Raschid vermutlich ebenfalls. Sie gewährten den Verliebten ein paar Momente der Zweisamkeit, doch ehe es ernst werden konnte, würde die Mutter auch schon im Innenhof erscheinen, die Erzürnte spielen und die Mädchen ins Haus schicken.

Raya stürzte sich sofort in Josefs Arme. Eng umschlungen fingen die beiden an, sich zu küssen. Als Ayscha auf ihn zukam, stand Jack auf. Sie trug ein bodenlanges weißes Kleid aus Kattun – ein Stoff, der aus Ägypten kam und den Jack erst in Spanien kennengelernt hatte; er war weicher als Wolle und glatter als Leinen. Bei jeder Bewegung schmiegte er sich um Ayschas Glieder, und seine weiße Farbe schien im Dämmerlicht zu leuchten. Ihre braunen Augen wirkten dadurch beinahe schwarz. Sie blieb vor Jack stehen und grinste wie ein Kobold. »Was hat er zu dir gesagt?« fragte sie.

Jack erriet, daß sie ihren Vater meinte. »Er bot mir an, mich als Baumeister ins Geschäft zu bringen.«

»Was für eine schäbige Mitgift!« rief sie erbost. »Ich kann es kaum glauben! Er hätte dir wenigstens auch Geld anbieten können!«

Die traditionelle arabische Umschweifigkeit lag Ayscha nicht, dazu war sie zu ungeduldig. Jack fand ihre Offenheit erfrischend. »Eigentlich mag ich keine Häuser bauen«, sagte er.

Mit einemmal wurde sie ernst. »Magst du mich?«

»Das weißt du doch.«

Sie machte einen Schritt vorwärts, hob den Kopf, schloß die Augen, stellte sich auf die Zehenspitzen und küßte ihn. Ein Duft nach Ambra und Moschus umfing ihn. Sie öffnete den Mund und stieß ihre Zunge spielerisch zwischen seine Lippen. Seine Arme legten sich beinahe ohne eigenes Zutun um sie, und er ließ die Hände auf ihrer Taille ruhen. Der Kattun war sehr dünn – Jack kam es vor, als berühre er ihre bloße Haut. Sie nahm seine Hand und führte sie zu ihrer Brust. Ihr Körper war schlank und straff und ihre Brust flach, ein kleiner fester Hügel mit einer winzigen harten Spitze. Ihr Brustkorb hob und senkte sich – sie war erregt.

Dann spürte Jack erschrocken, wie sich ihre Hand zwischen seine Schenkel schob. Hart drückte er den Brustnippel zwischen seinen Fingerspitzen. Ayscha japste auf und machte sich schwer atmend von ihm frei. Jack ließ die Hände sinken.

»Hab' ich dir weh getan?« flüsterte er.

»Nein!« antwortete sie.

Unwillkürlich mußte er an Aliena denken und fühlte sich schuldig, doch dann erkannte er, wie dumm das war. Wie sollte er eine Frau betrügen können, die einen anderen *geheiratet* hatte?

Ayscha sah ihm ins Gesicht. Es war schon beinahe dunkel, er konnte das Verlangen sehen, das sich in ihrem Gesicht spiegelte. Sie griff nach seiner Hand und legte sie wieder auf ihre Brust. »Mach das noch mal, aber fester«, drängte sie.

Er fand ihre Brustwarze und neigte sich vor, um sie zu küssen, doch sie bog den Kopf zurück und betrachtete sein Gesicht, während er sie streichelte. Sanft nahm er die Brustwarze zwischen die Finger, dann drückte er – wunschgemäß – fest zu. Sie bog ihren Rücken durch, so daß die kleinen Brüste vorstanden und ihre Brustspitzen sich wie kleine, harte Punkte durch den Stoff drückten. Jack neigte den Kopf, dann biß er, einer Augenblickseingebung folgend, zu. Er hörte, wie Ayscha heftig Luft holte.

Dann spürte er, wie ein Schauder ihren Körper durchlief. Sie nahm seinen Kopf von ihrer Brust, drängte sich an ihn, zog ihn wie wild an sich und küßte ihn so ungestüm, als wolle sie sein ganzes Gesicht mit ihrem Mund bedecken. Kurze, unbeherrschte Laute entrangen sich ihrer Kehle. Jack war erregt, verwirrt und sogar ein wenig erschreckt: So etwas hatte er noch nie erlebt. Schon glaubte er, sie wolle kommen, gleich hier, an Ort und Stelle – doch da wurden sie gestört.

»Raya! Ayscha!« schallte die Stimme der Mutter über den Hof. »Kommt sofort herein!«

Ayscha sah ihn an. Sie rang noch immer nach Atem. Dann küßte sie ihn noch einmal und preßte dabei ihre Lippen so fest auf die seinen, daß es ihm weh tat. Erst danach trat sie zurück. »Ich liebe dich!« flüsterte sie atemlos – machte kehrt und lief ins Haus.

Jack sah ihr nach, sah, wie Raya ihr mit ruhigeren Schritten folgte. Die Mutter funkelte ihn und Josef entrüstet an, bevor sie den Mädchen ins Haus folgte und die Tür mit unnachahmlicher Bestimmtheit hinter sich schloß. Jack starrte ihr eine Weile lang wie blind nach und fragte sich, was er von alledem halten sollte.

Dann kam Josef quer über den Hof auf ihn zu und setzte seiner Träumerei ein Ende. »Wie wunderschön die beiden sind«, sagte er und zwinkerte verschwörerisch mit den Augen.

Jack nickte geistesabwesend und wandte sich dem Hoftor zu; Josef folgte ihm. Kaum hatten sie den Torbogen durchschritten, tauchte schattengleich ein Diener aus dem Dunkel und verschloß hinter ihnen das Tor.

»So schön Verlobtsein ist«, sagte Josef, »eins ist von Übel: Wenn du heimgehst, hast du Schmerzen zwischen den Beinen.« Jack gab keine Antwort. »Vielleicht wird Fatima mich davon befreien«, fuhr Josef fort. Bei Fatima war das Hurenhaus, in dem trotz des arabischen Namens die meisten Mädchen hellhäutig waren; die wenigen maurischen Huren waren überaus teuer. »Kommt Ihr mit?« fragte Josef.

»Nein«, gab Jack zurück, »ich habe anderswo Schmerzen. Gute Nacht.« Rasch ging er seiner Wege. Für Josef hatte er selbst in bester Stimmung nicht viel übrig – und heute stand ihm der Sinn schon gar nicht nach dessen Gesellschaft.

Während er eilends auf das Kollegium zuschritt, wo ihm im Dormitorium ein hartes Bett zur Verfügung stand, kühlte sich die Abendluft spürbar ab. Jack hatte das Gefühl, an einem Wendepunkt angekommen zu sein. Vor ihm lag ein Leben in Wohlstand und ohne Mühsal – unter zwei Voraussetzungen: Er mußte Aliena vergessen und sich die Idee, die schönste Kathedrale der Welt zu bauen, ein für allemal aus dem Kopf schlagen.

In dieser Nacht träumte ihm von einer nackten Ayscha, die zu ihm kam, den Körper in duftenden Ölen gebadet. Verlangend rieb sie sich an ihm, doch *sein* Verlangen wollte sie nicht stillen.

Als er am Morgen erwachte, hatte er seinen Entschluß gefaßt.

Die Diener wollten Aliena nicht in Raschid Al-Haruns Haus einlassen. Wahrscheinlich sehe ich aus wie eine Bettlerin, dachte sie, die in staubiger Tunika und abgetragenen Stiefeln vor dem Tor stand, ihr Kind auf dem Arm. »Sagt Raschid Al-Harun, daß ich seinen englischen Freund Jack Fitzjack suche«, sagte sie auf französisch, nicht wissend, ob die dunkelhäutigen Bediensteten auch nur ein Wort davon verstanden. Nach einer gemurmelten Beratung in einer ihr fremden Sprache verschwand einer der Diener, ein hochgewachsener Mann mit kohlschwarzer Haut und einem Haarschopf wie das Vlies eines schwarzen Schafs, im Haus.

Aliena trat unruhig von einem Fuß auf den anderen, wobei die verbliebenen Diener sie unverhohlen anstarrten. Nicht einmal auf dieser endlosen Wallfahrt hatte sie gelernt, sich in Geduld zu üben. Nach der Enttäuschung in Santiago de Compostela war sie der Straße gefolgt, die ins Herz Spaniens führte, nach Salamanca. Auch dort konnte sich niemand an einen rothaarigen jungen Mann erinnern, der sich für Kathedralen und Spielleute interessierte, doch ein freundlicher Mönch erzählte ihr von dem Kollegium englischer Scholaren in Toledo. Sehr vielversprechend hörte sich das nicht an, aber Toledo lag nicht mehr allzu weit entfernt, und so ritt sie weiter.

Der quälenden Enttäuschungen war kein Ende. Ja, Jack war in Toledo gewesen – welch ein Glück! –, aber leider, leider hatte er es schon wieder verlassen. Immerhin – allmählich holte sie auf: Jack war ihr nur noch einen Monat voraus. Aber wiederum wußte niemand zu sagen, wohin er sich gewandt hatte.

In Santiago hatte sie erraten können, daß er nach Süden gezogen war, denn sie selber war aus dem Osten gekommen, und sowohl im Norden wie im Westen wurde die Pilgerstadt vom Meer begrenzt. In Toledo jedoch gab es unglücklicherweise viel mehr Möglichkeiten: Jack konnte sich nach Nordosten, gen Frankreich, gewandt haben oder nach Westen, Richtung Portugal. Vielleicht war er auch nach Granada im Süden gezogen oder hatte an der spanischen Küste ein Schiff nach Rom, Tunis, Alexandria oder Beirut bestiegen.

Aliena hatte beschlossen, die Suche aufzugeben, wenn sie in Toledo keinen brauchbaren Hinweis auf Jacks nächstes Ziel erhielt. Sie war bis auf die Knochen erschöpft und endlos weit von zu Hause fort. Nur um einer schwachen Hoffnung willen den Weg fortzusetzen – dazu fühlte sie sich zu entkräftet. In diesem Fall würde sie lieber nach England zurückkehren und versuchen, Jack endgültig zu vergessen.

Ein weiterer Diener erschien. Er war besser gekleidet als der erste und sprach Aliena höflich auf französisch an: »Ihr seid eine Bekannte von Monsieur Jack?«

»Ja, eine alte Freundin aus England. Ich würde gern Raschid Al-Harun sprechen.«

Der Diener warf einen Blick auf das Kind, und Aliena fügte rasch hinzu: »Ich bin mit Jack verwandt.« Das war nicht einmal gelogen – sie war immerhin, auch wenn sie sich inzwischen entfremdet hatten, die Ehefrau von Jacks Stiefbruder, und das war gewiß eine Art Verwandtschaft.

Der Diener machte das Tor weit auf und sagte: »Wenn Ihr mir bitte folgen wollt.«

Dankbar folgte Aliena ihm. Hätte man sie hier abgewiesen, wäre ihre Suche beendet gewesen.

Zunächst ging es durch einen schönen Innenhof, vorbei an einem plätschernden Springbrunnen. Was mochte Jack dazu bewogen haben, in diesem Hause zu verkehren? Hatte er vielleicht hier unter den schattigen Arkaden gesessen und seine Versepen für Raschid Al-Harun rezitiert?

Das Haus selbst – mit seinen hohen, kühlen Räumen, seinen Fußböden aus Stein und Marmor und den wunderbar geschnitzten, üppig gepolsterten Möbeln – war fast ein Palast. Sie schritten durch zwei Torbogen und eine hölzerne Tür, und schließlich hatte Aliena das Gefühl, sich in den Frauengemächern zu befinden. Der Diener bedeutete ihr mit erhobener Hand, zu warten; dann hüstelte er leise.

Einen Augenblick später glitt eine große, schwarzgewandete Sarazenin in den Raum. Sie griff nach einem Zipfel ihres Kleides und hielt ihn sich vor den Mund – eine Geste, die in jeder Sprache der Welt eine Beleidigung war. Dann sah sie Aliena an und fragte auf französisch: »Wer bist du?«

Aliena richtete sich zu voller Größe auf. »Ich bin Lady Aliena, Tochter des verstorbenen Grafen von Shiring«, gab sie in denkbar hochmütigem Tonfall zur Antwort. »Ich nehme an, ich habe das Vergnügen, mit der Gattin des Pfefferhändlers Raschid zu sprechen?« *Dieses* Spiel beherrschte sie ebensogut wie die andere.

»Was wollt Ihr hier?«

»Ich wünsche, Raschid zu sprechen.«

»Er ist für Frauen nicht zu sprechen.«

Aliena wurde klar, daß von dieser Frau keine Hilfsbereitschaft zu erwarten war. Aber an wen hätte sie sich sonst wenden können? Sie versuchte es noch einmal. »Vielleicht empfängt er eine Freundin von Jack.«

»Ist Jack Euer Ehemann?«

»Nein.« Aliena zögerte. »Er ist mein Schwager.«

Die Frau nahm ihr das nicht ab. Wahrscheinlich vermutete sie, wie die meisten Leute, Jack habe Aliena geschwängert und dann im Stich gelassen, und nun verfolge sie ihn mit dem Ziel, ihn zur Heirat zu zwingen und für ihr Kind sorgen zu lassen.

Die Frau drehte sich um und rief etwas in einer Sprache, die Aliena nicht verstand, und gleich darauf kamen drei junge Mädchen ins Zimmer. Ihrem Aussehen nach waren sie die Töchter der Sarazenin. Alle vier gafften Aliena an, die von ihrer Unterhaltung nichts weiter mitbekam als das Wörtchen *Jack*. Das kam allerdings ziemlich häufig vor.

Aliena fühlte sich gedemütigt. Am liebsten hätte sie auf dem Absatz kehrtgemacht und die Frauen einfach stehengelassen. Aber diese schlimmen Menschen hier waren ihre letzte Hoffnung. Sie räusperte sich, unterbrach die Unterhaltung und fragte: »Wo ist Jack?« Es hatte laut und deutlich herauskommen sollen, klang aber zu ihrer eigenen Bestürzung recht kläglich.

Die Töchter schwiegen. Ihre Mutter sagte: »Wir wissen nicht, wo er sich aufhält.«

»Wann habt Ihr ihn zum letztenmal gesehen?«

Die Frau zögerte. Sie hätte wohl am liebsten keine Antwort gegeben. »Am Tag nach Weihnachten hat er Toledo verlassen«, gab sie widerwillig Auskunft.

Aliena zwang sich zu einem freundlichen Lächeln. »Wißt Ihr auch noch, *wohin* er gehen wollte?«

»Ich sagte bereits, daß wir nicht wissen, wo er sich aufhält.«

»Vielleicht hat er es Eurem Gatten mitgeteilt.«

»Nein, auf keinen Fall.«

Aliena war nahe daran zu verzweifeln. Sie spürte genau, daß diese Frau mehr wußte, als sie ihr verriet, und fest entschlossen war, ihr Wissen für sich zu behalten. Sie hatte das Gefühl, alle Kräfte wollten sie verlassen. Mit Tränen in den Augen sagte sie: »Jack ist der Vater meines Kindes. Glaubt Ihr nicht auch, er würde seinen Sohn gern sehen?«

Die jüngste der drei Töchter wollte etwas erwidern, doch ihre Mutter hieß sie schweigen. Ein kurzer, heftiger Wortwechsel folgte – Mutter und Tochter hatten das gleiche feurige Temperament. Am Ende hielt die Tochter den Mund.

Aliena wartete, doch es fiel kein Wort mehr. Die vier starrten sie nur an. Ihre Feindseligkeit war unverkennbar, doch ihre Neugier war so groß, daß sie es unterließen, Aliena zum Gehen aufzufordern. Sie selbst sah keinen Sinn darin, noch länger zu bleiben. Am besten kehre ich in meine Unterkunft zurück und bereite mich auf den langen Heimweg nach Kingsbridge vor, dachte sie. Sie holte tief Luft und sagte mit ruhiger, kühler Stimme: »Ich danke Euch für Eure Gastfreundschaft.«

Die Mutter besaß immerhin soviel Anstand, ein etwas beschämtes Gesicht zu machen. Erhobenen Hauptes verließ Aliena das Zimmer.

Draußen drückte sich der Diener herum. Er paßte seine Schritte den ihren an und eskortierte sie durch das Haus. Aliena mußte blinzeln, um die Tränen zurückzuhalten. Der Gedanke, daß ihre lange, anstrengende Suche nur an der Bosheit dieser einen Frau zu scheitern drohte, war ihr unerträglich.

Der Diener führte sie über den Innenhof. Als sie das Tor erreichten, vernahm Aliena hastige Schritte hinter sich. Sie drehte sich um, sah die jüngste Tochter auf sich zulaufen und blieb abwartend stehen. Dem Diener war sichtlich nicht wohl in seiner Haut.

Das Mädchen war klein, schlank und überaus hübsch. Es hatte eine goldbraune Haut und dunkle, beinahe schwarze Augen. Es trug ein weißes Kleid, bei dessen Anblick Aliena sich schmutzig und ungewaschen vorkam. »Liebt Ihr ihn?« platzte das Mädchen in gebrochenem Französisch heraus.

Aliena zögerte. Dann erkannte sie, daß von ihrer Würde ohnehin nichts mehr übriggeblieben war. »Ja, ich liebe ihn«, gestand sie.

»Liebt er Euch auch?«

Aliena wollte die Frage schon bejahen, als ihr klar wurde, daß sie Jack schon über ein Jahr lang nicht mehr gesehen hatte. »Früher hat er mich geliebt«, sagte sie.

»Ich glaube, er liebt Euch noch immer«, gab das Mädchen zurück.

»Wie kommt Ihr darauf?«

Die Augen des Mädchens füllten sich mit Tränen. »Ich wollte ihn selber haben. Und ich hätte ihn beinahe bekommen.« Sie sah das Kind an. »Rote Haare und blaue Augen.« Tränen rannen über ihre glatten, gebräunten Wangen.

Aliena starrte sie an. Das also war die Erklärung für den frostigen Empfang! Die Mutter hätte Jack gerne zum Schwiegersohn gehabt! Das Mädchen konnte kaum älter als sechzehn sein, wirkte aufgrund ihrer frühreifen Sinnlichkeit jedoch älter. Aliena fragte sich, was zwischen den beiden vorgegangen war. »Ihr hättet ihn *beinahe* bekommen, sagt Ihr?«

»Ja«, kam die trotzige Antwort. »Ich wußte, daß er mich mochte. Als er fortging, hat es mir das Herz gebrochen. Aber jetzt ist mir alles klar.« Nun verlor sie doch die Fassung, und ihr Gesicht verzog sich kummervoll.

Mit einer Frau, die Jack geliebt und doch verloren hatte, konnte Aliena nur Mitgefühl empfinden. Unwillkürlich legte sie dem Mädchen die Hand auf die Schulter, als wolle sie es trösten. Doch dann fiel ihr ein, daß es Wichtigeres gab als Mitleid. »Hört!« sagte sie in drängendem Tonfall. »Wißt Ihr vielleicht, wohin er gezogen ist?«

Das Mädchen sah auf und nickte schluchzend.

»Sagt es mir!«

»Nach Paris«, kam die Antwort.

Nach Paris!

Aliena hätte jubeln können. Sie war wieder auf der richtigen Fährte! Paris war zwar weit weg, aber ein Gutteil des Weges war ihr schon vertraut. Und Jack war ihr nur einen Monat voraus! Sie fühlte sich geradezu verjüngt. Ich finde ihn doch noch, dachte sie, ich weiß es ganz genau!

»Werdet Ihr jetzt nach Paris ziehen?« fragte das Mädchen.

»O ja!« erklärte Aliena. »Ich bin ihm nun schon so weit nachgereist – jetzt gebe ich nicht mehr auf. Ich danke Euch, daß Ihr es mir gesagt habt – ich danke Euch vielmals!«

»Ich möchte, daß er glücklich wird«, war die einfache Antwort.

Der Diener trat mißmutig von einem Fuß auf den anderen. Er zog ein Gesicht, als befürchte er, dieses Zwischenspiel könne ihn seine Stellung kosten. Aliena fragte das Mädchen: »Hat Jack noch irgend etwas gesagt? Welche Route er einschlagen wollte – oder irgend etwas anderes, das mir weiterhelfen könnte?«

»Er wollte nach Paris, weil ihm jemand erzählt hat, dort würden wunderschöne Kirchen gebaut.«

Aliena nickte. Das war nichts Neues für sie.

»Und er hat die weinende Frau mitgenommen.«

»Die weinende Frau?« Aliena wußte nicht, was sie davon halten sollte.

»Mein Vater hat ihm die weinende Frau geschenkt.«

»Tatsächlich eine Frau?«

Das Mädchen schüttelte den Kopf. »Ich weiß nicht die richtigen Worte dafür. Eine Frau. Sie weint. Mit den Augen.«

»Ihr meint ein Bild? Eine gemalte Frau?«

»Das verstehe ich nicht.« Das Mädchen blickte sich jetzt ängstlich um. »Ich muß gehen.«

Wer oder was die weinende Frau auch sein mochte – die Geschichte klang nicht, als sei sie von besonderer Bedeutung. »Ich danke Euch vielmals für Eure Hilfe«, sagte Aliena.

Das Mädchen beugte sich vor und küßte Alienas Kind auf die Stirn. Ihre Tränen netzten seine runden Pausbäckchen. Dann blickte sie Aliena in die Augen. »Ich wünschte, ich wäre Ihr«, sagte sie, drehte sich um und lief ins Haus zurück.

Jacks Unterkunft lag in der Rue de la Boucherie in einem Vorort von Paris, am linken Ufer der Seine. Bei Tagesanbruch sattelte er sein Pferd, wandte sich am Ende der Straße nach rechts und passierte das Brückentor zum Petit Pont, der auf die Ile de la Cité führte.

Die Holzhäuser zu beiden Seiten ragten weit über den Rand der Brücke hinaus. Zwischen den Häusern standen Steinbänke, an denen am späteren Vormittag berühmte Lehrer ihren Unterricht im Freien erteilen würden.

Die Brücke führte Jack direkt zur Juiverie, der Hauptstraße der Insel, deren zahlreiche Bäckereien bereits voller Studenten waren. Sie besorgten sich dort ihr Frühstück. Jack erstand eine mit gekochtem Aal gefüllte Pastete.

Gegenüber der Synagoge wandte er sich nach links, am Königspalast wieder nach rechts und überquerte schließlich den Grand Pont, der zum rechten Seineufer führte. Die Goldschmiede und Geldwechsler auf der Brücke öffneten gerade ihre hübsch gebauten Lädchen. Jack passierte ein weiteres Brückenhaus und kam zum Fischmarkt, auf dem es schon überaus geschäftig zuging. Er drängte sich durch die Menge und fand die schlammige Straße, die nach dem Städtchen Saint-Denis führte.

Von einem Maurergesellen auf der Walz hatte Jack in Spanien erfahren, daß Abt Suger in Saint-Denis eine neue Kirche bauen ließ. Und wo immer er, um sich ein wenig Geld zu verdienen, ein paar Tage lang arbeitete – überall hatte man ihm von Saint-Denis erzählt. Anscheinend kombinierten die Steinmetzen dort bereits die neuen

Techniken, errichteten also sowohl Rippengewölbe als auch Spitzbogen, und erreichten damit erstaunliche Effekte.

Über eine Stunde lang ritt er an Feldern und Weingärten vorbei. Die Straße war ungepflastert, aber mit Meilensteinen gekennzeichnet. Sie führte über den Hügel von Montmartre, auf dem die Ruinen eines römischen Tempels standen, und mitten durch das Dörfchen Clignancourt. Drei Meilen weiter erreichte er die Stadtmauer von Saint-Denis.

Der heilige Dionysius war der erste Bischof von Paris gewesen. Nach seiner Enthauptung auf dem Montmartre hatte er seinen abgeschlagenen Kopf in die Hände genommen und ihn mehrere Meilen weit getragen, bis er schließlich tot umfiel. Eine fromme Frau hatte ihn dort begraben, und über seiner Grabstätte war ein Kloster errichtet worden. Die dazugehörige Kirche war die letzte Ruhestätte der Könige von Frankreich. Suger, der gegenwärtige Abt, war ein mächtiger und ehrgeiziger Mann, der das Kloster reformiert hatte und nun dabei war, die Kirche umzugestalten.

Auf dem Marktplatz von Saint-Denis zügelte Jack sein Pferd und betrachtete die Westfassade der Kirche. Von umwälzenden Neuerungen war hier nichts zu spüren: Es war eine schlichtweg altmodische Kirche mit Zwillingstürmen und drei Rundbogenportalen. Die aggressiv vorstehenden Torpfeiler gefielen ihm nicht schlecht, doch wäre Jack um ihretwillen keine fünf Meilen weit geritten.

Er band sein Pferd an einen Balken und trat näher. Die Skulpturen an den drei Portalen verrieten gute Steinmetzarbeit – lebensechte Figuren, sorgfältig gemeißelt. Jack betrat die Kirche.

Drinnen sah es ganz anders aus. Vor dem eigentlichen Mittelschiff befand sich eine niedrige, Narthex genannte Vorhalle. Als er den Blick zur Decke wandte, erfaßte ihn Erregung: Die Baumeister hatten tatsächlich ein Rippengewölbe mit Spitzbogen kombiniert – und sie paßten, wie Jack blitzartig erkannte, hervorragend zusammen: Die Anmut der Spitzbogen wurde durch die anschließenden Rippen zusätzlich betont.

Aber es gab noch mehr Neuheiten zu sehen. Statt der üblichen Mischung aus Mörtel und Bruchsteinen hatte der Baumeister zur Füllung der Räume zwischen den Rippen zugeschnittene Steine verwendet. Der Vorteil lag darin, daß die Steinschicht – da sie stärker war als das herkömmliche Material – dünner und damit auch leichter sein konnte.

Obwohl ihm allmählich der Nacken weh tat, starrte Jack unverdrossen in die Höhe, bis er Klarheit über einen weiteren bemerkenswerten

Vorzug der neuen Bauweise gewonnen hatte: Die Spitzbogen konnten unterschiedliche Weiten besitzen und dennoch die gleiche Höhe erreichen – man brauchte nichts weiter zu tun, als die Rundung des Bogens entsprechend anzupassen, zu überhöhen. Der Gesamteindruck, der dadurch entstand, war von einer Regelmäßigkeit, die mit Rundbogen nie zu erreichen war, mußte doch die Höhe eines halbkreisförmigen Bogens zwangsläufig der Hälfte seiner Breite entsprechen. Ein weiter Rundbogen mußte also sehr viel höher sein als ein schmaler. Das bedeutete, daß in einem rechteckigen Bauabschnitt oder Joch die schmalen Rundbogen, wenn sie die gleiche Höhe erreichten und die Decke gerade sein sollte, höher ansetzen mußten als die weiten. Die neue Lösung beseitigte dieses Problem.

Jack senkte den Kopf und verschaffte seinem schmerzenden Nacken Erleichterung. Ihm war, als wäre er gerade zum König gekrönt worden. Nach diesem Vorbild, dachte er, werde ich meine Kathedrale auch bauen!

Er wandte sich dem eigentlichen Kirchenraum zu. Das Hauptschiff war zwar ziemlich lang und breit, aber erkennbar alt und mit Gewißheit von einem anderen als dem derzeitigen Baumeister errichtet. In der Vierung allerdings befanden sich Stufen, die zur Krypta und zu den königlichen Grabstätten hinabführten.

Auch zum Altar führte eine kleine Treppe hinauf, wodurch der Eindruck entstand, als schwebe der Altarraum ein Stückchen über dem Boden. Die Bauweise war von Jacks Standort aus nicht genau zu erkennen, da ihn das durch die Ostfenster hereinströmende Sonnenlicht blendete. Es war so grell, daß er vermutete, die Außenmauer sei noch nicht vollendet und lasse daher so viel Licht ein.

Jack schritt das südliche Seitenschiff hinunter auf die Vierung zu. Je näher er dem Altarraum kam, desto deutlicher spürte er, daß er etwas ganz Besonderes entdecken würde. Trotz des einfallenden Sonnenlichts waren weder die Außenmauer noch das Gewölbe durchbrochen. Erst nachdem er aus dem Seitenschiff in die Vierung getreten war, erkannte Jack, woher das viele Sonnenlicht kam: Es schien durch mehrere Reihen hoher Fenster, von denen einige aus Buntglas waren. Die Strahlen füllten das weite, leere Kirchenschiff mit Wärme und Licht. Jack verstand nicht, woher der Baumeister den Platz für die Fenster genommen hatte – es sah aus, als bestünde die Mauer aus mehr Glas denn aus Stein. Überwältigt blieb er stehen. Wie war dieses Wunder entstanden, wenn nicht mit Hilfe von Zauberei?

Ein Anflug abergläubischen Schreckens wollte sich seiner bemächtigen, als er die Stufen zum Altar hinaufstieg. Oben angekommen, starrte er angestrengt in das Durcheinander aus Pfeilern und Steinen und farbigem Licht, das sich vor seinen Augen ausbreitete, bis ihm ganz allmählich dämmerte, daß er schon einmal etwas Ähnliches gesehen hatte, wenngleich nur in seiner Vorstellung: Dies war genau die Kirche, die zu bauen er sich erträumt hatte – mit großzügigen Fenstern und hoher Decke, ein Gebilde aus Licht und Luft, das von schierem Zauber zusammengehalten wurde.

Schon einen Augenblick später sah er es wieder anders. Alles hatte seinen Platz und seine Ordnung, und Jack erkannte in blitzartiger Erleuchtung, was Abbé Suger und sein Baumeister tatsächlich getan hatten.

Das Konstruktionsprinzip eines Rippengewölbes lag darin, daß eine Decke aus wenigen mächtigen Rippen zu bestehen hatte, deren Zwischenräume mit leichtem Baustoff ausgefüllt wurden. *Dieses Prinzip war hier auf die gesamte Kirche angewendet worden!* Die Chorraumwand bestand aus einigen wenigen mächtigen Pfeilern, die mit Fenstern verbunden waren. Die Bogengänge, die den Chorraum von den Seitenschiffen trennten, enthielten überhaupt keine Mauern – eine Reihe von Pfeilern, gekrönt von Spitzbogen, ließ weite Durchlässe für das Licht, so daß es durch die Fenster ungehindert ins Herz der Kirche strömen konnte. Die Seitenschiffe selbst waren jeweils durch eine Reihe schmaler Säulen in zwei Hälften geteilt.

Wie im Narthex waren überhöhte Spitzbogen und Kreuzrippengewölbe auch hier miteinander verbunden worden. Die Vorhalle – soviel erkannte Jack jetzt – war nur ein zaghafter Versuch gewesen; sie wirkte verkrampft, ihre Rippen und Tragsteine zu plump, und die Bogen zu klein. In der Kirche selbst war alles elegant, licht und luftig. Die einfachen Walzenformen waren schmal, die Säulen lang und schlank.

In seiner Gesamtheit wirkte das Gebäude beinahe zu zerbrechlich; man traute ihm kaum Standfestigkeit zu. Die Gewölberippen zeigten indes genau, wie das Gewicht von Stützpfeilern und Säulen getragen wurde – der schlagende Beweis dafür, daß ein großes Gebäude weder dicke Wände noch winzige Fenster noch plumpe Stützpfeiler brauchte. Vorausgesetzt, das Gewicht wurde präzise auf das tragende Skelett verteilt, konnte alles andere aus leichtem Mauerwerk, Glas oder sogar leeren Räumen bestehen. Jack fühlte sich wie verzaubert, wie neu verliebt. Schon Euklid war ihm wie eine Offenbarung vorgekommen; und um wieviel größer und vor allem schöner war dies hier! Bisher hatte er stets nur von einer solchen Kirche *träumen* können – nun

konnte er sie anschauen, anfassen, unter ihrem himmelwärts streben-
den Gewölbe stehen.

Wie betäubt umrundete er die Ostseite, unablässig zum Gewölbe
des Doppelschiffs hinaufstarrend. Die Rippenbogen kreuzten sich über
seinem Kopf wie das Astwerk eines Waldes aus ebenmäßigen steinernen Bäumen. Auch hier waren, wie schon im Narthex, die Zwischenräume der Gewölberippen mit zugeschnittenen Steinen verfugt, die
ihrerseits mit Mörtel zusammengehalten wurden. Man hatte also darauf verzichtet, die leichter herzustellende, aber vom Gewicht her
schwerere Mischung aus Mörtel und Bruchsteinen zu verwenden. Die
Außenmauern des Seitenschiffs enthielten, immer zu zweien gepaart,
große Fenster, die nach oben spitz zuliefen und genau den Spitzbogen
im Kircheninneren entsprachen. Gekrönt wurde diese wahrhaft revolutionäre Bauweise vom bunten Glas der Fenster. In England hatte
Jack kein einziges Mal buntes Glas gesehen, nur in Frankreich hatte
er einige Beispiele studieren können. In den kleinen Fenstern einer
herkömmlich gebauten Kirche konnte Buntglas ohnehin nicht seine
volle Wirkung entfalten. Doch hier, in dieser Kirche mit riesigen viel-
farbigen Fenstern, durch die die Morgensonne hereinstrahlte, war die
Wirkung mehr als nur schön – sie war einfach hinreißend.

Die Seitenschiffe trafen sich im abgerundeten Ostende des Baus
und bildeten dort einen halbkreisförmigen Wendelgang, den Jack,
noch immer ganz verzaubert, abschritt, bevor er zu seinem Ausgangspunkt zurückkehrte.

Dort stand eine Frau.

Er erkannte sie auf Anhieb.

Sie lächelte ihn an, und ihm war, als höre sein Herz auf zu schlagen.

Aliena beschattete ihre Augen mit der Hand. Das Sonnenlicht, das
durch die Ostfenster der Kirche drang, nahm ihr die Sicht. Da trat
aus dem bunten Feuer aus Sonnenstrahlen eine Gestalt, deren Haare
den Kopf umwaberten wie Flammen. Sie kam näher, und Aliena erkannte, daß es Jack war.

Sie fühlte sich einer Ohnmacht nahe.

Jack kam auf sie zu und blieb vor ihr stehen. Er war mager geworden, schrecklich mager, doch seine Augen glänzten vor Begeisterung.
Lange Zeit konnten sie einander nur schweigend ansehen.

Jack fand als erster seine Sprache wieder. »Bist du's wirklich?«
fragte er mit belegter Stimme.

»Ja.« Aliena konnte nur flüstern. »Ja, ich bin's wirklich.«

Ihre Anspannung war so groß, daß sie in Tränen ausbrach. Jack legte die Arme um sie und drückte sie mitsamt dem Kleinen an sich, tätschelte ihren Rücken und machte »Na, na«, als wäre *sie* ein kleines Kind. Aliena lehnte sich an ihn, atmete den vertrauten Steinstaubgeruch, lauschte seiner geliebten Stimme, die tröstliche Worte murmelte, und ließ ihre Tränen auf seine knochige Schulter tropfen.

Schließlich sah er ihr ins Gesicht und fragte: »Was tust du hier?«

»Ich suche dich.«

»Du suchst mich?« wiederholte er ungläubig. »Aber ... Wie hast du mich gefunden?«

Sie wischte sich die Tränen aus den Augen und zog die Nase hoch. »Ich bin deinen Spuren gefolgt.«

»Wie?«

»Ich habe alle möglichen Leute nach dir gefragt. Hauptsächlich Maurer und Steinmetzen, aber auch Mönche und Wirte.«

Er machte große Augen. »Willst du damit sagen, daß du bis nach Spanien gezogen bist?«

Sie nickte. »Nach Santiago, nach Salamanca – bis nach Toledo.«

»Wie lange bist du schon unterwegs?«

»Ein Dreivierteljahr.«

»Aber warum?«

»Weil ich dich liebe.«

Er war überwältigt, und seine Augen füllten sich mit Tränen. Er flüsterte: »Ich liebe dich auch.«

»Wirklich? Immer noch?«

»O ja, immer noch.«

Sie sah ihm an, daß er die Wahrheit sagte, und hob ihm das Gesicht entgegen. Er beugte sich vor, über das Kind, und küßte sie sanft auf den Mund. Die Berührung seiner Lippen machte Aliena schwindeln.

Da weinte das Kind.

Aliena trat zurück und wiegte ihren Sohn in den Armen, bis er sich wieder beruhigt hatte.

»Wie heißt das Kind?« fragte Jack.

»Er hat noch keinen Namen.«

»Wieso nicht? Er muß doch mindestens ein Jahr alt sein!«

»Ich wollte dich erst fragen.«

»Mich?« Jack runzelte die Stirn. »Wieso nicht Alfred? Das ist doch Sache des Vaters ...« Er hielt inne. »Willst du damit sagen, er ist ... es ist mein Kind?«

»Schau ihn dir an.«

Jack betrachtete das Kind. »Rote Haare ... Es muß ein ganzes und ein Dreivierteljahr her sein, daß ...«

Aliena nickte stumm.

»Gütiger Gott!« Er war wie vom Donner gerührt und schluckte. »Mein Sohn!«

Aliena beobachtete ihn voller Bangigkeit, während er die Neuigkeit zu bewältigen suchte. Vielleicht sieht er in dem Kind nur das Ende seiner Jugend und seiner Freiheit? dachte sie. Seine Miene wurde ernst. Gewöhnlich hatte ein Mann neun Monate Zeit, um sich an seine künftige Vaterschaft zu gewöhnen. Jack stand urplötzlich vor vollendeten Tatsachen. Erneut schaute er das Kind an, und endlich lächelte er. »Unser Sohn!« sagte er. »Ich freue mich so!«

Aliena seufzte beglückt auf. Endlich war alles wieder gut!

Jack kam ein ganz neuer Gedanke. »Was ist mit Alfred? Weiß er, da ...«

»Freilich weiß er's. Er brauchte das Kind ja bloß anzusehen. Außerdem ...« Aliena wurde verlegen. »Außerdem hat deine Mutter unsere Ehe mit einem Fluch belegt, und Alfred war niemals fähig – ach, du weißt schon.«

Jack lachte rauh auf. »Es gibt also doch noch Gerechtigkeit«, bemerkte er.

Aliena mißfiel seine offenkundige Schadenfreude. »Für mich war es alles andere als leicht«, sagte sie in leicht vorwurfsvollem Ton.

Sofort wurde er wieder ernst. »Entschuldige«, bat er. »Was hat Alfred denn getan?«

»Er warf einen Blick auf das Kind und schmiß mich hinaus.«

Ärgerlich verzog Jack das Gesicht. »Hat er dir weh getan?«

»Nein.«

»Trotzdem – er ist ein Schwein.«

»Ich bin froh, daß er uns hinausgeworfen hat. Denn deshalb habe ich mich nach einer Weile auf den Weg gemacht, um dich zu suchen. Und endlich habe ich dich gefunden! Ich kann dir gar nicht sagen, wie glücklich ich bin!«

»Du warst ungeheuer mutig«, sagte Jack. »Ich kann's noch immer nicht fassen. Diesen weiten, weiten Weg, den du mir gefolgt bist!«

»Ich würde es sofort wieder tun«, verkündete Aliena feurig.

Jack küßte sie noch einmal. Da sagte jemand auf französisch: »Wenn Ihr schon in der Kirche Unzucht treiben müßt, dann bleibt bitte im Mittelschiff.«

Es war ein junger Mönch. »Verzeiht, Vater«, sagte Jack und nahm Aliena am Arm. Sie schritten die Altarstufen hinunter und entfernten sich durch das südliche Querschiff. »Ich war selber eine Weile lang ein Mönch«, bemerkte Jack. »Ich weiß, wie schwer es für sie ist, mitansehen zu müssen, wie glücklich Liebende sich küssen.«

Glücklich Liebende! dachte Aliena. Genau das sind wir.

Sie verließen die Kirche und traten auf den belebten Marktplatz hinaus. Aliena konnte kaum glauben, daß sie Seite an Seite mit Jack im Sonnenschein stand. Ihr Glück war so groß, daß sie es kaum ertragen konnte.

»Schön«, sagte Jack, »und was tun wir jetzt?«

»Ich weiß nicht«, gab sie lächelnd zur Antwort.

»Wir könnten uns einen Laib Brot besorgen und eine Flasche Wein und dann in die Felder hinausreiten und dort unser Mittagsmahl essen.«

»Das klingt himmlisch.«

Sie gingen zum Bäcker und zum Weinhändler und kauften bei einer Meierin auf dem Marktplatz auch noch ein Stück Käse. Dann bestiegen sie ihre Pferde und ritten zum Dorf hinaus, den Feldern zu. Aliena konnte nicht anders, als ständig zu Jack hinüberzusehen – sie mußte sich einfach vergewissern, daß er wirklich und wahrhaftig bei ihr war, an ihrer Seite ritt, lebte und atmete und lächelte.

»Wie kommt Alfred mit dem Dombau zurecht?« fragte er.

»Oh! Das hab' ich dir ja noch gar nicht erzählt! Es gab ein schreckliches Unglück. Das Dach ist eingestürzt.«

»Was?!« Jacks lauter Ausruf erschreckte sein Pferd derart, daß es beinahe durchgegangen wäre und er es zunächst einmal beruhigen mußte. »Wie konnte das passieren?«

»Das weiß niemand. Sie hatten rechtzeitig für Pfingsten drei Joche überwölbt, und dann kam während des Gottesdienstes alles herunter. Es war grauenvoll! Neunundsiebzig Menschen haben dabei ihr Leben gelassen.«

»Das ist ja entsetzlich!« Jack war erschüttert. »Wie hat Prior Philip das verkraftet?«

»Schlecht. Er hat den Dombau aufgegeben. Er scheint all seine Tatkraft verloren zu haben. Als ich fortging, geschah jedenfalls überhaupt nichts.«

Philip und untätig? Diese Vorstellung fiel Jack schwer. Er hatte den Prior als einen stets begeisterten und entschlossenen Mann in Erinnerung. »Was ist aus den Handwerkern geworden?«

»Sie sind mit der Zeit alle fortgezogen. Alfred wohnt jetzt in Shiring und baut dort Häuser.«

»Kingsbridge muß ja halb entvölkert sein.«

»Es verwandelt sich wieder in das verschlafene Dorf zurück, das es einmal war.«

»Was Alfred wohl falsch gemacht hat?« fragte sich Jack halblaut. »Tom hatte ursprünglich gar keine Steindecke geplant. Alfred hat dann die Strebepfeiler verstärkt, damit sie das Gewicht tragen konnten. Da hätte im Grunde eigentlich nichts schiefgehen dürfen.«

Die bösen Nachrichten aus Kingsbridge dämpften seine Hochstimmung. Schweigend setzten die beiden ihren Ritt fort. Ungefähr eine Meile außerhalb von Saint-Denis banden sie die Pferde im Schatten einer Ulme fest und ließen sich am Ufer eines Bächleins nieder, das an einem grünen Weizenfeld entlangfloß. Jack tat einen tiefen Zug aus der Flasche und schmatzte zufrieden. »England hat nichts zu bieten, was mit französischem Wein zu vergleichen wäre«, meinte er. Er brach das Brot und reichte Aliena ein Stück.

Schüchtern schnürte Aliena ihr Mieder auf und gab ihrem Kind die Brust. Als sie merkte, daß Jack sie dabei beobachtete, wurde sie rot. Um ihre Verlegenheit zu überspielen, stellte sie schnell eine Frage. »Weißt du schon, wie du ihn nennen möchtest? Vielleicht Jack?«

»Ich weiß nicht.« Er blickte nachdenklich vor sich hin. »Jack war der Vater, den ich nie kennengelernt habe. Vielleicht bringt es Unglück, wenn wir den Kleinen nach ihm nennen. Der Mann, der für mich am ehesten einem Vater gleichkam, war Tom Builder.«

»Möchtest du ihn dann Tom nennen?«

»Ich glaube schon.«

»Aber Tom war ein solcher Hüne – wie wär's mit Tommy?«

Jack nickte. »Ja, Tommy. Er soll Tommy heißen.«

Besagter Tommy allerdings war, nachdem er sich satt getrunken hatte, der Bedeutung dieses Augenblicks gegenüber vollkommen unempfindlich – und einfach eingeschlafen. Aliena legte ihn auf den Boden und schob ihm ein zusammengefaltetes Schultertuch als Kissen unter den Kopf. Dann sah sie wieder Jack an. Sie fühlte sich unbehaglich – einerseits wünschte sie sich nichts sehnlicher, als daß er sie liebte, jetzt gleich, hier im Gras, andererseits fürchtete sie, ihn mit einer direkten Aufforderung zu verschrecken. Also sah sie ihn nur stumm an und hoffte.

Schließlich fragte er: »Versprichst du mir, nicht schlecht von mir zu denken, wenn ich dir jetzt etwas verrate?«

»Versprochen.«

Er wirkte verlegen, aber er sagte: »Seit ich dich wiedergesehen habe, kann ich kaum noch an etwas anderes denken als an deinen nackten Körper unter dem Kleid.«

Sie lächelte. »Deshalb denke ich doch nicht schlecht von dir«, sagte sie. »Ich freue mich darüber.« Er starrte sie gierig an, und sie fügte hinzu: »Es gefällt mir, wenn du mich so anschaust.«

Jack schluckte schwer.

Aliena breitete die Arme aus, und er kam zu ihr und umarmte sie.

Fast zwei Jahre waren vergangen, seit sie sich zum ersten und einzigen Male geliebt hatten, und damals hatten sie sich beide von Verlangen und Reue mitreißen lassen. Jetzt waren sie nichts weiter als zwei Liebende in einem Getreidefeld.

Seite an Seite ließen sie sich ins Gras gleiten und küßten sich. Aliena schloß die Augen und öffnete den Mund. Dann spürte sie, wie seine Hand ungeduldig ihren Körper erforschte und wie ihre Lenden zum Leben erwachten. Jack küßte sie sanft auf die Lider und auf die Nasenspitze und murmelte: »Es ist so lange her, und dabei habe ich mich so nach dir gesehnt, jeden Tag nach dir gesehnt.«

Sie zog ihn fest an sich. »Wie bin ich froh, daß ich dich endlich gefunden habe!«

Zärtlich und unbeschwert liebten sie sich auf dem freien Feld, während die Sonne auf sie herabschien und das Bächlein neben ihnen murmelte.

Tommy verschlief das Ereignis. Er wachte erst wieder auf, nachdem seine Eltern Erfüllung gefunden hatten.

Die hölzerne Dame hatte, seit Spanien hinter ihr lag, nicht mehr geweint. Da Jack nicht verstand, wie ihre Tränen zustande kamen, wußte er auch nicht, ob sie außerhalb ihres Heimatlandes überhaupt noch einmal weinen würde. Allerdings hegte er den Verdacht, daß die Tränen, die ihr in Spanien stets bei Einbruch der Nacht gekommen waren, mit der raschen Abkühlung der Luft zu tun hatten; daß die Tränen nun ausblieben, mochte vielleicht an der längeren Abenddämmerung in nördlicheren Gefilden liegen. Von ihr trennen wollte er sich nicht: Sie war eine Erinnerung an Toledo, vor allem an Raschid (und Ayscha, von der er Aliena freilich nichts erzählte). Als aber ein Steinmetz von Saint-Denis ein Modell für ein Standbild der Jungfrau Maria suchte, brachte Jack ihm die hölzerne Dame in seine Bauhütte und ließ sie dort stehen.

Die Abtei hatte ihn eingestellt, und so beteiligte er sich an der Wiederherstellung der Kirche. Der neue Altarraum, der ihn so hingerissen hatte, war noch nicht ganz vollendet und sollte rechtzeitig zur Weihe am Johannistag fertiggestellt werden. Der rührige Abt war indessen schon darauf aus, auch das Mittelschiff dem neuen, revolutionären Baustil anzupassen. Jack erhielt den Auftrag, die Bausteine dafür schon im voraus zu behauen.

Die Abtei vermietete ihnen ein kleines Haus im Dorf. In der ersten Nacht, die sie gemeinsam darin verbrachten, liebten er und Aliena sich nicht weniger als fünfmal – das Zusammenleben als Mann und Frau schien ihnen die natürlichste Sache der Welt. Nach einigen Tagen der Gemeinsamkeit hatte Jack das Gefühl, schon seit eh und je mit Aliena zusammenzuleben. Und niemand fragte sie, ob ihre Vereinigung von der Kirche gesegnet worden sei.

Der Baumeister von Saint-Denis war – mit Abstand! – der beste, den Jack je kennengelernt hatte. Während sie den neuen Hochaltar vollendeten und sich auf den Umbau des Kirchenschiffs vorbereiteten, ließ Jack ihn nicht aus den Augen, verfolgte jede seiner Bewegungen, merkte sich jeden seiner Handgriffe und eignete sich Schritt für Schritt seine Fähigkeiten an.

Abbé Sugers Interesse galt weniger dem Baustil als den Ornamenten, und sein Hauptanliegen war die Schaffung einer neuen Ruhestätte für die sterblichen Überreste des heiligen Dionysius und seiner beiden Begleiter Rusticus und Eleutherius. Suger wollte die Gebeine aus der Krypta in den neuen Altarraum heraufbringen lassen. Ihm schwebte für die drei Särge ein steinernes, mit schwarzem Marmor verkleidetes Grabmal vor, dessen Oberfläche von einer Miniaturkirche aus vergoldetem Holz gekrönt sein sollte; im Mittel- und in den Seitenschiffen dieser Kirche sollten drei leere Särge plaziert werden, für jeden Märtyrer einer. Das Grabmal sollte seinen Platz in der Mitte des neuen Chorraums finden, gleich hinter dem neuen Hochaltar. Sowohl der Altar als auch das Fundament des Grabmals befanden sich bereits an Ort und Stelle und die Miniaturkirche in der Bauhütte der Zimmerleute, wo ein unermüdlicher Handwerker das Holz aufs sorgfältigste mit unschätzbar wertvoller Goldfarbe überzog. Suger war kein Mann der Halbherzigkeiten.

Der Abbé erwies sich bei den Vorbereitungen für die Weihezeremonie als hervorragender Organisator. Alles, was Rang und Namen hatte, wurde geladen, und die meisten nahmen die Einladung an – darunter so hochstehende Persönlichkeiten wie der König und die Königin von

Frankreich sowie neunzehn Erzbischöfe, einschließlich des Erzbischofs von Canterbury.

Solcherlei Neuigkeiten machten natürlich die Runde unter den Bauleuten, die an und in der Kirche arbeiteten. Oft sah Jack Suger in seiner grobgewebten Kutte über das Klostergelände schreiten und seinen Mönchen Instruktionen erteilen. Sie folgten ihm auf Schritt und Tritt wie die Küken einer Glucke. Suger erinnerte Jack an Philip von Kingsbridge. Wie Philip war der Abbé armer Leute Kind und im Kloster aufgewachsen. Wie Philip hatte er die Finanzen des Klosters neu geordnet und die Verwaltung der Klostergüter gestrafft, so daß das Einkommen gewaltig gestiegen war. Und wie Philip verwendete auch Suger jeden überschüssigen Heller auf den Bau seiner Kirche. Er war erfindungsreich, tatkräftig und entscheidungsfreudig – genau wie Philip.

Nur daß Philip, wenn es stimmte, was Aliena behauptete, inzwischen alle diese Eigenschaften verloren hatte.

Jack vermochte es noch immer nicht so recht zu glauben – ein tatenloser Philip kam ihm so unwahrscheinlich vor wie ein urplötzlich zum Menschenfreund gewandelter Waleran Bigod. Allerdings hatte Philip viele schlimme Rückschläge hinnehmen müssen. Zuerst die Feuersbrunst in der Stadt – Jack schauderte heute noch, wenn er sich diesen entsetzlichen Tag in Erinnerung rief, den Rauch, die Angst, die furchtbaren Reiter mit ihren brennenden Pechfackeln, die blinde Panik der Menge. Möglich, daß Philip schon damals der Mut verlassen hatte; der Stadt jedenfalls war damals das Rückgrat gebrochen worden. Jack erinnerte sich noch allzu gut der Furcht und Unsicherheit, die über der Ortschaft lasteten wie Modergeruch. Philip hatte mit dem Weihegottesdienst für den neuen Chorraum gewiß ein Zeichen der Hoffnung setzen wollen – und nach der neuerlichen Katastrophe wohl selbst alle Hoffnung aufgegeben.

Nun waren die Bauleute fort, der Markt kaum noch der Rede wert, die Einwohnerzahl sank. Die jungen Leute – so sagte Aliena – wanderten alle nach Shiring ab. Im Grunde handelte es sich um eine Frage der geistigen Stärke, denn das Kloster verfügte ja immer noch über seine Güter und über seine großen Schafherden, die jedes Jahr Hunderte von Pfund einbrachten. Ginge es nur ums Geld, so hätte Philip seine Bautätigkeit gewiß längst schon wieder aufnehmen können, wenn auch erst nach Überwindung bestimmter Schwierigkeiten: Maurer und Steinmetzen waren oft abergläubisch und arbeiteten nicht gerne an einer Kirche, die schon einmal eingestürzt war. Auch ließ sich die Begeisterung der Bevölkerung für den Bau schwerlich noch einmal zur alten Glut entfachen ... Trotzdem: Der Plan stand und fiel mit Prior Philip, seinem Mut und seinem Einsatz. Jack hätte alles getan, um Philip seinen alten Mut zurückzugeben.

Die Weihezeremonie stand unmittelbar bevor. In Saint-Denis trafen die ersten Gäste ein: Bischöfe, Erzbischöfe, Herzöge und Grafen. Allen Würdenträgern wurde die Kirche von außen und von innen gezeigt. Die wichtigsten Persönlichkeiten geleitete Abbé Suger selbst, die weniger hohen Herrschaften wurden von Mönchen oder Handwerkern geführt. Alle zeigten sich gebührend beeindruckt von der neuen leichten Bauweise und von der Wirkung des Sonnenlichts, das durch die riesigen Buntglasfenster einfiel. Da kaum ein wichtiger Kirchenführer Frankreichs fehlte, kam Jack bald zu der Überzeugung, daß der neue Baustil rasch Schule machen würde – ein Steinmetz, der von sich sagen konnte, er habe in Saint-Denis gearbeitet, würde sich fortan nicht über Arbeitsmangel zu beklagen haben.

Und das galt nicht zuletzt für ihn selbst. Seine Aussichten, selbst einmal eine Kathedrale entwerfen und bauen zu können, stiegen in diesen Tagen ganz gewaltig.

Am Samstag traf König Ludwig in Begleitung seiner Gemahlin und seiner Mutter ein; sie bezogen das Haus des Abtes. In der Nacht zum Sonntag wurden bis zur Morgendämmerung ununterbrochen Messen gesungen. Bis zum Sonnenaufgang hatte sich bereits eine große Menschenmenge vor der Kirche eingefunden – Bürger aus Paris und Bauern von nah und fern –, die nun auf die vermutlich größte Versammlung mächtiger Persönlichkeiten aus Adel und Kirche wartete, die sie je in ihrem Leben zu Gesicht bekommen würden. Nachdem Tommy gestillt war, schlossen sich auch Jack und Aliena der Menge an. Eines Tages, dachte Jack, werde ich zu meinem Sohn sagen können: Du erinnerst dich zwar nicht mehr daran, aber als du gerade ein Jahr alt warst, hast du schon den König von Frankreich gesehen.

Sie hatten sich Brot und Apfelwein mitgebracht und vertrieben sich die Wartezeit vor Beginn der Spektakels mit einem herzhaften Frühstück. Dem Volk war das Betreten der Kirche natürlich untersagt, und dafür, daß dieses Verbot auch eingehalten wurde, sorgten die Waffenträger des Königs. Doch alle Kirchentüren standen weit offen, und wo immer sich ein Blick ins Innere erhaschen ließ, bildeten sich Menschentrauben. Im Mittelschiff drängten sich die Damen und Herren aus dem Adel. Dank der erhöhten Stellung des Altars über der Krypta konnte Jack die Zeremonie verfolgen.

Am anderen Ende des Langhauses rührte sich etwas. Die versammelte Noblesse verneigte sich tief. Über ihre gebeugten Köpfe hinweg sah Jack, wie von Süden her der König die Kirche betrat. Sein Gesicht war auf diese Entfernung nicht zu erkennen, aber die auffallende Farbe seines Purpurmantels kennzeichnete ihn deutlich genug. Er betrat die Vierung und kniete vor dem Hauptaltar nieder.

Unmittelbar darauf erfolgte der Einzug der Bischöfe und Erzbischöfe, alle in goldbestickten, strahlend weißen Gewändern, in den Händen den zeremoniellen Krummstab. Der Krummstab war im Grunde nur ein einfacher Hirtenstab, doch da die meisten von ihnen mit herrlichen Juwelen geschmückt waren, glitzerte die Prozession wie ein Bergbach im Sonnenlicht.

Gemessen schritten sie durch die Kirche und stiegen die Stufen zum Chor empor, wo sie die ihnen bestimmten Sitze um ein Becken einnahmen, in das man während der Vorbereitungen auf das Fest eimerweise Weihwasser geschüttet hatte. Dann wurden Gebete gesprochen und Choräle gesungen. Für die Menge draußen gab es dabei nichts zu sehen, so daß sie unruhig wurde. Auch Tommy begann sich zu langweilen. Schließlich erhoben sich die Bischöfe, und die Prozession setzte sich erneut in Bewegung.

Sie verließen die Kirche durch das Südportal und verschwanden zur Enttäuschung der Menge im Kreuzgang. Später verließen sie den Klosterbereich wieder und zogen in langer Reihe am Hauptportal vorbei. Jeder Bischof trug nun eine kleine Bürste – Weihwedel genannt – sowie einen Weihwasserkessel in den Händen. Singend zogen sie um die Kirche, tauchten die Weihwedel ins Weihwasser und besprenkelten damit die Mauern.

Die Zuschauermenge geriet in Bewegung – alles drängte sich vor, in der Hoffnung auf eine Segnung durch die heiligen Männer oder auf die Gelegenheit, eines der schneeweißen Gewänder zu berühren. Die Bewaffneten des Königs schlugen die Leute mit Stöcken zurück. Jack hielt sich in sicherer Entfernung – er wollte keinen Segen und zog es vor, den Stöcken nicht zu nahe zu kommen.

Majestätisch zog die Prozession an der Nordseite der Kirche vorbei, und die Menge folgte ihr ungeachtet dessen, daß sie dabei über den Friedhof trampelte. Manche Zuschauer hatten schon von vornherein hier Platz bezogen und stemmten sich nun dem Druck der Nachdrängenden entgegen. Hier und da kam es zu einem kleinen Handgemenge.

Die Bischöfe hatten das Nordportal hinter sich gelassen und setzten ihre Prozession um die halbkreisförmige, ganz neue Apsis fort.

Auf dieser Seite befanden sich die Bauhütten, die nun von der hereinbrechenden Menschenmasse hinweggefegt zu werden drohten, zumal die ersten Bischöfe der Prozession schon wieder im Kloster verschwanden und viele Zuschauer daraufhin noch entschiedener nach vorn drängelten. Die Ritter des Königs schlugen jetzt kräftiger zu.

Jack sah es mit Unbehagen. »Das gefällt mir gar nicht«, sagte er zu Aliena.

»Ich wollte eben das gleiche sagen«, gab sie zurück. »Sehen wir doch besser zu, daß wir hier rauskommen.«

Ehe sie sich jedoch entfernen konnten, brach ganz vorne eine Rauferei zwischen den Rittern und einigen Jugendlichen aus. Die Männer des Königs hieben blindwütig mit ihren Prügeln um sich, worauf die Jugendlichen nicht etwa kuschten, sondern zum Gegenangriff übergingen – genau in dem Moment, da der letzte Bischof eilends im Kreuzgang verschwand. Kaum waren die frommen Männer außer Sicht, galt die Aufmerksamkeit der Menge nur noch den Bütteln des Königs. Ein Stein traf einen der Männer an der Stirn. Die Zuschauer begrüßten seinen Sturz mit lautem Gejohle. Von der Westseite der Kirche stürmten weitere Bewaffnete herbei und eilten ihren Kameraden zu Hilfe.

Was als einfacher Raufhändel begonnen hatte, verwandelte sich zusehends in einen regelrechten Aufruhr.

Jack wußte, daß sich die aufgebrachte Menge auch von der bevorstehenden Zeremonie nicht mehr ablenken lassen würde. Die Bischöfe stiegen in diesem Augenblick mit dem König in die Krypta hinab, um die Gebeine des heiligen Dionysius heraufzuholen und feierlich durch den Kreuzgang zu tragen. Vor Ende des Gottesdienstes würde sich kein Würdenträger mehr der Menge zeigen. Abbé Suger hatte offensichtlich nicht mit dermaßen vielen Zuschauern gerechnet und daher auch für keinerlei Ablenkung gesorgt. Die Menschen waren unzufrieden und erhitzt – mittlerweile stand die Sonne schon hoch am Himmel – und suchten nach einem Ventil für ihren Ärger.

Zunächst kam den Männern des Königs zugute, daß sie – im Gegensatz zu ihren Widersachern – bewaffnet waren. Dann aber kam einer der Zuschauer auf die glänzende Idee, die Bauhütte aufzubrechen und nach Waffen zu durchsuchen. Zwei junge Leute traten die Tür der Steinmetzhütte ein und kamen kurz darauf mit Hämmern bewaffnet heraus. Mehrere Steinmetzen versuchten vergeblich, die Leute von ihrem Tun abzuhalten – sie wurden einfach beiseite gestoßen.

Jack und Aliena versuchten, sich aus der Menge zu lösen, fanden sich jedoch hilflos eingekeilt. Jack hielt Tommy fest an seine Brust gedrückt. Mit den Armen schützte er den Rücken des Kleinen und mit den Händen den Kopf. Gleichzeitig bemühte er sich, Aliena nicht zu verlieren. Er sah, wie ein kleiner Mann mit verschlagenem Gesichtsausdruck und schwarzem Bart die Statue der weinenden Dame aus der Steinmetzhütte entwendete. Die habe ich zum letztenmal gesehen! dachte Jack betrübt.

Auch die Hütte der Zimmerleute wurde aufgebrochen. Die Handwerker hatten inzwischen alle Hoffnung aufgegeben, ihre Hütten schützen zu können. Als uneinnehmbar erwies sich lediglich die Schmiede. An deren Statt zertrümmerte die Menge die dünnen Wände der Dachdeckerhütte und bemächtigte sich der schweren und gefährlich scharfen Werkzeuge, die zum Zurichten und Festnageln der Bleiplatten dienten. Wenn das so weitergeht, gibt es Tote, dachte Jack.

So sehr er sich auch dagegen sträubte – er wurde unaufhaltsam auf das Nordportal der Kirche zu gedrängt, wo die Kämpfe am allerheftigsten tobten. Dem schwarzbärtigen Dieb erging es nicht anders: Zwar versuchte er, mit seiner Beute zu entkommen, und drückte die Statue ebenso an die Brust wie Jack seinen Sohn, aber anstatt sich aus der Masse zu befreien, wurde er unaufhaltsam weiter in den Strudel hineingezogen.

Da hatte Jack einen Geistesblitz. Er übergab den kleinen Tommy Aliena und sagte: »Halt dich dicht bei mir!« Dann faßte er den Dieb beim Schlafittchen und entrang ihm die Statue. Der Mann leistete nur schwachen Widerstand, denn Jack war ein gutes Stück größer als er; außerdem wollte er jetzt seine Haut retten und war an der Statue gar nicht mehr besonders interessiert.

Jack hob die Statue hoch über seinen Kopf und schrie: »Erweist der Madonna die Ehre!« Zunächst beachtete ihn niemand, doch dann wandten sich ihm ein oder zwei Köpfe zu. »Rührt die Muttergottes nicht an!« brüllte er aus Leibeskräften. Den Umstehenden ward auf einmal unheimlich zumute; sie traten zurück und verschafften ihm damit ein wenig Freiraum. Jack seinerseits fand Gefallen an seiner Rolle. »Es ist eine Sünde, das Bildnis der Jungfrau Maria zu entweihen!« Er setzte sich, die Statue noch immer hoch über den Kopf haltend, in Bewegung und schritt auf die Kirche zu. Vielleicht klappt's! dachte er. Zahlreiche Raufbolde hielten inne, um zu sehen, was da vor sich ging.

Mit einem Blick vergewisserte er sich, daß Aliena ihm folgte – sie konnte ohnehin nicht anders, da sie von der nachfolgenden Menge geschoben wurde. Der Aufruhr kam rasch zum Erliegen. Die Menge folgte jetzt Jack, und manche Leute begannen, seine Worte ehrfürchtig zu wiederholen: »Es ist die Muttergottes«, murmelten sie. »Gegrüßet seist du, Maria ... Macht Platz für das Bildnis der Madonna ...« Sie hatten nur ein Schauspiel gewollt – und Jack erfüllte ihnen diesen Wunsch. Es gab nur noch ein oder zwei Rempeleien am Rande des Kirchplatzes. Jack war ganz verblüfft: wie leicht es ihm gefallen war, dem Aufruhr ein Ende zu setzen! Feierlich schritt er weiter. Die Menge wich ehrfürchtig zur Seite und ließ ihn ungehindert das Nordportal erreichen, wo er die Statue voller Ehrerbietung im Schatten abstellte. Sie maß nicht viel mehr als zwei Fuß und wirkte, da sie nun auf dem Boden stand, erheblich weniger beeindruckend als zuvor.

Das Volk versammelte sich erwartungsvoll um das Portal. Jack wußte nicht, was er tun sollte. Erwarten sie vielleicht, daß ich eine Predigt halte? dachte er. Mit seinem feierlichen Schritt und den klangvollen Mahnungen, die er von sich gegeben hatte, waren seine priesterlichen Fähigkeiten erschöpft. Hoffentlich tun sie mir nichts an, wenn ich sie jetzt enttäusche, dachte er beklommen.

Plötzlich ging ein Raunen durch die Menge.

Jack drehte sich um. Ein paar Adlige aus der Kirche waren ins Portal getreten und sahen hinaus, doch er konnte nichts an ihnen entdecken, was das offenkundige Staunen der Zuschauer gerechtfertigt hätte.

»Ein Wunder!« ertönte es plötzlich, und der Schrei vervielfältigte sich: »Ein Wunder! Ein Wunder!«

Jacks Blick fiel auf die Statue, und auf einmal war ihm alles klar: Wasser tropfte aus ihren Augen. Im ersten Moment war er ebenso verblüfft wie die Menschen; dann fiel ihm seine eigene Erklärung wieder ein: daß die Dame nur dann weinte, wenn sich die Luft rasch abkühlte. Die Statue war aus der vormittäglichen Hitze in die schattige Kühle des Nordportals getragen worden – und bestätigte mit ihren Tränen Jacks Vermutung. Die ahnungslosen Zuschauer sahen nur, daß eine hölzerne Statue Tränen vergoß – und hielten es für ein Wunder.

Eine Frau, die in vorderster Reihe stand, warf der Statue einen Denier zu Füßen, einen französischen Silberpfennig. Jack hätte beinahe laut herausgelacht: Welchen Sinn hatte es schon, einem Stück Holz Geld zu geben? Aber die Kirche hatte die Leute dazu erzogen, für alles, was heilig war, Geld herauszurücken, so daß es fast wie von selbst geschah. Viele andere folgten dem Beispiel der Frau.

Jack war noch nie der Gedanke gekommen, aus Raschids Spielzeug Geld zu schlagen. Auch war ihm sofort klar, daß kein Mensch auch nur einen Heller springen ließe, wenn er Anlaß zu der Vermutung hätte, das Geld flösse in Jacks eigene Taschen. Aber für eine Kirche war die Statue ein Vermögen wert!

Mit einemmal wußte er genau, was er zu tun hatte.

Noch bevor ihm die Folgen seiner Worte klar waren, begann er auch schon zu sprechen – so, wie es ihm gerade einfiel. »Die Weinende Madonna ist Gottes Eigentum, nicht meines«, begann er, und die Menschen lauschten ihm andächtig: Das war die Predigt, auf die die Leute gewartet hatten! Hinter Jack, in der Kirche, stimmten die Bischöfe ihren Gesang an, für den sich jetzt außerhalb der Kirche kein Mensch mehr interessierte.

»Viele hundert Jahre lang mußte sie im Land der Sarazenen darben und schmachten«, fuhr Jack fort. (Er hatte keine Ahnung, was es mit dem Schicksal der Statue wirklich auf sich hatte, aber das war ihm im Augenblick unwichtig: Selbst der Klerus hütete sich im allgemeinen davor, dem Wahrheitsgehalt von Wunderlegenden und Heiligenreliquien allzu genau auf den Grund zu gehen.) »Sie hat eine weite Reise über viele hundert Meilen hinter sich, aber sie ist noch immer nicht am Ende dieser Reise angelangt. Ihr Ziel ist die Kathedrale von Kingsbridge in England.«

Er fing einen Blick von Aliena auf und mußte sich beherrschen, um ihr nicht zuzublinzeln und damit zu verraten, daß seine Rede blanke Erfindung war, geboren aus einer Augenblickseingebung.

»Es ist meine heilige Mission, die Weinende Madonna nach Kingsbridge zu bringen. Dort, am Bestimmungsort ihrer Reise, wird sie ihre Ruhe und ihren Frieden finden.« Wieder sah er Aliena an, und dabei kam ihm die letzte und großartigste Eingebung, die er auch sogleich kundtat: »Ich bin zum Dombaumeister der neuen Kirche von Kingsbridge ernannt worden.«

Alienas Unterkiefer fiel herab, und Jack wandte den Blick ab. »Die Weinende Madonna hat befohlen, daß in Kingsbridge für sie eine neue, schönere Kirche errichtet werde, und mit ihrer gnädigen Hilfe werde ich einen Tempel erschaffen, der dem neuen Chorraum, der hier in Saint-Denis für die Gebeine des heiligen Dionysius gebaut worden ist, in nichts nachsteht.«

Er sah zu Boden, und beim Anblick der Münzen kam ihm der richtige Einfall für die Beendigung seiner Rede. »Eure Spenden«, sagte er, »werden zum Bau der neuen Kirche beitragen. Jedem Mann, jeder

Frau und jedem Kind, die mit ihren Opfergaben einen Beitrag zur Errichtung ihrer neuen Heimstatt leisten, erteilt die Madonna ihren Segen.«

Nach einem kurzen Schweigen klimperten zu Füßen der Madonna die Opfermünzen, die die Zuschauer ihr zuwarfen. Dabei murmelten sie »Halleluja!« oder »Gelobt sei der Herr!« oder baten um einen Segen, ja, sogar um ganz bestimmte Wundertaten: »Laß Robert wieder gesund werden!« – »Laß Anne schwanger werden!« – »Schenk uns eine gute Ernte!« Die Gesichter verrieten Aufregung, Hochgefühl und Glück. Sie drängten vorwärts und rempelten einander an in ihrem Eifer, der Weinenden Madonna Silberpfennige zu opfern. Und Jack sah staunend zu, wie der Geldregen allmählich seine Füße bedeckte wie angewehter Schnee.

In jeder Stadt, in jedem Dorf, die sie auf dem Weg nach Cherbourg passierten, erzielte die Weinende Madonna die gleiche Wirkung. Sobald die Prozession durch die jeweilige Hauptstraße begann, folgten die Menschen in Scharen. Vor der Kirche warteten sie, bis sich alle Leute versammelt hatten. Danach trugen sie die Statue ins kühle Innere der Kirche, wo sie ihre Tränen vergoß – mit dem Erfolg, daß sich die Menschen in ihrem Eifer, für den Bau der Kathedrale in Kingsbridge Geld zu spenden, beinahe überschlugen.

Gleich zu Beginn hätten sie die Statue beinahe verloren. Die in Saint-Denis versammelten Bischöfe und Erzbischöfe hatten sie eingehend untersucht und für wahrhaft wundertätig erklärt, worauf Abbé Suger sie für seine Kirche erwerben wollte. Er hatte Jack erst ein Pfund, dann zehn und schließlich sogar fünfzig Pfund geboten. Als ihm klar wurde, daß es Jack nicht um Geld ging, hatte er gar damit gedroht, ihm die Statue gewaltsam wegzunehmen, wurde jedoch vom Erzbischof Theobald von Canterbury daran gehindert. Theobald, der die Fähigkeit der Statue, Tränen in bares Geld zu verwandeln, nicht minder klar erkannt hatte, wollte, daß sie nach Kingsbridge kam, denn Kingsbridge gehörte zu seinem Erzbistum. Suger hatte sich ungnädig gefügt, nicht ohne dabei mit plumpen Andeutungen die Echtheit des Wunders erneut in Frage zu stellen.

Jack hatte unter den Handwerkern in Saint-Denis verbreitet, er werde jeden einstellen, der ihm nach Kingsbridge folgen wolle. Auch davon war Suger nicht eben erbaut. Die meisten von ihnen würden sich zwar an das Prinzip halten, daß der Spatz in der Hand besser ist als die Taube auf dem Dach, und bleiben; aber es gab auch einige unter ihnen, die aus England stammten und der Versuchung, in die Heimat zurückzukehren, nicht widerstehen mochten. Außerdem würden alle die Kunde vom Dombau verbreiten, denn es gehörte zu den Pflichten eines jeden Steinmetzen, seinen Zunftbrüdern von neuen Bauhütten zu berichten. Innerhalb weniger Wochen würden Steinmetze aus allen Ländern der Christenheit unterwegs nach Kingsbridge sein ... Aliena fragte Jack, was er zu tun gedenke, sollte ihn das Kloster von Kingsbridge *nicht* zum Dombaumeister ernennen. Er konnte ihr keine Antwort geben. Seine Ankündigung war einer Augenblickseingebung gefolgt, und er hatte noch keine Pläne für den Fall, daß etwas schiefging.

Erzbischof Theobald, der die Weinende Madonna für England beanspruchte, war nicht gewillt, Jack ohne Aufsicht weiterziehen zu lassen. Er stellte zwei Priester aus seinem Gefolge zur Begleitung von Jack und Aliena ab. Jack hatte das zuerst mißfallen, doch dann faßte er rasch Zuneigung zu den beiden. Reynold, ein streitbarer junger Mann mit aufgewecktem Gesicht und klugem Kopf, befragte ihn ausgiebig zu seinen mathematischen Studien in Toledo. Edward war ein schon älterer, sanfter Mann und ein großer Schlemmer. Die Hauptaufgabe der beiden bestand darin, zu verhindern, daß die Spendengelder in Jacks Tasche wanderten. Doch da die beiden Priester sich mit großzügig bemessenen Reisekosten aus der Spendenkasse bedienten (während Jack und Aliena für sich selbst aufkamen), hätte der Erzbischof am Ende besser daran getan, von vornherein nur Jack zu vertrauen.

Auf ihrem Weg nach Barfleur, wo sie ein Schiff nach Wareham besteigen wollten, kamen sie nach Cherbourg, eine kleine Stadt am Meer. Schon lange, bevor sie die Kirche im Herzen der Stadt erreichten, bemerkte Jack, daß irgend etwas nicht stimmte. Denn die Leute starrten nicht die Madonna an.

Sie starrten ihn selbst an.

Etwas später fiel es auch den beiden Geistlichen auf. Wie stets trugen sie die Statue auf einem hölzernen Gestell, und als die Leute hinter ihnen herzulaufen begannen, zischte Reynold Jack zu: »Was ist denn los?«

»Keine Ahnung.«

»Sie haben nur Augen für Euch, nicht für die Madonna! Seid Ihr schon mal hiergewesen?«

»Noch nie.«

»Nur die Älteren starren Jack an«, warf Aliena ein. »Die Jungen schauen die Madonna an.«

Sie hatte recht. Kinder und junge Leute waren neugierig auf die Statue – die älteren schienen sich sogar vor Jack zu fürchten. Einer bekreuzigte sich gar bei seinem Anblick. »Was haben die nur gegen mich?« fragte Jack laut.

Wie üblich zog die Prozession viele Menschen an, so daß sie den Marktplatz mit einem großen Gefolge erreichten. Vor der Kirche stellten sie die Madonna ab. In der Luft hing ein schwerer Geruch nach Salzwasser und Fisch. Ein paar Leute gingen in die Kirche hinein, um den Priester des Städtchens zu holen. Bisher hatte die Madonna nur einmal versagt – an einem kühlen Tag, an dem Reynold einer Warnung Jacks zum Trotz auf der Durchführung der Prozedur bestanden hatte. Seitdem hielt er sich an Jacks Ratschläge.

In Cherbourg war das Wetter in Ordnung, dafür stimmte etwas anderes ganz und gar nicht. In den windgepeitschten Gesichtern der Seeleute und Fischer spiegelte sich Aberglaube und Furcht. Die Jungen spürten die Beunruhigung der Älteren, so daß sich die Menschenmenge insgesamt mißtrauisch, ja beinahe feindselig verhielt. Niemand trat näher an die Gruppe heran, niemand stellte Fragen über die Statue. Alle hielten Abstand, tuschelten miteinander und warteten und warteten.

Endlich tauchte der Priester auf. Anderswo waren die Geistlichen mit vorsichtiger Neugier auf sie zugekommen, doch dieser hier stürmte aus der Kirche wie ein Exorzist, ein Kruzifix abwehrbereit in der Hand wie einen Schild, und in der anderen Hand einen Kelch mit Weihwasser. »Was hat er vor?« fragte Reynold. »Will er Dämonen austreiben?« Der Priester stimmte einen lateinischen Singsang an und ging auf Jack zu. Auf französisch sprach er ihn an: »Hebe dich hinweg, böser Geist, und kehre zu deinesgleichen zurück! Im Namen des –«

»Ich bin doch kein Geist, Idiot!« brach es aus Jack heraus.

Der Geistliche fuhr ungerührt fort: »... Vaters, des Sohnes und des Heiligen Geistes!«

»Wir sind hier in einer Mission des Erzbischofs von Canterbury«, protestierte Reynold. »Er hat uns seinen Segen erteilt.«

»Er ist bestimmt kein Geist«, meldete sich nun auch Aliena. »Ich kenne ihn schon seit seinem zwölften Lebensjahr!«

Der Priester blickte unsicher von einem zum anderen. »Ihr seid der Geist eines Mannes aus dieser Stadt, der vor vierundzwanzig Jahren gestorben ist«, sagte er. Zustimmende Rufe ertönten aus der Menschenmenge, und der Priester begann von neuem mit seinem beschwörenden Singsang.

»Ich bin erst zwanzig«, sagte Jack. »Vielleicht sehe ich dem Toten ähnlich.«

Ein Mann trat aus der Menge hervor. »Ihr seht ihm nicht nur ähnlich«, sagte er. »Ihr seid er – ganz genau wie an dem Tag, da Ihr gestorben seid.«

Abergläubisches, furchtsames Gemurr erhob sich. Jack, am Ende mit seinem Latein, betrachtete den Sprecher etwas genauer. Er war ein Mann von mehr als vierzig Jahren, mit ergrautem Bart, in der Kleidung eines gutsituierten Handwerkers oder Händlers. Er wirkte alles andere als überspannt. Jack wandte sich direkt an ihn. »Meine Begleiter kennen mich«, sagte er, wenngleich seine Stimme dabei etwas zitterte. »Diese beiden hier sind Priester. Die Frau ist mein Weib, das Kind ist mein Sohn. Sollen sie auch alle Geister sein?«

Der Mann wurde sichtlich unsicher.

Nun trat eine weißhaarige Frau neben Jack und sprach ihn an: »Erkennst du mich nicht, Jack?«

Jetzt bekam Jack es wirklich mit der Angst zu tun. »Wieso kennt Ihr meinen Namen?«

»Weil ich deine Mutter bin«, sagte die Frau.

»Das seid Ihr nicht!« mischte sich nun Aliena ein, und Jack hörte leichte Panik in ihrer Stimme mitschwingen. »Ich kenne seine Mutter, und sie sieht Euch nicht im geringsten ähnlich! Was geht hier eigentlich vor?«

»Ein böser Zauber«, meinte der Priester.

»Immer mit der Ruhe«, sagte Reynold. »Vielleicht ist Jack ja mit dem Toten verwandt. Hatte er denn Kinder?«

»Nein«, sagte der Graubart.

»Seid Ihr sicher?«

»Er hat nie geheiratet.«

»Das sind zwei Paar Stiefel.«

Ein paar Umstehende kicherten, und der Priester bedachte sie mit wütenden Blicken.

Dann meldete sich wieder der Graubart zu Wort. »Aber Jack ist vor vierundzwanzig Jahren gestorben, und *dieser* Jack hier behauptet, er sei gerade zwanzig.«

»Wie ist er denn gestorben?« fragte Reynold.

»Ertrunken.«

»Habt Ihr seine Leiche gesehen?«

Stille. Schließlich sagte der Graubart: »Nein, ich habe sie nie gesehen.«

»Hat sie überhaupt irgendwer gesehen?« fragte Reynold mit erhobener Stimme, da er sich einem Sieg schon nahe fühlte.

Niemand sagte ein Wort.

Reynold wandte sich an Jack. »Ist Euer Vater noch am Leben?«

»Er starb schon vor meiner Geburt.«

»Was war er denn?«

»Er war ein Spielmann.«

Ein Japsen ging durch die Menge, und die weißhaarige Frau sagte: »*Mein* Jack war auch ein Spielmann.«

»*Dieser* Jack hier ist aber ein Steinmetz«, gab Reynold zurück. »Ich habe schon Arbeiten von ihm gesehen. Immerhin, er könnte ja der *Sohn* des Spielmanns sein.« Fragend sah er Jack an. »Wie hieß Euer Vater? Jack Spielmann wahrscheinlich?«

»Nein, sie nannten ihn Jack Shareburg.«

Der Priester wiederholte den Namen, sprach ihn aber ein wenig anders aus: »Jacques Cherbourg?«

Nun fiel es dem jungen Steinmetz wie Schuppen von den Augen. Er hatte nie verstanden, warum sein Vater diesen seltsamen Namen trug, doch nun war es ihm klar – er hieß, wie so viele herumziehende Männer, nach der Stadt, aus der er kam. »Ja, natürlich«, sagte er verwundert. »Jacques Cherbourg ...«

Endlich – nachdem er die Suche schon längst aufgegeben hatte, fand er heraus, wer sein Vater war! Bis nach Spanien war er gezogen – doch das, was er suchte, fand er hier, an der Küste der Normandie! Seine Suche hatte ein Ende. Er war zutiefst zufrieden – und erschöpft. Ihm war, als hätte man ihm eine schwere Last von den Schultern genommen.

»Dann ist ja alles klar«, sagte Reynold und blickte triumphierend in die Runde. »Jacques Cherbourg ist nicht ertrunken. Er ging nach England, hat dort eine Zeitlang gelebt, ein Mädchen geschwängert – und ist dann gestorben. Das Mädchen hat einen Knaben geboren und ihn nach seinem Vater genannt. Jack ist jetzt zwanzig und sieht genauso aus wie sein Vater vor vierundzwanzig Jahren.« Er sah den Priester an. »Wir brauchen keinen Exorzismus, Vater. Es handelt sich nur um eine Familienzusammenführung.«

Aliena schob ihre Hand unter Jacks Arm durch und drückte die seine. Er fühlte sich wie betäubt. Hundert Fragen schossen ihm gleichzeitig durch den Kopf, und er wußte nicht, womit er beginnen sollte. Schließlich platzte er mit der erstbesten heraus. »Warum wart Ihr so sicher, daß er tot ist?«

»Weil niemand auf dem Weißen Schiff überlebt hat«, sagte der Graubart.

»Auf dem Weißen Schiff?«

»Ich erinnere mich daran«, sagte Edward. »Das war ein schlimmes Unglück, bei dem der Thronerbe ums Leben kam. Dann wurde Mathilde Thronerbin, und deshalb haben wir jetzt Stephan.«

»Aber was hatte er auf solch einem Schiff zu suchen?« fragte Jack.

Es war die weißhaarige Frau, die ihm Antwort gab. »Er sollte den Adel auf der Reise unterhalten.« Sie sah ihm ins Gesicht. »Dann bist du also sein Sohn. Und mein Enkel. Es tut mir leid, daß ich dich für einen Geist gehalten habe – aber du bist ihm wie aus dem Gesicht geschnitten.«

»Dein Vater war mein Bruder«, sagte nun der Graubart. »Ich bin dein Onkel Guillaume.«

Jack strahlte: Das ist also die Familie, nach der ich mich so lange gesehnt habe, dachte er – die Familie meines Vaters. Ich stehe nicht mehr ganz allein auf der Welt. Ich habe meine Wurzeln gefunden!

»Schaut, das ist mein Sohn Tommy«, sagte er stolz. »Seht euch bloß seine roten Haare an!«

Die weißhaarige Frau betrachtete den Kleinen mit Wohlwollen. Dann sagte sie mit unverkennbarem Schreck in der Stimme: »Meiner Seel', dann bin ich ja schon Urgroßmutter!«

Alles lachte.

Jack fragte: »Wie mag mein Vater nach England gekommen sein?«

»Und Gott sprach zu Satan: ›Sieh meinen getreuen Hiob. Er unter allen Menschen ist ohne Fehl.‹« Philip machte eine effektvolle Pause in seiner freien Nacherzählung der Bibelgeschichte. »›Er hat nicht seinesgleichen auf Erden, er ist fromm und rechtschaffen und gottesfürchtig und meidet das Böse.‹ Satan aber sprach: ›Warum sollte er dich auch nicht anbeten? Hast du ihm doch alles gegeben, was er besitzt: sieben Söhne und drei Töchter, siebentausend Schafe und dreitausend Kamele, fünfhundert Joch Ochsen und fünfhundert Esel. Kein Wunder, daß er so fromm und rechtschaffen ist!‹ Und Gott der Herr sprach: ›Nimm ihm alles, was er hat, und sieh, was geschieht.‹ Und Satan ging hin und nahm Hiob alles, was er besaß.«

Philips Gedanken schweiften immer wieder von seiner Predigt ab. Diesen Morgen hatte er einen äußerst rätselhaften Brief des Erzbischofs von Canterbury erhalten, der ihm zum Erwerb der wundertätigen Weinenden Madonna gratulierte. Philip hatte keine Ahnung von einer Weinenden Madonna, und ganz bestimmt befand sich nichts dergleichen in seinem Besitz. Er sei froh zu hören, fuhr der Erzbischof fort, daß Philip wieder mit dem Bau der neuen Kathedrale beginne wolle – doch Philip dachte gar nicht daran. Er wartete noch immer auf ein Zeichen von Gott, bevor er sich wieder ans Bauen wagte, und währenddessen hielt er den sonntäglichen Gottesdienst in der kleinen neuen Pfarrkirche. Erzbischof Theobald schloß sein Schreiben mit einem Kommentar zu Philips klugem Beschluß, einen Dombaumeister zu ernennen, der an dem neuen Chorraum von der Abtei zu Saint-Denis gearbeitet hatte. Philip hatte natürlich von der Abtei zu Saint-Denis und ihrem berühmten Abt Suger gehört – doch von dem neuen Chorraum dort hatte er keine Ahnung, und ganz gewiß hatte er auch keinen Dombaumeister ernannt, egal, woher er kam. Allmählich drängte sich ihm der Schluß auf, der Brief müsse an jemand anders gerichtet und nur durch ein Versehen an ihn gesandt worden sein.

»Was also sagte Hiob, als er seinen Reichtum verlor und seine Kinder starben? Hat er Gott verflucht und sich zu Satan bekehrt? Nichts dergleichen! Er sagte: ›Nackt bin ich geboren und nackt werde ich sterben. Der Herr hat's gegeben, der Herr hat's genommen – gelobt sei der Name des Herrn.‹ Da sagte Gott zu Satan: ›Na, was hab' ich dir gesagt?‹ Und Satan antwortete: ›Schön und gut, aber er hat immer noch seine Gesundheit, nicht wahr? Ein Mann nimmt es mit allem auf, solange er nur gesund ist.‹ Und Gott sah ein, daß er Hiob noch mehr leiden lassen mußte, wollte er sein Vertrauen in ihn rechtfertigen. Also sagte er: ›Nimm ihm seine Gesundheit und sieh, was geschieht.‹ Also schlug Satan Hiob mit Krankheit, mit Geschwüren vom Kopf bis zu den Füßen.«

Es war erst seit einigen Jahren üblich geworden, in der Kirche zu predigen. In Philips Kindheit war es noch sehr selten gewesen. Abt Peter hatte die Meinung vertreten, das Predigen verführte die Priester dazu, sich zu viel herauszunehmen. Er hing noch der altmodischen Ansicht an, die Gemeinde solle bloß zuschauen – schweigende Zeugen der rätselhaften heiligen Riten –, die lateinischen Worte hören, ohne sie zu verstehen, und blind auf die Wirkungskraft der priesterlichen Fürsprache vertrauen. Aber die Zeiten hatten sich gewandelt. Die fortschrittlichen Denker sahen in der Gemeinde nicht mehr nur stumme Diener einer mystischen Zeremonie. Die Kirche, meinten sie, solle ein integraler Bestandteil ihres Alltagslebens sein. Die Kirche setzte die Meilensteine in ihrem Leben – von der Taufe über die Eheschließung und die Taufe der Kinder bis hin zur Letzten Ölung und zum Begräbnis in geweihter Erde. Sie hätte ebensogut ihr Grundherr, Richter, Brotherr oder Auftraggeber sein können.

Auch von den einfachen Leuten wurde zunehmend mehr erwartet: Sie sollten sich nicht nur sonntags, sondern auch im Alltag als Christen erweisen. Dazu brauchten sie mehr als Rituale: Sie brauchten Erklärungen, Regeln, Ermutigung und geduldiges Zureden.

»Und wißt ihr, was ich glaube?« fuhr Philip fort. »Ich glaube, Satan hat mit Gott über Kingsbridge gesprochen. Ich glaube, Gott sagte zu Satan: ›Siehe meine Leute in Kingsbridge. Sind das nicht gute Christen? Fleißig arbeiten sie sechs Tage auf ihren Feldern und in ihren Werkstätten, und am Sonntag bauen sie den ganzen Tag an einem neuen Dom für mich. Diese Leute lassen sich nicht verderben.‹ Und Satan antwortete: ›Sie sind rechtschaffen, weil es ihnen wohl ergeht. Du hast ihnen reiche Ernten und gutes Wetter gegeben, Kunden für ihre Ware, Schutz vor üblen Grafen. Nimm all dies hinweg von ihnen, und sie werden sich zu mir bekehren.‹

Da sprach Gott: ›Was willst du ihnen antun?‹ Und Satan antwortete: ›Ihre Stadt verderben.‹ Und Gott sagte: ›Schön, versuche es und sieh, was geschieht.‹ Und Satan sandte William Hamleigh, der die Stadt in Brand setzte.«

In diesen Zeiten war Philip das Buch Hiob ein großer Trost. Nicht anders als Hiob hatte er, Philip, sein Leben lang rechtschaffen gearbeitet und sich bemüht, Gottes Willen zu gehorchen – und wie Hiob hatte er Unglück, Fehlschläge und Mißgunst geerntet. Seine Predigt sollte der Gemeinde Mut zusprechen – aber er sah deutlich, daß sie nicht wirkte. Nun, die Geschichte von Hiob war noch nicht zu Ende.

»Und Gott sagte zu Satan: ›Sieh hin! Du hast die ganze Stadt bis auf den Grund niedergebrannt, und noch immer baut sie mir eine neue Kirche. Diese Menschen sind wahrhaft rechtschaffen.‹ Aber Satan sagte: ›Ich habe sie nicht schwer genug geschlagen. Die meisten sind dem Feuer entkommen und haben ihre Häuser schnell wieder aufgebaut. Laß sie mit einem schweren Unglück heimsuchen und sieh, was geschieht.‹ Und Gott seufzte und sprach: ›Was also willst du ihnen antun?‹ Und Satan antwortete: ›Ich will ihnen das Dach ihrer neuen Kirche verderben und auf ihre Häupter herabfallen lassen.‹ Und so geschah's – wie wir alle wissen.«

Philip ließ den Blick über seine Gemeinde schweifen. Nur sehr wenige Leute hatten keinen Angehörigen bei jenem schrecklichen Einsturz verloren. Da war Witwe Meg, die an diesem Tag einen treusorgenden Gatten und drei wohlgeratene Söhne verloren hatte; seit jenem Tage hatte sie kein einziges Wort mehr gesprochen, und ihr Haar war über Nacht schlohweiß geworden. Andere hatten schwere Verletzungen davongetragen. Peter Pony hinkte jetzt, denn sein rechtes Bein war eingeklemmt worden; vor dem Unglück war er Pferdegänger gewesen, nun stellte er für seinen Bruder Sättel zum Verkauf her. Kaum eine Familie in Kingsbridge war gnädig davongekommen. Ganz vorn auf dem Boden saß gar ein Mann, der seine Beine nicht mehr bewegen konnte. Stirnrunzelnd fragte sich Philip, wer das sein mochte. Er hatte ihn nie zuvor gesehen – sein Unglück konnte ihm also nicht beim Einsturz der Kathedrale zugestoßen sein. Dann fiel ihm wieder ein, daß man ihm von dem Krüppel berichtet hatte, der in der Stadt zu betteln und in den Ruinen der Kathedrale zu schlafen pflegte. Philip hatte angeordnet, ihm ein Bett im Gästehaus zu geben.

Aber seine Gedanken schweiften schon ab, und er rief sich zur Ordnung. »Was tat Hiob? Sein Weib sagte zu ihm: ›Verfluche deinen Gott und stirb.‹ Tat er das? Nein, er tat es nicht. Verlor er seinen Glauben? Nein, er verlor ihn nicht. Und Satan mußte seine Niederlage eingestehen. Und ich sage euch –« – Philip hob die Hand, um seiner Rede größeren Nachdruck zu verleihen – »ich sage euch, Satan wird auch in Kingsbridge eine Niederlage einstecken müssen! Denn wir werden, wie einst Hiob, trotz all seiner Heimsuchungen, weiterhin dem wahren und einzigen Gott dienen!«

Er machte eine neuerliche Pause, um das Gesagte einsickern zu lassen – aber er konnte deutlich sehen, daß es ihm nicht gelungen war, seine Schäfchen aus ihrer Lethargie zu reißen. Ihre Gesichter zeigten Anteilnahme, aber keine Inspiration. Ich bin einfach kein mitreißender Prediger, dachte er. Dazu stehe ich zu fest mit beiden Beinen auf der Erde. Gewiß, ich habe sie dazu gebracht, daß sie mir treu ergeben sind – aber auch das brauchte seine Zeit, bis sie erkannten, wie ich lebe und was ich leiste. Ich kann sie nur durch Taten inspirieren – jedenfalls konnte ich das einst –, niemals durch Worte.

Unverdrossen fuhr er fort, denn das Beste an der Geschichte kam erst noch. »Wie erging es also Hiob, nachdem Satan von ihm abgelassen hatte? Gott gab ihm mehr, ja doppelt soviel, wie er zuvor besessen hatte! Wo er einst siebentausend Schafe hütete, waren es nun vierzehntausend. Statt der verlorenen dreitausend Kamele erhielt er sechstausend. Und er zeugte noch einmal sieben Söhne und drei Töchter.«

Auf den Gesichtern seiner Zuhörer malte sich Gleichgültigkeit. »Und auch Kingsbridge wird«, fuhr Philip redlich bemüht fort, »eines Tages wieder blühen und gedeihen. Die Witwen werden sich wieder einen Mann nehmen und die Witwer ein Weib. Wessen Kinder getötet wurden, die sollen wiederum Kinder haben. Unsere Straßen werden voller Menschen sein und unsere Läden voller Brot und Wein, Leder und Geschirr, Schnallen und Schuhe. Und eines Tages werden wir unseren Dom wieder aufbauen.«

Das Schlimme war, daß Philip selbst nicht so recht an seine eigenen Worte glaubte – wie sollte er also seine Gemeinde überzeugen? Kein Wunder, daß sie unbewegt blieb.

Aus der schweren Bibel, die vor ihm lag, übersetzte er die lateinischen Sätze ins Englische: »Und Hiob lebte noch weitere hundertundvierzig Jahre und sah seine Söhne, seine Enkel und seine Urenkel heranwachsen. Und als er starb, war er alt und lebenssatt.« Philip schloß die Heilige Schrift.

Im Eingang der kleinen Kirche gab es eine Störung, und Philip sah verstimmt auf. Gewiß, seine Predigt hatte nicht die erhoffte Wirkung gezeigt, aber dennoch durfte er zumindest erwarten, daß sich die Leute danach ruhig verhielten. Die Kirchentür stand offen, und wer sich dort befand, verrenkte sich den Hals. Philip sah eine Menschenmenge vor der Tür. Alle, die nicht zum Gottesdienst gekommen sind, dachte er, müssen da draußen zusammengelaufen sein. Was ging da vor?

Alles mögliche fuhr ihm durch den Sinn – einen Überfall, ein Feuer, Truppen Berittener und viele Tote hatten sie schon gehabt. Auf das, was nun geschah, war er vollkommen unvorbereitet. Erst traten zwei Priester ein, die eine weibliche Statue auf einem Gestell trugen, das mit einem bestickten Altartuch behängt war. Ihr feierliches Gehabe deutete darauf hin, daß es sich bei der Statue um ein Heiligenbild handelte, vermutlich um die Jungfrau Maria. Hinter den beiden Geistlichen traten zwei weitere Personen ein, und das war für Philip die größte Überraschung: Aliena und Jack!

Beim Anblick Jacks mischten sich Freude und Zorn in Philips Gefühlen. Dieser Knabe! dachte er. An dem Tag, als erstmals hier auftauchte, brannte die alte Kathedrale ab, und seitdem ging nichts mehr seinen gewohnten Gang, jedenfalls nicht, wenn Jack beteiligt war ... Doch die Freude überwog den Zorn – soviel der Knabe auch angestellt hatte, durch ihn war das Leben stets interessant gewesen. Der Knabe! Philip sah genauer hin. Das war kein Knabe mehr. Jack war nur zwei Jahre fort gewesen, aber um zehn Jahre gealtert – sein Blick war wissend und erfahren. Wo er sich wohl aufgehalten hatte? Und wie hatte Aliena ihn gefunden?

Die kleine Prozession kam auf ihn zu, und Philip entschied, einfach abzuwarten. Aufgeregtes Geflüster erhob sich, als die Leute die beiden jungen Menschen erkannten. Das Geflüster schwoll an, wurde zu ehrfürchtigem Gemurmel, und irgend jemand sagte laut und deutlich: »Sie weint!«

Der Satz wurde von anderen aufgenommen und wiederholt wie im Wechselgebet: »Sie weint! Sie weint!« Philip betrachtete die Statue. Richtig, aus ihren Augen floß Wasser. Der rätselhafte Brief des Erzbischofs über die wundertätige Weinende Madonna fiel ihm ein – das also war sie. Doch ob die Tränen ein Wunder waren? Das wollte er später beurteilen. Die Augen schienen aus einer Art Kristall gemacht, die Statue selbst war aus Holz – vielleicht lag darin des Rätsels Lösung.

Die Geistlichen drehten sich um und setzten das Gestell auf dem

Boden ab, so daß die Madonna der Gemeinde gegenüberstand. Und nun begann Jack zu sprechen.

»Die Weinende Madonna kam in einem weit, weit entfernten Land zu mir«, hub er an. Wie kommt er dazu, dachte Philip, einfach meinen Gottesdienst selber zu halten? Nun ja, soll er sagen, was er zu sagen hat. Immerhin hat er mich selbst neugierig gemacht ... »Ein getaufter Sarazene schenkte sie mir«, fuhr Jack fort, und wieder gab es überraschtes Gemurmel in der Gemeinde: Sarazenen waren in allen Geschichten eigentlich stets die barbarischen, schwarzhäutigen Bösewichte, kaum jemandem war bekannt, daß sich manche hatten taufen lassen. »Zuerst wunderte ich mich nur darüber, warum ausgerechnet ich die Madonna bekam. Dennoch habe ich sie viele, viele Meilen weit getragen.« Atemlos lauschte die Gemeinde Jacks Worten. Er kann besser predigen als ich, dachte Philip – die Spannung ist bereits zu spüren. »Endlich kam ich zu dem Schluß, daß die Weinende Madonna nach Hause gebracht werden wollte. Aber wo lag ihr Zuhause? Dann hatte ich eine Erleuchtung: Sie wollte nach Kingsbridge.«

Das Staunen der Gemeinde entlud sich in wirrem Durcheinandergerede, doch Philip blieb skeptisch. Es gab einen gewissen Unterschied zwischen den Wegen Gottes und den Wegen Jacks – und diese Geschichte roch ihm allzusehr nach Jack. Dennoch verhielt er sich weiterhin still.

»Dann überlegte ich: Wohin soll ich sie bringen? Welchen Tempel wird sie in Kingsbridge vorfinden? In welcher Kirche wird sie ihre Heimstatt sehen?« Sein Blick glitt über die schmucklosen, gemeißelten Wände der Pfarrkirche und sagte deutlicher als alle Worte, daß die Kirche nicht genug sei. »Es war, als spräche sie laut und deutlich zu mir: Du, Jack Jackson, sollst mir einen Schrein erbauen und eine Kirche errichten.«

Philip dämmerte nun, was Jack im Sinne hatte: Die Madonna sollte der Funke sein, der die Begeisterung der Leute für den Dombau aufs neue entzündete. Das gelang ihm wahrscheinlich besser als ihm, Philip, selbst mit seiner Predigt über Hiob. Dennoch blieb die Frage: Ist das Gottes Wille oder einfach nur Jacks Wille?

»Da fragte ich sie: Womit soll ich eine Kirche bauen? Ich habe kein Geld. Und sie antwortete mir: Dafür laß nur mich sorgen. Wir machten uns also auf den Weg, mit dem Segen des Erzbischofs Theobald von Canterbury.« Bei der Erwähnung dieses Namens sah er kurz zu Philip auf. Aha, dachte der Prior, er will mir zu verstehen geben, daß er eine Macht hinter sich weiß.

Jack wandte sich wieder der Gemeinde zu. »Und auf dem ganzen Weg hierher, von Paris aus durch die Normandie, über das Meer und durch den Süden Englands, haben uns viele, viele fromme Christen Geld gegeben, damit wir der Weinenden Madonna einen Tempel errichten können.«

Auf ein Zeichen von Jack zogen feierlich zwei Sarazenen ein, auf ihren Häuptern Turbane, auf ihren Schultern eine eisenbeschlagene Truhe.

Furchtsam wichen die Leute vor ihnen zurück, und selbst Philip versetzten sie in Erstaunen. Er wußte aus Büchern, daß Sarazenen dunkelhäutig waren, doch er hatte noch nie einen zu sehen bekommen, und die Wirklichkeit übertraf alle seine Vorstellungen. Sie trugen weit schwingende, schreiend bunte Gewänder, schritten durch die erstarrte Gemeinde, knieten vor der Madonna nieder und brachten ihr die Truhe dar.

Atemlose Stille herrschte, als Jack einen großen Schlüssel hervorzog, die Truhe aufschloß und den Deckel hob. Die Leute verrenkten sich die Hälse – und mit einemmal stieß Jack die Truhe um.

Ein heller Strom von Silbermünzen ergoß sich auf den Boden, und es klang wie ein Wasserfall – das mußten Hunderte, nein, Tausende von Pennies sein! Soviel Geld auf einem Haufen hatte noch keiner in seinem Leben gesehen.

Jack hob die Stimme und übertönte die erstaunten Ausrufe. »Ich habe die Weinende Madonna nach Hause gebracht, und nun übergebe ich sie dem Bauherrn der neuen Kathedrale.« Er drehte sich um, sah Philip in die Augen und neigte den Kopf, als wolle er sagen: Nun seid Ihr an der Reihe.

Jacks Vorgehen mißfiel Philip gründlich, wenngleich er sich insgeheim eingestand, daß der junge Mann die Sache meisterhaft in Szene gesetzt hatte. Doch das hieß noch nicht, daß Jack schon gewonnen hatte. Die Leute mochten ja die Weinende Madonna erfreut begrüßen; doch nur der Prior von Kingsbridge konnte entscheiden, ob sie neben den Gebeinen des heiligen Adolphus in der neuen Kathedrale ihren Platz fand.

Die Einheimischen bestürmten die Sarazenen mit Fragen, und Philip verließ sein Podest, um zuzuhören. »Ich komme aus einem weit, weit entfernten Land«, sagte der eine gerade. Erstaunt vernahm Philip, daß er das Englisch der Fischer aus Dorset sprach – allerdings wußten die Leute in Kingsbridge nicht einmal, daß Sarazenen eine eigene Sprache besaßen.

»Wie heißt Euer Land?« fragte jemand.

»Mein Land heißt Afrika«, war die Antwort. In Afrika gab es natürlich mehr als nur ein Land, und Philip fragte sich, aus welchem dieser Sarazene wohl stammen mochte. Vielleicht gar aus einem Gebiet, das in der Bibel erwähnt war – Ägyptenland oder Äthiopien?

Ein kleines Mädchen streckte einen Finger aus und berührte die dunkelbraune Hand. Der Sarazene lächelte es an. Von der Hautfarbe einmal abgesehen, dachte Philip, wirkt er keinen Deut anders als die Hiesigen.

Mutig fragte die Kleine: »Wie ist es denn in Afrika?«

»Dort gibt es große Wüsten und Feigenbäume.«

»Was ist eine Feige?«

»Das … das ist eine Frucht, die aussieht wie eine Erdbeere und schmeckt wie ein Pfirsich.«

Ein entsetzlicher Verdacht bemächtige sich Philips. »Sagt an, Sarazene«, sagte er, »in welcher Stadt seit Ihr geboren?«

»In Damaskus«, erwiderte der Mann.

Sein Verdacht war also gerechtfertigt! Wütend zog Philip Jack beiseite und fragte ihn ebenso leise wie zornig: »Was spielt Ihr für ein Spiel?«

»Wie meint Ihr das?« gab Jack mit gespielter Unschuld zurück.

»Diese Männer sind keine Sarazenen. Das sind Fischer aus Wareham mit braungeschminkten Gesichtern und Händen.«

Jack schien es nicht weiter zu stören, daß sein Betrug aufgedeckt war. Grinsend fragte er: »Wie habt Ihr das erraten?«

»Dieser Mann hat nie in seinem Leben eine Feige gesehen, und Damaskus liegt nicht in Afrika. Was soll der Betrug?«

»Es ist nur ein harmloser Schwindel«, sagte Jack und setzte sein gewinnendstes Lächeln auf.

»Einen Schwindel, der harmlos ist, gibt es nicht«, verwies ihn Philip frostig.

»Na schön.« Jack wurde klar, daß er Philips Zorn besänftigen mußte. »Es dient dem gleichen Zweck wie ein farbiges Bild in der Bibel. Es ist nicht die Wahrheit, aber es dient der Illustration. Meine braungeschminkten Fischer aus Dorset versinnbildlichen die Tatsache, daß die Weinende Madonna aus dem Land der Sarazenen kommt.«

Aliena und die beiden Priester traten zu ihnen. Philip ignorierte sie. »Man fürchtet sich nicht vor dem Abbild einer Schlange«, sagte er zu Jack. »Eine Illustration ist keine Lüge. Aber Eure Sarazenen sind keine Illustration, das sind Betrüger.«

»Seit wir sie haben, nehmen wir viel mehr Geld ein«, entgegnete Jack.

Philip betrachtete die aufgehäuften Pennies. »Die Leute denken vermutlich, das reiche, um eine Kathedrale zu bauen«, meinte er. »Mir scheint, das sind so um die hundert Pfund – und Ihr wißt genau, daß das nicht einmal reicht, um ein Jahr lang zu bauen.«

»Mit dem Geld ist es wie mit den Sarazenen«, sagte Jack. »Es ist ein Symbol. Und Ihr wißt, daß Ihr damit wieder anfangen könnt zu bauen.«

Das stimmt, dachte Philip. Nichts kann mich jetzt noch daran hindern. Die Madonna ist genau das, was Kingsbridge gebraucht hat. Sie wird eine Menge Menschen anziehen – Pilger und Scholaren und Neugierige. Und die Stadt wird sie als gutes Omen betrachten. Habe ich nicht auf ein Zeichen von Gott gewartet? Aber so gern ich daran glauben würde – das sieht mir eher nach einem Zeichen von Jack aus ...

Der jüngere der beiden Priester meldete sich zu Wort. »Ich bin Reynold, und dies hier ist Edward. Wir arbeiten für den Erzbischof von Canterbury. Er hat uns als Begleiter der Weinenden Madonna mitgeschickt.«

»Wenn Ihr den Segen des Erzbischofs habt, wieso braucht ihr dann noch zwei angebliche Sarazenen, um die Herkunft der Madonna zu bezeugen?« fragte Philip.

In Edwards Gesicht malte sich Beschämung, doch Reynold sagte: »Das war Jacks Idee, und ich habe nichts Arges daran gefunden. Zweifelt Ihr etwa an der Madonna, Philip?«

»Für dich *Vater*«, fuhr Philip ihn an. »Auch wenn du für den Erzbischof arbeitest, hast du kein Recht, dich unehrerbietig gegenüber Höherrangigen zu verhalten. Und die Antwort auf deine Frage ist ja. Ich hege Zweifel an der Madonna. Sie kommt mir nicht in meine Kathedrale, bevor ich nicht überzeugt bin, daß sie ein heiliges Artefakt ist.«

»Eine hölzerne Statue weint!« protestierte Reynold. »Wie viele Wunder braucht Ihr noch?«

»Warum sie weint, ist nicht geklärt – aber das allein macht es noch nicht zu einem Wunder. Daß Wasser zu Eis gefriert, können wir auch nicht erklären – trotzdem ist es kein Wunder.«

»Der Erzbischof wäre zutiefst enttäuscht, wenn Ihr die Madonna nicht annehmt. Er hatte sogar einen Streit darüber mit Abbé Suger, der sie für Saint-Denis reklamierte.«

Das war eine glatte Drohung. Der Junge, dachte Philip, wird sich ein bißchen mehr anstrengen müssen, wenn er mich einschüchtern will. »Der Erzbischof würde gewiß nicht wünschen, daß ich die Madonna annehme, ohne Fragen zu stellen.«

Zu seinen Füßen bewegte sich etwas – der Krüppel, der Philip schon vorher aufgefallen war. Der Unglückliche mit seinen lahmen Beinen zog sich über den Boden und wollte sich offenbar der Statue nähern, doch immer wieder war ihm die Menschenmenge im Wege. Philip trat beiseite, um ihn durchzulassen. Den Sarazenen, die die Leute davon abhielten, die Madonna zu berühren, entging der Krüppel, und Philip sah, wie er die Hand ausstreckte und das hölzerne Kleid berührte. Gleich darauf stieß er einen markerschütternden Schrei aus. »Ich spüre es! Ich spüre es!«

Alles wandte sich ihm zu.

»Ich spüre, wie das Leben in meine Beine zurückkehrt!« schrie er.

Fassungslos sah Philip ihn an. Er wußte genau, was nun kam: Der Mann beugte zuerst das eine Knie, dann das andere. Die Zuschauer japsten auf. Der Mann streckte eine Hand aus, und irgendwer nahm sie, so daß er sich mühselig aufrichten konnte.

Die Menge stöhnte auf.

»Versucht zu gehen!« erscholl es.

Noch immer die hilfreiche Hand haltend, versuchte der Mann, einen Schritt zu tun, dann noch einen. Totenstille herrschte. Beim dritten Schritt stolperte er, und alles seufzte. Doch dann hatte er sein Gleichgewicht wiedergefunden und ging weiter.

Die Menge schrie vor Begeisterung.

Der Mann ging aufs Kirchenportal zu, und alles folgte ihm. Schließlich begann er zu laufen, und das Geschrei steigerte sich zu Gejohle. Er trat aus der Kirche in die Sonne hinaus, und die Gemeinde tat es ihm nach.

Philip betrachtete die beiden Geistlichen. Reynold stand mit offenem Mund da, und Edward liefen die Tränen übers Gesicht; sie hatten offenkundig keine Ahnung gehabt. Schäumend vor Zorn wandte sich Philip an Jack: »Wie könnt Ihr es wagen, uns solch einen schmutzigen Streich zu spielen?«

»Was für einen Streich?«

»Dieser Mann dort ist erst vor ein paar Tagen in unserer Gegend aufgetaucht, und bis dahin hat ihn noch nie jemand gesehen. In ein oder zwei weiteren Tagen wird er auf Nimmerwiedersehen verschwinden, die Taschen voller Geld, das Ihr ihm gegeben habt. Ich weiß, wie solche Sachen gemacht werden, Jack. Ihr seid – bedauerlicher- weise – nicht der erste, der ein Wunder vortäuscht. Dieser Mann hat noch nie im Leben ein lahmes Bein gehabt, geschweige denn zwei. Er ist nichts anderes als ein weiterer Fischer aus Wareham, stimmt's?«

Jacks betretener Blick verriet ihn.

»Ich hab' dir gleich gesagt«, mischte sich Aliena ein, »daß das nicht gutgeht.«

Die beiden Priester standen wie vom Donner gerührt, und Reynold wurde wütend. »Dazu hattet Ihr kein Recht!« fuhr er Jack an.

Philip empfand eine Mischung aus Trauer und Zorn. Wie sehr hatte er gehofft, die Madonna werde sich als echt erweisen! Es sollte wohl nicht sein. Er wandte sich ab und ließ den Blick durch die Kirche schweifen. Nur wenige Betende waren dem Krüppel nicht ge- folgt, sondern starrten noch immer die Statue an. »Diesmal seid Ihr zu weit gegangen«, sagte Philip.

»Die Tränen sind echt«, sagte Jack. »Aber der Krüppel war ein Fehler.«

»Das war mehr als ein Fehler«, erwiderte Philip aufgebracht. »Wenn die Leute erfahren, daß sie an der Nase herumgeführt wurden, ist ihr Glaube an *alle* Wunder erschüttert.«

»Wieso müssen sie denn die Wahrheit erfahren?«

»Weil ich ihnen erklären muß, warum die Madonna nicht in der Kathedrale aufgestellt werden kann. Das kommt nun selbstverständ- lich überhaupt nicht mehr in Frage.«

»Ist das nicht ein bißchen voreilig gedacht?« wandte Reynold ein.

»Wenn ich deine Meinung hören will, junger Mann, dann sage ich dir Bescheid!« fauchte Philip.

Reynold war zum Schweigen gebracht, doch Jack ließ sich nicht so leicht das Wort verbieten. »Seid Ihr auch ganz sicher, daß Ihr den Menschen die Madonna vorenthalten dürft? Schaut sie Euch doch an.« Er wies auf die wenigen Betenden, die noch in der Kirche waren. Die Witwe Meg kniete direkt vor der Statue, und Tränen strömten über ihr Gesicht. Jack weiß nicht, fiel Philip ein, daß sie ihre gesamte Familie beim Einsturz von Alfreds Dach verloren hat. Ihre Tränen rührten ihn, und er fragte sich, ob Jack nicht doch recht haben mochte. Warum den Menschen so etwas nehmen? Weil es unehrlich ist, rief er sich streng zur Ordnung. Sie glauben nur deshalb an die Statue, weil sie ein falsches Wunder gesehen haben.

Jack kniete sich neben Meg und sprach sie an. »Warum weint Ihr?«

»Sie ist stumm«, sagte Philip.

Doch Meg antwortete auf Jacks Frage: »Die Madonna hat ebenso viel gelitten wie ich. Sie versteht mich.«

Philip stand wie vom Donner gerührt.

»Seht Ihr?« sagte Jack. »Die Statue lindert ihr Leid ... wieso starrt Ihr mich so an?«

»Sie ist stumm«, sagte Philip noch einmal. »Sie hat seit über einem Jahr kein einziges Wort mehr gesprochen.«

»Ja, ich erinnere mich!« fiel Aliena ein. »Als ihr Mann und ihre Söhne bei dem Einsturz umkamen, wurde sie stumm.«

»Diese Frau hier?« sagte Jack. »Aber sie hat mir doch gerade ...«

Reynold sah von einem zum anderen. »Ihr meint, dies ist ein Wunder? Ein *echtes* Wunder?«

Philip musterte Jacks Gesicht – der junge Mann war verblüffter als alle anderen. Das war keiner seiner Streiche!

Philip war zutiefst erschüttert: Hier war Gott selbst am Werk gewesen und hatte ein Wunder gewirkt! Mit unsicherer Stimme wandte er sich an Jack: »Trotz allem, was Ihr unternommen habt, um die Weinende Madonna in Verruf zu bringen, scheint Gott der Herr seine Wunder doch durch sie tun zu lassen.«

Jack gab keine Antwort. Es hatte ihm die Sprache verschlagen.

Als Jack der Kapitelversammlung seine Pläne für die neue Kathedrale vorlegte, kam es fast zu einem Aufruhr.

Philip hatte ihn schon im voraus gewarnt. Eines frühen Morgens hatte Jack zwei Holzrahmen, gefüllt mit Gips, in des Priors Haus gebracht und ihm seinen Grundriß und einen Aufriß gezeigt. Gemeinsam hatten sie die Entwürfe im klaren Morgenlicht betrachtet, und Philip hatte gesagt: »Jack, diese Kirche wird die herrlichste in ganz England – aber die Brüder werden eine Menge Einwände haben.«

Jack wußte noch aus seiner Novizenzeit, daß Remigius und seine Anhängerschar grundsätzlich gegen alles stimmten, was Philip am Herzen lag, obwohl es nun schon acht Jahre her war, daß der Subprior seine Wahlniederlage hatte einstecken müssen. Sie fanden nur selten volle Unterstützung bei den Mitbrüdern, doch in diesem Fall hegte selbst Philip Zweifel: Die meisten Männer waren konservativ bis ins Mark, und ein solch revolutionärer Entwurf wie der Jacks mochte sie durchaus abschrecken. Dennoch mußten sie ihnen die Pläne zeigen und sie zu überzeugen versuchen – denn wie sollte Philip eine Kathedrale bauen, wenn nicht die Mehrheit seiner Mönche voll und ganz hinter ihm stand?

Schon am folgenden Tag nahm Jack an der Kapitelversammlung teil und stellte seine Pläne vor. Er setzte sie auf einer Bank ab und lehnte sie gegen die Wand, und sofort wurden sie von den Mönchen umschwärmt. Kaum hatten die Brüder nähere Einzelheiten erkannt, entstand auch schon eine gemurmelte Diskussion, die rasch zum Tumult ausartete. Jack entnahm dem Tonfall, daß seine Pläne mit Mißbilligung, ja sogar mit Zorn aufgenommen wurden, und war enttäuscht. Der Tumult wurde noch lauter, als die Brüder nun auch untereinander zu streiten begannen, ob die Entwürfe nun gut oder schlecht seien.

Philip ließ sie eine Weile gewähren, bevor er sie zur Ordnung rief. Rasch kehrte wieder Ruhe ein, und Milius Bursar stellte eine im voraus verabredete Frage: »Wieso sind die Bogen so spitz?«

»Das ist eine neue Technik, die in Frankreich angewendet wird«, erwiderte Jack. »Ich habe sie dort in mehreren Kirchen gesehen und studiert. Der Spitzbogen ist stärker und tragfähiger, und aus diesem Grunde kann die neue Kathedrale so hoch werden. Das Hauptschiff wird wahrscheinlich das höchste in ganz England sein.«

Das gefällt ihnen, vermerkte Jack insgeheim.

»Die Fenster sind so unheimlich groß«, wandte einer ein.

»In Frankreich haben sie bewiesen, daß dicke Mauern gar nicht nötig sind«, erklärte Jack. »Was das Gebäude aufrecht hält, sind die Pfeiler, vor allem, wenn sie mit einem Kreuzrippengewölbe kombiniert werden. Und was die großen Fenster angeht – ihr Effekt ist einfach atemberaubend. In Saint-Denis ließ der Abt bunte Glasbilder einsetzen, mit dem Ergebnis, daß die Kirche voller Licht und Luft und Sonnenschein ist. Kirchen müssen heutzutage nicht mehr düster und lichtlos sein.«

Er sah, daß mehrere Mönche zustimmend nickten. Vielleicht waren sie doch nicht ganz so konservativ, wie er geglaubt hatte.

Doch dann meldete sich der Sakristan Andrew zu Wort. »Vor zwei Jahren noch wart Ihr ein Novize in unserer Mitte. Ihr wurdet bestraft, weil Ihr Euch gegen den Prior erhoben hattet, doch statt Eure Strafe hinzunehmen, seid Ihr davongelaufen. Und nun kommt Ihr zurück und wollt uns erzählen, wie wir unsere Kirche zu bauen haben.«

Noch bevor Jack antworten konnte, rief einer der jüngeren Brüder beinahe aufgebracht: »Was hat das denn mit dem Dom zu tun? Wir reden über den Bauplan, nicht über Jacks Vergangenheit!«

Daraufhin fühlten sich mehrere Mönche bemüht, ihre Meinung gleichzeitig kundzutun, so laut sie nur konnten, bis Philip sie alle zum Schweigen brachte und Jack bat, die Frage zu beantworten.

Jack hatte etwas Ähnliches erwartet und antwortete prompt. »Ich bin zur Strafe für diese Sünde nach Santiago de Compostela gepilgert, Vater Andrew, und ich hoffe, die Weinende Madonna, die ich Euch gebracht habe, wird mir als Buße zugutegehalten«, sagte er bescheiden. »Es ist gewiß nicht meine Bestimmung, ein Mönch zu werden, aber es ist mein sehnlichster Wunsch, unserem Herrgott auf andere Weise dienen zu können – als sein Baumeister.«

Das schien allen einzuleuchten.

Andrew allerdings hatte seine Pfeile noch nicht verschossen. »Wie alt seid Ihr?« begehrte er zu wissen, wiewohl er die Antwort genau kennen mußte.

»Zwanzig Jahre alt.«

»Das ist sehr jung für einen Dombaumeister.«

»Ich bin jedem von Euch bekannt. Ich habe seit meiner Kindheit hier gelebt.« Seit ich Eure alte Kirche in Brand gesteckt habe, dachte er schuldbewußt. »Meine Lehre habe ich bei unserem ursprünglichen Dombaumeister absolviert, und Ihr alle kennt meine Arbeiten. In meiner Novizenzeit habe ich unter Prior Philip und Tom Builder die Bauaufsicht geleitet. Ich bitte also die hier versammelten Brüder demütigst, mich nach meinen Leistungen beurteilen zu wollen, nicht nach meinem Alter.«

Auch diese Antwort hatte er sich im vorhinein überlegt. Als er nun einen der Mönche bei dem Wort *demütigst* breit grinsen sah, kamen ihm erstmals Bedenken ob der Klugheit seiner Strategie: Welche Vorzüge er auch sonst haben mochte, Demut gehörte gewiß nicht dazu – und das wußte hier jeder.

Bruder Andrew hatte nichts Eiligeres zu tun, als sich diesen Lapsus zunutze zu machen. »Demütigst?« fragte er mit gespielter Empörung und brachte es doch tatsächlich fertig, sein Gesicht zornesrot anlaufen zu lassen. »War es etwa *Demut*, die Euch veranlaßte, den Steinmetzen von Paris schon vor drei Monaten zu verkünden, Ihr wäret längst zum hiesigen Dombaumeister *ernannt*?!«

Erneutes Stimmengewirr mit höchst mißbilligendem Unterton – Jack unterdrückte ein Stöhnen. Wie mochte Andrew zu seinem Wissen gekommen sein? Reynold oder Edward, beschloß er, konnten den Mund nicht halten. Er versuchte, es mit einem Achselzucken abzutun. »Ich ging davon aus, daß ich damit einige ausgezeichnete Handwerker nach Kingsbridge locken könnte«, sagte er, nachdem sich das Durcheinander gelegt hatte. »Sie werden der neuen Kathedrale auf jeden Fall zugute kommen, ganz gleich, wer hier zum Baumeister ernannt wird. Ich glaube nicht, daß meine Voreiligkeit irgendwem geschadet hat.« Und mit einem gewinnenden Grinsen setzte er hinzu: »Es tut mir leid, daß ich nicht mehr Demut aufbringe.« Bisher lief die Sache nicht zu seiner Zufriedenheit.

Es war Milius Bursar, der ihn aus seiner Klemme befreite, indem er eine weitere abgesprochene Frage stellte: »Ihr wißt, daß der Altarraum teilweise eingestürzt ist. Was, meint Ihr, soll damit geschehen?«

»Ich habe ihn mir sehr genau angesehen«, erwiderte Jack. »Er kann durchaus wieder hergerichtet werden. Wenn Ihr mich heute zum Baumeister ernennt, wird er Euch in Jahresfrist wieder zur Verfügung stehen. Darüber hinaus könnt Ihr ihn benutzen, solange am Quer- und Hauptschiff nach meinen neuen Plänen gebaut wird. Erst danach, wenn das Langhaus vollendet ist, schlage ich vor, den alten Chorraum abzureißen und einen neuen zu errichten, der zum Stil der neuen Kirche paßt.«

»Aber wie können wir sicher sein«, wandte Andrew ein, »daß der alte Chor nicht noch einmal einstürzt?«

»Daß große Teile der Kirche einstürzten, lag daran, daß Alfred ein steinernes Deckengewölbe einzog, das in den ursprünglichen Plänen nicht vorgesehen war. Die Mauern konnten es nicht tragen – sie waren nicht stark genug. Ich schlage vor, zu Toms alten Plänen zurückzukehren und eine Holzdecke einzuziehen.«

Murmelnd äußerten die Mönche ihre Überraschung. Die Frage, warum Alfreds Dach eingestürzt war, war lange umstritten gewesen. »Aber Alfred hat doch die Stützpfeiler verstärkt«, meinte Andrew, »damit sie das höhere Gewicht tragen sollten.«

Das hatte auch Jack zu denken gegeben, aber nun glaubte er, die Nuß geknackt zu haben. »Sie waren immer noch nicht stark genug, vor allem ganz oben. Wenn Ihr Euch die Ruine genauer anseht, werdet Ihr erkennen, daß der Teil, der zuerst nachgegeben hat, der Lichtgaden war, und dort waren kaum Verstärkungen angebracht.«

Mit dieser Antwort schienen sie sich zufriedenzugeben. Jack hatte das Gefühl, daß seine sachkundigen, verläßlichen Antworten ihn dem begehrten Posten des Dombaumeisters ein gutes Stück näherbrachten.

Jetzt stand Remigius auf – Jack hatte sich schon gefragt, wo seine Einwände blieben. »Ich würde den Mitbrüdern gern einen Vers aus der Heiligen Schrift vorlesen«, sagte er bombastisch und sah zu Philip hinüber, der sein Einverständnis mit einem Nicken zu erkennen gab.

Remigius ging zum Lesepult und schlug die dicke Bibel auf. Seine schmalen Lippen, stellte Jack fest, waren in ständiger nervöser Bewegung, und seine wäßrig-blauen Augen standen ein wenig hervor, so daß er eine stets mißbilligende Miene zur Schau trug. Der Mann war ein einziger wandelnder Vorwurf. Vor vielen Jahren hatte er sich eingebildet, er sei dazu bestimmt, andere zu führen und zu leiten, doch in Wirklichkeit war er einfach charakterschwach, und da er seine Enttäuschung nie überwunden hatte, lebte er heute nur noch einem Ziel: besseren Männern wie er selbst einer war so viele Steine wie möglich in den Weg zu legen. »Das Zweite Buch Moses«, tönte er, während er die Pergamentseiten umblätterte. »Kapitel zwanzig, Vers vierzehn.« Jack fragte sich, was jetzt wohl kommen mochte. Remigius las vor: »›Du sollst nicht die Ehe brechen.‹« Er schloß den Folianten mit einem lauten Knall und kehrte zu seinem Platz zurück.

»Vielleicht verrätst du uns«, sagte Philip im Tone milder Verzweiflung, »warum du uns mitten in unserer Diskussion über die Baupläne ausgerechnet diesen kurzen Vers vorgelesen hast, Bruder Remigius?«

Der alte Mönch reckte anklagend den Zeigefinger und wies auf Jack. »Weil der Mann, der unser Dombaumeister werden möchte, in Sünde lebt!« donnerte er.

Jack vermochte es kaum zu fassen. Verdrossen gab er zurück: »Gewiß, der besonderen Umstände wegen wurde unsere Verbindung nicht von der Kirche gesegnet, aber wir können heiraten, sobald Ihr es wünscht.«

»Das könnt Ihr eben nicht«, sagte Remigius triumphierend. »Aliena ist bereits verheiratet.«

»Aber diese Ehe wurde nie vollzogen.«

»Nichtsdestoweniger wurde das Paar in der Kirche getraut.«

»Aber wenn Ihr mir nicht erlaubt, sie zu heiraten, wie soll ich dann *keinen* Ehebruch begehen?« versetzte Jack ärgerlich.

»Genug!« Das war Philips Stimme, und Jack wandte sich ihm zu. Der Prior sah wütend aus. »Jack«, sagte er, »lebt Ihr tatsächlich mit Eures Bruders Weib in Sünde?«

Die Frage erschütterte Jack. »Ja, wußtest Ihr das denn nicht?«

»Selbstverständlich wußte ich das nicht!« brüllte Philip. »Glaubt Ihr, ich hätte geschwiegen, wenn ich es gewußt hätte?«

Totenstille herrschte im Kapitelsaal. Es kam äußerst selten vor, daß Philip laut wurde, und Jack wurde klar, daß er in Schwierigkeiten war. Sein angebliches Vergehen war natürlich eine reine Formalität, aber Mönche sahen solche Dinge beträchtlich strenger, mußten sie wohl auch so sehen. Daß Philip keine Ahnung von seinem Zusammenleben mit Aliena gehabt hatte, machte das Ganze jedoch noch um einiges schlimmer. Und Remigius hatte ihn prompt auf dem falschen Fuß erwischt und als Narren hingestellt. Nun mußte Philip schon allein deshalb Unnachgiebigkeit an den Tag legen, weil das als Beweis für seine Strenge gewertet wurde.

»Aber Ihr könnt doch nicht eine falsche Kirche bauen, bloß weil Ihr mich bestrafen wollt«, sagte Jack unglücklich.

»Ihr müßt das Weib eben verlassen«, verkündete Remigius voll satter Selbstzufriedenheit.

»Schert Euch zum Kuckuck, Remigius! Sie hat ein Kind von mir, das schon ein Jahr alt ist!«

Remigius' Miene wurde noch um einiges selbstzufriedener.

»Jack«, sagte Philip, »wenn Ihr darauf besteht, eine solche Sprache in der Kapitelversammlung zu führen, so werdet Ihr gehen müssen.«

Doch Jack konnte sich wider besseres Wissen nicht so leicht beruhigen. »Aber das ist doch albern!« sagte er. »Mir zu befehlen, ich solle meine Frau und unser Kind im Stich lassen! Das ist keine Moral mehr – das ist Haarspalterei!«

Philips Ärger legte sich ein wenig, und Jack erkannte das vertraute, verständnisvolle Aufleuchten in den hellblauen Augen. »Eure Auslegung der Gesetze Gottes«, sagte er, »orientiert sich naturgegeben etwas mehr am Alltag, Jack. Wir jedoch ziehen eine strengere Haltung vor – schließlich ist das einer der Gründe, weshalb wir Mönche sind. Und wir können Euch nicht als Baumeister nehmen, solange Ihr Ehebruch begeht.«

Jack fiel ein Vers aus der Bibel ein: »Jesus sagte: Derjenige unter Euch, welcher ohne Sünde ist, werfe den ersten Stein.«

»Richtig«, sagte Philip, »aber Jesus sagte auch zu der Ehebrecherin: Gehe hin und sündige nicht mehr.« Er wandte sich Remigius zu. »Ich nehme an, du ziehst deine Einwände zurück, wenn kein Ehebruch mehr stattfindet.«

»Selbstverständlich«, sagte Remigius.

In all seiner Wut und Enttäuschung sah Jack doch klar, daß Philip Remigius säuberlich ausmanövriert hatte, indem er den Ehebruch zur entscheidenden Frage erhob und damit den neuen Entwurf gänzlich außer acht ließ. Darauf jedoch wollte Jack sich gar nicht erst einlassen. »Ich werde Aliena nicht verlassen!« sagte er.

»Es müßte ja nicht für lange Zeit sein«, meinte Philip.

Das kam für Jack völlig überraschend. »Wie meint Ihr das?«

»Wenn Alienas erste Ehe annulliert wird, könnt Ihr sie heiraten.«

»So etwas kann man machen?«

»Es sollte eigentlich sogar zügig gehen, wenn, wie Ihr behauptet, die Ehe nie vollzogen wurde.«

»Was muß ich dabei tun?«

»An ein Kirchengericht appellieren. Normalerweise sollte Bischof Waleran darüber entscheiden, aber in diesem Fall wendet Ihr Euch am besten direkt an den Erzbischof von Canterbury.«

»Und der Erzbischof – wird er die Annullierung aussprechen?«

»Wenn es gerecht zugeht, ja.«

Das war ja nun beileibe keine unzweideutige Antwort. »Und bis dahin müßten wir getrennt leben?«

»Ja – wenn Ihr zum Dombaumeister ernannt werden wollt.«

»Ich muß mich also zwischen Aliena und der Kathedrale entscheiden – und beide liebe ich mehr als alles andere auf der Welt.«

»Es ist ja nicht für lange.«

Der begütigende Ton ließ Jack abrupt aufsehen: In Philips Miene spiegelte sich ehrliches Mitgefühl. Philip empfand also tatsächlich Bedauern darüber, daß er diese Entscheidung treffen mußte! Dieser Umstand besänftigte Jack ein wenig, und er fragte: »Wie lange?«

»Möglicherweise ein Jahr lang.«

»Ein ganzes Jahr lang!«

»Ihr werdet nicht gezwungen sein, in zwei verschiedenen Städten zu leben«, erwiderte Philip. »Ihr könnt Aliena und das Kind täglich sehen.«

»Wißt Ihr, daß sie bis nach Spanien gezogen ist, um mich zu suchen?« fragte Jack. »Habt Ihr eine Ahnung, was das bedeutet?« Nein, natürlich nicht – Mönche hatten nun mal keine Vorstellung von weltlicher Liebe. »Und da muß ich ihr mitteilen, daß wir getrennt leben sollen!« fügte er erbittert hinzu.

Philip erhob sich und legte ihm eine Hand auf die Schulter. »Die Zeit wird schneller vergehen, als Ihr jetzt meint, das könnt Ihr mir glauben«, sagte er. »Ihr werdet viel zu beschäftigt sein – mit der neuen Kathedrale.«

Der Wald hatte sich in den vergangenen acht Jahren sehr verändert. Jack hatte gemeint, er könne sich unmöglich darin verirren, hatte er ihn doch einst gekannt wie seine eigene Hosentasche, doch nun mußte er einsehen, daß dies ein Irrtum war. Die alten Pfade waren überwachsen und überwuchert, Hirsche, Eber und Wildpferde hatten neue Fährten durchs Unterholz gezogen, die Bäche nahmen einen anderen Lauf, alte Bäume waren eingestürzt und die einst jungen in die Höhe geschossen. Alles kam Jack kleiner vor – die Entfernungen kürzer, die Hügel weniger steil. Am erstaunlichsten jedoch war, daß er sich wie ein Fremder fühlte. Als ihn ein aufgescheuchtes junges Tier über eine Lichtung hinweg mißtrauisch beäugte, hätte Jack nicht zu sagen gewußt, zu welcher Sorte Rotwild es gehörte noch wo seine Mutter zu finden war; als eine Schar Enten aufflatterte, war ihm nicht wie früher sofort klar, woher sie kamen und weshalb sie aufgeflogen waren. Und er war beunruhigt, denn er hatte keine Ahnung, wo sich die Outlaws aufhalten mochten.

Er hatte fast den ganzen Tag für seinen Ritt von Kingsbridge hierher gebraucht. Nach dem Verlassen der Hauptstraße hatte er absteigen müssen, denn die Zweige über dem Trampelpfad hingen zu tief für einen Reiter. Die Rückkehr zu den Schlupfwinkeln seiner Kindheit stimmte ihn seltsamerweise traurig. Er hatte das einfache Leben damals nicht richtig zu schätzen gewußt, da er kein anderes gekannt hatte. Nun erinnerte er sich, mit welcher Leidenschaft er die Erdbeeren gesucht hatte, die auf dem Waldboden wuchsen, mit welcher Freude er jeden Sommer ein paar Tage lang so viele gegessen hatte, wie er nur finden konnte. Heutzutage war nichts mehr einfach: Seine Freundschaft mit Prior Philip war schwierig, seine Liebe zu Aliena kritischen Spannungen unterworfen, sein Ehrgeiz, die schönste Kathedrale der Welt zu bauen, war übermächtig, und das Bedürfnis, die Wahrheit über seinen Vater herauszufinden, brannte ihm auf der Seele.

Ob seine Mutter sich in den vergangenen zwei Jahren, in denen er umhergezogen war, wohl sehr verändert hatte? Er freute sich auf das Wiedersehen mit ihr. Natürlich kam er längst allein zurecht, aber es war doch ein beruhigendes Gefühl, einen Menschen zu haben, der stets für einen da war, stets für einen eintrat – und dieses tröstliche Gefühl hatte er doch sehr vermißt.

Der kurze Winternachmittag war vorüber und die Dämmerung setzte ein, als Jack den Teil des Waldes erreichte, in dem sie früher zusammengelebt hatten. Wenn er ihre alte Höhle nicht bald fand, würde er sich nach einem geschützten Plätzchen für die Nacht umsehen müssen. Das würde eine kalte Nacht werden. Wovor habe ich eigentlich Angst? fragte er sich. Früher habe ich jede Nacht im Wald verbracht.

Am Ende war es Ellen, die ihn fand.

Er hatte seine Suche schon aufgeben wollen. Der schmale, beinahe unsichtbare Pfad, dem er gefolgt war, endete in einem Dickicht. Vermutlich wurde er nur von Füchsen und Dachsen benutzt. Das beste war wohl, wenn er den gleichen Pfad wieder zurückging. Er wendete sein Pferd – und wäre beinahe über seine Mutter gestolpert.

»Du weißt offenbar nicht mehr, wie man sich geräuschlos durch den Wald schleicht«, sagte sie zur Begrüßung. »Der Lärm, den du machst, ist eine Meile im Umkreis zu hören.«

Jack lächelte; sie hatte sich nicht verändert. »Hallo, Mutter«, sagte er und küßte ihr die Wange. Dann, von seiner Zuneigung überwältigt, schloß er sie in die Arme.

Sie streichelte sein Gesicht. »Du bist noch magerer als früher.«

Sie selbst, fand er, war braungebrannt und gesund, ihr Haar noch dicht und dunkel, ohne eine Spur von Grau darin. Ihre Augen hatten noch immer den alten Goldton, und sie schienen noch immer direkt durch ihn hindurchzusehen. »Und du bist immer noch dieselbe«, antwortete er.

»Wo warst du?« fragte sie.

»Ich bin bis nach Santiago gezogen, ja sogar noch weiter, bis nach Toledo.«

»Aliena hat sich auf die Suche nach dir gemacht.«

»Und sie hat mich gefunden – dank deiner Hilfe.«

»Das freut mich.« Sie schloß die Augen, als sende sie ein Dankgebet gen Himmel. »Ich kann gar nicht sagen, wir sehr mich das freut.«

Sie führte ihn durch den Wald zur Höhle, die kaum eine Meile weit entfernt lag – gar so schlecht war sein Gedächtnis also doch nicht. Drinnen brannten ein helles Feuer und drei sprühende Binsenlichter. Ellen gab ihm einen Krug Apfelmost, den sie aus Holzäpfeln und wildem Honig selbst machte, und sie rösteten sich Kastanien über dem Feuer. Jack hatte ihr verschiedene Dinge mitgebracht, von denen er aus Erfahrung wußte, daß sie von Waldbewohnern nicht selbst herzustellen waren: Messer, Schnur, Seife und Salz. Ellen begann, ein Wildkaninchen zu enthäuten. »Wie geht's dir, Mutter?« fragte Jack.

»Gut«, sagte sie, doch dann sah sie auf und erkannte, daß seine Frage ernst gemeint war. »Toms Tod macht mir immer noch Kummer«, erklärte sie, »aber daran ist nun mal nichts zu ändern, und ich werde mir keinen anderen Mann suchen.«

»Und sonst – fühlst du dich hier wohl?«

»Ja und nein. Ich bin das Leben im Wald gewohnt, ich bin gerne allein, und ich konnte es noch nie leiden, wenn mir aufdringliche Pfaffen vorschreiben wollten, wie ich mich zu verhalten habe. Aber ihr fehlt mir – du, Martha und Aliena, und es wäre schön, wenn ich mehr von meinem Enkelchen haben könnte.« Sie lächelte. »Aber ich kann nicht wieder nach Kingsbridge ziehen – nicht, nachdem ich eine christliche Hochzeit verflucht habe. Das verzeiht mir Prior Philip nie. Aber was soll's – wenn es dich und Aliena zusammengebracht hat, ist es mir das wert.« Sie sah von ihrer Arbeit auf und lächelte ihn fröhlich an. »Und wie gefällt dir das Eheleben?«

»Nun ja«, sagte er zögernd, »wir sind ja nicht verheiratet. In den Augen der Kirche ist Aliena immer noch Alfreds Frau.«

»Sei nicht albern. Was versteht die Kirche schon davon?«

»Nun ja, die Priester wissen, wen sie getraut haben, und sie wollten mich nicht den neuen Dom bauen lassen, solange ich mit der Frau eines anderen zusammenlebe.«

Ihre Augen funkelten zornig. »Du hast sie also verlassen?«

»Ja. Bis ihre Ehe annulliert wird.«

Ellen legte das Kaninchenfell beiseite und nahm ein scharfes Messer in ihre blutbesudelten Hände. Dann begann sie, das Fleisch von den Knochen zu lösen, und ließ die Stücke in den Kochtopf fallen, der über dem Feuer brodelte. »Prior Philip hat mir einmal das gleiche angetan, damals, als ich mit Tom zusammenlebte«, sagte sie, während sie das rohe Fleisch kleinschnitt. »Ich kann mir denken, warum er so durchdreht, wenn andere Leute sich lieben – einfach, weil es ihm selber verboten ist. Er gönnt anderen nicht die Freiheit zu genießen, was ihm nicht erlaubt ist. Wenn sie in der Kirche getraut wurden, kann er natürlich nichts dagegen tun. Aber wehe, sie sind nicht getraut! Dann verdirbt er es ihnen gründlich, bloß damit er sich ein bißchen wohler fühlen kann.« Sie schnitt dem Kaninchen die Füße ab und warf sie in einen Holzeimer voller Unrat.

Jack nickte. Er hatte das Unvermeidliche hingenommen, doch jedesmal, wenn er Aliena gute Nacht sagen und ihr Haus verlassen mußte, stieg die Wut auf Philip erneut in ihm auf, so daß er gut verstand, daß seine Mutter noch immer einen tiefsitzenden Groll gegen ihn hegte. »Es ist ja nicht für immer«, sagte er.

»Wie hält Aliena das aus?«

Jack zog eine Grimasse. »Gar nicht gut. Aber sie glaubt, es sei ihre Schuld, weil sie Alfred damals geheiratet hat.«

»Das stimmt. Es ist aber auch deine Schuld, weil du unbedingt Kirchen bauen willst.«

Schade, daß sie seine Vorstellungen nicht verstand. »Ich will nichts anderes bauen, Mutter – das ist mir einfach nicht genug. Kirchen sind größer und höher und schöner als jeder andere Bau, außerdem ist die Arbeit schwieriger, und sie werden mit mehr Ornamenten und Skulpturen ausgestattet.«

»Und mit weniger gibst du dich nicht zufrieden.«

»So ist es.«

Verdutzt schüttelte sie den Kopf. »Es wird mir wohl ewig ein Rätsel bleiben, wie du auf die Idee kommen konntest, du seist für etwas Großes bestimmt.« Sie gab das restliche Kaninchenfleisch in den Topf und machte sich an die Säuberung der Haut, denn sie wollte das Fell noch verwenden. »Von deinen Vorfahren hast du das jedenfalls nicht geerbt.«

Das war das Stichwort, auf das er gewartet hatte. »Mutter«, fing er an, »drüben in Frankreich habe ich einiges über meine Vorfahren gehört.«

Sie hörte auf zu schaben und sah ihn an. »Wovon sprichst du?«

»Ich habe die Familie meines Vaters gefunden.«

»Gütiger Gott!« Sie ließ das Kaninchenfell fallen. »Wie ist dir das denn gelungen? Wo sind sie? Sind sie nett?«

»In der Normandie gibt es eine Stadt, die Cherbourg heißt – daher stammt mein Vater.«

»Woher willst du das so genau wissen?«

»Ich sehe ihm so ähnlich, daß sie mich für seinen Geist gehalten haben.«

Mutter ließ sich ungeschickt auf einen Schemel plumpsen, und Jack fühlte Gewissensbisse aufsteigen: Er hatte nicht damit gerechnet, daß die Neuigkeiten sie so sehr erschüttern könnten. »Wie … wie ist seine Familie?« fragte sie stockend.

»Sein Vater ist tot, aber seine Mutter lebt noch. Sie war sehr nett zu mir, sobald sie erst einmal überzeugt war, daß ich nicht der Geist meines Vaters bin. Er hatte auch einen älteren Bruder – der ist Zimmermann und hat eine Frau und drei Kinder. Meine Vettern.« Er lächelte. »Ist das nicht fein? Wir haben tatsächlich Verwandtschaft.«

Doch seine Feststellung schien sie eher aufzubringen, und sie sah etwas niedergeschlagen drein. »O Jack«, sagte sie, »es tut mir so leid, daß ich dich nicht in einer normalen Familie großziehen konnte.«

»Nun, mir tut's nicht leid«, sagte er leichthin. Die Reueanfälle seiner Mutter brachten ihn jedesmal in Verlegenheit – sie paßten so gar nicht zu ihrem Wesen. »Aber ich bin froh, daß ich meine Vettern kennengelernt habe. Zwar werd' ich sie wohl kaum jeweils wiedersehen, dennoch ist es gut zu wissen, daß es sie gibt.«

Sie nickte traurig. »Ich verstehe.«

Jack holte tief Luft. »Sie dachten, mein Vater wäre bei einem Schiffsuntergang vor vierundzwanzig Jahren ertrunken. Das ›Weiße Schiff‹, auf dem er sich befand, sank vor der Küste von Barfleur, und man glaubte, alle, die an Bord waren, seien ertrunken. Mein Vater hat das Unglück offenbar überlebt, aber sie haben nie davon erfahren, weil er nicht nach Cherbourg zurückgekehrt ist.«

»Er kam statt dessen nach Kingsbridge«, sagte sie.

»Aber *warum?*«

Sie seufzte. »Er konnte sich an einem Faß festklammern und wurde in der Nähe einer Burg an Land gespült«, erklärte sie. »Er ging zur Burg und berichtete von dem Schiffsuntergang. Mehrere mächtige Barone auf der Burg wirkten bei seinem Auftauchen sehr betroffen. Sie setzten ihn gefangen und schafften ihn nach England. Nach mehreren Wochen oder Monaten – er hatte jedes Zeitgefühl verloren – landete er dann in Kingsbridge.«

»Hat er dir sonst noch etwas über den Schiffsuntergang erzählt?«

»Nur, daß sie sehr schnell sanken, als sei das Schiff durchlöchert gewesen.«

»Das klingt, als hätte man ihn unbedingt aus dem Weg haben wollen.«

Sie nickte. »Und als sie merkten, daß sie ihn nicht ewig gefangenhalten konnten, brachten sie ihn um.«

Jack kniete sich vor ihr nieder und zwang sie, ihm ins Gesicht zu sehen. »Aber wer sind *sie,* Mutter?« fragte er, und seine Stimme vibrierte vor unterdrückten Gefühlen.

»Das hast du mich schon einmal gefragt.«

»Und du hast mir keine Antwort gegeben.«

»Weil ich nicht will, daß du dein Leben damit verbringst, den Tod deines Vaters zu rächen!«

Sie behandelt mich, als wäre ich noch ein kleines Kind, dem man gewisse Dinge vorenthält, weil sie ihm schaden könnten, dachte er. Er versuchte es mit ruhiger Besonnenheit: »Ich werde mein Leben damit verbringen, daß ich in Kingsbridge eine Kathedrale baue und mit Aliena Kinder zeuge. Aber ich will wissen, warum sie meinen Vater gehängt haben. Und die einzigen Menschen, die die Antwort darauf kennen, sind jene, die falsches Zeugnis wider ihn ablegten. Daher muß ich wissen, wer das war.«

»Damals kannte ich ihre Namen gar nicht.«

Sie wich ihm aus, und das machte ihn wütend. *»Aber heute kennst du sie!«*

»Ja, ich kenne sie«, gestand sie, den Tränen nahe, und Jack erkannte, daß ihr das alles ebenso naheging wie ihm selbst. »Gut, ich nenne sie dir, denn ich merke, daß du sonst niemals Ruhe geben wirst.«

Sie schnüffelte und wischte sich die Tränen aus den Augen.

Jack wartete gespannt.

»Es waren drei: ein Mönch, ein Priester und ein Ritter.«

Jack sah sie unbarmherzig an. »Ihre Namen!«

»Willst du sie fragen, warum sie unter Eid falsch aussagten?«

»Jawohl.«

»Und du glaubst, sie werden es dir erzählen?«

»Wahrscheinlich nicht. Aber ich werde ihnen in die Augen sehen, wenn ich meine Fragen stelle, und das wird mir vielleicht alles verraten, was ich wissen will.«

»Selbst das wird vielleicht nicht möglich sein.«

»Ich möchte es wenigstens versuchen, Mutter!«

Sie seufzte. »Der Mönch war der Prior von Kingsbridge.«

»Philip?«

»Nein, Philip nicht, das war vor seiner Zeit. Es war sein Vorgänger, er hieß James.«

»Aber der ist tot.«

»Ich sagte doch, du wirst sie womöglich nicht mehr fragen können.«

Jacks Augen verengten sich. »Wer waren die anderen beiden?«

»Der Ritter war Percy Hamleigh, der spätere Graf von Shiring.«

»Williams Vater!«

»Richtig.«

»Der ist ja auch tot!«

»Eben.«

Waren sie alle drei tot und hatten das Geheimnis mit ins Grab genommen? Es durfte nicht sein! »Und wer war der Priester?« drängte Jack.

»Er heißt Waleran Bigod und ist heute Bischof von Kingsbridge.«

Jack tat einen Seufzer tiefster Erleichterung. »Und der ist immer noch am Leben«, sagte er.

Bischof Walerans Burg wurde zu Weihnachten fertiggestellt. William und seine Mutter, die eines schönen Morgens zu Beginn des neuen Jahres hinüberritten, sahen sie schon aus der Ferne über das ganze Tal hinweg. Sie stand auf dem höchsten Punkt der Hügelkette und schien die weite Landschaft unter ihr mit abweisenden Blicken zu bedecken.

Im Tal ritten sie am ehemaligen Bischofspalast vorbei, der nun als Lagerhaus für Schafvliese diente. Die Burg hatte ihre Existenz überwiegend den Erlösen aus dem Wollhandel zu verdanken.

Am anderen Ende des Tals führte die Straße sachte den Abhang hinauf, durch eine Öffnung im Erdwall und über einen tiefen, trokkenen Graben zum Torgang in einer steinernen Mauer. Erdwälle, Burggraben *und* Steinmauer machten diese Burg zu einem höchst sicheren Aufenthaltsort – sicherer noch als Williams eigene und viele der Burgen des Königs.

Den Innenhof beherrschte ein wuchtiger, quadratisch gebauter Wohnturm, der mit seinen drei Stockwerken die Kirche an seiner Seite wie ein Zwergenhaus erscheinen ließ. William half seiner Mutter beim Absteigen. Die Pferde überließen sie ihren Rittern und gingen die Treppe hinauf, die zum Saal führte.

Es war Mittagszeit, und Walerans Diener deckten die Tische. Mehrere Erzdiakone, Diakone, sonstige Angestellte und Anhänger des Bischofs standen herum und warteten auf das Essen. Ein Haushofmeister ging die Treppe hinauf, um Waleran in seinen Privatgemächern die Ankunft Williams und Regans zu melden.

William brannte inwendig vor Eifersucht, einer wilden, alles verzehrenden Eifersucht. Aliena war verliebt, und die ganze Grafschaft wußte es. Sie hatte ein Kind der Liebe geboren, und ihr Ehegatte hatte sie aus dem Haus geworfen. Danach hatte sie sich mit ihrem Wechselbalg im Arm auf die Suche nach ihrem Liebhaber gemacht und ihn tatsächlich auch gefunden, nachdem sie die halbe christliche Welt durchstreift hatte. Die Geschichte machte in ganz Südengland die Runde – und William machte es jedesmal krank vor Haß, wenn sie ihm noch einmal und noch einmal und immer wieder zu Ohren kam. Aber er hatte sich etwas einfallen lassen; er wollte seine Rache haben.

Man führte sie die Treppe hinauf in Walerans Kammer. Der Bischof saß mit Baldwin, jetzt Erzdiakon, an einem Tisch, wo sie Geld zählten, indem sie die Silberpennies zu jeweils zwölfen von den weißen auf die schwarzen Felder eines Tuches mit Schachbrettmuster schoben. Baldwin stand auf, verneigte sich vor Lady Regan und ließ das Tuch samt dem Geld schnellstens verschwinden.

Auch Waleran erhob sich und ging zu einem Armstuhl am Feuer. Er bewegte sich rasch wie eine Spinne, und William fühlte die altvertraute Abneigung in sich aufsteigen. Dennoch war er entschlossen, sich nichts anmerken zu lassen – erst kürzlich hatte er vom schrecklichen Tod des Grafen von Hereford gehört, der sich mit seinem Bischof gestritten hatte und im Status der Exkommunikation starb, worauf man ihn in ungeweihter Erde begraben hatte. William brauchte sich nur vorzustellen, er selbst läge in der nackten Erde, eine ungeschützte Beute für all die Teufel und Unholde, die die Unterwelt heimsuchten, und er wurde von Entsetzen geschüttelt. *Er* würde niemals einen Streit mit seinem Bischof vom Zaun brechen!

Waleran war so blaß und dünn wie eh und je, und seine Gewänder hingen an ihm herab wie zum Trocknen aufgehängte Wäsche. Er schien sich nie zu verändern. William selbst indessen hatte sich verändert. Da seine Hauptvergnügen gutes Essen und starker Wein waren, wuchs sein Umfang von Jahr zu Jahr, dem regen Leben, das er führte, zum Trotz, und das teure Kettenpanzerhemd, das ihm zum einundzwanzigsten Geburtstag angemessen worden war, hatte in den darauffolgenden sieben Jahren schon zweimal durch ein neues ersetzt werden müssen.

Waleran war erst kürzlich aus York zurückgekehrt, wo er sich fast ein halbes Jahr lang aufgehalten hatte, und William fragte höflich: »War Eure Reise von Erfolg gekrönt?«

»Nein«, war die Antwort. »Bischof Henry gab mir den Auftrag, einen nun schon vier Jahre währenden Streit zu schlichten – darüber, wer der nächste Erzbischof von York werden soll. Das ist mir nicht gelungen. Der Zank geht weiter.«

Darüber verliert man am besten kein Wort mehr, dachte William. »Während Eurer Abwesenheit«, sagte er, »hat sich hier viel verändert. Vor allem in Kingsbridge.«

»In Kingsbridge?« fragte Waleran überrascht. »Ich ging davon aus, dieses Problem sei ein für allemal gelöst.«

William schüttelte den Kopf. »Sie haben jetzt eine Weinende Madonna.«

Waleran sah ihn mißtrauisch an. »Was, zum Teufel, soll das denn sein?«

Williams Mutter ergriff das Wort. »Es geht um eine hölzerne Statue der Jungfrau Maria, mit der sie Prozessionen veranstalten. Zu bestimmten Zeiten vergießen ihre Augen Wasser, und das gemeine Volk hält es natürlich für ein Wunder.«

»Es *ist* ein Wunder!« protestierte William.

Waleran bedachte ihn mit einem abfälligen Blick.

»Wunder oder nicht«, fuhr Regan fort, »in den vergangenen Monaten waren schon Tausende von Leuten dort, um die Statue zu sehen. Und Prior Philip hat seinen Kirchenbau wieder aufgenommen. Sie stellen den Altarraum wieder her, der eine neue Holzdecke bekommen soll, und das Fundament für die Vierung wurde auch schon ausgehoben. Außerdem sind neue Steinmetzen aus Paris eingetroffen.«

»Aus Paris?«

»Die Kirche soll jetzt im Stil von Saint-Denis gebaut werden, was immer das heißen mag«, sagte Regan.

Waleran nickte. »Überhöhte Spitzbogen. Ich habe in York davon gehört.«

William, dem der Baustil der Kathedrale von Kingsbridge vollkommen gleichgültig war, erklärte: »Der springende Punkt ist, daß die jungen Männer meine Höfe verlassen und am Dombau Arbeit finden, daß der Sonntagsmarkt wieder stattfindet und die Einnahmen von Shiring vermindert ... Das Ganze geht also wieder von vorne los!« Verstohlen behielt er den Bischof und seine Mutter im Auge. Hatten sie Verdacht geschöpft, daß es ihm im Grunde um etwas ganz anderes ging? Es sah nicht so aus.

»Daß ich Philip zum Prior gemacht habe, war der größte Fehler meines Lebens«, sagte Waleran.

»Sie werden lernen müssen, daß sie damit nicht durchkommen«, meinte William.

Waleran sah ihn nachdenklich an. »Was wollt Ihr dagegen unternehmen?«

»Ich werde die Stadt noch einmal überrennen.« Und diesmal, dachte er und sah ins Feuer, damit die anderen nicht seine Gedanken lesen konnten, diesmal werden mir weder Aliena noch ihr Liebhaber entkommen ...

»So einfach wird das wohl nicht gehen«, wandte Waleran ein.

»Ich hab's schließlich schon einmal gemacht – warum nicht ein zweites Mal?«

»Damals hattet Ihr einen guten Grund dafür – die Wollmesse.«

»Diesmal liefert mir der Markt den Grund. König Stephan hat ihn nie genehmigt.«

»Trotzdem – das ist nicht das gleiche. Mit dem Wollmarkt hatte Philip den Bogen überspannt, und Ihr habt ihm sofort einen Riegel vorgeschoben. Aber der Sonntagsmarkt findet nun schon seit sechs Jahren statt. Und da Kingsbridge zwanzig Meilen von Shiring entfernt liegt, wäre es nur recht und billig, den Markt zu genehmigen.«

William schluckte seinen Ärger hinunter. Schade, daß er diesem Kerl nicht das Maul verbieten konnte! Der redete mal wieder daher wie ein altes Waschweib.

Ein Haushofmeister trat ein und blieb abwartend an der Tür stehen. »Was gibt's?« fragte Waleran.

»Da ist ein Mann, ehrwürdiger Herr Bischof, der darauf besteht, zu Euch vorgelassen zu werden. Jack Jackson ist sein Name – ein Baumeister aus Kingsbridge. Soll ich ihn abweisen?«

Alienas Liebhaber! Williams Puls beschleunigte sich. Wieso taucht der Kerl ausgerechnet jetzt hier auf? dachte er. Weiß er, was ich mit ihm vorhabe? Vielleicht besitzt er übernatürliche Fähigkeiten ... Furcht befiel ihn.

Waleran horchte auf. »Aus Kingsbridge?«

»Er ist der neue Dombaumeister«, erklärte Regan, »er hat die Weinende Madonna aus Spanien mitgebracht.«

»Wie interessant«, sagte Waleran. »Werfen wir doch einen Blick auf ihn. – Schick ihn herein«, befahl er dem Haushofmeister.

William starrte wie gebannt auf die Tür. In seiner abergläubischen Furcht erwartete er, einen hochgewachsenen, furchterregenden Mann eintreten zu sehen, der unverzüglich mit anklagend ausgestrecktem Zeigefinger auf ihn zugehen würde. Als Jack eintrat, versetzte es William einen Stich: Dieser Mann konnte kaum älter als zwanzig sein! Sein Blick aus lebhaften blauen Augen glitt über William hinweg, verharrte kurz auf Regan und blieb schließlich auf Waleran liegen. Die Gegenwart der beiden mächtigsten Männer der ganzen Grafschaft schien den Baumeister nicht einzuschüchtern – doch von dieser überraschenden Gleichgültigkeit einmal abgesehen, wirkte er ganz und gar nicht furchterregend.

Die unehrerbietige Haltung des jungen Mannes war auch Waleran nicht entgangen, und er begegnete ihr mit kühlem Hochmut. »Nun, Bursche, was ist Euer Begehr?«

»Die Wahrheit«, sagte Jack. »Wie viele Männer habt Ihr schon hängen sehen?«

William hielt den Atem an: was für eine unverschämte Frage! Mutter allerdings neigte sich stirnrunzelnd vor, als hätte sie den Mann schon einmal gesehen, wüßte aber nicht mehr wo. Waleran setzte seine übliche spöttische Miene auf.

»Sollen wir hier Rätsel raten?« fragte er. »Ich habe mehr Männer hängen sehen, als ich zählen kann, und ich werde bald noch einen weiteren sehen, wenn Ihr Euch nicht zu etwas mehr Respekt aufrafft.«

»Ich bitte um Entschuldigung, ehrwürdiger Herr Bischof«, erwiderte Jack, aber seine Stimme klang immer noch nicht, als erstürbe er in Ehrfurcht. »Entsinnt Ihr Euch jedes einzelnen?«

»Ich denke schon«, meinte Waleran. Es klang, als sei er gegen seinen Willen gefesselt. »Geht es Euch denn um einen ganz bestimmten?«

»Ihr habt vor zweiundzwanzig Jahren in Shiring an der Hinrichtung eines gewissen Jack Cherbourg mitgewirkt.«

William hörte, wie seine Mutter einen Aufschrei unterdrückte.

»Er war ein Spielmann«, fuhr Jack fort. »Erinnert Ihr Euch?«

Die plötzliche Spannung im Raum schien William beinahe greifbar. Dieser Jack Jackson hatte wahrhaftig etwas Furchterregendes an sich; wie sonst sollte er Mutter und dem Bischof einen solchen Schrecken einjagen können.

»Doch, ich glaube, ich kann mich erinnern«, hörte er Waleran mit mühsamer Selbstbeherrschung sagen, und das kam ihm nun vollends geheimnisvoll vor.

»Das will ich meinen«, versetzte Jack, nun wieder reichlich unverschämt. »Dieser Mann wurde damals auf das Zeugnis dreier Leute hin verurteilt. Zwei der Zeugen sind bereits tot. Ihr wart der dritte.«

Waleran nickte. »Er hatte etwas aus der Priorei zu Kingsbridge gestohlen – einen juwelenbesetzten Kelch.«

Jacks blaue Augen nahmen einen harten Ausdruck an. »Er hatte nichts dergleichen getan.«

»Ich habe ihn selbst ertappt – er trug den Kelch bei sich.«

»Ihr habt gelogen.«

Schweigen herrschte. Dann ergriff Waleran wieder das Wort – mit nachsichtiger Stimme, aber eisenhartem Blick. »Dafür könnte ich Euch die Zunge ausreißen lassen.«

»Ich möchte bloß erfahren, aus welchem Grund Ihr logt«, gab Jack zurück, als habe er die grausige Drohung nicht gehört. »Ihr könnt hier ganz offen sprechen. William ist keinerlei Gefahr für Euch, und seine Mutter scheint ohnehin Bescheid zu wissen.«

Wahrlich, dachte William, das ist Mutter nur allzu deutlich anzusehen. Das wird ja immer geheimnisvoller! Ist es möglich, daß dieser Jack gar nichts von meinen Mordplänen weiß? Er wagte es kaum zu hoffen.

»Ihr beschuldigt den Bischof des Meineids!« protestierte Regan.

»Eine Anklage, die ich nicht öffentlich zu wiederholen gedenke«, war Jacks kühle Antwort. »Dazu fehlen mir die Beweise. Auch ist mir nicht an Rache gelegen. Mir geht es nur um eines: Ich möchte wissen, warum Ihr einen Unschuldigen an den Galgen brachtet.«

»Raus mit Euch!« befahl Waleran frostig.

Jack nickte, als hätte er genau das erwartet. Er hatte keine Antwort auf seine Fragen bekommen – dennoch setzte er eine zufriedene Miene auf. Sein Verdacht mußte also bestätigt worden sein.

Noch immer verblüfft von dem geheimnisvollen Wortwechsel, warf William rasch ein: »Wartet einen Moment!«

Jack, bereits an der Tür, drehte sich um und warf ihm einen spöttischen Blick zu.

»Was …« William mußte schlucken, bevor er ruhig weitersprechen konnte. »Was liegt Euch an der Sache? Wieso kommt Ihr hierher und stellt solche Fragen?«

»Weil der Unschuldige, den sie damals hängten, mein Vater war«, gab Jack zurück und ging hinaus.

Eine ganze Weile lang sprach niemand ein Wort. Alienas Liebhaber ist also nicht nur Dombaumeister, dachte William, sondern auch der Sohn eines Diebs. Aber wieso macht das Mutter angst und bange – und Waleran nicht minder?

Endlich schien Waleran seine Sprache wiedergefunden zu haben. »Dieses Weib«, sagte er voller Ingrimm, »dieses Weib verfolgt mich nun schon seit zwanzig Jahren!« William erlebte zum erstenmal, daß der stets so beherrschte Bischof Gefühle zeigte.

»Sie verschwand nach dem Einsturz der Kathedrale«, sagte Regan. »Ich dachte, damit wären wir sie los.«

»Dafür haben wir nun ihren Sohn auf den Fersen.«

So furchtsam hatte Waleran noch nie geklungen, und William schlug vor: »Laßt ihn doch einfach in Eisen legen, wenn er Euch des Meineids beschuldigt.«

Waleran bedachte ihn mit einem strafenden Blick und sagte: »Regan, Euer Sohn ist ein Dummkopf.«

Die Beschuldigung war also nicht aus der Luft gegriffen, stellte William bei sich fest. Und wenn *ich* mir das zusammenreimen kann, dann kann es dieser Jack auch … »Weiß sonst noch jemand von dieser Sache?«

»Prior James«, erklärte Regan, »hat seinen Meineid auf dem Totenbett gebeichtet, und zwar seinem Subprior Remigius. Aber der hat uns stets gegen Philip zur Seite gestanden, er kann uns nicht gefährlich werden. Jacks Mutter weiß einiges, aber bestimmt nicht alles, sonst hätte sie ihr Wissen längst gegen uns verwendet. Nur dieser

Jack macht mir Sorge – er ist weit herumgekommen und könnte mehr erfahren haben, als seine Mutter wußte.«

Diese uralte Geschichte schien William direkt in die Hände zu spielen. Als wäre ihm der Gedanke eben erst gekommen, schlug er vor: »Am besten bringen wir also Jack Jackson um.«

Waleran schüttelte verächtlich den Kopf.

»Das könnte nur unnötige Aufmerksamkeit auf ihn und seine Beschuldigung lenken«, wandte Regan ein.

»Nicht unbedingt«, erwiderte William.

Die beiden sahen ihn skeptisch an.

»Man könnte Jack umbringen, ohne daß es besondere Aufmerksamkeit auf ihn lenkt«, sagte er stur.

»Na schön. Verratet uns, wie Ihr das machen wollt«, meinte Waleran.

»Er könnte beim nächsten Überfall auf Kingsbridge umkommen«, erklärte William und stellte mit Befriedigung fest, daß nun auf beiden Gesichtern ein Ausdruck verblüfften Respekts lag.

Es war später Nachmittag, als Jack mit Prior Philip einen Rundgang über die Baustelle machte. Die Ruine des Altarraums war inzwischen vom Schutt befreit, und die geborstenen Steine stapelten sich im Klosterhof. Das neue Gerüst stand, und die Maurer zogen bereits die Wände neu hoch. Neben dem Hospital lagerte ein großer Vorrat an Bauholz.

»Ihr kommt schnell voran«, meinte Philip.

»Nicht so schnell, wie ich gern möchte«, erwiderte Jack.

Sie inspizierten die Fundamente des Querschiffs. Vierzig oder fünfzig Tagelöhner waren in den tiefen Schächten dabei, Erde in Eimer zu schaufeln, die mittels einer Winde herausgezogen und entleert wurden. Gleich nebenan lagen große, roh behauene Steinblöcke für die Grundmauern bereit.

Jack führte Philip in seine eigene Bauhütte. Sie war weit größer als Toms einstige Hütte und nach einer Seite hin, des besseren Lichtes wegen, ganz offen. Die Hälfte der Fläche nahm Jacks Zeichenboden ein. Er hatte sich einen großen Rahmen aus Planken gezimmert und vollständig mit Gips ausgefüllt. In den hart gewordenen Gips ließen sich mit einem kurzen, zugespitzten Eisenstift Zeichnungen ritzen. Jack verwendete für seine Entwürfe Kompasse, einen Richtscheit und einen Winkelhaken. Frische Zeichnungen wiesen stets weiße, deutliche Linien auf, doch da sie rasch grau wurden, konnten neue Entwürfe darüber geritzt werden, ohne daß Verwechslungen entstanden – eine Erfahrung, die Jack in Frankreich gemacht hatte.

Den Rest des Platzes in der Bauhütte beanspruchte fast ausschließlich Jacks Werkbank, an der er seine Holzschablonen herstellte, nach denen die Steinmetzen ihre Blöcke bearbeiteten. Das Tageslicht schwand zusehends: Heute würde er nicht mehr daran arbeiten. Er räumte seine Werkzeuge auf.

Philip nahm eine der Schablonen zur Hand. »Wofür ist diese hier?«

»Für den Sockel eines Stützpfeilers, Plinthe genannt.«

»Ihr bereitet Euch sehr genau vor.«

»Ich kann's kaum abwarten, bis wir mit dem richtigen Bau beginnen.«

Jede Unterhaltung zwischen den beiden Männern schien sich nur noch um Fakten zu drehen.

Philip legte die Schablone wieder hin. »Ich muß zur Komplet«, sagte er und wandte sich ab.

»Und ich werde mal wieder meiner Familie einen *Besuch* abstatten«, sagte Jack giftig.

Philip verhielt den Schritt und drehte sich um, als wolle er etwas sagen. Doch er schwieg, sah Jack nur traurig an und ging hinaus.

Jack verschloß seine Werkzeugkiste. Er bereute seine Bemerkung bereits. Hatte er die Arbeit nicht zu Philips Bedingungen angenommen? Sinnlos, sich jetzt darüber zu beschweren! Dennoch fühlte er sich in des Priors Gegenwart ständig gereizt, und es gelang ihm nicht immer, das zu verbergen.

Im Zwielicht ging er zu dem kleinen Haus im Armenviertel, wo Aliena mit ihrem Bruder Richard wohnte. Bei Jacks Eintritt lächelte sie erfreut, doch sie küßten sich nicht zur Begrüßung. Ja, sie vermieden sogar jede Berührung, aus Sorge, es könne sie erregen – und dann mußten sie sich entweder enttäuscht und ohne Erfüllung gefunden zu haben trennen, oder sie gaben ihrer Lust nach und riskierten, dabei ertappt zu werden, wie sie das Philip gegebene Versprechen brachen.

Tommy spielte auf dem Fußboden. Er war jetzt eineinhalb Jahre alt, und gegenwärtig galt sein größtes Interesse Dingen, die sich ineinanderstapeln ließen. Vor ihm standen vier oder fünf Schüsseln, die er unermüdlich ineinander zu setzen versuchte – mal die kleineren in die größeren, mal umgekehrt. Jack sah verblüfft, daß Tommy nicht instinktiv wußte, daß eine große Schüssel niemals in eine kleine paßt – das mußten die kleinen Menschen offenbar erst einmal lernen. Tommy hatte mit den Raumverhältnissen ähnlich zu kämpfen wie er selbst, wenn er sich die Gestaltung eines bestimmten Steins im Gewölbe ausmalte.

Sein kleiner Sohn faszinierte Jack, machte ihn aber auch besorgt. Bislang hatte er sich nie Gedanken darüber machen müssen, ob er Arbeit fand oder nicht. Als er nach Frankreich aufgebrochen war, hatte er keinen Augenblick daran gedacht, das Geld könne ihm ausgehen und er müsse hungern. Jetzt war das alles anders, jetzt brauchte er Sicherheit – mehr aus Sorge um Tommy als um sich selbst. Zum erstenmal in seinem Leben trug er Verantwortung.

Aliena stellte einen Krug Wein und einen Gewürzkuchen auf den Tisch und setzte sich Jack gegenüber. Er goß sich Wein in seinen Becher und nippte dankbar daran. Aliena gab auch Tommy ein Stück Kuchen, doch der hatte keinen Hunger und zerkrümelte ihn auf dem Boden.

»Jack, ich brauche mehr Geld«, sagte Aliena.

»Ich gebe dir doch schon zwölf Pence die Woche«, erwiderte er überrascht. »Ich verdiene ja nur vierundzwanzig.«

»Tut mir leid«, sagte sie. »Du brauchst nicht so viel wie wir – du lebst schließlich allein.«

Jack fand das nicht sonderlich überzeugend. »Ein Tagelöhner hat bloß sechs Pence in der Woche – und ich kenne einige, die davon fünf oder sechs Kinder ernähren.«

Aliena sah ihn verstimmt an. »Ich weiß nicht, wie die Frauen von Tagelöhnern wirtschaften – ich habe es nicht gelernt. Und ich gebe das Geld ja auch nicht für mich aus. Aber du ißt jeden Tag zu Mittag hier, und Richard ist auch noch da –«

»Wieso bittest du dann nicht Richard um Geld?« warf Jack ärgerlich ein. »Der könnte schließlich selber für sich sorgen.«

»Das hat er noch nie müssen.«

Jack war der Meinung, es sei genug, wenn er für Aliena und Tommy zu sorgen hatte. »Ich wußte gar nicht, daß ich für Richard verantwortlich bin!«

»Bist du auch nicht, aber ich«, sagte sie ruhig. »Als du mich genommen hast, hast du ihn mit dazu bekommen.«

»Aber ohne daß ich gefragt wurde!« gab er wütend zurück.

»Sei mir nicht böse.«

Zu spät: Jack war ihr bereits böse. »Richard ist jetzt dreiundzwanzig – zwei Jahre älter als ich. Warum soll ich für ihn aufkommen? Soll ich etwa trocken Brot essen, aber für Richard Speck kaufen?«

»Ich bin wieder schwanger.«

»Was?«

»Ich kriege wieder ein Kind.«

Jacks Zorn war wie weggeblasen, und er griff nach ihrer Hand. »Das ist ja wunderbar!«

»Freust du dich wirklich?« fragte sie. »Ich hatte Angst, du könntest dich darüber ärgern.«

»Ärgern! Ich bin begeistert! Tommy habe ich ja erst zu Gesicht bekommen, als er schon ein Jahr alt war – jetzt kann ich das Versäumte nachholen.«

»Aber bedeutet das nicht noch mehr Verantwortung? Und was ist mit dem Geld?«

»Ach, zum Teufel mit dem Geld! Ich war bloß wieder schlechter Laune, weil wir uns nicht lieben dürfen. Das Geld wird schon reichen. Aber daß wir wieder ein Kind bekommen! Hoffentlich wird's ein Mädchen.« Stirnrunzelnd hielt er inne. »Aber wann …?«

»Es muß passiert sein, kurz bevor uns Prior Philip die Trennung befahl.«

»Wahrscheinlich an Allerheiligen.« Er grinste. »Erinnerst du dich an diese Nacht? Du hast mich ganz schön hergenommen –«

»Ich weiß«, fiel sie ihm errötend ins Wort.

Liebevoll sah er sie an. »Ich wünschte, wir könnten es jetzt gleich wieder tun.«

Sie lächelte. »Das wäre schön.«

Ihre Hände faßten sich auf dem Küchentisch und blieben ineinander verschlungen liegen.

Da platzte Richard herein.

Erhitzt und staubig, führte er sein verschwitztes Roß in die Stube. »Schlechte Nachrichten«, keuchte er.

Aliena hob schnell Tommy vom Boden, damit er dem Gaul nicht zwischen die Hufe geriet. »Was ist los?« erkundigte sich Jack.

»Wir müssen morgen alle aus Kingsbridge fort«, antwortete Richard.

»Warum denn?«

»William Hamleigh will die Stadt am Sonntag noch einmal brandschatzen.«

»O nein!« entfuhr es Aliena.

Jack lief es kalt über den Rücken. Sofort hatte er wieder die Szene vor Augen, wie damals, vor drei Jahren, William mit seinen Berittenen eingefallen war, mit Keulen und lodernden Fackeln. Die Panik, die

Entsetzensschreie, der Geruch des Todes! Das Bild seines Stiefvaters hatte sich ihm auf ewig eingeprägt, wie er ihn mit zerschmetterter Stirn gefunden hatte. Das Herz wurde ihm schwer.

»Woher weißt du das?« fragte er Richard.

»In Shiring habe ich gesehen, wie Williams Mannen sich beim Waffenschmied versorgten.«

»Das heißt aber noch nicht –«

»Das war noch nicht alles. Ich bin ihnen in die Schenke gefolgt und habe gelauscht. Einer erkundigte sich nach den Verteidigungsmöglichkeiten von Kingsbridge, und ein anderer sagte ihm, es gäbe keine.«

»O mein Gott, es ist also wahr!« stöhnte Aliena. Ihr Blick fiel auf Tommy, und instinktiv legte sie die Hand auf ihren Bauch, in dem das neue Kind wuchs. Sie sah auf und direkt in Jacks Augen. Beide dachten dasselbe.

»Später«, fuhr Richard fort, »hab' ich mich mit ein paar jüngeren Kerlen unterhalten, die mich nicht kennen. Hab' von der Schlacht um Lincoln erzählt und gefragt, für wen ich wohl in den Kampf ziehen könnte. Ich solle mich in Earlscastle melden, meinten sie, aber das müsse gleich heute sein, denn morgen brächen sie auf, um am Sonntag hier einzufallen.«

»Am Sonntag!« flüsterte Jack, von Furcht ergriffen.

»Dann ritt ich nach Earlscastle, um es nochmals zu überprüfen.«

»In welche Gefahr du dich gebracht hast!« stöhnte Aliena.

»Alle Anzeichen deuten auf einen bevorstehenden Überfall: Boten kamen und gingen, Waffen wurden geschliffen, die Pferde inspiziert, die Wege gesäubert … Kein Zweifel, was William vorhat. Diesem Teufel«, schloß Richard mit haßerfüllter Stimme, »reichen seine bisherigen Schandtaten noch nicht aus. Er muß immer und immer weiter wüten.« Unwillkürlich griff er sich ans rechte Ohr und berührte die gerötete Narbe.

Nachdenklich sah Jack ihn an. Gewiß, dachte er, Richard ist ein Faulpelz und ein Verschwender, aber was militärische Dinge betrifft, da ist er stets zuverlässig. Mit seiner Einschätzung von Williams Plänen hat er bestimmt recht … »Das wird eine Katastrophe«, murmelte er vor sich hin. Gerade erst hat sich die Stadt halbwegs von all den Übeln erholt, überlegte er. Vor drei Jahren der Brand, vor zwei Jahren der Einsturz der Kathedrale – und nun schon wieder eine Heimsuchung! Die Leute werden glauben, Kingsbridge bleibe vom Unglück verfolgt – selbst wenn wir alle fliehen und damit wenigstens neue

Opfer an Leib und Leben vermeiden. Das ist das Ende der Stadt. Kein Mensch wird noch hier wohnen und arbeiten, geschweige denn zum Markt kommen wollen. Und das könnte das Ende des Dombaus bedeuten ...

»Wir müssen Prior Philip unterrichten – ohne Verzug!« sagte Aliena.

Jack nickte. »Die Mönche sind gerade beim Abendessen. Gehen wir.«

Aliena nahm Tommy auf den Arm, und zu viert hasteten sie durch die Dämmerung zum Kloster.

»Wenn die Kathedrale erst fertig ist«, meinte Richard, »kann der Markt in der Kirche stattfinden. Das wird ihn vor weiteren Überfällen bewahren.«

»Aber bis dahin«, widersprach Jack, »brauchen wir die Einnahmen daraus, um weiterbauen zu können.«

Jack ging allein ins Refektorium. Ein junger Mönch hielt die Tischlesung – einen apokalyptischen Text aus der Offenbarung, wie Jack erkannte –, während die anderen schweigend aßen. Nach einer Weile entdeckte Philip den Besucher an der Tür; Jacks Anblick schien ihn zu überraschen, doch er stand sofort auf und kam zu ihm.

»Schlimme Nachrichten«, sagte Jack grimmig. »Richard soll Euch berichten.«

Sie zogen sich in den wiederhergestellten Altarraum zurück, den die untergehende Sonne mit ihren letzten Strahlen erhellte. Richard war schnell fertig mit seinem Bericht, und Philip sagte: »Aber wir haben doch nur ein paar Marktstände und keine Wollmesse mehr!«

»Wenigstens können wir morgen alle Stadtbewohner evakuieren«, meinte Aliena. »Es kann also diesmal ohne Tote und Verwundete abgehen, und danach bauen wir wieder auf.«

»Sofern William den Evakuierten nicht nachsetzt und sie zu Tode hetzt«, gab Richard zu bedenken. »Ich traue ihm das durchaus zu.«

»Das bedeutet das Ende des Markttags«, sagte Philip, »auch wenn wir alle fliehen. Denn danach wird es niemand mehr wagen, hier einen Verkaufsstand aufzuschlagen.«

»Ebensogut könnte es das Ende des Dombaus sein«, fügte Jack hinzu. »In den vergangenen zehn Jahren ist die Kirche einmal abgebrannt, einmal eingestürzt, und beim Überfall auf Kingsbridge kamen viele Maurer und Steinmetzen ums Leben. Noch solch ein Schicksalsschlag, und das wäre das Ende. Die Leute werden behaupten, Kingsbridge stünde unter einem schlechten Stern.«

Philip wirkte hin und her gerissen. Er ist noch keine vierzig Jahre alt, schätzte Jack, aber er hat schon Falten im Gesicht, und sein Haarkranz wird immer grauer ... Trotz alledem glomm ein gefährliches Licht in seinen blauen Augen, als er sagte: »Das werde ich nicht dulden. Das kann nicht Gottes Wille sein.«

Was für eine sinnlose Bemerkung! Wie konnte er von »nicht dulden werden« reden? Ebenso mochte eine Henne behaupten, der Fuchs gehe sie nichts an ... »Was wollt Ihr dagegen tun?« fragte Jack voller Zweifel. »Beten, daß William heute nacht aus dem Bett fällt und sich den Hals bricht?«

Richard griff den Gedanken an Widerstand sofort auf. »Ja, wehren wir uns!« sagte er. »Wir haben eine Chance. Wir sind Hunderte, während William fünfzig, allenfalls hundert Mann zur Verfügung hat – womöglich gewinnen wir die Schlacht nur, weil wir in der Überzahl sind.«

»Und wie viele von uns werden dabei umkommen?« protestierte Aliena.

Philip schüttelte den Kopf. »Mönche dürfen nicht kämpfen«, stellte er voller Bedauern fest. »Und ich kann die Stadtbewohner nicht auffordern, ihr Leben aufs Spiel zu setzen, solange ich es nicht selbst tue.«

»Mit meinen Bauleuten könnt Ihr auch nicht rechnen«, meinte Jack. »Das gehört nicht zu ihrer Arbeit.«

Philip fixierte Richard. Was militärische Aktionen betraf, war er der Versierteste von ihnen. »Gibt es denn irgendeine Möglichkeit, die Stadt zu verteidigen, ohne daß es zu einer Schlacht kommt?«

»Ohne Stadtmauer auf keinen Fall«, erklärte Richard. »Wir können dem Feind nur unsere eigenen Leiber entgegensetzen.«

»Eine Stadtmauer«, murmelte Jack nachdenklich.

»Wir könnten«, fuhr Richard fort, »William natürlich auffordern, den Ausgang der Schlacht durch Zweikämpfe herbeizuführen – Mann gegen Mann. Aber darauf wird er sich kaum einlassen.«

»Eine Stadtmauer könnte uns retten?« fragte Jack.

»Ein andermal vielleicht«, gab Richard ungeduldig zurück, »diesmal nicht. So etwas läßt sich nicht über Nacht errichten.«

»Meinst du?«

»Natürlich nicht, stell dich nicht so –«

»Moment, Richard«, fiel ihm Philip ins Wort. Er sah Jack erwartungsvoll an. »Was habt Ihr im Sinn?«

»Eine Mauer zu bauen, ist nicht schwer«, meinte Jack.

»Ja, und?«

Jacks Gedanken überschlugen sich, und die anderen warteten mit angehaltenem Atem, bis er sprach. »Keine Bogen, keine Gewölbe, keine Fenster ... Eine einfache Mauer *kann* über Nacht gebaut werden. Dazu braucht man nur Männer und Material.«

»Was könnten wir dazu verwenden?« fragte Philip.

»Schaut Euch um«, erwiderte Jack. »Alles da: zugeschnittene Steine, dazu ein Stoß Bauholz höher als ein Haus. Auf dem Kirchacker ein Haufen Bruchsteine, und am Flußufer die Blöcke aus dem Steinbruch. An Baumaterial ist kein Mangel.«

»Und Bauleute gibt es genug in der Stadt«, fügte Philip hinzu.

Jack nickte. »Die Mönche könnten die Organisation übernehmen, die Bauleute die Arbeit, die Können erfordert. Den Rest besorgt die gesamte Stadtbevölkerung.« Er dachte so weit voraus, daß er mit dem Sprechen kaum nachkam. »Die Mauer muß am diesseitigen Flußufer stehen. Die Brücke muß abgerissen werden. Dann muß sich die Mauer über den Hügel ziehen, ums Armenviertel herum, und auf die Ostmauer des Klosters stoßen ... dann in Richtung Norden ... und den Hügel wieder hinunter zum Fluß. Vielleicht reicht der Vorrat an Steinen doch nicht aus ...«

Richard unterbrach ihn. »Dafür brauchen wir nicht unbedingt eine Mauer. Dort tut's auch ein einfacher Graben, und die ausgehobene Erde wird zum Wall aufgeschüttet, vor allem dort, wo der Feind nur angreifen kann, wenn er seine Leute bergauf schickt.«

»Aber eine Steinmauer wäre bestimmt besser«, widersprach Jack.

»Besser ja, aber nicht unbedingt notwendig. Eine Mauer ist dazu da, den Feind in eine angreifbare Position zu bringen und den Verteidiger in die Lage zu versetzen, ihn aus seiner geschützten Position heraus zu treffen.«

»Zu treffen?« fragte Aliena. »Womit denn?«

»Mit Steinen, kochendem Pech, Pfeilen – wahrscheinlich verfügt beinahe jedes Haus hier über Pfeil und Bogen ...«

»Es läuft also doch auf eine Schlacht hinaus«, stellte Aliena schaudernd fest.

»Ja, aber nicht von Mann zu Mann.«

Jack zweifelte noch. Aller Wahrscheinlichkeit war es das Sicherste, wenn sich die ganze Bevölkerung in die Wälder verzog – in der Hoffnung, William werde sich damit begnügen, die Häuser abzubrennen. Blieb immer noch das Risiko, daß er und seine Mannen die Leute aufstöberten und niedermetzelten. Was war gefährlicher? Wenn sie alle hierblieben und die Stadt mit einer Mauer verteidigten? Ging alles schief und William fand einen Durchlaß, so gab es ganz gewiß ein grausames Gemetzel. Jacks Blick glitt unwillkürlich zu Aliena und Tommy, und er dachte an das Kind, das sie erwarteten. »Gibt es keinen dritten Weg?« fragte er. »Wir könnten die Frauen und Kinder fortschicken. Dann müßten nur die Männer die Stadtmauer halten.«

»Nein, danke«, sagte Aliena mit Nachdruck. »Das wäre das Dümmste von allem. Denn dann hätten wir weder eine Stadtmauer noch Mannsvolk, das sie verteidigt.«

Recht hat sie, dachte Jack. Was nützt eine Mauer, wenn keine Männer zu ihrer Verteidigung da sind, weil sie meinen, ihre Frauen und Kinder im Wald beschützen zu müssen? Und William ist ohne weiteres fähig, die Stadt in Ruhe zu lassen, wenn er dafür die Frauen umbringen kann …

»Jack«, sagte Philip. »Ihr seid der Baumeister. Läßt sich eine Stadtmauer in einem einzigen Tag errichten?«

»Ich habe darin keine Erfahrung«, gab Jack zu. »Allerdings brauchten wir einen Plan. Wir müßten nur für jeden Bauabschnitt einem erfahrenen Maurer die Verantwortung übertragen. Der Mörtel wird jedoch bis Sonntagmorgen nicht trocknen und die Mauer die am schlechtesten gebaute von ganz England sein. Trotzdem – ich glaube, wir können es schaffen.«

Philip wandte sich an Richard. »Ihr seid schlachtenerprobt. Was meint Ihr? Können wir William zurückwerfen, wenn wir eine Stadtmauer haben?«

»Bestimmt«, gab Richard zurück. »Bedenkt – er glaubt, er kann die Stadt im Sturm nehmen; er hat keine Belagerung geplant. Findet er jedoch eine Befestigung vor, kann er kaum etwas tun.«

Philip wandte sich an Aliena: »Ihr habt ein Kind zu beschützen. Was ist Eure Meinung? Schlagen wir uns in die Büsche in der Hoffnung, William setzt uns nicht nach – oder trotzen wir ihm mit einer Mauer?«

Jack hielt den Atem an.

Aliena ließ sich Zeit mit ihrer Antwort. Dann sagte sie: »Es geht nicht nur um unser nacktes Leben. Ihr, Philip, habt Euer Leben diesem Kloster geweiht; Jack träumt schon seit Ewigkeiten vom Bau dieser Kathedrale. Wenn wir jetzt davonlaufen, ist der Sinn Eures Lebens dahin. Und was mich angeht – ich habe einen ganz besonderen Grund, William einen Sieg zu mißgönnen. Ich meine, wir sollten bleiben.«

»In Ordnung«, stellte Philip fest. »Wir bauen die Stadtmauer.«

Bei Einbruch der Nacht schritten Jack, Richard und Philip die Stadtgrenzen mit Laternen ab und berieten sich, wie die Mauer verlaufen sollte. Kingsbridge lag auf einem niedrigen Hügel, der zur Hälfte vom Fluß eingerahmt wurde. Da das Flußufer zu seicht war, um dort eine Mauer ohne Fundamente errichten zu können, schlug Jack vor, Palisaden zu bauen. Richard war's zufrieden: Die konnte der Feind nur vom Wasser her überwinden, und das war fast unmöglich.

Blieben zwei weitere Stellen, die, wie Richard erklärte, teilweise mit Gräben und Erdwällen geschützt werden konnten: Das genügte überall da, wo der Feind zum Angreifen zunächst den Hügel überwinden mußte. Nur dort, wo kein Abhang Schutz bot, mußte eine Mauer her.

Jack trommelte seine Bauleute aus ihren Hütten, ihren Betten und aus der Schenke zusammen. Er schilderte die Lage und ernannte Verantwortliche für jeden Mauerabschnitt. Die Zimmerleute waren für die Palisaden, die Maurer für die Steinbauten, die Lehrlinge und die Tagelöhner für die Erdwälle zuständig. Er bat jeden einzelnen, seinen Bauabschnitt noch vor dem Schlafengehen mit Pfählen und Schnur zu markieren und sich zu überlegen, wie am raschesten und wirkungsvollsten gebaut werden konnte. Kurze Zeit später sah der Stadtrand aus wie eine punktierte Linie aus lauter blinkenden Lichtern, in deren Schein die Handwerker ihrem Auftrag nachgingen. Der Schmied schürte das Feuer in seiner Bauhütte und machte sich daran, Spaten herzustellen.

Die ungewohnte Geschäftigkeit störte die Stadtbewohner in ihren allabendlichen Ritualen, so daß die Bauleute den schläfrigen Neugierigen immer wieder erklären mußten, was sie taten. Nur die Mönche, die schon bei Nachtanbruch zu Bett gegangen waren, lagen im tiefen Schlaf gnädiger Unkenntnis.

Um Mitternacht, als die Bauleute ihr Werk beendet hatten und auch die Stadtbewohner wieder in ihre Betten gekrochen waren, wurden die Mönche geweckt. Die Gebete wurden abgekürzt, danach gab es Brot und Bier im Refektorium, und Philip erklärte die Lage. Die Mönche sollten am Tage die Organisation übernehmen, und zwar in Gruppen, die jeweils einem bestimmten Bauabschnittleiter zugeteilt waren. Dessen Anordnungen hatten sie auszuführen und darüber hinaus das Graben, Ausheben und Herbeiholen von Baumaterial zu überwachen. Das Wichtigste war, wie Philip betonte, daß die Zufuhr der benötigten Materialien – Steine, Mörtel, Bauholz und Werkzeuge – niemals eine Unterbrechung erfuhr.

Jack fragte sich währenddessen, was William wohl plante. Earls-castle lag einen guten Tagesritt von Kingsbridge entfernt, aber er glaubte nicht, daß William die Strecke an einem Tag zurückzulegen gedachte, denn sonst wäre sein Heer schon bei der Ankunft erschöpft. Sie werden sich bei Sonnenaufgang auf den Weg machen, überlegte Jack, und zwar in mehreren Gruppen und mit verdeckten Waffen, damit sie keinen Verdacht erregen. Am Nachmittag treffen sie sich dann ein, zwei Stunden von Kingsbridge entfernt, vermutlich auf dem Gut eines der Pächter Williams. Am Abend schärfen sie ihre Waffen, lassen sich mit Bier vollaufen und überbieten sich gegenseitig mit Gruselgeschichten von früheren Feldzügen. Angreifen werden sie erst am Morgen darauf ... Jack schauderte bei diesem Gedanken. Aber diesmal sind wir gut vorbereitet, dachte er. Diesmal werden wir sie Mores lehren! Dennoch ließ sich seine Furcht nicht beschwichtigen.

Die Mönche sorgten dafür, daß sie die Lage des Bauabschnittes, für den sie jeweils verantwortlich waren, genauestens kannten. Im ersten Dämmerlicht, das am östlichen Horizont sichtbar wurde, weckten sie die Stadtbewohner auf.

Als die Sonne aufging, war die Arbeit schon in vollem Gang. Die jungen Männer und Frauen taten die Schwerarbeit, während die Älteren für Essen und Trinken sorgten und die Kinder auf Botengänge schickten. Jack führte die Oberaufsicht und schien überall gleichzeitig zu sein. Einem Mörtelmischer gebot er, weniger Kalk zu verwenden, damit der Mörtel schneller trocknete. Einem Zimmermann empfahl er, statt des verwendeten Gerüstholzes zugeschnittenes Bauholz von einem anderen Stapel bringen zu lassen. Er vergewisserte sich, daß die einzelnen Abschnitte der Steinmauer sauber ineinandergefügt wurden. Und ununterbrochen witzelte und lächelte er und sprach allen Mut zu.

Die Sonne stieg höher, und es wurde ein heißer Tag. Die Klosterküche fuhr ganze Fässer Bier auf, das jedoch auf Philips Geheiß – und mit Jacks Zustimmung – verdünnt wurde, denn sie wollten vermeiden, daß die Leute bei der Arbeit einschliefen.

Trotz der drohenden Gefahr herrschte überall beste Laune, wie an einem Heiligentag, wenn die ganze Stadt gemeinsam etwas unternahm. Dennoch sah Philip einige, die sich verstohlen davonmachten; vielleicht versteckten sie sich im Wald oder suchten bei Verwandten in den umliegenden Dörfern Zuflucht. Aber das waren nur wenige, alle anderen arbeiteten fleißig mit.

Zu Mittag ließ Philip die Glocke läuten und Pause machen, während er mit Jack die Bauarbeiten inspizierte. Allem Fleiß zum Trotz schienen sie noch nicht weit gekommen zu sein – die Steinmauern reichten kaum über den Grund, die Erdwälle waren nicht höher als Maulwurfshügel, und in den Palisaden klafften noch große Lücken.

»Glaubt Ihr, wir werden rechtzeitig fertig?« fragte Philip am Ende ihrer Tour.

Jack, der den ganzen Vormittag über nur Zuversicht ausgestrahlt hatte, zwang sich nun zu einer realistischen Einschätzung. »Bei diesem Tempo nicht«, sagte er verzagt.

»Wie können wir es beschleunigen?«

»Schneller bauen heißt im allgemeinen schlechter bauen.«

»Dann bauen wir eben schlechter – wie geht das?«

Jack überlegte. »Derzeit tun alle das, was sie am besten können. Aber Zimmerleute können auch ein bißchen mauern, und Tagelöhner können auch allein ein Palisade errichten. Wenn die Zimmerleute also den Maurern zur Hand gehen und die Palisaden den Tagelöhnern überlassen, können die Bürger Gräben ausheben und Wälle aufschütten. Und sobald alles läuft, können die jüngeren Mönche bei der Arbeit helfen.«

»So sei es«, sagte Philip und gab die neue Order am Ende der Mittagspause aus.

Das wird die schlechtestgebaute Mauer von ganz England, dachte Jack. Die steht bestimmt nicht lange. Wenn sie im Laufe der nächsten Woche nicht zusammenfällt, dann grenzt das schon an ein Wunder …

Im Laufe des Nachmittags wurden die Leute müde, vor allem jene, die in der Nacht aufgeblieben waren. Die Feiertagslaune verpuffte, und es wurde wild entschlossen geschuftet. Die Steinmauer wuchs, die Gräben wurden tiefer, die Lücken im Zaun schlossen sich. Zum Abendessen, als die Sonne sich im Westen senkte, gab es eine neue Pause, danach ging es weiter.

Als die Nacht kam, war die Mauer immer noch nicht fertig.

Philip teilte Wachen ein, schickte alle anderen zu Bett und kündigte an, sie um Mitternacht zu wecken.

Jack ging zu Alienas Haus, wo sie ihn mit Richard erwartete.

»Nimm Tommy und versteck dich mit ihm im Wald«, sagte er zu ihr.

Dieser Gedanke war ihm schon den ganzen Tag über im Kopf herumgegangen. Zuerst wollte er ihn nicht wahrhaben, doch je mehr Zeit verstrich, desto deutlicher wurde die Erinnerung an jenen entsetzlichen Tag, da William die Stadt schon einmal in Brand gesetzt hatte. Am Ende war Jack überzeugt, es sei am besten, Aliena fortzuschicken.

»Ich bleibe«, erwiderte sie bestimmt.

»Ich weiß nicht, ob wir's schaffen«, sagte er. »Und ich will dich auf keinen Fall hierhaben, wenn William die Mauer überrennt.«

»Aber ich kann doch nicht einfach weglaufen, solange du hierbleibst und alle anderen sich wehren«, wandte sie ein.

Das war verständlich, aber er wollte nicht mehr verstehen. »Niemand wird's erfahren, wenn du dich jetzt gleich davonmachst.«

»Am Ende erfahren sie's doch.«

»Aber dann ist die Gefahr vorüber.«

»Denk doch nur, welche Schande das wäre.«

»Zum Teufel damit!« brauste er auf. Warum fand er nicht die richtigen Worte. »Ich will dich in Sicherheit wissen!«

Seine erhobene Stimme weckte Tommy, der zu weinen begann. Aliena nahm ihn in den Arm und wiegte ihn. »Im Wald bin ich vielleicht auch nicht sicherer aufgehoben.«

»William wird ihn nicht durchsuchen. Er will nur die Stadt treffen.«

»Vielleicht will er mich am meisten treffen.«

»Du könntest dich auf deiner Lichtung verstecken. Dort kommt nie jemand hin.«

»William könnte sie durch Zufall finden.«

»Hör doch auf mich! Dort bist du bestimmt besser aufgehoben als hier. Ich *weiß* es.«

»Trotzdem – ich will hierbleiben.«

»Aber ich will dich nicht hierhaben«, gab er schroff zurück.

»Ich bleibe auf jeden Fall«, erwiderte sie lächelnd und überhörte seine Schroffheit.

Jack unterdrückte einen Fluch. Hatte sie sich erst einmal etwas in den Kopf gesetzt, war sie durch nichts mehr davon abzubringen – stur wie ein Maulesel. Er verlegte sich aufs Bitten. »Aliena, mir graut vor morgen.«

»Mir auch«, gab sie zu. »Und ich meine, wir sollten unser Los gemeinsam tragen.«

Jetzt hätte er nachgeben können – aber seine Furcht war zu groß. »Dann geh doch zum Teufel!« fauchte er wütend und stürmte aus dem Haus.

Draußen blieb er stehen und sog tief die Nachtluft ein. Allmählich beruhigte er sich. Seine Angst war nicht geringer, aber es schien ihm töricht, Aliena zu zürnen: Womöglich starben sie beide schon am kommenden Tag.

Als er zurückkam, stand sie noch an der gleichen Stelle, mit traurigem Gesicht. »Ich liebe dich«, sagte er. Sie fielen sich in die Arme und blieben lange so stehen.

Als Jack wieder ging, stand der Mond bereits hoch am Himmel. Er wußte, daß er nicht würde schlafen können. Er hegte die närrische Befürchtung, alle anderen könnten verschlafen, bis William erneut mit seinen Mannen einfiel, Tod und Verderben um sich verbreitend. Ruhelos strich Jack um die Mauern, die ihm gerade bis zur Brust reichten. Das war nicht hoch genug! Und die Palisaden wiesen Lücken auf, die hundert Mann in kürzester Frist durchbrechen konnten. Selbst die Erdwälle waren von einem guten Pferd leicht zu überspringen – es gab noch so viel zu tun!

Dort, wo die Brücke sich befunden hatte, blieb er stehen. Sie lagerte, in Teile zerlegt, im Kloster. Sein Blick glitt über das Wasser, in dem sich das Mondlicht spiegelte. Dann sah er eine Gestalt an der Palisade entlangschleichen. Schon wollten ihn abergläubische Ängste überfallen – da entpuppte sich der Schatten als Prior Philip, der ebenso wenig schlafen konnte wie Jack.

Sein schwelender Groll gegen den Prior war angesichts der Gefahr wie verflogen, und er sprach ihn an. »Wenn wir das hinter uns haben, sollten wir die Mauer Stein um Stein wieder aufbauen.«

»Ganz meine Meinung«, sagte Philip begeistert. »Wir sollten eine regelrechte Stadtmauer bauen. In einem Jahr könnten wir das bewältigen.«

»An dieser Stelle hier, wo die Brücke über den Fluß führt, sollten wir ein Tor mit Pechloch errichten. Dann können wir uns wehren, ohne die Brücke abreißen zu müssen.«

»In solchen Dingen – bei der Verteidigung einer Stadt, meine ich – sind wir Mönche nicht viel nütze.«

Jack nickte verständnisvoll; Mönche durften nicht an Gewalttaten teilhaben. »Aber wenn Ihr Euch nicht darum kümmert, wer dann?«

»Wie wär's mit Alienas Bruder Richard?«

Im ersten Moment fand Jack den Gedanken verblüffend, doch dann sah er, wie hervorragend er war. »Das kann er, das kann er bestens! Das bewahrt ihn vor Müßiggang, und überdies läge er mir nicht mehr auf der Tasche«, stimmte er voller Begeisterung zu. Der Blick, mit dem er Philip bedachte, enthielt wider Willen Bewunderung. »Ihr seid unerschöpflich, wahrhaftig!«

Philip zuckte die Schultern. »Ich wünschte, alle Probleme wären so leicht zu lösen wie dieses.«

Jack wandte sich wieder der Mauer zu. »Nun wird Kingsbridge wohl auf ewig eine befestigte Stadt.«

»Nicht auf ewig, aber gewiß bis zur Wiederkunft unseres Herrn Jesus.«

»Wir werden sehen«, meinte Jack. »Es könnte eine Zeit kommen, da Barbaren wie William Hamleigh keine Macht mehr haben, da das Gesetz das Volk beschützt und nicht mehr unterdrückt, da die Könige Frieden schließen, statt Krieg zu führen. Denkt nur – eine Zeit, da die Städte in England keine Mauern mehr brauchen!«

»Was für eine Vorstellung!« gab Philip kopfschüttelnd zurück. »So etwas wird nicht geschehen vor dem Tag des Jüngsten Gerichts.«

»Nein, wahrscheinlich nicht.«

»Es geht auf Mitternacht zu. Zeit, die anderen zu wecken.«

»Ein Wort noch, Philip.«

»Ja?«

Jack holte tief Luft. »Wir haben immer noch Zeit, unsere Pläne zu ändern. Wir könnten die Stadt evakuieren.«

»Habt Ihr Angst, Jack?« fragte Philip verständnisvoll.

»Ja. Nicht um mich, sondern um meine Familie.«

Philip nickte. »Betrachtet es mal von dieser Seite: Wenn Ihr jetzt geht, seid Ihr in Sicherheit – morgen. Aber William könnte wiederkommen. Und wenn wir ihm morgen das Feld überlassen, werden wir immer und ewig in Furcht vor ihm leben. Ihr, ich, Aliena, der kleine Tommy. Euer Sohn wird in Furcht vor William – oder einem anderen wie ihm – aufwachsen.«

Er hat recht, dachte Jack. Wenn Kinder wie Tommy frei und furchtlos aufwachsen sollen, dürfen ihre Eltern nicht vor William davonlaufen.

Er seufzte. »So sei's denn.«

Philip ging die Glocke läuten. Ein Herrscher, dachte Jack, der den Frieden bewahrt, für Gerechtigkeit sorgt und die Armen nicht unterdrückt. Aber muß man wirklich keusch leben, um das zu können?

In den Häusern gingen die Lichter an, und die Bauleute krochen gähnend aus den Federn. Ihre Arbeit nahmen sie gemächlich auf, übellaunige Bemerkungen flogen hin und her – doch Philip hatte schon zu backen befohlen, und bald gab es frisches Brot mit Butter. Die allgemeine Laune hob sich.

In der Morgendämmerung machten Jack und Philip einen erneuten Rundgang. Ihre Augen suchten besorgt den Horizont nach den ersten Berittenen ab. Die Palisade am Fluß war beinahe fertig, die Zimmerleute stopften soeben die letzten Lücken. Die Erdwälle waren zu Mannshöhe gediehen, die Gräben davor sorgten für zusätzliche drei oder vier Ellen, die zu überwinden waren: Der eine oder andere mochte es mit etwas Mühe schaffen, mußte aber dazu absitzen. Auch die Mauer war nun mannshoch, doch die letzten Schichten war überaus nachgiebig, da der Mörtel sich noch nicht gesetzt hätte. Das allerdings erfuhr der Feind erst, wenn er sie zu überwinden suchte, und in diesem Moment mochte es sogar von Vorteil sein, ihm die Steine in den Weg zu werfen.

Philip gab neue Anordnungen: Die älteren Bürger sollten mitsamt den Kindern Zuflucht im Dormitorium des Klosters suchen. Sehr schön, dachte Jack, auf diese Weise sind Aliena und Tommy aus der Schußlinie, denn sie wird bei dem Jungen bleiben müssen. Die Handwerker bauten weiter, aber die Tagelöhner wurden Richard unterstellt, der ein Verteidigungsheer brauchte. Er teilte sie in Gruppen ein, deren jede einen bestimmten Teil der Befestigung bewachen sollte. Wer Pfeil und Bogen besaß, sollte an der Mauer bereitstehen, um den Feind zu beschießen. Wer keine Waffen hatte, sollte mit Steinen werfen, die derzeit gesammelt und aufgehäuft wurden. Kochendes Wasser war eine weitere nützliche Waffe, und ganze Kessel voll wurden davon bereitgehalten.

Jack war nun schon seit achtundvierzig Stunden ununterbrochen auf den Beinen. Sein Kopf schmerzte und seine Augen tränten. Er ließ sich auf dem Reetdach eines Hauses am Fluß nieder und hielt Ausschau über die Felder, während die Zimmerleute hastig die Palisade vollendeten. Da kam ihm der Gedanke, William könne seine Leute brennende Pfeile über die Stadtmauern schießen lassen – um die Stadt dergestalt in Brand zu setzen, brauchte er nicht einmal die Mauer zu überwinden. Eiligst machte Jack sich auf den Weg zum Kloster, wo er feststellte, daß Richard der gleiche Gedanke gekommen war: Mönche organisierten bereits mit Wasser gefüllte Fässer und Eimer, die an den empfindlichsten Punkten hinter der Mauer bereitgestellt wurden.

Jack wollte soeben das Kloster wieder verlassen – da ertönten die ersten Warnrufe.

Mit klopfendem Herzen sprang er aufs Stalldach und suchte mit den Augen die Felder im Westen ab. Auf der Straße, die zur Brücke führte, verriet eine Staubwolke die sich nähernden Berittenen – nicht weiter entfernt als eine Meile. Die Gefahr war nur allzu nahe!

Zeit, Aliena aufzusuchen, blieb ihm nicht. Jack sprang vom Dach und rannte den Hügel hinunter zum Fluß. Die Männer drängten sich um die letzte Lücke in der Palisade, hieben Pflöcke in die Erde, nagelten eiligst Verstrebungen dahinter und hatten im Nu den Zaun vollendet. Da kam auch schon Richard angelaufen und schrie: »Auf der anderen Seite ist niemand! Wenn sie einen Trupp von dort einfallen lassen, ist es zu spät! Los, alles auf die Posten!« Und als sich die Leute in Bewegung setzten, murmelte er Jack zu: »Keine Disziplin – sie haben keine Disziplin!«

Jack gab keine Antwort. Die Reiter waren nun deutlicher zu sehen. Wie Gesandte der Hölle, dachte er, nichts als Tod und Verderben im Sinn! Und das nur, weil Grafen und Könige meinen, sie seien ihnen nütze. So unwissend Philip auch in Liebes- und Ehedingen sein mag – zumindest weiß er, wie man eine Gemeinde regiert, ohne solche Barbarenhorden zu Hilfe zu rufen.

Ein seltsamer Gedanke, ausgerechnet in diesem Moment. Dachten so Menschen, die bald sterben mußten?

Es waren mehr als die fünfzig Reiter, mit denen Richard gerechnet hatte – eher hundert, schätzte Jack. Sie setzten auf die Brücke zu, die nicht mehr vorhanden war, dann nahmen sie ihre Pferde beim Zügel. In wirren Haufen sammelten sie sich auf der Wiese jenseits des Flusses, und Jack atmete auf. Als sie die nagelneue Stadtmauer anglotzten, lachte irgendwer auf. Ein anderer stimmte in das Lachen ein, ein dritter, ein vierter – und schon brüllten hundert, zweihundert Leute vor Lachen über die dummen Gesichter der Bewaffneten.

Die Reiter schlossen sich zum Kreis, einige stiegen ab. Jack meinte, Williams strohfarbenes Haar und rotes Gesicht inmitten des Haufens zu erkennen, doch sicher war er sich dessen nicht.

Schließlich sahen sie wieder auf, formierten sich neu und ritten davon. Die Stadtbewohner johlten ihnen befreit hinterher – doch Jack mochte nicht glauben, daß William klein beigab. Der ritt bestimmt nicht mit seiner Truppe nach Hause! Wahrscheinlich sammelten sie sich am Oberlauf des Flusses und beratschlagten sich. Richard, der eben kam, bestätigte Jacks Verdacht: »Sie suchen eine Furt. Dann kommen sie über den Fluß und durch die Wälder. Sag's den anderen!«

Jack machte sich auf seinen Botengang. Im Nordosten erstieg er den Erdwall. Von dort aus überblickte er die Felder bis hin zu dem Wald, aus dem William mit seinen Mannen auftauchen würde.

Die Sonne stieg höher. Der Tag war so wolkenlos wie der vergangene. Die Mönche brachten Brot und Bier, und Jack fragte sich, bis wohin sich William wohl zurückzuziehen gedachte. Eine Meile flußaufwärts gab es eine seichte Stelle, die ein gutes Pferd durchschwimmen konnte – doch die war vermutlich zu gefährlich für Ortsfremde. William würde vermutlich die Furt noch weiter stromabwärts durchqueren.

Wie es Aliena wohl ging? Jack wäre am liebsten ins Refektorium gegangen, um nach ihr zu sehen – aber wenn er jetzt seinen Platz verließ, gäbe er den anderen ein schlechtes Beispiel.

Da ertönte ein Schrei, und die Berittenen tauchten wieder auf.

Sie kamen aus dem östlich gelegenen Wald, so daß Jack, der ihnen entgegensah, die Sonne direkt in die Augen schien – was sie zweifellos einkalkuliert hatten. Dann erkannte er, daß sie in wildem Galopp angeprescht kamen – sie wollten also die Mauer im Sturmangriff überrennen.

Ein oder zwei Stadtbewohner schossen Pfeile ab. Richard, unweit Jacks postiert, brüllte sie an: »Aufhören! Das ist zu früh! Wartet, bis sie im Graben sind, dann könnt Ihr sie nicht mehr verfehlen!« Aber nur wenige hörten ihn, und ein Schauer sinnlos vergeudeter Pfeile ging auf das Gerstenfeld nieder. Wir sind ein hoffnungsloses Heer, dachte Jack; die Mauer ist unsere einzige Hoffnung.

In einer Hand hielt er einen Stein, in der anderen eine Schleuder, so wie in seiner Kindheit, wenn er auf Entenjagd ging. Ob er überhaupt noch treffen konnte? Seine Finger hatten sich um die Waffe verkrampft, und er zwang sich, den Griff zu lockern. Er schluckte trocken. Manche der Gegner führten Bögen und brennende Pfeile mit sich! Dann teilten sie sich auf: Die Bogenschützen hielten auf die Mauer zu, die anderen auf die Erdwälle. William glaubte also, die Mauer nicht erstürmen zu können, denn er hatte sich nicht klargemacht, daß der Mörtel noch feucht sein mußte. Er hatte sich an der Nase herumführen lassen! Jack gestattete sich einen winzigen Augenblick des Triumphes.

Dann waren die Angreifer da.

Die Stadtbewohner feuerten ihre Pfeile ab, die auf die Berittenen niederhagelten, doch nur wenige Opfer fanden. Die Pferde hatten den Graben erreicht, und viele scheuten, während andere hineinstürmten und auf der anderen Seite wieder herauskamen. Ein Hüne von einem Mann im Panzerkettenhemd setzte geradewegs über den Graben. Sein Pferd kam am Fuße des Erdwalls auf, und er trieb es sofort hügelauf. Jack hob seine Schleuder und zielte: Sein Schuß war so sicher wie eh und je. Der Stein traf das Roß mitten auf die Nase. Es wieherte vor Schmerz, bäumte sich auf und machte kehrt. Als es davontrabte, glitt der Reiter aus dem Sattel und zog sein Schwert.

Verschiedene Reetdächer hatten bereits Feuer gefangen, und die jungen Frauen, die zur Feuerwache abkommandiert waren, wurden der Flammen nicht mehr Herr. Das kann nicht gutgehen! dachte Jack entsetzt. Alle unsere Anstrengungen waren umsonst.

Die Berittenen formierten sich neu und griffen wieder an, manche nunmehr zu Fuß. Sie wurden mit einem Hagel aus Steinen und Pfeilen empfangen. Jack feuerte seine Schleuder mit der Regelmäßigkeit einer Maschine ab: laden und zielen, laden und zielen … Die Reihen der Angreifer lichteten sich merklich. Direkt unterhalb Jack stürzte einer der Reiter und verlor dabei seinen Eisenhut. Das hervorquellende Blondhaar verriet, daß es William persönlich war.

Keines der Pferde schaffte es, den rutschigen Erdwall zu erklimmen, doch zu Jacks Schrecken gelang es einigen ihrer Reiter. Mit Schwertern und Lanzen attackierten sie die Stadtbewohner, die sich mit Äxten und Stangen wehrten. Mehrere Angreifer gelangten gar über den Erdwall, und Jack sah ganz in seiner Nähe vier, fünf Männer aus Kingsbridge fallen.

Doch jeder der Eindringlinge wurde sofort von acht oder zehn Männern umringt, die erbarmungslos mit Stöcken und Äxten auf ihn einhieben, und wiewohl auch Bürger verwundet wurden, machten sie den Angreifern doch rasch den Garaus. Schließlich gelang es ihnen sogar, die Horde wieder hinter den Erdwall zurückzutreiben. Der Angriff verlief im Sand, und die Berittenen trabten ziellos umher. Dankbar für die Pause, atmete Jack tief durch.

William hob sein Schwert und stieß einen Schrei aus, um die Aufmerksamkeit seiner Mannen auf sich zu ziehen. Er schwenkte es im Kreis zum Zeichen, daß sie sich sammeln sollten, und deutete auf die Wälle. Er wollte also ein zweites Mal angreifen.

Da sah Jack eine Chance.

Er legte einen Stein in seine Schleuder und zielte sorgfältig.

Pfeilgerade flog der Stein durch die Luft und traf William mitten auf der Stirn – mit soviel Wucht, daß der Aufprall bis zu Jack zu hören war.

William ging zu Boden.

Seine Mannen standen zaudernd herum, der Angriff fiel in sich zusammen.

Ein großer, dunkelhaariger Recke sprang vom Pferd und eilte dem Gestürzten zu Hilfe – vermutlich Walter, Williams Pferdeknecht, der nie von seiner Seite wich. Er kniete neben William nieder, und Jack hoffte schon, er sei tot. Doch dann bewegte er sich, und Walter half ihm auf die Füße. Er wirkte stark benommen. Aller Augen – diesseits wie jenseits der Stadtbefestigung – waren unverwandt auf ihn gerichtet, der Hagel aus Steinen und Pfeilen versiegte.

Walter half seinem schwankenden Herrn aufs Pferd und saß hinter ihm auf. Dann schwenkte er sein Schwert zum Sammeln und deutete, zu Jacks tiefster Erleichterung, mit der Spitze auf den Wald.

Walter versetzte dem Pferd einen Tritt, und es setzte sich in Bewegung.

Die Berittenen folgten ihm. Wer noch auf den Erdwällen focht, machte nun ebenfalls kehrt und lief hinter seinem Anführer drein. Steine und Pfeile folgten dem Rückzug bis durch das Gerstenfeld.

Die Stadtbewohner brachen in Siegesgeheul aus.

Jack sah sich benommen um. War wirklich schon alles vorüber? Er konnte es noch gar nicht fassen. Die Frauen hatten die Brandherde mittlerweile unter Kontrolle gebracht. Auf den Wällen fielen sich die Männer in die Arme und tanzten siegestrunken herum. Richard kam angelaufen und schlug Jack auf die Schulter. »Die Mauer hat uns gerettet, Jack«, sagte er. »Deine Mauer!«

Stadtbewohner und Mönche drängten sich um die beiden. Jeder wollte jeden beglückwünschen – vor allem aber Jack.

»Haben wir sie endgültig zurückgeschlagen?« fragte er.

»O ja«, erwiderte Richard. »Die kommen nicht wieder. Die wissen jetzt, daß wir uns mit Zähnen und Klauen verteidigen. Vor allem aber weiß William, daß er eine Stadt mit Befestigungsanlagen nicht ohne ein gewaltiges Heer und monatelange Belagerung einnehmen kann.«

»Dann ist es also vorbei«, sagte Jack, noch immer nicht ganz bei sich.

Aliena kam mit Tommy auf ihn zu, und er schloß sie erleichtert in die Arme. Sie lebten, sie waren zusammen, und er empfand tiefe Dankbarkeit.

Urplötzlich machten sich die zwei schlaflosen Tage und Nächte bemerkbar, und am liebsten hätte er sich an Ort und Stelle hingelegt. Doch es sollte nicht sein. Zwei der jungen Männer ergriffen ihn und hoben ihn auf ihre Schultern. Jubel ertönte. Sie trugen ihn im Triumphzug durch die Stadt, die Menge an ihren Fersen.

Sie brauchen einen Helden, dachte Jack. Jahrelang haben sie in Furcht vor William gelebt, heute haben sie ihre Freiheit errungen ... Und während er ihnen zu Gefallen winkte und lächelte, hatte er nur noch einen Gedanken im Kopf: sich hinlegen und schlafen zu dürfen.

Die Wollmesse zu Shiring war größer und reicher bestückt denn je. William, der mit Bischof Waleran einen Rundgang über den Marktplatz machte, rechnete sich so hohe Einnahmen aus wie noch nie. Doch Freude darüber wollte nicht so recht aufkommen.

Die demütigende Niederlage in Kingsbridge fraß noch immer an ihm. Nichts hatte er erreicht – im Gegenteil, er hatte Verluste an Männern und Pferden hinnehmen müssen. Am schlimmsten aber quälte ihn das Wissen, daß die Stadtmauer ausgerechnet von Jack Jackson gebaut worden war, dem Liebhaber Alienas, den er, William, hatte umbringen wollen.

Fester denn je war er entschlossen, Vergeltung zu üben.

Walerans Gedanken schienen in ähnlichen Bahnen zu verlaufen, denn er sagte: »Es ist mir noch immer ein Rätsel, wie sie so schnell eine Mauer bauen konnten.«

»Eine wirklich gute Mauer war's wohl nicht«, meinte William.

Waleran nickte. »Aber Prior Philip ist mit Sicherheit schon wieder am Werk und läßt sie verstärken. Ich an seiner Stelle würde sie sogar noch höher ziehen, einen Wachtturm bauen und eine Wache aufstellen. Ich fürchte, Eure Überfälle auf die Stadt sind gezählt.«

Das war auch Williams Meinung, doch das hätte er nie zugegeben. »Ich kann sie immer noch belagern.«

»Das könnte der König wohl kaum noch übersehen. Die Stadtbewohner hätten genug Zeit, einen Boten zu ihm zu schicken und ihn um Schutz zu bitten. Das könnte übel für Euch ausgehen.«

»Stephan braucht mich. Er wird sich nicht gegen mich stellen.« William war selbst nicht davon überzeugt, aber der Bischof sollte den Eindruck gewinnen, er, William, ließe sich von ihm zur Vernunft bringen. Das verpflichtete – und dann konnte ihm William die Bitte unterbreiten, die ihm so sehr am Herzen lag.

Waleran schien in Gedanken verloren. Er nahm kaum wahr, wohin er ging, aber die Leute machten ihm so bereitwillig Platz, als schräken sie vor seinen schwarzen Gewändern zurück. Schließlich sagte er: »Habt Ihr schon gehört, daß der König Faringdon erobert hat?«

»Ich war dabei.« Das war der bisher einschneidendste Sieg Stephans im Laufe des langen Krieges. Er hatte Hunderte von Rittern gefangengenommen und Robert von Gloucester zur Flucht in den Westen gezwungen. Noch entscheidender war, daß Ranulf von Chester, Stephans alter Feind aus dem Norden, die Waffen gestreckt und dem König Treue geschworen hatte.

»Stephan sitzt jetzt fest im Sattel«, meinte Waleran. »Er wird künftig nicht mehr so nachsichtig mit den Privatfehden seiner Barone umgehen.«

»Vielleicht«, entgegnete William. Sollte er jetzt nachgeben und seine Bitte vortragen? Er zögerte. Ausgerechnet vor Waleran wollte er nicht seine Seele bloßlegen.

»Ihr solltet Kingsbridge in Ruhe lassen, wenigstens vorerst«, fuhr der Bischof fort. »Ihr habt die Wollmesse und den Wochenmarkt. Ihr habt den Wollhandel. Und Ihr habt das fruchtbarste Land der Grafschaft. Meine Lage hat sich ebenfalls verbessert. Ich konnte sogar meine Burg bauen. Der Kampf mit Philip sollte in den Hintergrund treten – jetzt, da es uns politisch gefährlich werden kann.«

Die Luft war erfüllt von den verschiedensten Gerüchen nach Kräutersuppe, frischgebackenem Brot, Zuckerwerk, gekochtem Schinken, gebratenem Speck, Apfelkuchen. William fühlte Übelkeit aufsteigen. »Gehen wir zur Burg«, schlug er vor.

Sie wandten sich dem Hügel zu. Der Vogt hatte sie zum Essen gebeten. Vor dem Burgtor blieb William stehen.

»Vielleicht habt Ihr recht mit Kingsbridge«, sagte er.

»Freut mich, daß Ihr das einseht.«

»Dennoch will ich auf meine Rache an Jack Jackson nicht verzichten, und Ihr könntet mir dabei helfen.«

Waleran hob eine Braue. Seine Miene besagte deutlich, daß er zwar bereitwillig höre, sich aber zu nichts verpflichtet fühlte.

»Aliena hat ersucht, ihre Ehe annullieren zu lassen«, erklärte William.

»Ja, das ist mir bekannt.«

»Was meint ihr? Wird sie Erfolg haben?«

»Die Ehe wurde anscheinend nie vollzogen.«

»Und das ist ausschlaggebend?«

»Wahrscheinlich. Gratian zufolge – ein Gelehrter, den ich im übrigen persönlich kenne – konstituiert sich eine Ehe aus dem gegenseitigen Einverständnis der beiden Parteien; er weist aber ausdrücklich darauf hin, daß es der Akt der physischen Vereinigung sei, der eine Ehe ›komplettiert‹ oder ›perfekt‹ macht. Er nennt insbesondere den Fall, daß ein Mann, der eine Frau heiratet, ihr aber nicht beiwohnt, danach eine zweite Frau heiratet, der er beiwohnt – in diesem Fall ist die zweite Ehe die gültige, also diejenige, die vollzogen wurde. Die hinreißende Aliena wird bei ihrer Appellation zweifellos diesen Fall ins Feld geführt haben, denn gewiß hatte sie in Prior Philip einen profunden Ratgeber.«

Soviel theoretisches Gefasel machte William kribbelig vor Ungeduld. »Dann wird sie also ihre Annullierung kriegen.«

»Solange Gratian nicht widersprochen wird, gewiß. Es gibt zwei Haupteinwände gegen seine Theorie: einen theologischen und einen praktischen. Der theologische besagt, daß Gratians Definition die Ehe zwischen Maria und Josef ungültig mache, da sie nicht vollzogen war. Der praktische Einwand ist mehr politischer Natur: Zur Zusammenlegung zweier Vermögen werden oftmals Ehen zwischen Kindern vereinbart, die körperlich gar nicht imstande sind, sie zu vollziehen. Wenn nun die Braut oder der Bräutigam noch vor der Pubertät stirbt, müßte nach Gratians Definition die Ehe für ungültig erklärt werden, und das könnte mitunter weitreichende Folgen haben.«

Das Klerikergezänk war William zu hoch, doch immerhin hatte er den Kern erfaßt: »Ihr meint also, es könnte so oder so ausgehen.«

»Richtig.«

»Und entscheidend dabei ist, *wer* den Druck ausübt.«

»Richtig. In diesem Fall ist der Ausgang gleichgültig – weder Besitzfragen noch Lehnspflichten noch militärische Bündnisse sind davon betroffen. Doch ginge es um mehr und – sagen wir – ein Erzdiakon legte begründeten Einspruch ein, so würde das Gesuch vermutlich abgelehnt.« Waleran bedachte William mit einem wissenden Blick, der dem Grafen mehr als unbehaglich war. »Ich glaube, ich weiß, worum Ihr mich jetzt bitten werdet.«

»Ich möchte, daß Ihr Einspruch gegen die Annullierung einlegt.«

Walerans Augen wurden schmal. »Ich weiß nie, ob Ihr dieses Frauenzimmer nun eigentlich liebt oder haßt.«

»Das«, sagte William, »weiß ich selber nicht.«

Aliena saß, grün beschattet von der mächtigen Buchenkrone, im Gras. Zu ihren Füßen sprühte der Wasserfall seine Tropfen wie Tränen auf die Felsen. Hier, auf dieser Lichtung, hatte Jack ihr einst seine vielen Geschichten erzählt. Hier hatte er ihr jenen ersten Kuß gegeben, so beiläufig und rasch, daß sie vorgegeben hatte, es sei nie geschehen. Hier hatte sie sich in ihn verliebt, ohne es zuzugeben, nicht einmal vor sich selbst. Heute wünschte sie sich sehnlichst, sie hätte sich ihm schon damals hingegeben und ihn geheiratet – dann wäre sie jetzt längst seine Frau.

Sie streckte sich aus, um ihrem schmerzenden Rücken etwas Ruhe zu gönnen. Es war Hochsommer, und kein Lüftchen milderte die Hitze. Ihre zweite Schwangerschaft machte Aliena schwerfällig. Sechs

Wochen lang sollte sie das noch ertragen! Manchmal meinte sie, sie bekäme Zwillinge, doch Martha hatte, als sie das Ohr direkt an ihren Bauch gelegt hatte, nur einen Herzschlag gehört.

Martha war es auch, die diesen Sonntagnachmittag Tommy hütete, so daß sich Aliena mit Jack treffen konnte, um ungestört über ihre Zukunft zu sprechen. Der Erzbischof hatte die Annullierung ihrer Ehe abgelehnt, anscheinend aufgrund einer Intervention seitens Walerans. Philip war der Meinung, sie solle es noch ein zweites Mal versuchen, doch sie müsse weiterhin von Jack getrennt leben. Er gab zu, daß das ungerecht war, doch er hielt es für den Willen Gottes. Aliena hielt es eher für Böswilligkeit.

An ihrer Reue trug sie ebenso schwer wie an ihrer Schwangerschaft. Sie bereute, daß sie Jack so weh getan, sie bereute, was sie sich selbst damit angetan, ja, sie bereute sogar das Leid, das sie dem ekelhaften Alfred zugefügt hatte. Der lebte mittlerweile in Shiring und ließ sich in Kingsbridge nicht mehr blicken. Sie hatte ihn nur aus einem einzigen Grund geheiratet – damit Richard weiterhin versuchen konnte, den Grafentitel zurückzugewinnen. Das hatte sie nicht erreicht. Sie war sechsundzwanzig Jahre alt, ihr Leben lag in Scherben, und sie konnte niemandem die Schuld daran geben – außer sich selbst.

Sie hörte Schritte, die sich näherten, und setzte sich rasch auf. Es war Jack, schmal und geschmeidig wie eine Katze. Er setzte sich neben sie und küßte sie zärtlich auf den Mund. Er roch nach Schweiß und Steinstaub. »Laß uns ein Bad nehmen«, schlug er vor. »Es ist so heiß.«

Die Versuchung war unwiderstehlich.

Jack zog sich aus, und sie sah ihm hungrig dabei zu. Es war Monate her, daß sie seinen Körper zum letztenmal gesehen hatte! Er warf ihr einen auffordernden Blick zu, und schüchtern begann sie, ihre Kleider abzulegen. Er hatte sie während keiner ihrer Schwangerschaften nackt gesehen, und sie befürchtete, ihr angeschwollener Leib könne ihn abstoßen. Ängstlich beobachtete sie seine Miene, doch darin war nichts als seine tiefe Zuneigung zu lesen. Ich hätte es wissen müssen! dachte sie.

Rasch kniete er vor ihr nieder und küßte sie auf den Bauch. Sie lachte verlegen auf, und er berührte ihren Nabel. »Er steht ja hervor«, sagte er verwundert.

»Ich wußte doch, daß du das sagen würdest!«

»Früher war er wie eine Einbuchtung – jetzt ist er wie ein Knopf.«

»Geh'n wir ins Wasser«, schlug sie vor. Dort würde sie sich weniger verlegen fühlen.

Der Teich unter dem Wasserfall war etwa drei Fuß tief, und Aliena ließ sich hineingleiten. Das Wasser kühlte wunderbar, und sie schauderte vor Entzücken. Jack glitt neben ihr in den Teich, der mit wenigen Fuß Durchmesser zum Schwimmen nicht groß genug war. Jack steckte den Kopf unter den Wasserfall und wusch sich den Staub aus den Haaren. Aliena tat es ihm nach, indem sie einfach untertauchte.

Als sie wieder an die Oberfläche kam, um Luft zu schnappen, wurde sie von Jack geküßt.

Atemlos spritzte und lachte sie und rieb sich das Wasser aus den Augen. Jack küßte sie erneut. Als sie die Hand ausstreckte, um Halt zu finden, berührte sie Jacks Glied, das hart zwischen seinen Lenden hochragte. Aliena seufzte vor Freude.

»Das hat mir so gefehlt«, flüsterte Jack ihr ins Ohr, mit einer Stimme, die brüchig klang vor Lust und Bedauern.

Alienas Verlangen machte ihr die Kehle eng. »Werden wir unser Versprechen brechen?«

»Jetzt und immerdar.«

»Wie meinst du das?«

»Wir werden nicht mehr getrennt leben. Wir gehen fort von Kingsbridge.«

»Aber was willst du dann tun?«

»In eine andere Stadt ziehen, an einer anderen Kathedrale bauen.«

»Aber dann wärst du nicht Dombaumeister. Es wäre nicht deine Kathedrale.«

»Eines Tages ergibt sich vielleicht eine neue Gelegenheit. Ich bin ja noch jung.«

Vielleicht – aber alles sprach dagegen. Aliena wußte es – und Jack auch. Das Opfer, das er ihr bringen wollte, rührte sie zu Tränen: Niemand konnte sie jemals mehr lieben als er! Doch sie konnte das Opfer nicht annehmen. »Das mache ich nicht mit«, sagte sie.

»Wie bitte?«

»Ich werde Kingsbridge nicht verlassen.«

»Wieso nicht?« gab er aufgebracht zurück. »Woanders können wir zusammenleben wie Mann und Frau, und kein Hahn kräht danach. Wir könnten uns sogar in der Kirche trauen lassen.«

Sie streichelte sein Gesicht. »Ich liebe dich viel zu sehr, um dich deiner Kathedrale wegzunehmen.«

»Das habe ich selber zu entscheiden.«

»Jack, es ist lieb von dir, aber es bricht mir schier das Herz. Daß du bereit bist, dein ganzes Lebenswerk aufzugeben, nur um mit mir zusammenleben zu können ... Wie sehr du mich lieben mußt! Aber du liebst auch deine Arbeit, und ich will sie dir nicht nehmen. So eine Frau bin ich nicht, und das ist auch keine Lösung. Es würde unser ganzes Leben überschatten, und ich könnte es mir nie verzeihen.«

Jack sah traurig drein. »Dein Entschluß steht also fest, und ich streite mich nicht mit dir. Aber was sollen wir tun?«

»Noch einmal die Annullierung beantragen. Getrennt leben.«

Er zog eine Grimasse.

»Und uns jeden Sonntag hier treffen, um unser Versprechen zu brechen«, beendete sie die Aufzählung.

Er drückte sie an sich, und sie spürte seine neuerliche Erregung. »Jeden Sonntag?«

»Jeden.«

»Du könntest wieder schwanger werden.«

»Darauf müssen wir es ankommen lassen. Und ich werde mich wieder mit der Tuchmanufaktur befassen, wie früher. Ich habe bereits Philips unverkaufte Wolle übernommen und will wieder Dorfbewohner fürs Spinnen und Weben anstellen. Danach wird es in der Walkmühle behandelt.«

»Womit hast du Philip bezahlt?« fragte Jack überrascht.

»Noch gar nicht. Ich werde ihn mit Tuch bezahlen, wenn es fertig ist.«

Jack nickte und sagte grimmig: »Damit war er nur deshalb einverstanden, weil du dann hierbleibst – und ich auch.«

»Und er kommt billig zu seinem Tuch«, bestätigte Aliena.

»Verdammter Philip! Immer bekommt er seinen Willen.«

Sie merkte, daß sie ihn überredet hatte. »Ich liebe dich«, sagte sie und küßte ihn.

Er erwiderte den Kuß und ließ seine hungrigen Hände über ihren Körper gleiten. Plötzlich jedoch hielt er inne und sagte: »Aber ich will dich jede Nacht bei mir haben und nicht nur am Sonntag.«

Sie liebkoste sein Ohr. »Eines Tages ist es soweit«, hauchte sie. »Das verspreche ich dir.«

Buch V 1152-55

Sieben Jahre später hatte Jack das Querschiff – den Querbalken im Kreuz der Kirche – vollendet, und es entsprach genau seinen Erwartungen.

Er hatte die in Saint-Denis gesammelten Anregungen fortgeführt und verbessert. Noch höher und schmaler waren Fenster, Spitzbogen und sogar das Gewölbe; über der Empore liefen anmutige Bündelpfeiler in Kreuzrippen aus, die sich in der Mitte des Gewölbes trafen. Durch die hohen Spitzbogenfenster flutete helles Licht in den Innenraum. Die hübschen Gesimsbänder waren üppig mit gemeißeltem Blattwerk ausgestattet.

Aber im Lichtgaden zeigten sich Risse.

Jack stand im Laufgang des Obergadens, starrte über die Kluft des nördlichen Querschiffs hinweg und grübelte. In seinem Empfinden mischten sich Bestürzung und Scham. Das Mauerwerk hätte, allen Regeln der Baukunst zufolge, stabil genug sein müssen; Risse jedoch waren Zeichen der Schwäche. Das Deckengewölbe war zwar höher als alle anderen Gewölbe, die Jack bisher gesehen hatte, aber keineswegs zu hoch. Auch hatte er nicht den gleichen Fehler wie Alfred gemacht und ein Steingewölbe auf einen Bau gesetzt, der gar nicht imstande war, ein solches Gewicht zu tragen. Und trotzdem zeigten sich Risse im Lichtgaden – ungefähr an der gleichen Stelle, an der auch Alfreds Konstruktion damals aufgebrochen war. Alfred hatte sich verrechnet; Jack hingegen war ganz sicher, daß ihm so etwas nicht unterlaufen war. Es mußte einen anderen, bisher unbekannten Grund für die Risse geben.

Gefahr bestand keine, jedenfalls vorläufig noch nicht. Die Risse waren mit Mörtel ausgefüllt worden und seither nicht wieder aufgetaucht. Das Gebäude war also sicher. Aber es war auch schwach –

und diese Schwäche nahm Jack alle Freude. Sein Ehrgeiz war es, eine Kirche zu bauen, die bis zum Tag des Jüngsten Gerichts erhalten blieb.

Er wandte sich ab und stieg die Wendeltreppe hinab zur Galerie, wo er sich dort, wo das Licht aus den Fenstern über dem Nordportal einfiel, einen Zeichenboden eingerichtet hatte. Er wollte die Plinthe für einen Strebepfeiler entwerfen. Zunächst zeichnete er eine Raute, dann in die Raute ein Quadrat und schließlich in das Quadrat einen Kreis. Die Hauptschäfte des Pfeilers sollten den vier Eckpunkten der Raute entspringen und sich an der Spitze der Säule nach Norden, Süden, Westen und Osten zu Jochbögen oder Gewölberippen verzweigen. Die Stützschächte sollten sich über den vier Ecken des Quadrats erheben und schließlich als Gewölberippen auslaufen, die auf der einen Seite das Mittelschiff-, auf der anderen Seite das Seitenschiffgewölbe diagonal durchliefen. Der Kreis in der Mitte stand für das Herzstück des Pfeilers.

Jacks Entwürfe beruhten sämtlich auf einfachen geometrischen Figuren und einigen nicht ganz so einfachen Proportionsberechnungen, wie zum Beispiel dem Verhältnis zwischen der Quadratwurzel aus der Zahl zwei zu der Wurzel aus der Zahl drei. Jack hatte das Wurzelziehen in Toledo gelernt. Die meisten Baumeister beherrschten es nicht und begnügten sich daher mit einfachen geometrischen Konstruktionen. Sie wußten, daß der Durchmesser eines Kreises, der um ein Quadrat gezogen wird, größer ist als eine Seite des Quadrats, und zwar im Verhältnis von der Wurzel aus zwei zu eins. Dieses Verhältnis – Wurzel aus zwei zu eins – war die älteste Berechnungsformel der Maurer, die bei einfachen Gebäuden das Verhältnis zwischen Außenbreite und Innenbreite und damit die Dicke der Mauern bestimmte.

Jacks Aufgabe wurde zusätzlich erschwert durch die religiöse Bedeutung verschiedener Ziffern. Prior Philip hatte die Absicht, die neue Kirche wieder der Jungfrau Maria zu weihen, weil die Weinende Madonna mehr Wunder wirkte als die Gebeine des heiligen Adolphus. Das Kloster hatte daher den Wunsch geäußert, Jack möge die Zahlen neun und sieben verwenden, die als die Zahlen der Jungfrau Maria galten. So hatte der Baumeister für das Langhaus neun Jochbögen geplant und für den neuen Chorraum, der erst ganz zum Schluß erstellt werden sollte, sieben. Die ineinandergreifenden Blendarkaden in den Seitenschiffen sollten sieben Bögen je Gewölbeabschnitt bekommen und die Westfassade neun Lanzettfenster. Jack hielt es nicht für nötig, sich über die theologische Bedeutung von Zahlen eine eigene Meinung zu bilden, doch ahnte er bereits, daß ihre regelmäßige

Verwendung den harmonischen Gesamteindruck des fertigen Baus nur noch verstärken konnte.

Er hatte die Zeichnung des Pfeilersockels noch nicht beendet, als er vom Dachdeckermeister unterbrochen wurde, der seine Hilfe brauchte. Er ging die Wendeltreppe hinauf und folgte dem Mann durch den Lichtgaden in den Dachstuhl. Sie passierten die runden Kuppeln an der Oberseite des Kreuzrippengewölbes. Über ihnen entrollten die Dachdecker große Bleimatten und nagelten sie an den Sparren fest. Sie arbeiteten von unten nach oben, so daß die obere Schicht jeweils die darunterliegende überlappte; auf diese Weise konnte das Regenwasser nicht in den Dachstuhl eindringen.

Jack erkannte das Problem auf den ersten Blick. Er hatte eine ornamentierte Fiale in die Senke zwischen zwei Dachschrägen gesetzt, Entwurf und Ausführung jedoch einem Steinmetzmeister überlassen. Der Mann hatte nun weder in der Fiale noch neben ihr für einen Regenwasserablauf gesorgt. Es war daher an ihm, Abhilfe zu schaffen. Der Dachdeckermeister erhielt den Auftrag, dem Steinmetzen dies zu sagen. Dann kehrte Jack wieder auf seinen Zeichenboden zurück.

Zu seiner Verblüffung stand dort Alfred und wartete auf ihn.

Sie hatten seit zehn Jahren kein Wort mehr miteinander gewechselt, obwohl Jack ihn ab und zu in Shiring oder Winchester von weitem gesehen hatte. Aliena, die nach dem Gesetz der Kirche noch immer mit ihm verheiratet war, hatte ihn seit neun Jahren nicht mehr zu Gesicht bekommen. Martha besuchte ihren Bruder gelegentlich in seinem Haus in Shiring und kehrte stets mit dem gleichen Bericht heim: Es gehe ihm glänzend, er baue Häuser für die Bürger von Shiring, er lebe allein und sei auch sonst ganz der alte geblieben ...

Der Alfred, der Jack nun gegenüberstand, entsprach dieser Beschreibung kaum noch. Er wirkte erschöpft und niedergeschlagen. Der große, bullige Alfred war abgemagert; seine Wangen waren eingefallen, und die einst so fleischige Hand schien nur noch aus Haut und Knochen zu bestehen.

»Hallo, Jack«, sagte er.

Seine Miene war angriffslustig wie eh und je, der Tonfall seiner Stimme jedoch eher vertraulich, fast kriecherisch.

»Hallo, Alfred«, gab Jack vorsichtig zurück. »Das letztemal, als ich dich sah, trugst du eine seidene Tunika und warst drauf und dran, fett zu werden.«

»Das war vor drei Jahren – noch vor der ersten schlechten Ernte.«

»Richtig.« Drei magere Ernten hintereinander hatten zu einer Hun-

gersnot geführt. Leibeigene waren verhungert, viele Pächter völlig verarmt, und vermutlich konnte sich auch in Shiring kann jemand mehr
ein prächtiges neues Steinhaus leisten. Das bekam Alfred offenbar
schmerzlich zu spüren. »Was führt dich nach so langer Zeit wieder
nach Kingsbridge?« fragte Jack.

»Ich habe von deinen Querschiffen gehört und will sie mir mal
ansehen.« Eine eher zähneknirschende Bewunderung schwang in seinen Worten mit. »Wo hast du das gelernt?«

»In Paris«, gab Jack kurzangebunden zurück. Alfred, dem er immerhin sein Exil zu verdanken hatte, war der letzte, mit dem er über
diesen Abschnitt seines Lebens zu reden gedachte.

»Ich würde ganz gern hier ein bißchen arbeiten«, sagte Alfred.
»Dümmer werd' ich davon bestimmt nicht.«

Jack blieb die Spucke weg. Ausgerechnet Alfred bittet mich um
Arbeit. Um Zeit zu gewinnen, fragte er: »Was ist mit deinem Trupp?«

»Ich bin jetzt allein«, antwortete Alfred, immer noch um einen
beiläufigen Ton bemüht. »Für einen ganzen Trupp reicht die Arbeit
nicht mehr.«

»Wir stellen derzeit ohnehin niemanden ein«, sagte Jack im gleichen Tonfall. »Unsere Mannschaft ist vollzählig.«

»Aber einen tüchtigen Maurer kann man doch gebrauchen, oder?«

Jack erkannte den flehenden Unterton, und ihm wurde klar, daß
Alfred der Verzweiflung nahe war. Er entschied sich für eine aufrichtige Antwort. »Nach allem, was wir miteinander erlebt haben, bin ich
der letzte, den du um Hilfe bitten solltest, Alfred.«

»Du *bist* der letzte«, gab Alfred ohne Umschweife zu. »Ich hab's
schon überall versucht. Nirgendwo werden noch Leute angeheuert.
Es liegt an der Hungersnot.«

Jack dachte an all die vielen Male, da Alfred ihn mißhandelt, geschlagen und gequält hatte. Es war Alfred, der ihn ins Kloster getrieben, und Alfred, der ihn in die Fremde getrieben hatte. Nein, er hatte
keinen Grund, Alfred zu helfen, im Gegenteil: Er hätte allen Grund,
sich an seinem Unglück zu weiden. »Ich würde dich nicht einmal
dann nehmen, wenn ich dringend Leute brauchte«, sagte er.

»Vielleicht doch«, gab Alfred mit der Sturheit eines Ochsen zurück.
»Es war immerhin mein Vater, der dich das alles gelehrt hat, ohne
ihn wärst du heute kein Dombaumeister. Willst du mir also nicht um
seinetwillen helfen?«

Um Toms willen. Jack verspürte plötzlich Gewissensbisse. Tom
hatte – auf seine Weise – versucht, ihm ein guter Stiefvater zu sein.

Er war weder zärtlich noch besonders einfühlsam gewesen, doch er hatte seine eigenen Kinder nicht anders behandelt. Mit viel Geduld und Großzügigkeit hatte er ihnen all das beigebracht, was er selbst wußte und konnte. Außerdem hatte er Ellen glücklich gemacht, jedenfalls die meiste Zeit über. Und da stehe ich nun, dachte Jack, ein erfolgreicher Dombaumeister, auf dem besten Wege dazu, mein Leben mit dem Bau der schönsten Kathedrale der Welt zu krönen – während Alfred arm ist, keine Arbeit hat und hungern muß. Ist das, nach alledem, nicht Vergeltung genug?

Nein, es ist nicht genug, dachte er.

Doch dann ließ er sich erweichen. »Na schön«, sagte er. »Du bist eingestellt – um Toms willen.«

»Danke«, sagte Alfred mit undurchschaubarer Miene. »Soll ich gleich anfangen?«

Jack nickte. »Wir legen gerade das Fundament fürs Mittelschiff, du kannst gleich mitmachen.«

Alfred streckte ihm die Hand entgegen. Jack zögerte zunächst, doch dann schlug er ein. Alfreds Händedruck war wie immer.

Nachdem Alfred gegangen war, starrte Jack noch eine geraume Weile auf seine Zeichnung für den Pfeilersockel. Er hatte ihn in Originalgröße gezeichnet, so daß der Schreinermeister direkt nach Jacks Zeichnung ein Modell aus Holz bauen konnte. Das Modell diente dann den Steinmetzen als Maß für die zu schneidenden Steine.

War das wirklich eine gute Entscheidung? fragte er sich. Er mußte daran denken, daß Alfreds Gewölbe eingestürzt war. Nun, ich werde Alfred gewiß nicht an meinem Kreuzrippengewölbe mitarbeiten lassen – gerade Wände und Bögen liegen ihm besser.

Jack war noch immer in Gedanken versunken, als die Mittagsglocke zum Essen rief. Er legte sein Zeicheninstrument nieder und ging die Wendeltreppe hinunter.

Die verheirateten Steinmetzen pflegten zum Essen nach Hause zu gehen, während die unverheirateten in ihrer Bauhütte speisten. Es gab sogar Bauherren, die die Mittagsmahlzeit von sich aus bereitstellten – um auf diese Weise zu vermeiden, daß die Handwerker zu spät, überhaupt nicht mehr oder womöglich betrunken zur Arbeit zurückkehrten. Die Kost der Mönche war freilich oft spartanisch, so daß die meisten Bauleute sich am liebsten selbst versorgten.

Jack, der in Tom Builders einstigem Haus wohnte, führte seine Stiefschwester Martha den Haushalt. Wenn Aliena in Geschäften unterwegs war, hütete Martha auch die Kinder Tommy und Sally. Martha kochte für Jack und die Kinder, und manchmal fand sich auch Aliena zum Essen bei ihnen ein.

Auf dem Weg nach Hause kam Jack plötzlich ein ganz neuer Gedanke: Ob Alfred sich wohl bei Martha einnisten will? Sie ist immerhin seine leibliche Schwester... Nein, das ist eine alberne Befürchtung, entschied er gleich darauf. Die Zeiten, da Alfred mich nach Lust und Laune schikanieren konnte, sind längst vorbei. Ich bin nun wohlbestallter Dombaumeister in Kingsbridge, und wenn ich bestimme, daß Alfred nicht in dieses Haus ziehen darf, so zieht Alfred eben auch nicht dort ein.

Dennoch rechnete er damit, Alfred am Küchentisch sitzen zu sehen, und war erleichtert, als sich seine Erwartung nicht bestätigte. Aliena sah den Kindern beim Essen zu. Martha stand am Feuer und rührte in einem Topf. Der Duft von geschmortem Lammfleisch ließ Jack das Wasser im Mund zusammenlaufen.

Er gab Aliena einen flüchtigen Kuß auf die Stirn. Sie war jetzt dreiunddreißig Jahre alt, aber sie sah nicht anders aus als vor zehn Jahren: Die üppige, dunkelbraune Lockenpracht war die gleiche, der Mund hatte noch immer den gleichen großzügigen Schnitt, und ihre dunklen Augen leuchteten wie eh und je. Nur wenn sie keine Kleider trug, waren die Veränderungen durch Alter und Kindsgeburten zu erkennen. Ihre herrlichen Brüste waren etwas herabgesunken, ihre Hüften ein wenig breiter geworden, und ihr Bauch war weder so straff noch so flach wie früher.

Voller Zuneigung betrachtete Jack die beiden Sprößlinge, die Aliena in ihrem Leib ausgetragen hatte – den neunjährigen Tommy, rothaarig, gesund und für sein Alter recht groß, der das geschmorte Lammfleisch in sich hineinschaufelte, als hätte er seit einer Woche nichts mehr zu essen bekommen; und die siebenjährige Sally, die die dunklen Locken ihrer Mutter geerbt hatte, über das ganze Gesicht strahlte und dabei eine Zahnlücke zeigte – genauso wie einst Martha, als Jack sie vor siebzehn Jahren zum erstenmal erblickt hatte. Tommy ging jeden Morgen in die Klosterschule und lernte dort Lesen und Schreiben. Mädchen nahmen die Mönche nicht auf; Sally wurde deshalb von Aliena unterrichtet.

Jack nahm Platz, und Martha stellte den Topf auf den Tisch. Sie war ein rätselhaftes Mädchen. Obwohl über zwanzig, zeigte sie noch immer nicht die geringste Neigung zu heiraten. Zu Jack hatte sie sich immer besonders hingezogen gefühlt; mit ihrem Leben als seine Haushälterin schien sie vollkommen zufrieden zu sein.

Jack führte ein höchst merkwürdiges Familienleben. Er, der Dombaumeister, und Aliena, die Besitzerin der größten Tuchmanufaktur außerhalb von Winchester, gehörten zu den angesehensten Bürgern der Stadt, und jedermann behandelte sie wie Mann und Frau. Dennoch war es ihnen untersagt, ihre Nächte gemeinsam zu verbringen, und sie wohnten in zwei verschiedenen Häusern – Aliena bei ihrem Bruder, Jack bei seiner Stiefschwester. An jedem Sonntag und jedem Feiertag pflegten die beiden des Nachmittags einfach zu verschwinden, und jedermann wußte genau, was sie dann taten – ausgenommen natürlich Prior Philip. Und Jacks Mutter hauste in einer Waldhöhle, weil sie als Hexe galt.

Von Zeit zu Zeit überkam Jack die kalte Wut darüber, daß er Aliena nicht heiraten durfte. Dann lag er hellwach im Bett, hörte Martha im Nebenzimmer schnarchen und dachte: Jetzt bin ich schon achtundzwanzig – warum muß ich immer noch alleine schlafen? Tags darauf ließ er dann seine schlechte Laune an Prior Philip aus, verwarf jeden Vorschlag und jede Forderung des Kapitels als undurchführbar oder zu teuer, weigerte sich, über Gegenvorschläge auch nur zu diskutieren, und ging keinerlei Kompromisse ein. In solchen Fällen pflegte Philip ihm einige Tage lang aus dem Wege zu gehen und zu warten, bis der Sturm sich gelegt hatte.

Aliena war über ihre Lebensumstände nicht minder unglücklich, und sie ließ ihre Unzufriedenheit an Jack aus. Da hatte sie dann an allem, was er tat, etwas auszusetzen, brachte die Kinder zu Bett, sobald er das Haus betrat, und weigerte sich mit der Behauptung, sie habe keinen Hunger, mit ihm zu essen. Nach ein oder zwei Tagen brach sie dann jedesmal in Tränen aus, entschuldigte sich, versprach, von nun an wieder lieb zu sein – bis zum nächstenmal, wenn die Belastung wieder zu stark wurde.

Jack schöpfte sich Schmorfleisch in eine Schüssel und begann zu essen. »Rate mal, wer heute vormittag bei mir aufgekreuzt ist«, sagte er. »Der liebe Alfred.«

Martha fiel ein gußeiserner Topfdeckel aus der Hand und polterte mit Getöse auf den Herdstein. Aliena erbleichte.

»Was will er in Kingsbridge?« fragte sie.

»Er sucht Arbeit. Die Kaufleute in Shiring bekommen die Hungersnot zu spüren und können sich keine schönen neuen Steinhäuser mehr leisten. Alfred hat seine Leute entlassen und findet selbst keine Arbeit.«

»Hoffentlich hast du ihn zum Teufel gejagt«, gab Aliena zurück.

»Er hat an mein Gewissen appelliert«, gestand Jack voller Beunruhigung. »Um Toms willen sollte ich ihm Arbeit geben.« Eine solch entschiedene Ablehnung seitens der beiden Frauen hatte er nicht vorausgesehen. »Und Tom bin ich immerhin einiges schuldig.«

»Kuhscheiße!« sagte Aliena bloß, und Jack dachte: Den Ausdruck muß sie von meiner Mutter haben.

»Wie dem auch sei, ich habe ihn jedenfalls eingestellt«, gab er zu.

»Jack!« schrie Aliena auf. »Wie konntest du?! Diesen – diesen Teufel darfst du doch nicht mehr nach Kingsbridge lassen!«

Sally brach in Tränen aus, und Tommy starrte seine Mutter aus großen Augen an. Jack sagte: »Alfred ist kein Teufel. Er ist am Verhungern und hat keinen roten Heller mehr in der Tasche ...«

»Wenn er dich dazu gezwungen hätte, neun Monate lang wie ein Hund auf dem Fußboden vor seinem Bett zu schlafen, täte er dir auch nicht mehr leid!«

»Mir hat er Schlimmeres angetan – frag Martha.«

»Mir auch«, bestätigte Martha.

»Der armselige Zustand, in dem er sich jetzt befindet, war mir Vergeltung genug«, sagte Jack.

»Wie schön für dich! Mir reicht das nicht!« tobte Aliena. »Herrgott im Himmel, was bist du für ein verbohrter Dummkopf, Jack Jackson! Es gibt Zeiten, da danke ich meinem Schöpfer dafür, daß ich *nicht* mit dir verheiratet bin!«

Das tat weh. Jack wandte den Blick ab. Er wußte genau, daß sie es nicht so meinte, aber es war schlimm genug, daß sie es aussprach. Er nahm seinen Löffel wieder auf und begann zu essen. Das Schlucken fiel ihm schwer.

Aliena tätschelte Sallys Hand und steckte ihr ein Stück Karotte in den Mund. Die Tränen des Mädchens versiegten.

Tommy starrte noch immer mit erschrockener Miene seine Mutter an. »Iß, Junge«, sagte Jack. »Es schmeckt gut.«

Der Rest der Mahlzeit verlief schweigend.

Im selben Frühjahr, da der Bau des Querschiffs vollendet wurde, unternahm Prior Philip eine Inspektionsreise zu den im Süden gelegenen Klostergütern. Nach drei schlechten Jahren war endlich wieder eine gute Ernte fällig, zudem wollte er sich über den Zustand der Güter in Kenntnis setzen.

Auf seiner Rundreise begleitete ihn Jonathan. Das Klostermündel war mittlerweile zu einem großen, linkischen und dabei sehr gescheiten Sechzehnjährigen herangewachsen. Wie Philip einst in diesem Alter, wußte er schon genau, was er mit seinem Leben anfangen wollte: Er hatte das Noviziat hinter sich gebracht und seine Gelübde abgelegt. Jetzt war er Bruder Jonathan. Und ebenso wie Philip war ihm hauptsächlich an den sachlichen Dingen gelegen, die der Dienst an Gott mit sich brachte. Er arbeitete als Stellvertreter von Cellerar Cuthbert Whitehead, der immer mehr in die Jahre kam. Philip war stolz auf den Jungen: Er war fromm, ein fleißiger Arbeiter und bei allen Mitbrüdern wohlgelitten.

Eskortiert wurden die beiden auf ihrer Reise von Alienas Bruder Richard, der in Kingsbridge endlich auch seinen Platz gefunden hatte. Nachdem die Stadtmauer gebaut worden war, hatte Philip der Kirchengilde vorgeschlagen, Richard zum Leiter der Stadtwache zu ernennen. Seitdem teilte Richard die Nachtwächter ein, sorgte für die Instandhaltung und Ausbesserung der Mauern und Wälle und war ermächtigt, an Markt- und Feiertagen Trunkenbolde und Störenfriede einzusperren. Seine Aufgaben, die mit der Stadt gewachsen waren, betrafen vor allem Tätigkeiten, die zu erledigen Mönchen untersagt war, und damit hatte sich die Gilde, in der Philip zunächst eine Bedrohung seiner Autorität gesehen hatte, als sehr nützlich erwiesen. Richard war glücklich in seinem neuen Amt. Er war mittlerweile um die Dreißig, doch das aktive Leben, das er führte, hatte ihm sein jugendliches Aussehen erhalten.

Auch für Aliena, Richards Schwester, hätte Philip gerne eine zufriedenstellende Lösung gefunden. Wenn jemand sich darüber beklagen konnte, von der Kirche im Stich gelassen worden zu sein, dann gewiß Aliena. Der Mann, den sie liebte, und der Vater ihrer Kinder war Jack, aber die Kirche hielt hartnäckig an ihrer Ehe mit Alfred fest, obwohl Aliena ihm niemals beigewohnt hatte. Die Ehe wurde nur deshalb nicht annulliert, weil der Bischof dagegen war. Es war eine Schande, und Philip fühlte sich schuldig, obwohl er nicht die Verantwortung dafür trug.

Gegen Ende ihrer Rundreise – sie waren schon auf dem Heimweg und ritten durch einen frühlingsbunten Wald – sagte Jonathan unvermittelt: »Ich frage mich, warum Gott es zuläßt, daß die Menschen verhungern müssen.«

Das war eine Frage, die jeder junge Mönch früher oder später zu stellen pflegte, und die Antworten darauf waren so zahlreich wie die Sandkörner am Meeresstrand. Philips Antwort lautete: »An dieser Hungersnot trägt Gott keine Schuld.«

»Aber Gott hat das Wetter gemacht, das die mageren Ernten hervorbrachte!«

»Die schlechten Ernten sind es nicht allein«, erwiderte Philip. »Schlechte Ernten gibt es alle paar Jahre wieder, und niemand muß deswegen verhungern. Zu dieser besonderen Not jetzt hat vor allem der lange Krieg beigetragen.«

»Inwiefern?« fragte Jonathan.

Diesmal war es Richard, der Krieger, der ihm antwortete. »Im Krieg leiden die Bauern immer am ärgsten«, meinte er. »Man raubt ihnen das Vieh, damit die Soldaten zu essen haben, dann werden ihre Getreidefelder niedergebrannt, um zu verhindern, daß sich der Feind an der Ernte gütlich tut, und schließlich vernachlässigen die Grundherren ihre Güter, weil sie selbst als Ritter oder Barone am Krieg teilnehmen.«

»Und wenn die Zukunft im Ungewissen liegt«, fügte Philip hinzu, »fehlt es allen an Mut, Zeit und Kraft, um Wälder zu roden, neue Weiden zu schaffen, die Herden zu vergrößern, Gräben zu ziehen und Scheunen zu bauen.«

»Aber wir haben doch auch nicht damit aufgehört«, wandte Jonathan ein.

»Bei Klöstern sieht das etwas anders aus. Die meisten einfachen Bauern aber ließen in den Kriegsjahren ihre Höfe verkommen, und als das schlechte Wetter einsetzte, waren sie nicht mehr in der Lage, die zusätzliche Belastung zu verkraften. Mönche sind da vorausschauender, obwohl auch das Kloster mit einigen Schwierigkeiten zu kämpfen hat. So sind wegen der Hungersnot zum Beispiel die Wollpreise verfallen.«

»Was hat das eine mit dem anderen zu tun?« fragte Jonathan.

»Wer am Verhungern ist, braucht keine neuen Kleider mehr. Das wird's sein.« Philip konnte sich nicht erinnern, daß es schon einmal einen solchen Preisverfall gegeben hatte. Bisher waren die Wollpreise Jahr für Jahr gestiegen. Die Krise wirkte sich unmittelbar auf die Geschäfte des Klosters aus: Philip hatte die Bauarbeiten am Dom einschränken müssen, konnte keine neuen Novizen mehr aufnehmen und mußte seinen Mönchen Wein und Fleisch vom Speisezettel streichen. »Es ist ein Jammer, daß wir ausgerechnet jetzt zum Sparen gezwungen sind, da immer mehr Verzweifelte in Kingbridge um Lohn und Brot bitten.«

»Und so stehen sie am Klostertor um ein bißchen Pferdebrot und Suppe an«, schloß Jonathan.

Philip nickte ernst. Es wollte ihm jedesmal schier das Herz brechen, wenn er sah, wie viele kräftige Männer um Brot betteln mußten, weil sie keine Arbeit fanden. »Aber merk dir, es liegt am Krieg, nicht am schlechten Wetter«, sagte er.

»Ich hoffe nur«, erwiderte Jonathan mit dem Feuer der Jugend, »daß man in der Hölle einen besonderen Platz für alle die Grafen und Könige bereithält, die soviel Elend heraufbeschwören!«

»Das hoffe ich – Herr und alle Heiligen, was ist das denn?«

Eine seltsame Gestalt war aus dem Unterholz gebrochen und stürzte Hals über Kopf auf Philip zu, die Kleider in Lumpen, die Haare wirr, das Gesicht schwarz vor Schmutz. Der arme Kerl, dachte Philip. Wahrscheinlich hat er einen wütenden Eber oder einen entkommenen Bären aufgestört und rennt nun um sein Leben.

Da war der Mann auch schon bei ihnen und stürzte sich auf Philip; und der war so überrascht, daß er vom Pferd fiel.

Sofort war der Angreifer über ihm. Er stank wie die Pest und gab grunzende Geräusche von sich wie ein wildes Tier. Der Mann schien es auf das Ledersäckchen abgesehen zu haben, das Philip an einem Riemen über die Schulter gehängt hatte. In dem Säckchen befand sich nichts weiter als ein Buch, *Das Hohelied Salomons*. Philip versuchte verzweifelt, sich zu befreien – nicht, weil ihm das Buch besonders ans Herz gewachsen war, sondern weil der Räuber so abstoßend stank. Am Rande bekam er noch mit, daß sein Pferd durchgegangen war.

Und dann war plötzlich Richard da und riß den Räuber von ihm weg. Philip setzte sich auf, kam aber noch nicht wieder auf die Füße. Er war völlig außer Atem und fühlte sich schwach. In tiefen Zügen sog er die frische Luft ein, froh darüber, der ungesunden Nähe des Räubers entkommen zu sein. Er tastete seinen Körper ab. Gebrochen war glücklicherweise nichts.

Richard hatte den Räuber zu Boden geworfen und stand nun über ihm, einen Fuß zwischen den Schulterblättern des Mannes, die Schwertspitze bedrohlich nahe an dessen Hals. Jonathan hielt die beiden verbliebenen Pferde am Zügel und schaute verwirrt von einem zum anderen.

Philip rappelte sich mühsam wieder auf. In Jonathans Alter, dachte er, hätte ich nach so einem Sturz sofort wieder aufsitzen können.

»Paßt auf diese Wanze auf, seid so gut«, sagte Richard. »Ich fange unterdessen Euer Pferd wieder ein.« Er hielt Philip sein Schwert hin.

»Danke«, sagte Philip und schob das Schwert beiseite. »Das brauche ich nicht.«

Nach kurzem Zögern steckte Richard es wieder in die Scheide. Der Räuber rührte sich nicht vom Fleck. Die nackten Beine waren dürr wie trockene Äste und von der gleichen Farbe; Schuhe trug er keine. Philip war nie ernstlich in Gefahr gewesen – diese arme Kreatur besaß nicht einmal die Kraft, einer Henne den Hals umzudrehen.

Als der Räuber sah, wie Richard sich entfernte, spannte sich sein Körper an. Philip, der erkannte, daß der Mann einen Fluchtversuch machen wollte, fragte ihn: »Willst du etwas zu essen haben?«

Der Mann hob den Kopf. Sein Blick schien zu sagen: Der ist wohl nicht ganz bei Trost!

Philip ging zu Jonathans Pferd, nahm einen Laib Brot aus der Satteltasche, brach's und bot dem Räuber die Hälfte an. Der Mann grapschte danach und stopfte sich umgehend den Mund voll.

Philip setzte sich auf die Erde und sah ihm zu. Der Räuber fraß wie ein ausgehungertes Tier, als befürchte er, das Brot könne ihm schon im nächsten Moment wieder entrissen werden. Philip hatte ihn anfangs für einen alten Mann gehalten, doch nun, bei näherem Hinsehen, wurde ihm klar, daß er allenfalls fünfundzwanzig Jahre alt war.

Richard, der mit Philips Pferd am Zügel zurückkam, reagierte unwirsch, als er den Räuber essen sah. »Wieso habt Ihr ihm unser Essen gegeben?« fragte er den Prior.

»Weil er kurz vor dem Verhungern ist.«

Richard antwortete darauf nicht, doch seine Miene verriet, daß er alle Mönche für übergeschnappt hielt.

Nachdem der Räuber das Brot verschlungen hatte, fragte Philip ihn nach seinem Namen. Der Mann zögerte. Wahrscheinlich hat er schon lange nicht mehr mit einem anderen Menschen gesprochen, dachte Philip. Endlich kam die Antwort: »David.«

»Was ist dir widerfahren, David?«

»Nach der letzten Ernte hat man mir meinen Hof genommen.«

»Wer war dein Gutsherr?«

»Der Graf von Shiring.«

William Hamleigh also, dachte Philip. Darauf hätte ich auch von selbst kommen können.

Nach drei aufeinanderfolgenden schlechten Ernten hatten Tausende von Hofpächtern ihre Pacht nicht mehr zahlen können. Auch vielen von Philips Pächtern erging es nicht besser, und so erließ er ihnen die Pacht aus der einfachen Überlegung, daß die Leute, wenn er sie dem blanken Nichts überließ, nur wieder im Kloster um Almosen bitten würden. Andere Gutsherren jedoch, vor allem Graf William, nutzten die schweren Zeiten aus. Sie warfen ihre Pächter hinaus und rissen die Höfe wieder an sich. Ergebnis war, daß die Zahl derer, die sich in die Wälder flüchteten und dort vom Raub lebten, bedrohlich anstieg – und daß Philip ohne Leibwächter nicht mehr auf Reisen gehen konnte.

»Was ist aus deiner Familie geworden?« fragte er den Mann.

»Meine Frau ist mit dem Kleinen wieder zu ihrer Mutter gezogen. Aber für mich ist dort kein Platz.«

Es war immer wieder dieselbe Geschichte. »Es ist eine Sünde, Hand an einen Mönch zu legen, David«, sagte Philip, »und es ist nicht recht, vom Diebstahl zu leben.«

»Aber wovon soll ich denn leben?« rief der Mann.

»Wenn du im Wald bleiben willst, solltest du dir wilde Vögel und Fische fangen.«

»Aber ich weiß doch nicht, wie man das macht!«

»Als Räuber bist du jedenfalls ein Versager«, stellte Philip fest. »Überleg mal, wie gering deine Erfolgsaussicht war – du allein und ohne Waffe gegen uns drei, darunter einer, der bis an die Zähne bewaffnet ist!«

»Ich war völlig verzweifelt.«

»Lassen wir's dabei bewenden. Aber wenn du wieder einmal völlig verzweifelt bist, dann geh zum nächsten Kloster. Dort gibt es allemal etwas zu essen für einen Armen, der um Hilfe bittet.« Philip erhob sich, im Mund den schalen Geschmack der Scheinheiligkeit. Er wußte nur zu gut, daß die Klöster gar nicht imstande waren, alle Outlaws durchzufüttern. Den meisten dieser armseligen Geschöpfe blieb gar nichts anderes übrig als zu stehlen. Andererseits war es für ihn als Mönch und Prior eines Klosters Pflicht, die Leute auf den Pfad der Tugend zurückzuführen.

Für diesen Unglücklichen konnte er nichts weiter tun. Er ließ sich von Richard die Zügel seines Pferdes geben und saß auf. Alles tat ihm weh; er wußte, daß er noch tagelang unter den Nachwirkungen des Sturzes zu leiden haben würde. Mit einem Zitat des Herrn Jesus schickte er David fort: »Gehe hin in Frieden und sündige fortan nicht mehr.« Dann trat er seinem Pferd in die Flanken und ritt davon.

»Ihr seid viel zu gut, wirklich«, bemerkte Richard, als sie wieder unter sich waren.

Philip schüttelte betrübt den Kopf. »Die traurige Wahrheit ist, daß ich nicht gut genug bin«, sagte er.

Am Sonntag vor Pfingsten heiratete William Hamleigh.

Dahinter stand, wie anders kaum zu erwarten, seine Mutter.

Jahrelang hatte sie ihm in den Ohren gelegen, er solle sich eine Frau suchen und einen Erben zeugen, doch er hatte es immer wieder hinausgeschoben. Frauen langweilten ihn einfach, und außerdem schüchterten sie ihn ein – auf eine Art und Weise, die er nicht so recht verstand und über die er auch nicht weiter nachdenken wollte. Also vertröstete er Mutter wieder und wieder mit der Bemerkung, er werde demnächst schon heiraten, tat aber nichts, um dieses Versprechen in die Tat umzusetzen.

Schließlich hatte sie ihm selber eine Braut ausgesucht.

Sie hieß Elisabeth und war die Tochter Harolds von Weymouth, eines reichen Ritters und bewährten Parteigängers von König Stephan. Regan Hamleigh hatte William zwar ausführlich dargelegt, daß er mit wenig mehr Mühe eine viel bessere Ehe hätte schließen können – etwa mit der Tochter eines Grafen –, doch da er sich darum nicht gekümmert habe, müsse er sich eben mit Elisabeth zufriedengeben.

William hatte sie zum erstenmal am königlichen Hof zu Winchester gesehen, und Mutter war aufgefallen, wie er das Mädchen anstarrte. Es hatte ein hübsches Gesicht, eine Fülle hellbrauner Locken, große Brüste und schmale Hüften – und damit alles, worauf William Wert legte.

Sie war vierzehn Jahre alt.

William war, als er sie damals fast mit den Augen verschlungen hatte, von ganz anderen Gedanken besessen gewesen. Er hatte sich vorgestellt, ihr in dunkler Nacht in einer einsamen Gasse von Winchester zu begegnen und sie mit Gewalt zu nehmen. Nie wäre ihm so etwas wie Heirat in den Sinn gekommen. Doch Mutter hatte die Sache in die Hände genommen und rasch festgestellt, daß der Vater des Mädchens ein annehmbarer Mann und das Mädchen selbst ein gehorsames Kind war. Nachdem sie William dann glaubhaft versichert hatte, es werde unter keinen Umständen zu einer Wiederholung jener Demütigung kommen, die Aliena der Familie zugefügt hatte, war von ihr ein Treffen zwischen ihrem Sohn und seiner jungen Braut vereinbart worden.

William war voller Zweifel und Bedenken hingegangen. Beim letztenmal, als er dergleichen getan, war er ein unerfahrener Jüngling gewesen, der zwanzigjährige Sohn eines Ritters, der auf eine hochnäsige junge Dame aus dem Adel traf. Heute jedoch war er ein gestandener, schlachtenerprobter Mann, siebenunddreißig Jahre alt und schon seit zehn Jahren Graf von Shiring. Es war einfach albern, wegen einer Vierzehnjährigen Herzklopfen zu bekommen.

Es hatte sich schließlich herausgestellt, daß Elisabeth noch viel aufgeregter war als er und sich verzweifelt darum bemühte, ihm zu gefallen. Unablässig hatte sie von ihrem Zuhause und ihrer Familie geplappert, von ihren Pferden und Hunden, ihren Verwandten und Bekannten, während er schweigend dasaß, ihr Gesicht betrachtete und ihr in Gedanken bereits genüßlich die Kleider vom Leibe riß.

Bischof Waleran vollzog die Eheschließung in der Kapelle der Grafenburg. Danach gab es ein großes Fest, das bis in die Nacht hinein währte. Der Sitte gemäß war alles eingeladen worden, was in der Grafschaft Rang und Namen besaß. William mußte auffahren, was Küche und Keller nur hergaben, anderenfalls hätte er sein Gesicht verloren. Im Burghof wurden drei ganze Ochsen nebst Dutzenden von Schafen und Schweinen gebraten, und die Gäste machten sich über Williams Keller her, bis kein Tropfen Bier, Apfelmost noch Wein mehr übrig war. Williams Mutter thronte über der Festgesellschaft, auf ihrem entstellten Gesicht einen Ausdruck des Triumphs, der bis zum Schluß nicht weichen wollte. Bischof Waleran, der so vulgäre Feiern ohnehin geschmacklos fand, empfahl sich, als der Onkel der Braut anfing, anzügliche Witze über junge Ehepaare zu erzählen.

Braut und Bräutigam zogen sich bei Einbruch der Nacht in ihr Gemach zurück und überließen die Gäste ihren lüsternen Phantasien. William hatte schon auf genug Hochzeiten getanzt; er wußte genau, was in den Köpfen der jüngeren Gäste vorging. Um Störungen jedwelcher Art auszuschließen, postierte er Walter vor dem Brautgemach und verriegelte die Tür von innen.

Elisabeth hatte Tunika und Schuhe ausgezogen und stand im Leinenhemd vor ihm. »Ich weiß nicht, was ich tun soll«, sagte sie. »Du wirst es mir zeigen müssen.«

So hatte William sich das nicht vorgestellt. Er trat vor sie hin, sie hob den Kopf, und er küßte ihre weichen Lippen. Doch es sprang kein Funke über. »Zieh dein Hemd aus und leg dich aufs Bett«, sagte er.

Sie war ziemlich rundlich, und ihre großen Brüste hatten winzige, tiefliegende Knospen. Hellbrauner Haarflaum bedeckte das Dreieck zwischen ihren Beinen. Folgsam ging sie zum Bett und legte sich auf den Rücken.

William schleuderte die Stiefel von den Füßen, setzte sich neben seine Braut aufs Bett und kniff ihre Brüste. Ihre Haut war ganz weich.

Dieses süße, nachgiebige, lächelnde Kind hatte so gar nichts mit seinem Traum von einer Frau gemeinsam, die, von Leidenschaft gepackt, schwitzend und stöhnend unter ihm lag. Er fühlte sich betrogen.

Er schob die Hand zwischen ihre Schenkel, und sofort spreizte sie die Beine. Sie stieß einen schwachen Schmerzensschrei aus und sagte gleich danach: »Schon gut, es macht nichts.«

Ihm kam der Gedanke, er könne die ganze Angelegenheit vollkommen falsch angegangen sein. Einen kurzen Moment lang ging ihm eine merkwürdige Vorstellung durch den Kopf: Sie lagen Seite an Seite, streichelten sich, sprachen miteinander und lernten sich allmählich besser kennen. Doch da sich bei ihrem Schrei endlich doch Verlangen in ihm geregt hatte, schob er seine Zweifel rasch beseite. Noch rücksichtsloser als beim erstenmal stieß er zu und weidete sich an ihrer Miene. Elisabeth bemühte sich verzweifelt, den Schmerz schweigend zu ertragen.

Nun stieg er aufs Bett und kniete sich zwischen ihre Beine. Sein Glied war noch nicht steif genug, und er rieb ohne großen Erfolg daran herum. Dieses verdammte Lächeln macht mich noch impotent! dachte er. Diesmal stieß er zwei Finger auf einmal in sie hinein, und sie schrie wieder auf. So war's schon besser. Doch dann fiel der blöden Kuh nichts Besseres ein, als wieder ihr Lächeln aufzusetzen! Das werde ich ihr austreiben, dachte er, und zwar sofort. Er schlug sie ins Gesicht. Sie schrie auf, und von ihrer Lippe tropfte Blut. So war's schon viel besser.

Er schlug noch einmal zu, und das Mädchen fing an zu weinen.

Dann war endlich alles in Ordnung.

Der folgende Sonntag war Pfingstsonntag, an dem sich eine riesige Menschenmenge in der Kathedrale versammeln würde. Bischof Waleran sollte den Gottesdienst abhalten. Da alle Welt das erst seit kurzem fertiggestellte neue Querhaus sehen wollte, wurde mit noch größerem Andrang als sonst gerechnet. Den Gerüchten zufolge handelte es sich um einen wahrhaft erstaunlichen Bau. William wollte die Gelegenheit dazu nutzen, dem gemeinen Volk seine Braut vorzuführen. Zwar war er, seit es die Stadtmauer gab, nicht mehr in Kingsbridge gewesen, doch Philip konnte ihn nicht hindern, in die Kirche zu gehen.

Zwei Tage vor Pfingsten starb seine Mutter.

Sie war um die Sechzig, und es geschah ganz plötzlich. Am Freitag, nach dem Essen, hatte sie sich etwas kurzatmig gefühlt und war zeitig zu Bett gegangen. Ihre Zofe weckte William kurz vor Morgengrauen und berichtete, seiner Mutter gehe es schlecht. Er stand auf und taumelte, sich den Schlaf aus dem Gesicht reibend, in ihr Zimmer. Mutter lag da, rang mühselig um Luft, brachte keinen Ton heraus, und in ihren Augen stand das nackte Entsetzen.

Ihr langgezogenes, schauriges Keuchen und ihr starrer Blick machten William angst. Sie sah ihn unentwegt an, als wolle sie ihn dazu bringen, irgend etwas zu tun. Sie jagte ihm so viel Angst ein, daß er schon wieder das Zimmer verlassen wollte, doch da sah er ihr Mädchen an der Tür stehen und schämte sich seiner Angst. Im unsteten Licht der einzigen Kerze schien Mutters Gesicht ständig neue Formen anzunehmen. Ihr rauhes, abgerissenes Keuchen wurde lauter und lauter, bis es seinen ganzen Kopf auszufüllen schien. Er verstand nicht, warum nicht die ganze Burg davon aufgeweckt wurde. Er hielt sich die Ohren zu, doch das gräßliche Geräusch war immer noch zu hören. Es kam ihm vor, als brülle sie ihn an, so wie sie es getan hatte, als er noch ein kleiner Junge war, eine irre, wütende Schimpftirade, und auch ihr Gesicht sah wütend aus, der Mund weit aufgerissen, die Augen starr, das Haar wirr. Die Überzeugung, sie stelle eine Forderung an ihn, bedrängte ihn mehr und mehr. Gleichzeitig hatte er das Gefühl, immer jünger und kleiner zu werden, bis ihn wieder jenes blinde Grauen packte, das er seit seiner Kindheit nicht mehr empfunden hatte – das Grauen, das aus der Gewißheit kam, daß der einzige Mensch, den er liebte, ein wutschnaubendes Ungeheuer war. Es war immer das gleiche gewesen: Sie sagte ihm, er solle zu ihr kommen oder weggehen oder sein Pony besteigen oder absitzen, und er folgte nicht schnell genug; daraufhin brüllte sie ihn an, und er bekam so große Angst, daß er nicht mehr verstand, was sie von ihm wollte. Schließlich artete das Ganze in hysterisches Geschrei aus. Ihre Stimme überschlug sich, während er nur noch blind, taub und stumm vor Entsetzen dastand.

Diesmal jedoch war es anders.

Diesmal starb sie.

Zuerst schlossen sich ihre Augen, und William beruhigte sich ein wenig. Dann wurde ihr Atem immer flacher, und ihr Gesicht verfärbte sich trotz der Geschwüre ganz grau. Sogar die Kerze schien nicht mehr so hell zu brennen, so daß die flackernden Schatten William nicht mehr ängstigten. Und dann hörte Mutter auf zu atmen.

»Na also«, sagte William, »jetzt geht's ihr wieder besser, was?«

Das Mädchen brach in Tränen aus.

William setzte sich neben das Bett und betrachtete Mutters stilles

Gesicht. Das Mädchen holte den Priester, der ärgerlich fragte: »Warum habt Ihr mich nicht früher rufen lassen?« William hörte ihm gar nicht richtig zu. Er blieb bis zum Sonnenaufgang bei der Toten, dann kamen die Dienerinnen und forderten ihn auf zu gehen, damit sie die Herrin »herrichten« könnten. William ging in den großen Saal hinunter, wo die Burgbewohner – Ritter, Waffenträger, Priester, Diener und Dienerinnen – trübselig beim Frühstück saßen. Er setzte sich neben seine junge Frau und trank ein paar Schluck Wein. Ein paar Ritter und der Hausmeister sprachen ihn an, doch William gab keine Antwort. Schließlich kam Walter herein und setzte sich neben ihn. Walter war schon so lange bei ihm, daß er wußte, wann er den Mund zu halten hatte.

Nach einiger Zeit fragte William: »Sind die Pferde bereit?«

Walter wirkte überrascht. »Wofür?«

»Für die Reise nach Kingsbridge. Die dauert zwei Tage – wir müssen heute vormittag los.«

»Ich dachte, wir blieben hier – unter diesen Umständen ...«

Der Vorschlag erregte Williams Zorn. »Hab' ich gesagt, wir bleiben hier?«

»Nein, Herr.«

»Also gehen wir!«

»Ja, Herr.« Walter stand auf. »Ich sehe gleich nach dem Rechten.«

Um die Mitte des Vormittags brachen sie auf, William und Elisabeth samt der üblichen Gefolgschaft von Rittern und Knechten. William war, als befände er sich in einem Traum. Nicht er schien durch die Landschaft zu ziehen – die Landschaft schien an ihm vorüberzugleiten. Elisabeth ritt neben ihm, wortlos und verwundet. Machten sie Rast, so war es Walter, der sich um alles kümmerte. Bei den Mahlzeiten aß William jedesmal nur wenig, trank aber mehrere Becher Wein. In der Nacht schlief er unruhig.

Als sie sich durch grünende Felder Kingsbridge näherten, erblickten sie den Dom schon von weitem. Die alte Kathedrale war ein geducktes, breitschultriges Gebäude gewesen, dessen kleine Fenster wie glänzende Äuglein unter rundbogigen Augenbrauen hervorlugten. Die neue Kirche sah, obwohl noch nicht fertig, völlig anders aus. Die Klostergebäude ringsum wirkten wie Zwerge.

Die Straße füllte sich allmählich mit zahlreichen Reitern und Fußgängern, die es gen Kingsbridge zog. Der Pfingstgottesdienst im Frühsommer, bei schönem Wetter und trockenen Straßen war seit jeher beliebt.

Auf der letzten Meile gingen William und seine Gesellschaft in kurzen Galopp über, der unachtsame Fußgänger von der Straße vertrieb. Dann polterten sie über die hölzerne Zugbrücke, die den Fluß überspannte. Kingsbridge war mittlerweile eine der am stärksten befestigten Städte in ganz England. Eine dicke Steinmauer mit bezinnter Brustwehr umschloß den Ort, und dort, wo die Brücke einst kerzengerade auf die Hauptstraße zugeführt hatte, verstellte nun ein steinerner Wachturm den Weg, dessen ausladende, eisenbeschlagene Tore bei Einbruch der Nacht fest verschlossen und verriegelt wurden. Diese Stadt, dachte William, werde ich wohl nicht noch einmal niederbrennen können.

Die Leute gafften, als er mit seinem Gefolge die Hauptstraße entlang auf das Kloster zuritt. William war daran gewöhnt – er war der Graf, da gafften die Leute immer. Diesmal allerdings galt ihre Aufmerksamkeit auch der jungen Braut zu seiner Linken. Zu seiner Rechten ritt, wie üblich, Walter.

Im Klosterhof saßen sie ab. William überließ sein Pferd Walter und wandte sich der Kirche zu. Die Ostseite, also die Spitze des Kreuzes, lag auf der anderen Seite des Klosterhofs und blieb somit seinen Blicken verborgen. Das westliche (untere) Ende des Kreuzes stand noch nicht, doch seine Umrisse waren bereits mit Pflöcken und Schnur markiert. Auch waren die Fundamente teilweise schon gelegt. Dazwischen ragte das neue, in Nord-Süd-Richtung erbaute Querschiff – der Querbalken des Kreuzes – auf. Die Mitte zwischen Quer- und Hauptschiff bildete die Vierung. Die Fenster waren wahrhaftig so groß, wie sie aus der Ferne gewirkt hatten. Nie zuvor in seinem Leben hatte William einen solchen Bau gesehen.

»Die Kirche ist traumhaft schön«, sagte Elisabeth, die bislang in unterwürfigem Schweigen verharrt hatte.

William wünschte, er hätte sie zu Hause gelassen.

Beinahe ehrfürchtig schritt er zwischen den Pflöcken und Seilen über den Grundriß des Langhauses. Elisabeth tappte hinterher. Vom Mittelschiff stand erst ein Joch, und auch das nur in Teilen, doch sah es so aus, als trüge es den riesigen Spitzbogen, der den westlichen Eingang zur Vierung krönte. Kaum war William unter diesem unglaublichen Bogen hindurchgegangen, da befand er sich auch schon inmitten der Menschenmenge, die sich in der Vierung zusammendrängte.

Der neue Dom wirkte wie aus einer anderen Welt – er schien viel zu hoch, zu schlank, zu anmutig und zu zerbrechlich zu sein, um Bestand haben zu können. Nirgendwo schien es solide Mauern zu geben, die das Dach tragen konnten – statt dessen eine Reihe von biegsam wirkenden Pfeilern, die beredt gen Himmel strebten. William tat es den andren nach: Er legte den Kopf in den Nacken und sah, daß sich die Pfeiler an der gewölbten Decke fortsetzten, um dort, wie die ineinandergreifenden Äste einer Gruppe hoher Ulmen im Wald, in der Mitte zusammenzulaufen.

Der Gottesdienst begann. Der Altar war an der Vorderseite des Chors errichtet worden. Die Mönche standen dahinter, so daß die Vierung sowie beide Arme des Querschiffs der Gemeinde vorbehalten blieben. Trotzdem fanden nicht alle Gläubigen Platz, sondern drängten sich auch auf dem Gelände des noch nicht erbauten Mittelschiffs. William kämpfte sich zum Altar durch und stellte sich, wie es sein Vorrecht war, zu den anderen Adligen. Man nickte ihm zu und unterhielt sich flüsternd.

Die bemalte Holzdecke des alten Chorraums wollte nicht so recht zu dem hohen Ostbogen der Vierung passen. Vermutlich hatte der Baumeister die Absicht, nach Fertigstellung der Kirche den Chor einzureißen und einen neuen zu bauen, der besser zu dem übrigen Gebäude paßte.

Kaum war William dieser Gedanke durch den Kopf gegangen, da sah er besagten Baumeister auch schon – Jack Jackson, ein gutaussehender Bursche mit roten Haaren, der eine an Saum und Kragen bestickte dunkelrote Tunika trug wie ein Edelmann. Er wirkte überaus zufrieden mit sich selbst – gewiß, weil er das Querschiff in so überraschend kurzer Zeit errichtet hatte und alle Welt nun sein Werk bestaunte. An der Hand hielt er einen ungefähr neunjährigen Jungen, der ihm wie aus dem Gesicht geschnitten war. Alienas Kind! schoß es William durch den Kopf, und die Eifersucht begann an ihm zu nagen. Und da war sie auch schon selbst: Sie stand seitlich hinter Jack und lächelte dezent, aber voller Stolz, William stockte der Atem: Sie war so schön wie eh und je ... Elisabeth war nichts als ein armseliger Ersatz, eine farblose Imitation der echten, lebendigen Aliena. Sie hatte den Arm um ein kleines Mädchen gelegt, das vielleicht sieben Lenze zählen mochte – ja, natürlich, sie hatte ja ein zweites Kind von Jack bekommen ... Und das, obwohl sie gar nicht mit ihm verheiratet war!

Bei näherem Hinsehen entdeckte er, daß Aliena offenbar doch ein wenig von ihrer früheren Lieblichkeit eingebüßt hatte: Um die Augen zeigten sich feine Kummerfältchen, und in ihrem stolzen Lächeln lag auch eine gewisse Traurigkeit. Kein Wunder, dachte William befriedigt.

Es muß ihr ja an die Nieren gehen, daß sie nach so vielen Jahren ihren Jack immer noch nicht heiraten kann! Bischof Waleran hatte sein Versprechen gehalten und die Annulierung ihrer Ehe mit Alfred zu Williams heimlicher Genugtuung wieder und wieder mit seinem Veto blockiert.

Waleran stand am Altar und hielt die Hostie hoch, so daß sie von der versammelten Gemeinde gesehen werden konnte. Nun knieten Hunderte von Menschen gleichzeitig nieder. In diesem Moment wurde das Brot zum Leib Christi, eine Wandlung, die William mit Ehrfurcht erfüllte, obgleich er keine Ahnung hatte, um was es wirklich ging.

Eine Zeitlang konzentrierte er sich auf den Gottesdienst, folgte den geheimnisvollen Handlungen der Priester, lauschte den lateinischen Sprüchen, die er nicht verstand, und murmelte ihm von irgendwoher vertraute, formelhafte Antworten mit.

Die Benommenheit, die er nun schon seit beinahe zwei Tagen empfand, war noch immer nicht von ihm gewichen, und die wundersame neue Kirche, auf deren erstaunlichen Säulen das Sonnenlicht spielte, verstärkte das Gefühl nur noch. Er glaubte zu träumen.

Kurz vor dem Ende des Gottesdienstes drehte Bischof Waleran sich um und wandte sich an die Gemeinde: »Lasset uns beten für das Seelenheil der Gräfin Regan Hamleigh, der Mutter des Grafen William von Shiring, die Freitagnacht von uns gegangen ist.«

Allenthalben erhob sich Gemurmel und Geraune, nur William starrte stumm und entsetzt den Bischof an: Endlich war ihm aufgegangen, was Mutter ihm hatte sagen wollen, bevor sie starb. Sie hatte nach dem Priester verlangt – *und er hatte nicht nach ihm geschickt!* Er hatte zugesehen, wie sie immer schwächer wurde, wie sie die Augen schloß, wie sie aufhörte zu atmen – und wie sie schließlich ohne Beichte starb. Wie hatte er das nur zulassen können? Nun befand sich ihre Seele schon seit Freitagnacht in der Hölle und litt dort all jene Qualen, die Mutter ihm so oft und so anschaulich geschildert hatte. Kein einziges Gebet war zu ihrer Erlösung gesprochen worden! Die Schuld wollte ihm schier das Herz zersprengen. Auch ich muß sterben, dachte er, gleich hier … Wie habe ich nur zulassen können, daß sie nun an diesem furchterregenden Ort dahinschmachten muß, ihre Seele von Sünden entstellt wie ihr Gesicht von Geschwüren … »Was soll ich bloß tun?« entfuhr es ihm unwillkürlich, und die Umstehenden sahen ihn erstaunt an.

Das Gebet war gesprochen, und die Mönche verließen die Kirche in Reih und Glied. William verharrte weiter auf Knien vor dem Altar.

Die Gemeinde verlor sich draußen im Sonnenschein. Nur der getreue Walter blieb in der Nähe, hatte ein Auge auf seinen Herrn und wartete auf ihn. William betete. Das Bild seiner Mutter vor Augen, bot er all seine Kraft auf und betete: das Vaterunser und alle anderen Gebete und Bekenntnisse, die ihm – oft nur bruchstückhaft – in den Sinn kamen. Doch, es gab noch Dinge, die er für seine Mutter tun konnte. Er konnte Kerzen stiften; er konnte Priester und Mönche gegen Bezahlung für Mutter Messen lesen lassen; ja, er konnte für ihr Seelenheil sogar eine Kapelle bauen lassen. Doch alles, was ihm einfiel, erschien ihm auch sogleich wieder unzureichend. Ihm war, als schüttelte sie den Kopf, gleichermaßen verletzt und enttäuscht von ihrem Sohn. Und sie sah ihm ins Gesicht und sagte: »Wie lange willst du deine Mutter noch diese Höllenqualen erleiden lassen?«

Er spürte, wie sich eine Hand auf seine Schulter legte, und sah auf. Bischof Waleran stand vor ihm, noch immer in dem prächtigen roten Gewand, das er ausschließlich zu Pfingsten trug. Seine schwarzen Augen schienen William durchbohren zu wollen, und William war, als gäbe es keine Geheimnisse mehr vor diesem Blick. »Warum weint Ihr?« fragte Waleran.

Erst jetzt merkte William, daß sein Gesicht tränenüberströmt war. »Wo ist sie jetzt?« fragte er.

»Ihre Seele wird durch das Feuer geläutert.«

»Leidet sie Schmerzen?«

»Ja, entsetzliche Schmerzen. Aber wir können die Zeit, die die Seelen unserer lieben Dahingegangenen an diesem furchtbaren Ort verbringen müssen, durchaus verkürzen.«

»Wie? Ich werde alles tun, alles!« schluchzte William. »Sagt mir nur, wie!«

Walerans Augen leuchteten vor Habgier. »Baut eine Kirche«, sagte er. »Baut eine Kirche wie diese hier. Aber in Shiring.«

Kalte Wut packte Aliena, so oft sie durch die ehemaligen Ländereien ihres Vaters kam. Die vielen verstopften Gräben, die geborstenen Zäune und die leeren, halbverfallenen Kuhställe erregten ihren Zorn; die verwahrlosten Weiden machten sie traurig; und die verödeten Dörfer wollten ihr schier das Herz brechen. Es lag nicht allein an den schlechten Ernten. Die Grafschaft hätte ihre Einwohner durchaus ernähren können, selbst in diesem Jahr noch, wäre sie nur ordentlich geführt worden. Doch William Hamleigh hatte keine Ahnung, wie Land zu verwalten und zu bewirtschaften war. Ihm bedeutete die Grafschaft nichts weiter als eine private Schatztruhe. Hatten seine Leibeigenen nichts zu essen, so verhungerten sie. Konnten seine Pächter ihre Pacht nicht mehr bezahlen, so warf er sie hinaus. Seit William Graf geworden war, hatte die bebaute Fläche mehr und mehr abgenommen. Die Natur eroberte sich die Höfe enteigneter Pächter zurück. Und William war so dumm, daß er nicht erkannte, wie sehr er sich mit seiner Politik auf lange Sicht ins eigene Fleisch schnitt.

Das Schlimmste an allem war, daß Aliena sich vorwarf, für die Misere mitverantwortlich zu sein. Richard und sie hatten versagt. Sie hatten keinen Versuch mehr unternommen, die Grafschaft zurückzugewinnen. Nachdem der König William zum Grafen ernannt und Aliena ihr gesamtes Vermögen verloren hatte, waren sie in Tatenlosigkeit verfallen. Dieses Versagen erbitterte Aliena noch immer, und der Eid, den sie ihrem Vater geschworen, war unvergessen.

Auf dem Weg von Winchester nach Shiring, unterwegs mit einer Ladung Garn und einem stämmigen Fuhrmann, der ein Schwert an seinem Gürtel trug, erinnerte sich Aliena eines gemeinsamen Ritts mit ihrem Vater auf derselben Straße. Indem er Wälder roden, Sümpfe trockenlegen und Hanglagen unter den Pflug nehmen ließ, hatte Vater beständig neues Ackerland geschaffen. Für schlechte Jahre hielt er stets genügend Saatgut bereit, um jenen auszuhelfen, die es aus Sorglosigkeit oder vor Hunger versäumt hatten, ihr eigenes aufzuheben. Nie hatte Graf Bartholomäus einen Pächter gezwungen, sein Vieh oder seinen Pflug zu verkaufen, um damit die Pacht zu bezahlen – wußte er doch zu gut, daß damit der Ertrag des folgenden Jahres erst recht nicht stimmen würde. Er hatte sein Land gepflegt wie ein guter Bauer seine Milchkuh – und auf diese Weise dafür gesorgt, daß es fruchtbar und ertragreich blieb.

Jedesmal, wenn Aliena sich der Zeiten erinnerte, da ihr kluger, stolzer, unbeugsamer Vater an ihrer Seite war, spürte sie den Schmerz über seinen Verlust wie eine offene Wunde. Nachdem man ihn damals fortgeschleppt hatte, war alles immer schlimmer geworden. Alles, was sie seither getan, kam ihr nichtig vor: daß sie sich in ihre Traumwelt versponnen und mit Matthew in der Burg geblieben war; daß sie in der vergeblichen Hoffnung, den König sprechen zu können, nach Winchester gezogen war; ja, sogar die Unterstützung, die sie Richard gewährt hatte. In den Augen anderer hatte sie viel erreicht, war eine wohlhabende Wollhändlerin geworden. Doch das Glück war rein äußerlich. Sie hatte einen Platz in der Gesellschaft gefunden, der ihr Sicherheit verlieh und Beständigkeit versprach, doch innerlich hatte sie sich stets verletzt und verloren gefühlt – bis Jack in ihr Leben getreten war.

Daß sie Jack nicht heiraten durfte, hatte seither alles verdorben. Prior Philip, ihr einstiger Retter und Mentor, war ihr mittlerweile verhaßt. Schon seit Jahren hatte sie kein freundschaftliches Gespräch mehr mit ihm geführt. Gewiß, es war nicht seine Schuld, daß ihre Ehe nicht annulliert wurde – aber er war es, der darauf bestanden hatte, daß Jack und sie getrennt lebten, und das konnte ihm Aliena nicht verzeihen.

Sie liebte ihre Kinder und machte sich Sorgen um sie, weil sie in so unnatürlichen familiären Verhältnissen aufwuchsen. In welcher Familie verließ schon der Vater zur Schlafenszeit das Haus? Glücklicherweise zeigten sich bislang noch keine schlechten Auswirkungen: Tommy war ein stämmiger, gutaussehender kleiner Bursche, der am liebsten mit seinen Kameraden Fußball oder Soldat spielte; Sally war ein liebes, aufmerksames Mädchen, das ihren Puppen kleine Geschichten erzählte, am liebsten aber bei Jack auf dem Zeichenboden saß und ihm bei der Arbeit zusah. Die täglichen Freuden, Sorgen und Wünsche ihrer Sprößlinge und ihre einfache, kindliche Liebe waren die einzigen Konstanten in Alienas ungewollt außergewöhnlichem Leben.

Natürlich gab es da auch noch ihre Arbeit. Über verschiedene Dörfer verstreut, standen Dutzende von Männern und Frauen in ihrem Lohn, die in Heimarbeit für sie spannen und webten. Noch vor wenigen Jahren waren es sogar Hunderte gewesen, doch auch Aliena hatte die Auswirkungen der Hungersnot zu spüren bekommen und fand es sinnlos, mehr Tuch herstellen zu lassen, als sie verkaufen konnte. Ihre Arbeit machte sie immerhin wirtschaftlich unabhängig; sie hätte sie selbst dann nicht aufgegeben, wenn sie Jack hätte heiraten können.

Prior Philip behauptete nach wie vor, die Annullierung könne jederzeit ausgesprochen werden, aber inzwischen waren sieben lange Jahre ins Land gezogen, ohne daß sich an Alienas und Jacks unerträglichen Lebensverhältnissen etwas geändert hätte: Noch immer zogen sie die Kinder gemeinsam auf, nahmen gemeinsam die Mahlzeiten ein – und schliefen getrennt.

Aliena empfand Jacks Unbehagen an diesem Leben schmerzlicher als ihr eigenes. Sie betete ihn an. Niemand ahnte auch nur, wie sehr sie ihn liebte – außer Ellen vielleicht, der nichts entging. Sie liebte ihn, weil er sie dem Leben zurückgegeben hatte. Sie hatte sich wie eine Raupe in ihren Kokon versponnen, und Jack hatte sie davon befreit und ihr gezeigt, daß sie in Wahrheit ein Schmetterling war. Ohne ihn wäre sie ihr ganzes Leben für die Freuden und Leiden der Liebe unempfänglich geblieben. Er aber war zu ihrer geheimen Lichtung gekommen, hatte sie mit seinen Verserzählungen unterhalten, hatte sie schließlich sanft geküßt und dann ganz allmählich und behutsam die Liebe geweckt, die tief in ihrem Inneren schlummerte. Wie geduldig und großzügig er gewesen war, trotz seiner Jugend! Allein deshalb würde sie ihn ewig lieben.

Auf ihrem Ritt durch den Wald mußte Aliena an Ellen denken, Jacks Mutter. Ob wir ihr vielleicht sogar begegnen? fragte sie sich. Die beiden Frauen trafen sich sonst nur hier und da auf einem Markt, und einmal im Jahr schlich sich Ellen bei einbrechender Dunkelheit durchs Stadttor und verbrachte die Nacht bei ihren Enkelkindern. Aliena empfand eine gewisse Verwandtschaft mit Ellen, denn sie waren beide Sonderlinge, Frauen, die nicht in den üblichen Rahmen paßten. Diesmal passierten sie den Wald, ohne Ellen zu Gesicht zu bekommen.

Danach fuhren sie durch Ackerland, und Aliena achtete genau auf den Fruchtstand der Felder. In diesem Jahr wird die Ernte einigermaßen zufriedenstellend ausfallen, dachte sie. Der Sommer war zwar nicht besonders schön gewesen, eher kalt und verregnet, doch die sintflutartigen Regenfälle und die Getreidekrankheiten, die die letzten drei Ernten verdorben hatte, waren ihnen glücklicherweise erspart geblieben. Mittlerweile nagten Abertausende von Menschen am Hungertuch. Bei einem weiteren strengen Winter würden sie wie die Fliegen hinweggerafft werden.

Die Ochsen mußten getränkt werden, so daß Aliena am Dorfteich von Monksfield Rast machte, einem recht ansehnlichen Ort, der zum Grundbesitz des Grafen gehörte. Er lag inmitten des fruchtbarsten Landstrichs der Grafschaft und besaß sogar einen eigenen Priester und eine gemauerte Kirche. Dennoch war nur ungefähr die Hälfte der Felder in diesem Jahr mit gelbem Weizen bebaut; auf den anderen Äckern wucherte schon wieder das Unkraut.

Am Teich im Herzen von Monksfield befanden sich bereits zwei andere Reisende, die ihre Pferde tränkten. Aliena beäugte sie vorsichtig. Mitunter war es von Vorteil, sich anderen Leuten anzuschließen, allein des gegenseitigen Schutzes wegen. Als Frau mußte man sich seine Begleiter allerdings sehr genau aussuchen. Aliena hatte festgestellt, daß ein Mann wie ihr Fuhrknecht zum Beispiel jeder ihrer Aufträge sofort und ohne zu murren ausführte, solange sie mit ihm allein war, in Gegenwart anderer Männer aber aufsässig wurde.

Einer der beiden Reisenden am Dorfteich war eine Frau, nein: ein Mädchen. Aliena hatte sie schon einmal gesehen, und zwar am Pfingstsonntag in der Kathedrale zu Kingsbridge. Es war Gräfin Elisabeth, William Hamleighs Frau.

Elisabeth machte einen unglücklichen, verschüchterten Eindruck und wurde von einem Bewaffneten mit hochfahrendem Gehabe begleitet, bei dem es sich offensichtlich um ihren Leibwächter handelte. Das hätte *mein* Los sein können, dachte Aliena. Gott sei Dank habe ich mich dagegen gewehrt.

Der Leibwächter nickte dem Fuhrknecht kurz zu, ignorierte Aliena jedoch geflissentlich. Nein, mit diesem Mann wollte sie nicht gemeinsam weiterreisen.

Noch während ihrer Rast bezog sich der Himmel mit dunklen Wolken, und ein heftiger Wind kam auf. »Sommergewitter«, brummte Alienas Fuhrknecht.

Aliena betrachtete forschend den Himmel. Ein bißchen Nässe machte ihr nichts aus. Bei einem heftigen Gewitter kam man jedoch nur noch langsam voran, und das bedeutete, daß sie womöglich im Freien nächtigen mußten. Schon fielen die ersten Regentropfen.

»Wir sollten lieber noch eine Weile hierbleiben«, sagte die Gräfin zu ihrem Begleiter.

»Das geht nicht«, lautete die schroffe Entgegnung. »Befehl vom Herrn.«

Aliena packte der Zorn, als sie hörte, wie er mit dem Mädchen umsprang. »Sei kein solch sturer Narr!« fuhr sie ihn an. »Nennst du das auf deine Herrin achtgeben?!«

Der Mann sah sie verblüfft an, dann fragte er grob: »Was geht's Euch an?«

»Gleich gibt's einen Wolkenbruch, du Narr!« sagte Aliena im Tonfall der Hochwohlgeborenen, den sie noch immer sehr gut beherrschte. »Bei derartigem Wetter kannst du doch eine Dame nicht durch die Gegend reiten lassen! Für diese Torheit wird dein Herr dich auspeitschen lassen.« Aliena wandte sich der Gräfin zu. Das Mädchen sah sie neugierig an, sichtlich erfreut, daß jemand ihrem großmäuligen Leibwächter die Stirn bot. Nun fing es richtig zu regnen an. Kurz entschlossen sagte Aliena zu Elisabeth: »Kommt mit.«

Bevor der Wächter noch reagieren konnte, hatte sie das Mädchen schon bei der Hand genommen. Elisabeth ging bereitwillig mit und grinste dabei wie ein Kind, das die Schule schwänzt. Aliena hegte den Verdacht, der Leibwächter könne ihnen folgen und sich die Gräfin wieder schnappen, doch da fuhr auch schon ein Blitz hernieder, und aus dem Regenschauer wurde ein Regenguß. Aliena fing an zu laufen und zog Elisabeth mit sich. Gemeinsam rannten sie über den Kirchacker auf ein Holzhaus neben der Kirche zu.

Die Tür stand offen, und sie liefen hinein. Wie Aliena richtig vermutet hatte, handelte es sich um das Pfarrhaus. Bei ihrem Eintritt erhob sich ein verdrießlich dreinblickender Mann, der eine schwarze Tunika und um den Hals eine Kette mit einem kleinen Kreuz trug. Aliena, die genau wußte, daß die Pflicht zur Gastfreundschaft von vielen Priestern – und besonders in diesen Notzeiten – als schwere Bürde empfunden wurde, beugte jedem Widerspruch vor, indem sie in bestimmtem Ton feststellte: »Meine Gefährten und ich brauchen einen Unterschlupf.«

»Ihr seid willkommen«, entgegnete der Priester zähneknirschend.

Das Haus besaß nur zwei Zimmer und einen angebauten Stall mit schrägem Dach. Obwohl die Tiere also draußen gehalten wurden, war es ziemlich schmuddelig in der Wohnstube. Auf dem Tisch stand ein Weinfäßchen, und als sie sich setzten, wurden sie von einem kleinen Köter angekläfft.

Elisabeth drückte Alienas Arm. »Ich danke Euch vielmals«, sagte sie mit tränenfeuchten Augen. »Ranulf hätte mich einfach weitergetrieben – er hört nie auf das, was ich sage.«

»Schon gut«, gab Aliena zurück. »Diese bulligen, starken Kerle sind im Grunde genommen bloß Feiglinge.« Sie sah Elisabeth jetzt aus der Nähe und erkannte erschrocken, daß das bedauernswerte Kind ihr ähnlich sah. Williams Ehefrau zu sein, war an sich schon ein arges Los, aber zeitlebens mit dem Makel der zweiten Wahl behaftet – das war gewiß die Hölle auf Erden!

»Ich bin Elisabeth von Shiring«, stellte sich das Kind vor. »Und wer seid Ihr?«

»Ich heiße Aliena und komme aus Kingsbridge.« Aliena hielt unwillkürlich den Atem an. Ob Elisabeth den Namen erkannte und mit der Frau in Verbindung brachte, die William Hamleigh einst zurückgewiesen hatte?

Aber die Gräfin war zu jung, um sich an den Skandal zu erinnern, und sagte nur: »Was für ein ungewöhnlicher Name.«

Aus dem zweiten Zimmer kam eine nachlässig gekleidete Frau mit einem gewöhnlichen Gesicht und nackten, fleischigen Armen. Mit trotziger Miene bot sie ihnen einen Becher Wein an. Aliena vermutete, daß sie das Weib des Priesters war, der sie vermutlich – da die Kirche

Priesterehen verbot – als seine Haushälterin bezeichnen würde. Das Verbot brachte der Kirche nichts als Scherereien ein. Zwang sie die Männer, ihre Frauen fortzuschicken, so empfand man dies als herzlos und schimpfte über die Kirche. Und obwohl die meisten von ihren Schäfchen der Meinung waren, Geistliche hätte enthaltsam zu leben, drückten doch viele in Fällen, da ihnen die Frau persönlich bekannt war, ein Auge zu. Notgedrungen stellte sich dann oft auch die Kirche blind und taub und nahm derartige Verbindungen hin. Aliena dachte unwillkürlich: Du hast allen Grund zur Dankbarkeit, Weib – denn wenigstens darfst du mit deinem Mann zusammenleben …

Nun kamen der Leibwächter und der Fuhrknecht herein, beide von Kopf bis Fuß durchnäßt. Ranulf baute sich vor Elisabeth auf und sagte: »Wir können nicht bleiben.«

Zu Alienas Verblüffung gab Elisabeth sofort nach. »Na schön«, sagte sie und stand auf.

»Setzt Euch wieder«, sagte Aliena und zog sie auf ihren Stuhl zurück. Dann richtete sie sich auf und fuchtelte dem Mann mit dem Finger vor der Nase herum: »Wenn ich noch ein Wort von dir höre, dann rufe ich die Dorfbewohner zusammen! Die wissen, im Gegensatz zu dir, genau, wie sie ihre Herrin zu behandeln haben.«

Ranulf wog seine Chancen, und man sah es ihm an: Im Ernstfall konnte er es wohl mit der Gräfin, Aliena, dem Fuhrknecht und dem Priester aufnehmen – mischte sich aber nur ein Dörfler ein, so wäre der Ausgang ungewiß.

»Vielleicht würde es die Gräfin *vorziehen,* weiterzureiten«, sagte er schließlich und sah Elisabeth herausfordernd an.

Das Mädchen war vollkommen verängstigt, und Aliena meinte: »Nun, Euer Gnaden – Ranulf bittet untertänigst, ihm Eure Wünsche mitteilen zu wollen.«

Elisabeth wandte ihr stumm den Blick zu.

»Teilt ihm einfach Eure Wünsche mit«, sagte Aliena aufmunternd. »Er muß Euch schließlich gehorchen.«

Alienas feste Haltung schien Elisabeth Mut einzuflößen. Sie holte tief Luft und sagte: »Wir bleiben hier. Geh und sieh nach den Pferden, Ranulf.«

Da fügte sich ihr störrischer Leibwächter mit einem merkwürdigen Grunzlaut und ging hinaus. Elisabeth sah ihm mit einem Ausdruck reinsten Erstaunens hinterher.

»Das schifft vielleicht!« bemerkte der Fuhrknecht.

Der Geistliche runzelte die Stirn ob der vulgären Rede. »Ich bin sicher, daß es sich nur um ganz gewöhnlichen Regen handelt«, sagte er im Tonfall eines Tugendbolds, und Aliena mußte unwillkürlich lachen. Sogar Elisabeth stimmte in ihr Gelächter ein. Aliena hatte das Gefühl, daß das Mädchen nur sehr selten lachte.

Das Geräusch des fallenden Regens wurde zu lautem Trommeln. Aliena warf einen Blick durch die offene Tür. Die nur ein paar Schritt entfernte Kirche war durch den Regenvorhang kaum noch zu sehen.

»Hast du die Fuhre gut abgedeckt?« fragte Aliena ihren Knecht. Der Mann nickte. »Die Tiere auch.«

»Gut. Ich will nicht, daß mein Garn filzig wird.«

Ranulf kam wieder herein, von oben bis unten klatschnaß.

Ein Blitz zuckte über den Himmel, gefolgt von langanhaltendem Donnergrollen. »Das wird den Feldern gar nicht gut tun«, bemerkte der Priester kummervoll.

Er hat recht, dachte Aliena. Wir brauchten eigentlich dringend drei Wochen Sonne und Wärme.

Wieder blitzte es, gefolgt von noch längerem Donnergetöse, und eine heftige Bö erschütterte das Holzhaus. Aliena spürte etwas Kaltes auf ihrem Kopf. Als sie aufblickte, sah sie das Regenwasser aus dem Strohdach heruntertropfen. Sie rückte beiseite. Der Wind trieb den Regen auch zur Tür herein, aber niemand traf Anstalten, sie zu schließen – Aliena war offenbar nicht die einzige, die sich das Unwetter ansehen wollte.

Elisabeths Gesicht war kreideweiß. Aliena legte ihren Arm um das Mädchen, das heftig zitterte, obwohl es gar nicht kalt war.

»Ich hab' solche Angst«, flüsterte Elisabeth.

Plötzlich wurde es draußen finster – und das, obwohl gerade Mittagszeit war. Aliena stand auf und trat an die Tür. Der Himmel war grau wie Stahl. Sie hatte noch nie ein solches Wetter mitten im Sommer erlebt. Der Wind kam in heftigen Böen. Ein weiterer Blitz erhellte eine Reihe von Gegenständen, die vor der Tür vorbeitrieben: eine Decke, einen kleinen Busch, eine hölzerne Schüssel, ein leeres Faß.

Stirnrunzelnd drehte sie sich um und nahm wieder Platz. Sie fing allmählich an, sich Sorgen zu machen, zumal das Haus schon wieder bebte und nun auch die Firststange in der Mitte des Raumes erzitterte. Dabei gehörte das Pfarrhaus noch zu den stabilsten in diesem Dorf; die ärmlicheren Hütten waren wohl schon ernsthaft gefährdet. Aliena wandte sich an den Priester. »Wenn's noch schlimmer wird, müssen wir wohl die Dorfbewohner holen und mit ihnen in der Kirche Zuflucht suchen«, schlug sie vor.

»Bei diesem Wetter bringt mich niemand vors Haus«, gab der Priester zurück und lachte kurz auf.

Aliena starrte ihn ungläubig an. »Diese Leute sind Eure Herde, und Ihr seid ihr Hirte!« erwiderte sie.

Der Geistliche bedachte sie mit einem unverschämten Blick. »Wenn mir hier jemand etwas zu sagen hat, dann ist das der Bischof von Kingsbridge«, fuhr er sie an. »Ich lasse mich doch nicht von Euch zum Narren machen.«

»So laßt wenigstens das Pfluggespann in Sicherheit bringen«, sagte Aliena. Das acht Ochsen zählende Gespann, das den Pflug zog, war in Dörfern dieser Größenordnung gemeinhin der kostbarste Besitz, denn ohne die Tiere konnte kein Bauer seine Felder bestellen. Das Pfluggespann war Gemeineigentum, denn kein Bauer konnte sich ein eigenes leisten. Aliena nahm daher an, der Priester wüßte wenigstens den Wert des Gespanns zu schätzen, hing doch sein eigenes Wohlergehen davon ab.

»Wir haben kein Pfluggespann.«

Damit hatte Aliena nicht gerechnet. »Wieso nicht?«

»Vier Ochsen mußten wir verkaufen, um die Pacht zahlen zu können, und im Winter haben wir die anderen vier geschlachtet, damit wir zu essen hatten.«

Deshalb also ist nur die Hälfte der Felder bestellt, dachte Aliena. Aus eigener Kraft oder mit Hilfe von Pferden hatten sie nur die leichteren Böden pflügen können. Geschichten wie diese regten Aliena maßlos auf. Nicht nur, daß es herzlos von William war, die Menschen zum Verkauf ihres Pfluggespanns zu zwingen – es war auch äußerst dumm, denn sie würden ja nun auch in diesem Jahr ihre Pacht kaum bezahlen können, selbst wenn das Wetter einigermaßen gut blieb. Aliena hätte William erwürgen können.

Ein weiterer Windstoß erschütterte das Holzhaus. Dann schien sich plötzlich das Dach zu verschieben, hob sich mehrere Zoll breit von der Außenwand, und Aliena konnte durch den klaffenden Spalt den schwarzen Himmel und das Zucken der Blitze sehen. Sie sprang auf, doch da legte sich der Wind auch schon wieder, und das Strohdach knallte zurück auf seine Unterlage. Der Ernst der Lage war nicht mehr zu verkennen! Sie hob die Stimme, um das tosende Unwetter zu übertönen, und schrie dem Priester zu: »So geht wenigstens und öffnet das Kirchenportal!«

Er fügte sich unwillig, holte den Kirchenschlüssel aus einem Kasten, hüllte sich in einen Umhang, verließ das Haus und war auch schon im Regen verschwunden. Aliena erteilte weitere Befehle: »Fuhrmann, du bringst die Ochsen mit der Fuhre in die Kirche. Ranulf, du holst die Pferde. Und Ihr kommt mit mir, Elisabeth.«

Sie legten ihre Umhänge um und traten ins Freie. Hand in Hand, die Oberkörper gebeugt, stemmten sie sich gegen den Sturm. Aus dem Regen war jetzt Hagel geworden, und große Eiskörner prasselten auf die Grabsteine vor der Kirche nieder. In einem Winkel des Gottesackers stand ein Apfelbaum – kahl wie zur Winterzeit: Der Sturm hatte ihn sämtlicher Blätter und Früchte beraubt. Diesen Herbst wird es wohl nicht viele Äpfel in der Grafschaft geben, dachte Aliena.

Kurz darauf hatten sie die Kirche erreicht und traten ein. Die plötzliche Stille schlug sie wie mit Taubheit. Draußen heulte zwar noch immer der Wind, der Regen trommelte aufs Dach, und ein Donnergrollen folgte dem anderen, doch klang alles gedämpft, entfernt. Die Dorfbewohner hatten ebenfalls schon Zuflucht in der Kirche gesucht und standen in ihren durchnäßten Umhängen herum. Ihren wertvollsten Besitz hatten sie mitgebracht: die Hühner in Säcken, die Schweine zusammengebunden, die Kühe an Stricken geführt. Kurz darauf brachte Alienas Knecht den Wagen herein, gefolgt von Ranulf mit den Pferden. Hin und wieder tauchte ein Blitz das Durcheinander von Menschen und Tieren in gespenstisches Licht.

»Schaffen wir doch die Tiere auf die eine und die Leute auf die andere Seite«, schlug Aliena dem Priester vor. »Sonst sieht die Kirche binnen kurzem wie ein Viehstall aus.« Mittlerweile schien der Gottesmann sich mit ihrer Führungsrolle abgefunden zu haben. Er nickte gehorsam und begann auf die Männer einzureden, während Aliena sich um die Frauen kümmerte, die ihre Kinder in den kleinen Altarraum führten. Die Männer banden die Tiere an den Pfeilern im Mittelschiff fest. Die schreckhaften Pferde rollten dabei mit den Augen und bäumten sich auf, die Kühe hingegen legten sich seelenruhig nieder. Die Dorfbewohner fanden sich zu Familien zusammen und labten sich an den mitgebrachten Vorräten. Sie hatten sich offenkundig auf einen längeren Aufenthalt eingerichtet.

Das Unwetter tobte so heftig, daß Aliena meinte, es müsse schnell vorübergehen, doch statt dessen wurde es immer schlimmer. Sie ging zu einem Fenster, das natürlich nicht verglast war, sondern mit feinem, durchsichtigem Leinen bespannt, das inzwischen zerfetzt im Rahmen hing. Aliena zog sich zur Fensterbank hinaus, doch alles, was sie draußen wahrnehmen konnte, war Regen, Regen, Regen.

Der Wind hatte noch zugenommen und heulte nun so laut um

das Gebäude, daß Aliena befürchtete, selbst die Kirche könne nur unzureichenden Schutz gewähren. Stillschweigend unterzog sie die Mauern einer kritischen Prüfung. Sie hatte genug von Jack gelernt, um gute Maurerarbeit von schlechter unterscheiden zu können, und stellte erleichtert fest, daß hier sorgfältig und ordentlich gearbeitet worden war. Nirgendwo zeigten sich Risse. Die Kirche war aus zugehauenen Steinblöcken errichtet worden und wirkte unerschütterlich wie ein Fels. Als die Haushälterin des Priesters eine Kerze anzündete, wurde Aliena klar, daß draußen nun tatsächlich die Nacht hereinbrach. Die Kinder wurden es allmählich müde, in den Seitenschiffen auf und ab zu rennen, rollten sich in ihren Umhängen zusammen und legten sich schlafen. Die Hühner steckten ihre Köpfe unters Gefieder. Aliena und Elisabeth ließen sich nebeneinander auf dem Fußboden nieder und lehnten den Rücken an die Wand.

Aliena brannte schon eine ganze Weile darauf zu erfahren, wie dieses arme Mädchen die Rolle als Williams Ehefrau bewältigte – eine Rolle, die zu spielen sie selbst vor siebzehn Jahren sich entschieden geweigert hatte. Sie gab nun ihrer Neugier nach und fragte: »Wie ist William denn heute so? Ich war als junges Mädchen mit ihm bekannt.«

»Er ist abscheulich«, sagte Elisabeth so heftig, daß Aliena tiefes Mitleid überkam. »Wie habt Ihr ihn kennengelernt?«

Das hab' ich nun von meiner Neugier, dachte Aliena und gestand: »Um die Wahrheit zu sagen – als ich ungefähr in Eurem Alter war, hätte ich ihn heiraten sollen.«

»Nein! Und wieso habt Ihr es nicht getan?«

»Ich habe seinen Antrag abgelehnt, und mein Vater hat mich dabei unterstützt. Allerdings gab es dann einen fürchterlichen Aufruhr und eine Menge Blutvergießen. Aber das liegt nun schon alles sehr lange zurück.«

»Ihr habt seinen Antrag abgelehnt!« Elisabeth wirkte beinahe begeistert. »Wie mutig Ihr seid! Ich wünschte, ich wäre genauso.« Mit einemmal sah sie wieder ganz niedergeschlagen aus. »Aber ich kann mich nicht einmal beim Gesinde durchsetzen.«

»Aber sicher könntet Ihr das«, meinte Aliena.

»Wie denn? Die übersehen mich einfach, weil ich erst vierzehn bin.«

Aliena dachte gründlich nach, bevor sie die Frage beantwortete. »Zunächst einmal müßt Ihr sozusagen das Sprachrohr für die Wünsche Eures Gatten werden. Fragt ihn gleich jeden Morgen, was er zu Mittag gerne essen würde, wen er im Lauf des Tages empfangen oder aufsuchen will, welches Pferd er zu reiten gedenkt – was immer Euch einfällt. Dann geht zum Küchenmeister, zum Haushofmeister und zum Stallaufseher und gebt die Befehle des Grafen weiter. Euer Gatte wird Euch dankbar sein und zornig gegen jeden werden, der Eure Anordnungen nicht befolgt. Mit der Zeit gewöhnen sich die Leute daran, daß sie zu tun haben, was Ihr ihnen auftragt. Dann habt ein Auge darauf, wer Euch bereitwillig dient und wer nur widerwillig. Macht deutlich, daß Ihr die Bereitwilligen belohnt – gebt ihnen die Arbeiten, die sie gern tun, und überlaßt die unangenehmen Arbeiten den Widerwilligen. Auf diese Weise wird bald allen klar sein, daß es sich lohnt, die Wünsche der Gräfin zu befolgen. Außerdem werdet Ihr ihnen bald sehr viel lieber sein als William, der ohnehin keine liebenswerte Person ist. Ihr werdet sehen, am Ende seid Ihr eine Macht aus eigenem Recht – wie viele andere Gräfinnen auch.«

»Es hört sich so leicht an, wie Ihr das sagt«, seufzte Elisabeth sehnsüchtig.

»Nein, leicht ist es nicht, aber wenn Ihr Euch in Geduld übt und Euch nicht allzu rasch entmutigen laßt, könnt Ihr es schaffen.«

»Ja, ich glaube, das kann ich«, sagte sie entschlossen. »Das kann ich bestimmt.«

Nach einer Weile fielen sie in einen leichten Schlaf. Nur der Wind, der hin und wieder aufheulte, weckte Aliena jedesmal auf. Im unsteten Licht der Kerze sah sie, daß die meisten Erwachsenen es ihr gleichtaten: Sie saßen aufrecht, nickten für kurze Zeit ein und schreckten immer wieder auf.

Es mußte schon um Mitternacht sein, als Aliena plötzlich hochfuhr und feststellte, daß sie diesmal beinahe eine Stunde oder noch länger geschlafen hatte. Um sie herum lag alles in tiefem Schlummer. Sie streckte sich auf dem Boden aus und wickelte sich fest in ihren Umhang. Der Sturm hatte noch immer nicht nachgelassen, doch die Müdigkeit hatte die Furcht der Leute besiegt. Das Geräusch des Regens, den der Wind gegen die Kirchenmauern trieb, klang wie Meereswogen, die mit der Flut über den Strand gespült wurden, und statt Aliena wachzuhalten, sang es sie nun in den Schlaf.

Irgendwann fuhr sie erneut auf und fragte sich, was ihr so ungewöhnlich vorkam. Sie lauschte: Stille. Das Unwetter hatte sich ausgetobt. Durch die Fenster schimmerte schwach ein graues Licht. Die Dorfbewohner lagen noch in tiefem Schlummer.

Aliena stand auf. Ihre Bewegungen weckten Elisabeth, die sofort hellwach war.

Sie hatten beide den gleichen Gedanken. Sie gingen zur Kirchentür und traten ins Freie hinaus.

Es hatte aufgehört zu regnen, und der Wind war kaum mehr als eine leichte Brise. Die Sonne war noch nicht aufgegangen, aber der Himmel schimmerte perlmutterfarben in der heraufziehenden Morgendämmerung. Die beiden Frauen sahen in das klare, wasserhelle Licht hinaus.

Das Dorf war verschwunden.

Außer der Kirche war kein einziges Haus stehengeblieben. Ein paar schwere Holzbalken waren an der Kirchenmauer angetrieben; ansonsten wiesen nur die gemauerten Feuerstellen inmitten der Schlammwüste darauf hin, daß hier einmal Häuser gestanden hatten. Am ehemaligen Dorfrand fanden sich fünf oder sechs ausgewachsene Bäume, Eichen und Kastanien, die das Unwetter zwar überlebt, aber nicht wenige Äste dabei eingebüßt hatten. Von den jungen Bäumchen war kein einziger mehr zu sehen.

Angesichts dieses Bildes vollendeter Zerstörung verschlug es Aliena die Sprache, und Elisabeth schien es nicht anders zu gehen. Gemeinsam bahnten sie sich einen Weg über das Schlammfeld, das einmal die Dorfstraße gewesen und nun übersät war mit zersplittertem Holz und toten Vögeln.

Am Rande des ersten Weizenfelds blieben sie stehen: Es sah aus, als hätte man darauf über Nacht eine Herde wilder Stiere eingepfercht. Was gestern noch wogendes Kornfeld gewesen, war heute niedergedrückt, geknickt, entwurzelt, davongeschwemmt, die Ackerkrume aufgewühlt, mit Wasserlöchern durchsetzt.

Aliena sah es mit Entsetzen. »O mein Gott!« murmelte sie. »Was sollen die armen Leute bloß essen?«

Sie überquerten das Feld, bestiegen einen kleinen Hügel und blickten von der Anhöhe ringsum ins Land. Wohin das Auge auch fiel – nichts als zerstörte Felder, tote Schafe, geknickte Bäume, überflutete Weiden und fortgewehte Häuser. Das Ausmaß der Tragödie war so entsetzlich, daß Aliena den Schmerz der Tragödie körperlich zu spüren glaubte. Es sieht aus, dachte sie, als wäre Gott persönlich auf England herniedergefahren und hätte das Land geschlagen. Und jedes Werk von Menschenhand vernichtet. Bis auf die Kirchen.

Elisabeth schien ihre Gedanken zu lesen. »Wie entsetzlich!« flüsterte sie. »Ich kann's nicht fassen! Nichts mehr da, gar nichts mehr.«

Aliena nickte grimmig. »Gar nichts mehr«, wiederholte sie. »Dieses Jahr wird es keine Ernte geben.«

»Was werden die Leute tun?«

»Ich weiß es nicht.« Und getrieben von Furcht und Mitleid fügte Aliena hinzu: »Der nächste Winter wird grauenvoll.«

Eines Morgens, vier Wochen nach dem Unwetter, bat Martha Jack um mehr Wirtschaftsgeld. Er war überrascht. Gab er nicht schon sechs Pence jede Woche? Und von Aliena bekam sie doch die gleiche Summe, oder? Damit kaufte sie Lebensmittel für vier Erwachsene und zwei Kinder und versorgte zwei Häuser mit Feuerholz und Binsen. Aber es gab andere, viel größere Familien in Kingsbridge, die mit sechs Pence in der Woche Nahrung, Kleidung und Miete bestreiten mußten. Jack fragte Martha nach dem Grund ihres Ansinnens.

Die Frage war ihr peinlich. »Alles ist teurer geworden«, sagte sie. »Der Bäcker verlangt jetzt einen ganzen Penny für einen Vierpfünder, und ...«

»Einen ganzen Penny! Für einen Vierpfünder?« rief Jack erbost. »Da bauen wir uns doch gleich selbst einen Ofen und backen unser eigenes Brot.«

»Aber das tu ich ja manchmal schon – ich meine, ich backe das Brot in der Pfanne.«

»Ja, ich weiß.« Jack erinnerte sich, daß er in der vergangenen Woche zwei-, dreimal selbstgebackenes Brot gegessen hatte.

»Aber das Mehl ist auch teurer geworden«, sagte Martha, »deshalb kann ich damit nicht viel sparen.«

»Wir sollten Weizen kaufen und ihn selber mahlen.«

»Das ist verboten. Wir müßten ihn in der Mühle der Priorei mahlen lassen. Aber auch das würde nichts helfen, denn der Weizen ist genauso teuer geworden.«

»Ja, natürlich.« Jack wurde klar, daß seine Vorschläge albern waren: Der Brotpreis war gestiegen, weil der Mehlpreis gestiegen war, und der Mehlpreis war gestiegen, weil der Weizenpreis gestiegen war, und der Weizen war deshalb so teuer, weil das Unwetter die gesamte Ernte vernichtet hatte – ein Kreislauf, dem nicht zu entkommen war. Wie bedrückt Martha aussah! Sie regte sich immer viel zu sehr auf, hatte immer Angst, er könne unzufrieden mit ihr sein. Um ihr zu zeigen, daß alles in Ordnung war, lächelte er sie an und tätschelte ihre Schulter. »Du kannst ja nichts dafür«, meinte er.

»Aber es klingt, als wärst du böse.«

»Nicht mit dir«, sagte er schuldbewußt, denn er wußte, daß Martha sich eher die rechte Hand abhacken ließe, als ihn zu betrügen. Er hatte keine Ahnung, weshalb sie so an ihm hing. Wenn sie mich liebt, dachte er, müßte sie eigentlich längst die Nase voll haben, denn inzwischen dürfte ihr und der ganzen Welt längst klar sein, daß die große Liebe meines Lebens Aliena heißt und ewig heißen wird. Er hatte sogar schon einmal erwogen, Martha aus dem Haus zu schicken, damit sie endlich einmal etwas anderes sah und sich vielleicht sogar in den Richtigen verliebte. Doch da er insgeheim ahnte, daß er Martha damit todunglücklich machen würde, ließ er alles, wie es war.

Er griff nach seiner Börse und nahm drei Silberpennies heraus. »Dann ist es wohl am besten, wenn du zwölf Pence in der Woche bekommst. Sieh mal zu, wie du damit wirtschaften kannst«, sagte er. Zwölf Pence waren eine Menge Geld – genau die Hälfte seines wöchentlichen Verdienstes, wobei man allerdings berücksichtigen mußte, daß er Kerzen, Stiefel und Kleidung gestellt bekam.

Er trank sein Bier aus und machte sich auf den Weg. Es war ein ungewöhnlich kalter Frühherbst. Das Wetter spielte immer noch verrückt. Als Jack den Klosterhof betrat, war die Sonne noch nicht aufgegangen. Gerade eine Handvoll Handwerker hatte bereits die Arbeit aufgenommen. Jack ging durchs Mittelschiff und inspizierte die Grundmauern, die zum Glück schon beinahe fertig waren. Angesichts der kalten Witterung war damit zu rechnen, daß die Maurerarbeiten in diesem Jahr schon früh eingestellt werden mußten.

Im neuen Querschiff waren am Tag nach dem schweren Unwetter neuerlich Risse zu erkennen gewesen. Sie nahmen Jack viel von der Freude an seiner Schöpfung. Gewiß, es war ein ganz außergewöhnliches Unwetter gewesen, doch eigentlich sollte seine Kirche Hunderte solcher Stürme aushalten können! Verwirrt schüttelte er den Kopf und stieg die Wendeltreppe zur Empore hinauf. Gerne hätte er sich mit einem Baumeister beraten, der eine ähnliche Kirche errichtet hatte, doch in England gab es keinen solchen, und selbst in Frankreich war noch nicht so hoch gebaut worden.

Aus einer Augenblickslaune heraus begab er sich nicht zu seinem Zeichenboden, sondern stieg weiter hinauf bis ins Dach. Die Bleiplatten waren nun alle verlegt, und das Türmchen, an dem sich das Regenwasser gestaut hatte, war mit einem breiten Abflußrohr versehen. Es war sehr windig. Jedesmal, wenn Jack der Dachkante nahe kam, sah er sich nach einem geeigneten Halt um – schon so manch einen Baumeister hatte der Wind vom Dach gefegt und in die Tiefe stürzen lassen! Hier oben kam ihm der Wild immer viel heftiger vor als unten auf der Erde, ja, es war, als stiege die Windstärke unproportional schnell an, je höher man stieg ...

Jack blieb stehen, den Blick ins Nichts gewandt. Der Wind wurde unproportional stärker, je höher man stieg. Das war die Lösung des Rätsels! Nicht das *Gewicht* verursachte die Risse, die *Höhe* war schuld! Er war ganz sicher, daß er die Kirche stark genug gebaut hatte, um das Gewicht zu tragen – aber er hatte den Wind vergessen. An diesen turmhohen Mauern rüttelte und zerrte er unablässig, und so kam es dann zwangsläufig zu Rissen. Auf dem Dach der Kirche stehend, spürte er die Gewalt, mit der der Wind an ihren Mauern zerrte, als wäre er mit ihr verschmolzen. Der Windstöße trafen die Kirche von der Seite, so wie sie ihn selbst trafen, und da sich der Bau unter den heftigen Böen nicht biegen konnte, bekam er Risse.

Das also war die Erklärung – aber was ließ sich dagegen tun? Der Lichtgaden mußte so verstärkt werden, daß er dem Wind standhielt. Nur wie? Wenn man die Außenmauern mit massiven Stützpfeilern verstärkte, war es um den alle Welt verblüffenden Eindruck von Anmut und Leichtigkeit, auf den Jack soviel Mühe und Sorgfalt verwendet hatte, geschehen.

Aber es blieb wohl nichts anderes übrig. Schließlich durfte seine Kirche nicht zusammenbrechen.

Auf dem Weg hinunter fühlte er sich, obwohl er endlich die Erklärung für das Rätsel gefunden hatte, niedergeschlagen und enttäuscht. Die Lösung des Problems zerstörte seinen alten Traum. Vielleicht war ich zu anmaßend, dachte er. Die schönste Kathedrale der Welt wollte ich bauen! Wie konnte ich mir nur einbilden, ich könne alles besser machen als andere, ich wäre etwas Besonderes! Ich hätte lieber die ausgereiften Pläne eines anderen Baumeisters kopieren und mich damit zufriedengeben sollen.

Beim Zeichenboden wartete Philip auf ihn. Seine Stirn war sorgenzerfurcht, der ergraunde Haarkranz um seine Tonsur ungekämmt. Der Prior sah aus, als hätte er die ganze Nacht kein Auge zugetan.

»Wir müssen unsere Ausgaben reduzieren«, sagte er ohne jegliche Einleitung. »Wir haben nicht mehr genug Geld, um im derzeitigen Tempo weiterzubauen.«

Das hatte Jack schon befürchtet. Die Windhose, die über das südliche England hinweggefegt war, hatte beinahe die gesamte Ernte vernichtet und damit natürlich auch das Kloster und seine Finanzen schwer getroffen. Jedesmal, wenn von Einsparungen die Rede war, wurde ihm angst und bange: Wenn sich die Arbeiten zu lange hinziehen, so fürchtete er insgeheim, dann werde ich die Fertigstellung meiner Kathedrale nicht mehr erleben ... Philip gegenüber ließ er sich nichts von seinen Befürchtungen anmerken. Eher beiläufig sagte er: »Der Winter kommt in diesem Jahr früh, da können wir ohnehin nicht so viel tun.«

»Für mich kommt er noch nicht früh genug«, verkündete Philip mit finsterer Entschlossenheit. »Ich will sämtliche Ausgaben auf die Hälfte beschränken, und zwar sofort.«

»Auf die Hälfte?« Das klang ganz und gar unmöglich!

»Die Winterpause beginnt mit dem heutigen Tage.«

Das war weit schlimmer, als Jack angenommen hatte! Die Saisonarbeiter verließen die Baustelle gewöhnlich Anfang Dezember und verbrachten die Wintermonate bei ihren Familien, wo sie Holzhäuser bauten oder Pflüge und Karren, sei's für ihre Angehörigen, sei's um Geld zu verdienen. In diesem Jahr würde sich über ihre Heimkehr niemand freuen. »Ist Euch denn nicht klar«, fragte er, »daß Ihr die Leute in Dörfer heimschickt, wo es schon jetzt nichts mehr zu beißen gibt?«

Philip bedachte ihn zur Antwort mit einem zornigen Blick.

»Entschuldigt die dumme Frage«, sagte Jack. »Natürlich ist es Euch klar.«

»Wenn ich sie jetzt nicht entlasse«, erklärte Philip mit Nachdruck, »dann stehen eines schönen Zahltags mitten im Winter sämtliche Arbeiter um ihren Lohn an, und ich kann ihnen bloß eine leere Truhe vorweisen.«

Jack zuckte hilflos mit der Schulter. »Dagegen läßt sich nichts einwenden.«

»Das ist noch nicht alles«, sagte Philip. »Von Stund an wird niemand mehr eingestellt, auch dann nicht, wenn dringend Ersatz gebraucht wird.«

»Wir haben schon seit Monaten niemanden mehr eingestellt.«

»Ihr habt Alfred genommen.«

»Das war ein Sonderfall«, gab Jack verlegen zurück. »Aber gut – es wird niemand mehr eingestellt.«

»Und niemand mehr befördert.«

Jack nickte bedächtig. Hie und da bat ein Lehrling oder Arbeiter darum, zum Maurer oder Steinschneider ernannt zu werden; befanden dann die anderen Handwerker, sein Können sei ausreichend, so wurde seiner Bitte stattgegeben, und die Priorei mußte ihm einen höheren Lohn zahlen. »Beförderungen sind das Vorrecht der Zunft«, sagte Jack.

»Daran will ich auch nichts ändern«, erwiderte Philip. »Ich bitte die Zunft lediglich darum, mit Beförderungen zu warten, bis die Hungersnot vorüber ist.«

»Ich werde es ihnen mitteilen«, sagte Jack, der sich keine Blöße geben wollte. Er hatte das ungute Gefühl, daß diese Forderung des Priors böses Blut machen könne.

Doch Philip war immer noch nicht fertig. »Von heute an wird an Heiligentagen nicht mehr gearbeitet.«

Es gab zu viele Heiligentage. Im Prinzip waren sie arbeitsfrei, und ob sie bezahlt wurden, hing von den Verträgen mit dem Bauherrn ab. In Kingsbridge galt die Faustregel, daß in dem Fall, daß zwei Heiligentage in dieselbe Woche fielen, der erste ein bezahlter freier Tag war und der zweite ein unbezahlter, der freigenommen werden konnte, aber nicht mußte. Philips Forderung bedeutete also, daß man sich künftig nicht mehr frei entscheiden konnte: Der zweite Heiligentag *mußte* freigenommen werden und blieb unbezahlt.

Die Aussicht, diese Änderungen den Zunftbrüdern mitteilen und erklären zu müssen, war nicht dazu angetan, Jacks Stimmung zu heben. »Die Männer würden diese Einschränkungen bestimmt viel leichter schlucken«, wandte er ein, »wenn sie darüber diskutieren könnten und nicht gleich vor vollendete Tatsachen gestellt würden.«

Philip schüttelte den Kopf. »Dann bilden sie sich bloß ein, es gebe noch Verhandlungsspielraum. Einer schlägt vor, an den Heiligentagen nur halbtags zu arbeiten, ein anderer will die Beförderungen auf eine bestimmte Zahl begrenzen ...«

»Aber ist das denn nicht verständlich?« fragte Jack.

»Natürlich ist es *verständlich*«, erwiderte Philip aufgebracht. »Aber ich habe einfach keinen Spielraum mehr! Ich muß jetzt schon befürchten, daß diese Maßnahmen bei weitem nicht ausreichen. Ich kann also keinerlei Zugeständnisse mehr machen.«

»Na gut«, antwortete Jack, dem klar wurde, daß Philip in dieser Stimmung nicht zu Kompromissen bereit war. »Gibt's sonst noch was?«

»Ja. Kauft keine Vorräte mehr ein. Baut Eure Vorräte an Steinen, Eisen und Holz allmählich ab.«

»Das Holz bekommen wir umsonst!« protestierte Jack.

»Aber wir müssen die Fuhrleute bezahlen, die es uns bringen.«

»Ja, ja. Ich verstehe.« Jack trat ans Fenster und ließ den Blick über die Stapel von Steinen und Baumstämmen schweifen, die im Klosterhof bereitlagen. Es war nicht viel mehr als eine Geste der Hilflosigkeit:

Er wußte aus dem Kopf, welche Vorräte er hatte und wie groß sie waren. »Das ist kein Problem«, sagte er nach einer Weile. »Wenn wir die Arbeitskräfte reduzieren, reichen die Materialien bis zum nächsten Sommer.«

Philip seufzte schwer. »Ich kann nicht garantieren, daß wir nächstes Jahr wieder Saisonarbeiter einstellen werden«, sagte er. »Es hängt vom Wollpreis ab. Am besten sagt Ihr es Euren Leuten schon jetzt, damit sie gewarnt sind.«

Jack nickte. »Steht's denn dermaßen schlimm?«

»Schlimmer, als ich es je erlebt habe«, bestätigte Philip. »Was dieses Land braucht, sind drei gute Sommer hintereinander. Und einen neuen König.«

»Amen«, erwiderte Jack.

Philip kehrte in sein Haus zurück. Jack grübelte darüber nach, wie er die drastischen Beschränkungen am besten bewältigte. Es gab zwei Arten, ein Kirchenschiff zu bauen: Joch um Joch, angefangen bei der Vierung in westlicher Richtung; oder aber Schicht um Schicht, indem man, beim Fundament beginnend, alles Mauerwerk gleichzeitig hochzog. Die zweite Methode war die schnellste, erforderte aber auch mehr Maurer und Steinmetzen. Jack hatte sich für sie entschieden und sah sich nun gezwungen umzudisponieren. Bei weniger Arbeitskräften war es besser, Joch um Joch zu bauen. Diese Bauweise hatte zusätzlich einen Vorteil: Jede Veränderung, die Jack, um dem Windwiderstand Rechnung zu tragen, an seinen Plänen vornahm, konnte zunächst an ein, zwei Bauabschnitten ausprobiert werden, bevor man sie auf das ganze Gebäude übertrug.

Auch die langfristigen Auswirkungen der Geldknappheit gaben ihm zu denken. Es war gut möglich, daß sich das Bautempo in den kommenden Jahren mehr und mehr verzögerte. Schon sah er sich selbst alt, grau und hinfällig werden, ohne sein Lebensziel zu erreichen. Am Ende trug man ihn auf dem Klosterfriedhof im Schatten einer noch immer unvollendeten Kathedrale zu Grabe ...

Als die Glocke Mittag läutete, ging Jack zur Bauhütte der Steinmetzen hinüber. Die Männer hatten sich soeben zu Bier und Käse an den Tisch gesetzt, und Jack fiel zum erstenmal auf, daß viele kein einziges Stück Brot hatten. Er bat die Steinmetzen, die sonst zum Essen nach Hause gegangen wären, noch eine Weile zu bleiben. »Der Priorei wird das Geld knapp«, verkündete er.

»Ich hab' noch nie ein Kloster gesehen, dem es nicht früher oder später so ergangen wäre«, meinte Edward Twonose, ein älterer Mann, der seinen Beinamen dem Umstand verdankte, daß er eine Warze im Gesicht trug, die beinahe so groß wie seine Nase war. Er war ein guter Steinmetz mit einem scharfen Auge für exakte Rundungen, so daß Jack ihn vor allem beim Bau der Säulen und Kuppeln einsetzte. »Ihr werdet zugeben«, erwiderte Jack, »daß hier in Kingsbridge besser gewirtschaftet wird als anderswo. Doch Prior Philip kann keine Unwetter umleiten und keine schlechten Ernten verhindern. Deshalb sieht er sich gezwungen, seine Ausgaben zu kürzen. Bevor Ihr eßt, will ich Euch Bescheid sagen. Zunächst einmal werden wir keine Steine und kein Bauholz mehr kaufen.«

Die Handwerker aus den anderen Bauhütten waren mittlerweile hereingekommen und hörten zu. Peter, ein älterer Zimmermann, bemerkte: »Das Holz, das wir hier haben, wird nicht den ganzen Winter über reichen.«

»Doch, es wird«, sagte Jack. »Wir werden nicht mehr so schnell vorankommen, weil wir weniger Leute haben werden. Die Winterpause beginnt mit dem heutigen Tage.«

Kaum hatte er die Ankündigungen gemacht, wurde ihm auch schon klar, daß er die Sache falsch angepackt hatte: Es hagelte Proteste von allen Seiten, und alle sprachen durcheinander. Ich hätte es ihnen behutsamer beibringen müssen, dachte er. Aber er hatte keinerlei Erfahrung in solcherlei Dingen. Zwar war er schon seit sieben Jahren Dombaumeister, doch bisher war das Geld nie knapp gewesen.

Die Stimme, die sich schließlich durchsetzte, gehörte Pierre Paris, einem jener Männer, die einst aus Saint-Denis gekommen waren. Nach sechs Jahren in Kingsbridge ließ sein Englisch immer noch zu wünschen übrig, was ihn jedoch nicht daran hinderte, sich zu Wort zu melden. »Ihr könnt aber niemanden an einem Dienstag entlassen«, sagte er.

»Genau!« stimmte Jack Blacksmith zu. »Das geht frühestens zum Wochenende.«

Auch Alfred, Jacks Stiefbruder, stimmte in den Chor ein. »Mein Vater baute einmal für den späteren Grafen von Shiring ein Haus. Da erschien Will Hamleigh und entließ alle Mann. Mein Vater sagte ihm, er habe jedem einen vollen Wochenlohn auszuzahlen, und hielt sein Pferd am Zaum fest, bis er das Geld herausrückte.«

Vielen Dank für deine brüderliche Hilfe, lieber Alfred, dachte Jack und sagte, dem Protest zum Trotz: »Ihr könnt auch gleich noch den Rest hören: Von heute an wird an Heiligentagen nicht mehr gearbeitet, und niemand wird mehr befördert.«

Das brachte die Handwerker erst recht in Rage: »Unannehmbar!«
rief einer, und gleich mehrere stimmten ihm lauthals zu: »Unannehmbar! Unannehmbar!« erscholl es von allen Seiten.

Jack geriet nun seinerseits in Wut. »Was denkt Ihr Euch eigentlich?
Wenn das Kloster kein Geld mehr hat, werdet Ihr überhaupt nicht
bezahlt! Was hat es also für einen Sinn, ›unannehmbar, unannehmbar!‹ zu tönen wie eine Horde Schuljungen, die lateinische Vokabeln
paukt?«

Edward Twonose ergriff das Wort. »Wir sind keine Horde Schuljungen, wir sind die Zunft der Steinmetzen«, stellte er richtig. »Die
Zunft hat das alleinige Recht, Beförderungen auszusprechen, und das
kann ihr niemand wegnehmen.«

»Und wenn das Geld für höhere Löhne nicht vorhanden ist?« gab
Jack in scharfem Ton zurück.

»Das glaube ich nicht«, sagte einer der jüngeren Steinmetzen, Dan
Bristol. Er gehörte zu den Saisonarbeitern, und das Steineschneiden
ging ihm nur mühsam von der Hand. Seine Stärke lag darin, daß er
sehr schnell und zuverlässig mauern konnte.

»Wie könnt Ihr einfach behaupten, Ihr glaubt das nicht?« fragte
Jack. »Was wißt Ihr schon von der Finanzlage des Klosters?«

»Ich weiß, was ich sehe«, gab Dan trotzig zurück.

»Müssen die Mönche hungern? Nein. Sind noch Kerzen in der
Kirche? Ja. Ist noch Wein im Keller? Ja. Geht der Prior barfuß? Nein.
Das Geld ist da. Er will es bloß nicht für uns ausgeben.«

Andere stimmten ihm lauthals zu. Zumindest in einem Punkt irrte
er, und zwar, was den Wein betraf – aber Jacks Glaubwürdigkeit war
schon so erschüttert, daß ihm eine Richtigstellung niemand mehr
abgenommen hätte.

In den Augen der Handwerker war er längst zum Handlanger der
Priorei abgestempelt. Es war ungerecht, denn schließlich war er nicht
verantwortlich für Philips Entscheidungen. »Schaut her«, sagte er,
»ich kann nur wiedergeben, was der Prior zu mir gesagt hat – daß es
der Wahrheit entspricht, kann ich nicht garantieren. Doch sagt mir:
Was können wir schon tun, wenn wir seiner Behauptung, der Priorei
gehe das Geld aus, nicht trauen?«

»Wir können *alle* die Arbeit niederlegen«, sagte Dan prompt. »Und
zwar sofort.«

»Richtig!« ertönte es irgendwoher.

Jack erkannte, daß ihm die Sache zu entgleiten drohte. »Moment
mal!« sagte er und suchte fieberhaft nach einem Argument, das schlag-

kräftig genug war, um die erhitzten Gemüter ein wenig abzukühlen. »Gehen wir jetzt wieder an die Arbeit, und heute nachmittag versuche ich, Prior Philip zu überzeugen, daß er seine Sparmaßnahmen ändern muß.«

»Ich bin dagegen, die Arbeit wieder aufzunehmen«, sagte Dan.

Es ist unfaßbar! dachte Jack. Mit den absonderlichsten Gefahren, die unter Umständen dem Bau seiner Traumkirche drohen konnten, hatte er sich im Laufe der Zeit beschäftigt – auf die Idee, die Handwerker selber könnten ihn verhindern, war er nie gekommen. »Wieso sollten wir nicht weiterarbeiten?« fragte er ungläubig. »Was macht das denn für einen Sinn?«

»So wie die Dinge liegen«, meinte Dan, »kann die Hälfte von uns nicht einmal sicher sein, daß sie bis zum Ende der Woche entlohnt wird.«

»Was jeder Sitte und Gewohnheit widerspricht«, sagte Pierre Paris. Der Begriff *Sitte und Gewohnheit* fiel häufig in der Rechtsprechung.

Der Verzweiflung nahe, sagte Jack: »Dann arbeitet wenigstens so lange, bis ich Prior Philip umgestimmt habe.«

»Wenn wir das tun«, fragte Edward Twonose, »könnt Ihr uns dann garantieren, daß alle bis zum Ende der Woche ihren Lohn erhalten?«

Bei Philips derzeitiger Stimmung ist das unmöglich, dachte Jack und erwog kurz, ob er nicht einfach ja sagen und die Löhne aus der eigenen Tasche bezahlen sollte, wenn es denn anders nicht ginge. Doch er verwarf den Gedanken sofort wieder: Dafür reichten seine Ersparnisse bei weitem nicht aus. »Ich werde alles tun«, versprach er statt dessen, »ihn zu überzeugen, und ich glaube, daß er mir zustimmen wird.«

»Das reicht mir nicht«, sagte Pierre.

»Keine Lohngarantie – keine Arbeit«, sagte Dan, und zu Jacks Bestürzung stimmten ihm die anderen zu.

Wenn ich weiterhin dagegenrede, dachte er, verliere ich noch mein letztes bißchen Autorität. »Die Zunft muß mit einer Stimme sprechen«, sagte er und zitierte eine gebräuchliche Formel. »Sind alle für eine Arbeitsniederlegung?«

Im Chor ertönte die Zustimmung.

»So sei es denn«, sagte Jack niedergeschlagen. »Ich werde es dem Prior mitteilen.«

Gefolgt von einem halben Heer von Begleitern ritt Bischof Waleran in Shiring ein, wo ihn Graf William im Portal der Kirche erwartete.

William, der nicht gerade mit einem Staatsbesuch gerechnet hatte, runzelte irritiert die Stirn: Worauf war der alte Ränkeschmied Waleran denn nun schon wieder aus?

Ein Fremder auf einem kastanienfarbenen Wallach fiel ihm auf: ein breitschultriger Mann mit buschigen schwarzen Augenbrauen und großer, gebogener Nase. Seine verächtliche Miene wirkte, als wäre sie ihm ins Gesicht gebrannt worden. Er ritt neben Waleran, als käme er ihm im Rang gleich, er aber trug keine Bischofskleidung.

Nachdem sie abgesessen waren, stellte Waleran den Fremden vor: »Graf William, dies ist Peter von Wareham, ein Erzdiakon in den Diensten des Erzbischofs von Canterbury.«

Keinerlei Erklärung, was dieser Peter hier soll, dachte William. Waleran hat bestimmt wieder etwas ausgeheckt.

Der Erzdiakon verneigte sich und sagte: »Euer Bischof hat mir von Eurer Großzügigkeit gegenüber der heiligen Mutter Kirche berichtet, Lord William.«

Bevor William antworten konnte, deutete Waleran auch schon auf die Pfarrkirche. »Dieses Gebäude wird abgerissen, Erzdiakon. So schaffen wir Platz für die neue Kirche.«

»Habt Ihr schon einen Baumeister ernannt?« fragte Peter.

Was interessiert den Erzdiakon von Canterbury eine neue Pfarrkirche in Shiring? wunderte sich William.

»Nein«, antwortete Waleran, »ich habe noch keinen gefunden. Zwar gibt es derzeit zahllose Bauleute, die um Arbeit nachsuchen, aber von den Parisern ist keiner zu bekommen. Es hat den Anschein, als wolle die ganze Welt die Kirche von Saint-Denis nachbauen. Steinmetzen, die sich auf diesen Stil verstehen, sind äußerst gefragt.«

»Auf den Stil könnte es in der Tat ankommen«, meinte Peter.

»Ich habe einen Baumeister an der Hand, der uns weiterhelfen könnte. Wir werden ihn später noch sprechen.«

Ein neuerliches Rätsel für William: Wieso hielt es dieser Peter für erforderlich, die Kirche im gleichen Stil wie die von Saint-Denis zu errichten?

»Die neue Kirche«, sagte Waleran, »wird natürlich viel größer. Sie wird ein gutes Stück weiter in den Marktplatz hineinragen.«

Walerans besitzergreifende Gestik mißfiel William so sehr, daß er nicht mehr an sich halten konnte. »Ich kann nicht zulassen, daß die Kirche auf den Marktplatz übergreift«, sagte er.

Walerans Miene verriet Verblüffung und Verärgerung. »Wieso denn nicht?« fragte er.

»An Markttagen ist jeder Fußbreit auf diesem Platz bares Geld wert.«

Waleran schien etwas einwenden zu wollen, doch Peter meinte mit verständnisvollem Lächeln: »Diese Geldquelle dürfen wir aber nicht verstopfen!«

»Richtig«, sagte William. Schließlich bezahlte *er* den Bau dieser Kirche. Glücklicherweise hatte die vierte schlechte Ernte hintereinander sein Einkommen kaum geschmälert. Die Kleinbauern zahlten ihre Pacht in Naturalien, und die meisten hatten ihm, während sie sich selber von Bucheckernsuppe ernährten, den Sack Getreide und das Paar Gänse abgeliefert, die ihm zustanden. Und da ein Sack Weizen inzwischen zehnmal soviel wert war wie vor fünf Jahren, wog das Einkommen daraus die säumigen Pächter und die Leibeigenen, die nichts mehr ablieferten, weil sie verhungert waren, gut und gerne auf. Die Mittel, die William zum Bau der neuen Kirche benötigte, waren also unschwer aufzubringen.

Sie machten einen Rundgang um die Kirche. Dahinter standen Häuser, die kaum etwas einbrachten. »Hier können wir alles niederreißen und die Kirche bauen«, sagte William.

Waleran widersprach. »Die meisten Häuser werden vom Klerus bewohnt.«

»Für den finden sich andere Behausungen.«

Waleran zog ein unzufriedenes Gesicht, sagte jedoch nichts mehr dazu.

Am Nordende der Kirche stand ein großer, breitschultriger Mann um die Dreißig, der sich vor den hohen Herren verneigte. William schätzte ihn der Kleidung nach als Handwerker ein. Erzdiakon Baldwin, der Vertraute des Bischofs, erklärte: »Ehrwürdiger Bischof, dies ist der Mann, von dem ich Euch berichtet habe. Alfred von Kingsbridge ist sein Name.«

Auf den ersten Blick wirkte der Mann nicht besonders einnehmend, eher wie ein Ochse: groß, stark und dumm. Betrachtete man ihn genauer, so erkannte man in ihm aber auch die Verschlagenheit eines Fuchses oder bestimmter Hunde.

»Alfred«, sagte Erzdiakon Baldwin, »ist der Sohn Tom Builders, des ersten Dombaumeisters zu Kingsbridge. Alfred war eine Zeitlang selbst Dombaumeister, bis sein Stiefbruder sich anmaßte, seine Stelle einzunehmen.«

Der Mann, der Aliena geheiratet hat! William wußte sofort Bescheid. Aber er hat die Ehe nie vollzogen! Wäre nie drauf gekommen, daß ein Kerl wie der impotent sein könnte, der sieht doch ganz gesund aus ... Aber William wußte aus eigener Erfahrung, wie sehr Aliena einen Mann verwirren konnte.

»Habt Ihr in Paris gearbeitet, und beherrscht Ihr den Stil von Saint-Denis?« fragte Erzdiakon Peter.

»Nein, ich –«

»Aber wir wollen, daß die Kirche in diesem Stil erbaut wird!«

»Zur Zeit arbeite ich in Kingsbridge, wo mein Bruder Dombaumeister ist. Er hat den neuen Stil aus Paris mitgebracht. Ich habe ihn bei ihm gelernt.«

William fragte sich, wie es Waleran gelungen sein mochte, Alfred, ohne Verdacht zu erregen, hierherzulocken, doch dann fiel ihm wieder ein, daß Remigius, der Subprior von Kingsbridge, auf Walerans Seite stand. Bestimmt hatte Remigius Alfred angesprochen.

»Aber das Dach, das Ihr in Kingsbridge gebaut habt, ist eingestürzt!« wandte er ein.

»Das war nicht meine Schuld«, erwiderte Alfred. »Prior Philip hatte darauf bestanden, den ursprünglichen Bauplan zu ändern.«

»Ich kenne Philip«, sagte Peter giftig. »Ein sturer, hochnäsiger Mann.«

»Woher kennt Ihr ihn?«

»Ich war vor vielen Jahren Mönch in der Zelle St.-John-in-the-Forest«, sagte Peter, und jedem seiner Worte war die Verbitterung anzuhören. »Philip war damals dort Prior. Als ich seine lasche Führung bemängelte, hat er mich zum Almosenpfleger ernannt, so daß ich ihm nicht mehr in die Quere kommen konnte.« Es war nur allzu deutlich, daß Peter seinen Groll gegen Philip seit jener Zeit hegte und pflegte. Welche Pläne Waleran auch ausgeheckt haben mochte – Peters Vorbehalte gegen Philip waren mit Sicherheit Teil seines Kalküls.

»Wie dem auch sei«, meinte William, »ich will keinen Baumeister haben, dessen Dächer einstürzen – ganz egal, welche Ausreden sich dafür finden lassen.«

»Ich bin«, wandte Alfred ein, »abgesehen von Jack Jackson, der einzige Baumeister in England, der den neuen Stil kennt.«

»Ich brauche keine Kirche, die aussieht wie die in Saint-Denis«, gab William zurück. »Dem Seelenheil meiner armen Mutter ist auch mit einem traditionellen Bauwerk gedient.«

Bischof Walerans und Erzdiakon Peters Blicke kreuzten sich, und Waleran sagte mit gesenkter Stimme zu William: »Diese Kirche könnte eines Tages die Kathedrale von Shiring werden.«

Plötzlich fiel es William wie Schuppen von den Augen. Vor vielen Jahren hatte Waleran schon einmal versucht, den Sitz der Diözese von Kingsbridge nach Shiring zu verlegen. Damals hatte Philip ihm einen Strich durch die Rechnung gemacht. Diesmal, so schien es, ging der Bischof listiger vor. Hatte er beim letztenmal lediglich den Erzbischof von Canterbury um seine Zustimmung gebeten, so plante er diesmal zunächst den Bau einer neuen Kirche. Sie sollte so groß und erhaben sein, daß man sie jederzeit zur Kathedrale weihen könnte. Gleichzeitig suchte sich Waleran Verbündete aus dem Umkreis des Erzbischofs, Leute wie diesen Peter von Wareham, bevor er sich direkt an das Oberhaupt der englischen Kirche wandte. Schön und gut, dachte William, nur: Ich will nichts weiter, als eine Kirche für meine Mutter bauen, damit ihrer Seele die Qualen des ewigen Höllenfeuers verkürzt werden … Walerans Versuch, die neue Kirche seinen eigenen Zielen unterzuordnen, ging ihm gewaltig gegen den Strich. Auf der anderen Seite konnte Shiring – und damit auch er selbst in seiner Eigenschaft als Graf von Shiring – von einer Kathedrale am Ort nur profitieren.

»Da wäre noch etwas«, sagte Alfred.

»Ja?« erwiderte Waleran.

William betrachtete die beiden Männer aufmerksam. Alfred war größer, stärker und jünger als Waleran, den er mit einer Hand hätte zu Boden schlagen können. Dennoch verhielt er sich wie ein Schwächling vor einem übermächtigen Gegner. Noch vor ein paar Jahren hätte der Anblick eines bleichgesichtigen, weibischen Priesters, der mühelos einen kräftigen Mann nach seiner Pfeife tanzen ließ, William zur Weißglut getrieben, doch mittlerweile regte er sich nicht mehr darüber auf: Das war nun mal der Lauf der Welt.

Alfred senkte die Stimme und sagte: »Ich kann Euch die gesamte Dombautruppe aus Kingsbridge bringen.«

Plötzlich besaß er die ungeteilte Aufmerksamkeit seiner drei Zuhörer.

»Sagt das noch einmal«, bat Waleran.

»Wenn Ihr mich als Baumeister einstellt, werde ich alle Handwerker aus Kingsbridge mitbringen.«

»Was garantiert uns, daß Ihr die Wahrheit sprecht?« fragte der vorsichtige Waleran.

»Ich habe Euch nicht gebeten, mir blind zu vertrauen«, gab Alfred zurück. »Ihr könnt Eure Entscheidung davon abhängig machen. Wenn ich mein Versprechen nicht halte, braucht Ihr mich nicht einzustellen.«

Die drei Männer haßten Prior Philip aus tiefster Seele. Jetzt sahen sie die Möglichkeit, ihm einen schweren Schlag zu versetzen.

»Einige der Steinmetzen«, fügte Alfred hinzu, »haben in Saint-Denis gearbeitet.«

»Aber wie wollt Ihr sie hierherlocken?« fragte Waleran.

»Das laßt nur meine Sorge sein! Sagen wir einfach, sie arbeiten lieber für mich als für Jack.«

William hielt diese Behauptung für eine glatte Lüge, und Waleran schien seine Meinung zu teilen, denn er legte den Kopf in den Nacken und maß Alfred mit prüfendem, herablassendem Blick. Was blieb, war Alfreds offensichtlich unverrückbare Überzeugung, mit sämtlichen Bauleuten aus Kingsbridge rechnen zu können.

»Die Arbeit in Kingsbridge wird gänzlich zum Erliegen kommen«, sagte William.

»Ja«, bestätigte Alfred, »genau das wird sie.«

William wandte sich an Waleran und Peter. »Das sollten wir ausführlicher besprechen. Am besten leistet er uns beim Essen Gesellschaft.«

Waleran nickte zustimmend und befahl Alfred: »Folgt uns zu meinem Haus. Es steht am anderen Ende des Marktplatzes.«

»Ich weiß«, sagte Alfred, »ich habe es gebaut.«

Zwei Tage lang weigerte sich Prior Philip strikt, über den Streik auch nur zu reden. Er war geradezu sprachlos vor Zorn. Sobald er Jacks ansichtig wurde, drehte er sich auf dem Absatz um und machte, daß er fortkam.

Am zweiten Tag trafen unter bewaffnetem Begleitschutz drei Fuhren Mehl von den klösterlichen Mühlen ein. Mehl war Gold wert in diesen Hungerzeiten. Bruder Jonathan, Stellvertreter des alten Cellerars Cuthbert Whitehead, nahm die Fuhren in Empfang. Jack sah ihm beim Zählen der Mehlsäcke zu. Das Gesicht des jungen Mönchs kam ihm seltsam vertraut vor, erinnerte ihn an irgendeinen Menschen, den er sehr gut kannte, aber er wußte nicht, an wen. Mit Prior Philip – klein, schmächtig und schwarzhaarig – hatte der hochaufgeschossene und ein wenig linkische Jonathan mit seinem hellbraunen Haar äußerlich nicht die geringste Ähnlichkeit. Dafür hatte er alle anderen Eigenschaften seines Ersatzvaters übernommen: Er besaß hohe moralische Grundsätze, arbeitete eifrig und unermüdlich, war entschlossen und ehrgeizig. Und wie Philip war er trotz seiner strengen Haltung in moralischen Fragen sehr beliebt.

Da Philip sich weigerte, mit Jack zu reden, konnte ein Gespräch mit Jonathan nicht schaden.

Jonathan entlohnte gerade die Bewaffneten und die Fuhrleute. Seine stille Tüchtigkeit war beeindruckend. Als die Fuhrleute – wie üblich – einen höheren als den vereinbarten Lohn verlangten, wies er sie ruhig, aber bestimmt zurecht. Die klösterliche Erziehung war allem Anschein nach eine gute Vorbereitung für künftige Führungskräfte.

Andere Menschen anleiten und führen: Jacks eigene Unwissenheit auf diesem Gebiet war in den letzten Tagen nur allzu deutlich zutage getreten. Nur weil ich die Leute falsch behandelt habe, ist aus dem Problem eine ernste Krise geworden, dachte er. Jedesmal, wenn die Erinnerung an jenes unglückselige Treffen wiederkehrte, verfluchte er seine eigene Unfähigkeit. Er war fest entschlossen, die Sache wieder ins Lot zu bringen.

Als die Fuhrleute murrend abzogen, schlenderte er zu Jonathan hinüber und sprach ihn an. »Philip ist schrecklich wütend über den Streik.«

Einen Moment lang sah es so aus, als wolle Jonathan ihn unfreundlich abfertigen – er war offenkundig selber wütend –, doch dann entspannte sich seine Miene, und er sagte: »Das scheint nur so. Im Grunde genommen tut es ihm einfach weh.«

Jack nickte. »Er betrachtet den Streik als Angriff auf seine Person.«

»Ja. Er hat das Gefühl, die Handwerker hätten sich in der Stunde seiner Not gegen ihn gewandt.«

»In gewisser Weise haben sie das wohl auch«, erwiderte Jack. »Aber es war Philip, der den entscheidenden Fehler machte. Er hätte nicht versuchen sollen, sie per Dekret vor vollendete Tatsachen zu stellen.«

»Was hätte er denn tun sollen?« gab Jonathan zurück.

»Er hätte mit den Handwerkern zunächst einmal offen über die Krise und ihre Hintergründe sprechen können. Dann hätten sie vielleicht sogar von sich aus Sparmaßnahmen vorgeschlagen. Allerdings bin ausgerechnet ich der letzte, der Philip daraus einen Vorwurf machen darf – schließlich habe ich den gleichen Fehler begangen.«

»Wie das?« Jonathans Neugier war geweckt.

»Indem ich den Männern die einzelnen Maßnahmen ebenso barsch und taktlos ankündigte wie Philip zuvor mir.«

Jonathan begann widerwillig einzusehen, daß der Streik sehr wohl von zwei verschiedenen Seiten betrachtet werden konnte. Jack beschloß, nichts mehr hinzuzufügen: Die Saat war gelegt.

Er kehrte zu seinem Zeichenbogen in der Kirche zurück. Dort suchte er seine Zeichengeräte zusammen und dachte weiter über die Auseinandersetzung nach. Der Streit war vor allem deshalb so unerfreulich, weil Philip in der ganzen Stadt als Friedensstifter galt: Er war der Richter der Irregeleiteten und Fehlenden, der Schlichter jeder Streitigkeit. Ihn nun selbst in einen Streit verwickelt zu sehen – parteilich, zornig, verbittert und unnachgiebig –, war sehr beunruhigend. Diesmal mußte wohl ein anderer die Streithähne dazu bewegen, sich gütlich zu einigen. Und Jack fiel nur ein einziger ein, der in die Bresche springen konnte: er selbst. Der Dombaumeister war sozusagen der geborene Vermittler zwischen den beiden Parteien, denn sein Beweggrund war über jeden Zweifel erhaben: Ihm lag ausschließlich daran, weiterbauen zu können.

Über seinen Grübeleien verging der Tag. Die entscheidende Frage war und blieb: Was würde Philip tun?

Erst am folgenden Tag fühlte Jack sich imstande, eine Aussprache mit Philip herbeizuführen.

Das Wetter war naßkalt und unangenehm. Am frühen Nachmittag machte Jack sich auf und huschte über die verwaiste Baustelle. Zum Schutz gegen den Regen hatte er die Kapuze seines Umhangs über den Kopf gezogen. Er tat, als prüfe er die Risse im Obergaden (ein noch immer ungelöstes Problem), und wartete, bis er Philip aus dem Kreuzgang kommen und auf sein Haus zueilen sah. Kaum war der Prior hinter der Tür verschwunden, heftete sich Jack auch schon an seine Fersen.

Philips Tür war nie verschlossen. Jack klopfte kurz an und trat ein. Philip kniete in der Ecke vor seinem Hausaltar. Man sollte meinen, dachte Jack, daß er in der Kirche schon genug betet – tagsüber bald jede Stunde, und dann noch mal die halbe Nacht lang –, so daß er zu Hause eigentlich darauf verzichten könnte … Es brannte kein Feuer: Philip sparte an allen Ecken und Enden. Jack wartete stumm, bis Philip aufstand und sich ihm zuwandte. Dann sagte er: »Das muß ein Ende haben.«

Philips sonst so liebenswürdige Miene verhärtete sich. »Das läßt sich ohne Schwierigkeiten bewerkstelligen«, erwiderte er kalt. »Die Männer können ihre Arbeit jederzeit wieder aufnehmen.«

»Zu Euren Bedingungen.«

Philip sah ihm schweigend ins Gesicht.

»Zu Euren Bedingungen werden sie die Arbeit nicht wieder aufnehmen«, erklärte Jack, »und sie werden auch nicht ewig warten, bis Ihr zur Vernunft kommt oder ...« Nach einer kurzen Pause fügte er hastig hinzu: »... zu dem, was sie für Vernunft halten.«

»Sie werden nicht ewig warten?« sagte Philip »Was wollen sie denn tun, wenn sie des Wartens überdrüssig sind? Arbeit finden sie anderswo auch nicht. Oder bilden sie sich ein, nur Kingsbridge hätte unter der Hungersnot zu leiden? Ganz England hungert! Jeder Bauherr im Land muß sparen, wo er kann.«

»Dann wollt Ihr also warten, bis sie auf dem Bauch zu Euch gekrochen kommen und Eure Vergebung erflehen«, sagte Jack.

Philip wandte den Blick ab. »Nein, das will ich nicht«, antwortete er. »Und ich glaube nicht, daß ich Euch jemals Grund zu der Annahme gegeben habe, ich würde dergleichen erwarten.«

»Nein, das habt Ihr nicht, und deshalb bin ich gekommen«, sagte Jack. »Ich weiß, daß Ihr die Männer nicht demütigen wollt – das könnt Ihr nicht wollen, weil es Eurer Natur widerspricht. Im übrigen würde ihre Leistung – müßten sie grollend und mit dem Gefühl, eine Niederlage erlitten zu haben, zur Arbeit zurückkehren – jahrelang zu wünschen übriglassen. Sowohl Euch wie mir muß also daran liegen, eine Lösung zu finden, bei der sie nicht ihr Gesicht verlieren. Und das heißt, daß wir in gewissen Punkten nachgeben müssen.«

Jack hielt unwillkürlich den Atem an: Das war sein überzeugendstes Argument, der entscheidende Punkt des ganzen Streits. Wenn Philip unnachgiebig blieb, sah die Zukunft düster aus.

Philip starrte ihn eine ganze Weile lang wortlos an, und in seiner Miene spiegelte sich seine innere Zerrissenheit wider. Dann endlich entspannten sich seine Züge, und er sagte: »Setzen wir uns erst einmal hin.«

Jack unterdrückte einen Seufzer der Erleichterung und nahm Platz. Er hatte sich seine Worte genau überlegt. Eine aus einer Augenblickseingebung entsprungene Taktlosigkeit wie gegenüber den Handwerkern sollte ihm nicht noch einmal unterlaufen. »Gegen Euren Befehl, kein Baumaterial mehr einzukaufen, ist nichts einzuwenden«, begann er. »Desgleichen nicht gegen das Verbot, neue Leute einzustellen. Außerdem glaube ich, daß die Handwerker sich auch mit den arbeitsfreien Heiligentagen abfinden werden – vorausgesetzt, wir sind ebenfalls zu Zugeständnissen bereit.« Er hielt inne, um Philip Zeit zu geben, über seine Vorschläge nachzudenken. Bislang hatte er nur nachgegeben und keine Forderungen gestellt.

Philip nickte. »Gebilligt. An was für Zugeständnisse denkt Ihr?«

Jack holte tief Luft. »Das Verbot, Beförderungen auszusprechen, hat die Männer arg verstimmt. Sie sehen darin einen Versuch, altherge-brachte Vorrechte der Zunft zu untergraben.«

»Ich sagte Euch bereits, daß dies nicht meine Absicht ist«, be-merkte Philip in einem Ton, der seine Empfindlichkeit verriet.

»Ich weiß, ich weiß«, beeilte sich Jack zu antworten. »Gewiß habt Ihr das. Und ich habe Euch auch geglaubt – aber die Handwerker nicht. Aber vergessen wir das. Ich will ihnen eine Vereinbarung vor-schlagen, die Euch keinen Penny kosten wird.«

Philip sah ihn neugierig an, und Jack fuhr fort: »Überlaßt die Entscheidung über Beförderungen ihnen, verschiebt jedoch die höhere Entlohnung um ein Jahr.«

»Werden sie das denn hinnehmen?« fragte Philip skeptisch.

»Es ist zumindest den Versuch wert.«

»Und was ist, wenn ich die höheren Löhne auch in einem Jahr noch nicht zahlen kann?«

»Darüber würde ich mir *heute* noch keine grauen Haare wachsen lassen.«

»Ihr meint, wir können in einem Jahr neu verhandeln?«

Jack zuckte die Achseln. »Wenn's sein muß.«

»Ich verstehe«, sagte Philip, ohne seine Meinung dazu durchblik-ken zu lassen. »Habt Ihr sonst noch Vorschläge?«

»Der größte Stein des Anstoßes ist die sofortige Entlassung der Saisonarbeiter«, bekannte Jack geradeheraus. Bei diesem Thema ließ sich nichts beschönigen. »Fristlose Entlassungen hat es in der ganzen Christenheit noch nicht gegeben. Das jeweils nächste Wochenende ist der früheste Zeitpunkt.« Um Philip die Einsicht leichter zu machen, fügte er hinzu: »Ich hätte Euch das vorher sagen sollen.«

»So muß ich die Leute also nur noch zwei Tage beschäftigen?«

»Ich glaube nicht, daß sie sich jetzt noch damit zufriedengeben«, meinte Jack. »Wären wir die Sache von Anfang an geschickter angegan-gen, dann hätte es vielleicht geklappt. Aber jetzt erwarten sie bestimmt ein größeres Entgegenkommen.«

»Zweifellos habt Ihr schon etwas Bestimmtes im Sinn.«

Dem war in der Tat so – es war das einzige echte Zugeständnis, das er von Philip erwartete. »Wir haben jetzt Anfang Oktober. Norma-lerweise entlassen wir die Saisonarbeiter Anfang Dezember. Kommen wir ihnen auf halben Wege entgegen und legen den Zeitpunkt der Entlassung auf Anfang November.«

»Das erfüllt nur die Hälfte meiner Forderungen.«

»Es erfüllt mehr als die Hälfte. Ihr profitiert davon, daß die Vorräte aufgebraucht werden, daß die höheren Löhne bei Beförderungen erst in einem Jahr zu zahlen sind und daß an Heiligentagen nicht mehr gearbeitet wird.«

»Das sind doch alles nur Belanglosigkeiten.«

Bedrückt lehnte Jack sich zurück. Er hatte sein Möglichstes getan. Er hatte all seine Argumente vor Philip ausgebreitet, seine gesamte Überredungskunst aufgewandt. Nun blieb nichts mehr zu sagen. Er war mit seinem Latein am Ende – und Philip zeigte noch immer keine Einsicht. Jack war nahe daran aufzugeben. Er sah in Philips wie versteinertes Gesicht und wartete.

Philip drehte sich um und ließ den Blick eine ganze Weile lang schweigend auf dem Hausaltar ruhen. Endlich wandte er sich Jack wieder zu und sagte: »Ich werde Eure Vorschläge der Kapitelversammlung unterbreiten müssen.«

Jack wurde vor lauter Erleichterung ganz schwach zumute. Das war zwar noch kein Sieg, aber ein wichtiger Schritt voran. Es war nicht Philips Art, die Mönche über Vorschläge diskutieren zu lassen, die er selbst nicht guthieß, und in den meisten Fällen entschieden sie genau so, wie er es wünschte. »Ich hoffe, die Mönche sind einverstanden«, sagte Jack matt.

Philip stand auf und legte ihm die Hand auf die Schulter. Zum ersten Male lächelte er. »Wenn ich ihnen die Sache so überzeugend darlege wie Ihr mir, dann sind sie einverstanden.«

Der plötzliche Stimmungsumschwung verblüffte Jack, und er sagte: »Je früher wir das hinter uns bringen, desto geringer sind die langfristigen Auswirkungen.«

»Ich weiß. Der Gedanke hat mich sehr erzürnt, aber an einem längeren Streit mit Euch liegt mir gewiß nicht.« Unerwartet reichte er ihm die Hand.

Jack schlug ein. Es war ein gutes Gefühl.

»Kann ich den Leuten sagen, sie sollen morgen früh in die Bauhütten kommen und die Entscheidung des Kapitels hören?« fragte er.

»Ja, das könnt Ihr.«

»Dann mache ich mich sofort auf den Weg.« Er hatte sich schon zum Gehen gewandt, als Philip ihn zurückrief: »Jack!«

»Ja?«

»Ich danke Euch.«

Jack nickte zum Zeichen des Verständnisses und trat hinaus. Er war so glücklich, daß er trotz des strömenden Regens nicht einmal die Kapuze aufsetzte.

Am Nachmittag suchte er die Handwerker in ihren Wohnhäusern auf und bat sie für den nächsten Morgen zur Besprechung. Wen er nicht zu Hause antraf – vorwiegend Junggesellen und Saisonarbeiter –, den fand er in der Schenke. Immerhin waren sie alle nüchtern, denn der Bierpreis war ebenso gestiegen wie alle anderen Preise. Niemand konnte sich mehr einen Rausch leisten.

Der einzige, den Jack nicht fand, war Alfred. Seit zwei Tagen hatte ihn niemand mehr zu Gesicht bekommen. Erst in der Abenddämmerung tauchte er in der Schenke auf, ein merkwürdig triumphierendes Grinsen in seinem tumben Gesicht. Weder erzählte er, wo er gewesen war, noch fragte ihn Jack danach. Er ließ ihn am Biertisch sitzen und ging nach Hause, um mit Aliena und den Kindern Abendbrot zu essen.

Die Besprechung am nächsten Morgen hatte er frühzeitig angesetzt, noch bevor Prior Philip zur Bauhütte kam. Er wollte den Boden gut vorbereiten und hatte sich seine Worte genau zurechtgelegt.

Die Handwerker kamen alle überpünktlich – immerhin ging es um ihre Existenz. Ein paar von den jüngeren Burschen hatten rotgeränderte Augen vom langen Aufbleiben und Zechen in der Nacht. Von den jungen Leuten und den Saisonarbeitern war am meisten Widerstand zu erwarten. Die erfahrenen Gesellen dachten eher an die Zukunft, und die wenigen Frauen unter ihnen waren vorsichtig und hingen am Bewährten. Bei ihnen konnte jeder Kompromißvorschlag mit Zustimmung rechnen.

»Prior Philip wird uns bitten, die Arbeit wieder aufzunehmen«, begann Jack, »und er wird uns dazu eine Art Kompromiß vorschlagen. Bevor er kommt, sollten wir vielleicht besprechen, in welchem Punkt wir ihm zustimmen, in welchem wir zu Verhandlungen bereit sind und wo wir auf gar keinen Fall nachgeben werden. Wir sollten Philip wie ein Mann entgegentreten. Stimmt Ihr mir darin zu?«

Mehrere Köpfe nickten.

Jack verlieh seiner Stimme einen halbwegs zornigen Klang und wetterte: »So kommt zum Beispiel nach meiner Meinung eine fristlose Entlassung überhaupt nicht in Frage!« Um seiner Kompromißlosigkeit in diesem Punkt Nachdruck zu verleihen, hieb er mit der Faust auf die Werkbank. Mehrere Männer bekundeten lauthals ihre Zustimmung. Jack, der ja wußte, daß Philip von dieser Forderung inzwischen abgerückt war, verfolgte damit die Absicht, die jungen Feuerköpfe unter den Handwerkern und Arbeitern noch zusätzlich anzustacheln. Gab Philip ihnen dann nach, so wäre ihnen rasch der Wind aus den Segeln genommen.

»Außerdem, meine ich, dürfen wir das Recht der Zunft, Beförderungen auszusprechen, nicht preisgeben. Nur ein Handwerker kann beurteilen, ob ein Lehrling geschickt und erfahren genug ist oder nicht.« Auch hier war er also nicht ganz aufrichtig, lenkte er doch die Aufmerksamkeit von der finanziellen Seite der Beförderungsfrage ab. Seine Hoffnung war: Blieb ihr Rechtsstandpunkt gewahrt, so ließen sie sich vielleicht bei der Bezahlung eher auf einen Kompromiß ein.

»Was die Arbeit an Heiligentagen betrifft – da fühle ich mich, wie ich gestehen muß, hin und her gerissen. Über freie Tage werden gemeinhin bei jedem Bauvorhaben eigene Vereinbarungen getroffen – es gibt da keine einheitlichen Richtlinien, soviel ich weiß.« Er wandte sich an Edward Twonose und fragte: »Was meint Ihr dazu, Edward?«

»Ja, das wird von Baustelle zu Baustelle anders gehandhabt«, erklärte Edward, sichtlich erfreut, daß man ihn um seine Meinung gebeten hatte. Jack nickte ihm ermutigend zu, worauf Edward begann, sich des langen und breiten über die verschiedensten Möglichkeiten auszulassen. Die Besprechung verlief ganz nach Jacks Wünschen: Die ausführliche Behandlung eines Punktes, der gar nicht sonderlich strittig war, langweilte die Männer mit der Zeit und nahm ihnen Kraft und Geduld für die eigentliche Auseinandersetzung.

Unversehens wurde Edward in seinem Monolog unterbrochen. Aus dem Hintergrund tönte es: »Das ist doch unwichtiger Kleinkram!«

Jack sah auf. Der Zwischenrufer war Dan Bristol. »Einer nach dem anderen bitte«, sagte er. »Laßt erst Edward ausreden.«

Doch Dan ließ sich nicht so leicht zum Schweigen bringen. »Das ist doch alles dummes Zeug«, sagte er. »Was wir wirklich wollen, ist eine Lohnerhöhung.«

»Eine Lohnerhöhung?« Die Forderung war so lächerlich, daß Jack nicht wußte, was er davon halten sollte.

Zu seinem Erstaunen jedoch fand Dan sogar Unterstützung. »Richtig!« meinte Pierre. »Eine Lohnerhöhung. Schaut – ein Vier-Pfund-Laib Brot kostet inzwischen schon einen Penny, und ein Huhn, das früher acht Pence kostete, gibt's mittlerweile nur noch für vierundzwanzig! Und ich gehe jede Wette ein, daß alle hier im Raum schon wochenlang auf gutes, starkes Bier verzichten müssen. Alles wird immer teurer, aber wir arbeiten noch immer für den Lohn, zu dem wir eingestellt wurden. Das sind ganze zwölf Pence in der Woche – und davon sollen wir unsere Familien ernähren?«

Jacks Zuversicht schwand. Bis hierhin war alles so gut gegangen, doch dieser Einwand machte seine Strategie mit einem Schlag zunichte. Er hielt an sich und vermied es, Dan und Pierre zu widersprechen; ihm war nur allzu klar, daß er ihren Sorgen Gehör schenken mußte, wenn er seinen Einfluß nicht verlieren wollte. »Ihr habt ja vollkommen recht«, sagte er zur offenkundigen Überraschung der beiden. »Allerdings frage ich mich doch, wie es mir gelingen soll, zu einem Zeitpunkt, da der Priorei das Geld ausgeht, Philip zu einer Lohnerhöhung zu bewegen.«

Darauf blieben die anderen eine Antwort schuldig. Dan aber wiederholte seine Forderung: »Wenn wir nicht verhungern wollen, brauchen wir vierundzwanzig Pence die Woche – und selbst damit sind wir noch schlechter dran als vorher.«

Bestürzt mußte Jack feststellen, daß ihm das Gespräch zusehends entglitt. Pierre rief: »Vierundzwanzig Pence die Woche!« Kopfnickend bekundeten zahlreiche Handwerker ihre Zustimmung.

Ich bin offenbar nicht der einzige, der sich auf diese Sitzung sorgfältig vorbereitet hat, dachte Jack und faßte Dan ins Auge. »Habt Ihr Euch etwa darüber abgesprochen?«

»Haben wir, gestern abend in der Schenke«, gab Dan selbstbewußt zurück. »Das ist ja wohl erlaubt, oder?«

»Selbstverständlich ist das erlaubt. Aber ich möchte Euch doch bitten, für alle hier Anwesenden, die nicht das Privileg hatten, an dieser Besprechung teilzunehmen, Eure Beschlüsse kurz zusammenzufassen.«

»Einverstanden.« Die Männer, die am Vorabend nicht in der Schenke gewesen waren, machten aus ihrem Unmut kein Geheimnis, doch Dan focht das nicht an. Er hatte gerade zu sprechen angesetzt, als Prior Philip den Raum betrat. Mit einem fast unmerklichen Kopfnicken gab er Jack zu verstehen, daß das Kapitel dem Kompromiß zugestimmt hatte. Welch ein Glück, dachte Jack und öffnete den Mund, um Dan am Sprechen zu hindern. Aber es war bereits zu spät. »Wir fordern vierundzwanzig Pence die Woche für gelernte Handwerker«, verkündete Dan, »zwölf für ungelernte Arbeiter und achtundvierzig für Meister.«

Philips eingangs so zufriedene Miene wich einem harten, kämpferischen Ausdruck. »Augenblick«, wandte Jack ein. »Das ist nicht die Meinung der Bauhütte. Das haben sich ein paar trunkene Hirne in der Schenke ausgedacht.«

»Das ist nicht wahr!« Unvermittelt meldete sich Alfred zu Wort. »Du wirst sehen, daß eine klare Mehrheit hinter diesen Lohnforderungen steht.«

Wutentbrannt starrte Jack ihn an. »Erst vor ein paar Monaten hast du mich noch buchstäblich um Arbeit angefleht«, rief er. »Und jetzt erdreistest du dich, eine derartige Lohnerhöhung zu fordern. Ich hätte dich verhungern lassen sollen!«

»Dieses Schicksal erwartet Euch alle, wenn Ihr nicht zur Einsicht kommt«, fügte Prior Philip hinzu. Provozierende Bemerkungen wie diese hatte Jack um jeden Preis vermeiden wollen – und jetzt fielen sie gleichsam zwangsläufig. Seine Strategie hatte vollkommen versagt.

»Vierundzwanzig Pence«, wiederholte Dan ungerührt. »Sonst nehmen wir die Arbeit nicht wieder auf.«

»Das kommt überhaupt nicht in Frage«, gab Prior Philip hitzig zurück. »Es ist reine Narretei. Ich weigere mich, darüber auch nur zu diskutieren.«

»Wir bestehen darauf«, erwiderte Dan. »Für weniger Lohn arbeiten wir nicht mehr, unter keinen Umständen.«

»Seid doch nicht blöde!« wandte Jack ein. »Wie könnt Ihr Euch hierhersetzen und behaupten, Ihr arbeitet nur um diesen Lohn und keinen anderen? Wißt Ihr, worauf das hinausläuft? Ihr werdet überhaupt keine Arbeit mehr haben. Wohin wollt Ihr denn gehen, wenn Euch hier keiner mehr will?«

»Wohin wohl?« fragte Dan.

O Gott, dachte Jack, sie haben tatsächlich eine andere Möglichkeit aufgetan. Er war dem Verzweifeln nahe.

»Wir können woanders anfangen«, sagte Dan und erhob sich. »Und was mich betrifft, so mache ich mich noch heute auf den Weg zu der neuen Arbeitsstelle.«

»Wovon redet Ihr?« fragte Jack.

»Man hat mir angeboten, in Shiring zu arbeiten«, erwiderte Dan mit triumphierender Miene. »An der neuen Kirche dort. Für vierundzwanzig Pence die Woche.«

Jack sah in die Runde. »Wurde auch noch anderen ein solches Angebot unterbreitet?«

Fast alle Gesichter senkten sich schamvoll.

»Allen«, sagte Dan.

Jack war zutiefst erschüttert. Das war ein raffiniert ausgeheckter Plan. Man hatte ihn nach Strich und Faden hintergangen – mit dem Ergebnis, daß er jetzt dastand wie der letzte Narr. Er hatte die Lage von Grund auf falsch eingeschätzt. Doch seine Betroffenheit verwandelte sich rasch in Zorn, und unwillkürlich suchte er nach einem Sündenbock. »Wer ist der Verräter unter Euch?!« schrie er die Handwerker an und ließ den Blick von einem Gesicht zum anderen wandern. Nur wenige wagten es, ihm in die Augen zu sehen. Ihre Beschämung war ihm kein Trost. Er fühlte sich wie ein betrogener Liebhaber. »Wer hat Euch dieses Angebot aus Shiring gebracht?« brüllte er. »Wer soll dort Baumeister werden?« Schließlich blieb sein Blick an Alfred hängen. Mit einem Schlag war ihm alles klar. Ihm wurde übel vor Ekel. »Alfred?« sagte er verächtlich. »Ihr wollt mich im Stich lassen, um ausgerechnet für *Alfred* zu arbeiten?«

Eine Weile lang herrschte Schweigen. Endlich sagte Dan: »Ja, das wollen wir.«

Jack erkannte, daß er machtlos war. »So sei's denn«, sagte er bitter. »Ihr alle kennt mich und Ihr alle kennt meinen Bruder – trotzdem habt Ihr Euch für Alfred entschieden. Ihr alle kennt Prior Philip und Ihr alle kennt Graf William – trotzdem habt Ihr Euch für William entschieden. Ihr habt Euch diese Suppe selber eingebrockt – nun seht zu, wie Ihr sie auslöffelt.«

»Erzähl mir eine Geschichte«, bat Aliena. »Du erzählst mir so wenig in letzter Zeit. Weiß du noch, früher ...«

»Ich weiß«, sagte Jack.

Sie waren im Wald, auf ihrem verschwiegenen Plätzchen am Bach. Der Herbst war ins Land gezogen, und so saßen sie nicht am schattigen Ufer, sondern im Schutz eines Felsvorsprungs, wo sie sich ein wärmendes Feuer angezündet hatten. Es war ein grauer, dunkler, kalter Nachmittag, aber sie waren noch warm von der Liebe. Das Feuer prasselte lustig. Unter ihren Mänteln waren sie nackt.

Jack öffnete Alienas Mantel und berührte ihre Brust. Aliena hielt ihre Brüste für zu groß und war traurig darüber, daß sie nicht mehr so hoch und fest waren wie vor der Geburt der Kinder. Jack schien sich daran glücklicherweise nicht zu stören – er liebte sie wie eh und je, und das half Aliena über ihren Kummer hinweg. »Ich erzähl' dir die Geschichte von einer Prinzessin, die hoch oben im Turm einer großen Burg lebte.« Zärtlich berührte er die Spitze ihrer Brust. »Und von einem Prinzen, der hoch oben im Turm einer anderen großen Burg hauste.« Er berührte die andere Brust. »Jeden Tag wechselten sie von den Fenstern ihrer hohen Verliese schmachtende Blicke miteinander und träumten davon, das tiefe Tal, das zwischen ihnen lag, zu überwinden.« Seine Hand, die mittlerweile in der Senke zwischen ihren Brüsten ruhte, glitt unvermittelt abwärts. »Doch jeden Sonntagnachmittag trafen sie sich im dichten Wald!« Aliena fuhr zusammen und quietschte auf – dann mußte sie über sich selbst lachen.

Sonntagnachmittag wie dieser waren goldene Augenblicke in einem Leben, das mehr und mehr aus den Fugen geriet.

Die schlechte Ernte und der Verfall der Wollpreise hatten eine wirtschaftliche Katastrophe heraufbeschworen. Kaufleute machten bankrott, Städter verloren ihre Arbeit, und die Bauern litten Hunger. Jack erhielt zum Glück noch seinen Lohn; zusammen mit ein paar anderen Handwerkern arbeitete er am ersten Joch des Hauptschiffs. Aliena hatte ihre Schneiderei fast völlig eingestellt.

Der gesamte Süden Englands war von der Hungersnot erfaßt. In der Grafschaft Shiring kam erschwerend hinzu, daß William sehr eigenwillig darauf reagierte.

Für Aliena war sein Verhalten das Schlimmste an der ganzen Sache überhaupt. Für den Bau seiner neuen Kirche in Shiring, die dem Andenken seiner bösartigen, halb wahnsinnigen Mutter gewidmet war, gierte er nach Bargeld. Er hatte so viele Pächter wegen Zahlungsrückständen von ihren Gütern vertrieben, daß einige der besten Ländereien in der Grafschaft inzwischen brachlagen. Der ohnehin schon prekäre Getreidemangel wurde dadurch noch verschlimmert. William hatte, das kam noch hinzu, große Getreidevorräte gespeichert, um die Preise hochzutreiben. Da er nur wenige Angestellte besaß und niemanden zu ernähren hatte, konnte er dank der Hungersnot in kurzer Zeit viel Geld verdienen. Langfristig führte sein Verhalten jedoch zu nicht wiedergutzumachenden Schäden auf den Gütern und drohte, die Hungersnot zum Dauerzustand werden zu lassen. Aliena mußte immer wieder daran denken, wie Shiring unter der Herrschaft ihres Vaters ausgesehen hatte – eine reiche Grafschaft mit fruchtbaren Feldern und prosperierenden Städten und Dörfern. Die Erinnerung an jene Zeiten brach ihr fast das Herz.

Einige Jahre lang war das Gelübde, das der sterbende Vater ihr und ihrem Bruder abgenommen hatte, nahezu in Vergessenheit geraten. Mit der Ernennung Williams zum Grafen und der Gründung ihrer eigenen Familie war das Ziel, die Grafschaft für Richard zurückzugewinnen, in weite Ferne gerückt. Richard hatte sich als Führer der Stadtwache ein Auskommen geschaffen und sogar ein Mädchen aus der Stadt geheiratet. Leider hatte sich nach einer Weile herausgestellt, daß es um die Gesundheit seiner Frau nicht zum besten bestellt war, und sie war im vergangenen Jahr kinderlos gestorben.

Seit Beginn der Hungersnot dachte Aliena wieder öfter an die Grafschaft und das Gelübde. Sie wußte, daß Richard, wäre er Graf von Shiring, mit ihrer Hilfe eine Menge zur Linderung der Hungersnot hätte tun können. Aber es war alles nur Träumerei: William stand bei König Stephan, der im Bürgerkrieg mittlerweile die Oberhand gewonnen hatte, hoch in Gunsten, und weit und breit sprach nichts für eine Änderung.

Auf der heimlichen Lichtung im Wald waren all diese Kümmernisse und Sorgen wie fortgeblasen, wenn Aliena und Jack im Gras lagen und sich liebten. Vom ersten Tag an waren sie wie besessen voneinander gewesen – nie würde Aliena vergessen, wie erschrocken sie anfangs über ihre eigene Lust gewesen war. Inzwischen war sie dreiunddreißig und durch die Geburten um die Hüften herum etwas breiter geworden, auch war ihr Bauch nicht mehr so flach und straff wie ehedem – und doch war Jack noch immer so wild auf sie, daß sie sich Sonntag für Sonntag drei- bis viermal hintereinander liebten.

Jacks scherzhafte Geschichte vom dichten Wald verwandelte sich nun in herrliche, wollüstige Zärtlichkeit. Aliena zog sein Gesicht an sich, um ihn zu küssen … Doch da hörten sie auf einmal eine Stimme.

Sie erstarrten. Ihre Lichtung lag ein gutes Stück von der Straße entfernt im Dickicht. Noch nie hatte jemand sie hier gestört, allenfalls mal ein unvorsichtiger Hirsch oder ein vorwitziger Fuchs. Sie hielten den Atem an und lauschten. Wieder diese Stimme – diesmal gefolgt von einer anderen. Als sie noch genauer hinhörten, vernahmen sie ein leises Knirschen oder Rascheln – es klang so, als marschiere eine größere Anzahl von Menschen durch den Wald.

Jack ergriff einen seiner Stiefel, die neben ihnen im Gras lagen, schlich zum Bach, füllte den Stiefel mit Wasser und leerte ihn über dem Feuer aus. Zischend erloschen die Flammen. Auf allen vieren, und ohne das leiseste Geräusch zu verursachen, verschwand Jack im Unterholz.

Aliena zog Unterhemd, Tunika und Stiefel an und wickelte sich wieder in ihren Mantel.

So leise, wie er verschwunden war, kehrte Jack auch wieder zurück. »Outlaws«, sagte er.

»Wie viele?«

»Sehr viele. Ich habe sie gar nicht alle sehen können.«

»Wohin gehen sie?«

»Nach Kingsbridge.« Er hob die Hand. »Horch!«

Aliena spitzte die Ohren. In der Ferne läutete die Glocke der Priorei Sturm. Aliena stockte das Herz. »Oh, Jack, die Kinder!« rief sie.

»Wenn wir durch den Sumpfgrund laufen und an der Furt beim Kastanienhain den Fluß überqueren, können wir vor den Banditen in Kingsbridge sein.«

»Gut, aber dann los!«

Jack berührte ihren Arm und hielt sie mit dieser Geste zurück. Er lauschte. Draußen im Wald hörte er immer Dinge, die sie nicht wahrzunehmen vermochte; es war das Vermächtnis seiner Jugend in der Wildnis. Sie wartete, bis er sagte: »Ich glaube, sie sind alle vorbei.«

Sie verließen die Lichtung und erreichten kurz darauf die Straße. Weit und breit war kein Mensch zu sehen. Sie überquerten die Straße und schlugen sich auf einem kaum erkennbaren Pfad durchs Gebüsch. Aliena hatte Tommy und Sally bei Martha gelassen, wo ein Feuer brannte und sie gut aufgehoben waren. Jetzt wurde sie von der furchtbaren Angst vorwärtsgetrieben, den Kindern könne während ihrer Abwesenheit etwas zustoßen. Wo immer es ihnen möglich war, rannten sie, doch über weite Strecken war das Gelände dafür zu unwegsam. In einer tiefen Senke lag der Sumpfgrund. Sie rutschten die steile Böschung hinab. Schon manch ein unvorsichtiger Fremder hatte sich hier verirrt und war unrettbar im Morast versunken. Ortskundige überquerten ihn gefahrlos, doch hemmte der tiefgründige, nasse Boden Alienas Lauf. Sie kam immer langsamer voran und wurde immer aufgeregter.

Hinter dem Sumpfgrund kam die Furt. Das kalte Wasser ging Aliena bis an die Knie und spülte ihr den Matsch von den Füßen.

Nach dem Fluß war der Weg ebener und es ging schneller voran. Je näher sie der Stadt kamen, desto lauter dröhnten die Sturmglocken. Irgend jemand muß Kingsbridge vor der heranrückenden Gefahr gewarnt haben, dachte Aliena und klammerte sich an diesen Hoffnungsschimmer. Als sie mit Jack aus dem Wald kam und über die Wiese vor dem Fluß lief, trafen gleichzeitig mit ihnen noch zwanzig oder dreißig Jugendliche ein, die in einem nahe gelegenen Dörfchen Fußball gespielt hatten. Trotz der Kälte stand den Jungen der Schweiß auf der Stirn.

Sie rannten über die Brücke. Das Tor war schon geschlossen, doch die Männer auf den Befestigungen hatten sie gesehen und erkannt. Eine kleine Ausfallpforte wurde geöffnet. Jack machte seine Autorität geltend und sorgte somit dafür, daß die Jungen ihm und Aliena den Vortritt ließen. Aliena war erleichtert, daß es ihnen gelungen war, rechtzeitig vor den Outlaws in die Stadt zurückzukehren.

Keuchend vor Anstrengung liefen sie die Hauptstraße entlang. Mit Speeren, Bogen und schweren Steinen bewaffnet besetzte die Bevölkerung von Kingsbridge die Wälle und Mauern. Die Kinder wurden zusammengetrieben und in die Priorei geschickt. Martha hat Tommy und Sally bestimmt schon hingebracht, dachte Aliena.

Im Hof der Klosterküche erblickten sie zu ihrem großen Erstaunen Ellen, Jacks Mutter. Sie war schlank und rank wie eh und je, die Haut gebräunt, doch mischten sich erste graue Strähnen in ihr langes Haar, und um die vierundvierzigjährigen Augen zeigten sich Fältchen. Ellen unterhielt sich angeregt mit Richard. In einiger Entfernung von ihr stand Prior Philip und dirigierte die Kinderschar ins Kapitelhaus. Er hatte Ellen anscheinend noch nicht gesehen.

Auch Martha stand in der Nähe, und bei ihr waren Tommy und Sally. Aliena atmete erleichtert auf und umarmte die beiden Kinder.

»Mutter!« rief Jack aus. »Was machst du denn hier?«

»Ich kam, um euch vor der Räuberbande zu warnen, die die Stadt überfallen will.«

»Wir waren im Wald und haben sie gesehen«, sagte Jack.

Richard spitzte die Ohren. »Ihr habt sie gesehen? Wie viele waren es?«

»Ich weiß nicht genau – aber ich schätze mindestens hundert, vielleicht auch mehr.«

»Wie sind sie bewaffnet?«

»Mit Keulen, Messern, auch ein paar Äxte habe ich gesehen. Aber vor allem Keulen und Knüppel.«

»Aus welcher Richtung kommen sie?«

»Aus Norden.«

»Dank dir. Ich muß jetzt hinauf auf die Mauern und Ausschau halten.«

»Martha, bring die Kinder ins Kapitelhaus«, sagte Aliena und folgte Richard. Auch Ellen und Jack kamen mit.

Auf ihrem Weg durch die Stadt wurde Richard mehrfach von aufgeregten Bürgern angesprochen. »Was ist los?« fragten ihn die Leute.

»Outlaws«, antwortete Richard knapp und ließ sich durch die Fragen nicht aufhalten.

Sieh mal einer an, dachte Aliena. Scheucht man ihn vom Lager und schimpft ihn einen Taugenichts, der endlich auf eigenen Füßen stehen soll, dann kommt er einem vor wie ein Versager. Aber in militärischen Notlagen behält er die Übersicht.

Sie erreichten die nördliche Stadtmauer und kletterten die Leiter zur Brustwehr hoch. In regelmäßigen Abständen lagen Steinhaufen bereit. Bogenschützen bemannten die Zinnen. Richard hatte den Rat der Stadt vor einiger Zeit gegen starke Widerstände dazu überredet, einmal im Jahr Notstandsübungen abzuhalten. Inzwischen hatten sich die Bürger daran gewöhnt; die Übungen waren zum Ritual geworden wie die alljährlichen Feiern zur Mittsommernacht, und jedermann hatte Spaß daran. Nun zeigte sich ihr wahrer Wert: Als die Sturmglokken läuteten, wußte jeder Bürger der Stadt, was er zu tun hatte; es gab keine unnötige Verzögerung, und man vertraute auf die eigenen Kräfte.

Angstvoll spähte Aliena über die Felder. Nichts war zu sehen.

»Ihr habt sie aber ganz schön abgehängt«, sagte Richard.

»Was wollen diese Banditen ausgerechnet *hier*?« fragte Aliena.

»Sie haben's auf die Vorratslager der Priorei abgesehen«, antwortete Ellen. »Das ist weit und breit der einzige Fleck, wo es noch größere Mengen Lebensmittel gibt.«

»Ach so.« Die Outlaws hungerten. Viele von ihnen waren erst durch William zu dem geworden, was sie waren: Er hatte sie enteignet oder vertrieben. Nun lebten sie von Diebstahl und Raub, weil sie anders nicht überleben konnten. In den unbewehrten Dörfern gab es wenig oder gar nichts zu stehlen – die Bauern hatten ja selbst kaum etwas zu beißen. Nur die Scheuern der Landbesitzer waren noch gefüllt.

Gerade hatte sich Aliena diesen Sachverhalt klargemacht, da sah sie auch schon die Outlaws kommen.

Sie kamen aus dem Wald wie Ratten aus einem brennenden Heuschober, überall, meist einzeln, und sie schwärmten aus über das freie Feld vor der Stadt, zwanzig, dreißig, fünfzig, hundert von ihnen, eine kleine Armee. Wahrscheinlich hatten sie darauf spekuliert, die Stadt zu überraschen und durch die offenen Tore hereinzukommen. Daß sie den Angriff nicht abgeblasen hatten, obwohl die Sturmglocken ihnen gesagt haben mußten, daß die Stadt gewarnt war, verriet das ganze Ausmaß ihrer aus Hunger geborenen Verzweiflung. Ein paar Bogenschützen schossen erste Pfeile auf die Angreifer ab, doch Richard rief ihnen zu: »Wartet! Verschwendet nicht eure Pfeile!«

Beim letzten Überfall auf Kingsbridge war Tommy achtzehn Monate alt gewesen, und Aliena ging schwanger mit Sally. Damals hatte sie zusammen mit den Kindern und den alten Leuten in der Priorei Zuflucht gesucht. Diesmal wollte sie auf den Zinnen bleiben und ihren eigenen Beitrag leisten zur Abwehr der Gefahr. Und weil auch die meisten anderen Frauen so dachten wie sie, befanden sich auf den Mauern fast so viele Frauen wie Männer.

Obwohl sie gut gerüstet waren, fühlte Aliena sich innerlich hin und her gerissen, und ihre Bedenken wuchsen, je näher die Angreifer kamen. Zum Kloster war es nicht weit – aber es war denkbar, daß die Angreifer irgendwo anders den Durchbruch schafften und die Priorei eher erreichten als sie. Und was ist, wenn ich verletzt werde und den Kindern nicht mehr helfen kann? fragte sie sich. Jack und Ellen stehen ebenfalls hier auf der Mauer – wenn wir getötet werden, muß Martha sich allein um Tommy und Sally kümmern ... Aliena zögerte; sie konnte sich nicht entscheiden.

Die Outlaws hatten die Mauern schon fast erreicht. Ein Pfeilhagel ging auf sie nieder, und diesmal gebot Richard den Bogenschützen nicht Einhalt. Die Pfeile hielten blutige Ernte. Die Angreifer waren durch keinerlei Rüstung geschützt, niemand führte sie, und sie verfügten über keinerlei Strategie. Wie eine in Panik geratene Rinderherde stürmten sie gegen die Mauer an, und als es dort nicht weiterging, wußten sie nicht, was tun. Die Verteidiger bombardierten die Outlaws mit schweren Steinen. Einige Angreifer warfen sich gegen das Nordtor und schlugen mit ihren Keulen dagegen – ein hoffnungsloses Unterfangen für jeden, der, wie Aliena, wußte, wie dick das aus massivem Eichenholz bestehende und obendrein eisenbeschlagene Tor war. Sie würden die ganze Nacht brauchen, um es einzuschlagen ... Alf Butcher und Arthur Saddler bugsierten inzwischen einen mit kochendem Wasser gefüllten Kessel auf die Zinnen über dem Tor.

Direkt unterhalb von Aliena bildeten ein paar Outlaws eine menschliche Pyramide. Jack und Richard merkten es sogleich und warfen Steine auf sie herab. Aliena dachte an ihre Kinder und tat es ihnen nach, und auch Ellen schloß sich ihnen an. Eine Weile widerstanden die Angreifer dem Steinhagel, dann wurde einer von ihnen am Kopf getroffen und die Pyramide brach zusammen.

Kurz darauf ertönten vom Nordtor her schrille Schmerzensschreie: Kochendes Wasser ergoß sich über die Köpfe der Männer, die das Tor zu stürmen versuchten.

Plötzlich entdeckten die Outlaws eine leichtere Beute als die wehrhafte Stadt: ihre eigenen Kameraden. Sie machten sich über die Toten und Schwerverwundeten her. Wer sich noch wehren konnte, wehrte sich nach Kräften, und bald schlugen auch rivalisierende Leichenfledderer aufeinander ein. Ein wahres Schlachten begann, ein widerliches, würdeloses Schlachten. Die Verteidiger brauchten keine Steine mehr zu werfen. Die Attacke war in sich zusammengefallen – und die Angreifer schlugen sich mit ihresgleichen, stritten sich wie Hunde um einen Knochen.

»Ein undiszipliniertes Haufen«, sagte Aliena zu Richard. »Die können uns nicht gefährlich werden.«

Richard nickte. »Gewiß – aber sie *könnten* zu einer Bedrohung werden, weil sie mit dem Mut der Verzweiflung kämpfen. Was ihnen fehlt, ist eine straffe militärische Führung.«

Aliena hatte auf einmal eine Idee. »Eine Armee, die auf einen Führer wartet«, sagte sie. Richard verstand nicht, worauf sie hinauswollte. Aliena hingegen war auf einmal ganz aufgeregt. Richard war ein guter militärischer Führer ohne Armee. Die Outlaws waren eine Armee ohne Führer. Und die Grafschaft war ein Scherbenhaufen ...

Wieder fielen Steine, wieder wurden ein paar Verfemte von Pfeilen durchbohrt. Die Angreifer hatten endgültig genug und wandten sich zur Flucht. Wie eine Meute geprügelter Hunde mit eingekniffenen Schwänzen rannten sie davon. Irgend jemand öffnete das Nordtor. Eine Horde junger Männer brach hervor und jagte, Schwerter und Äxte schwingend, hinter den Outlaws her. Die liefen um ihr Leben, aber einige von ihnen wurden schon bald erwischt und niedergemetzelt.

Ellen wandte sich angewidert ab und sagte zu Richard: »Du hättest die Burschen nicht rauslassen dürfen.«

»Junge Männer wollen Blut sehen nach so einer Auseinandersetzung«, sagte Richard. »Sie brauchen das einfach. Davon ganz abgesehen: Je mehr wir heute töten, desto weniger greifen uns das nächste Mal an.«

Die Philosophie eines Soldaten, dachte Aliena. Früher, in einer Zeit, in der sie Tag für Tag um ihr eigenes Leben bangen mußte, hätte sie vielleicht ähnlich gedacht wie die jungen Männer und alles darangesetzt, die fliehenden Outlaws zur Strecke zu bringen. Inzwischen dachte sie anders darüber: Sie wollte die Ursachen beseitigen, die Menschen zu Outlaws machten – und nicht mehr die Gesetzlosen selbst. Und außerdem wußte sie jetzt, wie sie die Outlaws für ihre eigenen Zwecke einspannen konnte.

Richard beauftragte jemanden, zur Entwarnung die Glocken läuten zu lassen, und verdoppelte die Sicherheitsvorkehrungen für die kommende Nacht. Neben den üblichen Wachposten wurden spezielle Patrouillen eingesetzt. Aliena ging zur Priorei, um Martha und die Kinder abzuholen. Dann trafen sie sich alle in Jacks Haus.

Aliena war heilfroh, daß sie die Ihren um sich scharen konnte: Jack, die Kinder, Jacks Mutter, Richard und Martha ... eine ganz normale Familie, dachte sie und hätte fast vergessen, daß ihr Vater in einem Verlies gestorben und sie selbst dem Gesetz nach mit dem Stiefbruder von Jack verheiratet war. Und Ellen – Ellen war eine Verfemte ...

Sie schüttelte den Kopf. Nein, gestand sie sich ein, das geht nicht. Ich kann nicht einfach so tun, als seien wir eine ganz normale Familie.

Jack ging zum Faß, zapfte einen Krug Bier und schenkte ihnen ein. Alle waren sie noch voll innerer Anspannung und Erregung nach der überstandenen Gefahr. Ellen schichtete ein Kaminfeuer auf, und Martha schnitt fürs Abendessen Steckrüben in einen Topf. In früheren Tagen hätten sie an einem besonderen Tag wie diesem ein halbes Schwein gebraten.

Richard leerte seinen Becher mit einem Zug, wischte sich den Mund ab und sagte: »Mit so was wie heute werden wir bis zum Beginn des Frühjahrs noch mehrfach rechnen müssen.«

»Sollen sie sich doch über Graf Williams Vorratsscheuern hermachen«, sagte Jack. »Schließlich haben sie es ihm – und nicht Prior Philip – zu verdanken, daß es ihnen so dreckig geht.«

»Da müssen sie sich aber eine andere Strategie ausdenken, sonst blitzen sie bei ihm genauso ab wie bei uns.«

»Sie brauchen einen Anführer«, sagte Aliena.

»Geb's Gott, daß sie nie einen finden!« rief Jack aus. »Sonst werden sie uns tatsächlich noch gefährlich.«

»Ein guter Anführer führt sie vielleicht gegen William – anstatt gegen uns.«

»Versteh' ich nicht«, sagte Jack. »Woher willst du das wissen?«

»Wenn er Richard hieße, wär' ich mir ganz sicher.«

Mit einemmal waren alle still.

Aliena hatte sich ihren Vorschlag genau überlegt und war inzwischen davon überzeugt, daß er einiges für sich hatte. Vielleicht können wir endlich unseren Schwur einlösen, dachte sie. Richard kann William vernichten und endlich Graf werden – und in der Grafschaft kehrt endlich wieder Frieden und Wohlstand ein … Je mehr sie darüber nachdachte, desto aufgeregter wurde sie. »Der Haufen heute zählte mehr als hundert Mann«, sagte sie und wandte sich an Ellen. »Wie viele hausen denn insgesamt da draußen in den Wäldern?«

»Man kann sie nicht mehr zählen«, sagte Ellen. »Hunderte, nein Tausende.«

Aliena beugte sich über den Küchentisch und blickte Richard an. »Du solltest ihr Anführer sein«, sagte sie hart. »Treib sie zusammen. Bring ihnen das Kriegshandwerk bei. Überleg dir die richtigen Angriffspläne. Und dann führe sie in die Schlacht – gegen William.«

Noch während sie auf ihn einredete, wurde ihr klar, daß sie ihren Bruder aufforderte, sein Lebens aufs Spiel zu setzen. Ihr war auf einmal angst und bange zumute. Statt der Grafenwürde erwartete Richard vielleicht der Tod.

Er selbst teilte ihre Bedenken überhaupt nicht. »Mein Gott, Allie, du könntest recht haben«, sagte er. »Ich könnte eine Armee gegen William führen ... meine eigene!«

Tiefsitzender Haß blitzte in seinen Augen auf. Unwillkürlich suchte Aliena die Narbe an seinem linken Ohr. Das Ohrläppchen fehlte. Sie mußte böse Erinnerungen niederkämpfen, die in ihr aufzusteigen drohten.

Richard fand immer mehr Gefallen an dem Gedanken. »Ich könnte mich zuerst über Williams Vieh hermachen«, sagte er mit sichtlicher Begeisterung. »Seine Schafe stehlen, sein Wild erlegen, seine Scheuern aufbrechen, seine Mühlen überfallen. Mein Gott, wenn ich eine Armee hätte, dann könnte ich dieses Aas piesacken ...«

Er ist schon immer Soldat gewesen, dachte Aliena. Jetzt sieht er eine Chance, sein Schicksal zu erfüllen ... Sie war so mitgerissen von der Idee, daß sie die Sorge um Richards Leben verdrängte.

»Die Sache hat einen Haken«, sagte Richard. »Wie komme ich an die Burschen ran? Die halten sich doch dauernd versteckt.«

»Ich kann's dir sagen«, bemerkte Ellen. »Von der Straße nach Winchester zweigt ein überwachsener Pfad zu einem ehemaligen Steinbruch ab. Das ist ihr Schlupfwinkel. Früher war er unter dem Namen ›Sallys Steinbruch‹ bekannt.«

»Ich hab' aber keinen Steinbruch«, verkündete die siebenjährige Sally.

Alle lachten, doch es wurde rasch wieder still.

Richard wirkte zu allem entschlossen. »Gut«, sagte er mit gepreßter Stimme. »Sallys Steinbruch.«

»Droben am Hügel war ein riesiger Baumstumpf, der mir schon lange ein Dorn im Auge war«, sagte Philip. »Wir hatten ihn an jenem Vormittag endlich entwurzelt. Als wir gegen Mittag zurückkehrten, stand mein Bruder Francis mit einem Säugling in den Armen dort am Ziegenpferch. Das warst du. Du warst gerade einen Tag alt.«

Jonathans Miene war ernst. Es war ein feierlicher Augenblick für ihn.

Philip inspizierte das kleine Filialkloster St.-John-in-the-Forrest. Vom Wald war nicht mehr allzuviel zu sehen: Über die Jahre waren große Flächen Landes von den Mönchen gerodet und urbar gemacht worden. Auch das Kloster selbst hatte sich verändert: Es gab erheblich mehr Steinhäuser als ehedem – ein Kapitelhaus, ein Refektorium und ein Dormitorium – sowie eine Ansammlung von Scheunen, Hütten und Melkschuppen aus Holz. Für jemanden, der den Ort vor siebzehn Jahren zum letztenmal gesehen hatte, war er kaum wiederzuerkennen. Auch die Bewohner waren nicht mehr dieselben. Einige der jungen Mönche von damals bekleideten inzwischen verantwortliche Positionen in Kingsbridge. William Beauvis – der weiland für einigen Wirbel gesorgt hatte, weil er während des Gottesdienstes dem Novizenmeister heißes Kerzenwachs auf die Glatze schnippte – war mittlerweile Prior. Andere Mitbrüder Philips aus der damaligen Zeit hatten die Priorei inzwischen verlassen: So war zum Beispiel der Unruhestifter Peter von Wareham nach Canterbury gegangen und arbeitete dort für einen ehrgeizigen jungen Erzdiakon namens Thomas Becket.

»Ich frage mich, was für Menschen sie waren«, sagte Jonathan. »Meine Eltern, meine ich.«

Philip verstand seine Not, schließlich hatte er selbst seine Eltern früh verloren. Aber er war eben doch schon sechs Jahre alt gewesen, als es geschah, und konnte sich noch recht gut an sie erinnern – an die sanfte, liebevolle Mutter und den hochgewachsenen Mann mit dem schwarzen Bart, der sein Vater gewesen war. Jonathan hatte nicht einmal diesen Trost: Alles, was er über seinen Eltern wußte, war, daß sie ihn nicht gewollt hatten.

»Es gibt durchaus einiges über sie zu sagen«, meinte Philip, »wenngleich wir natürlich auf Vermutungen angewiesen sind.«

»Tatsächlich?« Jonathan war ganz Ohr. »Was denn?«

»Sie waren arm«, sagte Philip. »Reiche Leute haben keine Veranlassung dazu, ihre Kinder auszusetzen. Sie hatten keine Freunde: Freunden kann man eine Schwangerschaft nicht verheimlichen. Sie waren verzweifelt: Nur verzweifelte Menschen ertragen den Verlust eines Kindes.«

Jonathans Gesicht wirkte verspannt; er hielt die Tränen gewaltsam zurück. Philip hätte gerne für ihn geweint – für diesen Jungen, von dem alle Welt sagte, er sei ihm in vieler Hinsicht sehr ähnlich. Und nichts hätte Philip lieber getan, als Jonathan ein paar warme, tröstliche Worte über seine Eltern zu sagen. Aber wie hätte er vorgeben können, daß sie ihr Kind geliebt hatten – schließlich war er von ihnen ausgesetzt und dem fast sicheren Tod preisgegeben worden.

»Warum läßt Gott solche Dinge zu?« fragte Jonathan.

Philip sah eine Chance und nahm sie sofort wahr. »Das ist eine Frage, die schon so manch einen in tiefe Verwirrung gestürzt hat«, sagte er. »In deinem Fall ist die Antwort aber, wie ich glaube, eindeutig: Gott wollte dich für sich selbst.«

»Ist das Euer Ernst?«

»Habe ich dir das noch nie gesagt? Es war von Anfang an meine feste Überzeugung. Schon am Tag, als du gefunden wurdest, sagte ich den Mönchen hier, Gott habe uns dich geschickt, weil er etwas ganz Bestimmtes mit dir vorhat. Es sei unsere Pflicht, sagte ich damals, dich im Dienste Gottes aufzuziehen, damit du eines Tages imstande seist, die Aufgabe, für die er dich ausgesucht hat, zu erfüllen.«

»Ob meine Mutter das weiß?«

»Wenn sie jetzt bei den Engeln ist, dann weiß sie es.«

»Worin könnte, nach Eurer Meinung, meine Aufgabe liegen?«

»Gott braucht Mönche als Schriftsteller, Aufklärer, Musiker und Bauern. Er braucht Männer, die anspruchsvolle Positionen in Kloster und Kirche übernehmen – Cellerare, Prioren, Bischöfe. Er braucht Männer, die mit Wolle handeln, Kranke heilen, Schulkinder unterrichten und Kirchen bauen können.«

»Ich kann mir kaum vorstellen, daß er ausgerechnet mir eine besondere Aufgabe vorbehalten hat.«

»Warum sollte er sich sonst soviel Mühe gegeben haben mit dir?« fragte Philip und lächelte dabei. »Es ist natürlich denkbar, daß die Rolle, die er dir zugedacht hat, nach weltlichen Begriffen nicht besonders groß und auffällig ist. Durchaus möglich, daß er in dir einen eher stillen Mönch sieht, der sein Leben demütig dem Gebet und der Meditation weiht.«

Jonathan machte ein langes Gesicht. »Durchaus möglich, ja.«

Philip lachte. »Allerdings glaube ich das nicht. Aus Holz macht der Herr keine Messer, und aus Schuhleder keine Frauenhemden. Für ein Leben in Ruhe und Beschaulichkeit bist du nicht geschaffen. Gott weiß das. Ich vermute, er erwartet von dir, daß du für ihn kämpfst – nicht singst.«

»Das wünschte ich mir auch.«

»Hier und jetzt erwartet er von dir freilich, daß du Bruder Leo aufsuchst und ihn fragst, wie viele Laib Käse er für unseren Keller in Kingsbridge erübrigen kann.«

»Ja, richtig.«

»Ich verfüge mich ins Kapitelhaus, um mich mit meinem Bruder zu unterhalten. Und denk daran: wenn dich die Mitbrüder über Francis ausfragen wollen, sag ihnen so wenig wie möglich.«

»Ich werde gar nichts sagen ...«

»Gut – und nun fort mit dir!«

Mit schnellen Schritten überquerte Jonathan den Klosterhof. Die ernste und getragene Stimmung war längst wieder seiner üblichen guten Laune gewichen.

Philip sah ihm nach, bis er in der Käserei verschwunden war. Ich war genauso, dachte er – nur nicht ganz so gescheit. Er begab sich ins Kapitelhaus. Francis hatte ihn in einer Botschaft um ein diskretes Treffen in St.-John-in-the-Forest gebeten. Die Mönche in Kingsbridge glaubten, Philip sei unterwegs auf einer seiner normalen Inspektionsreisen. Hier, am Ort der Begegnung, ließ sich das Treffen natürlich nicht vor den Mönchen verheimlichen. Aber St.-John-in-the-Forest lag noch immer so einsam, daß die Mönche kaum je in Verlegenheit kamen, mit Außenstehenden zu reden. Nach Kingsbridge kam lediglich der Prior gelegentlich, und den hatte Philip auf Diskretion eingeschworen.

Die beiden Brüder waren im Laufe des Vormittags eingetroffen, und obwohl sie ihre Begegnung kaum als Zufall darstellen konnten, pflegten sie nach außen hin den Schein, als handele es sich um ein rein privates Treffen. Gemeinsam hatten sie das Hochamt besucht und mit den Mönchen gespeist. Erst jetzt ergab sich die Gelegenheit zu einem Gespräch unter vier Augen.

Francis erwartete ihn im Kapitelhaus. Er saß auf einer Steinbank vor der Wand. Da Philip fast nie seine eigenes Konterfei sah – in Klöstern gab es keine Spiegel –, schloß er aus den Zügen seines nur um zwei Jahre jüngeren Bruders auf Spuren des Alters in seinem eigenen Gesicht. Francis war jetzt zweiundvierzig. Sein schwarzes Haar war mit einzelnen Silberstrahlen durchzogen, und um seine strahlend blauen Augen zeigten sich Krähenfüßchen. Er hatte seit ihrer letzten Begegnung erheblich zugenommen, vor allem an Bauch und Hals. Ich habe wahrscheinlich mehr graue Haare als er und weniger überflüssige Pfunde, dachte Philip bei sich. Aber wer von uns hat mehr Sorgenfalten?

Er setzte sich zu Francis auf die Bank und blickte versonnen in den achteckigen, leeren Versammlungssaal. »Nun, wie steht's?« fragte Francis.

»Die Wilden haben wieder Oberwasser«, sagte Philip. »Der Priorei geht langsam, aber sicher das Geld aus. Wir haben die Bauarbeiten an der Kathedrale nahezu einstellen müssen. Kingsbridge verfällt, die halbe Grafschaft leidet Hunger, und Reisen wird immer gefährlicher.«

Francis nickte. »Überall in England das gleiche!«

»Mag sein, daß die Wilden ewig das Sagen haben werden«, fuhr Philip trübsinnig fort. »Mag sein, daß in den Räten der Mächtigen die Habgier stets die Weisheit und im Kopf eines Schwertträgers die Furcht stets das Mitleid besiegt.«

»So pessimistisch kenn' ich dich gar nicht.«

»Vor ein paar Wochen wurden wir von einer Horde Outlaws überfallen. Es war erbärmlich! Kaum hatten die Bewohner der Stadt ein paar von den Angreifern getötet, da fielen die Outlaws auch schon übereinander her. Als sie kurz darauf den Rückzug antraten, setzten die jungen Männer aus der Stadt ihnen nach und metzelten jede dieser armseligen Kreaturen nieder, derer sie habhaft werden konnten. Es war widerlich.«

Francis schüttelte den Kopf. »Man begreift es nicht«, sagte er.

»Ich glaub' schon, daß ich es begreife. Die Outlaws hatten ihnen zuvor furchtbare Angst eingejagt. Diese Angst saß so tief, daß sie sie exorzieren mußten – mit dem Blut derer, die sie so erschreckt hatten. Ich sah das damals in den Blicken der Männer, die unsere Eltern töteten. Sie töteten aus Angst. Aber wie kann man sie von dieser Angst befreien?«

Francis seufzte. »Frieden, Gerechtigkeit, Wohlstand ... alles Dinge, die nur sehr schwer durchzusetzen sind.«

Philip nickte. »Richtig. Aber kommen wir zur Sache. Was kann ich für dich tun?«

»Ich arbeite für den Sohn der Kaiserin Mathilde«, sagte Francis. »Er heißt Henry.«

Philip hatte schon von diesem Henry gehört. »Was ist das für ein Mensch?«

»Ein sehr kluger und entschlossener junger Mann. Seit dem Tod seines Vaters führt er den Titel des Grafen von Anjou. Als ältester Enkel des alten Henry, der König von England und Herzog der Normandie war, ist er ebenfalls Herzog der Normandie. Und als Ehemann der Eleonore von Aquitanien ist er nun auch noch Herzog von Aquitanien.«

»Er gebietet über ein größeres Territorium als der König von Frankreich.«

»Genau.«

»Aber was ist er für ein *Mensch*?«

»Er hat eine gute Erziehung genossen, arbeitet sehr hart, zögert nicht lange, ist immer unterwegs und furchtbar aufbrausend.«

»Ich wäre manchmal auch ganz gerne etwas aufbrausend«, sagte Philip. »Manche Leute brauchen das, um nicht über die Stränge zu schlagen. Da alle wissen, daß ich stets ruhig bleibe, gehorcht man mir nicht so flink wie einem Prior, bei dem man jeden Augenblick damit rechnen muß, daß er in die Luft geht.«

»Bleib du nur so, wie du bist«, sagte Francis. Er lachte kurz auf, wurde aber gleich wieder ernst. »Erst dank Henry weiß ich, wie sehr es bei einem König auf die Persönlichkeit ankommt. Schau dir Stephan doch an: Sein Urteilsvermögen ist schlecht. Immer wieder zeigt er Anfälle von Entschlossenheit, nur im kurz darauf wieder aufzugeben. Sein Mut grenzt mitunter an Dummheit, und immer wieder verzeiht er seinen Feinden. Verräter riskieren bei ihm herzlich wenig, sie können sich auf seine Großmut verlassen. Es ist daher nur folgerichtig, daß er sich seit achtzehn Jahren erfolglos bemüht, ein Land zu regieren, das zur Zeit seiner Thronbesteigung ein vereinigtes Königreich war. Henry hat seine Sammlung bis vor kurzem noch unabhängiger Herzogtümer und Grafschaften schon heute besser unter Kontrolle als Stephan jemals in England.«

»Warum hat Henry dich nach England geschickt?« fragte Philip. Ihm war auf einmal ein Verdacht gekommen.

»Ich soll die Lage im Lande studieren.«

»Und was hast du für einen Eindruck?«

»Es ist ein Land der Hungernden und Gesetzlosen, sturmgepeitscht und vom Krieg verwüstet.«

Philip nickte nachdenklich. Der junge Henry war Herzog der Normandie, weil er der älteste Sohn Mathildes war. Mathilde war die einzige legitime Tochter des alten Henry, der sowohl Herzog der Normandie als auch König von England war.

Diese Abstammung rechtfertigte auch einen Anspruch auf den englischen Thron.

Schon seine Mutter hatte den Anspruch erhoben, doch da sie eine Frau war und ihr Mann aus dem Hause Anjou stammte, hatte man ihr den Thron verwehrt. Der junge Henry war nicht nur ein Mann, sondern konnte sich auch zugute halten, daß in seinen Adern sowohl normannisches als auch angevinisches Blut floß.

»Will Henry versuchen, den Thron von England zu erobern?« fragte Philip.

»Das hängt von meinem Bericht ab«, erwiderte Francis.

»Und was wirst du ihm sagen?«

»Daß die Zeit nie wieder so günstig sein wird wie jetzt.«

»Der Herr sei gepriesen«, sagte Philip.

Unterwegs zur Burg von Bischof Waleran machte Graf William Station an der Mühle von Cowford, die zu seinem Besitz gehörte. Der Müller, ein mürrischer Mann in mittleren Jahren, der auf den Namen Wulfric hörte, verfügte über das Privileg, das Getreide aus elf umliegenden Dörfern mahlen zu dürfen. Zwei von zwanzig Säcken behielt er als Gebühr – einen für sich und einen für William.

William suchte die Mühle auf, um den ihm zustehenden Anteil einzutreiben. Normalerweile kümmerte er sich nicht persönlich um solche Dinge, aber was war in diesen Zeiten schon normal? Man konnte ja kein Fuhrwerk mit Mehl oder anderen Lebensmitteln ohne bewaffneten Begleitschutz lassen! William hatte sich angewöhnt, bei jedem größeren Ausritt mit einer Entourage einen oder zwei Karren mitzuführen, um überall, wo er hinkam, einzusammeln, was einzusammeln war.

Die Outlaws waren zu einer Landplage geworden – eine unangenehme Begleiterscheinung seiner harten Linie gegen seine Pächter. Viele, die kein Land mehr hatten, wurden zu Dieben. Im allgemeinen waren sie freilich als Diebe genauso erfolglos wie als Bauern, und so hatte William darauf spekuliert, daß während des Winters die meisten von ihnen verrecken würden. Anfangs schien seine Rechnung auch aufzugehen, hielten sich doch die Wegelagerer hauptsächlich an einsame Wanderer, bei denen es kaum etwas zu stehlen gab, oder aber sie attackierten planlos Ziele, die gut verteidigt wurden. In jüngster Zeit hatten sie allerdings ihre Taktik verbessert. Sie griffen nur noch an, wenn sie zahlenmäßig mindestens doppelt so stark waren wie die Verteidiger. Sie kamen nur, wenn die Scheuern voll waren – was bedeutete, daß sie ihre Ziele vorher sorgfältig ausspähten. Sie schlugen unerwartet und schnell zu und waren getrieben vom Mut der Verzweiflung. Auf lange Kämpfe ließen sie sich nicht ein: Sie packten sich ein Schaf, einen Schinken, einen Käse, einen Sack Mehl oder eine Geldkatze und machten, daß sie davonkamen. Sie zu verfolgen, war sinnlos: Sie verschwanden sofort im Wald und zerstreuten sich in alle Richtungen. Irgend jemand mußte sich zu ihrem Anführer aufgeschwungen haben, und dieser Jemand führte sie genauso, wie William sie an seiner Statt geführt hätte.

Der Erfolg der Outlaws demütigte William. Sie degradierten ihn zum Hanswurst, der unfähig war, in seiner eigenen Grafschaft für Ordnung zu sorgen. Am schlimmsten war, daß die Kerle fast nur ihn selbst bestahlen. Es sah so aus, als hätten sie es ausdrücklich darauf angelegt, ihn herauszufordern. Nichts war William verhaßter als das

Gefühl, daß die Leute sich hinter vorgehaltener Hand über ihn lustig machten. Sein Leben lang hatte er den Menschen Respekt gegenüber ihm und seiner Familie eingebleut – und nun kam dieser Banditenhaufen und machte alles wieder zunichte.

Was William besonders bitter aufstieß, war, daß die Leute hinter seinem Rücken flüsterten, es geschehe ihm nur recht. Er sei mit äußerster Rücksichtslosigkeit gegen seine Pächter vorgegangen, und nun rächten sie sich dafür. Er müsse nun eben die Suppe auslöffeln, die er sich eingebrockt habe. Jedesmal, wenn William derartiges Gerede zu Ohren kam, fuhr er vor Wut fast aus der Haut.

Bestürzt und angstvoll beobachteten die Bewohner von Cowford die Ankunft Williams und seiner Ritter in ihrem Dorf. William bedachte die dünnen, verschüchterten Gesichter, die hie und da in den Hauseingängen zu sehen waren und rasch wieder verschwanden, mit finsteren Blicken. Es war noch gar nicht lange her, da hatten diese Leute ihren Priester zu ihm geschickt und ihn die Bitte vortragen lassen, in diesem Jahr ihr Getreide selbst mahlen zu dürfen, weil sie sich den Zehnten für den Müller nicht leisten konnten. William war versucht gewesen, dem unverschämten Pfaffen die Zunge herauszureißen.

Es war kalt, und ein Ring aus Eis säumte das Wasser im Mühlteich. Das Wasserrad stand still, der Mühlstein schwieg. Aus dem Haus neben der Mühle trat eine Frau. Begehren durchzuckte William, als er sie ansah. Die Frau war ungefähr zwanzig Jahre alt, hatte ein hübsches Gesicht und einen dunklen Lockenschopf. Trotz der Hungersnot waren ihre Brüste groß und ihre Schenkel kräftig. Beim Anblick Williams und seiner Ritter verflog der muntere Ausdruck in ihrer Miene. Sie zuckte zusammen, drehte sich um und verschwand wieder im Haus.

»Sie mag uns nicht«, sagte Walter. »Das heißt, sie hat Gervase gesehen.« Es war ein uralter Witz, aber sie lachten immer wieder darüber.

Sie saßen ab und banden die Pferde an. Seit Beginn des Bürgerkriegs hatte sich die Zusammensetzung von Williams Gefolge leicht verändert. Außer Walter waren Ugly Gervase und Hugh Axe von Anfang an dabei. Gilbert war in dem unerwartet blutigen Kampf gegen die Steinbrucharbeiter gefallen und durch Guillaume ersetzt worden. Miles hatte in einer Schenke in Norwich einen Arm verloren, als es überm Würfelspiel zu einem Schwertgefecht gekommen war. Für ihn hatten sie Louis aufgenommen. Sie waren alle dem Knabenalter längst entwachsen, redeten und handelten aber wie eh und je, lachten und soffen, spielten und hurten. Wie viele Schenken sie zertrümmert hatten, wie viele Juden gequält und wie viele Mädchen entjungfert, konnte William längst nicht mehr sagen.

Der Müller kam aus dem Haus. Seine Verdrießlichkeit war zweifelsohne unmittelbare Folge der ewigen Unbeliebtheit aller Müller, doch diesmal war die Angst noch größer als sein Mißmut. Recht so, dachte William. Ihm gefiel es, wenn die Leute bei seinem Erscheinen Angst hatten.

»Ich wußte gar nicht, daß du eine Tochter hast, Wulfric«, sagte er lüstern. »Du hast sie vor mir versteckt.«

»Maggie ist mein Weib«, erwiderte der Müller.

»Quatsch. Dein Weib ist eine angemalte alte Vettel, ich kenne sie doch.«

»Meine May ist im vergangenen Jahr gestorben, Herr. Ich habe mich neu verheiratet.«

»Du schmutziger alter Sack!« sagte William und grinste. »Die da drinnen ist doch mindestens dreißig Jahre jünger als du!«

»Fünfundzwanzig ...«

»Genug davon. Wo ist mein Mehl? Jeder zwanzigste Sack ist meiner!«

»Es steht alles bereit, Herr. Wollt Ihr bitte näher treten ...«

Der Weg zur Mühle führte durch das Haus. William und seine Männer folgten Wulfric in die Wohnstube, den einzigen Raum. Die junge Müllerin kniete vor dem Kamin und legte Holz nach. Die Tunika spannte sich über ihrem Rücken. Müllersfrauen waren immer unter den letzten, die eine Hungersnot zu spüren bekamen.

William blieb stehen und stierte auf ihren Hintern. Die Ritter grinsten, und der Müller zappelte unruhig hin und her. Da drehte Maggie sich um und bemerkte, daß alle sie anstarrten. Vollkommen verwirrt stand sie auf.

William blinzelte ihr zu und sagte: »Auf, Maggie, bring uns Bier. Wir sind durstige Männer.«

Durch einen kleinen Gang gelangten sie in die Mühle. Die Mehlsäcke waren vor dem kreisförmigen Dreschboden gestapelt. Viele waren es nicht. In guten Jahren stapelten sie sich übermannshoch. »Ist das alles?« fragte William.

»Die Ernte war so schlecht, Herr«, stammelte Wulfric.

»Wo sind meine?«

»Hier, Herr.« Er deutete auf einen Stapel von acht oder neun Säcken.

»Was?« brüllte William, und die Zornesröte stieg ihm ins Gesicht. »Das bißchen? Draußen stehen zwei Fuhrwerke, und du bietest mir *das*?«

Wulfric machte ein Gesicht wie ein geprügelter Hund. »Es tut mir leid, Herr.«

William zählte. »Das sind ja nur neun Säcke?«

»Mehr habe ich nicht für Euch, Herr.« Der Müller war den Tränen nahe. »Seht doch meinen Stapel daneben – das sind auch nicht mehr.«

»Du verlogener Hund!« schrie William. »Den Rest hast du unter der Hand verkauft!«

»Nein, Herr«, beteuerte Wulfric. »Es hat nie mehr gegeben.«

In diesem Augenblick betrat Maggie die Mühle. Sie trug ein Tablett, auf dem sechs mit Bier gefüllte Tonkrüge standen, und ging von einem Ritter zum anderen. Die Männer trankten gierig. William schenkte ihr keine Beachtung. Ihm war vor lauter Wut der Durst vergangen. Maggie blieb stehen und wartete, in der Hand das Tablett mit dem einsamen Krug.

»Was ist das da drüben?« fragte William den Müller und deutete auf einen Stapel von fünfundzwanzig oder dreißig Säcken, die vor der Wand aufgeschichtet war.

»Die warten auf ihre Abholung, Herr. Ihr seht ja das Zeichen der Eigentümer auf den Säcken ...«

Es stimmte: Jeder Sack trug eine Markierung, einen Buchstaben oder ein Symbol. Es konnte sich natürlich um einen Trick handeln, aber William war außerstande, das herauszufinden. Es war zum Verrücktwerden ... Aber er war nicht bereit, klein beizugeben. »Ich glaub' dir nicht«, sagte er zu dem Müller. »Du hast mich bestohlen.«

Wulfric antwortete mit respektvoller Beharrlichkeit, obgleich seine Stimme zitterte: »Ich bin ein ehrlicher Mann, Herr.«

»Ein ehrlicher Müller muß erst noch geboren werden.«

»Herr ...« Wulfric schluckte. »Herr, ich habe Euch nie auch nur ein Weizenkorn gestohlen«. Trotz der kalten Witterung lief ihm der Schweiß übers Gesicht. Er wischte sich mit dem Ärmel über die Stirn. »Ich bin bereit, bei Jesus und allen Heiligen zu schwören, daß ...«

»Halt's Maul!«

Williams Wut steigerte sich langsam zur Raserei, aber er wußte immer noch nicht, was tun. Er wollte Wulfric weh tun, richtig weh tun, und dachte schon daran, ihn von Walter mit den Kettenpanzerhandschuhen zusammenschlagen zu lassen ... Doch dann fiel sein Auge auf Maggie, die noch immer mit dem Tablett in der Hand dastand, das hübsche Gesicht vor Angst verzerrt. Jetzt wußte er die passende Strafe für Wulfric. »Pack dir das Weib!« raunte er Walter zu. Dann sagte er zu dem Müller: »Ich werde dir jetzt eine Lektion erteilen, Mehlsack.«

Maggie merkte zwar noch, daß Walter auf sie zukam, zur Flucht war es jedoch zu spät. Unwillkürlich drehte sie sich noch um. Im gleichen Moment packte Walter sie am Arm und riß sie zurück. Krachend fiel das Tablett zu Boden, und das Bier ergoß sich über die Dielen. Walter drehte ihr den Arm auf den Rücken und hielt sie fest. Maggie zitterte vor Angst.

»Laßt sie, ich bitte Euch!« flehte Wulfric.

William nickte zufrieden. Gleich wirst zu erleben, wie dein junges Weib ein paarmal hintereinander vergewaltigt wird, sagte er in Gedanken zu Wulfric. Das nächste Mal steht dann genug Mehl für deinen Herrn bereit … Laut sagte er: »Dein Weib wird fett und träge, Wulfric. Sie frißt zuviel Brot aus gestohlenem Mehl, während alle Welt den Gürtel enger schnallen muß. Wollen wir mal sehen, wie fett sie schon ist, wie?« Er nickte Walter zu.

Mit einer kräftigen Handbewegung riß Walter Maggies Tunika von oben bis unten entzwei, so daß sie auf den Boden fiel. Darunter trug Maggie ein knielanges Leinenunterhemd. Sie keuchte vor Furcht, und ihre großen Brüste hoben und senkten sich. William stand vor ihr. Walter verdrehte den Arm noch stärker, so daß Maggie vor Schmerzen ein Hohlkreuz machte und dadurch unwillkürlich William ihren Busen entgegenreckte. Nach einem Seitenblick auf Wulfric griff William mit beiden Händen zu und knetete ihre Brüste.

Wulfric machte einen Schritt vorwärts. »Du Teufel …«, sagte er.

»Halt ihn fest«, fauchte William. Louis war sofort zur Stelle und packte den Müller an beiden Armen, so daß er sich nicht mehr rühren konnte.

William riß der jungen Frau das Unterhemd vom Leibe.

Als er ihren üppigen weißen Körper sah, wurde ihm der Mund trocken.

»Nein, ich bitte Euch …«, sagte Wulfric.

Williams Begehren wuchs. »Runter mit ihr!« sagte er.

Maggie fing an zu schreien.

William schnallte sich den Schwertgurt ab und ließ ihn zu Boden fallen, während die Ritter Maggie an Armen und Beinen packten. Obwohl sie gegen vier starke Männer keine Chance hatte, wehrte sie sich nach Kräften. Sie wand sich hin und her und schrie aus vollem

Hals. William hatte seinen Spaß daran. Ihre Brüste zitterten, die Schenkel öffneten und schlossen sich und zeigten ihr Geschlecht.

Die vier Ritter zwangen sie auf den Dreschboden.

William kniete zwischen ihren Beinen und hob den Rock seiner Tunika. Wieder sah er sich nach ihrem Mann um. Wulfric starrte ihn an und war ganz außer sich. Er brabbelte um Gnade, doch Maggie schrie so laut, daß man ihn nicht hörte. Die Situation war so recht nach Williams Geschmack, und er kostete sie weidlich aus: die entsetzte Frau, die Ritter, die sie festhielten, der Ehemann als Zuschauer...

Da wurde der starre Blick des Müllers auf einmal unstet und schweifte ab.

William spürte die Gefahr. Alle Anwesenden starrten ihn und das Mädchen an. Wenn Wulfrics Aufmerksamkeit jetzt noch abgelenkt werden konnte, dann nur noch durch eines: die Aussicht auf Rettung. William drehte sich um und blickte zum Eingang. Im gleichen Moment traf ihn etwas Schweres und Hartes am Kopf.

Er brüllte auf vor Schmerz und brach über der Müllerin zusammen, sein Gesicht krachte gegen das ihre. Dann hörte er plötzlich zahlreiche Männerstimmen und bekam am äußersten Rand seines Blickfelds mit, daß auch Walter zu Boden ging, offenbar ebenfalls von einem Keulenschlag getroffen. Die Ritter gaben Maggie frei; in ihrer Miene spiegelten sich Schrecken und Erleichterung. Sie wand sich unter Williams Körper hervor. Er ließ sie laufen und rollte sich schnell zur Seite.

Dann war urplötzlich ein wild aussehender Mann mit einer Holzfälleraxt über ihm. Um Gottes willen, wer ist denn das? dachte er. Der Vater des Mädchens? Er sah, wie Guillaume aufstand und sich umdrehte. Im nächsten Augenblick fuhr die Axt in Guillaumes ungeschützten Nacken. Die scharfe Klinge drang tief ins Fleisch. Guillaume brach tot zusammen und fiel auf William, dessen Tunika von oben bis unten mit Blut bespritzt wurde.

William schob die Leiche von seinem Körper. Als er wieder imstande war, sich umzusehen, erkannte er, daß die Mühle von einer Bande wilder und ungewaschener Männer mit struppigem Haar und abgerissenen Kleidern überfallen worden war. Sie waren mit Keulen und Äxten bewaffnet und schienen überall zu sein. William erkannte den Ernst der Lage. Hatten sich die Dorfbewohner zusammengerottet, um die Müllerin zu befreien? Was fiel diesen Kerlen ein? Noch ehe der Tag sich neigte, würden die Rädelsführer an den Bäumen hängen! Wutentbrannt rappelte er sich auf und griff nach seinem Schwert.

Es war nicht da. Er hatte den Gurt abgenommen, um die junge Frau zu vergewaltigen.

Hugh Axe, Ugly Gervase und Louis waren in einen erbitterten Kampf verwickelt. Ihre Gegner waren weit in der Überzahl – eine tobende Horde außer Rand und Band geratener Bettler. Zwar lagen ein paar tote Bauern auf dem Boden herum, doch wurden die Ritter zusehends in die Enge getrieben. Der kreischenden nackten Maggie war es noch nicht gelungen, sich an dem Gedränge vor der Tür vorbeizuzwängen. Der Anblick ihrer fülligen weißen Hinterbacken erweckte in William, dem herrschenden Chaos zum Trotz, durch Bedauern getrübte Begierde. Doch da sah er plötzlich, daß auch Wulfric gegen einen der Angreifer kämpfte. Wieso schlug sich der Müller mit einem Mann, der seiner Frau zur Hilfe gekommen war? Was, zur Hölle, ging hier vor?

Aufgeregt suchte William nach seinem Schwertgurt und fand ihn, fast unmittelbar vor seinen Füßen, auf dem Boden liegend. Er hob ihn auf und zog die Waffe aus der Scheide. Dann sprang er zwei, drei Schritte zurück, um sich noch ein paar Augenblicke aus dem Getümmel herauszuhalten. Dabei fiel ihm auf, daß die meisten Angreifer gar nicht kämpften, sondern sich die aufgestapelten Mehlsäcke schnappten und mit ihnen davonliefen. Jetzt fiel es William wie Schuppen von den Augen: Das war *keine* Befreiungsaktion zorniger Dörfler, sondern eine Attacke von außen. Die Angreifer waren an Maggie überhaupt nicht interessiert, ja sie hatten anfangs gar nicht gewußt, daß William und seine Ritter in der Mühle waren, geschweige denn, was sie dort trieben. Sie wollten die Mühle überfallen und Williams Mehl stehlen – sonst gar nichts.

Es waren Outlaws.

Die heiße Wut überkam ihn. Endlich, dachte er. Endlich eine Gelegenheit zurückzuschlagen und mit dieser tollwütigen Bande abzurechnen, die meine Grafschaft terrorisiert und meine Scheuern ausraubt …

Die Angreifer – es waren ungefähr zwanzig – waren seinen Rittern zahlenmäßig weit überlegen, und William staunte über ihren Mut. Gemeinhin stoben die Bauern vor einem Rittertrupp wie ein aufgeregter Hühnerhaufen davon – ganz egal, ob sie zweifach oder zehnfach in der Überzahl waren. Diese Kerle hier schlugen sich wacker, und wenn einer aus ihren Reihen fiel, ließen sie sich dadurch nicht entmutigen. Sie waren offenbar zu allem bereit – notfalls auch zum Sterben. Aber was blieb ihnen auch anderes übrig? Ohne das Mehl drohte ihnen der Hungertod.

Louis focht gegen zwei Mann gleichzeitig, als ein dritter kam und ihm mit einem eisernen Zimmermannshammer auf den Hinterkopf schlug. Louis fiel um und stand nicht mehr auf. Der Mann warf den Hammer fort und ergriff Louis' Schwert. Jetzt kämpften zwanzig Outlaws gegen zwei Ritter. Allerdings hatte Walter sich inzwischen von dem Keulenhieb erholt. Er zog sein Schwert und griff in die Schlacht ein. Und dann hob auch William seine Waffe und stürzte sich ins Getümmel.

Zu viert ging es erheblich besser, sie waren ein kampferprobter Trupp. Die Outlaws versuchten verzweifelt, die blitzenden Schwerter mit ihren Keulen und Äxten abzuwehren, konnten aber nicht verhindern, daß sie in die Defensive gerieten. William dachte schon, ihr Kampfesmut wolle sie verlassen und es könne gelingen, sie in die Flucht zu schlagen, da rief auf einmal jemand: »Der rechtmäßige Graf!«

Es war wie ein Schlachtruf. Andere nahmen den Ruf auf, und unvermittelt verstärkte sich der Widerstand der Outlaws wieder. Und immer wieder ertönte der Schrei: »Der rechtmäßige Graf! Der rechtmäßige Graf!«

William, obwohl er um sein Leben kämpfte, wurde eiskalt ums Herz. Wer immer diese Banditenarmee befehligte, hatte es auf den Grafentitel abgesehen. Diese erschreckende Erkenntnis trieb auch William zu größeren Anstrengungen: Er kämpfte, als stünde in diesem Scharmützel seine eigene Zukunft auf dem Spiel.

Nur etwa die Hälfte der Angreifer beteiligte sich am Kampf – die anderen stahlen Mehlsäcke. Das Gefecht wogte hin und her – Angriff, Parade, Hieb und Stich, geschicktes Ausweichen. Wie Soldaten, denen bekannt ist, daß bald zum Rückzug geblasen wird, hatten sich die Outlaws auf eine vorsichtige, defensive Taktik verlegt.

Hinter dem Rücken ihrer kämpfenden Spießgesellen schleppten die Diebe gerade die letzten Mehlsäcke aus der Mühle. Die zurückweichenden Outlaws waren inzwischen in den schmalen Gang zwischen dem Dreschboden und dem Wohnhaus abgedrängt worden. William wußte, was ihm bevorstand: Binnen kürzester Zeit würde sich in der Grafschaft herumsprechen, daß ihm sein Mehl gleichsam vor der Nase weggeschnappt worden war. Die Leute würden sich ausschütten vor Lachen – und er wäre der Dumme. Der Gedanke brachte ihn derart in Rage, daß er seinen augenblicklichen Gegner mit einer Überraschungsattacke ausmanövrierte und mit einem klassischen Stich ins Herz tötete.

Hugh Axe erging es schlimmer. Dem Mann, der jetzt mit Louis' Schwert kämpfte, gelang ein glücklicher Stoß, der Hugs rechte Schulter durchbohrte und den Ritter außer Gefecht setzte. Zwei Outlaws im Gang hielten jetzt die drei noch kampffähigen Ritter in Schach. Dies allein war demütigend genug – doch dann geschah das Unglaubliche: Mit kaum zu überbietendem Hochmut gab der eine der beiden Angreifer seinem Kumpan zu verstehen, er möge sich davonmachen. Der Betroffene ließ sich das nicht zweimal sagen und verschwand, während der erste einen Schritt zurückwich und damit in die Wohnstube des Müllers trat.

Der Gang war so eng, daß nur jeweils ein Ritter in vorderster Front stehen und gegen den Outlaw kämpfen konnte. William drängte sich vor: Diesen Mann wollte er selbst erledigen. Als die Klingen ihrer Schwerter aufeinanderprallten, erkannte er sofort, daß sein Gegenüber kein enteigneter Bauer war. Es war ein kampfgestählter Krieger wie er selbst. Zum erstenmal sah William dem Mann ins Gesicht – und erschrak dermaßen, daß ihm um ein Haar das Schwert aus der Hand gefallen wäre.

Sein Gegner war Richard von Kingsbridge.

Richards Gesicht glühte vor Haß. William sah die Narbe an dem verstümmelten Ohr. Die Inbrunst von Richards Erbitterung machte ihm mehr angst als das blitzende Schwert seines Feindes. Er hatte geglaubt, ihn längst und unwiderruflich besiegt zu haben – aber auf einmal war Richard wieder da, an der Spitze einer Lumpenbande, der es gelungen war, William aufs Übelste zum Narren zu halten.

Richard nutzte den Schock des Erkennens aus und attackierte William schwer. William konnte dem Stoß jedoch ausweichen. Er hob sein Schwert, parierte einen Hieb und trat einen Schritt zurück. Richard drängte nach, doch William war durch den engen Gang jetzt besser geschützt und nur noch durch Schwertstöße, nicht aber mehr durch Hiebe zu erwischen. Trotzdem gelang es Richard, William immer weiter zurückzutreiben, bis hinaus auf den Dreschboden der Mühle. Dort aber wendete sich das Blatt, denn nun konnten auch Walter und Gervase ins Kampfgeschehen eingreifen. Richard blieb angesichts der Übermacht nichts anderes übrig, als sich wieder zurückzuziehen. Kaum war er wieder im Gang, blieben die Ritter zurück, und es entspann sich erneut ein Duell zwischen ihm und William.

William erkannte, daß Richard sich in einer kniffligen Lage befand: Sobald er Boden gewann, mußte er gegen drei Gegner kämpfen. Er, William, konnte das Feld Walter überlassen, wenn er ermüdete –

Richard hatte niemanden, der ihn entlastete; irgendwann mußten ihn im Kampf gegen drei Gegner die Kräfte verlassen. Er stand im Grunde auf verlorenem Posten. Vielleicht, dachte William, ist heute nicht der Tag meiner größten Erniedrigung, sondern der Tag, an dem ich meinem ältesten und ärgsten Feind endlich den Todesstoß gebe ...

Richards Überlegungen mußten sich in derselben Richtung bewegt haben, und möglicherweise war er sogar zu demselben Schluß gekommen. Von einem Nachlassen seiner Kräfte oder seiner Entschlossenheit konnte bisher allerdings keine Rede sein – im Gegenteil. Unvermittelt machte er einen Satz nach vorn und stieß das Schwert vor. William konnte dem Stoß ausweichen, geriet dabei aber ins Stolpern. Mit einem Hechtsprung warf sich Walter dazwischen, um den Todesstoß gegen seinen Herrn zu verhindern. Richard verzichtete jetzt auf ein Nachsetzen. Er machte auf dem Absatz kehrt und flüchtete.

William erhob sich und stieß mit Walter zusammen, während Gervase sich an ihnen vorbeizuzwängen versuchte. Die drei brauchten ein paar Augenblicke, um wieder zu sich zu kommen. Richard nutzte die Verwirrung. Im Nu hatte er die kleine Wohnstube durchquert und die Tür hinter sich zugeschlagen. William rannte ihm hinterher und riß die Tür wieder auf – um mit ansehen zu müssen, wie die letzten Outlaws – welch eine furchtbare Demütigung! – auf den Pferden seiner Ritter davonsprengten. Und im Sattel seines eigenen Pferdes, eines prächtigen Schlachtrosses, das ihn ein Vermögen gekostet hatte, saß Richard. Das Pferd war offensichtlich bereits losgebunden und für den Dieb bereitgehalten worden. Während William die furchtbare Erkenntnis durchfuhr, daß Richard ihm bereits zum zweitenmal sein Schlachtroß stahl, trat der ungewohnte Reiter dem Tier in die Flanken. Das Roß bäumte sich auf; es mochte keine Fremden, aber Richard war recht gewandt im Sattel und ließ sich nicht abwerfen. Es gelang ihm, den Kopf des Pferdes herunterzureißen. William sah noch eine kleine Chance: Er stürmte los und versuchte, Richard mit dem Schwert zu erwischen. In diesem Moment bockte das Pferd, der Stoß verfehlte sein Ziel, und die Schwertspitze fuhr in den hölzernen Sattelrahmen. Dann galoppierte das Roß über die Dorfstraße davon – den anderen fliehenden Outlaws hinterher.

William sah ihnen nach und wünschte sie alle zum Henker.

Der rechtmäßige Graf, dachte er. Der rechtmäßige Graf.

Er drehte sich um. Hinter ihm standen Walter und Gervase. Hugh und Louis waren verwundet – er wußte nicht, wie arg. Und Guillaume war tot. Sein Blut verschmierte die gesamte Vorderseite von Williams

Tunika. Die Erniedrigung war total. William wagte es kaum noch, den Kopf zu heben.

Glücklicherweise war die Dorfbevölkerung aus Furcht vor Williams Zorn geflohen. Natürlich hatten sich auch der Müller und seine Frau aus dem Staub gemacht. Die Outlaws hatten sämtliche Pferde mitgenommen und ihnen nur die beiden Ochsengespanne gelassen.

William sah Walter an. »Hast ihn erkannt, den letzten, wie?«

»Ja.«

Wenn sein Herr wütend war, beschränkte Walter sich gemeinhin auf das Nötigste.

»Richard von Kingsbridge«, sagte William.

Walter nickte.

»Und sie nennen ihn den ›rechtmäßigen Grafen‹«, schloß William.

Walter schwieg.

Durchs Haus kehrte William in die Mühle zurück.

Hugh hatte sich aufgesetzt und preßte die linke Hand auf die rechte Schulter. Sein Gesicht war blaß.

»Wie geht's?« fragte William.

»Nicht so schlimm«, antwortete Hugh. »Wer waren diese Kerle?«

»Outlaws«, beschied ihn William knapp. Er sah sich um. Sieben oder acht Verfemte lagen tot oder verwundet auf dem Boden. Louis lag flach auf dem Rücken. Seine Augen waren weit geöffnet. Im ersten Moment hielt William ihn für tot, doch dann blinzelte Louis.

»Louis?«

Der Angesprochene hob den Kopf, schien aber noch nicht mitzubekommen, was um ihn herum vorging.

»Hugh, hilf Louis auf eines der Fuhrwerke!« sagte William. »Du, Walter, legst Guillaume auf das andere.« Er ließ sie stehen und begab sich nach draußen.

Keiner der Bauern im Dorf besaß ein Pferd, wohl aber der Müller. Der kleine, gedrungene Schecke stand am Ufer des Flusses und nibbelte am spärlichen Gras. William fand auch den Sattel des Müllers und schnallte ihn dem Gaul auf.

Kurz darauf verließen sie Cowford. William ritt, Walter und Gervase trieben die Gespanne.

Ihr Ziel war nach wie vor die bischöfliche Burg. Williams Zorn legte sich auch unterwegs nicht; er wuchs vielmehr ins Unermeßliche, je länger William über die leidvollen Erfahrungen der vergangenen Stunde nachgrübelte. Schlimm genug, daß die Outlaws ihm so zugesetzt hatten. Schlimmer noch, daß sie von seinem Erzfeind Richard geführt wurden. Unerträglich aber, daß sie Richard den ›rechtmäßigen Grafen‹ nannten. Wenn es uns nicht gelingt, ihnen eine entscheidende Niederlage beizubringen, muß ich in allernächster Zeit mit einem direkten Angriff Richards rechnen, dachte William. Ein solcher Versuch, die Grafschaft zurückzuobern, verstieße zwar gegen jedes Recht und Gesetz – aber William hatte das unbestimmte Gefühl, daß eine Klage wegen unrechtmäßiger Enteignung in seinem Fall auf taube Ohren stoßen könnte. Daß Outlaws ihn überfallen und beraubt und zum Gespött der ganzen Grafschaft gemacht hatten, war gar nicht mehr sein Hauptproblem. Graf William war sich jetzt darüber im klaren, daß seine Herrschaft über Shiring gefährdet war.

Richard mußte sterben, soviel war gewiß. Die Frage war nur: Wo hielt er sich versteckt? Er grübelte den ganzen Weg darüber nach. Am Ziel der Reise glaubte er zu wissen, wer den Schlüssel zur Lösung des Problems in der Hand hielt: Bischof Waleran.

Wie eine Komödiantengruppe bei einem Festzug fuhren sie in den Burghof ein: der Graf auf einem kleinen Schecken, die Ritter als Ochsentreiber. William brüllte den Männern des Bischofs vorlaute Befehle zu – den einen schickte er nach einem Arzt für Hugh und Louis, einen anderen nach einem Priester, der für Guillaumes arme Seele beten sollte.

Gervase und Walter versorgten sich in der Küche mit Bier, und William ging in den Wohnturm. Waleran ließ ihn sogleich in sein Privatgemach führen. William haßte es, den Bischof um etwas bitten zu müssen. Aber er wollte Richard finden – und dazu brauchte er Walerans Unterstützung.

Der Bischof studierte eine Pergamentrolle mit seinen Einkünften – eine schier endlose Reihe von Zahlen. Bei Williams Eintritt blickte er auf und bemerkte sofort die furchtbare Erregung im Antlitz seines Besuchers. »Nun, was ist denn geschehen?« fragte er in jenem leicht ironischen Ton, der Williams Blut von jeher in Wallung brachte.

William bleckte die Zähne. »Ich habe jetzt endlich herausgefunden, wer der Kopf dieser verdammten Wegelagerer ist.«

Waleran hob die Brauen.

»Richard von Kingsbridge.«

»Ah ja.« Waleran nickte verständnisinnig. »Ja, natürlich. Das klingt plausibel.«

»Der Kerl kann uns gefährlich werden«, erwiderte William ärgerlich. »Sie nennen ihn den ›rechtmäßigen Grafen‹!« Er deutete mit dem Finger auf Waleran. »*Diese* Familie wollt Ihr doch gewiß nicht wieder in Amt und Würden sehen, wie? Die hassen Euch bis aufs Blut und sind zudem mit Prior Philip befreundet, Eurem Erzfeind.«

»Schon gut, schon gut«, sagte Waleran herablassend. »Ich gebe Euch ja recht. Daß Richard von Kingsbridge wieder Graf von Shiring wird, kann ich nicht dulden.«

William setzte sich hin. Er hatte Schmerzen und fühlte sich ganz zerschlagen. Noch nie hatten ihm die Nachwirkungen eines Gefechts so sehr zu schaffen gemacht. Er litt unter Muskelzerrungen, seine Hände waren wund, Prellungen und blaue Flecken zeigten, wo er getroffen worden war oder sich gestoßen hatte. Ich bin erst siebenunddreißig, dachte er. Beginnt jetzt schon das Alter? »Ich muß Richard töten«, sagte er. »Sobald er weg ist, verkommen die Banditen zu einem hilflosen Pack.«

»Ich stimme Euch zu.«

»Ihn zu töten, ist ein Kinderspiel. Das Problem ist, ihn zu finden. Aber dabei könnt Ihr mir helfen.«

Waleran rieb mit dem Daumen über seine scharfgeschnittene Nase. »Ich sehe nicht, wie.«

»Hört zu: Wenn sie sich organisiert haben, müssen sie irgendwo *sein*.«

»Ich weiß nicht, worauf Ihr hinauswollt. Die Outlaws sind im Wald.«

»Unter normalen Umstände kann man die Outlaws im Wald nicht finden, weil sie über das ganze riesige Gebiet verstreut sind. Die meisten von ihnen schlafen kaum zweimal hintereinander an ein und demselben Fleck. Sie machen sich einfach irgendwo ein Feuer und schlafen auf den Bäumen. Wenn man solche Leute organisieren will, muß man sie erst einmal sammeln. Man braucht eine Art Versteck.«

»Wir müssen also herausfinden, wo sich Richards Schlupfwinkel befindet.«

»So ist es.«

»Und wie wollt Ihr das anstellen?«

»Hier beginnt *Eure* Aufgabe.«

Waleran sah ihn skeptisch an.

»Ich wette, halb Kingsbridge weiß, wo er steckt.«

»Aber sie werden es uns nicht sagen. Die hassen uns beide doch wie die Pest.«

»Nicht alle«, sagte William.

Sally fand Weihnachten ganz großartig.

Die Speisen, die es zum Weihnachtsfest gab, waren überwiegend süß: Lebkuchenfiguren; Weizenbrei mit Eiern und Honig; Birnenmost, nach dem man immer so kichern mußte, wenn man ihn getrunken hatte; und Kuttelfleisch, das mehrere Stunden lang gekocht und dann in einem süßen Pastetenteig gebacken wurde. Wegen der Hungersnot gab es heuer von allem weniger als sonst, doch tat dies Sallys Vorfreude keinen Abbruch.

Sie schmückten das Haus mit Stechpalmenzweigen und hängten das Mistelsträußchen, unter dem man sich küssen mußte, über die Tür. Es hieß, daß der erste Mann, der über die Schwelle trat, Glück brachte – vorausgesetzt, er hatte schwarze Haare. Sallys Vater mußte am Weihnachtsmorgen im Haus bleiben, denn sein rotes Haar galt als unheilverkündend.

Sally war auch ganz begeistert vom Krippenspiel in der Kirche. Die Mönche hatten sich als Könige aus dem Morgenland, als Engel und Schäfer verkleidet. Das Mädchen platzte schier vor Lachen, als bei der Ankunft der Heiligen Familie im Ägyptenland alle falschen Götter umpurzelten.

Am besten aber war der kleine Bischof. Am dritten Tag des Weihnachtsfests legte der jüngste Novize des Klosters die Bischofsrobe an, und alle anderen hatten ihm zu gehorchen.

Fast die gesamte Stadtbevölkerung hatte sich auf dem Klosterhof versammelt und wartete auf den kleinen Bischof. Nach seinem Erscheinen pflegte er die würdigen älteren Herren der Gemeinde zu Handlangerdiensten abzukommandieren: Sie mußten zum Beispiel Feuerholz sammeln und Schweineställe ausmisten. Er stolzierte recht eingebildet einher und beschimpfte alle Autoritätspersonen aufs unflätigste. Im vergangenen Jahr hatte er den Sakristan ein Huhn rupfen lassen. Das Ergebnis war ein überwältigender Lacherfolg, denn der Sakristan hatte keine Ahnung, wie man so etwas machte. Überall flogen Federn herum.

Schon begann der feierliche Auftritt: Auf den Schultern von zwei Mönchen reitend, erschien ein ungefähr zwölfjähriger Knabe und blickte dreist in die Runde. Er trug eine purpurne Seidenrobe und hielt einen hölzernen Krummstab in der Hand. In seinem und seiner Träger Gefolge betraten die übrigen Mönche den Klosterhof. Die Zuschauer jubelten und klatschten. Die erste Amtshandlung des kleinen Bischofs bestand darin, mit ausgestrecktem Finger auf Prior Philip zu deuten und ihn anzuherrschen. »He, Bursche! Ab mit dir in den Stall! Du striegelst den Esel!«

Das Publikum brüllte vor Lachen. Der alte Esel war ein bekanntermaßen störrisches Tier, das sonst nie gestriegelt wurde. Prior Philip machte gute Miene zum derben Spiel und sagte: »Aber gewiß doch, hochverehrter Herr Bischof.« Dann trollte er sich, um die ihm zugewiesene Aufgabe zu erfüllen.

»Vorwärts!« kommandierte der kleine Bischof. Die Prozession verließ den Klosterhof, die Zuschauer liefen hinterdrein. Einige Leute versteckten sich und verschlossen ihre Türen, um nicht mit unangenehmen Aufgaben betraut zu werden – aber ihnen entging dafür auch der Spaß. Sallys Familie war vollzählig zur Stelle: Mutter und Vater, Tommy, Tante Martha und sogar Onkel Richard, der am Vorabend überraschend heimgekehrt war.

Altem Brauch entsprechend, führte der kleine Bischof seine Herde zunächst einmal zur Schenke, wo er für sich und seine Novizenbrüder Freibier verlangte. Der Wirt, der das Bier selber braute, fügte sich gutgelaunt.

Die Leute ließen sich auf den Bänken nieder. Neben Sally saß Bruder Remigius, ein hochgewachsener, unfreundlicher Mann, mit dem sie noch nie ein Wort gewechselt hatte. Plötzlich wandte er sich ihr zu, lächelte und sprach sie an: »Schön, daß dein Onkel Richard zu Weihnachten nach Hause gekommen ist.«

»Er hat mir eine Miezekatze aus Holz geschenkt«, sagte Sally. »Er hat sie mit seinem Messer selbst geschnitzt.«

»Na, das ist aber fein! Glaubst du, er wird länger hierbleiben?« Sally runzelte die Stirn. »Das weiß ich nicht.«

»Ich denke doch, daß er recht bald wieder fortgehen wird.«

»Ja. Er wohnt jetzt im Wald.«

»Weißt du denn auch, wo?«

»Ja. Der Ort heißt Sallys Steinbruch. Das ist mein Name!« Sie lachte.

»So ist es«, sagte Bruder Remigius. »Wie interessant.«

Als sie ausgetrunken hatten, sagte der kleine Bischof: »Und nun hört mich an: Sakristan Andrew und Bruder Remigius! Ihr zwei wascht für die Witwe Poll Wäsche!«

Sally quietschte vor Vergnügen und klatschte begeistert in die Hände. Die Witwe Poll, eine rundliche, rotgesichtige Frau, war Wäscherin. Muffige Unterhemden und stinkende Strümpfe waschen, die von ihren Trägern nur zweimal im Jahr gewechselt wurden – das war vielleicht eine Aufgabe für die beiden pingeligen Mönche! Gern taten sie das bestimmt nicht.

Die Menge verließ die Schenke und trug den kleinen Bischof zur Wäscherei der Witwe Poll an der Flußlände. Die Wäscherin bekam einen Lachkrampf und wurde, als sie erfuhr, *wer* ihr die Wäsche waschen sollte, noch röter im Gesicht, als sie ohnehin schon war.

Andrew und Remigius trugen einen schweren Korb mit schmutziger Wäsche vom Haus zum Flußufer. Andrew öffnete den Korb, und Remigius zog mit angewiderter Miene das erste Kleidungsstück hervor. Eine junge Frau rief: »Geht vorsichtig damit um, Bruder Remigius, das ist mein Unterhemd.« Remigius errötete, und alle Umstehenden lachten. Dann bissen die beiden alten Mönche die Zähne zusammen und wuschen die Wäsche im Wasser des Flusses. Die Bevölkerung von Kingsbridge gab ihnen gute Ratschläge und munterte sie mit Zurufen auf. Andrew machte aus seiner tiefen Abneigung gegen diese Arbeit keinen Hehl, das erkannte auch Sally. Remigius hingegen wirkte merkwürdig zufrieden.

An einem Holzgerüst, wie die Schlinge des Henkers am Galgen, hing eine Kette mit einer riesigen Eisenkugel. Auch ein Seil war an der Kugel befestigt. Es führte über eine Flaschenzugrolle am oberen Ende des höchsten Gerüstbalkens und wurde auf der anderen Seite von zwei Arbeitern gehalten. Zogen die Arbeiter an, so wurde die Kugel hochgezogen, bis sie die Rolle berührte, und die Kette lag waagerecht auf dem Arm des Gerüsts.

Fast ganz Shiring sah zu.

Die Männer ließen das Seil los. Die Eisenkugel fiel und krachte mit Schwung gegen die Kirchenwand. Es tat einen regelrechten Donnerschlag, die Mauer erzitterte, und William spürte, wie sich die Erschütterung auch noch im Boden unter seinen Füßen ausbreitete. Am liebsten hätte er genau an der Aufprallstelle Richard von Kingsbridge an die Wand geschmiedet – sein Feind wäre von der Kugel zerquetscht worden wie eine Fliege.

Die Arbeiter zogen das Seil wieder ein. Als die Eisenkugel am höchsten Punkt ihrer Fahrt anhielt und die Männer das Seil wieder losließen, hielt William unwillkürlich den Atem an. Diesmal schmetterte die Kugel ein Loch in die Steinmauer. Die Zuschauer applaudierten.

Es war ein genialer Mechanismus.

William freute sich darüber, daß die Arbeiten am Bauplatz der künftigen neuen Kirche voranschritten, doch hatte er an diesem Tag noch Wichtigeres im Sinn. Er sah sich nach Bischof Waleran um und erblickte ihn an der Seite Alfred Builders. William ging zu den beiden hin, zog den Bischof beiseite und fragte ihn: »Ist der Mann schon da?«

»Kann sein«, sagte Waleran. »Begleitet mich in mein Haus.«

Gemeinsam schritten sie über den Marktplatz. »Habt Ihr Eure Truppen mitgebracht?« fragte Waleran.

»Natürlich. Zweihundert Mann. Sie warten in den Wäldern draußen vor der Stadt.«

Sie betraten das bischöfliche Haus. Der Geruch von gekochtem Schinken stieg William in die Nase und ließ ihm trotz der drängenden Eile das Wasser im Munde zusammenlaufen. Die meisten Menschen gingen in schlechten Zeiten mit ihren Speisen sparsam um – für Waleran schien es dagegen eine Frage des Prinzips zu sein, auch in Zeiten der Not den Lebensstil nicht zu ändern. Der Bischof selbst war alles andere als ein Schlemmer, doch es machte ihm sichtlich Spaß, allenthalben kundzutun, daß er viel zu reich und zu mächtig war, um sich von trivialen Dingen wie schlechten Ernten beeindrucken zu lassen.

Das Stadthaus des Bischofs war ein typisches, schmales Gebäude mit einem großen Raum im vorderen Teil. Dahinter lag die Küche, an die sich ein Hof mit einer Versitzgrube, einem Bienenstock und einem Schweinekoben anschloß. Im Saal wartete ein Mönch. William fiel ein Stein vom Herzen.

»Guten Tag, Bruder Remigius«, sagte Waleran.

»Guten Tag, ehrwürdiger Herr Bischof. Seid gegrüßt, Graf William.«

William musterte den Gast aufmerksam. Er war ein unruhiger Mann mit hochmütigen Zügen und vorstehenden blauen Augen. Er kam William entfernt bekannt vor. Ich muß ihn irgendwann mal unter den geschorenen Brüdern in Kingsbridge gesehen haben, dachte er, bei einem Gottesdienst vielleicht. Seit Jahren war dieser Mann, wie William wußte, Walerans Spion im Lager von Prior Philip. Trotzdem hatten sie noch nie miteinander gesprochen. »Habt Ihr Neuigkeiten für mich?« fragte er ihn.

»Möglicherweise«, antwortete Remigius.

Waleran warf seinen pelzbesetzten Mantel ab und ging zum Feuer, um seine Hände zu wärmen. Ein Diener servierte heißen Holunderbeerenwein in Silberpokalen. William bediente sich, trank und wartete ungeduldig darauf, daß der Diener wieder verschwand.

Waleran trank den Wein in kleinen Schlucken und sah Remigius kritisch an. Nachdem der Diener sich entfernt hatte, fragte er den Mönch: »Unter welchem Vorwand habt Ihr die Priorei verlassen?«

»Unter gar keinem«, erwiderte Remigius.

Waleran zog eine Augenbraue hoch.

»Ich kehre nicht mehr nach Kingsbridge zurück«, sagte Remigius entschlossen.

»Wie das?«

Remigius holte tief Luft. »Ihr baut hier eine Kathedrale.«

»Es ist eine ganz normale Kirche.«

»Sie wird offensichtlich sehr groß. Eines Tages wollt Ihr sie zur Bischofskirche machen.«

Waleran zögerte, bevor er antwortete. »Angenommen – nur theoretisch, versteht sich – Ihr hättet recht ...«

»Die Kathedrale wird von einem Kapitel geführt werden müssen – entweder von Mönchen oder von Kanonikern.«

»Und das heißt?«

»... daß ich Prior werden will.«

Das hat was für sich, dachte William.

»Und Ihr seid Euch Eurer Sache so sicher, daß Ihr Kingsbridge ohne Prior Philips Erlaubnis verlassen habt?« fragte Waleran streng.

Remigius war nicht mehr ganz wohl in seiner Haut. William konnte das gut verstehen: Wer Walerans Unmut erweckte, hatte allemal nichts zu lachen. »Ich hoffe, meine Zuversicht ist nicht unbegründet«, sagte Remigius.

»Ihr könnt uns angeblich zu Richard führen.«

»Jawohl.«

»Ausgezeichnet, Mann!« fuhr William erregt dazwischen. »Wo steckt er?«

Remigius schwieg und sah Waleran an.

»Los, Waleran, laßt ihn in Gottes Namen Prior werden!«

Waleran zögerte noch. William wußte, daß er sich ungern in die Zange nehmen ließ. Doch dann gab sich der Bischof einen Ruck und sagte: »Einverstanden. Ihr sollt Prior werden.«

»Wo steckt Richard?« fragte William sofort.

Remigius' Blick ruhte unverändert auf dem Bischof. »Von heute an?« fragte er.

»Von heute an.«

Jetzt wandte sich Remigius an William. »Ein Kloster besteht nicht nur aus Kirche und Dormitorium. Es braucht Ländereien, Höfe und Pfarreien, die den Kirchenzehnt zahlen.«

»Sagt mir, wo Richard steckt, und ich gebe Euch fünf Dörfer mit ihren Kirchen. Da habt Ihr was für den Anfang.«

»Eine Klostergründung muß formgerecht beurkundet werden.«

»Keine Angst, Ihr bekommt Eure Urkunde schon«, sagte Waleran.

»Los jetzt, Mann!« drängte William. »Draußen vor der Stadt warten meine Soldaten. Wo hat der Kerl seinen Schlupfwinkel?«

»An einem Flecken namens Sallys Steinbruch, abseits der Straße nach Winchester.«

»Kenne ich!« William mußte an sich halten, um nicht in Triumphgeheul auszubrechen. »Der Steinbruch ist aufgelassen. Da kommt heute niemand mehr hin.«

»Ich erinnere mich«, sagte Waleran. »Die Arbeiten dort wurden schon vor Jahren eingestellt. Ein hervorragender Schlupfwinkel, muß ich sagen. Völlig unauffindbar, wenn man nicht direkt darauf zuläuft.«

»Und zudem eine Falle!« sagte William, von wilder Begeisterung ergriffen. »Die alten Bruchflächen ragen in drei Richtungen senkrecht in die Höhe. Da kommt keiner mehr raus. Und Gefangene werden diesmal nicht gemacht.« Mit wachsender Erregung malte er die Szene aus: »Ich mache sie alle nieder. Ich richte ein Blutbad an wie der Fuchs im Hühnerstall ...«

Die Blicke der beiden Gottesmänner verrieten eine gewisse Unbehaglichkeit. »Fühlt Ihr Euch nicht ganz wohl, Bruder Remigius?« fragte William verächtlich. »Dreht sich meinem hochverehrten Herrn Bischof beim Gedanken an ein Massaker der Magen um?« Die Mienen der beiden bestätigten ihm seine Vermutung. Sie waren großartige Ränkeschmiede, diese frommen Herrschaften – aber wenn's ans blutige Handwerk ging, waren sie auf Männer der Tat angewiesen. »Ich bin sicher, Ihr werdet für mich beten!« sagte er sarkastisch und ließ sie stehen.

Er ging zu seinem Pferd. Der schwarze Hengst hatte das von Richard gestohlene Schlachtroß ersetzt, erreichte aber bei weitem nicht dessen Klasse. William saß auf und verließ die Stadt. Er zügelte seine Vorfreude und versuchte, mit kühlem Kopf einen Angriffsplan zu entwickeln.

Wie viele Outlaws wird Richard in Sallys Steinbruch zusammengezogen haben? dachte er. Bei einigen Überfällen in jüngster Zeit sind sie in Horden von über hundert Mann erschienen. Insgesamt müssen es daher wohl mindestens zweihundert sein, vielleicht sogar bis zu fünfhundert. Wir müssen also damit rechnen, daß wir in der Minderzahl sind, und daher das beste aus unseren Vorteilen machen ...

Ein Vorteil war der Überraschungseffekt, ein anderer die Bewaffnung. Die Banditen verfügten über Keulen, Knüppel, Hämmer und, schlimmstenfalls, Äxte. Keiner von ihnen trug eine Rüstung. Der wichtigste Trumpf in Williams Händen war indes der Umstand, daß er und seine Leute zu Pferde kamen. Die Outlaws hatten nur sehr wenig Pferde, und daß sie zum Zeitpunkt des Angriffs kampfbereit im Sattel säßen, war nicht zu erwarten. Einen weiteren Vorteil erhoffte sich William von seinen Bogenschützen: Ein paar von ihnen wollte er vorausschicken. Sie sollten die Flanken des Steinbruchs hinaufklettern und das Banditenlager kurz vor Beginn der eigentlichen Attacke mit einem Pfeilhagel überschütten.

Das Wichtigste war jedoch, daß kein Outlaw entwischte – zumindest nicht, solange Richard nicht tot oder gefangen war. William beschloß, ein paar zuverlässige Männer auszusuchen, die hinter der Front mit all jenen aufräumten, denen es gelungen war, durch die Reihen zu schlüpfen.

Walter wartete mit den Rittern und Schergen dort, wo William sie ein paar Stunden zuvor verlassen hatte. Die Männer waren voller Tatendrang und bestens motiviert – schließlich rechneten sie mit einem leichten Sieg.

Sie schlugen den Weg nach Winchester ein. Walter ritt stumm an Williams Seite. Zu seinen besten Eigenschaften zählte die Fähigkeit, den Mund halten zu können. Bei anderen Leuten hatte William oft den Eindruck, sie redeten ununterbrochen auf ihn ein und das selbst dann, wenn es eigentlich gar nichts zu sagen gab. Angst und Aufgeregtheit mochten der Grund dafür sein. Walter respektierte William, war aber in seiner Gegenwart weder ängstlich noch aufgeregt: Dazu waren sie schon zu lange zusammen.

William spürte die vertraute Mischung aus brennender Erwartung und Todesfurcht. Nur im Kampf war er gut, und bei jedem Kampf setzte er sein Leben aufs Spiel. Heute jedoch ging es um alles, heute wollte er endlich jenen Mann erledigen, der ihm schon seit fünfzehn Jahren ein Dorn im Auge war.

Gegen Mittag unterbrachen sie ihren Ritt in einem Dorf, das groß genug war, um eine Schenke zu besitzen. William besorgte den Männern Brot und Bier, und die Pferde bekamen Wasser. Bevor sie ihren Weg fortsetzten, gab er seiner Truppe die letzten Instruktionen.

Ein paar Meilen weiter bogen sie von der Straße nach Winchester ab. Der Pfad, den sie einschlugen, war von außen kaum zu erkennen, und hätte William nicht aufmerksam nach ihm Ausschau gehalten, so wäre er gewiß an der Abzweigung vorbeigeritten, ohne etwas zu sehen. Nachdem sie den Pfad jedoch gefunden hatten, verriet die Pflanzendecke seinen weiteren Verlauf: Auf einem Streifen von fünf oder sechs Schritt Breite wuchs kein einziger alter Baum.

Er schickte die Bogenschützen los. Um ihnen einen Vorsprung zu geben, hieß er die übrige Truppe vorübergehend langsamer reiten. Es war ein klarer Januartag, und die blattlosen Bäume vermochten das kalte Sonnenlicht kaum zu dämpfen. William war schon seit vielen Jahren nicht mehr in dieser Gegend gewesen und konnte daher nicht genau sagen, wie weit es bis zum Steinbruch noch war. Ungefähr eine Meile nach der Abzweigung fielen ihm dann die ersten Anzeichen auf, die dafür sprachen, daß der Weg noch benutzt wurde: niedergetretene Pflanzen, abgebrochene Zweige und aufgewühlter Boden. William war heilfroh, bestätigten diese Indizien doch Remigius' Angaben.

Er war gespannt wie eine Bogensehne. Die Zeichen wurden deutlicher: zertrampeltes Gras, Pferdeäpfel, Abfälle. In diesem abgelegenen Teil des Waldes bemühten sich die Outlaws nicht mehr, ihre Gegenwart zu verbergen. Die letzten Zweifel verflogen: Man näherte sich dem Schlupfwinkel der Banditen. Die Schlacht konnte beginnen.

Es konnte nicht mehr weit sein. William lauschte angestrengt. Jeden Augenblick mußten die Bogenschützen das Lager unter Beschuß nehmen. Rufe würden ertönen, Flüche, Schmerzensschreie und das Gewieher verschreckter Pferde ...

Sie erreichten eine große Lichtung. Ungefähr zweihundert Schritt voraus entdeckte William den Eingang zu Sallys Steinbruch. Kein Laut war zu hören. Irgend etwas war faul. Die Bogenschützen schossen nicht. Ein Schauer fuhr William über den Rücken. Was war geschehen? Waren die Bogenschützen von Wachposten abgefangen und geräuschlos ins Jenseits befördert worden? Aber doch gewiß nicht alle, oder?

Für lange Überlegungen blieb keine Zeit mehr. William gab seinem Pferd die Sporen und galoppierte los. Seine Streitmacht folgte ihm. Wie Donnerhall klangen die Hufe, als sie über die Lichtung sprengten. Williams Beklommenheit wich der Angriffslust.

Der Weg in den Steinbruch war wie eine enge, gewundene Schlucht. Man konnte von außen nicht hineinsehen. Noch oben am oberen Rand des Abgrunds standen seine Bogenschützen und spähten hinunter. Warum schießen sie denn nicht? dachte William. Er befürchtete das Schlimmste und hätte am liebsten kehrtgemacht, doch ließ sich die anstürmende Truppe jetzt nicht mehr anhalten. Die Zügel in der Linken und das gezückte Schwert in der Rechten, galoppierte er in den aufgelassenen Steinbruch.

Doch der Steinbruch war leer.

Die Ernüchterung traf ihn wie ein Schlag. Um ein Haar wäre er in Tränen ausgebrochen. Er war sich seiner Sache so sicher gewesen – und nun das. Die Enttäuschung fuhr ihm in die Eingeweide wie ein stechender Schmerz.

Als die Pferde wieder ruhiger gingen, erkannte William, daß die Outlaws tatsächlich bis vor kurzem im Steinbruch gehaust haben mußten. Man sah zahlreiche einfach zusammengezimmerte Verschläge aus Schilf und Zweigen, alte Feuerstellen und einen Dunghaufen. Ein kleiner Fleck am Rande war mit ein paar Holzpföcken umzäunt; er hatte offenbar als Gehege für die Pferde gedient. Überall lagen irgendwelche Reste menschlicher Besiedlung herum: Hühnerknochen, leere Säcke, ein ausgetretener Schuh, ein zerbrochener Topf. Über einer Feuerstelle stand eine Rauchsäule. Ein Hoffnungsfunken keimte in William auf: Vielleicht waren die Kerle gerade erst fort und konnten noch eingeholt werden! Neben dem Feuer saß mit gekreuzten Beinen eine einsame Gestalt. Er ritt näher heran. Die Gestalt erhob sich. Es war eine Frau.

»Nun denn, William Hamleigh«, sagte sie. »Mal wieder zu spät gekommen, wie?«

»Unverschämtes Luder! Dafür reiß ich dir die Zunge aus dem Rachen!«

»Du rührst mich nicht an«, erwiderte die Frau gelassen. »Ich habe schon bessere Männer als dich verflucht.« Sie hielt sich die Hand vors Gesicht, drei Finger ausgestreckt, die Geste einer Hexe. Die Ritter wichen unwillkürlich zurück, und William bekreuzigte sich vorsichtshalber. Die Frau blickte ihm furchtlos ins Gesicht. Ihre Augen waren von auffallend goldener Farbe. »Kennst du mich noch, William?« fragte sie. »Du hast einmal versucht, mich für ein Pfund Silber zu kaufen!« Sie lachte. »Du kannst von Glück reden, daß der Handel nicht zustande kam ...«

William erinnerte sich an diese Augen. Vor ihm stand die Witwe Tom Builders, Jack Jacksons Mutter, die Hexe, die hier draußen in den Wäldern lebte. Ja, es war wohl ein Glück gewesen, daß er sie damals nicht bekommen hatte ... William wollte fort. Er wollte so schnell wie möglich fort – aber er mußte dieser Frau noch ein paar Fragen stellen. »Schon gut, Hexe«, sagte er. »War Richard von Kingsbridge hier?«

»Bis vor zwei Tagen, ja.«

»Und wo ist er hin? Kannst du mir das sagen?«

»Und ob ich das kann!« sagte sie. »Er und seine Mannen sind für Henry in die Schlacht gezogen.«

»Henry?« fragte William. Eine böse Ahnung sagte ihm, daß sie einen ganz bestimmten Henry meinte. »Mathildes Sohn?«

»Für eben diesen.«

William wurde kalt ums Herz. Der junge, tatkräftige Herzog der Normandie war imstande zu erreichen, was seiner Mutter versagt geblieben war – und wenn Stephan sürzte, so war es gut möglich, daß mit ihm auch William fiel. »Was ist denn geschehen?« fragte er ungeduldig. »Was hat Henry denn getan?«

»Er hat mit sechsunddreißig Schiffen das Meer überquert und ist in Wareham an Land gegangen«, antwortete die Hexe. »Mit ihm kam eine dreitausend Mann starke Armee. Wir haben es mit einer Invasion zu tun.«

Winchester war voller Menschen, Spannung und Gefahr. Beide Heere lagen hier einander gegenüber: Die Truppen König Stephans waren in der Burg kaserniert, während das Rebellenheer unter Herzog Henry – darunter auch Richard und seine Outlaws – außerhalb der Stadtmauern auf dem St.-Giles-Hügel ihr Lager aufgeschlagen hatte, dort, wo alljährlich der Jahrmarkt stattfand. Sich in der Stadt herumzutreiben war den Soldaten beider Seiten versagt, doch viele kümmerten sich nicht um das Verbot. Sie verbrachten ihre Abende in Schenken, beim Hahnenkampf und in Hurenhäusern, wo sie sich vollaufen ließen, die Weiber mißbrauchten und sich überm Würfelspiel in die Haare gerieten. Nicht selten gab es dabei Tote.

Im Sommer, nach dem Tod seines ältesten Sohnes, hatte Stephan das Kampfglück endgültig verlassen. Jetzt saß er in seiner Burg, und Herzog Henry residierte im Bischofspalast.

Ihre Diplomaten verhandelten derweil über einen Friedensschluß. Erzbischof Theobald von Canterbury vertrat den König. Bischof Henry von Winchester, jener alte Makler der Macht, den Herzog. Jeden Morgen trafen sich die beiden Unterhändler im Bischofspalast. Zur Mittagsstunde schritt Herzog Henry mit seinem Gefolge, zu dem auch Richard von Kingsbridge gehörte, durch die Straßen von Winchester zur Burg, um dort zu speisen.

Als Aliena den Herzog zum erstenmal sah, konnte sie nicht glauben, daß dieser Mann ein Reich von der Größe Englands beherrschte. Er war nicht älter als zwanzig Jahre und hatte ein sonnengebräuntes Gesicht mit vielen Sommersprossen, das eher zu einem Bauern gepaßt hätte. Er trug eine schmucklose dunkle Tunika ohne Zierat, und sein rötliches Haar war kurzgeschnitten. Er sah aus wie der hart arbeitende Sohn eines wohlhabenden Gutsbesitzers.

Es dauerte eine Weile, bis Aliena erkannte, daß diesen Mann die Aura der Macht umgab. Er war kräftig und untersetzt, hatte breite Schultern und einen großen Kopf. Der Eindruck roher körperlicher Stärke wurde indessen durch die wachen grauen Augen etwas gemildert. Die Männer in seiner Umgebung achteten darauf, ihm nie zu nahe zu kommen, sondern behandelten ihn mit vorsichtiger Vertrautheit als fürchteten sie, er könne jederzeit wild um sich schlagen.

Die gemeinsamen Mittagessen auf der Burg, bei dem die Führer der verfeindeten Armeen am gleichen Tisch saßen, mußten in einer sehr gespannten Atmosphäre stattfinden. Für Aliena war es jedenfalls anders kaum vorstellbar. Sie fragte sich, wie Richard es überhaupt ertragen konnte, mit Graf William an einem Tisch zu sitzen. Sie an seiner Stelle hätte mit ihrem Messer nicht das gebotene Wildbret attackiert, sondern William ... Sie selbst hatte William nur kurz und aus einiger Entfernung zu Gesicht bekommen. Er machte einen besorgten, übelgelaunten Eindruck, was Aliena als gutes Zeichen ansah.

Während die Grafen, Bischöfe und Äbte im Wohnturm zusammentrafen, versammelte sich der niedere Adel – die Ritter, Vögte, kleinen Landedelleute, Gerichtsverwalter und Kastellane – im Burghof. Es waren Leute, die zu einer Zeit, da wichtige Entscheidungen über die Zukunft des Königsreichs – und damit auch über ihre eigene Zukunft – getroffen wurden, der Hauptstadt nicht einfach fernbleiben konnten. Unter ihnen befand sich auch Prior Philip, dem Aliena meist vormittags im Burghof begegnete. Die Gerüchteküche brodelte und kochte jeden Tag etwas Neues aus. Einmal hieß es, alle Grafen, die Stephan unterstützten, sollten ihres Titels verlustig gehen (womit William erledigt gewesen wäre). Am nächsten Tag verlautete dagegen, es bliebe alles beim alten (womit Richard alle Hoffnungen hätte begraben können). Einmal hieß es, sämtliche Burgen Stephans sollten geschleift werden, das nächste Mal, die Burgen der Rebellen, beim übernächsten Mal waren *alle* Burgen im Gespräch und beim viertenmal keine einzige mehr ... Einem anderen Gerücht zufolge sollte jeder einzelne Verbündete Henrys geadelt werden und hundert Morgen Land erhalten. Richard war daran nicht interessiert – was *er* wollte, war seine Grafschaft.

Auch Richard konnte nicht sagen, was an den verschiedenen Gerüchten nun stimmte und was nicht: Er gehörte zwar auf dem

Schlachtfeld zu Henrys engsten Ratgebern, wurde aber bei den politischen Verhandlungen und deren Vorbereitung nicht zu Rate gezogen. Philip schien über den Stand der Dinge besser Bescheid zu wissen, wenngleich er sich über die Quelle seiner Informationen ausschwieg. Aliena hatte allerdings eine Vermutung: Sie erinnerte sich an den Bruder des Priors, der hin und wieder Kingsbridge besucht hatte. Er hatte einst für Robert von Gloucester und die Kaiserin Mathilde gearbeitet. Es war immerhin möglich, daß er inzwischen für Herzog Henry tätig war.

Philip berichtete, daß die Verhandlungen kurz vor dem Abschluß stünden. Man habe sich auf folgende Lösung geeinigt: Stephan sollte bis zu seinem natürlichen Ableben König bleiben, Henry sollte ihm auf den Thron nachfolgen. Aliena war über diese Lösung alles andere als erbaut: Es war ohne weiteres denkbar, daß Stephan noch zehn Jahre lebte. Was würde in der Zwischenzeit geschehen? Es war gewiß nicht anzunehmen, daß die Grafen und Barone, die Stephan unterstützten, abdanken mußten, solange er König war. Wie sollten Henrys Anhänger – also zum Beispiel Richard – zu ihrem gerechten Lohn kommen? Hoffte man auf ihre Geduld?

Philip erfuhr die Antwort auf diese Frage an einem Spätnachmittag, genau eine Woche nach Beginn der Versammlung in Winchester. Er schickte einen Novizen aus, der Aliena und Richard zu einer Unterredung bat. Die beiden machten sich sofort auf den Weg zum Klosterhof. Auf ihrem Gang durch die geschäftigen Straßen der Stadt beherrschte Richard finstere Entschlossenheit, während Aliena von Verzagtheit ergriffen war.

Philip erwartete sie auf dem Friedhof. Die Sonne stand schon tief am Himmel, so daß die Grabsteine lange Schatten warfen. Der Prior kam sofort zur Sache. »Sie haben sich geeinigt«, sagte er. »Allerdings ist das Ergebnis recht verwirrend.«

Aliena hielt die Spannung nicht mehr aus. »Wird Richard wieder Graf?« fragte sie aufgeregt.

Philip machte eine abwiegelnde Geste mit der Hand, die soviel besagte wie ›vielleicht ja – vielleicht nein‹. »Die Situation ist ziemlich kompliziert. Sie haben einen Kompromiß geschlossen. Ländereien, die Usurpatoren in die Hand gefallen sind, sollen an die ehemaligen Besitzer zurückgegeben werden – das heißt an jene, denen sie zu Zeiten des alten Königs Henry gehörten.«

»Das reicht mir doch!« rief Richard aus. »Zu Zeiten von König Henry war mein Vater Graf!«

»Halt den Mund, Richard!« fuhr Aliena dazwischen und fragte Philip: »Was ist der Haken bei der Sache?«

»In der Vereinbarung wird mit keinem Wort erwähnt, daß Stephan sie auch durchsetzen muß. Wir müssen also damit rechnen, daß sich erst nach Stephans Tod, wenn Henry die Thronfolge antritt, etwas ändern wird.«

Richard war zutiefst enttäuscht. »Damit kann ich die Grafschaft vergessen.«

»Ganz so schlimm ist es nicht«, sagte Philip, »bedeutet die Entscheidung doch, daß du als rechtmäßiger Graf anerkannt bist.«

»... und daß ich bis zu Stephans Tod das Leben eines Outlaws führen muß, während diese Bestie William meine Burg besetzt hält«, ergänzte Richard wütend.

Ein Priester ging vorüber. »Nicht so laut!« zischte Philip. »Das ist alles noch streng geheim.«

Aliena schäumte vor Wut. »Ich bin nicht bereit, mich damit abzufinden! Ich bin nicht bereit, Stephans Tod abzuwarten. Ich warte jetzt seit siebzehn Jahren und bin des Wartens endgültig überdrüssig!«

»Aber was wollt Ihr tun?« fragte Philip.

Aliena wandte sich an Richard. »Bei den meisten Menschen im Land giltst du als rechtmäßiger Graf. Stephan und Henry haben in ihrer Übereinkunft diese Ansicht bestätigt. Da ist es nur recht und billig, wenn du deine Burg zurückeroberst und auch als rechtmäßiger Graf regierst.«

»Ich kann die Burg aber nicht so ohne weiteres zurückerobern. William hat mit Sicherheit für eine strenge Bewachung gesorgt.«

»Wozu hast du denn dann eine Armee, he?« Wut und Enttäuschung gingen mit Aliena durch. »Die Burg gehört dir, und du hast die Macht, sie einzunehmen.«

Richard schüttelte den Kopf. »Ich habe jetzt fünfzehn Jahre Bürgerkrieg hinter mir. Weißt du, wie oft ich in dieser Zeit erlebt habe, daß eine Burg per Frontalangriff eingenommen wurde? Kein einziges Mal!« Wie immer, wenn er über militärische Dinge sprach, gewann er unvermittelt Reife und Überzeugungskraft. »So etwas geschieht so gut wie nie. Bei Städten manchmal schon, aber nicht bei Burgen. Burgen können durch Belagerungen zur Aufgabe gezwungen werden, manchmal werden sie aber auch durch Verstärkung von außen entsetzt. Ich habe auch schon erlebt, daß Feigheit, List oder Verrat zum Fall einer Burg geführt haben – nie aber ein Frontalangriff.«

Aliena war noch nicht zum Einlenken bereit. »Dann sag mir doch mal, was geschehen würde, wenn du morgen deine Streitmacht gegen Earlscastle führtest.«

»Bevor wir in die Burg hineinkämen, würde die Besatzung die Zugbrücke hochziehen und die Tore schließen. Das heißt, wir wären gezwungen, sie zu belagern. William würde von der Belagerung Wind bekommen und so schnell wie möglich zurückkehren und unser Lager attackieren. Selbst wenn es uns gelänge, ihn zurückzuschlagen, wäre die Burg noch lange nicht in unserer Hand. Burgen sind schwer anzu- greifen und leicht zu verteidigen – deshalb werden sie ja gebaut!«

Noch während er sprach, keimte eine Idee in Alienas aufgewühltem Geist. »Feigheit, List oder Verrat«, sagte sie.

»Was?«

»Du hast also schon mehrere Burgen durch Feigheit, List oder Verrat fallen sehen.«

»O ja.«

»Auf welche Weise hat William *uns* denn damals die Burg wegge- nommen?«

»Das waren ganz andere Zeiten!« warf Philip ein. »Damals, unter dem alten König Henry, herrschte seit fünfunddreißig Jahren Frieden im Land. William hat Euren Vater schlichtweg überrascht.«

»Ja – mit einer List«, sagte Richard. »Er hat sich, bevor Alarm geschlagen werden konnte, mit ein paar Männern in die Burg ein- geschlichen. Heutzutage, da gebe ich Euch völlig recht, würde ihm das kaum noch gelingen. Die Leute sind heute viel vorsichtiger.«

»*Ich* käme schon hinein«, sagte Aliena zuversichtlich, obgleich ihr das Herz bis zum Halse schlug.

»Ja natürlich, du schon«, sagte Richard. »Du bist ja auch eine Frau. Nur könntest du drinnen nicht viel ausrichten. Deshalb würden sie dich ja auch einlassen. Du bist harmlos.«

»Sei nicht so verdammt anmaßend!« fuhr sie ihn an. »Ich habe getötet, um dich zu schützen – und das ist weit mehr, als du jemals für *mich* getan hast, du undankbarer Mistkerl! Also untersteh dich, mich noch einmal als ›harmlos‹ zu bezeichnen!«

»Gut, gut, dann bist du eben nicht harmlos«, erwiderte Richard ärgerlich. »Was hast du denn vor, wenn du erst einmal in der Burg bist?«

Alienas Zorn verflog rasch. Was würde ich tun? dachte sie angst- voll. Verdammt – ich bin doch mindestens genauso mutig und erfinde- risch wie William, dieses Schwein ... »Was hat William denn getan?«

»Er hat dafür Sorge getragen, daß die Brücke nicht mehr hochgezogen werden konnte und daß das Tor offenstand, als die Hauptstreitmacht eintraf.«

»Dann mach' ich das auch!« sagte Aliena, ihrer Angst zum Trotz.
»Und wie?«

Aliena erinnerte sich an ein vierzehnjähriges Mädchen, das sich vor einem Unwetter fürchtete. Sie hatte es getröstet. »Die Gräfin ist mir noch einen Gefallen schuldig«, sagte sie. »Außerdem haßt sie ihren Mann.«

Sie ritten die Nacht hindurch – Aliena, Richard und fünfzig seiner besten Leute. Im Morgengrauen hatten sie Earlscastle fast erreicht. Im Schutz des Waldes hielten sie an; zwischen ihnen und der Burg lag freies Feld. Aliena stieg vom Pferd, zog ihren Mantel aus flandrischer Wolle und ihre weichen Lederstiefel aus. Statt dessen schlug sie das grobe Tuch einer Bauersfrau um sich und schlüpfte in ein Paar Holzschuhe. Einer ihrer Begleiter reichte ihr einen Korb mit in Stroh verpackten frischen Eiern, den sie sich über den Arm hängte.

Richard musterte sie von oben bis unten und sagte: »Tadellos! Eine Bäuerin, die der Burgküche ihre Eier verkaufen will.«

Aliena schluckte. Gestern noch war sie voller Feuer und Kühnheit gewesen – nun aber, da es ernst wurde, hatte sie nur noch Angst.

Richard gab ihr einen Kuß auf die Wange. »Wenn ich die Glocke höre«, sagte er, »spreche ich einmal langsam das Vaterunser. Danach setzt sich die Vorhut in Marsch. Du brauchst nichts weiter zu tun, als die Wachen in vermeintlicher Sicherheit zu wiegen, so daß zehn von meinen Leuten, ohne Verdacht zu erregen, über die Felder und in die Burg kommen.«

Aliena nickte. »Paß nur auf, daß die Haupttruppe die Deckung erst verläßt, wenn die Vorhut die Zugbrücke überquert hat.«

Er lächelte. »Mach dir darüber nur keine Sorgen, ich werde an ihrer Spitze stehen. Viel Glück!«

»Dir auch!«

Aliena ging.

Sie ließ den Wald hinter sich zurück und schritt über das freie Feld auf die Burg zu, die sie an jenem furchtbaren Tag vor nunmehr sechzehn Jahren verlassen hatte. Angesichts der vertrauten Umgebung kehrten auch die Erinnerungen zurück – lebhaft und schauerlich wie selten zuvor … Sie spürte die Luft jenes Tages, noch feucht vom Regen der vergangenen Nacht. Sie dachte an die beiden Pferde, auf denen sie in wilder Flucht davongesprengt waren – Richard auf dem

Schlachtroß und sie auf dem kleineren Tier –, und an die Todesangst, die ihnen in den Knochen steckte ... Ganz bewußt hatte sie sich darum bemüht, die furchtbaren Dinge, die ihr geschehen waren, zu vergessen, indem sie sich im Rhythmus der Hufschläge des Pferdes immer wieder einsagte: *Ich kann mich nicht erinnern, ich kann mich nicht erinnern, ich kann es nicht, ich kann es nicht ...* Es hatte tatsächlich geklappt. Auf lange Zeit hinaus war sie nicht imstande gewesen, sich an die Vergewaltigung zu erinnern. Sie wußte noch, daß etwas sehr Schlimmes vorgefallen war, doch die Einzelheiten waren wie fortgeblasen. Erst als sie sich in Jack verliebt hatte, war die Erinnerung zurückgekehrt – und dies mit so furchtbarer Macht, daß sie seine Liebe nicht erwidern konnte. Gott sei Dank hatte er soviel Geduld mit ihr gehabt. Es war für sie ein Beweis für die Stärke seiner Liebe: Er hatte soviel in Kauf nehmen müssen – und liebte sie immer noch.

Es war nicht mehr weit bis zur Burg. Um sich zu beruhigen, beschwor sie auch noch einige schöne Erinnerungen an Earlscastle herauf. Hier hatte sie ihre Kindheit verbracht, mit Richard und ihrem Vater, Graf Bartholomäus. Sie hatten in Wohlstand und Sicherheit gelebt. Sie hatte mit ihrem Bruder auf den Wallanlagen der Burg getollt, in der Küche herumgelungert und sich süßes Backwerk zustekken lassen und beim Abendessen im großen Saal neben ihrem Vater gesessen. Ich wußte damals gar nicht, daß ich glücklich war, dachte sie. Ich wußte nicht, was für ein großes Glück es ist, wenn es nichts gibt, wovor man sich fürchten muß.

Und wenn ich heute alles richtig mache, werden die guten Zeiten wieder zurückkehren.

Die Gräfin ist mir noch einen Gefallen schuldig, hatte sie zuversichtlich gesagt, und: *Außerdem haßt sie ihren Mann ...* Doch schon während des nächtlichen Ritts waren ihr Bedenken gekommen. Was konnte nicht alles noch schiefgehen! Zunächst einmal war keineswegs sicher, ob sie überhaupt in die Burg hineinkam – schließlich konnte die Besatzung eine Warnung erhalten haben. Vielleicht hatten die Wachen Verdacht geschöpft, vielleicht hatte sie auch bloß Pech und geriet gleich an einen Wachposten, der sie nicht einlassen wollte. Und selbst wenn zu Beginn alles nach Plan verlief – ob Elisabeth sich von ihr tatsächlich dazu überreden lassen würde, ihren Gatten zu verraten, stand auch noch in den Sternen. Seit jener Begegnung im Unwetter waren inzwischen anderthalb Jahre vergangen. Es war durchaus nicht selten, daß Frauen sich im Laufe der Zeit auch an die furchtbarsten Ehemänner gewöhnten.

Vielleicht hatte Elisabeth sich mit ihrem Schicksal abgefunden. Schließlich bestand auch noch die Möglichkeit, daß Elisabeth, selbst wenn sie Alienas Plan zustimmte, gar nicht die Autorität oder den Mut besaß, die erforderlich waren, um ihn in die Tat umzusetzen. In jener Sturmnacht war sie ein furchtsames kleines Mädchen gewesen; wer konnte schon sagen, ob die Wache überhaupt bereit war, ihren Anordnungen Folge zu leisten?

Als Aliena die Zugbrücke überquerte, waren ihre Sinne aufs äußerste gespannt. Mit geradezu übernatürlicher Klarheit sah und hörte sie alles, was um sie herum vor sich ging. Die Besatzung der Burg war gerade erst aufgewacht. Auf dem Schanzwerk lungerten ein paar trübsinnig dreinschauende, gähnende und hustende Wachen herum. Im Torbogen saß ein alter Hund und kratzte sich. Aliena zog sich die Kapuze tief ins Gesicht, um nicht erkannt zu werden.

Auf der Bank im Torhaus saß ein schäbig gekleideter Posten und kaute an einem riesigen Stück Brot. Sein Schwertgurt hing an der rückwärtigen Wand an einem Haken. Klopfenden Herzens bedachte ihn Aliena mit einem Lächeln, das über ihre Angst hinwegtäuschte, und zeigte ihm den Eierkorb.

Mit einer ungeduldigen Handbewegung winkte er sie durch.

Das erste Hindernis war überwunden.

Die Disziplin auf der Burg ließ sehr zu wünschen übrig. Kein Wunder: Die Besatzung war mehr oder weniger eine symbolische Truppe. Sie hatte man hiergelassen, während die besten Männer in den Krieg gezogen waren. Anderswo ging es hoch her – hier auf der Burg war nichts los ...

Bis heute.

So weit, so gut. Aliena durchschritt den unteren Burghof. Ihre Nerven waren zum Zerreißen gespannt. Es war ein merkwürdiges Gefühl, als Fremde einen Ort zu besuchen, der einst die Heimat gewesen war; sich einschleichen zu müssen in eine Burg, in der ihr früher jeder Winkel offengestanden hatte. Sie sah sich um, achtete aber darauf, ihre Neugier nicht zu deutlich hervortreten zu lassen. Die überwiegend aus Holz bestehenden Wirtschaftsgebäude waren neu oder hatten sich verändert: die Ställe waren größer, die Küche stand an einem anderen Fleck.

Neu war auch eine gemauerte Rüstkammer. Insgesamt wirkte die Anlage schmutziger als früher. Geblieben war die Kapelle – die Kapelle, in der sie und Richard bis zum Ende jenes furchtbaren Sturms ausgeharrt hatten – frierend, verschreckt und halb von Sinnen. Eine

Handvoll Diener machte sich an die allmorgendlich anfallenden Arbeiten. Ein oder zwei Bewaffnete patrouillierten im Burghof. Aliena empfand ihre Anwesenheit als sehr bedrohlich. Sie versuchte, sich zu beruhigen: das kommt wahrscheinlich daher, dachte sie, daß ich weiß, daß sie mich töten würden, wenn sie wüßten, was ich im Schilde führe ...

Wenn mein Plan aufgeht, bin ich schon heute abend wieder Burgherrin ... Der Gedanke war ebenso aufregend wie unwirklich – wie ein wundersamer, unmöglicher Traum.

Sie betrat die Küche. Ein Junge schürte das Feuer, ein junges Mädchen schnitt Karotten. Aliena schenkte ihnen ein strahlendes Lächeln, stellte den Korb auf den Tisch und sagte: »Vierundzwanzig frische Eier.«

»Der Koch ist noch nicht aufgestanden«, sagte der Junge. »Ihr werdet auf Euer Geld noch eine Weile warten müssen.«

»Kann ich irgendwo ein bißchen Brot für mein Frühstück bekommen?«

»Im großen Saal.«

»Danke.« Aliena wandte sich zum Gehen. Den Korb ließ sie in der Küche.

Sie überquerte die zweite Zugbrücke und lächelte dem Posten im zweiten Torhaus zu. Seine Haare waren ungekämmt, die Augen blutunterlaufen. Er sah sie von oben bis unten an und fragte: »Wohin des Weges?« In seinen Worten lag eine spielerische Herausforderung.

»Zum Frühstück«, antwortete Aliena, ohne stehenzubleiben.

»Ich hab' was zu knabbern für Euch«, rief er ihr anzüglich nach.

»Paßt nur auf, daß ich es nicht abbeiße!« rief Aliena über die Schulter zurück.

Niemand schöpfte auch nur den geringsten Verdacht. Sie kamen überhaupt nicht auf den Gedanken, daß eine Frau gefährlich sein konnte. Was für Narren sie doch sind, dachte Aliena. Frauen konnten fast alles, was Männer konnten: Wer hielt denn zu Hause den Betrieb aufrecht, wenn die Männer Krieg führten oder Kreuzzüge unternahmen? Es gab Färberinnen, Gerberinnen, Bäckerinnen, Brauerinnen und weibliche Zimmerer. Aliena selbst war eine der bedeutendsten Kauffrauen der Grafschaft. Die Pflichten einer Äbtissin unterschieden sich in nichts von denen eines Abts. Und war es nicht eine Frau, die Kaiserin Mathilde, die jenen nun schon seit fünfzehn Jahren tobenden Bürgerkrieg ausgelöst hatte? Doch all dies ließ diese holzköpfigen Wachsoldaten völlig kalt: Sie trauten einer Frau einfach nicht zu, eine feindliche Spionin zu sein – nur weil es ungewöhnlich war.

Sie rannte die Treppen zum großen Saal empor. Die Tür war nicht besetzt – vermutlich, weil der Burgherr nicht zugegen war. Ich werde in Zukunft dafür sorgen, daß stets ein Hofmeister an der Tür steht – ob die Burgherrin nun da ist oder nicht.

Fünfzehn oder zwanzig Personen hatten sich um einen kleinen Tisch zum Frühstück versammelt. Ein oder zwei blickten bei Alienas Eintreten auf, waren aber nicht weiter an ihr interessiert. Der Saal machte einen recht gepflegten Eindruck und verriet die weibliche Hand: Die Wände waren frisch geweißt, und süßlicher Kräuterduft mischte sich in den Geruch der Binsen auf dem Boden. Elisabeth machte, wenn auch nur in bescheidenem Maße, ihren Einfluß geltend – ein Zeichen, das Anlaß zur Hoffnung gab.

Ohne mit den Leuten am Tisch zu sprechen, durchschritt Aliena die Halle und begab sich zu der ins nächsthöhere Stockwerk führenden Treppe. Sie tat, als sei dies für sie die größte Selbstverständlichkeit, und schaffte es tatsächlich, den Fuß der Treppe zu erreichen, ohne daß sie jemand aufhielt. Erst als sie schon die Stufen hinaufhastete, hörte sie hinter sich jemanden rufen: »He, Ihr da – Ihr könnt nicht einfach so da hinauflaufen!« Sie achtete nicht auf die Stimme. Dann hörte sie, daß ihr jemand auf den Fersen war.

Schwer atmend kam sie oben an. In welchem Zimmer wird Elisabeth schlafen? In Vaters ehemaligem Schlafgemach? Oder hat sie in meinem Zimmer ein eigenes Bett? Aliena zögerte einen Augenblick. Wahrscheinlich hat William inzwischen kein Interesse mehr daran, jede Nacht das Lager mit ihr zu teilen, dachte sie dann, und wenn dem so ist, läßt er sie in ihrem eigenen Zimmer schlafen. Aliena klopfte an die Tür des kleineren Zimmers und öffnete sie.

Ihre Vermutung erwies sich als zutreffend. Elisabeth saß im Nachthemd am Feuer und kämmte sich die Haare. Sie schreckte auf und runzelte die Stirn. Dann erkannte sie Aliena. »Ihr seid es!« rief sie aus. »Was für eine Überraschung!«

Aliena hörte hinter sich Schritte auf der Treppe. »Darf ich hereinkommen?« fragte sie.

»Aber gewiß doch! Seid willkommen!«

Flink trat Aliena über die Schwelle, schloß die Tür hinter sich und ging auf Elisabeth zu. Da platzte ein Mann herein und rief: »He, Ihr da – für wen haltet Ihr Euch eigentlich?« Er kam auf Aliena zu, als wolle er sie festnehmen.

»Untersteht Euch, mir nahe zu kommen!« herrschte sie ihn mit befehlsgewohnter Stimme an. »Ich bin gekommen, um der Gräfin eine

Botschaft von Graf William zu überbringen, und wenn Ihr die Tür zum Saal bewacht hättet, anstatt Euch mit Brot vollzufressen, dann wüßtet Ihr längst Bescheid.«

Der Mann wirkte auf einmal sehr betreten.

»Schon gut, Edgar«, sagte Elisabeth. »Die Dame ist mir bekannt.«

»Sehr wohl, Gräfin«, sagte der Mann und entfernte sich.

Ich hab's geschafft, dachte Aliena. Ich bin bei ihr.

Ihr Herzschlag beruhigte sich langsam. Sie sah sich im Zimmer um. Es hatte sich nicht viel verändert seit der Zeit, da sie diesen Raum bewohnt hatte. In einer Schale lagen getrocknete Blütenblätter, an der Wand hing ein hübscher Gobelin, eine Kleidertruhe stand da, ein paar Bücher lagen herum. Das Bett – es war tatsächlich noch dasselbe – stand an der gleichen Stelle wie früher, und auf dem Kopfkissen lag eine Stoffpuppe von der Art, wie sie selbst eine besessen hatte.

Aliena fühlte sich auf einmal alt.

»Das war früher mal mein Zimmer«, sagte sie.

»Ich weiß«, antwortete Elisabeth.

Aliena war überrascht. Sie hatte Elisabeth nichts über ihre Vergangenheit erzählt.

»Ich habe mich seit jenem furchtbaren Sturm genauestens über Euch informiert«, erklärte Elisabeth und fügte hinzu: »Ich bewundere Euch so sehr!« Ihre Augen schimmerten vor Begeisterung; sie schien Aliena geradezu anzuhimmeln.

Das war ein vielversprechendes Zeichen.

»Und William?« fragte Aliena. »Vertragt Ihr Euch inzwischen besser mit ihm?«

Elisabeth wandte den Blick ab. »Nun ja«, sagte sie zögernd. »Ich habe jetzt mein eigenes Zimmer, und er ist ja oft unterwegs. Insofern ist tatsächlich alles viel besser geworden ...« Und dann brach sie in Tränen aus.

Aliena setzte sich zu ihr aufs Bett und legte die Arme um sie. Elisabeth schluchzte tief und jammervoll, und die Tränen flossen ihr die Wangen herunter. Sie weinte so sehr, daß sie nach Luft ringen mußte, und als sie sprach, kamen die Worte nur stoßweise: »Ich ... hasse ihn! Ich wollte ... ich wäre ... tot!«

Ihre Seelenqual und ihre Jugend waren so anrührend, daß Aliena beinahe selbst die Tränen gekommen wären. Ihr war schmerzhaft bewußt, daß Elisabeths Schicksal leicht ihr eigenes hätte werden können. Sie tätschelte der Gräfin den Rücken, so wie sie es bei Sally tat, wenn sie traurig war.

Mit der Zeit beruhigte sich Elisabeth ein wenig. Mit dem Ärmel ihres Nachthemds wischte sie sich die Tränen aus dem Gesicht. »Ich habe solche Angst, ich könnte ein Kind von ihm bekommen«, sagte sie bedrückt. »Ich weiß genau, daß er es mißhandeln würde.«

»Das kann ich gut verstehen«, sagte Aliena. Sie selbst hatte mit der furchtbaren Vorstellung leben müssen, von William schwanger zu sein.

Mit weit aufgerissenen Augen starrte Elisabeth sie an. »Stimmt es, was die Leute sagen … was er Euch angetan hat?«

»Ja, es stimmt. Ich war in Eurem Alter, als es geschah.«

Ihre Blicke trafen sich, der gemeinsame Abscheu brachte sie einander sehr nahe. Elisabeth kam ihr plötzlich sehr erwachsen vor.

»Wenn Ihr wollt, seid Ihr ihn heute abend los«, sagte Aliena.

Elisabeth starrte sie an. »Wirklich?«

Aliena nickte. »Deshalb bin ich hier.«

»Und dann darf ich wieder heim?« fragte Elisabeth, und ihre Augen füllten sich mit frischen Tränen. »Kann ich dann wieder heim nach Weymouth, zu meiner Mama? *Heute noch*?«

»Ja, aber vorher müßt Ihr sehr tapfer sein.«

»Ich bin zu allem bereit«, sagte sie, »zu allem! Ihr müßt mir nur sagen, was ich zu tun habe.«

Aliena erinnerte sich an die Ratschläge zum Umgang mit dem Personal, die sie Elisabeth damals gegeben hatte, und sie fragte sich, ob es der Gräfin wohl gelungen war, sie in die Tat umzusetzen. »Werdet Ihr noch immer vom Hauspersonal schikaniert?« fragte sie unverblümt.

»Sie versuchen's jedenfalls.«

»Aber Ihr erlaubt es Ihnen nicht …«

Elisabeth war die Frage sichtlich peinlich. »Doch, manchmal schon noch. Aber ich bin jetzt sechzehn Jahre alt und schon seit zwei Jahren Gräfin. Ich bemühe mich immer, Eure Ratschläge zu beherzigen, und es klappt ganz gut.«

»Hört zu, was ich Euch zu sagen habe«, sagte Aliena. »König Stephan hat ein Abkommen mit Herzog Henry geschlossen, demzufolge alle Ländereien denjenigen zurückzugeben sind, denen sie zu Zeiten des seligen König Henry gehörten. Das bedeutet, mein Bruder wird eines Tages Graf von Shiring. Er möchte es aber so bald wie möglich sein.«

Elisabeth riß die Augen weit auf. »Will Richard gegen William Krieg führen?«

»Richard liegt mit einer kleinen Truppe nicht weit von hier auf der Lauer. Wenn es ihm gelingt, die Burg noch heute zu erobern, wird man ihn allenthalben als Graf anerkennen – und dann ist William erledigt.«

»Ich kann es nicht fassen!« sagte Elisabeth. »Ich kann es einfach nicht fassen!« Ihre plötzliche Begeisterung war fast noch rührender als zuvor ihre tiefe Niedergeschlagenheit.

»Alles war Ihr zu tun habt, ist folgendes: Ihr müßt dafür sorgen, daß Richard kampflos in die Burg kommt. Wenn alles vorüber ist, bringen wir Euch heim.«

Elisabeth schien schon wieder zu verzagen. »Ich weiß nicht, ob die Männer mir folgen werden.«

Das war auch Alienas Sorge. »Wer ist der Hauptmann der Wache?«

»Michael Armstrong. Ich kann ihn nicht leiden.«

»Laßt ihn holen!«

»Gut.« Elisabeth putzte sich die Nase, stand auf und ging zur Tür. »Madge!« rief sie mit schriller Stimme. Von irgendwoher ertönte eine Antwort. »Geh und hol mir Michael. Er soll sofort kommen – es ist dringend. Beeil dich!«

Sie kam zurück, warf sich rasch die Tunika über ihr Nachthemd, schlüpfte in ihre Stiefel und schnürte sie zu. Aliena gab ihr noch schnell die nötigsten Anweisungen: »Sagt Michael, er möge die große Glocke läuten und alle Menschen auf dem Burghof zusammenkommen lassen. Sagt ihm, Ihr hättet eine Botschaft von Graf William erhalten und wolltet darüber zu allen Bewohnern der Burg sprechen, Bewaffneten wie Dienern gleichermaßen. Sie sollen sich, mit Ausnahme von drei und vier Wachen, die auf ihren Posten bleiben, im unteren Burghof versammeln. Sagt ihm ferner, daß Ihr in Kürze einen Trupp von zehn oder zwölf Reitern mit einer neuen Botschaft erwartet. Diese Leute müßten nach ihrer Ankunft unverzüglich zu Euch gebracht werden.«

»Ich hoffe, ich kann mir das alles merken«, sagte Elisabeth unsicher.

»Keine Angst – wenn Ihr etwas vergeßt, helfe ich Euch.«

»Da ist mir schon wohler zumute.«

»Was ist das für ein Mensch – dieser Michael Armstrong?«

»Ein Griesgram, gebaut wie ein Ochse, und er riecht nicht gut.«

»Ist er gescheit?«

»Nein.«

»Um so besser.«

Einen Augenblick später traf der Gerufene ein. Er hatte einen kurzen, gedrungenen Hals, breite Schultern und stank nachhaltig nach Schweinestall. Seiner verdrießlichen Miene war zu entnehmen, daß er ungern auf diese Weise gestört wurde. Fragend sah er Elisabeth an.

»Ich habe eine Botschaft von Graf William erhalten«, begann die Gräfin.

Michael streckte die Hand aus.

Verflucht, dachte Aliena, niemand hat daran gedacht, einen Brief an Elisabeth zu schreiben. Der ganze Plan kann an dieser dummen Nachlässigkeit scheitern ... Schon warf ihr die Gräfin einen hilfesuchenden Blick zu. Verzweifelt suchte Aliena einen Ausweg. Endlich fiel ihr etwas ein. »Könnt Ihr lesen, Michael?«

Die Frage ärgerte den Hauptmann. »Der Priester wird es mir vorlesen.«

»Eure Gräfin versteht sich aufs Lesen.«

»Ich möchte die Botschaft allen Bewohnern der Burg persönlich mitteilen, Michael. Läute die Glocke und ruf die Leute im unteren Burghof zusammen. Achte aber darauf, daß drei oder vier Mann auf den Posten bleiben.«

Wie Aliena schon befürchtet hatte, gefiel es dem Hauptmann ganz und gar nicht, daß Elisabeth ihm in dieser Form Befehle erteilte. Sein Widerspruchsgeist war geweckt. »Warum kann *ich* den Leuten nicht Mitteilung machen?«

Aliena spürte, daß der Mann sich nicht so ohne weiteres überzeugen ließ: Möglicherweise war er für vernünftige Argumente einfach zu dumm. »Ich habe der Gräfin folgenreiche Nachrichten aus Winchester überbracht«, sagte sie. »Sie möchte die Burgbewohner *persönlich* darüber in Kenntnis setzen.«

»Und was *sind* das für Nachrichten?«

Aliena gab ihm keine Antwort. Elisabeth wirkte auf einmal wieder sehr ängstlich. Aber da Aliena ihr über den Inhalt der fiktiven Botschaft nichts gesagt hatte, konnte sie Michaels Forderung gar nicht erfüllen. Sie entschloß sich, die Frage einfach zu ignorieren, und fuhr fort, als habe Michael gar nichts gesagt: »Sag den Wachen, sie sollen nach einer Gruppe von zehn oder zwölf Reitern Ausschau halten. Ihr Anführer wird eine weitere Botschaft von Graf William mit sich führen und muß unverzüglich zu mir vorgelassen werden. Und jetzt läute die Glocke.«

Michael war noch nicht bereit, klein beizugeben. Während Aliena vor Aufregung den Atem anhielt, runzelte er die Stirn und sagte:

»Noch mehr Boten? Diese Dame hier mit einer Botschaft – und zwölf Reiter mit einer anderen?«

»Ja – und nun geh bitte und läute die Glocke.« Aliena hörte deutlich ein leises Zittern in ihrer Stimme.

Michael gab seinen Widerstand auf. Er konnte nicht begreifen, was hier gespielt wurde – aber er wußte auch nicht, was er noch hätte einwenden können. »Sehr wohl, Lady«, sagte er schließlich mürrisch und entfernte sich.

Aliena atmete auf.

»Was wird jetzt geschehen?« fragte Elisabeth.

»Wir warten, bis sich die Leute im Burghof versammelt haben«, sagte Aliena. »Dann berichtet Ihr ihnen von dem Friedensschluß zwischen König Stephan und Herzog Henry. Dadurch werden sie abgelenkt. Noch während Ihr sprecht, wird Richards Vorhut eintreffen. Die Wachen werden sie für die angekündigten Boten von Graf William halten, das heißt, sie werden nicht sofort die Zugbrücke hochziehen. Ihr müßt versuchen, Euer Publikum so lange bei der Stange zu halten, bis die Vorhut die Burg erreicht hat. Habt Ihr das verstanden?«

Elisabeth war furchtbar aufgeregt. »Und was dann?« fragte sie.

»Sobald ich Euch Bescheid sage, verkündet Ihr, daß Ihr die Burg dem rechtmäßigen Grafen, also Richard, übergebt. Richards Streitmacht wird daraufhin ihre Deckung verlassen und die Burg erstürmen. Michael wird dann merken, was gespielt wird – seine Männer aber sehen sich urplötzlich vor einem Loyalitätskonflikt: Schließlich habt *Ihr* sie soeben zur kampflosen Übergabe der Burg aufgefordert und Richard den ›rechtmäßigen Grafen‹ genannt! Außerdem wird die mittlerweile auf dem Burghof befindliche Vorhut das Heraufziehen der Zugbrücke verhindern.« Die Glocke begann zu läuten. Alienas Magen verkrampfte sich vor Angst. »Wir haben keine Zeit mehr!« rief sie. »Wie fühlt Ihr Euch?«

»Ich fürchte mich so.«

»Ich mich auch. Gehen wir!«

Sie gingen die Treppe hinunter. Die Glocke am Turm des Torhauses läutete wie in unbeschwerten Kindertagen. Dieselbe Glocke, derselbe Klang – aber eine andere Aliena, dachte Aliena. Sie wußte, daß die Glocke weit über die Felder scholl und auch am Waldrand noch zu hören war. Richard würde nun leise das Vaterunser sprechen und damit die Zeit bis zur Entsendung der Vorhut messen.

Aliena und Elisabeth verließen den Wohnturm und begaben sich über die innere Zugbrücke zum unteren Burghof. Elisabeth war blaß

vor Furcht, doch die strenge Linie ihres Mundes verriet Entschlossenheit. Aliena lächelte ihr aufmunternd zu, zog sich dann aber schnell
wieder die Kapuze vors Gesicht. Zwar hatte sie bislang noch niemanden gesehen, den sie kannte, doch wußte sie, daß ihr eigenes Gesicht
in der Grafschaft weithin bekannt war, und rechnete über kurz oder
lang fest mit ihrer Entlarvung. Einige Leute musterten sie neugierig,
aber niemand sprach sie an.

In der Mitte des unteren Burghofs blieben die beiden Frauen stehen. Da der Grund zum Torhaus hin etwas abfiel, konnte Aliena über
die Köpfe der bereits versammelten Menge hinweg durchs Tor auf die
umliegenden Felder sehen. Die Vorhut mußte inzwischen schon aufgebrochen sein, doch war nirgendwo ein Zeichen zu erkennen. O Gott,
dachte Aliena angstvoll, hoffentlich ist nicht noch etwas schiefgegangen ...

Um zu den Menschen sprechen zu können, brauchte Elisabeth
eine Art Podest. Aliena wies einen Diener an, ihr aus dem Stall einen
Tritt aus Holz zu bringen, der kleinen Leuten leichter auf große Pferde
half. Während sie noch warteten, sprach plötzlich eine ältere Frau
Aliena an: »Meiner Treu! Lady Aliena. Wie schön, Euch zu sehen!«

Aliena erschrak. Die Frau war eine Köchin, die schon vor der
Besetzung der Burg durch die Hamleighs hier gearbeitet hatte. Aliena
zwang sich zu einem Lächeln und sagte: »Hallo, Tilly, wie geht es dir?«

Tilly gab ihrem Nachbarn einen Stoß. »He, du, Lady Aliena ist
wieder da, nach all den Jahren! Werdet Ihr wieder unsere Herrin sein,
Gnädigste?«

Aliena sah sich ängstlich um. Michael Armstrong hätte das jetzt
nicht hören dürfen, dachte sie. Glücklicherweise war der Hauptmann
der Wache nicht in Hörweite. Allerdings hatte einer seiner Bewaffneten
das kurze Gespräch mitbekommen und starrte Aliena jetzt mit gerunzelter Stirn an. Aliena erwiderte den Blick mit gespielter Arglosigkeit.
Der Mann hatte nur ein Auge (was zweifellos der Grund dafür war,
daß er nicht mit William ins Feld hatte ziehen dürfen). Aliena fand
es auf einmal furchtbar komisch, von einem Einäugigen angestarrt zu
werden. Sie mußte ein Lachen unterdrücken und spürte, daß sie fast
hysterisch war.

Der Diener brachte den Tritt, und die Glocke hörte auf zu läuten.
Aliena versuchte sich zu sammeln. Elisabeth bestieg das kleine Podest.
Die Menge verstummte.

»König Stephan und Herzog Henry haben Frieden geschlossen«,
sagte Elisabeth.

Sie machte eine Pause, und Jubelrufe ertönten. Aliena spähte durchs Tor. Jetzt, Richard, dachte sie ... jetzt! Du darfst nicht zu lange warten.

Elisabeth lächelte. Als der Jubel abgeebbt war, fuhr sie fort: »Stephan wird König sein, bis er stirbt. Henry wird sein Nachfolger.«

Aliena hielt nach den Posten auf den Türmen und über dem Torhaus Ausschau. Sie wirkten völlig entspannt. Wo blieb Richard?

»Der Friedensschluß wird unser aller Leben in vielfacher Hinsicht verändern«, sagte Elisabeth.

Die Posten fuhren plötzlich zusammen und konzentrierten sich. Einer beschattete die Augen mit der Hand und spähte über die Felder. Ein anderer sah in den Burghof hinab; es hatte den Anschein, als suche er seinen Kommandanten. Aber Michael Armstrong hörte interessiert Elisabeth zu.

»Der gegenwärtige und der zukünftige König haben gemeinsam beschlossen, daß alle Ländereien jenen zurückzugeben sind, denen sie zu Zeiten des seligen Königs Henry gehörten ...«

Diese Nachricht löste ein aufgeregtes Gemurmel aus. Die Leute spekulierten darüber, ob auch die Grafschaft Shiring von dieser Regelung betroffen war. Auch Michael Armstrong blickte nachdenklich vor sich hin. Und dann sah Aliena endlich die langersehnte Vorhut von Richards Truppe auf die Burg zukommen. Schnell! rief sie ihnen in Gedanken zu. Beeilt euch! Aber die Reiter dachten gar nicht daran. Sie ritten im gemächlichen Trab, denn sie wollten die Posten nicht mißtrauisch machen.

Elisabeth sagte: »Wir wollen alle dem lieben Gott für diesen Friedensschluß danken. Wir wollen beten, daß König Stephan in den Jahren, die ihm noch vergönnt sind, ein kluger und weiser Herrscher sein wird und daß der junge Herzog friedlich auf seine Stunde wartet, bis es dem Herrn gefällt, Stephan zu sich zu rufen ...«

Sie spielte ihre Rolle großartig, fürchtete aber offenbar, ihr könnten die Worte ausgehen.

Die Posten behielten die näher rückenden Reiter scharf im Auge. Sie waren auf ihre Ankunft vorbereitet und hatten den Befehl, den Anführer unverzüglich zur Gräfin zu bringen. Irgendwelche Abwehrmaßnahmen waren nicht erforderlich – aber neugierig waren sie trotzdem.

Der Einäugige spähte durchs Tor und sah sich wieder nach Aliena um. Offensichtlich grübelte er darüber nach, ob zwischen ihrer Gegenwart und der Ankunft der Reiter ein Zusammenhang bestand.

Einer der Posten auf den Zinnen schien sich zu einem Entschluß durchgerungen zu haben. Er verschwand im Treppenabgang.

Die Menge wurde langsam unruhig. Elisabeth verstand es sehr geschickt, ihre Rede in die Länge zu ziehen, doch die Leute waren nur an harten Fakten interessiert. »Dieser Krieg«, sagte sie, »begann im Jahr nach meiner Geburt, und wie so viele andere junge Menschen überall im Königreich warte ich mit Spannung darauf, den Frieden kennenzulernen ...«

Der Posten, der von der Brüstung heruntergekommen war, ging mit strammen Schritten auf seinen Kommandanten zu und redete auf ihn ein.

Die Reiter waren, wie Aliena durch das offenstehende Tor sehen konnte, noch immer gut zweihundert Schritt entfernt – also noch viel zu weit! Aliena hätte schreien können vor Wut und Verzweiflung. Lange halte ich es nicht mehr aus, dachte sie.

Michael Armstrong drehte sich um. Just in diesem Moment zupfte ihn der Einäugige am Ärmel, raunte ihm etwas zu und deutete auf Aliena.

Aliena war wie besessen von dem Gedanken, daß Michael noch vor Ankunft der Reiter das Tor schließen und die Zugbrücke hochziehen lassen könnte, und sie wußte nicht, wie sie ihn daran würde hindern können. Sie fragte sich, ob sie imstande wäre, sich im kritischen Augenblick, also bevor er die entscheidenden Befehle geben konnte, auf ihn zu stürzen. Sie dachte an den Dolch, der an ihren linken Arm gebunden war, und sagte sich: Notfalls kann ich ihn sogar töten. Da wandte sich Michael Armstrong mit einer entschlossenen Bewegung zum Gehen. Aliena berührte Elisabeths Ellbogen. »Haltet Michael zurück!« zischte sie ihr zu.

Elisabeth öffnete den Mund, brachte aber keinen Laut hervor. Sie war vor Angst wie versteinert. Dann wandelte sich ihr Ausdruck plötzlich. Sie holte tief Luft, reckte den Kopf und rief in einem Ton, der keinen Widerspruch zuließ: »Michael Armstrong!«

Michael kehrte um.

Jetzt gibt es kein Zurück mehr, dachte Aliena. Richard hat es immer noch nicht ganz geschafft – und uns hier geht die Zeit aus. Sie wandte sich an Elisabeth. »Jetzt müßt Ihr es ihnen sagen.«

Und Elisabeth sagte: »Ich übergebe diese Burg dem rechtmäßigen Grafen von Shiring, Richard von Kingsbridge.«

Michael Armstrong starrte seine Herrin ungläubig an und schrie: »Das kann doch nicht Euer Ernst sein!«

Elisabeth fuhr fort: »Ich befehle euch allen, auf der Stelle die Waffen niederzulegen. Es soll zu keinem Blutvergießen kommen.«

Michael drehte sich um und schrie: »Die Brücke hoch! Schließt die Tore!«

Die Bewaffneten sprangen herbei, um seinen Befehl zu erfüllen, aber Michael Armstrong hatte einen Augenblick zu lange gezögert. Als die Männer das schwere, eisenbeschlagene Tor erreichten, klapperte auf der anderen Seite gerade Richards Vorhut über die Zugbrücke und ritt unbehelligt in den Burghof ein. Michaels Leute trugen zum großen Teil keine Rüstung, und manche von ihnen hatten noch nicht einmal ihr Schwert parat. So stoben sie vor den anrückenden Reitern auseinander.

»Ruhe bewahren!« rief Elisabeth. »Diese Boten werden meine Befehle bestätigen!«

Von den Zinnen tönte ein aufgeregter Schrei: »Michael! Attacke! Wir werden angegriffen! Sie kommen zu Dutzenden!«

»Verrat!« brüllte Michael und zog sein Schwert. Aber da waren auch schon zwei von Richards Reitern über ihm. Klingen blitzten auf, Blut spritzte, und der Kommandant der Wache stürzte zu Boden. Aliena wandte sich ab.

Ein paar von Richards Leuten hatten inzwischen das Torhaus und den kleinen Raum mit der Zugbrückenwinde besetzt. Zwei weitere erstürmten die Zinnen, wo Michaels Posten sich kampflos ergaben.

Nun galoppierte Richards Haupttruppe über das freie Gelände vor der Burg. Ihr Anblick ließ Alienas Herz höher schlagen.

»Dies ist eine friedliche Übergabe!« rief Elisabeth, so laut sie konnte. »Niemandem wird ein Leid angetan, das verspreche ich euch. Bleibt, wo ihr seid!«

Die Menschen auf dem Burghof blieben stehen wie angewurzelt und lauschten dem Donnerhall der anstürmenden Armee. Michaels Bewaffnete waren sichtlich verwirrt und unsicher, aber keiner von ihnen rührte die Hand: Ihr Anführer war gefallen, ihre Gräfin hatte sie zur Kapitulation aufgerufen. Das Personal war von der Schnelligkeit der Ereignisse wie gelähmt.

Und dann ritt Richard von Kingsbridge auf seinem Schlachtroß zum Tor herein.

Es war ein großartiger Augenblick, der Alienas Herz mit Stolz erfüllte. Richard sah blendend aus; er lächelte und kostete seinen Triumph aus. Aliena rief: »Der rechtmäßige Graf!« Die Männer, die hinter Richard auf dem Burghof Einzug hielten, nahmen den Ruf auf, und auch in der Menge erhoben sich ein paar Stimmen, die ihn wiederholten – die meisten Menschen in der Runde waren auf William nicht gut zu sprechen. Im Schritt ritt Richard rund um den Burghof. Er winkte der Menge zu und bedankte sich für den freundlichen Empfang.

Aliena mußte daran denken, was sie um dieses glücklichen Augenblicks willen alles auf sich genommen hatte. Vierunddreißig Jahre war sie jetzt alt. Mein halbes Leben habe ich dafür gekämpft, dachte sie, meine besten Jahre dafür gegeben. Sie dachte daran, wie sie Wolle in Säcke gestopft hatte, bis ihr die Hände schwollen und bluteten. Sie dachte an die vielen Gesichter, die sie unterwegs gesehen hatte, von Gier, Grausamkeit und Lüsternheit verzerrte Gesichter von Männern, die sie beim geringsten Zeichen von Schwäche gewiß getötet hätten. Sie dachte daran, wie sich ihr Herz gegen den guten Jack verhärtet und sie an seiner Statt Alfred geheiratet hatte, und an die vielen Monate, in denen sie wie ein Hund vor der Bettstatt ihres Mannes hatte schlafen müssen, und dies alles einzig und allein deshalb, weil er versprochen hatte, Waffen und Rüstung für Richard zu kaufen ... »Hier hast du deine Burg zurück, Vater«, sagte sie laut, doch niemand hörte sie in der jubelnden Menge. »Dein Wille ist geschehen«, sagte sie zu ihrem toten Vater, und in ihren Triumph mischte sich Bitterkeit. »Ich habe es dir versprochen und mein Versprechen gehalten. Ich habe mich um Richard gekümmert, und er hat jahrelang gekämpft und gekämpft. Und heute kehren wir endlich heim, und Richard ist Graf von Shiring. Doch jetzt ...« Ihre Worte wurden zum Schrei, doch schrien jetzt alle, und niemand bemerkte die Tränen, die ihr die Wangen herunterliefen. »Doch jetzt, Vater, bin ich mit dir fertig. Fahr hinab in dein Grab und gib mir Frieden!«

Remigius war hochmütig, selbst in der Not. Hocherhobenen Hauptes betrat er das große Holzhaus in Hamleigh und blickte an seiner langen Nase vorbei auf die riesigen, grob behauenen Balken, die das Dach trugen, die Wände, die aus mit Lehm beworfenem Flechtwerk bestanden, und die offene Feuerstelle auf dem gestampften Boden.

William sah ihn hereinkommen. Ich mag ja gegenwärtig eine Pechsträhne haben, dachte er, aber so heruntergekommen wie du bin ich noch lange nicht ... Ihm entgingen weder die mehrfach geflickten Sandalen noch die schäbige Kutte des Mönchs, weder das unrasierte Kinn noch die verwahrlosten Haare. Remigius war nie besonders dick gewesen – doch jetzt war er so mager wie nie zuvor. Der hochmütige Zug, der seinem Gesicht eingebrannt zu sein schien, konnte weder die tiefen Spuren der Abzehrung noch die blutunterlaufenen Tränensäcke verhüllen. Remigius war noch nicht gebrochen, aber er hatte eine sehr schwere Niederlage erlitten.

»Gott segne Euch, mein Sohn«, sagte er zu William.

Komm mir bloß nicht so! dachte William und sagte: »Was willst du hier, Remigius?« Daß er den Mönch duzte und ihn zusätzlich noch durch die Verweigerung der Anrede »Vater« oder »Bruder« beleidigte, geschah in voller Absicht.

Remigius zuckte zusammen, als habe man ihn geschlagen, und William dachte: Dumm angeredet wurdest du sicher schon des öfteren, seitdem es mit dir so bergab geht ... Remigius sagte: »Graf Richard hat die Ländereien, die Ihr mir in meiner Eigenschaft als Dekan des Domkapitels von Shiring übereignet habt, wieder in seinen Besitz genommen.«

»Das überrascht mich nicht«, gab William zurück. »Alles wird den ehemaligen Eigentümern zurückerstattet.«

»Aber dadurch verliere ich meinen Lebensunterhalt.«

»Nicht nur du, viele andere auch«, erwiderte William leichthin. »Dir wird nichts anderes übrigbleiben, als nach Kingsbridge zurückzukehren.«

Remigius wurde blaß vor Wut. »Das kann ich nicht«, sagte er mit leiser Stimme.

William rieb Salz in die Wunde. »Warum nicht?«

»Das wißt Ihr ganz genau.«

»Was würde Philip denn sagen, he? Daß du kleine Mädchen nicht mehr nach Kriegsgeheimnissen ausforschen sollst? Er hält dich wohl für einen Verräter, weil du mir gesagt hast, wo die Outlaws stecken, wie? Oder ärgert er sich darüber, daß du Dekan einer Kirche werden solltest, die als Konkurrenzunternehmen zu seiner Kathedrale gedacht war? Tja, wenn's so ist, dann kann ich schon verstehen, daß du nicht mehr zurückwillst.«

»Gebt mir *etwas*«, bat Remigius. »Ein Dorf. Ein Gehöft. Oder eine kleine Kirche!«

»Verlierer werden nicht bezahlt, Mönch!« sagte William hart. Das Gespräch machte ihm Spaß. »In der Welt außerhalb der Klostermauern kümmert sich kein Schwein um dich. Die Enten fressen die Würmer, die Füchse töten die Enten, die Menschen erlegen die Füchse, und der Teufel jagt die Menschen.«

Remigius' Stimme verwandelte sich in ein Flüstern. »Was soll ich tun?«

»Betteln«, antwortete William lächelnd. Remigius machte auf dem Absatz kehrt und verließ das Haus. Immer noch stolz, dachte William, aber nicht mehr lange. Bald wirst du betteln ...

Es freute ihn, daß es Leute gab, die tiefer gefallen waren als er. Nie würde er die qualvolle Verzweiflung vergessen, die ihn befallen hatte, als man ihm am Tor seiner eigenen Burg den Einlaß verwehrte. Sein Mißtrauen war bereits geweckt worden, als er in Winchester erfuhr, daß Richard mit einigen seiner Leute die Stadt verlassen habe. Als die Bedingungen des Friedensvertrags bekannt wurden, hatte sich das Unbehagen in höchste Betroffenheit verwandelt. William hatte seine Ritter und Schergen zusammengetrommelt und war auf schnellstem Wege nach Earlscastle galoppiert. Da er eine Besatzung zurückgelassen hatte, rechnete er damit, daß Richard und seine Mannen die Burg belagerten und zu diesem Zweck auf dem freien Vorgelände ein Lager aufgeschlagen hätten. Als sie schließlich die Burg erreichten, war alles ruhig und nirgendwo ein Feind zu sehen. William fiel ein

Stein vom Herzen, und er machte sich schon Vorwürfe, daß er auf Richards plötzliches Verschwinden so überzogen reagiert hatte.

Doch dann sah er auf einmal, daß die Zugbrücke hochgezogen war. William ritt bis zum Rand des Burggrabens vor und rief: »Macht auf! Der Graf kehrt zurück!«

Da war oben auf den Zinnen Richard erschienen und hatte zurückgerufen: »Der Graf ist bereits anwesend.«

William hatte geglaubt, der Boden unter seinen Füßen tue sich auf. Immer hatte er Angst vor Richard gehabt, immer den gefährlichen Rivalen in ihm gesehen, vor dem man sich hüten mußte. Doch gerade zum damaligen Zeitpunkt hatte er die Gefahr nicht besonders hoch eingeschätzt. Später, hatte er gedacht, nach Stephans Ableben und Henrys Thronbesteigung, da mochte es wieder gefährlich werden, aber bis dahin hätten gut und gerne noch zehn Jahre ins Land gehen können ...

Nun saß er in seinem Landhaus und grübelte über seine Fehler nach. Verbittert gestand er sich ein, daß Richard mit großer Gerissenheit zu Werke gegangen war: Er hatte eine kleine Lücke erkannt und sofort ausgenutzt. Da der Krieg noch nicht offiziell beendet gewesen war, konnte man ihn nicht des Landfriedensbruchs anklagen. Sein Anspruch auf die Grafschaft war durch die Bestimmungen des Friedensvertrags legitimiert, und zudem hatte der geschlagene, alt und müde gewordene Stephan gar nicht mehr die Kraft für weitere Gefechte.

Großmütig hatte Richard alle Bewaffneten, die weiterhin für William Dienst tun wollten, freigelassen. Waldo Oneeye hatte William schließlich erzählt, wie die Eroberung der Burg vonstatten gegangen war. Elisabeths Verrat war unglaublich, doch das für William Demütigendste an der Sache war Alienas Rolle in dem Komplott. Das hilflose kleine Mädchen, das er vor vielen Jahren gefoltert, vergewaltigt und von der Burg vertrieben hatte, war zurückgekehrt und hatte sich gerächt. Jedesmal, wenn er daran dachte, brannte die Verbitterung in seinem Magen wie ein Essigtrunk.

Im ersten Impuls hatte er sogleich den Kampf gegen Richard aufnehmen wollen. Er hätte seine Armee behalten und sie von dem, was das Land noch hergab, ernähren können – den Bauern ließen sich schon noch Schutzgelder und Naturalien abpressen. Mit gezielten Schlägen aus dem Hinterhalt hätte sich der Kampf gegen Richard schon noch fortsetzen lassen. Andererseits: Richard hielt die Burg, und die Zeit war auf seiner Seite. Hinter ihm stand der junge Herzog und künftige König Henry, während er, William, nur mehr von dem alten, geschlagenen Stephan unterstützt wurde.

William hatte sich schließlich dazu durchgerungen, zunächst einmal den Schaden zu begrenzen. Er war ins heimatliche Dorf Hamleigh zurückgekehrt und hatte wieder in jenem alten Herrschaftshaus Wohnung genommen, in dem er aufgewachsen war. Hamleigh und die Dörfer in der Umgebung waren seinem Vater dreißig Jahre zuvor übereignet worden. Da das Gebiet nie zur Grafschaft Shiring gehört hatte, besaß Richard keinerlei Ansprüche darauf. William hoffte, Richard durch sein Stillhalten von weitergehenden Maßnahmen gegen ihn abzuhalten. Richard hatte seine Rache ausgekostet – mochte er sich nun damit zufriedengeben und ihn, William, in Ruhe lassen. Bisher war dieser Plan aufgegangen.

Was William jedoch nicht ausstehen konnte, war das Leben in Hamleigh. Alles war ihm verhaßt: die kleinen, schmucken Häuser, die aufgeregt schnatternden Enten auf dem Dorfteich, die Kirche aus blaßgrauem Stein, die Kinder mit ihren Apfelbäckchen, die breithüftigen Weiber und die starken, aufbrausenden Männer. Er haßte die Dürftigkeit, Langeweile und Armut des Dorfes, und er haßte es, weil es ein Symbol war für den Machtverlust seiner Familie. Im Frühjahr sah er den Bauern zu, wie sie mühsam hinter ihren Pflügen herschritten, schätzte, wie groß sein Anteil an der sommerlichen Ernte sein würde, und kam zu nur sehr mageren Ergebnissen. Er ging auf die Jagd in den paar Waldungen, die ihm noch verblieben waren, und störte nicht einen einzigen Hirsch auf. »Ihr müßt Euch mit Wildschweinen begnügen«, erklärte ihm der Forstmeister. »Den Hirschen haben die Outlaws während der Hungersnot den Garaus gemacht.« William hielt Gericht im großen Saal seines Hauses, wo der Wind durch die Löcher im Flechtwerk der Wände pfiff. Er urteilte und strafte hart und ganz nach Lust und Laune, aber besondere Genugtuung zog er aus seinem Richteramt nicht.

Den Plan, in Shiring eine neue, große Kirche zu bauen, hatte er natürlich aufgegeben. Er konnte es sich nicht einmal leisten, für sich selbst ein eigenes Steinhaus zu bauen – geschweige denn eine Kirche. Als er sie nicht mehr bezahlen konnte, hatten die Maurer und Steinmetzen ihre Arbeit eingestellt. William wußte nicht, was aus ihnen geworden war – vielleicht waren sie alle nach Kingsbridge zurückgekehrt und arbeiteten wieder für Prior Philip.

Was William Hamleigh zunehmend plagte, waren Alpträume. Sie waren immer gleich: Er sah seine Mutter im Reich der Toten. Sie blutete aus Ohren und Augen, und wenn sie den Mund öffnete, um zu sprechen, floß das Blut auch aus ihrem Mund. Ihr Anblick erfüllte ihn mit Todesangst. Tagsüber konnte er nie sagen, woran es lag, daß ihn dieser Traum so entsetzte, denn seine Mutter bedrohte ihn in keiner Weise. Bei ihren nächtlichen Erscheinungen jedoch überkam ihn blinde, hysterische Panik, die sich jeder vernünftigen Einsicht entzog. Als kleiner Junge war er einmal durch einen Teich gewatet und unversehens in eine Untiefe geraten. Er war untergegangen und hatte keine Luft mehr bekommen. Die übermächtige, alles verzehrende Gier nach Luft, die ihn damals überfallen hatte, gehörte zu seinen nachhaltigsten Kindheitserinnerungen. Das Entsetzen, das mit den Alpträumen kam, war um ein Vielfaches schlimmer. Stets wollte er vor Mutters Blutgesicht davonlaufen, aber es war hoffnungslos; er hätte ebensogut versuchen können, in einer Treibsanddüne um sein Leben zu rennen. Wenn er dann stöhnend und schweißgebadet aus dem Schlaf fuhr, war sein ganzer Körper verspannt und verkrampft von der durchlittenen Agonie, und Walter stand mit einer Kerze in der Hand an seinem Lager. (William schlief, da es im Haus kein eigenes Schlafgemach gab, in der großen Halle, von den Männern seines Gefolges nur durch einen Wandschirm getrennt.) »Ihr habt im Schlaf geschrien, Herr«, murmelte der Freund. Und während der Alptraum ihn langsam aus seinem furchtbaren Griff entließ, sah William sich schweratmend um, erkannte das richtige Bett, die richtige Wand, den leibhaftigen Walter … Die Angst begann zu schwinden, und er sagte: »Es war nichts, nur ein böser Traum. Geh fort!« Was blieb, war die Furcht, wieder einzuschlafen, und am nächsten Morgen sahen seine Männer ihn an, als sei er verhext.

Ein paar Tage nach dem Gespräch mit Remigius – William saß auf demselben harten Stuhl vor demselben rauchigen Feuer – betrat Bischof Waleran das Haus.

William war unangenehm überrascht. Er hatte die Pferde gehört, war aber davon ausgegangen, daß es Walter war, der von der Mühle zurückkehrte. Er wußte nicht, wie er sich dem Bischof gegenüber verhalten sollte. Waleran war immer anmaßend gewesen, hatte immer den Überlegenen hervorgekehrt, so daß William sich oft wie ein täppischer, ungehobelter Dorftrottel vorgekommen war. Es war ihm peinlich, daß Waleran sah, in welch bescheidenen Verhältnissen er jetzt lebte.

Er erhob sich nicht einmal, um den Besucher zu begrüßen. »Was wollt Ihr?« fragte er barsch. Er hatte nicht die geringste Veranlassung, höflich zu sein: Waleran sollte so schnell wie möglich wieder verschwinden.

Der Bischof sah über den unfreundlichen Empfang hinweg. »Der Vogt ist tot«, sagte er.

William verstand nicht, worauf Waleran hinauswollte. »Was schert das mich?« fragte er.

»Man braucht einen Nachfolger.«

Na und, wollte William sagen, schluckte die Worte aber im letzten Moment herunter. Waleran macht sich Gedanken über den neuen Vogt, dachte er – und er ist gekommen, um mit *mir* darüber zu sprechen. Das kann doch eigentlich nur eines heißen – oder? Hoffnung keimte auf in seiner Brust, aber er unterdrückte sie mit Gewalt: Wenn Waleran im Spiel war, endeten hochfliegende Hoffnungen oft mit herben Enttäuschungen. »An wen denkt Ihr?« fragte er.

»An Euch.«

Das war die Antwort, auf die William kaum zu hoffen gewagt hatte, und er hätte der Ankündigung liebend gern Glauben geschenkt. Ein kluger Vogt, der nicht zu viele Rücksichten nahm, konnte fast so bedeutend und einflußreich sein wie ein Graf oder ein Bischof. Für William lag darin eine Chance, wieder zu Macht und Wohlstand zu kommen. Aber die Sache hatte bestimmt ihren Haken ... »Wieso sollte König Stephan gerade auf mich verfallen?«

»Ihr habt ihn gegen Herzog Henry unterstützt und deshalb Eure Grafschaft verloren. Ich kann mir vorstellen, daß er Euch für erlittenes Ungemach entschädigen will.«

»Aus reiner Dankbarkeit hat noch nie jemand etwas getan.« William wiederholte einen Spruch seiner Mutter.

»Stephan kann nicht besonders glücklich darüber sein, daß der Graf von Shiring einst auf der Seite des Feindes gekämpft hat. Vielleicht sieht er in seinem Vogt eine Art Gegengewicht gegen Richard.«

Das gibt schon mehr Sinn, dachte William. Gegen seinen Willen war er plötzlich sehr aufgeregt. Bot sich da tatsächlich eine Gelegenheit, aus diesem Kaff namens Hamleigh herauszukommen? Schon sah er sich wieder als Anführer einer ansehnlichen Truppe aus Rittern und Bewaffneten ... Das wäre schon etwas anderes als der kümmerliche Haufen, über den er gegenwärtig noch gebot. Als Vorsitzender des Grafschaftsgerichts in Shiring wäre er imstande, Richard so manchen Knüppel zwischen die Beine zu werfen. »Der Vogt residiert auf der Burg zu Shiring«, sagte er sehnsüchtig.

»Ihr wäret wieder reich«, fügte Waleran hinzu.

»In der Tat …« Das Amt des Vogts konnte für jemanden, der sich nicht zu dumm anstellte, eine wahre Goldgrube sein. Williams Einkommen würde fast so hoch sein wie weiland als Graf. Aber wieso hatte Waleran ausgerechnet dieses Thema angesprochen?

Er brauchte nicht lange auf die Antwort zu warten. »Ihr könntet es Euch dann auch leisten, die neue Kirche zu vollenden«, sagte er.

Da also liegt der Hund begraben! dachte William. Waleran hat schließlich noch nie etwas ohne Hintergedanken getan. Er will mich zum Vogt machen, damit ich ihm eine Kirche baue … Von Williams Seite gab es gegen diesen Plan gar nichts einzuwenden: Vielleicht hörten die Alpträume auf, wenn er die dem Andenken seiner Mutter gewidmete Kirche fertigstellte. »Meint Ihr wirklich, es läßt sich machen?« fragte er begierig.

Waleran nickte. »Es kostet natürlich Geld – aber machen läßt es sich gewiß.«

»Geld?« wiederholte William, dem auf einmal ganz bange wurde. »Wieviel?«

»Das läßt sich schwer abschätzen. In größeren Orten wie Lincoln oder Bristol müßtet Ihr für das Amt wohl fünf- bis sechshundert Pfund bezahlen. Die Vögte dieser Städte sind allerdings auch reicher als Kardinäle. In einem kleineren Flecken wie Shiring – und unter der Voraussetzung, daß Ihr dem König ein genehmer Bewerber seid, wofür ich Sorge tragen kann – genügen wohl schon hundert Pfund.«

»Hundert Pfund!« Williams Hoffnungen waren dahin. Er hatte von Anfang an mit einem Pferdefuß gerechnet. »Wenn ich hundert Pfund hätte, würde ich nicht in diesen Verhältnissen leben«, sagte er bitter.

»Das Geld treibt Ihr schon auf«, sagte Waleran leichthin.

»Und wie?« William hatte auf einmal eine Idee. »Wollt *Ihr* es mir geben?«

»Seid kein Narr!« sagte Waleran in jener herablassenden Art, die William die Wände hochtreiben konnte. »Dafür sind die Juden da.«

William kannte die Mischung aus Hoffnung und Wut, die ihn jetzt erfüllte – und er wußte, daß, einmal mehr, der Bischof am Ende recht behalten hatte.

Zwei Jahre waren inzwischen vergangen, und Jack hatte noch immer keine Lösung für das Problem gefunden. Schlimmer noch: im ersten Joch des Hauptschiffs waren die gleichen Risse aufgetreten. In seiner Konstruktion steckte ein entscheidender Fehler. Zwar war der Bau stark genug, das Gewicht des Gewölbes zu tragen, doch konnte er auf

Dauer nicht den heftigen Winden widerstehen, die gegen die hohen Mauern bliesen.

Er stand auf dem Gerüst in luftiger Höhe, betrachtete sich die neuen Rissen und zerbrach sich schier den Kopf darüber. Er brauchte irgendeine Klammer, die verhinderte, daß der obere Teil der Mauer sich im Wind immer bewegte.

Er rief sich ins Gedächtnis zurück, wie der untere Teil stabilisiert wurde: in der Außenwand des Seitenschiffs befanden sich kräftige, dicke Pfeiler, die durch im Seitenschiffdach verborgene Halbbogen mit der Mauer des Hauptschiffs verbunden waren. Die Pfeiler und Halbbogen stützten die Mauer aus der Entfernung, ähnlich wie äußere Strebepfeiler. Da die Stützen nicht zu sehen waren, wirkte das Kirchenschiff leicht und anmutig.

Für den oberen Teil der Mauer mußte Jack sich etwas Ähnliches einfallen lassen. Eine Möglichkeit bestand darin, das Seitenschiff aufzustocken und die untere Konstruktion einfach zu wiederholen. Das hatte jedoch den Nachteil, daß dadurch der Grundgedanke des neuen Stils – mehr Licht in die Kirche – sich nicht mehr verwirklichen ließe.

Natürlich waren es nicht die Seitenschiffe als solche, die die Stützfunktion ausübten, sondern sie in die Wand eingelassene schwere Pfeiler sowie die verbindenden Halb- oder Schwibbogen im Dach. Am liebsten hätte Jack Pfeiler und Schwibbogen zur Stützung des Obergadens errichtet, ohne sie in die Seitenschiffe einzubeziehen: Wenn mir das gelingt, dachte er, dann ist das Problem mit einem Schlag gelöst.

Von unten rief eine Stimme seinen Namen.

Jack runzelte unwillig die Stirn. Bevor die Stimme ihn unterbrach, war ihm eine Idee gekommen – jetzt war sie wieder fort. Er sah hinab. Der Mann, der ihn gerufen hatte, war Prior Philip.

Jack verschwand im Treppenturm. Unten wartete Philip bereits auf ihn. Der Prior kochte vor Wut und kam sofort zur Sache. »Richard hat mich betrogen!« rief er.

»Wie das?« fragte Jack überrascht.

Philip ging nicht sofort auf die Frage ein. »Und das nach alldem, was ich für ihn getan habe!« tobte er. »Ich habe Alienas Wolle aufgekauft, als alle anderen sie übervorteilen wollten – ohne mich wäre sie wahrscheinlich nie ins Geschäft gekommen! Als der Handel zusammenbrach, habe ich dafür gesorgt, daß Richard die Stelle des Wachhauptmanns bekam. Und im November vergangenen Jahres steckte ich ihm vorzeitig die Nachricht vom bevorstehenden Friedensschluß zu und gab ihm so die Chance, Earlscastle zurückzuerobern. Und was macht er, kaum daß er seine Grafschaft wiederhat und in Glanz und Gloria regieren kann? Er kehrt sich gegen mich.«

Noch nie hatte Jack den Prior so wütend gesehen. Philips geschorener Schädel war rot vor Empörung, und er stieß seine Worte mit ungewohnter Hast hervor.

»Was hat er denn getan?«

Wieder ignorierte der Prior die Frage. »Ich wußte immer schon, daß Richard einen schwachen Charakter hat. Er hat Aliena in all den Jahren kaum unterstützt, sondern immer nur von ihr genommen, je nachdem, wie es ihm paßte. *Ihre* Bedürfnisse waren ihm immer gleichgültig. Was ich nicht wußte, war, daß er ein ganz durchtriebener Halunke ist.«

»Was genau hat er denn getan?«

Jetzt endlich ließ Philip die Katze aus dem Sack. »Er hat uns den Zugang zum Steinbruch verweigert.«

Jack war erschüttert. Das war in der Tat ein starkes Stück. »Wie rechtfertigt er sich denn?«

»Er behauptet, daß alle Güter wieder denjenigen gehören, die sie zu Zeiten des alten Königs Henry besaßen. Der Steinbruch wurde uns aber von König Stephan zugesprochen.«

Richards Habgier war beachtlich. Dennoch konnte sich Jack über die Geschichte nicht so aufregen wie Philip. Die Kathedrale war zur Hälfte fertig – überwiegend errichtet aus Steinen, die sie hatten kaufen müssen. Es würde schon irgendwie weitergehen. »Nun ja«, sagte er, »da ist er strenggenommen wohl im Recht.«

Philip war außer sich. »Wie kannst du so etwas sagen?«

»Es erinnert mich ein wenig an Euer Verhalten mir gegenüber«, sagte er. »Ich hatte Euch die Weinende Madonna mitgebracht, einen großartigen Entwurf für Eure neue Kathedrale erstellt und schließlich eine Stadtmauer errichtet, um Euch gegen Williams Übergriffe zu schützen … Und da verkündet Ihr auf einmal, daß ich mit der Mutter meiner Kinder nicht mehr zusammenleben darf. So etwas nenne ich Undankbarkeit.«

Philip war tief getroffen von dem Vergleich. »Das ist doch etwas ganz anderes!« protestierte er. »Ich will nicht, daß Ihr getrennt lebt. Es war Waleran, der die Annullierung Eurer Ehe verhindert hat. Und das Gesetz Gottes sagt: ›Du sollst nicht ehebrechen.‹«

Jack ließ sich nicht von seiner Meinung abbringen. »Ich bin sicher, Richard würde sich so ähnlich äußern. Schließlich hat ja nicht er die

Rückerstattung der Güter befohlen. Er ist lediglich der Vollstrecker des Gesetzes.«

Die Mittagsglocke läutete.

»Die Gesetze Gottes und die der Menschen sind nicht die gleichen«, sagte Philip.

»Aber wir müssen uns an beide halten«, erwiderte Jack. »So, und nun werde ich mit der Mutter meiner Kinder zu Mittag essen.«

Er ließ den empörten Philip stehen und ging. Im Grunde warf er Philip gar keine Undankbarkeit vor – doch die gespielte Entrüstung erleichterte ihn. Was den Steinbruch betraf, so wollte er darüber mit Aliena sprechen. Vielleicht ließ sich Richard ja doch noch zu seiner Freigabe überreden.

Er verließ das Klostergebäude und ging durch die Stadt zu dem Haus, das er mit Martha teilte. Wie üblich waren Aliena und die Kinder in der Küche. Mit einer guten Ernte im vergangenen Sommer war die Hungersnot zu Ende gegangen. Das Angebot an Lebensmitteln war so üppig wie lange nicht mehr; Weißbrot und geröstetes Hammelfleisch standen auf dem Tisch.

Jack küßte seine Kinder. Sally erwiderte seinen Kuß auf sanfte, kindliche Art – Tom hingegen, inzwischen elf Jahre alt und darauf brennend, endlich erwachsen zu werden, hielt ihm nur peinlich berührt die Wange hin. Jack lächelte, sagte aber nichts; er konnte sich noch gut an das Alter erinnern, in dem er Küssen furchtbar albern gefunden hatte.

Aliena wirkte beunruhigt. Jack setzte sich neben sie auf die Bank und sagte: »Philip ist sehr erbost, weil Richard ihm den Steinbruch streitig macht.«

»Ja, das ist schlimm«, sagte Aliena leise. »Wie undankbar von Richard.«

»Glaubst du, man kann mit ihm noch mal darüber reden?«

»Das kann ich dir wirklich nicht sagen.«

»Das Problem scheint dich nicht besonders zu interessieren.«

Sie sah ihn herausfordernd an: »Da hast du allerdings recht.«

Er kannte diese Stimmung. »Was bedrückt dich?« fragte er sie. »Willst du es mir nicht sagen?«

Aliena erhob sich. »Komm, wir gehen ins hintere Zimmer.«

Jack warf einen letzten verlangenden Blick auf die geröstete Hammelkeule. Dann stand auch er vom Tisch auf und folgte Aliena ins Schlafzimmer. Ihrer Gewohnheit entsprechend, ließen sie die Tür offen stehen, um bei unangemeldeten Besuchern keinen Verdacht zu erregen. Aliena saß auf dem Bett, die Arme vor der Brust verschränkt. »Ich habe einen wichtigen Entschluß gefaßt«, begann sie.

Sie sah sehr ernst aus. Was, um Himmels willen, hat sie vor? dachte Jack.

»Mein Leben wird, seitdem ich erwachsen bin, von zwei Dingen überschattet: einmal von dem Versprechen, das ich meinem Vater gab, als er auf dem Sterbebett lag, und zum anderen von meinem Verhältnis zu dir.«

»Aber du hast das Versprechen, das du deinem Vater gabst, inzwischen doch erfüllt«, wandte Jack ein.

»Ja. Und nun möchte ich mich auch von der anderen Last befreien. Ich habe beschlossen, dich zu verlassen.«

Jack fühlte sich wie vom Schlag gerührt. Aliena sagte so etwas nicht aus Lust und Laune, das wußte er. Sie meinte es ernst. Er starrte sie sprachlos an. Nie im Traum wäre er auf die Idee gekommen, Aliena könne ihn verlassen. Er wußte nicht mehr ein noch aus. Warum wurde ihm so übel mitgespielt? Ein böser Verdacht kam ihm, und er sprach ihn sogleich aus: »Gibt es einen anderen?«

»Red keinen Unsinn!«

»Aber warum dann?«

»Weil ich es einfach nicht mehr aushalte«, sagte sie, und ihre Augen füllten sich mit Tränen. »Seit zehn Jahren warten wir schon auf die Annullierung. Aber sie wird nie erfolgen, Jack. Wir sind dazu verdammt, ewig so weiterzuleben wie jetzt – es sei denn, wir trennen uns.«

»Aber ...« Er rang nach Worten. Ihr Entschluß hatte ihn völlig überrumpelt. Jeder Widerspruch erschien ihm sinnlos, wie der Versuch, vor einem Sturm davonzulaufen. Dennoch versuchte er es: »So, wie wir jetzt leben – ist das denn nicht besser als getrennt?«

»Auf lange Sicht nicht.«

»Aber was wird sich denn ändern, wenn du fortziehst?«

»Vielleicht finde ich einen anderen«, sagte sie unter Tränen. »Ich kann ihn liebgewinnen und dann endlich wieder ein normales Leben führen.«

»Deine Ehe mit Alfred bleibt weiterhin bestehen.«

»Aber woanders weiß das niemand. Ich kann mich von irgendeinem Dorfpriester trauen lassen, der von Alfred Builder noch nie etwas gehört hat – oder aber, *wenn* er von ihm gehört hätte, die Ehe für ungültig halten würde.«

»Das bist nicht du, die so etwas sagt. Ich nehme dir das nicht ab.«

»Zehn Jahre, Jack! Ich warte seit zehn Jahren darauf, endlich ein normales Leben an deiner Seite führen zu können. Ich bin nicht bereit, noch länger zu warten.«

Ihre Worte trafen ihn wie Schläge. Sie sprach und sprach, aber er hörte ihr nicht länger zu, er war vollkommen beherrscht von dem Gedanken, forthin ohne Aliena leben zu müssen. Er unterbrach sie: »Ich habe niemals eine andere geliebt, weißt du ...«

Sie zuckte zusammen wie bei einem plötzlichen Schmerz, ließ sich in ihrer Rede aber nicht aufhalten. »Ich brauche noch ein paar Wochen Zeit für die Vorbereitungen. Ich werde versuchen, in Winchester ein Haus zu finden. Auch möchte ich die Kinder nicht unvorbereitet lassen. Sie sollen sich mit dem Gedanken vertraut machen, bevor ihr neues Leben beginnt ...«

»Du willst meine Kinder mitnehmen«, sagte Jack stumpf.

Aliena nickte. »Es tut mir leid«, sagte sie, und zum erstenmal klang es so, als zweifele sie an der Richtigkeit ihrer Entscheidung. »Ich weiß, daß sie dich vermissen werden. Aber auch sie müssen endlich ein normales Leben führen können.«

Jack hatte genug. Er wandte sich zum Gehen.

»Bitte laß mich jetzt nicht allein, Jack«, sagte Aliena. »Wir haben noch eine Menge miteinander zu besprechen ... Jack!«

Er ging, ohne ihr eine Antwort zu geben.

Er hörte, wie sie hinter ihm herrief: »Jack!«

Ohne die Kinder auch nur eines Blickes zu würdigen, durchquerte er die Stube und verließ das Haus. Er war ganz benommen und wußte nicht wohin, deshalb ging er in die Kathedrale. Die Maurer und Steinmetzen waren noch beim Mittagessen. Weinen konnte er nicht – mit einfachen Tränen war sein Kummer nicht zu bewältigen. Ohne Ziel und Absicht stieg er die Wendeltreppe im nördlichen Querschiff empor und kletterte aufs Dach.

Unten war es fast windstill gewesen – hier oben, in luftiger Höhe, wehte eine steife Brise. Jack sah hinunter. Wenn ich springe, dachte er, lande ich auf dem schrägen Dach des Seitenschiffs, gleich neben dem Querhaus ... Kaum anzunehmen, daß ich den Sturz überlebe, auszuschließen ist es aber nicht ... Er ging vor bis zur Vierung, wo das Dach abrupt endete. Vor ihm gähnte der Abgrund. Die Konstruktion des Dachs ist nicht stabil, dachte er, und Aliena verläßt mich ... Wofür lohnt es sich noch zu leben?

So plötzlich, wie es den Anschein hatte, war ihr Entschluß freilich nicht gekommen. Ihre Unzufriedenheit war über die Jahre gewachsen – und nicht nur ihre, auch seine. Aber sie hatten sich beide an ihre unglückliche Lage gewöhnt. Nach der Zurückeroberung von Earlscastle war Aliena wie aus einer Betäubung erwacht und hatte sich daran erinnert, daß sie die Meisterin ihres eigenen Schicksals war, und diese Erkenntnis hatte in einer bereits kritischen Lage das Faß zum Überlaufen gebracht.

Sein Blick fiel auf die Querhausmauer und das Pultdach des Seitenschiffs. Er sah die schweren, aus der Seitenschiffwand hervorspringenden Strebepfeiler und rief sich den vom Dach verborgenen Schwibbogen ins Gedächtnis, der den Pfeiler mit dem unteren Teil des Obergadens verband. Bevor Philip ihn gestört hatte, war er der Lösung des Problems nahegewesen: Ein vielleicht um zwanzig Fuß höherer Strebepfeiler mußte her, mit einem zweiten Schwibbogen zur Stützung jenes Mauerabschnitts, an dem sich die Sprünge zeigten. Der Bogen und der hohe Pfeiler würden die obere Hälfte der Kirche wie eine Klammer zusammenhalten und bei Sturm die starken Schwankungen verhindern.

Ja, das war wahrscheinlich die Lösung. Sie hatte nur einen Schönheitsfehler: Wenn ich ein zweistöckiges Seitenschiff errichte, um den höheren Strebepfeiler sowie den zweiten Schwibbogen zu verbergen, geht Licht verloren, dachte er. Und wenn ich keines errichte ...

Wenn ich keines errichte, was dann?

Er war besessen von dem Gefühl, daß ohnehin alles gleichgültig war, denn sein Leben war dabei, zu zerbrechen und zu zerfallen. In einer solchen Stimmung fand er den Gedanken an ein *unverkleidetes* Strebewerk ganz in Ordnung. Von seinem dem Wind ausgesetzten Beobachtungsposten auf dem Dach konnte er sich recht gut vorstellen, wie es aussehen würde: eine Reihe stämmiger, aus der Außenmauer des Seitenschiffs emporwachsender Pfeiler, an deren oberen Ecken je ein Schwibbogen den Freiraum zum Lichtgaden überbrückte. Zur Zierde könnte man den Pfeilern jeweils auch noch eine hübsche Fiale aufsetzen, ja, das sähe gewiß besser aus ...

Es war ein revolutionärer Gedanke: ein starkes, offenes Strebewerk, welches das äußere Bild der Kathedrale entscheidend prägen würde. Die Idee entsprach durchaus dem neuen Stil, der die Statik des Gebäudes nicht mehr verbergen wollte.

Und außerdem sagte ihm sein Gefühl, daß es stimmte.

Je mehr Jack darüber nachdachte, desto besser gefiel ihm der Gedanke. Er stellte sich die Kirche von der Westseite her vor: Da sahen die Schwibbogen aus wie Vogelschwingen, ja, wie ein ganzer Vogelschwarm, kurz bevor er sich in die Lüfte erhob. Wer sagte, daß sie so massiv sein mußten? Schlank und elegant konnten sie sein, vorausgesetzt, sie waren gut gebaut, leicht und doch stark – wie Vogelschwingen eben. Geflügelte Strebepfeiler, dachte er – für eine Kirche, die so leicht war, daß sie fliegen konnte ...

Ob das klappt? fragte er sich. Ob das wirklich klappt?

Ein plötzlicher Windstoß packte ihn und brachte ihn aus dem Gleichgewicht. Er geriet ins Taumeln, hoch oben an der Kante des Daches. Schon sah er sich in den Tod stürzen, doch da gelang es ihm wie durch ein Wunder, sich wieder zu fangen. Rasch trat er einen Schritt zurück; sein Herz klopfte ihm bis zum Hals.

Langsam und vorsichtig trat er den Rückweg über das Dach an und erreichte unversehrt die Wendeltreppe.

Die Bauarbeiten an der Kirche in Shiring waren vollends zum Erliegen gekommen. Prior Philip ertappte sich dabei, daß er eine gewisse Genugtuung empfand. Nachdem er selbst so lange den trostlosen Anblick einer verwaisten Dombaustelle vor Augen gehabt hatte, konnte er einfach nicht anders, als sich heimlich darüber zu freuen, daß es seinen Feinden nun genauso erging. Alfred Builder hatte vor Williams Sturz gerade noch Zeit gehabt, die alte Kirche niederzureißen und die Fundamente für den Chorraum der neuen zu legen. Dann war von einem Tag auf den anderen das Geld ausgeblieben. Philip erkannte durchaus das Sündhafte an seiner Schadenfreude über einen unvollendeten Kirchenbau, sah andererseits darin aber auch ein Zeichen dafür, daß Gott die neue Kathedrale eben in Kingsbridge sehen wollte und nicht in Shiring. Daß Walerans Vorhaben von Anfang an unter einem unglücklichen Stern gestanden hatte, war ein deutliches Indiz für die göttlichen Absichten.

Das Grafschaftsgericht tagte, seitdem die größte Kirche der Stadt abgerissen war, im großen Saal der Burg. Mit Jonathan an seiner Seite ritt Philip den Burgberg hinauf.

Im Zuge der Umbesetzungen in der Klosterverwaltung nach der Flucht von Subprior Remigius hatte er Jonathan zu seinem Adlatus gemacht. Der Treuebruch seines Stellvertreters hatte Philip schwer getroffen, doch war er inzwischen froh, ihn endlich loszusein. Von jenem Tag an, da er ihn in der Priorwahl besiegt hatte, war Remigius ein Stachel in seinem Fleisch gewesen. Seit seinem Verschwinden war das Leben im Kloster angenehmer.

Neuer Subprior war Milius, der darüber hinaus, von drei Mitbrüdern unterstützt, sein Amt als Kämmerer behielt. Was Remigius den ganzen Tag über getrieben hatte, konnte sich nun, da er fort war, niemand mehr so richtig vorstellen.

Die Arbeit mit seinem Adlatus Jonathan erfüllte den Prior mit großer innerer Befriedigung. Es machte ihm Spaß, den jungen Mann in die Finessen der Klosterleitung und allgemein in weltliche Dinge einzuweihen. Auch bedurfte er noch der Führung im Umgang mit anderen Menschen: Zwar war der Junge überall recht beliebt, doch konnte er recht brüsk sein und weniger selbstbewußte Mitmenschen mit seinem Verhalten leicht vor den Kopf stoßen. Er mußte noch lernen, daß Feindseligkeit ihm gegenüber oft nichts anderes war als ein Ausdruck von Schwäche. Bisher sah er nur die Feindseligkeit und brauste auf – anstatt auch die Schwäche zu erkennen und aufbauend zu wirken.

Jonathan hatte eine rasche Auffassungsgabe, die Philip immer wieder überraschte. Ich war ganz ähnlich, dachte er manchmal, um gleich darauf zu bekennen, daß er sich der Sünde der Hoffart schuldig gemacht hatte.

An diesem Tag hatte er Jonathan mitgenommen, um ihm zu zeigen, wie die weltliche Gerichtsbarkeit der Grafschaft arbeitete. Der Prior wollte mit Hilfe des Gerichts seinen Anspruch auf Ausbeutung des Steinbruchs durchsetzen. Er war sich seiner Sache ziemlich sicher: Das Recht stand nicht auf Richards Seite. Denn die im Friedensvertrag festgesetzte Bestimmung, daß den ehemaligen Besitzern ihr Hab und Gut zurückerstattet werden mußte, berührte nicht die Rechte des Klosters. Ihr Ziel war es vielmehr, Herzog Henry die Möglichkeit zu geben, Stephans Grafen durch seine eigenen zu ersetzen und somit die Leute, die ihn in seinem Kampf unterstützt hatten, zu belohnen. Die Klöster waren davon eindeutig nicht betroffen. Es gab also durchaus Anlaß zur Zuversicht, wenngleich ein Punkt noch unklar war: Der alte Vogt war gestorben, der neue noch nicht bekannt. Seine Ernennung sollte gleich zu Beginn der Sitzung erfolgen. Vier einflußreiche Bürger von Shiring galten als Favoriten für das Amt: Der Seidenhändler David Merchant; Rees Welsh, ein Priester, der am königlichen Hof gearbeitet hatte; Glies Lionheart, ein Ritter, dessen Güter gleich vor den Toren der Stadt lagen, und Hugh Bastard, der illegitime Sohn des Bischofs von Salisbury. Philip hätte am liebsten Rees in dem Amte gesehen, nicht nur, weil er Waliser war wie er selbst, sondern weil von ihm ein offenes Ohr für die Anliegen der Kirche zu erwarten war.

Große Sorgen machte er sich nicht, denn auch bei den anderen konnte mit einem günstigen Urteilsspruch gerechnet werden.

Sie ritten in den Burghof ein. Die Anlage war nicht sonderlich stark befestigt. Da der Graf von Shiring außerhalb der Stadt auf einer eigenen Burg residierte, war Shiring schon seit einigen Generationen von Kampfhandlungen verschont geblieben. Die Burg in der Stadt war mehr ein Verwaltungssitz: Hier gab es Kanzleien, Unterkünfte für den Vogt und seine Leute und nicht zuletzt auch ein Verlies. Philip und Jonathan brachten ihre Pferde in den Stall und begaben sich in den großen Saal.

Die Tische, gemeinhin in T-Form ausgerichtet, waren umgestellt worden. Der Querbalken des T befand sich an der gewohnten Stelle, wurde jedoch durch ein Podium erhöht. Die anderen Tische flankierten die Wände: Auf diese Weise wurden die Kläger räumlich voneinander getrennt und die Versuchung, das Heil im Faustrecht zu suchen, eingedämmt.

Der Saal war bereits gut gefüllt. Oben auf dem Podium saß Bischof Waleran und sah aus, als führe er Böses im Schilde. Zu Philips Überraschung saß neben ihm William Hamleigh. Er sprach mit Waleran, schielte dabei aber immer zum Eingang, um die Neuankömmlinge im Auge zu behalten. Was treibt denn *der* hier? fragte sich Philip betroffen. Neun Monate lang war von William so gut wie nichts zu sehen und zu hören gewesen. Er hatte sein Dorf kaum verlassen und dadurch bei vielen Menschen – darunter auch Philip – die Hoffnung genährt, er möge bis zu seinem Lebensende dortbleiben. Aber jetzt saß er dort oben am Tisch und benahm sich ganz so, als wäre er noch immer Graf von Shiring. Warum ist er hier und was hat er vor? dachte Philip. Gewiß treibt ihn die Habgier, und er plant ein übles Ränkespiel ...

Philip und Jonathan ließen sich auf einer der seitwärts aufgestellten Bänke nieder und warteten auf den Beginn der Verhandlungen. Unter den Zuschauern herrschte eine geschäftige, zuversichtliche Stimmung. Der Krieg war vorüber, und die führenden Kreise im Lande wandten ihre Aufmerksamkeit wieder der Aufgabe zu, ihren Reichtum zu mehren. Das Land war fruchtbar und dankte ihnen rasch für ihre Bemühungen: Man rechnete in diesem Jahr mit einer Ernte, die alle früheren in den Schatten stellte; der Wollpreis hatte sich erholt, und Philip hatte mittlerweile fast alle Steinmetzen und Maurer, die Kingsbridge auf dem Höhepunkt der Hungersnot verlassen hatten, wieder eingestellt. Überall hatten vor allem die jungen, kräftigen und gesunden Menschen überlebt und waren jetzt voller Hoffnung und guten

Mutes. Man spürte diese Stimmung im großen Saal der Burg zu Shiring allenthalben – an der Kopfhaltung der Leute, am Tonfall ihrer Stimmen, an den neuen Stiefeln der Männer, den prunkvollen Kopfbedeckungen der Frauen und nicht zuletzt daran, daß sie alle wieder Reichtümer und Güter besaßen, für die es sich lohnte, vor Gericht zu ziehen.

Alle Anwesenden erhoben sich: Der Stellvertreter des Vogts und Graf Richard betraten den Saal. Die beiden schritten die Stufen zum Podium hinauf. Dann begann der stellvertretende Vogt, noch immer stehend, den königlichen Erlaß mit der Ernennung des neuen Vogts zu verlesen. Wie alle Urkunden dieser Art begann der Text mit einer wortreichen Präambel. Philip musterte die vier Favoriten. Er wünschte dem glücklichen Sieger schon jetzt viel Mut, denn es gehörte einiges dazu, dem Recht gegenüber so mächtigen örtlichen Würdenträgern wie Bischof Waleran, Graf Richard und Lord William Geltung zu verschaffen. Der erfolgreiche Bewerber wußte vermutlich schon von seiner Ernennung – es bestand kein Grund, daraus ein Geheimnis zu machen. Es war allerdings auffallend, daß keiner der vier besonders aufgekratzt wirkte. Normalerweise stand der Gewählte bei solchen Gelegenheit auch neben dem Mann, der die Ernennungsurkunde verlas. Auf dem Podium hielten sich außer dem stellvertretenden Vogt nur Richard, Waleran und William auf. Ein furchtbarer Gedanke keimte in Philip auf: Sollte etwa Waleran zum neuen Vogt ernannt worden sein ...? Kurz darauf verwandelte sich die böse Ahnung in schieres Entsetzen, denn der stellvertretende Vogt sagte: »... ernennen Wir zum Vogt von Shiring Unseren treuen Diener William Hamleigh und befehlen allen Unseren Untertanen in der Grafschaft, ihn in seinem Amte ihrer Unterstützung teilhaftig werden zu lassen.«

Philip sah Jonathan an und sagte: »William!«

Im Saal rumorte es. Die Leute aus der Stadt waren völlig überrascht; manche äußerten deutlich ihren Unmut über die Entscheidung.

»Wie hat er denn das zuwege gebracht?« fragte Jonathan.

»Er muß sich das Amt gekauft haben!«

»Und woher nimmt er das Geld dafür?«

»Er hat sich's wahrscheinlich geborgt.«

Lächelnd ging William zu dem hölzernen Thronsessel in der Mitte des Podiumstisches. Früher war er mal ein recht hübscher Bursche, dachte Philip. William hatte die Vierzig noch nicht erreicht, sah aber älter aus. Sein Körper war zu schwer, sein Gesicht vom Wein gerötet, und all die Lebenskraft und Zuversicht, die junge Gesichter so anziehend macht, war verschwunden und einem Ausdruck von Zügellosigkeit gewichen.

Kaum hatte William Platz genommen, da stand Philip auf.

Auch Jonathan erhob sich. »Gehen wir?« flüsterte er.

»Folge mir!« zischte Philip.

Die Menge verstummte. Aller Augen waren auf die beiden Mönche gerichtet, die auf den Ausgang zuschritten. Man rückte zur Seite, um ihnen Platz zu machen. Kaum fiel die Tür hinter ihnen ins Schloß, erhob sich aufgeregtes Gemurmel.

»Mit William als Richter sind unsere Erfolgsaussichten gleich null«, sagte Jonathan.

»Schlimmer noch«, erwiderte Philip. »Wenn wir auf der Behandlung unseres Falls bestanden hätten, wären wir womöglich noch ganz anderer Rechte verlustig gegangen.«

»Meiner Seel! Darauf wäre ich nie gekommen!«

Philip nickte verbittert. »Mit William als Vogt, Waleran als Bischof und dem treulosen Richard als Grafen hat die Priorei Kingsbridge so gut wie gar keine Möglichkeit mehr, hier in der Grafschaft zu ihrem Recht zu kommen. Die drei können mit uns machen, was sie wollen.« Während ein Stallknecht ihre Pferde sattelte, fuhr Philip fort: »Ich werde den König ersuchen, Kingsbridge zur Stadt zu erheben. Auf diese Weise bekämen wir unser eigenes Gericht, und die Steuern wären direkt an die Krone zu entrichten. Der Vogt wäre für uns dann nicht mehr zuständig.«

»Früher seid Ihr immer gegen eine solche Lösung gewesen«, meinte Jonathan.

»Ja, das stimmt. Ich war dagegen, weil in diesem Fall die Stadt ebenso mächtig wird wie die Priorei. Jetzt bin ich der Meinung, daß wir das hinnehmen müssen – es ist gleichsam der Preis für unsere Unabhängigkeit. Die Alternative heißt William.«

»Wird uns König Stephan das Stadtrecht gewähren?«

»Ja, vielleicht, wenn auch kaum umsonst. Und wenn nicht, dann möglicherweise Henry, wenn er die Nachfolge angetreten hat.«

Sie bestiegen ihre Pferde und ritten niedergeschlagen durch die Stadt. Hinter dem Tor, auf ödem Gelände gleich vor den Mauern, kamen sie am Müllplatz vorbei. Ein paar armselige Zeitgenossen durchwühlten den Unrat nach Eßbarem, alten Kleidern und Brennmaterial. Philip betrachtete sie ohne sonderliches Interesse. Dann, plötzlich, erregte jemand seine Aufmerksamkeit. Eine ihm wohlvertraute, hochgewachsene Gestalt beugte sich über einen Haufen alter Lumpen und kramte darin herum. Philip zügelte sein Pferd und wartete, bis Jonathan an seiner Seite war.

»Sieh mal, dort!«

Jonathan folgte seinem Blick. Kurz darauf sagte er ruhig: »Remigius.«

Philip behielt den ehemaligen Mitbruder im Auge. Waleran und William hatten ihm offenbar den Laufpaß gegeben, als die Gelder für die neue Kirche nicht mehr flossen. Sie brauchten ihn schlichtweg nicht mehr. Remigius hatte Philip verraten, die Priorei verraten und Kingsbridge verraten, alles in der Hoffnung, eines Tages Dekan von Shiring zu werden. Doch kaum hatte er sein Ziel erreicht, da war es zu Asche geworden.

Philip veranlaßte sein Pferd, die Straße zu verlassen, und ritt über das Ödland auf Remigius zu. Jonathan folgte ihm. Ein übler Geruch schien wie Nebel von dem Gelände aufzusteigen. Als sie näher kamen, sahen sie, daß Remigius bis auf die Knochen abgemagert war. Sein Habit war schmutzig, und er trug keine Schuhe. Er war jetzt sechzig Jahre alt und hatte sein gesamtes Erwachsenenleben in der Priorei Kingsbridge verbracht. Auf das rauhe Leben außerhalb der Klostermauern hatte ihn nie jemand vorbereitet. Philip sah, wie er ein Paar Lederschuhe aus dem Unrat zog. In den Sohlen waren riesige Löcher, doch Remigius starrte die Schuhe an wie ein Mann, der einen vergrabenen Schatz gefunden hat. Er wollte sie gerade anprobieren, als er Philip gewahrte.

Er richtete sich auf. Scham und Trotz kämpften in seinem Herzen, und seine Miene spiegelte die innere Zerrissenheit wider. Schließlich sagte er: »Seid Ihr gekommen, um Euch an meiner Not zu weiden?«

»Nein«, antwortete Philip milde. Sein alter Widersacher bot einen so erbärmlichen Anblick, daß er nur Mitleid mit ihm empfand. Er stieg vom Pferd und holte eine Flasche aus der Satteltasche. »Ich bin gekommen, um dir einen Schluck Wein anzubieten.«

Remigius wollte das Angebot eigentlich nicht annehmen, war aber zu ausgehungert, um lange zu widerstreben. Er zögerte nur kurz, dann riß er Philip die dargebotene Flasche aus der Hand und setzte sie an den Mund. Nachdem er erst einmal zu trinken begonnen hatte, konnte er nicht mehr aufhören. In wenigen Augenblicken war die Flasche leer. Leicht schwankend setzte er sie ab.

Philip verstaute die Flasche wieder in der Satteltasche. »Du brauchst auch was zu essen«, sagte er und reichte Remigius einen kleinen Laib Brot.

Remigius nahm das Brot entgegen und machte sich gierig darüber her. Brocken um Brocken stopfte er sich in den Mund. Es war unschwer zu erkennen, daß er schon seit Tagen nichts mehr gegessen hatte. Die letzte anständige Mahlzeit lag vermutlich schon mehrere Wochen zurück. Er ist dem Tode nahe, dachte Philip betrübt – und stirbt er nicht vor Hunger, so vor Scham.

Das Brot war schnell verzehrt. »Willst du zu uns zurückkehren?« fragte Philip.

Er hörte, wie Jonathan erschrocken die Luft anhielt. Wie viele andere Mitbrüder hätte der junge Mann Remigius am liebsten nie wiedergesehen. Wahrscheinlich hält er mein Angebot für vollkommen verfehlt, dachte Philip.

»Zurückkehren? In welcher Stellung?« Das war wieder ganz der alte Remigius.

Bedauernd schüttelte Philip den Kopf. »In meiner Priorei wirst du nie mehr ein Amt bekleiden, Remigius. Komm zurück als einfacher, demütiger Mönch. Bitte den Herrn um Vergebung deiner Sünden und verbringe die Tage, die dir auf Erden noch vergönnt sind, in Gebet und Meditation. Bereite deine Seele auf den Himmel vor.«

Remigius hob empört den Kopf, und Philip war auf eine verächtliche Antwort gefaßt, aber sie blieb aus. Remigius öffnete den Mund, um etwas zu sagen, dann schloß er ihn wieder und sah zu Boden. Still und stumm stand Philip vor ihm und wartete auf eine Reaktion. Lange Zeit gab Remigius keinen Ton von sich. Als er endlich wieder aufblickte, war sein Gesicht voller Tränen. »Ja, bitte, Vater«, sagte er. »Ich möchte wieder nach Hause.«

Glühende Freude ergriff Philip. »Dann komm!« sagte er. »Steig auf mein Pferd!«

Remigius wußte nicht, wie ihm geschah.

»Was sagt Ihr da, Vater?« rief Jonathan.

»Los, hinauf!« sagte Philip zu Remigius. »Tu, was ich dir sage!«

Jonathan war entsetzt. »Aber Vater, wie wollt Ihr denn reisen?«

»Ich gehe zu Fuß«, erwiderte Philip glücklich. »Einer von uns beiden muß ja laufen.«

»So soll Remigius laufen!« Jonathan war kurz davor, aus der Haut zu fahren.

»Er soll reiten«, sagte Philip. »Er hat Gott erfreut.«

»Und Ihr? Habt Ihr Gott nicht viel mehr erfreut als Remigius?«

»Jesus sagt, es ist größere Freude im Himmel über einen bußfertigen Sünder denn über neunundneunzig Rechtschaffene«, hielt Philip dagegen. »Erinnerst du dich nicht an das Gleichnis vom verlorenen Sohn? Als er heimkehrte, schlachtete sein Vater das gemästete Kalb. Die Engel im Himmel jubeln über die Tränen, die Remigius vergießt. Ihm mein Pferd zu geben ist das Geringste, was ich tun kann.«

Er nahm das Pferd am Zügel und führte es auf die Straße zurück. Jonathan folgte hinterdrein. Sie hatten die Straße kaum erreicht, als er absaß und zu Philip sagte: »So nehmt mein Pferd, Vater, und laßt mich zu Fuß gehen. Ich bitte Euch.«

Philip drehte sich nach ihm um. Seine Antwort war unmißverständlich: »Du steigst jetzt schleunigst wieder auf und widersprichst mir nicht mehr! Schweig still und denk darüber nach, *was* hier geschieht und *warum*!«

Verwirrt tat Jonathan, wie ihm geheißen: Er stieg wieder auf sein Pferd und sagte kein Wort mehr.

Nach Kingsbridge waren es noch zwanzig Meilen. Philip schritt munter voran. Er war voller Freude. Remigius' Rückkehr glich den Verlust des Steinbruchs mehr als aus. Ich habe vor Gericht eine Niederlage erlitten, dachte er, aber dabei ging es nur um Steine. Was ich bekommen habe, ist unvergleichlich wertvoller.

Ich habe heute eines Menschen Seele gewonnen.

Im Faß schwammen frische, glänzend rote und gelbe Äpfel, und die Sonnenstrahlen glitzerten auf dem Wasser. Sally, neun Jahre alt und leicht zu begeistern, beugte sich, die Hände auf dem Rücken verschränkt, über den Rand und versuchte, mit den Zähnen einen Apfel herauszufischen. Der Apfel spielte aber nicht mit: Er tauchte unter – und Sallys Gesicht ebenfalls. Prustend und quietschend richtete das kleine Mädchen sich auf. Aliena lächelte dünn und trocknete ihr das Gesicht ab.

Es war ein warmer Nachmittag im Spätsommer. Man feierte den Ehrentag eines Heiligen, und fast alle Bewohner der Stadt hatten sich auf der Wiese am anderen Ufer des Flusses eingefunden. Aliena hatte solche Festtage immer genossen, doch diesmal war ihre Stimmung gedrückt. Ständig mußte sie daran denken, daß es ihr letztes Fest in Kingsbridge war. Sie war noch immer entschlossen, Jack zu verlassen, doch litt sie seit jenem Tag, an dem sie ihren Entschluß getroffen hatte, an den Vorboten des Abschiedsschmerzes.

Auch Tommy trieb sich in der Nähe des Fasses herum. »Na, wie wär's, Tommy?« rief Jack. »Willst du's nicht auch mal versuchen?«

»Nein, noch nicht«, antwortete Tommy.

Tommy, inzwischen elf, wußte, daß er gescheiter war als seine Schwester, und er hielt sich auch für gescheiter als die meisten anderen Menschen, mit denen er es zu tun hatte. Er sah den Kindern genau zu und studierte vor allem die Technik derjenigen, die sich erfolgreich Äpfel aus dem Wasser schnappten. Aliena beobachtete ihn beim Beobachten. Tommy war ihr ganz besonderer Liebling. Als sie Jack zum erstenmal gesehen hatte, war er ungefähr so alt gewesen wie Tommy jetzt. Und die beiden waren sich so ähnlich! Ihm zuzusehen, entfachte in ihr die Sehnsucht nach der Kindheit, der Jugend. Jack hätte es gerne gesehen, wenn Tommy Baumeister geworden wäre, doch bisher zeigte der Junge noch kein besonderes Interesse an seinem Fach. Aber er hatte ja auch noch so viel Zeit ...

Endlich beugte sich Tommy über das Faß und öffnete den Mund. Er drückte den Apfel, auf den seine Wahl gefallen war, mit dem Gesicht unter die Wasseroberfläche und tauchte kurz darauf triefend wieder auf, den Apfel triumphierend zwischen den Zähnen.

Wenn Tommy sich etwas in den Kopf gesetzt hatte, dann schaffte er es auch. In ihm steckte etwas von seinem Großvater, Graf Bartholomäus. Er hatte einen sehr starken Willen und einen unbeugsamen Sinn für Gut und Böse.

Sally hatte dagegen Jacks unbekümmertes Wesen und seine Verachtung für alle von Menschen erfundenen Regeln und Gesetze geerbt. Wenn Jack den Kindern Geschichten erzählte, war Sally immer auf der Seite des Schwächeren, während Tommy ihn eher verurteilte. Die Eigenschaften der Eltern spiegelten sich in den Kindern wider: Die fröhliche Sally hatte Alienas ebenmäßige Züge und auch die dunklen, wirren Locken ihrer Mutter, der entschlossene Tommy Jacks karottenfarbenes Haar, weiße Haut und blaue Augen.

»Da kommt Onkel Richard!« rief Tommy plötzlich aus.

Aliena drehte sich um. Tommy hatte recht – da kam ihr Bruder, der Graf von Shiring, in Begleitung einer Handvoll Ritter und Knappen über die Wiese geritten. Aliena war entsetzt. Wie konnte er sich nach alldem, was er Philip angetan hatte, noch hier blicken lassen?

Richard ritt geradewegs auf das Faß zu und saß ab. Er lächelte nach allen Seiten und schüttelte Hände, die ihm entgegengestreckt wurden. »Versuch mal, einen Apfel zu schnappen, Onkel Richard!« sagte Tommy. »Ich glaub', du schaffst es!«

Richard tauchte seinen Kopf ins Faß und kam mit einem Apfel zwischen den starken weißen Zähnen wieder zum Vorschein.

Sein blonder Bart war durchnäßt. Im Spiel war er schon immer besser als im wahren Leben, dachte Aliena.

Sie war nicht bereit, ihn ungeschoren davonkommen zu lassen. Andere mochten sich vor ihm fürchten und lieber den Mund halten, schließlich war er der Graf ... Für Aliena hingegen war er der dumme kleine Bruder, sonst gar nichts. Er kam zu ihr, um sie mit einem Kuß zu begrüßen, doch sie schob ihn unwirsch von sich und sagte: »Warum hast du der Priorei den Steinbruch gestohlen? Was ist nur in dich gefahren?«

Jack spürte, daß Streit in der Luft lag. Er nahm die Kinder bei der Hand und trollte sich.

Richard war gekränkt. »Alle Besitztümer wurden jenen zurücker-stattet, die zu Zeiten ...«

»Komm mir bloß nicht damit!« unterbrach ihn Aliena. »Nach all-dem, was Philip für dich getan hat!«

»Der Steinbruch ist Teil meines Geburtsrechts«, erwiderte Richard, nahm seine Schwester beiseite und sprach in leisem Ton weiter, so daß die Umstehenden ihn nicht mehr verstehen konnten. »Abgesehen davon: Ich brauche das Geld aus dem Verkauf der Steine, Allie.«

»Kein Wunder bei einem, der nichts anderes tut, als auf die Hatz und die Beizjagd zu gehen.«

»Was soll ich denn sonst tun?«

»Dafür sorgen, daß das Land wächst und gedeiht! Es gibt so viel zu tun. Die Schäden, die Krieg und Hungersnot hinterlassen haben, sind noch längst nicht alle beseitigt. Wälder müssen gerodet, Sümpfe trockengelegt und die Bauern in neuen Anbaumethoden unterwiesen werden – so mehrt man seinen Reichtum, und nicht, indem man sich einen Steinbruch unter den Nagel reißt, den der König einst der Prio-rei Kingsbridge zugesprochen hat!«

»Ich habe mir nie fremdes Gut angeeignet.«

»Zeit deines Lebens hast du von anderen gelebt!« Aliena war jetzt so wütend, daß sie bereit war, Dinge zu sagen, die besser ungesagt blieben. »Nie hast du dir selbst etwas erarbeitet. Deine dämlichen Waffen hast du dir von *meinem* Geld gekauft. Du nahmst die Stelle, die Philip dir anbot, und deine Grafschaft bekamst du zurück, weil ich sie dir gleichsam auf einem Silbertablett präsentiert habe. Und jetzt kannst du sie nicht einmal regieren, ohne dich an fremdem Eigen-tum zu vergreifen.« Aliena machte auf dem Absatz kehrt und stürmte davon.

Richard lief ihr hinterher, wurde aber von irgend jemandem aufgehalten, der sich vor ihm verneigte und sich nach seiner Gesundheit erkundigte. Aliena hörte noch Richards höfliche Antwort und merkte, daß er sich in ein Gespräch verwickeln ließ. Um so besser, dachte sie. Ich habe ihm meine Meinung gesagt und will mich ohnehin nicht weiter mit ihm streiten ... An der Brücke blickte sie noch einmal zurück. Jemand anders redete jetzt auf ihn ein, und er winkte ihr zu, sie möge doch auf ihn warten, er wolle mit ihr reden. Aber er war jetzt so eingekeilt in der Menge, daß er gar nicht mehr vorankam. Jack, Tommy und Sally jagten mit Stöcken einem Ball hinterher, ein lustiges Spiel im hellen Sonnenlicht. Ich bringe es nicht über mich, sie von ihrem Vater zu trennen, dachte sie, aber es geht doch nicht anders. Wie sonst kann ich je wieder ein normales Leben führen?

Aliena überquerte die Brücke und betrat die Stadt. Sie wollte eine Weile allein sein.

Sie hatte ein Haus in Winchester angemietet, ein großes Gebäude mit einem Laden zu ebener Erde, einer Wohnstube und einem Schlafzimmer im Obergeschoß sowie einem großem Lagerschuppen im Hinterhof, in dem sie ihre Stoffe unterbringen konnte. Doch je näher der Umzugstag rückte, desto weniger war ihr nach einer Abreise zumute.

Die Straßen der Stadt waren heiß und staubig, und die Luft war voller Fliegen, die in den unzähligen Dunghaufen willkommene Brutstätten fanden. Alle Läden hatten zu, und alle Haustüren waren verschlossen. Die Stadt war menschenleer. Alle tummelten sich draußen auf der Wiese.

Sie ging zu Jacks Haus. Dorthin würden auch die anderen kommen, sobald das Apfelschnappen vorüber war. Die Haustür stand offen. Aliena runzelte ärgerlich die Stirn. Wer hatte vergessen, sie abzuschließen? Zu viele Leute besaßen einen Schlüssel: sie selbst, Jack, Richard und Martha. Viel zu stehlen gab es nicht: Ihr eigenes Geld bewahrte Aliena schon seit vielen Jahren mit Zustimmung von Prior Philip in der Schatzkammer der Priorei auf. Aber das ganze Haus würde voller Fliegen sein.

Sie trat über die Schwelle. Es war dunkel und kühl. In der Mitte des Zimmers tanzte ein Fliegenschwarm in der Luft, dicke Schmeißfliegen krabbelten über das Tischtuch, und zwei Wespen umsummten wütend den Honigtopf.

Und am Tisch saß Alfred.

Aliena stieß einen leisen Angstschrei aus, fing sich aber schnell wieder und fragte: »Wie kommst du hier herein?«

»Ich habe einen Schlüssel.«

Er muß ihn sehr lange aufbewahrt haben, dachte Aliena. Seine breiten Schultern waren knochig, sein Gesicht eingefallen. »Was willst du hier?« fragte sie.

»Ich wollte dich besuchen.«

Sie spürte, daß sie zu zittern begann – nicht vor Angst, sondern vor Wut. »Ich will dich nicht mehr sehen – weder heute noch in Zukunft«, schäumte sie. »Du hast mich wie einen Hund behandelt, und als Jack dir aus Mitleid eine Stelle anbot, hast du sein Vertrauen mißbraucht und all seine Handwerker nach Shiring abgeworben.«

»Ich brauche Geld«, sagte er in einer Mischung aus Flehen und Trotz.

»Dann arbeite.«

»Die Bauarbeiten in Shiring sind eingestellt worden. Und hier in Kingsbridge bekomme ich bestimmt keine Arbeit mehr.«

»Dann hau doch ab – nach London, nach Paris ...«

»Ich dachte, du könntest mir aushelfen.« Er ließ nicht locker, starrsinnig wie ein Ochse.

»Hier gibt's für dich nichts zu holen. Am besten verschwindest du jetzt.«

»Hast du denn gar kein Mitleid mit mir?« Der Trotz war verschwunden, das Flehen blieb.

Sie lehnte sich haltsuchend gegen den Tisch. »Alfred, kannst du eigentlich nicht begreifen, daß ich dich *hasse*?«

»Warum?« fragte er mit beleidigter Miene. Er wirkte geradezu überrascht.

Gott im Himmel, ist der Kerl dumm, dachte Aliena, das ist ja schon fast eine Entschuldigung. »Geh ins Kloster und bitte um eine milde Gabe«, sagte sie müde. »Prior Philip verfügt über einen schier übermenschlichen Fundus an Nachsicht und Verständnis – im Gegensatz zu mir.«

»Aber du bist meine *Frau*«, sagte Alfred.

Das war der Gipfel. »Ich bin *nicht* deine Frau«, zischte sie. »Und du bist nicht mein Ehemann. Du warst es auch nie. So, und jetzt mach, daß du fortkommst!«

Er packte sie an den Haaren. »Du bist meine Frau!« sagte er und zog sie am Schopf über den Tisch. Mit der freien Hand griff er an ihre Brust und drückte fest zu.

Das war das letzte, was Aliena von ihm erwartet hätte – von einem Mann, der neun Monate lang mit ihr das Zimmer geteilt hatte und nicht ein einziges Mal imstande gewesen war, mit ihr zu schlafen. Sie schrie unwillkürlich auf und versuchte sich ihm zu entziehen, aber er hatte ihre Haare fest im Griff und zerrte sie an sich. »Deine Schreie kann keiner hören. Die Leute sind alle unten am Fluß.«

Aliena hatte auf einmal furchtbare Angst. Sie war Alfred ausgeliefert, und er war sehr kräftig. Sie hatte weite Reisen gemacht und dabei auf Hunderten von Meilen Kopf und Kragen riskiert – und nun wurde sie zu Hause von dem ihr angetrauten Mann überfallen!

Alfred sah die Furcht in ihren Augen und sagte: »Angst, was? Es wär' besser für dich, wenn du ein bißchen lieb zu mir wärst.« Er küßte sie auf den Mund. Aliena biß ihn in die Lippe. Er brüllte auf vor Schmerz.

Sie sah den Fausthieb nicht kommen. Er traf ihre Wange mit solcher Wucht, daß sie fürchtete, der Knochen sei gebrochen. Ihr wurde schwarz vor Augen, sie verlor das Gleichgewicht und spürte, wie sie zu Boden stürzte. Die Binsenmatten auf dem Boden milderten den Aufprall. Sie schüttelte den Kopf, um wieder zu Sinnen zu kommen, und griff nach dem Messer an ihrem linken Arm. Doch ehe sie es hervorziehen konnte, umklammerte Alfred ihre Handgelenke und sagte: »Ich kenne den kleinen Dolch. Ich hab' dir ja schon beim Ausziehen zugesehen, erinnerst du dich?« Er gab ihre Hände frei, schlug ihr noch einmal ins Gesicht und nahm die Waffe an sich.

Aliena versuchte verzweifelt, sich unter ihm hervorzuwinden. Er saß auf ihren Beinen und legte die linke Hand um ihren Hals. Aliena schlug mit den Armen um sich, bis plötzlich die Dolchspitze unmittelbar vor ihrem rechen Auge auftauchte. »Gib Ruhe, sonst stech' ich dir die Augen aus«, sagte Alfred.

Sie erstarrte. Sie hatte furchtbare Angst um ihr Augenlicht. Mehrmals schon hatte sie Menschen gesehen, die zur Strafe für ein Vergehen geblendet worden waren. Sie tappten bettelnd durch die Straßen und richteten die leeren Augenhöhlen in grausiger Manier auf die Vorübergehenden. Die Gassenjungen hatten ihren Spaß mit den Blinden. Sie zwickten sie und stellten ihnen das Bein, bis die Geschundenen sich vor Wut nicht mehr zu helfen wußten und ihre Peiniger zu greifen suchten – wodurch für jene das Spiel erst richtig lustig wurde. Die meisten Geblendeten starben nach ein, zwei Jahren einen elenden Tod.

»Ich hab's doch gewußt, daß dich das zur Vernunft bringt«, sagte Alfred. Er beugte sich über sie, die Knie neben ihren Hüften auf dem Boden, den Dolch unverändert vor ihren Augen. Wieder zog er ihr Gesicht näher an sich heran. »So«, sagte er dann, »und jetzt sei lieb zu mir.« Er küßte sie.

Sein unrasiertes Gesicht schrammte über ihre Haut. Sein Atem roch nach Bier und Zwiebeln. Sie preßte die Lippen zusammen.

»Das ist nicht lieb. Küß mich auch.«

Er küßte sie erneut. Als die Messerspitze ihr Lid berührte, bewegte Aliena die Lippen. Ihr wurde übel vom Geschmack seines Mundes. Alfred stieß seine rauhe Zunge zwischen ihre Zähne. Aliena war zum Speien zumute. Verzweifelt versuchte sie, das Ekelgefühl zu unterdrücken. Wenn ich mich übergebe, wird er mich töten, dachte sie.

Er richtete sie auf, ohne den Dolch von ihren Augen zu nehmen, und sagte: »So. Faß an.« Er nahm ihre Hand und zog sie unter den Rock seiner Tunika. Sie berührte sein Geschlecht. »Nimm ihn in die Hand«, sagte er und fügte, als sie seinen Wunsch erfüllt hatte, hinzu: »Reib ihn. Aber sanft.«

Aliena gehorchte. Wenn ich ihn auf diese Weise befriedige, verschont er mich vielleicht, dachte sie. Angstvoll betrachtete sie sein Gesicht. Es war rot angelaufen, die Augen hielt er geschlossen. Sie streichelte sein Glied bis hinunter zur Wurzel und mußte daran denken, wie sehr Jack diese Liebkosung immer genoß. Es machte ihn ganz verrückt.

Sie fürchtete, nie wieder Spaß an dieser Zärtlichkeit zu haben, und Tränen stiegen ihr in die Augen.

»Nicht so fest!« sagte er und fuchtelte bedrohlich mit dem Messer.

Aliena riß sich zusammen, konzentrierte sich.

Und dann ging die Tür auf.

Ihr Herz füllte sich mit Hoffnung. Ein Keil strahlend hellen Sonnenlichts fiel ins Zimmer und funkelte verwirrend durch die Tränen in ihren Augen. Alfred erstarrte. Sie nahm ihre Hand fort.

Beide starrten sie auf die Tür. Wer war es? Aliena konnte nichts erkennen. Bitte, lieber Gott, erspar den Kindern diesen Anblick. Ich müßte vor Scham in den Boden versinken ... Dann hörte sie einen leisen Wutschrei. Es war die Stimme eines Mannes. Sie blinzelte die Tränen fort und erkannte ihren Bruder Richard.

Armer Richard! Es war fast noch schlimmer, als wenn es Tommy gewesen wäre. Richard trug eine Narbe am linken Ohr, die ihn für alle Zeiten an jene grauenvolle Szene erinnerte, die er als Vierzehnjähriger hatte miterleben müssen. Jetzt erlebte er es zum zweitenmal. Wie sollte er je darüber hinwegkommen?

Alfred versuchte sich aufzurappeln, doch Richard war schneller als er. Wie der Blitz stürmte er durchs Zimmer, holte aus und traf Alfred mit seinem stiefelbewehrten Fuß voll am Kinn. Alfred krachte rückwärts gegen den Tisch. Richard verfolgte ihn, trat dabei, ohne es zu merken, auf Aliena und drosch mit Händen und Füßen auf den Übeltäter ein. Aliena kroch aus der Gefahrenzone. Richards Gesicht war eine Maske aus zügelloser Wut. Er sah sich nicht nach Aliena um. Er beachtete sie überhaupt nicht. Es geht ihm gar nicht um mich, begriff sie. Seine Wut richtet sich gar nicht gegen Alfred und das, was er mir antun wollte, sondern gegen das, was William und Walter vor achtzehn Jahren ihm selbst angetan haben ... Damals war Richard ein schwacher, hilfloser Junge gewesen. Heute war er ein großer, starker Mann und ein kampferprobter Soldat, und endlich hatte er eine Zielscheibe für die rasende Wut gefunden, die er in all den Jahren in seinem Herzen genährt hatte. Unbarmherzig schlug er auf Alfred ein. Alfred suchte taumelnd hinter dem Tisch Zuflucht und machte mit erhobenen Armen zaghafte Abwehrversuche. Dann landete Richard einen Volltreffer auf seinem Kinn, und Alfred kippte nach hinten um.

Mit schreckgeweiteten Augen lag er auf den Binsenmatten. Aliena wurde die Raserei ihres Bruders unheimlich. »Genug jetzt, Richard!« rief sie. Richard hörte nicht auf sie und holte aus, um Alfred zu treten. In diesem Augenblick fiel Alfred ein, daß er noch immer den Dolch in der Hand hielt. Er wich dem Tritt aus, war im Nu wieder auf den Füßen und ging mit dem Messer auf Richard los. Der Graf hatte damit nicht gerechnet und sprang zurück. Alfred setzte sofort nach und trieb ihn vor sich her. Die beiden Männer waren ungefähr gleichgroß und gleichstark. Richard war ein erfahrener Kämpfer, Alfred aber war bewaffnet. Sie waren nun praktisch einander ebenbürtig. Aliena hatte auf einmal Angst um ihren Bruder. Was wird geschehen, wenn Alfred ihn überwältigt? dachte sie. Dann muß ich allein mit ihm fertig werden ...

Sie sah sich nach einer Waffe um. Neben der Feuerstelle lag ein Stapel Holz. Sie ergriff ein schweres Scheit.

Wieder ging Alfred auf Richard los. Richard wich aus, bekam das Handgelenk des noch ausgestreckten Arms zu fassen und zog Alfred zu sich her. Alfred verlor das Gleichgewicht und torkelte auf Richard zu, nur um von diesem mit einem Hagel von Faustschlägen auf Gesicht und Körper empfangen zu werden. Ein grausames Lächeln beherrschte Richards Miene – das Lächeln eines Rächers. Alfred fing an zu wimmern und hob wieder die Arme, um Kopf und Gesicht zu schützen.

Richard zögerte. Er atmete schwer. Aliena dachte schon, es sei alles vorüber, doch unvermittelt und mit überraschender Schnelligkeit stach Alfred wieder zu. Die Messerspitze streifte Richards Wange. Richard wich hastig zurück, doch Alfred setzte nach und hob das Messer zum entscheidenden Stoß ... Aliena erkannte, daß Richard in Todesgefahr schwebte. Sie holte aus und schlug mit aller Kraft zu. Das schwere Holzscheit verfehlte Alfreds Kopf, traf aber einen Ellbogen. Aliena hörte ein Knirschen, als Holz und Knochen aufeinanderschlugen. Der Schlag betäubte Alfreds Arm, und das Messer fiel ihm aus der Hand.

Schnell, entsetzlich schnell, kam dann das Ende.

Richard bückte sich, griff sich Alienas Messer und unterlief mit derselben, im Bogen aufwärts geführten Bewegung die Verteidigung seines Gegners.

Mit furchtbarer Gewalt fuhr die Klinge bis zum Heft in Alfreds Brust.

Aliena packte das Grauen. Alfred schrie wie ein gestochenes Schwein. Richard zog den Dolch wieder heraus, und Alfreds Blut sprudelte aus der Wunde. Alfred öffnete den Mund, aber es kam kein Schrei mehr. Sein Gesicht erbleichte und wurde dann fahl, die Augen schlossen sich, und er stürzte zu Boden. Blut sickerte in die Binsenmatten.

Aliena kniete neben ihm nieder. Seine Augenlider zitterten. Noch atmete er, doch das Leben verließ seinen Körper rasch. Aliena blickte zu ihrem Bruder auf, der schwer atmend auf die beiden herabsah. »Er stirbt«, sagte sie.

Richard nickte. Alfreds Tod rührte ihn wenig. »Ich habe schon bessere Männer sterben sehen«, sagte er und fügte hinzu: »Ich hab' auch schon Männer getötet, die's nicht so verdient hatten wie er.«

Aliena erschrak über seine Hartherzigkeit, doch verzichtete sie auf eine Gegenrede. Ihr fiel ein, wie Richard zum erstenmal einen Menschen getötet hatte – damals, nach der Eroberung der Burg durch William. Sie und Richard waren auf der Straße nach Winchester von zwei Wegelagerern überfallen worden. Aliena hatte einen der beiden mit ihrem Dolch schwer verwundet, dann aber ihren damals erst fünfzehnjährigen Bruder gezwungen, dem Kerl den Gnadenstoß zu versetzen. Wenn er wirklich so herzlos ist, dachte sie, dann bin ich dafür mitverantwortlich ...

Alfred öffnete die Augen und erwiderte ihren Blick. Aliena schämte sich fast, weil sie so wenig Mitleid mit ihm empfand. Sie sah ihm in die Augen und dachte, nie, Alfred, hast du auch nur eine Spur von Mitleid, Nachsicht oder Großzügigkeit gezeigt. Zeitlebens hast du in deinem Herzen nur Grimm und Haß genährt, und Freude hattest du nur an deinen Gehässigkeiten und kleinlichen Racheakten. Das hätte doch alles nicht sein müssen, Alfred … Du hättest ohne weiteres etwas netter zu deiner Schwester sein können. Und warum hast du deinem Stiefbruder nie verziehen, daß er gescheiter ist als du? Aus Liebe hättest du heiraten sollen, nicht aus Rache, und was hat dich bewegt, Prior Philips Vertrauen so zu enttäuschen? Du hättest glücklich sein können, Alfred …

Plötzlich riß Alfred die Augen weit auf und stöhnte: »Gott im Himmel, tut das weh …«

Wann stirbt er denn endlich? dachte Aliena.

Er schloß die Augen.

»Das wär's«, sagte Richard.

Alfred atmete nicht mehr.

Aliena erhob sich. »Jetzt bin ich Witwe«, sagte sie.

Alfred wurde auf dem Friedhof der Priorei Kingsbridge bestattet. Man entsprach damit einem Wunsch Marthas, der letzten überlebenden Blutsverwandten. Martha war auch die einzige Person, die um Alfred trauerte. Obwohl sie von ihrem Bruder immer schlecht behandelt worden war und deshalb schon früh bei ihrem Stiefbruder Jack Trost und Zuflucht gesucht hatte, bestand sie darauf, daß er in der Nähe begraben wurde, um ab und zu sein Grab aufsuchen zu können. Als der Sarg in die Grube gelassen wurde, weinte außer Martha niemand.

Jack nahm die Nachricht von Alfreds Tod mit finsterer Erleichterung auf. Tommy stand neben Aliena und war furchtbar neugierig: Es war das erste Familienbegräbnis, an dem er teilnahm, und er kannte die Rituale des Todes noch nicht. Sally war blaß und klammerte sich angstvoll an die Hand ihrer Mutter.

Auch Richard war anwesend. Während des Gottesdienstes sagte er zu Aliena, er sei gekommen, um Gott um Vergebung zu bitten. Er beeilte sich hinzuzufügen, das er nach wie vor nicht glaube, unrecht gehandelt zu haben, aber sicher sei sicher …

Aliena, deren Gesicht von Alfreds letztem Schlag noch ganz verschwollen war, rief sich ihre erste Begegnung mit dem Getöteten ins Gedächtnis: Er war in Begleitung seines Vaters, Tom Builder, Marthas und Jacks auf Earlscastle erschienen. Schon damals war Alfred der Raufbold der Familie gewesen – groß und stark wie ein Ochse, verschlagen und boshaft. Hätte Aliena damals jemand vorausgesagt, daß sie eines Tages seine Ehefrau werden würde, so wäre sie wohl versucht gewesen, sich aus Verzweiflung von den Zinnen zu stürzen. Als die Familie die Burg verließ, rechnete Aliena nicht damit, sie jemals wiederzusehen – doch das Schicksal hatte es gefügt, daß Tom und seine Familie später ebenso wie sie selbst nach Kingsbridge verschlagen wurden. Gemeinsam mit Alfred hatte sie die Kirchengilde gegründet, die inzwischen eine so bedeutende Rolle im Leben der Gemeinde spielte. Dann hatte Alfred ihr einen Heiratsantrag gemacht. Nicht im Traum wäre es Aliena damals eingefallen, daß er sie nicht begehrte, sondern nur seinem verhaßten Stiefbruder eins auswischen wollte. Trotzdem hatte sie seinen Antrag zurückgewiesen – bis es ihm dann mit dem Versprechen, Richard finanziell zu unterstützen, doch gelungen war, sie umzustimmen. Rückblickend, dachte Aliena, geschah es ihm nur recht, daß unsere Ehe ein solch entwürdigendes Debakel für ihn war. Seine Motive waren herzlos, sein Lohn ein Leben ohne Liebe.

Aliena war glücklich über Alfreds Tod, sie konnte es gar nicht verhehlen. Von dem geplanten Umzug nach Winchester war nun natürlich keine Rede mehr – vielmehr wollten Jack und sie so bald wie möglich heiraten. Zum Begräbnis setzte sie eine ernste und feierliche Miene auf, hatte wohl auch ein paar ernste und feierliche Gedanken – doch das Herz wollte ihr schier übergehen vor Freude.

Philip hatte sich bereiterklärt, Alfred zu bestatten, und damit einmal mehr seine anscheinend unerschöpfliche Nachsicht gegenüber Leuten unter Beweis gestellt, von denen er verraten und verkauft worden war.

Die fünf Erwachsenen und zwei Kinder standen noch am offenen Grab, als unvermittelt Ellen auftauchte.

Philip war alles andere als erbaut. Ellen hatte eine christliche Hochzeit verflucht und war seither auf dem Klostergelände unerwünscht. Andererseits konnte er ihr die Teilnahme am Begräbnis ihres Stiefsohns kaum verweigern. Da aber die Zeremonie ohnehin beendet war, drehte er sich einfach um und ging.

Aliena war sehr betrübt darüber, daß Philip und Ellen so verfeindet waren. Beide waren sie, jeder auf seine Weise, sehr gute Menschen, doch vertraten sie mit Überzeugung (und wenig Toleranz) vollkommen gegensätzliche moralische Vorstellungen.

Ellen war sichtlich gealtert: Sie hatte mehr Falten als früher, und in ihr Haar mischte sich mehr Grau, doch ihre goldenen Augen waren unverändert schön. Außer einer grobgenähten Ledertunika trug sie nichts am Leibe, nicht einmal Schuhe. Arme und Beine waren sonnengebräunt und muskulös. Tommy und Sally rannten sogleich auf sie zu und busselten sie ab. Jack folgte ihnen und schloß sie herzhaft in die Arme.

Dann hob sie Richard die Wange zum Kuß entgegen. »Du hast recht gehandelt«, sagte sie. »Mach dir keine Vorwürfe.« Vor dem offenen Grab blieb sie stehen und sah hinein. »Ich war seine Stiefmutter und hätte ihn gerne glücklich gemacht. Aber wie?«

Als sie sich vom Grab abwendete, nahm Aliena sie in die Arme. »Bleibst du zum Essen bei uns?« fragte sie.

»Gerne.« Ellen fuhr mit der Hand durch Tommys roten Schopf. »Ich möchte mal wieder mit meinen Enkeln sprechen. Sie werden ja so schnell groß. Als mir Tom Builder zum erstenmal begegnete, war Jack so alt wie Tommy heute!« Sie näherten sich dem Tor des Klosterbezirks. »Je älter man wird, desto schneller vergehen die Jahre«, sagte sie. »Ich glaube ...« Sie brach mitten im Satz ab und blieb stehen.

»Was ist los?« fragte Aliena.

Ellen spähte durch den Torbogen am Klostereingang. Die Holztore waren geöffnet. Die Straße vor ihnen war leer – bis auf ein paar Kinder, die dicht gedrängt beieinander standen und irgend etwas anstarrten, was von außen nicht zu sehen war.

»Richard!« rief Ellen in scharfem Ton. »Geh ja nicht raus!«

Nun blieben auch die anderen stehen, und Aliena begriff, was Ellen so beunruhigte: Die Kinder sahen so aus, als beobachteten sie jemand, der, von der Klostermauer verborgen, gleich hinter dem Tor auf der Lauer lag.

Richard reagierte schnell. »Eine Falle!« sagte er. Ohne ein weiteres Wort zu verlieren, drehte er sich um und lief davon.

Einen Augenblick später schaute ein behelmter Kopf hinter dem Torpfosten hervor. Er gehörte zu einem großgewachsenen Bewaffneten. Als der Mann sah, daß Richard auf die Kirche zulief, stieß er einen Alarmruf aus und jagte ihm nach. Drei, vier, fünf Männer sprangen auf und beteiligten sich an der Verfolgung.

Die Trauergemeinde zerstob, doch die Bewaffneten waren nur an Richard interessiert. Aliena war furchtbar erschrocken und hatte keine Ahnung, was die Männer beabsichtigten: Wer konnte es wagen, den Grafen von Shiring am hellichten Tag anzugreifen – noch dazu auf dem Gelände eines Klosters? Mit angehaltenem Atem verfolgte sie die Jagd. Richard sprang über eine niedrige Mauer, an der die Steinmetzen gerade arbeiteten, und seine Verfolger setzten ihm nach, ungeachtet der Tatsache, daß sie eine Kirche betraten. Die Handwerker erstarrten in der Bewegung, die Kellen und Hämmer erhoben. Ein junger Lehrling begriff am schnellsten, worum es ging; er streckte eine Schaufel aus und brachte dadurch einen der Bewaffneten zu Fall. Von den anderen rührte keiner eine Hand. Richard erreichte die Tür zum Kreuzgang. Der Mann, der ihm am dichtesten auf den Fersen war, hob sein Schwert ... Aliena durchzuckte ein entsetzlicher Schreck: Was ist, wenn die Tür verschlossen ist? dachte sie ... Der Bewaffnete schlug zu. Im selben Augenblick riß Richard die Tür auf und schlüpfte hindurch. Das niederfahrende Schwert biß tief ins Holz der zuschlagenden Pforte.

Aliena atmete auf.

Die Bewaffneten versammelten sich vor der Tür zum Kreuzgang. Sie waren sich über ihr weiteres Vorgehen offensichtlich unschlüssig und schienen erst jetzt zu merken, wo sie sich befanden. Die Maurer und Steinmetzen starrten sie feindselig an und ergriffen Hämmer und Äxte. Den fünf Bewaffneten standen fast hundert Handwerker gegenüber.

»Wer, zum Teufel, sind diese Kerle?« stieß Jack hervor.

Eine Stimme hinter ihm antwortete: »Es sind die Männer des Vogts.«

Entsetzt fuhr Aliena herum. Die Stimme war ihr nur allzu bekannt. Vor dem Tor, auf einem unruhigen schwarzen Hengst, saß William Hamleigh. Er trug ein Kettenhemd. Sein Anblick jagte ihr einen Schauer über den Rücken.

»Verschwinde, du abscheuliches Geschmeiß!« rief Jack.

Die Beleidigung trieb William die Zornesröte ins Gesicht, doch rührte er sich nicht von der Stelle. »Ich habe einen Haftbefehl zu vollstrecken.«

»Na dann los – Richards Männer werden dich in Stücke reißen!«

»Sobald er im Verlies hockt, hat er keine Männer mehr.«

»Für wen hältst du dich eigentlich? Ein Vogt hat überhaupt nicht das Recht, einen Grafen zu verhaften.«

»Wenn er einen Mord begangen hat, schon.«

Aliena rang nach Luft. Jetzt durchschaute sie Williams teuflischen Plan. »Das war kein Mord!« rief sie aus.

»Selbstverständlich war es Mord«, erwiderte William. »Graf Richard hat Alfred Builder ermordet. Und ich muß Prior Philip nun erklären, daß er einem Mörder Unterschlupf gewährt.«

William trat seinem Pferd in die Flanken und ritt an ihnen vorbei zum Küchenhof, wo die weltlichen Besucher des Klosters empfangen wurden. Aliena sah ihm fassungslos nach. Williams Tücke war kaum zu glauben. Was war schon der arme Alfred, den sie gerade beerdigt hatten, in all seiner Beschränktheit und fast schon tragischen Charakterschwäche gegen diesen Diener des Satans? Wann werden wir dieses Ungeheuer endlich los? dachte sie.

Im Küchenhof schlossen sich die Bewaffneten William an. Einer von ihnen hämmerte mit dem Schwertknauf gegen die Küchentür. Die Handwerker hatten die Baustelle verlassen und versammelten sich in angemessener Entfernung um die Eindringlinge – eine bedrohliche Streitmacht, bewaffnet mit scharfen Meißeln und schweren Hämmern. Aliena trug Martha auf, die Kinder nach Hause zu bringen, und gesellte sich zusammen mit Jack zu den Handwerkern.

Prior Philip öffnete die Küchentür. Ohnehin kleiner als William, wirkte er in seinem leichten Sommerhabit geradezu winzig vor dem feisten Mann im Kettenhemd, der ihm hoch zu Roß gegenübersaß. Doch der aufrichtige Zorn in seiner Miene verlieh seiner Erscheinung etwas Ehrfurchtgebietendes, dem William nichts entgegenzusetzen hatte.

»Ihr gewährt einem flüchtigen ...«, begann William.

Philip ließ ihn nicht ausreden. »Verschwindet!« brüllte er ihn an.

William versuchte es noch einmal. »Ein Mord wurde begangen, und ich ...«

»Raus! Verlaßt auf der Stelle das Gelände meiner Priorei!«

»Ich bin der Vogt von ...«

»Nicht einmal dem König ist es gestattet, Gewalttäter in ein Kloster eindringen zu lassen! Und jetzt fort mit Euch, raus!«

Ärgerliches Gemurmel erhob sich unter den Maurern und Steinmetzen. Die Bewaffneten sahen sich nervös nach ihnen um.

»Selbst der Prior von Kingsbridge muß dem Vogt Rede und Antwort stehen«, sagte William.

»Aber nicht unter diesen Bedingungen! Schickt Eure Leute sofort vom Klostergelände und deponiert Eure Waffen im Stall. Wenn Ihr bereit seid, als demütiger Sünder das Haus Gottes zu betreten, gewähre ich Euch Einlaß. Und *dann* wird der Prior Euch Rede und Antwort stehen.«

Philip verschwand wieder im Küchengebäude und schlug die Tür hinter sich zu. Die Bauarbeiter applaudierten.

Auch Aliena klatschte unwillkürlich Beifall. Ihr Leben lang hatte sie Williams Macht und Grausamkeit gefürchtet. Es war herzerfrischend zu sehen, wie Prior Philip ihm die Stirn bot.

William indes gab sich noch nicht geschlagen. Er stieg vom Pferd, schnallte sich umständlich sein Schwert ab und reichte es einem seiner Männer. Er wechselte ein paar ruhige Worte mit den Bewaffneten, worauf sie sich entfernten. William sah ihnen nach, bis sie das Tor durchschritten hatten. Daraufhin drehte er sich um und pflanzte sich vor der Küchentür auf.

»Öffnet dem Vogt!« rief er.

Es dauerte eine Weile, bis Philip wieder vor die Tür trat. Er musterte William, der nun unbewaffnet im Hof stand, von oben bis unten und hielt Ausschau nach den Bewaffneten, die vor dem Klostertor beieinanderstanden. Erst dann wandte er sich wieder William zu und sagte: »Nun?«

»Ihr gewährt einem Mörder in Euren Mauern Unterschlupf. Liefert ihn mir aus.«

»In Kingsbridge ist kein Mord begangen worden«, erwiderte Philip.

»Der Graf von Shiring hat vor vier Tagen Alfred Builder ermordet.«

»Das ist falsch«, gab Philip zurück. »Richard hat Alfred getötet, nicht ermordet. Alfred wurde in flagranti bei einer versuchten Vergewaltigung ertappt.«

Aliena schauderte.

»Vergewaltigung?« fragte William. »Wen hat Alfred denn vergewaltigen wollen?«

»Aliena.«

»Wie das? Sie ist seine Frau.« William triumphierte. »Wie kann ein Ehemann seine Frau *vergewaltigen*?«

Aliena merkte jetzt, worauf William hinauswollte, und heiße Wut brodelte in ihr auf.

»Diese Ehe ist niemals vollzogen worden«, sagte Philip. »Außerdem ist Aliena um Annullierung eingekommen.«

»Die niemals gewährt worden ist. Die Ehe wurde in der Kirche geschlossen und bestand dem Gesetz nach fort. Von Vergewaltigung kann also keine Rede sein. Im Gegenteil ...« William drehte sich plötzlich um und deutete mit dem Finger auf Aliena. »Seit Jahren schon will sie ihren Gatten loswerden – und nun ist es ihr endlich gelungen, ihren Bruder soweit zu bringen, ihn aus dem Weg zu schaffen. Er hat ihn mit *ihrem* Dolch erstochen!«

Angst legte sich wie eine kalte Hand um Alienas Herz. Was William hier vorbrachte, war eine ungeheuerliche Lüge – aber für jemanden, der den wahren Sachverhalt nicht kannte, klang seine Argumentation durchaus folgerichtig. Es sah nicht gut aus für Richard.

»Der Vogt kann den Grafen nicht festnehmen«, sagte Philip.

William zog eine Schriftrolle hervor. »Ich habe einen vom König unterfertigten Haftbefehl.«

Aliena war der Verzweiflung nahe. William hatte an alles gedacht. »Wie hat er das geschafft?« murmelte sie.

»Er hat sehr schnell reagiert«, antwortete Jack. »Er muß sofort nach Erhalt der Nachricht nach Winchester geritten sein und mit dem König gesprochen haben.«

Philip streckte die Hand aus. »Zeigt mir den Befehl.«

Auch William streckte nun die Hand aus, erreichte Philip jedoch nicht, da ein Zwischenraum von einigen Schritten sie trennte. Einen Augenblick lang standen sie reglos einander gegenüber. Dann gab William nach, ging auf Philip zu und überreichte ihm das Dokument.

Philip las den königlichen Erlaß durch und gab ihn William zurück. »Er gibt Euch nicht das Recht, ein Kloster anzugreifen«, sagte er.

»Aber er gibt mir das Recht, Richard festzunehmen.«

»Er hat um Asyl gebeten.«

»Aha.« William schien über diese Eröffnung nicht besonders überrascht. Er nickte nur, als hätte er darauf längst gewartet, und antwortete dann mit erhobener Stimme, so daß alle Umstehenden ihn deutlich hören konnten: »So laßt ihn wissen, daß er festgenommen wird, sobald er die Priorei verläßt. Meine Leute werden in der Stadt und vor seiner Burg stationiert sein, um ihn abzufangen. Und vergeßt nicht ...« Er blickte in die Runde. »Und vergeßt nicht, daß jeder, der sich an einem Mann des Vogts vergreift, einen Diener des Königs attackiert.« Er wandte sich wieder an Philip. »Laßt ihn wissen, daß er innerhalb des Freiraums, den ihm das Kloster gewährt, so lange bleiben kann, wie ihm beliebt. Wenn er jedoch von hier fortwill, wird er sich der Gerechtigkeit stellen müssen.«

Es herrschte Schweigen. William schritt gemessenen Schritts von dannen. Für Aliena hatten seine letzten Worte wie die Verhängung einer langen Freiheitsstrafe geklungen. Die Menge teilte sich und gewährte ihm Durchlaß. Als William an Aliena vorbeikam, warf er ihr einen selbstgefälligen Blick zu. Er ging zum Tor und bestieg dort, von den Blicken der Menge verfolgt, sein Pferd. Er erteilte seinen Leuten Order und ritt davon. Zwei Bewaffnete blieben am Tor zurück.

Aliena wandte sich ab und sah, daß Philip neben ihr und Jack stand. »Kommt in mein Haus«, sagte er ruhig. »Wir müssen darüber reden.« Mit diesen Worten verschwand der Prior wieder in der Küche. Aliena konnte sich des Gefühls nicht erwehren, daß Philip sich heimlich über etwas freute.

Die Aufregung hatte sich gelegt. Die Handwerker unterhielten sich angeregt und gingen wieder an die Arbeit. Ellen machte sich auf den

Weg in die Stadt; sie wollte noch etwas von den Enkeln haben. Aliena und Jack gingen auf schnellstem Wege zum Haus des Priors. Philip war noch nicht da. Sie ließen sich auf einer Bank nieder und warteten. Jack spürte Alienas Sorge um ihren Bruder und drückte sie tröstend an sich.

Als Aliena sich umsah, fiel ihr auf, daß Philips Haus mit jedem Jahr ein wenig gemütlicher wurde. Verglichen mit den Privatgemächern eines Grafen war es noch immer recht spärlich möbliert, doch war es längst nicht mehr so karg eingerichtet wie früher. Vor dem kleinen Altar in der Ecke lag inzwischen ein kleiner Teppich, der in langen Nächten des Gebets die Knie des Priors schonte. An der Wand hinter dem Altar hing ein juwelengeschmücktes silbernes Kruzifix, bei dem es sich offenbar um ein kostbares Geschenk handelte. Es schadet Philip gewiß nicht, wenn er mit zunehmendem Alter nicht mehr ganz so streng mit sich ist, dachte Aliena bei sich. Vielleicht wirkt sich das dann auch auf sein Verhältnis zu anderen aus ...

Philip kam kurze Zeit später zur Tür herein, im Schlepptau den sichtlich erregten Richard, der sofort zu reden begann. »Das ist doch das Letzte, was William da treibt!« rief er. »Er ist verrückt geworden! Ich überraschte Alfred dabei, wie er meine Schwester vergewaltigen will ... Er bedroht sie mit einem Dolch und bringt mich fast um ...«

»Beruhige dich«, sagte Philip. »Wir müssen uns in aller Ruhe darüber unterhalten und ganz klar sehen, wo die Gefahren liegen – vorausgesetzt, es gibt welche. Wollen wir uns nicht erst einmal alle setzen?«

Richard nahm Platz, doch sein Redefluß war ungebrochen. »Gefahren? Es gibt keine Gefahren. Ein Vogt darf einen Grafen nicht festnehmen, nicht einmal wegen Mordes.«

»Aber William wird es versuchen«, sagte Philip. »Er hat seine Leute vor den Toren der Priorei postiert.«

Richard machte eine abschätzige Handbewegung. »An den Burschen komm' ich mit verbundenen Augen vorbei! Das ist überhaupt kein Problem. Jack kann vor der Stadtmauer mit einem Pferd auf mich warten.«

»Und was machst du, wenn du nach Earlscastle kommst?« fragte Philip.

»Dasselbe. Ich schleich' mich an Williams Häschern vorbei oder schicke nach einer Eskorte aus der Burg.«

»Das klingt ja ganz gut«, meinte Philip. »Und was geschieht dann?«

»Gar nichts«, sagte Richard. »Was soll William denn tun?«

»Nun, er verfügt immer noch über einen königlichen Erlaß, demzufolge du dich wegen Mordes zu verantworten hast. Jedesmal, wenn du die Burg verläßt, hetzt er dir seine Häscher auf den Hals.«

»Ich werde überall eskortiert sein.«

»Auch wenn du in Shiring und anderswo Gericht hältst?«

»Auch dort.«

»Was meinst du – werden sich die Leute noch an deine Urteilssprüche halten, wenn sie herausfinden, daß du selbst auf der Flucht vor dem Gesetz bist?«

»Ich möcht's ihnen raten«, sagte Richard mit finsterer Miene. »Sie sollen nur daran denken, wie William, als er Graf war, seinen Urteilssprüchen Geltung verschafft hat.«

»Sie fürchten dich vielleicht nicht ganz so sehr wie William und halten dich vermutlich für weniger böse und blutrünstig. Ich hoffe, sie täuschen sich darin nicht.«

»Verlaßt Euch nicht darauf.«

Aliena runzelte die Stirn. Diese Skepsis, so dachte sie, ist so gar nicht nach Philips Art – es sei denn, er verfolgt damit einen ganz bestimmten Zweck. Wahrscheinlich dient dieses Frage-und-Antwort-Spiel lediglich zur Vorbereitung eines Plans, den er uns nachher präsentieren wird … Ich wette, es hat irgend etwas mit dem Steinbruch zu tun.

»Meine Hauptsorge«, sagte Philip, »ist der König. Indem du dich weigerst, auf den Mordvorwurf zu antworten, begehrst du gegen die Krone auf. Vor einem Jahr noch hätte ich gesagt, und wenn schon, dann tust du's eben. Aber inzwischen ist der Krieg vorbei. Die Grafen können nicht mehr so einfach tun und lassen, was ihnen gefällt.«

»So wie's aussieht, mußt du dich dem Verhör wirklich stellen, Richard«, meinte Jack.

»Aber das kann er doch nicht«, sagte Aliena. »Er hat nicht die geringste Chance auf ein gerechtes Verfahren.«

»Aliena hat recht«, sagte Philip. »Der Fall würde am königlichen Hof zur Verhandlung kommen. Der Tathergang ist ja bekannt: Alfred versuchte Aliena Gewalt anzutun und wurde dabei von Richard überrascht; es kam zu einem Kampf, in dessen Verlauf Alfred von Richard getötet wurde. Alles hängt nun von der Auslegung ab. Da aber William, der Ankläger, ein treuer Anhänger von König Stephan ist, Richard hingegen einer der engsten Waffenbrüder Henrys, wird das Urteil voraussichtlich ›schuldig‹ lauten. Warum hat König Stephan denn den

Haftbefehl unterzeichnet? Wahrscheinlich, weil er sich an Richard rächen will. Alfreds Tod verschafft ihm da einen ausgezeichneten Vorwand.«

»Wir müssen uns an Herzog Henry wenden«, sagte Aliena. »Er muß für Richard Partei ergreifen.«

Nun war es an Richard, seine Zweifel zu äußern. »Ich würde mich nicht darauf verlassen«, sagte er. »Henry ist gegenwärtig in der Normandie. Er kann ein Protestschreiben schicken – aber das ist auch schon alles. Gewiß, er kann auch mit einer Flotte übers Meer kommen, doch das wäre dann ein flagranter Verstoß gegen die Abmachungen des Friedensvertrags. Ich glaub' nicht, daß er das für mich riskiert.«

Aliena sah kaum noch einen Ausweg. »Oh, Richard«, sagte sie, »du bist in einem furchtbaren Netz gefangen, und das alles nur, weil du mich gerettet hast.«

Richard raffte sich zu seinem charmantestem Lächeln auf. »Ich würde es auf der Stelle wieder tun, Allie.«

»Ich weiß.« Er meinte es ernst. Richard war tapfer, all seinen Schwächen zum Trotz. Es war einfach unangebracht, daß er so kurz nach seinem erfolgreichen Aufstieg zum Grafen in eine solch unlösbare Zwickmühle geriet. Als Graf hatte er Aliena bisher enttäuscht – bitter enttäuscht sogar –, aber ein solches Schicksal hatte er nicht verdient.

»Das sind vielleicht Aussichten«, sagte er. »Entweder ich bleibe hier im Kloster und harre aus, bis Henry König ist, oder man hängt mich wegen Mordes. Ich würde ja sogar Mönch werden – aber ihr Mönche eßt mir zuviel Fisch.«

»Es gibt möglicherweise noch einen anderen Ausweg«, sagte Philip.

Aliena sah ihn erwartungsvoll an. Sie hatte von Anfang an vermutet, daß der Prior einen Plan ausbrütete. Inzwischen war sie für alles dankbar, was Richard aus seinem Dilemma befreien könnte.

»Du könntest Buße tun für die Tötung Alfreds«, fuhr Philip fort.

»Müßte ich dabei Fisch essen?« gab Richard respektlos zurück.

»Ich denke an das Heilige Land«, sagte Philip.

Alle schwiegen sie. In Palästina herrschte der König von Jerusalem, Balduin I., ein Christ französischer Herkunft. Das Land sah sich unablässig Angriffen seiner muselmanischen Nachbarn, namentlich Ägypten im Süden und Damaskus im Osten, ausgesetzt. Allein die Reise ins Heilige Land dauerte mindestens sechs Monate. Wer all die Strapazen auf sich nahm und vor Ort mit der Waffe in der Hand das Christliche Königreich verteidigte, leistete in der Tat eine Buße, mit der die Tötung eines Menschen gesühnt werden konnte. Dennoch war Aliena nicht ohne Angst: So manch einer, der zum Zug ins Heilige Land aufgebrochen war, kehrte nicht mehr zurück. Andererseits: Jahrelang war Richard von einem Schlachtfeld zum anderen gezogen, und sie hatte in ständiger Angst um ihn gelebt. Viel gefährlicher als England konnte das Heilige Land nicht sein. Die Sorge blieb ihr in jedem Fall, und sie hatte sich daran ja auch schon gewöhnt.

»Der König von Jerusalem braucht immer Leute«, sagte Richard. Alle paar Jahre zogen Abgesandte des Papstes durchs Land und versuchten mit großartigen Schilderungen ruhmreicher Schlachten, zur Verteidigung der Christenheit junge Männer zum Kampf im Heiligen Land zu animieren. »Aber ich bin doch erst seit so kurzer Zeit Graf«, fuhr Richard fort. »Wer würde sich denn während meiner Abwesenheit um die Güter kümmern?«

»Aliena«, sagte Philip.

Aliena stockte der Atem. Philips Vorschlag bedeutete nichts anderes, als daß sie die Stelle des Grafen einnehmen und wie einst ihr Vater die Grafschaft regieren sollte! Im ersten Moment war sie wie vor den Kopf geschlagen. Doch sobald sie wieder zu Sinnen kam, wußte sie: Ja, das ist die richtige Lösung! Wenn ein Adliger ins Heilige Land zog, war es durchaus üblich, daß sein Weib daheim die Geschäfte führte. Nichts sprach dagegen, daß bei einem unverheirateten Grafen dessen Schwester diese Rolle übernahm. Sie, Aliena, wollte die Grafschaft so regieren, wie sie sie schon immer regiert haben wollte – gerecht, vorausschauend und nicht ohne Phantasie. Ich werde all das tun, was Richard bisher schlimmerweise unterlassen hat. Je mehr sie darüber nachdachte, desto schneller schlug ihr Herz. Ich werde neue Methoden im Ackerbau ausprobieren – die Bauern sollen mal versuchen, mit Pferden zu pflügen statt mit Ochsen, und im Frühjahr auf brachliegenden Feldern Hafer und Erbsen säen. Ich werde Rodungen veranlassen, um neues Ackerland zu gewinnen, und neue Märkte einrichten – und selbstverständlich der Priorei wieder den Steinbruch zugänglich machen ...

Daran hatte Philip natürlich auch gedacht. Von all den raffinierten Plänen, die er sich im Laufe der Jahre hatte einfallen lassen, war dies vermutlich der genialste. Auf einen Schlag löste er drei Probleme: Er zog Richards Kopf aus der Schlinge, verschaffte der Grafschaft eine fähige Regentin – und bekam endlich wieder Zugang zum Steinbruch.

»Ich habe nicht den geringsten Zweifel, daß König Balduin über dein Kommen hocherfreut sein wird – vor allem, wenn du auch noch ein paar von deinen Rittern mitbringst, die sich wie du zur Reise ins

Heilige Land berufen fühlen. Du könntest deinen eigenen kleinen Kreuzzug führen.« Er machte eine kleine Pause, um seine Worte wirken zu lassen. »William kann dir dort drüben nichts anhaben«, fuhr er fort. »Und bei deiner Rückkehr wärst du ein Held – und niemand kann es wagen, einen Helden zu hängen!«

»Das Heilige Land«, sagte Richard, und in seinen Augen schimmerte ein verwegener Glanz. Tod oder Ehre ... Das ist genau das Richtige für dich, dachte Aliena. Ein guter Graf wird nie aus dir. Du bist ein Soldat, du willst kämpfen ... Sie sah den abwesenden Blick in seinen Augen und dachte: In Gedanken bist du ja schon dort und verteidigst in sengender Sonne eine Wüstenfestung gegen eine Horde anstürmender Heiden, verteidigst sie mit dem Schwert in der Hand und einem roten Kreuz auf deinem Schild ...

Richard war glücklich.

Zur Hochzeit kam die ganze Stadt.

Aliena war überrascht. Sie hatte angenommen, die Leute betrachteten die Trauung als reine Formsache – schließlich behandelten die meisten sie ohnehin schon mehr oder weniger als Ehepaar –, und von daher nur mit ein paar engen Freunden und Jacks Baumeisterkollegen gerechnet. Doch statt dessen war ganz Kingsbridge auf den Beinen, Männer, Frauen und Kinder gleichermaßen. Aliena rührte diese Anteilnahme. Und alle Menschen strahlten und freuten sich – für *sie*! Sie spürte jetzt, daß man in all den Jahren mit ihr und ihrer mißlichen Lage Mitleid empfunden hatte, es sie aus Taktgefühl aber nicht hatte wissen lassen. Und nun freute man sich mit ihr, daß sie endlich den Mann heiraten konnte, dem sie schon so lange in Liebe verbunden war. Am Arm ihres Bruders Richard schritt Aliena durch die Straßen, freudetrunken und ganz verwirrt von den vielen lächelnden Gesichtern um sie herum.

Am Tag nach der Hochzeit wollte Richard seine Reise ins Heilige Land antreten. König Stephan hatte diese Lösung akzeptiert – er schien heilfroh darüber zu sein, daß er Richard so leicht loswurde. Vogt William tobte – kein Wunder, hatte er doch sein Ziel, Richard die Grafschaft wieder abzujagen, verfehlt. In Richards Augen lag noch immer jener abwesende Blick: Er konnte es gar nicht abwarten, endlich fortzukommen.

So hat sich Vater die Zukunft von Earlscastle gewiß nicht vorgestellt, dachte Aliena, als sie das Klostergelände betrat – Richard als

Soldat in der Ferne und ich in der Rolle der Gräfin auf der Burg ...
Doch sie fühlte sich längst nicht mehr verpflichtet, ihr Leben nach
den Wünschen ihres Vaters zu gestalten. Er war nun seit siebzehn
Jahren tot und hätte gewiß nicht begriffen, was ihr inzwischen voll-
kommen klar war: daß sie, Aliena, weit eher zum Regieren taugte als
Richard.

Sie hatte die Zügel der Macht bereits in die Hand genommen. Die
Diener und das übrige Personal auf der Burg waren in den Jahren
unzureichender Führung faul und träge geworden; Aliena hatte sie
rasch wieder auf Trab gebracht. Sie hatte die Lager auf- und umräu-
men, den großen Saal streichen sowie das Backhaus und die Brauerei
säubern lassen. Die Küche war so verlottert und verdreckt gewesen,
daß Aliena sie niederbrennen und eine neue errichten ließ. Die wöchentlichen Löhne zahlte sie persönlich aus und gab damit allen zu
verstehen, wer jetzt das Sagen hatte. Drei Bewaffnete waren von ihr
wegen Trunkenheit entlassen worden.

Auch den Bau einer neuen Burg hatte Aliena bereits in die Wege
geleitet. Der Bauplatz war zu Pferd in einer Stunde erreichbar. Earlscastle lag zu weit entfernt von der Kathedrale; Jack hatte einen Bauplan gezeichnet. Sobald der Wohnturm stand, wollten sie einziehen.
Bis dahin gedachten sie, ihre Zeit zwischen Earlscastle und Kingsbridge aufzuteilen.

Fernab von Philips mißbilligenden Blicken hatten sie auch schon
einige gemeinsame Nächte in Alienas ehemaligem Schlafgemach verbracht. Wie Jungverheiratete auf der Hochzeitsreise hatten sie sich
gefühlt und sich fortreißen lassen von schier unersättlicher Leidenschaft, die möglicherweise daher rührte, daß sie zum erstenmal in
ihrem Leben in einem von innen verschließbaren Raum zusammenwa-
ren. Ungestörtheit war ein Luxus des Adels: Das Fußvolk schlief (und
liebte sich) in der großen Halle. Selbst Eheleute, die ein Haus besaßen,
mußten ständig damit rechnen, von ihren Kindern, Verwandten oder
Nachbarn überrascht zu werden. Man verschloß die Türen, wenn man
fortging, nicht wenn man zu Hause war. Aliena hatte sich nie daran
gestört – doch nun hatte sie den besonderen Reiz entdeckt, der in
dem Bewußtsein lag, alles tun und lassen zu können, was man wollte,
ohne dabei beobachtet zu werden. Als sie daran dachte, was sie und
Jack in den vergangenen zwei Wochen alles miteinander getrieben
hatten, errötete sie unwillkürlich.

Jack wartete auf sie im halbfertigen Schiff der neuen Kathedrale;
bei ihm waren Martha, Tommy und Sally. Das Ehegelübde sprach man

gemeinhin vor der feierlichen Messe im Portal der Kirche. In diesem Fall war man davon abgewichen: Als »Portal« diente der erste Bauabschnitt des Kirchenschiffs. Aliena war sehr glücklich, daß sie in der Kirche, die Jack errichtete, heiraten konnten. Die Kathedrale gehörte zu Jack wie seine Kleider und sein Liebesspiel. Man sah schon, daß sie ihm eines Tages ähneln würde – anmutig würde sie sein, freundlich, ideenreich, so ganz anders als alles, was es vorher gegeben hatte.

Voller Liebe sah Aliena ihren Jack an. Er war jetzt dreißig Jahre alt, ein ungemein gutaussehender Mann mit seiner roten Mähne und den funkelnden blauen Augen. Und wie häßlich er als Junge gewesen war! Sie hatte es damals, bei ihrer ersten Begegnung, für unter ihrer Würde gehalten, ihn auch nur zu beachten. Jack hingegen meinte, er habe sich auf Anhieb unsterblich in sie verliebt. Noch heute zuckte Aliena zusammen, wenn sie daran dachte, wie sie und die anderen Kinder Jack wegen seiner Behauptung, er habe keinen Vater, verlacht hatten. Das war jetzt fast zwanzig Jahre her. Zwanzig Jahre ...

Ohne Prior Philip, der soeben vom Kreuzgang her die Kirche betrat und lächelnd auf sie zukam, hätte sie Jack vielleicht nie wiedergesehen. Daß er sie endlich heiraten konnte, stimmte ihn sichtlich froh. Aliena konnte sich noch lebhaft an die Umstände ihrer ersten Begegnung erinnern, an die Verzweiflung, die sie erfaßt hatte, weil ein Händler sie um den gerechten Lohn für ihren mit unendlicher Mühe zusammengetragenen Sack Wolle bringen wollte ... und an die überwältigende Dankbarkeit, die sie ihrem Retter, jenem jungen, schwarzhaarigen Mönch entgegenbrachte, der zu ihr gesagt hatte.: »Ich kaufe Euch alle Eure Wolle ab ...« Inzwischen waren seine Haare grau.

Er hatte sie gerettet – und später fast zugrunde gerichtet, indem er Jack gezwungen hatte, sich zwischen ihr und der Kathedrale zu entscheiden. In Fragen der Moral war Philip ein harter, unbeugsamer Mann von ähnlichem Schlag wie ihr Vater, Graf Bartholomäus. Dennoch hatte er es sich nicht nehmen lassen, die kirchliche Trauung zu vollziehen.

Ellen hatte Alienas erste Ehe verflucht, und der Fluch hatte seine Wirkung getan. Im nachhinein war Aliena froh darüber. Wenn meine Ehe mit Alfred nicht völlig unerträglich gewesen wäre, dachte sie, würde ich vielleicht heute noch mit ihm zusammenleben. Man durfte gar nicht darüber nachdenken, was alles hätte geschehen können – ein kalter Schauer überlief sie. Sie dachte an das hübsche, liebeshungrige Arabermädchen in Toledo, das sich in Jack verliebt hatte: Was wäre geschehen, wenn er sie geheiratet hätte? Ich wäre mit meinem

Kind auf den Armen in diese Stadt gekommen und hätte Jack im Schoße einer arabischen Großfamilie vorgefunden – und in den Armen einer fremden Frau, mit der er Geist und Körper teilt ... Der Gedanke allein war ihr ein Graus.

Jack murmelte neben ihr das Vaterunser. Unglaublich, dachte sie, daß ich ihm, als ich damals nach Kingsbridge kam, zunächst nicht mehr Aufmerksamkeit schenkte als der Katze des Kornhändlers ... Ihm hingegen war sie sogleich aufgefallen: Er hatte sie all die Jahre hindurch heimlich geliebt – und mit welcher Engelsgeduld! Er hatte erlebt, wie die heiratsfähigen Söhne des Landadels um sie geworben hatten, einer nach dem anderen, und wie ein jeder von dannen geschlichen war, enttäuscht, beleidigt oder trotzig. Raffinierter Bursche, der er war, hatte er bald erkannt, daß Aliena mit herkömmlichen Formen der Werbung nicht zu gewinnen war, und sich ihr zunächst nur indirekt und unverfänglich genähert, als Freund eher denn als Verliebter. Bei ihren Treffen im Wald hatte er sie mit seinen Geschichten so umgarnt, daß sie sich in ihn verliebte, ohne es zu merken. Sie erinnerte sich an seinen ersten Kuß: Sanft und wie beiläufig auf ihre Lippen gehaucht, hatte er sie verbrannt, und das Feuer glomm wochenlang nach. Noch lebhafter war die Erinnerung an den zweiten Kuß: Jedesmal, wenn Aliena die Walkmühle rumpeln hörte, mußte sie an das so dunkle, unbekannte und unwillkommene Gefühl der Lust denken, welches sie damals überkommen hatte.

Bis heute litt Aliena darunter, wie ihre Gefühle danach erkaltet waren. Jack liebte sie mit Leib und Seele – sie aber war so verstört und verängstigt, daß sie sich von ihm abwandte und vorgab, sich nichts aus ihm zu machen. Ihr Verhalten verletzte ihn tief, und obwohl er sie auch weiterhin liebte und die Wunde inzwischen längst verheilt war, blieb, wie bei tiefen Wunden üblich, eine Narbe zurück. Manchmal konnte Aliena sie sogar sehen – in der Art, wie er sie anschaute, wenn sie sich wieder einmal stritten und sie ihn mit harten Worten anfuhr. Da schienen seine Augen zu sagen: Ja, ich kenne dich, du kannst so kalt und herzlos sein. Du kannst mich verletzen. Ich muß auf der Hut sein ...

War da ein Schimmer des Argwohns in seinem Blick? Jack gelobte ihr ewige Liebe und Treue bis in den Tod. Er hat Grund genug, an mir zu zweifeln, dachte Aliena. Ich habe Alfred geheiratet – gibt es überhaupt einen schlimmeren Treuebruch? Aber ich habe das wieder gutgemacht, bin ihm gefolgt bis ans Ende der christlichen Welt und habe ihn schließlich gefunden.

Enttäuschungen, Treuebrüche, Versöhnungen – das war das tägliche Brot der Ehe. Sie und Jack hatten all dies schon vor ihrer Hochzeit durchlebt. Inzwischen, endlich, konnte Aliena guten Gewissens von sich behaupten, daß sie ihren Jack kannte. Nein, große Überraschungen waren nicht mehr zu erwarten. Daß sie so spät ihren Lebensbund besiegelten, mochte ungewöhnlich sein – aber war es nicht besser so als umgekehrt? Wie viele sprachen die Ehegelübde und lernten einander erst nachher kennen! Den Priestern freilich war so ein Leben, wie sie beide es bisher geführt hatten, ein Dorn im Auge. Prior Philip würde der Schlag treffen, wenn er wüßte, was für Gedanken mir gerade durch den Kopf gehen, dachte Aliena – doch sei's drum: Priester verstehen halt nichts von Liebe!

Nun war sie an der Reihe mit dem Gelöbnis. Sie wiederholte die Worte, die Philip ihr vorsprach, und dachte bei sich, wie schön ist doch die Zeile *Mit meinem Leib huldige ich dir.* Was das bedeutete, würde Philip nie verstehen.

Jack schob ihr einen Ring über den Finger. Darauf habe ich mein Leben lang gewartet, dachte sie. Sie sahen einander in die Augen. Da war eine Veränderung in seinem Blick, die ihr nicht entging. Bis zu diesem Moment, erkannte sie, war er sich meiner nicht sicher. Jetzt sind seine Zweifel verflogen.

»Ich liebe dich«, sagte er, »auf alle Zeit.«

Das war sein Gelübde. Was nun noch kam, war Religion, doch mit diesen Worten hatte auch Jack sein Versprechen abgelegt. Auch ich, gestand Aliena sich ein, war mir seiner bisher nicht sicher ... Gleich würden sie nach vorne gehen und der Messe lauschen, danach die Gratulationen und guten Wünsche der Gäste entgegennehmen und sie zum fröhlichen Hochzeitsschmaus laden – gleich ... Doch dieser kleine Moment gehörte ihnen allein. Jacks Blick sagte *Du und ich – wir beide – immer.* Aliena dachte: *Endlich.*

Und tiefer Friede erfüllte sie.

Buch VI 1170-74

Kingsbridge wuchs und wuchs. Längst war es über seine ursprünglichen Grenzen hinausgewachsen; weniger als die Hälfte der Gebäude
lag innerhalb der alten Stadtmauer. Vor zirka fünf Jahren hatte die
Gilde eine neue Mauer errichten lassen, die auch die Vorstädte mit
einbezog, doch mittlerweile entstanden außerhalb der neuen Mauer
schon wieder neue Siedlungen. Die Wiese am anderen Ufer des Flusses, auf der seit alters her das Erntefest und die Mittsommernacht
gefeiert worden waren, hatte sich in ein kleines Dorf namens Newport
verwandelt.

An einem kühlen Ostersonntag kam hoch zu Roß Vogt William
Hamleigh durchs Dorf, überquerte die Steinbrücke und gelangte so
in jenen Teil von Kingsbridge, der seit einiger Zeit die »Altstadt«
genannt wurde. Die neue Kathedrale war fertig und sollte an diesem
Tag eingeweiht werden. William ritt durch das eindrucksvolle Stadttor
und betrat die seit kurzem gepflasterte Hauptstraße, die zu beiden
Seiten ausschließlich von Steinhäusern gesäumt war. Zu ebener Erde
waren die Läden, im Obergeschoß die Wohnquartiere untergebracht.
Kingsbridge ist größer, geschäftiger und wohlhabender als Shiring es
jemals war, gestand William sich zähneknirschend ein.

Am Ende der Hauptstraße erreichte er den Klosterbezirk, und dort
erhob sich vor seinen Augen die Ursache für Kingsbridges Aufstieg
und Shirings Fall: die Kathedrale.

Ihr Anblick war atemberaubend.

Das hoch in den Himmel ragende Hauptschiff wurde von einer
Reihe eleganter Schwibbogen gestützt. Über den drei riesigen Portiken
der Westseite erhob sich, von schlanken Türmen flankiert, eine Reihe
schmaler, hoher Spitzbogenfenster. Das Konzept war zwar bereits an
dem achtzehn Jahre zuvor fertiggestellten Querschiff erkennbar gewe-

sen, doch übertraf die endgültige Umsetzung der Idee alle Erwartungen. Nie zuvor war auf englischem Boden ein solches Gebäude errichtet worden.

Wie eh und je war der Sonntag in Kingsbridge Markttag. Dicht an dicht drängten sich auf der Domfreiheit die Buden und Stände. William saß ab, ließ die Pferde in Walters Obhut zurück und hinkte auf die Kirche zu. Er war jetzt vierundfünfzig Jahre alt und sehr schwer. Die Gicht in Beinen und Füßen bereitete ihm ständig große Schmerzen, und das hatte zur Folge, daß er fast immer schlechter Laune war.

Von innen wirkte die Kirche noch eindrucksvoller als von außen. Das Langhaus war im gleichen Stil errichtet wie das Querschiff, doch hatte der Dombaumeister seinen ursprünglichen Entwurf noch ausgefeilt: Die Pfeiler waren noch schlanker, die Fenster größer. Und es gab noch eine weitere Neuerung (William hatte die Leute schon davon reden hören): Die Fensterscheiben waren bunt. Sie stammten von Pariser Meistern, die von Jack Jackson nach Kingsbridge geholt worden waren. William hatte sich gefragt, warum soviel Aufhebens um diese Fenster gemacht wurde – ein buntes Fenster konnte doch nicht viel anders aussehen als ein Wandteppich oder ein Gemälde. Jetzt begriff er, was die Leute so begeisterte: Das Licht, das von außen durch die bunten Scheiben fiel, brachte die Farben zum Leuchten und rief eine geradezu magische Stimmung hervor. Die Kirche war voller Menschen, und alle reckten die Hälse nach den wundersamen Fenstern, auf denen Szenen aus der Heiligen Schrift, Himmel und Hölle, Heilige, Propheten und Jünger dargestellt waren – sowie einige Bürger von Kingsbridge, die vermutlich das betreffende Fenster bezahlt hatten: ein Bäcker mit einem Tablett voller Brotlaibe, ein Gerber mit seinen Häuten, ein Steinmetz mit Zirkel und Wasserwaage ... Ich gehe jede Wette ein, daß Philip beim Verkauf der Fenster einen dicken Gewinn gemacht hat, dachte William voller Ingrimm.

Die Kirche war inzwischen bis auf den letzten Platz besetzt. Die Ostermesse stand bevor. Hier und da griff der Markt auf die Kirche über: William wurden kurz hintereinander kaltes Bier, Lebkuchen und für drei Pennies ein kurzes Liebesvergnügen vor der Kirchenwand angeboten. Der Klerus versuchte immer wieder, die Kleinhändler und Huren aus der Kirche fernzuhalten, doch hatte sich diese Aufgabe längst als unlösbar erwiesen. William grüßte alle Leute von Rang und Namen oder erwiderte deren Gruß, doch schweifte sein Blick allen gesellschaftlichen und wirtschaftlichen Ablenkungen zum Trotz immer wieder ab, wurde von den aufwärtsstrebenden Linien der Arkade emporgezwungen. Bogen und Fenster, die Pfeiler mit ihren gebündelten Diensten, die Rippen und Segmente des Gewölbes – alles strebte nach oben, himmelwärts, als stete, unausweichliche Erinnerung an den ureigenen Zweck des Gebäudes.

Der Boden war gepflastert, die Pfeiler waren bemalt und jedes Fenster verglast: Kingsbridge und seine Priorei waren reich, und die Kathedrale kündete von ihrem Wohlstand. Goldene Leuchter und juwelenbesetzte Kruzifixe schmückten die kleinen Seitenkapellen im Querschiff. Auch die Bürger der Stadt hielten mit ihrem Reichtum nicht hinter dem Berge: Sie trugen farbenprächtige Tuniken, silberne Spangen und Schnallen und goldene Ringe.

William entdeckte Aliena.

Wie immer bei ihrem Anblick stockte ihm das Herz. Sie mußte inzwischen über fünfzig sein – und war noch immer schön wie eh und je. Noch immer hatte sie einen dichten Lockenschopf. Allerdings trug sie die Haare inzwischen etwas kürzer; sie waren auch von etwas hellerem Braun als früher, so als ob sie ein wenig ausgeblichen wären. In ihren Augenwinkeln zeigten sich attraktive Fältchen. Aliena war, obwohl inzwischen ein wenig fülliger, noch immer eine sehr begehrenswerte Frau. Sie trug einen blauen, mit roter Seide gesäumten Mantel und rote Lederschuhe und war von einer ehrerbietigen Menge umringt. Obgleich sie keine echte Gräfin war, sondern nur die Schwester eines Grafen, der sich im Heiligen Land niedergelassen hatte, wäre niemand auf den Gedanken gekommen, ihr die Reverenz, die einer Gräfin zustand, zu verweigern. Ihr Auftritt glich dem einer Königin.

Wie Galle brannte der Haß in Williams Magen, als er ihrer ansichtig wurde. Er hatte ihren Vater erledigt und sie selbst vergewaltigt; er hatte ihre Burg erobert, ihre Wolle verbrannt und ihren Bruder ins Exil gezwungen, doch jedesmal, wenn er glaubte, ihr den Rest gegeben zu haben, erholte sie sich von ihrer Niederlage und stieg empor zu neuen Höhen der Macht und des Wohlstands. William, fett geworden und gichtig und das Alter spürend, erkannte, daß sein ganzes Leben von einem furchtbaren Zauber beherrscht worden war.

Neben Aliena stand ein hochgewachsener Mann, den William im ersten Moment für Jack hielt. Bei näherer Betrachtung zeigte sich jedoch, daß der Mann zu jung war; es mußte sich also um Jacks Sohn handeln. Er war wie ein Ritter gekleidet und trug ein Schwert. Jack selbst stand neben seinem Sohn, der ihn um ein oder zwei Zoll überragte. Sein rotes Haar lichtete sich an den Schläfen. Wenn William sein Gedächtnis nicht trog, war der Mann jünger als seine Frau, um die fünf Jahre gar, doch waren auch seine Augen schon von feinen Linien umgeben. Er unterhielt sich angeregt mit einer jungen Frau – offensichtlich seiner Tochter. Sie ähnelte Aliena und war genauso hübsch wie sie, trug jedoch ihr reiches Haar streng zurückgekämmt und zu Zöpfen geflochten. Ihre Kleidung war recht unauffällig. Falls sich ein sinnlicher Körper unter der erdbraunen Tunika verbarg, so lag dem Mädchen nicht daran, ihn zur Schau zu stellen.

Der Anblick der wohlhabenden, ehrbaren und glücklichen Familie schürte die Glut in William. Alles, was diese Leute besitzen, gehört im Grunde mir, dachte er. Noch hatte er die Hoffnung auf Rache nicht aufgegeben.

Die Stimmen von mehreren hundert Mönchen erhoben sich zum Choral und übertönten sowohl die Gespräche als auch die Rufe der Händler. An der Spitze einer Prozession hielt Prior Philip Einzug in die Kathedrale. So viele Mönche wie heute hat es früher nie gegeben, dachte William. Die Priorei war mit der Stadt gewachsen. Philip, der die Sechzig überschritten hatte, war inzwischen fast völlig kahl. Er hatte kräftig zugenommen, und auch sein ehemals so schmales Gesicht war mittlerweile ziemlich rund. Er wirkte recht zufrieden mit sich selbst – kein Wunder, wenn man bedachte, daß er seit seinem Amtsantritt vor vierunddreißig Jahren auf die Weihe einer neuen Kathedrale hingearbeitet hatte.

Neugieriges Gemurmel erhob sich, als nun auch Bischof Waleran, gewandet in seinen üppigen Ornat, die Kirche betrat. Sein bleiches, eckiges Gesicht verriet eine steife, förmliche Neutralität. William allerdings wußte, daß es hinter der gefrorenen Miene brodelte, symbolisierte doch diese Kathedrale Philips endgültigen Triumph über Waleran. Und obwohl ihm Philip verhaßt war, konnte William nicht umhin, klammheimliche Freude über die Demütigung des immer so hochnäsigen Bischofs zu empfinden.

Waleran ließ sich nur selten in Kingsbridge blicken. Auch in Shiring war nun endlich eine neue Kirche errichtet worden – mit einer dem Andenken an Williams Mutter gewidmeten Seitenkapelle. Waleran hatte sie zu seiner Hauptkirche gewählt, obwohl sie nicht annähernd so groß und imposant war wie die Kathedrale in Kingsbridge.

Die offizielle Bischofskirche war, allen Bemühungen Walerans zum Trotz, nach wie vor Kingsbridge. In einer mehr als dreißigjährigen Fehde hatte er nichts unversucht gelassen, um Philip in die Knie zu zwingen, doch am Ende hatte der Prior obsiegt. Es war ein bißchen so wie bei William und Aliena: In beiden Fällen hatten sich – für William völlig unbegreiflich – Schwäche und Skrupel gegen Gewalt und Rücksichtslosigkeit durchgesetzt.

Seine Anwesenheit bei der Weihe des neuen Doms war für Waleran ein Muß. Es hätte sehr merkwürdig ausgesehen, wenn er der Zeremonie ferngeblieben wäre, und viele Festgäste hätten sich durch sein Nichterscheinen brüskiert gefühlt. Mehrere Bischöfe aus benachbarten Diözesen waren gekommen, des weiteren eine Vielzahl angesehener Äbte und Prioren.

Wer fehlte, war der Erzbischof von Canterbury, Thomas Becket. Er lag im Streit mit König Heinrich, seinem einstigen Freund. Mit solcher Erbitterung wurde der Streit ausgetragen, daß der Erzbischof gezwungen worden war, außer Landes zu gehen. Er hatte in Frankreich Zuflucht gesucht. Die Auseinandersetzung drehte sich um eine ganze Reihe juristischer Probleme, in deren Mittelpunkt jedoch eine einfache Grundsatzfrage stand: Konnte der König tun und lassen, was er wollte, oder war seine Machtbefugnis eingeschränkt? Der gleiche Streit hatte einst William und Philip entzweit. William war der Meinung gewesen, er habe in seiner Grafschaft völlig freie Hand; dies sei geradezu das Kennzeichen gräflicher Macht. Heinrich definierte sein Königtum genauso. Prior Philip und Thomas Becket wollten dagegen die Machtbefugnis der Herrschenden beschränken.

Bischof Waleran war ein Mann der Kirche, der sich auf die Seite der Herrschenden geschlagen hatte. Macht war für ihn da, um benutzt zu werden. Die vielen Niederlagen in den vergangenen drei Jahrzehnten hatten weder seinen Glauben, ein Instrument des göttlichen Willens zu sein, noch seine rücksichtslose Entschlossenheit, das zu tun, was er für seine heilige Pflicht hielt, erschüttert. William war überzeugt, daß der Bischof selbst noch bei der Durchführung der Weihezeremonie darüber nachsann, wie er Philip diesen glorreichen Tag verderben könne.

William war während der Messe ständig in Bewegung. Stehen war für seine Beine schlimmer als Gehen. Wenn er in Shiring den Gottesdienst besuchte, nahm Walter immer einen Stuhl für ihn mit. Hier in Kingsbridge gab es indessen viele interessante Leute zu sehen und zu sprechen; andere nutzten die Gelegenheit auch zu geschäftlichen Unterredungen. William ging von einem zum anderen, schmeichelte den Mächtigen, schüchterte die Schwachen ein und spitzte aufmerksam die Ohren. Anders als in seiner Glanzzeit als Graf trieb sein Erscheinen den Leuten nicht mehr den Angstschweiß auf die Stirn, doch war er auch als Vogt noch eine Respektsperson, vor der man sich besser in acht nahm.

Der Gottesdienst wollte und wollte kein Ende nehmen. Es gab eine längere Unterbrechung, die die Mönche dazu nutzten, außen um die Kirche herumzugehen und die Mauern mit Weihwasser zu besprengen. Zum Schluß verkündete Prior Philip die Ernennung eines neuen Subpriors: Seine Wahl war auf Bruder Jonathan gefallen, die Waise, die in der Priorei aufgewachsen war. Jonathan, inzwischen Mitte Dreißig und außergewöhnlich groß, erinnerte William an den alten Baumeister Tom Builder – das war auch so ein Hüne gewesen.

Dann war die Zeremonie endlich vorüber. Die hohen Würdenträger verfügten sich ins südliche Querschiff und wurden dort umschwärmt von den Angehörigen des niedrigen Adels. Auch William humpelte hinüber. Früher einmal hatte er mit Bischöfen von gleich zu gleich gesprochen – jetzt mußte er mit Rittern und kleinen Landbesitzern vor ihnen katzbuckeln.

Bischof Waleran zog ihn beiseite: »Wer ist dieser neue Subprior?« fragte er.

»Der Waisenknabe der Priorei«, erwiderte William. »Gehörte schon immer zu Philips Günstlingen.«

»Bißchen jung für einen Subprior, wie?«

»Philip war in seinem Alter schon Prior.«

»Der Waisenknabe …«, sagte Waleran nachdenklich. »Wie war das damals doch …?«

»Als Philip nach Kingsbridge kam, brachte er einen Säugling mit.«

Walerans Miene hellte sich auf. »Beim Kreuz, ja! Ich hatte Philips Mitbringsel ganz vergessen. Wie konnte ich!«

»Es ist über dreißig Jahre her. Wen kümmert das noch?«

William spürte den verächtlichen Blick, den er so haßte. *Du dummer Ochse,* besagte er, *siehst wohl den Wald vor lauter Bäumen nicht …* In dem vergeblichen Versuch, den stechenden Schmerz in seinem Fuß zu lindern, verlagerte er sein Gewicht von einem Bein aufs andere.

»Wo kam das Kind denn her?« fragte Waleran.

William unterdrückte seine Wut. »Wenn ich mich recht entsinne, fand man's ausgesetzt im Wald, unweit der kleinen Zelle, in der Philip damals Prior war.«

»Das klingt ja immer besser«, sagte Waleran eifrig.

William verstand immer noch nicht, worauf der Bischof hinauswollte. »Was soll das?« fragte er verdrossen.

»Kann man sagen, daß Philip den Knaben wie seinen eigenen Sohn großgezogen hat?«

»Ja.«

»Und jetzt hat er ihn zum Subprior gemacht.«

»Er wurde von den Mönchen in dieses Amt gewählt, nehme ich an. Ich glaube, er ist sehr beliebt.«

»Wer mit Fünfunddreißig Subprior wird, muß gewiß als aussichtsreicher Anwärter auf das Amt des Priors gelten ...«

William wollte nicht schon wieder *Was soll das?* sagen. Wie ein begriffsstutziger Schuljunge wartete er auf eine Erklärung.

Endlich ließ Waleran die Katze aus dem Sack. »Offensichtlich ist Jonathan Philips leiblicher Sohn.«

William brüllte vor Lachen. Er hatte mit einem tiefschürfenden Gedanken gerechnet – und nun das! Es war absolut lächerlich. »Niemand, der Philip kennt, würde so eine Geschichte glauben«, sagte er. »Der kam doch schon als vertrockneter Besenstiel auf die Welt. Das ist vielleicht eine Idee!« Er lachte wieder. Waleran mochte sich für wer weiß was halten – aber diesmal hatte er jeden Sinn für die Realität verloren.

Der Bischof reagierte mit eisiger Herablassung. »Ich behaupte, Philip hatte da draußen im Wald eine Geliebte. Dann wurde er zum Prior von Kingsbridge gewählt und mußte die Frau zurücklassen. Weil sie den Vater nicht mehr hatte, wollte das Weib auch sein Kind nicht. Sollte *er* doch sehen, wie er damit zurechtkam ... Philip, gefühlsduselig wie er nun einmal ist, fühlte sich verpflichtet, für das Kind zu sorgen, und gab es daher als Findling aus.«

William schüttelte den Kopf. »Unglaubhaft. Alle anderen – ja. Philip – nein.«

Waleran ließ nicht locker. »Wenn das Kind ausgesetzt wurde – wie will Philip dann beweisen, woher es kam?«

»Das kann er nicht«, gab William zu. Er sah hinüber zu Philip und Jonathan. Sie standen nebeneinander und unterhielten sich mit dem Bischof von Hereford. »Aber die beiden sehen sich überhaupt nicht ähnlich.«

»Ihr seht Eurer Mutter auch nicht ähnlich«, erwiderte Waleran. »Gott sei Dank.«

»Doch wozu soll das alles gut sein?« fragte William. »Was habt Ihr in der Sache vor?«

»Ich werde ihn vor einem kirchlichen Gericht anklagen«, antwortete Waleran.

Das war allerdings bemerkenswert. Niemand, der Philip kannte, hätte Walerans Anschuldigung auch nur einen Funken Glauben geschenkt. Bei einem Richter aus der Fremde lag die Sache schon anders. Widerstrebend sah William ein, daß die Idee doch nicht so dumm war, wie er zunächst angenommen hatte. Der Bischof, das zeigte sich einmal mehr, war weit raffinierter als er. Die plötzliche Aussicht, Philip doch noch zu Fall zu bringen, versetzte William in Begeisterung. »Bei Gott«, sagte er, »läßt sich da wirklich was machen?«

»Das hängt weitgehend von dem Richter ab. Aber da kann ich einen gewissen Einfluß nehmen ...«

Williams Blick fiel wieder auf Philip und seinen Schützling. Der Prior strahlte, er kostete seinen Triumph sichtlich aus. Die riesigen, bunten Glasfenster über ihnen tauchten die beiden in ein zauberisches Licht; sie wirkten wie Traumgestalten. »Unzucht und Nepotismus«, stieß William freudig hervor. »Mein Gott!«

»Wenn wir ihm das anhängen können«, sagte Waleran genießerisch, »dann ist der Kerl die längste Zeit Prior gewesen.«

Im Grunde war es unvorstellbar, daß ein Richter, der seine vier Sinne beisammen hatte, Philip schuldig sprach.

Es war Philip zeitlebens nicht allzu schwergefallen, den Versuchungen des Fleisches zu widerstehen. Als Beichtvater wußte er, daß manche Mönche einen verzweifelten Kampf gegen die fleischliche Lust führten, doch er selbst war weitgehend davon verschont geblieben. Als junger Mann, im Alter von achtzehn Jahren, war er eine Zeitlang von unkeuschen Träumen heimgesucht worden, doch hatte diese Phase nicht lange gedauert. Er hatte niemals den Geschlechtsakt ausgeführt und war inzwischen wahrscheinlich auch zu alt dafür.

Die Kirche indes nahm die Anklage sehr ernst und zitierte Philip vor das Kirchengericht. An der Verhandlung sollte auch ein Erzdiakon aus Canterbury teilnehmen. Walerans Antrag, den Prozeß in Shiring stattfinden zu lassen, hatte Philip erfolgreich angefochten. Zum Ort der Verhandlung wurde Kingsbridge bestimmt, wo ja immerhin die Kathedrale stand.

Philip räumte seine persönliche Habe aus dem Haus des Priors, das während des Prozesses dem Erzdiakon zur Verfügung gestellt werden sollte. Er wußte natürlich, daß er sich nie der Unzucht schuldig gemacht hatte und daher logischerweise auch nicht des Nepotismus schuldig sein konnte, denn wie kann ein Kinderloser seine Söhne bevorzugen? Dennoch erforschte er sein Herz gründlich und fragte sich, ob die Beförderung Jonathans vielleicht nicht rechtens gewesen war. Ebenso wie unkeusche Gedanken Schatten einer größeren Sünde waren, so mochte auch die Vorzugsbehandlung eines geliebten Waisenknaben ein Schatten des Nepotismus sein. Von Mönchen wurde erwartet, daß sie auf die Tröstungen des Familienlebens verzichteten, und dennoch war Jonathan für Philip in vieler Hinsicht wie ein Sohn gewesen. Schon in jungen Jahren hatte Philip ihn zum Cellerar ernannt, nun war Jonathan auf seine Veranlassung Subprior geworden. Habe ich das alles aus persönlichem Stolz und Vergnügen getan? fragte er sich.

Doch, ja.

Jonathan zu unterrichten, ihn aufwachsen zu sehen, mitzuerleben, wie er sich in die Klosterverwaltung einarbeitete – all dies hatte Philip mit großer Befriedigung erfüllt. Doch selbst wenn dem nicht so gewesen wäre, wenn die Fortschritte des jungen Mannes ihn kaltgelassen hätten – Jonathan wäre auch dann der fähigste junge Amtsträger in der Priorei. Er war hochintelligent, gottesfürchtig, einfallsreich und gewissenhaft. Im Kloster aufgewachsen, kannte er nur das monastische Leben und gierte nie nach Freiheit. Auch Philip war in einer Abtei großgeworden. Wir Klosterwaisen sind von dem Holz, aus dem die besten Mönche geschnitzt werden, dachte er.

Er packte ein Buch aus der Tasche, das Evangelium des Lukas, ein ungemein kluges Buch. Ja, er hatte Jonathan wie einen Sohn behandelt, aber er hatte sich keiner Sünde schuldig gemacht, die ein Kirchengerichtsverfahren rechtfertigte. Die Anklage war völlig aus der Luft gegriffen.

Unglücklicherweise war allein die Anklage als solche schon schädlich, beeinträchtigte sie doch seine moralische Autorität. Manche Leute, soviel stand fest, würden sich nur den Vorwurf merken, nicht das Urteil. Beim nächstenmal, wenn Philip sagte: »Begehre nicht deines Nächsten Weib«, würde so manch ein Gemeindemitglied heimlich denken: *Aber als du jung warst, hast du auch deinen Spaß daran gehabt ...*

Jonathan stürmte zur Tür herein. Er keuchte. Philip runzelte die Stirn. Es ziemte sich nicht für einen Subprior, völlig außer Atem irgendwo hereinzustürmen. Philip wollte gerade zu einer milden Moralpredigt über die Würde von Klosteroffizialen ansetzen, als Jonathan sagte: »Erzdiakon Peter ist bereits eingetroffen.«

»Gut, gut«, sagte Philip beruhigend. »Ich bin ohnehin gerade fertig.« Er reichte Jonathan die Büchertasche. »Bring sie ins Dormitorium, aber hetz nicht so! Ein Kloster ist ein Ort des Friedens und der Ruhe.«

Jonathan nahm Tasche und Tadel widerspruchslos entgegen, sagte aber: »Mir gefällt der Blick dieses Erzdiakons nicht.«

»Ich bin sicher, er wird ein gerechter Richter sein«, erwiderte Philip. »Mehr wollen wir nicht von ihm.«

Wieder öffnete sich die Tür. Der Erzdiakon kam herein. Er war ein großer, schlanker Mann in Philips Alter, mit schütterem grauem Haar und leicht überheblich wirkender Miene. Philip hatte den Eindruck, ihn schon irgendwo einmal gesehen zu haben.

Er reichte ihm die Hand und sagte: »Ich bin Prior Philip.«

»Ich kenne Euch«, gab der Erzdiakon ungehalten zurück. »Könnt Ihr Euch nicht mehr an mich erinnern?«

Die kollerige Stimme gab den Ausschlag. Philips Zuversicht schwand dahin. Vor ihm stand sein ältester Feind. »Erzdiakon Peter«, sagte er hart. »Peter von Wareham.«

»Er war ein Unruhestifter«, erklärte Philip Jonathan, nachdem sie den Erzdiakon im Haus des Priors allein gelassen hatten. »Er hatte an allem und jedem etwas auszusetzen: Wir arbeiteten nicht hart genug, unsere Mahlzeiten waren zu üppig, die Gottesdienste zu kurz – und so weiter. Mir warf er vor, zu nachgiebig zu sein. Ich bin sicher, er wäre selbst gerne Prior geworden – was für die Priorei natürlich eine Katastrophe gewesen wäre. Ich machte ihn damals zum Almosenpfleger. Dieses Amt brachte es mit sich, daß er die Hälfte der Zeit unterwegs war. Ich wollte ihn loswerden, ja. Es war für die Priorei und für ihn das Beste. Allerdings glaube ich, daß er mir das nie verziehen hat. Er haßt mich heute noch genauso wie vor fünfunddreißig Jahren.« Philip seufzte. »Als wir beide, du und ich, nach der großen Hungersnot St.-John-in-the-Forest besuchten, erfuhr ich, daß Peter nach Canterbury gegangen war ... Und jetzt ist er hier und sitzt über mich zu Gericht.«

Sie waren im Kreuzgang. Die Luft war mild, und die Sonne schien warm. Im Nordgang lernten fünfzig Schüler in drei verschiedenen Klassen Lesen und Schreiben. Der Wind trug das gedämpfte Gemurmel des Unterrichts herüber. Philip erinnerte sich an die Zeiten, da die ganze Schule aus fünf Knaben und einem senilen Novizenmeister bestanden hatte. Er dachte daran, wie sehr sich Kingsbridge unter seiner Führung verändert hatte: Er hatte eine Kathedrale errichtet, aus dem verarmten und verlotterten Kloster eine wohlhabende, geschäftige und einflußreiche Institution gemacht und der Stadt einen ungeahnten Aufschwung beschert. In der Kirche sang ein Chor von über hundert Mönchen die Messe. Von seinem Sitzplatz aus konnte Philip die herrlichen bunten Glasfenster im Lichtgaden der Kirche sehen. Hinter seinem Rücken, im Osten, erhob sich außerhalb des Kreuzgangs die aus Stein erbaute Bibliothek mit Hunderten von Bänden aus allen Wissensgebieten, darunter Theologie, Astronomie und Moralphilosophie. Außerhalb der Klostermauern ernährten die Güter der Priorei, die von fähigen, in aufgeklärtem Eigeninteresse handelnden Mönchen geleitet wurden, nicht nur die frommen Brüder, sondern auch Hunderte von Tagelöhnern. Und das alles sollte ihm durch eine Lüge genommen werden? Würde die prosperierende, gottesfürchtige Priorei Kingsbridge demnächst von jemand anders geführt werden – irgendeiner Marionette Walerans vielleicht wie dem kriecherischen Erzdiakon Baldwin oder Peter von Wareham, diesem selbstgerechten Narren –, nur um dann ebenso schnell, wie sie aufgeblüht war, wieder in Armut und Lasterhaftigkeit zu verfallen? Würden die großen Herden wieder zusammenschrumpfen auf eine Handvoll abgemagerter Mutterschafe, die Felder zu unrentablen Unkrautäckern verkommen, die Bücher in der Bibliothek ungelesen verstauben und die schöne Kathedrale verkommen und zerfallen? Mit Gottes Hilfe habe ich soviel erreicht, dachte Philip. Und da sollte es in seiner Absicht liegen, daß alles wieder zunichte gemacht wird? Nein, das kann ich einfach nicht glauben ...

»Wie dem auch sei«, sagte Jonathan. »Erzdiakon Peter kann Euch nicht schuldig sprechen, das ist einfach undenkbar.«

»Er wird's aber tun«, erwiderte Philip schweren Herzens.

»Auf Ehr' und Gewissen – wie *kann* er das?«

»Ich glaube, er hat mir ein ganzes Leben lang gegrollt. Jetzt bekommt er die Möglichkeit zu beweisen, daß all die Zeit in Wirklichkeit *ich* der Sünder war und *er* der Ehrenmann. Waleran hat das irgendwie herausgefunden und dann für gesorgt, daß Peter bei dieser Verhandlung das Richteramt ausübt.«

»Aber es gibt doch keine Beweise!«

»Er braucht keine Beweise. Er wird sich die Anklage- und die Verteidigungsrede anhören. Dann wird er Gott um Beistand bitten und sein Urteil verkünden.«

»Gott mag ihm den richtigen Weg weisen.«

»Peter wird nicht auf ihn hören. Zuhören war nie seine Stärke.«

»Was wird geschehen?«

»Man wird mich absetzen«, sagte Philip unverblümt. »Vielleicht wird mir gestattet, als einfacher Mönch im Kloster zu bleiben und Buße für meine Sünden zu tun. Wahrscheinlicher ist freilich, daß man mich aus dem Orden entläßt, um jegliche weitere Einflußnahme meinerseits zu unterbinden.«

»Und dann?«

»Dann kommt es natürlich zur Neuwahl. Unglücklicherweise spielt dabei die hohe Politik mit hinein. König Heinrich und der Erzbischof von Canterbury, Thomas Becket, sind miteinander verfeindet. Erzbischof Thomas und die Hälfte seiner Erzdiakone sitzen in Frankreich im Exil. Die anderen sind in England geblieben und haben sich auf die Seite des Königs geschlagen. Zu ihnen gehört offensichtlich auch Peter. Auch Bischof Waleran steht auf des Königs Seite. Sein Kandidat für das Amt des Priors wird demnach sowohl vom König als auch von den Erzdiakonen von Canterbury unterstützt werden. Dieser machtvollen Allianz haben unsere Mönche kaum etwas entgegenzusetzen.«

»Auf wen wird die Wahl fallen?«

»Waleran hat da gewiß schon seine Vorstellungen, darauf kannst du dich verlassen. Vielleicht heißt sein Kandidat Erzdiakon Baldwin, vielleicht sogar Peter von Wareham.«

»Wir *müssen* das verhindern!« rief Jonathan.

Philip nickte. »Aber alles spricht gegen uns. Die hohe Politik können wir nicht ändern. Die einzige Möglichkeit ...«

»Ja ...?« fuhr Jonathan ungeduldig dazwischen.

Philip sah keinen Sinn darin, in einer aussichtslosen Lage mit Ideen zu spielen, die aus Verzweiflung geboren waren. Sie würden bei Jonathan lediglich falsche Hoffnungen erwecken; die Enttäuschung wäre nachher um so bitterer. »Nichts«, sagte er.

»Was wolltet Ihr sagen, Vater?«

Philip wog seine Worte genau und sagte dann vorsichtig: »Wäre es möglich, meine Unschuld so zu beweisen, daß auch nicht der Schatten eines Verdachts mehr auf mir lastet – ja, dann wäre Peter wohl kaum imstande, mich schuldig zu sprechen ...«

»Aber was zählt als Beweis?«

»Du sagst es. Man kann ein Negativum nicht beweisen. Wir müßten deinen richtigen Vater finden.«

»Ja! Das ist es!« rief Jonathan aus. »Das tun wir!« Er war sofort Feuer und Flamme.

»Beruhige dich!« sagte Philip. »Ich habe das damals ja schon versucht. Das ist nach all den Jahren bestimmt nicht leichter geworden.«

Jonathan ließ sich nicht entmutigen. »Gab es denn keinerlei Hinweise auf meine mögliche Herkunft?«

»Nein, nichts, fürchte ich«, erwiderte Philip. Es betrübte ihn, daß er nun doch unerfüllbare Hoffnungen in Jonathan geweckt hatte. Obwohl sich der junge Mann an seine Eltern nicht erinnern konnte, hatte ihn die Tatsache, daß er von ihnen ausgesetzt worden war, immer bedrückt. Jetzt bildete er sich ein, das Rätsel seiner Herkunft lösen und vielleicht doch noch einen Beweis für ihre Liebe und Zuneigung finden zu können. Das mußte zwangsläufig zu einer herben Enttäuschung führen.

»Habt Ihr die Leute in der Umgebung befragt?« wollte Jonathan wissen.

»Da war niemand in der Umgebung. Die Zelle lag damals mutterseelenallein in einem riesigen Waldgebiet. Deine Eltern kamen wahrscheinlich von weither, vielleicht aus Winchester. Ich habe all diese Überlegungen damals auch schon angestellt.«

Jonathan gab sich noch nicht geschlagen. »Sind zu jenem Zeitpunkt irgendwelche Reisenden durch die Gegend gekommen?«

»Nein.« Philip runzelte die Stirn. Stimmte das? War da nicht ...? An jenem Tag, an dem das Kind gefunden wurde, brach ich auf zum bischöflichen Palast, dachte er. Und auf dem Weg dorthin unterhielt ich mich mit jemandem ... Plötzlich fiel es ihm ein. »Doch, in der Tat ... Tom Builder und seine Familie zogen damals durch unser Gebiet.«

»Das habt Ihr mir nie erzählt«, sagte Jonathan verblüfft.

»Es schien mir nie von Bedeutung, und ich weiß auch nicht, wie es uns heute weiterhelfen könnte. Ich traf sie ein oder zwei Tage später. Ich fragte sie, ob ihnen jemand begegnet wäre, und erzählte ihnen von dem Findelkind. Sie sagten, nein, sie hätten niemanden gesehen, keine schwangere Frau und auch sonst niemanden, der etwas mit der Kindesaussetzung zu tun gehabt haben könnte.«

Jonathan war sichtlich enttäuscht. Ihm steht eine doppelte Enttäuschung bevor, wenn wir so weitermachen, dachte Philip beklommen: Weder wird er etwas über seine Eltern erfahren, noch wird er den Beweis für meine Unschuld erbringen ... Aber Jonathan war inzwischen kaum noch aufzuhalten. »Was haben sie da im Wald eigentlich getrieben?« fragte er.

»Tom war unterwegs zum Bischofspalast. Er suchte Arbeit.«

»Ich will noch mal mit denen reden, die damals dabeiwaren.«

»Nun ja – Tom und Alfred sind mittlerweile tot. Ellen lebt im

Wald, und Gott allein weiß, wann sie wieder mal auftaucht. Aber du kannst dich ja mal mit Martha und Jack unterhalten.«

»Den Versuch ist es mir wert.«

Vielleicht hat Jonathan recht, dachte Philip. Er hat noch die Kraft der Jugend ... Er selbst war eher mutlos und pessimistisch. »Na, denn zu!« sagte er. »Ich werde langsam alt und müde, sonst wäre ich selber auf die Idee gekommen. Sprich mal mit Jack. Wir klammern uns an einen Strohhalm – aber er ist unsere einzige Hoffnung.«

Der Fensterentwurf war in Farbe und voller Größe auf einen riesigen Holztisch gezeichnet, den man, um ein Zerlaufen der Farben zu vermeiden, mit Bier gewaschen hatte. Dargestellt war der Baum von Jesse, ein Stammbaum Christi in Bildern. Sally nahm eine kleine, rubinrot gefärbte Glasscheibe zur Hand und legte sie auf den Körper eines der Könige Israels. Um welchen König genau es sich handelte, vermochte Jack nicht zu sagen: Er hatte sich den verdrehten Symbolismus religiöser Bilder nie merken können. Sally tauchte einen feinen Pinsel in eine Schale, in der sich mit Wasser angerührter Kalk befand, und zeichnete damit die Silhouette der Figur nach: Schultern, Arme und den Rock des Gewands.

Im Feuer auf dem Boden neben ihrem Tisch lag ein Eisenstab mit einem Holzgriff. Sie nahm den Stab heraus und zog mit ihm ebenso flink wie geschickt den vorgezeichneten Umriß nach. Das Glas brach genau entlang der Linie. Ihr Lehrjunge nahm es auf und begann die Ränder mit einer eisernen Feile zu glätten.

Jack sah seiner Tochter gerne bei der Arbeit zu. Sie arbeitete schnell und genau, mit sparsam bemessenem Bewegungsaufwand. Schon als Kind hatte sie sich für die Arbeit der Pariser Glaser begeistert, die Jack nach Kingsbridge geholt hatte. Das will ich auch machen, wenn ich groß bin, hatte sie immer wieder gesagt – und sich schließlich auch daran gehalten. Besucher, die zum erstenmal nach Kingsbridge kommen, so gestand sich Jack manchmal etwas wehmütig ein, sind von Sallys Glasmalerei oft stärker beeindruckt als von meiner Architektur.

Der Lehrbub gab Sally die Scheibe mit den geglätteten Rändern zurück, und sie begann, die Falten der königlichen Robe zu malen. Die Farbe bestand aus Eisenerz und Urin und war zur besseren Haftung mit Gummiarabikum angereichert. Unter Sallys Hand schien sich das flache Glas urplötzlich in weichen, locker um die Gestalt drapierten Stoff zu verwandeln. Ihr künstlerisches Geschick war beeindruckend. Rasch war sie fertig. Sie legte das frischbemalte Glas auf eine Eisenpfanne, auf der bereits einige andere Scheiben lagen und deren Boden mit Kalk bedeckt war. Die volle Pfanne würde später in den Ofen geschoben werden, die Hitze die Farben dann aufs Glas brennen.

Bevor sie die nächste Scheibe zur Hand nahm, blickte Sally kurz auf und schenkte ihrem Vater ein bezauberndes Lächeln.

Jack entfernte sich. Er hätte ihr den ganzen Tag zuschauen können, doch gab es auch für ihn noch einiges zu erledigen. Er war – das meinte Aliena zumindest – in seine Tochter ganz vernarrt. Wenn er sie ansah, überkam ihn immer wieder eine Art Staunen darüber, daß *er* für die Existenz dieser klugen, reifen und selbständigen Frau verantwortlich war. Er war ungemein stolz darauf, daß sie eine so hervorragende Handwerkerin war.

Merkwürdig: Jack hatte immer versucht, aus Tommy einen Baumeister zu machen, ja er hatte ihn regelrecht dazu gezwungen, ein paar Jahre lang auf der Dombaustelle zu arbeiten. Aber es hatte alles nichts gefruchtet: Tommy interessierte sich für Landwirtschaft, Pferde, Jagen und Fechten, also alles Dinge, die seinen Vater zeitlebens kaltgelassen hatten. Er hatte als Knappe bei einem Ritter gedient und schließlich selbst den Ritterschlag empfangen. Aliena hatte ihm daraufhin ein kleineres Landgut mit fünf Dörfern abgetreten. Das künstlerische Talent des Vaters hatte eindeutig Sally geerbt. Tommy war mit einer Tochter des Grafen von Bedford verheiratet; die beiden hatten drei Kinder. Sally mit ihren fünfundzwanzig Jahren war noch ledig; in ihr steckte viel von ihrer Großmutter Ellen. Sie war stolz auf ihre Unabhängigkeit und verteidigte sie offensiv.

Jack stand vor der Westfassade der Kathedrale und blickte hinauf zu den Zwillingstürmen. Sie waren jetzt fast fertig, und die riesige Bronzeglocke aus der Gießerei in London war bereits unterwegs. Allzuviel gab es für Jack nicht mehr zu tun: Hatte er einst über eine ganze Armee von kräftigen Steinmetzen, Maurern und Zimmerleuten geboten, so unterstand ihm inzwischen nur noch eine Handvoll Schnitzer und Maler, die auf kleinstem Raum Präzisionsarbeit leisteten: Sie schufen Statuen und kunstvolle Fialen und vergoldeten die Flügel der steinernen Engel. Auch zu planen gab es nicht mehr so viel wie früher, abgesehen von gelegentlichen Neubauten für die Priorei: eine Bibliothek, ein Kapitelhaus, bessere Unterkünfte für die Pilger, ein neues Waschhaus, verschiedene Wirtschaftsgebäude. Jack fand zum erstenmal seit vielen Jahren wieder Zeit für eigene Steinmetzarbeiten. Am liebsten hätte er sofort damit begonnen, Tom Builders alten Ostflügel abzureißen und durch einen neuen zu ersetzen. Dagegen sperrte sich allerdings Philip. Der Prior wollte die fertige Kirche wenigstens ein Jahr lang genießen, bevor er sie wieder den Bauleuten überließ. Philip spürte sein Alter, und Jack dachte bisweilen, hoffentlich wird der alte Knabe wenigstens so alt, daß er den Neubau des Ostflügels noch miterlebt.

Die hochgewachsene Gestalt Bruder Jonathans erschien im Küchenhof und steuerte auf Jack zu. Jonathan ist der Garant für den Fortgang der Bauarbeiten auch über Philips Tod hinaus, dachte Jack. Er wird gewiß ein guter Prior – vielleicht sogar ein so guter wie Philip. Ein Glück, daß die Nachfolgefrage geklärt ist – da weiß man, woran man ist, und kann entsprechend langfristig planen ...

Jonathan kam ohne Umschweife zur Sache. »Diese Kirchengerichtsverhandlung macht mir Kummer, Jack«, sagte er.

»Ich dachte, das wär' bloß viel Lärm um nichts.«

»Mir ging's genauso – nur hat sich inzwischen herausgestellt, daß der Erzdiakon ein alter Feind von Prior Philip ist.«

»Teufel auch! Aber das allein reicht doch wohl nicht aus für einen Schuldspruch.«

»Das steht in seinem Ermessen.«

Jack schüttelte angewidert den Kopf. Manchmal fragte er sich, wie Leute wie Jonathan es noch in einer so schamlos korrupten Kirche aushielten. »Was hast du vor?« fragte er.

»Es gibt nur eine Möglichkeit, seine Unschuld zu beweisen! Wir müssen herausfinden, wer meine Eltern waren.«

»Dafür ist's ein bißchen zu spät, meinst du nicht auch?«

»Es ist unsere einzige Hoffnung.«

Jack war sichtlich erschüttert. So ernst hatte er sich die Lage nicht vorgestellt. »Wo willst du denn mit der Suche anfangen?« fragte er.

»Bei dir. Ich wurde im Wald unweit von St.-John-in-the-Forest geboren. Zu jener Zeit hast du in jener Gegend gewohnt.«

»Hab' ich das?« Jack begriff nicht, worauf Jonathan hinauswollte. »Eins stimmt: Ich lebte bis zu meinem elften Lebensjahr im Wald – und bin ungefähr elf Jahre älter als du.«

»Prior Philip ist dir und deiner Mutter am Tag nach meiner Auffindung begegnet. Ihr befandet euch in Begleitung von Tom Builder und seinen beiden Kindern.«

»Ja, daran erinnere ich mich. Er gab uns etwas zu essen. Wir waren am Verhungern.«

»Nun denk mal genau nach: Hast du damals irgendwo in dem Gebiet jemanden mit einem neugeborenen Kind gesehen? Oder vielleicht eine hochschwangere Frau?«

»Moment mal ...« Jack war verwirrt. »Sagtest du nicht gerade, du seist in der Nähe von St.-John-in-the-Forest gefunden worden?«

»Ja. Hast du das nicht gewußt?«

Jack glaubte, seinen Ohren nicht zu trauen. »Nein, das habe ich nicht gewußt«, antwortete er langsam. Er zermarterte sein Gehirn. »Als wir nach Kingsbridge kamen, warst du bereits da. Ich bin natürlich immer davon ausgegangen, daß man dich hier in der Umgebung gefunden hat.« Er ließ sich auf einem Haufen Bauschutt nieder. Die Enthüllung hatte ihn so erschüttert, daß er sich unbedingt setzen mußte.

»Also – wie war's?« fragte Jonathan ungeduldig. »Hast du jemanden gesehen?«

»O ja ...«, erwiderte Jack. »Aber ich weiß nicht, wie ich dir das sagen soll, Jonathan ...«

Jonathan erblaßte. »Du weißt irgend etwas, nicht wahr? Was hast du gesehen?«

»Dich, Jonathan. Ich habe *dich* gesehen.«

»Was ...? Wie ...?« Jonathans Mund stand offen.

»Es war früh am Morgen. Ich war unterwegs, Enten jagen. Da hörte ich auf einmal Geschrei. Ich ging dem Geräusch nach und fand ein neugeborenes Kind. Es war in einen zerschnittenen Mantel gewickelt und lag neben der Glut eines ersterbenden Feuers.«

Jonathan starrte ihn mit weit aufgerissenen Augen an. »Was sonst?«

Jack nickte langsam. »Das Kind lag auf einem frischen Grab.«

Jonathan schluckte. »Meine Mutter?«

Jack nickte.

Jonathan begann zu weinen, hörte aber nicht auf zu fragen. »Was hast du da getan?«

»Ich habe meine Mutter geholt. Doch als wir zu der Stelle zurückkehrten, sahen wir einen Priester auf einem Zelter. Er trug das Kind auf den Armen.«

»Francis«, sagte Jonathan mit erstickter Stimme.

»Was?«

Jonathan schluckte heftig. »Ich wurde von Francis gefunden, dem Bruder von Prior Philip.«

»Was trieb der da draußen im Wald?«

»Er war auf dem Weg nach St.-John-in-the-Forest, wo er seinen Bruder besuchen wollte. Deshalb brachte er mich dorthin.«

»Mein Gott!« Jack starrte den hochgewachsenen Mönch an, dem die Tränen über die Wangen liefen. Du weißt ja noch gar nicht alles, dachte er.

»Hast du jemanden gesehen, der vielleicht mein Vater hätte sein können?«

»Ja«, sagte Jack mit feierlichem Ernst. »Ich weiß, wer dein Vater war.«

»Dann sag es mir«, flüsterte Jonathan.

»Tom Builder.«

»Tom Builder?« Jonathan setzte sich mit einem schweren Seufzer auf den Boden. »*Tom Builder war mein Vater?*«

»Ja.« Jack schüttelte fassungslos den Kopf. »Jetzt, da ich's weiß, erinnerst du mich auch äußerlich an ihn. Ihr beide seid die größten Menschen, denen ich je begegnet bin.«

»Er war immer sehr nett zu mir, als ich klein war«, sagte Jonathan mit belegter Stimme. »Hat oft mit mir gespielt und mochte mich sehr gerne. Ich sah ihn genausooft wie Prior Philip.« Jonathan ließ jetzt seinen Tränen freien Lauf. »Und er war mein Vater! Mein Vater!« Er blickte auf zu Jack. »Warum hat er mich ausgesetzt?«

»Sie dachten, du müßtest sowieso sterben. Sie hatten keine Milch für dich und waren selber am Verhungern, ich weiß es noch genau. Meilenweit im Umkreis war keine menschliche Siedlung – das Kloster kannten sie nicht. Das einzige, was sie noch zu essen hatten, waren Rüben – Rüben aber hätten dich umgebracht.«

»Also haben sie mich doch geliebt, irgendwie ...«

Jack hatte die Szene vor Augen, als läge sie erst einen Tag zurück: das erlöschende Feuer, die frische Erde auf dem Grab, das winzige, zappelnde rosa Kindchen in dem alten grauen Mantel. Und dieses kleine Wesen war jetzt herangewachsen zu dem großen Mann, der vor ihm auf dem Boden saß und hemmungslos weinte. »O ja, sie haben dich geliebt.«

»Warum hat nie jemand darüber gesprochen?«

»Tom hat sich natürlich geschämt«, sagte Jack. »Meine Mutter muß Bescheid gewußt haben, und wir Kinder haben es zumindest geahnt, glaube ich. Wie dem auch sei, es war ein Thema, über das man einfach nicht sprechen konnte. Und wir haben natürlich nie *dieses* Kind mit *dir* in Verbindung gebracht.«

»Tom doch gewiß, oder?«

»Ja, der schon.«

»Ich frage mich, warum er mich nie zu sich genommen hat.«

»Meine Mutter verließ ihn ziemlich bald nach unserer Ankunft in Kingsbridge«, sagte Jack und lächelte wehmütig. »Sie war recht anspruchsvoll, wie Sally. Für Tom bedeutete das, daß er für dich eine Kinderfrau hätte finden müssen. So hielt er es wahrscheinlich für das beste, dich in der Obhut des Klosters zu lassen. Er sah ja, daß du dort gut aufgehoben warst.«

Jonathan nickte. »Der gute alte Johnny Eightpence! Gott hab' ihn selig!«

»Gut möglich, daß Tom auf diese Weise mehr Zeit für dich fand. Du bist ja überall im Klostergelände herumgesprungen, tagaus, tagein. Und er arbeitete dort. Hätte er dich der Priorei weggenommen und bei einer Kinderfrau in Pflege gegeben, so hätte er nicht soviel von dir gehabt. Als du dann größer wurdest, erlebte er mit, wie glücklich du dich in die Rolle des Klosterwaisen gefügt hast. Und je glücklicher du warst, desto selbstverständlicher war es für ihn, dich im Kloster zu lassen. Es kommt ja oft genug vor, daß Eltern ihre Kinder dem Herrn schenken.«

»All diese Jahre habe ich über meine Eltern nachgedacht«, sagte Jonathan, und Jack konnte gut verstehen, wie ihm zumute war. »Immer wieder habe ich versucht, sie mir vorzustellen. Immer wieder habe ich Gott gebeten, mich zu ihnen zu führen, und mich gefragt, ob sie mich geliebt und warum sie mich verlassen haben. Jetzt endlich weiß ich, daß meine Mutter bei meiner Geburt gestorben ist und daß mein Vater bis zu seinem Tod immer bei mir war.« Er lächelte trotz seiner Tränen. »Ich kann dir gar nicht sagen, wie glücklich ich bin.«

Jack wollte es sich nicht anmerken lassen, daß auch er den Tränen nahe war. Zur Ablenkung sagte er: »Du siehst ihm sehr ähnlich.«

»Wirklich?« fragte Jonathan erfreut.

»Weißt du nicht mehr, wie groß er war?«

»Alle Erwachsenen waren damals groß.«

»Er hatte sehr markante Züge, genau wie du, ein gutgeschnittenes Gesicht. Wenn du dir einen Bart hättest wachsen lassen, wären wahrscheinlich auch andere darauf gekommen.«

»Ich erinnere mich noch gut an den Tag, an dem er starb«, sagte Jonathan. »Er ging mit mir zum Fest. Wir haben uns die Bärenhatz angeschaut. Dann bin ich die Chormauer hinaufgeklettert und habe mich dort verstiegen. Ich hatte furchtbare Angst. Tom trug mich hinunter, und dabei entdeckte er dann Williams Truppe. Er hat mich in den Kreuzgang gebracht. Das war das letzte Mal, daß ich ihn lebend sah.«

»Ich kann mich auch noch daran erinnern«, sagte Jack. »Ich sah, wie er mit dir in den Armen von der Mauer herabstieg.«

»Er brachte mich in Sicherheit.«

»Danach hat er sich um andere gekümmert.«

»Er hat mich von Herzen geliebt.«

Jack wechselte das Thema. »Das wird gewiß Auswirkungen auf das Verfahren gegen Prior Philip haben – oder?«

»Das hatte ich ganz vergessen!« rief Jonathan aus. »Ja, natürlich. Meine Güte!«

»Haben wir unwiderlegbare Beweise?« fragte Jack. »Ich sah das Kind und den Priester. Ich habe allerdings nicht mitbekommen, wie das Kind in der kleinen Priorei abgeliefert wurde.«

»Nun, das war Francis – aber Francis ist Philips Bruder. Seine Aussage gilt als voreingenommen.«

Jack dachte scharf nach. »An jenem Morgen«, sagte er schließlich, »sind meine Mutter und Tom einmal fortgegangen. Sie sagten, sie wollten den Priester suchen, aber ich wette, sie sind zur Priorei gegangen. Sie wollten wissen, ob es dem ... ob es dir gutging.«

»Ja, wenn sie das vor Gericht aussagen würde, dann wäre der Sack zu«, meinte Jonathan.

»Philip hält sie für eine Hexe«, gab Jack zu bedenken. »Würde er ihr Zeugnis akzeptieren?«

»Wir stellen ihn am besten vor vollendete Tatsachen. Aber sie kann ihn ja auch nicht leiden. Wäre sie überhaupt zu einer Aussage bereit?«

»Ich weiß es nicht«, sagte Jack. »Da fragen wir sie am besten selbst.«

»Unzucht und Nepotismus?« Jacks Mutter lachte schallend. »Philip? Das ist doch hirnverbrannt!«

»Die Sache ist bitterernst, Mutter«, sagte Jack.

»Und wenn ihr ihn zusammen mit drei Huren in ein Faß stecktet – da wär' nichts mit Unzucht. Er wüßte ja gar nicht, was tun!«

Jonathan errötete. »Prior Philip steckt in großen Schwierigkeiten«, sagte er. »Der Vorwurf mag noch so weit hergeholt sein.«

»Und warum sollte ich ihm aus der Patsche helfen?« fragte Ellen. »Er hat mich immer nur gepiesackt.«

Jack hatte es kommen sehen. Seine Mutter hatte Philip nie vergeben, daß er sie und Tom auseinandergebracht hatte. »Er hat mir dasselbe angetan wie dir«, sagte er. »Wenn ich ihm verzeihen kann, dann kannst du das auch.«

»Ich bin eben nachtragend.«

»Dann tu es nicht für Philip, sondern für mich. Ich möchte Dombaumeister in Kingsbridge bleiben.«

»Wie das? Die Kirche ist doch fertig.«

»Ich würde gern Toms Chor niederreißen und ihn im neuen Stil wiederaufbauen.«

»Herrgott noch mal ...«

»Mutter, Philip ist ein guter Prior, und wenn er einmal nicht mehr ist, wird Jonathan an seine Stelle treten – vorausgesetzt, du kommst jetzt mit nach Kingsbridge und sagst bei der Verhandlung aus.«

»Ich hasse Gerichtsverhandlungen«, sagte Ellen. »Da ist noch nie was Gutes dabei rausgekommen.«

Es war zum Verrücktwerden. Ellens Aussage war entscheidend für den günstigen Ausgang des Verfahrens. Aber sie war eine starrköpfige alte Frau. Jack begann ernsthaft an seinen Überredungskünsten zu zweifeln. Er probierte es durch die Hintertür: »Du hast ja recht, wenn du die lange Reise scheust. Für jemanden in deinem Alter ist es wirklich sehr weit. Wie alt bist du eigentlich mittlerweile – achtundsechzig?«

»Zweiundsechzig bin ich!« schimpfte sie. »Werd mir ja nicht frech! Ich bin besser zu Fuß als du, mein Junge!«

Das mag wohl sein, dachte Jack. Ihr Haar war schneeweiß und ihr Gesicht voller Falten, doch die seltsamen goldenen Augen sahen so viel wie eh und je. Ein Blick hatte genügt, um ihr zu sagen, wer Jonathan war. »Du brauchst mir nicht zu erklären, warum du gekommen bist«, hatte sie gesagt. »Du hast herausgefunden, wer du bist, nicht wahr? Bei Gott, du bist so groß wie dein Vater und fast so breit gebaut.« Auch ihr Wille und ihr Selbstbewußtsein waren ungebrochen.

»Sally ist nach dir geraten«, sagte Jack.

Das gefiel ihr. »Wirklich? In welcher Hinsicht?«

»Sie ist störrisch wie ein Maulesel.«

»Na, dann ist ja alles gut«, erwiderte Ellen spitz.

Jetzt kann ich mich nur noch aufs Betteln verlegen, dachte Jack. »Mutter, bitte! Komm mit uns nach Kingsbridge und stell klar, wie es damals war!«

»Ich weiß nicht ...«

Da mischte sich Jonathan ins Gespräch. »Ich habe noch eine weitere Bitte.«

Jack hielt den Atem an. Wenn er jetzt das Falsche sagt, ist alles verloren, dachte er. Zumal sie auf Männer der Kirche noch nie gut zu sprechen war ...

»Könnt Ihr mich zum Grab meiner Mutter führen?«

Jack atmete leise aus. *Diese* Frage war in der Tat unverfänglich, ja, im Grunde hätte Jonathan gar nichts Besseres einfallen können.

Alles Spöttische fiel von ihr ab. »Ja, natürlich kann ich das. Ich bin ziemlich sicher, daß ich es finden werde.«

Jack war ein wenig besorgt wegen des Zeitverlusts. Die Verhandlung sollte am nächsten Morgen beginnen, und sie hatten noch einen weiten Weg vor sich. Andererseits sah er ein, daß er dem Schicksal nicht ins Handwerk pfuschen durfte.

»Willst du sofort dorthin?«

»Ja, bitte, wenn's Euch möglich ist.«

»Gut.« Sie erhob sich und warf sich einen kurzen Umhang aus Kaninchenfell um die Schultern. *Das ist doch viel zu warm!* wollte Jack schon sagen, schluckte die Bemerkung aber hinunter: Alten Menschen ist immer kälter, dachte er.

Sie verließen die Höhle, in der es nach gelagerten Äpfeln und qualmendem Holz roch, bahnten sich einen Weg durch den dichten Pflanzenwuchs vor dem Eingang und traten in den hellen Frühlingssonnenschein hinaus. Ellen marschierte unverzüglich drauflos. Jack und Jonathan banden ihre Pferde los und folgten ihr. Da das Gelände zu dicht bewachsen war, konnten sie nicht reiten, sondern waren gezwungen, die Tiere am Zügel zu führen. Jack fiel auf, daß seine Mutter langsamer ging als früher. Sie war doch nicht mehr so gut zu Fuß, wie sie vorgab.

Allein hätte er die Stelle nicht mehr gefunden. Es hatte eine Zeit gegeben, in der er sich in diesem Wald so gut auskannte wie jetzt in Kingsbridge. Inzwischen sah eine Lichtung für ihn wie die andere aus. Seine Mutter folgte im dichten Unterholz ausgetretenen Tierpfaden. Gewisse Dinge, an denen sie vorbeikamen, riefen Kindheitserinnerungen in Jack wach: Da war die uralte Eiche, auf der er einmal vor einem wilden Eber Zuflucht gesucht hatte. Oder das »Kaninchenrevier«, das für so manch eine gute Mahlzeit gesorgt hatte. Auch an einen bestimmten Forellenbach konnte er sich erinnern. Manchmal wußte er genau, wo er war, dann kamen wieder Teile des Waldes, in denen er sich überhaupt nicht auskannte. Merkwürdig, dachte er, einmal war ich hier zu Hause – und jetzt kann ich mit all diesen Sümpfen und Dickichten genausowenig anfangen wie ein Bauer mit einem Gewölbe- oder Simsstein ... Ob ich damals schon irgendwelche Vorstellungen hatte, was einmal aus mir werden würde? fragte er sich. Vermutlich schon – nur mit der Wirklichkeit hatte das gewiß nichts zu tun.

So legten sie Meile um Meile zurück. Es war ein warmer Frühlingstag, so daß Jack nach einer Weile ins Schwitzen geriet. Seine Mutter behielt das Kaninchenfell an. Am Nachmittag machten sie auf einer schattigen Lichtung halt. Ellen atmete schwer, und ihr Gesicht war fahl. Es ist jetzt wirklich an der Zeit, daß sie zu mir und Aliena zieht, dachte Jack. Sie muß raus aus dem Wald ... Er wußte, daß seine Überredungskunst erneut gefordert war, wollte aber sein Bestes tun.

»Geht es dir gut?« fragte er.

»Natürlich geht es mir gut!« polterte sie. »Wir sind da!«

Jack sah sich um. Er erkannte die Stelle nicht wieder.

»Hier also?« fragte Jonathan.

»Ja«, sagte Ellen.

»Wo ist die Straße?« wollte Jack wissen.

»Dort drüben.«

Von der Straße aus gesehen kam ihm die Stelle dann doch irgendwie bekannt vor. Eine Flut von Erinnerungen strömte auf ihn ein. Die große Roßkastanie ... Damals war sie kahl; und überall lagen Kastanien herum ... Gegenwärtig stand der Baum in voller Blüte.

»Martha erzählte mir damals, was geschehen war«, sagte Jack. »Sie rasteten hier, weil deine Mutter nicht mehr weiterkonnte. Tom machte ein Feuer und kochte ein paar Rüben – Fleisch hatten sie keines. Genau hier, an dieser Stelle, hat deine Mutter dich geboren. Du warst gesund und munter, aber bei ihr hat irgend etwas nicht gestimmt. Sie starb.« Ein paar Fuß vom Stammgrund entfernt war eine kleine, flache Bodenerhebung zu erkennen. »Der kleine Hügel dort, siehst du ihn?«

Jonathan nickte. Seine Miene war angespannt; er bemühte sich, die Gefühle, die ihn zu überwältigen drohten, im Zaum zu halten.

»Das ist das Grab.« Bei diesen Worten Jacks wehte eine kleine Wolke Blütenblätter vom Baum und breitete sich über den Hügel.

Jonathan kniete nieder und begann zu beten.

Jack stand schweigend neben ihm. Er erinnerte sich an die Begegnung mit seinen Verwandten in Cherbourg und wie sehr ihn dieses Erlebnis aufgewühlt hatte. Das, was Jonathan jetzt widerfuhr, mußte noch erschütternder sein.

Nach einer Weile stand der Mönch wieder auf. »Wenn ich Prior bin«, sagte er feierlich, »werde ich hier ein kleines Kloster mit einer

Kapelle und einer Herberge errichten, auf daß fortan in diesem Gebiet nie wieder ein Reisender bei kalter Winternacht im Freien schlafen muß. Ich widme dieses Kloster dem Andenken meiner Mutter.« Er sah Jack an. »Wie sie hieß, hast du wahrscheinlich nie gewußt, oder?«

»Sie hieß Agnes«, sagte Ellen leise. »Deine Mutter hieß Agnes.«

Bischof Waleran war ein sehr beredter Ankläger.

Zu Beginn seiner Rede ging er auf Philips schnelle Karriere ein: mit Einundzwanzig Cellerar seiner Heimatabtei, mit Dreiundzwanzig Prior des Filialklosters St.-John-in-the-Forest, schließlich im bemerkenswert jungen Alter von achtundzwanzig Jahren Prior von Kingsbridge. Immer wieder hob er Philips Jugend hervor. Dabei gelang es ihm, den Eindruck zu erwecken, jemand, der in so jungen Jahren Verantwortung übernehme, müsse zwangsläufig eingebildet und hoffärtig sein. Anschließend beschrieb der die Zelle St.-John-in-the-Forest und betonte besonders ihre weltabgeschiedene Lage. Wer dort Prior sei, habe enorme Freiheit und Unabhängigkeit. »Wen kann es überraschen«, fragte er mit erhobener Stimme, »daß dieser unerfahrene, heißblütige junge Mann nach fünf Jahren, in denen praktisch niemand sein Tun und Lassen überwacht hat, Vater eines Kindes wurde?« Es klang fast wie eine unausweichliche Folge. Philip hätte Waleran erwürgen können.

Der Bischof schilderte daraufhin, wie Philip den kleinen Jonathan und Johnny Eightpence nach Kingsbridge gebracht hatte. Die Mönche seien bestürzt gewesen, sagte er, als sich ihr neuer Prior mit einem Säugling und einer männlichen Amme bei ihnen einfand ...

Da hat er sogar recht, dachte Philip, vergaß für einen Augenblick seine innere Anspannung und unterdrückte ein wehmütiges Lächeln.

Philip habe mit dem Kind Jonathan viel gespielt, ihn persönlich unterrichtet und später zu seinem Adlatus gemacht, fuhr Waleran fort, kurz: ihn genauso behandelt wie ein Vater seinen Sohn. Der Unterschied sei nur der, daß Mönche keine Söhne haben dürften. »Jonathan war frühreif, genau wie Philip. Als Cuthbert Whitehead starb, machte Philip Jonathan zum Cellerar, obwohl dieser erst einundzwanzig war. Gab es da wirklich in diesem Kloster von mehr als hundert Mönchen keinen anderen, der für das Amt geeignet gewesen wäre? War da wirklich nur dieser Knabe von gerade mal einundzwanzig Jahren? Oder begünstigte Philip bloß sein eigen Fleisch und Blut? Als Milius das Kloster verließ, um Prior von Glastonbury zu werden, hat Philip Jonathan zum Kämmerer ernannt. Er ist vierunddreißig Jahre alt. Ist er wirklich der klügste und gottesfürchtigste Mönch hier in der Priorei, oder ist er nur Philips Günstling?«

Philip sah sich um. Die Verhandlung fand im südlichen Querschiff der Kathedrale statt. Erzdiakon Peter thronte auf einem großen, mit reichem Schnitzwerk verzierten Sessel. Walerans Mitstreiter aus der Bischofskanzlei waren vollzählig versammelt. Auch die meisten Mönche von Kingsbridge waren zugegen – während des Verfahrens gegen den Prior blieb somit eine Menge Arbeit liegen. Alle Kleriker von Rang aus der Grafschaft waren gekommen, und sogar einige kleine Dorfpriester hatten sich eingefunden. Benachbarte Diözesen hatten ihre Beobachter entsandt. Die gesamte Kirchengemeinde Südenglands erwartete mit Spannung das Urteil des Gerichts. Philips Tugend oder Untugend interessierte dabei nur am Rande: Man sah in dem Verfahren die letzte entscheidende Schlacht zwischen Prior Philip und Bischof Waleran.

Nachdem Waleran wieder Platz genommen hatte, wurde Philip vereidigt und schilderte die Ereignisse jenes so lange zurückliegenden Wintermorgens aus seiner Sicht. Er begann mit der Unruhe, die Peter von Wareham damals verursacht hatte: Alle sollten wissen, daß Peter gegen ihn voreingenommen war. Dann bat er Francis zu erzählen, wie er den Säugling gefunden hatte.

Jonathan nahm an dieser Phase des Verfahrens nicht teil. Einer Nachricht zufolge, die er hinterlassen hatte, war er neuen Erkenntnissen über seine Herkunft auf der Spur. Da auch Jack verschwunden war, schloß Philip, es müsse etwas mit dessen Mutter, der Hexe Ellen, zu tun haben. Wahrscheinlich, so dachte er, hat Jonathan befürchtet, ich könnte ihm verbieten, diese Person aufzusuchen. Die beiden hätten eigentlich am Morgen zurückkehren sollen, waren aber bislang noch nicht eingetroffen. Daß Ellen Francis' Bericht noch wesentliches hinzufügen könnte, damit rechnete der Prior nicht.

Nachdem Francis seine Aussage beendet hatte, ergriff wieder Philip das Wort. »Das Kind war nicht von mir«, sagte er schlicht. »Ich schwöre es bei der Unsterblichkeit meiner Seele. Nie habe ich geschlechtlichen Umgang mit einem Weib gehabt. Bis auf den heutigen Tag lebe ich in jenem Zustand der Keuschheit, den uns der Apostel Paulus anempfiehlt. Nun fragt aber unser hochverehrte Herr Bischof, warum ich diesen Knaben wie meinen eigenen Sohn behandelt habe ...« Er sah sich im Kreis der Zuhörer um. Philip war zu dem Schluß gekommen, daß er nur eine einzige Chance hatte: Er mußte die reine, unverfälschte Wahrheit sagen und darauf hoffen, daß Gottes

Stimme laut genug war, um Peters spirituelle Taubheit zu überwinden. »Als ich sechs Jahre alt war«, begann er, »starben meine Eltern. Sie wurden von Soldaten des alten König Heinrich getötet, in Wales. Mir und meinem Bruder rettete der Abt eines nahe gelegenen Klosters das Leben, und von jenem Tag an wuchs ich unter der Obhut der Mönche auf. Ich war ein Klostermündel. Ich weiß daher, was es bedeutet. Ich weiß, wie sehr sich ein Waisenknabe nach der tröstenden Hand der Mutter sehnt, selbst wenn er die Brüder liebt, die sich um ihn kümmern. Ich wußte von Anfang an, daß Jonathan sich als Außenseiter, Sonderling und Wechselbalg fühlen würde, denn ich hatte es ja am eigenen Leibe erfahren, wie es ist, wenn alle anderen Eltern haben, nur man selber nicht. Wie ihm war es auch mir ein Greuel, von der Mildtätigkeit anderer abhängig zu sein, ihnen zur Last zu fallen. Immer wieder habe ich mich gefragt, warum mir das versagt wurde, was für meine Altersgenossen selbstverständlich war. Ich wußte, daß auch Jonathan des Nachts vom warmen, duftenden Busen und der weichen Stimme einer Mutter träumte, die er nie gekannt hat – von einem Menschen, der ihn von ganzem Herzen liebt und nur für ihn da ist.«

Erzdiakon Peters Miene war wie versteinert. Er gehört zur allerschlimmsten Erscheinungsform des Christenmenschen, dachte Philip. Überall pickt er sich nur das Negative heraus, denkt immer nur an Verbote und wie er sie durchsetzen kann, fordert bei jedem Delikt die schärfste Strafe … Er ignoriert das christliche Erbarmen und die Gnade, er mißachtet in flagranter Weise die Ethik der Liebe und verhöhnt in aller Offenheit die gütigen Gesetze Jesu. So wie er waren einst die Pharisäer. Kein Wunder, daß der Herr es vorzog, mit den Zöllnern und Sündern zu speisen …

Dann fuhr er fort, obwohl ihm jetzt klar war, daß er sagen konnte, was er wollte: Keines seiner Worte wäre imstande, den Panzer von Peters Selbstgerechtigkeit zu durchdringen. »Niemand, von seinen leiblichen Eltern abgesehen, hätte sich um diesen Knaben so kümmern können wie ich. Die Eltern aber waren unauffindbar. Wie hätte Gott seinen Willen deutlicher …« Er stockte. Soeben hatten Jonathan und Jack die Kirche betreten. Und bei ihnen war Jacks Mutter: die Hexe.

Sie war alt geworden: Ihr Haar war schneeweiß, ihr Gesicht zerfurcht. Aber ihr Gang war der einer Königin: den Kopf hocherhoben, die seltsam goldenen Augen voller Widerspruchsgeist. Philip war zu überrascht, um gegen ihr Erscheinen zu protestieren.

Das Gericht schwieg, als Ellen näher trat und vor Erzdiakon Peter stehenblieb. Ihre Stimme klang wie Trompetenschall und brach sich an den Mauern der von ihrem Sohn erbauten Kirche. »Ich schwöre bei allem, was heilig ist, daß Jonathan der Sohn meines verstorbenen Ehemannes, Tom Builder, und dessen erster Gemahlin ist.«

Unter den versammelten Klerikern erhob sich aufgeregtes Geraune, das alle Einzelstimmen übertönte. Philip war völlig überrumpelt. Offenen Mundes starrte er Ellen an. Tom Builder? Jonathan Tom Builders Sohn? Ein Blick auf Jonathan genügte, um ihn von der Richtigkeit der Behauptung zu überzeugen: Sie waren einander sehr ähnlich, nicht nur, was die Körpergröße betraf, sondern auch von den Gesichtszügen her. Jonathan fehlte nur der Bart.

Philips erste Reaktion war das Gefühl des Verlusts. Bisher war er für Jonathan *wie ein Vater* gewesen. Die Entdeckung seines leiblichen Vaters änderte alles – obwohl derselbe nicht mehr lebte. Philip konnte sich nun auch insgeheim nicht mehr als Jonathans Vater fühlen, und Jonathan nicht mehr als Philips Sohn. Von nun an war er Toms Sohn. Philip hatte ihn verloren.

Aufseufzend setzte sich Philip hin. Als die Zuschauer sich beruhigt hatten, berichtete Ellen, wie Jack damals das schreiende Kind gefunden hatte. Sie erzählte – und Philip lauschte ihren Worten wie in Trance –,wie sie und Tom sich im Gebüsch versteckt und die Heimkehr Philips und der anderen Mönche von der Morgenarbeit beobachtet hatten. Wie Francis die Brüder mit dem Neugeborenen im Arm erwartete und Johnny Eightpence versuchte, das kleine Wesen mit Hilfe eines Tuchzipfels zu füttern, den er zuvor in Ziegenmilch getaucht hatte.

Philip erinnerte sich deutlich daran, wie sehr der junge Baumeister ein oder zwei Tage später, als sie sich zufällig im Wald begegneten, am Schicksal des Findelkinds Anteil genommen hatte. Und wie freundlich er in späteren Jahren, als Jonathan zu einem frechen kleinen Bengel heranwuchs, zu ihm gewesen war. Aufgefallen war das niemand – war der Bub in jenen Tagen doch der Liebling der ganzen Priorei. Außerdem arbeitete Tom ja auf dem Klostergelände. Rückblickend betrachtet war es indes ganz klar, daß Tom dem kleinen Jonathan besondere Aufmerksamkeit geschenkt hatte.

Als Ellen ihre Aussage beendet hatte und sich setzte, wußte Philip, daß damit seine Unschuld bewiesen war. Ihre Enthüllungen hatten ihn derart erschüttert, daß er vorübergehend ganz vergessen hatte, wo er sich befand. Ihre Geschichte über Geburt und Tod, Verzweiflung und Hoffnung, uralte Geheimnisse und dauerhafte Liebe ließ die Frage nach Philips Keuschheit zweitrangig erscheinen. Was sie natürlich nicht war – hing doch die Zukunft der Priorei von ihrer Beantwortung ab. Ellen hatte sie allerdings so überzeugend beantwortet, daß an eine Fortsetzung der Verhandlung im Grunde nicht mehr zu denken war. Nach dieser Aussage kann mich selbst Peter von Wareham nicht mehr schuldig sprechen, dachte Philip. Waleran hat wieder einmal den kürzeren gezogen.

Der Bischof selbst war noch nicht bereit, die Niederlage einzugestehen. Anklagend zeigte er mit dem Finger auf Ellen und rief: »Ihr sagt, Tom Builder habe Euch erzählt, daß der Säugling, den man in die Zelle brachte, sein Sohn sei.«

»Ja«, bestätigte Ellen. Sie war auf der Hut.

»Die beiden anderen Zeugen, die das hätten bestätigen können – ich meine die Kinder Alfred und Martha –, haben Euch nicht zum Kloster begleitet.«

»Nein.«

»Und Tom Builder ist tot. Für Toms Worte seid Ihr demnach die einzige Zeugin. Eure Aussage kann nicht bestätigt werden.«

»Wieviel Bestätigung wollt Ihr denn noch?« fragte Ellen forsch zurück. »Jack sah das ausgesetzte Kind. Francis nahm es auf. Jack und ich begegneten Tom, Alfred und Martha. Francis brachte das Kind in die Priorei. Tom und ich beobachteten, was dort geschah. Wie viele Zeugen würden Euch denn zufriedenstellen?«

»Ich glaube Euch kein Wort«, sagte Waleran.

»So? Ihr glaubt mir kein Wort?« wiederholte Ellen, und Philip sah, daß sie unvermittelt von tiefem, leidenschaftlichem Zorn ergriffen war. »Ihr glaubt mir nicht? Ausgerechnet Ihr, Waleran Bigod, der Ihr mir als Meineidiger bekannt seid?«

Was, um alles in der Welt, hat das zu bedeuten? dachte Philip, und ein Abgrund tat sich vor seinem geistigen Auge auf. Waleran war bleich geworden. Da gibt es noch mehr Unausgesprochenes, Dinge, deren Enthüllung Waleran fürchtet. Die Aufregung schlug ihm auf den Magen. Waleran wirkte auf einmal schwer angeschlagen.

»Was meint Ihr damit?« fragte Philip Ellen. »Was veranlaßt Euch, den Bischof des Meineids zu bezichtigen?«

»Vor siebenundvierzig Jahren wurde hier, in dieser Priorei, ein Gefangener namens Jack Shareburg festgehalten«, sagte sie.

Waleran unterbrach sie. »Das Gericht ist an so lange zurückliegenden Ereignissen nicht interessiert.«

»Doch, hochverehrter Herr Bischof«, sagte Philip. »Die Anklage wirft mir ein Unzuchtdelikt vor, das angeblich fünfunddreißig Jahre zurückliegt. Ihr habt von mir den Beweis meiner Unschuld gefordert. Das Gericht wird an Euch nun die gleiche Forderung richten.« Er wandte sich an Ellen. »Fahrt fort!«

»Niemand wußte, warum er festgehalten wurde, am wenigsten der Gefangene selbst. Eines Tages wurde er dann freigelassen, und man schenkte ihm, wohl als Wiedergutmachung für die unschuldig erlittene Haftzeit, einen juwelengeschmückten Kelch. Jack Shareburg wollte den Kelch gar nicht haben, denn er konnte damit nichts anfangen. Auf dem Markt hätte ihm niemand einen so wertvollen Gegenstand abgekauft. Er ließ ihn also hier, und zwar in der alten Kathedrale. Kurz darauf wurde Jack wieder festgenommen – und zwar auf Veranlassung von Waleran Bigod, der damals ein einfacher Dorfpriester war, von niederem Stand, aber sehr ehrgeizig. Wundersamerweise fand sich der Kelch in Jack Shareburgs Gepäck wieder. Jack wurde zu Unrecht des Diebstahls angeklagt und nach den beeideten Aussagen von drei Männern zum Tode verurteilt und gehängt. Die drei Männer waren Waleran Bigod, Percy Hamleigh und Prior James von Kingsbridge.«

Einen Augenblick lang herrschte verblüfftes Schweigen. Dann fragte Philip: »Und woher wißt Ihr das alles?«

»Ich war die einzige, die damals zu ihm stand. Jack Shareburg war der Vater meines Sohnes, des Erbauers dieser Kathedrale.«

Ein Sturm der Erregung brach los. Waleran und Peter fingen gleichzeitig an zu sprechen, doch war weder der eine noch der andere im aufgeregten Stimmengewirr der versammelten Kleriker zu verstehen. Sie sind gekommen, um einen Entscheidungskampf zu sehen, dachte Philip – und *damit* haben sie nicht gerechnet.

Nach einer Weile gelang es Peter, sich Gehör zu verschaffen. »Aus welchem Grund sollten sich drei gesetzestreue Bürger zu einer falschen Anklage gegen einen unschuldigen Fremden verschwören?« fragte er skeptisch.

»Aus Eigennutz«, sagte Ellen. »Waleran Bigod wurde zum Erzdiakon befördert. Percy erhielt das Rittergut Hamleigh sowie ein paar andere Dörfer und wurde dadurch zu einem begüterten Mann. Was Prior James bekam, weiß ich nicht.«

»Diese Frage kann ich beantworten«, sagte eine Stimme, die sich bisher nicht hatte vernehmen lassen.

Verwundert blickte Philip in die Runde: Der Sprecher war Remigius. Er war inzwischen weit über Siebzig, hatte schlohweißes Haar und geriet beim Reden oft vom Hundertsten ins Tausendste. Auf einen

Gehstock gestützt, erhob er sich; seine Augen und seine wache Miene zeigten, daß er bei klarem Verstand war. Seit seinem Sturz und seiner Rückkehr ins Kloster hatte er ein ruhiges, demütiges Leben geführt und sich in der Öffentlichkeit nur noch selten zu Wort gemeldet. Auf welche Seite wird er sich jetzt wohl schlagen? dachte Philip. Wird er die letzte Gelegenheit nutzen, seinem alten Feind Philip in den Rükken zu fallen?

»Ich kann Euch sagen, welche Belohnung Prior James erhielt«, sagte Remigius. »Die Priorei erhielt die Dörfer Northwold, Southwold und Hundredacre sowie den Wald von Oldean.«

Philip war entsetzt. War es wirklich möglich, daß sein Vorgänger um ein paar Dörfer willen einen Meineid geschworen hatte?

»Prior James war nie ein guter Klosterverwalter«, fuhr Remigius fort. »Die Priorei steckte in finanziellen Schwierigkeiten. Er hoffte, das zusätzliche Einkommen würde uns aus der Misere befreien.« Er machte eine kleine Pause und fügte dann hinzu: »Unter dem Strich kam nicht viel dabei heraus. Das Geld half uns ein bißchen weiter, das schon. Aber Prior James hatte seine Selbstachtung unwiederbringlich verloren.«

Bei diesen Worten fiel Philip die gebeugte, resignierte Haltung des alten Priors wieder ein. Jetzt endlich wußte er, woher sie rührte.

»James' Schwur war strenggenommen kein Meineid, denn er hatte lediglich gesagt, daß der Kelch vormals der Priorei gehört hatte. Aber er hat geschwiegen, obwohl er wußte, daß Jack Shareburg unschuldig war. Darüber ist er bis an sein Lebensende nicht hinweggekommen.«

Das kann ich mir vorstellen, dachte Philip. Remigius' Aussage bestätigte Ellens Geschichte – und verurteilte Waleran.

Der alte Mönch war noch nicht fertig. »Ein paar von den Älteren hier in der Runde werden sich daran erinnern, in was für einem Zustand sich die Priorei vor vierzig Jahren befand: Sie hatte schlichtweg abgewirtschaftet. Es fehlte an Geld und moralischer Kraft. Mit ein Grund dafür war die schwere Last der Schuld, an der der Prior trug. Auf dem Sterbebett vertraute er mir seine Sünde an. Ich wollte ...« Remigius stockte. Niemand sprach ein Wort, alle warteten. Der alte Mann seufzte und sprach weiter. »Ich wollte sein Amt übernehmen und den Schaden wiedergutmachen. Aber Gott hatte für diese Aufgabe einen anderen Mann ausersehen.« Wieder hielt er inne. Der nächste Satz kostete ihn sichtlich Überwindung, und sein altes Gesicht wirkte zerquält: »Ich muß wohl sagen: Gott wählte den besseren Mann.« Er ließ sich auf seinen Stuhl fallen.

Philip war gleichermaßen erschrocken, verwirrt und dankbar. Zwei alte Widersacher – Ellen und Remigius – hatten ihn gerettet.

Bischof Waleran war fahl vor Wut. Er beugte sich zu Peter hinüber und flüsterte ihm etwas ins Ohr. Die ganze Kirche summte vom aufgeregten Geraune der Zuhörer.

Peter von Wareham erhob sich und rief: »Silentium!« Es herrschte sofort Stille. »Die Verhandlung ist beendet!«

»Einen Augenblick noch!« Es war Jack Jackson. »Das genügt mir nicht!« rief er leidenschaftlich. »Ich möchte wissen, *warum*!«

Peter ignorierte Jacks Einwurf. Gefolgt von Waleran, schritt er auf die Tür zu, die zum Kreuzgang führte.

Jack lief hinter ihnen her. »*Warum* hast du das getan?« schrie er Waleran an. »Du hast mit einem Meineid einen Menschen an den Galgen gebracht – und jetzt willst du dich ohne ein Wort der Erklärung aus dem Staub machen?«

Waleran stierte geradeaus, das Gesicht totenblaß, die Lippen zusammengepreßt, die Miene in stummer Rage erstarrt. Als er durch die Tür ging, brüllte Jack: »Antworte mir, du nichtswürdiger, korrupter, feiger Lügner! Warum hast du meinen Vater ermordet?«

Waleran hatte die Kirche verlassen. Krachend fiel die Tür hinter ihm ins Schloß.

Der Brief von König Heinrich traf während der Kapitelversammlung der Mönche ein.

Jack hatte ein großes neues Kapitelhaus errichtet, das allen einhundertfünfzig frommen Brüdern Platz bot. In keinem anderen Kloster Englands gab es so viele Mönche wie in Kingsbridge. Der Rundbau hatte ein steinernes Gewölbe und war mit treppenartigen steinernen Sitzreihen ausgestattet. Die Amtsträger saßen auf Steinbänken an der Wand, ein wenig höher als die anderen Mönche; für Philip und Jonathan waren gemeißelte Steinthrone an der Wand gegenüber dem Eingang reserviert.

Ein junger Mönch trug das siebte Kapitel aus der Regel des heiligen Benedikt vor: »Die sechste Stufe der Demut ist erreicht, wenn ein Mönch sich mit allem zufriedengibt, das niedrig ist und gering ...« Philip mußte sich eingestehen, daß er den Namen des Vortragenden nicht kannte. Kommt das daher, daß ich alt werde – oder ist das Kloster zu groß? fragte er sich. – »Die siebte Stufe der Demut ist erreicht, wenn ein Mann nicht nur mit eigener Zunge bekennt, daß er der Geringste ist und niedriger steht als alle anderen, sondern wenn er auch in der Tiefe seines Herzens daran glaubt.« Philip wußte, daß er diese Stufe der Demut noch nicht erreicht hatte. Er hatte eine Menge erreicht in seinen zweiundsechzig Lebensjahren, mit Mut, Entschlossenheit und Intelligenz, mußte sich aber immer wieder selbst daran erinnern, daß dies nur mit Gottes Hilfe möglich gewesen war.

Jonathan neben ihm rutschte unruhig auf seinem Sitz hin und her. Die Tugend der Demut bereitete ihm noch mehr Schwierigkeiten als Philip. Hochmut war die Achillesferse aller guten Menschenführer. Jonathan war bereit, das Amt des Priors zu übernehmen, und wartete voller Ungeduld. Er hatte sich mit Aliena unterhalten und brannte darauf, ihre landwirtschaftlichen Methoden wie das Pflügen mit Pferden und die Ausbringung von Frühsaat wie Erbsen und Hafer auch auf den Klostergütern auszuprobieren. So ähnlich war es damals, als ich mit dem Aufbau der Schafzucht begann, dachte Philip.

Er wußte, daß er eigentlich von seinem Amt zurücktreten und Jonathan ans Ruder lassen müßte. Ein friedlicher Lebensabend in Gebet und Meditation – wie oft hatte er anderen schon mit diesem Hinweis den Rücktritt nahegelegt! Doch nun, da er selbst ins Rücktrittsalter gekommen war, entsetzte ihn die Aussicht. Er war kerngesund, sein Verstand scharf und klar wie eh und je. Ein Leben in Gebet und Meditation würde mich in kürzester Zeit zum Wahnsinn treiben, dachte er.

Andererseits: Jonathan würde nicht ewig warten. Gott hatte ihm die Fähigkeiten verliehen, die zur Führung eines großen Klosters erforderlich waren, und er hatte nicht die Absicht, seine Talente zu vergeuden. Er hatte über die Jahre zahlreiche andere Abteien besucht und überall einen guten Eindruck gemacht. Es war jederzeit damit zu rechnen, daß man ihn nach dem Tod eines Abtes bat, sich als Nachfolgekandidat zur Verfügung zu stellen. Philip wußte, daß er ihm dann die Erlaubnis kaum würde verweigern können.

Der junge Mensch, dessen Namen Philip nicht einfallen wollte, beendete gerade seine Lesung, als es klopfte und der Türhüter den Saal betrat. Bruder Steven, der Cirkator, blickte unwillig auf: Derartige Störungen der Kapitelversammlung waren unerwünscht. Dem Cirkator oblag die Aufrechterhaltung der Disziplin, und wie alle Männer seines Amtes bestand auch Steven peinlich genau auf der Einhaltung der Regeln.

»Eine Botschaft des Königs!« flüsterte der Türhüter so laut, daß alle es hören konnten.

»Kümmere dich doch bitte darum«, sagte Philip zu Jonathan. Gewiß bestand der Bote darauf, seinen Brief einem führenden Mitglied der Klosterverwaltung persönlich auszuhändigen. Jonathan stand auf und ging. Die Mönche fingen an zu tuscheln. Philip sagte mit lauter Stimme: »Wir fahren fort mit dem Nekrolog.«

Die Gebete für die Toten begannen. Was hat der zweite König Heinrich wohl der Priorei Kingsbridge mitzuteilen? fragte sich Philip und beantwortete sich die Frage gleich selbst: Wahrscheinlich nichts Gutes ... Seit sechs Jahren lag Heinrich mit der Kirche im Streit. Es hatte begonnen mit einer Auseinandersetzung über die Zuständigkeit der geistlichen Gerichtsbarkeit. Heinrichs Starrsinn und der religiöse

Eifer des Erzbischofs von Canterbury, Thomas Becket, hatten dazu geführt, daß der Streit zu einer Krise eskalierte. Becket war ins Exil gezwungen worden.

Bedauerlicherweise stand die englische Kirche nicht einmütig hinter ihm. Bischöfe wie Waleran hatten sich auf Heinrichs Seite geschlagen, um der königlichen Gunst teilhaftig zu werden. Allerdings übte der Papst Druck auf Heinrich aus, mit Becket Frieden zu schließen. Die vielleicht schlimmste Folge des Streits bestand darin, daß machtgierige Bischöfe wie Waleran immer größeren Einfluß am königlichen Hof gewannen: Heinrich umwarb sie, weil er unbedingt Unterstützung aus den Reihen der Kirche brauchte. Aus diesem Grund hatte Philip, was den Brief des Königs betraf, mehr noch als sonst ein unangenehmes Gefühl.

Jonathan kehrte zurück und reichte Philip eine mit Wachs verschlossene Pergamentrolle. Das Wachs war mit dem Abdruck eines gewaltigen königlichen Siegels versehen. Alle Mönche blickten auf. Philip sah ein, daß er mit solch einem Brief in der Hand nicht mehr die für das Totengebet nötige Konzentration erwarten konnte. »Nun gut«, sagte er. »Wir werden das Gebet später fortsetzen.« Er erbrach das Siegel, öffnete den Brief und überflog die Grußformel. Dann gab er das Schreiben Jonathan, der jüngere und bessere Augen hatte. »Lies es uns vor, sei so gut.«

Nach der üblichen Anrede schrieb der König. »›Zum neuen Bischof von Lincoln schlagen Wir Waleran Bigod vor, gegenwärtig Bischof von Kingsbridge ...‹« Jonathans Stimme verlor sich im aufgeregten Gemurmel der Mönche. Philip schüttelte angewidert den Kopf. Seit den Enthüllungen beim Kirchengerichtsverfahren in Kingsbridge hatte Waleran in seinem eigenen Bistum sämtliche Glaubwürdigkeit verloren. Es war abzusehen, daß er sich nicht mehr lange im Amt würde halten können. Doch nun hatte er den König überredet, ihn zum Kandidaten für den Bischofsstuhl in Lincoln zu nominieren. Lincoln war eines der reichsten Bistümer der Welt und – nach Canterbury und York – die drittgrößte Diözese des Königreichs. Von dort war es nur noch ein kleiner Schritt zu einem Erzbistum. Vielleicht baute Heinrich Waleran sogar zum Nachfolger von Thomas Becket auf. Die Vorstellung, Waleran Bigod könne dereinst Erzbischof von Canterbury und Oberhaupt der englischen Kirche sein, war so entsetzlich, daß Philip vor Angst fast übel wurde.

Als sich die Mönche wieder beruhigt hatten, fuhr Jonathan mit der Verlesung des Schreibens fort: »›... und haben dem Kapitel von

Lincoln empfohlen, ihn zu erwählen.‹« Nun, das ist leichter gesagt als getan, dachte Philip. Eine königliche Empfehlung war fast ein Befehl, aber eben doch nicht ganz. Wenn das Kapitel in Lincoln Waleran ablehnte oder aber sich schon auf einen eigenen Kandidaten geeignet hatte, konnte es dem König Schwierigkeiten machen. Zum Schluß würde sich der König wahrscheinlich durchsetzen; selbstverständlich war es nicht.

»›Wir befehlen Euch, dem Kapitel der Priorei von Kingsbridge, einen neuen Bischof von Kingsbridge zu wählen, und empfehlen Euch für dieses Amt Unseren treuen Diener Peter von Wareham, Erzdiakon von Canterbury.‹«

Die versammelten Mönche quittierten diese Ankündigung mit einem Aufschrei der Empörung. Philip wurde kalt vor Entsetzen. Der hoffärtige, überall Unheil witternde, selbstgerechte Erzdiakon Peter sollte Bischof von Kingsbridge werden! Peter war genau der gleiche Typ wie Waleran. Beide Männer waren von echter Frömmigkeit und Gottesfurcht, aber sie besaßen kein Gespür für die eigene Fehlbarkeit. Sie hielten daher ihre eigenen Wünsche für den Willen Gottes und verfolgten ihre Ziele mit entsprechender Rücksichtslosigkeit. Mit Peter als Bischof stand dem künftigen Prior Jonathan eine harte Zeit bevor – ein lebenslanger Kampf um Gerechtigkeit und Anstand in einem Bistum, in dem mit eiserner Faust ein Mann ohne Herz herrschte.

Wurde dann auch noch Waleran Erzbischof, so gab es keine Hoffnung mehr auf eine Wendung zum Besseren.

Philip sah ein langes, dunkles Zeitalter voraus, nicht unähnlich der schlimmsten Phase des Bürgerkriegs, als Grafen vom Schlage Williams nach Gutdünken walteten, anmaßende Priester ihre Gemeinden vernachlässigten und die Priorei wieder in ein armes und geschwächtes Schattendasein verfiel. Die Vorstellung erregte seinen Zorn.

Er war nicht der einzige, der sich ärgerte. Cirkator Steven erhob sich rotgesichtig und schrie, so laut er konnte: »Soweit darf es nicht kommen!« Und das, obwohl er damit gegen ein Gebot Philips verstieß, nach dem im Kapitelhaus nur in ruhigem und besonnenem Ton gesprochen werden durfte.

Die Mönche stimmten ihm lebhaft zu. Jonathan hingegen bewies seine Umsicht, indem er die entscheidende Frage stellte: »Was können wir tun?«

Der dicke Küchenmeister Bernard sagte: »Wir müssen das Ersuchen des Königs zurückweisen.«

Mehrere Mönche taten ihre Zustimmung kund.

Steven sagte: »Wir sollten dem König antworten, daß wir selbst entscheiden, wen wir wählen.« Nach einer kurzen Pause fügte er einfältig hinzu: »Unter Gottes Führung natürlich.«

»Ich bin nicht der Meinung, daß wir seinen Vorschlag so brüsk zurückweisen sollten«, meinte Jonathan. »Je schneller wir den König herausfordern, desto eher beschwören wir seinen Zorn auf uns herab.«

»Jonathan hat recht«, sagte Philip. »Einem Mann, der eine Schlacht gegen seinen König verliert, kann vergeben werden. Wer aber eine solche Schlacht gewinnt, ist verloren.«

»Also gebt Ihr auf der ganzen Linie nach!« platzte Steven heraus.

Philip war nicht minder besorgt als die anderen, mußte jedoch nach außen hin die Ruhe bewahren. »Steven, mäßige dich!« sagte er. »Selbstverständlich müssen wir uns gegen diesen schlimmen Vorschlag des Königs zur Wehr setzen, doch werden wir unser Vorgehen sorgfältig planen und einen offenen Konflikt vermeiden.«

»Aber was wollt Ihr *tun*?«

»Ich weiß es noch nicht genau«, erwiderte Philip. Seine anfängliche Verzagtheit schwand, und der alte Kampfgeist erwachte. Die Schlacht, die es hier zu schlagen galt, kannte er; er hatte sie oft genug schlagen müssen, sein Leben lang: im Kloster, als er sich in der Priorwahl gegen Remigius durchsetzen mußte, aber auch in der Grafschaft bei den ständigen Auseinandersetzungen mit William Hamleigh und Waleran Bigod. Nun wurde die Schlacht auf höchster Ebene ausgetragen: Er, Philip, begehrte gegen den König auf.

»Ich glaube, ich werde nach Frankreich reisen müssen«, sagte er, »und mich mit Erzbischof Thomas Becket unterhalten.«

In allen anderen Krisen seines Lebens war es Philip gelungen, einen Plan zu entwickeln. Wann immer sein Kloster oder seine Stadt von den Kräften der Gesetzlosigkeit und roher Gewalt bedroht war, hatte er sich etwas einfallen lassen, sei es eine Abwehrmaßnahme oder eine Gegenattacke. Ob seine Bemühungen von Erfolg gekrönt sein würden, ließ sich nicht immer gleich absehen – auf jeden Fall war er nie um eine Strategie verlegen gewesen. Diesmal war es anders.

Als er in Sens, einer Stadt südlich von Paris im Königreich Frankreich, eintraf, war er noch immer ganz durcheinander.

Die Kathedrale von Sens war das breiteste Gebäude, das er je gesehen hatte. Das Hauptschiff hatte einen Durchmesser von gut und gerne fünfzig Fuß. Verglichen mit der Kirche in Kingsbridge beeindruckte in Sens eher der Raum als das Licht.

Auf seiner Reise durch Frankreich, der ersten in seinem Leben, war Philip die ungeheure Vielfalt in der sakralen Architektur aufgefallen. Sie überstieg alle seine bisherigen Vorstellungen, und er begriff jetzt den revolutionären Einfluß des Reisens auf Jack Jackson und dessen Baustil. Bewußt machte Philip von Paris aus einen Abstecher nach Saint-Denis und entdeckte in der dortigen Abteikirche manche Elemente wieder, die Jack zum Vorbild gedient hatten. Auch waren ihm unterwegs zwei Kirchen mit freiem äußerem Strebewerk begegnet; offensichtlich hatten sich andere Dombaumeister mit den gleichen Problemen wie Jack konfrontiert gesehen und waren zu derselben Lösung gekommen.

Philip stattete dem Erzbischof von Sens einen Höflichkeitsbesuch ab. William Whithands, ein Neffe des verstorbenen Königs Stephan, war ein hochbegabter junger Geistlicher, der Philip spontan zum Essen einlud. Obwohl er sich sehr geschmeichelt fühlte, lehnte Philip die Einladung ab: Er hatte eine lange Reise auf sich genommen, um Thomas Becket zu sprechen, und brannte nun darauf, ihn kennenzulernen. Nachdem er einem Gottesdienst in der Kathedrale beigewohnt hatte, verließ er die Stadt und setzte seinen Weg in nördlicher Richtung, dem Lauf der Yonne folgend, fort.

Für den Prior eines der reichsten Klöster Englands war die Reisegesellschaft eher bescheiden: Philip hatte zu seinem persönlichen Schutz zwei Bewaffnete mitgenommen sowie als Adlatus einen jungen Mönch namens Michael von Bristol. Außerdem führte er ein mit heiligen Büchern beladenes Packpferd mit. Die im Scriptorium von Kingsbridge kopierten, mit herrlichen Illustrationen versehenen Werke dienten als Geschenke für Äbte und Bischöfe, die man unterwegs besuchte. Die teuren Bücher standen in scharfem Gegensatz zur äußerlichen Erscheinung der Entourage. Philip hatte das beabsichtigt: Die Leute sollten die Priorei bewundern und respektieren, nicht ihren Prior.

Thomas Becket lebte seit drei Jahren nur eine kurze Strecke nördlich von Sens in der ehrwürdigen, auf einer sonnigen Wiese am Flußufer gelegenen Abtei von Sainte-Colombe. Philip wurde von einem Priester des Erzbischofs herzlich empfangen. Der Mann rief sogleich Diener herbei, die sich um die Pferde und das Gepäck kümmerten, und geleitete die Besucher zum Gästehaus, in dem der Erzbischof Wohnung genommen hatte. Die Exilierten waren offenbar sehr froh über die Besucher aus der Heimat – nicht nur aus sentimentalen Gründen, sondern auch, weil sie darin ein Zeichen für Unterstützung sahen.

Philip und seinem Adlatus wurde Wein kredenzt und ein gutes Mahl gereicht. Dann stellte man ihnen die Mitarbeiter des Erzbischofs vor. Es handelte sich samt und sonders um Priester. Sie waren überwiegend noch recht jung und – nach Philips Eindruck – durchwegs gescheite und helle Köpfe. Schon nach kurzer Zeit war Michael mit einem von ihnen in einen Disput über die Transsubstantiation verwickelt. Philip nippte an seinem Wein und hörte zu, ohne sich am Gespräch zu beteiligen.

Schließlich sprach ihn einer der Priester an: »Was meint Ihr dazu, Vater Philip? Ihr habt Euch bisher noch nicht geäußert.«

Philip lächelte: »Knifflige theologische Probleme bereiten mir am allerwenigsten Kopfzerbrechen.«

»Warum?«

»Weil sie sich im Jenseits von allein lösen. Man kann sie also ruhig auf die lange Bank schieben.«

»Wohl gesprochen!« sagte eine neue Stimme. Philip sah auf und erblickte Erzbischof Thomas von Canterbury.

Philip spürte sofort, daß eine bedeutende Persönlichkeit vor ihm stand. Thomas war ein hochgewachsener, schlanker und ausgesprochen gutaussehender Mann mit breiter Stirn, klaren Augen, heller Haut und dunklem Haar. Er war ungefähr zehn Jahre jünger als Philip, also an die Fünfzig oder knapp darüber, und hatte sich trotz des Unglücks, das ihm widerfahren war, eine muntere, fröhliche Miene bewahrt. Er war, wie Philip sogleich auffiel, ein sehr *attraktiver* Mann, und darin lag vermutlich auch eine Erklärung für seine bemerkenswerte Karriere. Thomas stammte aus einfachen Verhältnissen.

Philip kniete nieder und küßte die Hand des Erzbischofs.

»Welch eine Freude, endlich Eure Bekanntschaft machen zu dürfen!« sagte Thomas. »Immer schon habe ich Kingsbridge besuchen wollen. Ich habe soviel von Eurer Priorei und der wunderbaren neuen Kathedrale gehört!«

Philip war gleichermaßen bezaubert wie geschmeichelt. »Ich bin gekommen, weil alles, was wir in Kingsbridge erreicht haben, durch den König gefährdet wird«, sagte er.

»Ich möchte darüber sofort in Kenntnis gesetzt werden«, sagte Thomas. »Begleitet mich bitte in meine Kammer.« Er drehte sich mit einer schwungvollen Bewegung um und verließ den Raum.

Philip folgte ihm mit gemischten Gefühlen.

Thomas führte ihn in ein kleineres Zimmer, dessen Einrichtung von einem teuren, mit feinem Linnen bezogenen Bett aus Holz und

Leder beherrscht wurde. In der Ecke stand allerdings eine zusammengerollte dünne Matratze. Philip erinnerte sich an Gerüchte, denen zufolge Thomas niemals von der luxuriösen Einrichtung Gebrauch machte, die seine Gastgeber ihm zur Verfügung stellten. Er mußte an sein eigenes bequemes Bett in Kingsbridge denken und empfand es plötzlich als ungehörig, daß er sein Haupt auf Daunen bettete, während der Primas von England auf dem Boden schlief.

»Da wir gerade von Kathedralen sprechen«, sagte Thomas. »Wie gefiel Euch Sens?«

»Ein erstaunliches Bauwerk«, antwortete Philip. »Wer hat es errichtet?«

»William von Sens. Ich hoffe, ihn eines Tages nach Canterbury locken zu können. So setzt Euch doch. Berichtet mir von den Ereignissen in Kingsbridge.«

Philip erzählte ihm von Bischof Waleran und Erzdiakon Peter. Thomas folgte seinen Ausführungen mit großem Interesse und stellte eine Reihe kluger Fragen. Er war nicht nur charmant, sondern auch hochintelligent – anders wäre es ihm auch nie gelungen, in eine Stellung aufzusteigen, von der aus er einem der stärksten Könige, die England je hatte, Paroli bieten konnte. Unter der erzbischöflichen Robe, so hieß es, trug Thomas ein härenes Gewand – und hinter dem verbindlichen Äußeren verbarg sich ein eiserner Wille.

Als Philip seine Schilderung beendet hatte, sah der Erzbischof sehr ernst aus. »Dies darf nicht geschehen«, sagte er.

»Wohl wahr«, bestätigte Philip. Thomas' klares Wort machte ihm Mut. »Könnt Ihr es verhindern?«

»Nur, wenn ich wieder in mein Amt in Canterbury eingesetzt werde.«

Das war nicht die Antwort, die Philip sich erhofft hatte. »Könnt Ihr denn nicht an den Papst schreiben, von hier aus, meine ich?«

»Doch, das werde ich«, sagte Thomas. »Und zwar noch heute. Der Papst wird Peter nicht als Bischof von Kingsbridge anerkennen, das verspreche ich Euch. Aber wir können nicht verhindern, daß er sich im Bischofspalast einquartiert. Außerdem können wir keinen anderen Kandidaten ernennen.«

Philip war erschüttert von der Entschiedenheit, mit der Thomas ihm seine Illusionen raubte. Die ganze Reise über hatte er von der Hoffnung gezehrt, Thomas könne ihm einen Plan nennen, mit dem sich Walerans Strategie durchkreuzen ließe. Nun stellte sich heraus, daß selbst der brillante Thomas Becket nicht weiterwußte. Der einzige

Hoffnungsschimmer blieb seine Wiedereinsetzung in Canterbury, weil er dann natürlich gegen die königlichen Bischofskandidaten sein Veto einlegen könnte. »Besteht irgendeine Hoffnung auf Eure baldige Rückkehr?« fragte Philip niedergeschlagen.

»Bei einiger Zuversicht, ja«, erwiderte Thomas. »Der Papst hat einen Friedensvertrag ausgearbeitet und drängt sowohl mich als auch König Heinrich zur Zustimmung. Für mich sind die Bedingungen des Vertrags akzeptabel, denn meine Forderungen werden weitgehend erfüllt. Auch Heinrich sagt, er könne den Vertrag akzeptieren. Ich habe allerdings darauf bestanden, daß er seine Aufrichtigkeit unter Beweis stellen soll, indem er mir den Friedenskuß gibt. Und dazu ist er nicht bereit.« Die Stimme des Erzbischofs veränderte sich. Die natürlichen Höhen und Tiefen der Rede verflachten. Alle Lebhaftigkeit verschwand aus seiner Miene, und er wirkte auf einmal wie ein Priester, der einer gelangweilten Gemeinde die Tugend der Selbstentsagung predigt. Philip erkannte in seinem Ausdruck den Stolz und die Hartnäckigkeit des unermüdlichen Kämpfers. »Die Verweigerung des Friedenskusses«, fuhr Thomas fort, »ist für mich ein Zeichen dafür, daß er mich nach England zurücklocken und dann von den Bedingungen des Vertrags abrücken will.«

Philip nickte. Der Friedenskuß, der zum Ritual der Messe gehörte, war das Symbol des Vertrauens. Ohne ihn war kein Vertragswerk, vom Ehekontrakt bis zum Waffenstillstandsabkommen, vollständig. »Was kann ich tun?« sagte er, und die Frage war ebenso an Thomas wie an sich selbst gerichtet.

»Kehrt zurück nach England und werbt für mich und meine Sache«, antwortete der Erzbischof. »Schreibt Briefe an Eure Priorkollegen und an die Äbte. Schickt eine Delegation aus Kingsbridge zum Papst. Richtet eine Petition an den König. Predigt in Eurer berühmten Kathedrale, daß der höchste Priester des Landes vom König verstoßen worden ist.«

Philip nickte, obwohl er genau wußte, daß er nichts von alledem tun würde. Thomas forderte ihn unverblümt auf, sich der Opposition gegen den König anzuschließen. Das mochte der erzbischöflichen Kampfmoral Auftrieb geben, brachte aber für Kingsbridge überhaupt nichts.

Philip hatte eine bessere Idee. Wenn Heinrich und Thomas sich schon so nahegekommen waren, fehlte vielleicht nicht mehr viel, um sie endgültig zusammenzubringen. Darin liegt vielleicht eine kleine Chance, dachte Philip und war auf einmal wieder recht zuversichtlich.

Es war ein Strohhalm, an den er sich klammerte, aber er hatte nichts zu verlieren.

Schließlich stritten sich die beiden nur noch um einen Kuß.

Philip erschrak, als er sah, wie sehr sein Bruder gealtert war.

Francis' Haar war ergraut; er hatte ledrige Tränensäcke unter den Augen, und seine Gesichtshaut wirkte ausgetrocknet. Freilich war auch er inzwischen sechzig Jahre alt, und so durfte sein Aussehen wohl nicht allzusehr überraschen. Zudem waren seine Augen klar und heiter.

Philip merkte, daß es sein eigenes Alter war, das ihn so bestürzt hatte. So erging es ihm immer, wenn er seinen Bruder nach längerer Zeit wiedersah. Schon seit Jahren hatte Philip keinen Spiegel mehr zur Hand gehabt. Habe auch ich solche Tränensäcke? fragte er sich und tastete mit den Fingern über sein Gesicht. Die Frage ließ sich kaum beantworten.

»Nun, wie schmeckt die Arbeit bei Heinrich?« fragte Philip neugierig. Es gab niemanden, der nicht gerne erfahren hätte, wie es bei Königen privat zuging.

»Besser als bei Mathilde«, erwiderte Francis. »Sie war klüger, aber zu unaufrichtig. Heinrich ist sehr offen. Man erkennt immer gleich, woran man ist.«

Sie saßen im Kreuzgang des Klosters von Bayeux, in dem Philip untergekommen war. Der königliche Hof war in der Nähe einquartiert. Francis arbeitete seit über zwanzig Jahren für Heinrich. Er war inzwischen Leiter der Kanzlei, also jenen Amtes, dem die Ausfertigung aller königlichen Briefe und Urkunden oblag. Es war eine bedeutende Stellung mit großer Machtvollkommenheit.

»Offen?« fragte Philip. »Heinrich? Erzbischof Thomas ist da anderer Meinung.«

»Schon wieder so eine krasse Fehleinschätzung des Herrn Erzbischofs!« sagte Francis geringschätzig.

Philip war mit dieser verächtlichen Rede über den Erzbischof nicht einverstanden. »Thomas ist ein großer Mann«, sagte er.

»Thomas will Englands König sein«, gab Francis gereizt zurück.

»Und Heinrich anscheinend Erzbischof von Canterbury«, konterte Philip.

Erbost starrten sie einander in die Augen. Wenn *wir* uns schon streiten, dachte Philip, dann darf uns die bittere Auseinandersetzung zwischen Heinrich und Thomas nicht länger wundern. Er lächelte und sagte: »Nun, wir beide sollten uns darüber nicht den Schädel einschlagen.«

Francis' Miene entspannte sich. »Nein, natürlich nicht. Aber du darfst nicht vergessen, daß ich mich jetzt schon seit sechs Jahren mit diesem Streit herumquäle. Ich kann das nicht mehr so unvoreingenommen sehen wie du.«

Philip nickte. »Aber warum ist Heinrich nicht bereit, den Friedensvertrag des Papstes zu akzeptieren?«

»Er ist ja dazu bereit. Wir stehen ganz kurz vor der Versöhnung. Aber Thomas gibt sich damit nicht zufrieden. Er besteht auf dem Friedenskuß.«

»Was hindert den König daran, ihm zur Bestätigung den Friedenskuß zu geben – wenn er es denn aufrichtig meint?«

Francis hob die Stimme. »Das steht nicht im Plan!« sagte er gereizt.

»Na und wenn schon!«

Francis seufzte. »Er hätte ja im Grunde gar nichts dagegen. Das Problem ist nur folgendes: Er hat öffentlich geschworen, daß er Thomas niemals den Friedenskuß geben wird.«

»Es haben schon viele Könige Eide gebrochen«, wandte Philip ein.

»Schwache Könige, ja. Heinrich wird von einem öffentlich geleisteten Eid nicht abgehen. Das unterscheidet ihn eben von dem unglückseligen König Stephan.«

»Dann wäre es vielleicht besser, wenn die Kirche ihn nicht vom Gegenteil überzeugen wollte«, gestand Philip zögernd ein.

»Sag, warum besteht denn Thomas so hartnäckig auf diesem Kuß?« fragte Francis, neuerlich etwas gereizt.

»Weil er Heinrich nicht traut. Wer sagt denn, daß Heinrich sich an den Vertrag hält? Und was soll Thomas tun, wenn er's *nicht* täte? Soll er wieder ins Exil gehen? Seine Gefolgsleute stehen treu zu ihm, aber sie sind inzwischen müde. Thomas kann das nicht alles noch einmal durchmachen. Bevor er nachgibt, muß er eisenharte Garantien haben.«

Francis schüttelte traurig den Kopf. »Es ist zu einer Prestigefrage geworden«, sagte er. »Ich weiß genau, daß Heinrich nicht die Absicht hat, Thomas zu hintergehen. Aber er läßt sich nicht zwingen.«

»Ich glaube, bei Thomas ist es genauso«, sagte Philip. »Er hat nun einmal die Forderung nach dieser symbolischen Handlung gestellt und kann nun keinen Rückzieher mehr machen.« Er schüttelte resignierend den Kopf. Das Problem schien unlösbar.

»Das Verrückte an der Sache ist ja, daß Heinrich Thomas ohne weiteres küssen würde – aber erst *nach* der Versöhnung«, sagte Francis. »Er ist bloß nicht bereit, es als Vorbedingung zu akzeptieren.«

»Hat er das wirklich gesagt?« fragte Philip.

»Ja.«

»Aber dann sieht die Sache doch schon wieder ganz anders aus!« rief Philip aus. »Was hat er denn genau gesagt?«

»Er sagte: ›Ich küss' ihn auf den Mund, ich küss' ihm die Füße, und ich hör' mir seine Messe an – *nach* seiner Rückkehr.‹ Ich war dabei, als er es sagte.«

»Das werde ich Thomas berichten.«

»Meinst du denn, er ist damit einverstanden?« fragte Francis aufgeregt.

»Ich weiß es nicht.« Philip wagte es kaum zu hoffen. »Es ist ja eigentlich nur ein ganz kleiner Schritt zurück … Er bekommt seinen Kuß – nur eben ein wenig später, als er wollte.«

»Für Heinrich ist es auch nur ein kleiner Schritt«, sagte Francis mit wachsender Erregung. »Er gibt den Kuß – aber freiwillig, nicht unter Zwang. Bei Gott, ja – das könnte klappen!«

»Die Versöhnung könnte in Canterbury stattfinden. Die Bedingungen des Vertrages sollten vorher bekanntgegeben werden, so daß keine Seite im letzten Augenblick noch Änderungen verlangen kann. Thomas kann die Messe lesen, und Heinrich kann ihm dann, gleich dort in der Kathedrale, den Kuß geben.« Und dann, fügte Philip in Gedanken hinzu, kann Thomas Walerans böse Pläne durchkreuzen.

»Ich werde es dem König vorschlagen«, sagte Francis.

»Und ich schlage es dem Erzbischof vor.«

Die Klosterglocke läutete. Die beiden Brüder standen auf.

»Versuch, ihn zu überzeugen«, sagte Philip. »Wenn es klappt, kann Thomas nach Canterbury zurückkehren – und Waleran Bigod ist ein für allemal erledigt.«

Sie trafen sich auf einer schönen Wiese am Ufer eines Flusses, der die Grenze zwischen der Normandie und dem Königreich Frankreich bildete, unweit der Städtchen Fréteval und Vievy-le-Raye. Als Thomas in Begleitung von Erzbischof William von Sens eintraf, warteten König Heinrich und seine Entourage bereits auf ihn. Philip, der zu Thomas' Delegation gehörte, erblickte seinen Bruder Francis auf der anderen Seite der Wiese neben König Heinrich.

Heinrich und Thomas hatten sich geeinigt – in der Theorie.

Beide hatten den Kompromißvorschlag akzeptiert: Der Friedenskuß sollte nach Beckets Rückkehr anläßlich einer Versöhnungsmesse stattfinden. Als besiegelt konnte die Übereinkunft allerdings erst gelten, wenn die beiden miteinander gesprochen hatten.

Thomas gebot seinen Leuten stehenzubleiben und ritt allein ins Zentrum der Wiese. Heinrich tat das gleiche. Die Begleiter sahen mit angehaltenem Atem zu.

Die beiden unterhielten sich mehrere Stunden lang.

Niemand konnte verstehen, was sie im einzelnen sagten, doch jeder konnte es ahnen. Sie sprachen über Heinrichs Attacken gegen die Kirche, den Ungehorsam der englischen Bischöfe gegenüber Thomas, die umstrittenen Konstitutionen von Clarendon, die Exilzeit des Erzbischofs, die Rolle des Papstes ... Anfangs hatte Philip befürchtet, sie könnten in Streit geraten und in größerer Feindschaft denn je auseinandergehen. Schon einmal hatten sie kurz vor einer Vereinbarung gestanden und sich unter ähnlichen Bedingungen getroffen ... Bei irgendeinem Punkt waren sie sich uneinig gewesen, hatten sich in ihrem Stolz verletzt gefühlt; es war zu harten Worten gekommen, und schließlich waren sie davongestürmt und hatten einander Kompromißlosigkeit vorgeworfen.

Doch diesmal war es anders. Je länger die Unterredung dauerte, desto mehr wuchs Philips Zuversicht. Wenn einer von beiden es auf einen Eklat abgesehen hätte, so war der geeignete Zeitpunkt dafür längst verstrichen.

Der heiße Sommernachmittag kühlte langsam ab, und die Schatten der Ulmen über dem Fluß wurden immer länger. Die Spannung war unerträglich.

Da endlich geschah etwas. Thomas bewegte sich.

Wollte er fortreiten? Nein. Er stieg vom Pferd. Was hat das zu bedeuten? fragte sich Philip und hielt den Atem an. Thomas ging auf Heinrich zu und fiel vor den Füßen des Königs auf die Knie.

Nun saß auch der König ab. Er schloß Thomas in die Arme.

Die Höflinge auf beiden Seiten brachen in Jubel aus und warfen ihre Hüte in die Luft.

Philip traten die Tränen in die Augen. Der Streit war beigelegt – durch Vernunft und guten Willen. So sollte es sein.

Vielleicht war es ein Omen für die Zukunft.

Es war Weihnachten, und der König tobte vor Wut.

William Hamleigh fürchtete sich. Er hatte bisher nur einen Menschen von vergleichbarem Temperament gekannt, und das war seine Mutter. König Heinrich in seinem Zorn war fast genauso furchterregend wie sie.

Schon von Natur aus war er eine respektheischende Persönlichkeit, mit seinen breiten Schultern, dem mächtigen Brustkorb und dem unverhältnismäßig großen Kopf. Geriet er jedoch in Rage, so färbte sich sein sommersprossiges Gesicht tiefrot, und die blaugrauen Augen zeigten sich plötzlich blutunterlaufen. Wie ein wütender Bär in Gefangenschaft schritt der ohnehin rastlose Mann im Zimmer auf und ab.

Sie befanden sich in Bur-le-Roi, einer Jagdhütte des Königs in einem weitläufigen Park unweit der normannischen Küste. Eigentlich hätte Heinrich hier glücklich sein müssen, liebte er doch die Jagd über alles. Aber er war nicht glücklich. Er tobte vor Wut. Und die Ursache seines Zorns war Erzbischof Thomas von Canterbury.

»Thomas, Thomas, Thomas! Ich höre nur noch Thomas von Euch verteufelten Prälaten! Thomas tut dies, Thomas tut das, Thomas hat Euch beleidigt, Thomas hat Euch ungerecht behandelt! Mir reicht's jetzt, endgültig!«

William musterte verstohlen die Gesichter der Grafen, Bischöfe und anderen Würdenträger, die um die festlich gedeckte Weihnachtstafel versammelt waren. Die meisten fühlten sich sichtlich unwohl in ihrer Haut. Nur einer wirkte rundum zufrieden: Waleran Bigod.

Waleran hatte vorausgesagt, daß Heinrich und Thomas schon bald wieder aneinandergeraten würden. Der Sieg des Erzbischofs sei zu deutlich ausgefallen, meinte er. Der Friedensplan des Papstes habe dem König zu viele Zugeständnisse abverlangt; die Einforderung der königlichen Versprechen durch Thomas müsse zwangsläufig zu neuen Auseinandersetzungen führen. Waleran hatte sich freilich nicht damit begnügt, den Lauf der Dinge abzuwarten, sondern nach Kräften dazu beigetragen, daß seine Prophezeiungen sich auch erfüllten. Mit Williams Hilfe hatte er dafür gesorgt, daß dem König eine unablässige Flut von Beschwerden vorgelegt wurde, die allesamt Thomas Beckets Verhalten seit seiner Rückkehr nach England zum Inhalt hatten: Es hieß, er ziehe mit einer Ritterschar durchs Land, suche seine Spießgesellen auf und hecke ein Komplett nach dem anderen aus; auch nehme er Rache an Klerikern, die während seines Exils den König unterstützt hätten. Waleran schmückte diese Berichte aus, bevor er sie an den König weitergab, doch enthielten sie alle ein Körnchen Wahrheit. Waleran blies damit Wind in ein schon loderndes Feuer. All jene, die sich während des sechsjährigen Streits von Thomas losgesagt hatten und nun seine Vergeltung fürchteten, waren nun mit Eifer dabei, ihn beim König zu verleumden.

Waleran hatte also guten Grund, sich über die Wut des Königs zu freuen, aber er hatte auch hoch gereizt. Denn niemand hatte seit der Rückkehr des Erzbischofs soviel Anlaß zur Sorge wie er. Thomas hatte sich geweigert, Walerans Nominierung zum Bischof von Lincoln zu unterstützen, gleichzeitig aber Prior Philip zum neuen Bischof von Kingsbridge vorgeschlagen. Wenn er sich damit durchsetzte, hätte Waleran Kingsbridge verloren und Lincoln nicht gewonnen. Er wäre ruiniert.

Auch Williams Stellung war gefährdet. Mit Aliena als *de-facto*-Gräfin, Philip als Bischof und Jonathan als Prior hätte er in der Grafschaft keinen Verbündeten mehr. Aus diesem Grund hatte er sich Waleran angeschlossen und mit ihm am Königshof gegen den ohnehin auf wackligen Füßen stehenden Friedensvertrag zwischen Heinrich und Thomas intrigiert.

Die gebratenen Schwäne, Gänse, Pfauen und Enten auf dem Tisch waren nahezu unangetastet. Um seinen galligen Magen zu beruhigen, mümmelte William, der gemeinhin herzhaft aß und viel trank, an einem Stück Trockenbrot und nippte am Posset, einem mit Bier, Eiern und Muskat gewürzten Molkentrank.

Der unmittelbare Anlaß für Heinrichs Zorn war die Nachricht, daß Thomas eine Delegation zu Papst Alexander nach Tours geschickt hatte, die über angebliche Verstöße des Königs gegen den Friedensvertrag Beschwerde führen sollte. Einer der älteren Berater des Königs, Enjuger de Bohun, sagte: »Wahren Frieden wird es erst geben, wenn Ihr Thomas habt exekutieren lassen.«

William war entsetzt.

Heinrich, der inzwischen wieder Platz genommen hatte, brüllte: »Jawohl, so ist es!«

Für William war klar, daß Heinrich die Bemerkung eher als Ausdruck des Pessimismus denn als ernsthaften Vorschlag aufgefaßt hatte. Enjuger dagegen hatte nach Williams Dafürhalten den Satz nicht einfach so dahergesagt.

»Als ich auf dem Rückweg von Jerusalem durch Rom kam«, warf William Malvoisin gelangweilt ein, »hörte ich, daß man dort sogar schon einen Papst wegen unerträglicher Anmaßung exekutiert hat. Verflucht, daß mir sein Name gerade nicht einfallen will …«

»Es scheint, daß im Fall Thomas Beckets gar keine andere Lösung *möglich* ist«, bemerkte der Erzbischof von York. »Solange er am Leben ist, wird er zu Hause wie in der Fremde Aufruhr schüren.«

Nach Williams Eindruck waren die drei Bemerkungen sorgsam aufeinander abgestimmt. Als nächster meldete sich Waleran zu Wort: »An Thomas' Anstandsgefühl zu appellieren, ist gewiß zwecklos ...«, begann er.

»Ruhe!« brüllte der König. »Schweigt stille, ihr hundsföttisches Pack! Ununterbrochen jammert und klagt ihr – wann endlich kriegt ihr eure Ärsche hoch und *tut* etwas?« Er trank einen Schluck Bier. »Das Bier schmeckt wie Pisse!« röhrte er außer sich, schob seinen Stuhl zurück und stürmte – während alle Anwesenden sich hastig erhoben – zur Tür hinaus.

In das betroffene Schweigen hinein sagte Waleran: »Deutlicher könnte die Botschaft wohl kaum sein, meine Herren. Wir müssen endlich etwas gegen Thomas unternehmen.«

William Mandeville, Graf von Essex, sagte: »Ich glaube, wir sollten eine Delegation zu Thomas schicken und ihn zur Vernunft bringen.«

»Und was wollt Ihr tun, wenn er sich nicht zur Vernunft bringen läßt?« fragte Waleran.

»Dann sollten wir ihn im Namen des Königs festnehmen.«

Mehrere Herren begannen nun gleichzeitig zu reden, und die Versammlung löste sich in kleine Gruppen auf. Die Gefolgsleute des Grafen von Essex beratschlagten über die Entsendung der Delegation. Waleran unterhielt sich mit zwei oder drei jungen Rittern. Dann sah er sich nach William um und winkte ihn zu sich.

»William Mandevilles Delegation bringt uns nichts. Thomas erledigt sie mit links.«

Reginald Fitzurse sah William entschlossen an und sagte: »Einige von uns meinen, die Zeit sei reif für härtere Maßnahmen.«

»Was soll das heißen?«

»Ihr habt gehört, was Enjuger gesagt hat.«

»Exekutieren!« rief Richard le Bret, ein junger Mann von vielleicht achtzehn Jahren.

William wurde kalt ums Herz. Sie meinten es also ernst. Er starrte Waleran an. »Werdet Ihr den König um seinen Segen bitten?«

»Unmöglich«, sagte Reginald. »So etwas kann er nicht im voraus sanktionieren.« Er grinste böse. »Aber er kann seine treuen Diener *danach* belohnen.«

»Nun, William – macht Ihr mit?« fragte der junge Richard.

»Ich weiß nicht recht ...« William war erregt, fürchtete sich aber auch. »Ich muß mir das noch einmal durch den Kopf gehen lassen.«

»Dazu haben wir keine Zeit«, sagte Reginald. »Wir müssen uns sofort auf den Weg machen. Wir müssen vor William Mandeville in Canterbury sein, sonst kommen er und seine Bande uns noch in die Quere.«

Waleran wandte sich an William. »Sie brauchen einen älteren, erfahrenen Führer, der ihnen zeigt, wie man's macht«, sagte er.

Nur allzugern hätte William zugestimmt: Alle seine Sorgen konnten mit einem Schlag gelöst werden – und vielleicht gab ihm der König sogar wieder eine Grafschaft. »Aber die Ermordung eines Erzbischofs muß doch eine furchtbare Sünde sein«, sagte er.

»Zerbrecht Euch darüber nicht den Kopf«, erwiderte Waleran. »Ich erteile Euch die Absolution.«

Die Attentäter machten sich auf den Weg nach England. Wie eine Gewitterwolke lastete die Ungeheuerlichkeit ihres Vorhabens über William. Er konnte an nichts anderes mehr denken. Er hatte keinen Hunger und fand keinen Schlaf. Er handelte geistesabwesend und redete wirres Zeug. Als das Schiff in Dover anlegte, war er drauf und dran, den Plan abzublasen.

Drei Tage nach Weihnachten, an einem Montagabend, erreichten sie Saltwood Castle in Kent. Die Burg gehörte dem Erzbischof von Canterbury, war jedoch während dessen Exil von Ranulf de Broc besetzt worden, der nun die Rückgabe verweigerte. Zu den Beschwerden, die Thomas dem Papst vortragen ließ, gehörte unter anderem Heinrichs Versäumnis, ihm Saltwood Castle zurückzugeben.

Ranulf erfüllte William mit neuem Mut.

Er hatte während der Abwesenheit des Erzbischofs in der Grafschaft Kent ähnlich gehaust wie William weiland in Shiring und wollte seine Willkürherrschaft um jeden Preis erhalten. Der Mordplan erfüllte ihn mit Begeisterung. Er war sofort bereit mitzumachen und stürzte sich mit Feuereifer in die Details der Planung. Seine Art, Nägel mit Köpfen zu machen, vertrieb den Nebel aus Aberglauben und Angst, der sich auf Williams Gemüt gelegt hatte. Er sah sich schon wieder als Graf, der tun und lassen konnte, was er wollte.

Fast die ganze Nacht über hockten sie beisammen und besprachen die Einzelheiten ihres Plans. Ranulf ritzte mit seinem Messer einen Lageplan der Kathedrale, des Klosters und des Bischofspalasts in die Tischplatte. Die Klostergebäude befanden sich nördlich der Kirche. Das war ungewöhnlich; normalerweise lagen sie – wie in Kingsbridge – auf der Südseite. Der erzbischöfliche Palast grenzte im Nordwesten an die Kirche und war über den Küchenhof zu erreichen. Gleich zu Beginn der Vorbereitungen hatte Ranulf berittene Boten zu seinen in Dover, Rochester und Bletchingley stationierten Truppen geschickt. Die Ritter erhielten den Befehl, sich am nächsten Morgen an der Straße nach Canterbury einzufinden.

Als die Verschwörer sich endlich aufs Lager warfen, um wenigstens noch ein oder zwei Stunden Schlaf zu bekommen, dämmerte bereits der Morgen herauf.

Der Schmerz in Williams Beinen brannte nach der langen Reise wie Feuer. Dies wird hoffentlich mein letzter militärischer Einsatz sein, dachte er. Ich gehe wohl aufs fünfundfünfzigste Jahr zu. Ich bin zu alt für so etwas ...

Trotz seiner Müdigkeit und des Zuspruchs, den er von seiten Ranulfs erfahren hatte, fand er keinen Schlaf. Die Ermordung eines Erzbischofs erschien ihm nach wie vor als furchtbare Sünde, obgleich ihm Absolution bereits zugesichert worden war. Wenn ich einschlafe, kommen die Alpträume, dachte er und tat kein Auge zu.

Sie hatten einen hervorragenden Angriffsplan ersonnen. Er würde natürlich schiefgehen – *etwas* ging bei solchen Sachen ja immer schief. Es kam darauf an, flexibel genug zu sein, um auch mit Unerwartetem fertig zu werden. Aber was konnte schon viel geschehen? Eine Handvoll verweichlichter Mönche war kein ernstzunehmender Gegner für eine kampferprobte Truppe.

Durch die schießschartenartigen Fenster sickerte das trübe Licht eines grauen Wintermorgens. William erhob sich und wollte das Morgengebet sprechen, doch es kam ihm kein Wort über die Lippen.

Auch die anderen waren schon früh wieder auf. Gemeinsam frühstückten sie im großen Saal. Außer William und Ranulf waren dabei: Reginald Fitzurse, den William zum Anführer des Kommandos bestellt hatte; Richard le Bret, der Jüngste der Gruppe; William Tracy, der Älteste, und Hugh Morville, der Hochrangigste.

Sie legten ihre Rüstungen an und bestiegen Pferde aus Ranulfs Stall. Es war ein bitterkalter Tag. Düstere graue Wolken bedeckten den Himmel. Es sah nach Schnee aus. Sie folgten einer alten Straße, die unter dem Namen Stone Street bekannt war. Auf dem zweieinhalbstündigen Ritt gesellten sich einige Ritter zu ihnen.

Der Haupttreffpunkt war die Abtei Saint Augustine außerhalb der Stadt. Der Abt war, wie Ranulf William versichert hatte, ein alter Feind des Erzbischofs. William blieb dennoch vorsichtig und gab vor, man wolle Thomas nur festnehmen. Sie hatten vor, die Maske erst im letzten Augenblick fallenzulassen, auch vor den eigenen Leuten: Das wahre Ziel des Unternehmens kannten außer William nur noch Ranulf und die vier Ritter, die aus Frankreich mit herübergekommen waren.

Sie erreichten die Abtei gegen Mittag. Die von Ranulf herbeibefohlenen Männer warteten bereits auf sie. Der Abt ließ ihnen ein Mahl auftragen. Der Wein war ausgezeichnet, und sie ließen ihn sich schmecken. Ranulf gab den Bewaffneten, die die Domfreiheit umstellen und alle Fluchtversuche vereiteln sollten, die entsprechenden Anweisungen.

William schauderte, obwohl er unmittelbar neben der Feuerstelle im Gästehaus stand. Es war im Grunde eine einfache Angelegenheit – mit der Einschränkung, daß ein Fehlschlag wahrscheinlich mit dem Tode bestraft wurde. Der König würde schon eine Möglichkeit finden, die Ermordung Thomas Beckets zu rechtfertigen. Einen *versuchten* Mord könnte er dagegen nie gutheißen: Er würde jegliche Mitwisserschaft von sich weisen und die Frevler aufhängen lassen. William hatte in seiner Eigenschaft als Vogt von Shiring zahlreiche Menschen an den Galgen gebracht, doch die Vorstellung, selber am Ende des Stricks zu baumeln, ließ ihn ein ums andere Mal erzittern.

Er wandte seine Gedanken der Grafschaft zu, die er sich beim erfolgreichen Verlauf des Unternehmens erhoffen konnte. Es wäre zu schön, den Lebensabend als Graf verbringen zu können, als respektierter und gefürchteter Mann, dem widerspruchslos gehorcht wurde. Wenn Richard, Alienas Bruder, im Heiligen Land ums Leben kommen sollte, wird König Heinrich mir vielleicht sogar wieder Shiring geben, dachte er, und diese Hoffnung wärmte ihn mehr als das Feuer.

Als sie die Abtei wieder verließen, war der Trupp zu einer kleinen Armee angewachsen. Dennoch hatten sie keinerlei Schwierigkeiten, in die Stadt Canterbury hineinzukommen. Ranulf hatte diesen Teil des Landes sechs Jahre lang kontrolliert und seine Autorität bislang noch nicht preisgegeben. Noch galt sein Wort mehr als das des Erzbischofs (ein weiterer Grund für Thomas' bittere Klage vor dem Papst).

Kaum waren die Reiter in der Stadt, da schwärmten sie auch schon aus, umstellten das Gelände von Kloster und Kathedrale und versperrten alle Ausgänge.

Die Aktion hatte begonnen. Bis zu diesem Augenblick wäre es – zumindest theoretisch – noch möglich gewesen, die ganze Sache abzublasen. Doch nun waren die Würfel gefallen.

William überließ Ranulf das Kommando über die Blockade und sammelte eine klar Schar von Rittern und Bewaffneten um sich. Die Ritter teilte er in zwei Gruppen auf. Die größere Gruppe schickte er in ein Haus auf der anderen Seite des Durchgangs zum Domplatz, die kleinere begleitete ihn auf seinem Weg durchs Tor. Reginald Fitzurse und die drei anderen Verschwörer ritten in den Küchenhof, als seien sie offizielle Besucher und keine bewaffneten Eindringlinge. William jedoch stürmte das Torhaus und bedrohte den entsetzten Pförtner mit dem Schwert in der Hand.

Der Angriff nahm seinen Lauf.

William klopfte das Herz bis zum Hals. Er befahl einem seiner Bewaffneten, den Pförtner zu fesseln, ließ die anderen Männer ins Torhaus kommen und schloß das Tor. Nun konnte niemand mehr hinein oder hinaus. Er hielt jetzt ein Kloster mit Waffengewalt besetzt.

Dann folgte er den vier Verschwörern in den Küchenhof, der im Norden von den Ställen begrenzt wurde. Die vier hatten allerdings ihre Pferde dort nicht untergebracht, sondern mitten im Hof an einen Maulbeerbaum gebunden. Sie legten ihre Schwertgurte ab und setzten die Helme auf: Sie wollten die Fassade des Freundschaftsbesuchs noch ein wenig länger aufrechterhalten.

William holte sie ein und legte seine Waffen unter den Baum. Reginald sah ihn fragend an. »Alles in Ordnung«, sagte William. »Das Gelände ist isoliert.«

Über den Hof gingen sie auf den Bischofspalast zu. William hieß einen Ritter namens Richard, der aus der Umgebung stammte, im Portal Wache stehen. Die anderen betraten den großen Saal.

Das bischöfliche Personal saß gerade beim Essen. Das besagte, daß Thomas sowie den Priestern und Mönchen in seiner Begleitung bereits serviert worden war. Ein Diener erhob sich. Reginald sagte: »Wir sind die Männer des Königs.«

Die Gespräche verstummten. Der Diener, der aufgestanden war, sagte: »Willkommen, meine Herren. Ich bin der Haushofmeister des Palastes, William Fitzneal. Tretet ein. Darf ich Euch etwas zu essen anbieten?«

Der Kerl ist auffallend freundlich, dachte William, und das, obwohl sein Heer und der König so zerstritten sind. Vielleicht kann man ihn kaufen ...

»Ich danke Euch, nein, wir brauchen nichts zu essen«, antwortete Reginald.

»Wie wär's, nach der langen Reise, mit einem Becher Wein?«

»Wir haben eine Botschaft an Euern Herrn«, sagte Reginald ungeduldig. »Vom König. Bitte gebt ihm sofort Bescheid.«

»Sehr wohl.« Der Haushofmeister verbeugte sich. Da die Besucher nicht bewaffnet waren, hatte er keinen Grund, ihr Ansinnen zurückzuweisen. Er verließ den Tisch und begab sich zur Treppe.

William und seine vier Ritter folgten ihm, ihrerseits verfolgt von den Blicken der schweigenden Dienerschaft. William zitterte wie immer vor Beginn einer Schlacht. Hoffentlich dauert es jetzt nicht mehr so lange, dachte er. Ich fühle mich besser, sobald der Kampf losgeht ...

Sie stiegen die Treppe hinauf und gelangten in ein geräumiges Empfangszimmer. Die Wände waren mit Bänken gesäumt, und auf einer Seite stand in der Mitte ein großer Thron. Mehrere schwarzgewandete Priester und Mönche saßen auf den Bänken, doch der Thron war leer.

Der Haushofmeister durchquerte das Zimmer und blieb an einer geöffneten Tür stehen. »Botschafter vom König, hochehrwürdiger Erzbischof«, sagte er mit lauter Stimme.

Eine hörbare Antwort blieb aus. Doch offensichtlich hatte der Erzbischof sich mit einem Handzeichen verständlich gemacht, denn der Haushofmeister hieß die Gäste eintreten.

Thomas Becket, gekleidet in den erzbischöflichen Ornat, saß auf der Bettkante. Zu seinen Füßen saß ein Mönch und lauschte seinen Worten. Verblüfft erkannte William, daß es sich um Prior Philip von Kingsbridge handelte. Was hat denn der hier zu suchen? dachte er. Wahrscheinlich buhlt er um des Erzbischofs Gunst ... Philip war bereits zum Bischof von Kingsbridge gewählt worden, doch fehlte ihm noch die Bestätigung. Daraus wird jetzt nichts mehr, dachte William voller Ingrimm.

Philip war über Williams Erscheinen nicht minder überrascht. Indessen reagierte Thomas gar nicht auf die Gäste, sondern sprach ruhig weiter, als habe er sie nicht gesehen. Diese Unhöflichkeit ist reine Berechnung, dachte William. Die Ritter nahmen auf den niedrigen Bänken und Hockern Platz, die vor und hinter dem Bett standen. William hielt das für ungut: Auf diese Weise wurde die Attacke zum Besuch, der Impetus ging verloren. Vielleicht lag genau dies in Thomas' Absicht.

Endlich blickte der Erzbischof auf. Er erhob sich nicht zum Gruß. Bis auf William waren sie ihm alle persönlich bekannt. Sein Blick kam auf Hugh Morville, dem Höchstrangigen, zu ruhen. »Ah, Hugh«, sagte er.

William hatte Reginald mit dem Kommando betraut, und deshalb ergriff nun dieser – und nicht Hugh – das Wort. »Wir kommen aus der Normandie, vom König. Wollt Ihr seine Botschaft öffentlich oder unter vier Augen hören?«

Thomas blickte gereizt von einem zum anderen, als empfinde er es als Zumutung, mit einem untergeordneten Mitglied der Delegation verhandeln zu müssen. Seufzend sagte er: »Laßt mich allein, Philip.«

Philip stand auf und ging mit besorgter Miene an den Rittern vorbei zum Ausgang.

»Aber laßt die Tür offen!« rief Thomas ihm nach.

Als Philip fort war, sagte Reginald: »Ich ersuche Euch im Namen des Königs, Euch nach Winchester zu verfügen und dort zu der gegen Euch erhobenen Anklage Stellung zu nehmen.«

William hatte das Vergnügen, Thomas Becket erbleichen zu sehen. »Das also habt Ihr vor«, sagte der Erzbischof ruhig und sah auf. Der Haushofmeister drückte sich an der Tür herum.

»Schickt alle Wartenden herein. Ich möchte, daß jeder es hört.«

Die Mönche und Priester, unter ihnen Prior Philip, kamen herein. Einige setzten sich, andere nahmen an den Wänden Aufstellung. William hatte nichts einzuwenden – ganz im Gegenteil: je mehr Leute anwesend waren, desto besser, bestand das Ziel dieser Begegnung ohne Waffen doch darin, vor Zeugen zu demonstrieren, daß Thomas sich einem königlichen Erlaß widersetzte.

Als alle einen Platz gefunden hatten, wandte sich Thomas wieder an Reginald. »Noch einmal«, sagte er.

»Ich ersuche Euch im Namen des Königs, Euch nach Winchester zu verfügen und dort zu der gegen Euch erhobenen Anklage Stellung zu nehmen«, wiederholte Reginald.

»Was wirft man mir vor?« fragte Thomas ruhig.

»Verrat!«

Thomas schüttelte den Kopf. »Heinrich wird mich nicht vor Gericht stellen«, sagte er ruhig. »Gott weiß, daß ich keine Verbrechen begangen habe.«

»Ihr habt treue Diener des Königs exkommuniziert.«

»Das war nicht ich, sondern der Papst.«

»Ihr habt mehrere Bischöfe suspendiert.«

»Ich habe angeboten, sie auf dem Gnadenwege wieder einzusetzen. Das haben sie abgelehnt. Mein Angebot halte ich aufrecht.«

»Ihr habt die Thronfolge gefährdet, indem Ihr die Krönung des Königssohnes mißachtet habt.«

»Das habe ich nicht getan. Der Erzbischof von York darf überhaupt niemanden krönen. Dazu fehlt ihm das Recht. Der Papst hat ihn ob dieser Unverfrorenheit gerügt. Die Gültigkeit der Krönung hat kein Mensch in Frage gestellt.«

Reginald verlor die Geduld. »Das eine ergibt sich aus dem anderen, verdammter Narr, der Ihr seid.«

»Mir reicht es jetzt!« rief Thomas.

»Und uns reicht es auch, Thomas Becket!« brüllte Reginald. »Bei den Wunden Gottes, wir haben genug von Euch, Eurer Anmaßung, Eurer Unruhestifterei, Eurem Verrat ...«

Thomas stand auf. »Die bischöflichen Burgen sind von Gefolgsleuten des Königs besetzt!« schrie er. »Der erzbischöfliche Pachtzins wird vom König eingetrieben. Dem Erzbischof selbst befiehlt man, die Stadt Canterbury nicht zu verlassen. Und da sagt Ihr mir, *Ihr* hättet genug?«

Ein Priester versuchte zu intervenieren. »Ehrwürdiger Bischof«, sagte er zu Thomas, »laßt uns die Angelegenheit im kleinen Kreise besprechen.«

»Warum?« gab Thomas erregt zurück. »Diese Herren hier verlangen etwas von mir, das ich weder tun darf noch tun werde.«

Der Lärm hatte inzwischen den gesamten Bischofspalast alarmiert. Vor der Tür des bischöflichen Gemachs drängten sich die Neugierigen und spitzten die Ohren. Der Wortwechsel hat lang genug gedauert, dachte William. Keiner der Anwesenden kann abstreiten, daß Thomas einen Befehl des Königs mißachtet hat ... Er gab Reginald ein verstecktes Zeichen. Philip bemerkte es und runzelte überrascht die Stirn, ließ sich doch aus der Geste entnehmen, daß nicht Reginald, sondern William der eigentliche Anführer der Gruppe war.

»Erzbischof Thomas«, sagte Reginald feierlich, »Ihr genießt nicht länger Frieden und Schutz des Königs.« Er drehte sich um und befahl den Zuschauern: »Verlaßt diesen Raum.«

Niemand rührte sich.

»Im Namen des Königs befehle ich den hier versammelten Mönchen, den Erzbischof zu bewachen und jeden Fluchtversuch zu vereiteln.«

Es war klar, daß die Angesprochenen sich nicht daran halten würden. Aber das lag auch gar nicht in Williams Absicht. Er wollte Thomas vielmehr zu einem Fluchtversuch provozieren – auf der Flucht ließ er sich leichter töten.

Reginald wandte sich an den Haushofmeister, William Fitzneal, der von Amts wegen auch Leibwächter des Erzbischofs war. »Ihr seid festgenommen«, sagte er, packte den Mann am Arm und führte ihn zur Tür hinaus. Der Haushofmeister leistete keinerlei Widerstand. William und die anderen Ritter folgten ihnen.

Über die Treppen ging es hinunter und durch den großen Saal ins Freie. Ritter Richard stand noch immer im Portal Wache. William überlegte, was sie mit dem Haushofmeister anstellen sollten. »Bist du auf unserer Seite?« fragte er ihn.

Der Mann war außer sich vor Angst. »Ja, wenn Ihr auf seiten des Königs steht.«

Der hat die Hosen so voll, daß er keinen Schaden mehr anrichtet, dachte William. Ganz egal, auf welcher Seite er steht … An Richard gewandt, sagte er: »Paß auf ihn auf und halte die Eingangstür verschlossen. Niemand darf das Gebäude verlassen.«

Sie rannten über den Hof zum Maulbeerbaum und legten hastig Helme und Schwerter an. Jetzt wird es geschehen, dachte William voller Furcht, jetzt werden wir den Erzbischof von Canterbury töten, o mein Gott … Es war lange her, daß er einen Helm getragen hatte, und der Rand des Hals und Schultern schützenden Kettenpanzers kam ihm immer wieder in die Quere. Er verfluchte seine ungeschickten Finger. Ausgerechnet jetzt hatte er keine Zeit, so lange herumzufummeln. Da bemerkte er einen Jungen, der ihn mit offenem Mund anstarrte, und rief ihm zu: »He, du da! Wie heißt du?«

Der Junge sah sich nach der Küche um. Sollte er fliehen oder Williams Frage beantworten? Nach einer kurzen Pause sagte er: »Robert, Herr. Man nennt mich Robert Pipe.«

»Komm her, Robert Pipe, hilf mir mal schnell!«

Der Junge zögerte erneut.

William verlor die Geduld. »Komm sofort her, oder ich hack' dir mit meinem Schwert die Hand ab, das schwör' ich dir beim Blute des Herrn!«

Widerstrebend trat der Junge näher. William hieß ihn den Kettenpanzer hochhalten, setzte seinen Helm auf und befestigte ihn. Diesmal klappte es. Robert Pipe machte, daß er davonkam. Davon wird er seinen Enkelkindern noch erzählen, dachte William bei sich.

Der Helm besaß ein Visier, das über das Gesicht gezogen und mit einem Riemen befestigt werden konnte. Die anderen hatten die Visiere bereits heruntergeklappt und waren nicht mehr erkennbar. William wartete noch einen Augenblick. Alle hielten sie in der einen Hand ein Schwert, in der anderen eine Axt.

»Fertig?« fragte William.

Sie nickten.

Von nun an erübrigten sich weitere Gespräche. Keine weiteren Befehle waren nötig, keine weiteren Entscheidungen zu treffen. Zurück in den Palast und den Erzbischof töten – das war jetzt ihre Devise.

William steckte zwei Finger in den Mund und stieß einen schrillen Pfiff aus.

Dann schloß er das Visier seines Helms und zurrte es fest.

Ein Bewaffneter kam aus dem Torhaus gerannt und öffnete hastig das Haupttor.

Die Ritter, die William im Haus auf der gegenüberliegenden Seite hatte warten lassen, stürmten nun auf den Hof und riefen, getreu der Instruktion, die man ihnen erteilt hatte: »Soldaten des Königs! Soldaten des Königs!«

William rannte zum Palast zurück.

Ritter Richard und Haushofmeister William Fitzneal öffneten ihm die Tür des Portals, doch als er eintrat, nutzten zwei Diener des Erzbischofs den Umstand, daß die beiden einen Augenblick lang abgelenkt waren, und schmetterten die Tür zu, die das Portal mit dem großen Saal verband.

William warf sich mit seinem ganzen Gewicht gegen die Tür, doch es war zu spät – sie war von innen mit einer Stange verriegelt worden. Er fluchte. Ein Rückschlag – und schon so bald! Die Ritter begannen, mit ihren Äxten auf die Tür einzuhacken, kamen aber kaum voran – schließlich war die schwere Tür eigens zu dem Zweck gezimmert, Angreifer zurückzuhalten.

William spürte, daß ihm die Kontrolle über das Unternehmen entglitt. Er kämpfte eine beginnende Panik nieder, verließ den Palast und rannte um das Haus herum. Vielleicht gab es irgendwo noch eine zweite Tür. Reginald begleitete ihn.

Auf der Südseite des Gebäudes grenzte eine Obstbaumwiese an. Und dort befand sich tatsächlich eine Außentreppe, die zum ersten Stock hinaufführte. William grunzte vor Freude. Es sah ganz nach einem separaten Eingang zu den erzbischöflichen Gemächern aus. Das Gefühl der Panik ließ nach.

Die Treppe war auf halber Höhe beschädigt. Ein paar herumliegende Werkzeuge und eine Leiter deuteten darauf hin, daß sie gerade repariert wurde. Reginald lehnte die Leiter an die Längsseite der Treppe und kletterte hinauf. Oben erreichte er einen kleinen Erker und rüttelte an der Tür. Sie war verschlossen. Gleich daneben befand sich ein verschlossenes Fenster. Mit einem einzigen Axthieb zerschmetterte Reginald die Läden, langte mit dem Arm hindurch, tastete sich zur Klinke vor und öffnete die Tür.

Nun stieg auch William die Leiter hoch.

Die Furcht, die ihn befallen hatte, als er William Hamleighs ansichtig geworden war, ließ Philip nicht mehr los. Die Priester und Mönche in Thomas' Begleitung argwöhnten zunächst nichts Böses, doch als sie hörten, wie unten gegen die Saaltür gehämmert wurde, bekamen auch sie es mit der Angst zu tun. Einige schlugen vor, in der Kathedrale Zuflucht zu suchen.

»Zuflucht suchen?« fuhr Thomas sie voller Verachtung an. »Wovor? Vor diesen Rittern etwa? Ein Erzbischof kann doch vor so ein paar Hitzköpfen nicht einfach davonlaufen!«

Bis zu einem gewissen Grade hat er recht, dachte Philip. Wollte er sich von einer Handvoll Ritter einschüchtern lassen, so wäre sein Erzbischofstitel bedeutungslos. Ein Gottesmann, der sich beruhigt dem Glauben hingeben kann, daß ihm seine Sünden vergeben werden, sieht im Tod den glücklichen Übergang in eine schönere Welt und fürchtet sich nicht vor dem Schwert. Andererseits sollte aber auch ein Erzbischof sich nicht leichtsinnig in Gefahr begeben. Hinzu kam, daß die Heimtücke und Brutalität William Hamleighs Philip aus leidvoller Erfahrung bekannt waren. Als plötzlich das Erkerfenster eingeschlagen wurde, entschloß er sich daher zum Handeln.

Der Palast war ringsum von Rittern umzingelt, was durch die Fenster leicht zu erkennen war. Ihr Anblick verstärkte seine Befürchtungen noch: Es handelte sich um eine sorgfältig geplante Attacke, und die Eindringlinge waren zur Gewaltanwendung bereit. Hastig schloß er die Tür des Schlafgemachs und zog den Sicherungsbalken vor. Die anderen waren heilfroh, daß nun endlich jemand die Initiative ergriff. Erzbischof Thomas sah Philips Treiben mit nach wie vor verächtlicher Miene zu, versuchte aber nicht, ihm Einhalt zu gebieten.

Philip stand an der Tür und lauschte. Ein Mann war vom Erker her ins Empfangszimmer getreten. Hoffentlich hält die Tür, dachte Philip. Doch der Mann versuchte nicht, ins Schlafgemach einzudringen, sondern ging die Treppen hinunter. Wahrscheinlich wird er die Tür zum großen Saal öffnen und seine Spießgesellen hereinlassen wollen, dachte Philip.

Dadurch gewann Thomas eine kleine Atempause.

Auf der anderen Seite des Schlafgemachs befand sich, teilweise vom Bett verstellt, eine weitere Tür. Philip deutete darauf und sagte: »Wohin führt sie?«

»Zum Kreuzgang«, sagte jemand. »Aber sie ist fest verschlossen.«

Philip versuchte, sie zu öffnen, was ihm jedoch nicht gelang. »Habt Ihr vielleicht einen Schlüssel?« fragte er den Erzbischof.

Thomas schüttelte den Kopf. »Dieser Gang wurde, soweit ich mich entsinne, nie benutzt«, sagte er mit aufreizender Gelassenheit.

Besonders stabil wirkte die Tür nicht. Philip trat dagegen, ein Schmerz durchfuhr seinen Fuß, die Tür schepperte nur. Der Prior biß die Zähne zusammen und trat ein zweites Mal zu. Diesmal flog die Tür auf.

Philip sah Thomas an. Der Erzbischof zögerte offenbar noch immer. Er hatte anscheinend noch nicht begriffen, daß die große Zahl der Angreifer und die sorgfältige Planung der Attacke auf bitterernste Absichten gegen Leib und Leben hindeuteten. Doch es war aussichtslos, Thomas Becket mit drastischen Schilderungen der Gefahr zur Flucht bewegen zu wollen. Philip versuchte es auf andere Weise: »Es ist Zeit für die Vesper. Wir sollten uns nicht von ein paar Hitzköpfen die Gottesdienstordnung durcheinanderbringen lassen.«

Thomas lächelte, als er merkte, daß sein eigenes Argument gegen ihn gekehrt wurde. »Wohl gesprochen!« sagte er und erhob sich.

Erleichtert darüber, daß es ihm gelungen war, den Erzbischof zum Gehen zu bewegen, andererseits aber auch voller Furcht, die Flucht könne nicht schnell genug vonstatten gehen, setzte Philip sich an die Spitze. Der Gang führte zunächst eine lange Treppe hinunter und wurde nur durch das rasch schwächer werdende Licht aus dem erzbischöflichen Schlafgemach erhellt. Am Endes des Ganges versperrte ihnen eine weitere Tür den Weg. Philip versuchte, sie auf die gleiche Weise zu öffnen wie die obere, schaffte es jedoch nicht. Er trommelte mit den Fäusten dagegen und rief: »Hilfe! Öffnet die Tür! Eilt Euch, schnell!« Er merkte an seiner eigenen Stimme, daß er drauf und dran war, in Panik zu geraten, und zwang sich zur Ruhe. Doch sein Herz raste, und er wußte, daß Williams Ritter ihnen dicht auf den Fersen waren.

Die anderen hatten ihn eingeholt. Philip bearbeitete nach wie vor die Tür und schrie, was das Zeug heilt. »Würde, Philip, ich bitte Euch!« hörte er Thomas sagen, ließ sich aber davon nicht beeinflussen. Er wollte des Erzbischofs Würde bewahren – seine eigene war ihm jetzt vollkommen gleichgültig.

Ehe Thomas ein weiteres Mal protestieren konnte, wurde auf der anderen Seite für alle vernehmlich ein Sperriegel fortgeschoben. Ein Schlüssel drehte sich im Schlüsselloch, und die Tür ging auf. Philip stieß einen hörbaren Seufzer der Erleichterung aus. Vor ihnen standen zwei verblüffte Cellerare, von denen einer sagte: »Ich habe keine Ahnung, wo der Gang herkommt.«

Philip drängte sich ungeduldig an ihnen vorbei. Sie befanden sich im Vorratslager. Vorbei an Fässern und Säcken erreichte er die nächste Tür. Sie führte ins Freie.

Es wurde langsam dunkel. Philip stand im südlichen Kreuzgang. Am anderen Ende erspähte er die Tür zum Querschiff der Kathedrale von Canterbury.

Sie waren fast in Sicherheit.

Ich muß Thomas in die Kirche bringen, bevor William und seine Ritter uns einholen, dachte Philip. Hinter ihm verließen der Erzbischof und seine Entourage das Lager. »Los, in die Kirche!« rief Philip. »Schnell!«

»Nein, Philip, *nicht* schnell«, widersprach Thomas. »Wir werden meine Kathedrale mit der gebotenen Würde betreten.«

Am liebsten hätte Philip laut aufgeschrien. Er bezwang sich jedoch und sagte: »Selbstverständlich, ehrwürdiger Erzbischof.« Aus dem Gang am anderen Ende des Lagers hörte man das unheilvolle Geräusch rasch näher kommender Schritte. Die Ritter waren ins Schlafgemach eingedrungen und hatten den Fluchtweg entdeckt. Philip wußte, daß der beste Schutz des Erzbischofs dessen erzbischöfliche Würde war – was jedoch nicht ausschloß, daß er sich trotzdem besser aus der Gefahrenzone begab.

»Wo ist das Kreuz des Erzbischofs?« fragte Thomas. »Ohne Kreuz kann ich die Kirche nicht betreten.«

Philip stöhnte verzweifelt auf.

Da meldete sich einer der Priester aus seiner Begleitung zu Wort: »Ich habe daran gedacht. Hier ist Euer Kreuz.«

»Tragt es vor mir her, bitte – so wie der Brauch es will.«

Der Priester hielt das Kreuz hoch und schritt mit mühsam unterdrückter Eile auf die Kirchentür zu.

Thomas folgte ihm.

Wie der Brauch es verlangte, betrat die Entourge vor dem Erzbischof die Kathedrale. Philip war der letzte und hielt die Tür für Thomas auf. Kaum hatten sie die Kirche betreten, da stürzten auch schon zwei Ritter aus dem Vorratslager in den Kreuzgang und rannte auf die Kirche zu.

Philip schloß die Querhaustür. In der Mauer daneben steckte eine Stange zur Verriegelung. Philip zog sie heraus und legte sie vor.

Als Thomas das Geräusch hörte, blieb er unvermittelt stehen und drehte sich um.

»Nein, Philip«, sagte er.

Philip erschrak. »Aber ehrwürdiger Erzbischof ...«

»Dies ist eine Kirche, keine Burg. Entriegelt die Tür.«

Die Tür erbebte unter den Schlägen und Tritten der Ritter. »Ich fürchte, sie wollen Euch töten«, sagte Philip.

»Wahrscheinlich wird es ihnen sogar gelingen«, sagte Thomas, »ob Ihr nun die Tür verriegelt oder nicht. Wißt Ihr, wie viele Eingänge diese Kirche hat? So, und nun öffnet!«

Die Ritter hieben inzwischen mit Äxten auf die Tür an. »Ihr könntet Euch verstecken«, schlug Philip in seiner Verzweiflung vor. »Es gibt Dutzende von Schlupfwinkeln – da drüben ist der Eingang zur Krypta. Auch wird es zusehends dunkler.«

»Verstecken, Philip? Ich soll mich in meiner eigenen Kirche verstecken? Würdest Ihr das tun?«

Philip starrte Thomas wortlos an und sagte nach einer längeren Pause: »Nein.«

»So öffnet jetzt die Tür.«

Schweren Herzens entfernte Philip die Stange.

Die Ritter platzten herein. Es waren ihrer fünf. Sie trugen Helme mit Visieren, so daß ihre Gesichter nicht zu erkennen waren. Bewaffnet waren sie mit Schwertern und Äxten. Sie sahen aus wie Abgesandte der Hölle.

Philip wußte, daß Furcht ihm nicht anstand, doch der Anblick der scharfen Klingen ließ ihn unwillkürlich erzittern.

Einer rief: »Wo ist Thomas Becket, Verräter des Königs und des Königreichs?«

Es war mittlerweile schon recht dunkel. Nur matter Kerzenschimmer erhellte das Innere der großen Kirche. Alle Mönche trugen schwarzen Habit, und das Blickfeld der Ritter war durch die vorgeschobenen Visiere eingeengt. Hoffnung keimte in Philip auf: Vielleicht finden sie Thomas in der Dunkelheit nicht, dachte er. Doch die Hoffnung erwies sich schon im nächsten Augenblick als trügerisch. Erzbischof Thomas Becket schritt den Rittern entgegen und sprach: »Hier bin ich – kein Verräter, sondern ein Priester Gottes. Was wollt Ihr?«

Als Philip sah, wie der Erzbischof den fünf Rittern mit ihren gezückten Schwertern entgegentrat, wußte er auf einmal mit tödlicher Gewißheit, daß Thomas Becket an dieser Stelle und an diesem Tag sein Leben verlieren würde.

Den Männern aus Thomas' Entourage mußte es ähnlich ergangen sein, denn die meisten von ihnen suchten plötzlich das Weite. Einige verschwanden im düsteren Chor, andere mischten sich im Schiff unter die Gläubigen, die auf den Beginn des Gottesdienstes warteten. Einer öffnete eine kleine Tür und rannte die dahinter befindliche Wendeltreppe hinauf. Philip fand das Verhalten der Priester und Mönche empörend. »Beten sollt ihr«, rief er ihnen nach, »nicht davonlaufen!«

Auch ihm selbst drohte der Tod, wenn er nicht davonlief; er war sich dessen bewußt. Aber er konnte sich nicht von des Erzbischofs Seite losreißen.

Einer der Ritter sagte zu Thomas: »Sagt Euch los von Eurem Verrat!« Philip erkannte die Stimme von Reginald Fitzurse, der schon zuvor der Wortführer gewesen war.

»Es gibt nichts, von dem ich mich loszusagen hätte«, antwortete Thomas. »Ich habe keinen Verrat begangen.« Er war eiskalt und beherrscht, doch sein Gesicht war bleich. Er weiß, daß seine letzte Stunde geschlagen hat, dachte Philip.

»Los, rennt, sonst seid Ihr ein toter Mann!« schrie Reginald Thomas an.

Thomas rührte sich nicht vom Fleck.

Sie *wollen*, daß er fortläuft, dachte Philip. Sie bringen es nicht über sich, ihn kaltblütig abzuschlachten.

Aber Thomas Becket blieb stehen. Er zuckte mit keiner Wimper und trotzte den Rittern allein mit seiner Gegenwart. Eine ganze Weile standen sie sich stumm gegenüber, ein mörderisches, erstarrtes Tableau: die Ritter, von denen keiner bereit war, den ersten Schlag zu führen, und der Priester, dem es sein Stolz verbot, sein Heil in der Flucht zu suchen.

Thomas vollendete sein Schicksal, indem er den Zauber brach. »Ich bin bereit zu sterben«, sagte er. »Aber rührt sonst niemanden von meinen Leuten an – weder Priester noch Mönch noch Laien.«

Reginald reagierte als erster. Er fuchtelte mit seinem Schwert in der Luft herum. Die Spitze näherte sich dem Gesicht des Erzbischofs nur zögernd; es war, als koste es Reginald große Selbstüberwindung, mit seiner Waffe den Priester zu berühren. Thomas stand da wie eine Salzsäule, den Blick auf den Ritter gerichtet, nicht auf das Schwert. Dann schlenzte Reginald mit einer kurzen Bewegung aus dem Handgelenk Thomas die Bischofsmütze vom Haupt.

Wieder war Philip von Hoffnung erfüllt. Sie bringen es nicht über sich, dachte er. Sie wagen es nicht, Hand an ihn zu legen ...

Aber er irrte sich. Die Entschlossenheit der Ritter schien durch die alberne Attacke auf die Bischofsmütze gewachsen zu sein. Es war, als hätten sie im ersten Moment gefürchtet, von der strafenden Hand Gottes niedergeschmettert zu werden, und aus der Tatsache, daß dem nicht so war, neuen Mut für Schlimmeres gezogen. Richard sagte: »Greift ihn Euch und schleppt ihn raus!«

Die anderen Ritter steckten ihre Schwerter in die Scheiden und traten näher an den Erzbischof heran.

Einer von ihnen packte Thomas um die Taille und versuchte, ihn vom Boden zu heben.

Philip verzweifelte. Sie hatten die letzte Barriere überwunden und ihn berührt. Sie waren bereit, Hand an einen Mann Gottes zu legen! Philip schaute jetzt die ganze Tiefe ihrer Verrufenheit, und es drehte ihm schier den Magen um; ihm war, als luge er über den Rand eines bodenlosen Abgrunds. In der Tiefe ihres Herzens mußten diese Männer wissen, daß sie für das, was sie zu tun im Begriff standen, zur Hölle fahren würden. Und dennoch taten sie es.

Thomas verlor das Gleichgewicht, er ruderte mit den Armen und versuchte, sich zu befreien. Nun packten auch die anderen Ritter zu und wollten ihn fortschleppen. Von den Begleitern des Erzbischofs hatte außer Philip nur noch ein Priester namens Edward Grim ausgeharrt. Beide eilten sie Thomas nun zu Hilfe. Edward erwischte den bischöflichen Mantel und hielt sich daran fest. Einer der Ritter drehte sich um und schlug mit seiner gepanzerten Faust nach Philip. Der Hieb traf den Prior an der Schläfe. Philip taumelte benommen zu Boden.

Als er wieder zu sich kam, hatten die Ritter Thomas Becket wieder freigegeben. Der Erzbischof stand mit gesenktem Haupt da, die Hände wie im Gebet zusammengelegt. Einer der Ritter hob sein Schwert.

Philip, noch immer am Boden, stieß einen langen, hilflosen Schrei aus. »Nein!«

Edward Grim versuchte mit ausgestrecktem Arm, den Schlag abzuwehren.

Thomas Becket sagte: »Ich befehle mich in Gottes Ha …«

Das Schwert fiel.

Es traf beide, Thomas und Edward. Philip hörte sich schreien. Die Klinge hatte dem Priester den Arm abgeschnitten und war Thomas in den Schädel gefahren. Aus dem Arm spritzte Blut, und Thomas Becket sank in die Knie.

Entsetzt starrte Philip auf die furchtbare Kopfwunde.

Der Erzbischof fiel langsam vornüber, vermochte sich nur kurz mit den Händen abzustützen und sackte dann, das Gesicht voran, auf dem Steinboden zusammen.

Nun hob ein anderer Ritter sein Schwert und schlug zu. Philip in seinem namenlosen Kummer heulte unwillkürlich auf. Der zweite Schlag traf die gleiche Stelle wie der erste und trennte die obere Hälfte von Thomas' Schädel ab. Er war mit solcher Kraft geführt worden, daß die Klinge mit Wucht auf den gepflasterten Boden traf und dort in zwei Teile zersprang. Der Ritter ließ den Stumpf fallen.

Ein dritter Ritter verstieg sich nun zu einer Tat von furchtbarer Grausamkeit, die Philip bis an sein Lebensende verfolgen sollte. Er bohrte die Spitze seines Schwertes in den offenen Schädel des Erzbischofs, bis das Gehirn auf den Boden spritzte. Dann sagte er: »Der steht nicht mehr auf. Hauen wir ab!«

Die Mörder machten auf dem Absatz kehrt und rannten davon.

Philip sah, wie sie, wild mit den Schwertern fuchtelnd, die Menge im Hauptschiff auseinandertrieben.

Nachdem sie die Kirche verlassen hatten, herrschte einen Augenblick gelähmtes Schweigen. Die Leiche des Erzbischofs lag auf dem Boden, die abgetrennte Schädeldecke mitsamt den Haaren wie ein abgefallener Deckel neben dem Kopf. Philip barg sein Gesicht in den Händen. Das war das Ende aller Hoffnung. Die Barbaren haben gewonnen, schoß es ihm ein ums andere Mal durch den Kopf, die Barbaren haben gewonnen ... Ihn schwindelte. Es war ihm, als sinke er langsam hinab in einen tiefen See, als ertrinke er in Verzweiflung. Es gab nichts mehr, woran man sich halten konnte. Alles, was bisher fest und unverrückbar erschienen war, verlor auf einmal seine Konturen.

Sein ganzes Leben war gezeichnet vom ständigen Kampf gegen die Willkür und Machtbesessenheit böser Menschen. Und nun hatte er die letzte Schlacht verloren. Er mußte daran denken, wie William Hamleigh einst gekommen war, Kingsbridge ein zweites Mal in Brand zu stecken, und wie die Bewohner der Stadt in einem einzigen Tag eine Mauer erbaut hatten. Welch glorreicher Sieg das gewesen war! Die friedliche Kraft Hunderter von einfachen Leuten hatte die nackte Grausamkeit des Grafen William bezwungen. Auch an die Zeit, da Waleran Bigod versucht hatte, die Kathedrale in Shiring zu errichten, mußte Philip jetzt denken. Er hatte die Bevölkerung zu Hilfe gerufen, und so waren an jenem denkwürdigen Pfingstsonntag vor nunmehr dreiunddreißig Jahren Hunderte von Menschen nach Kingsbridge geströmt und hatten mit der bloßen Kraft ihres Arbeitseifers Walerans

Bestrebungen zunichte gemacht. Doch nun gab es keine Hoffnung mehr. Niemand in Canterbury, ja niemand in der gesamten Christenheit war imstande, Erzbischof Thomas Becket wieder zum Leben zu erwecken.

Kniend auf den Fliesen des nördlichen Querhauses der Kathedrale von Canterbury, erschienen ihm wieder die Männer, die vor sechsundfünfzig Jahren in sein Elternhaus eingedrungen waren und Mutter und Vater vor seinen Augen niedergemetzelt hatten. Und das Gefühl, das ihm aus dieser Erinnerung des sechsjährigen Knaben zuwuchs, war nicht Angst, nicht einmal Trauer, sondern Wut. Unfähig, den riesigen, rotgesichtigen, blutrünstigen Männern Einhalt zu gebieten, hatte er einen brennenden Ehrgeiz entwickelt, all diesen Schwertträgern ihr Handwerk zu legen. Ihre Schwerter wollte er stumpf machen, ihre Schlachtrösser zum Lahmen bringen und sie alle dazu zwingen, sich einer höheren Macht zu beugen – einer Macht, die stärker war als das Königreich der Gewalt ... Nach wenigen Augenblicken – seine Eltern lagen tot auf dem Boden – war Abt Peter auf der Walstatt erschienen und hatte ihm den Weg gewiesen. Ohne Waffen und ohne Rüstung hatte er das Blutvergießen beendet, allein kraft seiner Güte und der Autorität seiner Kirche. Dieses Bild hatte Philip sein ganzes Leben lang beeinflußt und geleitet.

Bisher hatte er geglaubt, er und seinesgleichen könnten den Sieg davontragen. Sie hatten im zurückliegenden halben Jahrhundert auch einige bemerkenswerte Erfolge errungen, doch nun, da sich sein Leben dem Ende zuneigte, war seinen Feinden der Beweis gelungen, daß alles beim alten geblieben war. Philips Triumphe waren nur von begrenzter Dauer gewesen, der Fortschritt erwies sich als Hirngespinst. Die Lage war aussichtslos, die paar gewonnenen Schlachten zählten nicht mehr. Männer vom Schlage jener Barbaren, denen einst seine Eltern zum Opfer gefallen waren, hatten einen Erzbischof in seiner Kathedrale ermordet, ganz als wollten sie über jeden Zweifel erhaben klarstellen, daß sich die Tyrannei eines Mannes mit seinem Schwert von keiner anderen Autorität besiegen ließ.

Nie hätte Philip sich träumen lassen, daß diese Männer es wagen würden, Erzbischof Thomas zu töten – schon gar nicht in einer Kirche. Aber er hatte es als Junge ja auch nicht für möglich gehalten, daß jemand kommen und seinen Vater ermorden könne ... In beiden Fällen hatten ihn dieselben blutrünstigen Helm- und Schwertträger eines Besseren belehrt, ihm die grauenvolle Wahrheit gezeigt. Und da saß er nun, ein zweiundsechzigjähriger Mann, vor dem entsetzlich zugerichteten Leichnam Thomas Beckets, und war besessen von der kindischen, unvernünftigen, alles verzehrenden Wut eines sechsjährigen Knaben, dessen Vater ermordet wurde.

Er erhob sich. In der Kathedrale herrschte eine ungemein bedrükkende Atmosphäre. Priester, Mönche und einfache Gläubige aus der Stadt kamen langsam näher und starrten voller Grauen auf die Leiche des Erzbischofs. Philip spürte, daß sich hinter ihren vom Schock gezeichneten Gesichtern ähnlich wie bei ihm selbst Wut verbarg. Ein oder zwei Menschen murmelten, kaum hörbar, Gebete vor sich hin. Eine Frau bückte sich rasch nieder und berührte den toten Körper, als verhieße eine solche Berührung Glück. Einige andere folgten ihrem Beispiel. Dann sah Philip eine Frau, die verstohlen ein kleines Fläschchen mit dem Blut des Erzbischofs füllte, als wäre er ein Märtyrer.

Die Geistlichen kamen langsam wieder zu Sinnen. Osbert, der Kämmerer des Erzbischofs, dem die Tränen über das Gesicht strömten, zog ein Messer hervor und schnitt einen Stoffstreifen aus seinem Hemd. Dann kniete er neben dem Leichnam nieder und band mit ungeschickten Fingern das abgetrennte Schädeldach wieder an den Kopf. Es war ein kümmerlicher Versuch, der auf so gräßliche Weise verunstalteten Person des Erzbischofs wenigstens ein Mindestmaß an Würde wiederzugeben.

Ein paar Mönche brachten eine Tragbahre, auf die sie Thomas vorsichtig betteten. Viele Hände boten ihre Hilfe an. Philip sah, daß die Miene des Erzbischofs friedlich war; als einziges Zeichen der Gewalt erkannte er ein dünnes Blutrinnsal, das sich von der rechten Schläfe quer über die Nase zur linken Wange zog.

Die Mönche hoben die Tragbahre hoch und machten sich auf den Weg. Philip nahm den Schwertgriff mit der abgebrochenen Klinge auf. Die Frau, die das Blut des Erzbischofs aufgefangen hatte, ging ihm nicht mehr aus dem Sinn. Er spürte, daß ihre Handlung ungemein bedeutungsträchtig war, wußte allerdings noch nicht, in welcher Hinsicht.

Wie von einer unsichtbaren Kraft getrieben, folgte die Menge der Bahre mit dem Ermordeten. Auch Philip ließ sich mitreißen, gefangen wie alle anderen in einem seltsamen Bann. Die Mönche trugen die Bahre durch den Chor und setzten sie vor dem Hochaltar vorsichtig auf dem Boden ab. Die Menschen, von denen viele jetzt laut beteten, sahen, wie ein Priester ein sauberes Tuch brachte und das bischöfliche Haupt sorgfältig verband. Zum Schluß stülpte er ihm eine neue Bischofsmütze über, die den Verband zum großen Teil bedeckte.

Ein Mönch zerschnitt den blutverschmierten schwarzen Mantel des Erzbischofs. Unschlüssig, was er mit dem Kleidungsstück tun sollte, drehte er sich um und wollte es achtlos fortwerfen. Da sprang aus der Menge ein Bürger hervor und riß es ihm aus der Hand, als wär's ein Gegenstand von größtem Wert.

Und da fiel es Philip wie Schuppen von den Augen. Er wußte auf einmal, was ihn die ganze Zeit so bewegte. Die Leute sahen in Thomas einen Märtyrer. Sie sammelten sein Blut und seine Kleider, als wohnten ihnen die übernatürlichen Kräfte von Heiligenreliquien inne. Philip hatte in dem Mord eine politische Niederlage der Kirche gesehen, doch die Menschen in Canterbury hatten ihre eigene Erklärung: Sie hielten den Tod des Erzbischofs für ein Märtyrium. Und aus dem Tod eines Märtyrers, so sehr er im ersten Moment auch als Niederlage erscheinen mochte, waren der Kirche noch immer neue Inspiration und neue Kräfte erwachsen.

Wieder mußte Philip an die vielen, vielen Menschen denken, die einst zum Kathedralenbau nach Kingsbridge gekommen waren, und an die Männer, Frauen und Kinder, die die halbe Nacht geschuftet hatten, um die Stadtmauer hochzuziehen. Wenn es gelingt, die Menschen jetzt in ähnlicher Weise zum Handeln zu bewegen, dachte er mit wachsender Erregung, dann wird sich ein Schrei der Empörung erheben, der überall auf der Welt zu hören sein wird ...

Philip beobachtete die Männer und Frauen, die sich mit vor Schmerz und Schrecken verzerrten Gesichtern um den Leichnam drängten. Das einzige was ihnen fehlt, ist einer, der ihnen die Richtung weist, dachte er.

War es möglich?

Irgendwie kam ihm die Situation vertraut vor. Eine übel zugerichtete Leiche, eine Zuschauermenge, in der Entfernung ein paar Soldaten: Wo habe ich das nur schon einmal gesehen? fragte er sich. Auch war ihm klar, was als nächstes geschehen mußte: Eine kleine Gruppe von Gefolgsleuten des Toten würde sich zusammenschließen und gegen die Macht und Autorität eines gewaltigen Reiches aufbegehren ...

Ja, natürlich! Das waren die Anfänge des Christentums!

Als Philip dies begriff, wußte er auf einmal genau, was er zu tun hatte.

Er stellte sich mit dem Rücken zum Altar vor die Menge, in der Hand noch immer das abgebrochene Schwert. Aller Augen richteten sich auf ihn. Selbstzweifel keimten auf: Kann ich es wirklich? Kann ich eine Volksbewegung ins Leben rufen – hier und jetzt? Eine Bewegung, die den Thron Englands erschüttern wird? Er blickte in die Gesichter der Menschen und erkannte neben unsäglicher Trauer und Wut in einer oder zwei Mienen auch einen Funken Hoffnung.

Er hob das Schwert in die Höhe.

»Dieses Schwert hat einen Heiligen getötet«, sagte er.

Zustimmendes Gemurmel war die Antwort.

Ermutigt fuhr Philip fort: »Wir alle wurden heute abend Zeugen eines Martyriums.«

Die Priester und Mönche wirkten überrascht. Ebenso wie Philip war ihnen die tiefere Bedeutung des Mordes nicht sofort aufgegangen. Die einfachen Gläubigen aus der Stadt wußten indessen genau Bescheid, und so stimmten sie ihm hörbar zu.

»Jeder von uns muß ausgehen und verkünden, was er gesehen hat.« Einige Zuhörer nickten heftig. Sie hörten ihm zu – aber Philip wollte mehr von ihnen. Er wollte sie inspirieren. Predigen war nie seine Stärke gewesen. Er gehörte nicht zu jenen Männern, die eine Menge in Begeisterungstaumel versetzen konnten, die sie lachen und weinen machen konnten und sie dazu bewegen, ihren Führern überallhin zu folgen. Philip wußte nicht, wie man seine Stimme zum Beben brachte und den Glanz des Ruhms in seine Augen zauberte. Er war ein praktischer Mensch, der mit beiden Beinen auf dem Erdboden stand – und hätte doch, in dieser Stunde, mit Engelszungen reden müssen.

»Bald wird jeder Mann, jede Frau und jedes Kind in Canterbury wissen, daß Erzbischof Thomas von Schergen des Königs ermordet wurde. Doch das ist erst der Anfang. Die Kunde wird sich alsbald über ganz England und danach über alle Länder der Christenheit verbreiten ...«

Er schaffte es nicht, die Menschen zu fesseln; er spürte es selbst. Auf manchen Gesichtern zeigten sich Unzufriedenheit und Enttäuschung. Ein Mann rief: »Aber was sollen wir tun?«

Sie brauchen ganz bestimmte Handlungsvorgaben, erkannte Philip, und zwar sofort. Man kann nicht einen Kreuzzug ausrufen und dann die Leute ins Bett schicken ...

Ein Kreuzzug. Das wäre eine Idee.

»Morgen werde ich dieses Schwert nach Rochester bringen«, fuhr er fort. »Und übermorgen nach London. Wollt Ihr mich begleiten?«

Die meisten Zuhörer starrten ihn nur mit leeren Augen an. Doch aus dem Hintergrund rief eine Stimme: »Ja!« Und ein oder zwei andere Rufer schlossen sich ihr an.

Philip hob die Stimme. »Wir werden unsere Geschichte in jeder Stadt und jedem Dorf in England bekanntmachen. Wir werden den Menschen das Schwert zeigen, das den heiligen Thomas tötete. Wir werden sie die Blutflecken auf seinen Priestergewändern sehen lassen ...« Er redete sich in Hitze und ließ seinen Zorn erkennen. »Und wir werden einen Aufschrei auslösen, der sich über alle Länder der Christenheit verbreiten und sogar im fernen Rom gehört werden wird. Wir werden dafür sorgen, daß sich die gesamte zivilisierte Welt gegen die Barbaren kehrt, die dieses unsägliche, gotteslästerliche Verbrechen begangen haben!«

Diesmal gab es kaum noch jemanden, der Philip die Zustimmung verweigerte. Alle hatten sie nach einer Möglichkeit gesucht, ihren Gefühlen Ausdruck zu verleihen, und da war nun einer, der ihnen diese Möglichkeit verschaffte.

»Dieses Verbrechen«, sagte Philip langsam, und seine Stimme erhob sich zu einem Schrei, »dieses Verbrechen wird nie, nie, nie vergessen werden!«

Und wie aus einer Kehle stimmten sie ihm zu.

Plötzlich wußte Philip, wohin ihn sein Weg führte. »Unser Kreuzzug beginnt sofort, hier und heute!«

»Ja!«

»Wir tragen dieses Schwert durch alle Straßen der Stadt!«

»Ja!«

»Und wir erzählen jedem Bürger in dieser Stadt, was wir heute abend hier gesehen haben!«

»Ja!«

»Nehmt euch Kerzen und folgt mir nach!«

Mit hocherhobenem Schwert marschierte er durch die Kathedrale. Und die Menschen folgten ihm nach.

Durch den Chor ging er, über die Vierung, durchs Schiff, flankiert von einigen Priester und Mönchen. Er brauchte sich nicht umzusehen: Seine Ohren sagten ihm, daß an die hundert Menschen hinter ihm herkamen. Er verließ die Kathedrale durch das Hauptportal.

Draußen fuhr ihm der Schreck durch die Glieder. Auf der anderen Seite des dunklen Obstgartens plünderten Bewaffnete den erzbischöflichen Palast. Wenn die Leute mit den Plünderern aneinandergeraten, dann endet unser Kreuzzug in einer Schlägerei, noch ehe er richtig begonnen hat, dachte Philip. Von plötzlicher Angst gepackt, wandte er sich scharf nach rechts und führte die Menge durch das nächste Tor in die Stadt.

Ein Mönch stimmte einen Hymnus an. Hinter den Fensterläden flackerten Lampenlicht und Feuerschein, doch als die Prozession näher kam, öffneten sich die Türen. Die Menschen wollten wissen, was los war. Sie fragten die Prozessionsteilnehmer. Manche marschierten gleich mit.

Hinter einer Straßenecke erblickte Philip unvermittelt William Hamleigh.

William stand in Begleitung einer Handvoll Ritter und Bewaffneter vor einem Pferdestall. Er hatte offenbar gerade seinen Kettenpanzer abgelegt und war im Begriff, sein Pferd zu besteigen und sich aus dem Staub zu machen. Alle blickten sie der Prozession erwartungsvoll entgegen. Sie hatten das Singen gehört und schienen sich zu fragen, was es damit auf sich hatte.

Dann erkannte William das abgebrochene Schwert in Philips Hand, und langsam ging ihm ein Licht auf. Von furchtbarer Scheu ergriffen, brauchte er eine Weile, bis er die Sprache wiederfand. »Hört auf damit!« rief er. »Ich befehle euch: Geht auseinander!«

Niemand beachtete ihn. Die Männer in seiner Begleitung blickten angstvoll um sich. Gegen eine über hundertköpfige, von heiligem Zorn erfaßte Trauerprozession halfen ihnen selbst ihre Schwerter nicht mehr viel.

William wandte sich nun direkt an Philip: »Im Namen des Königs befehle ich Euch, diesem Aufruhr Einhalt zu gebieten!«

Vorwärtsgetragen vom Druck der Masse rauschte Philip an ihm vorbei. »Zu spät, William!« rief er ihm über die Schulter zu. »Zu spät!«

Die kleinen Jungen waren die ersten, die zum Richtplatz kamen. Sie waren schon da, auf dem Marktplatz zu Shiring, als Aliena eintraf, bewarfen die Katzen mit spitzen Steinen, piesackten die Bettler und prügelten sich untereinander. Aliena war allein und kam zu Fuß. Ein schäbiger Mantel mit Kapuze bewahrte ihr Inkognito.

In einiger Entfernung vom Schafott blieb sie stehen. Ursprünglich hatte sie überhaupt nicht kommen wollen. Oft genug hatte sie in ihrer Eigenschaft als amtierende Gräfin von Shiring an Hinrichtungen teilnehmen müssen, und sie hätte gut und gerne darauf verzichten können, je wieder einen Menschen am Strick baumeln zu sehen. Aber bei diesem einen war es anders.

Sie war nicht mehr amtierende Gräfin, denn ihr Bruder Richard war in Syrien ums Leben gekommen – allerdings nicht auf dem

Schlachtfeld, sondern bei einem Erdbeben. Erst sechs Monate später hatte sie davon erfahren. Fünfzehn Jahre lang hatte sie ihn nicht gesehen; jetzt hatte sie die Gewißheit, daß sie ihn nie wiedersehen würde.

Hoch oben auf der Burg öffneten sich die Tore. Unter strenger Bewachung trat der Gefangene seinen letzten Gang an. Den Abschluß des kleinen Zuges bildete der neue Graf von Shiring, Alienas Sohn Tommy.

Da Richard kinderlos geblieben war, fiel der Grafentitel seinem Neffen zu. Der durch den Becket-Skandal erschütterte und geschwächte König hatte den Weg des geringsten Widerstands eingeschlagen und Tommy schleunigst bestätigt. Aliena hatte die Verantwortung bereitwillig an die jüngere Generation abgetreten. Was sie sich zu Beginn ihrer Regentschaft vorgenommen hatte, war inzwischen erreicht: Die Grafschaft Shiring war wieder ein blühendes, reiches Gemeinwesen, ein Land mit fetten Schafen, grünenden Feldern und emsigen Mühlen. Eine Reihe fortschrittlicher Gutsherren war Alienas Beispiel gefolgt und pflügte inzwischen mit Pferden statt mit Ochsen. Die Erträge hatten sich dank der neuen Dreifelderwirtschaft so verbessert, daß das Land inzwischen mehr Menschen ernährte als unter des alten Grafen Bartholomäus' aufgeklärter Herrschaft. Die Ackerpferde fraßen den Hafer aus der Frühsaat.

Daß Tommy ein guter Graf sein würde, daran hatte Aliena nicht den geringsten Zweifel. Er war für dieses Amt geboren. Jack hatte sich lange Zeit gegen diese Einsicht gesträubt und hätte nur allzugern einen Baumeister aus ihm gemacht. Tommys Unfähigkeit, auch nur einen einzigen Stein so zu schneiden, daß die Schnittkante gerade war, hatte ihn dann aber doch eines Besseren belehrt. Sein Sohn besaß andere Fähigkeiten, darunter eine natürliche Begabung zur Menschenführung. Tommy war inzwischen achtundzwanzig Jahre alt, entschlossen und entscheidungsfreudig, intelligent und gerecht. Er nannte sich nicht mehr Tommy, sondern Thomas.

Von Aliena hatten die meisten Leute erwartet, daß sie nach der Amtsübergabe im Schloß bleiben, ihre Schwiegertochter ärgern und mit den Enkelkindern spielen würde. Aber Aliena lachte alle aus, die ihr mit solchen Ideen kamen. Sie mochte Tommys Frau, eine hübsche jüngere Tochter des Grafen von Bedford, und war ganz entzückt von den drei Enkeln – nur: Um sich zur Ruhe zu setzen, fühlte sie sich mit ihren zweiundfünfzig Jahren noch nicht alt genug. Sie hatte mit Jack im ehemaligen Armenviertel von Kingsbridge, unweit der Priorei, ein großes Steinhaus erworben und war wieder ins Wollgeschäft eingestiegen. Sie kaufte und verkaufte, verhandelte mit der ihr eigenen, ungebrochenen Energie und verdiente schon nach kurzer Zeit wieder eine Menge Geld.

Der Zug mit dem Delinquenten betrat den Marktplatz und schreckte Aliena aus ihrer Tagträumerei. Sie faßte den Gefangenen näher ins Auge: Er stolperte am Ende eines Seils über den Platz, die Hände hatte man ihm auf dem Rücken gefesselt. Es war William Hamleigh.

Ein Gaffer aus der ersten Reihe spuckte ihn an. Inzwischen hatte sich eine große Menschenmenge versammelt. Die meisten Leute waren froh, daß es William nun endlich an den Kragen ging, und selbst wer keinen persönlichen Groll gegen ihn hegte, fand es immerhin bemerkenswert, daß ein ehemaliger Vogt am Galgen enden sollte. Doch William war Mittäter an der furchtbarsten Mordtat, die je bekanntgeworden war.

Die Reaktion auf die Ermordung von Erzbischof Thomas Becket hatte alle Erwartungen übertroffen. Aliena konnte sich nicht entsinnen, jemals etwas Vergleichbares erlebt oder gehört zu haben. Wie ein Flächenbrand hatte sich die Nachricht über die gesamte Christenheit verbreitet, von Dublin bis Jerusalem und von Toledo bis Oslo. Der Papst hatte sich zur Trauer zurückgezogen und den auf dem europäischen Festland liegenden Teil des Reiches von König Heinrich mit dem Interdikt belegt. Das bedeutete, daß die Kirchen geschlossen waren und außer der Taufe kein Gottesdienst mehr gehalten wurde. Canterbury war innerhalb kürzester Zeit zum Wallfahrtsort geworden, die Menschen strömten dorthin wie nach Santiago de Compostela. Und es hatte Wunder gegeben: Wasser, das mit einem Tropfen Märtyrerblut vermischt war, und Fetzen von dem Gewand, das Thomas Becket bei seinem Tod getragen hatte, heilten Kranke nicht nur in Canterbury, sondern überall in England.

Williams Männer hatten versucht, den Leichnam aus der Kathedrale zu stehlen, doch die Mönche hatten eine Warnung erhalten und ihn versteckt. Inzwischen lag er sicher verwahrt in einem steinernen Gewölbe; Pilger, die den Marmorsarg küssen wollten, mußten ihren Kopf durch ein Loch in der Mauer stecken.

Es war Williams letzte Schandtat gewesen. Hals über Kopf war er nach Shiring zurückgekehrt – um dort sogleich von Tommy festgenommen zu werden. Die Anklage lautete auf Sakrileg. Bischof Philips geistliches Gericht hatte ihn schuldig gesprochen. Unter normalen Umständen hätte kein Mensch es gewagt, einen Vogt, der immerhin in der Grafschaft die Krone vertrat, zu verurteilen, doch in diesem Fall waren die Vorzeichen genau umgekehrt: Niemand – nicht einmal der König – hätte es wagen können, einen Mörder Thomas Beckets zu verteidigen.

Williams Abschied war alles andere als ehrenvoll.

Die Augen traten ihm fast aus den Höhlen. Er glotzte um sich, aus seinem offenstehenden Mund troff Speichel. Er brabbelte unzusammenhängendes Zeug. Ein dunkler Fleck vorne auf der Tunika verriet, daß er sich besudelt hatte.

Aliena sah ihren alten Feind blindlings auf den Galgen zutorkeln. Sie mußte an den jungen, eingebildeten und herzlosen Burschen denken, der sie vor nunmehr fünfunddreißig Jahren vergewaltigt hatte. Es war kaum zu fassen, daß es sich bei der jämmerlichen, vor Angst wimmernden Kreatur dort vorne um ein und dieselbe Person handelte. Selbst der fette, gichtige und verbitterte alte Ritter aus späteren Tagen hatte mit diesem Wesen nichts gemein, das jetzt, im Angesicht des Galgens, zu strampeln und zu schreien begonnen hatte. Die Schergen schleiften ihn vorwärts wie ein Schwein, das ins Schlachthaus gezerrt wird. Aliena empfand kein Mitleid in ihrem Herzen; das einzige, was sie verspürte, war ein Gefühl der Erleichterung. Von heute an brauchte sich niemand mehr vor William zu fürchten.

Er trat mit den Füßen nach allen Seiten aus und kreischte wie am Spieß, als man ihn auf den Ochsenkarren hob. Rotgesichtig, wild und schmutzig sah er aus, wie ein garstiges Tier, doch die Töne, die er von sich gab, erinnerten eher an die eines Kindes: er plapperte, jammerte und heulte. Vier Männer mußten ihn festhalten, damit ihm ein fünfter die Schlinge um den Hals legen konnte. Mit seinen heftigen Bewegungen bewirkte er lediglich, daß der Knoten sich vorzeitig zuzog; er beraubte sich dadurch selbst der Atemluft, noch ehe man ihn hängen ließ. Die Schergen traten zurück. William wand sich und rang nach Luft. Sein feistes Gesicht verfärbte sich purpurn.

Entsetzt starrte Aliena ihn an. Selbst in ihrem tiefsten Haß und Zorn hätte sie ihm ein solches Ende nicht gewünscht.

Geräuschlos begann William zu ersticken, geräuschlos gaffte die Menge. Selbst den Gassenjungen hatte der grausige Anblick die Sprache verschlagen.

Dann versetzte jemand dem Ochsen einen Gertenhieb auf die Flanke, das Tier trottete vorwärts, und William stürzte ins Bodenlose. Doch sein Hals brach nicht. Er baumelte am Strick und starb einen langsamen, qualvollen Erstickungstod. Seine Augen blieben offen, und

Aliena hatte auf einmal das Gefühl, er starre sie an. Sein fratzenhaftes Grinsen kam ihr bekannt vor, und rasch fiel ihr ein, warum: So, genau so, hatte er sie angesehen, als er sie damals vergewaltigte, kurz vor dem Höhepunkt seiner Lust ... Die Erinnerung durchfuhr sie wie ein Messerstich, doch gestattete sie es sich nicht, den Blick abzuwenden.

Es dauerte lange, sehr lange, doch die Menge blieb stumm und rührte sich nicht. Williams Gesicht verfärbte sich immer dunkler, sein schmerzvolles Aufbäumen verkümmerte zu bloßen Zuckungen. Dann, endlich, verdrehte er die Augen, die Lider schlossen sich, die Zuckungen blieben aus – und plötzlich schob sich, ein gräßlicher Anblick, schwarz und verschwollen die Zunge zwischen den Zähnen hervor.

Er war tot.

Aliena fühlte sich vollkommen ausgelaugt. William hatte einst ihr Leben verändert – es ruiniert, wie sie früher gesagt hätte –, und jetzt war er tot und nicht mehr imstande, ihr oder einem anderen Menschen weh zu tun.

Die Menge zerstreute sich. Die Gassenjungen ahmten Williams letzte Zuckungen nach, verdrehten die Augen, streckten ihre Zunge heraus. Ein Scherge kletterte auf das Schafott und schnitt die Leiche herunter.

Aliena sah ihren Sohn, und er erwiderte ihren Blick. Ihre Anwesenheit schien ihn zu überraschen. Er kam sofort zu ihr und beugte sich zu ihr nieder, um sie zu küssen. Mein Sohn, dachte sie, mein großer Sohn. Jacks Sohn. Wie sehr ich mich damals fürchtete, Williams Kind in mir zu tragen ... Und so hat sich doch so manches zum Guten gewendet.

»Ich hätte nicht gedacht, daß du dir das antun würdest«, sagte Tommy.

»Ich konnte nicht anders«, erwiderte sie. »Ich mußte ihn tot sehen.«

Er sah sie bestürzt an. Er versteht mich nicht, dachte sie. Ein Glück, daß er's nicht tut. Hoffentlich wird er solche Dinge nie verstehen müssen.

Er legte seinen Arm um sie. Gemeinsam verließen sie den Platz. Aliena blickte sich nicht mehr um.

An einem heißen Hochsommertag saßen Jack, Aliena und Sally oben auf der Empore des Querschiffs beim Essen. Sie hockten auf dem zerkratzten Gips seines Zeichenbodens und genossen die Kühle, die in der Kirche herrschte. Wie das Geplätscher eines fernen Wasserfalls drang das Gemurmel der Mönche an ihre Ohren, die unten im Chor die Sexte zelebrierten. Es gab kalte Lammkoteletts mit frischem Weißbrot und einen Steinkrug voll mit goldenem Bier. Jack hatte den ganzen Vormittag damit verbracht, den neuen Chor zu entwerfen, mit dessen Bau er im kommenden Jahr beginnen wollte. Sally biß mit ihren hübschen weißen Zähnen herzhaft in ein Stück Fleisch und betrachtete dabei den Plan. Ich kann mich auf einen kritischen Kommentar gefaßt machen, dachte Jack, ich kenne meine Tochter ... Er sah Aliena an. Auch sie hatte Sallys Miene studiert und wußte, was zu erwarten war. Sie wechselten wissende Elternblicke und lächelten.

»Warum soll die Apsis abgerundet sein?« wollte Sally wissen.

»Ich habe mich an das Vorbild von Saint-Denis gehalten«, sagte Jack.

»Aber hat das irgendwelche Vorteile?«

»Ja, der Pilgerstrom wird nicht aufgehalten.«

»Es gibt also nur eine Reihe mit kleinen Fenstern?«

Jack hatte schon damit gerechnet, daß sie bald auf die Fenster zu sprechen kommen würde – schließlich war Sally Glaserin von Beruf. »*Kleinen* Fenster?« fragte er mit gespielter Entrüstung. »Die Fenster sind geradezu riesig! Als ich zum erstenmal Fenster dieser Größe in eine Kirche einbaute, prophezeite mir alle Welt den baldigen Einsturz des Gebäudes! So stark durchbrochene Wände, hieß es, seien nicht genügend tragfähig.«

Sally ließ nicht locker. »Wenn die Apsis rechtwinklig wäre, hättest du eine große, flache Wand zur Verfügung. Du könntest *wirklich* große Fenster einbauen.«

Da hat sie natürlich recht, dachte Jack. Bei einer abgerundeten Apsis mußte der gesamte Chorraum gleichmäßig in die traditionellen Gliederungselemente Arkade – Empore – Lichtgaden aufgeteilt werden. Eine rechteckige Apsis eröffnete neue architektonische Möglichkeiten. »Den Pilgerstrom kann man vielleicht auch auf andere Weise in Gang halten«, sagte er nachdenklich.

»Und die aufgehende Sonne würde durch die großen Fenster scheinen«, ergänzte Sally.

Das konnte Jack sich gut vorstellen. »Man könnte an eine Reihe hoher, schmaler Lanzettfenster denken«, sagte er.

»Oder an ein einziges, großes Fenster wie eine erblühte Rose«, sagte Sally.

Welch eine Idee! Dem Betrachter im Mittelschiff mußte das Rundfenster wie eine gewaltige, in unzähligen bunte Scherben zerspringende Sonnenscheibe erscheinen. Jack sah sie deutlich vor sich ...

»Ich frage mich, welches Motiv sich die Mönche wünschen.«

»Die zehn Gebote und die Propheten«, sagte Sally.

Er zog eine Braue hoch und sah sie an. »Du raffiniertes Luder hast schon mit Prior Jonathan gesprochen, wie?«

Er hatte sie offenbar ertappt, doch blieb ihr die Beantwortung seiner Frage erspart, weil in diesem Moment Peter Chisel, ein junger Skulpteur, zu ihnen trat. Peter war ein scheuer, linkischer Mann mit hellem Haar, das ihm immer wieder ins Gesicht fiel. Seine Skulpturen waren großartig. Jack war froh und glücklich darüber, ihn zu haben.

»Was kann ich für Euch tun, Peter?« fragte er.

»Mit Verlaub – eigentlich suche ich Sally.«

»Nun, die habt Ihr gefunden.«

Sally stand auf und klopfte sich die Brotkrümel vom Schoß. »Bis später«, sagte sie zu ihren Eltern und verschwand mit Peter in dem niedrigen Gang, der zur Wendeltreppe führte.

Jack und Aliena sahen einander an.

»Ist sie rot geworden, oder täusche ich mich?« fragte Jack.

»Ich hoffe«, antwortete Aliena. »Meine Güte, es ist auch wirklich an der Zeit, daß sie sich verliebt! Sie ist schon sechsundzwanzig!«

»Ganz recht. Ich hatte schon alle Hoffnung aufgegeben. Sie hat sich's in den Kopf gesetzt, als alte Jungfer zu enden, dachte ich mir.«

Aliena schüttelte den Kopf. »Nein, Sally bestimmt nicht. Sie ist genauso sinnlich wie alle anderen auch. Nur eben ein bißchen wählerischer.«

»Meinst du?« fragte Jack skeptisch. »Peter Chisel ist nicht gerade ein Mann, um den sich die Mädchen in der Grafschaft reißen ...«

»Die Mädchen in der Grafschaft reißen sich um große, gutaussehende Männer wie Tommy, die allen Sätteln gerecht sind und mit roter Seide verbrämte Mäntel tragen. Sally ist da anders. Sie sucht sich einen klugen, einfühlsamen Mann. Peter ist genau der Richtige für sie.«

Jack nickte. Obwohl er nie darüber nachgedacht hatte, spürte er, daß das, was Aliena sagte, stimmte. »Sally ist wie ihre Großmutter«, sagte er. »Meine Mutter verliebte sich damals auch in so einen Kauz.«

»Sally kommt auf deine Mutter raus – und Tommy auf meinen Vater«, sagte Aliena.

Jack lächelte sie an. Aliena war schöner denn je. Ihr Haar war mit grauen Strähnen durchzogen und die Haut an ihrem Hals nicht mehr von jener Marmorglätte wie ehedem. Aber da sie mit zunehmendem Alter die Rundungen der Mutterschaft verlor, traten ihre markanten Wangenknochen deutlicher hervor und verliehen ihrem hübschen Gesicht eine herbe, fast architektonische Schönheit. Jack fuhr mit der Hand die geschwungene Linie ihres Kiefers hoch. »Wie einer meiner Schwibbogen«, sagte er.

Sie lächelte.

Über den Hals glitt seine Hand in ihren Ausschnitt. Auch Alienas Brüste hatten sich verändert. Er konnte sich noch gut daran erinnern, wie sie einst ausgesehen hatten – stramm, scheinbar gewichtslos, mit aufwärts gekehrten Knospen. Während der Schwangerschaften waren sie größer, die Brustwarzen breiter geworden. Inzwischen waren Alienas Brüste niedriger und weicher und schwangen beim Gehen sacht hin und her. Jack hatte sie immer gemocht, in all ihren Erscheinungsformen. Wie werden sie aussehen, wenn Aliena alt ist? fragte er sich. Werden sie einschrumpfen und voller Falten sein? Sei's drum, ich werd' sie wahrscheinlich auch dann noch mögen ... Die Brustwarze versteifte sich unter seiner Berührung. Jack beugte sich vor, um Aliena auf die Lippen zu küssen.

»Jack, du befindest dich in einer Kirche«, murmelte sie.

»Und wenn schon«, sagte er, und seine Hand wanderte über den Bauch in ihren Schoß.

Von der Treppe her waren Schritte zu hören.

Wie ein ertappter Sünder zog Jack sich zurück.

Aliena mußte lachen. »Die Strafe Gottes folgt auf dem Fuß«, sagte sie respektlos.

»Wart's ab, du kommst später noch dran!« raunte er ihr in gespielter Entrüstung zu.

Die Schritten hatten den obersten Treppenabsatz erreicht. Prior Jonathan trat zu ihnen und grüßte sie mit ernster Miene. »Kannst du mal mit in den Kreuzgang kommen, Jack?« fragte er. »Da ist jemand, der mit dir sprechen möchte.«

»Ja, natürlich.« Jack erhob sich.

Jonathan war schon wieder auf der Treppe.

Jack drehte sich am Ausgang noch einmal um und drohte Aliena mit dem Finger. »Später!« sagte er.

Aliena grinste. »Ehrenwort?«

Durch die Tür im Südflügel des Querhauses erreichten Jonathan und Jack den Kreuzgang. Sie kamen an den Schülern mit ihren Wachstäfelchen vorbei und blieben an der nächsten Ecke stehen. Mit einer

Kopfbewegung machte Jonathan Jack auf einen Mönch aufmerksam, der im Westgang allein auf einer in die Mauer eingelassenen Steinbank saß. Der Kopf des Mannes war von der hochgezogenen Kapuze bedeckt, doch auf einmal drehte er sich um, sah zu ihnen auf und wandte dann rasch den Blick wieder ab.

Unwillkürlich trat Jack einen Schritt zurück.

Der Mönch war Waleran Bigod.

»Was will dieser Teufel denn hier?« fragte Jack.

»Er bereitet sich auf die Begegnung mit seinem Schöpfer vor«, sagte Jonathan.

Jack runzelte die Stirn. »Das verstehe ich nicht.«

»Er ist ein gebrochener Mann«, fuhr Jonathan fort, »ohne Stellung, ohne Macht, ohne Freunde. Er hat begriffen, daß Gott ihm nicht das Amt eines großen und mächtigen Bischofs zugedacht hat. Er hat seine Fehler eingesehen. Zu Fuß kam er hierher und bat um Aufnahme ins Kloster. Als einfacher Mönch möchte er die ihm noch verbleibende Zeit nutzen, Gott um die Vergebung seiner Sünden anzuflehen.«

»Es fällt mir schwer, das zu glauben«, sagte Jack.

»Mir ging es anfangs genauso«, erwiderte Jonathan. »Doch ich habe mich schließlich davon überzeugen lassen, daß er schon immer ein gottesfürchtiger Mann gewesen ist.«

Jack sah ihn skeptisch an.

»Ja, ich zweifle nicht an seiner Frömmigkeit. Nur machte er einen entscheidenden Fehler: Er bildete sich ein, im Dienste des Herrn rechtfertige der Zweck die Mittel – und leitete daraus die Freiheit ab, alles zu tun, was er für richtig hielt.«

»Einschließlich der Verschwörung zur Ermordung eines Erzbischofs.«

In einer abwehrenden Geste hob Jonathan die Hände. »Es liegt an Gott, ihn dafür zu strafen. Meines Amtes ist es nicht.«

Jack hob die Schultern. Diese Worte hätten auch von Philip stammen können. Jack sah keine Veranlassung, Waleran im Kloster aufzunehmen – aber Mönche hatten in diesen Dingen sicher andere Vorstellungen. »Warum bringst du mich hierher? Was habe ich mit ihm zu schaffen?«

»Er möchte dir sagen, warum dein Vater damals gehängt wurde.«

Ein kalter Schauer überlief Jack.

Reglos wie ein Stein saß Waleran da und stierte ins Ungewisse. Er war barfuß; unter dem Saum seiner härenen Kutte lugten die zerbrech-

1146

lichen Knöchel eines alten Mannes hervor. Vor diesem Mann braucht niemand mehr Angst zu haben, dachte Jack. Er ist schwach und traurig und von seiner Niederlage schwer gezeichnet.

Jack ging zu ihm hin und setzte sich, auf Abstand bedacht, neben ihn.

Waleran kam sofort zur Sache. »Der alte König Heinrich war zu stark«, sagte er, »und das gefiel verschiedenen Baronen nicht, denn er engte ihre Freiheiten ein. Der nächste König sollte schwächer sein. Aber Heinrich hatte einen Sohn, William.«

Uralte Geschichten ... »Das war doch alles lange vor meiner Geburt«, sagte Jack.

»Euer Vater starb vor Eurer Geburt«, erwiderte Waleran mit einem Hauch der alten Hochnäsigkeit.

Jack nickte. »Erzählt weiter.«

»Eine Gruppe von Baronen beschloß, den Sohn des Königs zu ermorden. Indem sie die natürliche Thronfolge zu verhindern trachteten, erhofften sich die Verschwörer mehr Einfluß auf die Wahl des neuen Königs.«

Jack studierte aufmerksam Walerans bleiches, schmales Gesicht. Der alte Mann wirkte müde, geschlagen und reumütig – von Arglist keine Spur. Wenn er dennoch etwas im Schilde führte, so war ihm jedenfalls nichts anzumerken. »Aber William starb doch beim Untergang des ›Weißen Schiffes‹«, sagte Jack.

»Der Untergang war kein Unfall.«

Jack erschrak. War das möglich? Der Thronerbe ermordet, nur weil sich ein paar Barone einen schwächeren König wünschten? Aber inzwischen war ja sogar ein Erzbischof ermordet worden ...

»Weiter«, sagte er.

»Die Barone versenkten das Schiff und entkamen in einem Boot. Alle anderen Passagiere ertranken – mit Ausnahme eines Mannes, der sich an einem Mast festklammerte und an die Küste getrieben wurde.«

»Und das war mein Vater.« Langsam erkannte Jack, worauf Waleran hinauswollte.

Walerans Gesicht war schneeweiß, seine Lippen blutleer. Er sprach ohne jede Gemütsbewegung und vermied es, Jack anzusehen. »Nicht weit von der Stelle, an der ihn die Wellen an den Strand spülten, lag die Burg eines Verschwörers. Sie nahmen ihn gefangen. Der Mann hatte nicht die Absicht, sie anzuschwärzen – was auch kaum möglich gewesen wäre, denn er hatte überhaupt nicht mitbekommen, daß das

Schiff versenkt worden war. Aber er hatte Dinge gesehen, die Kundigeren die Wahrheit verraten hätten. Und darum konnten ihn die Verschwörer nicht laufen und freimütig über seine Erlebnisse berichten lassen. Sie brachten ihn nach England und ließen ihn dort in der Obhut von Leuten zurück, die ihr Vertrauen besaßen.«

Jack überkam tiefe Traurigkeit. Seine Mutter hatte ihm erzählt, daß sein Vater immer nur eines im Sinn gehabt hatte: Er wollte die Menschen unterhalten, ihnen Freude machen. Irgend etwas an Walerans Geschichte kam ihm merkwürdig vor. »Warum haben sie ihn nicht gleich umgebracht?« fragte er.

»Sie hätten es tun sollen, ja«, gab Waleran kühl zurück. »Aber der Mann war unschuldig, ein Jongleur, ein Spielmann ... Er war unterhaltsam, und alle mochten ihn. Sie brachten es einfach nicht über sich.« Waleran lächelte freudlos. »Selbst die rücksichtslosesten Menschen werden gelegentlich von Skrupeln befallen.«

»Und warum haben sie später ihre Meinung geändert?«

»Weil der Mann ihnen dann doch gefährlich wurde, sogar hier. Anfangs war er harmlos – er konnte ja nicht mal Englisch. Aber mit der Zeit lernte er die Sprache und schuf sich einen Bekannten- und Freundeskreis. Man sperrte ihn daher in den Kerker unter dem Dormitorium – was zur Folge hatte, daß die Leute fragten, warum. Der Häftling wurde zu einer Belastung. Die Verschwörer merkten, daß sie, solange dieser Mann lebte, keine Ruhe finden würden. Schließlich trugen sie uns auf, ihn zu töten.«

So einfach war das also, dachte Jack. »Aber warum habt Ihr Euch gegen diesen Auftrag nicht gewehrt?«

»Wir waren ehrgeizig, alle drei«, sagte Waleran, und sein Mund verzog sich zu einer reumütigen Grimasse. »Percy Hamleigh, Prior James und ich. Eure Mutter hatte schon recht: Wir wurden dafür belohnt. Mit der Beförderung zum Erzdiakon eröffneten sich mir glänzende Zukunftsaussichten in der Kirche, Percy Hamleigh wurde zum wohlhabenden Landbesitzer, und Prior James konnte den Klosterbesitz mehren.«

»Und die Barone?«

»In den drei Jahren nach dem Schiffbruch wurde Heinrich von Fulk von Anjou, William Clito in der Normandie sowie dem König von Frankreich angegriffen. Eine Zeitlang stand es nicht gut um ihn. Aber er besiegte seine Feinde und regierte weitere zehn Jahre. Als er dann aber starb, ohne einen männlichen Erben zu hinterlassen, kam es unter Stephan dann doch noch zu jener Anarchie, auf die die Barone gehofft hatten. Während des zwanzigjährigen Bürgerkriegs herrschten sie in ihren Grafschaften wie kleine Könige, ohne daß eine zentrale Macht ihrer Willkür hätte Schranken setzen können.«

»Und dafür mußte mein Vater sterben.«

»Auch sein Tod half ihnen nichts mehr. Die meisten Barone kamen in den Kämpfen um, manche sogar mit ihren Söhnen. Und die kleinen Lügen, die wir in der Grafschaft verbreitet hatten, um Euren Vater getrost töten zu können, erwiesen sich als Geister, die wir nicht mehr loswurden. Eure Mutter verfluchte uns nach der Hinrichtung, und der Fluch tat seine Wirkung: Prior James ging an der Last, die auf seinem Gewissen lag, zugrunde – Remigius berichtete darüber während der Verhandlung gegen Philip. Percy Hamleigh starb, bevor die Wahrheit ans Licht kam – doch sein Sohn endete am Galgen. Und was mich betrifft, so braucht Ihr mich bloß anzusehen. Der Meineid, den ich vor fast fünfzig Jahren schwor, hat mich jetzt Stellung und Ansehen gekostet.« Waleran wirkte vollkommen erschöpft; offenbar kostete ihn die Aufrechterhaltung seiner strengen Selbstbeherrschung viel Kraft. »Wir hatten alle Angst vor Eurer Mutter, denn keiner von uns vermochte zu sagen, wieviel sie wußte. Wie sich am Ende herausstellte, war es gar nicht so viel – aber es hat gereicht.«

Auch Jack fühlte sich ganz ausgelaugt. Endlich hatte er die ganze Wahrheit über seine Vater erfahren – und nun empfand er weder Rachelust noch Wut. Seinen leiblichen Vater hatte er nie gekannt, aber er hatte Tom gehabt, dem er seine Liebe zum Baumeisterhandwerk verdankte – die zweitgrößte Leidenschaft seines Lebens.

Jack erhob sich. Die Ereignisse lagen so weit zurück, daß er darüber keine Tränen mehr vergießen konnte. Seither war so viel geschehen – und das meiste davon war schön und gut gewesen.

Er blickte hinab auf den alten Mann, der auf der Bank saß, ein klägliches Häufchen Elend, zermürbt von der Bitterkeit der Reue. Auf einmal empfand er Mitleid für ihn. Wie furchtbar es sein mußte, als alter Mensch zu erkennen, daß man sein Leben vertan hat. Waleran sah auf, und zum erstenmal trafen sich ihre Blicke. Der alte Mann zuckte zusammen und wandte sich ruckartig ab, als habe man ihn ins Gesicht geschlagen. Jack konnte in diesem Moment seine Gedanken lesen: Er hat das Mitleid in meinen Augen erkannt, dachte er.

Und für Waleran gab es keine schlimmere Erniedrigung als das Mitleid seiner Feinde.

Philip stand am Westtor der uralten christlichen Stadt Canterbury. Versehen mit den prachtvollen Insignien eines englischen Bischofs, trug er den juwelenbesetzten Krummstab mit königlicher Würde. Es goß in Strömen.

Sechsundsechzig Jahre zählte er, und die Kälte fuhr ihm in die alten Knochen. Es war das letzte Mal, daß er sich so weit von seinem Amtssitz fortwagte, doch um nichts in der Welt hätte er diesen Tag missen wollen. In gewisser Hinsicht bedeutete die heutige Zeremonie die Krönung seines Lebenswerks.

Dreieinhalb Jahre waren seit der geschichtsträchtigen Ermordung des Erzbischofs Thomas erst vergangen, doch hatte sich in dieser kurzen Zeit ein mystischer Kult um Thomas Becket über die ganze Welt verbreitet. Nie hätte Philip sich träumen lassen, was er mit der kleinen Kerzenprozession durch die Straßen von Canterbury damals ausgelöst hatte. Mit geradezu ungebührlicher Eile hatte der Papst Thomas heiliggesprochen. Im Heiligen Land nannte sich ein neuer Mönchsorden sogar *Die Ritter des heiligen Thomas von Acre*. König Heinrich war machtlos; gegen eine so mächtige Volksbewegung kam er nicht an. Sie war zu kraftvoll, als daß ein einzelner hätte Widerstand leisten können.

Für Philip lag die Bedeutung des Phänomens in dem, was es über die Macht des Staates aussagte. Thomas' Tod hatte gezeigt, daß sich der Monarch im Konflikt zwischen Kirche und Krone durch Anwendung brutaler Gewalt stets durchsetzen konnte. Doch der Kult des heiligen Thomas bewies, daß derartige Erfolge nichts als Pyrrhussiege waren. Absolute Macht besaß der König nicht; der Wille des Volkes vermochte sie zu beschränken. Es war ein Wandel, der sich zu Philips Lebzeiten vollzogen hatte, und er war nicht nur Zeuge dieser Veränderung gewesen, sondern hatte auch sein Teil dazu beigetragen. Die Feierlichkeiten an diesem Tag sollten daran erinnern.

Ein stämmiger Mann mit auffallend großem Kopf näherte sich, von Regenschwaden umwölkt, der Stadt. Er trug weder Hut noch Stiefel. In einigem Abstand folgte ihm eine große Zahl Berittener.

Der Mann war König Heinrich.

Während der durchnäßte König durch Schlamm und Matsch zum Stadttor schritt, verhielt sich die Menge so still, als trüge man jemanden zu Grabe.

Philip kreuzte, wie vorgesehen, den Weg des barfüßigen Königs und setzte sich nun an die Spitze des Zuges, dessen Ziel die Kathedrale war. Heinrich folgte ihm mit gebeugtem Haupt – er, der sonst so

Übermütige, bot nun in seiner ganzen Haltung das Bild des bußfertigen Sünders. In ehrfürchtigem Schweigen begriffen, starrte das Volk
den König von England an, der sich vor allen Augen demütigte. Des
Königs Hofstaat hielt sorgsam Abstand.

Bedächtig führte ihn Philip in die Kathedrale. Die mächtigen Tor-
flügel standen weit geöffnet. Sie schritten hindurch: eine feierliche
Prozession zweier Männer, Abschluß und Höhepunkt der politischen
Krise des Jahrhunderts. Übervoll war das Kirchenschiff. Die Menge
teilte sich, um die beiden durchzulassen. Überwältigt von diesem
Schauspiel, wagte man nur noch zu flüstern. Der stolzeste König der
Christenheit betrat, triefend vor Nässe, die Kirche wie ein Bettler!

Langsam schritten sie durch das Mittelschiff und die Stufen hinab
zur Krypta. Dort, neben dem neuen Grabmal des Märtyrers, warteten
die Mönche von Canterbury, an ihrer Seite die größten und mächtigsten Bischöfe und Äbte des Reiches.

Der König kniete auf dem Boden.

Seine Höflinge versammelten sich hinter ihm. Vor jedermanns Augen bekannte Heinrich von England, der zweite seines Namens, seine
Sünden – und auch, daß er unwissentlich Veranlasser der Ermordung
des heiligen Thomas gewesen sei.

Nach diesem Bekenntnis entledigte er sich seines Mantels; darunter trug er eine grüne Tunika und ein härenes Hemd. Abermals kniete
er nieder und beugte den Rücken.

Der Bischof von London bog ein Rohr.

Nun würde der König gegeißelt werden.

Von jedem Priester sollte er fünf Streiche bekommen, und drei
von jedem Mönch. Selbstredend beschränkte man sich auf die Symbolik, denn hätten alle achtzig ernstlich zugeschlagen, so hätte der König
die Zeremonie nicht überlebt.

Der Bischof von London berührte Heinrichs Rücken fünfmal sachte
mit dem Stock. Dann drehte er sich um und überreichte das Rohr
Philip, dem Bischof von Kingsbridge.

Philip trat vor, um den König zu geißeln. Er war glücklich, daß
er das noch erleben durfte. Von heute an, so dachte er, wird die Welt
eine andere sein.

Danksagung

Mein besonderer Dank gilt Jean Gimpel, Geoffrey Hindley,
Warren Hollister und Margaret Wade Labarge.
Sie ließen mich an ihrem enzyklopädischen Wissen
über das Mittelalter großzügig teilhaben.
Ich danke auch Ian und Marjory Chapman für ihre Geduld.
Sie haben mich immer wieder ermutigt und mir
viele Anregungen gegeben.